Concordance to the *Complete Works*

COMPLETE WORKS **XXVII** **CONCORDANCE**

Sangharakshita
Concordance to the *Complete Works*

COMPILED BY VIDYADEVI

Windhorse Publications
38 Newmarket Road
Cambridge CB5 8DT

info@windhorsepublications.com
www.windhorsepublications.com

First published in 2024.

Cover design by Dhammarati
Cover images: Front: *Itinerant Monk Accompanied by a Tiger,* China, 9th century, Musée Guimet, Paris (Pelliot Collection, EO 1141)
Back flap: Sangharakshita and Vidyadevi in Sangharashita's flat, London Buddhist Centre, early 1990s.
Photo: Dhammarati

Typesetting and layout Tarajyoti
Printed by Bell & Bain Ltd, Glasgow

British Library Cataloguing in Publication Data:
A catalogue record for this book is available from the British Library.

ISBN 978-1-915342-18-8

CONTENTS

ACKNOWLEDGEMENTS

I am so grateful for the contributions of all those who have helped with the creation of this concordance. My friend Satyalila has been a wonderful support both by creating the immensely helpful indexes of the *Complete Works* volumes (she began her work as indexer after the first three had been published) and by encouraging me at every step of the long way with zest, poetry, and cups of tea. Shantavira, who has faithfully copy-edited all the volumes of the *Complete Works*, surpassed himself to prepare this volume for publication at a time when he was facing the challenge of cancer diagnosis and treatment; I'm so grateful. Thanks also to Dhammarati for his nifty work on the design and to Tarajyoti, who took up the challenge of typesetting the volume (like pouring an ocean into a teacup) with grace and aplomb. Kalyanasri, our indefatigable and meticulous proofreader, brought all her experience of her work throughout the series to the demands of this final volume. Publishing the *Complete Works*, and especially this volume, has been a huge undertaking for Windhorse Publications. Many thanks to director Dhammamegha and publishing controller Michelle Bernard for all they've done to help it to happen. And thanks are due, too, to my husband Andy Johnson for his kindness and patience (and yes, more cups of tea) during the intensive period of work on this volume and indeed throughout the ten years of work on the *Complete Works*.

PICTURE CREDITS

Thanks to Aloka for the illustrations of Akṣobhya, Amitābha, Amoghasiddhi, Avalokiteśvara (*under* Triratna) and the Avalokiteśvara mantra, the bodhi tree, Brahma Sahāmpati's request, the Buddhas of the three times, cosmology, various *ḍākinīs*, devotion, the four *rūpa dhyānas*, the earth goddess bearing witness, the four sights, the initiation vase, Jambhala, Kukai, Kurukullā, *makara*, the mandala of the Five Buddhas, Manjuśrī, Māra's attack, Milarepa, the twin miracle, Mucalinda, *mudrās*, offering the mandala, seven offerings, *oṃ*, Padmasambhava, Prajñāpāramitā, Ratnasambhava, the Refuge Tree, Shinran, Siṃhamukta, *śrīpāda*, the stupa, Tārā, Tsongkhapa, Vairocana, the *vajra*, Vajrapāṇi, Vajrasattva, Vajrayoginī, the wheel of life, the windhorse, Xuanzang, and the *yab-yum*.

Thanks to Annie Leigh for the illustrations of Avalokiteśvara, Bhaiṣajyaguru, the Buddha, the elephant, Delphi (*under* Greece), growth and development, lotuses, Nāgārjuna, the woman and the fish-basket (*under* parables), bamboos (*under* trees), Vimalakīrti, and the Stupa of Abundant Treasures (*under White Lotus Sūtra*).

Thanks to the Urgyen Sangharakshita Trust for the photographs of Dr Ambedkar, Buddharakshita, U Chandramani, Chattrul Sangye Dorje, Yogi Chen, the Dalai Lama, Terry Delamare, Miss Delannoy, Dhardo Rimpoche, Anagārika Dharmapala, Dilgo Khyentse Rimpoche, Dinoo Dubash, Dudjom Khyentse Rimpoche, Allen Ginsberg, Lama Govinda, Christmas Humphreys, Jagdish Kashyap, Jamyang Khyentse Rimpoche, St Jerome, Jivaka, Kachu Rimpoche, Mahadhammavira, Ramana Maharshi, Swami Ramdas, Dr Mehta, Sachin, all the photos of Sangharakshita, Sangharakshita's mother, *Stepping-Stones*, Stonehenge, and Tomo Geshe Rimpoche.

Thanks to Khantipālo for use of his photo.

All other images are in the public domain.

USING THE CONCORDANCE

WHY 'CONCORDANCE'?

We started planning the *Complete Works* (CW) in the spring of 2014. (For more about that, see the restrospective in the appendices.) I don't know why it occurred to me that the series should end with a 'concordance', but when I consulted Sangharakshita about it, he immediately saw the need. I suppose that's not surprising, given the great value he placed on reference books. As you will know if you have read volume 20 of this series, confined to bed for two years as a child, he began his lifelong quest for knowledge upon the chance gift of the sixty-one parts of a children's encyclopedia, through which he could 'speak with the good and wise of all ages' and explore the secrets of nature (CW 20, p. 22). And throughout his life he relied on the dictionary – 'the most important book apart from the scriptures' – for the definitions that clarified his thinking and writing. It seems fitting to end his *Complete Works* with his own work of reference.

Why 'concordance'? A concordance is defined as an alphabetical list of the words used in the works of a particular author, together with quotations to give the context in which the words are used, and that roughly describes this volume, although it is also a sort of encyclopedia or dictionary or collection of anthologies or index, or something for which we don't quite have a word. 'Concordance' also means 'the state of there being agreement or similarity between things', and that suits

this volume, which brings together every aspect of Sangharakshita's writings, produced over more than seventy years.

Ten years after that first thought that a concordance would be needed, it's even more clear why. Next to me as I write this is a bookcase, two of whose shelves are filled with the elegant and vast volumes of the *Complete Works* (not quite all of them, as the last two are to be published alongside this one). Even I find them a bit daunting, and as series editor I know my way around them. How might a newcomer find a way into this vastness? This volume aims to answer that question, and thousands of others. In his poem about the *Blue Cliff Record* (a Zen text), Sangharakshita says, 'A thousand doors fly open' (CW 25 p. 342), and the concordance has thousands of doors. Whether you want to look up a person or place, explore a theme, track down a particular teaching, or find out more about Sangharakshita himself, the key to that door should be here somewhere. The compilation of a work like this is necessarily subjective, and there would be many possible ways of arranging it, but I hope that you'll quickly get the hang of how it is organized. Note that there are hardly any references to Volume 6; as it is an anthology, almost all its content also appears elsewhere in the *Complete Works*.

FINDING YOUR WAY AROUND

The concordance is simply a list of entries from A to Z, but some entries are one line while others run to several paragraphs or pages. The numbers refer to volume and page number, so 1.108 means volume 1, page 108. Any introductory material – descriptions, etymology, that sort of thing – will come at the start of the entry, while at the end there may be an invitation to 'see also' with links to other entries. Within an entry, there may be an element of alphabetical order, or if it's a subject that has a history of some sort, chronological order. In longer entries, subjects are grouped under helpful headings. Numbered lists will be found under the number, so it's 'four noble truths' (not 'noble truths, four') and 'seven *visuddhis*' (not '*visuddhis*, seven') – but there are cross-references to help with this sort of thing.

One of the challenges of creating the concordance has been to decide which terms need their own entry and which can be treated as synonyms, whether in English or in Pāli or Sanskrit. For example, if you look up *śraddhā*, you will be redirected to 'faith' (if you want to investigate faith

in a Buddhist sense) or 'Hinduism' (if it's the Hindu form of *śraddhā* you have in mind). Matters related to ethics, morality, and *śīla* are all grouped together under 'ethics'. Other terms, which though similar have their own flavour, are listed separately; courage and bravery are listed together, for example, but fearlessness has its own entry. Cross-references will help you find your way around. 'Buddhism' and 'Dharma' have been given their own entries, because although they are in a sense the same thing, there is a distinction between them. (If you look up 'Buddhism' and read about the term, you will discover where to find out what that distinction is.) If you can't find what you're looking for in one of these entries, I suggest looking at the 'see also' section at the end, to see if it's in the other one.

'Buddhism' and 'Dharma' are two of the five sections that are so long that there's a table of contents at the start of the section. (The other three are 'Buddha', 'Sangharakshita', and 'Triratna Buddhist Community'.) These sections are subdivided under roman numerals which are also used in cross-references. For example, a reference to Sangharakshita's visions would have the cross-reference '*see under* Sangharakshita VI/spiritual experiences'. To help you locate such references, in the margins of those sections the headings show the section title. To take the example just given, the heading in the margin is Sangharakshita VI/inner and emotional life. That heading confirms that you have found section VI, and within that section you can look for the heading 'spiritual and supernatural experiences', within which is the subheading 'visions'.

ABBREVIATIONS

You will notice that some entries relating to people have a reference such as V21 (rather than volume plus page number). This is an indication that relevant references are to be found in volume 21 by consulting the index of that volume.

I have usually abbreviated 'Triratna Buddhist Order and Community' to 'Triratna', 'Friends of the Western Buddhist Order' to 'FWBO', and 'Trailokya Bauddha Maha Sahayak Gana' to TBMSG.

APPROACHING THE CONCORDANCE

There's an idea in a book by Lewis Carroll, picked up in stories by other writers, of a map that's as big as the country it charts, and at

times in its preparation this concordance has threatened to resemble that map. But the map is not the territory. The main thing to remember is that these short references are intended to guide you to passages in the *Complete Works* volumes. The references will give you a sense of the original passage, or a range of perspectives on a subject, but shortened or paraphrased as they are, a glorious mixture as they are of writings of many genres produced over a long period of time, coming as they do from the words and experiences of so many people, they are no substitute for the real thing: Sangharakshita's own words and the context in which they were written. I find that looking things up is often like the moment in a film when black-and-white suddenly becomes colour. So to use the concordance effectively, you will need access to the other volumes in the series.

Although 'the nature of Buddhism is inevitably encyclopedic' (CW 11, p. 508), a little can go a long way, and in the pages of the concordance there are many reflections on how to approach the written word: look up 'more and more of less and less' or 'reading books on Buddhism' (under 'reading') or 'words and reality' (under 'words'), or 'Dharma study as a practice' (under 'study'), or 'advice for the Dharma student' (under 'Dharma III/teaching and learning the Dharma'). In that latter section you will also find a wealth of advice for the Dharma teacher. If you are teaching or studying the Dharma, you may want to follow any one of a thousand lines of inquiry, but for your own spiritual practice, you may only need the key to one of those thousand doors. Sangharakshita's advice is to start with an aspect of the teaching that arouses your interest (CW 19, p. 179, listed in the concordance under 'interest'), but I hope you will find your way to whatever you are seeking. As I have worked on Sangharakshita's writings for many years, I am often asked where to find this or that teaching, and I hope the concordance will help to answer that sort of question, but my own experience is that I have also found all sorts of things I wasn't looking for and didn't know were there, and that seems even more useful.

Vidyadevi
Herefordshire
July 2024

CONCORDANCE

A

a- (negative prefix) 14.347, 17.295, 17.565

abandonment abandoning habits of mind 17.359; abandoning the idea of attainment 26.175–6; abandoning oneself to the Dharma 9.455–6; abandoning the power mode 2.365, 17.583, 26.66; abandoning the raft 1.308; abandoning the search for happiness 17.360; abandoning slanderous speech 2.383; abandoning wrong views 2.392–3, 7.292–3; 'The abandonment of all is Nirvāṇa' (Śāntideva) 4.358; abandonment of respectability 1.201; abandonment of views 26.160; abandonment of worldly attachment 18.128; the Buddha contemplates the abandonment of *prapañca* 10.621; the Buddha's abandonment by his first five disciples, *see under* Siddhārtha; the categories of doctrine are ultimately to be abandoned 10.165, 14.362–3, 14.409; a cause of regret to abandon any being 5.152–5; the *ḍākinī*'s self-abandonment to the Three Jewels 13.242; the danger of abandoning positive conditions prematurely 18.34; desires can never be satisfied, but only abandoned 26.12; abandonment of self, *see under* self/getting rid of the self; it is doubtful whether wild abandon can be a spiritual quality 13.246; *śūnyatā* perceived only when all previous modes of thinking have been abandoned 15.187; ultimately there can be no abandonment of *saṃsāra* 1.268; views of the universe to be abandoned 26.154; the vigorous abandonment of unskilful states of mind 10.531; you can't abandon bad actions unless you have dealt with unskilful attitudes 19.10

Abdiel (angel) 3.569, 8.191

abhaya *see* fearlessness

Abhaya, Dharmachari (Mike) 23.xiii–xix, v24; brief introduction 24.623 (n88); chair of Norwich Buddhist Centre 24.6; compiler of aphorisms 26.xix; in Cornwall 26.615; in the New Forest 26.611; 'one of my closest friends' 26.611

abhaya mudrā *see under mudrās*

Abhayada, Dharmachari v24

Abhayanavita, Dhammacharini 10.lxv

Abhayarājakumāra Sutta *see under Majjhima Nikāya*

Abhidhammattha-saṅgaha introduction 1.102–3; 89 *cittas* 2.676 (n130); calculation of the lifespan of the four great kings 2.67; insistence on the wrong view that *dharmas* are ultimate realities 7.540–1; *paññattis* 19.85, 19.597–8; the smile of the *arhant* 4.137, 12.146

Abhidharma (Pāli Abhidhamma)

INTRODUCTION

the term 'Abhidharma'
the meaning of the word 3.86, 12.140–1; its use in the *Majjhima Nikāya* 14.72; how its usage developed and changed 14.73, 14.76, 17.444

what is the Abhidharma?
brief description 3.86, 3.667 (n267), 4.661 (n12), 7.502, 17.731 (n180); analysis of mental events, *see under dharmas*; Buddhist psychology, in a way 17.436; contrasting accounts by two modern Theravādins 1.223–4; 'the delight of the learned' 17.451; even the Abhidharma has loose ends 17.690; not a distortion of the Dharma, but an attempt to systematize it 1.223, 12.141–2; analysis in catechism form 14.84–5, 14.90–1; the analytical psychology of the Abhidharma 12.138–49; an exhaustive science of mind 17.436; it developed a scientific psychology of mystical experiences 12.151; it dominated Buddhism in India for about a thousand years 12.142; it studies *dharmas* in a way that precludes the possibility of thinking of a self 17.546; a valuable contribution to our understanding of Buddhism 7.539, 14.77; hundreds of texts 12.143; a massive cross-referencing operation 17.447; not really mysterious 12.140; its 'one notable constructive contribution to knowledge' 14.91; the 'psycho-ethical philosophy of Early Buddhism' 10.143, 14.75; studied by Tibetan *geshes* 13.45; a systematic presentation of the Buddha's discourses 15.160–1

expositions
Guenther's *Philosophy and Psychology in the Abhidharma* 8.510–11; Gyaltsen's *The Necklace of Clear Understanding* 8.510

its bearing on the spiritual life
be cautious about deciding you have gone beyond its perspective 17.592; is it necessary to the attainment of Nirvāṇa?

8.118–19, 8.129–30; its practical nature 17.454; it helps us sort out our mental states 12.149; it plays with operational concepts for practical purposes 17.494; it shows that the 'self' is just an ever-changing combination of mental states 12.149; it's not just about psychology 17.649; it was geared to the spiritual purpose of meditation 17.447; its key insight 17.498; its real purpose 17.697–8; why study the Abhidharma? 17.476

negative aspects
Abhidharma scholars' inflexible mental attitude 15.163; it can seem 'an unearthly ballet of bloodless categories' 14.85, 26.163; it banished the human element 3.86, 12.142, 17.441, 17.686; it suggested that the mind is just a complicated machine 15.187–8; it takes no account of personal inclinations 16.586–7 (n18); the limitations of its approach 17.686; losing sight of its original spiritual purpose 17.451; a mistake to think that any system could express the spirit of the Dharma 14.257, 17.686; omission of compassion from the Dharma 4.86; one can't really chop reality into little bits 17.493–4; thinking that ability to list its categories shows spiritual prowess 1.349

topics
analysis of *dharmas*, *see under dharmas*; the *brahma vihāras* and insight 15.337; a collection of doctrinal topics 14.79–80, 14.81–2, 14.93–4; cosmology 14.84; human types 14.81; the importance of distinguishing skilful from unskilful 17.617; investigation of the elements of existence 14.90–1; the Abhidharma and Nirvāṇa 1.225–6; spiritual life of laymen and monks 14.82–3; the ten fetters 15.203; three kinds of Stream Entrant 15.163; three stages in the practice of meditation 14.83; the twenty-four causal conditions 14.91–3

THE HISTORY OF THE ABHIDHARMA

how it began
the *Satipaṭṭhāna Sutta* as a basis 15.160–1; the Abhidharma and Sarvāstivādin thought 14.87–8, 14.93–5; classifying and cataloguing 14.360–1, 17.440–1; clear definitions of terms 17.441; developed by disciples with an analytical turn of mind 4.11; association with *mātṛkas* 2.197, 7.502, 14.72–3; association with Śāriputra, Ānanda, and Mahākaccāna 14.73; its connection with the Sāṃkhya school 17.439–40; Dharma became Abhidharma 2.203; association with the *vaidalya* aspect of the Sutta Piṭaka 14.24, 14.72–3; the starting point: 'Cease to do evil. Learn to do good. Purify your mind.' 17.435–6

the second stage
its three functions 12.141–2; a process of abstraction, analysis, and amplification 14.73; texts associated with this phase 14.73–4

the third stage
the apogee of its development 14.74; an attempt to create a special Buddhist language 14.74–5; the enumeration and classification of *dharmas* 14.73, 17.442–3; its categories criticized by Nāgārjuna 1.310–11; a 'gigantic card-index of the universe' 1.223, 14.75; analysis and classification of all existence 12.143; having analysed the bits, the problem is how to put them back together 19.236–7; it became a philosophy 14.75–6; originally metaphorical expressions became more literal 15.342; represented by the Abhidharma Piṭaka 14.74–88; thought that an analysis of *dharmas* would give a complete picture of reality 1.223

the fourth stage (post-Aśokan period)
the Abhidharma came to be regarded as embodying literal truth 3.359; carried an aspect of the original teaching to a logical conclusion 1.304; concern with the elaboration of technicalities 14.89; doctrinal systematization 14.88–91, 14.95; insistence that *dharmas* were real entities, *see under dharmas*/history/late Abhidharma; the Perfection of Wisdom challenged the Abhidharma's literalism 1.304, 3.359, 14.344; the story of the Buddha's response to the Great Book of the Abhidharma 14.91; their analysis contradicted the *anātman* doctrine 17.448–9; a transition from the practical and scholastic to the theoretical and philosophical 14.93; a work that reveals a synthetical and dynamic universe, like a motion picture 14.91; works associated with this stage 14.89–95

Mahāyāna and Vajrayāna
Nāgārjuna's refutation of the Abhidharma's analysis of *dharmas* 17.367–8; to counter the earlier doctrine, they taught the emptiness of all *dharmas* 17.448–9; the refinement of the Abhidharma vision of the universe 17.450–1; Tibetan and Chinese translations 14.82–4; the writings of Nāgārjuna and Asaṅga referred to as Mahāyāna Abhidharma 7.503; the Nyingma philosophers made a living experience of the Abhidharma 17.494; Zen has no time for Abhidharma studies 8.624

in modern times
the idea of formulating a modern Abhidharma 15.189; it is studied in an

academic way, not as a living thing 15.557; to be studied in its own critical spirit 17.447

ABHIDHARMA PIṬAKA

introduction
brief introduction 14.252; Abhidharma literature also includes works by Buddhaghosa and Vasubandhu 12.143, 17.447; an attempt to synthesize and elucidate the doctrines laid down in the *suttas* 1.223; composed over three centuries 14.78; an example of the scientific sort of Buddhist literature 14.110; the incorporation of the *Kathā-vatthu* 14.85; its place in the Tripiṭaka 12.142; two Abhidhamma Piṭakas, Theravādin and Sarvāstivādin 7.502, 12.142–3, 14.77–8, 17.441; difference between Theravādin and Sarvāstivādin 1.185, 17.441–2; some overlap with the Sutta Piṭaka 17.442; worship of the texts 2.225, 12.140

are the texts canonical?
not considered so by all Buddhist schools 14.77; those in the Chinese Tripiṭaka include works by Indian *ācāryas* 14.254, 14.261; those who saw the works as canonical 2.197, 7.502, 7.539, 14.76; refusal to accept them as the word of the Buddha 1.223, 14.77–8; treated as having canonical authority 14.76

Theravādin (Pāli)
introduction 1.102–3, 1.223, 12.142–3; taught by the Buddha to his mother 1.33, 1.255, 2.228, 12.143, 12.714–15 (n102), 13.586, 14.76, 17.442, 22.170; handed down by Śāriputra 12.143, 17.442; Buddhaghosa's commentary 12.143, 14.85; corrected what were seen as misrepresentations of the Dharma 14.85–6; list of works 14.78; the works contain no figures of speech (a proud boast) 16.16; *see also Dhammasaṅgaṇi*; *Vibhaṅga*; *Dhātu-kathā*; *Puggala-paññatti*; *Kathā-vatthu*; *Yamaka*; *Paṭṭhāna*

Sarvāstivādin (Sanskrit)
introduction 1.103, 1.174, 1.188, 1.223; accepted that the works were not by the Buddha himself 14.76, 17.442; devotion to the Abhidharma 7.504, 14.77; list of works 14.78; Vasubandhu's commentary 12.143; *see also Saṅgīti-paryāya*; *Dharma-skandha*; *Prajñapti-śāstra*; *Vijñāna-kāya*; *Dhātu-kāya*; *Prakaraṇa-pāda*; *Jñāna-prasthāna*

commentaries and summaries
Abhidhammattha-saṅgaha, see Abhidhammattha-saṅgaha; *Abhidharmasamuccaya, see under* Asaṅga; *Abhidharmakośa, see under* Vasubandhu; *Aṭṭhasalini, see under* Buddhaghosa; *Mahāvibhāṣāśāstra, see Mahāvibhāṣāśāstra*

Abhidharmasamuccaya *see under* Asaṅga

abhijjhā *see* covetousness

abhijñās **(Pāli *abhiññas*)** *see* six *abhijñās*

Abhimukhī **(Face-to-Face)** *see under* ten *bhūmis*

Abhinavagupta 26.327

abhinibbutatta 10.515

Abhiniṣkramaṇa Sūtra ('Discourse on the Great Renunciation') 12.182; astrologers predict the future of the Buddha-to-be 13.655; the Buddha expresses gratitude to the bodhi tree 3.596; a work belonging to the Dharmaguptika 2.13

Abhirati *see under* Akṣobhya

Abhirati community, Norfolk 4.225–7, 21.597

Abhisamayālaṃkāra *see* Maitreyanātha

abhiṣeka **(Tantric initiation)**

abhiṣeka
the meaning of *abhiṣeka* 2.169, 2.565, 4.266, 13.88, 13.159; a term from the ancient Indian coronation ceremony 2.169, 13.159–60, 22.502; bodhisattva *abhiṣeka* 7.477–8; four *abhiṣekas* 13.89–91

wongkur (or wangkur, Tibetan)
etymology 2.565, 5.575, 19.528–9; an *activation* of power 5.575, 13.88–9; bestowal of power whose source is in the founder of the lineage 7.474–5; a transmission of spiritual power from guru to disciple 13.88–9, 13.159; '*gelong-wongkur*' 7.483–4; what it really means 22.502

initiation ceremony
the disciple looks the teacher directly in the face 15.442; the hat worn 13.32–3; the initiation of body, speech, mind, and the unity of all three 12.20; initiation is an aspect of Going for Refuge 13.161; it is customary to make vows 18.161; introducing you and the Buddha or bodhisattva to each other 26.228–9; the mantra is given by the guru 13.290–1; ordeal 16.206; paying for initiations 4.611, 19.529–31, 26.34

the transmission
the activation of energies 18.75; if a lama without experience gives the initiation, not much happens 26.229; it is your own energy that you experience 13.161–2; like planting a seed 7.476; no lama can

transmit an *abhiṣeka* he has not been empowered to transmit 7.475; no one, not even the Buddha, can literally hand on their spiritual experience 13.161; not literally a transmission of power 19.529, 22.502–3; whether or not an initiation is 'Tantric' depends on the rapport between you 19.531–2; usually accompanied by the initiation of a guardian deity 13.208

the power of the initiation
better from someone who knows the practice than a rimpoche who doesn't 13.160–1; Gelugpas tease Nyingmapas about the power of their initiations 13.111, 18.498; great gurus are expected to have hundreds of *abhiṣekas* at their disposal 7.475–6; received from one's lama 12.17, 12.20

purpose and practice
a full initiation can be less effective than a simple blessing 4.266, 13.160; meditations are 'Tantric' only with initiation from a Tantric guru 13.89; only talking about the practice with someone with the same initiation 18.421, 18.476; some meditations are never practised without initiation 5.576; tantras can only be taken up after receiving the appropriate *abhiṣeka* 14.247; to embark on *sādhana* without the appropriate *abhiṣeka* is a waste of time 7.475; why have an initiation ritual at all? 13.160

differences and correlations
correlation between the *bardos* and the three Tantric initiations 12.206; difference between *abhiṣeka* and *saṃvara* ordination 2.447–8, 7.478; distinction between blessing (*chinlap*) and initiation 4.266–7, 13.160, 19.531

misuse of the tradition
commercialization 2.566, 19.530–1; 'empowerment' becoming fashionable 2.565–5; handing out initiations indiscriminately 19.488, 19.491, 19.546, 24.476; some people collect them like stamps 7.476, 18.468, 22.401; traditionally sacred, but devalued in modern times 3.331–2, 19.488; you don't need to go haring after Tantric initiations 19.544; *see also samaya*

Abhivinaya 2.203

abhūtaparikalpa (unreal imagination) 1.363–4, 1.369, 1.370

Abominable Snowman 25.246–7

abortion 8.610, 11.636–7, 13.451, 15.482–3, 17.196, 27.1072–3

absolute

what is the absolute?
the Higher Evolution is the conscious acceptance of its action 26.45; idealistic monism 1.87–8; it cannot be thought of as an object 'out there' 14.444–5; the Mahāyāna identifies the world of phenomena with it 1.268; the only affirmation possible is the negation of all affirmations 7.132; the phenomenal cannot in any way be related to it 7.132

the Buddha and the absolute
absolute and relative Buddha 14.211–12; in the notion of Buddha, humanity and the absolute coalesce 13.297; our conception of him must do justice to him as the unconditioned absolute 14.430

access to the absolute
absolute beauty 26.174, 26.176; 'doors' to the absolute 13.492; it responds to the beating of the golden drum 16.266; obscured by the unreal imagination 1.369; its reflection in the mirror of individual consciousness 1.283; a smash-and-grab raid 11.81; tension between religious and artistic absolutes 26.248–9; visualization practice as an approach 5.600; when the obscurations are removed, it shines forth 1.364

absolute and relative
the distinction is only relatively true 4.276, 16.454, 26.387–8; mind, *see under* mind/relative and absolute; switching between absolute and relative points of view 14.447–8; you need an absolute until you reach the point when you can do without it 4.590; *see also* reality/absolute reality; two truths

absorption you can forget your true purpose 19.9–10; absorbing the empirical self in the higher self 4.278–9; absorbing the experience of Enlightenment 2.22, 3.64–5, 10.262, 12.621; absorption in communication 18.478; absorption in quiet and evenmindedness is true happiness 18.343; Ālāra Kālāma is so absorbed that he didn't hear 500 bullock carts passing by 9.298; becoming absorbed in the Unconditioned 3.238; being so absorbed in what you're doing that there's no room for the ego 15.730–1; the competitive spirit can't function fully while your mind is absorbed in higher things 10.482–3; a musician completely absorbed in playing 15.731; only the more refined emotions can be absorbed into one's spiritual life 16.370; total absorption in the object of meditation 1.583, 3.352; the value of daily absorption

in a higher state of consciousness 12.555; we are absorbed in games, like the children in the burning house 16.74; when you are completely absorbed, there is no mental activity 10.602–3

abstract

abstract ideas
abstract thinking can run ahead of development, or even needs 26.39; abstraction has allowed us to reduce the chaos of our impressions to a cosmos 7.325; not very inspiring for most people 19.24–5; our positive emotions, not abstract ideas, keep us going 5.31, 26.30, 26.76; they can give us no idea of reality 14.588; they may not seem to impinge on 'real life', but we need to establish right view 3.292; we tend to take doctrines as abstract ideas 14.443

the Dharma and the abstract
the abstract medieval Indian mode of communication does not suit Buddhism 14.514; *ātman* is an abstraction, a mere name 10.159–60; don't use abstraction to set up fresh barriers between yourself and reality 1.88; we need to form a picture of suffering, not indulge in abstract speculations 1.128; the Buddha's thinking was not abstract and general, but concrete and particular 7.225; description of the goal in terms of abstractions may not carry conviction 2.127; the Dharma does not exist in the abstract 16.576; the Dharma is alive, not a system of abstract ideas 10.218; going from the more general and abstract to the more specific 18.413; an image gives a better idea of Buddhahood than an abstract definition 13.284–5; a middle way between an abstract ideal and one too close to where we are 19.182; reality is not abstract 5.596–7; the struggle between Buddhism and the abstract noun 3.398; the true nature of the Dharma cannot be comprehended abstractly 10.568

abstraction and emotion
it is easier to love 'humanity' than a single imperfect human being 7.328–9; one cannot adore an abstraction 2.128; you have to see the Transcendental not as dry and abstract, but as fascinating 19.24–5

dangers of abstraction
abstract terminology can introduce confusions that vitiate spiritual strivings 26.188; a general idea that does not correspond to anything you actually experience 14.588–9; preoccupying yourself with abstract ideas, you may lose your imagination 17.684–5; the problem with abstract analyses of world problems 3.613–14; the root error of humanity 7.325–7; the way things are conventionally divided up is a process of abstraction 19.240; the word 'Buddhism', like all abstractions, is a dangerous double-edged blade 7.225

see also
questions/abstract questions; concepts

absurdity fear of nuclear war appears absurd 7.343; from the perspective of reality the attainment of a goal becomes absurd 18.44–5; a shred of clothing caught on a branch shows Milarepa the absurdity of clinging 18.13; when you gain Enlightenment, you see that you always were Enlightened – absurd! 4.203, 18.45

Abū Sa'īd 25.381

abundance the abundance of Mahāyāna *sūtras* 16.336; achievements should be expressions of inner abundance 26.15; the earth made more abundant by the earth goddess 16.382; if you are truly generous you feel you are living in the midst of abundance 17.208; gold the colour of abundance 18.59; Ratnasambhava represents the abundance of the Enlightened mind 12.214

Abundant Treasures (Buddha) *see under White Lotus Sūtra*/the structure of the *sūtra*

abuse

physical
being sawn limb from limb without a thought of anger 1.437, 4.121, 13.577; the other person brought the stick, but you brought the body 4.119–20, 4.409, 10.482, 10.600; working on feelings about past abuse in the *mettā bhāvanā* 18.444

verbal
the Buddha explains how to deal with it 3.76, 3.546–7, 4.119, 10.481–2; the Buddha teaches the *bhikkhus* a verse with which to respond 10.539–40; 'the commotion will only last seven days' 10.539–40; one just has to bear it 10.541; Sangharakshita's sadness at being the object of abuse 22.172

academics *see* scholars

Acala *see* Achala

acalā (immovable) *see under* ten *bhūmis*

ācāryas (teachers)

Mahāyāna
were free to select whichever doctrines they were drawn to 1.367; included in the Tantric succession 1.382; most of them were born into brahmin families 1.381; not original thinkers but systematizers of traditional teachings 1.366–7; sages who had realized the transcendental import of the *sūtras* 1.298; Vasubandhu had equal prestige in Hīnayāna and Mahāyāna 1.365; venerated by the Mahāyāna 1.298–9; writers of *śāstras* (commentaries) 1.298, 1.359

other usage
responsible for training newly ordained *bhikṣu* 2.196–8; transmission of the Dharma through words 3.82, 14.17; your first *ācāryas* are your parents 3.70, 12.427

Accadhara, Ven. 10.131, 10.138

accanta (uninterrupted) 1.69

acceptance definitions of acceptance 8.585; despite disapproval 16.315; don't accept what is unskilful in your friends 12.481; the experience of being accepted and loved is deeply important to us 17.184–5; Dr Johnson's definition 12.480, 26.61; the quality of acceptance in the poetry of Sarojini Naidu 7.61; the unskilful in oneself is not to be accepted 8.584–6, 12.480–1, 15.520, 15.523, 26.61, 26.537

access concentration *see* neighbourhood concentration

Acchariya-abbhūta Sutta *see under Majjhima Nikāya*

accuracy difficulties arising from not defining terms accurately 7.289; Hogarth's satires are deadly accurate 3.508; importance of factual accuracy 2.376–7, 9.445; accustom yourself to accuracy of narration 10.576, 12.34; correcting children if they speak inaccurately 1.516–17, 12.34; inaccuracy of publishers' blurbs 16.491–2; make sure you convey what someone has said accurately in spirit and letter 2.377; Theravāda Buddhism's concern with verbal accuracy 16.240

accuta (deathless, immovable) 1.69, 15.58

Achala (bodhisattva) 4.194, 12.578

Achala, Dharmachari v24

achievement 'Achievement in meditation is the sprout' (Milarepa) 18.292–3; to attempt to achieve bodhisattvahood is heroic 4.445; feeling prematurely that you've really got there 18.252; how much one committed individual can achieve 23.405; be humble with regard to your spiritual achievements 18.165; even spiritual achievements can become fetters 15.341; the laws of thought are the foundation of every field of human achievement 26.201; meditation: the important thing is consistency, not the occasional brilliant achievement 4.149; ordination is not an achievement that sets you above other Buddhists 18.176; the path: not achievement of conscious goals but unfoldment of potentialities 2.111; people don't achieve much because they don't put all their emotions into what they are doing 13.242; religion: the achievement of a state of complete psychological wholeness 12.43; responding positively to people's pleasure in their achievements 4.319–20; should be expressions of inner abundance, not compensations for inner poverty 26.15; spiritual progress is not a matter of egoistically willed achievement 2.112; Stream Entry is an achievable goal 4.87; talking about something can make it happen 19.85, 25.104–5; never any flower of human achievement but some great sorrow lay at its root 7.389, 26.11; without unremitting effort nothing truly great is ever achieved 26.72

Achilles Achilles' heel 26.482; 'sing of the baneful wrath of Achilles' 3.513, 26.470, 26.481–2; the son of Thetis and Peleus 26.481–2; the purchase of a head of Achilles 23.266

Achrekar v22

acintya 16.448

acintya-vimokṣa, the 'inconceivable emancipation' 14.164, 16.445, 16.537

Acker, Hans 24.595

Ackerley, A. J. 24.389

acquisition the difference between acquisition and attainment 11.80–1; Enlightenment is not in the ultimate sense a personal acquisition 2.116; faith is innate, doubt acquired 26.35; it is taking something to ourselves which we haven't produced 11.81; the more we acquire, the less enjoyment our 'pleasures' bring 17.394; Rechungpa has acquired the teachings, but hasn't really 'got' them 18.491; remaining unmoved by acquisitions or fame 14.193; *samādhi* can't be acquired forcibly or artificially 2.260–1; spiritual practice reduced to the acquisition of merit 15.98, 15.647–50; when we learn a new language, we acquire a new soul 16.565

action and activity

IN THE DHARMA LIFE

Buddhism and action
action simplified into *mudrā* 7.320; the Buddha's actions were the overflow of his love for sentient beings 22.285; Buddhism has no means of enforcing uniformity of action in secular life 7.439; Buddhism is a religion of action 22.159–60; Buddhism says: 'Don't just react. Act!' 19.582; to be a Buddhist means to act, to speak out 8.xxxii; the five kinds of action 14.239–40; Going for Refuge is an action 8.573; association of certain reflections with certain actions (Vajrayāna) 19.329–30; the sacramental action of the Tantra 1.374; View, Practice, Action, Fruit 19.157–8, 19.380

action and Dharma practice
a balance of meditation, study, and external activities 4.461–3; combined with meditation 18.77; the constant repetition of positive actions is very important 17.525; every human activity has a spiritually demanding aspect 11.580; external activity and inner spiritual experience aren't necessarily incompatible 22.247–8; if you are busy with Dharma activities, keep up your meditation 19.550–1; knowledge of activity that is spiritually fitting 17.545; make whatever you are doing your spiritual practice 18.153–4, 19.330; most people naturally incline either towards activity or towards meditation 5.644, 5.648–9; no karmic retribution for actions performed out of great compassion 14.188; your life should be continuous practice 19.330

TAKING ACTION

preparing to act
becoming free to act with the help of someone else's advice 18.386; don't dwell so much on your limitations that you are inhibited from action 19.165; enter every activity having formed a clear intention 15.96; if you insisted on 'understanding' a sentence before acting, you would never act 14.566; spiritual friends can help you create a point of freedom from which to act 18.456–7; to stop someone acting in case they act wrongly removes their responsibility 7.245; transition between aesthetic contemplation and practical activity 14.523–4

what prompts action
animal instinct, child impulse, woman emotion, man reason 7.138; ideally we should act spontaneously, without self-recrimination 17.166; overcoming negative emotion by responding to what needs to be done 4.286–7; some actions are invariably the product of the ego-sense 7.282

acting
acting upon one's faith 18.219–20; aim to be fully and completely into what you are doing 10.602–5, 15.730–1; creative action 15.96; doing something for the first time and meeting obstacles 1.52; doing things, you can see where you have gone wrong 18.277; every action should be done with full mindfulness 10.158; goodwill must be expressed in action 1.533; give yourself wholly to what you are doing 15.115–16; prompt action 4.468; to feel alive, do something, experience yourself in action 26.62; to live we must act, so we are bound to make mistakes 17.434; total action, when one is fully involved in an act, with nothing left over 1.537; the transformation of action into service 7.302–3; we need productive activity for our physical and psychological well-being 15.280; you can be mindful and still act quickly 17.104–5; you learn what you are trying to do in the process of trying to do it 26.17

DECIDING WHAT TO DO

introduction
beware of the idea that our purpose is to fill our time with useful activities 16.522–4, 18.120, 26.16; don't depend on others to help you decide 18.388; every moment of awareness presents us with an opportunity to choose 15.174; the gods face the problem of what to do with their time, as do we 12.355; if you don't know, do something to help others 25.114; it might take a while to work it out 18.284–5; no one can really tell you what to do 19.555; people want someone to tell them what to do 12.232–3, 18.386; 'poems don't tell you what to do' 26.395, 26.399; some people are more interested in 'what is', others in 'what to do' 17.569; to begin with spiritual life is difficult because you don't know what to do 25.74; trying to decide before you have found out how to think and feel 7.373

what do you really want to do?
be honest with yourself 4.606; distinguishing between what we need to do to develop and what we want to do 4.91; do what you feel like doing 4.483–4, 10.604–5; everybody in the long run does what they want to do 15.361; exercising your own judgement 15.289; finding out 19.394–6; if someone is rationalizing, they give a lot of reasons for doing what they

want 19.334; it might be difficult, but it is what you deeply want to do 15.361; let your real desires surface 4.151–2; many people are alienated from what they really want to do 18.285; meditation helps you establish what you really want to do 18.522; the modern view that life, even spiritual life, is about doing what you feel like doing 17.638; notice your spontaneous reaction when you ask yourself 19.395; people want someone else to tell them 12.232–3; sit down quietly and ask yourself 18.452–3; on solitary retreat, ask yourself this question 19.276; if you don't know, stop doing anything until you know 4.483–7, 5.647, 10.603–4, 18.522–3; we are all free to do whatever we want to do 5.692, 12.232–3; 'What am I to do with my life?' 25.113–4; what if what you want to do is unskilful? 18.285

doing something you don't want to do
'It'll get in the way of my development' 11.451, 18.591; acknowledge the feeling and you may be able to transform it 19.395–6; if you don't feel like doing something, should you do it? 5.646–7, 10.604–5; if you don't want to do something, logical arguments to do it may irritate you 4.433; it isn't necessarily hypocritical to do something when you don't want to 5.374; knowing what you ought to do, but not wanting to do it 17.674; meditating when you don't want to 4.150, 5.373–5, 5.381–2

doing nothing
the choice is never action or inaction, but egoistic or empty action 7.407; doing nothing and engaging in activities are one and the same 5.646, 14.518–19; doing nothing is a creative activity 24.157; don't sit around imagining that the concept of emptiness exempts you from activity 7.414; for most people, creative work is 'doing nothing at all' 3.507, 18.267–8; happily doing nothing 5.645–6, 18.121, 26.16; having no emotional strength behind one's action 19.470; if you are sitting still doing nothing, at least you are causing no harm 18.342; the freedom of the gap between activities 4.486–7; 'Inaction in a deed of mercy becomes an action in a deadly sin' 8.215, 13.609; the 'job' of doing nothing in particular 14.522, 18.122; preferring to be active in a negative way than not active at all 18.457–8; remaining 'inactive' in the midst of action 7.410; sometimes it is better to do nothing 17.62, 19.355; we don't truly, authentically, do anything 11.50; without faith you can't do anything at all 17.17

REFLECTIONS ON ACTION

reflections
actions are neither good or bad, but 'thinking makes them so' 1.142, 7.282; actions may not be based on the afflictions of the past 10.622; consider how your actions stand in relation to Reality 26.17; emptiness, activity, and compassion: one thing seen from three points of view 7.413; everything we do is symbolical, or at least expressive 18.269; everything we experience is something that happens to us or something we do 17.476–7; if Man was a rational animal, knowing would be indistinguishable from doing 7.392; if you want something done, ask a busy man 10.176; it is wrong to distinguish between what a man is and what he does 26.18; karma is an action 8.573; peace is the seat of intensest activity 7.141; refusing to take responsibility for one's actions 13.609; solving the problem of egoless activity 7.408–9; taking stock of your actions 17.267; that one is able to do a thing is no reason for doing it 26.16; there is no person apart from their actions 15.318–19; we *are* our actions 11.47–8; what people think of as activity is often just passivity 19.582; you can tell what someone really believes by how they act 19.229–30; you can't ever be sure how somebody is going to act 18.382; you are what you do, and everything you do affects your being 15.374

action and thought
acting with the minimum of conscious thought one hurls oneself into rebirth 7.138; connection between thoughts and deeds 1.142–4; no action without thought (*Dhammapada*) 7.137–8; the power of mental actions 4.300; sometimes thought is luminous, but action is weak 7.138; there must be a balance between what you know and what you do 15.472; there needs to be continuity between thought and action 19.287; thought is a more fundamental fact of existence than action 7.137–8; thought and action are the static and kinetic aspects of will 7.138; thought is the intention of action 1.144

action and wisdom
action utterly divorced from wisdom is called *saṃsāra* 7.139; any action performed with *prajñā* can be considered a *pāramitā* 1.426; Nirvāṇa a state of harmonious and beneficent activity 2.102; wisdom utterly divorced from action is called *nirvāṇa* 7.139

PROBLEMS WITH ACTION

criticizing the actions of others
don't disparage people doing positive things, but try to help them 11.734; some people's only form of action is to get in the way of other people acting 10.604

neurotic activity
displacement activity 15.116; if you have become attached to activity for its own sake, you need some time off 4.479; masquerading as work 15.284; *vīrya* is not to be confused with neurotic activity or restlessness 4.478–9; we are neurotically busy, without any singleness of purpose 11.50

action in the world
actions society regards as good regardless of the state of mind behind them 7.282; everything done in this world is the action of a madman or madwoman 12.229; grasping is the most typical activity of worldly beings 1.232; most everyday actions are no better than the actions of a drunkard 3.195; shifting responsibility for one's actions from self to society 13.389; stupid and silly actions done by people befuddled and victimized by passion 4.407; you can act jargon as well as speak it 19.161

see also
ethics/actions have consequences; meditation/other aspects of life and practice; behaviour; four *saṃgraha-vastus*/beneficial activity (*artha-caryā*); bodhisattva/activity; compassion/compassionate activity; ethics/intentional or willed action; karma; Noble Eightfold Path/perfect action; right action; skilful action; unskilful action; *cetanā*

acting and actors the Buddha's condemnation of acting 1.547, 15.371; the danger for the actor of not being able to stop pretending 17.658; feeling as though one is acting a part 19.470; Sangharakshita acting in childhood 20.37

activism needs a basis of self-development 3.617; possible tactics, from petitions and marches to fasts and mass disobedience 12.346; protest against nuclear war must be non-violent 12.346–7; setting an example of impartiality, love for humanity, and non-violence 12.348–9; take an active interest in the material, moral, and spiritual welfare of your fellow citizens 7.439; the value of activism doubtful if it does not come from awareness 23.460–1

activity *see* action

Acton, Lord 13.555, 22.338

acupuncture *see under* medicine

Adam Kadmon 14.426

Adams, 'Samurai' William 26.677

adānaśīla **(a stingy person)** 11.307

adaptation adapting the Dharma, *see under* Dharma/relating to the Dharma; adapting spiritual practice to the character of the practitioner 7.313; Buddhism's spirit of adaptation 1.62–3, 1.189; the guru's personal precept adapted to the disciple's needs 18.393–4; the need to adapt to changing conditions 1.229, 12.470–1; *White Lotus Sūtra* adapted to suit the varying capacities of different people 16.42

adbhuta-dharmas **(Pāli** ***abbhuta-dhamma*****)** (marvellous events) 14.24–5, 16.235, 17.571

addiction Abhidharma analysis of addiction 17.512–14; the addictions of the people of Sāvatthi 10.616–18; a bodhisattva who appears as a courtesan to teach those addicted to carnal pleasure 1.448–9; from passion to greed to infatuation to addiction to intoxication 10.616–17; to drugs *see* drugs; self-deception in the way we justify our addictions 17.257

Addison, Joseph compared with Shakespeare 14.349; *Spectator* essays 8.169–72, 8.681 (n105), 14.292, 22.101, 22.171

adharma 7.256, 26.159

adhikaranaśamatha **or** ***adhikaraṇasamatha*** 2.195

adhimokṣa 17.535

adhiśīla, adhicitta, adhiprajñā 1.446

adhiṣṭhāna (roughly 'grace, blessing') a transmuting force or power that descends from above in the spiritual hierarchy 12.14; alternative translations 16.518–19; analogous to the Muses 16.519; the blessing of the guru 4.265–7; feeling the guru's *adhiṣṭhāna* in the guru yoga 13.217; flows from the Buddhas and bodhisattvas all the time 7.474, 16.519; equivalent to Tibetan *chin lab* 12.14, 16.519, 18.537; grace-waves, *see* grace-waves; the influence of a Buddha in the *dharmadhātu* or Buddha-field 3.243–4; it can affect you positively if you make yourself open to it 19.285; it is essentially this that is known as the teaching 12.14; 'sustaining power' 14.224, 14.261; and Mañjuśrī 16.520, 16.555; and spontaneity 16.520

Adhiṣṭhāna retreat centre *see under* Triratna IV/retreat centres

Adhyardhaśatikā *see Perfection of Wisdom in 150 lines*

adhyāsavāda *see under* Śaṅkara

Adhyāśayasasaṃcodana Sutra an inflated mind 17.663; 'Whatever is well said, that is the word of the Buddha' 3.168, 3.394, 7.457, 9.198

adhyeṣaṇa 1.412

Adi Granth 16.58–9

Ādibuddha all personalities are embraced by the One Personality, the primordial *ādi*-Buddha 7.304; correcting the misunderstanding of him as a Creator God 7.535–6; naked, because all veils have been removed 13.65; often depicted in the *yab-yum* position 13.65; on the top storey of a Tibetan temple 13.65; the originator of a lineage 18.94; the primeval, Absolute Buddha 13.65; Samantabhadra as Ādibuddha, *see under* Samantabhadra; symbolizes the timeless nature of Enlightenment 18.94; Vajradhara as Ādibuddha, *see under* Vajradhara

Ādibuddha Tantra *see* tantras/works

ādikarmika-bodhisattva *see under* bodhisattv/four kinds

Āditta-pariyāya Sutta (the Fire Sermon) *see under Saṃyutta Nikāya*/famous *sūttas*

Adivasi 10.178, 24.116–17, 24.632 (n138)

adjustment adjusting to other people's views at the expense of your own convictions 18.461; adjusting your lifestyle according to your own judgement 18.212–13; adjustment therapy and character therapy 12.226–7; adjustment therapy can't be a Refuge 15.588; the bodhisattva practises four virtues: creative adjustment, morality, tenderness, sacrifice 1.354; recognize what your observation tells you about yourself and adjust accordingly 18.11; Sangharakshita felt no need to 'adjust' to new surroundings 23.57, 23.453; a weakness of psychotherapy to think in terms of adjusting to existing conditions 12.100–1

Adler, Alfred 12.93

admiration Buddhism is prepared to respect and even admire other spiritual leaders 2.243; Buddhism's spirit of admiration 3.62–4; Going for Refuge to the Buddha is not just admiration of his personality 3.325; a lover may claim to admire the mind while thinking of the body 4.561; a nun who plucked out her eyes to give to the young man who admired them 4.557, 4.712 (n349); you can admire all the manifestations of the ideal, even those you don't follow 18.222–3

adornment the Buddha 'adorned with virtues' 17.326–7; the Mahāyāna *sūtras* magnificently adorned 16.530; on Goldsmith: 'He touched nothing that he did not adorn' 26.490; plates adorned with peacocks 24.104; 'That which we love, we adorn' 16.530, 26.300, 26.395

adosa *see* non-hatred

adultery *see under* precepts/third precept

Advaita Vedānta

introduction
brief introduction 23.490 (n128); the diluted Vedantism of the Ramakrishna Mission 20.148; an irascible ascetic: 'No one has given way to anger!' 14.565, 20.383–4; it gets along very well without God 12.7; knowledge rarely backed up with *dhyāna* 14.565; the main currents of Indian thought are derived from it 9.570 (n342); a muddled response to the idea that everything is God 18.632–3; negativity 7.134; one of the alternatives before mankind 13.513

teachings
attavāda view of reality 7.131–2, 7.586 (n228); *brahman* 7.78–80, 7.95, 7.98, 7.229, 16.449; change and changelessness 7.131–2; confusing use of the term self 7.211–12; dreamless sleep 17.340–1; the self 14.459, 16.173; four *mahāvākyas* 7.78, 7.572 (n141); *jivanmukta* 20.239–40; *māyā* (illusion) 16.454; Raja Yoga 21.461; taking the teachings the wrong way 12.268; *upāsana* 7.78, 7.572 (n142); *vikṣepa-śakti* and *āvaraṇa-śakti* 7.101

and Buddhism
their conceptions of absolute mind differ 14.200; Buddhist doctrines that were perhaps taken over by the Vedānta 10.50; contrast with Mahāyāna Buddhism 16.454; influenced by Madhyamaka school of Buddhism 1.323; is Nirvāṇa identical with the Vedantic *ātman*? 7.211–13; *Vedānta and Buddhism* (von Glasenapp) 8.383; what is the relation of the Vedānta to Buddhism? 7.72

see also
Gauḍapāda; Śaṅkara; Upanishads

advanced advanced meditation practices 5.686–7; are the *brahma vihāras* advanced

practices? 5.196; the desire for more advanced knowledge 18.166–7; don't stop doing the basic practices too 25.74; friendship with people who are more spiritually advanced than we are 3.604, 4.172, 11.506, 15.586; letting your natural desires flow freely is an advanced stage 4.625; the Madhyamaka is so advanced that you can't do much with it until *you* are very advanced 4.590; the more advanced the stage, the less there is to say about it 1.579–80; some religions are more advanced than others 16.77; the spiritual snobbery of only wanting advanced teachings 18.517–18, 19.531; spiritually advanced people die in the *dhyāna* state 2.231; successively advanced insight 7.509; the Tibetans' interest in advanced teachings 18.167, 19.531

advantage the advantages of meditation (*Samādhirāja Sūtra*) 14.193; the advantages of modern medicine 24.332; advantages of simplicity 10.396; the advantages of a supportive upbringing 15.270; the advantages you are born with 15.407; 'Great becomes the fruit, great the advantage …' 4.645, 7.507, 8.92; if you took full advantage of Buddhist centre facilities, you could become a Stream Entrant 12.377–8; taking advantage of meditation facilities 8.219; trying to see honestly which circumstances of our life are advantageous 18.148

advaya see 'not-two'

Advayacitta, Dharmachari v24

Advayavajra one of the 84 *siddhas* 1.382

Advayavajra (Arya Maitreya Mandala) 11.561, 11.563, 12.584

adventitious defilements *see* defilements

adventure the adventures of the soul among books 26.335; Buddhism is the beginning of a great spiritual adventure 7.186; have curiosity, a spirit of adventure: the lesson of the four sights 10.256; monastic life degenerated from a spiritual adventure to a safe investment 1.228; the sheer adventure of the spiritual life 16.487, 17.413

advertisements advertisements for the Catholic Church 8.252–4; advertisements obscene 25.186; advertising in a Buddhist magazine 8.153–4; designed to create mental pleasure 17.393; dismay at the advertisement of animal products 21.53; emotional blackmail: 'Now will you care?' 19.68; geared to stimulating craving 4.74, 4.384, 11.6, 15.288, 17.196–7; in the *Maha Bodhi* journal 8.644; practice of the fourth precept includes not sponsoring misleading advertising 26.669; their power 9.443; responding to them with the reactive mind 11.22; tell us what to think and feel 7.266–7; will the Buddhist world realize the importance of advertising? 8.253–4

advice

asking for advice
asking your *kalyāṇa mitra* for advice 18.369, 19.462; the difference between asking advice and putting yourself in someone's hands 18.385–6; if we hear the advice of a bodhisattva, best to consult our friends too 12.573; many people ask for spiritual guidance, but very few can act upon it 4.67; people may twist advice into approval 18.368; people want someone to tell them what to do 12.232–3, 18.386; wanting approval even when you are ignoring advice 18.363–4, 18.404; you can't give good advice to yourself, so ask your friends 19.355

responding to advice
becoming free to act with the help of someone's advice 18.386; consider your spiritual friend's advice very seriously 18.623; finding reasons to ignore advice 18.366; no one can really tell you what to do 19.555; Sangharakshita on the receiving end of advice as a young man 21.150; take a spiritual teacher's advice seriously, but take responsibility for yourself 17.308; you have to understand which advice applies to you 19.164–5

giving advice
advice at the moment of death 12.202; advice is often a gift best withheld 17.202; are you prepared to ask hard questions? 17.615; be clear about your own problems, or you won't be able to help 17.615; do we really know what is truly best for someone? 18.184; don't give advice unless you know what you're talking about 18.623–4, 19.355; empathy for someone to whom you are giving advice 18.625; giving advice to young people 18.624; giving advice too readily 19.555; if someone is likely to do whatever you say, be careful not to give an opinion 17.615; making it clear that the recipient is completely free to accept it or not 18.488–9; Sangharakshita's attitude to giving advice 18.623; 'Those who give help cannot refrain from offering advice' 22.104; to give specific advice you need to know the person well 18.369, 19.100, 19.491; well-meaning advice can do a lot of harm 19.355

givers of advice
the Buddha's advice to *bhikkhus*, *see under* *Udāna*/the people of the *Udāna*; a fool can give more advice in a day than a wise man can follow in a year 26.80; a friend who was fond of giving advice 26.559–60; Milarepa's handling of a disciple who won't take his advice 18.364–9; monks as givers of worldly advice 2.216–17, 3.410, 4.67; one's parents often give bad advice 19.355; some people are offended if their advice is not taken 19.364–5

Adyananda, Swami 7.107, 7.108

Adyar *see under* Madras

Aelred of Rievaulx 13.618–19, 24.387

Aeneas 24.548, 26.482

Aeneid *see* Virgil

Aeschylus 3.427, 23.292–3

Aesop fables 3.427; the fox and the grapes 22.87; the quarrelsome brothers and the bundle of sticks 8.182; similar stories in the *Jātakas* 14.64; the town mouse and the country mouse 22.348

aestheticism aestheticism is not enough 25.28–9; be careful the religion of art doesn't become aestheticism 26.396; spiritual life can become refined aestheticism 17.694–5

aesthetics

aesthetic appreciation
the aim is to bring it to whatever circumstances we meet 14.520, 17.227; akin to resting in pure awareness 17.227; artistic and culinary taste 15.294, 18.131–3; the aesthetic pleasure of the bodhisattva ideal 7.321; aesthetic self-indulgence: 'The Palace of Art' 26.149–51, 26.173–4; the aesthetics of a beautiful action 15.348–9; the bodhisattva's experience: the greater mandala 14.517–24, 26.64; to counteract craving for sensuous experience 5.344–6, 15.286–8, 17.271, 26.68; delighting in oneself and others 5.125; distinguishing objective from subjective aesthetic appreciation 17.695–6; a hierarchy of degrees of aesthetic development 18.132; the poet should be familiar with the philosophy of aesthetics 26.146; pure delight in the object of contemplation for its own sake 17.222, 26.68; Schiller's *Letters on Aesthetics* 12.695; seeing someone's inner beauty as well as their weaknesses 15.293–4; transition between aesthetic contemplation and practical activity 14.523–4

aesthetic experience
aesthetic enjoyment and artistic creation anticipate the Good Life 26.191; aesthetic experience is not everyday perception 26.327; aesthetic perception (*saṃjñā*) and the *dhyānas* 17.516–17; the aesthetics of order and cleanliness 23.169; analogies with religious or mystical experience 26.327–8; can be superficial and untransforming 16.285; contacting the *sambhogakāya* 4.208; in the god realm 13.130–1; how often is one really carried away by a work of art? 17.396; its diamond or *vajra* aspect 7.403; the difference between emotion and aesthetic experience 26.326–7, 26.362; it doesn't necessarily reflect the golden light of the Dharma 16.285; immersing ourselves in the aesthetic life 26.99–100; on the level of the *rūpaloka* 13.279; one is quickly surfeited by even the most refined aesthetic pleasure 17.395; part of its value is that it lifts you out of yourself 16.285; a relishing of things (*vidyā*) 14.516–17, 15.472, 17.608–9, 19.219; Schopenhauer on aesthetic and mystical experience 17.608; the state of mind of the god realm 13.130

approaches to aesthetics
aesthetic impoverishment (Far Eastern art) 7.321; the Aesthetic Movement 26.149, 26.710 (n82); the aesthetics of shrines 19.128; duality between the aesthetic and the ethical (Kierkegaard) 26.396; the state should help its citizens lead an aesthetic life 26.184; there is no incompatibility between the spiritual and the aesthetic approach 26.383; thinking of the process of Enlightenment in aesthetic terms 18.447

Indian aesthetics
kāruṇya rasa (pity) 24.564; *rasa-śāstra*, 'aesthetic relish' 10.567; the *rasas* of Indian poetics 26.324–8

affection affectionate speech, *see under* speech/four levels; combination of respect and affection: contrast in India and the West 4.610–11; 'From affection is born grief' (*Dhammapada*) 1.158; 'the holiness of the heart's affections' (Keats) 25.xxxiv, 25.17; sticky affection, *see sneha*, *pema*

affinity affinity with an old recluse: 'wings fluttering within me' 20.222; an affinity between intense mental suffering and Enlightenment 13.134; an affinity with Green Tārā 22.374–5, 22.395; avoid close association *only* with those with whom you feel affinity 26.31; craving at least indicates an affinity for other people 4.389, 17.601; 'the eye could not behold the sun unless

it had something in it that was like the sun' 3.58; an affinity with Enlightenment 3.301, 11.104; a friendship based on spiritual affinity 23.109–11; hatred has an affinity with wisdom 4.392–3, 13.132–3, 18.577, 26.478–9; karma-affinity, *see* karma-affinity; the meaning of the word 18.303; tolerance a point of affinity of the English with Buddhism 12.75; we can appreciate works of art because we have an affinity with them 3.57–8; we have within us something that has an affinity with the transcendental 16.561

Afghanistan Buddhas of Bamiyan 21.45, 26.475–9; the order to destroy all images 25.32

Africa Kenya 22.261–2; a study of spirit-possession in Africa 4.548–9; who is taking the Dharma there? 8.xxix, 8.277–8; the wildlife of Africa 18.23–4, 25.52; Zimbabwe 26.654

Agamananda, Swami 20.253, 20.265, 20.298

Āgamas Āgama passages cited and explained in the Abhidharma 14.83; Sanskrit texts corresponding to the first four Nikāyas of the Pāli Sutta Piṭaka 7.501, 7.526; *Ekottarikāgama* (= Aṅguttara Nikāya) 7.501; *Dīrghagama* (= *Dīgha Nikāya*) 7.501, 14.81, 14.84; *Madhyamāgama* (= *Majjhima Nikāya*) 7.501; *Saṃyuktāgama* (= *Saṃyutta Nikāya*) 7.501

Agastya (rishi) 26.224–5, 26.678

Agatha, St 13.631

the Age of Aquarius *see under* New Age

Aggañña Sutta *see under Dīgha Nikāya*

Aggivacchagotta Sutta *see under Majjhima Nikāya*

Aggivessana (Saccaka, the Jain ascetic) 2.110–11

aggregates *see* five *skandhas*

aggressiveness curbing as preparation for meditation 3.338; expressed through play 16.301; some people seem to invite aggression 4.410

agitation how one first aspires to become a bodhisattva 2.156; there is agitation for one who is dependent 10.637–8, 10.724 (n505)

agnosticism agnostic principle (18th century) 8.588; agnosticism with respect to rebirth 8.577; healthy agnosticism about knowledge 8.587–8; it is doubtful whether Socrates was an agnostic 8.588; it would be a mistake to conclude that the Buddha was agnostic 1.78–80; 'agnostic faith': term coined by T. H. Huxley 8.588

Agra introduction 21.521; Agra Fort 23.411–12; a Buddha Vihara in Agra 22.341–2; Sangharakshita visits 21.519, 22.340–2, 23.411–12; Taj Mahal 22.340–1, 23.412, 25.283; the tomb of Mirza Ghiyath Beg 23.412

agreement accepting only what is in agreement with reason and our own experience 21.505; agreement about the Dharma after the Buddha's death 11.369–70; agreement that a rose is beautiful 25.259; Buddhism and science agree that nothing in the world is solid 22.29; don't get bogged down in argument when there is substantial agreement 19.138–9; harmony cannot just consist in agreement 18.502; it should be possible to maintain harmony even when there is disagreement 12.677; receptivity doesn't necessarily mean agreeing 19.581; *samaya, see samaya*; to be tolerant does not mean you have to agree with what others say 12.677

agriculture *see* farming

Agrippa 8.560

āḥ (seed syllable) 18.321–2

ahaṃkāra (ego-maker) 4.630, 4.633

Ahicchatra 2.156

ahiṃsā *see* non-violence

Ahmedabad brief introduction 21.574–5; All-India Religions Conference (Dharma Parishad) 9.279, 9.449–50, 20.172–8; Bapunagar 9.459, 9.477; a brahmin-born Buddhist woman 23.345; celebration of Anandamayi's birthday 20.179–80; celebration of the Buddha Jayanti (1947) 9.450; Conference of Scheduled Castes Federation, 1945 9.63; factionalism in the Buddhist community 23.343; Ganpatnagar 9.476; Maha Bodhi Ambedkar Mission 10.160; Majuragaon 9.466; meeting with Jains 23.347; photograph 23.344; revival of Buddhism 9.158, 9.450–1; riots in 1985 10.62, 10.673–4 (n95); Sabarmati Ashram 23.347; Sangharakshita visits 9.158–9, 9.459–85, 10.155–9, 10.160, 10.296, 20.172–8, 23.334, 23.336, 23.343–7, 24.111–17; Saraspur 24.112; Sarkhej Roza 9.477–8; Sidi Sayeed Mosque 23.346–7; TBMSG developments 24.53, 24.117

Ahmednagar district, India 9.292, 10.143, 10.161–2

āhrīkya *see* shamelessness

Ahuja, Prof. N. C. v21

Aid for India *see* Karuna Trust

AIDS *see under* sickness

aims (well-being, happy rebirth, Enlightenment) *see* three aims

air element in the six element practice, *see under* six elements; associated with a pale green and a shallow bowl shape (stupa) 13.153, 16.147; the bodhisattva breathes reality 14.590; correlated with the psychic centre at the throat 16.147; experienced in the world 16.145; symbolism 13.154–5, 16.145–6

aiśvarya (autonomy) 10.592, 10.719 (n467)

Aitken, Roshi Robert 8.610, v24

Aivanhov, Omraam Mikhael v24, 25.418

Ajahn Sumedho v13

Ajakalāpaka the *yakkha* (*Udāna*) 10.451–4

Ajanta (Indian film) 21.399–413, 22.276

Ajanta caves *see under* caves

Ajātasattu (Ajātaśatru), Prince (King)

his political life
Devadatta urges him to seize the throne of Magadha 2.27; he imprisons his father, King Bimbisāra, and his mother, Queen Vaidehī 3.453, 3.571, 20.464; he kills his father 9.574 (n384), 16.274–5; he threatens to kill his mother 3.571; he plans the destruction of the Vajjians 2.28, 7.438

he visits the Buddha seeking peace of mind
the full text 26.156–7; Ajita Keskambalī tells him there is no karma and rebirth 12.757; he sets out on a moonlit night 3.77; he is afraid that Jīvaka is leading him into a trap 10.501; the silence fills him with a nameless dread 15.103; the sight of the Buddha and his disciples in silence 2.200, 10.274–5, 12.308–9; 'Oh that my son might experience such peace of mind!' 4.16, 10.287, 12.309, 12.676, 26.157; the fruits of the religious life 14.18–19; the Buddha tells him about mindfulness 1.150; Ajātaśatru's confession 16.274–5

in the Mahāyāna
his 12-year-old daughter (in a *sūtra*) 14.184; not present at the *parinirvāṇa* 14.233

ajātavāda *see under* Gauḍapāda

Ajita (bodhisattva) the Buddha warns him against harbouring doubts 1.331; another name for Maitreya 1.330

Ajita, Dharmachari v24, 24.637–8 (n158)

Ajita Kesa-Kambalin (Keskambalī) taught nihilism at the time of the Buddha 1.74; told King Ajātasattu there is no karma and rebirth 12.757

ājīva-pārisuddhi-sīla *see under* four *pārisuddhi sīlas*

Ajmer *see under* Rajasthan

akāliko *see under Tiratana Vandanā*

akaniṣṭha (Pāli ***akaṇiṭṭha***) *see under* heavens

Ākankheyya Sutta *see under Majjhima Nikāya*

ākāśa does it represent the transcendental? 16.160; etymology, 'to shine' 13.152, 16.145; halfway between matter and spirit or consciousness 16.145, 16.160; of the heart 16.160; one's inner visionary experiences take place within an inner, imaginal space 13.152; the 'living space' within which everything lives 3.350, 16.146; the primordial energy of which the other four elements are grosser manifestations 16.145; space is light and light is space 13.152; 'space' is a misleading translation 16.160; 'that which maintains all beings' 11.282–3; we all have some direct experience of *ākāśa* 13.152; *see also* space element

Ākāśadhātviśvarī (or Ākāśadhāteśvarī) 12.203, 12.222, 13.313

Ākāśagarbha 2.172

Akasati, Dharmacharini (Anne McAuley) v24

Akashadeva, Dharmachari (David Earl) 24.589, 24.760 (n781)

Akashagarbha, Dharmachari v24

Akashavana, women's retreat centre *see under* Triratna IV/retreat centres

akaṭa (increate, not compounded) 1.69, 15.58

akataññutā *see* ingratitude

Akbar, Jal-ud-Din Mohammed (emperor) 7.86, 12.245, 22.90

Akhenaten *see under* Egypt

akiñcana abides free of grasping 1.173, 10.634; he is no longer bound to conditioned existence 10.489; an early

term for the *arhant* in the *Sutta-Nipāta* 4.358, 10.486; in the *Dhammapada* 1.173, 15.53; one who has nothing because he is nothing 3.144

akiñcanyāyatana (sphere of no-thing-ness) *see under dhyānas/arūpa*

Akkosaka Bhāradvāja 3.693–4 (n477)

Akong Rimpoche 23.129, 25.92

Akṣayamati 17.773 (n548); his hymn to Avalokiteśvara in the *White Lotus Sūtra* 1.336, 2.176, 16.178–9

Akṣayamati-paripṛcchā Sūtra introduction 14.186–7; the bodhisattva's cultivation of vigour 17.69; five spiritual faculties as successive stages of the path 1.291–2; how the bodhisattva is to cultivate the ten perfections 14.186; *prajñā* without *upāya* fetters one to *nirvāṇa*, *upāya* without *prajñā* fetters one to *saṃsāra* 7.139–40; an account of the bodhisattva's qualities and a survey of the bodhisattva Vinaya 14.186–7

Akshobhya, Dharmachari v24

Akṣobhya brief description 4.207; his name means unshakeable, immoveable, imperturbable 13.308; Abhirati, his Pure Land 1.335, 14.166, 14.175, 16.459, 16.569; appears in Ruciraketu's house in the *Sūtra of Golden Light* 16.258, 16.261; association with Vajrapāṇi 2.172; head of the *vajra* family 13.309; his animal is the elephant 12.203, 13.309; his appearance in the *bardo* after death 12.203–4; his consort, *see* Locanā; his dark blue colour is like the midnight sky 12.213, 13.308; his emblem is the vajra 4.207, 12.213, 13.308; in a Five Buddha *caitya* in Nepal 20.430; in the mandala of the Five Buddhas 3.374, 4.207, 12.213–14, 13.308–9; mirror-like knowledge or wisdom (*jñāna*), *see under* five *jñānas*; *mudrā*, *see under mudrās*; the patron Buddha of people of choleric temperament 13.133; practically the only Buddha to appear in the Perfection of Wisdom *sūtras* 13.315, 14.138; Ratnoccaya in a previous life 16.390; he represents the adamantine, indestructible, *vajra* aspect of Enlightenment 13.169; represents overcoming the self 18.598–9; as *sambhogakāya* 2.42; seems to have been the central figure of a myth similar to that of Amitābha 1.335; the Tantra identified him with the *vijñāna-skandha* 1.376–7

Akṣobhya-vyūha 14.175

akuśala *see* unskilful

akuśala-mūlas *see* three roots

Alagaddūpama Sutta *see under Majjhima Nikāya*

alaṃkāras literary ornament 26.330; in commentaries, *see under śāstras*

Āḷāra Kālāma (Ārāḍa Kāḷāma) his teaching to Siddhārtha was not wrong but inadequate 1.58; taught Siddhārtha how to enter the sphere of no-thingness 1.166, 2.20–1; he invited Siddhārtha to share his leadership 2.21; the Buddha's instinct to teach him the Dharma 1.58, 11.413; so absorbed that he didn't hear 500 bullock carts passing by 3.667–8 (n271), 9.565 (n286)

Alaungyi (Burma Raja's son) v21, v22

Alaya, Dharmachari v24, 24.636 (n153), 26.565–6, 26.760 (n538)

ālaya-vijñāna *see* eight *vijñānas*

Al-Ghazālī (Sufi mystic) 3.429

Al-Ghazālī, Imam (*The Duties of Brotherhood in Islam*) 5.177–82, 26.688

Albers, Miss A. Christine 20.167–72, 20.213–14, 21.377

Alberti, Leon Battista 23.314, 23.523 (n359)

Albigenses *see* Cathars

alchemy an alternative Western tradition 13.374; the dross of mundane experience is transmuted into the gold of transcendental experience 7.403; the Great Work 4.370, 25.267; St Jerome as alchemist 2.527, 26.267; and Jung 12.184; the mythological system of alchemy: gnomes, undines, salamanders, sylphs 15.139; the union of fire and water: the marriage of the red king and the white queen 12.184–5, 26.267

Alcibiades compares Socrates to a satyr 10.619, 10.721–2 (n488); his influence over the Athenians 15.351–2

alcohol alcohol and *amrta* 19.332–3; alcohol used in Tibetan ritual 13.25, 22.399; drinking, *see* drinking

alertness the *bodhicitta* could arise without any preparation, so be alert 4.272–3; the Buddha like an alert, perfectly tamed elephant 4.706 (n313); on retreat, a combination of relaxation and alertness 23.134; one who is alert, active, and proud is invincible to the greatest foe 4.477; to expose wrong views requires practice, intelligence, alertness, and confidence 10.587; remain alert and mindful during everyday activities to support your meditation practice 5.652; suffering loss alerts us to our attachment 3.280–1

Alexander the Great 11.250–1

Alexandria *see under* Egypt

Alfred, King statue in Winchester [not King Arthur, as text states] 24.194, 24.253; he wrote *Consolation of Philosophy* in a time of darkness 4.658

Ali, Muhammad 15.413–14

Ali, Ramzam 26.692–4

Alice in Wonderland see Carroll, Lewis

alienation

what is alienation?
dictionary definition 18.608; *avidyā* as a sense of alienation and conflict 14.517; be careful to use the word in the strict sense 10.73; alienated energy 18.610; the alienated intellect 18.399–400, 19.178–83, 26.77; the alienated self 4.271, 10.602; alienated understanding and understanding with feeling 19.178–80; alienation and the language of potential 18.607; alienation from feelings, *see under* emotions/working with emotions; alienation from one's true nature (*White Lotus Sūtra*) 16.91–2, 16.173, 16.200, 16.219–20; alienation from reality 2.252, 16.93; alienation from society 18.335; confusion between alienation and non-attachment 17.509; many people are alienated from what they really want to do 18.285

causes of alienation
how does it arise? 12.264–8; the alienating effect of modern travel 18.337; alienation from nature in modern life 12.217, 15.236, 18.22–4, 25.54–5; applying metaphysical teachings psychologically 12.268; danger of alienation in the higher imaginative faculty 19.189–90; danger of developing it when we are new to Buddhism 12.266–7; does meditation cause it? 4.105, 5.459–60; meditating in a dangerously alienated way 12.267–8, 17.88–9, 23.45, 23.71–3; in modern times 'lack of attachment' may be due to alienation 18.331–2, 18.336–7; an inevitable stage in the development of the individual 15.743; living in a world in which we are foreigners and aliens 16.220; in the past aggravated by Eastern spiritual teachers 3.488, 12.267–8; repressions uncovered during analysis 16.97; 'watching' one's bodily movements 17.103–4

what is alienated awareness like?
introduction 3.487–8, 16.301; alienation from the body 12.265; being aware of ourselves without experiencing ourselves 3.487, 5.31, 12.263, 15.114–15; a cold, separated awareness 14.515–16; distinction from integrated awareness 12.263–4; an eerie feeling of not being at one with what you are doing 10.602–3; mistaking alienated awareness for mindfulness 4.602, 10.463, 12.259; non-experience of feelings and emotions 5.31, 12.265–6, 26.65; non-experience of thoughts 7.266–7, 12.266; quite a dangerous state 12.263; self-consciousness of an unhelpful kind 15.730

means of overcoming alienation
art 26.67; how to develop self-consciousness without alienation 19.181–2; professional help 12.268

Aligarh, India 9.151

alive all is not well with you simply because you remain alive 10.534; animism, *see* animism; being 'mindful' without really being alive 12.268, 23.463; the Dharma a shoreless ocean, alive with light and colour 11.43; the Dharma is fresh, alive 25.30–1; the Dharma is not a system of abstract ideas, it is *alive* 10.218, 14.98; Dudjom Rimpoche's delight in being alive 22.508; 'How wonderful it was to feel oneself alive in a world of living things!' 24.38; looking for experiences that make us feel more alive 11.78–9; to feel alive, do something, experience yourself in action 26.62; the universe is alive, magically so 4.14–15, 15.136–9; very sensitive, very alive 5.400; the Void is alive with unleashed energy 18.74

al-Kindi 8.604

Allahabad, India 10.627

Allan, Ian 24.31

Allen, Marguerite 22.131

Alles, Joseph (*Buddhist World*) 8.637, 22.168, 22.174–6

All-India Dharma Parishad *see under* Ahmedabad

Allen, G. F. (Y. Siri Nyana) introduction 8.698 (n264); *The Buddha's Philosophy* 2.188; *Buddhist Wisdom for the West* (review) 8.361–3; letter from a 'sincere European Buddhist' 8.129–31; suggestion that a uniform system of referencing Pāli quotations is needed 8.130–1; suggestions about working out a chronology of the Pāli canon 8.131, 22.170–3

Almora, India 10.160, 21.572, 21.575, 23.412–14

alms and almsfood (Sanskrit *bhikṣā*, Pāli *bhikkhā*) Anuruddha and his friends describe their almsround 12.606; 'bad food should not be put in a jewelled bowl' 14.161–2, 16.506–7; the *bhikkhus* are insulted when they go for alms 10.539; the Buddha vomited the first time he tried to eat almsfood 3.50, 3.633–4 (n48), 20.417; Buddhist conventions about begging for alms 10.518, 20.415–16; a Christian nun seeking alms in Italy 23.303; description of the monk's alms collection tour 3.589–90, 16.405; *madhukari bhikṣā*, collecting alms like the bee collects honey 3.590; giving alms to wanderers meritorious 10.479; Mahākassapa goes for alms among the weavers 10.447–9; Milarepa visits a village to get food 18.195–7; in modern times it is not possible to beg for alms 11.187–8; a monk shouldn't beg for alms outside a wine shop or a brothel 18.394; offered to monks as honoured guests 2.226; Sakka, ruler of the *devas*, gives almsfood to Mahākassapa 10.515–6; *samaṇa* and *bhikkhu* as overlapping terms for alms-mendicants 10.479; Sangharakshita goes for alms 7.426, 20.338, 20.414–18, 21.11–16; a set routine 10.556; to ask people to support you, you need faith and yearning for the Dharma 19.352–3; ulterior motives for going for alms 10.517–19; wise use of almsfood (as monastic requisite) 1.149; you've no right to be supported until you've destroyed your inner cravings 19.357

alobha *see* non-attachment

Aloka, Dharmachari 2.515, 8.xxxv, 13.ix–x, 13.671, 17.xv, 25.xxv

aloneness of the artist 3.509; the effect of living with no human contact but surrounded by animals 18.453–4; a good friend is someone with whom you can be alone 18.17, 18.395; individuality and interconnectedness: we are not alone 7.400; it can be a good thing to experience aloneness, but most people flee from it 4.531; of the genius 12.152; of the monk 2.201, 16.391; rejoicing in merits makes you realize that you are not alone, spiritually speaking 1.510; Sangharakshita's aloneness 11.xx, 11.598; Siddhārtha's aloneness 2.21, 3.30, 3.41, 3.472; of the true individual 3.472; unless one can live alone one can't really live with other people 26.27, 26.29; we are most likely to develop when we realize that we are on our own 16.202; willingness to go on alone 3.41–2; you have to be able to be alone 18.164; *see also* loneliness; solitude

Alpert, Richard *see* Baba Ram Dass

alphabet the *devanāgarī* alphabet, symbols of all *vajra* teachings 19.32; in mantras, the letters of the alphabet as representing deep knowledge 19.32; Siddham alphabet 14.237; Tibetan alphabet 12.570, 13.8, 16.15

altars the Christian altar 11.233; the Vedic altar and the stupa 16.70, 16.149–50, 16.162; the word altar is not appropriate for a Buddhist shrine 11.232–3

Altekar, A. S. 7.424

altruism

altruism and us
altruism can turn sour if one is not appreciated 14.424; devoting yourself to the good of all must include yourself 2.90–1, 17.190–1; don't just follow blind impulses, but think what is good for everybody 25.105; the exaggeratedly altruistic person may come to feel like the saviour of others 8.579; friendship is deep to the extent that it is altruistic and egoless 12.458; how genuinely altruistic are we? 4.89; it has to be learned, sometimes rather painfully 4.88–9; 'The most sublime act is to set another before you' (Blake) 26.655; one has to be able to afford to be altruistic 4.90; one is not necessarily altruistic because one is concerned with other people 18.591

altruism and spiritual practice
altruism as a path 4.18; altruism and *vīrya* 3.304; altruism stops the psychological dimension crowding out the ethical 17.645; the altruistic dimension of the spiritual life has no limits 4.64; altruistic orientation of the motivation to gain Enlightenment 3.452; Buddhist ethics based on altruism 7.486; can you be altruistic with no notion

of spiritual life? 4.89; Enlightenment is inseparable from great altruism 3.254; the ideal of spiritual altruism 16.214–15, 16.221; Perfect Vision arising through altruistic activity 1.481

altruism and individualism
'Altruism and individualism in the spiritual life' 4.84–117; altruistic spiritual life contrasted with egoistic 7.149; a division between the paths of altruism and individualism 1.236; the gap between transcendental altruism and spiritual egoism can be bridged 1.269; ultimately individual and altruistic ideals coincide 2.299–300, 11.319; in the *White Lotus Sūtra* 16.214

other-regarding
being the 'guide, philosopher, and friend' of mankind 7.149; contrast with cooperation 4.88; does *dhyāna* have an other-regarding aspect? 5.268; the other-regarding aspect of discipleship 19.208; other-regarding and self-regarding aspects of the spiritual life to be integrated 4.87–117; pay specific attention to the other-regarding aspects of spiritual practice 15.236–7; *shù* (Confucian term for altruism) 8.448; the six perfections are all other-regarding virtues 7.46; what does living for others really mean? 12.9–10; whatever one's spiritual context, one may adopt a self- or other-regarding attitude 4.25

altruism in the Buddhist tradition
'He who wishes to serve me, let him serve the sick' 4.11, 9.195, 11.443; in the *Jātakas* 1.233; in the Theravāda 4.86; in the Mahāyāna, *see under* Mahāyāna Buddhism/teachings and practices; Milarepa reminds Rechungpa of the altruistic aspect of spiritual life 18.369, 18.374; practising altruism 'like a bird' 19.319–20; emphasized on the day of the first WBO ordinations 2.471

see also
bodhicitta practice/altruism; *bodhicitta*/introduction; bodhisattva/what is a bodhisattva?; helping others; self and other; selflessness

amanojñam 2.144

amānuṣa ('no-men') 18.453

Amaradakini, Dharmacharini 11.xxii

Amaravati, South India 16.155

amata or *amatapadaṃ* *see under* deathless

Ambad, India 9.370

Ambalaṭṭhikarāhulovāda Sutta *see under Majjhima Nikāya*

Ambapālī or Āmrapālī how she met the Buddha and gave him a mango grove 16.624 (n310); her park in the *Vimalakīrti-nirdeśa* 14.158, 16.454, 16.464, 16.529

Ambaṭṭha Sutta *see under Dīgha Nikāya*

Ambedkar, Dr Bhimrao R.

HIS LIFE STORY

his life
introduction 2.437, 8.239–41, 10.186–7, 10.288–9, 10.310–11, 11.708, 25.123–4, 26.651–2; birth 6.610, 9.3; early life 6.610, 9.40–2, 9.179–80, 10.21–2, 10.399–400; his family's army background 6.610, 9.39–40; education 6.611, 9.4–5, 9.42–3, 9.46–7, 9.199, 9.373, 10.288, 10.310; his first contact with Buddhism 6.613, 9.45–6, 10.24, 10.127; his experience of caste prejudice 6.611, 9.40–4, 9.179–80, 10.22, 10.106–7; marriages 6.612, 9.7–9, 10.24, 10.660; Bombay residence, 'Rajagriha' 9.14, 10.4–5, 10.127; illness 9.17, 9.20–1, 9.210, 10.10, 10.17, 10.77; the last day of his life 22.361

his death
'His last waking thoughts must have been of the Buddha' 8.239, 10.106; a great shock 6.613, 8.239; people's response 10.xxxvii–viii, 10.312–13; 'A brilliant star appeared on the horizon and has vanished' 10.97; 'Dr Ambedkar is not dead. He still lives in your hearts.' 9.210, 9.223, 9.406, 10.97, 22.363; condolence meeting in Nagpur, *see under* Sangharakshita IX; cremation in Bombay 9.150; great as his influence was in life, it was greater still in death 8.241; his death should remind us that we too must die 10.321; honouring his memory by continuing his work 8.241;

Maha Bodhi journal articles 10.106–8, 22.366–7

WHAT HE WAS LIKE

his greatness
achieved by his own efforts 9.299; 'Dr Ambedkar's True Greatness' 10.xlix, 10.335–52; balanced faith and wisdom 9.325; a great Buddhist of the 20th century 6.610–15; great characteristics 10.167–9; like a mountain, his greatness appreciated from a distance 9.172–3, 9.427–8; his life shows what one man can do 25.129; a modern bodhisattva 10.xxxi, 10.319, 10.339, 25.129; modern Manu 9.9, 9.11, 9.173, 10.310; one of the greatest men in modern India 10.129, 10.378–9; a product of the best of the West and East 9.173; reasons for his greatness 9.321–6; true praise of Dr Ambedkar 10.343

his character and qualities
adherence to principle 10.168; appearance 9.15, 10.4–5; 'a bit of a fighter' 10.5; 'a bit of a sledgehammer' 10.76; blunt of speech 9.502, 9.510; bold 10.107; broad-minded 9.199; compassionate 9.322; energy and speed like a horse 9.368; faith 9.325; fearless (like a lion) 9.368, 10.167–8; formidable 10.14, 10.15–17; free from corruption 10.69; generous 10.318; he loved reading 10.400; he never wasted a minute 10.322; he said things that other people didn't dare to say 10.271; independent of thought 9.230; intellect ('as good as 500 ordinary graduates') 9.321–2, 10.319; like a great tree 10.406; like a mountain 10.129–30; his lion-roar 9.368; a man of extraordinarily varied interests and attainments 10.126; non-violence 9.411; one-pointedness of mind 10.319; patient, tolerant (like an elephant) 9.367, 10.318–19; powers of concentration 9.298–9; practical 9.172; a rationalist 10.38; self-confident 10.355; self-sacrifice 10.168; single-minded and fearless, unconventional and individual 12.561–2; strength of character 10.339; had the strength to break through obstacles (like a bull) 9.367–8); tender-hearted 9.322, 10.339; travel gave him a universal outlook 9.372; truthful 10.271, 10.318; wise 9.325, 10.319

his spiritual life
a deeply religious man 6.614, 10.25, 10.127; an exemplar of *vīrya*, hard work 10.168, 10.319; his bodhisattva-like vow 9.60, 9.149; his practice of the six perfections 10.318–19; to what extent was he leading a spiritual life? 10.69; a very strong moral sense 10.69, 10.318

THE JOURNEY TOWARDS BUDDHISM

politics
introduction 9.8, 9.62, 9.69, 9.125–6; Law Minister 6.613, 9.67, 10.14, 10.107, 10.289; the Hindu Code Bill, *see* Hindu Code Bill; he anchored his conception of democracy in the Buddha's *mettā* 10.xxvii–xxviii; he established the Republican Party of India (RPI) 10.693 (n228); he thought the Indian tendency to hero-worship was dangerous to democracy 10.37–8; his views on Marxism 9.411, 9.427, 9.508, 10.10, 10.70–2, 16.434, 22.361; on the committee that chose the Indian flag 8.xxviii; 'I have no future in India' 22.287; leaving politics gave him more time for Buddhism 10.76–7; 'Society must have the sanction of morality' 9.172, 9.182, 9.426, 10.63, 12.406

renouncing Hinduism
attitude towards brahmins 9.52, 9.63; the burning of the *Manusmṛti*, *see under* Mahad; the Chowdar Tank incident, *see under* Mahad; criticism of Gandhi 10.55; 'de-Sanskritization' 9.61; disapproval of the *Bhagavad Gītā* for its justification of the caste system 10.54; he appealed to the caste Hindus to change their ways 10.310–11; he needed a place to stand outside Hinduism 10.129; his threats to convert seen by Hindus as a political stunt 8.250, 22.150; 'Hinduism does not appeal to my conscience' 10.128; 'I am the most hated man in Hindu India' 10.167, 10.271, 10.319, 10.668 (n57); his renunciation of Hinduism 9.36, 9.53–61, 9.69; Yeola conference 9.54–5; 'I do not intend to die a Hindu' 6.612–13, 8.235, 9.54–5, 9.60, 9.179, 9.222, 9.292, 9.424, 10.94, 10.127, 10.289

on caste
The Annihilation of Caste 10.xxiv–xxvii, 10.xxx; the relief from caste prejudice in past Buddhist society 10.xxvii; breaking down Hinduism's division between social order and spiritual life 10.41; 'Caste has its roots … in religion with divine sanctity' 10.xxv; 'Caste is a notion, it is a state of mind' 10.xxx; the caste system assumes that people cannot change, but they can 10.54; the custom of endogamy 9.27, 10.xxv; 'How can people divided into castes be a nation?' 10.xxiv; 'I am now free from the hell of caste' 9.25, 10.xxx, 23.350; in the village the caste system is very strong 10.329; relative significance of Gandhi and Ambedkar in eradicating Untouchability 10.liii–iv

the search for a new religion
summary 10.289; turning points 9.44, 9.220–3; his assessment of other religions 9.424–5, 10.311; 'I consider the foundations of religion to be essential to life' 10.127–8, 10.205; why choose a religion at all? 6.614, 9.181–2, 9.426–7; why did he not choose Marxism? 10.71–2; approaches from the followers of various religions 9.55–6, 10.128; the search for roots 9.74; his attraction to Sikhism 9.57; rumours of his conversion to Islam 10.127; he saw that to change a community, you must change its religion 6.614, 10.342

three requirements of a religion
(1) it must be in accord with science 9.105, 10.362, 10.379; (2) it must recognize liberty, equality, fraternity 9.70, 9.105–6, 9.126, 9.144–5, 9.173, 9.183–6, 10.xxiii, 10.xxvi–xxviii, 10.362; (3) it must not sanctify or ennoble poverty 9.106–7, 9.400, 9.426, 10.362, 10.389, 27.1074

the decision to adopt Buddhism
'all this may sound very strange' 10.107–8; concern about what would happen to the Dalits after Indian independence 10.78; differences between Buddhism and Hinduism 9.72; did not attend an event at Sanchi 21.415; drawing up plans for the revival of Buddhism in India 22.287–8; Dr Mehta invites him to stay at his nature cure clinic 22.303; the influence of *The Light of Asia* 6.613, 9.181, 10.24; he didn't have much contact with other Buddhists 10.75–6; he distrusted Hindu interpretations of Buddhism 10.75; he saw the potential of the Dharma to change society 1.634 (n432); he was moved by an ancient Buddhist site at Mahad 10.127; his faith that Buddhism could be revived 9.171; his meetings with Sangharakshita, *see under* Sangharakshita IX; 'My master, the Buddha' (1936) 9.70; the process of making the decision 8.250, 9.44–73, 9.92–120; threefold classification: Dhamma, Not-Dhamma, and *Saddhamma* 9.142–4, 10.351; twenty-five years of preparation 8.235, 10.93–4; which form of Buddhism to adopt? 9.123–4; visit to Burma 9.11, 9.70, 9.119, 10.75; visit to Ceylon (Sri Lanka) 9.10, 9.65–7, 9.119, 10.75; the consequences of people's failure to understand the decision 9.431

reasons for adopting Buddhism
because a new society had to be founded on morality 9.182–3, 9.425; it does not condone man's inhumanity to man 6.613, 10.42; it is of Indian origin 6.613, 9.121–2, 10.24, 10.72, 10.128–9, 10.187; it has no caste system 9.124, 10.187; it is based on reason and experience 6.613, 9.425–6, 10.24, 10.129, 10.169; it is a humanistic, non-theistic religion 9.424–5; it teaches freedom of thought 10.187; its non-violence 9.411; a means of uplift 9.241; similar to the reasons that attract people to Buddhism in the West 10.209; his speech 'Reasons for Conversion' 9.40, 9.59–60; 'Why I Like Buddhism' (BBC talk) 9.72

CONVERSION TO BUDDHISM

introduction
brief description 3.669 (n280), 7.467, 10.8–9, 10.25, 10.311; an achievement for which Ambedkar will be remembered for hundreds of years 10.339; a deeply serious act 9.xi–xii; he wanted to take as many people with him as possible 9.64–5; his contact with Sangharakshita about conversion, *see* Sangharakshita IX; the act made Buddhism a mass movement 10.139; one of the events of a year of wonders 8.238; Ambedkar's pleasure at the conversion 9.134; the modern Aśoka 9.11–12; why did Dr Ambedkar leave conversion so late? 10.78–9

the conversion ceremony (Dhammadiksha)
brief account 6.613, 9.73; extended account 9.121–35; in the absence of lay ordination in the Theravāda, he created his own 2.597–8; Dr Ambedkar's original intention was to take only two Refuges 9.128; 'Ashok Vijayadashami Day' (October 14th) 10.676 (n117); eye-witness account 10.xxxv–vi; the greatest turning point in Dr Ambedkar's life 9.223; he held up the jewel of the Dharma for everybody to see 9.263; photograph 22.351; U Chandramani's role in the ceremony, *see* U Chandramani; created steps down to the river of Dhamma 9.458; Sangharakshita had to miss the ceremony 9.19, 10.19, 10.374, 22.350, 23.354; Sangharakshita's message to be read out on the occasion 22.350; showed people what they could really do 10.238

Dr Ambedkar's giving the Refuges and Precepts to his followers
a dramatic departure from tradition 2.495–6, 9.130; the inauguration of a new movement 23.354; monk and layman placed on an equal footing 9.130, 10.26–7; asserted the fact that it is Going for Refuge that makes one a Buddhist 6.615

the twenty-two vows (pratijñās)
devised by Dr Ambedkar himself 6.615, 9.73, 10.26; an assertion of the unity of the Buddhist community 9.129–33; given

to secure the integrity of the Refuges and Precepts 9.132–3, 10.363, 10.378; to separate the new Buddhists from Hinduism 6.615, 9.216, 9.240, 9.265, 10.9, 10.26; list of the vows 2.656, 9.541, 10.657–8; clarify that a lay Buddhist is a full member of the spiritual community 2.496, 2.597–8, 10.26; opposed by *bhikkhus* because they were not given by the Buddha 9.395; the three achievements of the vows 9.133

the response to the conversion
greeted with joy 10.94; Hindu hostility 9.123–5, 10.60, 10.187, 10.280; importance of enthusiasm 9.134–5, 9.199–200, 10.370, 10.388–9; inspired millions to convert to Buddhism 10.xxvii, 10.78–9; *Maha Bodhi* journal reports 10.93–4, 10.106–13; newspaper coverage 10.377; not 'Hīnayāna' or 'Mahāyāna', just Buddhist 9.361, 9.506–7, 10.169, 10.281, 10.362–3, 10.377; people who said it was just a change of label did not realize how deep religion goes 10.340; the reorientation of the whole of life 10.139; shouts of 'Sadhu!!!' throughout the Buddhist world 8.236

DR AMBEDKAR ON BUDDHISM

introduction
'The Buddha's way is a long way, but perhaps the surest way' 10.xxxii, 10.lxi; the Buddhist path in Dr Ambedkar's version: purity, righteousness, virtue 9.141; the function of the Buddha's teaching is 'to reconstruct an individual and a society' 10.xxvii; his ecumenical attitude 2.497; his view of meditation 10.68–9; 'a very difficult religion to practise' 9.269, 9.503, 10.386, 10.388, 12.654

the Buddha
did the Buddha claim infallibility? 10.40; his greatest achievement: to show that reform must be of the mind 10.xxii, 10.xxix; his emphasis on the Buddha's humanity, extraordinary in the Indian context 10.37; his view of the Buddha's character 9.148; his faith in the Buddha 9.181; his unconventional telling of the Buddha's life story 9.140–2, 10.40–1; wish to see an image of the walking Buddha 10.xxix

the Dharma
the Buddha's teaching of freedom 10.64–5; Buddhism and morality 9.144–5; Going for Refuge 2.494–7, 9.259, 10.27, 10.203; he did not regard Buddhism as a philosophy 9.241; he held up the jewel of the Dharma 9.263; he saw Buddhism in terms of the bodhisattva ideal 10.69, 10.82; he stressed the social bearing of the Buddha's teaching 10.41; he supported the publication of *The Essence of Buddhism* 7.158, 7.590 (n259); his approach was social and ethical rather than philosophical and mystical 9.139; his study of Buddhist scriptures 9.64; *oṃ maṇi padme hūṃ, see under oṃ maṇi padme hūṃ*; 'proposed gospel' 10.66–7; a recording of the *Dhammapada* made under his direction 15.436; religion is essentially ethics 10.355; a similar approach to Sangharakshita's 2.496–7, 10.xliii

the Sangha
disappointment at the mechanical practise of Buddhism 9.268; he decided there had to be a lay ordination 6.614–15, 10.26; he put his finger on the weak spot: the separation of monastic and lay 10.129; his followers had to be *bona fide* Buddhists, not just supporters of monks 2.597; his investigation into why Buddhism disappeared from India 6.614, 9.70, 10.25–6; his view of the Maha Bodhi Society, *see under* Maha Bodhi Society; it's not enough to be a blind follower of Buddhism 10.197; need to reform *bhikṣu* sangha 9.xiii–xiv, 9.112–17, 9.318, 9.392, 9.432, 9.510, 10.67–8, 10.271

HIS LEGACY

his achievements
the chief purpose of his life was the revival of Buddhism in India 10.127; compared to the father in the *White Lotus Sutra* 9.360; the effect of the Dhamma Revolution 9.428–9, 9.431–2; giving the gift of the Dharma 9.386, 10.318; he went for Refuge not just for himself or his own people, but for all people 10.203; his example 9.511, 10.168, 10.322; his dedication to propagating Buddhism 9.69; self-reliance was the keynote of his work 10.103; significance for the history of Buddhism 9.428–30; a vigorous Buddhist movement 10.157; his world Buddhist mission 9.393; worldwide significance of his work 9.509

anniversaries
of his birth 10.167, 10.169, 10.177, 21.630 (n121); of the conversion 9.190, 10.3, 10.149, 12.649, 23.355–6; death anniversary 8.268, 10.116, 10.316–19; the three anniversaries each have their special flavour 10.319

how he is remembered
association with the turning the wheel of the Dharma *mudrā* 9.385–6; becoming known in the West 9.241, 10.406; he is not sufficiently appreciated 10.379–80; he was omitted from an encyclopedia of Asian philosophy 8.605; '*Jai Bhim!*'

10.14; with gratitude 9.159, 10.xlii–xliii, 10.13–14, 10.313, 10.406; statues 9.159, 9.292, 10.xxxiv, 10.2, 10.140, 10.318; a talk in Malaysia about his work 24.40; a UK radio programme that didn't mention his conversion 25.123; Western Buddhists' appreciation of him 10.338–9, 10.380

his followers
followers in Bangalore 22.149–50; he belonged not only to India, but to the whole world 10.363, 10.379; their devotion 9.15, 9.208, 9.502; they insisted on hero-worshipping him 10.39; you can't refuse to take the *Dhammadiksha* and call yourself his follower 10.343

his vision
he wanted a world Buddhist mission 9.172; a conception of a deeply humanistic society 10.82; it fires the Buddhist movement in India 10.83; Triratna's attempt to fulfil Dr Ambedkar's vision 10.362

carrying on his work
appeals to the Buddhist world for help 8.176, 8.234, 10.79–80; group rivalries after Dr Ambedkar's death 10.187, 10.298; the need for funds and instruction 8.269–70, 10.108; the need for Buddhism to shed cultural baggage 2.603–4; needs to be accompanied by true understanding of the Dharma 8.241–3; the watering of tender shoots 8.244–5; need for a central institution and a training course for Dharma teachers 8.279; what the Buddhist movement needs is a chain of meditation centres 8.294; other countries will help, but India must stand on its own feet 10.139–40; taking on his work 10.89–90, 10.372–3; true homage to him 10.101, 10.103; unity is essential 10.169; without exemplars and teachers, progress was difficult 10.xlii; founding and history of TBMSG (Triratna), *see under* Triratna I/ Triratna in India

organizations and institutions he founded
Bharatiya Bauddha Maha Sabha, *see* Bharatiya Bauddha Maha Sabha; Republican Party of India (RPI), *see under* India/politics; Scheduled Castes Federation (SCF), *see* Scheduled Castes Federation; the People's Education Society, *see* People's Education Society; Milinda College, *see under* Aurangabad; Siddharth College, *see under* Mumbai

HIS WRITINGS AND SAYINGS

The Buddha and His Dhamma
brief introduction 2.741 (n676); full introduction 9.136–49; plans for the book 9.63–4; concentration while writing the book 9.298; he was working on the preface the night before he died 9.72, 22.361; the effect on the book of Dr Ambedkar's illness 10.660–1; publication 9.136, 9.224, 10.660–1; Dr Ambedkar's original preface was only published later 10.659–60; a manageable account of the Buddha's teachings 9.xiii; it contains his thoughts on Buddhism 9.92; his statue should show him with the book under his arm 9.12; breadth of approach 9.361

The Gospel of Buddha
9.138–9, 10.661; teachings 2.553, 9.52, 9.111, 9.145–6, 9.287–9, 10.219–21, 10.247, 10.351, 23.528 (n393); no special authority 9.136–7; studied at Range Hills 10.199; assessment of the book 10.661; suggestions for improvements 10.129, 10.661; what the book gave his followers 9.360

'Buddha and the Future of His Religion'
publication details 9.65, 10.31, 10.128; Sangharakshita first reads the article 10.3–4, 10.31; the style of the article 10.75; summary of the text 9.92–9, 10.362; full commentary 10.29–90; comparison of the Buddha with Jesus, Mohammed, and Krishna 9.94–7, 10.33–40; comparison of Buddhism with Hinduism 9.182, 10.43–50; 'The Hindu masses … are sure to turn to Buddhism' 9.171–2; 'The parent of the caste system' 10.51–6; 'The revival of Buddhism in India' 10.57–62; society must have the sanction of law or morality 9.181; 'Buddhism is the only religion the world can have' 10.63–9; 'The opium of the people' 10.70–4; 'The duty of a Buddhist is … to spread Buddhism' 10.xxxi; reorganization of the sangha 9.190, 9.223–4, 9.317; 'Why did the Buddha start a Sangha?' 10.270

other publications
summary 9.8; *Annihilation of Caste* 10.xxv, 10.xxvi, 10.xxx; *Buddha Puja Path* 9.10, 9.71–2, 10.174, 10.676 (n122); 'Castes in India: Their Mechanism, Genesis and Development' 9.4; *The Evolution of Provincial Finance in British India* 9.4; *Mooknayak* 9.5; *Revolution and Counter-revolution* 9.76; *Riddles of Hinduism* 9.76, 10.xxviii; *The Problem of the Rupee* 9.5; 'The Rise and Fall of the Hindu Woman' 9.68; *The Untouchables* 9.63, 9.76, 10.48–9, 10.54, 10.361; *What Congress and Gandhi Have Done to the Untouchables* 9.76, 10.311; *Who Were the Shudras?* 9.76–7, 10.361; writings and speeches 9.224

sayings
'The Buddhist *bhikkhu* has everything to do with the world' 7.230–1; 'Don't idealize the villages' 18.202; 'Hero-worship

is a sure road to degradation' 10.670 (n70); importance of enthusiasm 9.134–5, 9.199–200, 10.370, 10.388–9; '*Prajñā* is like a sword in the hand of a man' 3.354, 9.231; religion will decline if it doesn't have capable preachers 16.185, 16.602 (n132)

Ambedkar, Savita (Dr Ambedkar's second wife) 9.123, 9.127, 9.129, 10.6 (photo), 10.10, 10.17, 10.660

ambition the ambition to get hold of esoteric practices is a waste of time 5.50; the fulfilment of your life's ambition 15.214–15; the heroic ambition of the bodhisattva 16.312–13; misusing the Dharma as a screen for ambition 8.272; Siddhārtha's victory over spiritual ambition 11.398–9

ambrosia *see amṛta*

America *see* United States

American Buddhist Order 23.458

Amida *see* Amitābha

Amidism 7.43–4, 7.46

Amiel, Henri-Frederic 8.149–51, 8.678 (n84)

Amis, Martin 26.443–4

āmisa-pūja 16.568

Amita Nisatta, Sister 8.664, v22

Amitābha

INTRODUCING AMITĀBHA

introduction
brief description 4.207, 11.293; red: not a harsh bright red but a soft rosy glow 21.559; he presides over the Lotus family 1.263, 13.310; his animal is the peacock 13.310; his consort, *see* Pāṇḍaravāsinī; attendant bodhisattvas 16.462; his emblem is the deep red lotus 4.207, 11.293, 12.215, 13.309; *mudrā* (gesture), *see mudrās*; all-distinguishing knowledge, *see under* five *jñānas*; Iranian connections? 1.325, 16.57, 16.592 (n54); not a Creator God 7.535, 7.537; one of the most important *sambhogakāya* forms 2.42, 4.207, 19.318; protector of the present world-period 1.263

his qualities
Buddhahood in the most beautiful and adorable form conceivable 1.324–5; compassion 1.335, 1.341, 1.346; he exercises jurisdiction over ten thousand million worlds 2.42; he fulfils the functions of both Buddha and king 14.427; light and life immeasurable 1.329; the sublime beauty of Buddhahood in his radiant figure 2.554; a symbol of the *dharmakāya* 1.324, 21.559

associations
hrī (sense of shame) 17.558; the maturing power of love 12.215; other-power 1.346–7, 4.138; the setting sun 11.293, 12.215, 13.310; symbol of the *dharmakāya* 19.201; with Avalokiteśvara 1.263, 2.172, 16.180–1; with Tārā 5.578–9, 13.93, 17.147

Amitābha and Śākyamuni
association 1.263; Gautama his earthly reflex 2.177; personification of the Infinite in the Enlightened spiritual consciousness of Śākyamuni 7.537; Śākyamuni worships Amitābha 19.316; ultimately identical 2.567

HISTORY AND MYTH

Dharmākara and the 48 vows
Dharmākara, the monk eventually reborn as Amitābha 1.366–8, 15.95, 21.562; in the *Larger Sukhāvatī-vyūha Sūtra* 1.324, 1.327–9, 14.169; the 48 vows made under the Buddha Lokeśvararāja 1.324, 1.328, 1.421, 2.163, 14.169; Great Vow 2.745 (n693); he vowed that after attaining Buddhahood he would establish a Buddha-field 1.340; the power of his vows 14.104, 24.534

myth
according to scholarship, Amitābha is a myth, but what is it intended to teach? 1.325; the symbols of his myth engage our darkest and deepest desires 1.347

in Buddhist history
in the mandala of the Five Buddhas 3.374, 4.207, 12.215–16, 13.309–10, 18.599; in the *Larger Sukhāvatī-vyūha Sūtra* 1.324, 14.171; in the *sūtras*, *see Amitāyur-Dhyāna Sūtra* and *Sukhāvatī-vyūha Sūtras*; Padmasambhava is born from a lotus from a ray of light from Amitābha 1.382,

8.522, 12.288; Sukhāvatī, his Pure Land, *see* Sukhāvatī; Hōnen initiated Shinran into Amitābha 1.344; and the Jōdo Shinshū school, *see under* Jōdo Shinshū; Master Takuan does not invoke Amida 8.496; Amida in Japan 16.232; in Japanese paintings 13.284; in Vietnamese Buddhism 16.197, 23.124–5; the Panchen Lama an emanation of Amitābha 22.487

DEVOTION TO AMITĀBHA

worship
in China and Japan as the personification of the *dharmakāya* 1.324; in India, Nepal, Tibet, and Mongolia as one of the five principal *sambhogakāyas* 1.324; in a Five Buddha *caitya* in Nepal 20.430; in a three-floored shrine in Darjeeling 21.214, 22.467; taught by Nāgārjuna 1.324

faith in Amitābha
the old woman who prayed to him: 'Won't he let me have my little joke?' 3.249–50, 16.201–2, 17.354; a 'bad' man conscious of sin may be more receptive to Amitābha than a 'good' man 7.407; surrender to Amitābha 1.345–6; gratitude to Amitābha for the gift of Enlightenment 13.309–10; his appearance in the *bardo* after death 12.203

chanting his name (nembutsu)
the invocation of his name 1.340; the belief that a single heartfelt repetition of his name is enough 24.540; his merit transferred to us 1.343–4; it helps even one who has committed the five heinous sins 1.334, 7.42–3; leads to rebirth in Sukhāvatī 1.341, 1.343–4, 7.42–3, 7.123–4; identifying ourselves with Amitābha 1.343; Pure Land School practice 7.123–4

his mantra
namo amitābhāya buddhāya 1.334; Honen initiated Shinran into 1.344; like a narrow white path between fire and water 1.338; regarded not as a spiritual exercise but an expression of gratitude 1.348; seed syllable *hrīḥ* 16.180, 17.558; 'Who recites the Amitābha mantra?': a Zen question 18.239

prayers and hymns to Amitābha
Dr Ambedkar's 9.149; Chinese 9.139; Huiyuan's hymn of praise, the 'White Lotus Ode' 1.338; Vasubandhu's 9.149

meditation practices
as we identify ourselves with him, he identifies himself with us 1.347; in the guru yoga 13.217; on the Refuge Tree 13.208; the *phowa* practice of Amitābha 12.449, 22.554–5; visualizing yourself as Amitābha you contact hidden aspects of yourself 19.412

Sangharakshita
the Dalai Lama gives him an image of Amitābha 8.651; his devotion to Amitābha 22.301; his vision of Amitābha, *see under* Sangharakshita VI/spiritual experiences; seminar on *sādhana* 5.xxxi–ii

see also
Sukhāvatī/Pure Land

Amitamati, Dhammacharini 10.lix–lxiii

Amitaratna, Dharmacharini 2.737 (n653)

Amitāyur-Dhyāna Sūtra (or *Meditation Sūtra*)

Queen Vaidehī
the story of how she is imprisoned by her son Ajātaśatru 14.172; she calls on the Buddha to help her be reborn in a happier place 14.172; he teaches her how to visualize Sukhāvatī 1.332–4, 14.173; a vision of the Pure Land 3.453–5, 3.571–2, 14.173

other features of the sūtra
introduction 14.172–4; accepts but modifies the principle of karma 1.334; Amitāyus, Avalokiteśvara, and Mahāsthāmaprāpta 14.173; Avalokiteśvara in the *sūtra* 2.175; devotees born on thrones or in lotuses 1.334, 1.338; a guide to meditation 1.332–4; the invocation of Amitābha's name 1.340; 'since you have meditated on Buddha's body, you will see Buddha's mind' 2.125, 14.174; the sphere of the Buddha's radiance envelops a billion world systems 2.669 (n64)

Amitāyus appears in Ruciraketu's house in the *Sūtra of Golden Light* 16.258, 16.261; emanations as the Five Sisters 22.538; holds the *amṛta kalaśa* (vase containing the nectar of immortality) 2.58, 16.150; in the *Amitāyur-Dhyāna Sūtra* 1.333, 14.173; a mandala of Amitāyus 24.315; Sangharakshita is given his *abhiṣeka* 22.473; symbolized by a beribboned arrow 22.473; visualization included in the *phowa* practice of Amitābha 12.449, 22.554–5

amlaki *see under* fruit

Ammonius Saccas 26.368

amoeba 'Does an amoeba have karma?' 22.63; we progress for the same reason the amoeba evolves – from irritation 7.389, 26.11

Amoghasiddhi brief description 4.207; etymology of his name 12.216, 13.310; all-performing knowledge or wisdom (*jñāna*), *see under* five *jñānas*; appears as Dundubhīśvara in the *Sūtra of Golden Light* 16.258, 16.261; association with Viśvapaṇī 2.172; he is a deep green, like twilight 13.186; he is the head of the action or karma family 13.311; his animal is the *shang shang* bird 13.311; his appearance in the *bardo* after death 12.203; his consort, *see* Tārā/Green Tārā; his emblem is the double *vajra* 4.207, 12.216, 13.186; in a Five Buddha *caitya* in Nepal 20.430; in the mandala of the Five Buddhas 3.374–5, 4.207, 12.216–17, 13.310–11, 18.600; his *mudrā*, *see under mudrās*; as *sambhogakāya* 2.42, 4.207; symbolizes the mysterious practical activity of the Enlightened mind 1.536, 12.216, 13.186

Amoghavajra (Buddhist missionary to China) 1.383–4, 1.388

Amoghavajra, Dharmachari v24

amoha *see* non-deludedness

Āmrapālī *see* Ambapālī

Amritananda, Venerable 20.462, v21, 22.131

Amritapani *see* Phillips, Anna

Amritavacha, Dharmachari (Thomas Schwarte) v24

Amritlal (Gujarati Buddhist) 23.343–4, v24

Amritsar 1.382

amṛta (ambrosia, nectar) alcohol and *amṛta* 19.332–3; 'deathless' 13.681 (n48); the Dharma as nectar 10.231, 16.382, 17.364; brought from the Pure Land 'Sweetly Perfumed with All Perfumes' 16.457, 16.558, 16.559–60; the nectar of immortality 22.179; the nectar of mindfulness 18.51; nectar-like antidotes to the *kleśas* 19.228; 'the quintessence of milk and nectar' (Milarepa) 18.117

amṛta kalaśa (vase of immortality) 16.150

An Shigao 14.190

anābhāsa (imagelessness, shadowlessness) 14.219

anāgāmin *see* non-returner

anagārika Dharmapala becomes an *anagārika* 8.29, 8.93, 8.110; explanation 9.543; a freedom to follow the spiritual life and respond to others' needs 11.597; in the Triratna Buddhist Order, *see under* Triratna III/life in the Order; Sangharakshita as, *see under* Sangharakshita II/wandering days; Soṇa Koṭikaṇṇa becomes a sort of *anagārika* 10.573; use of the term in the *Dhammapada* 7.477; women ordained as *anagārikas* where monastic lineages are extinct 7.477

Anāgatavaṃsa (Theravādin poem) 10.263

anālaya (unattached) 1.69

Anālayo, Bhikkhu 14.335, 15.747 (n34, n35), 26.695–6

analysis the analysis of *dharmas*, *see under dharmas*; analysis of mental events, *see under* mental events; be careful not to take the analysis of mind too literally 17.493–4; psychoanalysis, *see* psychoanalysis; the purpose of Buddhist analysis 17.433, 17.489; and synthesis 1.102

analytical knowledges *see* four *pratisaṃvids*

Anand, Mulk Raj 10.xliv, 22.22, 22.573 (n30)

ānanda (bliss arising from the senses) 2.91

Ānanda (the Buddha's attendant)

IN THE PĀLI CANON

his background and character
born into the Kṣatriya caste 12.521; he joins the Order 2.26; an attractive character 4.18; an example of a faith-follower 11.453, 17.333; a bit of a gossip 11.369; a Mahāyānistic type of monk 4.569; his need for integration 13.359–60; an inquisitive, vivid, and lovable personality 11.450; 'the' St John of Buddhism' 12.520

as the Buddha's attendant
how he became the Buddha's attendant 11.435–6; he doesn't realize that the Buddha is communicating silently with

visiting *bhikkhus* 10.510–11; he gave up his own ego to serve the Buddha 4.18; did his service for the Buddha delay his own spiritual development? 4.18–19

his friendship with the Buddha
their mutual kindness 3.90, 11.434–7; they go for alms together 25.160–1; he was like the Buddha's shadow 4.17; his distress before the Buddha's *parinirvāṇa* 2.29–30, 3.118, 3.364–5, 4.17, 11.436, 13.146–7; his assessment of the Buddha's character: 'he who is so kind' 3.364–5, 4.17, 11.436, 13.146; the Buddha comforts him and praises his virtues 2.30, 3.118, 11.436–7; the Buddha praises his friendliness and popularity 3.179; being reborn together (*Jātakas*) 16.471–2; 'The Cave', a short story featuring the Buddha and Ānanda 24.371–2, 25.569–86

the recorder of the Buddha's teachings
the original hearer 26.627; the oral tradition by which the Dharma was memorized, *see under* oral tradition; the Ānanda within 16.61–2; he symbolizes our ordinary mind listening to our Enlightened consciousness 16.37

he asks the Buddha
about the body of the Tathāgata 1.255; about the leadership of the sangha 9.306; he fails to ask the Buddha to live longer 10.583–8, 11.276; to recite the *pāṭimokkha* (*Udāna*) 10.557, 10.561; why the Buddha's mother's life was so short 10.546–9; will there be disputes about the Dharma after he has gone? 11.369–70; what should be done with his body? 13.146

interactions between the Buddha and Ānanda
Ānanda marvels at the Buddha's ability to concentrate 3.288–9; Ānanda says that *pratītya-samutpāda* is easy to understand 1.95–6, 17.389, 17.750 (n325); spiritual friendship is 'the whole of the spiritual life', *see under kalyāṇa mitratā*; they care for a monk with dysentery 4.11, 9.194–5, 10.260, 11.434, 11.440–1, 14.414

Ānanda and women
the Buddha tells Ānanda how to behave in relation to women 8.444; he asks the Buddha whether they are capable of the highest spiritual attainment 11.421–2, 16.334–5; made it possible for women to join the sangha 2.27, 3.179, 4.712 (n352); women's gratitude to him 3.179, 4.569; he took water from an 'Untouchable' woman 10.260, 14.68–9

Ānanda and other disciples
the Buddha asks him to reassure Cunda 10.639–41; he arranges lodgings near the Buddha for Soṇa Koṭikaṇṇa 10.572–3; he asks Sāriputta about his shining face 3.409, 14.551–2; he explains the difference between the Buddha and all other monks 1.54–5; he teaches Subha the threefold way 7.434, 7.519; Mahākāśyapa transmitted the spirit of the Dharma to him 13.341; reluctant to admit Subhadda, the Buddha's last disciple 3.77, 13.147

after the Buddha's parinirvāṇa
excluded from the Council of Arhats because of his lack of meditative power 4.567–8; almost the last of the Buddha's disciples to attain Enlightenment 7.41; a scapegoat 4.567, 4.569; he had a large following 17.349; association with the Abhidharma 14.73; his disciple Śānavāsa 13.341

IN THE MAHĀYĀNA

in the Śūraṅgama Sūtra
he is rescued from the charms of Prakṛti by Mañjuśrī 13.358–60; his backslidings were the occasion for the *sūtra* 14.197; the Buddha asks him questions to be answered spontaneously 13.360–1; he sees the Buddha's beauty 12.307–8, 13.361, 15.556, 15.721, 17.337, 25.31; the Buddha shows him that his mind cannot be located anywhere 1.356, 13.362–3, 18.544

in other sūtras and contexts
the Buddha tells his life story in the *Mahāparinirvāṇa Sūtra* 14.241; he ordains Padmasambhava 8.522; in the *Larger Sukhāvatī-vyūha Sūtra* 1.327–30; in the *Vimalakīrti-nirdeśa* 16.459, 16.511–12; not present at the *parinirvāṇa* (Mahāyāna text) 14.233; predicted to Enlightenment in the *White Lotus Sūtra* 14.119; when he attained insight he wanted to share it (*Precious Garland*) 17.348–9; patriarch of the Zen school 13.341

Ananda, Dharmachari introduction 2.712 (n467), 3.xvi, 12.754 (n451), 24.648 (n202); compiler of aphorisms 26.xix; at first WBO ordination ceremony 2.403; friendship with Sangharakshita 2.404, 12.396, 12.653, 25.310–11, 26.352–3; Sangharakshita's poems to him 25.305, 25.420–1; leads a puja on an early FWBO retreat 12.367; in the New Forest 26.611; on the Sukhavati building site 24.165; comments on 'sixties-speak' 24.319; 'one of my closest friends' 26.611; the only one of the original 12 Order members

still in the Order (1986) 12.372; conducts *Urthona* interview 26.352–73

Ananda (Kalimpong Newar) 22.447–8

Ananda Bodhi (Canadian monk) at the Hampstead Buddhist Vihara 23.5–7, 23.26; flicked custard (or jelly) over an audience 19.161, 23.48; followers and critics 23.155–6; following at Cambridge University 23.155; in the Sangha Sabha 8.336; teacher of a controversial insight meditation method 17.88–9, 23.38, 23.66, 23.71; investigated by the police 23.85–7; becomes Namgyal Rimpoche, then Star One 23.440

Ananda Maitreya (Sinhalese monk) 22.231

Ananda Marga 15.490, 15.764 (n188)

Ananda Metteyya *see* Bennett, Allan

Anandajyoti, Dharmachari (Anthony Tribe) v24

Anandamayi Ma appearance 20.184, 20.186, 20.205; ashrams 20.183–218, 20.388, 23.13; and caste 10.41, 10.44, 20.196–7; celebration of her birthday in Ahmedabad 20.179–80; devotees 19.115, 20.186–9, 20.197, 22.73; and Sangharakshita 9.347, 20.179, 20.183–213, 23.13; singing 20.189; at Solon 20.220; spiritual status 20.202–3, 20.204, 20.206, 20.301; supernormal powers 20.204–5.20.220; her theory about happiness 10.475, 15.201

Anandashram *see under* Ramdas, Swami

Anand-ji *see* Kausalyayan

Anaṅga (Hinduism) 17.691–2

anaññaposī (not supporting anyone) 10.449, 10.454

ananta (infinite) 1.69

Ananta, the cosmic serpent (Hinduism) 16.398, 26.641

ānantarya-karma (disastrous karmic consequences) *see under* five heinous crimes

ānāpānasati *see* mindfulness of breathing

Ānāpānasati Sutta *see under Majjhima Nikāya*

anapatrāpya (lack of respect for wise opinion) 17.667–9

anarchy 14.543

anariyapariyesanā (ignoble quest) *see under ariyapariyesanā*

anāsa (freedom from longing) 1.69

anāsrava dharmas *see under dharmas/ analysis of conditioned dharmas*

Anāthapiṇḍika (or Anāthapiṇḍada) brief introduction 2.687–8 (n262); the meaning of Anāthapiṇḍika 10.472; his excitement at the prospect of meeting the Buddha 1.284, 13.683 (n57); he meets the Buddha for the first time and gains insight 1.635 (n439), 3.664 (n248); the Buddha's gradual teaching to him 8.592; 'Come, Sudatta' 2.687 (n258); contributed lavishly to the Buddhist cause 2.25, 4.454, 8.49; donation of the Jeta Grove to the Buddha 2.687–8 (n262), 8.671 (n44), 15.381; in Dr Ambedkar's account of the Buddha's teaching 9.142; embodiment of the lay Buddhist ideal 2.207; consoled on his deathbed by Śāriputra 2.204

Anāthapiṇḍika's Park *see* Śrāvastī

Anāthapiṇḍikovāda Sutta *see under Majjhima Nikāya*

anatimāni (humble) 15.274

anātman (Pāli *anattā*)

THE TRUTH OF INSUBSTANTIALITY

its essence
a simple account of insubstantiality 1.486–7; the absence of self in anything whatever 17.383; all phenomena are without self-nature or substantiality 7.193; a half-understood concept 3.17; Buddhism and science agree that nothing in the world is solid 22.29; the consciousness of the perceiver also changes all the time 7.208–10; insight into the truth of no-self 15.337; it pervades every particle of the Dharma 7.232; nothing has an own-being separate from everything else 3.317; nothing has any unchanging essence 18.179

the insubstantiality of everything
the body 16.493–4; a book 2.50–1; the conditioned 2.87–8; *dharmas* 1.172, 1.221; mind 1.175; thoughts 19.233; a lot of nothing still adds up to nothing 17.408; existence as a dream, an echo, a mirage, a reflection, a ball of foam 16.452; objects are like floating clouds, sea foam, a reflection 14.192; *sabbe dhammā anattā* 2.86–7; 'The things of this samsaric world are all illusion, like a dream' 5.602–8

relationship to other aspects of the Dharma
insubstantiality and impermanence 1.173, 2.86–8, 4.666 (n52), 7.49, 9.232; insubstantiality and interconnectedness 7.193–4; insubstantiality as *lakṣaṇa* 1.171–3, 2.87–9, 2.121, 3.217, 7.539, 15.111; a condensed and negative

statement of *pratītya-samutpāda* 7.191; don't make the mistake of seeing the *skandhas* as substantial 17.474–5; entrance to the *vimokṣa-mukha* of *śūnyatā*, *see under* three *vimokṣa-mukhas*; its positive counterpart is the interpenetration of all things 7.49, 7.312; the middle path in the sphere of psychology 1.139; nihilism and eternalism 1.139, 19.375–7; rebirth 3.111, 9.343–4; *śūnyatā* 1.139, 2.89, 7.213, 10.160; *tathatā* (thusness) 2.89

THE DOCTRINE

reflections
what is all the fuss about? 7.130; 'All things are devoid of unchanging selfhood' (*Dhammapada*) 1.171, 3.159, 3.217, 7.155; *anātman* and nominalism 2.88–9; an antidote to the delusion of a 'self' 7.257; the *dharmakāya* could be seen as its positive counterpart 14.604; difficult to explain: the structure of language is against us 10.159; friendship is its emotional equivalent 7.293; it envelops the whole world in a cloak of unity and love 7.133; it negates the Brahminical idea of a permanent, unchanging self 3.217, 3.492; it represents the possibility of radical change 26.85; its purpose is entirely practical, not a metaphysical statement 3.492; it just warns us not to abstract an entity behind 'own-being' 14.461; it implies the possibility of spiritual evolution 7.133; 'A Note on *Anattā*' (1949 article) 7.207–14, 20.228; a tendency to centre more and more on persons, less and less on things 7.538; the sense in which the Unconditioned is *anātman* 2.88–9; used in one sense for the conditioned and in another for the Unconditioned 2.89, 7.538

its place in Buddhist history
The Buddha's Teaching of Egolessness (Nyanatiloka) 8.379–80; central to Buddhism from the beginning 17.448; it permeates every phase of Buddhist philosophy and religious discipline 7.207, 7.399; some have said that the whole structure of Buddhism stands or falls with it 7.130; why the Buddha laid it down as the ultimate philosophical foundation 7.374; the idea that early Buddhists could not give up belief in the *ātman* 17.632; in the Perfection of Wisdom 14.150; developing insight into it on the Tibetan Buddhist path 12.296

opposition and contradictions
the Abhidharma analysis contradicted it 17.448–9; does recognition of the individual contradict the *anātman* doctrine? 3.492, 11.364; Hindu responses to it 7.232–3, 12.62, 20.228; opposed by the Rajpurohit of Nepal, 'Māra' 21.298–300; Sarvāstivādin repudiation 1.188–9, 1.221, 2.88

responding to the doctrine
the classical form of the doctrine is unhelpful 14.460; it's possible to adopt it in an aggressive, unskilful way 17.630; mistaking alienated awareness for insight into *anattā* 12.267–8; much misunderstood 10.142–3, 10.159; not a cold, alienated vision, but imbued with the Buddha's compassion 15.120; to one who has realized its truth everything becomes delightfully fluid and free 7.133; to understand it you have to understand the meaning of *attā* 3.492, 12.428–9, 17.630, 19.446–7, 20.447; to understand it your emotions have to get involved 7.293; using it to avoid personal responsibility 17.625; you can't accept it just theoretically 15.553; you need to be familiar with it, but don't cling to it 15.335; a young woman drawn to it by self-hatred 13.395–6, 16.200–1, 17.625, 17.629–30

see also
self/delusion of self; selflessness

Anavatapta, Lake 12.574, 14.538–9

Anaximander 3.427

ancient way leading to ancient city *see under* parables/a few more stories

Anderson, Abbot Tenshin 2.563, 2.567, 11.609–10, 12.506

Anderson, William 24.316–17

Andhra, India 1.300, 8.163–4, 8.210

Andrews, C. F. 22.179

Androcles 26.286

androgyny bodhisattvas aren't really male or female 13.186; in Hinduism a human figure, half male, half female 13.185–6; one should not think of oneself as a man or a woman in any absolute or exclusive sense 2.372; a Nepalese nun who 'was tired of all this business of masculine and feminine' 20.433–4; psycho-spiritual 2.371, 2.517, 11.582, 16.163–4, 16.539, 26.79; when meditating (in the *dhyānas*), one is leading an angelic, androgynous life 2.371, 13.453; *see also* transsexuality

aṅga (definition) 9.294

Aṅga, kingdom 2.25

Angelo, Dosi 22.257–8

angels

in literature
'An angel wakens in the drowsy beast' (Baudelaire) 26.173; the angel in Rilke's *Duino Elegies* 26.268; the angels and rebel angels of *Paradise Lost*, *see under* Milton; a jade tablet upheld by angels 25.436; for Milton angels had an objective existence 13.591; Shelley 'an ineffectual angel' 25.350

in art
contrast in depiction of angels and saints 16.7–8; depictions of angels 13.587–8, 26.237–8, 26.276; the angel in El Greco's *The Burial of Count Orgaz* 26.315–16; Fra Angelico's angels 13.585, 13.588, 26.240; in Islamic art 26.239–40; in medieval and Renaissance art 26.471; no angel is solitary 13.588; Reynolds' painting 13.585; the transformations of the image of the angel 26.276

in religion and philosophy
the angel has its counterpart in many religions and cultures 26.270; angels and the principle of non-violence 12.354, 26.55; in Christianity angels have no feminine equivalent 26.471; comparison with *devas* and bodhisattvas 13.586–7, 26.270–1; descriptions of them sound weak compared to devils 15.253; 'How many angels can dance on the head of a pin?' 14.76; musicians like Renaissance angels 24.249; 'Preach like an angel in the morning. Live like a devil at night!' 18.540; they correspond roughly to bodhisattvas 26.239; *Tobias and the Angel* 4.99, 13.589, 25.375, 26.269; as translators 26.239

guardian angels
related to 'genius' 3.513; Christian guardian angels 13.590–1; the Buddhist term is *puṇyadevatā* 14.423, 16.111; contacting and invoking guardian angels 16.111–12; Sangharakshita's guardian angel 26.616–18

becoming an angel
angels and androgyny 2.371, 26.620; cultivating positive emotions one becomes an angel 26.657; making Angels out of men 25.349; when one is in the *dhyānas*, one is leading an angelic life 2.371

Sangharakshita and angels
childhood fascination 13.585, 26.218, 26.239, 26.268–9, 26.616–17; a song about angels and 'Violet' 26.500; heard an angelic voice that said 'Don't' 13.591, 26.611, 26.617–18; 'The Angel in the House' (poem) 25.410–11; *Four Visitors*, a story about an angel 26.616–20, 26.662–3; 'My heart was held within an Angel's hands' 25.361; 'Angels are to men as men are to women …' 26.4–5, 26.27

anger (*krodha* or *kodha*, *pratigha*)

what is it?
anger as the ninth fetter 3.421; anger as a poison 3.340, 4.73–4; anger and hatred 16.295, 17.598–9; directly opposed to the spirit of compassion 4.74; frustrated desire 1.232, 16.295; *pratigha* 17.598–600; rage (*krodha*) 17.643–5

getting angry
cold anger 19.15; don't be afraid of anger 17.599; hard to imagine being without some element of it 3.241; a hot temper and a highly developed intellect often go together 13.133; 'I forgot myself' 12.264; like all things, it arises in dependence on conditions 4.424; losing one's temper at a vulnerable moment 8.73; momentary flash of rage (*rosanā*) 15.302–3; mostly directed towards our nearest and dearest 17.599; pretending we are not angry because we have been told anger is wrong 12.265; some people are hot-tempered, others are slower, but the process is the same 18.310; the unskilfulness is not the outburst, but indulging anger 17.270–1; you may not realize your capacity for anger 25.75–6

to express it or not?
bringing anger out into the open 5.353, 13.173; experiencing anger is better than repressing it 17.599; if anger is unexpressed, it becomes resentment or even hatred 15.303; it can be deployed quite skilfully 17.599; it's foolish to give way to anger 4.393–4, 4.406–7; learning to express it skilfully 17.599, 18.608–10

consequences of anger
all mental events that arise will be imbued with it 17.496; it dissipates merit 15.367; it makes a person in authority unpopular 4.389; one of its karmic consequences is to make you ugly 4.390, 4.400, 17.281, 17.602; resentment, hatred, and enmity all arise from it 17.268

justified anger?
'I've every right to be angry!' 17.601; the idea that one should 'embrace one's rage' is nonsense 26.537; in India it seems strangely excusable in the holy man 4.388–9; 'Let a child feel your healthy, hot anger' (Lawrence) 15.432; no justification for getting angry in defence of your ideals 17.602; spiritual personalities claiming they are exhibiting anger as a test 4.614; we don't need to keep exploring our anger 14.574

dealing with anger
antidote: the *mettā bhāvanā* 3.342–4, 4.390; be careful that anger does not develop into hatred 17.599; dealing with anger in meditation 10.226–7; integrating anger through visualizing the wrathful form of a bodhisattva 5.353; it's the product of frustrated desire, so a simpler lifestyle may help 17.271; *kṣānti* the antidote 4.390, 4.393, 17.270; mundane and transcendental ways of dealing with anger 14.475–6; stages of learning to deal with anger 15.441; there is energy in anger which you can't afford to throw away 18.77–8; why is setting up a goal of being good-tempered likely to fail? 3.226; 'Why on earth am I behaving like this?' 5.348

reflections on anger
the angry-minded man has no way to be happy 4.389; arguments against anger that are only effective if you hold certain beliefs 4.407; getting angry with a magical illusion 4.406–7; 'If I get angry sometimes, why should I accept that?' 12.480; if you believe in the interconnectedness of all beings, it's unreasonable to be angry 4.405; 'Since sorrow comes from my own offences, why be angry elsewhere?' 4.426; someone doesn't make you angry, but gives you the occasion for anger 17.99; 'Who is getting angry?' 5.637; why be angry at someone else's success? 4.430; why be angry with someone who is harming you? 4.407–8; you are at least partially responsible for your painful experience 10.482

anger in the Buddhist tradition
can the Buddha get angry? 19.429–30; Kāli the servant girl and her angry mistress 9.522, 25.76; the king of snakes who was tormented but had not the least trace of anger 4.394; not giving way to anger even when sawn limb from limb 1.437, 4.121, 8.200, 13.577, 14.475; Śāntideva on anger 4.74, 4.405–8, 15.316, 15.440; a bodhisattva precept to try to pacify any angry person in your vicinity 13.56–7; the sublimation of anger represented by Vajrapāṇi 13.174; 'the Great Anger' 13.69, 17.314; Akṣobhya is the patron Buddha of people of choleric temperament 13.133; some think it's possible to attain Enlightenment and still give way to anger 13.571; you couldn't be murderously angry after attaining insight 17.132

angry people
a bad-tempered fellow passenger 24.283–4; 'Beware the fury of a patient man' 18.610; Dharmapala helps Mrs Foster overcome her bad temper 8.49; an example of a person of angry temperament 21.158–9; a frustrated idealist's repressed anger 23.239; an irascible swami: 'No one has given way to anger!' 14.565, 20.383–4; a king whose enemies were anger and greed 13.654; a Malaysian disciple with a hot temper 24.41; the man who lost his temper when interrupted while 'radiating *mettā*' 5.175–6, 8.133, 17.645; Satyapriya, Sangharakshita's companion 20.302–3, 20.316–17, 20.378–9

Aṅgulimāla his encounter with the Buddha 3.147–8, 7.550 (n33), 9.142, 17.274; he couldn't catch up with the Buddha 8.290–1; conversion 2.238, 9.373–4; the karmic consequences of his actions 15.93; shows us that human beings can change 3.180, 12.512–13; an attempt to show that he was a worshipper of Shiva 8.621

Angulimala Buddhist Prison Chaplaincy 2.753 (n763), 12.489

Aṅgulimāla Sutta *see under Majjhima Nikāya*

Aṅguttara Nikāya

INTRODUCTION
introduction 3.85, 14.47–51; the principle of classification is numerical 14.47–9; parallels with the *Puggala-Paññatti* (Abhidharma) 14.81

BOOK OF THE ONES

Etadaggavagga
the Buddha praises the disciples 3.179, 4.170–1, 18.132, 18.222; Bhaddiya foremost of those who have a sweet voice 10.615; Piṇḍola Bhāradvāja foremost among lion-roarers 10.538; Sīvalī and Kuṇḍadhāna foremost in obtaining food 2.229, 3.179; Subhūti foremost among those who dwell in peace 14.450–1; Subhūti foremost among those worthy of gifts 10.607; Upasena foremost among those who are 'altogether charming' 10.542

other suttas
the mind is pure (luminous), but defiled by adventitious defilements 1.364, 1.389, 2.130, 7.527, 10.439, 11.656–7, 17.95, 19.97; four 'fruitions of monkhood' 15.679–80; ten recollections (*anussatis*) 1.154, 4.701–2 (n279), 4.710 (n337)

BOOK OF THE TWOS
'flesh may wither...' 11.16

BOOK OF THE THREES

Kālāma Sutta
introduction 2.565, 3.674 (n306), 9.470–1; text of the Buddha's advice 2.745 (n696);

the basis on which one should believe a statement 7.144; the Buddha's advice is not suggestive of respect for mere antiquity 2.648; 'Do not go by reasoning …' 15.562–3, 15.565; oft-quoted but much misunderstood 1.59–60, 15.562, 15.565; the Buddha answers the Kālāmas' question 1.60, 2.648 (n696), 7.381, 9.471, 10.691 (n215); submit all teachings to the test of personal experience 7.128, 7.381, 10.171; why not go by the thought, 'The Recluse is my teacher'? 15.563–4

Sukhamāla Sutta
Buddha's recollection of his youth 2.20; the four sights 2.35–6, 3.24; intoxication of youth, health, and life 15.422–4; Siddhārtha's palaces 3.24

Titthāyatanādi Sutta
effects of believing in a Creator God 2.695 (n338), 11.742 (n63), 12.710 (n67); the belief that experience is caused by 'God's creative activity' 10.712 (n413)

other suttas
right speech 8.173; donkey that said it was a cow 3.401, 9.192–3, 9.273; 150 rules of training 2.707 (n424); 'Laughter that shows the teeth is madness' 4.137, 12.450, 15.372; three secret things 9.419, 9.571–2 (n357)

BOOK OF THE FOURS

Rohitassa Sutta
full span of life a hundred years 10.584, 10.718 (n461); the origin of the universe cannot be perceived 13.567; one cannot reach the end of the world 14.606, 14.659 (n521); 'In this six-foot body is the origin and dissolution of the universe' 7.170, 10.597, 13.567

other suttas
four persons who shed lustre upon the Sangha 2.203; all four *vargas* illuminate the sangha 2.203, 2.722 (n559); 'great self' (*mahā-atta*), a mistaken translation 3.235, 3.659 (n226); Tathāgata: one who acts as he speaks and speaks as he acts 3.322; four purposes of the holy life 14.49; the Buddha like an alert, perfectly tamed elephant 4.706 (n313); Doṇa tries to understand what sort of being the Buddha is 13.297, 14.582–3; four ways of answering a question 4.335–6; four very distant things 14.49; four *viparyāsas* 17.767 (n484), 17.777 (n588); four qualities of husband and wife 14.49; those who help themselves, others, both, neither 4.5, 10.146, 14.50–1; spiritual life as training a mettlesome young horse 2.707 (n420); the literalist (*pada-parama*) 8.620, 8.708 (n345); four discriminations 16.626–7 (n336); four kinds of disciple: spiritual life is difficult at the start, at the end, both, neither 10.228, 17.252; people who gain Nirvāṇa with or without effort, in this life or upon death 10.228, 10.483, 15.353; Queen Mallikā asks the Buddha why she is so plain 10.544

BOOK OF THE FIVES
dāna – a list of potential gifts 3.679 (n336); benefits of walking meditation 5.81; the five hindrances 1.636 (n451); profitable reflections: on the law of karma, the benefits of spiritual effort etc. 10.598; *cetanā* equals karma 17.520, 17.765 (n462); wrong livelihood 1.635 (n442), 3.582–3, 3.666 (n262), 3.691 (n459), 13.709 (n253); five precepts 3.662 (n243), 3.668 (n275), 3.673 (n299), 16.584 (n9); list of wrong views 2.391; sexual misconduct 1.534; five hindrances, traditional similes 11.123

BOOK OF THE SIXES
turban on fire 1.124, 7.392; the six *gāravas* 3.639 (n77); *arhants* 'tell of their gain (*attha*), but do not bring in the ego (*attā*)' 1.180, 7.154; circumambulation of the Buddha 19.612 (n133); the Buddha advises Soṇa to attune the pitch of the five spiritual faculties 1.293, 9.561 (n232), 9.571 (n348), 14.42; *cetanā* equals karma 17.520, 17.765 (n462); volition and action 3.99; threefold conceit 4.675 (n101)

BOOK OF THE SEVENS
conditions under which the Sangha might grow 2.666 (n38); the Buddha did 'all that a teacher could do' 1.180, 1.236; advice to Mahāmoggallāna, who tends to fall asleep in meditation 19.614 (n155)

BOOK OF THE EIGHTS

Gotamī Sutta
Ānanda makes it possible for women to join the sangha 3.179; the effect of admitting women into the sangha 11.643

Saṅkhitta Sutta
the Buddha's teaching to Mahāpajāpati Gotami, *see under* Mahāpajāpati Gotami

other suttas
the eight worldly winds 3.650 (n155), 3.668 (n272); Devadatta's downfall 3.638 (n71); 'As the rivers lose their names in the great ocean, the Buddhist loses caste' 2.691–2 (n305), 9.473; eight liberations 4.692 (n225)

BOOK OF THE NINES
Enlightenment within seven lives 3.661 (n233); 'unconscious' gods (*asaññasatta*) 14.407, 14.639 (n382); Buddha becomes

Enlightened by traversing stages of meditation 8.584

BOOK OF THE TENS

Cunda Sutta
abandoning slanderous speech 2.383; wrong views: 'There is no gift ... no fruit ...' 2.391; ten precepts taught to Cunda the silversmith 2.330–1, 3.632 (n41)

other suttas
'The concentrated mind sees things as they really are' 2.113; lion a traditional epithet 11.383, 11.756 (n214); the lion's roar of the Buddha 3.635–6 (n57), 13.693 (n124), 16.598 (n100); the six senses are not the self 11.755 (n201); the effects of wrong views 7.523; observance and non-observance of the precepts, the light and dark paths 2.705 (n408); precepts practised (and not practised) by women, with or without confidence 2.347

BOOK OF THE ELEVENS

Mettānisaṃsa Sutta
eleven benefits of practising the *mettā bhāvanā* 4.394, 9.517, 10.725 (n511), 17.189

anicca *see* impermanence

anidassana (indiscernible) 1.69

Aniketa, Dharmacharini (Barbara Gill) v24

anima and animus *see under* Jung

animal nature (of human beings) *see under* human life

animal realm *see under* wheel of life

animals

human beings and animals
animals cannot make ethical choices in the way humans can 15.90–1; Christian belief that animals were created for the service of man 8.256; the effect of living in an environment with many animals 18.23–4, 18.453–4; the gulf between human beings and animals 18.24; hatred is a uniquely human quality 15.303–4; humans are conscious of the passing of time in a way animals aren't 15.304; in the ancient past, people could see divinity in animal forms 13.244; is it possible for an animal to be reborn as a human being? 2.93–4, 16.292; it is self-awareness that distinguishes at least some human beings from animals 12.46, 12.88; like animals, humans need to belong to a group 3.437; like an animal, use whatever faculties you have 19.165; like us, animals feel pain and want to live 8.256, 10.544; the line of demarcation between humans and animals 14.291; migration between human and animal states 14.203; psychical continuity with human beings 2.94; what distinguishes human beings from animals (Nabokov) 3.478

Sangharakshita
love of animals 20.27–9; 25.52, 26.418; the poignant sight of a monkey at the zoo 20.313–14, 26.424; support for donkey charity 25.52; toy animals 26.427

animals in the Buddhist tradition
on the Buddha's Enlightenment, enemy animals mated and produced hybrid beasts 13.184–5; animals that symbolize four events in the Buddha's life 9.364–6; the Buddha compared to various animals 4.469, 10.201; the animals wept at the time of the Buddha's *parinirvāṇa* 16.295; the four animals of Aśoka 9.363–9; Aśoka established hospitals for animals and birds 1.427, 8.257; Śāntideva referring to himself as an 'animal' may be unfair to animals 4.325–6; the Vajrayāna: the path on which you may appear to be like an animal 13.176; the duties of a Buddhist towards animals 8.256–7; how can a Buddhist beat an animal? 9.522–3; some Buddhists treat animals badly, but the potential to look after them is there 8.610–11

kindness to animals
the acceptance of evolution led to a kinder attitude 10.345–6; animal hospitals 8.224, 8.257; ants and worms requested to depart before the building of a temple 22.502; Buddhism teaches that animals should be treated with gentleness 2.94, 10.171, 10.537; celebrating a festival by showing kindness to birds and animals 8.222–4; charity towards animals 1.427, 4.72, 4.94; compassion towards animals 2.94, 7.124; the friendliness of the would-be bodhisattva to animals 4.68; love is necessary for their growth and development 12.215; *mettā* towards animals 8.224, 8.256, 9.323, 9.522–3; the practice of releasing animals and birds from captivity 12.660; preventing the destruction of wild animal life 8.257

cruelty
animal products 10.460, 21.53; animals in enclosures and cages 24.460; a boy who tormented the Vihara cat 22.441; the boys who tormented a crow (or snake or fish), *see under Udāna*/people; Burma Raja's enjoyment 'when I've *meditated* and when I've *killed* something' 21.135; buffaloes being driven to market 21.321,

25.235; can lead to cruelty to human beings (Shakespeare reference) 24.575; in Christianity 10.345–6; the cruel implications of eating meat 1.499–500; due to lack of empathy 26.653; Hogarth's 'The Four Stages of Cruelty' 1.499, 3.542; horrible souvenirs from kangaroo skin 24.98; in India 4.326; stems from dogma of an irreducible difference between man and other living things 2.94; the suffering of animals 4.51; the training of elephants 8.610–11; use of animals for experiments 8.213–15, 16.406–7

slaughter
a butcher who became vegetarian through an apparent miracle 22.31; closing slaughterhouses in the week of Vaiśākha Pūrṇimā Day 8.223; eating meat, *see* meat; effect on the mental states of slaughterhouse workers 1.545, 4.545, 5.290; the first precept includes not taking animal life 7.124; diverting its consciousness to a better rebirth (Tibetan belief) 4.111–12, 19.331, 19.527; the killing of whales 25.51; an offence against natural morality 13.608–9; poaching elephants 25.54; rescuing animals from the slaughterhouse 8.224; Sangharakshita protests against the slaughter of animals for a wedding 22.485–6; the terrible effect on Terry of being forced to kill rabbits 23.96–7; would be precluded by the practice of *ahiṃsā* 7.119; wrong views by which people seek to justify animal slaughter 17.195

sacrifice
animal sacrifice in the Karle caves 8.295–6, 8.302; animals 'butchered to make a Roman holiday' at the Colosseum 23.310; the Buddha comments on the practice 2.326–7, 3.76, 26.179–80; in the Buddha's day cows were regularly sacrificed 10.48–9; Buddhism opposed to animal sacrifice 3.76, 9.217, 10.49; given up when Buddhism was first adopted in India 9.236, 9.265, 10.45; sometimes still carried out by new Buddhists 10.9, 10.20, 10.45; in the *Kinnari Jātaka* 2.332–3; in Nepal 7.347, 10.46; performed by brahmins 12.522, 16.362–3; primitive idea that through sacrifices you keep nature stable 10.517; the reaction against killing animals was more the work of Jainism than Buddhism 8.451; ritual slaughter of animals in Islam 24.576; sacrifice of animals by Hindus in Buddhist sacred sites 22.458; sacrifice of buffaloes in Kalimpong 10.279; the sacrificial altar 11.233; Tantric sacrifice 10.45; the Vedic injunction to sacrifice animals 8.450–1

hunting
blood sports 1.427, 1.499, 11.78; hunting animals to extinction 25.447; prohibition of blood sports in Tibet 13.7; pheasants being hunted 24.151; a schoolteacher who delighted in shooting birds 8.12, 8.94; songbirds shot in continental Europe 23.246, 25.366–7, 25.516–19; a warning to a king of the spiritual dangers of hunting 17.179–80; *see also* individual animals

animism

the aliveness of things
better to think that things are alive than that they are dead 3.597–8; children are animists to whom nothing is dead 20.484; every living thing feels and is sensitive, and they are all connected 4.541; a healthy basis for spiritual life to feel that everything is alive 13.272; 'How wonderful it was to feel oneself alive in a world of living things!' 24.38; mountains are alive 22.12; 'Nature is not dead but alive with many voices' 1.28; one could not gain Enlightenment in a universe conceived of as dead 15.138–9; a pagan sense of connectedness with the life of the earth 4.108; personalizing things 13.273; poets persist in seeing the universe as alive 15.139; trees as living presences 4.540–1, 20.444; the universe is magically alive 15.136–9

Buddhism and animism
in ancient Indian, especially Jain, thought 14.539; the animism of the Buddha and his disciples 3.597; a strongly animistic background to early Buddhism 10.453; scholars disturbed to find Buddhism 'corrupted' by animism 13.272; Milarepa's animism 19.504; there is no incompatibility between Buddhism and animism 11.247–8; 'I wish we had more animism in Buddhism' 26.390

animistic feeling
'I feel like going on my knees to this old mountain and these trees' 25.233; 'I talked on Art with tulips' 25.194; keeping up a positive relationship with natural forces and energies 13.271–3; living in hills 'without a human past' 25.292; sharing the feelings of birds and beasts, trees, flowers, mountains, streams, and stones 26.140; we have to hunt for a real feeling for the life of things 15.138; worship of rocks and trees 11.247–8

see also
Sangharakshita's animism, *see under* Sangharakshita VI/emotional life

animitta (the 'signless') *see under* three *vimokṣas*

Aniruddha, king of Burma *see under* Myanmar

Aniruddha (Maha Bodhi Society monk) 22.63–4

Aniruddha, Venerable (monk in Kalimpong) v21, v22

anītartha 16.580

anītika (unendangered) 1.69

anitya *see* impermanence

aniyata 2.195

aniyatas (Abhidharma) *see under* mental events/unclassifiable

añjali *see under* devotion/salutations

Aññāta-Koṇḍañña *see* Koṇḍañña

Anne, Queen 16.424

anniversaries anniversaries form part of our history 12.649; Triratna (FWBO) anniversaries, *see under* Triratna II

Annunciation *see under* Virgin Mary

Anomarati, Dharmachari (Oliver Katz) v24, 25.3

Anopatapta, Lake 12.574, 14.538–9

answers the Buddha answers brahmins' questions on profound themes 2.205; the Dharma is not the source of answers to what are really scientific questions 8.586–8; how Zen answers abstract questions 13.356–7; if the Buddha was asked a question three times, he would always answer 10.458–9, 10.462, 12.157; an occasion when the Buddha answered Sangharakshita's questions 22.301–2; people want ready-made 'Buddhist' answers for their questions 17.627–8; people who find it hard to start spiritual life without all the answers 10.577; resolving doubts doesn't necessarily mean getting answers to your questions 10.578; the way the Buddha answers questions 18.357; when all the answers are in your being, you have no need to keep them in your head 26.52; when giving a talk, don't give the impression of knowing all the answers 17.207, 19.109

Antaeus 26.169

antarābhava *see bardo*

antevasika (young monk, disciple) 2.196, 15.667

anthimeria (rhetorical device) 12.241, 12.723 (n172)

anthology (definition) 14.43

Anthony the Great, St 7.155, 7.589 (n256), 25.376

Anthony of Padua, St 19.467, 23.258–9, 24.458

anthropology 1.31–2, 3.84

antima sanskar vidhi 9.336

antinomianism always a danger in India 2.168; the antinomial structure of reason 1.313; ethical relativism 1.143, 4.614, 7.377; Hōnen's awareness of its dangers 7.42; a Pure Land teaching which is not antinomian 1.332; D. T. Suzuki's antinomianism 8.610

antinomies definition 7.550–1 (n39); as to whether the universe is finite or infinite 10.596–7; of *arhant* ideal and bodhisattva ideal 7.40, 7.150–1; can be resolved only by attaining to a higher level of experience 7.363; contradictions with no third position 10.597; in Christianity 7.39; the endeavour to transcend antinomies constitutes the history of Buddhist thought 7.39; grace (or faith) and works 7.39, 7.42; how Kant uses them 14.422

Antinous 23.277–8, 25.258

Antyajas 9.31

anubhāva (influence, grace) 4.265, 14.539, 18.98, 18.537

anubhogacarya the life of spontaneity 14.521, 18.254

anubodhi ('after-Enlightenment') 2.126, 12.504, 14.571, 15.464, 19.313

anukampā 1.235–6; *see also* compassion

anumāna (reason) 26.198

Anupada Sutta *see under Majjhima Nikāya*

anupāya 1.428

Anupiya 10.500–1

anupubbi-kathā (progressive discourse) 8.592–3, 10.551

Anuruddha the Buddha visits Anuruddha and his friends 3.635 (n55), 19.599–600 (n55); Anuruddha and his friends live together 'blending like milk and water' 3.670 (n287), 12.606–7; the three friends are 'different in body, but of one mind' 12.607

anusayas (seven propensities) 14.81

anussatis *see* ten recollections

anutpādana (unproduced) 1.319

anutpattika-dharma-kṣānti *see under* *kṣānti*

anuttara 2.124

anuttara-samyak-sambodhi *see samyak-sambodhi*

Anuttara Yoga Tantra *see under* Tantric Buddhism/doctrines and practices

anuttaro 15.493–4

anxiety and worry

introduction
the age of anxiety 3.333; appropriate and inappropriate worry 17.688; a difference between worry and anxiety 17.688; Freud's explanation of anxiety 17.688–9; not acknowledging a strong feeling leads to anxiety 17.688–9; worry can be positive if it is a spur to positive action 17.688

anxieties
the future 18.340, 19.269; owning a property 18.334; planning 18.460–1; social situations 23.192; on solitary retreat 16.279–80

anxiety and the spiritual life
early Buddhism attached great importance to being free from anxiety 10.501; the bodhisattva counteracts anxiety with the gift of fearlessness 3.368; faith and worry are incompatible 14.557, 17.38; if you are anxious about the spiritual life, something has gone wrong 17.254; *kaukṛtya*, unclassifiable mental event (*aniyata*) 17.688–9; once you're committed, there's nothing to worry about 4.48–9; persistent doubt suggests insecurity and anxiety 10.578; you can't worry your way to insight 5.448

don't worry
having done everything you can about a situation, don't worry 17.689; if your energy isn't unified, don't worry, because that would waste more energy 26.77; much of our thinking is just needless anxiety 11.149; suddenly realizing the absurdity of worrying 4.203, 18.10–13; today people don't worry about losing things because they can be replaced 18.334–5; whether or not there is a remedy for unhappiness, there is no need to worry 4.422–3

Apadānas 14.68

apagabbho *see* modesty

apalokita (inextinguishable) 1.69

apāna 1.386

Apaṇṇaka Sutta *see under Majjhima Nikāya*

apara-vidyā 9.229

apatheia (Stoics) 2.117

apatrāpya (Pāli *ottappa*, fear of blame) being sensitive to the judgement passed upon you by the wise 15.417–18, 17.558–60; Buddha-pride as a form of *apatrāpya* 17.275; can one regard Buddhas and bodhisattvas as 'the wise' in this case? 17.560–1; connection with faith and *hrī* 17.559; it is not about bowing to external pressure 17.558–60; it protects oneself and one's spiritual practice 17.561; as a positive mental event (Abhidharma) 17.558–60; the opposite, *see anapatrāpya*; prevents you doing something of which your spiritual friends would not approve 17.560, 18.486; *hiri* and *ottappa* (shame and blame) are the guardians of the world 16.348, 17.558, 18.486, 19.406–7; the point of it is to get help to follow the path one has chosen for oneself 17.559–60; taking a vow before a shrine, one is drawing to oneself the protection of *apatrāpya* 17.561; to develop it one needs to be on good terms with friends in the sangha 17.560

apavagga (final deliverance) 1.69

aphorisms about the One Mind 14.209; an aphorism is like a firebrand 26.3; aphorisms for reflection (Batchelor) 8.575; cultivate an aphorism as you would a rose, but be careful not to remove the thorns 26.70; of Friedrich Nietzsche 3.494–5, 26.3–4; of William Blake 3.495; a guide to reading aphorisms 26.xv, 26.3–5; Sangharakshita's 15.701, 26.xv, 26.1–85; why Nietzsche wrote aphorisms 17.620; of Oscar Wilde 26.488

Aphrodite 25.395, 25.512, 26.469–70, 26.482

Apollinaire, St 23.261

Apollo *Apollo Belvedere* 23.308, 23.519 (n343), 26.593; *Discobolus* 23.307, 26.593; divine healer 16.190; the great and glorious figure 23.272; the Muses, the daughters of Apollo 16.363; patron of the arts and sciences 16.190; progenitor of poetry 25.433; John Ruskin on Apollo 4.685–6 (n188), 14.429; sculptures of the Kouros, the Archaic Apollo 26.593–4; the statue at Olympia 23.299; statue in Naples 25.512; the temple of Apollo at Delphi 8.259, 12.461, 13.351, 23.276; a young man compared to Apollo in a Trollope novel 26.595–6

Apollonius of Tyana 3.560

apologies after rainy season retreat 3.405; apologising for the ego as an inverted form of conceit 18.81–2; 'An Apology' (poem) 25.50–9, 25.447; an apology should come from the heart 25.51; if you have made a mistake, admit it, confess, and apologise 10.398; no need to be apologetic when giving a talk 12.587; parents may feel the need to apologise to their children 3.543–4

apophatic theology 26.478

appakicco 15.284

appamāda *see apramāda*

appamādena sampādetha ('With awareness, strive') *see under* Buddha I/ last days

appamañña (or *apramāṇa*, infinitudes, unbounded states) 1.159, 14.80, 14.83

appearances artists are not limited by appearances 14.418; the bodhisattva lives simultaneously in the world of appearances and the world of reality 2.159–60; bodhisattvas are not misled by appearances 14.440; the Buddha's birth and death nothing but appearances (Mahāyāna) 1.250; don't go by appearances, but pay close attention to them 14.429–30; monks keeping up appearances 8.246, 19.470; people go very much by outward appearances 10.618–19; 'the terrible doubt of appearances' (Whitman) 17.378

Appleton, George 23.215

appreciation associate with people who appreciate your qualities 17.654; the difference between ordinary appreciation and rejoicing in merits 18.494; difficulty in accepting others' appreciation 17.185; doing things in order to get appreciation 18.494; if you appreciate someone for what they are, you will never find them boring 18.159; Goethe and Rilke on the subject 4.593; lack of appreciation in childhood 17.654; when you are free of grasping, you become aware of things as never before 15.287; we should have a much more appreciative attitude towards things and other people 4.593–4; *see also vidyā*/appreciative awareness; rejoicing in merits

appropriation the appropriation of knowledge as a means of reinforcing the ego 18.167; of higher experience 16.520; principle of non-appropriation 3.320–1; 'taking' Refuge suggests appropriation 3.326, 12.596

approval all spiritual practices will help you to overcome desire for approval 18.639; dependence on approval 16.317; desire for the group's approval 17.184–5; the guru as approval-bestowing figure 18.363–4, 19.365; people may twist advice into approval 18.368; skilful actions performed for approval pave the way for unskilful actions 18.165; suppressing aspects of yourself because you want approval 19.17; the true individual does not require the approval of the group 3.470, 15.285; wanting approval even when you are ignoring advice 18.363–4, 18.404

apramāda (Pāli *appamāda*, non-heedlessness) *appamādena sampādetha*, *see under* Buddha I/last days/last words; an account by the poet Dasgupta 17.580–1; an aspect of *vīrya* 1.439; the way to immortality (*Dhammapada*) 7.118, 17.581; difference from mindfulness 17.581; the key to all Buddhist practice 3.70; to be respected (one of the six *gāravas*) 3.70; a combination of openness and vigilance 15.173–4; 'mindfulness in the midst of mental states' (*Maṅgala Sutta*) 15.422; not a quality that is achieved, but a process that one engages in 17.581; one of the eleven positive mental events (Abhidharma) 17.579–81; Śāntideva on *apramāda* 4.486; supported by mindfulness of purpose 17.581; watching out for unmindfulness 10.532; you have to maintain it constantly, with the help of your friends 17.677; a kind of zeal that never lets an opportunity go by 15.210–11

apraṇihita, the 'unbiased' *see under* three *vimokṣas*

apsaras 22.350

Aquinas, St Thomas introduction 7.575 (n157), 26.730 (n314); chapel dedicated to him in Rome 23.309; Christianized the philosophy of Aristotle 13.557; definition of beauty: that which when seen, delights 26.396, 26.596; depicted trampling on Averroes 24.431; at the end of his life he realized that his writings were worthless 14.599; and the intellectual emphasis 14.442; the monotheism of Thomas Aquinas may be no more developed than that of a tribesman 14.602; Sangharakshita reads 13.533; a scholar, and a mystic late in life 13.108; *Summa Theologica* 14.109; teaching theology in Naples 24.281; vilification of Islam 7.85; Zurbarán's *Apotheosis of Saint Thomas Aquinas* 24.441

Arabic learning 7.85

Ārāḍa Kāḷāma *see* Āḷara Kālāma

arahant *see arhant*

arahantship *see* arhantship

araṇya *see* forest

ārati 3.49

Archer, Jeffrey 24.319

archetypal Buddhas *see under* Buddhas

archetypal reality 16.529, 16.532

archetypal realm 4.36, 16.533–4

archetypes definition 12.181; activating 16.358; adding Buddhist meaning to your usage of the word 12.118; archetypes of the collective unconscious 19.409, 19.615 (n159), 26.269–70; the Buddha: archetype or ideal? 5.564; the difference between the bearer of an archetype and the exemplar of an ideal 5.564–5; the difference between Buddhist and Christian attitudes to archetypes 12.191–2; Divine Healer, *see* Divine Healer; a hierarchy of archetypes 26.270–1; Jung's approach to archetypes, *see under* Jung; is there a world of divine archetypes interpenetrating the realm of material existence? 20.315; they are present in us and need to emerge into consciousness 12.192

Archimedes 3.427, 10.129

architecture architectural forms of the stupa 1.192, 16.139; the architecture of Bhaja retreat centre 10.405; basilica 24.675 (n329); Churrigueresque style 24.415, 24.419; city planning: straight lines and curves 26.265; difference between gothic and neoclassical style 16.327; encouragement to aspire 25.277; follies: architectural fantasies with no function 18.276; a Gothic church in Pisa 24.224–5; Indian Buddhist centres in a neo-Buddhist style 26.257; Lalitpur, Nepal 21.286–8; Mogul 20.112; rococo 16.327, 24.450, 24.599, 24.724 (n568); Romanesque 24.596; South Indian 20.232–3; Tibetan architecture 13.62–6

Arciṣmati (Blazing) *see under* ten *bhūmis*

ardent 10.427, 10.433, 15.217, 15.251

arete (virtue) 15.404–5

arguments, disputes, and discussions

the Buddhist approach
the Buddha said that only disputes about the path or how to practise were disastrous 11.370; the Buddha's dignity and patience in discussion 8.168–9; 'wordy warfare' (*viggāhika*): how one should *not* speak in discussion 8.169, 8.172, 22.171; courteous discussion between the Theravādins and their opponents 14.86; Tibetan gradual mode of discussion 12.121–2, 22.373–4

methods from the Western tradition
Addison's essay 'Methods of Disputing' 8.169–72, 22.171; appealing to people's experience 15.196–7; 'arguing by abuse' 8.171–2, 22.171–2; 'arguing by torture' 8.170; argument through bribery 8.170–1; *Argumentum Basilinum*: knocking someone down if you can't confute them 8.169–70, 8.171; categorical argument 2.636–7; Socrates' catechetical method 8.169

arguments
arguing not for Truth but just to win 25.246; arguing without the basic desire to communicate 18.170; being tempted to switch from love mode to power mode 18.354–5; bitter disputes often arise over trivialities 13.137; the clergyman who wrote on his sermon 'Argument weak here: shout' 17.235, 19.292; coming to a wall which is someone's deeply ingrained conviction 19.18; covering weak arguments with expression of strong feelings 17.235–6, 19.292; the difference between evaluation and description 19.290–1; disagreement with a fellow Buddhist is painful 8.598; dispute can only be resolved on a higher level 19.149–50; for learning to think clearly, argument is better than agreement 15.193; immersing yourself in Dharma discussion without practising it is laziness 17.534–5; Milarepa criticizes the adoption of fixed positions 18.169; 'Nothing was ever learnt by either side in a dispute' (Hazlitt) 24.563; rational and emotional arguments 7.248, 19.290–3; Rechungpa explains how to 'win' a dispute 19.148–52; 'the saliva-splashing debate' 18.459; saying 'I feel' instead of 'I think' 17.235, 19.291–2; sympathizing with something to such an extent that one disagrees with it 26.5; the wise do not indulge in acrimonious disputes 1.60

good practice
accepting that you have lost an argument 18.189; be slow to take a stand on anything other than a real matter of principle 13.137; being able to disagree without rancour 26.539; the Buddhist tradition of courteous discussion 8.171; collaborative thinking 15.192–3; don't accuse someone who is trying to be logical of rationalizing 19.293–4; don't argue, discuss 12.483–4, 26.82; don't attribute someone's convictions to ego to counter

their argument 10.471; don't get bogged down when there is substantial agreement 19.138–9; don't let your mindfulness evaporate in the fervour of wanting to be right 18.172; don't rebut an argument by questioning motives 17.235, 19.292–3; extra mindfulness required to avoid harsh speech during a debate 17.229; if you argue, argue courteously, without heat 12.137; if you listen carefully, you may hear an ego – perhaps your own – behind the words 18.170–1; if you think someone's argument is irrational, raise it with them privately 19.292; keep a positive attitude and stay open 18.354; maintain harmony even when there is disagreement 12.677; objective, skilful discussion is a cooperative process 10.603; you can influence people more by listening than by meeting their views head on 18.169

being convincing
how to be convincing 15.195–7; it's the quality of your own being that is convincing 18.355–7; the reality of your life is its own argument 15.197; we don't need arguments to convince us of the truth 4.571; you may browbeat someone into submission, but you will not convince them 15.197, 17.602, 18.360; your aim is not to win the argument but to communicate the truth as you see it 18.170

see also
logic/logical arguments

arhant

the word arhant and other terms
etymology 2.139, 3.412, 10.445; definition 17.727 (n147); early usage 2.139, 9.480, 10.430, 10.445, 10.460, 10.465, 10.614, 10.628–9; theory that the term was preceded by *muni* 3.592 ; it came to be understood in a narrow, individualistic manner 1.447; *akiñcana* ('man-of-naught') an early term 4.358; 'incipient bodhisattvas' 11.254; New Man a possible translation 15.7

descriptions
association with the ocean 1.310; compared to a rhinoceros 4.469; danger of spiritual selfishness 1.404–5, 7.361; he finds it difficult to possess anything apart from his robe and bowl 10.630; the ideal realized under the limitations of time and space 16.7, 16.26; qualities 1.143–4, 1.285; one beyond training' (*asekha*) 10.616; portrayed as dry emotionless figures 4.21; selflessness 1.182; the serpent: one who has destroyed the *āsavas* 1.309–10; you can't imagine a foolish *arhant* 17.134–5

arhants and ethics
'beyond good and evil', but manifests as an ethical being 7.377; the difference between the *śīla* of an *arhant* and that of an ordinary person 1.144; the unskilful actions of which an *arhant* is incapable 1.143–4

becoming an arhant
attainment of Nirvāṇa 1.180; to become an *arhant* you had to go forth 10.628; can an *arhant* fall away from his attainment? 14.86; can one be called an *arhant* between perfecting concentration and perfecting wisdom? 2.145–6; full development of the five spiritual faculties 7.489; breaking the ten fetters 1.178, 2.149–50; is there a point at which you become an *arhant*? 10.614; it is not easy to know whether someone is an *arhant* 10.590, 19.100, 19.282; it results in a change of lifestyle, but not necessarily *vice versa* 10.629; continuing to meditate after becoming an *arhant* 10.538–9; if a layman becomes an *arhant*, he 'miraculously' becomes a *bhikkhu* 10.629; *prajñāvimukta* and *ubhayatobhāgavimukta*: distinction based on mode of attainment 2.145

arhants of the Buddha's time
the first sixty *arhants*, *see under* disciples/ the Buddha's disciples; Bāhiya wonders whether he is an *arhant* 10.458, 10.460; Bhaddiya 'the dwarf' becomes an *arhant* 10.613–16; response to the Buddha's *parinirvāṇa* 4.9–10; at first, many *arhants* and few rules, then many rules and few *arhants* 10.480, 10.563–4, 19.262

distinction from the Buddha
introduction 1.52–5, 1.179, 7.504; hardened into separate paths 12.504–5, 16.62–3, 19.314; they felt the difference between themselves and the Buddha 1.54; three kinds of Enlightenment: *arhant*, *pratyekabuddha*, *sammāsambuddha* 15.465

arhants in Buddhist history
as one (or rather two) of the eight holy persons 2.149–50; the sixteen *arhants* 2.316; the smile of the *arhant* 4.137, 12.146; those with whom Nāgārjuna studied 1.310; Theravādin belief that the age of *arhants* is past 8.20, 15.585–7

arhants in literature
Avādanas illustrating the deeds to perform to become an *arhant* 14.67; in the Pāli scriptures 2.139; in the *Sutta-Nipāta* 1.181–2; appearance in Mahāyāna *sūtras* 1.272–3; '*arhants*' walk out of the assembly, *see under White Lotus Sūtra*/

structure of the *sūtra*; a goddess showers the assembly with flowers which stick to the *arhants* (*Vimalakīrti-nirdeśa*) 16.538; in the *Large Prajñāpāramitā Sūtra* 2.140, 2.154

depictions
contrasted with that of bodhisattvas 16.7, 26.697; as wrinkled old men 16.7, 16.26, 6.464, 26.233; in Chinese art as caricatures 26.599

Mahāyāna view of the arhant
has a subtle self-awareness to be overcome by the bodhisattva ideal 2.149–50; in the Mahāyāna the *arhant* stands for spiritual individualism 2.140, 18.172, 19.210; not excluded from sangha 2.155; no Pāli *sutta* describes an *arhant* who lives down to the Mahāyāna's caricature 14.552; one who has not seen that *dharmas* are empty 14.413; possible for an *arhant* to develop the *bodhicitta* 2.168; reckoned as bodhisattvas of the sixth stage 1.273, 4.179–80

the arhant contrasted with the bodhisattva
introduction 1.400–5, 16.7, 16.25, 16.464; the *arhant* has attained wisdom, but the bodhisattva has attained more merit 19.44–5; the distinction between the *nirvāṇa* of the *arhant* and that of the bodhisattva 19.199; the two ideals are not as contradictory as they seem 16.472, 16.545; symbolic meaning of the contrast 16.26

respect for the arhant
a dream of an English woodland where *arhants* lived 26.683–4; in our unenlightened state, we are in no position to look down on the *arhant* 4.87; respect for *arhants* 4.246–7; visualized on the Refuge Tree 13.78, 13.205; we should feel the utmost reverence for them 4.631

***arhant* ideal**

the early ideal
its emergence 10.467, 15.241; an attempt to reconcile the philosophy of the rishis and the teaching of the Buddha 7.41–2; no reason for regarding it as different from the ideal of Buddhahood 1.179; to regard it as self-regarding is an inexcusable misinterpretation 1.180; unattainable by one who imagines that he has an individual self 7.362; when preached by the Buddha, the antithesis of spiritual selfishness 1.402; wisdom and the *arhant* ideal 1.168–82; the difference between the ideal and the discipline of individual liberation 17.268

degeneration
the doctrine that Nirvāṇa was not a personal gain was forgotten 1.403; degeneration 4.21; dissatisfaction with the Theravādin interpretation (Second Council) 1.186; a narrow interpretation of the ideal 11.286; 'selfish' 4.84; settling for a limited form of Enlightenment 17.682; solitary, negative 7.47

and the bodhisattva ideal
the *arhant* ideal a stepping stone to the bodhisattva ideal 16.39; the contrast between them 1.402, 3.133, 4.84, 9.115, 9.255; a difference developed because of no conception of historical development 4.22; individualistic and altruistic 1.271–2, 9.115, 11.318–19, 16.472, 19.314–15; no real distinction 14.555, 14.571, 19.49; the historical distinction is unfortunate 14.555; the two ideals cannot really be separated 4.240, 11.319, 16.472–3, 16.545; ultimately individual and altruistic ideals coincide 2.299–300, 4.87–117

***arhant* path**

description
the 'Open Path' 1.404–5, 7.361; 'quieting the pool of troubled thought which is the mind' 4.339

distinction from the path of the bodhisattva
development of two paths for two goals 1.404–5, 2.204, 26.207; in an absolute sense, no difference 2.168, 4.240, 11.254–5; in a sense, the path of the bodhisattva includes that of the *arhant* 13.38; the conception of insight on the *arhant* path is more limited 5.438–9; the goal is the same for both 7.361–2; an attenuated version of the same spiritual path 4.39; in the Perfection of Wisdom they are said to exclude each other 14.494

arhantship devaluation of the goal 4.38–9; gained in this life, at the price of complete withdrawal from all worldly concerns 7.504; the idea that it is no longer attainable 8.280; Mahāyāna views: a stage on the way or a spiritual cul-de-sac 4.38–9; a monastic ideal 2.209–21; two deliverances bound up with path and fruit 3.665 (n255)

Aris, Michael 24.388

Aristophanes 3.427, 23.111, 23.288, 23.290, 23.298

Aristotle

introduction
introduction 7.574 (n153), 23.517–18 (n332); emergence in the Axial Age 3.427; the originator of literary criticism

26.324; invention of syllogisms 8.169; classification of many kinds of information 7.84; defined Man as a rational animal 3.479; perhaps anticipates evolution 3.10, 3.626 (n5); for him 'who I am' tied to embodied existence 8.613; walking while teaching (peripatetic) 5.80; influence on Christianity and Islam 7.486, 13.557; Arabic translations 7.85; labelling things in the Aristotelian sense 18.287; Sir Francis Bacon tried to overthrow Aristotle 12.655; Sangharakshita's first reading of Aristotle 20.61

works
Ethics 12.406, 23.301; the four causes: material, efficient, formal, and final 18.269; on friendship 3.575, 7.294, 12.638–9, 12.644, 17.327; 'He who can bear to live alone is either a beast or a god' 7.276, 12.68; *Metaphysics* 14.109; *Nicomachean Ethics* 11.192, 26.164; the state should be organized to enable people to lead good lives 7.239, 26.184; 'There are many ways of being wicked, but only one way of being good' 3.554, 17.549

Ariṭṭha (who misunderstood the Buddha's teaching) 1.78

ariyadhanas (spiritual treasures) *see under* treasure

ariya-mona *see* silence/noble silence

ariyapariyesanā **and** ***anariyapariyesanā*** (noble and ignoble quest) Buddhism deflects the energies of the disciple towards the noble quest 1.129; definition of *esanā*, a very strong word 3.208, 10.637; *pariyesenā* relates to two kinds of desire 12.550–1; goal 3.236; noble and ignoble quest 3.207–8, 7.151, 9.528, 12.548–50, 12.619–20, 14.591, 16.389; not to be grasped intellectually, we need to learn to be moved by its beauty 12.551

Ariyapariyesanā Sutta *see under Majjhima Nikāya*

ariya-puggalas *see under* sangha/ traditional sangha

Ariyawamsa, Venerable 23.410

Arjuna *see under Bhagavad Gītā*

armour the bodhisattva putting on the armour of strenuousness 4.60, 4.69; 'A Bodhisattva puts on armour …' 4.97–8; character armour, *see* Reich; fighting in golden armour the battles of the sun 25.285; the great armour of a bodhisattva 14.141–2, 14.574–5; the 'heavy armour' of *vīrya* 17.575–6; 'Put on the whole armour of God' 13.595, 17.575; the sole armour of a warrior of the Dharma was reason 7.383; spiritual armour 4.547

arms trade *see* wrong livelihood

Armstrong, A. H. 23.311

Arnold, Sir Edwin

introduction
brief introduction 23.482 (n78); article about Bodh Gaya in the *Daily Telegraph* 8.44; meetings with Anagarika Dharmapala 8.46, 8.59

The Light of Asia
introduction 7.593 (n283); Arnold draws on his experience of India 26.636; based on the *Lalitavistara Sūtra* 12.182; Buddhism is 'the proudest assertion ever made of human freedom' 7.267; it might inspire one to go for Refuge 15.609–10; an indestructible element of faith in final good 7.343; its influence on Dr Ambedkar 6.613, 9.181, 10.24; its influence on Western Buddhism 10.139, 11.76; the most widely known English book on Buddhism 7.449; the poem's role in spreading knowledge of the Buddha 3.654 (n185), 9.137, 12.71; Sangharakshita takes a copy to India 20.108; Swami Ramdas reads 20.326; translation by Gurubaksh Singh 7.447–8

quotes from The Light of Asia
'ample shade' 8.96; 'The dewdrop slips into the shining sea' 4.80; 'Forgoing self, the Universe grows "I"' 5.656, 7.46, 26.141; 'Many a House of Life/ Hath held me' 1.113–14, 11.411; Suddhodana (the Buddha's father) 1.46, 13.709 (n257); Siddhārtha's going forth 3.686 (n393); 'What pleasure hast thou of thy changeless bliss?' 25.lvii; 'The wisdom that hath made our Asia mild' 7.280

see also
Bhagavad Gītā/Arnold's translation

Arnold, Matthew called Shelley 'an ineffectual angel' 25.350; *Dover Beach* 26.394, 26.397; *The Forsaken Merman* 26.397; literary critic 26.324; Oxford, the 'home of lost causes' 23.55; 'our sick hurry and divided aims' 11.49–50; quoted by Dr Ambedkar 9.199; religion as 'morality touched by emotion' 11.75; 'a stream of tendency making for righteousness' 15.631–2, 16.78; and the 'two cultures' 3.6, 13.479; 'We want all pleasant ends, but will use no harsh means' 25.83–4

arrogance (*māna*)

in Buddhism
the arrogance of identifying with the five *skandhas* 17.604–5; conditioning of pride

and arrogance (*Udāna*) 10.514; his powers made Devadatta arrogant 10.580; *māna* is arrogance as distinct from pride 17.604; as *mūlakleśa* (Abhidharma) 17.603–7

kinds of arrogance
difference from haughtiness 17.273; fearing anything that threatens your fixed idea of who you are 15.275–6; the greatest scholars are never intellectually arrogant 21.114; intellectual arrogance 1.293; intrinsic to arrogance is lack of awareness 17.607; inverted arrogance 17.606; a presumption of higher status 17.279–80; seven kinds of arrogance 17.604–6; sometimes it isn't arrogance but a wrong impression 17.280; thinking you know better than the guru 18.493; wallowing arrogantly in the world like a pig in his sty 19.494

causes and effects
it stems from a lack of contentment with who you really are 15.276; the consequences of arrogance 17.606, 18.472; the near enemy of confidence 14.405; a great spiritual handicap 14.405; the way to overcome it is to reflect on the Dharma 17.607

arrows being pierced with speech like an elephant in battle pierced with arrows 10.540; the flower-tipped arrows of Māra 15.14; the flowery bow and arrows of Kurukullā 19.24; the poisoned arrow 1.112, 4.374, 16.93–4, 16.192, 18.442; the second arrow 10.504; seeing self-agency and the agency of others as an arrow 10.600–1; 'To tell the truth and to shoot well with arrows' 2.376; *vedanā* symbolized by a man with an arrow in his eye, *see under* twelve cyclical links

Arseniev, Nicholas 23.209, 23.505 (n242)

art

WHAT IS ART?

introduction
all art is expression, but not all expression is art 26.21; *ars longa, vita brevis* 26.297; art for art's sake 26.118, 26.150; art is superfluous, which is why it's so necessary 14.521–2; the arts as disciplines 26.353–5; the arts as a field of creativity 12.637, 26.165–6; the arts as the bearers of values 26.376–8, 26.396; the arts are what you get when you eliminate the objective element 15.707; the asceticism of art 26.137–8, 26.170; a channel of spiritual content through form 26.384–5; the concentration and canalization of emotion is its lifeblood 7.403; it begins with sensory impressions 3.511; it can attract people to religion, but become an end in itself 19.469–70; it can become a kind of spiritual discipline 7.403; *lalitakāla* (the playful arts) 14.521–2; a means of overcoming alienation 26.67; no such thing as 'art', only works of art 26.112; not only expression but communication 26.166; an object through which we find our way back to the subject 26.67; the power of the visual medium 24.40; receptive and creative approaches 11.620; the Religion of Art: surrender to the Beautiful 26.174

Sangharakshita's definition: 'the organization of sensuous impressions …'
the full definition 26.xiii, 26.21; the completeness of this definition 26.167; a definitely spiritual perspective on art 3.510–11; how it relates to the fourfold classification of art 26.177; a 'persuasive definition' 26.94–5; a sort of hierarchy of experience 26.244–6; what does it mean? 3.514–15, 22.xv

other definitions
'Art is intuition' (Croce) 3.510; 'The attempt to create pleasing forms' (Read) 3.510, 26.167; it communicates a sense of values (Read) 26.166; fourfold: spiritual, conventional, both, neither 26.115–16, 26.164–5, 26.177–8, 26.259; 'significant form' (Bell) 3.510, 26.167; stretching the mind 26.113–14, 26.187–90; what a man does with his solitude 26.67

the effects of art
it anticipates what the Good Life would be 26.191; all true art in essence and effect is egoless 26.180; the different degrees of the effects of art 26.114–15, 26.181; the expansion or raising of consciousness 11.118–19, 26.114–17; glimpses of the Pure Land through the arts 25.389; a heightening of sensibility and a widening of sympathy 26.114; it can heighten consciousness more than science can 7.436; ideally it contributes to the experience of egolessness 26.67, 26.164; it gets the emotions flowing freely 4.256; it gives both pleasure and meaning 26.165–6; it gives work to our unemployed affections 26.195; it has a unifying effect on the psyche 8.445; it stretches the mind 4.353, 26.113–14; its effects remain a permanent part of our character 26.190; the passive enjoyment of the arts 11.78, 26.181; refinement of emotions through art, *see under* refinement; threats to humanity make the arts more relevant than ever 26.376; the transformative power of art 3.515, 26.188–9; 'values translated into immediately loved images' 26.189

BUDDHISM AND ART

perspectives on art in the Buddhist tradition
art has a place in Buddhism 10.208; belief that Buddhism will regenerate art and literature in the West 7.37; the bodhisattva should learn all arts and sciences 4.81, 18.414, 18.463–4; Buddhism has an intimate relationship with the arts 7.436; comparison between Buddhism and art 26.117–18; experiencing a conflict between Buddhism and art 26.xiii, 26.xvi–xvii; the inner connection between Buddhism and art 26.111–12; the inseparability of Buddhism and art 26.129; it is wrong to suppose that the Buddha was against art and culture 10.99; Mañjughoṣa the patron of art 2.174, 4.192; the meaning of Buddhism coincides with the value of art 26.118, 26.132; the monk who rejected art as 'the product of greed, hatred, and delusion' 12.393; a monk won't look: 'I am not allowed to appreciate beauty' 2.84, 21.397, 22.148; Sri Lankan Buddhists accuse a painter of polluting the Buddha 21.398–9; for those practising the Dharma the arts can be very helpful 26.396

Buddhist art
among the supreme flowerings of the human spirit 7.486; appreciation of the Dharma through art 9.383; art and the threefold way 7.435–7; art that is both formally and essentially religious 26.116; art produced by Western Buddhists 7.450–1; artists may represent a bodhisattva from tradition but not experience 4.195; attracts people to Buddhism 10.207–8; Buddhists should protest against pseudo-Buddhist works of art 8.131–3; characterized by spiritual elevation and sublimity 7.451; comparing Buddhist art to Christian art 24.243; a means of spiritual realization 7.510; flooded the whole Eastern world with radiance 7.382; gives us a non-historical picture 10.481; the heritage should be preserved 8.133; may be sacred or profane 7.436–7; a modern trend towards depictions with no spiritual significance 8.263; one can't consciously decide to produce a Buddhist work of art 26.356; performing the 'impossible' feat of portraying an Enlightened being 7.245; images from Buddhist mythology that have nothing to do with doctrine 7.437; it has to grow out of your practice of the Dharma 11.620–1; Mahāyāna art among the greatest treasures of mankind 1.262; not intended to depict Reality but to show the direction in which to seek it 7.244; not many great or even good artists in the field of Buddhism 26.389; not naturalistic, but intended to convey symbolic significance 8.262–3; primarily Buddhist and only secondarily art 7.511; shows the process of Buddhism's assimilation of the cultures to which it spread 7.396; traditional and modern 22.125; visual Dharma: the purpose of Buddhist art 8.530–1; work of monk-artists 2.212; a world of serene beauty 26.389

works of Buddhist art
Ajanta caves, *see under* caves; art exhibition in Delhi 22.349–50; Bhutanese 22.349; *Buddha's Life by Modern Indian Painters* (review) 8.367; a Buddhist art collection in Bombay 22.272; 'Buddhism, Art and Faith' exhibition at the British Museum 24.243; Central Asian murals which 'lingered in my mind for many years' 22.349–50; the colours of Tantric Buddhist art 13.285; craftsmanship in Nepal 7.344; depiction of the earth goddess 16.381; images of the Buddha, *see* Buddha images; a mural of the *Vimalakīrti-nirdeśa* 16.517–18; sentimental depictions of bodhisattvas 5.202; Sikkimese art 22.349; *White Lotus Sūtra* parables in painting and sculpture 8.478; woodblock prints from Kalimpong 23.395–7

THE ART OF OTHER TRADITIONS

Christian art
artists had freedom within the iron framework of the Church 13.668–9; being moved by the form while disturbed by the content 4.99; blood in Christian art 13.631–2; a Buddhist can appreciate Christian art 13.669; contrast between depiction of angels and saints 16.7–8; the Crucifixion 13.631–2, 26.270, 26.299; depictions of angels 13.587–8; Virgin Mary, *see under* Virgin Mary; icons 13.602–3, 26.598; one needs to understand the images for them to communicate values 26.377; a puritan attitude to art 26.118; seeing the archetypal significance 4.99–100; in their Christian sense, its images no longer have significance for us 26.279; through the centuries it gets bloodier and bloodier 26.388

Islamic art
angels in Islamic art 26.239–40; a ban on the representation of living things 26.245; beautiful patterns 26.245

sacred and secular art
art can attract people to religion, but become an end in itself 19.469–70; the art of a religion tends to flourish or decline with the religion 22.266; art which is

religious in sentiment but non-religious in subject 26.164; a 'glory' is a halo in religious art 19.185; most conventionally religious art strengthens the ego-sense 26.67, 26.164; pseudo-religious art 26.164; sacred and profane 7.436–7; the secularism of the British arts 12.76–7; when does a work of art become sacred? 26.258–9

ART AND SPIRITUAL LIFE

how does art help us spiritually?
aesthetic experience doesn't necessarily reflect the golden light of the Dharma 16.285; analogy with the creation of a Buddha-land 16.476; art and religion overlap 25.26, 26.148; art as a substitute for religion 3.515, 7.436–7, 12.45, 26.148–51; art as support to the spiritual life 1.262; art can develop sensitivities, refine emotions, and open the way to meditation 3.617, 12.672; arts transformed (through Zen) into paths to Enlightenment 2.555; arts workshops 26.355–8; the asceticism of art 26.137–8, 26.158; can art produce *dhyāna* or *prajñā*? 7.436–7; the combination of the inspiration of spiritual life and the expression of art 26.69; conscious surrender to the beautiful 26.98; a deep connection between the arts and spiritual life 21.250–1; future Dharma practitioners may have their energies aroused by art 18.412; spiritual inspiration from the arts 26.259; how can a work of art help us spiritually? 12.394, 15.158; the importance of the arts to the spiritual life 10.506–7; Perfect Vision arising from an experience of art 1.481; refinement of egoistic energy through the arts 26.67; to assess art, apply the Buddha's criterion: does it help you spiritually or not? 12.393–4; to find the Dharma in art, give yourself to the work 22.465; subjective and objective aspects of art 26.165–6; transforming the mind through art 26.188–9; truly religious art conduces to the experience of egolessness 26.164; until recent times art was not separate from religion 3.425; the relationship between art and meditation 21.251; we cannot confront reality directly, art is the medium 26.22; what is the connection between art and spiritual growth? 3.506; the wonders of art have the power to draw awareness to them 15.158

following the Religion of Art
be careful it doesn't become aestheticism 26.396; Blake's expression of the religion of art 26.385–6; distinguishing between 'good' and 'bad' art 26.182; does it have an ethical dimension? 26.396; following it can deliver us from the delusion that the mind is a fixed substance 26.188–9; for many, art is replacing religion 26.329; giving up cheap literature and shoddy artefacts 26.183–4; keeping one's home beautiful 26.183–5, 26.396; how to approach the beauty of nature 26.186–7; it has never preached a holy war or burned a heretic at the stake 26.195; it may allow some to experience the values in the past mediated by religion 26.195; wherever there is the touch of beauty is holy ground 26.196; recommended to modern men and women 26.196; surrender to the Beautiful 26.174; through creative activities 26.191–3

art and society
art is the Cinderella of education 26.194; the value of art to the whole community 26.194

art and beauty
aesthetic self-indulgence: 'The Palace of Art' 26.149–51, 26.173–4; confusion between true beauty and the merely pretty 17.225–6; modern art doesn't seem to value beauty 12.615, 17.225; a monk won't look: 'I am not allowed to appreciate beauty' 2.84, 21.397, 22.148

art as metaphor
the Dharma is a work of art that ranges up and down all the colours 1.31; the spiritual life as a work of art 7.321

WORKS OF ART

the appreciation of works of art
the absolute newness of a work of art 26.174; all great art contains an element of self-transcendence 7.403, 26.21; all works of art can guide and sustain all people of all periods of history 7.81; attempting to enjoy them without permitting them to change us 26.173–4; awe-inspiring 2.644; be honest with yourself about whether you find artworks inspiring 19.348–9; the better the work of art, the more fully it communicates spiritual qualities 18.132; creating a work of art: translating it from eternity into time 17.609; enjoying the world like a work of art 14.517, 26.64; enjoyment of works of art 5.346; gold leaf seeming to represent the transcendental breaking through 13.284; a great portrait is a spiritual biography 3.508; great works of art broaden and deepen our level of consciousness 3.515, 4.353; a hierarchy of value 18.132; the work of art is in some sense a liberation of the personality 26.191; individual artists and movements, *see* individual artists; learning to look

at works of art 12.259–60; not all are products of the creative mind 11.25; only a work of art can describe another work of art 14.99–100; the powerful feelings involved in creating a work of art 26.69; the raw material of art 26.165; receptivity to particular works of art 26.265–6; reflect the level of consciousness of the artist 3.511–12; to find spiritual values in works of art we usually have to go back to the past 26.395; visionary art is always made of pure, bright colours 13.284; we can appreciate works of art because we have an affinity with them 3.57–8; we have access to the *rūpaloka*, the archetypal realm, through works of art 12.559; when a work succeeds, it lifts us to the level of consciousness of the artist 3.514, 26.23; a work of art is a world 3.511; works of art are the product of their age 3.58–9; works of art that show us the qualities of humanity 26.370–1; they have two elements, substance and form 26.112–13

modern art
commercialism and kitsch 26.378; difficult to think of it in positive terms 14.293–4; experiments in the arts 26.374–6; the idea of rebellion in modern art 26.359–63; the influence of Buddhism on modern Indian art 7.448; mass availability of art may influence the population 3.515–16; modern art doesn't seem to value beauty 12.615, 26.244; Modernism in 20th century arts 26.378; nudity for shock value in the arts 18.634, 19.258; people can't tell the difference any longer between good and bad art 26.378; sets great store by being original 12.637; the Turner Prize 12.615

painting
Bengal school of painting 7.448; it may take two days to paint, but it is based on a lifetime's experience 12.581; born of empty space, and derives its significance therefrom 7.322; Impressionism as an illustration of the nature of phenomenal existence 1.104; the isolated figure in a huge landscape 26.255–6; only painting could do justice to the Buddha's teaching career 2.25; to paint bamboos, learn to see bamboos 1.571–2, 26.249; Persian miniature paintings 13.284; its raw material is visual impressions 3.511

crafts
the Buddha gives a place to handicrafts (*Maṅgala Sutta*) 15.404–5; the Buddha's metaphor of virtue in terms of craftsmanship (*Sāmaññaphala Sutta*) 15.405; calligraphy 25.373; creative instincts expressed through domestic crafts 26.192; difference between crafted and mass-produced objects 18.71; enamels and glassware 24.301, 24.681–2 (9n367); ethics like embroidery, a matter of delicate and sensitive craftsmanship 18.84; crafts and trades of the Buddha's day (*sippa*, *vijja*) 10.520

see also
artists; Chinese art, *see under* China; film as an art form, *see under* film; Japanese art, *see under* Japanese Buddhism; Sangharakshita's experience of art, *see under* Sangharakshita XII; *The Religion of Art*, *see under* Sangharakshita XIII/publication history; Tibetan Buddhist art, *see under* Tibetan Buddhism/culture; Zen, *see under* Zen/practices

Artaud, Antonin 3.471, 15.520

Artemis 23.305–6

artha see attha

artha-caryā see under four *saṃgrahavastus*

Arthadarshin, Dharmachari (Philip Veale) v24, 25.435

Arthapāda Sūtra see under Chinese Buddhism/literature

artha-pratisaṃvid 16.489–90

Arthur, King as archetypal figure 16.533, 19.410; compared to the four great kings 16.357; the Round Table 4.658, 25.99–100, 25.105, 25.107; Holy Grail 12.192, 16.221, 16.239, 16.558; *Idylls of the King* 25.99; *Mort d'Arthur* 25.99; a paynim admitted to the Round Table 4.639; a resemblance between the Arthurian cycle and Mahāyāna Buddhism 16.239; sending Lancelot to woo Guinevere 25.406; statue at Winchester not King Arthur (as text states) but King Alfred 24.194, 24.253; three Arthurian poems 25.97–9; Winchester identified with Camelot 4.638

Arthur, Prince 24.581

artists

the qualities of the artist
what is a 'true artist'? 26.177–80; aloneness 3.509, 26.354–5; has the characteristics of the true individual 3.506–17; aren't artists often depraved and selfish? 3.512; becoming an artist in fulfilment of one's gestalt 18.281; egoism 3.606–7; egolessness 26.177–80; genius 3.513–14; independence of spirit 3.509; individualism 3.606–7; instability and supposed immorality 26.177–80; longing

for beauty 26.176; more alive than other people 3.507; not limited by appearances 14.418; often unintegrated, deeply divided 3.512–13; uncompromising 19.60; sensitivity 26.169; sensitivity to colour and form 3.507

the artistic process
the artist produces forms that are more real than natural reality 5.598; contact with the earth strengthens the artist 26.169–70; contact with 'unknown modes of being' 26.169, 26.170; the great artist is not thinking, 'Here I am, painting a masterpiece' 14.548; the organization of raw material into pleasurable patterns 3.511, 26.113; sometimes the artist has to devote himself wholeheartedly to art 25.110; sublimation and the artistic experience 26.172–3; there is no value in breaking rules for the sake of it 26.249; they have to work on reducing input, just as meditators do 12.475; Tibetan artists regard striving for originality as an aberration 13.59; the true artist 'always substitutes a finer morality for a grosser' (Lawrence) 26.144, 26.179; what the artist tries to express is a new mode of being 26.166

artists and spiritual life
the artist invites you to look at his painting, the religious teacher to share his life 26.68; the artist's contribution to the higher evolution 26.23; *The Artist's Dream* (short story) 24.372, 25.xxx, 25.544–53, 26.252–3; artistic friendships 26.364–6; the artistic vision comes quite close to insight 5.428; artists as spiritual friends 3.603; can approach transcendental consciousness 3.511; difference from mystic 3.513; experience of the four levels of awareness 3.507–8; having control over his material analogous with control of the mind 4.355; highly evolved, and contribute to the evolution of other people 3.515; may be oblivious to religious motivation, but have a touch of the spiritual 12.117; monk-artists 2.212; the need for artists who are committed to the spiritual life 26.69; one cannot be an authentic artist without participating in the spiritual life 3.506, 26.21; participation in the Religion of Art 26.181; the spiritual development of great artists 26.258; Tibetan artist monks 13.52

creativity
the active, creative aspect of the artist's being 22.269; being carried away in artistic creation 4.265; compulsion to create 26.192–3; creative experience like a seed whose nature is revealed when the flower blooms 3.517; what happens when the artist creates? 3.516; the vision of the finished work of art and the process of creating it 17.609

inspiration
the artist and the muse 3.513; artistic inspiration and the second *dhyāna* 5.240; artists find that their inspiration dries up if they use their talent wrongly 18.119; inspiration 26.178–9

productivity
all the great artists seem to have been great workers 26.72; productivity 3.509, 12.645; to produce art, you have to put all your energies into it 19.523

difficulties and challenges
appealing to taste for sensuous beauty while aiming for something purer 17.222; the artist's struggle 26.363–4; the danger of dabbling 11.620, 26.357–9; dangerous for the artist to think of himself as a rebel 26.359–60; the difficulties an artist has to overcome 26.193–4; the effect of art critics 12.643; the effect of the breakdown of tradition 22.269; making compromises in their work 12.643–4; the two great difficulties facing the artist today 22.269

artists and the world
the artist risks unpopularity 3.472, 3.510; the artist safeguards privacy 3.512; artists may be more respected when they start making money 15.717; artists not being appreciated in their lifetime 26.360; the difference between the artist and the ordinary person 3.57–8; disappointment when an artist in person doesn't seem to live up to his work 3.513; gratitude towards artists 3.602; has two identities: an artistic self and an ordinary self 3.513; in revolt against conventional morality 3.512; painting as though with one eye fixed on an infinitely horrifiable public 19.258; support for artists 4.94–5

Arunachala, Hill of Light 20.337–46

Arundale, Rukmini 21.439, 26.383

arūpa dhyānas *see under dhyānas*

arūpaloka *see under trailokya*

arūpa-samāpatti *see under samāpatti*

ārya (Pāli *ariya*) 10.576, 14.81

Ārya (of Madhyamaka school) 1.323

Arya Maitreya Mandala established by Lama Govinda 6.617, 21.394, 21.630 (n120); its emphases 11.561; Lama Govinda performs the Mandala's puja

23.414; led by Advayavajra 11.561, 12.584; the nature of the movement 11.763–4 (n311), 24.61, 24.622 (n85); Sangharakshita visits them in Germany 12.584

Arya Samaj 12.427–8

Aryadaka, Dharmachari (Phil Miller) v24

Aryadeva (French *sāmaṇera* in Kalimpong) v22

Āryadeva (also Kānadeva, Nāgārjuna's Sinhalese disciple)

introduction
association with Padmasambhava 8.523; co-founder of the Madhyamaka school 13.342; a formidable debater 1.321; could Yalahankar Swami be Āryadeva? 20.361–2; Indian patriarch of the Zen school 13.342; one of the six ornaments of India 17.464–6; ordination lineage in Tibet 7.473–4

Catuḥśataka
a critique of Brahminical philosophy 1.321; Candrakīrti's commentary 1.322; 'Darkness is everywhere just as the skin covers the whole body' 17.509–10; 'The seeds for the possible worlds are concepts' 17.475

other works
commentary on the *Mūla-madhyamaka-kārikā* 7.200; possibly the author of the *Cittaviśuddhiprakaraṇa* 1.382, 17.748 (n313), 18.637; *Śata Śāstra* 1.311

āryajñāna *see under jñāna*

Aryaloka Retreat Center *see under* Triratna IV/retreat centres

āryamārga *see* Noble Eightfold Path

ārya-mārgas *see* four noble paths

Aryamitra, Dharmachari v24

āryan etymology 3.410; distinguished from *pṛthagjana* 3.434; Sangharakshita's preferred translation: individual, or true individual 3.416, 3.421–2; two kinds of human being: *pṛthagjana* and *āryan*, bound and free 10.140–1

Āryan Eightfold Path *see* Noble Eightfold Path

Aryan invasion *see under* India

Aryan Path (journal) introduction 22.584 (n105); editor Sophia Wadia 22.133–4; Sangharakshita starts contributing to the magazine 22.133; Sangharakshita's book reviews 8.xxxv, 8.343–54, 22.107

āryan **truths** *see* four noble truths

ārya-pudgalas (Āryasaṅgha) *see under* sangha/traditional sangha

Āryasaṅgha *see under* sangha/traditional sangha

Āryasiṃha 13.342

Aryasingha, Dharmachari v24

Āryaśūra (poet) 14.62, 14.66–7

Aryatara (Sarum House) *see under* Croydon Buddhist Centre

Āryatārābhaṭṭārikānāmāṣṭottaraśataka-stotra 1.336, 24.394

'As above, so below' *see under* Hermes Trismegistus

Aṣāḍha 3.403

asaṃjña 14.407

asaṃkhyeya *see under kalpa*

asaṃprajanya (inattentiveness) absorbed in watching *saṃsāra* unfold, you can forget the true purpose of your existence 19.9–10; a sort of neurotic introspection with no clear purpose 17.679; as *upakleśa* (Abhidharma) 17.678–80; we are neurotically busy, without any singleness of purpose 11.50; weak character: little continuity of purpose and easily distracted 3.567

asaṃskṛta (Pāli *asaṅkhata*) in the *Diamond Sūtra* 14.444; epithet for Nirvāṇa 1.69, 1.171; knowledge of the uncompounded 17.546; in the Abhidharma 1.225; in the *Udāna* 16.389; Sarvāstivādin assumption that Nirvāṇa is *asaṃskṛta* 1.319; two levels of existence, *saṃskṛta* and *asaṃskṛta* 13.438; translated as Unconditioned 3.206, 14.444, 16.452; *see also dharmas/ asaṃskṛta dharmas*; uncompounded; Unconditioned

asaṃskṛta-dhātu 13.492

asaṃskṛta-śūnyatā *see* emptiness

Asan, Kumaran (Malayalam poet) 7.448, 7.617 (n494)

Asaṅga

LIFE STORY

introduction
brief introduction 17.741 (n271); always a Mahāyānist 17.449; younger brother of Vasubandhu 1.365, 17.449; began his career as a Sarvāstivādin 1.365; how much do we really know about him? 12.562–3;

one of the six ornaments of India 17.464–6; originator of the ordination lineage that went to Tibet 7.473–4

the teachings of the Yogācāra
from the *ācārya* Maitreyanātha 1.359–60, 12.168, 17.464; from Maitreya in the Tuṣita *devaloka* 1.276, 1.359, 12.28, 12.169, 14.260, 17.325, 17.464, 26.239

WORKS AND TEACHINGS

overview
he accepted the whole Buddhist tradition 1.367; designation of *pratītya-samutpāda* as *jñāna* 7.199; sometimes referred to as Mahāyāna Abhidharma 7.503; commentaries 1.362

Abhidharmasamuccaya
an abridgement of the first two chapters of the *Yogācāryabhūmi* 17.449; its analysis of mental events differs from the Sarvāstivādin one 17.449; *adhimokṣa* 17.535; anger 17.598; arrogance 17.603; avarice 17.656; *avidyā* 17.607; *chanda* (interest) 17.532; deceit 17.657; distraction 17.680; equanimity 17.581; extreme views 17.623–4; five functional co-relations 17.496–7; five stages of *vīrya* 17.575–7; 'Give again and again' 1.628 (n386); gloominess 17.669; heedlessness 17.676; *hrī* and *apatrāpya* 17.558; ideologies 17.628; intoxication 17.663; laziness 17.674; malice 17.664; mindfulness 17.535; non-deludedness 17.566–7; non-hatred 17.563; non-heedlessness 17.579; *prajñā* 17.545; resentment 17.645; *samādhi* 17.542; *saṃjñā*: 'to know by association' 17.514; self-view 17.618; spite 17.651; third fetter 17.632; three aspects of faith 17.550–1; unmindfulness 17.678; wrong views 17.635

other works
The Bodhisattva Path to Unsurpassed Enlightenment 2.344, 2.707 (n423); *Dharmadharmatāvibhaṅga* 1.366; *Madhyāntavibhaṅgha*, *see under* Maitreyanātha; *Mahāyānasaṃgraha* 1.366; *Mahāyāna-uttaratantra* 1.366; *śāstra* on the *Diamond Sūtra* 1.301, 14.148, 14.372; *Sūtralaṃkāra* 1.366, 12.578; *Triśatikāya Prajñāpāramitāya Kārikā-saptati* 1.366; *Yogācāryabhūmi* 1.361, 1.366, 1.634 (n428), 12.578; *Yogaśāstra* 22.103, 22.584 (n100)

Asanga, Dharmachari 17.431–2

asaññasatta ('unconscious' gods) 14.407, 14.639 (n382)

Asatkāryavāda school *see under* causality/cause and effect

asceticism and ascetics

the term ascetic
negative connotations of the word 4.122; contrast with Sanskrit and Tibetan terms, which give a sense of radiant heat 15.447; *muṇḍaka* (shaven-headed ascetic, pejorative term for the Buddha) 10.623, 14.19

the Buddha
the Buddha comments on some ascetics and their ceremonial ablutions 10.457–8; the Buddha said that some of his disciples practised it, others didn't 18.222; he notices that King Pasenadi has employed spies disguised as ascetics 10.588–93

in Buddhism
Buddhism is ascetic in the Greek sense of training (*askesis*) 4.122, 17.253, 26.64, 26.158; in Buddhism asceticism has a provisional value 19.383–4; duties of an ascetic (*śramaṇakāraka-dharmas*) 2.194; for the 'safe' practice of the Vajrayāna you need some preliminary asceticism 19.382; what the yogi's hardships enable him to see 18.138

asceticism in the spiritual life
ascetic practices (*dhutāṅgas*) 1.62–3; ascetic practices are good, but not if you do them for the wrong reason 10.519; everyday life provides us with the same opportunities for practice as an ascetic life 4.422; a means to an end 26.158; the part played by asceticism 8.446

in other traditions and areas of life
in ancient India 4.121–2; the asceticism of art 26.137–8, 26.158, 26.170; brahmins' tendency to look upon ascetics (even Hindu ones) as a threat 20.235; the more you enjoy life the more ascetic you will be, and *vice versa* 26.64; a sort of capitalist asceticism 18.507–8

as an extreme
alignment with eternalism 1.138; becoming too ascetic 18.104; the middle way between hedonism and asceticism 10.609, 15.287, 24.467, 26.158–9; 'painful, unworthy, and unprofitable' 26.158; virtuous acts done to go to heaven can lead to the extreme of asceticism 10.608

examples of ascetics
Cheenia Baba, who lived in a tree and burned wax on himself, *see* Cheenia Baba; five ascetics (*parivrājakas*), *see under* Buddha/disciples; Jaṭila ascetics 2.23, 10.457; long-haired ascetics 10.589; Mother Lakshmi, cave-dwelling ascetic 20.366–7; naked ascetics 10.589; *nigaṇṭhas* 10.589; Zhaozhou, the Zen

master who mended a chair with firewood 8.488

see also
'Patience is the greatest asceticism', *see under Dhammapada*/chapter 14; Siddhārtha's practice, *see under* Siddhārtha; *tapas*; renunciation; giving up

Asch, Sholem 13.650

Asclepius *see* Asklepios

asekha ('one beyond training') 10.616

Ashoka *see* Aśoka

Ashokashri, Dharmacharini 24.172, 24.650 (n213), 24.668 (n299)

ashrams dreams of ashrams 12.685–6, 23.184, 26.223–5, 26.678–9; time spent in Indian ashrams, *see under* Sangharakshita II/wandering days; Wellawatta (Colombo), Ramakrishna Mission ashram 20.116–26, 23.11

Ashvajit, Dharmachari 4.225, 4.235, v24, 24.648 (n202), 24.666 (n287), 26.545

Asita (predictor of Siddhārtha's future) 3.23–4

asking asking the Buddhas for forgiveness 16.310–11, 17.650–1; asking for advice, *see under* advice; asking for a method that gives Enlightenment quickly without effort 19.284–5; asking for teachings 11.275–6; asking for ordination, *see under* Triratna III/ordination/seeking ordination; asking 'Why did the Buddha say this?' 1.7, 19.295, 26.43; asking questions, *see* questions; keep asking yourself, 'Am I just going through the motions?' 19.275–6

Asklepios (or Asclepius) 16.190–1, 23.294

asoka (free from grief) 15.452

Aśoka, Emperor

his conversion to Buddhism
introduction to Aśoka 16.614–15 (n234); Caṇḍāśoka (Aśoka the Fierce): his career of violence 1.541–2; the Kalinga war 8.192, 25.271; his remorse and conversion to Buddhism 1.542, 3.180–1, 7.237, 9.120, 9.363–4; his great ideal of *dharmavijaya*, conquest by righteousness 7.452, 7.512, 8.192; his lions 8.xxviii; a significant influence on the growth of Buddhism in India 15.184–5

his own Buddhist practice
link with Padmasambhava 8.523; Upagupta was his spiritual teacher 13.341, 14.68; worship of the bodhi tree 2.222

good works
built pillars 9.364–9, 20.390, 20.421, 22.343, 23.360, 25.243, 25.592 (n63); built the Great Stupa at Sanchi and other stupas 3.20, 3.628 (n19), 16.143; endowed and maintained monasteries 12.238; established hospitals for people and animals 1.427, 8.257

relationship with the sangha
commanded the sangha to hear and learn the doctrine of *pratītya-samutpāda* 7.193; decreed that messengers of the Dharma should go out into the world 15.184; exhorted his people to skilful actions 16.296; expelled *bhikkhus* found wearing sacred threads beneath their robes 8.247; patron of the Vibhajyavādin school 14.23; perhaps he didn't fully realize the Dharma's potential as a catalyst for social change 7.512; purged the sangha of unworthy elements 10.519; recommended that the monks should study seven scriptural passages 14.22

Rock Edicts
definition of noble deeds 16.615 (n234); how to treat prisoners 16.615 (n234); Edict XIII renounces war and proclaims the ideal of *dharma-vijaya* 1.541–2, 7.512; a warning against schism 23.360; 'Whatever the Buddha said was well said' 3.168, 3.394, 7.434

his empire
he made Pāṭali the capital 10.648; in what is now Bihar 7.423; he was in contact with the Persian empire 16.57; its history 10.473; its expansion 8.244

legends in the Divyāvadāna
the building of 84,000 stupas in a day 8.523, 16.143; the career of Aśoka's preceptor Upagupta 14.68

his example
Ashok Vijayadashami Day (October 14th) 10.676 (n117); an example of a wheel-turning king 7.512; 'the name of Aśoka shines almost alone, a star' 1.542; shows how human beings can change 3.180–1; the only example in history of a conqueror who changed his ways 1.542

see also
Sanghamitta (his daughter); Mahinda (his son)

Aśokadatta-vyākaraṇa 14.181, 14.184

aspiration Dr Ambedkar's aspiration 9.149; arising of the *bodhicitta*, *see bodhicitta*/arising; 'Aspiration' (poem) 25.181; the aspiration of the soul 25.271; aspiration to Enlightenment, *see under*

Enlightenment/goal; aspiration to get rid of ignorance 9.324; its principal expressions 23.244; the bodhisattva ideal 4.60–1, 16.229; the difference between craving and aspiring for spiritual experience 11.80–1; the distinction between aspiration and desire 7.289–91; encouragements to aspire 25.277; Enlightenment the cumulative effect of the efforts and aspirations of countless lives 1.48; *esana*: urge, desire, will, search, aspiration, quest, pursuit 3.208; the flame of spiritual aspiration 1.8; how aspiration to become a bodhisattva arises 2.156; how do we become established in our aspirations? 14.405; individuality involves individual aspiration to reach a higher level of development 16.24–5; a jump of faith, like a man jumping across a river (Nāgasena) 1.289–90; merit as the only aspiration of lay people 2.204; prayer: an aspiration for qualities we do not yet possess 4.130; the Pure Land is the product of a bodhisattva's intense aspiration 17.297; for the welfare of all living beings (*Sūtra of Golden Light*) 16.276, 16.333–4; Sangharakshita's aspirations, *see under* Sangharakshita VI/ emotional life; Shelley's skylark a symbol of the upward aspiration of the human spirit 23.244, 26.23; we are miserable because we have denied the aspirations of our souls 7.307

Asprashya 9.30

aśraddhā (lack of faith, non-faith) 17.671–4, 18.273

āśravas or ***āsavas*** *see* three *āśravas*

Assaji *see* Aśvajit

Assalāyana, lay follower of the Buddha 2.665 (n30)

Assalāyana Sutta *see under Majjhima Nikāya*

Assam Sangharakshita's tour of Assam 22.90–101; Tais, followers of Theravāda Buddhism 7.463, 21.86–7, 22.39, 22.91, 22.95

assumptions

reflections
Christianity is 'based on the assumption that God is a fool' 18.163, 19.246–7; a dogmatic assumption of equality prevents communication 15.536–7; look out for manifestations of the incoherence of our assumptions about life 17.378; speech based on assumptions 17.236; those who reject Christianity are still influenced by its ethical assumptions 4.105; we don't like changing deep-rooted religious assumptions 12.10; wrong views are not intellectual convictions, but unconscious assumptions 3.193

examples of assumptions
in psychology, the deeper you go, the worse it becomes 4.605; the cause of a phenomenon is inferior to its effect 8.230; everybody is as good as everybody else 'as a person' 4.170; the goal is a state or experience 7.168; if reality is not to be found among concepts it will be found nowhere 17.379; intolerance is sure to be followed by violence 22.529; morality requires belief in God 8.281–2; the self is a real entity 17.475; a separate self 1.232; wisdom is better expressed in concepts than images 14.430–1

see also
two veils/*jñeyāvaraṇa*

Assyria 26.290

Aṣṭadaśa *see Perfection of Wisdom in 18,000 lines*

aṣṭāṅgikamārga *see* Noble Eightfold Path

aṣṭapariṣkāra **or** ***aṭṭhaparikkhāra*** *see* eight requisites

Aṣṭasāhasrikā *see Perfection of Wisdom in 8,000 lines*

astral body 13.152, 16.136

astrology

Buddhism and astrology
'What can the stars do?' (*Jātaka*) 22.278; astrologers predict the future of the Buddha-to-be 13.655; the Buddha's astrological sign, the bull 9.365; Buddhism does not believe in astrology 9.365; Capricorn and the *makara* 13.184; a form of 'low art' from which the Buddha 'holds aloof' 8.116, 8.305, 22.307; a form of wrong livelihood 1.547; it came into popular Buddhism from outside 2.219; Kachu Rimpoche's belief in it 26.227; 'No need to read the stars' 19.266–71; Padmasambhava learns astrology from Mañjuśrī 8.522; precepts dealing with astrology could be applied today 11.316–17; setting the date of a festival for astrological reasons 8.116–17

different cultures and approaches
accurate astrological predictions of a refugee's experience 22.277–8; Dr Conze's interest in astrology 6.618, 11.531; Tamil belief in astrology that traces misfortunes back to sins of previous lives 20.280; Tibetan reliance on astrology 19.267–9,

19.357, 26.227; 'a high percentage of English Buddhists were Virgoans' 11.531; how to approach a horoscope 15.386; the manipulative power of astrology in India 8.303–5, 22.307; planetary conjunctions may influence, but they are not determining factors 19.269–70

Sangharakshita
birthchart 2.405–6, 22.306–7; prediction that he would never stay long in one place 24.3; Virgoan methodical ways 26.537

astronomy 1.39, 2.62–3

aśubha (ugly, impure, filthy) 2.82, 5.510, 17.219

aśubha bhāvanā

what is the practice?
recollection of the thirty-two bodily substances 15.123–4, 15.126, 18.128; meditation on the truly unattractive 4.270; the first of the eight *vimokṣas* 16.446

what is it for?
the aim is to reach a state of equanimity 4.564; emancipation from craving 16.446, 17.223; it prepares us for beauty 17.221–3; a medicine for a certain disease 4.563, 4.564, 4.627, 5.512, 18.558, 18.561; the practice of the 'body-witness' 2.144

advice
a case of 'bending the bamboo the other way' 15.124; must be balanced by contemplation of beauty 17.225–6; not to be viewed in a moralistic way 5.511; not seeing something as ugly, but seeing something else as more beautiful 5.346; one tries to see the body as it really is 17.220–1; should be done in a positive spirit 4.537–8; to take it literally would be to confuse method and doctrine 15.129–30

concerns
getting distracted by thinking of living bodies 17.681; isn't contemplating 'loathsomeness' off-putting? 5.511, 15.124; perhaps not a suitable practice for Westerners 15.130, 17.223–4; a way of thinking about the female body at odds with modern sensibilities 17.218–19

in the Pāli canon
canonical references 4.692 (n225); in the *Satipaṭṭhāna Sutta* 15.123–31; one of four 'things that are to be made to grow' (*Udāna*) 10.531; possibly practised by Aññāta-Koṇḍañña 10.620

in the Bodhicaryāvatāra
the vileness of the body 4.537; embracing excrement 4.625–6; Śāntideva is being deliberately difficult 4.558, 18.558; 'The vultures lift that dainty veil ...' 4.556; what's the difference between a live body and a dead one? a horrible paradox 4.557–8; you delight in a village full of walking skeletons 4.627

other Mahāyāna sources
described in the *Vimalakīrti-nirdeśa* 16.494; inability to perceive the body's impurity illustrates a low level of awareness (Nāgārjuna) 17.389; in the *Precious Garland*, to help men overcome sexual craving 17.217–19

see also contemplation of decay

asuras (titans) an aggressive, competitive state of mind 13.130; compared to the rebel angels in *Paradise Lost* 4.449; an encounter with an *asura* 26.621–2; fight the gods 11.323, 13.126, 16.349, 16.427; males are ugly, females are beautiful 16.349; our modern technological civilization said to be *āsura*-like 4.449; politicians tend to create *asura*-like worlds 17.298; sexual polarization 2.372; their world experienced at Napoleon's tomb 26.277; too competitive and possessive to be happy 4.449; *see also under* wheel of life/the third circle

Aśvaghoṣa

his life
brief introduction 2.690 (n296); he was a great musician who played the melody of impermanence 13.132; 'in the soul two aspects may be distinguished' 7.202; Indian patriarch of the Zen school 13.342; 'Knowing little, the blind men do not know how to bring contemplation to life' 17.573; one of the supreme poets and dramatists of India 2.13, 2.213; designation of *pratītya-samutpāda* as *ālaya-jñāna* 7.199

BUDDHACARITA

introduction to the work
in Dr Ambedkar's anthology 9.139, 9.140; a beautiful epic poem in classical Sanskrit 7.437, 12.109, 12.182; the Buddha's refutation of the Sāṃkhya school of Brahminical philosophy 17.440; exquisite language 9.111; 'how could liberation ... be expressed in words?' 17.741 (n268); last fifteen chapters lost in the original 2.13; Queen Maya 3.629 (n20); related to the story of Barlaam and Josaphat 13.662; the *vajrāsana* 12.186, 12.719 (n132)

Siddhārtha in the text
his birth 1.256, 10.36; Asita's encounter with the infant Siddhārtha 3.24; the four sights 2.35, 3.29, 10.256; his supposed disgust at sleeping dancing girls 2.33; he

goes forth and swaps his clothes 3.29, 9.191, 10.257; the attack of Māra's hordes 3.277

OTHER WORKS

The Awakening of Faith in the Mahāyāna
introduction 13.681 (n44), 16.560; Sangharakshita copied it out 20.332, 26.576; criticism of Dasgupta's reading 21.113; later scholars said it was at least partly Chinese 1.372–3, 11.752 (n166), 21.624 (n35); more 'metaphysical' than the *Bodhicaryāvatāra*, but also very positive 4.623; Sangharakshita discusses the text with a Japanese scholar 22.16; studied in the early days of the WBO 4.713 (n358); suchness (*tathatā*) 11.325, 14.502; *trikāya* 2.46; ultimate reality 'perfumes' conditioned existence 4.33, 7.317, 7.400, 13.313, 15.633, 16.560–1, 22.16–17, 25.32, 26.498; 'We use words to get free from words, until we reach the pure wordless essence' 8.498, 13.348, 14.325, 19.241, 19.447

Fo-Sho-Hing-Tsan-King (A Life of Buddha)
Siddhārtha's struggle to decide to go forth 3.208; how the emaciated Siddhārtha fell into a river 3.631 (n32)

Aśvajit (Pāli Assaji) his role in Śāriputra's spiritual life, *see under* Śāriputra

atakkāvacara (beyond the reach of reasoning) 1.17, 1.209, 8.589, 9.398

Āṭānāṭiya Sutta *see under Dīgha Nikāya*

atapa (*atappā*, world) 2.148

atheism the atheism of Buddhism, *see under* Buddhism I/what Buddhism is not; contemporary (the Bishop of Woolwich) 12.6–7; Francis Bacon's view of atheism 1.197–8; Bishop Berkeley saw materialism as synonymous with atheism 1.368; definition of an atheist: a man who does not believe in God but is afraid of him 11.341; inculcated by a schoolteacher 20.40; Shelley on atheism 11.343, 11.754 (n191)

Athene *see* Pallas Athene

Atīśa (Dīpaṅkara Śrījñāna)

life story
introduction: 'A Life for the Dharma' 12.563–79; biographies 12.563; birth and early life 12.564–5; he grew up in a Tantric atmosphere 12.565; perhaps some of his teachers were *mahāsiddhas* 12.565; he practised the Vajrayāna for years, but was not satisfied with his progress 12.565; said to have visited the land of Uḍḍiyāna and practised with the *ḍākinīs* 12.565; he was ordained and studied at Indian universities 12.567; to study the Mahāyāna, he spent twelve years in Sumatra 12.567, 12.569; he was inspired by the bodhisattva ideal 12.569; time at the monastic university of Vikramaśīla 12.569–72; protected defeated troops 12.569–70; invited to visit Tibet in dramatic circumstances 12.571–3, 13.13–14; Tārā advised him to go, though doing so would shorten his life 11.714, 12.572, 26.669; his journey to Tibet via Bodh Gaya and Nepal 12.574, 13.14; based at Tholing Monastery 12.574–7; wrote a poem in praise of Tibetan tea 12.574–5; his meeting with Rinchen Zangpo 12.575–6; composed devotional verses on the spot 12.575; his disciple Drömton 12.577–9; the founding of the Kadampa tradition 12.577–9, 12.594, 13.14; part of a renaissance for Buddhism in Tibet 13.14, 18.3; his self-sacrifice 11.714, 12.573, 12.578; his death in Nyetang, Tibet 12.578; on the Refuge Tree 11.714

Bodhipathapradīpa (Lamp of the Path to Enlightenment)
introduction 12.576–7; the basis of a work by Tsongkhapa 17.423–4; studied by the Kadam school 12.579; and the working out of the *triyāna* path of Tibet 13.106

other writings and teachings
all *sādhanas* are in principle the same 12.575–6; he emphasized the Mahāyāna, and played down the Tantra 12.576–7; Going for Refuge to the Three Jewels (the 'Refuge Lama') 2.442, 2.720–1 (n541), 12.577; he introduced ordination lineage in Tibet 7.473–4; 'The precept of the Lama is more important than the scriptures and commentaries' 8.528; the ten precepts and the development of the *bodhicitta* (*mettā* and *karuṇā*) 12.577; translations 12.577; encouraged the worship of Śākyamuni, Avalokiteśvara, Tārā, and Acala 12.578

atithi *see under* guests

Atiyoga along with the *mahāmudrā* and Zen, the peak of Buddhist spirituality 13.323; *atiyogayāna* 12.298; *dzogchen* in Tibetan Buddhism 12.299, 13.23; included in the Mahāmudrā 19.372

atmabhāvādi-parityāgaḥ (self-surrender) *see* self-surrender

ātman (Pāli *attā*)

introduction
definition 2.661 (n4); an abstraction, a mere name 10.159–60; and *aiśvarya* 10.592–3; *attā* contrasted with *attha*

1.180, 3.409, 7.154; attachment to the delusion of *ātman* 1.232; belief in *ātman* 7.327; the Buddha denied its existence 1.20, 7.211, 14.461; extreme view of eternal unchanging *ātman* 9.398–9, 19.375; Hīnayāna mistake that the analysis of *ātman* is sufficient for the attainment of Nirvāṇa 1.267; the idea that early Buddhists could not give up belief in the ultimate reality of the *ātman* 17.632; *mahā-atta* mistakenly thought to be used in Pāli canon 3.235; *mahātma*, the 'great self' (Mahāyāna) 3.234–5, 14.234–5; *paramātman* (supreme self) 2.130; rebirth does not involve it 9.343; in the Saṃkhya school of philosophy 4.424–5; if the term used in Buddhism, it is only as an accommodation to convention 2.14; to understand *anattā*, you have to understand *attā* 3.492, 12.428–9, 19.446–7, 20.447

in Hinduism
the *brahman* is to be sought in the *ātman* 7.98; confusing use of the word 'self' 7.211–12; a naive and literalistic attempt to convince brahmins that there is no *ātman* 19.101–2; is Nirvāṇa identical with the Vedantic *ātman*? 7.211–13; Upanishadic view 3.217; the views of Attavādins 7.130–2

Ātmanism introduction 7.165–8; the Buddha warned of its subtlety 7.211; Buddhism and Ātmanism are poles apart 7.213; limitations 7.167; and materialism 7.165–8; precluded the possibility of spiritual progress 7.213; the void of utter impersonality 8.260

ātmavāda (Pāli *attavāda*, noumenalism) introduction 1.99–100, 17.722 (n108); wrong belief in it 1.112; the idea of the final stage of development being present within is a form of *ātmavāda* 17.93

atmosphere

reflections on atmosphere
bringing children up in a loving, peaceful, supportive atmosphere 26.658; creating a positive atmosphere 17.297–8; creating the right atmosphere for a Dharma talk 22.245, 22.286; don't get precious about auras and atmospheres 4.547; importance of a peaceful atmosphere at the time of death 2.231–2; picking up the atmosphere of a place 17.511; places and objects can develop an atmosphere 14.463–5; *puṇya karma*, the skilful atmosphere you create around yourself 18.244–5; sensitivity to atmosphere 18.23; suffering can leave a vibration in the atmosphere of a place 18.312; you can get a lot of tough work done in a relaxed atmosphere 14.520

atmospheres
a community in New Zealand 24.67; created by a women's Order convention 12.591; during a talk about the *bardos* 23.93; retreats 23.137, 24.163; filled with hate 21.121; the College of Psychic Science 23.91; the cremation ground 13.224–5, 13.229, 13.247; in shops 4.573–4, 11.80; Glastonbury 18.23; at a Hindu festival 22.336; in big cities 4.571–4; in the Colosseum 23.255, 23.310; in a Roman Catholic cathedral 23.253; in shrine-rooms 19.328, 22.16, 22.239; rejoicing in the Buddha 17.337; the Sevenfold Puja 11.213, 11.234; the valley of the oracle of Zeus 23.266; of the *White Lotus Sūtra* 16.19

atom atom of divinity through which man attains union with the soul of the universe (Hinduism) 7.41; building a model of an atom is not to be taken literally 14.548; a continuously changing dance of forces 2.85; 'In every single atom/ Are all things of all places and times' 16.583 (n3); 'as many atoms as there are': life as a continuous salutation 11.246

atomic war *see* war/nuclear war

attā *see ātman*

attachment

what is attachment?
by no means positive, but a step up from nihilism 17.250–1; close relationship between hatred and attachment 17.564–5; 'the Dharma is difficult to see for those who delight in attachment' (the Buddha) 3.175–6; four kinds: to possessions, views, ethics as ends in themselves, belief in a fixed self 1.112, 3.199–200; it comes from desire 17.283; the near enemy of fidelity 3.567–8, 11.580; no self-awareness in attachment 3.568; pleasure is only succeeded by pain because of attachment 10.497–8; positive attachment is attachment that is a basis for non-attachment 19.241; those who are attached to a hundred things have a hundred sorrows 10.651–2; the truth is that worldly attachments are unsure and impermanent 17.363; we come up against it when we start trying to lead the spiritual life 14.570; the world is attached to the process of becoming 10.522–3

reflections
beware the idea that attachments are good because of the insight you get when they break up 11.540; concerning yourself with others' needs, you realize how attached you

are to your own 17.206; the discomfort of neurotic attachment produces further craving 15.231; fear indicates attachment to the self, and that implies duality 18.49; 'He who binds to himself a joy' 17.506, 26.598; hypocrisy: attachment to our faults and also to our reputation 17.284–5; in modern life, attachments are spread over easily replaceable objects 19.13, 19.19; in modern times lack of attachment may be due to alienation and lack of feeling 18.331–5; love and compassion are more blessed than attachment 7.291; suffering through the loss of something alerts us to the wrong view (*viparyāsa*) 3.280–1; we are born out of our attachment to conditioned things 3.200

attachment to …
a belief in a permanent unchanging self 3.200; the body 1.155; children 3.538–9, 10.455, 10.490–3; cloisters 8.312; comfort 19.13; ethics (*śīla*) and religious observance (*vrata*), *see* ten fetters/third fetter; existence 10.491; the food you're used to 19.252; family members who are not practising the Dharma 18.565–6; material things 17.284; the means to Enlightenment 1.303; mundane experience 17.512–13; our own community 18.139; particular families (monks) 15.284–5; people 18.330–1, 18.566–7; possessions, *see under* possessions; your native place 19.252, 19.362; your image of yourself 17.285; reputation 18.461; sex 11.573; the sights and sounds of the world 10.610–11; *śūnyatā*, *see under śūnyatā*/what it is/mistakes; views 3.199; worldly pleasures 18.130

attachment and pleasure
enjoy the *dhyānas* but don't become attached to them 14.563–4; enjoying beauty without making it an object of attachment 26.598; enjoying sense-pleasures and remaining unattached 17.221; pleasure is all right unless it becomes the basis for attachment 15.533; seeing that pleasures have their limitations, you're not attached to them 15.449; sense experience turned into attachment 18.345; some religions advise giving up pleasures, but better to give up attachment to misery 17.396–7

giving up attachment
the abandonment of worldly attachment 18.128; destroying something a person is attached to, to help them let go 19.12–14, 19.18; destruction of attachment to objects 1.100; feeling no attachment may be nihilism, not spiritual maturity 17.371; giving up narrow, exclusive attachment for the sake of a wider vision 18.215; if there was just one attachment, it would be terrible, but simple to get rid of 19.19; Milarepa renounces attachment to enjoy freedom 18.54; non-attachment has no meaning unless you're full-bloodedly capable of attachment 18.337; one can drop one's attachment because one is not holding onto it 17.408; the only way to see through the self is to be to some extent free from attachment 17.383; the stage of no attachments 4.625; think of attachment to the positive, not detachment from the negative 10.513, 18.332–3

practices to help with letting go
don't criticize people's attachment to lower realms, but show them higher ones 10.507; Nirvāṇa taught for those deeply attached to human desires 14.117–18; the teaching of *śūnyatā* is intended as a medicine to cure all attachments 3.237; those with strong attachments may need to practise the *aśubha bhāvanā* 4.564; Zen makes use of scriptures without becoming attached to them 13.343

see also
letting go; non-attachment; *pema* (sticky attachment)

attacks

physical
an elephant set to attack the Buddha, *see under* elephants; a Tibetan caravan is attacked by bandits 18.99–100; violent attacks on Indian Buddhists 10.301–2, 10.310; when the Śākyas were attacked, they offered no resistance 12.357; your attacker brought the stick (or sword), but you brought the body 4.119–20, 4.409, 4.425, 10.600, 15.440, 17.172

figurative and mythical
attacking distractions 15.177; the competitive world is like a hawk attacked by other hawks for the meat it is carrying 3.215; the danger of being attacked by Māra in worldly life 18.34; Māra's attacks on Siddhārtha, *see under* Māra; Nāgārjuna's attack on *asatkāryavāda* and *satkāryavāda* 1.315–16, 19.435; the six element practice attacks the notion of an ego 19.453

on views and beliefs
the bodhisattva ideal attacked by Theravādins 1.233; Buddhism attacked by a swami 22.10; 'Buddhists' who attack other forms of Buddhism without studying them 8.141; on Christianity, *see under* Christianity/attitudes; Christ's teachings attack group values 12.249; if

you don't regard an idea as yours, if it is attacked, you don't get upset 10.489; missionaries attacking Buddhism 12.136–7; need to attack traditions that hinder the development of the true individual 13.477–8; spiritual life is under attack 2.649–50; submissiveness can lead to people attacking you 4.477–8

attainment

reflections
for *arhants*, the idea of individual attainment has vanished 1.179, 14.450; 'attainment' is outside time 18.45; the attainment of liberating knowledge depends upon oneself 7.367; a balance between high spiritual attainment and wide compassionate activity 7.139; compassion the outward expression of all true spiritual attainment 7.290; confusion between ecclesiastical success and spiritual attainment 18.561–2; dedication to the attainment of supreme wisdom 7.320; the difference between wanting to attain and wanting to acquire 11.80–1; the highest attainment known to the Buddha's contemporaries 7.227; renunciation needed to attain both perfect love and perfect knowledge 7.95; spiritual attainments do not pour forth on the pressing of some yogic button 1.133; the *vajrāsana* the transcendental foundation of attainment 19.398; the whole conception of attainment is fundamentally wrong 7.412, 26.53; we need to be aware that there are states of consciousness we have not yet attained 15.163–4

making claims about attainment
attainments may harden into personal possessions 1.303; behaving as though one has attained more than one really has 18.473; conceit about your level of spiritual attainment 18.399–400, 18.405–6; Sāriputta does not lay claim to a meditative state 1.179, 3.409; laying false claim to attainment is a *pārājika* (defeat) 3.409; 'proving' spiritual attainment 18.108–9; so full of imagined spiritual attainments that you close your ears to the Buddha 16.64; testifying to your attainment is a risky procedure 14.450–1; those who lay claim to any attainment betray the hollowness of their pretensions 7.360

attainment and non-attainment
abandoning the idea of attainment 26.175–6; the bodhisattva courses in the idea of non-attainment while striving to attain 1.269, 14.562; attainment is not different from non-attainment 1.269; attainment of Enlightenment, *see under* Enlightenment/Enlightenment itself; rather than attaining the Transcendental, speak of the cessation of the mundane 19.435–6; in reality there is no striving and no attainment 7.45

Attar 26.687

attention (*manana*) the Buddha speaks about Nirvāṇa when the *bhikkhus* are listening attentively 10.632–3; the duality between distraction and attention 16.543–4; forcible fixation of attention 2.112–13; in communication, pay attention to the other person 1.519–21, 10.217, 16.579; the only way of knowing another person is through appreciative attention 14.582; paying attention to the small details of life 4.68; the *sambhogakāya*: seen when attention is withdrawn from the senses 2.41; a simple but creative shift of attention 18.53; spreading one's attention across the enjoyments of modern life 15.152–3; withdrawal of the scattered forces of the mind into a single unified focus of attention 7.358–9; unsleeping vigilant attentiveness 7.172; unwise attention 15.170, 15.204

attha (Sanskrit *artha*, essence, gain) the Buddha contrasts it with *attā* 1.180, 7.154; 'good' and also 'goal' 15.260–1; in Indian literary criticism 26.330; Moggallāna's pun about it 3.409; 'seeing the meaning of it' (*Udāna*) 10.556–7; used by the Buddha to describe the goal (rather than *bodhi*, *nirvāṇa*) 15.261

atthakusalena 15.260–1

aṭṭhāṅgikamagga *see* Noble Eightfold Path

Atthārasarāsī Dīpanī 2.60

Aṭṭhasalini *see under* Buddhaghosa

atthi 2.123

attitudes conceptualizations are intimately related to our basic attitudes to life 19.106; conflict between different attitudes to Buddhism 22.150; the difference between an attitude and an idea 19.105–7; the Tantric mental attitude 19.532–3; a wrong view is a conceptual concretization of an unskilful attitude 19.106; you can't abandon bad actions unless you have dealt with unskilful attitudes 19.109; verbally adopting certain attitudes but not really thinking in those terms 19.289

Attlee, Clement 23.202

attraction to another person can be emotional, not sexual 17.217; to Buddhism

for the wrong reasons 1.19–20; to another person for their sake, not just your own: *mettā* 5.170–1; distinguishing between biological attractiveness and aesthetic beauty 17.221–2; the *gaurīs*' hooks of attraction, to keep us in the mandala 16.362; the innumerable forms of attraction to pleasure 7.392; important that the bodhisattva should have an attractive appearance 15.465; attraction to Nirvāṇa 15.567–8; attraction to Reality, like a moth to a flame 10.610; attraction to the spiritual path turns to discomfort 10.610; attraction to the transcendental 1.419–20; attractive Dharma teachers 19.498–500; sexual attraction 1.160, 15.125–6

Atula (layman mentioned in the *Dhammapada*) 15.34, 15.745 (n15)

Atula, Dharmachari v24

auddhatya *see* restlessness

Auden, W. H. 4.69

Augustine of Canterbury, St 12.75

Augustine of Hippo, St introduction 2.675 (n123), 23.504 (n239); compared to Milarepa 18.160–1; *Confessions* 23.207; 'in blaspheming false things are spoken of God himself' 11.331; in El Greco's *The Burial of Count Orgaz* 26.310–11; for him the animal elements are excluded from the human essence 8.613; from sensualist to saint 18.160; 'God's thundering commands must be obeyed' 11.338, 12.228; 'Oh happy sin!' 4.289, 4.693–4 (n231); 'Oh Lord, make me chaste, but not yet' 17.354; and St Jerome 25.312; 'The more interpretations the better' 14.336, 16.546; 'Thou hast made us for Thyself' 2.92, 11.105

Aung, U Thaung 20.419–21

aura there is an aura at every level of your being 16.136–7; the Buddha's aura and what it represents 18.536–7; don't get precious about auras and atmospheres 4.547; everyone needs space around them, to accommodate their aura 4.538–40; the fourth *dhyāna* as though one were surrounded by a powerful aura 11.126; Sangharakshita's aura 23.xiv

Aura (magazine) 26.214

Aurangabad, India introduction 9.565 (n291); Ajanta caves, *see under* caves; caste violence 10.xli; Milind College (People's Education Society) 9.302, 9.312–13, 9.320, 9.327–46, 10.128; Vishwa Hindu Parishad 9.347

Aurangzeb 9.312

Aurobindo, Sri introduction 3.671 (n292), 7.592 (n269); accuses the Buddha of nihilism 1.74, 13.514; Clare Cameron's interest 21.481; his disciple Dilip Kumar Roy 22.77; on evolution 13.513–15; integral yoga 3.312; literary criticism 26.115; and non-violence 8.453; on reading novels 26.121; Sangharakshita abandons the idea of visiting him 20.350; Sangharakshita did not have a high opinion of his poetry 22.131; on Śankara 16.454; the spiritual function of poetry 26.118–20; Swami Ramdas likens him to Shiva 20.334; *The Life Divine* 7.167, 13.514; *Thoughts and Aphorisms* 13.515

Auschwitz 26.451, 26.736–7 (n363)

Austen, Jane 11.634, 26.355, 26.490

Auster, Paul 24.374

austere the austere beauty of India 20.111–12; the austere beauty of the Tibetan landscape 18.158–9; the austere figure of the *arhant* 7.504; 'Love's Austerity' 25.223; a rather austere type of Buddhism 8.362; the sober, austere beauty of Florence 23.314

austerities monks' practice of austerities a means of magical protection and blessing 2.215; Swami Ramdas advises Dharmapriya (Sangharakshita) and Satyapriya of their dangers 20.322; taking up austerities to frustrate yourself might be an expression of self-will 19.167; Siddhārtha's austerities, *see under* Siddhārtha; *see also* asceticism

Austin, Jack at the Buddhist Society's Wesak party 23.232; collection of ecclesiastical robes 23.52–3; correspondence with Sangharakshita 11.546, 21.338; his desire to be not a monk, but an ordained person 23.53; editor of the *Western Buddhist*, a Mahāyāna magazine 8.123, 23.53–4; at first WBO ordination ceremony 2.403

Australia

Dharma activity
Buddhism in Australia 24.373–4; FWBO activities started 9.171, 9.172, 9.189, 9.492, 24.51; Khantipālo's Dharma activities 12.647, 12.753 (n445); Sangharakshita visits 10.276, 12.543, 24.56–64, 24.532–45

Melbourne
Ballarat 24.536; Buddhist Centre 24.xxi–xxii, 24.545; Greek population 24.545; National Art Gallery of Victoria 24.536

Sydney
Buddhist Centre 24.5, 24.60, 24.534, 24.621 (n84); Buddhist Society of New South Wales 24.57–8; Immigration and Customs 24.56, 24.64; impressions of the city 24.59–60; Mount Annan Botanical Garden 24.534; the Opera House 24.59, 24.621 (n83); Royal National Park 24.62–4; staying with Rie and Sten 24.46–54; Vijayaloka retreat centre and community 24.532–3

general
Blue Mountains 24.535; the Diggers 24.373; political and economic conditions 24.545; wildlife 24.533, 24.536

authenticity

personal authenticity
authentic communication 19.224–6; authentic contact with the essence of the Buddha 19.222–3; being yourself, *see under* self/further perspectives on 'self'; depression through living under false pretences 23.191–2; people will always be convinced by honesty and sincerity 18.184; salutations depend on an authentic feeling of faith 9.337–8; Sangharakshita and authenticity 25.91–2; to live the life of renunciation authentically you must love the Dharma passionately 18.133; we are full of ideas we do not truly think and emotions we do not sincerely feel 7.266–7; we don't truly, authentically, do anything 11.50; we will not feel authentic on the level of the mundane 1.487

authenticity in the Buddhist tradition
the authenticity of Mahāyāna *sūtras* 14.399–400; a belief that only the Pāli canon represented authentic Buddhism 7.31; the authenticity of any Buddhist school is its capacity to produce Enlightened beings 1.205; Milarepa's songs express authentic Buddhist practice 18.6; a transcendental teaching's authenticity 1.327; validating the authenticity of Enlightenment 1.204; the *vajrakula*, the authentic, naked community 13.178–9; what is the proof that the scriptures are the authentic word of the Buddha? 16.240; spiritual authenticity of Perfection of Wisdom scriptures 14.139; a World Buddhism that accepts the authenticity of the whole tradition 7.484

authoritarianism authoritarian religious groups 15.490; authoritarianism and spiritual life are incompatible 26.80; if everyone takes responsibility, there will be no room for authoritarianism 26.75; in Christianity 3.430–1; the language of authoritarianism 8.596–7; a story about disobeying the Buddha, not to be interpreted in an authoritarian way 10.650; no authoritarianism in Buddhism 12.246; in religion 7.246, 12.227–8

authority

what is authority?
the meaning of the term 3.445–6; full introduction 3.445–51; dealing with someone in authority 3.446; distinction between natural and artificial authority 16.577; intoxication of authority 16.299; 'Man, proud man, dressed in a little brief authority' 15.424; the power of authority 3.447, 15.618; traditional authority and charismatic authority 13.468–74

Buddhism and authority
authority and Buddhist scriptures 7.334, 16.443, 19.186; the Buddha's spiritual authority comes from his experience 15.266–7; the Buddha repudiated the pretensions of authority 7.144; the Buddhas and bodhisattvas are not authority figures 17.662–3; Buddhist monks' subservience to people in authority 17.212; deliberate decentralization of authority in the Sangha 7.438; if we are going to accept some authority unquestioningly, why bother with Buddhism? 16.553; in the spiritual community, we cannot deal with others as representatives 3.446; it appeals to intelligence rather than authority 15.266–7; it lacks 'the warlike voice of authority' (Humphreys) 22.126; looking for authority: 'Would a Buddhist do this? Would a Buddhist do that?' 19.102; Sangharakshita's 'authority' as a teacher 11.655, 11.667, 13.469; the Three Refuges are not an authority 19.285; to appeal to science on behalf of Buddhism is to appeal to authority 17.330–1; who decides what is right view? 11.654–5

authority in other religions
the authority of the book 12.233; the authority of God 1.528–9; belief in the authority of the Bible 15.264–5; religions of discovery appeal not to infallible authority but to reason and experience 7.367; theistic religions 15.617–21, 15.720

authority in the modern world
discomfort with authority 12.689; the habit of lumping true and false authority together 8.573–4; someone with a problem with authority 23.67–8; submission to authority in the contemporary world 15.489

personal authority
most people are afraid to stand on their own feet 12.232–3; the ultimate authority

is your own mind 19.284; wanting the approval of authority 18.366, 18.404; we must use our own judgement 10.150; we should not rely on authority 16.576–8

autobiography (genre) *see under* biography

autonomy of the true individual 3.470; *see also aiśvarya*

autumn autumn festival 18.379; autumn flowers in the Himalayas 7.335; autumn foliage 25.305; autumn in a cloister in Naples 24.279–80; the autumn lily 25.221; autumn moon 25.306; autumn poems 25.liv–lv, 26.398; 'Autumn Vignette' 25.343; the beauty of autumn 7.335–7, 22.322; chrysanthemum of autumn and orchid of spring 2.130; the face and body of the Tathāgata shining like the autumn moon 1.327; the great burning of leaves in autumn 25.436; the season of friendship 22.322–3; yellowing autumn woods 25.233

avādanas (glorious deeds)

introduction
fables about the Buddha's disciples 3.85; an example of the imaginative kind of Buddhist literature 14.110; one of the twelve *aṅgas* of the Sarvāstivādin school 14.25, 14.61, 17.571; how they came into existence 14.61; relationship to *Jātakas* 14.61–2, 14.67

Divyāvadāna ('Divine Heroic Feats')
introduction 14.68–9; Ānanda and Prakṛti (the outcaste girl) 10.260, 10.672–3 (n86), 14.68–9; the *Gaṇḍavyūha Sūtra* is based on one of the stories 14.218; legends about King Aśoka 8.523, 14.68, 16.143; Māra is converted and assumes the form of the Buddha 14.68; mention of Maitreya 2.179; refers to the *reading* of the Dharma 14.22; Upagupta and the courtesan 14.68; the wheel of life 2.73–4, 13.681–2 (n49)

other avadānas
Avadāna-kalpalatā 14.69; *Avadāna-śataka* 14.67–8; *Damamukha* 14.69; *Karma-śataka* 14.69; *Mahāvastu Avadāna*, *see Mahāvastu Avadāna*; *Sahasodgata Avadāna* 2.673 (n104)

avadhūti *see* central channel

availability the beauty we experience through the senses is not the highest beauty available to us 15.131; Enlightenment is dependent on energy being totally available on all levels 18.77; the good fortune that the Dharma is available to us 10.263; 'The greatest virtue is availability' 17.202; if your energy is totally available to you, you become a smooth, harmonious flow 3.372; making the Buddha's teaching available 26.650; mass availability of art 3.515–16; Sangharakshita available to 'anyone who wants to talk to me about anything' 24.158–9; to be available to others is to be ready to give yourself 17.202, 17.204; trapped in sexual channels, our energy may be unavailable for spiritual life 1.390

avaivartika *see* irreversibility

Avalokiteśvara, the bodhisattva of compassion

INTRODUCTION

his place in the Buddhist tradition
introduction 2.175–7, 11.292; attendant bodhisattva of Amitābha 1.330, 1.333, 2.172, 2.177, 16.462; correspondence between Avalokiteśvara, Vajrapāṇi, Mañjughoṣa, and Green Tārā 26.663–4; one of a group of eight bodhisattvas 2.172; chief bodhisattva of the lotus family 11.292, 13.310; sometimes placed at the centre of the mandala 18.602; he appears in the six realms of the wheel of life 2.74, 3.382–3, 13.228, 19.59; association with Putuoshan, a sacred mountain in China 2.224; and Tārā, born from a lake of his tears 1.263, 1.503, 2.178, 5.577, 13.92–3, 16.177–8; one of the three principal bodhisattvas of the Tibetan pantheon 7.304; patron of Tibet 7.397; Samye monastery's temple to Avalokiteśvara 12.292; the Dalai Lama said to be his manifestation 2.183, 3.134, 4.687 (n196), 13.39, 16.421, 22.487, 26.233

his compassionate activity
approachable and compassionate 2.229; concerned with the temporal as well as the spiritual welfare of his devotees 2.176; he corresponds to compassion, purified emotion 2.173, 7.303–4; he is what

compassion would look and sound like if we could see and hear it 13.288; the form in which Śākyamuni continues to work in the world 4.190; delivers those who call on his name from dangers 2.176; descends into hell to help beings 3.182; protector of the present world-period 1.263; protects even from the fear of being timid 4.632; the quintessence of compassion 11.292; ready to step out into the world 5.646; responsible for the spiritual evolution of humanity between Buddhas 2.177, 4.85; turns back on the brink of Enlightenment to help living beings 3.132–3, 4.581, 13.37–8; it's limiting to regard him as the personification of a particular quality 19.564

in literature
his myth told in the (partly Hindu) *Kāraṇḍavyūha Sūtra* 1.336, 2.176; in the *Heart Sūtra, see under Heart Sūtra*; the *Mahāvastu*'s two *Avalokita Sūtras* have nothing to do with Avalokiteśvara 2.175; in the *White Lotus Sūtra, see under White Lotus Sūtra*/characters

myths and stories
Agastya (Hindu rishi) was taught by him 26.225; a *ḍākinī* who swallowed Padmasambhava, then gave him the Avalokiteśvara initiation 12.287, 22.471; human beings are descended from Avalokiteśvara and a monkey (Tibetan myth) 2.65; the legend of Avalokiteśvara 13.37–8; the Potalaka, his abode 24.394, 24.400; in a story by Lama Govinda, 'Look Deeper!' 15.130

in spiritual practice
Akṣayamati's hymn of praise ('O you, whose eyes are clear') 1.336, 2.176, 14.177, 16.178–9; Atīśa encouraged his worship 12.578; the figure in Sangharakshita's study, seeming to point to the jewel in the lotus 24.146; an object of devotion 1.335–6, 16.232; offerings made to him by women wanting babies 2.176, 26.668; 'the wonderful Avalokita, who labours for the weal of all beings' 23.270; meditation on sound 14.197; *sādhana* practice 16.179–81, 19.453–4; Sangharakshita's devotion to him 22.301–2; visualizing Avalokiteśvara 16.179–81; we each have to be our own Avalokiteśvara 16.399

NAMES AND FORMS

names
Avalokiteśvara: 'the lord who looks down' 2.175, 11.292, 13.38, 14.177, 16.178, 19.564; Chenrezi 25.164–5, 25.280; hundreds of other names 2.175

iconography
description 4.190–1; his original colour seems to have been red, but he became white 13.305; a young prince, his beautiful face alive with tenderness and compassion 2.176; what compassion would look like if we could see it 13.288

thousand-armed form
iconography 2.176, 4.657, 13.69; he 'looks down on every place' 25.269; his eleven heads 13.69; in the guru yoga 13.217; the legend of the figure's origin 1.503, 4.191, 16.177; an image in a Tibetan shrine room 1.196; in a three-floored shrine in Darjeeling 21.214, 22.467; one can aspire to be one of his thousand arms, or even a finger 4.191, 26.655; pure shining white 11.292; represents absolute compassion, operating in all directions and in all ways 13.69; and the Triratna Buddhist Order, *see under* Triratna III/what is the Order?; Sangharakshita deeply distressed by the origin of the figure 26.599; in a shrine in Nepal 21.295; symbol of the *sambhogakāya* 19.201; the thousand eyes symbolizing awareness 13.69

other forms
108 forms 4.191, 13.285, 26.233; Amoghapāśa ('Unfailing Lasso') 14.658 (n517); the form of a cuckoo 22.457; Guanyin or Kwannon (female form), *see* Guanyin; Mahākāla, wrathful form, ('Great Time') 16.178; Mahākārunika 2.175, 5.xxxi–ii, 10.227, 15.529; Nīlakaṇṭha ('blue-throated') 7.580 (n190). 16.398–9, 26.641–2; Padmanarteśvara his emanation 2.178; Padmapāṇi, 'lotus in hand' 4.84, 5.202, 9.313, 11.292, 26.233–4, 26.384, 26.697; *Ṣaḍakṣarī* ('possessing six syllables'), the four-armed form 16.178, 23.400; Samantamukha 2.176; Shinje, the Lord of the Dead 8.559

MANTRA, *OṂ MAṆI PADME HŪṂ*

introduction
Ṣaḍakṣarī ('possessing six syllables') 16.178; illustration 13.289; the *Kāraṇḍavyūha Sūtra* relates how the mantra was obtained 2.176, 10.144; did the mantra come from the Buddha? 10.227; the *Maṇi Kabum* (Tibetan) is a sort of encyclopedia about the mantra 13.8; chanted to invoke Avalokiteśvara's

presence 4.632; in the *White Lotus Sūtra* 12.502, 16.165–88

meaning
'meaning' 9.520, 10.151, 16.176; the hidden meaning flowering before one's eyes 8.391; misunderstandings 16.601 (n123); only a partial translation is possible 19.134; *maṇi* stands for mind or *bodhicitta* 10.145, 10.175; *padme* and *hūṃ* represent the ten perfections 10.147; translation of *padme* 10.145, 16.601 (n123); and the priceless jewel 16.221; includes the whole of Buddhism, in a sense the whole of knowledge 10.147, 10.174; repeating it we seek to contact our innate compassion 13.287; there is no magical value in a particular sound 19.134; Tibetan pronunciation 11.289; the usefulness of chanting the mantra 10.227; what compassion would sound like if we could hear it 13.288

the jewel in the lotus
feminine and masculine principles 22.28; gesture of salutation representing the jewel in the lotus 16.179–80; the jewel within the lotus of sentient existence 7.316, 7.400, 26.51; Lopez' translation in *Prisoners of Shangri-La* 13.290; one must never take one's eyes off the jewel in the lotus, the potential of all 24.146; and the priceless jewel 16.173, 16.221; the potential for Enlightenment in our own heart 12.502; range of interpretations 22.28–9; reminds us that our dualistic way of looking at things is a delusion 22.29; related to the three levels of wisdom 16.186–7; to say that the mantra *means* that is a mistake 11.288, 13.290, 26.233; the two symbols (jewel and lotus) together fully represent the path 16.186; symbolism 16.176; you yourself become the jewel in the lotus 16.181

connections and associations with the mantra
Dr Ambedkar's connection 10.xliv, 10.144, 10.147, 10.676 (n122), 25.45; article by George Roerich 21.49; Dhardo Rimpoche had a mynah bird who would recite it 12.96, 22.522; an Indian woman who entered *dhyāna* through chanting it 25.44–5; on *maṇi* walls in Tibet 10.144, 16.165–6, 21.202; 'May the lotuses awake!' 10.xliv; Swami Ramdas gave it to Sangharakshita (then Dharmapriya) 20.325–6; Sangharakshita chants it in response to black magic 22.261; Sangharakshita gave talks on it in India 10.xliv, 10.144–7, 10.151–2, 22.265–6; a series of meditations on its significance by Lama Govinda 8.391–2; Sangharakshita's initiation, *see under* Sangharakshita V/ *sādhanas*

Avalon, Arthur *see* Woodroffe, Sir John

Avanti, India 10.572–3

āvaraṇas *see* two veils

avarice (*mātsarya*) 17.284, 17.656–7

Avarnas 9.28

āvāsa (local group or chapter of *bhikṣus*) 2.189, 2.193–4, 2.198, 2.203

Avataṃsaka school *see* Japanese Buddhism/Kegon Shū

Avataṃsaka Sūtra **('Flower Ornament Scripture')**

introduction
brief introduction 1.352–4, 22.627 (n402); fuller introduction 14.216–29

description
not so much a *sūtra* as a family of *sūtras* 7.501, 14.216; the consummation of Buddhist thought, sentiment, and experience 14.216; 'the king of the *sūtras*' 1.352, 16.17; replete with dramatically organized symbolic elements 14.201; D. T. Suzuki on the *sūtra* 1.353–4, 14.216; to understand it, six contemplations are needed 1.354; value of reading it 16.22–4

history
its origin is a mystery 14.216; if this extraordinary works doesn't go back to the Buddha, who did produce it? 16.241; occupies an intermediate position between the Madhyamaka and the Yogācāra 1.352; a link between the Yogācāra and the Tantra 1.375–6; Mr Chen's interest in the chapter on pure conduct 22.536–7; Zhiyi said that it was the Buddha's first teaching 11.716

translations
Chinese translations 14.216–17; by Upasika Chihmann (Miss P. C. Lee) 2.454; Thomas Cleary's translation 14.9, 16.587 (n20)

doctrine of mutual interpenetration
the text's principal theme 1.353, 14.219; 'A Buddha … is contained in every grain of dust' 7.344, 21.287; and the recognition of the Divine everywhere in the universe 7.575 (n161); comparison with Blake's vision 16.23–4, 19.215; conception of the universe as a gigantic system of correspondences 1.376, 26.209; 'In every single atom/ Are all things of all places and times' 16.583 (n3); Indra's net, *see* Indra's net; innumerable beams of light, all intersecting 2.55, 4.31

other content
absolute mind is the sole reality 1.352–3; 'All the Buddhalands rise from one's own mind 2.78; the One Mind 1.353; prayer of taking refuge in the Three Jewels 2.5; sees that unity and diversity are both just concepts 16.21; ten *bhūmis* 3.679 (n341); the vows of the bodhisattva Samantabhadra 2.454, 22.541; Vairocana's tower, *see under Gaṇḍavyūha Sūtra*; *see also Daśabhūmika Sūtra*; *Gaṇḍavyūha Sūtra*

Avennir, King 13.654–5, 13.659, 13.664

Averroes (also Ibn Rushd, Islamic philosopher) 24.430–1

aversion (*vyāpadā*) meaning and synonyms 2.388; and the difficulty of breaking emotional fetters 2.147–8; aversion can be useful if directed towards *saṃsāra* 17.290; in relation to sexual desire 15.525; the more insight you have, the less craving and aversion you have 18.576; nihilism is the philosophical expression of aversion to the world 17.250; reaction to pain 7.380, 15.151; when aversion is predominant, we tend to think of the other as the agent 10.601; wish to get rid of disliked objects of sensuous cognition, in hope of security 11.130; as the fifth fetter, *see under* ten fetters; as a hindrance to meditation, *see under* five hindrances; reframing from it, *see under* precepts/ten precepts/(9); *see also* hatred

avidyā (Pāli *avijja*) *avidyā* is intrinsic to arrogance 17.607; as one of the *mūlakleśas* (Abhidharma) 17.493, 17.607–11; it is what perceives 'described fact' 17.493; lack of intrinsic awareness 17.608–9; 'lack of pure awareness' (*ma-rigs-pa*) 17.494, 17.763 (n436); not all bad, because its confused actions are skilful as well as unskilful 17.610; of two kinds: lack of practical wisdom and lack of *prajñā* 17.607–8; relationship with the *saṃskāras* 1.108, 2.75; the root of *saṃsāra* 17.610; a sense of alienation and conflict (the opposite of *vidyā*) 14.517; specifically ignorance of the doctrine of conditioned co-production and other tenets 1.108; as the tenth fetter, *see under* ten fetters; as the first *nidāna*, *see under* twelve cyclical *nidānas*; *see also* ignorance

avidyāsrava *see under āsrava*

avihiṃsā *see* non-violence

avippaṭisāra (non-remorse) 11.320

avṛhā world (Pāli *aviha*) 2.148

avyākṛtavastūni *see* undetermined questions

avyāpāda *see* non-hatred

avyāpajjha (unoppressed) 1.69

awakening an alternative term for Enlightenment 3.149–50, 8.572, 10.442; awakening is an individual thing 8.586; the awakening of the heart 7.316–18; the awakening of faith, *see under* faith/arising and development; *The Awakening of Faith in the Mahāyāna*, *see* Aśvaghoṣa; awakening wisdom by appealing to the heart 26.198; before awakening from a dream, we can't know that what we saw in it doesn't exist 1.369; *bodhicitta*: the awakening of a new spiritual aspiration 2.160; the bodhisattva's experience like awakening from a dream 14.228–9; the body as the citadel of awakening 18.49; the Buddha as the awakened one 12.501; a 'culture of awakening' 8.580; the Dharma enables us to awaken to our dormant Buddha nature 7.313; in the parable of the jewel in the garment 16.170–1, 16.218; reaching a higher level of consciousness is like waking up in the morning feeling happy 18.298; the seed of awakening hidden in the heart 7.316–17; shock may have nothing to do with awakening 26.362; spiritual dawn 26.173; ultimately what we want is not book learning but spiritual awakening 11.716; waking up to the fact that you are Buddha 12.234; writing awakens within us something ... we failed to recognize before 13.367

awareness (*sati-sampajañña*)

DIFFERENT PERSPECTIVES

introduction
awareness of any kind is not easy to develop 15.101; an aware attitude will be a responsible, ethical one 13.456; difference from consciousness 9.514–15; for human beings growth means growth in awareness 11.109–10; mind and matter: a continuity of awareness patterned in different ways 15.138; perhaps awareness is a better term than mindfulness 17.88; to the extent there is awareness, there is the higher evolution, and *vice versa* 3.478; very sensitive, very alive 5.400; we take it for granted that we can be aware 16.252; you can fantasize, daydream, as long as you are aware 10.463

developing awareness
can your level of awareness be raised by the touch of a teacher? 9.528; the first fruit of one's development as an individual 18.300–1; it can be learned by observing

silence 9.519; supported by receptivity and curiosity 17.xxi; to be practised whatever we are doing 3.286, 9.295; through overcoming distraction you become more aware 17.260; trying to do two things at once is incompatible with true awareness 1.573; why the cultivation of awareness has a central place in Buddhist practice 11.36

awareness of being aware
awareness of being aware 11.115; becoming aware that we have been unaware 15.213–14; distinctly human: being aware of being aware of being (Nabokov) 3.478; one is not really human unless one has a spark of awareness 26.7; the true individual is intensely, luminously aware 3.469

integrated awareness
bringing our projections into awareness 15.307–8; developed by learning to experience yourself more fully 3.488, 12.268–9; experience without awareness, awareness without experience, integrated awareness 12.263–4; has a very powerful emotional component 5.209; the unification of energy and awareness 18.322

transformative awareness
is awareness transformative? 17.539; by transforming our level of awareness, we transform the world we live in 15.128; continuing to be aware, all day, all night, even in dreams, will transform us 1.575; 'a man transforms himself into a kind of living statue made up of awareness' 1.151; the most powerful transforming agent we know 1.575

the effects of awareness
differentiates subject and object 14.420; every moment of awareness presents us with an opportunity to choose what to do 15.174; the more aware you are, the more sensitive you are to sense impressions 15.287; releases creativity 11.32; revolutionary 26.20

other kinds of awareness
the awareness of the artist 3.507–8; the awareness that comes with rejection 17.225; bringing energies into harmony with awareness 18.322; participatory awareness 14.581; transcendental awareness 3.480–1

FOUR DIMENSIONS OR LEVELS OF AWARENESS OR MINDFULNESS

introduction
general introduction 1.570–8, 3.469, 17.536–9; characteristics of the true individual 3.469; at the end of his life the Buddha urged his disciples to practise them 2.28; and the four kinds of consciousness (simple, self-, transcendental, absolute) 12.262–3; each has its distinctive effect on the person practising it 1.578; not to be confused with the four foundations of mindfulness, for which *see under* mindfulness

(1) awareness of self
as soon as you become aware of yourself you have in some sense changed 15.167; it begins with awareness of what we are doing and saying 3.286; awareness of the changing empirical self 17.537; awareness of self (body, feelings, thoughts) should be practised all the time 1.575; awareness of your own uniqueness 3.469; we need to be aware of what we're doing, saying, and thinking 11.731–2; *see also* mindfulness/four dimensions; self-awareness

(2) awareness of nature or awareness of things
appreciative awareness of what is around us 17.227; as something completely other 3.469; awareness of our environment through the senses 17.536; awareness of works of art and music 12.259–60, 17.537; being aware of how we are influenced by our environment 15.153, 15.392–5; ecological awareness 11.733, 17.87; environment, *see* environment; how long do we spend really looking at things? 1.570–1; Milarepa's awareness of his environment 18.53–4; the poet's awareness of the unique individuality of things 26.135–6, 26.170; includes all the senses 12.259; there's always scope for awareness 5.77, 5.399; *vidyā*, *see vidyā*; we have to learn to look at and listen to things 1.571, 12.259–60

(3) awareness of other people
appreciative attention 14.582; the artist's awareness of others 3.508; aware of the nature and quality of your relationships 3.469; awareness of their bodily presence 5.399; awareness that they are subjects as well as objects 17.521; being aware of other people's mental states 15.164–6; being aware of a person, not just our reactions to them 1.519–21, 12.36, 17.229; children must be taught 9.439; in communication, pay attention to the other person 1.519–21, 10.217, 16.579; a comparatively rare thing 17.538; considering other people as much as you consider yourself 15.120–1; deep in communication, you become aware of someone's total pattern 18.285–6; awareness of the nature and quality of your

relationships 3.469; the ethical dimension of awareness of someone 17.661; the idea of 'seeing' another person is metaphorical 19.122; in communication, pay attention to them 1.519–21, 10.217, 16.579; learning to look at people 17.539; only if we are aware of them can we love them 12.262; putting oneself in other people's shoes 4.68, 5.175–6, 11.724; really looking at them 1.519, 1.575, 12.262, 18.216; seeing people with warm and clear awareness 17.227; tendency to objectify other people, as a baby does its mother 12.262, 17.538–9; true receptivity to other people requires us to see them as they really are 15.164; vivid awareness of the existence of other people 8.452; we're rarely aware of what they are in themselves 11.732; you can be with another person and still not be aware of them 17.101

(4) awareness of reality
awareness of *śūnyatā* 1.577; it's very difficult to say what this is 17.539; the most difficult level of awareness to maintain 1.577–8; the mysterious thread of unity that runs through the fabric of things 3.469; recollection of the Buddha 1.577; repetition of a mantra 1.578; synonymous with meditation as contemplation 12.262, 17.539

see also
mindfulness; alienated awareness, *see under* alienation; appreciative awareness, *see vidyā*; four foundations of awareness or mindfulness (*satipaṭṭhānas*), *see under* mindfulness; a hierarchy of awareness, *see* consciousness/four levels; as one of the five spiritual faculties (*indriyas*), *see under* five spiritual faculties; as one of the seven *bodhyaṅgas*, *see under* seven *bodhyaṅgas*; other people; pure, *see* pure awareness; self-awareness; self and other; the story of the young man and the umbrella, *see under* umbrella; total awareness, *see under* *Bodhicaryāvatāra*/chapter 5

awe a translation of *gāravo* 15.426; a species of fear 26.153; awe-inspiring Christian images 2.644; the awe-inspiring landscape of the Himalayas 2.644, 18.158–9; awe-inspiring works of art 2.644; Buddhism's fundamental state of mind is not a sense of awe 26.152–3; Buddhist philosophy discloses awe-inspiring perspectives 7.486; the Dharma's awe-inspiring perspective 3.17; Mozart's awe-inspiring symphonies 2.644; what we feel when confronted by nature, works of art, heroism, and religious images 2.644; wisdom sublime and awe-inspiring 14.xvi; the *yakṣa* an awe-inspiring natural force 10.451

Axial Age Karl Jaspers' conception of the Axial Age 3.424, 3.426–8, 11.354, 12.592; the emergence of true individuals 3.426–8, 10.229, 11.354–5, 12.592; in Greece, an outpouring of philosophical, spiritual, and artistic creativity 3.427; human beings 'dared to rely on themselves as individuals' 3.428; its importance 24.500; in India, the Buddha 10.229; myths remoulded in Axial Age 3.427–8; a tremendous cultural and spiritual change in human affairs 10.229

āyatanas *see* twelve *āyatanas*

Ayer, A. J. 24.319

Ayling, Mr and Mrs 26.574

āyurveda 16.193–4

Ayya Khema attitude to Vinaya rules about eating 26.536; correspondence with Sangharakshita 24.484–5, 26.536–9; a fan of Agatha Christie 26.536; for her, spirituality and common sense were not incompatible 26.536; a good friend 26.537, 26.539; her character 26.539; her disciples 24.588, 24.593; meeting in London 26.536; Sangharakshita visits Buddha Haus in Bavaria 24.593–4; her death 24.593, 26.539; Sangharakshita's tribute to her 26.408, 26.535–9

Ayyappan (Tamil god) 7.461, 20.249–50, 20.282–3, 20.318

Aztecs 13.602

B

Baba, Hari 20.203, 20.209

Baba Lal 8.167

Baba Ram Dass (Richard Alpert) 3.561

Baba Saheb *see* Ambedkar

babies ceremony of the bathing of the infant Buddha 2.228, 11.239; the instincts a baby is born with 17.14; a man who caused an accident to his baby and interpreted the result as a miracle 17.63–4; offerings made to Avalokiteśvara by women wanting babies 2.176, 26.668; tendency to objectify other people as a baby does its mother 12.262; thinking of the Buddha as your baby! 4.305; unconsciously being a little child, or even a baby 26.37; the unnervingly direct and honest gaze of a baby 18.140

Babylon 1.543, 10.460, 12.338, 12.694

Bach, J. S. *Mass in B Minor* 13.669; Pāli discourses like a Bach fugue 14.36; 'Sheep May Safely Graze' 23.261; Sangharakshita writes a stanza on Bach 26.503; sublimity of his music 16.285; *Toccata and Fugue in D Minor* 20.72, 26.503; you might never become a Bach but you can become a Buddha 16.286

backwards approaching the Unconditioned backwards 15.569, 15.575, 15.579–80, 18.580

Bacon, Sir Francis brief introduction 12.708 (n52), 23.542 (n500), 26.743 (n413); *The Advancement of Learning* 1.197–8; association with Highgate 23.473; Blake's view of Bacon 8.561, 19.179–80, 26.350; 'He that hath wife and children hath given hostages to fortune' 9.114, 21.325; 'Histories make men wise and the study of the poets makes them witty' 10.474; induction and the scientific method 12.77; 'men's business and bosoms' 7.388, 8.221; 'Money is like muck, the better for being spread' 4.102, 16.402; 'Nature is often hidden, sometimes overcome, seldom extinguished' 21.344; *New Atlantis* 1.539, 12.355; *Novum Organum*, the four idols 11.612–14, 12.655–6, 26.478, 26.480; 'The world's a bubble' 14.508

Bacon, Francis (artist) 13.425

Bacon, Roger 7.85–6, 7.364, 7.575 (n158)

Bacot, J. 8.222

Badley, Bishop 9.55–6

Bagdatopulos, W. S. 25.228

Bagdogra 21.507, 21.510

Bagehot, Walter 26.144

Bahadur, Dil v21

Bahadur, Man v21, v22

Bahadur, Nucche v21

Bahadur, Padam (cook-bearer) v22

Bahá'í faith 9.348, 9.449, 22.280

Bāhiya of the Bark-cloth *see under Udāna*

Bahm, A. J., *Philosophy of the Buddha* 8.538–9

Bahudhātuka Sutta *see under Majjhima Nikāya*

Bahujan Samaj Party 10.xlviii

bahujana ('manyfolk') 2.138

bahujana hitāya *see* 'for the welfare of the many'

bāhuśruta 15.403–4, 15.436

Baines, Joy (landlady) 26.600, 26.606–7, 26.610–11

Baizhang (Zen master) 2.555, 8.487, 11.318, 12.497, 17.73

Baker, Dame Janet 24.370

Baker, Mrs 20.56–7, 20.59–60

Baker, Richard v24

Bakhtiapur 7.425

Bakula, Dhammachari 24.22, 24.609–10 (n39)

Bakula, Kusho (Ladakhi lama) 21.107, 23.363

Baladitya, Dharmachari v24

balance

a balance between …
effort and relaxation 18.584–5; free energy and mindfulness 18.581; head and heart 1.240, 1.294, 9.322, 12.65, 26.40; imagination and discipline 18.372–3; love and knowledge 10.224; pleasure without craving and non-craving without

eliminating pleasure 19.382; reason and the scriptures (and personal experience) 18.416, 19.186, 19.203; subjective and objective approaches to the spiritual life 10.12–13, 10.41–2, 15.707; theory and practice 9.274; vision and pragmatism 4.62–3; what you know and what you do 15.472–4

balance and Buddhist life
balance in nature represented by the four great kings 16.357; balance of meditation, study, and external activities 4.461–3; the balanced approach of Tibetan Buddhism 13.108–9; a balanced view of the bodhisattva ideal 4.224; balancing the model of the path with the model of unfolding 4.201–3; balancing *samādhi* and *vīrya* 19.551; Buddhism and art are both indispensable to a balanced spiritual life 26.117; Buddhism attaches great importance to harmony and balance 13.328; cultivate faith to achieve a balanced approach 23.151; developing balancing qualities 4.41, 26.129; Dharma study is probably essential, in balance with other practices 17.573–4; everyone has phases, but in the end you hope to achieve a balance 25.110; feeling balanced, poised, and calm in meditation 10.638; green represents the balancing aspect of the Enlightened mind 13.282; the guru needs to find a balance of encouragement and criticism 18.144; the idea of balancing reason and faith is not useful 14.442–3; if the need to develop insight gets lost, look again at the balance of your life 15.97–8; mindfulness is so pivotal to Buddhism because balance is so pivotal 3.310; the six perfections 16.12; a state of poise and balance and at the same time spontaneous action 18.344; taking a balanced approach to Buddhism 12.65; we can take a balanced view of the Dharma only if we become balanced 3.187; *see also under* five spiritual faculties

Bālapaṇḍita Sutta *see under Majjhima Nikāya*

balas (powers) *see* five *balas*

Balendraketu, King *see under Sūtra of Golden Light*

Balfour, Crispin 24.333

Balik, Michal *see* Nityabandhu

ballads 25.334, 26.394

ballet *Everyman* in wartime London 13.658–9, 20.86; *Petroushka* in New York 23.462

Balrampur *see* Śrāvastī

Balsekar, Gautam 10.367

Balthasar, Hans Urs von 13.424

Balzac, Honoré de 23.452, 23.539 (n474), 24.96–7, 24.629 (n123), 26.354

Bamboo Grove *see under* Rajgir

bamboos *see under* trees

BAMCEF 9.499–512, 9.526–7, 9.575–6 (n394), 10.xlviii

bananas *see under* trees

Bancroft, Anne *see* Lobstein

band of six 10.520, 10.712–13 (n417)

Bandaranaike, S. W. R. D. 2.756 (n781), 7.567 (n121), 8.283–4, 8.474, 22.458

Bandaranaike, Sirimavo 8.283, 8.694–5 (n227)

bandits, robbers, and thieves the Bodhisattva as a robber (*Jātakas*) 3.85; Buddhaghosa's story of an equanimous decision as to who should be sacrificed to bandits 15.322; falling into the hands of bandits but not being affected by the eight worldly winds 18.325; Milarepa and the night-time robber 18.139; the monk who told the bandits a lie to save someone 3.323, 7.118; the monk whose bowl is broken by robbers 10.649; the passions are a brotherhood of thieves 4.380–1; a pickpocket on the Tube train 26.563–4; Rechungpa's gems cannot be stolen because they are within him 19.441; Sangharakshita is robbed in Kalimpong 22.562; the savage bandits of hope and fear 19.398; the saw, and the bandits who carve you limb from limb 1.437, 4.121, 13.577; Thai monk charged with murder and robbery 2.551; a Tibetan caravan is attacked by bandits 18.99–100

Banerjee, Dr Anukul Chandra Ani-la studies with him in Calcutta 22.223; 'Dasadhyayavinaya' (*Maha Bodhi* article) 8.643; message of goodwill to the Maha Bodhi Society 22.126; on the 'deification' of Buddhas and bodhisattvas 7.537; *Sarvāstivāda Literature* 7.629 (n575), 14.33, 14.81, 14.90, 14.614 (n62)

Banerjee, Rabindra Kumar *see* Buddharakshita

Bangalore dispute (based on caste) over the building of a vihara 22.149–50; followers of Dr Ambedkar 22.149–50; Lal Bagh 22.144, 22.588 (n135); lectures at the Indian Institute of World Culture, *see under* Sangharakshita XIII/*Survey*; local

intelligentsia 22.141–2, 22.147; a tolerant, cosmopolitan place 22.146–7

banishment the Abhidharma banished Buddhism's human element 3.86, 12.142; the horror of banishment (Shakespeare) 17.185; the true brahmin is one who has banished evil states 10.439

banner of victory a banner for Dhardo Rimpoche 10.408–9; a banner of victory on the vihara roof, *see under* Kachu Rimpoche; in Buddhist cosmology 13.262, 16.346; its significance 22.477

Banshilal (Kalimpong trader) 21.141–2

Bapat, P. V. *2,500 Years of Buddhism* 22.249, 22.596 (n209), 22.305; review 8.348–9, 8.376–8; 'to know what Buddhism is we must look elsewhere' 8.349, 8.378

Barclay, Miss Helena arrives in Kalimpong to study Tibetan 21.442–4; the funeral of her cat 22.47, 22.85; memorial service 22.89; proof that she was a Buddhist 15.146, 22.80–1, 22.86–7; quarrels 22.11, 22.45; her death and cremation 12.220–1, 15.146, 16.277–8, 22.80–5

bardo (*antarābhava*, intermediate state)

INTRODUCTION

the nature of the bardo
one of the most profound aspects of Buddhism 12.197; references to an intermediate state in the Pāli canon 10.723–4 (n504); in relation to cyclical conditionality, the point between effect and cause 12.197–8; the intermediate state, a point of rest, like that of a pendulum 10.638; Milarepa as a guide to the *bardo* 18.569–70; Milarepa's 'Song of the *Bardo*' 18.82–6; birth in the *antarābhava* 14.407; Root Verses of the Six Bardos 5.388, 12.206–8; 'This life, the next life, and the life between – Regard these all as one' 7.305; wandering the *bardo*, we are buffeted by the winds of evil karma 18.83–4; the light that illuminates the *bardo* 13.152

the length of time between death and rebirth
when karmas come into effect 3.108; related to the tenth of the twelve cyclical *nidānas* 3.200; in Sarvastivāda and Tibetan Buddhism 2.76, 3.196, 10.638; no interval, says the Theravāda 1.109, 2.75–6, 3.196, 10.638, 12.200; forty-nine days (*Tibetan Book of the Dead*) 12.200

the opportunity for Enlightenment
gaining Enlightenment in the after-death state (one of Nāropā's six yogas) 13.28; gaining Enlightenment in the *bardo* 15.592, 18.85–6; it is said that you can gain Enlightenment at the moment of death 18.221; when the rope of clinging is cut, the *bardo* disappears 'like the uncoiling of a snake' 18.612–13; the correlation of the last three *bardos* with the three bodies of the Buddha 12.205–6, 23.93; with the three Tantric initiations 12.206

THE SIX BARDOS

(1) the bardo of life
according to this teaching, life itself is an intermediate state 12.199; root verse 12.206

(2) the bardo of dreams
intermediate between waking and deep sleep 12.199–200; root verse 12.206; sleep as a *bardo* state 19.321–2

(3) the bardo of meditation
intermediate between two states of 'normal' consciousness 12.200; root verse 12.207; connection with the *bardos* between death and rebirth 12.206

(4) the bardo of the moment of death (chikhai bardo)
root verse 12.207; what happens at the moment of death? 12.201; we learn the lesson of impermanence too late to apply it 7.131; consciously preparing for it 8.143–4; faith in Amitābha will act as a condition for the realization of Nirvāṇa 1.345; fear 12.201–2; a great opportunity, if one does not shrink from the clear light 12.201–2, 16.96, 16.108, 18.250, 18.570–1, 23.93; importance of a peaceful atmosphere at the time of death 2.231–2, 8.143; meditation helps one to prepare for that moment 4.80, 12.201–2; the monk offers spiritual consolation at the time of death 2.217; rebirth in accordance with the nature of the last thought 2.231; the value of having a friend or spiritual teacher beside you to offer advice 12.202; we get a glimpse of the clear light, but we can't sustain it 17.678; what use is a friend? 4.329

(5) the bardo of reality (chönyi bardo)
root verse 12.207; you have to be told by the friend at your side that you are dead 12.202–3; the appearance of the five Buddhas and lights of the six realms: choices 12.203–6; the order in which the Buddhas appear 8.558; the appearance of the *vidyādharas* and wrathful deities 12.204–5; if one has meditated on the archetypal Buddhas, one will not shrink from their radiance 23.93; you have a body, albeit not like the one you had when you were alive 17.622; an opportunity for spiritual attainment we cannot assimilate 18.30

(6) the bardo of rebirth (sidpa bardo)
root verse 12.207–8; the colours associated with rebirth in the six realms 13.283; experiences according to past karma 12.205; seeing your future parents and the moment of conception 12.205, 23.93

Bardo Thödol *see Tibetan Book of the Dead*

Barlaam and Josaphat

introduction
both are included in the calendar of saints 13.663–4, 23.307; evidence of the influence of Buddhism on medieval Christian Europe 8.398; the saint buried at St Peter's in Rome is a different Josaphat 23.307; St Josaphat's commemoration is on 26 August, Sangharakshita's birthday 23.307

medieval story
based on a version of the life of the Buddha 11.297, 13.523, 13.653–64, 23.307; Arabic version (*The Book of Balawha and Budasf*) 13.662–3; different versions of the story 8.397; the four sights as described in the story 8.398, 13.655–7; a link with the medieval play *Everyman* 13.658–9; Josaphat is converted to Christianity 13.659; 'Josaphat' is a corrupted form of 'bodhisattva' 13.655; Josaphat's dream of heaven and hell 13.660–1; Josaphat's 'going forth', similar to Siddhārtha's 13.661; related to works like the *Lalitavistara* and the *Buddhacarita* 13.662; Shakespeare used the story 13.653, 13.657, 13.663; a version by St John of Damascus 8.397, 13.662–3; *The Wisdom of Balahvar – A Christian Legend of the Buddha* 8.397–8

Barlaam of Antioch 13.664

Barnet, Mrs (Kalimpong) 22.191

Barnett, L. D. 1.411, 1.620 (n323), 22.129

Baroda, India 9.4, 9.42–4, 9.180

Barrett, Verne *see* Satyadevi

Barrie, J. M. 17.274

barriers barriers set up between one class, one nation, one religion and another 7.274; breaking down the barrier between self and other (*Bodhicaryāvatāra*) 3.574; the danger of building barriers with concepts meant to pull them down 15.335; a double barrier between us and reality: perceptions and words 14.421; *mettā*: removing the barriers between self and other 5.188, 15.325; friendship an opportunity to break down the barrier between self and other 3.321, 11.698–9; we need a Buddhist movement that transcends national and cultural barriers 10.90; without breaking down the subject–object barrier there can be no happiness on earth 7.273–4

Barth, Karl 13.449

Barthélemy, Jules St Hilaire 7.32, 7.549 (n25)

Bartók, Béla 24.521, 24.589

Barua Buddhists *see under* Bengal

Barua, Dr Beni Madhab

introduction
brief introduction 7.592 (n270); rescued in Calcutta riots 20.166; Sagaramati's critique 7.597 (n307); Sangharakshita meets in Calcutta 20.135

'Buddhism as Personal Religion'
'Buddhism as Personal Religion' 7.25, 7.596 (n305), 20.124; of the two trends within the order of becoming, it is up to us to decide which to seek 7.206; the positive *nidānas* as an infinite series 10.614, 26.174–6; *pratītya-samutpāda* and Nirvāṇa 1.116–19, 7.198; *saṃsāra* and *nibbāna* are both possibilities in the same reality 7.167, 7.202, 7.203–4

other works
'Early Buddhism' 7.172; *Prolegomena to a History of Buddhist Philosophy* 7.198–9

Barua, Kali Kinker v22

Barua, Munindra 23.367

Barzini, Luigi 23.312, 23.522 (n354)

bases *see* six bases

Bashō, Matsuo 2.555, 4.646, 4.717 (n382), 26.262

Basiasita 13.342

basilica *see under* architecture

Batchelor, Stephen aphorisms for reflection 8.575; *Buddhism Without Beliefs* (review) 8.xxxvi, 8.571–99; on the shrinking of the Buddhist world 2.550; translation of the *Bodhicaryāvatāra* 11.219

Bates v21

Bath, England 23.206

bathing bathing not in the Ganges but in the Dharma 1.62; belief in the purifying effect of bathing in the Ganges 3.194, 10.457–8, 26.179; the bliss of a man who travels through the desert and then bathes in a lake 2.107–8; the ceremony of the bathing of the infant Buddha 2.228; the idea that nuns should wear bathing dresses 10.498–9, 19.250, 19.262; a magical herb

bath (the *Sūtra of Golden Light*) 16.370; you don't become pure by bathing (*Udāna*) 10.457–8

battles Battle of Waterloo 10.222, 24.149; the battleground of the spiritual life: a telling metaphor 3.294, 18.103; being pierced with speech like an elephant in battle pierced with arrows 10.540; between conditioned and Unconditioned 16.428; between gods and asuras 11.323, 13.126, 16.349, 16.427; existence as a conflict between the forces of light and the forces of darkness 8.525–6; 'Māra has been overcome, the battle has been won' 10.522, 10.524; metaphor for human life 16.85; a rule prohibiting *bhikkhus* from 'looking at armies' 18.105; seeing spiritual life as a battle 4.372; subduing the army of the five poisons 18.103; 'There is no doubt I shall win the battle' (Milarepa) 18.104; the transition between sensation and craving: the battlefield of the spiritual life 1.111–12

Battisford, Suffolk 26.508–10

Baudelaire, Charles

Fleurs du Mal
introduction 25.73; a resonance with 'The Flowers of Evil' 25.117; 'L'Albatros' 21.170, 21.625 (n40), 22.103, 22.584 (n101); 'Une Charogne' 1.522; 'Hymne á la beauté' 25.269, 25.592 (n65); 'Les Phares' 20.72, 26.503; 'L'Aube Spirituelle' 26.173

other work
'Les Yeux des Pauvres' 15.164

Bauls 7.461

Bāvarī 1.82

Baxter, James K. 24.549–54

Bayle, Pierre 8.180, 8.681 (n106)

Bays, Gwendolyn *see Lalitavistara Sūtra*

BBC (British Broadcasting Corporation) *The Brains Trust* 23.136; Dr Ambedkar gives a talk: 'Why I Like Buddhism' 9.72; Order members who were formerly employees of the BBC 24.615 (n58); Sangharakshita speaks on 'Self-Denial and Self-Affirmation' 11.496–9, 23.330; shipping forecast 26.589; two interviews for the BBC 23.xv, 23.32

Beal, Samuel 12.70

Beat Poets 22.565–6, 22.630 (n417), 23.123–4, 24.580–1, 26.375

Beatles, the influenced by Indian classical music 26.258; a magistrate affects ignorance of the Beatles 18.153; a photographic portrait 24.359; revolutionary 15.492

Beaumont and Fletcher 26.365

beauty

BEAUTY IN THE BUDDHIST TRADITION

the beauty of Enlightenment
the aesthetic aspect of reality 5.597; Ānanda is converted to Buddhism by seeing the Buddha's beauty 12.307–8, 13.361, 15.556, 15.721, 17.337, 25.31; a Beauty without form and void 25.223, 26.666; the beauty of the ideal should be allowed to manifest 15.353; the beauty of the Unconditioned 2.82, 2.84–5, 15.568, 16.329; being drawn into the spiritual life by the beauty of the ideal 18.580, 22.199; the bodhisattva draws us to Enlightenment with beauty 16.352; enhancing the beauty of existence through gaining Enlightenment 18.447; Enlightenment described as pure beauty 13.278, 16.362; the faith-follower drawn to the joy and beauty of Enlightenment 18.129; Ratnasambhava represents the beauty of the Enlightened mind 12.214; the tranquil beauty of the life of the Enlightened One 7.33

in the Pāli canon
Bhaddiya is like a beautiful royal chariot 10.618–19; the Buddha saw everything as pure beauty 14.516; the Buddha's appreciation of beauty 1.125, 10.586, 12.616, 26.126–9; Buddhism applied an ancient Indian conception of ideal beauty 2.42; the idea that the *theras* sought the forest for aesthetic reasons 26.128; only the Buddha sees the true beauty of the world 12.616; the Release called the Beautiful 2.84, 5.511, 10.506, 13.279, 14.311; Sappaka, who was sent into ecstasy by the beauty of a white bird and a dark cloud 26.242; in the story of Nanda and the nymphs, *see* Nanda; traces of the ideal of beauty in the Pāli canon 13.279

and the Theravāda
Hīnayāna misunderstanding about beauty 1.125; suspicion of beauty 13.279; a monk says that he is not allowed to appreciate beauty 2.84, 21.397, 22.148; 'What frescoes?' 13.279

and the Mahāyāna and Vajrayāna
the beauty of the *dharmakāya* 14.236; the dazzling beauty of the Pure Land 14.168; the beauty of the *Sūtra of Golden Light* 16.246; it emancipates Buddhism into a celestial context of dazzling beauty 1.183; Milarepa's poetic sensibility attuned to beauty 18.54; Mañjughoṣa's beauty

17.462; the *White Lotus Sūtra*: drawing attention to the beautiful side of Buddhism 12.503; Zen poetry's appreciation of natural beauty 2.555

beauty and doctrine
appreciation of beauty to counter *kāmacchanda* 5.344–6; do what is morally beautiful (*Dhammapada*) 15.348–53; the emphasis of the path of the seven *visuddhis* on beauty 3.295; the *rūpaloka* is the world of pure beauty 12.559; seeing what is ugly as beautiful (*viparyāsa*) 2.82, 3.281, 12.614–16; *śubha, see śubha*; things are impermanent but they are also beautiful 26.241–2

beauty and Buddhist practice
appreciate beauty, but relinquish desire to possess it 17.271; the *aśubha bhāvanā* as preparation for beauty 17.222–3; beauty and *mettā* 5.592–3, 13.279, 14.516, 17.222; beauty and the refinement of positive emotion 5.43; beauty as preparation for meditation 18.159; the beauty of the spiritual quest 12.551; the Buddhist path is a path of beauty 3.295, 10.248, 26.382–3; the cultivation of beautiful states of mind 25.46; the element of beauty in Going for Refuge 15.554–6; finding beauty outside the objects of craving 17.271; going in the direction of an ideal beauty 15.156; historically Buddhism has not developed a path of beauty, but it could 26.665; *karuṇā* (compassion) is one of the most beautiful words in Buddhism 1.235, 7.383; the *kasiṇa* exercises to enhance our appreciation of beauty 12.615; the mandala: 'Take any prominent aspect of reality and surround it with beauty' 14.518; perhaps Western Buddhists could develop the Buddha's teachings about beauty 14.311; the refined beauty of the opening of the Sevenfold Puja 11.232–3; refining desire by contemplating beauty 5.511; reflection on the beauty of the state of non-craving 16.447; the *samādhi* of pure beauty, associated with Green Tārā 26.664; Sangharakshita hears a talk on Buddhism and beauty (1947) 21.439, 26.383; in visualization practices, *see under* visualization/introduction

BEAUTY IN WESTERN CULTURE AND OTHER TRADITIONS

philosophy
absolute beauty 26.174, 26.176; the ascending scale of beauty (*Symposium*) 13.279, 14.310, 19.24, 26.137–8, 26.312–15; 'Beauty is the splendour of form reflected on the proportioned parts of matter' 26.167; for the Greeks the beautiful was linked with the ethical 13.279; the Greek *to kalon* 4.269; Aquinas' definition of beauty: that which when seen, delights 26.396, 26.596; 'a beautiful soul' (Schiller) 7.33, 7.549 (n27); is beauty in the eye of the beholder? (Schopenhauer) 12.613, 15.533, 17.222; Plato on beauty 25.232, 26.312

Neoplatonism
in a Neoplatonic sense: something shining in a world of its own 2.82; in Neoplatonism 13.279; it induces 'a trembling that is all delight' (Plotinus) 23.318; 'On Beauty', *see under* Plotinus

other spiritual traditions
beauty in Sufism 13.279, 14.311; 'the beauty of holiness' (Bible) 17.337; emphasis on beauty in Manicheism 3.432; 'the gate which is called Beautiful' (Bible) 26.181; Jesus said of a dead dog, 'What beautiful teeth!' 1.521–2

art
appealing to taste for sensuous beauty while aiming for something purer 17.222; 'Beauty is a unity of formal relations among our sense perceptions' (Read) 26.167; modern art doesn't seem to value beauty 12.615, 26.244, 26.395; the pre-Raphaelites set out to create it 26.395; the Religion of Art: surrender to the Beautiful 26.174; Wilde, 'the House Beautiful' 26.395

poetry
the beautiful flights of the mind of poetry and science 26.686; 'Beauty is truth, truth beauty' 12.308, 16.257, 22.180, 24.547, 25.xxxiv; beauty of expression in literature 26.330; 'Beauty's face is aye unveiled' 25.185; Bridges' *Testament of Beauty* 20.124; 'Exuberance is beauty' (Blake) 24.584; finding no word for beauty 25.237; 'He hath a daily beauty in his life/ That makes me ugly' 17.280, 17.654; D. H. Lawrence: 'we also need our Beauty' 9.444; 'The Moon of Beauty' 25.168; 'Our meddling intellect/ Mis-shapes the beauteous forms of things' 7.242; 'that which, from instant to instant, is always new' 17.462, 26.174

RESPONDING TO BEAUTY

appreciation of beauty
agreement that a rose is beautiful 25.259; appreciate beauty, but relinquish desire to possess it 17.271, 26.186; appreciating the beauty of nature 18.158–9, 26.185–7; appreciation of beauty to counter *kāmacchanda* 5.344–6; the Buddha's appreciation of beauty 1.125, 10.586, 12.616, 26.126–9; conscious surrender

to the beautiful 26.98; 'Elusive Beauty' 25.269; enjoying beauty without making it an object of attachment 26.598; grief that the so beautiful should be so brief 25.281; the *kasiṇa* exercises to enhance our appreciation of beauty 12.615; a monk says that he is not allowed to appreciate beauty 2.84, 21.397, 22.148; the more you appreciate beauty, the more selfless you become 26.244; 'muse not that Beauty passes, but that she stays at all' 25.270; seeing someone's weaknesses and still appreciating their inner beauty 15.293–4; the Temple of Beauty 26.195; Zen poetry's appreciation of natural beauty 2.555

beautiful people
the beauty or ugliness of a face depends on mental and emotional state 26.594; being intoxicated by your own good looks 15.423; the most beautiful aspect of a human being is their spiritual potential 15.130–1; 'beautiful people' 4.270, 18.447; beautiful young men 20.344, 26.471, 26.562–3, 26.594–9; distinguishing between biological attractiveness and aesthetic beauty 17.221–2; the male human form more beautiful than the female 23.289, 26.594; woman as the embodiment of ideal beauty 26.593; a person's beauty can be as a result of their disposition, or previous lives 4.390; seeing someone's weaknesses and still appreciating their inner beauty 15.293–4; taking delight in the spiritual beauty of our dear friend 11.440, 26.79; 'Your beauty, in repose, is like a vase ...' 25.264; 'Your beauty is like the inaccessible beauty of the stars' 25.489

beautiful places, sounds, and things
India 20.111–12; bamboos 22.431–2, 25.217; Bodh Gaya 20.453–6, 23.365; candlelight 11.240; Indian villages 26.183–4; Thailand's eight principal places of worship 8.139; the world as seen by the first human beings 13.165; jewels 13.165–6; the Taj Mahal 23.412; the world (described by Rovelli) 26.686; beauty spots 24.448; a cremation by the river 12.221, 15.143, 22.202–3; Indian music 7.83; mathematical equations 15.577; the natural world (in the *Book of Job*) 13.540–1; travelling by air 19.93–4, 24.112; Aldous Huxley on beauty spots 24.448, 26.185; 'I loved all flowers for their beauty' 22.433; people who can't enjoy a flower's beauty until they know its Latin name 13.347, 25.242, 25.538; the sober, austere beauty of Florence 23.314; Tirumal Nayak's palace 20.233; the way beauty spots are spoiled by mass tourism 26.185; when the imagination is activated the beauty of the world is enhanced 8.579; wherever there is the touch of beauty is holy ground 26.196

the effect of beauty
Beauty is not merely Truth, but Goodness as well 26.196; the contemplation of beauty gives rise to love, and when sublime, to faith 2.554; the death of beauty in modern life 26.131–2; the enjoyment of beauty makes you happy 26.396; experiences of 'shattering beauty' 26.372–3; fear of being left alone with beauty 18.42–3; the importance of keeping our surroundings beautiful 9.444–5, 26.183–5, 26.396; it can help bridge the gap between emotion and reason 8.445; the link between beauty and positivity 13.279; the purifying and refining power of a thing of beauty 7.437; Sangharakshita's response to beauty helped him realize he was a Buddhist 23.317–18; a single smile of beauty 26.189; the sublime moves us in a way that the simply beautiful cannot 14.472; transcending the limits of doctrine and belief 26.96

our need for beauty
the artist's longing for beauty 26.176; attraction to intellectual beauty or sensuous beauty 15.577; beauty has an important place in the spiritual life 12.672–3; there has to be external, visible beauty in our lives 9.444; we need beauty to nourish and inspire us 12.559; we should never forget the importance of beauty in the spiritual life 12.308; without beauty we cannot lead a truly human life 10.368

reflections on beauty
'the beautiful is that which from moment to moment is always new' 18.159; beauty is not only bodily 15.131, 23.317–18; beauty worshipped for beauty's sake: 'horrible putrefaction' 26.148–9; the danger of susceptibility to beauty 13.279; the Eternal Beauty which walks in brightness behind all the shows of the world 7.83; is beauty limited to that which has form? 13.279; the good, the true, and the beautiful 13.278–9; the hierarchy of beauty 14.310–11, 26.597; an intermediary between unreality and reality, an agent of transformation 18.158; judging from modern art, people seem to have lost their sense of beauty 12.615; the limitations of words to express beauty 14.15, 14.297; relationship to purity and goodness 4.269–70, 15.348–53; scientists in search of 'elegant' truths 13.279, 15.349; there are degrees of beauty 12.615; we see

something as beautiful when we see it without desire 12.613–14, 15.533

Bechardas, Amritlal 8.657, 8.662, 23.343–5, 24.24–5, 24.114, 24.117, 24.610 (n42)

Beck, L. Adams 3.30, 3.631 (n31)

Becket *see* Thomas Becket

becoming (*bhāvanā*) Buddhism views existence as a single grand becoming 7.152; is the Highest Good aimed at by religion is a becoming? 7.197; the identity of being and not-being 7.195–6; Reality = Becoming = *paṭicca-samuppāda* 7.203; the spiritual life as essentially a willed process of becoming 7.204; twofold 1.112, 1.118–19; we should say 'becoming' rather than 'being' 3.187; the wisdom of the realization of a dynamic Becoming 7.375; the world is attached to the process of becoming 10.522–3; the universe as a gigantic process of becoming 3.475, 12.84

see also
rebirth; as tenth *nidāna*, *see under* twelve cyclical *nidānas*;

Bécquer, Adolfo 24.438

Bede, the Venerable 3.231

Bedingfield, Sir Thomas 26.515–16

beef *see under* meat

Beerbohm, Max 24.557

bees the bee takes the honey from the flower 25.380; environmental concerns 25.54; 'Haste, O wild-bee hours' 7.58; the element of Buddhahood like 'honey covered by a swarm of bees' 13.389; 'I felt as if I were a tiger-cub, or a bee' 18.582; 'let the silent sage move about the village as the bee goes taking honey from the flower' 3.589–94; *praśrabdhi* like a bee within a flower 3.288, 15.117; the queen bee and the hive mind 18.227–8; St Teresa uses a bee metaphor 13.392–3; 'singing masons building roofs of gold' 26.195

Beethoven, Ludwig van

introduction
Beethoven at his worst is will pretending to be power 26.22, 26.249; the *Heart Sūtra*'s artistic unity, like a Beethoven quartet 14.152; 'To the heart it came, to the heart may it go' 7.83; his music is religious in sentiment, though non-religious in subject 26.164; *Missa Solemnis* 7.83; *Pastoral Symphony* 26.671; Ninth Symphony 26.377; the opera *Fidelio* 3.570–1; the sublimity of his work 14.472; symphonies and overtures 26.502

Sangharakshita
his favourite composer 20.73, 26.502; writes a dramatic idyll about Beethoven's meeting with Goethe 7.573 (n149), 20.72, 26.503; sees as hero 20.68; writes a stanza on Beethoven 26.503

beggars Baudelaire's story of lovers who respond completely differently to a beggar 15.164; the beauty of an old blind beggar 25.269; beggars as guarantors of your favourable rebirth: a grotesque idea 17.211; beggars in big cities 25.126; beggars in Granada 24.443; blaming someone for making you impatient is like blaming a beggar for making you mean 14.597; a blind man (or beggar) finding a jewel on a dungheap 1.420, 2.126, 4.42, 4.44, 10.145; experiencing the beggar as a Buddha 19.538–9; hippies begging at Sarnath 23.364; 'How can I scorn the beggar's lot?' 25.207; Milarepa, disguised as a beggar, arouses Rechungpa's compassion 19.513–14; Siddhārtha's exchange of clothes with a beggar 3.29, 3.40, 10.257, 13.661; as a teenager, Sangharakshita (following St Francis) gave all his money to a beggar 13.533, 13.624; treating a beggar as you would your dearest friend 17.205; useless to aspire to universal charity when the beggar on our doorstep remains unfed 7.328

begging-bowl (*bhikṣāpātra*) description 16.405; analogous to the Holy Grail 12.192; 'bad food should not be put in a jewelled bowl' 14.161–2, 16.506–7; bowl and robe the two wings of the monastic life 1.152, 16.405; the Buddha begs in the streets of Kapilavastu 13.461; the Buddha sometimes returned with an empty bowl, due to Māra's intervention 1.228; as one of the eight requisites, *see* eight requisites; imaginary hairs in one's begging-bowl (illustration of reality) 14.505; 'The Message of the Bowl' 25.204–5; a monk is dependent on others not only for food but even for his bowl 16.405; the monk whose bowl is broken by robbers 10.649; the rule that *bhikkhus* mustn't put their begging-bowl on bare ground 12.429, 20.447; Sangharakshita is shown how to lacquer his bowl 20.413; Sīvali, the Buddha's disciple whose begging-bowl was never empty 2.229; Śrī gives a bowl to the monk in the *Sūtra of Golden Light* 16.404–5; symbolism in Buddhist art 7.396–8; turning the bowl upside down to express disapproval 19.483

beginners and newcomers to Buddhism

the beginner
allowing the blaze of initial enthusiasm to subside into a glow of half-interest 8.313; as a beginner you need positive conditions 15.394; better not to be Buddhistically inclined at the start, so you can discover it within yourself 4.352; the Dharma can be practised by a beginner 17.159–60; disheartened and confused by all the different schools 13.326–7; tends to want to discuss general things – 'Nirvāṇa', 'Enlightenment' 18.413; put off by traditional Buddhist language 16.137; latches onto whichever form of practice seems most inspiring and helpful 11.221; some are more interested in 'what is', others in 'what to do' 17.569; spiritually amphibious 11.131; the story of John's experience of starting to practise Buddhism 11.59–62; we need doctrinal supports to begin with 14.547; why some beginners struggle with devotional practice 15.391–2; you need to build self-confidence before you can take the Dharma seriously 25.142

welcoming beginners
the Buddha would put newcomers at their ease 16.15; make newcomers feel welcome 4.338, 11.238–9, 12.60–1, 12.487, 12.539, 12.680; Śāntideva's way of putting things is not always appropriate 4.623; what they need when they first become interested in spiritual life 17.159; when teaching Buddhism, begin with a degree of generality 19.102

beginner's mind 'the beautiful is that which from moment to moment is always new' 18.159; the bliss of beginner's mind 23.xiv; in meditation 5.328, 5.694–5, 15.503–4, 16.439–40; in relation to Buddhism 12.39–41; it's important to keep our beginner's mind with respect to ideas 12.465; keep going back to what you think you understand 18.183; keeping alive our sense that the *Dharma-Vinaya* is a wonderful thing 11.44; looking at the world with a fresh, new mind 15.504–5, 18.159, 19.457; not seeing new sights with old eyes, but seeing old sights with new eyes 7.295; we don't want to lose the fresh inquiring mind of a child 18.167; when we say, 'Now, finally I understand', we are really only just beginning 17.413; with regard to everything you do 12.422–3

beginning 'All beings are from the very beginning the Buddha' 1.269, 2.742 (n682), 18.44–5, 19.537; beginnings of the human quest 3.4–5; Buddhism comes from the beginningless past 7.342; Buddhism does not recognize an ultimate first beginning 16.100; Buddhism is the beginning of a great spiritual adventure 7.186; every event can be regarded as an end or a beginning 8.225–6; 'The fear of the Lord is the beginning of wisdom' 16.277; 'I have no before or after, neither beginning nor end' 26.53; 'In the beginning was the Word' 13.567; *saṃsāra* has no beginning 16.388; unknowingly a Buddha from the very beginning: the jewel in the garment 18.44–5; whatever has a beginning must have an end 11.446, 11.449; you are pure from the beginningless beginning 5.33–4, 5.537, 26.52

behaviour

Buddhist behaviour
the bodhisattva vows outline how all Buddhists should behave 4.63–4; Buddhism's values eroded by the behaviour of its traditional custodians 2.551; how an Enlightened being would behave 1.531; however a *bhikkhu* behaves he is treated as a *bhikkhu* by virtue of his ordination 2.590–4; a layman may behave better than a *bhikkhu* and still defer to him 2.591–2; not teaching the Dharma to someone who is not behaving respectfully 4.342; Order members behaving as though they are not really Buddhist 2.570–1

patterns of behaviour
energy locked away in habitual patterns of thought, feeling, and behaviour 18.77; patterns of behaviour that meditation doesn't affect 16.114; we create patterns as we move over the surface of things 18.283

changing behaviour
behaviour motivated by ego's resistance 16.24; change may or may not manifest in external behaviour 18.204–5; is Buddhist practice reflected in changed behaviour? 9.192; we don't accept that we might need to change the way we behave 4.128; we must want to change group behaviour 3.452

assessing our behaviour
interpreting one's own behaviour positively, other people's negatively 19.573; one's own behaviour should be the primary object of one's scrutiny 4.25; we must be clear about what is behind our behaviour 19.527; 'Why on earth am I behaving like this?' 5.348

how to behave
adopting rules isn't artificial, just behaving like everyone around you 10.529–30; behave towards others as you wish them to behave towards you 2.359; ethical behaviour is habitual good action 11.308; religious people's behaviour based on

principles opposite to those they profess 2.80–1; *śīla* means behaviour, especially ethical behaviour 2.147; the ten precepts the norm of ethical behaviour for all human beings 2.348; whatever religious beliefs people profess, their behaviour is usually similar 19.229–30

behaving badly
all sorts of factors in the world almost oblige us to behave unskilfully 16.323–4; cruel behaviour 16.294, 26.653–4; demolishing the wrong views that undergird morally evil behaviour 26.678; disrespectful behaviour in the name of informality 4.345–6; fear of seeming to condone unsavoury behaviour 22.131; self-indulgent wacky behaviour 18.178; there's nothing you can't do with the wrong motive 18.361; thinking that people are behaving most characteristically when they are behaving most badly 26.35; violence is the most extreme form that unethical behaviour can take 2.359; we ourselves will feel the effects of unskilful behaviour 3.323

see also
action; ethics; skilful, unskilful

being

introduction
in essence consciousness 2.77; no perception of being 1.395–6; not a very Buddhistic word 3.187; the possibilities of being are infinite 18.227; whether Enlightened or unenlightened, you're always in a state of being 15.592–3; 'Why do you harp on "being"?' 1.100

and non-being
reducing conditioned things to a flow in which 'being' and 'non-being' are meaningless 2.121; the bodhisattva above the extremes of being and non-being 4.240, 17.411; for Heracleitus being and not-being are equally real 7.195–6; 'I sense within this "being" a "not-being" more profound' 25.435; without the 'I' you have neither being nor non-being 17.342

being oneself *see under* self/further perspectives on 'self'

beings *see* living beings

Belgium 26.404

belief believing what everyone else believes 17.52–4; 'I believe that it is a weakness to believe anything … or nothing' 7.38; born of fear 1.20; *Buddhism Without Beliefs* 8.571–99; difference between Buddhist and Christian belief 13.570–1; 'an emotional satisfaction that no argument could be allowed to disturb' 20.217; faith is active, whereas belief is passive 19.581; find something to believe in, then you can do it with all your energy 10.603; genuine belief, not just saying something as spiritual good manners 19.538–9; hopefully we'll start actually believing in something 19.413; 'idols of the theatre' (Bacon) 12.656; provisional belief 8.591–2; the temptation to believe something because it feels comfortable 12.655; we owe it to ourselves to ask ourselves what we really believe 12.690; wrong beliefs spring up again like weeds 8.303; you can tell what someone really believes by how they act 19.229–30

Bell, Clive 3.510, 26.166

Bellini, Giovanni v24

Belloc, Hilaire 15.489

bells bells in the puja 11.226; 'Never send to know for whom the bell tolls' 4.472, 25.422; the temple bell at Arunachala: symbol of spiritual change 20.340–1

Belsen 18.321

Beluva 2.28

Benares (Varanasi) Dr Ambedkar visits the city 9.11; Anandamayi Ashram 20.387; Bharat Mata Mandir 20.387; Burmese Rest House 20.442; Hindu University 9.13, 9.281, 9.468, 9.489, 20.442–53, 20.458; Isipatana, *see* Sarnath; Ramakrishna Mission 20.386–8; Sangharakshita and Terry visit the city 23.360–1; Sarnath, *see* Sarnath; Sri Ramakrishna's vision 20.387; Theosophical Society 20.387, 20.388; Vizianagaram Palace 20.453

Bendre, N. S. 21.558

Benedict, St 13.597

benefactors contention that all benefactors of humanity are bodhisattvas 2.183–4; directly or indirectly everybody is a benefactor 4.435; 'the greatest benefactor is a spiritual friend in the form of an ordinary human being' 2.700 (n370), 3.604, 4.172, 15.586; one of the greatest benefactors of Buddhism, Mrs Mary E. Foster 8.49, 8.99

benevolence 'Attachment may be mistaken for benevolence and compassion' 5.169–72; the benevolence of bodhisattvas 4.180–1, 5.186; Confucian *shù*, Godwinian 'benevolence' 8.448; extending benevolence to the universe as a whole 13.271

Bengal Barua Buddhists 7.460–1, 22.9, 22.26; Bengali Buddhists in Assam and Darjeeling 22.92–3, 22.97–8, 22.108–10;

a journey through Bengal 22.50–1; Shantiniketan, *see under* Tagore

Bennett, Adrienne assists with the *Maha Bodhi* journal 8.636, 23.54; describes I. B. Horner's work as 'the last ounce of dust in desiccation' 5.248, 23.225; 'I Went to Them and Said' 8.643; *Long Discourses of the Buddha* 8.662; translation of the *Bodhicaryāvatāra* (basis of Sevenfold Puja) 8.636, 11.218–19, 23.55

Bennett, Allan (Ananda Metteyya) introduction 3.410, 3.682 (n368), 23.481 (n72); death in London two years before Sangharakshita was born 12.71, 20.4, 20.480, 23.41; has an important place in the history of Western Buddhism 23.41; prospective biography 20.101; resemblance between him and Sangharakshita 23.41; returns as a monk to introduce Buddhism in England 10.139, 11.xvi, 11.485, 12.71

Benninger, Christopher 10.367, 26.257, 26.722 (n211)

Beowulf 3.96, 12.641–3, 16.85–6

bereavement *see under* death

Bergson, Henri-Louis 7.209, 7.599 (n321)

Berkeley, Bishop George brief introduction 7.554 (n58), 12.708 (n53), 14.642 (n395); Christianity cannot be detected in his work 12.77; *esse est percipi* (to exist is to be perceived) 1.351, 1.368, 7.45, 12.172, 14.420; *The Principles of Human Knowledge* 1.375; saw materialism as synonymous with atheism 1.368; and Vasubandhu 1.368–9, 12.78; 'We have first raised a dust and then complain we cannot see' 8.616

Berlin Buddhist Centre *see under* Germany

Bernard, Michelle 14.xx, 17.xv

Bernard, St, of Clairvaux introduction 17.720 (n94); devotion to the Virgin Mary 13.600–1; ignoring the Alps on the way to Rome 13.279; involvement in the Second Crusade 13.629; keen nose for heresy 13.629; On Consideration 17.86; sermons on the Song of Solomon 13.544, 13.715–16 (n319)

Bernardette, St 13.601

Berniak Kazi *see* Rai Bahadur Densapa

Bernini, Gian Lorenzo 23.308, 23.520 (n345)

Berruguete, Pedro de 13.666–7, 24.410

Berry, John 22.55

Besant, Annie introduction 22.587 (n129); dressed in white 22.140; leadership of the Theosophical Society 8.24; a lecture finding a scientific basis for the practice of Untouchability 20.218; meeting with Anagarika Dharmapala 8.46; Sangharakshita reads 20.148

Besthorpe *see under* Norfolk

Betjeman, John brief introduction 23.542 (n500); association with Highgate 23.473; good accessible poetry 26.379; Miss Joan Hunter-Dunn 24.566; 'Norman fonts' ('The Wykehamist') 21.373

betrayal betrayal of the spirit of Buddhism 8.475–6; the French nun betrays George Roerich 22.427–8; the invalidity of Sangharakshita's ordination an act of betrayal 2.611; minimizing the importance of devotion betrays Buddhism 26.629–30; the theme of *David Copperfield* 24.555–7; turning Buddhism into an ethnic religion: the worst of betrayals 8.471

beyond

terms and references
arhant: 'one beyond training' (*asekha*) 10.616; *atakkāvacara* (beyond thought) 1.17, 1.209, 8.589, 9.398, 11.8; *lokuttara*, literally 'world beyond', *see lokuttara*; 'a man of the beyond' 18.68; *pāra* (beyond) 1.69; 'The Way to the Beyond' 1.82

going beyond …
conditioning 18.147–8; the ego 22.374–5, 22.394–5, 25.xli, 25.183, 26.668–9; good and evil 15.367–8, 17.636; the idea of progress 18.397; pairs of opposites 1.294, 3.308, 10.464–5, 15.155–6, 16.543–8; psychology 5.355, 17.649; *see also under* concepts; *dhyānas*, 'I'; individuality; limitations; Nirvāṇa/Nirvāṇa and *saṃsāra*; self and other; senses; speech/introduction; subject–object; mind/rational mind; opposites; reason; thought; time/and space; yourself; words

going beyond in practice
'Am I looking beyond what I already know?' 17.348; challenge yourself to move beyond your habitual sources of pleasure 15.158; the delusion that you've gone beyond all concepts 18.399–400; do something to go beyond your conditioning 18.147–8; the goal is to go beyond the individual self, not regress from it 17.625; going beyond your comfort zone 25.77–8; growing beyond the limits of your knowledge 17.206; growing beyond roots, not severing them 26.60; in spiritual friendship you try to get beyond your selfishness 12.669; looking beyond

the present moment 25.22; practices serve a purpose that lies beyond them 2.265, 17.306; reaching out beyond personal happiness to benefit others 17.166; resistance to going beyond a certain point in meditation 5.695; to go beyond intellectual understanding, we must possess it 2.244–5, 12.515, 26.199; we can evolve beyond the point of self-consciousness 3.477; we have to create something that goes beyond what we are 25.73; widening the mind beyond its natural boundaries 1.563

reflections
'allowing myself to be a channel for something beyond me' 11.687; beyond the Buddha's smile there is only silence 26.385; the conservation of spiritual values beyond death 4.63; the 'beyond within' 2.41; 'The grace of the Gurus is beyond our comprehension' 18.554; a life 'beyond all that is comprehensible and embraceable here' 26.176; 'he lives having passed beyond uncertainty' 5.283–5; the meaning of life is to be found only beyond life 26.13; the nature of the world is beyond categorization 17.387; 'the otherness that lies beyond the boundaries of man's conscious mind' 26.169; the poet responds to the world beyond 26.137; the profound Dharma beyond ideas of existence and non-existence 17.364

Bhaddiya (aristocrat turned *bhikkhu*) 10.500–1

Bhaddiya 'the dwarf' (Lakuntaka Bhaddiya Thera) 'foremost of those who have a sweet voice' 10.615; how he became a dwarf 3.105–6; in the *Theragātha* 3.105–6; in the *Udāna* 10.618–19

Bhadra the Magician 14.187

bhadracārin 2.729 (n614)

Bhadracari-praṇidhāna-rāja (vows) 14.227

Bhadrajyotis, bodhisattva 16.543

Bhadramāyākāra-paripṛcchā Sūtra 14.187

Bhadrapāla-śreṣṭhi-paripṛcchā Sūtra 14.187–8

Bhagat, Taranath 23.356–7

Bhagavad Gītā

introduction
regarded as a revealed work 14.374; the book as a goddess 20.175–6; Arnold's translation (*The Song Celestial*) 20.62–3; a radical new translation 22.154; compared with the *Sūtra of Golden Light* 16.424–5; Sangharakshita read when young 9.466, 9.487, 20.62; 'There you are, rotting under your *Bhagavad Gītā*!' (Krishnamurti) 18.632, 26.558; 'the Vedas are the cows, the Upanishads the milk, the teaching the butter' 18.220; verses read to the workers on a tea estate 22.22; *Yoga of Bhagavad Gītā* (Prem) 20.61

teachings
the four kinds of yoga 7.588 (n248); *guṇas* (theory of psychological types) 7.579 (n187), 10.53–6, 12.277–8; Kurukṣetra (the battlefield) 7.149, 7.588 (n248); on caste 9.102–3, 9.266, 9.482, 10.53–6; roots in the sky 14.590; used to justify violence 8.449, 20.164, 22.76

Arjuna
has no memory of past lives 16.424; 'Vision of the Universal Form' 2.644, 10.56, 20.62; reluctance to fight 10.55–6, 20.164

Krishna
the All-Destroyer, Time 10.56, 26.296; 'The caste system is of my creation' 9.102–3, 10.54; claim to be God Supreme 9.95; embodiment of absolute consciousness 3.484; exhorts Arjuna to fight 20.164; gives Arjuna a complete course in Hinduism 13.569; 'I am born age after age' 13.569, 16.424–5; on rebirth: like putting on a new set of clothes 3.196–7, 7.165, 19.375; 'Out of a thousand who seek him, only one will find him' 3.484; 'There is danger in the duty of another' 10.55–6; 'Whenever unrighteousness prevails, I will take birth to restore righteousness' 10.37

Bhagavān 12.529, 15.461–2, 15.470

Bhaggava (recluse) 2.84, 5.511, 10.506, 13.279, 26.597

Bhagwat, Dr N. K. v21, v22

Bhai, Panch 10.383

Bhaiṣajyaguru, Bhaiṣajyarāja, or Vaiḍūryaprabha introduction 16.193–5;

Dhardo Rimpoche initiates Sangharakshita into the practice 22.557; explains Dharma-worship (*Vimalakīrti-nirdeśa*) 16.572–4; how he establishes a Pure Land 14.175; King of Healing 12.228; the Medicine Buddha 22.557; and myrobalan fruit 16.620 (n276); as *sambhogakāya* 2.42; *sūtra*, *see Sūtra of the Lord of Healing*; in the *White Lotus Sūtra*, *see under White Lotus Sūtra*/characters in the *sūtra*; his worship immensely popular 1.335

Bhaja caves *see under* caves

Bhaja retreat centre, India *see under* Triratna IV/retreat centres

bhājanaloka (world of things) 1.342

bhajans (Hindu devotional songs) *see under* Hinduism

bhakti sacred music as a path to the divine 22.294; the term occurs for the first time in Indian literature in a Buddhist treatise 1.290; yoga, *see under* Hinduism/yogas 7.61

Bhallika and Tapussa (Sanskrit Trapuṣa) merchants go for Refuge 2.727–8 (n600), 3.681 (n356); the Buddha's first two lay disciples 2.22, 3.64, 14.611 (n29); they offer the Buddha honey and rice cakes 3.64; they took a relic of the Buddha to Orissa 10.lvi; *The Travellers from Orissa* 26.xvii

Bhāmaha 26.330

bhaṇanaśīla (one in the habit of speaking) 11.307

Bhandare, R. D. 10.122–3

Bhandari, Mr (SCF) 10.8

bhang 20.162

bhantacitta (wandering mind) 10.532, 15.116–17, 17.97

Bhante (meaning) 18.315, 26.xi

Bhāradvāja (brahmin disciple of the Buddha) 2.692 (n305), 3.76

Bhāradvāja the farmer *see* Kasi-Bhāradvāja

Bharate family 10.355, 10.367

Bharati, Swami Agehananda (Leopold Fischer) introduction 8.434–5, 21.585; how a cartoonist would depict him 8.446; *A Functional Analysis of Indian Thought* 8.435; *The Light at the Center* (review) 8.434–46; *The Ochre Robe* 8.435, 8.437, 8.439, 21.583; *The Tantric Tradition* 8.435

Bharatiya Bauddha Mahasabha 9.293, 9.526, 9.564–5 (n280), 10.148

Bhari Lotsawa (Tibetan translator) 18.156–9

bhasma 9.345

Bhaswarananda, Swami 7.108, 7.110, 20.148

Bhaṭṭa, Kumārila 8.359–60, 9.183, 9.482, 9.575, 10.624

Bhattacharya, Dr Benoytosh 2.174, 2.176, 22.30

bhāva *see* becoming

bhava-tṛṣṇā *see under tṛṣṇā*

bhāvanā 1.364, 1.561, 7.152, 7.436

Bhāvanā-krama 16.445

bhāvanā-mārga 2.141

bhāvanā-mayī prajñā *see under* three levels of wisdom

bhavaṅga-sota (life-stream) 17.523

Bhavasaṃkrānti Sūtra Vṛtti 1.311

bhavāsrava *see āsrava*

Bhāvaviveka 1.321–2

Bhave, Vinoba introduction 19.601 (n66); building a temple at Bodh Gaya 8.147, 8.179–81, 22.128–9, 22.159, 23.367; Gandhi's chief disciple 21.615; he compares himself to the Buddha 8.147–8; his *bhūdan* (land donation) programme 17.199–200; his disciples' claims about his 'greatness' 19.162–3; a new Buddhist not wanting to do what Bhave does 9.519–20; Sarvodaya movement 8.178–9, 22.158–9

Bhayabherava Sutta *see under Majjhima Nikāya*

bhikkhu (Sanskrit *bhikṣu*)

INTRODUCTION AND EARLY DAYS

introduction
what *bhikkhu* means 9.543; it can be translated 'one who shares' 11.188; comparison between priest and *bhikṣu* 26.160–1; and lay people, *see under* lay people/lay people and monks; literally someone who lives on almsfood 10.479, 16.404–5; not just a yellow-robe wearer but anyone who practises the precepts 7.69, 7.566–7 (n117); originally imagined to be part of the ordination of the Western Buddhist Order 2.469; seniormost nun subordinated to juniormost monk 2.602–3; *saddhivihārika* (newly ordained monk) 2.196; they have everything to do with the world (Ambedkar) 7.230–1; Tibetan

equivalent (*gelong*), *see under* Tibetan Buddhism/monks and nuns

in the early days of Buddhism
ability to ward off malign forces 3.409–10; altruism 2.213; the 'band of six' 10.520, 10.712–13 (n417); conception in *Dhammapada* (Ambedkar) 9.146; 'division of labour' between study and meditation 2.201; duties 3.409–10, 7.230; encouraged by *devas* to get on with their meditation 19.413; gathered twice a month to chant Dharma stanzas, and later the *prātimokṣa* 7.496; glimpsed in Pāli texts: 'the pristine, ascetic stage' 2.188; a *bhikkhu* has control over his hands and feet (*Dhammapada*) 20.122; the pattern of a *bhikkhu*'s daily life at the time of the Buddha 10.582; being a *bhikkhu* became respectable, and people took it up for dubious reasons 10.519–20; the term equated with *brāhmaṇa* and *samaṇa* in the *Udāna* 10.515, 10.554; the most junior *bhikṣu* takes precedence over kings 2.214; poets and artists 2.213

ORDINATION

introduction
does not signify a particular depth of Going for Refuge 3.408; effected by a *saṅgha-karma* (resolution of local sangha) 2.193; two phases reflect going forth and joining the sangha 3.461–2; it became the ceremony of ordination within a monastic order 2.189; now has a quasi-magical character, though the traditional practice was plain 2.594; the importance of proper screening and training 8.296–7, 8.307–8; it is joining a group 2.415; lifestyle requirements 2.191; as 'rite of passage' 2.641–3; the impossibility of validity of ordination 2.579–650

ceremony
the form of the ceremony 2.193–4, 21.107–9; *karmakāraka-bhikṣu* (master of ceremonies) 2.194; *karmavācanā* or *kammavācā* (declaration) 2.194; *pārisuddha*, purity of *bhikkhus* of ordaining chapter 2.580–1, 2.582; 'not the done thing' to question a *bhikkhu*'s *pārisuddha* 2.586; *sīmā*, area in which the ordination takes place 2.580, 2.586, 2.587, 2.590; difference between ordination in the technical Vinaya sense and lived experience 2.641–2

'lower' (pabbajjā or pravrajyā, śrāmaṇera)
going forth 3.462; Refuges and Precepts 7.473; set of ten precepts taken by the *śrāmaṇera* 11.258, 11.747 (n117); conditions 2.193, 21.96; ordaining people but not teaching them anything 22.458; Sangharakshita's *śrāmaṇera* ordination, *see under* Sangharakshita V/ordination; Tibetan equivalent, *getsul* 12.14, 13.45, 22.520

'higher' (upasaṃpadā)
conditions, which do not include any caste restrictions 2.193; quorum of a chapter of monks required for ordination 2.623, 2.628–30, 13.339; the highest importance is attached to proper ordination 8.246–7; in Japan became bodhisattva ordination 2.209, 8.246; leaves the *bhikṣu* dependent on his own spiritual efforts 7.474; originally the acceptance (*upasampadā*) of the Buddha's teaching 2.187–8; the practical difficulty of assembling a chapter of ten monks 10.572–4; someone who tried to get ordained by bribery 8.307–8; two main lineages, Theravāda and Sarvāstivāda 7.472–3

the life of the newly ordained monk (saddhivihārika)
niśraya (Pāli *nissaya*, period of spiritual tutelage) 2.196, 18.388; obligations and duties 2.194; *raho 'nuśāka-bhikṣu* (privy admonisher) 2.194; repetition of the Going for Refuge formula 11.420; two teachers 15.667; *upādhyāya* (or *upajjhāya*, preceptor) 2.193, 2.194, 2.196–7, 2.629, 2.634, 15.667

disrobing
bhikkhus who disrobed 22.52–3, 23.76; one can disrobe and be ordained again up to seven times 2.519, 18.541

MODERN *BHIKKHUS*

status
are *bhikkhus* really regarded with awed inspiration? 2.645–6; avoiding the translation 'monk' 15.7; a *bhikkhu* is treated as one by virtue of his ordination, however he behaves 2.590–4; *bhikkhus* who become academics 19.486–7; *bhikkhus* who pride themselves on adherence to the Vinaya, but break it secretly 7.263; certainty about their superior status 22.332, 22.338–9; going through the motions of being a *bhikkhu* 19.274–5; irreverence towards a *bhikkhu* who was expecting reverence 19.308–9; the 'jargon' of being a *bhikkhu* 19.294; junior *bhikkhus* paying respect to elder *bhikkhus*: a pleasant thing to see 4.327; like social workers or professors 10.225, 19.486–7; may be unwilling to compromise their dignity 4.86–7, 14.556; one is not necessarily a *bhikkhu* because one wears a yellow robe 2.560, 9.271; only the most senior are allowed to give advice on worldly affairs 4.67; they believe they are

bhikkhus because they have been ordained 2.598; salutations to *bhikkhus* 9.337–8; to be a poor *bhikkhu* is a disgrace 18.333

problems
being given unsuitable gifts 2.214; conflict between desire to propagate the Dharma and monastic rules 4.117; confusion about how to teach the Dharma 19.497; dispute between celibate *bhikkhus* and married priests in Korea 8.292–3, 22.458; the extreme veneration shown to them is bad for them 2.599–601, 2.646; negatively disposed towards *bhikkhunīs*? 11.645; robes (*ticīvara*) give an impression of Buddhism as archaic 9.316; someone who became a *bhikkhu* so his parents could get merit 10.267; the thought of devoting themselves to Enlightenment barely occurs to them 8.280; trapped in an out-of-date system 9.224; unhelpful to New Buddhists in India 9.155–6, 20.252

need for reform
can be good Buddhists but bad monks 2.581–2, 2.587–8; if indifferent to the woes of mankind, not a *bhikkhu* (Ambedkar) 9.147; a new kind needed (Ambedkar) 9.318, 9.392, 9.432, 9.510; the role of *bhikkhus* (Ambedkar) 9.112–13, 9.208; 'Wanted: A New Type of Bhikkhu' 2.448–9, 8.327–30, 10.271; what is a real *bhikkhu*? 9.536; which is the *upāsaka* and which is the *bhikkhu*? 10.225; could borrow from Jesuits (Ambedkar) 9.318

see also
monastic tradition; monks

bhikkhunī (or *bhikṣuṇī*)

introduction
explanation of term 9.543; Burmese 'nuns', not being considered as providing merit, are neglected 2.215; commitments after ordination 13.339; *dasasilamata* ('ten precept nuns') in Sri Lanka 2.744 (n689); desire for equal status with *bhikkhus*: based on egalitarian notions, not Buddhism 2.602–3; duties 3.409–10; wearing bathing dresses (*Udāna*) 10.498–9, 19.250, 19.262; observe a much larger number of *vinaya* rules than *bhikṣus* 2.196, 2.602–3; *maechis*, Thai 'nuns' 2.601–2; Malaysian nuns chanting 24.36–7; seniormost nun subordinated to juniormost monk 2.602–3, 11.442

ordination
the Buddha's reluctance to let women go forth 7.496–7, 11.420–31; the Buddha ordained women to overcome 'the gospel of inequality' (Ambedkar) 9.101; countries where ordination survives 3.408; desirability of reinstating ordination 3.408; does not signify a particular depth of Going for Refuge 3.408; emphasis on ordination shows more concern with status than monastic life 2.602; extinction of *upasampadā* ordination lineage in Japan 2.209; having died out in Theravādin countries, temporary ordination not open to women 2.210; originally simply a difference of lifestyle 9.131; subordination to monks 11.422–3, 11.425–7; women ordained as *anagārikās* where monastic lineages are extinct 7.477; why bother with *bhikkhunī* ordination? 11.641–2; would the ordination of women cause a deterioration of the sangha? 2.27, 11.642–5; is the tradition extinct? 2.196, 2.469, 2.688–9 (n274), 12.667; sangha *see under* sangha/traditional sangha

bhikṣā *see* almsfood

bhikṣāpātra *see* begging-bowl

bhikṣuṇī sangha *see under* sangha

bho (greeting) 10.438

bhojana-dāna (food offering) 2.212, 22.26–7, 22.28, 22.93, 22.99, 22.109, 23.364

Bhoodan Yajna v8

Bhūmija Sutta *see under Majjhima Nikāya*

bhūmis ten *bhūmis*, *see* ten *bhūmis*; thirteen *bhūmis* (or *viharas*) 4.646, 16.150

bhūmisparśa mudrā *see under mudras*

Bhumiveda, Mr 21.431–2, v22

Bhusawal, India 10.177

bhūtakoṭi ('pinnacle of existence') 2.43

Bhutan assassination of the 'Prime Minister' 23.118–19; Bhutanese Buddhists in Kalimpong 21.210, 22.33–4; Buddhism in Bhutan 2.548–9; Pemalingpa (controversial Bhutanese *tertön*) 24.388; royal family 23.118–22; Sangharakshita visits the border 21.21

bhūtapubbam 10.596

bhūtas (evil spirits) introduction 17.729 (n157); Tārā conquers them 17.144; the world protected from them by the four great kings 16.349–50

Bhutia, Dawa Tsering (student) v21, v22, 23.384

Bhutia, Dorje v22

bias false speech based on unconscious bias 17.234–5; scientific thinking now less biased towards materialism than it

was 2.33; three biases, *see* three *āsravas*; wrong views held in accordance with an unacknowledged emotional bias 14.572

Bible

INTRODUCTION

introduction
belief that Old and New Testaments come from different sources 13.622–3; belief in the Bible's authority 9.109, 9.426, 14.374, 15.264–5; the Bible you don't read does you more good than the Bible you read 19.135; Biblical phrases are part of our culture 4.35; black market Bibles in Soviet Russia 9.349; 'deposit of faith' 14.453; doesn't explain how to practise 9.470, 9.494; inspired in the way some poets are inspired 13.547; references to homosexuality 13.611–12, 13.616; the whole text is a revelation 18.495; wisdom writings 13.544

translations and interpretations
Authorized Version 8.13, 9.111, 13.535, 13.644, 14.289, 16.444, 16.479; *The Bible Designed to be Read as Literature* 14.298–9; mistranslations 13.576; 'The more interpretations the better' 14.336, 16.546; the symbolism of St Jerome's Bible 26.299–302

Bible stories
Cain and Abel 12.642; Daniel in the lion's den 26.287–8; Elijah fed by ravens 18.33; Jacob's Ladder 12.185; Judas 12.513, 13.594; the influence of St Paul 12.695–6; Martha and Mary 4.114, 7.98, 7.149, 22.296–7, 22.603 (n246); Moloch 7.364, 7.608 (n408); Moses and the burning bush 25.18; Samson slaying the lion 26.287–8; Satan 12.513, 18.27; speaking in tongues 13.576; Tobias and the Angel 4.99, 13.589–90, 25.375, 26.269

Sangharakshita and the Bible
reading the Bible as literature 13.521–2, 13.535, 14.298–9, 14.300–1, 25.19–20; family Bible 13.526, 20.9–10, 26.287–8; favourite books 13.535–44; learning to read from the Bible 20.9–10, 20.495–6, 26.287; reading of Psalms and Proverbs 13.544–6; struck by the image of gates that were 'one pearl' 13.532, 26.221

OLD TESTAMENT

introduction
association of religiosity with mundane well-being 17.20; God of Power 3.449; Moses and the Ten Commandments 1.528; some good stories, but much that is abhorrent 13.546–7; 'this savage Bronze Age literature' (Huxley) 11.362, 13.546; stoning people for blasphemy 11.336

Genesis
the Creation 1.528; Adam and Eve in the Garden of Eden 1.528, 15.619

The Book of Job
composed in the 5th century BCE 13.536; the story 13.536–42; the author had a painter's eye for the beauty of nature 13.540; Blake's illustrations 13.536, 26.485; comes close to being a tragedy 16.423; its author emerged in the Axial Age 11.355; its God is the God of power 13.542; the masterpiece of Hebrew literature 13.542; the Book of Job moves us more than the Book of Leviticus 14.303; sees human life as a problem 16.86; suffering as the punishment of God 16.86; 'Behold now Behemoth' 13.541; 'in my flesh I shall see God' 13.576; 'Hast thou given the horse strength?' 13.540–1; 'Let the day perish, wherein I was born' 13.537; 'Who is this that darkeneth counsel?' 13.539

The Song of Solomon
the celebration of the coming of spring 13.543; connection with the poetry of St John of the Cross 13.544; the description of the lover 13.543–4; interpreted as an allegory 13.544; lovely poetry 13.542–4; St Bernard's sermons 13.544, 13.715–16 (n319); 'How beautiful are thy feet' 13.543–4; 'Rise up, my Love, my fair one' 13.543; 'Set me as a seal upon thy heart' 13.544

Psalms
'the beauty of holiness' 17.337; 'The fear of the Lord is the beginning of wisdom' 16.277, 26.155; 'He giveth his beloved sleep' 7.100; 'As the hart panteth after the water brooks' 23.106; 'Put not your trust in princes' 12.239, 17.552; 'vale of tears' 2.80; the wicked man flourishes like the green bay tree 17.263

Proverbs
appreciation 13.544–6, 14.343; 'Go to the Ant, thou sluggard' 13.545–6; heaping coals of fire on your enemy's head 4.411, 17.172; 'The eyes of the Lord are in every place' 14.581, 17.560, 17.662, 19.276; 'The fear of the Lord is the beginning of wisdom' 16.277, 26.155; 'The soft answer that turneth away wrath' 15.441; 'He that walketh uprightly walketh safely' 26.522; 'Where there is no vision the people perish' 11.161, 25.144

Ecclesiastes
the tragedy of human life 3.96; 'Eat, drink, and be merry' 16.302; 'There is no new

thing under the sun' 7.163; 'Whatsoever thy hand findeth to do, do it with all thy might' 10.603, 11.711

other Old Testament books
'After the fire a still small voice' 14.535; 'the beauty of holiness' 17.337; 'Can a leopard change his spots?' 22.174; 'The goat shall bear upon him all their iniquities' 2.753 (n756); 'Love thy neighbour' 9.494, 25.239; man shall not lie with a man as with a woman 13.611; 'Now go and smite Amalek' 13.546–7; 'The people that walked in darkness have seen a great light' 10.319; 'A stranger in a foreign land' 23.111; 'Thou shalt not suffer a witch to live' 11.361; 'A Virgin shall conceive, and bear a son' 13.576

NEW TESTAMENT

introduction to the Gospels
different portrayal of Jesus in synoptic gospels and John's gospel 13.567; Gnostic gospels, *see under* Gnosticism; in church these days you might not hear the gospel being expounded 19.489; intolerance in the gospels 4.123; the inclusion of the raising of Lazarus in John's gospel 13.645–6; Irenaeus championed John's gospel 13.621; Marcion regarded Luke's gospel as the only reliable account 13.623; the New Testament teaches a God of Love 3.449; parables 13.643–4; the Sermon on the Mount, *see under* Jesus; speak repeatedly of hell 13.572–3; stories about possession by devils in the gospel of St Mark 13.594–5; St Mark's gospel says nothing about Jesus's conception and birth 13.642; written not by the Apostles but by their disciples 14.399

Matthew
'Depart from me, ye cursed' 13.573; 'Take care that ye despise not one of these little ones' 13.590; 'Don't let your left hand know what your right hand is doing' 14.418; 'An eye for an eye' 16.310; 'He that findeth his life shall lose it' 2.130; 'By their fruits ye shall know them' 7.291, 8.116, 13.644; 'Get thee hence, Satan' 13.554; 'I did not come to bring peace but a sword' 8.153; 'Inasmuch as ye have done it unto the least of these my brethren' 21.355; 'Judge not that ye be not judged' 13.644; 'If we seek first the Kingdom of Heaven, all things will be added unto us' 7.307; 'Let your light so shine' 7.35; 'The lilies of the field' 18.105, 21.303; 'No man can serve two masters' 13.644; 'Man shall not live by bread alone' 25.437, 26.382–3; 'If Satan cast out Satan, he is divided against himself' 18.27; 'They that sit in the shadow of death' 7.68; 'new wine in old bottles' 1.62, 10.429, 23.178, 26.474; 'Whatsover ye would that men should do to you ...' 13.614; 'Which of you, if your son asks for bread, will give him a stone?' 1.22, 25.9–10, 25.420; 'Where your treasure is, there will your heart be also' 16.98, 16.346, 25.103; 'Whoever looks at a woman to lust for her' 2.70

Mark
'The fire that never shall be quenched' 13.572; Jesus's family said, 'He is out of his mind' 13.457; 'A prophet is not without honour, but in his own country' 22.298; 'new wine in old bottles' 1.62, 10.429, 23.178, 26.474

Luke
'Eat, drink, and be merry' 16.302; 'Father, forgive them, for they know not what they do' 4.394–5; 'Judge not that ye be not judged' 13.644; 'The Kingdom of God (or Heaven) is within you' 7.98, 7.369; 'A light to lighten the Gentiles' 7.68; 'No man can serve two masters' 13.644; 'Man shall not live by bread alone' 25.437, 26.382–3; 'new wine in old bottles' 1.62, 10.429, 23.178, 26.474

John
'Behold the Lamb of God' 13.577; 'Greater love hath no man than this, that he lay down his life for his friend' 7.293, 12.457; 'He that abideth in me' 7.550 (n34); 'I am the way, the truth, and the life' 13.621; 'I have overcome the world' 16.393; 'In the beginning was the Word' 13.567; in the world, but not of it 7.291; 'The light shineth in darkness' 7.33, 7.69; 'The truth shall set you free' 16.499; 'Unless a kernel of wheat falls to the ground and dies ...' 22.588–9 (n150)

Acts
'The gate which is called Beautiful' 26.181

St Paul's letters
'Be not deceived ...' 13.573; 'Being all things to all men' 1.448, 7.33, 12.523, 16.479; heaping coals of fire on your enemy's head 4.411, 17.172; 'In flaming fire taking vengeance' 13.573; 'The letter killeth, but the spirit giveth life' 7.159, 13.437; 'Doing evil that good may come' 26.292, 26.724 (n231); 'Men with men working that which is unseemly' 13.612; 'O death, where is thy sting?' 4.331; 'The peace of God which passeth all understanding' 13.283, 23.98; 'The powers that be are ordained of God' 17.212; 'To the pure all things are pure' 7.99; 'Through a glass darkly' 7.295, 17.24–5, 17.28; the

vice not to be named among Christians 13.451; 'Whatsoever is lovely and of good report' 4.269; 'The whole armour of God' 13.595, 18.81

Revelation
the Great Whore of Babylon 13.555; the vision of the new Jerusalem 1.539; 'And every several gate was of one pearl' 1.539, 13.532, 26.221; 'Behold, I make all things new' 7.163, 13.428

Apocrypha
its function is to illustrate faith and morals, not define doctrine 14.61; obviously pseudonymous 14.399; the wisdom of Solomon 14.343

Biddulph Old Hall *see under* English Sangha Trust

Bigandet, Bishop P. 12.70

bigotry 1.293

Bihar, India Bargaon 7.428, 20.460; Bhikkhu Kashyap and Sangharakshita visit 7.423–32, 20.457–66, 22.387–8; Bihar Sharif 7.424–5, 20.459; Dipnagar 7.426, 20.459; Fatehpur 7.429; Kul 7.427, 20.460; Nalanda, *see* Nalanda; Patna (Pataliputra), *see* Patna; Rajgir, *see* Rajgir; Sarichak 7.429; Vulture's Peak (Gṛdhrakūṭa), *see* Vulture's Peak

bīja (seed syllable) acting as summaries in Perfection of Wisdom text 14.155; *see also* individual seed syllables

Bimbisāra, King

introduction
addressed as *deva* 16.416; in Dr Ambedkar's account 9.142; in Pāli canon and the *Jātaka* stories 9.574n, 16.621 (n287); ruler of Magadha 2.25; his rivalry with King Pasenadi (*Udāna*) 10.472–3; suggested the *uposatha* days (regular meeting of *bhikkhus*) 10.559, 10.716 (n441); at Vulture's Peak 7.431; his story is not really a tragedy, because he was a Stream Entrant 16.423; his previous birth as a *yakkha* 16.621 (n287)

and the Buddha
their first meeting 2.24, 12.712 (n86), 16.621 (n287); he ascertains that the Buddha converted Uruvelā Kāśyapa, not *vice versa* 2.24; gives the Buddha the 'Bamboo Grove' 2.24; he sees the Buddha going forth 9.478; which is happier? 3.271–2

and his son Prince Ajātaśatru
imprisoned 3.453, 3.571, 16.621 (n287), 20.464; kept alive by his wife's fidelity 3.571; used to gaze towards the Vulture's Peak, where he could see the Buddha 20.464; murdered 16.274–5; Bimbisāra's Jail, Bihar 20.464

bindu (Thig Le, sexual energy) 18.76, 18.91, 19.52

biography and autobiography (as a genre) the ancient Indians didn't go in for biography, but the Chinese and Tibetans did 12.563; biographies of Enlightened beings and Buddhist saints 4.53, 15.93–4, 15.164; the difficulty of writing truthful biography 24.148; the genre 20.490–1; even the fullest autobiography is a thin cross-section 24.148; 'higher autobiography' 26.443; 'It is impossible to trace [a life] steadily through successive years' 22.xvi, 22.281; its closeness to fiction 26.443–4; 'Life's memories are not life's histories' 22.xv; of great men 9.219; outer, inner, and secret 22.535–40, 23.xiii, 23.181–2, 23.387; the 20th century an age of great biographies 26.375; *see also* Buddha I/introducing his life/biographies; writing/writing biography

biology biological evolution and hierarchies of spiritual development aspects of a single principle 3.11; the biological function of the group 3.437; biological sex, *see* sex; biology is not necessarily committed to a mechanical theory of life (Sheldrake) 24.209–10; Buddhism teaches psychical as well as biological heredity 1.108; *homo sapiens* the conjunction of a descending spiritual order and an ascending biological one 2.64–5; if you stay in the biological group you make it more difficult for yourself to evolve 18.485–6; life isn't valued so much in wartime – a biological significance? 16.302; the metabiological sciences 12.87; the vast process of biological evolution 3.480

birds

A MISCELLANY OF BIRDS

stories and legends
the arrival of a pure white bird – a good omen? 23.154; the beauty of a white bird and a dark cloud (Pāli canon) 26.242; a bird in Rechungpa's dream 19.566; 'Birds and Their Gods' (poem) 25.395–7, 26.439; 'Birds of a feather flock together' 3.398; the birds still don't sing in Belsen 18.312; the bodhisattva like the kalaviṅka bird 14.180; *The Buddha's Law Among the Birds*, *see under* Conze; the instinct that makes a magpie build its nest 24.540; a letter in the form of a bird

('Hymn of the Pearl') 16.91; Milarepa's heart 'turns into numerous small birds' 19.23, 19.25; Mount Kanchenjunga in the form of a white bird guided a lama to Sikkim 22.244; the partridge, the monkey, and the elephant 14.64; practising altruism 'like a bird' 19.319–20; 'St Francis and the Birds' 25.366–7; 'When the iron birds fly in the sky ...' 12.196, 12.720 (n144), 12.300

free and captive birds
feeding birds: a delightful way of practising *maitrī* 8.224; fortune-tellers with little birds in the bazaar in India 15.386; the freed song-bird 25.192; the practice of releasing birds from captivity 12.660; set free at Chinese Buddhist festivals 1.427

hunted birds
pheasants finding a refuge from being hunted 24.151; a schoolteacher who delighted in shooting birds 8.12, 8.94; songbirds shot in continental Europe 23.246, 25.366–7, 25.516–19

singing and speaking birds
birds sing the Dharma in Sukhāvatī 1.343; 'a wild bird is crying out Truth' 1.28, 7.395, 26.243; 'The Darkling Thrush' 26.398; a mynah bird who recited *oṃ maṇi padme hūṃ* 12.96, 22.522; a sweet singing bird 25.281

birds in different places
Australia 24.533; Guhyaloka 24.394; India 22.295, 22.431–2, 24.114–15; New Zealand 24.70, 24.82–3, 24.501; Padmaloka 24.150–1, 26.438

SPECIES OF BIRDS

blackbirds
Apollo's bird 25.395; singing at dawn 25.lx, 25.391; singing in East London 26.438–9

cock
at the hub of the wheel of life, *see under* wheel of life/first and second circles; the lusts of Chanticleer 25.194

crows
according the Vinaya you can be ordained if you are old enough to scare crows 2.193, 13.31; the boys who tormented a crow, *see under Udāna*/the people of the *Udāna*; despised in Indian folklore 4.477; the Ganges so full that a crow standing on the bank could drink from it 10.643; how your sins become crows and fly back to you 3.194; 'impudent as a crow' (*Dhammapada*) 15.36; pecking to death a white crow 25.445

cuckoos
Avalokiteśvara in the form of a cuckoo 22.457; cuckoo calls in Kalimpong 21.543–4; the cuckoo's double cry 25.240; Norfolk cuckoo 26.438; the sad song of the cuckoo 18.53

eagles
the golden eagle and Milarepa 18.29–30, 19.340; joy like an eagle 25.266; the soul winged as an eagle 25.271; Zeus's bird 25.397

geese
Saravatī seated on a goose 16.361; wild geese in Norfolk 26.438

gulls
albatross 24.71–2; flying inland for winter 25.307; the gull's lonely flight 25.266; white gulls on the greensward 25.306

hawks
'the falcon cannot hear the falconer' 7.311; harrier hawks in New Zealand 24.68; a hawk attacked by other hawks (Pāli canon) 3.215; the symbolism of keen eyesight 19.76

nightingales
Ode to a Nightingale, *see under* Keats; the glorious unseen nightingale 25.266; singing in London 23.231; the sorrow of the nightingales 25.194

owls
Athene's bird 25.397; an owl down the chimney at Padmaloka 24.151; owls in Moseley 26.438; the solitary owl 25.366; 'A wise old owl sat in an oak' 14.494

parrots
in Australia 24.64; the 'green parrot with red eyes' (Upanishads) 23.311; kias in New Zealand 24.77; macaws 26.424, 26.441; the parrot who let out his natural squawk 12.96, 18.249; patrons gossiping like parrots 19.478

peacocks
Amitābha's animal 13.310; at Sangharakshita's old family home 26.523–4; dancing for joy when the monsoon comes 12.477; eating snakes 25.396; Hera's bird 25.396; Jagdish Kashyap used to feed the peacocks at Nalanda 12.430, 22.389; their colours 26.441; in the trees near the Ganges 20.385, 25.243; wealthy lay Buddhists who 'swagger like peacocks' 19.477–8; in a woodland garden in New Zealand 24.72

pigeons
the colours of a pigeon's neck 7.301–2, 26.129; in the elms in Tuscany 25.380; white pigeons in Seville 24.439

ravens
at the Tower of London 25.396; Elijah fed by ravens 18.33; Milarepa the raven's neighbour 18.54

skylarks
the ecstasies of skylarks 25.194; *Ode to a Skylark*, *see under* Shelley; Sangharakshita's first poem was about a lark 23.244

sparrows
Aphrodite's bird 25.395; the *bodhicitta* like the cry of a baby sparrow still in the egg 4.273; the clinging mind like a short-lived sparrow in the woods 18.262, 18.562–3; 'If a sparrow come before my window I take part in its existence' (Keats) 26.139–40; song like a little sparrow 25.353; sparrows in Poland 25.442, 26.447; the ubiquitous, democratic sparrow 24.72

storks, herons, and cranes
'a wild crane cries out the Truth' 26.243; the milk-drinking heron leaves the water (*Udāna*) 10.649–50; ibises in New Zealand 24.535; storks in Greece 23.269; storks in Poland 25.442

swallows
dark blue swallows by the river 25.157; in the willow-bowers 25.164; flights of swallows through the skies 25.221; returning swallows 25.302; newly arrived 25.337; preparing for flight 25.344; swallow-flights of song 25.353

swans
a boat's sails like a swan 25.249; *The Dying Swan* 25.61, 25.69–70; Sri Ramakrishna as *Paramahaṃsa*, Great Swan 7.88; 'swanlike, many a shining boat' 25.264; 'swanlike, upon the Sun-Path let me soar' 25.182–3; swans in poetry 25.xlviii–xlix, 25.lv, 26.398; the symbolism of the swan in India 7.577 (n166); 'The Wounded Swan' 25.200–1

vultures
in Milarepa's Song of Meeting and Parting 19.504; symbolism: the vulture soars higher than any other bird 19.75–6; at the towers of silence 12.692; vulture's feather 12.334, 19.76; 'The vultures lift that dainty veil …' 4.556; Vulture's Peak, *see* Vulture's Peak

Birla, Durgadas v21, v22

Birla, Jugal Kishore 16.396, 20.114, 20.458, 21.316–17, 22.104

Birmingham Adrian Boult Hall 24.589; Birmingham Oratory 13.562; Buddhist Centre 12.649, 12.678, 12.691; Cannon Hill Park 24.582; Hippodrome 24.589; Madhyamaloka 12.637, 24.578, 26.403–6; Midlands Arts Centre 24.582; Oscott College 13.562; Symphony Hall 24.589

Birmingham, George 17.66

birth (*jāti*) apparitional birth 1.339, 14.407, 15.342, 16.169, 16.462; the appearance of the five *skandhas* in the mother's womb 1.113; ceremony, *see under* ceremonies; conception 1.108–9, 4.633; a form of *duḥkha* 3.210, 16.321; as the eleventh *nidāna*, *see under* twelve cyclical *nidānas*; interval between past and present 1.109; remembrance of former births, *see under* rebirth/how it works; the very notion is self-contradictory (Vimalakīrti) 16.502; the oppression of birth 16.321; the pain of birth 10.496–7; rarity of birth as a human being 1.417–18, 2.94, 4.367, 7.170, 13.139; worth and not birth is the measure of man 10.351

birth and death *see* cycle of birth and death

bisexuality of the bodhisattva 4.142, 4.192; psychological and spiritual 4.142–3; of *yab-yum* figures 4.143; *see also* transsexuality

bitterness bitter disputes often arise over trivialities 13.137; the bitter fruit of desire 7.291; a bitter man whose preoccupation with spiritual teachings did him no good 24.101; bitter words between Sangharakshita's parents 20.70; bitterness at being looked down on 15.716; the Dharma: 'bitter in the mouth but sweet in the stomach' 18.133; frustrated craving leads to bitterness and hatred 1.498; love is bitter-sweet 25.259; a man whose bitterness came from an inferiority complex 22.416–17

Bizet, Georges 24.360

black associated with the Tantric rite of destruction 13.280, 19.24; stands for spiritual death, and the destruction of all that stands in the way of Enlightenment 13.283; symbolizes the destruction of spiritual ignorance 13.68; a white dot against a black background 26.84

'Black Salvation' *see* Tarpa Nagpo

Blacker, Carmen 11.495, v23, v24

Blackwood's Magazine 21.51

Blaenddol *see* Vajrakuta

Blake, William

INTRODUCTION

his life
his life story 8.553–4, 26.342–3; he never lost contact with his childhood 17.470; he rejected orthodox Christian belief 8.559–60, 26.349; he experienced conflict, but he was a very happy man 26.364; his expression of the religion of art 26.385–6; his inspirations 8.560; independence, originality, joy 8.554, 26.485; a revolutionary 26.646–7; his happy death 8.554, 26.343, 26.486

assessments
'Academics in their ivory tower discuss Blake's worth' 25.423; art critics have mixed feelings about him 26.254; 'Blake Walked Among the Stones of Fire' (poem) 25.360; a great artist and a great poet, a rare combination 26.485, 26.660; 'He beat upon the wall/ Till Truth obeyed his call' (Yeats) 15.520, 16.266; he was faithful to his creative powers and they to him 8.560, 13.640; his genius probably owed as much to spiritual enemies as spiritual friends 8.561; 'a man without a mask' 19.122, 24.176; a source of inspiration 13.639–40; Swinburne's *William Blake* 20.332, 26.484–5

influences
Rossetti's connection with Blake 26.485, 26.661; Allen Ginsberg's 'guru' 23.123, 25.lvi, 26.485; one of Sangharakshita's literary heroes 26.484–6, 26.659, 26.661

Blake and Buddhism
Blake and the *Avataṃsaka Sūtra* 16.23–4; 'Buddhism and William Blake' 8.552–61, 26.341–50, 26.490; compared to the Buddha, even Blake was ordinary 11.371; he made some approach to the Dharma 16.375; a seminar and exhibition held at Adhisthana 26.659

art
the 'bounding line' 26.254, 26.721 (n206); colour in his work 13.284, 26.254; *Christ Refusing the Banquet* (illustration) 24.574; 'Death's Door' (engraving) 26.659; his drawing of Michelangelo's Laocoon statue 26.386; illustrations to *The Divine Comedy* 26.661; illustrations to the Book of Job 13.536, 26.485, 26.659; illustrations to *Paradise Lost* and *Paradise Regained* 13.592, 24.519, 24.574; *The Reunion of the Soul and the Body* (engraving) 26.254

poetry
Allen Ginsberg used to sing the poems 23.123, 26.485; included among the romantic poets 8.554; musical settings of his poems 24.242, 24.666–7 (n241); 'The Rossetti Manuscript' 26.661; what stars mean in his poems 25.78

HIS VIEWS AND VISIONS

views
modern civilization: Newton, Bacon, Locke 8.561, 17.117–18, 19.179–80, 26.350; Newton 15.139, 16.630 (n364), 17.117–18, 19.178–9; political views 8.555, 26.344; science 19.180; Swedenborg 13.639–40

his own philosophy
all religion is 'decayed poetry' 8.560, 26.349; and 'alternative traditions' 8.560, 26.349–50; the casting out of error 18.277; fallen man 8.558, 26.347; his conception of liberty 8.555; his emphasis on the importance of individuality 8.555, 8.558; his great doctrine of the forgiveness of sins 8.558, 16.473, 26.347, 26.647–9; it can be useful to study Blake and his irreconcilable contradictions 17.685; Nobodaddy, the 'angry God' 8.559–60, 26.348; Satan the Accuser 8.559, 26.348; the theme of energy 18.78

vision
comparable to the *Avataṃsaka Sūtra*? 16.23–4; the enemies of his Divine Vision were Bacon, Newton, and Locke 8.561, 26.350; a non-theistic imaginative vision of rare intensity 8.560, 13.639–40, 26.349; single vision and Newton's sleep 15.139; the fourfold vision 8.555–6, 10.596, 10.719 (n469); visionary faculty 16.23; he warned against the loss of the 'divine vision' 16.533

imagination
he achieved the final casting out of error from the imagination 8.561; his emphasis on its importance 26.486; his understanding of the Imagination 8.458, 14.589, 17.685; 'The Imagination is the

Human Existence itself' 8.559, 26.348; the Imagination not a faculty, but the operation of the whole man or woman 14.589; Jesus as the imagination 8.559, 26.348, 26.385; the ratio of the senses contrasted with the Imagination 17.484

PROPHETIC BOOKS

introduction
compared to *The Life and Liberation of Padmasambhava* 8.521; explore the deeper levels of human experience 16.533; descriptive passages of astonishing beauty and spiritual insights 26.486; struggling to understand them 26.485–6

The Four Zoas
introduction 8.556; an attempt at creating a myth 13.583; the myth of how the Zoas fell 8.556–7; Blake's correlation of the Zoas with other sets of four 8.557, 26.346; correlations between the Zoas, the *kleśas*, and the Five Buddhas 8.556–8; the Zoas enter time in anticlockwise order 8.558; Luvah (emotions) 8.556; Tharmas (sense) 8.556; Urizen (reason) 8.556, 8.559, 12.331–2, 19.179–80, 25.423, 26.77; Urthona (Imagination) 8.556; 'Homage to William Blake' 25.340; the Emanation 8.555–6, 12.314, 12.727 (n220), 19.409, 19.615 (157); the Female Will 11.427–8; the Spectre 8.556, 17.685

Milton
'Bring me my bow of burning gold' 17.575; England's green and pleasant land 8.545, 26.647; 'I go to Eternal Death!' 26.486; 'Jerusalem': battle as metaphor 18.103–4

Jerusalem
Bacon, Newton, and Locke 16.630 (n364); Golgonooza 25.342, 26.363; 'I give you the end of a golden string' 2.649, 11.19, 26.664–5; Los and Enitharmon 25.342; 'Minute particulars' 14.589; 'Religion is politics', 'Politics is brotherhood', 'Brotherhood is religion' 3.575, 11.700; system of correspondences 8.557, 26.346

other works
The Book of Thel 26.395, 26.485; *America: a Prophecy* 7.284

THE MARRIAGE OF HEAVEN AND HELL

introduction
a Blakean devil 15.435; bold reversal of conventional values, seeming to anticipate Nietzsche 26.485; the integration of abstract understanding and inchoate energy 12.29; 'The Proverbs of Hell' 3.495, 13.515; reason and emotion 15.257–8; Sangharakshita copied it out as a teenager 20.332, 26.485

quotations
the body: 'that portion of the soul ... perceptible by the senses in this age' 17.622; 'The cut worm forgives the plough' 26.646; distinction between the 'prolific' and the 'devouring' 12.644–6; 'Drive your cart and your plough over the bones of the dead' 26.646; 'Energy is eternal delight' 19.381, 26.659; 'Everything possible to be believed is an image of the truth' 10.595; 'Exuberance is beauty' 24.584; 'A fool sees not the same tree that a wise man sees' 19.80; honouring God's gifts in other men 8.555, 17.275, 26.344; Milton was 'of the Devil's party without knowing it' 13.592, 18.78; 'The most sublime act is to set another before you' 2.361, 26.655; 'If the doors of perception were cleansed ...' 15.205–6; 'Improvement in sensual enjoyment' 18.417; 'Opposition is true friendship' 16.525; 'The priest lays his curse on the fairest joys' 13.618; 'The roaring of lions ... and the destructive sword' 26.652–3; 'The tigers of wrath are wiser than the horses of instruction' 18.78

OTHER WORKS

Auguries of Innocence (Pickering Manuscript)
'Joy and woe are woven fine' 2.73, 13.139; 'To see a World in a Grain of Sand' 1.376, 7.400, 14.219, 16.4, 16.11, 16.23, 19.215

'The Everlasting Gospel'
'Thine own humanity learn to adore' 8.559, 26.348; 'The vision of Christ that thou dost see' 8.560, 11.343, 26.349

Songs of Innocence and Experience
'Ah! Sun-flower' 25.lvi; 'The Clod and the Pebble': 'builds a Heaven in Hell's despair' 11.25; 'London': 'marks of weakness, marks of woe' 3.228, 11.78, 18.424; 'Tyger, Tyger, burning bright' 19.56

quotations from other works
'He who binds to himself a joy' 17.506, 26.598; 'Mutual forgiveness of each vice: Such are the gates of paradise' 8.558, 16.473, 26.347, 26.647–9; 'To hinder another is not an act' 10.604; 'To the Muses' 26.485; 'When the Sun rises do you not see a round Disk of fire ...?' 11.725

blasphemy

law of blasphemy
different religions consider different things blasphemous 11.346–7, 12.477; the *Gay News* blasphemy trial 11.326–8; laws 11.327–31, 11.344, 11.347, 16.500

blasphemy in Christianity
its history 11.328–31; it is a terrible offence because God is seen as so powerful, 11.334–6; severe punishment 11.336; Christians' compulsion to blaspheme 11.336–7; rational and irrational blasphemy 11.337–8

Buddhism and blasphemy
Sangharakshita's essay 11.326–47, 13.468, 24.619–20 (n77), 24.142, 26.640; review in the *New Humanist* 24.53; blasphemy as the entrance into non-duality 16.548; blasphemy does not exist in Buddhism 11.331–3, 11.338; the idea of Buddhist texts being blasphemous 11.329

the use of blasphemy
blasphemous poetry 11.343; the individual has the right to blaspheme 11.346; therapeutic blasphemy 11.341–2, 11.345, 13.468, 26.640

Blavatsky, Madame H. P.

life
in Sri Lanka (Ceylon) 8.17–24; conversion to Buddhism 8.18; accused of being a fraud 8.23–4; connection with Anagarika Dharmapala 8.18–32; Sangharakshita's gratitude towards her 20.64; her 'original' theosophy 22.134; her revelations on prehistoric giant races 24.214; her death 8.38; *H. P. Blavatsky, Her Life and Work for Humanity* 8.24

The Voice of the Silence
brief introduction 26.716 (n149); the Buddha 'like a white pillar to the west' 26.210; 'Can there be bliss when all that lives must suffer?' 1.405; Christmas Humphreys gets the Dalai Lama to 'authenticate' the text as Buddhist 22.354–5; dedicated to the few 7.360; 'Do not believe that lust can ever be killed out if gratified' 7.358; the Doctrine of the Eye and the Doctrine of the Heart 7.359; images 26.210; 'Inaction in a deed of mercy becomes an action in a deadly sin' 8.215, 13.609; compassion is 'the Law of laws, eternal harmony' 7.362, 7.457, 26.205; 'Learn to separate Head-learning from Soul-wisdom' 26.198; literature of power, not literature of knowledge 26.197–8; the Open Path and the Secret Path 1.404–5, 7.361, 26.207; 'Remain unselfish till the endless end' 26.207–8; rhythm in its poetry 26.210–11; 'the sweet but selfish rest of quiet wilds' 1.213; 'Paradox and Poetry' 26.197–212; 'The Path is one for all, the means to reach the goal must vary with the Pilgrims' 7.363; Sangharakshita gives a lecture on the text 22.147; 'Thou canst not travel on the Path until thou hast become that Path itself' 1.136, 4.646, 7.359, 26.205–6; the title's paradox 26.202; the two paths 26.207; the voice of the silence 16.73; 'the voidness of the seeming full' 7.375

other works
Isis Unveiled 13.533–4, 14.xi, 20.63–4; *The Secret Doctrine* 13.304, 13.693 (n123)

blessings (*adhiṣṭhāna*) being in such a good mood that you feel like blessing everything 19.503–4; blessings and vibes at the Mind Body Spirit Festival 18.428–9; *chinlap* 13.160; distinction between blessing and initiation 4.266–7; the effect of a guru blessing a thangka 19.326; feeling the guru's blessing (*adhiṣṭhāna*) in the guru yoga 13.217; the guru as the giver of initiations and blessings 4.265–7; in his time, most people thought the Buddha's function was to give blessings 10.497; holy men believed to be a means of magical protection and blessing 2.215, 10.496–7; religious people giving their blessing to government or royal activities 19.463; medicine that has been blessed by a guru 19.366; seeing the Buddha image as a source of blessing 2.229–30; 'To please one's Guru is to gain his blessings' 18.511; *see also adhiṣṭhāna*

blind men and the elephant *see under Udāna*/other key teachings

blindness the brahmins and their teachers like the blind leading the blind 14.42; perhaps Jesus healed blindness in a spiritual, not literal, sense 10.555–6; the reasons for our (metaphorical) blindness 2.55–6; until you have insight, you can only act blindly and foolishly 19.354–5

bliss

different kinds of bliss
ānanda (bliss arising from the senses) 2.91; the *bhikkhu* (a former king) who said 'Ah, what bliss!' 10.500–1; the bliss arising from goodness (Krishna) 7.100; the bliss of a man who travels through a desert, then bathes in a lake 2.107–8; bliss in the *Taittirīya Upaniṣad* 8.438–9; 'Bliss-Illumination' (Milarepa) 19.378–80; 'Can there be bliss when all that lives must suffer?' 1.405; communication with a spiritual companion is intensely blissful 18.419; four stages of bliss (Vajrayāna) 2.91; great bliss, *see mahāsukha*; may love and passion be transformed to brilliance and bliss 25.278; *see also sukha*

in meditation
awareness of bliss in meditation 17.518; 'Bliss, bliss' 17.518; don't allow meditative bliss to overpower mindfulness 2.109; full bliss only experienced with the integration of all unconscious energies 15.219; the meditative life is the blissful life 8.440; *paramānanda* (bliss arising from the *dhyānas*) 2.91; the process of gathering and unifying one's energies is inherently blissful 18.91, 19.52; a 'quintessential, keen, ethereal bliss' 20.145, 26.193

the bliss of Nirvāṇa
the bliss and contentment of the Void 18.90–1; bliss and insight 18.416; the bliss of the *dharmakāya* 14.236; the bliss of Enlightenment 10.262, 18.90, 19.424–6; the Bliss-Void (*mahāsukha*) 18.415–16; even the blissful higher realms are painful compared to the bliss of Enlightenment 18.589; Nirvāṇa is the highest bliss 2.124, 3.235, 7.68–9, 7.120, 11.85–6, 18.90, 19.424; the Unconditioned: blissful, permanent, and ultimately real 4.161; the imperishable bliss of Nirvāṇa 26.159; the union of bliss and emptiness 13.75, 17.364, 18.61, 19.155, 19.196–7; *viramānanda* (bliss arising from Nirvāṇa) 2.91

bliss and us
bliss is not to be rejected 19.52; different degrees of bliss, from ordinary to Enlightened 19.424–6; if you think of the spiritual life as a way to attain bliss, you haven't understood 7.412, 26.53; it's important to cultivate detachment towards bliss, as the Buddha did 2.108, 18.581; no form of Buddhism requires you to give up bliss 19.379

Blofeld, John introduction 2.692 (n312), 22.503; an admirer of the *Survey* 21.589, 22.503; at the Buddhist Society's summer school 23.32–3; initiation from Dudjom Rimpoche 22.503–7; photographs 11.474, 23.33; stays with Sangharakshita in Kalimpong 8.664, 22.503; translation of the *I Ching* 21.589; *The Way of Power* 22.506; *The Wheel of Life* 2.224, 21.589

blood blood in Christian art 13.631–2; 'felt in the blood, and felt along the heart' 3.361; 'A good book is the precious life-blood of a master-spirit' 19.70; how can Buddhism be in your blood? 19.474; 'Let blood dry up, let flesh wither away', *see under* Siddhārtha/his resolve; 'More than the seas he gave his blood, more than the stars his eyes' 1.430; occult properties of blood 21.446; red is the colour of blood and hence the colour of life 13.280; ties of blood and soil 3.435, 3.437; 'Work out the secret of your blood' 25.277

Bloom, Harold *The American Religion* 24.519; *Shakespeare: The Invention of the Human* 3.602; *Yeats* 25.liii–liv

blue blue-throated Avalokiteśvara 7.580 (n190), 16.398–9, 26.641–2; the blueness of the real 25.284; 'the deep and dark blue ocean' 2.644; represents the Enlightened mind 13.282; represents knowledge of the Truth, of *śūnyatā* 13.67; Sangharakshita's eye condition meant he saw blue more vividly 26.441; *see also* sky/blue sky; lotus/*utpala*

Blue Annals *see* Roerich

Blue Cliff Record a collection of one hundred anecdotes of masters and disciples 2.555, 8.485–6; each chapter consists of anecdotes, poems, and commentary 8.486; essentially a collection of koan 8.486–7; 'Every day is a good day' 25.342; a major contribution to our knowledge of primary sources 8.489; review of a new translation 8.484–9; Bodhidharma and the emperor: 'Vast emptiness and nothing holy' 12.531, 14.575–6; a 12th-century master who, seeing that students were infatuated with the text, destroyed it 8.500; a work of extraordinary richness, variety, and beauty 8.487; in its world Buddhism is the only thing that matters 8.488

'Blue Rider' school 24.588, 24.759 (n779)

Bly, Robert 24.362

Blyth, Reginald Horace introduction 12.708–9 (n57), 17.716 (n67); *Zen in English Literature and Oriental Classics* 12.78, 17.64–5, 17.66–7

Bo, Mr v21, v22

Boadicea 23.468

boasting *see under* pride

Boccaccio, Giovanni 24.271, 24.410, 24.675 (n331)

Bodh Gaya (Buddha Gaya)

history
the Buddha's Enlightenment, *see under* Buddha I/Enlightenment; in the *Udāna*, *see under Udāna*/settings; Padmasambhava visits Bodh Gaya 12.290; Atīśa's visit 12.574; excavated by British archaeologists 9.237; temple restored by General Sir Alexander Cunningham 20.454; description of its state in 1891 8.35–6; International Buddhist Conference (1891)

8.39–40; Hindu presence 8.xiv, 8.51–3, 8.178, 20.454–5, 22.344; a controversial Japanese Buddha image 8.51–3, 8.60–1; Anagarika Dharmapala's campaign to save it, *see under* Dharmapala; Vinoba Bhave's controversial temple 8.147, 8.179–81, 22.128–9, 22.159, 23.367; Māra's possession of the diamond throne 8.181; requests to the Indian government about facilities 22.342; renovation 8.260–1; a tourist attraction 19.470

pilgrimage
the Buddha's recommendation 2.223; accommodation for pilgrims 7.465; effect of going there 4.325; the focus of devotion on Vaiśākha Pūrṇimā Day 8.177–8; Tibetan pilgrims 7.415–18, 19.335, 20.455–6; Triratna Order convention held there 6.xxi, 11.718

features of Bodh Gaya
the Buddha's footprint 2.223; Maha Bodhi (Burmese) Rest House 8.36, 8.39, 8.60–1; temple complex 20.454–5, 23.366; Thai temple 8.664, 23.365–6; water-lilies 23.366

Sangharakshita and Bodh Gaya
visits for the first time 20.453–6, 23.365; Dhardo Rimpoche sees him there 12.432, 12.452, 21.453, 22.419, 22.542; visit with Dhardo Rimpoche (photo) 22.345; a visit with Terry 23.365–9; 'The Birthplace of Compassion' (poem) 25.210

Bodhananda, Maha Sthavira 19.164, 21.46–7, 21.111

Bodhanandi, Dharmacharini v24

Bodhaniya, Dharmacharini 26.463

bodhi definitions 1.87, 2.266, 9.294; defined as 'true non-attachment' 14.570; has three main aspects: cognitive, volitional, and emotional 13.297–8; if words to describe *bodhi* sound baffling, they are just words 13.298; *prajñā* and *upāya* are one, which is *bodhi* 7.139; *pratyātmagocara* preferred to *bodhi* as a term for Enlightenment (*Laṅkāvatāra Sūtra*) 12.173; saturating the entire psychic contents 2.114; Mahāyāna separation of Nirvāṇa from *bodhi* 8.620; the source and goal of *prajñā* and *upāya* 7.139; of three kinds: *sāvaka-bodhi*, *pacceka-bodhi*, and *sammā-sambodhi* 1.85–6, 2.266–8; traditional pre-eminence of the term as description of the Goal 2.126; *see also* Enlightenment

bodhi tree (*aśvattha* or pīpal, *ficus religiosa*) the Buddha's gratitude towards the tree 3.74, 3.596; a stupa erected to mark the spot where the Buddha gazed at the tree 3.596; association with the symbolism of the world tree 11.30, 12.185; Sangharakshita and Khantipālo plant a bodhi tree in Kalimpong 22.543–4, 25.302; Sanghamittā takes a cutting of the tree to Sri Lanka 2.222; symbol of the Buddha's Enlightenment 3.137, 11.30, 16.564; 'The Tree of Wisdom' (poem) 25.252–4; 'the true Buddhist carries his bodhi tree around with him' 9.206; worship 2.219–22; a bodhi tree in a hot-house in London 8.151

bodhicarya 15.448

Bodhicaryāvatāra *see under* Śāntideva

bodhicitta (will to Enlightenment, Tibetan *changchub sems*)

INTRODUCTION

etymology and meanings
altruistic intention 8.611; the awakening of a new spiritual aspiration 2.160; the *bodhi*-heart 3.452, 4.28, 18.102; *changchub sems* in Tibetan 18.226; 'cherishing the desire for Enlightenment' (Suzuki) 2.160; its denotation is not metaphysical but psychological 1.416–17; 'Enlightened attitude' (Guenther) 4.28, 4.257; 'Enlightenment-mindedness' 4.257; problems of translation 4.241–2; to name it is to falsify it 14.546–7; to understand it, we must understand the three kinds of *bodhi* 2.266–9; 'will' or 'aspiration', not 'thought' 1.417, 2.160, 3.365–6, 4.27–8, 4.241–2, 14.546; the urge of one's whole being in the direction of Enlightenment 3.366; 'will to Enlightenment' appropriate because it is an active force 4.32, 11.650, 12.537–8

descriptions
introduction 3.365–6; an active force at work in the world 4.32, 4.263; as long as you're in touch with it, you can

amuse yourself with sensuous pleasures 14.188; aspiration to Enlightenment without a shadow of selfhood 2.268; the *bodhicitta* ('Friend Bodhi-Heart') is Milarepa's companion 18.225–6; the *brahma vihāras* are connected with reality through the *bodhicitta* 18.103; Buddhas and bodhisattvas gather round it 4.263; characterized by perpetual emptiness 4.29; a committed volition to perpetual self-transcendence 3.17; conversion from individualistic to non-individualist conception of Enlightenment 2.269; cosmic will to Enlightenment 2.478; the creative mind *par excellence* 4.283; it can be developed by both monk and layman 11.570–1; it fills up the gap between unenlightenment and Enlightenment 14.604; immanent in all forms of life, as illustrated in the *Jātakas* 2.15; it has the power to overcome evil 4.268; a liberation principle 3.17; love is the essence of the *bodhicitta* 4.70; *mettā* is wonderful, and the *bodhicitta* is even more wonderful 14.556; the myth that inspires the Buddhist spiritual community 4.36; no words can do it justice 4.28, 4.278; on the lowest level, one's understanding before real spiritual experience 4.260; one of the most important terms in Mahāyāna Buddhism 4.27, 14.546; one of the three roots of the bodhisattva ideal 17.174; its purpose is to transcend spatio-temporal models 3.16–17; a sort of higher power which works through you when you are receptive 4.241; a sort of cosmic will, a spirit of Enlightenment (poetically) 4.34; a supra-personal force 4.259–60, 11.285, 14.575; transcendence of self and other 4.40; we must want to relate on the basis of the *bodhicitta* 3.452

what it is not
not the life-force of the universe or a causative first principle 3.17; not to be confused with *tathāgata-dhātu* 1.416–17; not a philosophical doctrine, but has the truth of a symbol, a myth 4.36, 4.262–3; not included in the five *skandhas* 4.28–9, 4.241; we must be careful not to reify it 4.263, 14.594

personal or collective?
it arises within the spiritual community as a whole 2.474–5, 4.29–30, 4.278; not anybody's individual will 3.366; if you possess it, it isn't the *bodhicitta* 4.34, 4.241; it is us, but not us 4.265; not just 'my' little subjective idea of the goal of 'my' spiritual life 4.263; not a personal act of will 4.28; not a product of the mundane consciousness, not 'my' *bodhicitta* 4.28, 16.289; pride in the *bodhicitta* not as yours, but in a sense as everybody's 4.623; the principle governing the spiritual community 3.451; a private and personal experience 1.422; the sangha and the arising of the *bodhicitta* 3.451, 4.30; the sangha as the reflection of the 'personified' *bodhicitta* 2.474–5; supra-individual, but not collective 4.30; supra-personal 4.259–60, 11.285, 14.575; think of it as arising within the spiritual community 11.285; without *mettā* in the sangha, no chance of the *bodhicitta* arising in its midst 17.186

only one bodhicitta
all bodhisattvas participate in one *bodhicitta*, but express it in their own way 4.57; only one, which manifests through different receptive individuals 3.366, 4.248

images and metaphors
'the Bodhichitta flowers in me' 25.xli, 25.302; the flaming drop at the tip of the Tantric stupa 13.163; in the *Gaṇḍavyūha Sūtra* 2.165–6, 4.35, 4.165; a golden thread 13.587; a jewel 12.214; like a blind man (or beggar) finding a jewel on a dungheap 1.420, 2.126, 4.42, 4.44, 10.145; like the full moon 4.31; like the cry of a baby sparrow still in the egg 4.273; manifesting through the ten *bhūmis* like gold refined and made into a crown 4.177–8; Milarepa weaves cloth from the *bodhicitta* into the liberation path 18.136–7; the thousand-armed Avalokiteśvara 2.474; the wish-fulfilling gem 16.174–5; the womb of wisdom and compassion 4.276

the bodhicitta in the Buddhist tradition
anticipation in the Pāli canon 4.39; implied in the *mettā bhāvanā* 4.39, 5.188; Atīśa encouraged its development 12.577; attained after magical occurrences (*Vimalakīrti-nirdeśa*) 16.451; in the *Bodhicaryāvatāra, see under* Śāntideva/*Bodhicaryāvatāra*/Chapter 1; described in Tsongkhapa's *Three Chief Paths* 17.424, 17.427; a bodhisattva precept not to give up the *bodhicitta* 13.56, 14.186, 14.188; praise in the Mahāyāna *sūtras* 4.35; refers to semen in Tantric Buddhism 1.391–2

the altruistic dimension of Going for Refuge
brief references 2.433, 2.448, 2.465, 2.471, 2.500, 9.255–6; the *bodhicitta* emphasized at the expense of Going for Refuge 2.441–2, 2.564; the individual subjectively goes for Refuge and objectively manifests the *bodhicitta* 13.399; the lives of Order members have an other-regarding aspect 2.516, 12.373; motivation to gain Enlightenment has an altruistic

orientation 3.452; no distinction between Going for Refuge and the arising of the *bodhicitta* 2.465; one of five aspects of a single spiritual experience 2.300–1, 2.483; 'personified' by the thousand-armed Avalokiteśvara 2.474–5; the real *bodhicitta* is neither individualistic nor altruistic 12.600; we should see the altruistic dimension of Going for Refuge more clearly 12.405; whatever is said of Going for Refuge can be said of the *bodhicitta* 2.475

THE ARISING OF THE *BODHICITTA* (*BODHICITTOTPĀDA*)

introduction

summary 2.266–74, 4.27–54; a breakthrough to a higher level of experience 4.92; one of the Mahāyāna's most important terms 4.27, 4.39; first of three important events in the bodhisattva career 2.160; not 'producing a thought' 14.406; a powerful impulse that becomes the master-current of your being 2.300, 9.255; it doesn't occur only once but grows as the bodhisattva progresses 2.164; it is better if it occurs early on in one's spiritual life 2.270; levels of arising: cultural, provisional, effective, and real 2.431, 4.197, 12.599; the most important event that can occur in the life of a human being 1.416, 25.xli; one of five different aspects of a single crucial spiritual experience 2.301, 2.464, 2.483; rejoicing in the arising of the *bodhicitta* 11.269; a talk on the subject in 1966 23.232; together with withdrawal from the mundane produces Enlightenment 18.102

preparation for its arising

considerable preparations are needed 2.160–1; developed out of the seed of the *mettā bhāvanā* 4.39, 5.189; doing the Sevenfold Puja 4.278; it isn't like making a cake: you don't know what the ingredients may be 4.44; saying to the Buddhas and bodhisattvas, 'Take me over' 4.293–4; observing the precepts and developing compassion 18.517; sometimes one happens to 'tune in' accidentally 4.272; through receptivity and removing obstacles 4.224; resistance to the *bodhicitta* 4.263–4; a waste of time to think of developing it, but you can set up the conditions 4.43; you don't feel that 'you' are making the effort 4.242

factors in its arising (Vasubandhu)

introduction 1.417–20, 2.271–4, 4.49–54; (1) seeing the faults of conditioned existence 1.419–20, 2.271, 4.50–1, 4.593; (2) observing the suffering of sentient beings 2.271–2; (3) recollecting the Buddhas 2.272–3, 4.49–50; (4) contemplation of the virtues of the Tathāgatas 2.273, 4.52–3

how does it arise?

'creating' the *bodhicitta* 4.283; it can arise even if one's belief in individuality is as high as Sumeru 4.272–3; it arises out of the conjunction of serene withdrawal and compassion 2.116, 18.52; it could arise without any preparation, so be alert 4.272–3; it could not arise in us if there was not already something like it in us 4.33; it takes you over when you are ready 4.241–2; like everything, it arises in dependence on conditions 4.42; one might be shocked in its arising in an unlikely person 4.274; sudden or gradual? 4.242

what produces it

the coalescence of two different trends of thought and emotion 1.417–20, 2.271–4; the coming together of desire for salvation (*vairāgya*) and compassion 10.175; the desire for Nirvāṇa joined with *maitrī* 10.145; the fusion of wisdom and compassion 1.420; an initial experience of wisdom and compassion as one, not two 4.515; longing for the Unconditioned and compassion for those suffering 2.161–2, 2.271–4; tension between withdrawal and involvement 2.271–4; the union of wisdom and compassion gives birth to the *bodhicitta* 18.296–7; when wisdom and compassion are not two things but one, it has arisen 2.274

the effects of its arising

between its arising and the attainment of Enlightenment lie years of exertion 1.421; bodhisattva ordination is its natural expression 4.197; conflict before the *bodhicitta* is solidly established 4.274–5; consciousness permeated by the living experience of Enlightenment 4.260–1; the devotee rejoices that his birth has become fruitful 1.416; the emergence within our ordinary experience of something quite different 4.28; difficult to know whether or not it has arisen in a particular individual 4.198; how can it arise without being expressed in action? 4.284; it abolishes the tension between self and not-self 17.192–3; it transforms the devotee or ordinary person into a bodhisattva 1.416, 2.126; it turns everything upside down 4.261–2; one doesn't stop doing devotional practices when the *bodhicitta* has arisen 4.53; only when it has arisen is one really on the spiritual path 4.70; a statement on its arising 2.207–8; what is the next step?

4.55; what was once a simple aspiration becomes a cosmic force 2.164; you don't enter upon the Vajrayāna unless the *bodhicitta* has arisen 18.463; you still act, but you will not be subjectively disturbed 19.193; *you* (your will, your thought and emotion) are transformed into the *bodhicitta* 4.35; your external life might remain exactly the same 4.261–2

comparisons and connections
all the different terms revolve around one spiritual experience 4.40; an analogy (*only* an analogy) with the descent of the Holy Spirit 4.29, 4.241–2, 4.263; its arising in Ruciraketu (*Sūtra of Golden Light*) 16.288; compared to the *parāvṛtti* 4.261; comparison with Stream Entry 4.38–41, 4.264, 11.285–6; comparison with Nietzsche's Will to Power 3.503; connection with the *Vimalakīrti-nirdeśa* 4.31; how does it relate to insight? 4.515

RELATIVE AND ABSOLUTE *BODHICITTA*

relative (saṃvṛti)
aspiration or vow aspect (*bodhipraṇidhicitta*) 2.162, 3.366–7, 4.55, 4.284, 14.412; the *bodhicitta* as manifesting in time 4.261; the bodhisattva vow as a support to the *bodhicitta* 4.65–6, 14.412, 18.161; establishment aspect (*bodhiprasthānacitta*) 2.162, 3.367–75, 4.55, 4.283–4, 14.412, 15.82; the reflection of the absolute *bodhicitta* in the web of conditioned existence 4.32; relationship between absolute and relative *bodhicitta* 4.32–4, 4.55; in the teachings of the *White Lotus Sūtra* 16.58; twofold, like the decision to walk and the act of walking 2.164

absolute (paramārtha)
'absolute' may give the wrong impression 4.32; the *bodhicitta* viewed as it were out of time 4.261; beautifully described by Gampopa 2.162; its essence expressed in the 'Confounder of Hell' verses 4.211–13; not static or fixed 4.32; pulses with the spiritual life and activity we call compassion 4.31; like pure light, radiant and immaculate 4.31; realizing that Buddha and bodhisattva are different aspects of the same reality 4.211; *saṃbodhicitta* 4.268; in the teachings of the *White Lotus Sūtra* 16.58; transcends space and time 4.31

see also
bodhicitta practice; Nāgārjuna/works/Nāgārjuna's discourse on its transcendentality; *śūnyatā*/*śūnyatā* and compassion

***bodhicitta* practice** altruism and the *bodhicitta* practice 5.556, 13.81–2; the foundation of the Vajrayāna 18.463; having an effect on others like moonlight 13.82; how does it fit into the system of meditation? 5.541; inasmuch as you recognize the altruistic dimension of spiritual life, you are doing the practice 5.556; as one of the four *mūla yogas* 12.19–20, 13.80–2; the practice of *bodhicitta* surpasses all ethical practices 8.612; recitation of the bodhisattva vow 12.19, 13.81–2; reflections between sessions of practice 13.82; should it be more widely performed? 5.542

Bodhicittavivaraṇa 4.28–9, 4.70

Bodhicittotpādasūtra *see under* Vasubandhu

Bodhidharma asked what he teaches, tells the emperor, 'Vast emptiness and nothing holy' 12.531, 14.575–6; tells the emperor that the Dharma is so simple a child can understand it 1.492–3, 3.241–2, 7.134, 7.292; is said to have taken the *Laṅkāvatāra Sūtra* from India to China 2.276, 12.173; took the spirit of Buddhism to China 13.342; 28th Indian patriarch of the Zen school 13.342; wafted to China on a reed 12.173, 13.342; 'Who are you that is standing before me?' 'I don't know' 12.531, 14.576; Zen verse attributed to him 14.611 (n27)

Bodhidharma, Dhammachari 10.367

bodhimaṇḍa (place of Enlightenment) *see vajrāsana*

Bodhimitra, Dharmachari v24

bodhipakṣya-dharmas *see* thirty-seven *bodhipakṣya-dharmas*

Bodhipathapradīpa (*Lamp for the Path to Enlightenment*) *see under* Atīśa

bodhipraṇidhicitta *see bodhicitta*/relative

bodhiprasthānacitta *see bodhicitta*/relative

Bodhiraja, Dharmachari v24

Bodhiruci (translator) 14.151, 14.201–2, 14.227

bodhisakta ('one bent on Enlightenment') 4.4, 4.239, 14.569–70

bodhisattva

WHAT IS A BODHISATTVA?

the term
definition 3.365, 9.255; etymology 3.365, 4.4, 16.229; *bodhisattva-mahāsattvas* 13.281, 14.571; a link with *bodhisakta*

(*sakta* meaning 'striving')? 4.4; Mahāyāna usage 14.570; 'one who is bent upon Enlightenment' 14.569–70; originally referred to the Buddha in his pre-Enlightenment days 4.652, 26.667; used by early schools for rulers whose prospects of Enlightenment were distant 2.210

the bodhisattva in Buddhist history
the Buddha in previous lives 1.257–8, 4.652–3; the Buddha refers to himself as the *bodhisatta* in the *Ariyapariyesanā Sutta* 14.569; only one Bodhisattva, the Buddha himself (Theravādin view) 1.272, 1.402, 2.477; only one bodhisattva in whom different people participate (Mahāyāna view) 4.247–8; the ideal Buddhist (Mahāyāna) 4.5, 16.441; the Mahāyāna insisted that *everybody* should aim to be a bodhisattva 2.300

the bodhisattva and the Buddha
the bodhisattva encouraged to contemplate the Buddha's unconditioned aspect 2.44; a bodhisattva should be honoured far more than a Tathāgata 14.181; bodhisattvahood necessarily precedes Buddhahood 1.49; the Buddha and the bodhisattva, eternity and time 4.199–213, 13.39; the Buddha principle at work in the activities of the bodhisattva 13.141; easier for us to identify with the bodhisattva than the Buddha 5.621

descriptions
above the extremes of being and non-being 4.240, 17.411; a balance between high spiritual attainment and wide compassionate activity 7.139; the bodhisattva suffers, but there is no suggestion of martyrdom or humiliation 4.14; Buddhism's highest expression and ultimate meaning 4.655; charts a course between the extremes of *nirvāṇa* and *saṃsāra* 7.139; coalescence of contradictory tendencies to produce 'not a third note but a star' 2.162; description in the Perfection of Wisdom 14.140–1; the difficulty of describing a bodhisattva 4.240; embodiment of the Higher Evolution 13.516, 16.7; enumerating virtues and stages will never reveal the secret of bodhisattvahood 2.155; expresses the evolutionary principle of self-transcendence 3.17, 4.655; a force let loose in the universe for the good of all 4.262; free of self-consciousness 14.411, 14.548; a glimpse of the bodhisattva's mind 2.157–9; how is one to describe the bodhisattva's experience? 18.590; the individual *par excellence* 14.580; the life of the bodhisattva is the sublimest that can be lived upon earth 8.369; lives simultaneously in the world of appearances and the world of reality 2.159–60; a living paradox 4.92, 17.609, 26.202; the living embodiment of the *bodhicitta* 14.546; one dedicated to the attainment of Enlightenment for the sake of all 2.126, 4.5; one in whom the urge to grow has become self-conscious 16.7; one who has consciously devoted their life and work to helping others 25.113; one who sees that living beings have no reality without falling into nihilism 17.411; part of the 'spiritual economy' of the world 13.39; personification of a cosmic principle 2.477; a real individual 14.572; represents the abstract, transcendental spiritual ideal 16.7, 16.26; represents the living unity of altruism and emptiness 14.150; the spirit of Enlightenment at work in the world 4.63, 13.141; spiritual friend (Gampopa) 2.161; stillness of wisdom, storm of activity realized as twin aspects of emptiness 7.140–1; a supra-personal cosmic force 4.61, 7.155; the supreme exemplar of the devotional life, and the highest object of devotion 1.395; symbolizes both the lower and the higher evolution 4.210; two types: one fond of literary ornament, the other unafraid of profound teachings 14.166; the unifying factor of the whole Buddhist tradition 1.397; Vimalakīrti's poetic description of the true bodhisattva 16.540–1; a 'white magician' 4.607

what a bodhisattva is not
not a being in search of the highest perfection 14.547; not an abstract concept but a spiritual reality 4.92, 4.139; not literally a person, but a 'supra-personal' stream of spiritual energy 4.63, 14.575, 16.229; not a saviour in the Christian sense 4.246–7; they do not belong among the *dharmas* 14.492; you can't imagine a foolish bodhisattva 17.134–5

images and metaphors
emerging from the eggshell of ignorance 3.231; every bodhisattva is a sort of Christ 4.599; like a candle that lights thousands of other candles 16.487; like a deeply rooted tree 14.587–8; like an elephant 4.135, 4.468–9; like the melodious kalaviṅka bird inside the egg 14.180; likened to the new moon 1.395, 3.54; plunging into the ocean of Enlightenment 14.548; their 'family', as described in the *Vimalakīrti-nirdeśa* 16.457; their relationship with all beings is like that of a mother with her baby 17.193

characteristics
aesthetic appreciation: the greater mandala 14.517–24; 'all things to all men' 16.481–

3; answers questions on his own terms 25.127; benevolence 5.186–7; bisexuality 4.142; both introvert and extrovert 1.396; characteristics described in the *Large Perfection of Wisdom sūtra* 2.153–5; commitment to the happiness of all sentient beings 13.271; contentment 15.290; courage to speak 16.491; devotion 4.53; embodiment of energy 4.135; embodiment of wisdom and compassion 7.290; fearlessness 1.429, 2.157, 4.293–4, 13.230, 14.166, 14.560, 14.575; fidelity 3.572; 'Like a fire his mind constantly blazes up' 1.396, 8.xvii, 8.95, 20.124; fond of diverse phraseology and literary ornament 14.166; four qualities bodhisattvas preserving the *White Lotus Sūtra* must have 16.47; important that the bodhisattva should have an attractive appearance 15.465; loving speech 16.486–7; magical powers 4.552–3, 16.450; never tires of working for universal salvation 4.85–6, 4.279; no sentimentalist 2.156, 4.84, 4.243; not afraid of suffering 1.133, 7.391; self-confidence 4.446, 4.468; spontaneity 4.135–6; takes the initiative 4.477; takes things very lightly 4.136–7; willing to take risks 16.421

compassion
aims at a goal in which wisdom and compassion are not separate 1.420; based on the realization of emptiness 14.562; difficult to describe, because one sees existence in a completely different way 4.181; on Enlightenment he participates in the compassionate activity of the *dharmakāya* 14.554; experience of compassion and wisdom as non-different 16.522; if the bodhisattva learns only compassion, that is quite enough 1.504, 2.125–6, 5.199–200; always brings compassion into Dharma teaching 2.168–9, 4.65, 4.189, 15.630, 18.588; his compassion radiates naturally from his realization of non-duality 7.140; 'looking upon living beings as upon an only son' 14.235; no conception of compassion, having no conception of 'you' and 'I' 7.140; for the suffering of living beings 2.156, 2.161–2, 18.590

altruism
an analogy with Hercules 23.270; the bodhisattva doesn't have to make an effort to help people 18.254; rejecting Nirvāṇa as something attainable for oneself alone 1.213–14, 7.41, 14.551, 26.207–8; the bodhisattva wants to share his skilful mental states 15.371–2; compassion conjoined with wisdom 2.159; expressed in the bodhisattva ordination 2.207; on a grand scale 1.395; the Great Being's resolution (*Diamond Banner Sūtra*) 2.157–8; he includes himself, but only as one among many 2.300, 9.255; he makes the effort to develop spiritually so that he can help other beings 13.22; how bodhisattvas help beings 14.144; 'I will place all beings in suchness' 1.233; if he just *is* a bodhisattva, that will influence people 25.128; like the sun, that radiates over all 1.230; represents the living unity of altruism and emptiness 14.150; to say his emphasis is on helping others is wrong, because it isn't 'him' doing it 4.246; why should the bodhisattva be concerned with others? 16.472–3; wish to be of service to all, like the elements 11.282

as hero
conquering spirit 14.537; heroic ambition 4.445, 16.229, 16.312–13; historical heroes 2.181–2; in the *Jātakas* 4.652–3; in the *Perfection of Wisdom in 8,000 Lines* 2.156–7, 3.55–6

love and hatred
a bodhisattva should not be afraid of the passions 14.186; the bodhisattva 'is allowed to hate' – obviously open to misunderstanding 4.613; hatred obstructs the bodhisattva more than anything 4.389; the love of the bodhisattva for living beings 16.538; 'Love springs into the Bodhisattva's eyes' 25.156; wants to do the complete opposite to hatred 4.392; you can't be a bodhisattva if you've got even a little bit of hatred left 16.295

the bodhisattva and wisdom
connections with reality described in terms of the elements 14.590; courses in the idea of non-attainment while striving to attain Enlightenment 1.269; 'his practice of wisdom, the highest perfection 14.587–8; in realizing *śūnyatā* the bodhisattva transcends the self–other distinction 16.232; perceives the world as a mock show without plunging into madness 14.576; sees all phenomena like a mirage in the desert 14.562; takes emptiness for the basis 1.269–70; their home is meditation on the meaning of the Void 16.457; their 'reading' of signs and symbols 14.566; their wisdom is rooted in both head and heart 14.516, 14.559; they do not mistake perceptions for reality 14.440; they see existence as inconceivable 16.449; they understand the nature of all things 14.563

BODHISATTVA CAREER

how does one become a bodhisattva?
don't think of it as a sort of career move 4.43; four necessary qualities 14.189;

how the aspiration arises (Perfection of Wisdom) 2.156; the metaphysical answer 3.365–6; not everybody wants to be one, so skilful means must be employed 16.229–30; not directly, but through the cosmic *bodhicitta* 4.224; starting on the path by trying to see what people need 14.413–14; upon the awakening of the bodhi heart (*bodhicitta*) 4.27, 4.42

bodhisattva ordination (bodhisattva-saṃvara)
can be taken by *bhikṣus*, *śramaṇeras*, lay followers 7.474, 7.479–80, 13.339; can it really be an individual affair? 4.278; ceremony 2.207–9; commitments after ordination 13.339; does not confer any spiritual status 4.198; emphasis on altruism 2.207; ideally conferred by a Buddha or bodhisattva, but self-ordination is permitted 13.339; ideally takes place in the first *bhūmi*, but can be taken in anticipation 4.197; natural expression of the arising of the *bodhicitta*, or a means to it 4.197; no meaningful ordination unless the *bodhicitta* has arisen 4.277–8; not a separate ordination, but the altruistic dimension of Going for Refuge 12.373; originally part of the structure of the Western Buddhist Order 2.469, 2.471, 12.371; Sangharakshita gives the bodhisattva ordination 23.232; Sangharakshita's, *see under* Sangharakshita V/ordination; transmitted in Japan 7.483; the two lineages of bodhisattva ordination 22.509; vows (*bodhicitta-utpāda*) and precepts (*bodhisattva-śīla*) 4.196–7, 7.473–4

bodhisattva training and practice
the aspiring bodhisattva is advised not to look down on the ordinary *bhikṣu* 17.664; the idea of following a path is a metaphor, not to be taken literally 4.199–200; a duty to be joyful 17.182; the bodhisattva has a teacher and aspires to have disciples 13.22; no goal to train for 14.599; needs a foundation of merit 19.44–5; should not keep a cat 16.295; the bodhisattva's practice (Perfection of Wisdom) 14.153; confession 16.289–90; determination to be reborn in the human realm 1.443–4; the 'domain' of the bodhisattva (*Vimalakīrti-nirdeśa*) 16.523–4; the effects of self-realization 14.206; eliminates selfishness by dedicating merit to Enlightenment 16.332; going all out for Enlightenment while realizing that no one attains it 11.14; training by way of a no-training 14.143; how a bodhisattva should regard beings 16.538; learns to meet people halfway 16.230; naturally comes to dwell in the *dhyānas* 14.563; needs knowledge of words 16.490; practises both self-power and other-power 4.141; sees all bodily states and processes with complete equanimity 4.563; should acquire as many supernormal powers as possible 1.443; should learn all arts, sciences, and even crafts 4.81, 13.134, 18.414, 18.463–4; skilful means (*upāya*) 1.432, 14.188, 16.230; studies all schools of Buddhism and other religions, secular subjects, and trades 4.81; tested by Māra 16.525–6; should be able to rid all beings of their wrong views 17.465; trains in non-attachment to all *dharmas* 14.141

bodhisattva career
it begins with taking a vow 3.366; the bodhisattva gains Enlightenment by relying on Perfect Wisdom 14.363; the bodhisattva has a long career because he needs time to accumulate merit 19.45; the bodhisattva putting on the armour of strenuousness 4.60, 4.69; described in various texts 1.401; described in the *Larger Sukhāvatī-vyūha Sūtra* 1.329, 1.401; divided into higher and lower stages 1.270; doesn't stop even at Enlightenment 14.596; has three periods, related to the practice of the perfections and *bhūmis* 2.16–17; infinitely long 1.260; it has an 'endless end' 26.208; the origin and nature of the bodhisattva career 14.189; the past deeds of bodhisattvas who fail in Perfect Wisdom 14.144; the single subject of the *Ratnaguṇa-saṃcayagāthā* 14.513; takes three *kalpas*, an unthinkable length of time 3.55, 3.375–6, 19.47; ten stages, *see* ten *bhūmis*; three key events: the *bodhicitta*, irreversibility, and realization of *trikāya* 2.160–71; 'He goes to Nirvāṇa', but no one can say where he went 14.582

BODHISATTVA PRECEPTS

introduction
breaking them out of desire or out of hatred 2.389, 14.186, 16.294–5; concerned at least as much with thoughts as with acts 7.477; connected with self-purification 4.104; corresponds to the *samaya* of Tantric Buddhism 7.476; the difference between bodhisattva precepts and *śrāvaka* precepts 14.186; ego-driven practice of ethics hinders the bodhisattva in three ways 1.435–6; explained to Sangharakshita by Dhardo Rimpoche 2.455, 22.543; the heart of the bodhisattva expressing itself 1.536; the 64 precepts (18 major and 46 minor) 1.535–6, 2.208, 2.657–9, 7.473, 13.56, 13.339; a variant in the *Brahmajāla-bodhisattva-śīla Sutra* 2.208; practice of

the five precepts 16.9–10; readiness to commit a sin out of desire to help beings to salvation 1.145; reciting them in the Sevenfold Puja 12.405; the ten precepts as the Buddha-field of the bodhisattva 2.334

major precepts
not to disparage the 'Hīnayāna' 13.56; not to give up the *bodhicitta* 13.56; not to glorify oneself and disparage others for gain 11.319; not to instruct an unprepared person in *śūnyatā* 13.56, 14.576

minor precepts
don't neglect the sick 13.57; if someone in your vicinity is angry, try to pacify their anger 13.56–7; show respect for your seniors in bodhisattva ordination 13.56; don't despise evildoers 13.56; don't fail to worship the Three Jewels three times a day 11.319; don't follow after desires 11.319; don't laugh heedlessly 13.56; work for your own circle of disciples and students 13.57

BODHISATTVA ACTIVITY

introduction
activity and meditation 4.160; the bodhisattva neither comes nor goes 18.341; the function of cutting off mistaken views 14.572; everything they do is an expression of *bodhimaṇḍa* 16.503; the fearful task of plumbing the depth of existence and transforming despair 2.180; four *caryās* (courses of conduct) 1.406, 1.422–3; doing nothing and engaging in activities are one and the same 5.646, 14.519; incapable of self-referring or other-referring activities 7.155; is it impossible for the bodhisattva to conform to the conventions of social life? 1.442; it's an offence to hinder them in their work 4.364–5; just doing what needs to be done 19.193; keeping reviving the Dharma 14.433; the Pure Land is the product of a bodhisattva's intense aspiration 17.297; should acquire merit spontaneously 14.502; unable to rest so long as one grain of dust remains undelivered 7.317; their 'purpose' is to make the universe into a mandala 14.517–18; their whole life becomes play (*līlā*) 4.135–8, 4.240, 4.262, 14.501, 14.521–2, 19.193; their work is never done 11.272–3; they act without haste and without delay, serene, cheerful, and optimistic 1.440, 4.135; they do good rather than just eschewing evil 1.395; they don't separate others' needs from their own 17.661; they teach by communicating the sheer adventure of the spiritual life 16.487; they help people spontaneously while having no notion of people 14.411, 14.501–2; they see their actions, and their own merit, as empty 14.417; working in our world you have to have strong compassion and determination 16.558

the liberation from suffering of all beings
the aim is both the spiritual and material amelioration of human life 1.429; all they can do is help people to help themselves 14.577; they help all beings to enter the city of Nirvāṇa 8.452; dedicated to the attainment of Enlightenment of all beings 2.126, 4.5; don't think of the bodhisattva as leading passive people to Nirvāṇa 14.577; 'five stores': methods by which the bodhisattva liberates beings 14.181–2; in hell for millions of years to help one living being 4.60–1; like a mother helping people to grow up spiritually 15.324; like rescuing them from drowning themselves 14.129; vows to lead all beings to Nirvāṇa realizing there are no beings to lead 1.396, 11.14, 14.141; a painless sympathy with pain 4.52, 4.581, 7.290, 16.523, 17.304, 17.511; paradox: because there are no beings to be delivered, he vows to deliver them 2.131; rebirth for the benefit of all beings 3.132–4; resolve to rescue all beings 2.158–9; sees an enormous cloud of suffering and must respond 4.580–1; seeks to gain Enlightenment so that all beings may also gain it 3.365; the sentimental idea of the bodhisattva ladling out Enlightenment is un-Buddhistic 14.578–9; shouldn't be so caught up with saving all beings they forget those around them 7.329; their relationship with all beings is like that of a mother with her baby 17.193; they should be able to rid all beings of their wrong views 17.465; the work is never done 15.499

'postponing' Enlightenment
be careful not to sentimentalize that idea 4.243; 'The Bodhisattva' (poem) 25.220; not to be taken literally 14.555, 19.47; a distortion of the bodhisattva ideal 4.84, 4.223; don't take the bodhisattva for granted 11.277; for a bodhisattva, Nirvāṇa is a failure 4.188, 26.8; for the sake of accumulating merit 19.46–7; how can he be Enlightened until everybody is Enlightened? 18.216; the idea appears in the Pāli canon 4.676 (n107), 4.688 (n200); the mystery of the bodhisattva's 'renunciation' of Nirvāṇa 7.291; on a plateau, within view of Nirvāṇa but acting for the benefit of others 4.553, 4.681; rejects individual emancipation 1.270; 'renunciation' of a personal Nirvāṇa 4.592; they have passed beyond the duality between *saṃsāra* and *nirvāṇa* 17.411; in

Tibet it was believed that lamas could do this 17.411–12; until every blade of grass is Enlightened: what could that possibly mean? 4.243–4; why the bodhisattva continues to work in the world after 'Nirvāṇa' 7.400, 11.273

the bodhisattva spirit
advice from Nāgārjuna that doesn't express the bodhisattva spirit 17.301; the bodhisattva vow an expression of the bodhisattva spirit 4.191, 14.412; exposing yourself to difficult conditions 15.394; everyone can act in the bodhisattva spirit to some extent 11.286; Gotami's bodhisattva spirit 4.445; helping others needs a touch of the bodhisattva spirit 4.70, 4.246; 'I am able to do it' 4.468; its presence makes the perfections into dynamic realities 1.425–6; a Malaysian monk with a touch of the bodhisattva spirit 24.41–2; Milarepa tries to awaken Rechungpa's bodhisattva spirit 18.369

the bodhisattva and the spiritual community
building a buddha-field 1.341–3, 16.467–8; gathering a sangha together 4.97–8; leading the spiritual community on the path to Enlightenment 4.657; rejoicing in the bodhisattva 11.273

THE PRACTICE OF THE PERFECTIONS

introduction
the bodhisattva should exert himself in them 14.153; the fruits of the practice (in the *Śūraṅgama-samādhi Sūtra*) 14.196–7; how the bodhisattva is to cultivate them 14.186; one of four *caryās* (courses of conduct) 1.406, 1.422–3; practice of the perfections (*pāramitās*) 2.164, 4.645–6, 13.399; in practising them, the bodhisattva becomes aware of weaknesses and faults 16.289–90; practised by the bodhisattva on a heroic scale 1.213, 3.54–5

(1) dāna
introduction 1.426–34, 16.8, 16.400; giving courteously, happily, without distinction, with discretion 1.432–3; he can sacrifice his life only for one who can do more than himself 1.430–1; *dāna* in all its forms 1.429; gives fearlessness, self-confidence, encouragement, inspiration 4.97–8; gives his or her life 4.100–1; gives without entertaining the idea of a 'being' 7.330; giving alms with *mahākaruṇā* equals serving the Buddhas of the three times 19.537; giving 'unsupported' 14.416–24; a list of gifts in the *Bodhicaryāvatāra* 3.679 (n336); can no more receive without giving than breathe in without breathing out 1.448; shares himself with people 15.371–2, 16.487; radiates himself or herself out towards others, not holding anything back 3.369; spreads confidence and happiness wherever he or she goes 4.97; why should the bodhisattva give without any ulterior motive? 14.411

(2) śīla
actions for the good of others based on compassion 1.245; the bodhisattva might disregard rules in the interests of teaching the Dharma 4.386; commits a grave offence by doing anything against their own potential 4.364; practises four virtues: creative adjustment, morality, tenderness, sacrifice 1.354; wears his righteousness as lightly as a flower 1.436

(3) kṣanti
practice of patience 1.437–9; undisturbed by dualistic concepts 1.269

(4) vīrya
cultivation of vigour (*Akṣayamati Sūtra*) 17.69; next to wisdom and compassion, vigour is his most prominent characteristic 1.441; without *vīrya*, he will attain to nothing but defeat 4.469

(5) samādhi
the bodhisattva does not relish the *dhyānas* 1.443; needs solitude for meditation 1.442, 4.528; reflects that even the *dhyānas* are painful, transitory, and insubstantial 1.444; temptation to stay in higher meditative realms 4.521–2

(6) prajñā
attainment of a transcendental body 1.259, 1.443; by means of wisdom, liberates a purely transcendental force: compassion 1.387–8; comes to see that 'beings' are mere abstractions 7.330, 14.408–12; doesn't allow the terms of a question to limit the reply 14.417–18; the life of a bodhisattva is the union of wisdom and skilful means 14.164; 'My own self I will place in Suchness' 1.230; should train in the Perfection of Wisdom 1.73; takes nothing whatever as the basis 1.269

see also
perfections/six perfections

THE BODHISATTVA HIERARCHY

introduction
comparison with the orders of angels 13.586–7; the hierarchy of unenlightened beings right up to the Enlightened Buddha 4.171–98; the glorious company of bodhisattvas 2.153–84; ordinary humans, bodhisattva ideal accepters, the *bodhicitta*, archetypal 4.222; 'The Guardian Wall'

(poem) 13.587, 25.293; throughout the hierarchy runs the golden thread of the *bodhicitta* 13.587

historical and living bodhisattvas
could the spiritual masters of other religions, or benefactors, be bodhisattvas? 2.183–4; distinction between historical and archetypal 3.678 (n334), 16.167; dwells among beings on earth 'as father, mother, wife, or child …' 4.520–1; lama as bodhisattva 12.15–16; makers of Buddhist history and moulders of Buddhist thought 2.181–2; may be a monk or a layman 1.244, 1.442; Sangharakshita's meetings with living bodhisattvas 26.234; St Francis as a bodhisattva? 4.607

FOUR KINDS OF BODHISATTVA

(1) novice bodhisattvas (ādikarmika-bodhisattva)
also called bodhisattvas in precepts 4.178; devoted to the bodhisattva ideal, but the *bodhicitta* has not yet arisen 2.171, 3.413, 4.178; their dominating sentiments: love and compassion 1.241; possibility of taking refuge in monastic formalism is precluded 1.245; practices: study, copying scriptures, the *brahma vihāras*, the perfections, puja 4.178–9; their position in the hierarchy 1.241

(2) bodhisattvas of the path
mentioned in the *Diamond Sūtra* 14.404; those traversing the first six of the ten *bhūmis*, the *bodhicitta* having arisen 2.171, 3.414, 4.179; the Stream Entrant, once-returner, non-returner and *arhant* 4.179–80; three kinds of benevolence 4.180–1

(3) irreversible bodhisattvas
characteristics 2.168–9; difficult to describe 2.167, 4.181; dreams 2.169; experiencing life like a game 14.501; how does a bodhisattva become irreversible? 2.166, 4.188, 14.228–9; how to recognize an irreversible bodhisattva 2.168–9, 4.65, 4.189, 15.241, 15.630, 18.588; imagine what it would be like to be an irreversible bodhisattva 14.501; the move to irreversibility in terms of the *bhūmis* 3.414, 4.184, 4.322–3; in the Perfection of Wisdom, *see under Perfection of Wisdom in 8,000 Lines*; proving irreversibility by conjuring a ghost to depart 2.169; the spiritual ideal on an unlimited or cosmic scale 14.404; tempted by Māra 2.168–9; their truthfulness can produce tangible results 2.169; until that point, the bodhisattva can fall back 4.264, 4.322; in the *White Lotus Sūtra*, *see under White Lotus Sūtra*/the structure of th *sūtra*

(4) bodhisattvas of the dharmakāya
between them and the Buddhas there is no real difference 2.172; the bodhisattva's Enlightenment depicted as a ceremony of consecration 2.169; on Enlightenment they participate in the compassionate activity of the *dharmakāya* 14.554; personalized aspects of Buddhahood itself 3.414, 16.167; a far-off goal, but we can form an intention to travel that distance 4.196; the top of the bodhisattva hierarchy 4.190; transformation into the *trikāya* 2.169–70; of two kinds 2.171–2, 4.189–90

ARCHETYPAL BODHISATTVAS

what are they?
all are manifestations of the Great Void, and not different from each other 21.559; both *dharmakāya* and *sambhogakāya* 4.208; different embodied aspects of the same Enlightenment 4.330; distinction between human and divine bodhisattvas 2.172; different forms like the rainbow when light passes through a prism 1.261; emanations 2.178; embodiment of Enlightened qualities 16.167; embodiments of the bodhisattva principle 4.657; emergence in the Mahāyāna 1.241; five '*dhyānī*' bodhisattvas 2.172; hardly historical figures in the scientific sense 2.181; have no history 1.260–1, 4.190, 26.667; the ideal in the process of realization within space and time 4.191; manifestation as a *tulku* 2.183; manifestations of the *dharmakāya* 5.34; new bodhisattva forms could emerge in Western Buddhism 4.194; not quite the same as an archetypal Buddha 4.191; not really male or female 13.186; the most popular constitute two well-known groups 2.172; personifications of the stages of the path 1.243; protectors 17.560; sometimes misleadingly referred to as gods 2.172; visualized on the Refuge Tree 13.78, 13.205; we could say that all the bodhisattvas are one bodhisattva 4.193–4

iconography
beautiful princes, eternally young 1.273, 2.154–5, 12.308, 26.471, 26.599, 26.667; depictions contrasted with those of *arhants* 16.7, 26.697; Indian Buddhists see iconography as resembling that of Hindu gods 10.81; significance of their being depicted as 16 years old 2.316, 13.293, 18.238, 26.233

our relationship with them
appealing to bodhisattvas for protection 4.312–13; 'The bodhisattvas are also necessary' 12.429, 20.448, 26.666–7; bodhisattvas are within us, potentially

13.287; contact with an archetypal bodhisattva is contact with the *dharmakāya* 12.572–3; consulting one means acting with awareness of what is highest 12.573; for the devotee, each possesses a distinct spiritual personality 2.173; hymns of praise to the bodhisattvas 2.554; meditating on their perfections the devotee hopes to obtain their grace 7.123; one has to create the form out of one's experience of the principle 4.195; outside or within? 4.130–1, 5.34, 19.141; they draw us to Enlightenment with beauty 16.352; we have to work from the traditional appearance to what it represents 4.195; what is the connection between ourselves and the bodhisattvas? 4.139; worship of bodhisattvas 4.246–7, 26.667–8; you can close yourself to the influence of a bodhisattva if you want to 4.247

see also
arhant/the *arhant* contrasted with the bodhisattva; *bhūmis*; hierarchy/bodhisattva hierarchy; *dāna*/generosity; three family protectors; Tibetan Buddhism/*tulkus*; bodhisattva vow; wrathful deities

bodhisattva ideal

INTRODUCTION

descriptions
the aesthetic pleasure of contemplating the ideal 7.321; all can become Buddhas: this is the bodhisattva ideal 10.171; the altruistic dimension of the desire to gain Enlightenment 1.245, 1.395, 3.365; a beautiful 'spiritual pipe dream'? 3.133, 8.100, 8.157–8, 13.38–9; the Buddhist spiritual ideal in its loftiest form 13.36; contemplate it to know the heart of Buddhism 1.398; the cosmic context of Going for Refuge 2.477–8; the cosmic significance of the bodhisattva ideal 3.376; dedication to the Enlightenment of 'all sentient beings' taken quite literally 3.376; the doctrine of conditionality in terms of human life and spiritual action 1.272; the equilibrium of the five spiritual faculties 1.395; the finest flower of Buddhist spirituality 3.376; a force at work throughout space, in all worlds 3.384; a heroic aspiration 16.229; it depends upon a profound conception of the inmost nature of things 7.44; it has a double aspect: living the life of a bodhisattva and worship of the bodhisattvas 26.667; Nāgārjuna describes it to the king in the *Precious Garland* 17.173–4; one of the sublimest spiritual ideals that humankind has ever seen 4.221; the perfectly ripened fruit of the whole vast tree of Buddhism 1.394, 8.xvi–xvii, 22.279; the practical aspect of the entire Buddhist tradition 1.445, 13.515–16; principal unifying factor for the entire Buddhist tradition 1.397, 2.432; a restatement of the Sangha Jewel 14.166–7; 'the right ideal in life' 10.101; the salvation of all sentient beings, a mutual interpenetration of being 7.41; the term has only a relative validity 16.545; the translation of the Buddha's teaching into lay terms 12.123–4; the Unconditioned at work in the midst of the conditioned 3.384; the way to Enlightenment (*White Lotus Sūtra*) 16.67; we 'mingle with this world of pain,/ As on roses fall the rain' 25.43

what it is not
cruelty is the behaviour most directly opposed to it 16.294; not a dogma, but an attitude to life 10.122; not literally about saving others as opposed to saving oneself 4.88, 4.221; not humanitarianism, but the wisdom of the voidness breaking through 16.232; not to be equated with the secular concept of social service 8.460–1

characteristics
absolute non-attachment to worldly things 1.399; courageous (Govinda) 21.313–14; the *Gaṇḍavyūha Sūtra* describes it in terms of interpenetration 1.354; pragmatic: to facilitate the realization of the ideal 1.400; progressive: ready to adopt fresh formulations as necessary 1.394–5; sublime 2.455, 22.541–2

universality
universal in its aim, its scope, and its frame of reference 16.229; not limited by time or space 3.383; the possibility of its realization by the layman 14.104; to be followed by all Buddhists, monk and lay, male and female 1.402; the view that it is not universally applicable 1.422

Sangharakshita and the bodhisattva ideal
its attraction from an early stage of Buddhist life 2.454, 22.541–2; 'an example on the grandest possible scale of what I was trying to do' 2.455, 22.542; a point of contact with a Tibetan abbot 21.178–9; an early article 7.39–46; chapter on the ideal in *A Survey of Buddhism* 1.394–454; analysis of the chapter in the *Survey* 2.429–30, 22.144

THE HISTORY OF THE BODHISATTVA IDEAL

origin of the bodhisattva ideal
full introduction 4.3–213; academic discussion of possible origins 26.667; as ancient as Buddhism itself 2.209; in Ananda's remark about the Buddha: 'He

who is so kind' 3.364–5, 4.17–18; derived from the Buddha's example as well as the record of his teachings 2.206–7; the *Jātakas* and *Avadānas* are its scriptures 1.398; 'Origins of the Bodhisattva Ideal' (Lama Govinda) 1.233, 1.398–400, 21.313; in the Pāli canon 4.5; response to the degeneration of the *arhant* ideal 4.21; stressed the altruistic dimension of spiritual life at a time when it had been lost 4.85; not a dividing but a uniting factor in Buddhist life and thought 21.314

Early Buddhism and the bodhisattva ideal
comparison with the *arhant* ideal, *see under arhant* ideal; rejection of the ideal 2.152; adoption of the ideal for lay people 2.209; strengths and weaknesses of the 'Hīnayāna' view of the ideal 4.223–4; the bodhisattva ideal in Theravāda Buddhism 16.29–30; attacked by Theravādins 1.233, 21.313

the bodhisattva ideal and the Mahāyāna
the central teaching of the Mahāyāna 18.463; development 1.243–4; connections 1.394–5; the *Bodhicaryāvatāra* one of the ideal's sublimest statements 4.224; effect of the emphasis on the bodhisattva ideal 1.264; its highest ideal 7.472; the ideal in the Mahāyāna *sūtras* 14.97; positive and negative aspects exemplified by Śākyamuni 14.189; the practical aspect and unifying factor of all Mahāyāna schools 1.397, 3.429; strengths and weaknesses of the Mahāyāna's view of the ideal 4.223–4; stress on the ideal of attaining Enlightenment for the sake of all 9.254–5; translates the Buddha's teachings into lay terms 12.123–4

the bodhisattva ideal in Tibetan Buddhism
the bodhisattva vow taken by both monks and lay people 13.56; for Tibetan Buddhists the ideal is a real, living thing 13.38–9; 'the presiding idea of Tibetan Buddhism' (Marco Pallis) 3.133–4, 13.38; accepted by all Tibetan Buddhists, whether monk or lay 13.55–7; the response of a Tibetan abbot 21.179; the Tantric form of the ideal 4.607; they follow the bodhisattva ideal in an intensely practical way 13.109–10; Tibetans see logic as part of the bodhisattva ideal 13.46

in Triratna (FWBO)
an essential aspect from the beginning 2.471; its influence on the young FWBO 4.237

exemplars and embodiments
the example of the Buddha's life 2.206–7, 4.222, 16.14–15; Ānanda its first exemplar 4.18; the bodhisattva ideal exemplifies the potential for Enlightenment of humanity 3.384; communicating the Dharma through setting an example 12.580–1; Dhardo Rimpoche 2.585; Kusho Bakula, Ladakhi incarnate lama 21.107; Milarepa 3.180; Dr Ambedkar 9.421; one can find exemplars in practitioners of all schools of Buddhism 4.25, 19.208; exemplification stops doctrinal tradition degenerating into scholasticism 2.155–6; a vihara in India as an example of the bodhisattva ideal 9.421

PRACTISING THE BODHISATTVA IDEAL

taking it as inspiration
Atīśa was inspired by it 12.569; Dr Ambedkar saw Buddhism in terms of it 10.68–9; an inspiration to Buddhists through the ages 25.113; monks inspired by the ideal 2.213; more inspiring than the idea of giving things up 4.62; support to one 'working for the good of Buddhism' 2.455, 22.541–2; taking it seriously 18.463; we can't literally think of being a bodhisattva, but we can be open to the ideal 4.61–2; we need it to break the bonds of our individualism and the tendencies of modern life 26.56

aspects of practice
adopting an attitude in which 'self' and 'other' have become indistinguishable 4.221–2; at the highest level, transference of merit becomes the bodhisattva ideal 4.47–8; a connection with the *mettā bhāvanā* 3.376–7; eating and the bodhisattva ideal 19.325–6; two responses: become a bodhisattva or have faith in the bodhisattva's vow 1.400

misunderstandings and misuse
distortion: the bodhisattva as the perfect gentleman 4.84; if the unreality of others is lost sight of, the ideal degenerates into profane sentiment 1.404; to think that one could personally form that aspiration is to misunderstand it 4.60; unattainable by one who imagines that there are separate beings to save 7.362; use of the ideal as an excuse for a weak and cowardly life 1.443; without transcendental insight, it degenerates into an ideal of secular humanism 2.160

doubts and reservations
extremely challenging 4.187–8; giving a talk on the bodhisattva ideal, then not finding volunteers to wash up 18.163; how can it be a workable aspiration for a real live human being? 4.61; if one accepts the ideal, how will one follow it while living in the world? 4.525–6; is it impossible in

concrete historical circumstances? 16.25–6; it could become a rationalization for attachment to the world 3.133, 13.38

bodhisattva path the path of the six perfections 9.249; central to Mahāyāna Buddhism 15.80; divided into three stages 1.406; for householders as well as monks 17.291; and the path of the *arhant*, *see under arhant* path; the 'Secret Path' 1.404, 7.361, 26.207; without the *arhant* path, it may be a rationalization of attachment to the world 13.38

bodhisattva principle 4.637–58

bodhisattva-saṃvara *see under* bodhisattva/ordination

bodhisattva-śīla (code of conduct) *see* bodhisattva/precepts

bodhisattva vow (*praṇidhāna*)

introduction
brief introduction 3.366–7; longer introduction 4.55–83; alternative translations 4.56; acting as if you have taken the vow 14.485; analogy with mundane and transcendental Eightfold Path 3.367; a down-to-earth account 14.413–15; emphasis that moving towards Enlightenment is inseparable from altruism 3.254; the essential revolution called for by the vow 14.413; an expression of the bodhisattva spirit 4.191; being drawn to the *Diamond Sūtra* suggests having taken the vow in past lives 14.482–5; Going for Refuge and bodhisattva vow as self-regarding and other-regarding 12.373; like the light of the *bodhicitta* shining through many prisms, creating rainbows 4.57; Sangharakshita spoke about it on the day of the first ordinations into the WBO 2.471; sparks struck from the bodhisattva's total being 4.57–8; supports the arising of the *bodhicitta*, or expresses it once arisen 4.65–6, 14.411–12; a transcendence of limitations 4.64; twofold: to attain Enlightenment and to deliver all sentient beings 1.259, 1.422; the universe responds to the vow 4.66; the vow and the prediction to Enlightenment (*vyākaraṇa*) 1.422, 2.163, 4.66; we have to be careful that the vows don't just become fantasy 4.60; what distinguishes the vow from the *bodhicitta* 1.422

traditional set of four vows
expression of the Mahāyāna attitude 11.318; outline how all Buddhists should behave 4.63–4; they illustrate the inseparability of ethics and metaphysics in Buddhism 7.35; the vows in verse: 'However innumerable beings are, I vow to save them ...' 2.163, 2.274; (1) May I deliver all beings from difficulties 1.422, 3.366–7, 4.66–72, 16.229, 16.441; (2) May I eradicate all passions 4.73–81; (3) May I master all dharmas 4.81–3, 18.413–14, 19.45; (4) May I lead all beings to Buddhahood 4.83, 14.411–12

other sets of vows
forty-eight taken by Dharmākara, *see* Dharmākara; ten *praṇidhanas* of the *Daśabhūmika Sūtra, see under Daśabhūmika Sūtra*; threefold: worship the Buddha, make spiritual progress, make others happy 4.435–6

vows made by figures in Buddhist history and myth
the bodhisattva's vows in the *Vajra-dhvaja Sūtra* 2.158; a set of vows which vary from one bodhisattva to another 4.57; the vow of Sumedha, who became Gautama the Buddha 2.17; the vows of Samantabhadra in the *Avataṃsaka Sūtra* 2.454, 22.541; vows in the *Sūtra of Golden Light* 16.288–9; the great vows of the cosmic bodhisattvas 18.161; Milarepa's bodhisattva vow 18.215; Dr Ambedkar's version 9.149; Mr Chen vowed to connect with those who cut themselves off from Buddha nature 4.275

formulating one's own vows
to express an ultimate, all-comprehensive aim 4.64; 'I never felt that I could venture to formulate any such vows' 4.197; 'I place no limit on what I am prepared to do for other living beings' 4.64; people make specific, practical vows 4.65; Yogi Chen recommended this 4.197

why take the vow?
the bodhisattva's motivation is the perception of the need of beings for Enlightenment 14.412; the motivation is to bring about the arising of the *bodhicitta* 18.161; taken to strengthen one's resolve, give oneself some spiritual backbone 1.421, 4.65

taking the vow
the bodhisattva makes the vow in the presence of a Buddha 2.163; devalued by casual recitation 4.64, 18.488; an example of vows made 2.207–8; not irreversible 4.322; a very serious kind of promise 4.56; a public declaration with universal significance 1.422, 4.66; take it, but remember there are no beings to be saved, no passions to eradicate 7.413; transference of merit paves the way for taking it 1.511

the vow in practice
as part of visualization practice 16.179; if you have taken the vow, you won't be happy until all beings are happy 19.547; reciting it 100,000 times (in the second *mūla yoga*) 12.19–20, 13.81–2; unflagging fulfilment of the vows through infinite time and infinite space 2.454; it can be broken at any point up to irreversibility 14.412–13

Bodhisattvabhūmi description of the bodhisattva's career 1.401; ethics and manners 11.309; 'I shall rejoice at staying in hell for thousands of aeons ...' 4.60

Bodhisattvāvadāna *see under* Āryaśūra

bodhisattvayāna *see under yānas*

Bodhisri, Dharmacharini 24.618 (n68)

Bodhivajra, Dharmachari 11.466–7

bodhyaṅgas *see* seven *bodhyaṅgas*

body

THE BODY AS WE USUALLY EXPERIENCE IT

the body's needs
the attention we give the body is often unnecessary, even harmful 12.554–5; clamping down on bodily sensations 3.487; detached and objective attitude 4.609; forbearance 4.120; a healthy body 18.447–8; importance of exercise 9.442, 15.280, 20.303; it clamours for what it needs 4.532; its ability to balance and heal itself 16.357; look after your practice as you look after your body 17.306; need for bodily contact 4.562–3

the consequences of having a body
the body and karma 10.481–2, 18.46; an example of something pleasant that binds us to something that brings suffering 3.215; oppression of bodily existence 16.321; to be associated with the body is to be associated with the possibility of pain 18.557–8; you have sensual desire because you have a body, the product of your karma 15.204

identifying with the body
the body is not the self 1.172; the body is 'that portion of the soul which is perceptible by the senses in this age' (Blake) 17.622; death is terrifying because one identifies so completely with the body 15.145; identifying the total self with the body 4.76; to love the body but not the soul or spirit is perversion 12.230; meditating reminds us not to identify exclusively with the physical body 12.555; is the physical body (*sarīra*) identical with the vital principle (*jīva*)? 1.74, 17.622–3

attachment to the body
giving up attachment through contemplation of decay 1.155; overcoming attachment to the body 4.563; tendency to over-identify with the body 15.147

the bodies of others
a lover may claim to admire the mind while thinking of the body 4.561; our craving casts a sort of glamour over someone's body 17.220; treating the bodies of others as you treat your own 4.632

dead body
'as the ocean rejects a dead body', *see under Udāna*/great ocean; Burma Raja's dead body 22.204–6; chopped up in the *chöd* practice 13.268–70; coming close to a dead body brings us face to face with impermanence 15.141–2; embalmed or gilded 2.232; Hindu belief that contact with a dead body is polluting 21.282; how to treat a body after death 15.145–6; missionaries refuse to view Miss Barclay's dead body 22.83–4; what's the difference between a live and a dead body? 4.557–8; you don't get the feeling that the person is actually there 17.622

THE BODY FROM A SPIRITUAL PERSPECTIVE

body and mind
are the mind and the body the same or different? 10.225–6, 17.621–3; a bigger mistake to identify oneself with the mind than with the body 3.216, 17.687; the body belongs to the lower evolution, but the mind has the potential for the higher evolution 3.479; the body is conscious only in relation to the mind 18.236–7; the body is innocent, it's in the mind that everything tends to go wrong 10.307; can more than one mind occupy the same body? 18.227–8, 26.85; division between body and mind 3.479; the effect on the body of negative mental states 17.290; even the most refined mental pleasure is felt in the body 17.393; the flesh is more than raiment 1.266; if there's a great change in the mind, that will literally change the body 18.535–6; like two ends of a stick 3.111; *manomaya* (mind-made body), *see manomaya*; mind and matter are dynamically related 7.137; perhaps we shouldn't make our usual distinction between physical and mental 5.182, 17.xxiii; related health of mind and body 1.163–4, 17.xxiii; a sensation does not impinge on the body without an idea arising in the mind 7.137; strong emotions affect the body as well as the mind 19.135; Western twofold classification 12.33

the body in the Buddhist tradition
we are determined not by the physical body but by consciousness 15.127–8; 'In this six-foot body is the origin and dissolution of the universe' 7.170, 10.597, 13.567; 'Within this body is the arising and passing away of the world' 10.597; the impermanence and insubstantiality of the body (Vimalakīrti) 16.493–4; the other person brought the stick, but you brought the body 4.119–20, 4.409, 10.482, 10.600, 17.173; Tantric Buddhism glorifies it as the vessel of salvation 1.375, 1.388; the Vajrayāna concretizes the Dharma in direct experience of the body 18.74–5; the Vajrayāna gives it special emphasis 18.75–6, 18.535–7

metaphors
'the divine fortress of your own body' 18.48–9; like a bag of mixed grains (*Satipaṭṭhāna Sutta*) 15.123–4, 15.187; a many-storeyed pagoda on each floor of which is a shrine to a Buddha 19.41–2; a 'mirage-city' 18.558–9; spinal column identified with Mount Sumeru by the tantras 2.67; 'Within the temple of your body is your own Buddha mind' 18.618–19

its preciousness
because through it one can attain Enlightenment 3.601, 13.78–9, 18.46; the citadel of awakening 18.49; having obtained it, one should not fritter away its strength 8.219; as one of the four preliminary meditations 5.547; method, not doctrine 15.130

subtle body
direct experience of the body, including the subtle body 18.74–5; 'mind-formed' 18.75; the nerves of the subtle body 18.76–7; out-of-body experience 17.622, 23.84, 23.129–30, 24.337–9

the body and spiritual practice
bodily composure through mindfulness 1.151; the body is simply a vehicle for spiritual development 15.122; the body we perceive to be in the process of change is illusory 18.154; bringing the body into spiritual practice through prostrations 13.78–9; contemplation of the elements of the body 1.160–1; effect of the *dhyānas* on the body 1.162–4; experience of the first four releases 2.144; experimenting with locating consciousness in different parts of the body 18.545–6; getting in touch with feelings through bodily activity 14.573; getting in touch with your body before meditating 5.302–3, 15.429–30; going forth in respect of the body 12.553–6; insight into the body 5.410; purifying the body through ethics 9.287; reflection on the arbitrariness of dividing the body into parts 19.240; the transformation of body 18.535–7; 'watching' one's bodily movements can lead to alienation 17.103–4; wisdom begins at home, in the body 17.389; you may feel that the body is not yours after deep meditation 4.409

the Enlightened body
after Enlightenment, the body becomes an instrument of Enlightenment 4.512; the bodhisattva deploys his body for the benefit of others 4.608–9; the body of a Tathāgata, *see under* Tathāgata; the Buddha's *rūpakāya* and *dharmakāya* 3.150–1; the divine body of a Buddha 19.58; 'enjoyment body', *see trikāya/sambhogakāya*; the physical body compared with the body of a Tathāgata 16.494–5; while the Enlightened mind is associated with the body, suffering is possible 18.47

see also
astral body; mindfulness/four dimensions/mindfulness (or awareness) of the body; *aśubha* bhāvanā/meditation on the loathsomeness of the body; rainbow/'rainbow-body'

body, speech, and mind

in Buddhism
Buddhism's threefold division 1.514–15, 2.335–6, 12.33; the Buddha perhaps derived this analysis from Zoroastrianism 2.337–8; association with the *trikāya* 1.380, 2.336, 18.87, 18.293, 19.30, 19.222–3; Dharmapala strove for their complete purity 8.90

actions of body, speech, and mind
analysing them 17.165; they are not detachable from you 15.374; we are all three, so things should be given utterance and bodily expression 18.378–9; we are usually not aware that they will have consequences 18.84

in spiritual practice
all three must participate for any spiritual exercise to be effective 4.45; bringing them into line with discriminating awareness and faith 17.679; framework for the ten precepts 2.337; Going for Refuge with body, speech, and mind 18.383; perfecting them 18.613; practices bring them into harmony 13.418; in the prostration practice 13.79; they are acknowledged when we bow before the Buddha 1.514–15, 17.228; transformed into something totally skilful 17.164, 18.293

in Vajrayāna Buddhism
association with three psychic centres 1.514–15; emphasis on their total transformation 18.535; those of Milarepa become the three *kāyas* 19.23; their transmutation into those of the Tathāgata 1.380, 7.506, 17.546; their initiation and unity 12.20; *vajra* body, speech, and mind 19.30, 19.43

body-witness (Sanskrit *kāyasākṣin*, Pāli *kāyasakkhin*) description 25.13; on becoming an *arhant* is an *ubhayatobhāgavimukta* ('doubly-liberated one') 2.145; career does not exclude wisdom 2.145; considers the aggregates as painful 2.144; Dharma study 25.14; a faith-follower may become a body-witness 2.144; one of the seven holy persons 2.143; practice of the eight *vimokṣas* (releases) 2.143–4; progressively dissociates himself from his grosser personality 15.562; realizes the true nature of levels of concentration 2.144

Boehme, Jacob 7.98, 7.579 (n184), 8.560

Boer, Charles 24.396

Bohm, Professor David v24

Boin, Emile (Upaya) at first WBO ordination ceremony 2.403; contributions to *The Buddhist* 23.239; a frustrated idealist 23.239–40; owner of 'Sakura', the first centre 12.365, 23.131, 23.426, 26.607; presents Sangharakshita with a yellow kimono 23.169

Boin, Sara (Sujata) at first WBO ordination ceremony 2.403–4; photograph 23.441; translation of the *Vimalakīrti-nirdeśa* 16.445

boldness Dr Ambedkar's boldness 10.107; follow the path boldly 25.33; 'I heard Chapman speak out loud and bold' 26.470; 'I want disciples who are bold, self-confident, and independent' 26.80; speaking with boldness, courage, and wit (*pratibhāna-pratisaṃvid*) 1.449, 16.491; 'Valmiki's heroes bold' 7.57

Bole, S. K. 9.45, 9.47

Bole resolution 9.47–8

Boleyn, Anne 12.697

Bombay *see* Mumbai

Bön (religion of Tibet) circumambulation 'widdershins' 19.329; contact with Buddhism when the Dharma spread to Tibet 7.144, 7.485; and the Nyingma school 1.383; Padmasambhava brought the Bön demons under control 13.9–10; shamanism 13.10; the struggle for ascendency with Buddhism 8.351–2, 8.523; when the Dalai Lama needed money, he asked Bön priests to worship black Jambhala 22.557

bondage belief in the real existence of self or other is a source of bondage 2.159, 26.52; the Biblical story of Israel's bondage and oppression 16.220; essentially a state of impeded volition 2.127; freedom has no meaning except in relation to a previous state of bondage 16.448; peace from bondage 2.124; a reliable teaching will lead towards freedom, not bondage, *see under* Mahāpajāpati; the secret of bondage is also the secret of liberation 1.113; those in the bondage of *saṃsāra* don't see anything wrong with it 10.617; to be truly free one has to escape not only from bondage but from liberation 2.56, 2.118

bones the crown of skulls of the monster of Impermanence 13.128; difference between theoretical knowing and knowing in our very bones 12.612; the dry bones of concepts rubbing against one another 12.314; a garland of skulls 13.240, 13.243, 26.297; keeping skulls and bones as a reminder of death 4.76, 4.536, 16.28; skull-cup 12.335, 13.240, 13.242, 13.246, 13.258–9; the symbolism of the skull in St Jerome's study 26.297–8; Tantric ritual objects made of bone 13.243; Vajrayoginī's ornaments of human bones 13.217, 13.240, 13.243; vows taken to give oneself some spiritual backbone 1.421, 4.65; 'without a monastic order Buddhism has no backbone' (Conze) 3.410; 'your skin for paper, ... your bones for a pen' 2.213

Bonhoeffer, Dietrich 12.5, 12.7–8, 12.9, 12.701 (n3), 23.211

Book of Common Prayer introduction 19.600 (n59); its archaic language gives it a kind of sanctity 19.133; 'an outward and visible sign of an inward and spiritual grace' 8.203, 14.542; prosecutions against clergy introducing rituals not in the book 11.208; 'Read, mark, learn, and inwardly digest' 22.438; the Thirty-nine Articles 23.25

books

the archetypal book
represented by St Jerome's Bible 26.299–302; shown to the animals in the wheel of life 2.74, 3.382–3, 13.134, 14.291, 26.300–1; what Mañjughoṣa's book represents 1.432, 13.367

the sacred book
'All manifestations are holy books' (Milarepa) 19.69–70; belief in the authority

of the Bible 15.264–5; Buddhism has no 'revealed' sacred book 4.642, 10.138, 14.453; Buddhism is free of bibliolatry 8.220, 14.375; Buddhism possesses not one sacred book but many 7.525–9, 14.375; one of the most dangerous authorities is the Sacred Book 12.233, 14.375

the value of books
'Books in the running brooks' 18.182, 18.619, 19.69; the adventures of the soul among books 26.335; the book is the golden key to the treasury of human culture 26.301; 'A good book is the precious life-blood of a master-spirit' (Milton) 19.70; a real book doesn't refer you elsewhere, but is itself existence, an end in itself 19.70–1; a window opening onto a wider world 10.400; why a book is a better teacher than a tree 18.633; you don't really possess a book until you get its spirit 19.143–4

the limitations of books
the difference between book knowledge and experience 10.223–4, 10.440, 19.88; the dust of close-printed volumes 25.194; the primacy of personal, oral teaching over mere book learning 18.14; slavish dependence on the authority of a book 12.233; some books do you good by *not* reaching you 19.135; the wrong idea that religion is found in musty books, not in flowers, or music 7.283

burning and banning books
at Nalanda, *see under* Nalanda; the burning of heretical books 7.380; *Index Expurgatorius* (list of books banned by the church) 7.246; Milarepa burns Rechungpa's books 18.xvii, 19.12–14

book worship
described in the *Perfection of Wisdom in Eight Thousand Lines* 4.307; Dharma books should be treated with reverence 1.407; in the Mahāyāna 2.224–5, 4.306; in parts of the Buddhist world books are worshipped rather than read 14.299–300; on the shrine to represent the Dharma jewel 1.407, 16.59; in Sikhism 4.306–7, 16.58–9; in Tibetan Buddhism 4.308, 14.257; veneration of the *White Lotus Sūtra* 14.130, 16.58; veneration for the scriptures in Buddhism 2.224; visualized on the Refuge Tree 13.78, 13.205; might be a bit artificial for Western Buddhists 4.307, 16.58–9

Tibetan books
printed from wood blocks 7.75, 19.13; hiding a book under your arm 14.247, 19.367; Tibetans' great respect for books 4.308, 13.107; in hell, people who didn't show respect for books crushed beneath them 13.20

books on Buddhism
authors who don't study Buddhism before writing about it 8.242–3; bibliography of Buddhist books 14.272–84; books about Zen 2.284, 11.9, 13.332, 14.515, 14.576; books on meditation 4.519–20, 4.711 (n339); books on mindfulness that are excellent but rather dull 17.88; Buddhism exists not in books, but in its devotees' hearts 7.226; words in a title that arouse curiosity: 'secret', 'magic', 'sex', 'Tantra' 11.181–2, 13.276; dry, off-putting books 25.9; good books written by scholars who are practising Buddhists 25.9; many books 'about' Buddhism have an air of unreality 15.578; many books to read and little time for practice 18.166; most take a lot of understanding 18.459; the need for them to be entertaining 8.361; none the worse for being written by someone who believes in the Dharma 8.539; not many worth reading 4.352; one-sided presentations 12.103; outdated books 12.103; over time books published have shown a deeper understanding 8.512–13; so widely available one must discriminate 8.409–10; sponsored by the governments of Buddhist countries 8.208–9; Theravādin Buddhism is shut up between the pages of a book 1.222; there's a danger of taking the teachings too lightly 18.246; they can make Buddhism seem complicated, but it's really quite simple 12.611; times when books were rare 19.13; the true esoteric path is not found in any book 7.360, 26.49; very few authors can actually write 24.388; writers can be careless with their use of terms 7.515–17; you can tell when a book is based on *śruta-mayī-prajñā* 17.128–9

see also
scriptures/a Buddhist 'Bible'; *ganthadhura* (the way of study); reading/reading Buddhist books

bookshops 'the best Buddhist bookshop I have come across' 24.527; a bookshop as a kind of Pure Land 12.492; in Calcutta 21.589, 22.74, 23.371, 23.440, 25.132; in Melbourne 24.536; in America 24.515–16, 24.527–8; a Buddhist bookstall in Malaysia 24.34; Chetana's bookshop, Mumbai 24.11–12; dreams about bookshops 26.681; in Glasgow 24.140; Indian bookstalls 20.111; in Australia 24.xxii, 24.99; in Colchester 24.166; in London 11.80, 20.32, 20.49, 20.51, 20.81, 20.84–5, 23.9, 24.193, 24.577; in New Zealand 24.85, 24.96, 24.573–4

Boonman, Nai 23.45

Borabadur 16.143

Boral, Dr (Kalimpong) 22.10

boredom boredom of family life 15.479–81; boredom leading to spiritual search 13.351–2; boring, repetitive, non-creative work 1.548, 16.412, 17.194, 17.399–400, 18.201; don't approach life as endless repetition 15.504–5; don't try to fill the emptiness, but experience it 15.427–8, 17.399; feeling bored can be quite productive 18.452–3; finding the mindfulness of breathing boring 5.67–8; if you delight in someone for what they are, you will never find them boring 18.159; it's connected with frustrated energy and not being able to be yourself 17.400; an intermediate state between distraction and being in touch with deeper levels within oneself 17.399; looking round for something to fill the gap 18.334; media input can lessen our ability to deal with boredom creatively 15.174; *mettā* saves you from emotional ups and downs, but isn't that boring? 5.155–6; not getting bored when there is nothing to do 5.645; nothing is intrinsically boring 17.400; the search for relief from boredom 11.78–9; on solitary retreat 16.280; an opportunity to experience the energy usually drained away by distractions 17.399; the opposite of *santuṭṭhi* 15.xx; overcoming spiritual ennui through entering a Mahāyāna *sutra* 16.440; the passivity of heaven becomes boring after a while 19.580; the time to go into town is definitely not when you're feeling bored 18.424; ways of dealing with boredom 15.428–30; when you're bored, sit down and let yourself experience it more fully 17.xxiii

Bosch, Hieronymus 24.409, 24.413, 26.293

Bose, Nandalal (artist) 7.448, 7.618 (n497), 8.367, 26.635, 26.765 (n592)

Bose, Subhas Chandra 7.111–12, 7.582–3 (n208), 20.141–2, 20.153, 21.43, 23.408, 23.535 (n449)

Boswell, James 14.489, 20.51, 23.137, 23.495 (n165)

bother the Buddha tells Ānanda not to bother about the disposal of his remains 16.154; disciples who 'did not bother me with questions about the Dharma' (the Buddha) 10.578; feeling shame about deeds and activities which wouldn't bother most people 18.136; if *śūnyatā* is always present, why bother ascending the stages of the path? 1.363–4; if we are going to accept some authority unquestioningly, why bother with Buddhism? 16.553; Jagdish Kashyap 'simply did not bother with material things' 20.444; let's get rid of suffering without bothering too much which bit is 'mine' and which bit is 'yours' 4.592; make some progress every day, but don't bother about exactly where you are 4.500–1; our inspirations may be sabotaged by something in us that says 'Why bother?' 17.460; a real koan is something that really bothers us 4.245; should Western Buddhists bother with Tantric teachings? 18.494–5; sometimes one may think 'Why bother about personal development?' 26.11; whatever people say to you or about you, don't bother 4.394; why bother about religion? 10.58; why bother getting into the *dhyānas*? 5.278–9; why don't we attain emancipation without the bother of following the path? 1.363–4

Botticelli, Sandro 13.425, 17.222–3, v23, v24, 26.245, 26.252, 26.592–3

Boughen, Ronald v22

Bouic, Matthew v24

Bouquet, A. C. 7.369–70

Bouts, Dieric 24.450

bowl Milarepa's broken bowl 13.27, 24.426; *see also* begging-bowl

Bowles, Paul 24.362, 24.374, 24.389

Box Hill, Surrey 20.100

Boy Yogi 20.330–1

Boyce, Mrs Hilla v21

Boyd, Arthur (Australian artist) v24

Bradley, F. H. 14.85, 20.446, 26.163

Brahmā (Hindu god) appears in a hymn to Tārā 17.146; in the *trimūrti* (Creator) 16.364, 16.415, 17.729 (n162); his place in the Buddhist tradition 9.344, 13.274; his wife is Saravatī 16.364; a spiritual adviser (*purohit*) to the gods 16.415; Swami Ramdas said to be like 20.334

Brahmā (in Buddhist tradition) admits that he is not as all-knowing as people think 2.245, 2.695 (n338), 12.97–8; could not stop the wheel of the Dharma from rolling 8.227, 9.384; explanation of the presence of the god in Pāli canon 9.344; a god, but neither omniscient nor omnipotent 1.158; heaven 16.345; Mahābrahma as a *deva*, escorting the Buddha 13.586; not even Brahmā together with Māra could shake your faith 3.329, 12.505; in the *Sūtra of Golden Light* 16.416–31

Brahmā Sahāmpati's request

the Buddha's hesitation to teach
the Dharma is profound and hard to see 1.90, 2.22, 3.72, 8.589, 11.366; his vision was so out of this world 14.317; the first presentation of the Buddha's insight into conditionality 3.175–6, 7.191–2; how could he possibly get through to people? 9.479–80, 11.161, 11.406, 15.467, 17.389; a supreme spiritual crisis 12.152; the decision to teach 9.220, 10.307

Brahmā Sahāmpati asks the Buddha to teach the Dharma
full text 3.176–8; he appeared like a great golden light 11.412; people are perishing through lack of the teaching 11.412, 15.467; corresponds to the God of Christian mythology in a way 12.191; his attitude of respectful entreaty 11.275; his request echoed in the Sevenfold Puja 1.412–13, 1.510; 'In Magadha there has appeared till now/Impure law' 10.117, 10.678 (n130); 'Open wide the Door of the Deathless' 1.180, 10.678 (n130), 15.467–8; represents the forces of the Buddha's compassion 3.73, 12.188–9; shows the kind of influence a god could have 17.167; so does compassion depend on wisdom? 19.33; there are at least a few who will understand 11.406; 'There are some with little dust on their eyes' 1.181, 2.23, 3.73, 3.596, 11.161, 12.189, 12.407, 15.468, 17.324, 17.389, 18.57, 23.366, 24.3; the wise old man archetype 12.191

the Buddha's vision of humanity as a bed of lotuses
the full text 3.177; the Buddha opened his divine eye and recognized the potential of all human beings 11.725, 12.189; the Buddha thus overcame spiritual individualism 11.406–7; he saw all beings as individuals 11.366–7; he saw that everyone is capable of development 9.185, 9.232–3, 10.206; he saw that some would understand 3.73–4, 11.161; compassion arose 2.22, 3.177–8, 7.143, 11.412, 15.467–8; an example of the Buddha's sensitivity to the environment 26.242–3; the lake at Bodh Gaya 23.366–7; plant symbolism 16.120–1, 16.463–4; that is how Buddhism has seen humanity ever since 11.109, 15.579; that vision of growth developed in Buddhist history to take many forms 11.87–8; we are free to develop as we wish 3.181

brahma vihāras *see* four *brahma vihāras*

Brahmā voice *see under* voice

brahmacārin 2.729 (n614)

brahmacarya (*brahmacariya*)

general use of the term
as used in early Buddhism 10.549, 14.521; *brahmacarya*, *dharmacarya*, and *bodhicarya* 15.448; the Buddha said to his disciples: 'Make known the perfectly pure *brahmacariya*' 10.439; the divine life 11.704, 26.634–5; 'faring in the divine, noble faring' 13.452, 14.547, 15.447–8; in the phrase 'Spiritual friendship is the whole of the spiritual life' 3.579, 11.704; it connotes both chastity and the spiritual life 9.114; it means a great deal more than abstention from sexual activity 2.605; it originally referred to the whole spiritual life 10.439, 11.536; that life which leads to the *brahmaloka* 3.579, 11.704

as celibacy
the connection between celibacy and the broader use of the term 11.537–8; Dharmapala's practice of *brahmacarya* 8.11–12, 8.93–4; unless you love the Dharma passionately, sexual renunciation will be a struggle 18.127; moving towards complete *brahmacarya* 12.487–8; no point in avoiding sexual involvement if you can't find pleasure elsewhere 17.226–7; observation by lay Buddhists and monks 11.536–7; one who practises it will tend to limit possessions, live simply, do without paid work 2.605; it sometimes means celibacy or chastity 3.579, 9.114, 26.635; *brahmacarya* and transcending sexual dimorphism 2.371, 2.605; that way of life that leads to the *brahmaloka* 3.579; training-rule: abstention from non-chastity 2.605; *see also* celibacy

Brahmadatta (wanderer) 3.546–7

Brahmadatta, King 14.63–4

Brahmajāla Sutta *see under Dīgha Nikāya*

Brahmajāla-bodhisattva-sīla Sutra 2.208, 2.213

brahmalokas *see* heavens

brahmam (sublime) 15.330

***brahman* of the Vedānta** *see under* Advaita Vedānta

brāhmaṇas antagonism with *śramaṇas* 20.234–5; language 16.367; should not be translated 'brahmin' 9.537

brāhmaṇa-śramaṇa appear as a pair of terms in the *Dhammapada* 10.479; a collective designation for all those following the Threefold Way, whether monastic or lay 1.427; the contrast likened to that between friar and priest in Europe 10.488; 'Outside my teaching there is no true *brāhmaṇa* or *śramaṇa*' 14.241; at present refers primarily to the monastic sangha 1.428; *śramaṇa* wanderers contrasted with settled *brāhmaṇas* (*Udāna*) 10.487–8; in the *Udāna* the Buddha equates the two ideals with *bhikkhu* 10.515

Brahmaputra, River 22.90–1, 22.98–9

Brahmās, highest of gods *see under* heavens

Brahmasūtras 14.374

Brahmavamso, Bhikkhu (Phra Ajahn Brahm) 2.617, 2.620–50, 2.753–4 (n764)

Brahmāyu Sutta *see under Majjhima Nikāya*

brahmins

BACKGROUND

history
the original meaning of the word 10.430; appearance with the Aryan invasion of India 16.362; hereditary priests 12.521–2; the Sarasvatī river 16.362–3

brahminical rituals and sacrifices
accompanied by the recitation of Vedic hymns 16.362; controlling the gods through rituals 10.516–17; specifications led to arithmetic and geometry 16.362–3; importance of grass 16.373; *nityakarma* 7.100, 7.580 (n192); performance of rituals 7.180–1, 7.183, 12.240, 12.521–2; performed on the bank of a river 16.362; the one performing ritual contrasted with those devoted to spiritual practice 10.488; sacrifices 12.522, 16.362–3

attitudes
attempt to restrict world-renunciation to brahmins 20.235; belief in their superiority over other castes 1.501, 12.239; contempt for 'Untouchables' 9.84, 9.87; Hinduism organized to their social and economic advantage 20.251; opposition to equality 9.68; place in caste system 9.26, 9.30; tendency to look upon ascetics (even Hindu ones) as a threat 20.235

modern brahmins
Maharashtrian brahmins 22.155; Nambudiri brahmins of Travancore (Kerala) 20.285–7; Telegu brahmins 20.368–9

BRAHMINS AND BUDDHISM

brahmins at the time of the Buddha
among those taught by the Buddha in the eight assemblies 12.521–2; the brahmins and their teachers like the blind leading the blind (Pāli canon) 14.42; the brahmins tried to monopolize spiritual truth, but the Buddha gave it freely 10.624; in the Buddha's day, they had lost connection with the transcendental 16.354; the Buddha defines the term afresh, but a new word would have been better 10.441–2; the Buddha had no quarrel with individuals, only those who adhered to caste 10.381–2; the Buddha's first visitor after his Enlightenment was a brahmin 2.22, 10.436–8; conditioning of pride and arrogance (*Udāna*) 10.514; the conflict between the real brahmin and the pseudo-brahmin 10.440; 'lovers of secrecy' (Pāli canon) 9.419; their attempts to outsmart the Buddha with tricky questions 12.239–40; they contemptuously called the Buddha and his disciples *muṇḍaka* 10.623; they disturbed the minds of the Kālāmas 1.60; they objected to the Buddha's teaching because he was not a brahmin 10.446–7, 10.624; to think they had secret teachings which the Buddha made available is a misreading 10.625; why did a brahmin intervene in the quarrel over the Buddha's relics? 16.153

term used in early Buddhism
brahmin (or *brāhmaṇa*) in the *Dhammapada* 10.430, 23.178, 23.498–9 (n206); the Buddha used it in his first teachings, according to the *Udāna* 10.439–42, 10.465; one becomes a brahmin not by birth but by deeds 8.358, 10.xxvi, 12.727 (n218), 14.56; used interchangeably with *bhikkhu* 16.153, 16.265; what makes a true brahmin? 10.xxvi, 10.430, 10.436–47, 10.457–8, 10.514, 14.57; when the Buddha first became Enlightened, he referred to himself as a brahmin 10.429–30

brahmins in later Buddhism
Aśoka expelled *bhikkhus* found wearing sacred threads beneath their robes 8.247;

most Mahāyāna *ācāryas* were born into brahmin families 1.381; in the *Sūtra of Golden Light* a brahmin beat the drum in Ruciraketu's dream 16.265–6

brahmins and Buddhists in modern times
Dr Ambedkar's attitude towards brahmins 9.52, 9.63; a brahmin-born Buddhist woman in modern Ahmedabad 23.345; a naive and literalistic attempt to convince brahmins that there is no *ātman* 19.101–2; political alliance with Dalits 10.62; Sangharakshita's satirical sketch on Brahminism 22.10

hostility to Buddhism
their role in Buddhism's decline in India 7.233–5, 8.122–3, 9.236–7, 10.565, 12.239–40; hostility in a poem by Tulsidas 8.358; the hostility of a brahmin to Sangharakshita 10.446–7; insistence that Buddhism is part of Hinduism, *see under* Hinduism; reasons for their hostility 10.308, 10.624, 12.239–40

Brahmo Samaj 7.189, 8.167, 8.299, 8.680 (n98)

Brahms, Johannes 26.505

bravery *see* courage

breakthrough

introduction
symbolized by the wrathful Vajrapāṇi 11.17–18; thinking of spiritual life in terms of breaking through 11.4–5

what one has to break through
the arising of the *bodhicitta* is breaking through contradictions 4.92; caste conditioning 10.lviii–ix; individualism and modern anti-spiritual tendencies 26.56; mechanical time 11.9–10; negative emotions 11.5–6; psychological conditioning 11.6–8; rational thinking 11.8–9; reactive patterns 17.434; resistance to meditation 13.171, 18.618; self-will 19.166–7; tiredness 18.617

breaking out
'I Want to Break Out' (poem) 25.xxxiii, 25.xxxv, 25.309; of the closed circle of self-interest 17.342; of the cocoon of the present 17.403; of the cycle of reactivity 15.205; of the 'self' 17.348

bursting through
bursting the bonds of phenomenal existence 4.244–6; bursting the bonds of relativity 7.102; the *vajra* bursts through limitations 16.504

the experience of breaking through
'breaking fetters' may suggest sudden breakthrough, but progress is gradual 3.420; breaking through gently 5.424; the *vajra* breaking through compared with psychological breakthrough 13.171–2; breaking through via only meditation is quite rare 5.635; it can be very joyful 13.171; it is most likely to happen at a time of crisis 11.16–17; not everyone makes a breakthrough when attachments break down 11.539–40; one's secret life breaking through into lower levels 23.183–4; partial and total breakthrough 19.19; a pattern of breakthroughs and plateaus 12.626; pushing someone to break through may lead them to break down 17.653; sensations of a light trying to break through 22.302; sudden breakthrough 18.613

how to break through
how did the Buddha make his breakthrough? 19.313–14; breaking through negative emotions 11.13; breaking through psychological conditionings 11.13–14; breaking through rational thinking 11.14–16; breaking through the time sense 11.16; breaking through to the absolute mind through the six element practice 3.350; making a breakthrough at work 13.172; a path of regular steps 11.12–13; taking the opportunity for a breakthrough 5.602; the twentieth blow 2.282–3, 11.13, 12.177–8, 12.626, 14.456–7; the way of mindfulness 11.12; when the rational mind really gives up 18.189; when something is a real question for you 4.245; you need to practise with intensity 13.171

breaking through into what?
'Breaking Through Into Buddhahood' 11.4–18; Enlightenment is a breakthrough beyond time and space 3.146; everything that happens is a breakthrough to something you couldn't envisage 17.233; gold leaf in works of art representing the transcendental breaking through 13.284; a higher dimension of consciousness 2.274; love, freedom, non-rationality, the eternal now 11.11; Stream Entry 2.146; the transcendental 17.458

breath the bodhisattva can no more receive without giving than breathe in without breathing out 1.448; the breath of the *ḍākinīs*, *see under ḍākinī*; 'Every flower enjoys the air it breathes' 7.388; every time you breathe in, you take life 4.355–6; the inherent fragility of breathing 15.110–11; our life depends upon the breathing process 18.565; reflecting on the breath 15.110–12; the span of a man's life a single breath 14.60, 26.296–7; *see also* mindfulness of breathing; *prāṇa*

Breathworks 5.xxiv, 24.634 (n148)

Brett, Dorothy 8.546, v24

Brewer, Roy 2.403

Brewster, Earl H. 7.451, 8.543, 21.261

bribery argument through bribery 8.170–1; someone who tried to get ordained by bribery 8.307–8; Yama doesn't take bribes 10.321

Bridges, Robert 20.124, 26.379

Bridget, St, of Sweden 13.638

Brighton Buddhist Centre (FWBO) 11.39, 24.128–9, 24.315–16; Buddhist group 23.151–2.23.244, 23.330; the Royal Pavilion 11.141, 24.379–80, 26.477

Brindaban Forest *see under* Krishna

Bristol, England 23.206

British Buddhism *see under* Western Buddhism

British history anniversaries form part of our history 12.649; the Barons' Wars 24.558–9; the Battle of Agincourt 24.560–1; the Gunpowder Plot 13.548; the Ridolfi Plot 13.548–9; the Tudors 13.548–51; the Diggers 3.431, 8.416, 10.232; Civil War 9.408, 23.481 (n75), 24.567; periods of moral licence and repression 11.497; view of kingship 16.423–4; conditions of workers in Victorian England 25.121–2; British Empire 7.86; British rule in Sri Lanka 8.469–70

Brittain, Vera 26.637

'Broken Men' 9.81–91, 9.121, 9.132

Brontës admired and enjoyed 26.490; Charlotte 20.19–20; Emily 2.418, 16.597 (n92); Parsonage Museum, Haworth 24.584

Bronzino 23.219–20, 23.507 (n252)

Brooke, Rupert 26.397

Brooks, Andrew 8.615

Brooks, Kevin 23.465–70, 23.466 (photo), 23.473, 23.543 (n501)

Broomhouse Farm 4.540–1, 26.624–5

brotherhood brothers and sisters in the Dharma 10.351; among Buddhists 9.422; *The Duties of Brotherhood in Islam*, *see under* Al-Ghazālī; Mass Movement Buddhist Brotherhood 9.422; the passions are a brotherhood of thieves 4.380–1; 'Politics is brotherhood', 'Brotherhood is religion' (Blake) 3.575, 11.700; sentient existence a great brotherhood of suffering 7.388; the Theosophical Society aims to create a nucleus of universal brotherhood 12.81

Broughton, B. L. 8.642

Brown, Mick 8.607–8

Brown, Norman O. 8.597

Browne, Thomas introduction 8.678 (n85); his life 26.587; his ideas like fishes moving around in a pool 8.149; the only writer Sangharakshita ever wanted to imitate 26.587; *The Garden of Cyrus* 12.218; *Hydriotaphia* 20.52, 26.332; *Religio Medici* 7.324, 26.587

Browning, Elizabeth Barrett 20.36

Browning, Robert 'Abt Vogler' 2.162, 22.462, 26.144; *The Mask of Robert Browning* 24.535; a recital in India 22.55; *A Soliloquoy of the Spanish Cloister* 1.412, 4.430, 19.277, 19.329–30

Bruegel, Pieter the Elder v24

Brunelleschi, Filippo 23.314, 23.523 (n359), 24.268, 24.674 (n325)

Brunner, Elizabeth 21.398

Bruno, St 13.629–30, 15.141, 17.25–6, 24.454

Brussels 23.246–7

Buchan, John 26.337–8

Buchman, Frank 7.238, 7.602 (n341), 23.88, 26.132

Bucke, Maurice Richard 1.480, 1.623 (n363)

Buddha (general term) *see* Buddhas

Buddha, Gautama (or Gotama)

contents for this section
(I) life story: introducing his life – his background and early life – Enlightenment – the period just after Enlightenment – the Buddha's life after Enlightenment – last days; (II) what the Buddha was like: characteristics – descriptions – symbols and myths; (III) communication: how he communicated and with whom – his ways of communicating – the Buddha as teacher – teachings; (IV) who is the Buddha?: responses to the Buddha – who is the Buddha?

(I) Life story

introducing his life

notes on the Buddha's biography
brief introduction 7.491, 10.326, 11.491–2, 12.131–4; biographies deal with two quite different people: Siddhārtha and the Buddha 3.145; the Buddha's twelve principal acts a framework for biographies 4.59, 14.25; contrast between historical view and cosmic significance 1.46–8; the major events of his life took place beneath trees 4.10, 10.330, 15.137, 26.242; the mandala of the five Buddhas is based on episodes in his life 13.302–4; *mudrās* based on incidents in his life 13.302–3; the mystic marriage of the human and the divine 1.49; the pattern of his life 10.546–9; pilgrimage to the places associated with him, *see* four holy places; the question of who he is cannot be answered in a biography 3.3; reconciling historicity and metaphysics 13.300; turning points 9.219–20

reading about his life
distinguishing which incidents are of spiritual significance 15.590, 19.54–5, 22.124; getting a sense of Enlightenment from reading about his life 11.103; getting a vivid sense of his life 26.635; gives us a sense of the Buddha as our spiritual friend 26.636; inspiration from his life 11.711, 12.507–8, 19.55, 26.511

how legendary and mythical elements are handled
compilers don't make an absolute distinction between fact and symbol 2.34–5; a source of embarrassment to Eastern monks 12.110; tend to be disregarded by Western scholars 11.15–16, 12.110, 12.182

biographies
introduction 2.12–13, 12.109–10; *Abhiniṣkramaṇa Sūtra*, *see Abhiniṣkramaṇa Sūtra*; *adbhuta-dharmas* (Pāli *abbhūta-dhammas*, miraculous events) 14.24–5, 17.571; Dr Ambedkar's unconventional account of the Buddha's life 9.140–2, 9.146–7; *Ariyapariyesanā Sutta*, *see under Majjhima Nikāya*; in the Vinaya Piṭaka, *see under* Vinaya Piṭaka stories; 'The Buddha' (poem) 25.296; *Buddha's Life by Modern Indian Painters* (review) 8.367; *Buddhacarita*, *see under* Aśvaghoṣa; Christianized version used by Shakespeare 13.653; *Lalitavistara*, *see Lalitavistara*; *The Light of Asia*, *see under* Arnold; *Mahāparinibbāna Sutta*, *see under Dīgha Nikāya*; *Mahāparinirvāṇa Sūtra*, *see Mahāparinirvāṇa Sūtra*; *Mahāvastu*, *see Mahāvastu*; Marathi publication by Krishnaji Keluskar 9.45; *Nidānakathā*, *see Nidānakathā*; Pāli canon sources 6.xxv, 13.143–4, 14.264–5, 17.402, 26.511, 26.635–6; the principal events of his life told in a Mahāyāna *sūtra* 14.241; Vishvapani's biography of the Buddha 6.xxv–xxvi; a wish to see the Buddha's life illustrated 11.621

his background and early life

cosmological background
introduction 1.46–8, 16.343–4; as Bodhisattva 2.477, 19.313–14; described by Bodhisattva doctrine 1.257; the idea that he was Enlightened before his present birth, *see under* Lokottaravādins; the fourth of the five Buddhas of this *kalpa* 8.201; lineage of previous Buddhas 1.43–50, 1.49, 4.669 (n63), 7.227; merit accumulated over a series of lives 19.44; traditionally speaking he was following the bodhisattva path 15.644; when he is reborn, he has only to open his hands to find them full of jewels 17.200

previous lives
as the bodhisattva Never Direct (*White Lotus Sūtra*) 4.418, 14.129; as Prince Candracchattra 16.572–4; as Puṇyaraśmi 14.189; as Sakka, Lord of

the Devas 1.49–50; as King Susaṃbhava (*Sūtra of Golden Light*) 16.245, 16.389–90; in the *Jātaka* stories, *see Jātakas*; prediction to Enlightenment as Sumedha, *see* Sumedha

birth and early life
astrological sign, the bull 9.365; the *devas* rejoiced at his birth 8.202; his birth and death dates debated 2.662 (n12), 7.491, 11.491; of the Kṣatriya (warrior) caste 3.49, 9.185, 9.191, 9.482, 10.624, 12.521; one could say that his wealth was a disadvantage 10.236; his physical birth, *see under* Siddhārtha; his spiritual birth took place at Bodh Gaya 10.261

ENLIGHTENMENT

introduction
quest for Enlightenment, *see under* Siddhārtha; brief account 2.21–2, 3.31, 8.xiii; the preparation, *see under* Siddhārtha; his Enlightenment was reckoned to have taken three *asaṃkhyeya* aeons 13.299; all his energy poured into it, like a waterfall falling from a great height 10.428; the alpha and omega of the entire system of Buddhism 7.309; it had its origins in his practice of the ten perfections 8.232; it was gained through meditation 9.202; he may have been doing the mindfulness of breathing 15.102

what he saw
the answer to the problem that had tormented him 12.134; that when craving ceases, birth ceases, and when birth ceases, death ceases 12.359; his previous lives 2.21, 3.32, 10.434, 18.444; how all beings are reborn according to their karma 1.487, 3.32, 4.373, 10.434, 14.497; beings tormented by feverish longings born of passion 10.521–5; his vision of human existence 11.161–7; the twelve links of conditioned co-production 1.91–3, 3.676 (n316), 10.428–9; knowledge of the destruction of the *āsravas* (biases), *see* three *āsravas*

what happened
a Buddha's face shines on Enlightenment and when about to enter *parinirvāṇa* 13.144; he broke at last the chain of birth and death 25.341; inconceivable to us 14.442; a many-faceted experience which took place over weeks 4.168, 15.467–8; he entered a new dimension of being 3.148; his tremendous relief 12.151–2; more than an 'intellectual penetration into the nature of the human situation' 5.426; Siddhārtha died and the Buddha was born 3.149; 'There arose in me light' 1.86, 1.93, 7.600 (n331), 12.519; three aspects: purity, compassion, wisdom 12.546–7; when dawn came a Supreme Buddha sat beneath the tree 2.22

reflections
celebrating his Enlightenment, *see* festivals/Buddha Day; a great turning point 9.220; he transcended the duality between conditioned and Unconditioned 14.596; his Enlightenment compared to that of his disciples, *see under* disciples; his Enlightenment was unique 8.232; it cannot be undone 4.182–3, 11.161; it was not conditioned by thought and speech 14.15; the luxury of doubting whether the Buddha was really Enlightened 15.176; not a personal gain, but for the sake of all 1.403; recognizing our own versions of his experience 3.42–3; why didn't he 'postpone' Enlightenment, as bodhisattvas are said to do? 4.85

THE PERIOD JUST AFTER ENLIGHTENMENT

the first few days
absorbing the experience 2.22, 3.64–5, 10.262, 12.621; after his Enlightenment, he did not cease to function as a person 2.128–9; the bliss of Enlightenment 10.262, 10.469–70; his instinct to pay honour and respect, *see under* reverence; looking at the world 25.398–9; sitting under the bodhi tree for seven days: literal or symbolic? 10.427–8; seven days later his experience followed the pattern of Enlightenment 10.434–5; people must have been supplying him with food 10.437; he sees that no-one has achieved more than he has himself 3.66, 26.630; under the goatherd's banyan tree 10.437; Vinaya accounts of how he spent the first four weeks 10.428; later accounts describe him sitting under seven trees for seven weeks 10.437

deciding to teach
mysteriously, Enlightenment begins to communicate itself 11.411; his first words: 'House-builder, (now) you are seen!', *see Dhammapada*/chapter 11; Brahmā Sahāmpati's request, *see* Brahmā Sahāmpati; vision of humanity as a bed of lotuses, *see under* Brahmā Sahāmpati's request; 'Wide open are the doors of the Deathless', *see under* deathless; 'Let those who have ears to hear release their faith' 3.74, 3.640 (n80), 11.413

first encounters
meeting with Upāka, *see* Upāka; a haughty brahmin 2.22, 10.436–43; first

lay disciples, Tapussa and Bhallika, *see* Bhallika

first discourse
given to his first five disciples, *see under* disciples/first five disciples; an account with no reference to content 3.641 (n83); the appearance of the second Jewel 3.395; in the *Ariyapariyesanā Sutta*, *see under Majjhima Nikāya*; in the *Dhammacakkappavattana Sutta*, *see under Saṃyutta Nikāya*; inadequacy of account (Ambedkar) 9.141; association with wheel-turning gesture 16.124; celebration of anniversary (Dharmachakra Day), *see under* festivals; echoed in a Mahāyāna *sūtra* 14.181; the rejoicing of the gods 1.36; sets rolling the wheel of the Dharma 1.36–7, 9.384, 16.613 (n221)

THE BUDDHA'S LIFE AFTER ENLIGHTENMENT

almsround
he vomited the first time he tried to eat almsfood 3.50, 20.417; begging in Kapilavastu 13.461; his practice of remaining silent on his almsround 12.157; sometimes other monks begged on his behalf 14.401; as seen in the *Diamond Sūtra* 14.396; initiated a social revolution through setting the conditions for collecting alms 20.416; he sometimes returned with an empty bowl, due to Māra's intervention 1.228

attendants
Ānanda as the Buddha's attendant, *see under* Ānanda; Meghiya wants to leave the Buddha for a mango grove 3.577–8, 10.526–8, 11.702–3, 18.367; Nāgasamāla, the Buddha's companion at one time 10.649–50; why did the Buddha need an attendant? 11.435–7

incidents in his life
brief account of his life after Enlightenment 2.22–8; attempts to kill him, *see under* Devadatta; the Buddha and Ānanda as exemplars of spiritual friendship 3.90, 11.436–7; deals with criticism 3.76, 3.546–7; even the Buddha made mistakes 3.90, 4.360; he was not prepared to put up with just anything 10.537; discusses ploughing with Kasi-Bhāradvāja, *see under Sutta-Nipāta*/chapter 1; he gives in to public opinion 19.262; he had to suffer according to the law of karma 15.93, 16.310; he is abused by a wanderer 3.76; he goes to live alone in the jungle (with an elephant) 10.323–4, 10.429, 10.536–7, 14.401; he intervenes in conflict between Śākyas and Koliyans 7.238, 9.140, 10.260, 12.338–9; he pacifies a mad elephant 2.27, 3.63, 4.13, 10.260, 11.162, 13.280, 17.188; he says that he will no longer participate in *uposatha* days (*Udāna*) 10.557, 10.562; he scandalizes brahmins by disparaging ceremonial bathing and animal sacrifice 26.179–80; he sends the first disciples out to teach, *see* 'for the welfare of the many'; he travels on foot 10.229, 10.330; his appreciation of a *gandharva*'s music 26.122–4; his daily habits 15.381–2; his experiences of pain 3.184, 10.236, 14.239, 15.368–9; his response to insults 3.693–4 (n477), 13.683 (n57); why should he need a friend? 11.437

his relationship to the India of his day
at that time, Buddhism made its greatest appeal in the urban areas 18.203; the Buddha appeared at a time of intense spiritual enquiry 3.59; cultural and economic conditions in north-eastern India at his time 13.144; the geographical area of his personal influence 2.25; he had to risk unpopularity 3.472; he lived in a world populated by nature spirits and supernatural beings 15.136; he refrained from commenting on politics 7.438; he saw the teachings of his day as rationalizations of craving 12.99; he seemed to throw overboard the religious practices of an entire nation 7.102; he spent twenty-five rainy seasons in Śrāvastī 14.401; he was accused of destroying families 2.24; he was well informed about things 15.491; his influence on other religions 2.11–12; his influence so strong that other teachers said he used spells to charm people 2.26, 11.492; his open air life 11.452, 14.398, 15.136–7, 26.242; the simplicity of life in his day 10.561, 14.398–9; slander 3.606, 4.311; social egalitarianism 7.438; some of his contemporaries had no idea of the reality he represented 18.89; what language did the Buddha speak? 14.12–14; the world he lived in, as depicted in the Pāli canon 10.465–6, 16.236, 16.529, 17.402

meditation
'the Buddha was always in *samādhi*' 5.743 (n431); 'the happiness which arose in me could not obsess my mind' 2.108, 18.581; he meditates in the *Diamond Sūtra* 14.398, 14.401; he reviews his state of mind 10.593–4; why does a Buddha meditate? 14.401–2, 19.421–6

LAST DAYS

an overview of the story
different accounts 2.27–8, 3.117–20, 9.146, 12.357, 13.144–8

his last tour
advice to the Vajjians, *see under* Vajjians; the threefold way 2.28, 3.354, 4.334, 4.644–5, 7.507, 8.92, 11.306; *āsavas* (four) 3.665 (n257); Sāriputta declares that the Buddha is the greatest Enlightened One 1.54, 1.293, 3.144; prediction of a great city at Pāṭaligāma 18.24; powerful *devatās* bend the hearts of kings and ministers to build on their ground 24.81; 'Through not understanding the four noble truths, we have wandered a long journey' 1.96; the Mirror of the Dharma 3.650 (n156) 3.683 (n371), 11.449–50; the *Tiratana Vandanā* 2.343, 3.627 (n13), 4.683–4 (n172), 15.493, 19.600 (n60); 'the wise have crossed the stream' 7.315; a company of Licchavis whom the Buddha compares to gods 26.126–7; Ambapāli 16.624 (n310)

last rainy season retreat
the Buddha observed it with Ānanda 13.145; the pain of his final illness 3.117, 15.369; a depiction of the Buddha in old age 26.635–6; only free of pain when in *dhyāna* 15.156, 19.422; 'I am not one who has the closed fist of the teacher' 10.624; 'I do not consider that I lead the sangha' 2.28, 9.306, 10.580, 25.107; body like an old cart held together with straps 3.117, 11.102; why should the Buddha be subject to old age and death? 4.205

an island unto oneself
'Be ye islands unto yourselves, refuges unto yourselves' 2.142, 2.593, 7.50, 7.268, 15.583; one takes refuge in oneself *and* in the Dharma 11.451; 'Hold fast to the Dharma as a lamp' 2.28, 9.306, 12.675

length of life
given all his skilful actions, why didn't he have an immeasurably long life? 16.254; he could have lived longer if asked 1.254, 1.413, 11.276–8, 21.584–5; Ānanda's failure to ask him to live longer 10.583–8, 11.276–8; Māra suggests to the Buddha that he should attain *parinibbāna* (*Udāna*) 10.584, 10.587; he needed to die so that his disciples could become independent 10.324–5, 16.202; he remained alive because there was something to be done 10.585; he said he would not pass away until his monks could 'refute any wrong view arising' 10.587; Ruciraketu questions the Buddha's short life (*Sūtra of Golden Light*) 16.244–5, 16.253–61

the final part of the journey
teaching the Dharma to those in the eight assemblies 2.647, 12.521–32; advice in Vesālī: master, practise, meditate upon, and spread these truths 2.29; seven *bodhyaṅgas* 2.126; thirty-seven *bodhipakṣya-dharmas* 1.86, 2.126, 12.466; the Buddha's 'elephant look' 4.706 (n313), 10.461, 12.157; the Dharma is based on reason and experience 9.97, 10.40; water churned up by wagons becomes clear when he asks for a drink 10.639; ability to concentrate while 500 bullock carts pass by 3.288–9, 9.298; a presentation of robes made of cloth-of-gold 2.29, 13.144; a Buddha's face shines at Enlightenment and when about to enter *parinirvāṇa* 13.144

the Buddha's last meal
given to him by Cunda the smith 2.29, 3.117–18, 10.639–40; the Buddha asks Ānanda to tell Cunda not to feel remorse 2.29, 3.118, 10.640–1

in the Sāl Grove
artists' depictions of the scene 3.119, 4.10; the Buddha lay with his head to the north and his feet to the south 11.452, 12.357; the falling of untimely blossoms beneath the *sāl* trees 2.29, 3.119, 4.10, 11.451–3, 13.145–6; 'He who would worship me, let him follow my teaching' 2.29, 11.452–3, 13.146; advice to visit the four holy places 2.223, 8.193–4, 23.358; how to behave in relation to women 8.444; the Buddha tells Ānanda not to bother about the disposal of his remains 2.29, 13.146, 16.154

Ānanda's distress
'He who is so kind' 2.29–30, 3.364, 4.17–18, 13.146; the Buddha comforts and praises Ānanda 2.29–30, 3.118, 13.147

last interactions
why gain *parinirvāṇa* in the wattle-and-daub township of Kusinārā? 4.37; teaching to Subhadda, his last disciple 1.178, 2.30, 3.77, 10.678 (n130), 11.453–4, 13.147; the Buddha said he needed no successor: 'The Dharma will be your teacher' 11.662–3, 11.736; permission to abolish minor rules 9.97–8, 12.678; many people were present 13.145–8; the Buddha asks the monks if they have any last questions or doubts 2.29–30, 3.119

last words (appamādena sampādetha)
the circumstances in which they were spoken 2.30, 3.119; Dr Ambedkar quotes them 9.61; determination and perseverance 18.411; go on making an effort 4.183; knowing these words, why are people still unmindful? 10.84; stay awake to the truth of impermanence 13.147; these two things encapsulate everything we need to do 3.251, 18.12; 'With mindfulness, strive on' 17.579

the parinirvāṇa itself
attainment of 'Nirvāṇa without remainder' 10.566–7, 11.403, 14.407; synonymous with *skandha nirvāṇa* 3.658 (n216); nothing significant about it from the Buddha's point of view 13.144; even the Buddha had to die 11.449, 12.357–8; he doesn't really die 10.654–5; he would only be reborn out of compassion, not out of compulsion 11.403; an extension of the experience of Enlightenment 4.8; the Buddha is now purely Unconditioned 10.654; going over the horizon as regards the physical body 10.615; impossible to describe his state 3.645 (n126), 4.205, 10.655–6, 13.393, 14.408, 14.583; by comparison, 'resurrection' is a clumsy attempt to negate the fact of death 12.357–8; it reminds us to review our meditation practice 3.120; in the *Udāna* the Buddha comments on someone else's *parinirvāṇa* 10.653–6; significance in relation to the *trikāya* doctrine 7.455–6; the Buddha's *parinirvāṇa* as skilful means (Mahāyāna) 1.443, 4.85, 4.205–6, 14.236; Mahāyāna *sūtras* associated with the *parinirvāṇa* 14.230–41; use of the word *parinirvāṇa* 3.658 (n216), 8.273, 12.520, 15.463–4, 21.582; the date of the *parinirvāṇa* 22.304; Parinirvana Day, *see under* festivals

grief
'The Eye of the World has disappeared!' 4.10; some disciples were upset, but the *arhants* sat calmly 4.10, 13.147–8, 14.233–4, 14.470; all the animals wept (except the cat) 3.119, 4.10, 16.295; a monk who was pleased when the Buddha died 14.432

relics
instructions about disposal of relics 16.141–2; the funeral pyre 16.141; a quarrel over the relics 13.148, 16.141–2, 16.153; eight stupas built over them 16.142, 16.153–4; the burial mound (origin of the stupa) 13.148, 16.142; relics presented to the vihara in Sarnath 8.69–70, 21.191; a sacred relic of the Buddha in Madras 8.64; worship of the Buddha's relics 14.144, 16.571

afterwards
disciples faced various problems 2.188; the Buddha's confidence in agreement about the Dharma after his *parinirvāṇa* 11.369–70

(II) WHAT THE BUDDHA WAS LIKE

CHARACTERISTICS

appreciation of beauty
he is moved by the beauty of the Licchavi youths 26.126–7; he saw everything as pure beauty because he saw everything with compassion 14.516; his appreciation of art and nature 1.125, 10.586, 26.122–4; only the Buddha sees the true beauty of the world 12.616

beauty
Ānanda is converted to Buddhism by the Buddha's beauty 12.307–8, 13.361, 15.556, 15.721, 17.337, 25.31; the tranquil beauty of the life of the Enlightened One 7.33

compassion
the *anattā* doctrine is imbued with the Buddha's compassion 15.120; 'A being has arisen … out of compassion' 1.236; the basis of the bodhisattva ideal 3.363–5, 4.17–18; bequeathed the canonical literature out of compassion 14.271; boundless 13.566, 15.319; brings the Enlightened mind into communication with the unenlightened mind 2.58; the Buddha-Heart 25.173; it encompasses the whole universe 25.262; the Buddha's 'escape' from *nirvāṇa* back into *saṃsāra* 2.56–7; he cares for a monk with dysentery 4.11, 9.194–5, 10.260, 11.161, 14.414; did the Buddha always look upon living beings as upon an only son? 14.235–6; the golden Lotus of the Lord's Compassion 25.208; he saw everything as pure beauty because he saw everything with compassion 14.516; a heartfelt desire for the well-being of all beings 11.102; his compassion overflows without any consideration of merit 14.403; his mind was full of compassion 12.547; 'The Lord of Compassion' (poem) 25.202; so compassionate that the broken-hearted fled to him for refuge 2.26; deciding to teach the Dharma out of compassion, *see* Brahmā Sahāmpati's request; the guiding spirit behind his activities 1.236; his compassion as he looked out at the world from Vulture's Peak 7.431; his will to live was replaced by compassion 10.585; towards Kisāgotamī, *see* Kisāgotamī; concerned with the realities of the human situation 1.123; towards all those beings who are not yet Enlightened 1.180–1, 3.73, 9.234; unwavering 16.309; 'Whatever is to be done by a teacher with compassion … has been done by me' 1.180, 1.236, 3.670 (n287); the word gives just a glimmering of what the Buddha felt 19.429–30; wouldn't he want to be reborn in the world out of compassion? 4.205

fearlessness
among his outstanding characteristics 2.26; dismissed the monks who wanted to guard him 4.14, 12.216; he faced

hostility with a calm smile 11.492; he had the courage to face the forces of darkness and evil 12.529; how he overcame fear in the forest, *see under* Siddhārtha; only the Buddha is completely fearless 16.279; perhaps his fearlessness kept him from harm 4.15; in relation to Devadatta's attack on him 4.13–14; when threatened by a *yakkha* 10.453–4

generosity
the gifts he gave are incalculable 3.594; he and his disciples gave the Dharma freely 10.624; 'I am not one who has the closed fist of the teacher' 10.624; 'More than the seas he gave his blood, more than the stars his eyes' 1.430

gratitude
he was instinctively full of gratitude 3.609; towards his first two teachers 3.74, 3.597; towards his first five disciples 3.74, 3.597; towards the bodhi tree 3.74, 3.596

happiness
'the happiness which … arose in me could not obsess my mind' 2.108, 18.581; his happiness just after Enlightenment 10.469–70; people sought to learn the secret of his radiant happiness 3.315; he proved he was happier than a king 3.271–2

heroic qualities
he was of a prompt, decisive character, like a military commander 11.440–1; resemblance to a wheel-turning king 14.427–8; self-confidence 2.26, 10.471, 11.415, 11.492, 12.529; strong, fierce, even controversial 10.14

kindness and love
Ānanda and the Buddha's mutual kindness 3.90, 11.436–7; friend to all beings 17.327–8; friendly and informal 10.574; he asks Ānanda to reassure Cunda, who gave him his last meal 2.29, 3.118, 10.640–1; 'he who is so kind' 3.364, 4.17–18, 13.146, 11.436; his actions the spontaneous overflow of his love for sentient beings 22.285; love for all beings, knowledge of what is good for them, and resolve to help them 7.295; the original spiritual friend 26.634; the supreme exemplar of love for all humanity 12.343

knowledge
distinction between sphere of knowledge and sphere of influence 16.461; he has no views 2.391, 3.164, 3.549, 15.334; he knows the true nature of all things 17.328–9; how the Buddha knows the world and minds of sentient beings 14.144; the source of his authority 15.266–7

omniscience and infallibility
he did not claim infallibility 9.425; he never claimed to possess omniscience 1.78, 17.328; he was omniscient only with regard to the path to Enlightenment 17.463; he was spiritually omniscient, but scientifically ignorant 17.328–30; his 'omniscience finds room in the Great Book' 14.91; infallible but not omniscient or omnipotent 10.40, 13.566; omniscient in the sense of knowing whom to teach and what to teach them 17.369; *sarvajñā* (omniscient) 17.328; three kinds of omniscience 14.146

other qualities
'adorned with virtues' 17.326–7; aloneness 3.472; calm and controlled, like a perfectly trained elephant 10.458, 10.461, 11.492; character (Ambedkar) 9.148; characteristics 2.26, 4.11–17; common sense 2.26; dignity and affability, wisdom and kindliness 7.491, 11.491; the embodiment of the scientific spirit 7.160; greatness 1.50–6, 2.34; identical with emptiness 14.495; imperturbability 10.370; incomprehensibility 1.64; inconceivable 16.450, 22.124; inconceivable power (Mahāyāna) 14.218–19; infinitely wise 13.566; love of peace, solitude, and silence 4.15–16; patient 2.26; perfectly pure 13.566; qualities 1.286, 2.26, 13.566, 14.25; radiant personality 7.123; sense of humour 2.26, 14.49; sense of irony 10.514, 11.492, 12.33; transcendental innocence 14.240; virtues immeasurable 16.328

DESCRIPTIONS

his physical body
his human body and historical existence like rags thrown over his spiritual glory 1.264, 14.98; material existence 2.40–1; material or apparitional (early Buddhist views) 1.253–4; he didn't sleep much 10.573, 10.574; his appearance was very impressive due to his merit (Mahāyāna view) 4.20; his aura and what it represents 18.536–7; his 'elephant look' 4.706 (n313), 10.461, 12.157; his face as bright as a golden cloud (*Sukhāvatī-vyūha Sūtra*) 14.169; his humanity illustrated by his suffering from backache 3.184, 10.236, 14.239; his smile 4.137, 11.492, 26.385; imagining what the Buddha looked like 22.463; represented by the Buddhist flag 22.92; the result of karma 1.253; should be identified with the *dharmakāya*, not the physical body 13.150–1, 16.512; the 'thirty-two marks' 14.426–32; *ūrṇā* (between eyebrows), *see ūrṇā*

descriptions of his nature
all things to all men 2.647, 7.33, 12.523; animist 3.597–8, 10.453; embodiment and symbol of the truth 11.492–3; father to his disciples 2.138; gives guidance in doubt, support in crisis, impetus in stagnation 2.11; 'guide, philosopher, and friend' 7.124; he does not sit in judgement over people 11.263, 16.309–10, 17.662–3; a guide, not a leader 2.27, 3.63, 4.13, 9.305–6, 10.580, 14.541, 25.107; like an unexpected guest 1.508, 9.419, 11.238, 13.256, 18.430, 25.86–7, 26.494; he matures or ripens living beings 16.463, 19.24; he never asked anybody to have faith in him 3.562; he functioned vigorously as an unmistakably individual person 10.471, 17.625; he shines through the spiritual hierarchy 4.175; he was impatient with the formalistic element in religion 2.202; healer 10.555–6, 16.192–3; his genius lay in his imagination 8.579–80; the highest being in the universe 3.152, 12.134; his own greatest work of art 3.471; an infinitely wise and boundlessly compassionate Teacher 14.19; an initiator rather than laying something down once and for all 14.351; an irruption from a higher dimension into your ordinary life 25.87; the Julius Caesar of the spiritual life 12.529; king 3.48–9; living proof of the possibility of Enlightenment 15.197; one who speaks only to help beings 17.342; philosopher 7.196–8; physician 3.213, 7.115; pioneer 4.20, 4.21, 10.xxvii, 25.256–7; a poet 26.128, 26.386; a stranger in an ultimate sense 11.xvii, 11.43; superman 3.61–2; to say he was democratic is inapposite 8.462; a 'thinking Soul' 14.291; a true individual 11.358–9, 26.72; a unique being 7.227; a very mysterious, distant 'personality' 12.657; warrior 3.49–53, 12.529; was the Buddha a *bhikkhu*? 2.646–7

epithets and titles (A–Z)
akiñcana (man of naught) 1.173, 3.144, 10.486, 10.489; *arhant* 15.462–3; the awakened one 12.501; *Bhagavān* 12.529, 15.461–2; bull-man (*nārapuṃgava*) 4.469; conqueror of the three worlds 3.48; *dharmarāja* (King of the Law) 3.48, 13.149; the Elder Brother of Mankind 7.295, 10.252; the Good Friend 7.295–6; the great magician 10.497; the great physician 3.657 (n205), 7.115, 12.98, 12.710 (n70), 26.645; the great *yakkha* 10.451–2; Jina, 'Conqueror' 3.48, 11.407, 12.528–9, 14.404; *karmavādin* 7.121; the Leader 14.541; *Lokajyeṣṭha* (the first-born of the world) 3.61, 11.107–8, 12.530–1; *Lokavidu* (knower of the world) 12.528, 15.491–3; 'Lord Buddha' doesn't have the right sort of resonance 10.442–3; *Mahābhaiajya* (Great Physician) 16.192–3; *mahāpuruṣa* ('superman') 3.62, 14.426–7; *Mahāsamaṇa* 2.646, 12.522; Mahāvīra (Great Hero) 3.48, 12.529, 19.313; Mārajit (the conqueror of Māra) 3.52; *mārgadattā* (the shower of the way) 3.163, 9.97, 9.425, 9.474–5, 10.35, 10.150, 10.247, 11.359–60, 15.267, 15.546, 15.547–8, 26.181–2; *narasīha* or *narasiṃha* (lion among men) 4.469, 9.365, 11.383, 11.757 (n214); *pudgala* 17.631; *purisadamma-sārathi* (charioteer for the training of persons) 2.343, 2.706 (n419), 15.493, 17.466; Śākyamuni (sage of the Śākya tribe) 3.591; *śāntināyaka* (the one who leads to peace) 15.262, 15.267; *sarvajñā* (omniscient) 17.328; *satthā devamanussānam* (teacher of gods and men) 1.33, 3.69, 15.495–6, 25.402, 26.603; *śramaṇa* 3.93; *Sugata* (the happy one, the 'Well-Gone') 3.315, 10.198, 14.404, 14.548, 15.477–8; Tathāgata, *see* Tathāgata; the Trackless One 3.143, 4.21, 11.12; *varado* (the giver of the highest and best) 9.385; *varaharo* (the bringer of the highest and best) 9.385; *varaññū* (the one who knows) 9.385; *vibhajyavādin* (one who analyses) 4.335–6, 14.23; *vijjā-caraṇa-sampañña* (the one fully endowed with knowledge and practice) 2.127, 15.471–5

SYMBOLS AND MYTHS

images and symbols
animals that symbolize four events in his life and four great attributes 9.364–6; compared to the moon, which only appears to wax and wane 14.238; footprint, *see* *śrīpāda*; the golden drum 16.264; like a forest grove putting forth its flowers 15.65; like the full moon on a cloudless night or the sun shining in a clear blue sky 26.125; like a storm cloud pouring rain on the earth 26.126; his lion's roar 3.53, 9.365–6, 10.201, 11.383, 13.307, 16.125; Mount Sumeru 16.464; the newly arisen Buddha 'like a white pillar to the west' 26.210; a priceless jewel 9.262–3; the sun 16.464; symbolic representations before Buddha images were made 3.137–8, 7.123, 16.156, 26.476

myths and legends
archetypal symbolism in the biography of the Buddha 12.181–93; assumed in the West to be fictional 7.491, 11.15, 11.492; on the Buddha's Enlightenment, enemy animals mated and produced hybrid beasts 13.184–5; Brahmā Sahāmpati's request, *see*

Brahmā Sahāmpati; have their counterparts in the metaphors, similes, and parables of the *suttas* 14.42; he was escorted to earth down a jewelled staircase or ladder 11.15, 11.30, 12.185, 13.586; Mucalinda the serpent king, *see* Mucalinda; Sangharakshita's approach to the mythic element of the Buddha's life 24.537; some were illuminations from the impact of the Buddha's personality 7.492; some legends probably based on actual occurrences 7.492, 11.492; the story of his response to the Great Book of the Abhidharma 14.91; a story that the Buddha was eighteen feet tall 13.427; three categories of legend 2.32–8; the twin miracle, *see under* miracles; we come closest to the historical Buddha when we include the legendary 2.552–3, 11.15–16

(III) Communication

HOW HE COMMUNICATED AND WITH WHOM

introduction
the amount he communicated a handful of leaves, his knowledge a forest 4.3, 7.50, 25.xxxviii; *Buddhavacana*, *see Buddhavacana*; compassion brings Enlightened mind into communication with unenlightened 2.58; from the day of his Enlightenment he did not utter a word, *see Laṅkāvatāra Sūtra*/chapter 7; he means exactly what he says 14.302; he speaks the truth in the sense of ultimate reality 14.477–8; his speech was music 25.402; perhaps he didn't think of himself as teaching something called the Dharma 14.498; what the Buddha 'really said' 2.50–1; 'Whatever the Buddha said was well said' 3.168, 3.394–5, 7.434; 'Whatever is well said, that is the word of the Buddha', *see under Buddhavacana*

communicating his experience
although he uses ordinary language he is not misled by it 14.477; Buddhist philosophy began with his effort to communicate 8.498, 19.353–4; contact with human beings had to be made – so how did he do it? 3.182; had to use old words to describe a new experience 10.429–30, 11.512, 15.463; he found the linguistic resources of his day inadequate 14.14; he just hinted at it, pointed in its direction 14.318; he used the best words he could find 19.452; his awareness of the limitations of words 14.15–16; his desire to communicate 3.73–4; if he is to teach, he needs others to listen 11.277–8; the inadequacy of language to describe his experience 10.522, 19.429–30; levels of communication, of which words were the lowest level 3.79–81; more concerned with spiritual reality than the factual truth of references 2.65; revealing the Law that leads to Peace 25.181; teaching the *devas* 1.33, 4.16–17, 15.382, 26.635; what he communicated was essentially an experience 11.482, 19.403

his effect on the people he met
'Don't accept what I say just out of respect for me' 3.15; he adopted the appearance and language of those to whom he spoke 12.523; he influenced people more by what he was and did than what he said 4.8, 14.16, 26.46; he taught a great range of people 2.25, 3.76–7, 3.178, 3.330, 8.444, 10.483–7, 12.306, 12.511; he taught thousands of people, but in reality nothing had been said 13.348; he would put people at their ease 16.15; how he established communication with people 13.248–50; the kinds of people he taught, *see under* disciples/the Buddha's disciples; 'Let any reasonable man come to me, and I will teach him the Dharma' 3.562, 15.362; most people thought his principal function was to give blessings 10.497; not everyone was grateful to him 3.605–6; people were astounded and overwhelmed by him 2.291–2, 9.247, 12.306, 13.249–50; people who failed to recognize him 14.431–2; people used to be drawn to his teachings because of their life circumstances 4.351; Upāka's response, 'May it be so', *see* Upāka

responses to his teaching
'as if something had been set upright …' 2.291–2, 3.330, 10.553, 12.307, 13.249; Going for Refuge 11.383–4, 12.307; as though a great weight had been lifted 3.330; people gaining insight on hearing him teach 3.272; what he says opens up a new world 12.306; stories of some of his encounters 14.18–19; voice of Brahmā: each understands him in their own way 16.281–2; what his contemporaries thought of him 13.143

HIS WAYS OF COMMUNICATING

different methods of communication
a variety of methods 3.161, 11.161–2; he knows how to put things so that people will understand 10.243; concepts and images 4.144–8, 12.106, 12.503, 16.15–16, 16.416–17; everything he did would communicate his vision 11.162; simile and metaphor 8.621, 26.209; he could not read or write 9.271, 9.356, 10.229–30, 12.529, 14.18, 16.233; he wrote nothing, but taught orally, *see under* oral tradition; his use of words, *see under* words; holding

up a golden flower, *see under* flowers/golden flower; in silence 10.510–11, 11.162; *svākkhāto* ('well taught'), *see under Tiratana Vandanā*; in this world he must make use of ordinary human speech 14.207; public lectures: perhaps the Buddha invented them 10.551–2; through poetry 26.128, 26.386; we do not know what language he spoke 7.498

his style of communication
he did not speak *about* the Dharma, he simply spoke Dharma 17.159; he reveals himself and inspires the disciple to be his own Enlightened self 14.453; he seems to have been more able to communicate than his disciples 4.20–1; he spoke the cultural language of his day 10.430, 10.438–44, 10.465–8, 12.322, 16.367; he spoke the language of reason 16.417; he took great precautions against literalism 3.167, 8.620; he used ordinary language to explain what was happening 10.434; his lion's roar (*siṃhanāda*) 3.53, 9.365–6, 13.307, 16.125; his sense of irony 10.514, 11.492, 12.33; if he was asked a question three times, he would always answer 10.458–9, 10.462, 12.157; not 'teaching', just talking with the people he happens to meet 10.307, 12.306; what he communicated through his personality outweighed his words 14.296–7

THE BUDDHA AS TEACHER

the kind of teacher he was
he declares that he no more teaches than *śūnyatā* does (*Mahāparinirvāṇa Sūtra*) 14.239; for him to teach, people have to be listening 11.277–8; he knows whom to teach and what to teach them 17.369; his first five disciples, *see under* disciples/of the Buddha; 'All that a teacher could do have I done for you' 1.236, 3.53; his attitude towards women, *see under* women/in the Buddhist tradition; an infinitely wise and boundlessly compassionate teacher 14.19; only painting could do justice to his teaching career 2.25; the quality of his being transcends what he says 18.357

teaching methods
general description 3.330, 9.226; abstract terms 3.161; according to different needs 9.359; all the different ways he taught the Dharma 10.243–4; apparent severity to make a point 14.235–6; communicating his vision through concrete images 14.41–2; he created lists of teachings to make them easier to remember 10.230; he knew that a positive method of teaching was more appealing 1.62; he didn't wait for people to come to him 16.15; empirical, with a difference 1.59; graduated discourse or public lecture (*ānupubbi-kathā*) 8.592–3, 10.551–2; he encouraged his followers to think for themselves 16.553; he is said to have foreseen future disputes and laid down methods 14.85; gradual approach, *see* gradual; he often taught in response to questions 10.552, 15.80; he preferred the 'negative' method of determination 1.74; he taught orally, *see under* oral tradition; he tried to give existing beliefs and traditions a positive twist 1.62–3, 3.522–3, 15.380; his peremptory dismissal of a group of *bhikkhus* did them good 10.509–11; images 3.161; long expositions 3.161, 9.226; many of his teachings were Pith-Instructions 19.205–6; no one, not even the Buddha, can literally hand on their spiritual experience 13.161; one teaching at a time 16.75; poetry 9.226, 14.19; he presented the Dharma more often under the aspect of method than doctrine 1.123; Sāriputta rejoices in the way the Buddha teaches the Dharma 3.144, 3.648 (n144); short sayings 9.226; silence 3.161, 9.226, 13.393–4; skilful means 9.233–4; stories 3.161, 9.226, 10.596; 'intelligent people through a parable reach understanding' (*White Lotus Sūtra*) 12.110–11, 16.215; the *suttas* may suggest the Buddha's teaching style 10.552; words, *see under* words

TEACHINGS

what his teachings were for
he taught what would help people transcend suffering and attain Enlightenment 4.3; asking oneself why the Buddha taught a particular doctrine 1.7, 19.295; concerned with the development of the individual 26.39; only one aim: to point out the way to Enlightenment 13.566

the nature of the teaching
feeling through words, concepts, and images that which gives life to them all 16.126; he concentrated on 'doing it now', and spoke little about rebirth and karma 4.373; he gives Ānanda a list of practical teachings, nothing theoretical 11.369–70; he says his teaching is not to be paid for 3.76; he taught his disciples specific meditation practices 1.380, 12.466–7; he taught the spiritual life as essentially a willed process of becoming 7.204; his psychological teachings subtler and more comprehensive than Western ones 7.229; more concerned to describe the path than the goal 1.68; the message is simple, but has been elaborated for different people 18.495; nothing to teach 3.164, 3.549; very general, even abstract, and aimed at the intelligence

12.322; not abstract and general, but concrete and particular 7.225; not to be identified with any one formulation 16.126; original in the sense of never being out of date 1.55; they can never be reduced to a specific formula or set of doctrines 11.417; they cannot be abstracted from the context in which they arose 11.513

emphases
his early emphasis on the impermanent and conditioned nature of existence 15.180; the importance of the rational as well as the mystical approach 12.515–16; the need to maintain momentum in one's practice 3.305; truth and righteousness are more important than externals of religion 1.274; uncompromising insistence on personal realization of Nirvāṇa 2.202–3

some famous teachings
'The concentrated mind sees things as they really are', *see under* concentration; 'He who sees the Dharma sees me' 1.251, 3.150, 3.191, 7.493, 10.678–9 (n132); 'He who would serve me, let him serve the sick' 4.11, 9.195, 11.443; 'I teach only suffering and the cessation of suffering', *see under dukkha*/the Buddha; 'Test my words as the goldsmith tests gold in the fire', *see under* gold

responses and reflections
criteria for reliable teachings, *see* Mahāpajāpati Gotami; he taught some monks who committed suicide 3.346, 4.67, 4.360; his teachings didn't always lead to the arising of insight 10.534; how to distinguish between Māra's teaching and the Buddha's 14.237; the Theravāda concerned with what he said, the Mahāyāna with what he meant 7.541; the Abhidharma's systematization of his teaching 12.140–2; take the Buddha's statements poetically rather than scientifically 19.242; taking on trust only teachings about ultimate reality 17.33; fake Buddha quotes 8.128–9, 8.140–1, 8.493

see also
Buddhism I/ essential principles; Dharma II/teachings

(IV) Who is the Buddha?

responses to the buddha

perspectives
Buddhism's unity stems from the Buddha 11.690; Buddhists who have never heard of the Buddha 12.180–1, 12.507–8, 13.20–1; central figure of the Hīnayāna 1.262; described in the *Sūtra of Golden Light* 16.326; diminished by modern perspective 1.33; don't regard the Buddha as having come to a full stop called Buddhahood 10.615; enlisting the Buddha in support of one's own movement 8.180; his authority repudiated by the Hīnayāna 1.314–15; 'no man ever lived so godless yet so godlike': a paradox for Western admirers 4.90; 'scientific' view of the Buddha 1.33; shift of interest from the person of the Buddha to his teachings 3.191; 'a sort of oriental Jesus' 13.296–7; unknown in India in the 1940s 22.163–4; Victorian view 3.45

relating to the Buddha
be prepared to see the Buddha's footprints in unlikely places 25.33; being seen by the Buddha 14.479; 'Burn as a Fire for men!' 25.296; closeness to the Buddha comes from following his teachings 2.137–8; confession to the Buddha 16.313–14; disrespect to the Buddha 13.683 (n57), 16.303; don't take him for granted 11.277; gratitude towards the Buddha 3.609, 13.250–1, 13.255, 14.143; how to get a sense of the Buddha as your spiritual friend 26.634–7; if one is thinking of the Buddha, one is occupied with something positive 4.50; if you don't accept the Buddha as Buddha, better to leave his Dharma alone 7.310, 11.483; one should place one's reliance on the words of the Buddha 1.23; positive pride at being born into the family of the Buddha 4.275–6, 4.359; receptivity to the Buddha 4.7–8, 25.181; remembering the Buddha 9.478–9; Sangharakshita's sense of really being present in the Buddha's day 17.402–3; you follow his example, not commands or orders 15.266

praise of the Buddha
declared by Śāriputra to be the greatest of the Enlightened Ones 1.54, 1.293, 3.144; different ways of showing respect 4.295, 9.337; gratitude, *see under* gratitude; homage to the Buddha 1.179; honouring the Buddha 1.52, 15.629; 'How pleasant is thy shadow, O Śramaṇa!' 2.11; Piṅgiya's praises 1.288–9; recollecting his qualities 16.283; rejoicing in his merits 11.269, 16.326; in the *Sutta-Nipāta* 14.57; in the *Tiratana Vandanā*, *see Tiratana Vandanā*; hymn of praise in the *Vimalakīrti-nirdeśa* 16.466; hymns of praise in the *Sūtra of Golden Light* 16.246, 16.326, 16.328; tributes to the Buddha (Ambedkar) 9.148; true praise of the Buddha is praise for his attainment of Enlightenment 10.343; 'we should be very proud that there was such a person' 4.465

faith in the Buddha
acknowledging the Buddha as the Buddha prompts one to act 17.553–4; confidence

in the historical fact of his Enlightenment 11.482–3; contrasted with faith in God 1.38; as an Enlightened being 17.27–8; an emotional response, not just an intellectual assent 17.34–5; expressed in the Pāli canon 1.240; essential for spiritual development 1.290; the faith of the faith-follower and the doctrine-follower 17.35; faith in the Buddha is inseparable from faith in yourself 17.37; if your faith has faded, how are you going to get it back? 17.90; Going for Refuge to the Buddha, *see under* Going for Refuge; the merit of developing faith in his eternal life 14.127; the motivating power of the disciple's life 1.290; the principal object of the Buddhist's devotion 22.285; resorting to the Buddha 15.628–9; some Buddhists seem not to have faith in the Buddha 13.571; to have faith in the Buddha is to have faith in humanity 17.37

worshipping and respecting the Buddha
analogous to worship of the Creator in theistic religions 11.493; 'Before an image of the Buddha' 25.158–9; Buddha worship in the Mahāyāna 11.225–6; Buddhists worship him as an Enlightened being, not God 3.64, 3.152, 11.107, 12.527, 12.621; in his lifetime, his radiant personality served as a focus for devotion 7.123; different approaches, elaborate and simple 4.306–8; different people saluted him in different ways 4.295, 9.337, 11.250; do we revere him as a Buddha or see him as just one of us? 17.276–7; for devotional purposes the Buddha's attributes have to be allowed to stand 14.496; giving ourselves to the Buddha 11.223–4; 'He who would worship me, let him follow my teaching' 11.452–3, 13.146; his disciples 'sat to one side' 14.402; image worship, *see under* Buddha images; is it Gotama the Buddha to whom you go for Refuge? 15.588–90, 15.593, 15.628–9; is there not a better way of worshipping the Buddha? (*Vimalakīrti-nirdeśa*) 16.568–71; the *Mahāvastu* is suffused with an atmosphere of rejoicing in the Buddha 17.337; must go beyond the worship of his relics 14.144, 16.571; one truly honours him by honouring the Dharma 16.571; refusing to respect him: 'He is not more but differently developed' 17.606; serving the Buddha 25.124–5; spiritual projection 13.353; a stupa dedicated to the Buddha is better than one dedicated to world peace 14.447; in the *Sūtra of Golden Light* 16.326, 16.328; thinking of the Buddha as your baby 4.305; worship of the Buddha with incense 14.193

meditating on the Buddha
an occasion when the Buddha answered Sangharakshita's questions 22.301–2; recollection of the Buddha, *see* recollection of the Buddha; Queen Vaidehī's vision 1.332–4, 3.454–5, 3.571–2, 14.172–3, 20.464; visualizing the Buddha 1.251, 1.284, 3.516, 10.207

emulating the Buddha
the gap between him and ourselves can be closed 9.248; the gulf that separates us from the Buddha 3.181–2, 26.479; identifying with or imitating the Buddha 14.539–40, 19.54–6, 19.296; 'kinship with a star' 25.286; lessons from the life of the Buddha 10.255–60; no point saying you believe in the Buddha unless you try to close the gap 4.202; an ordinary person sees the Buddha as someone like himself 2.40; a man who married, had a child, then went forth, to emulate the Buddha 25.9–10, 26.562; something in oneself corresponds to what is fully developed in the Buddha 4.201–2; we have to will to be like the Buddha 11.651, 12.538, 26.62; we ourselves are the Buddha – potentially 3.152–3; what he did, we can do, if we make the effort 10.252–3; what the Buddha became, we too can become 2.272–3, 15.95–6

the example of the Buddha's life
because he was human we can learn from his life 10.255; exemplar of the other-regarding aspect of the spiritual life 4.5; he exemplified the bodhisattva ideal 4.222; he shows us what we can all become 3.393, 9.418–19; his living example 16.15; how literally to follow his example? 19.54–6; it is vital that he becomes a living figure and exemplar for us 11.690; lessons from the life of the Buddha 3.34–43, 10.254–60; monastic interpretation of his teaching ignored his personal example 2.205; we can follow in his footsteps 16.495

WHO IS THE BUDDHA?

knowing the Buddha
in what sense do we know the Buddha? 3.139, 12.531–2; knowing the Buddha means knowing the mind in its Unconditioned state 3.152; Śāriputra makes a claim about the Buddha's nature and is challenged 1.54, 1.293, 3.144; we speak of him in familiar terms, but this is a sort of profanity 3.181–2

identifying him
an author who sees the Buddha as a messenger from God, like Mohammed 26.690–1; best to read about his life,

not do a lot of subtle theorizing 14.430; the Buddha transcends all conditionings 3.142–3; he cannot be classified 3.141–5; a third category missing from Western thought 3.152, 12.527, 12.621–2, 14.430, 23.178; 'deification' 7.492, 7.535–7, 11.106, 11.492–3, 12.527; did he project a human form from the Tuṣita heaven? 14.86; different from others not in kind, but in degree of development 3.60–1; distinguished from Jesus, Mohammed, and Krishna 9.94–9, 10.33–40; an entirely new species of being 3.478; even to call him *a* Buddha is inaccurate 14.583; to be identified with the *dharmakāya*, not the physical body 16.512; he transcends the subject–object distinction 12.530–1; an independent category of existence 11.107–8; Lokottaravādin view that he was wholly transcendental, *see under* Lokottaravādins; our conception of him must do justice to him as the unconditioned Absolute 14.430; people who fail to recognize him 14.431–2; we try to categorize him by applying to him terms we already know 12.526–8; words could never fully express what he was 4.7; you can neither say that he is alive, nor that he is dead 4.206

a human being
an account of the Buddha's backache reveals his humanity 3.184, 10.236, 14.239; Dr Ambedkar's view 9.94–7; an extraordinary human being 10.242–3, 14.239, 11.114; not 'just a man' 3.61, 3.151, 9.212, 10.234, 11.105–6, 12.527, 12.622, 22.124; when asked 'Are you a human being?', he said 'No' 3.141, 13.297, 14.582; from his appearance, no wonder some people didn't recognize him 22.463; a great message of hope 10.235–6; he is the exemplar of what a human being can be 11.310; the highest being in the universe is an Enlightened human being 15.81; his Enlightened humanity had undreamt-of dimensions 22.321; the human embodiment of insight, freedom, happiness, and love 13.298; the living embodiment of the highest human perfection 11.384–5; in the notion of Buddha, humanity and the absolute coalesce 13.297; the most important thing to realize about him is that he was human 12.134; regarded as such in the Hīnayāna 1.250; to have faith in him is to have faith in humanity 17.37; who gained Enlightenment by his own efforts 9.18, 9.265, 9.474, 10.103, 11.107, 16.495; who has become one with reality 12.8–9

he was not God or a god
although he is responsible for the spiritual welfare of the universe 16.460; the Buddha cannot save you, but shows you how to save yourself 9.212; the Buddha has no power to punish 15.621; and did not ask anybody to regard him as such 3.562, 12.134; compared with Jesus 12.592–3; confusion between the Buddha and God 11.253, 15.621, 16.309–10; no point in getting rid of the old god and installing the Buddha as a new one 9.418; not a god or a spiritual dictator 7.124; 'the God who did not create the universe' 2.129; he didn't claim divine authority 10.35–6; in Buddhism the distinction between God and man is false 10.234; a *mārgadatta* (shower of the way), not a *mokṣadattā* (Ambedkar) 10.35; not an *avatāra* of Vishnu 3.151–2, 3.325, 7.228, 9.18, 9.46, 9.265, 9.365, 9.474, 10.235; not central to Buddhism doctrinally in the way Jesus is to Christianity 15.266; not 'the Great Gawd Budd' 12.527; simply a man who differed from others not in kind but in degree 7.227–8; so why do Buddhists worship him? 11.107, 11.492–3, 12.527, 12.621; Westerners try to fill a God-shaped space 3.151–2, 13.566; the *White Lotus Sūtra* is not suggesting theism 14.130–1

other things he was not
not an agnostic, or social reformer, or humanitarian 1.80, 7.310, 8.180, 11.483; not a rationalist like Bertrand Russell 12.618; not a religious reformer like Luther 12.618; not just an ethical teacher 7.228, 12.134; not just a philosopher or wise man 3.164, 3.325; not just a social reformer 8.205; not a scholarly intellectual delivering lists of terms and definitions 15.250; not a sort of boss or party leader 10.580–1; not a spiritual dictator 7.124; the theories about what he was are to be dismissed as impertinent 11.493

conclusions about who the Buddha was
his achievement 9.95–7; analogy with cultural hero 3.60; a balance between the historical Buddha and the archetypal Buddha 16.207–8; breaking through without a guide 1.52; the Buddha *is* Buddhism 4.8; he discovered, or rediscovered, the Dharma 1.55, 3.4, 7.254, 8.201, 19.313; he found the path to the ancient city 1.53–4, 3.18, 11.408–9; he can't fully express his realization due to the limitations of history 4.191; he exists on the level of time, eternity, and the archetypal level in between 4.204; he is known to be a symbol of Enlightenment, but how do we know that? 13.119; he represents a higher evolutionary development 12.622; he saw things not in a limited or distorted way, but as they are 12.547; his attainment a

confirmation of a law which acts wherever conditions permit 1.55; the Buddha of the present 1.44–5; he dominates the entire history of Buddhism 2.11; the earthly reflex of Amitābha 2.177; embodiment and symbol of the truth 11.492–3; the historicity of the Buddha 11.482, 13.570–1; the living embodiment of the spiritual ideal 7.485, 9.249, 11.101; the most successful propagandist the world has ever seen 2.25; one who has reached the Unconditioned 16.328; originator of the Perfection of Wisdom tradition 3.358–9; the path he revealed was unknown to the other religious teachers of his time 7.227; reality is fully realized by the Buddha and revealed in and through him 2.43

see also
Ānanda/his friendship with the Buddha; *Laṅkāvatāra Sūtra*/the Buddha laughed; caste system/the Buddha; Buddha images; three *āsravas*/destruction of the *āsravas*; Devadatta/Devadatta and the Buddha; *arhants*/distinction from the Buddha; Going for Refuge/Going for Refuge to the Buddha; Siddhārtha Gautama/going forth; Vishnu/Hindu claim that he was an incarnation of Vishnu; Mahāyāna/teachings and practices/historical Buddha in the Mahāyāna; images/Buddha; insight/sources of inspiration; logic; supernormal powers; Mahāyāna/doctrines/Mahāyāna view of the Buddha; Mahāyāna *sūtras*; miracles; *trikāya*/*nirmāṇakāya*; Nirvāṇa; parables and stories; Śākya Seng-ge; Śākyamuni; Suddhodana; Sumedha; Tathāgata/ten powers; threefold knowledge; undetermined questions; Vulture's Peak; five heinous crimes/wounding the Buddha

'Buddha and the Future of His Religion' *see under* Dr Ambedkar/publications

Buddha and His Dhamma *see under* Dr Ambedkar/publications

Buddha Day *see under* festivals

Buddha images

significance
can art convey the Buddha's experience? 26.598–9; the coalescence of the meaning of Buddhism and the value of art 26.116; depictions of the supreme beauty of human spiritual reality 26.384; 'the face, they say, of the Enlightened One' 26.391; the image *par excellence* of the Wisdom of the East 7.485; in popular Buddhism, a source of blessing and magical protection 2.229–30; an image will give us a better idea of Buddhahood than an abstract definition 13.284–5; the interiority of the Buddha image 26.390; it's significant that the most characteristic form is in meditation posture 8.254; not naturalistic, but an attempt to convey the nature of Enlightenment 8.262–3; one of the best known of all the religious symbols of mankind 4.641; people aren't always clear why we have Buddha images 18.430–1; they give us an opportunity of developing devotional feelings 18.431; they show us what we can become 9.418–19, 9.460, 18.431; what the image of the Buddha conveys 11.98

history
Buddhist Sculptures and Monuments 8.349, 8.366–7; the Buddha was not depicted in the years after the *parinirvāṇa* 16.155–6, 18.431, 26.476; people felt that the Buddha could not be represented 3.137–8, 13.148–9; the idea was to convey that the Buddha was a transcendental being 12.530; the first appearance of the Buddha image 13.251; a carving mentioned in commentarial literature 2.221–2; depicted with the gods of the Hindu pantheon waiting on him 18.25; first introduced among the Sarvāstivādins of Mathura 2.222; early Mahāyāna figures perhaps modelled on images of *yakkhas* 10.452; Mathuran sculptures 2.222, 3.53–4; Graeco-Roman Buddhas 25.326; Gandhāran sculptures 3.51, 3.53, 7.396, 16.190, 22.124; Khmer style 3.300; the different cultural styles can be of great doctrinal significance 7.396; destruction of images 21.45, 21.622 (n10), 25.32, 26.475–9; how will Western Buddhists treat images? 4.304

particular images
Ahicchatra image of Maitreya 2.156; angular Buddhas with multi-coloured haloes 22.350; Buddha image in Nagpur (1954) 22.156–7; the Buddhas of Bamiyan 21.45, 21.622 (n10), 26.475–9; Nandalal Bose's painting *Buddha as Ascetic* 26.635–6; a controversial Japanese image at Bodh Gaya 8.51–3, 8.60–1; a golden Buddha in a Tibetan monastery 7.74–6; an image that shone with a green light 14.464, 19.327–8, 21.460; images of the emaciated Siddhārtha 3.51, 15.353; ivory and sandalwood figures in the shops in Delhi 23.334; Maitreya statue at Ghoom 20.134; meditating Buddha statue at Shantiniketan 22.54; a standing Buddha given by Lama Govinda (photograph) 22.6–7; standing Buddhas at Kanheri Caves 20.382, 23.334; Thai paintings in which the Buddha's disciples are identical to him 2.647, 14.567; two *rūpas* that created a strong atmosphere in a London flat 14.463; images owned by Sangharakshita 21.261; images made

by Triratna artists 9.382, 11.621; at the London Buddhist Centre, *see under* London Buddhist Centre

responses to Buddha images
at the beginning we may find that the Buddha image is not a symbol for us 13.122; the Buddha's face speaks to people who have never heard of Buddhism 26.384; don't feel obliged to be inspired just because it's labelled a Buddhist image 19.349; finding another way of connecting 4.196, 5.617; for some people, the Buddha image *is* Buddhism 13.251; images that leave you cold 4.100, 5.617; 'the mind becomes purified if it looks at this picture for a few minutes' 7.161; people whose lives have been changed after seeing a Buddha image 12.624; really trying to get a feeling for what the image represents 2.273; the response of the French nun to an image in the Guimet 3.300, 22.48, 26.116; they can give rise to faith 3.300

worship and respect
worship emerged comparatively late in the Buddhist tradition 2.221–2, 4.298; unclear whether popular worship arose from within or outside Buddhism 2.219; images should be treated with care 1.407, 4.327; images treated as a living person 4.302–4; 'life force' of images that have been worshipped 4.304–5; *The Parable of the Talking Buddha* (short story) 25.540–3; 'They gilded Him till He was sick with gold' 25.296; will Western Buddhists retain image worship? 4.298–9; choosing a beautiful Buddha image for a shrine 11.232; showing only part of the Buddha's body regarded as wounding him 21.56–7; superstitions about breaking a Buddha image 22.7–8; Tibetans' great respect for images 13.107; used as decorations by people with no interest in the Dharma 19.477

making images
artists who don't use the correct *mudrās* 8.132; embodying the Buddha in aesthetically pleasing and inspiring forms 15.351; the 'life-establishing' ceremony, including the painting in of the eyes 14.464; make sure their form does justice to their content 15.353; a modern trend towards depictions with no spiritual significance 8.263; protest against Hindu-influenced depictions of the Buddha 8.131–3; they are usually idealized 11.691

Buddha 'families' *see under* Buddhas

Buddha Jayanti *see* festivals

Buddha Maharaj (Ramakrishna Mission) 20.141, 20.386–7

Buddha nature 'All beings possess the Buddha nature' 14.239; the Dharma is the means to awaken us to our dormant Buddha nature 7.313; 'If one does not know the Buddha nature one cannot be called a man' 14.238; no-nature is Buddha nature 2.676 (n132); one Buddha nature functioning on three levels: the *trikāya* 4.204; one Buddha nature with many aspects and many forms 4.247; the Buddha nature within oneself clamouring for recognition 4.270–1; exists potentially in every living being 7.312–13; 'Has a dog Buddha nature?' 8.499, 13.356; in the *Laṅkāvatāra Sūtra* 14.215; in the *Mahāparinirvāṇa Sūtra* 14.237–8; in a sense innate within us, but we have to follow a path to realize it 4.9; mirrored in the depths of everything 7.317; extremely subtle 14.237; its compassion aspect brought out in the *tulku* doctrine 7.397; Mr Chen's vow to connect with those who had cut themselves off from their Buddha nature 4.275; penetrating your own true nature, you emerge into Buddhahood 12.234; realized when the energy of which we are the expression no longer craves manifestation 2.100; reflected in every natural object 20.102; seeing one's friend's Buddha nature 4.176; 'This very body the Buddha' 16.37; within us all 26.385; the *yidam* is the practitioner's particular expression of Buddha-nature 8.531; 'you' and not 'you' – a great paradox 4.271

Buddhabhadra (translator) 14.217, 14.231

Buddhacarita *see under* Aśvaghoṣa

Buddhadasa, Bhikkhu (Thailand) 6.621

Buddhadasa, Dharmachari 11.518, 11.729, 24.xix–xxvii, v24, 26.549

Buddhadatta, A. P. 7.445, 7.616 (n484), 17.632

Buddha-field (*buddha-kṣetra*) *see* Pure Land

Buddhafield festival a safe place for children 11.709; Sangharakshita speaks at the festival 11.xix–xx, 11.706–12

Buddhaghosa

introduction
brief biography 3.289–90, 15.645; a native of India, but lived and worked in Sri Lanka 12.143, 17.447; his right to be called the Voice of the Buddha 1.99; his writing guards against the dangers of spiritual individualism 1.233; paradoxes 7.133; *Buddhaghosuppatti* (biography) 15.645, 15.773 (n254)

VISUDDHIMAGGA ('PATH OF PURITY')

introduction
a collection of all the Buddha's teachings on meditation 17.441; a complete exposition of Theravāda teaching 3.290; based on the seven *visuddhis* 10.578; evidently in Buddhaghosa's day the practice of meditation had almost died out 15.734–5; Buddhaghosa aspires to attain arhantship in Maitreya's presence 2.178; its double framework 4.645; translations 3.668 (n273); Dharmapala and the *Visuddhimagga* 8.34, 8.91, 8.102

on meditation in general
antidotes to the hindrances to meditation 15.171; for one busy with recitations, books are an impediment to *samādhi* 2.201; forty *kammaṭṭhānas* 1.154–61, 4.519, 13.409; a passage that became a sort of initiation 15.733–5; the section on *samādhi* particularly useful 2.552; two meditation practices suitable for everyone 5.390–1; we must know exactly what we need to do to help us go forward 12.280–1; formless *dhyānas* 1.638 (n456)

five meditation factors
pīti or *prīti* 3.288, 9.297; *vitarka* and *vicāra* 9.200, 16.601 (n119), 17.518, 17.689

the brahma vihāras
introduction 3.628 (n16), 4.710 (n337), 5.196, 9.537; called the four infinitudes 5.215; *mettā bhāvanā* 3.676 (n313), 3.685 (n382), 4.74, 5.36, 5.148, 5.181–2, 15.300; was Buddhaghosa wrong to correlate them with the *dhyānas*? 5.274

the mindfulness of breathing
method 3.676 (n312), 9.516; keeping the mind on the breath like tethering a calf with a rope 15.106; like a carpenter keeping his attention on one spot 15.107

other meditations
contemplation of the decomposition of a corpse 4.536; contemplation of the four elements 1.160–1, 15.133; *kasiṇa* practice 5.568; the loathsomeness of food 2.65, 15.129, 24.725 (n573); ten recollections (*anusattis*) 1.155, 4.701–2 (n279), 11.306

character types
Buddhaghosa's descriptions show he might have made a good novelist 12.279; the habits of those of different temperaments 21.624 (n31); how those of different character types relate to insight 18.577; how they walk, eat, speak, dress, and sweep a floor 10.172, 12.279–80; linked with three kinds of experience of the world 12.279; meditation according to character type 2.83–4, 4.518–19, 5.390–1, 12.280; the types mustn't be taken too rigidly 5.390–1; seven kinds of follower, *see* seven kinds of follower; six kinds of temperament 4.710 (n335), 5.46, 5.709 (n37)

greed type (lobhacaritra)
description 17.602–3; artistic temperament 21.496; attracted to the Unconditioned 18.580; contemplation of decay helpful for greed types 2.83, 12.280, 18.561; greed types and complacency 13.139; the kinship between faith and greed 17.42–3; Rechungpa as a greed type 18.561; the refined version is the faith type 17.603

hate type (dveṣacaritra)
description 17.603; affinity with wisdom 4.392–3, 13.133, 18.577, 26.478–9; should practise the *mettā bhāvanā* 10.173, 12.280; *kaṣina* meditation suitable for hate types 2.83; the refined version is the wisdom type 17.603; repelled by *saṃsāra* 18.580; susceptibility to complacency 13.139

deluded type
description 17.603; should practise the mindfulness of breathing 12.280; finds it difficult to get into *dhyāna* and difficult to get out 18.577; 'has formerly drunk a lot of intoxicants ...' 2.673 (n102); the refined version is the 'intelligence type' 17.603

on monastic life
assertions that represent a *reducto ad absurdum* of Vinaya rules 2.630; the eighteen faults of a monastery 2.201; medicine: urine and gallnuts 16.620 (n276); 'one-mealer' 2.630

other teachings
on anger 8.78–9; definition of *dhammas* 1.97–8; the difference between disgust and withdrawal: getting rid of the snake 2.115–16; the digestive processes 2.65; Enlightenment does not involve a transition of a real person 1.268; five spiritual faculties 9.571 (n348); 'He who is concentrated sees what really is' 1.87; mindfulness is useful everywhere 17.85; grasping a poisonous snake: metaphor for the *lakṣaṇas* 3.276; the eight worldly winds 3.650 (n155), 3.668 (n272); the ten ways of skilful actions 11.309; morality giving precedence to self, the world, the Dharma 11.325; mistaking a snake for a fish: metaphor to describe *nibbidā* (disgust) 2.116; near and far enemies 3.690 (n443); the power of virtue 11.320–1; *pratītya-samutpāda* 1.117–18, 1.120, 7.198–9, 7.200–1; story of an equanimous

decision as to who should be sacrificed to bandits 15.322; ten impurities 1.155; three *vimokṣas* 3.219, 3.658 (n213); 'No doer of the deed is found' 1.103–4, 3.656 (n193); the *Tiratana Vandanā* 19.600 (n60); the wheel of life 13.680–1 (n49); wisdom disperses the darkness of delusion 17.131–2; 'The worldling is like a madman' 4.711 (n342), 5.659, 12.229, 16.192–3, 26.75

COMMENTARIES

Aṭṭhasalini (The Expositor, commentary on the Dhammasaṅgaṇi)
the Buddha teaches the Abhidharma to his mother, then to Sāriputta 12.714–15 (n102), 14.76; the Buddha creates a number of mind-formed Buddhas 1.255; connotations of wisdom 17.130–1, 17.726 (n131–4); description of *sukha* 2.107–8, 17.518; five kinds of *prīti* 2.106; five *niyamas* 2.672 (n96), 3.644 (n113), 3.672 (n296), 16.422; four wonderful and marvellous things 14.24–5; *prajñā* as analytical appreciative understanding 17.767 (n483); the story of the Buddha's response to the Great Book of the Abhidharma 14.91; *vedalla suttas* 14.25

Majjhima Nikāya commentary
a passage on the Refuges 15.627–9; alternative formulas for Going for Refuge 15.696; a bit too cut and dried 15.690; his very broad definition of the Dharma 15.630–1, 15.646; *Satipaṭṭhāna Sutta* 15.106–7, 15.169–70, 15.226, 15.235

Paramatthajotikā (The Illustrator of Ultimate Meaning)
a seven-year-old *śrāmaṇera* answers the question 'What is the one thing?' 10.230–1, 13.31

Sumaṅgala-Vilāsinī
the Buddha's daily habits 15.381–2; infinite radiant consciousness identical with Nirvāṇa 2.130

other commentaries
he identified *veyyākaraṇa* with the Abhidhamma Piṭaka 14.24; *visabhāga-paṭibhāga* and *sadisa-paṭibhāga* 1.120, 7.200–1; *Kathā-vatthu* commentary 14.85; *Nidānakathā* (commentary on the *Jātakas*) 2.13, 12.182; Abhidharma commentary 12.143

Buddhahood

its qualities
Amitābha: Buddhahood in the most beautiful and adorable form conceivable 1.325, 2.554; the archetypal Buddhas all represent the same ideal 19.404–5; both immanent and transcendent 25.33; an image gives a better idea than an abstract definition 13.284–5; in its essence it has no beginning 18.94; reflected in everything 7.312–13, 7.317

and all beings
all beings are in possession of the Element of Buddhahood 1.283–4; all sentient beings are capable of Buddhahood 13.135; a hierarchy between Buddhahood and unenlightened humanity 1.49, 3.410–11; 'How is it that we have not already attained Buddhahood?' (Gampopa) 13.138; it exists within the spiritual aspirant as the impulse behind their quest 7.312; it has a special correspondence with the human condition 2.96; it may be immanent in potential, but we still have to make the effort to realize it 4.33; the Mahāyāna maintained that every Buddhist ought to aspire to it 1.214; reflected in the heart of every sentient being 7.400; we don't have potential for evil in the way we have potential for Buddhahood 16.305; 'when to the eternal life of Buddhahood we all awake' 23.446

how to attain it
all the ways are different aspects of the path to it 16.76; attained with a fraction of the effort expended over millions of years of rebirths 4.629; if anyone offers a single flower, they are in principle on the path to it 14.114, 16.41; 'If you want Buddhahood, forget all pleasures of this life' 19.585; it's not an entity 'out there' ready to be grasped 14.143; it's ridiculous for the mind to try to realize it 13.364; its gradual flowering 3.481; the one thing to be concerned with: your resolve to gain it 19.131; 'Seeing into one's own nature and realizing Buddhahood' 12.234; to be gained by the actual practice of the six perfections, not abstract contemplation 7.329; *see also under* Enlightenment/ Enlightenment itself

reflections
a Buddha doesn't have to justify his Buddhahood 18.122; the danger of appropriating it as a mental possession 19.98; experiencing the eternal life of Buddhahood 4.331; as a goal, it can be understood in temporal as well as spatial terms 4.33; it exists not in time, but in eternity 4.204, 12.234; 'May I lead all beings to Buddhahood' (bodhisattva vow) 4.83, 14.411–12; no reason for regarding the *arhant* ideal as different from the ideal of Buddhahood 1.179; terms like 'Buddhahood' can be used

only provisionally 13.348; a theoretical concept of it superimposed on the ego has disastrous results 2.97

Buddha-kappas 1.44–5

buddha-kṣetra *see* Pure Land

Buddha-lands *see* Pure Land

Buddhamitra 13.341

Buddhanandi 13.341

Buddha-nature *see* Buddha nature

Buddhapālita (Madhyamaka school) 1.321

Buddhapalita, Dharmachari v24

Buddha-pride *see under* pride

Buddharakkhita, Thera *Dhammapada* (trans.) 8.385–6

Buddharakshita (previously Rabindra Banerjee, Satyapriya)

character
'everything to him was black or white' 20.158, 20.300; mischievousness 20.201; over-sensitivity to differences of opinion 20.306–7, 20.378–9; outspoken about caste prejudice 20.147, 20.194–8, 20.200–1, 20.212–13; sensitivity to slights 20.163; strong tendency to anger 20.302–3, 20.317, 20.378–9, 20.392–3, 24.41, 26.492; truth-loving nature tending to censoriousness 20.152

his spiritual life
brahmin background 20.146–7, 20.158–9; renouncing the view that Buddhism was a branch of Hinduism 20.158–9; given the name Satyapriya by Anandamayi 20.207; conducts *bhajans* at Muvattupuzha ashram 20.291; ambitious programme of spiritual activities 20.300–1, 20.303; was his mental balance affected by his spiritual practices? 20.316–18; enamoured of Spiritualism 20.351–3; attempts but fails to observe silence 20.376–8; ordained as Buddharakshita 20.410

his life after ordination
administers Refuges and Precepts for the first time 20.425–6; continues to struggle to control anger after ordination 20.443–4, 26.492; effect of the practice of *prāṇāyāma* 23.17; gives a Dharma talk after his first almsround 20.417; reproves a Nepalese nun for speaking Hindi incorrectly 20.433–4; what he did after leaving Sangharakshita in Benares 20.452, 22.231–2; in Burma 21.438, 22.232; Khantipālo's teacher 12.647

friendship with Sangharakshita
'an attraction of opposites' 20.153; decision to lead life together 20.159, 23.12; a strong mutual attachment 20.160; their travels together in India 20.227–444; a visit to his home village, at risk of caste pollution 20.161–2; together at Anandamayi's ashram 20.193–210; Satyapriya asks to be taught better writing style 20.261–2; his views about caste and Hinduism affect their friendship 20.279–80; he undermines a talk, to Sangharakshita's mortification 20.294–5; he is violent towards Sangharakshita 20.316, 20.379; personal differences become acute, to mutual distress 20.318; photographs 20.148, 20.290, 20.412, 20.431; Swami Ramdas stresses the need for brotherly love between them 20.324–5; he accompanies Sangharakshita on the quest for ordination 20.388–413; parting 20.443–4, 23.16–17; gratitude towards him 20.444

Buddhas

the meaning of the word Buddha
'awakened' 10.445, 10.554; even the notion 'Buddha' is a limitation in respect of the ultimate spiritual ideal 16.27; it once had a more general meaning than it later assumed 10.429–30, 10.445, 10.555, 15.463–4; a mere word 1.308; the old meaning of the word 'Buddha' 9.480; not a name but a title 7.227, 11.511, 12.131, 12.528; 'one who knows' 11.511, 14.342

all Buddhas
are the embodiment of the highest ideal of spiritual life 2.153; are manifestations of the Great Void, and not different from each other 21.559; are phenomena of the unconditioned reality of absolute mind 2.67; are within you 19.40–2; gain Enlightenment through Perfect Wisdom 14.363–4; in a manner of speaking are identical 19.43; teach the same thing,

because they have all realized the same reality 14.474; 'when they started on their way ... were not quite free from passions ...' 4.49–50

the Buddhas of the three times: past, present, and future
the Buddhas of the Three Eras 11.246; Dīpaṅkara, Gautama, and Maitreya 1.44; giving alms with *mahākaruṇā* is equal to serving the Buddhas of the three times 19.537; represented by Green Tārā's blue lotuses 13.69; in the *Tiratana Vandanā* 15.498; visualized on the Refuge Tree 13.78, 13.205

archetypal Buddhas
appear in different forms in the Mahāyāna tradition 7.505–6; different forms like the rainbow when light passes through a prism 1.261; entry into the realm of undefined meanings 16.532; having meditated on them, one will not shrink from their radiance after death 23.93; the historical Buddha was overshadowed by them in the Mahāyāna 16.207–8; a personification of the principle in accordance with which Buddhas become Buddhas 19.316; Buddhahood as realized in an ideal manner 19.404–5

Buddha 'families'
systems of classification vary 1.263; the complex system on which Vajrayāna practice is based 2.172; meditating on different figures within the same family 5.610–11; the *sambhogakāya* classified into five Buddha 'families' 1.263, 2.172, 4.206–7

eternal Buddhas
Buddhahood in its essence has no beginning 18.94; compassion embraces the whole universe 2.128, 25.262; eternally Enlightened 1.250; teach the Mahāyāna *sūtras* 16.241; in the *White Lotus Sūtra, see under White Lotus Sūtra/* doctrines

primordial Buddhas
Abundant Treasures 16.152; all personalities are embraced by the primordial (*ādi*)-Buddha 7.304; *see also* Ādibuddha

appearance
a rare event 1.44, 1.327; not limited to present world-period or world-system 1.338–9; they appear to different beings in different ways 1.261; they appear to others as a child, a madman, a ghost 11.11–12; when the way to Enlightenment has been lost 8.201, 12.318–19

many Buddhas
an infinity or plurality of Buddhas 1.43–50, 11.246, 14.583, 16.460; in number incalculable as the sands of the Ganges 1.43–4; it's not possible for one person, even a Buddha, to embody all aspects of the ideal 18.221–2; *relatively* unique: there have been other Buddhas before and there will be others after 12.593; visualizing the innumerable Buddhas 14.193

only one Buddha
how can Padmasambhava be a 'second Buddha?' 12.318–19; there's really only one Buddha 4.247; why there can only be one Buddha in a world system at any time 19.312–16, 26.699; you can think of the whole of existence as one great Buddha 4.589

lineage of twenty-nine Buddhas
the Theravādin tradition 1.45; the *Diamond Sūtra*'s declaration that the succession is empty 14.453

the pattern of a Buddha's career
the life of every Buddha follows a standard pattern 4.59, 10.546–9; he is born fully conscious of his past lives and his future greatness 1.256; born not for his own sake, but for the sake of all beings 1.50; he discovers the path to Nirvāṇa by his own efforts 7.227, 12.321–2; his cosmic function: rediscoverer of the Way 1.253, 8.201–2, 15.498, 19.313; the Manu prepares the way for the Buddha 12.321; twelve great acts in a Buddha's life 4.59, 4.670 (n74), 14.25; vowing to see all the incidents in the career of a Buddha 4.58–9

what makes a Buddha a Buddha
eighteen special qualities or attributes of a Buddha 3.144, 14.448–9; he is the inheritor of the results of actions performed during many lives 1.49; Perfect Wisdom 14.343; the union of the highest

conscious thought and the acme of thought-expressive activity 7.138–9

characteristics
a Buddha's characteristics 11.11–12; eight qualities 1.401; eternal happiness radiated by all the Buddhas 8.452; in a Buddha's attributes there is nothing that is not wonderful 11.43; the dignity of the Enlightened person 4.14; may appear remote, even a little unreal 2.214; omniscience 1.339, 17.328; the power of non-discrimination: the compassion of all the Buddhas 1.347; three kinds: those in whom wisdom, or love, or activity predominate 12.512

truths about Buddhas
a Buddha's work is never done once and for all 15.498–500; it is against the nature of things that a Buddha should be killed 4.14; a Buddha becomes his own refuge 19.316; a Buddha doesn't have to justify his Buddhahood 18.122; a Buddha gains something when others become Enlightened 18.216; a Buddha has the same attitude of *mettā* towards beings whatever they do 15.319–20; his inner experience is expressed in what he is and does, then in what he says 4.7; if you are a Buddha, you are a Buddha all the time 19.230–1; they can be 'seen' only in the way that *śūnyatā* is to be 'realized' 1.307; Reality itself in human form 3.149; they are protectors 11.252, 17.561; they are the unconditioned absolute reality 2.43; they are the vehicle for the rediscovery of universal consciousness 1.48; they render the attainment of Nirvāṇa practicable 1.51; they reveal their true self if they are praised 4.176; when a Buddha 'thinks', Perfect Wisdom comes into operation 14.536–7; when you hurt beings, you indirectly cause sorrow to the Buddhas 4.435

doctrines about Buddhas
Absolute and relative Buddha 14.211–12; 'Cosmic Person' (*puruṣa*) 4.589–90; the Mahāyāna conception of the Buddha-nature 1.250; *nimitta* (mind-made) Buddhas 1.255–6; their nature is wholly transcendental (Lokottaravādin doctrine) 1.189–90; view that the Buddha is not merely a human being, but reality itself 1.250

all beings are potentially Buddhas
'All beings are from the very beginning the Buddha' 1.269, 2.742 (n682), 18.44–5, 19.537; Enlightenment is within us all, but shrouded by ignorance 3.340; the logical corollary of the bodhisattva ideal 1.274; all *will* attain Enlightenment (in the language of eternity) 1.274; not much point thinking that in your ultimate mind you are Buddha if it's just words 19.284; unknowingly a Buddha from the very beginning 18.44–5; waking up to the fact that you are Buddha 12.234, 13.364; we can become Buddhas if we make the necessary effort 19.97–8

Buddhas and us
'The bigger the heap of mud, the bigger the Buddha' 4.467, 25.73; don't think too much about becoming a Buddha 18.165; his being can impinge on that of the ordinary person, if they are receptive 4.7; how the Buddhas see us 17.662–3; 'I am Buddha' – a dangerous statement 2.96–7, 10.440; the nondifference between Buddhas and ordinary beings 4.587–91; 'one who sees the Truth sees the Buddha' 1.97; the only difference between the Buddha and an ordinary man 1.274–5; recollecting the Buddhas (one of Vasubandhu's four factors) 2.272–3; rendered always accessible to us by the *trikāya* doctrine 18.86–7; 'There is no Buddha other than one's mind' 19.283–4; the ultimate authority is your own mind 19.284; 'using the Buddha to realize the Buddha' (Zen) 13.364; to want to become a Buddha is the surest way of remaining an ordinary man 7.412

see also
Buddha (Gautama) Enlightenment/potential; families; five female Buddhas; *samyak-sambuddha*; *pratyekabuddha*; *trikāya* doctrine

Buddhas of confession *see under* confession

Buddha's Law Among the Birds *see under* Conze

Buddhavacana, 'Enlightened speech'

introduction
definition 16.592 (n62); *Buddhavacana* and Buddhadharma are inseparable 14.266; can only come to life in the context of the sangha 3.90; a communication from the Enlightened mind to those not yet Enlightened 3.78–81, 14.302; everyone should be taught in their own dialect, *see under* language/language and Buddhism; fundamentalist concern with what the Buddha 'really said' 2.50–1; a guide to the *Buddhavacana* 14.5; listening receptively to the *Buddhavacana* 15.436, 22.226; Mahāyāna approach to *Buddhavacana* 14.261; Mañjughoṣa the embodiment of *Buddhavacana* 3.90–1; one should place one's reliance on the words of the Buddha 1.23; our most reliable guide to the nature of Buddhism 14.265; reproduced in stanza form by Vaṅgīsa 14.20, 15.347; 'Whatever

the Buddha said was well said' 3.168, 3.394, 7.434; when an Enlightened disciple speaks 14.540; 'The Word of the Buddha' (poem) 25.193; words find their ultimate expression in *Buddhavacana* 14.xii

scriptures
the entire Tripiṭaka regarded as *Buddhavacana* 13.336; just one aspect of *Buddhavacana* 3.83; perhaps later compilers added to the original lines 10.522; what is the proof that the scriptures are the authentic word of the Buddha? 16.240; the zenith of literature 14.xiii

what is accepted?
are the Mahāyāna *sūtras Buddhavacana*? 16.52–4; at one time it was believed that the tantras were *Buddhavacana* 12.577; doubting whether a Pāli canon teaching is really the word of the Buddha 1.84–5; distinction between poetry and the word of the Buddha 2.168; fake Buddha quotes 8.128–9, 8.140–1, 8.493; Mahāyāna *sūtras* not accepted by Hīnayānists as genuine 14.96, 16.55; not to be identified with any one linguistic version 14.14; we need to remember the spirit of *Buddhavacana* 3.89, 17.157; the term can be understood in a wider primary or narrower secondary sense 14.11

'Whatever is well said, that is the word of the Buddha'
an argument for the authenticity of Perfection of Wisdom scriptures 14.139; does Buddhism have to be confined to what is labelled 'Buddhism'? 11.370–1; hesitation in practice to accept teachings that conflict with the scriptures 14.11–12; if you find a helpful teaching, even in the Bible, accept it and put it into practice 19.543; a link with the Buddha's teaching to Mahāpajāpatī Gotami 7.434; we have to be careful about what we take to be 'well said' 3.394

see also
Buddha III/communication; scriptures

Buddhavaṃsa the bodhisattva career 1.401; the four sights 3.630n, 10.698 (n268); lives of previous Buddhas 1.49; the pattern of a Buddha's life 2.59, 10.715 (n435)

Buddhayan (magazine) 9.164, 9.170–1, 9.218, 9.393, 9.401, 9.543, 10.xli, 10.liv, 10.299, 10.316

Buddhayāna 7.362, 9.359–62, 14.116

buddhi the faculty of integration and unification 8.289; intelligence 4.290

Buddhism

contents for this section
(I) the essence of Buddhism: starting points – essentials – essential principles and practices – ways of describing Buddhism – what Buddhism is not – perceptions and misconceptions; (II) further perspectives: challenges of Buddhism – emotional and intellectual aspects – approaches and attitudes – knowledge, spirit, activities; (III) history of Buddhism: an overview of the history – schools and sects – the spread of Buddhism – decline and renewal – Buddhism and the rest of the religious world

(I) The essence of Buddhism

starting points

the term
Dharma-Vinaya is the traditional term 11.42; the distinction between 'Buddhism' and 'the Dharma' 13.401; we could have been Jinists (followers of the conqueror) or Sugatists ('Happies') 11.407, 14.404; no need to think of 'Buddhism', just whatever helps the individual evolve 19.543; a product of scientific modes of thought 1.18; a quite recent Western coinage 4.640–1, 11.364; wiser not to use the word 'Buddhism' at all 7.38. 11.42, 24.xxiii; the word 'Buddhism', like all abstractions, is a dangerous double-edged blade 7.225

where Buddhism begins
with a feeling rather than an idea 1.123; it begins and ends with the fact of the Buddha's Enlightenment 7.309, 11.482; it grew out of meditation 5.29; it started with the Buddha beneath the bodhi tree 9.235–6; it starts with human life 12.120–1; logically it begins with the 'existence' of a transcendent Absolute 8.581–2; the original Buddhist ideal was not of liberation for oneself alone 4.5; suffering is where Buddhism begins 7.388–9, 12.120–1; it *may* start with 'anguish', but that is not the only way 8.581–2; where Buddhism begins and why it begins there 7.385–92

questions about Buddhism
ask yourself what in Buddhism appeals to you and examine your motives 13.361, 16.201; is Buddhism escapist?, *see under* escapism; is it a religion at all? 4.641–2, 7.331, 12.94; is it self-indulgent?, *see under* self-indulgence; is knowing about Buddhism any help at all? 19.507; people want ready-made 'Buddhist' answers for their questions 17.627–8; we need to ask: what was the Buddha getting

at? 1.7, 1.515–16; we need to examine our fixed ideas about what 'Buddhism' is 16.128; what is Buddhism? – an essentially practical question 4.8–9; what is Buddhism? – the teaching of the middle way 12.387; *What Makes You Not a Buddhist?* 12.656–8; why follow Buddhism in preference to any of the other great religions? 12.54–7; why is it so difficult to put into practice? 3.241–4; why are there so many forms? 4.124

ESSENTIALS

what is essential?
distinguishing between what is essential and what is not 1.8, 12.78; distinguishing essence from cultural expression 3.45, 13.470–4; rejecting the idea of an 'essence' of Buddhism 13.509

Buddhism in one word (or phrase)
change 10.327–8, 17.94–5; conditionality 3.182–3, 14.607; an experience 2.54; impermanence 11.445–6; suffering (*dukkha*) 7.388, 15.233; 'This being, that becomes' 3.183

what is Buddhism, essentially?
the bodhisattva is its highest expression and ultimate meaning 4.655; the Buddha and his compassionate spirit cannot be left out 4.25–6; Buddhism *is* the Buddha 4.8; a Buddhist *is* Buddhism – in miniature 11.xix, 26.55; the crystallization of the Dharma into methods and teachings 14.434–6; the cultivation of awareness 11.36; a do-it-yourself religion 3.14, 3.163, 12.135; the elucidation of spiritual laws and the inculcation of a way of life based on them 8.283; half of it is in what Ananda said about the Buddha: 'He who is so kind' 4.17–18; it consists of two things: a path and a goal 11.72; its essence is morality (Ambedkar) 9.100; the keywords of Buddhism 8.273, 22.458–9; the means to Enlightenment 7.433; a meditation on time 26.296; a method of resolving the disharmonies of life 26.154; only a means to an end 3.164, 3.232, 16.514–16, *see also* raft; a path of beauty 3.295, 10.248, 26.382–3; a process of growth 11.87–9, 15.578–9; a progressive deepening of Going for Refuge 11.175; the process of the higher evolution 15.632; a reflection on the preciousness of human life 26.296–7; a rich and complex thing 12.610–11; a spiritual community 3.429; thousands of things, but all with the same mysterious seal 2.53; the transition from conditioned to Unconditioned 26.645–6; a twofold method for destroying delusion 1.99–100; unhelpful ways of answering the question 'What is Buddhism?' 25.15–17; a way of life that leads to spiritual experiences 26.104–11; 'whatever conduces to the Enlightenment of the individual' 16.76; whatever frees us from the grip of the ego 17.391; whatever helps us to grow 3.168, 9.198 (*see also under* Mahāpajāpatī Gotami); whatever helps us transform the real into the ideal 11.109, 11.114; wisdom and compassion are the twin pillars 3.158

its essential nature
always in the making 2.39; the *Buddhavacana* is our most reliable guide to its nature 14.265; communicated through friendship 21.475; definite methods 10.156; direct experience 12.56, 14.206; thinking for oneself 9.494; a felt experience 17.331; explores who we are in relation to ourselves, to others, and to reality 12.43; great confidence in the potential of the individual 11.359–60, 11.362; has to transform every aspect of our lives 26.20; it tends towards peace of mind and heart, and peace in the world 7.278, 13.447; not in essence intellectual 15.197, 15.250; not to be understood by words alone 14.17, 25.8–9; seeks to transform world as well as self 12.554, 16.223; spiritual freedom 8.579; a transcendental essence and a mundane expression 7.514

emphases
the analysis of *dharmas* 17.86; meditation 10.156; mindfulness 3.310, 17.86–7; non-violence 3.318; personal experience 9.470–1; right motive 1.15; the supreme value of spiritual experience 7.143–4; the value of direct, personal experience of reality 12.56–7; wholeness 15.625

characteristics
balanced 12.65; dualistic 11.312, 15.634–5; empirical 3.167, 9.343, 12.74–5; familiar (along with a sense of newness) 16.217–18; inevitably encyclopedic 11.508–9; intelligent 8.305; can seem self-absorbed, and in a way it has to be 15.221; critical, and self-critical 14.565; empirical, open-minded enquiry 3.10; humanistic attitude 9.352, 9.425; infallibly produces the right results 3.14; it may seem complicated, but it's quite simple 12.611; melioristic (rather than pessimistic or optimistic) 2.90, 26.10; outward-looking 9.66; practical 7.117, 10.156–8, 11.109, 17.106; progressive, *see under* progressive; quite a bit of it is just common sense 15.362; radically optimistic 12.526, 15.81; revolutionary 26.20; social helpfulness 7.127; spirit of adaptation 1.62–3, 1.189; spiritual vitality 14.251

images and symbols
Buddhism is presented as a path, but the path is a symbol 17.435; a drama enacted on a vast stage 7.342; a finger pointing to the moon 7.44–5, 7.158–9; a great river 2.39; a great tree with wide branches and deep roots 12.111; the lotus 26.242–3; a map of the human territory 3.7; path and mandala 18.525, 18.584, 19.436–7; a pure stream 7.8–12, 7.34

ESSENTIAL PRINCIPLES AND PRACTICES

introduction
its fundamental principles need to be defended 2.649; it delineates principles, but leaves their practice to individuals 11.185; it will not prescribe practices which are not truly helpful 7.185; practice is to be judged by whether it is in accordance with the scriptures 14.265; primarily concerned with experience 19.378; use doctrines and practices appropriately, not as something to hide behind 15.335; we have to distinguish between what is central and what is peripheral 8.580; with some teachings, it might be better to reformulate the basic principle 15.189

essential principles
the aspiration to make people happy 17.182; the attainment of perfection 1.133; the concept of spiritual evolution 13.515; conditionality 12.21; consciousness is not fixed but subject to change 15.161; development of higher states of consciousness 4.440–1; the distinction between wrong and right view 11.160; distinguishing *jñāna* from *vijñāna* 3.356, 14.315–16; everything is connected with the Three Jewels 1.250, 11.394–5; the expansion of consciousness 26.111; *The Foundations of Buddhism* 8.623; Going for Refuge is the highest common factor 2.323–3; hierarchy a fundamental concept 4.169; integrating head and heart 15.558–9; its centre of reference is the human being 11.334; it places the individual at the forefront of its teaching 9.285, 11.358, 11.362; 'Man is nothing else but that which he makes of himself' 2.100; Nirvāṇa and the whole point of being a Buddhist 3.222–3; only wisdom cuts through everything: in a sense *the* basic point 4.371; the right to evolve 9.334; self-help 12.135; states of consciousness are the product of conditioning factors 15.242; the transcendental verities 1.39, 26.57; the value of the individual 17.21–2; we are conditioned beings with an affinity for ultimate reality 12.43; a vision of constant transformation 16.488

essential practices
based upon the realization of emptiness, egolessness, unselfishness 7.278; the bodhisattva ideal 1.397, 1.445, 10.171; the constant repetition of positive actions 17.525–7; impossible to imagine Buddhism without worship 26.476; its lifeblood is *mettā* 7.275; the key to all Buddhist practice: *appamāda* 3.70; meditation is at its heart 8.200, 11.498; to practise effectively we need to learn to reflect 15.191; the transformation of mental states 18.511–12; transference of merit 2.269; ultimately a waste of time (Zen) 13.364

WAYS OF DESCRIBING BUDDHISM

the difficulty of describing it
the abstract medieval Indian mode of communication does not suit it 14.514; the difficulty of finding words to describe it 10.476–8; it cannot be described in terms of Western thought 11.312; it makes use of words but can never be reduced to them 11.418; the relation of Buddhism to language 14.12–15; trying to communicate a mystery 12.106

descriptions nonetheless
it acts primarily on the intellect, but makes a powerful appeal to the emotions 26.118; an ascetic religion in the Greek sense of getting into training 26.64; to Buddhism, all human beings are brothers and sisters 9.186, 9.496, 10.172; cessation is far from being the last word 11.310; its cosmic perspective 1.32–3, 1.37–43, 1.325; it has a popular aspect and a philosophical aspect 11.395; it prefers to speak the language not of identity but of analysis and change 2.97; a chain of events 8.617–18; close connection with the natural world 26.242; a complete account could come from denying how non-Buddhist writers describe it 26.161; a comprehensive system of thought 3.8; the dominating influence of the whole of life 26.43; it could be described as a therapy 12.98–9; it doesn't accept anything that is not part of human experience 19.187; it doesn't recognize an ultimate first beginning 16.100; its concern for material as well as spiritual well-being 8.460; an equilibrium between literalizing and liberalizing influences 1.249; an experiment 7.186–8; firmly grounded on the facts of psychology 8.262; a fully integrated teaching: take up one aspect of it and all the others follow 12.139; the least organized of religions 8.188–9, 10.187; the link between ethics and good manners, *see under* manners;

middle ground between Marxism on one hand, Christianity and Islam on the other 13.514; a middle way between authoritarianism and individualism 10.609, 16.553; naive assertions of the scientific character of Buddhism 13.436; more concerned with the heights than the depths of the mind 3.334–5; it obliterates distinctions of colour, creed, social position, and all other polarities 7.33–4; it proclaims freedom from religion 26.155; the religion of evolution on a cosmic scale 13.516; 'the religion of here and now' 7.169–73; seeing Buddhism in terms of duty 11.90–1; seeing Buddhism in terms of work 11.89–90; sees itself as subject to the same cyclical process as everything else 12.594; sets up and discards one indication of reality after another 1.83; simple for a child to understand, difficult for an old man to practise, *see* Bodhidharma; a solar religion 16.163; there existed from the beginning a tradition of idealism 2.130; three parables that illustrate its meaning 26.105–10; the timelessness of Buddhist truths and traditions 13.439; its truths are of such a nature that to understand them is to act on them 15.553; view of social reform 13.390; the way leading from private trial and public turmoil to peace of mind 8.217

'negative' presentation of Buddhist teachings
the *via negativa* approach considered the best way to describe Nirvāṇa 1.67, 1.114; the charge of nihilism 1.72–80; a one-sided presentation of the Dharma 3.15, 3.45–6, 12.626–7; the apparent negativity of the Buddha's teaching 7.132, 10.432–3, 19.227; better to speak of a new dimension of consciousness than getting rid of the ego 10.471; considering Buddhism positive rather than negative 7.203, 7.312; Indian language grammatically negative when meaning positive 10.635, 17.295–6, 17.565; the language of many Buddhist texts is negative, though the implications are positive 10.513; the Mahāyāna rectified the one-sidedly negative presentation of the Dharma 10.432; the negative approach to reality 16.328–9; the strong hold of the negative needed an exaggerated emphasis on the positive 7.204; the Theravādin emphasis on the negative 19.200; there cannot be a purely negative conception of the spiritual life 10.635; we must have a strong emphasis on the emotionally positive 10.432, 17.291, 17.296; why use a grammatically negative word to express something positive? 17.566

descriptions of the goal
the Buddha placed more emphasis on the path than on the goal 15.241; different ways of seeing the goal 11.72; Enlightenment, *see* Enlightenment; poetical descriptions 2.131–2; the positive goal: Nirvāṇa, the highest bliss 7.120; its purpose is to bring about insight into the true nature of things 15.260; release from the endless round of rebirth 8.565; to replace a mechanistic universe with one that has meaning 3.11; the transformation of consciousness 15.98; the Unconditioned 2.149; the difference between Nirvāṇa and Supreme Perfect Enlightenment 26.698; what is the goal of Buddhism? – don't answer too slickly 12.121–2

WHAT BUDDHISM IS NOT

deciding what is or is not Buddhism
the Buddha's words to Mahāpajāpatī Gotami, *see* Mahāpajāpatī Gotami; the criterion is ultimately pragmatic 1.204; does Buddhism have to be confined to what is labelled 'Buddhism'? 11.370–1; does it have the taste of freedom? 11.51; making the distinction 9.272–3; having the authority to decide 13.469, 13.472–4; how to work out what the essence of Buddhism is 13.399–401; it has to be determined empirically, so an encyclopedic approach is necessary 11.508–9; the Pāli canon is not the sole criterion 7.31, 7.499; there is no ecclesiastical authority to decide 11.508; unless we accept a 'Buddhism' there can be no Buddhists 13.509

what Buddhism is not
is Buddhism a religion?, *see under* religion/what is religion?; it isn't a service industry, its role is not to bless worldly activities 15.701–4; it doesn't demand belief 10.156, 11.110, 15.265; it doesn't encourage morbid obsession with suffering 1.132, 15.228; it doesn't exist in the abstract 9.187; it doesn't impose itself to the exclusion of other creeds 7.34; it doesn't teach that all the phenomena of existence are reducible to one 16.449; it has no creeds 14.375; it is no more a metaphysical dualism than a metaphysical monism 26.645–6; it isn't 'a form of Naturalism' 21.84; it isn't gloomy 11.155; it isn't just a means of obtaining social justice 8.205; it isn't sceptical 11.110; its fundamental state of mind is not a sense of awe 26.152–3; neither ancient nor modern, but *sanātana* Dharma, the eternal truth 7.115, 8.217; neither monistic nor pluralistic, but both and more than both 3.374, 12.215–16; neither religion nor philosophy 7.493;

not authoritarian 12.246; not a system of philosophy in the modern academic sense 8.604, 26.103–4; no excuse for describing it as a system of self-torture 8.146; no form of Buddhism requires you to give up bliss 19.379; no official party line, only the standpoint of the individual Buddhist 3.614, 12.246; not dogmatic 7.128; not intellectually woolly 12.515; not just about learning philosophy – we have to change every aspect of our lives 3.370; not recognizing as Buddhism anything that can't be related to Going for Refuge 1.8; not just an ethical teaching 8.231; not just intellectual, but involves the emotions at every step 15.250–1; not the daydream of a beautiful soul, but a carefully thought-out scheme 7.33; not a product of its environment, though the environment was a factor 1.57; not a religion, but the path of the higher evolution 3.477–8, 13.515; not science, or speculative philosophy, or religion 26.154–5; talking about monks and monasteries gives a wrong impression of Buddhist life 26.43; it has some 'religious form' which is not of value to the individual 13.422; universal: no more Eastern than Western 8.552–3, 10.341–2, 12.78, 26.341

Buddhism is non-theistic
and no metaphysical principles run the universe 14.444; attempts to assert that Buddhists 'really' believe in God 8.167–8, 11.108; its atheism affects the whole character of Buddhism 10.138; Buddhism and God 9.344–5, 9.425, 9.469, 9.494, 16.425; Buddhism is the sole non-theistic universal religion 4.641–2, 7.485, 12.55; the Buddhist position may come as a shock 7.9–10; Christianity could learn from Buddhism's non-theistic approach 12.113; consequences of not believing in God 10.150; disappointing when Buddhist teachers play down its non-theism 4.125; don't mistake Mahāyāna Buddhism for a kind of theism 7.535–7, 11.106, 14.602–3; how can it be both non-theistic and a religion? 11.509, 12.621–2; the highest being is not a god but an Enlightened human being 15.81; the most important non-theistic religion 11.296; no need to assume that spiritual renewal must involve God 8.431; no place for God in Buddhism 8.xix, 12.55, 12.135, 14.444, 22.78; a non-theistic system of spiritual self-development 12.57; the perfect example of a spiritual way of life without reference to God 12.7; saying Buddhism is non-theistic defines it in unhelpfully theistic terms 14.603; to discuss it in Christian terms is to distort it 11.509; a union of the non-theistic and the spiritual 13.514; wanting to fill a God-shaped hole in the Buddha's teaching 3.151–2, 13.566; we should make it clear that Buddhism is a non-theistic religion 8.282–3, 12.56; 'what God is to other religions morality is to Buddhism' (Ambedkar) 9.99; why Buddhism does not believe in God 10.138

PERCEPTIONS AND MISCONCEPTIONS

different views of Buddhism
Buddhists shouldn't let other people tell them what they 'really' believe 8.168; confusion and conflicting messages 1.201–2; the divergence of views is semantic in origin 9.143–4; diverse views of Buddhism 9.197–8; explaining away whatever aspects are in conflict with preconceived ideas 1.19–20; it has suffered from the misrepresentations of critics 26.153; like the blind men examining the elephant 12.103; one-sided views of Buddhism: sectarian, fundamentalist, encyclopedic 2.49–52; prejudice against Buddhism 19.207

misperceptions and misrepresentations
the allegation that Buddhists are indifferent to human suffering 2.69; 'cold, bleak, inhuman, antisocial' 4.643; considering that it is concerned only with the removal of suffering 7.390; the danger of its becoming trivialized or psychologized 17.454; don't reduce it to materialism or nihilism through misunderstanding *śūnyatā* 14.459–60; equating worship of bodhisattvas with polytheism reduces Buddhism to a pagan cult 2.172; the error of considering that its quintessence is contained in this or that doctrine 7.144; giving up wrong views about Buddhism 9.265–6; the idea that it appeals primarily to reason 12.104–6; is Buddhism nihilistic? 1.72–80, 17.362–3, 17.444; its near enemies can be more dangerous than its far ones 8.599; it's wrong to assume that it can be reduced to one of its forms 13.514; a mistake to confuse Buddhism with its cultural expressions 13.495–6; misunderstandings based on thinking of Buddhism as a philosophy 26.102–4; modern expositions make it seem one-sidedly intellectual 4.147; pessimistic, *see under* pessimism; 'sayings' falsely attributed to the Buddha 8.128–9, 8.140–1; seen as a passive, negative, gutless tradition 3.45, 3.287; selfish and individualistic 3.245, 5.209–10, 17.191–2; the silliest of all the silly things that have been said about Buddhism 7.524; specifically oriental

3.45; 'strange, exotic, colourful, weird, mysterious' 4.644, 13.495; textbooks can give the impression that Buddhism is dry bones 10.211; Western misconceptions 3.44–5, 7.31–3, 11.142–3

does Buddhism exist at all?
are we justified in speaking of Buddhism at all? 1.202; it exists not in books or monuments, but in the faithful hearts of its devotees 7.226; no such thing as Buddhist tradition 14.453; there's no such thing as Buddhism 3.164, 14.362–3

(II) Further perspectives

challenges of buddhism

difficulties
dangers, *see under* dangers; a difficult religion, the Buddha said 7.41; difficult to practise 3.579, 9.269; it is difficult because it is a product of the Enlightened mind 11.373; it's easier to live a Buddhist life in a traditional society 7.395; it may not be easy, but it should certainly not be miserable 17.338; it isn't easy to regard Buddhism as provisional 14.441; practising Buddhism without belief in karma and rebirth is difficult 3.113–14; we should be ashamed not to attempt that which is difficult 11.408

challenges
it is based on principles which admit of no exception 10.171; it exhorts, but it does not command or force 7.439, 16.72; even little old ladies have to become lions in Buddhism 4.469; if you lose sight of the transcendental element, you lose sight of Buddhism 26.57; if we take it seriously, we may be required to make sacrifices 4.100–1; if we're just playing at it, we won't get far 11.407; it brings the darker side of life into view to correct our one-sided view of it 2.90–1; it exhorts us to perform our duties rather than struggle for our rights 7.280; it means change 9.192, 9.525–6; it says: 'Don't just react. Act!' 19.582; its besetting sins are laziness and indifference 26.15; keep seeing Buddhism afresh 12.39–41; make the experiment, live the life: that's all that Buddhism asks us to do 7.128, 11.110; not for 'old ladies' (of both sexes and all ages) 1.553; it points out the opposite of everything to which we cling 7.35; practised with a sense of urgency 10.303; a religion of action 22.159–60; sane and vigorous ascesis, far from refined hedonism 1.129; a serious enterprise 23.463; a whole-time religion, not a once-a-week religion 7.117, 10.147

emotional and intellectual aspects

emotional aspects
why Buddhism begins with a feeling rather than an idea 1.124, 7.392, 26.77; the Buddhism of Faith and Devotion 1.323–336, 2.128; Buddhism started with reason and only later spoke the language of emotion 12.107; the importance of enjoying being a Buddhist 11.45, 16.284–5; the importance of emotion (the parable of the raincloud) 16.129–30

intellectual and rational aspects of Buddhism
the Buddha's teaching appeals initially to the intellect 8.297; Buddhism appeals to innate reasonableness 10.170–1; Buddhism began with reason, then emotion: vision and transformation 12.107–8; Buddhism's rational element is very strong, but it isn't *purely* rational 12.106, 12.180; Buddhism needs to appeal both to rational mind and unconscious depths 12.181; Buddhism upholds the equal validity of reason and experience 26.198; characterized by clarity, honesty, and rigour of thought 4.144; discords at the intellectual level 1.198; intellectual and doctrinal side represented by *prajñā* 3.303; the keen-eyed hawk of intellect need not be hoodwinked 7.128; rationalist presentations of Buddhism 12.104–6, 26.242; reason has an honoured place, but is not the governing principle 3.397–8; a reasonable intellectual understanding can be useful in the early stages 14.405

approaches and attitudes

how to approach Buddhism
the approach should be synoptic, not sectarian 12.65, 13.326; are you approaching it as the way to Enlightenment? 12.63; better to be attracted to it because it refutes your ideas 26.9; the ideal approach 2.52; it cannot be practised mechanically 9.193–4, 9.266; it must be approached on its own terms 12.61–3; approach it with openness, or you will learn nothing 19.106; it must be approached as a whole 1.296–7, 1.348, 12.63–5; our approaches are one-sided, so we need to juxtapose contradictions 13.327–8; a realistic facing of the facts 8.143; seeing Buddhism in its breadth and depth 1.6–8; shape your understanding to Buddhism, not Buddhism to your understanding 7.310, 11.483; turning the ideas of Buddhism into effective attitudes 19.105–6; turning yourself upside-down is

a good Buddhist way of looking at things 14.590

contrasting approaches
the academic approach is hostile to the possibility of Enlightenment 7.310, 11.483; armchair Buddhism 16.285; contrast between Indian and Western approaches 10.41–2; dabbling in Buddhism 11.58, 11.467; fundamentalist approach concerned with what the Buddha 'really said' 2.50–1; hostility towards Buddhism 1.19, 8.227–8; one's reasons for being a Buddhist may change 14.599; the psychological approach 11.549–50; the social dimension of Buddhism 11.550; some people are more interested in 'what is', others in 'what to do' 17.569; a tendency to pick and choose between teachings 11.58, 11.209; we approach Buddhism with mixed motives 11.81–2

KNOWLEDGE, SPIRIT, ACTIVITIES

knowledge of Buddhism
it's no good thinking that one has 'got' Buddhism 3.165, 11.417; all our knowledge is second-hand 13.346; Buddhism stresses that knowledge should be shared with everyone 1.501; Buddhism is inevitably encyclopedic 11.508–9; Buddhism is a religion of knowledge 2.126; complete factual knowledge about Buddhism is impossible 2.51–2; confusing knowledge *about* with knowledge *of* Buddhism 2.51; fearlessness in pursuit of the truth about Buddhism 1.20; having exhaustive knowledge about Buddhism does not make one a Buddhist 11.467; how much do you need to know about Buddhism to be a Buddhist? 17.391; if we think we understand Buddhism, we do not understand it *at all* 11.56–8; make sure that familiarity doesn't breed indifference 11.44; the rationale: knowledge of dependent origination and the four noble truths 19.577; to know the heart of it, contemplate the bodhisattva ideal 1.398; 'knowing this for oneself': a characteristic Buddhist emphasis 10.465; knowledge of Buddhism does not come automatically, so we need to study 2.244; we know too much, but our knowledge is theoretical 15.508–9, 19.506–9; an understanding of Buddhism goes with a knowledge of the sacred books 14.7; *see also* more and more of less and less; understanding/ understanding Buddhism

the spirit of Buddhism
Bodhidharma took its spirit to China 13.342; expressed by different cultures but not to be identified with them 11.374; its spirit can be studied in the light of its letter 1.240; the living spirit of the Dharma 14.17; the Mahāyāna restored it 14.555; it needs to be backed up by doctrines and scriptures 14.435; our methods of propagating it must be in accordance with its spirit 8.276; repudiating doctrines prematurely, one may lose the spirit 2.58; its transmission 13.340–3; which languages are best able to give expression to it? 14.14–15

Buddhist activities
remember that all activities are means to an end 8.196–8; better live a 'worldly' life in a Buddhist spirit than do 'Buddhist' activities in a worldly way 8.276; Buddhist activities as a means of making money 7.246; organizational activities are no substitute for practising the Dharma in one's own life 8.280; like isolated rays of sunshine, but to make fire, a lens (a central institution) is needed 8.278–9; they should be judged according to their effect on the individual 8.197–8; they should include meditation 8.283–4; a world of meaningless 'Buddhist activities' 24.138

(III) HISTORY OF BUDDHISM

AN OVERVIEW OF THE HISTORY

introduction
Buddhism has a cyclical vision of history 12.593–4; Enlightenment is the one constant factor 7.313; a historical perspective is one of the biggest dangers 19.279; a historical perspective on Buddhism 4.22–3, 10.554–5; the historical phenomenon of Buddhism 1.31–7; ideas that occupy an important place in the history of Buddhism 12.464; in its essence Buddhism has no history 1.17; interconnectedness of teachings and historical forms 1.6; it can get so weighed down with cultural forms that the Dharma gets lost 14.435–6; it would have been very different if it had included the Vedas 13.623; lifted far above the plane of mere historicity 1.264; a long history in which Buddhism has changed: major reformations 12.116–17; misleading generalizations about Buddhist history 7.71; the need for an entirely new consideration of the history of Buddhism 7.72–3; a process of the solidification and dissolution of concepts 4.38; the student of the Dharma must recapitulate in his spiritual life the history of Buddhism 1.393; a vast reworking every few hundred years 19.51–2; you don't need to know the history of Buddhism to understand Buddhism 19.51; Buddhist

history may seem remote and unreal to some, but not in Nepal 7.341–2

beginnings of Buddhist history
the historicity of the Buddha 13.570–1; the days when 'Buddhism' did not yet exist 10.422–3; the ideas and ideals of India the best conditions for Buddhism's development 1.57; not a product of the 6th century BCE, but comes from the beginningless past 7.342; 'pre-Buddhistic' Buddhism 10.429–31, 26.474; when the Buddhist era began 22.304; Buddhism and its original cultural environment 11.511–13; Buddhism's historical and spiritual importance 4.641; what is the origin of Buddhism? 8.230–2; early Buddhists didn't distinguish between history and myth as we do 16.241; in the early days, people had no conception of historical development 4.22; taking over material from Indian ethnic religion 16.182; unintentional literalism in the early history 8.620

developments
how Buddhism developed 14.351–2; the Indian mind getting to work on Buddhism 1.61, 11.512–13, 12.241, 17.95; Nāgārjuna could be regarded as its second founder 1.310; as it developed, people asked more sophisticated questions 14.351–2; from being a religion of the mind, Buddhism became a religion of faith 7.41–2; testimony to the vigour with which contradictory opinions were opposed 7.382–3; the categorization of the elements of existence for the first time 14.93; Chinese classification of the Buddha's teachings into five periods 4.22, 14.103; underwent radical change, but mainly faithful to the spirit 7.122, 7.585 (n221), 12.678; *The History of Buddhism in India and Tibet* (Büton) 13.29, 13.674 (n9); periods of renewal 10.564; rarely has theology been allowed to subvert ethics 13.623; royal patronage of Buddhism 12.238–9; a tendency towards deterioration 8.312–13

popular Buddhism
introduction 2.218–32; astrology, *see* astrology; Buddhism as a cultural phenomenon without the Dharma is not helpful 14.469; devotion 2.220–3; festivals, *see* festivals; hospitality and good manners 2.232; household shrines 2.229–30; neither wholly sacred nor wholly profane 2.218; non-rational elements 12.105–6, 12.180; a bridge between ordinary existence and spiritual life 2.218, 16.230–1; popular Mahāyāna Buddhism 16.231; sees the Buddha image as a source of blessing and magical protection 2.229–30; should be made more and more a religion of meditation 8.294; as a skilful means 2.218, 2.219; worship in popular Buddhism 2.219–20

see also
Indian Buddhism; *yānas*/three *yānas*; Western Buddhism/history

SCHOOLS AND SECTS

introducing them
summary of the forms of Buddhism 8.502–3, 12.63–5; the schools of Early Buddhism, *see under* Early Buddhism; 'eighteen schools', *see under* Early Buddhism; Indian schools 2.49–50, 13.15–17, 13.340; Mahāyāna schools are not sects 1.296; regional traditions eventually emerged as independent sects 7.497; extant Eastern schools 8.502–3, 11.371–3; the rise of schools and sects a sign of health, not decay 8.462; to be judged according to their richness of transcendental attainments 1.205, 7.313–14

divisions
adherents of one school may assert that only theirs is true 1.198, 12.64–5; calling into question the division between Theravāda and Mahāyāna 8.624; different sects do not recognize each other 2.595–6, 19.547; divided by sects professing the same beliefs 7.273; let us do away with divisions 26.56; there is room for criticism of different schools 19.584; tolerance and respect for one another 1.205–6, 7.490; *see also* Mahāyāna Buddhism/contrasts with Early Buddhism

sectarianism
'Buddhists' who attack other forms of Buddhism without studying them 8.141; 'Clinging to one's school ... is the certain way to waste one's learning' 19.543–4; fortunately on the wane in the Buddhist world 2.50; identifying Buddhism with one form like identifying an oak with an acorn 11.143, 26.10; identifying oneself with a particular form of Buddhism 18.380; it makes it difficult to know what Buddhism is 9.197; no Buddhist consigned to hell by their opponents for holding unorthodox views 7.490; not one 'Buddhist world' but a number of sectarian worlds 2.548; problems of identifying Buddhism with one version 2.50, 12.64–5; produced by fixed attitudes 16.127–8; quite foreign to the spirit of Buddhism 13.326; relation between two principal doctrines divided Buddhist teachers 1.117; sectarianism sometimes ran high, but differences were

settled peacefully 7.490; schools tend not to know much about each other's teachings 3.8; schools that have lost faith in Enlightenment criticize those that have it 1.205; today a sectarian approach is scarcely possible 16.75–6; trying to reconstruct 'original' Buddhism from knowledge of one school 21.245; whether you are a follower of this or that school doesn't matter much 19.177

what the schools have in common
all expressions, under different conditions, of the Buddha's teaching 12.595–6; all schools of Buddhism have a great deal of common ground 13.324; devotion as an aspect of all schools 1.336–7; doctrines held in common by all schools of Buddhism 7.531–42; the hallmark of a Buddhist school: does it try to solve the problem of pain? 7.126–7; is Buddhism one or many? 1.191–202; a liberal view of all Buddhist traditions 22.532; no one school has the whole Buddhist teaching 16.422, 22.126; ritual is part of the heritage of all schools of Buddhism 2.147, 11.208–9; syncretist movements 1.295, 1.360–1; there does exist a common foundation to all schools 1.198

a positive approach
accepting what is useful from tradition and rejecting what is not useful 9.402–3; by eschewing sectarianism the Buddhist world can become a living spiritual reality 8.274; it would be better not to think in terms of schools at all 8.496, 19.543; no need to be Theravādin or Zen or Mahāyānist – why not just be Buddhist? 16.76; Western Buddhists should study and appreciate them all 11.89, 13.325–6

the whole Buddhist tradition
Asaṅga accepted the whole tradition 1.367; the bodhisattva is the unifying factor 1.397; Buddhism is so vast that one cannot literally accept it *in toto* 13.408; Buddhism is a whole and must be followed as a whole 1.296–7, 1.348, 12.63–5; direct experience is the emphasis of the whole tradition 12.56, 14.206; it can't really be spilt up into ethics, philosophy, psychology, etc. 17.433; knowledge of Buddhism must be based on the entire tradition 8.274, 14.265; Sangharakshita's vihara in Kalimpong dedicated to the total Buddhist tradition 8.652, 22.376; seeing Buddhism as a whole 1.6–7; the *triyāna* system is a framework for the whole Buddhist tradition 7.479, 11.89; we can accept the whole tradition, but not all of it may be equally useful to us 18.495

THE SPREAD OF BUDDHISM

the history
first sixty disciples exhorted to spread the Dharma, *see under* disciples/the Buddha's disciples; Aśoka decreed that messengers of the Dharma should go out into the world 15.184; it began on foot 9.496; it penetrated practically the whole of Asia 16.5; maintained tolerance for indigenous faiths in the countries to which it spread 7.144–5; missionary activity of monks 2.212, 10.264–5, 12.252–3; merged with pre-existing spiritual traditions 18.174; the Dhamma Revolution, *see* Dhamma Revolution; increasing in the West and India 9.429–30; interest in Buddhism in Europe (1954) 8.136, 8.138, 8.617; until recently Tibetan lamas didn't think of spreading the Dharma 19.209, 19.532–3

how it is spread
Buddhism cannot be spread by purely organizational means 9.526; Buddhism learns the language of the places it reaches 3.161, 7.395–6, 12.116–18; to spread Buddhism you must practise Buddhism 8.281, 9.526; entirely by peaceful means 7.486; like the migration of a living species 17.155; by non-violent means 9.236, 9.496; three steps to be taken (Ambedkar) 9.108, 9.117–18, 9.223–4, 9.317–18

exhortations
exhortation to spread the Dharma throughout the world 22.311; the Great Work of the dissemination of the Dharma 8.xxix, 8.192; if we don't want to spread the Dharma we won't get far 11.407; it's better to draw people into spiritual life than drive them into it 15.573; it is so important to make the Buddhist path known to others 15.94–5; lassitude, indifference, neglect, and procrastination retard progress 8.272; make a resolution to do something specific to help spread the Dharma 8.192–3; the need for resources to spread the Dharma throughout the world 8.176; the opportunities to spread the Dharma in the modern world 8.267–8; our methods of propagating the Dharma must be in accordance with its spirit 8.276; proselytization 9.116–17, 10.85, 16.28–9; reaching out to people who are neglected by others, out of human concern 10.86–7; remaining friends with culture and civilization 7.443; a vow to spread the Dharma worldwide 8.226

the influence of Buddhism
on Aśoka 7.237; on Confucianism 2.11, 7.485; on Daoism 2.11; on Eastern culture 7.125, 7.128, 16.35; on Hinduism

2.11, 7.485, 9.236, 9.265, 10.45, 10.48, 12.241–2; on primitive Islam 7.370; on modern Indian art 7.448; on other systems of belief 7.485; on Tibetan culture 7.442; on Western culture 7.448–51, 14.267; wherever the Buddha leaves his footprints there is an efflorescence of culture 25.27–8; why did Buddhism not use political influence to enforce religious conformity? 7.383

DECLINE AND RENEWAL

degeneration
contamination of ideals with mundane considerations 18.174–5; cotton candy Buddhism: sweet, sticky, but it doesn't last long 11.610, 12.515; degeneration of some Buddhists into violence in modern times 26.631; the devaluation of Going for Refuge 11.69–70; seeing Buddhist history as a degeneration is like seeing an oak as a degeneration of an acorn 1.249, 1.612 (n203); hardening of categories of Buddhist thought 2.131, 4.38; if Buddhists agree to become 'respectable', Buddhism ceases to be Buddhism 18.135; sometimes there is a real degeneration of the teaching 17.595; turning Buddhism into an ethnic religion: the worst of betrayals 8.471; values eroded by the behaviour of some of Buddhism's traditional custodians 2.551

decline
as a spiritual principle the Dharma cannot possibly decline 14.434; in all its forms, Buddhism is born, develops, matures, declines, and dies 12.594, 18.497; Buddhism in a state of decline 2.550–1, 2.556, 2.603; counterfeit Dharma 16.82–3; disappearance from India, *see under* Indian Buddhism; the Dharma will not disappear so long as people practise it 18.497; the great forms of Buddhism have a fourfold process of development and decline 18.496–7; the idea first mentioned by the Buddha as a spur to practise the Dharma 14.434; the idea that the teaching of one Buddha will disappear before the arising of another 11.622; in the Buddhist East 7.512, 12.594–5, 13.104, 15.499–500; laying down rules is always a sign of decline 10.563–4; the periodic disappearance of the Dharma calls for the appearance of a Buddha 1.231; phases of decline and renewal 10.564, 14.433–7, 15.498–500; a spiritual hardening of the arteries 14.441; we are fortunate to live in a time and place when the Dharma is still known 11.409; what was originally a spontaneous act becomes a laborious chore 14.436; when the Buddhist world is in communication it flourishes, but in isolation it declines 8.244; where there is no Sangha, there is no Dharma 8.245

predictions of decline and disappearance
Buddhist texts that predict decline 12.594, 12.747 (n400), 19.597 (n37); discussed in the *Diamond Sūtra* 14.433–41, 14.472–3; how the idea of the Kali Yuga (age of decline) crept into Buddhism 11.621, 14.433–4, 19.83; as human beings become more degenerate 1.50–1; Padmasambhava predicts the growth and decline of the Dharma 8.523; prophecies of decline in Buddhist texts 14.189–90, 14.433–4; three periods: true Dharma, counterfeit Dharma, destruction of the Dharma 8.574; a time will come when no one will remember a single verse of the Dharma 10.263; you can't say the Dharma will inevitably decline 8.574, 11.621, 14.434–7, 19.83

threats to Buddhism
Communism 8.309–10, 8.317, 8.320–1; hostile forces 25.32; a threat to any minority is a threat to Buddhism 26.74; militant Marxism and Christianity 8.313–14; in the 20th century 9.319

the future of Buddhism
'Buddha and the Future of His Religion', *see under* Ambedkar/works; in India (envisaged in 1953) 7.235; 'The Present State and Future Prospects of Buddhism in Asia' (Conze) 8.538; in the West, *see under* Western Buddhism; indebtedness to the past and responsibility to the future 8.580; the future of Tibetan Buddhism (as seen in 1966) 13.99–112; it depends on every Buddhist 8.305–6

see also
world/modern world/Buddhism in the modern world

BUDDHISM AND THE REST OF THE RELIGIOUS WORLD

other traditions
as we make sense of Buddhism, we may understand our former religion better 2.245; Buddhism and Ātmanism are poles apart 7.213; Buddhism attacked by a swami 22.10; Buddhism and the Cathars 8.424; Buddhism and Christianity, *see under* Christianity/Christianity and Buddhism; Buddhism and Islam, *see under* Islam; Buddhism as an anticipation of Marxism (Ambedkar) 9.412; Buddhism now the smallest and least influential of the three world religions 2.550–1; Buddhism and other religions: a comprehensive approach 2.245; Buddhism's influence on other systems of belief 7.485; Buddhist critique

of other religions 14.459–60; distinction between Buddhism and Taoism 16.163–4; and Hinduism, *see under* Hinduism; influenced by Manicheism? 3.431–2; a middle way, neither indiscriminately accepting nor rejecting wholesale 2.245–6; prepared to respect and even admire other spiritual leaders 2.243; seeing that the truth is beyond words distinguishes Buddhism from other religions 7.331; struggle with Shaivism 7.72; Tibetans shocked to hear the follower of one religion running down another 12.137, 13.111; a true Buddhist will behave with courtesy and goodwill towards those of other faiths 26.631; why did Buddhism ally itself with Vaiṣṇavism? 7.72

mixing Buddhism with other things
Ambedkar's twenty-two vows guard against mixing Buddhism with Hinduism 9.216, 9.265; attempts to bring Buddhism together with other ideologies 12.656; Buddhism is not to be mixed with other religions for a purely theoretical syncretism 12.369; the Dharma could be corrupted by the ethnic traditions with which it merged 18.174; the Dharma must not be mixed with anti-Dharmic elements 3.314, 12.516; don't mix Buddhism with Christianity 24.485; don't mix up Buddhism and psychology 12.117–18; don't mix fashionable isms and ideologies with the Dharma 11.603, 12.455, 12.476; the meaning of Buddhism coincides with the value of art 26.118; mixing different kinds of Dharma teaching 17.390; muddling Buddhism with theistic ideas 14.602–3; the effect of Buddhism being mixed with Hinduism in Nepal 14.435; 'Protestant Buddhism' 13.398–423; temptations to mix the Buddha's teachings with something else 12.404–5

see also
art/Buddhism and art; caste system/Buddhist responses; Buddhists/becoming a Buddhist; Western Buddhism; women/women in the Buddhist tradition; Myanmar/Buddhist practice; communication, *see under* Dharma; contradictions/in the Buddhist tradition; conversion; culture/Buddhism; Dharma; evolution/and Buddhism; freedom/and Buddhism; four holy places; Indian Buddhism; Mahāyāna Buddhism; myth/and Buddhism; oral tradition; orthodoxy/in Buddhism; path; peace/and Buddhism; philosophy/Buddhist philosophy; psychology/Buddhist psychology; reading/books on Buddhism; Sangharakshita V/Buddhist life; science/Buddhism and science; scriptures; study; Dharma; tolerance/in Buddhism; unity; universality; Western Buddhism; writing/about Buddhism

Buddhism in Translation *see* Warren

Buddhist Bible assessment of the need for a Buddhist Bible, *see under* scriptures/introducing the Buddhist scriptures; *A Buddhist Bible* (Goddard's compilation), *see* Goddard

Buddhist centres, Triratna (FWBO) *see under* Triratna IV

Buddhist countries

traditions
Mahāyāna 1.211; Sarvastivāda Buddhism 3.408; Theravāda Buddhism 2.548–9, 3.407; Buddha Day customs 3.19–20; ethics according to custom rather than personal scrutiny 11.568; making children salute monks 10.495; the tradition for the eldest son to become a monk 19.475; the traditional approach starts with devotion 11.206; Western and Indian Buddhists have no wish to follow customs 9.507–8

Going for Refuge
devaluation of Going for Refuge 11.69–70; emphasis on becoming a *bhikkhu*, not Going for Refuge 10.267; no Going for Refuge ceremony in Theravādin countries 15.710–12; not Going for Refuge but just seeking the Buddha's protection in worldly life 19.484–5

monastic and lay
being a monk becomes a sort of profession 17.111; countries where *bhikkhunī* ordination survives 3.408; lay people like to listen to monks chanting 15.437; the minor role played by the laity 12.123; monastic–lay split, *see under* sangha; no serious expectation that the lay person will lead a spiritual life 11.568

Buddhism in Buddhist countries
books sponsored by the governments 8.208–9; Buddhism has become just part of the national culture 19.474; a 'Buddhist state' is a contradiction in terms 14.543; complacency 12.113; a country cannot be called Buddhist unless it provides an environment for practice 7.258; the effect of birth in a Buddhist country 7.258, 12.58–9, 13.486–8; encumbered by 'dead wood' 9.98; formerly Buddhist countries now Communist 2.551, 9.238–9; in some there's not much difference between Buddhists and non-Buddhists 19.229; laws do not always spring from Buddhist principles 16.434; the life of Buddhism choked 8.xxxi; money is wasted in the

name of *dāna* 8.175; people think they are Buddhist although they are not practising 19.477; prosperity 4.439–40; in relation to India 7.464–5, 9.118–19; scandals 2.551; they condemn and prohibit slavery 3.582–3

is Buddhism practised in them?
decline of Buddhism 12.594–5; the problem of restating the truths of Buddhism for the modern world 11.600; right livelihood is not much observed 19.473; sometimes people miss what the Dharma is all about 11.670; 'the true spirit of Buddhism has fled' 8.50; what use is propagating Buddhism if harmful influences are allowed to continue? 8.214; young people have very little time for Buddhism 8.212–13, 12.118–19

see also
Buddhist world; individual countries; lay people

Buddhist flag *see under* flags

Buddhist Hybrid Sanskrit *see under* Sanskrit

Buddhist Legends *see Dhammapada Commentary*

Buddhist movements all their activities have only one purpose: to help people grow and develop as individuals 3.457; have to consist essentially of committed Buddhists 2.467, 12.374; have to steer a middle course between 'Buddhism says you must do this' and 'Anything goes' 10.609; have two parts: a spiritual community and a positive group 3.457, 19.467–8; should provide material support without strings for those fully committed to spiritual life 18.121–2; they have to operate within society's rules 19.261; they must develop all five spiritual faculties 11.478–9; *see also* Triratna Buddhist Order and Movement

Buddhist Research Centre 9.527

Buddhist Review 10.139

Buddhist societies conditions for joining 9.307–8; the danger of having a subscription to join 9.307, 12.374; the difference between a Buddhist society and a Buddhist order 12.374, 12.497–8; founded in Britain 12.74–5; the limitations of Buddhist societies 13.510

Buddhist Society (London)

introduction
brief history 2.714 (n481), 23.496 (n182); the oldest surviving Buddhist organization in the West 3.396, 12.72; originally the Buddhist Lodge of the Theosophical Society 10.139, 23.46; move to Eccleston Square 23.49; links with Thai royal house 23.157–8; controlled by people who were sympathetic to Buddhism but not Buddhist 11.468–9; Ajahn Sumedho as president (1980s) 13.382–3; receptions for visiting Asian Buddhists 23.157; thirtieth anniversary 8.196, 8.390–1; Wesak celebration 20.102

Christmas Humphreys,
founded the Society 10.139, 12.72; president 20.100; saw the Society as secular and middle class 23.404; tendency to dominate 20.103; ends Dharma Group (studying Mahāyāna) 21.339

and the English Sangha Association (and Trust)
contrast 13.383; differences 11.546–7, 23.23, 23.45–9, 23.143–4, 23.240; trying to heal the rift 11.547, 23.44–5, 23.49–50, 23.144, 23.200–1, 23.326, 26.579–80; working in collaboration 23.335

and Sangharakshita
in 1943–4, *see under* Sangharakshita V; gives talks at the Society on his return from India 23.49

summer schools
atmosphere 27.1071; 'cheaper than going to a hotel' 23.199; Sangharakshita reproved for being two minutes late 9.499, 11.542–3, 23.36, 25.382; 'enjoyable, because I felt myself to be part of the English Buddhist scene' 23.329; the introduction of puja 11.213, 23.151; newcomers became disheartened and confused 13.326–7; photograph 11.474; Sangharakshita's attendance 23.32–8, 23.151, 23.329–30

Buddhist Text Society 9.46

Buddhist texts *see* scriptures

Buddhist Texts through the Ages *see* Conze

Buddhist world awakening to new life 7.275; the Buddhist world is one world 8.244, 8.274; Buddhists everywhere need to consider how to preserve the Dharma 2.551–2; the customs, practices, and beliefs that have grown up around the Dharma 25.31–2; demands of consumerism 2.551; the dream of a World Buddhism 7.484, 8.274, 8.402; five Buddhist 'worlds', according to the five spiritual faculties 2.549–50; the importance of advertising 8.253–4; no such thing as 'a Buddhist world' 2.548; only growing in India and in the West 2.551; the Buddhist world's need for

a concrete spiritual basis 23.160; has shrunk dramatically in recent times 2.550–1; in much of the Buddhist world drinking is an accepted part of social life 8.313; its great weakness is lack of unity 8.217–18, 22.308; a self-contained Buddhist world 26.630; there needs to be more active cooperation 8.297–8; three Buddhist 'worlds', based on Theravāda, Mahāyāna, and Vajrayāna 2.548–9, 7.482; to withstand materialism, the Buddhist world must stand together 8.182; Triratna's relationship with the Buddhist world 2.543–74, 12.664–5; when it is in communication it flourishes 8.244

Buddhist World *see under* Sri Lanka/ publications

Buddhists

the word 'Buddhist'
a quite recent Western coinage 4.640–1; the word could have been 'Sugatists' – 'Happies' 14.404

becoming a Buddhist
better not to be inclined to Buddhism at the start, so you can discover it within yourself 4.352; better to be attracted to Buddhism because it refutes your ideas 26.9; does it help you materially? 9.534; does it mean giving up caste? 9.532–3; changing one's way of life 9.192; first contact with Buddhism 12.624–5; it's possible to be drawn to Buddhism for the wrong reasons 1.19–20, 4.186–7, 17.629–30; people are free not to want to have anything to do with Buddhism 4.248, 26.9; people who profess interest in Buddhism may be the least suitable to practise it 18.412; people who say they're not interested may be interested in what Buddhism really is 4.102–3; we catch hold where we can, but the bit we get hold of is not actually Buddhism 17.674; when you become a Buddhist you cease to be a Christian – as simple as that 14.602

what does becoming a Buddhist involve?
Buddhists don't have to live in the same way or do the same things 6.621; don't imagine that being a Buddhist puts you in a category 17.628; for most people, it just involves participation in popular Buddhism 2.218; Going for Refuge to the Three Jewels 7.225–6, 9.212, 10.385, 11.383–6, 11.467–8, 11.662; how much, if anything, do you need to know about Buddhism? 17.391; looking for authority: 'Would a Buddhist do this? Would a Buddhist do that?' 19.102; the only thing you have to believe is that you can grow 17.28; the greatest task is to insist on the difference between *jñāna* and *vijñāna* 3.356; to eliminate the sense of separative selfhood is the first and last duty of the Buddhist 7.312; traditionally being of good social position was regarded as helpful 14.405; you can't be a Buddhist unless you are free not to be a Buddhist 8.471, 10.281, 26.9; 'You don't even have to call yourself a Buddhist' 3.14, 12.136; you don't have to be highly educated 9.338–9, 11.716; you have to see the Buddha as a Buddha, and understand what that means 7.227–8

being a 'good Buddhist'
Dharma life is not about following some theoretical principle to be a good Buddhist 17.364; don't curb your courage and confidence for the sake of being a 'good Buddhist' 4.444; Going for Refuge as a formality: 'the sort of thing that a good Buddhist did' 2.438; it is possible to be a good Buddhist but a bad monk 2.581–2, 2.587–8; Order members being 'good Buddhists' and not being themselves 4.603

'born Buddhists'
you can't be a 'born Buddhist' 2.302, 2.480–1, 7.226, 8.xxi, 9.486, 9.506, 10.lix, 12.246, 13.489, 15.554; a Buddhist is not someone who has simply been born into a Buddhist family 11.467; a born Buddhist can hardly help having wrong views about the Dharma 14.436; feeling that Buddhism is their birthright however they neglect its teachings 8.313; how can Buddhism be in your blood? 19.474; the kind of Buddhism of those brought up in a traditional environment 7.341; most 'born Buddhists' don't meditate 15.735–6; no sense of being in a sangha 15.648; pride in being a born (rather than converted) Buddhist 12.310–11; Sangharakshita's rejection of the idea 13.480–1; the sense in which one could be reborn a Buddhist 15.687–8

the Buddhist life
honouring the expansive richness of the Buddhist life 3.71; it's not easy to be a Buddhist 11.362; the life of giving 16.400; a new kind of Buddhist worker 9.173–4, 9.224, 9.258, 9.392–3, 9.432–4, 9.510; 'No Buddhists, no Buddhism' 9.187; one-hundred-percent Buddhists 9.211, 9.243, 9.307, 9.432, 10.333, 10.378; Stream Entry is a serious ideal for every Buddhist 18.578; unity among Buddhists 6.621, 9.422–3, 26.82; a vast network of golden lotuses 11.88; what are Buddhists trying to achieve? 3.222–3; when you get together

with other Buddhists, discuss Buddhism 12.81

characteristics of the Buddhist
Buddhists are not 'special' people, but come to have a special view of life 11.503; happiness 10.198, 17.226–7; ideally should feel *mettā* towards everyone they meet 2.569–70; joy is their hallmark 3.265, 17.79–80; living happily 19.426; the embodiment of energy 3.287; a real Buddhist should grow a little every day 26.56; someone who vibrates with presence, with wakefulness to life 3.296; they can be gentle and humble, but also firm, sure, determined, and confident 4.444; they never forget that the real business of their life is to make an end of pain 7.117–18; they should state their views clearly 4.124–5; they should try to live their social and political life in accordance with the Dharma 7.439; to be a Buddhist means to act, to speak out 8.xxxii; truly passionate involvement with the Dharma 26.57; what a Buddhist really is 8.203–5

reflections on being a Buddhist
any Buddhist has to fight to sustain their principles 3.534; the average Buddhist is not usually noticeably radiating *mettā* 19.229; the authoritarian mentality of some Buddhists 7.246; a Buddhist cannot 'represent' Buddhism 3.446–7, 14.542, 26.55; a Buddhist *is* Buddhism – in miniature 11.xix, 26.55; Buddhists are free to make use of good things whatever their source 10.319; Buddhists shouldn't let people of other religions tell them what they 'really' believe 22.78; 'coming out' as a Buddhist 12.126–7; concealing the fact that you are a Buddhist 10.630, 11.378, 12.540, 19.500; if you don't agree that everybody is a Buddhist to some extent, you are called elitist 19.476; like *nāgas*, someone may know a lot about Buddhism but neglect to practise it 16.351; monks coming to be regarded as the 'real Buddhists' 12.388–9, 12.666; the more scholarly a Buddhist is, the more the need to base himself on practice 26.58; participating in the functions of other religions 10.278–9; to think they should be independent of external aids is a misunderstanding 7.258–9; an unenlightened Buddhist is still a Buddhist 19.129; unless we accept a 'Buddhism' there can be no Buddhists 13.509; very few Buddhists are devoted to Buddhism as a means to Enlightenment 21.261

what a Buddhist is not
summary 11.467; false Buddhist like a donkey pretending to be a cow 3.401, 9.192–3, 9.273; false and true (donkey and horse) 9.273–5; if you don't feel psychologically and spiritually free, you're not really a Buddhist 10.188; it's not about being surrounded by Buddhist artefacts 19.477; people who profess to be Buddhist but don't believe in Buddhist teachings 8.205; to be a Buddhist in name only is worse than useless 26.56; to the extent that you have unskilful states, you're not a Buddhist 15.651–3; you can't be a nominal Buddhist 19.468

see also
great lives/great Buddhists; sangha; unity

Budhkumar (or Budha Kumar) v22, 23.384

Buffalmacco 24.224

Bulger, James 3.541–2

bulls *see under* cows

Bullock, Mr and Mrs v22

bullock-cart *see under* transport

Bulwer-Lytton, Edward 20.19–20, 23.8, 23.304

bumpa 16.150

bundle of selves *see under* self/experience of self

Bunyan, John

Pilgrim's Progress
'He that is down need fear no fall' 16.279; one of the best-known allegories in English 16.103; life seen as a journey 16.86, 18.80, 26.262; similarities to one of Milarepa's songs 18.80; takes place in the context of a dream 16.263; Vanity Fair 18.567

other works
Grace Abounding to the Chief of Sinners 2.719 (n519); *The Holy War* 13.531, 20.44

Burckhardt, Jacob 23.312, 23.315

burden the bodhisattva bears the burden of all beings 2.178; the burden of the five *khandhas* (*Saṃyutta Nikāya*) 13.386–7; the 'burden' of insight, *see vipassanādhura*; 'the burden of self' 13.384–97; *ganthadhura* (literally 'the burden of books'), *see ganthadhura*; Going for Refuge as if a great burden had been lifted 3.330, 11.384; 'Love cannot bear the burden of wisdom' 25.442; modern life burdened with more knowledge and less wisdom than our forefathers 1.231, 4.147;

people don't want to carry the 'burden' of responsibility 12.232–3

Burghley House 24.383–4

Burke, Thomas 21.481

Burleigh, Patrick *see* Dharmika

Burlingame, Eugene Watson *see Dhammapada Commentary*

Burma *see* Myanmar

'Burma Raja' *see* Latthakin, Prince K. M.

Burne-Jones, Edward 11.77, 25.438, 25.452, 26.661–2

burning Fire Sermon, *see under Saṃyutta Nikāya*/famous *suttas*; burning oneself 16.195–7, 16.604 (n142); the world is burning, *see under* world

burning grounds *see* cremation grounds

Burnouf, Eugene introduction 7.618 (n499); pioneer of translation of Buddhist works into Western languages 3.654 (n185), 7.449, 8.478; translated the *White Lotus Sūtra* into French 8.478

Burns, Robert brief introduction 24.624 (n96); 'Holy Willie's Prayer' 14.451; 'pleasures are like poppies spread' 25.lvi, 26.398; seeing ourselves as others see us 1.555, 3.565, 15.91, 19.317; Tam o'Shanter's wife 'nursing her wrath to keep it warm' 17.645

Burra, Edward 24.251, 24.670 (n306)

Burton, Richard 11.336–7

Burtt, E. A. 8.217, 9.137

Bury St Edmunds 26.507

business the Buddha meets a businessman 10.483–7; the Buddha sympathizes with the difficulties of business life 10.499; business ethics 1.433, 3.581–2, 13.455; business letters 12.694–5; the business lunch – incompatible with true awareness 1.573, 4.113, 12.557; constant activity in pursuit of business is laziness 4.132, 17.534, 18.390, 19.582; 'May the businessmen and bankers rule over us no more!' 25.437; *see also* right livelihood

busyness beware of the idea that our purpose is to fill our time with useful activities 15.284, 18.120; can one be mindful in a busy life? 5.76–8; doing things slowly, you may get more done than someone who looks busy 1.573; don't be too busy to heed the whispers of inspiration 19.305; for one busy with recitations, books are an impediment to *samādhi* 2.201; if busy, don't do anything until you know what you want to do 4.483–4, 5.646–7, 10.603–4; it's hard to meditate in the midst of busy, worldly life 4.527–8, 5.651–2; people think of themselves as busy, but there may be an underlying passivity 19.582; we are neurotically busy, without any singleness of purpose 11.50; we are so busy going after things we don't really want 16.283–4; when busy with worldly things we have neither strength nor freedom 17.96; Tibetans don't need lectures on meditation, they're too busy practising it 5.576; you can technically be a monk but be busy with all sorts of worldly things 10.629

'but little dust' *see under* dust

Butaol *see under* Nepal

Butler, Bishop Joseph 12.77, 12.708 (n54)

Butler, Samuel 2.604, 13.533, 15.197, 18.360

Büton 13.29, 13.674 (n9)

byāpāda *see vyāpāda*

Byng, Geoffrey v24

Byron, Lord

life story
brief introduction 23.512 (n295); philanderings 26.177; called Euphorion in *Faust* 25.400; carved his name on the temple of Poseidon 23.287; the creation of a protective persona 19.122; letters 12.698; in Ravenna 23.261, 26.660–1; in Shelley's poem 'Julian and Maddalo' 26.660–1; Trelawny's *Records of Byron, Shelley and the Author* 24.571; his death in Missolonghi 23.270, 23.515 (n316)

'Childe Harold's Pilgrimage'
animals 'butchered to make a Roman holiday' at the Colosseum 23.310; 'the deep and dark blue ocean' 2.644; the landscape of the poem compared to New Zealand 24.29–30

other works
'Don Juan' 24.441, 24.163; *She walks in beauty* 26.395

Byzantium *see under* Turkey

C

Cabbalists *see under* Judaism

cabochons *see under* jewels

Cairo, Francesco 23.511 (n292)

caitta-dharmas *see under dharmas*/ analysis of conditioned *dharmas*

caitya (Pāli *cetiya*) as shrine 10.452, 14.462–3; as stupa, *see* stupa

Cakkavattisīhanāda Sutta *see under Dīgha Nikāya*

Cakrasaṃvara 13.309

Cakrasaṃvara Tantra *see under* tantra/ works

cakravartin-rāja (wheel-turning king) *see under* king

Calcutta (Kolkata)

locations
airport 21.510; Ballygunge 20.131; Belur Math 20.131; bookstalls, *see under* bookshops; city centre 22.58; Dakshineshwar 20.131; Dharmapala Institute 21.592; Kalighat 20.134–5; Maha Bodhi Society, *see under* Maha Bodhi Society; Ochterlony Monument 22.578–9 (n64); railway station 22.57; Ramakrishna Mission, *see under* Ramakrishna Mission; Sri Gauranga Press 22.120–1, 22.132; St Paul's College 22.311; Victoria Memorial 22.578–9 (n64)

sights and events
Anagarika Dharmapala interned there for five years 8.63–4; celebration of the Buddha's birthday (1896) 8.53–4; concerns about education in the city 8.176–7; dreadful heat 22.120–2; Hindu–Muslim riots (in 1945) 15.387–8, 20.166, 23.12; night sleepers 25.265; a political procession (1953) 25.258; Pujas 20.134–5; 'this grey city' 25.262

Sangharakshita
stays there while in the Army 20.130–7, 23.11, 23.370–1; lives in Calcutta after demobilization 20.158–72; 'the only thing I really like is the book-stalls' 21.589; living there while editing 22.120–32, 22.166–78, 22.228–32, 22.307–11, 22.377; teaches the Dharma 10.177, 16.507; shopping for Buddhist requisites 23.399–400

Calderón, Pedro 24.410

Caligula 19.19

Cālika Hill *see under Udāna*/settings

call, divine *see under* divine

calm

examples
the Buddha calm and controlled, like a perfectly trained elephant 10.458, 10.461; Dilgo Khyentse Rimpoche was always relaxed and calm 12.446, 12.448; Dudjom Rimpoche was like an ocean: calm depths and a sparkling surface 22.508; the Enlightened disciples' calm after the Buddha's *parinirvāṇa* 4.660–1 (n11), 13.147–8

developing calm
better to say we can develop calm than in our depths we *are* calm 17.93–4, 17.123; by looking into the mind we make it still and calm 17.282; calming the mind in relation to sense experience 15.287–8; calmness can be the result of repressed energy 15.219; developing calm 17.96; feeling balanced, poised, and calm in meditation 10.638; insight 'surrounded by a calm and gentle aura' 5.423–4; mindfulness as the protector of inner calm 17.96

expressions
green the colour of peace, calm, and tranquillity 2.387, 13.67, 18.59; the soothing calm imparted by the Enlightened mind 13.280; white represents the calming aspect of the Enlightened mind 13.282–3; Wordsworth's 'Tintern Abbey' expresses calm like that of meditation 12.672

see also
praśrabdhi

Calvin, John 7.39, 7.551 (n41), 13.387

Cambodia Cambodian monk 22.231; children orphaned by the Khmer Rouge 8.602; a conference of the World Fellowship of Buddhists held there 23.162; its ex-king, Prince Norodom Sihanouk Varma v22, v23; Pol Pot 26.654; revival of Buddhism 7.445–6; Theravāda Buddhism practised 2.548, 3.407

Cambridge Fitzwilliam Museum 26.97–8; King's College Chapel 16.211, 26.95–6; sangha 24.317; Sangharakshita's talks 16.211–23, 23.155, 23.174–5, 24.317

Camden, William 2.238, 2.694 (n331), 15.363–4

camels in a traffic jam with camels 24.111; 'Too long have I been a camel' 25.319; under a flyover in Spain 24.460

Cameron, Clare

her life
tender as a flower and hard as a diamond 20.100, 21.480; a combination of elf and sibyl 20.103; gifts from Dinoo Dubash 21.592; became lost in universalist mysticism 23.40; last years 21.481–2

friendship with Sangharakshita
first meeting 20.100; criticism of Sangharakshita's poetry 20.103, 22.183, 26.583; correspondence 11.547, 12.59; dedicatee of *Messengers from Tibet* 20.103, 21.481, 22.182–3; its depth and significance 7.13, 21.338; visit after returning to England 21.582, 21.592, 23.39–40; introduces Sangharakshita to Sir George Trevelyan 24.195; 'one of the best and sweetest persons I have ever met' 21.586–7

works
editor of *The Middle Way* 7.6, 12.59–60, 20.87, 20.150, 26.583; editor of *Here and Now* 21.338, 21.481, 23.39; editor of the *Science of Thought Review* 21.582; poetry 20.103, 21.480–1, 21.594, 25.87; *A Stranger Here* 21.481; autobiography, *A Rustle of Spring* 21.479, 23.40

Cameron, Julia Margaret 24.358–9

Campanella, Tommasso 1.539, 12.355

Campbell, Alistair Te Ariki (New Zealand poet) 24.563–5

Campbell, Malcolm 26.615

Campbell, Thomas 7.169, 17.358

Canada Joe Cann's early life in Canada 21.447; Sangharakshita's ancestors there 26.525–6, 26.756 (n509); Vancouver 24.531; visiting Canada 12.543, 24.491

caṇḍālī *see under kuṇḍalinī*

candles the beauty of candlelight 11.240; the bodhisattva like a candle that lights thousands of other candles 16.487; Dhardo Rimpoche's mindfulness: incense and candles for everyone 12.433–4, 22.339–40, 22.424; offering thirty-seven candles symbolizing the thirty-seven *bodhipakkiyadhammas* 8.55, 13.252; interconnectedness explained using candles and mirrors 16.22; the symbolism of offering candles 3.340, 9.324, 9.461–2, 11.240, 13.252, 13.417

Candracchattra, Prince 16.572–4

Candragomin (7th-century Indian poet) introduction 17.728 (n150); 'Flower-Garland Hymn to the Goddess Tārā' 17.141–7; a layman 11.571

Candragupta *see* Chandragupta

Candrakīrti

Prasannapadā
commentary on the *Mūlamadhyamakakārikā* 1.311, 1.321; the absence of being as a dogmatic view 3.660 (n227); if the medicine becomes poisonous, where will you turn for treatment? 17.630; imaginary hairs in one's begging-bowl 14.505; verses on Nirvāṇa are directed against the Sarvāstivādins 1.319

other works and sayings
'a city razed to the ground': his nihilist description of Nirvāṇa 14.407–8; commentary on Āryadeva's *Catuḥśataka* 1.322; critique of Vijñānavāda and Sautrāntikas 1.322; failing to wonder every day about existence and non-existence, you're scarcely human 17.570; the king who couldn't bear being the only sane person in a mad kingdom 4.526–7; *Madhyamakāvatāra* 1.322, 5.719 (n186)

Candraprabha 14.191, 14.194

Candrapradīpa Sūtra *see Samādhirāja Sūtra*

caṅkamana *see* walking meditation

Caṅkī Sutta *see under Majjhima Nikāya*

Cann, Joseph E. ('Joe') what he was like 21.45–8, 21.63–5, 22.7–8, 22.87–8; accidentally breaks a Buddha image 22.7–8; bitterness and hatred because of an inferiority complex 22.416–17; commissions a Vajrapāṇi thangka 21.231–2; conflict with Miss Barclay 21.444, 22.11; he makes contact with Dhardo Rimpoche 21.307–8; his critical side 21.64, 21.162–3, 21.428–9; criticizes a book of Sangharakshita's poems 22.183; early life in Canada 21.447; forms his own circle in Kalimpong 21.310–11; friendship with Roderick Langford Rae 22.479; gives a priest his Christmas dinner 21.356; he and Sangharakshita meet in 1966 23.384; helps Sangharakshita sell his thangkas 22.118–19; illustration of one of Sangharakshita's poems 8.646; in Lucknow 21.109; pen-picture of the Buddha 21.56; photographs 21.257, 22.251–2; pursued by two ladies of Kalimpong 22.191; quarrel with Ani-la ('the French nun') 22.236–8; said that Sangharakshita knew nothing

about Buddhism 21.589, 22.503; a Tibetan boy goes to live with him 21.429–30; as a tutor of English 21.166–7

Cannan, Mary 8.549

canonical literature *see under* scriptures

Cantwell Smith, Wilfred 13.429

capability being truly capable (*sakko*, *Mettā Sutta*) 15.269–71; beings are not all equally capable of becoming Enlightened from their present state 13.135; the bodhisattva is incapable of self-referring or other-referring activities 7.155; don't do less than you can, don't compromise 18.622; don't underestimate the degree of rationalization that people are capable of 18.366; even the best of things is incapable of giving permanent satisfaction 2.121; if the ideal is pitched beyond people's reach, they do what they are capable of 18.638; 'I'm capable of doing it, so why should I leave it to other people?' 4.477; the implication of a rule of training is that one is capable of learning 2.343; in India, memories were capable of preserving teachings for a hundred generations 1.379; the mind is capable of change for the better 9.399; most people are not capable of enjoying the company of Buddhas and bodhisattvas 18.635; non-attachment has no meaning unless you're full-bloodedly capable of attachment 18.337; often your spiritual friends have a better idea of your capabilities than you do yourself 18.622–3; one has to be capable of fear of death 16.278, 18.341; one who has realized the perfection of emptiness is incapable of acting unethically 7.377; religion will decline if it doesn't have capable preachers (Ambedkar) 16.185; reverence for all beings for what they are capable of attaining 3.62–3; a Stream Entrant is incapable of ingratitude 3.607; that one is able to do a thing is no reason for doing it 26.16; truthfulness is a power capable of producing tangible results 2.169; to embark on the spiritual life you need to be a capable human being 15.269–71; the unskilful actions of which an *arhant* is incapable 1.143–4; very few people are capable of truly following a universal religion 12.251; women's spiritual capacity, *see under* women

Cape Comorin, India 7.593 (n282), 20.237–42

capitalism 16.412, 18.507–8, 26.20

Caple, Dr v23

Capote, Truman 24.374, 24.389, 26.380

Caravaggio 23.308, 23.520 (n346), 24.323 (film), 24.420

caravan 'battered caravanserai' 2.80; 'the caravan of humanity moving along the road of being ...' 4.361; Sangharakshita stays in a wooden caravan in New Zealand 24.48–9; Sangharakshita's sister lives in a gypsy caravan 23.29, 25.69, 25.449; a Tibetan caravan is attacked by bandits 18.99–100

Cardinal, Roger 24.568

carelessness 7.515–17, 17.91

Carey, William v22

Cariappa, General Kodandera Madappa v22

caritas or *caritras* *see* character types

cariya *see caryā*

Cariyāpiṭaka ('Basket of the Bodhisattva's Conduct) 14.66–7

Cariyāpiṭaka Aṭṭhakathā 16.584 (n6)

Carlyle, Thomas commenting on the seriousness with which people took Christianity 4.125; *The French Revolution* 8.588, 8.706 (n333); the 'great man' theory of history 10.167; *On Heroes and Hero-Worship* 3.46, 26.178, 26.482; his need for solitude 26.354; a picture in Sangharakshita's flat 26.406; the poet as prophet and seer 26.209; ridiculed for his lengthy use of words to praise silence 1.525; 'the Thought of thinking Souls' 14.291, 26.321; 'We are all poets when we read a poem well' 26.191

Carney, Julia Abigail Fletcher 18.411

Carpaccio, Vittore 25.377

carpe diem 17.163

Carpenter, Dorothy v23

Carpenter, Edward 9.xxi, 13.610

carpets life like unrolling a Persian carpet to see the pattern 18.283; pushing unskilful mental states under the carpet (alienated awareness) 12.267; Western tendency to sweep death under the carpet 4.76, 12.194–5, 15.144, 15.147

Carr, Brian 8.603

Carrithers, Michael 2.589, 2.590, 2.592, 5.366

Carroll, Lewis (*Alice's Adventures in Wonderland*) 'Drink Me' 8.594–5; the Mock Turtle and the walrus 23.67; 'I felt like Alice at the Mad Hatter's tea party' 23.355; not some kind of Zen text 8.594,

14.481, 17.65–6; Sangharakshita first reads 20.16–17; takes place in the context of a dream 16.263; Queen Victoria's response 17.65

Carter (American friend) he sets Sakura on fire 26.608; his girlfriend Andrea 26.613–15; his sexual relationship with Sangharakshita 26.608; living with him 26.607–16; losing him 26.616; taking drugs with him 26.496–7, 26.609–10

Carter, Lee *see* Sucharita

Cartland, Barbara 23.98, 23.489 (n121)

Carus, Paul introduction 7.619 (n503), 8.676–7 (n76); founder of the American Maha Bodhi Society 8.54; *The Gospel of Buddha* 7.548 (n23), 8.140–1, 9.137, 9.138–9, 10.661, 12.750 (n417)

Cārvākas (materialists) 1.314, 19.185

carya (Pāli *cariya*) meaning 14.547; *cariya* (conduct) in the *Patisambhidā-magga* 14.74; the *carya* series (from *brahmacarya* to *anubhogacarya*) 14.521; four *caryās* (of the bodhisattva), *see* four *caryās*

Castañeda, Carlos 24.257, 24.672 (n313)

caste system

THE SYSTEM

introduction
brief description 10.287, 10.308–9, 12.50; definition of caste 9.27–8; four castes (*caturvarṇa*) 14.532; 'graded inequality' 9.28, 9.30, 9.101, 9.134–5, 9.184–5, 9.353–4; harsh and divisive spirit 20.301; the hell of caste 9.25–44, 9.179; hereditary principle 9.354–5; compared to the burning house 9.360; a sanitized account 8.605; the consequences of belief in the caste system 8.xxiii; distinctions of caste are made by the mind 10.232–3

history
the myth of the 'cosmic man' and the origin of the four castes 9.77, 12.239, 14.426; the *Bhagavad Gītā* links *guṇas* (character types) with castes 10.53–6, 12.278; Tulsidas' *Rāmacaritamānasa* 8.xix, 8.358, 20.199; *Dharma Śāstras*: regulate relations between castes 20.263; religious knowledge kept away from the lowest castes 10.625; practice of Untouchability made a penal offence 3.629 (n22), 20.264

aspects of the system
caste *dharma* 9.544, 10.55–6, 15.463; caste negated by crossing the ocean (*kālapāni*) 9.315–16, 21.275; higher castes' projection onto lower castes 12.223; imperative to belong to a caste 9.353; impossibility of acquiring caste 10.44; impossibility of repudiating caste 20.199; incompatible with secular state 9.354; marriage within castes 9.27, 10.363; pollution 20.161–2

terms
Mlechchha 20.199, 20.339, 20.433; Scheduled Castes 9.31, 9.124–5; 'Untouchables', *see* Dalits

enquiries about caste status
so people know where they stand in relation to you 17.286; questioning strangers aggressively about their background 20.263–4; Sangharakshita challenged to declare his caste 3.142, 9.280, 12.245, 20.267–9, 20.306

caste prejudice
against Dalits, *see under* Dalits; against a doctor in Mumbai 10.lx–xi; against Europeans 20.194–5, 20.198–9; against students at the Nagarjuna Training Institute 10.lvi–vii; among children in Travancore 20.291; in Indian villages 10.12, 10.288; violence in Aurangabad 10.xli; against the YMBA in Kalimpong 21.80

Hinduism
brahmin obfuscation about 'untouchability' 15.175; brahmins, *see* brahmins; Hindu ideas of karma and rebirth institutionalized in the caste system 17.211–12; Hinduism is inseparable from the caste system 9.53–4, 12.245; Hinduism's division between social order and spiritual life 10.41; orthodox Hindu belief in the caste system 22.162–3; high-caste Hindus may be in danger of arrogance 14.405

speaking out against caste
Banerjee's repudiation of caste 20.194–6; Dharmapala speaks out against 'the abominations of caste' 8.57, 8.103; diverging views 20.278–9; Dr Mehta's opposition to the caste system 22.303; Muslim reaction to caste 21.106; some Hindus recognize caste as an evil 9.429

observance of caste
in Anandamayi's ashram 20.193–203; by Christians 9.62, 9.315

BUDDHIST RESPONSES

the Buddha
he allowed no caste distinctions within the sangha 14.405; *Buddha and Caste System* (book review) 8.359–60; he saw everybody simply as a human being 10.326; his teaching about caste 2.691–2 (n305), 19.545–6; he was criticized for not living according to his caste 9.185, 10.624, 12.50, 12.239; he was the pioneer and founder of casteless society 10.xxvii;

his disciples came from all castes and none 13.699 (n163); Kshatriya 3.49, 9.185, 9.191; no distinction to be drawn between members of different castes 2.692 (n305), 3.77; only the Buddha could remove the evils of caste 22.163; opposition to the caste system 1.541, 9.72, 9.142, 9.473, 12.239, 13.699 (n163); reassures two brahmin disciples who have been abused for renouncing their caste 3.76–7; rejected the system of hereditary caste 7.511; said that as a fire can be kindled from any fuel, all castes can grow spiritually 14.42; 'when someone joins the sangha, he loses his caste' 2.691–2 (n305), 9.473, 12.521; the system wasn't as rigid at the Buddha's time as it later became 10.446

Buddhism
a *bhikkhu* who called other *bhikkhus* outcastes due to brahmin conditioning 10.514–15; renunciation of caste by wanderers 3.461; as Buddhism declined in India, the caste system hardened 10.186; does becoming a Buddhist mean giving up caste? 9.532–3; Buddhism does not believe in caste 9.496–7, 20.196; in the realization of the highest truth, difference of caste is obliterated 7.103; *bhikṣu* ordination does not include caste restrictions 2.193; the symbolism of the low-caste woman in Tantric Buddhism 13.359, 13.699 (n163); in the past Buddhist society experienced a relief from caste prejudice 10.xxvii; in the sangha differences of caste and nationality should actively be discouraged 10.565; Varrier community of Travancore – connection with Buddhism? 20.287; Nepali low-caste students' attraction to Buddhism 21.75

caste and the modern Buddhist community
breaking free from the caste system 9.428, 22.289–90; Buddhist localities in Indian cities and the caste system 24.17; difficulties around official declarations of caste status 9.523–5; dispute over the building of a vihara in Bangalore 22.149–50; the eradication of caste 9.341; moving to the city to escape the caste system 10.329; Sangharakshita insists on receiving food from a low caste woman 20.399–400; the system applied to Buddhists 9.416

see also
Ambedkar/on caste; Dalits; Nepal/caste system in Nepal

Castle Acre, Norfolk 19.493

castles Dover Castle 23.245; Sforza Castle, Milan 23.253–4; turning one's house into a (metaphorical) castle 18.284–7; the ultimate material refuge, and the ultimate expression of fear 18.49

Castro, Don v24

cat association with Krishna 20.281; a black cat at Guhyaloka 24.394–5; a bodhisattva should not keep a cat 16.295; the cat's unteachable obstinacy 19.17; a childhood emotional response to kittens 26.418; Cleopatra, Sangharakshita's cat in Kalimpong 21.317; cats did not weep at the Buddha's *parinirvāṇa* 3.119, 16.295; Miss Barclay's cat 22.47, 22.85; an enormous cat's jaws form the Mouth of Hell in a fresco 24.383–4; Mrs Fifi Greywhiskers 22.617 (n339); a frightened kitten on the Tube 26.564; the guru who tied a kitten to a post 19.55; a relative who hated cats 26.553; the spiritual life is to develop heroes, not pussycats 19.360; talking to the cat 9.520; Tiger, the Padmaloka community cat 24.151; 'Tread softly as a cat' 25.231; the Vihara cat in Kalimpong 22.441; the War Office cat 20.486, 26.426; the young Sangharakshita firing his water pistol at a cat 26.655–6

Catena of Buddhist Scriptures *see* Beal

Cathars (Albigenses) introduction 8.420–1, 15.771–2 (n241); against marriage as a sacrament 8.423; the Albigensian crusade 11.361; Arthur Guirdham's *The Great Heresy* 8.420–5, 16.472; Cathar revival in the 20th century 24.189; Cathar teachings 8.423; comparison with Buddhism 8.424; *perfecti* burnt alive 8.421, 13.580, 13.667; rebirth 16.472; and spiritual community 24.xxiii; their practice of a form of right livelihood 8.424; their rejection of the Church 8.420, 15.623; vilification by the Catholic Church 8.421–3

cathedrals admired for their beauty, but not their spiritual message 19.469; an idea for a short story about a cathedral 26.273–6, 26.282; Aachen 24.370; Bristol 23.206; Bury St Edmunds 26.507; Canterbury 14.465, 23.253–4, 23.321; Chartres 13.602; Chichester 23.116; Cologne 24.369; Coventry 23.139; Durham 24.584; Essen 24.367; Florence 23.312; Granada 24.449–50, 24.455–6; Guildford 24.194; Kraków 26.449; Lichfield 23.137; Lugana 23.250; Luxembourg 23.247; Metz, France 23.247–8; Milan 23.252–3; Murcia 24.458–9; Naples 24.267–9; Norwich 23.116, 26.490; Padua 19.467, 23.259, 24.458; Peterborough 24.365; Pisa 24.224; Salisbury 23.116; St Albans 24.310 (n379); St Peter's, Rome 23.309; Seville 24.435–6; Siena 13.634, 13.637; Toledo

24.417–20; Tours 23.452; Ulm 24.594–5; Uppsala 13.639; Westminster 13.549–50; Westminster Abbey 8.560, 26.680; Worcester 24.581; York Minster 24.386

Cather, Willa 24.389

Catherine, St, of Siena canonization 13.637; *Dialogue* 13.637; her house in Siena 13.634–5; life story 13.634–8; burial in Rome 13.637–8, 23.309; portrait 13.635–6; relics 13.635, 13.637–8; she comforts di Tondo at his execution 13.637; she encourages women to be heroic 11.633–4; she persuades the pope to move back to Rome 11.633; a woman from whom we can learn 11.633–4

Catholicism, Roman *see under* Christianity

cattle *see* cows and buffaloes

Catuḥśataka *see* Āryadeva

Catuḥstava 1.311

caturvarga 2.138, 14.532

caturvarṇa *see under* caste system

catuṣkoṭi (four logical alternatives, the fourfold negation) explanation 10.689–90 (n202); held in common by Theravāda and Mahāyāna 7.531; Nāgārjuna's use of the *catuṣkoṭi* 10.690 (n202); useless to preoccupy oneself with them 10.598

Caulfield, Patrick 24.134, 24.637 (n155)

causality, causation, and causes

causes
do we need to know the cause of our unskilful state? 18.442–4; the example of the conditions that have 'caused' a loaf of bread 3.317; the four causes, *see under* Aristotle; nothing arises without at least two causes 7.259; our tendency to think in terms of one agent, not a complex of conditions 10.601; philosophy shows the importance of investigating the causes of things 3.261, 7.115; think in terms of causes and conditions, not 'I did this' or 'He did that' 10.600–2; to free ourselves from the limitations of existence we must ask its cause 7.115

causation and causality
the Buddhist distinction between causality and conditionality 1.110, 14.607–8, 19.435; causal (*kāraṇa*) designations in the Abhidharma 14.83; causality in the spiritual life 25.77; a complex web with multiple nature 3.316–17, 9.389; 'formative causation' (Sheldrake) 24.209–10; the idea of conditionality is the idea of causation employed in modern science 17.637; 'Deep indeed is this Causal Law, and deep it appears to be' 1.95–6, 17.389, 17.750 (n325); it is better to think of conditionality than causation 17.636; the law of causation, *see* 'This being, that becomes'; a nihilist refuses to accept that things are causally connected (Nāgārjuna) 17.250; the principle of causality the conceptual formulation of the truth of *śūnyatā* 1.343; Sangharakshita troubled by the nature of causality 20.159; twenty-four causal conditions, *see* twenty-four causal conditions

cause and effect
the assumption that the cause of a phenomenon is inferior to its effect 8.230; better to think of cause and effect than getting rid of the ego 17.352; essentially a relation between two things 1.315; the five effects (*pañca-phala*) 14.212; great events can come from seemingly insignificant causes 8.73–4; the law of cause and effect works itself out in a complex way 15.370; Nāgārjuna on the middle way between them 1.315–16, 14.607, 17.247–9, 17.637, 19.435; Nirvāṇa is empty of the whole cause–effect process 14.561; one aspect of Enlightenment is the ability to see cause and effect 18.85; our ideas of cause and effect subtly determine how we interpret experience 17.247; primitive people's lack of understanding of it 15.382; relative terms 17.248; *satkāryavāda* and *asatkāryavāda* 1.314–16, 3.197, 10.142, 10.160, 14.607, 17.362, 17.636–7, 19.435; unreal: a thought-construction imposed upon existence 1.316

Cavafy, C. P. 23.472, 23.541 (n496)

Cavalieri, Tommaso 24.316

Cavell, Edith her life 12.728 (n231), 26.590; she died for others 12.9, 12.701–2 (n7), 23.211; a heroine 26.490;'Patriotism is not enough' 12.343, 26.490, 26.590

caves

Ajanta caves
introduction 10.704 (n335), 26.389–90; how were the monks who painted the images free of sexual desire? 17.226, 21.403–4; illustrations of the *Jātakamāla* 14.66; mural paintings 2.212, 4.84, 7.396, 7.448, 8.302–3, 9.313, 9.363, 9.383, 26.233; the Padmapāṇi figure 9.313, 26.234, 26.384, 26.599, 26.697; *My Pilgrimages to Ajanta and Bagh* (Dey) 21.402; a plan for a film 17.226, 21.403–6; show that Buddhism must have been widespread in the area 9.313, 10.372

Bhaja caves
'The Caves of Bhájá', *see under* Mahadhammavira; lit up by the evening sun 26.390; photograph 10.334; relationship to Bhaja retreat centre 10.405–6

Kanheri caves, near Mumbai
depiction of the twin miracle 12.184; Sangharakshita leads a pilgrimage to the caves in 1959 10.122, 10.335; Sangharakshita visits 20.381–2, 23.16, 23.334; standing Buddhas 20.382; vandalism by a film crew 8.287–8, 8.300

Karle (or Karla) caves
introduction 24.607 (n25); Buddhists are not allowed to make offerings in the caves 8.295; animal sacrifice within the caves 8.295–6, 8.302, 10.171; vandalism 8.294–6, 8.300–2, 22.458; a visit to the caves 24.13

other caves
cave temples with paintings at Ipoh, Malaysia 24.43–4; cave viharas of Maharashtra 9.53, 9.236, 10.333, 10.406; beneath Nottingham 24.580; Dunhuang caves, *see* Dunhuang; Ellora caves 9.313, 10.293, 10.701 (n295); rock-cut dwellings along the Loire 23.452–3; Virupaksha Guha cave 20.337–46, 26.225–6

cave dwellers
Ani-la lives in an electrified cave 22.233–4; caves in which Padmasambhava meditated 22.468; Mother Lakshmi, cave-dwelling ascetic 18.328, 20.366–7; Milarepa meditates in the tiger-cave of Singa-dzong 18.41–2, 18.51–2

cave dwelling
no point living in a cave and wondering what's going on in the world 4.555; why is a cave regarded as an ideal place to meditate? 4.542; why stay in a cave unless you make use of the opportunity? 19.557

metaphorical and fictional caves
'The Cave' (short story) 24.371–2, 25.569–86; the cave of the heart 26.284–5, 26.305–6; 'I carry my cave around with me' (Gandhi) 19.492; living in a metaphorical cave in the city 19.492–3; the prisoners in the cave, *see under* Plato/*Republic*; symbolism 4.542

Caxton, William 13.653–62, 13.726 (n454), 26.662

'Cease to do evil, learn to do good, purify the heart' *see Dhammapada*/chapter 14

Cecil, William, Lord Burghley 24.383

Cecilia, St 23.308

celibacy

introduction
Buddhism's emphasis on celibacy 17.221; distinction from chastity 2.709 (n444); everybody is celibate to some extent 11.589; how it was seen in the Buddha's day 11.568–9; if your sex life is restricted you need more simple bodily contact 4.562; men's and women's responses 17.219, 26.30; neurotic and non-neurotic celibacy 11.587–8; the principle of celibacy 11.589; *Sex is Not Compulsory* 24.313; the celibacy of the monk 11.570, 16.391; celibates not appreciating the difficulties of those who are not celibate 17.303

choosing celibacy
accusation that taking this vow makes one almost a murderer 7.218; as lifestyle 3.566; if one can live happily celibate, that is really best 12.402; if you're attracted to that lifestyle, talk with others who live it 17.364; it may not be a good idea to repress strong sexual feelings and take up celibacy 17.217; it must be a voluntary decision 11.587, 11.597; moving in the direction of celibacy 11.588–90, 13.452–3; not much point in giving up sex when neurotic craving is still there 26.30; taking a vow of celibacy 19.145; to be seriously considered by the time you're 45 12.402

the value of celibacy
being physically celibate by itself has little value 11.588; celibacy for the sake of a higher interest or ideal 11.588; conserving energy 15.153; the entrance into non-duality 16.548; in the spiritual life 27.1073–4; an indication that one's sex life is under control 17.221; not an end in itself 17.221; prerequisite to any form of higher spiritual life 1.10, 1.348, without celibacy Enlightenment is unattainable 1.442

see also
brahmacarya; chastity

Cellini, Benvenuto 23.313, 23.522 (n356)

Celsus 13.717–18 (n341)

cemetery *see* cremation ground

cenobitical *see under* monasticism

central channel (*avadhūti*, sometimes 'median nerve') the aim of visualizing the central channel 19.31; energy rising through the central channel 18.91; feeling the guru descend through the central channel in the guru yoga 13.219; *lalanā* and *rasanā* running through the central channel 1.389, 13.163, 18.76; Milarepa's energy: a horse galloping wildly along the central channel 18.72–3; Tantric practice of bringing the 'breath' (*prāṇa*) into the central channel 18.76; in Tantric yoga 19.30–1; visualizing energy rising up the central channel 19.412

Centre House first ordinations into the Western Buddhist Order 23.440; home to a New Age group called Centre 23.416; Sangharakshita and Terry stay there 23.416–17; autumn lectures 23.463

centres *see under* Triratna IV

ceremonies

reflections
even the most sacred ceremonies can degenerate into entertainment 24.531; for some an earthly reflection of an archetypal realm, for others a distraction 24.530–1; ideally combine richness with simplicity, aesthetic appeal with significance 24.531; the importance of ceremonies: an enactment of body, speech, and mind 18.378–9; keep ceremonies simple 19.535

name-giving ceremony (namkaran-vidhi)
in India, potential contribution to unity 9.336; eight name-givings 24.23; a joyful occasion 12.588; a name-giving in New Zealand 24.617 (n66); Sangharakshita's first name-giving ceremony in England 23.150; sorry to hear that a ceremony was conducted behind closed doors 10.167–8

other ceremonies
birth 2.230; *paritrāna* (protection) ceremonies 10.124, 10.140, 10.147, 10.681 (n141); *paritta* or *pirith* (protection) ceremony 8.532, 22.250–1; Thai tonsure ceremony 2.230–1

see also
funerals; *kaṭhina* ceremony; marriage; Triratna II/teachings and practices/Triratna ceremonies

ceremoniousness 12.486–7

certainty (and uncertainty) the certainty of beauty, love, and pain 25.259; a culpable state of uncertainty 2.147; direct, unmediated experience, characterized by absolute certainty 2.54; 'he lives having passed beyond uncertainty' 5.283–5; in study, moving from clarity to uncertainty and back to clarity 19.101; *kaṅkha* (uncertainty) 10.577; people would rather have absolute certainty than think for themselves 17.627; sometimes we want more certainty than life can give us 17.689; speculation, creed, and dogma lead to uncertainty 7.145; wanting certainty, people are apt to believe those with very definite views 17.627

Cervantes, Miguel de (*Don Quixote*) credulous faith exemplified by Don Quixote 17.62–3, 17.67; Don Quixote country 24.407; Don Quixote and Zen 17.64–5, 17.66–7; the Plaza del Potro, Córdoba 24.430; praise of sleep 3.338

cessation (*nirodha*) of the cycle of birth and death 1.92–3; of desire 1.131; of distinction between 'self' and 'not-self' 1.64; far from the last word in Buddhism 11.309; *khandha-nirodha* 7.151; *loka-nirodha* 7.151; *nirodha* an epithet of Nirvāṇa 1.69; spiritual life may be seen as cessation or development 7.151; of suffering (*dukkha-nirodha*) 1.131–4, 7.151; of thought-constructions 1.64

cetanā (volitional consciousness)

introduction
introduction 17.723 (n113); broader than ordinary volition, a bit like a life-force 17.522; the Buddha found it a feeble word to describe 'will' 14.14; it plays a crucial role in Buddhist life 11.650, 12.537–8; classified in terms of the ten precepts, ten channels for *cetanā* to flow through 17.528–9; contrast with *bhavaṅga-sota* 17.523; 'directionality of mind': the pressure forward of the whole subject towards its object 17.521; in relation to the *ālaya-vijñāna* 1.369; as an omnipresent mental event (Abhidharma) 17.520–9; and rebirth 1.112

karma-cetanā (volitional actions)
cetanā is the aspect of mind which is not the result of karma, but karma itself 17.524; different types of volitional activity 14.84; one's level of being is determined by whether they are skilful or unskilful 17.679; and *saṃskāras* 1.108; important equation: karma = *cetanā* = *saṃskāras* 2.68, 17.520–1; sometimes

karma is said to be equivalent to *cetanā* 3.9, 8.576

see also
will

cetasika-dhammas *see* mental events

cetiya *see* stupa

ceto-vimutti or *ceto-vimukti* *see under vimukti*

Ceylon *see* Sri Lanka

Cézanne, Paul 26.98, 26.309

chaang 18.403

Chagna Dorje *see* Vajrapāṇi

chains breaking the chains of folly, hate, and greed 25.381; breaking the chain of birth and death 25.341; the chain forged by Jacob Marley in *A Christmas Carol* 15.205; chains of prisoners of the Moors 24.422; the 'great chain of being' (medieval idea) 12.463; *nidāna* chain meditation, *see nidāna* chain meditation; people going round and round like dumb chained cattle 25.301; spiritual hierarchy a living chain of spiritual beings 12.14

chairs 'Are you here for the Dharma or are you here for a chair?' 16.535–7; armchair Buddhism 1.553, 8.497, 16.285, 19.96; Maitreya often shown not cross-legged, but seated as though upon a chair 2.179; Zhaozhou, the ascetic Zen master who mended a chair with firewood 8.488

Chaitanya 1.166

Chaitanya, Sri (Gouranga) 7.61, 7.98, 7.563 (n99)

chaitya *see stupa*

Chaityavādins 16.154–5

chakras (psychic centres) associated with the elements 18.77; awakened by energy rising up the central channel 16.121, 18.91; the basis for transformation 19.37, 19.40–1; in Buddhism usually three or four chakras 18.619; correlated with the elements of the stupa 13.155–7, 16.145–8, 16.161–2; difference between Buddhist and Hindu chakras 4.258–9, 18.619; different ways of seeing 16.135; the distinction between the organic heart and the heart chakra 4.259, 16.135; higher and lower chakras 18.619; identification of chakras with the nerves of the physical body 19.31; illustration 13.156; *kuṇḍalinī*, *see kuṇḍalinī*; Lama Govinda's description 16.134; as lotus flowers 18.76; the Lord's Prayer related to the chakras at a New Age event 24.202; Mr Chen's view 16.135; release of energy 16.134–5; in the subtle body 16.135–6; and the symbolism of Mucalinda 2.37; the throat-centre 4.314, 19.43; Tibetan tradition of visualization 16.135; visualizing energy rising up the central channel 19.412; wariness of employing the language of chakras 22.301

Chakravarty, Dr Gyanendranath 20.184

chaḷabhiñño (possessor of the six superknowledges) 14.81

challenge anger when our views are challenged is a sure sign of attachment 3.199–200; the challenge of the four gifts 25.147–8, 25.335; the challenge of real communication 3.618; challenges of Buddhism, *see under* Buddhism II; challenges of change, *see under* change; challenges of spiritual life, *see under* spiritual life; a challenge to literalistic thinking 3.361, 14.318–19, 14.321; challenging people out of their passivity 19.581; doesn't necessarily make you stronger 16.324; facing up to the challenge of existence 13.356; the four noble truths are challenges to act 8.572–3; 'It's very challenging to change yourself' 10.lxi; persisting through the challenges of spiritual practice 18.161–2; the true test of spiritual practice is how we relate to the challenge of 'other people' 3.521

Chamberlain, Neville 20.46

Chan Zong 1.372

chance having found out as much as we can, we always have to take a chance 14.550; in Buddhism, *mettā* isn't left to chance, but consciously developed 1.502; our lives don't represent just a series of chances 18.283–4; spiritual life doesn't depend on chance or fate 8.202; the wrong view that everything happens by chance 3.292, 10.249

chanda eagerness, the opposite of laziness 17.533; intense will, a sort of concentrated volition 10.586, 17.457; an object-determining mental event (Abhidharma) 17.532–5; one of the four *iddhipādas* 10.586, 17.457, 17.766 (n472); a very strong term 12.550; *dhammachanda* or *dharmachanda*, *see dharmachanda*; *kāmacchanda* (desire for sensuous experience), *see kāmacchanda*

chandali (*caṇḍālī*) *see under kuṇḍalinī*

chandas (Vedic Sanskrit) 16.365

Chandra, Arun 20.419–21

Chandrabodhi, Dhammachari 24.366

Chandragupta Maurya 7.423, 10.648, 20.374

Chandramani, U

his life
brief introduction 2.717 (n502); character 20.404; disciples 22.258–60; his ordination of many women 11.427; photograph 20.405; spent fifty years restoring shrines at Kusinārā 2.417–18, 20.407–8; administers Refuges and Precepts to Dr Ambedkar 2.495, 9.73, 9.127–9, 22.335–6; receives a visit from the Eminent Buddhists 22.335–6

and Sangharakshita
Jagdish Kashyap encourages Sangharakshita to ask him for ordination 20.395; *śrāmaṇera* ordination 2.418–19, 9.280, 9.467–8, 9.488–9, 9.501, 10.7, 20.404–11; he asks Sangharakshita to preach the Dharma in Nepal 20.413, 23.16; Sangharakshita recommends him to Dr Ambedkar 9.17, 9.209, 9.405, 9.502–3, 10.7, 22.288; Sangharakshita writes to him requesting *bhikṣu* ordination 21.98; unable to attend Sangharakshita's *bhikṣu* ordination 2.748–9 (n713)

Chandrasila, Dhammachari 24.366

Chang, Garma C. C.

introduction
travelled to Tibet in the 1930s 18.xii; *The Hundred Thousand Songs of Milarepa*, *see under* Milarepa/translations

A Treasury of Mahāyāna Sūtras
a bodhisattva who breaks precepts out of desire 2.389; the gaining of Enlightenment was a play 4.136; *Ratnakūṭa sūtras* 4.663 (n24), 14.179

changchub sems *see bodhicitta*

change

change and Buddhism
becoming a Buddhist means changing 9.192, 9.525–6, 18.485; Buddhism does not just exhort you to change, but shows you how 11.153; Buddhism in one word: change 10.327–8; Buddhism is not just learning philosophy – we have to change our lives 3.370; a Buddhist does not think that anything is exempt from the law of change 7.131; change and going forth 9.191; the changes you might want to make when you start practising the Dharma 10.630–1; the doctrine of no-self represents the possibility of radical change 26.85; has the practice of Buddhism changed your way of life? 9.192; 'The Importance of Change in the Buddhist Spiritual Life' 24.44–5; the path is a symbol representing the fact that we can change 17.435; the sangha should encourage people to change 17.239; spiritual practices are important because it is important to change the mind 12.466–7; when people change as a result of Buddhist practice: the greatest miracle 3.463–4; when the unenlightened man becomes Enlightened, what changes? 11.114–15; within the sangha, change should be in the context of continuity 12.677–8; your reasons for being a Buddhist may change 14.599

the philosophy of change
change, but nothing that changes 7.133, 10.160, 18.154, 19.376; the changing nature of experience 7.37; 'Even in one and the same moment, things are and are not the same' 7.195; everything is in constant flux 18.179; 'Existence (or Reality) = Change (or Becoming)' 4.647; the language of change implies that a substance can exist without attributes 2.87; life teaches us the lesson of change all the time 7.132, 25.195; an unchanging element at the heart of becoming would make change impossible 7.153

the potential offered by change
all things change, and this can become a source of joy 15.250; the *anattā* doctrine implies the possibility of spiritual evolution 7.133, 7.153; change is not just about decay, it can be for the better 9.398–9, 13.228; change your consciousness to see a different world, or see the world differently 26.84; contrast between change and progress 7.163; directing change of consciousness towards positive growth 15.161; everything can change, and mental states are no exception 15.178; how

terrible if in a year's time we were the same as we are today! 11.147, 26.10; it can be hard to assess whether change is good or bad 10.555; it contains the promise and potentiality of development 11.29; making change into transformation 13.228; one supremely important fact is that we *can* change 26.9; openness to people can make it possible for them to change 17.239; reflecting that one has changed, and further change is possible 17.378; spiritual progress is based upon the truth that the mind can change 19.235; steering change through mindfulness 15.243; there is nothing about us that cannot be changed 19.235; we can change, help others to change, together change the world 26.57; we need not just change, but change for the better 15.509–10

external and internal change
awareness brings change, but perhaps not how we expect 17.xx–xxi; bringing about change through changing your environment 11.117, 12.553–4; change may or may not manifest in external behaviour 18.204–5; changing society through establishing single-sex communities 15.473–4; danger of mistaking external change for internal change 16.122–3; external changes can bring about internal changes, but they are not the same 18.640; it is usually possible to change the situation you're in 15.117; one's environment must cooperate with inner change 4.183; tendency to think that the world changes, but 'I' persist unchanging 7.208–9; things that change us 9.370–8; we need to change ourselves, not just our conditions 19.89; when you start changing, you may feel you can't live in the same old way 3.464; you can't practise spiritually without changing how you live and work 15.114; your whole pattern of life has to change once you change your mind 4.508

the challenges of change
for most of us, change doesn't go very deep 3.148–9; it's very difficult to change 10.lxi, 10.277–8, 11.552, 11.710–11, 19.89; resistance to change 3.293–4, 4.150, 11.710, 15.520; other people don't want you to change 4.271, 9.418, 11.48, 18.485; overcoming fear of change is the function of all spiritual practices 16.110; people do not want to change 26.173; to imagine radically changing involves letting go of our idea of self 3.418; unconscious resistance to change you are consciously trying to make 17.255; we prefer to settle down in the familiar 12.10, 14.409–10, 18.204–5; we don't accept that we might need to change how we think and behave 4.128; when you are determined to change, a label can be removed 17.238–9

rate of change
the pace of change in the modern world 10.xxii, 10.328, 11.111; a real Buddhist should change a little every day 26.56; the self is constantly changing 3.492; slow rate of change in prehistoric times 9.178–9; sometimes change is very sudden 4.271–2; spiritual change can happen almost straightaway 3.162, 15.363–4

the effects of change
a change should mean a change 10.14; changing religion 10.342, 14.602; a genuine change of consciousness will express itself in one's whole life 25.47; people can see that you've changed 5.251

Channa (Siddhārtha's charioteer) 3.25–9, 3.118–19

Channovāda Sutta see under Majjhima Nikāya

chanting *The Book of Protection* (*Pirith Potha*) in Sri Lanka 8.532–3; chanting texts to learn them by heart 17.417; developing devotion through chanting 4.298, 4.305–6; the effect of the ceremonial chanting of Pāli texts 15.436–7; in Buddhist countries lay people like to listen to monks chanting 15.437; chanting mantras, *see under* mantras; chanting *suttas* 14.37, 22.89; chanting together, *see saṅgīti*; quality and styles of chanting in puja 11.227

chaos the bodhisattva transforming chaos into a cosmos 4.98; creating a cosmos out of the chaos of human experience 4.82; through abstraction we have reduced the chaos of impressions to a cosmos 7.325; Mahāyāna Buddhism a chaos full of life and movement 1.277–9; in the modern world 16.351, 16.356; whereas Pāli literature is a cosmos, Sanskrit literature is a chaos 1.277

Chapters (*Skandhakas*) *see under* Vinaya/other sets of rules

character character armour, *see under* Reich; character building 10.119; the effects of art remain a permanent part of our character 26.190; 'giving style to one's character' (Nietzsche) 3.500–1; meditation according to character, *see under* meditation/methods/general points; variables in the mathematics of character 7.271; adapting spiritual practice to the character of the practitioner 7.313; weak:

little continuity of purpose and easily distracted 3.567

character types (*caritas* or *caritras*) the Buddha's designation of the literalist (*pada-parama*) as a distinct type of person 8.620; identified by Buddhaghosa, *see under* Buddhaghosa/*Visuddhimagga*

characteristics of conditioned existence *see* three *lakṣaṇas*

Chari, A. S. R. 8.370, 22.149–50

chariot chariot-craft 10.520; horses drawing the chariots of the sun and moon in Buddhist cosmology 16.346; the ill-fitting chariot wheel (*dukkha*) 3.209–10, 3.260; the seven *visuddhis* as the 'Relay of Chariots', *see* seven *visuddhis*; simile of the composite nature of being 1.100

charioteer the Buddha as 'the charioteer for the training of persons' 2.343, 2.706 (n419), 15.493, 17.466; Siddhārtha's charioteer, *see* Channa; the 'six ornaments of India' as the Great Charioteers 17.466

charisma obliterates the distinction between reliance on a person and reliance on truth 13.477; 'the rhetoric of the person' 13.476–7; Roman Catholic doctrine of charisma 13.477; Sangharakshita described as having 'charismatic authority' 13.469, 13.472–3; understandings of charisma 13.475–6; 'Take charisma and wring its neck' 13.476, 26.78; 'We should be wary of being seduced by charismatic purveyors of Enlightenment' 8.578; you can get carried away by your own popularity and influence 15.399–400

charity begins at home but does not end there 1.426, 7.327–9; 'charity' perhaps has the wrong connotations for *dāna* 4.336, 7.324; emotional blackmail 4.341, 19.68; the giving of buns and blankets 1.428; helping people by giving to charity 4.72; identifying strongly with a good cause, you become self-important 17.285; a man who had grandiose schemes to improve people's lot, but no *mettā* 7.327–8; a man who thought that the only good cause was to help lepers 4.72, 17.285, 25.52; towards animals as well as people 1.426–7; useless to aspire to universal charity when the beggar on our doorstep remains unfed 7.328; we select our charities according to our own feeling 25.52; *see also dāna*

Charles I 16.424, 24.566–7, 24.580

Charles V (Holy Roman Emperor) 13.551, 16.565

Charles XII of Sweden 26.483

charnel ground *see* cremation ground

Charumani, Dharmacharini (Carol) 26.507, 26.514, 26.754 (n494)

chastity chastity, spiritual androgyny, and a vision of the Truth 26.79; degrees of chastity 11.571; distinction from celibacy 2.709 (n444); 'Oh Lord, make me chaste, but not yet' 17.354; some people have a natural gift for chastity 17.216; what defines a monk 2.604–5, 2.609; *see also brahmacarya*; celibacy

Chatterjee, Pandit Jagadish Chandra ('Pandit-ji') Hindu representing Buddhism 20.178–82, 23.12; character 20.178, 20.180, 20.185, 20.195, 20.214; on caste 20.194–6; his plans for the revival of Buddhism in India 23.13; duplicity 20.223–6, 20.249, 23.13; outcaste on return from travels 9.315–16; persuades Nehru to visit Anandamayi 20.190; a resemblance to a speaker in England 24.210; *Kashmir Shaivism* 22.253, 22.597 (n210)

Chatterjee, Dr Suniti Kumar v21

Chatteron, Thomas 23.206, 23.504 (n235)

Chattopadhyaya, Aghorenath 7.56, 7.556–7 (n71)

Chattopadhyaya, Harindranath (poet) 7.56, 7.557 (n72)

Chattrul Sangye Dorje

his life

introduction 22.372–3, 22.390–1; meaning of 'Chattrul' 22.372, 22.390–1; appearance 12.436, 12.659, 22.373, 22.391–2; photograph 22.393; eccentricity 12.436–7, 12.494–5; emphasized the practice of releasing animals and birds from captivity 12.660;

removed *ribus* from an ancient stupa 12.436, 22.395, 25.443; vegetarianism 12.660–1; a wanderer who wandered with his two wives in later years 12.437, 12.661; death (at 102) 12.734 (n287), 12.738 (n321)

respect for him
he met Thomas Merton, whom he greatly impressed 12.437; one of three great Nyingma gurus 3.551, 12.443, 18.109–10, 19.310–11, 22.373, 22.384, 22.391; a remarkable man, with depths that were difficult to fathom 12.437; very highly respected by Dharma practitioners 12.495

and Sangharakshita
first meeting 12.436, 12.659–60, 22.391–2; discussion of meditation 22.374; gifts 25.443; Green Tārā initiation 5.754 (n554), 12.436, 12.659–60, 22.374–5, 22.392, 25.443, 26.228, 26.669; names the Triyana Vardhana Vihara 8.653, 12.437, 22.376–7, 22.390, 22.393–4, 23.18; 'To My Teacher, Chattrul Sangye Dorje' (poem) 25.443; verses in honour of the vihara 8.653, 22.376–7, 22.394; looking up to him 26.629; they stayed in touch 11.691

***chaturvarna* system** 9.68, 9.72, 9.77, 9.101–3, 10.51–3

Chau, Thich Minh v23

Chau, Thich Thien 8.662, 11.494, 22.515, 23.193, 23.228–30

Chaucer, Geoffrey 12.76, 21.266, 25.341c

Cheenia Baba (wax-burning ascetic) 16.197, 20.406–7, 22.334–5

cheerfulness all practice should be performed in a cheerful and easy-going manner 14.451; the bodhisattva is serene, cheerful, and optimistic 1.440, 4.135; the cheerfulness that arises from being aware of following the path of virtue 2.105; in some company you get the impression that cheerfulness is almost an offence 4.321; Sangharakshita's cheerfulness 22.86; Sangharakshita's father's cheerful disposition 25.68; 'You used to be so cheerful. What's happened?' 4.383

Chekhov, Anton 24.390

Chelliah (friend in Sri Lanka) 20.121

Chen, C. M. ('Yogi Chen')

life story
brief introduction 26.231; born in China 12.443; family and education 22.535–6, 22.537–8, 22.539–40; Taixu's disciple 22.536; interest in the chapter of the *Avataṃsaka Sūtra* on pure conduct 22.536–7; oscillation between Buddhism and Taoism 22.537; practice of the four foundation yogas 22.537; a pupil of Gelu Rimpoche 22.537; a prediction from Lola Hutuktu Rimpoche 22.537; gurus, personal and non-personal 22.537–8; instruction from the Heruka Ḍākinī 22.538; dreams and *abhiṣekas* 22.538–9; pilgrimage to the holy places 22.540; a disciple of Jamyang Khyentse Rimpoche 12.443, 22.538; renunciation and hermit life 22.540; in Kalimpong, lived in a bungalow which he never left 12.443–4, 22.533, 23.383; his devotion 22.540–1; refused to consider himself a teacher and wouldn't accept disciples 12.444, 13.325, 23.384; eccentric dress sense, including a cowboy costume 12.444, 22.532, 23.383; he wept bitterly on reading a Western article on Zen 12.444, 13.331; his encounters with local deities 18.22–3; outward, inward, secret, and most secret biographies 22.535–40; photograph 22.539; a prolific writer 13.325; he had absolute clarity of understanding 12.444; a thorough knowledge of the Buddhist scriptures 23.383; read all 1,656 works of the Chinese Tripiṭaka twice 12.443, 23.383; he took his Vajrayāna quite literally 12.448; took the bodhisattva ordination from Dhardo Rimpoche 22.541; he meets and is shocked by Allen Ginsberg 22.568; left Kalimpong for Thailand 22.541; eventually he settled in America 12.444–5

teachings and practices
bodhisattva vows 4.197, 4.275; he devised hundreds of little mantras for every conceivable activity 19.330, 19.612 (n136); he didn't have much time for Zen 12.443; explained *mahā* as meaning having been transformed by *śūnyatā* 14.571–2; explanation of *xin* (mind) 13.350; five methods of meditation as antidotes to five poisons 3.646 (n134), 3.675 (n311), 5.29; the function of the Tantra to transform the body as well as the intellect and the emotions 18.75; a great believer in the *phowa* practice of Amitābha 12.449; the prophecy about Padmasambhava: 'When iron birds fly in the sky ...' 12.720 (n144); he said that Padmasambhava had been in Kalimpong 22.468; images for reality, 2.133, 2.680 (n179); the system of meditation 5.37; teaching on chakras 16.135–6; the visualization of the stupa 5.573; without realizing *śūnyatā* Vajrayāna visualizations are vulgar magic 5.35, 5.579–80, 19.356, 19.531

writings and translations
books in Chinese 22.533; *Buddhist Meditation, Systematic and Practical* 5.xxi, 12.636, 22.533–41; comment on contemporary Tibetan practice 5.541; version of the 'Flower-Garland Hymn to the Goddess Tārā' 17.141

and Sangharakshita
first meeting 22.532–3; allows Sangharakshita to visit him 12.444, 12.636, 23.383; discussions 5.xxi, 12.444, 12.636, 22.533–41, 23.383–4; gives Sangharakshita the six element practice 5.484; learning the spirit of Zen from Mr Chen 13.324–5; Sangharakshita came to see Yogi Chen as one of his teachers 23.384; suggests asking Dilgo Khyentse for the Jambhala and Kurukullā initiations 12.448; consulting Mr Chen about returning to England 23.385; looking up to him 26.629

Ch'en, Kenneth, 10.565–6

Cheng Weishi Lun *see under* Xuanzang

Chengguan 1.353

Chennai *see* Madras

Chesterfield, Lord 12.697

Chesterton, G. K. brief introduction 23.515 (n317); became Catholic 15.489; an essay on songs for modern activities 18.192; 'It is because we no longer believe in the gods that we no longer believe in ourselves' 3.11; 'Lepanto' 23.271; story about the man who always brought the conversation round to the Church 2.382, 4.102; 'What a horrible word 'worker' is' 18.390

Chevalier, Nicholas 24.536

Chhawara, Rahul Suman 9.486, 9.489, 9.497–8

Chiang Kai-shek, General v22

Chiang Kai-shek, Madame 15.352

Chichester, England 20.46, 21.582, 21.587

Chih-I *see* Zhiyi

Chihmann, Upasika (Miss P. C. Lee) 2.454

Chikhalwadi, India 9.415

Childers, Robert Caesar 2.344, 2.707 (n422), 12.70

childhood adult memories of childhood may vary from children's experience 17.401; the advantages of a supportive upbringing 15.270; capacity for delight in simple pleasures 18.130; getting in touch with early childhood feelings 16.101–2; how we learn to repress emotions 12.265–6; lack of appreciation in childhood 17.654; relationship with mother 12.262, 16.101–2; re-experiencing a moment in childhood of a transcendence of time and space 17.402–3; resentment left over from childhood 14.573, 15.305, 19.58–9; self-hatred stemming from childhood can be difficult to dislodge 17.254–5; sentimental ideas of childhood innocence 8.586, 17.470; 'a soul raged in their child' 23.97; the trauma of being weaned 16.102; when we are young, we may be in touch with a previous life 17.470–1

childishness belief in a personal God an infantile attitude in Freud's view 12.95; fear of nuclear war appears childish and absurd 7.343; infantile demands of a lover 18.208; letting go of childish attitudes 16.317; 'To laugh excessively is childish' – what did the Buddha mean? 4.137; the need to resolve an attitude of infantile dependence 12.232; Western people sometimes think that devotion is childish 3.301; when visiting one's parents, the danger of slipping back into infantile attitudes 3.37

childlikeness a Buddha appears to others as a child, a madman, a ghost 11.11–12; Jagdish Kashyap quite childlike 12.431; the childlikeness of the truly spiritual man 7.285–6; Milarepa's shepherd disciple is quite childlike 18.234

children animists to whom nothing is dead 20.484; bringing up children, *see under*

parents; the Buddha's innocence analogous to that of a child 14.240; Buddhafield a safe place for children 11.709; children need the Dharma (Milarepa) 11.368, 18.589; children's natural tendency to admire 15.715; a crèche on a Spanish train 24.425; education, *see* education; egoism 9.439–40; epitaph for a young child 25.379; an experiment in which children were deprived of human contact 12.215; the idea that children are innocent is socially conditioned 15.204–5; the influence of horror comics 8.206–9; Mañjuśrī tests an eight-year-old girl's understanding of *śūnyatā* 14.185; and meditation 4.503; relationship with parents, *see under* parents; self-confidence 3.541; a seven-year-old *śrāmaṇera* answer the question 'What is the one thing?' 10.230–1, 13.31; sons, *see* sons; taking to new technology 24.424–5; 'Too long have I been a child' 25.319; young children are very honest about their likes and dislikes 15.432

Children of God 17.40, 17.711 (n43)

chin lab (Tibetan) *see under adhiṣṭhāna*

China

history
Tang dynasty 10.565–6; the burning of the books in the time of Qin Shi Huang 25.10; persecution of Manicheans 3.432; the Middle Kingdom 11.297; first contact with Western powers 11.297–8; Boxer rebellion 20.485–6, 26.289–90; Kuomintang government 22.53; Chairman Mao's regime 22.349; Cultural Revolution 26.477; Chinese people of Kalimpong interned 22.546, 22.557; and India, *see under* India; and Tibet, *see under* Tibet/history; and the Dalai Lama 2.572–3, 13.39, 22.371; Beijing Olympics 12.674–5

art
chrysanthemum of autumn and orchid of spring 2.130; cloisonné vases 24.416; depiction of *arhants* 26.599; depictions of Xuanzang 26.304; depictions of natural subjects and the Pure Land 16.184–5; in the deepest sense spiritual 26.116, 26.164; influence on Tibetan art 13.58–9; the rapport between the artist and the object of his contemplation 26.249–50; *White Lotus Sūtra* illustrations 16.46

connections with Buddhism
Buddhist influence on Chinese culture 7.442; the emperor commands the monk Jojin to make rain 2.216; pilgrimage associated with the bodhisattva and the starving tigress 4.324; presentation of Buddhist artefacts to Burma 7.446

other aspects of China
I Ching, *see I Ching*; incense 26.495; language 13.358; the need for a son 10.455; pagoda 16.150, 16.156; the people have great self-respect, and express appreciation for others 4.318–19; sages 3.427; Sangharakshita's love for China and the Chinese people 22.211; saying: the leaves return to the root 7.297

Chinese Buddhism

INTRODUCTION

history
Bodhidharma 2.276, 13.342; the restatement of Buddhism in terms of Chinese culture 11.513, 12.116–17, 13.116; transformed Indian modes of expression into something more Chinese 4.601, 4.624; came into contact with Daoism and Confucianism 7.144, 12.117; problem caused by compromise with Confucians 12.516; influence on culture 7.125, 16.35; monks made their own clan, the Śākyas 10.565–6; popularity of travelling to learn about Buddhism 2.198; popularity of ordination at one time 16.205; revival under the influence of Taixu 7.444–5, 12.594; decline 12.594–5, 15.499; Sangharakshita's contact with Chinese Buddhists 9.279, 9.488, 9.501

the flavour of Chinese Buddhism
brief introduction 11.372; art 22.349–50; *bhikṣunī* ordination 3.408; bodhi tree identified with a sacred tree connected with Taoism 2.222; bodhisattva ordination 2.209; costly funeral rites 8.175; Dunhuang Caves 14.258, 16.518, 16.628 (n352); faith and devotion 2.128; festivals: the setting free of birds and turtles 1.427, 8.223; good seeds, bad seeds, and Buddha seeds, *see under* seeds; keeping the coffin in the sitting room 12.195; monasteries and temples 7.465, 19.478–9; the Perfection of Wisdom called 'The Dark Wisdom' 14.514; practical and earthy 4.578, 4.624, 14.584; pure and impure merit 16.331–2; rites for the dead 1.384, 2.232; sacred mountains 2.224, 2.692 (n312); the Three Jewels are called the Three Treasures 11.394; worship of Amitābha 1.336–7; *wuxin* (mental state) 1.354

forms of Buddhism
Mahāyāna 1.211, 2.549, 11.372; Sarvastivāda Buddhism 3.408; Madhyamaka teaching, *see* Madhyamaka; Tantric Buddhism 1.384–5; Chan, *see* Zen; Buddhist Association of China 22.349

bodhisattvas
Guanyin, *see* Guanyin; names for Mañjuśrī: Man-shu-shi-li, Wénshū 2.173; Samantabhadra 2.180; Ti-tsang (Kṣitigarbha) 2.181

SCHOOLS

Tiantai (Japanese Tendai)
brief introduction 4.663 (n31); association with the *White Lotus Sūtra* 8.478, 8.480–1, 13.16; classified the Buddha's teachings into five periods and eight doctrines 4.22, 14.103; a comprehensive outlook 4.495–6; historical perspective 4.22; literature about the school 4.495; the path of regular steps and the path of irregular steps 4.495, 11.54; Sangharakshita's wish that Triratna should resemble the Tiantai 4.495; transmits the *bodhisattva-saṃvara* 7.483; view of the universe as one gigantic Buddha 4.589; Zhiyi, the founder, *see* Zhiyi

other schools
Chan Zong 1.372; Faxiang Zong 1.371; Huayan Zong 1.353, 7.401, 14.409; Kusha Shū 1.365; Yogācāra school 1.371; Zhenyan Zong or Mijao Zong 1.384

LITERATURE

sūtras and śāstras
each school selected a particular work as a working basis 14.255; *Arthapāda Sūtra* 7.527; Chinese Tripiṭaka (San Zang), *see under* Tripiṭaka; *Dharmapada*, *see Dharmapada*; *Prajñāpāramitā Śāstra* 7.527; *Vimalakīrti-nirdeśa* 16.444; Vinaya (*Shisong-lü*) 14.30, 14.33

translations
1.326, 16.444; Abhidharma 14.82–4, 14.93, 14.94–5; Chinese Tripiṭaka 1.384, 7.503; *Daśabhūmika Sūtra* 14.227; *Dhammapada* 9.111, 14.52, 15.4; *Diamond Sūtra* 14.148, 14.151; *Laṅkāvatāra Sūtra* 14.201; Mahāyāna *sūtras* 14.102; the *Samādhirāja Sūtra* 14.190; *Sandhinirmocana Sūtra* 14.200; *Sukhāvatī-vyūha sūtras* 1.328, 14.168; *Śūraṅgama-samādhi Sūtra* 14.195; *Śūraṅgama Sūtra* 14.197; *Sūtra of Golden Light* 14.241; the *Sūtra of Forty-Two Sections* 14.60, 14.253; Vajrabodhi and Amoghavajra bring and translate tantras 1.383–4; very early material in the Chinese canon 1.612 (n200); *Vimalakīrti-nirdeśa* 14.157; *White Lotus Sūtra* 14.108–9, 16.35

see also
Taixu; Xuanzang; Yinkuang

Chinese poetry *see under* poetry

Chinia Lama (or Chini Lama, Nepal) v13, v19, v21

chinlap *see under* blessings

Chintamani, Dharmachari 10.195, 10.694 (n230), v15, v24

chinthes 9.127, 9.556 (n146)

Chitnis, M. B. 9.312, 9.566 (n296)

chivalry 4.337, 4.465

Chivers, Vanda (later Vanda Harvey) v24

Chiyo-ni (Japanese poet) 19.70, 19.595 (n28)

***chöd* practice** etymology 13.267; concerned with the cutting off of ego 13.267–8; history 4.362; how the practice is done 13.268–70; relationship to the *Bodhicaryāvatāra* 4.362; systematized by Phadampa Sangye and Machig Labdron 4.362, 13.268, 18.432

Chodags, Thubden (the Yellow Monk) 21.331–6

choice actually the guru chooses the disciple 3.557–8; can you really say that marriage is a result of free choice? 18.457; the central principle of spiritual life is that we are free to choose how to be here and now 17.212–13; the choice before us is one world or no world 12.342; the choice between feeling and craving, *see under vedanā*; the choice between meditation and study 4.568–9; a choice – evolution or regression – is before us every minute 13.129; the choice facing us: (higher) evolution or extinction 3.617; choices in the *bardo* of reality 12.203–6; choosing the right practice for you: don't be too precious 18.192–3; choosing to enter the cremation ground 13.231; choosing to be reborn 13.37–8; every individual is responsible for their own destiny, and you need freedom to choose 4.124; every

moment of awareness presents us with an opportunity to choose what to do 15.174; extra precepts are a personal choice representing more intensive practice 2.347; freedom to choose one's religion 9.118–19, 9.184; freedom to choose the world we live in 16.478; freedom to make up one's mind 26.19; fulfilling family or 'tribe' duties from personal choice, not group pressure 18.149–50; in life there are certain situations in which we have apparently only one choice 17.192; making a choice between values set in opposition to each other 18.103; one can choose whether to magnify or minimize intellectual doubt 17.48; one should choose one's enemies with care (Nietzsche) 4.412; our fate is in our own hands 11.167; the point of choice that confronts us at every instant of our lives 2.103; ultimate spiritual choices are not to be determined by cultural considerations 26.13; we can't choose our starting point, but we can choose what to make of our situation 17.434; when you and others are suffering, choose to help the other 4.579–80

Chokei, Master 8.496

Chopin, Frédéric 23.173, 26.448

chorten *see stupa*

chös 13.12–13

Chos grub (Tibetan translator) 14.202

Chototsang, Aggen v16, v21

Chou Hsiang Kuang 8.374

Chowdar Tank *satyagraha* *see under* Mahad

Christ *see* Jesus

Christianity

HISTORY

introduction
it dominated Western culture for a thousand years 13.406–7; the history of the Roman Catholic Church inseparable from European history 13.550; linear vision of history, from Creation to Last Judgement 12.592–4; seeds of degeneration present from the beginning 3.430; violence of Christians towards non-Christians 13.619–23

early history
Bible stories, *see under* Bible; appealed at the beginning more to the heart than the head 12.107; the Catacombs: contrast between early simplicity and later triumphalism 23.310–11; in the early days a kind of spiritual community 3.448–9; 'The early Christians were criminals' 25.330; hundreds of little groups of believers 13.621; influence of Judaism 13.622–3; much of 'Christianity' is Mediterranean paganism or Roman imperialism 12.241; persecution by the Romans 13.552; Roman roads were built for the triumphant feet of Christianity 7.86; the history of Christian spiritual communities 3.430–1, 3.448–9; the effect of Constantine's recognition of Christianity 13.552, 13.579, 13.622–3; Nestorianism 11.297, 12.289; Irenaeus divided Christians into orthodox and heterodox 13.621; the coming into existence of the Holy Catholic Church 13.622

medieval history
at first an exotic religion in the West 13.494; Christians' criticism of Manuel II Paleologus of Byzantium 15.624; Christianity and paganism, *see under* paganism; contrast between depictions of angels and saints 16.7–8; introduction of meditation methods from the East (14th century) 8.126; medieval fear of criticizing the Church 7.85; martyrs 4.316, 13.266–7, 13.631; religion became a trade on a grand scale 10.593; contrast between friar and priest 10.488; Dance of Death (medieval Christianity) 2.85, 13.230–1, 25.415; fear of falling into heresy 16.82; the holy fool 11.129, 15.350; the Knights of St John 26.509, 26.511–12; largely responsible for divisions in Europe 2.613–14, 10.282; persecutions and wars, *see under* Christianity/Roman Catholicism; rationalist assaults upon other faiths 7.85; sale of indulgences 4.600, 18.428, 19.278; scepticism and fanaticism 15.565; the scholastic period of medieval philosophy 17.465; the scientific attitude as protest against medieval Christianity 26.103–4; split between religious faith and intellectual growth 14.443

16th and 17th centuries
Gunpowder Plot 13.548; Protestant Reformation, *see under* reformation; Ridolfi Plot 13.548–9; the burning of Protestants in the reign of Mary I 13.549; the Massacre of St Bartholomew's Eve 13.549–50; the destruction of 'superstitious' art by Puritans 26.276, 26.476–7; the seriousness of belief in 17th-century Britain 4.125; wars of religion 11.361

more recent history
Oxford Movement or Group 3.419, 11.207–8, 12.253; Christian swindling 12.251–2; Dead Sea Scrolls 14.258; the effect of Darwin's theory of evolution 11.75; ritualist controversy 11.208; made

more humanistic 9.352–3; friendly relations with new Buddhists in India 10.60–1; Second Vatican Council 2.457–8, 12.4, 13.552, 13.555; regime in Vietnam 16.196–7; with respect to divisions in Europe, Christianity is part of the problem 2.614

decline
bound up with accretions which are foreign to its spirit 7.34; the decline of intellect in its original sense 14.558; disenchantment with Christianity 13.374–6; loss of faith 3.603, 9.181, 9.283–4, 9.493, 12.5, 12.48, 16.355; post-Christianity 3.191; sceptical clergy 12.105; 'When Roman Catholicism died in Britain, English literature was born' 26.259

THE SPREAD OF CHRISTIANITY

introduction
Christian propagandists with the answer to everything 19.109; could the Church's proselytizing zeal extend to other planets? 8.157; emotional blackmail 19.68–9; invitation to Dr Ambedkar to become Christian 9.55–6; spread of Christianity (Ambedkar) 9.125; spreading the gospel of love by means of the sword 7.384, 22.529

missionaries
aggressive methods 4.447; attacking Buddhism 12.136–7; attempts to convert Tibetan refugees 8.319–20; being rude to followers of other faiths 15.671; confusing Christianity and national culture 12.252; connection with Western imperialism 8.285–6; the danger of Christian missions 22.153; Jesuits 9.116; in Kalimpong, *see under* Kalimpong; in Sri Lanka 8.5–6, 8.27, 8.470; missionaries' shocking methods 8.115–16, 23.207–8; narrow-minded and intolerant 22.138; putting people off Buddhism 22.45–6; Sangharakshita warns against it in Nepal 21.278–9; saying that material prosperity shows that God favours you 17.19–20; shortcomings 22.167; their missionary zeal 10.84–5; use of bribery 8.171; what does missionary work mean? 21.355

conversion
a Christian convert who continued to observe the caste system 9.315; conversion by logic and the sword 7.85; 'conversion through pregnancy' 21.364–6, 21.426, 22.25–6; converting the 'heathen' 2.237; forcible conversion of thousands of Hindus to Catholicism 8.318; Josaphat is converted to Christianity 13.659; St Augustine's conversion of the British from paganism 12.75; St Paul's conversion 2.238

CHRISTIAN BELIEFS

doctrines
Annunciation, *see under* Virgin Mary; Ascension, *see under* Jesus; based on a fallacy 2.87; belief that the body of Jesus was only apparent (docetism) 4.135; beliefs about cosmology 2.62–3; central tenet a 'speculative view' according to Buddhism 13.442; Commandments 1.528, 8.15; Creation 1.528, 16.388; the descent of the Holy Spirit 4.29, 4.241–2, 4.263; its doctrine is love, but it broke out into persecution and vengeance 8.167–8; eternal damnation 13.572–4, 16.78; faith (or grace) and works 7.39, 7.551 (n40), 20.40; faith is not to be associated with pleasure 17.673; forgiveness of enemies 3.449; the grace of God 4.7, 4.139, 18.538; Holy Ghost 13.567–9, 13.576; the idea of the descent of the Divine to earth is not only Christian 13.569–70; immortality of the soul 2.85; introduction to teachings 12.42–3; justification (or salvation) by faith 1.291, 1.346; Last Judgement 13.573, 17.469; life everlasting 13.578; Limbo 17.469; 'Love thy neighbour' 9.494, 25.239; the nature of faith in Christianity 7.96, 13.571; purgatory 13.573–4; redemption 13.577; Resurrection, *see under* Jesus; suffering as the punishment of God 16.86; three offers: the person of Christ, an ethical code, and hope of life after death 3.189; Traductionism 17.468–9; transubstantiation 2.87; Trinity 2.87, 11.296, 16.77

miracles
interpreting an event as a miracle rather than one's own foolishness 17.63–4; a miracle in a church that turns out to be due to natural causes 8.608; the miracles of Jesus, *see under* Jesus

original sin
unhelpful conditioning 9.495; Christian predicament 16.508; belief in original sin 26.376; Buddhism by contrast speaks of forgetfulness, unmindfulness, and ignorance 16.90; idea that your natural impulses are sinful 4.597; and irrational guilt 2.260; the sin of Adam 4.289

other beliefs about sin
Christ taking on himself the sins of the world 4.599; disobedience to the commands of God 15.619–22; forgiveness of sins 13.576–8; punishment 3.99–100; putting the fear of God into people, gratifying a desire for power 17.181–2

CREEDS

Athanasian Creed
not regarded as authoritative by the Eastern Orthodox Church 13.563, 13.579; contains a stern warning 13.579

Apostles' Creed
introduction 13.563–81; an ancient formula, the basis of mainstream Christianity 13.522; baptismal creed 13.564; Sangharakshita's declaration of the opposite of the Apostles' Creed 13.434; highlights doctrines, not ethical principles 13.578; recited by Sangharakshita for the first (and last) time 13.563; nothing but myth 13.302; the oldest of the three authorized creeds 13.563; 'I believe in God …' 13.442, 13.564–7; 'And in Jesus Christ …' 13.567; 'Who was conceived by the Holy Ghost …' 13.567–70; 'Suffered under Pontius Pilate …' 13.570–1; 'He descended into hell …' 13.571–5; 'The third day he rose again …' 13.575; ' I believe in the Holy Ghost …' 13.575–8

Nicene Creed
one of three creeds officially authorized 13.563; its adoption by those favoured by Constantine 13.579; differences from the Apostles' Creed 13.565, 13.567, 13.568–9

MYTHS AND PARABLES

myths
allegorical interpretations of Old Testament myths and legends 16.102; awe-inspiring images (Burning Bush, Last Judgement) 2.644; Christian mythology 13.522, 13.582–604; Christianity spoke the language of myth from the beginning 12.107, 13.302; depiction of the Evangelists in semi-animal form 13.244; the descent of Jesus into hell 13.571–4; literal belief in myths and symbols 3.230–1, 12.106–7, 13.434, 13.522, 16.528; a lunar religion 16.163; mysteries 3.230–1; the myth of the virgin birth 12.106–7, 13.568–9, 13.576; mythological figures disguised as saints 16.182; perhaps its mythology will prove to be the most enduring part of Christianity 13.584; taking the *Genesis* story literally 10.554; the value of myths, perhaps better communicated by art than creed 13.575

parables
introduction 13.643–4; the good Samaritan 13.643, 14.478; the lost piece of silver 16.221; the mustard seed 13.643; not essentially Christian, part of Western cultural heritage 13.644; the parable of the sower (Buddhist parallels) 13.644, 13.724–5 (n442); the prodigal son 13.643, 13.725 (n442), 16.90–1, 16.215, 16.220

ATTITUDES

general attitudes
attitude to animals 10.345–6; attitude to death and dying 4.76, 8.142–4; attitude to Greek and Roman myth 16.103; attitude to non-Christians 13.619–23; attitude to pornography 13.448; attitude to usury 13.616; 'based on the assumption that God is a fool' 18.163, 19.246–7, 19.607–8 (n107); 'Christianity and Communism are the same thing!' 12.136, 13.111; 'Christianity has never really suited the English' 12.75–7; Christianity is on the side of the group 11.361; considering Christianity to be the one true faith 17.19; dogmatism 13.434–5; ecclesiastical authority 15.720; encourages an unnecessarily abject view of ourselves 18.120; the end justifies the means 8.153, 8.253; extremes of attitudes to colourful ceremony 24.531; fear 16.276–7; fierce bigotry 8.166; fundamentalism 14.298–9; hostility towards communalism 8.417–18; infliction of emotional damage 11.342–3; intolerance 4.123–4, 9.183–4, 9.472, 9.495–6, 13.623, 13.666–7, 17.51–2, 22.138, 26.15; it has done a great deal of harm in the world 11.342–3; makes people think in detrimental ways, or not think at all 11.338–9, 16.500; no respect for the individual 11.361; observation of caste system 9.62, 9.315; Christians seeking laws to compel non-Christians to conform to their ideas 11.361; projection of unconscious reaction against Christianity 11.339–41; restrictive and coercive nature 11.338–40; set great store by prophecies and revelations 13.576; social conscience 10.347; tendency to identify religion too closely with the material order 14.443; tendency to think of poverty as a virtue 10.347; they seem to think it good to hate and persecute those of different beliefs 13.666; trades on irrational guilt 16.307–8; triumphalism 2.458, 13.556; why did the Church become so violent? 13.620–3; why should Christians be so afraid of death? 13.230; the will of God created rich and poor 15.681, 17.212

attitude to homosexuality
violence directed against homosexuals 13.522; abhorrence felt as a result of Christian attitude 13.617; Bible references 13.611–12, 13.613–14, 13.615; choosing Jesus's teaching of human solidarity or Biblical condemnation 13.615; Dante's attitude 13.615–16; implacable hostility 13.617; the moral danger of 'particular friendships' 13.618; St Paul's denunciation 13.611–12, 13.615; shifts in the Church's

position 13.612–13; 'the vice not to be named among Christians' 13.451; 'a vulgar vice, or rather a crime' 13.611; what Jesus said about how to treat others 13.615–16

Christian conditioning
freedom from it in moral matters 12.254; getting rid of it 10.277, 18.443; it affects even those who no longer think of themselves as Christians 11.107, 11.341; it may encourage us to think of spiritual life as a struggle 17.337; its effect on devotional feelings 14.534; Sangharakshita's experience 13.606; taking up an Eastern religion as a substitute for Christianity 26.256–7; therapeutic blasphemy, *see under* blasphemy; and Western Buddhists 10.277, 11.106–7, 11.378, 11.509, 17.337, 18.443

positive aspects of Christianity
awareness of 'the beauty of holiness' 17.337; imagining a better Christianity 11.361–2; social conscience 10.347

attacks on Christianity
blasphemy, *see* blasphemy; the *Freethinker* 11.344; Kierkegaard's attack on Christianity 12.251–2; a published attack by a swami on the Virgin Mary 20.298; ridicule and sarcasm 11.344–5

THEORY AND PRACTICE

practices
the average Christian is not usually turning the other cheek 19.229; baptism 11.296, 12.249, 13.564, 15.711–12; Christian names 18.150; Christmas, *see* Christmas; church-going to create a good impression 3.420; confession 11.260; confirmation service 15.712; Easter 3.230–1; the emphasis is not generally on methods 17.606–7; ethics, *see under* ethics/general ethical consideration; forgiveness of sins 13.576–8; 'Give until it hurts' 16.402–3; harvest festivals 11.239; it has no scheme of systematic self-development 7.369, 9.470, 9.494; just going to church on Sunday 12.23; the Lord's Prayer 13.577, 24.202, 26.647; penance 16.510; prayer 4.131, 12.10; the sacraments 11.296; self-mortification 1.140, 13.267; social service 4.440–1, 18.120–1; strict Sabbath rules 19.67; the use of music in liturgy 11.227–8; walking meditation 15.190

theology
analysis of human being into body, soul, spirit 2.335, 14.558; apophatic theology 26.478; a belief that the Magi came from India 13.557; the docetic heresy, *see under* Gnosticism; Christianity as theological monarchism 11.335–41; Christianization of Plato and Aristotle 7.486, 13.557; conflict with Karl Marx 10.347; 'death of God' theology 11.361, 12.130, 12.135; 'father' and 'son' in Christian terminology 18.315; reconciling man's free will with God's foreknowledge 4.66, 19.84; less intellectually acceptable after Darwin 3.189; difficulty of accepting evolution 3.9; the *felix culpa*, the 'Happy Fall' 14.606, 14.659 (n522); the higher criticism 3.189, 13.426–7, 14.374; the influence of secular philosophies 10.344–50; modernism 7.34, 7.549–50 (n30), 13.424–7; preoccupation with precise theological expression to fundamental beliefs 13.578; Ritualist controversy 2.147, 2.682 (n201); salvation by faith and works 13.531, 20.44; scientific discoveries have disproved the Church's dogmas 7.381; a non-theistic Christianity? 12.10, 12.94, 12.113; theologians on the possibility of life on other planets 8.157; theological language 11.298; a universal religion 12.55, 12.249

PROTESTANTISM

general entries
the case for 'Buddhist Protestantism' 13.402–23; Christians of Muvattupuzha, India 20.284–5; contrast between Catholics and Protestants 2.613; devaluation of ritual 11.206, 11.215; diluted by secular humanism 13.407; emphasis on self 13.385; High Church ceremony 13.532; a hospital chaplain 24.353; in a sense no such thing as Protestantism 13.407; liberal Protestantism 13.403–4; origin 18.428; 'pan-religious protestantism' 13.403–5; Protestant martyrs 13.549–50, 13.555; a Protestant view of Roman Catholicism 23.253; Protestants and Catholics largely responsible for divisions in Europe 2.613–14; the real Vicar of Hampstead 23.213; the rebel child of Roman Catholicism 13.407; Reformation, *see under* reformation; rival claims of mutually hostile sects 7.380; Society of St John the Evangelist (Cowley Fathers) 13.556, 21.353–4; why the FWBO criticizes Catholicism and not Protestantism 13.406–7

churches
applying the word 'church' to a Buddhist place of worship 24.529; the association of the altar with sacrifice 11.232–3; the atmosphere in old churches 19.328; the church as metaphor 26.397; churches in Suffolk (associated with Lingwood family) 26.508–9, 26.512–13, 26.532; often built on the sites of old temples 14.463; Sangharakshita's childhood

visits to churches 20.33, 26.532; visiting the shrines of England 20.33; *see also* cathedrals

denominations
Anabaptists 8.416; Baptists 20.21, 20.42–4; Brethren of the Free Spirit 3.430–1, 8.416; Calvinism 4.140, 18.538, 18.663–4 (n194), 24.531; Church of England, 3.373, 13.619, 20.20; Jehovah's Witnesses 17.469; Huguenots 13.549; Hutterites 8.416; Liberal Catholic Church 24.57, 24.60–1, 24.621–2 (n85); Lollards 3.430, 24.538; Lutheranism 3.431, 13.620, 24.531; Mennonites 8.416; Methodism 10.85–6, 11.342–3, 12.4, 12.253–4, 23.153, 23.208–9; *see also* John Wesley; Pentecostal church 24.124–5; Puritanism 12.254, 19.67, 24.292, 24.531, 26.276; Quakers 3.431, 12.8, 13.619, 15.699, 16.327, 18.394, 24.531; Salvation Army 19.68, 20.20–1; Seventh Day Adventists 8.183, 15.264–5, 17.469, 21.224–5, 21.349–50; Taborites 3.431, 8.416; Unitarians 11.337, 12.8; Universalism 16.595 (n71)

ROMAN CATHOLIC CHURCH

introduction
attitude to ceremonies 24.531; a change of heart? 13.562; contrast between Catholics and Protestants 2.613; English literature began with the rejection of Catholicism 13.511; how it came into existence 13.622; its iron framework 13.668; it does not recognize that anyone ever leaves it 9.353, 10.280–1; obligations on Catholics 11.338–9; a pagan atmosphere in a cathedral 23.253; 'Petrine communion' 13.426, 13.705 (n220); 'The Priest's Dream' (poem) 25.347; readiness to supply answers 3.6; rococo style 16.327; the 'Roman racket' 16.308, 22.286; split with the Eastern Orthodox Church 13.622; tolerance of the frailty of the priest 13.477; the true legatee of the Roman Empire 13.667–8; why the FWBO criticizes Catholicism and not Protestantism 13.406–7

Catholic doctrines and practices
apostasy 9.353; automatic efficacy of sacraments 18.428, 18.520; Calendar of Saints 13.426–7, 23.307; charisma 13.477–8; confession 13.558, 16.269, 16.308–9; devotion 24.454; excommunication 13.553, 13.556; 'Hail Holy Queen' 2.674 (n112); holy relics 13.427; interdicts 13.553, 13.555–6; the Mass 18.430; the Nicene Creed 13.579; the treasury of merits of the saints 4.599–600

publications
advertisements for the Catholic Church 8.252–4; *Concilium* 11.295; in Lampedusa's *The Leopard* 13.427; *Index Expurgatorius* 7.246, 7.603 (n346); *Reserve in Communicating Religious Knowledge* 16.55–6, 16.592 (n53); *Studia Missionalia* 11.305

papacy
'Babylonian Captivity' in Avignon 13.636, 13.638; calling on the statesmen of the world to ensure peace 8.152; Catherine of Siena persuades the pope to move from Avignon to Rome 11.633; temporal power 13.552, 13.554–5; *ex cathedra* pronouncements 7.602–3 (n346); popes have gone to war 3.450; claimed to be vicegerents of God 3.449–50; collapse of papal supremacy 7.380, 13.555; corruption 13.555; criticized for not representing the God of Love 3.449; Anagarika Dharmapala almost has an audience with the pope 8.55–6; Great Schism 13.554, 13.630; horrifying that massacres should have the blessing of the pope 13.550, 13.580–1; how did the papacy come to have so much power? 13.551–5; kissing the pope's toe 11.251; 'liberal' popes 8.315–16; a pope is not necessarily a saint 19.359; the pope's dismissal of Buddhism as 'an excellent human teaching' 12.62, 17.556–7; the pope's response to the persecution of Buddhists in Vietnam 8.315–16, 8.318; a pope who said that both Catholicism and Buddhism work for the peace of mankind 8.315; popes styled 'the Great' 13.554; Protestants identified the papacy with the Great Whore 13.555; putting aside the triple crown 'too late' 25.347; 'triple Tyrant' 13.580–1

individual popes
Peter, the first Bishop of Rome 13.552–3; Alexander VI 13.626–7; Alexander VII 13.583; Clement V 25.544; Clement VII 13.551, 13.637; Gregory I 13.554, 13.636; Gregory XVI 11.339; Innocent III 8.425, 13.553–4; John 8.315; John Paul II 25.90; Leo I 13.554; Nicolas I 13.554; Paul 8.315; Paul III 24.265, 24.274–6; Pius II 13.637; Pius V 13.549; Pius IX 8.316; Pius X 11.339, 13.425; Pius XII 3.449; Silvester I 13.552; Urban IV 25.428; Urban VI 13.637

monastic orders
Austin Friars 3.430; Carthusians 13.629–31, 24.302, 24.454–5; Cistercians 3.430, 24.386–7; Dominicans 3.430, 13.635, 24.281; Franciscans 3.430, 4.603, 18.480; islands of civilization in the Dark

Ages 3.430; Jesuits, *see* Jesuits; Merced order, devoted to ransoming Christian captives from Moors 24.441; monastic communities of the Dark and Middle Ages 8.416; the noonday demon 5.351–2; Poor Clares 3.430, 24.279, 24.678 (n340); Spiritual Franciscans 13.619; Trappists 23.488 (n116)

persecutions and wars
authoritarian mentality leads to persecution 7.246; auto-da-fé 22.626 (n395); the burning of heretical books leading to the burning of heretics 7.380; burning people alive 7.380, 7.384, 9.353, 11.340, 13.549, 13.596–7, 13.666–7, 22.529, 25.376; burning of witches 11.340, 11.361; a cardinal is annoyed at tolerance of non-Catholics in Spain 8.117–18; cruel suppression of the Templars 11.340; Crusades 3.450, 13.622, 13.629, 13.636, 13.666, 17.462; the ghosts of the Inquisitors are still very much abroad 8.425; heretical movements stamped out 3.430–1; the Inquisition 3.450, 7.380, 11.361, 13.550, 13.666–7; how the church became so violent 13.622; how does that bloodstained history relate to morality? 8.282; invoking divine blessing on troops and tanks 8.152–3; a man who had his daughters burned at the stake 13.620–1; the massacre of the Waldensians 13.580–1; parallel between the Inquisition and the Nazi Gestapo 8.422; persecution of the Cathars (Albigenses) 8.420–3, 11.361, 13.580, 13.667; persecution of the followers of other religions throughout Church history 9.184; persecution of Manicheans 3.432; persecution of the Spiritual Franciscans 13.619; Portuguese persecution and conversions in Sri Lanka 8.468; Protestants tortured to death in Colombia 7.380, 8.116, 8.170; torturing and burning in the name of religion 26.653; in Vietnam, *see under* Vietnam; wars of religion 9.472; were the inquisitors and crusaders true Christians? 13.564

power
authoritarianism 3.430, 12.228, 13.622; inheriting the political power of the Western Roman Empire 3.449–50; it controls people through fear 26.20; political power 3.430, 7.380; the power of cardinals 26.291–2; power taking over a spiritual community 3.450; temporal power 3.449, 13.555

and people
Catholics who believe that they will be damned for missing Mass 19.277; the church demands superficiality 19.278; contemplatives 4.582; converts 22.148; ex-Catholic Buddhists troubled by Catholic symbolism 24.366; friction with Hindus in South India 20.298; a Jesuit priest in India who was persecuted for his views 13.558–9; a mission in New Zealand 24.511; Mr Bo, a 'sworn enemy' of the Church 22.297; painful experience of Roman Catholicism 13.409; a priest who thought the Church should become culturally more Indian 13.557–8; quite a high proportion of Western Buddhists are ex-Roman Catholics 17.556; staying on the orthodox path 17.109; terror of punishment 11.260; warning against 'particular friendships' 13.618

OTHER TRADITIONS

Orthodox Christianity
creed 13.563; decision to allow two-dimensional, but not three-dimensional images 26.477; Greek Orthodox Church 4.582, 26.384; Hesychasm 8.126–7; icons 13.602–3, 26.598; Mount Athos 8.126; Russian Orthodox Church 7.380, 24.530; saints' days of Barlaam and Josaphat 13.663–4; Sophia, the Divine Wisdom 13.603–4, 14.343, 26.388; split with the Roman Catholic Church 13.622; 'very congenial' 26.388

alternative traditions
alternative traditions to Christianity in the West 8.415–28, 13.373–6; list of alternative traditions 13.580; viewed as heretical 13.579–81; Cathars, *see* Cathars; Waldensians, *see* Waldensians

CHRISTIANITY AND BUDDHISM

Christian attitudes to Buddhism
attempts to identify Maitreya with Christ 2.179; Buddhists not allowed to criticize Christianity 9.212; the Catholic church's depreciation 12.61–2; a Christian assessment of Zen 8.500–1; Christian interpretations of Buddhism 3.44–5; Christian writers' view of the Buddha 3.151; claim that all Buddhist doctrines are to be found in Christianity 23.213; difficult for Christians to understand Buddhism 4.125–6; the pope's dismissal of Buddhism as 'an excellent human teaching' 12.62, 17.556–7; suspicion that Buddhism is selfish and individualistic 5.209–10; strange ideas about Buddhism taught to university students 11.378

Buddhist attitudes to Christianity
Buddhism denies what Christianity affirms 13.375; Buddhism might consider Christianity to be a pseudo-religion 17.18–19; 'Buddhism the most profound

and fundamental antithesis to Christianity' 7.366; a Buddhist can appreciate Christian art, music, and poetry 13.669; attitudes of Buddhist ex-Christians 11.345–6, 13.490, 13.501; can a Buddhist appreciate Christian poetry? 26.397; Christian 'dangers for the individual' 13.468; Christianity as a culture may be part of the heritage of the Western Buddhist 25.19–20; defending Christianity 11.345–6; Dharmapala's views on Christianity 8.93; for some, Buddhism is simply more attractive 13.404; a greater affinity with Orthodoxy than with Roman Catholicism 23.209; how can Christian images be of significance to Buddhists? 26.269–70; an incarnate lama who became a Christian 22.492; it is wrong of a Buddhist to offend Christian sentiment 8.13; one is not being untrue to one's heritage if one rejects Christianity 26.14; painful experience of Roman Catholicism 13.409; possibility of Buddhist influence on early Christianity 20.292; 'Puritan Buddhism' 13.403; when you become a Buddhist you cease to be a Christian – as simple as that 14.602

influences and attitudes
Buddhism treated as a Christianity-substitute 3.190; Christian attitudes in Buddhism 16.127, 16.416; evidence of the influence of Buddhism on medieval Christian Europe 8.398; spiritual impulses from the Buddha through Neoplatonism 2.11–12; their ignorance of each other throughout most of their existence 11.296–7; threads of influence between Buddhism and heterodox Christian movements 8.127; to discuss Buddhism in Christian terms is to distort it 11.509

comparison
Christian and Buddhist archetypes 12.191–2, 26.269–70; Christian practices similar to mindfulness? 17.86, 17.720 (n94); Christianity compares people to sheep, the Buddha to nobler animals 10.201; Christianity stresses historicity whereas Buddhism stresses interiority 26.390; comparison of practices 11.296; contrast between Buddhist and Christian miracles 1.168, 4.12–13, 9.344–5; comparison of Buddhist meditation with Christian mysticism 4.513; contrasting attitudes to death 8.143–4; contrasting attitudes to the religion being criticized 11.333–4; contrasting attitudes to sin 13.576–7; the difference in respect to peace is not fortuitous 7.444; difference in belief 13.570–1, 15.25–6; difference in conception of hell 13.572–3, 16.282; differences between them 22.96; different approaches to myth 12.107; different responses to animals 8.256; in Buddhism there is no such thing as fundamentalism in the Christian sense 14.299; one cannot become Christ, but all can become Buddhas 10.171; the only real advantage that Christianity has over Buddhism is that it is more poetic 26.58; to reconcile them, you have to know them both very deeply 26.58; resemblance between Christian meditation and the mindfulness of breathing 8.126; their different attitudes to awareness of difference 13.665–6; their visions of history compared 12.592–4; they are as different from one another as they can be 11.296; they are both universal religions 11.295–6

contact
contact between them 11.296–8; 'Dialogue between Buddhism and Christianity' 11.295–304; Nestorian Christians in contact with Padmasambhava 11.297, 12.289; they have to communicate, but don't have a common language 11.298–300, 11.496

SANGHARAKSHITA'S RELATIONSHIP WITH CHRISTIANITY

introduction
full account 13.521–670; an idea for a short story about a cathedral's images coming to life 26.273–6, 26.282; 'If forbidden to speak of Buddhism in Buddhist terms, I could use Christian terms' 26.387; his book on how he saw Christianity (*From Genesis to the Diamond Sūtra*) 11.691, v13, 26.442; intention to write a comparative study of Buddhism and Christianity 13.521; reading the Bible, *see under* Bible; response to Jesus, *see under* Jesus

early memories of Christianity
awakening of moral consciousness 13.522; baptism 13.525; first being taught a prayer ('Now I lay me down to sleep') 13.525–6; Bible stories and prayers at school 13.527–8; childhood nightmare of a cross 13.525–6; encyclopedia articles 13.529; an essay on the disestablishment of the Church of England 20.56; family Bible 13.526, 20.9–10, 26.287–8; godparents 13.526–7; 'How big is God?' 26.475, 26.479; *Paradise Lost*, *see under* Milton; prayed to the Buddha, Christ, and Mohammed in turn 13.531, 20.44; 'seeing the Holy Ghost' 13.527; Sunday school 13.527, 20.20, 20.43

church-going
Baptist 13.530–1, 20.45; Boys' Brigade 7.12–13, 13.530–1, 13.609–10, 20.40–4; dreams of a deserted church 26.679–80;

experience of Church of England and Baptist church compared 13.532, 20.48; enjoyment of visiting old churches 20.33; parents' interest in sects 20.20–2; parish church in Torquay: saw the place of ritual in religion 13.532; prayer meetings 20.44; his declaration that salvation was by faith and works 13.531, 20.44

positive feelings for Christian figures and traditions
admiration for Christian mystics 26.387; as a teenager, influenced by St Francis, he gave all his money to a beggar 13.533, 13.624; inspiration from St Catherine of Siena 13.634–8, 26.387; inspiration from St Jerome 2.526–7, 13.633–4, 26.267–8; sympathy with the Eastern Orthodox tradition 26.388

rejection of Christianity
an assessment of his views 8.xxvi–vii; 'Back to where the paths divided' 25.288; better to worship the Bull of Memphis 25.287; 'Better that Mary's Son had ne'er been born' 25.377; continuing to appreciate it aesthetically without assenting to its doctrinal content 26.532; declaration of the opposite of the Apostles' Creed 13.434; 'From sages, sects and churches, Good Lord, deliver me' 25.239; an image of 'two men who nailed upon a cross a third' 25.274; realizing that he was not a Christian 12.493, 12.682, 13.534, 20.63–4, 23.10, 23.207; rejection of Christianity on principle 13.375–6, 13.434; the Christian centuries were a bad dream from which we've woken up 12.405; 'Buddhism is (on the whole) true and Christianity is (on the whole) false 13.433–4; the 'Enemy of the Church' 8.xxvii, 21.363–4; 'I believe that Christianity is dead … But I mourn it, for I owe it much' 7.38; 'I think I must never have believed in God' 13.565; not rejection in the sense of seeing it as having been superseded 13.441; Triratna attitude to Christianity 13.490, 13.501, 13.503; conclusions about Christianity 13.523

encounters with Christians
an animus developed due to the behaviour of missionaries in India 23.207–8; the Bishop of Woolwich, *see* Robinson; contact with Christians in India 13.556–9, 21.345–66; cordial contact with Christians of many denominations 12.3–4, 13.562; encounter with Indian Christians 20.284–5, 21.345; Father Mascarenhas, *see* Mascarenhas; Father Monchanin, *see* Monchanin; friendly contact with Roman Catholics in later years 13.562; a Jesuit priest in India who was persecuted for his views 13.558–9; meeting a farmer who literally believed in Adam and Eve 13.532; his experience of Christians quite positive 13.375–6; meeting Christians in Kalimpong 21.345–66; missionaries in Kalimpong, *see under* Kalimpong; reading of Thomas Merton, *see* Merton; sympathetic dialogue with Christians 23.215–16; those met at the Baptist Church when he was a teenager 13.530–1

interest in Church history
interest in Church history 13.548–62; the question of whether Jesus really existed 13.641–3; the effect of two illustrations of horrifying episodes 13.549–50; investigation of how the papacy became so powerful 13.551–5

see also
art/Christian art; Bible; Robinson (Bishop of Woolwich); blasphemy; cathedrals; cosmology; Devil; Fall of Man; Gnosticism; God; Jesus; miracles; mysticism; paganism; individual saints; sin; tolerance

Christie, Agatha 20.64, 26.536

Christmas abolished by Puritans 19.67; a Buddhist approach to Christmas 24.169–70; difficult for Western Buddhists to avoid 9.417, 10.279; a doctor's work on Christmas Day 24.332; for many people just a matter of eating and drinking 19.485; going on retreat during Christmas 9.417; Nativity scenes in Naples 24.282–3; a priest who hated Christmas because of the confessions he had to hear 13.558, 16.308–9; Sangharakshita's childhood experience 20.12, 20.14

Christopher, St 24.369, 24.419

chrysanthemums *see under* flowers

Chu La Swordsmanship 19.156

chuba 22.242

Chulalongkorn, King 23.157

church *see under* Christianity/Protestantism; *see also* cathedrals

Churchill, Winston 20.49, 23.89, 23.487–8 (n115), 26.478

Cicero, Marcus Tullius brief introduction 24.680 (n356); on gratitude 3.604–5, 3.693 (n475); his dialogue *On Friendship* 12.406, 24.294; *On Old Age* 24.294; visiting his villa at Pompeii 24.293–4

cinema *see* films

cintāmaṇi *see under* jewels/wish-fulfilling jewel

cintā-mayī prajñā *see under prajñā*

circle the circle of flames around the mandala 12.220; circles of oceans and mountains 13.261, 16.342; the circle tries to become a spiral 16.383–4; the circles of the greater mandala 18.318; expanding the limited circle of self-interest 17.342; generosity an ever-expanding circle 1.426; peace symbolized by a circle 5.213; time is unable to square the circle of eternity 26.83

circumambulation Bön circumambulation 'widdershins' 19.329; of the Buddha 19.329–30; a custom associated with the solar cult 19.329; external and internal circumambulation 19.338; Milarepa circumambulates the Buddhas 19.328–9; Rechungpa circumambulates Milarepa 19.418–19; Tibetans circumambulating Lhasa 19.335

circumstances the aim is to bring aesthetics to whatever circumstances we encounter 14.520; being constrained by circumstances 25.116–18; circumstances are so complex that what is skilful for one person may not help another 15.291; contact with the *dharmakāya* can occur under mysterious circumstances 14.438; developing in unfavourable circumstances 3.329, 3.456; Enlightenment is responding creatively to all the circumstances that may arise 15.468–9; the equanimity of Milarepa's mind in all circumstances 18.48; favourable circumstances for growth 3.313–14, 12.513–14; human nature is highly resilient even under difficult circumstances 4.423; 'In what circumstances may the practice of mindfulness exist?' 4.480–1; insuperable circumstance 25.281; misery of feeling so restricted by circumstances one cannot grow 16.71; people used to be drawn to the Buddha because of their life circumstances 4.351; *prajñā* can arise under any circumstances whatsoever 4.533; refuse to be the victim of circumstances 15.174–5; something is bound to happen to upset your comfortable circumstances 25.77; trying to see honestly which circumstances of our life are advantageous 18.148; a vow to be reborn in more favourable circumstances 18.147–8; you can completely trust only one whose virtues can survive any circumstances 17.327

citizens children should learn their rights and duties as citizens 9.440; gratitude for the benefits of being a citizen 12.488; our first duty as citizens is to be honest in all our dealings 17.231; remember you're a citizen 11.624, 12.488–9; the responsibility of exercising one's vote 11.635; 'a true citizen of the world should aim at a broad acquaintance with all that is best' 20.61; to achieve world peace we shall have to regard ourselves as citizens of the world 12.353; the relationship between the Buddhist citizen and the state 7.439

citta (heart-mind) Abhidharma types of consciousness 1.102–3; the ambiguity of the term, both heart and mind 14.209–10, 15.197; 'capital' and 'diminutive' meanings 4.431; luminosity of *citta* 1.84; *māyā-citta* 16.544; mental attitude 16.544; as one of the four *iddhipādas*, *see* four *iddhipādas*; the power of *citta* 4.551–3; the term applied to the two poles of the perceptual situation, mind and matter 17.482–3; translations 13.350–1

citta visuddhi *see* seven *visuddhis*

cittadhārā 19.187

cittamātra *see* Yogācāra/doctrines/One Mind

Cittapala, Dharmachari 2.737 (n653), 5.xxii, v24, 26.458

Cittaprabha, Dharmacharini 2.733 (n628), v24

citta-santāna (Sanskrit *citta-saṃtāna*) the stream (waterfall) of thoughts dissolved temporarily and permanently 19.188–9; the Abhidharma analysed the apparently continuous flow into a succession of bits 19.235–7; one seems to have a constant stream of thoughts 'and yet they ne'er exist' 19.232–9; with insight, circling thoughts become a spiral 19.237; and rebirth 2.14; Yogācāra doctrine 19.237, 19.606 (n99)

cittass' ekaggatā *see* one-pointedness

cittata *avidyā* in the sense of not knowing mind-as-such 17.607–8; 'mind as pure fact' 17.493; mind-as-such 17.491–2, 17.761–2 (n430–1); mind-essence, Tibetan *sems nyid* 18.338; a sort of equivalence with transpersonal feelings 17.510–11

city

city life
at the Buddha's time, Buddhism made its greatest appeal in the urban areas 18.203; being in the city is an opportunity to witness the human condition 18.424; the Buddha speaks of noisy cities 10.330, 10.702–3 (n315); city life draws out energy and wastes it senselessly 15.152; clouds of suffering in cities 4.572–4, 4.583; the distractions of city life 12.421; getting over the desire for city life 19.578–80;

how human beings are treated in big cities 25.126; impermanence in the city 17.378; independence 9.413; is it conducive to an initiative-taking attitude to one's mental states? 18.423; living in a metaphorical cave in the city 19.492–3; noise in the city 12.474; people moved to build in particular places by psychic forces, or deities 10.647–8, 18.24; planting trees in cities 18.23; pros and cons 11.196–7; shrines to local gods in cities 18.24; the ugliness of city life 26.184–5; violence is on the increase in cities 11.358; you have to estimate your ability to sustain life in the city 4.583, 19.342

city and country
alternate between life in the country and in the city 14.520, 15.394–5; is the countryside or the city the better situation? 15.394–5; population shift from country to city 10.328–9; village people may regard the city as a place of liberation 11.196

figurative cities
magic city, *see under White Lotus Sūtral* parables; no abiding city 3.261; the path to the ancient city 1.53–4, 1.81, 3.18, 10.567, 11.408–9; Yeats on Byzantium as the perfect city 26.386

civilization the beginnings of civilization 3.95; exposed as savagery in time of war 7.163; a frail structure superimposed on virtual barbarism 11.197, 11.270–1; it goes through cycles 11.271; it is not difficult to wipe out a whole civilization 11.270; a middle way between changing outer conditions and working on the mind 7.238–9; modern civilization 7.325, 19.179–80; the problem of death emerges in civilization 3.95–6; a sense of the ancient world as being almost one civilization 10.467

claims claiming to be in continuously skilful states without meditating 5.645; the Buddha didn't claim divine authority 10.35–6; the Buddha never claimed to possess omniscience 1.78, 17.328; did the Buddha claim infallibility? 9.425, 10.40; a false and perverse 'I' claims one name or another 4.579; the incongruity of the ego claiming anything for itself 14.598; laying false claim to attainment as a *pārājika* (defeat) 3.409; a lover may claim to admire the mind while thinking of the body 4.561; making claims which by their nature cannot be verified 24.214; the man who thinks 'I am Enlightened' 7.407; no need for anybody to claim spiritual superiority 15.535–7; perception that a nun hadn't done the practice she claimed, *see under* Kachu Rimpoche; 'Pure Dharma': organizations that claim to possess it 7.314; real spiritual teachers do not make claims 16.577–8; Rechungpa makes claims about himself 19.388–9; the self's tendency to lay claims to attainment 3.409; this is what *I* have gained 2.268, 7.406; those who lay claim to spiritual attainment 7.360

clairaudience (*divya-śrota*, supernormal faculty) 1.167, 1.584, 12.559, 20.308–9

clairvoyance 1.584

clarity being clear about what you stand for 18.153; Buddhism is characterized by clarity, honesty, and rigour of thought 4.144; as Buddhists we seek to keep our minds clear 10.395; characteristic of a true individual 3.468; the clarity about the Dharma that emerges from the *dhyānas* 18.580; clarity about the Dharma: invigorating or humiliating 8.xxiv–v; clarity about doctrines and practices 17.616–17; clarity of mind is hard to achieve 15.115; communication with those with greater clarity to counter wrong views 2.392–3; the effect of medical treatment on mental clarity 16.407; experiencing the world without unskilfulness is an experience of complete clarity 19.192; faith brings clarity to one's life and mind 17.551; the hindrances cloud the clarity of perception 18.11; intellectual clarity is a condition for spiritual growth 3.314, 12.515–16; intellectual clarity is not attained by education, reading, or becoming an intellectual 4.146–7; intellectual clarity is not everything, but it counts for a great deal 26.84; lack of clarity is a sort of laziness 26.251; many of us have a deep resistance to clarity in our approach to the Dharma 17.391; meditating on Mañjuśrī to aid clarity in writing 26.250–1; one of the fruits of spiritual practice: seeing things as they are 17.168; skilful mental states are characterized by contentment, love, understanding, and clarity of mind 3.102; in study, moving from clarity to uncertainty and back to clarity 19.101; there can be no intellectual clarity without awareness of emotion 15.197–8; we are not usually clear about what is shaping what we do, feel, and think 17.11; your own clarity can make someone else more confused 17.615; *see also* thinking/clear thinking

Clarke, Sir Humphrey 18.xi–xii

Clarke, Jeremiah 26.506

class barriers set up between one class, one nation, one religion and another

7.274; bitterness at being looked down on 15.716; class loyalties breaking down 3.441; class system in England 9.240–1; distinctions at London Buddhist Society 20.101; intoxication of class 16.299; Jilly Cooper's *Class* 24.124, 24.127; middle-class abhorrence of homosexuality 23.393, 23.404; middle-class respectability 23.404, 23.406; one tries to break down class barriers to relate to others as individuals 26.73

Cleary, Thomas 8.484–9, 14.9, 16.587 (n20)

Cleather, Alice Leighton 8.24

Cleopatra Cleopatra the cat 21.317; drawn by Sangharakshita 20.27; 'If Cleopatra's nose had been shorter the history of the world would have been different' 8.73; women who claimed they had been Cleopatra in a past life 17.31, 23.41; Sangharakshita and a friend in London: 'Look, mate, 'ere comes Julius Caesar and Cleopatra!' 23.174

clerisy (Coleridge term) 8.466, 8.472, 8.475

Clifton, Robert Stuart 8.674–5 (n66), v13, v21, v22, v23

clinging

objects of clinging
the clinging mind like a short-lived sparrow in the woods 18.262, 18.562–3; clinging to a 'higher self' 7.211; clinging to orthodoxy 16.82; clinging to the means to Enlightenment as though they were ends in themselves 7.264–5; clinging to a remnant of a raft while hurling abuse at those who are crossing 7.314; clinging to the turmoil of thoughts 18.452; ego-clinging and the five consciousnesses 19.156; pleasure is to be enjoyed, but not made the occasion of clinging 19.380–1; subtly clinging to one's identity as a member of a group 18.27; practising non-violence while clinging to the notion of self like rowing a boat tied to the shore 7.375; worldly desire as clinging 19.156

the consequences of clinging
becoming frozen in a posture of clinging 10.637–8; clinging to one-sided views is a waste of time 10.598; the five *skandhas* are subject to clinging, hence are suffering 3.655 (n189); it's due to clinging that people are reborn 18.612; a right view to which you cling turns into a wrong view 17.259, 18.172; we fear death because we cling to 'self' 23.92

getting rid of clinging
conquering the demon of ego-clinging 19.156; ego-clinging is a demon which can be tamed by mindfulness 18.12; getting rid of ego-clinging should not be confused with feeble self-effacement 18.81–2; if you get rid of desires and clinging, joy will spontaneously arise 19.579; when the rope of clinging is cut, the *bardo* disappears 'like the uncoiling of a snake' 18.612–13; with no distinction between subject and object, how can there be clinging? 18.344; words alone can never free one from ego-clinging 19.158–9

practices to overcome clinging
the integration of the outer world and the non-clinging self 18.102; Milarepa observes his ego-clinging 18.11; a shred of clothing caught on a branch shows Milarepa the absurdity of clinging 18.13; the *śūnyatā* of *śūnyatā* is taught to counter the tendency to cling 23.320; where does clinging come from? – an insight exercise 4.376–7

see also
twelve cyclical *nidānas/upādāna*

Clive, Robert (of India) 22.59

clothes an analogy between perfuming clothes and the perfuming of Suchness 22.17; a brown woollen cloak is made for Sangharakshita 23.203; dressing with care for a puja 11.233; dressing brightly has a positive effect 11.13; it can be skilful to take care of your appearance 19.526; a middle way between puritanism and hedonism needed 24.467; not spending too much on clothes 12.554–5, 12.671; rebirth like putting on a new set of clothes (Hindu view) 3.196–7, 7.165, 19.375; robes were once ordinary clothes 16.404; Sangharakshita colours clothes with *gerua-mati* on going forth 20.225; Sangharakshita finds buying clothes difficult after return to civilian dress 23.190–1; Siddhārtha's exchange of clothes with the beggar (or hunter) 3.29, 3.40, 10.257, 13.661; wearing appropriate clothes as skilful means 19.526

Cloud of Unknowing (medieval text) introduction 23.332; he who knows himself is near to knowing God 7.98; influenced by Christian Neoplatonism 7.578 (n180); 'short prayer pierceth heaven' 24.540; we must strive to unite our will with the will of God 7.97

clouds

beautiful clouds
the beauty and impermanence of clouds 26.241; the beauty of clouds seen on a flight, 'like the gossamer scarf of a *ḍākinī*' 24.112; the beauty of a white bird and a dark cloud (Pāli canon) 26.242; white clouds lying asleep 25.219

clouds as symbols of impermanence
life is a dream, a cloud, a drop of dew 25.390; objects are like floating clouds, like sea foam, like a reflection 14.192; we should view what is conditioned as a cloud 14.509–10

clouds of suffering
clouds of suffering hanging over cities 4.572–4, 4.583; dark clouds of unawareness 17.613; *dukkha*: a cloud has to float across the face of the sun 26.12; not 'mine' or 'yours', but to be dispelled 4.592, 4.630; one wants to replace them with clouds of joy for everybody 4.624; so bound up with negativity that one's life is passed in a dark cloud 3.270; to be dispelled by the united efforts of us all 4.634

joyful clouds
clouds of joy created by spiritual emancipation 4.584, 4.592; making people happy like a rain cloud watering the dry land 17.182; 'the moon freed from clouds' (*Dhammapada*) 2.625–7

dispelling clouds
dispelling the clouds obscuring the pure light of the mind 23.104, 23.110; the mind like a clear blue sky, free of clouds of conceptualization 1.586; watching an unskilful thought like a cloud in the sky 11.689

more metaphorical clouds
blue-black elephants of heaven 25.296; the Buddha compared to a storm cloud pouring rain on the earth 26.126; 'Cloud of the Dharma' (Dharmameghā), *see under* ten *bhūmis*; 'The grey clouds are my friends' 25.446; 'Huge cloudy symbols of a high romance' 1.28, 13.120; 'Indra's cows' (storm clouds) 13.167; the *nirmāṇakāya* like rain from the cloud of the *sambhogakāya* 4.204; rainbow-coloured cloud 13.204; *The Way of the White Clouds*, *see* Govinda/works

Clough, Arthur Hugh 24.140, 24.640 (n167)

coarseness abstention from coarse speech 2.379–80; coarse emotions 4.134; coarse energy 4.134, 11.202–3; a coarsening of the visual arts in the Renaissance 24.273; trying to translate the subtleties of spiritual experience into the coarse language of thought 7.134

cock *see under* birds

Cocteau, Jean 25.378

Coe, Stella 11.474, 23.33, 23.36

coenobitical monasticism *see under* monasticism

coercion *see* force

cognition the Buddha's cognition of reality was expressed in his teaching of conditionality 1.264; converting intellectual recognition of something's rightness into an ardent desire to do it 4.150, 26.399; Indian Buddhist texts' emphasis on the cognitive 5.267–8; longing desire to possess objects of sensuous cognition in hope of security 11.129–30; a profound 'metaphysical' cognition 2.117; transcendental cognition (*vidyā*) 2.127

Colantonio, Niccolò 24.276

Colchester, England 24.165–6

Colenso, John, Bishop of Natal 12.6–7, 12.701 (n4)

Coleridge, Samuel Taylor

his life
brief introduction 23.542 (n500); Dr Ambedkar's non-resemblance to Coleridge 9.92; appreciation of nature 16.387; association with Highgate 23.473, 26.495; Coleridge as a thinker 26.21–2; experience of inspiration from outside 19.141; his feelings of being unloved and a failure 26.487; letters: 'a very rich collection' 12.698; literary critic 26.324; one of Sangharakshita's literary heroes 26.486–7; weaknesses of character 19.122; Richard Holmes' study of Coleridge 24.563

thoughts and quotations
clerisy (a word he coined) 8.466, 8.472, 8.475; his use of the term imagination 8.458, 12.559, 12.744–5 (n378), 26.487; the greenness of the evening sky 26.136, 26.709 (n66); 'a light in sound, a sound-like power in light' 16.267; on Wordsworth 25.591–2 (n62); spring 'comes slow up this way' 23.133; 'There is now no reverence for any thing' 11.56, 15.392; 'to see Charles Kean act is like reading Shakespeare by flashes of lightning' 3.495, 13.73, 19.450; on Sir

Thomas Browne and quincunxes 12.218; we can reverence only what we cannot understand 11.56–7, 17.276, 18.167

The Rime of the Ancient Mariner
the albatross falls from the mariner's neck 19.503; ends with a simple homily 26.395; 'has always formed a part of my imaginative landscape' 26.486; has the quality *kāvya* 26.332; its deeper, darker themes of sin and guilt 26.486–7; 'like one that hath been stunned/ And is of sense forlorn' 21.381; the mariner sees beautiful sea creatures and 'I blessed them unaware' 19.503, 26.487; the silent sea and emerald ice 26.394; 'to the sleeping woods all night/ Singeth a quiet tune' 1.153; Wordsworth's contribution 26.366

'Kubla Khan'
'as though I've always known it' 26.486; the 'person from Porlock' 25.135; 'ancestral voices prophesying war' 22.341; 'A savage place!' 24.399

other works
Biographia Literaria 26.487; 'Christabel' 26.486; 'Cologne' 24.369, 24.698 (n437); *On the Constitution of the Church and State* 24.144

collective unconscious *see under* Jung

College of Psychic Science *see under* London

Collins, Cecil 24.316–17, 26.240

Collins, Rodney 23.135

collusion 12.481, 26.33

colour

the experience of colour
the bright colours of Kalimpong 11.171, 18.158, 20.469–70; the light and colour of visionary experience 14.170; in dreams 16.259; no colour exists in the abstract 13.283; 'only a beautiful soul can perceive beautiful colours' 21.162; a sensation produced by light from the object upon the retina – interconnectedness 1.31; there are all sorts of beautiful colours to be seen in the spiritual life 13.284; we experience everything in the universe as possessing colour 13.283–4; the vivid colours of the Tibetan landscape 13.66

colour in art
the brilliant colours of a thangka and what they represent 13.66–8; colour came back into Western art with the advent of a new age of faith 13.284; the colours of Tantric Buddhist art 13.285; the five basic colours of Tibetan iconography 13.67–8; natural dyes 5.569, 13.66, 21.162; Renaissance mastery of colour 26.253

the effect of colour
colour therapy 5.570; the emotional effect of colour 13.283–5; in a meditation space 5.302; painting shrine rooms different colours 5.570; the positive effect of surrounding oneself with bright colours 11.13; they have a psychological and spiritual significance of their own 2.601, 16.185

colour in spiritual practice
higher worlds described in terms of brilliant colours 26.221; in the *kasiṇa* practice 1.154, 5.566–9; the Tantric symbolism of colour 13.280–5; think of reality as colourful rather than as colourless 13.284–5, 19.25; in visualization, *see under* visualization/doing the practice

Sangharakshita
colour sense atrophied after return to England 23.470; the effect of colour in early experiences of art 26.218; the experience of colour in the Himalayas 26.218–19; meditation an ascent into a more colourful world 25.42–3

see also
individual colours

Columbus, Christopher 24.420, 24.436

Combastet, Mme 21.445–6, 22.52

comfort

comfortable life
not allowing our lives to become too comfortable 16.207; the comfort of modern life 25.77; comfort and sloth 4.470–1; the comfortable life of the West 17.253; comfortable monastic life 25.76; doesn't provide the possibility of mental freedom that hardship does 18.138; makes spiritual breakthroughs more difficult 19.18–19, 19.21; you can make yourself comfortable in hell if you know how to go about it 4.423, 23.10

attachment to comfort
attachment to comfort 19.13; believing in God because one wants to feel comfortable 12.655; the difficulty of giving up comfort 19.95–6; objecting to spiritual practice because of its imagined discomforts 17.302–3; over-concern with comfort 16.536–7; Rechungpa's wish for comfort to increase devotion 18.260, 18.560, 18.566; we prefer comfort to truth 12.655

giving up comfort
dangerous to deprive oneself of comfort on the basis of rational understanding 16.284; discomfort doesn't in itself mean that anything spiritual is happening 17.253; going beyond your comfort zone 25.77–8; precepts 'cutting away the bond formed by a life of comfort' 11.316; the sangha is not a cosy place to be 10.573; sometimes you have to absorb things, though it might be uncomfortable 4.573; spiritual life may be uncomfortable and difficult at first, but it's worth it 4.370

commercialization the commercial instincts of Tibetan people 21.241; the commercialism of Tantric 'empowerment' in the West 2.565–6; the 'commercialization' of Buddhism 7.246; commercialized sacramentalism 18.428–9, 19.532; one must be on one's guard against humbug 18.429

commitment

TO THE THREE JEWELS

introduction
the term 'commitment' 2.301, 18.563–4; the Buddhist life is a *committed* life 3.396; a committed lay person can do a great deal 12.126–7; commitment of yourself to the 'Highest' 2.292; commitment to the spiritual ideal 1.509, 3.153, 3.458; a commitment for life 15.497–8; festivals remind us of our commitment 3.405; once you're committed you're free from worry 4.48–9, 4.293; a shift in the centre of gravity; what that commitment means 3.396–7, 9.246; why 'commitment' might be preferable to 'Going for Refuge' 9.256; *see also* Going for Refuge

commitment is primary, lifestyle secondary
commitment must precede lifestyle 16.495–6; monk or lay, all part of the sangha 2.299, 9.254, 9.340, 11.135, 11.389, 12.388–9, 12.498; but that doesn't mean that lifestyle is unimportant 2.351–2, 2.517; commitment primary, ten precepts secondary, lifestyle tertiary 2.352, 12.666; definition of an orthodox Buddhist 2.557–8; Dr Ambedkar's belief 2.497, 10.27; friendship with other Buddhists for whom commitment is primary 2.502, 2.547, 2.558; the idea of 'family-based' Buddhism emphasizes lifestyle over commitment 24.489; lifestyle can edge commitment out of its primary place 24.489; in the Mahāyāna 11.571; Sangharakshita's first understanding of this 2.456, 2.499, 21.343–4, 23.145; a slogan in the early days of the FWBO 23.xvi; be cautious of speaking in terms of full-timer and part-timer 10.486; Triratna Order members constantly questioning commitment and lifestyle 12.389; whether you are monastic or lay doesn't matter so much 10.268

FURTHER REFLECTIONS ON COMMITMENT

becoming committed
you could start with the feeling that you ought to be committed 15.706; commitment is the opposite of *moha* 17.47; commitment to growth 15.98; committing oneself to the spiritual life 11.50; conscious individual commitment to religion 15.711–12; extrovert and introvert approaches to commitment 18.171; freedom is found in commitment, not in refraining from commitment 12.484

the mystery of commitment
it is always commitment to the unknown 14.550, 14.566, 14.602, 16.448, 26.31; it involves risk 17.46–7; it's impossible to explain fully what commitment is 15.578

commitment to a promise or vow
a day-to-day commitment may feel more spontaneous than a vow 19.146–7; doing something you've said you'll do requires a firm resolution 19.286–7; don't commit yourself for a specific period until you're ready 19.362–3; the importance of honouring commitments 18.487–8, 19.524

total commitment
how much one committed individual can achieve 23.405; if you're a committed Dharma practitioner, you're always on duty 19.500; intense spiritual practice requires powerful commitment 18.161; make an effort to give yourself wholly to what you are doing 15.115–16; only commit yourself to a plan that can absorb all your energies and interests 19.522–4; ordination as total commitment 15.660–1; the relationship between the more committed and the less committed 26.44; settling down in a way that is committed and also provisional 17.371; support for those fully committed to spiritual life 12.679–80, 18.121–2; work that can only be done if one is fully committed 10.359

what does spiritual commitment require?
commitment to friendship is made possible by shared commitment to ideals 17.328; freedom from mundane ties and responsibilities 16.390–1; integration 5.30–1, 26.40; to achieve something substantial, commit yourself for a long time 12.485; the work and responsibility of spiritual commitment 11.xxii

lack of commitment
accusing someone of failing in commitment 17.234, 17.236, 19.290; cultural interests can be a 'near enemy' to commitment to spiritual life 19.350; failing to commit yourself suggests underlying doubt and indecision 17.616; unwillingness to commit oneself 2.147, 3.255, 3.418

Common Era (CE) 12.564, 12.592

common sense common sense posits an 'I', but the Eye of Enlightenment sees no such unchanging entity 2.86; the fact of impermanence is obvious to common sense, but we don't act on it 17.136; faith needs to be corrected by common sense 17.63; for Ayya Khema, spirituality and common sense were not incompatible 26.536; Milarepa teaches plain straightforward Buddhism – or just common sense 18.565; quite a bit of Buddhism is just common sense 15.362; three levels of ethics: common sense, 'scientific', spontaneous 14.547

communication

unsatisfactory communication
communication with our own mental projections 1.520; don't relate to people in a group-like way 19.501; the dry bones of concepts rubbing against one another 12.314; either one communicates or one is blocked 26.80; the failure of communication between superpowers 12.349–53; it can be exhausting 19.550; jargon doesn't communicate anything 19.294; likely to be less deep when between more than two people 18.478, 23.214; masks communicating with other masks 25.96; modern facilities are used for purposes of non-communication 12.340; most people find it very difficult to communicate 12.37–8; no need to try to talk about the latest fashions 18.153; sex doesn't play much part in communication 11.585; sometimes we talk to avoid communication 12.557; sorting out communication difficulties through practising the *mettā bhāvanā* 5.149; superficial communication 19.107; things left unspoken build up a barrier to communication 26.80

real communication
authentic communication 19.224–6; the challenge of real communication 3.618; characteristics of real communication: relief, energy release, concentration 18.478; drinking together mustn't become a substitute for real communication 19.333; effective communication is like finding the right way to lead a calf 18.169; if everyone is covering up, there's no real communication 10.570; the expression of the creative mind 11.25–6; genuine communication is only possible with warmth and friendliness 12.314; the gift of communication as part of Enlightenment 4.21; going deeper 3.140, 18.153; if you've got genuine feelings you will be able to articulate them 19.293; it has an energizing, almost electrifying effect 4.133; it is necessary to human development 3.556; it is not polarized in the way most communication is 15.527–30; meaningful communication 2.249; 'ordinary communication is not real communication at all' 3.140; people within the sangha will do what they can to spark off real communication 3.439; possible only on the basis of openness and receptivity 16.579; talking exhausts energy, but real communication heightens energy 4.482

what makes communication possible
only possible under certain conditions 18.422; people who set up conditions which make communication impossible 18.357; rational framework needed 16.490; setting up the right conditions for communication 18.477–8; to express yourself is to take a risk 18.278; when one becomes aware that other people are subjects as well as objects 17.521; why is it important to look like others to communicate with them? 12.523–4

advice about communication
all we can communicate is ourselves 16.488; the basis should simply be communication, not point-scoring or verbal kung fu 18.170; communicating with children 3.535; it starts with being aware of the other person 14.582; never talk down to young people 18.238; pay attention to the person speaking 1.519–21, 1.575, 10.217, 16.579; pay attention to the substance of someone's communication, not their manner 26.80; try to get a sense of what words and thoughts are trying to communicate 19.159; use whatever knowledge you've got to establish contact 18.414; we need communication, so we may need to seek it out 17.190, 18.205

communication with spiritual friends
communication plays a vital part in spiritual life 3.402, 10.217; communication with a spiritual companion is intensely blissful 18.419; communication with spiritual peers is radical, no-holds-barred, dangerous 18.420; 'creating light for one another' 16.335; pleasing a spiritual friend

makes it easier for them to communicate with you 4.176; spiritual experience that demands to be communicated 2.268

in the spiritual community
communication in study groups 18.478–80; connection with the single-sex idea 2.517; Going for Refuge to the Sangha is essentially a matter of communication 2.247–8; horizontal communication 3.554–6; the importance of communication in the spiritual life 11.258; importance of learning how to get on with other people 9.189; 'May our communication with one another be sangha' 3.521; people will do what they can to spark off real communication 3.439; relating to others on the basis of what you have in common *as Buddhists* 2.571; represented by the *ḍākinī* 12.314–15; the sangha as communication: 'a vital mutual responsiveness' 2.247–8, 2.461–2, 23.xvi; special use of the term communication in Triratna 19.294–5; trustful and open communication 16.315; what's the use of being in a spiritual community if you don't try to communicate?

forms of communication
alternative means of communication (*Vimalakīrti-nirdeśa*) 16.562–6; giving 17.202; grace waves 4.139, 18.98; it can be so subtle as to be telepathic 1.576; the more means we have at our disposal, the better 4.83, 16.566; objective, skilful discussion 10.603; one person's being impinging on that of another 4.7; perfume 16.558–62, 26.498; silence 12.557; words are not the only means of communication 16.562–6; writing is no substitute for face-to-face communication (unless you write a book) 26.70

effects of communication
deeply in communication with someone, you become aware of their pattern 18.285–6; energy generated in communication 18.478; insight resulting from intense communication 19.328; intense communication reflects you to yourself 19.571; it can help us to change 9.377; it helps us to know ourselves better 3.400; mutual modification of being 3.555; the right sort of talk can have the same effect as meditation 10.530; talking about something can make it happen 19.85, 25.104–5; we become more whole, more ourselves 3.556

mystery
concepts are the means of communicating something incommunicable 15.334–5; the fact that we can't communicate our experience doesn't mean it isn't there 18.357; how to communicate *samādhi* when language comes from the experience it transcends? 26.199–200; intelligence is the ability to express what wisdom sees 17.603; much of our experience is incommunicable 14.595–6; mutual responsiveness across a chasm 18.16–17; the mystery of human communication 16.551–66; a sudden communion between mystery and mystery 26.336; translating experience at one level of consciousness into the terms of another 26.305

see also
Buddha III/communication; guru/relationship with the disciple; *ḍākinī*/as the principle of communication; Dharma III/communicating the Dharma; communication exercises; McLuhan/'The medium is the message'; openness; speech

communication exercises their origin 4.690–1 (n215), 12.704 (n25), 14.656–7 (n501), 25.590 (n46), 26.561–2; the effect is like the angels merging in *Paradise Lost* 4.691 (n325); encouraging people to look at each other 1.519, 1.575–6; not staring, but just looking 15.443; to get the emotions flowing freely 4.256, 11.200, 12.651, 14.573, 15.732, 17.80; in an all-male group at Yale: 'a herd of stampeding young bulls' 23.455; a stately academic does the exercises with a young ex-coalminer 24.213; try to see one another without masks 25.94–5; the usefulness of the practice 9.518–19, 12.38

Communism the American fight against Communism 22.517; Buddhist delegates from Communist bloc countries 22.348–9; changing according to the party line out of insecurity 16.82; 'Christianity and Communism are the same thing!' 12.136, 13.111; Communist strategies 23.86–7; concern about Communist influence in the Himalayas 22.261; to create an ideal society there is no need to turn to Communism 10.348; formerly Buddhist countries now Communist 9.238–9; 'Communists should study Buddhism' (Dr Ambedkar) 9.72; Dr Ambedkar's rejection of Communism 9.411; it controls people through hatred 26.20; a pseudo-religion 17.18; respect for public property in communist countries 18.335; Russian 9.409; Sangharakshita suspected of being a Communist spy 13.559, 22.25; Sangharakshita's response to Communism 8.308–10, 22.209–13; a threat to Buddhism 8.309–10, 8.317, 8.320–1; welcomed by poor people 9.340;

a wrong view that inflicts terrible suffering 12.616–17

communism (libertarian) 8.416–20

community (residential)

HISTORY OF COMMUNITIES

communities in the West
communes and intentional communities 8.416–20, 26.649–50; D. H. Lawrence's idea of living in community ('Rananim') 8.543–51; Oneida Community 24.486–8

communities in Buddhist history
Anuruddha and his friends as exemplars (Pāli canon) 12.606–7; studied different kinds of Buddhism while following the same way of life 4.24; not an Eastern Buddhist institution 11.464

TRIRATNA COMMUNITIES

introduction
the first communities, *see under* Triratna I/early days; the need for a whole spectrum of kinds of community 15.763 (n181); the principles behind residential communities 3.622; living and working together 12.608; living in a residential community as a form of discipleship 15.668; large-scale communities 15.480–1

what a community is like
apprehension about living in a community turns to joy at living there 14.474; the gentle, friendly atmosphere of a community in New Zealand 24.67; it should have a happy, friendly, and peaceful atmosphere 17.182; a sort of hermitage in the middle of *saṃsāra* 19.341; your goodwill needs to be expressed in specific helpful actions 19.557

advantages of community living
the advantages of living in a community 11.189; the advantages for women of communal living 8.418; being changed by community life 15.477; encourages closer personal contact and mutual helpfulness 3.439; a positive alternative to family life 3.623, 12.469, 15.197, 15.473–4; responsibility is spread across many people 15.474; a way of breaking up the existing social setup 15.473–4; you can't always have things your own way 12.669–70, 19.21

challenges
can be vulnerable to the gravitational pull of the group 3.443; don't assume that your community is always a spiritual community 18.497–8; going through the motions of community life 19.275; more difficult when community members get old? 24.61; not being ready to live in a community 19.275; usually not yet true spiritual communities 18.358

single-sex and mixed
couples living in separate communities 11.579–80; mixed communities 11.464, 15.474; need of monks for a 'closed' residential community 2.607; single-sex communities 11.464, 15.474, 24.247; a view of single-sex and mixed communities 24.61

community (spiritual), *see* sangha

companions and companionship avoid unsuitable company (*White Lotus Sūtra*) 16.47; the *bodhicitta* ('Friend Bodhi-Heart') is Milarepa's companion 18.225–6; the Buddha's attendants, *see under* Buddha I/life after Enlightenment; communication with a spiritual companion is intensely blissful 18.419; craving for company, desire for contact, and aspiration for spiritual fellowship 26.24; 'I wish I had a companion in my search for the Way' 18.656–7 (n153); 'it was as though the trees were my silent companions' 21.322; marriage for the sake of close human companionship 2.607; most people, not capable of enjoying the company of Buddhas and bodhisattvas, need friends 18.635; is it true that cutting off ties will be your best companion? 18.621, 18.635; the relationship between friends and companions 11.698–700, 16.300; the spiritual community is companionship that helps you grow, not a group to conform to 18.35; study with the help and companionship of spiritual friends 16.578, 18.xvii; take any opportunity for spiritual companionship 18.425; 'There is no companionship with the spiritually immature' 10.650, 15.385; treating our friends and companions like our own self (*samānārthatā*) 3.575; we need the companionship and support of other members of the sangha 12.514; 'Work makes the companion' (Goethe) 25.400, 26.16; *see also kalyāṇa mitra*; *ḍākinī*

comparison comparison of reason and emotion 5.248–9; the comparison of science with Buddhism is an *upāya* 1.39; comparison between science fiction and Mahāyāna *sūtras* 3.381, 12.503, 16.37, 16.237, 22.463; comparisons, if not odious, are otiose 17.274; hungry ghosts are so hungry they don't think about how they compare with others 4.77; knowledge is essentially comparison 12.130; if you don't agree that everybody is a Buddhist to some extent, you are called an elitist

19.476; no riches can compare with the Tathāgata 15.63; spiritually fruitful to compare Early Buddhism and the Mahāyāna 4.25; we make the effort to compare things when their existence is a problem for us 12.91; Western literature in comparison with *sūtras* 16.443–4

see also
comparing Buddhism and Christianity, *see under* Christianity/Christianity and Buddhism; comparing oneself to others, *see under* pride

compassion (*karuṇā* or *anukampā*)

introduction
the essence of the Dharma 9.147; at the heart of the spiritual community 3.451; it arises when *mettā* contacts suffering 5.158, 5.171–2, 5.197, 5.198, 9.323, 9.537; *karuṇā* is one of the most beautiful words in Buddhist vocabulary 1.235, 7.383; the outward expression of all true spiritual attainment 7.290; perhaps Buddhism's most important teaching 22.285; personified as various Buddhas and bodhisattvas 7.361; the word 'compassion' gives just a glimmering of what the Buddha felt 19.429–30; article by I. B. Horner 1.235–6

the nature of compassion
a hierarchy of compassion: for beings, for *dharmas*, for *śūnyatā* 5.201–2, 26.204–5; freedom is recognizable, and manifests as compassion 10.141; if it causes you distress, it isn't real compassion 5.172; if one is in the *saṃsāra* out of compassion, one doesn't experience it as *saṃsāra* 4.473; informed by awareness 4.193; it must be matched by inner tranquillity 4.393; it must never be confused with sentimental pity 2.125, 4.193, 5.202, 12.661; it requires that everyone shall love and serve (Ambedkar) 9.147; it says: 'Can there be bliss when all that lives must suffer?' 1.405; its boundless nature 5.218–19; its near enemy is contempt, and its far enemy cruelty 5.200–1, 10.173; the nature of compassion 9.323; not an inert principle but a purely transcendental activity 7.361; not mere ratiocination, but involves one's whole being 21.314; nothing blind, sentimental, or foolish about it 4.193, 5.202; one does not feel it for beings because they suffer, one simply feels it 26.53; the positive counterpart of the ninth precept, abstention from hatred 2.389; purified emotion, correspondence with Avalokiteśvara 2.173; a state of no distinction between self and others 12.547; there is nothing emotional about compassion 14.444; the way one acts when one has a deep realization of non-selfhood 12.9

its arising
if we feel as though all living beings are intimately related to us, compassion arises 13.81; it springs up in the emptiness when you are not there 25.215; living ethically is essentially about developing compassion 17.158; love and desire becoming compassion 25.493–8; once self and other have been transcended 5.187

compassion in practice
being compassionate to your weaknesses 10.524–5; compassion can transmute our hate 25.256; 'an expression of compassion such as I had seen on no other human face' 20.369; it can be a sort of emotional indulgence 15.613; it could lead to all other aspects of practice 5.200; it's difficult for us to feel even a glimmer of real compassion 12.547; reflecting on the evils of mundane existence to intensify compassion 1.419; the tension between the claims of compassion and renunciation 4.567–8; why should a disciple have to have compassion? 19.208

compassionate activity
of the Absolute is perceived in different ways, so assumes different forms 1.261; acting with compassion is an essential part of one's spiritual life 25.116; action in which there isn't a trace of self-interest or egoism 12.661; arises when the self–other distinction is transcended 16.214; cultivate a sense of unity, not involvement in fussy charities 7.140; based not on any 'humanitarian' ideal but the emptiness of all *dharmas* 1.269; beneficial activities spontaneously manifesting with no ego-sense 7.409; the fifth and final stage of the spiritual path 5.44; of Green Tārā 12.660–1; not limited by time 1.347; not a sort of do-gooding divorced from awareness or wisdom 13.69; rebirth out of compassion 3.132–4; the spiritual life and activity we call compassion 4.31; spontaneous 5.44, 7.376; teaching the Dharma on the basis of compassion 1.181, 7.383–4, 19.204–5; to speak to the heart, compassion must be shown revealing itself 1.326

compassion in Buddhist history
the compassion that led the Buddha to teach, *see* Brahmā Sahāmpati's request; the Buddha did 'all that a teacher could do out of compassion' 1.180, 1.236; go forth and teach 'out of compassion for the world' 1.26, 1.33, 1.180–1, 1.236, 2.23, 2.58. 3.174, 9.220, 9.235–6, 10.83;

for the Theravāda just one state of mind among others 1.235; eliminated from their conception of Buddhahood by the Uttarapāthakas 2.152; hyperbolical glorification of compassion 1.145; it is of central ethical importance in the Mahāyāna 8.452; Milarepa attempts to dispel demons with 'compassion' 18.26; Rechungpa's sight of a beggar arouses his compassion 19.513–14; the compassion aspect of Buddha-nature brought out in the *tulku* doctrine 7.397

Enlightened and archetypal compassion
the Buddha's compassion, *see* Buddha II/compassion; compassion and the arising of the *bodhicitta* 1.419–20; compassion breaking through from the Unconditioned 2.119; embodied by Padmapāṇi 9.313, 26.384; in an Enlightened person, the will to live is replaced by compassion 10.585; not only the positive but also the dynamic aspect of Enlightenment 1.387; of Avalokiteśvara, *see under* Avalokiteśvara; represented by the masculine in Buddhist iconography 18.373; transcendental compassion of the eternal Buddha 2.128; the unconditional compassion of Amitābha 1.335; wouldn't the Buddha want to be reborn in the world out of compassion? 4.205

compassion and wisdom
analogy with *mārga* and *phala* 15.644–5; the *bodhicitta* as the point at which they start coming together 4.515–16; a Buddha's wisdom and compassion create a Buddha-field 17.298; compassion is the flower of wisdom 12.9; a danger of thinking that compassion is dependent upon wisdom? 19.33–4; the Dharma a bird, the two wings wisdom and compassion 3.355, 3.365, 9.231, 16.15; Enlightenment is not only wisdom but compassion 11.511; the expansion of consciousness through developing wisdom and compassion 26.111; the ideal can be thought of in terms of wisdom or compassion 11.318; indissoluble union (the Tantra) 1.388–90; and the metaphor of a lute 25.286; must be cultivated simultaneously (*Diamond Sūtra*) 1.395–6; one has the qualities of the other, if you look deeply enough 18.373–4; the perfect integration of wisdom and compassion 13.76; not two but one 7.140, 7.362; paradox of compassion for beings recognized as in reality non-beings 2.116; the same thing looked at from different points of view 12.229, 18.588; true wisdom is always accompanied by compassion 3.355, 14.565; the twin pillars of the edifice of Buddhism (Suzuki) 3.158; the Mahāyāna regards the two as coordinate 1.235; they are ultimately non-different 26.208; they coalesce in non-dual reality 17.694; the two-in-oneness of wisdom and compassion 13.75; when teaching the Dharma, trying to reflect wisdom, compassion is also reflected 7.317; wisdom is not enough, compassion is also needed (Ambedkar) 3.354–5; 'Wisdom with Mercy met' 25.181; withdrawal (*nirveda*) must be conjoined with compassion (Tsongkhapa) 2.116, 18.52

images and metaphors
'The Alms of Compassion' 25.213; the Law of Laws (*The Voice of the Silence*) 7.362, 7.457, 26.205; 'The Lamp of Compassion'(poem) 25.215; 'The Lotus of Compassion' 25.208; symbolized by perfume 16.560–1, 25.214; 'pour down like rain' 25.214; the unseen flower 25.215

see also
Amitābha; animals/kindness to animals; Avalokiteśvara, the bodhisattva of compassion; bodhisattva/what is a bodhisattva?/compassion; Buddha II/compassion; *karuṇā bhāvanā*; *mahākaruṇā* (great compassion); Tennyson/'painless sympathy with pain'; *śūnyatā* and compassion; parables and stories/the young man who learned compassion through chess

competition and competitiveness among the Buddha's disciples, everybody excelled at something 4.170–1; the competitive spirit can't function fully while your mind is absorbed in higher things 10.482–3; the competitive world is like a hawk attacked by other hawks for the meat it is carrying 3.215; competitiveness in the spiritual community should be playful, not about power 18.17–19; competitiveness with your spiritual companion, your *ḍākinī* 18.418; competition helps people to give of their best 4.170; competition in the spiritual life 4.500, 13.136–7; cut-throat competition 17.293; in a competitive state, the next step is to develop intellectual insight into truth 13.132; joviality sometimes masks competitiveness 26.78; outside the sangha, criticism can be fraught with competitiveness 15.295; the realm of the *asuras*, an aggressive, competitive state of mind 13.130; true competition is a form of collaboration 26.79; unlike the Olympics, for the followers of the Buddha there is no question of competition 12.675

complacency about not occupying oneself with things of higher value 17.534; about

practising one's religion without fear 16.198; complacent lethargy is not to be mistaken for blissful peace 15.219; in Eastern Buddhist countries 12.113; the good qualities you have developed can lead to complacency and pride 17.285; greed types are more prone to complacency, but hate types are also susceptible to it 13.139; in the grip of self-complacency, you are satisfied with yourself as you are – a great obstacle 13.138–9; it stems from a lack of contentment with who you really are 15.276; the near enemy of contentment 15.275; Siddhārtha's victory over spiritual complacency 11.398–9; sometimes the spiritual community supports complacency 18.164; you ought to get a bit impatient with yourself sometimes 4.368

complexity Buddhism is a rich and complex thing 12.610–11; Buddhist conversion is a complex and arduous task 2.285; of causality 3.316–17, 9.389; circumstances are so complex that what is skilful for one person may not help another 15.291; the complex nature of guilt 16.306–9; the complexity of life and experience 15.690; the complexity of modern society 16.432; existence is an infinitely complex, constantly shifting network 4.648; ordinary life is much richer and more complex than we realize 24.148–9; the senses: a complex network of conditions 1.109–10; systems of correspondences are subtle, complex, and changing 19.43

composite or compounded (Pāli *saṅkhāra*, Sanskrit *saṃskṛta*) compounded and uncompounded 13.193, 16.389; the meaning of *saṅkhāra* 1.171; the conditioned 3.206; two levels of existence, *saṃskṛta* and *asaṃskṛta* 13.438; seeing the component parts of something 1.100; things are compounded, but how? 1.173

comprehension of purpose *see* mindfulness of purpose

compromise adjusting to other people's attitudes and views at the expense of your own convictions 18.461; artists making compromises in their work 12.643–4; the Buddha's uncompromising insistence on the need to personally realize Nirvāṇa 2.202–3; compromise is the enemy of the spiritual life 26.63; don't confuse skilful means with capitulation to the pressure of the group 19.261; don't do less than you can, don't compromise 18.622; giving talks: 'I beat the drum of the Dharma vigorously and without compromise' 23.79; it's good that at least a few people are totally uncompromising 18.639; the importance of uncompromisingly maintaining the FWBO's principles 24.167; the middle way involves neither moral compromise nor intellectual eclecticism 7.299; Milarepa adopts a compromise with a wayward disciple 18.365–6; Milarepa's uncompromisingness 18.221, 18.246, 18.638–9; perhaps it's better to be pedantic than risk compromising the ideal 19.463; to work together we have to learn to discuss things, compromise, listen 10.397–8

Conan Doyle, Arthur 23.490 (n127)

concealment

general reflections
with spiritual friends, you no longer have to hide anything 18.420; concealing the fact that you are a Buddhist 10.630, 12.540, 19.500; concealment is often unavoidable 25.89; hiding things in polite society 19.256–7; hypocrisy's connection with concealment and dissimulation 17.278; 'I do not conceal whatever evil I may have done' 16.314–15; in Buddhism great importance is attached to not concealing any thought 18.515; do words conceal or reveal thought more? 7.378; four aspects of concealed suffering 3.213–15; Milarepa doesn't hide anything 19.256–7; out of fear 10.570–1; when giving a talk, don't conceal your ignorance 12.582

slyness-concealment (mrakṣa)
an attempt to cover up your weaknesses is a serious matter 19.152–3; covering up what you consider shameful 19.259–60; hanging on to your weaknesses 17.647–8; in concealing something from others, you are concealing it from yourself 17.648; it arises only when you have committed yourself to certain spiritual standards 17.647–8; the main antidote is confession of faults 17.648–51; as *upakleśa* 17.647–51

conceit (*māna*) *see* pride

concentration

the nature of concentration
the body-witness realizes the true nature of levels of concentration 2.144; 'The concentrated mind sees things as they really are' 1.87, 1.168, 2.113, 3.274, 12.566; 'A concentrated person is happy, a happy person is concentrated' 2.109, 3.271, 15.221, 26.46; the concentration of a murderer is very different from true mindfulness 1.91; deep concentration without mental activity 5.438; it continues

the work of mindfulness, but they are quite different 17.114; the mandala as the archetypal image of concentration 18.125; not an end in itself 1.168; not forcibly fixing the mind, but the gradual unification of energies 5.49–50, 17.116; preparatory, intermediate, and full 2.109; of two kinds, depending on karmically wholesome or unwholesome state 1.149–50; a unifying, synthesizing activity 17.116–17; a union of the forces of the depths with the forces of the heights 26.47; the whole art of life is being able to do one thing at a time 5.681, 26.17; withdrawing the scattered forces of the mind into a single focus of attention 7.358–9

ability to concentrate
the Buddha's ability to concentrate 3.288–9; a mind disturbed by recalling a breach of precepts cannot concentrate 2.105; why is our concentration so weak? 1.569

objects of concentration
breath, coloured discs, concepts, a flame, psychic centres, the Buddha 11.123; everyday activities transformed from hindrances to helps to concentration 1.151–4; four kinds of mental objects, relating to the threefold path 17.542–3; how can concentrating on a sense object lead beyond the *kāmaloka*? 5.570–1; *kammaṭṭhānas*, *see* forty *kammaṭṭhānas*; reflection on the Dharma 5.438; they are of various kinds 10.158

in meditation
concentrating on the right thing (we are always concentrating on something) 12.148; having cultivated the preceding *nidānas*, moderate practice will produce profound *samādhi* 2.112–13; if you do the practice, concentration will follow 17.115; meditation begins with concentration 3.272; pure concentration in the *kasiṇa* practice 5.643; stupa visualization as a concentration exercise 5.486–7

effects of concentration
the aim of meditation is to make us more concentrated, unified beings 17.116–17; concentrated mental activity can produce physical effects 14.463–5; without study, concentration is no more use than a sharpened pencil to one who can't write 1.170; you can be aware of everything around you, but no sense desire arises 17.123

see also
Noble Eightfold Path/Perfect or right concentration; *samādhi*

conception *see* birth

concepts

THE USE OF CONCEPTS

the nature of concepts
any concept owes its 'existence' to its opposite 17.368; essentially dualistic, silence being the entrance to non-duality 16.548; the means of communicating something essentially incommunicable 15.334–5; 'The seeds for the possible worlds are concepts' 17.475–6; they arise in two ways: by postulation and by intuition 17.437; they are the creation of the *kliṣṭa-mano-vijñāna* 16.542; they are vital, but they do not exhaust the whole of life's mystery 15.137

using concepts
conceptual commentary on one's experience in meditation 5.629–30; handling abstract concepts 19.39–40; ideas and concepts rest upon you, not you upon them 14.566; intelligence is the creative use of concepts 14.549, 15.187, 17.603, 18.238; the nature of concepts and how one employs them 17.248–9; to communicate the Dharma you need some skill in handling concepts 14.575; understanding concepts to get back to the transcendental experience they express 4.145; using words clearly to express concepts 4.145, 16.490–1; we should use concepts but not settle down in them 14.417

limitations and dangers
conceptual symbols, treated as reality, turn from helps into hindrances 1.303–4; beware of the temptation to produce concepts too readily 1.483; concepts – 'the State', 'Wealth' – are useful, but they can become dangerous 7.326; danger of converting concepts of relative validity into entities of ultimate reality 1.224; endowing concepts with a life of their own leads to disastrous consequences 7.326; even the concept of experience has its limitations 19.378; indications for practical spiritual purposes of that which they cannot express 1.243; intellectual conversation: the dry bones of concepts rubbing against one another 12.314; spiritual experience can be expressed through concepts but is not identical to them 1.482; the spiritually disastrous habit of treating concepts as ends in themselves 21.314; they can wreak havoc, like a constellation of malignant stars 7.326; they may convince the head, but they will not move the heart 26.163; an 'unearthly ballet of bloodless categories' 14.85, 26.163

operational concepts
can Nirvāṇa be attained, or is its attainment just an operational concept? 19.47; the difficulty of disposing of them 18.396–400; the distinction between mind and mental events 17.493–4; natural purity only an operational concept 17.98; they cannot define suchness, but designate it for practical purposes 7.299; using dirt to get rid of dirt 17.366, 17.494; we need them as the basis of the spiritual life 18.397–8, 19.508; viewed from the perspective of *śūnyatā*, any concept is an *upāya* 15.186–7; you can't postulate them 'in cold blood', you have to believe them 19.38–9

literal and symbolic use
beware of taking conceptual formulations of exalted experiences too literally 1.259; literalism with regard to concepts 15.334; to give precedence to the conceptional mode over imagination is an error 14.430–1; they must be understood not literally but symbolically 1.234

playing with concepts
best treated in the spirit of poetry, not logic: playful juggling, not grim calculation 2.54; our reflections and questions should be our own, not a game of rearranging concepts 4.147; playwords (Milarepa's name for concepts) 18.66; real koan must be distinguished from playing around with reified concepts 14.422

going beyond concepts
bypassing concepts with koan 8.499; the difficulty of disposing of them 18.396–400; distinction between concepts and realities 1.72, 2.114, 26.84; the emptiness of all concepts, including emptiness 16.11–12, 19.377; getting rid of concepts with concepts 17.xx, 17.366; having meaningful dreams suggests being tired of the conceptual framework 19.564; it's easy to juggle refined concepts but difficult to stop thinking in those terms 19.373; myths and legends help to convey the trans-conceptual truth of Enlightenment 11.15–16; the truth is beyond words and concepts 7.331, 14.297

CONCEPTS AND BUDDHISM

in Buddhist tradition
Buddhist history is a process of the solidification and dissolution of concepts 4.38; the Theravāda identifies them with reality 1.235; conceptual medieval Indian communication does not suit Buddhism 14.514; the Mahāyāna on concepts 1.219–20, 1.242; the Madhyamaka's refined concepts need the Yogācāra 's meditative context 19.374; the *Heart Sūtra* as an extended conceptual formulation 5.449; the conceptual formulation of the truth of *śūnyatā* 1.343; the idea of conceptual expression contradicted by the Mahāmudrā 19.271–2; connections between Buddhist ideas and Western concepts 11.463

concepts and Dharma teaching
Buddhism is expressed in concepts, and therefore in terms of opposites 16.542; Buddhism speaks the language of concepts and of images 4.144–8, 12.106, 12.503, 16.15–16, 16.416–17; communication between the Enlightened and non-Enlightened mind 3.232; concepts going round and round like a wheel and the ratchet never gripping 19.216–17; conceptual symbols like the moon's reflection 10.159; if we don't practise the Dharma, we will only have ideas, concepts, words 12.455; knowing concepts to communicate the truth (*artha-pratisaṃvid*) 16.489–90; the means of transition from intellectual to intuitive understanding 18.399; a medium for communicating a unique and ineffable experience 2.59; mere words: only when we discard them in meditation will we realize *śūnyatā* 1.308; non-conceptual modes of doctrinal instruction 1.219; the relationship between Buddhist concepts and the realization behind them 11.653–4; to begin with, right view is just a conceptual understanding 12.616; they address the conscious mind 16.16; a transcription into conceptual symbols of the Buddha's ineffable experience 7.309; treated as though they possessed absolute validity 1.222; you can't convey the Dharma conceptually 10.568

concepts and reality
as long as we are dealing with concepts we are not dealing with ultimate reality 14.547; assuming that wisdom is better expressed in concepts than images 14.430–1; concepts cannot encompass the whole of reality 15.187; the concepts of existence and non-existence can't deal with the flow of reality 19.376–7; concepts personified as Buddhas, bodhisattvas, and other divinities 1.243; conceptual symbols coming in between the unenlightened mind and reality 8.498–9; conceptual verbal signposts, like the description of an orange 7.510; conditioned consciousness attempts to catch reality in the net of concepts 17.379; conceptual symbols of things contrasted with reality (Abhidharma) 14.83; confusing the realization of truth with the concepts that communicate

it 19.354; Thomas Merton could not distinguish words and concepts from realities 8.491–2; reality can be mediated as much by images as by concepts 19.189; reality is as much fascinating and alluring as it is a matter of concepts 13.284; reflection on concepts to get back to the transcendental experience 4.145; the transcendental truth shines just as brightly through myth as through concepts 1.326; the Unconditioned transcends all concepts whatsoever 2.121; wisdom may not necessarily take conceptual forms 17.134–5

see also
insight/how to gain insight/insight and conceptual thinking; *śūnyatā/śūnyatā* as concept and teaching

conceptualization conceptualization of Enlightenment leads to distortion 2.54; conceptualizations are intimately related to our basic attitudes to life 19.106; does insight require conceptualization? 5.629; the mind like a clear blue sky, free of clouds of conceptualization 1.586; two kinds of wrong conceptualization 19.106

conclusions arriving at general conclusions from limited experience 10.612; the Buddha didn't jump to conclusions 11.441–2; don't jump to conclusions about people 10.500–1, 11.441–2, 19.282; drawing conclusions from experience 9.343; in the spiritual life, it's important to come to your own conclusions 19.164–5; taking responsibility for one's conclusions 17.626

concubine *see under* prostitution

conditionality

law of conditionality
all things, from cells to galaxies, and all thoughts and feelings, are governed by it 2.251, 3.94; everything arises and ceases in dependence on conditions 1.47, 4.42, 8.xxiv, 17.246; the idea of conditionality is the idea of causation used in modern science 17.637; perhaps the most important principle of Buddhist thought 12.21; not just an idea: can have a transformative effect 3.279; the principle of conditionality makes transformation possible 15.81; a universal principle, for the universe without and the world within 8.243–4

Buddhism and conditionality
the Buddha gained Enlightenment as a result of his insight into it 1.93, 1.226; the Buddha's cognition of reality was expressed in his teaching of it 1.264; each step of the Noble Eightfold Path is based on it 15.250; the guiding principle of the Buddhist path 15.81; the universal principle of Buddhism 14.607; the whole of Buddhism is founded upon it 2.251, 3.182; the Buddhist distinction between causality and conditionality 1.110, 14.607–8, 19.435; Hīnayānists neglected the principle in favour of a specific application 1.266; handled differently by different Buddhist schools 10.143; if the *dharmakāya* is the ocean, conditionality is the waves 14.607; conditionality and emptiness are the same thing 1.267

understanding conditionality
the idea of conditionality brought about a tremendous spiritual upheaval 12.464; not understanding it, human life is 'like a tangled ball of string' 2.696 (n342); right view: understanding the conditionality of all phenomena 7.521; understanding the principle more important than understanding any application 1.266

cyclical and spiral
the Buddha's discovery of the two main orders of conditionality 3.97, 11.163–4; Buddhism sees itself as subject to the same cyclical process as everything else 12.594; cyclical *nidānas*, *see* twelve cyclical *nidānas*; cyclical, progressive and regressive, irreversibly progressive 4.650; oscillation or augmentation 2.252, 3.97, 3.184–5, 4.648, 12.21, 12.153–4; relationship to the *trikāya* 4.650–1; a switch from the cyclical to the spiral type of conditionality 11.xxii, 13.432–3; whatever happens, is our reaction cyclical or progressive? 3.279

see also
five *niyamas*/orders of conditionality; twelve positive *nidānas*

conditioned co-production *see pratītya-samutpāda*

conditioned existence

THE NATURE OF CONDITIONED EXISTENCE

the nature of conditioned things
all are phenomena of the unconditioned reality of absolute mind 2.67; all phenomena are conditioned 3.94, 3.176; any conditioned thing can be transformed into any other, over time 18.295; any conditioned thing comes into being in dependence on its own non-existence 17.384; Conze's article on the conditioned 1.102, 22.124–5; as delicately contingent as a candle in the wind 14.506; distinction

between how it is in reality and as the unenlightened mind interprets it 2.80; illusory from a metaphysical point of view 14.505; nothing conditioned can fully satisfy the deepest longings of the human heart 4.51; speaking in terms of illusion draws attention to what the conditioned is like 5.603

what conditioned existence is like
the *bodhicitta* in the web of conditioned existence 4.32; the conditioned in pursuit of the conditioned, the ignoble quest 3.207–8, 9.528, 16.389, 16.394; the *Diamond Sūtra*'s similes ('As stars, a fault of vision ...'), *see under Diamond Sūtra*; divided into three great planes, *see under trailokya*; in a sense Māra rules over it 11.402, 26.645–6; it means suffering 17.173; its characteristics, *see* three *lakṣaṇas*; loneliness is inherent in it 18.16; reducible to the five *skandhas* 2.124, 11.401; subject to the danger of desire 18.172; symbolized by the wheel of life 3.243; there are no absolutes 17.626; wandering through the realms of conditioned existence 8.558–9, 26.347–8

release from conditioned existence
the first five *pāramitās* are a refinement of the whole conditioned nature 4.550; freedom from conditioned existence 2.56; what prompts one of high status to seek to realize its true nature? 17.160–1; withdrawing from it as a fisherman lets go of a poisonous snake 3.275–6; you don't get released from it by means of the conditioned 10.523

THE CONDITIONED AND THE UNCONDITIONED

differences and distinctions
all conditioned things are phenomena of the unconditioned reality of absolute mind 2.67; are they different in an ultimate sense? 15.633–4; the battle between them 16.428; the conditioned in any form is infinitely remote from the Unconditioned 14.454–5; the discontinuity between them 14.172; distinction between them 3.234; don't transfer to the Unconditioned categories from experience of the conditioned 14.442; in its depth, the conditioned 'is' the Unconditioned 14.397; a misunderstanding to see the conditioned and the Unconditioned as separate 'things' 3.218; no transformation of the conditioned can be the Unconditioned 25.73–4; the non-duality of conditioned and Unconditioned 4.587–91; nothing conditioned can deserve the Unconditioned 14.403; pleasure from conditioned things can't satisfy our longing for the Unconditioned 3.215; *śūnyatā* as a term for the total process 15.637; the term conditionality used to refer to both 'conditioned' and 'Unconditioned' 15.637; transcending the distinction 2.56–7; two sides of the same coin 3.218; the Unconditioned as the higher principle 16.388–9; unconditioned identity of the conditioned and the Unconditioned 1.305

and the spiritual life
the Buddha transcended the duality 14.596; the Buddhist life is transition from conditioned to Unconditioned 26.645–6; by knowing the conditioned in its depth we also know the Unconditioned 2.89; can one see through the conditioned without a glimpse of the Unconditioned? 15.576; the conditioned mind asks questions, but for the Unconditioned the answer is unnecessary 17.355; the conditioned in pursuit of the Unconditioned 3.207–8, 9.528, 16.389; draw nourishment not from your conditioned being, but from the Unconditioned 14.588; household shrines: the presence of the Unconditioned in the midst of the conditioned 2.229; insight can be developed into any conditioned object, even a matchbox 18.88; insight: seeing conditioned existence as it really is, as a living experience 4.498; one's centre of gravity shifts from conditioned to Unconditioned 2.263; only by 'grasping hold of' the Unconditioned can you escape the conditioned 10.634; seeing through the conditioned to the Unconditioned 3.274–5; why not try to go from the conditioned to the Unconditioned? 26.369; without the Unconditioned escape from the conditioned would be impossible 14.54

see also
three *āśravas*/craving for conditioned existence; *pratītya samutpāda*; *bodhicitta*/the arising of the *bodhicitta*/seeing the faults of conditioned existence

conditioning the *ālaya vijñāna* is what makes conditioning possible 18.292; breaking through conditioning 11.6–8, 11.13–14; the Buddha transcends all conditionings 1.65, 3.142–3; by becoming aware of conditioning we become free of it 11.13–14, 17.538; Christian conditioning, *see under* Christianity attitudes; conditioning by nationality, class, work, social system, religion 11.6–7; conscious rejection of conditioning 23.187; deconditioning (Gnosticism) 8.426–7; deeply ingrained convictions connected with deep conditioning 19.18;

freedom from group conditioning an aspect of the true individual 3.468; our minds are conditioned in many unskilful ways, but spiritual practice undoes that 12.467; our psychological conditioning 11.6–8, 12.262; positive conditioning eventually unravels all conditionings 17.475; to practise the Dharma, we have to go against the whole weight of our conditioning 12.455; recognize any disadvantage of your conditioning and do something to go beyond it 18.147–8; travel as a way of overcoming one's conditioning 11.13–14; unconscious conditioning derives largely from the exigencies of primitive life 3.425

conditions

difficult
the bodhisattva does not shrink from working in the most difficult conditions 2.180; the bodhisattva spirit is exposing yourself to difficult conditions 15.394; life itself is a difficult condition 11.622; the need to adapt to changing conditions 12.470–1; practising contentment in an unsatisfactory situation 15.289–90; you can respond positively even to difficult conditions 11.622

positive
can we surround ourselves with conditions that support our spiritual aspirations? 18.36; creating favourable conditions for spiritual life 4.481; the danger of abandoning the safeguard of positive conditions prematurely 18.34; early FWBO retreats demonstrated the importance of positive conditions 12.652; the effect of positive conditions on retreat 4.183, 5.683; good conditions aren't necessarily peaceful or easy 15.393–6; it is the presence of certain objective conditions that makes the Dharma life possible 5.259–61; making best use of good conditions for Dharma practice 4.365–7, 12.513–14, 15.365; Milarepa makes best use of a beneficial environment 18.41–2; the need to set up positive conditions to support practice 4.183; perhaps we place too much importance on having good conditions 11.622–3, 18.630–1; you need a positive, creative, supportive environment until you enter the Stream 12.315

reflecting on conditions
being aware of how we are influenced by our environment 15.153, 15.392–5; conditions for mindfulness 4.480–1; think in terms of causes and conditions, not 'I did this' or 'He did that' 10.600–2

see also
four conditions; twenty-four causal conditions

confession (*pāpa deśanā*)

confession in the Buddhist tradition
it translates *deśanā*, 'pointing out' 16.290; importance in all Buddhist schools 1.509; part of Buddhist spiritual life from the beginning 26.642; Ajātaśatru's confession 16.274–5; its origins: the rainy season retreat 1.410, 16.272–4; in the Vinaya 1.410, 2.195; recitation of *prātimokṣa* on *uposatha* days 1.146, 2.187; development of ceremony of confession 2.189; in Theravāda Buddhism 1.410–1, 4.46; in Mahāyāna Buddhism 1.411, 4.46–7, 16.275; in the *Bodhicaryāvatāra*, *see* Śāntideva/*Bodhicaryāvatāra*/chapter 2; in the *Sūtra of Golden Light*, *see under Sūtra of Golden Light*; purification ritual described in *Dhyāna for Beginners* 2.105, 14.486; Rechungpa's confession 19.548–9; the 35 Buddhas of confession 4.314, 14.185, 17.650–1; degeneration in the Buddhist tradition 16.273–4, 25.642

other traditions
confession in psychoanalysis 16.269, 16.318; difference between Christian and Buddhist 1.411, 11.260, 16.269, 16.308–9, 17.650; a priest who hated Christmas because of hearing confessions 13.558, 16.308–9; Swami Ramdas received confession like an ocean receiving a river 20.325

reasons for confession
an antidote to slyness-concealment 17.648–51; an aspect of openness 16.316; crucial to the spiritual life 16.319, 26.62; it means accepting responsibility 16.323; preparation for meditation 2.105; reason (Ambedkar) 9.146; to the extent to which we do not confess, we do not grow 16.293

what to confess
best to confess specific things 16.304, 16.314, 17.649; confess acts of omission as well as commission 11.262; confess little things, because they keep us away from Enlightenment 4.309–10; confession of evil 16.290–319; confession to a failure to live up to our ideals 17.649; cruelty 16.294–6; disrespect to the Three Jewels 16.303; faults through lack of *vīrya* 4.474; if you're not sure whether to confess something, best to confess it 17.649; neglect of parents 16.296–8; things done out of greed, hatred, delusion 2.260

how to confess
as soon as possible 16.319; before a shrine 3.265–6; a cry uttered from the very depths of a heart on fire with remorse 1.411; the difference between confession and admission 11.261–2, 17.649–50; a heartfelt pouring forth of regret and a fierce determination 4.46–7; it must include resolution to change 16.313; it requires trust 10.570–1, 16.315–16; it takes effort 16.316; its hallmark is a feeling of intense regret 11.262–3; learning how to confess breaches of the precepts 2.343; not breast-beating, but a realistic appraisal and a resolve to do better 4.46; not a mechanical procedure 16.315; not something you do once and for all 16.319; out of awareness and confidence that one can develop skilful states 2.260; a saint's confession: sensitivity to things most people think don't matter 4.309–10; spewing up poison (impurities) 10.450–1, 16.292–3; steps of confession 16.509; without guilt 11.262, 16.306–11, 26.33; writing down your confession 16.313, 16.318

to whom should we confess?
to whom should we make confession? 16.313–14; confessing to those one respects most 17.651; confession to a stranger 16.318; the disciple's confession to their teacher 4.46, 16.274, 17.650; ideally you confess to the person you've offended 17.649, 17.651; to the Buddha 16.313–14; to spiritual friends 16.314, 16.317–18, 17.650, 18.516; within the sangha 11.268; you can't effectively confess to yourself, though it may be a start 17.651

difficulty with confession
fear of confession 10.570–1, 16.316–17; fear that people would no longer accept us 16.315; finding it challenging is a good thing 16.318; it is not easy to confess everything 11.261–2; a woman who talked too much because she had something to confess 15.116–17

the effect of confession
balanced by rejoicing in merits 4.317, 4.332; developing more mindfulness with regard to unskilful actions 16.311; it does not absolve you from the consequences of your actions 1.509; it helps us live without a mask 25.95; it helps you to experience your karma in a different perspective 4.314–15; it may have consequences 10.571–2; it's inspiring 16.309; primarily an ethical (not a psychological) act 17.649; psychological value 4.310–1; purification 16.315, 16.325; restoring a clear conscience 3.265–6, 12.160; Śāntideva doesn't mention any therapeutic value 4.310; to clear away darkness and evil so we can experience freedom and joy 16.337; to eliminate remorse and replace it with delight 2.259; true openness allows you to make a fresh start 10.570; a way of overcoming obstacles 16.290; why stress that it has a *spiritual* significance? 16.269–71; you objectify what you have done 16.313

after confession
getting back onto the right path 16.508; making reparation for breaking precepts 3.409; having confessed, put it out of your mind 4.332, 11.264; penance 16.510; really to confess something is to give it up, not just verbally but in fact 16.293

see also
devotion/Sevenfold Puja/confession; forgiveness; *pariṣuddhi*; Sangharakshita V/ personal practice

confidence

confidence
in Going for Refuge 7.309; interpreting faith or confidence as dogmatism 19.102–3; needed to refute wrong views 10.587; that you are on the right path 4.202; when talking about the Dharma 12.587; you need confidence to approach Enlightenment 12.216–17

self-confidence
of the bodhisattva 4.446, 4.468; of the Buddha 2.26, 10.471, 12.529; can be enhanced by wearing the right clothes 19.526; developing self-confidence 10.506; the difference between egoism and self-confidence 18.464; don't label someone else's self-confidence as ego 10.471; education can give self-confidence 14.405; faith in the Buddha is inseparable from faith in yourself 17.37; in meditation 5.336; Milarepa's confidence is not subject to external conditions 18.45; openness with spiritual friends leads to confidence and fearlessness 18.420–1; over-confidence 16.299, 18.34, 18.465; the self-confidence of Milarepa's shepherd disciple 18.234; self-confident people won't feel at home in a meek, submissive sangha 4.469; taking the initiative requires self-confidence 9.303; we need a healthy self-confidence 10.470–1; when you see that something helps you, have confidence to go ahead with it 19.350; without self-confidence one can do nothing 10.355; you don't ignore the dangers, but you know that you are more than equal to them 4.446; you need to build self-confidence before you can take the Dharma seriously 25.142

lack of confidence
confronting lack of self-confidence (the crucial situation) 13.232; looking for praise reveals a lack of confidence in what you have done 18.165; overcoming lack of confidence to attain *dhyāna* 4.96, 5.327, 5.452–3; self-deprecation 17.654; undermining someone's confidence: a bleak thing 17.660–1

developing confidence
by doing things 4.287, 15.602–4; the key to success in meditation 5.453; a translation of *pahitatta* 10.506; various methods 15.271

confidentiality 2.208

conflict

conflict between ...
attachment to self and rejection of self 13.396; Buddhist traditions and the forces of the modern age 8.538; Buddhists in Kalimpong 22.235–6; the claims of compassion and renunciation 4.568–9; creative and other energies 16.286–7; *dāna* and *śīla* 4.92, 4.116–17, 4.386–7; desire and fear 25.85; different attitudes to Buddhism 22.150; the ego-centred intellect and the deeper, transpersonal spiritual life 12.217–18; the gravitational pull of the conditioned and the Unconditioned 17.612; the group and the true individual 13.457, 13.461–2; incorporating and surrendering 16.520; keeping something and giving it away 4.181; the mundane and the spiritual 13.396; the emptiness of everything (ontologically) and the struggle for Enlightenment 14.146

conflict within oneself
avidyā as a sense of alienation and conflict 14.517; before the *bodhicitta* is solidly established 4.274–5; for a long time we are just a bundle of conflicting impulses and ideas 19.98; no conflict between what you know you should do and what you actually do 18.459; often much of our energy is tied up in internal conflict 15.216; a real question springs out of one's own conflict 4.147; resolution of conflict between rational and emotional on the spiritual path 26.77; sloth and torpor in meditation may be produced by conflict 10.533; unconscious conflict can be a great drainer of energy 19.394–5; without it, it's easier to deal with external pressures 16.323, 26.59

other elements of conflict
conflict as metaphor for human life 16.85–6; conflict in the Order should be resolved as quickly as possible 2.522–3; conflict between people and nations from the belief in separate selfhood 26.168–9; Milarepa avoids conflict with a wayward disciple 18.364–5; working towards harmony through positive conflict 26.7

see also
argument

conformity the common man must conform or perish, so he naturally conforms 7.148; conforming for the sake of peace and quiet 17.559; the conformity imposed by the family 15.484; the group requires conformity 3.438, 3.440, 12.253; the individual has to stand up for himself in the face of pressure to conform 19.261–2; the middle way between conformity and rebellion towards parents 12.390–2; the middle way between individualism and conformity 18.35; rules can become an external conformity, neglecting the spirit 10.563, 18.324; why did Buddhism not use political influence to enforce religious conformity? 7.383

'Confounder of Hell' verses *see under* Vajrasattva

Confucianism civic responsibilities 12.247; a Confucian scholar praises the etiquette in a Chan monastery 12.309; contact with Buddhism when the Dharma spread to China 7.144; and Daoism 7.150; an ethnic religion 11.296; filial piety 3.523, 11.696–7, 12.247, 18.505–6; five relationships 3.523; influenced by the Buddha 2.11, 7.485; mainly a code of social morality 12.53; on the whole an ethnic religion 12.247; problem when Confucianism is mixed with Buddhism 12.516; a spiritual teaching without reference to God 12.7; 'virtually extinct' 13.513

Confucius *Analects* 3.426; 'The rectification of terms' 2.376, 3.489, 7.289, 9.479; 'At seventy I could follow the desires of my heart without fear' 4.485; appearance in the Axial Age 3.426, 11.355; his own greatest work of art 3.471; human-heartedness (*jen* or *ren*) 5.174–5, 15.256; the respect of Chinese Buddhists for him 2.243; *shù* (reciprocity or altruism) 8.448; a true individual 12.247; unpopularity 3.472

confusion the bodhisattva transforming confusion into a beautiful mandala 4.98; the confused actions of *avidyā* 17.610; confusion about Buddhism 1.201–2; confusion about how to teach the Dharma 19.497; confusion arising from mixing facts with value judgements 12.477; confusion and chaos of the West 16.351; confusion between the Buddha and God

16.309–10; confusion of Going for Refuge with becoming a monk 2.433; confusion of intellect and wisdom 7.242–3; confusions that vitiate spiritual strivings 26.188; the difference between holding a wrong view and confused thinking 19.106; freedom from confusion 8.579; if we are mentally confused, we have to go back to meditation 12.566; 'joyous in confusion of diversity' (Milarepa) 18.45–6; a synonym for ignorance 10.631; these days there is a great deal of mental confusion 12.566; 'Tied up in confusion, the world is seen as agreeable in nature' (*Udāna*) 10.627, 10.631; wandering the *bardo* in confusion 18.83; your own clarity can make someone else more confused 17.615; *see also* delusion

Connla *see under* Ireland

conquest the bodhisattva's conquering spirit 14.537; the Buddha as conqueror (Jina) 3.48, 11.407, 12.528–9, 14.404; conquering the demon of ego-clinging 19.156; conquest of Māra, *see under* Siddhārtha; conquest over oneself 1.178–9; the *ḍākinī* called Adamantine Conqueror of Demons 12.325; desiring the conquest of the three worlds 4.477; 'He who conquers himself', *see under Dhammapada*/chapter 8; a king who is convinced by a wise man that there is no point in conquest 19.337–8; thinking about death to conquer the demon of laziness 18.555; 'To conquer an army you need many weapons, but to commit suicide a pin is enough' 14.348

conscience a sort of inner monitor 19.459; blunted through habit 16.311; *hrī* and conscience 17.558; the joy of a clear conscience 2.259, 12.160; lack of conscience 9.274

conscious mind *see under* mind/what is the mind like?

consciousness

THE NATURE OF CONSCIOUSNESS

introduction
definitions 3.479–80; the accumulated inheritance of all that man has ever thought and felt and done 7.364–5; compared to a seed 14.187–8; the difference between consciousness and wisdom 14.260; a sort of power 4.379; a human being is a stream of consciousness imbued with the dye of craving 26.63; it arises in dependence on conditions 1.139; it arises from the interaction of the senses with their objects 17.404; it can be inferred from its functions, like the wind from the swaying of trees 14.187; it can either contract around a 'self' or break out of that view of things 17.348; it precedes and determines being (*Dhammapada*) 2.67, 2.77; the word usually signifies something more basic than awareness 9.514–15; luminous, but defiled by adventitious defilements 1.84, 1.275, 1.364, 2.130, 7.527, 10.439, 13.389; not fixed but subject to change 15.161; Padmasambhava: human consciousness face to face with death, fear, reality 13.247; the phenomena that appear to consciousness likened to a mirage 17.379–80; religious consciousness is not a separate kind of consciousness 26.14; all objects of perception are transformations of consciousness 1.377; to believe that consciousness can be explained by brain function is materialism 8.581; time is part of our structure of consciousness 26.49; the transcendental aspect of every phenomenon of consciousness 7.403; we are active participants in consciousness 15.136; we are what our state of consciousness is 3.123; you are part of the web of consciousness 15.707

ordinary consciousness
household shrines stand for the presence of the Enlightened mind behind it 2.229; how it differs from meditative consciousness 11.148–9; its limitations 17.376; it tends towards superficiality 17.xviii–xix; looking into ordinary consciousness in a non-dualistic way 18.242; the state of consciousness in which things appear separate is an illusion 7.299; you don't go from it directly to insight 10.562–3

development of consciousness
the concern of the arts and psychology 3.484; in meditation 13.73; difficult 3.484; through evolution 3.16, 3.477–85, 11.114–15; requires *all* our energy 3.484–5

transforming, expanding, raising consciousness
the aim of the Buddhist path 15.98; change your consciousness to see a different world, or see the world differently 26.84; changing our state of consciousness 3.123; 'the consciousness of man expands like light' 25.162; don't identify thought processes with consciousness 5.229; an exalted state of consciousness produced by giving a talk 13.132, 23.xvii; expansion of consciousness 3.350, 3.353, 4.80, 17.341, 26.110–11; experiencing dimensions of consciousness unknown to our everyday self 14.462; experimenting with locating consciousness in different parts of the body 18.545–6; if consciousness is raised,

it brings about the transformation of the whole being 19.57; not just noticing states of consciousness but transforming them 15.166–7; the point of discriminating between states of consciousness is to transform them 15.166; practices that prolong consciousness into the dream state 19.307; purified in the fourth *dhyāna* 3.307; raising the level of consciousness on retreat 11.462; speak of a new dimension of consciousness rather than 'getting rid of the ego' 10.471; spiritual practice is whatever conduces to expansion of consciousness 26.129; subtle enjoyments that are the fruits of the effort to transform consciousness 15.158–9; in the Tantra 18.77; three transformations of consciousness (Yogācāra) 1.369; to solve problems one needs to rise to a different level of consciousness 7.299; to understand reality we must change the structure of our consciousness 14.593; transferring your consciousness to other people 4.633–4; translating experience at one level into the terms of another level 26.305; ways (other than meditation) of raising our level of consciousness 11.116–20; what we are trying to do in all our practice is to refine consciousness 18.157–9

higher states of consciousness
attained through meditation 11.120, 11.461; bringing all the bands of the spectrum of consciousness together 17.341; Buddhism's main purpose is to develop them 4.440–1; dimensions of higher consciousness 4.514; the doctrine of rebirth becomes clear in higher states of consciousness 3.114, 17.45–6; having an idea of a higher consciousness without the ego appropriating it 14.460–1; individualistic enjoyment of higher states (Ambedkar) 9.114–15; lower consciousness receptive to higher consciousness within us 16.37; most practices don't lead to them directly but remove the obstacles 4.160, 11.120; an unpleasant experience may be the result of *karma vipāka* 17.497

collective consciousness
the bodhisattva principle is the key to collective consciousness 4.656; creates the universe 2.77; multiple consciousnesses associated with single bodies 17.523, 18.227–8, 26.85; no really suitable English term, but the Russian *sobornost* comes close 4.656; a kind of consciousness shared by individuals with the same spiritual ideals 4.656; 'self' is really a tiny fraction of limitless multidimensional consciousness 17.522

third order of consciousness
the spiritual community 2.474–5, 4.278, 4.656–7, 12.676; neither 'we' nor 'I' 11.224

consciousness after death
awareness of the multidimensional nature of consciousness helps 17.688; freed from the body 3.350

FOUR LEVELS OF CONSCIOUSNESS

introduction
summary of the four levels 3.480–1, 7.421–2, 11.115–16, 11.131; connected with the four dimensions of awareness 12.262–3

(1) simple consciousness
the level of consciousness we share with animals 3.480, 11.115; sense consciousness 11.31; the vast process of biological evolution 3.480

(2) self-consciousness, individual consciousness, reflexive consciousness
how it works 11.32, 15.169; awareness of being aware, *see* self-awareness; consciousness and self-consciousness at the margin of disappearance 4.512–13; developing a life of one's own 19.180–1; developing self-recollection in a dream 19.572; the development of self-consciousness 19.81; faith is only possible when self-consciousness has emerged 18.274; from conscious to self-conscious 12.46; how is one to develop a healthy self-consciousness? 19.181–2; the human being, a conscious being in the process of becoming self-conscious 12.46; if we are self-conscious, it is only in the most vague and intermittent way 3.435; if you have it, you will understand that actions have consequences 15.359; in it our humanity resides 3.480; the individual is someone who has developed it 11.363; it brings about the development of ethical ideas 8.447–8; it brings vivid awareness of the existence of other people 8.452; it is what sparks off the process of spiritual growth 15.215; it may lead to isolation and a sense of superiority 4.77; its emergence in the Axial Age 11.354; the intellect that grows out of it is a dangerous weapon 19.181–2; life has swept us onto the shores of self-consciousness and left us there 3.482; in man the universal dissatisfaction becomes self-conscious 7.114–15; to move to the next stage, needs to be negated as a self-contained entity 4.511–12; needs mindfulness of purpose as a basis 15.96; once it has begun to develop, one can't forget about the higher evolution 26.11;

once you have attained it, you're unlikely to lose it 16.291; one in whom the urge to grow has become self-conscious 16.7; one of its characteristics is that it can destroy itself 16.292; self-consciousness in a social sense, *see* self-consciousness; a sense of ourselves as continuous entities moving through time 15.306; using the mind to watch the mind 17.xvii; the watershed between lower and higher evolution 3.480, 4.653–4; we have the capacity to evolve beyond the point of self-consciousness 3.477

(3) transcendental consciousness
also spoken of as objective consciousness 3.481; direct personal contact with reality 11.115; functioning through the ego 4.512; some artists approach 3.511; where philosophy and religion come into their own 3.480–1; 'transcendental' as it transcends the subject–object distinction 3.481; transcendental awareness 11.31

(4) absolute or universal consciousness
a Buddha is the vehicle for its rediscovery 1.48; description of the goal 2.129; Enlightenment 2.96; frees us from the whole cycle of human life and death 3.481; the gradual flowering of Buddhahood 3.481; how does this differ from a conception of an absolute being? 3.686 (n402); 'infinite, invisible, radiant on all sides' (*Kevaddha Sutta*) 2.129–30; influences karma and all five *niyamas* 2.70; it has focused itself in you 3.469; it is the individual that expresses the universal 16.132; Perfect Awareness 11.31; full realization of ultimate reality 11.115–16; the sole reality 1.268; when the subject–object distinction disappears, consciousness remains 1.364

see also
citta; *vijñāna*; eight *vijñānas/ālaya-vijñāna*; as the third *nidāna*, *see under* twelve cyclical *nidānas/vijñāna*; consciousness and the unconscious, *see under* unconscious; letting go of consciousness in the six element practice, *see* six element practice; linking, *see paṭisandhi*; *parāvṛtti*, the 'turning about in the deepest seat of consciousness', *see parāvṛtti*; self-consciousness as psychological state, *see* self-consciousness; transference of consciousness, *see phowa*

conscita 7.208, 7.599 (n320)

conservation the central problem: how to conserve and unify our energies 1.390, 4.133–4, 5.571; conserving energy by observing silence 4.134, 18.482; the imprint of actions is conserved in the *ālaya vijñāna* 18.291–2; the conservation of spiritual values beyond death 4.63

conservatism conservative and literal-minded aspects of Early Buddhism 1.187, 1.221–2, 7.540–2; becoming consciously conservative 15.489; religion is always conservative, it would seem 16.365

consistency the *Bodhicaryāvatāra*: paradoxes and inconsistencies at every turn 4.426; fidelity involves consistency over time 3.564–5, 3.567–8; 'A foolish consistency is the hobgoblin of little minds' 13.328; children need consistency 16.429; meditation: the important thing is consistency 4.149

Constantine, Emperor his recognition of Christianity 13.552, 13.579, 13.622–3; Decretal 2.35, 2.668 (n56)

Constantinople *see under* Turkey

consumerism advertisements, *see* advertisements; as consumers of products produced by cheap labour, we are not 'easy to support' 15.282–3; attractions of Western consumer society for Indian students 21.67–8; consumer mentality even at the Buddhist centre 15.433–4; consumerism and the power of the state 11.357; eroding the values of the traditional Buddhist world 2.551; danger of pseudo-spiritual consumerism 3.327; don't fall into the trap of consumerism 10.lxii; 'Frozen Tulips' 25.416; giving up consumerism 16.412; a glittering net to catch the Yankee dollar 24.33; the goal is to be a creator of a Pure Land, not an endless consumer of spiritual goodies 17.243; the lure of consumer goods 11.78; no room for consumerism in a right livelihood business 12.608; to be a consumer of Buddhism is the antithesis of transformation 3.327; rampant consumerism in the modern world 12.654; respectability in an age of consumerism 18.134; see not how much you can consume, but how little you can live on 10.396; symbolized by the animal realm 3.348; the throw-away society 25.121; the versions of Buddhism peddled to the consumer society 18.135

contact *see sparśa*

contemplation the contemplation of any phenomenal object can develop *prajñā* 19.70; the contemplation of beauty 2.554; meditation as contemplation 12.262, 17.539; to think of the life of service *or* the life of contemplation is a mistake 7.155–6; *see also* reflection

contemplation of decay (ten corpse meditations)

introduction
description 3.344–6, 5.346, 15.14; the body reverts to the elements of which it consists 12.639; illusion and decay 18.154; responses to corpses 4.558–9

traditional sources
among the forty *kammaṭṭhānas* 4.519; *Satipaṭṭhāna Sutta* 1.155, 15.140–8; *Mahāsatipaṭṭhāna Sutta* 3.676 (n314, 4.674 (n96); Buddhaghosa's account of the practice 4.536, 15.142; Śāntideva's account of the practice 4.536

doing the practice
apparently intended to be done literally 15.142; how could it be done in the West today? 3.127, 15.144–5; if it makes you depressed, don't do it 4.537; it should be done on the basis of a strong experience of *mettā* 3.346; less drastic alternatives to deepen awareness of impermanence 13.227–9; not a good idea to do it in relation to someone you knew 15.145; this type of practice is not suited to everybody 13.227; you must estimate how much you can take 4.536, 13.229, 15.144–5

its purpose and effects
antidote to craving 4.75, 5.29, 17.543; antidote to neurotic sexual desire 4.75, 5.510; it should be exhilarating 3.346, 4.537–8; nothing morbid, but has a tonic effect on the system 1.155; overcomes fear, as the Buddha found 3.346; a practice for greed types 2.83, 12.280, 13.227, 18.561; a quiet, almost gentle seeing of the facts as they are 4.536; a reminder that you too will die 11.448; through it, one can attain the first *dhyāna* 1.155; to assist the unfolding of the golden flower of Awakening 7.171; a way of eradicating covetousness 2.387

see also
aśubha bhāvanā (contemplation of the loathsomeness of the body, a different practice)

contemplation of the *nidānas* *see nidāna* chain meditation

contempt the aspiring bodhisattva is advised not to look down on the ordinary *bhikṣu* 17.664; be careful that discarding respect for convention isn't rationalizing contempt for others 17.667; near enemy of compassion 5.200–1; self-intoxication can manifest as contempt for others 17.664

contented gods *see under* gods

contentment (Sanskrit *saṃtuṣṭi*, Pāli *santuṭṭhi*)

the nature of contentment
the contented person is both inspired and an inspiration to others 15.309; the contentment of a bodhisattva 15.290; contentment with oneself 5.125; the greatest wealth (*Dhammapada*) 1.152, 18.96; if you are contented, you can find delight in the world around you 15.310; the more someone has, the less likely he is to be contented 1.152; a very important quality 15.427; why can't we stay contented? 10.475, 15.201; you're consciously in the present 15.428

where does it come from?
contentment on retreat 25.311; feeling *mettā* for oneself is the keystone 15.309; in the wake of mindfulness and self-possession 1.152; it can only come from within oneself 15.277; it presupposes a degree of individuality 15.275; producing inner warmth becomes contentment 18.90–1

cultivating contentment
in marriage 15.276; in an unsatisfactory situation 15.289–90, 18.34; to overcome craving and hatred 17.271; with practice it will not be dependent on living simply 15.288; the third precept 1.534, 2.371, 3.321–2, 9.267, 15.276; working with its opposite, boredom 15.xx

contentment and other mental states
complacency 13.138, 15.275–6, 15.427; faith 3.264; receptivity 15.427–8

see also
Mahāpajāpatī Gotami/the Buddha's teaching

continuity the *ālaya vijñāna* represents the possibility of continuity 18.289–90; continuing to have faith 25.42; continuity between old and new ways of teaching the Dharma 12.471, 12.677–8, 19.211; continuity of effort 19.438; continuity of mindfulness 5.399, 17.xx; continuity of purpose, *see* mindfulness of purpose; continuity of spiritual lineage 19.403–4; are the *rūpa* and *arūpa dhyānas* continuous or not? 2.111–12; craving for continued existence 1.111, 3.199, 3.202, 3.278; craving for eternal life leads to continued rebirth 2.149; of empirical experiences 7.165–7; the lamp-flame an analogy for the continuity of the five *skandhas* 7.210–11; not existence or non-existence, but continuity 19.376–7; personality: a continuity of a series of experiences, subjective and objective 7.209; the

psychical life is an absolutely continuous flow 7.209; of the religious quest 7.212

contradictions

contradictions in the Buddhist tradition
'A is A because it is not-A' (*Diamond Sūtra*) 10.165, 14.151; apparent contradictions between space-type and time-type models of reality 4.203; the arising of the *bodhicitta* 4.91–2; the bodhisattva – a living contradiction 4.92; the conceptual expression of the Dharma contradicted by the Mahāmudrā 19.271–2; contradictions between doctrines 1.198–9, 1.208–210, 1.215; contradictory passages in the scriptures 19.165; describing an ineffable state by juxtaposing contradictory attributes 2.130; the idea of self as self-contradictory 17.377–8; the Mahāyāna's fearless acceptance of contradictory propositions 1.245–6; Nāgārjuna demonstrated that views are self-contradictory 1.313; Nirvāṇa is the solution of an insoluble contradiction 7.45; to meet a one-sided approach to the Dharma, juxtapose contradictions 13.327–8; the paradoxes of the Buddhist scriptures are real contradictions 26.200; the safest way to communicate transcendental realities 26.207; transcending logic, one reaches the realm of contradiction 1.309; translogical matters can only be expressed in contradictions (*Diamond Sūtra*) 14.467; vowing to lead all beings to Enlightenment while reflecting that no beings exist 1.348

other contradictory matters
an abstract or theoretical ideal is a contradiction in terms 18.569; antinomies, *see* antinomies; the concept of God is self-contradictory 3.448; the contradictory nature of human beings 26.398–9; 'contradictory' projections of the globe 26.201; deeply satisfactory to find contradictions 16.469; feeling two contradictory emotions at the same time 18.143; 'A foolish consistency is the hobgoblin of little minds' 13.328; it can be useful to study Blake and his irreconcilable contradictions 17.685; the limitations of thought force us into contradictions 7.133; reflecting on contradictions to find insight into them 1.210, 16.469; spreading the gospel of love by means of the sword 7.384, 22.529

control being ready to learn to control oneself (*damma*) 15.493; confusing control with repression 15.494; controlling people by manipulating their negative emotions 26.20; losing mental balance due to forcible breath control 20.324; the demon money, a power which has got out of control 12.333–4; the desirability of controlling yourself 19.17; ethics inculcates a habit of self-control 15.173; friendship becomes unhealthy when one friend controls the other 12.644; gaining control over your own life 10.249–50; the gods of higher realms too refined to control chaotic energies 16.349; the *indriyas* as controlling principles 3.297; the love mode in control of the power mode 16.432; mind control, *see under* mind; most of the time we are controlled by the senses 3.298; nature within human beings has got out of control 16.394; objective self-control 15.494; preparing for meditation: controlling food, sex, and sleep 3.337–8; taking control of your responses to sensory stimuli 17.102–3; we need more exuberance and less 'self-control' 4.321; society's insistence on self-control can lead to its being a habit 11.195; speech is difficult to control because it is so close to thought 2.375

convention be careful that discarding respect for convention isn't rationalizing contempt for others 17.667; the Buddha tells his monks how to respond when somebody sneezes 19.608–9 (n112); conventional as a philosophical term 19.234; conventional existence, *see under* existence; Alexandra David-Néel's willingness to defy convention 6.609–10; the dropping of all conventional social activities 3.38; freeing oneself from the power of social conventions 18.134–6; one's conventional life is sustained by reactivity 4.508; conventional mind 19.234–5, 19.237; conventional religion 3.419–20; can the bodhisattva conform to the conventions of social life? 1.442; the residential community as an alternative to conventional family life 3.623; sometimes you have to go along with social conventions 9.524; the view that conventional experience (in a philosophical sense) has an absolute value 19.234

conventional morality *see under* ethics/in the Buddhist tradition

conventional truth (or reality) *paratantra*, *see under* three *svabhāvas*; *saṃvṛti-satya*, *see under* two truths

conversation 'Argument is the death of conversation' (Hazlitt) 24.563; merely intellectual conversation is the dry bones of concepts rubbing against one another 12.314; story about the man who always brought the conversation round to the Church 2.382, 4.102; thinking and feeling at the same time 17.333–4

conversion (Buddhist)

introduction
what is conversion? 2.237–9; the word 'conversion' has unpleasant associations 8.183, 8.203, 10.314, 11.699

conversion to Buddhism
of Dr Ambedkar and his followers, *see* Ambedkar/conversion to Buddhism; Buddhism and conversion 8.203–5; Buddhists are not anxious to make converts 12.11; conversion of possessing entities or demons 4.548; difference from 'Dhamma Revolution' 9.407–8; Padmasambhava's conversion of the demons of Tibet, *see under* Padmasambhava/his life story; don't push your view onto someone 4.248–9; don't think about 'converting' someone, but just being a friend 3.575, 11.700; if you've changed yourself through Dharma practice you can convert others 18.362–3; logic as a means of conversion 1.372; material profit and mundane advantage should have no place in conversion 8.205; remarkably, the British converted themselves to Buddhism 11.485, 12.71; two types (Ambedkar) 9.141; Westerners' reasons for conversion, *see under* Western Buddhism/the future

conversion within Buddhism
a complex and arduous task 2.285; literally 'turning around': the *parāvṛtti* 2.237–8, 12.174; a turning around not just *to* Buddhism, but *within* our practice 2.250, 2.263, 2.462–4; *The Meaning of Conversion in Buddhism* 2.235–85, 2.460–5, 13.480, 23.79–80; as the arising of the *bodhicitta* 2.266–74, 10.175; the breaking of the fetters 2.265; from an individualistic to a non-individualist conception of Enlightenment 2.269; Going for Refuge as conversion 2.7, 2.239, 2.240–9, 2.460–2, 2.465, 8.203–5, 9.17, 23.79–80; a shift in the nature of our experience of the world 2.275; the transition from the ignoble quest to the noble quest 7.151; the transition from the wheel to the spiral 2.259

see also
Christianity/spread; four *saṃgrahavastus*

conviction are you convinced that the Dharma works? 19.228–9, 19.246; be careful not to attribute someone's convictions to ego 10.471; becoming convinced of an eternal spiritual reality 7.69–70; being convinced of the essential truth of the teachings 2.244; the difference between healthy conviction and attachment to views 3.199–200; the importance of teaching religion in schools with conviction 12.51; important to know the doctrinal principles thoroughly and be convinced of their truth 2.245; no conflict between what you're convinced you should do and what you actually do 18.459; people respond to clear-cut principles, lived out and expressed with conviction 18.153; people will always be convinced by honesty and sincerity 18.184; we want the transcendental not just to convince us, but to coax, even seduce us 13.284, 19.25; have courage not of your intellectual convictions but your transcendental realizations 1.209

Conze, Dr Edward

HIS LIFE AND CHARACTER

his life
introduction 8.699–700 (n272), 21.545, 23.483–4 (n87); his life story 6.618–20, 8.539; his wife Muriel 6.619, 11.530–1, 23.56; discovery of Buddhism 6.619; association with San Francisco Zen Center 6.620, 12.492; his death 6.620, 11.534

his character and interests
his character 6.620, 11.529, 12.562, 13.133, 14.329, 23.55; an outsider 17.41–2; both scholar and devotee 6.620, 8.539; deeply aware of the limitations of a purely theoretical approach 8.535; Theravādin or Mahāyānist? 17.112; meditation 6.619, 6.620; his field was the Perfection of Wisdom 8.537, 8.540, 13.510, 14.328–9; politics 6.618–19, 6.620, 8.538; acceptance of magic 8.539; his interest in astrology 6.618, 11.531; a great Buddhist 6.618–20; 'one of the great translators' 8.537, 14.xx; talking to a Tibetan lama makes him realize how little he knows 13.107; a very hard worker 17.78

and Sangharakshita
'kindred spirits' 11.530; dedicatee of *Alternative Traditions* 8.407; gratitude to him 11.535; he recommends Sangharakshita to teach at Yale 11.531, 26.674; his review of *A Survey of Buddhism* 11.530, 21.543; their correspondence 6.619; they meet in Oxford 11.529, 11.530, 12.169–70, 23.55–6; 'Dr Conze: a personal appreciation' 11.529–35

WORKS

quotations and teachings
comparison of Buddhist meditation with Christian mysticism 4.513; 'Conditions and the Unconditioned' 1.102, 22.124–5; four aspects of concealed suffering 3.213–15; he coined the term 'conditioned co-production' 4.676 (n105); 'It is foolish

to expect too much advance information about spiritual states' 8.539; on love and compassion in Buddhism 1.157–8; the nearer one is to a religion's geographical centre, the nearer one is to its spirit 13.106; 'no greater menace than a mere grammarian set loose on a sacred text' 8.539; on Oxford philosophers and linguistic analysis 11.530, 12.170, 23.55–6; 'A religion's unworldliness is its greatest asset' 8.539; translation of *dhyāna* as 'trance' 17.118, 17.124; his translation of *indriyas* as 'cardinal virtues' 3.298; 'without a monastic order Buddhism has no backbone' 3.410; sanctity needed to do good to others without harming or irritating them 8.535

Selected Sayings from the Perfection of Wisdom
introduction 21.314; 'Beings, beings' 1.209; the bodhisattva's training 1.230; the *Diamond Sūtra*'s appeal to a spiritual intuition 1.301; being guided by the five spiritual faculties 1.280; the Prajñāpāramitā as the antidote to self-seeking 1.303; *Mahāprajñāpāramitā Śāstra* 1.311; review 8.386–7; in *Stepping-Stones* 21.314–15; unconditioned identity of the conditioned and the Unconditioned 1.305

Perfection of Wisdom sūtras (translations)
a critical reading 14.328–35; the *Diamond Sūtra* 14.372, 14.377–94; a monumental labour of love 12.103–4, 12.561; one of the great pioneering works of Buddhist history 6.619, 11.535, 12.72–3, 14.328; 'Hate, Love, and Perfect Wisdom' 4.392, 11.530, 13.132; *Perfection of Wisdom in Seven Hundred Lines* 8.534; review of the *Diamond Sūtra* translation 8.387; *see also* individual *sūtras*

Buddhism: its Essence and Development
Sangharakshita's book review 8.343–4; avenues of approach to the spiritual 5.51; the book exemplifies a synoptic approach to Buddhism 7.487; an example of a really reliable presentation 8.141; the Buddha-Dharma: all those teachings linked to the original teaching 1.205, 2.50; the Buddha's 'glorious body' 1.264; the doctrine: those teachings ... whose methods lead to the extinction of ego 22.376; the Buddhism of Faith and Devotion 2.128; consciousness and self-consciousness at the margin of disappearance 4.512–13; the doctrine and the extinction of individuality 8.652, 14.267; how the idea of the Kali Yuga (age of decline) crept into Buddhism 11.621, 19.83; karma and the Pure Land 1.342; the monastic sangha 'the only constant factor in the history of Buddhism' 8.245; later Buddhist history – a degeneration? 1.249; on the *siddha* 7.506; a successful book 6.619; on the Tantra 1.373, 1.375; the woman who worshipped a dog's tooth 2.71, 19.327; on the Yogācāra 1.350

Buddhist Texts through the Ages
1.279–80, 9.137, 22.142; care taken with translations 7.515–16; a hymn to Tārā 1.336; 'Mila Repa and the Novices' (trans. Snellgrove) 18.41

Buddhist Thought in India
Conze viewed it as his greatest achievement 11.534–5; account of the Pudgalavādins 17.631–2; translation of *sambhogakāya* 2.41; Western approach to tantras 14.248

Further Buddhist Studies
book review 8.536–40; 'Buddhism and Gnosis' 8.537–8, 16.606 (n170); 'Love, Compassion, and Sympathetic Joy' 8.537; 'The Philosophical Background' 8.538; 'The Present State and Future Prospects of Buddhism in Asia' 8.538; review of the *Hevajra Tantra* 12.104

A Short History of Buddhism
the Protestant character of Buddhism in the West 13.510; published by *The Buddhist Library* 8.662, 11.530; a shift towards the writing down of esoteric teachings 14.27

The Way of Wisdom: the Five Spiritual Faculties
publication details 17.112; five cardinal virtues 3.298, 3.670 (n282); Sangharakshita's commentary 17.5–137

other works
articles on love and compassion, which 'every Buddhist should read' 8.139; book reviews 8.538–9; *The Buddha's Law Among the Birds* (trans. Conze) 5.602–8, 8.222; *Buddhist Scriptures* (Penguin) 8.387–8; *A Buddhist Students' Manual* 8.390–1; 'Conditions and the Unconditioned' 8.643; *Buddhist Wisdom Books* 8.387, 14.430; *Memoirs of a Modern Gnostic* 11.532–4; *The Prajñāpāramitā Literature* 14.145, 14.146, 14.149, 14.153; *The Principle of Contradiction* 6.618; *Der Satz vom Widerspruch*: 'modelled a bit on Schopenhauer' 8.536, 8.538; *Stepping-Stones* articles 6.619, 11.529–30, 21.314–15; *Thirty Years of Buddhist Studies* 8.534–5; *White Lotus Sūtra* (chapter 5) 8.479, 8.482, 8.534–5

Cook, Captain 24.529

Cook, Miss (Sangharakshita's colleague at LCC) 20.76

Cooke, Alistair 12.695

Cooke, Hope 12.442

coolness how does a monk become 'cool'? 14.58; the 'self that has become cool' (*abhinibbutatta*) 10.515; a sense of coolness in meditation 25.45; 'Those who are free from defilements become utterly 'Cool' 10.515, 10.614, 19.204

Coomaraswamy, Ananda 2.17, 7.445, 8.461

Cooper, Dr David v23, 26.605–6

Cooper, Jilly 24.124, 24.127, 26.596

Cooper, Pam *see* Saddhajivini

cooperative businesses *see* right livelihood businesses

cooperation cooperation is the foundation stone of the Dharma Revolution 10.398; cooperation is needed to build the Buddha-land 16.473; the cooperation of unconscious energies 3.41, 12.23; cooperative effort 9.305; the more wholehearted and warm the cooperation, the better it is for everyone 13.137; objective, skilful discussion is a cooperative process 10.603; organizer and organized are two: cooperation is the Dharma-door to non-duality 16.548; the success of a venture is due to everybody's cooperation 19.536; to work together we have to learn to discuss things, compromise, listen 10.397–8; without cooperation human life is impossible 10.397

Corbin, Henri 26.688

Corelli, Marie 26.575

Cornuel, Madame 3.633 (n42)

Cornwall, England camping trip (1970) 23.470; sabbatical (1973) 2.474, 4.225, 4.463, 4.572, 11.514–17, 11.525–6, 11.552, 25.139, 25.147; the *Udāna* seminar 10.420–3

corpse meditation *see* contemplation of decay

Correggio 24.273, 24.676 (n333)

correspondences conception of the universe as a gigantic system of correspondences 1.376, 26.209; between Blake's emanation and the *ḍākinī* 12.314; between the *arūpa dhyānas* and the emancipations 16.447; between Buddhist and Christian archetypes 12.191–2; between the *dhyānas* and the heavenly realms 1.159, 2.66–7, 16.345; correspondence of the first four duties towards a friend with the four *saṃgrahavastus* 3.574–5; correspondences with the *vimokṣa-mukhas*, *see* three *vimokṣa-mukhas*; Hermetic correspondences, *see under* Hermes Trismegistus; images are perceptions of real correspondences 26.209; an ingenuity for detecting 'correspondences' 22.255; a special correspondence between the human condition and Buddhahood 2.96; systems of correspondences are subtle, complex, and changing 19.43

Cosmic Consciousness *see* Bucke

Cosmic Person *see puruṣa*

cosmogony 14.84

cosmology

the traditional Buddhist view
introduction 2.62–7, 2.672 (n90), 16.342–53; in the Abhidharma 14.83–4; the Buddha probably believed in the traditional view 17.329; background to the Buddha's teaching 16.343–4; *Buddhist Cosmology* 16.624 (n311); cosmic perspective 1.32–3, 1.37–43, 1.325, 2.62; the cosmos as a hierarchy 4.169, 14.309; the Dalai Lama instructs monks that they need not teach traditional cosmology 13.427; discrepancies between Buddhist traditions and modern science 2.64–6; impermanence 2.85–6; an important part of Buddhist tradition 8.624–5; Indo-Tibetan and Western 'useful for different purposes' 16.343, 19.505–6, 22.497; not just one world but a plurality, even infinity, of worlds 3.376–7, 18.227–8; 'all sentient beings' implies intelligent life elsewhere 3.377; literalism responsible for Buddhist cosmology (controversial view) 8.620; Māra's place in the cosmology 11.402; in Milarepa's 'Song of Meeting and Parting' 19.504–6; morality is of cosmic

significance 11.323; sees space as infinite 16.460; the cosmic process of evolution and involution 14.605–6; the view sometimes embarrasses modern Buddhists 8.624; and the third precept 2.370–3; views of the universe, *see* universe; you can never identify a point where it all begins 14.606

world systems
the Buddha teaching in many 16.199; Buddhas teaching in and travelling between worlds 2.64, 16.38–9, 16.45–8; an infinity of world-systems 1.39; involution 1.40–3, 14.84, 14.605; Pure Lands, *see* Pure Land; small, middling, and great universes 16.460

picture of the cosmos
a bit like Dante's system 19.505; circles of oceans and mountains 13.261, 16.342; four continents 13.261, 16.342; eight subsidiary continents 13.261; iron wall 13.261, 16.342; Mount Meru (or Sumeru) 2.65, 13.168, 13.261, 16.342, 19.504; inhabitants 13.261, 16.344–6; heavens and hells 19.505–6; rests on crossed *vajras* 16.341; shares features with the Tibetan wheel of life 13.261; three-tiered universe, *see trailokya*; visualized in the mandala offering practice 13.260–2, 18.446–7

cosmological principle
pratītya-samutpāda could be invoked as a cosmological principle 3.13; reality is not a sort of cosmological principle present in the world 14.603–6

Council of Buddhist Monks of Great Britain *see* Sangha Sabha

councils, Buddhist

First Council
account in the Vinaya 4.660 (n9), 10.706 (n358); convened mainly for the recitation or recording of the teachings 7.521; the chanting of the Dharma (*saṅgīti*), *see under* oral tradition; Upāli recited the Vinaya Piṭaka 14.186

Second Council (Vaiśālī)
the Mahāsaṃghikas and the arising of the Mahāyāna movement 8.183; considered the question 'What is Buddhism?' 4.8–9; disputes after the Council 8.462, 14.82; schism in the sangha ('Vaiśāli schism') 1.186, 2.192, 4.9, 4.18, 8.183, 10.682 (n155), 14.21

Third Council (at the time of Aśoka)
considered whether there is an interval between death and rebirth 10.723–4 (n504); the Tipiṭaka rehearsed 14.85

Fourth Council (Theravāda, at Alu-vihāra, Ceylon)
Pāli canon first written down 4.24

Fourth Council (Sarvāstivāda, held in Kashmir by Kaniṣka)
Pārśva was its president 13.342

Sixth Council (Rangoon, Burma)
introduction 8.684 (n125); attended by Buddharakshita 22.232; determining whether a certain letter of the texts was a 't' or a 'd' 1.222; importance of correct pronunciation when the Tipiṭaka recited 8.119–20; important work of textual revision 8.184; insistence of Burmese monks on eating meat and fish 22.232; no doctrinal or disciplinary question was raised 7.631 (n594); treatment of the Mahāyāna sangha 8.184

counterfeit Dharma 8.574, 16.82–3

countryside allowing the influence of nature to remind us of the greater mandala 14.519; alternate between life in the country and in the city 15.394–5, 14.520; the British countryside has been denuded of gods 19.413; the Buddha walks through the Magadha countryside one spring morning 10.310; countryside Maharashtra 10.292–3; don't fall into 'back to the land' romanticism 11.196; escaping into rural life 12.394; impermanence in the countryside 17.378; important because it produces food, and because it is quiet 10.329–30; the Malaysian countryside 24.38, 24.42–3; the New Zealand bush 24.29; spending a day in the country to lift your mood 15.153; temptation to stay in the peaceful countryside rather than going back to the city 4.521–2; village people may regard the city as a place of liberation 11.196; you can be walking along and suddenly find yourself full of rapture 15.220; you can sometimes find more solitude in the city 19.492–3

courage and bravery the bodhisattva's courage to speak 16.491; bravery distinguished from fearlessness 16.27–8; the Buddha had the courage to face the forces of darkness and evil 12.529; the courage of the Bishop of Woolwich 12.5–6, 12.11; the courage of the bodhisattva ideal (Govinda) 21.313–4; courage is not necessarily dissociated from gentleness 4.446; the courage it takes to defend institutions, and to create them 26.73; the courage to be inspired by sublimity 14.473; courage to face the things about ourselves we would rather not see 17.xxv; the courage to receive

the Mahāmudrā teaching 18.245; don't curb your courage for the sake of being a 'good Buddhist' 4.444; one should have the courage of one's positive emotions 26.65; speaking with boldness, courage, and wit (*pratibhāna-pratisaṃvid*) 1.449, 16.491; we should have courage not of our intellectual convictions but our transcendental realizations 1.209; in the world today, we need courage to uphold spiritual values 12.518; *see also* fearlessness

courtesans *see under* prostitution

courtesy *see* manners

Cousins, Dr James Henry 20.248, 22.457

Cousins, Lance 23.155

covetousness (*abhijjhā*) the Buddha's teaching to Mahāpajāpatī Gotami, *see* Mahāpajāpatī Gotami; connection with hatred 2.388; links to *jhāyati* (to meditate) 2.386; *abhijjhā* approximately synonymous with *lobha*, *taṇhā*, *ragā* 2.386; coveting religious experience to relieve inner emptiness 11.79–80; getting what you covet and then not enjoying it 18.568; 'having put away covetousness and grief for the world' 15.202; meditation practices to eradicate it 2.387; mental state of brooding over something to which we are attracted 2.386; often combined with *domanassa* (grief) 2.386; a state in which the self tries to appropriate the non-self to fill its inner emptiness 2.386; undertaking to refrain from it, *see under* precepts/ten precepts

Cowley, Abraham 26.339

cows and buffaloes

cows
All-India Cow Protection Society 22.31–2; as though a butcher had killed a cow, a *bhikkhu* reviews the elements of the body 15.132–3; Bāhiya killed by a cow 10.464; being lassoed like a reluctant steer by reality 14.597; better to have sacred cows, even literally, than to hold nothing sacred 26.36; the body of a cow can pass through a door, but the tail cannot 8.248; the Buddha talks to a cowherd 10.533–4; in the Buddha's day cows were regularly sacrificed 10.48–9; cow of plenty (*kāmadhenu*) 4.361, 16.398, 26.641; cow's urine, *see under* medicine; cows garlanded on festive occasions 8.222–3; the goal isn't reached by wrong means any more than milk comes from a cow's horn 14.42; 'Indra's cows' (storm clouds) 13.167; a cow's products like one who strives for his own welfare and that of others 14.50; sacred cows (Hinduism) 12.246, 16.371; Suppabuddha trampled to death by a cow 10.550, 10.555; 'the Vedas are the cows, the Upanishads the milk, the teaching the butter' 18.220, 18.408; wish-fulfilling cow 13.261

bulls
the Buddha as bull-man (*nārapuṃgava*) 4.469; Bull of Memphis 25.287; connection with the Buddha's birth 9.365; a dream of an angry black bull 26.681; the effect of spring on the bull 24.151–2; symbolism 9.366, 12.183

calves
keeping the mind on the breath like tethering a calf with a rope (Buddhaghosa) 15.106; moving closer to ageing and death like a calf drinking its mother's milk 10.617–18; a talking calf 22.31–2; those who walk in faith like a calf carried across a stream 1.291; 'The White Calf' 25.xxxvi, 25.206–7

buffaloes
American bison 25.53–4, 25.447; buffaloes being driven to market 25.xxv, 21.321, 25.235; sacrifice of buffaloes 10.46, 10.279

Cowper, William 'the cup that cheers but not inebriates' 22.23, 23.275; 'The Solitude of Alexander Selkirk' 18.454, 24.83, 24.627 (n112)

Crabbe, George 4.471–2, 26.339

crafts *see under* art

Cranach, Lucas the Elder 23.308, 23.520 (n346), 24.273, 24.592, 24.676 (n333)

Cranach, Lucas the Younger 24.591

Cranmer, Archbishop 13.549

craving

WHAT IS CRAVING?

the nature of craving
craving dominates our life, and it doesn't want to be transformed 12.626; craving to crave, as though you want to be dissatisfied 10.475; the difference between craving and aspiring for spiritual experience 11.80–1; distinguishing between healthy needs and neurotic craving 10.605; a human being is a stream of consciousness deeply imbued with the dye of craving 26.63; it usually expresses itself as a desire to prolong pleasure 19.383; longing desire to possess objects of sensuous cognition in hope of security 11.129–30; may be in relation to past, present, future, *kāmaloka*, *rūpaloka*, *arūpaloka* 17.597; may be represented by mother in Buddhist myth

3.35; neurotic craving 11.79–80, 11.538–9, 15.276, 17.398–9, 18.207, 26.24; once you get what you want, you no longer want it 17.258; the poison of craving 3.125, 3.340; sexual craving 11.573–4, 17.218–21, 17.271; a strong word found mainly in poetry, not philosophy or psychology 1.111; there is no end to human craving 17.161; trying to get from outside something you should be getting from inside 18.218; the urge to devour something, whether another person, an idea, or a thing 12.646

how does it arise?
'adding to the cemeteries': increasing craving 10.608; advertisements geared to stimulating craving 4.74, 4.384, 15.288; how craving arises 15.200–1; it doesn't arise while in *dhyāna*, but one can crave *dhyāna* 17.597; popular culture offers a constant invitation to indulge our cravings 17.271; the thirty-six streams of craving (*Dhammapada*) 15.46, 15.746 (n22); this sense of emptiness arises in dependence on causes and conditions 15.231; what makes pleasure lead to craving? 19.92–3; wherever there is a wish to repeat an experience there is craving 26.63

its effects
frustrated craving leads to bitterness and hatred 1.498; hanging on to craving 19.59; heedlessness out of craving 17.677; it casts a sort of glamour over someone's body 17.220; violence due to sensuous craving 7.238; when craving is predominant, we tend to think of the self as the agent 10.601

GETTING RID OF CRAVING

meditation practices
aśubha bhāvanā, *see aśubha bhāvanā*; contemplation of decay (corpse meditation), *see* contemplation of decay; modern difficulty of taking traditional practices in the way they're intended 4.563; recollection of impermanence, *see under* impermanence/lessons in impermanence; uprooting the weeds of craving 25.32–3; selecting the appropriate antidote 4.75–7; threefold antidote 19.227

other approaches
aesthetic appreciation reduces the pressure of craving 17.227; the aim is not to eliminate desire, but to eliminate craving 26.63; better to aim for a gradual destruction of craving than a sudden one 2.104; better to think of cultivating the positive *nidānas* than getting rid of craving 10.513; the *Bodhicaryāvatāra* helps the strong craving type 4.623; cultivate contentment to overcome craving 17.271; cutting the root of craving, like cutting the banana plant 18.579; don't try to get rid of craving by getting rid of pleasure 19.381; discipline as a method of reducing craving 17.169; to eradicate it, try using your imagination 17.597–8; if one tries to live simply, craving will be diminished 12.608; it is not the case that 'Enlightened Beings could still have cravings' 26.537; one could speak in terms not of getting rid of craving, but of just relaxing 18.584; practising experiencing pleasure without craving 19.383; craving puts up a tremendous fight when you try to transform it into faith 12.626; we need to be prepared simply to experience it 15.231–2

the effect of getting rid of craving
happiness comes not from satisfying craving, but from not having it at all 10.474–5; having cut off craving at the root, for what would one go in search? 10.625, 10.627; the idea that suffering ceases when craving ceases is counterintuitive 15.231–2; one who manages to destroy craving doesn't rejoice in that destruction 10.524–5; release by the destruction of craving 10.619–21; to give up craving is Dhamma (Ambedkar) 9.288; 'What would life be without craving?' 19.227–8; when craving ceases, birth ceases, and when birth ceases, death ceases 12.359; when craving ceases, positive mental events arise 17.590; when the pain caused by craving is eliminated, one is left with blissful emotion 19.126; you've no right to be supported until you've destroyed your inner cravings 19.357

see also
āsrava; *vedanā*/breaking the link between feeling and craving; hatred/craving and hatred; craving for sensuous experience, non-existence, continued existence, *see tṛṣṇā*; twelve cyclical *nidānas*/eighth *nidāna*; four noble truths/second truth

creativity

the nature of creativity
compulsion to create 26.192–3; confusing it with reactivity 4.340; a creative life is a happy life 12.641, 26.64; 'Fields of creativity' 12.634–48; the forces of death and destruction requires an equally strong creative response 4.638; if you're not allowed to create, you'll destroy 18.458; it always takes some form of expression 16.475–6; it means bringing something new into existence, but new isn't always creative 12.637; mindfulness of purpose makes us capable of creative action 15.96;

primitive humanity reproductive, modern humanity productive, the individual creative 3.471; the terms creative and creativity have become clichéd 12.637; to create something new one has to build on something old 4.282; volition is a creative force 17.479

creativity and the Buddhist path
awareness releases creativity 11.32; *bodhi*: uninterrupted creativity and spontaneity 13.298; the Buddhist vision is a vision of creativity 16.488; the constant effort to keep Buddhism creative 10.480; contacting deeper creative energies on solitary retreat 5.682; creating institutions 12.639–40, 18.277–8; creative work instead of meditation? 5.636–7; creativity as spiritual childbirth 26.316–18; the creativity of the true individual 3.471; the creativity of visualization practice 5.591; after the point of irreversibility, whatever you do can only be creative 18.268; the *dhyāna* states are just as tangible as things made by potter or carpenter 5.251; faith is the first movement of creativity 19.580; from our present being we must create something that goes beyond what we are 25.73; it is possible to live creatively in the householder lifestyle 19.582; meditation as a field of creativity 12.637–8; Milarepa sees his situation with creativity 18.13; responding creatively to the present 17.406; the *trikāya*: the product of supreme creativity 18.293; waking up to the fact that you are Buddha releases tremendous creativity 12.234

everyone is creative
all the time we are creating patterns according to our state of mind 18.270; creating the world we live in 1.342, 16.478; the creative, outward-looking momentum of your being 17.345; creative speech 16.363, 16.475; domestic creativity 26.192; everyone is creative 16.475; 'I hate and renounce as a coward every being who … does not wish to have recreated himself' 3.471, 15.520; 'I'm not very creative' 16.474; latent spiritual-creative powers 7.268; media input can lessen our ability to deal with boredom creatively 15.174; no one can be absolutely uncreative 26.192; our relationship with the world is essentially creative 16.475; you are creating a world around you all the time 17.299; you are potentially creative all the time 5.683

the creative arts
the creativity of the artist 3.509; the arts as a field of creativity 12.637, 26.165–6; arts workshops have little to do with creative activity 26.355–8; for most people, creative work is 'doing nothing at all' 3.507, 18.267–8; the powerful feelings involved in creating a work of art 26.69; the receptiveness and creativity of the poet 26.171; the unpredictable nature of a creative writer 15.505; the vitality of the creative person 11.26

the creative process
a creative activity into which all your energies can flow 10.602; creative experience like a seed whose nature is revealed when the flower blooms 3.517; the creative gap 4.487; creativity will find its own uses, so don't try to direct it 18.119–20

doing nothing is a creative activity
don't just aim to get your work finished, but immerse yourself in the process 18.164–5; if you really want to create something you'll do it 19.59–60; the movement of creation 26.113; the release of feeling from creative activity 26.191–3; sitting in an armchair doing absolutely nothing 24.157; sudden inspiration when doing creative work 19.307; totally absorbed in something creative, you and the energy are one 14.588; whatever you are creating, you are really creating yourself 3.471; without structure the individual can't be creative 19.545; working creatively with moods 18.53

creative thinking
creative power of thought 1.342; creativity is stopped by self-conscious thought 14.548; intelligence is the creative use of concepts 14.549, 15.187, 17.603, 18.238; requires the bringing together of intellect and emotion 19.189

see also
mind/creative mind; Sangharakshita's creativity, *see under* Sangharakshita VII/ temperament

credulity don't go through your life with credulity 17.47; the near enemy of faith 17.43; exemplified by Don Quixote 17.62–3, 17.67; if faith is strong and wisdom weak 1.293; a middle course between credulity and scepticism 8.607–8

Creighton, Mandell 13.550, 20.32

cremation grounds and cemeteries 'adding to the cemeteries' (metaphor for craving and ignorance) 10.607–8; the atmosphere of the cremation ground 13.224–5; a body used by a yogi as a seat 22.48; choosing to enter the cremation ground 13.231; and the contemplation of decay 1.155,

4.75, 13.225–9; the eight great cremation grounds of the mandala 12.220–1, 13.232–6; the crucial situation, *see* crucial situation; facing loneliness in the cremation ground 13.231; in Hinduism the domain of Śiva the Destroyer 16.71; an inspiring place 4.627; a moonlit night by the Ganges 20.384–5; overcoming fear by visiting the cremation ground 13.229–31; practising in the cremation ground 16.590 (n36); Śāntideva dwells on their loathsome aspects 4.627; symbol of the gateway between lower and higher worlds 12.220–1; a symbol of transformation 13.231–6; the symbolism of the cremation ground 13.223–36; the Tibetan cremation ground at Tirpai 22.84; visiting as a way of overcoming fear 16.28

cremations *see* funerals

Cresswell, Jamie 11.660–72

crest jewel *see under* jewels

crime the crime of passion 18.208, 18.309–10; criminal type 21.139–40; criminals can have a healthy energy 15.435; five heinous crimes, *see* five heinous crimes; monks suspected of committing offences against criminal law 7.440–1; murder, *see* murder; pandering to lust for sex and crime 26.115; premeditated crime 18.310; resentment at modern life expressed in criminal activities 11.78

crisis the Buddha gives support in crisis 2.11; breaking through at a time of crisis 11.16; the Cuban missile crisis 23.87; living at a time of crisis in world history 8.272; Maitreya's significance at the present crisis in history 21.558; Suez Canal crisis 14.543, 22.341

Crisp, Esmond v21

Crisp, Mrs Flossie 3.6–7, v21

critical faculty 'test my words as the goldsmith tests gold in the fire' (the Buddha), *see under* gold; weigh and test all the thoughts and emotions that come pouring in 7.268

criticism

dealing with criticism
the Buddha explains how to deal with criticism 3.76, 3.546–7, 10.477, 10.481–2; criticism aimed at oneself 4.428, 4.595; dropping the habit of self-criticism 15.309, 15.424; the effect of the criticism of a spiritual friend 15.295–6; exposing oneself to criticism 18.278; handling criticism 3.546–8; reacting defensively to our friends' criticism 17.651–2; receiving criticism 11.431; take no notice (like the elephant ignoring barking dogs) 9.366, 10.201, 18.420

criticism of others
criticism of others' spiritual practice 11.267; criticizing someone behind their back 17.237; don't just criticize people's way of life, but offer a better alternative 18.302; Mahāyāna precept against disparaging others 2.208; no need to go around humbling people 'for their own good' 14.491; out of frustrated craving 1.498; people tend to think that it is an expression of dislike 5.208–9; it's easier to criticize others than conduct our own affairs ethically 17.231; it's easy to see the faults of others, but pointing them out can be unskilful 17.653; its purpose is to help someone grow and develop 16.505; sometimes people do it to pay homage to the ideal without having to practise it 26.81; what masquerades as criticism may be a form of one-upmanship 15.295

criticism in Buddhism
appeal for a critical spirit in Western Buddhism 7.73; Buddhist critique of other religions 14.459–60; criticizing the sangha without realizing that one is oneself part of it 18.475; 'A disciple should be critical …' 14.327; the psychology of the criticism of Buddhism 7.185; the stifling of honest criticism 19.543; there is room for criticism of different schools of Buddhism 19.584

criticism in religion
criticism of religion 16.515, 19.546; the higher criticism of theology 3.189, 13.426–7, 14.374; religion based on realization smiles at criticism 7.145; the transcendental critique of religion 16.499–516

criticism in the arts
an author may be dissatisfied, but that doesn't mean critics have the right to be 26.67; cultural critics do our thinking and feeling for us 7.266–7; destructive criticism in the arts 12.643–4; the effect of art critics 12.643; literary criticism, *see* literary criticism

Croce, Benedetto 3.510, 26.166

Cromwell, Oliver introduction 7.603 (n348); 'A man never flies so high as when he doesn't know where he is going' 4.500; 'Think it possible you may be mistaken' 7.247–8, 16.40; his death 4.674 (n97)

Crosbie, Robert 22.140

Crosland, Anthony 23.88

crosswords 17.66

Crowley, Aleister mentored by Allan Bennett 3.682 (n368); an obscene poem 23.52; 'the Wickedest Man in the World' 18.xiii

crows *see under* birds

Croydon Buddhist Centre Arts Centre 26.357; Aryatara (originally Sarum House) 4.704 (n294), 12.653, 15.517, 24.67, 24.129, 24.254; flourishing after upheavals 24.327; Kalpadruma 24.67; Khadiravani community 24.67, 24.248–9; the need for change 24.317; Order members (mid-1980s photograph) 24.255; Sangharakshita gives a poetry reading on 'Friendship' 24.329, 24.359–60; Sangharakshita visits 24.314–15; St Michaels Road project 15.517, 15.765 (n197)

crucial situation symbolized by the cremation ground 13.231–2, 13.236; confronting lack of self-confidence 13.232; the *ḍākinīs* are the energies that arise in the crucial situation 13.246–7; death is the most crucial situation of all 11.17; in difficult conditions 15.394

Crucifixion *see under* Jesus

cruelty (*nirdaya*)

the nature of cruelty
delighting in inflicting suffering on others 15.350, 26.653; delighting in the suffering of others 16.295–6; the behaviour most directly opposed to the bodhisattva ideal 16.294; it may arise from one's unhappiness 10.477; the opposite of compassion 16.294; worse than hatred or anger 16.295

human cruelty
'Man is the cruellest animal' (Nietzsche) 26.654; what human beings are capable of doing to each other is horrifying 25.54; why does one human being enjoy inflicting pain on another? 26.653–8, 26.677–8

instances of cruelty
being cruel to yourself prevents the process of sublimation occurring 10.524; cruel speech 1.499; the cruelty of cats 16.295; William Hogarth's 'The Four Stages of Cruelty' 1.499, 3.542; Japanese cruelty in the war 26.677

becoming less cruel
avoiding cruel occupations 8.450; confession of cruelty 16.294–6; the *karuṇā bhāvanā* as the antidote to cruelty 10.173; a person given to cruelty has non-cruelty to lead him upwards 11.658; 'Since I took up Buddhism have I become less cruel? 1.499

see also
animals/cruelty to animals; malice

Crusades 3.450, 13.622, 13.629, 13.636, 13.666, 17.462

crying *see* weeping

crystal a crystal ball showing the past 25.403; a crystal lotus 24.250; 'The Crystal Rosary' (poem) 25.304; the perfect crystal sphere of the Buddha cut into five facets 5.596–7, 13.304, 18.601–2; 'the new-born lotus smiles beside the crystal fountains' 25.345; a pillar of crystal (third precept) 2.373; the Pure Land: flowers of jade and crystal flecked with gold 25.372; a silver crystal ball 24.143, 24.146

crystallization as soon as we have crystallized an idea in language we have to dissolve it 14.447–8; the crystallization of the Dharma into a system of methods and teachings 14.434–6; the crystallization of orally transmitted teachings into scriptures 12.232, 14.26

Csoma, Sándor Körösi (de Körös) introduction 7.618 (n498); the inaugurator of Buddhist studies in the West 7.449; translator of the *Mahāvyutpatti* 16.617 (n257); on the Vinaya Piṭaka 7.500

Cuchulain *see under* Ireland

cūḍamaṇi *see* jewels/crest jewel

Cudworth, Ralph 1.527

Cūḷa-assapura Sutta *see under Majjhima Nikāya*

Cūḷadhammasamādāna Sutta *see under Majjhima Nikāya*

Cūḷadukkhakkhandha Sutta *see under Majjhima Nikāya*

Cūḷagopālaka Sutta *see under Majjhima Nikāya*

Cūḷagosinga Sutta *see under Majjhima Nikāya*

Cūḷahatthipadopama Sutta *see under Majjhima Nikāya*

Cūḷakammavibhaṅgha Sutta *see under Majjhima Nikāya*

Cūḷamālunkya Sutta *see under Majjhima Nikāya*

Cūḷapanthaka (*bhikkhu*) 8.119, 10.581–2

Cūḷasakuludāyi Sutta *see under Majjhima Nikāya*

Cūḷasihanāda Sutta *see under Majjhima Nikāya*

Cūḷasuññata Sutta *see under Majjhima Nikāya*

Cūḷavaṃsa 2.225

Cūḷavedalla Sutta *see under Majjhima Nikāya*

cults 2.172, 2.176, 11.248, 13.304–5, 19.329, 21.49, 23.424, 25.279, 26.222

culture

ASPECTS OF CULTURE

what is culture?
definitions 12.392; etymology 7.435; a frail structure superimposed on virtual barbarism 11.197, 11.270–1; an idea of culture 13.479; it enriches our lives and contributes to our development 26.66; it can be looked at from three points of view 7.435; a rainbow bridge thrown from the material to the spiritual world 26.66; *saṃskṛti* as opposed to *prakṛti* 16.364–5; what is culture? 16.364–5

the refining effect of culture
involvement with culture refines the emotions 16.375, 19.469; the effect of the mass availability of high culture on the population 3.515–16; general raising of cultural sensibility 3.58; like *samādhi*, culture refines consciousness 7.436; no spiritual life is possible without culture in the sense of refinement of spirit 3.368

culture and religion
cultural interests can be a 'near enemy' to commitment to spiritual life 19.350, 19.474; culture is the greatest friend of religion and also its greatest enemy 19.469; the need to know classical and Bible stories to connect with culture 23.256–7; not Western culture but Western religion in a state of decay 13.511; a purely secular culture is a contradiction in terms 16.355; a ritual symbolizing the integration of cultural activity into spiritual life? 16.376; there can be no healthy culture without a basis in transcendental values 16.355

reflections on culture
the break-up of culture 3.5–6; communication shouldn't depend on the cultural flotsam of the time 18.153; cultural heritage 3.606–7; cultural transferral and cultural translation 13.505–8; a culture often doesn't have a word for its most important principle 4.168–9; European culture can have a cramping effect 19.348–9; everyone should have an appreciation of the traditions of other countries 12.51, 20.61; genius is the product of a favourable cultural milieu 3.59; gratitude towards those who have created our collective cultural heritage 3.602; the language of culture as an expression of truth 7.394–5; a middle way between unthinking acceptance and unthinking rejection 12.392–4; no culture without memory 16.363; take care that it doesn't become an end in itself 19.469–70; the 'two cultures' 3.6; the yield of culture to commercialism 23.452

popular culture
fear is fed by it 17.181; folk culture, high culture, and mass culture 13.484; is our current cultural decline due to television? 14.434; it offers a constant invitation to indulge our cravings 17.271; malice finds expression in Western culture 17.665; the unhealthy influence of horror comics 8.206–8

Sangharakshita and culture
feeling the lack of a Western Buddhist culture 13.669–70; he hears F. R. Leavis speak on T. S. Eliot 23.419; love for Renaissance Italy 23.249–50; reclaiming cultural roots by immersing himself in Western culture 23.256; his wish to write on the relationship between Buddhism and culture 13.479, *see also* Sangharakshita XII

BUDDHISM AND CULTURE

culture and the spread of Buddhism
Buddhism and Indian culture 11.512–13, 13.116; China and the West already had highly developed cultures 13.116; Buddhism and its cultural environment 11.511–13; Buddhism learned to speak the language of different cultures 11.512–13, 16.367; Buddhist practice and the development of Buddhist culture go together 16.375–6; a 'culture of awakening' 8.580; wherever Buddhism goes, culture goes too 19.469

Buddhist and Eastern culture
Buddhism has accumulated much cultural baggage 2.603; Buddhism must be distinguished from Eastern culture 13.104–5, 16.374; the coming together of Mahāyāna Buddhism and Indian culture 16.366–7; the cultural heritage of Buddhism 7.441–3; distinguishing essence from cultural accretions 3.45, 13.470–4; is knowledge of Eastern culture necessary to understand Buddhism? 16.374–5; no need to follow cultural customs 9.507–8; unabsorbed elements of ethnic culture in *Sūtra of Golden Light* 16.370

the engagement of Buddhism with culture
the bodhisattva gives the gift of education and culture 1.501, 3.368; a cultural context

of some kind is needed for the practice of Buddhism 16.375; culture as a means to Enlightenment 7.435; culture is part of Buddhism 7.441; the Dharma teacher needs to speak the language of culture 16.366–7; the distinction between *jñāna* and *vijñāna* is important to culture 14.315; incorporation of culture into the Dharma engages the emotions fully 16.370; links with our own culture prepare us for the deeper insights of Buddhism 16.42; refined, humanistic culture provides a foundation for the spiritual life 13.134

BUDDHISM AND WESTERN CULTURE

integration
as Buddhists we cannot ignore our great Western cultural heritage 25.18–20; avoid the extremes of unthinking acceptance or rejection of culture 12.392–4; how can Western culture place itself at the service of Buddhism? 16.375; the integration of Buddhism into Western culture 11.466–7; need to find ways of integrating the Dharma with Western culture 3.45, 4.98–100; to absorb Buddhist culture we must know the roots of our own 6.617, 11.564; we must harness the 'demons' of our culture 13.273

a new culture
the creation of a new Western Buddhist culture 11.377, 11.466–7, 13.484, 13.670; culture being changed by Western teachers of Eastern religions 8.627–9; culture in need of renewal which Buddhism can provide 13.511–12; early days for the influence of Buddhism on culture 7.448–51; may need a radical revaluation of Western religion and culture 8.561; wherever the Buddha leaves his footprints there is an efflorescence of culture 25.27–8

language
Buddhism must learn Western culture's language 4.638–41, 4.657–8, 11.620, 16.368–9; the influence of Buddhist literature on Western culture 14.267; the interaction of the Dharma and the language of secular Western culture 13.512, 26.66; presenting Buddhism through the medium of Western culture 26.252

points of contact
bringing Buddhism into contact with Western culture 8.553, 13.512, 26.66; Buddhism must link up with Buddhistic elements in British culture 12.78–9; culture as supportive of spiritual growth 13.483–4; establishing points of contact with great artists and other creative figures 16.375; Goethe: one of its noblest examples of self-discipline and self-development 23.473; Indian Buddhists' interest in Western culture 10.81; links with Nietzsche 3.493–504; our thinkers and artists have anticipated some of Buddhism's ideas 7.37–8, 24.xxii–xxiii; the story of *Everyman* is a remarkable anticipation of Buddhist teaching 15.375; using points from Western philosophers and poets 11.370–1, 16.422

differences
Buddhism and Western culture seen as completely opposed to each other 12.393; a clash between Buddhist culture and the one into which we were born 13.166; competing claims on our emotions 26.96–7; even the greatest figures are ordinary compared to the Buddha 11.371; a Mahāyāna *sūtra* goes completely beyond the best of Western culture 19.350, 25.lix; much Western culture is an obstacle and a hindrance 13.484; perhaps Western Buddhists need to get right away from Western culture 19.349; Western culture as a whole is quite incompatible with Buddhism 11.377; 'working against the grain of Western culture' 13.459

culture shock 19.252, 23.340

Cummins, Major v22

Cunda the novice 1.143–4, 1.285

Cunda the silversmith the Buddha teaches him the ten positive precepts 2.330–1, 2.391, 3.632 (n41); he gives the Buddha his last meal 2.29, 3.117–18, 10.639–41; in the *Mahāparinirvāṇa Sūtra* (Mahāyāna) 14.231, 14.233–4

Cunningham, Alexander 9.46

Cupitt, Don 23.215, 23.506–7 (n250), 24.500

curiosity about whether someone is Enlightened 10.590; an attitude of warm curiosity 17.261; certain words in a book title arouse curiosity: 'secret', 'magic', 'sex', 'Tantra' 13.276; curiosity supports awareness 17.xxi; Dharma practice presented as a sort of exotic curiosity 11.509; have curiosity, a spirit of adventure: the lesson of the four sights 10.256; make sure the rain of the Dharma doesn't go down the drain of intellectual curiosity 8.535; in modern people, intellectual curiosity is more awake than transcendental wisdom 1.231; without disciples' curiosity and receptivity, no teaching can take place 11.277–8

curse 'Depart from me, ye cursed' 13.573; nationalism is the curse of modern history 12.342; 'The priest lays his curse on the fairest joys' 13.618; a very serious thing, especially among primitive peoples 18.309

Curzon, George Nathaniel 17.604

cuti-citta (death-consciousness) 2.75

cycle of birth and death the bodhisattva vows to rescue all beings from its terrors 2.158; breaking the cycle 15.207, 15.228; 'Exert yourself and cut off the stream' (*Dhammapada*) 15.51; freedom from birth and death 12.202; the round of birth and death 1.39, 1.113, 1.130–1, 17.378; the sharks of birth and death 7.68; stepping outside the endless round 17.351; whatever is born must die 11.446; *see also* rebirth; wheel of life

cyclical conditionality *see under* conditionality; twelve cyclical *nidānas*

cynicism the cynic feels less than is justified, the sentimentalist more than is justified 26.23; the hateful cynicism of the West 24.401; the cynicism of a Buddhist monk 22.213–14; it arises when there's a lack of positivity to guard against it 11.553; the tendency to cynicism is a vice 3.62; 'There's nothing to believe in' 17.23; towards people engaged in positive activities 4.317, 11.734–5; we assume that the more we know about people, the less we will find to respect 17.276

Cyrus the Great 12.338

D

da Vinci, Leonardo introduction 23.511 (n287), 23.523 (n359); a great man of Florence 23.314; his drawing of the Virgin and St Anne vandalized 26.477; his work compared to the Padmapāṇi figure at Ajanta 26.234; *The Last Supper* 13.648–9, 23.254; *Portrait of a Lady with an Ermine* 26.448; the *Mona Lisa* 14.99

Dabba Mallaputta (*Udāna*) 10.653–6

Dadu Dayal 8.167, 8.680 (n100)

Dagmema (Marpa's wife) 14.488, 18.14

dagoba *see* stupa/*dhātugarbha*

Dai Nippon Bukkyō Zencho 14.263

daily life *see* everyday life

daimon (or daemon) daimonic 2.218; 'demon' as 'devil' is a Christian usage of the Greek *daimon* 18.24–5; Eros as a daemon in the *Symposium* 18.158; a *yakkha* (nature spirit) could be translated *daimon* 10.451

Dainichi *see* Vairocana

Dak bungalows 21.515

ḍākas introduction 12.294, 17.133; symbolism 18.425; visualized on the Refuge Tree 13.207; you may think you have found a *ḍāka* or *ḍākinī* when you have only fallen in love 13.203

ḍākinīs (sky-dancers)

INTRODUCING THE *ḌĀKINĪ*

the word
'she of space' or 'sky-being' 13.202, 13.236, 18.58–9, 19.143; 'those who belong to the sky' – sky-dancers 12.294, 18.66, 19.143; *khadroma* (Tibetan, 'sky-goer') 13.236, 18.425; Śāntideva's non-Tantric use of the word 4.378; sometimes used very loosely 19.409; used in different senses 18.372

descriptions of ḍākinīs
embodied prayers 19.143; the embodiment of freedom 11.52; the embodiment of the spiritual energy of the Buddha 11.52; an essay on the *ḍākinī* 24.389; her self-abandonment to the Three Jewels 13.242; illustrations 13.218, 13.241, 13.269; the physical appearance of a *ḍākinī* and what it symbolizes 13.240–3; the primordial forces to be subdued by Padmasambhava 12.324–5; a thangka of a white *ḍākinī* 25.443

different ḍākinīs from the tradition
similar figures in the Pāli canon 19.413; Atīśa is said to have visited Uḍḍiyāna and practised with the *ḍākinīs* 12.565; the *ḍākinī* called Adamantine Conqueror of Demons 12.325; a *ḍākinī* who swallows Padmasambhava 12.287, 22.471; Heruka Ḍākinī 22.538; the 'knowledge *ḍākinī*' in the *chöd* practice 13.268–70; Milarepa's dream of a green *ḍākinī* 18.58–9; in Tantric legend ugly old women are sometimes *ḍākinīs* in disguise 13.203–4; transcendental *ḍākinīs* 18.370–1; wrathful *ḍākinīs* 13.244–6

as esoteric Refuge
brief introduction 2.481, 13.237; the company of *ḍākinīs* with whom one can be in living contact 4.175; in Tantric tradition selected by the guru 13.202–3;

the *ḍākinī* within 12.313–15; a 'horizontal' relationship to balance the 'vertical' one with the guru 13.204

forces of inspiration
the appeal of *ḍākinīs* to Western Buddhist women 13.244–6; the breath of the *ḍākinīs* 18.119, 18.180–1; contacting those forces of inspiration 19.135; *ḍākinīs* can be a sort of siren or muse 18.59; if you are busy listening to your own voice you won't hear the *ḍākinī* within 18.178–9; a force of inspiration welling up from unconscious depths 18.59; the forces of inspiration that arise in the depths of the Enlightened mind 12.294; inspiration from the heights 11.151; *mātṛkās* (inspiration from below) and *ḍākinīs* (inspiration from above) 18.469; misusing your inspirations 'disturbs and offends' the *ḍākinīs* 18.475–6; they are there to be served, not used, and will desert you if exploited 18.118–19; we must see the goal of Enlightenment as inspiring and invigorating 18.372

symbolism
complemented by the *heruka* 18.373; the *ḍākinī* is that which arouses your passion for the Dharma 18.371; no connection with the passions aroused by sexual attraction 18.425; one can take them literally or symbolically 18.424; the subjugated *ḍākinī* principle symbolized by Padmasambhava's staff 12.335; the symbolism originally belonged to Indian Buddhism 18.425; a symbol for an aspect of transcendental reality 18.372

where are ḍākinīs found?
a black hat 'literally woven out of the hair of *ḍākinīs*' 18.429; cloud formations like *ḍākinīs*' scarves 19.94, 24.112; in the cremation ground with Padmasambhava 13.246–7; in the sky 12.294, 18.66, 19.143; reality as the realm of the *ḍākas* and *ḍākinīs* 17.133; visualized on the Refuge Tree 13.207

the Formless Ḍākinī Dharma Series (Tantric texts)
introduction 18.364–5; cherished by goddesses 18.472; an enigmatic description of the text 18.400–2; 'formless' meaning absolute or transcendental 19.10; good if put into practice, but misunderstood, can do harm 19.11; for you, texts that produce a creative response are Ḍākinī Dharmas 18.372–3; Milarepa burns the copies Rechungpa brought back from India 19.10–14; those Tantric teachings that have an exhilarating effect on you 18.371–2; wisdom teachings 18.371; you haven't got the books until you've got their spirit 18.472, 18.517, 19.143–4

THREE KINDS OF *ḌĀKINĪ*

(1) female Buddha forms
introduction 13.237, 13.313–15; five great *ḍākinīs*, *see* five female Buddhas

(2) embodiment of energy
ḍākinīs and *dharmapālas*: feminine and masculine energies 19.408–9; *ḍākinīs* as moods 13.238–9; the *ḍākinī* is meant to energize all your spiritual energies 18.371; the *ḍākinī* offers a way of integrating one's unconscious contents 13.239–40; the embodiment of one's own upsurging energy 13.237; the energies that arise in the crucial situation 13.246–7; the free-moving energies of the mind 13.236, 18.180; integrating primordial forces 12.324; the more passionate side of our nature, helpful if brought under control 13.237–8

(3) spiritual companion
beautiful, with intense faith and devotion, spiritually inspiring 13.237; corresponds to William Blake's emanation 12.314, 19.409; could the presence of a *ḍākinī* prolong a lama's life? 22.404–6; Terry Delamare's interest in finding a *ḍākinī* 23.172, 23.328; Jamyang Khyentse Rimpoche kept a *ḍākinī* with him 19.553–4, 22.401, 22.404–6; the mirror that implies revelation by *ḍākinīs* 19.566; not a pseudo-spiritual girlfriend 12.314, 17.638, 18.371; openness to the *ḍākinī* – keeping in communication with spiritual friends 18.318; the principle of communication 19.409; rather than a particular person, a possibility in communication 13.203–4; a spiritually stimulating friendship 13.203; the third esoteric refuge 13.237; warm, friendly communication, kindling a spark 12.314–15, 13.202, 18.418; you may think you have found a *ḍākinī* when you have only fallen in love 13.203

see also
Siṃhamukta; Vajravārāhī; Vajrayoginī

Dakkināvibhaṅga Sutta *see under Majjhima Nikāya*

dakṣiṇi 9.481, 9.575 (n388)

Dalai Lamas

INTRODUCING THEM

introduction
the 'reincarnations' of the Dalai Lama 13.35–42; the Dalai Lamas are the reincarnations of the third abbot of Ganden 13.36; given careful training, but not regarded as a doctrinal authority 13.40; manifestation of Avalokiteśvara 2.183, 3.134, 4.687 (n196), 13.39, 13.42, 16.421, 22.487, 26.233; the Potala in Lhasa 13.41; rebirth as *tulku* 2.183, 13.49, 22.488; the temporal and spiritual head of Tibet 13.39, 14.427; what could cause a Dalai Lama to be murdered? 16.421

names
'Dalai Lama' is a title, not a personal name 25.92; *dalai lama*, 'the teacher who is great like the ocean' 13.40; *galwa rimpoche*, 'precious ruler' 13.40; *yeshe norbu*, 'jewel of knowledge' 13.40

THE LINEAGE OF DALAI LAMAS

the Third
converted the Mongols 13.40; the first to receive the title 'Dalai Lama' 13.40

the fifth
the 'Great Fifth' 13.40–1; started building the Potala 13.41; sympathetic to the Nyingma school 13.41; wrote several books 13.41

the Sixth
his dissolute life 22.488; biography 24.388; love poems 13.59

the Seventh
The Song of the Four Mindfulnesses 8.507–8

the Thirteenth
'Death and the Bodhisattva Trainings' 24.310–11; a great Buddhist 6.621; meeting with Alexandra David-Néel 6.608; reasserted Tibet's independence from China 13.41; took refuge in Mongolia when Younghusband came to Tibet 13.41

THE FOURTEENTH DALAI LAMA

his life
brief introduction 2.746–7 (n704), 22.609 (n296); account by Lobsang Phuntsok Lhalungpa 2.183; misunderstandings about him 13.35; discovered and identified (in 1935) 13.41; his mother (Gyalmo Chenmo) 21.229; his brother, *see* Jigme Norbu; affiliated with the Gelug school 13.35–6; his *geshe* examination 8.504, 13.46–7; danger from Chinese invasion 21.200; his flight from Tibet 13.41, 13.99, 22.488–9; arrival in India 8.236–7, 8.238, 13.39, 22.364–6; the effect of his presence in India 7.467; attends Buddha Jayanti celebrations in Delhi 22.353–7; exile in Dharamsala 13.41–2; and the Chinese 2.572–3, 13.39, 22.371; visits Gangtok 21.201, 22.240; how Tibetans and Mongolians see him 8.236–7, 13.42; photographs 22.370, 23.341; 'our Chintamani of the Himalayas' 22.551; prophecies that he will be the last of the line 13.41, 13.99–100

teachings and practice
The Buddhism of Tibet and the Key to the Middle Way 8.504–5; a conference with Western Buddhist teachers (1993) 12.468; distinguishes between theistic and non-theistic religions 12.677; foreword to *Common Ground Between Islam and Buddhism* 26.691; he declares that unity among Buddhists is essential 23.335; he has faith in reason, and a willingness to use it to its limits 8.505; instructs monks that they need not teach traditional cosmology in the West 13.427; not vegetarian 22.365; stance on non-violence 7.11; *Transforming the Mind: Teachings on Generating Compassion* 8.611–12

anecdotes
asked to 'authenticate' *The Voice of the Silence* as Buddhist 22.354–5; a *bhikkhu* who maintained that he was superior to the Dalai Lama 22.354; an expensive haircut 22.365; he asks to see a Marx Brothers film 22.365; he meets Dinoo Dubash 21.465–6, 21.527; his deep chanting in the Japanese Buddhist temple in Bombay 13.50–1; when he needed money, he asked Bön priests to worship black Jambhala 22.557

and Sangharakshita
the Dalai Lama visits Kalimpong 8.651, 21.529–30, 22.366, 22.368–72; gifts for Sangharakshita 8.651, 22.371; meetings

22.354, 22.365–6, 22.371, 23.334–5, 23.341–2; Sangharakshita's appreciation of him 11.626; Sangharakshita helps with the English of a book on Tibetan Buddhism 23.204; he congratulates Sangharakshita on a Tsongkhapa celebration 8.659, 22.511; the translation of Tsongkhapa's 'Three Chief Paths' 8.529, 10.131

Dalhousie, India 23.335–6

Dalits

BACKGROUND

history
brief introduction 11.707–8; heredity 9.26–7, 9.30; origins 9.74–91, 9.121, 10.54; 'Broken Men' 9.81–91; descent from Nagas 9.121; past connection with Buddhism 9.121–2

the plight of 'Untouchables'
what is 'Untouchability'? 9.25–6, 10.21–2; denial of rights 9.6, 9.32–7; leaving the village to escape the caste system 23.351; living conditions 10.186, 10.288, 10.309–10, 20.297–8; not allowed to draw water from the village well 22.160–1, 25.124; not allowed to use Hindu names 20.298; 'pollution' 9.26–7, 9.30, 10.308–9; poverty 9.107; punishment for listening to the Vedas 10.186; slavery 9.135, 9.222; sufferings 9.1, 9.37–9, 9.54–5, 9.222, 10.xxxvi, 10.xli; 'Unseeables' 10.186, 20.256, 20.284, 25.115

names
'Dalit' 9.544; 'Depressed Classes' 9.31, 9.48; 'ex-Untouchable' is an objectionable term 10.307; 'Harijans' (rejected term) 9.31, 22.160; Scheduled Castes 9.31, 23.346; Shudras 9.31

caste Hindu attempts to justify their treatment
claim of scientific basis 20.218; the effect of the Hindu claim that Buddhism is part of Hinduism 22.150; their tragedy the result of centuries of cruel conditioning 7.469; the law of karma used to rationalize injustice 4.396, 4.400, 15.681, 17.211–12; a lecture finding a scientific basis for the practice of Untouchability 20.218

attempts to change the situation legally
Untouchability is a penal offence according to the constitution of India 10.309; Untouchability 'on its last legs', according to Gandhi 9.59, 10.361; positive discrimination 11.639; reserved jobs, scholarships etc. 9.124–5, 9.152–3, 9.524

communities
Chamars 9.195; Eazhavas, Untouchable community 20.251–2, 20.295; fisher-folk of Travancore Christianized 20.253; Mahars, *see* Mahars

THE DALITS AND BUDDHISM

conversion to Buddhism
with Dr Ambedkar, *see* Ambedkar/ conversion to Buddhism; ceremonies 9.73, 9.130, 9.150–1; confusion after Dr Ambedkar's death 9.22–3, 9.155, 9.158–9, 9.177, 10.313; development of Buddhist movements 7.469–70; a gathering at Worli 9.18; if anyone needed something like Buddhism, it was them 11.596; importance of enthusiasm (Ambedkar) 9.134–5, 9.199–200, 10.370, 10.388–9; 'Neo-Buddhists' 8.250, 10.109, 10.281–2; not 'Hīnayāna' or 'Mahāyāna', just Buddhist 9.361, 9.506–7, 10.169, 10.281, 10.377; significance 9.135

response of the rest of the Buddhist world
bhikkhus from South-east Asia often did more harm than good 2.458, 20.252; lack of success in learning from *bhikkhus* 9.156, 10.79–80, 12.252–3; the new Buddhists didn't want their customs 9.317, 11.593; reluctance of Buddhist countries to support them 8.268–9, 9.118–19, 10.79; some *bhikkhus* didn't want to accept 'poor people' as Buddhists; temples built mainly in the Buddhist holy places to cater for pilgrims 10.80

Sangharakshita's involvement
Dharma teachings, *see under* Sangharakshita IX; advised to act as Manu for them 12.320–1, 26.560; a fellow feeling because like them, he was a New Buddhist 25.125; given river water to drink because the Dalits could not use the well 25.124; he organizes work for Dalits in the UK 23.81–2; his influence because, like them, he was an Outsider 26.578–9; his sense of closeness to them because of shared Going for Refuge 2.439; strong feelings for them 10.306–7, 11.596; witnessing their plight 22.160–1; the founding of TBMSG, *see under* Triratna I/history

progress of conversion movement
growth 8.268, 9.151–4; for a while the movement slowed down 9.151–2, 9.158–9, 9.509–10; why is change slow? 9.194, 9.201, 9.223–5, 9.264, 9.509–10, 24.23; progress in Triratna (TBMSG), *see under* Triratna I/ history

life after conversion
Buddhism has given them back their self-respect 10.303, 10.314–5; Dalit literature

and folk culture 10.81; family life 15.484–5; friendly relations with Christians and Muslims 10.60–1; going forth from the old life to the new 10.257; gratitude to Dr Ambedkar 9.159, 10.xlii–xliii, 10.13–14, 10.313; hopefulness 8.251, 10.297–8; is Buddhist practice reflected in changed behaviour? 9.192; 'Now I am a Buddhist I feel free' 6.613, 7.469, 9.340, 9.428, 9.508, 10.12, 10.25, 10.61, 10.188, 10.314, 11.671, 11.708–9; one-hundred-percent Buddhists 9.132, 9.211, 9.243, 9.307, 9.432, 10.333, 10.378; political alliance with brahmins 10.62; population 8.268, 9.152–3, 10.58–9, 10.673 (n93); position of women 10.161; prosperity 10.19, 10.303–4, 10.314–15, 10.407–8, 10.410–11, 24.23, 27.1075; sense of confidence 10.61; shouldn't be afraid to become Buddhists 10.167–8; social training 10.180; their Buddhism has an edge, a sense of urgency 10.303; they like the idea of being financially self-supporting 10.300–1; they see the Buddha's teaching as the key to uplift as well as a spiritual path 10.13; thrilled that religious knowledge not withheld as in Hinduism 10.625–6; tribespeople in India turning towards Buddhism 10.178

their approach to the Dharma
challenging conditions for Dharma practice 3.313; conditions for meditation 18.630–1; Going for Refuge to the Three Jewels 2.438–9; it will be generations before they can think of spiritual hierarchy positively 10.82; keenness to hear the Dharma 10.296–7; learning about the Dharma for the first time 10.xlvii; reluctance to practise non-violence 10.302; social rather than psychological 10.41–2, 10.303; their energies are engaged because their disadvantages are felt every day 10.87–8; they can lack self-confidence 14.405; thirteen duties 10.161; vibrant and full of life and positivity 3.296–7, 10.315

relationship with Western Buddhists
comparison with new Buddhists in the West 9.506–8, 10.12–14, 10.41–2, 10.300–4; does an affluent audience have any idea what their life was like? 24.40; interest in Western culture 10.81; it's shameful that so few people know about the Dalits' plight 10.89; message of solidarity from the Buddhists of the West 10.337; their situation is pitiful, but in some ways the situation in the West is worse 10.315; views of Western culture 15.485; what can Western Buddhists do to help? 10.88–90

relationship to old Hindu customs
animal sacrifice 9.236, 9.265, 10.9, 10.20, 10.45; change to domestic ceremonies 10.187; don't want anything to do with Hinduism 9.264–5, 10.80–2; difficulty with giving up customs 9.417, 10.257, 10.277–8; difficulty with iconography of bodhisattvas 10.81; 'How are we to perform the marriage ceremony?' 26.560; sometimes they don't want to be vegetarian because Hindus are 10.81–2

the response of caste Hindus
violent attacks on Buddhists, rape and murder 10.59–62, 10.301–2, 10.310, 24.23–4; Buddhists threatened by Hindus when making a new vihara 9.417; a change of heart on the part of Hindus 10.302–3; Dalit resistance to caste oppression 10.59–60; a gulf of hatred and misunderstanding 8.252; Hindus unhappy that Dalits should be taught Buddhism 10.626; Hindus used 'New Buddhist' as a pejorative term (*narva bolta*) 9.506; prejudice against the new Buddhists 9.107, 10.187; protests at the proposal to name a university after Dr Ambedkar 10.xli, 24.23; responses of Hindus to the conversion 10.18–19; still forced to live outside the village 9.416, 10.309

other difficulties
difficulties around official declarations of caste status 9.523–5; forced to forfeit facilities to which they had been entitled 10.110–11; government stops giving positive discrimination to Buddhists 8.250–2, 9.153, 10.61–2; material difficulties and spiritual needs 10.123; in modern India, Dalits have less freedom than other people 10.65; too much emphasis on politics 10.169, 10.298, 10.313

see also
Ambedkar

Damamukha 14.69

Daman Hongren (Zen patriarch) 13.342

Dameki, Mr 22.73–4

Damrong, Prince 23.157

dāna (giving)

THE PRACTICE OF GIVING

what is giving?
'charity' perhaps has the wrong connotations 4.336, 7.324; *dāna* is a free gift 25.139; *dāna* means the act of giving and also that which is given 4.336; a form of communication 16.486, 17.202; four aspects: to whom, what, how, and why

1.426–34, 4.94–104, 10.175; giving is innate 14.424; a matter of imagination 17.598; the natural interchange of one's energy with that of others 26.35; a virtue in itself 17.210; acting with a fixed idea of what it is supposed to be 14.421

the basic Buddhist virtue
even if you can't meditate or study, you can give 14.574–5, 16.9; giving is the basic Buddhist virtue 1.500, 4.93, 17.200, 17.210; giving is important, but *mettā* is even more important 17.186; a gradual training 4.460–1; if our practice of ethics is not very successful, we can practise *dāna* 12.566–7; if you can't give, you're scarcely a Buddhist at all 25.114; where there is no giving, there is no Buddhism 11.169; without a spirit of giving, there is no spiritual life 3.369; traditionally giving is threefold 8.199; the place of *dāna* in Buddhist life 4.612–13, 16.400; mindfulness and total awareness are more important (Śāntideva) 4.380

giving in the Buddhist tradition
exemplified by the Buddha 3.594; in the Buddhist scriptures 4.93–4; in the Theravāda it precedes the threefold way 8.174; a lay practice, *see under* lay people/practice; the tradition of giving *dāna* on Buddha Day 8.173–6; 'superior to any form of rigid discipline' (Śāntideva) 4.354; Śāntideva puts his finger on the essence of *dāna* 4.358–9; practising step by step (Śāntideva) – from vegetables to one's own flesh 4.457–60; one of the four *saṃgrahavastus* 16.485–6, 17.174; one of the three 'items of meritorious action' 11.306; Mahāyāna precept against giving nothing to the destitute 2.208; Nāgārjuna in *The Precious Garland* 17.198–213; as *dāna pāramitā*, the first of the six perfections, *see under* perfections; description of giving in the *Śikṣā-Samuccaya* 8.174; Tibetans divide income between necessities, pleasure, and the Dharma 13.53, 16.401, 18.62–3, 21.329

the practice of giving
as practised in the East 4.254–5, 16.8–9; antidote to greed 8.199; a habit to be cultivated 18.115; in Triratna more attention should be paid to *dāna* 12.467; a lessening of the conflict between keeping something and giving it away 4.181; 'renouncing a gift' 14.478; taking the practice seriously 19.544; two ways of practising: one conjoined with wisdom, the other not 14.478

to whom?
charity begins at home – but doesn't end there 7.324–30; the giving of robes to the sangha, *see kaṭhinacīvaradāna*; giving to the poor with compassion 19.537; giving to support the Dharma 9.267, 9.393, 16.402, 18.375–7; giving to support the sangha 1.427–8; the giving of lay people to monks, *see under* lay people/lay people and monks; friends and family 1.426, 15.120, 16.485–6; the guru 18.113–15; is it more efficacious to give to the spiritually developed than the needy? 19.539; the poor, the sick, the afflicted, the helpless 1.426–7, 4.70–2, 4.94; those engaged in spiritual and creative activity 4.94–5; we select our charities according to our own feeling 25.52

what to give
different kinds of giving depending on temperament 17.202; 'Four Gifts' (poem) 25.138–48; giving away what we're attached to 4.460–1; giving benefits 3.606; giving flowers 4.297–8; giving gifts at ordination ceremonies 13.417; giving the opportunity of practising *dāna* 18.271; wanting to give everything you have to the Dharma 13.275

how to give
according to people's real needs, not their apparent wants 4.103; courteously, happily, promptly, without regret, without boasting 1.432–3, 4.103; in whatever way you can 9.216; just give for the sake of giving 17.208; to friend and foe alike 4.103; 'Give till you swoon with joy!' 16.403; a spirit of mutual giving, as between parents and children 3.593–4; we don't have to wait until we feel generous 14.423–4, 17.204; with awareness of the recipient's needs 17.205; with no sense of a distinction between self and other 5.186; with no strings attached 17.200–1, 18.123–4

why give?
dāna is given ultimately for the *spiritual* good of humanity 8.175; for the sake of bringing Enlightenment to all beings 1.433; the giving of gifts plays an important part in social life 1.533, 14.423; why give? 4.103–4

giving and receiving
the desire to be given something 21.583; give what you can, take what you need 3.581, 3.592, 13.462, 15.282–3, 16.391, 17.199; receive rather than take, give rather than impose, share rather than divide 26.35; think not of what people should be giving you, but of what you can give them 26.81; what is the relationship between giving and getting? 17.200–1; you can't separate giving from receiving 4.601

the effects of giving
it is axiomatic for Buddhism that merit is gained by giving 13.86, 14.422–3; the layman's motivation 2.214–15; the more you give, the happier and freer you will feel 16.403

problems with giving
businessmen giving with the expectation of material reward 17.211; the difference between giving and paying 16.403; flattery in the hope of a gift 17.278; giving out of guilt 4.341; hardly anybody is willing to give 26.34; in all Buddhist countries money is being wasted in the name of *dāna* 8.175; is there a difficulty about giving in the West? 4.254–7; it's easy to say you've given everything to God and then hang on to it 4.358; perhaps it is immoral to give something for nothing 26.34; ulterior motives for giving 8.173–6, 19.484–5

dāna and śīla
dāna must always accompany *śīla* 4.93; is there a contradiction? 4.92; contradiction can be resolved by doing everything mindfully 4.116–17, 4.385–7; the king who gave to monks but had relatives killed by elephants 12.124–5, 15.521, 21.126

THE TRADITIONAL KINDS OF GIVING

(1) material things
being asked to give money reveals people's real attitude to giving 4.611–13, 18.113–14; *bhojana-dāna* (food offering), *see under* offerings; create a shrine-room before setting up a soup kitchen 14.447; feeding the poor, providing for the sick, digging wells, planting shady trees 3.315; to friends and family, to the poor, and to the sangha 1.426–7; the gift of land for the Mahavihara in Dapodi 10.355; giving for the sake of fame 19.484; giving money is often the best way to practise *dāna* 14.417; giving possessions away for the sake of the Dharma 18.219–20; the gift of a single *mālā* bead 18.116, 22.337; the greatest spiritual gift is offered in devotion to the spiritual idea 14.447; good, but not sufficient 1.428–9; hospitality, *see* hospitality; list of potential gifts in the Pāli canon 3.679 (n336); the merit gained 14.446–7; Milarepa's disciple tries to give him all kinds of material things 18.70–137; obvious but important 3.367, 16.8; offering three hundred pots of food is less than an instant of love 17.185–6; one of three aspects of giving 2.164; some people make it a practice to give something every day 1.500, 4.95; 'It means … transcending the boundaries of heaven and earth' 1.428; whatever can be possessed can be given away 4.95; 'With rains of food and drink may I dispel the anguish of hunger and thirst' 4.358

(2) time, energy, and thought
giving can be of time and energy, health and strength, life itself 8.175, 8.199; giving people space 4.69; time is a very precious thing to give 1.500; one can sacrifice time and energy no less than money 8.199

(3) fearlessness
Dr Ambedkar gave the gift of fearlessness 10.318; the bodhisattva's gift 17.180; the development of self-confidence 10.355; not so much given as sparked off 4.95; through positivity you create confidence and freedom from anxiety 3.367–8; resolving people's feelings of insecurity 16.8; a uniquely Buddhist conception 1.429–30; in a sense an aspect of giving the gift of the Dharma 16.27; ultimately the gift of insight into egolessness 16.27; why does the Buddha mention this in particular? 4.95–7; you give fearlessness to others by being fearless yourself 16.27

(4) education (śikṣa) and culture
always highly ranked in Buddhist countries 1.501, 3.368; culture is the gift of Buddhism wherever it has gone in the world 4.98; the gift of the bodhisattva 16.8; given through a library 10.355; included in *dāna* for two reasons 1.430; one of three aspects of giving 2.164

(5) life and limb
dāna can go as far as this 1.501; giving can be of life itself 8.175; if practising Buddhism was dangerous, would we do it? 4.100–1; in the *Jātakas*, *see Jātakas*; the importance of an element of self-sacrifice 4.459–60; the self-immolation of Vietnamese monks, *see under* Vietnam; something that surpasses the scope of most of us today 3.368; we should be prepared to sacrifice our lives for the Dharma 16.198; a young monk offering himself in the place of a condemned man 8.157–8; *see also* self-sacrifice

(6) merit
don't hug your virtue to yourself 4.101–2; the transference of merit 1.431, 3.368–9; *see also* merit/transference of merit

(7) the gift of the Dharma
the bodhisattva shares with others whatever truth he acquires 1.448; communicating the Dharma, *see under* Dharma III/teaching and learning the Dharma; Dr Ambedkar's gift of the Dharma 9.385–6, 10.318; any material gift is incomparable with the smallest gift of the Dharma 8.267, 14.445–7; 'The gift of the Dharma surpasses all gifts', *see under Dhammapada*/chapter 24; given by

the Buddha 17.328; the greatest of all gifts 3.369; compared to the giving of *amṛta* (nectar) 10.231; it requires the support of the other perfections 14.416–17; it requires sensitivity and discernment 4.102–3; if we can't give the Dharma ourselves, we can help others to do so 17.206; monks braved the deserts and seas to bring the gift of the Dharma 8.246; preserving a sense of wonder at the *gift* of the Dharma 14.403–4; no distinction between our Dharma practice and communication to others 17.174; one of three aspects of giving 2.164; you haven't started practising the Dharma until you have started giving it 17.206

(8) oneself
being available to others is to be ready to give yourself 17.202, 17.204; blessed is he who can wear out his body in the service of the Dharma! 8.175; giving oneself in the *chöd* practice, *see chöd*; the greatest virtue is availability 17.202; radiating yourself out towards others, not holding anything back 3.369, 4.600–1; not to be practised before one has developed the inner resources 3.369; offering oneself 18.188; Śāntideva's teaching of giving oneself 4.357–62; people find it difficult to give themselves totally to the spiritual life 13.242; 'When I give, I give myself' (Whitman) 2.365, 3.369, 4.93, 4.357, 11.169, 16.8; you can just give a smile 25.114

GENEROSITY

as an attitude
the antidote to possessiveness 17.657; an attitude of one's whole being 4.93; characteristic of a skilful mental state 15.263; the connection of generosity to gratitude 17.201; the equitable distribution of resources 2.368–9; an ever-expanding circle 1.426; an expression of love 2.365; a flow of energy 17.202, 26.35; if you are truly generous you may feel you are living in the midst of abundance 17.208; it comes from psychological security 17.199; it is intrinsic to non-attachment 17.562; must be wise 4.341–2; mutual (in Shakespeare's *The Phoenix and the Turtle*) 2.365–6; treating a beggar as you would your dearest friend 17.205

the Buddhist tradition on generosity
the aspect of Enlightenment that gives spiritual gifts without discrimination 12.214; the *varada mudrā* represents unlimited generosity 13.309; if you are generous there is hope for you yet (Mahāyāna) 14.573; many *Jātakas* show the generosity of the Buddha-to-be in previous lives 17.200; Nāgārjuna's arguments in favour of generosity 17.209–13; in the bodhisattva, giver, gift, and recipient are indistinguishable 2.366, 17.202; to gain wealth in future lives, be generous now 17.210–12

the practice of generosity
the best kind of returns for generosity 17.202; generosity to a friend 3.573, 3.579, 11.698; part of the practice is awareness of how much one is given 17.201; the real importance of generosity 13.271; responding to the desire to give 14.423–4; the spirit of sharing in the sangha 10.273–4; wanting to give is often the first manifestation of the spiritual life 1.500

generous people
Americans 4.255; fundraising: appealing to people's natural generosity 17.199–200; generosity in Malaysia 24.35; the ideal donor, *see* Mrs Mary E. Foster; the quiet generosity of those who possess almost nothing 18.115–16; Tibetans 13.53, 16.401, 18.62–3, 21.329

failing to be generous
deciding to give and then changing your mind is demeritorious 4.363–4; if you are not giving, you are stagnating 4.613; giving a talk on the bodhisattva ideal, then not finding volunteers to wash up 18.163; failing to act on a generous impulse 15.349; we injure ourselves by suppressing our impulse to be generous (Hazlitt) 24.562

see also
bodhisattva/practice of the perfections; perfections/*dāna*

Danaë 26.481

Dānapāla (translator) 14.138, 14.152

Danasamudra, Dharmacharini 26.550

Danavira, Dharmachari v24

dance and dancing the ballet *Everyman* 13.658–9, 15.375–6, 20.86; the Dance of Death (medieval Christianity) 2.85, 13.230–1, 25.415; dancing to get the emotions flowing freely 4.256; dancing to rock music 11.196; 'Dancing Round the Maypole' 25.430–1; Jamyang Khyentse Rimpoche: 'Do you know anything about dancing?' 12.437–8, 13.108, 22.399; Krishna calls the *gopīs* to dance in the forest by playing the flute 16.73; Lama Dances 12.438, 13.108, 19.384, 22.399; the Order as a dance 25.145; the relation between human beings like the movement of dancers 7.276–7; the sky of the One Mind in which *ḍākinīs* and *ḍākas* dance

12.294; the Theravāda's prohibition of dance 19.384

danger

physical dangers
Avalokiteśvara delivers us from dangers 2.176; a dangerous drive through the Greek mountains 23.271; if practising Buddhism was dangerous, would we do it? 4.100–1; the proximity of danger can make you practise harder 18.52

positive dangers
communication with spiritual peers 18.420; 'Live dangerously' (Nietzsche) 19.57

dangers of language and concepts
being preoccupied with words and missing the meaning 19.158–9; believing that unskilful action does not result in suffering 17.250; Buddhism may be smothered by information 'about' Buddhism 1.8; confusing the realization of truth with the concepts that communicate it 19.354; converting concepts of relative validity into entities of ultimate reality 1.224; military metaphors 18.104–5; reifying any abstract noun 11.656; sinking into scholasticism 2.142; taking metaphors literally 16.133, 18.606–8, 26.206–7; theoretical understanding 18.167; using the language of psychology 10.440–1

dangers in relation to Dharma practice
appropriating Buddhahood as a mental possession 19.98; attempting to gain Enlightenment by manipulating *prajñā-upāya* 1.389; democratization 11.612–13; developing alienated awareness 12.266–7; the Dharma could be corrupted by ethnic traditions 18.174; Dharma life becoming a routine 10.241–2; feminization 11.613; getting used to the Dharma 19.477; identifying with the Buddha 19.53; its being presented as a sort of exotic curiosity 11.509; no safe way of practising the Dharma 4.186–7, 19.57; nothing more dangerous than pseudo-Dharma 18.172; a one-sidedly negative approach 3.15; practising the Dharma the wrong way 19.56–7; seeing Buddhism as a transcendental sweet shop 11.62; settling down in a partial experience of Enlightenment 16.524; sophisticated or psychological approaches 17.454; speaking of Buddhism almost exclusively in terms of mindfulness 17.87–8; spiritual selfishness 1.404–5; that your preoccupation with the Unconditioned is purely theoretical 15.576; thinking that one is already Buddha 10.438–40, 11.657, 11.689, 14.594, 17.390, 17.594

dangers of spiritual life
abandoning the safeguard of positive conditions prematurely 18.34; allowing your mindfulness to evaporate through wanting to be right 18.172; associating spiritual life with fear and revulsion 18.129; avoiding the truth of the immediate situation 15.272; formalism 2.559, 19.279; getting sidetracked 16.536; getting too far away from your needs 19.50; meditation 3.456, 4.503–5; mistaking external change for internal change 16.122–3; positive intentions being overwhelmed by the gravitational pull 19.61–2; 'pride of priesthood' 18.176; pseudo-spiritual consumerism 3.327; rejecting or passing judgement on the guru 18.111–12; small entanglements 17.283; thinking of the self as having experiences while remaining unchanged 16.122; thinking that you are pure already 10.439–40

inner dangers
self-consciousness is a dangerous weapon 19.181; unskilful mental states are dangerous things, like poison 15.367

dangers and other people
criticizing a vulnerable person can be dangerous 17.653; drying up emotionally without spiritual friendship 2.607; the exaggeratedly altruistic person may come to feel like the saviour of others 8.579; latching onto a sense of martyrdom or self-sacrifice 18.592; sexual relationships hindering one's development as an individual 3.39; 'There is danger in the duty of another' 10.55–6; women disrupting men's friendships 24.542–4

dangers of the world
becoming more positive but ignoring the difficulties of society 10.73; Christian missions 22.153; immersion in worldly life 18.422–4; pleasure becoming the basis for attachment 15.533; remaining in the world, being stuck (*White Lotus Sūtra*) 16.71; success is always dangerous 17.272; susceptibility to beauty 13.279

Daniell, David 26.337

Daniélou, Alain 24.528–9

Däniken, Erich von 24.69, 24.623–4 (n92)

Dantabhūmi Sutta *see under Majjhima Nikāya*

Dante Alighieri

introduction
introduction 7.563–4; the *Convivio* 24.546; *La Vita Nuova* (Dante's love for

Beatrice) 7.402–3, 20.84, 23.314, 23.522 (n358), 24.546

The Divine Comedy (Divina Commedia) Sangharakshita's first reading of the poem 20.84, 24.547–8; *Inferno* 13.592–3, 13.615–17, 19.619 (n188); *Purgatorio* 24.547–8; *Paradiso* 13.600–1, 26.318, 26.660; Blake's illustrations 26.661; Doré's illustrations 13.593; *terza rima* 24.547; translations 24.546–7; compared to Einstein 26.686; comparison with *Paradise Lost* 13.583; Dante's relationship with Beatrice 24.548; doctrinal elements are part of the story 13.669; it came to be styled 'divine' 2.645; affection and respect for homosexuals 13.615–16; 'Love which moves the sun in heaven, and all the stars' 7.61, 26.150; permeated by Christianity 12.76; the poet's treatment of the relationship between himself and Virgil 24.548; sees life as a journey 16.86, 26.262; similarities to Buddhist cosmology 19.505; sorrowful reproach of Constantine 13.552

paintings and writings featuring Dante 'Dante in Verona' (Rossetti) 26.660; Holiday's painting *Dante and Beatrice* 24.224, 24.546; Maria Rossetti's *The Shadow of Dante* 24.546; Rossetti's painting *Dante's Dream* 24.547, 24.584–5, 26.660

Dao De Jing *see under* Laozi

Daochu 1.337

Daoism (or Taoism) Mr Chen's oscillation between Buddhism and Taoism 22.537; and Confucianism 7.150; contact with Buddhism when the Dharma spread to China 7.144; the Daoist sage who went fishing without using any bait 14.518–19; degeneration 12.53; distinction from Buddhism 16.163–4; an ethnic religion 11.296; the homely mysteriousness of a Daoist sage 7.396; influenced by the Buddha 2.11; knowledge that sense experience is only part of the spectrum of human experience 5.51; potentially a universal religion, but quickly degenerated 12.247; preaches a return to nature 12.247; sacred tree 2.222; a spiritual teaching without reference to God 12.7; 'The Taoist Teacher' 25.165; transcendental primitivism 12.247; 'virtually extinct' 13.513

Dapoli, India 10.399–400

Darīmukha (the monk who saw a leaf fall) 3.272, 3.664 (n249)

Darjeeling, India advice on visiting 21.513–14; Aloobari Gompa 22.106; Bhutia Busti YMBA 22.195–6; Cooch Behar House 22.401; Anagarika Dharmapala's visit 8.42; first visit 20.132–4; the Gandhamadan Vihara 22.26, 22.27–8, 22.47–8, 22.108, 22.195; Ghoom monastery, *see* Ghoom; Observatory Hill 20.133; reminiscent of Japan 22.16; Sangharakshita and Terry visit Darjeeling in 1966 23.392–4; steam train 13.101, 18.63, 21.331; Tamang Gompa 8.520, 12.285–6, 21.91–4, 22.27–30, 22.466–8, 22.469, 26.673; a trip to borrow a projector 22.105–10; a visit to a tea estate with Sachin 22.18–27; visits to give public lectures and organise printing 21.233–5; visit to Jamyang Khyentse Rimpoche 12.438, 22.401–2; a visit with Lama Govinda 21.259–61; the Yellow Monk 21.331–6

dark night of the soul *see under* mysticism

darkness 'Darkness is everywhere just as the skin covers the whole body' 17.509–10; the darkness of ignorance, *see under* ignorance; dazzling darkness 2.130, 16.329, 23.103, 26.201; developing positivity so that you feel like a radiant lamp, not overwhelmed by darkness 18.575; dispelled by the radiant Wisdom Lamp 19.156; 'embalmèd darkness' 22.21–2; existence as a conflict between the forces of light and darkness 8.525–6; and light 16.388; reality is neither light nor darkness 16.329; 'The light shineth in darkness' 7.33, 7.69; the mind's action, now dark, now light 19.455–6; Milarepa in darkness 18.20; a principle of Darkness in the world 12.354–5; the Tathāgata is like the sun arising to dispel darkness 1.53

Darlington, Cyril 11.323

darśana (Pāli *dassana*) an important word in India 11.158, 15.441–2; in the *Maṅgala Sutta* 15.441; taking *darśan* 1.576, 15.441–2, 20.320, 20.341–3; 'that which is seen' 11.158; in philosophy, *see under* philosophy/Indian

Darshan, Lok (Nepal) v21

Darwin, Charles the principle of evolution 3.10, 3.12, 3.475, 10.345–7, 12.84; application of the principle of conditionality 12.153; its effects on life in the West 10.345–7, 11.75; natural selection 10.345; he lost his capacity to enjoy Shakespeare 16.532, 17.684; *On the Origin of Species* 3.189, 3.475; Shaw's witty summary of the Darwinian controversy 23.371; Spencer, not Darwin,

coined the phrase 'the survival of the fittest' 10.691 (n216)

Das, Bhagavan 20.388, 26.174

Das, Ishwar 8.367

Das, Sarat Chandra 8.37, 8.45

Das, Sri S. R. (Chief Justice of India) 8.658, 22.318

dasa sīla upāsaka* or *upāsika early name for Triratna Order members (replaced by Dharmachari/ni) 9.165, 9.174, 9.190; explanation 9.544; practice 9.309–10, 9.510–11

Daśabhūmika Sūtra (also *Daśabhūmīśvara*)

about the sūtra
introduction 1.401, 14.227–9; an early Mahāyāna *sūtra* 16.239; one of nine *sūtras* venerated in Nepal 14.100; a portion of the *Avataṃsaka Sūtra* 14.227; preoccupied with doctrinal categories 14.201; set in Indra's paradise 14.228; translations 14.227, 16.607 (n177); a veritable encyclopedia of Buddhism 2.170

the bhūmis
among them all the more important doctrines and practices are distributed 2.170; correlation of the ten perfections with the ten *bhūmis* 1.447–8; described in bewildering, dazzling detail 1.450; how the bodhisattva passes from the seventh to the eighth 14.228; the eighth *bhūmi* 1.258–9, 1.260, 1.439; the *bodhicitta* manifests through them like gold made into a crown 4.177–8, 19.198–9

ten bodhisattva vows (praṇidhanas)
introduction 1.421, 4.58; third vow: how could one 'see all the incidents in the career of a Buddha'? 2.58–60; sixth vow – to perceive the universe – can be taken not literally but imaginatively 4.59–60

other teachings
upon the attainment of the *dharmakāya* the bodhisattva attains a glorious body 1.260; *dharma-pratisaṃvid* 1.449, 16.489, 16.627 (n337); knowledge of how the different *yānas* merge together 16.489

Daśabhūmikavibhasa *see under* Nāgārjuna/works

Dasgupta, Shashi Bhusan (*An Introduction to Tantric Buddhism*) the Kālacakra Tantra 1.386, 1.619 (n307); Mantrayāna 1.384–5, 1.619 (n305); the Sahajiya School 1.386, 1.619 (n308); sexual practice in the Tantra 1.391–2, 1.619 (notes 310 and 311)

Dasgupta, Surama 21.112–15

Dasgupta, Surendranath 7.202, 21.112–14

dassana 15.333

Dasuttara Sutta *see under Dīgha Nikāya*

dates the Buddha's birth and death dates 2.19, 2.662 (n12), 7.491; question about the date of Jesus's birth 12.591; when the Buddhist era began 22.304, 22.318

Datta, Michael Madhusudan 26.325–6

daughters the attempt by Māra's daughters to seduce Siddhārtha 3.277, 12.187; the cruelty of King Lear's daughters 18.210–11; duty: 'Stern daughter of the Voice of God' 7.277; the earth goddess represents the same forces as Māra's daughters, now tamed 12.188; Milarepa's view of daughters 18.211–13; the Muses, the daughters of Apollo 16.363

Daund, India 9.277, 9.292

daurmanasya *see under* sorrow

dausprajñā *see duppañña*

Davendra, D. T. 8.643, 21.499

David of Dinant 23.247, 23.510 (n281)

David-Néel, Alexandra brief introduction 22.597–8 (n212); her life story 6.607–10; her character 12.561–2; a great Buddhist 6.609–10; the first woman to make the trip to Lhasa 6.609–10, 12.561; disciple of the Gomchen of Lhachen 6.608–9; meeting with the Thirteenth Dalai Lama 6.608; adoption of Lama Yongden 6.609; a message of goodwill to the Maha Bodhi Society 22.126; has an argument with a fellow Buddhist in Paris 22.255–6; 'The Buddha and His Modern Disciples' 8.362; contact with Sangharakshita 6.609; description of *tummo* heat 24.113, 24.623 (n135); 'On Anicca' 8.643;

The Secret Oral Teachings in Tibetan Buddhist Sects (review) 8.349

Davidson, John 24.520

Davies, W. H. 1.570, 24.389

Daw, Muriel v23

Dawa *see* Bhutia, Dawa Tsering

Dawa-Samdup, Lama Kazi 12.197, 18.98, 21.71,

dawn the beauty of dawn contrasted with the ugliness of outcaste work 25.123; blackbirds singing at dawn 25.lx, 25.391; 'the Caravan starts for the Dawn of Nothing' 26.395; the dawning sun of Buddhism in the West 12.383–4; a New Zealand dawn 24.82; spiritual dawn 26.173; Uṣas, goddess of the dawn 16.418

Dawson, Leslie *see* Ananda Bodhi

dāyaka *see* lay people

Dayal, Har (*The Bodhisattva Doctrine in Buddhist Sanskrit Literature*) the bodhisattva emerging from the eggshell of ignorance 3.231, 3.658 (n219); on the *bhūmis* 1.450; on the *bodhicitta*, here called the 'thought' of Enlightenment 4.27; on *bodhisakta* 2.659 (n3), 4.239; on the bodhisattva vow 4.56, 4.58; on faith 1.290–1; how to give 4.678 (n127); kinds of giving 4.94; 'May I attain supreme Enlightenment' 1.420; on the rarity of human birth and the truth of death and suffering 1.417–18; Sangharakshita's view of the book 4.239; on skilful means 1.448

Dayaraja, Dharmachari (Wolfgang Schroeder) v24

Dayasri, Dharmacharini v24

daydreams some daydreams are blueprints for the future 1.538–40; spiritual daydreaming 4.60; you can fantasize, daydream, as long as you are aware 10.463

Dayi Daoxin (Zen patriarch) 13.342

Dazu Huike (Zen patriarch) 13.342

De, Sushil Kumar 26.331

de Chardin, Teilhard 3.9, 3.625 (n4), 13.513–15

de la Mare, Walter 22.181–2, 26.379, 26.393

de la Vallée Poussin, Louis 7.486

de Laszlo, Violet 3.491

De Quincey, Thomas 'The English Mail Coach' 26.332; 'everlasting farewells!' 23.394; literature of knowledge and literature of power 10.153, 14.302–4, 26.197–8

de Silva, Dr C. L. A. 7.435–6, 26.129

dead, the can we help the dead by doing the *mettā bhāvanā*? 5.179–82; Chinese rites for the dead 1.384, 2.232; contact with people after death 10.492–3; the dead restored to life by the Greek god Asklepios 16.191; the departed consciousness can be helped by the positive thoughts of the living 4.560; the living should not be sacrificed to the dead (Blake) 26.646; Japanese rites for the dead (O-Bon) 2.232; Jogis, gatherers of the souls of the dead 11.456–7, 12.439, 23.391; a Nepalese nun who had a vision of her dead brother as a skeleton 20.434; offerings to the dead (*Tirokuḍḍa Sutta*) 15.67–8; praying for the dead (Islam) 5.177–82; rice balls offered to the dead in after-death ceremonies 4.478; Shinje, the Lord of the Dead (Tibetan) 8.559; *Tibetan Book of the Dead, see Tibetan Book of the Dead*; we need not forget the dead 5.180–1

death

OPENING THOUGHTS

reflections on death
death as a form of *duḥkha* 3.211; death is the most crucial situation of all 11.17; death is out to ensnare you 10.492; death is not an abstraction, but a concrete reality 11.401; death is the test of Dharma practice 18.249–50; from a higher spiritual point of view there is 'no more death' 4.331; heedlessness is the way to death 7.118; impermanence is a death sentence, but also our hope of freedom from death 17.163; in reality birth and death are inseparable 8.224–5; the mystery of death 3.4–5, 3.94–8, 3.113; the other side of the coin of birth is death 4.76, 10.652, 23.93; the paradigm of the inescapable situation 15.376–7; the problem of death 3.95–7, 12.356–61, 23.91–3; we are the only beings for whom death is a problem 12.358

images and metaphors
'The Ballad of Journeyman Death' 25.334; the blind old king riding bravely to meet Death 25.411; the Dance of Death 2.85, 13.230–1, 25.415, 26.297; Death and Orpheus 25.257; in Greek imagery death was represented as a beautiful winged youth 13.230–1; the Triumph of Death (Pisa) 26.298

TRYING TO AVOID DEATH

fear of death
effects of suppressed fear of death 1.155; in the West 16.276–8; all insight meditation

practices are methods of coping with the fear of death 26.75; a *bhikkhu*'s fear of death 22.41–2; it is essentially fear of loss of ego 18.245; fearlessness in the face of death is central to the practice of Buddhism 16.278; a horrifying idea for most people 3.211; it's terrifying because one identifies so completely with the body 15.145; lack of fear can be lack of imagination 16.278, 18.341; people may talk about the Dharma, but faced with death they forget all about it 18.249–50; we fear death because we cling to 'self' 16.97, 23.92; why should Christians be so afraid of death? 13.230

not thinking about death
euphemisms 12.194–5, 23.92; fondness for sleep despite the reality of death 4.471–2; forgetting the lesson of death 10.320–1; the idea of 'resurrection' a clumsy attempt to negate the fact of death 12.357–8; in vain we flee before the King of Death 25.445; it is morbid *not* to think about death 12.358, 23.91–2; most men whistle their way through life as though they had never heard of death 7.171; 'O procrastinating one, who thinketh not of the coming of death' 12.208; refusing to face death deprives us of knowing what we truly are 12.358; we are usually able to ignore any number of corpses 12.360; we prefer not to think about death 19.16; we try to forget that we will die 8.575; Western tendency to sweep death under the carpet 4.76, 12.194–5, 15.144, 15.147

RECOLLECTING DEATH

facing death
all beings are 'on their way to their slaughter' 2.156; the Buddha faced death quite early in his life 12.358–60; coming to terms with our own impermanence 15.145; 'Death is no different whined at than withstood' 26.439; developing awareness of the multidimensional nature of consciousness helps 17.688; Anagarika Dharmapala faces death 8.13, 8.55; *Do not go gentle into that good night* 26.398; eternalist and nihilist ways of approaching death 17.243–3; facing the monster of death, *see under* wheel of life; if you love life, you will love death 4.76–7, 12.195; going looking for death in the cremation ground 13.231; in the East people accept death more readily than in the West 4.120, 12.195, 15.144; in the form of a Tibetan wrathful figure 1.196–7; inability to accept the death of a saint 24.280–1; life and death are both to be accepted: reflections at an Indian funeral 13.223; messengers of death 4.330–1, 12.358; mindfulness in the face of death 8.144; only one deep in love with life will find that death gives a keener edge to joy 1.129; practising forbearance towards death 4.120–1; Sangharakshita learns that death shows no respect for earthly privilege 15.144; seeing the shadow of mortality 25.470; seizing pleasure in the face of death 16.302, 18.151; to be self-aware is to be aware of death 3.568–9, 12.358; those who are used to being close to death can be close to the spiritual path 18.245; to speak of death is just being realistic 15.147; we are going to die and it is not morbid to be mindful of the fact 17.180; we cannot afford to forget that human life is an unstable, fragile thing 15.146–7; whether your life has been long or short, it's the same from death's perspective 4.427; with mindfulness and *mettā* 11.629

death may come to us at any time
at any moment you could breathe out and not breathe in again 18.565; moving closer to death like a calf drinking its mother's milk 10.617–18; 'No one can tell when death will fall upon him' 18.362; no special set of conditions for death 3.128; the older we get, the more the odds are stacked against us 11.651–2, 12.543; reconcile your quarrels, for death may come at any time 11.458; Sangharakshita's near-death experiences 23.129–30, 24.337–9, 26.645; so take every opportunity to create merit 18.551, 18.555; we may die at any moment 2.536, 26.75; we may think we're ready to die at any time, but are we? 17.354

realizing we must die
acceptance of death (Pompeii) 24.293; are you convinced that you are going to die? 19.246; Buddhists of all schools are exhorted to be mindful of death's inevitability 12.195; the effect on us of the death of a powerful or rich man 10.321; English old ladies natter about death, having come to terms with it 24.127–8; even the Buddha had to die 11.449, 12.357–8; even heroes and great artists must die 11.448–9; 'Going to work, I walk past the mortuary, and that puts life in perspective' 10.lxii; 'I *knew* that I would die' 22.199, 23.91; insight into the universality of death (Kisā-Gotamī) 3.357–8, 9.233–4; Not in the sky, nor in the ... sea ... can one escape [death] (*Dhammapada*) 15.376–7; a lot of old people don't mind the idea of dying 15.376–7; one fallen rose petal teaches the lesson of mortality 25.372; the realization that one is going to die: the story of St Bruno 15.141; that we must die is the

one thing about ourselves we really know 10.320–1, 12.358, 12.396, 18.151; three epitaphs (poems) 25.379; you can't take it with you when you go 18.472; 'You cannot evade the Lord of Death' 19.103

preparing for death
appreciating life as much as we can and appreciating death when it comes 17.244; conscious preparation 8.143; a great opportunity for which we have to prepare *now* 23.93; 'Life is nothing but a preparation for death' 10.320; make the most of opportunities to hear the Dharma 9.291; making a will 15.146; meditation is a preparation for death 18.154; only those who experience death in life can experience life in death 26.83; preparation for death 15.147–8, 18.250; 'The Ship of Death' 25.liv, 26.398, 26.490; what would you regret not doing before you die? 16.302

death's four reminders:
(1) we too must die 10.320–1; (2) we should make the best use of our life 4.75, 10.322–3, 19.244–5, 23.465; (3) we should end our quarrels 10.323–4, 11.458; *see also under Dhammapada*/chapter 1; (4) we have to rely on our own efforts 10.324–5

recollection of death meditation practice
antidote to craving 4.75, 12.195; bearing in mind that we will die, things once important become unimportant 23.92; Buddhism offers us a number of practices to remind us of death 11.448; everyone has to die 3.128, 11.448; helps one to lead the spiritual life 18.551; helps us to face the facts 23.92; helps us to see impermanence 18.128; how to make use of the practice 19.103–4; it can take you a long way towards insight 19.453; keeping skulls and bones as a reminder 4.76, 4.536, 16.28; meditating on the certainty of death and the uncertainty of its time 8.575; should be exhilarating, if taken up at the right time 3.346; no special set of conditions for death 3.128; overcomes fear 3.346, 16.28; the precariousness of life 1.418, 3.127–8, 18.564; reflect on death to prepare you for when the time comes 15.147–8; since death must come, why not make the best use of your life? 4.75; people can take the practice the wrong way 19.246; thinking about death to conquer the demon of laziness 18.555; Tibetan Buddhists reflect on death and decay in a very positive spirit 4.537–8; to be undertaken on a foundation of mindfulness and emotional positivity 3.126; in use in the Buddha's time 5.35; use it to keep up good relations with other people 19.104; a way of breaking up individuality 5.32; a way of eradicating covetousness 2.387; what death reminds us of 10.316–25; whatever is born must die 11.446

DYING, DEATH, AND AFTERWARDS

ways of dying
William Blake's happy death 8.554; death by car accident 24.513; dying in catastrophes 4.51; the forces of death have assumed noxious forms in modern life 4.638; a man who died at the age of 146 23.242–3; sudden death described in a poem by Crabbe 4.471–2

the process of dying
according to Buddhism death takes place in five stages 23.92; the breath, like the body, arises and passes away 15.110; Buddhists believe dying well is almost as important as living well 8.142; do whichever practice you are most familiar with, or have most faith in 26.75; importance attached to making 'a good death' 2.231; instructions at the time of death 2.231; learn to renounce during your life and you will be happy in the hour of death 8.199; *mettā* for the dying 5.176–7; pain relief when dying 16.407; spiritually advanced people die in the *dhyāna* state 2.231; dying can be a pleasant experience 23.465; dying peacefully because of ethical practice 10.645; the mystery of the dying process 15.145; should a patient be warned of approaching death? 8.142–4; the smell of death 16.562; traditions that hold that the dying process takes place over a long period 15.145; when you are dying you can speak the truth without fear 15.376–7

time of death
death-consciousness (*cuti-citta*) 2.75; mistaking psychic illumination for transcendental wisdom can cause difficulty 18.251; meditation is a kind of death, death is a kind of meditation 12.206, 12.555–6; post-mortem emancipation 2.149; a state of enforced meditation 5.34, 18.154, 26.49; the Tibetan belief that your consciousness passes out of the top of your head 18.154; the time of death can be a wonderful opportunity 18.250; unless we have freed ourselves from ignorance, our death is a prelude to rebirth 3.131; why not see death as wiping the slate clean and forgetting everything? 17.244

what happens after death
after death you have desires but no senses through which to satisfy them 17.15; all

one needs is a faith in the conservation of spiritual values beyond death 4.63; Christian belief in life after death 3.189–90; the condition of the Tathāgata after death, *see under* Tathāgata; could a 'glorified spiritual form' exist after death? 20.311; descending into the Underworld 25.345; does Going for Refuge continue after death? 15.687–91; how to treat a body after death 15.145–6; life after death is not such a burning issue as it used to be 3.192; the long and weary round of life after life and death after death 7.49; a mental experience of a dead person (not seeing a ghost) 17.622; no need to wait until after death to experience the results of positive action 9.287–8; 'The sun shines out to light us after death' (Aristophanes) 23.290; according to the *Tibetan Book of the Dead* 3.110–11, 11.17, 12.201–6, 16.532, 17.15; different views: heaven and hell, materialist, rebirth 17.468–9; a middle way between nihilism and eternalism 19.375; nihilism: the view that there is nothing after death 17.245; we are right to be concerned about it, for it may be a traumatic experience 17.286; what happens after death could be culturally determined 26.537–8; you have desires but no senses through which to satisfy them 17.15

bereavement
feeling loss unselfishly rather than selfishly 12.612–13; feeling resentful when someone dies 17.564; losing someone near and dear 26.25; Parinirvāṇa Day: remembering friends and relatives who have died 11.457–8; the Path of Vision arising as a result of 1.480; an opportunity to come to terms with our own impermanence 15.145, 18.560–1; when someone close to you dies, life starts teaching you about impermanence 18.560–1

see also
bardo; contemplation of decay; death by black magic, *see under* magic; funerals; ghosts and apparitions; the 'great death', *see under* spiritual death; *jarā-maraṇa* (decay and death), *see jarā-maraṇa*; the length of time between death and rebirth, *see under bardo*; *Māra* as the personification of death, *see under Māra*; the moment of death, *see under bardo*; the monster of death, *see under* wheel of life; as one of the four sights, *see* four sights; one of Yama's three messengers, *see* Yama; sacrificing one's life for the sake of the Dharma, *see under* self-sacrifice; spiritual death, *see* spiritual death; the death of the Tathāgata, *see* Tathāgata; Vajrasattva mantra when someone has died, *see under* Vajrasattva

deathless (*amṛta* or *amata*) *amata* is an example of a word that is grammatically negative but means something positive 10.635; the Buddha's attainment of the deathless state 11.403, 13.681 (n48); 'I beat the drum of the Deathless' 8.xviii, 11.415, 16.264; the nectar given to beings in hell 13.134; the sapphire Lake of Deathlessness 25.183; a synonym for Nirvāṇa 1.171, 11.413, 15.57, 26.473; The Undying 25.291; 'Wide open are the doors of the Deathless' (*amatapadaṃ*) 1.90, 3.74, 3.176–7, 7.153, 11.406, 11.412–13, 23.367

debate *see under* Tibetan Buddhism/ teachings and study

debt Enlightenment like release from debt 13.192–3, 14.42; epitaph for a debtor 25.379; freedom from hindrances is like freedom from debt 2.56; unskilfulness of indebtedness 2.367–8

deceit or pretence (*māyā*) the Buddha pretended to enter *parinirvāṇa* as skilful means (Mahāyāna) 4.85, 4.205–6; the danger for the actor of not being able to stop pretending 17.658; deceit, fraud, hypocrisy 10.514; a donkey pretending to be a cow 3.401, 9.192–3, 9.273; five forms of pretence 17.658–9; in cheating others, one cheats oneself 17.172; pretending to be what one is not; keeping up the pretence of being a monk while not keeping the rules 18.487; pretence is a magic show, a sort of trick 17.657; pretended, culpable doubt 10.577; pretending we are not angry because we have been told that anger is wrong 12.265; pretending to be what you're not 17.657–8, 19.259; pretending to let go of the 'rope' of self 9.457; pride in qualities you have, or imagine or pretend you have 17.273; as *upakleśa* (Abhidharma) 17.657–9; within the sangha there is no need to pretend 11.137–8

deception bad faith 17.17, 17.708 (n25); hypocrisy: an element of conscious deception 17.647, 18.515; the *kleśas*, the inner deceptions 18.574; self-deception, *see* self-deception; work frequently involves deception of some kind 17.194–7; you can't be deceived if you enter into a situation with integrity 26.35

decisions allowing someone else to make a decision for you 18.383–4; the conscious mind forcing the decision to gain Enlightenment on the psyche 3.40–1;

consulting the *I Ching* 17.614; decision-making in the spiritual community 18.35–6; do not keep too many options open too long 12.484–5; helping people to reach the point of decision 18.625–6; if you keep your options open indefinitely, you avoid having to do anything 15.175–6; making a choice between values that oppose each other 18.103; making a decision free of irrational guilt 18.455–7; objectifying the situation by talking about it with a friend 17.614–15; we are vague when we don't want to decide 11.49; you cannot avoid making decisions, so use whatever faculties you have to make them 19.165

see also
action/deciding what to do; indecision, *see* ten fetters/second fetter

decline of Buddhism *see under* Buddhism III/decline and renewal

decomposition of a corpse *see* contemplation of decay

dedication ceremony composed by Sangharakshita 3.521, 12.366, 23.429; draws on traditional material 13.419; 'Here may no idle word be spoken' 11.651, 12.541; used to dedicate the FWBO's first centre 12.366, 13.705 (n220), 23.429

deer apology for hunting them 25.447; the Banyan deer sacrifices himself for a pregnant doe (*Jātaka*) 14.65; Deer Park, *see under* Sarnath; the deer who need to stay safe up in the mountains (Pāli canon) 18.34; friendly deer in New Zealand 24.79

defilements adventitious 1.84, 1.275, 1.364, 2.130, 7.527, 10.439–40, 13.389–90, 17.95, 19.97; 'defiled-mind-consciousness', *see under* eight *vijñānas*; *kleśa nirvāṇa* (the extinction of all defilements), *see under* Nirvāṇa/Nirvāṇa in practice; the Māra of the defilements, *see under* Māra/four Māras; purification of defilements on the Tibetan Buddhist path 12.296–7; purifying the defilements like removing a stain from a pure white cloth 26.642; seeds of defilement and purity (*bījas*) within the *ālaya-vijñāna*, *see under* eight *vijñānas*; 'Those who are free from defilements become utterly 'Cool' 10.515, 10.614, 19.204

definition (definition of) 13.400

degeneration

degeneration of …
the *arhant* ideal 1.403, 4.21; Bengali Buddhism 22.93; the bodhisattva ideal 2.160; Christianity 3.430; confession in the Buddhist tradition 16.273–4; Daoism 12.247; the dialectical method 1.350; the ideal 1.404; Nichiren Buddhism 7.370; popular Mahāyāna Buddhism 16.231; pseudo-Tantric schools 1.274; sacred ceremonies 24.531; the spiritual community 3.440; unskilful mental states 18.208

reflections on degeneration
a coalescence between material progress and spiritual degeneration 1.42; could the ideal of Enlightenment degenerate? 4.20–1; degeneration into spiritual individualism 1.404; the Dharma disappears as human beings become more degenerate 1.50; the emergence of the tantras not a degeneration but a rebirth 12.219; a mistake to think of Tantric Buddhism as a degeneration 1.377, 1.381; monastic life degenerated from a spiritual adventure to a safe investment 1.228; preventing the doctrinal tradition from degenerating into scholasticism 2.155–6; regarding later Buddhist history as a degeneration 1.249, 1.612 (n203); Theravāda Buddhism regards the Mahāyāna as a degeneration 1.249, 1.436; though someone may degenerate, they are still recognizably a human being 16.291; Triratna must be careful not to degenerate into something wishy-washy 10.14

Delamare, Terry

his life story
introduction 23.xviii–xix, 23.95–105; childhood suffering at being made to kill rabbits 23.96–7; distress at lack of education 23.255–7, 23.275; his relationship with his parents 23.97, 23.100, 23.170, 23.442, 25.65; sculpture 'Mother' or 'Woman' or 'Death' 23.442, 25.318; sense of inferiority 23.97, 23.268, 23.275; persona ('Golden Balls') 23.108;

work in advertising 23.97–8, 23.169–70, 23.191–2; his relationships 23.98–101, 23.171–2, 23.221–2; his daughter 23.99, 23.101, 23.170, 23.221–2, 23.328; friends 23.100–1, 23.107–8; photographs 23.50, 23.96, 23.230, 23.262, 23.330, 23.413, 23.415; photographer 2.404, 23.269, 23.278, 23.298, 23.333–4, 23.355; psychoanalysis 23.101–4, 26.605; drug-induced experience 23.103–4, 23.442–3; the experience of the pure white light 23.93–4, 23.109; seeking the help of different spiritual organizations 23.104–5; he moves to a flat in Lancaster Grove, the 'Other Vihara' 23.170–1, 23.184–5; depression 23.191–2, 23.218–19, 23.255–7, 23.275, 23.278, 23.287, 23.337–9, 23.342, 23.362, 23.415, 23.427; death 23.104, 23.440–6, 26.505

Terry and Buddhism
belief that robes had nothing to do with Buddhist practice 23.190; he reads the *Laṅkāvatāra Sūtra* 23.244; preoccupation with finding a *ḍākinī* 23.172, 23.328, 23.342, 23.397, 23.427; Vajrasattva practice 23.xviii–xix, 23.139–40; visited Dilgo Khyentse Rimpoche 12.450

friendship with Sangharakshita
first meeting 23.93–4, 26.505; anniversary of their first meeting 23.218; based on spiritual, even transcendental affinity 23.109–11; 'Could you drive me to India?' 23.94, 23.106, 23.235; the gift of a copy of the *Sūtra of Wei Lang* 23.107; 'he treated me not as a monk but as a fellow human being' 23.111–12; long discussions 23.107, 23.109, 23.112, 23.114, 23.251; meditating together 23.169; Terry's wish to be of service 23.112; a journey to Greece and Italy 23.234–5, 23.242–321, 26.237–8, 26.266–7, 26.417; listening to music together 26.505; 'one of the most important friendships of my life' 23.94, 26.442, 26.505; a trip to Stonehenge 23.113–16; they both talk to Terry's suicidal friend (Ivan) 4.543–5, 23.116–17, 26.623–4; they go to India together 23.333–414; deepening friendship a factor in the decision to stay in England 23.326; others' suspicions that it was a homosexual relationship 11.583–4, 23.393–4, 23.402–3; an assessment of their friendship 23.403; Sangharakshita needing to talk to someone about the friendship 25.89; they share a flat 23.427, 26.599–604; Terry's final letters 23.443–4; Terry 'called to me for days after his death' 4.560, 23.444; Sangharakshita's poem 'For the Record' 23.444–5, 25.314–15; regret that he didn't live to see the FWBO as it developed 24.507

Delannoy, Miss ('the French nun', 'Ani-la')

introduction
brief introduction 26.734 (n342); her response to an image in the Guimet 3.300, 22.48, 26.116; her complex temperament 22.222–4; restless and demanding 22.184, 22.223; the physique of a peasant 22.222, 22.426

life as a nun
as Anagarika Dharmarakshita 22.73; as Thupten Chhokyi 22.184, 22.219, 22.424–7; she hits a taxi driver 22.219–21, 22.425; is horrified when advised to learn to waste time 14.520–1; hasn't done the practice she claims 12.440–1, 13.25, 22.326–7, 22.396–7, 26.227; learns Tibetan from Lobsang Phuntsok 22.221, 22.251; lives in an electrified cave 22.233–4; more eager to discuss sexual topics than a nun should be 22.194–5; photographs 22.117, 22.251–2, 22.326; quarrel with Joe Cann 22.236–8; studied with A. C. Banerjee 22.223; sympathy for her 22.221, 22.426; troubles 22.108–110, 22.115–16, 22.193–4, 22.197–8, 22.220–1; suicidal feelings 22.220, 22.325, 22.426; return to lay life 22.428

and Sangharakshita
concern about how she can be helped 22.194, 22.221–2; she gives him advice 22.104; English lessons 22.184; evenings in the shrine-room 22.226–7, 22.233; he teaches her the mindfulness of breathing 22.195; she is concerned about his health 22.249; she takes the Refuges and Precepts from him 22.15; she reads him French poetry 22.89; his account of her could have come from a novel 26.443; she takes over at his residence 22.193; they had a lot in common intellectually 22.222–3

her gurus
asks Jamyang Khyentse Rimpoche for help 22.399; meets Chattrul Sangye Dorje 22.375; Dhardo Rimpoche 22.184, 22.219, 22.424–7, 26.227; Kachu Rimpoche 12.440–1, 13.25, 22.326–7, 22.396–7, 22.398–9; teaching them how to teach her 11.250, 18.492–3, 19.365–6, 22.220, 22.426

Delhi (New Delhi)

locations and history
Aśok pillar, Feroz Shah Kotla 22.343; Ashok Vihara, Mehrauli 22.342; Connaught Circus 20.112–13, 22.348; the Delhi riots of 1947 23.384; Laxminarayan Temple (Birla Mandir) 16.396, 20.114–15, 22.346, 23.410; Maha Bodhi Society, *see under* Maha Bodhi Society/branches; Old Fort (Purana Khila) 20.112; Red Fort (Lal Khila) 20.112; Sher Shah's mosque 20.112; Symposium 21.513, 21.516; UNESCO seminar 21.519

Sangharakshita
first visit to Delhi 20.110–15; talks 9.499, 10.157–60; visits the city with the Eminent Buddhists 22.342–55; visits the city with Terry 23.410, 23.414

delight

delight in …
Dharma practice 11.45, 18.130; the beauty of the Unconditioned 2.84–5; Dharma study 4.448; the *Dharma-Vinaya* 10.562; harmony (the Buddha) 2.384; impermanence 18.54; an inner vision 26.597; the spiritual beauty of your dear friend 26.79; the world around you 15.310

delight in the Dharma
the Buddha's hearers are 'instructed, inspired, fired, and delighted' 12.525–6; the delight of studying the Buddha's teaching in 'his own words' 20.445–6; 'The Dharma surpasses all delights' (*Dhammapada*) 25.29–30; doctrinal differences ought to delight us, not dismay us 1.209; having realized *anattā*, everything becomes delightfully fluid and free 7.133; Nirvāṇa, the delightful stretch of level ground 1.81–2

other delights
beauty induces 'a trembling that is all delight' (Plotinus) 23.318; delighting in where we are leads us to more subtle delights 17.370–1; delighting in oneself and others 5.125; delighting in someone for what they are 18.159; Dudjom Rimpoche's delight in being alive 22.508; 'Fortunate are those on delightful rock terraces …' 4.629; gods that take delight in the creations of others 16.344; Milarepa's delight in solitude 18.41–5, 18.52–4; our capacity for delight in simple pleasures in childhood 18.130; 'Rarely, rarely, comest thou, Spirit of Delight' 3.512; the seventh heaven of delight inspired by organ music in Metz 23.248; the three delights (Milarepa) 18.417–20

unskilful delights
the difference between delighting in the skilful and in the unskilful 15.350–1; the academic mind delights in 'contradictions' and 'difficulties' 7.310, 11.483; delighting in inflicting suffering on others 15.350, 26.653, 26.678; delighting in the suffering of others 16.295–6; the Dharma 'difficult to see for those who delight in attachment' 3.175–6; 'unrest which men miscall delight' 2.124; you delight in a village full of walking skeletons 4.627

see also
delight in good, not evil, *see under* Mahāpajāpatī Gotami

deliverances (*ceto-vimutti* and *pañña-vimutti*) *see under vimukti*

Della Casa, Giovanni 4.336, 4.696 (n252)

Delors, Jacques 2.612

Delphi *see under* Greece

deluded type *see under* Buddhaghosa/*Visuddhimagga*/character types

delusion (*moha*) canonical source 16.616 (n242); the delusion that you've gone beyond concepts 18.399–400; Enlightenment: freedom from all delusion 3.31; Enlightenment is the cessation of the delusion that any kind of self exists 1.179; Buddhism's twofold method for destroying the delusion of the fixed nature of things 1.99–102; the deluded mind divides things into opposites, pursues some and rejects others 7.299; imagining one has realized what one has not 2.113; Māra: a baleful star in the firmament of man's delusion 7.327; meditation practices to eradicate delusion 2.392; the opposite of *moha* is commitment 17.47; the paradoxical nature of human self-delusion 17.163; a stubborn closed-mindedness about learning anything that would threaten ego-identity 11.130; subdivided into ignorance, conceit, and distraction 18.449; wandering in the suffering of delusion 11.276; the whole firmament of man's delusion 7.327; wisdom disperses the darkness of delusion 17.131–2

see also greed, hatred, and delusion; three roots; *viparyāsas*

Dem Chog *see* Śaṃvara

Dembu, Lady *see under* Rechungpa

dementia *see under* mental health

Demeter 16.385, 16.386

Demetrius 20.61

democracy *see under* politics

democratization 11.612–13

Democritus 17.439

demons becoming a demon through hatred 17.602; 'demon' as 'devil' comes from the Greek *daimon*, a tutelary deity 18.24–5; the demon of egotism 13.267–8; a demon-created storm, a metaphor for ego-clinging 18.12; the 'demoniacal' in Buddhist art 8.117; demons as inner processes 17.643, 19.411; depicted on the wall of a Tibetan monastery 7.75; economic, sociological, political, religious, and philosophical demons 11.715, 12.334; experiencing someone who had been taken over by a demon 26.623–4; the demon of Death (or Impermanence) 2.76, 2.85, 12.356, 12.359–60; Manichees' distinction between the God of this world (a demon) and the spiritual God 15.623; how Milarepa deals with five Indian demons 18.21–32; 'Let the demons come!' 12.335; Sangharakshita's experience of demons 11.715, 26.623–4; thinking about death to conquer the demon of laziness 18.555; we are living in a world of demons, and we ourselves are half demon 12.334; the demons of Tibet subdued, *see under* Padmasambhava/life story; possession by demons, *see* possession

Demosthenes 23.296, 23.518 (n332)

Den Pag 8.525

denial behind every friendship is the denial of the selfish individual will 7.293–4; 'The fruit does not deny the flower' (Hegel) 1.182; denial of the continuity of empirical experiences 7.165–7; the denial of the existence of the world of appearance 7.194; denial of one's own spiritual potential 4.78, 4.248; denying the truth of *śūnyatā* 7.213, 10.158; the materialist denial and the ascetic refusal 7.167

Denmark 25.437

Deolali *see under* Lama Govinda

Deoli, India 10.177

dependence dependence on others for material things 18.387–8; dependence on the very person you can't depend on: yourself 18.387; dependency in friendship 15.312; don't depend on others for happiness, or to help you decide what to do 18.388; don't look to others to support your image or experience of yourself 18.388; don't rely on an outside source for something you should be developing within yourself 18.300; emotional dependence 3.549–51; legitimate dependence: for material things, for inspiration, for protection 18.388–9; men's emotional dependence on women 26.28; the need to resolve an attitude of infantile dependence 12.232; people sometimes need a period of dependence 26.44; reasonable and unreasonable dependence 18.387–9, 19.360; slavish dependence on the letter of the teaching 1.239–40, 7.471, 7.540; *śūnyatā* shows us there is nothing to depend on 14.409–10; there is agitation for one who is dependent 10.637–8, 10.724 (n505); things are mutually dependent and therefore lack 'selfhood' 14.608; you never really depend on anybody except yourself 19.284; dependence on rules and religious observances, *see under* ten fetters/third fetter; everything arises in dependence on conditions, *see pratītya-samutpāda*; 'No dependence on words and letters', *see under* Zen/Zen teachings

dependent origination *see pratītya-samutpāda*

Depressed Classes *see* Dalits

depression asking oneself how one has got into that state 5.348–9; the difference between sadness and depression 18.556; empathy with depression 23.275; helping someone overcome it can be exhausting 19.550; manic depression 17.670; not allowing loneliness to turn into depression 18.53; one may be resistant to being helped 17.669; practices like the contemplation of decay should not be depressing 4.537; rejoicing in merits (in puja) counters any feeling of depression after confession 1.412; Sangharakshita and depression 22.86, 23.275; spending a day in the country to lift your mood 15.153; Terry Delamare's depression, *see under* Delamare

deprivation dangerous to deprive oneself of all comforts on the basis of rational understanding 16.284; an experiment in which children were deprived of human contact 12.215; experimenting with depriving oneself of sense satisfaction 5.677; if we take things for granted, we deprive

ourselves of a rich source of satisfaction 17.202; if you are imprisoned, don't let it deprive you of your mental freedom 18.458; in modern society, people have everything they need and still feel deprived 17.269–70; not to think about death is to deprive ourselves of our humanity 12.358; spiritual deprivation 17.269; to enter the higher *dhyānas* is to enter a state of sensory deprivation 4.154, 5.641–3; you don't necessarily get closer to happiness by depriving yourself of pleasure 19.244

depths *see* heights and depths

deśanā ('pointing out') 16.290

Descartes, René 7.387, 8.613

desert 'an arid desert of negation' 1.114, 7.204; the bliss of a man who travels through the desert and then bathes in a lake 2.107–8; every drop of the Dharma is precious, like water in the desert 9.291; life is like a desert 9.453; the merchant in the desert 9.264; mirages, *see* mirages; Sangharakshita in the wilderness (or desert) 2.610–12, 13.633–4; St Jerome in the desert 13.633, 26.283–4; turning Love loose in the desert 25.230

deserving a belief that you are undeserving will inhibit your practice of the Dharma 17.166; the Dharma cannot be earned or deserved 14.403; every human being deserves to be happy 5.184, 17.165–6; nothing conditioned can deserve the Unconditioned 14.403; only those who are pure deserve to wear the yellow robe 9.271; refusal to recognize someone as deserving of respect 12.13–14, 15.714–20; who deserves our help? 19.539

Desideri, Ippolito 11.297

desire

the nature of desire
desire and hatred are rooted in the ego-sense 26.153; its characteristic is to grasp one thing and reject another 7.411; a knot of psychic energies which seek to remain tied as the 'self' 8.492; the problem of desire 7.288–91; the root of desire is ignorance 7.126; a sort of neurotic craving, a clinging 19.156; treasure as symbol of desire 16.346; wrong views are symptomatic of wrong desires 8.231; you have sensual desire because you have a body 15.204

a world of desire
creatures of desires, we are concerned with things only to serve our own ends 2.55; human beings are desiderative rather than rational 1.123–4, 7.392; if you do not meditate on impermanence in the morning, by midday you will have many desires 4.265, 8.528; Indra's palace, where you can find everything you could desire 16.346; slaves to the compulsion of our unaware and ignorant desires 16.220; 'the stream of my desire' 25.264; the symbols of the Amitābha myth engage our darkest and deepest desires 1.347; we're a bundle of conflicting desires tied together with a name and an address 5.30; the whole of conditioned existence is subject to the danger of desire 18.171–2; the world of the hungry ghosts, a state of neurotic desire 13.130; you create your world, the network of your desires 17.14–15

consequences of desire
anger is the product of frustrated desire 17.271; attachment comes from desire 17.283; 'Desire dashed from my hands the chalice that love raised to my lips' 26.65; desires are immediately translated into deeds 1.151; the fruit of desire, even for Nirvāṇa, is pain, if the desire is selfish hankering 7.291; our desires bring all kinds of rationalizations in their wake 17.629; the stronger the desire, the more the suffering 3.212

skilful and unskilful desire
'At seventy I could follow the desires of my heart without fear' (Confucius) 4.485; the energy in healthy desire is needed for aspiration towards Enlightenment 17.290; few desires are so negative that they can't be connected with spiritual life 4.152; higher ideals are often lower instincts and desires in disguise 10.349; it can be selfish (as in sex-love) or selfless (as in friendship-love) 7.293; letting your natural desires flow freely – an advanced stage 4.625; no conflict between desire and duty 14.451; suppressing it is appropriate to *kāmacchanda*, but not *dharmachanda* 7.306–7; two forms of desire, one escapist, the other not 7.218–24; of two kinds: the desire to unite and the desire to separate 7.293; a wish to help others motivated by desire 4.89; the word has two contrary hemispheres of meaning 7.289

happiness and desire
happiness upon satisfied desire is on account of the desire's cessation 10.475, 26.12; happiness when existence accords with desires or *vice versa* 1.172; happy is the man whose needs and wants coincide 26.12; view that happiness consists in the full satisfaction of desires 7.116; you can never get happiness if you go about it at the blind dictate of desire 7.48

desire and other mental states
craving usually expresses itself as a desire to prolong pleasure 19.383; difference between breaking precepts out of desire and out of hatred 2.389, 4.702 (n283), 14.185–6, 16.614 (n232); the distinction between desire and aspiration 7.289–91; love and desire becoming compassion 25.493–8

mistakes about desire
desire for the transitory is doomed to disappointment 7.307; most people spend their life in pursuit of things they do not want 7.294; the problem is not getting what we want, but the wanting 18.187; the tragedy is not that we don't get what we want, but that we get it 26.11; unsatisfied because we are so busy going after things we don't really want 16.283–4; what we think we want is often not our heart's desire, just a habit 16.286; when we get what we've set our heart on, often we no longer want it 17.258

what do we really desire?
all unillumined desire is a groping in the dark for Enlightenment 7.307; allowing one's real desires to surface 4.151–2; discover what you really desire, and where that desire is coming from 13.134; nothing conditioned can fully satisfy our deepest longings 4.51

getting rid of desire
after death you have desires but no senses through which to satisfy them 17.15; cutting the ties of worldly desire 19.156; desires can never be satisfied, but only abandoned 26.12; 'Do not believe that lust can ever be killed if gratified' 7.358; ended by penetration into the truth of the transience of all phenomena 1.171; how a bodhisattva liberates the lustful 14.182; in a state of desire, we need to get back to the present moment 13.133–4; joy will spontaneously arise 19.579; no need to try out everything for confirmation of unsatisfactoriness 16.284; refining desire through beauty 5.511; stilling the turbulence of the wild winds of desire 7.125; the sublimation of desire and reorientation of emotion 1.390; we can cross the stream of suffering only by crossing the stream of desire 7.253; 'Wheresoever desires arise, there must they be overcome' 7.171; won't we get rid of the desire for pure and holy things as well? 7.288

sublimation and transformation
if you have solved the problem of desire, you have solved the problem of love 7.291; sublimated desire generates the energy to keep the spiritual life going 26.130; the Tantra and sexual sacramentalism 1.391; the transformation of desire 25.248

absence of desire
absence of desire equals absence of desired object 19.65; the cessation of desire is the cessation of phenomenal existence 1.131; as desire lessens, one can live more in the present 7.285; desire briefly ceasing to operate 10.475, 15.201; in a concentrated state, you can be aware of everything, but no desire arises 17.123; desire need not go on forever 25.277; quenched (*Ratana Sutta*) 15.65; we see something as beautiful when we see it without desire 12.613–14, 15.533

see also
desire for approval, *see under* approval; desire for existence, *see* three *āśravas*; desire for sensuous experience, *see kāmacchanda*, *kāma-rāga*; desire for the Dharma, *see dharmachanda*; eradicating desire through the four *vimuttis*, *see under* four *vimuttis*; sexual desire, *see under* sex; what do you really want to do?, *see under* action/deciding what to do

despair building a heaven in hell's despair (Blake) 11.25; do people in modern life feel despair? 18.556–7; the fearful task of plumbing the depth of existence and transforming despair 2.180; 'Lives of quiet desperation' 26.398; 'My son, despair not' 25.197; the Pure Land emerged from a sense of spiritual despair 17.298–9; shrill despairing cry: 'One single self we shall tame' 1.231; the would-be bodhisattva's temptation to give up on people in despair 4.187–8

despondency spreading 'alarm and despondency' ('Dismal Jimmy') 11.201, 17.181–2; we shouldn't feel despondent about the state of the world 11.271, 25.57–9

destruction

destructive forces
the All-Destroyer, Time 10.56; destruction does not bring the same joy as creation 26.194; destruction when 'the king overlooks an evil deed' (*Sūtra of Golden Light*) 16.430–1; destructiveness a characteristic of hatred and also wisdom 13.132–3; the forces of death and destruction 4.638, 7.512; a grain of dust in the wrong place can destroy us 4.76; hatred is a destructive force 4.392, 15.311; if humanity is not to destroy

itself, there must be a revival of spiritual life 16.394; if you're not allowed to create, you'll destroy 18.458; pagan roots destroyed by Christianity 4.106–7, 12.253–4; reflexive consciousness can destroy itself 16.292

skilful destruction
the *arhant*: one who has destroyed the *āsavas* 1.309–10; be proud of nothing except destroying pride 4.467; the destructive aspect of the Enlightened mind 13.278; eternalism is destroyed by the *animitta vimokṣa-mukha* 2.122; it is not enough to destroy evil passions, the Truth must be learned 7.35; of ourselves as we are at present 13.171; of attachment to objects 1.100; of craving 10.524–5; of the hosts of Māra 3.54; of limitations 16.504; of negative mental states (by Vajrapāṇi) 13.173; of spiritual ignorance 13.68–9, 13.278; of the wrong belief in self 1.103; only one way to the destruction of suffering 1.218; rebirth destroyed 1.95; seeing that the hindrances are destroyed, one feels joy 5.342–3; twofold method for destroying delusion 1.99–100

see also
knowledge of the destruction of the *āsravas*, *see under* three *āśravas*; Shiva the destroyer, *see* Shiva; Yamāntaka, 'The Destroyer of Death', *see* Yamāntaka

detachment detachment as taught by the Buddha transcends ordinary attachment and detachment 22.301; think of attachment to the positive, not detachment from the negative 10.513, 18.332–3; the idea that we can practise detachment anywhere 4.554–5; the Buddha's teaching to Mahāpajāpatī Gotami, *see* Mahāpajāpatī Gotami; a detached and objective attitude towards the body 4.609; cultivate detachment towards bliss 2.108; it means caring for others as much as you care for yourself 15.121; physical conditions need to be favourable for mental detachment 4.566; you can't speak of detachment from a place or people unless there is feeling there 18.332

deterioration Buddhist history has a tendency towards deterioration 8.312–13; committing teachings to writing a sign of spiritual deterioration 1.222; the factors leading to spiritual deterioration 14.56; without the constant intervention of spiritual forces human affairs tend to deteriorate 8.312; would the ordination of women cause a deterioration of the sangha? 2.27, 11.642–5

determination

determination to …
act to transform ourselves and our bit of the world 10.315; be a real friend 26.26; gain Enlightenment (represented by Padmasambhava) 13.247; go for Refuge (developed in the prostration practice) 13.211; meditate, *see under* meditation/preparation/regularity; overcome the hindrances 5.328; practise the Dharma 12.513–14, 19.223, 19.228

reflections
adhimokṣa 17.535; 'Be determined and persevering' 18.411; being determined in a relaxed way 5.389; commitment to following the Buddha with urgency and determination 25.29; determination applied to the Three Jewels becomes faith 17.535; from the bottom of one's heart 18.618; the determination of the elephant 4.469; how does one determine to rest one's mind on the Dharma? 19.466; Siddhārtha's resolve to reach the goal of Enlightenment, *see under* Siddhārtha; if you are really determined, why is a vow necessary? 19.146; some people try all the harder if they face opposition 4.423–4; very different from self-will 19.16

Deutscher, Isaac 24.157

deva as esoteric Dharma Refuge, *see under* three esoteric Refuges; as the mode of address for a king 16.416; for *devas*, *see devas*

Devadatta (the Buddha's cousin)

his life
brief introduction 4.661 (n15); in the *Jātakas* 4.361, 16.471–2, 17.480; joins the Order 2.26; miracles 4.13; psychic or supernormal powers 2.27, 3.63, 10.36, 10.580, 10.669 (n66), 19.117; traditionally the villain of the Pāli canon 4.13; tries to instigate a split in the sangha (*saṅghabheda*) 2.27, 3.63, 10.579–81; incites Ajātaśatru to seize the throne of Magadha 2.27; downfall, death, and rebirth 2.27, 3.63; prediction to Buddhahood in the *White Lotus Sūtra* 3.63, 12.513, 14.122

Devadatta and the Buddha
praised by the Buddha for his exemplary practice 10.669 (n66); he offers to take charge of the sangha 2.27, 3.63, 4.13, 9.305–6, 10.580, 14.541; he closes himself to the Buddha's influence 17.188, 18.538; becomes the Buddha's enemy 9.305–6; he rolls a boulder downhill towards the

Buddha 2.27, 3.63, 4.13–14, 4.311, 15.93, 16.616 (n244); the injury caused shows how the Buddha had to suffer *karma-vipāka* 15.93, 16.310, 16.616 (n244); he sets a mad elephant to attack the Buddha 2.27, 3.63, 4.13, 10.260, 11.162, 13.280, 17.188; Queen Vaidehī asks the Buddha how his life has been connected with Devadatta's 3.454

Devadatta Sutta *see also Aṅguttara Nikāya/Book of the Eights*

Devadūta Sutta *see under Majjhima Nikāya*

devālaya *see* Sri Lanka/temples

Devamitra, Dharmachari general entries v24; interviews Sangharakshita (1977) 11.518; on the *Bodhicaryāvatāra* seminar 4.225, 4.233–7; president of FWBO centres 12.631

devanāgarī **(*Nāgarī*) script** 9.36, 14.456, 19.32, 21.510

Devapriya Valisinha *see* Valisinha

Devaraja, Dharmachari v24

Devaraja, N. K. 24.546

devas (or *devatās*)

the nature of devas
definition 3.141, 15.495–6, 16.416; comparison with angels 13.586; not on the same level as those leading the spiritual life 10.516; personifications of natural phenomena (Vedas) 16.418; self-satisfied rather than conceited 4.77; sexual gratification progressively refined 16.344–5; their experience is subtle but not dhyānic 17.527; their life is blissful, but passive 1.444; their positive karma only sustained by a vision of the transcendental 16.354; they appear spontaneously 16.345; they are unable to create fresh karma 17.527; they belong to the natural world and are subject to its laws 2.34; they face the problem of what to do with their time, as do we 12.355; they have no envy 10.621; they inhabit higher and happier realms than the human realm 1.32

relating to devas
an attack by *devas* 26.624–5; the fragrance of *devas* in a house in Kalimpong 11.236–7, 21.132–6; from projecting the *deva* 'out there' to experiencing the *deva* 'in here' 15.496; in Burmese Buddhism 21.132–4, 21.136; scholars regard scriptural references to them as interpolations 1.34, 2.33–4; their influence on the building of cities, according to folklore 10.646–8, 24.81; traditional to show respect to them 2.34; twenty-two classes of *devas* in the Buddhist tradition 13.586; worship of the gods in Hindu folklore 10.516–17

devas around the Buddha and his followers
appearances in the Pāli canon 14.45–6; the Buddha teaches them 1.33, 4.16–17, 15.382; a *devatā* speaks to Bāhiya 10.461; the first disciples urged to teach them 1.33; the *Large Prajñāpāramitā Sūtra* preserved in their king's realm 14.145; the meaning of their appearance: the magical side of existence 10.447–8; their interaction with Kassapa in the *Udāna* 10.448–9, 10.515–16; their offerings make a jewelled canopy in the *White Lotus Sūtra* 14.129–30, 16.50; they encourage *bhikkhus* to get on with their meditation 19.413; they offer Siddhārtha celestial nourishment, but he refuses 10.448, 22.285; they often visit the Buddha, usually at night 13.586; they worship and praise the Buddha 10.516, 10.621

see also
the *devas* of the god realms, *see under* heavens; in the wheel of life, *see* wheel of life/the third circle

Devaśarman 14.87

development spiritual, *see* growth and development; no sense of development until quite recently in human history 10.554–5

Devendra, D. T. 2.227, 22.126

Devil 'the Devil is the busiest bishop in the land' 18.177; *Diabolus Deus inversus est* 12.295, 26.155; the Enemy of Mankind – fulfils a useful role 4.412; Milton was 'of the Devil's party without knowing it' 13.592, 18.78; theological view 18.149; the voice of the Devil 15.620; *see also* Māra; Satan; temptation in the wilderness, *see under* Jesus

devils becoming a devil under the influence of intense negative emotions 26.657; descriptions of angels often sound weak in comparison with devils 15.253; depictions of devils in art 13.597–8; Jesus casting out devils 13.594–5; pagan gods and goddesses seen as devils 13.595; 'Preach like an angel in the morning. Live like a devil at night!' 18.540; Sangharakshita sees a devil on the Tube train 4.546–7, 13.597–8, 26.565

devotion, worship, ritual

INTRODUCTION

general introduction
an aspect of all schools of Buddhism 1.336, 2.147, 11.208–9; atheism and devotion have never presented a contradiction 7.538; Buddhism developed its devotional aspects in parallel to Hindu devotionalism 7.123; fundamental to Buddhism 3.64, 3.71, 26.476; in Buddhism you worship anything you look up to 12.621; the instinct to worship is deep-rooted in the human psyche 2.213–14; the more highly developed the religion, the richer its ritual expression 11.214; much better to worship a tree than not worship anything 26.390; the traditional Eastern Buddhist approach starts with devotion 11.206; Dr Ambedkar's anthology of devotional texts 9.71–2

definitions and ideas
etymology of worship 15.389; 'Buddhism and Worship' 8.362; ideally an expression of faith in thoughts, words, and deeds 17.553–4; 'Love and Devotion in Buddhism' 22.285; neurotic ritual is solitary, but rational ritual is shared 11.210; 'The Psychology of Ritual' 11.205–15, 13.420; scholarly misunderstandings 7.535; 'shared action, expressive of common strivings, rooted in common values' 11.209–14, 13.420; 'a symbolic expression of thoughts and feelings by action' (Fromm) 11.212; worship and projection 15.390–2

Early Buddhism
the Buddha's instinct to worship after his Enlightenment 3.64–9; expressions of devotion in the Pāli canon 1.240, 7.537–8; scriptures of Devotional Buddhism 3.323–36; true worship (*Sigālaka Sutta*) 3.522–3, 10.167; the devotional element developed through lay influence 2.220; Theravādin ritual 1.242, 22.93

the Mahāyāna and Vajrayāna
devotion in the Mahāyāna 1.241–2, 1.262–3, 11.225–6, 16.232–3; Atīśa's composition of devotional verses 12.575; Dharma-worship, 'the supreme worship' (*Vimalakīrti-nirdeśa*) 16.572–5; Tibetan Buddhism is highly intellectual and deeply devotional 13.106–8; the devotion of Tibetan Buddhists to an image of the Buddha 4.177; devotional songs of the Newars of Nepal 20.435, 21.272

REFLECTIONS ON DEVOTION

how it arises
as one treads the path of the positive *nidānas* 12.160; the transformation of emotion into devotion 7.302–3; when *mettā* touches something higher and nobler than ourselves 15.327, 26.26; when our potential for Enlightenment resonates with actual Enlightenment 3.301

the nature of Buddhist devotion
more akin to poetry than logic 1.323–6; the burning monk a vivid reminder of what devotion to the Dharma means 22.518; the difference between worship and Going for Refuge 11.247–8; even offering a flower with devotion puts one on the path to Buddhahood 16.41; exclusive by its nature 2.243, 2.461; it can go to extremes, to become superstition, fanaticism, or intolerance 3.301; it is not about showing respect to symbols of religious authority 15.327–8; it is not 'emotional' as opposed to 'intellectual' 4.516–17; it is not propitiatory 11.223, 26.155–7; it's perpetual, to be done every day 6.xxviii; it must involve an element of joy and spontaneity 15.604–5; it needs to be balanced with wisdom 3.301, 16.59, 22.285; its essence is thinking about the Buddha 11.216, 11.224; perhaps not possible to separate the devotional and the aesthetic 20.259; a practical and realistic response to the nature of things 18.117; recognizing the sublimity of the ideal 4.45; worship of rocks and trees as part of Buddhism 11.247–8

devotion to whom or what?
the goal is the object of worship 2.128; in worshipping one figure, indirectly you worship all 7.304–5; one's teachers 3.63–4, 12.160; devotion towards Sangharakshita: 'What had I done to deserve it?' 22.165; the man from whom one learns the Dharma 22.385; worshipping the Buddha, *see under* Buddha IV/responses to the Buddha

Westerners and devotion
developing forms of devotional practice 4.296–300; the transformative effect on a sceptic of bowing to the shrine 11.215;

enthusiasm of American students 4.296; it's a mistake to play down the devotional side of Buddhism 15.550–1, 15.557; the introduction of puja at a Buddhist Society summer school 11.213, 23.151; our need for devotional practice 11.453; reasons for adverse reactions 11.57–8, 13.418, 14.534; ritual in the FWBO 13.415–20, 24.61–2; some think that devotion is childish or superstitious 3.301; we haven't yet evolved our own devotional forms 4.296; warm response 10.216–17, 12.24, 14.534, 15.392

the value of devotion
minimizing its importance betrays Buddhism 26.629–30; devotion to the goal in only some of its forms is scarcely devotion 15.328; its importance 4.297–300, 13.271; the importance of worship in a non-traditional society 1.30; in a sense, the most important element of the spiritual life 2.242–3; it integrates instinct and emotion with understanding 12.24; it reduces the tension between conscious and unconscious 11.212; it provides the driving power of spiritual life 2.243; leaving out devotion closes the door on engagement with the ideal 3.301; the need for distinctively Buddhist rituals in India 9.340; the need for ritual can be transcended 11.206; only a means to an end 7.102; a reminder that the Buddha's compassionate spirit cannot be left out 4.25; to get the emotions flowing freely 4.256; there to be useful, not to use us 3.419; there must be part of your spiritual life in which you feel devotion 4.297; a time-honoured way of raising the level of consciousness 11.119; a way of developing a non-egoistic attitude 7.408

devotional feelings
any approach that expresses genuine devotion is justified 4.305; Buddha images give us an opportunity of developing them 18.431; Christianity's effect on them 14.534; developing through chanting 4.298, 4.305–6; the difference between reverence and worship 15.425–7; the difference between worship and feelingful understanding 19.179; it's a big step to put our trust in these feelings 11.213; an occasion when devotional feelings rise up like a fountain 24.117; repressed in a secular society 14.534; the supra-personal emotions associated with devotion 11.228–9

devotion and bodhisattvas
meditating on their perfections, the devotee hopes to obtain their grace 7.123; preliminary devotional practices 1.405–16; the bodhisattva as exemplar of the devotional life and highest object of devotion 1.395

ASPECTS OF DEVOTIONAL PRACTICE

who practises it and who doesn't
bhikkhus who say puja and worship is just for lay people 11.214, 15.557–8, 19.125; deeply learned people are often also highly devotional 15.390–1; dismissive attitudes to ritual 11.205–6; don't feel under pressure to do it 11.221; exclusion of devotional practice from a Buddhist conference 23.159–60; earthly reflection of an archetypal realm for some, a distraction for others 24.530–1; popular devotional observances 2.219; reasons for devaluation of ritual 11.206–8; the repression of devotional feelings in a secular society 14.534; why newcomers to Buddhism may struggle with it 15.391–2

the effects of devotional practice
it carries us to regions of light and fire 13.418; could an apparition be created by the power of worship? 20.311; genuine devotion dissolves whatever is not genuine 26.35; it may assuage the wandering mind 15.116; it enlists the cooperation of unconscious energies in growth and development 3.41; it strengthens devotion 11.453; losing the effect through unmindful chatter afterwards 5.307–8; it may lead to the arising of insight 5.640; preparing to become receptive to the Perfection of Wisdom 14.437; refining the emotions 11.197–8

PUJA AND RITUAL

introduction
description 9.324, 16.611 (n204); an *action*, which produces great consequences 4.300; the connotations of the word *pūjā* 1.408, 15.389; the consecration of the senses to the attainment of Enlightenment 1.408; difference from Hindu puja 9.481; different people's responses 4.294–7; a foretaste of the Pure Land 11.241; keeping the ideal of Buddhism at the forefront of one's consciousness 4.52–3; *The* FWBO *Puja Book* 11.218, 13.418–19; a kind of *śraddhā bhāvanā* 5.158; outward expression of faith 9.323–4; its powerful effect on the writer John St John 15.392; it needs a touch of magic 18.321; Tantric 1.377; a way of self-surrender 4.294; the words *pūjā* and *vandanā* are more or less interchangeable 11.248–9; why bother with puja? 11.220–1

ritual
an acting out of symbol or myth 11.212; alcohol used in Tibetan ritual 13.25,

22.399; *āmisa-pūja* (worship with material things) 16.568; as preparation for meditation 2.105, 3.340, 4.42–3, 6.xxviii; be cautious about insisting on any particular expression 4.298–300; experimenting with ritual 11.229, 13.292, 13.419–20; Fromm's definition applied to the ritual of Going for Refuge 11.214–15; going through the motions to get into a devotional mood 4.296, 11.242–3, 15.706–7; the importance of aids to devotion 20.259; in Buddhism you do the ritual yourself, and it is demanding 11.210; in ritual we create a specific atmosphere 11.213; it has a spirit of *mettā* and solidarity 11.210; perhaps all ritual works through correspondence of higher and lower 13.292; the qualities of a good ritualist 11.210–12; what is ritual trying to achieve? 11.205

notes on the practice of puja
all times of day are good for pujas 11.225–6; authenticity is the important thing 11.229; doing puja on one's own 11.224–5; doing a reading in the puja 11.280; don't feel under pressure to do puja 11.221; going through a period where you don't experience anything much 11.229; if you do it, do it regularly 11.221; it could be thought of just as a devotional exercise, though this is limited 11.225; it is easy to forget that it is something *you* are doing 11.229; it doesn't call for long faces and a 'dim religious light' 14.523; an elaborate puja keeps one engaged and unselfconscious 15.615; just enjoy it 11.221; everybody present should join in 11.225; making offerings 11.242–4; prostrations in pujas 11.249–50; a puja must be done for or to the Buddha 11.224, 18.321; if you don't feel in the mood, that's the time to do a puja 17.417–18; 'mental puja' 11.224–5; no one can do puja on your behalf 10.217; one is not just in contact with an idea in one's own ordinary mind 18.320; one may bow or prostrate at any appropriate moment 13.416; the quality of chanting 11.227; the role of the person leading the puja 11.226; try to absorb and really feel what you are chanting and saying 18.167; using music in pujas 11.227–9; why a bell is rung at the end of each section 11.226

preparing for a puja
the merits of meditating before or after the puja 11.227; preparing the shrine 11.232–3; dress with care: you are there representing the Sangha jewel 11.233; seating arrangements 11.233–4

Threefold Puja
its composition 11.746 (n107); description of the Three Jewels 2.462; the 'Short Puja' 11.224; 'What the Buddha overcame, we too can overcome' 4.50, 11.293

THE SEVENFOLD PUJA

introduction
descriptions 1.408–14, 1.507–11, 2.719 (n525), 4.45–8; commentary 11.216–94; each section builds on the one before 11.246–7; the effect of listening to a recording 15.437; Sangharakshita's composition of the puja used by Triratna 11.218, 11.235; how should we understand its reference to Buddhas and bodhisattvas? 11.223; its recitation in Triratna 11.376; the Triratna version includes elements of all three *yānas* 11.291; an important and demanding practice 4.49; it has a distinctive atmosphere 11.213; it has a subjective and an objective aspect 11.223; an act of giving, not receiving 11.223–4; the act not of a single person but of the spiritual community 11.224; a microcosm of all our efforts towards Enlightenment 11.223; a *nirmāṇakāya* puja 11.225–6; a sequence of seven devotional moods 11.216; should it include recitation of the bodhisattva precepts? 4.64, 12.405; a wish for a musical setting 11.621

the practice in the Buddhist tradition
derived from Śāntideva's *Bodhicaryāvatāra* 1.406, 1.413, 2.429, 4.45, 11.216, 13.705 (n220); in the *Precious Garland* 17.414–17; supreme worship (*anuttara puja*) 1.406, 2.429; in the *Sūtra of Golden Light* 11.219, 16.267–8, 16.275; Nāgārjuna recommends reciting it three times a day 17.417; performed by the novice bodhisattva 4.179; an esoteric sevenfold puja recited when offering the mandala 13.262–3

practice in the West
considering that mentioning 'lamps encrusted with jewels' is untruthful 11.222; an experiment with composing an English poetic version 11.221; objection that one doesn't literally offer *mandāravas* etc. 11.746 (n107), 24.49; a puja in Germany 24.368

its purposes and effects
an antidote to hatred 2.389; it aids the process of Going for Refuge 11.220; it may restore your enthusiasm for Buddhism 11.220; it refines the emotions through devotion and art 11.204; the preliminary practice of the bodhisattva path 1.406; encouraging the arising of the *bodhicitta*

4.45–9, 4.197, 4.278, 11.216–17, 11.220, 11.284; it isn't a spiritual practice if you're not in tune with it 18.428

practising the puja
get in touch with the spirit of the words 11.222; 'How to approach the Sevenfold Puja' 11.220–30; relate to it as a timeless process 11.219; placing symbols of the *trikāya* on the shrine 11.226; it takes some getting used to 11.221–2; study the text of the puja 11.230

(1) offerings (pūjā)
two translations 11.231–2; the verse sets the scene of refined beauty 11.232–3; saying '*mandārava*' creates an archetypal atmosphere 11.234; as to an honoured guest 1.507–8, 11.237–9; material and mental 1.408; the qualities of incense 11.235–7; we recognize the sublimity of the ideal 4.45

(2) worship (vandanā)
two translations 11.245; 'as many atoms as there are': life as a continuous salutation 11.246; the Buddhas of the Three Eras 11.246; may include hymns of praise 1.407–8; paying respect with the body 1.508, 4.45, 11.246, 11.249–51; places in which the bodhisattvas have been 4.324–5, 11.249; profound obeisance to the Teachers 11.249; *saddharma* 11.246; we see the gulf between us and the ideal 11.246–7

(3) going for refuge (śaraṇa-gamana)
two translations 11.252; the culmination of the practice 4.308–9; the refuge formulas repeated thrice 1.410; the powerful protectors 11.253, 16.288; the Dharma they have ascertained 11.253; the abode of security 11.253–4; the host of bodhisattvas 11.254; commitment to the Three Jewels 1.509, 4.45–6; recitation of the precepts 11.255–8

(4) confession of faults (pāpadeśanā)
two translations 11.259–60; 'the evil that I have heaped up' 11.260–1, 25.75–6; its significance at this stage of the puja 11.260; an observance dating from early Buddhism 1.410–12; a realistic appraisal 4.46–7, 11.260; psychologically important 1.509; the significance of the verse 26.643–4; terrified of suffering 11.263–4; 'What is not good, I shall not do again' 4.332, 4.480–1, 11.264; writing down your confession 16.318–19

(5) rejoicing in merit (puṇyanumodanā)
two translations 11.265–6; the converse of confession of faults 1.412, 11.266–7; encouragement and inspiration 4.47; recollecting the noble lives of others 11.266; rejoicing in the nature of the Bodhisattva and the Buddha 11.269–73; rejoicing in the arising of the *bodhicitta* 11.269; taking delight in good 26.644

(6) entreaty (adhyeṣaṇa) and supplication (yācanā)
two translations 11.274; it's significant that it comes after rejoicing in merits 11.278; it recalls Brahmā Sahāmpati's request to the Buddha 1.412–13, 1.510, 11.275; developing receptivity 11.274–6, 11.278–9; entreat the Buddhas in all the quarters 11.276; the Buddhas don't need to be reminded of their duty 1.413, 4.47; the lamp of the Dharma 11.276; wandering in the suffering of delusion 11.276; the reading that follows this section 11.279–80; the recital of the *Heart Sūtra* 11.280

(7) transference of merit (pariṇāmanā) and self-surrender (atmabhāvādi-parityāgaḥ)
two translations 11.281–2; you give up *all* your merit 11.282, 11.283; 'just as the earth and other elements are serviceable ...' 11.282; that which maintains all beings 11.282–3; at the highest level, the bodhisattva ideal 1.413–14, 4.47–8; for Nāgārjuna the point of the whole practice 17.418; no room for religious individualism 1.510–11; similar verses in Nāgārjuna's *Precious Garland* 17.203–5, 17.415–16; the practice of a young Indian Buddhist 10.lxii–xiii; self-surrender 11.284; a training in egolessness 11.284; concluding mantras 11.288–94

PHYSICAL EXPRESSIONS OF DEVOTION

salutations (vandanā)
añjali salutation 15.669; different people saluted the Buddha in different ways 4.295, 9.337–8, 11.250; expressing reverence with the body can take different forms 1.508, 11.250; gesture of salutation representing the jewel in the lotus 16.179–80; Early Buddhist and Mahāyāna 1.407–8; may be made at any appropriate moment in the puja 13.416; joining the hands at head, throat, and heart 1.514–15, 17.228; the words *pūjā* and *vandanā* are more or less interchangeable 11.248–9

prostrations
of the bodhisattva-to-be 1.407; bringing the body into the practice 13.78; curb pride and make one more receptive to spiritual influences 1.407, 13.416; elaborate prostrations to curb egotism 14.489, 20.353–4; Going for Refuge and Prostration practice, *see* Going for Refuge and Prostration practice; homage by

prostration to the Three Jewels 15.669, 15.672–3; in India prostrations are part of everyday life 15.672; *pañcāṅga-praṇama* in some modern languages 1.478; reverence for the ideal 3.63–4; prostrating from Lhasa to Bodh Gaya 13.79, 19.335; lay followers prostrating to *bhikkhus* 2.214, 19.490; *bhikkhus* teaching new Buddhists to prostrate to them 2.458; different cultural responses 11.249–51; Theravādin remonstrations about prostrating 'in the wrong way' 21.301–2

see also
Hindu worship, *see under* Hinduism; offerings; rituals as ends in themselves, *see under* ten fetters/third fetter; Sangharakshita's devotion, *see under* Sangharakshita V/personal practice; stupa worship, *see under* stupa; Tantric ritual, *see under* Tantric Buddhism; worship of the bodhi tree, *see under* bodhi tree; worship of the book, *see under* book; worship of a dog's tooth, *see under* parables and stories; worship of the Buddha's footprint, *see śripāda*; worshipping the Buddha, *see under* Buddha IV/responses

dew 'The dewdrop slips into the shining sea' 4.80; life is a dream, a cloud, a drop of dew 25.390; the White Rose bright with morning dew 25.226

Dewsay (Hindu festival) 21.100–2

Dey, Mukul Chandra 21.402

Dhamma Mamaka v22

Dhamma Revolution

history
the background to the revolution 10.186–7; eye-witnesses 10.xxxv–xxxix; meditation the seed 9.202–3; started in Nagpur 10.376–7

its nature
characteristics 9.411–13; the aim was a complete transformation, individual and collective 10.389; cooperation is the foundation stone 10.398; difference from 'conversion to the Dhamma' 9.407–8, 9.508; entirely non-violent 9.411, 26.651; involves radical change in every aspect of life 6.614, 9.410, 9.511, 10.25; it took place suddenly 9.411; related to the idea of the new society 2.516

significance
effect on India as a whole 9.428–9, 9.431–2; it has made a total revolution in the lives of millions of people 9.410, 10.14; it must not be limited to one group 10.125; it shows that a whole society can change through a spiritual vision 10.315; the most important revolution of the 20th century 10.339; of great human as well as religious and sociological interest 10.185–6; a revolution that has succeeded 9.431, 10.19; the significance of the revolution 10.379; significance for the world 9.431, 10.379; the turning of the tide of the revival of Buddhism in India 8.234–6, 10.93–4

see also
Dalits; Dr Ambedkar's role, *see* Ambedkar

Dhammacakkappavattana Sutta *see under Saṃyutta Nikāya*/famous *suttas*

dhammacariyā *see dharmacarya*

Dhammachari/ni *see under* Triratna III/what is the Order?/nomenclature

Dhammadāyāda Sutta *see under Majjhima Nikāya*

Dhammadiksha (conversion) explanation 9.544–5; 'initiation into the Dharma' (Ambedkar) 9.133; means changing your whole life 9.415–16; means Going for Refuge 9.392, 9.411, 9.474; reluctance to take it arising from confusion about the word *dharma* 10.351; significance 9.428, 9.509; you cannot refuse to take it and call yourself a follower of Dr Ambedkar 10.343

Dhammadinnā (Buddha's disciple) on the Refuge Tree 13.209; teaching on *pratītya-samutpāda* 1.117–18, 3.68, 7.198–9, 7.494, 26.175

Dhammadinna, Dharmacharini brief introduction 24.650 (n212); in the early days of the FWBO 11.729; introduction to *The FWBO Puja Book* 13.418; member of the Preceptors' College 12.597, 12.631; on the *Udāna* seminar 10.421–2; on retreat at Padmaloka 24.172

dhammadūta 9.332–3

Dhammajoti, Bhikkhu v21, v23

dhammakathā *see dharmakathā*

Dhammaloka (Sinhalese monk in India) v21

Dhammaloka (Sinhalese monk in London) v23

Dhammaloka, Dharmachari v24

Dhammaloka, Ven. (Bombay) 10.123

Dhammamegha, Dharmacharini 17.xv

Dhammamitra *see under* Triratna II/the people involved

Dhammananda, Ven. H. 10.123, 10.335

Dhammapada

INTRODUCTION TO THE TEXT

introduction
brief account 12.31–2, 14.52–3; its freshness and relevance 25.30–1

history
part of the *gātha*, one of the nine *aṅgas* of the Pāli canon 14.24; one of the older portions of the Pāli canon 15.347; Prakrit and Sanskrit versions 15.4; a section of the *Dhammapada* in the *Mahāvastu* 14.71; Jain equivalent 20.449; *Udānavarga* (Sanskrit version), *see Udānavarga*; possible link with the *Bodhicaryāvatāra* 4.378; compared to the *Diamond Sūtra* 10.164; 'Chinese' *Dharmapada* 9.111, 10.66–7, 14.52, 15.4; Dr Ambedkar's anthology 9.145, 10.66; verses read to the workers on a tea estate 22.22; among three texts most popular with Western Buddhists 14.268–9

comments on the text
can hardly be accused of a tendency to sensuality 2.124; greatly needed by the modern world 15.8; has an honoured place in world literature 14.53, 15.5; inspiration and guidance from the text 2.552, 15.5; it contains as much as we need to know to progress towards Enlightenment 15.5; its teachings are literal truth, to be engraved on our hearts in letters of gold – or fire 26.45; not a Buddhist 'gospel' (Ambedkar) 9.109; 'not fastened around a story' (Ambedkar) 9.110, 10.66; the Pāli text is pungent and pointed 15.348; one could see the whole truth in a verse of the *Dhammapada* 16.59; the verses are fresh, appropriate, relevant, as though spoken yesterday 25.30–1

translations
assessment of different translations 15.347–8; Dr N. K. Bhagwat's edition, which Sangharakshita carried with him in India 22.133–4; Buddharakkhita's translation 8.385–6; first translation into a Western language (Latin) 12.31–2, 14.53, 15.4; list of translations and commentaries 15.59; many English translations 14.53; Nepali translation 8.660, 21.238–9; Russian translation 23.158; the title could be translated 'footprints of the Dhamma' 25.30

Sangharakshita and the Dhammapada
buys a copy in the first Buddhist temple he ever saw (1944) 15.5, 20.115; tries to learn the text by heart 15.5–6, 20.328–9; studies the text with Bhikkhu Kashyap 15.6, 20.445, 21.9; gives a training course on the text to illiterate workers in Poona (1956) 10.179, 15.6; absorbs the beauty of a recording made under Dr Ambedkar's direction 15.436; conducts seminars in the 1970s and 80s 15.6; the experience of translating the text 15.xiii–xiv, 23.469, 25.30–1; the process of translating: 'a directness and sense of urgency' 15.xiv–vi, 15.6–7; translation decisions 15.xiv, 15.7–8; full translation 15.9–56

THE TEXT
Verse numbers are displayed thus (1)

introduction
glimpses of the *bhikṣu* sangha 2.18; poetry 9.226; structure of text 9.271; use of the term *anagārika* 7.477

brahmins
the Buddha's insistence that you are only a brahmin if you act like one 2.701–2 (n383); *bhikkhu* and brahmin, terms used almost interchangeably 16.153, 16.264–5; *brāhmaṇa*, *samaṇa*, and *bhikkhu* 10.479, 10.554, 15.7–8; the use of the word brahmin 10.430, 15.7–8

chapter 1, 'pairs'
introduction 9.271–2; full text 15.9–11; (1) Experiences are preceded by mind, led by mind, produced by mind: the basis of Buddhist ethics 3.317, 7.138, 7.270; the epigraph of *Buddha Mind* 11.3; the germ of the doctrine set forth in Mahāyāna *sūtras* 2.67; everything depends on mind 10.145; it is clear that the starting-point of Buddhism is the mind 11.20; the importance of the mental state over the action 17.186; 'Mind is the first of things' 12.466; there is a connection between our mind and the nature of our future life 17.473; the word translated 'experiences' is *dhammas* 15.422; (2) If one acts with a pure mind, one will experience happiness 9.291; (5) Hatred ceases only by non-hatred: the eternal law 3.159, 9.314–15, 15.505–6: have we found this out from our own experience? 18.166; the importance of making distinctions 9.271; a reminder in Edith Cavell's words: 'Patriotism is not enough …' 26.590; the Sangha's message to rulers and politicians 7.440; a teaching of explicit meaning 11.718–19, 15.227, 16.579–80; (6) Others do not realize that we are all heading for death 10.xlvii, 10.323, 18.563, 19.104, 23.92; (7) As the wind blows down a weak tree, so Māra overthrows one … 14.587; (10) He is worthy of the yellow robe who has made an end to all impurity 7.566–7 (n117); (11) antithesis between *sāra* and *asāra*, 'real' and

'unreal' 10.450; (**12**) 'Those who, having known the real as the real ...' 13.654

chapter 2, 'mindfulness'
full text 15.11–12; heedfulness is its theme 1.439; (**21**) Mindfulness is the way to immortality 7.118, 17.581, 26.473; (**25**) An island that no flood can overwhelm 15.580; (**29**) The wise man forges ahead 8.25–6, 9.367

chapter 3, 'the mind'
full text 15.13–14; (**33**) The trembling, unsteady mind 10.226, 18.231; (**34**) A fish floundering on the bank 18.542, 22.223; (**40**) The Dharma-farer destroys the hosts of Māra with the sword of wisdom 3.54; (**42**) Whatever foe might do to foe ... 10.534

chapter 4, 'flowers'
full text 15.14–15; (**49**) Gathering alms in the village as the bee collects honey from the flower 3.491–4, 3.589, 21.13; (**54–6**) The fragrance of ... aromatic resin ... 6.xxviii; (**58**) As pink lotuses ... spring from ... rubbish 10.145, 18.583

chapter 5, 'the spiritually immature'
full text 15.15–17; translation of *bāla* 15.xv–xvi, 15.8, 15.384–5, 17.324; (**61**) There is no companionship with the spiritually immature 10.650; (**62**) Even his self is not his own. How then a son? How wealth?: attachment to individuality 10.455; in the ultimate analysis we have no self 1.173; nothing in the whole world is yours 18.219; regarding others as possessions 10.490; selfishness 10.146, 15.384–5; (**63**) The spiritually immature person who recognizes his immaturity ... 15.xv–xvi; (**64**) The spoon does not detect the taste of soup 18.516; (**65**) The wise man can detect the flavour of the Dharma as the tongue detects the taste of soup 10.568; (**75**) One path leads to worldly prosperity, quite another to Nibbāna 7.171–2

chapter 6, 'the spiritually mature'
full text 15.17–19; translation of *paṇḍita* 15.8, 17.324; (**80**) The spiritually mature discipline themselves 15.493, 17.529; (**87**) Forsaking dark ways, the spiritually mature person cultivates the bright 19.455

chapter 7, 'the worthy'
full text 15.19–20; (**96**) His mind becomes peaceful, so also his speech and deeds 7.376

chapter 8, 'the thousands'
full text 15.20–22; a Nāgārjuna verse reminiscent of this chapter 17.185–6; (**100**) Better than a thousand meaningless words... : commentary 12.32–8; the Buddhist attitude towards mere number 8.198; the meaningful words of the *Dhammapada* itself 15.5; Perfect Speech 3.282–3; (**103**) He who conquers himself: the battlefield of the spiritual life 1.112, 3.294, 3.502: the Buddha as the Conqueror 3.48, 12.529; conquering himself the disciple conquers the universe 1.178–9; self-conquest 13.351; true spiritual victory 3.382

chapter 9, 'evil'
full text 15.22–3; Sangharakshita's commentary 15.348–77; (**116**) Be quick to do what is (morally) beautiful 15.348–53, 15.359; (**117**) Should a man (once) do evil, let him not make a habit of it 15.353–4, 15.360; (**118**) Should a man (once) do good, let him make a habit of it 15.355–7, 15.360; (**119–20**) As long as it bears no fruit ... 15.357–62; (**121**) Do not underestimate evil 15.362, 17.283; (**122**) Drop by drop, a man fills himself with good 11.397, 15.362–6, 18.411; (**123**) As a merchant (travelling) with a small caravan ... 15.366–7; (**124**) If one has no wound in one's hand one may (safely) handle poison 15.367–70; (**125**) Whoever offends against an innocent man ... 15.371–3; (**126**) Those who are free from defilements become utterly 'Cool' ('Nirvānized'): difficulty of translating 15.373–4; a typical idiom of Pāli Buddhism 10.515; the verb *parinibbanti* 10.614–15, 19.204; (**127**) Not in the sky, nor in the ... sea ... can one escape the fruits of one's evil deeds: the bitter harvest of the seeds one has sown 7.221; the consequences of actions are inescapable 8.144; examples from English literature 15.374–6; the law of karma does not forgive 13.578; (**128**) Not in the sky, nor in the ... sea ... can one escape [death] 15.376–7

chapter 10, 'punishment'
full text 15.23–5; (**129**) Neither kill nor cause to kill 2.359; (**131**) He who, seeking his own happiness, strikes with a stick beings who also long for happiness 8.257; (**133**) Do not speak roughly to anyone 2.374–5; (**142**) Even though a man be richly attired ... living a holy life, he is a brāhmaṇa: the Buddha did not identify spiritual life with monasticism 1.244, 2.203, 2.432, 2.451, 23.188; what a *bhikkhu* is 2.591, 10.554

chapter 11, 'decay'
full text 15.25–6; (**145**) The spiritually mature discipline themselves 15.493;

(146) What mirth can there be ... when all the time (everything) is blazing? 15.xiv–xv; (153–4) Housebuilder, I have seen you now: the Buddha's first utterance to himself 11.411–12, 15.745 (n11); the Buddha's song of victory 22.190; the Buddha is addressing his own ignorance 18.269; the cessation of suffering 1.113–14; the world is the illusory creation of an illusory self 17.328–9

chapter 12, 'self'
full text 15.26–7; (160) Don't rely on anyone outside yourself 12.97; (161) The evil done by oneself crushes oneself 7.171; (165) No one can purify another: Buddhism is a do-it-yourself religion 3.14, 10.346, 12.135; a favourite text of modern Theravādins 1.199; one can only advise 10.136

chapter 13, 'the world'
full text 15.27–8; (168) Get up! Don't be heedless! 18.390; The *dhammacāri* lives happily, (both) in this world and in the world beyond 2.491; (175) the 'path of the sun' 15.28, 15.745 (n12), 25.182–3; (176) There is no wrong that cannot be committed by a lying person 2.376; (178) Better is the fruit of entering the Stream than sole sovereignty over the earth 2.140

chapter 14, 'the Enlightened One'
full text 15.29–30; (179) That Enlightened One whose victory is irreversible 4.182–3; By what track will you lead him (astray), the Trackless One? 3.143, 4.21, 7.73; (182) Difficult is the attainment of the human state 3.484, 7.170, 13.139; (183) Cease to do evil, learn to do good, purify the heart: also found in the *Dīgha Nikāya* 2.187; before thinking about doing good, we could stop doing mischief 18.342; expressed in a statement by Milarepa 18.512; the occasion on which the Buddha said these words 22.93–4; as *prātimokṣa* 2.187, 10.560; Dudjom Rimpoche connects this verse with the Vajrasattva practice 5.555–6; spoken by the sage to the emperor 1.492–3, 3.241–2, 7.134, 7.292, 18.360; the starting point of the Abhidharma 17.435–6, 17.549; we must cease to do evil before we learn to do good 1.145, 7.183; (184) Forbearance (or patience) is the greatest asceticism 4.121–2, 4.422; (185) Not to speak evil, not to injure ... 10.538; (188) Many people, out of fear, flee for refuge to sacred hills ... 8.304, 13.194; (190–2) He who seeks refuge in the Buddha, in the Dharma, and the Sangha ... 8.305; (194) Happy is the birth of the Buddhas 22.239; The blaze of spiritual practice of those on the same path is happy or blessed 3.xi, 3.402

chapter 15, 'happiness'
full text 15.31–2; (197–200) Happily indeed we live: Buddhism doesn't require you to give up bliss 19.379; chanting these verses from our heart for world peace 12.362; a characteristic of the Buddhist is happiness 10.198, 10.202, 19.426; fewness of possessions 2.605–6; 'like the Gods of Sonant Light' 8.440; the spiritual life is indeed happy, but are you living it? 15.360; verses recited to the Śākyans and Koliyans after their conflict was ended 12.362; (200) Feeders on rapture shall we be 18.50; (204) Contentment is the greatest wealth 1.152, 18.96; Nirvāṇa is the highest bliss, *nibbāṇaṃ paramaṃ sukhaṃ*: a contrast to the idea of a cool, emotionally astringent Nirvāṇa 18.90; not bliss as we understand it 2.124, 3.235, 11.85–6, 19.424; a state to which the whole creation is tending 7.68–9, 7.120; (207) The meeting of friends to hear about the Dharma is a very pleasant thing 10.251

chapter 16, 'affections'
full text 15.32–3; (213) From affection is born grief 1.158

chapter 17, 'anger'
full text 15.33–4; it is axiomatic that hatred is to be rejected 8.585; (223) Overcome anger with non-anger 7.173

chapter 18, 'stains'
full text 15.35–7; (243) Worst of all stains is the stain of ignorance 7.126

chapter 19, 'the man of principle'
full text 15.37–9; translation of *dhammaṭṭha* as 'man of principle' 15.8

chapter 20, 'the way'
full text 15.39–40; (275) Walking this path you shall make an end of suffering 4.644; (276) You yourself must make the effort. The Buddhas only show the way: the Buddha shows the way, but you must tread it 3.163, 10.35, 10.247, 12.135; the fact that the Buddha points the way makes a great difference 15.547–8; perhaps showing the way is all the Buddha can do 15.267; we are our own saviour 10.141, 13.577; we have to make the effort 12.622; you have to decide for yourself 9.475, 15.546; (277–9) Impermanent are all component things: *lakṣaṇas* 1.171, 2.81–2, 3.657 (n200), 9.562 (n246); (279) All things are devoid of unchanging selfhood 2.81–2, 3.159; (285) Cut off your sticky affection 1.158, 4.526, 4.711 (n343); (286) Here shall I pass the monsoon, here shall

I dwell during winter ... thus reflects the fool 7.171

chapter 21, 'the miscellaneous'
full text 15.41–2; (294) Having killed mother and father, the brāhmaṇa goes blameless 11.719, 15.41, 16.580; (295) Having slain ... two learned kings ... and having killed a tiger 15.41

chapter 22, 'the woeful state'
full text 15.42–4

chapter 23, 'the elephant'
full text 15.44–5; (320) I shall patiently endure abuse, as an elephant in battle endures the arrow 9.366; (330) Live alone and do no evil 7.150

chapter 24, 'craving'
full text 15.46–8; (339) the thirty-six streams of craving 15.46, 15.746 (n22); (348) Renounce what lies in the future, give up that which is past ... 7.285, 13.468, 25.22; (353) Whom should I point out as my teacher? 15.48, 15.746 (n23); (354) The gift of the Dharma surpasses all gifts 1.431, 2.212, 3.369, 3.604, 8.267; Delight in the Dharma surpasses all delights 25.30

chapter 25, 'the almsman'
full text 15.49–51; 2.625–7; (362) a *bhikkhu* has control over his hands and feet 20.122; (370) Cut away five, abandon five 15.50, 15.746 (n24)

chapter 26, 'the brāhmaṇa'
full text 15.51–6; (383) Exert yourself and cut off the stream 15.51, 15.746 (n24); (391) I call him a brāhmaṇa by whom no evil is done ... 13.712 (n278); (393) Not by family or birth does one become a brāhmaṇa 7.226; He in who there exists both truth and principle ... he is a brāhmaṇa 10.458, 10.708 (n382), 14.57; (417) human and celestial bonds 15.55, 15.746 (n27)

Dhammapada Commentary (*Buddhist Legends*, trans. Burlingame) the battle of the Śākyans and the Koliyans over water 7.238, 9.140, 10.260, 12.338–9, 12.362; the Buddha begs in the streets of Kapilavastu 13.461; the Buddha's descent to earth down a jewelled staircase or ladder 11.15, 11.30, 12.185, 13.586; Cūḷapanthaka, who attained arhantship though he couldn't memorize one Dharma verse 8.119; kept separate from the verses 10.66; the story of Devadatta 3.638–9 (n71); Moggallāna's murder 4.662 (n19); parallel story to the parable of the sower 13.724–5 (n442); the Śākyans massacred by Viḍūḍabha, King of Kosala 12.357, 12.729 (n236); the story of Nanda 3.557–8, 12.614–15, 14.310, 23.317; the story of Rāhula 16.627 (n346); the story of Vakkali 3.150; the twin miracle 4.16, 10.37, 10.654, 12.183, 14.111, 16.528

Dhammaratana, Bhikkhu (Calcutta) 8.635

Dhammaratana, U (Sinhalese monk) general entries v8, v21, v22, v23, v24; brief introduction 24.665 (n285); *Buddha and Caste System* 8.359–60; General Secretary of the Maha Bodhi Society 11.562

Dhammarati, Dharmachari brief introduction 24.638–9 (n158, n159); book designer 2.752 (n752), 14.xx, 14.320; in Glasgow 24.136–7; president of FWBO centres 12.631

dhammas *see dharmas*

***Dhammasahayak* (Friend) of Triratna** 9.308, 9.545, 10.268, 11.178, 11.391

dhammasākacchā (discussion about the Dharma) 15.443–4

Dhammasaṅgaṇi (*A Manual of Buddhist Ethics*) introduction 14.78–9; connotations of wisdom 17.130–1; different types of karma 2.70; the foundation of the Abhidharma 14.78; synonyms for *vīrya* 1.439

Dhamma-shibirs *see* retreats

Dhammāsoka 7.424

dhammaṭṭha (man of principle) 15.8

Dhamma-Vinaya *see Dharma-Vinaya*

Dhammawara, Venerable Veera (Cambodian monk) 22.231

Dhammika (in the *Theragātha*) 10.718 (n453)

Dhammika, S. 23.xvii

dhana (or *dhānā*, riches or grain) 16.409

Dhanapala, D. B. (Sri Lankan art historian) 7.445, 7.616 (n488)

Dhanaskuti, India 20.229

Dhaniya (potter) 9.142

dhāraṇī etymology 16.369; contrasted with mantras 16.497; the *dhāraṇīs* the bodhisattva will attain 14.186–7; *dhāraṇis* to protect the *White Lotus Sūtra* 14.130; generally taught to the bodhisattva by benevolent deities 1.449; the Great Dhāraṇī recited by Mañjuśrī 13.359–60; importance in Tantric Buddhism 1.374; as magic spell 2.216; as skilful means 1.449, 16.496–7; in the *Sūtra of Golden Light*

14.245, 16.369; a touch of magic 16.497; very short Perfection of Wisdom texts 1.301, 2.216, 14.154, 14.347; *see also* mantras

Dhardo Rimpoche

HIS LIFE

life story
brief introduction 16.611–12 (n208), 17.707 (n18); born in Dhartsendo, on the border between Tibet and China 12.431, 22.542; his mother gave him quite a lot of trouble 12.431; when he was young he could remember his past lives 12.431–2, 12.688; a monk of the Gelug school 22.419, 23.382; he was Nyingmapa, but studied at Gelugpa colleges 12.432, 22.542; he was told he was an incarnate lama and acted accordingly 14.484–5; his brief stay at a rigorous Tantric college 13.48; a dispute from his time at Bodh Gaya 21.451–3, 22.419–20; at Ghoom monastery 21.309; he moves to the Old Bhutan Palace in Kalimpong 22.192, 22.420; he was often consulted by Western scholars 12.435–6; preceptor of the 'French nun' (ordained as Thupten Chhokyi) 22.184, 22.424–7; admired by Mr Chen 22.541; Tibetan officials 12.435, 22.499; photographs 21.452, 22.343, 22.345, 22.421, 23.380

Indo-Tibetan Buddhist Cultural Institute (ITBCI)
brief introduction 4.690 (n214), 12.733–4 (n283); a colourful account 22.530; he wanted the children to learn that actions have consequences 15.358; initial plans 22.192; Dhardo loved the school and its pupils 12.453; founded in 1954 12.452; its new home near the bazaar in Kalimpong 23.381; Sangharakshita's help with the Institute 4.253, 12.433, 22.422–3, 23.380; Terry takes photographs at the school 23.381; threatened by Tibetan officials 22.499; what the school day was like 12.453

his death and commemorations
death 2.739 (n661), 12.435, 24.381–2; video of his funeral 24.391; the first anniversary of his death 12.452, 24.402; the enshrining of his ashes at Sudarshanaloka, New Zealand 24.513–14; stupa at Padmaloka 25.457; stupa at Guhyaloka 26.455; a banner of victory for him 10.408–9; biography by Suvajra 12.435; 'The Guru of Dharsendo' (poem) 25.392; 'Rejoicing in the Merits of Dhardo Rimpoche' (poem) 12.459–60

his character
a completely mindful and compassionate person 11.666; bodhisattva-like qualities 12.662; goodwill, candour, and integrity 21.453; sense of humour 12.435–6, 22.424; he manifested the six perfections 22.543; his almost supernatural mindfulness 12.433–4, 22.339–40, 22.424; his appearance 22.421; kind and generous 22.339, 22.424, 23.380–1; rather reserved 22.339; a living embodiment of the bodhisattva ideal 2.585, 23.18, 26.234; a very good public speaker 22.550–1; a very good ritualist 11.211–12; 'a very human kind of incarnate lama' 21.309

anecdotes and details of his life
he had a mynah bird who would recite *oṃ maṇi padme hūṃ* 12.96, 22.522; he had a reputation for being good at fortune-telling 19.268; he helped to alleviate a black magic attack 22.523; he was very fond of photography 12.434; his pets 22.522, 26.231; how he handled a scholar's question about the highest tantra 12.436

his teachings and thoughts
'Cherish the doctrine. Live united. Radiate love.' 12.453–9, 25.457; he didn't write books or give formal lectures 12.452; his view that very few *tulkus* are really incarnate bodhisattvas 17.412; if you don't know what to do, do something to help others 25.114; things like hydroelectric dams don't solve the problem of human suffering 22.331; on Nirvāṇa 26.368; teachings on Going for Refuge 2.435–6

RELATIONSHIP WITH SANGHARAKSHITA

first meetings
brief introduction to their connection 12.452, 22.542–3, 23.379–81; Dhardo saw him for the first time at Bodh Gaya 12.432, 12.452, 21.453, 22.419, 22.542; first meeting in Kalimpong 21.451–3, 22.137, 22.420; inviting Dhardo to give a

talk at the Vaiśākha Purṇimā celebrations 22.1379; contact through work on *The Path of the Buddha* 2.434–6, 12.432–3

together in Kalimpong
celebration of festivals 8.658, 22.237–9; collaboration over how best to help the 'French nun' 22.194–5, 22.427; consecration of a Buddha image 21.307–9; Dhardo blesses the Triyana Vardhana Vihara 23.381; help with the Indo-Tibetan Cultural Institute 4.253, 12.433, 22.192; Dhardo blesses Sangharakshita's new residence 22.192–3; they collaborate to prevent violence at the Vaiśākha Pūrṇimā festival 22.235–6; he gives Sangharakshita a dog 22.522; travelling together with 'Eminent Buddhists' 12.433–4, 22.338–47, 22.423–4, 23.380; taking a Tibetan novice as a helper on Dhardo's advice 22.521; they speak against Chinese aggression 12.434–5, 22.548–50; Sangharakshita and Terry visit (1966) 23.381–4

working on translations together
Tharpe Delam 2.443, 22.474; concluding prayer of the guru yoga 13.219–20; an esoteric sevenfold puja recited when offering the mandala 13.262–3; mandala offering verse 17.1; invocation to the wrathful deities 17.317–18; White Tārā *sādhana* 7.1, 22.562, 23.382

friend and teacher
Dhardo instructs Sangharakshita in the *Guhyasamāja Tantra* 22.234–5; a dream of jewels and Dhardo Rimpoche 23.110; 'I came into contact with his mind and his deep understanding of the Dharma' 12.433; 'I never knew what his personal name was' 25.92; shared language 22.421–2; confession 16.274; gratitude 4.253; bodhisattva ordination 2.455–6, 12.435, 13.587, 22.420, 22.541–4, 23.18; White Tārā initiation 12.435, 12.662, 22.420; Dhardo explained the *tummo* heat practice 19.570; consulting Dhardo about returning to England 11.519, 23.385; Dhardo's parting gifts 23.398; 'I could never really be parted from him' 23.398; 'I was to be in contact with him, in a sense, for the rest of my life' 21.453; inspired by him 11.666; looking up to him 26.629

Dharma (Dhamma)

contents for this section
(I) what is the Dharma?: what does the word 'Dharma' mean? – the nature of the Dharma; (II) teachings and practices: doctrines and teachings – approaching the Dharma – emotional responses – knowledge, understanding, reason – misunderstandings and misrepresentations – practising the Dharma; (III) teaching and learning the Dharma: communicating the Dharma – methods of communicating the Dharma – Dharma teachers

(I) What is the Dharma?

what does the word 'dharma' mean?

introduction
the distinction between 'Buddhism' and 'the Dharma' 13.401, 14.435–6, 26.159; it probably has more meanings than any other term in Buddhism 7.492–3; Dhamma or Dharma? – complexities in India 9.537–8; key word of Buddhism 1.97; in Buddhism and Hinduism 3.158, 9.18, 9.100–1, 9.266, 9.482; called *karmavāda* by the Buddha's contemporaries 7.120; *chös* the standard translation into Tibetan 13.12–13; Norm or normative as (unsuccessful) translation of 'Dharma' 5.175, 9.538, 12.112, 15.255

etymology and definitions
etymology: 'to support, to bear' 1.28, 1.99, 12.501, 15.630–1; literal interpretation 1.251; list of definitions 1.97–8, 3.158–60, 3.393–4, 15.501; two principal meanings: (1) law, truth, reality, (2) the teaching of the Buddha 12.454; in Sanskrit you can't use capitals to distinguish between meanings 14.441–2, 14.498; both the Reality the Buddha experienced and his expression of it 3.158; cosmic (or eternal) law 3.159, 8.201–2, 12.501, 15.505–6, 15.631, 16.84; duty is one meaning of the word 7.278, 13.447; the real truth 3.394–5; the word has much in common with the word 'principle' 2.339

the nature of the dharma

briefly put
a current of spiritual energy 12.14; a grid (pattern) that frees you from grids 19.241; it can be applied to all people whatsoever 7.158; it can be practised by a beginner 17.159; it can be truly understood only by means of transcendental awareness 16.582; it is capable of assuming a thousand forms 1.63; it is fresh, alive 25.30–1; it is to be realized in every fibre of one's being 17.158–9; it constantly changes but remains the same 9.452, 9.453; it has the taste of freedom, *see under Udāna*/great ocean; it poses a threat to the ego 17.337; it quenches our thirst 9.453; elusive 14.257; frightening 14.566–7, 17.324; its awe-inspiring perspective 3.17; its essence can be contained in a single verse 18.495; its principles are few, and can be explained

in a few pages 7.333; its true nature can only be comprehended by experience 10.568; its true nature is your own nature 14.588; a living spiritual force 14.342, 17.159, 25.197; overwhelming 9.247; pragmatic 7.50, 7.69, 7.434; 'profound and hard to see' 1.90–1, 3.175, 3.181, 17.324; morality is its essence 9.100, 9.425; probably closer to poetry than science 14.549; 'a stream of tendency making for Enlightenment' 15.631–2, 15.636; sublime 14.471–2, 14.474; transcendental psychotherapy 16.193; what is its essence? 2.54–7

what is its purpose?
to awaken us to the reality of our dormant Buddha nature 7.313; the eradication of the three roots 7.221–2, 7.256; its goal is *bodhi* 9.452; a means of entrance to ultimate truth 16.542; it is simply the means to Enlightenment 1.63, 7.256–7, 7.520; to help us see ourselves more clearly 17.342; it helps us to change 9.373–4, 9.525–6; it purifies us 9.452; to inculcate aversion to, and consequent renunciation of, the *saṃsāra* 1.124; to make us aware of reality 26.361; two things: the goal and the path 11.385; whatever helps the individual grow 3.15, 3.167–8, 8.566, 9.198, 9.249–50, 9.474, 10.211–13, 10.227, 10.567, 11.365–9, 12.369

further poetic and mysterious descriptions
all statements about it are provisional 3.169; *anattā* pervades every particle of it 7.232; at a certain level, poetry and the Dharma are the same thing 21.78–9, 26.393; the Buddha's Enlightenment objectified and therefore falsified 26.43; the Dharma of words and speculation is the same as the Dharma of realization 19.88; the Dharma on which the Buddha depends is a mystery to the unenlightened 26.631–2; the eight wonderful qualities of the *Dharma-Vinaya*, *see under Udāna*/the great ocean; a force that makes possible your skilful activities 15.631; friendship *is* the Dharma 3.575, 11.700; it says the state of consciousness in which things seem separate is illusory 7.299; it exists only to the extent that it is practised and realized 16.576; it is embodied primarily in things you actually do 11.370; it presents itself to human understanding under a double aspect 1.122–3; terrifying to worldly people, awe-inspiring to bodhisattvas, beautiful to the Buddha 14.474; there needs to be some element of it that is not 'relevant' at all 14.481; transcendental cognition is conterminous with the whole Dharma 2.127; the truth is the whole (as per Hegel) 2.50; to people immersed in worldly states of mind, it will appear negative 26.44; to 'realize' the Dharma and to 'see' the Buddha are the same thing 1.251; we can't fully understand any of it unless we understand the whole of it 16.4–5; the whole of the Dharma is a skilful means 16.497; without a pinch of it, everything else is flavourless 10.568; the words that make it up hint at a certain kind of reality 19.452

more practical descriptions
above all it is something to be practised 10.247; the Buddha's conception of it was positive growth 3.15–16; *Buddhavacana* and Buddhadharma are inseparable 14.266; the conceptual and verbal formulation of the Buddha's Enlightenment 8.232; feeling through words, concepts, and images that which gives life to them all 16.126; a means to an end 1.265, 2.59, 7.244, 7.433, 7.520, 10.141; the practical usefulness of the Dharma 7.228, 17.106, 18.375–7; the process of the higher evolution 15.632; it can only be given, not bought 18.113, 18.188; it crystallizes into a system of methods and teachings we call Buddhism 14.434–6; it finds expression in many formulations 15.80–1; its starting point is the mind 11.20; the sum total of insights and experiences conducive to Enlightenment 11.19–20; that which is profitable to oneself as well as to others 7.256; a transcription into conceptual symbols of the Buddha's ineffable experience 7.309; truth as communicated in a teaching from the Enlightened mind 11.364–5; the underlying principle of all paths 1.51; without the ten precepts it could not exist 2.318, 2.395, 13.444

traditional descriptions
what the Buddha says the Dharma is 11.364–6; Dr Ambedkar's six definitions 9.287–9; Dr Ambedkar's threefold classification 9.142–4, 10.351; 'Bitter in the mouth but sweet in the stomach' 18.133; Buddhaghosa's very broad definition 15.630–1, 15.646; lovely in the beginning, lovely in the middle, and lovely at the end 1.33, 2.23, 10.264; traditionally said to consist of 84,000 teachings 12.313

the Dharma in images and metaphors
analogy with the law of gravity 15.631–2; a bird, the two wings wisdom and compassion 3.355, 3.365, 9.231, 16.14–15; the Dharma jewel represented by a book on the shrine 16.59; as difficult to grasp

rightly as a water snake 1.78, 18.180; every drop precious, like water in the desert 9.291; a golden net symbolizing its interconnectedness 25.142–3; 'Hold fast to the Dharma as a lamp' 2.28, 9.306; inexhaustible reservoir 14.xvii; the lamp of the Dharma 7.332, 11.276, 12.674–5; like an invisible perfume in a musty chamber 1.22; like a mighty spreading tree 1.63, 1.394; like a stream or river 9.451–3, 9.455–8, 14.539; medicine 16.192, 16.201–2, 26.645; nectar (*amṛta*) 10.231, 16.382; an ocean 8.599, 11.39–52; a shoreless ocean, alive with light and colour 11.43; our picture of the Dharma must not be a sharp silhouette from one point of view 1.31; the rain of the Dharma 3.314, 10.218, 12.511, 12.516–17, 25.156; a raft, *see* raft; the seed of the Dharma 1.57, 1.63; tie the mad elephant of the mind to the pillar of the Dharma 4.384–5; a work of art that ranges up and down the whole gamut of colours 1.31

what the Dharma is not
the Buddha made it clear what the Dharma is not, as well as what it is 7.382–3; in many ways the Dharma is opposed to aspects of modern thinking and belief 12.679; not to be identified with any one formulation 2.293–4; not infallible 9.97; not the development of any previous teaching 1.56; not fixed, but its proceeding in a certain way is fixed 16.84; not a product of the 6th century BCE, but comes from the beginningless past 7.342; not speculative philosophy or a set of theories 7.256; not the source of answers to what are really scientific questions 8.586–8; not just abstract ideas and lists, but *alive* 1.56, 2.59–61, 2.291, 9.247, 10.218, 14.98; not a vague, general process, but specific action 11.370, 12.280–1, 15.83; not a way among ways, but The Way 1.51

the Buddha and the Dharma
he set the wheel of the Dharma rolling in Sarnath 1.175; he did not speak *about* the Dharma, but simply spoke Dharma 17.159; his followers are 'heirs of the Dharma, not heirs of worldly things' 1.236, 2.138, 15.155; he discovered, or rediscovered, the Dharma 1.53–5, 3.4, 3.18, 7.254, 12.501, 19.313; 'He who would worship me, let him follow my teaching' 11.452–3, 13.146; 'He who sees the Dharma sees me' 1.251, 3.150, 3.191, 7.493; the Dharma emerged from the depths of his experience 2.291, 9.247; he is the Dharma's source 9.452; he honoured and respected the Dharma 3.65–7, 4.168, 4.346, 19.316, 26.627–8

need for the Dharma
'Everybody needs the Dharma' (Milarepa) 9.170, 11.367–8, 18.589–90; giving the gift of the Dharma, *see under dāna*/kinds of giving; only the Dharma will and can bring true peace 26.538; people need the Dharma 12.455, 12.489; people who are perishing for not hearing the Dharma 12.407, 18.589–90; reaching out to people who need the Dharma 12.489; a terrible and tragic need at a crisis in world history 8.272; the world needs the Dharma 12.600

(II) TEACHINGS AND PRACTICES

DOCTRINES AND TEACHINGS

character
the Dharma is not quite 'doctrine' and it's not quite 'teaching' 3.159; all doctrines are just components of the raft 3.232; all the most important formulations include mindfulness 17.86–7; always expressed in terms of opposites 16.542; apparent formal negativity 7.132–4, 17.291; applications of the law of the higher evolution 15.632; a balanced spiritual ideal 4.25; basic teachings about the nature of reality 17.33; 'Difficult to see for those who delight in attachment' 3.175–6; each teaching contains the whole Dharma 19.215–16; for some, the doctrines of the Dharma are absolute truth 1.83, 1.265; foreshadowed in earlier teachings and capable of further development 2.39; not just ideas but experience, a way of living 17.391; not to be taken literally, but point towards experience 14.442; the product of argument and debate 8.618–19; the systematic presentation of the teaching 13.340; not definitions of reality but symbols, intellectual supports for realization 1.303; not speculative, but state the conditions of spiritual progress 10.158; they contradict themselves when taken literally 14.608; to be refined to such transparency that Enlightenment shines through 2.61

purpose
however sublime, a teaching only has meaning if it can effect transformation 8.483; you need to ask 'Why did the Buddha say this?' 1.7, 19.295, 26.43; simply for communicating the Enlightened mind, the 'raft' 3.232, 7.158; to help human beings to become free from their conditioning 16.125; to help us towards Enlightenment 3.169

complexities
being 'in two minds' about the teachings 17.290; categories of doctrine are ultimately to be abandoned 10.165,

14.362, 14.409; the danger of a one-sidedly negative approach 3.15, 17.291, 17.295–6; the Dharma can't be reduced to a specific formula or set of doctrines 11.417–18; 'doctrine' may suggest something intellectual 14.443, 17.158; the heart is more profoundly moved by ideals than doctrines 1.397; if everybody gets the same teaching, why don't all become Enlightened? 11.359–60; repudiating doctrines prematurely, one may lose the spirit of Buddhism 2.58; the social teaching of Buddhism is on the periphery of the Dharma 8.205; sometimes one-sided, presented without reference to other doctrines 3.8; doctrines cannot be abstracted from the context in which they arose 11.513; to be evaluated on the basis of efficacy, not mere truth 7.50; to understand any Buddhist doctrine you have to identify it as relative truth 17.383; viewed under the aspects of wisdom and of method 1.122–3; what does it mean that a teaching is 'difficult'? 17.48

history
see it against a background of historical events and geographical conditions 1.31; the historical uniqueness of the Dharma 1.56–63; doctrinal differences 1.199–202, 1.209; doctrines held in common by all schools of Buddhism 7.531–42; heroes who have given the Dharma a fresh impetus 2.181–2; historical doctrinal development 4.40; it is all teachings linked to the original by historical continuity 8.652, 14.267; it was not long before it was treated as something that could be grasped 1.232; one cannot say that any one presentation is best 15.80; the sixty disciples are urged to go forth and teach, *see under* disciples/of the Buddha; oral tradition, *see* oral tradition; without the sangha the Dharma would quickly have been forgotten 8.245; written down, *see under* scriptures/canonical literature

adapting the Dharma
adapting the teachings to our needs 3.169; the Dharma must adapt to different characters, times, and places 7.313; Mahāsāṃghikas believed its spirit could be preserved by willingness to adapt it 1.189; not trying to 'adapt' it, just trying to make it understandable 13.379, 13.423; organizations that claim to exclusively possess 'Pure Dharma' 7.314

the relative nature of the Dharma as a teaching
apparently different teachings are different ways to express the same truth 18.369–70; Buddhists are convinced of the relativity of their own doctrines 22.268; doctrines possess only relative validity 1.316–17; the Mahāyāna relegated the whole doctrine to the domain of conventional truth 1.265; Mahāyāna teachings are conscious of their own relativity 1.239; not descriptions of Reality but indications of the direction in which to seek it 7.244; the only way to understand any doctrine is to identify it as relative truth 17.383; what is the use of retaining doctrines if they are only relatively true? 1.265

preserving the Dharma
Buddhists everywhere need to consider how to preserve the Dharma 2.551–2; the difficulty of preserving Buddhism in the hostile environment of modern life 7.446; gratitude to the Theravāda for preserving the Tipiṭaka 2.553; in India, memories were capable of preserving teachings for a hundred generations 1.379; the only way to preserve the Dharma is to practise it 18.474–5, 18.494, 18.498; the preservation of the *Dharma-Vinaya* 2.188; preserving the *White Lotus Sūtra*, *see under White Lotus Sūtra*; scriptures preserved by both monks and lay people 16.242; the spirit of the Dharma best preserved by a willingness to adapt it 1.189

APPROACHING THE DHARMA

approaches
'Cherish the doctrine' (Dhardo Rimpoche) 12.454–6; Dharma teachings are all good, but not equally relevant here and now 19.545–7; different temperaments need different approaches 4.372; a liberal attitude 1.251; Sangharakshita's approach: rational understanding plus emotional response 23.15; the teachings mean little without the sangha's knowledge of practising them 17.364; turn aspects of the Dharma over in your mind whenever you can 17.207; we need a teacher to guide us 3.89–90; when something isn't clear, interpret it in the light of what *is* clear 11.643–4; you are drawn to a teaching when you are ready for it 14.483

where to start?
no question of 'higher' and 'lower' teachings 10.171; rebirth and *pratītya-samutpāda* is one of the hardest ideas to grasp 1.109; step by step approach 5.41–2, 9.494, 16.56; thinking one can afford to neglect the 'elementary' teachings 2.318; Western Buddhists' tendency to pick and choose 11.58, 11.209

questions
disciples who 'did not bother me with questions about the Dharma' 10.578; how does one determine to rest one's mind on the Dharma? 19.466; the nature of questions about the Dharma 9.327–8, 9.513–14; what does working hard at the Dharma boil down to? 18.316–18; why does the Dharma draw attention to painful experience? 1.124; why should you master all the teachings? 18.413–14; *see also under* questions

EMOTIONAL RESPONSES

total immersion
abandoning oneself to the Dharma 9.455–6; aspects we appreciate or want to ignore may suggest an imbalance in ourselves 3.187; becoming completely attuned to the Dharma, like Milarepa 18.340; the benefits of hearing the Dharma being recited 8.532; being willing to die for the Dharma 10.271, 10.342, 11.384, 12.573, 16.198; a bodhisattva always weeping because constantly moved by the Dharma 14.470; the Buddha's hearers are 'instructed, inspired, fired, and delighted' 12.525–6; the Dharma's emotional impact: *saṃvega* 14.470–1; evidence from early FWBO retreats that the Dharma really does work 12.652; Going for Refuge: response to the overwhelming effect of the Dharma 9.247–8; gratitude for the Dharma 3.604, 10.263; if something helps you spiritually, it is by definition part of the Dharma 3.168–9; the incorporation of culture into the Dharma engages the emotions fully 16.370; loving the Dharma 12.581–2; 'One who loves the Dharma passionately, progresses' 13.274–5; plunging into the Dharma 9.455, 9.458–9; preserving a sense of wonder at the *gift* of the Dharma 14.403–4; to ask people to support you, you need faith and yearning for the Dharma, 19.352–3; the spiritual community helps maintain your genuine interest in the Dharma 18.542; to be truly Buddhist, our involvement must be truly passionate 26.57; taking delight in the *Dharma-Vinaya* 10.562, 11.45; taking in the Dharma is like taking in food 17.389–90; total immersion in the serene, radiant, and majestic world of the Dharma 22.225; working for the Dharma 10.396–7, 11.89–90, 14.xvi, 14.522–3, 16.207; you need to be receptive to the Dharma 4.359–60, 11.175–6, 14.403

not feeling inspired
aspects of the Dharma we tend to ignore 3.187; dipping in and out of the Dharma 9.454–5, 9.457; if it doesn't inspire you, it isn't the Dharma, at least not for you 15.509, 18.180; not being wholly devoted because you value something else more 25.103; paying lip service to the Dharma 19.246–7; seeing the Dharma as something dull which is supposed to do you good 13.274

respect and disrespect
'ascertaining' rather than 'mastering' the Dharma 11.253; disrespect to the Dharma 16.303; if you think you've mastered the Dharma, how can you reverence it? 11.56, 18.167; misusing the Dharma as a screen for personal and collective ambition 8.272; paying respect to a Dharma teaching 4.327; seeing the Dharma as a thing to be exchanged for worldly advantage 18.175–7; vilifying the Dharma 4.311

Dharma worship
Dharma-worship, 'the supreme worship' (*Vimalakīrti-nirdeśa*) 16.572–5; honouring and respecting the Dharma 3.65, 4.168, 4.346, 19.316, 26.627–8

KNOWLEDGE, UNDERSTANDING, REASON

knowledge
being unenlightened, our knowledge is fragmentary, faint, and distorted 15.593–4; the difference between what you know and what you believe 8.587; even when the teachings are familiar to us, they are still a mystery 25.133; how much Dharma do we really know for ourselves? 13.345–7, 18.166; a little Dharma known deeply is best, *see* more and more of less and less; no need for formal education 9.338–9, 11.716

understanding
arrive at true understanding with difficulty rather than false with ease 1.25; coming to understand it after many years 25.136; dragon's head, snake's body: understanding but not practising 1.493–4, 15.473, 16.351, 26.38; to understand and explain the Dharma sincerity is not enough 8.599; if we think we understand Buddhism, we do not understand it *at all* 11.56–8; strengthen your understanding by giving talks 19.453; it may appear abstruse 2.214; obstacles to understanding 1.22; a peasant with faith more likely to understand than a scholar without 7.310, 11.483, 17.331; 'To enter the Dharma Essence' 18.413; understanding the Dharma is more like eating than thinking 10.568; understanding is common, but practice is rare 15.558–9, 18.107–8; you can almost forget about it if you're in contact with a sangha 15.610–12; you have to wait until your experience catches up to really understand 4.500

the Dharma and reason
the Dharma is reasonable 9.96; accepting only what is in agreement with reason and our own experience 9.97, 21.505; the Dharma is 'beyond the reach of reasoning', *see atakkāvacara*; the importance of a correct intellectual grasp of the Dharma 1.112, 19.453; it is an appeal to one's intelligence, not one's willingness to believe 15.266; 'Let any reasonable man come to me, and I will teach him the Dharma' 3.562, 15.362; many of us have a deep resistance to clarity in our approach 17.391; only when reason is confounded can we enter the wisdom that goes beyond 14.xiv; our first encounter with the Dharma is usually through words and reason 19.88; the scholastic aspects have an iciness that some find repellent, others refreshing 7.133; thinking clearly about doctrines and practices 17.616–17; transposition from the intellectual mode to the emotional 1.325; you need a conceptual support for your Dharma practice 19.508

MISUNDERSTANDINGS AND MISREPRESENTATIONS

misunderstandings
an abstract Dharma is a non-existent Dharma 16.576; failure to see it in its true context 1.31–7; failure to view it in correct perspective 1.37–43; it is possible to take in the teaching in a way that causes us suffering 17.389–90; misled by the apparent simplicity of the Dharma, people stay on the surface 12.34; mistaking rational comprehension for actual realization 1.222, 2.113; misunderstanding the Dharma 18.180; misunderstandings arising from semantic confusion 14.86; misuse of the Dharma can harm us 16.200–1; monastic interpretation failed to do justice to its depth and universality 2.205; sometimes the Dharma is disguised by Eastern culture 11.598

misrepresentations
attempts to elucidate Buddhist doctrines leaving out Enlightenment will fail 7.309–10; the adulteration of the Dharma 3.314, 11.610–11, 12.516, 19.584; attempts to reduce the Dharma to modern isms and ologies 1.25; belittling Buddhism by saying that *all* it teaches is non-violence 8.179–80; Anagarika Dharmapala would not tolerate misrepresentation of Buddhism 8.102; it is important to protest against any misrepresentation 4.127, 8.xxiv, 24.206; misrepresentations 1.19–20; misrepresentations of Buddhism 8.140–1

PRACTISING THE DHARMA

the nature of Dharma practice
the Dharma is above all something to be practised 3.294; even perhaps practised in other worlds 2.64, 16.462; it can be practised by everybody, wherever they live 1.56, 3.162, 9.289; it can embrace a range of purposes 8.577; it requires periods of silence and solitude 7.239; it's more like artistic creation than technical problem solving 8.579; the raw material is ourself and our world 8.579; there is no safe way of practising the Dharma 4.186–7; the training is gradual 1.176, 10.145

conditions for Dharma practice
conditions for practice 7.259–61; 'Did you come for the sake of the Dharma or for the sake of a chair?' 16.535–7; difficult political conditions for Dharma practice 4.100–1, 12.490; the Pure Land provides ideal conditions to practise the Dharma 1.340–1; you don't need special conditions 18.342, 18.473–4

starting to practise
the changes you might want to make when you start practising 10.630–1; don't think in terms of results, just immerse yourself in the Dharma 11.736; the earlier the better 10.230; latch onto whichever form of practice seems most inspiring and helpful 11.221; no one can practise for you, but you don't have to practise alone 3.578, 10.267–8, 11.703; we should practise teachings that correspond to the stage we have reached 11.65; you must want to practise 9.475

theory and practice
the difference between theory and practice 3.242; overwhelmed by ideas about it, forgetting to see whether you're practising it 4.284–5; translating the ideal into practice 9.264; *vijjacarana* could almost be translated as theory and practice 15.472; why our theoretical understanding and practical realization isn't commensurate 1.390

difficulties
the danger of practising the Dharma the wrong way 16.200–1, 19.56–7; Dharma practice all too easily becomes pseudo-Dharma practice 19.456; if you're not convinced it works, you won't really practise it 19.228–9; ensuring that the practice functions not as a hindrance but as a help 1.404; it's not easy to practise the Dharma 12.455; mechanical practice 9.266, 17.306; practising alternative

therapies as a substitute for practising the Dharma 24.327–8

reflections on Dharma practice
be careful not to develop an exam mentality 9.230, 9.328; the desire to find 'special' teachings 18.473–4; determining and applying the Dharma according to the Dharma 16.574–5; 'the Dharma protects him who practises the Dharma' 10.570; the effects of Dharma practice 17.335–6; if we don't practise and cherish the Dharma, it won't really live 12.455; if you wonder why others don't practise more, ask why *you* don't 10.84; the only way to preserve the Dharma is to practise it 18.474–5, 18.494, 18.498; our practice cannot be proved, only demonstrated by how we live 7.264; our practice must be specialized, but our approach should be broad 13.326; the roles of intellect, feeling, and will in Dharma practice 11.650, 12.538; we are not Buddhist unless we practise 10.158; 'Wouldn't you rather be practising the Dharma?' 8.593–4; you haven't really started practising the Dharma until you have started giving it 17.206

the Dharma and meditation
clarity about the Dharma emerges from being immersed in the *dhyānas* 18.580; contemplating the Dharma 5.438; teaching the Dharma goes hand in hand with meditation 9.202; there is only one way to realize the Dharma: meditation 8.219; thinking about the Dharma is transformed by *śamatha* experience 5.420

(III) Teaching and learning the Dharma

communicating the dharma

the need to communicate
the Buddha's communication, *see under* Buddha III; all Buddhist schools were aware of the need to communicate it 1.402; communicating the Dharma 'one of the great joys of my life' 22.528; the Dharma is never confounded with its verbal expression 8.220; everyone to hear the Dharma in their own language, *see under* language/Buddhism; given the world's need for the Dharma, we should want to communicate it 12.380–1; helping the communication of the Dharma 17.206; it doesn't mean dragging in Buddhism on every occasion 4.102; it's no longer possible to keep people from teachings until they're ready 16.75–6; it is our duty to teach the Dharma 9.215, 11.600; it is so important to make the Buddhist path known to others 15.94–5; making the effort to communicate 14.446; no distinction between our own practice and communication to others 17.174; one cannot overestimate how meritorious it is to teach the Dharma 14.446–7; reaching out to people who need the Dharma 12.489; religion will decline if it doesn't have capable preachers (Ambedkar) 16.185; sharing your own understanding of the truth as far as it goes 16.8; we should be able to bear hardship for the sake of spreading the Dharma 16.206–7; we teach the Dharma because we cannot help it 7.317–18; you will only try to bring the Dharma to people's notice if you see they need it 18.589

methods of communicating the dharma

how can the Dharma be taught?
any attempt to elucidate it without Enlightenment will fail 7.309–10; the communication of a mystery through reason and myth 12.106; the Dharma is beyond communication 3.164; how to communicate doctrine 15.335; however difficult it is, the Dharma can be communicated 3.178; if asked to explain it from our own experience, what could we say? 18.166; if the Dharma is inexpressible, how is it to be taught? 16.450; more like conveying the beauty of art than explaining scientific laws 14.549; no use looking for rules and procedures 14.436; teaching the Dharma 'in the wrong way' 16.505–6; to communicate transcendental realities, use logical contradiction 26.207; traditionally two aspects: propagating the truth and dispelling error 1.432, 4.125; words and concepts a medium for a unique and ineffable experience 2.59

methods of teaching the Dharma
the abstract, conceptual medieval Indian mode does not suit the Dharma 14.514; the best situation is one-to-one communication 18.96–7; the Buddha's method: going around talking to people 17.635; continuity between old and new ways of teaching 12.471, 12.677–8, 19.211; the Dharma is best communicated in a shared mother tongue 22.527–8; in our world it has to be taught in very blunt terms 16.556–7, 26.399; little artifices to communicate the Dharma 19.439; Thai *bhikkhus* teaching through story-telling 15.445–6

teaching the Dharma through …
English poetry 21.77–9; harnessing people's energies 17.161; images 12.580; language which is familiar verbally and

ideologically 7.159, 13.438; lectures, books, classes, and supporting those activities 12.455; lights in the sky 16.563; magical action (*Vimalakīrti-nirdeśa*) 16.450–4; many means (*Vimalakīrti-nirdeśa*) 16.563–6; music (in the Pure Land) 3.455; non-conceptual modes of instruction 1.219; perfume 16.458, 16.554, 16.558–63, 26.498; reason and persuasion, not force 7.383; setting an example 12.580–1; speech and mantras 19.32; sound 8.531–2; the symbolism of art and poetry 22.124; visual Dharma 8.530–1

preaching the Dharma
'An old pine tree is preaching wisdom' 1.28, 7.395, 26.243; the Buddha is always preaching the *White Lotus Sūtra* 4.206, 16.203; preaching the Dharma (not just 'teaching') 19.73–4; preaching the Dharma as skilful means (*Sūtra of Huineng*) 7.34; preaching to women 4.348; an unskilful love of preaching 19.489

DHARMA TEACHERS

the qualities you need to teach the Dharma
a certain depth of spiritual practice 17.207; a clear understanding of Buddhist terminology 8.272–3; depth of meditation experience 17.268; developing your communication skills 10.224; eloquence and effectiveness of expression 16.185–6, 16.368; eloquence, good memory, well-ordered material, understanding 16.368–9; a good command of language and culture 19.45; inspiration and *mettā* 17.182–3; it requires all sorts of skills 4.81–2, 19.45–6; just a small stock of knowledge 17.207, 18.184; a lot of energy 16.356; love and compassion 19.204–5; a magical, Padmasambhava-like quality 16.369; openness and directness 17.232–3; some insight into human character 16.506–7, 19.490–1; some skill in handling concepts 14.575; sometimes you have to be a bit rude 12.660–1

Dharma teachers
adding Buddhist meaning to your usage of words 12.118; communicating the Dharma to children 3.533; developing a more 'embodied' wisdom by teaching 17.307; the Dharma teacher needs to speak the language of culture 16.366–7; don't think of speaker and audience as two different things 12.83; for a Dharma teacher, to reveal truth and dispel falsehood are one process 7.382; four types of preachers (Abhidharma) 14.81; if you know anything of the Dharma, pass it on to others 10.274; in a sense, anyone who teaches Buddhism functions as a Tantric guru 13.199; instruction in the Dharma by monks 2.212; Milarepa's genius in being able to teach different kinds of people 18.255; must produce a disciple better than they are, *see under* guru/relationship with the disciple; needs to speak the language of culture 16.366–7; people respond to clear-cut principles, lived out and expressed with conviction 18.153; a poor talk about Buddhism could still inspire someone 13.199, 14.545; seeing the potential for Enlightenment in those we are teaching 7.318; speakers' classes 12.377, 13.327, 23.83, 23.134, 23.144; teaching the Dharma shows you how inadequately you understand it 17.206–7; teaching the Dharma without the medium of culture 16.375; teaching the Dharma is just one human being talking to another 10.243; when teaching, trying to reflect wisdom, compassion is also reflected 7.317; you have to grow beyond the limits of your knowledge 17.206; teaching by example 19.230–1; teaching by one's mere presence in the world 12.17; teaching isn't laying down the law, it's a heart to heart communication 12.524; you can be confident about the Dharma even if you can't explain it well 18.360–1; you can only teach Buddhism out of your own experience 18.475; *see also* guru; teachers/spiritual

advice for Dharma teachers
adopt the appearance and language of your audience 12.523–5; airing your own views ... is just empty noise 14.544–5, 18.178; allow your commitment to Buddhism to show in what you say 19.500–1; avoid literalness by saying 'as it were' 19.102, 24.18; check whether the methods you recommend are working for people 4.102; distinguish between personal experience, evidence, and what you accept 8.587–8; be honest about what you know and don't know 17.207; communicate in response to people's needs, not for your own sake 19.489; create the right atmosphere 22.245, 22.286; the difficulty of teaching an unreceptive audience 16.64; don't assume that you can represent Buddhism in its entirety 14.544; don't cause offence, but don't lose sight of what you're trying to communicate 18.135; don't get carried away with your own rhetoric 17.658; don't give the impression of knowing all the answers 17.207, 19.109; don't fall back on entrenched Buddhist positions

19.108–9; don't give talks full-time, your inspiration will dry up 18.481–2; don't teach the Dharma to someone who is not behaving respectfully 4.342; don't try to explain profound teachings if you have only partial knowledge 19.356–7; draw on past experience, but there's room for creative variation 17.635; give talks based on the second level of wisdom, not just the first 17.129; the golden light must shine through you 16.369; how to be convincing 15.195–7; how to inspire people 19.74; if your understanding is weak, try strengthening it by giving talks 19.453; the important thing is to teach from your own experience 10.223–4; learn the array of teachings to place them at others' disposal 18.413–14; make sure you have sufficient solitary time 4.535–6, 5.652; make yourself acceptable, but don't try to impress with your personality 19.499–500; speak from your own experience 18.482, 19.206–7; speak plainly about the impact of the Dharma on your life 14.446; speaking at short notice, choose a topic you know well or feel strongly about 10.306–7; teach with awareness of the inclinations of those listening 16.506–7; use the Dharma to communicate your experience 19.206–7; use any medium you can to communicate the Dharma 19.206; use traditional language as far as possible 12.455; when teaching Buddhism to beginners, begin with a degree of generality 19.102

fifteen points for giving a Dharma talk
(1) know and love your subject 12.581–2; (2) prepare well 12.582; (3) don't conceal your ignorance 12.582; (4) know your audience 12.583–4; (5) be genuine 12.584–5; (6) don't be too concerned to communicate the Dharma 'your way' 12.585; (7) avoid fashionable terminology 12.585; (8) dress appropriately 12.585–6; (9) watch your gestures 12.586; (10) don't talk down to people 12.586–7; (11) don't be apologetic 12.587; (12) be aware of the occasion 12.587–8; (13) be systematic 12.588; (14) don't be afraid of (intentionally) repeating yourself 12.588–9; (15) speak clearly 12.589–90

difficulties and problems for teachers
being asked about issues that you haven't addressed yourself 17.206–7; being Enlightened but not articulate 19.204–5; communicating the Dharma to someone who is suspicious of religion 19.207; communication of the Dharma by charisma is not encouraged 13.477; crossing the gulf that separates the worldly mind from the Enlightened mind 18.57; difficulties with language 1.402, 1.404, 18.57; finding natural expression for genuine feelings in appropriate words 16.368; giving a talk based on Buddhist scriptures that is not about the Dharma 14.540; giving a talk not having experienced what you are talking about 14.544, 19.296–8; if you aren't getting anything from teaching, you shouldn't be doing it 18.216–17; if you teach the Dharma a lot, it can all become a bit meaningless 18.482; indigestion from mixing different kinds of Dharma teaching 17.390; instructing someone in the Dharma with a wrong motive 18.421; introducing people to teachings for which they are not ready 16.55–6; is it hypocritical to withhold teachings that may put people off? 16.55–6; it is not skilful to present a pupil with teachings they are sure to reject 16.55–6; it's unwise to go out to teach others just because you feel like it 16.29; make sure you don't undermine doctrine by the way you communicate it 15.335; the message of the Buddha can't be delivered in the language of Māra 12.455–6; a naive and literalistic attempt to communicate the Dharma 19.101–2; people who don't practise what they preach 8.271–2; the problems of using words inherited from other traditions 10.438–43; realizing that you are no longer in touch with what you are saying 18.178–9; 'To instruct an idler brings misfortune' 18.421

advice for the Dharma student
could there be a wrong time to listen to the Dharma? 15.437–9; Dharma study, *see* study; a disciple who asked for a teaching every twenty years 19.507, 19.619 (n189); don't allow yourself to forget it 17.261–2; everyone is to learn it in their own language, *see under* language/Buddhism; following the Buddha's teaching means gaining his experience for yourself 19.403; the ideal student 1.20–1; learning starts with an aspect of the teaching that arouses your interest 19.179; one should rely on the Dharma, not on any person 16.576–8; opportunity of hearing the Dharma 9.291; to learn the Dharma, you need *kalyāṇa mitras* 9.317; learning about the Dharma means learning to listen 17.208; learning from the events of the Buddha's life 3.20–1; the nature of questions about the Dharma 9.327–8; the need for an individual teaching tailored to your needs 18.393–4; the need for a teacher with personal experience to interpret

the teachings 19.172–4; one teaching at a time 16.75; people ask for a teaching, but it is often the last thing they want 16.201–2; a religious discourse shouldn't just instruct us, but inspire us with delight 12.525–6; remaining open to the teaching that is all around you, wherever you are 18.182; some want an overview of the whole Dharma before they start practising 19.507; training in the Dharma is gradual 1.176, 10.145, 10.388, 10.562–3; very often people don't want to be taught the lesson they need 18.493; we must be careful to apply what we hear to ourselves 12.83; we take from the Dharma whatever is helpful to us here and now 10.282; what's the use of going to a Dharma talk if you're not going to listen? 19.557; worshipping the person from whom one learns the Dharma 22.385

paying for the Dharma
the 'commercialization' of Buddhism 7.246; it cannot be earned or deserved 14.403; making communicating the Dharma a livelihood can turn it into a commodity 18.176; paying for the Dharma 16.403, 18.375–7; perhaps it is immoral to give something for nothing 26.34; suggestion to spend money not on shrines but on propagating the Dharma 22.171; 'trading on religion': using the Dharma as a sort of secular profession 10.593

see also
books; Buddhism; concepts; *Tiratana Vandanā*; Going for Refuge/Going for Refuge to the Dharma; study; decline and disappearance of the Dharma, *see under* Buddhism III/decline and renewal; esoteric Dharma Refuge, *see under* three esoteric Refuges; focus on a very few teachings, *see* more and more of less and less; 'From the Dharma should one see the Buddhas', *see under Diamond Sūtra*; has one taste (*ekarasa*), *see under Udāna*/great ocean; 'how to determine what is the Dharma, *see* Mahāpajāpatī Gotami; lists of doctrinal terms; mixing the Dharma with other things, *see under* Buddhism III/and other religions; oral transmission of teachings, *see* oral tradition; Pith-Instructions; *sanātana*; self-sacrifice for the Dharma, *see under* self-sacrifice; so simple a child can understand, *see under* Bodhidharma; something to be left behind, *see* raft; the spirit and the letter, *see* spirit and letter; systematizing the Dharma, *see* systematization; talking about the Dharma, *see dharmakathā*; to be tested as gold in the fire, *see under* gold

dharma (Hindu) caste occupation determined by *dharma* 9.18, 9.28, 9.184–5, 10.55–6, 12.50, 15.463; difference from Buddhist Dharma 9.212, 9.266, 9.482, 13.569, 22.289; why new Buddhists in India use Dhamma instead of Dharma 9.537

dharma (phenomenon) *see dharmas*

Dharma Day *see under* festivals

dharma deśanā (exposition of the Dharma) 3.159

Dharma Eye (*dharma-cakṣus*) *see under* five eyes

Dharma Life (magazine) *see under* Triratna/publications

Dharma Mata (mother in religion) 20.411, 22.259

dharma mūdras *see* four *dharma mūdras*

Dharma Publishing *see under* publishing

Dharma Wonshu *see* Milarepa/disciples/Shiwa Aui

Dharmabandhu, Dharmachari v24

Dharmabodhi (translator) 14.231

dharmacakra (Pāli *dhammacakka*) golden eight-spoked wheel 22.xv–xvi; on the Indian flag 8.xxviii, 9.355; set rolling by the Buddha 1.36–7, 9.384, 16.613 (n221); solar symbolism in the *Sūtra of Golden Light* 16.282; symbol of the Buddha's first discourse 3.137; Vairocana's emblem 4.207, 13.306; 'The Wheel of Dharma' 25.169

dharmacakra-pravartana mudrā *see under mudras*

dharma-cakṣus *see under* five eyes

Dharmacandra (translator) 14.152

dharmacarya (Pāli *dhammacariyā*) 14.521, 15.416, 15.448

Dharmachakra Tapes 24.371

dharmachanda (desire for the Dharma) all unillumined desire is a groping in the dark for Enlightenment 7.307; the *ḍākinī* is that which arouses your passion for the Dharma 18.371; desire for the eternal 7.306–8; desire for the pleasures of the Buddhist path 18.129–30; the distinction between *kāmacchanda* and *dharmachanda* 15.156, 26.63; Enlightenment is what everybody truly desires, whether they know it or not 13.278; the difference between desires and real wishes 19.28; 'humanity clamouring for admission on the threshold

of the Divine' 20.127; a powerful emotion, an act of concentrated will, not just an idea faintly tinged with emotion 12.551; it does not eliminate craving, but transforms it into enjoyment 15.156; it powers us on our spiritual quest 12.550; suppressing desire is appropriate to *kāmacchanda*, but not *dharmachanda* 7.306–7; we can't enjoy what we seem to desire because what we really want is insubstantial 15.276–7; we have to gradually replace desire for conditioned things with desire for Nirvāṇa 12.551

Dharmachari or Dharmacharini *see under* Triratna III/what is the Order?/ nomenclature

Dharmadharmatāvibhaṅga *see* Maitreyanātha and Asaṅga

dharmadhara (doctrine-holder) 17.208, 18.474

Dharmadhara (Donald Miller) 8.656

Dharmadhara, Dharmachari (Keith Downer) v24

dharmadhātu (sphere of ultimate reality) etymology 3.243, 12.212; *dharmadhātu* and *lokadhātu* are identical 14.226; the *dharmakāya* the principle that allows everything to be woven into its harmony 14.604; and the doctrine of interpenetration 7.401, 14.218–20, 26.51; in the *Gaṇḍavyūha Sūtra* 14.219–20, 14.226; the idea of the *dharmadhātu* as a mandala is not to be taken literally 14.604–5; indicates reality's characteristic of totality and all-embracingness 2.43; and Indra's net 7.274; the mandala (of the Five Buddhas) depicts the *dharmadhātu* 3.243, 16.581, 18.447; represented by Vairocana's Tower 14.220; sangha gives us the possibility of inhabiting the *dharmadhātu* 3.402; symbolized by the Pure Land 3.244; the wisdom of the *dharmadhātu*, *see under* five *jñānas*; the world of suffering and the Realm of Truth are not different places 7.274

Dharmadhirarajamahamuni, Ven. 8.664

Dharmadipa, Dharmachari (Robert Lusch) v24

Dharma-door (*dharma-mukha*) of non-duality 16.541–50

dharmadūta (messenger of the Dharma) 4.535, 7.384

Dharmagupta (translator) 14.109, 14.151

Dharmaguptika (one of the eighteen early schools) 2.13

Dharmajyoti, Dharmachari (Lim Poi Cheng) v24

Dharmākara *see under* Amitābha/history and myth

dharmakathā (Pāli *dhammakathā*) Anuruddha and his friends get together once every five days to talk about the Dharma 12.606; the Buddha advises nattering monks to talk about the Dharma or stay quiet 10.472–5, 10.517–21, 10.561, 15.191; 'good talk' 14.296; if you go into any subject deeply enough, that could be said to be *dhammakathā* 10.474; the right sort of talk can have the same effect on one's mental state as meditation 10.530; stories and plays as a form of *dharmakathā* 15.445–6; talk about the means to Enlightenment 2.381–2; 'talking about the Dharma' 3.159; the third thing that conduces to spiritual maturity 3.578, 10.530; the use of the word *Abhidhamma-kathaṃ*, a discussion about the Dharma 14.72; *see also dhammasākacchā*

dharmakāya ('body of Truth') *see under trikāya*

Dharmakīrti Dignāga's disciple 1.372; one of the six ornaments of India 17.464–6; *Pramāṇavarttika* 17.544

Dharmakīrti of Sumatra 12.569

Dharmakṣema (translator) 14.201, 14.231, 14.241

Dharmakṣetra (Hinduism) *see under* Hinduism

Dharmalakṣaṇa school *see* Chinese Buddhism/Faxiang Zong

Dharmalocana, Dhammacharini (previously Mrs Maheshkar) brief introduction 10.701 (n294), 24.608 (n28); meets Sangharakshita in Pune, 1979 24.15–16; ordination 10.290; organization of lectures 23.339, 23.351; translates for Sangharakshita 24.18

Dharmameghā (the Cloud of the Doctrine) *see under* ten *bhūmis*

dharma-mukha (Dharma-door) 16.541–50

Dharmananda, Swami 20.263–5, 20.294

Dharma-niyāmatā 16.84

dharmānusārin *see* doctrine-follower

Dharmapada (Chinese *Dhammapada*) 10.66–7, 14.254

Dharmapāla, abbot of Nālandā 1.366, 1.371, 17.770 (n516)

Dharmapala, Anagarika

introduction
brief summary of his life story 21.380–1; brief summary of his work in India 7.464–5; his appearance 8.47, 8.107; the first Buddhist missionary to take the whole world for his parish 8.110; a great life 6.603–7, 8.105; his life was an unceasing battle against injustice 8.10; photograph 21.383

his character
fearlessly speaking out 8.57, 8.102; fearlessness 8.13, 8.55; the greatest Buddhist missionary of our times 8.3, 8.51; his pious Sri Lankan upbringing was the foundation of his character 8.8–9; his gift for friendship 8.15, 8.33, 8.94; he tolerated no lowering of standards in himself or in others 8.313; honesty 8.33, 8.55–6, 8.102–3; integrated and harmonious 8.9–10; mindfulness 8.98–9; 'a modern bodhisattva' 8.xvi–xvii, 8.95, 8.100–4; patriotism 8.109; revealed vividly in his diary 21.381–2; 'the servant of the Lord Buddha' 8.48; single-minded and fearless, unconventional and individual, a hero 12.561–2; spirit of controversy 8.15–16; sympathy for so-called 'Untouchables' 8.57, 8.103; tireless energy in doing good (*vīrya*) 8.25–6, 8.41–2, 8.98, 8.102; total dedication 8.99; unshakeable resolution 8.103; very particular about cleanliness 8.11

his early life
his parents 8.7–8, 8.21–2, 8.24, 8.45, 8.59–60; his birth 8.8; his childhood in Sri Lanka 8.5–16; he evolved his own convictions from an early age 8.105–6; a schoolteacher who delighted in shooting birds 8.12, 8.94; his younger brother Edmund 8.63; encounters with Christianity 6.603, 8.10–13; the influence of Keats and Shelley 6.604, 8.19–20; insistence on celebrating Wesak 6.603–4, 8.14; 'Reminiscences of my Early Life' 8.11, 8.20, 8.23, 8.91, 21.372; connection with Colonel Olcott and Madame Blavatsky 6.604–5, 8.18–34, 8.56, 8.106; the Theosophical Society 8.xvi, 8.17–34; going forth 8.24–5; brief employment 8.26–8

his work for Buddhism
his activities were the outward expression of an intense inner life 8.95; took Buddhism seriously from a young age 8.11–12, 19.474; a connection with Schopenhauer 8.284–5; the message that the Buddha is the only refuge 6.607, 8.xx, 8.21, 8.90, 8.106, 22.76; attempted to set the wheel of the Dharma rolling again 9.384; believed that if he became a *bhikkhu*, he could not work for the Dhamma 9.318; the revival of Buddhism in India 8.42, 8.97–8, 8.109–10, 9.237–8, 12.561; the effect of a talk he gave in New York 8.66; an example of a lay (for most of his life) full-time worker for Buddhism 8.110; he founded *The British Buddhist* (journal) 8.66, 8.107; he was free to work for Buddhism 8.93–4; he put Buddhism back onto the map of India 8.233; he would not tolerate the least misrepresentation of Buddhism 8.102; his lifelong labours enable the seeds of Buddhism to shoot and flower 8.285; his message 8.49; his vow to spread the Dharma throughout the world 8.192; 'I will do this great work' 8.55; on the lookout for news of *arhants* 8.20, 8.91; organized an international Buddhist conference at Bodh Gaya 8.39–40, 8.186; regarded as exemplar of 'modernist' Buddhism 13.403; the role in his work of his benefactor, *see* Mrs Mary E. Foster; a summary of his work 8.89; supported the publication of *The Essence of Buddhism* 7.158, 7.590 (n259); working for the unity of Buddhism 8.110

Dharma work in Sri Lanka
founding educational establishments 8.56, 8.59–60, 8.107; his ideas for the regeneration of the nation 8.61–2; lecture tour of Sri Lanka with Olcott and Leadbeater 8.26–8, 8.106; return after his world tour, the first native of Ceylon to travel round the world 8.50–1; travelling from village to village by bullock cart 8.56, 8.59

campaign to save Bodh Gaya
his first visit 6.605, 8.35–7, 8.97; his vow to protect the sacred spot 8.xvi, 8.35–6, 8.103; hoisting the Buddhist flag there

8.39; first Buddhist monks installed 8.38–9; an international Buddhist conference 8.39–40, 8.186; a legally complicated but morally simple matter 8.110; loss of a law suit 8.60–1; the mahant's opposition 8.35, 8.37, 8.39–40, 8.42–4, 8.51–3, 8.60–1, 8.71, 8.181; Sir Edwin Arnold's article in the *Daily Telegraph* 8.44; struggle against powerful vested interests 6.605–6, 8.94, 8.107; his vow to be reborn to continue the battle 8.71; his work reminded people of India's Buddhist heritage 9.46

Sarnath
building of Mulagandhakuti Vihara 6.606, 8.66, 8.67, 10.699 (n274), 20.390, 22.331; founding an Industrial School 8.58–9

the Maha Bodhi Society
he founded the Society 6.605–6, 7.444, 7.464, 8.38–9, 8.107; founding of the *Maha Bodhi* journal 6.606, 8.40–2, 8.107, 8.631–2, 9.93, 23.370

his own spiritual life
while at school, determination to attend Buddhist festivals despite punishment 8.14; *brahmacarya* 8.11–12, 8.93–4; becomes an *anagārika* and takes the name Dharmapala 6.606–7, 8.29, 8.93, 8.110; discovery of a manuscript about meditation in Ceylon 8.34, 15.736; he faces death for the first time 8.13; he found practising equanimity difficult 8.103; he strove for complete purity of body, speech, and mind 8.90; his practice of the ten perfections 8.100–4, 8.233; invoking the *devas*' blessings on those helping with his work 8.80; love of solitude and meditation 8.12; meditation practice 6.606, 8.34, 8.90–2; meditation teachers 6.606, 8.91–2; moderation of food and sleep 8.12, 8.93; resisting attempts to seduce him 8.54; no Sinhalese *bhikkhu* could teach him meditation 8.34, 8.91, 15.736; practice of the *mettā bhāvanā* 8.94, 8.103; lower (*pabbajja*) and higher (*upasampada*) ordinations 6.606, 8.69, 8.107; study of the *Satipaṭṭhāna Sutta* and the *Visuddhimagga* 8.34, 8.91; vegetarianism 8.94

friendships and meetings
he nearly meets the Pope 8.55–6; with Sir Edwin Arnold 8.46, 8.59; with Mrs Mary E. Foster, *see* Foster; with William James 8.58; with Nanda Kishore Lall 8.42–3; with Peter Kropotkin 8.59; with Nirodanath Mookerjee 8.43; with Maji (Reverend Mother) 8.35, 8.91–2; with Max Müller 8.54; with Moung Hpo Hyhin 8.91; with T. W. Rhys Davids 8.46, 8.54

travels
his response to Niagara Falls 8.10; America 8.44–5, 8.47–9, 8.54–5, 8.58; Burma 8.37–8, 8.43, 8.58; England 8.45–6, 8.54, 8.59, 8.65–7; continental Europe 8.55–6, 8.59; Hawaii 8.49, 8.74; India 8.42, 8.56–8; Japan 8.29–33, 8.49–50, 8.62–3, 8.106; Korea, China, and Java 8.63; the story of how he travelled with the Bible and the *Visuddhimagga* 8.102; the World's Parliament of Religions (Chicago) 6.606, 8.44–5, 8.47–9, 8.74, 8.110

his views and teachings
defence of Swami Vivekananda 8.33, 21.386–7; he spoke out against 'the abominations of caste' 8.57; he thought the Western university system was without ethical value 8.56; 'Immortal Sayings' 8.xvi, 8.82–8; to him, religion was intimately connected with every part of life 8.62; views on Christianity 8.93

later years
interned in Calcutta for five years 8.63–4; mission work in London 8.65–7; the breakdown of his health 8.64–5, 8.67–72; criticism of him 8.68; his death 8.72, 8.81, 8.107, 21.381

after his death
birth centenary 8.311–12; birthday celebrations 8.104–5, 8.108, 8.109–11, 8.232–4, 8.284–5, 8.658, 22.34, 22.264; a claim that after his death and rebirth, he communicated via a medium 23.368; he appears on the Triratna 'Refuge Tree' 8.xvii

Sangharakshita
found in Dharmapala a kindred spirit 8.xv, 21.380–1; inspired by his devotion to spreading the Dharma 8.3–4; a photograph in Sangharakshita's flat 26.406; writings on Dharmapala, *see under* Sangharakshita XIII/publication history/*Flame in Darkness*

Dharmapala, Bhikkhu (Sinhalese scholar) 7.565

Dharmapala, Dharmachari v24

dharmapālas (guardian deities)
comparison with *lokapālas* 16.348; converted local demons, turbulent natural energies 19.407–8; defenders of the faith 2.178; looking for Western equivalents to *dharmapālas* 19.410–11; the initiation of a *dharmapāla* to ward off undesirable influences on your practice 13.207–8; in the mandala of the five Buddhas 18.601; meditating on and making offerings to them 19.409–10; protectors of the Dharma 19.406–7; that aspect of oneself which is

hard on the weaknesses that prevent one's Dharma practice 19.407; their conversion from turbulent energies to protectors of the Dharma 19.408; visualized on the Refuge Tree 13.77, 13.207–8

Dharmapali, Anagarika Martha 24.490

dharma-paryāya 14.98

dharma-pratisaṃvid 16.489

Dharmapriya (translator) 14.138

Dharmapriya (Sangharakshita's name at one time) 7.5, 20.207, 20.332

Dharmapriya, Dharmachari (Mike Scherk) v24

Dharmarakṣa (Chinese translator) 14.108, 14.227

Dharmarakshita (briefly Sangharakshita's name) 20.410–11

Dharmarakshita, Dhammachari (previously Mr Maheshkar) brief introduction 10.701 (n294), 24.608 (n28), 24.610 (n39); at the time of Dr Ambedkar's death 10.xxxvii–viii; accompanies Sangharakshita on preaching tours in India 10.xxxviii–ix, 10.277, 23.339, 23.349; 'my faithful translator' 10.179, 23.351; ordination 10.290, 24.22; meets Sangharakshita in Pune, 1979 24.15–16; translates Sangharakshita's talk 10.181; visits Sangharakshita in Kalimpong 8.657

Dharmarakshita, U (disciple of U Chandramani) v21

Dharmarāja *see under* kings

Dharmaratna (Nepal) v21

Dharmaruci, Dharmachari v24

dharmas (Pāli *dhammas*, phenomena)

WHAT ARE *DHARMAS*?

definitions and explanations
ideas 18.604; Pāli dictionary and Buddhaghosa 1.97–8; phenomena, mental object 3.159; the 'realities' into which the Buddhist schools analysed the world 1.103, 12.143–4; ultimate psychophysical elements or events 14.344; what are *dharmas*? 1.97–104, 12.143–4

characteristics
absolute quiescence 14.562; all *dharmas* are One Mind (Yogācāra view) 19.371; all supposedly real, the building blocks of existence 17.447; they arise in dependence on conditions 1.89; compared to scientific atoms 14.344, 17.443–4; the attributes of Tathāgatahood applied to all *dharmas* 14.144; cognized by the eye of truth 14.314; 'conceptually constructed' and 'more than conceptually constructed' existence 17.445; egoless 1.264–72; emptiness of all *dharmas*, *see under śūnyatā*; eternally unproduced 1.269; have no separate characteristics 16.449; have only a nominal existence 2.88–9; illusory 14.141; Impressionism as an illustration of the nature of *dharmas* 1.104; inexpressible 1.65–6; insubstantial 1.221; like a mirage in the desert 14.562; neither existent nor non-existent 16.448–9, 16.452; *nairātmya* (non-ego) of all *dharmas*, *see nairātmya*; 'Nirvanized' 16.449; they are non-*dharmas*, therefore they are *dharmas* 2.131; peaceful from the beginning 16.449; quiescent 1.269; the sameness of all *dharmas* (*sarvadharma-samatā*) 1.268, 14.192

THE HISTORY OF *DHARMAS*

introduction
the analysis of *dharmas* is distinctive to Buddhism 17.86; reducing existence to a flux of *dharmas* 1.489, 14.344

Early Buddhism (pre-Abhidharma)
the Buddha's analysis 1.221, 17.444; *Satipaṭṭhāna Sutta*'s list of *dharmas* as mental objects 15.168–9; the Vinaya is truly observed by one who knows that *dharmas* are unreal 14.162

Abhidharma
analysis of the phenomenal world 1.102–3; analysed in the *Dhamma-saṅgaṇi* 14.78–9; the enumeration and classification of *dharmas* 14.73, 14.93, 17.442–3; fourfold classification, different from the earlier five *skandhas* 12.144, 14.360; over-preoccupation with analysis of *dharmas* 1.222–5; the *dharmakāya* as a succession of *dharmas* 1.252; reality as the realm of *dharmas* 17.133; Sarvāstivādin thesis that past, present, and future *dharmas* are equally real 14.87; thought that an analysis of *dharmas* would give a complete picture of reality 1.223; two classifications (Theravāda and Sarvāstivāda) 2.98–9, 12.145–8, 14.73, 14.360; wisdom penetrates into *dharmas* as they are in themselves (*Atthasālinī*) 17.131

late Abhidharma view that dharmas have a permanent, real existence
absolutely existent entities 1.304, 14.439, 17.248, 17.443; it used *dharmas* to deny the reality of *pudgalas*, then treated *dharmas* as real 17.248; came to stand for the very substantialism the Buddha rejected 1.305; the consequence of seeing *dharmas*

as ultimate realities 1.264–5, 14.476; a heretical view 7.539–40; a disastrous deviation from orthodoxy 7.539; ontological difficulties 1.304; pluralistic realism 1.221, 7.539–40, 12.143, 14.360, 17.443–4; Sarvāstivādin *sarvam asti* doctrine 1.188, 1.221; a tendency to reify them emerged 15.183–4; don't reify the non-existence of *dharmas*, they have a relative existence 14.439

Mahāyāna
'All *dharmas* spontaneously freed as mists of rain vanish into air' 18.596–7; bodhisattvas do not belong among the *dharmas* 14.492; compassion which has *dharmas* for its object 5.202; it sees *dharmas* not as entities but as concepts 17.546; Mahāyāna teachings about *dharmas* 1.489, 18.597; the Mahāyāna's view of the Hīnayāna's conception of *dharmas* 15.186; the realization of the non-arising of *dharmas* 14.183; reducing *dharmas* to *śūnyatā* 1.489; a school of thought that *dharmas* appear for a split second, then disappear 17.367; they are perceived by bodhisattvas as provisional intellectual constructions 14.439

CONDITIONED AND UNCONDITIONED *DHARMAS*

conditioned (saṃskṛta)
empty 1.267; equivalent to one meaning of *saṃskāra* 2.67; include the whole phenomenal universe 2.62; recognizable by such signs as painfulness and impurity 1.267

unconditioned (asaṃskṛta)
the Theravāda identified one, the Sarvāstivāda three 12.144, 17.443, 17.446; epithet of Nirvāṇa 1.69, 1.171, 1.267, 2.62; inclusion in the Sarvāstivādin fivefold classification of *dharmas* 14.93

relationship between them
alike mere thought-constructions 1.306; dependent on each other 1.267–8; distinction between permanence and impermanence 9.527–8; not a distinction between real and unreal 12.144, 17.443

ANALYSIS OF CONDITIONED *DHARMAS*

introduction
analysis of the flow of thoughts into a succession of mental states 19.235–6; summary of the Abhidharma analysis 12.143–5; distinction between *citta* and *caittas* 18.207; *anāsrava dharmas* (Sarvāstivāda) 18.295–6; the Sarvāstivādin classification, to replace the older one 14.93

(1) rūpa (material form)
an investigation of what we would call matter 12.145; Sarvāstivādin count of eleven 17.446; Theravādin count of 28 *rūpas* 14.79, 15.183, 17.446; *see also rūpa*

(2) citta (mind or mental state)
analysis of mental states 1.174–5; skilful, unskilful, and neutral (*avyākata*) 12.146, 14.79; the smile of the *arhant* 4.137, 12.146; according to the plane (*loka*) on which they occur 12.146–7; analysis of the mental states present in the *dhyānas* 12.147; pyramid of consciousness (Govinda) 12.147; the Sarvāstivādins recognized only one 17.446; Theravādin analysis of 89 *cittas* 1.174–5, 12.146–8, 14.79, 17.446, 17.496

(3) caittasikas (Pāli cetasikas)
functions associated with mind, *see* mental events

(4) cittaviprayukta saṃskāras
elements independent of mind: in Western terms, a mix of philosophy, psychology, epistemology 12.145; Sarvāstivādin category 17.446

dharmasala (village hall) 10.472, 10.641–3

Dharmasaṅgīti Sūtra 1.504, 2.126

Dharmashura, Dharmachari 12.693

Dharma-skandha ('Compendium of Doctrines') 14.82–3

dharmaskandhas (84,000) 12.313

dharma-sthitiṃ 16.84

Dharmatā-niṣyanda-Buddha 14.211

Dharmatāśīla (translator) 14.190

dharma-vicaya (Pāli *dhamma-vicaya*, investigation of mental states) etymology 3.287; akin to *citta visuddhi* 3.291; be precise, or a positive mental state can be confused with a negative one 17.670; being aware at any moment whether what you are doing is beneficial or harmful 17.265; being aware of whether thoughts are rooted in skilful or unskilful states 11.37; connection with the Abhidharma list of positive mental events 17.550; distinguishing skilful states from unskilful ones 3.287, 9.272, 9.296, 17.617; doesn't constant evaluation of mental states detract from spontaneity? 17.265–7; as one of the seven *bodhyaṅgas*, *see under* seven *bodhyaṅgas*; one's own behaviour should be the primary object of one's scrutiny 4.25; look at your own mind 10.201; meditation is necessary to the process of

examining the mind 17.438; the mindful observation of our own mental processes 17.260; noticing the arising of unskilful states is a step towards overcoming them 17.270; the purpose of Buddhist psychology (Abhidharma) 17.433, 17.489; scrutinizing emotions to see their effect 7.290–1; a stocktaking of mental states 1.555; taking stock of your actions from time to time 17.267

dharmavijaya 7.452, 9.120

Dharma-Vinaya (Pāli *Dhamma-Vinaya*) term for the Buddha's teaching 1.184, 11.42, 11.706; teaching and practice 1.122, 10.562, 14.28; Dharma developed into Abhidharma, Vinaya into Abhivinaya 2.203; the expression of the Dharma in a carefully formulated way of life 14.434; it is strange to us 11.42–3; makes the distinction between personal religion and institutional religion 1.191; preservation 2.188; taking delight in the *Dharma-Vinaya* 10.562; a vast ocean, strange and wonderful 10.569, 11.42–4, 11.707

Dharmavira, Dharmachari (Brian) v24

Dharmawansa, Venerable (Bihari *bhikkhu*) 20.166, 22.91–2

Dharma-worship, 'the supreme worship' (*Vimalakīrti-nirdeśa*) 16.572–5

Dharmika, Dharmachari (Patrick Burleigh) 24.27, 24.611 (n45)

Dharmodaya Sabha v21

Dharmogata (bodhisattva) 2.224–5

Dharmottara, Dharmacharini 18.xiv

dhātu garbha 16.150

dhātus

eighteen
introduction 17.404; doctrine held in common by Theravāda and Mahāyāna 7.531; in the Abhidharma 14.74, 14.79, 14.84; give us a close analysis of experience 15.200; the interaction of eye with visual form 17.510; only mental constructions 1.267

other enumerations
seven 2.692–3 (n225); six: inconsistencies exposed 1.320

Dhātu-kathā (Pāli Abhidharma text) introduction 14.84–5; classification of doctrinal categories 14.84; literature of knowledge 14.303

Dhātu-kāya (Sanskrit Abhidharma work) 14.88–9

Dhātuvibhaṅga Sutta *see under Majjhima Nikāya*

dhīḥ (Pāli *dhi*) seed syllable 2.127, 13.295; term for transcendental cognition 2.127

Dhirananda, Dharmachari v24

Dhivan, Dharmachari *see* Jones, Dhivan Thomas

Dhivati, Dharmacharini 2.737 (n653), 17.432

dhṛ 16.369

Dhṛtaka 13.341

Dhṛtarāṣṭra (great king) 16.346

dhṛti 1.439

Dhruva (Order member) 4.225, 4.235

dhutāṅgas *see* ascetic practices

dhuva (stable) 7.191

dhyāna

INTRODUCTION

definitions, synonyms, translations
definitions 4.489; the difference between *dhyāna* and *samādhi* 9.205–6; the English language doesn't have words for them 17.436; insensibility with regard to sense perceptions 4.489; superconscious state 11.149; 'trance' (Conze) 11.112, 17.118, 17.124; (unsatisfactory) translations 1.162

its nature
an abundance of blissful feeling 15.156; central to the spiritual life, and not confined to meditation 4.156; essentially a skilful mental state 5.435; a flowing together and concentration of all our energies 4.152; Lama Govinda's paintings of *dhyāna* states 4.155; just as tangible as things made by potter or carpenter 5.251; just labels for experience 4.158; like the first stage of a rocket taking you out of the earth's gravitational field 4.521; a natural state 4.160, 5.252, 5.284; the nature of *dhyāna* 5.237–42; not methods of attaining anything, but states you experience 17.123; a pleasurable state of pure mental energy 4.481–2; pure will 4.481; a temporary getting away from the world 4.566, 18.575; an uninterrupted flow of skilful mental states 2.392, 18.423; withdrawal from sense experience 5.641–3

more complex descriptions
the aim of meditation described in terms of the four *dhyānas* 5.242; the integration of the conscious mind with the superconscious 11.124; *mahaggata* (expanded consciousness) 5.52, 15.163,

17.608; mental activity with positive karmic consequences 11.650, 12.538; mundane, taking place in space and time 19.437; not a 'state' in which 'we' are, but a way we reorganize our being 26.48; not transcendental, but not 'worldly' 4.157; paradoxically, *dhyāna* is both active and passive 17.123–4; passing beyond the process of integration into true concentration 15.108; 'subjective' equivalents of corresponding planes of 'objective' existence 7.228–9; 'to pass through the door of the mind' 4.488–9; the traditional descriptions don't always relate to people's experience 17.108; weighty karma 3.107, 5.269, 15.92, 15.108

TRADITIONAL ACCOUNTS

the Buddha's experience
a description which doesn't convey the full import of the experience 5.244–5; from going forth to Enlightenment, he experienced *arūpa* but not *rūpa dhyānas* 2.111; the happiness that arose in him could not lay hold of his mind 2.108, 17.528, 18.581; his ability to stay in *dhyāna* for as long as he wished 19.423; spontaneous *dhyāna* under the rose-apple 2.110–12, 18.31; why the Buddha enters *dhyāna* 18.576, 19.422–6

traditional perspectives on dhyāna
well known in India before the time of the Buddha, and still taught there 1.165–6; the Abhidharma's analysis of the mental states present in the *dhyānas* 12.147; Hindus are familiar with them 14.563–4; in the *Vibhaṅga* (Abhidharma) 14.80; some Theravādins say they are unattainable, but Mahāyānists disagree 7.532; a topic in the *Śāriputra-abhidharma-śāstra* 14.74; the traditional analysis doesn't give the whole picture 5.275; Yogācāra emphasis on *dhyāna* 1.350

A GUIDE TO DHYĀNA

preparing for dhyāna
the *kasiṇa* practice 5.643; the observance of the five precepts 7.125; preparing a basis for *dhyāna* experience 5.269, 11.123–4; think deeply about the implications of attaining *dhyāna* 17.534

obstacles
the five hindrances 17.119–21, 18.575–6; for some people meditation without *dhyāna* has great attractions 5.445; nothing is so inimical to *dhyāna* as anger and hatred 5.325–6

entering the dhyānas
the bodhisattva naturally comes to dwell in the *dhyānas* 14.563; deluded types find it difficult to get into *dhyāna* and difficult to get out 18.577; entering the god realms through the *dhyānas* 1.443–4, 15.239–40, 17.527; the importance of having experience of them 9.343; it's hard to enter the higher *dhyānas* because we want to hang onto the familiar 4.153; having reached *passaddhi*, you should dwell in *dhyāna* whenever you meditate 15.221; an Indian woman who experienced *dhyāna* though knowing nothing about Buddhism 25.44–5; lack of confidence in attaining *dhyāna* 5.452–3; one experiences first *saṃskāra* and then *vedanā* 17.527–8; for some people it's easy, while others find it difficult 5.452; through mantra recitation 5.595–6, 5.631–2; through the mindfulness of breathing 5.571; through visualization practice 5.594–6, 5.630–1; turning from the lower mind to the higher mind 13.354–5; passing from the conscious mind to the superconscious (*dhyānas*) 10.349–50; sustaining awareness of the everyday mind while in *dhyāna* 17.518; within the reach of everybody who meditates systematically 26.46; you have to turn away from sense experience 4.154, 5.324–5

enjoying the dhyānas
craving doesn't arise while in *dhyāna*, but one can crave *dhyāna* 17.597; enjoy them but don't become attached to them 14.563; enjoying *dhyāna* 19.421–6; the higher hedonism of Buddhism 12.542, 15.532–3; so enjoyable that in a sense you don't have to make an effort 5.270–1; *paramānanda* (bliss arising from the *dhyānas*) 2.91

the effect of dhyāna
resting one's whole being 5.418, 19.422–3; clarity about the Dharma 18.580; a direct experience of relaxation and tranquillity 17.263; the effect on the body 1.162–4; the experience can quickly fall away 5.450; gives the mind more powerful thrust for purposive thinking 5.464; a temporary state 8.441, 19.448–9; the power of *dhyāna* 4.520–1; produces positive karmic consequences 4.481; to dissolve doubts 10.577

the ensuing dhyāna stage (or samādhi)
the after-effect of successful meditation 18.72; keeping the *dhyāna* experience all day, especially on retreat 18.595–6

dhyāna in everyday life
the beginner may need to go away to practise *dhyāna* 5.680–1; difficult to get into *dhyāna* while moving about 5.80; if

you are fairly well integrated, you are in a slightly dhyānic state 5.639; modern life is incompatible with the maintenance of dhyānic consciousness 18.499

questions about dhyāna
are the *rūpa* and *arūpa dhyānas* continuous? 2.111–12; can art produce *dhyāna*? 7.436–7; can you enter *dhyāna* while chanting a mantra? 5.595–6; can you enter *dhyāna* through reading, or appreciating painting? 5.640–3; do the *dhyānas* have an other-regarding aspect? 5.268; is *dhyāna* a detour? 5.445–6; is *dhyāna* different depending on the method by which you reach it? 5.265; isn't talk of *dhyāna* rather self-obsessed? 5.450; how do you know you've attained it? 9.522; were the *arūpa dhyānas* added to the first set after the Buddha's *parinirvāṇa*? 2.110; why bother getting into the *dhyānas*? 5.278–9

GOING BEYOND THE *DHYĀNAS*

the limitations of the dhyānas
being mundane, they can't conduce directly to liberation 26.198–9; the bodhisattva does not relish the *dhyānas* 1.443; the bodhisattva's temptation to stay in them 4.522; developing repugnance for the *dhyānas* 1.165, 1.444; *dhyāna* prepares you for wisdom, but doesn't take you there 14.564–5; don't linger in the *dhyānas* 1.168, 14.563–4, 15.208, 18.577; each *dhyāna* is positive, but it's important to move on 17.682; there must be wisdom too 18.252–3; they are not the goal of spiritual life 2.108; they are part of the mundane world 13.355, 15.240; even the *dhyānas* are inherently painful, transitory, and insubstantial 1.444; getting 'stuck' in the *dhyānas* 1.168, 14.563–4; the unsatisfactoriness of the *dhyānas* 18.589; until *prajñā* arises, negative mental states could reassert themselves 17.597; a vast improvement on everyday self-interest, but continue to be self-referential 15.336

dhyāna and the heavenly realms
absorption in *dhyānas* without allowing them to be the basis of celestial rebirth 2.164; aesthetic perception (*saṃjñā*) and the *dhyānas* 17.516–17; correlation with heavenly realms (*brahmalokas*) 16.345, 17.263; *dhyāna* has to be invested with the clear recollection of your purpose 15.223; and the three planes of the *trailokya* 1.159, 2.66–7

dhyāna and insight
alternation between *dhyāna* and *vipaśyanā* 5.438–9, 5.446, 5.464, 18.576–7; attempt a deeper experience of the *dhyānas* before developing insight 5.461; bringing insight-type reflections to the *dhyānas* 18.577–8; *dhyāna* experience may have to be sacrificed temporarily 19.190; *dhyāna* gives the mind more powerful thrust for purposive thinking 5.464; *dhyāna* is an intermediary between alienated intellect and insight 19.189; *dhyāna* is not an end in itself, but a means to the development of insight 5.434; the *dhyānas* refine the whole being so that insight can develop 4.494, 5.418; *dhyāna* unifies one's energies, a basis for insight 15.108, 18.576; *dhyānas* without insight 19.159; the difference between the *dhyānas* and insight 18.615; don't associate the arising of insight just with *dhyāna* 5.639–40; don't think too literally in terms of leaving the *dhyānas* to gain insight 4.493, 5.267, 16.161; insight includes a subtle mental activity, incompatible with *dhyāna* experience 4.514; insight without the *dhyānas* 1.168, 1.349, 5.445, 5.450, 5.461; merging *dhyāna* and insight 19.454; once you have insight, you can enter *dhyāna* when there is an opportunity 18.575–6; returning to the first *dhyāna* as a basis for insight 5.417–18, 5.434, 18.576, 19.451–2; soak yourself in *dhyāna* before trying to develop insight 5.458–9; to sustain insight you need a basis in the *dhyānas* 5.446; when the mind in *dhyāna* turns to the transcendental 4.159

dhyāna and prajñā
alternating between contemplating the Dharma and *dhyāna* 5.438–9; if *dhyāna* is the first stage of a rocket, *prajñā* is the second stage 4.521; *dhyāna* as a support for *prajñā* 1.444; the great difference between *dhyāna* and *prajñā* 4.511; the 'surface experience of *dhyāna*' compared to the depth of *prajñā* 18.251–2; to go from *dhyāna* to *prajñā*, invoke the Three Jewels 18.252; two methods 4.493

THE FOUR *RŪPA DHYĀNAS*

introduction
brief description 11.149–50; the absence of all negative emotions, suspension of the five hindrances 4.149; a comparison with falling in love 17.126; a description from the Pāli canon 1.162–3; don't take the idea that there are four too literally 1.163, 4.149; don't think about them, but get a feeling for them through images 11.124; each *dhyāna* represents a whole range of psychic territory 17.124–5; the experience of approaching the first *dhyāna* 17.122–3;

II
III
I
IV

developing repugnance for the four lower stages 1.165; the Buddha's experience of them 2.111; can you reflect in them? 16.161; could they be brought about by will power? 5.268–9; correspondence with four of the eight emancipations 16.447; do they 'shade into' the Transcendental? 5.265–6; if the fetter of self-view isn't yet broken you will still have a strong sense of ego 17.608; experiences depicted through shapes and colours of the world of form 7.297; the fifth group of classical 'supports' of concentration 1.159–60; in the *Precious Garland* 17.262–3; and insight 5.451–2; known as *nirvikalpa-samādhi* in India 1.166; 'mundane' or quasi-transcendental? 4.158; not becoming attached to them 4.520; in the Pāli canon 4.682 (n165); Nirvāṇa is beyond all of them 10.632–3; Ramana Maharshi had experience of them but not wisdom 14.565; their names tell us little about their nature 13.355; they render the fully conscious mind subtler and more 'transparent' 2.110; relationship to the fourth *rūpa dhyāna* 1.563, 4.492–3, 5.265, 17.517; aesthetic perception (*saṃjñā*) and the *arūpa dhyānas* 17.517; a pure singleness of mind without defilements 17.494–5; a transcendence of individuality 5.656; a mysterious body of experiences 5.249–51

first arūpa dhyāna
the sphere of infinite space (*ākāsānatyāyatana* or *ākāsānañcāyatana*) 1.165, 2.110, 16.160; difference from sphere of infinite consciousness 16.161; has the effect of widening the mind beyond its natural boundaries 1.563; a feeling of not being obstructed, infinite expansion 4.509–10, 17.495; imagining the space left behind if one abstracts oneself from the senses 4.156; the inner *experience* of infinite space 16.161

second arūpa dhyāna
the sphere of infinite consciousness (*vijñaṇānantyāyatana* or *viññaṇānañcāyatana*) 1.165, 2.110; the Buddha speaks in terms of infinite consciousness 4.158; difference from sphere of infinite space 4.156–7, 4.510, 16.161; one realizes that the mind itself is infinite 1.563, 17.495

third arūpa dhyāna
the sphere of no-thingness (*ākiñcaññayatana* or *akiñcanyāyatana*) 1.165, 2.110; the Buddha learned the technique from Āḷara Kālāma 1.166, 2.20–1, 2.111; 'nothing in particular' 4.510; one doubts whether there is an object, and therefore whether there is a subject 17.495; the possibility of discriminating between things doesn't exist 4.157; reflection on no-thingness 16.447; things lose their sharp edges 1.563

fourth arūpa dhyāna
the sphere of neither-perception-nor-non-perception (*n'eva-sañña-nāsaññayatana* or *naivasaṃjñānasaṃjñāyatana*) 1.165, 2.110, 14.406; the Buddha learned the technique from Uddaka Rāmaputta 1.166, 2.21, 2.111; the highest attainment known to the Buddha's contemporaries 7.227; the highest worldly attainment of the path of practice 17.495; consciousness and self-consciousness at the very margin of disappearance 4.512; Conze's comparison with Christian mysticism 4.513; the subject–object duality has been practically transcended 1.563, 4.157, 4.510

***dhyāna* factors** *see* five *dhyāna* factors

Dhyana for Beginners *see under* Zhiyi

'*Dhyāni* Buddhas' 13.304, 13.692–3 (n123), 18.601; *see also* mandala of the Five Buddhas

Diabolus *see under* Devil

dialectics Āryadeva's application of the dialectical method to the Sāṃkhya school 1.321; Buddhapālita's dialectical method 1.321; the dialectical exchange between Vimalakīrti and Mañjuśrī 16.524–6; Nāgārjuna's, *see under* Nāgārjuna; those of Socrates and Nāgārjuna compared 1.312

diamond or vajra aspect of existence *see under vajra*

Diamond Banner Sūtra (*Vajra-dhvaja*) 2.158–9

Diamond Sūtra (*Vajracchedikā*)

INTRODUCTION
brief introduction 2.713 (n476), 3.232, 11.170, 16.16, 22.610 (n300); longer introduction 14.178–51, 14.371–6; full text 14.377–94

the sūtra's name
etymology: 'the wisdom that cuts like a diamond thunderbolt' 14.xvi, 14.148, 14.372; the Diamond Cutter of Doubts (Hanshan) 14.535; gives a clue to the significance of the *sūtra* 14.372–3; also 'the Perfection of Wisdom in Three Hundred Lines' 14.148; the significance of the title (Hanshan Deqing) 14.149; 'Wisdom which has gone beyond' 14.466

the history of the sūtra
the attitude of the author or compiler 14.399–400; it emerged from the third of the Prajñāpāramitā's four phases 14.347; its historical importance 10.164; the oldest printed book known to us 1.301, 8.387, 8.700 (n273), 10.166; analogous to the *Dhammapada* 10.164; Asaṅga wrote a *śāstra* on the *sūtra* 1.301; an essential current in Mahāyāna Buddhism 14.371–2; popular in Tibet 13.45; chapter divisions introduced in Kumārajīva's Chinese translation 14.148; influence on Zen 2.555, 10.164, 14.367, 14.453, 19.372; the exact words on hearing which Huineng became Enlightened 14.456–7; torn up by Huineng 12.233, 19.372; its popularity 14.151; among three texts most popular with Western Buddhists 14.268–9; modern scholarship suggests it is among the earliest Perfection of Wisdom texts 14.333

descriptions
a breath of nonsense 14.480–2; a dialogue between the Buddha and Subhūti 14.148; the essence of Buddhism can be known from the *sūtra* 9.109; an expression of the Enlightened mind 14.373; the 'hidden meaning' (*saṃdhā*) 14.153; a Mahāyāna *sūtra* that summarizes the Prajñāpāramitā teachings 10.163–4, 16.239; from an ordinary beginning it becomes more and more uncompromising 14.xv; not a systematic treatise but a challenge to the logical mind 10.165, 14.150–1, 14.376; it addresses the intuition rather than logical intelligence 1.301, 14.148; a sort of elaborate koan 14.468; through it we make contact with reality 14.373

approaching the text
being drawn to the *Diamond Sūtra* suggests having taken the bodhisattva vow 14.482–5; it's quite a good sign if you're terrified of it 14.474; no reason why we should not approach it critically 14.375–6; to be approached cautiously 14.373–4; with receptivity and gratitude 14.402–4; the temptation to reject it 14.480

the sūtra's effect in practice
association with the *vajra*: it destroys us as we are at present 13.170–1, 14.373; those who take up the *sūtra*, 'well humbled they will be!' 14.486–8; used to support a fundraising appeal 21.311–12; the value of its teaching, ontologically, logically, and psychologically 10.165, 14.150–1; we can benefit from the *sūtra* only when we meditate on it 10.165

translations
range of English translations 2.713 (n476); great difference between different translations 7.515; the ambiguity of the word *dharma* 14.441–2, 14.498; *Dorje Chopa* (Tibetan translation) 22.414; Chinese translations 14.148, 14.151; translations into Western and Asian languages 14.151, 14.372

commentaries
Asaṅga, Vasubandhu, Kamalaśīla 1.301, 14.148, 14.372; a great number of commentaries 14.141; Hanshan Deqing 14.148–9, 14.367, 14.376; Edward Conze 14.372; Sangharakshita's seminar 14.320; alternative readings of terms (by Dharmachari Śraddhāpa) 14.329–33

first read by Sangharakshita
a first glimpse of Perfect Vision 3.389, 11.170; going for Refuge to the Dharma 2.407–8, 2.499; gratitude to the translator 3.361; 'I at once embraced it' 8.xxii; 'I had an immediate apprehension of its ineffable truth' 13.324, 23.10; 'I had known and believed and realized it ages before' 2.407, 16.218, 20.85, 23.109–10; 'on reading it I realized I was a Buddhist' 9.13, 9.278, 9.382, 20.85, 22.414; an overwhelming experience that changed the course of my life 2.408, 14.371

THE TEXT

introduction
part 1 is fairly coherent, but part 2 is complicated 14.148–9, 14.374, 14.375–6; to understand it you have to include Subhūti's unspoken doubts 14.149, 14.376; to understand it you need to have a lot of merit and wisdom 14.437

the opening of the sūtra
an unusually ordinary opening for a Mahāyāna *sūtra* 14.395–8; the Buddha meditates 14.398, 14.401; 'Thus have I heard at one time' 14.399; set in Śrāvastī 14.400–1

Subhūti in the sūtra
his attitude of receptivity and gratitude 14.402–4; 'the impact of the Dharma moved the Venerable Subhūti to tears' 2.713 (n478), 14.470–2; his tone of progressive reasoning 14.447; he mentions his attainments 14.450–2; he comes across as quite the Mahāyānist 14.452; he asks the same question, but it elicits a different answer 14.473

themes in the sūtra
are we prepared for spiritual death? 14.408–9; do the Buddha's five eyes exist?

14.496; eight ways we may misinterpret our experience 14.438–40; giving 14.416–24, 14.446–7, 14.477–8; harmonious Buddhafields 14.453–6; honouring the place where the *sūtra* is revealed 11.429; it doesn't include what we usually think of as Dharma teachings 14.481; the merit gained from not rejecting the *sūtra* 14.480–1; the merit gained from teaching or studying the *sūtra* 14.468–9, 14.478–9, 14.482; no formulated teaching to announce 11.417–18; 'the notion of a being' 14.408–15; the parable of the raft 14.440–1; the patience of Kṣāntivādin, who enraged the king of Kaliṅga 1.437–8, 14.475; the perfection of patience 14.475–9; the prediction to Enlightenment of Sumedha 14.452–3, 14.492–4; the sacredness of the place where the *sūtra* is expounded 14.462–5; 'some beings are more empty than others' 14.498; *śūnyatā*: ontological, psychological, logical, and soteriological aspects 14.150–1, 14.409–10; taking up the *sūtra* at a time of the Dharma's decline 14.472–3; the Tathāgata 14.502–3; will the Dharma decline? 14.433–41; 'Those who by my form did see me …' 1.307, 2.44, 3.150, 12.531, 14.499–500; 'From the Dharma should one see the Buddhas …' 1.307, 2.44, 3.150, 4.208–9; 'I have nothing to teach' 3.549

its most famous verse
'As stars, a fault of vision, as a lamp …' 2.81, 14.394, 16.623 (n308); analysis of the verse line by line 14.505–10; things are impermanent but they are also beautiful 26.241–2; reflect on it to provoke the arising of insight 14.505

the sūtra's contradictions
'A is A because it is not-A' 10.165, 14.410, 14.448; beings taught as non-beings, and therefore called beings 1.209, 14.498, 26.202; self-identical through the absence of a self 14.499; switching between absolute and relative points of view 14.447–8; 'That which is supported has no support' 1.438–9, 14.477, 26.83; translogical matters can only be expressed in contradictions or paradoxes 14.467; 'why', 'therefore', and 'because' are like ghosts of a reason-bound world 14.422, 14.447

leading beings to Nirvāṇa with no perception of beings to save
quotation of the text 1.395–6, 2.159, 14.150, 26.201–2; the activity of emptiness 7.409; an example of the *sūtra*'s logic 10.165; how does a bodhisattva do this? 14.410–11, 19.66; in the ultimate sense there exists no individuality 7.154–5

the bodhisattva
a bodhisattva who has 'fallen among things' 14.478; 'No Bodhisattva … cherishes the idea of an ego-identity' 7.362; 'should produce an unproduced thought' 10.165, 14.477; 'How should a bodhisattva progress?' 10.165, 14.149–50, 14.404–5; as living paradox 26.202; they do not belong among the *dharmas* 14.492

diamonds *see under* jewels

Diana of the Ephesians 13.602, 16.386; the many-breasted statue in Naples 24.257, 24.672 (n313); Princess 16.424; Temple of Diana at Ephesus 24.672 (n313)

diaries diaries can be very misleading 26.69; it can be helpful to keep a diary 17.402; meditation diary, *see under* meditation/the effects of meditation

dibba-sota *see* clairaudience

Dickens, Charles

introduction
his miserable childhood 26.364; the development of his personality 26.258; even Dickens couldn't be inspired all the time 15.152; a genius: his works are full of tremendous zest 15.194; the importance of the family in his time 10.73; surrounded by his characters: analogy with the *sambhogakāya* 15.397–8; he used to laugh and cry when he was writing 14.471; unlocking his memories through writing *David Copperfield* 15.87–8

characters and works
American Notes 24.78, 24.626 (n105); Jacob Marley (*A Christmas Carol*) 15.205; Uriah Heep (*David Copperfield*) 12.217, 15.274, 17.605, 18.325, 18.511; Mr Micawber (*David Copperfield*) 12.271, 24.556; the theme of betrayal in *David Copperfield* 24.555–7; the death of Little

Nell (*The Old Curiosity Shop*) 3.189–90, 14.471; *Dombey and Son* 14.471, 16.597 (n92); *Hard Times* 22.464; *The Haunted Man* 15.85–7; 'Meditations in Monmouth-Street' 12.365, 12.729 (n241); Mr Bounderby (*Hard Times*) 3.601; Mr Chadband (*Bleak House*) 20.21; Sir Leicester Dedlock (*Bleak House*) 26.370; Mrs Gamp (*Martin Chuzzlewit*) 13.582; Mrs Nickleby mentions the Cock Lane Ghost 2.667 (n53); Mr Pecksniff (*Martin Chuzzlewit*) 22.341; Sam Weller (*The Pickwick Papers*) 3.525, 22.225

Dickinson, G. Lowes 11.146–7

dictionaries dictionaries are full of interesting surprises 4.145; the dictionaries Sangharakshita consulted 26.7; Dr Johnson's dictionary 12.476, 14.309, 25.7; Pāli-English 1.97, 12.70; the most useful book in the world, leaving aside the scriptures 12.476, 14.308–9, 26.70; the reader's, and writer's, best friend 25.8; we should consult them much more than we do 26.6–7; *Webster's New International Dictionary* 21.219–20

diet *see under* food

difference the aim is not to reduce all difference to unity, but to see things as interfused 14.409; barriers set up between one class, one nation, one religion and another 7.274; a difference must make a difference 26.154; human beings' difficulty with difference 25.445; in the realization of the highest spiritual truth all sense of difference is obliterated 7.103; people attach a lot of importance to purely external differences 19.229–30; there's no use *trying* to be different 4.281; unity doesn't obliterate difference, and difference doesn't obscure unity 12.215–6; people get more different from each other as they grow spiritually 14.451, 16.131–2

'difficult' giving of robes *see kaṭhinacīvaradāna*

difficulty

the bodhisattva's approach to difficulties one does not shrink from working in the most difficult conditions 2.180; 'May I deliver all beings from difficulties' 3.366–7; wish to help others is so intense that one doesn't mind difficulties 4.69

difficulties relating to Enlightenment absorbing the experience of Enlightenment 3.64; attempting to gain Enlightenment by manipulating *prajñā-upāya* 1.389; difficulties encountered by Siddhārtha 3.51; expressing Enlightenment to those who are unenlightened 3.158, 3.178, 3.181–2; gaining Enlightenment from a state of unadulterated happiness 13.137; getting any idea of what the Buddha-mind is like 3.78; grasping the nature of Enlightenment 3.148; imagining the Enlightened state 12.546–7

the difficulty of being a Buddhist being a Buddhist in the West is difficult 12.128; Buddhism is a difficult religion, the Buddha said 7.41; Buddhism may not be easy, but it should certainly not be miserable 17.338; Buddhist life in this difficult world 12.113–14; desire for an easier practice 7.185; the Dharma is as difficult to grasp rightly as a water snake 1.78, 18.180; 'Difficult is the attainment of the human state' 3.484, 7.170, 13.139; difficult political conditions for Dharma practice 4.100–1, 12.490; difficulties facing Western Buddhism 11.521–2; the difficulty of leading a spiritual life 4.370, 11.705, 12.489–90, 12.654–5, 19.278; the difficulty of simply being a Buddhist 12.389; the difficulty of the way to Enlightenment 3.42; don't make attaining Enlightenment more difficult than it already is 5.260–1; four kinds: spiritual life is difficult at the start, at the end, both, or neither 10.228, 17.252; the higher evolution is the most difficult thing a human being can attempt 12.258; if you're trying to live a spiritual life, you face external and internal difficulties 12.623; it is not easy to be a Western Buddhist 8.598, 11.362, 12.128; it is not easy to regard Buddhism as provisional 14.441; simple for a child to understand, difficult for an old man to practise, *see* Bodhidharma; why is Buddhism so difficult to put into practice? 3.241–4

difficulties that arise in Dharma practice applying 'insights' to oneself 26.61; awareness of any kind 15.101; becoming aware of emotions 3.343; being ethical in an unethical society 3.283; being truly selfless 15.336; exposing yourself to difficult conditions (the bodhisattva spirit) 15.394; changing 3.123, 10.277–8, 12.107–8, 16.488, 19.89; concentrating 3.271–2; continuous effort 19.438; developing in unfavourable circumstances 3.329, 3.456; developing love towards ourselves 3.342; doing the *mettā bhāvanā* 12.24–5; following a middle path between blocking and free expression of what one feels 5.133; giving money for the Dharma 18.113–14, 18.376–7; giving oneself totally to the spiritual life 13.242; having an idea of a higher consciousness without

the ego appropriating it 14.460–1; knowing oneself 12.233–4, 12.461–2, 19.97–100, 25.74; leading a spiritual life in isolation 12.67, 15.612; learning to let go, 'the most difficult thing in the world' 3.250; living in a society whose values you do not share 4.524–5; maintaining your principles and also remaining on friendly terms with people 18.502; making sense of fragmented knowledge 3.6; making spiritual progress 4.181–2; making the transition from interest to commitment 24.58; in meditation, a teacher can help us with difficulties 3.339; mindfulness of the body is difficult, but brings Nirvāṇa very close 10.513; overcoming craving 3.125; personal development is not an easy matter for anyone 26.66; positive energy can be more difficult to deal with than negative energy 18.78; practising Buddhism without belief in karma and rebirth 3.113–14; practising right livelihood 19.473; practising something that runs counter to our habits 7.182; realizing that you are going to die 3.126–7, 19.246; reflecting is difficult 15.191; refining one's emotional nature 12.28; resisting modern values and temptations 3.39, 3.621; seeing things as they are on the everyday level 12.655; seeing the true nature of mind 19.97–8; seeing the truth of *pratītya-samutpāda* 1.95, 3.175–6; sticking to your principles 19.463–4; total transformation 19.18–19; transcending subject–object duality 19.103; transforming craving into faith 12.626; what does it mean that a teaching is 'difficult'? 17.48; without spiritual androgyny, it is difficult to experience a vision of the Truth 26.79

conceptual difficulties
the academic mind delights in a sticky web of 'difficulties' 7.310, 11.483; difficulties arising from not defining terms accurately 7.289; disposing of concepts 18.396–400; *duḥkha*, the most difficult of the three *lakṣaṇas* to come to terms with 3.209; it's easy to juggle refined concepts but difficult to stop thinking in those terms 19.373; eradicating misconceptions 3.44; people who find it hard to start spiritual life without all the answers 10.577; the idea of non-duality 14.592–3; raising difficulties as a way of avoiding action 3.293; understanding the *anattā* doctrine 7.293; understanding the emptiness of all *dharmas* 16.449; understanding karma 3.99

difficulties and other people
actively helping another person to grow 17.178–9; are we becoming more positive but ignoring the difficulties of others? 10.73; assessing others' spiritual attainment 10.588, 10.590–1, 19.101; being truly open 25.89; ceasing to identify with the group 3.475; knowing other people, *see under* other people; knowing whether or not the *bodhicitta* has arisen in a particular individual 4.198; putting yourself imaginatively in the place of others 10.476, 17.304; sorting out communication difficulties through the *mettā bhāvanā* 5.149; sympathy for someone having a difficult time 26.24; difficulty of understanding other people, *see under* other people; we don't realize what a difficult life so many people have in the world 18.202

things that aren't as difficult as you might think
the difficulty of doing evil, ease of doing good 4.289; no reason for thinking of spiritual life as difficult and worldly life as easy 4.48–9; 'There is nothing whatever which is difficult after repetition' 4.423; we see spiritual life as difficult and worldly life as easy, but it's *vice versa* 4.292–3

what to do about difficulties
the difference between problems and difficulties 3.551, 16.255; the difficulties an artist has to overcome 26.193–4; turning a difficulty into an opportunity 17.302; we should be ashamed not to attempt that which is difficult 11.408

Diggers in Australia, *see under* Australia; in the UK, *see under* British history

Dīgha Nikāya

introduction
introduction 3.84, 14.37–9; Buddhaghosa's commentary 2.130; translations 7.515, 8.662

Aggañña Sutta
introduction 14.39; the Buddha explains that no distinction can be drawn between castes 2.692 (n305); a comparable text in the Abhidharma 14.84; the evolution of the universe 1.41–2, 3.13, 16.100; and the myth of the Fall 1.42, 16.100; 'Not even Brahmā together with Māra ... could shake your faith' 3.674 (n307), 12.505

Ambaṭṭha Sutta
introduction 14.38

Āṭānāṭiya Sutta
the Buddha repeats a spell he learned from the four great kings 14.39

Brahmajāla Sutta
introduction 14.38; the Buddha draws distinctions between others' beliefs and his own 10.678 (n130); the Buddha explains how to deal with criticism and abuse 3.76, 3.546–7, 11.332–3; commentary (by Dhammapala) 14.657 (n502); 'extra' precepts: abstaining from untimely meals, handling money, etc. 2.350; significance of its being the first *sutta* in the *Dīgha Nikāya* 17.640–1; inauguration of comparative religion 7.364; prohibition of astrology, fortune-telling, etc. 1.547, 2.691 (n304), 3.583, 8.116, 8.305, 19.609 (n114), 22.307; the 'Perfect Net' in which wrong views are caught 2.392, 17.641; praise of the Buddha 10.343, 10.703 (n321); religious teachings as rationalizations of craving 12.99, 12.711 (n76); sixty-two wrong views 1.62, 2.392, 2.670 (n79), 7.382, 10.249; critique of theism 13.435, 14.603; 'eel-wrigglers' (who evade the issue) 10.587; everything happens by chance, is made by God, is the result of fate 3.292, 10.249; *issara-nimmāna-vāda* (belief in a creator God) 10.138, 13.442, 17.641–2; a great net of wrong views dragged up out of the ocean of misunderstanding 10.587; the sixty-two schools of philosophy divided into eternalists and nihilists 7.196–7; sports and games 16.236; thirty-two kinds of frivolous talk 2.381, 12.33

Cakkavattisīhanāda Sutta
the advent of Maitreya foretold 1.47, 2.178, 12.747 (n400), 14.39, 19.597 (n37); the Dharmarāja 1.635 (n434), 19.597 (n37); the disappearance of the practice of the ten precepts 11.322; a dreadful 'sword-interval' 11.322, 12.747 (n400), 19.597 (n37)

Dasuttara Sutta
brief introduction 14.39; resemblance to *Saṅgīti-paryāya* (Abhidharma) 14.81; 'The concentrated mind sees things as they really are' 1.168, 2.113, 3.274, 12.566

Kevaddha Sutta
the Buddha explains that only one kind of miracle is of any use 3.76, 12.749–50 (n417); consciousness is invisible, infinite, radiant on all sides 2.129; Great Brahmā admits that he is not all-knowing 2.695 (n338), 12.97–8, 23.500 (n200); the miracle of instruction 3.686 (n394), 8.655, 14.38

Kūṭadanta Sutta
introduction 14.38; the Buddha speaks against animal sacrifice 2.326–7, 3.76, 10.45, 26.179–80, 26.715 (n130); 'Sharp Tooth' 23.173; ten precepts 1.633 (n423), 2.327, 3.690–1 (n448); various salutations made to the Buddha 9.567 (n312)

Lakkhaṇa Sutta
brief introduction 14.39; the qualities of the Buddha 3.61, 3.637 (n67)

Lohicca Sutta
introduction 14.38

Mahāgovinda Sutta
four *brahma vihāras* 4.39, 5.189, 5.218; 'How does a mortal reach the immortal *brahma* world?' 1.237, 3.209, 3.579, 11.704–5, 26.472, 26.498; indicates the shape of things to come in the form of the Mahāyāna 4.39, 5.189–90; Sanankumāra's teaching 5.218

Mahānidāna Sutta
introduction 14.38–9; 'Deep indeed is this Causal Law, and deep it appears to be' 1.95–6, 17.389, 17.750 (n325); not understanding conditionality, human life is 'like a tangled ball of string' 2.696 (n342); twelve cyclical *nidānas* 3.647–8 (n135), 3.654 (n184), 13.682 (n54), 19.614 (n151)

Mahāpādana Sutta
abstention from all evil – antique verses also in the *Dhammapada* 2.187; the pattern of the Buddha's life 10.547; Vipassī Buddha and the four sights 3.630 (n27), 10.698 (n268)

Mahāparinibbāna Sutta
brief introduction 12.520, 14.39; 'for pathos, sublimity, and beauty unexcelled in Buddhist literature' 14.39; literature of power 14.303; in *The Buddha and his Dhamma* 9.146–7; for the story of the Buddha's last days, *see under* Buddha I/ last days

Mahāsamaya Sutta
'magical' or 'mythical' material 8.532

Mahāsatipaṭṭhāna Sutta
introduction 14.38; the contemplation of decay 3.676 (n314); four foundations of mindfulness 3.667 (n263); four noble truths 15.234, 15.753 (n88); four right efforts 1.636 (n448), 3.670 (n286); meditation on impurity (of the body) 4.692 (n225); the mindfulness of breathing 1.156, 3.675 (n312), 3.694 (n478), 9.516, 9.576 (n281); the seven *bodhyaṅgas* 3.667 (n265), 4.717–18 (n385), 9.565 (n396); the seven kinds of suffering 1.127–8, 1.604 (n113); suffering 1.111, 1.127–8, 3.657 (n201); worship of the *sutta* in Theravāda Buddhism 2.225

Mahāsudassana Sutta
anticipates Pure Land imagery 1.183, 4.37, 16.57; the Dharmarāja 1.635 (n434), 7.512; the noisy city of Kusāvati 10.702–3 (n315)

Pāsādika Sutta
the Buddha tells Cunda the precepts practised by an *arhant* 1.143–4, 1.285; rejoicing in merits 4.695 (n241), 15.774 (n269)

Pāṭika Sutta
Bhaggava and the Release called the Beautiful 2.84, 5.511, 10.506, 13.279, 14.311; the idea of a Creator is a wrong view 2.695 (n338), 11.107, 11.742 (n63)

Poṭṭhapāda Sutta
introduction 14.38; although the Buddha uses ordinary language he is not misled by it 14.477

Sakkapañha Sutta
the Buddha teaching the *devas* 4.662 (n22); a song by Pañcasika the musician and the Buddha's appreciation of music 26.121–3

Sāmaññaphala Sutta
introduction 14.38; King Ajātasattu visits the Buddha, *see* Ajātasattu; the *abhiññas* 19.595 (n25); abstaining from music and 'improper shows' 23.173, 23.175; Ajita Keskambalī says there is no such thing as karma and rebirth 12.757 (n481); the Buddha's metaphor of virtue in terms of craftsmanship 15.405; the development of equanimity 5.211; the four *dhyānas* 1.162–4, 5.251–2, 18.81; mindfulness 1.150; destruction of the *āsavas* 1.170; 'Dusty is the household life' 10.724 (n507); Makkhali Gosāla's eternalist views 17.242; *manomayakāya* 13.299, 17.622; a parallel in the (Mahāyāna) *Mahāparinirvāṇa Sūtra* 14.240; release from the five hindrances 2.56, 5.341–3; 'he lives having passed beyond uncertainty' 5.283–5; the monk's robe and bowl, like the bird's two wings 1.152; a path for the dust of passion 1.58; 'the purpose of perfect insight' 5.409–10; supernormal powers 2.750 (n728)

Sampasādanīya Sutta
Sāriputta rejoices in the way the Buddha teaches the Dharma 3.648 (n144); *viññāna-sota* (stream of unconscious mental activity) 12.710–11 (n72)

Saṅgīti Sutta
brief introduction 14.39; parallels with the *Puggala-Paññatti* (Abhidharma) 14.81; resemblance to *Saṅgīti-paryāya* (Abhidharma) 14.81–2; the Buddha's backache 3.184, 10.236; four right efforts 16.585 (n11); the fourfold sangha 3.683 (n371); Sāriputta's organization of a *saṅgīti-paryāya* so that 'this holy life may persist' 14.20–1; skilful means 16.626 (n330); the ten fetters 3.662 (n238), 3.684 (n377), 4.667 (n54), 16.595 (n75); three levels of *prajñā* 1.169, 3.670 (n284), 4.683 (n170), 9.229, 12.515, 16.603 (n136)

Sigālaka or Sigālovāda Sutta
introduction 3.522–3, 11.695–6, 14.39; advice to a layman 12.713 (n93); the Buddha giving existing traditions a positive twist 15.380, 15.756 (n126); the ethics of the lay Buddhist 11.317; overview of the relationships the *sutta* mentions 12.603, 13.450–1; fidelity between husband and wife 3.563; the relationship between friends and companions 3.573–4, 11.698–700, 16.300; the relationship between employers and employees 3.581–8, 9.571; the relationship between parents and children 3.529, 3.531, 3.600–1; the relationship between teacher and disciple 3.545; the *sutta* considers reciprocal duties, not rights 12.603–4; true worship 3.522–3, 10.167

Soṇadaṇḍa Sutta
introduction 14.38; different people's ways of showing respect to the Buddha 4.295

Subha Sutta
Ānanda teaches Subha the threefold way 7.434, 7.519

Tevijja Sutta
introduction 14.38; extending *mettā* in all directions 3.684 (n382); Going for Refuge 3.674 (n308), 4.686 (n189), 12.726 (n212); the four *brahma-vihāras* 3.628 (n16), 4.710 (n337); three levels of wisdom 16.585 (n12)

Udumbarika-Sīhanāda Sutta
brief introduction 14.39; 'Let any reasonable man come to me, and I will teach him the Dharma' 3.562, 15.362

Dīghāya, Prince 14.63–4

Dignāga 1.372, 17.464–6

dīkṣā-guru (Hinduism) 18.508

Diksha Bhumi *see under* Nagpur

Dikshit, Sudhakar 24.101–2

Dilgo Khyentse Rimpoche

life story
the brother *tulku* of Jamyang Khyentse Rimpoche 12.442, 22.554; instigated collected edition of *termas* (*Rinchen Terdzö*) 12.719 (n143); in Kalimpong, lived at the Bhutanese gompa 12.442, 12.447, 22.553–7; his wife and daughters 2.722 (n548), 12.448; a great reader 12.447, 12.450; poverty and wealth 12.447, 12.449–50; photograph 22.556; went to the United States and became famous 12.442, 12.450; became head of the Nyingma school 12.735 (n291); his writings 5.556, 5.753 (n535), 12.450–1, 12.735 (n297); died in Bhutan 12.735 (n291)

character and appearance
extremely tall 12.448, 23.409; a gentle, kindly person, and a great scholar 12.442, 12.447; always relaxed and calm 12.446, 12.448; the characteristics of Kurukullā, a subtle attractiveness 12.450; his attention passed seamlessly from one thing to another 22.554–5; a very sweet smile 12.447, 12.450; 'one of the most subtly impressive people I have ever met' 12.451

and Sangharakshita
their first meeting 22.553–4; their connection 5.563; discussion of the *Tharpe Delam* 22.555; Sangharakshita's gratitude towards him 5.563; initiations into Jambhala and Kurukullā 12.448–9, 22.555–7, 23.409, 26.228; the *phowa* practice of Amitābha 12.449, 22.554–5; Sangharakshita visits him in Darjeeling 12.449; the gift of a knife 12.449, 23.409; Sangharakshita and Terry Delamare visit him in Calcutta 12.450, 23.408–9; looking up to him 26.629

diligence 18.274–5

Dillon, Michael *see* Jivaka

Din Ri *see under* Tibet

Dinesh (Anand-ji's protégé, ordained as Naginda) v22

Dionysius the Areopagite brief introduction 13.585–6, 23.504 (n239); *Celestial Hierarchies* 13.585–7; Christian Neoplatonist 13.585; 'deep but dazzling darkness' 23.103; *Mystical Theology* 23.207

Diotima (in the *Symposium*) 2.691 (n303), 26.312–15, 26.316–18

Dīpaṃkara Śrījñāna *see* Atīśa

Dīpaṅkara the Buddha of the past 1.44; predicts the Enlightenment of Sumedha (later Gautama the Buddha) 2.17, 14.70, 14.143, 14.492–4; Sumedha resolves to attain Enlightenment as a result of meeting him 13.299; visualized on the Refuge Tree 13.78, 13.205

Dipankara, Dharmachari v24

Dīpavaṃsa 7.491

Dipupa *see* Tiphupa

direct experience all we directly experience is the present 8.289; Buddhism conceives of mind as what we experience directly 17.438; direct experience in visualization practice 17.544; direct experience is the emphasis of the whole Buddhist tradition 12.56; direct experience of what we truly are: the Buddha points the way beyond the wheel 13.140–1; the direct, immediate recognition of the One Mind (on the Tibetan Buddhist path) 12.298; direct knowledge is transcendental in character 13.492; direct realization of the highest spiritual truth 2.555, 13.22; direct seeing 1.479; the emphasis of Zen 12.75; 'finding out and knowing directly' 13.490–2; glimpsed through the symbols of the Tantra 13.118; knowledge and vision of things as they really are, *see* knowledge and vision …; in the *Laṅkāvatāra Sūtra* 12.173, 13.492, 14.206–7, 19.374; Milarepa's direct experience 18.125; mindfulness as 'the direct way' (*Satipaṭṭhāna Sutta*) 15.79–81, 15.243; our knowledge depends so much on words and so little on direct experience 13.345; one of the most vivid and vital elements in Buddhism 14.206; reductionist to equate 'knowing directly' with stress on immediate experience 13.492; the theme of *The Way to Wisdom* 17.xxiv; the *vajraguru* aims to introduce the disciple to the direct experience of their own nature

13.176, 18.61; the Vajrayāna concretizes the Dharma in direct experience of the body 18.74–5; the Vajrayāna reasserted the primacy of direct spiritual experience 17.465; the value of direct experience of reality 12.56–7; your path is simply a path of direct experience 19.377–8

direct method (meditation) 2.387, 11.120

direct pointing 'Direct pointing to the mind', *see under* Zen/Zen teachings; in the Mahāmudrā, *see under* Mahāmudrā; it means referring everything back to the mind 13.356

direction art showing the direction in which to seek reality 7.244; *bodhicitta*: the urge of one's whole being in the direction of Enlightenment 3.366; Buddhist teachings don't describe Reality but show the direction in which to seek it 7.244; encouraging unenlightened minds to grow in the direction of Enlightenment 13.280; getting your emotions flowing in the direction of Enlightenment 13.242; making the effort to develop in a positive direction 17.435; 'Is what I am doing really helping me in the direction of Enlightenment?' 3.256; it is as though your life has a direction of its own, independent of conscious volition 15.94; a mental state without any inclination in any direction 3.219, 12.506; moving in the direction of non-duality 14.479; once your direction is established, you don't need conceptual support 5.252; seeing the spiritual direction your life is taking 15.91–2

dirt 'the dirty devices of this world' 13.31, 17.470; using dirt to get rid of dirt 17.366, 17.494; receiving a transfer of energy 'like dirty dishwater' 19.327

disappointment desire for the transitory is doomed to disappointment 7.291, 7.307; if you feel disappointed with yourself, look to your spiritual friends for help 25.33; fear of disappointment 7.285; having our expectations disappointed may be good for us 18.464; opportunity for insight 5.638; suffering is disappointed desire 7.116–17

disapproval acceptance despite disapproval 16.315; *apatrāpya* prevents you doing something of which your spiritual friends would not approve 18.486; Buddhas and bodhisattvas don't regard us with disapproval 17.662–3; fear of disapproval 16.317; fear of the group's disapproval 15.285, 16.307, 18.134–5; imagining that people disapprove of us 17.652; turning a bowl upside down to express disapproval 19.483

disciples

INTRODUCTION

words
the etymology of 'disciple' 18.xviii; some believe that *muni* was the original term 3.592; the *śrāvaka*, the one who listens, 12.296

kinds of disciple
a 'disciple with capacity' 19.208–9; the disciple who began with a strip of cloth and ended up with a farm 18.199–201; the disciple's career, according to the Pāli canon 1.96; four kinds of disciple compared to four kinds of pot 17.160; four kinds of disciple: like patients, friends, sons, lovers 22.xvi, 26.36; the good disciple is not necessarily the best or the closest disciple 18.433; heart-disciples 18.59–60, 18.190, 19.171–2; 'It requires a disciple possessing merit to receive the teaching' 18.244–5; living in a residential community as a form of discipleship 15.668; son-disciples 19.171–2; three kinds: disobey, obey, know without being told 12.19

the qualities of disciples
Āryan disciples see things not as they seem but as they are 1.104; 'A disciple should be critical …' 14.327; faith in the Buddha is the motivating power of the disciple's life 1.290; 'I want disciples who are bold, self-confident, and independent' 26.80; the true disciple is like a bulldog puppy – won't let go 3.555–6; a 'very good disciple' who 'doesn't hesitate to disagree' 10.367; why should a disciple have to have compassion? 19.208

THE BUDDHA'S DISCIPLES

the first five disciples
introduction 11.415–18; their abandonment of Siddhārtha 2.21, 3.30, 3.41, 3.472; the Buddha's first teaching to them 2.22–3, 3.74–6, 9.383, 11.416–18; they can't help showing him respect 2.22, 3.75, 10.263, 11.415–16, 11.446–7; they need to be convinced 8.585, 8.592, 10.263–4; it's not certain what he taught them 3.75–6, 11.417–18; not a 'sermon', but personal discussion 11.418, 22.331; the opening of the Dharma-Eye 11.447–8; they talked for a whole rainy season 11.416–17, 11.447; the first ever retreat 9.383; the Buddha's gratitude to them 3.74; Dr Ambedkar's version of the story 9.140–2; Koṇḍañña (or Kauṇḍinya), *see* Koṇḍañña

the first sixty disciples whom the Buddha urged to teach the Dharma
the text quoted 2.23, 3.174, 9.220, 9.235–6, 14.292; the best purpose to which language can be put 14.292; given this exhortation, why are Buddhists lazy? 10.83; 'lovely at the beginning, the middle, the end' 1.33, 2.23, 10.264; out of compassion for the world 1.26, 1.180–1, 1.236, 2.58, 2.150; 'for the welfare of the many' (*bahujana hitāya*) 1.181, 2.23, 2.204, 4.86, 8.xviii, 8.444, 9.185, 14.537, 16.530, 21.473; 'Make known the perfectly pure *brahmacariya*' 8.460, 10.439; no question of the teaching only being for monks 8.444; an other-regarding emphasis 4.5; they journeyed all over India 10.264

other disciples
his first two lay disciples, *see* Bhallika and Tapussa; his two chief disciples, *see* Śāriputra and Maudgalyāyana; a disciple who disobeys the Buddha and comes to grief 10.649–50; the 'band of six' (a notorious group of monks) 10.520, 10.712–13 (n417); he praises Vaṅgīsa for his verses 26.125–6; Subhadda, his last disciple, *see* Subhadda; women disciples, *see* Ambapāli, Dhammadinnā, Kisāgotamī, Mahāpajāpatī, Gotami, Mallikā, Paṭacārā, Subhā, Visākhā

the Buddha's relationship with his disciples
he praised them for their qualities 3.179, 4.170–1, 10.573, 10.576, 18.132, 18.222; he took a personal interest in them 11.438; the way the Buddha communicated with them 11.441–2; 'heirs of the Dharma, not heirs of worldly things' 1.236, 2.138, 15.155; 'Here are the roots of trees. Sit down, meditate' 1.236, 3.53, 18.368; 'We are warriors' 3.53, 11.407; 'You are my own true sons, born of my mouth' 2.138, 8.476, 11.108, 14.444, 19.171–2; disciples who 'did not bother me with questions about the Dharma' 10.578; *suttas* preached by disciples 14.261

who were they?
conversion of thirty pleasure-seeking young men 2.23; a cowherd 10.533–4; examples of the people the Buddha taught 3.76–7; the introduction of disciples in the *Udāna* 10.444, 10.480; lay disciples included bankers and businessmen 1.543, 10.483–7; mainly recruited from among the wanderers (*parivrājakas*) 3.461; a mistaken view of the Buddha's lay disciples 8.461; the people the Buddha met in his wanderings 3.330, 12.306, 12.511; the range described in the *Majjhima Nikāya* 8.444; there was hardly any kind of person the Buddha didn't teach 16.236; young and old, men and women, of all castes 2.25, 3.178

what were they like?
all were 'new Buddhists', like us 10.423; compassion their motivating force 1.236; envied for their success by wanderers of other views 10.477–8; supremely happy people 7.120

the difference between the Buddha and his disciples
their Enlightenment compared 1.213, 3.61, 4.20, 13.298–9, 14.570–1, 15.464–6; the Buddha proclaimed the way and they followed it 26.181–2; difference of mental faculties (Abhidharma) 14.84; he definitely had something they did not 4.20, 13.298–9; he reveals himself and inspires the disciple to be his own Enlightened self 14.453; he was first 3.61; when Enlightened disciples speak, in what sense is it the Buddha speaking? 14.539–40

see also
gurus/relationship between guru and disciple

discipline

introduction
the etymology of the word 19.110; what discipline really is 19.109–10; a means to an end, not an end in itself 23.187; not necessarily a dirty word 4.340–1; discipline through perfume 16.558; positive and negative connotations 4.122–3

who needs it?
the arts as disciplines 26.353–5; most people need to go through a period of discipline 4.341; needed at the beginning of spiritual life 4.485; people who can do without it are very rare 17.459

self-discipline
Goethe as an exemplar of self-discipline 23.473; learning self-discipline like calming the ocean 8.266; learning some self-discipline will support your meditation practice 15.173; Westerners confuse self-mortification and self-discipline 17.253–5

the value of discipline
adopting a lifestyle that lets you give full expression to your ideals 18.516; a disciplined way of life protects one against ups and downs 17.573; it may help you develop the appropriate attitude 4.296, 19.458; leading a disciplined life can raise your level of consciousness 11.118; a method of reducing craving 17.169; to prepare the way for individuality 18.359; people need structure 5.378, 19.548; 'A regulated life gives strength' 16.207,

16.552, 20.281; spiritual practice is to be done regularly, not just when you happen to feel like it 12.467; spontaneity may be the ideal, but reaching it may need discipline 17.268, 17.459–60; success depends on establishing a disciplined and committed lifestyle 15.97

reasons to be cautious
a balance between imagination and discipline 18.372–3; the danger of discipline becoming fixed habit 23.187; a day-to-day commitment may feel more spontaneous than a vow 19.146–7; discipline dished out by some spiritual teachers 16.72; external discipline without the appropriate inner attitude 19.457–8; in the spiritual life there can be no question of regimentation 16.127; it doesn't necessarily have spiritual value 16.552; its purpose should be understood before its restraints are accepted 7.268; remember that it's a retraining, not a punishment 16.510; you can't produce an individual through discipline 18.357–8; you shouldn't have to impose the spiritual life on yourself 5.285

see also
meditation/working in meditation

discontent the clearness of mind and the goad of discontent to see Enlightenment 4.448; 'divine discontent' 17.676

Discourse on the Ten Wholesome Ways of Action 2.334

discovery better not to be Buddhistically inclined at the start, so you can discover it within 4.352; the Buddha discovers the path to Nirvāṇa 1.53–5, 3.4, 3.18, 7.227, 7.254, 12.321–2, 19.313; 'To discover that within myself which I *must* obey' 2.401; to discover the cause of suffering one has to go very deep 12.98–9; discovering the emotional equivalents of spiritual truths 5.295, 12.110–11; religions of discovery, *see under* religions; Sangharakshita's process of spiritual discovery 2.498–502, 2.579–80; self-discovery, *see* self-discovery; truth: divine revelation or human discovery? 9.63

discrimination Buddhism obliterates distinctions of colour, creed, social position, and all other polarities 7.33–4; the characteristic of ignorance is to perceive things as mutually exclusive 7.411; 'How to Develop Discrimination' 22.32; in the third *arūpa dhyāna* the possibility of discriminating between things doesn't exist 4.157; it isn't wrong to discriminate, but our discrimination must be objective 17.282; studying the Dharma with discrimination 17.447; to make spiritual progress, we have to discriminate between dualities 18.85; words are bound up with discrimination 14.208

see also
caste discrimination, *see* caste system; discrimination between mental states, *see dharmavicaya*; discriminating wisdom, *see under* five *jñānas*; non-discrimination

discussion *see* arguments, disputes, and discussions

disenchantment disenchantment with Christianity 13.374–6; people may think they are disenchanted when they just want a change 10.456–7

disgruntlement difference from dissatisfaction or disillusionment 4.450–3, 15.572–3, 15.575–6, 17.592; if your starting point is disgruntlement, aim for real disillusionment 18.555–6; lack of power brings corruption in the form of envy, disgruntlement, and negativity 17.654–5; those who are disgruntled will not necessarily take to the Higher Evolution 4.453

disgust *see* revulsion

disharmony being out of harmony with the guru 18.483, 18.504; being out of harmony with the Three Jewels 18.483; Buddhism is a method of resolving the disharmonies of life 26.154; disharmony with a *kalyāṇa mitra* 15.294–5; disharmony in the sangha 12.456–7, 21.202–3; in the Order 2.522–3, 12.676–7; a person who is out of harmony with everyone 18.503; putting yourself out of harmony with the Order 15.418; what gets in the way of harmony in the sangha? 15.515–17

dishonesty (*śaṭhya*) the consequences of telling lies 17.236–7; the dishonesty of the legal profession 20.275; the four bleak things 17.660–2; it is not that one is dishonest, but that one is only honest up to a point 26.59; lying to one's teacher, or any member of the sangha 17.660; most of us live with a kind of background dishonesty 18.140; praising others insincerely 17.662; saying nothing in praise of those who practise the spiritual life: dishonesty by omission 17.661–2; the second precept: abstention from any kind of dishonesty 1.533; 'There is no wrong that cannot be committed by a lying person' 2.376; undermining the skilful intentions of others 17.660–1; we can't know the karmic effects of dishonesty 17.263; you won't get away with it 17.659–60; as an *upakleśa* (Abhidharma) 17.659–63

see also
speech/four levels of skilful speech/truthful speech; untruthfulness

disillusionment can it work as a way into spiritual life? 15.570–1; difference from disgruntlement 4.450–3, 15.572–3, 15.575–6, 17.592; disillusionment with self 16.304; if your starting point is disgruntlement, aim for real disillusionment 18.555–6; it is easy for hatred of the mundane to disguise itself as disillusionment 17.594; it's salutary to experience disillusionment with oneself 16.304; positive disillusionment 15.576, 15.609; Sangharakshita's tendency to think that the world was a pleasant place disillusioned 4.415–16

disintegration the condition of modern human beings 12.217; disintegrated energy 3.120–1; extreme fear can lead to a disintegration of our sense of self 17.180; the more one looks at the stable ego, the more it is seen to disintegrate 17.687

disinterest the difference between *dis*interested and *un*interested 15.314; disinterested action: sinister implications of philosophy 20.164; disinterested friendship 15.293; disinterested love 15.314–15

Diskul, Princess Poon v23

dislike contact with what one dislikes is a form of *duḥkha* 3.211–12; it seems there will always be someone we dislike among our acquaintances 15.305–6; likes and dislikes, *see* preferences; people tend to think that criticism is an expression of dislike 5.208–9

disobedience Buddhism speaks of ignorance rather than sin, disobedience, and guilt 16.90; disobedience in theistic religions 15.619–21; disobedience to the guru 18.483; mass disobedience 12.346

dispassion *see vairāgya*

disputes *see* arguments

disrespect disrespectful behaviour in the name of informality 4.343–4, 15.438; if you have some spiritual awareness, disrespect towards you won't upset you 19.518; in India, touching something with your feet is a sign of disrespect 19.568; for the Buddha 13.683 (n57), 16.303, 17.606; for the Dharma 4.342–4; for the Three Jewels 4.326–7, 16.303; for the sangha 9.131; lack of respect for wise opinion (*anapatrāpya*) 17.667–9; refusal to recognize someone as deserving of respect 12.13–14, 15.714–20

dissatisfaction

reflections
craving to crave, as though you want to be dissatisfied 10.475; dissatisfaction with your circumstances 15.174–5; distinction from disgruntlement 3.463; however much we learn, we can learn more 10.258; in man universal dissatisfaction finds expression as religion 7.114–15; nothing that is conditioned, worldly, impermanent, can give us lasting satisfaction 12.624; the path of dissatisfaction 3.459–64; a powerful and positive impulse 3.463; what produces dissatisfaction? 15.287; we may be dissatisfied with the world, but are we dissatisfied enough? 11.182; 'we should cherish our dissatisfaction' 3.262; we start on the path because of dissatisfaction with worldly things 10.157–8, 13.396

dissatisfaction with oneself
feeling you cannot go on living in the same old way 3.464; get impatient with your weaknesses and failings 4.368; like the arrival of a disappointing parcel 3.462–3; 'If you're not dissatisfied with what you are, you will never strive to be what you aren't' 3.224–5, 12.623; a reason why people adopt Buddhism 13.396; spiritual friends won't let you settle down in what you now are 18.639–40; the way of overcoming ourselves (Nietzsche) 3.498; we may be dissatisfied but not know what to do about it 11.148; we become dissatisfied with ourselves when we get a glimpse of our potential 3.463

see also
dukkha

distinctions the Buddha draws clear distinctions between others' beliefs and his own 10.678 (n130); distinctions of caste are made by the mind 10.232–3; the distinctions the mind makes 18.179; importance of making clear distinctions 9.271–2; many philosophies make black and white distinctions, rather than seeing things in colour 13.284; provisional, not final or ultimate 3.237; the relationship between things we distinguish in the world is impossible to pin down 17.377; to make spiritual progress, we have to make dualistic distinctions 18.85, 18.179

distractions (*vikṣepa*)

what is distraction?
definition: something that forces itself on our attention 3.567; the claims of other 'selves' 3.418–19, 5.655; distracted mind 15.163, 26.657; the far enemy of fidelity 3.567; 'fondness for diversion' 18.452–3;

it manifests in different ways 15.116–17; lack of integration 18.522

traditional references
six kinds of 'desultoriness' (Abhidharma) 17.680–2; the poison of distraction 3.124, 3.340, 11.405; as *upakleśa* (Abhidharma) 17.680–2

distraction in everyday life
displacement activity 15.116; distraction at work 15.117–18; the distractions of workaday life 1.345; getting sidetracked 16.536; the letter to post and the boiling kettle 1.567–9, 15.115; life without distractions in the Buddha's day 14.398–9; modern life multiplies the distractions from the sensory world 17.44; most of us are occupied with matters unworthy of our attention 3.35; our tendency to get enmeshed in distractions 15.174–5; the sensory distractions of everyday life 15.288; symbolized by the burning house 3.35, 16.74; ways we distract ourselves from the tedium of normal life 17.393

distracting things
city life 12.421; mental activity 19.194; the opposite sex 12.422; reading 26.42; sexual distraction 3.567; television 10.251, 12.421; Western lifestyle 10.251

looking for distraction
looking for distraction in religion 19.468–9; seeking diversions while on solitary retreat 19.491–3; seeking something with which to distract yourself 18.333–4; there's a strange side of the mind that almost wants to be distracted 5.394; wanting to bring distractions into the Pure Land 16.471

what's going on?
'distracted from distraction by distraction' 4.73; our energies are not unified 5.654–5; where do distractions come from? 15.170; why are we so easily distracted? 1.568–9

practices to overcome distraction
absorbed in retreat life, you don't feel the need of any distractions 19.254; *dhyāna* experience allows one to contemplate reality without distraction 4.494; don't deliberately expose yourself to distraction 4.384; the doorway to non-duality beyond distraction and attention 16.543–4; if you are distracted, ask yourself whether you are enjoying your situation 15.117; the *mettā bhāvanā* and devotional practices 15.116; the mindfulness of breathing 3.124–5, 3.341–2, 4.73, 5.29, 11.405, 15.116, 19.227; the *nāḍis* and *prāṇas* dispel drowsiness and distractions 19.155; only insight can 'kill' the longing for diversion 19.518; preventing ideas from floating away 17.89–91; spiritual life: no longer papering over discomfort with distractions 15.232; sustaining mindfulness of purpose on a trip to town 18.422–4; through overcoming distraction you become more aware 17.260; to strengthen motivation, avoid distractions 12.381; vigilance with regard to distractions 18.46–7

see also
distraction in meditation, *see under* meditation/dealing with difficulties

diṭṭhi *see* views

diṭṭhi visuddhi *see* seven *visuddhis*

Divatia, Sir H. V. 22.270

diversions *see* distractions

diversity *Avataṃsaka Sūtra* sees that both unity and diversity are just concepts 16.21; the Enlightened mind sees things in their unity and their diversity 3.374; 'joyous in confusion of diversity' (Milarepa) 18.45–6; true religion makes for unity, not diversity 7.103

divine call of the divine 16.73–4; divine ear (*dibba-sota*), *see* clairaudience; divine eye, *see under* five eyes; Divine Healer (archetype) 16.189–209; divine kingship, *see under* kingship

Divine Light Mission 15.490, 15.764 (n188), 17.40, 17.711 (n43)

divya-cakṣus *see under* five eyes

Divyagiri mountains 20.375–80

divya-śrota (divine ear) *see* clairaudience

Divyāvadāna *see under Avādanas*

Dix, Otto 26.379

Dobbs-Higginson, M. S. 24.509, 24.563

docetism *see under* Gnosticism

doctrine *see under* Dharma II/teachings and practices

Doctrine of Mere-Consciousness *see under* Xuanzang

doctrine-follower (*dharmānusārin*)

introduction
an 'island unto himself' 2.142; approach to Buddhism 17.332–3; may want an overview of the whole Dharma before practising 19.507–8; their emotions have to catch up gradually 15.743; they get their inspiration from the Dharma via its 'philosophy' 15.561, 25.13; they have broad sympathies, but mustn't spread

themselves too thinly 17.333; they will want to understand a practice before taking it up 11.157–8; they need to understand intellectually before they can go for Refuge 18.272–3; taken to extremes, this approach can leave one high and dry 17.573–4; typifies the predominantly intellectual approach 2.142, 15.561; will make a careful examination of the Dharma 11.157–8, 17.614

traditional references
canonical definition 2.142–4; canonical references 2.737 (n651), 15.767 (n210); distinction from faith-follower 2.143, 11.158, 17.333, 18.133; does not attain arhantship by wisdom alone 2.145; examples from the tradition 2.143, 17.333; on becoming an *arhant*, known as a *prajñāvimukta* ('wisdom-liberated one') 2.145; one of the seven holy persons of the Āryasaṅgha 2.141–3, 17.710 (n39; 29,565 kinds identified by the Sarvāstivādins 2.152

the practice of a doctrine-follower
approaches the Unconditioned backwards 15.569, 15.575, 15.579–80; faith 17.35; Going for Refuge 15.546, 15.567–8, 15.600–1, 15.605, 15.610, 15.720; knowledge comes first, then love 10.224; recollection of the world's unpleasant qualities 18.128; reflections on impermanence for the doctrine-follower 18.154; rejoicing in merits 11.268; the way of study 2.143, 25.13–14

dogs

physical dogs
an argument of dogs in Spain 24.415; a dog at the first Wesak celebration at Sakura 23.430; a fierce dog for the Vihara 22.522; howling dogs in Pune 24.15; 'lion-dogs' (Pekingese) 26.289–90; a relative who bred bulldogs 26.553; Roy, the dog who liked chocolate 26.413; dogs' sense of smell 16.559, 26.498; two poems about dogs 24.564–5; Uncle Leonard's Sealyham Terriers 26.431, 26.569; 'What beautiful teeth!' 1.521–2

symbolic and imaginary dogs
'Barking dogs all round me ...' 25.423; a dog in Rechungpa's dream 19.562–3; discussion like dogs barking at each other 19.178–9; the elephant ignoring barking dogs 9.366, 10.201, 18.420; 'Has a dog Buddha nature?' 8.499, 13.356, 13.699 (n161); 'milk put in the skin of a dog' (Kumārila Bhaṭṭa) 8.359–60, 10.624; sensual pleasures don't satisfy any more than a meatless bone satisfies a dog 14.42; the shadow appearing in our dreams as a black dog snapping at our heels 12.192; the true disciple is like a bulldog puppy – won't let go 3.555–6; the universe struggling away from pain like a dog in a treadmill 7.47; worship of a dog's tooth 2.71, 19.327

Dōgen the wise man who said to the man of power 'Cease to do evil' 3.660 (n228); 'always take refuge in Buddha, Dharma, Sangha' 2.567, 3.331, 12.506; 'Instructions for the Cook' 17.732 (n184); death anniversary 2.228

dogmatism the Buddha rejected dogmatism 7.144; creating a Buddhist 'Bible' would pollute the pure Dharma with dogmatism 7.334; can be caused by insecurity 16.82; in Christianity 13.434–5; the cold ice of dogmatism blocks the river of life 7.145; a dogmatic attitude turns right views into wrong views 17.631; the dogmatism of art and religion 26.249; if faith is strong but wisdom weak 1.293; 'the Great Perfection has no dogmas' 19.271–3; interpreting faith or confidence as dogmatism 19.102–3; not necessarily a bad thing 1.15; people's desire for dogmatic statements 19.102; static and dead, a matter of definitions merely 7.144; a tiny crack of dogmatism and intolerance 7.246; word used in non-derogatory sense 1.297

do-gooders compassionate activity is not a sort of do-gooding 13.69; a do-gooder clergyman 5.201; do-gooders want to make themselves happy using others as the means 17.597; the harm sometimes caused by do-gooders 17.597; when helping others, beware of a sense of 'do-gooding' 18.592

Dohākoṣa 1.27, 1.306, 1.382, 1.392, 13.179

Dolma *see* Tārā

domanassa (distress, dejectedness, melancholy, grief) 2.386

domestic life being tied down by domestic life 23.99; the lure of domesticity 25.445; 'narrow domestic walls' 7.273, 7.399; people often just drift into domestic life 19.582; pursuit of wisdom vitiated by domestic responsibilities 1.340; retreat centres should not suggest domesticity 19.96

Dominic, St 13.600

Don Juan 24.441–2

Doṇa (a brahmin) asked the Buddha, 'Who are you?' 3.140–3, 3.647 (n139); intervened in the quarrel over the Buddha's relics 16.142, 16.153

Donatello 23.259, 23.314, 23.513 (n300), 23.523 (n359)

Dongshan 8.488

donkeys and mules abbot reborn as a donkey 3.102–4; Buraq, Mohammed's intelligent mule 26.689; converting to Hinduism would be like making a donkey into a horse 10.44, 12.245; the donkey who said he was a cow 3.401, 9.192–3, 9.273; a married man is like a donkey tethered to a post 26.29; Sangharakshita's support for a donkey charity 25.52

Donne, John introduction 21.632 (n141); 'Donne's Bell' (poem) 25.422; 'Letters mingle souls' 12.694, 21.457, 25.421; 'No man is an island, entire of itself' 4.707 (n316), 12.68, 26.633; 'Never send to know for whom the bell tolls' 4.472, 25.422; Sangharakshita reads 20.100, 26.392; sermons 12.519

Donnelly, Ignatius 20.32

Dooars, India 21.33, 21.540–1, 22.377, 22.440, 22.456

doors begging door to door 10.518; Dharma-doors to non-duality 16.541–50; 'The door of the Truth is covered by a golden disc' 12.384; 'doors' to the absolute 13.492; doors to emancipation, *see* three *vimokṣas*; 'If the doors of perception were cleansed ...' 15.205–6; if we walk into a door, it is more than a 'linguistic fiction' 17.445; karma according to 'door' – body, speech, and mind 2.70–1, 3.104–5; leaving out devotion closes the door on emotional engagement with the ideal 3.301; a thousand doors fly open 25.324; like an unwanted, faithful dog, the ego-sense, kicked out of the front door, creeps in the back 7.406; the man who forgot which side of the door he'd left his umbrella, *see under* umbrella; the teaching about *dukkha* opens the door to progress 10.158; 'to pass through the door of the mind to other regions of experience' 4.488–9; a universal symbol, signifying passing from a lower to a higher state of existence 26.664–5; the Virgin Mary opened the back door to hell 13.601; 'Wide open are the doors to the Deathless', *see under* deathless

Doraiswamy, Dr and Mrs v22

Doré, Gustave 13.593

dorje *see vajra*

Dorje Chopa *see under Diamond Sūtra*/translations

Dorje Lamo (female *tulku*) *see* Samding Dorje Phagmo

Dorje Phagmo *see* Vajravārāhī

Dorje Phagmo (female *tulku*) *see* Samding Dorje Phagmo

Dorje-Chang *see* Vajradhara

Dorje-lek-pa *see* Vajrapāṇi

Dorji, Jigme (Bhutan) v22, v23

Dorji, Kesang v23

Dorji, Lhendup v23

Dorji, Raja Sonam Topgay (Kalimpong) v21, v22, 23.119

Dorji, Rani Chuni (Kalimpong) v21, v22, v23

Dorji, Tashi v21, v22, v23

Dorsey, Isaac v24

dosa *see* hatred

dosa (medical term) 10.451

Dossi, Dosso 23.308, 23.520 (n346)

Dostoevsky, Fyodor *The Brothers Karamazov* 13.478, 22.120; his conception of the spiritual life is Eastern rather than Western 8.379; *The Jātaka Stories and the Russian Novel* (Wickramasinghe) 8.378–9

double *vajra* *see viśvavajra*

doubt

the nature of doubt
avoiding having to do anything 15.175–6; doubt with regard to the Three Jewels 17.632; doubting whether you are on the right path 15.360; faith is innate, doubt acquired 26.35; a kind of camouflage 15.176; not really wanting to know what one thinks 17.290–1, 26.60; resistance to the positive spirit of the path 15.176

how does it arise?
doubt and perplexity about doctrines 17.23; persistent doubt suggests insecurity and anxiety 10.578; sometimes just because of lack of energy 10.578; speculation, creed, and dogma lead to doubt, hesitation, uncertainty 7.145; we are usually in a state of doubt on account of our dependence 10.637

traditional references
'crossing over by the overcoming of doubt', *see under* seven *visuddhis*; doubt as a hindrance to meditation, *see under* five hindrances; one of the *mūlakleśas* (Abhidharma) 17.612–17; a tiger to be killed (*Dhammapada*) 15.41; rebirth

in Sukhāvatī in a closed lotus because of having entertained doubt 1.331; the enemy of effective Tantric practice is doubt 18.181

getting rid of doubt
the antidote is mindfulness 5.29; don't indulge someone in their self-doubt 18.624–5; the doubting mind can never be laid to rest outside of practice 18.182; make sure you're doing what you really want to do 4.483–7; one can choose whether to magnify or minimize intellectual doubts 17.48; resolving doubts may not mean getting answers to your questions 10.578; we practise only to the extent that we are free from energy-sapping doubt 14.586; you can't resolve it theoretically and then start on the spiritual life 10.577–8; your doubts don't go until you see things as they really are 10.431

positive doubt
Buddhism teaches that there is nothing wrong with doubt 15.265; experiencing while trying to understand something more clearly 17.613; the 'Great Doubt' (Zen) 17.378; honest doubt 2.146–7, 3.418; objective, cool, critical enquiry – the sort of doubt that Buddhism encourages 4.185

see also
vicikitsā (doubt and indecision); ten fetters/second fetter

Dougan, Abdullah 24.576–7

Douglas, Bill 24.490

dove-footed nymphs *see under* Nanda

Dover, Kent 23.244–5

Downer, Keith *see* Dharmadhara

dowry system *see under* marriage/Indian

Dowson, Ernest 7.131, 7.586 (n230), 13.630

dragons (*nāgas*, sometimes serpents)
association with water and treasure 16.348; at Glastonbury Tor 25.499; 'The Clouded Dragon' 25.172; dragon's head, snake's body 1.493–4, 15.473, 16.351, 26.38, 26.705–6 (n19); dragons on Anglo-Saxon helms 25.287; the forces of inspiration emerging from the depths 14.346; *garuḍas* feed on them 16.349; guarding the golden apples 25.281; keepers of the Perfection of Wisdom texts 14.345–6, 16.16–17; magical powers 16.348; the painted dragon who flew away as soon as his eyes were painted 2.213; paper-and-tinsel dragons 25.319; the Kraków dragon 26.448–9; ruled by Virūpākṣa 16.346; Sangharakshita's childhood fascination with dragons 20.484; symbolism 16.351–2, 20.2, 20.484; Tibetans refused to mine for gold, believing it was guarded by dragons 15.138; understand the teaching but don't practise it 16.348, 16.351–2

Drake, Francis 25.431

drama *see* theatre

drapa (Tibetan monk) 12.14, 13.50

Draupadi *see under Mahābhārata*

dravya 14.83

dravyasat 17.445

Drayton, Michael 24.558–61

Dṛḍhā *see under* earth goddess

Dṛḍhāmati (bodhisattva) 14.195

dreams

the nature of dreams
ancient Greek tradition of healing through dreams 16.191; archetypal dreams 12.199, 12.685, 19.306; aspect of the *mano-vijñāna* 12.175; before waking, we can't know that what we saw in our dream doesn't exist 1.369; 'big' dreams 16.259, 19.306, 26.682; a connection with a realm of experience we ignore at our peril 17.686; a dream has its own reality 19.305; the dream is you, though a part of yourself you do not usually experience 26.84; evidence that the mind is not limited to waking consciousness 17.341; inspiration from deeper sources 19.304–5, 19.562; 'little dreams' 19.324, 19.566–7, 26.682; our dream experience has a life of its own 17.686–7; our dream life may be more vivid than our waking life 4.36, 19.564–5; our waking activities supply the seed from which we reap the harvest of dreams 7.100; they can be about two things at the same time 4.203; they can be full of power and interest and fascination 19.323; they play an important part in the individuation process 12.199; they play an important part in our lives 12.685; a way of staying in touch with the imagination 17.684; we have parallel lives, a waking life and a dream life 26.223

working with dreams
asking what dreams 'mean' is beside the point 17.687; dreams are their own explanation 19.563, 26.84; the interpretation of dreams 16.204–5, 19.324–5, 19.562–3; learning how to direct your dreams 17.340; some dreams need to be paid particular attention 19.564; very

often one has to take dreams at face value 25.64; writing dreams down 19.324

reflections
dreamless sleep (Vedic tradition) 17.340–1; having meaningful dreams suggests being tired of the conceptual framework 19.564; if one does not dream, one becomes a monster 26.19; images reflect your cultural background 16.266; as literary convention 16.263; one could think of a spiritual movement as having a dream life 4.37; practising the *mettā bhāvanā* gives happy dreams 9.517; the shadow appearing in our dreams 12.192

dreamers
a bodhisattva's dreams 2.169; Josaphat's dream of heaven and hell 13.660–1; Maitreya appeared in a dream to Master Hanshan Deqing 14.260; Milarepa interprets Rechungpa's dreams 19.561–73; Milarepa's dream of a *ḍākinī* 18.58–9; Ruciraketu's dream (*Sūtra of Golden Light*) 16.253, 16.262–7, 16.287–8; Siddhārtha's dreams before Enlightenment 12.685

spiritual life in dreams
analogous to the archetypal realm 4.36, 16.534; the *bardo* of dreams 12.199–200, 18.83; being given a mantra in a dream 13.291; blending waking practice with dreams 19.323–4; confessing ill will in a dream 4.46; connected with the Vajrasattva practice 14.487; contacting the *sambhogakāya* in dreams 4.208; continuing to be aware, all day, all night, even in dreams, will transform us 1.575; different states of consciousness in dreams 16.252–3, 16.263; dimensions of consciousness in dreams unknown to our everyday self 14.462; developing self-recollection in a dream 19.572; dream yoga (Nāropā) 13.28, 17.340, 17.744 (n292), 18.65; dreaming about gurus, Buddhas, and *ḍākinīs*: a deeper level 19.303–5; dreaming of going for Refuge 15.689; dreams and *vipaśyanā* 19.305–6; gaining insight in a dream 19.571–2; gaining Enlightenment in the dream state 12.199, 19.306; integration in dreams 19.565; meditation and the dream state 12.172–3, 12.199–200, 26.46; mindfulness in the dream state 12.199–200; one can contact reality directly from the dream state 19.305–6; Perfect Vision arising in dreams 1.481; practices that prolong consciousness into the dream state 19.307; proof that something can be perceived without objective reality 12.172; reaching higher states of consciousness from the dream state 26.224; a sign of progress if insight experiences and dreams influence each other 19.306–7; spiritual experiences in dreams 19.565; the value of the dream state (Mahāyāna and Vajrayāna) 16.252–3; access to the *rūpaloka*, the archetypal realm 12.559

life is like a dream
life is a dream, a cloud, a drop of dew 25.390; life is like a dream 4.427, 18.555–6; realizing that the whole of existence is like a dream (one of Nāropā's six yogas) 13.28; 'The things of this samsaric world are all illusion, like a dream' 5.602–8; view what is conditioned as a dream 14.509

awakening from a dream
the bodhisattva's experience 'like awakening from a dream' 14.228–9; getting rid of the sense of self like waking up from a dream 10.470; without translation into conceptual terms, insight is like a fading dream 5.449; you may get a glimpse that there is no ego 17.340

see also
daydreams; Sangharakshita's dreams, *see under* Sangharakshita VI/emotional life

Drepung 2.191, 13.33, 22.476

Driberg, Tom 23.87–9

Drikung Kyabgön Chetsang 24.473

drinking (alcohol)

abstention from drinking (fifth precept)
does it mean complete abstention or moderation? 3.323, 15.422, 19.331–3; a little alcohol can have a positive role within definite limits 4.603, 19.331–2; one who indulges regularly has little right to be called Buddhist 8.226–7; the precept taught in India 9.19, 9.129, 9.216, 9.410, 9.463; 'restraint in drink' (*Maṅgala Sutta*) 15.422

selling alcohol as a form of wrong livelihood
one does not keep a liquor shop, or produce liquor 9.216; Mahāyāna precept 2.208; one of the prohibited occupations in the Pāli canon 1.546, 3.283, 13.454; state revenue from liquor sales 8.213, 8.227

concerns
Buddhists should reach out to people with drinking problems 24.154; the desire for oblivion 17.256; drinking to relieve boredom 11.78; drinking together mustn't become a substitute for real communication 19.333; the effects of drunkenness 17.256–7; loss of mindfulness through drinking 9.216, 13.401; the problem of alcoholism 10.86

drinking in different cultures and religions
banning alcohol from state functions (Sri Lanka) 8.227; the drinking habits of an English nun 22.519–20; drunken Tantric teachers 1.200; the excessive drinking of two Indian lawyers 20.276; a guru who was always drunk, but said to be very wise 13.177, 19.160–1; it is not part of the Dharma, but may be part of a Buddhist culture 13.401; often an accepted part of social life in Buddhist countries 8.313; regarded as disreputable in India 17.257; regarded as a sin in the Boys' Brigade 13.609–10; temperance (Rechabites) 20.21

wine
at Vajrayānic feasts 19.486; Cicero's Falernian 24.294; a monk shouldn't beg for alms outside a wine shop or a brothel 18.394; 'putting new wine in old bottles' 1.62, 2.58–9, 9.480, 10.429, 23.178, 26.474; relaxing through drinking a little wine (in early FWBO days) 14.573, 17.257, 19.331–2; tantras on wine 1.383

Sangharakshita's experience of drinking
a drunken step-grandfather 26.553; drinking with his father 20.88, 20.90; black and tans in the Army 20.99; a pub crawl with a fellow Buddhist 20.101; bhang in India 20.162; alone in the pub (60s London) 11.xx, 26.604; sangria in Spain 24.433–4

drunkenness as metaphor
symbol of ignorance or unawareness 1.108, 3.195–6, 16.170–1, 16.218, 17.434; intoxication of mind 16.298–9; *saṃskāras* likened to actions committed while drunk 1.108, 3.195–6, 17.434

Driver, John introduction 17.728 (n149), 22.403, 22.503; collaboration on the 'Flower-Garland Hymn to the Goddess Tārā' 17.141–7; collaboration on *The Three Chief Paths* 8.529, 8.661, 17.425; initiation from Dudjom Rimpoche 22.503–7; translation of *sādhanas* 2.174–5, 22.403, 22.506–7; visits the vihara in Kalimpong 8.664

Driver, Prof. and Alu 23.351–2

Drokmi 13.28

Dromtön Atīśa's chief Tibetan disciple 12.577; founder of Reting Monastery 12.578; began the Kadam school of Tibetan Buddhism 8.528, 12.577–9; never became a monk, but was a man of deep spiritual realization 12.577; 'Wouldn't you rather be practising the Dharma?' 8.593–4

drowsiness drowsiness on retreat 5.678–80; if you feel drowsy, try going to sleep and see how you feel when you wake up 19.395; in meditation, *see under* five hindrances/sloth and torpor; as a mental event, *see middha*

dṛṣṭi *see* views

drugs abstaining from taking or dealing in drugs 3.583, 9.216, 10.395, 26.669; altered states of consciousness 5.271–2, 17.341; article by Lama Govinda 5.272; Hare Krishna followers smuggling drugs into Australia 24.56; a drug-taker in Seville 24.436; drug addiction 10.395, 17.256–7, 17.285; ganja 20.348, 20.399–400, 20.414; opium 8.208, 10.72; in the Sixties and Seventies 12.654; taking drugs to relieve boredom 11.78; Terry Delamare is given ether 23.103–4; taking drugs compared to meditation 5.269–74; dimensions of consciousness unknown to our everyday self 14.462; experience of *samāpattis* in 4.514; one's capacity for karma is swamped by *vipāka* 17.527; Sangharakshita taking LSD 23.465–9, 25.81–2, 26.496–7, 26.609–10; the possibilities of experience 5.51; trying to see things as they are through taking drugs 17.132–3

drum of the deathless, *see under* deathless; golden, *see Sūtra of Golden Light*/golden drum; *Golden Drum* (magazine), *see Golden Drum*

drunkenness *see* drinking

Drunye Chenmo 22.499–500

dry an anthology of stories to correct any impression of Buddhist teaching as dry 10.569; *arhants* portrayed as dry emotionless figures 4.21; the danger of drying up emotionally 2.607; 'dry' insight, *see under* insight/how to gain insight; dryness as a mental state 19.90; early Buddhism wrongly represented as a dry, rationalistic system 1.290; if your approach to the Dharma is dry, you need inspiration from its more colourful aspects 18.372; insight is not dry and barren, but a deeply emotional experience 19.379; 'Let blood dry up, let flesh wither away' 3.52, 4.370–1, 5.389, 10.259, 11.16; merely intellectual conversation is just the dry bones of concepts rubbing against one another 12.314; reading some works might give the impression that Buddhism is dry 19.125; scholars' dry approach to Buddhism 9.230–1; we mustn't be dry-as-dust intellectuals, but we mustn't be cotton candy Buddhists either 12.515–16; we need beauty: without it we tend to dry up 12.559; Western Buddhism can

be presented in a very dry, academic way 16.129, 19.126; without knowledge of truth, our world is a dry and barren place 16.219; you can't have a cold spiritual life any more than you can have a dry spiritual life 12.514; you have to consider your interests, or your Buddhism will be dry and abstract 19.50–1; you have to see the Transcendental not as dry and abstract, but as fascinating 19.24–5

Dryden, John *Alexander's Feast* 26.373; 'Beware the fury of a patient man' 18.610; 'chemist, fiddler, statesman, and buffoon' 1.569; 'Great wits are sure to madness near allied' 24.422; *The Hind and the Panther* 26.395; 'in order to their stations leap' 26.113; the inappropriateness of the term 'literary criticism' 26.324; as literary critic 26.324; 'Pity melts the mind to love' 26.613; 'Smooth the descent, and easy is the way' 1.25; translation of the *Aeneid* 26.469; translation of the *Decameron* 24.410

Dsudbhu 19.31

du Pin, Patrice de la Tour 24.389

dualism or duality

our dualistic life
the division between inner and outer worlds is produced by dualistic thinking 15.138; dualistic consciousness splits experience into 'me' and 'the world' 15.210; dualistic views can lead to individualism 1.267, 4.188; fear indicates attachment to the self, and that implies duality 18.49; interdependent dualities 17.368–9; represented in the parable of the return journey 16.98; we are creatures of duality 16.542; the whole framework of our knowledge is dualistic 14.441

the dualistic nature of spiritual life
all systems founded on a dualistic philosophy create a split in the psyche 7.401; Buddhism is dualistic in character 11.312, 15.634–5; a dualistic approach is the necessary working basis 4.162, 14.591; in negating duality you are setting it up 14.593; the mind interprets dualistically even the bodhisattva's realization of non-duality 7.140; reality seen as an object from within the framework of the dualistic mind 19.142–3; spiritual practice is necessarily dualistic, though its goal is non-dualistic 2.282; when doing a puja, best to go back to some old-fashioned dualism 19.508–9

how do we transcend duality?
the bodhisattva undisturbed by dualistic concepts 1.269; crossing the mountain of dualism 19.81; Early Buddhist and Mahāyāna approaches 1.274, 14.591–4, 15.634; how can the transition from dualism to insight be 'a matter of time'? 16.112–13; how can we realize duality by means of the dualistic? 16.542–50, 17.xx, 17.365–6; the Perfection of Wisdom breaks down the dualistic basis of religious life 14.104

beyond duality
dualistic experience is transcended in the experience of Enlightenment 12.613–14; in the last analysis the duality between mundane and transcendental disappears 19.49; in reality all dualisms are transcended 14.361; primordial: earth and sky 16.385; realizing that duality is created by our own minds, we become Enlightened 22.29

see also
subject–object

Dubash, Dinoo

her life and work
introduction 21.456–73; early life 21.461–2; her character 21.505, 22.283; assists with publication of 'Is Buddhism for Monks Only?' 7.189; considers taking a cottage at the Vihara in Kalimpong 21.549, 21.552; deafness 12.692–3, 21.596; and Dr Mehta 21.466–8, 22.356–7; gifts for Clare Cameron 21.592; illness 21.579; meets the Dalai Lama 21.465–6, 21.527; meets Jagdish Kashyap 21.464–5; Montessori school 21.557–8, 21.578, 22.283; paintings of Maitreya 12.692, 21.462–3, 21.558–9; photograph 21.456; receives the FWBO newsletter 21.595; spiritual experiences 21.559; trouble with servants 21.552, 21.555; visits Kalimpong 21.565–6, 21.569–70; last years 12.693, 21.470–1

and Sangharakshita
first meeting 12.692, 22.270, 22.283; she finances publications 22.364; letters 12.693, 21.471–3, 22.363–4; misunderstandings 21.571–2; support 21.469–70, 21.539–40, 22.378, 24.12; he visits her in 1979 24.12

dubdor (fighting monk) 22.521

Duccio's *Maestà* 13.634, 13.646

Dudjom Rimpoche

life
delight in being alive 22.508; he is arrested 22.509–10; his style of dress 22.508; a great Nyingma master 22.501–2; formed a group with Chattrul Sangye Dorje and Jamyang Khyentse Rimpoche 12.443; 'which of the three gurus is the greatest?' 3.551, 12.443, 18.109–10, 19.310–11, 22.384; like a great ocean, with calm depths and a sparkling surface 22.508; liveliness and spontaneity 22.508; marriage 2.722 (n548), 12.442, 13.26; met Allen Ginsberg 22.568; photograph 22.505; rather unapproachable, lived in regal style, and was fond of whisky 12.442–3; built a temple at Rinkingpong 22.501–2; celebrated festivals at the vihara in Kalimpong 8.658–9; established the Zangdokpalri Monastery, Kalimpong 12.684, 12.757 (n476); the Sherpa community were devoted to him 22.507, 22.509; spoke at an event commemorating Tsongkhapa 22.510–11; the stillness of his mind 22.501, 22.508; his death 12.443

teachings and works
Counsels from my Heart 5.555–6; explains three types of meditation practice for three types of practitioner 22.510; a work on the history and teachings of the Nyingma school 12.443

and Sangharakshita
questions about *sādhanas* 22.508–9; Green Tārā initiation 12.661; Vajrasattva *abhiṣeka* 13.161–2, 22.504–7; looking up to him 26.629

duḥsīla 11.307

dukkha or ***duḥkha*** (unsatisfactoriness, suffering)

introduction
where Buddhism begins 7.388–9, 8.581, 12.120–1

etymology and translations
exploitation (Ambedkar) 9.412, 9.427; harm 15.302; the ill-fitting chariot wheel 3.209–10, 3.260, 26.12; *jarā-maraṇa* a figure of speech for *dukkha* 1.115; peace (*santa*) is its positive counterpart 15.262, 15.302

the Buddha
his experience of suffering 3.261; he made it clear that suffering is not integral to spiritual life 15.353; he wanted us to form a picture of *dukkha*, not indulge in abstract speculations 1.128; 'I teach only suffering and the end of suffering' 1.78, 3.213, 7.115, 7.134, 7.222, 26.154, 26.158–9

the teaching of dukkha
the allegation that Buddhists are indifferent to human suffering 2.69; both the world of suffering and the Realm of Truth are in the mind 7.274; Buddhism recognizes suffering and evil, but also the power of positive forces 4.267–8; the difference between relative and absolute unsatisfactoriness 17.593; the doctrine is a corrective to a one-sided view of existence 2.90; the hallmark of a Buddhist school: does it try to solve the problem of pain? 7.126–7; is the teaching pessimistic?, *see under* pessimism; it is placed at the heart of Buddhism because it stimulates us to act 15.233; a reminder not to imagine that suffering can be avoided altogether 17.252; there is suffering, but nobody suffers: a paradox 7.133; three kinds: pain, change, conditioned existence 11.104–5, 17.427, 17.754 (n358); to be understood as method, not doctrine 1.124–5, 1.129–30, 15.129–30, 15.227–30; to think that Buddhism is only about removing suffering is a mistake 1.132, 7.390

descriptions of dukkha
a feeling, not a concept 7.389; hell is suffering, and suffering is passivity 19.580; illustrated by St Augustine and Goethe 2.91–2; nothing quite lives up to our expectations 3.260, 26.12; a sign that we

are not living as we ought to live 1.132, 7.390–1; some descriptions gloss over the uncomfortable fact of suffering 7.389; an unenlightened state of dissatisfaction and muddle 15.262

images, myths, and metaphors
the cloud of suffering 4.572–4, 4.624, 4.634; no flower of human achievement but some great sorrow lay at its root 7.389, 26.11; over many lifetimes: the flood of tears 1.130–1; poison drunk by Avalokiteśvara 16.398; we can cross the stream of suffering only by crossing the stream of desire 7.253

the experience of dukkha
an affinity between intense mental suffering and Enlightenment 13.134; all experience short of Enlightenment is a subtle form of suffering 1.486; being subject to clinging, the five *skandhas* are suffering 3.213; confusing the experience with insight into it 5.460, 16.407, 23.73; from an absolute perspective pleasant experience is *dukkha*, but it is still pleasant 17.592; the innocent can suffer 15.368, 16.422; it can leave a vibration in the atmosphere of a place 18.312; no need to try out everything for personal confirmation of unsatisfactoriness 16.284; suffering and joy not experienced as separate (Milarepa) 18.47; suffering from one's psychic state 5.657, 5.659–70, 12.225–6, 13.396; three kinds: actual, potential, and metaphysical 1.486, 12.623–4; self-inflicted suffering 13.137–8; seven kinds (birth, old age, etc.) 1.127–8, 3.210–13, 7.47–8, 7.116, 7.219; *sukha* (pleasant experience) is painful (*dukkha*) because it has its limitations 15.449, 17.592; suffering from the lack of a philosophy of life 5.663–4; suffering helps you understand the suffering of others 17.303; suffering in the modern world 12.381; suffering in the spiritual life, *see under* spiritual life/challenges; the suffering of the body 18.557–8; the unsatisfactoriness of pleasant worldly experiences, and even the *dhyānas* 18.589; when you are suffering, you have an urge to retaliate 15.304; you can suffer evil but stay skilful 15.368–70

concealed dukkha
(1) something that is pleasant for oneself may involve suffering for others 3.213–14; (2) fear of losing pleasant experience 3.214–15; (3) something pleasant that binds us to something that brings suffering 3.215; (4) conditioned things cannot satisfy our longing for the Unconditioned 2.91–2, 3.215

awareness of dukkha
a catalyst for spiritual progress 13.137–8; fear of suffering 11.263–4; facing our own suffering – 'swallowing the pot of poison' 16.398–9; a factor in spiritual growth 3.556; how to sustain a realization brought by painful experience? 4.13; if one does not reflect on unsatisfactoriness, sloth will arise 4.470; 'If you are suffering, don't just reach out for another chocolate' 3.227; insight into the truth of suffering can be gained even when one is happy 26.62; it may prompt us to think that there must be something more 12.647; our infatuation with transitory pleasures prevents us from seeing it 7.388–9; people undergoing illness or distress may have intense spiritual experiences 13.137; people who suffer are not necessarily nearer realizing the truth of suffering 26.12; some people only learn when they suffer 15.358; spiritual life: no longer papering over discomfort with distractions 15.232; spiritual life starts with experiencing it 7.391, 18.400, 22.259; 'we should cherish our dissatisfaction' 3.262; when we experience *dukkha*, we should try to develop faith 12.646–7; when we realize the fact of *dukkha*, the pleasures of the senses lose their relish 7.50–1

the causes of dukkha
all our suffering is *indirectly* the result of past unskilful volitions 17.173; craving (described in the *Mahāsatipaṭṭhāna Sutta*) 1.111; due to the failure to transcend ignorance 16.219; even the best of things cannot give permanent satisfaction to the human heart 2.121; the 'I'-concept is the root cause of the suffering of sentient beings 7.273; impermanence as the occasion of suffering 1.172, 7.116; it is the inevitable fruit of craving 15.202; it is true that unskilful action leads to suffering, but this shouldn't be made a threat 15.621–2; not accidental or caused by God or fate, but may be connected with karma 7.219, 26.159; not all sufferings are due to karma 3.184, 4.408, 7.19, 7.599–600 (n326), 16.422, 17.173; our guarding of the self is the root cause of our suffering 15.263; people ask 'Why do I suffer?' but not 'Why am I happy?' 5.640; pleasure is good, but if you can't enjoy it mindfully, it will lead to suffering 18.151; preponderant factors are ignorance and craving 7.219; 'the punishment of God' 16.86; the result of karma: that view may not be acceptable to Western Buddhists 4.395–6; selfish desires 26.162; sometimes suffering may be the consequence of spiritual practice 14.487–8; suffering caused by the mind 18.236,

18.237; the suffering that must follow unskilful actions 17.294; the suffering that results from evil 26.642; the suffering you bring on yourself when you ignore the truth 26.46; a symptom of disease (lust, hatred, and ignorance) 7.222; through attachment we bring about our own suffering 10.611; to discover the cause of suffering one has to go very deep 12.98–9; to free ourselves from suffering, we must find out its cause 7.115–16; two views of cause, one mundane, one transcendental 7.116; we can't say it's caused by the *kleśas*, but we suffer when we are subject to them 17.637; we cause ourselves suffering through our own mental states 4.51–2; we suffer because we have not realized our potential for Enlightenment 12.613; 'Whether Buddhas come or not, one thing is fixed: out of craving arises suffering' 15.266

the suffering of all beings
all beings are equally susceptible to suffering 4.569–70, 15.237; all our suffering is unnecessary 16.287; analysing the problem of human suffering 3.261–2; the Buddha who listens to the fears and anxieties of suffering beings 14.212; 'Can there be bliss when all that lives must suffer?' 1.405; 'every blade of grass feels with pain the sting of rain' 7.388, 25.220; feeling compassion for beings 26.53; no objective reason to be more concerned with our own suffering than others' 4.570; not 'my' suffering or 'your' suffering, just suffering 4.630; observing the suffering of sentient beings (Vasubandhu) 2.271–2, 4.51–2; overcoming indifference to the world's suffering 13.81; Padmasambhava's teaching on the sufferings of the six realms 8.524; realizing that others can suffer as one does oneself 8.447–8; reflection on the suffering of human beings 1.419; *sabbe saṅkhāra dukkhā* ('all conditioned things are suffering') 2.89–90; sentient existence is a great brotherhood of suffering 7.388; some people naturally feel the sufferings of others, while others don't 4.571; the suffering of the whole saṃsāric process 1.130, 7.220; using imagination to feel someone else's suffering as our own 4.570; we're in the same boat, so we should feel solidarity with all living beings 19.540; when you and others are suffering, choose to help the other 4.579–80; the world's sufferings are probably far greater since Western scientific discovery 7.115

the alleviation of suffering
Buddhists are urged to make every effort to remove suffering in all forms 2.69–70; by eradicating craving for continued existence 26.159; 'digging up the root of suffering' (*Udāna*) 10.492; helping to relieve suffering for money 24.349; let's get rid of it, without bothering which bit is 'mine' and which is 'yours' 4.591–2; liberation from suffering is not an 'experience' in the ordinary sense 11.303; the more you develop spiritually, the more pain and suffering are eliminated 19.426; solving the problem of human suffering 26.299; things like hydroelectric dams don't solve the problem of human suffering 22.331; the Three Refuges are a refuge from suffering 2.241; try to relieve suffering, including your own, but some must be borne patiently 4.120; what are we going to do about it? 25.113; wrongly thinking that you can escape suffering by changing your situation 7.220

practices to help alleviate it
bearing it and endeavouring to prevent the arising of future suffering 7.223; meditation as a power to help dispel the cloud of suffering 4.582; motivating oneself to relieve suffering through the *karuṇā bhāvanā* 5.198

the bodhisattva's response
bearing the burden of all beings 2.178; feeling *for* beings rather than suffering *with* them 16.523; how the bodhisattva sees suffering 18.590; liberating beings from suffering, *see under* bodhisattva/ bodhisattva activity; a painless sympathy with pain 4.52, 4.581, 7.290, 16.523, 17.304, 17.511; torn between withdrawal and involvement: the arising of the *bodhicitta* 2.161–2

the cessation of suffering (dukkhakkhaya)
the bliss of relief from physical suffering 24.331–2; described in the *Dhammapada* 1.113–14; described in the *Udāna* 1.68–9, 2.123, 10.632; *dukkha* can only end on the basis of a realization of the Unconditioned 10.635–6; in the four noble truths, *see* four noble truths/third truth; the eighth emancipation 16.447; the goal of Buddhism, though cessation is not the last word 11.309; the idea that suffering ceases when craving ceases is counterintuitive 15.231–2; liberation from suffering 15.438–9; 'Neither here nor there nor in between exist.' 10.463, 10.724 (n505); Nirvāṇa as the cessation of suffering 11.310, 17.368; solving the problem of suffering 15.249–50; a state of ineffable repose, beyond words to express 7.69; staying at the point of rest, the intermediate state 10.638; suffering is

disappointed desire 7.116–17; suffering [shall be transmuted] into ecstasy 23.446; there can be no complete end of suffering for living beings 11.272; the Three Jewels represent the possibility of complete liberation from suffering 2.241–2; through acting unskilfully we lose sight of the path away from suffering 17.172; 'Walking this path you shall make an end of suffering' 4.644; while you hold on to the idea of an end to suffering, there can be no end to suffering 17.368–9

misunderstanding the teaching
'If it hurts it must be doing me good' is not a Buddhist attitude 10.503, 15.450–1; the wrong idea that to make progress we will have to suffer 17.166, 17.251–2

see also
dukkha and the four noble truths, *see under* four noble truths; and the positive *nidānas*, *see under* twelve positive *nidānas*

dullness an atmosphere of dull, heavy greed in a shop 4.573–4; dry and dull literature in Sri Lanka 20.124; dull discussions in Dharma study 4.419–20; if you're pleasure-free as well as craving-free, you're going to end up dull 19.381; in the early days in England people thought of Buddhism as arid, dull, and lifeless 19.126; Mahāyāna *sūtras* give a more vivid, attractive experience than a dull discourse 19.26; as a negative mental state 17.686; why might the precepts seem dull? 7.184–6; with no insight, *śamatha* can become dull and drowsy 19.159

Dumont, Louis v13

Dundubhīśvara, Buddha (later Amoghasiddhi) 16.258, 16.261, 16.264

dungheap better to end up on the dungheap than in a museum 26.13; a blind man (or beggar) finding a jewel on a dungheap 1.420, 2.126, 4.42, 4.44, 10.145

Dungkar Gompa 1.342–3, 26.229

Dunhuang Caves 14.258, 16.518, 16.628 (n352)

Dunlop, Mark (Vajrakumara) 4.225, 24.75, 24.625–6 (n103)

Dunne, John S. 8.431–3

Dunne, John William 7.100, 7.580 (n193)

Dupchen Lama v21, v22

duppañña (Sanskrit *dausprajñā*) 16.557

Dūraṃgamā (Far-Going) *see under* ten *bhūmis*

Dürer, Albrecht 24.596–7

Durgā 4.391, 4.703 (n287), 10.46, 16.384, 20.134–5

Durgaprasad (student in Kalimpong) v22, v23

Durrell, Lawrence 8.425–6, 8.428

Duse, Eleonora 26.166

dust

the dust of the world
the bodhisattva can't rest so long as one grain of dust remains undelivered 7.317; bodies as 'so many grains of dust in the wide expanse of the universal void' 1.356; the body a corpse crumbled to dust (*Satipaṭṭhāna Sutta*) 15.141–2; the dust of the world's roads 26.181; 'Dusty is the household life' 2.688 (n266), 10.644; the number of particles of dust in the world-system (*Diamond Sūtra*) 14.466; the dust of India 10.291, 10.305, 10.381, 23.336; the wayside dust 25.207; the world a cloud of fine particles of dust blown about by invisible winds 7.49

each grain of dust
contains a Buddha and his company of bodhisattvas 7.344, 21.287; contains all the Buddha worlds of the ten directions and the three times 16.4; contains the *dharmadhātu* 1.353, 14.218; contains the secrets of the universe, the reason of *śūnyatā* 1.353–4

dusty books
'Ah, what a dusty answer gets the soul' 1.23; a copy of the Kangyur made with ink from the dust of precious stones 14.255; the dust of close-printed volumes 25.194; 'the dust of books was blown away' 25.170; a scholar's work described as 'the last ounce of dust in desiccation' 5.248, 23.225; 'unnecessary dust' raised by scholars 22.458

metaphorical dust
beings with 'but little dust' on their eyes, *see under* Brahmā Sahāmpati's request; a *bhikkhu* 'shaking off the dust (*rajas*) of what he has done' 10.503; the dust of a hundred dreams 25.222; evil committed 'fine dust thrown against the wind' (*Dhammapada*) 15.371; the dust on the surface of the mind 18.323; the element of Tathāgatahood 'a precious statue covered in dust' 13.389; a path for the dust of passion 1.58; to be 'dust-freed' the greatest luck (*Maṅgala Sutta*) 15.452; we must live as best we can, or be accounted less than dust 25.406

philosophical dust
a grain of dust in the wrong place can destroy us 4.76; if you knew a grain of dust thoroughly you would know everything 19.215; a tiny speck of dust in the eye can prevent one from seeing 26.50; 'We have first raised a dust and then complain we cannot see' (Berkeley) 8.616; 'We mutter "All is dust"' 25.185; what has been gained and what is to be gained are strewn with dust 10.607–8; the wrong idea that reality is the dust to which everything is reduced 17.444

dusty stories
a boy ground into dust by a *vajra* for not observing the precepts 14.235; the fly who sits on a chariot saying, 'My! Aren't I kicking up a dust?' 18.367

duties *see* duty

Dutt, Dr Nalinaksha introduction 8.674 (n65); Sangharakshita meets in Calcutta 20.135; and the *Maha Bodhi* journal board 8.635, 22.166; *Aspects of Mahāyāna Buddhism* 1.65, 1.189, 1.251–4, 1.450, 21.385; *Buddhist Sects in India* 3.638 (n70); *Development of Buddhism in Uttar Pradesh* 2.195; *Early Monastic Buddhism* 2.144; on the four noble truths 1.96–7, 1.121; *Gilgit Manuscripts* 7.632 (n606); 'Why Buddhism Disappeared from India' 8.120–3

Dutt, Sukumur

Early Buddhist Monachism
bhikkhu ordination 2.648; critique of Vinaya literature 2.627; *Dhammapada* verses 10.560; the four *nissayas* 2.191; the eight releases 2.198; *parivrājakas* 2.186; *pāṭimokkha* 10.560; *Vinaya-saṅgīti* 2.188

other works
The Buddha and Five After Centuries 2.221, 2.648, 14.22; *Buddhist Monks and Monasteries of India* 2.648

Dutt, Toru (Indian poet) 7.55–6, 7.58, 7.555–6 (n69)

Dutt-Majumdar, Sri v22

Dutugamunu, King (Sri Lanka) 7.512, 8.463–5

duty and duties

what is your duty?
'The demands of the day' (Goethe) 11.90; it relates to the principles you believe in and the situation you're in 26.73; to be happy 4.97, 26.25; to take stock of your position and responsibilities 3.619

going about your duties
conscientiously performing duties leads to loosening selfishness and egotism 7.277; duties are reciprocal 12.604; duties of employers and employees 3.585–8; the duties of friendship 3.573–5; if you're too dutiful, don't you end up with an odd life? 25.110; fulfilling family or 'tribe' duties from personal choice, not group pressure 18.149–50; not the 'Stern daughter of the Voice of God' 7.277; often we've taken on so many duties we don't know what we feel like doing 4.486; peace springs naturally from duties quietly done 7.279; the unobstructed flow of love and compassion 7.277

Buddhist duties
a Buddhist's duty: to eliminate the sense of separative selfhood 7.312; as a Dharma practitioner, you're always on duty 19.500; the duties of an ascetic (*śramaṇakāraka-dharmas*) 2.194; the duties of a *bhikkhu* 2.194, 3.409–10, 7.230; duty is one meaning of the word 'Dharma' 7.278, 7.37, 13.447; in the Buddha family, no conflict between desire and duty 14.451; failing in the duty to preserve and disseminate the Dharma 8.271–2; parents' duty to bring up their children in knowledge and practice of the Dharma 22.94; seeing Buddhism in terms of duty 11.90–1; the ten duties of the lay Buddhist 23.352; to begin with you need a strong sense of duty 4.485; when a monk feels it is his civic duty to get involved in politics 7.441, 26.576

see also
rights and duties

Dvādaśanikāya Śāstra *see under* Nāgārjuna/works

Dvedhāvitakka Sutta *see under Majjhima Nikāya*

dveṣa *see* hatred

dwarves Bhaddiya the dwarf, *see* Bhaddhiya; Sangharakshita threatened with rebirth as a dwarf 8.682 (n113), 22.171

Dyer, Edward 25.357, 25.593 (n86)

dying *see under* death

dynamic Buddhism envisages the universe not as static but as dynamic 7.208; compassion is not only the positive but also the dynamic aspect of Enlightenment 1.387; compassion is the dynamic aspect of *śūnyatā* 7.457; the dynamic aspect of Reality symbolized by the flowering bowl 7.397; events considered to be intrinsically dynamic 7.196; meditation is something

dynamic, challenging, shattering 3.107; the middle way between spatio-analytical and dynamic-synthetical methods 1.103; the mind conceived of dynamically as a force, an energy 12.99; mind and matter are dynamically related 7.137; the mind in a very active, powerful, dynamic state 5.651; the path of the inner life to be seen dynamically 7.357–8; the positive and dynamic elements of Enlightenment brought out by the Tibetans 7.397; Sangharakshita's view of spiritual life as dynamic criticised 21.114; the spiritual dynamism of Buddhism has never been exhausted 7.392; the wisdom of the realization of a dynamic Becoming 7.375

dysentery *see under* sickness

dzogchen ('Great Perfection' teaching) *ati-yoga* in Tibetan Buddhism 12.299, 13.23; included in the Mahāmudrā 19.372; interpretation of the sense of self 8.616; some practitioners say it has no essential connection with Buddhism 2.565; 'staring' 24.393, 24.712 (n492); taking up a simplified form of the practice 5.613

Dzongsar Khyentse Rimpoche believed to be a tulku of Jamyang Khyentse Rimpoche 12.656; his book *What Makes You Not a Buddhist* 12.656–8; director of *The Cup* 12.656

E

E MA O! *see under* Vajrasattva

Earl, David *see* Akashadeva

Early Buddhism

introduction
brief summary 7.504–5, 12.167

names
also called basic, original, ancient (Conze), pure 1.182–3; coinage of the term 'Hīnayāna' 1.214–15, 3.413; 'Hīnayāna' as the limited ideal that may be espoused by any practitioner 18.172–3; 'Hīnayāna' represents an attitude rather than a particular doctrinal school 16.31; the term 'Hīnayāna' should not be understood in a pejorative sense 14.342; what did the 'Hīnayāna' schools call themselves? 1.211, 16.30

history
began as a broad spiritual movement 15.186; origin in those of the Buddha's disciples who focused on the teachings 16.14; origins of early schools obscure 1.185; Upanishadic influence on early Buddhism? 10.545–6; it does not necessarily coincide with the Pāli canon 16.60; eighteen schools 1.185–6, 7.472, 7.497; emergence from the Sthaviravādins 2.206; lineage 1.275; and 'Mahāyāna', *see* Mahāyāna/contrasts with Early Buddhism; by Aśoka's time there were four independent monastic corporations 7.497; Zen and Early Buddhism 19.48

and the Buddha
its central figure is the historical Buddha Śākyamuni 1.262; repudiated the Buddha's authority 1.314–15; said that there is only one bodhisattva in the world at a time 4.223; tendency to lose the archetypal Buddha in the historical 16.208

ideal
the austere figure of the *arhant* 7.504; the monk who observes the Vinaya, meditates, and gains arhantship 7.472; plurality of religious ideals 2.209–10; sees the ideal Buddhist as the *arhant* 16.7; stunting of spiritual ideals, implying that arhantship is the highest goal 2.151–2

attitudes and teachings
attached great importance to being free from fear 10.501; approach to duality 14.591, 14.593, 15.634; a close connection between Early Buddhism and the natural environment 26.242; conception of Going for Refuge 13.195; conservative and literal-minded 1.221–2, 7.540–2; 'hearing' is very important in Early Buddhism 15.436; how it pursued the cultivation of arts and sciences 7.437; the idea that they could not give up belief in the ultimate reality of the *ātman* 17.632; importance of faith 1.290; imposition of conditions under which the Dharma can be taught 16.14; innocent of paradox 2.131; the 'metaphysical reticence' of early Buddhism 10.507; no reference to Enlightenment as experience 11.73; no short cuts in the spiritual life 1.274; pluralistic realism 1.103, 1.224, 1.313–14; primarily cognitive 4.517; regarded *Jātakas* as edification, not exemplification 2.210; as represented by Śāriputra in the *White Lotus Sūtra* 1.271, 16.81–2; should be happy to realize that the *skandhas* don't exist 17.353–4; spiritual individualism 1.180, 1.229–36, 1.245, 1.269, 16.97; a strongly animistic background 10.453; the subtlety of their quest to understand the mystery of impermanence 15.183; teaches reflection on the *lakṣaṇas* to gain insight 19.453

'negativity'
emphasis on the negative resulted in distortion of the Doctrine 1.226; negative view of Nirvāṇa 1.225–6, 16.63–4; why its spiritual practice is, logically speaking, exclusively negative 7.133–4; wrongly represented as a dry, rationalistic system 1.290

mistakes and shortcomings
assertion that though personality was unreal its constituent elements were real 1.304; belief that the analysis of *ātman* is sufficient for the attainment of Nirvāṇa 1.267; 'the blissful Hīnayāna peace': Milarepa's critique 18.172–3; charges against the 'Hīnayāna' 1.220–31; danger of mistaking rational understanding for insight 1.349, 7.532; neglect of the practice of meditation 1.225; neglect of the principle of conditionality 1.266; over-attachment to the formal aspects of monasticism 21.377; over-emphasis on the four noble truths 1.226; over-preoccupation with analysis of mental states 1.222–5; scholasticism 1.222–5, 1.277; shortcomings when teachings taken literally 16.502; slavish dependence on the letter of the teaching 1.229–31, 1.239–40

see also
Abhidharma; and the bodhisattva ideal, *see under* bodhisattva ideal/history; Mahāsāṃghikas; monastic formalism, *see under* formalism; Sarvāstivāda; Theravāda; *trikāya*; two truths; Vibhajyavādins

earth (element) associated with the colour yellow and the shape of a cube 13.153, 16.147; association with the stupa 16.149; correlated with the lowest psychic centre 16.147; meditation upon earth 3.349, 8.269–70; what we conventionally call 'earth' is always a mixture of elements 17.377; *see also* six element practice

Earth (the planet) apology to the earth for pillaging its riches 25.447; contact with the earth strengthens the artist 26.169–70; the earth itself will have to come to an end one day 12.356–7; gratitude to the earth 16.382; the earth has no light of its own 16.388; the portent of the earth shaking 8.481; praise to our patient Mother Earth 25.177; primordial dualism of earth and sky 16.385; represented by Jambudvīpa in Buddhist cosmology, *see* Jambudvīpa; strengthened and made more abundant by the earth goddess 16.382; a time when the powers of earth served religion and the forces of religion blessed the earth 23.265

earth (symbolism) as a form of physical energy 16.144; instead of covering the earth with leather, wear shoes 4.379, 18.80; as a person 8.270, 16.146; in terms of blocked psychical energy 13.153–4, 13.155, 16.145

earth goddess (Dṛḍhā)

introduction
all goddesses are earth goddesses 16.384; compared to the Neolithic Venus 16.386; correspondence with the Virgin Mary 12.191; Dṛḍhā the original Indian earth goddess 16.386; earth-mother 19.141; everyone should be grateful to her 16.382; has her limitations 16.384; in the jewel family of Ratnasambhava 13.309; in Jungian terms, she represents the anima 12.190–1; *mātṛkās* (the Mothers): forces of inspiration coming from the earth 18.469; Mother Nature 16.385; not worshipped in modern India 16.384–5; receives her light from a higher principle: Enlightenment 16.388–9; represents cyclical change 16.385; we have to summon her, to free ourselves from the anima or animus 12.192–3

bears witness to Siddhārtha's practice
the story 9.382, 12.187–8, 13.308–9, 16.380–1; account in the *Lalitavistara Sūtra*, *see under Lalitavistara Sūtra*/Siddhārtha; as depicted in Buddhist art 12.188, 16.381; like Hertha in Swinburne's poem 12.188; like Mother Erda in Wagner's *Ring* 12.188, 16.380–1; reminds him of the long road he has travelled over many lifetimes 18.19; represents the same forces as Māra's daughters, now tamed 12.188

in the Sūtra of Golden Light
aspirations and prayers 16.384; makes a promise 16.379; is nourished by the *sūtra* 16.383; promises to make the earth stronger 16.382; a shadowy figure 16.384, 16.386; what she symbolizes 16.378–94

earthquake at significant times in the Buddha's life 3.100–1, 10.588; a reminder of the insignificance of human intentions to elemental powers 18.12; in the *Perfection of Wisdom in 8,000 Lines* 14.144; in the *Udāna* 10.584, 10.588

earth-touching the Buddha touches the earth with his toe 16.468; *mudrā*, *see under mudras*

East, the a journey to the East is a journey towards the light, a spiritual journey 26.263; light comes from the East (*ex Oriente lux*) 8.128, 26.102; materialism in the East 11.373, 13.489–90, 15.683–5; the Orientals (*ishrāqīya*) of medieval Iran 26.263, 26.722 (n216); today in the East most Buddhists don't meditate 15.735–6

East and West no sharp distinction between materialistic West and spiritual East 11.373, 13.489–90; 'ever the twain shall meet' 25.432; if something differentiates them, it is embodied in Buddhism 7.443; 'Perplexed between the East and West' 25.468, 26.392; there is no difference between the 'Eastern mind' and the 'Western mind' 11.373; there is

no division between them because we are all human beings 10.341; unanimity of religious ideals in East and West 7.105

Easter 3.230–1

easy

reflections and references
Ānanda says that *pratītya-samutpāda* is easy to understand 1.95–6, 17.389; easy and difficult path to *nirvāna* 1.341; the easy path of dependence on the Buddhas' compassion 1.324, 1.400–1; it's easier to be fascinated by the mundane than the transcendental 17.692; the middle way between being too easy-going and being too strict 9.440; no reason for thinking of spiritual life as difficult and worldly life as easy 4.48–9; 'Smooth the descent, and easy is the way' 1.25; the solution to the problem of wilfulness is not to take things easy 16.520; the Tantra is a short and easy path only if practised long and hard enough 13.74; the Vajrayāna called the easy path 19.379; we are fortunate to have such easy access to the Dharma 12.579; we tend to give ourselves a fairly easy time 18.617; you suffer at first, but after a while renunciation becomes easy 4.423

it's easy …
to be seduced by the attractions of the middle-class lifestyle 12.555; to blame your parents, but do you do the best for yourself? 18.521–2; to forget basic things like the precepts, but we do so at our peril 3.331; to forget that every moment of our life is unique 16.439–40; to juggle refined concepts but very difficult to stop thinking in those terms 19.373; to make the mistake of postponing one's spiritual endeavours 7.169; to misunderstand another person 10.500–1, 10.591; to say you've given everything to God and then hang on to it 4.358; to stop making a real effort 19.456

eating *see* food

Eazhavas (toddy-tappers) 20.283–4

Eberhardt, Father 22.45–6

ecclesia 3.448–9

Eckermann, Johann Peter 3.471, 22.464

Eckhart, Meister 2.143, 2.681 (n193), 23.25, 23.480 (n62)

eclecticism the middle way involves neither moral compromise nor intellectual eclecticism 7.299; Triratna does not identify with any one school of Buddhism, but it is not eclectic 11.376–7; usually involves an evasion of the real issues of the spiritual life 12.52

ecology the development of an ecological dimension to Triratna 12.409–10; ecological awareness 17.87; right or perfect livelihood is ecologically sound 3.283; *see also* environment

economics Buddhist 16.413, 16.399–400, 16.410–11; complexity of modern economics 3.283; the cost to the environment of economic development 22.100; 'The Economic Argument' 25.437; economic individualism 11.604; the history of banking 12.694–5; idols of the market place 26.480; of Karl Marx 3.423–4, 10.167, 10.347–8; part of the Noble Eightfold Path in the form of right livelihood 1.543–51; production of wealth, *see under* prosperity; represented by Śrī (Lakṣmī) 16.399, 16.411; the search for an alternative form of socio-economic organization 8.417; the second precept implies abstaining from economic exploitation 26.669

ecstasy *Ecstatic Religion* (a study of spirit-possession) 4.548–9; *mettā* is blissfully ecstatic 15.254; a monk sent into ecstasy by the beauty of a white bird and a dark cloud 26.242; 'Reason dies in giving birth to ecstasy' 14.358–9, 25.82; *samāpatti*, *see samāpatti*; Sangharakshita's states of ecstasy 2.408, 20.62, 20.85, 23.xvii; suffering [shall be transmuted] into ecstasy 23.446

ecumenism Dr Ambedkar's ecumenical attitude 2.497; Buddhists need to find a more appropriate term 11.713–14; principle in the Triratna Buddhist Order 2.547–56, 9.362, 11.470, 11.713–14, 12.368–9, 12.668–9; Sangharakshita's ecumenical attitude 2.547–56, 12.437, 21.246, 23.238; the use of the term 'dialogue' 11.297

Eden 1.528, 15.619, 25.390

Edgerton, Professor Franklin 3.651 (n158), 14.181, 14.193, 22.74

Edinburgh National Gallery of Scotland 24.585–6; Rosslyn Chapel 24.584; Writers' Museum 24.586

Edman, Irwin 26.189, 26.191

education

purposes
to enable you to develop your understanding and capacity to learn 18.182; to learn to be a responsible member of society 9.439–40, 26.71; to

learn the skills to earn one's living 9.440–1; to help one develop one's potential 9.442–6; to teach you to think for yourself 9.443

education of children
aesthetic and artistic education 9.444–5, 26.131–2; 'Buddhism and Education' 9.435–48; a Buddhist education with no modern subjects (Nepal) 7.353–4; Buddhist schools 7.258, 9.438–9, 21.280–1; children of Buddhist families being educated by the enemies of Buddhism 1.427; children should be corrected if they speak inaccurately 1.516–17; Plato's view that educating a pupil also educates the teacher 18.419; teaching religion in schools with conviction 12.51; increasing our knowledge of the world, the human race, and ourselves 9.372–3; the most important thing is that it does no harm to the child 18.285; the period when the foundations of life are laid 10.102; responsibility towards the environment 9.440, 9.445–6; a step towards fullness of life 10.101

education and Dharma practice
education and the spread of Buddhism 2.213; the helpfulness to Dharma practice of education 14.405; no need for formal education to understand Buddhism 9.338–9, 12.587; religion 'cannot be taught, it can only be caught' 9.446, 26.56

see also
the Buddha's education, *see under* Siddhārtha Gautama; Dhardo Rimpoche's School (ITBCI), *see under* Dhardo Rimpoche; giving education, *see under* *dāna*/traditional kinds of giving; Sangharakshita as tutor, *see under* Sangharakshita II/in Kalimpong

Edward II, King 24.558–9

Edward III, King 24.538, 24.559

Edward VI, King 13.551

'eel-wrigglers' 10.587

effort

the need for effort
the best time for endeavour is now, and the best place is here 7.169; the constant effort to develop *vīrya* 17.70; the constant effort to keep Buddhism creative 10.480; double and treble your efforts, but remember that all your efforts are void 7.413; 'Here are the roots of trees. Sit down, meditate' 1.236, 3.53, 18.368; let us spare no effort until we find the priceless jewel 16.223; the opportunity you let slip if you relax the effort to be mindful 18.155; the minute you stop trying, you start slipping back 3.443, 4.264–5, 4.380, 7.100; the need to keep up effort all the time 18.324; no short cuts in the spiritual life 2.284–5; make a definite effort in some area of practice all the time 4.44; the path of self-effort that underlies all forms of Buddhism 26.669–70; *prajñā* is not to be gained, but don't relinquish efforts to gain it 1.306–7; progress depends on our own individual effort 10.346, 11.84; putting in the necessary spiritual work 25.83–4; someone's death reminds us that we have to rely on our own efforts 10.324–5; sometimes we hold back when it would be better to make more effort 10.604; there is no spiritual welfare state 17.243; we need to make a constant effort until the point of irreversibility 4.183; 'With mindfulness strive', the Buddha's last words 2.30, 3.251, 4.183, 13.147; without unremitting effort nothing truly great is ever achieved 26.72; working hard at the Dharma 18.316–18; you may fail, but the important thing is that you should try 1.553

the results of effort
anyone who makes the effort can attain the goal 12.135–6; gaining Enlightenment through one's own efforts 1.348, 15.81; *if* you make the effort, spiritual success is inevitable 4.323; if you put in effort on working on yourself, the effect is cumulative 15.364, 18.290; it is profitable to reflect on the benefit of spiritual effort 10.598; making the effort to develop, your life becomes more meaningful 17.435; the person you could become if you make the right kind of effort 13.317; subtle enjoyments are the fruits of the effort to transform consciousness 15.158–9; with a fraction of the effort expended over many lives you could gain Enlightenment 4.629

difficulties with effort
asking for a method that gives Enlightenment quickly without effort 19.284–5; the Buddha's exhortations to self-effort taken literally 1.245; difficulty of making effort 3.484; don't spread your effort over unskilful mental states and activities 10.592; it's difficult to keep up a steady effort 19.438; it's very easy to stop making a real effort 19.456; effort can be boosted by Buddha-pride 4.464–5; resistance to making effort 5.679–80; we don't make the effort to grow because we don't really want to 12.622–3; why bother making the effort to evolve? 11.147

effort is about more than effort
aiming for Nirvāṇa solely by self-effort like trying to lift oneself by one's own

bootstraps 7.259; effort is impossible without self-awareness 12.46; effort needs to be directed towards the growth of the whole psyche 3.41; the effort to live so that progress will come 'without effort and striving' 19.578–9; the effort to be receptive 16.519; the effort to create positive conditions 4.183; just effort is no use, it must be an illumined effort 19.165–6; just stop trying 19.136; relaxed effort 5.302; 'resting one's mind at ease' 18.584; spreading effort over a broad spectrum of interests 16.520; supportive conditions allow change without much effort 5.252; watching an unskilful thought like a cloud in the sky is a way of applying right effort 11.689

balanced effort
alternating between exertion and relaxation, work and meditation 26.19; a balance between effort and relaxation 18.584–5; effort and self-power and other-power 4.141, 17.243; middle way between making no effort at all and intellectually directed effort 2.111–12; the example of Siddhārtha's childhood experience under the rose-apple tree 3.31

willed effort
wilful exertion 16.520; stop forcing things 5.300–1; willed, forceful effort doesn't get you very far 10.507; you can use willed effort either sensibly or foolishly 18.618

see also
four right efforts; in meditation, *see under* meditation/working in meditation; Perfect Effort, *see under* Noble Eightfold Path; the twentieth blow, *see under* parables and stories

egalitarianism contemporary ideology 11.603, 11.611; a dogmatic assumption of equality prevents communication 15.536–7; we need to acknowledge that some people are better than others in certain respects 18.132, 18.189; influences people to believe that no one is superior to them 16.106; a form of conceit or arrogance 4.78, 13.183, 17.606; 'honouring the honourable' is against our egalitarian principles 13.270, 17.276–7, 26.628; it undermines the whole idea that one may develop into a better human being 17.640; obsession with the idea that people are equal: a *micchā-diṭṭhi* of modern times 17.640, 18.439; pseudo-egalitarianism 4.126, 4.345, 15.389, 15.715, 18.441; reciting the Refuges and Precepts in a 'pseudo-egalitarian' way (London 1964) 12.304; respect for elders is not very popular these days 12.678–9; true egalitarianism is the faith that all beings everywhere have the capacity to develop 4.126; in the West we don't like to think of anybody as being spiritually superior 12.13

egg the bodhisattva emerging from the eggshell of ignorance 3.231; the Buddha like the first chick to hatch from a clutch of eggs 3.61, 11.108; 'I feel my body and soul break forth/ Like the crushing of an egg' 18.605; 'Keep quiet, you egg!' 15.413, 18.489; symbolism 3.231

ego

the nature of ego
ego in the Freudian sense 12.99–100; it appropriates experience wherever it can 17.341; it is not a thing, but a way of being 17.348; it is simply the wrong idea of separate individuality 26.167–9; a metaphor, like 'it' in 'it's raining' 13.268, 19.111; neurotic individuality 18.219; not a thing, but a faulty interpretation 17.625; a selfish, reactive way of functioning 17.344–5; there's nothing there, it's just like a knot to be untied 17.344–5; what is meant by ego? 13.267–8; you adopting a particular attitude 13.267–8

ways the ego functions
apologising for the ego is an inverted form of conceit 18.81–2; the appropriation of knowledge as a means of reinforcing the ego 18.167; behaviour motivated by ego's resistance 16.24; better a positive, happy ego than a sour, carping, critical one 4.320; don't be too quick to judge that others are being egoistic 4.319–20, 10.471, 19.111; the ego hiding in Going for Refuge 15.729–31; the ego is still there even in a passive person 15.387–8; ego 'loss' in sex or sleep 11.575; the ego thinking that it is Buddha 19.53; ego's merry masquerade 7.282; it can appropriate 'good' actions and 'religious' practices 7.282, 7.406–7; it can inflame an argument 18.170–1; it gets in the way of knowing other people 3.140; murder is the assertion of one ego at the expense of another 2.359; the rebellion of the ego 18.367–8; so long as there is an ego ... there will be rebirth 17.475; to work with others, learn to keep your ego under control 10.397

the ego and fear
the Dharma poses a threat to the ego 17.337; ego dissolved through fear 20.355; fear arises from the desire to protect the ego 17.340; fear of the death of the ego 17.339, 17.354; fear of death is essentially fear of loss of ego 18.245; fear is an indicator of ego 16.27; fear on

behalf of the ego is an unskilful mental state 17.180–1; overcoming ego through overcoming fear 16.28; symbolized in the parable of the return journey 16.97

the illusory ego
experiencing the truth that ego is an illusion emotionally 17.xxiv; the illusoriness of the ego-conception 7.290; a turning about takes place when one realizes its illusory nature 14.315; perceiving in one's mind the existence of an ego 14.183; the problem of the illusory ego is partly linguistic 17.352

ego and Buddhist doctrine
arhants 'tell of their gain (*attha*), but do not bring in the ego (*attā*)' 1.180; as long as the ego is there, one cannot receive the Dharma 18.188; Buddhism is whatever frees us from the grip of the ego 17.391; a concept of Buddhahood superimposed on the ego has disastrous results 2.97; the ego dissolved into the *dharmakāya* at the time of death 18.250; if *śūnyatā* is not clearly understood, the result is an ego-based life 17.391; 'No Bodhisattva … cherishes the idea of an ego-identity' 7.362; not much difference between ego in the psychological and Buddhist sense 4.511; using the *anātman* doctrine unhelpfully 17.625

the ego and spiritual life
conflict between ego-centred intellect and transpersonal spiritual life 12.217–18; the ego-dominated intellect can't penetrate the mystery of egoless activity 7.376; having an idea of a higher consciousness without the ego appropriating it 14.460–1; make sure that the transcendental consciousness functions through it 4.512; a sense of humour brings out the incongruity of its claiming anything for itself 14.598; sitting back from the ego is not as easy as it sounds 5.300–1; we need to realize how much we are identified with ego-consciousness 12.560; you attain some genuine spiritual experience but then your ego intervenes 18.174

getting rid of the ego
being so absorbed in what you're doing that there's no room for the ego 15.730–1; 'How can the ego get rid of itself?': not a useful question 17.349; in a way the ego wants to be annihilated 25.83; it is most likely to die by 'the death of a thousand cuts' 11.735–6; one can't think of getting rid of one's ego 'up to a point' 4.64; saying 'You must get rid of your ego' is bound to irritate people 10.471; the six element practice directly attacks the notion of an ego 19.453; speaking of getting rid of it can be unhelpful 17.343–5; use the language of 'getting rid of ego' with caution 19.111; ways to eliminate it: devotion and self-awareness 7.407–8; we need to see ourselves in the universal perspective of the Buddha 21.88; what the destruction of ego is like in practice 14.487–8; you are not out to smash the ego, but to change its way of functioning 4.512; you can't get rid of the ego until you've got an ego to get rid of 4.511; you can't get rid of ego with ego 18.27

wearing the ego away
the ego disintegrating 25.81–3; in spiritual friendship it gets gradually worn away 12.669; it has to exhaust itself against some impenetrable object 18.189; the more one looks at it, the more it is seen to disintegrate 17.687; you need actual practices to help weaken the ego 18.636–7

going beyond ego
the best and most reliable guidance comes from beyond one's own ego 22.374; don't ask 'Do I have an ego?' but 'Am I looking beyond what I already know?' 17.348; the ego and the subject–object distinction 18.241–2; how to go beyond the ego? 26.668–9; overcoming ego is not just an idea but an experience: a way of life 17.342; *sādhana* as a way of getting beyond the ego 22.374–5, 22.394–5; Swami Ramdas discovers that his ego has disappeared 20.329

ego and Enlightenment
Enlightenment negates ego, not individuality 12.512; speech as the spontaneous expression of the non-dual state 18.48; when you become Enlightened, what happens to your ego? 17.351–2; you can't get to Enlightenment by the ego accumulating good actions 11.283

ego-clinging *see* clinging

ego-directedness or -centredness 3.491

ego-identity delusion is a stubborn closedmindedness to anything that threatens ego-identity 11.130; the five *skandhas* are not nucleated by a permanent, unchanging ego-identity 1.139; 'No Bodhisattva … cherishes the idea of an ego-identity' 7.362; the primordial error that 'self' represents an eternal, unchanging ego-identity 7.327

ego-sense a class of actions inseparably connected with it 7.409; practice that heightens it or attenuates it 7.375, 26.49; attenuating it 1.133, 7.302, 7.361–2; it battens upon any thought or action,

even those regarded as good 7.281–2; desire and hatred are rooted in it 26.153; to engage in compassionate action, work on transcending it 12.661; most conventionally religious art strengthens it 26.67, 26.164; observing the precepts without it 10.175; only by uprooting it will we stop the growth of hatred and violence 7.374; renouncing it 7.406; some actions are invariably produced by it 7.282; a subtle ego-sense attaching itself to spiritual experience 18.580–2; it transfers itself to the very practices intended to eliminate it 7.406; weakening it 18.250; when it is removed, compassionate activities stream forth spontaneously 7.376, 7.409

egoism or egotism (*asmi-māna*)

the nature of egoism
'the demon of egotism' 13.267–8; the difference between egoism and self-confidence 18.464; hatred has a lot to do with it 17.600; not an entity but an attitude 13.268; 'the only real obstacle to the realization of Truth' 20.362; the tendency to rigidity 19.111

kinds of egoism
dualistic views can lead to egotism 1.267; egoism in the arts 3.606–7; egoism in religion 3.607; fixed self view is the rationalization of ordinary human egotism 26.188; humility is just as much a form of egotism as pride 4.78, 14.489, 20.362; it lurks in the desire for eternal life and for communion with a personal god 7.405; a reason for ingratitude 3.606–7

ways of eradicating or transcending egoism
the central task of spiritual life 7.405; the conscientious performance of one's duties 7.277; the elaborate prostrations of Yalahankar Swami's disciples 14.489, 20.353–4; friendship is a mutual transcendence of egotism 12.638; by surrendering one's will to that of another 13.628, 20.463–4, 22.394–5; the gap between transcendental altruism and spiritual egoism can be bridged 1.269; progression from egoism to selflessness 26.111; reflecting on the six elements 10.532; reflecting on impermanence 10.531; reflection on the web of causes and conditions weakens it 10.601–2

reflections on egoism
absence of the egoistic 18.613; accepting responsibility for your egotism 19.111; egoistic spiritual life contrasted with altruistic 7.149–51; freedom from egoism equated to fearlessness 16.278; having no egoistic motive for doing anything, one is free to respond 17.521–2; the more egoistic you are, the less likely you are to realize it 18.464; spiritual progress is not a matter of egoistically willed achievement 2.112; using the teachings in a way that increases egotism 19.178–83; when your self-will is frustrated you realize how egoistic you are 19.16

égoïsme à deux 1.159, 3.39

egolessness the aim of the *mettā bhāvanā* 15.338; Anuruddha and his friends as exemplars 12.606–7; art and egolessness 26.67, 26.83–4, 26.97–8, 26.177–80; the awakening of faith: an instant of pure egolessness 1.346; better to sweep a floor egolessly than meditate with the prideful thought 'I am meditating' 7.284; dragging egolessness down to the level of egotism 11.483; egos coming together with the objective of achieving egolessness: a paradox 12.605–6; the gift of fearlessness is ultimately the gift of insight into egolessness 16.27; it has positive content despite being negative in form 26.167; most people can't be fully egoless because of limitations of character 26.180; one who 'bears on his soul the stamp of egolessness' 26.190–1; we can radiate love only from egolessness 12.458; realizing the truth of egolessness simply means being truly and deeply unselfish 15.339; rejoicing in one's own merits without egotism 10.542; religion is essentially the experience of egolessness 26.14; the Sevenfold Puja as a training in egolessness 11.284; solving the problem of egoless activity 7.408–9; spiritual friendship a training in egolessness 3.579, 7.293–6, 12.458; that point within ourselves which has position without magnitude 12.458; the truly religious life is the life of egolessness 26.163; when the personality becomes egoless, it shines with wisdom, compassion, and skilful activity 7.302; *see also nairātmya*

Egypt

introduction
civilization only survives in its monuments 3.424; imagining living in ancient Egypt 26.467–8; the national character, affected by the Nile 4.576–7; they had one philosophy, religion, way of life 10.612

history
Akhenaten 16.264; Hermopolis 26.368; the pyramids 23.415; mummification of pharaohs 16.159–60; the Ptolemies 26.468, 26.740 (n392); the Egyptians criticized the Greeks for their exercise regimes 14.419; the burning of the library at Alexandria

15.617, 26.476; Israel's bondage in Egypt 16.220; Napoleon's soldiers using the Sphinx for target practice 26.476; Egyptian artefacts at the British Museum 26.470; Egyptian museum collections 24.266, 24.416; Christmas Humphreys' belief that he had lived in ancient Egypt 17.31, 23.41

gods
the Buddha thought to be the Egyptian god Apis 12.69; for the Egyptians the gods were real 14.419; comparison between Greek and Egyptian gods 26.470–1; learning to see gods in animal forms as the Egyptians saw them 13.244; Hathor 16.386, 26.494; Horus 16.190; Isis 16.190, 16.386, 24.294–5, 24.680 (n358); Osiris 16.190, 25.352; Ra, the sun god 25.56; Sekhmet, the lion-headed goddess 13.244; Thoth (Greek Hermes) 16.189–90, 26.406, 26.466–9

symbolism
Egyptian Book of the Dead 12.197; the Egyptian setting of *The Magic Flute* 24.385; Gnostic symbolism 16.220; the 'Hymn of the Pearl', *see under* Gnosticism; Neoplatonists influenced by Egyptian magic and symbolism 13.292–3; temple offerings of frankincense, myrrh, and *kifr* 26.494; symbol of the 'other country' 16.220

Sangharakshita
childhood introduction 20.23, 26.466–7; gives a talk in Cairo 23.415; short story set in ancient Egypt 26.467–8; visit in 1967 4.576–7, 23.415

ehipassiko *see under Tiratana Vandanā*

Eichhorn, J. C. 2.627

Eicho, Tōyō 1.28, 7.395, 26.243

eidetic images 5.598–9, 12.172, 19.28

Eidmann, Philipp Karl 1.345–7, 2.690 (n291, n294)

eight assemblies 2.647, 12.521–3

eight auspicious symbols 17.145, 17.729 (n160)

eight emancipations 16.446–7

eight individuals or holy persons (*ariyapuggalas*) *see* holy persons

eight opportunities 17.427, 17.753–4 (n354)

eight requisites (*aṣṭapariṣkāra* or *aṭṭhaparikkhāra*) all the wanderer possessed 14.398; everything else the monk uses is the property of the monastery 19.551, 27.1074; carrying a water strainer to avoid harming life in water 17.583, 17.584; four necessities, *see* four necessities; given upon ordination 2.194; listed 2.198, 2.605–6, 16.405, 17.584, 22.592 (n172); the probable reason why the Buddha made the stipulation 22.188; the Sarvāstivādin Vinaya adds a few more 2.605; Sangharakshita is instructed in them 2.418, 21.108

eight special conditions (*garudhammas*) for women's ordination 2.27, 11.422–8, 11.638–9

Eight Verses on Transforming the Mind (Langri Thangpa) 8.611–12

eight *vijñānas*

THE EIGHT *VIJÑĀNAS* AS A WHOLE

introduction
summary 2.278–82, 14.314–15, 16.581; sources 2.676 (n130), 2.698 (n357); the depth psychology of the Yogācāra 18.604–5; a hierarchy of consciousness 14.315; the term *citta* used to cover the whole system 14.210

transformed into the five jñānas or wisdoms
description 2.280–1, 14.315, 17.483–4; connection with the arising of the *bodhicitta* 4.261; the mandala of the Five Buddhas 17.487–8, 18.605–6; the order in which they are transformed 8.558; symbolized by the eight cremation grounds of the mandala 12.221, 13.234–6; the work of the spiritual life 16.581

ĀLAYA-VIJÑĀNA (STORE CONSCIOUSNESS, UNIVERSAL CONSCIOUSNESS)

introduction
and six element practice 3.350; an attempt to explain why we think matter exists 1.369; comparison with psychoanalysis 12.99; a sort of collective memory, but not really a box of memories 18.607–8; to be treated metaphorically, not metaphysically 18.292; a teaching of explicit or implicit meaning? 17.488–9; a verse on the *ālaya-vijñāna* (*Sandhinirmocana Sūtra*) 14.200–1; what makes conditioning possible 18.292; 'When the Ālaya consciousness dissolves into the Dharmakāya' (Milarepa) 18.605

absolute
etymology 2.279; introduction 12.174–7; all the time immanent in the system of impure consciousness 14.210; equivalent to the wisdom of the *dharmadhātu*, *see under* five *jñānas*; reality itself, free from subjectivity and objectivity 17.486; acts on all five

niyamas 2.70; also called the *mūla-vijñāna* 14.188; compared to the ocean, and *vāsanā* to the wind blowing across it 14.210; designated as *pratītya-samutpāda* 7.199; the doctrine explains how we take the self and the world to be real 1.369, 17.488; the imprint of actions is conserved in the *ālaya vijñāna* from life to life 18.291–2; at the level of the *ālaya* the turning about (*parāvṛtti*) takes place 2.279, 12.176; the *ālaya* is normally hidden from us 2.281–2; and the *tathāgatagarbha* 14.210–11; not to be confused with the non-Buddhist idea of the supreme self 14.200; not to be reified, but a concept that clarifies the possibility of growth 18.291; one of the most obscure questions of Buddhist thought 18.282; recognizes reality as the principle of potentiality 2.43, 18.607; relationship between relative and absolute *ālaya* 18.292

relative
analogy with Jung's collective unconscious 2.279, 8.458, 12.176, 18.606; contains traces of all of our previous experiences 17.486; 'the good earth' (Milarepa) 18.288–90; like a mirror to which reflections stick 18.605–6; represents the possibility of continuity 18.289–90; tension between the *manas* and the relative *ālaya* 12.218; transformed into the mirror-like wisdom, *see under* five *jñānas*

seeds of defilement and purity (bījas) within the ālaya-vijñāna
active impressions, like seeds ready to sprout 17.486; the *ālaya* stores them until circumstances permit them to sprout 1.120, 14.314–15; the impure seeds are the causes of our future rebirth 12.176; pure seeds push impure seeds out of the *ālaya* 2.280, 12.176, 17.486–7; and rebirth 18.290–2; related to the comparison of consciousness to a seed 14.187–8; related to the four noble truths 7.202; these seeds develop into the five *skandhas* 1.369; 'a twofold seed from which spring up *saṃsāra* and *nirvāṇa*' 7.202; *vāsanā* (habit-energy): the impressions conserved 1.369, 14.209–10

PARĀVṚTTI-VIJÑĀNA (EVOLVING CONSCIOUSNESS)

five sense consciousnesses
ego-clinging and the five consciousnesses 19.156; five modes of discriminating awareness 2.278, 12.174, 14.314, 16.581; five 'perceptions' (Guenther) 17.484; the self-purity of the senses 19.191; the third transformation of consciousness 1.369; transformed into the all-performing wisdom, *see under* five *jñānas*

mano-vijñāna (ego-consciousness)
consciousness of mental objects or ideas 14.314; distinction from *manas* 17.484; mind as sixth sense, *see under* senses; the second transformation of consciousness 1.369; two types: 'ideas of sense' and ideas that arise from the mind 2.278, 12.175, 17.485; meditation, imagination, dreams 12.175, 17.485; transformed into distinguishing wisdom, *see under* five *jñānas*

kliṣṭa-mano-vijñāna or manas ('defiled-mind-consciousness')
concepts are its creation 16.542; distinctions made by the mind 10.232–5; constructs a dualistic world revolving around subject and object 12.175, 17.485; defiled by the sense of mine and yours, me and you 18.604; faces two ways: towards the senses and towards the *ālaya-vijñāna* 12.175, 17.486; gives rise to greed and hatred 14.314; the highest operative principle of human consciousness 8.289; how it becomes defiled 14.210; it is the faculty of abstract thought 12.559; it may be described as ethically neutral 14.210; going forth from *manas* to *āryajñāna* 12.559–60; it has taken humanity a long time to develop it, but one can go further 12.559; reversing the process of defilement, *see parāvṛtti*; sees things in terms of opposites 2.278–9, 10.232, 16.545; it is the scientific mind, in a sense 12.559; spiritual practice takes place at this level 2.282; tension between the *manas* and the relative *ālaya* 12.218; two modes: space and time 8.289; turns sense experience into attachment 18.345; the way we usually live our lives 17.485; we need to realize how we are dominated by it 12.560; transformed into the wisdom of equality, *see under* five *jñānas*

eight *vimokṣas* introduction 16.446–7; in the Abhidharma 14.81; meditator's experience of the first four releases 2.143–4; perhaps extinct as a practice, but may have been incorporated by the Vajrayāna 2.144; practised by the body-witness 2.143–4; the third release, 'called the beautiful' 2.84, 5.511, 10.506, 13.279; Master Tu Lun's discussion of them 8.481

eight worldly winds (or conditions, *lokadhammas*)

introduction
summary 3.159–60; drifting on the winds and tides of the world 15.233; falling into the hands of bandits but not being affected by the eight worldly winds 18.325; Kipling's *If* and the worldly winds 26.395; in the *Maṅgala Sutta*

2.117, 3.159–60, 15.452–3, 22.183; Sangharakshita's experience of them 2.499, 25.425; 'understanding the wrongness of the eight worldly winds' 18.343; *upekṣa* (equanimity) guards against them 3.289

pleasure and pain
nirāmisa: a mode of feeling beyond pleasure and pain 15.155–6; you can't have one without the other, so you have to be ready to give up both 10.482

praise and blame
the Buddha explains how to handle them 3.76; as a child cries at a broken sandcastle, the mind reacts to the loss of praise and fame 4.431; the door to non-duality: transcendental individuality 16.545–6; if your happiness is dependent on others' praise, you are in an insecure position 4.432

success and failure
becoming upset by failure and uplifted by success 15.99, 15.452; our tendency to take the credit for success and blame others for failure 10.601; treating Triumph and Disaster just the same (Kipling) 22.183

loss and gain
it is a great blessing to learn to be unmoved whether we win or lose 3.160

eighteen *dhātus* *see under dhātus*

eighteen schools *see under* Early Buddhism/history

eighteen special qualities of a Buddha 3.144, 14.448–9

eightfold path *see* Noble Eightfold Path

eighty-four (*mahā*)*siddhas* (Perfect Ones) introduction 1.381–3; *dohās*, the rhymed couplets the *siddhas* sang 1.382; famous *siddhas* 1.381–2, 7.507; frequently belonged to degraded and despised communities 1.381; the origin of the lines of spiritual transmission 7.507; Padmasambhava the most famous 19.214; perhaps some of them taught Atīśa 12.565; and the tantras 14.249–50

Einstein, Albert compared to Dante 26.686; 'How will the next war be fought?' 9.497; if any religion could cope with modern scientific needs, it would be Buddhism 1.471; space is curved 19.437

ekagrata (Pāli *ekaggatā*) *see* one-pointedness

Ekajaṭī 22.506

Ekākṣari *see Perfection of Wisdom in One Letter*

ekalakṣaṇa-samādhi 1.587

ekarasa (one taste) *see under Udāna*/great ocean

eka-seyyā (sleeping alone) 10.573

Ekaśloka Śāstra *see* Nāgārjuna

ekayāna *see yāna*

El Greco

life and works
his life (in Veronica de Osa's *The Mystic Finger Symbol*) 24.570–1; his house in Toledo 24.422; spiritual outlook 26.253–4; underlying Neoplatonic philosophy 26.245, 26.314–15; used inmates of an asylum as models 13.648; paintings in Spain 24.413, 24.415, 24.419–21, 24.441; *The Agony in the Garden* (school of El Greco) 26.308, 26.675

The Burial of Count Orgaz
the painting itself 24.418; Sangharakshita's first encounter with the painting 24.417; viewing it in Toledo 24.417; the angel in the painting 26.315–16; comments on the painting by Veronica de Osa 24.570–1; Michener's critique 26.308–10, 26.316; a monograph 24.425–6; 'the painting impressed me very deeply' 26.373; Sangharakshita's critique 26.307–18; the symbolism of the baby 26.316–18; the symbolism of the young man 26.311–12, 26.315–16, 26.318

Sangharakshita
described some of the paintings in a novel (1943) 24.417, 26.307, 26.444; acquaintance with El Greco's work 26.307–8

Eleatic philosophers 7.195

eleemosynary (one who subsists on charity) 7.496

elegance 13.279

elements

what are they?
association with the chakras 13.155–7, 18.77; Buddhaghosa defines them not as substances but as tendencies 15.133; the English word element doesn't suit Buddhist concepts 15.133; *mahābhūtas* ('great ghosts') 2.97, 13.151–2, 15.133, 17.446; as metaphors for reality 14.590; mythological elements of alchemy: gnomes, undines, salamanders, sylphs 15.139; 'neither earth nor water nor fire nor wind' ... 1.68, 10.459, 10.632–6, 16.389; seen as living beings, *jīvas* 14.539; 'serviceable in many ways ...' 11.282;

neither different from one another, nor the same 17.408; they cannot be said either to exist or not to exist 17.377; thinking of the elements as gods and goddesses 15.139

experiencing the elements
contact with the elements (an open-air shower) 24.398–9; counterbalance excessive thinking through contact with Nature and the elements 26.37; an experience of being suspended between water, air, and fire 22.50; gratitude for the elements 17.201; mastering the elements 19.65; the presence of the elements at a cremation 12.220–1; Turner's paintings capture the dramatic qualities of the elements 26.254; we do not experience them directly, only sensations of resistance, wetness, etc. 15.135

four elements
identified as aspects of *rūpa* by the Abhidharma 2.97, 13.151–2, 15.133, 17.446; represented by four of the female Buddhas of the five-Buddha mandala 15.139; seeing the elements as psychological rather than material states 15.137–8; unlike the elements of science, these great elements are alive 15.136, 17.445–6

five elements
associations with colours and geometrical forms 16.147; in the body 16.494; conceived of by the Sāṃkhya school 17.439; correlations with five psychic centres 16.147–8; correspondences with the five Buddhas of the mandala 13.184; symbolizing different kinds of people 16.146–7; represented by one of the *vajra*'s sets of five spokes 13.183; represented in the stupa 13.63, 13.153, 15.139; representing different states of energy 13.153–5, 16.144–6; representing mental energies 16.145–6

contemplating the body with regard to four elements
among the forty *kammaṭṭhānas* 4.519; awareness of the elements as qualities extending through and beyond the body 15.135–6; Buddhaghosa's commentary 1.160–1; in the *Satipaṭṭhāna Sutta* 1.160, 15.132–9

see also
earth, water, fire, air, space; six elements, *see* six element practice

Elenjimittan, Father Anthony v21

elephants

and the Buddha
the Buddha-to-be descends in the form of a white elephant 13.570; his mother's dream of the white elephant 9.364–5; response to the first sight: 'like an elephant struck by a thunderbolt' 3.26; the Buddha and an elephant seek solitude in the forest 10.323–4, 10.429, 10.536–7, 14.401; Nālāgiri, the elephant pacified by the Buddha 2.27, 3.63, 4.13, 11.162, 13.280, 17.188; the Buddha like an alert, perfectly tamed elephant 4.706 (n313), 10.458, 10.461; his 'elephant look' 4.706 (n313), 10.461, 12.157; his virtues compared to those of a majestic elephant 4.706–7 (n313)

from the Pāli tradition
Ajātasattu takes a party on 500 elephants to see the Buddha, *see* Ajātasattu; being pierced with speech like an elephant pierced with arrows 10.540; the blind men and the elephant, *see under Udāna/* other key teachings; descend from one pool to another 3.663 (n246); *Dhammapada* chapter, *see Dhammapada/*chapter 23; elephant-craft 10.520; a man on an elephant offering a reward for one Dharma verse 10.263; the partridge, the monkey, and the elephant 14.64; plunges from one lotus pool to another 1.440, 3.287–8, 4.135, 4.478–9, 9.297, 23.223; *praśrabdhi* like an elephant stepping into a huge lake 3.269, 12.161; take no notice of criticism (as an elephant ignores barking dogs) 9.366, 10.201, 18.420; young elephants poisoned by unwashed lotus roots 17.447, 19.296, 21.552–3

Mahāyāna and Vajrayāna elephants
the 'elephantine work' of the yogi 18.419–20; elephants and Akṣobhya 12.203, 13.309; an illusory elephant conjured by a magician 14.501, 14.562, 16.452–3, 17.385–7, 19.79; the image

of *vīrya* (Śāntideva) 4.468–9; a piece of wood in the form of an elephant (Vasubandhu illustration) 1.370; the precious elephant 13.262; Samantabhadra rides a white elephant 2.180; tie the mad elephant of the mind to the pillar of the Dharma 4.384–5

Hinduism
the earth supported on the back of four elephants 19.437; Ganesha 16.361; heavenly elephant produced from the cosmic ocean of milk 16.398

stories
the elephant and the frog 15.423–4, 16.299; a foolish man and a mad elephant 18.632–3

elephantine qualities
determination 4.469; playfulness 4.469; symbol of strength 9.366

sundry other elephants
blue-black elephants of heaven (clouds) 25.296; in Burma, execution by elephant-trampling 12.124–5, 15.521, 21.126; clearing jungle 20.283–4; dancing at an Indian fair 20.294; depicted on Aśoka's pillars 9.364; making a symbolic link through an attraction to elephants 13.121; mindfulness: 'Life proceeds at a pace like that of a mild and majestic elephant' 1.151; poaching elephants 25.54; the sound of elephants in Kusāvati 10.702–3 (n315); in Sri Lanka 1.194; stuck in a traffic jam behind an elephant 23.346, 24.111

Eleusinian Mysteries 23.289–90

Elgar, Edward 23.173, 26.505

Elijah 14.535

Eliot, Charles (*Hinduism and Buddhism*) the *Avataṃsaka Sūtra* 14.216–17; the Chinese Tripiṭaka 14.254–5; infiltration into Buddhism of superstitious rites and beliefs 2.220; Kṣitigarbha 2.181; Mahāyāna *sūtras* 14.100; the Tendai school 4.495; the *trikāya* doctrine 1.260; the 'wearisome and mechanical iteration' of the Pāli canon 14.23

Eliot, George ability to realize with absolute conviction the life of another human being 3.508; admiration for her writing 11.634; invention of the word 'melioristic' 2.90, 26.10; *The Mill on the Floss* 16.597 (n92), 20.10, 20.496; partner of George Lewes 7.571 (n135)

Eliot, John 23.152–3

Eliot, T. S.

his life and work
became Anglo-Catholic 15.489; John Middleton Murry and Eliot 13.511, 26.332; contemporary poetry difficult because modern life complex 26.378; on culture 13.479; overrated 26.339; poetic drama 26.375; Sangharakshita hears F. R. Leavis speak on Eliot 23.419

Four Quartets
'distracted from distraction by distraction' 4.73; 'Human kind cannot bear very much reality' 3.110, 12.201, 14.373, 15.210, 16.96; 'the intersection of the timeless moment' 3.145; 'Music heard so deeply/ That it is not heard at all' 14.517; 'the thing one no longer has to say' 17.249; 'Teach us to care and not to care' 18.337

The Waste Land
'April is the cruellest month' 22.104; the Buddha's Fire Sermon 7.450; modern life as a wasteland 25.146; the removal of teeth 26.433

other works and quotations
'The winter evening settles down' 20.11, 20.500; 'And the wind shall say: "Here were decent godless people"' 12.45; to transcend the intellect, one must have an intellect 2.244, 12.515, 26.199; *The Family Reunion* 25.61; 'The lengthened shadow of a man/ Is history' 3.423, 3.685 (n383); 'the skull beneath the skin' 15.125; *The Use of Poetry and the Use of Criticism* 22.30

elitism 18.441, 19.476

Elizabeth I, Queen called St Mary Redcliffe 'the fairest parish in England' 23.206; denounced as a heretic 13.549; the difficulties of travel in her day 19.96; 'frequently ruder than queens are today' 25.432; the investments of her courtiers 18.95; 'my favourite historical character' 26.425, 26.490; the Ridolfi Plot 13.548–9; *Sayings* 24.xxii; sketched by the young Sangharakshita 20.27

Elizabeth II, Queen 22.12–14, 25.432

Elizabethan age 3.10

Elliott, John 11.495

Ellis, Havelock 13.610–11, 22.57

Ellmann, Richard 24.404, 26.375

Ellora caves *see under* caves

eloquence 16.185–6, 16.368–9

elucidate 2.525

elusiveness 'Elusive Beauty' 25.269; the elusiveness of the Dharma 14.257; the elusiveness of the Enlightened person 11.12; the elusiveness of the Perfection of Wisdom 1.65–7, 14.535–6; the elusiveness of pleasure and pain 17.506

Elwin, Father Verrier 22.179

emancipation *Acintya-vimokṣa*, the 'inconceivable emancipation' 16.445; drama of universal emancipation 1.325; through faith 1.291; 'the Destructible and the Indestructible' 16.458; all emancipations are inconceivable 16.448; of Dr Ambedkar and his followers 9.54, 9.60; has no meaning except in relation to a previous state of bondage 16.448; only possible because there is no absolute duality between duality and non-duality 16.542; post-mortem emancipation 2.149; if someone gains spiritual emancipation, it affects everybody 4.584; why don't we attain emancipation without the bother of following the path? 1.363–4

see also
freedom; of mind (*cetovimutti*), *see under vimukti*; through wisdom (*paññāvimutti*), *see under vimukti*

emancipations *see* eight emancipations

embarrassment embarrassment about nakedness 19.250–1, 19.256; God as an embarrassment to Christians 12.113

embodiment *ḍākinīs* are embodied prayers 19.143; doing things that are practically embodied, you can see where you have gone wrong 18.277; Enlightenment must be embodied in some form of sentient existence 15.591; the ideal embodied by the wheel-turning king 7.512; transition from intellectual understanding to embodied experience 16.186; we are reborn because we want to be embodied 10.482

Emerson, Ralph Waldo brief introduction 22.276, 22.600 (n222), 24.619 (n74); 'Self-Reliance' 3.685 (n383), 13.328; 'Social Aims' 4.6; 'Thoreau' 24.52–3; 'wisdom literature' 14.343

emetic, spiritual 16.292–3

Emin, Tracey 12.615, 12.749 (n412), 26.478

'Eminent Buddhists from the Border Areas' brief account of their tour 22.423; an exhibition of Buddhist art 16.517–18; meet Pandit Nehru 22.344–5; meet the president of India 22.342–4; participate in 2,500th Buddha Jayanti 9.19; pilgrimage to the holy sites 9.xii, 9.19–21, 12.433–4, 21.519, 22.329–40; Dr Radhakrishnan gives them a homily, to their puzzlement 22.344; Sangharakshita remonstrates with the Hindu speakers at a reception 22.346–7; visit to Dr Ambedkar 22.352–3

Emotion, Perfect *see* Perfect Emotion

emotional blackmail an aspect of the power mode 11.701, 17.583; charity advertising 4.341; the *fait accompli* 11.424, 11.427; making someone feel guilty 14.522–3, 15.622; telling someone your expectations of them mustn't be emotional blackmail 15.364–5; manipulating other people 3.577, 17.234, 19.67–8

emotions

INTRODUCTION

the nature of emotions
the word means movement 1.289; are all emotions painful? 12.657; children need to learn to consider other people's feelings 3.537; the difference between feeling (*vedanā*) and emotion, *see under vedanā*; the education of the emotions 9.443–4; emotion is such an important part of our lives 25.106; every emotion is directed towards inferior, equal, or superior 1.241; innumerable forms of attraction to pleasure and repulsion from pain 7.392; it is emotion that binds things together 5.248–9; the most important emotional experience of our life: with our mother 16.102; nothing wrong with emotions, it's their misuse that causes the trouble 16.200; out of the depths come our energies of emotion 12.23; strong emotions affect the body as well as the mind 19.135; there is no question of getting rid of emotions 19.126; you've got to keep close to your emotional experience 19.143

how emotions arise
enjoyment is passive, but emotion is active, expressive, even creative 15.155; they are not produced automatically, but are actions of mind 17.503; *vedanā* (feeling) combines with *saṃskāra* to produce emotion 15.150; whether you create harmful or helpful emotions out of feelings is up to you 15.305

emotions in the Buddhist tradition
Buddhism involves our whole emotional nature from the outset 7.392, 15.250–1; Buddhist literature is more truly canonical the more deeply it moves us 14.303–4; the importance of emotions (the parable of the raincloud) 16.129–30; the incorporation of culture into the Dharma engages the

emotions 16.370; the place of emotion in Buddhism 7.241–3; shift of the Dharma from intellectual to emotional mode 1.325–6, 1.347; in Mahāyāna Buddhism 1.240–1; freedom of emotion in Tibetan Buddhism 19.124–5; emotional engagement in the visualization practice 5.601

emotions and the spiritual life
beware of being precious about tender feelings 10.571; the concentration of emotion: the lifeblood of religion and art 7.403; discovering the emotional equivalents of spiritual truths 5.295, 12.110–11; emotional freedom to respond to an ideal or vision produces faith 18.273; emotions spring up between us and others: sangha 1.511; if our emotions are tied up with worldly life, our Dharma life can only be superficial 26.57; the importance of emotions in spiritual life 9.322–3; *mettā* saves you from emotional ups and downs – but isn't that boring? 5.155–6; the misunderstanding that there is no place for emotion in the spiritual life 17.594; no more possible without emotion than without understanding 7.290; perceiving the spiritual significance of our ordinary emotional experiences 7.295; the point of contact with reality is really neither thought nor feeling 4.516; putting all one's emotions onto the spiritual ideal 5.619; the second of the five stages of the spiritual path 5.43; the spiritual life is above all concerned with the reorientation of emotion 1.390; taking responsibility for our feelings 15.159; the transformation of emotion into devotion 7.302–3; transmuting lower into higher emotions 10.174, 18.619

emotion and intellect or reason
a balance of head and heart 1.240, 1.294, 9.322, 12.65, 26.40–1; Blake on reason and emotion 15.257–8, 17.685; Buddhism acts primarily on the intellect, but makes a powerful appeal to the emotions 26.118; Buddhism is not just intellectual, but involves the emotions at every step 15.250–1; the combination of over-developed intellect and under-developed emotions 26.37, 26.41; comparison 5.248–9; concepts may convince the head, but only emotions can move the heart 26.163; dressing up emotions as reasons 14.557–8; emotional equivalents for intellectual understanding 1.494, 7.292–3, 11.192–4, 12.110–11, 15.154, 26.399; the heart is moved more powerfully by a myth than by an argument 1.325; in a healthy person feeling and thinking are virtually identical 15.257; faith integrates emotions and intellect 3.304, 17.674; the function of intellectual structures is to stimulate the corresponding feelings 14.566; the gap between them can be bridged with the help of the fine arts and natural beauty 8.445; integrating them 5.248–9, 14.431, 14.557–8, 15.549, 17.673–4, 17.685, 18.77, 26.38; it's important to develop a positive emotional counterpart to intellectual understanding 26.37; like the wings of Shelley's skylark 26.132; the Mahāyāna is rigorously intellectual and also deeply emotional 1.240; *mettā* is the synthesis of reason and emotion 15.258; once on the spiritual path, conflict between rational and emotional is virtually resolved 26.77; our emotional life tends to lag behind our intellectual development 15.317; Going for Refuge: emotional, rational, volitional 2.487, 11.194, 12.536–41, 15.607, 15.615, 15.727–9; the problem of how to combine reason and emotion 26.76; rational and emotional arguments 7.248; the rational and the emotional: the two aspects of personality 15.607; reasoned argument in support of emotion, and emotional appeal on behalf of reason 8.125–6; relationship to the path of vision and the path of transformation 12.107–8; the simultaneous expansion of understanding and emotions 26.132; a split between the intellect and the emotions 14.442–4, 19.114–15, 26.130; there can be no intellectual clarity without awareness of emotion 15.197–8; Tibetan Buddhism is highly intellectual and also deeply devotional 13.106–8; to become an individual, restrain your intellectual side and cultivate your emotional side 26.40; union between intellect and emotion 14.431

emotion and the arts
the difference between emotion and aesthetic experience 26.326–7, 26.362; the fine arts as a way to bridge emotion and reason 8.445

NEGATIVE EMOTIONS

what they are
at the back of all negative emotion is the thought 'What's in this for me?' 15.336; they are all expressions of the wish to do harm to others 15.303; they are much stronger than positive emotions 26.20; we have a baseline of negative feeling that never altogether goes away 17.397

their effect
being poisoned by someone else's negative emotions 11.6, 22.416–17; controlling people by manipulating their negative emotions 26.20; the energy locked up in them is your raw material 5.394; they get

in the way of our appreciation of things 18.42; indulgence in them weakens us 11.6; people seem to set up situations to express them 18.276; passing one's life in a dark cloud 3.270; negative feelings towards relatives 15.305; negativity wastes energy at a catastrophic rate 4.133–4, 11.200–2; a negative twist has been given to positive energy 4.596; one of the biggest obstacles to the spiritual life 12.391; sectarian organizations tend to express them 16.76; they close us in upon the private, self-regarding 'I' 15.326

dealing with them
avoiding them 15.263; breaking through negative emotions 11.5–6, 11.13; must be confronted, not dismissed or ignored 5.394; checking negative emotions without opening outlets for positive ones 26.131; cultivate the opposite 4.134, 4.382, 13.174; dealing with them skilfully 18.610–12; finding a way to work directly on and with our emotions 15.317; one should be quick to prevent them from arising 3.270; our task is to experience them and then find a way to change them 15.312; repression of negative emotions, *see under* repression; not repressing them but putting them aside for the time being 4.287; their eradication is just the beginning of the spiritual path 16.67; trying to help people overcome them can be exhausting 19.550

POSITIVE EMOTIONS

introduction
all positive emotions have an expansive, other-regarding tendency 15.326, 15.328; developed by the true individual 3.472; emotion which is pleasurable and at the same time skilful 26.77; English words for them do not give a true idea of their strength 15.253; *mettā* is the fundamental positive emotion 17.186; in modern life we are not adept at dealing with strong emotion 15.343; negative emotions are stronger than positive emotions 26.20; not soft or sloppy, but Abhidharma positive mental states 12.315; one should have the courage of one's positive emotions 26.65; three dimensions: *mettā*, *śraddhā*, and *muditā* 11.733–5; the three great emotions of Buddhist life: faith, compassion, and love 4.174, 11.507

the need for them
at the heart of the spiritual community 3.451; better to have positive emotions tinged with ego than negative ones 4.320; the bridge between the lower and the higher self 19.28; emotional sustenance from our relationships 17.271; express positive feelings for others frequently, fully, and unmistakably 24.383; one should actively cultivate and encourage positive emotion 3.270; their development crucial for our development as individuals 5.31; they are the lifeblood of the Order 26.24; they have an absolutely central place in the spiritual life 5.188, 19.125–6; they need to be consciously developed 3.472; they (not abstract ideas) keep us going 5.31, 26.30, 26.76; they need to be strong and deep, rooted in loyalty and commitment 14.471; we need to shield ourselves from negative influences 15.152–3; we owe it to ourselves and others to be positive whenever possible 3.270; whatever you are doing 5.43; without a basis of positivity, little spiritual development is possible 10.432, 26.25; you can't suppress your own better nature indefinitely 4.267

developing them
actively pursuing sources of positive feeling 15.158–9; arousing positive emotion in someone gives them a wider perspective 19.514; cultivating positive emotions one becomes an angel 26.657; cultivating unselfish feeling 12.612–13; definition of moral skilfulness 15.263; developing mettā, *see mettā bhāvanā*; developing positivity through meditation 18.574–5; guide positive feelings rather than suppressing them 5.617; insight 'fixes' emotional positivity 18.449; one positive emotion gives birth to another 19.515; our capacity for positive emotion is necessarily limited 15.152; positive emotions are latent within you, to be called forth 14.533–4

WORKING WITH EMOTIONS

introduction
not being afraid of emotion, but using it to the advantage of the spiritual life 7.290; showing respect for people's feelings 25.17; why are our emotions not freely available to us? 11.194–204; we need to recognize that our emotional experience is self-created 3.472

experiencing emotions
being 'with' our emotions, not cut off from them 11.121; bodily activity, the arts, or even alcohol may help you get in touch with them 14.573; carry your basic and primitive emotions along with you 16.102; the cynic feels less than is justified, the sentimentalist more than is justified 26.23; doing what you don't feel like doing 5.646–7, 10.604–5; the effect of becoming aware of our emotions 12.261; establish contact with your emotions, whatever they are 5.31,

26.65; experiencing emotions while remaining conscious of them 12.268–9; feeling two contradictory emotions at the same time 18.143; getting in touch with early childhood feelings 14.573, 16.101–2; getting in touch with feelings 18.608–10; if you really see, you really feel 18.590; inspiring people by getting them in touch with their emotions 19.228; making contact through the *mettā bhāvanā* 5.105; not acknowledging a strong feeling leads to anxiety 17.688–9; once you acknowledge a feeling there is a possibility of transforming it 19.395; one doesn't need sex to keep in touch with one's emotions 26.28; to be aware of one's feelings one must allow oneself to experience them 11.36–7; we need to be able to recognize the ethical content of our emotions 15.157; we need to feel them, but make sure they are appropriate to objective reality 15.307–8; working on feelings about past abuse in the *mettā bhāvanā* 18.444; writing it down can help you to face up to how you feel 18.453

expressing feelings
eloquence: easy, natural expression for the genuine feelings of the heart 16.368; emotion has a natural tendency towards self-expression 26.191, 26.194; if you have genuine feelings, you can articulate them in a rational way 19.293; it is impossible to communicate feeling 17.503; the more freely we express positive emotion, the better we deal with instinctual urges 17.217; poetry gives expression to feelings that could find no other outlet 2.423; saying 'I feel', not 'I think' 17.235, 19.291–2; through words, concepts, and images 16.126; women's conditioning around the expression of feelings 4.597–8

strength of emotion
only when a man feels strongly will he act effectively 1.124, 7.392, 26.77; to feel strongly calls for energy 15.152; very often there isn't enough oomph in people's emotions 15.431

refining emotions
through the arts 11.195–6, 11.204; by practising the *brahma vihāras* 10.173; lyric poetry lifts our emotions to a high pitch of intensity 26.114; only the more refined emotions can be absorbed into spiritual life 16.370; as preparation for meditation 3.617; refining them 5.43; sublimating sexual feelings 12.402; through contact with a *ḍākinī*, inner or outer 12.314–15; through nature 11.195–6; through faith and devotion 11.197–8, 11.203, 12.24–5; you need to find your own way of doing this 15.157

inhibiting and suppressing emotions
be careful to direct positive feelings rather than suppress them 5.617; consciously checking emotions to allow them more subtle expression 26.138; the difference between acknowledging emotions and expressing them 18.610–12; don't use activities to escape from feelings of anxiety 16.280; the English tendency to shrink from showing emotion 20.500; inhibiting emotions 18.609–10; a middle way between suppressing them and free expression 5.133, 5.618; repression, *see* repression; scrutinizing emotions to see their effect 7.290–1; some emotions need to be suppressed in everyday society 11.194–5; suppressing the expression of emotions enables us to practise the precepts 19.17; we need more exuberance and less 'self-control' 4.321

blocked emotions and how to deal with them
genuine communication may help 11.196–7; getting your emotions flowing in the direction of Enlightenment 13.242; they find another outlet 18.610; it may be unskilful to express emotion, but it is also unskilful to block it 18.611–12; methods to get the emotions flowing freely 4.256, 11.200; preventing the expression of gratitude 4.255–6; reasons for emotional blockage 11.198–200; the teaching of mindfulness may need to be supplemented by something else 17.88; you may need to investigate past relationships 14.573

alienation from feelings
alienated understanding and understanding with feeling 19.178–80; being alienated from emotions means being alienated from one's energy 17.599; 'being good' without experience one's true feelings 11.267; being out of touch with feelings 15.150, 18.608; how we become alienated from our emotions 12.265–6; if you are out of touch with your feelings, try doing what you enjoy 17.166; it's important to re-contact your emotions however you can 17.599; inhibiting feelings 18.609; non-experience of feelings and emotions 12.265–6, 18.608–10; losing contact with our feelings, we lose contact with ourselves, and with life 11.78; our hearts are full of emotions we do not truly feel 7.266–7; the synthetic emotions of modern culture make genuine feeling superfluous 7.266; why people today feel less strongly than people did in the past 15.149–50

difficulties
being carried away by untransformed emotional energy 8.489; danger of drying up emotionally 2.607; emotion confused with prejudice 1.495–6; emotional neediness 15.283; finding it difficult to put all your emotions into what you are doing 13.242; having no emotional strength behind one's action 19.470; in English, difficulty of associating strength with positivity 5.169; investing all our emotional energies in one person 19.19; the manipulation of emotions by mass media 15.288

see also
for feeling as *vedanā*, *see vedanā*; four right efforts

empathy for animals and plants as well as people 3.542; the Buddha teaches empathy to boys tormenting an animal, *see under Udāna*; cruelty to animals due to lack of empathy 26.653; empathize more 4.624; empathy with Cardinal Newman's religious difficulties 23.208; empathy with depression is not easy if one has not suffered from it 23.275; ethical integrity is rooted in empathy 8.577–8; for someone to whom you are giving advice 18.625; identifying ourselves with all living things 12.353; teaching children empathy 1.498, 3.542–3, 10.477, 26.71; identifying imaginatively with others 17.523; in the end you don't understand how it feels to be another person 18.16; in skilful states we act out of awareness and empathy 15.263; as well as knowing the difference between right and wrong, one has to be able to empathize 3.542; learning empathy through suffering 17.303; one empathizes with the more refined emotional side of oneself 19.409; realizing that others can suffer as one does oneself 8.447–8; through imagination 11.724–5, 17.598; transcending subject and object in communication through empathy 17.521; using imagination to feel someone else's suffering as our own 4.570, 10.476, 10.544; violence betrays the failure of empathy 3.318; a willingness to put oneself in other people's shoes 4.68, 5.175–6, 11.724; wondering if an affluent audience had any idea what it was like to be an ex-Untouchable 24.40; 'Your sadness is my sadness, friend' 25.275

emperors an emperor who commanded the monk Jojin to make rain 2.216; the emperor who decided to convert to Hinduism 12.245; the emperor's new clothes 12.6; the emperor who wanted to know what Buddhism was, *see under* Bodhidharma

empire empires mean that different peoples come into contact with one another 15.489; the growth of empire leads to the spread of religion 7.86–7; Western imperialism 8.285–6

empirical absorbing the empirical self in the higher self 4.278–9; a characteristic of the Dharma 3.167, 9.343, 12.74–5; continuity of empirical experiences 7.165–7; empirical self, *see under* self/further perspectives on 'self'

emptiness inner emptiness 2.386, 11.79–80, 15.309, 17.668, 26.24; *see also śūnyatā*

encouragement the bodhisattva's encouragement to live the spiritual life 16.230; four qualities wherefrom the bodhisattva gains encouragement 14.189; the guru needs to find a balance of encouragement and criticism 18.144; in the spiritual life we need plenty of encouragement 16.230; rejoicing in merits gives one encouragement 1.412, 4.47, 16.329; to encourage others you need to be inspired yourself 17.189–90

encyclopedias Harmsworth's *Children's Encyclopaedia* 9.487, 12.681, 13.528–9, 20.22–4, 23.8, 26.416, 26.482, 26.689; *Daśabhūmika Sūtra* a veritable encyclopedia of Buddhism 2.170; *Encyclopaedia Britannica* 24.400; encyclopedic approach to Buddhism 11.508–9; *Oriya Encyclopaedia*, *see under* Sangharakshita XIII/articles; *Tattvasaṅgraha* a kind of encyclopedia of refutations 1.323

endless round *see* cycle of birth and death

endogamy 9.27, 10.xxv

ends and means *see* means to an end

ends in themselves art can attract people to religion, but become an end in itself 19.469–70; clinging to the means to Enlightenment as though they were ends in themselves 7.264–5; the Dharma is not an end in itself 2.59, 7.244, 7.433, 7.520, 7.540, 7.542; discriminating between states of consciousness is not an end in itself 15.166; the *Heart Sūtra* eliminates religion as an end in itself 14.362–3; in some Buddhist circles the study of philosophy became an end in itself 8.498; it is difficult to have faith in something without regarding it as an end in itself 14.441; make sure even

positive habits don't become ends in themselves 15.356–7; renunciation is not an end in itself 16.511; rites and rituals as ends in themselves, *see* ten fetters/third fetter; the spiritually disastrous habit of treating concepts as ends in themselves 21.314; thinking about reality should be a springboard for the experience, not an end in itself 19.166; take care that culture doesn't become an end in itself 19.469–70; treating doctrines and disciplines as ends in themselves 7.261; what are meant to be means to an end become ends in themselves 19.134–5; you are an end in yourself 14.522

enemies

external
being 'without any enemy' 15.324, 15.430; enemies of the Buddha 9.146; enemies of the Dharma 10.240–2; an enemy who is out to harm you can do more for you than even a guru 4.411–13; Christian forgiveness of enemies 3.449; essentially a helpless creature 4.412; the evildoer making himself that which his enemy would wish him to be 4.390; gives the opportunity for the exercise of patience 4.413–4; gratitude towards enemies 4.417; heaping coals of fire on your enemy's head 4.411, 17.172; honour and respect the enemy for helping you, even though they don't intend to 4.434; may have many good qualities 4.416; non-violent strength against enemies 9.366; our friend, the enemy 4.415; one should choose one's enemies with care (Nietzsche) 4.412; 'One's enemies are to be prized and treasured' (Śāntideva) 4.410–11; one who is alert, active, and proud is invincible to the greatest foe 4.477–8; 'regard all enemies as passers-by on the road' – but you may need protection 18.621, 18.636; Sangharakshita's enemies 4.412–16; the *vajra* destroys enemies, everything that stands in the way of Enlightenment 13.168; you can be your own worst enemy 10.534–6, 18.521; if you try to defeat enemies using their means, you become like them 19.129; your friend in disguise 4.437

inner
compromise is the enemy of the spiritual life 26.63; external enemies go, but enemies within stay until you get rid of them 4.369; 'I will not bow before my everlasting enemies, the passions' 4.370; the inner enemy of routine 10.240–2; internal enemies are useful 4.467; a king whose enemies were anger and greed 13.654

see also
mettā bhāvanā/the practice/fourth stage; near and far enemies, *see* near and far enemies

energy

the nature of energy
'Energy is eternal delight' (Blake) 19.381; energy is primary, form secondary 2.93, 26.52; the energy of matter and mind 2.86; energy, like the wind, bloweth where it listeth 11.515; the five *skandhas* are temporary condensations of energy 14.548; human beings are embodiments of energy 2.93–4, 3.120, 26.653; human life is a transformation of energy 2.101–2; impermanence as streams of energy 2.86, 26.48; is thought dependent on physical energy? 24.347–8; the Void is alive with unleashed energy 18.74; we *are* energy 4.133

REASONS WHY ENERGY ISN'T AVAILABLE TO US

blocked energy
alienated energy 18.610; being sexually blocked 17.638, 17.776 (n573); blocked by inner conflict 15.216; blocked emotions, *see under* emotions/working with emotions; blocked energy symbolized by earth 13.153–4; the difference between being passive and being blocked 15.387–8; the effects of the release of blocked energy 11.200, 18.581–2; either one communicates or one is blocked 26.80; energy locked away in habitual patterns of thought, feeling, and behaviour 18.77; a balance between blocked energy and over-exuberance 15.732; it is unskilful to block energy 18.79; *prīti* is the sense of relief upon the release of blocked energy 2.105, 3.268, 15.218; reasons for energy being blocked 4.133; ways of unblocking our energy 3.372, 11.23; you may need to go back to find out the cause 18.443

the draining away of energy
the energy usually drained away by distractions 17.399; the draining nature of frivolous speech 17.229–30; modern life seems almost designed to drain energy 8.290, 15.151–2; unconscious conflict can be a great drainer of energy 19.394–5

waste of energy
conserving energy through celibacy 15.153; if your energy isn't unified, worrying about it would waste energy 26.77; the hindrances: energy that is going to waste or getting stuck 15.216–17; the *kleśas* and *āsravas* obstruct and waste energy 14.534; how to conserve energy 3.372; negativity

wastes energy at a catastrophic rate 4.133–4, 11.200–2

lacking energy
for many people the first task is to realize that they *have* energy 18.412; most people live far below the level of optimum vitality 11.33; of our total energy we only use about ten percent 4.599; often much of our energy is tied up in internal conflict 15.216; people lacking in energy accusing those with a lot of being insensitive 17.76; sometimes you can have doubts just because of lack of energy 10.578; we tend to be preoccupied with energy because we don't have it 17.78; you don't necessarily counter laziness by being more energetic 17.675

other kinds of unavailable energy
being carried away by untransformed emotional energy 8.489; boredom is connected with frustrated energy 17.400; energy that's too coarse 4.134, 11.202–3; repressed energy 18.78; suppressing energy 4.598–9; unconscious energy 3.41

WORKING WITH ENERGY

energy and Buddhist practice
Buddhism deflects the energies of the disciple towards the noble quest 1.129; a Buddhist should be the embodiment of energy 3.287, 3.372, 10.201; *dhyāna* is a state of pure energy without thought 4.481–2; energy is needed to practise all the disciplines leading to Enlightenment 16.11; energy, not laziness, the Buddha's teaching, *see* Mahāpajāpatī Gotami; the Goal: a release of energy back into the world 2.125; over-use of the word energy 17.77–8; the radiant energy of asceticism 15.447; spiritual energy needs to be cultivated and periodically renewed 15.152; we must dedicate *all* our energy to the development of consciousness 3.484–5

turbulent energies
energies compressed into a space too small for them 22.223; from the depths come our energies of instinct, emotion, and will 12.23; how to bring saṃsāric energies into line? 19.378–80; one cannot just cut off unsublimated energy 10.507; should be accepted as essentially positive 18.78; there is energy in anger which you can't afford to throw away 18.77–8; the transformation of turbulent energies within the psyche (*dharmapālas*) 19.408; the turbulent energies of non-human beings 16.349; working with turbulent energies: mantra chanting 18.78–9; without employment, energies may turn destructive 12.380; if wrathful forms put us in touch with primal energies, that is a good start 13.246

activation of energies
activation of energies through initiation 18.75; the *ḍākinī* is meant to energize all your spiritual energies 18.371; the energies of future Dharma practitioners may be aroused by art or sport 18.412; everyone needs the Dharma presented in a way that harnesses their energies 17.161; for the Tantra spiritual life starts with the activation of one's energies 13.157; the guru activates your dormant energies 18.67–8; helping people to access their energy 17.175; incorporating our deeper energies into the spiritual quest 12.335; the Vajrayāna is concerned with arousing and applying energies 18.371

getting your energy going
the energizing effect of going on retreat 15.153; energy generated in real communication 4.133, 4.482, 18.478; the energy locked up in negative emotions is your raw material 5.394; the energy released by Going for Refuge 13.161; find something to believe in, then you can do it with all your energy 10.603; freeing psycho-spiritual energy, symbolized by the stupa 13.153–5; getting rid of doubt gives one energy 4.482; getting your energy going through exercise 17.72; if we are interested in something, we will find the energy to do it 4.150; sexual energy 19.52–3, 19.412; the source of pleasure is the engaging of our energies 18.158; you produce energy by resisting inertia 15.403

energy and work
if one has energy one wants to work 26.72; inspiration is needed as well as energy 10.202; put as much energy as you can into what you are doing 18.79; work as the application of human energy 16.411; work stimulates energy 17.71–4

positive energy
cultivating emotional energy 15.152–5; energy that formerly found a negative expression expressed in positive ways 13.173; expressing positive energy is always pleasurable 15.217; truly positive energy can be more difficult to deal with than negative energy 18.78

refining energy
gradually refining gross energy 17.75; refinement of egoistic energy through the arts 26.67; refining energy 4.134

energy and other people
the effort to avoid blocking, misusing, or manipulating the energy of others 15.217;

giving is the natural interchange of one's energy with that of others 26.35; the unskilfulness of taking someone's energy against their wishes 2.367, 18.79

directing energies
directing emotional energies to practical help 23.337; energy cannot be programmed indefinitely 11.515; how to harness our energy to the Dharma 19.409–11; only through directing all one's energies can one gain Enlightenment 13.309; the powerful energies that produce *saṃsāra* channelled towards Enlightenment 19.378; understanding how to employ one's energy 17.175

subtle energy
becoming sensitive to subtle energies 15.216; working in meditation with the subtle energy system 18.322

the flow of energy
artists' energy flows with extraordinary vitality 3.509; bringing energies into harmony with awareness 18.322; the deeper the realization, the broader and stronger the outflow of energy 26.17; *dhyāna*: a flowing together of all the energies of our being 4.152; ethics consists in giving a certain direction to energy 17.529; if your energy is totally available to you, you become a smooth flow of energy 3.372; if you're interrupted too much your energy gets discouraged 5.681–2; free-flowing energy to support awareness 18.322; getting our energies flowing in the same channel through meditation 1.312; how to get your energy flowing in accordance with the truth 19.17; massage shifts the flow of energy 18.611; a natural flowing together of all one's energies in meditation 11.148–9; observing the natural rhythm of your energies 5.352; only commit yourself to a plan that can absorb all your energies 19.522–4; situations into which all your energies can flow 10.602

male and female energy
ḍākinīs and *dharmapālas*: feminine and masculine energies 19.408–9; is there a difference between 'male' and 'female' energy? 17.74–6

free energy
the experience of liberated energy is very pleasurable 11.149; five element practice in which the energies are progressively released 5.487; having enough free energy to direct towards the ideal 18.443–4; powerful, positive, free energies represented by the four great kings 16.353; the untrammelled energies of the *ḍākinīs* 18.180

integrating energies
integrating our disintegrated energies 3.120–1; integrating our energies 17.459–60; keeping unintegrated energy out of the mandala 16.352; the process of gathering one's energies is inherently blissful 18.91; a regular lifestyle helps to clarify and concentrate one's energies 15.154; subduing and integrating primordial energies 12.325; they come together in the practice of meditation 4.513; we live in a world of scattered energies which we have to bring together 12.336

transforming energy
energy can always be transformed 18.78; the transformation of psycho-spiritual energy is central to spiritual life 13.162; the Vajrayāna approach 5.352–3, 18.75

unification
concentration is the gradual unification of energies 5.49–50; *dhyāna* unifies one's energies, a basis for insight 18.576; drawing the energies into the central channel (Tantra) 19.31; gradual, without forcing 5.49–50; how to unify our energies – the central problem of the spiritual life 1.390, 4.133–4, 5.571, 7.292–3; increasingly an experience of bliss 19.52; involves enlisting the cooperation of unconscious energies 3.41, 12.23; a particular need in the modern world 18.417; in the Tantra 1.389; the unification of energy and awareness 18.322; unified energy oriented in the direction of the Transcendental 26.77; the union of *nāḍis* and *bindus* 19.52; the Vajrayāna's emphasis on the total unification of energies 18.411–12, 18.416–17; when all your energies are united, you are meditating 18.579–80; when you are absorbed in something creative, you and the energy are one 14.588

see also
transmission of energy, *see under* transmission; *vīrya*

Engels, Friedrich 25.121

England Buddhism in England, *see under* Western Buddhism/Buddhism in Britain; history, *see under* British history; Parliament, *see under* politics; royal family 22.12–14; Sangharakshita's impressions after twenty years away, *see under* Sangharakshita III/return to England

English, the

characteristics
characteristics of the English which may mesh with Buddhism 12.74–9; 'Christianity

has never really suited the English' 12.75–7; empirical pragmatism 12.74–5; fatalism 20.69–70; punctuality 10.101, 10.239, 23.36; secularism 12.75–7; tolerance 12.75

aspects of Englishness
class system 9.240–1; double standards in India 20.159; English law 11.327, 12.75–6; the sea figures in the imagination of all English people 26.393–4, 26.589; 'The English take their pleasures sadly' 15.172; the significance of the oak 13.274, 18.25; so organized it's hard for the individual to feel free 9.284–5; not entirely secular 9.349; perhaps only in the field of poetry have the English been truly great 26.21; the type of Englishman who was obnoxious in many parts of the world 22.130

English Sangha Association and Trust

introduction
its founding 12.73, 12.707 (n48); invites Sangharakshita to England 2.457, 9.157, 21.578–80, 22.560, 23.xv, 23.19–20; differences with the Buddhist Society, *see under* Buddhist Society; financial matters 23.127–8; journal (*The Buddhist*) 13.495–6; made up of shadowy figures 23.126–9; Hampstead Buddhist Vihara, *see* Hampstead Buddhist Vihara; a stormy meeting 23.110–11; letter to Sangharakshita advising him not to return 12.364–5, 23.376–8, 23.407; AGM at which Sangharakshita was defended by John Hipkin 23.401–4; Sangharakshita forbidden from setting foot in Sangha Trust properties 23.424; General Meeting confirming Sangharakshita's dismissal 23.424–5; the Association became a lay Theravādin organization 23.436

Biddulph Old Hall, Staffordshire
introduction 23.45; residence for monks 12.80, 23.127; meditation courses 11.499, 12.125; neglect of the place 23.231; plans to sell it 23.201; Sangharakshita leads retreats there 23.118, 23.132–41; Sangharakshita's plan to live there part-time 11.495; Trungpa Rimpoche invited to teach there 23.206; the warden and his wife 23.135, 23.231; after Sangharakshita's dismissal, new management 23.436–7

at Amaravati
Ajahn Sumedho as leader 13.382; attitude to culture 13.502–3; contrasted with FWBO 13.381–3, 13.407–23, 13.435–65, 13.473–4, 13.485–98, 13.507–10; a monastic order 13.445; moral values 13.448–9; related to forest monasteries of Thailand 13.381, 13.408, 13.508; relationship to tradition 13.469–74; supported by Thai laity 13.381–2

English language *see under* language

English, Elizabeth *see* Locana

enjoyment

the 'enjoyments' of worldly life
the 'Hīnayāna' Nirvāṇa for those bent on the enjoyment of trifling things 14.117–18; the more we acquire, the less enjoyment our 'pleasures' bring 17.394; Rechungpa's wish to take 'some comfort and enjoyment' 18.260, 18.560, 18.566; the superficial enjoyments of modern life 15.152–3; 'What essence has remained mine from things I once enjoyed?' 18.131

enjoying life
Darwin lost his capacity to enjoy Shakespeare 16.532; don't use needing enjoyment to rationalize not giving up anything at all 16.285; enjoyment is passive, but emotion is active 15.155; enjoyment of works of art 5.346, 17.396; 'Every flower enjoys the air it breathes' 7.388; if you are distracted, ask yourself whether you are enjoying your situation 15.117; if you are out of touch with your feelings, try doing what you enjoy 17.166; make sure there is room in your life for enjoyment 19.93; the more you enjoy life the more ascetic you will be, and *vice versa* 26.64; enjoying the world like a work of art 14.517, 26.64; the passive enjoyment of the art-lover 26.181; some people almost have to teach themselves to enjoy life 26.63; 'Sometimes I think work is the greatest enjoyment in life' 26.72

enjoying spiritual life
as much enjoyment from spiritual life as from mundane life, or more 19.379; bringing the enjoyment of daily life into spiritual practice 15.155; Buddhism is enjoyable in every way 11.45; enjoyment is not a luxury, but central to the spiritual life 18.133; enjoyment that helps the process of growth 15.156; an essential element of the spiritual life 15.158, 19.91–2; importance of enjoying being a Buddhist 16.285; Milarepa's enjoyment of his life 18.48, 18.54; our worldly enjoyments are to be blended with the spiritual (Vajrayāna) 19.379; to really enjoy yourself, get involved with the spiritual life 19.67; we need to take responsibility for our enjoyment 18.130

enjoying the elements of Buddhist life
enjoying *dhyāna* 5.270–1; enjoy Mahāyāna *sūtras* like poetry or a novel 16.57; enjoy

puja 11.221; faith is a deep enjoyment of the contemplation of the ideal 17.336; important to associate meditation with enjoyment 5.375–6; the Order as an enjoyable dance 25.145; read Buddhist literature for enjoyment 14.300–1; subtle enjoyments from the effort to transform consciousness 15.158–9; *vīrya* and enjoyment 9.297

see also
'body of mutual enjoyment', *see trikāya/ sambhogakāya*

Enlightened mind

its qualities
beauty, richness, and abundance 12.214; it abides not in anything, least of all in itself 7.35; it exerts on all living beings an unrivalled fascination 13.278; inexhaustible wealth 18.59; playful and inexhaustible manifestation 18.48; pure, perfect objectivity 4.165, 12.214; the wish-fulfilling gem 12.214

its aspects
the aspect that regards all things as beloved 12.222; its calming, pacifying aspect 13.282–3; its destructive aspect 13.278; the harmonizing, reconciling aspect 13.282; Kurukullā represents its passion aspect 13.68; the wisdom aspect 13.295

its activity
bridging the gap between Enlightened and unenlightened mind 12.152, 14.302, 17.389; devotes itself to the welfare of all beings, acting spontaneously 4.166, 12.217; it cannot 'fall' 17.97–8; it does not try to pin reality down to any particular manifestation 18.44; it imparts soothing calm 13.280; it sees not only the unity of things but also their uniqueness 4.166; it shines its love and compassion on 'good' and 'bad' alike 4.165; one of its principal functions is the destruction of ignorance 13.278; only an Enlightened mind can act with the whole of itself 1.536; total action, mysterious practical activity 1.536, 12.216; wrathful forms the only way it can operate in this deluded world 13.68–9

Enlightenment

INTRODUCTION

introducing Enlightenment
all experience short of Enlightenment is a subtle form of suffering 1.486; by definition it must be embodied in some form of sentient existence 15.591; the central fact of the Buddha's life and the principal theme of his teaching 7.157; the difference between Enlightened individual and principle of Enlightenment 13.300–1; different conceptions of Enlightenment 11.72; the essence of Enlightenment 1.88–97; the one constant factor in the history of Buddhism 7.313; it is not anybody's personal possession 18.314–15, 26.208; it is the same for all, but there are many ways of manifesting it 18.222–3; it negates ego, not individuality 12.512; it offers the only lasting solution to universal human problems 15.261; it transcends existence and non-existence 17.242, 17.251; no such thing as Enlightenment, only Enlightened people 16.502, 16.576, 18.58; not individual salvation, but for the welfare of all beings 3.245–6, 4.21–2; ordinary life is Enlightenment, and Enlightenment is ordinary life 14.397, 26.63; words can give us no idea of Enlightenment 3.250–1

questions about Enlightenment
are you missing the possibility of Enlightenment here and now? 18.155; can lay people gain Enlightenment? 10.225; can the *mettā bhāvanā* take you all the way to Enlightenment? 5.188–9; can the sexual act possibly be conducive to Enlightenment? 1.390; could the ideal of Enlightenment degenerate? 4.20–1; does Enlightenment take you beyond the working out of karma? 18.84–5; is it possible to explain how one can become Enlightened? 5.266; 'Is what I am doing really helping me in the direction of Enlightenment?' 3.256; why does an Enlightened being meditate? 14.401–2, 19.421–6

POTENTIAL FOR ENLIGHTENMENT

the potential of all for Enlightenment
an affinity with Enlightenment 3.301, 11.104; 'All beings are from the very beginning the Buddha' 1.269, 2.742 (n682), 18.44–5, 19.537; all beings are potentially Buddhas 1.274, 3.316, 9.285, 16.7; the bodhisattva ideal exemplifies humanity's potential 3.384, 10.175; the Buddha or bodhisattva represents what you can become 5.621; Enlightenment is within us all, but shrouded by ignorance 3.340; every human being has the capacity for Enlightenment 11.324, 15.250, 15.568–9; every phenomenon in the universe contains the potentiality of *bodhi* 7.344; however degraded their present condition 3.63, 12.512–13, 19.540–1; human beings seen not as sinners and heretics, but as the Buddha saw them 7.318; human consciousness, wherever it arises, shares the same spiritual potential 15.81; the human realm alone is where a Supreme

Buddha can arise 1.32; the idea related to interconnectedness 7.317; the logical corollary of the bodhisattva ideal 1.274; Mahāyāna Buddhism sets no limits on potential for Enlightenment 16.440; people in a much worse condition than we are have gained Enlightenment 4.448; a permanent possibility at the heart of every living being 7.311; a permanent possibility in the universe 2.163; the person incapable of Enlightenment, *see icchantika*; possible for 'the common man'? 9.113, 9.248–9, 9.266; the potential of body, speech, and mind to become the *trikāya* 19.30; the qualities of Enlightenment are present in everyone in germinal form 11.103–4; 'the quality of Enlightenment is inherent in the universe' (Govinda) 1.48; reflect on the teaching that every human being is potentially a Buddha 4.176; something in oneself corresponds to what is fully developed in the Buddha 4.201–2; a special correspondence between the human condition and Buddhahood 2.96; this belief is the reason for tolerance 7.318; the *trikāya* is potentially present in every human being 21.215; 'we are frail ... but embody the universal possibility of Enlightenment' 3.17; 'You might never become a Bach, but you can become a Buddha 16.286

actualizing the potential
celebrating Wesak is a reminder to think of our own Enlightenment 3.21; faith is the stirring of our potential for Enlightenment 3.300–1; the human mind has the *potential* to embark on the higher evolution 3.479; it has to pass through many steps and stages 26.479; 'Many who are Buddhas today were once worms' – a convincing argument? 4.448; the mind is the raw material, the stuff of Enlightenment 18.234; objectified through visualization of the Buddha 3.516–17; the precious human body as vehicle for Enlightenment 3.601, 7.170–1; *śamatha* actualizes all the positive potentialities of the mind 5.425; some would view the prospect of becoming a Buddha with dismay 14.484; talk of gaining Enlightenment is fine on the level of conventional truth 1.245; we cannot be truly and fully happy until we have realized that potential 12.613; we don't have to become Enlightened if we don't want to 26.52; we will have to follow a path to realize our potential 4.9

symbols of our potential
the 'golden treasure underground' 19.497; human beings like a bed of lotuses, *see under* Brahmā Sahāmpati's request; the jewel in the garment 9.262; the jewel in the lotus 12.502; like the seed of a plant 3.313, 7.316–18; parable of the raincloud, *see under White Lotus Sutra*/parables and stories

dangers of the language of potentiality
the Buddha did not use it 16.61–2, 17.92, 18.608; the danger of thinking that Enlightenment is within 18.606–8; the dangers of the metaphysics of potentiality 16.61–2, 16.221–2, 17.92–5, 17.97–8; don't see the element of Tathāgatahood as a potentiality in the mundane self 13.390–1; the idea of the final stage of development being present within is *ātmavāda* 17.93; if one thinks one is near Enlightenment, one is far from it, and *vice versa* 26.479; it may be the metaphysically-inclined Indian mind getting to work on Buddhism 17.95; it should come with a health warning 4.33, 15.583, 18.607–8, 19.97–8; more helpful to think in terms of growth and development 17.93–5; that language may be helpful for someone suffering from guilt 17.95; thinking 'I am Enlightened' you are as far from Nirvāṇa as thinking 'I am rich' 7.407; you're not like a box with Buddhahood at the bottom 18.607

the timeless nature of Enlightenment
above and beyond the world of time and particularity, all beings *are* Enlightened 13.135; all living beings *will* attain Enlightenment (in the language of eternity) 1.274; at this very moment we are as close to Enlightenment as we shall ever be 4.213; culmination of evolutionary process or breakthrough beyond time and space 3.146; a meeting of two dimensions: eternity and time (story of Aṅgulimāla) 3.145–50; Enlightenment is eternal (*White Lotus Sūtra*) 4.209–10, 16.60–1, 16.199; Enlightenment is instantaneous in that it takes place outside time 19.435; eternally young, because it's always new, always fresh 12.308; 'the intersection of the timeless moment' – but no point of intersection 3.145; to see Enlightenment as being attained within time is to speak conventionally 4.204; symbolized by the Ādibuddha 18.94

THE GOAL

the goal of Enlightenment
the goal is to go beyond the individual self, not regress from it 17.625; a higher goal than simply the eradication of negative emotions 16.67; it may seem very far off, so we need intermediate goals 15.95; projected as non-attachment 14.570; the true goal of human life 1.80; we must see it as inspiring and invigorating 18.372

aspiration
aspiration to Enlightenment (*Sūtra of Golden Light*) 16.435; the energy in healthy desire is needed to develop the aspiration 17.290; Enlightenment is the cumulative effect of the aspirations of countless lives 1.48; a prayer for the Enlightenment of all, made on the Vulture's Peak 20.466; the wish-fulfilling jewel gives us what we really desire: Enlightenment 13.166

the urge to Enlightenment
the altruistic orientation of the motivation to gain Enlightenment 3.452, 11.282; a blind urge, present in every living being 16.7; *bodhicitta*, *see bodhicitta*; a conflict with the ego's resistance to new experience? 16.24; few strive for Enlightenment, for most are concerned with other things 2.218; imagine Enlightenment in such a way that you are energized and inspired 18.372–3; we have to satisfy it by developing Enlightenment within ourselves 13.353

the ideal of Enlightenment
the aim of Enlightenment is the unifying factor of Buddhism 1.202; all unillumined desire is really a groping in the dark for Enlightenment 7.307; could the ideal degenerate? 4.20–1; encouraging unenlightened minds to grow in the direction of Enlightenment 13.280; Enlightenment is what everybody truly desires, whether they know it or not 13.278; having an abstract idea of Enlightenment 18.443; if we really wanted Enlightenment in the future, we would really want it now 17.354; if you don't feel that you can develop Enlightenment, it isn't an ideal for you 18.569; the natural ideal for human beings 11.103–5, 11.110; the need of beings for Enlightenment 14.412; the true individual is not satisfied with anything less 11.104–5; if you are aiming at Enlightenment, you are relating to everybody else who is 26.27; take it as a working hypothesis 11.110; we're aiming for Enlightenment in every lifetime 25.136; where does the ideal come from? 11.105–9

THE PATH

the path to Enlightenment
the Buddha's teachings' only aim is to point out the way to Enlightenment 13.566; it leads to a precipice: not even the 'right' path will take us to Enlightenment 4.200; the most worthwhile thing to which we can possibly devote ourselves 3.562; a middle way 11.481; must include all stages and degrees of the spiritual life 1.269

the process of gaining Enlightenment
as people grow towards it, they grow more different from one another 3.180; by renouncing self desires and views based on them 1.20; the Buddha's Enlightenment had its origins in his practice of the ten perfections 8.232; conflict between emptiness (ontologically) and the struggle for Enlightenment 14.146; dedicating one's merit to Enlightenment 16.331–2; dedicating the senses to Enlightenment 13.258–9; the *Dhammapada* contains all we need to know to progress towards it 15.5; enhancing the beauty of existence through gaining Enlightenment 18.447; Enlightenment is difficult – we need to take what help we can get 3.42; the ethical and spiritual qualities needed 15.81; by one's own effort 1.348, 4.533–4, 15.81; by manipulating *prajñā-upāya* in the individual 1.389; gaining more skill and experience, like a doctor after qualification 15.469; how does the flower of Enlightenment come from the black root of *kleśas*? 25.73–4; how rejoicing in merits can be transmuted into Enlightenment 14.144; in the *bardo* state between death and rebirth 13.28, 18.85–6; in the dream state 12.199, 19.306; it is dependent on energy being totally available on all levels 18.77; it is difficult to gain Enlightenment from a state of unadulterated happiness 13.137; it is less effort to gain Enlightenment than to be successful in the world 4.292–3; it's easier to attain to Enlightenment from Sukhāvatī than from anywhere else 7.43; it is thought of as the culmination of a process, but that's problematic 4.33–4; not even the 'right' path will take us to Enlightenment 4.200; one could not gain Enlightenment in a universe conceived of as dead 15.138–9; through concentrating and directing all one's energies 13.309; the powerful energies that produce *saṃsāra* channelled towards it 19.378; practice of the *mūla yogas*, if thorough, will bring one close to Enlightenment 13.87; it requires heroic qualities 3.46; setting up the conditions for the attainment of Enlightenment 17.589; spiritual life is like the plant and Enlightenment is like the flower 11.88; thinking of the process in aesthetic terms 18.447; through friendship we perceive Enlightenment itself 7.295; through insight into the true nature of phenomena 1.87–8; trying to gain Enlightenment by force of will 3.40–1; until it is attained, a conflict between appropriating and experiencing 16.520; 'In vigour lies Enlightenment' 1.440; we don't need all the teachings

to gain Enlightenment 18.369; without celibacy Enlightenment is unattainable 1.442; women's capacity to gain Enlightenment, *see under* women; you've always got to be vigilant 4.532

the means to Enlightenment
apparently contradictory 1.209; Buddhist doctrines are a means to the end of Enlightenment 14.608; culture as a means to Enlightenment 7.435–6; to be determined by the test of experience 7.520; the Dharma is the Buddha's Enlightenment objectified and therefore falsified 26.43; doctrines to be refined to such transparency that Enlightenment shines through 2.61; ethics as a means to Enlightenment 1.200, 3.324; the limitations of the means to Enlightenment 16.503–4; the teachings of the Dharma are the means to that end 1.316–17

quick and slow routes to Enlightenment
asking for a method that gives Enlightenment quickly without effort 19.284–5; Bāhiya, *see Udāna*/Bāhiya; the 'Council of Lhasa': does Enlightenment come gradually or all at once? 13.11–12; gradual Enlightenment 3.146; 'Never hope quickly to attain Enlightenment' 18.164–5; one does not attain Enlightenment either slowly or quickly 13.11–12; the quick route to Enlightenment 18.164; there is no such thing as the quick path and the slow path (Huineng) 16.183; Enlightenment has nothing to do with speed within time 1.176, 3.146; the *parāvṛtti* teaching implies that it is sudden, but the preparation is long 2.284–5; *satori* 1.176; sudden Enlightenment in the *Sūtra of Huineng* 3.146, 16.602 (n131); splitting the rock may seem sudden, but it has been taking place at deeper levels 2.284; stories of its arising on hearing the Buddha or seeing a leaf fall 3.272, 4.7; why doesn't sudden Enlightenment happen to us? 3.272–3, 4.7

obstacles to Enlightenment
belief that terms such as *attā* refer to unchanging realities 1.99; craving 12.623; conventional religiosity 3.256; the destruction of all that stands in the way 13.283; the dichotomy between self and other 23.18; Enlightenment is within us all, but shrouded by ignorance 3.340; the five poisons 18.448; the sexual urge 3.321, 11.572; only through ignorance do we think of ourselves as unenlightened 1.347; ossification of the ideal 4.21; when the means to Enlightenment becomes an object of attachment 1.303; the *vajra* destroys everything that stands in the way 13.168; the ego's accumulation of good actions 11.283

misunderstandings and mistakes
the Buddha did not inherit it, but gained it through struggle and mistakes 3.20; conceptualization of Enlightenment leads to distortion 2.54; grasping at the concept of Enlightenment 14.451; having read about Enlightenment, people think they've realized it 19.506–7; to think of it as a psychological experience is to misunderstand it completely 16.270; thinking of it as an object waiting to be realized 14.445; misconstrued as something to be gained 1.303; mistakenly thinking you're Enlightened 4.586–7; mistaking *śamatha* experience for Enlightenment 19.159; it is much more than an 'intellectual penetration into the nature of the human situation' 5.426; taking descriptions of Enlightenment too literally 15.230, 17.459; using the word 'enlightened' as a synonym for 'intelligent' 8.152

ENLIGHTENMENT ITSELF

attainment
at what point in time is somebody said to be Enlightened? 15.466–7; the idea that Enlightenment can be attained without meditation 8.620–1; there is the attainment of Enlightenment, but nobody who attains it 19.376; to be attained for its own irresistible sake 1.133, 7.391; eternally in the process of attainment 15.470; gaining Enlightenment for the benefit of all beings 11.282; going all out for Enlightenment while realizing that no one attains it 11.14; if everybody gets the same teaching, why don't all become Enlightened? 11.359–60; if you think you're near to it, you're far, and if you think you're far, you're near 25.136; inseparable from the entire cessation of greed, hatred, and delusion 13.571; it can be attained whenever and wherever circumstances permit 11.246; language makes us speak as though it could be an individual attainment 1.233; not even thinking of trying to attain Enlightenment 18.451; not attainment of a fixed position, but a continuous and irreversible process 14.596; organizing one's entire life to subserve the attainment of Enlightenment 2.323; out of time 1.347, 19.34; in the ultimate sense there can be no attainment 1.268; speaking of this or that person attaining Enlightenment is only relatively true 1.179; 'What a silly Buddha I was!' 4.203, 18.45; when we realize that duality is the creation of our own minds 22.29; within seven lives 3.251

experience of Enlightenment
better to speak of it not as an experience but as a state of being 2.55; a constantly expanding and unfolding experience 15.226, 15.230; different for different people 19.203–4; Enlightenment as experience and non-experience 11.72–91, 19.378; an experience in which, paradoxically, there is neither subject nor object 12.614; the experience of Enlightenment transcends happiness 19.244; an experience that seeks to communicate itself 11.511; how did we come to think of Enlightenment as 'experience'? 11.73–4; imagine a day of complete creative freedom 15.230; for Zen, the only thing that ultimately matters 13.343; inconceivable to us 14.442; it cannot be described at all 2.251, 3.32; it contains an element of communication, an element of spiritual friendship 26.78; it involves a shift to a higher level of understanding 16.270; it is 'felt in the blood, and felt along the heart' 11.73; it might not be what one expected, but it would be much better 17.380–1; the limitations of language to describe the experience of Enlightened beings 19.429–30; more like death 3.149; not self-contained, but has an element of communication, of friendship 11.437; not to be compared with anything else whatsoever 12.322; often described in negative terms 17.520; a process of Enlightening, not a state of Enlightenment 19.204; a subtle sense of self only disappears completely upon Enlightenment 14.413; we naturally think of it in terms of our own experience 3.148, 14.441–2

names and synonyms
absolute consciousness 2.96; the *amṛtapada*, the deathless state 13.134. 15.63; *anuttara-samyak-sambodhi* (unsurpassed, perfect Enlightenment) 2.267; 'awakened' 8.572, 10.442; awakening to the truth of things 3.149–50; described in terms of 'the three true knowledges' (*Mahāsaccaka Sutta*) 3.631 (n34); described in terms of what it is not (Pāli canon) 15.228–9; the Enlightened One described in the Abhidharma 14.81; 'Enlightenment', 'Nirvāṇa', 'Buddhahood' are only provisional terms 13.348; 'the great death' (Zen) 3.149, 3.230, 12.174; great passion, great anger synonyms for Enlightenment in Tantric Buddhism 3.235; *vajrabodhi* 13.178

what is Enlightenment like?
acting with the whole of oneself 1.536; awareness, love, and energy 11.101–2; an awareness of things *as they really are* 3.31; any kind of Enlightenment experience must have a compassionate dimension 4.86; better to think Enlightenment is red or blue or green than a state of nothing 12.218–19; beyond conception 12.546; blissful 10.262, 18.90, 19.424–6; the cessation of the delusion that any kind of self exists 1.179; compassion is its positive and dynamic aspect 1.387; complete spontaneity 19.258–9; even the blissful higher realms are painful compared to it 18.589; freedom from all defilements and their consequences 13.298; freedom from all delusion, all prejudice 3.31; freedom from greed, hatred, and delusion 12.546–7; not gaining any object, but realizing the immaculate nature of mind 1.364; not only wisdom but compassion 11.511; indescribable, unclassifiable 17.242; ineffable 3.31, 3.181; inexhaustible energy, total spontaneity, uninterrupted creativity 3.32, 11.102; inseparable from great altruism 3.254; the inseparable unity of ineffable Bliss and transcendental Awareness 8.445; inspiration from the lives of Enlightened individuals 15.164; the joy and beauty of Enlightenment 18.129; like opening the closed fist of the ego 17.351–2; magical (according to the Vajrayāna) 19.214; not only illumination and freedom, but also infinite and inexhaustible love 2.57; an overflowing of profound love and compassion 3.32, 11.102, 22.285; *prajñā-upāya*, the unity of wisdom and compassion 1.386; primarily a state of knowledge, then emotional experience and action 7.271; pure beauty 13.278; the realization of the essential non-difference of the universe and the Absolute 1.306; a seeing of 'things' unmediated by any separate subject doing the seeing 3.31; selflessness 7.296; self-regarding and other-regarding aspects 4.21–2; beauty, harmony, colour, spiritual life, and spiritual activity 12.219; pure, clear, radiant awareness, no distinction between oneself and others 3.31, 11.101; the union of opposites at the highest possible level 12.185; unwavering happiness 10.655–6; we have no idea of what it is like 17.631; a way of functioning 19.203

traditional perspectives on Enlightenment
arts transformed (through Zen) into paths to Enlightenment 2.555; described in terms of freedom in the *Ariyapariyesanā Sutta* 3.631 (n34); Enlightenment and lay followers 2.203–5; gratitude to Amitābha for the gift of Enlightenment 13.309–10; 'how could liberation … be expressed in

words?' (*Buddhacarita*) 17.741 (n268); the idea of individual Enlightenment 1.403, 1.405; the lineage of Enlightenment 1.204; the Mahāmudrā stresses its non-conceptual character 19.271; its positive and dynamic elements brought out by the Tibetans 7.397; the Pure Land: Enlightenment as a 'social experience' 18.305–6; a state of non-duality (Mahāyāna) 15.592, 17.483; Tantric Buddhism regards the world as a help to Enlightenment 1.375; the Theravādin view of it as a state in which the self has been eliminated 15.338; three kinds: *arhant*, *pratyekabuddha*, *sammāsambuddha* 1.85–6, 15.465; the universal cosmic principle in the *White Lotus Sūtra* 16.48–9; the wrong time for Enlightenment (*Vimalakīrti-nirdeśa*) 16.523–4

aspects of Enlightenment
aspects represented by the five-Buddha mandala, *see* mandala of the Five Buddhas; 'aspects' of Enlightenment an accommodation to our limitations 19.34; the healing aspect of Enlightenment 13.282, 16.193–4; we split it into different aspects to understand it 11.102–3, 18.599, 18.606; its power aspect 7.397; the seven constituents of Enlightenment 14.81, 14.83; three principal aspects, *see* bodhisattvas/archetypal/three family protectors

proving Enlightenment
the academic approach to Buddhism is hostile to the possibility 7.310, 11.483; the Buddha was living proof of the possibility of Enlightenment 15.197; curiosity about whether someone is Enlightened 10.590; the luxury of doubting whether the Buddha was really Enlightened 15.176; rational proof 1.285; there is no way of inferring that someone is Enlightened 14.431–2; validating its authenticity 1.204; a worldly person can't possibly tell whether someone is Enlightened 19.282, 26.49

symbols, metaphors, and similes
Enlightenment is itself a metaphorical term 13.122; the Full Moon of Enlightenment 25.176; the glorified human body as the most fitting symbol of Enlightenment 1.388; an illumination in which things become visible in their reality 2.55; myths and legends help convey the trans-conceptual truth of Enlightenment 11.15–16; personified by the Buddha 5.621; escape from jungle, freed from debt, release from prison 2.56, 10.262, 13.192–3, 14.42; like a great ocean 14.548; like a river flowing into an ocean we can't see 3.145–6; a *mudrā* is essentially Enlightenment expressed by the hands 13.306; the sun-smile of Enlightenment 25.257; symbolized by the flaming drop at the top of the Tantric stupa 13.163; the true wish-fulfilling gem 16.174–5; the vibration of the music of Enlightenment in one's heart 1.283–4

after Enlightenment
any given moment expresses the whole of the Enlightened personality 19.231; being Enlightened but not articulate 19.204–5; the body is still there, but it becomes an instrument of Enlightenment 4.512; by gaining Enlightenment you can escape karma 4.292, 15.92–3; characteristics of an Enlightened person: a child, a madman, a ghost 11.11–12; the difference it made to the Buddha's outlook on existence 2.251; the difference between Nirvāṇa and Supreme Perfect Enlightenment 26.698; differences of temperament would seem to persist 12.511–12; does the process continue? 3.68–9, 10.614–15, 15.226, 15.230, 15.466–70; 'ensuing' Enlightenment 18.87; the happiness of an Enlightened person 19.525–6; how Enlightenment positively changes our experience 17.380–1; it is impossible that an Enlightened one could act unethically 7.408–9; it is not the case that 'Enlightened Beings could still have cravings' 26.537; the mental activity of an Enlightened one 5.421; not a fixed position but a way of operating 15.468–9; not a full stop 4.21, 16.524, 17.459; the arising of positive mental events once Enlightenment has been attained 17.590; the personality of an Enlightened being is a succession of pure *dharmas* 1.252; responding creatively to all the circumstances that may arise 15.468–9; there is no fall from the state of Enlightenment 16.100; to be Enlightened is to be such that you could not use Enlightenment wrongly 13.168; to understand an Enlightened One, we have to see Enlightenment's qualities 2.132–3; when you become Enlightened, what happens to your ego? 17.351–2; when you are Enlightened the law of karma doesn't get in your way 14.593; when you have gained Enlightenment, what the Buddha has said, you have said 19.33; while the Enlightened mind is associated with the body, suffering is possible 18.47; the world is the same but you see it differently 17.483; you experience others in a completely different way 17.483; you see that you always were Enlightened –

absurd! 4.203, 18.45; you won't become solemn, but joyful, or unpredictable 18.254

see also
arhant; arhantship; Buddha nature; the Buddha's Enlightenment, *see* Buddha/I life story/Enlightenment; Enlightened communication, *see* Buddha III; limbs of Enlightenment, *see* seven *bodhyaṅgas*; prediction to Enlightenment, *see under* prediction; *satori*, *see under* Zen; Siddhārtha's determination to reach Enlightenment, *see under* Siddhārtha; thought of or will to Enlightenment, *see* *bodhicitta*; three doors to Enlightenment, *see* three *vimokṣas*

enlightenment (18th-century philosophy) introduction 4.659 (n2); agnostic principle 8.588; emphasis on self 13.385; the idea of enlightenment 12.463; possible confusion with the Buddhist sense of the word 4.4, 8.152, 10.442, 21.450; rejective of the normative power of tradition 13.467–8

enmity in cultivating *mettā*, you protect yourself from thoughts of enmity 18.80; the persistent desire to harm another person 17.269; a sort of vengeful hatred 16.295; *vaira* (Pāli *vera*) 2.388

Ens and non-Ens 1.317–19

ensuing *dhyāna* (or *samādhi*) *see under* *dhyāna*/a guide to *dhyāna*

entanglement disentanglement from mundane experience 17.512–13; a conscious effort to break away from entanglements and murkiness 13.191–2; the danger of small entanglements 17.283

entering the Stream *see* Stream Entry

entertainment the Dharma student should abstain from activities which stimulate the lower mind 1.30; the entertainment of the spiritual life 19.22, 19.73–4; even the most sacred ceremonies can degenerate into entertainment 24.531; the *Jātaka* stories are not told merely for entertainment 1.233; the need for Dharma books to be entertaining 8.361; Rechungpa is entertained by the play of wild goats 19.9–11, 19.77–80

enthusiasm allowing the blaze of initial enthusiasm for the Dharma to subside into a glow of half-interest 8.313; certain pages of the Pāli canon thrill with quiet enthusiasm 1.240; dampening someone's enthusiasm 17.660; enthusiasm is not necessary to keep up a steady progress 17.576; find something to believe in, then you can do it with all your energy and enthusiasm 10.603; reasons for lack of enthusiasm 9.199; Sangharakshita sharing his enthusiasm for the Dharma 14.xvi; to be developed by practising meditation 9.201; to generate enough enthusiasm to break our bonds we need the bodhisattva ideal 26.56; 'without enthusiasm, life becomes drudgery' (Ambedkar) 9.134–5, 9.199–200, 10.370, 10.388–9; without enthusiasm, no progress 9.200; why aren't Order members full of enthusiasm for the Dharma? 10.84, 10.87; why does enthusiasm for the spiritual life wear off? 1.554–5; enthusiasm for the good, *see* *vīrya*

environment

environmental concerns
apparently small actions can have a devastating cumulative effect 3.321; destruction when 'the king overlooks an evil deed' (*Sūtra of Golden Light*) 16.430–1; the dreadful destruction of rainforests and many species of living things 12.409; the effect of environmental destruction on tribal people 25.58; the effect of the loss of forests 18.23, 25.52; an irrigation scheme threatening an ancient Buddhist site 8.163–4; man ruining Nature's peace 25.237; noise pollution 10.291, 12.474, 16.387, 24.465–6; oil fields in India: a black blight on the green earth 22.100; plastic 25.53; a poem apologising for human destruction of the environment 25.50–9; pollution 10.291, 25.53, 25.447; the ravages of open-cast mining in Malaysia 24.42–3; sadness at the construction of new roads through 'the living green' 24.426; things like hydroelectric dams don't solve the problem of human suffering 22.331; wasting natural resources 15.283, 16.386–7

taking care of the environment
the Buddhist tradition has potential to contribute to environmental ethics 8.611; Buddhists need to play an active part in protecting the environment 12.409–10; concern for the environment is no substitute for leading the spiritual life 24.501; environmental awareness 11.733; the environmental effect of vegetarianism 25.58; the first precept covers environmental concerns 26.669; Greenpeace 10.83; having an effect on our immediate environment 11.623; its tendency to balance itself 16.357; preventing the destruction of wildlife 8.257; realizing one's responsibilities towards the environment 9.440; the principle of non-violence can be applied

to environmental problems 8.453; right livelihood is ecologically sound 3.283; a sensitive, almost reverential attitude towards one's environment 10.647; taking care of one's surroundings 9.445–6; using as few of the earth's resources as possible 12.670; teaching children to care for the environment 3.541; we have to think what we can do to save the planet from human beings 25.57–8; we should take no more than we need, and give what we can 15.283; we shouldn't feel despondent 11.271, 25.57–9

awareness of our environment
awareness of the environment 3.284, 3.469, 9.294–5, 13.456; awareness through the senses 17.536; bringing about change through changing your environment 11.117, 12.553–4; the environment in which beings live is largely determined by their deeds 1.342; 'In a fair land to dwell': the importance of one's environment 15.392–5; living in an environment populated by many animals 18.23–4; Milarepa makes best use of a beneficial environment – a tiger's cave 18.41–2; the mind made clear and tranquil by a beautiful environment 7.337; responsiveness to the natural environment 18.52–4; the responsiveness of primitive cultures 18.21–2; spirit of place 18.21–4; unpleasant environmental conditions can be a form of *duḥkha* 3.212; we are usually not really aware of our environment 1.570

envy bodhisattvas preserving the *White Lotus Sūtra* need to be unaffected by envy 16.47; the Buddha's disciples envied by wanderers of other views 10.477–8, 10.539–41; corruption in the form of envy 17.654–5; countered by rejoicing in merits 16.329–30, 17.654; envy of the merits of others 4.430, 16.330–1; 'He hath a daily beauty in his life/ That makes me ugly' 17.654; *īrṣyā* (*upakleśa*) 17.653–5; as a poison 13.183; to counter it, associate with people who appreciate your qualities 17.654; without *muditā* there is envy 5.203; you only afflict yourself by being envious 4.431

Epicurus 17.507

Epidaurus 16.192, 23.293–5, 26.238

epistemology confusion of ontology with epistemology (Upanishads) 8.619; for Buddhism there is no question of an ontology as distinct from an epistemology 8.442–3; a mix of philosophy, psychology, epistemology 12.145; the Yogācāra's philosophy is epistemological and its method psychological 7.201

Epstein, Jacob 22.54, 26.379

equality all things are equally *śūnyatā* 19.191; Ambedkar's views on equality 9.101–2; the anti-hierarchical concept of equality is very restricting 4.169; the assumption that everybody is as good as everybody else 'as a person' is questionable 4.170; beings are not all equally capable of becoming Enlightened from their present state 13.135; the Buddha's advocacy of equality 9.68, 9.101; concepts of equality and inequality are inappropriate with regard to women and men 26.56; democracy means equality before the law, not that everyone is equal 15.715–16; the Dharma as expressive of equality (Ambedkar) 9.143, 9.144, 9.426; the Dharma must promote equality between human beings 10.351; a dogmatic assumption of equality prevents communication 15.536–7; does not mean that everyone is exactly the same 9.184; equality is a concept that has a place only in arithmetic 26.72; in Buddhism it means that everyone has the same right to develop 9.184, 9.496–7; 'Inequality is life. Equality is death.' 26.74; the Mirror of Equality 19.152; 'the outspread pinions of Equality' 9.xxi; *parātmasamatā* (equality of self and others) 2.361, 4.584, 4.587–9, 4.599; there are always inequalities between people, and they need to be acknowledged 17.274; treating our friends and companions like our own self (*samānārthatā*) 3.575; the yogi sees all beings with the eye of absolute equality 7.102

see also
egalitarianism; sameness; thinking of oneself as superior, inferior, or equal, *see under* pride; wisdom of equality, *see under* five *jñānas*

equanimity *see upekṣā*

eradication effort to eradicate unskilful states of mind 3.304, 7.172; Enlightenment is a higher goal than simply the eradication of negative emotions 16.67; eradicating craving for continued individual existence 26.159; eradicating misconceptions 3.44; the eradication of egoism 7.405–10, 26.668; the eradication of the three roots 7.221–2, 7.256; 'May I eradicate all passions' 4.73–81; meditation practices to eradicate delusion 2.392; to eradicate craving, try using your imagination 17.597–8

see also
eradicating wrong views, *see under micchā-diṭṭhis*; eradicating negative emotions, *see under* emotions/negative; eradicating passions, *see under* five *kleśas*

Erasmus 5.249, 5.724–5 (n234), 24.275

Erasmus, St 13.631

Erastrianism 18.339, 18.653 (n129)

Erda, Mother (Wagner) 12.188, 16.380–1

eremitical *see under* monastic life

Eric (ordained as Viriya) *see* Viriya

Eros 2.218, 18.158

eroticism 5.131–3, 24.292

error Blake and the casting out of error 18.277; considering that Buddhism is contained in this or that doctrine 7.144; the Dharma traditionally has two aspects: propagating the truth and dispelling error 4.125; doing things that are practically embodied, you can see where you have gone wrong 18.277; the primordial error that 'self' represents an eternal, unchanging ego-identity 7.327; regarding the fictions of thought as having an independent real existence: a root error 7.325–6; the root error of humanity is abstraction 7.325–6; thinking in terms of Buddhism's appeal to 'the intellectual classes' 7.241, 7.243–4; see *also* mistakes

esanā see under ariyapariyesanā

escape (*nissaraṇa*) being with others as an escape from yourself 26.29; difference between escape and escapism 13.191–2, 16.78–9; don't let work become an escape from your true self 15.284; escape from becoming 10.523–4, 13.193; escape is no longer possible: modern societies will not leave anyone alone 18.34; escaping into a private world: rural life, mystical or aesthetic experience, fantasies, madness 12.394; helping others as a way of escaping the demands of your self-development 18.592–3; the idea of Going for Refuge as escape doesn't do justice to the spiritual life 13.194–5; one has to escape not only from bondage but from liberation 2.56; 'Rather than trying to escape from ourselves, we need to … acknowledge the reality of what we are' 3.226–7; religion is escape but not escapism 7.224; spiritual practice is actuated by a desire to escape from something 7.218, 13.191–3; trying to escape from the truth 13.356–7

escapism acceptable as a description of what Buddhists seek to do 4.438–9; if you find yourself in a situation that has a negative effect on you, run away 15.369; is Buddhism escapist? 4.440–1, 19.360; craving for talk is a form of escapism 19.493; the criticism of religion as escapist is ridiculous 26.57; the difference between escape and escapism 13.191–2, 16.78–9; does the parable of the burning house teach escapism? 16.78–9; due to wrong views 7.220–1; escapism is 'the tendency to seek distraction and relief from reality' – very unlike Buddhism 13.191; the escapist wants to have his cake and eat it too 7.221; found in all spheres of human activity 7.220; in meditation, if you're just trying to escape an aspect of your experience, you won't get far 17.369; is going on retreat escapism? 5.676; any kind of life that involves no positive effort to evolve is escapism 4.440, 16.79, 26.10; legitimate and illegitimate reasons for wanting to escape, in relation to the four noble truths 7.219–24; our difficulty today is not escapism, but the impossibility of finding escape at all 8.259; is religion escapism? 7.217–24; religious and non-religious escapism 13.193

esoteric the ambition to get hold of esoteric practices is a waste of time 5.50; *Esoteric Buddhism*, *see* Sinnett; esoteric integration of body, speech, and mind with that of the Tathāgata 1.380; nothing in the religious life is truly esoteric except spiritual experience 7.359; a shift towards the writing down of esoteric teachings 14.27; the tantras are the most highly esoteric of the canonical texts 7.503; you don't make something esoteric by keeping people out 18.425

esoteric path 7.345–63, 26.49

esoteric Refuges *see* three esoteric Refuges

Esperanto 11.298

essence

essences
distinguishing essence from cultural expression 3.45; essence precedes existence 19.57; nothing has any unchanging essence 18.84, 18.179; the pure wordless essence 8.498, 13.348, 14.325, 19.241, 19.447

the essence of Buddhism …
a brief description 12.43; can be known from the *Diamond Sūtra* 9.109; the eradication of the three root poisons 7.221–2; in its essence it has no history 1.17; is the attainment of perfection 1.133; is communicated through friendship 21.475; is compassion 9.147; is ethics

9.100, 9.425; can be contained in a single verse 18.495; in Hakuin's 'Song of Meditation' 9.109; in the *Hundred Thousand Songs of Milarepa* 9.109; like the flame of a lamp which kindles other lamps 7.332; a transcendental essence and a mundane expression 7.514; *see also* Buddhism I/ the essence of Buddhism

the Three Jewels
the Three Jewels as essence of mind 2.408; the Three Jewels the expression of the essence of existence 7.317; authentic contact with the essence of the Buddha 19.222–3; what is the essence of the Dharma? 2.54–7; the essence of sangha 3.416–22; 'To enter the Dharma Essence' 18.413

more essences
being is in essence consciousness 2.77; the 'bright essence create' (*Paradise Lost*) 1.261; the *bodhicitta*: *śūnyatā* endowed with the essence of compassion 2.162; Buddhahood in its essence has no beginning 18.94; the essence of the absolute *bodhicitta* in the 'Confounder of Hell' verses 4.211–13; the essence of Enlightenment 1.88–97, 1.386; the essence of religion is to recognize the Divine everywhere in the universe 7.86–7; the essence of transcendental life is realizing that the self is unreal 1.402; going forth is of the essence of the spiritual life 22.209; introducing into your life a little of the essence of Sukhāvatī 18.121; Marpa 'had experienced the mother-like Essence of Mind' 18.64; Śāntideva puts his finger on the essence of *dāna* 4.358–9; *śūnyatā* and *rūpa* are of the same essence 1.489–90, 16.534; 'What essence has remained mine from things I once enjoyed?' 18.131; the will is the constitutive essence of man 7.138; you could study and still miss the essence of the matter 19.158

see also
attha; *cittata*; *nissatta*; *sāra*

Essenes 3.429, 13.650–1

essential Buddhism is essentially an experience 2.54; Buddhism is essentially trying to communicate a mystery 12.106; the challenge is to distinguish the essential in Buddhism from the nonessential 12.78; 'Deep is the essential original nature of *dharmas*' 1.66–7; delight in the beauty of the Unconditioned is essential to spiritual life 2.84–5; the direct experience of one's own essential nature 18.75; distinguishing between what is essential and what is not 1.8; the essential characteristic of the Dharma is that it conduces to freedom 10.567; the essential definitive qualities of the spiritual life 2.552; the essential non-difference of the universe and the Absolute 1.306; the essential non-difference between Buddhas and all beings, oneself and others 4.587–8; the essential religious question 3.209; fear of death is essentially fear of loss of ego 18.245; *The Four Essential Doctrines of Buddhism* 7.435–6; 'I consider the foundations of religion to be essential to life' (Ambedkar) 10.127–8, 10.205; losing sight of what is essential 19.61; our essential need is freedom 16.499; experiencing yourself by yourself: an essential human need 5.670, 12.419; reflection that all things are pure, including one's own essential nature 16.179; the simple life glows with significance, the unessential having melted away 7.320–1; the spiritual life as essentially a willed process of becoming 7.204; we must recognize ourselves as essentially spiritual beings 7.308; whatever we learn, the Dharma is always essentially a mystery 3.232

Estonia 11.xxii

eternal *see* eternity

Eternal Legacy *see under* Sangharakshita XIII/publication history

eternalism (*sassata-diṭṭhi*, *śāśvatavāda*) definition 17.242; alignment with asceticism 1.138; association with *bhava-taṇhā* (craving for existence) 14.572, 17.243; division of schools of philosophy into eternalists and nihilists in the *Brahmajāla Sutta* 7.196; Christian view of the soul 17.624; the Dharma is not fixed in the sense of eternalism 16.84; eternalism and attachment 17.250–1; an eternalist believes that life has a meaning and tends to be ethically scrupulous 17.250; an eternalist view of Nirvāṇa: on the right track to an extent 17.245; eternalist view of reality 7.386; and the fetter of personality-view 2.146; a general term for all doctrines that posit the existence of an unchanging principle 7.522–3; includes all forms of theism, including belief in a Creator God 7.523; in relation to *pratītya-samutpāda* 7.495; in relation to what happens after death 19.375–6; immanence: one doesn't want to adopt a substantialist or eternalist outlook 19.387; related to the *tathāgatagarbha* doctrine 14.594; opposed and destroyed by the *animitta vimokṣa-mukha* 2.122; psychological, metaphysical, and ethical aspects 17.624–5; represented by the four *viparyāsas* 14.594; the self continuing unchanged from life to life

17.624; sometimes 'realism' 19.369, 19.375, 19.377, 19.391, 19.393; to say that living things are interrelated is Buddhism, but to say they are one stuff is eternalism 8.372; we *believe* we are eternal because we *want* to be eternal 14.572; eternalism and nihilism, *see under* nihilism

eternity

introduction
desire for the eternal 7.306–8, 7.405; the Eternal gives itself freely to those who freely give themselves to it 7.307; the eternal life of Buddhahood 4.331, 23.446; the eternal nature of things preached 'in order to refute the bigoted belief of noneternity' 7.34; the eternal now 7.286, 11.11, 19.84; eternity and Enlightenment 3.146; 'Eternity's sunrise' 17.506, 26.598; is the universe eternal or not? (Yogācāra) 17.641–2; only Eternity can glut the heart 25.390; reality in its eternal, unconditioned aspect 13.282

eternity and time
according to the Tantra, we need to realize both simultaneously 4.211; Buddhahood exists not in time, but in eternity 4.204; each of us is falling from eternity at every instant 17.611; eternity considered as transcending time rather than infinitely prolonging it 4.204, 4.210; the goal is attained out of time, eternally attained 4.201; limitations of language when considering 4.204; passing from time to eternity in the *Larger Sukhāvatī-vyūha Sūtra* 1.327; symbolized by the Buddha and the bodhisattva 4.210–11; 'Time and Eternity' (poem) 25.393; time never reaches eternity, no matter how long it goes on 4.213; time is eternity 16.534; time is unable to square the circle of eternity 26.83; translating a work of art from eternity into time 17.609; we swivel round and round in time on the pivot of eternity 26.49

ethics (*śīla*, morality)

TERMINOLOGY AND DEFINITIONS

ethics and principles
broad and narrow senses of the term ethics 2.350; definitions of the word principle 2.339–40; ethics is synonymous with *kuśala* 2.340

morality
derivation of the word morality, and its relation to *śīla* 1.141; no such word in Buddhism 3.244; perhaps the term is to be avoided, having unhelpful connotations 3.370, 4.104–5

śīla
actions associated with karmically wholesome mental states 7.507–8; almost identical with 'morality' 1.141; behaviour, especially ethical behaviour 2.147; 'immersed in Dharma life' 4.104; habitual skilful action of body, speech, and mind 9.187; literally 'uprightness' 4.104, 16.9; primary and secondary meanings 1.140–1, 11.307–8; translation as ethics and manners 6.xxxi

GENERAL ETHICAL CONSIDERATIONS

reflections on ethics
an aware attitude will be a responsible, ethical one 13.456; circumstances are so complex that what is skilful for one person may not help another 15.291; the cultivation of a moral sense is the first thing to be attended to (Hazlitt) 24.562; the development of a code of morality is a degeneration (Laozi) 14.419; does art have an ethical dimension? 26.396; Dharmapala on morality 8.92–3; difference between ethical and legal rights 13.451; duality between the aesthetic and the ethical (Kierkegaard) 26.396; ethical behaviour is habitual good action 11.308; ethical integrity is rooted in empathy 8.577–8; ethics inculcates a habit of self-control 15.173; going out of oneself, not being limited by one's present mode of being 17.598; the good is the beautiful 15.352–3; 'The great secret of morals is love' 2.360, 15.249, 17.598, 26.139, 26.189–90; a happy person is more likely to behave ethically 26.396; injustice is morally wrong 13.609; it consists in giving a certain direction to energy 17.529; materialist view 7.165; memory and ethics 15.86–7; moral decisions must be individual 13.447; moral life interpreted in terms of the accumulation of moral property 1.436; morality is born of natural human solidarity 13.615, 13.621; morality is of cosmic significance 11.323; mundane and transcendental morality 11.313–14; not everything that is legal is moral, and not everything that is illegal is immoral 26.60; not just about our own mental state but about how we treat others 11.723–4; not keeping a tight rein on oneself, but freeing one's imagination 17.598; in terms of liberty, equality, and fraternity 9.182–6; the influence of Seneca's 'ethical sublimity' on the young Sangharakshita 13.611, 20.61; literature and ethics 10.153–4; only an individual can be ethical 15.359; psychologically based 3.102; reflexive consciousness brings about the development of ethical ideas 8.447–8;

searching for moral messages in poetry 26.394–5; substituting a finer morality for a grosser 26.144, 26.179–80; the universe is an ethical universe 3.100; the way you live relates to your capacity to apprehend Truth 1.21; what induces us to start leading a moral life? 11.324–5

ethics in the modern world
the collapse of traditional morality 1.527; the need to modify presentation of ethics in the modern West 13.410–13; 'If it feels good, do it' 1.527, 3.104; immorality tends to be associated with sexuality 15.204; 'Morality Without Religion' (Knight) 8.281; people are no longer looking for an ethical code 3.191; pseudo-liberal denial that there is such a thing as ethics 13.413; shifting responsibility for one's actions from self to society 13.389; we have to discuss ethics in secular terms 12.117

Judaeo-Christian ethics
introduction 1.527–9, 13.605–23; assumption that society's ethics must be Christian 12.406–7; complex, because it has more than one source 13.606; ethical absolutism 17.593; ethical principles do not feature in the Apostles' Creed 13.578; a matter of law: the Commandments, authority, original sin 1.528; doing or not doing things by command of someone in whom we don't believe 1.529, 26.59; freedom from Christian conditioning in moral matters 12.254; is it possible to be moral without believing in God? 8.281–2; morality 1.527–9, 3.99–100; punishment of sin and reward of virtue, judgement 3.99–100; those who reject Christianity still influenced by its ethical assumptions 4.105

moral crusaders
holier-than-thou castigators of people's moral shortcomings 17.285; Mrs Whitehouse, *see* Whitehouse; unbending moralists to whom art and immorality are practically synonymous 26.179

ETHICS IN THE BUDDHIST TRADITION

introduction
one of the richest and most fascinating fields in Buddhism 11.307; the essence of Buddhism 9.100; Buddhist history a living tapestry of skilful actions 11.315; Buddhist ethics and the Greek 'ethics of virtue' 8.610; habitual good action of body, speech, and mind 11.308; living ethically is essentially about developing compassion 17.158; a long list of dos and don'ts? 7.181, 7.373, 15.348, 18.324, 19.558; contrast with the attitude of not doing this, not doing that 16.296; more about personal growth and progress than about rules 15.291; non-exploitation is a fundamental principle 3.592; only an integrated person has an ethical identity 17.697; the subject is full of light, life, warmth, and colour 2.319; patterns of morality 11.315–20; the positive ethical value of joy 2.98; what is the sanction of morality? 9.333–4; *śīla* must always be accompanied by *dāna* 4.93; sublimation of desire is perhaps the central problem of ethics 26.130; three levels: common sense, 'scientific', spontaneous 14.547; *Aspects of Buddhist Morality* 2.319, 11.305–25, 13.443; *Contemporary Buddhist Ethics* (review) 8.609–11; Sangharakshita's writings on ethics 13.443–4

the nature of Buddhist ethics
actions are ethical according to state of being or mind 1.529, 3.102 –4; actions expressive of skilful mental states 11.63; based on altruism 7.486; Buddhism exhorts, it does not command 7.439; cannot be grounded on the concept of rights 8.611, 26.19; carrots and sticks to encourage or provoke ethical effort 17.158; a continual renunciation of the self 26.111; the creative power of ethically relevant actions 1.342; the effort to avoid blocking, misusing, or manipulating the energy of others 15.217; ethics according to degree of spiritual development 11.315–17; ethics is there to be useful, not to use us 3.419; essentially a morally healthy attitude towards life 2.71; the ethics of Buddhism founded upon its metaphysics 7.33, 7.35; the important place of precepts does not mean that *śīla* is just ethical formalism 1.142; the inseparability of ethics and metaphysics 7.35; an intricate net woven to catch the passions 7.117; it exists only when people practise it 9.187; it is very important to see the ethical ideal in positive terms 15.360; makes intelligible the secrets of spirituality 1.144; may seem commonplace in theory, but devastating in practice 7.172–3; the measure of moral actions is whether they're done out of concern for others 17.171; a psychological ethics 13.605; 'something that you have to practise yourself' 9.187; traditionally includes much no longer seen as pertaining to ethics 7.261–2

references from the tradition
the Buddha's ethicization of the world a turning point in history 8.619; how *śīla* fits into different formulations of the Buddhist path 11.306–7; 'Be quick to do

what is morally beautiful' (*Dhammapada*) 15.348–53; the ethics of the lay Buddhist (*Sigālovāda Sutta*) 11.317; leaving righteous (and unrighteous) ways behind (parable of the raft) 1.203, 14.440; ethical choices as one of the five *niyamas* 17.478–9; the morality of the *pṛthagjana* 11.314; lay and monastic ethics 11.317–18; three grades of morality (Pāli canon) 11.315–17; Buddhaghosa on morality 11.309, 11.325; Aśoka's attitude to ethics 16.296; mindfulness and total awareness are more important (Śāntideva) 4.380; ethics and manners in *The Jewel Ornament of Liberation*, *see under* Gampopa; the Mahāyāna would say that the basic principle of ethics is helping others 17.154; 'What God is to other religions morality is to Buddhism' (Ambedkar) 9.99, 9.144; religion is essentially ethics (Ambedkar) 9.99, 10.355

ethics as a basis
the indispensable foundation of the whole spiritual life 8.199; an absolute value because it is a means to Enlightenment 1.200; the basis on which wisdom may be developed 17.158; the reciprocal relationship between ethics and wisdom 17.154; the ethical foundations of *mettā* 15.268–96; the connection between morality and Going for Refuge 3.325, 11.310–12; only makes sense in the context of commitment to the spiritual path 3.324; our past and our future the product of our ethical decisions 17.637; a means of weakening unwholesome states of mind 1.144–5; preparation for the inward life of spirit 7.124–5; traditionally ethics is said to cast out craving and distraction 15.173; we are to be ethical not by divine command, but so we can practise *samādhi* 7.228

ethics and the threefold way
ethics as the first stage of the threefold path 3.315–32, 11.306, 13.605–6; if your meditation isn't going well, go back to ethics 12.566–7, 15.345; preparation for meditation and wisdom 3.321, 3.338, 7.124–5, 7.187, 7.508; the stepping-stone to meditation 1.144–5; the way begins with ethics (*śīla*), but does not end there 7.181; why it's only the first stage 3.324

actions have consequences
action is significant for ourselves and also affects others 1.191; awareness of this is a characteristic of the true individual 3.468; bearing in mind that one's actions have consequences 16.427, 26.61; described in the *Dhammapada* 15.373; Dhardo Rimpoche wanted the children at his school to learn this 15.358; the effect of behaviour on rebirth 11.321; the effect of unskilfulness on our mental states 3.321, 3.323; even small actions have a cumulative effect 3.321; following the path of ethical action from which happiness arises 17.360; heeding the ethical implications of mental states 17.679; the idea of rebirth follows logically 17.468; imagining that you can escape the consequences of your actions 15.358; individual actions have social effects 25.105; how far do our actions conduce to egolessness? 1.435; knowing this gives rise to fear 16.311; knowledge of the relationship between actions and their consequences 17.545; the law of conditionality applied to the ethical sphere 3.183, 3.317, 8.xxiv; and the law of karma 3.99–104, 16.309, 16.419, 17.293, 17.480, 18.60, 18.146; parents teach children an understanding of this 16.428–9; principle of the moral order 16.426–7; refusing to admit that our actions affect others 17.637; the regret experienced when bad deeds have unpleasant consequences 17.290; that connects us to both past and future 11.657; this can seem like a threat 15.621; two people could do the same things with different consequences 17.525; unethical actions have unpleasant consequences 11.263–3; we are usually unaware of this 18.84; we ourselves will feel the effects of unskilful behaviour 3.323; what we do now will have a decisive effect on the future 15.89; the wrong view that actions don't have consequences 2.391, 12.616, 17.594, 17.635–40; you cannot be an individual unless you realize this 15.358; you need strong reflexive consciousness to be aware of this 15.359

an ethics of intention
an action's ethical status determined by the level of purity of the mind 7.373; actions are neither good nor bad, but 'thinking makes them so' 1.142; any action will only have a karmic effect if it is intentional 2.68, 3.105, 15.90; it doesn't mean an ethics of 'good intentions' 11.308, 13.605; deliberately doing something leaves an imprint on a certain level of your being 18.291; a doctrine of ethical relativism fraught with dangers 1.200–1; ethical behaviour hoping for reward in heaven comprises purity of intention 17.171; every willed action produces an effect, a *vāsanā* (Yogācāra) 1.369; the importance of the mental state over the action 7.373, 17.186; the imprint of willed action is conserved in the *ālaya vijñāna* 18.291–2; interpret texts

which seem to countenance breaking moral law symbolically 1.145; it is the intention behind your actions that constitutes karma 17.292; a matter of intelligence and insight as much as good intentions 1.530; mindfulness of purpose and ethical sensitivity 15.96–7; the role of things done through lack of mindfulness 17.292; there's nothing you cannot do with the wrong motive 18.361–2; this doesn't mean they're just about how we feel 17.679–80; varying degrees of volition brought to an action 2.71, 17.589; your goodwill needs to be expressed in specific helpful actions 19.557

the ethics of advanced beings
the Buddha denies that you can 'go beyond good and evil' 15.367–8, 17.636; Enlightened beings do not have to try to act skilfully, it's their nature 14.440; an Enlightened person may act unethically out of compassion 1.200–1, 14.188; one who has realized emptiness is incapable of acting unethically 7.377

the benefits of ethics
Buddhaghosa's verse on the subject 11.320–1; five benefits for the householder 10.644–6, 11.320; Gampopa on the results of perfecting morality 11.321; a means to an end 3.245–6, 3.320–1, 7.257, 14.440–1; non-remorse (*avippaṭisāra*) 11.320; practised for rebirth in heaven: spiritual materialism 3.315–16, 4.104, 17.171; the second of five things that conduce to spiritual maturity 3.578, 10.529–30; virtue is its own reward 15.370, 15.375, 17.171

THE PRACTICE OF ETHICS

practising ethics
adopting skilful modes of action 17.613–15; assessing the ethical status of mental states 15.160–3; the Buddha tells villagers five practical reasons to lead an ethical life 10.644–6; developing ethical sensitivity 16.311–12; developing a plan to become more ethical 10.222–3; ethics and good manners 2.232, 4.336–8; if our practice of ethics is not very successful, we can practise *dāna* 12.566–7; in behaving ethically we are refining and purifying our mental states 3.321; the ethical dimension of awareness of someone 17.661; an ethical life arises naturally from faith 3.264–5; knowing the theory is very different from habitually behaving skilfully 11.324; learning what to be and not to be 25.367; like embroidery, delicate and sensitive craftsmanship 18.84; the 'negative' side of ethical life: disentangling yourself from the unskilful 15.421; the practice is key to a healthy human existence 17.168; a sense of moral continuity 15.90–1; the senses are ethically neutral 19.191; some people find ethics more difficult than others 10.222–3; tacitly assumed to be the prerequisite of spiritual practice 1.218; three levels of practice: in supportive, unsupportive, and whatever conditions 18.84; we can practise being less deliberately, 'heavily' virtuous 14.418; your relationship with your spiritual friends show you where you stand ethically 15.296

problems with ethical practice
actions performed with wrong views 1.435–6; acts become immoral when done in an egoistic way 1.435; being more interested in 'what is' than 'what to do' 17.569; don't be discouraged when you notice the arising of unskilful states 17.270; ethical relativism 1.200–1, 7.377, 15.291, 15.488–9; 'I see the better and approve it, but the worse is what I pursue' 7.391; people lose sight of the difference between right and wrong 9.272–3; the spirit and the letter 11.480–1; trying to determine what to do before one has found out how to think and feel 7.373; virtuous actions ... can lead to the extreme of self-torture 10.608; why are we unable to act in accordance with what we know is right? 1.493–4

conventional and natural morality (paṇṇatti-sīla and pakati-sīla)
introduction 3.245, 7.529–30; be careful to distinguish between them 11.262; compulsion to shatter moralities out of sheer intensity of spiritual life 26.179; distinction between them 1.145, 4.109–10, 13.608, 13.704 (n210); actions society sees as good whatever state of mind inspired them 7.282; the artist in revolt against conventional morality 3.512; the conventionally 'bad' person may be sympathetic and unselfish 7.282; conventionally moral acts alongside cruelty 21.128; conventionally moral acts become immoral when performed egoistically 1.435; the fetter of conventional morality 3.419; it's not that having transcended good and evil one is indifferent to ethics 7.377, 7.408; don't confuse natural morality with prejudices about right and wrong 4.110; an example from the Vinaya Piṭaka 7.530; guilt about not observing matters of conventional morality 4.109–10, 13.608; and monastic rules 4.385, 17.633–4; the most serious offence against natural morality is deliberate killing 13.609–10; natural morality and artificial morality 19.458; natural morality an integral part of the order of the universe 1.145; natural morality creates karma, but conventional morality doesn't 3.102, 4.385;

rational and irrational guilt 13.608–9; in relation to orthodoxy 7.529–30, 7.544–5; the sense of human solidarity is the basis of natural morality 13.615, 13.621; talking of etiquette rather than rules reduces natural to conventional morality 13.413; Victorian conventional morality compared to Theravāda 19.384; the Theravāda's rigid adherence to conventional morality 7.544–5

social ethics
ethics and society 9.181–3; Hīnayānists more interested in personal, Mahāyānists in social 1.207; it's not enough to be personally ethical, we have to try to transform society 3.283; an opportunity to break down the barrier between self and other 3.321; two aspects of ethics, social and individual 10.142

see also
attachment to *śīla*, *see under* fetters; *bodhisattva-śīla* (code of conduct), *see under* bodhisattva/bodhisattva career; ethical formalism, *see under* formalism; the ethics of eating, *see under* food; the ethics of marriage, *see under* marriage; ethics of work, *see* right livelihood, work; four *pārisuddhi sīlas*; killing, *see* precepts/first precept; moral order, *see under* society; *pātimokkha saṃvara-sīla*, *see* vinaya/ *saṃvara-śīla*; precepts, *see* precepts; *śīla pāramitā*, one of the six perfections, *see under* perfections; *śīla visuddhi*, *see under* seven *visuddhis*; unskilful action, *see under* unskilful

Ethiraj, Dhivya 10.lvi–ix

ethnic religion *see under* religion/universal and ethnic religion

Etruscans 3.231

etymology *see under* words

Euclid 3.427

Eumachia 24.295

Euripides introduction 3.427, 23.509 (n276); *Andromache* 23.281; *Bacchae* 23.243–4, 23.286; *Helen* 23.297; *Ion* 23.279–81; *Iphigenia in Tauris*, *Hecuba* 23.243–4; *The Madness of Herakles* 23.269–70; *The Trojan Women* 23.293; 'sad Electra's poet' 23.244

European Buddhist Union introduction 2.746 (n702), 26.757 (n517); an experience of sangha 12.624–5; *Lotusblatter* (German newsletter) 24.588; membership open only to bona fide Buddhist organizations 11.469; Sangharakshita speaks at their conference 11.459–70, 12.602–9, 26.535–6, 26.757 (n519); Triratna active in the EBU 2.568

Eurydice 25.254, 25.257, 25.312

Evans, Jane *see* Santacitta

Evans-Wentz, W. Y.

The Tibetan Book of the Dead
on the Adibuddha 7.536; description of Sikkimese death ceremony 2.231; gave the translation that title 12.197; launched the Oxford Tibetan series 12.72

The Tibetan Book of the Great Liberation
introduction 22.106–8; its account of Padmasambhava's life doesn't do him justice 8.345–6; Jung's psychological commentary on the text 8.346–7; Lama Govinda's review 1.378; Sangharakshita's review 8.344–8, 22.107–8, 22.471–2

Tibetan Yoga and Secret Doctrine
reading it at the ashram 20.340; developing *tummo* heat 12.297–8

Eve 1.528, 13.244, 15.619, 25.386

ever-smouldering anthill 11.719, 16.586 (n16)

Everest 4.349, 7.450, 22.11–12

everyday life

the nature of everyday life
based on subject–object dualism 2.275, 12.173–4, 17.481; a battering experience 5.694; Buddhism has no means of enforcing uniformity of action in secular life 7.439; the deadening routine of daily life 10.241; distractions in everyday life: the letter to post and the boiling kettle 1.567–9; the distractions of workaday life 1.345; everyday life as a *bardo* 18.83–4; experience everything all the time under its diamond (*vajra*) aspect 7.401–2, 13.180; an experience ultimately no more real than the Indian rope trick 14.507; in everyday life it doesn't matter that we know so little from direct experience 13.345; in the modern world everyday activity lacks any clearly spiritual dimension 15.157; look out for manifestations of the incoherence of our assumptions about life 17.378; Milarepa rearranges the everyday world 18.66; the mind regarded as sixth sense is our everyday mind 1.556; most everyday actions are no better than the actions of a drunkard 3.195; most of the people you meet entertain false values 4.524–5; much richer and more complex than we realize 24.148–9; the psychopathology of everyday life, *see under* Freud; Sangharakshita returns to life in

the workaday world 23.191; the sensory distractions of everyday life 15.288; ways we distract ourselves from the tedium of normal life 17.393

everyday life and spiritual practice
aesthetic experience is not perception as in everyday life 26.327; aim for not too much contradiction between 'spiritual' activities and daily life 15.155; before you start meditating, take a look at how you behave in daily life 15.343; better sweep a floor egolessly than meditate with the thought 'I am meditating' 7.284; bringing the enjoyment of daily life into spiritual practice 15.155; the Buddhist in public life incognito 12.126–7; carrying the effects of meditation into the rest of life 5.308–9, 5.649–50; clear comprehension of daily activities (*Satipaṭṭhāna Sutta*) 15.97, 15.113–22; don't isolate yourself from everyday experience 15.288; everyday activities transformed from hindrances to helps to concentration 1.151; everyday life for Anuruddha and his friends 12.606; everyday life in the *Udāna* 10.499; everyday life spilling into meditation 18.499; five things to practise every day 5.45–6; if ordinary life was enough, the Buddha would not have founded an order 8.490; if religion is not inherent in ordinary life, there is something amiss 14.419; it provides us with the same opportunities for practice as an ascetic life 4.422; keeping the *dhyāna* experience going all day 18.595–6; kindness needs to be cultivated in everyday dealings, not just in meditation 5.175; make whatever you are doing your spiritual practice 8.490, 18.153–4; making connections with the *sādhana* in everyday life: don't force it 5.616–17; methods of making a bridge between ordinary existence and spiritual life 16.231; mindfulness in daily life 10.150, 12.403; mindfulness of purpose in day-to-day living 15.214; the need for faith in everyday life 5.76–8, 17.23–4, 17.36, 17.46–7; not a new kind of life, but the same old life lived in a new way 7.295; an ordinary life lived in a Buddhist way is a good advert for the Dharma 8.276; permeated with a sense of reverence for sacred things 1.407; 'Pots and pans are my instruments of prayer' (St Teresa) 7.102; *prīti* can arise in everyday life 15.220; sometimes one can be aware of karmic effects in everyday experience 18.146; to enjoy positive mental states, pay attention to your everyday activities 15.298; trying to find more significance in our daily lives: what the spiritual life is about 13.120; waking up feeling happy and enjoying all your experiences 18.298; walking meditation as a transition from spiritual practice to the ordinary world 5.82–3; we can see impermanence at work every day 10.327; with intrinsic awareness, everything one does transforms the everyday world 17.608–9; the would-be bodhisattva sympathetic and helpful in the affairs of everyday life 4.68

everyday life and insight
insight in everyday life 1.154, 5.431–2, 5.637–8, 15.112; cooking pots, the extinction of a lamp 1.154; everything that happens to you is a breakthrough 17.233; if you have an insight, try to embody it in your day to day life 12.29; inevitably the routine of life is sometimes interrupted by a vajric situation 13.172

everyday life and reality
the Buddha as an irruption from a higher dimension into your ordinary life 25.87; considered to be the Pure Land 16.181; 'How wonderful! How miraculous! I draw water and I carry fuel' 14.397, 16.252; ordinary life is Enlightenment, and Enlightenment is ordinary life 14.397, 26.63; reality is to be experienced in the midst of ordinary life 14.xv; you are presented with the ultimate truth every moment of your life 16.184

Everyman introduction 22.579–80 (n72); the ballet 13.658–9, 15.375–6, 20.86; connection with the story of Barlaam and Josaphat 13.658–9; the deep impression the story made on Sangharakshita 13.659, 20.86; 'Everyman, I will go with thee and be thy guide' 13.659; Good Deeds 22.68; Govinda (the Buddha's disciple) speaks as Everyman 26.473; a remarkable anticipation of Buddhist teaching 15.375

Everyman's Library 13.659, 13.726–7 (n461)

evil

the nature of evil
the conventionally 'bad' person may be sympathetic and unselfish 7.282; delighting in inflicting suffering is the worst form of evil 26.653, 26.678; the English word: an unskilful mental state or an unpleasant experience 15.368; evil done in the belief that one is in the right 16.305; how can people act so evilly to one another? 26.xv; many ways of being wicked, but only one way of being good (Aristotle) 3.554, 17.549; not just actions or just intentions, but a combination of both 17.589; not usually done deliberately

16.305; the potentiality for evil is in all of us 25.75–6; the principle of evil 26.655; Sangharakshita's feeling that there are evil beings around 4.331; the suffering that results from evil 26.642; to say that matter is evil is to say that it is not material 26.48; translation of *pāpa* 16.290

Buddhist reflections on evil
a bodhisattva precept not to despise evildoers 13.56; the Buddha denies that you can 'go beyond good and evil' 15.367–8, 17.636; 'Even the good man will be saved. How much more so the evil man!' 1.199; no question of irredeemable evil 2.260; one should not dishonour any evil person who has offended 4.436; the power of evil is terrible, but can be overcome by the *bodhicitta* 4.267–8; restraining the mind from evil (*Dhammapada*) 15.349–50

evil and us
the best way to keep it out is to have something inspiring to do 15.350; doing good rather than just eschewing evil 1.395; the doing of good is meaningless apart from the ability to do evil 7.245–6; 'the evil that I have heaped up' 11.260–1, 25.75–6; projecting the evil that is within ourselves 26.654; shun evil like poison 15.367; we don't all have potential for evil as we all have potential for Buddhahood 16.305; we must demolish the wrong views that undergird morally evil behaviour 26.678; we shouldn't be afraid to use the word 25.117–18; we underestimate evil – and we also underestimate good 15.362; you can suffer evil but stay skilful 15.368–70

see also
confession; delight in good, not evil, *see under* Mahāpajāpatī Gotami; Māra

evocation the difference between invocation and evocation 18.319–20; the evocation of Nirvāṇa 2.132; in Tibetan Buddhism 1.194–7; in connection with visualizing Buddhas and bodhisattvas 18.319

Evola, J. *The Doctrine of Awakening* 1.151, 1.164, 11.316–17, 26.158; 'Zen and the West' 8.362

evolution

THE IDEA

introduction
what is evolution? 12.85; principle 3.9–17, 3.475–6; the evolution of the world 8.265–6; the mechanistic model 3.11, 3.476, 12.85; monkey and typewriter theory 12.85; probably the most important general concept of modern thought 12.83–4; the term can be applied to almost anything, as a general principle 1.564, 3.475; teleological and vitalist perspectives 3.476, 3.625 (n4), 12.85–7; the universe is a gigantic process of becoming 1.564, 12.84

history
the idea discovered in the 19th century 12.464; anticipated by Kant, Hegel, and perhaps Aristotle 3.10; the effect on religion of Darwin's theory of evolution 11.75; the language of evolution used to express new understanding 13.431; evolution and mutual aid (Kropotkin) 4.88; it never stops (Nietzsche) 3.498; it dominates the modern world 1.564, 3.10

reflections
absolute reality manifesting through the evolutionary process 12.86–7; any evolving phenomenon can be studied genetically or teleologically 1.565, 3.12, 12.87; a being may be forced to evolve in order to survive 16.24; a coalescence between material progress and spiritual degeneration 1.42; conflation of biological evolution and spiritual development 17.242–3; the desire to evolve is innate within us 3.486; diagram of the evolutionary process 12.87–90; distinction between evolution, progress, and development 13.465–6; evolution and the artist 3.515–16; evolution or extinction – the alternatives before us 3.169, 3.617; the evolutionary urge and cosmic ignorance 7.47; human existence as the crown of the evolutionary process 14.522, 18.120; human gestation and early life recapitulates evolution 3.481–2; it applies to the individual, not the religious tradition to which they belong 8.457; those who prefer evolution to revolution 26.18

EVOLUTION AND BUDDHISM

introduction
Buddhism is not a religion, but the path of the higher evolution 3.477–8; the Buddhist approach is broadly 'vitalist' (not mechanistic) 3.16, 12.85–6; the concept of spiritual evolution is central 13.465, 13.515; evolution aligns with the Buddhist system of thought 3.9; evolution as a metaphor or temporal model for Buddhism 3.16, 3.477; for Buddhism the evolutionary narrative is not single but dual 13.433; fully in accordance with the Buddha's teaching 2.476; not the way we usually think of Buddhism 2.475–6; one could say that the Dharma is the process of the higher evolution 15.632; the process of spiritual development and the course of human evolution 4.652–7; a restatement

in contemporary terms of the Buddha's teachings 5.664; we need not think of 'Buddhism', just whatever will help the individual to evolve 19.543

Sangharakshita's use of the evolutionary model
introduction to his approach 3.9–17, 12.82–7, 13.517, 23.463; he researches the subject 23.371; his realization that Buddhism was the higher evolution 13.516–17; he speaks on it for the first time, in Kalimpong 21.83–4; first talk in the West 23.226; his use of the evolutionary model 11.550; it was to play an increasingly important role in my thinking 23.226–7; 'the evolutionary approach, which some people like and others don't' 4.248; using the concept as a medium for the exposition of Buddhism 13.430–1

illustrations from the Buddhist canon
Buddhist stories and parables illustrating evolution 2.476; depicted in the *Jātaka* stories 4.210–11, 4.653; the evolution of the Buddha in terms of his past lives 4.652–3; the evolution of the universe described in the *Aggañña Sutta* 1.41–2, 3.13, 16.100; the Yogācāra on how the seemingly objective universe evolved from absolute mind 1.351

links with Buddhist doctrines and practices
the bodhisattva 4.210, 16.7; the *brahma vihāras* 3.16; faith is the driving force of the higher evolution 18.275; the four noble truths 3.14; Going for Refuge 2.475–6, 2.482–3; the Going for Refuge and Prostration Practice 13.212–13; 'growth and development' 19.201; the lotus as a symbol of the evolutionary process 25.139–40; *pratītya-samutpāda* 3.12–14, 13.431; the spiral path 13.432–3; spiritual hierarchy 4.171; the stupa as representation of evolution 16.163

HIGHER AND LOWER EVOLUTION

introduction
any kind of life that involves no positive effort to evolve is escapism 4.440, 16.79, 26.10; comprehended in one gigantic sweep 12.89, 23.227; a crucial discontinuity between the two: individual awareness 1.566, 3.478; crucial to our understanding of the Buddha 3.12; the relationship of higher evolution to lower evolution 13.432–3; stages: biological, human, trans-human, Stream Entrant, Buddha 3.59–61

lower evolution
from amoeba to ordinary man 11.115; from non-living to living, sensitive to conscious, conscious to self-conscious 12.46; the evolutionary principle of self-transcendence 3.17, 4.655–6, 12.86–7; governed by the cyclical trend of conditionality 13.433; how is the lower evolution the basis of the higher evolution? 15.632–3; human beings at the point where higher evolution emerges from lower 3.477; lower incorporated into higher 16.163–4; results in the healthy, happy human being 18.275; we must not lose contact with the rhythms of the lower evolution 11.395

higher evolution
the Buddha represents a higher evolutionary development 12.622; the development of consciousness, not in an abstract way, but yours and mine 11.146; the Dharma a direct vision of the higher evolution 15.594; it comes about through individual effort 11.146–7; the higher evolution becoming conscious of itself is effective Going for Refuge 2.482; it has two stages 13.465; not necessarily religious 16.129; once self-consciousness has begun to develop, one can't forget about it 26.11; the process of development from unenlightened to Enlightened 11.115; universal religion and the higher evolution 12.250–1; within this life and over successive lives 15.401

the path of the higher evolution
we can see Buddhism as the path of the higher evolution 3.477–83, 9.249; by far the most difficult thing a human being can undertake 12.258; despite different approaches, we are all participating in it 16.77; a formidable proposition which will take all our energy 3.484–5; governed by the spiral trend of conditionality 13.433; and growth and development, *see* growth and development; the conscious acceptance of the action of the Absolute 26.45; the evolution of the individual 3.475–85, 13.456–7; an individual process 3.482, 3.483, 3.499, 16.24–5, 17.243; the importance of Perfect Effort as an aspect of the spiritual path 1.566; it has to happen in association with others 16.473; putting your shoulder to the wheel of higher evolution 15.351; religions should be about not converts and buildings, but evolving beings 12.90; self-awareness the starting point 3.14–16, 3.477–8, 12.88–90; a specific process requiring a particular course of action 5.46; to the extent that there is awareness, there is the higher evolution, and *vice versa* 3.478; the stages of the process

1.565–6; symbolized by the parable of the return journey 16.99; traditionally the concern of the universal religions 3.483–4; very quick compared to the time the lower evolution takes 12.47; a voluntary process 16.72; we can evolve only by our own efforts 8.202, 12.46–7, 16.202, 17.243

see also
Evolution in Religion, *see under* Zaehner; the universe's evolution, *see under* universe

exaggeration exaggerating mental states 18.581; exaggerating numbers at a meeting 1.517, 8.136–7, 12.34; Indian people tend to exaggerate 13.5; making exaggerated statements about the guru 18.410; myths created through exaggeration 2.32; saying 'You're *always* doing that' 17.652; truth is the middle way between exaggerating and minimizing 14.573; exaggerating the importance of what we do and minimizing what others do 10.601, 17.587; we tell lies, exaggerate, minimize, or embroider 2.376–7

examination the Dalai Lama's *geshe* examination 8.504, 13.46–7; the doctrine-follower will make a careful examination of the Dharma 11.157–8, 17.614; don't develop an examination mentality to the Dharma 9.230, 9.328; Nāgārjuna's examination of Nirvāṇa 1.317–19; the six element practice: a minute examination of the components of our material existence 14.418; students' exam anxiety 21.95

excrement 4.560–1, 4.625–7

exemplification (*samānārthata*) activism: setting an example 12.348–9; the benefits of skilful actions are exemplified by the great Buddhist saints 15.93; and the bodhisattva ideal, *see under* bodhisattva ideal/history/exemplars; monks exemplifying the Dharma 8.245; one of the four *saṃgraha-vastus* 1.449, 3.575, 11.700, 16.487–8; teaching the Dharma by example 19.230–1; the team running a retreat 12.625; we mustn't follow even a good example unthinkingly 17.447; we never forget the lessons given us by a good life 7.35

exercise the Greeks and exercise 14.419; getting your energy going 17.72, 17.669; the importance of exercise 9.442, 15.280, 20.303; monks unhealthy from lack of exercise 15.280; as preparation for meditation 3.339; the prostration practice is good exercise 13.79; Sangharakshita should have taken more exercise 9.442

exhilaration contemplation of decay should be exhilarating 3.346, 4.537–8; the exhilarating exaltation of the spirit above the letter which characterizes Buddhism 7.331; for a Buddhist impermanence can be a source of exhilaration 14.508–9; meditation is full of exhilaration, buoyancy, and joy 5.651; John Stuart Mill 'exhilarating in the extreme' 20.446; the near enemy of *muditā* is exhilaration 5.204

exile *Born in Exile* (Gissing) 24.374; the Dalai Lama's exile 13.41–2; Dante on exile 26.660; *A Drama of Exile* (Barrett Browning) 20.36; Napoleon's exile 26.277

existence

the nature of existence
all things have no inherent existence 12.657; any kind of existence is relative 17.411; becoming (*bhāvanā*) is a more Buddhistic word 7.152; the bodhisattva's view of existence as inconceivable 16.449; a collective hallucination 14.507, 16.452; a congeries of interrelated becoming 7.152; indefinable (Mahāyāna) 1.65; not only mind-preceded and mind-determined but made up of mind 2.67; the oppression of existence 16.320–1; sentient existence is a great brotherhood of suffering 7.388; the three *lakṣaṇas*, *see lakṣaṇas*; the whole of existence is contained in every part 19.216

the mystery of existence
a conflict between the forces of light and the forces of darkness 8.525–6; divine archetypes interpenetrating the realm of material existence? 20.315; 'How extraordinary it is to be here at all!' 8.575; it seems strange that anything should continue to exist at all 14.506–7; love arises out of the perception of the impersonality of existence 8.200; the mystery of existence 25.487; not comprehensible to the mundane intelligence 1.104

phenomenal existence
arises in dependence on causes and conditions 16.452; based on the wrong assumption of a separate self 1.232; an infinitely complex, constantly shifting network of phenomena 4.648; neither absolutely real nor absolutely unreal 16.452, 19.233–4; no things exist apart from their attributes 14.439–40

philosophical and Dharmic perspectives
Abhidharma investigation of the elements of existence 14.90–1; conventional existence (philosophical term) 1.265, 19.234; 'Existence (or Reality) = Change (or Becoming)' 4.647; 'Neither here nor there nor in between exist. Just this is the end of suffering' 10.463; philosophy and Buddhism

both consider existence as a whole 7.191; Mahāyāna Buddhism is not trying to tell us that nothing exists at all 16.454; speaking conventionally, individual beings do exist 1.245; *śūnyatā* is to existence as a whole what *anātman* is to the individual 10.160; words indicative of existence have a disagreeably substantialist flavour 2.55; wrong notion of objective and subjective existence 1.370

the Buddha and existence
the difference Enlightenment made to his outlook on existence 2.251; enhancing the beauty of existence through gaining Enlightenment 18.447; even if the Buddha were to say that beings existed, that would not make it true 14.601; you can think of existence as one great Buddha 4.589

images of existence
a dream, an echo, a reflection, a ball of foam 16.452; the jewel within the lotus of sentient existence 7.316, 7.400, 26.51; like a dream (one of Nāropā's six yogas) 13.28; like a magical illusion 14.183, 14.507, 16.454; like a rainbow 19.234; a magic show, an illusion 14.562, 16.451, 19.79–80; a mandala 18.446–7; a mirage 4.181, 5.187, 14.562, 16.452; a great ocean without beginning and without end, without boundaries 12.593–4; a vast ocean of changes in which nothing is changed 7.133

spiritual practice relating to existence
before we can experience it as 'baseless' we must rest our weight on that base 17.370; facing up to the challenge of existence 13.356; gearing our existence to the clock means not really living at all 11.10; human beings are impelled to find a means of transcending relative existence 7.170; letting go of 'a view of existence' 17.247; reflecting on the evils of mundane existence to intensify pity 1.419; the Three Jewels the expression of the essence of existence 7.317; we do not often get time to be still and feel our own existence 12.82

existence and non-existence
any conditioned thing comes into being in dependence on its own non-existence 17.384; just ideas in our mind 16.449; the desire for continuing existence 15.208; Enlightenment transcends them both 17.242, 17.251; failing to wonder about them every day, you're scarcely human 17.570; the fundamental abstract concepts 19.377; middle way between them 10.609, 19.280; perceiving the non-existence of something 17.519–20; the profound Dharma goes beyond ideas of existence and non-existence 17.364; refusing to think of reality in those terms 1.139, 1.363, 10.142–3; these concepts are inadequate to deal with the flow of reality 19.376–7; the terms have no validity, according to the Mahāyāna 19.377; the truth of your existence is neither unchanging existence nor non-existence 19.376; we mistakenly treat them as absolutes 17.626; you don't escape the conditioned through either 10.523

see also
sarvam asti ('everything exists'); the *vajra* or diamond aspect of existence, *see under vajra*

existential situations dilemmas 4.92–3; Dr Johnson's existential question 26.484; fear 4.97; the four sights 3.34–6; the parable of the burning house, *see under White Lotus Sūtra*/parables

existentialism for the existentialists the idea of freedom is fundamental 25.116–17; Indian philosophy has much in common with modern existentialism 8.457; Jean-Paul Sartre on existentialism 2.100

exogamy 9.27

exorcism 4.548, 19.550

exoticism definitions 13.494; the danger of Buddhism's being presented as a sort of exotic curiosity 11.509; Christianity was in the past an exotic religion 13.494; distinction between primary and secondary meanings 13.499; the exoticism of Buddhism in the West 11.82–3, 11.374–5, 13.493–8; the exoticism of a Tibetan puja 11.229; Mellor's critique 13.492–504; sometimes the Dharma is disguised by Eastern culture 11.598

expansion the air element as expanding physical energy 16.145; the Buddhist movement must expand if it is the real thing 5.218–19, 19.417; continually expanding *mettā* 5.218–19; *dhyāna* cannot expand the mind permanently 19.448–9; expanding the closed circle of self-interest 17.342; expansion of consciousness 3.350, 3.353, 4.80, 26.110–11; a feeling of not being obstructed, infinite expansion 4.509–10; expansion of the Triratna Buddhist Community, *see under* Triratna II/further developments; generosity is an ever-expanding circle 1.426; a period of expansion for Sangharakshita (1970) 23.451; Rechungpa's offerings of meat for Milarepa expand to fill a whole valley 19.515; Ruciraketu's house expands and four Buddhas appear in it 16.257–61; the spiralling outwards of one's being 17.345; three levels of meditation: *dhyānas*, intensification, expansion 3.121–2, 3.246,

3.617, 5.655; through life, periods of contraction alternate with periods of expansion 23.451

expectations appealing to bodhisattvas for protection, what is one expecting? 4.312–13; don't ask glib questions about profound things and expect an answer on the spot 21.121–2; expecting someone else to practise the Dharma for you 18.520–1; the four things the monk has a right to expect from lay people 16.408; a great mistake to expect from a guru what we can only get from ourselves 3.561; 'I expect every Order member to do better than I have done' 12.545; having our expectations disappointed is probably quite good for us 18.464; human beings are not rational, and it would be irrational to expect them to be 12.11; *mettā* is the response to be expected from one human being to another 5.174; nothing quite lives up to our expectations 3.260, 26.12; Siddhārtha's courage in giving up his disciples' expectations 3.52, 3.472; we should not expect from others more than they are able to give 18.16

experience

the nature of experience
what is an 'experience'? 11.72–3; changing, ungraspable 7.37; direct, unmediated, characterized by absolute certainty 2.54; ineffable 7.359, 14.595; it is not real in the way we think it is 17.358; in a sense it can't be duplicated 19.203; 'having' an experience is really a situation in which perception takes place 13.151; many-layered, many-faceted 24.xxvi, 24.4

limitations and difficulties
even the concept has its limitations 19.378; an abstract term that we tend to take literally 14.595–6; experiences are not possessions, but states and modifications of our being 26.166; experiences are rarely satisfying in themselves 26.13; the neurotic need for experience 11.79; reducing things to intellectual formulas is an attenuation of one's experience 18.287; some experiences are incompatible with mindfulness 17.100–1; trying to appropriate higher experience 16.520; wherever there is a wish to repeat an experience there is craving 26.63

interpreting experience
drawing conclusions from experience 9.343; from the flux of experience we abstract bits and pieces and imagine a continuity 19.376; language conditions experience 17.248–9; one's so-called present experience actually consists of 'present' plus 'past' 24.4; our ideas of cause and effect subtly determine how we interpret experience 17.247; people always want to affix ready-made labels to their experiences 13.347; take care with the interpretations you put on your experience 19.572–3; taking the self as the absolute reality of things has a negative effect on experience 15.335; the way to Enlightenment is the present experience without interpretation 10.463–4

'kinds' of experience
bare experience 2.257; ordinary experience based on subject–object dualism 2.275, 12.173–4, 17.481; 'pure experience' 19.377; zero-experience (Bharati) 8.436–7, 8.442–3, 8.445

Dharmic perspectives on experience
analysis of experience (eighteen *dhātus*) 15.200; *bodhicitta*: the emergence within ordinary experience of something quite different 4.28; deepening present experience 4.201; the Dharma's true nature can only be comprehended through experience 10.568; eight ways we may misinterpret our experience (*Diamond Sūtra*) 14.438–40; Enlightenment as experience and non-experience 11.72–91, 19.378; *gatigocara* (experience) 11.73–4; it's important that you should *know* that you experience something 10.542; Buddhism upholds the equal validity of reason and experience 26.198; the Mahāmudrā keeps people on experience, not descriptions of experience 19.272; the means to Enlightenment to be determined by the test of experience 7.520; the relationship between sense-experience and spiritual experience 2.54, 26.198–9

communicating experience
the fact that we can't communicate our experience doesn't mean it isn't there 18.357; human experience is much richer than any 'map' (text) describing it 17.108–9; if asked to explain the Dharma from our own experience, what could we say? 18.166; much of our experience is incommunicable 14.595–6; some things, though capable of being experienced, transcend thought and speech 13.348; 'To speak of one's experience leads to loss' – in some circumstances 18.421–2; we can only talk in terms of experience to talk about what transcends it 14.441–2; use the Dharma to communicate your experience 19.206–7

personal experience
the arising of the *bodhicitta* as a private and personal experience 1.422; the

arising of the *bodhicitta* is not a personal experience 4.29–30, 4.278; Buddhism's emphasis on the value of direct, personal experience of reality 12.56–7; the Dharma is not all about what is relevant to 'me' 14.480–1; does all experience include some kind of subtle vocalizing? 5.629; don't parrot others' words, but speak from personal experience 17.308; focus on the quality of your responses to experience 15.155; if we can think 'This is my experience', that experience is not ultimate 26.8; learning from our own experience 17.xxii; Milarepa's emphasis on personal experience 18.228; our experience is so limited 25.136; ordination as a matter of personal experience 2.640–2; personal experience (with reason and scriptures) as validation of the path 19.186–7; the rainbow spectrum of our experience 17.xxi–xxii; test all teachings in personal experience 7.128, 7.381, 10.171, 10.691 (n215); taste is a matter of personal experience 2.641, 10.568; the truth is indescribable, hence a matter for personal experience 1.206; very little in our experience is really free and spontaneous, really us 11.7; we try to repeat the same old pattern of experience 26.168–9; widening experience of external world, deepening experience of internal 26.169–72; you alone can have your experience, another person's will be quite different 14.593; you've got to keep close to your emotional experience 19.143

consult your own experience
a connection between *dhyānas* and *brahma vihāras*?: consult your experience 5.216–17, 5.274; like the shepherd in the Milarepa story 5.668; 'knowing this for oneself': a characteristic Buddhist emphasis 10.465; the means to Enlightenment to be determined by the test of experience 7.520; let us test all views in the fire of our own reason and experience 12.617; relate your experience of meditation to what the texts say 5.250–1, 5.687; watch your own experience and see what happens 5.629, 5.630; we know what will help us grow from our own experience 12.369–70; weigh and test all the thoughts and emotions that come pouring in 7.268; when you read the *sūtra*, how do you feel? 16.66; you've got a source of knowledge within you, and you should use it more than you do 5.624

lived experience
difference between ordination in the technical Vinaya sense and lived experience 2.641–2; the distinction between concepts and lived experience 17.307; translating rational understanding into lived experience 15.95

visionary experience
dwelling on it 5.44; it takes place within an inner, imaginal space 13.152; its light and colour 14.170

see also
direct experience; personal experience; sense experience; spiritual experience

experiments as an experiment, try doing something without finding reasons for it 14.556–7; Buddhism is an experiment 7.186–7; definition of 'experiment' 26.374; experiment as a pillar of the FWBO 12.469–71; an experiment in semantics 14.566; how to conduct an experiment 12.470–1; make the experiment, live the life: all that Buddhism asks us to do 7.128, 11.110; an experiment in which children were deprived of contact 12.215; an experiment to find out how much – or how little – you know 13.345–6; experiments in the arts 26.374–6; experimenting with depriving oneself of sense satisfaction 5.677; experimenting with ritual 11.229, 13.292, 13.419–20; experiment with the order in which the *brahma vihāras* are practised 5.205; the need to adapt to changing conditions 12.470–1; Sangharakshita's first experiment in guided meditation 23.37–8, 27.1071; trying out a commitment 19.146

explanation the difference between explanation and interpretation 11.720; if asked to explain the Dharma from our own experience, what could we say? 18.166; trying to explain something through metaphors 18.282; we want explanations, so we find pseudo-explanations 14.606; with trust, explanations are unnecessary, but without it, explanations are useless 26.81

exploitation fear of being exploited for what you reveal about yourself 10.570–2; if you allow yourself to be exploited, sooner or later you will resent it 26.17; if you take symbolism literally, you are open to exploitation in the name of Buddhism 18.429; in business 1.433, 3.581–2; exploiting people through their guilt and sense of obligation 18.121; most 'gurus' are simply exploiters 26.80; exploiting nature 10.647, 26.243; not giving in to exploitation and still keeping the second precept 17.199; exploitative orientation (Erich Fromm) 12.276; the second precept implies abstaining from economic exploitation 26.669; the suffering of

exploitation (Ambedkar) 9.412, 9.427; at work 3.565–6, 25.121–3

Expositor, The (*Aṭṭhasalini*) *see under* Buddhaghosa/commentaries

expression (*vyañjana*) *see under* four reliances

expulsion the anguish of those who felt they might be living in a state of expulsion 2.589; expulsion or suspension from the Order 2.194–5; monks who are observing the precepts expelling those who are not 14.236; *pārājikas*, *see under* Vinaya/ *prātimokṣa*

external

external conditions
can help or hinder us in our development 11.183; are important 15.289–90; Milarepa's confidence is not subject to them 18.45; all elements, both material and mental, arise in dependence on external conditions 1.266; the reactive mind does not act, but only *re*acts to external stimuli 23.428; some people depend on them less than others 11.183–4; there has to be external, visible beauty in our lives 9.444; we should accustom ourselves to become less dependent on them 18.630–1

external pressure
apatrāpya is not about bowing to it 17.558–60; it's easier to deal with when there is no conflict within oneself 16.323, 26.59; people attach a lot of importance to external differences 19.229–30, 19.308–10; solitary retreat is an opportunity to be free of them 5.637

externals and spiritual life
a balance of meditation, study, and external activities 4.461–3; Buddhism is against the externality that may grind spiritual life out of existence 7.267–8; change may or may not manifest in external behaviour 18.204–5; concerned with spiritual life, no need to know what will happen externally 19.270–1; even the Tibetans can be misled by externals 13.161; freedom from restrictions imposed by our minds, not external circumstances 2.127; mental states are affected by external factors 16.223, 19.527; one cannot go by externals 19.281–2; right motive is more important than external consequences 21.314; rules can become an external conformity, neglecting the spirit 10.563; spiritual life is difficult, so people try to reduce it to external practice and money 19.278; to think Buddhists should be independent of external aids is to misunderstand 7.258–9; the trap of understanding religious practice in a purely external way 15.99; truth and righteousness are more important than the externals of religion 1.274; when the *bodhicitta* arises your external life might remain exactly the same 4.261–2; why Buddhism takes up an independent attitude towards the external world 7.266–8

outer and inner
activity and meditation, external and inner dimension 4.160; the Buddhas and bodhisattvas are as much outside oneself as within 4.131; contemplating mind internally and externally 15.164–7; the division between inner and outer worlds is produced by dualistic thinking 15.138; every man has both an internal and an external 7.581 (n197); external activity and inner spiritual experience may not be incompatible 22.247–8; external and internal difficulties of the spiritual life 12.623; external changes help internal changes, but they're not the same thing 18.640; external enemies and enemies within 4.369; external and internal circumambulation 19.338; going forth means changing, not just externally but internally 9.191; how to bring about peace – through outer or inner change? 7.237–8; if you're trying to live a spiritual life, you face external and internal difficulties 12.623; 'joining the inward and the outward man' 25.348; making the transition from external to internal life 18.302–3; the *mettā bhāvanā*'s two aspects: inner intensification and external radiation 1.158; mistaking external change for internal change 16.122–3; non-violence: the external expression of an internal realization 7.373; outer and inner renunciation 7.397; personal myth is experienced as outside oneself as well as within 18.318–19; phases of spiritual life: periods of internal activities, then external 4.461–4, 4.568–9; phenomena are internal as well as external 1.102; renunciation is significant only if it reflects an inner experience 18.36; Siddhārtha's going forth: not just an external but an internal change 9.191; the six senses the bases for our experience of the external world 3.198; a split between external observances and inward state of being 2.298; widening experience of the external, deepening experience of the internal 26.169–72

extremes deliberately choosing an extreme example 13.473; extreme views, *see under* nihilism/nihilism and eternalism; 'Extremes meet' 11.497; middle way between extremes, *see* middle way; a person who

goes to extremes at least has a certain amount of energy 4.448–9; a tendency to go to extremes in all human activities 8.167

extrovert *see under* introvert

exuberance asceticism prunes the exuberance of nature into the restraint of art 26.158; a balance between blocked energy and over-exuberance 15.732; 'Exuberance is beauty' (Blake) 24.584; silent periods on retreat to calm down over-exuberance 18.581; we need more exuberance and less 'self-control' 4.321, 4.604

'ex-Untouchables' *see* Dalits

Eye of Truth *see* five eyes/Dharma Eye

Eye, Suffolk 26.512

eyes divine eye (*dibba-cakkhu* or *divya-cakṣu*) 1.33, 1.167; the downcast eyes of the monk 4.383–4, 15.173, 21.14–15; the eye of the artist 26.170; the eye of intelligence 17.595; the eye-base (*āyatana*) 14.80; the interaction of eye with visual form 17.510; the king of the Sivis (or Śibis), who gave away his eyes 1.430, 2.16, 14.65; the 'life-establishing' ceremony, including the painting in of an image's eyes 14.464; meditating with the eyes open 17.543; 'More than the seas he gave his blood, more than the stars his eyes' 1.430; myth that the moon and the sun were produced from the eyes of Avalokiteśvara 2.176; the eyes of Nepalese stupas 13.157, 14.479, 16.148, 16.161–2; not seeing new sights with old eyes, but seeing old sights with new eyes 7.295; one cannot be what one should be merely by closing one's eyes to what one is 26.34; opening your inner eyes 10.595; the painted dragon who flew away as soon as his eyes were painted 2.213; 'Pure are your eyes' (hymn to the Buddha) 16.466; symbolizing awareness 13.69; 'they that have eyes to see can see shapes' 10.556; when the Eye of Reality opens 25.309

see also
five eyes; Subhā, who plucked out her eyes, *see* Subhā; those with little dust on their eyes, *see under* Brahmā Sahāmpati's request; White Tārā's seven eyes, *see under* Tārā/White Tārā

F

Faber, Geoffrey 23.208

Fabian Society 23.104, 23.489 (n127)

faces Ānanda asks Sāriputta about his shining face 3.409, 14.551–2; Avalokiteśvara's beautiful face alive with tenderness and compassion 2.176; the beauty or ugliness of a face depends on mental and emotional state 26.594, 26.657; the Buddha's face as bright as a golden cloud (*Sukhāvatī-vyūha Sūtra*) 14.169; the Buddha's face shines like burnished gold (*Mahāparinirvāṇa Sūtra*) 14.239; a Buddha's face shines on Enlightenment and when about to enter *parinirvāṇa* 13.144; the calm, pure face of the Buddha 25.241; the face and body of the Tathāgata shining like the autumn moon 1.327; the face of the Buddha speaks to people who have never heard of Buddhism 26.384; the face of a monster 20.225–6; 'The Face of Silence' (poem) 25.198–9, 26.595; from the perspective of the gods the loveliest human face is repulsive 2.83; one is supposed not to shave one's head without shaving one's face (Vinaya) 17.587; seeing your original face before you were born 13.141, 16.92–3; in the Tantra the disciple looks the teacher directly in the face 15.442; a standing Tārā image with a beautiful face 22.476; women have more beautiful faces than men 26.594

Fachang (translator) 14.152

facts distinguish facts from value judgements 12.477; indistinguishable from events 1.102; a realistic facing of the facts is characteristic of Buddhism 8.143; Herbert Spencer's idea of a tragedy was a theory killed by a fact 8.242, 12.274

factors *see* five factors

factors of Enlightenment *see* seven *bodhyaṅgas*

faculties five spiritual faculties, *see* five spiritual faculties; imaginal faculty, *see* imaginal faculty; life-faculty, *see jīvita-indriya*; the *manas* is the faculty of abstract thought 12.559; pay attention to your weakest faculty 3.311; the perfection of wisdom is the spiritual faculty that intuits *śūnyatā* 16.232; use whatever faculties you have, as an animal would 19.165; visionary faculty 16.23

Fa-hsien 8.374–5

failure better not to make a vow than to make it and fail to keep it 4.476–7; confronting fear of failure 13.232; failure to see the Dharma in its true context and correct perspective 1.31–7; for a bodhisattva, Nirvāṇa is a failure 4.188, 26.8; having attained Stream Entry, you cannot be regarded as having failed in life 16.423; our tendency to take the credit for success and blame others for failure 10.601; refusing to face up to the fact of failure: a modern wrong view 19.343–4; we should not be discouraged if sometimes we fail 7.101; you get results after you put all your energy into something, fail, and give up 18.189; you may fail, but the important thing is that you should try 1.553; you need to risk the humiliation of failure to be successful 14.489–91; *see also* eight worldly winds

fairness *see* justice

fait accompli 11.424

faith (Sanskrit *śraddhā*, Pāli *saddhā*)

INTRODUCTION

definitions
brief introduction 1.507, 3.299–301; dictionary definition of faith 1.282

translations of śraddhā
confidence-trust 17.550; confidence in one's own potential 17.576; a lifting up of the heart 3.263–4; to place the heart upon 1.282, 2.104, 2.243, 12.625; relationship to Latin *cor*, 'the heart' 17.35; translation as 'confidence': not the whole meaning 17.334–5

the nature of faith
an attitude of serenity, an extremely positive state 17.37–9; the capacity to be moved by what transcends the senses and the rational mind 26.60; a deep enjoyment of the contemplation of the ideal 17.336; described by Wordsworth 17.557; faith and worry are incompatible 14.557, 17.38; faith is action, karma 17.557; faith is innate, doubt acquired 26.35; the difference between someone with faith and someone without 17.36; an integral part of the spiritual life 25.47; it integrates emotions and intellect 17.674; it is comparatively rare 11.413; it is difficult to have faith in something without

regarding it as an end in itself 14.441; it lends itself to emotional excitement 17.81; its near enemy is credulity 17.43; our life is grounded on faith at every step 17.23–4, 17.36, 17.46–7; its quality of mind compared to the original meaning of 'religion' 17.554; rejoicing in the Buddha's realization and trusting that you can do the same 17.336; sometimes we have to go on until experience confirms, or does not confirm, our belief 8.591; there's no faith without faith in yourself 17.37

FAITH IN BUDDHISM

the history of faith in Buddhism
'Let those who have ears to hear release their faith' 3.74, 3.640 (n80), 11.413; the ardent response of Piṅgiya in the *Sutta-Nipāta* 1.287–9; 'By faith the flood is crossed' (*Saṃyutta Nikāya*) 1.290, 25.15; 'Faith is the wealth here best for man' (*Sutta-Nipāta*) 1.290; in the *Kālāma Sutta* 9.470–1; liberation by faith (Pāli canon) 1.291, 4.516; an integral part of the Buddhist ideal from the earliest times 1.290; in the early days, faith was a 'somewhat frozen sort of devotion' 7.122–3; the Buddhism of Faith and Devotion 1.323–336, 2.128; the merit of developing faith in the Tathāgata's eternal life 14.127; the Theravāda tends to underrate 'mere faith' 4.516, 15.723–6; all we should seek to attain is an awakening of faith in Amitābha 1.345

faith in the Three Jewels
avetyaprasāda (firm faith) in the Three Jewels 14.82; in Buddhism, this is what faith means 1.282, 3.263, 3.299, 12.159–60; confidence that they represent the ultimate values of life 15.328; confirmed and strengthened by seeing monks 2.214; contemplating the Three Jewels 14.586; determination applied to the Three Jewels becomes faith 17.535; does faith in the Three Jewels come into sexual experience? 17.639; faith consolidated into confidence 2.104–5; faith becomes unshakeable on real Going for Refuge 3.329, 12.505; four kinds of firm faith (*avetyaprasāda*) in the Three Jewels 14.82; as the highest values of existence 2.477; not blind faith 10.331–2; placing our heart on them 2.259; unshakeable faith is very rare 18.219

reflections on Buddhist faith
an affinity with Enlightenment 3.301; appreciation of and trust in spiritual friends 17.553; the capacity for being moved by something that transcends the senses 17.18; directed to those above us in the spiritual hierarchy 11.507; the driving force of the Higher Evolution 18.275; the element of receptivity in Buddhist faith 15.5[illegible]1–3; exclusive as in concentrated, but not intolerant or fanatical 2.243; faith in the four noble truths 17.551; faith in spiritual friends 17.673; a gift and a virtue 17.42–3; the healthy counterpart of craving 2.104, 2.259; if you have faith you cease to worry about life 17.38–9; it asks us to have faith in ourselves 11.110; the kinship between faith and greed (Buddhaghosa) 17.42–3; people can be devoted Buddhists for years without any idea what faith means 17.671–2; primarily faith in the Buddha as an Enlightened being 11.483, 17.27–8, 17.38; the only thing you have to believe as a Buddhist is that you can grow 17.28; retaining a clear and conscious belief in Buddhist values 17.2[illegible]0; some people are surprised that there is faith in Buddhism 3.299; taking on trust basic teachings about the nature of reality 17.33; *vīrya* depends on faith, and faith depends on inspiration 17.71; a whole culture can be a culture of faith 17.5[illegible]6; you need faith if you are to lead the spiritual life 17.335

comparison with other traditions
Buddhist faith contrasted with faith in God 1.38, 9.342, 17.25–6; Buddhists shouldn't be upset to think that others don't believe what they do 4.124; critique of theistic definition 1.282–3; 'Every great religion has been based on faith' (Ambedkar) 9.11[illegible]; 'faith-decisions' (Mellor) 13.480–2, 13.4[illegible]6–7, 13.490–2

the grounds for faith
faith based on book learning is always vulnerable to being challenged 18.185; the faith of the Buddhist is capable of verification 13.570–1; faith is only possible when self-consciousness has emerged 18.2[illegible]4; grounds: intuition, reason, and experience 1.283–7; no faith and devotion without wisdom, effort, concentration, and mindfulness 3.310; patient and trusting acceptance 17.23; verifying faith through discussion 17.45; you can verify faith in this life 17.26

what faith is not
it's not emotional self-indulgence 15.612–15; faith distinguished from pleasure 17.5[illegible]2–3, 17.672–3; interpreting faith or confidence as dogmatism 19.102–3; it's not an investment plan 17.336; not a belief, or even just a feeling 2.104, 3.299, 17.554; not a tepid 'confidence' 15.550–1; not a substitute for knowledge, but based on knowledge 1.38

images for faith
a 'jump' of faith like a man jumping across a river 1.289–90; 'Faith is the firm foundation of my house' 18.271–4; 'Faith is the seed' 10.331–2, 13.571, 15.625, 17.17–19, 26.648–9; incense 25.42; like the rising sun 1.286–7; like a sunflower turning towards the sun 21.463; swimming across the river 17.36; those who walk in faith are like a new-born calf carried over a stream 1.291; the vibration of the music of Enlightenment in one's heart 1.283–4

THE ARISING AND DEVELOPMENT OF FAITH

the awakening of faith
a reflection of the Transcendental in the mundane 18.280; following your emotional interest into the spiritual life 15.600–1; having faith and taking risks go hand in hand 17.47; a leap in the dark 14.602; a leap of faith 26.60; when it awakens, we make the 'crosswise leap' 1.347; when with *mettā* we look up to one who is more spiritually developed 5.158, 9.323; on meeting the Tantric guru 18.67; in dependence on suffering, *see under* twelve positive *nidānas*; it arises when *mettā* touches something higher than us 11.155, 11.734, 15.327–8; to awaken faith, one needs the imaginal faculty: emotion plus intellect 17.673–4

a response
the authentic, living response of the whole being to something greater 11.413; an emotionally healthy person must respond to the ideal with faith 18.273–4; the existential response of one's total being when confronted by perfection 14.114; experiences that might provoke that response 12.624–5; a heartfelt response to the spiritually attractive 17.326; a response of delight and fascination 17.336; a response to something higher 3.263, 22.285; a response which brings relief and clarity to one's life and mind 17.551; to the embodiment of Enlightenment, in a person, biography, or image 3.299–300; of our potential Enlightenment to the actual Enlightenment that confronts us 3.300–1; to the Three Jewels 9.342; a total emotional response to the spiritual ideal 17.335; the response of what is ultimate in us to what is ultimate in the universe 12.159, 26.35; you need to have an idea or vision, and be emotionally free to respond to it 18.273

developing and sustaining faith
confirmed and strengthened by embodiments of one's ideals 2.214; the consolidation of faith into confidence 15.602–4; continuing to have faith 25.42; cultivating faith to get our energy going 14.586; the difference between *mettā* and *śraddhā* 5.158; even offering a flower with devotion puts one on the path to Buddhahood 16.41; faith and worry are incompatible 14.557, 17.38; faith can wax and wane 3.264; faith 'needs something on which the imagination can fasten' (Ambedkar) 9.110; faith stirred up through the faith of other people 3.400; as faith strengthens, one becomes less self-centred 3.264; how to cultivate faith 17.43; may be confused to start with, but gradually strengthens 2.259; the sangha keeps your faith alive 15.657, 17.71; *śraddhā bhāvanā* 5.158; strengthened by experiencing the results of Dharma practice 19.286; strengthened by self-discipline 17.44–5; when we experience suffering, we should try to develop faith 12.646–7; you need an environment that sustains your faith: the sangha 15.657; you yourself are responsible for your own faith 10.495

ASPECTS OF FAITH

faith as a positive mental event (Abhidharma)
'a deep conviction for those things which are real, have value, and are possible' 17.550–1; faith is present in every skilful state of mind 1.291, 17.43, 17.557, 18.207, 26.36; faith, trust, and pleasure 17.552–3, 17.672–3; if one has it, one is happy despite any difficulties 17.555; it is a very precise mental event, and very rare 17.671–3; the significance of its being listed first 15.650, 17.550

no blind faith
faith distinguished from blind faith 17.290; is faith irrational? 14.550; in Buddhism there is no association of faith with uncertainty 17.555–6; no such thing as blind faith in Buddhism 1.283, 9.342, 10.331–2, 11.413; reaction against blind faith 11.205; religions of discovery require not blind faith but clear-sighted understanding 7.367; we shouldn't just accept the tradition unthinkingly 16.553

simple faith
the faith of Tibetan pilgrims, full of nerve and vigour 7.417–18; Langland's respect for the simple faith of shoemakers and shepherds 24.540; a peasant with faith compared to a scholar without 7.310, 11.483, 17.331; simple faith in the saving power of the Buddha's vow 14.104

faith and reason
accepting only what is in agreement with reason and our own experience 21.505; an assent to doctrines not substantiated by immediate evidence 17.22–3; the borderline between reasonable faith and pathological faith 17.63; faith is the emotional counterpart of reason 3.299; 'Faith is far more a matter of the heart than of the intellect' 17.35–6; faith needs to be corrected by common sense 17.63; having found out as much as we can, we always have to take a chance 14.550; the idea of balancing reason and faith is not useful 14.442–3; reason cannot create faith 18.273; using reason to distinguish between faith and mundane emotion 1.285; we need to be convinced 8.595–6; will, understanding, and emotion as aspects of faith 15.616; you are bigger than your reason, hence the need for faith 14.557

faith and wisdom
balanced 1.240, 1.293, 3.301–4, 9.213, 9.325–6, 9.342, 22.285; development of faith is equivalent to wisdom (*White Lotus Sūtra*) 16.49; faith is the emotional counterpart of wisdom 1.347, 4.515, 14.172, 14.431, 15.616–7; faith is gradually transformed into knowledge 13.571; faith is provisional until wisdom arises 17.24–6; faith, not wisdom, will be your lifeline when your practice goes off course 18.181; faith occupies the position traditionally assigned to wisdom (China and Japan) 2.128; at a higher level there is no distinction 17.333–4; scholars who don't see them as equal 17.334–5; without wisdom faith can become fantasy 17.63–4

the dynamism and expression of faith
acting upon faith 14.566, 18.219–20; the consequences of faith 3.263–5; devotion is ideally an expression of faith in thoughts, words, and deeds 17.553–4; different people express faith in different kinds of salutations 4.295, 9.337–8, 11.250; directing our emotions towards the objects of faith: the Three Jewels 14.586; faith is active, whereas belief is passive 19.581; faith is the first movement of creativity 17.36, 19.580–1; 'I will' and 'I can': a creative and powerful thing 17.36–7; if you have faith in the Dharma, you will make the most of chances to practise it 17.168; it expresses itself in generosity and ethical behaviour: the first two *pāramitās* 2.105; the placebo effect of faith 19.327; there is no *vīrya* without faith 17.70; to decide your next spiritual step you need not just faith but a definite goal 18.272–3; volitional faith (faith and the will) 17.35–7; when there is no pleasure, faith must be sustaining your practice 17.554–5; where there is faith there will be energy 5.327; without faith you can't do anything at all 17.17

see also
devotion; faith as one of the five spiritual faculties, *see under* five spiritual faculties; faith as one of the positive *nidānas*, *see under* twelve positive *nidānas*; faith in the Buddha, *see under* Buddha IV/responses to the Buddha; faith in the Dharma, *see* Dharma II/emotional responses; lack of faith, *see aśraddhā*

faith-follower, faith-type (*saddhānusārin*, *śraddhā-carita*)

what the faith-follower is like
drawn to the joy and beauty of Enlightenment 18.129; love comes first, then knowledge 10.224; may be enjoying life, but then finds that Buddhism is even better 15.574–5; not inclined to study the Dharma much 17.332; a person of predominantly devotional temperament 2.142; response to the spiritual teacher 2.142, 11.157, 15.561–2, 25.13; their approach to Buddhism 17.332–3; their enthusiasm gets spiritual life off to a good start 17.43, 17.614; they are attracted by the Unconditioned from the beginning 15.569–70; they can get started on practice with minimal explanation 11.157, 14.349; they love to go on pilgrimage 25.12; they manage with the minimum of intellectual formulation 17.35, 18.272; they may not seem to experience doubt, but still need to develop clarity 17.614; they take their emotions with them out of the group 15.743

the tradition
'the one freed by faith' 10.685 (n172); Going for Refuge 15.546, 15.567–8, 15.600–1, 15.608, 15.720; a faith-follower on the path of Stream Entry may become a body-witness 2.144; faith-follower and doctrine-follower 11.158, 17.333, 18.133; one of the seven holy persons of the Āryasaṅgha 2.141–3, 17.710 (n39); on becoming an *arhant*, called an *ubhayatobhāgavimukta* ('doubly-liberated one') 2.145; term found in the Tipiṭaka 1.291; canonical references 2.737 (n651), 15.767–8 (n210); 147,825 kinds identified by the Sarvāstivādins 2.152; lay Buddhists tend to be faith-followers 2.220, 15.562; exemplars from

the Buddhist tradition 14.349, 17.333, 17.553, 18.308–9

the faith-follower's practice
considers the aggregates as impermanent 2.144; do they need to study the Dharma? 25.14; even faith-followers need a basic level of intellectual understanding 17.333; faith only slightly predominates over wisdom 1.291; gaining insight through visualization 5.465; reflections on impermanence for the faith-follower 18.154–5; their career does not exclude wisdom 2.145; they follow the way of contemplative insight 2.143; they run the risk of becoming unable to understand others' practice 17.333; taken to extremes, this approach can leave us high and dry 17.573–4

Fall of Man Buddhist conceptions 1.42, 12.109, 16.100–1; Christian myth 1.528, 15.619, 16.100–1, 17.97; each of us is falling from eternity at every instant 17.611; fallen man (Blake) 8.558, 26.347–8; it takes place every time we follow the dictates of our lower nature 12.109; thinking about the 'fallen mind' is problematic 17.97–8; the transition from sensation to craving is the psychological fact behind it 1.111–12

fame doing meritorious deeds for the sake of fame 19.484; the fame of Siddhārtha's austerities 3.30; remaining unmoved by acquisitions or fame 14.193; as a worldly wind, *see under* eight worldly winds

family

nuclear family
embarking upon family life is usually a passive thing 18.457; disadvantages 15.xx; claustrophobic 3.540–1, 15.475–6, 15.481–2, 16.297; happiness does not depend on it, as living in a community shows 15.197; one-parent families 10.73–4; psychological tensions 11.188–9; rationalized as unselfish 15.476–7; a trend towards the nuclear family in India 10.411–12

extended family
family life in ancient India 15.408–9; the family man's responsibilities in ancient India 10.449, 10.485; in the East, the family still rules people's lives 3.441; more positive than the nuclear family 15.480; the extended family has lost importance in the West 3.441, 11.188; the extended family in India 10.411–12

positive perspectives
considering your family is a step towards being non-egoistic 17.345; a group, but that a necessary stage in the individual's development 10.73–4; learning about one's ancestry 26.530–1; making the most of family relationships 18.394–5; the network of family relationships 3.521–2, 11.695; relationships can be deepened and made closer as a result of spiritual practice 3.528–9; retaining individuality within the family 3.37

difficulties with family life
anger is mostly directed towards our nearest and dearest 17.599; attachment to one's family is not always positive 18.330–1; avoid any feeling that you're trapped in the family situation 18.455–8; the conformity imposed by the family 15.484; differences of religion could divide families in the 19th century 12.464; 'disgracing the family name' 13.459–62; the dysfunctional family 25.65; family quarrels and conflict 10.323, 18.330–1; generational split 25.72–3; the myth of the happy family 25.65; negative feelings towards relatives 15.305; the poet and family life 26.144; why isn't family life happy? 15.478–85; your family tends to see you as you have always been 11.48, 18.485

leaving the family
the Buddha accused of destroying families 2.24; the Buddha's disciple Saṅgāmaji, who left his wife and son 10.454–7; freeing oneself from psychological ties 19.520–1; is it selfish to leave your family? 10.455–6; kinsmen as a tribe from which you may need to go forth 18.150–1; making a decision free of irrational guilt 18.455–7; people don't find it easy to leave 18.330–1; Shiwa Aui renounces his family 18.186; Siddhārtha's leaving of his wife and son 10.456, 13.445; staying in the biological group makes it more difficult to evolve 18.485–6; what does Milarepa mean by 'renouncing one's kin'? 18.484–6

the spiritual family
be cautious about using family terms to describe the spiritual family 17.40; 'brother and sister, mother and father, to one another' 4.11, 11.442–3, 14.414; the Buddha as Father, the Dharma as Mother, and the Sangha as son 2.138; discontinuity between biological and spiritual family 11.442; the idea of 'family-based' Buddhism emphasizes lifestyle over commitment 24.489; if you love family life, imagine a much wider 'spiritual family': sangha 17.363; residential communities

as a positive alternative 11.189, 12.469, 15.473–4; in the spiritual life everybody becomes kin 15.416; making the whole of humanity your family 18.214–15; a spiritual family, not a substitute social family 17.40–2; the spiritual hierarchy like a spiritual family 4.177

the family of the Buddha
Mañjuśrī explains in the *Vimalakīrti-nirdeśa* 16.457; positive pride at being born into the family of the Buddha 4.275–6

see also
Buddha families, *see under* Buddhas; parents

fanaticism the besetting sin of Islam 26.15; devotion can go to extremes, to become fanaticism 3.301, 17.81; persecution, fanaticism, and dogmatism 7.145–6; religions' faith in infallibility leads to fanaticism and persecution 7.366–7; scepticism and fanaticism in medieval Christianity 15.565

fantasy fantasies in meditation 3.567; fantasy and the imagination 11.724–5; Sangharakshita's fantasy of living as a monk at Sarnath 20.346; science fiction fantasies 25.320; we have to be careful that the bodhisattva vows don't become fantasy 4.60; without wisdom faith can become fantasy 17.63–4; you can fantasize, daydream, as long as you are aware 10.463

far enemy *see* near and far enemies

Faraday, Michael 26.686–7

farming and agriculture the Age of Agriculture 3.426; agricultural life producing an emotionally healthy state, responsive to the Dharma 18.273–4; the crops that grow without cultivation (mandala visualization) 13.261–2; the countryside and food production 10.329; farming in Maharashtra 10.292–3; goddess of agriculture 16.409; human development of agriculture 3.425–6; Kasi-Bhāradvāja the farmer discusses ploughing with the Buddha 3.76, 10.330–2, 18.294, 26.648–9; Milarepa uses farming as an analogy for spiritual practice 18.288–93; Sangharakshita the farmer 21.551, 21.553, 22.429–33, 22.624, 24.463, 26.530–1; the hard work of farming perhaps not compatible with spiritual life 18.202–3; 'the slave-labour of the hungry' (Milarepa) 18.294

Farnese, Alessandro (Pope Paul III) 24.265, 24.274–6

fascination dreams can be full of fascination 19.323; the Enlightened mind exerts on all living beings an unrivalled fascination 13.278; it's easier to be fascinated by the mundane than the transcendental 17.692; faith is a response of delight and fascination 17.336; reality is as much fascinating and alluring as it is a matter of concepts 13.284; rite, *see under* four Tantric rites; the *sambhogakāya*: peaceful, fascinating, stern, even terrible 2.42; unhealthy fascination with supernormal powers 3.584; you have to see the Transcendental not as dry and abstract, but as fascinating 19.24–5

fascism 12.616, 17.629

fatalism astrology may indicate an influence, not an inevitable outcome 19.269–70; a characteristic of the English 20.69–70; fatalism about the decline of the Dharma is against the Buddha's teaching 19.83; kinds of fatalism 19.85–6

Fates (Greek myth) 22.14, 25.407

fathers

introduction
blissful experience 'like my father' (Milarepa) 18.298–9; in Christian terminology 18.315, 19.123; if fathers perform their duties, their children need not clamour for their rights 7.280; the compliment of leaving one's children alone to make their own mistakes 16.202; faith in God is like having an angry father 17.337; father figures 12.233, 17.40; father-light and son-light 18.251; father-substitutes 3.549–51; feelings of hatred towards your father 18.609–10; and mother, *see* parents; traditionally the father had complete right over his children 15.482–4

relationship between fathers and sons
advice about the way a father should treat his son 3.539, 15.412, 16.297; cultures in which it's considered to be the most important relationship in life 18.505–6; destructive love between father and son, 'noble pathos' 26.372; father's expectations of his son 15.419–20, 15.482–4; the 'father–son' relationship of Milarepa and Rechungpa 19.27, 19.114, 19.123; Nepali fathers' strictness 22.451; using the language of father and son in a religious context 18.315–16, 19.123; the way the relationship changes 16.298

symbolism
in the parable of the burning house 16.71–2; in the parable of the return

journey 16.90–8, 16.107; in the parable of the good physician 16.199–200, 16.202

Faulkner, William 22.276, 22.600 (n223), 24.389

faults better to think of cultivating virtues than correcting faults 17.291, 17.296; the faults of conditioned existence, *see under bodhicitta*/arising/factors; don't just put up with your own faults 4.368; hypocrisy: attachment to our faults and our reputation 17.284–5; it's always easy to see others' faults, but pointing them out can be unskilful 17.653; laughing at others' faults to show that we are free of those faults 17.279; our tendency is to see others' faults rather than virtues 17.278–9, 18.112; seeing oneself as full of faults and others as oceans of virtue 4.592–3

Fausbøll, Michael Viggo 3.589, 12.31–2, 14.53, 15.4

Faxian (pilgrim and translator) 7.32, 14.231

Faxiang Zong 1.371, 17.770 (n516)

Fazang 1.353–4

fear

the nature of fear
all fear is basically hatred of death 26.153; all fear is ultimately fear of annihilation 18.46; existential fear 4.97; it comes from desire to protect the ego 12.661, 16.27, 17.180–1, 17.340; it indicates attachment to the self, and that implies duality 18.49; it is fed by popular culture 17.181

fear of …
the arrival of the Stranger 25.81, 25.84; being alone 8.260; being fearless 17.352–3; being found out 16.306; being open 10.570–1, 16.316; breaking the rules 17.635; breaking a taboo 21.225; censure 19.344; confronting people with the truth of yourself 15.272; death, *see under* death/trying to avoid death; the death of the ego 17.339, 17.354; disappointment 7.285; the disapproval of the group 15.285, 16.307; emotion 7.290; freedom 12.232–3; giving things up 16.74; God 10.205–6, 11.361–2, 15.620, 15.719, 16.308–9; hell 18.71; hunger and thirst 18.50–1; hypnosis 4.507; living 17.47; loneliness 18.42–3, 18.49–50; losing one's way 18.51; madness 11.9, 16.278–9; the natural world 18.42–3; non-violence 17.353; nuclear war 4.95–6, 7.343; poverty 18.50; public speaking 13.232; punishment 3.322, 11.260, 16.306–7; Reality 16.39–40, 16.96–7, 16.112; saying you're a Buddhist 10.259; sexual feelings 17.216–17; strong emotions 11.9; suffering 11.263–4; the unfamiliar (relating to entering the *dhyānas*) 4.154; the unknown 14.566, 17.370; the withdrawal of love 16.307

other fears
don't be afraid of anger 17.599; enjoying creating fear in others 4.97, 17.181–2; 'The eternal silence of these infinite spaces terrifies me' 14.504; the group's fear of other groups 3.435; hopes and fears 7.285, 18.344, 19.398; the intent to harm brings fear 17.258; Milarepa considers the various kinds of human fears 18.49–52; modern fears 4.95–6; pleasure is not something to be feared 8.446; the unskilfulness of frightening others 17.179–81; xenophobia (fear of alien places and peoples) 18.137–9

feeling and responding to fear
as fear approaches, we realize it is not really this that we are afraid of 26.76; either repressed or allowed to diffuse through one's whole experience 26.75; extreme fear can lead to a disintegration of our sense of self 17.180; facing fear 11.399; fear in the *bardo* between death and rebirth 12.201; fearful times for Sangharakshita 20.104, 20.169–70; 'I failed to venture in' 25.211; living under the influence of fear 4.96, 16.278; 'perhaps the psychic is nothing to be afraid of, whereas the spiritual is' 20.310; realizing the peril of death, a wise man should feel fear 1.418; something that shakes you so much that you are never the same again 14.598; when you are dying you can speak the truth without fear 15.376–7

religious fears
beliefs born of fear 1.20; the Catholic Church controls people through fear 11.338, 26.20; 'The fear of the Lord' is *not* the beginning of wisdom 26.155; putting the fear of God into people 17.181–2; religion is based on fear 26.155

fears and Dharma practice
the Dharma can be frightening 14.566–7, 17.324; fear of anything that holds us back is a positive thing 17.180; fear on solitary retreat 16.279–80; for some people it is a necessary part of spiritual development 26.47; getting a true sense of transcendental wisdom is frightening 17.370; supernatural beings perhaps rationalized fears of pre-Buddhist India 26.153; the touch of *śūnyatā* 4.162, 5.32, 26.48

overcoming fear
Avalokiteśvara protects from fear 4.632; the best way of getting rid of fear is self-surrender 15.735; by visiting the cremation ground 13.229–31, 16.28; can be done only by eliminating the ego-sense 1.429, 17.340, 20.355; green is the colour of freedom from fear 13.282; one of the most important teachings of the Buddha 10.259; overcoming fear of change is the function of all spiritual practices 16.110; removed by the sound of the golden drum (*Sūtra of Golden Light*) 16.276–9; spiritual friends can help 3.574, 4.96, 16.109–10

see also
fear in meditation, *see under* meditation/dealing with difficulties; Siddhārtha's fear in the jungle, *see under* Siddhārtha

fearlessness (*abhaya*)

the nature of fearlessness
absolute fearlessness is synonymous with Enlightenment 1.429, 16.278; distinguished from bravery 16.27–8; equated to freedom from egotism 16.278; it can come from lack of imagination 14.474, 16.278; it doesn't mean that you never feel fear 14.474, 18.52; we fear being fearless 17.352–3; the willingness to give everything 18.115

fearlessness and Dharma practice
contemplating Vajrapāṇi 2.177; development of fearlessness, especially of death, central to Buddhism 16.278; Early Buddhism attached great importance to being free from fear 10.501; emphasized in all forms of Buddhism 13.310; fearlessness in pursuit of the truth about Buddhism 1.20; fearlessness is one of the fruits of spiritual practice 18.49; the fundamental religious state of mind is a sense of absolute fearlessness 26.162; if you're not confident, you can make no approach to Enlightenment 12.216; it figures prominently in the Buddhist scriptures 13.230; it is emphasized much more in Buddhism than Christianity 16.276–8; the Mahāyāna's fearless acceptance of contradictory propositions 1.245–6; openness with spiritual friends leads to confidence and fearlessness 18.420–1; required to sustain insight into reality 14.576; symbolized by a lion 9.367; in the Tantra, associated with the cremation ground 13.311; we shouldn't be afraid to become Buddhists 10.167–8, 10.259; the would-be bodhisattva 'becomes without fear of being or becoming' 4.48, 4.293–4

exemplars of fearlessness
a *bhikkhu* who lived fearlessly in the forest 10.500–1; the bodhisattva 1.429, 2.157, 3.55–6; Dharmapala's fearlessness 8.13; represented by Green Tārā 12.661; the yogi 18.420–1

see also
mudras/abhaya mudra; the Buddha's fearlessness, *see under* Buddha II/characteristics; courage; giving the gift of fearlessness, *see under dāna*/traditional kinds of giving

feelings awareness of feelings, *see under* awareness/four levels of awareness; feelings as synonymous with emotions, *see* emotions; feelings as *vedanā* (pleasant, unpleasant, neutral), *see vedanā*

feet the Buddha lay with his head to the north and his feet to the south 11.452, 12.357; everything is slipping from beneath our feet 7.49, 25.324; feet injured through walking barefoot 20.382–3, 20.432; Indian customs involving feet 16.381–2, 19.568; most people are dependent on authority, afraid to stand on their own feet 12.232–3; our only refuge is at the feet of the Buddha 2.424, 25.250–1; placing your head on someone's feet 16.381; the true individual can stand on their own two feet 18.136; Vimalakīrti's advice to laymen is not an exhortation to put your feet up 16.492–5

female Avalokiteśvara's female form, Guanyin, *see* Guanyin; only one female *tulku* 12.16, 13.53, 18.109; 'Female beauty can overbear even the wise' 25.438; female Buddhas, *see* five female Buddhas; Female Will (Blake) 11.427–8; is there a difference between 'male' and 'female' energy? 17.74–6; male *āsuras* are ugly, females are beautiful 16.349; the monstrous Female 25.280; the word *prajñā* is of feminine gender, so wisdom is spoken of as female 19.434; worship of female gurus as Mother 3.550, 20.197

feminine and femininity (*strīndriya*) among the secondary qualities of *rūpa* 2.97; *ḍākinīs* and *dharmapālas*: feminine and masculine energies 19.408–9; developing the whole range of human qualities, 'masculine' and 'feminine' 11.582; difference between Gurkhas and Newars like the difference between masculine and feminine 7.345; feminine forces (red channel) 19.31; feminine and masculine are different mentalities and may need different spiritual practices 12.283; a feminine ideal, receptive and cooperative – but don't take this literally 18.105–6; feminine and

masculine are two, and individuality is the Dharma-door 16.548; 'feminine' and 'masculine' Buddhist art 22.349; 'feminine' and 'masculine' in the symbolism of the stupa 13.163; the feminine principle represented by the lotus 22.28; *heruka* and *ḍākinī* 18.373; knowledge of a man's unrealized 'feminine' side through Tantric practice 13.90; and *kṣānti* 4.118, 4.142–4; masculine and feminine in the mandala of the five Buddhas 18.601; Prajñāpāramitā, personalized as feminine 7.139, 16.163; represents wisdom in Buddhist iconography 18.373; seeing the form and hearing the mantra: 'masculine' and 'feminine' 26.39; a shift from feminine to masculine values in Judaism 19.414; taking the initiative to develop feminine qualities 16.164

feminism a book by Buddhist women little beholden to feminism 24.373; the difference between feminism and Feminism 11.638–9; extreme developments in Feminism 11.603, 11.611; 'feminist' Mahāyāna *sūtras* 14.175; inclusive language 11.640–1; the prevention of its irruption in the Order of the Buddha's time 11.426, 11.638; a question to a Zen roshi from a feminist perspective 24.476–7; reflections on feminism 24.72–3; the tendency to see woman as victim and man as victimizer 11.639

feminization 11.613

Fénelon, Archbishop 13.626

Ferdowsi (Persian poet) 4.411, 4.704 (n298)

festivals

INTRODUCTION

the nature of festivals
adding a pagan element 4.108, 18.379; direct, spontaneous, and colourful 2.226–9; festivals remind us of our commitment 3.403; hard to imagine having a party as part of a Buddhist festival 16.370–1; they should be joyful 3.20, 3.265, 17.338; take children to festivals 3.540; they draw attention to exemplars of the attainment of Enlightenment 17.640; the three most important festivals are associated with the Three Jewels 11.395; use of the vihara for festivals 9.465; wrong to set the date for astrological reasons 8.116–17

full moon festivals
celebrated by different cultures on different days 12.119–20; remind us to maintain a harmony between ourselves and nature 11.395; guidelines for celebrating a festival 8.657–8

BUDDHA DAY (WESAK)

names
in India it is 'Buddha Jayanti', the celebration of the Buddha's victory 11.395–6; 'Saga Dawa' is the Tibetan name 11.488; threefold or 'Thrice Sacred' festival 2.226–7, 3.19, 11.488, 22.5, 22.595 (n199); Vaiśākha is the Sanskrit source of the Sinhalese 'Wesak' 3.18, 11.395, 11.488, 23.238

the nature of the festival
campaign for it to be a public holiday in India 8.164–6, 8.247–9; 'colour and serene joy' 2.227; great rejoicing 3.20, 23.122; include meditation in the celebrations 8.293–4; a day of heart-searching for all sincere Buddhists 8.176; determination to practise the six perfections is good preparation 8.199; different ways of celebrating 8.173; essentially celebrates the rediscovery of the path 8.202; its deeper significance 7.454–7; meditation as preparation 22.309–10; must never become a purely social or cultural occasion 19.486; rejoicing in the Buddha Jewel 11.395; reflecting on its true meaning 8.279–81, 11.489; a reminder to think of our own Enlightenment 3.21, 3.403; should be celebrated on a grand scale 9.465; to celebrate, consider how to make the Buddha's teaching of peace effective 8.262; a time of moral and spiritual stocktaking 11.489, 23.238; the tradition of giving *dāna* 8.173–6; Vaiśākha publications 8.137–9; Western Buddhists used to forget it should be joyful 1.506, 17.337, 23.121–2

in Kalimpong
2,500th celebration 8.650–1, 21.497, 21.506, 21.508–9; a big occasion at the Hermitage 22.5–9; celebrated by the Newars 21.37; a collaboration to prevent violence at the festival 22.235–6; Dhardo Rimpoche performs a puja at Craigside 22.238; first celebration at the Triyana Vardhana Vihara 8.658; a procession from the Dharmodaya Vihara 22.238–9

in London
1944 12.301–2, 20.102, 23.121; 1960s 12.304–5, 23.121–3, 23.235–7; London Buddhist Centre, 1990 24.388

in other places
customs in Buddhist countries 2.226–7, 3.19–20; Ahmedabad 9.450; Auckland, NZ (1979) 24.95–6; Bodh Gaya 8.177–8; Nagpur (1946) 22.163; Paris 22.256; Sri Lanka 2.226; Dharmapala's insistence on celebrating Wesak 6.603–4, 8.14; first ever celebration in the United States (1897) 8.55; at the FWBO's first centre

(photograph) 23.430; giving a Dharma talk at Wesak 12.588; procession at Kusinārā 20.411, 20.413

Sangharakshita and the festival
asked for the day off Army duties in Singapore 20.156; ordained at Kusinārā 20.408–13; reads poems for five short TV programmes for Wesak 24.388; 'The Tree of Wisdom' (a poem for Wesak) 25.252–4; 'Wesak Joy' (poem) 25.184; 'Wesak Thoughts' (poem) 25.188–91

PARINIRVĀṆA DAY

the nature of the festival
contact the Buddha's compassion through meditation 7.457; the chanting of the Vajrasattva mantra 11.455–6; giving a Dharma talk 12.588; how the day might be marked 11.455–8; it focuses our minds on the fact of death 3.119–20; its significance 7.454–7; remembering friends and relatives who have died 11.457–8; reminds us to meditate 3.120

2,500th anniversary of the Buddha's parinirvāṇa
introduction 22.304–28; art exhibition in Delhi 16.517, 22.349–50; bringing Buddhists together 8.244–5; *Buddha Jayanti* special publications 8.367–8, 8.369–70, 8.373, 8.375–6; celebrated by the whole Buddhist world 7.454–5, 12.610; celebration (the next year) in Thailand 8.249–50; celebrations in Kalimpong, *see under* Kalimpong; an opportunity and a challenge 8.217; commemorative volume, *see under* Bapat; delegates to the Delhi celebrations from Communist countries 22.348–9; inner preparation 8.218–19; it can be seen as marking an end or a beginning 8.225–6; *Maha Bodhi* journal editorials 8.216–30, 22.308–11; the Maha Bodhi Society's celebrations 22.306; the need for inner preparation: meditation 22.309–10; the tour of the Eminent Buddhists, *see under* Eminent Buddhists; preparations 8.216–17; prophecy that it would mark a revival for Buddhism 8.216, 22.315; publications marking the event 8.367–8, 8.369–70, 8.373, 8.375–6, 25.5; renovation of the holy places 8.260; sponsored by the government of India 7.466–7, 8.228–30, 8.238, 9.133, 22.304–6; why not celebrate by showing kindness to birds and animals? 8.222–4

OTHER FESTIVALS

Dharma Day (Dharmacakra-Pravartana Day, Aṣāḍha)
celebrating the impact of the Buddha on us 11.418–19; celebration in Kalimpong 8.658; celebration of the Buddha's first discourse 2.228, 3.75, 3.403, 11.410; in London (1971) 11.410; putting a book on the shrine 16.59; rejoicing in the Dharma jewel 11.395; Sangharakshita reads 'The Caves of Bhájá' 24.237; the second most important festival of the Buddhist year 22.151

Sangha Day (Kārttika)
it commemorates the end of the rainy season retreat 3.403–5; celebration at the London Buddhist Centre (1979) 24.161; rejoicing in the Sangha jewel 11.395

Padmasambhava Day
celebration following the Tibetan tradition 12.286; celebration in New Zealand 24.129–30; unveiling the Nālandā crest at the London Buddhist Centre 12.317; why it is celebrated 12.323, 12.334–6; widely celebrated at Triratna centres 26.673

the Buddha's birthday
celebration in Calcutta (1896) 8.53–4; celebration in Japan 2.227–8; Sangharakshita's campaign to have it recognized as a holiday in India 21.394; later (2017) a public holiday in about half of the Indian states 21.630 (n121)

FWBO (Triratna) Day
beginning to see ourselves, what do we see? 12.462; the importance of the celebration 12.649–50, 12.676, 12.678; 'A Buddhist Dawn in the West' 12.xvi, 12.363–84; launch of *Living Ethically* 11.722; 'Twenty Years on the Middle Way' 12.385–95

other brief references
celebration of the Buddha's descent from the Trayastriṃśa Heaven 2.228; Magha Pūrṇimā 22.93–4; New Year festivals 2.179, 2.219, 4.108

fetishism religious 22.93; sexual 12.230

fetters *see* ten fetters

feudal system *see under* medieval

Feuerstein, Georg 24.531

fever-spirits *see pūtanās*

Ficino, Marsilio introduction 2.739–40 (n662), 23.524 (n359); *Commentary on Plato's Symposium on Love* 24.389; a great man of Florence 23.315; Sangharakshita drawn to him 2.536

fiction Aurobindo on reading novels 26.121; Buddhaghosa might have made a good novelist 12.279; detective stories 17.66; enjoy Mahāyāna *sūtras* like poetry or novels 16.57; epistolary novels 12.696–7; 'faction' is an illegitimate, even immoral,

literary genre 24.566; fiction can enlarge our sympathies 26.114; give up reading cheap fiction 26.183; a good novel can widen our mental horizon and indirectly teach a moral lesson 24.541; imaginary characters: essence without existence 13.582–3; magic realism 24.529, 24.745 (n694); the novel as a thought adventure (Lawrence) 26.256; the novel is an occasion for a kind of wisdom 19.70; Sangharakshita's attempt at writing a novel 20.88, 24.417, 24.525; Sangharakshita's reading of fiction, *see under* Sangharakshita XII/books read; science fiction, *see* science fiction

fidelity the difference between fidelity and attachment 11.580; in friendship 14.471, 18.336; in love and marriage 3.563, 15.155; to oneself 3.563–4, 3.572; to ideals 3.564, 3.572, 14.471; to other people 3.564, 3.567–8, 3.572; examplars of fidelity 3.570–2, 20.464; the faithful Tārā 14.471; how is fidelity tested? 3.568–72; involves consistency over time 3.564–5, 3.567–8; lack of self-awareness stops us being faithful 3.565; a quality of the true individual 3.563, 3.565; sexual fidelity 3.566–8, 11.579–80

Fields, Rick 24.374

films

introduction
appreciation of cinema 23.471–2, 24.38–9; cinematic anti-heroes 19.410; the emotional muck-heaps of the popular film 26.130; film as an art form 23.471–2, 24.38–9; a film as an illustration of the nature of things 1.104; horror, violent, and pornographic films 17.181, 17.666, 26.362–3; the limitations of the genre are inherent in all art 7.244–5; 'a love for the stage which I never felt for the screen' 20.86; a major art form 23.472, 24.39; nights at the cinema: 'We had a really good cry' 14.471; potentially a power for good 8.212; purveyors of pseudo-artistic trash 26.115; their morally corrupting influence 8.212–13; their value is in their capacity to enlarge our sympathies 24.390; the unskilfulness of some humorous films 15.372

the Indian film industry
Jairaj, an actor in Tamil films 22.279–80; meeting people in the Bombay film industry 22.279–82; Sangharakshita is consulted on the making of *Ajanta* 21.399–401, 22.267

Buddhism and films
an Abhidharma view of the universe like a motion picture 14.91; the Dalai Lama asks to see a Marx Brothers film 22.365; film shows in Kalimpong 21.57–8, 22.104–5, 22.113–18; the filming of the Buddha's life can never achieve perfection, but what can? 7.246–7; a monk tries to get into Bengali films 21.375; monks not supposed to see films 22.13; the Panchen Lama asks to see *War and Peace* 22.365; 'The Question of Buddhist Films' (1954 article) 7.240–8; Tibetans are great cinema-goers 22.114–15; to make or not make Buddhist films? 8.125–6

FWBO and Sangharakshita films
'An Opening of the Heart' 12.513, 12.739–40 (n335); appearance on Thames Television's *Night Thoughts* 24.243–8; Clear Vision Trust 24.583, 24.615 (n58); *The Enlightened Englishman* 24.319; a film about the LBC building project 24.164–5, 24.647–8 (n201); film of Il Convento retreat 24.256; *In the Footsteps of Ambedkar* 10.lii, 10.liii–iv, 10.353, 24.312, 24.319; *In the Realm of the Lotus* 26.215–16; Lights in the Sky Films 24.615 (n58); Mokshapriya's video for the Karuna Trust 24.319; poetry readings (five short TV programmes) 24.388; reluctantly accepting film as a medium of communication 2.535–6; 'Why are we here?' (TV programme) 24.319–20; a wish to have a film cooperative 24.39

films seen
Africa Speaks 25.52; *The American Friend* 24.390; Antonioni's *Red Desert* 23.471; Arnold Schwarzenegger 24.461–2; *Battleship Potemkin* 24.582; *Buddhism in China* 24.38; Buñuel's *Simon of the Desert* 24.318–19; *Caravaggio* 24.323; *Citizen Kane* 24.582; *Close Encounters of the Third Kind* 24.104; *The Cup* (Tibetan film) 12.656; Walt Disney's *Fantasia* 26.504, 26.670–1; films of D. H. Lawrence stories 24.525; *Gandhi* 10.311, 10.337–8; *Gone With the Wind* 21.409, 21.630 (n125); *Henry V* 23.206, 24.390; *Jesus of Montreal* 24.390; *The Law of Desire* 24.323; *Lawrence of Arabia* 24.390; *The Lord of the Rings* (animation) 24.66; *Marie Waleska* 21.409, 21.630 (n125); *McCabe and Mrs Miller* 24.390; *The Moderns* 24.323, 24.390; *The Navigator* 24.390; *Paris by Night* 24.390; Pasolini's *The Gospel According to Matthew* 13.650; Pasolini's *Theorem* 16.504; *Rob Roy* 26.363; Ken Russell's *Women in Love* 23.472; the Russian film of *Hamlet* 23.175; *Salaam Bombay* 24.323; *Sinbad the Sailor* 24.429; Tarkovsky, Andrei 24.389, *Stalker* 24.582; *Torch Song Trilogy* 24.390; *Walkabout* 24.98; Westerns 22.114; *The Woodlanders* 24.582; *Yeelen* 24.390

Findlay, Professor F. N. 26.674

a finger pointing to the moon Buddhism 3.359, 7.34, 7.44, 7.158; disciples who fastened their attention on the finger 14.318; mistaking the finger for the moon in relation to Zen 13.333; no less foolish than carrying the raft 1.205; the Perfection of Wisdom texts make us look at the moon 14.321, 14.584; religions frequently mistake the finger for the moon 7.159, 13.437; Sangharakshita's statement about his beliefs (1944) a finger pointing to the moon 7.38; thinking that thoughts *are* reality, we mistake the finger for the moon 19.377; you pass from a religious teaching to a spiritual experience 3.166–7; your view is a finger pointing to the moon 15.334, 19.446

Finland Marxism 4.442; the composition of the Threefold Puja 11.xviii, 24.49; poem prompted by a painting in Helsinki 25.334; reticence 10.240; Sangharakshita's visit 24.78, 26.214; 'Sequence in a Strange Land' (poem) 25.336–7; translations into Finnish 11.xvi–xvii, 26.214

Fintry Trust 23.525 (n366)

fire

physical fire
the brahmins who claimed they could kindle fire through reciting mantras 19.62–3; fire and Christianity 13.596–7; a fire during a lecture 26.621–2; the Indian belief that an extinguished fire passes from a gross to a subtle state 10.655–6; is sitting watching a fire meditation? 5.49; it is an offence for a *bhikkhu* to kindle a fire 18.390; 'Meditation on a Flame' 8.264–5, 22.458, 25.291

element
associated with the colour red and the shape of a cone 13.153, 16.147; correlated with the psychic centre at the heart 16.147; giving back the fire element 3.349; neither earth nor water nor fire nor wind' … 1.68, 10.459, 10.632–6, 16.389; symbolism 13.154, 16.145–6; *see also under* six element practice

as metaphor
'all beings in the Three Realms enslaved in a prison of fire' 18.588–90; as a fire can be kindled from any fuel, all castes are capable of spiritual attainment 14.42; being on fire with reality 14.590; the bodhisattva: 'Like a fire his mind constantly blazes up' 1.396, 8.xvii, 8.95, 20.124; to the Buddha: 'Burn as a Fire for men!' 25.296; the *Dhammapada* should be engraved on our hearts in letters of fire 26.45; the flame of spiritual aspiration 1.8; a halo of flames round a Tibetan Father-Mother figure 1.197; a heart on fire with remorse 1.411; Milton's inspiration like a great furnace 26.69; peace is a fire 26.53; 'Test my words as the goldsmith tests gold in the fire', *see under* gold; 'Yet shall my soul burn upward like a fire' 25.271

symbolism
Amitābha's mantra like a narrow white path between fire and water 1.338; the Buddha walking in the air emitting fire and water, *see under* miracles/twin miracle; the circle of flames around the mandala 12.220; contrast between tending the sacred fire and the light of inner practice 2.697 (n350); energy moving upwards (stupa symbolism) 13.154–5; falling into the fire of attachment, like moths in the flame 10.610–11; fire and water are cosmic opposites: alchemy 12.184–5; in the *White Lotus Sūtra* 16.70–1; one flame being lit from another 12.646, 12.753 (n444); Pāṇḍaravāsinī's robe on fire 19.570; positive symbolism of fire: change, transformation, spiritual rebirth 16.70; *rasanā* corresponds to fire 18.76; the symbolism of the burning of the body of Dabba Mallaputta 10.653–4; symbolism of the flames that surround wrathful deities 11.18, 16.71; tending the sacred fire of reflection 26.145; the fire of transmutation 12.221; the true fire burns within, on the fuel of meditation 1.62; turban on fire 1.124, 7.392; the union of fire and water, *see under* alchemy; 'When the Sun rises do you not see a round Disk of fire …?' (Blake) 11.725

fire altar *see under* altars

Fire Sermon *see under Saṃyutta Nikāya*/ famous *suttas*

firebrand an aphorism is like a firebrand 26.3; a whirling firebrand as a metaphor for how senses perceive objects 17.406–8; the world like a ring produced by a firebrand 14.204, 17.350–1

fire-worshipper (Uruvelā Kāsyapa) *see* Uruvelā Kāsyapa

First Council *see under* councils

First World War the destruction of the heroic ideal 3.47; D. H. Lawrence's response to the war 8.542–3; poets 26.393; Sangharakshita's father in the war 20.488, 25.68

Fischer, Leopold *see* Bharati, Swami

Fischer, Norman v24

fish the boys who tormented fish, *see under Udāna*; the Daoist sage who went fishing without using any bait 14.518–19; 'a fish floundering on the bank' (*Dhammapada*) 18.542, 22.223; the fish and the turtle 10.685–6 (n175); the fish who were reborn as gods 16.246; 'Goldfish' (poem) 25.225; golden-eyed fish in the ocean 19.340; the great fish Timiratipiṅgala finds room in the great ocean 14.91; Jalavāhana saves 10,000 fish from dying of drought (*Jātaka*) 14.244; the king of fishes (in Milarepa's songs) 18.29–30; monks 'spreading Buddhism' by teaching people to eat fish 12.252–3; trapped by craving like fish in the mouth of a net 10.617–18; the visualized form emerging and disappearing like a fish leaping from the sea 5.583, 5.600, 13.96

fish-basket 16.470–1

Fisher King 16.219

Fiske, Mother Adele v23

fist becoming Enlightened like opening the closed fist of the ego 17.351–2; 'I am not one who has the closed fist of the teacher' 10.624

Fitzgerald, Edward 14.289, 26.445, 26.661, 26.735 (n346)

Fitzgerald, F. Scott 24.374

five ascetics (*parivrājakas*) *see under* disciples/of the Buddha

five *balas* (powers) canonical source 1.279, 11.369; the five spiritual faculties in their fully developed state 1.280, 10.568

Five Buddha mandala *see* mandala of the Five Buddhas

five *dharma-skandhas* 13.463

five *dharmas* (categories) 14.89, 14.213–14

five *dhyāna* factors list of the factors 9.200, 17.725 (n126); canonical references 4.708 (n321), 13.698 (n158), 16.601 (n119), 17.725 (n126); Buddhaghosa's description 17.518; the factors as present in the first *dhyāna* 5.238, 17.122–3; not to be taken too literally 2.110; their presence, and progressive absence, in the four *dhyānas* 4.490, 5.242–4, 10.159, 13.355, 17.582; they don't give the whole picture of what *dhyāna* is like 5.275; *see also vitarka-vicāra*; *sukha*; *prīti*; one-pointedness

five *dṛṣṭis* (views) 14.89

five elements *see under* elements

five eyes

introduction
description 2.295–6; as a hierarchy 14.314; do the Buddha's five eyes exist? (*Diamond Sūtra*) 14.496; Pāli sources 2.700 (n373); and perceptions of the Buddha 14.429, 14.430

(1) the eye of flesh (māṃsa-cakṣus)
the organ of physical sight 2.295, 14.314

(2) the divine eye (divya-cakṣus)
one of the supernormal powers 2.295–6; the Buddha uses his divine eye 10.456, 11.725; perceives the decease and rebirth of beings 14.314; Sangharakshita's experience 20.85–6; through it we experience the *rūpaloka* 12.559

(3) the eye of truth (dharma-cakṣus)
cognizes the true characteristics of *dharmas* 14.314; correlation with real Going for Refuge 2.482, 12.505; Koṇḍañña's 'Eye of Truth' was opened 2.700 (n372), 11.446–8; its opening is insight, Stream Entry 2.296, 3.330, 9.251–2, 9.253, 11.446; the realization that whatever has an origin has an end 11.446; shows the depth of the cognitive content of spiritual experience 2.301, 2.483, 9.256

(4) the eye of wisdom or Dharma Eye (prajñā-cakṣus)
arises when one becomes an *arhant* 2.296; knows by which teaching people will find the path to liberation 14.314; 'to attain the eye of the Dharma' 17.349

(5) the universal eye (samanta-cakṣus)
the 'Buddha Eye' 2.296; the direct intuition of the ultimate elements of existence 14.314; faculty of direct perception into the future 14.479

five factors (of meditation) *see* five *dhyāna* factors

five female Buddhas the five *prajñās*, the five great *ḍākinīs* 12.222, 18.59; four of them represent the four elements 15.139; *see also* Ākāśadhāteśvarī; Locanā; Māmakī; Pāṇḍaravāsinī; (Green) Tārā

five functional co-relations 17.495–7

five heinous crimes called 'deadly sins' 1.334, 1.343; consequences of committing them (*Itivuttaka*) 3.637–8 (n70); descending scale of offences 4.364, 18.503–4; and karma 2.72, 7.523; killing one's parents 15.409, 18.503–4; rebirth in Sukhāvatī despite having committed them 7.42–3; impossible to commit for someone possessing right view 3.637 (n70); a picture that didn't show the whole of the Buddha

regarded as wounding him 21.56–7; suggests an almost pathological state of antagonism to spiritual values 18.504

five hindrances (*nivaraṇa*)

WHAT ARE THEY?

introduction
description 1.152, 4.73, 11.122, 13.72; canonical sources 1.153, 13.677 (n27), 15.168–78; traditional images describing water in different states 1.152, 1.559, 10.159, 11.122–3

the nature of the hindrances
the battle with them personified by Māra 15.178; each clouds the lightness and clarity of perception 18.11; energy that is going to waste or getting stuck 15.216–17; the overlap between the hindrances and the fetters 15.203–4; they can be very subtle 5.337–8, 18.11; they prevent you from entering the *dhyānas* 17.119–21, 18.575–6; temporarily eradicated in *dhyāna* 15.203–4, 17.121; they tend to arise when we react mechanically to situations 15.172–3; the ultimate answer is that they are void 18.637

(1) craving for sensuous experience or material things (kāmacchanda)
arises from the accumulated force of your own karma 15.204; counteracting it 5.344–6; a hindrance with deep roots 13.72; so long as sense desires are present, absorption is not possible 5.323–5, 11.122; craving for material things, a very strong craving 1.557; you are aware of sense objects to some extent, but there must be no desire 17.119–20; *see also kāmacchanda*

(2) hatred (vyāpadā)
it's of the utmost importance that we get rid of it 12.391; the feeling of ill will when desire for sense experience is frustrated 11.122; includes antagonism of any kind 1.557–8, 13.72, 17.120; nothing so inimical to *dhyāna* as ill will 5.325–6

(3) restlessness and anxiety (uddhacca-kukkucca)
a nagging sense of insecurity 13.72; a hindrance of modern times 1.558; if you are prone to distraction, meditate in a slightly darkened room 15.171, 19.394; mental restlessness 5.327, 17.681; one of meditation's two great enemies 4.288–9, 19.380; oscillating between drowsiness and distraction 19.394–5; a state of continual fussing and bothering 11.122; you mustn't be agitated or worried about anything 17.120

(4) sloth and torpor (thīna-middha)
the afternoon is when one is most likely to feel sluggish 4.574–5, 4.578, 5.678–9; being overcome by lethargy and sleep, one falls into the power of Māra 10.532–3; the Buddha's advice about dealing with sleepiness in meditation 19.614 (n155); causes of drowsiness 5.678–80, 19.394–5; half-heartedness 5.326–7; if prone to drowsiness, surround yourself with brightness 15.171, 19.394; if you're of sluggish temperament, think in terms of following the path 18.525; inertia and stagnation 1.558–9, 11.122, 13.72; may be produced by conflict 10.533, 19.394; the *nāḍis* and *prāṇas* dispel drowsiness and distractions 19.155; resistance to making effort 5.679–80; resisting sloth brings joy 5.382; one of meditation's two great enemies 4.288–9, 19.380; oscillating between drowsiness and distraction 19.394–5; overcoming sleepiness in meditation 5.332, 5.387–8, 15.171; without wisdom, *śamatha* can become dull and drowsy 19.159; you must be very alert, light, aware, bright 17.120

(5) doubt and indecision (vicikicchā)
basically a lack of trust 11.122; almost pretended, culpable doubt 10.577; dealing with not wanting to meditate 5.373–7; 'Ought I really to be meditating at all?' 5.283, 5.327–8, 17.120; an unwillingness to make up one's mind, commit oneself 1.559, 13.72, 15.175–6, 26.60; wondering whether some other meditation might be better 11.711

DEALING WITH THEM

tackling the hindrances
don't rationalize them, but be honest with yourself 1.558; insight will eventually cut the root of the five hindrances 17.121; it is essential to keep the initiative 15.174; the language of overcoming the hindrances 11.658; make sure that none of them is present before starting to meditate 5.283–4; overcoming them with determination 5.328; some people wonder how anyone could be happy without them 5.342; the joy of release from the hindrances 5.342–3; what a mind free of all hindrances is like (traditional images) 2.670 (n80), 5.341–2

antidotes
a summary of ways to deal with the hindrances 18.637; canonical references 1.559, 1.637 (n453), 4.702 (n280), 5.347, 19.110, 19.599 (n52); described in Buddhaghosa's *Visuddhimagga* 15.171; awareness should be enough to shift mild hindrances 15.171; becoming aware of

them before they take hold 15.178; the effort of meditation is to remove the hindrances 4.160; an example of how to apply the antidotes 10.226–7; they are useful first aid, but you also need to consider your lifestyle 15.171–2; ways to 'denourish' the hindrances 1.637 (n453)

(1) consider the consequences
reflect on the consequences of the unskilful mental state 1.559–60, 19.110; Śāntideva's advice 4.382

(2) cultivate the opposite
introduction 5.344–7; canonical reference 13.685 (n70); is it similar to the Tantric approach? 5.352; an alternative: reflecting that both hindrance and its opposite are *śūnyatā* 13.174; example: cultivating *mettā* to counteract hatred 1.560, 4.381–2, 5.326, 19.110; aesthetic appreciation to counteract craving for sensuous experience 5.344–6

(3) sky-like attitude
cultivate a witness-like attitude 1.560; don't enjoy it or gloat over it, just let it float away 4.382; let it go 19.110; this is one way of applying right effort 11.689

(4) suppression
just say 'No!' 4.382; quite a positive method 19.110–11; suppression, not repression 1.560, 4.382; the suppression of the hindrances (second stage of meditation) 13.72

(5) Go for Refuge to the Buddha
if all else fails 1.561, 5.354–5; this is Sangharakshita's own addition to the list 5.347; the Vajrayāna approach 5.352–3

(6) ask yourself why you are feeling like this
seeing the state as incompatible with what you really want 5.347–9

five *indriyas* *see* five spiritual faculties

five *jñānas* (wisdoms, knowledges)

introduction
eight *vijñānas* transformed into the five *jñānas* 2.280–1, 16.581; the five aspects of fully developed *prajñā* 10.176; the five 'awarenesses' (Guenther) 18.598; in a hymn to Tārā 17.143; insight into the five wisdoms 11.126–7; naming five aspects illuminates the wisdom of the Buddha 13.304; realizing the five knowledges (on the Tibetan Buddhist path) 12.297; represented in the *vajra* 13.182–3; transforming negative mental states into the five wisdoms 5.352; why the wisdoms are identified separately 18.599, 18.606, 19.152

(1) the wisdom of the dharmadhātu
Vairocana's wisdom 3.373, 16.581; corresponds to consciousness (*skandha*), space (element), and ignorance (poison) 13.184; the equivalent of the absolute *ālaya* 2.281, 12.177, 17.488, 18.605–6; knowledge of the whole cosmos as being pervaded by one reality 4.164, 12.213, 13.182; knowledge of the totality of things 11.127; form is emptiness, emptiness is form 4.164, 14.397; the 'Wisdom of Reality' 18.597–8

(2) the mirror-like wisdom
Akṣobhya's wisdom 3.374, 16.581; be like a mirror, reflecting everything without distortion 11.127, 12.158, 18.598–9; corresponds to water (element), form (*skandha*), aversion (poison) 13.184; doesn't mean reflecting without feeling 10.463–4, 18.599; the Enlightened mind understands the nature of things, as a mirror reflects objects 4.165; like the tower Sudhana reaches in the *Gaṇḍavyūha Sūtra* 4.165; not a cold hard surface, but a deeply responsive awareness 15.202–3; the pure, perfect objectivity of the Enlightened mind 4.165, 12.214, 13.182; relative *ālaya* transformed into 2.281, 12.177, 14.315, 17.488, 18.605–6; the senses are a mirror 19.192–6

(3) the wisdom of equality (samatā-jñāna)
Ratnasambhava's wisdom 2.117, 3.374, 16.581, 19.191; beyond all dualism 15.224; the Enlightened mind sees things with no preferences, no reactions 12.214–15; *kliṣṭa-mano-vijñāna* transformed into 2.280–1, 12.177, 14.315, 17.488, 18.605; like the sun, the Enlightened mind shines its compassion on 'good' and 'bad' alike 4.165; seeing that all things are *śūnyatā* 11.127, 13.182, 18.599; similar to *upekkhā* (equanimity) 5.215

(4) the all-distinguishing or discriminating wisdom
Amitābha's wisdom 3.374, 16.581; the Enlightened mind sees the diversity of things 4.166, 11.127, 12.215–16; *mano-vijñāna* transformed into 2.281, 12.177, 14.315, 17.487–8, 18.605; objective discrimination at the highest level 17.282; you see the unique features of every individual thing 13.182–3, 18.599–600

(5) the all-performing wisdom
Amoghasiddhi's wisdom 3.375, 16.581; the Enlightened mind devotes itself to the welfare of all beings 4.166, 12.217; five sense *vijñānas* transformed into 2.280, 12.176–7, 14.315, 17.487, 18.605; the knowledge of what is to be done for the

spiritual welfare of living beings 11.127; spontaneous activity, like play or dance 13.183; wisdom is active 18.604

five *kāyas* 17.146, 17.729 (n164)

five kinds of action 14.239–40

five (or ten) *kleśas* (poisons, passions)

the nature of the kleśas
what *kleśa* means 11.401, 17.596; all Buddhas 'when they started ... were not quite free from passions ...' 4.49–50; the bigger the heap you start off with, the greater your realization 4.467; a bodhisattva should not be afraid of them 14.186; a brotherhood of thieves 4.380–1; emotional and intellectual aspects of the *kleśas* 18.449–51; how does the flower of Enlightenment come from their black root? 25.73–4; 'I will not bow before my everlasting enemies, the passions' 4.370; the inner deceptions 18.574; the fever of the passions 10.515; most people are subject to them from time to time 26.657; our states of mind most of the time 18.103; people might think of them as only natural 19.227–8; a rather negative way of looking at the spiritual life 19.227; rightly called five poisons 26.645; they are very nasty things, and they go right down deep 25.75; they stand between you and Enlightenment 18.448; try to see where they come from 4.374–6; we are reborn because our minds are dominated by them 11.401; we suffer when we are subject to them 17.637

traditional references
an elaboration of the three roots 18.449; defined in the Abhidharma 14.89; Avalokiteśvara swallowed the poison of the *kleśas* 7.580 (n190), 26.641–2; in the *Bodhicaryāvatāra* 4.370, 4.373–5, 4.380–1; in the *Śāriputra-abhidharma-śāstra* 14.74

correlations
correlation with Blake's four Zoas 8.556–8, 26.345–7; correspondence with the wisdoms of the five Buddhas 13.184; relationship with the three *āsravas* 18.449; represented by one of the *vajra*'s sets of five spokes 13.183

conquering the kleśas
at least the grosser *kleśas* have been eliminated once insight is attained 17.132–3; the bodhisattva should forsake them 14.153; the bodhisattva's vow 4.73–81; the Buddha's teaching as medicine for the five poisons 26.645; Buddhist ethics: an intricate net woven to catch the passions 7.117; ceasing to offer any resistance to them 17.676–7; experience it, then ask where is it coming from? 4.376; facing them directly by visualizing a wrathful form 5.353, 13.173–4; the Hīnayāna idea of Nirvāṇa 16.7, 16.63; how they are overcome 11.403–5; it is not enough to destroy evil passions 7.35; 'May I eradicate all passions' 4.73–81; preventing the waves of passion rising 8.266; rooted out by wrathful deities 17.318; subduing the army of the five poisons 18.103; to be killed, not just suppressed 25.445; to be transformed into the five *jñānas* 19.227; transformed from hindrances to helps 1.385–6; they must be removed because they obstruct and waste energy 14.534; we need to really feel that they're to be got rid of 4.374–5; wisdom is designed to cut off the *kleśas* 17.131; would also involve the attainment of *bodhi* 16.63; you have to learn to control them to see their emptiness 13.174

antidotes (meditation practices)
full introduction 3.123–31, 3.340–51, 4.73–81; include both *śamatha* practices and 'insight' practices 18.449; nectar-like antidotes 19.228; recollection of the Buddha 4.381; source (Mr Chen) 3.646 (n134), 3.675 (n311), 5.29–30

see also
distraction; aversion; craving; ignorance; conceit; Māra the personification of the *kleśas*, *see under* Māra/four Māras

five *niyamas* introduction 3.98–101, 3.316, 4.396–9, 17.55; sources 3.644 (n113), 3.672 (n296), 16.422, 16.621 (n285); all act on each other, and are acted on by the *ālaya-vijñāna* 2.70; can be depended upon not to change 16.84; can be divided into three groups, governed by cyclical and/or spiral reactions 12.547–8; counter the allegation that Buddhists are indifferent to human suffering 2.69–70; example of a fever to show the different *niyamas* in operation 2.69, 3.316, 4.398, 17.714 (n59); five types of conditionality, only one of which consists of ethical choices 17.478–9; the nibbānic order of existence 7.151, 7.588 (n252); the *niyamas* and the *nidānas* 12.547–8; the *niyamas* guard against a tendency to see karma in a mechanical way 3.xiv; only a Buddha can know whether or not karma is a cause 4.398; only found in Theravāda 16.422; Mrs Rhys Davids' exposition 3.672 (n296), 4.399, 16.596 (n78), 16.621 (n285)

five pillars of the FWBO/Triratna *see under* Triratna II/introduction

five poisons *see* five *kleśas*

five powers *see* five *balas*

five *skandhas* (Pāli *khandhas*)

introduction
definition 1.173–4, 3.655 (n189), 15.57, 15.181, 15.187; description 2.97–100, 4.28, 11.401; analysis of the human being 2.335; as a Buddhist one needs to be very familiar with the list 15.188; why did the Buddha analyse existence into five *skandhas*? 17.444, 17.448

their nature
boundless 14.600; emptiness 1.175, 3.217, 14.561–2; the keynote is impermanence 15.183; the lamp-flame an analogy for their continuity 7.210–11; like a mirage 17.359; middle way between ultimately real and illusory 17.626; no aspect of personality that does not fall into one of these categories 3.655 (n189); not nucleated by a permanent, unchanging ego-identity 1.139; not separable components but five sets of processes 15.188; not unchanging 'things' but a congeries of related processes 2.97; only mental constructions 1.267; painful 1.130; a provisional model that is not ultimately valid 14.548; the psychophysical organism 1.109, 3.198; temporary condensations of energy 14.548; their identity depends on to their relationship with things other than themselves 17.347; they are subject to clinging, hence are suffering 3.655 (n189); they arise from the conception of 'I' 17.343, 17.347; they cannot be said either to exist or not to exist 17.377; they do not represent absolute realities 14.563; they represent the whole of conditioned existence 4.28–9, 7.130–1, 11.401; unoriginated, like a magical show 14.577; the world of the *skandhas* is under the sway of death 11.401

correlations
correlations with other sets of five, both microcosmic and macrocosmic 2.336; correspondence with the wisdoms of the five Buddhas 13.184; the doctrine at the hub of the wheel of the Dharma 1.175; and the five elements 13.150

the history of the teaching
their importance in the Buddhist tradition 15.180–1, 15.188; doctrine held in common by Theravāda and Mahāyāna 7.631; *Alagaddūpama Sutta*: 'Form is not yours, O monks' 1.173; *Dhammacakkappavattana Sutta*: 'the five aggregates subject to clinging are suffering' 3.655 (n189); *Heart Sūtra* 1.175, 3.655 (n189), 4.29, 14.359–60; *Satipaṭṭhāna Sutta* 1.101, 15.179–89; the burden of the five *khandhas* (*Saṃyutta Nikāya*) 13.386–7; Abhidharma 14.79, 14.83, 14.84, 14.90, 15.187, 17.448; the Yogācāra said that there is only one *skandha*, *vijñāna* 17.482; the *skandhas* and the 'seeds' of the *ālaya-vijñāna* 1.369; the Buddha's *khandavāda* logically suggests Nāgārjuna's *śūnyavāda* 7.132; Perfection of Wisdom 14.153, 14.577, 14.587, 14.600; represented by one of the *vajra*'s sets of five spokes 13.183; symbolized by a boat and passengers on the wheel of life 1.109, 2.75, 15.200, 17.502

the limitations of the teaching
the Abhidharma adopted a different classification 12.144; inadequate to the complexities of the psychophysical organism 15.187; inconsistencies exposed 1.320; perhaps not the best formulation of the principle it is meant to convey 15.188

self-view and the skandhas
the arrogance of identifying with the five *skandhas* 17.604–5; don't make the mistake of seeing them as substantial 17.474–5; identifying with the five *skandhas* 10.481; misconception of the true nature of the *skandhas* (as subject to the *lakṣaṇas*) 17.350; none of the five *skandhas* is self 11.755 (n201); right view: understanding the impermanence of the five *skandhas* 7.521; self-view means identifying with a cross-section of the flow of *skandhas* 17.625; twenty forms of self-view associated with the five *skandhas* 17.620–1; the wrong view of a self that exists outside or within the *skandhas* 14.438; the wrong view of thinking that the *skandhas* are the self 13.393, 14.439; you see an 'I' in them like seeing a reflection in a mirror 17.346–8

nāma-rūpa
place in the twelve *nidānas* 3.198; *skandhas* divided into *rūpa* and *nāma* 15.187; we need to pay attention to both our mental state and our physical condition 10.317; *rūpa* is body and *nāma* is mind, divided into *vedanā*, *saṃskāra*, *samjñā*, *vijñāna* 10.231

reflecting on the skandhas
as considered by different character types 2.144; as part of the process of analysis 1.101, 1.109; practising contemplating them separately 15.181; reflection on the *skandhas* (*Satipaṭṭhāna Sutta*) 15.181–2; contemplating them 'internally' and 'externally' 15.182–3; mind dissociated from the *skandhas* to become free 18.614–15

no skandhas
bodhicitta not included in the *skandhas* 4.28; Hīnayāna followers should be happy to realize that they don't exist 17.353–4; no trace of them remains in Nirvāṇa 7.168; the Tathāgata cannot be identified with the five *skandhas* 14.550

see also
rūpa; *vedanā*; *samjñā*; *saṃskāras*; *vijñāna*

five spiritual faculties (*indriyas*)

introduction
description 1.279–94, 3.296–314, 9.213–14, 9.396–7, 10.201, 11.477–9, 12.65, 13.328; etymology of *indriya* 3.297; Conze's translation 'cardinal virtues' misses the connection with the senses 3.298; canonical sources 1.281, 3.669 (n281), 11.369, 17.757–8 (n391); all five must be regarded as one whole, which is *you* 17.59–60; Abhidharma analysis 14.84; analogy with five senses 3.297–8, 9.213; the bodhisattva as exemplar 1.395; the Buddha gave the teaching to integrate and unite the faculties 14.443; Buddhist movements must develop all five 11.478–9; a complete harmonious unfoldment of all the aspects of the human being 12.283–4; embryonic and in need of development 3.298–9; from being dominated by the senses, one is guided by the five spiritual faculties 1.280; illustrated by a man jumping across a river 4.474; they constitute the whole of the Buddha's teaching 1.295; spiritual progress depends on their emergence 17.10–13; the teaching makes clear Buddhism's emphasis on wholeness 15.625

balancing the faculties
all-round development 26.40; in two pairs, with mindfulness as the balance 1.292–3, 1.393, 11.477–9, 12.65, 13.328, 23.37; balancing *samādhi* and *vīrya* 17.60–8, 19.551; the Buddha advises Soṇa to tune them like a lute 1.293, 7.489, 9.561 (n232); equalization through mindfulness 1.293–4, 3.309–10, 12.25, 13.328; perhaps after all mindfulness can go to extremes 17.82–3; the importance of balance 12.25; the work of spiritual life 26.629; you have to develop all of them, not just one (more the Hindu view) 17.134

cultivating the faculties
full development of them makes one an *arhant* 7.489; nurturing them: five conditions for spiritual growth, as for a plant 3.312–14; recapitulating the history of Buddhism 1.393; the sangha provides opportunities to develop them 3.312; when you cultivate them, you're not seeing a mechanical universe 17.118

as a path
as successive stages of the path 1.291–2, 7.489–90; developed in sequence: a path of regular steps 17.83–4, 17.136–7; in relation to a path of five stages 5.45–6, 17.458; Western conditioning leads us to think of developing them in parallel 14.443

in relation to other systems
compared to the four principal yogas of Hinduism 3.310–12, 14.443; correspondence between the five senses and the five spiritual faculties 17.13; correspondence with the schools of the Mahāyāna 1.277–393, 13.328–9; the first four compared to Blake's fourfold vision 8.555; in the *bodhipakṣya-dharmas* 1.279; held in common by Theravāda and Mahāyāna 7.531; the same group, fully developed, appears as the five *balas* (powers) 1.279, 10.568; a schema to differentiate schools of Buddhism 1.279, 1.292–9, 1.393, 7.489

see also
faith (*śraddhā*); wisdom (*prajñā*); *vīrya* (vigour); *samādhi* (one-pointedness); mindfulness (*smṛti*)

five stages *see* path of five stages

five stores (methods by which the bodhisattva liberates beings) 14.181–2

flags Buddhist flag 8.39, 9.292, 18.536, 22.92; *dharmacakra* on the Indian flag 7.447, 8.xxviii, 8.323, 9.355; spiritual life is like climbing a greasy flagpole 4.200, 4.213

flattery flattery in the hope of a gift 17.278, 17.659; a monk flatters a king in Nepal 21.302–3; monks feel they must flatter lay people 19.481; its part in a hierarchical society 17.278; we flatter people to win approval and also out of fear 17.278

Flaubert, Gustave 11.335

Fletcher, John 24.374

flexibility and pliancy acting with ease and flexibility 17.166; meditation makes the mind more flexible and pliable 19.89–90; mindfulness: a certain pliancy of mind 15.106; flexibility in everyday life 19.59–60, 19.62; flexibility of mind 15.274; the parts of speech of English are interchangeable, giving it great flexibility 19.238–9; plan things provisionally and flexibly 19.525; the pliancy of *praśrabdhi* 17.579; soak yourself in *dhyāna* to make

your mind pliable before trying to develop insight 5.458–9

flirtation Anandamayi's with her devotees 20.197; flirtation and the third precept 17.216; flirting on retreat 19.465; an old man flirts with much younger women 24.245–6

floods 'By faith the flood is crossed' 1.290, 25.15; campaign to stop the flooding of Nāgārjunikoṇḍa 8.163–4, 8.210, 8.680 (n95); 'flood of tears shed upon this long way' 1.130–1; floods, typhoons, and tidal waves 8.266; 'The Haystack in the Floods' 20.108; 'Let the wise man make for himself an island that no flood can overwhelm' 15.580; Nirvāṇa as an island in the flood 1.82; relief work after floods (Poona, 1961) 10.181

flow the concepts of existence and non-existence are inadequate to deal with the flow of reality 19.376–7; 'the feast of reason and the flow of soul' 3.71; the flow of energy, *see under* energy/working with energy; self-view means identifying with a cross-section of the flow of *skandhas* 17.625; freely flowing energy 18.322; how to get your energy flowing in accordance with the truth 19.17; letting your natural desires flow freely – an advanced stage 4.625; a natural flow from one stage to the next 3.278–9, 5.392–3; our lives are dedicated to seeking fulfilment by stemming the flow of experience 17.370; the psychical life is an absolutely continuous flow 7.209; sustaining a flow of skilful mental states while active 5.645, 5.649–50; an uninterrupted flow of skilful mental states 2.392, 18.423; the unobstructed flow of love and compassion 7.277; *see also citta-santāna* (flow of thoughts)

Flower Ornament Scripture *see Avataṃsaka Sūtra*

flowers and plants

IMAGINARY AND IMAGINATIVE FLOWERS

metaphorical and symbolic flowers
symbolism of flowers 9.324; a flower is a wonderful symbol, but it cannot be a teacher 18.632–3; the bodhisattva wears his righteousness as lightly as a flower 1.436; the Buddha like a forest grove putting forth its flowers 15.65; compassion, 'the unseen flower' (poem) 25.215; the corrupt flowers of evil 25.117; faith is like a sunflower turning towards the sun 21.463; the four main Mahāyāna schools represent the four petals of a flower 1.296–7; a goddess showers the assembly with flowers which stick to the *arhants* 16.538; imagery of plants 16.464; imagining yourself growing in a garden, unfolding your petals 18.105; living free from haste, like walking in the garden among tranquil flowers 8.291; Māra's weapons turn to flowers 3.277; mind-made flowers 14.143; receptivity to those above us, opening like a flower in the sun 4.174; self-awareness 'pure and bright as a flower' 18.252; the seven *bodhyaṅgas* emerge like the petals of a flower from the bud 15.225; sometimes you may feel as though you are unfolding like a flower 4.202, 18.105; spiritual life is like the plant and Enlightenment is like the flower 11.88; the ten precepts, the ten petals of a magnificent flower 2.396; the warrior ideal and the ideal of the flower 18.106

golden flower
of Awakening 7.171; of love 25.379; held up by the Buddha 1.523, 3.82, 4.148, 8.73, 8.484–5, 11.162, 12.231–2, 13.341, 14.16, 25.320, 25.404; trying to tie the golden flower of Enlightenment to the barren branches of our lives 11.81

poetic flowers
afternoon flowers 25.294; 'Every flower enjoys the air it breathes' 7.388; 'a flower, and the scent of a flower' 25.181; 'Flower in the crannied wall', *see under* Tennyson; the flower that will survive the destruction of the world 25.404; 'flowers that turn their faces to the sun' 25.277; 'Petals' (poem) 25.316; 'pleasures are like poppies spread' 26.398; shadows of flowers 25.352; stars unfolding like flowers 25.181; 'We hasten to gather our flowers' (Tagore) 1.129; 'with odours visited and annual flowers' 8.271; 'Yesterday's Blossoms' (poem) 25.402

FLOWERS TO OFFER AND REFLECT ON

appreciating flowers
autumn flowers in the Himalayas 7.335; Bach flower remedies 26.457–8; a bush surviving a storm 25.242; D. H. Lawrence on the love of flowers 26.186; needing to know a flower's Latin name 13.347, 25.242, 25.538; floral splendour in Rhyl 24.133; flowers in New Zealand 24.8; 'I loved all flowers for their beauty' 22.433; *samādhi* upon seeing a flower 2.113; Sangharakshita's life described in flowers 25.282; vandalism of breaking off armfuls of flowering branches 8.287; the wrong idea that religion is found in musty books, not in flowers, or music 7.283

reflecting on flowers
a flower is sacred, a tree holy, if you look at it with an illumined mind 7.284; 'Flowers' (*Dhammapada* chapter), *see* *Dhammapada*/chapter 4; flowers develop a 'soul' as a result of attention paid to them 8.423; hold up a flower to someone, and their experience will be different from yours 14.595; knowledge of a flower: classifying it or seeing it as a reminder of impermanence 17.351; the law which watches over the development of a flower 8.201; lunar influences on trees and plants 4.576; perceiving a flower 15.134; plants react to what is going on around them 4.541; the sum total of sensations 1.368

offering flowers
Flower Festival in Japan, celebrating the Buddha's birthday 2.227–8; flowers for the shrine 4.253; giving flowers 4.297–8; growing flowers for the shrine 22.432; *ikebana* 8.390, 11.118, 23.36, 23.420; *mandārava* flowers 11.234; offer a single flower and in principle you are on the path to Buddhahood 14.114, 16.41; offering flowers 3.340, 4.297–8, 8.161–2, 9.461, 11.234–5, 13.252–3, 20.259; *vajrapuṣpa*, the flower of Tantric ritual 13.180; 'white flower' (Tibetan offering) 13.255

PARTICULAR FLOWERS

lilies
the autumn lily 25.221; clasped in youth 25.282; 'Lilies that fester smell far worse than weeds' 1.443, 26.631

orchids
bamboo orchids 25.224; dealing bliss 25.282; the orchid-gatherer 22.432–3, 25.xxxviii, 25.130–7, 25.241; galaxies of waxen orchids 25.285; orchid collection 21.450; 'the orchid of spring' 2.130; too high to pluck 25.222

roses
agreement that a rose is beautiful 25.259; 'as on roses falls the rain' 6.xxix; can we describe even the colour of a rose? 2.54; cultivate an aphorism as you would a rose, but be careful not to remove the thorns 26.70; 'If you have a loaf of bread, sell half and buy a rose' 22.432; 'the Lady of the Three Roses' 26.619–20; members of the sangha are like roses blooming on a single rose bush 11.507; one fallen petal teaches the lesson of mortality 25.372; the perfect rose of Buddhahood 25.219; in the painting of the *Birth of Venus* 26.593; in the poem 'The Root Speaks' 25.72; the red rose doesn't boast of its beauty 25.240; the red roses of summer 25.lv; in Sangharakshita's painting of the Virgin Mary 26.593; set round with thorns 25.282; the scent of roses in India 26.493; the snow-white rose of celestial love (*Paradiso*) 26.318; the Summer rose 25.221; 'this red rose too sickly to live' 25.230; *The Two Roses* (short story) 25.524–32; we 'mingle with this world of pain,/ As on roses fall the rain' 25.43; the White Rose bright with morning dew 25.226; 'white rose of Mary's gift' 24.511

sunflowers
aureole of yellow flames 25.287; Blake's sunflowers 25.lvi; faith is like a sunflower turning towards the sun 21.463; and D. H. Lawrence 24.523–4; 'The Sunflower's Farewell' 25.lvi, 25.345

water-lilies
the water-lilies at Bodh Gaya 23.366; water-lilies at Padmaloka 24.66, 24.157, 25.lvii–lviii; water-lilies on the shrine in New Zealand 24.50

weeds
better to have the weeds of superstition than the sterile garden of rationalism 12.105; 'Lilies that fester smell far worse than weeds' 1.443, 26.631; lives that spring up 'as weeds between wet stones' 25.117; uprooting the weeds of craving 25.32–3; the weeds of practices and customs that grow up around Buddhism 25.31–2; wrong beliefs spring up again like weeds 8.303

other flowers
the aloes-bud, which flowers once a century 7.84; blue poppy 25.337; bluebells 25.282, 25.285, 25.456; cactuses 24.469, 24.475, 24.477; carnations in Italy 24.284; cherry-blossom 25.238; chrysanthemums 2.130, 20.34, 25.282; coral trees 24.13; crocuses 25.221; daffodils 14.507–8, 23.133, 23.231, 25.303; datura 25.282; delphiniums 26.441; gardenias 22.5, 22.8–9, 26.493; gentians 26.441; hibiscus 25.282; the holy Passion Flower 25.194; ivy 25.387; jasmine in Spain 24.439–40; lotuses, *see* lotuses; morning glory 19.70, 19.595 (n28); periwinkle flowers 25.294; red-hot pokers 25.434; rhododendrons 23.231; spring flowers 24.150, 25.282, 25.337; sprigs of wild thyme 23.291; tulips 25.194, 25.416; violets 23.457, 25.336, 26.184, 26.500

flute Aryadeva (French *sāmaṇera*) plays the flute 22.254–5; Krishna's flute 16.73, 16.594 (n66); Marsyas the flute-playing satyr 10.721–2 (n488); the novice monk who learned to play the flute 16.231; *The Sceptred Flute*, *see* Naidu

fly-whisk 3.48–9

folklore Buddhist 3.86; in the *Jātakas* 14.62–3; Indian 16.399; the primitive folklore of our indigenous culture 13.273

food

our dependence on food
'the one thing': all sentient beings depend on food 10.230–1; our dependence on the countryside for food 10.329; our dependence on other people for food 12.653; our need for food shapes our whole life 17.11–12

ethics of eating
basic but crucial – we eat every day 3.370, 4.110–11; eat without causing harm 3.370, 4.111–12; eating and the bodhisattva ideal 19.325–6; eating in moderation 16.552, 22.225, 23.188; eating without desire, hatred, or folly (*Vimalakīrti-nirdeśa*) 3.679 (n338); eat without neurotic craving 3.370, 4.113; the practices of different Buddhist traditions 19.325–6; the translation of monastic rules about eating in terms of lay life 12.124; vegetarianism, *see* vegetarianism

mindful eating
applying mindfulness of purpose to eating 15.361; bringing to mind a little verse, perhaps reflecting on the source of the food 4.113; the business lunch – incompatible with true awareness 1.573, 4.113, 12.557, 15.119; could symbolize the incorporation of gross energies into the spiritual life 18.427–8; eating should be quiet, peaceful, even meditative 4.113; Japanese tea ceremony 1.572–3, 4.113; mealtimes give us a good opportunity to practise mindfulness of the body 15.119; one should eat with full awareness of what one is doing 4.113; one eating mindfully every day might gain as much spiritually as from meditation 4.113; an opportunity to 'contemplate arising and vanishing factors in the body' 15.119; sensitivity to the tastes and textures of food 15.287; Theravādin practice 19.325–6; unmindful eating 11.625–6, 18.426

attitudes to food
attachment to the food you're used to 19.252; being able to tell the mental state of the person who cooked the food 18.312; best to shop for food when you are not feeling hungry 15.288; changing attitude to food as you start practising the Dharma 10.630; controlling intake in preparation for meditation 3.337; culinary taste 18.131; Dharmapala's practice with regard to food 8.12; eating 'only for the purpose of crossing over suffering' 24.725 (n573); eating the right kind of food helps one break through negative emotions 11.13; eating sweets 15.276–7; food and sex are likely to arouse almost everyone's interest 15.154; healthy diet for children 3.536–7; 'If you are suffering, don't just reach out for another chocolate' 3.227; neurotic desire for food 4.74, 12.554, 13.130, 18.633–4; 'The painted picture of a dumpling does not take one's hunger away' 8.496; practising indifference towards food 17.585; practising loving kindness towards oneself by eating wholesome food 4.112; sometimes we forget that the purpose of eating is just to keep the body going 4.112; the waste of food 10.322; we should never eat so much that our appetite is fully satisfied 17.290

Sangharakshita
learns to eat with his fingers in India 20.119; becomes vegetarian, *see under* vegetarianism; almost misses his lunch 22.348; gazpacho 24.428; over-zealous invitations in India 9.401–2

fasting
Abdullah Dougan 24.576–7; an important practice because it frees you from having to spend time eating 17.12; to practise experiencing pleasure without craving 19.383; Sangharakshita's experience of fasting 17.12, 20.303–4

prasad ('sacred' food)
at Anandamayi's ashram 20.186, 20.200; at the ashram of Swami Ramdas 20.329; does it really have a special effect on your mind? 18.429–30, 19.325–7; Sangharakshita distributes in Nepal 20.426; in South Indian temples, food offerings make meals for brahmins 20.251; symbolic and consumer value 11.240; *jutha* (leavings of food in Hinduism) 20.200

Buddhist traditions
almsfood, *see* almsfood; *bhojana-dāna* (food offering), *see under* offerings/the nature of offerings; 'A day of no working is a day of no eating' 2.555, 8.487, 11.318, 12.497, 17.73; feeding on rapture 18.50; the food of the Dharma 10.333; 'The food of *samādhi* is sufficient to sustain one' 18.620; four kinds of nutriment (Pāli canon) 22.285; monastic rules about eating, *see* Vinaya/other sets of rules/eating rules; offerings of food and drink in the puja 11.237; the pros and cons of eating in the shrine-room 18.426–8; the secret or sacramental feast 18.424–6, 19.485–6; taking in the Dharma compared to taking in food 10.231, 17.389–90; Ucchuṣma, the deity of the toilet 18.426; 'With rains of food and drink may I dispel

the anguish of hunger and thirst' 4.358; the way to sacramentalize eating and drinking 18.427–8, 19.485; you may feel hungry after meditating 18.634

contemplation of the loathsomeness of food
a means of attaining neighbourhood concentration 1.160; antidote to craving 4.77; among the forty *kammaṭṭhānas* 4.519; Buddhaghosa's graphic description 15.129, 24.725 (n573); designed to break attachment to eating 18.128; a doctor who pointed out the delicacy of the digestive process 2.65, 15.129; eating is quite a gross physical activity 18.426–7, 18.634; a parallel in Catholicism 24.455; Sangharakshita's experience 26.452

fools and foolishness anyone this side of Enlightenment is something of a fool 4.526; in Buddhism there is no such thing as the holy fool of Christianity 11.129, 15.350; in the *Dhammapada* ('spiritually immature'), *see Dhammapada*/chapter 5; 'The fear of the Lord' is not the beginning of wisdom but the crown of folly 26.155; a fool can give more advice in a day than a wise man can follow in a year 26.80; the fool is the wilful person, motivated by egoistic will 15.385; a fool may live with a wise man, but won't learn anything from him 18.516; the fool rushing about 'helping' the world without remembering emptiness makes things worse 7.414; 'A fool sees not the same tree that a wise man sees' 19.80; fooling other people can be dangerous, but fooling oneself is fatal 26.83; foolish talk 19.380; ignorance and foolishness 11.261; to know if someone is an *arhant*, you must be a wise man and not a fool 10.590, 19.100, 19.282; like King Lear's fool, a fool may have things to say 17.238; the oppression of foolishness 16.321; the painful experience of keeping company with a fool 10.649–50; someone can be highly intelligent but still a fool because his 'I'-sense is strong 15.385; there is no foolproof situation because into it you bring the fool, namely yourself 19.363; unskilful actions committed through foolishness 16.300; until you have insight, you can only act blindly and foolishly 19.354–5; you can't imagine a foolish *arhant* or bodhisattva 17.134–5; Zen stories and the tendency to laugh at the stupidity of others 17.279

Foot, Michael 24.216, 24.664 (n272)

football *see under* sport

Foote, G. W. 11.344

footprints the Buddha's footprint, *see śrīpāda*; 'footprints in the sands of time' 8.232; tigers' footprints 20.380, 20.398

'for the welfare of the many' (*bahujana hitāya*) the Buddha's words to his first sixty disciples 1.181, 2.23, 2.204, 4.86, 8.xviii, 8.444, 9.185, 14.537, 16.530, 21.473; and democracy 10.xxviii–ix; Dharmapala recites the words to his benefactor Mrs Foster 8.78; the motto of the *Maha Bodhi* journal 8.40–1; one of the Buddha's last teachings echoes the same phrase 2.29

forbearance *see kṣānti*

force the conscious mind tries to force the decision to gain Enlightenment on the rest of the psyche 3.40–1; don't force the *mettā bhāvanā* 5.617; *The Force of Character and the Lasting Life* 12.699, 12.760 (n499); the limitations of thought force us into contradictions 7.133; making connections with the *sādhana* in everyday life: don't force it 5.616–17; if *mettā* is present, force is unnecessary 3.450; the minority in society who try to harm others and need to be restrained 26.73; one is not following the path if one feels forced to follow it like a driven sheep 17.435; the quietest hints can have the force of commands 18.110; 'Relax – do not force your mind or body' 5.299–302; sometimes it would be better to make more effort, but don't force yourself too often 10.604–5; spiritual coercion is a contradiction in terms 3.447; teaching the Dharma through reason and persuasion, not force 7.383, 15.266–7; why did Buddhism not use political influence to enforce religious conformity? 7.383; you can't compel anyone onto the spiritual path 18.357; you can't create a spiritual community through coercion 18.488–9; you can't force people to follow your religion 15.623, 17.21–2; you can't force people to grow 16.72, 18.357–8

forces

inimical forces
the anti-creative force in meditation 12.644; *bhikkhus*' ability to ward off malign forces 3.409–10; the forces of death and destruction 4.638, 7.512; the forces of inertia within us are very strong 1.554–5; the forces of Māra 7.172; forces inimical to growth 16.349–50; occult forces 2.215–16

primordial, archetypal, elemental forces
the atom is a continuously changing dance of forces 2.85; William Blake's concern

with archetypal forces 16.533; *ḍākinīs*, forces of inspiration 12.294, 12.324–5, 18.59; elements: the forces of cohesion, undulation, radiation, and vibration 2.97; human beings are a battleground of opposing forces 16.393; integrating primordial forces 12.292–4, 12.323–5; jewels are produced only by the collision of immense forces 26.42; the samsaric force of the sexual urge 3.321; the scattered forces of the mind 7.358–9; subdued by Padmasambhava 12.323–32; to be brought within the sphere of spiritual life 12.332; the *yakṣa* an awe-inspiring natural force 10.451

forces for good
adhiṣṭhāna, a transmuting force 12.14; the arising of the *bodhicitta* 2.164, 4.32, 12.537–8; the bodhisattva 4.262, 7.155; the bodhisattva ideal 3.384; the Buddha's compassion 12.188–9; the Dharma as a living spiritual force 14.342; faith is the driving force of the higher evolution 18.275; the four great kings represent forces of balance and harmony 16.357; love is the only force strong enough to overcome hatred 3.319; Mahāyāna Buddhism a living spiritual force 1.187; rejoicing in merits: recognizing that there are positive forces at work 4.317; you can open yourself to spiritual forces, but *you've* got to respond 4.302

Forest Hermitage, Warwickshire 2.619–20, 2.753 (n763)

forest monasticism of Ajahn Chah 13.439–40; forest monasteries of Thailand 13.381, 13.408, 13.474; forest renunciants 3.407, 4.554–5

forests and jungles *araṇya* 14.452; a *bhikkhu* who lived fearlessly in the forest 10.500–1; the Buddha and an elephant seek solitude in the jungle 10.323–4, 10.429, 10.536–7, 14.401; Buddhism 'a hacked path, roughly made, through densest jungle' 25.xxxix, 25.278; 'The Call of the Forest' (poem) 25.xlii–xliii, 25.137, 25.408–9; charcoal-burners 25.236–7; Dharma practice like hacking one's way through a jungle 11.408; destruction of the forests 18.23, 25.52, 25.447; the encroaching jungle of modern life 11.409; elephants clearing jungle 20.283–4; Enlightenment like escape from a jungle 2.56, 10.262, 13.192–3, 14.42; eulogies to the forest-dwelling monk 14.193; the experience of standing alone in a forest 15.257; going off into the forest makes sure that you are really an individual 5.680; did the *theras* seek the forest for aesthetic reasons? 26.128; Krishna calls the *gopīs* to dance in the forest 16.73; orchid-hunters in the forest, literal and metaphorical 25.136–7; Siddhārtha's fear in the forest, *see under* Siddhārtha; the Tantra 'a jungle' 13.92, 13.116–17, 17.685–6, 21.176–8; the true individual not king of the jungle but an indefatigable earthworm 3.619

see also
Forest Monks of Sri Lanka, *see under* Carrithers; trees

forgetting

forgetfulness
a feeling that we've forgotten something 17.540; forget all about making progress 5.46; forgetting about worldly life 19.253–4; forgetting as we get older 17.541; if in the end we forget the self, what is the use of meditation? 10.223; once aware of your higher purpose, you can never forget it completely 15.94; once you've confessed something, forget it 3.265; rather than original sin, Buddhism speaks of forgetfulness 16.90; to help others, forget about yourself, at least for the time being 18.592; we never forget the lessons given us by a good life 7.35

things we forget
benefits received 3.607, 3.608–9; the danger of nuclear weapons 10.87–8; deliberately forgetting spiritual experience 4.272; faced with death people forget all about the Dharma 18.249–50; the lesson of death 10.320–1; prosperity might lead people to forget about Buddhism 10.410–11; that every moment of our life is unique 16.439–40; that pleasure is bound up with pain 10.497–8; that the purpose of eating is just to keep the body going 4.112; the true purpose of our existence 19.9–10; to notice whether we are practising the Dharma 4.284–5

things never to forget
the bodhisattva should not forget those around him 7.329; the Dharma 19.330; if you have an insight, don't forget it 12.29; that human beings are only human and may make mistakes 10.398; the importance of beauty in the spiritual life 12.308; that people in a much worse condition than us have succeeded in spiritual life 4.448; that the real business of this life is to make an end of pain 7.117–18; we need not forget the dead 5.180–1

see also
unmindfulness

forgiveness asking the Buddhas for forgiveness 16.310–11, 17.650–1; don't ask for forgiveness, just confess unskilfulness and forgive others 26.647–8; don't forget that human beings are only human and make mistakes 10.398; 'Forgive me if I have stained your beauty with my desire' 25.230; forgive your parents if necessary 18.510; forgiveness of enemies 3.449, 4.410–1; forgiveness of a fellow Sangha member 21.202–5; forgiveness of sins in Christianity 13.576–8, 26.647; the forgiveness of Vajrasattva 16.325; it doesn't mean escaping the karmic consequences of one's actions 13.578, 17.651; forgiving people their vices can be easier than forgiving them their virtues 26.33; a loyal friend may say there is nothing to forgive 15.319; Mahāyāna precept against not forgiving those who ask for pardon 2.208; 'Mutual forgiveness of each vice' (Blake) 8.558, 16.473, 26.347, 26.647–9; Sangharakshita asks his teacher's forgiveness for that day's offences 20.445; sometimes we have to forgive without understanding 26.83; 'To err is human, to forgive divine' 26.647; 'To understand all is to forgive all' 4.425, 14.476, 26.83; trusting people to have a forgiving attitude 16.315

form as *skandha*, *see rūpa*; energy is primary, form secondary 26.52; form is emptiness, emptiness is form, *see under Heart Sūtra*

formalism

dangers of formalism
a feature of much traditional Buddhism, and a danger to the religious life 2.559; the only way of guarding against formalism is individual effort 19.584; thinking any situation guarantees spiritual progress is a kind of formalism 19.362

ethical formalism
in Britain in the 1960s 17.634; confining oneself to applications of precepts mentioned in the scriptures 2.366; ethical formalism and the third fetter 17.633; one of the greatest enemies of the spiritual life 2.366; the important place of precepts does not mean that *śīla* is just ethical formalism 1.142; rigid observance of obligations without ethical significance 1.200

monastic formalism
attack on it 2.449; avoiding the extremes of formalistic monasticism and lax laicism 12.389; for the bodhisattva, no possibility of taking refuge in monastic formalism 1.245; in Early Buddhism and the Theravāda 1.10–11, 1.227–9, 1.244, 2.432–3, 2.558–62, 21.301–4; formalism of confession practice 1.410, 21.300–1; formalism in relation to merit 2.152; in Sri Lanka 20.447–8; in Zen 1.11, 2.433; tendency to identify the monastic life with the spiritual life 7.504, 17.633; Mahāyāna monks don't attach as much importance to it 1.244; over-attachment to the formal aspects of monasticism 1.227–9; Sangharakshita separating himself from it 2.415, 23.xv; the Vajrayāna as a movement of protest against it 19.109

formless formless *dhyānas*, *see under dhyānas*; formless meditation 11.688; the formless is not necessarily closer to reality than that which has form 18.88; formless world (*arūpaloka*), *see under trailokya*

Forster, E. M. 8.545, 8.548, 26.380

fortitude (*dhṛti*) *see* steadfastness

fortune-telling the experience of seeing what was going to happen 19.84, 20.85–6; fortune-tellers with little birds in the bazaar in India 15.386; fortune-telling Sinhalese monks 22.254; monks prohibited from fortune-telling in Pāli canon 1.547, 3.583; lay people rely on monks to tell fortunes throughout the Buddhist world 3.583; Tibetan lamas telling people's fortunes 19.268–9, 19.357; you don't need fortune-telling if you live in accordance with the Dharma 19.267–71

forty *kammaṭṭhānas* (objects of concentration, places of work) introduction 1.154–61, 12.607; a *bhikkhu* who used to lecture on them but never meditated himself 4.618, 19.354; the Buddha himself instructed his disciples in their practice and asked after their progress 1.380; enable us to see the structure of the whole system of practice 1.154; no more necessary to use them all than for the sick to take all medicines 1.161, 10.172; listed by Buddhaghosa 1.154, 4.519, 12.280, 13.409, 19.354

Fo-Sho-Hing-Tsan-King (*A Life of Buddha*) *see under* Aśvaghoṣa

Foster, Mrs Mary E. (Dharmapala's benefactor) her family background 8.74; her meetings with Dharmapala in Honolulu 8.49, 8.62, 8.74–5, 8.78–9, 8.99; Dharmapala helps her overcome her bad temper 8.49, 8.75, 8.78; Dharmapala recites the words 'for the welfare of the many' to her 8.78; annual donations 8.60, 8.76; donations used for the Maha Bodhi Society in London 8.64–5, 8.78; one of the greatest benefactors of Buddhism 8.49,

8.99; funding for a hospital in Colombo 8.62, 8.76; funding for an Industrial School at Sarnath 8.58–9, 8.75; funding for a Maha Bodhi Society vihara in Calcutta 8.64, 8.76–7; her donations were the mainstay of Dharmapala's work 8.103, 8.105; her gratitude to Dharmapala 8.77; gratitude to her 8.49, 8.80, 8.99; the ideal donor 8.79–80; memorial issue of the *Maha Bodhi* journal 8.80; 'Queen of the Empire of Righteousness' 8.73–81, 21.385; she made her life sublime through giving 18.234; her death 8.68, 8.80; annual celebration of her birthday 8.80, 8.104, 8.234

foundation, path, accomplishment *see under* Mahāmudrā

foundation yogas *see* four *mūla yogas*

four bases of psychic power (*ṛddhipādas*) *see* four *iddhipādas*

'Four Bodies' 19.201, 19.214–15, 19.336–7, 19.387–8

four *brahma vihāras*

introduction
brief description 1.157, 3.15–16, 10.196–7, 15.251; meaning of term 9.537; the 'infinities' 18.103; the four infinitudes 5.215; the four unbounded states 1.159, 14.80, 14.83; the 'illimitables' 5.218–19; they are closely interconnected 15.326–7

their place in the tradition
based on the Three Refuges 5.214; canonical references 1.157, 3.85, 4.677 (n113), 4.710 (n337), 5.189; in the *Mahāgovinda Sutta*, *see under Dīgha Nikāya/Mahāgovinda Sutta*; evidence that the Buddha saw the Dharma in terms of positive growth 3.15–16; may belong to an earlier phase of Buddhism 5.217; the Abhidharma on the *brahma vihāras* and insight 15.337; doctrine held in common by Theravāda and Mahāyāna 7.531, 8.444; even *paccekabuddhas* are said to practise them 4.86; among the forty *kammaṭṭhānas* 4.519; in Buddhaghosa, *see under* Buddhaghosa/*Visuddhimagga*; in the *Precious Garland* 17.262–3; *The Four Sublime States: Brahma-Vihara* (Nyanaponika) 8.384; the bodhisattva's practice 2.157, 4.179, 14.153; in the context of the heroic ideal 18.103–5; 'Love, Compassion, and Sympathetic Joy' (Conze) 8.537

the practice
the basis of practice 5.214; *mettā* must be the basis 5.196, 5.219, 11.155, 15.251, 17.183, 26.26; in a way *mettā* is the only *brahma vihāra* 5.197; and beauty 5.592; changing the order in which the practices are done 5.204–5; could they permeate one's life? 4.585; emotional aspects of the state of psychic wholeness 2.125; and evolution 3.16; an expansion of feeling 14.459; they develop and refine the emotions 10.173; developing the same attitude towards all 10.171; and the *dhyānas* 5.216–17; different levels 4.585; 'May all beings possess happiness and its causes' 5.719 (n179); near enemies 5.196; practising all four 5.219; they have to be consciously developed 3.16; a way of refining emotion 12.24

an advanced practice?
are they an advanced practice? 5.196; as an approach to the transcendental 5.217–18; as they deepen, we come to understand them differently 15.256–7; the cultivated emotions passing through the fires of *śūnyatā* 15.339; and insight 5.210–11, 5.215–18; mundane, not transcendental 2.125; preparation for the arising of the *bodhicitta* 5.189, 5.214; their connection with ultimate reality through the *bodhicitta* 18.103; they give access to the realms of the gods 26.271; undervalued 5.214–15; and visualization practices 5.579, 5.592–3

see also
mettā bhāvanā; *karuṇā bhāvanā*; *muditā bhāvanā*; *upekkhā bhāvanā*

four *caryās* (bodhisattva's courses of conduct) 1.406, 1.422–3

four conditions (*pratyāya*) 14.88

four *Dharma mūdras* *see* four seals

four dimensions of mindfulness *see under* mindfulness

four foundation yogas *see* four *mūla yogas*

four great kings

introduction
the Buddha repeats a spell he learned from them 14.39; calculation of their lifespan 2.67; control non-human beings 16.346, 16.349; as *devas* 13.586; heavenly beings of the lowest order 16.348; to invoke their power, you have to be interested in them 16.358; on Mount Meru 16.346; represent powerful, positive, free energies 16.353; represent forces of balance and harmony in the cosmos 16.357; as represented in art 16.346; strength comes from the transcendental 16.355; in the *Sūtra of Golden Light* 16.346–58; can be said to symbolize the principle of spiritual hierarchy 16.356–7; in what sense can they be said to exist? 16.357; Western

counterparts: King Arthur, St George? 16.357

guardians
of the gates of the mandala 16.352; *lokapālas* (guardians of the world) 16.348; protect the world from the *bhūtas* (evil spirits) 16.349–50; of the spiritual community 16.352–3; of the temple 16.346, 16.350

four great reliances *see* four reliances

four holy places (of Buddhism) the Buddha's advice to visit them 2.223, 8.193–4; their decay after the Muslim invasion 8.194; their state in the 19th century 8.xiv, 9.237; their renovation 7.466–7, 8.194–6, 8.260; temples built to cater for pilgrims 10.80; each has its own atmosphere 16.567; the effect of pilgrimage to them 4.325, 10.397, 11.690, 26.511; for us, hallowed ground 14.465; Mr Chen's pilgrimage 22.540; pilgrims rarely think of helping Buddhism in India 8.176; Sangharakshita's connections with them 11.717–18; still preserved and visited 9.478–9; Tibetan pilgrims 2.223, 7.415–18, 13.54, 13.79, 20.455–6; ambition to have Triratna centres there 11.527

see also
Eminent Buddhists from the Border Areas visit, *see under* Eminent Buddhists; Lumbinī; Bodh Gaya; Sārnāth; Kusinārā

four *iddhipādas* (bases of psychic power, Sanskrit *ṛddhipādas*) introduction 10.586–7, 17.457; canonical references 10.717 (n451), 11.369; in the *Vibhaṅga* (Abhidharma) 14.80; an obscure aspect of the path 10.568; operate on the basis of the fourth *dhyāna* 10.586

four idols *see under* Sir Francis Bacon

four kinds of nutriment (Pāli canon) 22.285, 22.601–2 (n233)

four mindfulnesses (Tantric) 8.508

four mind-turning reflections 1.418, 5.388

four *mudrās* (the *yogayāna* of Tibetan Buddhism) 12.297

four *mūla yogas* (foundation *yogas*) introduction 12.19–20, 13.75–87; all Order members should practise them 5.555–6; the meaning of *mūla* and *yoga* in this context 13.74–6; Mr Chen's practice 22.537; in a copy of the *Tharpa Delam* bought in the bazaar 2.443; the entrance to the Vajrayāna 13.76; if practised thoroughly enough, will bring one close to Enlightenment 13.86–7; introduced to Sangharakshita by Kachu Rimpoche 22.473; preceded by the four preliminary meditations 5.547; relevance 5.542; and the system of meditation 5.540–1; teaching the practices to the 'Three Musketeers' 23.231–2; they begin the process of integration of one part of our nature with another 13.76; they precede the whole system of Vajrayāna meditation 13.74, 13.86–7

see also
Going for Refuge and prostration practice; *bodhicitta* practice; Vajrasattva practice, *see under* Vajrasattva; offering of the mandala

four necessities (for which the *bhikkhu* depends on lay people) 10.172, 16.408, 18.387–8, 22.103

four noble paths (*ārya-mārgas*) 12.27

four noble truths

introduction
summary 7.218–19, 15.235; enumerations 1.121, 1.485, 3.281, 4.660 (n10), 9.213, 15.58, 12.121, 16.613 (n219); introduction 1.120–36; the briefest synthesis of the entire doctrine of Buddhism 1.121, 7.126; to know them (and the *nidānas*) is to know Buddhism's whole rationale 19.577; distinction between general formula and specific application 1.120–2; can be divided into two causes and two effects 7.193; four 'ennobling' truths 8.572–4, 8.589; faith in the four noble truths 17.551; the first and second truths 7.494; a kind of blueprint for Buddhist practice 15.249–50; method, not doctrine 1.124–5, 15.227–33; applying method and doctrine 17.593; positive formulations? 1.115, 1.134; propositions or injunctions to act? 8.572–3, 8.589–96; seeing the truth of the truths 7.222–3; understanding each of the truths 'as it actually is' 15.232–3; unless we understand them in detail, we know little about Buddhism 1.477

their place in the tradition
the subject of Buddha's first discourse 1.477, 3.76, 3.281; based on an ancient Indian medical formula? 5.660, 12.98, 12.228, 16.192; canonical sources 1.94–5, 1.121, 1.126–8, 3.627 (n11), 16.613 (n219); in the *Dhammacakkappavattana Sutta* 1.36, 1.127, 1.477, 8.589–91, 16.613 (n219); 'Through not understanding them, we have wandered a long journey' 1.96; discourse on the analysis of the four noble truths (MN 141) 8.532; in the *Udāna* 10.552; reflection on the four noble

truths (*Satipaṭṭhāna Sutta*) 15.227–37; the Fourfold Āryan Truth of things (*Ratana Sutta*) 15.64; perhaps a relatively late formulation 10.552; agreement between Mahāyānists and Hīnayānists on them 1.96–7; Hīnayāna schools' lopsided interpretation 1.121, 1.226–7; Abhidharma analysis 14.80, 14.84; in the *Mahāparinirvāṇa Sūtra* 14.237; the *Heart Sūtra* restates them in the light of emptiness 14.152; in the *yānas* of Tibetan Buddhism 12.296; Dr Ambedkar's doubts about them 9.141; drew Sangharakshita's attention during his wandering days 20.302

the truths and other aspects of doctrine and practice
best-known formulation of the principle of conditionality 3.183–4, 8.243; correspondence to the wheel of life 1.485, 2.102; and evolution 3.14; related to karma and *karma-vipāka*, *mārga* and *phala* 2.102; and *pratītya samutpāda* 1.94–5, 1.120–1, 1.266, 3.14, 7.494; related to the seeds stored in the *ālaya-vijñāna* 7.202; right view as right understanding of the four noble truths 7.521; the third and fourth truths corresponds to the path to Nirvāṇa 7.494

(1) the truth of suffering (dukkha)
canonical description not a definition but a list of examples 1.127; the content of the first truth can be varied 1.121; how you see things when you have transcendental vision 15.448–9; ignorance of this truth 7.220; insight into this truth can be gained even when one is happy 26.62; *karma-vipāka* corresponds to it 2.102; people who suffer not necessarily nearer realizing the truth of suffering 26.12, 26.62; recognition of it comes as a terrible shock 1.124, 7.392; the teaching of *dukkha* needs to be located in the context of the noble truths 3.8; the truths come from applying the principle of conditionality to suffering 1.266; the universality of suffering 7.389; why is suffering the first noble truth? 1.123–4, 15.228; *see also dukkha*

(2) the truth of the cause of suffering (dukkha-samudaya)
karma corresponds to this truth 2.102, 7.219; although we run after pleasure for a million years, we shall never find it 7.48; craving is the origin of suffering 1.111, 3.184, 3.199, 7.219, 12.623–4, 15.202; craving not being present, suffering does not arise 3.184, 7.219; the idea that suffering ceases when craving ceases is counterintuitive 15.231–2; the desire for things to be other than they are 15.249–50; through attachment we bring about our own suffering 10.611; we should pay particular attention to this truth 15.231

(3) the truth of the end of suffering
introduction 1.131–4; corresponds to Nirvāṇa 1.131, 7.494; deduced from the first truth by immediate inference 1.131; ignorance of this truth results in anxious prayers 7.221; it will not be achieved through trying to avoid *dukkha* 15.231; your own thoughts, words, and deeds will eventually free you 7.219

(4) the truth of the path to the end of suffering
introduction 1.134–6; *see also* Noble Eightfold Path

four pairs of persons *see under* sangha/Āryasaṅgha

four *pārisuddhi sīlas* 1.146, 10.172, 10.692 (n218)

four *pratisaṃvids* (Pāli *paṭisambhidā*, analytical knowledges)

introduction
description 1.449, 16.488–91; an aspect of the perfection of skilful means 10.147; in the *Vibhaṅga* (Abhidharma) 14.80; embodied by Mañjughoṣa 1.491

(1) dharma-pratisaṃvid (knowledge of phenomena)
knowledge of how the different paths of Buddhism merge (*Daśabhūmika*) 1.449, 16.489; knowledge of phenomena in their appearance and reality 1.449; knowledge of principles 16.489

(2) artha-pratisaṃvid (knowledge of meaning)
knowing the characteristics of phenomena and the categories of the Doctrine 1.449; knowing conceptual formulations as a medium of communicating the truth 16.489–90

(3) nirukti-pratisaṃvid (knowledge of etymology)
avoiding confusing the letter and the spirit of the teaching 1.449; knowing linguistics, public speaking, literary composition 1.449, 16.490; using words clearly to express concepts 16.490–1

(4) pratibhāna-pratisaṃvid (knowledge of courage)
speaking with boldness, courage, and wit 1.449, 16.491

four preliminary meditations (precious human body, impermanence, karma, shortcomings of *saṃsāra*) 5.547

four reliances (*pratisāraṇa*)

introduction
outline 14.315–16; longer introduction 16.575–82; the teaching occurs in a number of Mahāyāna texts 3.355, 14.315; in the *Mahāparinirvāṇa Sūtra* 14.236–7; in the *Vimalakīrti-nirdeśa* 16.575

(1) relying on the Dharma, not on any person
charisma obliterates the distinction between person and truth 13.477; rely on the teaching, not on the person who teaches 3.355; what this means is that we should not rely on authority 16.576–8

(2) relying on the meaning, not on the expression
try to find out what is really meant 3.355; the danger of becoming a mere scholar of Buddhism 16.578–9; we have to rely not merely on words, but on the spirit of the Dharma 14.297

(3) relying on discourses of explicit meaning (nītārtha), not implicit meaning (neyārtha)
applying this to the Pāli canon and to Mahāyāna *sūtras* 11.719–20; examples from the *Dhammapada* 11.718–19, 15.227, 16.579–80; one interprets the obscure in the light of the clear 3.355; your interpretations must not contradict the discourses of explicit meaning 16.580–1

(4) relying on transcendental awareness, not discriminative consciousness
the approach to the fourth reliance 8.505; the Dharma can be deeply understood only by transcendental awareness 16.581–2; making this distinction is our greatest task 14.316; very few people really rely on *jñāna* 3.355–6

four right efforts (or exertions)

introduction
brief description 3.304, 8.585, 10.202, 15.170, 17.456; canonical sources 3.670 (n286), 10.694–5 (n236), 11.369, 16.584–5 (n11); longer introduction 1.554–64; description in the *Udāna* 10.531; the Buddha reviews his practice 10.593–4; an extremely important aspect of spiritual life 3.283–4; and the *mettā bhāvanā* 17.456; in the *Vibhaṅga* (Abhidharma) 14.80; the practice requires complete honesty with oneself 1.555; and *vīrya* 1.374, 1.440. 3.304, 8.200, 16.10–11

(1) effort to prevent the arising of unskilful states of mind
be very quick to prevent negative emotions from developing 3.270; guarding the doors of the senses 1.556–7; prevented from arising through mindfulness of the body 10.622; you have to keep evaluating your situation 4.480–1

(2) effort to eradicate unskilful states of mind
the effort to eliminate all states based in greed, hatred, and delusion 3.304; eradicating the hindrances 1.557–61; no talk of the unskilful being 'accepted' 8.585; strenuous spiritual practice 7.172–3; watching an unskilful thought like a cloud in the sky is a form of effort 11.689

(3) effort to develop unarisen skilful states
actively cultivate and encourage positive emotions 3.270, 3.304; can be measured by the attainment of the *dhyānas* 1.561–4

(4) effort to maintain skilful states of mind
it is easy to slip back 1.564; the Buddha must have noticed people letting things slide 3.305

four *saṃgrahavastus* (elements of conversion)

introduction
descriptions 1.449, 16.485–8, 17.174–5; alternative translations 16.485; correspond to the first four duties of friendship 3.574–5, 11.699–700; Nāgārjuna recommends them to the king in the *Precious Garland* 17.173–4; the positive mental events arise through them 17.590; relevant at every stage of spiritual development 17.175; and the seventh perfection, *upāya-kauśalya-pāramitā* 1.449, 3.575, 10.147, 11.699

(1) dāna
in this context it is a means of establishing contact between people 16.485–6; we let go of our tight grip on what belongs to us 17.174

(2) loving speech
affectionate speech to create the spiritual community 16.486–7; consciously cultivating it 17.174–5

(3) beneficial activity
doing whatever helps people spiritually 16.487; encouraging others to lead the holy life 1.449; knowing what would be of most benefit 17.175

(4) exemplification
being the embodiment of the qualities you encourage others to develop 16.487–8; the

courage to be honest about where we stand 17.175

four *satipaṭṭhānas* *see* awareness/four kinds of awareness

four seals (*Dharma mūdras*) 8.611, 12.656–8, 12.754–5 (n456)

four sights

introduction
accounts 3.25–9, 10.256–7, 12.131–3, 12.358–9, 14.291; did it really happen? 2.35–6, 3.25; Dr Ambedkar's inability to accept the tradition 9.140; as described in the story of Barlaam and Josaphat 13.655–7; 'The Four Sights' (poem) 25.178–80

sources
introduction 3.630 (n27), 10.698 (n268), 12.713–14 (n98); Aśvaghoṣa's *Buddhacarita* 2.668 (n55), 10.698 (n268); described in connection with the Buddha Vipassi 3.630 (n27), 10.698 (n268); no mention of the four sights in the *Ariyapariyesanā Sutta* 3.207, 3.630 (n27); a passage in the *Aṅguttara Nikāya* shows the psychological basis 2.35–6

lessons
Siddhārtha saw that perhaps there was a solution to the problem of death 12.359; existential reality breaks in on our little world 3.34–6; the first three sights caused the loss of intoxication of youth, health, life 15.424; the facts of old age, sickness, and death 12.133, 24.229–38, 24.501; have curiosity, a spirit of adventure: the lesson of the four sights 10.256

see also
fourth sight

four supports (*nissayas* or *niśrayas*) 1.146, 1.149, 2.191, 2.421

four Tantric rites

introduction
each associated with a different Buddha family 13.278; each symbolizes a certain activity of the Enlightened mind 13.278; how they developed from Indian magical rites 13.276–80; began to be used as a means of supporting a family 1.383, 18.174–5

(1) pacification
associated with the colour white 13.280, 19.24; connected with the soothing calm imparted by the Enlightened mind 13.280

(2) maturation, prospering
associated with the colour yellow 13.280, 19.24; the Enlightened mind's capacity to encourage unenlightened minds to grow 13.280

(3) destruction
associated with the colour black 13.280, 19.24; the destruction of the real enemy: ignorance 13.278; the Tibetans used it to try to halt the Chinese invasion 22.372, 26.700; the wrathful deities are manifestations of this aspect of the Enlightened mind 19.24

(4) fascination
associated with the colour red 13.280, 19.24; associated with Kurukullā, Red Tārā 19.24–5; the Enlightened mind exerts a subtle fascination 13.278–9; the *gaurīs* who keep us in the mandala by hooks of fascination 16.352; why not be seduced by reality? 14.597

four *vargas* (*bhikkhu*, *bhikkhunī*, *upāsaka*, *upāsikā*) 2.203, 2.205–6, 2.208

four *vimuttis* (faith, ethics, meditation, wisdom) 7.122–6

four *viparyāsas* (topsy-turvy views, mental perversities, Pāli *vipallāsas*)

introduction
descriptions 2.80–1, 3.280–1, 12.612–17, 15.127, 17.219–20, 17.545; attitudes as deeply rooted almost as sentient existence 2.81; being drawn to practices based on topsy-turvy views 17.681–2; can have disastrous consequences for us and for other people 12.616; the characteristics of the Unconditioned falsely applied to the conditioned 14.590–1; great importance is attached to overcoming them 14.591; extirpated by meditating on the fact that the world as we know it is unreal 2.81; to overcome them requires the development of *prajñā* 2.92; superimposing on conventionally existent the attributes of absolutely existent 19.233–4; they represent eternalism 14.594; this teaching rests on a dualistic basis 14.591; we have to turn them the right way up 12.616–17

sources and correspondences
Pāli canon sources 3.666 (n258), 14.658 (n513), 17.767 (n484), 17.777 (n588); *vipallāsa* included as a topic in the *Patisambhidā-magga* 14.73; in the *Mahāparinirvāṇa Sūtra* 14.237; correspondence with the three *lakṣaṇas* 2.81, 3.281; correspondence with the three *vimokṣas* 2.114–15

(1) seeing the impermanent as permanent
not a thought but an emotional attitude 2.80–1, 3.280–1, 12.612–13; whatever has been put together must one day be taken apart 1.172–3; 17.370

(2) seeing what is painful as pleasurable
we imagine that what is unsatisfactory is giving us satisfaction 3.280; we search for happiness in the wrong place 12.613

(3) seeing what is not possessed of unchanging selfhood as being so
the reason why we act selfishly 12.613–14; seeing what is really insubstantial as having a self 3.281

(4) seeing what is ugly as beautiful
that is, in comparison to the beauties of a higher plane 3.281, 12.614–16; an example of method, not doctrine 1.125, 5.511–12

four yogas (*kriyāyoga*, *ubhayayoga*, *yoga tantra*, *anuttara yoga*) 13.91

fourfold path (morality, meditation, wisdom, emancipation) 16.446

fourteen (or ten) inexpressibles (*avyākṛtavastūni*) *see* undetermined questions

fourth sight Barlaam in the story of Barlaam and Josaphat 13.657; the Buddhist incognito in public life 12.126–7; don't let people think that Buddhists are rude or ill-mannered or thoughtless 12.404; a happy person will communicate the happiness of the Buddhist ideal 15.353, 17.226–7; seeing a Western Buddhist might show someone that they could do that too 19.309–10; Siddhārtha's experience, which moved him to go forth 3.28–9, 12.551, 15.424; you may be the first Buddhist that somebody has ever seen 12.60–1, 12.309–10

foxes the howling of foxes at Guhyaloka 24.394; rebirth as a spirit fox 14.593, 18.85; Sangharakshita's wish to inherit his godfather's stuffed fox 20.482–3, 26.417; the story of the fox who lost his tail 19.358

Fra Angelico v13, v23

'Fragrant with all Fragrances' (Buddhaland) *see* Sarvagandhasugandhā

France

Buddhism
Les Amis du Bouddhisme 22.219, 22.255–6; translation of the *White Lotus Sūtra* into French 8.478; Wesak celebration in Paris 22.256

history
false hierarchy replaced not by true hierarchy but by anti-hierarchy 4.170; 'Liberty, Equality, Fraternity' 4.170; the Revolution 4.169–70, 9.408

Paris
Alexandra David-Néel has an argument with a fellow Buddhist 22.255–6; Anagarika Dharmapala visits 8.55; 'Culture had not been forced to yield to commercialism' 23.452; Montmartre at midnight 23.452; the Louvre 23.452; Musée Guimet 3.300, 8.55, 22.48, 22.576 (n49), 23.452, 26.116; Napoleon's tomb 26.277–8; the pattern of the streets 26.265

other places
a journey through France 23.247–8; Sangharakshita visits in 1970 4.443, 4.705 (n307), 23.451–3; Avignon 24.7; Carcassonne 13.580, 24.xxiii, 24.7 24.189–91; Chartres Cathedral 13.602; Lourdes 13.601; rock-cut dwellings along the Loire 23.452–3; Tours 23.452

Francis, St and the bodhisattva ideal 4.607; *Canticle of the Sun* 4.594, 14.109; compared to Milarepa 13.625, 18.xi, 18.xvi, 18.160; experienced joy when turned away on a cold dark night 4.316, 13.625, 17.555; a great spiritual soul, but probably knew nothing about theology 13.108; a joyful person 15.353; *The Little Flowers of St Francis* 13.625; 'St Francis and the Birds' 25.366–7; under his influence, the teenage Sangharakshita gave all his money to a beggar 13.533, 13.624; wedded to Lady Poverty 13.624

Francis Xavier, St 8.318, 11.297, 18.562

Franco, General 24.412

fraternity 9.185–6, 9.426

freedom (*vimukti* or *vimutti*)

the nature of freedom
the distinction between 'freedom from' and 'freedom to' 10.567; distinction from and connection with liberty (internal and external) 9.183; inconceivable 16.448; much of the sense of *vimutti* is conveyed by 'growth and development' 10.567; peace

from bondage 2.124; a state of unimpeded volition 2.127

restricted freedom
freedom is the aim of religion, but it keeps us enslaved 16.499–500; having no freedom of action 25.116–17; if for the time being you can't get free, hang on to your spiritual practice 19.418; in a modern democracy, does anyone really feel free? 10.65; to be truly free one has to escape from bondage and also from liberation 2.56, 2.118; to free yourself from the limitations of human existence, ask its cause 7.115; you can never be really free if you treat ideas as corresponding to realities 2.118; you're not free if you're at the mercy of every passing whim and fancy 18.489

looking for freedom
allow others freedom to grow spiritually in their own way 3.15; desire for freedom to develop oneself 13.410–12; do you ask 'What will make me happy?' or 'How can I become free?' 17.164–5; fear of freedom 11.17–18, 12.232–3; freedom to choose religion 9.183–4; happiness is a by-product of the quest for freedom 17.165, 26.64; the mistake of thinking that freedom means doing just as you like 10.567; our essential need 16.499; we are all free to do whatever we want to do 5.692, 12.232–3; whatever your situation, remind yourself that you are free to leave 18.458

freedom and Buddhism
the Buddha is not the giver of *mokṣa*, but the shower of the path of *mokṣa* 10.247; the Buddha's teaching of freedom (Ambedkar) 10.64–5; Buddhism is the interplay between a free man and the unfree 10.141; Buddhism is the means to freedom 10.160; Buddhism is 'the proudest assertion ever made of human freedom' 7.267; Buddhism recognizes the freedom of the individual 10.281; Buddhism teaches social, intellectual, economic, and political freedom (Ambedkar) 9.426; the Buddhist conception of freedom 26.19; as a Buddhist you are free to practise however you want 12.246; the central principle is that we are free to choose how to be 17.212–13; the essential characteristic of the Dharma is that it conduces to freedom 10.567; the freedom of Enlightenment is absolute and unconditioned 2.56; freedom of mind and heart is the aim and object of Buddhist life and practice 3.277; freedom to practise Buddhism not guaranteed 4.100–1, 12.490; freedom to question Buddhism 9.494; the goal of the Buddhist path 2.127, 3.277–8, 9.183, 26.19; if you don't feel free, you're not really a Buddhist 10.188; 'Now I am a Buddhist I feel free' 6.613, 9.340, 9.428, 9.508, 10.12, 10.25, 10.61, 10.188, 10.314, 11.671, 11.708–9; 'O monks, I am freed from all bonds, human and divine …' 4.20, 15.464–5; the spiritual community is founded on the basis of individual freedom 18.488–9; spiritual freedom is of the essence of Buddhism 8.579; you can't be a Buddhist unless you are free not to be one 4.248, 8.471, 26.9

elements of freedom
freedom from confusion, to realize our potential, to be for others 8.579; freedom from theories and from conditioned existence 2.56; freedom from wrong views 3.277; freedom in terms of breaking the fetters 11.709–12; freedom is recognizable, and manifests as compassion 10.141; freedom of speech 4.125, 4.127; freedom to close yourself to spiritual influence 4.247; freedom to choose the world we live in 16.478; the freedom of the creative mind 11.25; the freedom of the first *arūpa dhyāna* 4.510; the freedom of the gap between activities 4.486–7; freedom and the spiral path 16.446; freedom that arises from knowing oneself 17.434; freedom and spiritual friends 18.456–7, 26.633; one has freedom, but there is still a pattern to life 18.284; twofold: *ceto-vimukti* and *prajñā-vimukti* 12.164, 16.446

how to become free
confession 16.337; freedom is found in commitment, not in refraining from commitment 12.484; how can we become free? – the Dharma is the answer to the question 10.140–1; the method by which freedom is attained must be left behind 10.152–3; really seeing the process of passing from one state to another 13.140; methods to obtain freedom 9.342–3; mind dissociated from the *skandhas* to become free 18.614–15; renouncing group identity in favour of the freedom of absolute emptiness 18.139; your thoughts, words, and deeds, which caused suffering, will free you from it 7.219

true freedom
the *ḍākinī* as the embodiment of freedom 11.52; if you have surmounted attachment even to your son, you are free indeed 10.455; there is no real freedom without insight 11.47; where there is no world and no freedom from the world 17.368; the yogi lives in perfect freedom 7.102

see also
four *vimuttis*; freedom as one of the positive *nidānas*, *see under* twelve positive

nidānas; freedom of thought, *see under* thought; a reliable teaching will lead towards freedom, *see under* Mahāpajāpati Gotami; the taste of freedom, *see under* *Udāna*/great ocean; *vimukti*

Freeman, John 24.577–8

Freemasonry 13.374

Freethinker 11.344

French nun *see* Delannoy

Freud, Sigmund analysis of humour 2.636, 4.137, 15.372; application of conditionality to the workings of the subconscious mind 12.153; arrested development 12.272; death wish 8.127, 12.99; founder of psychoanalysis 12.93; a Freudian interpretation of a missionary's experience 21.362–3; Freudian psychologists put their own names to their writings 14.399; Freudian slips 5.658; God is a father-substitute 3.549, 12.94–5; his analysis of human experience compared to the five skandhas 15.188; explanation of anxiety 17.688–9; id, ego, super-ego 10.524, 10.713 (n419), 12.99–100, 24.577; *Jokes and their Relation to the Unconscious* 2.636, 4.137; not so popular among Western Buddhists 4.606; the pioneer of psychoanalysis 10.348–50; placed psychology on a scientific basis 3.333; pleasure principle and reality principle 5.658, 10.483; the repression of emotions 5.657–8, 10.608, 12.265–6, 15.494; *The Psychopathology of Everyday Life* 2.636, 5.658; three stages of sexual development (oral, anal, genital) 12.272, 12.281; use of hypnotism 4.507; 'What does a woman want?' 22.221, 22.594 (n192); without instinctual repression there could be no civilization 24.463–4

Friedman, Lenore 24.373

Friedrich, Caspar David 26.255–6

Friend (Dhammasahayak) of Triratna (FWBO/TBMSG) 9.308, 9.545, 10.268, 11.178, 11.391

friendliness the Buddha praises Ānanda's friendliness 3.179; the Buddhist ideal is to be the friend of all 10.283; courtesy paves the way for friendly communication 12.404; the *ḍākinī*: warm, friendly communication, kindling a spark 12.314–15; the difference between friendliness and friendship 15.311–12; extolled in the *Mahāparinirvāṇa Sūtra* 14.240; genuine communication is only possible with warmth and friendliness 12.314; the importance of being friendly to visitors to a Buddhist centre 12.60; not incompatible with *seeming* violence (Mahāyāna) 14.236; one cannot always be happy, but one can be friendly 26.757 (n519); people drawn to the Triratna Buddhist Community by its friendliness 12.457–8; *Suhṛllekha* (Friendly Epistle), *see under* Nāgārjuna/works; suspected by psychology 4.605; there is no equanimity without friendliness 26.26; to maintain your principles and also remain on friendly terms with people is difficult 18.502; towards those who practise other religions 10.278–9

Friends, Andy *see* Subhadra

Friends of the Western Buddhist Order (FWBO) *see* Triratna (Buddhist Community)

friendship

INTRODUCTION

etymology
the English word friend is cognate with the word free 3.575, 11.700; the Pāli word for friend, *mitta*, is related to *mettā* 3.576, 3.604

the nature of friendship
an area of freedom 26.633; artistic friendships 26.364–6; a gift for friendship 8.601; having once met, we can never really be separated 26.26; it implies a degree of mutual knowledge 22.339; it is of the most profound possible significance 7.295; it takes time 19.99, 23.149, 26.27, 26.79; non-exclusiveness is a vital part of friendship 26.78; ordinary friendship 10.394, 16.315, 16.318; a very powerful positive emotion 1.502

the perspectives of writers and philosophers
autumn the season of friendship 22.322–3; 'Friends rarely know how much they love until it is too late' 25.407; it can only exist between virtuous persons (Aristotle) 7.294, 12.638–9, 17.327; it can only exist between free people (Aristotle) 3.575, 12.644; 'Keep your friendships in constant repair' (Johnson) 12.640, 18.336, 22.322, 26.78, 26.537; 'Greater love hath no man than this, that he lay down his life for his friend' 7.293, 12.457; the poetry of friendship 24.359–60, 25.407; story of a lifelong friendship 24.316; ten verses on the Advantages of Friendship 8.532; true friendship (Hazlitt) 24.561; we can learn a lot from Cicero's dialogues on friendship 12.406; wish to live on a planet where friendship is the rule of life 25.454

THE DUTIES OF FRIENDSHIP

five duties we have towards a friend (Sigālaka Sutta)
(1) generosity 1.502, 3.573, 3.579, 11.698; (2) always to speak kindly and compassionately 3.573, 3.575, 3.579, 11.698; (3) to look after our friend's welfare, especially spiritual welfare 3.574, 3.579, 11.698; (4) to treat our friend as we would treat ourself 3.574, 3.579, 11.698–9; (5) to keep our promises 3.574, 11.699; the first four are identical with the four *saṃgraha-vastus* 3.574–5, 11.699–700

other aspects
rejoicing in friends' merits 1.509–10; taking care of your friends' needs 15.121; think not of what people should be giving you, but of what you can give them 26.81

five duties our friend has towards us (Sigālaka Sutta)
(1) to take care of us when we are sick 3.574; (2) to watch over our property when we are neglectful 3.574; (3) they are our refuge in times of fear 3.574; (4) they do not forsake us when we are in trouble 3.574; (5) they show concern for our dependants 3.574

BECOMING AND BEING A FRIEND

making friends
the bodhisattva treats all sentient beings as his friends 1.426; committing yourself to a friendship has to be an act of faith 14.550–1; creating a network of friends 12.645–6, 12.675; extending the hand of friendship to all 2.570; if you are committed to the Dharma, friendships will have that element 19.500

the characteristics of friendship
behind every friendship is the denial of the selfish individual will 7.293–4; a blessing to share our thoughts and feelings with another human being 11.440; committed friendship requires openness 15.311; even the closest friends could have different perceptions of the same thing 24.433; even with an old friend we should feel we don't know who we're meeting 17.239; expressive of the love (or *mettā*) mode 11.701; friends are like midwives, who draw forth what is waiting to be born 8.578; the function of a friend is to encourage individuality 16.25; getting to know another human being is like exploring another world 26.25; a good friend is someone with whom you can be alone 18.17; it manifests as a readiness to sacrifice one's own pleasure for that of another 7.293; it's helpful to have a few friends to whom you can say absolutely anything 18.516; the need to have friends with whom you can be yourself 25.89–90; the panacea for psychological problems 26.78; they encourage us to do good 7.294; you cannot become friends with proud and haughty people 18.141

spending time with friends
a friend may offer a glimpse of something beyond the problem-oriented mode 14.403; a friend's help with making a decision 17.614–15; introduce your children to your Buddhist friends 3.540–1; keeping friendship alive 25.421; make sure it isn't all devoted to practical matters 14.520

real friendship
determination to develop real friendship and be a real friend 26.26; finding out who your real friends are 17.327; very rare 26.26; one can be a true friend to the extent that one has a spiritual life 17.328; the qualities of a real friend 26.78; a true friend (from an epistle of the Sincere Brethren of Islam) 24.569–70; very few people know the real meaning of friendship 26.23; without the capacity to recollect the past, there can be no real friendship 15.86; you don't bolster up each other's little weaknesses 18.389

depth of friendship
friendship is deep to the extent that it is altruistic and egoless 12.458; how to create depth in friendship 12.458; the more deeply you can rely on someone, the less predictable they become 14.551; our deepest friendships will be with others who Go for Refuge 2.570, 10.630

fierce friendship
introduction 11.758 (n238), 12.732 (n271); communication with spiritual peers is radical, no-holds-barred, dangerous 18.420; criticism that is concerned with our welfare 11.431; misunderstanding of fierce friendship 12.416–17

single-sex friendship
'buddyship' 24.542–4; effect of fear of homosexuality 11.583–5, 13.452, 13.618, 23.438; friendship between women: Vera Brittain and Winifred Holtby as exemplars 26.637; physical contact in friendship 11.583–4; in the Western world, friendship has lost its traditional significance 2.569

sex and friendship
can one's sexual partner be one's best friend? 11.576; emotions of friendship are skilful but weak, of sex unskilful but strong 26.79; friendships and sexual relationships 12.458

complexities
avoid close association *only* with those with whom you feel close affinity 26.31; enemies are really friends 16.525; evil friends 16.300, 16.322; friends can find it hard to accept that you have changed 4.271; in the misfortunes of our friends we find something not displeasing to us 15.311–12; it becomes unhealthy when one friend dominates or controls the other 12.644; no amount of friendship can alleviate existential loneliness 18.16–17; obstacles to friendship 12.458; often there is too much emphasis on sentiment and too little on action 26.23; the unconscious influence of friends with conventional and materialistic ideas 18.152

see also
Greece/history and culture/friendship; spiritual friendship, *see kalyāṇa mitratā*; 'the whole of the spiritual life', *see under kalyāṇa mitratā*

frivolousness a near enemy to playfulness 19.397; not spending too much on frivolous things 12.554–5, 12.671; the production of frivolous things 1.548, 16.412; robs you of energy, awareness, mindfulness, stability, equanimity 19.396–7; the *vajra* cannot be used frivolously, so a *vajra*-like person is not frivolous 13.168; what makes people frivolous? 19.397; *see also* frivolous speech, *see under* speech/unskilful

frogs and toads the frog and the elephant 15.423–4, 16.299; frog haiku 25.294; pet and favourite frogs and toads 20.28–9, 25.426, 26.418; the snake who could neither swallow a frog nor throw it up 10.490, 11.279, 15.94; the well-frog and the ocean-frog 1.198, 9.372, 10.256, 26.105–6, 26.110

Fromm, Erich biophilia and necrophilia 12.99; ritual: 'shared action, expressive of common strivings, rooted in common values' 11.209–14; ritual is 'a symbolic expression of thoughts and feelings by action' 11.212; *The Heart of Man* 23.206; his school 12.93; humanistic and authoritarian religion 12.227–8; the individual relates to the world in five different orientations 12.275–7; influenced by D. T. Suzuki 12.72; interest in Zen 5.665; more sympathetic to religious ritual than Freud had been 11.207; popularity 4.606

Froude, J. A. 13.576, 21.434

frugality the Buddha's teaching to Mahāpajāpatī Gotami, *see* Mahāpajāpatī Gotami

fruit *amlaki* fruit 16.193; 'Better is the fruit of entering the Stream than sole sovereignty over the earth' 2.140; the bitter fruit of desire 7.291; the bodhisattva ideal: the perfectly ripened fruit of the vast tree of Buddhism 1.394, 8.xvi–xvii, 22.279; 'By their fruits ye shall know them' 7.291; 'The fruit does not deny the flower' (Hegel) 1.182; fruits of a life well used and not wasted 8.270; 'Great becomes the fruit, great the advantage ...' 4.645, 7.507, 8.92; myrobalan fruit 16.620 (n276); 'Not in the sky, nor in the ... sea ... can one escape the fruits of one's evil deeds' 7.221; ordination is a rich and fruitful growing thing 12.423; rejoicing that one's birth has become fruitful 1.416; the sweet fruit of [unselfish] love is liberation for all sentient beings 7.291; 'There is no gift ... no fruit or ripening of deeds well done or ill done ...' 2.391; the three golden apples 26.469–70; two deliverances bound up with path and fruit 3.665 (n255); View, Practice, Action, Fruit 19.157–8

see also
fruit of karma, *see under karma vipāka*; a man gathering fruit, *see* twelve cyclical *nidānas*/(9) *upādāna*; *phala*

frustration all terror and frustrations come from the mind 17.476; frustrated craving leads to bitterness and hatred 1.498; frustrated desire 1.232, 16.295; 'Frustration' (poem) 25.221; boredom is connected with frustrated energy 17.400; frustrating the course of one's spiritual life 7.290; the frustration children feel when they are not believed 19.20–1; the frustration of not being believed when you are speaking the truth 19.19–20; looking for ways of relieving frustration 11.78–9; most people have never experienced the salutary effects of frustration 19.21; taking up austerities to frustrate yourself might be an expression of self-will 19.167; thinking about something objectively can be frustrating 17.626; total frustration and total transformation 19.18–19; when your self-will is frustrated you experience how egoistic you are 19.16; you can't impose frustrations on yourself 19.167; young people's sense of frustration leading to violence 18.457–8

Fry, Elizabeth 1.509, 1.630 (n399)

Frydman, Maurice (friend in Bombay) his life 12.320, 26.556–60; he and Sangharakshita met in Gangtok 24.101; fond of giving advice 26.559–60; said that Mahāyāna *sūtras* are like science fiction 3.381, 12.503, 16.37, 16.237, 22.463; told

Sangharakshita he needed to be a Manu to the new Indian Buddhists 12.320–1, 26.560; visits Kalimpong 8.665, 23.376; his death 24.101

Frye, Northrop 19.615 (n157)

Fugen Bosatsu *see* Samantabhadra

Fugger banking family 24.591

Fukuyama, Francis 3.424

Fuller, Buckminster 3.561, 23.458, 23.539 (n478)

Fuller, Peter 2.609, 24.313, 24.374, 24.685 (n388)

fun the bodhisattva doesn't have to make an effort to help people, it's just fun 18.254; looked at from the outside, spiritual life might not look like much fun 17.381; the Pure Land: all transcendental fun and games 19.26; the spiritual life has to be fun 19.22

fundamentalism in Buddhism 7.314, 7.471, 21.246; in Buddhism, a sort of quasi-fundamentalism 14.299–300; fundamentalist approach concerned with what the Buddha 'really said' 2.50–1; fundamentalists' insistence on the observation of irrelevant rules 7.262–3; modern aggressive fundamentalism 21.246; Pāli fundamentalists among Western Buddhists 11.379

fundraising appealing to people's natural generosity 17.199–200; Friends of the Triyana Vardhana Vihara 23.82–3, 23.324; fundraising for the Karuna Trust 10.88; fundraising for the London Buddhist Centre 3.622–3; fundraising for the FWBO 4.612–13, 12.407, 12.663; support for the ITBCI school in Kalimpong 12.435; with the support of the *Diamond Sūtra* 21.311–12

funerals

general
the absurdity of a Christian funeral service 24.378–9; ceremony in Nepal 21.276; Chinese rites for the dead 1.384, 2.232; for famous monks and holy persons, death rites may last for a year or two 2.232; Indian funerals 3.27, 13.221–3, 15.142; not necessarily solemn affairs 13.221; rice balls offered to the dead in after-death ceremonies 4.478; Sikkimese death ceremony 2.231; Tibetan sky burial 15.142–3; wind or air burial 12.692

Buddhist funerals
the domestic ceremony most closely associated with Buddhism 2.231–2; funerals at the Buddha's time 10.490–3, 10.651–2; costly funeral rites in Chinese Buddhism 8.175; performing funerals 15.702–3; rejoicing in merits at a funeral 11.734

Sangharakshita and funerals
the beauty of a cremation by the river 12.221, 15.143, 22.202–3; funerals in London when he was a child 15.143; Uncle Jack's 24.122–8; Burma Raja's 15.143–4, 22.206–7; Miss Barclay's 15.146, 22.83–5; Raja Dorji's 22.35–8, 23.119; Mrs Rao's 22.201–3; the funeral of Miss Barclay's cat 22.47; a *puṇyanumodanā* (after-death ceremony) in Pune 10.xlvii, 24.19

Furlong, Monica 10.306–7, 24.204, 24.208, 24.661–2 (n261)

future

reflections
if our future lies anywhere, it lies in the mind 3.479, 25.390; imagination loses itself in the future and in the past 7.285; imaginatively linking with past and future, break out of the cocoon of the present 17.403; a neurotic preoccupation with what is going to happen 18.460–1; assuming that certain events will follow from what you do, they often do 17.161; our past and our future are the product of our ethical decisions 17.637; past and future exist only as concepts 8.289; past, present, and future are only relatively real 17.405; 'Renounce what lies in the future, give up that which is past …' (*Dhammapada*) 7.285; we can be sure that what we do now will affect the future 15.89; the will-o'-the-wisp, Tomorrow 25.308; worrying about the future 18.340

the future of Buddhism
the future of the sangha 10.261–75; the future of Tibetan Buddhism (as seen in 1966) 13.99–112; looking back at Buddhist history to prepare for the Dharma's future 8.226; without a spiritual community, there is no future for Buddhism in the West 3.xi–xii

Sangharakshita
his experience of future events 19.84, 20.85–6; an occultist's vision of his future 20.25

G

Gabb, W. J. 8.370–1

Gabriel (angel) 13.599–600

Gabrieli, Giovanni 24.589

Gadgadasvara (bodhisattva) 14.130, 14.176

Gadgil, N. V. 10.177

Gadrabha Sutta *see Aṅguttara Nikāya*

Gaganagañja Sūtra 7.41

Gaikwad, A. 10.357

Gaikwad, B. K. 23.88

Gainsborough, Thomas 12.76, 26.361

Gaitskell, Hugh 23.493 (n152)

Galileo Galilei 23.315, 23.524 (n359)

Gallagher, Shaun 8.613

gallnuts 3.590, 16.406

gambling 17.257, 24.541

games bodhisattva activity is like playing a game 19.193; if you are Enlightened, worldly 'bliss' is like a grown man playing with toys 18.589; listed in the Pāli canon 16.236, 16.606 (n168); we are absorbed in games, like the children in the burning house 9.358–9, 16.74; no longer caught up in the games people play 3.276; the true revolutionary does not play other people's games 26.18

Gampopa

who he was
brief introduction 2.744 (n685); lack of historical perspective 2.442; Milarepa's 'sun pupil' 18.260–1, 19.510

THE JEWEL ORNAMENT OF LIBERATION

introduction
Sangharakshita's reading, *see under* Sangharakshita/reading; inspiration to the Triratna Buddhist Order 2.555, 11.377; study seminars 24.172, 24.225; Kagyu text 2.555–6; preface (by Guenther) 2.440

the text
the *arūpa dhyānas* 5.249–51; the benevolence of bodhisattvas 5.186; the *bodhicitta*: *śūnyatā* endowed with the essence of compassion 2.162; the bodhisattva precepts 11.319; 'A Bodhisattva puts on armour/ In order to gather all beings around him' 4.97–8; bodhisattvas of the path 4.180; the Buddha is the ultimate refuge 2.425, 2.441, 11.310; the bodhisattva as spiritual friend 2.161; constant activity in pursuit of politics and business is laziness 4.132, 17.534, 18.390, 19.582; *dāna* 14.657 (n502), 16.584 (n6); developing *mettā* 5.184–5; 'Enlightened attitude' 4.257; ethics and manners 4.336, 11.309; 'How is it that we have not already attained Buddhahood?' 13.138; 'I shall rejoice at staying in hell for thousands of aeons ...' 4.60; one should 'think of a spiritual friend as the Buddha' 4.175–6; pleasing spiritual friends 4.176; the results of the perfection of morality 11.321; sheds light on Going for Refuge 2.425, 2.441; spiritual exercises instead of sleep 5.305–6; 'a spiritual friend in the form of an ordinary human being' 2.700 (n370), 3.604, 4.172, 11.371, 15.586; the stage of Buddha activity 17.459; 'Whatever immeasurable offerings there may be ...' 13.271

THE SUPREME PATH OF DISCIPLESHIP: THE PRECEPTS OF THE GURUS

introduction
brief introduction 22.610 (n300); an important source of inspiration for Sangharakshita 22.375; seminar 24.159–60

the text
'Attachment may be mistaken for benevolence and compassion' 5.169–72; a cause of regret to abandon any being, for all have been our kindly parents 5.152–5; 'Cessation of thought-processes mistaken for quiescence of infinite mind' 5.228–9, 5.421–3; 'Having experienced spiritual illumination, commune with it in solitude' 5.671–5; 'Should there be great drowsiness, persevere in thine efforts' 5.678–80; 'Those who outwardly profess, but do not practise, religion' 5.373–5; 'Thought-forms, being the revelry of Reality, are not to be avoided' 5.596–9; 'To differ from the multitude in every thought and action is the sign of a superior man' 3.470; spiritual armour 4.547

Gamre, Krishna 23.81–2

gaṇa 10.479

Gaṇakamoggallāna Sutta *see under* *Majjhima Nikāya*

Gaṇapati (elephant-headed god in Hinduism) 10.46

Gaṇḍavyūha Sūtra

introducing the sūtra
introduction 1.354–5, 3.88, 7.501–2, 14.217–27, 16.17; based on one of the legends of the *Divyāvadāna* 14.218; the last of a group of three *sūtras* known as the *Avataṃsaka* 1.352; a disreputable lama who nonetheless taught it effectively 13.177–8, 19.163; grand inscrutable mystery 14.218; set in a concrete world of glowing particulars 1.355; the history of the inner religious consciousness of Samantabhadra 2.179, 14.218; a passage resembling Prajñāpāramitā paradox 14.225–6; 'a sort of Buddhist *Pilgrim's Progress*' 14.218, 16.17; D. T. Suzuki on the *sūtra* 14.217–18, 14.222–3; one of nine *sūtras* venerated in Nepal 14.100; Guenther's translation 21.147; its vision of the Buddhist life 14.223

the story
the opening: the Buddha at Śrāvastī 14.218–19; Sudhana's pilgrimage 1.354–5, 3.88, 4.646, 14.218–27, 16.17, 21.147; Mañjuśrī in the *sūtra* 1.355, 2.161, 2.173–4, 14.220; the teachers Sudhana meets on the way 14.220–22; Samantabhadra in the *sūtra* 1.355, 2.179, 14.218, 14.226–7; *Bhadracari-praṇidhāna-rāja* (vows) 14.227

the Vairocana Tower of Maitreya
Maitreya in the tower 14.222–6; how Sudhana enters the tower 14.223; the dwelling place of all who understand the meaning of emptiness … 14.222; description of the tower 14.223–4; contains all the phenomena of the universe, perfectly interpenetrating 1.355, 3.88, 16.17; and Glastonbury Tor 26.613; a Jewel-Tower 25.213; marvellous offerings 14.224–5; mirrors reflecting myriad worlds 14.224; the ravishingly beautiful sounds of the tower 14.224; stands for the *dharmadhātu* 14.223; a symbol of the *bodhicitta* 4.165

doctrines
the role of good friends in the spiritual life 2.161, 14.218, 14.220–2; the bodhisattva career 2.165; description of the *bodhicitta* 2.165–6, 4.35, 4.165, 14.223; the fundamental insight: the mutual interpenetration of everything 14.219; the *trikāya* doctrine 2.45

Gandhāra the Buddha's footprint 2.223; sculptures, *see under* Buddha images/ history

gandharvas in the *Dhammapada* 15.55; Doṇa wants to know if the Buddha is one 3.141; the *Large Prajñāpāramitā Sūtra* preserved in their king's abode 14.145; live on perfume 16.348; musicians in the palace of Indra 16.349; ruled by Dhṛtarāṣṭra 16.346; a song by Pañcasikha the celestial musician 26.121–3; uxorious 16.349

Gandhavyūhāhāra deities 16.554

Gandhi, Indira 10.301, 20.191, 22.344

Gandhi, Mohandas Karamchand

his life
introduction 7.584 (n215); Salt March 23.347, 23.582 (n387); fasting 6.612, 9.7, 10.24, 20.303, 22.291; financial support 16.396; association with Sarojini Naidu 7.56, 7.57; stayed at Dr Mehta's Nature Cure Clinic in Poona 22.291, 23.349; *Mahatma* (Tendulgar) 22.276, 22.600 (n221); mind-reading 22.481; Mirabehn, *see* Mirabehn; assassination 10.540–1, 20.292–3; birth anniversary celebrations 22.196; Satyapriya invokes his spirit through the Ouija board 20.352; the film *Gandhi* 10.311, 10.337–8; *Gandhi and his Critics* 10.55; *Gandhi Marg* (review) 8.382–3; harsh criticism of Gandhi 24.528; *Hind Swaraj* 22.159, 22.588 (n144)

and the Dalits
he called them 'Harijans' 9.31, 9.59; disliked by Dalits 6.612, 10.311; he claimed to represent the Dalits, but they did not recognize him in that role 10.23; Gandhi and Dr Ambedkar 9.5, 9.53, 9.75–8, 9.125, 10.liii–iv, 10.24; Untouchability is 'on its last legs' 9.59, 10.361; *What Congress and Gandhi Have Done to the Untouchables*, *see* Ambedkar/publications

thoughts, sayings, and character
'All virtues to be practised in a spirit of humility' 4.118, 17.605; argued that the Buddha must have believed in God 23.200; 'The end is the extreme of the means' 13.75, 19.100, 25.83; his economic ideals appealed to Sangharakshita 22.159; 'I carry my cave around with me' 19.492; on vivisection 8.214; non-violence (*ahiṃsā*) 7.119, 8.453; outwardly humble and meek, but very bold 4.446

Gandhi, Rajiv 10.301, 10.702 (n299), 22.344

Gandhi, Sanjay 22.344

Gandhinagar, India 9.498, 24.115–17

Ganesha 16.361, 16.411

Ganga Guru 22.538

Ganges, River bathing not in the Ganges but in the Dharma 1.62; belief in the purifying effect of bathing in the Ganges 3.194, 10.457–8; the Buddha crosses the Ganges by means of supernormal power 10.643, 10.648; Buddhas incalculable as the sands of the Ganges 1.44; crossing the Ganges 22.167, 22.232; the Gotama Gate and the Gotama Ford 10.643, 10.648; Hindus having to get Ganges water sent to them for ceremonies 10.245; peacocks in the trees near the Ganges 20.385; pilgrims at Benares (Varanasi) 20.387, 23.360–1; Sakaligali Ghat 22.50; Sangharakshita spends the night on the river bank near Lucknow 20.384–5; the sun rising above the river 22.49–50

Gangeshwarananda, Swami (Ramakrishna Mission) v21, v22

Gangtok *see under* Sikkim

Ganhar, J. N. and P. N. 8.380–1

ganthadhura (the way or burden of study) 2.143, 4.568

Ganymede 25.397

gārava meaning 26.628; *gāravas*, *see* six *gāravas*

Gārava Sutta *see under Saṃyutta Nikāya*/ famous *suttas*

garbha 14.210–11

garbha-dhātu (womb-element) 1.388

gardens and gardening the archetype of the garden 24.72, 25.146; better to have the weeds of superstition than the sterile garden of rationalism 12.105; the Garden of Eden 1.528, 15.619, 25.390; *The Garden of Cyrus* 12.218; the garden of Gethsemane 3.52; the ideal of the gardener 18.105; imagining yourself growing in a garden, unfolding your petals 18.105; Order members like trainee gardeners 11.516; 'My Secret Garden' (poem) 25.393; pruning one's thoughts like pruning a rose 25.219; the sangha as a garden in a wilderness 25.145–7; Sangharakshita gardening 21.534; *see also* farming

Gardiner, Rolf 8.545, 8.546–7

garlic abstention from 2.208, 19.559

Garrie, John v23

garuḍas (mythological winged creatures) 4.477, 16.349

garudhammas *see* eight special conditions

garuka-kamma *see* karma/weighty

Gaskell, Mrs 26.490

gate gate pāragate *see under Heart Sūtra*

Gateless Gate *see Mumonkan*

gātha (verses) 14.24, 16.234–5

gati (sphere of existence) 14.73

gatigocara (experience) 11.73–4

Gauba, K. L. 9.55

Gauḍapāda brief introduction 7.569 (n127); *ajātavāda* 7.132, 7.587 (n233); borrowed from the Mādhyamikas 1.323; the denial of the existence of the world of appearance 7.194; 'No *jīva* is ever born' 7.134; was he a Buddhist? 7.72

Gaulle, Charles de 23.453, 23.539 (n475)

gauris (fair ones) 16.362

Gautam, Jungi Bahadur (student) v21

Gautam, Munishilal 10.381

Gautier, Pierre Jules Théophile 23.182

Gay News 11.326–8

Gayā Head Hindu temple 10.437; in the *Udāna*, *see under Udāna*/settings; where the Buddha taught the Fire Sermon 10.457

Gayā Kāśyapa *see* Kāśyapa brothers

Gayasata 13.342

Gazamair, Lachuman (student) v21, v22

Gedun, Prince 8.528

Geering, Lloyd 24.499–501, 24.563

gelong 7.481, 7.483–4, 12.14, 13.45

Gelu Rimpoche v22

Gelug *see under* Tibetan Buddhism/schools

Gemmell, William 3.361, 14.3

gender 16.538–9, 23.438

gender fluidity *see* transsexual

Gendun Drup 13.35–6

general arriving at general conclusions from limited experience 10.612; the Buddha's teaching is general, even abstract, and aimed at the intelligence 12.322; the Buddha's thinking was not abstract and general, but concrete and particular 7.225; going from the more general and abstract to the more and more specific: the Dharma essence 18.413; misleading generalizations about Buddhist history 7.71; the path is not a

vague, general process, but specific action 11.370, 12.280–1, 15.83; the term evolution can be applied to almost anything, as a general principle 1.564, 3.475; you can't practise meditation and mindfulness in a general way, you need specific methods 12.467; you need three things: the general teaching, the Pith-Instruction, and your own judgement 18.408

General Strike 20.498

generosity *see under dāna*

Genghis Khan 8.518, 26.59

genius of the artist 3.513–14; different from an ordinary person by degree, not kind 3.57–8, 26.181; often very simple 12.152; originally guardian deity 3.513; and evolution 3.59–60; hard for a man of some genius to be associated with a man with more 26.333; at first works alone, then there is a general raising of cultural sensibility 3.58; marked out by individuality 3.59–60; the problem of communicating their insight 12.152; the qualities of genius 15.193–4; Turner was a great genius 26.254–5; we can appreciate works of genius because of an affinity with them 3.58

Genko (Shinran's teacher) 1.328

geography 20.387

George, St 16.357

George V, King 20.27, 26.578

George, Stefan 25.279

Gerke, Robert v24

Germany

general references
audiences like an intellectual presentation of Buddhism (Govinda) 3.303–4; damage in the Second World War 24.597–8; German Romantic movement 24.568, 24.587, 26.255–6; Second World War, *see under* Second World War; a young man with an interest in the Nazi movement 19.101

Berlin
botanical gardens 24.587; Buddhist Centre 11.695, 12.610, 12.618, 24.361, 24.587; Charlottenburg Palace 24.587; Hakuin's restaurant 26.535; a piece of the Berlin Wall 24.361; visits 12.602–27, 25.3, 26.405, 26.451, 26.505

Cologne
Romano-German Museum 24.369; School of Painting 24.369; Wallraf-Richard Museum 24.369–70

Essen
Akashadhatu men's community 24.600–1; FWBO 11.563, 24.361, 24.367–9; Sangharakshita resolves to lead a puja in German 24.368; Sangharakshita visits 11.727–36, 24.367–9, 24.599–600, 24.600–1; Sumandala women's community 24.599; Windhorse Evolution shop 24.601

Munich
art galleries 24.587–8; Bavarian State Opera 24.589; Botanical Garden 24.589; churches 24.589–990; Englischer Garten 24.588–9; Stuck Villa 24.590–1

Nuremberg
the castle 24.596; Dürer's House 24.596–7; the German Museum 24.597; Nuremberg trials 10.56, 20.150, 26.396; Edwin Muir's description of the city 24.597

Sangharakshita visits
support for the growth of the FWBO in Germany 24.383; visit in 2001 26.404; Mainfrankisches Museum 24.599; Old Main Bridge 24.598; the Residenz 24.599

other places
Aachen 11.729, 24.7, 24.370; Augsburg 24.591–2; Dresden 24.526, 24.592; Düsseldorf 24.370, 26.255, 26.505; Memmingen 24.594; Minden 24.600; Recklinghausen 24.600; Ulm 24.594–5; Weimar 11.729; Würzburg 24.597–9

geruamati 3.404, 20.225

Gervaise, Nicolas 2.635

gestalt the gestalt hindered from being given full expression 18.280–1; the gestalt is in terms of space what the continuum is in terms of time 19.239–40; the gestalt of a Buddhist text 14.301; the meaning of the word 18.650 (n107), 19.239; not a metaphysical entity, not static or inert 18.282; the reflection of the *dharmakāya* in the individual 18.281–2; the truth is a sort of gestalt, a whole, complete in itself 10.595–6; our whole life is the working out of a pattern, a gestalt 18.279–87; we impinge on the world in accordance with the pattern which is ourselves 16.475; your view is not quite the same as your gestalt 19.212

gesture *see mudrā; kāyavijñāpti*

Gethin, Rupert 8.623–5

getting sidetracked 5.445, 16.231, 19.9–10; *see also* distraction

geya (Pāli *geyya*) 14.23, 16.235, 17.571

Ghaṭīkāra Sutta *see under Majjhima Nikāya*

Ghiberti, Lorenzo 23.312, 23.522 (n353)

Ghoom monastery and Dhardo Rimpoche 21.309; Sangharakshita's first visit 7.16, 7.74–6, 20.133–4, 21.258; and Tomo Geshe Rimpoche 13.78; visit with Lama Govinda and Li Gotami 21.256–9

Ghosh, Eta (Kalimpong) 21.156–7

ghosts and apparitions

introduction
the alienated self, a fictitious, rather ghostly little self 10.602; being haunted by ghosts of the past (*White Lotus Sūtra*) 16.70; a bodhisattva may prove irreversibility by conjuring a ghost to depart 2.169; a Buddha appears to others as a child, a madman, a ghost 11.11–12; the Cock Lane Ghost 2.34, 2.667 (n53); confronting the ghosts of your past life 18.203–4; the ghost of a Bengali lady in Kalimpong 22.323–4; ghosts in a graveyard 13.229; haunted by fear of death, like a man who sees a ghost but pretends it isn't there 23.92; hungry ghosts, *see* hungry ghosts; *mahābhūtas*, 'great ghosts', see *mahābhūtas*; a mental experience of a dead person (not a ghost) 17.622; to perceive the Buddha, we have to dispel the ghost of God 3.152; on the Vajrayāna path you may appear to be mad, or like an animal, or like a ghost 13.176

Sangharakshita's experiences
experiences of people after their death 4.559, 26.622–3, 26.674; feeling of being insubstantial in a world of ghosts 20.74; an apparition of a dead friend in a pit 5.xxx, 11.455–7, 12.438–9, 23.387–91; *see also* Sangharakshita VI/spiritual and supernatural experiences

Gibbon, Edward 13.533, 21.365

Gibran, Kahlil (*The Prophet*) 1.129, 1.604 (n114–5)

Gide, André discovery of his homosexuality 22.588–9 (n150); he had to teach himself to enjoy life 26.63; quotations 8.156–7; *Corydon* 13.612; *Fruits of the Earth* 22.135–6; *If It Die* 22.166, 22.588–9 (n150); *The Immoralist* 22.135

Gilbert and Sullivan 20.37, 26.365, 26.501

Gilgamesh (epic) 3.96, 24.359, 26.481

Gilgit Sanskrit texts 7.503, 7.528, 7.632 (n606), 14.30, 14.108, 14.147, 14.190, 16.35; *Gilgit Manuscripts* 7.632 (n606), 20.135

Gill family *see* Aniketa, Ratnamala, Silaprabha, Suvajri

Ginés, José 24.416

Ginsberg, Allen

his life
brief introduction 2.738 (n656); Albert Hall poetry reading 22.568, 23.123, 23.493 (n151), 24.652 (n219); the best-known American Buddhist of his time 23.123; chanting Blake's poems 26.485; contrast with Christmas Humphreys 24.178–80; as guru 3.561; a man without a mask 24.176, 25.93; he once stripped naked to demonstrate the naked truth 13.243, 19.260, 25.93; he was greater than his poetry: sincere, selfless, even saintly 24.175–6; his guru was William Blake 23.123, 24.176; his view of 'academic' poetry 2.534, 24.176; his 'wife' Peter 13.612, 22.566–8, 23.123, 25.93; photographs 22.564, 24.177; tour of India 23.123

his work
compared with Whitman 26.376; an experiment that failed 26.375–6; *Howl* and *Kaddish* 22.565, 22.567, 22.629–30 (n416); *Poems All Over the Place, Mostly Seventies* 24.178, 24.653 (n224); *Reality Sandwiches* 23.123; 'Sunflower Sutra' 25.lvi

Ginsberg and Buddhism
curiosity about Tantric sexual practices 13.612, 22.568; meets Dudjom Rimpoche 22.568; meets Yogi Chen 22.568; preoccupation with Tantric initiation 22.566–8; and Chögyam Trungpa 24.176–7

Ginsberg and Sangharakshita
'In Memory of Allen Ginsberg' (poem) 25.413; surprise that a radical Buddhist like Sangharakshita wrote traditional poetry 26.640; Sangharakshita admired his honesty 11.626; Sangharakshita's

view of his poetry 11.626, 24.175; their meetings in London 22.568, 23.123, 24.175–8, 26.485; 'With Allen Ginsberg in Kalimpong' 22.565–8, 22.630 (n423)

Giordano, Luca 24.300, 24.681 (n366)

Giorgione 23.258, 23.512–13 (n296)

Giotto 13.593–4, 13.646, 23.259, 23.314, 23.513 (n301), 23.523 (n359)

Gissing, George 12.643–4, 24.374, 26.339

giving *see dāna*

giving up

giving up in relation to people
don't give up on someone you find difficult 17.185; not giving up family life, but making all humanity your family 17.363, 18.214–15; Siddhārtha's courage in giving up his disciples' expectations 3.52, 3.472; when you join the sangha, you give up your separate identity 9.195; the would-be bodhisattva's temptation to give up on people in despair 4.187–8

other kinds of giving up
the breakthrough when the rational mind really gives up 18.189; difficulty of giving up customs 9.417, 10.277–8; don't give up your principles, even at the cost of sacrificing life 10.168; to give up craving is Dhamma (Ambedkar) 9.288; 'I don't believe in encouraging people to give up their worldly commitments' 4.455; it's not easy to give up your own will 4.302; the monk doesn't 'give up the world' 15.492–3; the more you give up yourself, the more perfectly yourself you become 5.656; no form of Buddhism requires you to give up bliss 19.379; not giving up, but growing up 1.497; not giving up rules, but following them without attachment 4.186; 'Renounce what lies in the future, give up that which is past …' 7.285; results come when you try very hard, fail, and truly give up 18.189; the spiritually committed can never give up hope on anyone 16.434; we hope we can achieve peace without giving up violence 12.360; you can't have pleasure without pain, so you must be ready to give up both 10.482

see also
renunciation

Gladstone, William 8.703 (n302)

Glasenapp, Helmuth von 8.383, 13.413, 13.566

Glasgow

Sangharakshita visits
Art Gallery and Museum 24.141–2, 24.322; a talk at Glasgow University 23.177–80, 23.182–3; a tour around the city 23.178–9, 24.140–1; the Voltaire and Rousseau bookshop, Otago Street 24.140

Buddhist Centre
centre in Sauchiehall Street 24.140; premises and community, Heruka, in Kelvinside 24.135–6, 24.638–9 (n158); questions and answers 24.142–3; Susiddhi's involvement 17.8; taken more seriously once it had its own property 15.718

Glastonbury, England the atmosphere of the place 18.23; 'On Glastonbury Tor' 23.469, 25.xxxvi, 25.liii, 26.612–13, 26.640; Glastonbury Tor 19.413, 24.70, 24.624 (n94), 26.613; visit with Carter 26.612–13, 26.615; visit with Paramartha 26.547

globalization 3.615

globe 'contradictory' projections of the globe 26.201; 'When silence settles on the globe …' 25.404; *see also* world

glorious deeds *see Avadānas*

glory the Buddha's human body like rags thrown over his spiritual glory 1.264; 'The Glory of the Literary World', *see under* Sangharakshita XIII/publication history; 'going from glory to glory' (Bible) 16.109; a halo in religious art 19.185; morning glory, *see under* flowers; seeing the Buddha as actually present in a glorious form 2.41–2; the undimmed glory of Nirvāṇa 2.150; the yogi's glory 19.185

glow-worms 1.230, 10.611–12, 25.495–6

Gnosticism

introduction
brief description 16.606 (n169); an alternative Western tradition 8.426–7, 13.374; a pre-Christian religion 8.425; ascetic and licentious Gnostics 8.427; deconditioning 8.426–7; doctrine of the Alien whose true home is Elsewhere 8.426, 8.428, 23.111; drunkenness and sleep as symbols for lack of awareness 16.170; Egypt as Gnostic symbol 16.220; 'fallen into the world' 14.478; Gospel of Thomas 4.142, 16.22; *The Gnostic Religion*, *see* Jonas; *The Gnostics*, *see* Lacarrière; Gnostics and the spiritual community 8.428; the 'Hymn of the Pearl' 4.646, 16.91, 16.170, 16.220; knew that sense experience is only part of the spectrum

of human experience 5.51; of Aivanhov 24.531; the Lazy Men (Enchites or Messalians) 8.427; *Pistis Sophia* 8.425, 16.238; 'a stranger here' 14.492, 23.111, 25.87; Valentinius 13.596

docetism
the docetic heresy 13.300, 13.692 (n118); relating to the Buddha's life 1.189–90, 1.250, 4.85, 4.135–6, 13.300, 14.188, 26.636

Gnosticism and Buddhism
an almost Gnostic world view from the life of Padmasambhava 8.525; 'Buddhism and Gnosis' (Conze) 8.537–8, 16.606 (n170); comparison between Gnosticism and Buddhism 8.426, 16.238–9; the sense of a connection to Mahāyāna Buddhism 16.238–9; Sophia, the Divine Wisdom (compared to Prajñāpāramitā) 13.603–4, 14.343

Goa, India 9.319, 11.297

goal

what is the goal?
introduction 2.120–33; we need to be clear what 'goal' means 17.355; the Pāli word *attha* means 'good' and also 'goal' 15.260–1; what is the goal of Buddhism? – don't answer too slickly 12.121–2; any goal becomes a new starting point 17.356–7; described as consciousness 2.129; described as though personal for practical reasons 2.129; different conceptions of the goal of Buddhism 11.72; the assumption that it is a state or experience 7.168; danger of describing it in abstract terms 2.127; the goal of the Vajrayāna 7.506, 18.75; the goal as the object of worship 2.128; how is it possible to describe it in terms of personality? 2.127–9; Indian Buddhism sees it more in terms of knowledge than emotion 2.126; need to counteract a tendency to think of it as existing 'out there' 2.131; poetical descriptions 2.131–2; thinking of it as an experience 11.72; to harmonize thoughts, words, and deeds and raise them higher 7.141

the goal and the path
the Buddha placed more emphasis on the path than on the goal 15.241; the end is the extreme of means 2.122; the goal is implicit in the path 18.164–5; the path is the goal 25.83; 'The Path is one for all, the means to reach the goal must vary with the Pilgrims' 7.363, 24.49; to determine the next step in your spiritual life you need a definite goal 18.272–3; the spiritual life has no goal, the means is the goal 7.412; the two things with which the Dharma is sconcerned 11.385; we need a clear idea of both the goal and the steps necessary to achieve it 15.95–6

working towards the goal
being goal-oriented 25.83; consciousness of the goal helps you free yourself from unskilful mental states 18.443; consists in the permanent eradication of all unhealthy mental attitudes 2.122; developing the habit of recollecting one's goal often and deeply 15.96; the goal isn't reached by wrong means any more than milk comes from a cow's horn 14.42; goal-orientation 5.389, 5.404–5; goal-setting 3.224–9; little by little 18.411; 'A man never flies so high as when he doesn't know where he is going' 4.500; short-term goals give us something to work on and a measure of progress 15.95–6; Stream Entry is the most worthwhile goal in this life – and it is *achievable* 4.87; without a goal, no progress in the spiritual life 3.398; your arrival at the goal depends on intensity of effort 15.241–2

the ultimate goal
attained out of time, eternally attained 4.201; *bodhi* 2.126; the cessation of the whole process of phenomenal existence 2.123; from the perspective of reality the attainment of a goal becomes absurd 18.44–5; peace 2.124–5, 5.213, 15.262; the positive goal: Nirvāṇa, the highest bliss 7.120; positive qualities affirmed of the goal to a superlative degree 2.128; the ultimate goal of the spiritual life is the Unconditioned 2.149; 'the ultimate unborn voidness' 18.102–3; when the goal is reached, things are seen as they really are 7.412

see also
the goal of Enlightenment, *see under* Enlightenment

goats a goat cooked at Lumbini: violation of the first precept 20.420; the goatherd's banyan tree 10.437; Marpa requires a disciple to give everything, even a lame goat 12.18–19, 19.530; Rechungpa is distracted watching the play of goats 19.9–11, 19.76, 19.77–80; scapegoat, *see* scapegoat

God

ASPECTS OF GOD

the concept of God
based on a fallacy 2.87; different ideas about God (Christian, Hindu, Muslim) 10.233–5; as father-substitute 3.549–50, 7.93, 12.94–5, 12.233; 'How big is God?' 26.475, 26.479; self-contradictory 3.448; societies that have no word for such a

concept 13.565; 'a stream of tendency making for righteousness' 15.631; whose centre is everywhere and whose circumference is nowhere 7.103

Creator God
the belief that experience is caused by 'God's creative activity' 10.712 (n413); the consequences of the view that God created Nature for man 8.xxiii–iv; the effects of believing in a Creator God 2.695 (n338); 'Gods can create themselves, but not others' (Dharmapala) 8.15; God was not created by anybody 9.228; called by Hindus *Saguṇa Brahman* 9.228; the idea is usually enough to satisfy the ordinary man or woman 14.602; praising God for the beauty of creation 4.594; the voice symbolizing the creation of the world by God 26.204

personal God
the conception of a personal God 7.92–3; the difficulties of theologians attempting to prove that God is personal 7.212; egoism lurks in the longing for communion with a personal God 7.405; if there is no personal God, what becomes of prayer and worship? 12.10; the split between reason and emotion produces demand for God's existence 14.444

God of Power
the demands of the God of Power 11.339; in the Book of Job 13.542; because God is seen as so powerful, blasphemy is a terrible offence 11.334–6; difficult to get free of the concept of God as judge 7.97; divine authority 1.528–9; fear of God 10.205–6, 11.361–2, 15.620, 15.719, 16.308–9; God's representative 3.448–9; in a sense the God of Nature 15.618–21; the judge 3.99–100; making God angry 16.307–8; the most powerful member of the group 19.277; putting the fear of God into people 17.181–2; a tree as a demonstration of the power of God 7.94; the will of God 7.97, 15.620–1

God of Love
God as lover 7.96–7; having an ideal of the God of love without feeling love at all 19.182; love of God 7.93–5; New Testament teaching (the Old Testament teaches a God of Power) 3.449, 15.623; popes criticized for not representing the God of Love 3.449; representatives of God represent the God of Power, not the God of Love 3.448–9

other aspects of God
acts of God 3.448; does God dare look St Francis in the face? 25.367; it's easy to say you've given everything to God and then hang on to it 4.358; for Christianity God and man are entirely different beings 11.106; the grace of God 4.7, 4.139, 18.538; giver of prosperity 17.19–20; a glimpse of a higher dimension – 'call it God if you must' 3.275; God has become an embarrassment for modern Christians 12.113; 'God is friendship' 13.619; infallible word of God 9.99; the 'mind of God' 17.437; a muddled response to the idea that everything is God 18.632–3; not an attractive character in *Paradise Lost* 13.584; practice of awareness of the presence of God 13.627; prophets hearing 'the voice of God' 11.151; worship 7.97–8

belief in God
an example of ignorance 3.193–4; faith in God 9.342; an infantile attitude in Freud's view 12.95; is it really necessary to believe in an almighty Creator? 13.566; like having an angry father 17.337; often associated with fear 10.205–6, 15.620, 17.336–7; *regressus ad infinitum* 9.333; a survival from pre-scientific times 8.282; because people want to feel safe, comfortable, loved 12.655; one who assents to the idea is 'a coward' 3.471; the result of rationalization 26.155; to believe in God *and* obey him is pitiable 26.13; theists can struggle to understand why God lets them suffer 15.370; the traditional image of God must go 12.130; why people feel the need for God 8.260

not believing in God
the Bishop of Woolwich on the decline of traditional theism 12.5–6, 12.45; God is dead (Nietzsche) 3.497, 12.44; 'I think I must never have believed in God' 13.565; is it possible to be moral without believing in God? 8.281–2; it doesn't indicate religious deficiency 13.565; the onus is on people who believe in God to prove he exists 9.344–5, 10.150, 13.565; religion without belief in God 12.7; without God, no religion? 9.493

GOD AND BUDDHISM

introduction
a spiritual way of life without reference to God 9.283–4, 9.493, 12.7; theism referred to in the Pāli texts 1.158, 10.517; in Buddhism morality takes the place of God 9.99; Buddhism's rejection of the idea of God 8.xix, 12.55; the Buddhist position on the non-existence of God 7.9–10; Buddhists who find the idea of God ridiculous 4.126, 12.622; Dharmapala's argument for God being

a Buddhist 8.15; disappointing when Buddhist teachers play down Buddhism's non-theism 4.125; to perceive the Buddha, we have to dispel the ghost of God 3.152; wanting to fill a God-shaped hole in the Buddha's teaching 3.151–2, 13.566; why Buddhism cannot believe in a First Cause 9.389; why Buddhism does not believe in God 10.138

belief in God a wrong view
an example of ignorance 3.193–4; like the horn of a rabbit, a non-existent entity cannot have attributes 17.641–2; Pāli canon references 2.695 (n338), 10.138, 13.442; the question of belief in God in the fourteen inexpressibles 17.641; a wrong view that prevents us from developing as individuals 10.138, 11.361, 12.97; it hinders the attainment of Enlightenment 1.20, 2.245, 7.523, 11.107

misunderstandings
'the Buddha who created the universe' (missionary's neologism) 2.129, 13.565; correcting the misunderstanding of the Adibuddha as a Creator God 7.535–6; it's understandable to confuse 'God' with the transcendental 14.605–6; the misunderstanding that the Buddhas of the Mahāyāna were creator gods 7.535–6; no Buddhist text attributes to the Buddha the creation of the universe 2.129

see also
Buddhism is non-theistic, *see under* Buddhism I/what Buddhism is not; God as Nobodaddy, *see under* Blake/his views; monotheism, *see* monotheism

Godāniya (continent) 16.342

Godbole, W. R. 10.116–17

Goddard, Dwight (*A Buddhist Bible*) 1.356, 9.137, 9.138, 18.xii, 20.151, 22.241

Godden, Rumer 21.73

goddesses all goddesses are earth goddesses 16.385, 16.409; earth goddess, *see* earth goddess; eight offering goddesses, *see* offering goddesses; a night goddess in the *Gaṇḍavyūha Sūtra* 14.220–1; in the *Sūtra of Golden Light* 14.243–4, 16.245, 16.371; in the *Vimalakīrti-nirdeśa* 14.164–5, 16.456, 16.538–9, 22.435; the White Goddess, the poet's Muse 25.433; *see also* individual goddesses

Godhika (Pāli canon monk) 8.451

gods the gods of the underworld 25.345; marble gods in the gallery 25.400; originally it seems that all gods were gods of the soil 19.414–15; people living a happy, god-like life may not want to hear about the Dharma 19.496; saviour gods: the human tendency to manufacture divinities who might help 7.43–4; 'these gods and goddesses that men have framed' 25.xxxv, 25.290; unconscious worship of Greek and Egyptian gods 12.52; worship of gods 11.248

see also
Buddhist gods, *see devas*; the god realm in the wheel of life, *see under* wheel of life; god realms, *see under* heavens; Hindu gods, *see under* Hinduism; local deities, *see* local deities; pagan gods, *see under* paganism; rebirth as a god, *see under* rebirth/where one will be reborn

Godse, Nathuram (Gandhi's assassin) 20.293

Godwin, William introduction 8.702 (n291); benevolence 8.448; 'Literature … forms the … line of demarcation between human and animal kingdoms' 14.291, 26.321; relationship between Shelley and Godwin 26.223–3

Goenka, S. N. 5.445, 5.742–3 (n428)

Goethe, J. W.

his life
Dr Ambedkar's appreciation of him 9.199; compared to the Buddha, even Goethe was ordinary 11.371; an example of someone who gave style to his character 3.500–1; friendship with Schiller 26.365; he deliberately kept people at a distance 19.122; his greatest poem was his life 3.471; made some approach to the Dharma 16.375; meeting with Beethoven 7.573 (n149), 20.72, 26.503; Napoleon's view of him: 'Look, there is a man!' 3.501; one of the noblest examples of self-development in Western culture 23.473

thoughts and quotations
admiration of Goldsmith's *The Vicar of Wakefield* 24.582; the male human form more beautiful than the female 23.289; on appreciation 4.593, 4.713 (n360); on letters 21.457; on self-education and self-transformation 11.463; the 'open secret', the sacred mystery of the universe 26.178; something sun-like … 3.58; 'to have fathomed the fathomable, and quietly to revere the unfathomable' 11.57; 'What is one's duty? The demands of the day.' 11.90; 'Work makes the companion' 25.400, 26.16

Faust
Faust's pact with Mephistopheles 2.92, 2.675 (n125); 'a Helen medievalized, a Euphorion with wings' 25.400; illustration of the unsatisfactoriness of the conditioned 2.91–2, 12.613, 17.397–8; Mephistopheles' function 4.412; Sangharakshita's first reading 20.49; the union of Faust and Helen of Troy, set in Mistra 23.297; use of Christian images 13.583; we are all Faust and we are all Mephistopheles 12.613

other works
Conversations with Eckermann 3.471, 22.464, 23.473; *Italienische Reise* (*Italian Journey*) 23.249, 23.473, 23.510 (n282), 24.284–5, 24.299; *The Sorrows of Young Werther* 12.697; *Theory of Colours* 3.58; *Wilhelm Meister* 7.549 (n27), 8.545, 16.86

going for alms *see* almsfood

Going for Refuge to the Three Jewels

WHAT IS GOING FOR REFUGE?

introduction
brief introduction 3.393–6, 10.266, 11.467–8, 16.593 (n59); description 2.240–9, 3.324–31, 8.203–5, 9.18, 9.212–15; overview 3.324–31, 9.244–59

etymology and terminology
alternative Refuge-going formulas 2.487; the meaning of *gacchāmi* 3.326; the meaning of *śaraṇa* 15.646, 18.563–4; difference between the Three Jewels and the Three Refuges 2.241–2, 10.266–7; Going for Refuge as 'commitment', *see under* commitment; *Going* for Refuge no linguistic accident: a total reorientation of one's life 2.242; not *taking* Refuge 2.241, 3.326, 3.397, 12.596, 15.545; the Refuge-going formula (in Pāli and English) 2.503; in some languages it is linguistically impossible to say 'I go for Refuge' 2.695 (n334); use the full phrase, not just 'Going for Refuge' 12.535; the term 'refuge' is liable to be misunderstood 11.468

perspectives on Going for Refuge
allowing oneself to be attracted to the highest and best within one's experience 15.675; cosmic context 2.477–8, 12.316; the difference between worship and Going for Refuge 11.247–8; the element of beauty in Going for Refuge 15.554–6; establishing contact with a higher dimension and thus being 'saved' 4.330–1; Going for Refuge and the definition of an orthodox Buddhist 2.558–9; Going for Refuge and 'finding out and knowing directly' 13.491; Going for Refuge as 'conversion' 2.7, 2.239, 2.240–9, 2.460–2, 2.465, 9.17, 23.79–80; Going for Refuge in the midst of the ruins of Christian culture 26.279; it cannot be overvalued 9.250; it is important to bring out its positive implications 13.195; it is of two kinds, intellectual and spiritual 2.461; it leads to the attainment of Enlightenment 17.589; many do not see any need for a refuge 15.566–7; a matter of belief 11.482–3; a Refuge doesn't improve *saṃsāra*, but enables you to transcend it 15.587–8; the social context: the spiritual community 2.474–5; what Going for Refuge means 9.212, 11.384–6

the act of Going for Refuge
the act is individual but takes place in a wider context 2.473; an act of will and understanding 15.559; an act the significance of which continually deepens 19.58; the basic declaration of commitment to the Buddhist path 11.67–8; between the act of Going for Refuge and the context is an organic connection 2.478; 'a conscious act of determination, understanding and devotion' 2.485; determination applied to the Three Jewels becomes faith 17.535; individual but not individualistic 2.516; it cannot be done once and for all 1.408, 2.429, 3.397, 11.431, 15.582, 18.564, 19.57–8; it is an individual, conscious *action* 4.300, 8.573, 15.546, 15.693–4; it requires a leap of faith 26.60; a matter of total commitment 15.616, 15.625, 15.660; motivation for Going for Refuge 15.567–8; a new decision to go for Refuge is taken every minute 15.688; takes place within the context of the sangha 2.474–5; there is no collective Going for Refuge, it's an individual act 12.535–6, 15.651; we can never go for Refuge 'again', we just go for Refuge here and now 12.40; you have to go for Refuge by your own effort 15.547

the central and definitive act of the Buddhist life
introduction 12.665–7; all Buddhist ordinations have Going for Refuge in common 11.68–70; all who are

committed are equally members of the spiritual community 11.135; the basis of everything else 2.295, 10.271–2; a Buddhist is one who goes for Refuge to the Three Jewels 3.69, 7.225–6, 9.212, 10.385, 11.383, 11.662; the central act of the Buddhist life 3.325, 3.331, 10.440; clear enough from the Pāli canon 12.306–7; the common factor for all Buddhists 10.486–7, 12.506; the evolution of Sangharakshita's thinking 2.450, 2.500, 11.383, 11.388, 15.xxi, 21.343–4, 23.160, 26.669; if you have gone for Refuge, you are just as much a Buddhist, whether monastic or lay 11.475; the fundamental unity among Buddhists 2.323, 2.451–2, 2.463, 10.267–8; it is what makes one a Buddhist 9.215, 9.340, 11.467–8, 15.545; 'the most fundamental belief and most widespread practice in Buddhism' 2.435; 'one who does not take the Triple Gem is not a Buddhist' 2.436; one's whole Buddhist life is a progressive deepening of Going for Refuge 11.175, 11.431; overlooked in Zen 12.506; recognition in different Buddhist schools 2.566–7; refusing to recognize as Buddhism anything not related to Going for Refuge 1.8; the place of the idea in the Western Buddhist Order (Triratna) 2.472, 2.515, 12.665–7; we need a Buddhism that is neither monastic nor lay, but based on this centrality 11.613; whether you are monastic or lay doesn't matter so much 10.268; you don't go for Refuge because you're a Buddhist, you're a Buddhist because you go for Refuge 2.431

Going for Refuge as a practice
can we go for Refuge to the Three Jewels 'within our mind'? 15.580–2; Going for Refuge itself purifies our motivation for Going for Refuge 17.287–8; it is the absolute bedrock of our spiritual life 26.32; not just a preliminary practice 2.431; taking the Triple Gem as your guiding ideal 15.651, 15.663–5; three aspects: volitional, rational, emotional 15.600–6; you can't have a merely theoretical Going for Refuge 15.553–4

THE BUDDHIST TRADITION

introduction
the language of refuge used in Buddhism since early times 3.681 (n356); all later developments in Buddhist history based on the Going for Refuge 13.200; all schools of Buddhism recognize its decisive importance 1.410, 2.430; the approach to Going for Refuge of the three *yānas* 13.195–204; the origin of the tradition 9.247–8; originally the most important thing in Buddhism 9.389

in Early Buddhism
canonical references 2.727–8 (n600), 8.305; clear about the centrality of Going for Refuge 12.306–7; Going for Refuge in Early Buddhism 13.195; response to the Buddha 11.383–4; its significance is clear from the Buddhist scriptures 2.480

expressions of Going for Refuge
the classic phrases 2.292, 3.77, 3.329–330, 4.686–7 (n189), 10.553, 11.383–4, 12.307, 12.665–6, 13.250; different ways of expressing it 15.666–7, 15.693, 15.696–700, 15.708–9, 15.724–9; it needs to be publically acknowledged 15.704–5; showing respect to the Three Jewels 15.668–9

in the Mahāyāna
the arising of the *bodhicitta*, not Going for Refuge, the central act 2.441–2; *Avataṃsaka Sūtra* prayer 2.5; the Mahāyāna's conception of Going for Refuge 1.409–10, 9.254, 13.195–6; sought a fresh formulation, the original significance having been lost 2.431–2; the universalization of Going for Refuge 13.195–7

in the Tibetan tradition
in Tibetan Buddhism 2.435–6, 2.440–2, 12.296, 12.305, 13.76; Atīśa (the 'Refuge Lama') 2.442, 2.720–1 (n541), 12.577; emphasis on the good intention preceding Going for Refuge 2.435; the lama (or guru) as fourth refuge 1.409, 12.17; light shed by personal contact with Tibetan Buddhists 2.445–6; Milarepa combines the Going for Refuge with the Mahāmudrā teaching 18.239

in the Zen tradition
Dōgen: 'Always take refuge in Buddha, Dharma, Sangha' 2.567, 3.331, 12.506; Going for Refuge overlooked 2.563; 'Let us take refuge to the Three Gems within our mind!' 15.580–2

Going for Refuge and other teachings
along with the bodhisattva vow, self-regarding and other-regarding aspects 12.373; the connection between morality and Going for Refuge 11.310–12; doctrine-followers and faith-follower 15.546, 15.567–8, 15.600–1, 15.610, 15.720; emphasis on Going for Refuge compared to Mahāyāna's emphasis on *ekayāna* 16.63; Going for Refuge and the Higher Evolution 2.475–7; Going for Refuge and Stream Entry are the same thing 15.532; Going for Refuge, Stream Entry, *bodhicitta*, *parāvṛtti*

2.464, 14.479; Going for Refuge and the three *yānas* 11.255; initiation is an aspect of Going for Refuge 13.161, 15.15.694–5, 15.704; it is identical with the following of the spiritual path 13.194; right view is an integral part of Going for Refuge 12.616; we start practising the path of regular steps by going for Refuge 11.67; whatever is said of the *bodhicitta* can be said of Going for Refuge 2.475; you subjectively go for Refuge and objectively manifest the *bodhicitta* 13.399

Going for Refuge as a formality
the devaluation of Going for Refuge 11.387–8; the dying out of its significance 2.299, 15.694, 15.709–10; people started thinking of the Buddhist life as just the *bhikkhu* life 10.267–8; confusion of Going for Refuge with becoming a monk 2.433, 11.69–70, 21.342–3; the devaluation of Going for Refuge in the East 11.69–70; helping other Buddhists by pointing out Going for Refuge in their tradition 2.572; if they have gone for Refuge, laity are as much Buddhist as monastics 23.xv; in the East, something you recite to show that you are a Buddhist 11.388, 12.305–6, 15.626; it has become a formality in many Buddhist cultures 2.240–1, 5.541, 12.665, 15.546–7; it lost its central position in Buddhist spiritual life 4.85; often undervalued in the Buddhist countries of Asia 2.295, 2.299; 'the sort of thing that a good Buddhist did' 2.438; Theravāda countries lost sight of Going for Refuge 2.431–2, 2.560, 2.596–7, 9.254; there is no point in 'taking' the Refuges if one is not prepared to commit oneself 11.69; Tibetan lamas often don't bother to teach the Refuges and Precepts 19.489; undervalued in some Buddhist traditions 3.331, 9.250, 12.506

the restoration of Going for Refuge
Dr Ambedkar's emphasis on Going for Refuge 2.494–7, 6.615, 9.259, 10.27; the Going for Refuge of new Buddhists in India 2.438–9; the basis for a new Buddhist movement (Triratna) 10.266, 10.268, 11.376, 15.695; let us base ourselves firmly on our common Going for Refuge 26.56; restoring its original significance 2.295

taking and reciting the Refuges and Precepts
Dr Ambedkar administered the Refuges and Precepts 2.495–6, 6.615, 9.130, 10.26–7; ceremonies in Buddhist countries 1.410; in *bhikṣu* ordination 2.193; it's not enough just to recite the verses 5.541, 10.260; mechanical recitation 10.241–2, 15.692–5, 15.698, 15.700; no Going for Refuge ceremony in Theravādin countries 15.710–12; reasons for chanting them in Pāli 19.133; recite them as often as possible, as a reminder 15.690; reciting the precepts in the Sevenfold Puja 11.255–8, 12.405; reciting the Refuges and Precepts in a 'pseudo-egalitarian' way, London 1964 12.304; reciting the verses with no clear idea of their meaning 7.67; the relationship between Refuges and Precepts 2.323–5, 9.187, 11.311–12; the ritual of Going for Refuge 11.214–15; Sangharakshita administers them for the first time 12.303, 20.425–6; Sangharakshita first takes Refuges and Precepts 2.410–11, 12.301–2, 20.102; taking *pansil* (Sinhalese *pañcasīla*) 2.410–11, 2.419, 2.438, 12.302, 20.102

Going for Refuge and the sangha
the act of Going for Refuge takes place within the context of the sangha 2.474–5; a basis of Going for Refuge, not attaching too much importance to our differences 26.82; witnessing Going for Refuge 2.512–13, 15.698, 15.704, 15.708, 15.738–9; if you want to join the sangha, you want to go for Refuge 15.668; Going for Refuge in the presence of the sangha supports spiritual progress 4.66; Going for Refuge needs the support of the sangha 15.738; move from the group to the spiritual community 3.452; without the idea of the New Society, Going for Refuge may be individualistic 2.517

GOING FOR REFUGE IN PRACTICE

what it involves
are you going for Refuge when you are asleep? 15.688–9; responsibility to others 14.446; it isn't easy to go for Refuge 10.385–6; it isn't easy to sort out genuine and less genuine motivations 15.609–10; it requires the surrender of at least a little independence 5.259; it takes place in a threefold context: social, higher-evolutionary, cosmic 2.473–8; much more is implied by it than people usually think 2.301; no qualifications are needed 9.215; not just turning to the Three Jewels, but being transformed into them 2.462; organizing one's life around the Three Jewels 2.461; showing respect for the Three Jewels 4.326–7; subjective and objective Going for Refuge 11.451; surrender of self 2.486–8, 15.660–79, 15.698, 15.722–3, 15.733–40; three aspects: emotional, rational, volitional 2.487, 11.649, 12.536–41, 15.607, 15.615, 15.727–9; a turnabout in our whole way of life 10.14; virtually synonymous with

ordination, spiritual life, being a Buddhist 11.68, 21.343; we rely on others to support our Going for Refuge 15.560–1, 15.657–9; what matters is not lifestyle, but depth and intensity of Going for Refuge 2.446; when you go for Refuge you do so with your whole being 11.67, 15.606–7, 18.383

the heart's response
a response to whatever is highest within your experience 15.673, 15.676; confidence in Going for Refuge 7.309, 15.602; the emotional basis 15.600–5; emotional and volitional aspects 2.301, 2.483, 9.256, 15.607–10; an emotional response needs support through contact with a spiritual community 15.610; feeling it in our heart 9.267; real devotion culminates in Going for Refuge 4.308–9; reflections on the poem 'Taking Refuge in the Buddha' 2.423–6, 2.439; a response to the overwhelming effect of the Dharma 9.247–8; some people are drawn to it, others are disillusioned by life 15.574–5, 15.578, 15.609–10; some people respond to the Buddha, others the Dharma, others the Sangha 12.624–5; supported by the Sevenfold Puja 11.220; 'We needs must love the highest when we see it' 2.292; when faith is strong enough, we go for Refuge 2.259

understanding Going for Refuge
becoming convinced of an eternal spiritual reality and trying to realize it 7.69–70; the Buddha's teachings teach us to take refuge where it can be found 7.51; feeling like going for Refuge is more powerful than thinking it's a good idea 15.607–8; one has to understand what one is going for Refuge to 15.610, 22.289; a one-sidedly intellectual approach 2.485–6; to go for Refuge, one has to understand what the Three Jewels are 1.409, 3.325–7; Going for Refuge as a conscious act of understanding 15.559; reflect on what it means to go for Refuge and try to live in accordance with it 18.167; understanding the Three Jewels in accordance with tradition 7.408–9

is it about escape?
the idea of Going for Refuge as escape doesn't do justice to the spiritual life 13.194–5; as a means of escape 13.194; nothing to do with running away 2.301, 9.256; some people see it as an escape 15.609

Going for Refuge and ethics
'Buddhism's in the life and in the heart' 25.20–1; Going for Refuge must find ethical expression 12.499; one cannot truly go for Refuge while leading an unethical life 3.331; if Going for Refuge is the Buddhist's lifeblood, the precepts are its circulation 3.331; the relationship between Refuges and Precepts 2.323–5, 9.187; to the extent that you have unskilful states, you're not going for Refuge 15.651–3

Going for Refuge and meditation
in prostration practice, *see* Going for Refuge and prostration practice; in visualization practice 5.578–9, 13.93–4

the effect of Going for Refuge
the energy released by Going for Refuge 13.161; the fruits of Going for Refuge 15.679–91; it must find its expression in total transformation 2.325; it must involve external change 9.534–5; it transforms one's whole life 2.7; a turning point in one's spiritual life 1.509; one who goes for Refuge will become more of a human being 16.355; a profound inner experience, change of heart 2.7, 3.397, 22.461; we cannot be truly human without going for Refuge 16.354–5

continuing to go for Refuge
developing confidence in the Three Refuges over time 15.602; does it continue after death? 15.687–91; fluctuations 15.651–2, 15.657; it should deepen all the time, 'with every day that passes' 2.502, 3.397–8; it grows with one's understanding of Buddhism 1.408–9, 2.429; the main thing is to go on deepening it 26.57; the Refuge grows by the process of going to it 15.580; self-interrogation: has one's Going for Refuge slipped? 2.512–13

potential problems
breaking the Refuge 15.676–9, 15.688–91; the ego hiding in Going for Refuge 15.729–31; it's a mistake to think of Going for Refuge 'in the secrecy of one's own heart' 15.738–9

LEVELS OF GOING FOR REFUGE

introduction
introduction 2.479–83, 3.328–31, 9.483, 10.386–7, 12.371–2, 13.481; Sangharakshita's first statement about the levels 12.310–16; degrees of Going for Refuge 26.33; according to tradition there are two levels: mundane and transcendental 2.479, 15.653–9; trying to ascertain the level of Going for Refuge of another Buddhist 2.572

(1) formal (cultural, ethnic)
being attracted to the Buddhist movement as a positive group 12.311; distinction between formal and effective Refuge 1.408, 2.429–30; reciting the Refuge-

going formula as part of culture 2.300–1, 2.479–80, 15.546–7, 15.625–6; need to replace this 'old' form of Going for Refuge with a 'new' one 2.488; not to be depreciated, a starting point 3.328; not really Going for Refuge at all 12.666; the level of a 'born Buddhist' 2.302, 2.480–1, 9.486, 9.506, 10.386, 12.310–11, 15.554; a purely theoretical understanding 15.553–4

(2) provisional
Going for Refuge up to a point 3.328; level of a Mitra within Triratna 2.481, 12.311–12, 13.481; 'provisional' isn't a satisfactory term 12.311; the stage of trying out Buddhism 12.666; you're not committed, but you're thinking of committing yourself 12.311; [cultural and provisional conflated at 2.301–2, 9.256–7, 10.386]

(3) effective
can be deflected or destroyed 15.610; a conscious commitment to the Buddha, Dharma, and Sangha 2.302, 2.481; corresponds to ordination in the Triratna Buddhist Order 2.481, 12.312, 12.666, 13.481, 15.676; corresponds, though not perfectly, to Nyanaponika's 'surrender of self' 2.487–8, 15.660–1; the deeper one's understanding of the Refuges, the more effect one's refuge 1.408; illustrated by examples from the Buddha's time 3.329; the level of the majority of sincere practising Buddhists 3.329; a means of stimulating real Going for Refuge 4.197; not effective unless one tries to make it real 3.356, 11.430–1, 12.372, 12.596, 14.316; one who goes effectively for Refuge is *ipso facto* an individual 2.568; the practical question is at what point one's Going for Refuge is effective 10.486; progressing from effective to real 14.312; self-surrender, total commitment 15.737; taking hold of a golden string which will lead one to Nirvāṇa 2.649; this is the Going for Refuge described in the scriptures 12.312; to go for Refuge effectively you must intend to aim for the transcendental 11.257; in the Vajrayāna, effective Going for Refuge is twofold 12.312–14; you sincerely wish to go for Refuge with your whole heart 9.257, 12.666; you think very seriously about the significance of Going for Refuge 10.386–7

(4) real or transcendental
correlated with the opening of the Dharma Eye 2.482, 12.505; an element of *vipaśyanā* 3.329, 12.505; examples from the Pāli canon 3.330, 10.387; faith becomes unshakeable 3.329, 12.505, 15.771 (n235); free from defilements 15.686; Going for Refuge to the Unconditioned 15.653–7; the Going for Refuge ceases to be 'my' Going for Refuge 12.599; if your Going for Refuge is transcendental, you can't *not* go for Refuge 15.657; one enters upon the transcendental Path 13.491; the permanent destruction of unskilful mental states 15.651–2; the real Going for Refuge of a faith-follower 15.720–4; a spiritual community needs some people who have gone for Refuge at this level 15.658–9; synonymous with Stream Entry 2.296–7, 2.302, 2.481–2, 3.329–30, 9.253, 9.257, 12.315, 12.505, 13.481; the threshold of the Transcendental 26.280; you've passed the point of no return 10.387, 12.372, 12.666–7

(5) Absolute or Ultimate
the Enlightened One is his own refuge 1.409, 12.315; you go for Refuge to the Buddha, but you are yourself the Buddha 2.302, 2.482, 9.257

(6) cosmic
the evolutionary process 2.482–3, 12.315–6; may seem impossibly poetic, but it is what one sees 2.482, 12.315–16; the whole cosmos goes for Refuge 12.316

THE THREE REFUGES INDIVIDUALLY

Going for Refuge to the Buddha
introduction 11.384–5; acknowledging the Buddha as the Buddha prompts one to act 17.553–4; being seen by the Buddha 14.479; a Buddha becomes his own Refuge 19.316; the Buddha is ultimately the only Refuge 2.302–3, 2.424–5, 9.258, 11.310–12; 'Buddhaṃ Saraṇaṃ Gacchāmi' (poem) 25.209; can you go for Refuge to a Buddha you have never seen? 12.313, 13.197; commitment to following the Buddha with urgency and determination 25.29; devotion to the Buddha finds its fulfilment in Going for Refuge 2.452; the Dharma and the Sangha are contained within the Buddha 2.424–5; Dharmapala's emphasis 8.xx, 8.21, 8.90, 22.76; the Early Buddhist conception 13.195; faith in the Buddhist sense 1.282; as the Buddha 15.628–9; Going for Refuge to his historical life, archetypal forms, and absolute nature 11.255; 'I know and understand him to be the refuge' 15.629; intermediate between knowledge of the Buddha and experience of Unconditioned mind 3.153; is it Gotama the Buddha to whom you go for Refuge? 15.588–90, 15.593, 15.628–9; it means Going for Refuge to the Buddha alone 8.203–4; the living embodiment of an ideal which is an ideal *for us* 2.242, 2.293, 9.248–9; from knowing of the Buddha

to feeling for him, willing to become like him 12.536–7; one goes for Refuge to the Buddha *as* the Buddha 1.56–7, 3.325, 7.227–8, 15.673–5; not blind faith 7.67–9; our object of Refuge must be an Enlightened human being 15.591; placing the Buddha at the centre of one's mandala 2.325; to accept the Buddha Jewel as an ideal is to acknowledge its relevance to us 3.393; shift from limited ideals to a transcendental ideal 2.248–9; Śreṇika goes for Refuge to the Buddha as an act of faith 14.550; 'Taking Refuge in the Buddha' (poem) 2.423–6, 2.439, 8.xxvii, 21.429, 22.143, 25.xxxvii–viii, 25.250–1; in the *Tiratana Vandanā* 15.497–8; we say 'I go for Refuge to the Buddha', not the idea of the Buddha 26.369; why not go for Refuge to *all* great spiritual teachers? 2.242; you gradually transform yourself into a Buddha 15.583

Going for Refuge to the Dharma
introduction 11.385; we take Refuge in the Dharma, not the teachings of this or that school 13.326; comes after Going for Refuge to the Buddha 7.69; a commitment to the Path of the Higher Evolution 2.293–4; a commitment to whatever helps us grow spiritually 2.294; described in the *Tiratana Vandanā* 15.511–12; the Dharma to which we go for Refuge is not the faint glimmer in our unenlightened mind 15.593–4; the Early Buddhist conception of the Dharma as Refuge 13.195; 'Hold fast to the Dhamma as a Refuge' 9.306; in this context 'Dharma' means the Buddha's teaching and the spiritual law 2.243–4; involves accepting it with no subtractions or additions contrary to its spirit 7.230; it means accepting the Dharma as the only means of attaining Nirvāṇa 8.204; it's the Dharma we've actually experienced to which we go for Refuge 12.313; on the intellectual plane, it means being convinced of the truth of the teachings 2.244; it means the actual practice of the Dharma 2.245, 7.69; shift from 'little systems that have their day' to a path of unchanging truths 2.249; as the transcendental path to Enlightenment 3.325; not just a source of interesting and useful ideas 3.326; we take Refuge in ourselves *and* in the Dharma 2.750–1 (n733), 7.261, 7.317, 11.451, 15.583–4

Going for Refuge to the Sangha
brief introduction 11.385; essentially communication: 'a vital mutual responsiveness' 2.247–8, 2.461–2, 23.xvi; has an equal place with the other two great ideals of Buddhism 3.390, 11.90; in early Buddhism seen as twofold: Āryasaṅgha and *bhikkhu* sangha 13.195; for most Buddhists the Refuge is the other Buddhists with whom they are in contact 15.612; going for Refuge is the uniting factor that creates a sangha 15.599; going for Refuge to the Āryasaṅgha 1.178, 3.326, 9.128–9, 15.585–6; inspiration comes from the Sangha, which is why the Sangha is one of the Refuges 17.61; means becoming a *bhikkhu* – not a yellow-robe wearer but a practising Buddhist 7.69; members of this Sangha are not necessarily monks 15.599, 15.640–1; must be understood in the context of the Three Jewels as a whole 2.247; going for Refuge to the *bhikkhu* sangha 3.326, 7.231, 7.601 (n335), 10.554; Nyanaponika's conception of Buddhism without spiritual community 2.488; part of the very definition of being a Buddhist 12.69; in practical terms it means we help one another 9.215; resorting for spiritual guidance only to those in the Sangha 8.284; the sangha as the social context of Going for Refuge 2.474–5; shift from meaningless worldly contact to meaningful communication 2.249, 2.462; spiritual fellowship with one another, helping one another on the path 2.294, 9.250; threefold sangha: transcendental, *bhikkhus*, Mahāsaṅgha 2.246–7, 2.294, 2.461; in practice we go for Refuge to only a few sangha members: the *ḍākinī* 12.313–14; when people explore together a spiritual dimension they couldn't explore alone 2.248; why go for Refuge to the sangha? 3.398–402; you're able to go for Refuge to the Sangha because you can become a member of it 15.585

see also
altruistic dimension, *see under bodhicitta*; antidote to hindrances in meditation, *see* five hindrances/antidotes; commitment is primary, lifestyle is secondary, *see under* commitment; esoteric or Tantric Refuges, *see* three esoteric Refuges; and going forth, *see under* going forth; Sangharakshita's experience, *see under* Sangharakshita V/ personal practice

Going for Refuge and Prostration practice description 12.19, 13.76–80; develops determination to Go for Refuge 13.211; its effect is impossible to describe 13.79; as a Going for Refuge practice, it is the fundamental act of a Buddhist 13.209; good exercise 13.79, 13.212; has a powerful effect 2.445; how can the practice be regarded as 'therapy'? 10.441; how you prostrate 13.211; imagining the practice as the cosmic Going for Refuge

13.212–13; imagining prostrating with your parents 13.212; includes repetition of the Refuge-going formula 2.445; involves body, speech, and mind 13.79; intensifies devotion to the Dharma expressed through the body 22.528; introduced to Sangharakshita by Kachu Rimpoche 22.473, 26.673; as one of the four *mūla yogas* 13.76–80; Padmasambhava practice 2.444, 13.204–13; part of the point of extended practice is to keep going when inspiration dries up 17.554; the practice in the Triratna Buddhist Order 2.445, 2.514, 2.721 (n544, 546), 13.209, 13.416, 22.xx–xxi, 26.673; the practice has mental, verbal, and physical aspects 13.77–9; the practices of the different schools of Tibetan Buddhism 13.213–15; represents a restoration of Going for Refuge to its original place in Buddhist life 2.445; Sangharakshita takes up the practice, *see under* Sangharakshita V/meditation; and the system of meditation 5.540–1; the Tibetans believe that it is a cure for tuberculosis 13.79; traditionally you do 100,000 prostrations 13.80, 13.211, 13.416, 17.554; *see also* Refuge Tree

going forth

introduction
cultural, provisional, effective, and real going forth 12.552; going forth with body, speech, and mind 12.553–60; reflections on going forth 12.545–60

exemplars of going forth
in the Hindu tradition, one symbolically performs one's own funeral 4.75; Siddhārtha's going forth, *see* Siddhārtha/going forth; Soṇa Koṭikaṇṇa wants to go forth, but is advised by his teacher to wait 10.572–3; Yaśa goes forth, *see under* Yaśa; to become an *arhant* you had to go forth 10.628; bodhisattvas skilled in going forth 2.154; Anagarika Dharmapala's going forth 8.24–5

going forth and Going for Refuge
in the Buddha's time, the two sometimes coincided 2.298; an integral part of Going for Refuge 18.36; we can go forth without Going for Refuge, but not *vice versa* 12.552

literal and metaphorical
going forth literally as well as metaphorically 9.534–6, 11.131–2, 26.279; how literally to follow the Buddha's example? 19.54–5, 25.9–10, 26.562; it means changing not just externally but internally 9.191

going forth from ...
the *kāmaloka* to the *rūpaloka* 12.558–9; kinsmen as a tribe 18.150–1, 18.330–1; *manas* to *āryajñāna* 12.559–60; the group 3.36–9, 3.460–1; the old life to the new 10.257; one's native country 9.330–1, 9.371–2, 12.553–4, 18.331; the social group 3.38, 7.217–18; speech into silence or song 12.557–8; your native language 12.556–7, 18.331

notes on going forth
connection with single-sex idea 2.517; draws attention to the reorganization spiritual experience brings 2.301, 2.483; going off into the forest makes sure that you are really an individual 5.680; going forth may be easier than giving up comfort 19.95; must be carried out by every Dharma practitioner (Conze) 17.711 (n41); need for ceremony (Ambedkar) 9.148; going forth *to* the spiritual community 2.415, 11.133, 11.442–3, 17.111–1218.36–7; going forth viewed as a cowardly flight from reality 7.218; of the essence of the spiritual life 22.209; and ordination 3.461–2, 9.253–4; the result of starting to lead a spiritual life 11.131–2; sometimes it's the only option 17.192

see also
going forth from the family, *see under* family; leaving home, *see under* home; *parivrājaka* ('one who has gone forth'), *see parivrājaka*; Sangharakshita's going forth, *see* Sangharakshita II/going forth

going through the motions

going through the motions of ...
accepting receptivity as an ideal 19.289; being a *bhikkhu* 19.274–6; Going for Refuge, *see under* Going for Refuge/the Buddhist tradition/a formality; listening to the Dharma 15.438–9; meditating 5.293, 5.335–7, 15.532, 19.57; practising the precepts 19.455–6; religion 7.148; spiritual practice 3.420, 3.457–8; work 17.196

reasons for going through the motions
because you're not really convinced the Dharma works 19.228–9; can it be good to do the right thing for the wrong reason? 5.373, 11.430; for the sake of group conformity 19.459; to get into a devotional mood 4.296, 15.706–7; to help yourself develop the appropriate attitude 4.296, 11.267, 19.458

don't just go through the motions
Dharma talks which were just 'babble and jabber' 19.295–6; don't just practise mechanically 9.192–3, 9.266; don't mistake acting with part of yourself for acting with

the whole 19.276; involve more and more of yourself 19.276, 19.278–9; keep asking yourself, 'Am I just going through the motions?' 19.275–6; remaining unchanged when going through the motions 15.521; a solitary retreat may help you to see that's what you're doing 19.276–7; there's no security in it 19.274–5; to help others, there must be real kindness in your heart 19.287

see also
ten fetters/third fetter

gold

gold in the Buddhist tradition
the *bodhicitta* manifesting like gold made into a crown 4.177–8, 19.198–9; the Buddha's face as bright as a golden cloud (*Sukhāvatī-vyūha Sūtra*) 14.169; the Buddha's face shines like burnished gold (*Mahāparinirvāṇa Sūtra*) 14.239; brightening gold, brightening *śūnyatā* 19.199; the *Dhammapada* should be engraved on our hearts in letters of gold 26.45; the element of Buddhahood 'like gold within impurities' 13.389; the golden colour of Ratnasambhava 12.214; the golden statue covered in dirt 11.689; the 'golden treasure underground' 19.497; the inexhaustible wealth of the Enlightened mind 18.59; Jambunada gold (*Dhammapada*) 15.34, 15.745 (n16); Milarepa is given gold in return for the useful Dharma 18.375–6; Nāropa rejects Marpa's gold 16.625 (n321); a Tibetan king whose captors asked for his weight in gold 12.571–2, 13.13–14; Tibetans used to refuse to mine for gold 15.138

'test my words as the goldsmith tests gold in the fire'
the Buddha is the only founder of religion to say this 9.494, 10.246, 26.111; even the Buddha did not consider his words sacrosanct 11.667; Dr Ambedkar's use of the Buddha's simile 9.62, 9.425; very different from the idea of the lama as infallible 2.565; come and see for yourself 3.15, 12.136; let us test all views in the fire of our own reason and experience 12.617; neither accept nor reject the Buddha's words without examination 7.268, 9.471

Sangharakshita's use of golden metaphors
a golden net symbolizing the interconnectedness of the Dharma 25.142–3; the golden thread that connects us to reality 4.171–2; the second precept as a pillar of gold 2.369; 'They gilded Him till He was sick with gold' 25.296; 'While the vein lasted, it was gold' 25.281; 'You remind me of whatever's made of gold' 25.287

other gold, real and mythical
the gold Columbus brought from the New World 24.420; gold leaf in works of art 13.284; the gold standard 12.694–5; golden apples 25.281; golden artefacts in Athens 23.289; Jason and the Golden Fleece 26.262; Mexican gold in Seville 24.436; produced by alchemy 4.370; religions are gold mixed with ore 26.13; 'roofs bright with a million tiles of gold' 8.194; the three golden apples 26.469–70; valued for its beauty 13.165; Zeus descending on Danaë in a shower of gold 26.481

see also
Sūtra of Golden Light/the golden drum; *Sūtra of Golden Light*/golden light; not handling gold and silver, *see under* money

Goldberg, Herb 24.541–4

Goldberg, Natalie 24.518–19

Golden Drum (magazine) 11.565–630, 12.383, 12.488

Golden Legend v13

Golden Lotus (magazine) 8.139, 8.155, 21.341

Golden Rosary of the Precepts of the Gurus *see under* Gampopa

Goldsmith, Oliver 'He touched nothing that he did not adorn' 26.490; 'Let not his frailties be remembered, he was a very great man' 24.582; *Citizen of the World* 24.582; *The Deserted Village* 10.129–30; *She Stoops to Conquer* 24.582; *The Vicar of Wakefield* 24.582

Gomateshwara (Jain tradition) 20.373–4

Gombrich, Richard *Buddhism Transformed* 13.403; *How Buddhism Began* 8.573, 8.584, 8.617–22

Gomchen of Lhachen 6.608–9

Gompu, Tashi v21

good and goodness

doing good
Miss Albers: 'herself wholly good, she saw nothing but good around her' 20.168; the attractiveness of goodness 4.269–70; Beauty is not merely Truth, but Goodness as well 26.196; cultivating goodness as a skilful means 7.35; 'definite goodness' (Nāgārjuna) 17.160–1, 17.339, 17.352; the king 'the parent of those who do good deeds' 16.418; the good is the enemy

of the best 2.149, 26.36; meditation is essentially the willing of the Good 26.75; not just actions or just intentions, but a combination of both 17.589; ordinary goodness is too weak to overcome evil 4.268, 4.270; secularized version of the jewel motif: man is fundamentally good 16.222; we are naturally attracted by goodness 7.35; we become good only by thinking, speaking, and doing good 7.99

good and evil
the Buddha denies that you can 'go beyond good and evil' 15.367–8, 17.636; doing good rather than just eschewing evil 1.395; doing good is meaningless apart from the ability to do evil 7.245–6; human beings urged to fight on the side of good 26.655; it's sometimes hard to do something evil, easier to do good 4.289; 'many ways of being wicked, only one way of being good' (Aristotle) 3.554, 17.549; we often find it easier to hate the wicked than to love the good 26.66

problems with doing good
all the wisdom of the wise to undo the harm done by the merely good 4.193, 13.69; before thinking about doing good, we could stop doing mischief 18.342; being sluggish in doing the good 15.349–50; beware good deeds which beget too acute an awareness of your own goodness 7.282; 'being good' but not feeling good 11.267; the conventionally good man or woman may be harsh and unsympathetic 7.281–2; counter the tendency to do good for your own benefit by dedicating merit 16.332; doing 'good' with an egotistic consciousness binds you to the wheel of life 7.409–10; don't interpret the Buddha's example in a goody-goody way 10.650; neglecting the good 16.298; religious people can be weak because to be 'good' they have repressed their energy 18.78; trying to get away from a narrow, puritanical idea of goodness 4.270; when helping others, beware of a sense of 'do-gooding' 18.592; wisdom and goodness are incompatible with individualism 13.463

see also
do-gooders; good man; a reliable teaching will lead towards delight in good, *see under* Mahāpajāpati Gotami; skilful

good life aesthetic enjoyment and artistic creation anticipate what the Good Life would be 26.191; 'friends in the good life' 2.161, 14.220–2; 'I learned to love the good life and strive after it' 20.61; we never forget the lessons given us by a good life 7.35

good man 'Even the good man will be saved. How much more so the evil man!' 1.199; 'A good man always loves his parents' 16.297; 'A good man sometimes helps to perpetuate a bad system, and *vice versa*' 26.74; a 'good' man's core of separative selfhood is often harder than that of a 'bad' man 7.407; Socrates' definition of the good man, who 'produces' virtue (*arete*) 15.404–5

good manners *see* manners

good works *bhikkhus* more interested in meditation than good works 7.65; good works ... not worth a sixteenth part of *mettā* 2.315, 14.54–5; a spirituality that is sterile in respect of good works is highly suspect 26.17

goose (*haṃsa*) *see under* birds

Gopaka Moggallāna 1.54

Gopakamoggallāna Sutta *see under Majjhima Nikāya*

Gopal (cook) v21

Gopal, Ram (dancer) v21

gopīs 16.73, 16.361

Gorakhpur, India 22.336

Gorboduc 13.425

Goregaon, India 9.40–1, 9.179–80

Goshosokushu *see under* Shinran

Gospel of Buddha *see under* Carus

Gosse, Sir Edmund 7.63, 7.564–5 (n107)

gossip *see under* speech/unskilful speech

Gotami (Order member) 4.225, 4.280–2, 4.235–6, 4.320, 4.445

gotrabhū (intermediate state) definition 2.142–3, 18.578; 'lightning-like transitional stage' between average person and Stream Entrant 2.142, 15.643; an obscure aspect of the path of fives stages 17.457; Sarvāstivādin discussion 15.643–4, 18.578

Gott, W. J. 11.327–8

Gottmann, Armin 8.657

Goulstone, George v23

Goulstone, Mrs v23

Gour, Sir Hari Singh 22.163

Gouranga *see* Chaitanya

government *see under* politics

Govey, Arthur and Roy 26.684

Govinda (the Buddha's disciple) has a vision of Brahmā Sanankumāra 3.209, 26.472; 'How may the mortal obtain the immortal Brahmā world?' 1.237, 3.209, 3.579, 26.472, 26.498; speaks as Everyman 26.473

Govinda, Lama

HIS LIFE

introduction
brief introduction 1.622–3 (n360), 6.616–18, 8.700–1 (n275), 24.665 (n285); photographs 21.257, 23.413; his belief that he had been the poet Novalis in a previous life 12.688, 26.256; his early life (as Ernst Lothar Hoffman) 6.616; appearance 21.248–9; the direction of his life and work 6.617; marriage to Li Gotami 6.617, 21.418–20, 21.423–4, 22.51; styling himself 'Anagarika' 6.616, 22.122–3; his guru was Tomo Geshe Rimpoche 6.616, 22.493, 22.496–7; representing Tibetan Buddhism at a parliament of religions 5.209–10; disagreement with Devapriya Valisinha 22.122–3; establishes the Arya Maitreya Mandala, *see* Arya Maitreya Mandala; ill health 11.560; his death 6.617, 11.560, 24.237; a distorted account of his life 24.528

places of residence
residence in Italy 6.616, 11.562, 11.564, 25.429; time in Ceylon 6.616; at Shantiniketan 6.616, 22.51; interned at Dehradun 6.616–17, 22.297; at Almora 6.617, 23.413–14; at Deolali 21.417–25; in San Francisco 6.617, 12.492

his character and interests
an exemplar of constructive speech 12.36–7; a great Buddhist 6.616–18; he concentrated on Tibetan mysticism 12.561; he stressed the importance of meditation and art 6.617–18; the influence on him of the *Tibetan Book of the Dead* 14.263, 16.107; interested in recollections of previous lives 6.616; single-minded and fearless, unconventional and self-motivated 12.561–2

art
he believed that religion and art were closely connected 22.180; paintings 7.451, 21.252–3, 21.421; *Capri at Night* 25.429; his depictions of Tibetan landscapes 13.62; paintings of the *dhyānas* 4.155, 21.421; his use of pastel colours 21.421, 26.221; on the relationship between art and meditation 21.251, 26.93; a Theravādin tells him, 'I am not allowed to appreciate beauty' 2.84, 21.397, 22.148

expedition with Li Gotami to Tsaparang
introduction 6.617, 21.252–3, 21.418–22; astonished by the colours of the Tibetan landscape 13.66; a distinct stage in the evolution of Buddhist art 21.420; it transpired that Tucci had visited the site before Govinda 21.421–2; Li Gotami's photographs 23.414, 24.12

friendship with Sangharakshita
brief introduction 23.536 (n456), 25.596 (n112); he corrects a talk given by Sangharakshita 22.30; he gives Sangharakshita a Buddha image and books 21.261–2, 22.6–7; introduction to *The Veil of Stars* 22.180, 25.l, 25.477–80; Lama Govinda advises him to speak less and write more 23.414; letters 4.444–5, 6.617, 11.560–4; 'more in common with him than with any other Buddhist I had met' 6.617, 11.563, 21.250; reunion at Sanchi 21.392–401; Sangharakshita visits him in Almora 10.160, 21.572, 23.413–14; he visits Sangharakshita in Kalimpong 21.244–62, 26.220; precious memories 11.561

WORKS

Creative Meditation and Multi-Dimensional Consciousness
critique of the New Burman Satipaṭṭhāna method 11.740–1 (n47); paintings of the *dhyānas* 4.155, 21.421

Foundations of Tibetan Mysticism
ākāśa 16.599 (n111); Amoghasiddhi 13.186; chakras 16.134, 16.161–2, 16.599 (n103); the association of Amitābha with *hrī* (sense of shame) 17.558; a *ḍākinī* who swallows Padmasambhava 12.287; the efficacy of mantras is not just about sonic vibrations 11.288, 13.288, 22.30; literary classic 6.617, 12.561; partly based on a *Stepping-Stones* article 21.147; the plurality of Buddhas 11.246; the qualities of Enlightenment 2.132–3; read on a train

in Surrey 25.333; review 8.391–2; stupa 16.600 (n112); The *Tibetan Book of the Dead* is a book of the living 16.107; to understand the nature of an Enlightened One 2.132–3; 'The Universal Attitude of the Mahayana and the Bodhisattva Ideal' 16.228

The Psychological Attitude of Early Buddhist Philosophy
hedonic indifference 17.508, 17.764 (n451); the possibilities of bliss 19.426; pyramid of consciousness 12.147; refutation of the criticism that Buddhism is pessimistic 2.108–9

Stepping-Stones
'Buddhism as Living Experience' 21.247; 'Look Deeper!' 15.130, 21.88; 'On the Right Concentration of Effort' 19.104–5; 'Origins of the Bodhisattva Ideal' 1.233, 1.398–400, 21.313; 'The Relativity of Perfection' 26.176; 'The Significance of "OM" and the Foundations of Mantric Lore' 21.147, 21.244–5; 'The Temple of Sunyata' 21.147; 'The Universal Perspective of the Bodhisattva Ideal' 21.88

The Way of the White Clouds
a chapter on colour 26.220–1; description of Lake Manasarovar 12.574; literary classic 6.617; sacred mountains 22.12; Tomo Geshe Rimpoche 22.497; the Tsaparang expedition 21.252, 21.419

other works and teachings
Art and Meditation 26.93; 'The Buddha as the Ideal of the Perfect Man' 1.47–8, 8.643, 22.123–4; *Buddhist Reflections* 11.560; comment on Germans' preference for intellectual presentation of Buddhism 3.303–4; *Drugs or Meditation?* 5.272; human beings and the rediscovery of the transcendental nature of mind 3.17, 3.628; *The Inner Structure of the I Ching* 11.560–1; introduction to *The Tibetan Book of the Dead* 14.262–3; *A Living Buddhism for the West* 11.560; poem: 'The Buddha's Seat' 22.123; 'Principles of Tantric Buddhism' 7.536; *Psycho-cosmic Symbolism of the Buddhist Stūpa* 3.48, 16.599 (n112); review of *The Tibetan Book of the Great Liberation* 1.378; the spiritual life in terms of building up a mandala 21.259; a story about the Noble Truthers and the Holy Truthers 1.478; 'Time and Space and the Problem of Free Will' 8.362

Govinda, Li Gotami *see* Li Gotami

Gown, Gladys 26.420–1

Goya, Francisco de v24

grace *anubhāva*, *see anubhāva*; the grace of God 4.7, 4.139–40, 18.538; 'The grace of the Gurus is beyond our comprehension' 18.554; the gravitational pull of the Unconditioned 3.252; 'the outward and visible sign of an inward and spiritual grace' 3.373; the 'rain of grace' 19.27–8; what is meant by grace in the Buddhist context 18.538

grace (or faith) and works 7.39, 7.42, 20.40

grace-waves arise essentially within oneself 4.139; Buddhas and bodhisattvas are always sending out grace-waves 18.98; 'gift-waves' 11.507; the influence of a highly developed being 18.537–8; it may be that you are protected by them in the sense of being open to positive influences 18.98; nothing special: the possibility of communication 4.139; *see also adhiṣṭhāna*

gradual better to aim for a gradual destruction of craving 2.104; 'breaking fetters' may suggest sudden breakthrough, but progress is gradual 3.420; the Buddha taught in a gradual, progressive way 3.330, 8.256, 8.592–3, 10.551; concentration: the gradual unification of energies 5.49–50; danger of terms 'gradual' and 'sudden' 16.183–4; 'Drop by drop', *see under Dhammapada*/chapter 9; faith gradually strengthens 2.259; gradual Enlightenment 3.146, 13.11–12; the gradual flowering of Buddhahood 3.481; the gradual method in terms of the twelve positive links 2.258–60, 12.158; the gradual nature of human development 19.125; the gradual approach in the *White Lotus Sūtra* 16.39; gradual training 1.176, 2.343, 10.145, 10.388, 10.562–3; the guru uses the gradual or sudden method depending on the disciple 16.171–2; instantaneous and gradual purification of the *āsravas* 14.215; *Laṅkāvatāra Sūtra* not a gradual but an abrupt realization of the truth 14.207; progress on the path is gradual 1.176, 3.420, 15.363–4; spiritual qualities are developed gradually 11.396–7; sudden and gradual conversion 2.238; there is no such thing as the quick path and the slow path (Huineng) 16.183; working towards the goal little by little 18.411; *see also* sudden

Graham, Billy 8.157, 12.119

Graham, Brian v21

Graham, Dr (founder of Dr Graham's Homes) v21

grail *see under* King Arthur

grammar *see under* language

graphology 22.253

grasping any kind of existence is relative, and when one sees this, there is no more grasping 17.411; egoistic, grasping attitude to meditation 4.504; grasping a poisonous snake: metaphor for the *lakṣaṇas* 3.276; grasping at spiritual states 14.451; the habit of grasping 15.263, 18.218; Milarepa lets go of grasping at his few remaining possessions 18.9–11; misunderstanding the Dharma is like grasping a water snake the wrong way 1.78, 18.180; only by 'grasping hold of' the Unconditioned can you escape the conditioned 10.634; our habitual grasping for worldly things is like a gravitational pull 18.177; *prapañca*, the manifold grasping, *see prapañca*; the most typical activity of worldly beings 1.232; seeing without grasping 19.192; when you are free of grasping, you become aware of things as never before 15.287; 'Where there is nothing to grasp there is no more grasping' 1.368

grass *dūrvā* grass 16.373–4; *kuśa* grass 3.31, 3.42, 15.16, 16.373–4; *muñja* grass 15.733

gratitude (*kataññutā*)

introduction
definitions 3.598; introduction 3.595–609; an auspicious sign that you are making spiritual progress 3.598; the connection of generosity to gratitude 17.201; felt when you take what you need from someone who is willing to give 2.367; in Buddhism, traditionally three objects: parents, teachers, spiritual friends 3.599; it opens us up to the fact of our interconnectedness with others 18.93; it involves knowledge of what has been done for our benefit 3.598–9, 3.605; it should be a natural, spontaneous feeling 15.433; it's difficult to have a practice for gratitude 15.435; *kataññutā* 3.598, 3.605; a neglected virtue 3.361; very much a Buddhist virtue 3.360, 8.98, 14.319; Cicero's view 3.604–5

the Buddha's gratitude
as expressed in the *Perfection of Wisdom in 8,000 lines* 3.360, 14.319; he acted upon his gratitude 3.598–9; towards the bodhi tree 3.74, 3.596; towards his first five disciples 3.74, 3.597; towards his teachers 3.597; he was utterly and instinctively full of gratitude 3.609

other examples from the Buddhist tradition
in the *Maṅgala Sutta* 3.598, 15.433; not everyone felt grateful to the Buddha 3.605–6; in the *Bodhicaryāvatāra* 4.250, 4.257; Subhūti's gratitude in the *Diamond Sūtra* 14.402–3

gratitude to …
Dr Ambedkar 9.159, 10.xlii–xliii, 10.13–14, 10.313, 10.406; Amitābha 13.309–10; Anagarika Dharmapala 8.98; the Buddha 3.609, 13.250–1, 13.255, 14.403; the Buddhas and bodhisattvas 4.313; the compilers of the Pāli canon 15.234; composers 3.602; the earth 16.382; an enemy 4.417; Mrs Mary E. Foster 8.49, 8.80, 8.99; the guru, cultivated in the guru yoga 18.93; Maharishi Mahesh Yogi for popularizing meditation 12.645; one's preceptors 26.630; other people, for all the things they do for us 5.154–5; our spiritual friends, because from them we receive the Dharma 3.604, 14.319; parents 3.529, 3.600–1; Sangharakshita 3.607–8, 10.xl, 10.xliii; teachers 3.601–3; the Theravāda for preserving the Tipiṭaka 2.553; those who are more committed 26.44; whoever introduced us to the Dharma 14.319, 18.93

gratitude for …
all the things we are given freely 17.201; the benefits of being a citizen 12.488, 17.201; the elements 17.201; the inevitable word 25.436; the FWBO (Triratna) 12.386, 12.489; having people to look up to 17.274–5; help received 3.42; the spiritual teachings of the East 11.83

expressions of gratitude
three ways of expressing gratitude to spiritual friends 3.604; through offering the mandala 13.260, 16.343, 18.125; through the three traditional offerings 13.417; you can always find things to do to show gratitude 4.253

why do Western Buddhists find it difficult to feel grateful?
egoism 3.606–7; forgetfulness 3.607, 3.608–9; if we don't feel that someone or something has benefited us 3.599, 3.605; in the early days of the FWBO people didn't feel grateful 15.433; it puts us in an inferior position 3.361; many people find it difficult to give or receive thanks gracefully 17.201–2; not that people *ought* to feel grateful, but why don't they? 4.255–6; perhaps cultural reasons make it difficult 4.251–2; sometimes people are ashamed to feel grateful 14.319–20; we take things for granted 3.606, 4.250

see also
Sangharakshita's gratitude, *see under* Sangharakshita VI/emotional life

Graves, Robert 25.433, 26.320, 26.379

graveyard *see* cremation ground

gravitational pull

introduction
'The Gravitational Pull and the Point of No Return' 3.241–57; introducing the metaphor 2.263, 19.595 (n24)

the gravitational pull of the conditioned
brief introduction 15.759 (n144); being in conflict with the gravitational pull 15.402; the best of intentions can be overcome by the gravitational pull 19.61–2; *dhyāna* like the first stage of a rocket to take you out of the gravitational field 4.521; it can turn Dharma practice into pseudo-Dharma practice 19.456; it is at work all the time 19.456, 19.462; do not underestimate its power 3.251; if you don't keep making an effort, you will slip back 3.248, 4.264, 4.322–3, 4.380, 18.324; important to see its workings in human history and in our own lives 3.251; its effect on meditation 3.247–8; laziness is a manifestation of its effect 18.555; the individual struggles to emerge in the middle of the group 12.253; our habitual grasping for worldly things 18.177; the part of oneself that is not integrated 15.399; the pull of the round of existence 2.261; universal religion pulled back into ethnic religion 12.253

the pull of the Unconditioned
the conflict between the pull of the conditioned and the Unconditioned 17.612; fear when we feel it 3.249; the gravitational pull of Enlightenment 15.470; grace 3.252

gravity analogy between the Dharma and the law of gravity 15.631–2; analogy with the law of karma 3.100; a religious person makes spiritual experience their centre of gravity 2.185, 16.98, 18.541; a shift in the centre of spiritual gravity 23.185

Gray, Thomas

'Elegy in a Country Churchyard'
'Full many a gem of purest ray serene' 8.148, 11.41–2; has the quality *kāvya* 26.332; a longing, lingering look behind 7.162, 11.397; 'The paths of glory lead but to the grave' 3.96, 26.394; there are no 'mute inglorious Miltons' 26.18

other works
'Ode on a Distant Prospect of Eton College' 21.59; 'The Progress of Poesy' 24.395

Gṛdhrakūṭa *see* Vulture's Peak

great bliss *see mahāsukha*

Great Britain *The British: Their Identity and Their Religion* (review) 8.429–31; its spiritual renewal need not be Christian 8.430–1; *see also* Western Buddhism/Buddhism in Britain; British history; England; Scotland; Wales

great lives

introduction
the biographies of great men 9.219; the 'great man' theory of history 10.167; great men are like mountains 9.172–3; lives no longer consider great 25.431; 'I think continually of those who were truly great', *see* Spender; in the lives of all great men, there is a certain pattern 10.127; not honouring their memory as we should 25.447; 'The Truly Great' 7.423; we should celebrate the lives of great men and women by following their example 10.167

great Buddhists
'Great Buddhists of the Twentieth Century' 6.600–21; in the lives of great Buddhists a noble pattern emerges 15.93–4; what is a great Buddhist? 6.601–2; what we may learn from their inspiring lives 6.621

great reliances *see* four great reliances

Great Sideways Leap 12.86, 12.709 (n64)

'Great Wisdom' (*Mahaprajna*) v9, v21

Great Work in alchemy, *see under* alchemy; in the *Bodhicaryāvatāra*, *see under* Śāntideva; the Great Work of the dissemination of the Dharma 8.xxix; the Great Work of Enlightenment is accomplished 7.403–4; 'The Great Work' (poem) 25.267

greatness Buddhas to be are born fully conscious of their past lives and their future greatness 1.256; great lives, *see* great lives; a guru whose 'greatness' was just inconsiderate behaviour 19.161–2; *mahatta* (greatness) 3.235

Greece (ancient)

HISTORY AND CULTURE

introduction
the ancient Greeks did not know themselves 12.462; philosophical, spiritual, and artistic creativity in the Axial Age 3.427, 11.355; perhaps a kinship between ancient India and ancient Greece 10.467–8; asceticism 1.140; the beauty of the male form 26.594; for them the beautiful was unquestionably linked with the ethical 13.279; the Egyptians criticized them for

having to set up ways of taking exercise 14.419; *to kalon*: the good, the true, and the beautiful 4.269, 13.279; interpretation of dreams 16.191, 16.204–5; philosophy, *see under* philosophy; prejudice against physical work 15.404; schools of philosophy 3.427, 3.428–9; sanctuaries of healing 16.191–2; statues in the archaeological museum in Athens 23.289; artefacts at the British Museum 26.470; the teaching tradition 18.409; their humanistic dislike of prostrating before kings 11.250–1; 'To me Greece meant *ancient* Greece' 23.295–6

friendship
only possible between virtuous persons (Aristotle) 7.294, 12.638–9, 17.327; people took their friendships very seriously 15.149–50; there could be no friendship between a free man and a slave 3.575, 11.700, 12.644

classical literature and song
making parallels with the Buddhist tradition 12.406; Order members should study the classics 12.406; Orphic hymns 26.494; pre-Euripidean Greek tragedy 14.109; *see also* individual writers

gods
associations of certain gods with specific types of incense 26.494–5; comparison between Greek and Egyptian gods 26.470–1; even more real than the characters of Shakespeare or Dickens 26.469; *see also* individual gods

myths and mythology
allegorization 16.103; Asclepius (or Asklepios), *see* Asklepios; Atlas 7.379; death was represented as a beautiful winged youth 13.230–1; Hercules, *see* Hercules; *Homeric Hymns* 24.396; Jason and the Golden Fleece 26.262; King of the Dead 16.191; Melampus and Chiron 24.379; might Western Buddhism adopt Greek mythology? 19.128, 19.410; Muses, *see* Muses; Odysseus's journey home 26.262; Olympus 25.520; Orpheus, *see* Orpheus; Perseus and Medusa, *see* Perseus; Prometheus, *see* Prometheus; Sirens 25.348; the three Fates 22.14, 25.407; the three golden apples 26.469–70

ANCIENT SITES

ancient Athens
the beauty of the 'city of the violet crown' 26.184–5; the Parthenon 2.644, 23.284–5; the Tyrannicides 24.265, 24.673 (n320); visiting the ruins with Terry 23.284–5

Delphi
Castalian Spring 3.157, 23.274–5; Henry Miller's description 23.234–5, 23.272, 23.276; in Euripides' *Ion* 23.279–81, 26.238; a holy place 23.273, 25.55; museum 23.276–8; Sangharakshita's visit 3.157, 12.461, 23.272–82, 26.238; the temple of Apollo: 'Know thyself' 8.259, 12.461, 13.351, 23.276; the Tholos 23.273–4, 23.278

other sites
Dodona, the oracle of Zeus 23.266–7; Eleusinian Mysteries 23.289–90; Elgin Marbles 24.491, 24.731 (n610); Epidaurus 16.192, 23.293–5, 26.238; Lauros 23.269; Mycenae 23.291–2; Olympia 23.298–9, 26.238; Tiryns 23.292–3

Greece (modern) Athens 23.283–90; Cape Sounion 23.286; a dangerous drive through the mountains 23.271; the effects of the Second World War 23.268; the friendliness of Greeks 23.267–8; Lepanto (sea battle) 23.271; Missolonghi, where Byron died 23.270; Mistra 23.296–7; Nauplio 23.295; the Peloponnese 23.290–300; Sangharakshita and Terry travel in Greece 23.264–300

greed (*lobha*) canonical source 16.616 (n242); an *arhant* free from greed 14.450; an atmosphere of dull, heavy greed in a shop 4.573–4, 11.80; attenuated through spiritual practice 7.360; capitalism plays on people's greed 26.20; to be confessed? 16.311; countered by rejoicing in merits 16.329–30; difference from *rāga* 17.596; don't give free rein to sensory stimuli 15.288; from passion to greed to infatuation to addiction to intoxication 10.616–17; the kinship between faith and greed 17.42–3; *lobha* synonymous with *abhijjhā* 2.386; 'No hurried path of success, forcibly cut by the greed of result, can be the true path' 2.112; fed by incentives at

work 3.586; generosity as the antidote to greed 8.199; 'the greediest and most selfish person I had ever met' 22.257–8; the greedy brahmin 9.288; a king whose enemies were anger and greed 13.654; the most typical mental attitude (along with anger) of worldly beings 1.232; strengthened through accumulated karma 15.204; voraciousness 18.559; *see also* craving

greed, hatred, and delusion *see* three roots

greed type *see* Buddhaghosa/ *Visuddhimagga*/character types

green association with the air element 16.147; Amoghasiddhi is deep green, the merging of the gold of day and the blue of night 13.186; the colour of balance and healing, and thus restorative action, justice, and karma 13.282; the colour of peace, calm, and tranquillity 2.387, 13.67, 18.59; the colour of nature, refuge, shelter, protection 13.281–2; dark green Osiris 25.352; green suggests something springing up with a fresh energy 18.59; greenstone 24.79, 25.353; a Buddha image that shone with a green light 14.464, 19.327–8, 21.460; Milarepa depicted as green in colour 18.4; Milarepa's dream of a green *ḍākinī* 18.58–9; represents the harmonizing, reconciling aspect of the Enlightened mind 13.282; Vaiśravaṇa (great king) 16.346; *see also* Tārā/Green Tārā

'Gregory' 22.260–1

Gregory the Sinaite 8.126

Grendel 12.642–3

Gretton, Miss (colleague at LCC) 20.76–7

gṛhapati* or *gahapati (householder) *see under* lay people

grief *asoka* (free from grief) 15.452; bereavement, *see under* death; the death of a beloved son (*Udāna*) 10.490–3; 'digging out the root of grief' 10.492; *domanassa*, *see domanassa*; 'From affection is born grief' 1.158; the grief of the Buddha's disciples: 'The Eye of the World has disappeared!' 4.10; the grief of three queens: a quality of archetypal tragedy 22.13–14; grief so deep that it is dumb 25.281; grief that the so beautiful should be so brief 25.281; and impermanence, *see under* impermanence/ responses; not always a negative state 26.65; suffering the deaths of loved ones over many lifetimes 1.130; Visākhā's grief on the death of her granddaughter 10.651–2

Grieg, Edvard 23.173

Grierson, G. A. v8

Griffiths, Bede 13.557

Grimm, George 12.104

Grosz, George 26.379

the 'ground of being' *see under* Robinson/ *Honest to God*

group

introducing the group
the history of the group 3.437, 11.352–6; a basic human need 3.444, 20.41; biological function 3.437; from birth to death the human being only survives because of the group 26.633; Christianity is on the side of the group 11.361; a collectivity organized for its own survival, a power structure 26.71; the corporate state is the group *par excellence* 11.356–7; cultural group 3.39; economic group 3.38–9; family group 3.37, 3.436, 3.441, 10.73–4; the group nature of most ostensibly religious people 7.148; the group's requirements of religion 19.468; handling criticism of the group 3.547–8; if you offend group susceptibilities, you have to take the consequences 15.678; it is breaking up in the modern world 3.441–2; sexual relationship, *égoïsme à deux* 3.39; social group 3.38, 3.436; subtly clinging to one's identity as a member of a group 18.27; symbols and slogans 3.436; ties of blood and soil 3.435, 3.437; undermined by encouraging members to think for themselves 3.618; we almost always accept the norms and values of the groups to which we belong 3.435; we are born into some and consciously join others 3.436, 3.438

characteristics of the group
characteristics of group members 3.435–8; conformity 3.438, 3.440, 12.253, 19.459; egocentricity 24.461; fear of individuality 3.438; fear of other groups 3.435; the group is always wrong 3.435, 26.42; group mentality 11.xxi, 19.456, 26.71; it does not know itself 12.462; loyalty 3.436

group pressure
desire for the group's approval 16.545, 17.184–5; don't confuse skilful means with capitulation to the pressure of the group 19.261; even in the sangha we must take care not to put pressure on 'difficult' people 17.184–5; fear of the group's disapproval 16.307, 18.134–5; fulfilling family or 'tribe' duties from personal choice, not group pressure 18.149–50; the individual has to resist the pressure of the group 19.261–4; looking after the sick and elderly: personal choice, not group pressure 18.149–50; praise and blame 16.545–6;

similar to the pressure of belief in God 19.277; someone trying to make you feel guilty is functioning as a group spokesman 15.622

the power of the group
its most powerful members confused with its most developed individuals 15.719–20; based on power 3.438; cannot be overestimated 3.440; God as the most powerful member of the group 19.277; the group consists of people who relate to one another in terms of power 3.447, 3.452; the power of the group is the power of Māra 11.359; power hierarchies 18.17–18

leaving the group
introduction 3.459–61; the Buddha's 3.460, 11.398; if you stay in it you make it more difficult for yourself to evolve 18.485–6; going forth as a transition from group existence to the spiritual community 2.415; means shaking off your identification with humanity as a mere collectivity 3.37; renouncing group identity for the freedom of absolute emptiness 18.139; usually emancipation from the group occurs via independent thinking 26.40–1; victory over the internalized group 11.398

positive group
introduction 3.452–8; a church as a positive group 24.128; how can it defend itself against the negative group? 15.624; the importance of the positive group 11.197; and moral order 16.432–3; needs rules 19.559; open to anyone who wishes to take part in its activities 3.457; the positive group has a definite place in Triratna 11.392, 24.128; progressing from society to the positive group 18.359; and the spiritual community 3.457, 8.419, 16.433, 17.41, 17.673, 19.467–8; it won't last for long without some sustaining spiritual principle 19.467–8

the group and the spiritual community
introduction 3.434–44; battle 3.432; the difference between them 2.474, 13.429, 17.559; the group exerts a gravitational pull on the spiritual community 3.443; the group tries to incorporate into itself those committed to the spiritual life 18.198–9; the lowest common denominator and the highest common factor 26.31; positive influence of 3.444; the pull of the group on the spiritual community 15.498; the group has rights but the spiritual community has duties 26.73; the monk does not belong to the group 16.391; seeing the teacher as the head of a group 15.564; a spiritual community is not a group 8.549, 10.573, 13.485, 17.559, 26.7; Triratna (FWBO) and the group 2.568, 13.485; we must want to shake off group mentality 3.452

see also
going forth; the group and the individual, *see under* individual

growing up the bodhisattva like a mother helping people to grow up spiritually 15.324; a child unable to imagine growing up like clinging to self-view 17.626; giving up the toys and tales of childhood 3.36; 'It's time you grew up' 19.59; most people never grow up 3.549–51; people sometimes need some help to grow up spiritually 26.44; 'What do you want to be when you grow up?' 26.582, 26.591

growth and development

introduction
distinction between evolution, progress, and development 13.465–6; the essence of Sangharakshita's teaching: human spiritual development 11.730–6; 'A Method of Personal Development' 11.145–56; people think of developing land, money, their house, but not themselves 18.569; what does 'development' mean? 11.145

the nature of spiritual growth and development
an active process which requires *vīrya* 16.164; advancing from stage to stage, or deepening present experience 4.201; analogy with the construction of a house 11.65; bringing the whole of our life up to the level of its highest moments 1.482; each exploration sheds light on the whole process 16.5; every living being wants to fulfil the law of its own being: to develop 11.147, 26.10; everyone grows according to their own nature 3.178, 16.126–7; for human beings, growth means growth in awareness 11.109–10; for most people

intellectual development comes first 26.40–1; the gradual nature of human development 19.125; growth is not just up, but takes place in all directions 17.343; an individual affair 12.622, 16.97; it happens not automatically but by pursuing specific steps 2.100, 12.467, 15.83; it has to begin with a healthy human individual 18.18; it is conscious and deliberate 11.64–5; it must take place at all levels of one's being or not at all 26.129; it takes time 19.99; the law of impermanence guarantees the possibility of development 2.296, 17.444; a natural process of growth 3.278, 11.87–9, 15.578–9; 'Nirvāṇa' indicates the unlimited nature of the process 17.357; not an easy matter for anyone 26.66; perpetual self-transcendence 3.17; possible only for one who understands consciousness to be intrinsically undefiled 1.84; reflexive consciousness is what sparks it off 15.215; the shedding of dead leaves and the blossoming of buds 10.567; sometimes a long and painful process 26.61; spiritual life may be seen as cessation or development 7.151; the whole of space filled with flowers 11.88; you need an ideal which is, as it were, ahead of you 10.636

growth and development as a way of thinking about spiritual life
the more advanced the stage of development, the less there is to say 1.579–80; the Buddha's conception of the Dharma 3.15–16, 10.211–18, 15.229–30; the concept of *ālaya* clarifies the possibility of growth 18.291; dependent origination 12.151; the Dharma has one flavour, the flavour of growth and development 10.567; emphasis on developing what is positive rather than crushing what is negative 10.525; it fits in with the evolutionary way of looking at things 2.476, 10.567, 19.201; practising the first precept allows people to grow in their own way 17.178–9, 18.183–4; growing into Nirvāṇa 10.635; more helpful to speak of growth than getting rid of the self 10.471, 14.462; much of the sense of *vimutti* (freedom) is conveyed by 'growth and development' 10.567; the only thing you have to believe as a Buddhist is that you can grow 17.28; the parable of the raincloud, *see under White Lotus Sūtra*; a positive emphasis is very important 10.513, 17.291, 17.296, 19.227; the rite of prospering: encouraging growth towards Enlightenment 13.280; two ways to think about it: removing imperfections or trying to develop 26.61; Western people respond better to growth and development than renunciation 19.200–1; willingness to grow: the breaking of the first fetter 15.519; within each of the six realms there is the potential for development 13.135

personal growth
as we develop, we find that we can think and feel, act and be still, simultaneously 12.65; better to grow in a natural way rather than forcing yourself 4.566, 18.31; concentrate on positive growth and development, not just looking back into the past 18.444; the crucial question: is it helping me to develop? 16.515–16, 19.544; 'Do I really want to grow?' 15.610; distinguish between what you need to do to develop and what you want to do 4.91; the effort to grow needs to be directed towards the whole psyche 2.112, 3.41, 3.491; four qualities to be 'made to grow' (*Udāna*) 10.527, 10.531–2; it depends on rediscovering spiritual truths for ourselves 21.245; it is important that we should actually feel ourselves growing 16.130, 18.105; the last thing you think of as a stage of development may be just what you need 19.343; many ways in which we can grow and develop 11.419; the more we develop, the more creative will be our effect on others 15.237; out of our present being we have to create something that goes beyond what we are 25.73; people get more different from each other as they grow 14.451, 16.131–2; a real Buddhist should grow a little every day 26.56; suspend thoughts of your development and put yourself at others' disposal 18.592; a type of person who aims at the growth and development of all their potentialities 12.277; we all work on different aspects of ourselves at different times 4.41; we can change consciousness towards positive growth 15.161; we have a responsibility for our own growth 26.12; we know what will help us grow from our own experience 12.369–70; we need development from which we don't fall back: insight 19.449; when a situation is no longer helping you to grow, be ready to move on 17.371; the whole of us is growing all the time 11.87–8; why bother with personal development? 11.147; you can't ensure further growth by staying in the same situation 19.362; you don't have to keep tearing yourself up by the roots to see if you have grown 17.267; you don't need to know what is going on externally 19.270

what supports growth
association with others 11.385–6, 16.473; the body 1.122; communication 3.555; contact with someone more highly

developed 3.556; culture 13.483–4; emotional positivity 10.432, 15.396, 15.399; enjoyment 15.156; ethics: more about personal growth and progress than about rules 15.291; the experience of suffering and contact with more developed people 3.556; fear (for some people) 26.47; friendship 7.294; individual effort 10.346; it is only helpful at the start to speak of growth depending on definite conditions 1.133; love 12.215; living in a conducive situation 3.464; meditation, with support from indirect methods 5.635; ordination: a rich and fruitful growing thing 12.423; renunciation 12.479–80; perfect conditions for development in a pure Buddha-land 16.462; serving others 4.18; *śūnyatā* 17.95

conditions needed, as for a plant
(1) the potentiality for Enlightenment (the seed) 3.313, 12.512–13; (2) favourable circumstances (the soil) 3.313–14, 8.270, 12.513–14, 15.365; (3) spiritual friendship (warmth) 3.314, 12.514, 25.140; (4) intellectual clarity (light) 3.314, 12.515–16; (5) the rain of the Dharma 3.314, 10.218, 12.516–17; other conditions the plant might need 11.89–90

obstacles to growth
be careful that your thinking doesn't develop disproportionately 26.38; confession removes obstacles to growth 16.508; even in pursuit of spiritual training one can entrap oneself further in time, place, personality 18.31; forces inimical to growth 16.349–50; helping others as a way of escaping the demands of self-development 18.592–3; the idea that any attempt at development is spiritual materialism 17.594; if everything's peaceful and happy there's less growth 4.419; the limitations of the psychological model of development 17.670–1; making a directed effort to remove obstacles 15.95; the metaphysics of potential negates the concept of growth 17.94–5; misery of feeling so restricted by circumstances one cannot grow 16.71; not all phases are a stage of development, some are a waste of time 19.343; sloth is the weight of one's existence resisting further evolving 26.47; sometimes one may think 'Why bother about personal development?' 26.11; trying to develop spiritually without giving up one's affluent lifestyle 11.613

mistakes
misusing the developmental model 11.451, 12.404–5, 12.478–9, 18.591; making use of your spiritual development to aggrandize yourself 10.448; getting an inflated idea of one's development 17.681–2; thinking that a 'revised version' of a certain stage is a higher stage 2.431; regarding the spiritual community as a convenience to your development 11.286; talking about 'my spiritual development' 15.340; you cannot force people to grow 16.72, 18.357–8

growth movement 14.574, 18.591

Gruber, Peter 18.xii

Guān Jing 16.621–2 (n287)

Guanyin (or Kwannon, Kwanyin, Kuan Yin) an image in Cambridge 26.97; an image in Penang 24.54; and the Madonna 26.599, 26.620; Sangharakshita as a child encounters a figure of Guanyin 20.2, 20.485; Sangharakshita buys a figure for his mother 23.130; the transformation of Avalokiteśvara into female form 1.336, 2.175, 7.124, 26.599, 26.655

guard the Buddha dismisses the monks who want to guard him 4.14, 12.216; the danger of abandoning the safeguard of positive conditions prematurely 18.34; guarding the gates of the senses, *see under* senses; 'Guarding of Total Awareness' (*Bodhcaryāvatāra*) 4.378–87; one should always be on one's guard against Māra 15.366–7; one must be on one's guard against humbug 18.429; safeguarding one's insights 4.13; the self we guard so jealously is no more than an idea 15.263; the Tibetans believed gold was guarded by dragons 15.138; 'the trembling, unsteady mind, which is difficult to guard' (*Dhammapada*) 10.226, 18.231

guardian angel *see under* angel

guardian deities *see dharmapālas*

guardians of the temple *see* four great kings

Guénon, René 12.32, 21.159, 21.161, 23.121, 23.492 (n145)

Guenther, Herbert V.

introduction
Sangharakshita's first meeting with him in Lucknow 21.111–14; visits Kalimpong 21.310–1

Philosophy and Psychology in the Abhidharma
the best modern exposition 8.510–11; difficulty of breaking emotional fetters 2.147–8; no distinction between path and goal 2.122; ethics 4.336, 4.696 (n251); mental attitude 17.496; numbers of faith-followers and doctrine-followers

2.152; the 'objective content of the perceptual situation' 2.97, 13.151, 15.134, 17.445, 17.482; *pīti*: 'a driving and even overwhelming emotion' 2.106; *prajñā*: 'analytical appreciative understanding' 14.516, 19.219

Stepping-Stones articles and translations 'Ahankara and Selflessness' 21.147; excerpts from the *Gaṇḍavyūha Sūtra* 21.147; 'The Origin and Spirit of Vajrayāna' 1.374; 'Our Position in Life' 21.310; review of Conze's *Buddhism* 21.313

other works
The Dawn of Tantra 19.38; *Mind in Buddhist Psychology*, *see* Gyaltsen; 'The Origin and Spirit of the Vajrayāna' 1.374, 7.536; *The Jewel Ornament of Liberation* (translation) 2.440; *The Tantric View of Life* 5.43, 5.523, 14.560, 18.29, 19.38; *Tibetan Buddhism in Western Perspective* 19.38–9, 19.236, 19.592 (n12); translation of *The Necklace of Clear Understanding* 17.453; *Treasures of the Middle Way* 19.230

Guenther, Sarojani v21

Guercino v24

Guest, David 22.210

guests alms offered to monks as honoured guests 2.226; the Buddha as honoured guest 9.419, 13.255–7; the Buddha just turned up, like an unexpected guest (*atithi*) 11.238, 13.256–7, 25.86–7; hospitality to guests, *see* hospitality; seven (or eight) offerings, as to the honoured guest 1.507–8, 11.237–9, 13.254–6, 18.430; treating guests kindly 4.68

guhya 12.312

Guhyaloka, Spain *see under* Triratna IV/ retreat centres

Guhyananda, Dharmachari v24

Guhyapāda (deity) 14.235

Guhyaratna, Dharmachari v24

Guhyasamāja (Tantric deity) 19.37

Guhyasamāja Tantra *see under* tantras/ works

guidance all works of art can guide and sustain all people of all periods of history 7.81; the best and most reliable guidance comes from beyond one's own ego 22.374; the Buddha as a guide, not a leader 7.149, 14.541; the Buddha gives guidance in doubt, support in crisis, impetus in stagnation 2.11; from being dominated by the senses, one is guided by the five spiritual faculties 1.280; guide and direct positive feelings rather than try to check or suppress them 5.617; meditation techniques can guide, but one should allow unfolding to happen naturally 18.31; Dr Mehta's guidance, *see under* Mehta; many people ask for spiritual guidance, but very few can act upon it 4.67; Nyingma lamas guided by what came to them in their meditation 13.24; precepts guide the application of ethical principles to all aspects of life 4.110; take the Theravāda for daily practice and the Mahāyāna as a guide to the ideal 4.62–3; we need a teacher to guide us through the teachings 3.89–90

Guhyavajra, Dharmachari (Murray Wright) v24

guilt assuming that someone is guilty before establishing the facts 11.442; burn incense before a Buddha image and recite *sūtras* until you feel free of guilt 1.509; and Christianity 2.260, 16.90, 16.307–8, 18.160–1; confession without guilt 16.306–11; confusing rational and irrational guilt 13.608–9; if someone is trying to make you feel guilty, they are functioning as a group spokesman 15.622; the etymology of the word is unknown 16.306; and fear 16.306–7; feeling guilty about being happy 17.165–6; getting rid of guilt through confession 16.312; don't feel guilty if you have made mistakes as a parent 3.543; giving out of guilt 4.341; the guilt that surrounds sex 17.638–9; the idea that we are pure by nature comes as a positive shock if one is from a guilt-ridden culture 5.34; importance of feeling rational guilt 13.608–9, 16.311; it's important to free oneself from guilt 1.509; inappropriate in relation to the Buddha 16.309–10; irrational guilt 2.260, 3.265, 16.307–8, 18.455–6, 21.224–5; the language of potential may help someone suffering from guilt 17.95; lingering guilt leads people to think that pain in meditation is necessary, but it is not 10.503; purged through the practice of generosity and ethics 2.105; some people even feel guilty if they are quite skilfully happy 10.609; unconscious guilt leads to a tendency to justify oneself 3.214; in the West, with our background of sin and guilt, we need much more praise and appreciation 4.622; when the unconscious mind knows that our pleasure is at the expense of another's pain 3.214

Guimet, Musée *see under* France/Paris

Guinevere 25.101–8, 25.438–9

Guirdham, Arthur 8.420–5, 16.472, 16.625 (n323)

Gujarat the Buddhist Society of Gujarat 10.182, *see also* Ahmedabad

Guṇabhadra (translator) 14.201–2

Guṇamati (*ācārya*) 1.371

Guṇananda, Migettuwatte 7.444, 8.16–18

Gunapala, Dharmachari (Bernie Tisch) v24

Guṇaprabha (authority on the Vinaya) 8.403

Gunaprabha, Dharmachari v24

Gunaratana, Henepola v24

Gunavati, Dharmacharini v24

guṇas (Hinduism) aspects of *prakṛti* 10.53; the *Bhagavad Gītā* links the *guṇas* with the different castes 10.53–6; character types in which each of the *guṇas* predominate 12.278; the kinds of food liked by people of each type 10.54–5; used to justify the caste system 9.102–3, 10.55–6, 12.278; three *guṇas* (*sattva*, *rajas*, *tamas*) 10.53, 12.278, 24.114

gunnaw 20.432

Gupta, Das (CIB) v23

Gupta, Keshub Chandra 8.643, 22.175–7

Gurdjieff, G, I. introduction 16.604 (n146), 22.617 (n340), 23.490 (128); 'A good man always loves his parents' 16.297; he insisted that everything must be paid for 26.34; 'Pain helps you remember' 16.206; a teacher of Gurdjieff's ideas 24.576

Gurdjieff Society 23.104, 23.490 (n127)

Gurkhas *see under* Nepal

guru

GURUS OF DIFFERENT TRADITIONS

history in Buddhism
the Buddha made no claims to be a guru 3.163; far more important in the Mahāyāna than in the Theravāda 7.543; the bodhisattva has a teacher and aspires to have disciples 13.22; a bodhisattva precept to work for your own circle of disciples 13.57; one's most important relationship is the vertical one with the guru 18.504–5; Amitābha regarded as the guru in the Avalokiteśvara visualization practice 16.180–1; the guru as esoteric Refuge 2.481, 4.175, 12.17, 12.313, 19.221–2; visualized on the Refuge Tree 13.77, 13.207

gurus in Hinduism
claims to be God, or *avatāras* of God 3.163, 9.304, 10.246; the expectation that the guru will be revelling in divine bliss 19.244; the gurus make a distinction between devotees and disciples 15.682–3; mutual backscratching of gurus and disciples 20.202; the most successful gurus promise worldly success 19.460; people are all too ready to claim God-realization 14.564; *vidyā-guru* and *dīkṣā-guru* 18.508

the vajraguru (or vajrācārya, Tantric guru)
absolute obedience is required 12.18–19; any guru will find only a few disciples 18.97; as far as the Tantra is concerned, the guru is the Buddha 13.197–9, 17.277, 18.93; devotion to the guru is fundamental to Tantric practice 18.14; as esoteric refuge, *see under* three esoteric refuges; the guru activates your dormant energies 18.67; the guru embodies the Buddhadharma itself 18.220; the guru's important place in the Vajrayāna 7.507; in a sense, anyone who teaches Buddhism functions as a Tantric guru 13.199; the intimate and personal link between teacher and disciple in the Vajrayāna 14.402; the no-nonsense guru who can make you do anything – open to abuse 13.176–8; Tantric meditation cannot be practised without a guru 13.89; you never find fault with your Tantric guru 12.17–18; Tibetan lamas are gurus in a threefold sense, relating to the three *yānas* 12.15–19; the *vajraguru* introduces the disciple to the direct experience of their own nature 18.61; why the Vajrayāna stresses the importance of the guru 19.173–4

WHAT GURUS ARE AND ARE NOT

the nature of the guru
an interpreter, a translator, rather than a Buddha or even a teacher 18.67; by definition someone with whom we have a direct personal relationship 19.163–4; crest jewel 19.176, 19.568–9; *dharmakāya* 19.222–4; the embodiment of the ideal 18.220, 19.176; a 'guru with lineage' 19.203; gurus of different temperaments 18.145; gurus who are involved with worldly life 19.462; he operates in the love mode, not the power mode 18.410–11; living Buddha, living Dharma 18.495–6, 19.120, 19.221–2; the middlemen of religion 26.36; *nirmāṇakāya* 19.230–1; on a higher level of being and consciousness than ourselves 3.554; real spiritual teachers do not make claims or seek power 16.577–8, 19.118; the teacher as archetype or exemplar 5.563–4; they cannot be

pinned down as being either conventional or unconventional 19.163; they don't necessarily have to be based in monasteries 19.208–9; unconventional gurus 19.160–4

how gurus function
be cautious about the idea that the guru is testing the disciple 19.118; the Buddha principle active within the field of our own experience 18.67, 19.137–9; the danger for the guru of demanding cash for teachings 18.118–19; gradual and sudden methods 16.171–2, 16.183–4; the Guru follows the Buddha to transform the depths 12.323; a guru's teaching is not a commodity, it is always an exchange 18.114–15; hard gurus 14.488; he can see your individual pattern and help you to work it out 18.284; he holds up a mirror to you 19.570–1; married gurus 18.410; the need for a teacher with personal experience to interpret the teachings 19.172–4; he needs to find a balance of encouragement and criticism 18.144; his role is primarily to activate the disciple's energies 18.93–4; 'The precept of the Lama is more important than the scriptures and commentaries' 8.528; in principle the guru is an interpreter 13.198; is he simply someone who helps you to see, or is he an Enlightened being? 19.231; their humiliation of their disciples 14.488–9; they may function in many ways 3.553–4; they should communicate *through* their temperament, not just express it 14.567–8

how gurus are seen
the danger of considering the guru as leader 3.546–8, 9.303–4; the disciples can end up leading the guru by the nose 19.464; a great mistake to expect from a guru what we can only get from ourselves 3.561; a guru is partly responsible for how people regard him 19.164; often people are on the lookout for a great guru, but that is not what they need 2.295; one has to be able to see in the guru what is of universal significance 19.120–1; people can attach false and inflated value to the guru 2.529, 3.558–9; projection onto a guru 11.83–4; respect for gurus 19.465–6; seeing the guru as the Buddha is seeing his deepest nature 19.288; seeing the guru as Enlightened, or at least more Enlightened than you 19.231; seeing the guru's *sambhogakāya* 19.120–1; seen as an approval-bestowing figure 18.363–4; they cannot be overvalued 3.558; Western conceptions of the guru 3.560–1; the Western tendency to identify with the master, not the disciple 8.497; you have to experience him as he really is 19.121

faith in the guru
adulation of a guru is not good for him or his disciples 11.666–7; the difference between faith and blind belief 18.410–11; don't turn your faith in the guru into a limiting factor 18.182; the faith-follower's response to the guru 2.142, 15.561–2; 'The grace of the Gurus is beyond our comprehension' 18.554; a 'guru on whom you can rely' 19.577–8; his disciples' unshakeable faith in Milarepa rather than in the Dharma 18.220; imbibing the guru's words like salt into water 18.593–4; making exaggerated statements about the guru 18.410; 'My guru's words are absolutely true' 19.137–9; 'O my own immediate holy guru' 13.219–20; putting yourself in the hands of the guru 18.383–7, 18.392–3, 18.410, 19.529; the quietest hints can have the force of commands 18.110; revering one's teacher 17.277; visualize the guru above your head at all times 18.92–3

what a guru is not
summary 2.528, 3.545–54; he cannot represent the spiritual community 14.541–2; not a group leader or a boss or an authority figure 18.411; not the head of a religious group 3.546–8; not an ecclesiastical superior 3.548; not a teacher 3.548–9, 18.346–7; not a father-substitute 3.549–51, 18.411; not a problem-solver 3.551–3; to think of him as someone who gives out initiations is to miss the point 13.198

pseudo-gurus
be wary of being seduced by charismatic purveyors of Enlightenment 8.578; blaming their vanities on their disciples 19.164; disciples who are fooled by deceptive gurus 19.161–3; express their own ideas or feelings as higher insight 19.293; the monk who exhorted Sangharakshita to meditate on 'the Light of the Self' 20.177; most 'gurus' are simply exploiters 11.84, 26.80; people would rather have a nominal guru than a real one 19.462–3; pseudo-spiritual claptrap 8.437; the rationalizations of pseudo-teachers 19.430; those who boss psychologically weaker people around 18.386–7; you're at liberty to criticize them 19.546

is a guru necessary?
introduction 3.545–62; contact with someone more highly developed is necessary for spiritual growth 3.556; debasement of the term 2.528, 9.304, 16.577–8, 24.177; an enemy could do more for you than a guru can 4.411–12; in the last analysis the true guru is your

own mind 18.619, 18.631; it might be best to drop the guru concept 2.529, 13.198; to grow spiritually without a guru is extremely difficult 3.556; 'we always need a guru' 18.631; you need a personal connection with one who has experienced the transcendental 16.354

guru stories
a guru who flicked custard (or jelly) over an audience 19.161, 23.48; a guru who was always drunk, but was said to be very wise 13.177, 19.160–1; a guru who tied a kitten to a post 19.55

RELATIONSHIP BETWEEN GURU AND DISCIPLE

'choosing' a guru
the search for a guru 9.250; actually the guru chooses the disciple 3.556–8; can you have two gurus at the same time? 19.544; flitting from guru to guru 18.109–10, 19.316; giving money is what makes a meeting between teacher and disciple possible 18.114; gradual or immediate connection with gurus 22.419; no question of choosing a guru 18.65

the nature of the relationship
being regarded as a disciple by the teacher 15.668; it needs to be close if the Dharma is to be taught without the medium of culture 16.375; the disciple cannot really understand the guru's actions 18.112; the disciple's mode of being needs to be in harmony with the guru's 19.557–8; an intensely personal relationship 18.162; the guru's difficulty in knowing the disciple's mental state 19.555; 'the guru's rules' 19.557–8; living with the teacher (Indian tradition) 15.667–8, 15.724–5; love and friendship, not authority or power 3.556; a mutual responsiveness 2.248; a mutual vow 18.146–7; the need for mutual generosity 18.115; the rebellious disciple 18.363–8; remembering the guru 19.137, 19.175–6; the terms guru and disciple only make sense in relation to each other 18.xviii; working on your relationship with the guru 18.318

communication
authentic communication 19.223–6; being out of harmony with the guru 18.483, 18.504; breaking off contact 18.366–7; a disciple who asked for a teaching every twenty years 19.507; disciples who want to teach the guru how to teach them 11.250, 18.492–3, 19.365–6, 22.220, 22.426; 'existential' contact 3.554; the guru's personal precept exactly adapted to the disciple's needs 18.393–4; harmony with the guru 18.502–3; in the past, disciples were given teachings when they were ready 10.440; no need to establish before communication starts who is guru, who disciple 24.177; the transmission of spiritual power from guru to disciple 13.88–9; vertical communication 3.555–6, 13.216, 18.418–19, 18.504; without disciples' curiosity, no teaching can take place 11.277–8

offerings and blessings
the blessing of hairs from the guru's head ('Like a dog's hair!') 19.366, 22.491; the effect of a guru blessing a thangka 19.326; the giving of initiations and blessings 4.265–7; making offerings to the guru 19.529–30; Marpa requires a disciple to give everything, even a lame goat 12.18–19, 19.530; medicine that has been blessed by a guru 19.366; offering yourself to the guru 18.61, 19.529–30; serving the teacher 16.106; 'To please one's Guru is to gain his blessings' 18.511

complaints and criticisms
complaining that the guru's teachings are unreasonable 18.493; criticizing the guru 19.546; the dangers of rejecting or passing judgement on the guru 18.111–12; finding fault with the teacher 18.111

disciple overtaking guru
disciples who are more distinguished than their gurus 19.210–11; if disciples don't do better than their teacher, the sangha will decline 12.545; guru and disciple may appear to be giving completely different teachings 14.568; the guru must produce disciples who are better than him 12.377, 18.255, 19.210, 19.416–17, 26.81; a reversal of roles 3.556; you best imitate your teacher by being yourself 14.568

see also
teacher/spiritual; Padmasambhava as guru, *see under* Padmasambhava/introduction; Pith-Instructions; Sangharakshita's gurus and teachers, *see under* Sangharakshita V/ early years

Guru Maharaj 12.654, 15.490

Guru Nanak 8.167, 8.680 (n100), 20.401

Guru Rimpoche *see* Padmasambhava

guru yoga brief introduction 5.558–9, 18.92–3; be aware of your guru above your head all the time 18.92–3; can one do the practice in relation to a guru one has never met? 5.562–3; concluding prayer ('O my own immediate holy guru') 13.219–20; the cultivation of gratitude – a formal version of what we should feel anyway 18.93; a description of the Tantric practice 13.216–

20; Dilgo Khyentse Rimpoche 5.563, 5.556; doing the practice as Vajrayoginī 13.217; does doing the practice treat the teacher as an archetype or an exemplar? 5.563–5; feeling the guru's blessing, his *adhiṣṭhāna* 13.217; *kalyāṇa mitra yoga* 5.xxvii, 5.753 (n538); Milarepa's practice 18.15, 18.92; not to be confused with the *mettā bhāvanā* 5.158; one places oneself in alignment with the whole lineage of gurus 4.619; Padmasambhava in the practice 5.562; its purpose is to help you attune yourself to the mind and heart of the guru 12.19; treating a living guru differently when visualizing them and when actually meeting them 5.564; Tsongkhapa in the practice 5.562; visualizing the guru above your head 13.217, 18.92–3, 19.175–6

Gurupriya (at Anandamayi's ashram) 20.196, 20.200

Guyon, Mme 13.626, 26.203–4

Gyalmo Chenmo *see under* Dalai Lama

Gyaltsen, Tenzin (Khunu Lama) v22

Gyaltsen, Yeshe

Mind in Buddhist Psychology (Necklace of Clear Understanding)
introduction to Yeshe Gyaltsen 17.xii, 17.452; summary of the text 8.508–10; awareness of the author's kindness and patience 8.510; the best traditional exposition of the Abhidharma in English 8.510; book review 8.508–11; is it a helpful text? 17.108; Sangharakshita's commentary 17.431–698; translation of *śūnyatā* as nothingness 3.658 (n220), 5.32

Gyan Jyoti v21, v22

Gyepa Dorje *see* Hevajra

gypsies gypsy music in Poland 25.442, 26.447–8; Sangharakshita's sister lived in a gypsy caravan 23.29, 25.69; their ancestors from India 25.442; they are harassed because they represent the untameable 11.9

H

Habermann, Anne (Lama Govinda's foster-mother) 21.256

habits

how habits arise
actions that started deliberately can become habitual 17.524; be careful not to let unskilful actions become habits 15.354; from the repetitive nature of the reactive mind 11.23–4; indulgence in harmful habits indicates lack of self-love 5.126; learned through one's culture 9.371; our habitual grasping for worldly things, a gravitational pull 18.177; we *are* our habits 11.48

the effects of habits
conscience blunted through habit 16.311; don't underestimate the power of habit 15.362; energy locked away in habitual patterns of thought, feeling, and behaviour 18.77; habitual karma 2.72, 3.108, 17.526–7; keeping on with something out of habit 18.207; moving along deep ruts of unconscious habit 14.551; other people tend to see us in a habitual way 11.48; they keep us immersed in trivial pursuits 3.35; they seem to drive all the freshness and spontaneity out of life 16.439; without mindfulness of purpose we just base our actions on habit 15.96–7

habits and spiritual life
dealing with our habits 17.663; develop the habit of recollecting your goal often and deeply 15.96; don't carry your ordinary habits over into the spiritual life 18.106; ethics: habitual skilful action 9.187; religious life can become a matter of habit 11.23–4; something is difficult to practise when it runs counter to our habits 7.182; the spiritually disastrous habit of treating concepts as ends in themselves 21.314

changing habits
abandoning ingrained habits of mind 17.359; 'Am I exploring new avenues or going round the treadmill of my habits?' 17.348; breaking down habitual ways of responding to the world 17.267; changing habits 15.355; giving up bad habits and adopting good ones 9.410, 9.418; if you can get into a habit, you can get out of it 11.48; make sure even positive habits don't become ends in themselves 15.356–7; scrutinize all your habits and see whether they are still relevant 5.334, 15.355–6; they may seem to plough on, but like the Titanic they are sinkable 15.242

see also
habit as the first fetter, *see under* ten fetters; *vāsanā* ('habit-energy')

Hachiman *see under* Japanese Buddhism/ bodhisattvas

Hafez 25.26, 26.687

Haggard, Rider 24.566

haiku *see under* poetry

Haklena 13.342

Hakuin Ekaku

his life
introduction 1.630 (n398), 2.742 (n682), 16.591 (n40), 16.625 (n325); he was accused of fathering an illegitimate child: 'Is that so?' 11.283, 14.490; he said the best time for spiritual progress is when sick or suffering 15.393, 15.395, 15.403; rejoicing in his merits 1.509; the revitalizer of Rinzai Zen 12.594

'Song of Meditation' ('Song of Zazen', 'Song of Enlightenment')
'All beings are from the very beginning the Buddha' 1.269, 2.742 (n682); contains the essence of Buddhism 9.109; emphasis on direct realization of the highest spiritual truth 2.555; inspiration for the Triratna Buddhist Order 2.555, 12.368; 'Outside living beings, no Buddhas' 16.473; 'This very body the Buddha' 16.37

Halford, Bill 23.176–7

Hall, Radclyffe 13.612

Hall, Stephen *see* Shantideva

haloes angular Buddhas with multi-coloured haloes 22.350; a 'glory' is a halo in religious art 19.185; haloes of coloured light surrounding the Buddha or bodhisattva 16.260; a portrait with a halo 19.164, 21.47; through mindfulness, the most trivial occasions are invested with a halo of sanctity 1.151; the two haloes of the Buddha represent the two accumulations 14.425, 17.463

Ham Wol (Stacey Krause) v24

Hamblin, Henry Thomas v21

Hamilton, Lady 26.589

Hamilton, Mrs (Kalimpong) v21

Hammarskjöld, Dag 23.81, 23.486 (n107)

Hampstead Buddhist Vihara

introduction
all Buddhist traditions honoured at the Vihara 23.238; an assessment of the Vihara's progress 11.489–90; Beth, who attended the Vihara 23.23; *bhikkhus* hostile to the Mahāyāna but drawn to Christian mysticism 23.24–5; *The Buddhist* (English Sangha Association magazine) 11.475–99, v23; caretaker 23.127–8; the community at the Vihara 23.21–6, 23.167–9; the extravagant lifestyle of its occupants 23.7, 23.64–5, 23.136; the library 23.209; owned by the English Sangha Trust 23.127; the purchase of the property 23.48; Ratanasara is asked to leave 23.138; the shrine room 23.26, 23.137; speakers' classes 11.476, 11.495, 13.327, 23.83, 23.144, 23.194; Thai monks at the Vihara 23.43, 23.162–3; triumphalism 2.459, 13.414–15; why it was built in that part of London 13.410, 23.58–9

Sangharakshita at the Vihara
arrival 23.6–7; 'the Buddhist equivalent of the vicar of Hampstead' 11.543, 17.634, 18.347, 23.80–1, 23.213; concerned with Buddhism not just theoretically but practically 12.67; first talk 23.7; found that people's 'Buddhist' life was mainly reading 4.351, 11.378; gives more than a hundred lectures on Buddhism 13.321; giving lectures, teaching meditation, and giving personal interviews 2.457; people's expectations 18.347; a reception at the Vihara 23.241; talks 23.78–83; secretarial help 23.165–7; sensing a shift to the Other Vihara (Terry's flat) 23.185; his letter explaining the reason for his journey to India 11.494–5; arranging for people to cover his responsibilities while he was away in India 23.331; farewell reception before departure 23.332; a letter from Sangharakshita in India to the Vihara regulars 23.333–6; Maurice Walshe and George Goulstone try to prevent his return 23.373–4; an attempt to oust him 23.401–2, 23.407; the case for reinstatement 11.520, 23.402–3; Phra Maha Prasit, his replacement 23.427, 23.437; reasons for his dismissal 23.432–7

haṃsa (goose) *see under* birds

Hamsun, Knut 24.397

Handel, George Frederick performances of three operas and two oratorios 24.182; his aptitude for music from an early age 17.589; *Julius Caesar* 24.370, 26.505; *The Messiah* 2.645, 13.669, 23.261; *Water Music* played at birthday celebration 24.240

Hanshan (poet) 1.509, 1.630 (n398), 18.656–7 (n153), 23.124

Hanshan Deqing (enlightened Chan master) autobiography 14.260; on the *Diamond Sūtra* 14.148–9, 14.367, 14.376, 14.535; on the *Heart Sūtra* 14.367

Hanuman 16.361, 22.483

happiness

THE NATURE OF HAPPINESS

what is happiness?
absorption in quiet and even-mindedness is the true happiness 18.343; a creative life is a happy life 11.25, 12.641, 26.64

the importance of happiness
'Happiness is the perfume of the soul' 8.156; a happy ending is not necessarily an artistic disaster 24.183; if you feel you don't deserve to be happy, you must look into that 5.184, 17.165–6; it is our duty to be happy 4.97, 11.155, 26.25; people ask 'Why do I suffer?' but not 'Why am I happy?' 5.640, 12.646–7, 26.11; there is nothing wrong with wanting to be happy 17.165–6; we are not being asked to put our own happiness to one side altogether 17.165; we have a responsibility for our own happiness 26.12

the search for happiness
abandoning the search for happiness for the ethical path from which it arises 17.360; all things strive after happiness 7.68; 'Call no man happy until he is dead' (Sophocles) 6.601; do people search for happiness consciously or unconsciously? 19.243–4; every human being deserves to be happy 5.184, 17.165–6; happiness is a by-product of the quest for freedom 17.164–5, 26.64; looking out for signs that happiness is on its way 15.383–4; the more you try to be happy, the less likely you are to be so 17.208; setting up a goal of happiness to get away from unhappiness is ineffective 3.225–8; there can be no happiness on earth while there is division of subject and object 7.273–4; where goodness, truth, and beauty abound, happiness is not far to seek 7.321; you may have a happy life but still feel that something is missing 12.624

looking in the wrong places
conventional (and wrong) view that happiness comes through pursuing

desires 3.261; depending upon others for happiness 4.432, 18.388; getting everything you thought you wanted and still not feeling happy 17.269–70; the illusion that contact of sense object with sense organ brings happiness 19.234; mistaken view that happiness consists in the full satisfaction of desires 7.116; the self is the sole obstacle to the 'attainment' of happiness 7.412, 26.53; to find true happiness, you have to be convinced you won't find it in *saṃsāra* 19.242–4; we look for it in the wrong places, but we can find it if we search 12.613, 17.359–60; we try to convince ourselves we *must* be happy 3.262; you can't be happy unless you are active 19.583–4; happiness and desire, *see under* desire

finding happiness
does it depend on your own effort, or on your environment? 10.599; even within painful experience there can be deep happiness 15.221, 19.583; happily doing nothing 5.645–6, 18.121; happiness to stay where you are 18.341; happy is the man whose needs and wants coincide 26.12; instead of running from it into guilt or intoxication, understand its true nature 3.227; the less you own, the happier you are 10.488–90; happiness attained when existence accords with desires or *vice versa*: the second difficult, the first impossible 1.172; if we work, it should be because it makes us happy 18.121; if you can't be happy alone, you can't be happy with others 26.29; it comes from allowing oneself to be penetrated by everything that exists 7.412, 26.53; it comes not from satisfying craving, but from not having craving at all 10.474–5; it comes only when we desire and are attached to – nothing 1.172; it depends on our attitude towards things and what we do 17.507; it's stabilized by equanimity 5.211; 'Man hands on happiness to man' 25.423; one cannot always be happy, but one can be friendly 26.757 (n519); a paradox: he only is happy who does not care for happiness 7.412; produced by integration 5.238–9; *samādhi* arises naturally when you are perfectly happy 15.221; a short cut to happiness through poise and equilibrium 7.238; through restraint of the senses 1.148; we experience true happiness when we are active, including when we are meditating 26.63; when we are truly happy we tend not to think more than necessary 11.149; you will never find happiness if you go about it in a haphazard way 7.48

happiness and pleasure
pleasure is a passive state, happiness an active one 19.583, 26.63; we must distinguish between happiness and pleasure 17.166; why sacrifice real happiness for transitory pleasure? 17.163; you don't necessarily get closer to happiness by depriving yourself of pleasure 19.244

skilful happiness
skilful action *is* happiness 3.102; some people feel guilty if they are quite skilfully happy 10.609, 17.165–6

the happiness of others
the aspiration to make people happy is central to Buddhism 17.182; do-gooders want to make themselves happy using others as the means 17.597; finding your happiness in working for others' happiness 19.547; how strange that we do not naturally wish others the deepest happiness! 15.308; obstructing others' happiness may lessen your own chances of happiness 10.476; one should make people happy 4.97, 17.18; reaching out beyond personal happiness to benefit others 17.166; striking with a stick those who also long for happiness 8.257; thinking of happiness as a 'thing' which one person can give another 24.94–5; when happy oneself, one naturally rejoices in the happiness of others 16.333

happiness and the spiritual life
the Buddhist is a paradox: happy without what's said to bring happiness 17.226–7; going from happiness to happiness: the spiral path 4.475; happiness is a characteristic of progress 2.109; the happiness of the Dharma 10.251, 19.242; the happiness of monastic life 4.628–9, 11.590, 16.392, 17.337–8, 19.74; if you can't be happy on the spiritual path, how will you ever be happy? 17.338; if you're not happy you can hardly say that you're a Buddhist 19.426; insight into the truth of suffering can be gained even when one is happy 26.62; its role in the spiritual life 2.108–9; once on the path, you feel deeply happy 12.626; the spiritual life is happy, but getting into it may be a struggle 15.360, 17.252–3; spiritual practice brings happiness, which produces further positive results 17.168; the worldly-minded person thinks of happiness, the spiritually-minded of liberation 26.64

HAPPINESS AND ENLIGHTENMENT

the Buddha's happiness
the Buddha's solution to the problem of happiness 15.249; 'the happiness which

… arose in me could not obsess my mind' 2.108, 18.581; his happiness just after Enlightenment 10.469–70; people sought to learn the secret of his radiant happiness 3.315; he proved he was happier than a king 3.271–2

happiness in the Buddhist tradition
'a concentrated person is happy, a happy person is concentrated' 2.109, 3.271, 15.221, 26.46; 'The *dhammacāri* lives happily' (*Dhammapada*) 2.491; 'Happily we live', *see Dhammapada*/chapter 15; 'May all beings be happy' (*Karaṇiya Mettā Sutta*) 15.297–8; perfect happiness (*Maṅgala Sutta*) 15.453; bodhisattvas preserving the *White Lotus Sūtra* need happy states of mind 16.47; happiness after death 8.257; happiness and the bodhisattva vow 19.547; 'May sentient beings possess happiness with its causes' 5.197, 5.719 (n179); Milarepa's happiness 18.296, 18.328–45

the happiness of Enlightenment
eternal happiness radiated by all the Buddhas 8.452; the experience of Enlightenment would transcend happiness 19.244; the happiness of an Enlightened person 19.525–6; 'Nirvāṇa is the supreme happiness', *nibbānaṃ paramaṃ sukhaṃ* 2.124, 3.235, 7.68–9; the only real happiness is an unconditioned happiness 19.280–1; the unwavering happiness of Enlightenment 10.655–6

Hardenberg, Friedrich von *see* Novalis

Harding, Douglas 23.122, 23.492–3 (n148)

hardships be prepared to undergo hardships, but don't subject yourself to them for the sake of it 19.493; the hardship of life in medieval times 19.96; a life of great hardship 22.259; the possibility of freedom for the mind offered by hardship 18.138; Milarepa seeks inspiration in the very hardship that seems to be drying up his inspiration 18.20; working for the Dharma with vigour and indifference to hardship 16.207; the yogi's hardships enable him to see how experience is not 'out there' but one's response 18.138

Hardwick Hall 24.365

Hardy, Robert Spence 10.139, 12.69–70

Hardy, Thomas criticism of Christianity in his work 11.343, 11.754 (n191); 'The Darkling Thrush' 26.398; 'Great Things' 25.lx, 25.391; *The Woodlanders* 24.582

hare in the moon 8.392, 13.141

Hare Krishna movement 17.40, 17.711 (n43), 24.56

Hare, E. M. 19.374, 26.210

Haribhadra (of Madhyamaka School) 1.300, 1.323, 1.362, 2.167

'Harijans' *see under* Dalits

Harivarman (Satyasiddhi school) 1.252–3

harm

approaches to harm in the Buddhist tradition
dukkha translated as harm 15.302; the first precept covers abstention from harm of all sorts 17.178; 'Harm cannot befall the wise man' 10.536; the highest rule of Dharma is not to cause harm (*Mahāvastu*) 2.332, 2.358, 3.318–19; *mettā* protects one from harm 17.189; perhaps the Buddha's fearlessness kept him from harm 4.15

things that may cause harm
alcohol 3.323; animal slaughter (harm to animal and slaughterer) 1.544–5, 3.583; the attention we give the body 12.554–5; do-gooding 17.597; indulgence in habits that harm health 5.126; it takes all the wisdom of the wise to undo the harm done by the merely good 4.193, 13.69; misuse of the Dharma 16.200–1; production of harmful or frivolous things 1.548, 16.412; renunciation (if you pride yourself on your abstentions) 7.281; thinking without *prajñā* 9.231; well-meaning advice 19.355

avoiding causing harm
analysis of whether what you are doing is beneficial or harmful 17.265; carrying a water strainer to avoid harming life in water 17.583, 17.584; eating without causing harm 3.370, 4.111–12; every time you breathe in, you take life, but avoid intentional harm 4.355–6; 'The first requirement of a hospital is that it should do the sick no harm' 18.285; how to help someone get out of a harmful situation 19.514; if you are just sitting still, at least you are causing no harm 18.342; the most important thing about education is that it does no harm to the child 18.285; right livelihood does no harm to oneself or to others 3.371, 9.441, 15.415; with the best will in the world, you can't avoid doing some harm somewhere 4.355–6; you can perfect your will not to harm, but your performance will fall short 4.355–6

harming others
enmity is the persistent desire to harm another person 17.269; harming others is always dangerous 17.293; if you try

to harm another, you are really harming yourself 15.371; the intent to harm brings fear 17.258; the mental state of one who is bent on harming others 17.294; negative emotions are all expressions of the wish to do harm to others 15.303; not doing harm, or causing annoyance or inconvenience, to other people 4.336–7; there will always be a minority in society who try to harm others 26.73; you need a high degree of sanctity to do good to others without harming them 8.535

being harmed
an enemy who is out to harm you can do more for you than even a guru 4.411–13; if people harm you and suffer because of that, it's your fault (Śāntideva) 4.410, 4.426; why be angry with someone who is harming you? 4.407–8; your own unskilful mind can do you more harm than any foe 10.534

harmikā *see under* stupa

harmony

the harmony of reality
the *dharmakāya* as the principle of harmony 14.605; green symbolizes the harmonizing aspect of Enlightenment 13.282; harmony in the cosmos represented by the four great kings 16.353, 16.357; reality should be considered not as a homogeneity but as a harmony 7.167; *siddha*: a man who is in harmony with the cosmos 7.506

the practice of harmony
'Bliss-Illumination': harmonizing emotion and awareness at every level 19.378–80; the bodhisattva transforming chaos into a cosmos 4.98; bringing energies into harmony with awareness 18.322; bringing your life into harmony with the Dharma 25.103; harmony arises when looking with compassion on the suffering of sentient beings 7.347; harmony between ourselves and nature 11.395; harmony cannot just consist in agreement 18.502; having a harmonious effect on one's surroundings 4.98; mindfulness harmonizes and unifies every aspect of Buddhist practice 15.83; psychologically Buddhism attaches great importance to harmony 13.328; skilful mental states are characterized by harmony of consciousness 15.115; working towards harmony through positive conflict 26.7

harmony in the sangha
exploring the path with others in complete harmony 2.462; harmony between Buddhist schools 7.490; harmony with the guru 18.502–3, 19.557–8; 'horizontal harmony' and 'vertical harmony' 18.502–3; the importance of harmony in the spiritual community 12.676–7, 15.515–17, 18.15; maintaining harmony with people is not an easy matter 18.501–2; providing an example of how human beings can get on together 25.58–9; the team running a retreat an example of working together harmoniously 12.625, 25.128; whatever we do together as Buddhists, let it be done in harmony 10.273

see also
harmonious speech, *see under* speech/four levels of skilful speech

Harper, Alison *see* Lilavati

Harrer, Heinrich v21

Harris, Tom 11.495, 23.401

Harṣa 12.238

Harshaprabha, Dharmachari v24, v26

Hartmann, Franz 20.63

Hartmann, Mrs 23.171, 23.419

Haslemere Keffolds 2.404, 2.712 (n471), 12.246, 12.651, 23.464–5, 25.333; Quartermaine 2.404, 2.712 (n471), 12.367, 12.651

Hasta, Bahadur Lama v22

haste the bodhisattva acts without haste and without delay 1.440, 4.135; the feverish haste of modern life 8.290; living free from haste, like walking in the garden among tranquil flowers 8.291; 'Haste, O wild-bee hours' 7.58; time is short, but that is no reason for being in a hurry 26.49; 'We hasten to gather our flowers' (Tagore) 1.129

Hastings, Sussex 23.244, 23.330

Hastings, Warren 22.59

hate type *see under* Buddhaghosa/ *Visuddhimagga*/character types

Hathor *see under* Egypt

hatred (*dveṣa* or *dosa*)

WHAT IS HATRED?

the nature of hatred
a basic human trait, evolved to protect our ego from attack 15.306–7; a fixed idea 16.295; the greatest of defilements (Mahāyāna) 4.389, 4.391–2; hatred wants to destroy – the complete opposite to the bodhisattva ideal 4.392; it is not something that happens to you, but something you do 15.304–5; it often occurs between those who are supposed to be close 17.269;

as much an idea as a feeling (Spinoza) 15.304; not just a psychological state, but a spiritually destructive force 15.311; political hatred 25.258; a uniquely human quality 15.303–4; we only too often find it easier to hate the wicked than to love the good 26.66

hatred and craving
at least you get some pleasure out of craving 4.388; craving at least indicates an affinity for other people 4.389, 17.601; the link between them 17.271; breaking precepts out of desire or hatred 2.389, 4.702 (n283), 14.185–6, 16.614 (n232); the more insight you have, the less craving and aversion you have 18.576

hatred and other mental states
an affinity with wisdom 4.392–3, 13.132–3, 18.577, 26.478–9; close relationship between hatred and attachment 17.564–5; connection between *dosa* and *vyāpāda* 2.388; contrast with anger 16.295; the enemy of *mettā* 15.303; hatred and being in love 16.295; hatred and violence 7.373, 7.380; it has a lot to do with egotism 17.600; it is easy for hatred of the mundane to disguise itself as disillusionment 17.594; love and hate are near akin 25.432; relationship to covetousness 2.388

self-hatred
don't hate yourself, but see through your experience of selfhood 4.621–2; an important function of the sangha is to let us know that we are cared for 17.185; nihilism a rationalization of self-hatred 17.243–4; it may reinforce one's emotional investment in the self 17.250; not valuing oneself as one should 25.78; often the residue of hatred within us is directed towards ourselves 15.308–9; self-hatred stemming from childhood can be difficult to dislodge 17.254–5; taking a self-punishing attitude towards oneself is a sort of suicide 10.524–5; texts advocating hating self and praising other can be misunderstood 4.614–15; we hate others because we hate ourself 10.173, 17.189; being drawn to the *anattā* doctrine out of self-hatred 13.395–6, 16.200–1, 17.625, 17.629–30

ITS ARISING AND ITS EFFECTS

how does hatred arise?
hatred arising from paranoia 17.601; hatred for religious opinions contrary to one's own 7.380; if anger is unexpressed, it becomes resentment or even hatred 15.303, 17.268–9, 17.599; it is a feeling of pain and an idea of its cause (Spinoza) 15.304, 17.269, 17.503; it may have its roots in frustrated desire 17.271; to identify with a self is to be susceptible to the arising of hatred 15.306–7; misunderstanding the idea of having 'potential' for hatred 18.606–8; why do we hate? 15.303–7; why does love turn to hatred? 18.309–10

the effects of hatred
an atmosphere filled with hate 21.121; becoming a demon through hatred 17.602; Communism controls people through hatred 26.20; enough religion to make us hate, but not enough to make us love one another 10.283, 26.195; expressing hatred under the pretext of encouraging others to be heroic 18.104–5; a hateful thought can work untold harm in the world 3.319; heedlessness out of hatred 17.677; it hurts the person doing the hating 17.602; it leads to more hatred 17.564; it takes away one's sleep 17.602; things seem to go wrong for those who are full of hatred 17.189

HOW TO GET RID OF HATRED

approach
changing hatred into loving-kindness 13.173; compassion can transmute our hate 25.256; cultivate contentment to overcome hatred 17.271; 'Destroy all fear of the Yamarāja of hatred 17.317; handling hatred 18.611–12; the inhibition of hatred 18.609; it ceases only through love, *see Dhammapada*/chapter 1; it is to be rejected 8.585; it's easier to transform hatred into love than to transform indifference into love 15.431; love is the only force strong enough to overcome hatred 3.319; only by uprooting the ego-sense will we stop the growth of hatred and violence 7.374; the only way to avoid hating one's fellow men is to love them 26.65; transferring animosity towards people to annihilation of wrong views 4.151–2

antidotes
the *brahma vihāras* 2.389; *kṣānti* 4.390, 4.393; the *mettā bhāvanā* 3.125, 3.342–4, 4.74, 5.29, 5.326, 9.494–5, 19.227; rejoicing in merits 2.389; the Sevenfold Puja 2.389

see also
abstention from: the ninth precept, *see under* precepts; as one of the three roots or poisons, *see* three roots; malice; one of the five hindrances to meditation, *see* five hindrances

hats (Tibetan) 5.565, 13.32–3, 13.117

haughtiness difference from arrogance 17.273; a haughty brahmin 2.22, 10.436–43; you cannot become friends with proud and haughty people 18.141

Havell, Alec 26.418

Havell, E. B. 7.448

Havens, Joe and Teresina 23.457

Hawking, Stephen 26.xvi, 26.685–6

Haydn, Joseph of *The Creation*: 'Not I, but a Power from above created that!' 3.513, 16.519; 'Drum' Mass 24.589; Kodály, *In Memory of Haydn* 24.521; one of Sangharakshita's favourite composers 20.73, 24.521, 26.505

Hayward, Jeremy 8.616

Hazlitt, William 'Argument is the death of conversation' 24.563; the cultivation of a moral sense is the first thing to be attended to 24.562; 'Give a man a motive to work, and he will work' 24.562; on Wordsworth 25.591–2 (n62); 'Nothing was ever learnt by either side in a dispute' 24.563; *The Plain Speaker* 24.561–3; that which appeals to the imagination can only perish with it 24.561; there is no language that can come up to the truth and force of reality 24.562; true friendship 24.561; we injure ourselves by suppressing our impulse to be generous 24.562

'He who sees the Dharma sees me' 1.251, 3.150, 3.191, 7.493, 10.678–9 (n132)

head the Buddha lay with his head to the north and his feet to the south 11.452, 12.357; dragon's head, snake's body 1.493–4, 15.473, 16.351, 26.38, 26.705–6 (n19); heaping coals of fire on your enemy's head 4.411, 17.172; in India, to place something on your head is a sign of respect 16.381–2, 19.568; our heads are full of ideas we do not truly think 7.266–7; 'sex in the head' (D. H. Lawrence) 5.619; symbolism of the head 16.381, 19.175–6; the Tibetan belief that at death your consciousness passes out through the top of your head 18.154

see also
head and heart, *see under* heart; visualizing the guru above your head, *see under* guru yoga; a *yakṣa* hits Sāriputta on the head, *see under* Sāriputta

Healer, Divine *see* Divine Healer

healing the Buddha as healer 10.555–6, 16.192–3; the Buddha of healing, *see* Bhaiṣajyaguru; chanting mantras for healing 18.311; Greek god of healing, *see* Asklepios; Greek sanctuaries of healing 16.191–2; green as the colour of healing 13.282; the healing aspect of Enlightenment 13.282, 16.193–4; 'healing powers descend and bless' 25.43; the ideal of the healer 18.105–6; perhaps Jesus didn't literally heal the sick, but brought spiritual healing 10.555–6; spiritual healing: an analogy with initiation 13.89; in the *Sūtra of Golden Light* 16.246; the Tārā of Healing 18.311; a tradition of spiritual healing in Buddhism 18.313

health being healthy doesn't necessarily make you more receptive to the Dharma 17.163–4; the health benefits of hearing the Dharma being recited 8.532; importance of physical exercise 9.442; looking after as support for meditation 3.617; *mens sana in corpore sano* 26.594; practise the Dharma when you've got good health 4.367; Swami Ramdas advises the need to take care of one's health 20.322–4; the true meaning of health 18.447–8

healthy (in ethical sense) *see kuśala*

healthy, happy human being *see under* human being

Heape, John and Marlene 24.200

Hearn, Lafcadio 6.619, 7.549 (n29), 13.495, 22.273, 22.277

heart

the heart's possibilities
the awakening of the heart 7.316–18; awakening wisdom by appealing to the heart 26.198; the heart in quest of love and wisdom 25.270; the heart's possibilities 25.274; the inexhaustible richness of the potentialities of the human heart 7.307; the language of myth speaks very effectively to the heart 12.109–11; 'may my heart unfold' 25.181; prayer: an invitation to prepare an open heart 19.71; 'To the heart it came, to the heart may it go': applied to art and religion 7.83; the starting point of the 'real you' 4.259–60; we *are* our heart 25.103; whatever you do, put your whole heart into it 11.711–12; 'Where your treasure is, there will your heart be also' 16.98, 16.346, 25.103; words that make the heart beat faster 25.373; you sincerely wish to go for Refuge with your whole heart 12.666; your heart must be in your spiritual life 11.193–4

the sensitive heart
developing a compassionate heart 14.193; an empty heart 25.290; 'The ever-beating heart' 25.159; a few words are enough to say what the heart means 25.336; 'The

Heart's No' 25.230; not wearing your heart on your sleeve, you may be accused of having no heart 26.82; 'the perilous stuff that weighs upon the heart' 1.412; purity of heart 5.211; the silence of the heart 7.134, 25.167; take care not to tread upon hearts 25.231; 'The Wondering Heart' (poem) 25.xxxvii, 25.368–9

heart and head
balance between head and heart 1.240, 1.294, 9.322, 12.65, 26.40; the bodhisattva's wisdom is rooted in both head and heart 14.516, 14.559; concepts may convince the head, but only emotions can move the heart 26.163; the heart is moved more powerfully by a myth than by an argument 1.325; 'heart wisdom' and 'head wisdom' 19.542–3; the ideal is to integrate head and heart, thought and action 7.127; learning poetry by heart 26.393, 26.439; the letter learned from books, but the spirit transmitted heart to heart 7.543; reading that goes straight to the head without passing through the heart 22.438; today our head races ahead of our heart 15.558

heart metaphors
the cave of the heart 26.284–5, 26.305–6; 'the fountains of my heart' 25.264; the lotus of my heart 25.181; 'thine own heart's citadel' 25.197; 'the unlocked cage of my heart' 25.163

heart and the Buddhist tradition
the Buddha-Heart 25.173; the Doctrine of the Eye and the Doctrine of the Heart 7.359; a heart bound up or infatuated (*paṭibhaddacitta*) 10.490; 'The Heart of the Doctrine' (Abhidharma) 14.80; Heart-Doctrine (*Hṛdaya Dharma*) 7.360; understanding the *bodhicitta*'s nature one sees everything with a loving heart 4.70; *vīrya* which does not lose heart 17.576

learning the scriptures by heart
the Buddha's disciples learned his teachings by heart 2.197, 10.230; chanting texts to learn them by heart 17.417; oral tradition, *see* oral tradition; the novice bodhisattva learns the scriptures by heart 4.178–9; the practice began during the Buddha's lifetime 10.575; Sangharakshita learns the *Dhammapada* by heart 15.5–6, 20.328–9; Soṇa Koṭikaṇṇa learns the *Aṭṭhaka-vagga* by heart 10.573–6, 14.20; the value of learning by heart 15.6; in Zen monasteries scriptures are studied and learned by heart 13.338

Heart Sūtra (*Prajñapāramitāhṛdaya Sūtra*)

introducing the sūtra
introduction 1.70, 3.233, 14.151–2, 16.16; full text 1.444–5, 14.355–6

what is its nature?
the deepening of a limited understanding 14.366; a dialogue between wisdom and Perfect Wisdom 14.358–9; the heart, the essence, of the Perfection of Wisdom 1.300, 4.163, 14.100; it speaks both to the unconscious and to the conscious mind 14.359; its artistic unity, like a Beethoven quartet 14.152; the literary form and the spiritual content are of equal importance 14.357, 14.359; 'one of the finest and most profound spiritual documents of mankind' 1.70, 1.444; a restatement of the four noble truths in the light of emptiness 14.152; a sort of extended conceptual formulation 5.449; the *sūtra* and the wisdom of the *dharmadhātu* 4.164; transcendental iconoclasm 26.478

history
it emerged from the third of the Prajñāpāramitā's four phases 14.347; two recensions, one long, one short 14.151; a Tantric counterpart to the *Heart Sūtra* 14.154; the basic view of the Kagyu school, and the Triratna Buddhist Order 19.371–2; discovery by modern scholarship that it was originally a Chinese text 14.333–5; meditated on in Japanese Buddhism 14.367; beautiful commentary by Han Shan 14.367; Zen connection with the *Heart Sūtra* 14.362; scholarly revaluation of some terms 14.334–5; the discovery of an ancient copy 14.366–7; translations 14.152, 14.367; Sangharakshita's seminar 14.320; reciting it in the Sevenfold Puja 11.280

Avalokiteśvara and Śāriputra in the sūtra
a drama, dialogue, or clash, between them 14.xv, 14.151–2, 14.357–8; a debate between the 'Hīnayāna' and the 'Mahāyāna' 14.152; Avalokiteśvara 1.70, 2.175–6, 4.190, 14.357–8, 14.361, 14.397; why Śāriputra doesn't say a word 14.358–9; the implication of the situation for us 14.359, 14.366

the sūtra's six great statements
(1) the emptiness of the five *skandhas* 1.175, 3.655 (n189), 4.29, 14.359–60; (2) the emptiness of all *dharmas* 1.70, 14.360–1; (3) in *śūnyatā* no *dharmas* exist 14.361–2; (4) in effect there is no such thing as Buddhism 14.363–4; (5) the bodhisattva gains Enlightenment by relying on Perfect Wisdom 14.363; (6) all Buddhas

gain Enlightenment through Perfect Wisdom 14.363–4

śūnyatā and rūpa
'Form is emptiness, emptiness is form' 2.133, 4.164, 4.188, 14.397, 15.591; in the Green Tārā visualization practice 5.583, 13.96–7; non-duality of *śūnyatā* and *rūpa* 5.523, 19.371; the philosophical basis of the possibility of transformation 5.352–3; *śūnyatā* and *rūpa* are of the same essence 1.489–90, 16.534; symbolized by the blue sky 5.603–4; it may sound abstruse, but it is what makes transformation possible 13.173; we cannot experience *śūnyatā* except through *rūpa* 13.119; whenever we are in contact with *rūpa* we are in contact with *śūnyatā* 13.120

'holding to nothing whatever'
'One who sees holds on to nothing' (*Udāna*) 10.627, 10.631, 10.633–4

mantra: gate gate pāragate pārasaṃgate bodhi svāha
chanted in the Sevenfold Puja 11.294; distinction from *oṃ āḥ dhih hūṃ svāhā* 11.294, 14.365; the mantra *par excellence* of the Prajñāpāramitā 1.301; properly intoning these words one's heart is opened to Perfect Wisdom 14.152; could be said to refer to the four degrees of *śūnyatā* 4.163; translation 4.163, 14.364–5

the sūtra as practice
if you studied the *Heart Sūtra*, you would end up with the whole Dharma 19.215; in a way you have to recapitulate Śāriputra's progress 14.366; learning to listen to the voice of Avalokiteśvara in our own hearts 14.367; a path of regular steps 14.365–6; a way of analysing *dharmas* 14.365; a way of reflecting on *śūnyatā* 5.523

heart-disciples 18.59–60, 18.190, 19.171–2

heaven building a heaven in hell's despair (Blake) 11.25; helping others in the hope of heaven 4.89; 'If we seek first the Kingdom of Heaven, all things will be added unto us' 7.307–8; if you are Enlightened, you have gone beyond heaven 10.455; the imaginal world 26.271; impermanence (Buddhist tradition) 2.86, 3.315–16, 7.120–1, 13.578, 26.47; literal or symbolic 3.672 (n295); Mohammed never explained that talk about heaven's delights was skilful means 3.167; no marriage in heaven 16.392; the passivity of heaven becomes boring after a while 19.580; you don't have to wait for heaven, you can see the effects of practice in this life 3.162

heavens (*devalokas*)

introduction
Buddhist cosmology 16.344–5; descriptions in the Pāli canon 16.109, 16.597 (n94); higher and happier realms than the human realm 1.32; progressive refinement 16.344–5; beings in them are too intoxicated by pleasure to focus on Nirvāṇa 7.170; accessed through meditation 26.271; one reaches them by giving up egoism and selfishness 1.237, 3.579

the Heaven of the Thirty-three (Tāvatiṃsa-devaloka)
the Buddha's descent from it on a magnificent staircase 11.15, 12.185, 13.586; celebration of the Buddha's descent from it 2.228; from the perspective of its residents the loveliest human face is repulsive 2.83; King Indra's palace 16.344; Nanda's visit to the nymphs there, *see under* Nanda; the battle of the gods there with the *asuras* 16.349; offering goddesses 16.345–6; it could be seen as the world of the arts, or of meditation 10.505–6; where the Buddha taught his mother the Abhidhamma 1.33, 1.255, 2.228, 12.143, 12.714–15 (n102), 13.586, 14.76, 22.170

Tuṣita Heaven
the heaven of the contented gods 16.344; did the Buddha project a human form from the Tuṣita heaven? 14.86; referred to in the *Udāna* 10.548; and Maitreya, *see under* Maitreya

the Brahma heavens (brahmalokas)
correspondence between them and the *dhyānas* 16.345, 17.263; inhabited by different classes of Brahma gods 16.345; the gods of brilliant light 15.30, 15.745 (n13), 16.345; gods of light 16.345; the Gods of Sonant Light (*Dhammapada*) 8.440; gods of purity 16.345; gods that take delight in the creations of others 16.344; gods that take delight in their own creations 16.344; the lifespan there 2.67; 'The Brahmas and the Sages' (poem) 25.451–2; 'unconscious' gods (*asaññasatta*) 14.407, 14.639 (n382)

pure abodes (suddhavāsa)
their names 2.148, 15.239; *akaniṣṭha* (Pāli *akaṇiṭṭha*) 2.148, 14.211, 15.239; difficult to say whether they are mundane or transcendental 15.240; the gods there too refined to control chaotic energies 16.349; inhabited by angels 16.345; realms of increasing brilliance 16.109; rebirth of non-returner in them 1.341, 2.148–9, 3.254, 14.167–8, 15.239–40, 15.342; a Pure Land resembles them 1.341, 14.167–8

see also
wheel of life; *devas*

Hebe 25.520

Heber, Bishop 8.5

Hebrew 20.64

hedonism alignment with nihilism 1.138; being apologetic about one's hedonism 10.609; the *dhyānas* are the higher hedonism of Buddhism 12.542, 15.532–3; hedonism, asceticism, and bliss 8.438–9; a hedonistic Thai layman 22.45; the higher hedonism of the Vajrayāna 19.379; the higher hedonism that coincides with asceticism is an integral part of spiritual life 8.445; the middle way between hedonism and asceticism 15.287, 24.467; and the perpetuation of *saṃsāra* 10.608

heedlessness (*pramāda*) a bodhisattva precept not to laugh heedlessly 13.56; heedlessness out of craving, hatred, or ignorance 17.677; 'letting yourself go', spiritually speaking 17.676; like not bothering to keep your house in repair 17.676–7; the way to death 7.118; as *upakleśa* (Abhidharma) 17.676–7

Heep, Uriah *see under* Dickens

Hegel, Georg Wilhelm Friedrich introduction 7.554 (n55); absolutes 4.32; on evolution 3.9; the axis of history 3.426; crushed religion and stretched physics on the Procrustean bed of his dialectic 7.387–8; the fruit does not deny the flower 1.182; identified the dialectical process of thought with the dialectical movement of history 7.387; *Lectures on the Philosophy of History* 23.40; 'History moves from east to west' 12.426; and Marx 20.83, 22.210; 'The Truth is the whole' 2.50, 7.44, 7.385, 8.225; *geist* 14.309; history as the progressive manifestation of Spirit 3.423; *Philosophy of Religion* 20.70; Sangharakshita's Neo-Hegelianism 20.81, 20.83; thesis and antithesis 4.91; universals 16.186, 16.602 (n134)

heights and depths Buddha nature is mirrored in the depths of everything 7.317; Buddhism emphasizes heights rather than depths 11.657–8; Buddhism needs to appeal to both the rational mind and the unconscious depths 12.181; Buddhism's mythical approach to the unconscious depths 12.109–11; Buddhist psychology explores both 7.486; Buddhists are more concerned with the heights than the depths of the mind 3.334–5; translating what one has experienced in the heights or depths 25.li, 26.305; concentration is a union of the forces of depths and heights 26.47; 'contact with Buddhism was contact with the depths of my own being' 16.218; in the depths of your own being, you are Buddha 12.234; don't take talk of surface and depth too literally 17.136; different ways of using the language of heights and depths 11.657–8; draw your nourishment from the depths of the Unconditioned 14.588; everything is in its ultimate depths the same 1.587; Height mates with Depth 25.248; the heights and depths of the spiritual life 12.21–30, 19.76; heights symbolized by texts from heaven, depths by texts from the deep ocean 12.28–9; it's not enough to think, one must feel, and plumb the depths 12.295; it's not enough to scratch the rational surface of the mind, we need to drop a depth charge 12.323; *kleśas* are very nasty things, and they go right down deep 25.75; the need to unite the heights and depths in one's spiritual life 12.29; philosophy titillates the rational surface of our being, poetry stirs it to its depths 1.347; religion must penetrate the desiderative depths of the psyche 1.124, 7.392; Śāntideva knew both the heights and depths of spiritual experience 1.322; subduing and integrating the primordial energies in the depths of the unconscious mind 12.325; *sūtras* are a revelation issuing from the depths of the Enlightened consciousness 16.33; symbolized by an iceberg, a mountain 12.22; we can't ignore the depths: from them come our energies of instinct, emotion, and will 12.23

Heine, Heinrich 24.157, 24.644–5 (n187), 26.508

heinous crimes *see* five heinous crimes

heirs the disciples: heirs of the Dharma, not heirs of worldly things 1.236, 2.138, 15.155; we are the heirs of our own actions 11.263

Heissig, Walther 8.517–19

Helen of Troy 23.297, 26.470

hell

the idea of eternal punishment in hell
the Christian idea of hell 13.572–4; in Buddhism, no one is condemned to hell for ever 3.316, 7.121, 12.513, 15.621, 16.282; one of the most horrible ideas ever 13.572–5; the Virgin Mary opened the back door to hell 13.601

do we need to think about hell?
building a heaven in hell's despair (Blake) 11.25; fear of hell as spiritual motivation

17.472, 18.71; if you find it a bit much, transfer it to painful experiences in this life 4.372; mindfulness restored by 'full recollection of the pain of hell' 4.381; only the spiritual individualist 'loves God' for the sake of escaping hell 7.391; what is going on in the world is so terrifying that we can do without hell 4.447; you can make yourself comfortable even in hell, if you know how to go about it (Tibetan proverb) 4.423, 23.10

Buddhist teachings about hell
all the phenomena of hell are created by one's own mental states 4.369, 17.497; beings in hell are too depressed by pain to be able to focus on Nirvāṇa 7.170; Buddhist teachings about hell should not be made to seem threatening 15.621–2; 'Hell is the lama of all the Buddhas' (Padmasambhava) 8.526; hell is suffering, and suffering is passivity 19.580; hell itself is falling into further wrong views 17.259; if someone goes to hell because they harmed you, it's your fault (Śāntideva) 4.426–7; literal or symbolic? 3.672 (n295); people who didn't show respect for books crushed beneath them in hell 13.20; rebirth in hell 2.333, 16.282, 17.525, 26.700; 'those who speak falsely go to hell' 10.539; the time it would take one born in a hell realm to regain the human state 13.682 (n53); the world of the tormented beings, a state of acute mental suffering 13.130

descriptions from the Buddhist tradition
in the *Sutta-Nipāta* 14.57; in the *Majjhima Nikāya* 15.771 (n240); a *yakṣa* hits Sāriputta on the head and falls into the great hell 1.639 (n469), 10.534–5; in the *Bodhicaryāvatāra* 4.476, 4.633; in the *Sūtra of Golden Light* 16.287; on Mount Meru 16.344

bodhisattvas descending into hell to help beings
Avalokiteśvara 3.182; can we imagine going to hell for millions of years to help one being? 4.60–1; like wild geese into the lotus pond 4.582–3, 4.631; Kṣitigarbha, *see under* Kṣitigarbha

Heller, Erich 26.195

help importance of being able to accept help (symbolized by Siddhārtha's acceptance of it) 3.42; mutual 16.473; seeking help to alleviate one's mental suffering 5.659–70

helpful speech *see under* speech/four levels of skilful speech

helping others

introductory reflections
the Buddha as one who speaks only to help beings 17.342; difference between the idea of helping others and actually feeling love for them 21.43; don't disparage people doing positive things, but try to help them 11.734; if you don't know what to do, do something to help others (Dhardo Rimpoche) 25.114; 'It is hard to help others towards Enlightenment according to their various needs' 4.67; the knowledge of what is to be done for the spiritual welfare of living beings 11.127; practise thinking about others' needs 14.414–15; Tārā helps people to help themselves 13.315; there's a limit to what you can do for other people 14.577–9

how to go about helping
attend to practical needs before spiritual ones 4.67, 4.72; a basic rule is to help in ways that are as simple as possible 4.67–8; beware of a sense of martyrdom, self-sacrifice, or 'do-gooding' 18.592; by listening 4.67; by not getting in their way 4.69; direct your energy to practical help rather than sentimental lamentations 23.337; don't think that your way of helping is the only way 4.72, 17.285, 25.52; forget about yourself, at least for the time being 18.592; it needs a touch of the bodhisattva spirit 4.70, 4.246; mockery is not generally a good way to help people 10.506; taking an interest where others have not yet done so 4.72; 'Those who give help cannot refrain from offering advice' 22.104; very often the best thing you can do for other people is leave them alone 18.342

who needs help?
choosing to look after the sick and elderly 18.149–50; the group of others to whom our concern extends can grow 14.415; helping one another in the sangha 9.194–5, 9.215, 10.273–4; 'It is the strong who need help' 15.538–9, 26.5, 26.35, 26.489; ministering to the sick 21.354–6; old people 4.70; people in mental distress 4.71; prisoners 2.753 (n763), 4.70–1, 12.489; the strong helping the weak 26.655; there are so many ways to help, directly and indirectly 4.72; those within one's sphere of influence 4.191; who deserves our help? 19.539

what do you need to be able to help?
be clear about your own problems, or you can't help others with theirs 17.615; the more means of communication one has at one's disposal the better 4.83; one has

to develop a degree of spirituality before trying to help others 25.116; our only need before helping others is to love ourselves and feel loved 14.415; there must be real kindness in your heart 19.287; to be able to help living beings you need to have no obstacles 19.66; a few teachings are enough for you, more are needed to help others 14.348, 18.413–14; to really help others, you need insight as well as love 19.287–8; unless you really see people suffering, you won't want to help them 18.589; we need not put off helping until our motivation is pure 4.89

helping others and helping yourself
the best way to help ourselves is to help others 17.296–7; the danger of insisting that practices that help us will help others 16.127; do-gooders want to make themselves happy using others as the means 17.597; don't help others as an indirect way of helping yourself 18.592; experiencing pain while trying to help others 17.303; finding your happiness in working for others' happiness 19.547; getting something out of helping others 4.89; helping others also benefits you 4.591, 11.286; helping others as a way of escaping the demands of self-development 18.592–3; reaching out beyond personal happiness to benefit others 17.166; when you and others are suffering, choose to help the other 4.579–80; you become less able to distinguish between helping yourself and helping others 14.555; you can't help helping others when you are truly helping yourself 26.17; you can't help yourself without helping others, and *vice versa* 16.472–3, 18.591–2, 21.314

how does it fit in with other aspects of practice?
the basic principle of ethics is helping others (Mahāyāna) 17.154; doing things for others, you are moving towards the aim of spiritual practice 17.694; helping others based on meditation 9.206; helping others to see that there is a spiritual dimension to life 4.52; no distinction between the life of service and the life of contemplation 7.155–6; Perfect Vision arising through helping others 1.481; to be truly compassionate, cultivate a sense of unity, not involvement in charities 7.140; to renounce everything is necessary, but what about your wish to help others? 4.568–9; rushing about trying to help without remembering emptiness makes things worse 7.414; a way of raising your state of consciousness 11.119; we can help people by developing *mettā* towards them 4.69

how bodhisattvas help
the bodhisattva's emphasis isn't on helping others, because it isn't 'him' doing it 4.246; starting on the bodhisattva path by trying to see what people need 14.413–14; they don't have to make an effort to help people, it's fun 18.254; they have consciously devoted their life and work to helping others 25.113; they help people spontaneously while having no notion of people at all 14.411; their wish to help others is so intense that they don't mind difficulties 4.69

see also
altruism; other people

helplessness from an Enlightened point of view all beings are helpless 15.324; giving to the poor, the sick, the afflicted, the helpless 4.70–2, 4.94; 'May I be a guide to the helpless' 7.150

Hemingway, Ernest 22.276, 22.599 (n221)

Henri, Adrian 25.320

Henry VII (Holy Roman Emperor) 25.544

Henry VIII, King 12.697, 13.551, 13.630–1, 26.509, 26.514

Henson, Bruce 24.27, 24.611 (n45)

Hera 25.396, 26.469–70

Heracleitus (Heraclitus) introduction 7.596 (n300); 'Everything flows' 7.195–6; for Heracleitus being and non-being are equally real 7.195; you don't step into the same river twice 7.596 (n300), 12.422

Herbert, George 'A verse may find him who a sermon flies' 26.394; 'Who sweeps a room as for Thy laws …' 25.80

Hercules (or Herakles) the son of Zeus and Alcmene 26.481; alone among the heroes he was received by the gods 26.481; the embodiment of altruism, like the bodhisattva 23.270; connection with Tiryns 23.293; Euripides' *The Madness of Herakles* 23.269–70; Hercules Farnese 23.305, 25.513–20; founder of Pompeii 24.295; the four great kings compared to Hercules 16.353; 'Hercules and the Birds' (poem) 25.4, 25.20, 25.512–20; Hercules and the Nemean lion 26.288; the infant Hercules strangling a snake (Pompeii) 24.291; Michelangelo's Hercules-like Christ 26.475; patron of pugilists 24.674 (n320); shows how strength, directed by love, changes the world 25.519–20; statue of Hercules and Pallas Athene at Olympia 23.299; 'was to occupy a special place in

my imagination' 23.269; the twelve labours of Hercules 25.513–15

here and now are you missing the possibility of Enlightenment here and now? 18.155; Buddhism is 'the religion of here and now' 7.169–73; Dharma teachings are all good, but not equally relevant here and now 19.545–7; it is not elsewhere that the nature of reality becomes apparent, but here and now 17.353; the *nirmāṇakāya*: 'your actual being here and now' 19.230; Nirvāṇa is attainable here and now 1.345; today people are more interested in the here and now than in rebirth 3.192, 17.32–3; 'the way I see things here and now' 4.600–1; we can never go for Refuge 'again', but just here and now 12.40; we take from the Dharma whatever is helpful to us here and now 10.282

heredity the advantages you are born with 15.407; Buddhism teaches psychical as well as biological heredity 1.108

heresy (Buddhist) definition 7.524; the heresy of the Pudgalavādins 7.524, 17.631; the 'heresy' of referring to the 'great self' 14.234–5; the heretical view of *dhammas* as ultimate realities 7.540; there is such thing as heresy in Buddhism 11.360, 19.129; to translate *tīrthika* as heretic is wrong 7.524

see also
Christian heretics, *see under* Christianity/Roman Catholic Church/persecution; docetic heresy, *see under* Gnosticism

Heritage of Buddhism 8.661

Hermes equivalent of the Egyptian god Thoth 26.468–9; Hermes carrying Dionysus, statue by Praxiteles 23.299; in Virgil's *Aeneid* 26.469; the messenger of the gods in Greek mythology 16.350, 26.468–9; Raphael compared to Hermes 26.471

Hermes Trismegistus between the realm of conditioned and the realm of unconditioned existence 2.96; the Smaragdine Tablet: 'As above, so below' 1.28, 7.295, 7.400, 12.181, 16.23, 18.77

Hermetic Order of the Golden Dawn 3.682 (n368)

Hermeticism 13.374

hermits and hermitages aloof from organized monasticism 2.201; developing a spiritual community that can support hermits 18.36; eremitical sangha (being recluses or hermits) 7.496; express the feeling that if they haven't got a spiritual friend they are alone 18.395; the hermit of Lotus Flower Peak 8.488; hermitage life 19.578–80; 'Hermits upon Mount Meru or Everest' 7.450; if you're not living in a hermitage, how do you make do? 19.341–2; it's better to have the support of your 'hermitage', whatever form it takes 19.346–7; lingering in the hermitage due to a lack of outgoingness 19.342; supportive conditions for a hermit lifestyle are hard to find today 18.33–4

Herodotus brief introduction 15.763 (n186), 23.518 (n332); one of the first modern historians 3.427; a traveller 15.489; *Histories* 7.84, 7.573–4 (n152), 10.467

heroes the bodhisattva as hero 3.54–6; the Buddha as hero 3.49–54; 'The Cult of the Young Hero' 25.279; cultural heroes – an analogy with the Buddha 3.60; Drake, Francis 25.431; five literary heroes 26.481–90; Greek heroes 26.481–2; Hercules 23.269–70; heroes of Buddhist history 2.181–2; honouring the memory of great men and women 25.57; the inspiration of the lives of heroes 15.353; in the *Jātakas* 4.653; Lord Nelson 25.431, 26.588–9; past heroes are now villains 25.431; the sinner as hero 4.467; the spiritual life is to develop heroes, not pussycats 19.360; we need to cherish our heroes and heroines 6.621; where are the modern heroes? 25.57

heroism the bodhisattva ideal a heroic aspiration 16.229; Buddhism attaches great importance to the heroic virtues 13.230; as Buddhists, we need to be heroic for our own sake and to spread the Dharma 12.489–90; to attempt the achievement of bodhisattvahood is heroic 4.445; the dangers of encouraging oneself or others to take up the heroic ideal 18.104–5; the demands of the Perfection of Wisdom are to be met only by a heroic spirit 14.537; the destruction of the heroic ideal in the First World War 3.47; be heroic 12.489–90; in Buddhism 3.44–56, 4.438, 4.444–7; St Catherine of Siena encourages women to be heroic 11.633–4; Siddhārtha's going forth heroic, a great wrench 3.49–50; having become patient, one should become heroic 4.470; a heroic step to go abroad to teach the Dharma 12.554; in a situation you find hard to handle, it may be better to run away than try to be heroic 15.369; Milarepa draws attention to the heroic ideal 18.245; people can do much more than they think they can, as in time of war 4.445–6; 'people need something to live for, and, if necessary, to die for' 3.56,

10.342; popular in Victorian times 3.46–7; unfashionable today 3.46–7; Vajrapāṇi represents heroic, fearless energy 3.54; the Vajrayāna as the heroic path 19.382

hero-worship Dr Ambedkar spoke against the Indian tendency to hero-worship 10.37–8; a good thing when directed to those who are higher than us 3.62; *Heroes and Hero-Worship* (Carlyle) 3.46–7; hero-worship is not in fashion, but we need heroes 6.600; people 'worshipping' pop stars and footballers 15.389–90

see also
the bodhisattva as hero, *see under* bodhisattva/what is a bodhisattva?/hero; *Divyāvadāna* ('Divine Heroic Feats'), *see under* Avadānas

Herrick, Robert 'Gather ye rosebuds while ye may' 14.508, 18.151; Sangharakshita reading Herrick 20.100, 26.392, 26.577; 'To Daffodils' 14.507–8

Hertha *see* Swinburne

heruka 18.373

Heruka Ḍākinī 22.538

Herzberg, Alexander 7.77

Hesiod 23.295, 23.517 (n332)

Hesse, Hermann 24.575–6, 26.263, 26.380

Hesychasts 8.126–7

heterosexuality 11.581–3

Hettiarachchi, Sujatha (Kalimpong, later Sujata Nataraja) v21, v24

Hetuvādins 14.86

Hevajra (Tibetan Jeba Dorje or Gyepa Dorje) 13.309, 19.37

Hevajra Tantra *see under* tantras/works

Hewavitarne family 8.6–8

Hewavitarne, Dr C. A. 8.67–8

Hewavitarne, Don David *see* Dharmapala (Anagarika)

Hewavitarne, Edmund 8.63

hidden the element of Tathāgatahood present in all, 'like a treasure hidden in the soil' 1.275; the jewel hidden in the heart-lotus of every being, and the world-lotus of existence 7.400, 26.51; 'Nature is often hidden, sometimes overcome, seldom extinguished' 21.344; the seed of awakening hidden in the heart 7.316–17; *termas* hidden in the body of Tarpa Nagpo 8.526, 12.333; visualizing yourself as Amitābha you contact hidden aspects of yourself 19.412

hierarchy

introduction
definition 4.171, 14.309; the 'great chain of being' (medieval idea) 12.463; the concept dominated the Elizabethan age 3.10; Lucifer and the celestial hierarchy 1.16; true and false hierarchies 4.169–70; existence like a ladder on which we occupy the lowest rung 7.12–13

the hierarchy of …
the Āryasaṅgha 3.410–11, 3.413; awareness 14.314–16; beauty 13.279, 14.310, 19.24, 26.137–8, 26.312–15; beings within the cosmos 14.309–10; compassion 5.201–2; love 25.223; nature: rocks, plants, animals, humans 15.138; power 18.17–18; the sangha 3.403–15; Shakespeare 12.463; spiritual states (the *brahma vihāras*) 5.217; symbolism 13.121; the ten *bhūmis* 14.571; Tibetan Buddhism 13.54–5; value in the arts 18.132

the idea of hierarchy
Buddhism is saturated with hierarchy, but has no word for it 4.169; Buddhist hierarchy contrasted with political hierarchies 7.451–2; for Sangharakshita it was natural to think in terms of hierarchy 13.425; the idea that some people are more developed than others 3.561, 4.170–71; we can all grow, so none of us have to accept a fixed position 4.170

spiritual hierarchy
being sensitive to the degree of Enlightenment in others 4.365; the Buddha shines through the spiritual hierarchy 4.175; created by spontaneous emotion 4.176–7; from 'worldling' to Buddha 14.311–12; a hierarchy of degrees of awakening 8.573–4, 26.181; and the Higher Evolution 3.11, 4.171; inspiring 14.312–14; it will take years before Dalits can think of spiritual hierarchy positively 10.82; it would be under threat if Buddhism was democratized 11.612–13; a living chain of spiritual beings up and down which run spiritual influences 12.14; natural seniority avoids disputes 15.535, 18.18; no question of any 'official grading' 11.507; pervaded by freedom, light, and warmth 11.507; power has no place in the spiritual hierarchy 15.619; some people have difficulty with the idea 4.525, 14.308, 14.313; receptivity to those above, kindness to those below, reciprocity to peers 4.174, 11.507; respect those who are more experienced in the Dharma

than yourself 10.273; the scale of spirit 14.309–12; symbolized by the four great kings 16.356–7; a very important principle 4.171; a thin veil through which we see the light of reality 4.172, 11.506; when we enter upon the spiritual life, we take our place in a hierarchy 12.13–14

see also
bodhisattva hierarchy, *see under* bodhisattva/the bodhisattva hierarchy

higher self *see under* self

Hikata, R. 14.133

Hill, Christopher 24.193

Hill, Michael 13.440

Hillary, Sir Edmund 22.11

Hillman, James *Archetypal Psychology* 24.380; *The Dream and the Underworld* 24.397; *The Force of Character and the Lasting Life* 12.699, 12.760 (n499); *Loose Ends* 2.753 (n757); *Re-Visioning Psychology* 24.389, 24.397; a seminar, 'Towards an Aesthetic Ecology of Soul' 24.380; *Suicide and the Soul* 24.389

Hills, Christopher v23

Himachala 21.437

Himalayan Buddhist Association v21

Himalayas the awe-inspiring landscape of the Himalayas 2.644, 18.158–9; 'the congealed laughter of Shiva' 21.437; inspiration 21.436–7; personified as a deity 21.437; Prajñāpāramitā *sūtras* tower over 'Hīnayāna' *sūtras* like the Himalayas over foothills 14.137; seen from an aeroplane 21.269; 'Shine on, O Himalayas!' 7.80; the unsullied snow peaks of the Himalayas 13.282

Himavantavasi *see under Maha Bodhi* journal

Himmelfarb, Gertrude 26.337–8

hiṃsā *see* violence

'Hīnayāna' ('little way') *see* Early Buddhism

Hincks, Jos 17.9

Hindemith, Paul 4.282

Hindi the Association for the Advancement of the National Language 21.449; one of every three dreams in India, speaking Hindi 24.395; Sangharakshita gives his first sermon in Hindi 22.31; Sangharakshita learns literary Hindi 22.40–1; Sangharakshita remembers Hindi on his return to India 24.16; Sanskrit's relationship to Hindi 9.480–4

hindrances (*nivaraṇa*) *see* five hindrances

Hindu Code Bill 9.9–10, 9.14, 9.16, 9.67, 9.68, 10.3–4, 10.76, 20.452

Hinduism

HINDUISM AND HINDU PRACTICE

introduction
differences between followers of different gods and systems 10.283; has no human founder – a strong point for its apologists 10.34; an ethnic religion 10.245, 12.54, 12.244–6, 16.364; origin in ancient civilization 3.424; continuity of tradition 4.105; argument about what a Hindu is 20.279–80; its basis is social 10.43–4; four aims of life 4.556; no conversion to Hinduism 10.44, 12.245; 'not founded on morality' (Ambedkar) 9.99, 9.182, 9.425; the religion of a nation 13.513; religion of revelation or discovery? 7.368; so long as you follow the caste system it doesn't matter what you believe 10.58; division between social order and spiritual life 10.41; Christian antipathy towards Hindus 20.284–5; forcible conversion of Hindus to Catholicism 8.318; lapse (according to Ambedkar) 9.103; not to be equated with the Vedantism of the Ramakrishna Mission 20.148; taught in the West 12.52

characteristics
the attitude that all religions are the same 10.58, 17.52–4; confusing and misleading ideas about tolerance 22.528–9; devotionalism 7.123; injustice 9.134–5; intolerance 17.53–4; its besetting sin is inhumanity 26.15; recognition of the authentic utterance of spiritual experience 20.176; universalist 22.67; 'You can't be a Hindu without believing in the caste system' 10.44

beliefs and attitudes
beliefs about pollution 9.49, 9.221, 21.282; character types (*tāmasika*, *rājasika*, *sāttvika*) 7.99, 7.579 (n187); *dharma*, *see dharma* (Hindu); Dharmakṣetra 7.149, 7.588 (n248); disinterested action: sinister implications of philosophy 20.164; fatalistic view of karma 2.69; group values 12.245–6; *guṇas* 9.102–3; Kashmir Shaivism 8.605, 22.253, 22.597 (n210); knowledge that sense experience is only part of human experience 5.51; Mīmāṃsās 7.368, 8.450; muddled discussion of philosophical topics 20.273–4; the need for a son 10.455; non-violence 10.48; that modern science was anticipated by ancient

Hindu saints 20.217–18; *sanātana-dharma* 9.314–16, 22.162, 22.346, 22.607 (n284); a sin not to have children 12.245–6; *śraddhā* (faith) 7.96; stages of life 20.235; stress on prosperity 16.398; tend to consider they understand any religion better than its adherents 20.178; *trimūrti* 16.77, 16.364; understanding of *mokṣa* 9.539; Yogadarśana 7.368

sects
Mahanubhava sect 22.161–2; Narayana Swami sect 20.178–9; represented at Dharma Parishad 20.174–5; Vallabha sect 20.174–5

organizations
All-India Hindu Mahasabha 9.56, 9.57, 22.579 (n65); Arya Samaj (Hindu reform organization) 12.427–8; Rashtriya Swayamsevak Sangh 9.122; Vishwa Hindu Parishad 9.347

gods
Ambedkar's renunciation of Hindu gods 9.130; *avatāras* (incarnations of God) 9.18, 9.248, 9.265, 9.365, 9.484, 16.425; the gods of the Hindu pantheon depicted waiting on the Buddha 18.25; local deities that were incorporated into the Brahminical system 19.413–14; married gods 15.677–8; the presence of Hindu gods in Buddhist texts 9.344; some of the best-known gods are said not to be of Aryan origin 19.414; worship of the gods 16.360–1, 16.395–7, 16.411; *see also* individual gods

myths
the churning of the cosmic ocean 7.580 (n190), 16.398, 22.179, 22.589–90 (n158); creation myth 16.398, 19.437; the cosmic man 9.77, 14.426

rituals, ceremonies, and customs
arati 20.351; bathing in the Ganges 3.194, 10.457–8; *bhajans* 20.187–90, 20.291, 20.329; a dancing *devadasi* 20.245; Hinduism is only ritual 9.100; going forth ritual 3.460–1; *jutha* (leavings of food) 20.200; Kumari-Puja 20.135; the need of Ganges water for rituals 10.245; *pindadan* ceremonies 9.216, 9.410; *prāṇipratiṣṭhā* ('life-giving ceremony') 4.302–5, 20.246; Puja season 20.134–5, 21.513, 21.516; sacred cows 9.49, 9.221, 12.246, 26.36; *shraddh* ceremonies 9.216, 9.410; *talwa puja* 9.217; weddings 20.181–2; *yajñas* and *homas* (sacrifices) 8.304

festivals
an atmosphere of deep peace at a Hindu festival 22.336; a Buddhist approach to Diwali 24.169; Buddhist retreat during Diwali 9.418; Dussehra 9.120, 10.46; *kathā* (religious performance) 15.445; Shivaratri 20.162; Vijayadashami 8.235, 8.690 (n186), 10.93, 10.676 (n117)

temples
Kanya Kumari temple 7.593 (n282), 20.238–9; temple at Suchindram 20.245; untidiness 20.121

spiritual practices
distinction between *bhakta* and *jñānin* 2.143; does not distinguish between *samādhi* and *prajñā* 21.506; familiarity with the *dhyānas* 1.166, 14.563–4; mindfulness not stressed 3.312; renunciation 19.201; *sannyasin* 7.95, 9.112–13; *satsangh* 20.123–4; *Vāmācāra* 7.72, 7.568 (n123)

four principal yogas (bhakti, jñāna, karma, rājā)
brief introduction 17.727 (n146); *bhakti* yoga 7.61; compared to the five spiritual faculties of Buddhism 3.310–12, 14.443, 17.134; each is contained in all the others 7.79; explained in the *Bhagavad Gītā* 7.588 (n248); *jñāna* and *bhakti* meet 7.103–4; *jñāna* and *karma* yoga contrasted 7.149; Nishkama Karma-Yoga 20.164; in the Upanishads 7.79

HINDUISM AND BUDDHISM

the relationship
appearance of Hindu mythological figures in Buddhist *sūtras* 16.415–6; brahmins' social position threatened by Buddhism, *see under* brahmins; 'Buddhism is the rebel child of Hinduism' 10.279–80; Buddhism speaking the language of Hinduism 12.241; Buddhism's influence on Hinduism 2.11, 7.485, 10.48, 12.241–2; Buddhist monks are not expected to salute Hindu gods 15.677–8; comparison of *trimūrti* with the Buddhist *trikāya* doctrine 16.77; difference between Hindu *sannyasin* and Buddhist *bhikṣu* 9.112–13; the differences 9.72, 10.117, 10.126, 22.153; doing injustice to Buddhism 8.145–7; Hindus argue that the Buddha did not teach the *anātman* doctrine 7.232–3, 12.62; Hindu incorporation of elements of Buddhist monasticism 20.235; Hindu writers who have been moved by the Buddhist ideal 7.448; Hindus at Bodh Gaya, *see under* Bodh Gaya; Hindus' belief that they have an innate understanding of Buddhism 22.67; Hindus gave up animal sacrifice through Buddhist influence 9.236, 9.265, 10.45, 10.48; Hinduism borrowing from Buddhism 9.237, 10.48–50; the Hinduization of Buddhist India 22.200; Hinduization of a Buddhist shrine 7.461,

22.97–8; infiltration of Mahāyāna Buddhism 16.370; influenced Buddhist lay people 9.391, 9.394; knowledge of Buddhism spread among Hindus by Dharmapala 9.239; much of what we think of as Buddhist is actually Hindu, or simply Indian 12.241

claim that Buddhism is part of Hinduism
but the doctrine of *anattā* is unacceptable 7.232–3, 12.62; a census taker is adamant 9.174–5; claim that the Buddha is an *avatāra* of Vishnu, *see under* Vishnu; claim that Buddhism has been absorbed by Hinduism 7.9, 7.232–5, 12.240–1; claim that the Dharma is identical with the teachings of the Upanishads 7.234; claim that Hinduism encompassed Buddhism 8.xix–xx; claim that Hinduism influenced Buddhism 7.537; 'Hinduism is like the great ocean, Buddhism is just a little stream' 6.615, 10.26, 22.76; 'Hinduism killed Buddhism with a loving embrace' (Vivekananda) 8.xx; like maintaining that Shakespeare 'copied' his plays 2.58–9; minimizing Buddhism's historical importance and spiritual significance 8.231; Dr Radhakrishnan overstates his case 8.348; Sangharakshita (aged 21) is urged to say this in a talk 20.174; Sangharakshita has to remonstrate 22.48, 22.346–7; seen by Scheduled Castes as designed to make it impossible for them to escape 22.150; therefore no need for anyone born a Hindu to 'convert' to Buddhism 22.149–50; to insist that they are the same and fight Buddhism tooth and nail is illogical 8.229; why does Brahmanism maintain this with such vigour? 7.233–6, 20.158–9

Sangharakshita's contact with Hinduism
contact during wandering days in India 2.414–15, 9.279–80; conflict with Hinduism despite meetings with impressive individuals 20.301; involvement with Ramakrishna Mission, *see under* Ramakrishna Mission; stay at Anandamayi's ashrams, *see under* Anandamayi; regarded as anti-Hindu 8.xix–xx; the monk who tried to become Sangharakshita's guru 20.177; guru Masala Dosai! 20.358–9; contact with Ramana Maharshi, *see* Ramana Maharshi; Swami Ramdas, *see* Swami Ramdas; Yalahankar Swami, *see* Yalahankar Swami; the young Sangharakshita's response to Hindu scriptures 20.62

see also
Dr Ambedkar's renunciation of Hinduism, *see under* Ambedkar/the journey towards Buddhism; *Bhagavad Gītā*; brahmins; caste system; *chaturvarna*; cosmology; graded inequality in Hinduism, *see under* caste system/the system; gurus; Manu; Mohini; *Nirguṇa Brahman*, *see* Śaṅkara; *Purāṇas*; *Saguṇa Brahman*, *see under* God/Creator God; *Skanda Purāṇa*; Upanishads; Vaiṣṇavism; Vedas

Hipkin, John general entries v23; at first WBO ordination ceremony 2.403, 23.440; friendship with Sangharakshita 23.152–5; clearing Sangharakshita's name 23.433–4; gives a lecture 11.495; joins the Sangha Association 23.153; photograph 23.330; rejoices in Sangharakshita's merits 23.xix,

hippies begging at Sarnath 23.364; preferred drugs over meditation 18.584; their need to replace conventional values by real ones 23.xix; were lots of hippies involved in the early FWBO? 11.550–1

Hippocrates 3.427

hiri *see hrī*

Hirohito, Emperor 26.602

Hirst, Damien 26.360–3

'His Holiness' (Maha Bodhi Society *bhikkhu*) *see under* Maha Bodhi Society

history

what is history?
is there such a thing as history? 24.149; the history of mankind 3.424–8; history as a downward spiral 13.458; history as opposed to myth 1.327, 16.526–34; large-scale overviews of history 3.423–8; linear and cyclical visions of history 12.592–4; an attempt to be objective about the past that has no real hope of success 3.423; 'Histories make men wise and the study of the poets makes them witty' 10.474; historical judgement must consider events both as ends and beginnings 8.225; effect of gravitational pull on history 3.251; the 'great man' theory of history 10.167; much of what is thought of as history is really myth 26.72; no longer simply 'the lengthened shadow of a man' 3.423; periods of purification and decay 13.440; the product of material factors (Marx) 10.167; study of world history 9.235; there was no sense of development until quite recently 10.554–5; the true individual is aware of history 3.468; value of studying history 9.235, 9.372–3; we are less confident of history as uninterrupted progress than we used to be 12.593

Buddhist perspectives
history versus tradition 1.31–43; the ideal can't be manifested fully within

the historical process 16.26; historical reality represented by Vimalakīrti 16.527; leaving history far behind in the *Larger Sukhāvatī-vyūha Sūtra* 1.327; lack of historical perspective in Indian and Tibetan Buddhists 2.442; Nyingmapas, not being historically minded, don't look *back* but *up* 22.467

see also
British history; the history of Buddhism, *see under* Buddhism III; the history of the Church, *see under* Christianity; the history of religion, *see under* religion; the history of Western Buddhism, *see under* Western Buddhism; medieval; prehistory

Hitler, Adolf Pope Pius XII refused to condemn Hitler's massacre of the Jews 3.449; someone suggests that he should be attacked by London's East Enders 20.47; the killing of the Jews 26.33, 26.538, 26.654

Hitopadeśa (Hinduism) 14.343

Hiup, the Venerable Siak Kiong 20.142–3, 20.149

Hobsbaum, Philip 26.337

Hobson, Mr v22

Hochhuth, Rolf 3.449

Hoddle, Glenn 25.16–17

Hodgkinson, Lizji 24.313

Hodgson, Brian Houghton 13.304, 13.692–3 (n123)

Hoffman, Helmut 8.351–3

Hofford, Donald 21.44–5

Hogarth, William 'The Four Stages of Cruelty' 1.499, 3.542; his satires are deadly accurate 3.508; the secular nature of his paintings 12.76

Hogg, Quintin 23.88

Hokusai 24.512

Holbein, Hans the Elder 24.592

Holbein, Hans the Younger 13.230, 24.273, 24.676 (n333), 26.297

Holiday, Henry 24.224

holidays be clear about whether you're going on solitary retreat or on holiday 5.673–4, 19.492; Bodh Gaya as a tourist attraction 19.470; culture-guzzling package holidays 17.395–6; the way beauty spots are spoiled by mass tourism 24.448, 26.185; you are still a Dharma practitioner when you are on holiday 19.500

holiness 'All manifestations are holy books' (Milarepa) 19.69–70; everything that lives is holy 7.281–4; a flower is sacred, a tree holy, if you look at it with an illumined mind 7.284; four purposes of the holy life 14.49; growth in holiness is essentially growth in emptiness 7.375, 26.53; 'the holiness of the heart's affections' (Keats) 25.xxxiv, 25.17; the holy fool 15.350; the holy ground of the human soul 25.xxxiv, 25.17; 'holy indifference' 4.489; 'holy' isn't a very Buddhistic term 17.135; if we eliminate desire, won't we get rid of desire for pure and holy things as well? 7.288; is 'holy' or 'noble' a better translation of *ārya*? 1.478; link with wholeness 1.30; no 'holiness devoid of wisdom' 17.134; the quest for holiness 26.44; 'Vast emptiness and nothing holy' 12.531, 14.575–6; you cannot see anything as holy until you see everything as holy 7.284

Holland Dutch occupation of Sri Lanka 8.468–9; Sangharakshita visits 4.485, 24.367, 24.371;

Holman Hunt, William *The Scapegoat* 2.609–10, 24.65, 24.134, 26.255, 26.283, 26.465

Holmes, Richard 24.563, 26.375

Holocaust *see under* Second World War

Holtbernd, Luise *see* Ratnadevi

Holtby, Winifred 26.637

holy grail *see under* Arthur, King

holy persons

eight holy persons or individuals, four pairs of persons
introduction 2.146–50, 4.683 (n172–3), 10.717 (n452); canonical references 4.683 (n172–3); 'arising' from the Unconditioned 14.444–5; as beings in the ocean of the Dharma, *see under Udāna*/great ocean; described in the Abhidharma 14.81; described in the *Tiratana Vandanā* 15.517–18, 17.631; doctrine held in common by Theravāda and Mahāyāna 7.531; the list can scarcely capture their true nature 15.240–1; listed 2.682 (n199); one need not take the number of rebirths too literally 15.531; path and fruit, *see mārga* and *phala*; this set regarded by the Hīnayāna as definitive 2.151; we don't know whether the list was introduced by the Buddha 10.569; 'worthy of offerings' (*Ratana Sutta*) 15.64; *see also* Stream Entrant; once-returner; non-returner; *arhant*

other enumerations
seven holy persons 2.141–6; nine holy persons 2.150–1

holy and sacred places the holy places of Buddhism, *see* four holy places; Delphi 23.273; Nepal 7.341–2; paying respect to holy places 1.407, 4.324–5, 14.463; the sacredness of the place where the *Diamond Sūtra* is expounded 14.462–5

Holy Roman Empire 13.551, 16.565

homage *see* reverence

home

reflections
be careful not to think of the Buddhist Refuges as a sort of home 18.563–4; bodhisattvas' home is meditation on the meaning of the Void 16.457; charity begins at home 7.324; home and land like a rasp filing away one's body, word, and mind 18.201; keeping one's home beautiful 26.183–5; practising the Dharma at home 10.573; you just go on multiplying whatever is unskilful at home 18.206; you think of *my* home, but nothing in the whole world is yours 18.219

leaving home
children leaving home 15.410–11, 15.480; different levels of leaving home 9.535–6; examining your motivation for leaving your family 10.456–7; getting a better view of your parents 3.37; leaving behind a bad temperament is harder than leaving home 19.89; so that you meet people who *see* and know you as you are now, not stuck in the past 18.204; only do it when you're ready 9.535; probably best to literally leave home as soon as you can 3.37; *see also* going forth

wandering without a home
in the *Ratnaguṇa-saṃcayagāthā* 14.548–9; not just literal but having nothing in which to mentally settle down (*Udāna*) 10.520–1

homelessness the ideal of homelessness 14.549; in the modern world you can get away from home, but not the state 11.624

Homer

introduction
brief introduction 23.514 (n306); assertions about gods and goddesses 13.669; an expressive head of Homer in Munich 24.587; his works began as oral compositions 14.290; in the Axial Age 3.427; recommendation to read 12.406; respect for objects in his accounts of the ancient Greek world 18.71

the Iliad
introduction 17.740 (n260); the consequences of Helen's adultery with Paris 17.294; delight in the episodes in which the gods appear 23.266; the distinct individuality of the gods 26.469; Hermes 16.350; Homeric Hymns 24.396; 'I sided with the Greeks' 26.469; the perception of rebirth 3.96; sees human life in terms of conflict 16.85; part of our cultural heritage, not our religious heritage 25.19; 'the price of a hundred oxen for the price of nine' 20.449; 'sing of the baneful wrath of Achilles' 3.513, 26.481; Sangharakshita reads Chapman's translation 20.49, 23.xviii, 23.266, 26.469; the story 26.469–70; *The Story of the Iliad* 26.482; Zeus 23.266–7

the Odyssey
Hermes 16.350; 'The justling rocks where fierce Charybdis raves' 7.46; life seen as a journey 16.86; Neoplatonist commentators 8.607; Odysseus's journey 26.262; Pope's translation 26.371; 'Tell me, Muse, of the man of many wiles' 3.513

homo sapiens 2.64–5; *see also* human life

homosexuality

introduction
abhorrence 13.611, 13.617; André Gide on homosexuality 13.612, 22.588–9 (n150); of Allen Ginsberg 13.612, 22.566–7; Carpenter's *The Intermediate Sex* 13.610; Dante's expression of affection and respect for homosexuals 13.615–16; Ellis, *The Psychology of Sex* 13.610–11; English middle-class abhorrence of homosexuality 23.393–4, 23.404, 23.438; fear of homosexuality 3.527, 11.583–4, 13.452, 13.618, 23.438; the FWBO founded in the same year that homosexual acts were decriminalized 26.580, 26.672; the *Gay News* blasphemy trial 11.326–31; homophobia 13.451–2, 13.617–18, 26.577–8; Housman's poem ('the colour of his hair') 13.613; 'I thought men like that shot themselves' (George V) 26.578; idealized in ancient Greece 13.611; increased tolerance 13.617; *Jung, Jungians, and Homosexuality*: 'required reading' 24.389; King's *A Domestic Animal* 24.389; labelling people 'heterosexual' or 'homosexual' 11.583; 'The Love That Dares to Speak its Name' 11.327–8; rainbow as symbol of the gay rights movement 26.672; relationships 11.482; violence towards homosexuals 13.617; Oscar Wilde's prison term 13.611, 26.149, 26.177, 26.489; repeal of the law under which Oscar Wilde was convicted 13.612

and Buddhism
attitudes in traditional Buddhist circles 13.612; the Buddha made no pronouncements about sexual orientation or behaviour 3.322; 'going with boys' in Tibetan monasteries 13.612, 22.521; the Buddhist movement must be free of homophobia if friendship was to flourish 23.438; *The Love of the Samurai*: first book in English on Buddhism and homosexuality 24.388–9; reaching out to gay people 11.596; retreats for gay men 26.xiv; Triratna does not discriminate 12.668, 12.675, 13.451–2; viewed in Buddhism in the same light as heterosexuality 3.371

see also
Christian attitude, *see under* Christianity/attitudes/attitude to homosexuality; Sangharakshita's, *see under* Sangharakshita VII/characteristics/sexuality

homunculus (medieval idea) 17.94

Hōnen Shōnin initiated Shinran 1.344; taught a combination of faith and works 7.42

honesty

honesty with oneself and about oneself
about the importance we give to pleasure 17.302; about what we believe 4.125; about what you want to do 4.606; about whether you find artworks inspiring 19.348–9; about the limitations we need to overcome to make progress 18.147–8; about one's struggles to live in accordance with one's vision 16.488; honest doubt 2.146–7, 3.418; it is difficult to find an honest witness of his mind 19.459; practising the four right efforts requires complete honesty with oneself 1.555; to speak the truth we must be honest, be ourselves 1.518–19; try to see honestly which circumstances of your life are advantageous 18.148

honesty with other people
be as honest as you can be in your dealings with people 19.501; don't insist on your preference, but be honest about what you prefer 18.36; exploring the path with others in complete harmony and honesty 2.462; the importance of honesty 1.555; in sexual relationships there might be intimacy but not much honesty 15.164; only being honest up to a point 26.59; our first duty as citizens is to be honest in all our dealings 17.231; people will always be convinced by honesty and sincerity 18.184; the stifling of honest criticism 19.543; when teaching the Dharma, be honest about what you know and don't know 17.207

examples of honesty
Buddhism is characterized by clarity, honesty, and rigour of thought 4.144; the honesty of Anagarika Dharmapala 8.33, 8.55–6, 8.102–3; the unnervingly direct and honest gaze of a baby 18.140; young children are very honest about their likes and dislikes 15.432; work is right livelihood if you work honestly and conscientiously 1.548

see also
speech/four levels of skilful speech/truthful

honey and rice cakes offered to the Buddha 3.64

Hong Kong 8.480

honour the Buddha wonders whom he can honour and respect 3.65, 4.168, 4.346, 19.316, 26.627–8; cultures in which men fight to defend their honour 18.101; honour and respect the enemy for helping you, even though they don't intend to 4.434; honoured guests, *see under* guests; honouring all the great schools of Buddhism 12.369; honouring the Buddha 1.52, 3.64, 3.152; honouring the expansive richness of the Buddhist life 3.71; 'honouring the honourable' (Nāgārjuna) 13.270, 17.276–7; honouring the memory of great lives 25.447; one truly honours the Buddha by honouring the Dharma 16.571; the six *gāravas* 3.67–70; we honour Dr Ambedkar as a modern bodhisattva 10.318–19; 'honour those worthy of honour' (*Maṅgala Sutta*) 8.511, 8.704 (n307), 10.318, 13.270, 17.276–7

Hooker, Richard 18.653 (n129)

Hookham, Mike 11.495, v23, 23.50 (photograph)

hooks the bodhisattva represented with a hook of compassion 14.597, 14.658 (n517); of the *gaurīs*, associated with fascination 16.352; Tārā's hook of compassion 17.146

Hopcke, Robert H. 24.389

hope don't lose heart about the harm being done to the natural world 25.57–9; every kind of hope is essentially desire for life 26.153; a great message of hope 10.235–6; helping others in the hope of heaven 4.89; 'Hope' (poem) 25.349; 'Hope' (sonnet) 25.275; 'Hope springs eternal in the human breast' 7.162; 'Hope triumphs over experience' 10.496; the hopefulness of Dalit Buddhists 8.251,

10.297–8; hopes and fears 7.285, 18.344; if you are generous there is hope for you yet 14.573; impermanence is a death sentence, but also our hope of freedom from death 17.163; making offerings in the hope of merit 19.311; meditating on the bodhisattva's perfections, the devotee hopes to obtain their grace 7.123; no hope of Enlightenment if there was another samsaric force as strong as the sexual urge 3.321; the only hope for beings in hell: Enlightenment 2.96, 13.134; the only motive for Dharma study is the hope that through it Enlightenment may be attained 1.15–16; the savage bandits of hope and fear 19.398; the spiritually committed can never give up hope on anyone 16.434

Hopkins, E. W. 4.90

Hopkins, Gerard Manley 24.365, 26.379, 26.397

Hopkins, Jeffrey 17.152, 17.322

Horace (Roman poet) poets are born, not made 26.133; *Sermones* 2.366, 2.709 (n440)

Horner, I. B. brief introduction 23.507 (n259); article on compassion 1.235–7; claim that the Theravāda is 'the most orthodox form of Buddhism' 2.556, 7.516–17, 7.530–45, 23.225; her work described as 'the last ounce of dust in desiccation' 5.248, 23.225; reviews Sangharakshita's poems 22.182; *Ten Jātaka Stories* (review) 8.392–3; 'Women in Early Buddhism' 2.744 (n687) 7.516

Horney, Karen 12.93, 12.273–4

Hornung, E. W. 26.574–5

horses association with Ratnasambhava 13.309; converting to Hinduism would be like making a donkey into a horse 10.44, 12.245; controlling the mind like riding a horse 4.354; denying the truth of *śūnyatā* is like a man on a horse denying he is on horseback 7.213, 10.158; drawing the chariots of the sun and moon in Buddhist cosmology 16.346; 'Hast thou given the horse strength?' (Book of Job) 13.540–1; hearses drawn by plumed black horses in London 15.143; 'a horse of Prāṇa-Mind' 18.72, 18.322, 19.437–8; the horse Shiwa Aui offers Milarepa, and the symbolic horse Milarepa already has 18.70–3; in the New Forest 25.329; life is as precarious as a single hair of a horse's tail on the verge of breaking 18.564; the precious horse 13.262; Rechungpa like a young horse that needs training 18.346; sensitivity 24.460; Siddhārtha's horse Kanthaka 3.208, 3.656 (n197), 13.309, 13.693 (n126); the spiritual life like the training of a horse 2.343, 4.460–1, 16.557; symbol of the Buddha-to-be's leaving home 3.137, 9.365, 10.201, 13.309; symbol of *vīrya* 9.366–7, 10.200–2; in the Tantra the embodiment of speed and energy 13.309; 'The tigers of wrath are wiser than the horses of instruction' 18.78; the wild horse of the mind 15.286; windhorse, *see* windhorse

Horus *see under* Egypt

hospitality of a brahmin in Madura 20.234–5; in Eastern Buddhist countries 4.95; a feature of popular Buddhism 2.232; Indian hospitality 11.237–9, 13.254; Punjabi 20.221; to members of the spiritual community 15.534; when someone visits, make sure they feel at ease 4.68; *see also* guests

Hossō Shū *see under* Japanese Buddhism

Houlder, Dominic (Dharmachari Mahaprabha) 11.765 (n323)

housebuilder *see Dhammapada*/chapter 11

household life 'Dusty is the household life' 2.688 (n266), 10.644; being tied up with household life 10.484–6; the Mahāyāna gave increased importance to household life 1.273; offerings to the household shrine 2.229, 26.494; Vimalakīrti, a bodhisattva who appears as a layman out of skilful means 16.492–3; *see also* lay people; everyday life

householders *see* lay people

houses burning house, *see under White Lotus Sūtra*; creating the new self compared to building a house 18.271–2; 'Faith is the firm foundation of my house' (Milarepa) 18.271–4; going for alms, stop at all houses 20.415–16; keeping your house in good repair, like looking after your mind 17.676–7; living without a house 18.628–9; the symbolism of houses 18.275; turning one's house into a castle (metaphorically) 18.284–7

Housman, A. E. brief introduction 23.542 (n500); association with Highgate 23.473; 'Loveliest of trees, the cherry now' 20.36, 26.392; poem ('the colour of his hair') 13.613

Howe, Dr E. Graham 23.72, 23.217

Hṛdaya Sutra *see Heart Sūtra*

hrī (Pāli *hiri*, sense of shame) as one of the positive mental events (Abhidharma) 17.557–8; association with Amitābha 17.558; conscience 17.558; *hiri* and *ottappa* (shame and blame) are the guardians of the world 16.348, 17.558, 18.486, 19.406–7; feeling shame about deeds and activities which wouldn't bother most people 18.136; it is salutary to feel ashamed of one's unskilful actions 9.275, 16.304; self-respect, Buddha-pride 17.558; shame of heart 18.459; we tend to be most ashamed of matters over which we have no control 18.136

Hridaya, Dharmachari v24

hrīḥ (seed syllable) 16.180, 17.558

Hsüan Tsang *see* Xuanzang

Huainanzi 23.40

Huángbò (Huang Po) 8.487, 12.170–1

Huayan Zong 1.353, 7.401, 14.409

Hua-yen Buddhism 3.672 (n297), 16.3–4

hubris 17.272, 18.142–3

Hudson, Dr Irene Bastow v21, v22

Hudson, W. H. 26.332

Hügel, Baron von 26.142, 26.709 (n74)

Hughes, Ted 12.641

Huguenots 13.549

Hui-Hai 1.598 (n63)

Huineng brief introduction 1.629–30 (n398); biography 14.349, 19.593 (n15); an example of a faith-follower 14.349; faith can arise through reading his life story 3.299, 11.716; insight on first hearing the Dharma 18.544; the words (from the *Diamond Sūtra*) on hearing which he became Enlightened 14.456–7; 'Grain threshed and ready?' 25.414; he was illiterate 11.716, 14.349; he was not necessarily illiterate 19.45; his inspiring example 1.509; on the Refuge Tree 11.715–16; Sixth Patriarch 13.342; such was his spiritual genius that he was able to transmit the spirit of Buddhism to 43 disciples 13.342; tearing up the *Diamond Sūtra* 12.233, 13.337–8, 19.372; *see also Sūtra of Huineng*

Huiyuan 1.337–8

Hull, England 24.387

hūṃ (seed syllable) concrete universal 16.176, 16.186; Consciousness dissolves into – ? 25.441; 'descent': associated with the last four *pāramitās* 10.151, 10.176; the Five Buddhas as parts of the visualized *hūṃ* in the yoga of the long *hūṃ* 8.558; relationship to *oṃ* 10.147, 16.176, 16.186; roared by the wrathful deities 17.318

human body *see* body

human life

what is a human being?
what makes us human? 10.251–2, 13.139–40; an amalgam of mind and matter (*nāma-rūpa*) 7.137; a battleground of opposing forces 16.393; the child of earth and the offspring of heaven 16.393; conjunction of descending spiritual and ascending biological orders 2.64–5; a conscious being in the process of becoming self-conscious 12.46; a creature of duality 12.605, 16.542; an embodiment of energy 2.93–4, 3.120, 26.52, 26.653; first and foremost a human being 9.351–5; indefinable, as Jean-Paul Sartre says 2.99–100; neither miserable sinner nor stainless immortal spirit 2.99; a 'normal' human being 5.175; not only risen ape but fallen angel 1.42; one manifestation of a current of psychophysical energy 2.93; 'the roof and crown of things' 1.32; root and flower and star 25.78; something transitional (Nietzsche) 3.499; sometimes not much more than animals 12.46, 12.88–9; a spiritual being striving to fathom the mystery of existence 26.306; a stream of consciousness deeply imbued with the dye of craving 26.63; we are archetypal beings 16.532–3; we are what our state of consciousness is 3.123

and what is human life?
constantly changing 10.327–8; the destruction of human life 25.404; liable to unexpected termination 4.76, 10.320; like the flame of a candle, or a wave of the ocean 7.165; 'like a tangled ball of string' 2.696 (n342); metaphors 16.85–6; a mixture of pleasure and pain 2.73, 2.95, 7.170, 13.139, 19.497–8; the most important subject we could ever concern ourselves with 12.82; a spark of pleasure between the terminals of two eternities of non-existence 7.311; a tragedy 3.96; a transformation of energy 2.101–2; a vale of soul-making 12.698, 26.399

but what is it to be really human?
being human is an achievement, not something we're born with 3.477; an element of risk to being truly human (Nietzsche) 3.499; failing to wonder every day about existence and non-existence, you're scarcely human 17.570; in a truly human state, devote yourself to spiritual development 13.135; most 'human beings'

rarely experience the truly human state 13.131; one is not really human unless one has a spark of awareness 11.24, 26.7; *śīla* makes you a true human being 9.187; the state of artists, philosophers, and saints (Nietzsche) 3.499; to become a true human being is very difficult, and we usually need help 16.170; to go for Refuge 16.354–5; to live in accordance with the principle of non-violence 12.354, 26.55; ultimately only the Enlightened human being is the true human being 16.355; you are not automatically a human being, you have to become one 10.252–3

what do humans need?
contact with the true self is the most important thing 16.173; an element of pleasure 19.91; human needs 15.309–10; the nourishment of both emotion and reason 16.129–30; our essential need: freedom 16.499; solitude 5.670, 8.260; without beauty we cannot lead a truly human life 10.368

the human experience
abstraction has let us reduce the chaos of our impressions to a cosmos 7.325; being in the city is an opportunity to witness the human condition 18.424; the *bardo* of human existence 12.199; the contradictory nature of human beings 26.398–9; creating a cosmos out of the chaos of human experience 4.82; desiderative rather than rational 1.123–4, 7.392; governed by power until reflexive consciousness is developed 8.447–8; history of human development 3.424–8, 9.178–9; the human predicament 15.249, 16.79, 17.433–4; living life as best we can 25.406; messier aspects of human life 3.567; most human beings are content to be human, as a pig is content to be a pig 26.173; not that man wills, but rather that will 'mans' 2.93, 26.52; our place in the evolutionary process 12.87–90, 14.522; until recent times we had to spend much of our time just surviving 12.379–80; three aspects, rational, emotional, and volitional 15.606–8; we are human by accident, or just for a short time 16.354; we are in danger (*White Lotus Sūtra*) 16.71; we are naturally attracted by goodness 7.35; we are really machines rather than human beings 11.7; we are ruled to a great extent by pleasure 18.129; we exist in both history and myth 16.534; we have access to all the planes of existence 2.96; we have a natural tendency to grow 16.71; we occupy a middle place between heaven and hell 2.94–6, 7.170

human beings and animal nature
Buddhism does not see sentient beings as divided into different forms of life 2.93–4; don't try to hide the animal side of yourself 19.250–1, 19.256; humanity does not exclude the animal 3.62; it is literature that distinguishes man from the animals 14.291; man insignificant in the midst of nature 26.284; oscillation between animal level and level of reasoning 7.421–2; our animal instincts are still very strong 11.197; self-awareness distinguishes at least some human beings from animals 12.46; though someone may degenerate, they are still recognizably a human being 16.291; we need to recapture the sense that to be human is to be part of nature 15.136

human solidarity
human beings are only human and may make mistakes 10.398; the human race tending to become more and more one great family 12.129–30; *mettā* is the response to be expected from one human being to another 5.174; murder: the absolute negation of the solidarity between humans 2.358; the natural solidarity between human beings 2.358, 13.615, 13.621, 19.540; to be human is to be related to other human beings 3.521; we are all brothers and sisters 9.186, 9.496, 10.172; we are at different stages of development 3.561; we are essentially social 16.427; you can't ignore the spiritual nature of human beings when dealing with them 16.113

the rare opportunity of being human
the *bardo* of life is a marvellous opportunity 12.199; the blind turtle putting its head through a yoke in the sea 1.418, 4.367, 7.170, 13.139; Buddhism as a reflection on the preciousness of human life 26.296–7; 'It is difficult to attain the human state' (*Dhammapada*) 3.484, 7.170–1, 13.139; the pebble of life which we fail to see as the precious stone it is 16.251; the precious human body as vehicle for Enlightenment 2.94, 3.601, 7.170–1, 18.46; a brief and precious opportunity, not to be wasted 17.163, 17.474; our lives are too precious an opportunity to be wasted in a comfortable twilight zone 15.159; the preciousness of life 7.171, 17.168; the preciousness of human life wasted 7.131, 10.322; rare conditions for Dharma practice (Śāntideva) 4.365–8; the rare gift of human life 7.311; the rarity of birth as a human being 1.417–18, 2.94; resolve never to lose sight of the valuable opportunity you have been given 14.404; 'Unless Man strives for Truth

and loves, he is ... merely brute' 25.203; why risk one's precious human life on dangerous sports? 24.503

the healthy, happy human being
described in the *Karaṇīya Mettā Sutta* 15.274; from being a healthy, happy human being to something more 18.160; confronted by the ideal must respond with faith 18.273–4; head and heart work together 14.559; one can become one through spiritual training 4.107; not a 'natural' state, despite speculation about how a child would develop alone 4.107; the practice of ethics is key to a healthy human existence 17.168; the result of the process of the lower evolution 3.477, 18.275; spiritual development has to begin with a healthy human individual 18.18; would ideally dwell in the first *dhyāna* all the time 4.156

two kinds of human being: pṛthagjana and āryan
bound and free 10.140–1; ordinary and extraordinary 10.235; progressing from one to the other 14.312; those whose view is limited and those whose view is unrestricted 11.160

the human quest
'Any attempt to treat man as other than a spiritual being distorts him' 26.10; the beginnings of the quest 3.4–5; the duty of every human being is to take stock of their responsibilities 3.619; following the spiritual path is the best thing you can possibly do 12.626; human beings urged to fight on the side of good 26.655; humans are more important than religion 9.352, 10.252; the ideal human being 11.100–1; the ideal of the non-specialized human being 14.522, 17.202; impelled to find a means of transcending all conditions of relative existence 7.170; is man a spiritual being with a spiritual destiny? 4.637–58; our true nature is to develop 9.232–3, 16.71; to embark on the spiritual life you need to be a capable human being 15.269–71; to free ourselves from the painful limitations of human existence we must ask its cause 7.115; the most beautiful aspect of a human being is their spiritual potential 15.130–1; the possibilities of human experience 5.51; we are not here *for* anything 14.522, 18.120; we have to understand ourselves afresh, now that 'God is dead' 3.497–8; we have within us something that has an affinity with the transcendental 16.561; we must recognize ourselves as essentially spiritual beings 7.308; we progress for the same reason the amoeba evolves – from irritation 7.389, 26.11

the human being and Buddhism
blessed with clearness of mind and goad of discontent to see Enlightenment 4.448; the Buddha was a human being, so we have that in common with him 4.201–2; Buddhism doesn't accept anything that is not part of human experience 19.187; Buddhism offers us the possibility of developing 10.206; Buddhist organizations must remember that it is the human being that matters 18.121–2; the Dharma disappears as human beings become more degenerate 1.50; Enlightenment is the true goal of human life 1.80, 2.120; however depraved we are, there is some reflection of the *dharmakāya* 18.286; 'If one does not know the Buddha-nature one cannot be called a man' 14.238; we are too absorbed in our games to listen to the Buddha 9.358–9, 16.74

see also
for Buddhist analysis of the human being, *see* five *skandhas*; 'Humankind cannot bear very much reality', *see* T. S. Eliot; illustrated by the wheel of life, *see* wheel of life; Enlightenment/potential for Enlightenment

human nature the capacity to look up to someone or something higher is inherent in human nature 26.629; claim that Shakespeare is 'the creator of human nature as we know it' 3.602; compartmentalization 10.154; the dissipation of a naive Rousseauistic view of human nature 26.376; essentially the same in spite of the variety of its manifestations 7.257, 7.327; the 'Fall of Man' embodies an eternal truth about human nature 12.109; highly resilient even under difficult circumstances 4.423, 5.125; human nature is in reality a no-nature 2.99–100, 2.120; positive and negative views of human nature 14.534; religions of revelation emphasize the weakness and sinfulness of human nature 7.366; tolerance of human frailty 13.477–8

human rights Buddhism and 8.611, 9.334; denied to Untouchables 9.30, 9.32–7, 9.184; right to develop as a human being 9.184; rights and duties, *see* rights and duties; *The Rights of Man* (Paine) 26.587–8

humanism Dr Ambedkar's conception of society was deeply humanistic in the most ideal sense 10.82; Blake's spiritual humanism 8.559; and the bodhisattva ideal

2.160; and Buddhism 9.352, 9.425, 12.98, 21.450; the Greeks' humanistic dislike of prostrating before kings 11.250–1; humanistic religions 12.42; Protestantism is diluted by secular humanism 13.407; refined, humanistic culture provides a foundation for the spiritual life 13.134; Rousseauism as a form of secular humanism 13.407; what is secular humanism? 13.407

humanitarianism the bodhisattva ideal is not a kind of humanitarianism 1.269, 4.608, 16.232; not introducing a note of humanitarianism into the symphony of Buddhism 8.175; superficial: religion summed up as the giving of buns and blankets 1.428; the warm glow of humanitarianism is not enough to fuse the world's differences into unity 7.271

humanity the bodhisattva ideal exemplifies the potential for Enlightenment of humanity 3.384; the Buddha's vision of humanity as a bed of lotuses, *see under* Brahmā Sahāmpati's request; 'the caravan of humanity moving along the road of being ...' 4.361; if humanity is not to destroy itself, there must be a revival of real spiritual life 16.394; in the notion of Buddha, humanity and the absolute coalesce 13.297; it is easier to love an abstraction like 'humanity' than a single imperfect human being 7.328–9; an Enlightened humanity is a contradiction in terms 11.271–2; the forces of the collective unconscious have to be tackled if humanity is to be transformed 12.323; humanity becoming aware of its contingent nature 26.473; leaving the group means shaking off your identification with humanity as a mere collectivity 3.37; Nietzsche's vision of humanity as a bridge between the beast and the overman 3.499; not giving up family life, but making the whole of humanity your family 18.214–15; not to think about death is to deprive ourselves of our humanity 12.358; one who habitually breaks the first precept without guilt sinks below truly human level 13.609; primitive humanity is reproductive, modern humanity is productive, the individual is creative 3.471; quarrelsome through their views 10.600; to have faith in the Buddha is to have faith in humanity 17.37; 'Thine own humanity learn to adore' (Blake) 8.559, 26.348; true humanity consists in vivid awareness of the existence of other people 8.452; we have to love humanity as ourselves 12.343; without the capacity to recollect the past, our humanity ebbs away 15.86; works of art that show us the qualities of humanity 26.370–1

humanities Sangharakshita inclined to the humanities rather than the sciences 2.531–2, 11.663, 26.638; split from sciences 3.6

Hume, Allan Octavian 7.557–8 (n75)

Hume, David awoke Kant from his 'dogmatic slumber' 24.586; his *Treatise on Human Nature* fell 'dead-born from the press' 26.442, 26.733 (n340); how he arrived at concepts 17.437; reduction of the so-called self to a stream of perceptions 8.613; statue in Edinburgh 24.586

humiliation the bodhisattva suffers, but there is no suggestion of humiliation 4.14; fear of humiliation 16.279; gurus' humiliation of their disciples 14.488–9; the humiliation that springs from *puṇya* 14.487–91; it might even be the way Perfect Vision might arise 14.490, 26.61; make the most of humiliating situations 14.490; no need to go about humbling people 'for their own good' 14.491; setting up humiliating conditions 14.488; those who take up the *Diamond Sūtra*, 'well humbled they will be!' 14.486–8; you need to risk the humiliation of failure to be successful 14.489–91

humility 'All censure of a man's self is oblique praise' (Dr Johnson) 14.489; *anatimāni* (humble, *Mettā Sutta*) 15.274; be humble with regard to your spiritual achievements 18.165; a 'bad' man shattered into humility and repentance 7.407; the Buddha had no false humility 10.471; can be a strategy for avoiding humiliation 14.489; an exemplar of lack of humility 8.147–8; following the guru's precepts shows a kind of humility 18.483; Gandhi on humility 4.118, 17.605; humility in comparison to the grandeur of the ideal 15.426–7; humility is necessarily unselfconscious 17.605; humility is the pride of the weak 26.61; it naturally comes with reverence 17.605; just as much a form of egotism as pride 4.78, 14.489, 20.362; if you practise humility self-consciously, it becomes hypocrisy 4.118; modesty is somewhat more positive than humility 18.514; the odious humility of Uriah Heep, *see under* Dickens; real humility is not to think of oneself as superior, inferior, or equal 18.511; 'To be humble is to succeed' 18.511; 'When it comes to humility, we Franciscans are tops!' 4.603, 17.605, 18.480; Yalahankar Swami exposes humility 14.489, 20.362

humour the Buddha's sense of humour 2.26, 14.49; Dhardo Rimpoche's sense of humour 12.435–6; does a sense of humour have a part to play in Buddhist life? 4.137; the freeing effect of laughter 4.137; Freud's analysis of humour 2.636, 4.137, 15.372; 'To laugh excessively is childish' – what did the Buddha mean? 4.137; 'Laughter that shows the teeth is madness' (the Buddha) 4.137, 12.450, 15.372; laughing at others' faults to show that we are free of those faults 17.279; making someone a scapegoat in the name of humour is very unskilful 17.653; Moggallāna's sense of humour 10.405; negative humour 4.137, 15.372–3; a sense of humour can bring out the incongruity of the ego claiming anything for itself 14.598; a sense of proportion 4.136–8; Zen stories and one's tendency to laugh at the stupidity of others 17.279

humours (identifying different types of people) 12.271–2

Humphreys, Christmas

life story
introduction 2.714 (n481), 8.685 (n132), 10.673 (n91), 23.482 (n78), 24.653–4 (n225); he believed he had been an officer in Pharaoh's bodyguard 17.31, 23.41; his father was a prosecutor at Oscar Wilde's trial 23.393; his participation in the Nuremberg Trials 10.56, 20.150; ; founder of the Buddhist Society, *see* Buddhist Society; Britain's best-known Buddhist in the 1960s 23.46; his wife 11.542; attends the seventh World Fellowship of Buddhists conference 23.159; gets the Dalai Lama to 'authenticate' *The Voice of the Silence* as Buddhist 22.354–5; the Dalai Lama enquires after him 23.335; insists on reciting the Refuges and Precepts in a 'pseudo-egalitarian' way 12.304; nicknamed 'the Pope of Eccleston Square' 11.543, 23.67–8; speaks to the Society of the Servants of God 22.359; photograph 23.35

views and character
appreciation for him 27.1071; 'basically a Theosophist' 10.56, 22.354, 23.68; thought Western Buddhists should adhere to middle-class respectability 23.404, 23.406; contrast with Allen Ginsberg 24.178–80; spoke of 'hacking off great bleeding lumps of self' 3.490, 10.524, 23.35; his coldness of manner 11.542, 22.354, 22.359; not vegetarian 23.34; on the English attitude to homosexuality 23.393–4, 23.404; on waning interest of Western Buddhists in karma and rebirth 4.403; quoting Kipling 8.196; regarded psychic powers as dangerous 4.517, 23.48; said that meditation was dangerous for Westerners 3.456, 4.504, 11.378, 23.48; tendency to be dictatorial 23.80; the true Buddhist 'wears the yellow robe within' 23.190, 23.322; 'twelve principles of Buddhism' 1.222, 14.375; on Zen 8.495; 'Zen class' 23.35, 23.46, 23.69

works
Both Sides of the Circle (autobiography) 11.534, 23.159, 23.439; *Buddhism* 12.72, 23.46; *Concentration and Meditation* 12.682, 12.756–7 (n473); 'The Menace of Belief' 8.643, 22.126; *The Mountain Side* (poems) 24.179; *The Pilot* (poem) 24.360; an edition of the *Sūtra of Huineng* 24.321; 'Why Are We Afraid?' 8.375; *The Wisdom of Buddhism* 2.126, 5.199–200, 8.394–5; *Zen Buddhism* 12.444, 14.481, 17.65–6

and Sangharakshita
'Toby as I Knew Him' 11.xxi, 11.541–4; their first meeting 11.541, 20.100; their correspondence 11.542; meeting in New Delhi 11.542; he visits Kalimpong 8.664, 11.546; 'You're two minutes late' 9.499, 11.542–3, 23.36, 25.382; he gives Sangharakshita a watch 9.499, 11.542–3, 23.36; 'Think of yourself as the Buddhist equivalent of the vicar of Hampstead' 11.543, 17.634, 18.347, 23.80–1, 23.213; he writes to Sangharakshita about his being asked to leave the Vihara 23.392–4; they meet in London in 1980 24.178–80; resuming their friendship 11.xxi, 11.543, 23.439, 24.179; his fascination with the FWBO 11.543–4, 23.439

Hungary Hungarian music 24.520–1; Sangharakshita's ancestry 26.531

hunger best to shop for food when you're not feeling hungry 15.288; compelling hungry refugees to listen to a sermon

23.208; 'The painted picture of a dumpling does not take one's hunger away' 8.496; 'the slave-labour of the hungry' (Milarepa) 18.294; 'With rains of food and drink may I dispel the anguish of hunger and thirst' 4.358; you may feel hungry after meditating 18.634

hungry ghosts (*pretas*) can be helped through contact with human beings 2.96; the environments in which one might encounter them 4.545; they're so hungry they don't think about how they compare with others 4.77; one needs to reflect deeply on the symbolism 16.350; *pretas* in the form of Indian demons inhabit Milarepa's cave 18.27; rebirth as a hungry ghost 14.67; ruled by Virūḍhaka 16.346; Sangharakshita's vision of a hungry ghost in an Indian ashram 20.310; if you see them, the tradition is to ask whether you can do anything for them 20.310; so miserable that they cannot think about the Dharma 19.497–8; a state of neurotic desire 13.130, 17.285; susceptibility to their influence 4.542; they're like people in a state of paranoia, under attack by their own projections 19.497; thieves are *preta*-like people who are never satisfied with what they have 17.294; in the wheel of life, *see under* wheel of life; the world of drug addiction or intense emotional dependency 17.285

Hunt, Ernest Shinkaku 8.372

Hunt, Sir John 22.11

Hunt, Leigh 21.434

hunting *see under* animals

Hus, Jan 13.666–7

Husserl, Edmund 8.615

Huxley, Aldous on beauty spots 24.448, 26.185; *Brave New World* 15.487; a catalogue of the states of mind and actions recognized as religious 26.151–62; on El Greco 24.417, 26.307; five Latin words that sum up moral history 7.391; on D. H. Lawrence 26.137, 26.169; D. H. Lawrence's attempt to persuade him to join a spiritual community 8.545; his writings include appreciative references to Buddhism 7.450; the light and colour of visionary experiences 14.170; on precious stones 26.221, 26.718–19 (n179); our psychophysical organism is designed to shield us from the impact of reality 12.201; 'The Substitutes for Religion' 26.148–9; 'this savage Bronze Age literature' 11.362, 13.546

Huxley, Julian brief introduction 12.705 (n29), 23.531–2 (n419); *The Living Thoughts of Darwin* 23.371; *Religion Without Revelation* 12.55–6; the universe is one gigantic process of becoming 1.564, 12.84

Huxley, T. H. coined the term agnosticism 8.588; 'Follow your reason as far as it will take you' 8.588–9; the 'two cultures' 3.6, 3.625 (n2)

Huysmans, Joris-Karl 17.395

hymns

Buddhist
Catuḥstava: a kind of hymn in four parts 1.311; prayers and hymns to Amitābha 1.338, 9.139, 9.149; hymn to Avalokiteśvara 1.336, 2.176, 16.178–9; hymn of praise to the Buddha in the *Vimalakīrti-nirdeśa* 16.466; hymn of praise to Mañjuśrī 2.174–5; hymn to Prajñāpāramitā 3.362; hymn to Sarasvati 16.372–3, 16.384; hymn of praise to Śrī 16.384; a hymn to Tārā 1.336; hymns to the Buddha in Mahāyāna *sūtras* 11.225–6

Christian
'Away in a Manger' 26.500; 'From Greenland's icy mountains' 8.5; 'Hymn of the Pearl', *see under* Gnosticism; 'Jerusalem' 18.103–4; 'Little drops of water, little grains of sand' 18.411; 'New every morning is the love' 12.423; 'O God, our help in ages past' 26.294, 26.500; 'Onward Christian Soldiers' 18.103, 26.439, 26.502; 'The rich man in his castle' 15.681, 17.212; 'Sun of my soul, Thou Saviour dear' 25.56

Hindu
hymns to Indra 7.59, 7.561 (n92); hymns to Laksṃi 7.59, 7.561 (n92); Vedic hymns 7.570 (n131), 16.362, 20.62

Hypatia *see* Kingsley

hypnosis 4.502–3, 4.506–9

hypocrisy the adoption of a way of life designed to make you appear other than you are 17.659; attachment to our faults and also to our reputation 17.284–5; being without hypocrisy was considered very important by Tantric yogis 19.385–6; connection with concealment and dissimulation 17.278; deliberately trying to give an impression that your mental state is other than it is 11.267–8; an element of conscious deception 17.647, 18.515; an example: adopting a Buddhist lifestyle for the sake of mundane rewards 17.278; of monastic life 1.229, 8.246; in

relation to merit 2.152; if you can't feel the breath of the *ḍākinīs* your spiritual life is just hypocritical posturing 18.180; if you feel like murdering someone but you don't do it, you are not being a hypocrite 11.268; if you practise humility self-consciously, it becomes hypocrisy 4.118; it is always possible to adopt a lifestyle out of hypocrisy 18.176; it isn't necessarily hypocritical to do something when you don't want to do it 5.374; leading a double life, an element of conscious deception 18.515; a monk is accused of hypocrisy 22.312–15; Tartuffe, the archetypal hypocrite 17.285; those who maintain that all religions are gates to Heaven are hypocrites 7.88; we are quick to expose hypocrisy 17.276; why do people indulge in hypocrisy? 18.460

hypostasis 12.507

I

'I'

belief in 'I'
the belief that 'I' am real 2.263; the biggest *kleśa* 4.376; Buddhism does not encourage one to imagine 'I am Enlightened' 14.460–1; common sense posits an 'I', but the Eye of Enlightenment sees no such entity 2.86; difference between psychological and spiritual conceptions of 'I' 4.620; a false and perverse 'I' claims one name or another 4.579; the five *skandhas* arise from the conception of 'I' 17.343; 'I am Buddha' – a dangerous statement 2.96–7; 'I am nothing ... I am something' 7.38; '*I* am praying', '*I* am meditating' – the intrusion of the ego-sense 7.406; the 'I'-concept is the root cause of the suffering of sentient beings 7.273; the idea of an 'I' (Śāntideva) 2.360–1; locating the I-consciousness in the heart 4.259; negative emotions close us in upon the private, self-regarding 'I' 15.326; saying 'This is me', we are limiting ourselves by identifying with who we are now 17.406; still thinking in terms of me, myself, and I, we can't have developed much insight 4.185; tendency to think that the world changes, but 'I' persist unchanging 7.208–9; this is what *I* have gained 2.268; when you experience a process as static, the 'I' comes into existence 17.349; who am I? 3.489, 3.490, 3.497, 17.66, 17.623; the wise man doesn't have a strong 'I'-sense, but the fool does 15.385; the world of suspicion and fear is the inevitable result of the 'I'-concept 7.274; you see an 'I' in the *skandhas* like seeing a reflection in a mirror 17.346–8

'I' and 'mine'
around the seed of 'I' develops the world of 'mine' 17.342; the average man is dominated by this in its grossest form 2.149; determined by the 'defiled-mind consciousness' 18.604; 'I' and 'mine' are real experiences with a provisional validity 17.343; if 'my' realization is real then 'I' must be a reality 1.232; if you don't have a conception of 'I' you won't have a conception of 'mine' 10.489; in the future there will not be anything that is taken as 'I' and 'mine' 10.622; how the Enlightened consciousness experiences 'I' and 'mine' 17.343; let's get rid of suffering, without worrying which bit is 'mine' and which is 'yours' 4.592; Milarepa has an insight into the experience 18.10; you think of *my* home, *my* wife, but nothing in the whole world is yours 18.218–19; one reaches the *brahma* world by giving up all thoughts of 'I' and 'mine' 3.579; renunciation of the ideas of 'I' and 'mine' 7.361; renunciation of 'mine' is not possible without renunciation of 'me' 1.414; since there is no 'me', there can be no 'mine' 17.339; two sides of a single coin 7.360; violence is based on 'I' and appropriation is based on 'mine' 3.320; we have to act without the sense of 'I' or 'mine' – but how? 7.407–10; 'What essence has remained mine from things I once enjoyed?' 18.131

beyond 'I'
the electric urge to thrust beyond the 'I' 25.xli, 25.183; 'Forgoing self, the Universe grows "I"' 5.656, 7.46, 26.141; getting rid of the subtle 'I' sense that persists after Stream Entry 4.187; how the conception of an 'I' ceases 17.350–1; the Ocean of Nirvāṇa swallowed the droplet 'me' 25.195; practise ethics, meditate, develop wisdom, knowing that there is no 'I' to do it 1.402–3; removing 'conceit of self' doesn't mean annihilating functional sense of 'I' 10.470; sloughing off the outworn skin of 'thou' and 'I' 7.156; thinking not of 'I', 'me', and 'mine', but of the impersonal procession of dharmas 12.149; try to see where 'I' starts 4.376; what should we do about 'I'? 3.490

no 'I'
the bodhisattva has no conception of 'you' and 'I' 7.140; the Buddha's happiness because there is no 'I' 10.470; the deepest religious action is one with no feeling that 'I am the doer' 7.408; no 'I' apart from my constituent parts 4.51; the ordinary person is frightened to be told there is no 'I', but it is liberating 17.339–40; the test of whether an experience is spiritual is whether it is 'my' experience 7.360–1; there is no 'me' apart from the flow of physical and mental events 17.623; 'There is no such thing as *my* realizations or *your* realizations' 7.155; when the 'I' is found in the 'thou' 7.46; 'When you sought the 'I' ... you could not find it' 18.246; without the 'I' you have neither being nor non-being 17.342

I Ching 12.184, 17.614, 21.589

Iamblichus 13.292–3, 23.136, 23.494 (n162)

Ibn Arabi (Sufi master) 24.431

Ibn Rushd *see* Averroes

Ibsen, Henrik brief introduction 15.764 (n192); *Brand* 15.505; the unpredictable nature of his writing 15.505; *The Wild Duck*, 24.390

icchantika (a person incapable of Enlightenment) 14.81, 14.215, 14.238, 14.240, 14.627 (n261)

iceberg our 'knowledge' is the tip of the iceberg 12.22–3; the mind is like an iceberg 3.334; the self, only a small part of which we let ourselves experience 12.266

iconoclasm the iconoclastic nature of wisdom 26.478–9; of Islam 12.242–3, 26.475–80; of Nietzsche 3.502; of Zen Buddhism 14.436, 16.514; iconoclasm about Zen 26.57

iconography of bodhisattvas, *see under* bodhisattvas/archetypal bodhisattvas; despite iconography, forms are not subject to ordinary spatial limitation 2.42; *also see under* individual Buddhas and bodhisattvas

iddhi *see ṛddhi*

iddhipādas *see* four *iddhipādas*

ideal and ideals

introduction
what the word 'ideal' means 11.99–100; what is the ideal human being? 11.100–1; dismay that for some, idealism had become a dirty word 24.393, 24.401; distinction between natural and artificial ideals 11.103; dead ideals are simply ideas 3.564; higher ideals are often lower instincts and desires in disguise 10.349; how the bearer of an archetype differs from the exemplar of an ideal 5.564–5; it seems important that the ideal is pitched beyond people's reach 18.638; the snows of the Ideal 25.284; the spiritual ideal only matters to a few people 10.497; to be able to grow, you need an ideal which is, as it were, ahead of you 10.636

Buddhist ideals
the bodhisattva ideal is the Buddhist spiritual ideal in its loftiest form 13.36; for Buddhism to succeed in the West, people need a positive ideal 15.571; a happy person will communicate the happiness of the Buddhist ideal 15.353; the ideal of Enlightenment 11.103–10; the ideal of individuality 19.182; indications that the original Buddhist ideal was not of liberation for oneself alone 4.5; one person, not even a Buddha, cannot embody all aspects of the ideal 18.221–2; the spiritual ideal can be thought of in terms of wisdom or compassion 11.318; Stream Entry is a serious ideal for every Buddhist 18.578; taking the Triple Gem as your guiding ideal 15.651, 15.663–5; we should admire all the different manifestations of the ideal 18.222–3; why did Buddhism end up with different ideals? 4.22

relating to ideals
'backing into' the ideal 15.569, 15.575, 15.579–80, 18.580; fidelity to ideals 3.564, 3.569; the gulf between us and the ideal 11.246–7; having enough free energy to direct towards the ideal 18.443–4; responding to the ideal with faith 17.336, 18.273–4; human beings seek to avoid being derided on account of their ideals 3.569; the human heart is more profoundly moved by ideals than doctrines 1.397; humility in comparison to the grandeur of the ideal 15.426–7; if you feel uninspired, make contact with someone who shares your ideals 15.153; no justification for getting angry in defence of your ideals 17.602; putting all one's emotions onto the spiritual ideal 5.619; thinking of the ideal in terms of silence or magical potency 11.320; the universe we know and love ... puts heart into our highest ideals 13.274; we may be devoted to an ideal in principle, but attracted to something quite different 25.102–4; you can know what your ideal is only when you know yourself 22.293; you're not collecting ideals like cigarette cards 18.223

embodying ideals
an abstract or theoretical ideal is a contradiction in terms 18.569; the difficulty of not being able to live up to ideals 16.488; an ideal has meaning for us only to the extent that it is embodied in our lives 4.227; an ideal isn't an abstract thing, but an ideal for life 19.182; the ideal has to be kept close to the needs of the living person 19.181; a middle way between an ideal that is too abstract and one that is too low 19.182; paying homage to the ideal without having to practise it 26.81; translating ideals into practice 9.264; worship requires as concrete an embodiment of one's ideals as possible 2.214; you are trying to work out an ideal in your spiritual life, or *as* your spiritual life 18.282

see also
bodhisattva ideal

idealism (philosophy) all forms of idealism mistakenly see mind as the unifying factor of consciousness 19.237; the idealism of Buddhism was there from the beginning, but cannot be the last word 2.130; in Buddhist philosophy pluralistic realism, absolutism, and idealism all flourished in turn 7.488

ideas

the nature of ideas
bodhisattvas' 'flashes of ideas uninterrupted' 2.154; built up around a particular sensuous perception 2.121; the difference between an attitude and an idea 19.105–7; the evolution of ideas 14.602; ideas as mental objects 3.159; 'ideas of sense' (Locke) and ideas that arise from the mind itself 2.278, 7.137, 12.175; a list of ideas that have been important in the West 12.463–4; the mystery of how they emerge into consciousness 7.137; nothing exists except ideas 12.171–2; we get used to ideas, but once they would have been new, exciting, controversial 12.464; whatever world we find ourselves in owes its origin to ideas in the mind 17.476

our own ideas
better to be attracted to Buddhism because it refutes your ideas 26.9; even ideas like 'Buddha' and 'bodhisattva' must be given up to realize *śūnyatā* 10.165; 'giving back' ideas that you normally think of as your own 19.39–40; ideas and concepts rest upon you, not you upon them 14.566; if you don't regard ideas as yours, if an idea is attacked, you don't get upset 10.489; the mind has a certain responsibility for its own ideas 19.195; our heads are full of ideas we do not truly think 7.266–7; some people live much more in ideas than in practical reality 19.287; stopping positive ideas from 'floating away' 17.89–91; your positive ideas can be overwhelmed by reactive tendencies 19.61

ideas becoming real
as soon as we have crystallized an idea in language we have to dissolve it 14.447–8; coming to regard ideas as entities 17.247–8; ideas move people to action, even to change the world, even to die for an idea 12.463; if we don't practise the Dharma, it won't live, and we will only have ideas ... 12.455; one can never be free so long as ideas are treated as corresponding to realities 2.118; turning the ideas of Buddhism into effective attitudes 19.105–6; the way ideas spread and become realities 19.85–6; we don't realize the power of ideas 12.465; when ideas are given concrete expression, it is easier to cast them out 18.277; your life as the working out of the idea which is you 18.269

see also
concepts

identification

identifying with ...
all living things 12.353; Amitābha 1.343, 1.347; the beloved, or social position 19.87; the body 3.216, 4.76, 12.555; the Buddha 19.53–8; the five *skandhas* 10.481; the master, not the disciple 8.497; our ideal image of ourselves 17.285; a particular form of Buddhism 18.380; the senses 3.298; what we think we know rather than direct knowledge 18.107; who we are now 17.406

further notes on identification
ceasing to identify with the group 3.475; easier for us to identify with the bodhisattva than the Buddha 5.621; identifying with the spiral trend, we 'escape' the cyclical trend 4.312; if peace is to be achieved, we have to identify ourselves with both parties 12.343–4; important not to identify thought processes with consciousness 5.229; not identifying rigidly with the form we find ourselves in 17.523; problems of identifying Buddhism with one version 2.50, 12.64–5; reflecting, 'How real is the self with which I identify?' 17.378; self-view means identifying with a cross-section of the flow of *skandhas* 17.625; you might not identify with any group, but others will want to identify you 12.652

identity Buddhism prefers to speak the language not of identity but of analysis and change 2.97; going through the door of *śūnyatā* you see that nothing has any self-identity 3.219–20; ego-identity, *see* ego-identity; the identity of being and not-being 7.195–6; rivers lose their separate identity in the ocean 2.691–2 (n305), 9.195, 9.473, 10.565–6, 11.41, 12.521; Siddhārtha's exchange of clothes with the beggar symbolized the giving up of social identity 3.40; when you join the sangha, you give up your separate identity 9.195

ideologies all kinds of ideologies by which we may be ensnared 12.654–6; clinging to ideologies 17.628–30; contemporary ideologies that are inimical to the Dharma 11.603; don't mix fashionable isms and ideologies with the Dharma 12.455,

12.476; the ideology behind the question 'Is Buddhism escapist?' 4.441; the truth must be conveyed in language which is familiar ideologically 7.159, 13.438; wrong views in the form of political ideologies 12.616–17

idleness *see* laziness

idols four idols, *see under* Bacon; idols can be metaphorical as well as literal 26.478

ignorance (Sanskrit *avidyā*, Pāli *avijja*)

the nature of ignorance
the cause of the human predicament 17.433–4; the cause of suffering 7.219; cosmic ignorance endeavours to satisfy its ceaseless craving for pleasure 7.47; the direct antithesis of *bodhi* 1.107, 3.193; however far back we go in time, we will never find where it began 16.219; ignorance and foolishness 11.261; the intellectual counterpart of lust-and-hate 1.19; it underlies the whole saṃsāric process 1.112, 18.180; its characteristic is to perceive things as different, mutually exclusive 7.411; made up of wrong views 1.112, 3.193–4; a natural condition of man, but not necessarily a permanent one 16.219; not an ultimate first cause of things 5.516–17; a primordial state 16.219; the root of all hindrances and obstacles to the spiritual life 18.180; the root of desire 7.126; the root-illusion that we are individual selves 7.360, 7.374–6, 7.383, 26.53; the schism between subject and object 15.524; twinborn with desire 1.232; we identify it for practical purposes, but it has no independent reality 17.377; when analysed, found to consist of five mental poisons 3.340

metaphors
'adding to the cemeteries': increasing craving and ignorance 10.608; the bodhisattva emerging from the eggshell of ignorance 3.231; darkness 3.130, 3.193; drunkenness 17.434; like the darkness in the egg before it's hatched 3.61; represented by father in Buddhist mythical literature 3.35; sleep 11.24, 16.170, 16.218–19; 'Worst of all stains is the stain of ignorance' (*Dhammapada*) 7.126

ignorance of what?
conditioned co-production 1.108; right view 1.107–8; the truth of suffering 7.220

the effects of ignorance
the Absolute is obscured by ignorance 1.364; avoiding doubt and indecision in a cloud of unawareness 17.613; belief in a personal God an example of ignorance 3.193–4; evil committed through ignorance 16.305; heedlessness out of ignorance 17.677; if you doubt that this world is the result of ignorance, is that due to your ignorance? 17.50; the ignorance of primitive humans 3.424–5, 3.468; in the depths of our being is another dimension of which we're mostly unaware 12.234; a little learning is more dangerous than complete ignorance 1.198; nihilism represents the worst tendencies of spiritual ignorance 17.243; only through ignorance do we think of ourselves as unenlightened 1.347

the Buddhist approach to ignorance
the start of the entire teaching 1.107; in Buddhism, ignorance, not sin, is the root evil 16.90, 17.134; ignorance in the sense of misunderstanding the Dharma 18.180; Siddhārtha Gautama confined by it 3.35; a very basic category of Buddhism 15.472

the poison of ignorance
refusal to see things as they really are 3.129; unawareness of reality, the basic poison 4.80; overcome by developing wisdom 11.404; sluggish and at the same time chaotic 13.183

getting rid of ignorance
antidote, see *nidāna* chain meditation; aspiration to get rid of ignorance 9.324; *avidyā* is very strong, so progress is gradual 10.152; becoming aware of our unawareness 11.24; dismantling the overall framework of ignorance 15.525; ignorance is you as you are totally, and must be totally transformed 19.18; one of the principal functions of the Enlightened mind 13.278; removing the jewel from the garment 16.222–3; symbolized by wrathful forms 13.68–9; 'teach me, being ignorant' 25.181; transforming it into *bodhi* 22.529; Vajrapāṇi trampling on ignorance 13.173; we can only get rid of it because it is not there 17.408; when giving a talk, don't conceal your ignorance 12.582; without transcending it there can be no escape from suffering 16.219

freedom from ignorance
the cessation of ignorance is the attainment of Enlightenment 1.114; freedom from ignorance 9.343; knowledge of the destruction of ignorance (*avidyāsrava*) 3.278; a progression from ignorance to knowledge 8.592

see also
as first *nidāna*, *see under* twelve cyclical *nidānas*; 'Housebuilder, I have seen you now', *see Dhammapada*/chapter 11; veil of ignorance, *see* two veils

Ihimaera, Witi v24

ikebana 8.390, 11.118, 23.36, 23.420

Il Convento, Tuscany introduction 2.730 (n619), 24.664 (n273); annual men's pre-ordination course 9.173, 9.189–90, 11.xvi, 24.7, 26.238, 26.261–2, 26.440; 'Eight Tuscan Haiku' 25.380; its history 26.276–9, 26.282; *The Journey to Il Convento* 26.261–80; a quantum leap 11.556; Sangharakshita's residence there 2.494, 11.562, 24.221–2, 24.225–8, 26.440; 'Tuscany 1983' (poem) 25.367

Ildefonso, St 13.600

ill will confessing ill will in a dream 4.46; the feeling of ill will when desire for sense experience is frustrated 11.122; a feeling of victimization coming from unacknowledged ill will 17.258; nothing so inimical to *dhyāna* as ill will 5.325–6; *see also* hatred

illiteracy *see* literacy

illness *see* sickness

illumination all four *vargas* illuminate the sangha 2.203, 2.722 (n559); all unillumined desire is really a groping in the dark for Enlightenment 7.307; Enlightenment: an illumination in which things become visible in their reality 2.55; Enlightenment is not only illumination and freedom, but also infinite and inexhaustible love 2.57; a flower is sacred, a tree holy, if you look at it with an illumined mind 7.284; 'Having experienced spiritual illumination, commune with it in solitude' 5.671–5; The Illuminating Voidness, the Illuminating Wisdom, and the Illuminating Manifestations' 18.614; illuminations from the tremendous impact of the Buddha's personality 7.492; 'the Illuminator', *see* Vairocana; mistaking psychic illumination for transcendental wisdom 18.251; Nirvāṇa: a state of absolute illumination 7.510; *Prabhākari* (Illuminating), *see under* ten *bhūmis*; the scientific approach tends to accumulate facts rather than illuminate principles 7.486–7; 'The shining Wisdom of Reality illumines all like the cloudless sky' 18.603; stories can be more illuminating than pages of psychological analysis 2.71

illusion (*māyā*)

introduction
the nature of *māyā* 14.215; can be used positively or negatively 5.606–7; speaking in terms of illusion draws attention to what the conditioned is like 5.603; the term can create misunderstanding when discussing Buddhism 16.453–4; in the highest sense the spiritual life is an illusion 14.592; using illusion to get rid of illusion 19.241; getting rid of illusion, reality is like a stained-glass window 5.606–7

magical illusions
a great crowd of people, conjured up at the crossroads 14.575; everything is like a magical illusion (Tibetan Buddhism) 12.296; the illusory elephant 14.501, 14.562, 16.452–3, 17.385–7, 19.79; the Indian rope trick 4.374–5, 12.185, 14.507, 19.80; so-called objective facts are like a magical illusion 14.143; 'The things of this samsaric world are all illusion' 5.602–8; the whole of existence is like a magical illusion 14.183, 14.187, 19.80

illusions
the ego-conception 17.xxiv, 7.290; ideas 19.233; illusion and decay 18.154; the passions 4.373–4; the sense in which the contemporary world view is based on illusion 14.506; the state of consciousness in which things appear separate 7.299

metaphysical illusions
the illusion in the Perfection of Wisdom must be understood precisely 14.575–6; in Advaita Vedānta 7.194–5, 7.596 (n299), 16.454; it is from a metaphysical point of view that the conditioned is illusory 14.505; it is metaphysically true that people are illusions, but they are pretty solid 13.300

relative and absolute
experiencing an illusion as an absolute reality gives rise to unskilful states 16.453; if we regard the relatively real as illusory our spiritual life falls to the ground 14.576; the illusory nature of relative experience 16.453, 19.233–4

Illustrated Weekly of India publishes Sangharakshita's poems 21.250, 22.103; review of Sangharakshita's poems 22.181–2; sponsors Tsaparang expedition 21.252, 21.421–2

images

introduction
definition of 'image' 26.208–9; archetypal images 3.80; any image has its limitations 4.31; being drawn to particular images 26.265–6; broken images 26.276, 26.278–9; different images appeal to people of different temperaments 14.589–90; how can Christian images be of significance to Buddhists? 26 269–70, 26.278–9; images are perceptions of real correspondences 26.209; in perceiving an image what one

perceives is in a sense oneself 26.271; reality can be mediated as much by images as by concepts 19.189; the significance of images can change 26.273–6; vehicle of psychological and spiritual truth 2.132

the language of images
communication through images 3.80–1; to describe the goal 2.132; emotions, poetry, myth and symbol, simile and metaphor 14.589, 16.16–19; the essence of poetry is imagery 26.208–10

see also
Buddha images; Buddhism speaking the language of images, *see under* language

imaginal faculty danger of alienation 19.189–90; has a conceptual side and an imaginative side 19.189; helps us bridge the gap between self and other 11.724–5; distinction between ordinary imagination and the imaginal faculty 12.559; the expression should not be taken too literally 26.271; a fusion of reason and emotion 3.11; image perceiving image 26.171; imaginal space 13.152; the journey through the imaginal world 26.265–6, 26.271; needed for the awakening of faith 17.674; our desire to satisfy instinct can be stronger than the desire to develop the imaginal faculty 15.359; Sangharakshita's imaginal faculty 26.268; vertical imagination and the divine eye 11.725

imagination

what is imagination?
an aspect of the *mano-vijñāna* 12.175; 'the capacity to emancipate oneself from one's present experience' (Johnson) 17.598; Coleridge's use of the term 8.458, 12.559, 12.744–5 (n378), 26.487; distinction between ordinary imagination and the imaginal faculty 12.559; the higher imagination developed by bringing together intellect and emotion 19.189; horizontal and vertical imagination 11.724–6; the imagination uses images 19.189; it is aroused by images based on a system of correspondence 26.210; that which appeals to the imagination can only perish with it (Hazlitt) 24.561; the truth of the imagination 12.182–3; what we imagine today we may do tomorrow 11.181; what the word meant to Blake and Coleridge 8.458; your own imagination will tell you 12.472

what imagination can do
egolessness through art and the imagination 26.190; from the flux of experience we abstract bits and pieces and imagine a continuity 19.376; the importance of the imagination 26.486; it can enhance the beauty of the world 8.579; it helps to enlist the cooperation of unconscious energies 3.41; linking with past and future to break out of the cocoon of the present 17.403; to eradicate craving, try using your imagination 17.597–8; a sense of the vastness of space through imagination 2.63; wandering imaginatively in high and remote regions 24.xxiv

using and developing the imagination
a balance between imagination and discipline 18.372–3; be more imaginative 4.624; fine as long as you are aware of what is happening 10.462–3; poetry 'enlarges the circumference of the imagination' 26.190; reading: an imaginative identification with a larger consciousness 4.353

Buddhism and the imagination
Buddhism views the evidence of the senses in the light of imagination 3.11; imagination and the Mahāyāna *sūtras* 1.355, 12.501; imagination as a pillar of Triratna (the FWBO) 12.472; imagination is needed for faith 9.110; the imaginative, archetypal element is very important in the spiritual life 19.25–6; imagine Enlightenment in such a way that you are energized and inspired 18.372–3; the kind of imagination that can access the *sambhogakāya* 18.88; poetic epithets for Nirvāṇa appeal to imagination 1.81; a section of a book on Buddhism devoted to the imagination 8.579–80; to understand what an Enlightened being really is requires an effort of imagination 4.6; using the imagination when taking the bodhisattva vows 4.59–60; we experience the *rūpaloka* by means of the imagination 12.559

imagination and other people
giving is a matter of imagination 17.598; imagination is the Dharma door to non-duality beyond self and other 11.726; often the way we treat other people is due to lack of imagination 5.153, 17.598; putting yourself imaginatively in the place of others 2.361, 4.570, 10.476, 11.724–5; with a vivid imagination, when you think of people, it's as though they're present 23.61

lack of imagination
can be mistaken for fearlessness 14.474, 16.278; indulging ourselves without considering the consequences 17.598; to see that actions have consequences 15.359; to spread the Dharma 8.268, 8.272

dangers of and to imagination
damage to the imagination in our modern era 26.240; the (horizontal) imagination tethered to worldly activity 11.724–5; giving precedence to the conceptional over the imaginative approach 14.430–1; if you preoccupy yourself with abstract ideas, you may lose your imagination 17.684; impaired by watching television 3.536; the readiness with which it loses itself in the future and in the past 7.285

see also
Blake on imagination, *see under* Blake; unreal imagination, *see abhūtaparikalpa*

imasmiṃ sati *see under pratītya-samutpāda*

imitation the difference between imitation and copying 19.56; imitating the Buddha 14.539–40, 19.54–6, 19.296; imitating Padmasambhava 19.55; imitating Vimalakīrti 16.495–6; you best imitate your teacher by being yourself 14.568

Imji Gelong ('English monk') 13.31, 22.224, 22.498

immanence all the Buddhas are within you 19.41–2; the *bodhicitta* is immanent in all forms of life 2.15; 'bright wisdom' is immanent, already contained within the ordinary human being 18.606; Buddhahood existing within the spiritual aspirant as the impulse behind their quest 7.312; Buddhahood is both immanent and transcendent 25.33; in the Buddhist tradition 11.656–7; the danger of taking metaphors about immanence literally 18.606–8; deep metaphysical waters 15.632–3; the danger of thinking that one is 'already Buddha' 10.438–40, 11.657, 11.689, 14.594, 17.390, 17.594; the language of immanence should come with a spiritual health warning 4.33, 11.657; not much point thinking that in your ultimate mind you are Buddha if it's just words 19.284; one doesn't want to adopt a substantialist or eternalist outlook 19.387; 'poised in the natural realm of Immanence' 18.344; polarization with transcendence 20.234; reality's mysterious immanence 2.43; *sahaja, see sahaja*; scratching the surface of one's being with a little meditation will not reveal the Buddha within 26.479; Tantric Buddhism sees reality as immanent in all phenomena 1.385

immersion being immersed in the *dhyānas* 18.580; the dangers of immersion in worldly life 18.422–4; don't just aim to get your work finished, but immerse yourself in the process 18.164–5; even if you're immersed in a Buddhist lifestyle, you still need to study 19.508; habits and social pressure keep us immersed in trivial pursuits 3.35; lotus flowers immersed in water 1.164, 3.307, 4.155, 5.240; pure awareness like that of a musician immersed in a symphony 15.202–3; *śīla*: immersion in Dharma life 4.104; to people immersed in worldly states of mind, the Dharma will appear negative 26.44; total immersion in the serene, radiant, and majestic world of the Dharma 22.225

immortality (*amata*) *amata* as a synonym for Nirvāṇa, *see under* deathless; *apramāda* is its basis 17.581; example of a word that is grammatically negative but means something positive 10.635, 17.565; how shall a mortal attain the immortal state? 1.237, 3.209, 3.579, 11.704–5, 26.472, 26.498; 'Immortality Ode', *see under* Wordsworth; immortality of the soul (Christianity) 2.85; mindfulness (*apramāda*) is the way to immortality (*Dhammapada*) 7.118, 17.581; self-transcending 3.208–9; 'Truth is immortal (or deathless) speech' 13.644, 14.293, 19.294–5; vase of immortality, *see amṛta kalaśa*

impact the Buddha's impact 7.492, 14.16; Dharma Day celebrates the impact of the Buddha upon *ourselves* 11.418–19; the Dharma's emotional impact: *saṃvega* 14.470–1; 'My lectures had far more impact than I realized at the time' 24.16; our psychophysical organism shields us from the impact of reality 12.201; Padmasambhava's impact on Tibet 13.10–11; poetry's emotional impact 26.118; speak plainly about the impact of the Dharma on your life 14.446

impartiality activism: setting an example of impartiality 12.348–9; love 'impartial as the sun' 25.203; symbolized by the raincloud and the sun in the *White Lotus Sūtra* 16.125; Upasena rejoices impartially in his own merits and those of others 10.541–2; *see also upekṣā*

impatience blaming someone for making you impatient is like blaming a beggar for making you mean 14.597; don't be impatient, especially with other people 26.81; the more committed should help the less committed rather than feeling impatient with them 26.44; you ought to get a bit impatient with yourself sometimes 4.368; the young getting impatient with the old 17.523; your enemy isn't making you impatient, but

giving you the chance to practise patience 4.413–14

impermanence (Sanskrit *anitya*, Pāli *anicca*)

THE NATURE OF IMPERMANENCE

introduction
simple account 1.486; law of impermanence 8.xxiv, 9.251–2; a truth which squares with our experience 7.131; we can see it at work every day 10.327

Buddhist tradition
Buddhism in one word: impermanence 11.445–6; the whole of Buddhism can be reduced to this principle 10.327; you're not a Buddhist if you don't accept that all compounded things are impermanent 12.657; Buddhism's relentless thoroughness in exploring impermanence 2.85; the subtlety of early Buddhists' quest to understand its mystery 15.183; cosmological background 2.85–6; 'Impermanent are all component things': *sabbe saṅkhāra aniccā* 1.171, 2.30, 2.85; it implies the whole of the Buddha's teaching, both practical and theoretical 11.446; its relation to conditionality 3.183; the keynote of the five *skandhas* 15.183; in relation to the three levels of wisdom 17.129–30; to believe that all compound things are impermanent is Dhamma (Ambedkar) 9.288–9

what is impermanent?
breaking the idea down in detail helps to hammer it home 15.180; all conditioned things, including the human race and the solar system 12.356–7; all phenomena will tell you that they are impermanent if you attend to them 19.70; all things are transitory 7.48–9; association with people can only last a short time 18.566–7; either everything is permanent or everything is changing 7.132; every state and form of phenomenal existence must one day end 1.171; everything is slipping from beneath our feet 7.49; how delicately contingent are all conditioned things 14.506–7; impermanence applies to the subject as well as the object of experience 7.208–9; impermanence of the body 15.110–11, 16.493–4; it is all around us 11.448; 'Life Is King' 25.324; nothing unchanging in the mind 3.216; only the Truth endures 7.343; *sic transit gloria mundi* 22.206; since everything is fleeting, life is fleeting 19.244; the span of a man's life a single breath 14.60, 26.296–7; we cannot hear, see, smell, touch, taste or think of anything which is not impermanent 7.132

RESPONSES

failing to see it
the fact of impermanence is obvious to common sense, but we don't act on it 17.136; the gods don't want to realize that what they are enjoying is impermanent 19.496; holding awareness of impermanence at bay 17.397; it's hard to realize the truth of impermanence 3.216–17; it cannot be fully understood as a concept, for in our heart we are afraid of it 17.378; powerful measures are needed to break through one's resistance to this simple idea 15.180–1; seeing what is impermanent as permanent (*viparyāsa*) 3.280, 12.612–13, 16.453; we must respect the power of this truth and recognize how deeply we resist it 17.378; we say we 'know' it, but if the house burns down, we don't shrug 12.612–13

grief
desire for the transitory is doomed to disappointment 7.307; feeling loss unselfishly rather than selfishly 12.612–13; grief that the so beautiful should be so brief 25.281; impermanence and suffering 7.116; only one exceptionally deep in love with life will find it sweeter for its transitoriness 1.129; when someone close to you dies, life starts teaching you about impermanence 18.560–1

the positive aspect of impermanence
change is not just about decay, it can be for the better 13.228; for a Buddhist it can be a source of exhilaration 14.508–9; it implies not only change, but the potential for transformation 2.296; it is a death sentence, but also our hope of freedom from death 17.163; it is what enables us to turn our lives towards Enlightenment 15.147; it makes growth and development possible 9.232, 9.251–2, 9.288, 17.444; a source of delight 18.54; things are impermanent but they are also beautiful 26.241–2; while the vein lasted, it was gold 25.281; worldly things pass away, but spiritual things do not 9.478–9

taking it to heart
changing an intellectual understanding into an actual experience 5.425; coming to terms with our own impermanence 15.145; could singing a hymn at school have instilled the truth of impermanence? 26.294; insight into the truth of impermanence 2.296, 5.463–4, 15.147, 18.579; transforming the concept into embodied experience 16.186; 'When the transiency of life strikes deeply into one's heart' 18.554

LESSONS IN IMPERMANENCE

symbols and metaphors
the burning house 16.69–70; Dance of Death 2.85, 13.230–1, 25.415; everything will flow away, like the water of a great river 13.147; flowers 9.324, 11.240–1, 13.252–3, 17.331; hourglass and skull 26.297; the melody of impermanence 2.74, 3.382, 13.131–2; an unbounded, unbroken flow 15.205

in nature
'Life is sweet, the windbells seemed to be saying, but not lasting' 21.126; seen in the changing seasons 3.345; seen in the city and in the countryside 17.378; in the countryside 13.227–8

seeing a leaf fall
could be an experience that permanently changes you 5.432; Enlightenment arising on seeing a leaf fall 3.272, 4.145, 8.119; seeing a leaf fall, you see everything fall 5.464, 18.13; the teaching of the leaves that change must come to all 25.195; the world is full of falling leaves 25.221

in poetry
'all things ripen toward the grave' 7.51; expressed in English poetry 14.507–8; in the writings of non-Buddhist poets 5.641; in Japanese poetry 3.345; in Keats' odes 3.345; poems about impermanence 26.398; reflections on transitoriness in poetry 13.228

recollection of impermanence
antidote to craving 3.128–9, 3.345, 4.75–6; for the breaking up of individuality 5.32; considering the precariousness of life 17.161–4; contemplating impermanence as the antidote to possessiveness 17.657; contemplation of decay, *see* contemplation of decay; different contemplations for the faith-follower and the doctrine-follower 18.154–5; during the practice starting to relish the object as though it were permanent 17.680–1; for the uprooting of egoism 10.531; if you do not meditate on impermanence in the morning, by midday you will have many desires 4.265; leading to insight 4.145, 5.431, 15.147; might it give rise to a negative feeling that nothing really matters? 5.433; in everyday life 5.431–2, 17.100; not abstract contemplation but applied to everything around you 17.99–100; as one of the four preliminary meditations 5.547; reflecting on impermanence when you are young 13.228–9; through observing a tree outside the window 13.227–8, 24.xxiv, 24.66; in use in the Buddha's time 5.35; weakens the illusion of a separate self 15.147; as *lakṣaṇa*, *see* three *lakṣaṇas*

see also
the Buddha's last words, *see under* Buddha I/the Buddha's last days/last words; entrance to the *vimokṣa-mukha* of *animitta*, *see* three *vimokṣa-mukhas*; the monster of impermanence, *see under* wheel of life

importance

IMPORTANT THINGS IN GENERAL

importance itself
considering important things that don't matter much 17.283–4; a culture often doesn't have a word for its most important principle 4.168–9; exaggerating the importance of what we do and minimizing what others do 10.601, 17.587; human beings are more important than religion 9.352, 10.252; human life is the most important subject we could concern ourselves with 12.82; investing oneself with importance by being the bearer of what is important 18.493; knowing we will die, things regarded as important become unimportant 23.92; *praśaṃsā* (eulogy) draws attention to importance, not to be taken literally 5.199

important things in everyday life
being at ease socially 10.644–5; bring a spirit of non-harming to sexual activities 3.322; the countryside 10.329–30; don't let the business of living get in the way of what's important 26.34; exercise 9.442, 20.303; a good relationship with parents 3.599–60, 4.328–9, 9.447–8, 12.391–2, 16.296–8; the importance of lifestyle 2.351–2, 2.517; keeping a good reputation when living in a village 10.644; keeping our surroundings beautiful 9.444–5; livelihood 3.582; making a will 15.146; meeting material needs 9.340; the relative unimportance of lifestyle 2.587–8; the sense of smell 24.567; speaking properly 3.539

important things in relation to children
education should do no harm to the child 18.285; physical education 9.442; teaching empathy 1.498, 3.542–3, 10.477; teaching religion in schools with conviction 12.51

important Western concepts
evolution as a concept of modern thought 12.83–4; a list of ideas that have been important in the West 12.463–4

questions about important things
'What is the most important question in your life?' 18.508–9; why do people feel it's so important to be right? 19.293;

why is friendship so important? 9.309; why is it important to look like others to communicate with them? 12.523–4

IMPORTANT THINGS ABOUT ONESELF AND OTHER PEOPLE

important emotional matters
be aware of your feelings 15.151–2; be honest about the importance you give to pleasure 17.302; being accepted and loved 17.184–5; carry your basic and primitive emotions along with you 16.102; contentment is a very important quality 15.427; cultivate detachment towards bliss, as the Buddha did 2.108; develop a positive emotional counterpart to intellectual understanding 26.37; emotion is such an important part of our lives 25.106; enthusiasm (Ambedkar) 9.134–5, 9.199–200, 10.370, 10.388–9; establishing what you really want to do 4.151–2, 10.604–5, 17.674; feeling rational guilt 16.311; freedom from fear and anxiety 10.501; the importance of emotions in spiritual life 9.322–3, 16.129–30; a positive emphasis 10.513; we should actually feel ourselves living, feel ourselves growing 16.130

important aspects of personal experience
being able to discern what is relevant to oneself 18.517–18; contact with the true self 16.173; don't attach too much importance to your own strengths 4.41; dreams 12.199, 12.685; keeping in contact with spiritual experience 4.272; knowing ourselves 1.555, 12.100; learning to think 12.475–6; making 'a good death' 2.231–2; a mythic aspect 25.100; pleasure 5.327, 19.91; a store of merit 15.396; the workings of the gravitational pull in our lives 3.251; you may fail, but the important thing is that you should try 1.553

important things in relation to other people
accepting help 3.42; as well as feeling *with* people, it is important to feel *for* them 4.68; being able to hear the truth is as important as being able to tell it 17.239–40; being positive towards others in spite of all their failings and your own 4.180; being friendly to visitors to a Buddhist centre 12.60; being imprisoned by giving importance to being a successful person 18.101–2; having a network of long-standing relationships 13.450, 18.336–7; honouring commitments 18.487–8; learning how to get on with other people 9.189; making the Buddhist path known to others 15.94–5; other people play an important part in our lives 12.602; our relationship with our mother 16.102; paying attention to the person speaking 1.519, 1.575, 16.579; teaching from your own experience 10.223–4; 'vertical' contact, to strengthen motivation 12.382

IMPORTANT THINGS ABOUT BUDDHIST LIFE AND PRACTICE

important things in Buddhism
advertising 8.253–4; all the important doctrines and practices are distributed among the *bhūmis* 2.170; Buddhism's historical and spiritual importance 4.641; common mental states and ideals more important than common rules 10.561; the constant repetition of positive actions 17.525–7; distinguishing skilful from unskilful 17.617; dying well 8.142; freedom of individual judgement 11.508–9; the heroic virtues 13.230; homage 15.720; knowing about the life of the Buddha 11.711, 12.507–8, 19.55, 26.511; Nāgārjuna's *Mūlamadhyamakakārikā* 1.311; the Pāli canon 16.531–2; protesting against misrepresentation of the Dharma 4.127; right motive 1.15; unity among Buddhists 9.268, 10.282–3

important terms and teachings
conditionality 12.21; the distinction between *jñāna* and *vijñāna* 3.356, 14.315–16; Going for Refuge 1.410, 2.430, 13.195; harmony and balance 13.328; *kuśala*: 'clever, skilful, expert' 2.340; the positive *nidānas* 1.114; right doctrine 7.524; right view 11.160, 11.653–4, 12.616; spiritual hierarchy 4.171; Stream Entry 15.531–2; *termas* 12.300; 'This being, that becomes' 10.142; transference of merit 2.269; the Vinaya 8.307–8

important practices
being determined and persevering 18.411; ceremonies 18.378–9; communication 11.258; confession 1.509, 4.309–10; devotion 2.242, 4.297–300, 12.24; Dharma study 1.169–70, 9.267–8; an element of self-sacrifice 4.459–60; faith 1.290; giving words their correct meaning 9.479; investigating the causes of things 3.261, 7.115; *kalyāṇa mitratā* 3.578, 10.527, 18.367; listening to one's *kalyāṇa mitra* 9.515; magical practices 2.215; making clear distinctions 9.271–2; *mettā* 5.39–40, 10.173, 10.653, 12.24–5; mindfulness 10.349; openness 10.217, 10.570; overcoming fear 10.259; perfect effort 1.566; prompt action 4.468; receptivity 19.219; right livelihood 11.376; right motive 1.425, 21.314; right view 1.112; sacramental actions: mantras and *mudrās* 1.374–5; the Sevenfold Puja 4.49, 11.221; silence 11.202; spiritual friendship

12.669–70, 12.675; taking refuge in Amitābha 2.566; total awareness 4.378–87; worship 1.30, 3.69

important things about ethics
awareness of the consequences of one's actions 26.61; ethical acts in relation to egolessness 1.435; factual accuracy 2.376–7, 9.445; the first precept is the most important manifestation of Going for Refuge 2.358; honesty about oneself 1.555; more important than more glamorous teachings 3.331–2; right speech 1.513–14, 2.374, 12.33

important things about meditation
associating meditation with enjoyment 5.375–7; the distinction between mundane and transcendental meditation 26.199; emphasis on direct personal experience 12.56–7; meditating with others 10.274–5; protecting the mind is more important than protecting the body 18.80–1; refresh your meditation practice from time to time 12.644; quality is more important than quantity 5.54; regular meditation 5.375–6, 5.378–9

important things in spiritual life
aids to devotion 20.259; appreciation of nature 16.387; the arts 10.506–7; awareness of whether your tendency is towards eternalism or nihilism 3.202; beauty 12.308; changing the mind 12.466–7; changing ourselves 19.89; a correct intellectual grasp of the Dharma 1.112; distinguish between what you need to do to develop and what you want to do 4.91; don't carry your ordinary habits into the spiritual life 18.106; don't develop an examination mentality to the Dharma 9.328; enjoy your spiritual life 16.284–5, 19.91–2; free yourself from guilt 1.509; get on with practising the Dharma 22.477; keep your promises, so don't make them lightly 4.484, 12.485, 18.487; keep a balance between what you know and what you do 15.472–4; *know* that you experience something 10.542; maintain momentum in your practice 3.305; material progress is good, but spiritual progress is more important 10.346–7; the more important something is, the less there is to say 1.579–80; myth, imagination, emotions 16.129–30, 26.486; positive conditions 12.652, 15.289–90; preparation 3.272–3, 4.42–3; rational and mystical approaches 12.515; relate traditional accounts of the scriptures to your own experience 5.250–1; see the ethical ideal in positive terms 15.360; silence and emptiness 7.322, 12.557–8; the spiritual faculties 3.298; the stage of irreversibility 1.260; take full advantage of your spiritual opportunities 26.532; truth and righteousness are more important than the externals of religion 1.274

important things about the sangha
the Buddha regarded the sangha as being of supreme importance 3.395; the creation of sangha in the West 3.396, 12.81; a good relationship between teachers and students 9.447; harmony 15.515–17, 18.15; helping one another 9.194–5; to let us know that we are cared for 17.185

Impressionism 1.104

imprisonment *see* prison

impulses an animal acts from instinct, a child from impulse, a woman from emotion, a man from reason 7.138; the *bodhicitta*: a powerful impulse that becomes the master-current of your being 2.300; Buddhahood is the impulse behind the spiritual aspirant's quest 7.312; the Christian idea that your natural impulses are sinful 4.597; dissatisfaction is a powerful and positive impulse 3.463; don't just follow blind impulses, but think what is good for everybody 25.105; the early stages of spiritual life are a struggle between lower and higher impulses 7.358; even a healthy sexual impulse pertains to a relatively lower level of consciousness 1.10; for a long time we are just a bundle of conflicting impulses and ideas 19.98; becoming more aware of passing emotional states, we're less likely to act impulsively 11.732; Sangharakshita's life determined by impulse and intuition, not reason and logic 2.406, 11.584–5; we should resist the impulse to make a commodity of ourselves 18.122

impurity can the Buddhas take away impurity? 16.312–13; a condition of non-integration 19.385; impure mind, *see under* mind/what is the mind like?/purity; meditation on impurity of the body, *see aśubha bhāvanā*; *rajas* 10.503; spewing up your impurities 10.450–1; ten impurities, *see* ten impurities

Inamdar family v24

inattentiveness *see asaṃprajanya*

in-between practice 19.321

incense burn incense before a Buddha image and recite *sūtras* until you feel free of guilt 1.509; burning frankincense, myrrh, and *kifr* 26.497; burning Tibetan incense in the morning, Indian in the evening 11.237, 26.493; Dhardo Rimpoche's mindfulness:

incense and candles for everyone 12.433–4, 22.339–40, 22.424; the effect of incense in a puja 11.235–6; guide to the practical use of incense 24.567–8; incense has a meaning 26.497–8; incense in ancient Greece 26.494–5; incense in Egypt 26.494–5; Indian, Tibetan, Chinese, and Japanese 26.495–6; 'Let my life burn like incense/ Before thy precious shrine' 25.219; one of the three traditional offerings 1.408, 3.340, 9.324, 9.462, 13.253, 13.417; Sangharakshita used to hold incense parties in London 24.567, 26.495–6; just burning a little incense at the shrine of religion 12.23; Montaigne on incense 24.567–8; 'one whose thoughts have been burned up like incense' 10.606; 'perpetual incense' 6.xxviii; representing faith 25.42; Sangharakshita fond of tuberose-scented incense 22.74; the scent of incense in Indian houses 26.493–4; the smoke of the incense stick 25.305; worship of the Buddha with incense 14.193

incest the case of a man imprisoned for committing incest 23.195–6; incest and human society 11.322–3

inclusiveness extreme 8.167; inclusive language 11.640–1; to include someone in too conscious a way is to exclude them 11.641

incomposite *see asaṃskṛta*

indecision *see under* ten fetters/second fetter; *see also* decisions

indefinability human beings are indefinable, as Jean-Paul Sartre says 2.99–100; the indefinability of the real nature of things 1.65; the nature of existence is indefinable 1.65; pain is a sensation, and hence indefinable 1.127; reality's unique indefinable essentiality 2.43; the realm of myth is a realm of indefinable meanings 16.528; spiritual experience is a living and electric thing, utterly indefinable 7.144; *śūnyatā* is a synonym for the indefinable mystery of the true nature of things 13.119

independence the independence of the creative mind 11.25; reasonable and unreasonable independence 18.387; some people would apparently rather preserve their independence and remain in *saṃsāra* 7.261; there's no such thing as independence 4.424; to think that a true Buddhist should be independent of external aids is a misunderstanding 7.258–61; why Buddhism takes up an independent attitude towards the external world 7.268; you need to be prepared to stand on your own two feet 15.283

indescribable Enlightenment is indescribable, unclassifiable 17.242; paradoxes used to describe the indescribable 26.201; reality is logically indescribable 10.142; the truth is indescribable, hence a matter for personal experience 1.206

Index Expurgatorius 7.246, 7.603 (n346)

India

HISTORY

ancient India
Jambudvīpa 11.297; Aryan invasion 16.362; fertility of the Indian mind 1.61; no democratic political life 10.478; no welfare state 10.449; perhaps a kinship between ancient India and ancient Greece 10.467; prosperity 10.478; what family life was like 15.408–9; writing considered profane 16.363

later periods
Gupta period 12.239, 16.367; Pala dynasty 7.471, 12.239, 12.569–70; Muslim invasion, *see under* Indian Buddhism/ decline of Buddhism; the British in India and the introduction of English 7.55; British Indian Association 8.53; the Inner Line Permit (ILP) 22.240–1, 22.596 (n202), 23.374; North-East Frontier Agency 7.462

twentieth century
Vinoba Bhave's land donation scheme 17.199–20; Dacca communal riots 20.159; Anglo-Indian orphans 21.346–8; relations with China 8.308–10, 9.69, 12.434–5, 21.200, 22.211, 22.545–52; McMahon Line 22.545, 22.549

Independence
Dr Ambedkar's activities at that time 9.62; brought freedom of speech 21.348–9; can be seen as an end or a beginning 8.225; the promise of an egalitarian society 10.xxiii–iv; Sangharakshita speaks to a crowd in Kausali on Independence Day 20.222–3; sympathy for Buddhism after Independence 8.xxviii; talks about 20.190; use of Buddhist symbols in flag and official seal 7.447, 8.xxviii, 8.323, 9.355; Partition 20.168–71, 21.69, 21.104–6, 22.577 (n56)

INDIAN LIFE AND CUSTOMS

the country
austere beauty 20.111–12; changes that have taken place 10.328; Himalayas, *see* Himalayas; hydroelectric dams 22.330–1; pollution 10.291; seasons 16.116–17; visiting an Indian village 3.296–7, 10.292–3

Indian life and character
character of Indian people 13.4–5, 16.421, 16.423; contrast between Indians and Tibetans 13.3–5, 17.556, 17.627, 19.399; the decency of relations between the sexes 24.18, 24.116; drinking alcohol regarded as disreputable 17.257; family life 15.102, 15.484–5, 19.253; Indian houses 23.344–5, 26.493–4; poverty 10.lvii, 20.109–10; prosperity 10.297; rich people's attitude to the poor 17.212; the attitude that work is inherently unspiritual 15.278–9; sexual morality 15.485; tendency to look down on physical work 10.216, 15.404; an understanding of personal service 4.609–10; violence against women 10.lvii, 10.lxii, 20.382–3

customs
customs involving heads and feet 16.381–2; dowry system 9.217; eating customs in different areas 20.120; marriage ceremonies 9.217, 9.335, 20.181–2; other ceremonies, *see under* ceremonies; sanitary habits 20.235–6

religion and culture
aesthetics 10.567, 16.326–7; the belief that worldly benefits can be obtained by magical means 15.682; continuity of religious tradition 12.254; a cultural renaissance linked to the revival of Buddhism 7.447–8; dialects share words with Buddhism, with different meanings 9.480–2, 9.484; the idea of *ahiṃsā* permeates Indian religious consciousness 8.448; in India prostrations are part of everyday life 15.672; the *jivanmukta* at Cape Comorin 20.240–1; mythology and folklore 16.399; the power of astrology in India 22.307; religious diversity 9.348–9; stereotyped view 3.45; spiritual life has a traditional underpinning almost entirely lacking in the West 24.401

Indian classical music
Ali Akbar Khan at the Royal Festival Hall 24.372; Asian Music Circle (London) 23.327; the *bhairava* mode 14.472; a concert in Benares 24.528; the difference between Indian and Western music 7.83; greatest when its inspiration is most spiritual 7.83; an influence on the Beatles 26.258; *kirtan* 17.81, 17.719 (n87), 20.185–90; learning to listen to it 7.14, 7.81–3, 20.120–1; Northern and Southern styles 7.82; a performance of devotional songs that approached the divine 22.293–4; ragas 20.187; a recital of devotional music 22.77; *sistrum* 22.293, 22.602 (n241); Tukloji Maharaj plays at Vaiśākha Purṇimā in Nagpur 22.163

Indian popular music
film music 20.350; folk songs 7.59

POLITICS

a secular state
caste system incompatible with a secular state 9.354; *Is the Republic of India Secular?* 8.228–9, 8.689 (n176); more secular as a result of mass conversion to Buddhism 9.429; what that means 8.228–9, 9.349, 9.351, 10.414–15, 22.305

politics
Constitution 9.xii, 9.9, 9.32; foreign policy 22.341; political boundaries 7.462; politicians almost deified by their followers 10.37–8; Republican Party of India (RPI) 10.188, 10.693 (n228)

government
census 8.291–2, 9.152, 9.174; the Eminent Buddhists' requests to the government 22.342–3; failure to acknowledge Dr Ambedkar's conversion 9.133; Indian National Congress 7.56, 7.60, 7.557–8 (n75); Lok Sabha 9.10, 9.69, 9.126, 9.553 (n66); on missionaries' methods 8.115–16; response to the campaign for Vaiśākha Pūrṇimā to be a public holiday 8.164–6; withdrawal of grants from Dalit Buddhists 8.250–2

see also
Ambedkar; art; Dooars; festivals, *see under* Hinduism; Hindu Code Bill; Hinduism; hospitality to guests, *see under* hospitality; Indian Buddhism; individual cities and towns; Manu; marriage; Sangharakshita in India, *see* Sangharakshita II 2; tribal people, *see* Adivasi

Indian Buddhism

introduction
'A Bird's-Eye View of Indian Buddhism' 2.452–3, 7.485–513, 22.461, 26.585; Buddhism and Indian culture 1.57–8, 11.512–13; for Buddhists India is the *puṇya bhūmi*, the sacred land 10.381; India as the *buddha-kṣetra* 10.254

THE DISAPPEARANCE OF BUDDHISM FROM INDIA

the background and the consequences
Atīśa finds texts in Tibet no longer available in India, a sign of decline 12.577; the destruction was taking place at the time of Milarepa 18.402; the Hinduization of Buddhist India 22.200; the loss of sacred texts 14.264, 15.185; some Indian monks sought refuge in Tibet 18.402; the ramifications extended far beyond the history of Buddhism 12.236–7; Buddhism

was not entirely lost 7.71; 'India dates her misfortunes since the disappearance' 8.41, 8.632; Buddhism was almost completely forgotten for 800 years 10.166

reasons for the disappearance
brief summary 10.308, 22.329; Dr Ambedkar's account and distress 9.66–7, 9.70; an account of the reasons by Dr Nalinaksha Dutt 8.120–3; Sangharakshita spent a long time reflecting on the reasons 12.236; (1) the centralization of monastic life 7.459–60, 9.237, 9.390, 12.237–8; (2) dependence on patronage 9.390–1, 9.393, 12.238–9, 19.481–2; (3) the hostility of the brahmins 7.233–5, 8.122–3, 9.236–7, 10.565, 12.239–40; (4) the partial absorption of Buddhism by Hinduism 7.459, 8.122, 9.237, 12.240–2; (5) the Muslim invasion of India 7.460, 9.236–7, 9.391–2, 11.270, 12.242–3, 14.264, 17.155, 18.3, 25.32, 26.276; (6) separation between monastic and lay Buddhists 8.122, 9.390, 9.392

THE BUDDHIST REVIVAL IN MODERN INDIA

the situation before Dr Ambedkar's conversion
rediscovery in 19th century 9.46; contribution of Anagarika Dharmapala 8.42, 8.97–8, 8.109–10, 8.244, 9.237–8, 12.561; the founding of the Maha Bodhi Society (1891) 7.444, 8.38–40; the tide of revival 20.419–20; 'Is there Buddhism in India?' (1953 article) 7.225–35; small Buddhist population 7.231–2, 7.601 (n336), 8.158, 8.197, 8.203, 22.304, 22.329; attempts to promote Buddhism pre-Ambedkar 22.270–2; 'It was not going to be easy to revive Buddhism in the land of its birth' 21.169; pilgrims to the Buddhist holy sites rarely think of helping Buddhism in India 8.176; the tree of Buddhist revival can only grow as high as its roots are deep 8.218–19; the effect of the return of the sacred relics 7.466, 10.93; effect of the Dalai Lama's presence in India 7.467, 8.237; the 2,500th Buddha Jayanti, *see under* festivals; until Dr Ambedkar it was a minority movement 8.234–5

survivals of ancient Buddhism in the modern era 7.460–5
Bauls, singers of mystic songs 7.461; Bengali (or Barua) Buddhists, *see* Bengali Buddhists; Orissa villagers who worship the *Śūnya Puruṣa* 7.461; worshippers of Ayyappan, *see* Ayyappan

revival in modern India
1956 as a 'year of wonders' 8.237–8; the Dhamma Revolution, *see* Ambedkar, Dalits, Dhamma Revolution; one of the strangest events in the history of religions 7.446–7; study of Pāli, Sanskrit, Tibetan, and Chinese 7.447; lights the way to a better life for India 7.470; a rising wave 12.595; challenging conditions for Dharma practice 3.313; objective of spreading Buddhism throughout India 9.341; 'Buddhism in India Today' (1959) 7.458–70; the 'ethnic overlap': Ladakhi, Tamang, Tais, Sikkimese 7.462–4; founding and history of TBMSG (Triratna), *see* Triratna I/Triratna in India; number of Buddhists 8.291–2, 9.152, 9.476–7, 12.400–1

see also
India at the time of the Buddha, *see under* Buddha I/life after Enlightenment; Mahāsāṃghikas; Sarvāstivādins; Tantric Buddhism; the three great phases of Indian Buddhism, *see yānas*/three *yānas*

Indian Buddhist Society 9.151

Indian rope trick 4.374–5, 12.185, 14.507, 19.80

indifference becoming indifferent to objects of perception 7.358–9; the besetting sin of Buddhism 26.15; Christian tolerance is a product of impotence and indifference 7.381; the danger of *upekṣā* being mistaken for indifference 5.209–10, 19.527; distinguishing detachment from indifference 23.60; four things to which the bodhisattva must be indifferent 14.189; the hateful indifferentism of the West 24.401; the indifference of a lover 25.489; indifference to hardship 16.207; in the modern world, non-attachment could be confused with indifference 18.331–3, 18.336–7; it's easier to transform hatred into love than to transform indifference into love 15.431; tolerance does not mean indifference 1.428, 10.83; a way of overcoming indifference to the world's suffering 13.81; 'The worst feeling you can have towards somebody is indifference' 15.431–2

indignation at the problems of the world 3.616; righteous indignation 1.557–8, 17.601–2

indirect methods they can become ends in themselves 19.469; how far can indirect methods take us? 25.140–1; as well as meditation (the direct method), indirect methods are also needed 5.635; a list of indirect methods 11.116–20, 11.148; of

raising the level of consciousness 2.387, 5.635–6, 11.466

individual

introducing the term
three senses of the word individual: statistical, psychological, and true 15.534; the English language has no word for true individuality 2.474; distinction between individual and true individual 3.417; to William Blake the individual was sacred and inviolable 8.555; the modern view of the individual as 'quasi-sacred absolute' 13.385, 13.459, 13.464

THE TRUE INDIVIDUAL

the nature of the true individual
the artist as true individual 3.505–17; the *bodhicitta* arises out of the interaction of true individuals 4.30–1; committed to the Three Jewels 3.473; distinguished from the individualist 3.470, 13.457, 13.460, 13.464, 13.483; each individual is a pattern 18.286; encourages individuality in others 3.473; every true individual is a whole species in himself 3.470, 26.41; he doesn't put pressure on people, but can't be pressurized 14.578; his own greatest work of art 3.471; implication of the ultimate reality of the individual 1.343; individuals are incommensurable 26.41; it is the individual that expresses the universal 16.132; keeping promises requires individuality 12.485; not king of the jungle but an indefatigable earthworm 3.619; not psychologically dependent on others 3.470; nothing but a succession of *dharmas* 1.252; only an individual can be ethical 15.359; the reflection of the Absolute in the mirror of individual consciousness 1.283; someone who has developed reflexive consciousness 11.363; standing up for what one believes in 3.618; their emergence in the Axial Age 3.426–8, 10.229, 11.354–5, 12.592; they stand on their own two feet and maintain harmony with the way things are 18.136; through the individual is seen the universal 3.469; you never really depend on anybody except yourself 19.284

qualities of the true individual
aloneness 3.472–3; cannot easily be labelled 17.239; characteristics 3.468–73, 16.308; contentment 15.275; fidelity 3.563; free of group conditioning 3.468; moral sensitivity 15.96; not an eccentric 3.470; positive emotions 3.472; self-awareness 3.468–70, 18.136; they can live without a mask 25.95; unfathomable 14.580–6; unique, unrepeatable 14.581; unpopular 3.471–2

examples
the bodhisattva as the individual *par excellence* 14.580; the Buddha as an example 11.358–9, 26.72; great Buddhists as exemplars of true individuality 6.621; Milarepa 18.136; Ruciraketu, *see under Sūtra of Golden Light*

HOW TO BECOME AN INDIVIDUAL

becoming an individual
awareness is the first fruit of one's development as an individual 18.300–1; become more aware of self, others, the environment, Reality 3.60; becoming more individual, one has more in common with other individuals 17.550; being able to go forth shows that you are an individual 5.680; the characteristics of the consciously evolving individual 4.656, 26.71; confession motivated by desire to develop as an individual 16.308; development of true individuality 4.30; discipline to prepare the way for individuality 18.359; doing your best to become a true individual 13.462; the happy, healthy individual you have become must die (spiritual death) 5.32; how does one become an individual? 8.550; in terms of the breaking of the fetters 3.416–22; more likely to arise at times of social unrest? 15.488–91; need to attack traditions that hinder their development 13.477–8; realize that actions have consequences 15.358; restrain your intellectual side and cultivate your emotional side 26.40; the true individual and integration 3.486–92; the true individual and the spiritual community 3.416–22, 8.547–8; what makes one a true individual 3.416–22; you can't produce an individual by force 18.357–8; you differ from others simply by being yourself 3.470

Buddhism and the individual
alienation seems to be an inevitable stage in their development 15.743; Buddhism is whatever conduces to the Enlightenment of the individual 16.76; the Buddhist movement exists to support the individual's development 3.457; the decision to follow the spiritual path can be made only by an individual 3.417; the Dharma is concerned with the development of the individual 26.39, 26.72; does recognition of the individual contradict the *anātman* doctrine? 3.492, 11.364; for *arhants*, the idea of individual attainment has vanished 1.179; four kinds of individual in *Tiratana Vandanā* 3.412–13, 3.416; the individual-in-relation-to-Buddhahood 13.391–2,

13.399, 13.412, 13.456, 13.460, 13.477; has great confidence in the potential of the individual 11.359–60; deeply convinced of the value of the individual 11.362, 17.21–2; one who goes effectively for Refuge is *ipso facto* an individual 2.568; places the individual at the forefront of its teaching 9.285, 11.358; recognizes the freedom of the individual 10.281; the spiritual life is dedicated to the development of the individual 15.266–7; we need not think of 'Buddhism', just whatever helps the individual to evolve 19.543–4

recognizing an individual
accepting someone's individuality means accepting they may think differently from you 17.53–4; organizations don't see people as individuals 11.359; to the extent that you are individual, you can recognize another as more individual 15.717; to know an individual, you need individuality, and a warm, empathizing regard 14.581

THE INDIVIDUAL AND OTHERS

the statistical individual
happy with what the group provides 11.357–8; he does not think for himself 11.353–4; a member of the group 3.417, 3.437; most of us are individual only in a statistical sense 3.60, 3.434–5, 13.458; powerlessness 9.284–5, 18.457–8; *pṛthagjanas*: people who are not individuals 3.434

the individual and the group
the Buddha was concerned with the development of the individual, not the group 26.39; the significance of the individual above the group 13.448; conflict between the group and the true individual 11.xxii, 13.457, 13.461–2; creative tension 11.355–6; distinguishing between what you do as an individual and as a group member 15.674; encourage individual development in groups to which you have to belong 3.618; the group came before the individual 11.352; the group can swallow up the individual 12.644; 'the individual is swallowed up in Leviathan' 13.485; the group is the enemy of the true individual 11.48; one can legislate for the group, but not for the individual 26.42; the individual has to resist the pressure of the group 19.261–4; the individual is threatened with extinction by the group 11.352–7; an individual doesn't comply with the group's norms 15.290; the individual struggles to emerge in the middle of the group 12.253; the power of interlocking groups over the individual 11.357; statistical individuals in the group 3.60, 3.417, 3.434–5, 3.437, 13.458; the term evolution applies to the individual, not their religious tradition 8.457; the true individual does not need the group's approval 3.470, 15.285; we have to restore the balance between individual and group 11.358; you can create a healthy group member by force, but not an individual 18.357–8

complexities of individuality
am I an individual or just a social unit? 3.467; being in a minority of one doesn't necessarily mean you're more of an individual 26.40; Christianity has no respect for the individual 11.361; danger of sexual relationships hindering one's development as an individual 3.39, 26.29; distinction between individual and social 1.191; don't throw your weight about imagining you're expressing individuality 17.563; if you are not an individual yourself, you can't understand someone who is 14.580–1; the individual cannot be a representative or authority 3.446; it is difficult to be an individual 3.484; one can generalize about people only to the extent that they are not individual 26.42; people may experience themselves as individuals however others see them 4.248; respect and lack of respect for the individual 11.359; we like to think that we are individual, but most of the time we are not 3.60; we exist as individuals, but also as members of society 4.89, 26.71; the world's biggest problem is the survival of the individual 11.352

individualism

what is individualism?
the difference between individuality and individualism 11.363, 18.359; every mundane thought, word, and deed is individualistic 1.232; individualist distinguished from true individual 3.470; examples of individualists 3.606; an individualist is simply a stronger member of the herd 15.534; individualists are mentally free of the group but still belong to it emotionally 26.41

individualism in the modern world
economic individualism 11.604; exaggerated individualism 7.264; extreme individualism in modern times 25.105; finding a middle way between authoritarianism and individualism 16.553; the forces of individualism in the modern world 12.654; the freedom of modern individualism 13.412; the individualism of Western society 13.458–64; 'unworldly' and 'outworldly' individualism (Christianity) 13.387

spiritual individualism in Buddhism
Siddhārtha overcomes spiritual individualism 11.406–7; not to be found in the Pāli canon 1.233; some think the *Khaggavisāṇa Sutta* upholds an individualistic ideal 8.259; it developed because the Buddha's exhortations to self-effort were taken literally 1.245; the *arhant* represents it (in the Mahāyāna) 2.140; the individualism of the 'Hīnayāna' 1.229–31, 4.223; thinking that one can gain Enlightenment solely by one's own efforts 5.259–61; Going for Refuge is individual, but not individualistic 2.516; individualistic attitude to merit 4.101; individualistic talk of attainment 1.133; individualism can carry us only part of the way 1.405; individualism in the sangha 12.456–7; the FWBO accused of individualism 13.457, 13.464–6

spiritual individualism and spiritual altruism
both are necessary 11.319; a sharp divergence in the Buddhist tradition 1.236, 16.214; in the long run they coincide 2.299–300, 9.255; in the spiritual life 4.84–117

guarding against spiritual individualism
Buddhaghosa guards against it 1.233; conversion from individualistic to non-individualist conception of Enlightenment 2.269; countered by dedication of merit to Enlightenment 16.332; the danger for the would-be bodhisattva 4.187–8; degeneration into it if the unreality of self is forgotten 1.404; dualistic views can lead to it 1.267, 4.188; escaping from individualism can mean giving up individuality 13.464; guarding against it in British Buddhists 2.471; not settling down in it 2.270; only the spiritual individualist 'loves' God for the sake of escaping hell 7.391; a possibility even after Stream Entry 4.187; some people withdraw into it 2.272; spiritual friendship is the enemy of individualism 12.670; there is no room for individualism in the spiritual life 1.510; to overcome it, (1) transfer merits, (2) pursue individualism to an extreme 2.270; transcending pseudo-spiritual individualism 11.386, 18.172–3; wisdom and goodness are incompatible with individualism 13.463

individuality

notes on individuality
Blake's emphasis on its importance 8.555, 8.558; development of individuality, as opposed to abandonment of the self 3.59; the difference between individuality and individualism 11.363, 18.359; Enlightenment negates ego, not individuality 12.512; entrance into non-duality beyond masculine and feminine 16.548; even in the group one need not surrender one's individuality 3.618; gestalt: the interaction between phenomenal individuality and higher principle 18.285; the idea is incompatible with the idea of a permanent unchanging self 19.234–5; the ideal of individuality 19.182; individual aspiration to reach a higher level of development 16.24–5; individuality and evolution 3.475–85; individuality and genius 3.59–60; individuality and interconnectedness: we are not alone 7.400; individuality in the modern negative sense 25.63; it is unfathomable and inexhaustible 3.468; the keen eye for individuality of the Renaissance 23.315; the middle way between individualism and conformity 18.35; people express it differently, but can overlap with others in a wider pattern 18.286

we may have no real individuality
the ego is neurotic individuality 18.219; a number of personalities fighting for supremacy 26.258; the three fetters: wrong belief concerning the nature of individuality 1.177; true or false individuality relates to the degree of integration 3.491; we are a succession of different people 1.569; we are just a bundle of conflicting desires tied together with a name and an address 5.30; you can't commit yourself unless there is just one individuality to commit itself 26.40

what supports individuality
the anonymity of city life 9.413; discerning a clear thread running through your life 15.91–2; the function of the teacher or friend is to encourage individuality 16.25; the more you give up yourself, the more perfectly yourself you become 5.656; insisting on being treated as an individual in the family 3.37, 13.461; it must come from one's direct spiritual experience 11.xix; one individuality sharpening itself on another 14.581; participation in public life 11.635; taking the initiative 9.303–6, 9.366, 9.395; we begin to create it through mindfulness 5.30; we will not find it on the level of the conditioned 1.487

beyond individuality
the doctrine of the Buddha and the extinction of individuality (Conze) 14.267; the six element practice dissolves the idea of individuality in a narrow sense 4.80; transcendental individuality: the

Dharma-door beyond praise and blame 16.546

Indo-Tibetan Buddhist Cultural Institute *see under* Dhardo Rimpoche/life story

Indra (or Sakra) as a *deva*, escorting the Buddha 13.586; brandishes the *vajra* 13.167–8; explanation of the presence of the god in Pāli canon 9.344; he is given his place in the Buddhist tradition 13.274; god of rain and thunderstorms 13.167, 16.418; as the gods worship Indra ... 22.385; hymns to Indra 7.59, 13.167; 'Indra's cows' (storm clouds) 13.167; king of the thirty-three gods 16.344; palace, where you can find everything you could possibly desire 16.346; praises the teaching of the inconceivable emancipation (*Vimalakīrti-nirdeśa*) 16.458; 'a rather unedifying god' 12.427; relationship of the god to the term *indriya* 3.297; and the squirrel, *see* parables and stories

Indra's net association with the *Avataṃsaka Sūtra* 1.353, 1.376, 2.733 (n631), 3.672 (n297), 16.3–4, 16.17; development in the Triratna Buddhist Order as Indra's net 2.513; every jewel reflects the whole net 3.317, 7.159, 7.274, 13.438; in Hua-yen Buddhism 2.733–4 (n631), 3.672 (n297); symbolism 1.353, 2.733–4 (n631), 16.3–4

Indrabhūti (*siddha*) 1.381, 1.385

Indrabodhi, Dharmachari v24

Indrajala, Dharmachari v24

indriya-saṃvara-sīla *see under* four *pārisuddhi sīlas*

indriyas etymology 1.280, 3.297; Pāli texts contain a list of 22 *indriyas* 1.280, 14.80, 14.83; term given to the five, or six, senses 3.297–8; *see also* five spiritual faculties

indulgence the animal realm of the wheel of life represents sensual indulgence 13.130; the Buddha didn't want us to indulge in abstract speculations 1.128; consuming Buddhist books as a sort of indulgence 17.672–3; don't indulge in Buddhist sentimentalism 4.244; don't indulge people in their feelings of self-pity 18.624; a fine line between acknowledging your weaknesses and indulging them 17.657–8; indulging in craving, you get some pleasure out of it, but hatred is unpleasant for you too 4.388; indulgence in habits which harm health is an indicator of lack of self-love 5.126; indulging negative mental states 4.368–9, 18.79; neither ignoring one's unskilful side nor indulging it 10.608–9; occasional pleasures easily turn into regular indulgences 17.253; one should never indulge in purely negative, destructive criticism 4.125; popular culture offers a constant invitation to indulge our cravings 17.271; self-indulgence, *see* self-indulgence; 'To indulge in luxury and pleasure is the cause of poverty and death' 18.472; why give yourself a hard time by indulging in unskilful mental states? 5.349; the wise do not indulge in acrimonious disputes 1.60

Indus Valley civilization 10.460

industry industrial activity in New Zealand 24.81; Industrial Revolution 1.28, 9.409, 14.443, 16.387, 26.131; industrialization as a threat to Buddhism 11.522; industrialized society 12.563–4; Sangharakshita using knowledge of the coal industry as skilful means 18.414; victims of industrialization 25.121–3

ineffability all experiences are ineffable 7.359; can we describe even the colour of a rose? 2.54; concepts and words communicating a unique and ineffable experience 2.59; the Dharma is a transcription into conceptual symbols of the Buddha's ineffable experience 7.309; the *Diamond Sūtra*'s ineffable truth 13.324, 23.10; an experience may be ineffable, but the idea of the experience can be recognized 17.520; the inseparable unity of ineffable Bliss and transcendental Awareness 8.445; of Nirvāṇa 1.63–72, 1.131; of reality 2.131, 7.299; reality being ineffable, positive and negative definitions are equally out of the question 1.119; *śūnyatā* is the ineffable non-dual Reality which transcends all apparent oppositions 7.505; of the Tathāgata 1.64; the 'thusness' of things is their ineffable essence 14.595; of the Transcendental 1.238–9; the truth is ineffable 1.64–5; we can be positively drawn even to the ineffable emptiness of *śūnyatā* 18.129

inequality the graded inequality of the caste system, *see under* caste system; class inequality 15.716–17; concepts of equality and inequality are inappropriate with regard to women and men 26.56; 'Inequality is life. Equality is death.' 26.74; the remedy is insistence not upon one party's rights, but on the other's duties 7.279

inertia the forces of inertia within us are very strong 1.554–5; the hindrance of inertia and stagnation 1.558–9, 11.122,

13.72; sloth arises through inertia 4.470; a state is governed by a combination of force and inertia 26.20; you produce energy by resisting inertia 15.403

inexhaustible jar (*kumbha*) 4.361

inexpressibility the Buddha's virtues are inexpressible 16.328; if the Dharma is inexpressible, how is it to be taught? 16.450; fourteen inexpressibles, *see* undetermined questions; *niṣprapañca*, *see niṣprapañca*; of all *dharmas* 1.65–6

infallibility the Buddha and infallibility, *see* Buddha II/omniscience and infallibility; 'Infallible Success', *see* Amoghasiddhi; lamas disastrously regarded as infallible 2.565; religions of relation and discovery 7.366–7; to create an infallible authority would be to pollute the pure Dharma 7.334

infantile *see* childishness

infatuation from passion to greed to infatuation to addiction to intoxication 10.616–17; a heart bound up or infatuated (*paṭibhaddacitta*) 10.490; *pema*: a sort of infatuation which can be very painful 10.652; our infatuation with transitory pleasures prevents us from seeing the fact of suffering 7.388–9; synonym for intoxication 16.298

inference *see under* logic

inferior assumption that the cause of a phenomenon is inferior to its effect 8.230; confidence gives the strength to break through inferiority complex and caste conditioning 10.lviii–ix; don't feel inferior because you're not scholarly 19.521–2; every emotion is of a triune nature, directed towards inferior, equal, or superior 1.241; feeling inferior 15.717, 16.330; the idea of oneself as superior, inferior, or equal to others is conceit, *see under* conceit; 'pseudo-scientific' approach: attempts to demonstrate Buddhism's inferiority 7.487

infidelity a breach of continuity in our relationship with another person 3.567; seeing evidence of your partner's infidelity 18.579

infinity *ananta* (infinite) 1.69; antinomies as to whether the universe is finite or infinite 10.596–7; any moment is infinitely divisible 17.367; bodhisattva vows through infinite time and infinite space 2.454; the bodhisattva's career as infinitely long 1.260; the Buddha an infinitely wise and boundlessly compassionate Teacher 14.19; 'Cessation of thought-processes mistaken for quiescence of infinite mind' 5.228–9, 5.421–3; 'The eternal silence of these infinite spaces terrifies me' 14.504; 'everything would appear as it is, infinite' (Blake) 15.205–6; existence is an infinitely complex, constantly shifting network 4.648; 'For the Boundless, the Unlimited, the Infinite I long' 25.229; 'God is an absolutely infinite substance with infinite attributes' 4.203, 14.603; in the *arūpa dhyānas*, *see under dhyānas/arūpa dhyānas*; the infinite light (*amitābha*) which shines within 7.510; infinity or plurality of Buddhas 16.460; the infinity of space 5.485; an infinity of world-systems 1.39, 3.376–7; is space finite or infinite? 16.161; mathematicians may be moved by the concept of infinity, but it leaves most of us cold 13.284; the positive *nidānas* as an infinite series 10.614, 26.174–6; the possibilities of being are infinite 18.227; the reflection of infinity 25.175; reflection on infinity of consciousness 4.80, 16.447; trying to ascertain whether the world is finite or infinite is a mistake 17.385; when the centre of the self expands to infinity 7.412, 26.51; the *White Lotus Sūtra* attempts to convey infinity through images 14.112, 16.38

inflexibility contrast between inflexible and distracted mind 15.163; doubt is an inflexible attitude of scepticism and indecision 15.207

influence

the Buddha's influence
adhiṣṭhāna: the influence of a Buddha in the *dharmadhātu* or Buddha-field 3.243–4; *anubhāva* (influence, grace) 4.265, 14.539, 18.98, 18.537; 'the blessed influence of Jinas': like tuning the radio 4.272; Devadatta closed himself to the Buddha's influence 18.538; distinction between a Buddha's sphere of knowledge and sphere of influence 16.461; the geographical area of the Buddha's personal influence 2.25; he influenced people more by what he was and did than what he said 4.8, 26.46; the influence of the Buddhas and bodhisattvas, like perfume 16.559–60; it was so strong that other teachers said he used spells to charm people 2.26, 11.492; the sphere of influence of a Buddha 16.460–1

influence and Buddhism
Aśoka's influence on the growth of Buddhism in India 15.184–5; the Buddha used old words but was not influenced by old teachings 2.58–9, 10.133, 23.178; Buddhism depends on equilibrium between literalizing and liberalizing

influences 1.249; claim that Hinduism influenced Buddhism 7.537, 9.391, 9.394; the devotional element of Buddhism developed through lay influence 2.220; did Manicheism influence Buddhism? 3.431–2; the *devas*' influence on the building of cities 10.646–8; a king is advised to become king of the gods, to have even greater influence 17.167; if a bodhisattva just *is* a bodhisattva, that will influence people 25.128; incense symbolizes the widespread influence of the precepts 9.324; the influence of Buddhism, *see under* Buddhism III/expansion; the influence of the *Jātakas* on Buddhist countries 1.398, 14.65–6; *termas*: highly important teachings which exert profound influence 12.300; Theravādin efforts to enlarge the sphere of Buddhist influence 1.345; Upanishadic influence on early Buddhism? 10.545–6; vegetarianism came to India due to the influence of Buddhism and Jainism 10.48–9; consolidating the influence of the Dharma in the West 12.609; Western Buddhists need to assimilate Buddhism's influences in their own way 4.281

the influence of the spiritual community
the influence of Order members working together 12.309, 12.625, 25.128; a network of spiritual communities could perhaps influence world events 3.619; spiritual hierarchy: a living chain up and down which run spiritual influences 12.14; those who reject Christianity are still influenced by its ethical assumptions 4.105

positive influences
being open to positive influences enables you to make progress 18.98; bringing the world under the influence of the golden light 12.395; the influence of *mettā* 15.329–30; literature can exert a tremendous influence for good 8.208; lunar influences on trees and plants 4.576; mass availability of art may influence the population 3.515–16; the positive influence of the spiritual community 3.444

negative influences
the brutalizing influence of horror comics 8.206–9; Māra's influence in this world 14.484; the influence not of distractions but our tendency to get enmeshed in them 15.174–5; the influence of an 'evil friend' 16.300; susceptibility to the influence of hungry ghosts 4.542; we don't realize the extent to which we are under the influence of fear 16.278; we need to shield ourselves from negative influences 15.152–3; a whole nation living under the influence of fear 4.96

receptivity
allowing the influence of nature to remind us of the greater mandala 14.519; freedom to close yourself to spiritual influence 4.247; opening oneself to the influence of Buddhas and bodhisattvas in puja 11.223; prostrations make one more receptive to spiritual influences 1.407, 13.416; receptivity to the Buddha's influence 4.7–8; receptivity to higher spiritual influences 4.127–8, 4.339, 16.10; receptivity to the influence of a bodhisattva 16.230; Rechungpa resists Milarepa's influence 18.538–9

our own influence
charisma: you can get carried away by your own popularity and influence 15.399–400; don't underestimate the effect of personal influence 25.128–9; influencing the society you live in by being vegetarian 17.585; one does one's bit by helping those within one's sphere of influence 4.191; one should feel that one's influence upon others is beneficent, like moonlight 13.82; you can influence people more by listening than by meeting their views head on 18.169

ways we are influenced
analysing motives before allowing them to influence conduct 1.151; astrology may indicate an influence, not an inevitable outcome 19.269–70; by our environment 15.153, 15.392–5; by friends with conventional and materialistic ideas 18.152; by likes and dislikes of personality 15.516–17; by sense experience 3.422; coming from every object, whether material or mental, there is an influence 18.537; *dharmapālas*' ability to ward off undesirable influences on your practice 13.207–8; make sure that the influences impinging on you are positive 12.474, 26.62; mindfulness: freeing the conscious mind from the influence of the unconscious 10.349; not spiritually developed, your mental state is greatly influenced by other people 15.369; not yet a bodhisattva, worldly people will affect you more than you affect them 18.152; the way we look at things exerts a strong influence on how they appear to us 17.xix; when insight experiences and dreams influence each other 19.306–7

see also
grace waves

informality an excuse for disrespect 4.343–4, 15.438; 'On Formality and Informality' 15.438, 15.759–80 (n157); people's preference for informality 12.533

Inge, Dean William brief introduction 23.489 (n122); 'a disguised Buddhist' 7.370; his experience of marriage 23.98; *The Philosophy of Plotinus* 23.317, 23.328, 24.248, 24.311, 24.361, 26.590

Ingersoll, Colonel 8.166

ingratitude (*akataññutā*) Dickens' Mr Bounderby as an exemplar of ingratitude 3.601; the housewife who served boots to her ungrateful family 17.201; ingratitude towards parents 3.601, 3.607; Jivaka's ingratitude 22.445; one of the four great offences that bring about *niraya* 3.605, 3.693 (n476); reasons for ingratitude 3.605–9; 'sharper than a serpent's tooth' 15.253; a Stream Entrant is incapable of ingratitude 3.607

initiation initiation and Going for Refuge 13.161, 15.15.694–5, 15.704, 15.733–4; Sangharakshita's initiations, *see under* Sangharakshita V/*sādhanas*; Tantric initiation, *see abhiṣeka*

initiation vase 13.157–62

initiative *see* taking the initiative

injustice Dharmapala's life was an unceasing battle against injustice 8.10; an experience of injustice in hospital 13.609; caste injustice, *see under* caste system; karma used as a rationalization for social injustice 15.681; the remedy is insistence not on one party's rights, but on the other's duties 7.279, 26.73; why is it wrong to take from multinationals in an unfair system? 3.320–1, 3.323

Inkpen, Gerald 26.417

inner life achievements as expressions of inner abundance, not compensations for inner poverty 26.15; the bodhisattva becomes aware of weaknesses and inner darkness 16.289–90; a Buddha's inner experience is first expressed in what he is and does, then in what he says 4.7; a close relationship between your inner experience and what you do with your life 25.48; compassion must be matched by inner tranquillity 4.393; covetousness: the self tries to appropriate the non-self to fill its inner emptiness 2.386; a deep inner connection between the arts and spiritual life 21.250–1; difficult to get into the bodhisattva's inner experience 4.240; having a cultivated and creative inner life 17.341; a healthy person's principal support is always within 26.29; the inner enemy of routine 10.240–2; the inner *experience* of infinite space 16.161; inner nourishment 18.50; inner resources 18.300; inner warmth becomes contentment 18.90–1; inner yogas 18.76; opening your inner eyes 10.595; the path of the inner life (*nivṛtti mārga*, esoteric path) 7.357–63; a phase of inner activity after a very active period 4.462; receptivity to the inner teaching: listening not just with the ears 18.290; refinement of emotions through contact with a *ḍākinī*, inner or outer 12.314–15; struggle between the golden light and one's inner poisons 16.290–1; 'To feel this internal world as an organic whole working out its own destiny' 2.401; turning the five senses inside out like a glove, to merge into a single inner sense 7.358, 26.37; use your warrior's strength to fight the inner, spiritual battle 18.103, 18.106; *see also* external/inner and outer life

innocence *Auguries of Innocence*, *see under* William Blake/works; the body is innocent, it's in the mind that everything tends to go wrong 10.307; the Buddha's transcendental innocence analogous to a child's natural innocence 14.240; the idea that children are innocent is socially conditioned 15.204–5; an ideal of innocence 18.105; the knowledge that comes with the innocence of youth 18.30–1; the loss of innocence 25.120; the innocent can suffer 15.368, 16.422–3; the innocence of nature 4.108; the innocence of the senses 10.610–11, 15.200–1, 15.286–8, 18.345; sentimental ideas of childhood innocence 17.470; two kinds: ignorance and natural goodness 25.120; you are not a philosophical innocent, your mind is full of *micchā-diṭṭhis* 19.508

innovation; the Mahāyāna: a movement not of innovation but of development and unfoldment 1.247; tradition was once innovation 26.20

insanity *see* madness

insects ants and worms requested to depart before the building of a temple 22.502; bees, *see* bees; black scarab beetles 23.262; dragonflies 20.100–2, 25.240; the fly who sits on a chariot saying, 'My! Aren't I kicking up a dust?' 18.367; glow-worms, *see* glow-worms; impossible to avoid crushing grasshoppers on the road 23.297; moths in the lamp's flame 10.610–11; noxious insects among the few beings not present at the *parinirvāṇa* 14.233; providing food for ants 8.506; Sangharakshita moving insects out of the way before lying on the ground to sleep 10.xxxix; wasps 24.86; 'Wisdom is a butterfly' 2.405, 26.265

insecurity *see under* security

insight (*vipaśyanā* in Sanskrit, *vipassanā* in Pāli)

INTRODUCING INSIGHT

introduction
introduction to the use of the term 4.498, 11.126–7, 16.589 (n32); insight is a spatial term 18.607; it can be attained *in this life* 1.225, 4.493–4; not within the sphere of causality 2.262; perhaps the more active and causally efficacious aspect of wisdom 1.170; relationship of *vipaśyanā* with *prajñā* 2.114; Sangharakshita's preference for using the term *vipaśyanā* rather than *vipassanā* 5.485; synonymous with knowledge and vision of things as they really are 2.113–14; *vipaśyanā* and real Going for Refuge 3.329, 12.505

what is insight like?
like a sharp knife 18.574; like making a hole in the shell of the mundane 19.435; not dry and barren, but a deeply emotional experience 19.379; no nearer to intellect than it is to emotion 4.516, 19.189, 26.77; not just intellectual understanding, a direct intuitive perception 3.218, 19.454; not seeing into, but seeing through 18.579; a suffusion of our whole being with reality 13.73; 'surrounded by a calm and gentle aura' 5.423–4; a total experience, both cognitive and emotional 5.427–8; if your life is rather uneven, insight might be almost unpleasant 4.499

why develop insight?
because all worldlings are mad 26.75; it allows the bodhisattva to see all beings as on their way to their slaughter 2.156; cultivating insight is the fifth of five things that conduce to spiritual maturity 3.578; developing insight is the only way to permanently remove unskilful states 5.450; the purpose of Buddhism is to bring about insight into the true nature of things 15.260; to go out into the world without spiritual support you need a degree of insight 19.347; to really help others, you need insight as well as love 19.287–8; until you have insight, you can only act blindly and foolishly 19.354–5; without insight you are liable to become attached to the place where you live 19.362

the history of insight
people meeting the Buddha and gaining insight 3.663–4 (n248), 5.640; 'when things become clear' in very early texts 10.434; women of the harem gain insight (*Udāna*) 10.627–9; the Buddha saw no difference between his own insight and that of his disciples 1.213; the Buddha's teachings didn't always lead to the arising of insight 10.534; the difference between that of an *arhant* and that of a bodhisattva 5.438–9; levels of insight in the Āryasaṅgha 1.177, 3.412–13; Early Buddhist and Mahāyāna approaches 5.458, 19.453; and the Madhyamaka school 19.373; described in Tsongkhapa's *Three Chief Paths* 17.424, 17.427

how and where insight might arise
the artistic vision comes quite close to insight 5.428; it can arise equally in dependence on all three levels of wisdom 12.541–3; committing yourself to your practice, insight may arise at any time 18.154; 'definite goodness': qualities that make for insight 17.160–1; in dependence on intellectual activity 18.580; in a dream 19.305–6, 19.571–2; in everyday life 1.154, 5.431–2, 5.637–8, 15.112; it demands a powerful and positive emotional commitment 15.208; from *mettā* 5.172–3; from reflecting on contradictions 16.469; on the basis of concentration 1.154, 2.262; on the basis of strong devotion 5.640; on the basis of suffering 5.640; on seeing a leaf fall 3.272; resulting from intense communication 19.328; spontaneous insight 2.262; through contemplating the idea of Nirvāṇa 2.262–3; through contemplation of the three *lakṣaṇas* 2.262; when the bottom drops out of a bucket (Zen story) 5.449; with the aid of very subtle mental activity 16.161; at work 13.172; you don't have to be officially meditating to gain insight 5.431; you don't need perfect intellectual understanding to gain insight 18.359–60;

you have that extraordinary experience because you are susceptible to it 17.126

insight into what?
all things as an illusion 4.374–5; any conditioned object, even a matchbox 18.88; five *skandhas* 1.175; the body 5.410; conditioned co-production 1.89, 17.427; the dependently arisen nature of *vedanā* 10.482; the four noble truths 17.458; the three *lakṣaṇas* 1.170–3, 4.498, 11.126; the true nature of phenomena 1.87–8; the true nature of reality 5.417; the Unconditioned: the five wisdoms (*jñānas*) 11.126–7; conditioned existence as it really is 2.114, 4.498; the conditioned nature of sense experience 3.218

the effect of gaining insight
a growth and development from which we don't fall back 19.449; how one with insight into the nature of conditioned things sees the Buddha 2.43; if insight is sufficiently powerful, you will never lose it 5.425, 18.575; insight 'fixes' emotional positivity 18.449; insight into Truth gives a feeling of certitude 7.145; insight will eventually cut the root of the five hindrances 17.121; it can hit you hard or gently, depending on how much meditation you do 4.499; a little insight can set you against the grain of the world 17.164; the more insight you have, the less craving and aversion you have 18.576; not seeing new sights with old eyes, but seeing old sights with new eyes 7.295; only insight can 'kill' the longing for diversion 19.518; it permanently destroys unskilful mental states 18.575; the qualities that things around you seemed to possess fade away like a mirage 17.358–9; the thinking process functions more purposefully 19.151–2; true selflessness is not separable from insight 17.208; when you attain it you want to share it with others 17.348–9; you can enter the *dhyānas* whenever there is an opportunity 18.575–6; you can move around in the world without being affected by it 18.575; you couldn't be murderously angry after attaining insight 17.132–3; you experience as *śūnyatā* anything that comes within your spiritual vision 14.561; your being is transformed in accordance with an insight 18.554; your attitude to sense experience is different 5.447, 5.643

HOW TO GAIN INSIGHT

developing insight
at least the grosser *kleśas* would have been eliminated if you had attained insight 17.132–3; the classic pattern of development 5.418, 5.448, 5.458–9, 5.464, 5.524; it can be developed only by a prepared mind 5.409–10, 15.83; the conditions for its arising can be developed 2.262; Dharma study's importance to the development of insight 19.449; fearlessness is required to sustain insight into reality 14.576; if the need to develop it gets lost, look again at the balance of your life 15.97–8; it is not difficult to have 'insights', but it is very difficult to apply them to oneself 26.61; make the most of opportunities to develop insight 5.451; you don't go directly from perception to insight, always a conceptual stage 4.146; the point at which insight begins to arise 5.409–10; positive discussion can prepare you for the arising of insight 10.530; to develop *vipaśyanā*, you only need a thorough grasp of certain basic things 19.453; through the practice of mindfulness, insight unfolds of its own accord 15.206; through reflecting on the Dharma 17.543; you can have a degree of insight in the form of intelligence 15.549; you can't worry your way to insight 5.448; you don't go from an ordinary state of consciousness directly to insight 10.562–3

insight and meditation
the arising of insight is the fifth and final stage of meditation 13.73; developing insight through meditative practice 3.218; different kinds of insight meditation 5.613; formal meditation isn't necessarily needed for the arising of insight 19.451; insight and the *brahma vihāras* 5.210–11, 5.215–18, 15.337; *kasiṇa* meditations as insight practice 18.513; *mettā* and insight, *see under mettā*; the mindfulness of breathing as an insight practice 15.109–12; meditation is the best way to insight, though it isn't automatic 5.450; the process is a sort of active receptivity 15.111–12; the role of *samādhi* 2.145; Sangharakshita's experiences of insight in meditation 22.227; visualization 4.618–19, 5.448

insight and conceptual thinking
capacity for insight not necessarily associated with intellectual understanding 18.544; the conceptual element of the process of developing 4.145–6; the danger of mistaking rational understanding for insight 1.349–50, 7.532; the difference between intellectual understanding and insight 5.424–5; discursive thought as a basis for developing insight 5.429; does insight require conceptualization? 5.629–30; insight is based on a certain kind of

conceptual activity 5.417; insight is nothing to do with conceptual construction 1.88; intellectual study has its limits, but don't underestimate its importance to insight 15.198; mistaking book knowledge for transcendental insight 11.481; for most people insight is mediated by conceptual symbols 5.463–4; the process of reflecting on concepts to develop insight 19.190; using concepts to develop insight 5.447, 5.448–50; when intellectual understanding passes over into insight 18.545; why does insight have to be translated into conceptual terms? 5.449; without translation into conceptual terms, insight is like a fading dream 5.449; you need a conceptual support 19.508

insight and the fetters
the concept of breaking fetters is a measure of our progress towards insight 4.185; do you break the fetters and thus develop insight or *vice versa*? 4.41, 5.446–7; to begin with, your insight may not be strong enough to break them 18.578–9; the stage of wisdom depends on intensity of insight 1.177; upon insight the fetters are permanently broken 5.426–7

flashes of insight
a flash of understanding, but not permanent insight 19.217; glimpses at first 5.431; in relation to Stream Entry 19.450; like a flash of lightning 1.176, 11.64, 13.73; not like a lightning flash in the physical world 19.450–1; as part of the path of five stages 17.458; Sangharakshita's experience 20.302, 23.15; *vipaśyanā* (rather than *prajñā*) 2.114, 4.498, 12.25–6; when the flashes consolidate, they become wisdom 4.515, 13.73, 14.564–5

'dry' insight (or bare insight, sukkha-vipassanā, suddha-vipassanā)
can one experience *vipaśyanā* without a basis of *śamatha*? 5.419–20; the central tradition of Buddhism maintains that it is not possible 8.444–5, 19.453; the classification presents a danger 1.349; acknowledged by the tradition, but a relatively rare attainment 5.461, 7.532; seems to rest on confusion between actual insight and recollecting doctrinal categories 8.445; traditionally experienced by a certain type of disciple 1.168; the whole idea seems suspect 5.420

partial insight
insight can be cumulative 18.578–9; you can't fall back from a limited experience of insight, you can add to it 18.578; moving from insight to *prajñā* 14.564–5

remembering insight
if you have an insight, don't forget it but try to embody it in your day to day life 12.29; making notes can help 17.261–2; a memory of insight 5.432; safeguarding one's insights 4.13

mistakes and misconceptions
being in too much of a hurry to rush on to so-called *vipassanā* 5.445; the mistaken idea that pain in meditation shows that insight is being achieved 23.73; mistaking a thought about reality for insight into reality 19.165

questions
can insight only be developed in formal meditation practice? 18.514, 18.579–80; does it come naturally? 5.428; does it require conceptualization? 5.629; how can the transition from dualism to insight be a matter of time? 16.112–13; how does it relate to the *bodhicitta*? 4.515; is scientific insight the same as Buddhist insight? 26.687; sudden or gradual? 1.176, 4.498–9, 10.562–3; we may think we want insight right now, but do we really? 17.354

see also
bhāvanā-mayī prajñā, *see under* three levels of wisdom; the 'burden' of insight, *see vipassanādhura*; and *dhyāna*, *see under dhyāna*; and the intermediate state, *see gotrabhū*; knowledge and vision of things as they really are; and *śamatha*, *see under śamatha*; six element practice as insight practice, *see under* six element practice; through visualization practice, *see under* visualization

insight meditation *see vipaśyanā*

insight meditation movement *see* vipassanā movement

inspiration

what is inspiration?
definition 2.645, 5.240; how inspiration works: like a series of interconnected reservoirs 15.156; one's most important relationship is with one's source of inspiration 18.504–5

sources of inspiration
beauty 12.559; communication in the sangha 17.189–90; dreams: inspiration from deeper sources 19.304–5; the experience of reality itself 18.180; finding our own sources 17.466; from Dharma texts 12.382, 16.443–4; from the life of the Buddha 11.711, 12.507–8, 15.164, 15.548, 19.55, 26.511; from the life and teachings of Dr Ambedkar 10.337; from the lives of great Buddhists 6.621; from

outside 19.140–1; from the Sangha 17.61; the goal of Enlightenment 18.372; if they dry up, your Dharma-related activities will become just activities 5.652; 'Inspiration – Whence?' (talk in Bombay) 12.692, 22.269; it comes to Buddhists in the form of *nāgas* 11.151; *mātṛkās* (the Mothers): forces of inspiration from the earth 18.469; not from theories about life but from life itself 1.398; paradoxically, from discipline and regular practice 17.459–60; a religious discourse shouldn't just instruct us, but inspire us with delight 12.525–6

losing inspiration
don't give Dharma talks full-time, your inspiration will dry up 18.481–2; falling away from one's original inspiration 12.679; how inspiration fluctuates 18.540–2; how to deal with a spiritually barren period 26.58; if the powers of inspiration are not honoured, they can be lost 18.119; if you feel uninspired, make contact with someone who shares your ideals 15.153; if you're busy listening to your own voice you won't hear the *ḍākinī* within 18.178–9; keeping going with extended spiritual practices when inspiration dries up 17.554; losing touch with inspiration so that you can only communicate ideas 18.477; Milarepa seeks inspiration in the hardship that is drying up his inspiration 18.20; no one can be inspired all the time 15.152; our inspirations may be sabotaged by something in us that says 'Why bother?' 17.460; renewed by confession 16.509

notes on inspiration
an abstract idea is not very inspiring for most people 19.24–5; be honest with yourself about whether you find artworks inspiring 19.348–9; the contented person is both inspired and an inspiration to others 15.309; a Dharma teacher's most important qualities are inspiration and *mettā* 17.182–3; don't be too busy to heed the whispers of inspiration 19.305; inspiration and the second *dhyāna* 5.240, 11.151–2; inspirational power experienced by poets and prophets 11.151; inspiring people by getting them in touch with their emotions 19.228; it can keep you going when strength of will fails 18.618; it is needed as well as energy 10.202; it will arise as long as we just get on with the job 17.576; latch onto whichever form of practice seems most inspiring and helpful 11.221; not acknowledging sources of inspiration 3.607; the sacredness or profaneness of a thing depends on the state of mind it inspires 7.283; singing suggests freedom of communication and inspiration 18.462; Tantric practice relies on energy, positivity, and inspiration 18.181; to generate enough to break our bonds we need the bodhisattva ideal 26.56

see also
ḍākinīs/forces of inspiration

instinct an animal acts from instinct, a child from impulse, a woman from emotion, a man from reason 7.138; biological instincts seem to come before the senses 17.13–14; the Buddha's instinct to pay honour and respect, *see under* reverence; our desire to satisfy instinct can be stronger than the desire to develop the imaginal faculty 15.359; devotion: a way to integrate instinct and emotion with mental understanding 12.24; group instinct 3.437; higher ideals are often (but not always) lower instincts and desires in disguise 10.349; the instinct that makes a magpie build its nest 24.540; the instinct to revere and worship is deep-rooted in the human psyche 2.213–14; sexual instinct (Freud) 10.349; some rare people seem able to lead a spiritual life by sheer instinct 4.90; we are governed by sense-based instincts 17.11–16; we can't ignore the depths: from them come our energies of instinct, emotion, and will 12.23; we don't need arguments to convince us of the truth, we develop an instinct for it 4.571; without instinctual repression there could be no civilization 24.463–4

institutions the courage it takes to defend them, and to create them 26.73; distinction between personal religion and institutional religion 1.191; essentially individuals working in a particular way, whether negative or positive 18.277–8; a field of creativity 12.639–40, 18.277; in Triratna (FWBO), *see* Triratna/IV institutions; the institutionalization of sexual relationships 3.528; institutions are not necessarily worthy of respect due to mere antiquity 2.648; mundane and spiritual institutions 12.468; not necessarily a dirty word 18.277–8; taking charge of a spiritual institution does not imply spiritual superiority 18.18; the usefulness of institutions 12.468

insubstantiality *see anātman*

integration

introduction
'The Integrated Individual' 3.486–92; 'horizontal' and 'vertical' integration 3.486–7, 5.239, 5.249, 11.120–2, 18.412; the ideal is to integrate head and heart,

thought and action 7.127; the mandala as a symbol of integration 12.218–23

lack of integration
being divided within oneself 3.120–1, 16.323, 18.441–2; being 'in two minds' about the teachings 17.290; distraction is really lack of integration 18.522; and doubt 3.418–19; the gravitational pull of the parts of oneself that are not integrated 15.399; keeping unintegrated energy out of the mandala 16.352; a loose congeries or bundle of selves 3.418–19, 3.486, 3.501, 5.655, 11.120–1, 19.81, 26.39; not being able to keep a promise 17.696–7, 18.487; until we become integrated there is no real progress 5.30–1

and meditation
the aim of meditation is to make us more concentrated, unified beings 17.116–17; distraction resolved through integration 16.544; in first *dhyāna* 3.307, 5.238; inability to integrate meditation experience 5.364–5; meditation pulls all the different bits of yourself together 3.120–1, 3.487, 18.522; the *mūla yogas* begin the process of integration of one part of our nature with another 13.76

other methods of integration
achieved by the most self-conscious part of us taking control of the rest 19.81–2; aim to be fully and completely into what you are doing 10.602–5, 15.730–1; art and beauty have a unifying effect on the psyche 8.445; faith and devotion integrates emotions and intellect 12.24, 17.674; helped by meditation, devotional practices, and Dharma study 3.487; integrating one's unconscious contents with the help of the *ḍākinīs* 13.238–40; integration in dreams 19.565; integration through mindfulness 3.487, 5.30–1, 11.731–3

becoming integrated
as you become integrated, you feel less pulled around by the oppressions 16.323; bringing the scattered bits of oneself together 5.43, 5.655, 10.605, 11.120–1; don't put off doing things until you're completely integrated 5.374–5; establishing a foundation of integration 17.455–6; if you are fairly well integrated, you are in a slightly dhyānic state 5.639; incorporating our deeper energies into the spiritual quest 12.335; integrating heights and depths 12.23–30; integrating primordial forces, so our spiritual life glows with the *ḍākinīs*' energy 12.324; integrating reason and emotion 14.557–8, 15.549; the integration of faith and wisdom 14.431; integration of 'male' and 'female' 16.163; the integration of the outer world and the non-clinging self 18.102; the integration of what you esteem and what you love 25.110; the integration of unconscious and conscious 18.77, 19.307; the making of a true individual 3.488, 3.492; no conflict between what you're convinced you should do and what you do 18.459; a rebirth of the whole personality 17.119; taking a vow requires a high degree of integration 17.170, 19.145; we gain a foothold, then gradually pull the rest of ourselves up to that level 5.375; you can't be sure what sort of person will develop as a result of the process 19.99

what being integrated is like
bliss in the full sense experienced with the integration of all unconscious energies 15.219; the capacity for directed thinking is a characteristic of the integrated personality 15.193; equanimity is the strength that comes from complete emotional integration 17.582; the integrated person acts as a total person 26.38; it leads to happiness 5.238–9; it is followed by spiritual death and spiritual rebirth 5.41–2; only an integrated person can be trusted 17.697; the process culminates in the perfect integration of wisdom and compassion 13.76; purity and integration 19.385; total integration 26.38; we become one whole 26.38

see also
wholeness

integrity development of integrity 3.487; ethical integrity is rooted in empathy 8.577–8; in refusing to accept someone's judgement one is not questioning their integrity 26.82; Jagdish Kashyap a model of personal integrity 2.582; you can't be deceived if you enter into a situation with true integrity 26.35

intellect and intellectual

distinctions
confusion of intellect and wisdom 7.242–3, 17.135; confusing the intelligent and the intellectual 15.565; danger of mistaking intellectual knowledge for real experience 16.122–3; distinction between intellect and reason (Macmurray) 15.255; distinction between 'head-learning' and 'soul-wisdom' 7.359; distinguishing wisdom from mere cleverness 17.131; Kant's distinction between intellect and understanding 14.558

Buddhism and the intellect
the ego-dominated intellect cannot penetrate the mystery of egoless activity 7.376; for all its subtlety, the Buddha's

teaching is not in essence intellectual 15.197, 15.250; the intellect cannot fathom the nature of the Tathāgata 1.64; the intellect cannot penetrate the inner meaning of Buddhism 1.20; intellectuals misunderstanding Zen 13.332; a mistake to think that Buddhism is just for intellectuals 15.556–7; mistaking intellectual reminiscence of the Dharma for penetration of its import 2.113; intellectual people find it hard to start spiritual life without all the answers 10.577; the more intellectual a person is, the less they may take in Buddhism's essence 17.331; Perfect Vision arising by means of the intellect 1.481; scrambling up the tree of one's intellect to try to reach the Palace of the Dharma 1.184; shift of the Dharma from intellectual to emotional mode 1.325–6, 1.347; thinking about Buddhism's appeal to 'the intellectual classes' 7.241, 7.243–4, 23.58–9; transmuted intellect corresponds to Mañjuśrī 2.173; we mustn't be dry-as-dust intellectuals, but we mustn't be cotton candy Buddhists 12.515–16; why an intellectual presentation of the Dharma angered the gods of Tibet 12.291–3; you don't have to be highly educated to be a Buddhist 9.338–9, 11.716

strengths and weaknesses
the alienated intellect 18.399–400, 19.178–83; 'Am I speaking from being or just from intellectual knowledge?' 19.507; the decline of the word 'intellect' 14.558, 17.673–4; a hot temper and a highly developed intellect often go together 13.133; the intellect can clarify your thinking, but it cannot be ultimately decisive 18.360; intellectual arrogance 1.293; intellectual clarity is not attained by education, reading, or becoming an intellectual 4.146–7; intellectual discussion's one aim is to generate the flame of transcendental life 1.400; an intellectual has a strong creative element in his thought 26.45; intellectuals whose understanding of the intellect's limitations is intellectual 26.43; intellectual knowledge (like a car) needs the motivating spark of devotion 2.243; intellectual study has its limits, but don't underestimate its importance to insight 15.198; a lot of intellectual revving up, but never moving forward 19.217; not regarding ideas as intellectual possessions 10.489; 'Our meddling intellect/Mis-shapes the beauteous forms of things' 7.242; qualifying the devotional by the intellectual, or *vice versa* 15.629; reducing things to intellectual formulas attenuates reality and one's experience 18.287; today, intellectual curiosity is more awake than transcendental wisdom 1.231; using the word 'enlightened' as a synonym for 'intelligent' 8.152; we have a compulsive need to make everything comprehensible to our intellect 19.563; we need the courage not of intellectual convictions but of transcendental realizations 1.209; we need not reject intellectual models, but we shouldn't put our security into them 14.548–9

see also
intellect and emotions, *see under* emotions

intellectual understanding

its uses
even faith-followers need a basic level 17.333; it can be useful in the early stages of practice 14.405; to go beyond it, we have to possess it 2.244–5, 12.515, 26.199; transformed into transcendental wisdom 1.169; when it passes over into insight 18.545

limitations and dangers
can you have intellectual understanding without an emotional aspect? 5.420; capacity for insight is not necessarily associated with it 18.544; the difference between intellectual understanding and insight 5.424–5, 17.331; the difference between intellectual understanding and wisdom 18.438–9; it's not enough, there must be a radical transformation 2.284; it is not the same as 'knowledge and vision of things as they really are' 12.163; it takes a long time for our emotions to catch up 12.322; 'Learn to separate Head-learning from Soul-wisdom' 26.198; thinking that because you have understood you have developed wisdom 11.481; thinking you are qualified to practise whatever you understand intellectually 18.517–18; you don't need perfect intellectual understanding to gain insight 18.359–60

understanding the Dharma but not practising it
avoid a false antithesis with spiritual experience 19.541; dragon's head, snake's body 1.493–4, 15.473, 16.351, 26.38, 26.705–6 (n19); the gap between our understanding and our Dharma practice 1.390, 1.493–4, 5.374–5; understanding is common, but practice is rare 18.107–8

practice
develop a positive emotional counterpart 26.37; devotion as a way of integrating it with instinct and emotion 12.24; finding emotional equivalents 1.494, 7.292–3,

11.192–4, 12.110–11, 15.154, 26.399; keep a balance between what you know and what you do 15.472–4; the transition from intellectual to intuitive understanding 18.399; transition to embodiment in experience 16.186, 16.221–2

intellectualism intellectualism in Buddhism and Hinduism 18.417; the Mahāyāna never went to the extreme of anti-intellectualism 1.240; the Vajrayāna's reaction against intellectualism 18.417

intelligence the ability to express what wisdom sees 17.603; the bodhisattva is like an elephant: strong, intelligent, trainable 4.468–9; *buddhi* (intelligence) 4.290; Buddhist ethics: a matter of intelligence and insight as much as good intentions 1.530; confusing the intelligent and the intellectual 15.565; the creative use of concepts 14.549, 15.187, 17.603, 18.238; developing a clearer understanding of our situation (Nāgārjuna) 17.260; an exceptionally intelligent and unpretentious scientist 24.210–11; to expose wrong views requires practice, intelligence, alertness, and confidence 10.587; if intelligent beings are discovered elsewhere, did Christ die for them too? 3.377; intelligence as a kind of mundane insight or vision 15.549, 15.564–5; 'intelligence type' (the refined version of the deluded type) 17.603; 'intelligent people through a parable reach understanding' 12.110–11, 16.215; karmic cause of intelligence 2.72; meditation is a union of purified emotion and clarified intelligence 4.146; the nature of existence is not comprehensible to the mundane intelligence 1.104; *prajñā* is produced from the coalescence of clarified intelligence and purified emotions 7.242; the Tathāgata's wisdom cannot be measured by the yardstick of human intelligence 1.20; teenagers are as intelligent as any adult you will ever meet 18.238–9

intensity a bodhisattva's wish to help others is so intense that they don't mind difficulties 4.69; *chanda* is intense will, a sort of concentrated volition 10.586; concentration so intense that 'I would practically lose consciousness of my body' 20.72–3; desire for ordination 'unbearably intense' 20.346; 'I would experience an intense joy' 21.322; insight resulting from intense communication 19.328; intense relationships 19.116; intense spiritual practice requires powerful commitment 18.161; intensification of practice 5.542; intensification of skilful mental states in meditation 5.650–1; intensity through close communication 18.380, 18.478, 19.571; Milarepa's intense experiences, his 'wives' 18.300; a more intense and vibrant experience of spiritual community 18.425; peace, which is the seat of intensest activity 7.141; the relationship between guru and disciple is intensely personal 18.162; remembering exactly where you were when you had a certain intense experience 18.400–1; Śāntideva might be in favour not of relieving tension but of letting it build up 4.310; Śāntideva's intense confession of sin 1.411; solitary retreat: an intensified experience of yourself 5.673; to break through, you need to practise with intensity 13.171; there is room for more intensity in the lives of most Western Buddhists 13.171; the true individual is intensely, luminously aware 3.469; *upekṣā* has an intense, definite, dynamic character 5.212–13; usually one is more intense when in difficulties, though it need not be so 4.313

intentions the best of intentions can be overcome by the gravitational pull 19.61; Buddhism teaches us that it is the intention that counts 13.86; *cetanā* (will or conscious intention) plays a crucial role in Buddhist life 11.650, 12.537–8; enter every activity having formed a clear intention 15.96; every time you breathe in, you take life – the practice is to avoid intentional harm 4.355–6; forming an intention to become a bodhisattva of the *dharmakāya* 4.196; the insignificance of human intentions to elemental powers 18.12; intention in an abstract sense is not enough 19.129; thoughts is the intention of action 1.144; undermining the skilful intentions of others 17.660–1; a world of difference between intending to follow the precepts and doing so 18.101; your intention to meditate may be at variance with the overall purpose of your life 5.387–8; *see also* ethics/ethics in the Buddhist tradition/an ethics of intention

interconnectedness and interpenetration

the nature of interconnectedness
birds and flowers and mountains are seen to be mutually interfused 14.219; existence is a congeries of interrelated becoming 7.152; existence is like a vast spider's web 4.581; explained using candles and mirrors 16.22; like the interpenetration of innumerable coloured lights 7.274, 7.401, 14.409; the mutual interpenetration of all things 7.302, 7.399–400, 14.219; the web of consciousness 15.707

in the Buddhist tradition
Buddhism teaches the mutual interpenetration of all things 7.278, 13.447; a distinctive Buddhist way of expressing a certain insight 16.20–2; taught by *pratītya-samutpāda* 14.608; the positive counterpart of the *anattā* (no-self) doctrine 7.49, 7.193–4, 7.312; to say things are interrelated is Buddhism, but to say they're one stuff is eternalism 8.372; Buddhahood reflected in everything 7.312–13, 7.317; that aspect of existence is called the *Dharmadhātu* or *Vajradhātu* 7.401, 26.51; and Mahāyāna Buddhism 16.6–7; interconnectedness and the bodhisattva ideal 7.41; depicted in Mahāyāna *sūtras* 7.274, 14.219; the Tantra's bold application of the doctrine to sexual union 1.388, 1.389–90; in the Far East fostered an attitude of interconnectedness towards nature 1.376

other perspectives
Sufi approach 16.22–3; 'Nothing in this world is single', *see* Shelley; in Plato 16.23; the theory of evolution demonstrates the truth of interconnectedness 10.346; the world-view of traditional societies 3.10–11

examples and applications
any unselfish act acknowledges the interconnectedness of self and other 17.696; colour as an example 1.31; degrees and levels of interconnection 5.182; every atom of the universe reflected in my heart 25.497; every living thing is connected with every other living thing 4.541; if you are aiming at Enlightenment, you are relating to everybody else who is 26.27; if you believe in interconnectedness, it's unreasonable to be angry 4.405; interconnectedness among the people of the world 12.129–30; the interconnectedness of the Buddhist world 7.458; the interconnectedness of the Dharma 25.142–3

reflections
does a world of divine archetypes interpenetrate the realm of material existence? 20.315; happiness comes from allowing oneself to be penetrated by everything 7.412, 26.53; if we feel that all living beings are intimately related to us, compassion arises 13.81; if you know one thing deeply you know everything 19.215; interconnectedness and individuality: we are not alone 7.400; interrelation is the law of life, isolation is death 8.244; it does not mean extinction of individuality 1.353; it is impossible to imagine a phenomenal thing existing in splendid isolation 7.132; nothing moves by its own power 1.102; things do not stand alone 17.xix; a transcendental reality only imperfectly represented by human thought 1.391; the whole of existence is contained in every part 19.216

contemplation and practice
achieving a state of consciousness in which things exist in interpenetration 7.300; the aim is not to reduce all difference to unity, but to see things as interfused 14.409; might be better to read a text than reflect on the doctrine 16.22; more useful than reflecting on *śūnyatā*? 16.21; as a practice 16.22

see also
in the *Avataṃsaka Sūtra*, *see under Avataṃsaka Sūtra*; Indra's Net; 'To see a World in a Grain of Sand', *see under* Blake/other works/*Auguries of Innocence*

interdependence between the Buddha and his disciples 11.278; interdependent dualities 17.368–9; spirit and letter are interdependent 2.59; underlying impermanence is the law that all things are interdependent (*anattā*) 7.49

interest approaching meditation with interest 5.328; behind many of our interests is a psychological need 19.48; bringing the energy of our interests into harmony with our spiritual ideal 25.102–3; it is crucial to notice what we find genuinely interesting 18.xvii; find something to believe in, then you can do it with all your energy and interest 10.603; following your interest into the spiritual life 15.600–1; food and sex are likely to arouse almost everyone's interest 15.154; to invoke the power of mythological figures you have to be interested in them 16.358; lack of interest is one of the greatest difficulties of the spiritual life 5.327; latch onto whichever form of practice seems most inspiring and helpful 11.221; only commit yourself to a plan that can absorb all your energies and interests 19.522–4; out of boredom can come a genuine interest 18.453; people who profess interest in Buddhism may be those who are least suitable to practise it 18.412; the spiritual community helps you to maintain your genuine interest in the Dharma 18.542; the spiritual life has to be interesting 19.22; start with an aspect of the teaching that arouses your interest 19.179; try to follow the rhythm of your natural interest 4.569; you have to consider your interests, or your Buddhism will be dry and abstract 19.50–1; *see also* action/deciding what to do

internal *see* inner

International Buddhist Conference, Sanchi 12.374, 21.393–5

International Network of Engaged Buddhists (INEB) 26.691–2

interpenetration *see* interconnectedness

interpretation be careful how you interpret people's actions 19.290–1; the difference between explanation and interpretation 11.720; the interpretation of dreams 16.204–5, 19.324–5, 19.562–3; literal interpretation of the Dharma 1.251; the Mahāyāna is just as prone to misinterpretation as the original teaching 1.404; monks as the preservers of the correct interpretation of texts 13.339; 'The more interpretations the better' 14.336, 16.546; reading the teachings is not enough, one has to learn the correct interpretation 13.340; we must take care with the interpretations we put on our experience 19.572–3

interrogation how interrogation works 17.184; self-interrogation: has one's Going for Refuge slipped? 2.512–13

intolerance are some religions intolerant by their nature? 22.138; the assumption that intolerance is sure to be followed by violence 22.529; characteristic of all forms of monotheism 4.124; of the Christian Church, *see under* Christianity/attitudes/general attitudes; has no place in Buddhism 2.243; hatred for religious opinions contrary to one's own 7.380; how does a tolerant belief or teaching or organization protect itself from an intolerant one? 4.127; in ancient India 7.378–9; intolerance of others' faith suggests doubt about one's own 17.51–2; saying that all religions are the same is intolerance 17.53–4

intoxication or mental inflation (*mada*) being intoxicated by your own good looks 15.423; beings in heaven are too intoxicated by pleasure to be able to focus on Nirvāṇa 7.170; craving for emotional intoxication 20.72–3; freeing one's energy can lead to a kind of intoxication 18.581; instead of running from happiness into intoxication, understand its true nature 3.227; intoxicated with pleasure, we tend to lose our mindfulness 10.532; intoxication of youth, health, and life 15.422–3, 17.663–4; intoxication with possessions 15.423–4; it arises when we are so pleased with ourselves that we become unmindful 17.663–4; it can manifest as contempt for others 17.664; karmic consequences 17.292; on seeing the four sights, the intoxications of youth, health, and life left Siddhārtha 2.36, 15.424; of youth, authority, class, wealth 16.298–9; from passion to greed to infatuation to addiction to intoxication 10.616–17; as *upakleśa* (Abhidharma) 17.663–4; watch out for it when you're doing something at which you're expert 17.664

introverts and extroverts the bodhisattva is both introvert and extrovert 1.396; the distinction is transcended by the bodhisattva's non-dual experience 22.247–8; extroverts: what about an occasional retreat from social activities? 12.125; introverts could be encouraged to go out and meet people more 12.125; Jung's classifications 12.274–5; lingering in the hermitage due to a lack of outgoingness 19.342; obsession: a neurotically extrovert attitude 19.396; once an individual has made spiritual progress, they are beyond this classification 1.294, 3.308; and relating to reality as subject or object 19.143; it's wrong to think that Buddhism is just for introverts 3.308

intuition an ambiguous word 14.558; 'Art is intuition' (Croce) 3.510; concentrating more on the undertones of intuition than on the overtones of reason 7.133; the *Diamond Sūtra*'s appeal to a spiritual intuition 1.301; the direct intuition of the ultimate elements of existence 14.314; an element of faith 1.283–4; 'I had an intuitive apprehension that this was the truth' 12.59; Jung's psychic functions (thinking, sensation, feeling, intuition) 12.273–5, 12.281; 'a perpetual upholding of the intuitive element in religion' 14.207; Sangharakshita's life determined by impulse and intuition, not reason and logic 2.406; a strict sense of duty in earlier life, then more trustful of intuition 4.485; transition from intellectual to intuitive understanding 18.399; Zen: realizing the truth not through thought but a flash of intuitive insight 7.125

invocation the invocation of Amitābha's name 1.340; *Paradise Lost* begins with the invocation of the heavenly muse 3.513; a tapping of energy 18.320; in the visualization of Buddhas and bodhisattvas 18.319–20

involution of the world system *see under* cosmology

involvement in life, we are involved in something we do not fully understand

15.94, 18.83; the tension between involvement and withdrawal 2.161–2, 2.271–3; to be truly Buddhist, our involvement must be truly passionate 26.57; to really enjoy yourself, get involved with the spiritual life 19.67; total action, when one is fully involved in an act, with nothing left over 1.537

Ipswich 26.507, 26.510–11, 26.754 (n493)

Iqbal, Mohammed 24.433

Iran

Persian empire
contact with Aśoka 16.57, 16.593 (n54); the Orientals (*ishrāqīya*) of medieval Iran 26.263; the Persian custom of prostrating before kings 11.250; Persian historian Minhaj-i-Siraj, who described the destruction of Nālanda 12.723 (n173); Zoroastrianism 3.427

Persian arts
angels in Persian art 26.239–40; Ferdowsi (poet of the *Shahnameh*), *see* Ferdowsi; influence on Sarojini Naidu 7.58; literature 14.289; Mahāyāna imagery owes something to Iranian influences 16.57; miniature paintings 13.284, 26.218; the *rubáiyát* of the Persian poets 1.382; the Sufis of medieval Iran were true poets 26.209; Zeb-un-Nisa, *see* Zeb-un-Nisa

other references
Bahá'í followers murdered 9.18; 'Oh for a Persian garden …' 25.373; Time God Zurvan, and Amitābha 16.592–3 (n54); Zoroastrians 12.53

Ireland 4.411, 4.704 (n298)

Ireland, John (or Jack) 10.422, 11.495, v23, 23.50 (photo)

Irenaeus 13.596, 13.621

Irene, Princess of Greece v21, v22, 25.258, 26.493

Iris (Greek goddess) 26.671

Iron Grindstone Liu 8.487

irony the Buddha's sense of irony 10.514, 10.548, 12.33; dramatic irony in a story from the *Udāna* 10.540; the irony of advocating *mettā* in an aggressive way 8.133

irrational or non-rational the exclusion of non-rational elements in Sri Lanka 12.105–6; fear of the non-rational 11.9; harnessing non-rational forces, the gods and demons of Tibet 12.291–3; human beings are not rational, and it would be irrational to expect them to be 12.11, 19.107–8; it degrades Zen to think of it as a kind of irrationality 17.65–6; irrational guilt, *see under* guilt; the Kagyu school's emphasis on speaking to people deeply, their irrational side as well 19.109; rational and irrational are complementary 12.294; irrational wisdom 26.266; irrationality in women and men 14.535–6, 19.108; Socrates' ethical theory fails to consider 'the irrational parts of the soul' 11.192, 26.164

irreversibility (*avaivartika*) of the bodhisattva, *see under* bodhisattva/four kinds of bodhisattva; found in the earliest Buddhist texts e.g. *Dhammapada* 4.182; this fundamental concept has been lost sight of 4.183–4; of the Stream Entrant, *see under* Stream Entry; until the point of irreversibility, you may not make the spiritual effort necessary 4.323

irritation becoming irritable when you are ill 17.282; getting irritated with people for spurning our '*mettā*' 17.188; if you don't want to practise something, logical arguments to do so may irritate you 4.433; saying 'You must get rid of your ego' is bound to irritate people 10.471; to dispel irritation, practise the *mettā bhāvanā* 17.183; we progress for the same reason the amoeba evolves – from irritation 7.389, 26.11; you need a high degree of sanctity to do good to others without irritating them 8.535

Irving, Washington 24.444

Isenheim Altarpiece 26.675–6

Ishtar 16.386

Isigili 8.532

Isigili Sutta *see under Majjhima Nikāya*

Isipatana *see* Sarnath

Isis *see under* Egypt

Isis Unveiled *see under* Blavatsky

Islam

the nature of Islam
brief introduction 12.53–4; ethical absolutism 17.593; horror at ritual slaughter of animals 24.576; iconoclasm 12.242–3, 26.276; the idea that the richness of Arab countries is due to God's favour 17.20; Imam Bara 7.59; intolerance of Muslims 9.184, 9.472; its besetting sin is fanaticism 26.15; mercilessness towards non-Islamic religions 8.168; Muslim pilgrims on the road between Bombay and Poona 24.104; no monastic life 12.249; no scheme of systematic self-development 7.369; on friendship 26.688; one of the

alternatives before mankind 13.513; orthodox view of Sufism 3.429–30; surrendering one's will to God 15.661; a universal religion with some ethnic features 11.296, 12.249; apostasy 9.353, 10.280; being forced to become a Muslim 10.414; world-view 3.6

history
for Islam, history is a single story, with beginning and end 12.593; the burning of the library at Alexandria 15.617, 26.476; Moharram (Shiah festival) 7.59, 7.561 (n91); Muslim architectural remains in Maharashtra 10.293; the Muslim invasion of India 7.460, 9.236–7, 12.242–3, 14.264, 25.32, 26.276; a Muslim king kidnaps the king of Tibet 12.571–2, 13.13–14; invitation to Dr Ambedkar to become Muslim 9.55; the destruction of the Buddhas of Bamiyan 26.475–9; Jihadists and 9/11 26.479–80, 26.688; persecution of Rohingya Islamic minority in Myanmar 26.687, 26.691–2

mosques
Islamic architecture 26.688; the Mezquita at Córdoba 24.427–8, 24.429–30; Sher Shah's mosque, Delhi 20.112; Sidi Sayeed Mosque, Ahmedabad 23.346–7

the Koran
the final authority for Muslims 12.54, 14.374–5; gives a confused impression 26.687; light upon light 16.108; rationale for burning the library at Alexandria 15.617; the whole text is a revelation 18.495

books on Islam
The Book of Balawha and Budasf 13.662–3; *The Duties of Brotherhood in Islam*, *see under* Al-Ghazālī; *The Epistles of the Sincere Brethren* 24.568–70; *Mystical Dimensions of Islam* 24.311

Islam and Buddhism
the influence of Buddhism and Vedānta on primitive Islam 7.370; the *Kālacakra Tantra* contains references to Mecca and Islam 14.249; tempered by spiritual impulses from the Buddha through Sufism 2.11–12, 7.485; tolerance of Muslims in Burma (1953) 8.124–5; a Muslim assists Sangharakshita on his first almsround 20.416–17; a Muslim who had visions of the Buddha 14.438; Muslims in Sri Lanka 8.62; friendly relations between Muslims and new Buddhists in India 10.60–1; a Muslim friend 26.692–4; *Common Ground Between Islam and Buddhism* 26.688–92

Islam and the West
Islamization of Plato or Aristotle 7.486; St James depicted slaughtering Muslims 24.419; a paynim once admitted to King Arthur's Round Table 4.639, 4.715 (n370); vilified by St Thomas Aquinas 7.85; Iqbal's indictment of Indian and European civilization 24.433; turned back from Poland 26.450

see also
Averroes; Islamic art, *see under* art/the art of other traditions; Mohammed; Sufism

island

'Be ye islands unto yourselves, refuges unto yourselves'
the appeal to the doctrine-follower 2.142; the Buddha's words shine out like a beacon 7.50; no conflict with having the Dharma as a refuge 2.750–1 (n733), 15.583–4; unless we are self-reliant, we cannot live 'islands unto ourselves' 2.592–3

other island references
the Buddha tells Kappa about an island of refuge 1.82; the Dharma as our light (or island) 7.261; the doctrine-follower an 'island unto himself' 2.142; if you spent your whole life alone on a desert island, you'd never really know yourself 3.400; Nirvāṇa as an island in the flood 1.82; 'No man is an island, entire of itself' 4.707 (n316)

isolation interrelation is the law of life, isolation is death 8.244; it can be a good thing to experience isolation, but most people flee from it 4.531; an isolated Buddhist is a contradiction in terms 15.612; 'Isolation for limited periods appears to be always desirable' 4.535; the test of fidelity, especially fidelity to ideals 3.569; through solitary retreat 4.530; of a wandering monk 4.530; when travelling 4.530–1; *see also* solitude; aloneness

issariya (Sanskrit *īśvarīya*) 10.592

iṣṭa-devatā *see yidam*

īśvara (God) 10.592

Italy

introduction
history 13.636–7; reflections on Italy 24.228; Symonds's *The Renaissance in Italy* 13.550, 20.32, 23.249–50; Sangharakshita's love for Renaissance Italy 11.562, 23.249–50; why do you really want to go to (say) Italy? 19.347–8

Florence
'bonfire of vanities' 13.626–7; Brancacci Chapel 13.646; the Duomo 23.312; Giotto's Tower 24.436; impressions of the city 23.314–15; San Miniato 13.597; the Uffizi 23.313

Naples
visiting 23.305–6, 24.256–305; Basilica of Santa Chiara 24.278–9; Bourbon rulers 24.290, 24.679 (n348); Capodimonte Museum 24.272–7; Castel Nuovo 24.263, 24.672 (n316); Certosa di San Martino 24.302–3, 24.450, 24.453; Duomo 24.267–9; Jesu Nuovo 24.280–1; Monastery of the Gerolomini 24.268–9; National Archaeological Museum 23.305, 24.257, 24.265–7, 24.673–4 (n320), 25.512; Porta Capuana 24.161, 24.672 (n315); Royal Palace 24.263–5, 24.673 (n316); St Januarius, *see* Januarius; San Domenico Maggiore 24.281–2; San Lorenzo Maggiore 24.270–1; San Paolo Maggiore 24.269–70, 24.674–5 (n328); 'see Naples and die' 24.302; Villa Floridiana 24.299–301

Pisa
buying pottery 24.223–4; Campo Santo 11.562, 13.593, 26.298; the cathedral 24.224, 24.664 (n275); Santa Maria della Spina 24.224–5

Pompeii
23.304–5, 24.285–97, 24.674 (n321); artefacts in Naples 24.266, 24.290; Cicero's villa 24.293–4; erotic paintings 24.292; founded by Hercules 24.295; fresco from the House of Terentius Neo 24.288; the infant Hercules strangling a snake 24.291; the Temple of Isis compared to an FWBO centre 24.294–5

Rome
Catacombs 12.495, 23.308, 23.310–11, 26.237; churches 23.306–9, 24.280, 24.678 (n342); the Colosseum 23.310; Anagarika Dharmapala visits 8.55; the Pantheon 23.310, 24.263, 24.673 (n317); Pyramid of Caius Cestius 23.309, 23.520–1 (n347); rebirth as one of the Caesars 16.420; the roads Rome built were built (unknowingly) for the triumphant feet of Christianity 7.86; Roman remains 23.306, 23.309; Santa Maria sopra Minerva 13.637–8; Sistine Chapel 2.644; a visit to Rome 23.306–11

Siena
cathedral 13.634; 'my favourite Italian city' 11.562, 13.634, 26.238; St Catherine's birthplace 13.634–5

Venice
visit with Terry 2.752 (n753), 23.257–8, 26.465–6; the Frari: awareness of a meeting of spiritual importance 200 years ago 24.228; the doge 23.258, 23.513 (n298); Europe's gateway to the East 23.258; 'Genius of Venice' exhibition (London) 25.375–7; the Lion of St Mark 25.377; mosaics at St Marks 26.237; Scuola di San Rocco 13.649; Turner's *Bridge of Sighs, Ducal Palace and Custom-House, Venice* 2.609, 2.612

other places
Amalfi coast 23.303–4; crossing the Alps 23.249–51, 23.316; Matera 23.301; Milan 13.648–9, 23.252–4; Padua 13.593, 19.467, 23.258–9; Pliny's description of the coast of Campania 24.284–5; Ravello 23.302–3; Ravenna 23.260–1, 26.237, 26.389, 26.660–1; Salerno 23.302; Taranto 23.301; Verona 23.254–5, 26.660; Vicenza 23.257; *see also* Il Convento

itivṛttakas 17.571

Itivuttaka (Sanskrit *ityuktaka*) brief introduction 14.54–5; etymology of the term 14.24; 'Bhikkhus, I am a brahmin' 2.646; the Buddha as physician 3.657 (n205), 7.115, 12.710 (n70); the Buddha's former lives in *deva* realms 1.49–50; closeness to the Buddha comes from following his teachings 2.137–8; inspiration and guidance from 2.552, 22.320; *mettā* 'burns and shines and blazes forth' 15.253; negative presentation of spiritual life 16.64; as one of the nine *aṅgas* of the Pāli canon 14.24; a schism in the sangha described 3.637–8 (n70); 'that goodwill which is the heart's release' 2.315, 14.54–5; the three unwholesome roots 13.686 (n77); wrongly Sanskritized as *itivṛttaka* 14.24; 'You are my own true sons, born of my mouth' 2.138, 8.476, 11.108, 14.444, 19.171–2

Itylus 25.194

Ixion 24.291

Iyer, Ramaswami 20.255

Iyer, Sir C. P. Ramaswamy 20.241, 20.248, 20.250, 20.370

Iyer, Sundaram 20.281

Iyer, Venkateshwara (Muvattupuzha lawyer) v20

Izumi, Hokei 13.337

J

Jabalpur, India 23.356–7

Jackson, R. J. (co-founder of the UK's first Buddhist society) 8.362, 10.139, 12.71

Jackson, R. L. 20.101

Jacobi, Jolan 11.340

Jacobus de Voragine v13

Jaffna, Yoga Swami of *see* Yoga Swami

Jagatīṃdhara, bodhisattva (also Vasuṃdhara) 14.162–3, 16.512–13

jagrat 14.464, 20.246

Jaikwadi, India 9.363

Jain, Suresh Chandra 21.53–4

Jainism animism 14.539; approval of self-mortification 8.451; arising of communities 3.429; attendance of Jains at Dharma Parishad 20.173; brief description 12.53; and causation 1.314; doctrine of karma 23.347; doesn't mention God 12.7; emergence in the Axial Age 3.427, 11.355; enumeration of 432 types of *hiṃsā* 8.448; even involuntary actions create karma 2.68, 17.584; Gomateshwara 20.373–4, 23.15–16; in principle a universal religion 11.296; Jain equivalent of the *Dhammapada* 20.449; Jain friends 9.348; a Jain who sold his merit to set up in business 14.423; Jaina Tantra 10.46; Jains could have been called Buddhists 14.404; Mahāvīra (founder), *see* Mahāvīra; Manniyar Math 20.464; meeting with Jains in Ahmedabad 23.347; Nirgranthas 17.362; practice of non-harm 4.356; Sangharakshita introduced to Jainism by Bhikkhu Kashyap 20.449; Sangharakshita visits a Jain community 22.144–5; Sravana Belgola (centre of Jainism in Mysore) 20.373–4, 23.15–16; Svetambar ('white-robed') and Digambar ('sky-clad') Jains 20.460; their order perhaps the oldest in the world 7.496; wrangling after Mahāvīra's death 14.21

Jairaj (Rashk's friend) 22.279

jakris **or** ***jhakkhris*** (magicians) 13.277, 22.523

Jalavāhana (physician in the *Sūtra of Golden Light*) 14.244, 16.246

Jalgaon, India 9.53

Jambeyang (Tibetan name for Mañjuśrī) 2.173

Jambhala (bodhisattva) introduction 12.735 (n293); grasps a mongoose 13.166–7; iconography 13.166–7; illustration 13.167; of Ratnasambhava's jewel family 13.166, 13.309; represents wealth 12.448, 18.523; Sangharakshita's initiations, *see under* Sangharakshita/meditations; three forms of Jambhala 22.556–7; when the Dalai Lama needed money, he asked Bön priests to worship black Jambhala 22.557

Jambu (river) 17.145

Jambudvīpa ('Rose-Apple Island') Ancient India 11.297; one of the four continents in ancient Indian Buddhist cosmology 16.342, 16.344, 19.504; 'the known material world, the human world' 16.356; made peaceful and prosperous by the earth goddess 16.382; Queen Vaidehī is not satisfied with this 'world of depravities' 3.454; protected by the four great kings 16.347, 16.356; represents our earth, constituting one plane of existence 2.65; in the *Ratnaguṇa-saṃcayagāthā* 14.538; in the *Sūtra of Golden Light* 16.332

James, Henry brief introduction 23.513–14 (n302); *The Bostonians* 23.260; Nabokov's view of James 3.514; *The Spoils of Poynton* 24.374

James, St (Santiago) 24.419

James, William and the 'block-universe' 7.194, 7.385; introduction 7.595 (n296); a

difference must make a difference 26.154; distinction between personal religion and institutional religion 1.191; meeting with Anagarika Dharmapala 8.58; a religious person makes spiritual experience their centre of gravity 2.185, 11.475, 16.98, 18.541

Jamyang Khyentse Rimpoche

his life
brief introduction 26.742 (n405); appearance 22.399; belonged to the Tibetan Rimé tradition 12.437; considered to be a manifestation of Mañjughoṣa 26.474; his consort or *ḍākinī*, Tsering Chodron 19.553–4, 22.401, 22.404–6, 23.172; Dzongsar Khyentse Rimpoche believed to be Jamyang's *tulku* 12.656; famous as both a yogi and a scholar 4.568, 12.437; formed a group with Dudjom Khyentse Rimpoche and Chattrul Sangye Dorje 12.443; 'which of the three gurus is the greatest?' 3.551, 12.443, 18.109–10, 19.310–11, 22.384; the French nun asks him for help 22.399; his ownership of a thangka of Nāgārjuna 6.xxx; not a dry-as-dust bookworm, but both a scholar and a meditator 13.108; one of five reincarnations of the original Khyentse Rimpoche 17.523, 22.487, 22.554; performs a Lakshmi puja 22.401; photograph 22.405; stays at Arunachal in Kalimpong 22.403–4; a very kindly, regal person 12.439; visits the Triyana Vardhana Vihara 8.663; Yogi Chen was his disciple 12.443; his death 12.439, 22.406

and Sangharakshita
asked Sangharakshita, 'Do you know anything about dancing?' 12.437–8, 13.108, 22.399; directs Kachu Rimpoche to give him the Padmasambhava *abhiṣeka* 22.469; gives him a thangka 22.406–7, 23.390, 24.12–13; initiated him into the Avalokiteśvara, Vajrapāṇi, Mañjughoṣa, and Green Tārā practices 2.685 (n238), 12.438, 12.661, 22.402, 23.390, 26.228, 26.474, 26.663; told him about the Vajrasattva mantra 11.455–6, 12.438–9, 22.407, 23.390–1; he visits the Triyana Vardhana Vihara 22.406; looking up to him 26.629

Jamyang Khyentse Wangpo 22.554

jaññā 10.513

Janov, Arthur 4.605

Janssens (Kalimpong) v21

Januarius, St 24.269, 24.674 (n327)

Jāṇussoṇī (follower of the Buddha) 15.627–8

jap-māla 9.357, 9.568n

japa (Hindu mantra recitation) 7.100

Japan art and culture 23.169; Anagarika Dharmapala visits 8.29–33, 8.49–50; the endless view, like removing the window of a Japanese house 19.184–5; English Buddhists visit Japan 23.164; *ikebana*, *see under* flowers; Japanese incense 26.495–6; Kabuki v24; *The Love of the Samurai* 24.388–9; Noh plays 20.61; reflections of impermanence in Japanese poetry 3.345; post-war religious revivals 3.442–3; in Second World War, *see under* Second World War; whaling industry 25.51; work providing a group for people to belong to 3.442

Japanese Buddhism

history
brief introduction 11.372; Kōbō Daishi introduced Buddhism to Japan 1.384; disestablishment of Buddhism at the start of the Meiji Era 7.444; the monks of medieval Japan who fought in their own armies 7.443; in the Nara period the *bodhisattva-saṃvara* was introduced 7.483; in Japan the Buddhists were leaders in every sense 7.442; influence on culture 7.125; the ancient Buddhist city of Kyoto 8.31–2; all three *yānas* once flourished 7.483; *bhikṣu* ordination replaced by bodhisattva ordination 2.209, 3.408, 8.246; *kesas* 24.529–30; Mahāyāna 2.549; Tantric Buddhism 1.384–5; 'The bigger the heap of mud, the bigger the Buddha' 4.467; Shinran's work, *see* Shinran; contact with the Buddhists of Sri Lanka 8.30–4; critical Buddhism in Japanese Buddhist scholarship 7.567 (n119); difficulty of preserving Buddhism in the hostile environment of

modern life 7.446; communicated in the West by Suzuki 7.446; efforts to enlarge the sphere of Buddhist influence in the West 1.345; Higash Honganji 8.123–4; 'Buddhism and the Japanese Character' 8.643, 22.125–6

schools
Hossō Shū 1.371; Kegon Shū 1.353–4; Rinzai school, *see under* Zen/schools; Ritsu Shū/Risshū (Vinaya) 2.209, 7.473, 7.483; Shin Buddhism, *see* Jōdo Shinshū; Shingon Shū 1.388, 4.589; Tendai (Chinese Tiantai) 4.495, 11.89, 25.207; Zen Shū 1.372

bodhisattvas
Achala 4.194, 12.578; Hachiman 4.194; Jizo (Kṣitigarbha), *see* Kṣitigarbha; Jōgyō, *see* Viśiṣṭacāritra; Kannon Kwannon, *see* Guanyin; Monju (name for Mañjuśrī) 2.173; Samantabhadra 2.180; Fugen Bosatsu (form of Samantabhadra) 1.448–9, 14.182

faith and devotion
aesthetics 4.308; faith and devotion 2.128; worship of Amitābha 1.336–7; temple at Kobe 8.30; chanting in Mumbai 9.507; Japanese Pure Land temple, Seattle 24.491; stupa in England 9.507–8; symbols have been converted into objects of emotion 26.38

festivals and commemorations
bathing an image of the infant Buddha in tea 11.239; celebration of the Buddha's birthday 2.227–8; celebration of the Buddha's Enlightenment 2.227; memorial services for aborted babies 8.610; observation of the death anniversaries of prominent religious personages 2.228; rites for the dead (O-Bon) 2.232; tea ceremony 1.572–3, 4.113

art
aesthetic impoverishment (Kanso) 7.321–2, 7.607 (n385); Amitābha in Japanese paintings 13.284; depictions of natural subjects and the Pure Land 16.184–5; frescoes at Sarnath by Kosetsu Nosu 10.699 (n274); should be as popular in the West as Tibetan iconography 2.556; the Sixth Patriarch tearing up the scriptures 12.233

literature
the academic work on Tibetan texts of Japanese scholars 17.453; augmentation of Chinese Tripiṭaka 7.526–7, 11.372; availability of Buddhist literature in Japanese 14.266–7; *Dai Nippon Bukkyō Zencho* 14.263; the *Heart Sūtra* 14.366–7; relationship of Japanese literature to that of other languages 14.289; system of writing invented by Kōbō Daishi 2.213; *Taishō Shinshū-Daizōkyō* 14.255

see also
Shōtoku Taishi; *Tanni Shō*, *see* Shinran; Zen; Zhiyi

jarā-maraṇa (decay and death) a figure of speech for all experiences of *duḥkha* 1.115; as the twelfth *nidāna*, *see under* twelve cyclical *nidānas*

jargon false speech often hides behind jargon 17.234; jargon doesn't communicate anything 19.294; the 'jargon' of being a *bhikkhu* 19.294; using words loosely, and using jargon, does not conduce to clarity 12.476; verbally adopting certain attitudes but not really thinking in those terms 19.289; the word judgemental is pseudo-liberal jargon 13.413; you can act jargon as well as speak it 19.161

Jason 26.262

Jaspers, Karl conception of the Axial Age 3.424, 3.426–8, 11.354, 12.592; definition of psychotherapy 5.657, 12.225–6; 'feeling ill and suffering from one's psychic state' 5.657, 5.659–70, 12.225–6, 13.396; *Way to Wisdom* 23.311

Jātakamāla *see* Āryaśūra

Jātakas (birth stories)

WHAT ARE THE *JĀTAKAS*?

introduction
introduction 1.49, 3.85–6, 4.652–3, 8.393, 14.61–7, 16.235; etymology of the word 14.24; an example of the imaginative kind of Buddhist literature 14.110; regarded by the Hīnayāna as edification, not exemplification 2.210; they exert a deep influence on the religious life of all Buddhist countries 1.398, 14.65–6; if people today aren't moved, it's because they see them as doctrines, not ideals 1.400; non-canonical Jātakas give folklore a Buddhist context 14.62–3; not 'a mere jumble of metamorphoses' 4.653; 'not told merely for entertainment' (Govinda) 1.233; they illustrate how the urge to Enlightenment is immanent in all forms of life 2.15; they illustrate the law of karma 14.61–2, 17.480; fairy tales, humorous sketches and picaresque tales 14.64; 'the most complete, authentic, and ancient collection of folklore in the world' 3.86, 14.63; to be read like poetry 1.399; telling the stories in villages 15.445; their function is to illustrate faith and morals rather than define doctrine 14.61; they have fascinated generations of Buddhist

children 8.209; *Oldest Short Stories of India* 8.378–9; *Ten Jātaka Stories* (review) 8.392–3

their place in the Buddhist canon
one of the nine types of literary composition in the *Āgamas* and *Nikāyas* 14.24, 14.61; *Jātakas* in the Vinaya Piṭaka 14.66; relationship to the *Avadānas* 14.61–2; distinction between canonical and non-canonical Jātakas 2.15, 14.24, 14.62; among the texts of the Sarvāstivāda 17.571; fifty *Jātakas* referred to in a Mahāyāna *sūtra* 14.189; in the *Sūtra of Golden Light* 16.246; studied by the Kadam school 12.578

other resonances
some similarities to Aesop's fables 14.64; stories that also occur in the *Mahābhārata* 14.65; *The Jātaka Stories and the Russian Novel* 8.378–9

themes
stories to illustrate the Bodhisattva's practice of the perfections 2.16, 14.63, 14.65; record the whole series of the Buddha's previous existences 2.477; the Buddha's disciples being reborn together again and again 14.455, 16.471–2; many *Jātakas* show the generosity of the Buddha-to-be in previous lives 17.200; twelve *Jātakas* said to explain the Buddha's suffering after Enlightenment 16.616 (n244); self-sacrifice 1.430, 2.16, 4.100, 14.65, 16.246, 16.254; they do not account for all the Buddha's previous existences 4.719 (n390); depictions of evolution 4.210–11, 4.652–3; altruism 1.233; the bodhisattva ideal 1.398, 10.122; Devadatta in one of the stories 4.361; 'the Dharma protects him who practises the Dharma' 10.717–18 (n453); 'Greater love hath no man than this, that he lay down his life for his friend' 7.293

THE STORIES

the starving tigress
the confidence of the Buddha-to-be in the law of karma 7.329; a reminder of the need to make sacrifices for one's ideals 4.100; the story has no Pāli equivalent 14.66–7; the story lives in the popular Buddhist imagination 1.430; Lama Govinda's comments 1.399–400; pilgrimages to the place where the bodhisattva sacrificed himself 4.324, 7.342; in the *Sūtra of Golden Light* 14.244, 16.246, 16.254

other stories about animals
the Banyan deer sacrifices himself for a pregnant doe 14.65; the fish who were reborn as gods 16.246; the hare in the moon 8.392, 13.141; Jalavāhana saves 10,000 fish from dying of drought 14.244; the king of snakes who was tormented but had not a bit of anger 4.394–5; a hawk attacked by other hawks for the meat it is carrying 3.215; Indra and the squirrel 3.305, 10.356; the monkey-chief makes himself into a bridge 4.361, 14.65; the partridge, the monkey, and the elephant 14.64; *Sivijātaka* (the Bodhisattva sacrifices his flesh to ransom a bird) 2.16

stories about humans
the Bodhisattva as a robber 3.85; Darimukha gains insight on seeing a leaf fall 3.664 (n249); *Kalandaka* (Sri Lanka) 3.670 (n288); Prince Kaṇha renounces all he possesses 14.65; King Kuśa subdues seven armies with a terrible shout 14.71; a king who goes forth when his barber finds his first grey hair 18.13; the king of the Sivis (Śibis) who gave away his eyes 1.430, 2.16, 14.65; *Kinnari Jātaka* 2.332–3; Kṣāntivādin, who enraged the king by preaching patience 1.437, 2.16, 8.392, 14.65, 15.439; Siddhārtha's leaving home 3.630–1 (n29); Jimūtivāhana, who allowed himself to be sacrificed 1.430; *Nakkhatta Jātaka*: 'What can the stars do?' 22.278; in the *Nanda Jātaka* the Bodhisattva functions like a psychoanalyst 8.378–9; Prince Dīghāya, who pulls back from avenging his parents' murder 14.63–4; the story of Ghaṭikāra and Jotipāla 14.62, 14.63; the *Śyāmaka Jātaka* (in the *Mahāvastu*) 14.71; *Vessantara Jātaka* 1.399, 1.619 (n316), 4.100, 14.65

see also
Rhys Davids, T. W./*Buddhist Birth-stories*

***Jātaka* Commentary** (*Jātakāṭṭha-vaṇṇanā*) 4.662 (n19), 14.63

jāti *see* birth

Jaṭila ascetics 2.23, 10.457

javana 17.499–500

Jayachandram, R. 20.273, 22.152

Jayachitta, Dharmacharini v24

Jayadev (protégé of Anand-ji, ordained as Sumedha) v22

Jayadevi, Dharmacharini v24

Jayamati, Dharmachari v24

Jayaprabha, Dharmacharini v24

Jayapushpa, Dharmacharini 21.479, 24.617 (n64), 25.369

Jayaratna, Dharmachari (Harvey) v24

Jayarava, Dharmachari v24

Jayata 13.342

jayati 11.406

Jayatilleke, K. N. 8.383–4, 8.399

Jayawardhana (Mitra) v24

Jaynes, Julian 24.208–9

Je Rimpoche *see* Tsongkhapa

jealousy as the crucial situation 13.232; the far enemy of *muditā* 10.174; 'He hath a daily beauty in his life/ That makes me ugly' 17.280; it comes from a basic insecurity which can lead to murder 17.655–6; jealousy in an Indian ashram 19.115, 20.197; jealousy of someone else's holiness 1.412; Śāntideva brings out the irrationality of jealousy 17.280; sexual jealousy 13.232, 13.238–40; as an *upakleśa* (Abhidharma) 17.655–6; a very unpleasant emotion, but it can be transformed 13.232; we resent others for possessing qualities we feel we do not 17.280

Jeba Dorje *see* Hevajra

jen (or *ren*, human-heartedness) *see under* Confucius

Jenkins, Daniel 8.429–31

Jenkins, Owen 11.495, 23.323, 23.331

Jenks, Beryl v23

Jennings, J. G. 2.34, 2.667 (n52), 4.405, 9.137

Jerome, St

history
alchemist 2.527, 26.267; and St Augustine 25.312; his disciples 26.305; not a very saint-like person 13.634; parallels in Buddhist tradition 26.303–4; Sangharakshita's connection with him 2.526–7, 26.238–9, 26.267–8, 26.281–306; 'St Jerome in the Desert' (poem)13.633, 25.312; his separation of himself from the social order 26.292; translator of the Vulgate Bible 2.526, 11.xvi, 13.633–4, 25.312, 26.267, 26.301; Wise Old Man archetype 2.526–7, 13.633–4, 26.267

depictions
in the desert 13.632, 24.441, 24.458, 26.282–4, 26.296; in his study 2.526, 13.632–3, 26.267, 26.284–302; by Caravaggio 23.308, 23.520 (n346); by Colantonio (illustration included) 24.276–7; by El Greco 24.415; left to the artist's discretion 13.668

iconography
introduction 2.526, 13.632; the Bible 26.299–302; crucifix 26.298–9; his hourglass 26.292–6; his red cardinal's hat 26.290–2; his faithful lion 24.224, 26.283, 26.285–90; the skull in his study 26.297–8; the symbolism of his study, the 'cave of the heart' 26.285, 26.305–6

Jesuits history 9.318–19; a Jesuit Father reports Sangharakshita as a spy 13.559, 22.25–6; a Jesuit priest in India who was persecuted for his views 13.558–9; Jesuits in Goa 9.319, 11.297; a model for the sangha (Ambedkar) 9.116–17, 9.318–19; *The Secret Instructions of the Jesuits* 20.52; Stonyhurst College 24.365–6

Jesus

INTRODUCTION

beliefs about him
for Christians, Jesus is unique, the incarnate *logos* 12.592, 13.567; 'Christ' means 'the anointed one' 12.131, 13.567; a Jewish religious teacher 13.567; the 'man for others' 12.8–10, 23.211; a man or a myth, or a combination of the two? 24.149; many other people have also died for others 12.9, 23.211; not only the *christos* or the Messiah, but also God 13.567; regarded as God incarnate 12.8–9, 13.621, 13.645–6; regarded as a sacrifice 11.233; taking on himself the sins of the world 4.599; Marcion's view of Jesus as a purely spiritual being 13.623, 13.641–2; belief that his body was only apparent (docetism) 4.135; if intelligent beings are discovered elsewhere, did Christ die for them too? 3.377; he never warned his disciples not to take his words too literally 3.167

different traditions
the imitation of Christ 14.540, 14.654 (n481), 19.53, 19.593 (n18); the visions

of Julian of Norwich 26.587; depiction in art 13.646–49; a Greek sculpture that resembled Christ as the Good Shepherd 23.285; Michelangelo's Hercules-like Christ 26.475; Asch, *The Nazarene* 13.650; Moore, *The Brook Kerith* 12.696, 13.650–2; Schweitzer, *The Quest of the Historical Jesus* 13.643; different imagined versions of Jesus 13.643; films about Jesus 13.650

Buddhist perspectives
attempts to identify Maitreya with Jesus 2.179, 21.559; 'Betrayal' (poem) 25.388; connection with India? 13.642, 13.651–2; could he be a bodhisattva? 2.183; difference between Christian and Buddhist response to miracles 4.12–13; distinguished from the Buddha 9.94–7, 9.424–5, 10.33–40; the good shepherd compared with the Buddha, the great physician 12.98; the Buddha is not central to Buddhism doctrinally as Jesus is to Christianity 15.266; Buddhists could not countenance the idea of the Buddha's being killed as Jesus was 4.14; in many ways the faithful disciple of the Buddha 7.291; Jesus in Milton's *Paradise Regained* seems at times more like the Buddha 24.572–3; Western Buddhists find it difficult to get rid of Jesus 9.417

THE ACCOUNT OF HIS LIFE

Nativity
St Mark's gospel says nothing about Jesus's conception and birth 13.642; question about the date of his birth 12.591; story that Jesus was the son of a Roman soldier 13.568, 13.718 (n341); the question of his historical existence 13.523, 13.570, 13.641–3; 'Better that Mary's Son had ne'er been born' 25.377

raising Lazarus from the dead
showed power over death 13.575; contrast with the Buddha's response to Kisāgotamī 4.12–13; we can't do any such thing, so the incident has no meaning for us 10.255; you can only believe it if you believe that Jesus was God Incarnate 13.645–6

other miracles
how might a Buddhist relate to them? 4.12–13, 13.645; miracles showing power over the elements 13.645; miracles of healing 13.644–5; perhaps he didn't literally heal the sick, but brought spiritual healing 10.555–6; the loaves and the fishes 13.645; the miracle of the tax money 13.646–7

other incidents
temptation in the wilderness 3.449, 13.554, 13.594; rejection of temporal power 3.449; his family were convinced that he had gone mad 13.461; his response to Martha and Mary 4.114; casting out devils 13.594–5; and the money-changers: 'righteous indignation' 1.557–8; rebuked by the Pharisees for letting his disciples pick corn on the Sabbath 26.179–80; writing characters on the ground in the dust 12.529; in the garden of Gethsemane 3.52, 26.675

teachings and sayings
'Be ye perfect' 3.252; better if Christianity's emphasis had been on his sayings, not those of St Paul 12.696; emphasizes the spirit rather than the letter of morality 13.614; he developed the insights of Jewish prophets 3.427; he insisted that his disciples should give up mother and father 12.249; he seems not to have regarded the family as an important institution 13.445; he seems to set the Mosaic Law utterly at naught 7.102; 'The Sabbath was made for man, not man for the Sabbath' 3.419, 4.186; said of a dead dog, 'What beautiful teeth!' (Muslim tradition) 1.521–2; sayings 13.644; the Sermon on the Mount 13.614–15, 13.619; 'Split the wood and there am I' (Gnostic) 16.22; use of metaphor and simile 26.209; they attack group values 12.249; 'We must lose our life in order to find it' 2.130; what he said about how to treat others 13.615–16; 'What is a man profited, if he shall gain the whole world, and lose his own soul?' 16.173; 'Woman, what have I to do with thee?' 12.249

Crucifixion
the common mode of execution for criminals 13.570–1, 26.675; Mary's presence at the Crucifixion 13.599; increasingly bloodthirsty depictions 13.631–2; in depictions of St Jerome 26.299; the haunting depiction of the Isenheim Altarpiece 26.675–6; his descent into Hell 13.571–4

Resurrection
associations with the pagan god of harvest 16.163; a clumsy attempt to negate the fact of death 12.357–8; the effect of Christians' belief in it 16.528; El Greco's painting 24.409; mythology, not history 13.575; a possible explanation? 20.311

Ascension
one of the Articles of Faith 13.575, 26.25; mythology, not history 13.575; the

disciples who witnessed his transfiguration 8.126, 12.523

see also
Bible/Gospels; Christianity

Jeta Grove *see* Śrāvasti

Jetsun Dolma *see* Tārā

jewels and precious stones

physical jewels
cabochons 22.93; a copy of the Kangyur made with ink from the dust of precious stones 14.255; jade 3.206, 19.513–14, 24.574, 25.415, 25.436; give us a glimpse of some higher archetypal realm (Huxley) 26.221; jewels are produced by the collision of immense forces 26.42; lapis lazuli 1.332–3; looking at gemstones almost a spiritual experience 24.322; no satisfaction to be gained from ordinary jewels 18.296; a search for a collection of precious stones 24.141; their beauty 13.165–6; their colours 26.441

metaphors
the arising of the *bodhicitta* like finding a jewel on a dungheap 1.420, 2.126, 4.42, 4.44, 10.145; associated with higher states of consciousness 16.259; in Kalimpong everything seemed to be made of jewels 11.171; the mandala of the five Buddhas like cutting facets in a diamond 13.304; mistaking the precious stone of life for an ordinary pebble 16.251; the ten precepts described as pillars of precious stone or metal 2.318, 13.444; Rechungpa's gems cannot be stolen because they are within him 19.441

symbolism
flame-coloured jewel at the top of the stupa 16.151; the guru as crest jewel (*cūḍamaṇi*) 19.176, 19.568–9; jewel (Buddha) family 13.309; the jewel that elevates your mind 17.595; the masculine principle and the jewel 22.28; the mountain of jewels in the mandala 13.261; the priceless jewel, not to be sacrificed for anything whatever 16.173; Ratnasambhava's emblem 4.207, 12.214, 13.166, 13.309; a solar symbol, embodiment of yang 16.175; the symbolism of the jewel in Buddhism 13.166–7; the *vajra* or *dorje* as a jewel 13.167, 16.175; when the Buddha is reborn, he opens his hands to find them full of jewels 17.200

see also
the jewel in the lotus, *see under* mantras/ *oṃ maṇi padme hūṃ*; parable of the jewel in the garment, *see under White Lotus Sutra*; *Ratana Sutta*; Three Jewels; wish-fulfilling jewel

Jewish prophets *see under* Judaism

jhakkhri (sorcerer) 22.523

jhānas *see dhyānas*

jhāyati 2.386

Jibananda 21.432

Jigme Norbu 22.558–9

Jimūtivāhana *see Jātakas*

Jina 'the blessed influence of Jinas': like tuning the radio 4.272; epithet of the Buddha 3.48, 11.407, 12.528–9, 14.404; the five Buddhas called the five *Jinas* 13.304; the 'vessel of the Supreme Jinas' 14.575

Jinamātā *see* Prajñāpāramitā

Jinamata (Order member, Gisela Szagun) 4.225, 4.234–5

Jinamitra (translator) 14.242

Jinamitra, Dharmachari 17.xv

Jinananda, Dharmachari introduction 17.xiv; photograph 17.xiv; the Spoken Word Project 2.737–8 (n654), 14.xv, 14.320, 17.152, 17.431, 18.xiv, 24.687 (n393)

Jinananda, Venerable (Madras) v22

Jinaraja, Dharmachari v24

Jinarajadasa (Theosophical Society) v21

Jinaratana, Venerable general entries v20, v21, v22, v23; introduction 8.635–6; a meeting in London 26.601; 'A Retrospect' (*Maha Bodhi* article) 8.643; his death 11.562

jing *see under* scriptures

Jinnah, Muhammad Ali 7.57

Jinorasa, Bhikkhu v20

jiriki *see* self-power

jīva (vital principle, living being) no unchanging substantial entity 2.99; the so-called living being lacks a basis in reality 17.411; wrong view that it is identical with the physical body (*sarīra*) 1.74

Jīvaka (royal doctor) his conversion 9.142; accompanies Ajātaśatru to see the Buddha, *see* Ajātaśatru

Jivaka (Michael Dillon) life story 21.583, 22.439–40, 22.444–5; a disciple of Lobsang Rampa 22.436–7, 23.388–9; *An English Buddhist in a Tibetan Monastery* (review) 8.398–9; *The First Man-Made Man* 11.710; gives financial support 21.583; Sangharakshita names him 20.475; he read about Buddhism without understanding the need for reflection 22.438; Jivaka's sex change 11.710, 22.434–6, 22.439, 22.519–20, 23.388; *The Life of Milarepa* 22.444; operates on Prajnaloka 22.449–50; ordained as a *sāmaṇera* but not as a *bhikkhu* 22.441–3; *Out of the Ordinary* 22.439; photograph 22.437; *Practising the Dhammapada* 8.661; his relationship with Sangharakshita 22.438–44; seeks to learn psychic powers 3.584–5, 8.626, 22.434, 22.438; he beats a young resident at the vihara with a shoe 22.441, 23.389; at the vihara 8.656; time in a monastery in Ladakh 23.389; his death 22.445, 23.389; after his death Sangharakshita chanted the Vajrasattva mantra to help him out of a pit 5.xxx, 11.455–7, 12.438–9, 23.387–91

Jivaka (later Khantipālo) *see* Khantipālo

Jīvaka Sutta *see under Majjhima Nikāya*

jīvita-indriya (life-faculty) 10.585

Jiyu Roshi *see* Kennett, Peggy

Jizo *see under* Japanese Buddhism

jñāna (transcendental wisdom)

introduction
etymology 3.355, 18.604; translated as awareness 17.610; brief introduction 16.603 (n135); term for transcendental cognition 2.127; how is it developed? 3.356, 14.316; if we truly get a sense of it, we are frightened by it 17.370; it cuts through conditioning like a diamond-thunderbolt 14.373–4; mistaking psychic illumination for *jñāna* can cause difficulty at death 18.251; today, intellectual curiosity is more awake than transcendental wisdom 1.231; passing from wisdom to transcendental wisdom 1.308–9, 14.358–9; Śākyamuni is a Buddha in whom *jñāna* predominates 12.512

āryajñāna
going forth from *manas* to *āryajñāna* 12.559–60; knowledge without a subject and without an object, non-dual awareness 12.560; noble knowledge or cognition 2.127, 26.198; three aspects 14.215

the distinction between jñāna and vijñāna
as a Buddhist one's greatest task is to insist on this distinction 3.356, 14.316; of fundamental importance for Buddhism, spiritual life, and civilization 14.315–16; *jñāna* is non-dualistic knowledge, *vijñāna* is dualistic 18.604; one should rely on *jñāna*, not on *vijñāna* 3.355–6, 16.581–2; only Stream Entrants and the greatest poets and thinkers rely on *jñāna* 3.355–6

difference from prajñā
as a perfection, it stands for the subtlest type of *prajñā* 2.164–5; the *Platform Sūtra*'s analogy: like a lamp and its light 1.587–8, 3.356–7

and other Buddhist terms and texts
the distinction between *puṇya* and *jñāna* 19.46–8; inclusion as a topic in the *Patisambhidā-magga* 14.73; the relationship between *vidyā*, *prajñā*, and *jñāna* 17.610–11; the sword of *prapañca*-free *jñāna* 17.147

see also
five *jñānas*; *jñāna-pāramitā*, *see* perfections/tenth perfection

jñāna-dhātu 14.83

Jñānagupta (translator) 14.109

Jñānakumāra (translator) 14.242

Jñānaprabha, king of western Tibet 12.571–2

Jñāna-prasthāna the encyclopedic 'Establishment of Knowledge' 7.502; introduction 14.94–5; commentary 1.365, 14.95, 14.254; encyclopedic in content, but unsystematic in form 14.95; said to be the key work of the Sarvāstivāda Abhidharma 14.82; six accessory treatises 14.254; translations 14.94–5

jñāna-sambhāra *see* two accumulations

jñānasattva *see under* visualization

Jñānasiddhi *see* Indrabhūti

Jnanasiddhi, Dharmacharini 13.523

Jnanasuri, Dhammacharini at Dr Ambedkar's conversion ceremony 10.xxxv–vi; memories of Dr Ambedkar's death 10.xxxvi; caught up in caste violence in Aurangabad 10.xli; ordination 10.lii; teaching meditation in prison 10.xli

Jñānottarabodhisattva-paripṛcchā Sūtra 14.188

jñeyāvaraṇa *see* two veils

Job *see under* Bible

Jōdo Shinshū (Shin Buddhism)

history
founded by Shinran 1.344–5, 3.651 (n165), 7.42; the largest of the Japanese branches of the Mahāyāna 1.345; Pure Land doctrine 1.337; prominence given to compassion 2.126; the eighteenth vow of Dharmākara, the 'King of the Vows', foundational 2.163; the monk–layman dichotomy has no significance 8.624; not orthodox because of its emphasis on lay life 2.562; two levels of ordination, including the Threefold Refuge 2.566–7; Rennyo, second founder 2.566, 2.746 (n698); divergence from Zen 1.208; Zen and Shin both ultimately tend towards liberation, but they take different routes 17.390; teaches salvation by faith against the background of a profound metaphysic 1.241, 1.346; the awakening of faith: not mere belief but an instant of pure egolessness 1.346; faith as the emotional counterpart of wisdom 15.616–17; church in Seattle 24.529; a novel on the subject, *The Buddha Tree* 24.532; relations of Triratna Buddhist Order with Shin 2.562, 2.566

and Amitābha
attention concentrated on Amitābha 1.134, 1.199, 1.208, 1.344–5, 2.562, 13.309–10, 19.405; the belief that a single heartfelt repetition of Amitābha's name is enough 24.54; gratitude to Amitābha for the gift of Enlightenment 13.309–10; the importance of taking refuge in Amitābha 2.566; spiritual life centres around Amitābha's vows 1.329

see also
and Jōdomon, *see under* Pure Land Buddhism; Nakayama; Otani; Kanamatsu, Kenryo, *see* Kanamatsu; self-power and other-power; Shinran

Jōdomon (path of other-power) *see under* Pure Land Buddhism

Jogis, gatherers of the souls of the dead 11.456–7, 12.439, 23.391

Jōgyō *see Viśiṣṭacāritra*

John, King 13.553–4, 24.581

John the Baptist, St 13.631, 23.257, 25.376

John of the Cross, St brief introduction 13.716 (n319); the dark night of the senses 17.673; the dark night of the soul 7.101, 7.580 (n195), 17.109, 17.673, 17.724 (n116); *The Spiritual Canticle* 13.544, 13.716 (n319)

John of Damascus, St 13.662–3

John Sobieski (Polish king) 26.450

Johnson, Jane (Padmasiddhi's wife) 24.72–3, 24.624–5 (n97 and n99)

Johnson, Mike 24.548–9

Johnson, Dr Samuel

life
brief introduction 23.495 (n165); born in Lichfield 23.137; as a child, he was touched by Queen Anne 16.424; his Christian outlook 26.484; lack of musical faculty 3.57; literary critic 26.324; his fear of being alone 18.16; his laziness 26.484; amorous propensities' 23.196; desire to 'spend his life driving briskly in a post-chaise with a pretty woman' 24.522; the perceptiveness of his psychological analysis 12.77; his view of Oliver Goldsmith 24.582; portrait 26.565; his summer house 24.165; helped to prove that the Cock Lane Ghost was a fraud 2.667 (n53); his death 26.484; underrated 26.339; Boswell's *Life of Johnson* 20.51, 23.137, 26.4, 26.483–4; Dr Ambedkar's resemblance to Dr Johnson 9.92

sayings and writings
'All censure of a man's self is oblique praise' 14.489; 'Clear your mind of cant' 4.244, 25.372, 26.484; 'Hope triumphs over experience' 10.496; 'If you were to read Richardson for the story, you'd go and hang

yourself' 12.697; 'If a young man forgets his hat, no one thinks anything of it' 24.346; imagination: 'the capacity to emancipate oneself from one's present experience' 17.598; 'Keep your friendships in constant repair' 12.640, 18.336, 22.322, 26.484, 26.537; 'mankind, from China to Peru' 22.142; 'Mercy I asked, mercy I found' – saying he perhaps made popular 2.238, 15.363; on accuracy of narration 1.516–17, 12.34; on Goldsmith: 'He touched nothing that he did not adorn' 26.490; travellers' narratives: 'general accounts which leave no distinct idea' 23.250; 'wisdom literature' 14.343; 'A woman preaching is like a dog walking on its hind legs' 14.419

dictionary
introduction 12.476, 14.309, 25.7, 25.371; definition of 'accept' 12.480, 26.61; definition of 'gratitude' 3.598; definition of 'scholar' 25.5

other works
'Letter to Chesterfield' 12.697; *The Lives of the Poets* 25.370; *Life of Swift* 26.371–2; *Rasselas* 11.724; *The Vanity of Human Wishes* 25.371, 26.483–4; 'An Ode on Friendship' 24.315; 'On the Death of Dr Robert Levet' 24.314–15, 26.399, 26.483, 26.745–6 (n429)

and Sangharakshita
'By the time I was fifteen I was an ardent Johnsonian' 20.51, 26.483; considers Johnson a literary hero 26.483–4; first reads 20.46, 20.51, 23.137, 26.483; goes to Lichfield on pilgrimage 23.137–8; 'Johnsonian studies' 23.427; writing a poem about Dr Johnson 26.490; 'Lines Composed on Acquiring the Works of Samuel Johnson' 25.370–2

Jojin (Japanese monk) 2.216

Jonas, Hans 23.111, 23.491 (n139)

Jones, Dhivan Thomas assistance with Pāli sources 17.xv, 17.152; foreword to Pāli commentaries 15.xi–xxii; introduction to *The Religion of Art* 26.xix, 26.90–100; translation of *Udāna* verses 10.419–656

Jones, Eli Stanley 21.345, 21.628 (n97)

Jones, Roger *see* Vajradipa

Jonson, Ben 8.298, 20.62

Jorhat, India 22.92–3, 22.95, 22.97

Josaphat *see* Barlaam and Josaphat

Joseph of Arimathea 13.650–1

Joshua 16.143

journeys calling the path a journey 3.254; crooked journeys 26.264–5; the heroic bodhisattva takes his family on a fearful journey 2.157, 3.55–6; an imaginal journey through the three realms (*trailokya*) 26.271–3, 26.279; the journey through the imaginal world 26.265–6; the journey from conditioned to Unconditioned existence 3.244; the journey from death to rebirth 3.110–11, 12.201–6, 16.532, 23.93; 'A journey of a thousand miles starts with a single step' 7.397; life as a journey 15.366–7, 16.86, 18.80, 26.262; the mythical journey towards ordination 26.272–3, 26.279; Night Journey, *see under* Mohammed; the parable of the return journey, *see under White Lotus Sūtra*/parables; Rechungpa compares his journey to the spiritual life 19.370–89; the spiritual path as a mythical journey 4.646, 18.80, 26.262–6; the symbol of the journey 16.123–4; 'Through not understanding the four noble truths, we have wandered a long journey' 1.96; translation as a journey 11.xvii–xviii

Journey to the West (*Monkey*) *see under* Xuanzang

joviality 26.78

Jowett, Benjamin 1.197, 17.605

joy (*pamojja* or *prāmodya*)

the arising of joy
the cheerfulness that arises from being aware of following the path of virtue 2.105; feeling *mettā*, you feel an airy and weightless joy 15.331; finding in the present an inexhaustible satisfaction and perennial joy 7.286; if you get rid of desires and clinging, joy will spontaneously arise 19.579; a joyous response to a Perfection of Wisdom *sūtra* 14.533; the *mettā bhāvanā* is a guide to recovering our inheritance of joy 15.345; the natural consequence of faith is joy 18.143; resisting sloth brings joy 5.382; upon release from the hindrances 5.342–3; what do you do with joy? 18.78; when you become Enlightened, you'll bubble with joy 18.254

joy whatever the conditions
even when undergoing pain 4.316–17; joy despite discomfort 17.252–3; joy is not dependent on circumstances 18.47; only joy will keep us going in the spiritual life 18.133; 'Pain shall be transmuted into joy …' 23.446; sensitivity to the joys and sorrows of others 8.452

joy and other mental states
devotion must involve an element of joy 15.604–5; 'Give till you swoon with joy' 16.403; if there's no joy in your spiritual life, there's no faith either 17.336; the line between joy and intoxication 16.301; *saumanasya*, an aspect of *vedanā* 2.98; there is no feeling of joy without a feeling of strength 26.35; 'When you are joyous, look deep into your heart ...' (Gibran: *The Prophet*) 1.129

the joyful Buddhist
the bodhisattva has a duty to be joyful 17.182; Dudjom Rimpoche's delight in being alive 22.508; the faith-follower drawn to the joy of Enlightenment 18.129; four things that cause the bodhisattva joy 14.189; the hallmark of the true Buddhist 3.265, 17.79–80; the joy of Mahāyāna *sūtras* 16.336; joy on a retreat in England (1966) 23.232; joyfully rising to the height of seven palm trees 14.183; Milarepa's joy 17.302, 18.45–6, 18.129, 18.345; we have to be honest about how much spiritual joy we experience 17.302

other joys
'He who binds to himself a joy' 17.506, 26.598; joy in flight 25.266, 25.284; joy in solitude, and in society 19.518; the joy of St Francis 4.316, 13.625, 17.555; joy's fountain 25.xxxiv, 25.163; the planets' dance of joy about the sun 25.497; 'Writing is in itself a joy' 14.294, 14.299

see also
twelve positive *nidānas/prāmodya*; sympathetic joy, *see muditā*

Joyce, James 3.514, 26.339

Juan Diego 13.602

Judaism brief description 12.53; anti-Semitism 24.73, 26.337–8; the cabbala and *Adam Kadmon* 14.426; Cabbalists 7.369; conversion to Judaism 12.248; emergence of Jewish prophets in the Axial Age 3.427, 11.355; an ethnic religion with some universal features 11.296, 12.248; has no scheme of systematic self-development 7.369; the Holocaust, *see under* Second World War; how a great rabbi tied his shoelaces 11.162; iconophobia 26.477; in India 9.348; influence on Christianity 13.622–3; Jewish prophets believed to be sent or inspired by God 12.134; the journey from Egypt to the Promised Land 26.262; linear vision of history 12.593; Maimonides (12th-century philosopher) 24.427; a purge of nature spirits, shift from feminine to masculine values 19.414; the religion of a nation 13.513; story that Jesus was the son of a Roman soldier 13.568, 13.718 (n341); strong identification with Palestine 12.248; synagogues 24.422–3, 24.430; their recognition of only one God 19.414

Judas 12.513, 13.594

Judge, W. Q. 8.51

judgement

introduction
distinguish fact from value judgement 12.477; sound judgement is a rare quality 26.82; who is to judge what is profound? 16.59; the word judgemental is pseudo-liberal jargon 13.413

judging other people
don't be too quick to judge that others are being egoistic 4.319–20, 10.471, 19.111; in refusing to accept someone's judgement one is not questioning their integrity 26.82; it's always advisable to reserve one's judgement 10.590–1, 19.100, 19.538; misjudging other people 19.107; our tendency is to see faults rather than virtues 18.112; people judge others by quite superficial standards 19.308–10; take care not to bring a judgemental attitude to unskilfulness 17.xxiv

using your own judgement
exercising your judgement about what to do, based on your self-knowledge 15.289; the importance in Buddhism of freedom of individual judgement 11.508–9; an individual makes their own judgements 15.290; there is no authority, we must use our own judgement 10.150; three things needed: the general teaching, the Pith-Instruction, and your own judgement 18.408

judgment in religious matters
the Buddha does not sit in judgement over people 16.309–10, 17.662–3; Buddhist schools to be judged according to their transcendental attainments 1.205; the danger of passing judgement on one's teacher 18.112; daring to sit in judgement on the wisdom of Buddhas and bodhisattvas 7.311, 11.484; difficult to get free of the concept of God as judge 7.97; judgement in Judaeo-Christian ethics 3.99–100

judo 23.419, 23.421

juggling concepts are best treated like playful juggling, not grim calculation 2.54; is all the intellectual juggling of the Perfection of Wisdom really necessary? 14.584; it's easy to juggle refined concepts but difficult to stop thinking in those terms

19.373; keeping up *vīrya* is like juggling 17.70

Julian, Emperor 20.61

Julian of Norwich 26.586–7

Julius Caesar compared with the Buddha 12.529; divorced his wife because 'she ought to be above suspicion' 23.385; the historical fact of his assassination 10.222; Sangharakshita out in London in his robes: 'Look, mate, 'ere comes Julius Caesar!' 23.174

Jung, C. G.

HIS WORK

introduction
influenced by D. T. Suzuki 12.72; has inspired modern interest in myth and symbol 12.508; interest in Eastern religions 5.665; more sympathetic to religious ritual than Freud had been 11.207; said that the problems of all his patients were ultimately religious 5.664; said this is the age of 'interiorizing' symbols 26.389; alchemy 12.184; all reality is psychical, nothing exists except ideas 12.172; analytical psychology 12.93; use of images 2.132; *Jung, Jungians, and Homosexuality* 24.389; *Experiment in Depth* 23.130; psychological commentary on 'The Yoga of Knowing the Mind' 8.346–7

Jung and Buddhism
his interest in Buddhism well known 7.450; learning to express Buddhism in Jungian terms 12.117–18; Jungian symbolism of the twin miracle 12.619; response to the *Tibetan Book of the Dead* 12.197

collective unconscious
Jung's first use of the term 2.698 (n358); approximate analogy to the *ālaya vijñāna* 2.279, 8.458, 12.176, 18.606; archetypes of the collective unconscious 19.409, 19.615 (n159), 26.269–70; symbolized by the ocean 14.346; descriptions of the forces Padmasambhava subdued 12.323–32

psychic functions
thinking, sensation, feeling, intuition, extrovert, introvert 12.273–5, 12.281; extraverted and introverted thinking types 18.145–6; extrovert and introvert approaches to commitment 18.171

other key Jungian terms
definition of the self 3.491, 16.173; the individuation process 12.190–2, 12.199, 12.218; persona 3.40, 13.299; projection, *see* projection; psyche 3.41; synchronicity 22.475

ARCHETYPES

introduction
Jung's shifting use of the word 12.181, 16.189; universal archetypes 13.121

the anima and animus
the *ḍākinī* as anima 18.59; the earth goddess 12.190–1; interesting discussion 23.138; the unintegrated animus 13.238; we have to integrate our unconscious femininity (or masculinity) 12.192–3

the shadow
appears in our dreams 12.192; Māra 12.190; 'It's not a romantic shadow but a smelly stain' 16.304; we have to integrate the shadow into our conscious attitude 12.190, 12.192

the wise old man
Brahmā Sahāmpati 12.191; consulting the *I Ching* 17.614; St Jerome 2.526–7, 13.633–4, 26.267; we have to learn from the wise old man 12.193

the young hero
Mucalinda 12.191; we have to give birth to the young hero, that is, to ourselves 12.193

Jungi *see* Gautam, Jungi Bahadur

jungle *see* forest

Jupiter 16.385

just sitting meditation introduction 5.xxvi–vii, 5.395–405; analogous to the relaxation of the Mahāmudrā 18.584, 19.137; different meanings, different practices 5.404–5; a difficult practice 18.584–5; not strictly speaking a practice 5.403, 19.137; radical receptivity 5.xxxiv; Zen term *shikantaza* 5.400

justice Buddhism is not just a means of obtaining social justice 8.205; green as the colour of justice 13.282; the idea of justice (Plato) 12.463; 'Justice and Pity' (poem) 25.437; pseudo-liberalism is the belief that fairness can be achieved by unfair means 26.74; without truthfulness there could be no justice 2.375–6, 3.322

justification are we justified in speaking of Buddhism at all? 1.202; a Buddha doesn't have to justify his Buddhahood 18.122; caste Hindus' justification of the caste system 9.103, 10.51–3, 10.54–6, 12.278; the Church saying that the end justifies the means 8.153, 8.253; the cynic feels less than is justified, the sentimentalist more than is justified 26.23; justifications for anger, *see under* anger; justifying what you want to do 3.577–8, 10.526–8, 18.366–7; no justification for getting

angry in defence of your ideals 17.602; no question of justifying any war 3.583; the parable of the burning house is not saying that the end justifies the means 16.83–4; the scriptures shouldn't be invoked to justify unBuddhistic practices 14.265; self-deception in the way we justify our addictions 17.257; the spiritual life doesn't have to be justified in worldly terms 14.522, 18.121; unconscious guilt leads to a tendency to justify oneself 3.214; we don't have to justify our human status by being useful 14.522, 18.120

Justinian 11.336

Juvenal 26.761 (n558)

Juzhi, Master 8.487, 8.493

Jyoti brothers v21, v22

Jyotipala, Dharmachari 5.xxxv, 24.132, 24.636 (n153)

K

Kabir brief introduction 8.167, 8.680 (n100); *Dijak* 20.449; the levitation of a Kabirapanthi 3.267–8; 'the unstruck sound' 2.130

Kachu Rimpoche

his life
brief introduction 21.553–4; incarnation of Lhatsun Chempo Rimpoche 22.471; his character 12.441, 26.226; abbot of the Pemayangtse Gompa in Sikkim 2.445, 12.440, 22.398; answered Americans' questions before translation 12.441, 13.25–6, 22.327–8, 22.397–8, 26.227–8; belief in astrology 26.227; devoted to Jamyang Khyentse Rimpoche 12.441–2, 22.400, 23.382, 26.228; he makes a silver image of Padmasambhava 22.471, 26.228; his nephew, Namzey 21.576, 22.472; and levitation 13.25; saw that a nun hadn't done the practice she claimed 12.440–1, 13.25, 22.326–7, 22.396–7, 26.227; performed the coronation ceremonies of the Maharaja of Sikkim and his wife 12.442; photographed demonstrating the eight offering *mudrās* 23.383; photographs 22.326, 22.400; death in Sikkim 12.442

Sangharakshita's teacher
the bond between them 22.328; gave him the name Urgyen 22.474, 23.171, 26.673; gave him the Padmasambhava practice 2.442, 12.441, 22.469, 22.472–3, 23.383, 26.673; introduced him to the four *mūla* yogas 2.443, 22.473, 22.477, 23.383; made a banner of victory on the roof of the vihara in Kalimpong 12.298, 12.441, 13.24–5, 13.177, 19.160, 22.477, 23.383, 26.226–7; visits to the vihara 8.663, 21.552, 22.469, 22.477, 23.382; Sangharakshita dreams of Kachu Rimpoche 23.319; 'very much the guru' 23.382–3; looking up to him 26.629; Sangharakshita visits him at the Pemayangtse Gompa 22.470–1

Kadam precepts 18.393

Kadam school *see under* Tibetan Buddhism/schools

Kadamthorbu 8.528, 8.593

Kah Tong *see* Shin Yeung

Kahn, Marghareta 2.403

Kaikini, Dr v22

Kaila (cook) 22.524

Kailash *see under* mountains

Kailashananda, Swami 22.138

kaivalya *see under* Sāṃkhya school

Kajiyama, Dr 22.270–1

Kakacūpama Sutta *see under Majjhima Nikāya*

Kakusandha Buddha 1.45

kāla-cakra (wheel of time) 1.386

Kālacakrayāna *see under* Tantric Buddhism

Kālāmas of Kesaputta the Buddha's advice to them, *see under Aṅguttara Nikāya/Book of the Threes*; republic 2.25

kālapāni 9.315–16

Kalaram Temple campaign 9.55

Kālī (goddess) introduction 7.561 (n92); awe-inspiring images 26.383; and Calcutta 22.59; form of mother goddess 10.46; her appearance 16.384–5; her devotees included thugs (assassins) 10.55; hymns 7.59; temple at Kamakhya, Assam 22.91, 22.582 (n91); worshipped by animal sacrifice 10.45; wrathful consort Shiva 22.91

Kali Yuga 11.621, 19.83

Kalidasa 20.62, 25.26

Kalimpong

introduction
brief introduction 22.383–4; advice on visiting 21.513; terminal of the Lhasa–

India trade route 21.441; trading centre 21.139; visitors 21.441–2; a special place with a special atmosphere 22.468–9; where Padmasambhava met the King of Tibet 22.468; repeating a mantra once in Kalimpong 22.468–9; its bright colours: 'a world of jewels' 11.171; the scents of Kalimpong 26.493–4; the surrounding forests 25.131; Dailo Hill 21.13, 21.347, 21.436–7; rainy season 21.40; poetic description of the town 22.180–1; an exotic place 25.134; the magic of the *jakri* 13.277; colour and music 20.469; its name means 'a skull capsized' 25.389; different nationalities of the town 20.468, 21.8; Bhutanese Buddhists in Kalimpong 21.210, 22.33–4; 'The Town of the Seven New Years' 22.384; lack of brothels 22.45; map of Kalimpong 22.xiii

events during Sangharakshita's time there
Buddha Jayanti 21.506, 21.508–9, 21.547–8, 22.299–300, 22.306, 22.311–18; commemoration of Tsongkhapa's death anniversary 22.510–11; other Buddhist festivals 8.658–9; the Dalai Lama visits 8.651, 21.529–30, 22.366, 22.368–72; the visit of the Sacred Relics, *see* Sacred Relics; Hindu festivals 21.98–101; the brahmins who tried to kindle fire through reciting mantras 19.62–3; film shows 21.57–8, 22.104–5, 22.113–18; an earth tremor 18.12; divisions in the Buddhist community 22.235–6; Chinese people of Kalimpong interned 22.546, 22.557; military build-up in the area 22.557–8; consequences of Chinese incursion (1962) 22.545–51, 22.559–60

buildings and institutions
Arunachal 22.403–4; Bhutan House 21.142, 21.210, 22.33, 22.35, 22.371; the Blind School 21.34–5; Chinese-language school 22.546; Dr Graham's Homes 21.346–8, 22.13, 22.115, 22.137–8, 22.371–2; *Himalayan Times* 22.213; Indo-Chinese Friendship Society 22.211–13; Indo-Tibetan Buddhist Cultural Institute, *see under* Dhardo Rimpoche; Lepcha Association 21.365–6; Mani Press 21.234–5; Mela Ground 22.317–18; Old Bhutan Palace 22.192; police station 21.122–3; St Philomena's Convent and School 21.351–2; Tsechu Offering Association 8.658

Tharpa Choling Gompa
abbot 8.659, 22.511; ceremony of reconciliation 21.228–9; conflict in 21.185; and the Dalai Lama's visit 22.368–9; the lamas participate in funerals 22.201–2, 22.205–6; procession for Tsongkhapa's death anniversary 8.659; Sangharakshita's contact with the monastery 23.395–7; visiting the gompa 21.32–3, 21.176–82, 23.384; Terry makes woodblock prints there 23.396–7; Tomo Geshe Rimpoche's residence 21.213, 23.397; 2,500th Buddha Jayanti procession 22.315–18

other monasteries and gompas
Bhutanese gompa 12.442, 12.447, 21.210, 22.553–7; Dharmodaya Vihara v21, v22; Ramakrishna ashram 21.158–9; Zangdokpalri Monastery 12.684, 12.757 (n476)

missionaries
the exaggerated bonhomie with which they dealt with their converts 24.304; compelling hungry refugees to listen to a sermon 23.208; 'conversion through pregnancy' 21.364–6, 21.426, 22.25–6; praying for the conversion of the 'heathen' 2.237; bribing people to become Christian 19.468; Sangharakshita's contact with missionaries 13.556–7, 21.21–2, 21.345–66; a young student of Buddhism is scared into leaving 22.45–6; missionaries are forced to receive the Dalai Lama 22.371–2; offensive posters 22.530–1; taking children from their parents 23.208

see also
Sangharakshita II/in Kalimpong; Newars; Tibetan refugees, *see under* Tibet/people

Kalinga king 1.437, 14.475; war 8.192, 25.271

kalpa (Pāli *kappa*, measurement of time) the Buddha would stay until 'the end of the *kalpa*' if asked 11.276; the current *kalpa* is the *bhadra* (auspicious) *kalpa*, because it is to have five Buddhas 8.201; time taken for a piece of silk to wear away a rock 1.39–40, 2.64, 3.679 (n342), 4.60, 19.593 (n16); divided into four periods (*asaṃkhyeyas*) 1.40, 13.299, 17.472; four 'incalculable' *kalpas*, twenty 'intermediate' *kalpas*, and eight *yugas* 2.64

kalpa-vṛkṣa *see* wish-fulfilling tree

kalyāṇa definition 2.529; etymology 3.603; an important term 15.348

kalyāṇa mitra yoga *see under* guru yoga

kalyāṇa mitratā (spiritual friendship)

THE TRADITION

introduction
what the words mean 3.399, 3.603–4, 11.704; brief explanation 9.545–6, 15.765 (n195); the term has a richer connotation than the English 'spiritual friend' 3.604;

the meaning of spiritual friendship 3.573–80; difference from ordinary friendship 10.208, 16.315; disinterested friendship 15.293; distinction between spiritual friendship and ethnic solidarity 21.261; distinction between good friendship and spiritual friendship 26.633–4; distinction between *kalyāṇa mitratā* and 'mundane' personal relationships 4.522–4; friendship infused with *mettā* becomes *kalyāṇa mitratā* 15.252; 'The Good Friend' 7.292–6; spiritual friendship *is* the Dharma 3.575, 11.700; the crucial importance of friendship in spiritual life 24.360; what makes a friendship spiritual 21.463

'Friendship is the whole of the spiritual life'
although the Buddha said this, books on Buddhism rarely mention friendship 8.578; and also the panacea for ordinary psychological problems 26.78; the image of Tobias and the angel 13.589; the Buddha denies that there is a purely individual spiritual life 26.632–3; the importance of the Sangha refuge 10.208, 12.514, 15.742; no tradition has ever taken that extraordinary utterance seriously 12.669, 13.619; the right livelihood context 12.608; a similar statement by Aelred of Rievaulx 13.619; so important and delightful is spiritual friendship 3.90; understanding this depends on understanding the words the Buddha used 11.703–4; Westerners beginning to take it seriously 13.619; what this means 3.399–400, 3.578–80, 9.309, 11.704–5, 12.669–70, 23.438; the word used for 'spiritual life' is *brahmacarya* 11.704

other reference points in the Buddhist tradition
reliance on spiritual friends stressed throughout the Buddhist tradition 11.506; the Buddha and Ānanda as exemplars of spiritual friendship 3.90, 11.436–7; the first of five things that conduce to spiritual maturity 3.578, 10.529; described in the *Gaṇḍavyūha Sūtra* ('friends in the good life') 2.161, 14.220–2; Milarepa's song of spiritual friendship 18.13–15; 'the greatest benefactor is a spiritual friend in the form of an ordinary human being' 2.700 (n370), 3.604, 4.172, 15.586, 17.307; one should 'think of a spiritual friend as the Buddha' (Gampopa) 4.175–6; Ayya Khema's belief in the value of spiritual friendship 26.538–9

references in other cultures
the importance of spiritual friendship in ancient Greece 3.524; *The Duties of Brotherhood in Islam* 5.177–82, 26.688; St Aelred's *Spiritual Friendship* 13.618–19, 24.387; 'Tobias and the Angel' 4.99, 13.589, 26.269; 'Opposition is true friendship' (Blake) 16.525; 'An Ode on Friendship' (Johnson) 24.315

Buddhas and bodhisattvas and spiritual friendship
the Enlightenment experience contains an element of spiritual friendship 26.78; how to get a sense of the Buddha as your spiritual friend 26.634–7; the Buddha as a friend to all beings 17.327–8; the Buddha was the original spiritual friend 26.634; the bodhisattva as spiritual friend 2.161; the bodhisattva should tend good friends 14.153; if we hear an archetypal bodhisattva's advice, best to consult our friends too 12.573

THE BASIS OF *KALYĀṆA MITRATĀ*

the need for kalyāṇa mitratā
it is needed to learn the Dharma 9.317; its importance for someone who is spiritually immature 3.578, 10.527, 18.367; *kalyāṇa mitratā* is crucial to the education process 9.446; need for spiritual friendship of those practising chastity 2.606–7; the need of the spiritually committed for friendship 23.403; our need for spiritual friends 11.703; spiritual friendship and fear of homosexuality 3.527, 23.438; you can't really be a spiritual friend to yourself 18.395, 19.355; you get something from it that you get from no other relationship 12.639; you need a connection with someone with experience of the transcendental 16.354

spiritual friends and levels of development
don't assume which of you is more developed 11.666; don't think of leading or guiding another person, but just being a good friend 16.25; just be friends, and any teaching will happen naturally 26.81; from counsellor to guide to bodhisattva to Buddha 7.295; overlap between teachers and spiritual friends 3.603; someone who is more developed than you *as a human being* 9.446; spiritual friendship developed through living and working together 12.608, 16.413; those who are spiritually more advanced than we are 32.700 (n370), 3.604, 4.172, 11.506, 15.586; 'the wise': a truly spiritual community, not just a social group 15.292

'horizontal' and 'vertical' friendship
introduction 3.554–6; Buddhism's approach to vertical and horizontal relationships 18.507–8; the guru is the ideal vertical, with the *ḍākinī* the ideal

horizontal 13.204, 18.418; the importance of vertical *kalyāṇa mitratā* 14.313–14; in some Buddhist sanghas horizontal spiritual friendship is neglected 12.514, 24.485; it can tend towards horizontal or vertical 18.505; the more developed of the two can learn something from the less developed 18.216; 'vertical' contact is a very important way of strengthening motivation 12.382; we need both 3.314

kalyāṇa mitratā in the Triratna Buddhist Community
spiritual friendship is one of the cornerstones 12.457–8; when choosing a *kalyāṇa mitra*, don't think too much about accidental qualities 19.61; *kalyāṇa mitra* ceremony 18.379; learning from both your *kalyāṇa mitras* 19.544; the system 2.514; two *kalyāṇa mitras* should work together to advise a third person 19.316–17

THE WORKING GROUND

the nature of spiritual friendship
accustoming ourselves to prefer another's will 7.296; based on having a higher ideal 18.508–9; connection with single-sex idea 2.517; depth of communication between spiritual friends 2.248; an effective way of sustaining mindfulness of purpose 17.541; the emotional equivalent of understanding the no-self doctrine 7.293; a field of creativity 12.638–9; following the path with spiritual friends like mountaineers roped together 25.34; a good friend is someone with whom you can be alone 18.17, 18.395; in the course of spiritual friendship the ego gets worn away 12.669; it can never involve any kind of power relationship 3.576, 3.579, 11.701–2; it enables us to be true to our individuality 15.332; it helps us overcome fear of or resistance to change 16.109–10, 17.255; it is based upon *mettā*, not *pema* 3.576; mutual responsiveness across a chasm 18.16–17; a mutual transcendence of egotism 4.633–4, 12.638; no lies or emotional blackmail, just concern for happiness and well-being 3.577; one of the conditions for spiritual development 3.314; real communication 3.439; richly endowed with the potential for spiritual development 7.294; through it we perceive the pure and tranquil lineaments of Enlightenment 21.476; a training in unselfishness 3.579, 10.394, 11.705

how spiritual friendship works
if you feel downhearted, you need the help of your spiritual friends 25.33; commitment to it is made possible by shared commitment to ideals 17.328; in communication with friends, we turn the theory of the Dharma into practice 3.90; no pressure, but helps you create a point of freedom from which to act 18.456–7; often your spiritual friends have a better idea than you of what you can do 18.622–3; sometimes they are a better friend to you than you are to yourself 18.521; you can entrust your mental state to your spiritual friends 15.369; your friend won't see your welfare in quite the same way you do 15.293; your spiritual friends can remind you of what you're like at your best 18.521; when all else fails, it is spiritual friendship that keeps us going 17.309

support for your spiritual life
adopting the lifestyle of your spiritual friends 10.529–30; at the moment of death 12.202; during difficult times our friends are our main source of help and inspiration 26.80; a factor in spiritual growth 3.556; friends help us identify where to put our effort 3.312, 12.370, 18.369; friendship helps us throughout our spiritual life 3.580, 11.703, 11.705; giving things up need not involve hardship if you are in contact with spiritual friends 17.364; have as much contact with them as possible, to strengthen your motivation 12.381–2; it supports the development of the emotions 9.443–4; making a practice of helping and encouraging one another 3.578; someone who can help you at the stage you're at now 9.250; observing the progress of a spiritual friend 15.363; sharing our experience of the Dharma, enthusiasm, inspiration, mistakes 11.440; spiritual friends can sometimes act as stimulating *ḍākas* or *ḍākinīs* 13.203–4; spiritual friendship is what helps us practise, not distant spiritual superstars 16.578; support for our Going for Refuge 15.560–1; study with the help and companionship of spiritual friends 9.376–7, 16.578; they can help you let go of neurotic craving 18.207

openness
appreciation of and trust in spiritual friends 17.553; confession 16.314; consider your spiritual friend's advice very seriously 18.623; the effects of concealing things from one's friends 17.648; the importance of listening to one's *kalyāṇa mitra* 9.515; openness in spiritual friendship 16.315–16; openness to the *ḍākinī* – keeping in communication with spiritual friends 18.318; receptivity to friends 4.43, 11.507; trusting spiritual friends 17.560; with your spiritual friends you're accustomed to being completely open 18.420–1

rejoicing, gratitude, fidelity
gratitude towards our friends, because from them we receive the Dharma 3.604; having faith in spiritual friends 17.673; *muditā* (sympathetic joy) between spiritual friends 4.176; pleasing spiritual friends makes it easier for their true nature to emerge 4.176; serving spiritual friends 4.174–5, 15.384–5; taking delight in the spiritual beauty of our dear friend 11.440, 26.79; a vow to be reunited in future lives 18.146–7; we need to make the most of time with our spiritual friends 18.567

tackling difficulties
apatrāpya stops you doing things of which friends wouldn't approve 15.296, 18.486; disharmony with a *kalyāṇa mitra* 15.294–5; the effect of being told the truth by a friend 16.504–5; the effect of the criticism of a spiritual friend 15.295–6; in modern life, friendship is not meant to go deep enough to produce problems 3.527; it is difficult to develop 3.579; its near enemy is mere socializing 12.540–1; reacting defensively to our friends' criticism 17.651–2; pointing out one's friend's reactive patterns 5.653; spiritual friends can help you overcome weaknesses 19.153; 'stickiness' in women's spiritual friendships 11.637–8; tackling psychological problems and reactive patterns of behaviour 16.114–15; using your *dharmapāla* aspect to help your friend overcome their weaknesses 19.407

see also
fierce friendship, *see under* friendship

Kalyanaprabha, Dharmacharini forewords 8.xiii–xxxvii, 22.xv–xxiv, 26.xix, 26.403–8; an account of Sangharakshita, women, and friendship 21.476–9; launches *A Moseley Miscellany* 26.549–50; visit in Manchester 24.381; work with Sangharakshita on *Dear Dinoo* 12.693

Kalyanasri, Dharmacharini 14.xx, 18.xiv

kāma importance of not confusing with *kamma* 10.576; *see also* pleasure

Kāma Sūtras 20.287

kāmacchanda (desire for sense experience) countered by aesthetic appreciation 5.344–5; desire for worldly pleasures 18.129; the distinction between *kāmacchanda* and *dhammachanda* 15.156, 26.63; the energy that keeps the wheel of life turning 12.550; sexual relationships a form of organized *kāmacchanda* 5.348; suppressing desire is appropriate to *kāmacchanda*, but not *dharmachanda* 7.306–7; 'urge in the direction of sense experience' 5.323–5; we have to gradually replace desire for conditioned things with desire for Nirvāṇa 12.551; *see also* five hindrances

Kāmadeva (Hindu love god) 17.691–2, 25.458

kāmadhenu *see* cow of plenty

Kamala (Kay, niece) *see under* Sangharakshita/IV family/other relatives

Kamalashila (Bhikkhu Kashyap's disciple) 21.85–7, 22.91

Kamalashila, Dharmachari brief introduction 24.636 (n153); advice 17.xv, 17.431–2; conducts ordinations for the first time 2.510–12, 12.379; 'The Death of the Order' 24.382; foreword 5.xxix–xxxv; president of FWBO centres 12.631; works on the building of Vajraloka 5.xxxiv–v, 24.132; writes a book 12.379

Kamalaśīla (Śāntarakṣita's disciple) accepted the Yogācāra as relative truth 1.371; *Bhāvanā-krama* 16.445; commentary on the *Diamond Sūtra* 14.148, 14.372; commentary on the *Tattvasaṃgraha* 1.322; the 'Council of Lhasa', his debate with a Chan monk 13.11–12; at the University of Odantapuri 7.425

kāmaloka *see under trailokya*

kāma-rāga (desire for sensuous experience) and the difficulty of breaking emotional fetters 2.147–8, 15.524; imagining blindness or deafness to understand the strength of longing for sense experience 3.421; in relation to the subject–object distinction 15.524–6; sexual desire 15.525–6; what causes desire for rebirth 3.421; *see also* ten fetters/fourth fetter

kamāsrava *see āsravas*

Kamble, N. M. 10.357

kamma importance of not confusing with *kāma* 10.576; *see also* karma

Kammāsadhamma, India 15.80

kammaṭṭhānas *see* forty *kammaṭṭhānas*

Kamptee *see under* Nagpur

Kaṇaḍa 17.362

Kānadeva *see* Āryadeva

Kanamatsu, Kenryo (Jōdo Shinshū scholar) 7.537

Kanchenjunga, Mount its beauty and colours 7.336, 11.171, 12.235, 20.469–70, 26.219; first climbed in 1955 21.624 (n30); the 'Five Treasures of the Snow'

11.171, 21.98, 26.219; ‘the great white peak … seemed to speak to me’ 20.470; an inspiration 23.17; the legend that the mountain in the form of a white bird guided a lama to Sikkim 22.244; ‘one white wave of snow’ 25.219; photograph 20.470; a sacred mountain 25.55

Kandaraka Sutta *see under Majjhima Nikāya*

Kandinsky, Wassily 24.588, 26.379

Kangyur *see under* Tripiṭaka

Kanhangad *see* Ramdas, Swami

Kaṇhapāda 1.382, 1.392

Kanheri Caves *see under* caves

Kaniṣka, King 7.512, 12.238, 14.94

kaṅkha (uncertainty) 10.577

kankhāvitaraṇa visuddhi *see* seven *visuddhis*

Kaṇṇakatthala Sutta *see under Majjhima Nikāya*

Kannon *see* Japanese Buddhism

Kanso *see under* Japanese Buddhism/art

Kant, Immanuel

works
although knowledge begins with impressions of sense it is not circumscribed by them 7.138; anticipates evolution 3.9; awoken from his ‘dogmatic slumber’ by David Hume 24.586; Copernican Revolution 7.388; critical philosophy 10.597; on taking interest in the beauty of nature 26.185; the thing in itself 19.239–40

Critique of Pure Reason (Kritik der reinen Vernunft)
antinomies 7.550–1 (n39), 10.597, 14.422; compared to Nāgārjuna’s *Mūlamadhyamakakārikā* 1.310–11; distinction between intellect and understanding 14.558; Sangharakshita reads 7.551 (n39), 20.70, 24.248; time is part of our way of perceiving reality 19.85

Kantaraj (Ramakrishna Mission) v20, v21

Kaṇṭhaka (Siddhārtha’s horse) 3.208, 3.656 (n197), 13.309, 13.693 (n126)

Kapila 17.439

Kapilavaddho (William Purfurst) 12.707 (n48), 23.46–7

Kapilavastu the Buddha was born and brought up there 17.439; the Buddha begs in the streets of Kapilavastu 13.461; the Buddha visits, and intervenes in the conflict between Koliyans and Śākyans 12.338–9

Kapimala 13.342

Kapleau, Roshi Philip the influence on him of attending the Nuremberg trials 26.396; invites Sangharakshita to visit him in Santa Fe 24.324; notes the appropriation of Zen by psychotherapists 2.564, 11.611, 12.517–18

Kaplinski, Jaan 16.xiv

Kapoor, Prithviraj 21.412

Kapoor, Raj v21, v22

Kappa (pupil of Bāvarī) 1.82

Kappatakura (grass-seller) 9.142

kāraṇa (causal) 14.83

Kāraṇḍavyūha Sūtra introduction 14.177–8; and Avalokiteśvara 1.336, 2.176, 4.713 (n355), 10.176, 14.178; a composite work with Hindu features, including how a bodhisattva created the world 2.176; English translation, *The Basket’s Display* 10.685 (n174); reputedly the first Buddhist text translated into Tibetan 2.176, 14.178; summarized in Thomas’s *History of Buddhist Thought* 1.336

Karaṇīya Mettā Sutta

introducing the sutta
brief introduction 15.258; chanted during an ordination ceremony 23.146; a kind of poem, a kind of meditation 15.259; its metrical form 15.xiii; where it occurs in the Pāli canon 15.258

Sangharakshita and the sutta
he reads it on the radio 24.360–1; his approach to the text 15.xix; his commentary 15.247–345

translations
Saddhatissa 15.247–8; Sangharakshita 3.319–20, 7.119–20, 15.xiii, 15.71–2; Vipassi 24.361

the text
statement of the aim of Buddhism 15.260–1; description of the happy, healthy human being 15.268–74; contented, easily supported … 15.274–96; not pursuing things for which the wise might censure you 15.291–3; ‘May all beings be happy’ 15.297–8; the Buddha’s instructions on how to do the *mettā bhāvanā* 15.297–332; extending *mettā* in all directions 3.684 (n382), 9.517, 15.325–6; reference to an intermediate state (born and to-be-born) 10.723–4 (n504); cultivating the love a mother feels for her only child 11.102,

14.57, 15.321–4, 26.692; 'whether he stands, walks, sits or lies down' 15.328–9; the results of perfecting the practice 15.333–45; 'Never again is he reborn' 15.335

Karki, Arun 22.211–12

Karle (or Karla) caves *see under* caves

karma

INTRODUCTION

definitions and descriptions
introduction to karma and rebirth 3.92–115; every willed action produces an effect, a *vāsanā* 1.369; it creates the world 1.342; it is action, both physical and mental 8.619; it is what you do 15.90, 17.476; simply a description of the way things happen 16.309

what creates karma?
an action will only have a karmic effect if it is intentional 2.68, 3.105, 15.90, 17.200, 17.292; does unmindfulness have karmic consequences? 17.524; the first stirring of fresh karma 17.499; involuntary actions do not produce karma i.e. do not modify character 2.68; mind and mental events 17.476; natural morality creates karma, but conventional morality doesn't 4.385; no karmic retribution for actions performed out of great compassion 14.188; not everything that happens to you is the result of karma 4.408; the role of lack of mindfulness or intoxication in the creation of karma 17.292; the senses are karmically or ethically neutral 19.191

how karma works
an introduction 3.99–104; although all willed actions produce an effect, not all effects are products of karma 2.69; as one's mind is, so is one's karma 17.480; the effect is always proportionate to the cause 21.582; the effect is not separate from the cause 17.57; the exhaustion of karma 13.578; forgiveness does not mean escape from the karmic consequences of actions 13.578, 17.57; the gods are unable to create fresh karma 17.527; if people harm you and suffer because of that, it's your fault (Śāntideva) 4.410; if you accidentally swallow a fly, that is not bad karma 17.584; in a way, everything we experience is a result of karma 17.479; it applies to all sentient existence 16.419; it concerns a living human mind and character, not a dead mechanism 2.70; it is the intention behind your actions that constitutes karma 17.292; it is not always conscious, actions that started deliberate become habitual 17.524; it is produced at the *javana* (volition) stage of the perceptual process 17.499–500; karmic obstacles 18.60; life is not entirely determined by karma 8.576–7, 15.94, 17.208; no accumulation of karma can get you to Nirvāṇa 26.52; non-karmic factors in human experience (Pāli canon) 8.577; not a machine of cogs and wheels, but a play of healthy and unhealthy volitions 2.73; not some sort of bad luck or fate about which nothing can be done 15.89; on a higher spiritual level karma works in a different way 4.301; operates over a series of lives 17.292; suffering is not always due to karma 3.184, 4.408, 7.19, 7.599–600 (n326), 16.422, 17.173; we can't stand back from karma as though separate from it, we *are* karma 15.375–6, 17.524–5; we have a common perception to the extent that we have a common karma 17.483; 'whatever we do to other people, we are in the long run doing to ourselves' 3.106; you reap the consequences of what you have allowed yourself to think 2.70–1; you tend to draw to yourself karmically appropriate experiences 4.402, 10.476

the law of karma
introduction 3.100–4, 3.316–18; affirmation in the *Sūtra of Golden Light* 16.425; analogy with the law of gravity 3.100; introduction (by Buddhism and Jainism) 16.419; the Dharma cannot be deserved under the law of karma 14.403; does not forgive 13.578; even the Buddha had to suffer according to the law of karma 15.93, 16.310, 16.616 (n244); green is the colour of justice, so karma is, as it were, green 13.282; illustrated by the *Jātakas* 14.61–2, 17.480; karmic consequences are simply the natural consequence of your mental state 17.56–7; a law but no lawgiver 3.100; the *nidāna* chain a reflection on the workings of the law 4.81; no 'iron law' of karma 2.72, 3.106; non-individualistic interpretation provided by transference of merits 1.343–4; not administered by the Buddhas 11.263, 16.309, 17.662–3; not fatalistic 3.111, 3.317, 10.56; not to be thought of in a mechanical way 2.72, 16.310, 17.55–7; not punishment 11.263, 17.56; not the universal principle of Buddhism 14.607; nothing mysterious or mystical about it 18.146; nowhere to run to escape karma 16.312; it is profitable to reflect on it 10.598; as an object of faith 17.551, 17.553; results of karma are in keeping with actions 16.254, 16.419; should be mirrored by the social order 16.426; a

simple fact of life 11.263; some people's view of karma fails to acknowledge that the innocent can suffer 16.422; a special case of the principle of causality 1.343; taking it too literally 17.479; teaching to children 16.428–9; there is no cosmic policeman handing out speeding tickets 17.292; universal 7.121; used as a rationalization for social injustice 15.681; we can rely on the karmic level of conditionality 17.473; when you are Enlightened the law of karma doesn't get in your way 14.593

karma and the body
'a body free from harmful karma' (Milarepa) 18.45–6; the body is produced by past karma 10.481–2, 15.204; 'He brought the stick, but I brought the body' 4.119–20, 4.409, 4.425, 10.482, 10.600

examples of karma at work
breaking vows is considered to be damaging karma 18.161; experiences in the *bardo* after death according to one's karma 12.205; how Bhaddiya became a dwarf – a story of karmic consequences 3.105–6; the karma of actors 1.547; the karma of children 3.543; the karmic consequences of Aṅgulimāla's action 15.93; karmic consequences of arrogance 17.606; karmic links between people 18.255; one cannot tell from people's experience precisely what is going on karmically 17.526; one of the karmic consequences of anger is to make you ugly 4.390, 17.281, 17.602; Milarepa's karma 4.292, 4.448, 15.93, 18.61, 18.128–9; the positive karma of the gods only sustained by a vision of the transcendental 16.354; a robbery, payment of a karmic debt 22.562; a woman who was so unfortunate that perhaps karma was the cause 4.401

THE HISTORY OF KARMA

karma in Buddhist history
of central importance to all schools 3.187; Siddhārtha saw beings' rebirth in accordance with their karma 1.487, 3.32, 3.115; did the Buddha himself teach karma and rebirth? 4.405, 12.689; the Buddha didn't say much about it 4.373; *Majjhima Nikāya* descriptions of the different kinds of karma 16.254; the Dharma was called *karmavāda* by the Buddha's contemporaries 7.120; *Amitāyurdhyāna Sūtra* accepts but modifies the principle of karma 1.334; karma lies at the heart of the Buddha's world-view 8.573; the path of the understanding of the truth of karma (Mahāmudrā) 18.243; the teaching developed as a reaction to Brahminism (Gombrich) 8.619; a topic in the *Śāriputra-abhidharma-śāstra* 14.74; reification of karma 8.620

karma in other traditions
Dalits told that their suffering was due to bad karma 4.396, 4.400, 15.681, 17.211–12; the teaching was perhaps taken to Hinduism from Buddhism in garbled form 10.50; Hindu ideas about karma 4.396, 10.56, 15.681, 17.211–12; Jain doctrine of karma 17.584, 23.347, 23.528 (n388); Tamil belief in astrology that traces misfortunes to sins of previous lives 20.280

Westerners and the teaching of karma
handling traditional texts about karma carefully 4.396; is the traditional view that suffering is caused by karma acceptable? 4.395–6; an unsatisfactory aspect of Buddhist teaching from a Western point of view 4.402; Westerners' attitude to karma 4.402–5; attitudes to rebirth, *see under* rebirth

karma and other Buddhist teachings
dhyāna produces positive karmic consequences 4.481; the first two verses of the Dhammapada 17.473; the imprint of willed action is conserved in the *ālaya vijñāna* 18.291; *kamma-niyama*, *see under* five *niyamas*; karma and *cetanā*, *see under cetanā*; karma and mindfulness of purpose 15.90; karma and the *nidānas* 1.111; middle way between determinist and casualist views 7.585 (n220); the wheel of life 17.476–8; wandering the *bardo*, we are buffeted by the winds of evil karma 18.83–4

QUESTIONS AND MISUNDERSTANDINGS

questions about karma
could pain be due to past karma? 10.502–4, 16.407; did the Buddha teach karma and rebirth? 4.405; does an amoeba have karma? 22.63; does it explain discrepancies in fortune? 7.121, 7.585 (n219); what is the proof of karma? 3.111–15; why be surprised if you suffer under the law of karma? 4.428–9

misunderstandings
misunderstandings of karma 2.68–9, 2.72, 8.353, 24.484; a much misused word 15.89; thinking of it in a rigid, literalistic way 4.301; traditional doctrine needs reformulation 3.112–13; when people talk about karma, they usually mean *karma-vipāka* 15.90

KINDS OF KARMA

seven classifications
(1) according to ethical status 2.70, 3.101–2; (2) according to 'door' – body, speech, and mind 2.70–1, 3.104–5; (3) according to the appropriateness of resultant experiences 2.71–2, 3.105–6; (4) according to time of taking effect 2.72, 3.106; (5) according to relative priority of taking effect 2.72, 3.107–9; (6) according to function: reproductive, supportive, counteractive, destructive 2.72–3, 3.109–10; (7) according to the plane on which the karma matures 2.73, 3.110

weighty karma (garuka-kamma)
introduction 2.72, 3.107–8; can mantra chanting produce weighty karma? 17.526; faith is weighty karma, though not technically classified as such 17.557; karma whose effects cannot be counteracted by any other karma 7.523; meditation as weighty karma 3.107, 5.269, 15.92, 15.108; one is unlikely to have performed any weighty karma by the time of death 17.526; takes precedence over death-proximate and habitual karmas 2.72; unlikely to pop up from the remote past 15.691; the weighty karma of deliberately taking life 3.107; wrong view as weighty karma takes precedence over the five heinous offences 7.523

other kinds of karma
death-proximate 2.72, 3.107–8, 13.36–7; habitual 2.72, 3.108, 17.526–7; indirect or collective 17.479; residual 2.72, 3.108; ripening 2.72

KARMA IN PRACTICE

how to handle karmic consequences
bearing the consequences of one's actions with patience 10.502–4, 15.92; the Buddhas cannot take away the effects of karma 16.310; by gaining Enlightenment you can escape karma 4.292, 15.92–3; learning to create positive karma even while experiencing pain 15.151, 15.304–5; neutralizing bad karma 4.291–2, 4.399; ways of counteracting the future effects of past unskilfulness 15.92–3; when we experience the effects of bad karma, why not take it as a warning? 17.163

practices
assessing the karmic significance of mental states 15.160–3; confession helps you to experience your karma in a different perspective 4.314–15; creating fresh karma 17.478; it is profitable to reflect on the law of karma 10.598; modifying the karmic flow through repeating positive actions 17.525–7; reflection on karma as one of the four preliminary meditations 5.547

see also
ānantarya-karma (disastrous karmic consequences), *see* five heinous crimes; karma and rebirth, *see under* rebirth; karmic consequences, *see karma vipāka*; *kuśala-karma*, *see* skilful action

karma formations (*saṃskāras*) *see saṃskāras*

karma vipāka (fruit of karma)

how it relates to karma
any action will only have a karmic effect if it is intentional 2.68, 3.105, 15.90; at any time we are reaping the fruits of past actions 15.231; ethically skilful actions will eventually bear positive fruit 15.92–3; in the wheel of life 1.112, 17.476–8; it begins functioning at the instant of conception 1.109; karmic fruits have to be taken on trust 17.263–4; the karmic results of any action are quite uncertain 14.494, 15.90; the result of willed action 18.291–2; the results of karma are in keeping with actions performed 16.254; only one of the types of cause and effect relation 2.69, 3.111, 3.317; a thought produces a karmic result even if not acted on immediately 17.264; upon Enlightenment there is no karma and therefore no *vipāka* 15.592–3; when people talk about karma, they usually mean *karma vipāka* 15.90; you understand the *vipāka* better if you are aware of the karma 15.165

how we experience vipāka
fear of karmic consequences 1.411; in a way, everything we experience is a *vipāka* 17.479; pleasure is a *vipāka*, so neither skilful or unskilful 18.528, 19.93; sometimes one can be aware of these karmic effects in everyday experience 18.146; an unpleasant experience in higher states may be the result of *karma vipāka* 17.497; suffering the results of loss of mindfulness 15.213–14; *vedanā* is the feeling tone of our experience of *vipāka* 17.502; we experience *karma-vipāka* in terms of feeling 17.524; when taking psychedelic drugs, capacity for karma is swamped by *vipāka* 17.527; the wrong view that there is nothing after death, therefore no *karma vipāka* 17.245; *see also* ethics/actions have consequences

karma-affinity 18.303

karma-bhāva 1.112

karma-cetanā (volitional actions) *see cetanā*

'karma-exhausted' 18.60, 18.71

karmakāraka-bhikṣu 2.194

karma-niyama *see* five *niyamas*

Karmapa v22

karma-process and result-process 2.75–6

Karma-śataka 14.69

karmavācanā* or *kammavācā 2.194

karmavādin 7.121

Karpelles, Suzanne 20.171

Kārttika 3.403–5

Kārttikeya 16.411

karuṇā *see* compassion

karuṇā bhāvanā Atīśa encouraged the practice 12.577; a deepening experience 15.256; *mettā* mantled with the sober shades of *karuṇā* 15.327; the point is to motivate oneself to relieve suffering 5.198; the practice 5.198–9, 10.173; recommended for cruel people 10.173; removing suffering with its causes 5.197; whether you find it or the *muditā bhāvanā* easier is a matter of temperament 5.204; *see also* four *brahma vihāras*

Karuṇā Puṇḍarīka Sutra 14.175, 16.51, 16.592 (n47)

Karuna Trust (formerly Aid for India) introduction 12.731 (n261); description of work in India 10.li; fundraising 10.88, 12.401; Lokamitra's contribution 12.482; Mokshapriya's video for the Karuna Trust 24.319; a quantum leap 11.556; support for the ITBCI school in Kalimpong 12.435

Karunabandhu, Dharmachari v24

Karunamati, Dharmachari 26.463

Kasauli, Punjab 20.219–26

Kashmir *Buddhism in Kashmir and Ladakh* 8.380–1; discovery of copies of the *White Lotus Sūtra* in Kashmir 14.108, 16.35; Fourth Council (held in Kashmir by Kaniṣka) 13.342; Kṣmendra (Kashmiri poet) 14.69

Kashmir Shaivism *see under* Hinduism

Kashyap, Jagdish

LIFE STORY

introduction
brief description 21.509–10, 23.493–4 (n156), 26.231; photographs 20.450, 22.389

early years
born in Bihar as a caste Hindu 12.427, 20.458; as a teenager joined the Arya Samaj (Hindu reform) 12.427; disillusioned by the Vedas 10.236, 12.427–8; decided to take up Buddhism 12.428; the story of the Buddha's backache revealed to him the Buddha's humanity 3.184, 10.236

ordination in Ceylon
ordination 20.447–8; studied Pāli at the Vidyalankara Pirivena 12.428; *bhikkhus* remonstrate with him about *anattā* 3.492, 12.428–9, 17.630, 19.446–7, 20.447; struggled to wear his robe properly 12.429; told off by an old woman for putting his bowl on the ground 12.429; when asked which Nikāya he belonged to, he replied 'Buddha Nikāya' 12.428, 20.447–8

Penang and Benares
lived in a temple in Penang 20.448; learned to revere the bodhisattvas 12.429, 20.448, 26.666–7; professor at Benares Hindu University 12.429–30, 20.394–5, 20.442–53; resigns and meditates in the jungles of Bihar 20.470

Nālanda
decides to devote the rest of his life to reviving the university 12.430, 21.38; meets Dinoo Dubash 21.464–5; his *mettā* tested by a cobra? 9.521; rediscovers the possibility of living a traditional monk's life 20.459–60; founds the Nalanda Pāli Postgraduate Institute 12.430–1, 22.16, 22.320; edits the entire Pāli canon 22.320; teaches at Nava Nalanda Mahavihara 23.124

CHARACTER, WORKS, AND CONTACT WITH SANGHARAKSHITA

character
an exceptionally tolerant and open-minded person 20.448; he used to feed the peacocks at Nalanda 12.430; the mildest person imaginable, but had a sharp and penetrating mind 4.393; a model of personal integrity 2.582; never got restless if there was nothing to do 5.645; quite childlike, simple in his way of life 12.431; 'simply did not bother with material things' 20.444; unconventional manner of teaching 12.431, 20.446–7

views, works, and teachings
The Abhidhamma Philosophy: the Psycho-Ethical Philosophy of Early Buddhism 14.75; belief in naturopathy 20.444–5; *Buddhism for Everybody* 20.452; disillusionment with the sangha 21.202–4; edits the entire Pāli Tipiṭaka in Nagari script 12.430, 21.507; interpretation of the first verse of the *Dhammapada* 15.422; 'Origin and Expansion of Buddhism' 2.720 (n535); to understand *anattā*, you have to understand *attā* 3.492, 12.428–9, 17.630, 19.446–7, 20.447

and Sangharakshita
'my first teacher' 26.231; their first meeting 20.122; Sangharakshita is encouraged to seek ordination at Kusinārā 20.394–5; Sangharakshita practises doing the teacher's will 13.628, 20.463–4, 22.394–5; Sangharakshita studies with Kashyap-ji 7.23–4, 9.281, 9.468, 9.489, 9.501, 12.430, 20.444–9; Sangharakshita asks Kashyap-ji's forgiveness for any offence committed 20.445; they go on a tour of Bihar 7.423–32, 20.457–66, 22.387–8; 'Stay in Kalimpong and work for the good of Buddhism' 9.281, 9.468, 9.489, 9.501, 10.3, 12.430, 20.470, 21.7–8, 22.388, 23.17; Kashyap-ji takes part in Sangharakshita's *bhikṣu* ordination 2.581, 21.108; they meet in Gangtok for the visit of the Sacred Relics 21.190–7; their last meeting, at the Nalanda Pāli Institute 12.430, 23.368–9; Kashyap-ji gives his blessing to Sangharakshita's plan to return to the West 23.368–9; looking up to him 26.629

Kasi-Bhāradvāja (the farmer) 3.76, 10.330–2, 18.294, 25.174–5, 26.648–9

***kasiṇa* meditation practice** *see* ten *kasiṇas*

Kassapa (the Buddha's disciple) *see* Mahākassapa

Kassapa (English novice) 23.72, 23.74–5

Kasulis, Tom 23.453

Kāśyapa or Kassapa brothers (Gayā, Nāḍi, and Uruvelā, fire worshippers) Uruvelā not impressed by the Buddha's supernormal powers 2.23, 2.668 (n54); converted to Buddhism 2.23–4, 9.142; King Bimbisāra ascertains that the Buddha converted Uruvelā Kāśyapa, not *vice versa* 2.24

Kāśyapa or Kassapa Buddha 1.45, 7.341

Kāśyapa (bodhisattva) 14.231, 14.235–41

Kāsyapa-parivarta (Mahāyāna text) introduction 14.180–1, 14.189; 'a Bodhisattva should be honoured far more than a Tathāgata' 14.181; an echo of the Buddha's first discourse? 14.181; an imaginative collection of similes 14.180; its interpretation of *śūnyatā* in terms of the Middle Way 14.181

kataññutā *see* gratitude

kathā 15.444–6

Kathā-vatthu (*Points of Controversy*) introduction 14.85–7; argument that worldlings possess no real knowledge refuted 14.86; attributes to the 'Andhakas' (Mahāsaṅghikas) Mahāyāna-type doctrines 14.135; it grew by a process of accretion 14.85–6; between concentration and wisdom can one be called an *arhant*? 2.145; contains references to the beliefs of the Chaityavādins 16.154–5; corrected what the Theravāda regarded as misrepresentations of the Dharma 14.85–6; the courtesy of discussion between the Theravādins and their opponents 14.86; in many cases the topic of discussion is left unsettled 15.444, 17.442; logical arguments 14.87; on the intermediate state 10.723 (n504); 'discussion' would be a better translation than 'controversy' 15.444; the points of discussion range from the trivial to the fundamental 14.86; *samayavimukti* 2.682 (n198); records discussions between Theravāda and proto-Mahāyāna schools 4.24; stupa worship 16.143

kaṭhinacīvaradāna ('difficult' ceremony) at the end of the rainy season 2.199–200, 3.405–6; an affirmation of the mutual obligation of the monastic and lay community 8.307; expression of the devotion of the sangha 2.226; an important festival 8.306–8; in the Vinaya 14.32; a reminder of the importance of the Vinaya 8.307–8; Sangharakshita takes part in the ceremony in Calcutta 23.371–2

Kathmandu *see* Nepal

Kati 26.604–5

Katō, Bunnō 16.36

Katsimbalis, George 23.234

Kātyāyana 14.83

Kātyāyanīputra 14.83

Kaufmann, Walter 3.687 (n408)

kaukṛtya *see* anxiety

Kauṇḍinya (one of the Buddha's first five disciples) *see* Koṇḍañña

Kauṇḍinya (brahmin in the *Sūtra of Golden Light*) 16.258, 16.372

kaupin (ascetic's loin cloth) the disciple who began with a *kaupin* and ended up with a wife and farm 18.199–201; the swami whose *kaupin* was washed by princesses 20.347–8

Kausali 9.279

kauśalya-ekāgratā-citta 2.109

Kausalyayan, Bhadant Anand ('Anand-ji') brief introduction 24.637 (n156); accompanying the Sacred Relics 21.271, 21.297–304; a *bhikkhu* whom Ambedkar said his followers should trust 9.549 (n4); his background 21.449–50; a complex figure 22.217–18; in controversy in Nagpur 24.138; a cynical, worldly-wise Punjabi monk 21.449; dismisses the threefold way as 'old-fashioned' 22.214; his picture on the wall of an institute in Nagpur 10.381; manipulates a poor layman into giving him new sandals 22.215–17; no knowledge of the Three Jewels 24.139; an 'outstanding contributor to Hindi *belle-lettres* 7.448; Sangharakshita meets him in Glasgow 24.135–9; a tall striking figure 21.266; tries to get Sangharakshita involved in a political meeting 22.211–13; translated Ambedkar's *The Buddha and his Dhamma* into Hindi 7.618 (n496); visits Sangharakshita in Kalimpong 8.664

kausīdya *see* laziness

Kauśikaprajñāpāramitā 1.71

Kavitha, India 9.58–9

kāvya (literary term) 26.330–2

Kawade, Shri 10.97

Kawinda Sayadaw, U 21.107–10

kāya *see under trikāya*

kāyasākṣin *see* body-witness

kāyavijñāpti (gesture) 2.97

Kazemi, Reza Shah 26.688–92

Kazi (cook) 22.524

Kazi Lhendup Dorje-Khangsarpa of Chakhung introduction 21.483–5, 23.378; his aristocratic background 22.479–9; the Maharaja of Sikkim's main political opponent 23.204; photograph 23.379; his time as a lama in a monastery 22.413–14; his marital difficulties 22.410–13

Kazi, Sonam Topgay v22, v23

Kazini of Chakhung (Elisa-Maria Dorje-Khangsarpa, or Marie-Elise Langford Rae) introduction 21.483–5; becomes a Buddhist 22.414–15; critical of India 22.559; difficulties with her third marriage 22.408–13; escape plan if the Chinese should reach Kalimpong 22.547; 'a fabulist' 22.613 (n323); friendship with Sangharakshita 21.485, 22.413–15, 22.478–86, 22.519–20, 23.378–9; and Gandhi 22.481; gives gruesome details of the Delhi riots (1947) 23.384; her character 22.413, 22.484–5; the Kazini is apparently attacked 22.412–13; life story 21.483–4, 22.415, 22.478–9, 22.622–3 (n372); perceptiveness 22.439; photograph 23.379; politics 22.480–4, 23.204; Sangharakshita initiates her into Buddhism 8.656; she doesn't take to Terry Delamare 23.379; her sixth sense for enmity 4.414–15; consulting the Kazi and Kazini about returning to England 23.385

Kean, Charles 3.495, 13.73, 19.450

Keats, John

his life and work
a secular poet but sometimes expresses the spirit of religion 16.138; Keats House in London 24.311–12; association with Winchester 24.203; early death but many creative works 11.448, 12.32; influence on Anagarika Dharmapala 8.19–20; odes evoke impermanence 3.345; the odes have the quality *kāvya* 26.332

Endymion
description of Circe 20.36; 'Some shape of beauty moves away the pall/ From our dark spirits' 4.96; 'A thing of beauty is a joy forever' 7.437, 26.211; 'universal tinge of sober gold' 24.32

Ode on a Grecian Urn
'Beauty is truth, truth beauty' 22.180, 24.547, 25.xxxiv; beauty may or may not be truth, but truth is certainly beauty 12.308; a sort of koan 16.257

Ode to a Nightingale
studying the poem with Sachin in Kalimpong 21.434; 'a beaker full of the

warm South' 23.275; 'embalmèd darkness' 22.21–2; the nightingale became a symbol for Keats 5.642; nightingales in Highgate 23.231; paraphrasing the poem takes you further away from it 19.563

other works and quotations
'The Eve of St Agnes' 26.513; 'the holiness of the heart's affections' 25.xxxiv, 25.17; 'Huge cloudy symbols of a high romance' 1.28, 13.120; human life as a vale of soul-making 12.698, 26.399; *Hyperion* 20.36, 26.323; letters 12.698, 14.71, 26.139–40; *Ode to Autumn* 26.398; *Ode to Psyche* 23.278; 'On First Looking into Chapman's Homer' 24.129, 26.470; 'To Sleep' 1.22; sonnets 20.36; 'Veil'd Melancholy has her sovran shrine' 3.13; 'When I have fears that I may cease to be' 1.28

Keble, John 'New every morning is the love' 12.423; 'Who runs may read' 16.75, 18.246

Kedari, Miss K. V. 10.181

Keer, Dhananjay 10.725 (n514), 18.646–7 (n69)

Keffolds *see* Haslemere

Kegon Shū *see under* Japanese Buddhism

Keluskar, Krishnaji Arjun 9.45–6

Kendo, Master 8.496

Kenko, Rev. 19.599 (n50)

Kennedy, John F. 8.318, 22.517–18

Kennedy, Pagan 11.710

Kennett, Peggy (Jiyu Roshi) introduction 26.762–3 (n570); attempts to practise 'mirroring' in the West 11.375–6, 23.164, 26.604; her English students refuse to do a puja 11.375; writes to Sangharakshita describing life in a Japanese monastery 3.308; she visits Sangharakshita in London 26.602–4

Keown, Damien 8.609–11

Kern, Hendrik 8.478–9, 13.337, 16.36

kesa *see* TriratnaIII/ordination ceremonies/ *kesas*

Kevaddha (one of the Buddha's lay followers) 3.76

Kevaddha Sutta *see under Dīgha Nikāya*

kevala (absolute) 1.69

Kevala, Dharmachari (Clive Pomfret) v24

keys *apramāda*: the key to all Buddhist practice 3.70; the bodhisattva principle is the key to collective consciousness 4.656; the Buddha's teaching as the key to uplift 10.13; confidence is the key to success in meditation 5.453, 25.142; *darśana* (view) is the key to Indian philosophy 7.78, 11.158; ethics is key to a healthy human existence 17.168; feeling *mettā* for oneself is the keystone to contentment 15.309; four *śūnyatās*: keys to unlock the experience the Buddha had 18.399; the key of right motive opens the portals of the Palace of Wisdom 1.22; the keywords of Buddhism 8.273, 22.458–9; learning key terms 1.24, 2.60; the Mahāmudrā's relaxed attitude: a key to the realization of your true nature 19.387

Keyserling, Arnold v24

Keyt, George (Sri Lankan painter) 7.445, 7.616 (n486), 8.139

khadroma *see ḍākinī*

khakkhara (ringed staff) 2.181, 19.366–7

Khamtul Rimpoche 8.659, v22, v23

Khaṇḍadeva 8.450

khandhas *see* five *skandhas*

Khantipālo (previously Laurence Mills, Jivaka, Sujiva)

life
brief introduction 23.488 (n117); his life was full of creativity 12.647; his mother 23.239; his friendship with Bhikkhu Vivekananda 12.635, 12.647; his friendship with Buddharakshita 12.647; at one time called Sujiva 10.149, 12.636; talk on 'The Centre Point of Mind-Control' 10.155; his friendship with Sangharakshita 8.656, 11.545, 12.635–7, 22.526–8; joined in discussions with Yogi Chen 12.636; assisted on a Buddhist training course in Poona 10.179, 23.488 (n118); ordained by Buddharakshita 22.526; Sangharakshita

asks him to come to England 23.239; Dharma activities in Australia 12.647; photograph 22.527

works
literary works written in Kalimpong 8.661–2; *The Buddha's Middle Way* 8.662; *Noble Friendship* 5.xxi, 12.635–7, 12.647–8, 22.526, 22.528, 22.532; *Tolerance, a Study from Buddhist Sources* 22.528

Khantivādī *see* Kṣāntivādin

Kharagpur 3.267

khata (ceremonial scarf) 22.83, 22.582 (n85)

Khayyám, Omar 'Alas, that Spring should vanish with the Rose!' 21.291–2; 'battered caravanserai' 2.80; 'A Hair perhaps divides the False and True' 8.599; 'One Moment in Annihilation's Waste' 26.395; the phantom of a false morning 7.162; You asked, 'What is this transient pattern?' 20.xvii

khecārin 2.729 (n614)

Khedup, Geshe Jampa 8.516

khema 15.452–3

Khema, Ayya *see* Ayya Khema

Khemadhammo, Phra Ajahn 2.619–20, 2.753 (n763)

Khemadhammo (young Aurangabad monk) 24.108

Khemanandi, Dharmacharini v24

Khemapala, Dharmachari 5.xxxv

Khemasiri (Thai monk) 8.656, v21, v22

Khemavira, Dharmachari v24, 26.458

Kheminda Thera 21.313–14

khenpo 7.474, 13.48–50

khitta ('contracted' or 'shrunken' mental state) 15.162–3

Khubilghanic succession 13.36

Khuddaka Nikāya (minor collection) introduction 1.401, 14.51–60; inclusion of early Abhidharma work 14.73–4; as a collection it has no Sanskrit counterpart 14.43; contains the oldest texts 10.220; list of works 7.501, 14.52; individual works, *see Khuddakapāṭha, Dhammapada, Udāna, Itivuttaka, Sutta-Nipāta, Vimānavatthu, Petavatthu, Theragāthā and Therīgāthā, Jātaka, Niddesa, Patisambhidāmagga*

Khuddakapāṭha *Khuddakapāṭha* commentary (*Paramatthajotikā*), *see under* Buddhaghosa; Nepali translation 8.660, 21.503, 21.531; Sangharakshita's translations 15.xiii, 15.61–72; *see also Karaṇīya Mettā Sutta*; *Maṅgala Sutta*; *Nidhikaṇḍa Sutta*; *Ratana Sutta*; *Tirokuḍḍa Sutta*

Khunu Lama *see* Gyaltsen, Tenzin

Kierkegaard, Søren attack on Christianity (*The Present Moment*) 12.251–2, 18.163, 19.246–7, 19.607–8 (n107); *Either/Or* 26.396; *Fear and Trembling* 20.124

Kierski, Werner 24.383

killing abstention from killing, see precepts/first precept; murder, *see* murder; the slaughter of animals, *see under* animals

Kimbila (Anuruddha's companion) 3.635 (n55), 3.670 (n287)

kiṃnaras 16.349

kindness Ānanda and the Buddha's mutual kindness 3.90, 11.436–7; the Buddha, 'he who is so kind' 3.364, 4.17–18, 11.436, 13.146; celebrating a festival by showing kindness to birds and animals 8.222–4; going out to the world in kindness 18.52; in Tibetan Buddhism a transcendental kindliness 14.555–6; is it possible for me to develop more kindness? 4.202; the kindness of a neighbour in Sangharakshita's childhood 26.413–14; kindness needs to be cultivated in one's everyday dealings with people, not just in meditation 5.175; 'little, nameless, unremembered acts of kindness and of love' 11.736; the most beautiful of all the music of the soul 8.156; people are not kind enough to one another 15.343; perhaps in our culture we have forgotten basic human kindness 4.68; Sangharakshita's memory of his teachers' great kindness 26.443; sometimes people are more concerned to appear kind than actually to be so 18.624–5; 'to ten persons' (Auden) 4.69; there should be an element of kindness in our attitude to everyone we meet 4.69; to those below us in the spiritual hierarchy 4.174, 11.507; we need to practise kindness in little ways 4.68–9; to help others, there must be real kindness in your heart 19.287; *see also mettā*

Kindred Sayings of the Buddha *see Saṃyutta Nikāya*

King, Charles William 24.248, 24.667 (n298)

King, Francis 24.389

kings and kingship

the Buddha and kings
and King Ajātasattu, *see* Ajātasattu; and King Bimbisāra, *see* Bimbisāra; the Buddha as a king 3.48–9; the Buddha shows that he is happier than a king 3.271–2; kings who offered their kingdoms to the Buddha 13.86; kings' support for Buddhism (after the Buddha's time) 9.390–1, 12.238–9

stories of kings
Bhaddiya, the king who gave up royal life for bliss in the forest 10.500–1; the blind old king riding into battle 25.411; a king is advised to become king of the gods, to have even greater influence 17.167; a king goes forth as a wanderer when his barber finds his first grey hair 18.13; a king is convinced by a wise man that there is no point in conquest 19.337–8; a king to whom Nāgārjuna gives his 'Precious Garland' of advice 17.153, 17.158

kingship
collapse of society when 'the king overlooks an evil deed' 16.418, 16.429–32; divine kings 3.48–9, 3.426, 16.416–21, 16.423–4; 'even an infant king must not be despised ...' 3.62–3; hereditary 16.421; idealized view of kingship 16.420–1; the initiation ritual based on the ancient ritual to consecrate a king 13.159–60, 22.502; 'Instruction concerning Divine Kings' 16.414–15, 16.426; the king as *deva* 16.416–21, 16.425; the king will protect those who do good deeds 16.426; the *ṛddhi* (power) of the king 10.586, 11.152–3, 14.539; rebirth as a king 16.417, 16.420–1; religious people giving their blessing to whatever the king wants to do 19.463

wheel-rolling or wheel-turning king (cakravartin-rāja, dharmarāja)
Aśoka an exemplar 7.512; the Buddha as *dharmarāja* 3.48, 13.149; Milarepa like a wheel-turning king 18.50; parable in *White Lotus Sūtra* 16.47–8; his principal function is to create an ethical society 1.541, 7.512, 13.390, 16.477–8; resemblance to a Buddha 14.427–8; the seven jewels of the wheel-turning king 13.262, 18.50; and the thirty-two marks 14.427

metaphorical kings
eternalism and nihilism as 'two learned kings' (*Dhammapada*) 15.41; 'Life is King' 25.324, 26.445

see also
four great kings

Kingsley, Charles *The Heroes* 26.482; *Hypatia* 20.20; *The Water Babies*: 'do as you would be done by' 10.476

kinnarī 2.332–3

kinsmen *see* family

Kipling, Rudyard 'The Disciple' 7.264; 'If' 13.172, 22.183, 26.395; 'The Ladies' 1.198; 'Mandalay' 12.527, 21.25; 'the race is won by one and one, and never by two and two' 8.196; Sangharakshita's appreciation of him 26.393; 'What should they know of England who only England know?' 3.5, 8.274, 12.130

Kirkhalwadi, India 23.350–1

Kirkup, James v11

Kisāgotamī the Buddha's responds to her loss of her child 3.357–8, 4.11–13, 4.698 (n260), 9.233–4, 14.18, 16.483; gained insight by reflecting on a lamp that was extinguished 8.119

Kīṭāgiri Sutta *see under Majjhima Nikāya*

Kitamori, Kazoh 26.602

Kittima, U (U Chandramani's disciple) v21, v22

Klee, Paul 26.379

kleśas (passions) *see* five *kleśas*

kleśāvaraṇa *see* two veils

Klíma, Ivan 26.380

kliṣṭa-mano-vijñāna *see* eight *vijñānas*

Kloetzli, Randy 16.624 (n311)

Knight, Margaret 8.281

knights the knights of the Round Table 25.99–100; Knights of St John 26.509, 26.511–12; 'Stanzas' 25.285

Knoch, Pat 26.509–10

knowledge

what is knowledge?
what is knowledge? 14.580–1; knowledge is relating things to their principles 4.82; knowledge is essentially comparison 12.130; the whole framework of our knowledge is dualistic 14.441; investigations into the cause of things occupies an important place 7.115; if you know one thing deeply you know everything 19.215; the difference between knowledge and wisdom 1.170; to know something seems to call for a 'knower', but not so 15.206–7; how does one translate knowledge? 26.301–5; the book as symbol of knowledge 26.300–1

kinds of knowledge
archetypal knowledge, a fusion of reason and emotion 3.11; a Buddha's sphere of knowledge and sphere of influence 16.461; horizontal and vertical differentiation of knowledge 26.302; Kant criticizes the form of our knowledge 10.597; from the Reformation a breakdown of knowledge into specializations 10.154; knowledge par excellence 26.302; the knowledge we have when we are young 18.30; knowledge of what has been done for our benefit 3.598–9; 'right' knowledge (*samyag-jñāna*) 14.213; two degrees of knowledge, sense-based and suprarational 3.10–11, 13.438; two independent sources of valid knowledge 19.185–6; three kinds of knowledge (Spencer) 10.171; four kinds of knowledge to be cultivated for the attainment of *prajñā* 17.545–6; ten kinds of knowledge (Abhidharma) 14.94

theoretical and experiential knowledge
the difference between book knowledge and knowledge from experience 10.223–4; difference between subjective and objective knowledge 2.640–2; Enlightened knowledge, a state of direct spiritual vision 11.101; hard for us to distinguish between theoretical and experiential knowledge 4.147–8; impossible today to keep people away from theoretical knowledge 5.41–2; knowing, feeling, and willing 2.487, 11.194, 12.536–41, 15.607, 15.615, 15.727–9; 'knowing this for oneself': a characteristic Buddhist emphasis 10.465; knowledge of the highest kind is identical with its object 26.302, 26.304–5; mistaking intellectual understanding for true knowledge 16.40; our knowledge depends so much on words and so little on direct experience 13.345; the problem of how to translate knowledge into being 11.192; a progression from ignorance to knowledge 8.592; theoretical knowledge mistaken for wisdom 1.225; there must always be a balance between what you know and what you do 15.472–4; we have to remember that our knowledge outstrips our being 19.412, 19.506–7

not knowing
as well as time and space, infinitely more attributes of which we know nothing 14.603; brought up against the limits of your knowledge, you are forced to grow 17.206; the collectivity – nations, spiritual movements – do not know themselves 12.462; the craving for more advanced knowledge 18.166–7; religion is for those who know they don't know, and desperately want to know 12.47; Sangharakshita troubled by the question 'How is true knowledge possible?' 20.159; the value of saying 'I do not know' 8.587

thinking we know
airing one's knowledge to impress 18.178; almost all our knowledge is second-hand 3.302–3, 13.344–5, 18.166; the appropriation of knowledge as a means of reinforcing the ego 18.167; but our 'knowledge' is based on what we have read and heard 13.344–5; but we know it only with the rational part of ourselves 1.494; difference between theoretical knowing and knowing in our very bones 12.612; don't try to explain the profound teaching with only partial knowledge 19.356–7; the greatest obstacle to knowledge is to think that we know 13.346; 'He who knows does not speak, he who speaks does not know' 7.37, 7.44; modern life has more knowledge and less wisdom than our forefathers 1.231, 4.147; our 'knowledge' is the tip of the iceberg 12.23; realizing that you know what you did not know you knew 17.307; that we must die is the one thing about ourselves we really know 12.358; we don't know anything about anything, but we think we do 16.449–50; we identify with what we think we know rather than direct knowledge 18.107; we may have to *un*know what we know 4.147; we need to become more worthy of knowledge, more open to it 17.50; 'What I don't know isn't knowledge' 1.197, 17.605; what we know is infinitesimal compared with what we do not know 8.576; being able to weigh the stars is useless if you don't know your own mind 12.233

knowing about Buddhism
the danger that Buddhism may be smothered by information 'about' Buddhism 1.8; the deep knowledge represented by mantras 19.32; the encyclopedic knowledge of Tibetan lamas 13.108; how much Dharma do we really know for ourselves? 13.345–7, 18.166; how much do you need to know about Buddhism to be a Buddhist? 17.391; is knowing about Buddhism any help at all? 19.507; learning a new teaching, you must look again at everything you already 'know' 16.5; mistaking book knowledge for transcendental insight 11.481; one can amass knowledge about Buddhism while hardly practising it at all 18.107–8; we know a lot, but our knowledge is only theoretical 15.508–9, 15.558, 19.506–9; we need less Dharma knowledge than we think 17.xix, 17.332; you can't 'know'

that you're on the path to Enlightenment 4.201

see also
attained by Koṇḍañña, *see* Koṇḍañña; of the destruction of the *āśravas*, *see* three *āśravas*; of etymology (*nirukti-pratisaṃvid*), *see* four *pratisaṃvids*; 'Know thyself', *see under* self-knowledge; knowledge of Buddhism, *see* more and more of less and less; knowledge of meaning (*artha-pratisaṃvid*), *see* four *pratisaṃvids*; knowing other people, *see under* other people; knowledge of phenomena (*dharma-pratisaṃvid*), *see* four *pratisaṃvids*; *ñāṇa-dassana visuddhi*, 'knowledge and insight', *see* seven *visuddhis*; self-knowledge; wisdom

knowledge and vision of things as they really are (*yathābhūta-jñānadarśana*)

introduction
'Seeing Things As They Really Are' 12.610–17; what *yathābhūta* means 12.611; term for transcendental cognition 2.127; the point of transition from the mundane to the transcendental 2.113, 2.115; it coincides with Stream Entry 2.140, 2.263; and the Point of No Return 3.253; relationship with *prajñā* 2.114, 14.344

the nature of the experience
the Buddha saw things not in a distorted, limited way, but as they are 12.547; a direct perception which changes one's whole outlook 12.163; an experience of the ultimate nature of things 2.113–14; harmony with the way things really are 18.136; if you really see, you really feel 18.590; it is to see everything as *śūnyatā* 18.599–600; one 'feels all Dharmas spontaneously freed' 18.596; 'One who sees holds on to nothing' (*Udāna*) 10.627, 10.631, 10.633–4; 'seeing' emphasizes the noetic character of the experience 2.55; seeing things not only as they seem, but as they are 1.104; there are not two worlds, one of appearance, one of reality 7.412; things as they really are, transcending subject and object 11.101; turning with delight to the Things That Are 25.195; twofold, corresponding to the first two kinds of *śūnyatā* 12.163; your doubts go 10.431

how do we achieve it?
the concentrated mind sees things as they really are 1.87, 1.168, 2.113, 3.274, 12.566; it can arise in dependence on intellectual activity 18.580; it is one of the fruits of spiritual practice 17.168; learning to see 1.571–2; seeing things differently through mystical experience 4.245; things are seen as they truly are not by the intellect, but by *prajñā* 7.242–3; trying to see things as they are through taking drugs 17.132; we must learn to retire within 7.268; when the adoption of positive conditioning unravels all conditionings 17.475

seeing things as they are not
belief in self 7.360, 26.53; the experience of all unenlightened beings 2.55; people think they already see things as they are, but Buddhism disagrees 12.611–12; there must be a hindering factor in our mind 14.209; we may be worldly-wise, but we do not know the world as it really is 12.528

see also
in the positive *nidānas*, *see under* twelve positive *nidānas*; insight

knowledge-holding deities *see vidyādharas*

Knox, John 24.71, 24.624 (n96)

Knox, Father Ronald 24.374

koan *see under* Zen

Kōbō Daishi *see* Kūkai

Kodály, Zoltán 24.520–1

kodha *see* anger

Koestler, Arthur 8.538

Koirala brothers, Nepal v21

Koliyans conflict with the Śākyas over water 7.238, 9.140, 12.338–9; a tribe or community in north-western India 10.496

Konāgamana Buddha 1.45

Könchok Gyalpo 13.28

Koṇḍañña (Kauṇḍinya, one of the Buddha's first five disciples) his 'Eye of Truth' was opened 2.700 (n372), 11.446–8; the first to realize the truth of the Dharma 1.37, 2.23, 10.620; he asked for ordination 11.447; his name Aññāta-Koṇḍañña (Ajñāta Kauṇḍinya), 'one who has understood' 10.620, 11.447; he contemplates his release by the destruction of craving (*Udāna*) 10.619–21

Koṇḍañña Buddha 1.45

Kongtrul, Jamgon *Tharpe Delam*, *see* *Tharpe Delam*; *The Torch of Certainty* 5.547; *The Ornament of the Guru's Realisation* 22.622 (n370)

Koperagaon 9.292

Koran *see under* Islam

Korea dispute between celibate *bhikkhus* and married priests 8.292–3, 22.458; Mahāyāna Buddhism 2.549; Sarvastivāda Buddhism 3.408

***kośa* system** *see under* Upanishads/ *Taittiriya Upanishad*

Kośala, kingdom its geographical position 2.25; King Viḍūḍabha, *see* Viḍūḍabha; ruled by King Pasenadi (Sanskrit Prasenajit), *see* Pasenadi; the Sākyan territory was incorporated into it 14.400–1; swallowed up by Magadha 10.471–2; when in Kośala the Buddha must have spoken Kośalese 14.12–13

Kosambī, India the Buddha leaves crowded Kosambī in search of solitude (*Udāna*) 10.536–7, 14.401; the Buddha stays at the Ghosita monastery 10.627; the quarrel at Kosambī 3.77, 10.323–4; King Udena's palace burned down, killing the women of the harem 10.627; present-day Allahabad 10.627

Kosambi, Dharmananda (writer in Marathi) 7.448, 7.617 (n495)

Kosambiya Sutta *see under Majjhima Nikāya*

koṭis 1.327

Kovida, Dharmachari (John Hunter) general entries v24; the play *A Face Revealed* 11.466–7; president of FWBO centres 12.631

kōvil *see* Sri Lanka/Hindu temples

Krauskopf, Peter *see* Karunabandhu

Krishna

introduction
description 7.562 (n94), 10.33–4; in the *Bhagavad Gītā*, *see Bhagavad Gītā*; claimed to be an incarnation of God 12.134; defines the bliss arising from goodness 7.100; distinguished from the Buddha (Ambedkar) 9.10, 9.64, 9.99; and *chaturvarna* 9.102–3, 10.51–3; fondness for cats 20.281; lifting a mountain with one finger: has no lesson for our own life 10.255; the madness of his adherents (*bhaktas*) 7.94; not considered as a god (Dr Ambedkar's 22 vows) 9.541; and Radha 20.188; role he claimed for himself 9.94–7, 9.424–5; subtle form of Krishna 20.315

calls the gopīs to dance in Brindaban forest
the story 16.361; the *gopīs* saw him as infinite Love 7.93; in the poetry of Sarojini Naidu 7.59, 7.561–2 (n94); symbolism of the divine call and the human heart 16.73–4; where is Brindaban? 7.593 (n282)

Krishna (small boy at Muvattupuzha) 20.312–15

Krishna (coach tour operator of Mysore) 20.363–4, 20.376–7, 20.379–80

Krishna, Devayani v21

Krishna, Kanwal v21, v22

Krishnabai, Mother 20.319, 20.321–2, 20.324, 24.576

Krishnamurti (Madras poet) v22

Krishnamurti, Jiddu brief introduction 2.685 (n242), 2.695 (n336), 23.482 (n77), 24.630 (n126); attitude to gurus and scriptures 18.632; *Commentaries on Living* 26.22; he was against ideals 19.181; his books 'slices of experience' 26.559; identified with Maitreya 2.179; followers of Krishnamurti 12.320, 18.632; a link with the scientist David Bohm 24.211; 'The Soul' 8.362; a talk in Bombay 26.557–9; 'There you are, rotting under your *Bhagavad Gītā*!' 18.632, 26.558; vitiating influence on Theosophists 21.58, 23.46; the woman who followed him for forty years, but 'hadn't got anywhere' 2.244, 26.558–9

Krishnan, Mr (toddy-tapper) 20.283–4

krodha (Pāli *kodha*) *see* anger, rage

Krodheśvari 13.316

Kropotkin, Peter meeting with Anagarika Dharmapala 8.59; *Mutual Aid* 4.88, 4.677 (n114)

Krusenstierna, Rie and Sten von (Theosophist friends) meeting in Singapore 17.569, 20.147–8; reunion in Australia 10.276, 24.56–64

kṣānikavāda 17.367

kṣānti (patience, forbearance)

introduction
full introduction 4.118–131; one of the most beautiful of all the Buddhist virtues 3.372; one of the most beautiful words in Buddhism 4.118; range of translations 4.118, 16.10

the nature of kṣānti
a balance with *vīrya* 4.132–3, 4.141; you need *vīrya* to develop it 16.164; becoming steadfast like a mountain 14.193; essentially an attitude of love 4.121, 8.200; expressed as non-violence

17.582–3; includes *mettā* 4.390; intellectual humility: the recognition that you don't know anything 4.129; *kṣānti* and 'femininity' 4.118, 4.141–3; much more than stoical endurance, unsupported by anything 1.437–8, 14.476; mundane and transcendental kinds of patience 14.475–6; the positive counterpart of hatred or anger 4.390, 17.270, 17.566; receptivity to higher spiritual influences 4.127–8, 4.339, 16.10; three kinds: patience with harsh words, physical suffering, *śūnyatā* 10.175–6

references in the Buddhist tradition
the Buddha's response to verbal abuse 4.119; being sawn limb from limb without a thought of anger 1.437, 4.121, 8.200, 13.577; the greatest asceticism (*Dhammapada*) 4.121–2, 4.433; Śāntideva's advice, *see* Śāntideva/ *Bodhicaryāvatāra*/chapter 6; your attacker brought the stick, but you brought the body, *see* Śāntideva; in the *Diamond Sūtra* 1.437–8; three kinds of *kṣānti* in the *Samādhirāja Sūtra* 14.192–3; *gambhira-dharma-kṣānti* (patient acceptance of the profound Dharma) 14.192; the Mahāyāna's metaphysical interpretation 14.192; and other-power 4.138–41

anutpattika-dharma-kṣānti (patient acceptance of the non-arising of dharmas)
the acceptance of the egolessness and impersonality of all phenomena 8.200; bodhisattvas who have accepted that all entities of reality have no origin 5.186–7; connected with the first fetter 14.501–2; one sees the whole of existence as like a mirage 4.181; patient acceptance of the essential nature of all *dharmas* 1.439, 14.562; 'allowing reality to have its way with you' 14.597–8; so difficult not to resist that it is a characteristic of the 'irreversible' bodhisattva 4.129; the transition from the seventh to the eighth *bhūmi* 14.228; why should seeing things in this way constitute irreversibility? 14.500–2

opportunities to practise
absence of retaliation 15.439–40; avoiding quarrels 14.193; regard all enemies as passers-by on the road 18.621; remaining unmoved by acquisitions or fame 14.193; 'renouncing a gift' as a form of *kṣānti* 14.478; when looking after children 5.638; when people annoy or threaten us 15.263; when people speak evil of you 1.437; when we are doing social and religious work 10.356; when you are criticized 4.428; with our friends and relatives 10.356

forbearance ...
of being interrupted 5.681–2; of the consequences of one's actions 10.504; of the weather 4.120, 4.423; of our own body 4.120; of old age and death 4.120–1; of other people 4.121, 4.180; of pain in meditation 10.502–3

reflections on practice
accepting your own mistakes 4.360; being fussy about how you practise patience 19.60, 19.167; blaming someone for making you impatient is like blaming a beggar for making you mean 14.597; if it's difficult, don't be discouraged 17.270; the practice benefits you by keeping your mind free from anger and hatred 4.393; obstacles that *kṣānti* needs to overcome 16.10; the patience of the positive outlasts the obstinacy of the negative 19.36; the patience of uncomplaining nurses 24.349–50; people who give you a hard time are helping you practise *kṣānti* 17.566; the person obstructing you is making you patient 4.434, 14.597; seeing that a 'negative' situation is actually positive 4.418; sometimes we must bear with others, and sometimes they must bear with us 26.66; Tomo Geshe Rimpoche's response to his imprisonment in Lhasa 22.495; we are usually able to bear much more than we think we can 26.45; we may think we're being patient when we're only being persistent 26.34; your enemy is giving you the chance to practise patience 4.413–14

see also
as one of the six perfections, *see under* perfections; tolerance

Kṣāntivādin (who enraged the king of Kaliṅga) in the *Diamond Sūtra* 1.437–8, 14.475, 15.439; in the *Jātakas* 1.437, 2.16, 14.65, 15.439

Kṣemīśvara (*Naiṣadhānanda*) 26.326–7

Kshatriya or Kṣatriya caste (Pāli *Khattiya*) Arjuna (*Bhagavad Gītā*) a Kshatriya 10.55–6; in the eight assemblies 12.521; the sangha created by the Buddha to preserve the freedom and democracy of the Kshatriyas? 10.501; Siddhārtha Gautama (the Buddha-to-be) born into that caste 3.23, 3.49, 9.185, 9.191, 12.521; the Buddha's family 9.185, 9.482

kṣetra (literally 'field') 4.435

Kṣitigarbha, 'Earth-Womb', bodhisattva Ākāśagarbha his celestial counterpart 2.181; in China called Ti-tsang, *see* Chinese Buddhism/bodhisattvas; embodiment of spiritual optimism 2.180–1; descends into hell to help beings 2.180–1, 3.182, 3.383, 4.583, 16.232; etymology, 'earth-womb' 3.383; iconography 2.181; in Japan called Jizo 2.181; Kṣitigarbha is the principle of spiritual sublimation 2.180; occupies a prominent place in Devotional Buddhism 1.337, 2.180; one of a group of eight bodhisattvas 2.172; the task of reclaiming what seems irretrievably lost 2.180–1; vows to refrain from becoming Enlightened until every region of hell is empty 15.342

Kṣmendra (Kashmiri poet) 14.69

Kublai Khan introduction 7.575 (n160); religion spread due to his conquest 7.86, 13.29; told: 'Everybody should be free to follow the form of Buddhism they like' 4.123, 13.29–30

Kübler-Ross, Elisabeth 24.310

Kuiji 1.371

Kūkai (Kōbō Daishi) introduction 1.384, 2.690–1 (n297); credited with inventing the Japanese system of writing 2.213; death anniversary 2.228; 'To a Nobleman in Kyoto' 24.xxiv

Kukkuripāda 1.382

Kul, Moggallāna's birthplace *see under* Bihar

kula 13.178

Kuladeva, Dharmachari 15.437

Kulamitra, Dharmachari 15.437

Kulananda, Dharmachari *Mindfulness and Money* 11.765 (n323); on the Tiratana Vandanā seminar 15.457; president of FWBO centres 12.631; proves his worth in the Order Office team 24.313; reply to Philip Mellor's 'Protestant Buddhism?' 13.371; starts Windhorse Trading 24.6

Kulanandi, Dharmacharini v24

kulaputra 14.405

Kularatna, Dharmachari brief introduction 24.633 (n148); general entries v24; in India 10.xl; medical advice 26.463; on the *Tiratana Vandanā* seminar 15.457

Kularatne, H. de S. 8.643

Kulkarni, A. R. hosts Sangharakshita on his first visit to Nagpur (1954) 10.116–17, 22.154–65; account of Sangharakshita's visit to Nagpur at the time of Dr Ambedkar's death 10.95–105; campaigns to make India 'Buddha-minded' 22.161–4; a connection with the Kulkarni family 10.99, 10.105, 22.165; 'The Dhamma or Doctrine' (*Maha Bodhi* article) 8.643; at the time of Dr Ambedkar's death 10.17; on tour with Sangharakshita 10.116–18, 10.123; Sangharakshita and Terry stay with him (1966) 23.355–7; meets Lokamitra 10.xxxix

Kulkarni, G. G. 10.99

Kumar, Maharaj, of Sikkim *see under* Sikkim

Kumārabhūta 2.173, 17.462

Kumārajīva (Chinese translator) brief introduction 2.686 (n246); considered as bodhisattva 2.181; *Daśabhūmika Sūtra* 14.227; *Diamond Sūtra* 14.148, 14.151; *Heart Sūtra* 14.152; parallel to St Jerome 26.303; Perfection of Wisdom 14.138; *Vimalakīrti-nirdeśa* 14.157, 16.444; *White Lotus Sūtra* 8.479, 14.108–9, 16.35

Kumārata 13.342

kumbha *see* inexhaustible jar

kumbhāṇdas 16.346

kuṇḍalinī ('coiled-up' power, Hinduism) or ***caṇḍālī*** ('the fiery path', the tantras) potential energy 16.121; psychic heat 19.439; represented by the serpent king Mucalinda 2.37, 12.190; wariness of employing the language of *kuṇḍalinī* 22.301; a way of relating to our meditation experience? 5.250

Kuṇḍiya 10.493–8

Kurseong, India 22.26, 22.197, 22.337

Kuru people 15.79–80

Kurukullā (Red Tārā) brief introduction 12.735 (n293); connection with Hindu love god Kāmadeva 17.778 (n594); her flowery bow and arrows, hook and noose 14.658 (n517), 19.24; illustration 13.286; of the lotus family 13.310; the love aspect, the passion aspect, of the Enlightened mind 13.68; represents the Tantric function of fascination 12.448, 19.24–5, 22.556; Sangharakshita's initiation 12.448–9, 22.555–7

***kuśa* grass** 3.31, 3.42, 15.16, 16.373–4

Kuśa, King 14.71

kuśala *see* skilful

kusala-dhammas 9.546

kuśala-karma *see* skilful action

Kusāvati (city) 10.702–3 (n315)

Kusha Shū *see* Chinese Buddhism

Kusho Bakula (Ladakhi lama) 2.756 (n783), 22.509–10

Kusinārā or Kuśinagara

the Buddha's parinirvāṇa
in the *sāl*-tree grove of the Mallas 2.29–30; why gain *parinirvāṇa* in this wattle-and-daub township? 3.118–19, 4.37; *see also* Buddha I/last days

history
sacked at the time of the Muslim conquest 20.402; excavated by British archaeologists 9.237; formerly the capital of a great kingdom 4.37; restored by Mahavir Swami and U Chandramani 8.194, 20.407

features of the town
Angar Caitya (on the spot where the Buddha's body was cremated) 20.406, 22.342; Mahaparinirvana Stupa 16.567, 20.405; the *sāl*-tree grove of the Mallas in the *Udāna*, *see under Udāna*/settings; Temple of the Recumbent Buddha 8.138, 20.406, 22.334, 25.196–7

pilgrims
Dr Ambedkar visits 9.11; Cheenia Baba, the ascetic *see* Cheenia Baba; pilgrimage to Kusinārā 2.223, 21.511, 22.334–6

Sangharakshita
śrāmaṇera ordination 2.418, 9.280, 20.403–13; 'the Stupa and the Temple became the twin centres of our spiritual existence' 20.406

Kūṭadanta Sutta *see* under *Dīgha Nikāya*

Kuwait 24.406

Kwan Yin *see* Guanyin

Kyd, Thomas 20.56

L

La, Sardar Bahadur Laden 21.260

labels

the process of labelling
conceptual verbal signposts, like the description of an orange 7.510; labelling things in an Aristotelian sense 18.287; *saṃjñā* labels a temporary condensation of conditions as an object 17.547; people always want to affix ready-made labels to their experiences 13.347; 'People like things labelled' (poem) 25.402; read them for the information, not 'what they really mean' 14.566

misleading labels
don't be misled by labels 2.572–3, 16.30, 18.498; labels can be useful, but we have to be careful with them 17.238; most things we label 'pleasure' are really a mixed experience 17.400–1; we think that if we can label a thing we have understood it 13.347; what you think of as the self is only a label 7.327, 10.602

labelling people
be very careful before labelling anyone else as egoistic 10.471; don't label people 19.155; labelling people 'heterosexual' or 'homosexual' 11.583; take care not to label people unfavourably 17.184; to ask someone's name is not just asking for a label 18.238; a true individual cannot easily be labelled 17.239; when you are determined to change, a label can be removed 17.238–9

Buddhism and labels
Buddhism under different labels 18.498; Buddhist texts label experience, to be related to one's own experience 4.158; does Buddhism have to be confined to what is labelled 'Buddhism'? 11.370–1; in Buddhism, some labels for experience may have got mixed up 5.451–2; the titles of teachings are just labels 18.402; Triratna needs time to develop before being labelled 19.52

Lacarrière, Jacques 8.425–8

lack

lack of …
attachment 18.331–5; awareness 16.170; awareness of the beauty of the Unconditioned 2.84–5; confidence 13.232, 18.165; energy 10.578; enthusiasm 9.199; fear 16.278, 18.341 ; integration, *see under* integration; inner security 19.269; mindfulness 12.382, 12.403; a philosophy of life 5.663–4; receptivity 18.115, 18.117; respect 17.667; self-love 5.126, 17.667–9; *vīrya* 4.474; vision 17.676

other lacks
avidyā: lack of practical wisdom and lack of *prajñā* 17.607–8; is lack of faith a psychological problem? 18.273; suffering the consequences of lack of awareness 15.214, 17.292; Nanda's lack of zest for spiritual life 2.82–3; often the way we treat other people is due to lack of imagination 5.153, 17.598; reasons for lack of motivation in the modern world 12.379–80; a sense of lack 13.396; the weakness of the Buddhist world is lack of unity 22.308

Lack, David 23.371, 23.531 (n419)

Ladakh *Buddhism in Kashmir and Ladakh* 8.380–1; described in *Peaks and Lamas* 7.462; *An English Buddhist in a Tibetan Monastery* (review) 8.398–9; followers of Tibetan Buddhism 7.462, 9.171; Kusho Bakula, incarnate lama 21.107, 23.363; Ladakhi Buddhist boys 22.518

ladder the Buddha escorted to earth down a jewelled staircase or ladder 11.15, 11.30, 12.185, 13.586; Jacob's Ladder 12.185; a ladder stretching up from earth to heaven 11.167; logic cannot reach *brahman* any more than a ladder can reach the stars 7.79; the path is more like a growing thing than a ladder 1.478, 1.590; the whole of existence like a great ladder on which we occupy the lowest rung 7.12–13

lagna-vidhi *see under* marriage/Indian

Laing, R. D. 23.101, 23.102, 23.489 (n124), 26.605

laity *see* lay people

Lake District, England 24.143–5

Lakkhaṇa Sutta *see under Dīgha Nikāya*

lakṣaṇas* or *lakkhanas *see* three *lakṣaṇas*

Lakshmi, Mother (cave-dwelling ascetic) 18.328, 20.366–7

Lakṣmī (or Lakshmi, goddess of wealth) etymology 16.396; absorbed into the Buddhist pantheon 22.401; her birth from

the cosmic ocean of milk 16.398, 26.641; her consort is Viṣṇu 16.396, 16.398; depiction 16.396; her image on a Buddhist shrine 7.461, 11.253, 22.98; hymns 7.59, 7.561 (n92); in India a good wife is called a Lakṣmī 16.397; Jamyang Khyentse Rimpoche performs a puja to her 22.401; legends 16.398; popularly worshipped in India 16.361, 16.384, 16.395–7, 16.411; represents prosperity, wealth, economics 16.399, 16.411; *see also* Śrī

Lakuṇṭaka Bhaddhiya Thera *see* Bhaddhiya

lalanā *see under* central channel

lalitakāla (playful arts) 14.521–2

Lalitavajra, Dharmachari (John Wadkin) v24

Lalitavistara Sūtra

introduction
its title ('the extended sports or games') 3.88, 4.135, 12.109, 14.521, 16.18; translation 16.587 (n22); the basis of *The Light of Asia* 12.182; the Buddha expresses gratitude to the bodhi tree 3.640–1 (n81), 3.692 (n468); calculated to produce faith and devotion 2.12; depicts the Buddha as a transcendental being reborn out of compassion 2.13; includes some teachings of the historical Buddha 16.53; mention of Maitreya 2.179; one of nine *sūtras* venerated in Nepal 14.100; a poetic work with devotional and literary appeal 12.182; presents the Buddha's life as a kind of charade or play 13.300; related to the story of Barlaam and Josaphat 13.662; speaks the language of images 16.18; tells the story of the Buddha's life from a docetic point of view 26.636; ten *bhūmis* 14.227; twelve great (or principal) acts in a Buddha's life 4.59, 4.670 (n74), 14.25

Siddhārtha's story
takes seven steps after he is born 2.38, 2.668 (n61), 11.15, 11.738 (n20); Asita's encounter with the infant Siddhārtha 3.629 (n23); has to prove himself by fighting Yaśodharā's kinsmen 3.49; adopts and then gives up self-mortification, Sujata and the milk rice 9.399–400, 10.437; settles to meditate by the river before his Enlightenment 3.631 (n33); 'Let blood dry up, let flesh wither away' 3.524, 4.370–1, 5.389, 10.259, 11.16; the attack of Māra's hordes 2.36, 3.665 (n254); the earth goddess bears witness to Siddhārtha's practice 9.569n, 13.693 (n125)

Lalitpur *see* Nepal

Lalkaka, Major and Mrs v22

Lall, Nanda Kishore v8

Lam, Wong Mow 1.24, 3.361, 14.3

Lam rim *see under* Tsongkhapa/works

Lama of Shang 8.354

Lama, Hasta Bahadur *see* Hasta

Lama, Karka Bahadur (student) v21

Lama, P. T. v22

Lama, Shantabir (Kalimpong) v21

Lama, Venerable Fu Chin (Chinese monk at Nalanda) 20.460

Lamaism 8.514–15

Lamarck, Jean Baptiste 3.626 (n5)

lamas *see under* Tibetan Buddhism/lay people and lamas

Lambert, Cuthbert 21.481

Lamotte, Étienne 13.337, 16.445

Lampedusa, Giuseppe 13.427

lamps

physical lamps
enormous amounts spent on butter lamps in Tibet 8.175; offering lamps in the puja 11.222, 11.240; reading the Dharma by lamplight 14.22; thousands of lamps burning at Bodh Gaya 23.366

lamps in the Buddhist tradition
an oil lamp in a dark place: Going for Refuge 3.xv, 3.77, 3.330, 13.249; moths in the lamp's flame 10.610–11; Kisāgotamī gained insight by reflecting on an extinguished lamp 8.119; Śāntideva would like to be like Aladdin's lamp 4.361; wisdom is like a lamp (*Questions of King Milinda*) 17.726 (n139); a monk makes himself into a living lamp (*White Lotus Sūtra*) 22.516; self-awareness, 'shining like a brilliant lamp' 18.252; 'I felt as if I were a radiant lamp' – a resonance with the fourth *dhyāna* 18.584–5; the Teaching of the radiant Wisdom Lamp (Milarepa) 19.156; *The Transmission of the Lamp of the Dharma* 12.675; 'so should one view what is conditioned' 14.506–7; *jñāna* and *prajñā* like the light and the lamp, *see Sūtra of Huineng*

metaphorical lamps
individuality grows clearer, like the pattern on a lamp as it's turned up 14.451, 16.131; the lamp of the Dharma 11.276; handing on the lamp of the Dharma like the Olympic torch 12.674–5; through the ages monks have kept the lamp of the Dharma burning 8.245–6

Lancaster, England 24.584

Lancelot 25.101–6, 25.406, 25.438–9

landscape the awe-inspiring landscape of the Himalayas 2.644, 18.158–9; the isolated figure in a huge landscape 26.255–6; a Norfolk winter landscape 4.225; reading Nietzsche like making out the landscape of human existence by flashes of lightning 3.495; the Tibetan landscape 13.66, 18.158–9; Turner's way of looking at the landscape 5.642; visions of landscapes 20.208

Lane, Mark v24

Lang, Andrew 23.8

Lang, David Marshall 8.397–8

Langdarma, anti-Buddhist king of Tibet 13.13

Langford Rae, Mme Marie-Elise *see* Kazini of Chakhung

Langford Rae, Roderick v22

Langland, William (*Piers Plowman*) his feeling for the poor and respect for their faith 24.540; Lady Meed 24.538–9; old age and death 24.539–40; the poem takes place in the context of a dream 16.263; Piers wonders at the instinct that makes a magpie build its nest 24.540; set in the Malvern Hills 24.581; written in a racy style 24.538

Langri Thangpa 8.611

language

general reflections on language
inclusive language 11.640–1; it has to be either personal or impersonal, but in reality it's neither 18.613; language conditions experience 17.248–9; a language needs to be rich in ambiguities to serve our needs fully 17.686; language run wild 18.608; linguistic convention as implying a real distinction between things 2.87, 2.123; the nature of language has a reifying tendency 19.238–9; not limited to the expression of thoughts and desires in verbal form 7.394; our relationship with it is similar to our relationship with symbols 13.123; sense-based 19.436; sign language 24.246; speaking the same language as someone else, literally and metaphorically 12.523; subject to a gravitational pull 1.404; translation, *see* translation; use it clearly and precisely 4.145; a very subtle, elastic thing 12.118; we have to learn to use language against the grain of its original purpose 17.249; we need to use language and not let language use us 18.611; when we learn a new language, we acquire a new soul 16.565

language and Buddhism
as soon as we have crystallized an idea in language we have to dissolve it 14.447–8; bad philology, good doctrine, but good philology, bad or no doctrine 1.17; Buddhism's sophisticated use of language 19.437; the Buddha spoke the language of reason 16.417; the danger of using other people's language 10.440, 13.431; the danger of using the language of psychology 10.440–1; the Dharma is best communicated in a shared mother tongue 22.527–8; the Dharma is beyond communication 3.164; the different effects of a logical exposition and a story 12.110; difficulty of finding words to communicate the Dharma 1.402, 1.404, 2.117; don't imagine that the Buddha carefully defined his terms from the beginning 14.350–1; the English language doesn't have words for higher states of consciousness 17.436; everyone should be taught the Dharma in their own language 3.161–2, 7.393, 7.498, 8.220–2, 9.480, 10.244, 14.13, 16.15–16, 16.365, 22.10; finding English equivalents of Buddhist terms 8.596–7; finding natural expression for genuine feelings in appropriate words 16.368; how to express *samādhi* when language comes from the experience it transcends? 26.199–200; Indian language grammatic negatives with positive meaning 10.635, 14.347, 17.295–6, 17.565; language has its origins in mundane experience, so cannot describe Nirvāṇa 2.123; the language of Buddhism becoming part of Western vernacular 11.xviii; language must be looked at no less clearly than its content 8.599; the language of Western writers coinciding with the language of Buddhism 2.393; learning at least one canonical language 11.510; no need for Western Buddhists to use Tibetan, Chinese, or Japanese terms 19.134; old language used to express new understanding 10.429–30, 11.512, 13.431, 15.463; prefers to speak the language not of identity but of analysis and change 2.97; the profundity of the teaching has nothing to do with written language 1.222; the relation of Buddhism to language 14.12–15; a sanctity attached to archaic language 19.133; speaks the language of concepts and of images 4.144–8, 12.106, 12.503, 16.15–16, 16.416–17; the assumption that wisdom is better expressed in concepts than images 14.430–1; speaking the language of Western culture 4.638–41, 4.657–8; has no one sacred language 3.161; speaking the

language of Hinduism 12.241; speaks the language of myth 12.102–11, 12.179–80; to be conveyed in language which is familiar verbally and ideologically 7.159, 13.437; to begin with, the Buddha used ordinary language to explain his experience 10.434; trying to communicate in a language which negates wisdom is confusing 2.393–4; using the world's language, be careful it doesn't overcome you 12.476, 16.415–16; we need to develop an indigenous yet faithfully Buddhist language 16.138; we need to use language poetically rather than scientifically 19.447; what language did the Buddha speak? 14.12–14

the limitations of language
be aware of the limitations, to avoid artificial problems 18.608; Buddhism's awareness of the limitations 19.437; created for practical purposes, not philosophical discussion 10.144; due to the nature of language 12.655; to describe the experience of Enlightened beings 19.429–30; to describe reality 5.597; the fish and the turtle, *see under* parables and stories; the *Laṅkāvatāra Sūtra*'s awareness of the limitations of language 14.207; the limitations of analogy 7.210–11; and prayer 19.139–41; the problem of the illusory ego is partly linguistic 17.352; Shakespeare had no problems with limitations 16.579; no language can come up to the truth and force of reality (Hazlitt) 24.562; to speak about *śūnyatā* we have to do violence to language 14.467; use language imaginatively, not too literally 19.436–7; we speak in space- and time-bound language 18.607, 19.436–7; when considering time and eternity 4.204

the language of the world
the cultural language of humanity 7.394; different languages allow us to say different things 16.565; don't increase negativity by using language suited to other cultural contexts 4.622–3; going forth from your native language 12.556–7; having to speak a language whose underlying ideology you don't accept 4.524–5; imperative and conditional statements 15.264–7; language arises out of man's experience of the mundane 2.124; language is the child not of transcendental knowledge but of mundane necessity 1.234; modern European languages are deficient in religious and philosophical terms 1.24; nations can only speak the same 'language' if they believe in objective truth 12.352; secular language 12.117; when nations don't speak the same language literally or metaphorically 12.349–50

metaphorical and poetic language
all language is metaphorical 13.122, 19.436–7, 26.70; the language of images speaks to some more intimately than concepts 4.156; in metaphor language begins to transcend itself 14.589, 26.70; metaphor: the language of the soul, the universal language 7.394; metaphorical language is indispensable 11.659; poetry can get closer to reality than prose 19.238–9; poets use ordinary language to communicate something new 16.138; we shouldn't be too afraid of the language of the 'true self' 4.283

English language
the availability of Buddhist literature in English 14.266–7; the contrast between exuberant Elizabethan and 'correct' Queen Anne English 14.108; the mingling of the English language with Indian culture 7.55; number of words 25.7; its parts of speech are interchangeable, giving it great flexibility 19.238–9; Sangharakshita's gratitude to have been brought up speaking it 26.531; singular and plural forms of address 15.699

grammar
aspect of monastic studies 2.197; grammar gives something quasi-metaphysical objectivity 26.369; Indian language may be grammatically negative when the meaning is positive 10.635; one shouldn't linger too long over grammar 19.132–3; study of language in relation to spiritual teaching 1.17; 'no greater menace than a mere grammarian set loose on a sacred text' 8.539; why use a grammatically negative word to express something positive? 17.566

Laṅkāvatāra Sūtra (the *Ārya-saddharma-Laṅkāvatāra*)

THE *SŪTRA* AS A WHOLE

introduction
brief introduction 22.610 (n300); introductions to the *sūtra* 1.356–9, 2.276–7, 3.87–8, 16.17; full introduction 14.201–15; full title 14.201

the history of the text
dating the text 14.201–2; a late Mahāyāna *sūtra* 16.239; Mañjuśrī in the *sūtra*, as Mahāmati 1.238–9, 2.173, 14.204–6; rejected by the Theravāda as uncanonical 7.534; the *sūtra* and the Yogācāra 1.357, 12.168, 19.373–4; alleged reference to Nāgārjuna 14.203, 17.466; one of nine *sūtras* venerated in Nepal 14.100; Bodhidharma took the text from India to China 2.276, 12.173; Zen (or Chan)

seems to have arisen among Chinese students of the *sūtra* 2.555; influence on Zen 2.276, 12.173, 19.372; translations 7.548 (n23), 13.337, 14.201–2, 16.587 (n19); *East-West Fire: Schopenhauer's Optimism and the Laṅkāvatāra Sūtra* (review) 8.365–6

what the sūtra is like
almost entirely psychological in content 14.201; aware of the limitations of language 14.207; 'a collection of notes unsystematically strung together' 14.202–3; a heap of jewels mixed with bits of glass and stone 1.356–7; impossible to give an account by a résumé of contents 14.204; an inner perception of the deepest truth 14.206; 'a memorandum kept by a Mahāyāna master' 1.357; not to establish a system of thought but to discourse on a religious experience 1.357, 14.208; not a gradual but an abrupt realization of the truth 14.207; one of the most difficult of all the *sūtras* 16.17; 'a perpetual upholding of the intuitive element in religion' 14.207; a repository of nearly all the principal tenets of the Mahāyāna 14.214

subject matter
absolute mind 2.67; the *akaniṭṭha* heaven 15.239; *āryajñāna* (noble knowledge) 26.198; correspondences with the *trikāya* 14.212–13; devoid of symbolism 14.201; distinction between Absolute Buddha and relative Buddha 14.211; the doctrine of the twofold *nairātmya* 2.674–5 (n119); the eight *vijñānas* 14.210; emphasis on direct personal experience 12.173, 13.492, 14.206–7, 19.374; emphasis on One Mind 1.260, 3.87, 7.502, 12.170, 14.204–6, 14.208, 14.215, 19.374; the five *dharmas* (categories) 14.213–14; *gatigocara* (experience) 11.73–4; metaphors for conditioned existence 2.81; 'noble wisdom' 11.73–4; *parāvṛtti* doctrine, *see parāvṛtti*; *pratyātmagocara* preferred to *bodhi* as a term for Enlightenment 11.74, 12.173, 14.207; a radical transformation in our consciousness 2.284; three *svabhāvas* 14.214; two *nairātmyas* 14.213; *vasanā* (habit-energy) 14.209–10; words are but signs, and should not be mistaken for realities 14.234

Sangharakshita and the sūtra
it confirmed his mystical experience: 'the world as being like a dream' 20.74; influence on early writing 7.550 (n36); an important source of inspiration 22.375; he revisits the *sūtra* 22.241; Terry Delamare reads the *sūtra* 23.244, 23.275

CHAPTER BY CHAPTER

chapter 1, 'The Invitation of Rāvaṇa'
the foundation of the Yogācāra 1.357; summary of the chapter 1.357–9; Rāvaṇa 1.357–9, 2.277; the Buddha laughed 1.358

chapter 2, 'Collection of All the Dharmas'
erroneous views of worldly philosophies 14.204; long passage on the Mind in itself 14.204–6; to see the stars after the sun has risen 2.81; 'words are not the highest reality' 1.238–9; 'The world is nothing but mind' 12.170

chapter 3, 'On Impermanency'
the bodhisattva is not to become attached to the words of the texts 1.612 (n199); the distinction between the *nirvāṇa* of the *arhant* and that of the bodhisattva 19.199; 'Is all created? Is all uncreated?' 7.534–5; myriad names of the Tathāgata 1.261

chapter 4, 'On Intuitive Understanding'
how *śrāvakas*, *pratyekabuddhas*, bodhisattvas handle the happiness of *samādhi* 1.259; the effect of seeing that the world is no more than Mind itself 1.260

chapter 6, 'On Momentariness'
three degrees of practising each of the six perfections 1.425

chapter 7, 'On Transformation'
from his Enlightenment until his death the Buddha spoke not one word 1.67, 2.251, 3.164, 3.549, 11.418, 13.348, 14.207, 14.297, 14.477, 25.8

chapter 8, 'Meat-Eating'
giving up meat 1.357, 3.370, 4.111, 10.49; 'It is not true that meat is proper food ...' 17.585; 'like devouring one's own relatives ...' 14.203–4

chapter 9, 'Dhāraṇis'
reflects a phase of Tantric influence 14.203; 'the triple world of existence is no more than thought-construction' 2.679 (n170), 12.170

chapter 10, 'Verses'
entirely in verse 14.203; ' a heap of rubbish and gems' 14.203

Laos revival of Buddhism 7.445–6; Theravāda Buddhism practised in 2.548, 3.407

Laozi (Lao-tzu)

introduction
appearance in the Axial Age 3.427, 11.355; the respect of Chinese Buddhists for him 2.243

Dao De Jing (Tao Te Ching)
a perennial best-seller 3.426–7; the development of a code of morality is a degeneration 14.419; 'He who knows does not speak, he who speaks does not know' 7.37, 7.44, 24.206; it is only because of empty space that the wheel is able to revolve 7.323; 'He who knows others is wise, he who knows himself is enlightened' 13.351; 'A journey of a thousand miles starts with a single step' 7.397; 'Looked at, it cannot be seen, listened to, it cannot be heard' 2.53; Sangharakshita's appreciation of the text 20.87; a tree that is too big to be used? 14.524, 19.219, 19.605 (n90); 'Without looking out of the window, one can see the Way of Heaven' 26.279

Lapotaire, Jane 24.582

Large Prajñāpāramitā Sūtra brief introduction 14.145–6; consists of three texts 14.146; description of *arhants* 2.140, 2.154; description of the characteristics of bodhisattvas 2.153–5; includes parts of the *Perfection of Wisdom in 8,000 Lines* 14.146; a late Mahāyāna *sūtra* 16.239; Maitreyanātha's commentary, the *Abhisamayālaṃkāra*, *see* Maitreyanātha; subject matter 14.146; texts it is represented by today 1.300; that the *nāgas* received it from the Buddha need not be taken literally 1.310; transmitted to Nāgārjuna by the *nāga* kings, so legend says 1.309; twenty kinds of *śūnyatā* 14.560; versions of different lengths preserved in different mythical realms 14.145

Larger Sukhāvatī-vyūha Sūtra *see under Sukhāvatī-vyūha Sūtras*

Larkin, Philip appreciation of his poetry 26.379, 26.439–40; 'Death is no different whined at than withstood' 26.439; letters 12.698; 'This Be The Verse' 3.600, 25.423

Last Vandanā 2.491, 2.729 (n616), 24.18

Latimer, Hugh 'the Devil is the busiest bishop in the land' 18.177; his last words when burned at the stake 13.549

Latin five Latin words that sum up moral history 7.391; people who can't enjoy a flower's beauty until they know its Latin name 13.347, 25.242, 25.538; translation of the *Dhammapada* into Latin 12.31–2, 14.53, 15.4

Latthakin, Prince K. M. ('Burma Raja') 11.236–7, v15, v21, v22

Lattimore, Richard 23.288, 23.516 (n325)

Latur, India 9.396

Laugharne, Wales 26.615

'Laughing Buddha' *see* Mi-lo Fu

laughter a bodhisattva precept not to laugh heedlessly 13.56; the Buddha laughs (*Laṅkāvatāra Sūtra*) 1.358; the freeing effect of laughter 4.137; 'Laughter that shows the teeth is madness' (the Buddha) 4.137, 12.450, 15.372; 'To laugh excessively is childish' – what did the Buddha mean? 4.137; reflectiveness turning into happy laughter 18.53; therapeutic laughter caused by *ikebana* 23.36; Zen masters laughing at the absurdity of ever imagining that they weren't Enlightened 4.203, 18.45

laukika *see* mundane

laurels one never rests on one's laurels 8.226, 17.577; 'Rest on your laurels and they will wither' 26.59

Lavater, Johann Kasper introduction 7.574 (n155); classified human character 7.84; influence on Blake 8.560, 26.349

law the Dharma as law 3.159, 8.201–2, 12.501, 15.505–6, 15.631, 16.84; dishonesty of legal profession (in the view of two lawyers) 20.275; to fight intolerance, use the law when it is on your side 4.127; the law of conditionality, *see under* conditionality; the law of karma, *see under* karma; the law of the universe 8.201

Law, Bimala Charan *Designation of Human Types, see Puggala-Paññatti*

Lawrence, Brother (Carmelite lay brother in Paris) his devotion to God 7.93–4; a mystery to his contemporaries and perhaps to himself 7.104; sees a tree as a demonstration of the power of God 7.94; *The Practice of the Presence of God* 7.92–105, 7.577–8 (n172), 13.627, 23.207

Lawrence, D. H.

life
introduction 23.512 (n294), 24.651 (n215), 26.489; his lack of education 19.521–2; his response to the First World War 8.542–3; his meeting with Earl Brewster in Capri 8.543, 21.261; nomadic lifestyle 26.489; his time in Ceylon and response to Buddhism there 8.543–4; his idea for a spiritual community, 'Rananim' 8.543–51; in New Mexico 11.627, 24.491, 24.518, 24.522–6, 26.444, 26.489; his emblem, a phoenix 24.523; his death 8.542–3; the trial about the publication of *Lady Chatterley's Lover* 10.153; the fiftieth anniversary of his death 8.541; Sangharakshita's connection with

Lawrence 24.525; one of Sangharakshita's literary heroes 26.489–90

biographies and studies
Luhan's *Lorenzo in Taos* 24.525, 26.489; Middleton Murry's *Son of Woman* 23.473, 24.525; Sagar's *Life of D. H. Lawrence* 8.541–51, 24.174, 24.525; Shukman's *Savage Pilgrims on the Road to Santa Fe* 24.518

character
his character 19.118; he didn't have a persona 19.122; he meant what he said 18.347; he repudiated leadership 8.549; he saw himself as a preacher rather than a writer 26.256; he touched nothing that he did not bring to life 26.490; he was against ideals 19.181; out of sympathy with the age in which he lived 26.488; 'the outstanding creative force of his generation' 26.444

writings
'a capacity of experiencing unknown modes of being' 26.137; a good poet 26.379; 'grand and cakey style' 22.346; his writings are not works of art, but the work of an artist 26.22; made some approach to the Dharma 16.375; the novel as a thought adventure 26.256, 26.380; novellas better than novels 26.380; on the Etruscans 8.425; on the love of flowers 26.186

quotations
'Art for my sake' 26.150, 26.710 (n85); 'The first principle of good parenting is to let the child alone' 18.184; 'Let a child feel your healthy, hot anger' 15.432; 'A man in his wholeness, wholly attending' 14.291, 15.198, 15.257; 'There is no point in work unless it absorbs you like an absorbing game' 19.26; 'the otherness that lies beyond the boundaries of man's conscious mind' 26.169; 'The true artist always substitutes a finer morality for a grosser' 26.144, 26.179; 'We also need our Beauty' 9.444

works
'The Argonauts' 23.264; 'Art and Morality'; 'Bavarian Gentians' 26.441; *Fantasia of the Unconscious* 5.619, 15.443; *Kangaroo* 24.373, 26.489–90; letters 12.698; paintings 8.542, 24.491, 24.518, 24.525–6; *The Man Who Died* 26.490; *The Plumed Serpent* 26.489–90; *The Rainbow* 8.543, 21.261, 24.525, 26.444; 'The Ship of Death' 25.liv, 26.398, 26.490; *St Mawr* 24.324, 26.332; *The Woman Who Rode Away* 26.490

Lawrence, Frieda 19.256–7, 24.524

lay people (*dāyakas*, *upāsakas*)

LAY LIFE IN THE BUDDHIST TRADITION

introduction
the place of the laity 2.202–17; the meaning of *dāyaka* 8.682 (n112); 'Was the Buddha a *bhikkhu*?' 2.615–50

in the Pāli canon
the Buddha's description of a devoted householder 4.346, 4.697 (n256); exclusion of laity from spiritual life 2.204; the first few verses of the *Maṅgala Sutta* are about Dharma practice as a householder 15.407; the four *vargas* placed on terms of complete equality (*Aṅguttara Nikāya*) 2.203; householders (*gṛhapati* or *gahapati*) in the eight assemblies 12.522; a layman's difficulty in assessing spiritual attainment 10.588, 10.590–1; lay disciples becoming non-returners, once-returners, and Stream Entrants 11.450; lay people in the Pāli canon 2.665 (n30); names of lay disciples who attained Release 2.203; teachings not communicated to lay people (contradicted in *Sutta-Nipāta*) 2.204–5

in the Mahāyāna
the *bodhicitta* can be developed by both monk and layman 11.570–1; devotion to the bodhisattva ideal 1.442, 2.209; the Pure Land *sūtras* are part of the laity's response to exclusion from the spiritual life 14.168; recognition that being a bodhisattva was easier for a monk than a layman 2.211

prospects of Enlightenment
can become Enlightened 2.203, 9.389–90, 10.225; declared incapable of becoming Enlightened 2.204; gain Enlightenment 9.390, 9.570n; lay life may be said to be any situation that prevents higher development 26.31; make good progress on the path, though not fully Enlightened 2.716 (n492); a place for the laity's aspirations: Hīnayāna and Mahāyāna solutions 2.206–11; persisted in regarding Enlightenment as their proper goal 2.205; the possibility of the bodhisattva ideal's realization by the layman 14.104

status
the great majority of Buddhists throughout history 2.202; if a layman becomes an *arhant*, he 'miraculously' becomes a *bhikkhu* 10.629; in effect second-class Buddhists 2.299, 2.597, 9.254; lay ordination 13.338–9; lay people playing a more responsible role 12.126–7; 'not-so-real' Buddhists 2.559; originally known as part-timers 3.404

practice
benefits of practising ethics 10.641–6, 11.320; a committed lay person can do a great deal 12.126–7; the Buddha's teachings for them (Ambedkar) 9.147; giving 2.204, 9.390, 18.175; a household shrine a reminder of higher spiritual values 2.230; it is possible to live creatively in the householder lifestyle 19.582; lay ceremonies: birth, marriage, and death 2.230–2; living a 'worldly' life in a Buddhist spirit 8.276; monastic rules about eating and retreats in lay terms 12.124–5; more emotionally than intellectually inclined 2.220; need for solitary time 4.535; practice expected of lay people 2.204; precepts 11.317; reformulating the principles of Buddhism in terms of lay life 12.123–6; their low expectations of their own practice 11.568, 15.486; Vimalakīrti's advice to laymen: not an exhortation to put your feet up 16.492–5; 'Wanted: A New Type of Upāsaka' 2.448–9, 8.331–5, 10.271

limits to practice
came under influence of Hinduism 9.391; hard to meditate in the midst of worldly responsibilities 4.527–8; historical weakness (Ambedkar) 9.339–40; the insecurity of a spiritual life based on supporting *bhikkhus* 2.592–4; more interested in material gains than spiritual attainments 2.215; not yet willing to give up pleasures 4.564–5; spiritual practice reduced to the acquisition of merit 15.98, 15.647–50; they possess hereditary traditions about the Buddha's life and teachings 2.205; think they don't have to take Buddhism seriously 10.267, 19.309–10; tied up with worldly responsibilities 10.483–7

LAY PEOPLE AND MONKS (*BHIKKHUS*)

devotion
bhikkhus teaching laity how to pay them proper respect 2.600; given what monks have done in the history of Buddhism, no wonder they are revered 8.245–6; a layman may behave better than a *bhikkhu* and still defer to him 2.591–2; monks as objects of devotion 2.213–14, 2.225–6; the extreme veneration shown to *bhikkhus* is bad for them 2.599–601; reverence of lay people for monastic sangha 1.407, 2.211–17, 7.231; salutation of *bhikkhus* 16.381

support
disproportionate emphasis on making offerings to monks 13.419; for support, you need faith and yearning for the Dharma, 19.352–3; the four things the monk can expect, *see* eight requisites/four necessities; householders should support wanderers before making offerings to *devas* 10.648; lay followers' duty to support *bhikkhus* 9.390, 18.175; lay people almost pay *bhikkhus* to practise for them 10.267, 18.520–1, 19.472; making offerings to monks to acquire merit 15.647–50; a mean patron 18.549–50; monks are supported in the hope of material benefit 19.472–3; monks' reliance on lay people 15.278, 19.481–2; some *bhikkhus* would love to work, but the lay people won't let them 17.73; support of monastic community 16.408–9; supporting *bhikkhus* to become academics 19.486–7

how they relate to each other
the basis of the relationship 16.106–7; a *bhikkhu* manipulates a poor layman into buying him sandals 22.215–16; common devotion to the Buddha 2.451; cynical support for *bhikkhus* 15.652; a division of labour, not necessarily healthy 10.267, 12.125–6, 18.389; for lay people, it would be unthinkable for a monk to wear civilian clothes 23.188; lay people like to listen to monks chanting 15.437; the laity see monks as an embodiment of their ideals 2.214; lay people are more likely to listen to handsome young monks 19.498; lay people think of monks in terms of conventional morality 7.545; lay people think they are the boss 15.649, 19.478; lay people's disappointment at *bhikkhus*' bad behaviour 2.593, 2.635–6, 18.520; monks and laity seem to have little in common 11.570; monks are the focus of the projections of the laity 19.310; monks are happier than lay people 4.628–9, 11.590, 16.392, 17.337–8, 19.74; monks don't look down on the laity 4.565–6; monks feel they must flatter lay people 19.481; the mutual obligation of the monastic and lay community 8.307; the need for monks and hermits to please lay supporters 18.338–40; not a very positive arrangement 18.390; the patronizing attitude of some patrons towards monks 18.137–8; relations were cordial during the Buddha's lifetime 2.202, 2.451; the relationship can produce a desire to keep up appearances 8.246; Sri Lankan monks in thrall to the laity 17.587; they are mutually dependent 11.476; the unwritten contract between them 15.98; wealthy lay Buddhists who 'swagger like peacocks' 19.477–8

see also
monastic–lay split, *see under* sangha/monastic–lay split; neither monastic nor lay, *see under* sangha/monastic–lay split

Laycock, Steven 8.615–16

Lazarus 4.12–13, 10.255, 13.575

Lazarus, Malcolm v24

laziness (*kausīdya*)

introduction
what is laziness? 5.326–7; a deep-rooted and terrible thing which requires drastic treatment 18.555; the near enemy of peacefulness 10.83; not doing something when it has to be done 5.646; it can arise if *samādhi* is not balanced by *vīrya* 3.307–8; it prevents continuity of concentration in meditation 17.533–4; it's associated with ignorance because what is lacking is vision 17.676; being busy doing something that is not conducive to skilful mental states 17.534

from the Buddhist tradition
a reliable teaching will lead towards energy, not laziness, *see* Mahāpajāpatī Gotami; 'Get up! Don't be heedless!' (*Dhammapada*) 18.390; 'Here are the roots of trees. Sit down, meditate.' 1.236, 3.53, 14.19, 18.368; as *upakleśa* (Abhidharma) 17.674–6; difference from *styāna* 17.675; activity in pursuit of politics and business is laziness (Gampopa) 4.132, 17.534, 18.390, 19.582; Vimalakīrti's advice to laymen is not an exhortation to put your feet up 16.492–5; 'To instruct an idler brings misfortune' 18.421

examples
Dr Johnson's regrets about being lazy 17.675; the Lazy Men (Gnosticism) 8.427; 'Satan finds work for idle hands to do' 15.350, 17.675; the scholar who uses his learning to engage in controversies 19.545

lazy Buddhists
the attraction of Zen for people who think practising it needs no effort 17.675; laziness about practising the Dharma 17.671; the laziness of monks 4.438, 4.443; a lazy person doesn't develop very easily as a human being 10.213; most Western Buddhists take things rather easy 13.171; saying 'I don't feel inspired to do this' as a rationalization for laziness 17.576; urging lazy Buddhists to bestir themselves 8.268, 22.458; we tend to give ourselves a fairly easy time 18.617; a weakness that Buddhists need to guard against 8.268, 10.83, 17.675, 26.15

reflections
the Great Work of spiritual transformation may appear to be idleness 25.267; lots of people think that meditating is not doing anything 18.268; to overcome it we need to be able to distinguish what is worthwhile 17.534; you don't necessarily counter it by being more energetic 17.675

Le Brun, Charles 7.63, 7.564 (n105)

Leadbeater, Charles Webster 8.26–8, 20.148, 22.587 (n129), 24.59, 24.213, 24.621 (n82)

leaders and leadership 'I do not consider that I lead the sangha' (the Buddha) 2.28, 9.306, 10.580–1, 25.107; Buddhism is prepared to respect and even admire other spiritual leaders 2.243; dangers of leadership 9.303–6; the guru is not a group leader or boss or authority figure 18.411; the human desire to preserve a leader 16.159; it's a great quality for a leader to be able to hear and respond to difficult truths 17.240; in Japan the Buddhists were leaders in every sense 7.442; D. H. Lawrence repudiated leadership 8.549; the paranoia of absolute rulers 17.258–9; protection of political leaders by the four great kings 16.356; the role of the person leading the puja 11.226; Sangharakshita didn't want the Triratna Buddhist Order to have a leader 25.107; a spiritual movement can have a teacher, but not a leader 25.107, 26.31

Leal, Valdés 24.441

leap, crosswise 1.347

Lear, Edward 14.481

learning

learning to …
get on with other people 9.189; make and keep vows 2.343, 4.56–7, 18.161; accept reality 16.216; be dissatisfied with ourselves 3.498, 12.623; enjoy poetry 9.444; experience yourself more fully 3.488, 12.268–9; let go, 'the most difficult thing in the world' 3.250; listen to music 12.260; look at works of art 12.259–60; love oneself, *see* self-love; see 1.571–2; stand on your own feet 12.232–3; take delight in Dharma practice 18.130

learning from …
lots of different teachers 19.544–5; nature 18.182, 18.619, 19.69; our own experience 17.xxii; the phenomenal world 19.69

different aspects of learning
analogy between the pianist practising scales and the Buddhist learning doctrines 2.60; confusion between ordinary and spiritual learning 15.726–8; don't try to learn everything all at once 19.544–5; distinction between 'head-learning' and 'soul-wisdom' 7.359; however much we learn, we can

learn more 10.258; the implication of a rule of training is that one is capable of learning 2.343; it isn't easy to find people who really want to learn in a spiritual sense 11.275; learning a lot from small incidents 15.718; learning transformed into wisdom 1.169–70; a little learning is more dangerous than complete ignorance 1.198; the mistake of thinking you've got nothing more to learn 4.128, 16.40; the path of no more learning 17.459; the purpose of learning is to support the faith that comes from practice 18.185; worshipping the man from whom one learns the Dharma 22.385; learning not to react to feeling with craving 2.256–9, 3.202–3, 3.259, 12.157–8

see also
learning the Dharma, *see under* Dharma III/advice for the Dharma student; learning from books, *see under* books; learning the scriptures by heart, *see under* heart

Leary, Timothy introduction 23.491 (n134); a kind of guru figure 3.561; 'Turn on, tune in, drop out' 11.551, 11.763 (n305); *The Psychedelic Experience* 23.109

Leatherhead, Surrey 20.91, 20.100

leaves changing colour, illustration of three *lakṣaṇas*, *see* three *lakṣaṇas*; falling leaves and impermanence, *see under* impermanence/lessons in impermanence; insight gained on seeing a falling leaf 3.272; the great burning of leaves in autumn 25.436; the red leaf falls 25.300; *siṁsapā* leaves, see *siṁsapā*

leaving home *see* going forth

Leavis, F. R. introduction 26.723 (n245); his literary criticism 26.320; Sangharakshita hears him speak on T. S. Eliot 23.419; and the 'two cultures' 3.6, 3.625 (n2)

Legenda Aurea 13.653, 13.663

legends of the Buddha, *see under* Buddha II/symbols and myths; the difference between myths and legends 12.108; *see also* myths

Leggett, Trevor 8.494, 13.332

Leibenthal, Dr 8.664

Leibniz, Gottfried Wilhelm 8.705 (n321)

Leishman, J. B. 26.166–7, 26.172

leisure the eight conditions of non-leisure 17.168, 17.731–2 (n183); leisure in this life is rare 19.244–5; making the most of 'leisure' to practise the Dharma 17.168; until recent times human beings had to spend much of their time just surviving 12.379–80; in the West we are fortunate to have leisure 3.313–14, 15.365–6

Lemon, Denis VII

Lenin, Vladimir 22.210

Leo, Friar 13.625

Leonidas 23.295, 23.517 (n331)

leopards 9.467, 9.488, 20.376. 20.378, 20.380, 23.16

leprosy *see under* sickness

lesbianism an emotionally charged relationship 11.582; blurring of relationship and spiritual friendship 11.637; Jivaka's feelings about lesbianism 22.439; *The Well of Loneliness* 13.612

Lester Smith, E. 24.213–14

letter and spirit *see* spirit and letter

letters (as a genre) business letters 12.694–5; didactic letters 12.695–6; epistolary novels 12.696–7; the first letters, found in ancient Babylon 12.694; 'for some reason I feel more like writing long letters on rainy days' 21.560; Goethe on letters 21.457; 'Letters mingle souls' 12.694, 21.457, 25.421; the newsletter 12.695; personal letters 12.697–8

letting go destroying something a person is attached to, to help them let go of attachment 19.12–14, 19.18; *kalyāṇa mitratā* can help you let go of neurotic craving 18.207; learning to let go, 'the most difficult thing in the world' 3.250; learning to let go of fear 10.259; as a fisherman lets go of a poisonous snake 3.276; in the self-liberating Mahāmudrā 19.156; into the absolute 19.137; of childish attitudes 16.317; of consciousness in the six element practice, *see* six element practice; of sense experience 19.156; of our idea of self 3.418; of 'a view of existence' 17.247; wondering whether to let go of the 'rope' of self 9.456–7; *see also* renunciation

levitation brought about by excess of *prīti* 3.267–8; Kachu Rimpoche says he can levitate 13.25; the levitation of a Kabirapanthi 3.267–8

Levy, Paul 8.350

Lewes, George 7.571 (n135)

Lewis, C. S. 19.141

Lewis, Helen (Dharmacharini Pasadanita) 17.xv

Lewis, I. M. 4.548–9

Lewis, Percy Wyndham 26.339

Lewis, Sinclair 24.374

ley lines *see* Watkins

Lhalungpa, Lobsang Phuntsok arrested in connection with Lhasa politics 4.338; 'Buddhism in Tibet' 2.434–6, 22.192–3, 22.265; discusses Tibetan Buddhism with Sangharakshita 22.234–5; taught by Sangharakshita 22.112; translation of *The Life of Milarepa* 24.396–7; his wife 22.112–13

Lhatsun Chempo Rimpoche (bringer of Buddhism to Sikkim) 22.244, 22.470–1

Lhendup, Dhondup v22

Li Gotami general entries v21, v24; an artist of repute 8.391; her journey to Tsaparang, *see under* Govinda

Li Po 20.61

liberal and liberalism Buddhism depends on equilibrium between literalizing and liberalizing influences 1.249; the difference between liberalism and pseudo-liberalism 26.74; liberal attitude to the Dharma 1.251; a liberal view of all Buddhist traditions 22.532; Mahāyāna carried to extremes 1.249; pseudo-liberalism, *see* pseudo-liberalism

liberation the ambiguity of the term 13.462–3; devoting yourself to liberating self or other believing that they are real 2.159, 26.52; the difference between the ideal and the discipline of individual liberation 17.268; essentially about liberating energies 18.77; four things leading to liberation (*Aṅguttara Nikāya*) 3.85; individual liberation as *prātimokṣa* 2.344; four ways that will never lead you to liberation (Milarepa) 19.491–4; liberation by faith 4.516; the individual must be liberated from the past 13.468; it consists in seeing processes rather than things 17.355; liberation by wisdom 17.187; liberation from the first three fetters 13.463–4; liberation from suffering 15.438–9; liberation is not so much of the self as from the self 7.412, 26.53; liberation through love (*mettā*) 17.186–7; minor liberations 13.464; opportunities for liberation in the *bardos* after death 12.199–205; the secret of bondage is also the secret of liberation 1.113; the Tantric yogi is liberated by practices by which others are bound 7.402; the worldly-minded think of happiness, the spiritually-minded of liberation 26.64

see also
doors of liberation, *see* three *vimokṣa-mukhas*; freedom

liberty Blake's conception of liberty 8.555; control of the senses is liberty, according to the Buddha 10.520; distinction from and connection with freedom 9.183; 'Licence they mean when they cry liberty' 13.462; 'Who loves [liberty], must first be wise and good' 13.463; *see also* freedom

liberty, equality, and fraternity 4.170, 9.105–6, 9.126, 9.144–5, 9.173, 9.183–6, 10.xxiii

libido 12.99

libraries

Sangharakshita Memorial Library (previously the 'Order library')
based at Sarum House (Aryatara) 4.397; books from Australia 24.xxii; the hundred books brought back from India 25.12, 25.132–3; Sangharakshita rearranges the library at Padmaloka 24.166; Sangharakshita's ideas about the library 11.616; the library at Adhisthana 15.xi, 15.xvii, 26.550

other libraries
the Dr Ambedkar memorial library at Dapoli 10.400; ashram library 20.331–3; Barnstaple Public Library 20.51; the burning of the library at Alexandria 15.617, 26.476; the burning of the library at Nālandā 1.381, 12.243, 14.264, 25.10–11; the Institute library in Bangalore 22.141; Padmaloka library 12.418; Ruskin Memorial Library at Lancaster University 24.584; Streatham Public Library 20.70, 24.248; Tooting Public Library 20.32, 20.38, 23.9–10; Torquay Public Library 12.493, 20.61, 20.63; Triyana Vardhana Vihara library 8.660–1

Licchavi youths *see under Vimalakīrti-nirdeśa*

Licchavis (republic) 2.25

Lichfield, England 23.137–8

Lichtenberg, George Christoph 13.367

Liebenthal, Dr and Mrs v22

Lieou you tsi king 1.428

life

the examined life
conspicuously, life constantly changes, but people seem not to notice 7.411; learning from life 25.203; not taking responsibility for your own life 19.580; 'This life, the next life, and the life between – Regard these all as one' 7.305; trying to see honestly which circumstances of our life are advantageous 18.148; 'An unexamined

life is not worth living' 18.164; 'What am I to do with my life?' 25.113–4; what would you do if you had three months to live? 16.302; Zen and the art of living 16.475–6

life's difficulties
all is not well with you simply because you remain alive 10.534; the darker side of life 2.90–1, 11.260; even the pleasant things, being ephemeral, are potentially sources of pain 1.128–9; let your life be a heroic symphony 8.157; life itself can start teaching you about impermanence 18.560–1; life itself is a difficult condition 11.622

delight in life
Dudjom Rimpoche's delight in being alive 22.508; every moment of our life is unique, but it's easy to forget this 16.439–40; 'How wonderful! How miraculous! I draw water and I carry fuel' 14.397, 16.252; life as a continuous salutation 11.246; mistaking the precious stone of life for an ordinary pebble 16.251–2; some people almost have to teach themselves to enjoy life 26.63; some think worldly life is interesting, but Dharmic life is much more exciting 10.239

mystery and meaning
it is as though your life has a direction of its own 15.94; making the effort to develop, your life becomes more meaningful 17.435; a means to an end – the end being *bodhi* 7.320; the meaning of life is to be found only beyond life 26.13; mystery of life 3.4–5; religion is what you are prepared to die for, it is your life 10.342; a thread of meaning running through our lives 15.94; we are involved in something we do not fully understand 15.94, 18.83; what is life for? 7.320; the working out of a pattern, a gestalt 18.279–87; your life as the working out of the idea which is you 18.269; your life reveals yourself to yourself 18.280

qualities
born of silence and stillness, and derives its significance therefrom 7.322–3; in practical terms, life is a constant struggle 11.273; its precariousness 3.127–8, 18.564; life is transient, but it is also beautiful 26.241–2; meaningless and meaningful 7.322–3, 20.133; pleasure is our life, pleasure is our energy 19.381; its sacramental character 7.295; spontaneity is life 3.297; stillness makes our lives truly useful 7.323

images
a dream, a cloud, a drop of dew 25.390; a prison 11.709–10; a desert 9.453; a dream 4.427, 18.555–6; life's experiences strung out like washing on a line 11.10; 'Life's Furnace' 25.221; a river flowing faster and faster 24.89; unrolling a Persian carpet to see the pattern 18.283

don't waste your life
don't let the business of living get in the way of what's important 26.34; a life well used and not wasted 8.270; 'I wasted time and now doth time waste me' (Shakespeare) 3.419; it's a pity to waste time on anything that doesn't enhance the quality of your life 26.68; 'How do we obtain long life?' 14.235; life is given to us to recreate ourselves 3.471; through procrastination 7.172; throughout life periods of contraction alternate with periods of expansion 23.451; too precious an opportunity to be wasted in a comfortable twilight zone 15.159; wake up, for life in this world is short (Dharmapala) 8.57; watching television 10.322

trusting life
an attitude of faith and trust towards life 14.596; life is conquered when we yield to it 25.217; 'Life is King' 25.324, 26.445; life requires faith at every step 17.23–4; living without forethought 18.460–1; to live from one day to the next requires a leap of faith 26.60

see also
giving one's life, *see under* self-sacrifice; inner life, *see* inner life; modern, *see* modern life; private, *see* private life

life force Dhardo Rimpoche's concern that Sangharakshita shouldn't be held back by threat to life force 22.562; 'life force' of images that have been worshipped 4.304–5; the life force that holds things together from birth until death 14.439

life stories listening to the life stories of others 15.165; telling your life story shows the pattern of your life 17.470, 18.283; telling your life story can help you become more objective 15.91–2, 18.283; a useful and powerful practice 17.470

life-faculty *see jīvita-indriya*

lifespan calculation of the lifespan of the four great kings 2.67; full span of life a hundred years (Vedic and Buddhist tradition) 10.584–5; Tibetan long-life ceremony 10.585; the span of a man's life a single breath 14.60, 26.296–7; why didn't the Buddha live longer?, see under Buddha I/last days

lifestyle

does lifestyle matter?
dictionary definition of lifestyle 2.351; different lifestyles of monk and lay in Tibet didn't make much difference 2.445–6; the effect on your mind of the way you live 5.290; living in a situation that is conducive to your growth is a rare opportunity 3.464; the relative unimportance of lifestyle 2.587–8; a suitable lifestyle isn't necessarily easy 15.393–4; very few lifestyles are neutral in character 2.352; what matters is not lifestyle, but the depth and intensity of Going for Refuge 2.446; whatever one's chosen lifestyle, *saṃsāra* is always present 18.177; you can't have one lifestyle which is the ideal for everybody 18.222; you can't identify the spiritual life with any particular lifestyle 19.272–4

a Buddhist lifestyle
adopting a Buddhist lifestyle for the sake of mundane rewards 17.278; Buddhism is above all a way of life that leads to spiritual experiences 26.104–11; Buddhism is a spiritual way of life without reference to God 12.7; *Dharma-Vinaya*: expressing the Dharma in a carefully formulated way of life 14.434; 'doctrine' is not just ideas but experience, a way of living 17.391; even immersed in a Buddhist lifestyle, you still need to study 19.508; Going for Refuge: a turnabout in our whole way of life 10.14; the need to create a specifically Buddhist way of life 18.34–5; overcoming ego is not just an idea but an experience, a way of life 17.342; what the Buddhist way of life is about 16.228

monastic, lay, semi-monastic
brahmacarya: that way of life that leads to the *brahmaloka* 3.579; choosing a lifestyle outside of social norms 17.192; it's easy to be seduced by the attractions of the middle-class lifestyle 12.555; it is possible to live creatively in the householder lifestyle 19.582; lifestyle with respect to sexuality 3.566; part-time monastic 1.549–50; plans for the vihara in Kalimpong to be a 'semi-monastic' community 21.535, 21.537; seeking to go for Refuge, the best lifestyle has a strong single-sex element 2.517; wandering as a lifestyle 12.237–8, 19.549

regular
allow your skilful lifestyle to have its effect over a number of years 19.579; from a skilful way of life, *siddhis* will come without effort 19.578–9; a regular lifestyle helps to clarify and concentrate one's energies 15.154; to strengthen motivation, lead a regular lifestyle 12.381; success depends on establishing a disciplined and committed lifestyle 15.97; sustain a way of life so that progress will come 'without effort and striving' 19.578–9

changing lifestyle
adopting the lifestyle of your spiritual friends 10.529–30; adopting a lifestyle to give full expression to your ideals 18.516; adjusting your lifestyle according to your own judgement 18.212–13; becoming an *arhant* results in change of lifestyle, but not always *vice versa* 10.629; a determined shifting of perspective in the way we live 18.130; don't just criticize people's way of life, but offer a better alternative 18.302; has the practice of Buddhism changed your way of life? 9.192; it is always possible to adopt a lifestyle out of hypocrisy 18.176; spiritual change may compel you to change your lifestyle 3.464, 10.629; talk with others in the sangha with experience of the way you want to live 17.364; if your lifestyle doesn't change, is anything happening inside? 10.630; trying to develop spiritually without giving up one's affluent lifestyle 11.613

see also
commitment is primary, lifestyle is secondary, *see under* commitment; community living, *see* communities; hermit lifestyle, *see under* hermits; simple lifestyle, *see under* simplicity

light the archetypal significance of light 11.240–1; the Buddha: 'There arose in me light' 1.86, 7.600 (n331), 12.519; the Buddha bathes Cunda in multi-coloured light 14.238; the clear light of the Void 13.28, 18.43–4, 18.570–1; 'creating light for one another' 16.335; light and darkness 8.525–6, 16.329, 16.388; light and Enlightenment 2.55; golden light, *see under Sūtra of Golden Light*; a kind of light that is not that of the sun, moon, and stars 13.152; the light and colour of visionary experiences 14.170; light as an offering 11.240; the light that illuminates the *bardo* 13.152; the light that pervades the astral world 13.152; lights in the sky 16.563; the mind's action, now dark, now light 19.455–6; mother-light (*dharmakāya*) (or father-light) and son-light 18.251; the mystic's perception of a subtle brilliance 15.239; mystics and meditators speak of seeing everything as being lit up from within 13.120; rays of coloured light issuing from the Buddha's body 14.91; space is light and light is space (*ākāśa*) 13.152; subject and object are suffused

by the light of reality 18.614; as a symbol of reality 16.108–9; the symbolism of the evenness of light, not from any particular point 16.109, 18.603; symbol of *prajñā* (wisdom) 9.324, 9.462; a universal symbol, found in all spiritual traditions 12.518–19

Light of Asia *see under* Arnold, Sir Edwin

The Light of the Dhamma *see under* Myanmar

lightning conditioned existence is like a lightning flash 14.509; insight like a flash of lightning 1.176, 11.64, 13.73; 'lightning-like transitional stage' between average person and Stream Entrant 2.142; 'Like lightning in a dark sky, the thought of the world may be turned to good' 4.282; receptivity like a lightning conductor 4.43–4; 'to see Charles Kean act is like reading Shakespeare by flashes of lightning' 3.495, 13.73, 19.450

likes and dislikes *see* preferences

līlā (play) the activity of the bodhisattva 4.135–8, 14.521; a spontaneous welling-up of spiritual energy 14.521

Lilavati, Dharmacharini (Alison Harper) 24.361, 24.392

Lilith 25.390

Lim Poi Cheng *see* Dharmajyoti

limbs of Enlightenment *see* seven *bodhyaṅgas*

limitations

the limitations of …
analogy 7.210–11; character 26.180; the concept of experience 19.378; images 4.31; intellectual study 1.22–3, 2.244–5, 26.43; materialism and Ātmanism 7.167; metaphor 18.282–3, 18.606–7; the mundane 17.676; mundane goals 15.95; pleasure 15.449, 17.397, 17.592; the psychological model of development 17.670–1; a purely theoretical approach 8.535; *śamatha* experience 8.440–2; *saṃsāra* 19.10; solitary practice 3.401; words 14.15–16

limiting oneself
be careful about setting limits to what is possible 12.300; the difficulty of being content with a limited perfection 7.166; don't dwell so much on your limitations that you are inhibited from action 19.165; don't just settle down and accept limitations 19.279; don't place limitations on your positive emotions 14.533–4; don't superimpose on spiritual experience your limited modes of thinking 10.614; don't turn your faith in the guru into a limiting factor 18.182; rather than thinking of getting rid of the self, think of yourself as limited 17.342; the self-limitation of reducing things to intellectual formulas 18.287; settling for limited progress 17.682; we limit ourselves minute to minute by our own thoughts, words, and actions 10.141

getting free
being honest about the limitations we need to overcome 18.147–8; criticism is to help us move on from limitations 16.505; destruction of limitations 16.504; to free yourself from the limitations of human existence, ask its cause 7.115; the *vajra* bursts through limitations, like Vimalakīrti 16.504

beyond limitations
all limitations are removed by the experience of wisdom 18.594; the altruistic dimension of the spiritual life has no limits 4.64; consciousness freed from limitations 5.485; the *dharmakāya*: limitations disappear such that the Buddha himself disappears 16.27; the endless view: the removal of all limitations 19.184–5; the mysterious 'preachings' of the *dharmakāya* transcend all limitations 14.259; the 'self' is not a thing, but a limitation that is removed 10.470; *śūnyatā*: no fixed or final limitation 18.294

reflections
accepting limitations that cannot be changed and changing those we can 18.148; 'aspects' of Enlightenment: an accommodation to our limitations 19.34; the limitations of describing reality either as experience or as non-experience 17.548; up against the limits of your knowledge, you have to grow beyond them 17.206; to the extent that things are experienced as entities, there are limitations 19.66; intellectual study has its limits, but it's still important to insight 15.198; doing a visualization practice in a limiting way 5.607; the limitations placed on *mettā* by the sense of a separate self 15.336–7; modern literature is aware of its limitations and in search of wholeness 10.154; the personal limitations of human beings: prejudices, preferences 12.655; the limitations of thought force us into contradictions 7.133; meeting the limitations of ordinary consciousness is frustrating but necessary 17.376; remind yourself constantly that your understanding is limited 17.412–13

see also
language/limitations of language

limitless according to the Buddha's teaching there is no limit to the human mind 17.437; 'A bodhisattva stays for a limitless time in the world' 4.61; Buddhist scriptures: far horizons and limitless vistas 1.38; limitless compassion 15.319; limitless merit accrued from the wish to help limitless beings in limitless worlds 17.306; 'lord over the limitless' 17.379

limpid *see* transparent

Lin Yutang 14.484

Lincoln, Abraham 1.546, 1.635 (n443)

Lincolnshire, England 24.387

Lindsay, Norman (Australian writer) 24.535

Lindsey, Jenine 24.31

lineage the Ādibuddha the originator of a lineage 18.94; behind one's spiritual friend stands their teacher, all the way back to the Buddha 4.175; in Early Buddhism, traced back to the Buddha's *nirmaṇakāya* 1.275; faith in the authenticity of lineage 18.181; the four noble lineages 14.83; lineage is not just an idea, but a truth 13.216; the lineage of previous Buddhas 1.43–50; a lineage that has petered out can be revived 13.199; in the Mahāyāna, sometimes traced back to the *sambhogakāya* 1.276; in Tantric Buddhism 13.215; is the Triratna Buddhist Order a lineage? 11.667–8; a metaphor derived from biological life, not to be taken too literally 19.403; passing the meaning of a text down a lineage 17.156; three lines of lineage: mind-lineage, sign-lineage, word-lineage (Tibetan Buddhism) 3.82, 14.16–17

see also
Milarepa's lineage, *see under* Milarepa/life story; transmission; the 'whispered lineage', *see under* Tibetan Buddhism/schools; Zen lineage, *see under* Zen

linear linear and cyclical visions of history 12.592–4; people tend to think about spiritual life very linearly 18.280, 18.287; we mustn't superimpose on spiritual experience our limited linear modes of thinking 10.614

Ling, Trevor introduction 24.660 (n250); *The Buddha* 5.244–5, 5.426, 15.381, 18.203; *Buddhist Revival in India* 24.193

Ling Rimpoche v23

lingering don't linger in the *dhyānas* 18.577; lingering guilt 10.503; lingering in the hermitage due to a lack of outgoingness 19.342; lingering (or malingering) in the realm of action 19.177–8; a longing, lingering look behind 7.162, 11.397; Rechungpa lingers in the village 19.265–6

linguistics an aspect of *nirukti-pratisaṃvid* 1.449, 16.490; Oxford philosophers and linguistic analysis 11.530, 12.170, 23.55–6

Lingwood, Dennis *see* Sangharakshita

Lingwood, Philip (father) *see under* Sangharakshita IV/family

Linji Yixuan 14.362, 14.636 (n356)

Linnaeus 7.84

lions

the Buddha
lion among men (*narasīha* or *narasiṃha*) 9.365; his lion's roar 3.53, 9.365–6, 10.201, 11.383, 13.307, 16.125; would the Buddha ever have heard a lion roar? 3.636 (n57)

other mythical and symbolic lions
Androcles and the Lion 26.286; Aśoka's lions 8.xxviii; association with Mañjuśrī 2.174, 18.19, 26.289; association with Vairocana 12.203, 16.125, 26.289; biblical lions 26.287; even little old ladies have to become lions in Buddhism 4.469; Hercules and the Nemean lion 26.288; 'I feel as if I were a lion' (Milarepa) 18.613; 'I have sometimes bleated like a sheep when I should have roared like a lion' 4.445; the Lion of St Mark 25.377; 'lion-dogs' (Pekingese) 26.289–90; lion-headed Egyptian goddess, Sekhmet 13.244; Marpa appear to Milarepa in the form of a lion 18.19; a mythical Assyrian lion 26.290; 'The roaring of lions ...' (Blake) 26.652–3; the significance of St Jerome's faithful lion 24.224, 26.283, 26.285–90; snow lion 18.29–30; 'Too long have I been a lion' 25.319; the white lion on the mountain 19.340; lion-headed *ḍākinī*, *see* Siṃhamukta

lip service paying lip service to the Dharma 19.246–7; why do people pay lip service to religious and political ideals? 19.247

listening

listening to the Dharma
Ānanda: our ordinary mind listening to our own Enlightened consciousness 16.37; the Buddha speaks on Nirvāṇa when the *bhikkhus* are listening attentively 10.632–3; the benefits of hearing the Dharma being recited 8.532; the difference between listening to a logical exposition and to a story 12.110, 16.215; the first characteristic of a good disciple is that

he listens 12.296; if you're not listening, how can the Buddhas and bodhisattvas be said to teach? 277–8; learning about the Dharma means learning to listen 17.208; listening to the Dharma with one's whole being 10.197, 15.436; merits of listening to the *White Lotus Sūtra* 16.49–50; receptive listening to the *Buddhavacana* 22.226; receptivity to the inner teaching: listening not just with the ears 18.290; teach the Dharma with awareness of the inclinations of those listening 16.506–7; teaching the Dharma when no one is listening 16.507; the true Buddhist listens carefully 9.275; what's the use of going to a Dharma talk if you're not going to listen? 19.557

listening carefully
be careful to listen to people and give an honest reply 9.445; before writing, the learned man was the man who had heard much 15.403–4; being able to hear the truth is as important as being able to tell it 17.239–40; the Buddha who listens to the fears and anxieties of suffering beings 14.212; a good way of helping people 4.67; hearing is passive, but listening is active 19.581; the importance of listening to one's *kalyāṇa mitra* 9.515; listening to the silence 16.203; listening to what people are trying to say 18.169, 19.138–9; a song beginning 'Listen' 19.219; to the words of the sages 17.50–1

see also
divine ear (*dibba-sota*), *see* clairaudience

lists of doctrinal terms Abhidharma list-makers, *see Mātṛkadharas*; *Atthārasarāsī Dīpanī*, *see Atthārasarāsī Dīpanī*; the Buddha came up with some of the lists himself 4.334–5; the Buddha created lists of teachings to make them easier to remember 10.230; Buddhism can seem to be all lists 15.240; compared to the jewels of the great ocean 10.568; the Dharma is not just a matter of lists 2.291, 14.98; early lists are lists of methods, not philosophical doctrines 10.568; the lists became almost an obsession for some of the Buddha's followers 2.60; lists of lists compiled after the Buddha's death 13.340; the lists don't necessarily relate to actual spiritual experience 4.277; just the Indian mind at work 12.241; not to be taken too literally 3.193, 4.277; the origin of the lists and their use 4.333–6; what is one to do with all of them? 2.60–1

Liszt, Franz 24.537, 24.555

literacy and illiteracy the Buddha probably wasn't literate 2.20, 3.23, 9.271, 9.356, 10.229–30, 12.529, 14.18, 16.233; 'the bugbear of literacy' 8.461; Huineng and illiteracy 11.716, 14.349, 19.45; to be illiterate in the Buddha's day did not imply any lack of education or culture 8.461; literacy is almost a Buddhist virtue 2.213; ultimately what we want is not book learning but spiritual awakening 11.716

literalism and literalness

INTRODUCTION

about literalism
the designation of the literalist (*pada-parama*) as a distinct type of person 8.620; half the questions Sangharakshita was asked arose from literalism 3.361, 14.321; the human mind has an inbuilt tendency to slip into literalism 11.xviii, 11.654; a teacher's problem: literal-minded people want literal answers to literal questions 26.83; literal-mindedness is a great handicap in the spiritual life 15.230; the Māra of literalism 2.511; the metaphysical problems that arise from taking language too literally 19.437; the part of the mind that tends to take things literally 14.366; people tend to think about spiritual life very literally 18.287; people's capacity to be literal-minded 11.689; *praśaṃsā* (eulogy) draws attention to importance, not to be taken literally 5.199; reification is the child of literalism 8.620

avoiding literalism
avoiding literalness by saying 'as it were' 19.102; paradoxes are useful because you can't take them literally 19.242

LITERALISM AND ENLIGHTENMENT

taking the Buddha literally
Brahmā's request that the Buddha should teach is not to be taken literally 12.188–9; the *Dhammapada* is literal truth 26.45; don't literally regard the Buddha as having come to a full stop called Buddhahood 10.615; he explained that some of his earlier teachings are not to be taken literally 14.238; he took great precautions against literalism 3.167, 8.620; how literally to follow the Buddha's example? 19.54–6; some of his stories have been taken too literally 10.596; take the Buddha's statements poetically rather than scientifically 19.242; taking his exhortations to self-effort too literally 1.245; taking literally a statement which may have been meant ironically 10.548

taking Enlightenment literally
all positive statements about Nirvāṇa are analogies, not to be taken literally 3.235;

don't be misled by the literal translation of *śūnyatā* as 'emptiness' 16.232; don't take attempts to express reality literally, but try to see the point of them 4.204; even birds and flowers will gain Enlightenment: beautiful but not literal 7.585 (n218); if we take statements about transcendental reality literally we go off the rails 14.605; taking descriptions of Enlightenment too literally 15.229–30, 17.459

LITERALISM AND BUDDHIST HISTORY

introduction
Buddhism needs an equilibrium between literalizing and liberalizing influences 1.249; Buddhism's tendency towards literalism reflects the mind's tendency 14.367; development of literal-mindedness in Buddhism 2.131; literalism in the three *yānas* 19.49–50; the need to take Buddhist philosophy literally to begin with 19.38–9

Early Buddhism
literal-mindedness of Hīnayāna Buddhism 1.221–2, 1.233–4, 1.423, 7.540–3; in the Abhidharma originally metaphorical expressions became more literal 15.342; the Abhidharma's insistence that *dharmas* were real entities 1.304, 17.248; Nāgārjuna shattered the shell of literalism in which Buddhism was imprisoned 1.316; a naive and literalistic attempt to communicate the Dharma 19.101–2; unintentional literalism was a force for change in the early history of Buddhism 8.620

Mahāyāna
avoid literalism when reading *sūtras* 4.63, 16.57; the Mahāyāna's correction of literalism 16.537; the Mahāyāna's shortcomings when taken literally 14.163, 16.503; in the *sūtras* Śāriputra represents a literal interpretation of the Dharma 1.271; 'the bodhisattva need master only compassion': to be taken literally? 5.199–200; Mahāyāna teachings may be protests against taking earlier doctrines literally 1.221–2; the metaphor of the bodhisattva following a path is not to be taken literally 4.199–200; no need to take the bodhisattva vows literally, use your imagination 4.59–60; subdivisions of the bodhisattva path are not to be taken too literally 2.170; taking the Mahāyāna's dualistic language literally 19.49

Perfection of Wisdom
texts challenge literalistic thinking 3.361, 14.318–19, 14.321, 14.366; that the *nāgas* received it from the Buddha need not be taken literally 1.310; to be understood in the context of tendency towards literalism 1.307

Tibetan Buddhism
difference between literal meaning and symbolical interpretation of the *tantras* 1.380; disastrous consequences of Nyingma literalism 1.383; a literal-minded interpretation of the Tantra 1.386–7; should we take the *Tibetan Book of the Dead* literally? 16.107–8

TAKING DOCTRINES LITERALLY

general reflections
Buddhist doctrines contradict themselves when they are taken literally 14.608; doctrinal categories are not to be taken literally, but point towards experience 14.442; don't take 'doctrine' too literally, it is not just ideas but a way of living 17.391; don't take 'Master all teachings' too literally 18.414; grasping a doctrine with intellect powered by craving can lead to literalism 12.551; the lists of canonical Buddhism are not to be taken too literally 3.193; literal interpretation of the Dharma 1.251; regarding formulations of Doctrine as valid in the ultimate sense 1.221, 7.542; some are literally true, others require interpretation 3.355, 15.227, 16.579–81; shortcomings of teachings when taken literally 16.502–3; literally possessing books and teachings doesn't mean you've 'got' them 18.491; there is always the danger of taking theoretical teachings literally 11.654; writing about Buddhism should use doctrinal terms, but not too literally 2.60–1

specific doctrines and practices
the *skandhas* 14.548; the analysis of mind 17.493–4; talk of 'annihilating self' 10.470–1; going forth literally as well as metaphorically 26.279; the idea of the *dharmadhātu* as a mandala 14.604–5; the six element practice 5.481–2, 5.484; the stages of the positive *nidānas* 5.275; leaving the *dhyānas* to gain insight 4.493, 5.267; the four *śūnyatās* 4.163–4; if you get too scrupulous about the term self, you are taking it too literally 14.549; the list of ten fetters 15.209–10; merit 1.414, 4.101; puja 11.222, 11.746 (n107), 24.49; rebirth 17.286; *abhijñās* (superpowers) 19.62; the middle way 7.298–9; karma 3.106, 4.301, 17.479; the three *lakṣaṇas* 2.87; two methods of spiritual growth, neither to be taken too literally 26.61

WORDS AND SYMBOLS

words and concepts
after some Dharma study you realize that you can't take words literally 19.508; confusion between literal and symbolic

interpretations of the same terms 1.423; don't take the language of Indian Buddhist texts too literally 5.268; experience is an abstract term that we tend to take literally 14.595–6; if you take words and concepts literally, your view becomes 'word-conditioned' 19.446; literal terminology can introduce confusions that vitiate spiritual strivings 26.188; literalism with regard to concepts 15.334; spirit and letter, *see* spirit and letter; taking a statement literally, not looking *through* it for truth 26.4; words and concepts must be understood not literally but symbolically 1.234

taking metaphors literally
the danger of taking metaphors literally 16.133, 18.606–8; the danger of understanding the metaphor of the path too literally 3.254, 26.206–7; don't think too literally in terms of a linear model for the spiritual life 18.280; lineage is a metaphor derived from biological life, not to be taken too literally 19.403; a metaphor may be taken literally, a paradox never 26.207; 'surface' and 'depth' to be taken poetically, not literally 17.136; treating a figure of speech too literally and logically leads to misunderstanding 7.481; in a way the spiritual life is not at all like following a path 1.589

myths and symbols
Christianity takes its myths literally 12.106–7; the expression 'imaginal faculty' should not be taken too literally 26.271; if you take symbolism literally, you are open to exploitation 18.429; is one to take the twin miracle literally? 10.37; literal-mindedness holds back understanding of Vajrayāna myths and symbols 18.88; myths: psychological experiences, spiritual truths, not to be taken literally 12.108–9; an over-literal reading of the parable of the jewel in the garment 16.218, 16.221; the parables of the *White Lotus Sūtra* 16.105; taking myths and parables literally 16.528; the wise physician and the prohibited cure: a demonstration of literalism 14.235

literary criticism the characteristics of the literary critic 26.323–4; 'Criticism East and West' 26.319–39; concerned primarily with enjoyment, not analysis 26.320–1; the concerns of literary criticism 26.323; differences and similarities between Indian and Western traditions 26.328–32; higher criticism 2.627; the inappropriateness of the term 'criticism' (Dryden) 26.324; the literary critic should enjoy what they are reading 26.338; literary critics as 'mere pickers up of pence' 25.lix; Middleton Murry's way of assessing a work 26.334–6; mistakes in literary criticism 26.336–8; originated by Aristotle 26.324; the *rasas* of Indian literary criticism 26.325–8; the *rasika* in India 26.324; a vocation, not a profession 26.338; what it ought to be doing 26.336–9

literature

definitions and descriptions
as designated in Indian literary criticism 26.330–2; a bearer of values, a means of access to reality 26.329–30; finding a better word? 14.293; it can be an expression of the literary personality or the whole personality 10.154; it follows a 'curved' route 26.330; it points us in the direction of life 26.339; 'the Thought of thinking Souls' (Carlyle) 14.291, 26.321; 'like mist and rain, it permeates and nourishes' 14.295; 'line of demarcation between human and animal kingdoms' (Godwin) 14.291, 26.321; *Littera Scripta Manet* (the written word *remains*) 23.414, 26.70; 'language put to its best purpose' (Mackail) 14.xiii, 14.292–4, 26.321; 'language charged with meaning to the utmost possible degree' (Pound) 14.296, 26.321; Sangharakshita's definition 26.322–3; 'the shadow of good talk' (Stevenson) 14.296, 26.321; a sudden communion between mystery and mystery 26.336; the symbol and the flower of the universe of life (Murry) 26.336; 'the use of literature lies in its conveyance of every truth' (Lu Ji) 14.295, 26.321–2

the function of literature
the difference between 'profane' literature and 'scripture' is less than supposed 14.299; English literature began with the rejection of Catholicism 13.511, 26.259; 'faction' is an illegitimate, even an immoral, literary genre 24.566; it is capable of exerting a tremendous influence for good 8.208; 'The Joy of Writing' (Lu Ji) 14.xii, 14.294, 14.299; has an effect commensurate with the effort one makes to understand it 16.444; human frailty is not the only possible subject 16.443; literature and ethics 10.153–4; literature of knowledge and literature of power 10.153, 14.302–4; minor literature and great literature 10.154; modern literature is aware of its limitations and in search of wholeness 10.154; modern literature is a record of symptoms of disease 14.294; performing a function that used to be fulfilled by religion 26.329; religious literature has two modes, one intellectual,

the other emotional 14.109–10; wisdom (or gnomic) literature 14.343; with so many masterpieces it's a pity to waste one's time on trivia 26.68

Buddhist literature
an account of Sukhāvatī one of the most gorgeous writings in world literature 1.329; canonical literature, *see under* scriptures; a classic in one language is often a classic in another 14.289; a creative response to the influx of Buddhist literature into Western culture 17.453–4; demand for Buddhist literature in Indian languages 8.220–2; examples of scientific and imaginative literature 14.110; free literature distributed by the Buddhist Publication Society, Kandy 8.275–6; an invitation to explore the world of Buddhist literature 14.xvi; *Mahāparinibbāna Sutta*, 'for pathos, sublimity, and beauty unexcelled' 14.39; the parables of the *White Lotus Sūtra* unsurpassed in Buddhist literature 14.112; the specific purpose of Buddhist literature 14.xiii; two divisions, canonical and non-canonical 14.289–90

Western literature
discussions on Buddhism and English literature 22.323; 'Eastern Thought and English Literature' 22.321; English literary works which have the quality of *kāvya* 26.332; novels, *see* fiction; the idea of literary property is rather modern 14.399; imagining you can see Zen in the classics of English literature 17.67; in comparison with *sūtras* 16.443–4; insights which are close to those of Buddhism 12.672; letters, *see* letters; literature and ethics 10.153–4; making links between Buddhism and Western literature 12.78; moralists in English literature 12.77; one can encounter the Dharma in Western literature 22.464–5; 'Reason and Emotion in English Literature' (unfulfilled project) 26.537; the revival of poetic drama 26.375; some of the greatest English literature takes the form of sermons 12.519; a talk on English literature at The Hermitage 22.52; we should make use of apposite passages from a Buddhist point of view 4.472; *Zen in English Literature and Oriental Classics*, *see* Blyth

Liu Fu Ken 22.503–4

livelihood *see* right livelihood; wrong livelihood; work

Liverpool, England 24.584–6

living beings all 'on their way to their slaughter' 2.156; aspirations for the welfare of all living beings 16.276, 16.333–4; the bodhisattva is careful not to injure even the humblest of living beings 16.9; the Buddhafield, a field of living beings 16.467, 16.473; compassion for the suffering of living beings 1.405, 2.161–2; even if the Buddha were to say that beings existed, that would not make it true 14.601; every living being wants to fulfil the law of its own being: to develop 26.10; every living thing feels and is sensitive, and they are all connected 4.541; 'Everything endeavours to persist in its own being' (Spinoza) 26.168; how a bodhisattva should regard living beings 16.537–8; *mettā* is about your emotional attitude towards living beings, including yourself 5.380; natural solidarity with all living beings 19.540; 'Outside living beings, no Buddhas' 16.473; teaching children not to be cruel to other living beings 1.498–9, 10.477; there can be no complete end of suffering for living beings 11.272; they can be very tiresome 14.413; when you hurt beings, you indirectly cause sorrow to the Buddhas 4.435; *see also* sentient beings

Living Silence *see* Dr Mehta

Lloyd, Selwyn 23.202

loathsomeness of the body, *see aśubha bhāvanā*; of food, *see under* food; isn't contemplating 'loathsomeness' off-putting? 5.511; things are neither loathsome nor attractive: they are as they are 4.579

lobha *see* greed

lobhacaritra (greed type) *see* character types

Lobsang Norbu ('fighting monk') v21, v22

Lobsang Rampa *see* Rampa

Lobsang, Gelong (Dhardo Rimpoche's attendant) v22

Lobsang, Lama (Ladakhi monk) v22

Lobstein, Anne (later Bancroft) v23, v24

local deities, gods, and spirits the Buddha's followers staying in the shrines of local gods 10.452, 16.272; being on good terms with local spirits 10.647–8, 18.24–6; Mr Chen's encounters with local deities 18.22–3; local deities that were incorporated into Hinduism 19.413–14; offerings to local spirits at *caityas* (folk shrines) 10.452; sacrifices to local gods (Hindu custom) 10.9; shrines to local gods in cities 18.24; the spirit of a place in a personalized form 18.21–4; taken over by the Vajrayāna 19.413–14; a woman who worshipped a milestone 13.272; 'Ye local

demons, ghosts, and gods/ All friends of Milarepa' 13.273; Yolmo, a local deity who visits Milarepa 18.41

Locana Buddha 2.213

Locanā (female Buddha) brief description 17.729 (n166); appears in verses to Tārā 17.146; consort of Akṣobhya 12.222, 13.315; the embodiment of clear awareness 13.315

Locana, Dharmacharini (Elizabeth English) 24.249

Locke, John introduction 7.587 (n239); Blake's view of Locke 8.561, 19.179–80, 26.350; discussion of the problem of personal identity 8.613; 'ideas of sense' 7.137; *tabula rasa* 12.99, 17.499

Lodro Thaye 23.419

logic

introduction
a highly irrational phenomenon 26.76; illogical to be too logical 7.37; modern suspicion of logical argument 17.375; 'one of the most fascinating ... stretches of the intellectual terrain' 14.90, 20.446; transcending logic 1.309, 26.200

logic in Buddhism
the Buddha spoke of four possible modes of predication 1.313; the Buddha's abjuration of views transposed from metaphysical to logical mode 1.313; how Buddhist logic began: as a means of conversion 1.372; logical arguments in the Abhidharma 14.87; the science of logic: a shock to non-Buddhist schools 1.372; the Madhyamaka is renowned for its relentless logic 17.326; Nāgārjuna tries to prove the non-existence of the self by logical argument 17.373–8; enthusiasm for logic in Indian Buddhism 17.375–6, 17.465–6; the Prajñāpāramitā's rejection of logic 1.209; contradicted in the *Diamond Sūtra* 10.165, 14.150–1, 14.376; Milarepa's advice about logical argument 18.352–61; studied by Tibetan *geshes* 13.46; Tibetans see logic as part of the bodhisattva ideal 13.46; Gelugpa faith in the power of logic to convey the truth of the Dharma 17.376; battles of logic 12.241–2; logical contradiction the safest way to communicate transcendental realities, 26.207; the bodhisattva courses in a realm transcending logic 1.396

other schools of logic
ancient Greeks and logic 17.376; European medieval philosophers and logic 17.376, 17.465; Nyāya school of Indian logic 17.519–20

logical arguments
analysis of a logical argument 2.640; applied to faith 1.284–5; the four logical positions on the metaphysical status of things 17.384–5; if you don't want to do something, logical arguments may irritate you 4.433; logical thinking 15.195–6; putting forward a logical argument 18.171

fallacies
conception of God as absolute being based on a fallacy 2.87; the ambiguous middle term 7.243; 'subsequent to, therefore because of' 15.382; the higher can be explained in terms of the lower 8.230–2; linguistic convention about change denotes a real distinction between things 2.87; pathetic fallacy 4.243, 4.689 (n210)

further categories and methods
deductive and inductive methods 1.123, 7.85; inference 19.186–7; the *infima species* 14.581; laws of logic 1.209–10, 14.448, 26.200–2; *reductio ad absurdum* (*prasaṅgha*) 1.321; syllogisms 8.169, 19.186–7; terms of logic 1.284

Lohicca Sutta *see under Dīgha Nikāya*

Lok, Tan Keng (friend in Singapore) 7.17, 20.142–3, 20.149

loka dhammas *see* eight worldly winds

Lokakṣema (translator) 14.138

Lokamitra, Dharmachari brief introduction 2.728–9 (n611), 12.736–7 (n311), 24.605 (n15); at work in India v9, v10, v24; connection with Taiwan 10.li; deputizes as a speaker when Sangharakshita is unwell 24.113, 24.115; doubts about teaching the Dharma in India 10.xli–xliii; facilitates Sangharakshita's tour of India, 1979 24.9–125; goes to India in 1977 2.490, 10.xxxix–xl, 10.290; handing on responsibilities 10.416; a hero 12.490; in the early days of the FWBO 11.729; his achievements in India 12.482, 24.19; launches publications 10.299; meets Dinoo Dubash 21.470–1; member of the Council 12.632; photographs 10.xlix, 10.194; in Poona 10.255; Sangharakshita's teaching 'awakened me to the vision I had been seeking' 10.xxxix; spearheads the Mahavihara project 10.367; tours UK Buddhist centres with news of India 10.337; a 'very good disciple – he doesn't hesitate to disagree' 10.367

Lokanātha 2.175

Lokanāthavyākaraṇa Sūtra 4.578

lokapālas (guardians of the world) comparison with the *dharmapālas* of the Vajrayāna 16.348; tradition that the infant Siddhārtha was bathed by the four *lokapālas* 2.228; *gaurīs* as the fascinating aspect of the *lokapālas* 16.352; *hiri* and *ottappa* (shame and blame) 16.348, 19.406–7, 24.575; four great kings as *lokapālas* 16.348

Lokarakṣa (Chinese translator) 1.326

Lokāyatikas (materialists) 17.362, 17.747–8 (n308)

Lokeshvara, Dharmachari 26.549

Lokeśvararāja, Buddha 1.324, 1.327

lokiya *see* mundane

lokottara *see lokuttara*

lokottara-dharmas 1.39

Lokottaravādins *Mahāvastu Avadāna*, *see Mahāvastu Avadāna*; non-violence is the supreme *dharma* 3.318–19; *rūpakāya* 1.253–4; a subsect of the Mahāsaṃghikas 7.500; taught that the Buddha's nature is wholly transcendental 1.189–90, 1.256–7, 13.299–300, 14.71; their transcendentalist doctrines a statement of early traditions 1.254

lokuttara (Sanskrit *lokottara*, literally 'world beyond') ultimate reality is *lokuttara* 9.398; in contrast to *laukika* (mundane) 1.232, 10.586, 16.607–8 (n178), 26.198–9; inclusion as a topic in the *Patisambhidā-magga* 14.73; translated as 'transcendental' 3.236, 11.170, 15.637–8, 16.271

lokuttara-magga *see* path, transcendental

Lola Hutuktu Rimpoche 22.537

London Dr Ambedkar studies 9.4; the beauty of a London morning 23.226; bookshops, *see under* bookshops; British Museum 24.243, 26.290, 26.470–1; Buddhist Society, *see* Buddhist Society; the changes in the city during Sangharakshita's twenty years away 23.61–2; Christ Church, Spitalfields 24.373; Civil Nursing Reserve 20.77–8; Cock Lane Ghost 2.34, 2.667 (n53); College of Psychic Science, South Kensington 23.90–1, 23.490 (n127); County Hall 20.75–87; crossing the road 4.509; Crystal Palace 20.34–5; customs during Sangharakshita's childhood 20.7–9, 20.494; Derby Day 20.492; the East End 23.217; Eros, Piccadilly 25.320; Fulham 20.499; Grub Street 12.643–4; Hampstead Heath 23.466–7, 23.468–9, 24.130, 24.165, 24.311; Hampton Court 23.113; 'happy because we were together' on Westminster Bridge 25.276; Highgate 23.473, 26.604; Keats House 24.311–12; 'London' (Blake) 3.228, 11.78, 18.424; 'London Bridge is falling down' 25.404; London in spring 25.303; Maha Bodhi Society, *see under* Maha Bodhi Society/branches; Mitcham Common 20.27, 26.425; Monmouth Street, *see under* Triratna/history/Sakura; Muswell Hill (first FWBO men's community) 23.473, 24.241, 24.666 (n289); Natural History and Science Museums 26.425–6; Royal Academy 25.375–7; in the Second World War, *see under* Second World War; sightseeing 23.124, 24.311–12; the smells of London in the 1960s 26.495; St James's Church, Piccadilly 12.518; the Thames 25.53, 25.276, 26.424–5; Tooting 20.9, 20.12, 20.37, 20.494–5, 23.205–6, 26.426–7; the Tower of London 23.113, 25.396; the Underground 4.546–7, 13.597–8, 26.562–5; very quiet compared to Indian cities 23.57–8; Victoria and Albert Museum 10.93, 16.156, 20.453, 21.27, 21.171, 23.457; Wandsworth Cemetery 24.126; Wimbledon Common 20.27–9, 26.684

London Buddhist Centre (Sukhavati)

the building of the centre
introduction 12.726–7 (n216), 15.757 (n135), 24.648–9 (n203); the beginnings of the plan 11.525; Alaya as part of the team 26.566; appreciating the value of the work 10.215, 17.73; a film about the building project 24.164–5, 24.647–8 (n201); fundraising for the centre 3.622–3; a gathering of those who worked on the building 24.163–5; given the name Sukhavati 3.455–6; a great creative achievement 12.640; if it had been funded by a big organization it wouldn't have been the same 15.434; opening 3.455–6, 10.195, 25.346; a quantum leap 11.556; a slideshow which overdid the 'rags to riches' element 24.39–40; supported by establishing right livelihood businesses 11.465; warnings about establishing the centre in Bethnal Green 18.141

Buddha images
description 9.382, 10.195; gesture of fearlessness 10.259; supplementing inadequate words with silent communication 24.320; their impact on Sangharakshita's mother 24.181–2; thinking about the lessons we can learn from the Buddha 10.255; to make it easier to think of the Buddha 10.208

other features
the mural of lotuses 10.694 (n233); the mural of the windhorse 9.275, 10.199–201,

10.200 (photograph), 24.18; Nālandā crest 12.317, 12.335–6, 24.660 (n251)

festivals
Padmasambhava Day (1979) 12.317, 12.336; Dharma Day (1985) 24.237; Sangha Day (1979) 24.161; Wesak (1990) 24.388

businesses and communities
Friends Foods 24.181; Friends Trading 24.181; right livelihood businesses 10.195, 10.215–16; Approach Road women's communities 24.579; Amritakula (men's community) 26.455; Beulah (women's community) 24.162

what the centre is like
like a Buddhist colony 9.492; like a complex of urban caves 19.493; making use of the centre over the Christmas period 24.312–13; a newcomer's impression of the centre 26.xi–xii; visitors impressed by the way the sangha worked together 12.309

Sangharakshita at the centre
a poetry reading on friendship 24.359–60; book launches 24.388, 24.580; reading 'The Caves of Bhájá' on Dharma Day 24.237; his mother visits 24.180–2; his residence there, *see under* Sangharakshita III/places of residence

London Buddhist College v23

London Buddhist Vihara, Chiswick (Sri Lankan) 23.44, 23.72, 23.75–6

loneliness based on the duality of self and other 18.17, 18.54; facing loneliness in the cremation ground 13.231; inherent in conditioned existence 18.16; the gull's lonely flight 25.266; Milarepa's loneliness 18.13–17, 18.53; not allowing loneliness to turn into depression 18.53–4; as a result of social groups breaking down 3.441–3; Samuel Johnson's fear of being alone 18.16; of Siddhārtha 1.59; it is not physical solitude that engenders loneliness, but mental isolation 18.16

Long, Miss (Kalimpong) 21.358–63

Longchenpa 24.12

longevity Āryadeva and Yalahankar Swami 20.361–2; of the Buddha, *see* Buddha I/the Buddha's last days/length of life

Longfellow, Henry Wadsworth 'The Arsenal at Springfield' 17.116, 17.118; 'footprints in the sands of time' 8.232; *Hiawatha* 24.235; poems on Spanish themes 24.405; 'Torquemada' 24.405

longing *anāsa* (freedom from longing) 1.69; the artist's longing for beauty 26.176; feverish longings born of passion 10.521–5; 'For the Boundless, the Unlimited, the Infinite I long' 25.229; 'I … longed to pluck those mauve sprays' 25.222; lonely longing 25.226; longing for intellectual exchange 23.106; longing for the Unconditioned and compassion for those suffering 2.161–2, 2.271–4; a longing, lingering look behind 7.162; loving, longing heart 25.381; nothing conditioned can fully satisfy the deepest longings of the human heart 4.51; only insight can 'kill' the longing for diversion 19.518; pleasure from conditioned things cannot satisfy our longing for the Unconditioned 3.215; the strength of longing for sense experience 3.421

Longinus 20.61

Long-Lived Deva *see* Tsering, Lha

looking up to people *see* reverence

Lopez, Donald S. *Buddhism in Practice* 24.515–16; *Prisoners of Shangri-La* 13.290, 16.601 (n123)

Lopon, Claude d'Estrée v24

Lord of the Rings *see* Tolkien

Lorrain, Claude 26.250

loss the degree of distress suggests the degree of emotional investment 19.243; equally painful whether you've had something for a long or a short time 4.427–8; even if you lose everything, if you meditate you have inner resources to draw on 17.341; fear of death is essentially fear of loss of ego 18.245; fear of losing pleasant experience 3.214–15; feeling loss unselfishly 12.612; if you don't have anything, there's no fear of losing it 18.341–2; losing enthusiasm for meditation practice 1.554–5; losing everything doesn't necessarily lead to spiritual growth 19.21–2; losing one's 'edge' in meditation 4.181–2; losing someone near and dear 26.25; losing trust in existence 18.579; the loss of the 'divine vision' (Blake) 16.533; loss of face 23.163; loss of faith in Christianity, *see under* Christianity; loss and gain, *see under* eight worldly winds; the loss of praise and fame 4.431; pleasures are tied up with anxiety because we fear losing them 2.91; suffering through losing something alerts us to our attachment 3.280–1; today people don't worry about losing things because they can be replaced 18.334–5, 19.19

lost Enlightenment like finding your way after being lost 13.192–3, 14.42; the lost piece of silver 16.221; reclaiming what

seems irretrievably lost 2.180–1; when the way to Enlightenment has been lost 8.201, 12.318–19; young people's sense of being lost 7.421

Loti, Pierre 13.495, 13.712 (n282)

Lotto, Lorenzo 24.273, 24.676 (n333)

Lotus Sūtra *see White Lotus Sūtra*

lotuses

in Buddhist tradition
the true disciple is like a lotus (*Dhammapada*) 10.145; a lotus whose spirit told a monk not to steal its scent 26.243; 'The Abundance of Lotuses' chapter in the *Sūtra of Golden Light* 16.245; rebirth in Sukhāvatī in a closed lotus 1.331, 1.334; bodhisattvas 'plunge into the worst hell like geese into a lotus pond' 4.582–3, 4.631; association with Amitābha 4.207, 12.215, 13.309; lotus family 1.263, 13.310; the circle of lotuses around the mandala 12.220; the lotuses of the Lotus Throne and the Refuge Tree 11.87; Green Tārā's three blue lotuses 13.69; the three lotuses of White Tārā 16.121–2; Padmasambhava born from a lotus 1.382, 12.288; the two lotuses of the *vajra* 13.180–2; the White Lotus school 1.337–8

kinds of lotus
puṇḍarīka (white lotus) 12.502, 16.32, 16.51–2; thousand-petalled lotus 14.239, 16.561, 18.76; *utpala* (blue lotus) 1.338, 16.51–2; *The White Lotus* (short story) 25.533–9

lotus as metaphor
'the Buddha in a faded lotus flower' 13.389; the Buddhist life as a vast network of golden lotuses 11.88; compassion springs up in the Void as a lotus in water 1.239; the cosmic golden lotus floating on the waters of existence 12.220; it unfolds gradually, like the bodhisattva 10.175; the lotus blooming from the mud 18.84, 18.583; 'The Lotus of Compassion' (poem) 25.208; the lotus of my heart 25.181; the white unfading lotus of old age 25.282; 'A Wreath of Blue Lotus' 11.420–31

symbol
of awakening 7.316–17; considering the symbolism of the lotus 13.118–20; has both a macrocosmic and microcosmic significance 7.400, 16.175; of the Buddha's birth 3.137; of Buddhism 26.242; of different stages of spiritual development 10.145; of evolution 16.175; of the feminine principle 22.28; of natural growth 10.146; in the world but not of it 7.291; of the lotuses that sprang up as Siddhārtha took his first steps 2.38; of love 12.215; of purity 12.502, 16.32–3, 19.571; of rebirth 4.207, 10.145, 12.220; signifies something happening on a higher plane of existence 12.184; of spiritual growth 13.309; of spiritual rebirth 4.207; of the whole evolutionary process 25.139–40; seeing the lotus as a symbol, you see it in a deeper and truer way 13.120

see also
the Buddha's vision of humanity, *see under* Brahmā Sahāmpati's request; the elephant plunging into lotus pools, *see under* elephant; the lotuses of the *chakras*, *see under chakras*

Louie (art student) 26.496–7

Lounsbery, Mme G. Constant 8.643, 22.219, 22.222, 22.256, 22.597 (n212)

love

the word love
often a weak term 12.551; ambiguous 3.450, 4.526, 10.652, 11.701, 12.457; an unsatisfactory equivalent to the more precise *mettā* 1.157–8, 5.189

the nature of love
the awareness of the being of another person 12.36; Confucian *shù*, Godwinian 'benevolence' 8.448; difference from generosity 2.365; an expression of spiritual insight 16.487; love and hate are near akin 25.432; 'Love cannot bear the burden of wisdom' 25.442; 'Love is love of beauty' (*Symposium*) 26.312; the most powerful weapon in the world 3.319; only fools think it is something that happens between a man and a woman 25.497; the only force strong enough to overcome hatred 3.319; 'Pity melts the mind to love' (Dryden) 26.613; the secret of love is love 25.498;

a self-giving of person to person 2.365, 26.66; spirit of self-abnegation 26.150; truly loving someone does not mean seeing them as perfect 15.320; the vigorous expression of imaginative identification with other beings 2.361, 26.66

impartial love
anattā envelops the whole world in a cloak of unity and love 7.133; the aspect of the Enlightened mind that regards all things as beloved 12.222; being in love with everybody and everything 5.618; 'free as the air, impartial as the sun' 25.203; love in Buddhism arises out of the perception of the impersonality of existence 8.200; love is love only when felt impartially for all 1.159, 8.256; 'Love which moves the sun in heaven, and all the stars' (Dante) 7.61, 26.150; the need of boundless love 25.210; the sweet fruit of [unselfish] love is liberation for all sentient beings 7.291; we can radiate love only from egolessness, from *śūnyatā* 12.458; you can no more confine love within human hearts than catch the moonlight ... 26.65

kinds of love
the cherishing, protecting, maturing love meant by the first precept 2.361; Enlightenment is infinite and inexhaustible love 2.57; love is of three kinds, directed towards superior, inferior, or equal 22.285; a mother's love for her only child 11.102, 14.57, 15.321–4, 26.690; moving from grosser to finer forms of love 7.61; possessive love 15.253, 15.254; true love (Shelley) 1.158; unconditional love 5.146–8, 15.319–20

love and spiritual life
all religions say 'love others', but only Buddhism explains how 10.156, 10.173; the difference between earthly love and spiritual love 26.598; for all human beings, and all animals, love is necessary for growth 12.215; Mme Guyon's doctrine of pure love 13.626; having an ideal of the God of love without feeling love at all 19.182; the integration of what you esteem and what you love 25.110; Kurukullā represents the love aspect of the Enlightened mind 13.68; love and passion transformed to brilliance and bliss 25.278; love of God 7.93–5; 'Love's Austerity' 25.223; loving the Dharma 12.581–2, 13.274–5; the object of love is invariably a person, not 'wisdom and compassion' 2.128; religion: enough to make us hate, but not to make us love one another 10.283, 26.195; Rilke's philosophy of love and sublimation 26.172–3; to communicate the Dharma you need love and compassion 19.204–5

the expression of love
ahiṃsā is a state of love, so practising it means cultivating that state 7.373; 'The great secret of morals is love' 2.360, 15.249, 17.598, 26.139, 26.189–90; in the world today, love isn't enough, we need courage to act upon it 12.518; it must be expressed in words and deeds 1.533; the only way to avoid hating one's fellow men is to love them 26.65; 'Radiate love' 12.457–8; 'That which we love, we adorn' 16.530, 26.300, 26.395

what love depends on
the creative mind loves where there is no reason to love 11.25, 23.xvi; if we do not really know people, we cannot love them 1.520; mutual awareness, mutual love 1.521; one can love people only as far as one understands them 26.65; only if we are aware of people can we love them 12.262; our only need before helping others is to love ourselves and feel loved 14.415; to really help others, you need insight as well as love 19.287–8; without the capacity to recollect the past, there can be no real love 15.86

falling in love
being in love may be fleeting or may last a lifetime 15.155; a comparison between entering the *dhyānas* and falling in love 17.126; falling in love while leading a retreat 19.342; a golden flower of love 25.379; having the misfortune to fall in love 13.277; if someone is in love, their beloved defines them 19.87; it is possible to fall in love instantly, but friendship takes time 23.149; a look of love on the Underground 26.563; with a bodhisattva 5.617–18; off with the old love and on with the new 22.409; our craving casts a sort of glamour over someone's body 17.220; the *śamatha* aspect of *sādhana* compared to falling in love 5.595; the worst thing you can do to someone is fall in love with them 11.576–7; you may think you've found a *ḍāka* or *ḍākinī* when you've only fallen in love 13.203; a young woman who fell in love with a monk 19.471

problems of love
bitter-sweet 25.259; destructive love in family relationships 26.371–2; easier to love 'humanity' than one imperfect human being 7.328–9; if you have solved the problem of desire, you have solved the problem of love 7.291; looking for love to fill your inner emptiness 15.309, 17.668, 26.24; the more you insist you love

people, the less likely they are to believe you 17.208; the pain of loving 25.492; the search for security of love 13.386; why does love turn to hatred? 18.309–10

see also
the difference between love and *mettā*, *see under mettā*/translation; difficulty of loving oneself, *see under* self-love; fear of the withdrawal of love 16.307; 'God of Love', *see* God/God of Love; Kāmadeva (Hindu love god), *see* Kāmadeva; love charms and love magic, *see under* magic; loving speech, *see under* speech/four levels of skilful speech

love charms *see under* magic

love mode being tempted to switch from love mode to power mode in argument 18.354–5; confidence that someone you trust will act from the love mode 18.387; in control of the power mode 16.432; and the first precept 2.361–2; friendship is expressive of the love (or *mettā*) mode 11.701; if the love mode is not possible, the power mode must be subordinated to it 2.362, 12.415; Order members should relate to each other in the love mode 12.415; relating in the love mode to people in negative states 15.351; the spiritual community is based on the love mode 2.362; switch from the power mode to the love mode as much as possible 2.362–3; *see also* power mode

Lovelace, Richard 25.357, 25.593 (n86)

lovers the description of the lover in the Song of Solomon 13.543–4; four kinds of disciple: like patients, friends, sons, lovers 22.xvi; God as lover 7.96–7; 'he sighed as a lover, obeyed as a son' 21.365; the infantile demands of a lover 18.208; a lover may claim to admire the mind while thinking of the body 4.561; 'Nature had not meant me for a lover' 20.88; *samādhi* like the absorbed experience of the musician or the lover 11.34; a sort of magnetic energy between lovers 4.558, 4.562; the urge of lovers to become one through the sense organs is doomed to failure 24.517

Lovett, Estelle 24.250

lower self *see under* self/higher self and lower self

Lowry, Malcolm 24.323, 24.374, 26.380

loyalty be careful not to set up a situation in which people's loyalties are divided 19.316–17; class loyalties breaking down 3.441; group loyalty 3.436; 'I cannot feel that I owe an exclusive loyalty to any nation or race' 20.230; in your personal spiritual world there can be only one focus of absolute loyalty 19.315; 'With loyalty to my teachers' 2.525

Lu Ji 'The Joy of Writing' (Lu Ji) 14.xii, 14.294, 14.299; 'the use of literature/ Lies in its conveyance of every truth' 14.295, 26.321–2

Lubac, Henri de 1.428–9, 26.204–5

Lucas, E. V. 7.55, 7.555 (n68)

Lucian 20.61

lucidity 17.551

Lucifer *see* Satan

luck auspicious signs, *see Maṅgala Sutta*; bringers of good and bad luck in India 16.397; bringing about your own good luck 15.385–6; karma is not some sort of bad luck about which nothing can be done 15.89; making your own luck 15.385–7; sometimes we don't realize how lucky we are 12.543–4; superstitions about good and bad luck 15.382–3; the use of an exalted teaching as a lucky charm 2.216

Lucknow 21.46, 21.109–15

Luhan, Mabel Dodge *Lorenzo in Taos* 24.525, 26.489

Luk, Charles *Chan and Zen Teaching* 13.332, 14.149, 14.621 (n174); translation of the *Heart Sūtra* 14.367; translation of the *Śūraṅgama Sūtra* 13.337; translation of the *Vimalakīrti-nirdeśa* 16.445

Lumbini

introduction
advice on visiting 21.512; Aśoka Pillar: 'Here the Blessed One was born' 8.195, 20.421, 25.232; at one time called Rummindei 23.529 (n403); birthplace of Siddhārtha Gautama (the Buddha-to-be) 3.21–2; excavated by British archaeologists 9.237; in a way the most sacred spot of all 8.196; the Nepalese government's recognition of the Buddhists' right to the sacred place 8.195; pilgrimage 2.223, 22.336; renovation 8.194–6; Rummindei Temple 20.420–1; shrines representing in the Japanese celebration of the Buddha's birthday 2.228; suitable as the venue for an international Buddhist movement 8.195–6; the World Fellowship of Buddhists' resolution about it 8.195

Sangharakshita visits
walking there 9.468, 9.489, 20.419–21; distress at seeing the first precept violated there 20.420; joy to be there and regret at how it had been neglected 20.419–20;

'Lumbini' (poem) 25.232; devotional feelings 20.421

Lumbini (magazine) 22.214, 22.249

luminous the *Gaṇḍavyūha Sūtra* depicts everything as luminous 14.219–20; luminosity of *citta* 1.84; *pabhassara* (luminous) 1.84; self-luminous mind 17.410–11; sometimes thought is luminous, but action is weak 7.138; 'This consciousness is luminous' 1.84, 1.275, 1.364, 2.130, 7.527, 10.439, 13.389, 19.97; 'This mind of yours is inseparable luminosity' 2.672 (n93); the true individual is intensely, luminously aware 3.469

lunar symbolism *see under* moon

lung (permission to read) 7.543, 13.340, 22.406

Lung (Tibetan) *see prāṇa*

lungta *see* windhorse

Lusch, Robert *see* Dharmadipa

lust *see* desire

Luther, Martin introduction 8.706 (n332); and Erasmus 5.249, 5.724–5 (n234); faith and works 7.39, 7.551 (n40), 13.388; his protests against the Church's sacramental system 18.428, 18.520, 19.278; inaugurated the Reformation 3.194, 9.318, 12.114; introduction 7.551 (n40); the mistaken idea that the Buddha was a reformer like Luther 12.618; the nailing of his ninety-five theses to a church door 13.550; portrait by Cranach 24.591; preached in Augsburg 24.591; 'Reason is a whore' 8.588; 'Sin on bravely' 4.563, 4.712 (n351); he wrote best when he was in a rage 5.249; 'unworldly individualism' 13.387

Luxembourg 23.247

luxury at a Buddhist conference in Tucson, Arizona 24.470–1; enjoyment is not a luxury, but central to the spiritual life 18.133; in a luxury culture, people should work because they want to 3.587; the rule to refrain from sleeping in high and luxurious beds 19.275, 21.370; Siddhārtha's disgust at a life of luxury 1.58; 'To indulge in luxury and pleasure is the cause of poverty and death' 18.472

Lycurgus 23.295, 23.517 (n331)

Lye, Len 24.510

Lyell, Charles 10.554, 10.715–16 (n439)

Lynn, Vaddhaka 11.765 (n323)

M

Ma-ism *see* Anandamayi

Macarius, St 26.298

Macaulay, Colman v22

Macaulay, Rose 11.634

Macaulay, Lord Thomas 1.524

Macdonald, 'Daddy' v21

Machado y Ruiz, Manuel 24.432

Machig Labdron 13.268, 13.690 (n103), 18.432

machines the Abhidharma gave the impression that the mind is just a complicated machine 15.187–8; karma is not a machine of cogs and wheels, but a play of healthy and unhealthy volitions 2.73; modern civilization: a complicated machinery of supply and demand 7.325; we are really machines rather than human beings 11.7

Mackail, J. W. 14.xiii, 14.292–4, 26.321

Mackenzie, Dr (heart specialist) 20.24–5

Macmillan, Harold 23.61, 23.87

Macmurray, John (philosopher) 15.254–5

Macpherson, James (Scottish poet) 2.668 (n56)

Macquarrie, John 13.449–50

mada *see* intoxication

Maderno, Stefano 23.308, 23.520 (n344)

madhukari bhikṣā 3.590

Madhuribehn (singer) v22

Madhva 1.166

Madhyamakavāda or Madhyamikavāda (New Wisdom school)

introduction
introduction to the school 1.309–23; also called the *śūnyavāda* 17.360; always called 'the profound Madhyamaka' 17.325; it emerged from the depths 12.28–9, 17.325; it was founded by Nāgārjuna 13.342, 17.450; Nāgārjuna's *Mūlamadhyamakakārikā* is its foundational text 17.153; its inspirational source is Mañjughoṣa 17.463; it was a reaction against the extreme views of the Hīnayāna 7.538; influence on Advaita Vedanta 1.323; Prāsaṅgika school became the norm of Madhyamaka teaching 1.322; teachers, *see* Nāgārjuna, Āryadeva, Buddhapālita, Bhāvaviveka, Candrakīrti, Śāntideva; School of the Three Śāstras 1.311; its last phase: the Yogācāra-Svātantrika Madhyamaka school 1.323; it sank into scholasticism 1.374, 19.373; it's so advanced that to relate to it you need to be very advanced yourself 4.590; a good idea to read the original works 17.465–6

views and teachings
concerned to show that reason is self-contradictory 10.143; conditioned and Unconditioned are non-dual 4.587–91; the distinction between relative and absolute is only relatively true 4.276; interpretations of *śūnyatā* teaching 16.20; it designated *pratītya-samutpāda* as *śūnyatā* 7.199; it saw the Dharma as conventional truth 1.265; its basic teaching: the conditioned is itself the unconditioned reality 23.320; its basic view is the emptiness of all *dharmas* 7.540, 19.371; its philosophy is metaphysical and its method dialectical 7.201, 7.506; Madhyamaka and *rūpakāya* 1.253; Madhyamaka and *vipaśyanā* 19.373; the middle way is its characteristic teaching 1.313, 8.504–5, 10.609; the negation of all views 19.372–3; not so much a doctrine as a method 1.312; one of four systematic transmissions of the doctrine 13.340; preoccupation with the conditionality of *dharmas* 1.103; realization of *śūnyatā* not indispensable for attainment of Nirvāṇa 1.321; renowned for relentless logic 17.326; repudiation of all views 1.322; view that the Path and the Goal cannot be separated 2.122

and the Yogācāra
a potential danger in the Madhyamaka led to the Yogācāra 1.349–50; closely interconnected, but a difference of emphasis 17.449–50; a difference not of doctrine but of method 1.350–1, 7.201, 7.506, 12.168, 19.372; the Madhyamaka relied on philosophical thinking, the Yogācāra on meditation 17.450; the Madhyamaka's refined concepts need the Yogācāra meditative context 19.374; Tibetan Buddhism almost a blend of the two 17.451–2, 19.373; the Yogācāra represented the relative and the Madhyamaka the absolute truth 7.506

relationship to the rest of the Buddhist tradition
anticipated in the Pāli canon 7.527, 19.374; the *Bodhicaryāvatāra* gives information on Madhyamaka metaphysics 1.322; connection with Buddhist schools that upheld the supremacy of faith 1.323; not a rival to other systems of thought but an expression of advanced insight 7.509; the Perfection of Wisdom *sūtras* 1.298, 1.309, 12.168; China and Japan 1.311; influence in Tibet, Mongolia, China, and Japan 1.323; how it relates to Tibetan Buddhism 8.503; Tibetan *geshes* and the Madhyamaka 13.45, 19.374; the Vajrayāna 'a working out of the Madhyamaka in practical terms' 19.372

Madhyamakāvatāra *see* Candrakīrti

Madhyāntivibhaṅga *see* Maitreyanātha

madness the bodhisattva perceives the world as a mock show without plunging into madness 14.576; a Buddha appears to others as a child, a madman, a ghost 11.11–12; and meditation 5.363–5; to attempt Tantric practice without a teacher risks insanity 1.389; the king who couldn't bear being the only sane person in a kingdom of madmen 4.526–7; the near insanity of the conflict between conscious and unconscious 12.217; 'The ordinary man is like a madman' 4.711 (n342), 5.659, 12.229, 16.192–3, 26.75; people like to think that they're sane, but it isn't really so 12.229–30; poetic inspiration as a kind of madness (Plato) 25.4; the Vajrayāna: the path on which you may seem mad, or like an animal, or like a ghost 13.176; zaniness: wanting to impress others with 'crazy wisdom' 18.178; Zen masters who appear to be quite mad 11.279; *see also* mental illness

Madras, India (Chennai) excellent English spoken 22.151–2; landscape 22.136; Maha Bodhi Society, *see under* Maha Bodhi Society/branches; Mylapore beach 20.228; Ramakrishna Math, Mylapore 20.227–8, 22.138–9; Rationalist Society 9.63; Sangharakshita's visit to Adyar in 1947 20.228, 21.439; Theosophical Society, Adyar, *see under* Theosophical Society; Vivekananda College 22.153

Madura, India 20.231–5

Maeterlinck, Maurice 7.56, 7.557–8 (n73), 13.533

Mafalda *see* Reis, Mafalda

Magadha (kingdom) becomes the Magadhan empire of Aśoka 10.473; birthplace of Buddhaghosa 3.289; the Buddha walks through the Magadha countryside one spring morning 10.310; its geographical setting 2.25; glorious Magadha 7.423; the expansion of the kingdom 10.646; need to revive Buddhist culture 7.425–6; ruled by King Bimbisāra, *see* Bimbisāra; swallows up the state of Kosala 10.472–3

Māgadhī (language) 14.12–13

Magandiya, Anagarika v22

Māgandiya Sutta *see under Majjhima Nikāya*

magazines and journals Buddhist titles that are like local parish magazines 15.703; comics 20.22, 23.8; *Everybody's* 26.416; the functions of a Buddhist journal 8.187–9, 8.646; high standard of Buddhist magazines (1955) 8.155; horror comics 8.206–9; *Time* (American magazine) devoted an issue to Buddhism (1955) 8.217; *see also* individual titles

Magee, Bryan 26.xiv

magga-amagga-ñāna-dassana visuddhi *see* seven *visuddhis*

Māgha (young brahmin who becomes a lay disciple) 2.665 (n30)

Magha Pūrṇimā *see under* festivals

magic

magic in the Buddhist tradition
the Buddha's 'magic' is superior to that of Bhadra the Magician 14.187; don't misuse your magical powers (*Udāna*) 10.448; *devas*: the magical side of existence 10.447–8; *dhāranī*, *see dhāraṇī*; the magical transformations of *rūpa* (*mahābhūtas*) 13.151–2; magical practices an important aspect of Buddhist life throughout history 2.215; performed by bodhisattvas 16.451; an illustration of what existence is really like 16.454; a magical herb bath (the *Sūtra of Golden Light*) 16.370; Vimalakīrti's magical powers 16.450–1, 16.555; magical acts as demonstrations of the Dharma 16.451; magical rites adopted by the Indian Buddhist Tantra 13.278–80; monks' austerities a means of magical protection and blessing 2.215; the Buddha image as a source of magical protection 2.229–30; magic power of the Tathāgata, like thistledown on the wind 1.255; Enlightenment is magical according to the Vajrayāna 19.214; without realizing *śūnyatā* Vajrayāna visualizations are vulgar magic, *see under* Chen; supernormal powers, *see*

supernormal powers; thinking of the ideal in terms of magical potency 11.320

the magic show
existence compared to a magic show 14.562, 16.451, 19.79–80; the five *skandhas* like a magical show 14.577; an illusory elephant 14.501, 14.562, 16.452–3, 17.385–7, 19.79; the Indian rope trick 4.374–5, 12.185, 14.507, 19.80; a magician conjures up a crowd, then makes them vanish 14.141

beliefs and superstitions about magic
a cook who wanted to be a sorcerer 22.524; in India 4.374–5, 13.276–8, 16.451–2; *jakri* or *jhakkhri* (sorcerer) 13.277, 22.523; in the past people avoided wearing animal products for magical reasons 10.460; love charms and love magic 2.216, 13.277, 18.432; rain-making 2.216

black magic
could be skilful means, though that is open to misuse and misunderstanding 18.361–2; Dhardo Rimpoche helps to alleviate a black magic attack 22.523; Milarepa gives Rechungpa advice about 'wicked occultism' 19.355–6; Milarepa's use of black magic 18.64, 18.362; suspicion of a death by black magic 22.37; the Vajrayāna viewed as black magic by a missionary 21.357; a visitor describes the battles of black magic in the cities of the world 22.260–1; a young man with an interest in black magic 19.101, 23.197

a touch of magic
all our actions and communications need a touch of magic 16.498; the preacher of the Dharma needs something magical, a *dhāraṇī* 16.369; a puja needs a touch of magic 18.321

relating to magic
don't exclude the magical, but be on your guard against humbug 18.429; expecting some sort of magic to transform you without any work 18.520; helpful as a way of thinking about the Dharma for Western Buddhists? 4.374–5; nothing magical about the wise, they've just got on with the spiritual life 10.648; psychologically, magic may be better for you than technology 15.685; replaced by technology in the East 15.682–5; Sangharakshita meets a witch 23.196–7

'Magical Buddhism' *see under* Tantric Buddhism

Magritte, Rene 26.379

mahā- (prefix) 13.69, 13.280–1, 14.571–2, 15.257, 17.314, 18.65, 18.597

***Maha Bodhi* journal**

the founding of the journal
founded by Anagarika Dharmapala 8.40–2, 8.107, 8.631–2, 9.93, 23.370; its motto: 'Go ye, O Bhikkhus, and wander forth …' 8.40–1, 8.631; struggles in the early days 8.632

contributors
Dr Ambedkar 9.14, 9.68, 10.3–4, 10.29–90; Anagarika Dharmapala 8.41, 8.63–4, 8.631–2; Lama Anagarika Govinda 8.362, 8.643, 22.122–4; Colonel Olcott 8.41, 8.632; previous contributors to *Stepping-Stones* 22.122; to the Vaiśākha issue (1954) 8.642–4

how it developed
advertisements 8.644; cover 8.641–2, 22.128; memorial issue for Mrs Mary E. Foster 8.80–1; a historical resource for information about the Buddhist world 8.645; changes to the journal over the years 8.258–9; its governing body dominated by caste Hindus 8.xix; editorial board 8.634–9; claim that it was a purely Theravāda publication 8.638, 22.168–74; 'Non-Theravāda Articles in the Journal' 22.173, 22.177; problems with renewal of its licence 22.228–30; decline 22.174

Sangharakshita's articles under the name 'Himavantavasi'
introduction 22.69–70; the choosing of the name 8.xvii; 'an extension of my personality' 22.69; Himavantavasi could say things that Sangharakshita could not 8.xviii; 'In the Light of the Dhamma' 8.xvii, 8.115–58, 22.171, 22.589 (n153); responses to Himavantavasi's writings 8.144–5

Sangharakshita's editorship
introduction 21.525; asked to take on Diamond Jubilee issue 21.384–5; he agrees to take it on 8.xviii–xix, 8.633, 22.62; disappointed not to be editorial chair 8.xix, 8.xxi, 22.70–2; conditions in which the journal was edited 22.120–2; his editorship challenged 22.174–8; page proofs in Calcutta 23.370–1; questions over his appointment 8.638, 22.169–70; relationship with the editorial board 8.636–9, 22.129–30, 22.166–7; Dr Ambedkar's challenge 9.502; attacked for bringing Mahāyāna Buddhism to the journal 8.637–9, 22.168–78; what it was like during his time 8.646–7; the first issue he edited 8.639–41, 22.122–9; Vaiśākha issue (1954) 8.642–4; difficulties in bringing out the journal 22.229–30; the assistance of Adrienne Bennett 8.636, 23.54–5; book reviews 8.xxxiii–v, 8.357–403; continued to edit

after returning to England 23.54, 23.118, 23.428–9

editorials
introduction 8.xxii–xxxii, 22.70; summary of editorials 8.xxiii, 8.xxix–xxxii, 22.458; horrified to realize that triumphalism may have crept in 2.458; 'Ancient Buddhist Site in Danger' (first editorial) 8.xxx, 8.163–4; 'Buddha Gaya' 8.177–81, 22.127–8; 'Buddha Jayanti Among the Birds' 8.222–4, 22.310; 'Buddhism and the Indian Languages' 8.220–2, 22.310; 'Buddhism and the Parliament of Religions' 8.166–8, 22.78; the Great Work of the dissemination of the Dharma 8.xxix, 8.216–18; Dr Ambedkar's conversion to Buddhism 8.234–6, 10.93–4, 22.350–2; Dr Ambedkar's death 8.239–41, 10.106–8, 22.366–7; the challenges facing the Neo-Buddhists 10.109–11; 'Controversy' 8.xxiii, 8.168–73, 22.171; the World Fellowship of Buddhists 8.154–5, 8.185–7, 23.160–2; on the Diksha Bhumi 8.270–1, 10.112–13; editorials about Anagarika Dharmapala 8.96–111, 8.232–4; 'The Inner Preparation' 8.218–19, 22.309–10; 'Meditation Upon Water' 8.xxxi, 8.265–6; money to be spent not on shrines but on teaching the Dharma 8.175, 22.171; the 2,500th Buddha Jayanti 8.216–30, 8.237–8, 8.244–52, 22.308–11; 'Ring in the New' 8.224–5, 22.310–11; 'Wanted: A New Type of Bhikkhu' 2.448–9, 8.xxxii, 8.327–30, 8.661, 10.271; 'Wanted: A New Type of Upāsaka' 2.448–9, 8.xxxii, 8.331–5, 8.661, 10.271

articles about Sangharakshita
Bhikshu Sangharakshita's lecture tour in Nagpur' 22.156–65; report of the first meeting of the Sangha Sabha in Great Britain 8.336–8

Maha Bodhi Society

THE SOCIETY

introduction
brief introduction 21.524; the founding of the society 8.38–40, 9.208, 9.239; all schools of Buddhism welcomed 2.173, 2.175; the first office bearers 8.38; presidents 8.xx–xxi; run by Hindus 8.xix–xx, 9.16, 9.211, 9.239, 11.174, 11.381; first Buddhist president 8.xxi, 9.209, 10.76, 22.64–7; effectively the only Buddhist organization in India at one time 22.61; missionary work 7.464–5; kept a low profile during the war years 22.60; Dr Ambedkar on 8.xx, 9.15–16, 9.208–9, 9.502, 10.5, 10.16, 10.76, 21.415–16, 22.65; expression of shock at Dr's decision to renounce Hinduism 9.56–7; celebrations of the 2,500th Buddha Jayanti 22.306; messages of goodwill towards the Society 22.126; accused of hostility towards the Theosophical Society 21.439; struggle to control the Society 22.61–2; suspicious of poverty 9.280, 20.390, 22.60–1; 'virtually defunct' (1984) 11.562

Sangharakshita and the Society
summary of his association with the Society 22.60–2; his misgivings about it 11.380–2

BRANCHES

Calcutta
architecture 21.369; change of atmosphere 21.369–70; committed to non-violence, so no forceful eviction of squatters 21.373–4; governing body predominantly Hindu 21.389; His Holiness 20.165–6, 20.170–1, 23.12; in Hindu–Muslim riots 20.166; how it changed over the years after Dharmapala founded it 21.382–4; *kaṭhina* ceremony 23.371–2; location 21.566; the madwoman's wail 21.374; monastic practice 21.374–5; Sangharakshita there 19.295–6, 20.162, 20.165–72, 21.368–89, 22.320, 23.12, 23.371; Sri Dharmarajika Vihara 8.64, 20.136, 22.57; a tiny island of Buddhism in the vast ocean of Hinduism 8.xxviii, 22.59; the visit of a Muslim who had visions of the Buddha 14.438

Mumbai
Ananda Vihara 10.335, 21.545, 22.267–8, 22.270–3; Bahujana Vihara 22.271

Sarnath
Sangharakshita is refused ordination, *see under* Sangharakshita/V Buddhist life/ ordination; a friendlier reception en route to Kusinārā 20.396–7; a press campaign against Maha Bodhi Society monks 23.365

other branches and activities
American Maha Bodhi Society 8.54; Delhi 9.500, 20.115, 23.410; Kalimpong 8.650, 8.655, 21.427–31, 22.62; London 8.65–7; Madras 8.57–8, 22.138, 22.151–3; Nautanwa Guest House (en route to Lumbini) 20.418–19; plans for a branch on a tea estate in Darjeeling 22.24; *Sinhala Bauddhaya* (Sri Lanka publication) 8.64

Maha Prom 22.514

Mahā-Assapura Sutta *see under Majjhima Nikāya*

mahā-atma or mahā-atta *see under atman*

Mahābhaiajya *see under* Buddha/epithets

Mahābhārata and Dr Ambedkar 9.111; the *Bhagavad Gītā* is part of it 16.424;

Draupadi 7.58, 7.559 (n81); Mahabharata War 8.303; Savitri 7.58, 7.559 (n81); sees human life in terms of conflict 16.85; stories that also occur in the *Jātakas* 14.65

Mahābhijñājñānābhibhū (Tathāgata) 14.117

mahābhūtas 'great ghosts', great magical transformations 13.151–2, 15.135, 17.445–6; the elements 15.135, 17.445; ways of classifying *rūpa* 2.97

Mahācattārīsaka Sutta *see under Majjhima Nikāya*

Mahad, India Buddhist ruins near Mahad, visited by Dr Ambedkar 9.53, 10.127, 10.681 (n144); the burning of the *Manusmṛti* 6.612, 9.6, 9.50–1, 9.222, 10.27, 10.127, 10.295; Chowdar Tank *satyagraha* 6.611–12, 9.45, 9.47–50, 9.220–1, 10.22–3, 10.127; Sangharakshita gives a talk in Mahad 9.292, 10.xlviii, 10.294; second conference 9.52

Mahādeva (Hindu god) *see* Shiva

Mahādeva (Mahāsāṃghika scholar monk) 1.186

Mahadhammavira, Dhammachari the poem 'The Caves of Bhájá' 24.234–7, 25.505–11; his suicide 24.233–8; photograph 24.234

Mahādukkhakkhanda Sutta *see under Majjhima Nikāya*

mahaggata 5.272, 5.726 (n261), 15.163, 17.608

Mahāgosiṅga Sutta *see under Majjhima Nikāya*

Mahāgovinda Sutta *see under Dīgha Nikāya*

Mahāhatthipadopama Sutta *see under Majjhima Nikāya*

Mahākaccāna advises his disciple Soṇa Koṭikaṇṇa to delay going forth 10.572–3; association with the Abhidharma 14.73; practises mindfulness of the body 10.621–2

Mahākāla ('Great Time') the rebirth of Tarpa Nagpo 8.525; wrathful form of Avalokiteśvara 16.178

Mahākammavibhaṅgha Sutta *see under Majjhima Nikāya*

mahākaruṇā the bodhisattva should master just one virtue: great compassion 2.125–6, 5.199–200; the bodhisattva's experience of (*Vimalakīrti-nirdeśa*) 16.522–3; the Buddha's 'escape' from *nirvāṇa* back into *saṃsāra* 2.56–7; the difference between compassion and great compassion 2.125, 18.590; equal to *mahāprajñā* 2.125; 'Great compassion is called Buddha-nature' 2.125; has for its object the ultimate emptiness of living beings 2.125; like being fully absorbed in something despite pain 16.522–3; no karmic retribution for actions performed out of great compassion 14.188; what makes it *mahā* is *śūnyatā* 19.537

Mahākārunika 2.175, 5.xxxi–ii, 10.227, 15.529

Mahākassapa (or Mahākāśyapa) being reborn with the Buddha in the *Jātakas* 16.471–2; an encounter with the *devas* 10.448; famous for his practice of asceticism 10.447–9; given almsfood by Sakka, the ruler of the *devas* (*Udāna*) 10.515; goes to the streets of the weavers in Rājagaha for almsfood (*Udāna*) 10.447–9; how he met the Buddha 2.698 (n363), 15.665–6; a leper's finger falls into his bowl 17.771 (n534); in the *Vimalakīrti-nirdeśa* 14.161, 16.525–6, 16.539; not present at the *parinirvāṇa* (Mahāyāna text) 14.233; patriarch of the Zen school 13.341; tells the story of the return journey *White Lotus Sūtra*) 16.42, 16.215; transmitted the spirit of the Dharma to Ānanda 13.341; understands when the Buddha holds up a golden flower 1.523, 3.82, 4.148, 8.73, 8.484–5, 12.231–2, 13.341, 14.16, 25.404; in the *White Lotus Sūtra* (one of four elders) 14.115, 16.41–2

Mahākātyāyana 14.115, 16.41–2

Mahalingam, Indira 8.603

mahāmaitrī 3.451, 15.257

Mahāmālunkya Sutta *see under Majjhima Nikāya*

Mahāmaṅgala Sutta *see under Sutta-Nipāta*

Mahāmati (Mañjuśrī in the *Laṅkāvatāra Sūtra*) 1.238–9, 2.173, 14.204–6

Mahamati, Dharmachari general entries v24, v26; brief introduction 17.7, 24.622 (n88); foreword writer 13.xi–xviii; at Mañjughoṣa stuti *sādhana* retreat 26.663

Mahāmaudgalyāyana *see* Maudgalyāyana

Mahāmāyā (the Buddha's mother) *see* Māyādevī

Mahāmoggallāna *see* Maudgalyāyana

Mahāmudrā

introduction
the meaning of the term 13.28, 18.65–6, 18.243, 19.271; along with *atiyoga* and Zen, the peak of Buddhist spirituality 13.323; 'the Bliss, the Illumination, and Non-thought' 19.415; encourages you to adopt a relaxed attitude of not desiring anything 19.387; foundation, path, accomplishment 18.243–4; glib talk about the Mahāmudrā 18.246; the highest teaching of the Kagyu tradition 13.28, 18.65, 18.243; if you aren't ready to die, leave the Mahāmudrā alone 18.246; 'In the Mahāmudrā there is no acceptance or rejection' 19.274; includes Atiyoga and Dzogchen practices 19.372; it tries to keep people on experience, not descriptions of experience 19.272; the point of the Mahāmudrā 18.231; requires the 'courage of fearlessness' 18.245–6; the self-liberating Mahāmudrā 19.156; stresses the non-conceptual character of Enlightenment 19.271; the union of bliss and emptiness 18.61; Zen and Mahāmudrā 13.28, 19.272

teaching and practice
if you know how to see nothing, something will be seen 18.242, 18.244, 18.253; 'It requires a disciple possessing merit to receive the teaching' 18.244–5; it's not a teaching, but a non-verbal pointing out 19.271–2; Milarepa's practice 18.13, 18.29–30, 18.61, 18.239; not anything that can be practised 19.136–7; the pointing-out ceremony 18.233–4, 18.243, 19.552, 19.570–1; relaxation at the deepest level of one's being 18.451–2, 18.584, 19.136–7; spontaneity 18.253–4, 19.156; teaching about the four kinds of teacher 18.631; there's no fixed path to it, no definite lifestyle 19.272–3; we can benefit from the Mahāmudrā only when we meditate on it 10.165

Mahānidāna Sutta *see under Dīgha Nikāya*

Mahant (definition) 8.668 (n1)

Mahanubhava sect *see under* Hinduism

Mahāpadāna Sutta *see under Dīgha Nikāya*

Mahāpajāpatī Gotami (Mahāprajāpati Gautami)

the Buddha's aunt and foster-mother
she was his mother's sister 2.19, 3.22, 11.421; he converted her to Buddhism 9.142

'What do you teach?'
the story 2.726 (n592), 11.365–6; the full text 1.60–1, 1.203–4, 2.294, 7.381–2, 7.434, 7.519, 9.197–8, 9.249, 11.366; the Buddha's criterion used to assess Western art 12.393–4; the Buddha's description of the Dharma 13.401; spiritual pragmatism 1.204, 3.167, 9.198, 11.109; the Dharma conduces to solitude, not company 26.156; the essential characteristic of the Dharma is that it conduces to freedom 10.567; an illustration of Buddhism as the path of the higher evolution 2.476; keep applying these criteria to distinguish the right from the wrong path 3.293–4; makes clear the Buddha's attitude towards contemporary teachings 1.61; a similar approach in the Perfection of Wisdom 14.139; these teachings are the Dharma *when put into practice* 3.394; a way to work out for yourself which of the available teachings are the Dharma 3.15, 7.50; we take from the Dharma whatever is helpful to us here and now 10.282; whatever conduces to the spiritual development of the individual 9.249–50, 11.366, 11.417; whatever helps you to grow 9.474, 10.206, 10.212–13, 12.369

her request for ordination
refused 2.26–7, 11.421–2, 16.334–5; her behaviour after the refusal 11.421, 11.424; ordination granted under eight special conditions 2.27, 11.422–31

Enlightenment
her attainment of Enlightenment 11.428; predicted to Enlightenment in the *White Lotus Sūtra* 16.47; verses after her Enlightenment (*Therīgāthā*) 11.428–9

Mahāparinibbāna Sutta *see under Dīgha Nikāya*

Mahāparinirvāṇa Sūtra

introduction
introduction 14.230–41; does not describe the Buddha's death 13.683–4 (n58); *dramatis personae* 14.231; included in the Mūlasarvāstivādin Vinaya 14.34; one of the longest Mahāyāna *sūtras* – but very little happens 14.231; a late Mahāyāna

sūtra 16.239; the *parinirvāṇa* is not described 14.232; remarkable for the extent to which it refers to other canonical texts 14.238; the story of the *sūtra*, chapter by chapter 14.232–41; the *sūtra*'s light surpasses the light of all other *sūtras* 14.238; ten qualities that result from the practice of the *sūtra* 14.240; translations 14.231

themes
Ānanda's life story 14.241; the Buddha compared to the moon, which only appears to wax and wane 14.238; the Buddha's backache, when he lies down 'like any child ill in bed' 14.239; clarification of points of doctrine 14.241; a denunciation of meat-eating 14.236; the Dharma explained in terms of the Siddham alphabet 14.237; *ekayāna* 14.238; a eulogy on *mettā* 14.240; the four noble truths 14.237; the four positive aspects of Nirvāṇa 14.234; the four reliances (*pratisāraṇa*) 14.236–7; the four *viparyāsas* 14.237; the four ways a bodhisattva expounds the *sūtra* 14.236; the 'great self' 3.235, 14.234–5; 'How do we obtain long life?' 14.235; how to distinguish between Māra's teaching and the Buddha's 14.237; the implications of the Middle Way 14.240–1; King Ajātaśatru visits the Buddha (a parallel to the Pāli *Sāmaññaphala Sutta*) 14.240; Tathāgatagarbha doctrine 3.659 (n223); the wise physician and the prohibited cure 14.235

Mahāprajāpati Gautami *see* Mahāpajāpatī Gotami

mahāprajñā *see under prajñā*

Mahaprajna ('Great Wisdom', Nepalese monk) *see* Great Wisdom

mahāpraṇidhāna *see* bodhisattva vow

Mahāpratibhāna (bodhisattva) 14.120, 14.122

mahāpuruṣa (superman, great man)

introduction
an important idea in India at the Buddha's time 3.61; in *Lakkhaṇa Sutta* 3.61–2; resonances in Nietzsche 3.61; taken over by Buddhism for spiritual purposes 2.42

marks or signs
could the Buddha literally have these marks? 14.428–9; doctrine held in common by Theravāda and Mahāyāna 7.631; thirty-two major marks 2.45, 3.62, 7.531, 14.84, 14.425–32, 19.31; eighty-four minor marks 3.62, 7.531; Pāli canon references 14.426; the same marks appear on a Buddha and on a *cakravartin rāja* 14.427; the transcendental counterpart of the thirty-two marks 14.448–9

mahā-rāga a spiritualized, even transcendentalized passion 13.280–1; a stream of positive feeling from the heart of Enlightenment to living beings 13.281

Mahārāhulovāda Sutta *see under Majjhima Nikāya*

Maharaja Kumar of Sikkim *see under* Sikkim

Maharajgunj, India 20.417

Maharashtra (Indian state) as the *dharma-kṣetra* 10.254–5; Buddhist movement v9, v10; cave viharas 9.53, 9.236, 10.406; countryside 10.292–3; Maharashtrian brahmins 22.155; map of Maharashtra 9.167; Muslim architectural remains 10.293; Sangharakshita's tours, *see under* Sangharakshita IX/Dr Ambedkar; the state 10.287–8; unrest in Bombay in connection with the demand for a separate Maharashtra state 22.295

Mahāratnakūṭa Sūtra 2.389, 14.186

Maharatnapriya *see* Ratnapriya

Maharishi Mahesh Yogi introduction 19.618 (n179), 23.490 (n128); and Advaita Vedanta 23.105; and the Beatles 12.654, 15.674; gratitude to him for popularizing meditation 12.645; he promised people that TM would make them millionaires 19.460; his visit to Yale 23.454

Mahars caste discrimination against the Mahars 9.37–9, 10.288, 10.309–10; their suffering under Peshwa rule 9.37–9; recruitment by the East India Company 9.39–40; conversion to Buddhism 9.151–4; Dr Ambedkar was a Mahar 9.39–42, 10.288; *see also* Dalits

Mahāsaccaka Sutta *see under Majjhima Nikāya*

Mahāsakuludāyi Sutta *see Majjhima Nikāya*

Mahāsamaya Sutta *see under Dīgha Nikāya*

Mahāsāṃghikas (or Mahāsaṅghikas) asserted that the Buddha was always in *samādhi* 5.743 (n431), 19.423; Atīśa was ordained as a Mahāsāṃghika monk 12.567; believed that the spirit of the Dharma could be best preserved by a willingness to adapt it 1.189; connection with the *Mahāvastu* 14.188; connection with the *Ratnakūṭa Sūtras* 14.188; the

Kathā-vatthu attributes to the 'Andhakas' (Mahāsaṅghikas) Mahāyāna-type doctrines 14.135; link between the orally transmitted Dharma and the Mahāyāna *sūtras* 14.96; the Lokottaravādins were a subsect 7.500, 16.607 (n178); *Mahāvastu Avadāna, see Mahāvastu Avadāna*; maintained that the Dharma had been taught for everyone, monastic and lay 2.205–6; the majority party at the Second Council 1.189, 8.183; no evidence that their traditions are less reliable than those of the Theravādins 1.190; the Mahāyāna originated among them 2.192, 2.206, 8.183, 13.44; and the Prajñāpāramitā 14.135; preserved traditions that went back to the Buddha 16.241–2; repudiation of Sarvāstivādins' *sarvam asti* doctrine 1.188–9; and *rūpakāya* 1.253–4; scholars call them Hīnayānists, but Sangharakshita regards them as Mahāyānists 1.212; split from Sthaviravādins (Theravādins) 1.186–9, 2.192, 13.44

mahāsampanna 19.271

mahāsaṅgha *see under* sangha

Mahāsatipaṭṭhāna Sutta *see under Dīgha Nikāya*

mahāsattva 13.281, 14.404, 14.571

mahāsiddhas *see* eighty-four *siddhas*

Mahāsīhanāda Sutta *see under Majjhima Nikāya*

Mahāsthāmaprāpta ('Attained to Great Strength') attendant bodhisattva of Amitābha (or Amitāyus) 1.330, 1.333, 2.180, 14.173, 16.462; largely superseded Vajrapāṇi in the Far East 2.180; occupies a prominent place in Devotional Buddhism 1.336; one of the eight bodhisattvas 2.172; in the *White Lotus Sūtra* (twentieth chapter) 2.179

Mahāsudassana Sutta *see under Dīgha Nikāya*

mahāsukha (the Bliss-Void, the great bliss) bliss united with the experience of the Void 18.415–16; 'One secures the great bliss through viewing' 18.596; synonymous with the Mahāmudrā 19.280; its teachings will 'burn all wandering thoughts' 19.155

Mahāsuññata Sutta *see under Majjhima Nikāya*

mahā-śūnyatā *see under śūnyatā*/four *śūnyatās*

Mahātaṇhasaṅkhaya Sutta *see under Majjhima Nikāya*

mahatta (greatness) 3.235

mahā-upāsaka **and** ***upasīka*** (Triratna) 2.469

Mahāvacchagotta Sutta *see under Majjhima Nikāya*

Mahāvairocana *see* Vairocana

mahāvākyas *see under* Advaita Vedānta/teachings

Mahāvaṃsa *see under* Sri Lanka

Mahāvastu Avadāna

introduction
description 14.70–1; 'a bulky and rather chaotic work' 2.12–13, 14.70; the Buddha depicted as a transcendental being reborn out of compassion 2.13, 14.71; connection with the Mahāsaṅghika school 14.188; contrast with the Pāli Vinaya 15.185–6; a fine and important early work 21.582; its foundation among the oldest Buddhist documents we possess 14.71; held to reflect beliefs current among the laity 21.582; it exhales an aroma of exalted devotion 14.70; it is suffused with an atmosphere of rejoicing in the Buddha 17.337; its joyful and poetic tone 15.185; the insertion of *Jātakas* and *Avadānas* 14.71; the insertion of *suttas* 14.71; a life of the Buddha into which legends have been inserted 7.500, 12.181–2, 14.70; mention of Maitreya 2.179; written in Mixed Sanskrit 14.70; the twelve principal acts of the Buddha provide a framework 14.25; a Vinaya work of the Lokottaravādins 7.500, 14.69, 14.71, 16.155

Volume 1
eighteen special qualities or attributes of a Buddha 3.144, 14.448–9; the 'genesis of the world' 3.627 (n8); Maudgalyāyana's visits to various worlds 14.70; the ten *bhūmis* (stages of the path) 1.401, 1.447, 14.70; Megha [Sumedha] predicted to Enlightenment by the Buddha Dīpaṅkara 14.70

Volume 2 (Siddhārtha's story)
the rose-apple tree 3.629 (n21); the four sights 3.630 (n27); his supposed disgust at sleeping dancing girls is a misattribution 2.33; his horse Kanthaka leaves the palace on muffled hooves 3.656 (n197), 13.693 (n126); the practice of austerities 3.631 (n31); the *devas* offer him celestial nourishment, but he refuses 10.448, 22.285; how he settled to meditate before his Enlightenment 3.631 (n33); the routing of Māra 14.71; 'Siddhārtha's Dream' 25.295

Volume 2 (other aspects)
non-violence is the supreme *dharma* 3.318–19; story of Queen Maya 3.629 (n20); stupa worship 2.221, 13.251, 13.689 (n97), 14.144, 16.155; the two *Avalokita Sūtras* have nothing to do with Avalokiteśvara 2.175

Volume 3
the Buddha's propagation of the Dharma and the rise of the sangha 14.70; the Buddha sends his followers out to teach the Dharma 3.640 (n79); the twin miracle (the Buddha walking in the air emitting fire and water) 4.16, 12.183, 16.528

Mahāvibhāṣā 1.365, 14.95

Mahāvibhāṣāśāstra 1.103, 7.504–5, 14.254

Mahāvihāra (ancient monastery) 2.191

Mahavir Swami (Kusinārā) 20.407

Mahāvīra (founder of Jainism) appearance in the Axial Age 3.427; an elder contemporary of the Buddha 12.53; called Nātaputta in Pāli texts 10.479, 11.369; claim of omniscience 10.40, 17.328; doctrine of karma 23.347; a wanderer 10.479; wrangling among Jains after his death 11.369, 14.21

Mahāvyutpatti 16.342, 16.617 (n257)

Mahaweera, Venerable M. M. 20.143

Mahāyāna Buddhism ('great way')

WHAT IS THE MAHĀYĀNA?

introduction
brief summary 12.167; summary of its teachings 1.387–8; fuller introduction 1.237–49; etymology 13.281, 16.440; the 'great way' 4.19, 16.229; the term Mahāyāna 1.214, 3.413, 16.31; literary basis 1.211–12; countries where it is practised 1.211

descriptions
brings to fulfilment the original teaching 1.183, 14.351–2, 14.555; a chaos full of life and movement 1.277–9; characteristics 1.238; deeply emotional and rigorously intellectual 1.240; described in metaphors 1.183; an easing of tension between mundane and transcendental 1.274; *ekayāna*, the one way (*White Lotus Sūtra*) 1.218, 14.555, 16.41; emancipates Buddhism to a celestial context of dazzling beauty 1.183; emphasis on getting rid of suffering, whether 'mine' or 'yours' 4.591–2; four major approaches: faith, Madhyamaka, Tantra, and Zen 1.277–99, 13.328–9; the goal is a person in whom wisdom, compassion, and power are united 2.127–8; it declares indefinability of the real nature of things 1.65; it had to invent a myth to do justice to its vast ideal 1.325, 4.37; it is set on a stage of infinite space and infinite time 1.325; it opens up ever wider approaches to the Truth 1.239; it sees itself in terms of cosmic evolution 13.516; it sets no limits on the spiritual potential of the individual 16.440; its optimism about our spiritual condition 14.483–5; a living spiritual force 1.187, 14.342; a movement not of innovation but of development and unfoldment 1.247; 'mysticism tinged with rationalism' 12.515, 26.367; not a sect or school of Buddhism but a particular attitude to Buddhism 16.228; a profound metaphysical principle and its application in spiritual life 14.142–3; spirit reflected in the Arthurian cycle? 16.239; spiritual vitality 1.276; progressive in the sense of awareness that the Transcendental is ineffable 1.238; a restatement of Buddhism 14.103; a synonym of immeasurableness (Perfection of Wisdom) 14.142; the two-in-one path of wisdom and compassion 18.102; 'in this vehicle there is room for incalculable beings' 14.142; the *yāna* of *śūnyatā* 5.33

history
indicated in the Pāli canon 5.189–90; factors leading to the emergence of the Mahāyāna 1.83, 1.219–37; Mahāyāna-type views had their antecedents early in Buddhist history 15.184; descended from the Mahāsāṃghikas 1.189, 1.212, 2.192, 2.206; influenced by the Sarvāstivāda school 1.188; lineage 1.276; it never went to the extreme of anti-intellectualism 1.240; not just a movement of reaction 15.186; Nāgārjuna's Perfection of Wisdom teaching a factor in its rise 16.17; systematization 1.366–7; its failure to absorb ethnic culture allowed the infiltration of Hinduism 16.370; the Tantra indissolubly connected with the Mahāyāna 1.377; the Vajrayāna irrupts into the Mahāyāna 16.369

schools
full introduction 1.278–393; according to the schema of the five spiritual faculties 1.278–9, 1.294–9, 1.393; each school an accretion upon doctrines of earlier schools 1.373; it embraces and ultimately transcends all schools 1.220; like the four petals of a flower, to be followed as a whole 1.296, 1.393; magnificent temples – but it's not certain who was the architect of which bit 1.367; not sects, not mutually

exclusive but complementary 1.296; pass through three stages: dogmatism, systematization, scholasticism 1.297; of philosophy 1.241

ordination
bodhisattva ordination, *see under* bodhisattva/bodhisattva career; self-ordination 2.208; strictly speaking, 'Mahāyāna monk' represents a confusion of categories 7.473; *upasampadā* lineage 2.192, 7.472–3

popular Mahāyāna
introduction 16.230–2; it may be popular, but it is also very profound 16.232; represents a degeneration only when it becomes an end in itself 16.231; taking in elements of indigenous culture 16.231–2

TEACHINGS AND PRACTICES

Mahāyāna attitudes and approaches
adaptation to changing conditions 1.229; all sentient beings are destined for Enlightenment 13.516; anti-literalism 1.221–2, 1.239, 2.131, 16.537, 19.49–50; approach to developing insight 5.458, 19.453; attaches more importance to the spirit than the letter 1.239, 7.541, 14.101, 16.390; balanced methods 1.412; broad and liberal attitude 14.220; a Buddha whose resolve is to help those who cannot accept the Mahāyāna 14.117; commitment primary, lifestyle secondary 11.571; every Buddhist ought to aspire to supreme Buddhahood 1.214; every Mahāyāna Buddhist is a sort of Christ 4.599; fearless acceptance of contradictory propositions 1.245–6; stresses both wisdom and compassion 3.355, 3.365, 9.231, 16.14–15; 'If you can do nothing else, at least practise *dāna*' 14.574–5; insisted that *everybody* should aim to be a bodhisattva 2.300; it can get a bit theatrical – the Theravāda stays closer to our situation 4.61–2; it has *śūnyatā* as background 1.243; it makes use of conceptual formulations but is not limited by them 1.219–20; it sees existence in terms of *dharmas* 16.448–9; it sees hatred as much worse than greed 16.294–5; it transformed the distinction between monastic and lay 14.167; it values scriptural studies 7.543; it was negligent towards the textual integrity of its scriptures 14.101; it wanted to free the Dharma from the limitations of historical existence 16.530; negations (*dharmas*, Perfect Wisdom) 1.69; no short cuts 1.274; positivism 1.242–3; protest against the concept of Stream Entry 4.38; recognition of the plurality of Buddhas 11.246; rectified the one-sidedly negative presentation of the Dharma 10.432; refused to regard the spiritual and the monastic life as synonymous 1.244; Sangharakshita's faith in the Mahāyāna attitude 18.347; the success of the practice depends on realizing that success is impossible 1.239; threefold emotion: compassion, love, and devotion 1.241; universal perspective 16.228–9, 16.530

altruism
it developed the altruistic aspect of Buddhism 1.238; the basic principle of ethics is helping others 17.154; to counter the Hīnayāna's individualism 1.245, 1.258, 4.223, 7.150, 9.254–5; does its claim to altruism make a practical difference? 4.86; incorporated Hīnayāna individualism as a stage of the path of altruism 1.271; the living unity of altruism and emptiness 14.150; Mahāyānists will try to help without standing on their dignity 4.86–7, 14.556; no such thing as self-development without concern for others 1.237, 3.245–6, 16.6; the origins of the Mahāyāna's altruism 4.85–8; unbounded altruism of Mahāyāna precepts 2.208; vision that helping people develop is part of the spiritual life 16.229; went to an extreme of altruism 4.223; *see also* bodhisattva ideal

how to approach the Mahāyāna
shortcomings when taken literally 14.163, 16.503; study of texts must be preceded by study of the Pāli canon 1.184; the Theravāda for daily practice and the Mahāyāna as a guide to the ideal 4.62–3

ethics
actions must be based on compassion 1.245; the self-regarding and other-regarding aspects of moral life 1.207, 4.87; confession 16.275; gentleness, patience, not giving way to anger 16.296; handling money ('gold and silver') to be useful to others 22.103, 22.584 (n100); more aware of the instrumental nature of ethics than the Theravāda 1.147–8; sometimes absurdly charged with having 'no morality' 1.244

faith and devotion
devotional practice 1.238, 1.262–3, 11.225–6; emphasis on wisdom does not mean a neglect of faith and devotion 16.232–3; objects of devotion 1.241–2; transference of merit the traditional conclusion to any practice 18.102; worship of the bodhisattvas 1.397

the historical Buddha in the Mahāyāna
inspired by his life as well as his teachings 16.14–15; his life a sort of play (*līlā*) 1.189–90, 1.250, 4.85, 4.135–6, 13.300, 14.188, 14.236, 26.636; it believed its teachings were taught by the Buddha 1.247; overshadowed by the archetypal Buddha 1.263–4, 12.507–8, 16.207–8; reconciling historicity and metaphysical nature 13.300; said that the Buddha's appearance was impressive due to his merit 4.20; a *sūtra* in which he bursts from the ground 14.185

doctrines and teachings
adheres to the middle way 7.532; all conceptions of reality are equally invalid 1.242; all beings are equally susceptible to suffering 4.569–70; all teachings appear in germinal form in Theravādin scriptures 1.247; compares existence to a dream, an echo, a mirage, a reflection, a ball of foam 16.452; conception of the Buddha-nature 1.250; confidence in the spirit of the teaching 1.239; the doctrine of the *bhūmis* allowed the antedating of the Buddha's Nirvāṇa 1.261; elucidation of the true meaning of Buddha, Dharma, and Sangha 14.103–4; equated *saṃsāra* and Nirvāṇa 1.268, 1.274; held in common with Theravādins 7.531–40; how the Mahāyāna tackles dualism 14.591–2, 15.634; identifying the world of phenomena with the Absolute 1.268; in philosophy, represented by the Madhyamaka and the Yogācāra 7.506; incorporated the 'Hīnayāna' 1.246, 1.249; its fundamental Buddhist doctrines wrapped in glorious extraneous trappings 23.225; interconnectedness 16.6; the *Laṅkāvatāra Sūtra* a repository of nearly all its principal tenets 14.214; the Mahāyāna's hierarchy, the ten *bhūmis* 14.571; a metaphysical interpretation of the parable of the raft 1.265; one sees the mind by not seeing: one of its most important teachings 13.363–4; the path of the bodhisattva is central 15.80; potentially all beings are Buddhas 1.274; relegated the whole of the Doctrine to the domain of conventional truth 1.265; separation of Nirvāṇa from *bodhi* 8.620; systematic and unsystematic 1.367; transparent, inviting the eye to look through it to pure consciousness beyond 1.239; the Unconditioned as the 'great self' 3.234–5; universal conditionality 1.264; why does it hold skilful means in such high regard? 16.481–5; wisdom (*prajñā*) and skilful means (*upāya*) as the twin aspects of the Dharma 1.122

meditation
it transformed paradoxes into meditation subjects 1.82; the same practices as early Buddhism combined with the practice of *śūnyatā* 7.508; tendency to rely on the Theravāda for methods 5.461; what *śamatha* means for the Mahāyāna 17.187

culture
absorbed elements of ethnic culture as a skilful means 16.370; art among the greatest treasures of mankind 1.262; the integration of as many arts and sciences as possible 7.437

misunderstandings
don't mistake the Mahāyāna for a kind of theism 7.535–7, 11.106, 14.602–3; imagining the Mahāyānist as a model of transcendental politeness 16.6; it is not trying to tell us that nothing exists at all 16.454; it is just as prone to misinterpretation as the original teaching 1.404

CONTRASTS BETWEEN THE MAHĀYĀNA AND EARLY BUDDHISM (THE 'HĪNAYĀNA')

introduction
summary 1.246; at bottom a difference of attitude 1.447; the Mahāyāna uses terms from earlier traditions in a debased sense 14.552; relations between 'Hīnayāna' and 'Mahāyāna' 22.321–2; the terms 'Hīnayāna' and 'Mahāyāna' show an antagonism 1.214–15; like comparing Everest and Kanchenjunga: we have to look up to both 4.349; spiritually fruitful to compare the two approaches 4.25; we can't afford to neglect either of them 11.255; why Sangharakshita's early writings stressed the Mahāyāna, later the Pāli scriptures 6.xxv

different attitudes and approaches
distinctions 1.211–13; between 'Hīnayāna' *suttas* and Mahāyāna *sūtras* 1.272–3, 16.235–7; contrast between solitary and altruistic practice 7.150–1; difference of opinion about what accordance with the scriptures means 7.541; different approaches to formal monasticism 1.244, 9.254–5; different uses of the same terms 1.447; if put crudely, distinctions can be misleading 16.6–7; illustrated by a parable about a famine 16.12–14; individualism and universalism 1.403; the Mahāyāna has more faith in human nature 15.570; the Mahāyāna has a much more positive ideal of spiritual life 1.243, 15.568–71; the Mahāyāna has a spiritual warmth which is not there in the Theravāda 4.86; the

Mahāyāna places more importance on the guru 7.543; nobody is always Mahāyānist or always Hīnayānist 4.25; not so much difference of doctrine as evaluation of doctrine 1.225; protest against the Hīnayāna's spatio-analytical method 1.103; they correspond to two tendencies of the mind, centripetal and centrifugal 10.134; the Hīnayāna relies on human concepts, the Mahāyāna on cosmic myth 1.401; one adhered to what the Buddha said, the other to what he meant 7.541; there is something in the Mahāyāna which is not there in the Theravāda 14.555–6; Theravāda missionaries outnumbering Mahāyāna ones 14.554–5

doctrinal and conceptual distinctions
contrasting conceptions of the Āryasaṅgha 1.273; different idea of the 'non-returner' 15.239–40; discussions recorded in the *Kathā-vatthu* 4.24; Early Buddhism starts from the 'self', the Mahāyāna from the 'non-self' 1.403; the Mahāyāna has a more positive view of Nirvāṇa 1.238, 1.317; the Mahāyāna's view of the Hīnayāna's conception of *dharmas* 15.186; Nāgārjuna's refutations 1.314–15; *prajñā* seen in different ways 17.546–7; on *bodhi* 1.85–6; radically different conception of Enlightenment 1.268, 4.25; the two are not lower and higher stages of a single path 2.586

points of connection
a bodhisattva precept not to disparage the 'Hīnayāna' 13.56; calling into question the division between Theravāda and Mahāyāna 8.624; common philosophical basis: all things are *anattā/nairātmya* 7.155; doctrines held in common 7.531–40; each has its own ideal, but both are undergirded by karma and rebirth 26.695; early Pāli texts contain little trace of what the Mahāyāna calls the Hīnayāna 17.547; 'Hīnayāna' and 'Mahāyāna' followers living side by side 1.246, 4.23, 7.490, 10.282; 'Hīnayāna' practices included in the Mahāyāna 1.423; the Mahāyāna proclaims the same truths as early Buddhism 1.183; the Mahāyāna recognizes the truth of Hīnayāna teachings 7.40; the Mahāyāna a systematic development of Early Buddhist teaching 1.240; points of agreement about Nirvāṇa 1.65; Vasubandhu bridged the gap between them 7.504–5

Early Buddhist views of the Mahāyāna
accusation of materialism 8.183–4; the Hīnayāna's rejection of the Mahāyāna 1.246, 4.24, 21.245–6; the idea that Mahāyānists are not Buddhist at all 8.182–4; that the Mahāyāna was the work of Māra 16.81–2; Mahāyānists 'have dared to go beyond the words of the Master' 21.313; the *Laṅkāvatāra Sūtra* rejected by the Theravāda as uncanonical 7.534; Western *bhikkhus* hostile to Mahāyāna but drawn to Christian mysticism 23.24–5

Mahāyāna views of Early Buddhism
the Mahāyāna regarded the Hīnayāna not as wrong but as inadequate 7.505; a story about a princess expresses the Mahāyāna's rejection of Hīnayāna ideals 14.184

see also
ācāryas; *bodhicittotpāda*, *see bodhicitta*/arising; bodhisattva ideal, *see under* bodhisattva ideal/history; emphasis on skilful means, *see* skilful means; and Going for Refuge, *see under* Going for Refuge/perspectives; Madhyamakavāda; Mantrayāna; Perfection of Wisdom; sangha/the history of the sangha; *sarvadharma-śūnyatā*; Jōdo Shinshū; Mahāyāna *sūtras* and individual texts; two veils; three *yānas*; Vijñānavāda; Vinaya/history

Mahāyāna *sūtras*

introduction
an outline 3.86–8; 'the largest body of sacred writings extant anywhere in the world' 14.100, 16.442

their history
origins 14.96, 16.52–4, 16.530, 17.156–7; difficult to date them 14.101–2; the oldest are roughly contemporary with the Pāli canon 1.297; no definitive collection or fixed canon 14.100; affiliated to the orally transmitted Dharma through Mahāsaṅghikas and others 14.96; could they have been transmitted orally? 1.326, 14.102; some were written down at the same time as the Pāli canon 14.102; literary accretions 14.102; written down in Sanskrit, the language most widely understood 16.365–6; produced at a time when writing was more common than in the Buddha's day 16.54; made their appearance in the 5th century CE 1.380; classified as 'early' or 'late' i.e. before or after Nāgārjuna 16.239; early *sūtras* a repudiation of the Hīnayāna and a restatement of Buddhism 14.103–4; the difference between early and late *sūtras* 14.199–200; Hindu *Purāṇas* perhaps modelled on Mahāyāna *sūtras* 10.50; the Mahāyāna was negligent towards the textual integrity of its scriptures

14.101; *vaipulya sūtras* 12.210, 14.97–8, 14.102, 16.241–2; *alaṃkāras* the link between the *sūtras* and the Yogācāra 1.361–2; each Mahāyāna school derives its inspiration from a particular *sūtra* or *sūtras* 1.298; different recensions, translations, titles 13.337, 14.101–2; merit to be derived from copying and distributing them 16.54; 'your skin for paper, ... your bones for a pen' 2.213; divided into six great collections 7.501–2; Nepalese collection of nine *sūtras* (listed) 14.100; most of them are common to Tibetan and Chinese canons 7.527; literary history in China 16.242; some *sūtras* have not survived, or exist only in translation 14.100

the teachings of the Buddha?
the authenticity of Mahāyāna *sūtras* 14.399–400; the communication of an Enlightened mind 16.53–4; for Mahāyānists *Buddhavacana par excellence* 14.96; if not, they must have been produced by remarkable spiritual personalities 16.241; not accepted by Hīnayānists as genuine *Buddhavacana* 14.96, 16.55; it is open to us to believe that they were not literally taught by the Buddha 16.241; the people who composed them must have been highly imaginative 12.501; relationship to the Buddha's original teaching 4.19–20; revealed by the Buddha in his *sambhogakāya* form 1.272–3, 14.99; some may have originated in someone's meditation 14.259–60; taught by the eternal Buddha 16.241; they begin 'Thus have I heard' 14.99, 14.399; they may not have been taught by the Buddha, but they reflect his spirit 17.156–7; they try to recast the words of the Buddha in contemporary form 12.501; two approaches to the question, one more subtle than the other 1.247–8; in what sense might a Mahāyāna *sūtra* be apocryphal? 16.52

the nature of Mahāyāna sūtras
accessible to all who can ascend to their plane in meditation 14.99; comparison with Gnostic texts 16.238; a cure for spiritual ennui 16.440; each responds to the needs of a particular mentality 14.97–8; an effort to achieve a complete reconstruction of the teachings 4.19; emancipated from history 14.99; 'feminist' Mahāyāna *sūtras* 14.175; grandeur and sublimity 1.298; joy and rejoicing on a grand scale 16.336–7; like transcendental science fiction 3.381, 12.503, 16.37, 16.237; magnificently adorned 16.530; mode of instruction intuitive rather than explanatory 1.297; not to convince minds but awaken transcendental intuition 1.297–8; only another *sūtra* can do them justice 14.99–100; set in a transformed, beautiful, and mysterious world 16.237–8; some conceptual, others poetic and mythical 12.211, 12.503, 16.16–18; a spiritual world which transcends thought and speech 1.73; their dominant interest is not rhetorical but spiritual 1.333; they are instinct with a sense of their own inadequacy 1.239; they contact something in us of which we were unaware 16.532; they give a more vivid, attractive experience than a dull discourse 19.26; they go completely beyond the best of Western culture 19.350, 25.lix; they grew around a nucleus, a centre of spiritual energy 16.243; they recast in contemporary form the spirit of the Buddha's teaching 12.501; they transport you out of yourself into some other world 19.26, 22.463, 25.11; universality of outlook 2.553, 14.98–9

notes about content and intentions
settings 14.396–7; cosmological background 16.343–4; the bodhisattva ideal is an important theme 14.97; the Buddha appears in his archetypal form 1.272–3, 1.297, 14.99, 16.461, 16.531–2; concerned not with the historical Buddha but with his archetypal life 4.19; concerned to transmit the spirit of the Buddha's teachings 14.26, 16.240–1; describe the bodhisattvas' acts of worship 4.53; bodhisattvas praising the Buddha with beautiful hymns 11.225; each contains the whole Dharma 14.98; each is a *dharma-paryāya*, means for full realization 14.98; the great vows of the cosmic bodhisattvas 18.161; strangely silent with regard to meditation methods 1.379; intended for the novice bodhisattva 1.241; later *sūtras* warn not to confuse their doctrines with non-Buddhist ideas 14.200

audience
beings who exist on a level of spirituality beyond all we can imagine 11.57; bodhisattvas are more numerous and prominent than *arhants* 1.273, 2.153–5; difference between early and late *sūtras* 14.532–3; taught to a great assembly of many kinds of beings 1.272–3, 1.297; sometimes the visitors have to reduce their dimensions to make room 1.273

how to read and study them
avoid literalism, enjoy them like poetry or a novel, experience them as a whole

16.57; the bodhisattva is not to become attached to the words 1.612 (n199); don't take them too seriously 16.57; not to be taken literally 4.63, 16.57; one should read them *without thinking of their meaning* (Yinkuang) 24.533; read them, then use a commentary to throw light on them, not the other way round 16.57; some 'revelations' to be treated with reserve 14.260; studied in the Triratna Buddhist Community 2.553, 12.368; they need interpretation in the light of the Pāli *Nikāyas* 11.720; the traditional view is that one should read them with a teacher 17.156–7

see also
Chinese translations, *see under* Chinese Buddhism/translations; comparison with Pāli canon *suttas*, *see under* Pāli canon; individual *sūtras*

Mahāyānasaṃgraha 1.366

Mahāyāna-sūtra-alankāra-śāstra 7.201

Mahāyāna-uttaratantra 1.366

Mahāvyutpatti 13.26, 13.673 (n2)

Mahendra, Crown Prince (Nepal) v21

Maheshkar, D. R. *see* Dharmarakshita

Maheshwara *see* Shiva

Mahinda (*arhant* son of Aśoka) 2.228, 8.462–3, 15.184–5

Mahinda, Bhikkhu 8.360–1

Maimonides (12th-century philosopher) 24.427

Maison, Clare 20.101, 23.40–1

Maitreya (the future Buddha, 'The Friendly One')

the future Buddha
belief that his advent will be preceded by the reappearance of Nāgārjuna 2.179; *bhikkhus* piously hoping to be reborn in the days of Maitreya 8.280; the fifth of the five Buddhas of this *kalpa* 8.201; prophecies about his return 21.49–51; Nicholas Roerich's devotion to the cult of Maitreya 26.222; strictly speaking a bodhisattva of the ninth *bhūmi* 2.179; in the Tuṣita heaven before his final rebirth 1.190, 1.324, 2.18, 2.179, 4.136–7, 10.548; gives Yogācāra teachings to Asaṅga 1.276, 1.359, 12.28, 12.169, 14.260, 17.463–4; simultaneously an ineffable spiritual being and a recognizable historical figure 14.226; Ajita is another name for him 1.330

depicted in art
Ahicchatra image 2.156; Dinoo's painting 21.462–3, 22.283; frequently depicted as a Buddha 2.179; often shown not cross-legged, but seated as though upon a chair 2.179; a statue symbolizing Sangharakshita's dedication to the Dharma 20.134, 21.258

in literature
his advent foretold in the Pāli canon 1.44–5, 1.47, 2.178, 12.747 (n400); appearance in the *Large Perfection of Wisdom sūtra* 2.154; he lives in the Vairocana tower in the *Gaṇḍavyūha Sūtra*, *see Gaṇḍavyūha Sūtra*; *Maitreya-vyākaraṇa* 2.179; mentioned in earlier Sanskrit and mixed Sanskrit works 2.179; in the *Samādhirāja Sūtra* 14.194; Vimalakīrti tells him there is no such thing as a future Buddha 14.162, 16.502–3; in the *Visuddhimagga* Buddhaghosa aspires to attain arhantship in his presence 2.178; in the *White Lotus Sūtra* 2.179, 16.39

worship
could devotion be a unifying factor in modern Buddhism? 1.324, 2.178, 26.699–700; the only bodhisattva recognized through the entire Buddhist world 1.324, 2.178; sometimes as a Buddha, sometimes as a bodhisattva 1.335; taught by Nāgārjuna 1.324; visualized on the Refuge Tree 13.78, 13.205

other associations
appeared in a dream to Master Hanshan Deqing 14.260; attempts by non-Buddhists to identify him with their spiritual heroes 2.179; the five books of Maitreya 14.260, 17.464, 17.489; horse races held in his honour during the Tibetan New Year 2.179, 4.108; as 'Laughing Buddha' 2.182; 'Maitreya' (poem) 25.233; not to be identified with Christ 21.559; one of a group of eight bodhisattvas 2.172; possesses tremendous spiritual significance at the present crisis in history 21.558; Tomo Geshe Rimpoche created a vision of him 1.342

Maitreyabandhu, Dharmachari 'Art For Our Sake' 26.xi–xvii; paints the mural of lotuses at the LBC 10.694 (n233); *The Travellers from Orissa* 26.xvii

Maitreyanātha (*ācārya*, sometimes called Maitreya)

life
Asaṅga's teacher 1.359; confused or conflated with the bodhisattva Maitreya 1.359, 12.168; and the five books of Maitreya 14.260, 17.464; inclined to

synthesis, tried to conciliate various tendencies of Buddhism 1.360; his biography obscure, so can only be gathered from his works 1.359–60; the inspirer of the Yogācāra 1.301, 1.359, 12.168–9

Abhisamayālaṃkāra
introduction 1.301, 14.147–8; commentary on the *Perfection of Wisdom in 25,000 lines* 1.362, 14.147–8; attempt at synthesis 1.361; dominated the exegesis of the *Large Prajñāpāramitā* for centuries 1.362; for Haribhadra's commentary on the text, *see* Haribhadra; recognizes the three *yānas* (*śrāvakayāna* etc.) as grades of one path 1.362; still studied in Tibet and Mongolia 1.362

Madhyāntavibhaṅga
distinction between mind and mental events 17.489–90; one of the five books of Maitreya 17.489; one of Maitreyanātha's five *śāstras* 1.361; reality is both existent and non-existent 1.363; taught by Asaṅga to Vasubandhu 17.489; its title provokes a comparison with Nāgārjuna's *Madhyamakārikā* 1.363; the unreal imagination (*abhūtaparikalpo*) 1.363–4, 1.369

other works
Dharmadharmatāvibhaṅga 1.361; *Sūtralaṃkāra* 1.361, 1.362; *Yogācārabhūmi* 1.401; *Bodhisattvabhūmi* 1.401, 1.420

Maitreyanatha, Dhammachari 10.367

Maitreyaratna, Dhammachari 10.lvi–ix

Maitreya-vyākaraṇa 2.179

maitrī *see mettā*

Maitri Sangha (Bengali) 22.9

Maitrīpa *see* Medripa

Maitriveer Nagarjuna, Dhammachari (Dr Santosh I. Raut) 10.xxii–xxxii, 10.15–20

Maji (Reverend Mother) v8

Majjhima Nikāya

introduction
introduction 3.84, 14.39–42; asceticism described in the *Majjhima Nikāya* 4.679 (n139); descriptions of the different kinds of karma 16.254; Sangharakshita's study of the text 20.302; Sāriputta's teachings 1.121, 4.663 (n26); similarities to the *Vibhaṅga* (Abhidharma work) 14.80; translations 6.xxv, 7.590 (n260), 14.9, 20.302, 23.14, 24.515

Abhayarājakumāra Sutta
the Buddha's meeting with a prince 2.699 (n363); 'As if one should set up again that which had been overthrown' 2.292; a plot to refute the Buddha's doctrine 12.239–40; the time to say what is true, correct, and beneficial 8.xxiv

Acchariya-abbhūta Sutta
the Buddha's marvellous qualities 14.25; story of Queen Māyā 3.629 (n20)

Aggivacchagotta Sutta
does the Buddha exist after death or not? 17.621; the fourfold negation (*catuṣkoti*) 10.689–90 (n202), 13.393; fourteen inexpressibles 13.684 (n61), 17.621; the questions of the wanderer Vacchagotta 1.75–7, 3.647 (n140), 4.700 (n275), 10.696 (n251); the Buddha's silence when Vacchagotta asked if the self exists 13.393–4, 14.461; whether the mind and the body are the same or different 10.225–6, 17.621–3; the Tathāgata has no views 2.391, 3.164, 3.549, 15.334, 17.617; the Tathāgata is deep, immeasurable, unfathomable, like the ocean 2.44, 10.141, 10.449, 10.655

Ākaṅkheyya Sutta
four formless *dhyānas*: 'liberations that are peaceful' 1.563; six *abhijñās* 3.645 (n125)

Alagaddūpama Sutta
eternalism 14.656 (n500); 'Form is not yours, O monks' 1.173; misunderstanding the Dharma is like grasping a water snake the wrong way 14.40, 18.180; hierarchy of Āryasaṅgha 3.684 (n374); 'I teach only suffering and the cessation of suffering' 1.78, 3.213, 7.115, 7.134, 7.222, 26.154; the Parable of the Raft, *see* raft

Ambalaṭṭhikarāhulovāda Sutta
the Buddha's admonitions to his son Rāhula 2.665–6 (n34)

Ānāpānasati Sutta
the mindfulness of breathing 3.675 (n312), 3.694 (n478), 9.516, 9.576n; the seven *bodhyaṅgas* 3.667 (n265), 9.565n

Anāthapiṇḍikovāda Sutta
Sāriputta consoles Anāthapiṇḍika on his deathbed 2.204

Aṅgulimāla Sutta
brief introduction 14.41; the story of Aṅgulimāla 2.238, 3.147–8, 7.550 (n35), 9.142, 9.373–4, 17.274; the *karma-vipāka* Aṅgulimāla had to endure 15.93, 15.747 (n39)

Anupada Sutta
the five mental factors experienced in the first *dhyāna* 4.490, 9.299; anyone speaking truly of me would say, 'A being has arisen ... out of compassion' 1.236

Apaṇṇaka Sutta
the Buddha's description of a devoted householder 4.697 (n256); if you have to choose between eternalism and nihilism, eternalism is better 17.243

Ariyapariyesanā Sutta
brief introduction 14.40; noble and ignoble quest 2.413, 3.207–8, 9.528, 10.636, 11.312, 12.548, 12.619–20, 14.591; the going forth 2.663 (n15), 3.107, 3.685–6 (n393), 11.397, 12.549, 12.620, 12.624; Siddhārtha masters the teachings of the teachers he consults 3.51, 10.257–8; Siddhārtha's experience of *arūpa-dhyānas* 2.111; the possibility that someone might enjoy sense-pleasures and remain unattached 17.221; description of Enlightenment 3.631 (n34); gaining the doctrine 'profound and hard to see' 1.90–1, 3.175, 3.181, 17.324; 'Whom should I point out as my teacher?' 15.48, 15.746 (n23); Brahmā Sahāmpati's request, *see* Brahma Sahāmpati's request; vision of humanity as a bed of lotuses, *see under* Brahmā Sahāmpati's request; 'Wide open are the doors of the Deathless', *see under* deathless; 'I beat the drum of the Deathless', *see under* deathless; the meeting with Upāka, *see under* Upāka; teaching the first five disciples 3.641 (n83), 11.415–17; the four noble truths 3.627 (n11); implication of the positive nature of Nirvāṇa 10.633, 10.636; the Buddha to the monks: either keep silent or talk about the Dharma 3.38; other monks begging food on the Buddha's behalf 14.401; the Buddha refers to himself as the *bodhisatta* 14.569

Assalāyana Sutta
Assalāyana tries to argue against the Buddha, but ends up a lay follower 2.665 (n30)

Bahudhātuka Sutta
it would be impossible for someone possessing right view to commit the five heinous crimes 3.637 (n70), 18.661 (n182)

Bālapaṇḍita Sutta
the time it would take one born in a hell realm to regain the human state 13.682 (n53)

Bhayabherava Sutta
the Buddha describes his fear in the forest 3.51, 3.634 (n50), 12.620, 16.590 (n36), 26.153; he describes his mind as malleable 19.598 (n42); he experiences Enlightenment in the watches of the night 2.663 (n17), 3.632 (n35); he sees his previous existences and those of other beings 2.15, 3.115, 12.689; 'There is no more existence for me in conditions such as these' 1.179

Bhūmija Sutta
the goal isn't reached by wrong means any more than milk comes from a cow's horn 14.42

Brahmāyu Sutta
Going for Refuge to Gotama the Buddha 15.589; the thirty-two marks 14.426, 14.642–3 (n399)

Caṅkī Sutta
the brahmins and their teachers like the blind leading the blind 14.42

Channovāda Sutta
there is agitation for one who is dependent 10.724 (n505)

Cūḷa-assapura Sutta
the *brahma-vihāras* 1.157

Cūḷadhammasamādāna Sutta
a tree spirit is threatened by a creeper 10.708 (n377)

Cūḷadukkhakkhandha Sutta
the Buddha is happier than the king 3.271–2, 3.663 (n247)

Cūḷagopālaka Sutta
faith-followers and doctrine-followers 11.157, 11.748 (n122); those who walk in faith, like a calf carried across a stream 1.291, 15.767 (n210), 17.710 (n39)

Cūḷagosinga Sutta
the Buddha visits Anuruddha and his friends 3.635 (n55), 3.670 (n287), 12.606–7

Cūḷahatthipadopama Sutta
a brahmin plot to disprove the Buddha's doctrine 12.239–40; Jāṇussoṇī becomes a lay follower of the Buddha 15.627–8

Cūḷakammavibhaṅgha Sutta
the evil-doer making himself that which his enemy would wish him to be 4.390; karma 4.396, 16.254, 16.616 (n245); karmic consequences of actions in terms of rebirth 2.71–2; ugliness is a karmic consequences of anger 4.390

Cūḷamāluṅkya Sutta
brief introduction 14.40; the fourfold negation (*catuṣkoti*) 10.689–90 (n202); the ten inexpressibles 17.750 (n322); the parable of the poisoned arrow 1.112, 4.374, 16.93–4, 16.192

Cūḷasakuludāyi Sutta
'This being, that becomes' 1.89, 2.700 (n374), 4.647, 14.650 (n452), 17.710 (n38)

Cūḷasīhanāda Sutta
'Destroyed is (re-)birth' 2.139

Cūḷasuññata Sutta
the four *arūpa dhyānas* 4.682 (n165); a principal locus of the *śūnyatā* teaching 14.136; remaining in an 'attitude of emptiness' 4.682 (n165); the word *suññatā* used in general terms 14.350–1

Cūḷavedalla Sutta
the Buddha gives his blessing to Dhammadinnā's teaching 7.494, 16.590 (n37); Dhammadinnā's teaching on conditionality 3.68, 15.466

Dakkiṇāvibhaṅga Sutta
the giving of robes to the sangha 3.395

Dantabhūmi Sutta
'Teach the Dharma that is good in the beginning, good in the middle, and good at the end' 21.473

Devadūta Sutta
description of hell 15.771 (n240)

Dhammadāyāda Sutta
the disciples: heirs of the Dharma, not heirs of worldly things 1.236, 15.155, 15.750 (n68)

Dhātuvibhaṅga Sutta
six element practice 5.484–5

Dvedhāvitakka Sutta
'Here are the roots of trees' 3.635 (n54)

Gaṇakamoggallāna Sutta
spiritual life as training a mettlesome young horse 2.706 (n420), 4.460–1

Ghaṭīkāra Sutta
the *Jātaka* story of Ghaṭikāra and Jotipāla 14.62, 14.63

Gopakamoggallāna Sutta
the Buddha as the shower of the way 11.359–60, 15.546; no monk has the qualities of the Buddha 1.54–5

Isigili Sutta
the Discourse at Isigili 8.532

Jīvaka Sutta
conditions in which monks were permitted to eat meat 10.49, 14.40, 17.585; no counterpart to this *sutta* in the Chinese version of the *Majjhima Nikāya* 14.40

Kakacūpama Sutta
brief introduction 14.40; the parable of the saw (patiently sawn limb from limb by bandits) 1.437, 4.121, 8.200, 13.577; the story of the servant girl and her angry mistress 9.522, 9.577 (n402); 'we will suffuse the whole world with loving thoughts' 4.121

Kandaraka Sutta
'Teach the Dharma that is good in the beginning, good in the middle, and good at the end 21.473, 21.632 (n145)

Kaṇṇakatthala Sutta
as a fire can be kindled from any fuel, all castes are capable of spiritual attainment 14.42

Kīṭāgiri Sutta
a *bhikkhu* who is freed in both ways (*ubhatobhāgavimutta*) 2.682 (n196); seven kinds of followers (one freed by faith etc.) 2.737 (n651), 4.709 (n333), 10.685 (n172)

Kosambiya Sutta
the quarrel at Kosambi 3.77, 10.323–4

Māgandiya Sutta
Māgandiya the wanderer 2.716 (n492)

Mahā-Assapura Sutta
the Buddha's three similes for Enlightenment 13.192–3, 14.42; description of the four *dhyānas* 3.671 (n289), 4.154–5, 4.708 (n322), 9.201, 11.124–6, 13.315; the period after the Buddha's Enlightenment 10.262

Mahācattārīsaka Sutta
the mundane and transcendental Noble Eightfold Path 15.597; right view 7.522; pernicious views: actions don't have consequences, no one is highly developed 17.594

Mahādukkhakkhanda Sutta
violence due to sensuous craving 7.238

Mahāgosiṅga Sutta
monks have an *Abhidhamma-kathaṃ*, a discussion about the Dharma 14.72

Mahāhatthipadopama Sutta
six element practice 3.647 (n138), 19.617 (n175)

Mahākammavibhaṅgha Sutta
karmic consequences of actions in terms of rebirth 2.71–2

Mahāmāluṅkya Sutta
the fourteen (or ten) inexpressibles 2.63, 17.750 (n322)

Mahārāhulovāda Sutta
six element practice 3.676–7 (n318)

Mahāsaccaka Sutta
Siddhārtha's experience under the rose-apple tree 2.20, 2.110–11, 3.629 (n21), 5.391–3, 15.222; his experience of the

arūpa-dhyānas 2.111; his practice of austerities 2.21, 3.51, 9.219–220; the *devas* offer him celestial nourishment, but he refuses 10.448, 22.285; he gives up austerities 3.686 (n398); his disciples leave him in disgust 3.52, 3.634; the pleasure that arose could not obsess [lay hold of] his mind 2.108, 17.528, 18.581; the Buddha's Enlightenment experience 1.94–5, 3.631–2 (n31); he sees his previous existences and those of other beings 3.115, 4.373, 10.434; he sees everything as being subject to conditionality 3.97; he sees how all beings are reborn according to their karma 3.32, 14.650 (n453); Saccaka is impressed by the Buddha, but does not go for Refuge 2.716 (n492); Saccaka is insolent to the Buddha 13.683 (n57)

Mahāsakuludāyi Sutta
images for the *dhyānas* 3.671 (n289), 4.708 (n322), 11.124–6, 13.315

Mahāsīhanāda Sutta
the ten powers of a Tathāgata 1.59, 3.665 (n255), 10.40, 10.670 (n71); *cetovimutti* and *paññavimutti* 13.695–6 (n142), 17.733 (n196)

Mahāsuññata Sutta
a principal locus of the *śūnyatā* teaching 14.136; the word *suññatā* used in general terms 14.350–1

Mahātaṇhāsaṅkhaya Sutta
the hindrances 1.153; list of attributes of the Dharma 3.627 (n13); restraint of the senses 1.148; 'This being, that becomes' 3.183, 16.587 (n24); the twelve cyclical *nidānas* 13.682 (n54), 19.614 (n151)

Mahāvacchagotta Sutta
lay followers gain Enlightenment 9.390, 9.570 (n344); lay followers make good progress on the path, though not fully Enlightened 2.716 (n492)

Naḷakapāna Sutta
women's capacity for Enlightenment 16.617 (n255)

Nivāpa Sutta
monks, like deer, should not stray from their pastures, or they may come to harm 18.34

Potaliya Sutta
sensual pleasures don't satisfy any more than a meatless bone satisfies a dog 14.42

Rathavinīta Sutta
the 'Relay of Chariots' 3.291, 10.248; teaching of the seven *visuddhis* 3.290–1, 4.716 (n375), 10.248–51, 10.578–9, 11.306

Sabbāsava Sutta
avoiding the question of whether the self exists or not 11.755 (n201); wise use of monastic requisites 1.149

Saccavibhaṅgha Sutta
profound 'philosophical' exposition 8.532

Sāleyyaka Sutta
a court case as an illustration of truthfulness 3.322; heavenly realms 16.597 (n94); the ten precepts 11.747 (n118)

Sallekha Sutta
all wholesome states lead downwards and all wholesome states lead upwards 11.657–8

Sāmagāma Sutta
the Buddha's confidence on agreement about the Dharma after his death 11.369–70

Sandaka Sutta
nihilism 14.656 (n500)

Satipaṭṭhāna Sutta
history 15.79–80, 15.234–7; the meaning of *satipaṭṭhāna* 15.82, 15.747 (n34); all its teachings have one goal: transformation 15.242; the basis of the Abhidharma 15.161; Buddhaghosa's commentary 15.106–7, 15.169–70, 15.226, 15.235; translation by Bhikkhu Bodhi 15.79–243; the *bhikkhu*: 'ardent, fully aware, and mindful' 15.217; definitions of mindfulness 15.80–2; Dharmapala's study of the text 8.34, 8.91; the four foundations of mindfulness 15.82–4, 17.87; clear comprehension of the activities of daily life 15.97, 15.113–22; mindfulness of the body 10.512, 15.82, 15.101, 15.111, 15.119–22, 15.243; the right place, time, and posture for meditation 15.102; the mindfulness of breathing 3.675 (n312), 3.694 (n478), 15.101–12; the monk 'lives detached' 15.121; 'having put away covetousness and grief for the world' 15.202; contemplation of the impurities of the body 15.123–31; the body like a bag of mixed grains 15.123–4, 15.187; contemplation of the elements 1.160, 15.132–9; contemplation of decay 1.155, 15.140–8; contemplation of feelings 15.149–59; contemplation of the mind and mental objects 15.160–89; description of mental states 15.160–3; *mahaggata* 5.272, 5.726 (n261), 15.163; contemplating mind internally and externally 15.164–7; the five hindrances 15.168–78; 'Set up mindfulness in front of you' 15.104, 15.173; the five

skandhas 1.101, 15.179–89; recollection of the six sense bases and their objects 15.199–211, 18.10–11; contemplation of the seven *bodhyaṅgas* 15.212–26; the liberated state of consciousness 15.226; contemplation of the four noble truths 15.227–37; the reason for 'internal' and 'external' contemplations 15.235–7; 'the direct way to the transcending of sorrow' 1.218, 15.79–81, 15.241, 15.243, 17.87; the fruit of developing the foundations of mindfulness for seven days 15.238–9, 15.242

Sekha Sutta
the Buddha gives his approval to a disciple's teaching 16.590 (n37)

Sela Sutta
the Buddha says that Sāriputta is his general 3.633 (n46)

Sevitabbāsevitabba Sutta
ten precepts 1.633 (n423), 2.327–8, 2.347–8

Tevijjavacchagotta Sutta
the threefold knowledge 1.78–9, 10.670–1 (n73)

Upakkilesa Sutta
the Buddha visits Anuruddha and his companions 19.599–600 (n55)

Upāli Sutta
the Buddha as a *yakkha*, a mighty spirit 10.708 (n375); the Buddha is said to attract people by means of spells 2.665 (n31); Jains dispute doctrine with the Buddha 23.528 (n388); Upāli 'attained the Dhamma' 2.701 (n378)

Vammika Sutta
the ever-smouldering anthill 11.719, 16.586 (n16); the serpent: one who has destroyed the *āsavas* 1.309–10, 14.346

Vatthūpama Sutta
'The mind of the happy one becomes concentrated' 2.109, 15.221

Vekhanassa Sutta
'I go for Refuge' 2.728 (n600)

Vīmaṃsaka Sutta
the noble disciple believes in the Enlightenment of the Buddha 15.588

Vitakkasaṇṭhāna Sutta
antidotes to the five hindrances, with similes 1.559, 4.382, 13.685 (n70), 19.599 (n52); the fifth antidote: ask yourself 'Why am I feeling like this?' 5.347

makara (mythological beast) 13.184–5

Makkhali Gosāla (contemporary of the Buddha) 17.242

mālā (rosary) the giving of a single *mālā* bead 18.116, 22.337; Sangharakshita gives Terry Delamare his *mālā* 23.141

Malabar 20.298

Malalasekara, Dr Gunapala Piyasena
introduction 8.682 (n108); an active lay Buddhist, and High Commissioner for Sri Lanka 12.126; Ambassador for Ceylon in the USSR 23.158; as a scholar 7.445, 7.616 (n483); attacked by the *Buddhist World* 8.172, 22.178, 23.158; author of the *Dictionary of Pāli Proper Names* 23.158; 'Buddhism and Worship' 8.362; defence of the making of Buddhist films 7.240; *Encyclopaedia of Buddhism* 8.400–2, 14.82, 14.88, 14.618 (n111); founder of the World Fellowship of Buddhists 2.746 (n702), 23.158; a great Buddhist 6.621; introduction 7.565 (n109), 7.604 (n344); a mutual friend in London 24.245; photographs 11.474, 23.33; *Thus Have I Heard* 7.65

Malaysia Alor Star 24.37–9; the FWBO (later Triratna) in Malaysia 24.46, 24.617 (n64); officially Muslim 9.350–1, 10.280; Malaysian Buddhist Association 24.36–7, 24.38; the Malaysian countryside 24.38, 24.42–3; Malaysian nuns chanting 24.36–7; Ipoh 24.43–6; its beautiful traditional culture 11.352; Penang 24.34–7, 24.53–5, 26.668; publications 24.34–5; Ramakrishna Mission 7.106–13; Sangharakshita visits 10.276, 24.34–46; talks given in Malaysia and their effects 24.35, 24.40, 24.44–6, 24.54; talks on the Noble Eightfold Path published 12.367, 24.35–6; Young Buddhist Association of Malaysia 10.li, 24.34–5, 24.38

male is there a difference between 'male' and 'female' energy? 17.74–6; positivity and male conditioning 4.597; Pure Land inhabited by male bodies 1.339; *see also* masculine

malice a cruel desire to inflict pain, the opposite of *mettā* 15.302–3 17.665; the

most unskilful of all mental states 16.296, 17.269, 17.666; it finds expression in Western culture 17.665; the malice of little boys 1.498–9, 3.688 (n429), 9.573n, 10.476–7, 10.556–7, 16.429, 17.665; *vihiṃsā* as *upakleśa* (Abhidharma) 17.664–6

Malini, Dharmacharini 2.734 (n633), 11.729

Malla, Dr (Nepal) 20.435, 20.440

Mallander, J. O. brief introduction 24.643 (n185); contact with Sangharakshita 24.154, 26.214–16; *In the Realm of the Lotus* 26.213–59

Mallas republican tribe in ancient India 10.533; the Buddha travels among the Mallas 10.622–7; lay claim to the Buddha's relics 16.141–2; a Nepalese descendant of the Mallas 20.435

malleable the Buddha describes his mind as malleable 19.598 (n42); through meditation the mind becomes more malleable, more *ḍākinī*-like 19.143

Mallikā, Queen asks the Buddha why she is so plain 10.544; discusses with King Pasenadi whether one holds anyone dearer than one's own self 10.543–6

Mallinātha 11.406

Malory, Thomas 15.221–2, 25.99

Māluṅkyaputta (the Buddha's disciple) 10.709 (n382)

Malva, Zarin 21.xv, 21.462

Malvern *Piers Plowman* set in the Malvern Hills 24.581; Sangharakshita visits (1997) 24.580–1

Māmakī ('mine-maker') brief description 17.729 (n166); appears in verses to Tārā 17.146; consort of Ratnasambhava 12.222, 13.315; the aspect of the Enlightened mind that appreciates all equally 12.222, 13.315, 14.495, 15.121

Mamaki (Order member) 4.286

Mammon 8.xxiv, 8.197, 18.507

māṃsa-cakṣus *see under* five eyes

Man *see* human being

man of naught *see akiñcana*

māna *see* arrogance

manana *see* attention

manas *see* eight *vijñānas*/*kliṣṭa-mano-vijñāna*

manaskāra (Pāli *manasikāra*, mental activity) and the *ālaya-vijñāna* 1.369; as omnipresent mental event (egocentric demanding) 17.531

Manasarovar, Lake 12.574, 14.538–9

Manchester, England an evening in the city 24.131–2; the City Art Gallery 12.533, 24.134; Lady Lever Art Gallery, Port Sunlight 24.381; modern art gallery 24.134

Manchester Buddhist Centre opening of the new centre 12.533, 12.543–4; dedication of the shrine-room 12.533; the effect of a bomb in Manchester 11.651, 12.544; Gridhrakuta community 24.67, 24.130–2, 24.134, 24.145; history of the centre 12.533; a poetry reading on friendship 24.381

Manchester Buddhist Society 23.141

mandala

what is a mandala?
brief introduction 19.516–17; the archetypal image of concentration 18.125; a circle of symbolic forms (Snellgrove) 2.96, 12.211, 18.125; combining the clear, pure conscious mind and the rich, colourful unconscious 12.218; essentially a group of things surrounding something in the centre 18.446; mandala-like patterns produced by musical sounds 18.283; sometimes translated as 'magic circle', but it is not magic but spiritual 1.513, 12.211; 'Take any prominent aspect of reality and surround it with beauty' 14.518; we find mandalas everywhere: Jung, quincunxes, rose windows 12.218

symbolism
the palace as three-dimensional mandala 18.525; the path implies time, the mandala implies space 18.584, 19.436–7; seeing the whole of existence as a mandala 18.446–7; symbol of integration 12.218–23, 18.522–5; universal symbol 12.218

Buddhist mandalas
the mandala emerged at a critical stage in Indian Buddhism 12.219; all Buddhist mandalas follow the same pattern 12.211; created by the positive effect of a bodhisattva 4.97–8; a diagram of a mandala 13.235; finding one's place in the mandala of the sangha 4.98; *gaurīs* stop people leaving by means of hooks of attraction 16.362; the idea of the *dharmadhātu* as a mandala is not to be taken literally 14.604–5; integration on the highest possible level, Enlightenment 12.218–19; mandalas need space 25.336; Milarepa's body is like a mandala, embodying all aspects of Buddha nature

19.517; a picture of the contents of our own mind 12.219; the Pure Land as mandala 2.132, 18.525; spiritual life is finding your true place in the mandala 18.447; their gates guarded by the four great kings 16.352; work in a similar way to *kasiṇa* practice 1.154–5

the greater mandala
the bodhisattva's rearrangement of the universe into a mandala 14.518; nature can remind us of it 14.519–20; you may have realized it, but for the world it is still an ideal to be realized 17.609; three concentric circles: mandalas of usefulness, work on yourself, and myth 18.318; learning to live within a greater mandala of aesthetic appreciation 14.518–24, 17.609

personal mandalas
almost everything can be included 13.317–18, 18.524–5; the mandala of our own life can become the mandala of the five Buddhas 13.318; simple and complex mandalas 13.317; how to create a personal mandala 13.316–18, 18.522–6; incorporating your gestalt into a higher pattern 18.279–80; putting yourself at the centre – the real you, the person you could become 13.317; the spiritual life in terms of building up a mandala 12.223, 21.259; placing the Buddha at the centre 2.324–5, 13.316–17, 18.509, 18.524; sexual relationships 11.578–80, 11.587, 12.488, 13.449–50, 18.509, 19.475; the Theravādin approach 13.317; two mandalas: a present one and an ideal one 18.523–5

see also
offering the mandala

mandala of the Five Buddhas

introduction
brief introduction 11.127, 13.83, 19.405; description 12.212–17; illustration 13.303, 17.487; one of the most beautiful and meaningful patterns in the Tantra 13.316; getting a feeling for the mandala through its concrete details 18.601; called the five *Jinas* or the five *Tathāgatas* 13.304; the term '*Dhyāni* Buddhas' is not used by Buddhists 13.304, 18.601; correlations between the Five Buddhas and Blake's four Zoas 8.556–8, 26.345–7; a three-dimensional model of a mandala palace 22.471

history
the nucleus out of which the mandala was developed 2.173, 13.298–304; how the mandala arose 13.303–4; based on episodes in the historical Buddha's life 13.302–4; prefigured by the four-Buddha mandala of the *Sūtra of Golden Light* 16.260–1; the diamond sphere of the Buddha cut into five facets 5.596–7, 13.304, 18.601–2; the development of the symbolism of the five Buddhas 13.296–305; many of its Buddhas and bodhisattvas became the object of cults 13.304–5; initiation into the mandala (on the Tibetan Buddhist path) 12.297

symbolism
the palace of the mandala 12.221; the path and the mandala or palace the two great images of Buddhism 18.525, 18.584; all its elements represent different aspects of the Enlightenment experience 13.318; playing around with the symbolism of the mandala 13.311; symbol of integration 12.218–23; eventually the whole of existence, the whole psyche, becomes a great mandala 12.221; the path connecting the wheel of life to the mandala of the Five Buddhas 1.484; the mandala of our own life can become the mandala of the five Buddhas 13.318; appearance of the mandala in the *bardo* after death 8.558, 12.204

central figure
identifying with the deity at the centre of the mandala 14.461; not Śākyamuni, but one of the *sambhogakāya* forms 13.307–8, 18.602; that the central figure is usually Vairocana or Akṣobhya is historical accident 13.307; Vairocana in many early forms 13.305–6; when figures move towards the centre they become white 13.305–6; place in the centre the figure at the centre of your practice 13.307–8, 18.602–3

the Buddhas and their consorts
association of each Buddha with a different time of day 16.598 (n99); correlation with five elements, *skandhas*, senses, etc. 1.263, 2.706 (n418), 8.557; the relationships between the *mudrās* (gestures) of the Buddhas 13.311, 18.600; the five Buddhas,

'male' and 'female' 13.296–318; male and female forms in sexual union 13.311–13; masculine and feminine aspects, the feminine bringing warmth 18.601; sexual symbolism 12.221–2

other elements of the mandala
you enter the mandala from the east 13.311; aspects of each Buddha represented by attendant bodhisattvas 13.304; bodhisattvas and *dharmapālas* 18.601; the eight cremation grounds 12.220–1, 13.233–6; the guardians of the gates of the mandala 12.221; surrounded by three circles: flames, *vajras*, and lotuses 12.220, 13.234; wrathful forms of the Buddhas 13.315–16; the 'sixth Buddha', Vajrasattva 13.83, 22.504

see also
Buddha families, *see under* Buddhas; five knowledges or wisdoms, *see* five *jñānas*; Vairocana; Akṣobhya; Ratnasambhava; Amitābha; Amoghasiddhi

Mandalay 9.70

Mandapam, India 20.230

mandārava 11.234

Mandeville, Bernard de 11.604, 11.765 (n322)

Manegaon, India 10.116–17

Maṅgala Sutta

introduction
the meaning of the title 15.380; addressed to a *deva* 1.33, 4.662 (n22), 13.586; chanted at the first ever celebration of Buddha Day in the United States (1897) 8.55; its meaning explained in Nagpur 22.161; its metrical form 15.xiii; *Life's Highest Blessing* (commentary by Soni) 8.384–5; Sangharakshita's translation 15.xiii, 15.61–2; seminar (*Auspicious Signs*) 15.xx, 15.379–454; subject of a sermon in Mulund, India 10.141; the Buddha seeking to give existing beliefs a positive twist 15.380–1; the *sutta's* verses represent the substance of the Buddha's teaching 15.381; Tibetan translation 8.660

the text
the first few verses are about Dharma practice as a householder 15.407; serving the wise, not serving fools 15.384–5; the worship of the worshipful 15.388–92; in a fair land to dwell 15.392–5; meritorious works done in the past 15.395–400; to have set oneself on the right path 15.400–3; a path of regular steps 15.400, 15.406; learning and skill, being trained in discipline, well-spoken words 15.403–6; family and occupation 15.407–15; generosity and good deeds 15.416–21; 'He whose firm mind ... is void of sorrow' 11.35; restraint 15.421–4; reverence and gratitude 3.598, 10.318, 15.425–36; timely hearing of the Dharma 15.436–9; forbearance and conversation 15.439–46; 'a godly life' 15.446–51; the eight worldly winds 2.117, 3.159–60, 15.452–3, 22.183; undefeated 15.453; 'we should honour those worthy of honour' 8.511, 8.704 (n307), 10.318, 13.270, 17.276–7

Mangala, Dharmachari (Eric Wright) 23.465, 23.540 (n486), v24

Mangalo (English *bhikkhu*) 8.336, 12.80, v23

mango *see under* trees

Mani 3.429, 3.431–2

Maṇi Kabum *see under* Tibetan Buddhism/literature

***maṇi* wheel or cylinder** 11.27, 22.27

Manicheism contact with Padmasambhava 12.289; its destruction 13.103; distinction between the God of this world (a demon) and the spiritual God 15.623; emphasis on beauty 3.432; influenced Buddhism? 3.431–2; persecution of Manicheans 3.432; principles 3.431, 13.103; rise and fall 3.431–2; the story of Barlaam and Josaphat 13.662; Sufism's connection with Manicheism 3.429

Mañjughoṣa (or Mañjuśrī), the bodhisattva of wisdom

introduction
description 1.432, 2.174–5, 13.293–5, 16.376; the etymology of his name 17.462, 26.232; where does he come from? 16.529; sixty-four-fold voice 2.174; 'To Mañjuśrī' (sonnet) 25.275

iconography
description 4.192, 4.657, 13.293; Arapacana form 2.174, 26.232; eternal youth 16.527–8; like wisdom, he is beautiful and never grows old 17.462; holds the book of wisdom to his heart 1.432, 11.292, 13.295; holds the sword of knowledge 1.432, 2.174, 3.54, 10.81, 11.292, 13.367, 17.462; lotus 1.432, 2.174; put aside the traditional iconography and ask yourself, 'What is Mañjughoṣa?' 4.195; wearing a wreath of five blue lotuses 26.474; *yab-yum* form never popularized 16.376–7; illustration 13.294; a thangka given by Jamyang Khyentse Rimpoche 22.406–7

names
the gentle-voiced one 16.232; introduction to his many names 2.173–4; Sanskrit: Kumārabhūta, Mañjunātha, Vagīśvara, Mahāmati 2.173, 17.462, 26.474; Tibetan: Jambeyang 2.173; Chinese: Man-shu-shi-li, Wénshū 2.173; Japanese: Monju 2.173

what he represents
he corresponds to wisdom, transmuted intellect 2.173; the embodiment of *Buddhavacana* 3.90–1; the embodiment of the four analytical knowledges (*pratisaṃvids*) 16.491; the embodiment of wisdom 11.292, 26.232; his gentle wisdom 17.462; a hypostasis of the Buddha's transcendental wisdom 26.474; he represents archetypal reality, myth 16.528; he represents spiritual wisdom as communicated 24.xix; in him, culture is fully absorbed 16.377; the personification of the transformation of thought into wisdom 7.303–4

associations and comparisons
association with the lion 2.174, 18.19, 26.289; association with the *Saptaśatikā*, *see Saptaśatikā*; association with writing and public speaking 16.490, 26.250–1; patron of arts and sciences 2.174, 4.192, 13.134, 24.xix, 26.474; and the sacred mountain Wutaishan 2.224; comparison with the Egyptian god Thoth 26.474; comparison with Pallas Athene 16.385

his place in the tradition
Sanankumāra (Brahmā) in the *Mahāgovinda Sutta* perhaps corresponds to him 5.218; link with Avalokiteśvara, Vajrapāṇi, and Green Tārā 26.663–4; occupies a prominent place in Devotional Buddhism 1.336; one of a group of eight bodhisattvas 2.172; in the Śākya Trinity 2.180; the inspirational source of the Madhyamaka 17.463; and the Perfection of Wisdom 1.70–1, 1.73; a Perfection of Wisdom text attributed to him 14.153; Sarasvatī regarded as his consort in Tantric Buddhism 16.376; he taught Padmasambhava astrology 8.522; one of the three principal bodhisattvas of the Tibetan pantheon 7.304; Yamāntaka his emanation 2.178; his Buddha-field 14.176; in Vajrayāna texts 2.174; an important figure for the Gelugpas 17.463; a work revealed by him to Tsongkhapa 8.508; Tsongkhapa regarded as a manifestation of Mañjuśrī 2.182, 13.34; Jamyang Khyentse Rimpoche considered to be a manifestation 26.474; dialogue with Wuzhuo (Zen) 8.488

in the Mahāyāna sūtras
association with the Perfection of Wisdom 2.174; he asks why Vinaya regulations are necessary 14.186; he engages in discussion with a girl who turns herself into a boy 14.183; he tests an eight-year-old girl's understanding of *śūnyatā* 14.185; he rushes towards the Buddha with a sword to kill him 14.182–3; in the *Mahāparinirvāṇa Sūtra* 14.231; in the *Śūraṅgama Sūtra* 13.358–60, 14.197; in the *Śūraṅgama-samādhi Sūtra* 26.546; in the *White Lotus Sūtra* 2.173, 16.39, 16.47; *see also under Diamond Sūtra*; *Gaṇḍavyūha Sūtra*; *Laṅkāvatāra Sūtra*; *Smaller Sukhāvatī-vyūha*; *Vimalakīrti-nirdeśa*

stuti sādhana
description of the practice 13.293–5; for many years one of Sangharakshita's main practices 26.546, 26.663; Going for Refuge and the *brahma vihāras* 5.541–2, 5.578–9; hymn of praise 2.174–5, 2.685 (n238); Mañjughoṣa as 'kind sun of speech' 25.56; 'May sentient beings possess happiness with its causes' 5.197; the colophon: the four *pratisaṃvids* 16.491; resolution of the tension between subject and object 15.529; a way to insight 5.448; a retreat held at Adhisthana 26.663; seminar on 5.xxxi–ii

his mantra, oṃ a ra pa ca na dhīḥ
as you recite it, you feel that you are absorbing wisdom 13.295; last syllable, *dhīḥ* 2.127, 13.295; repeating his mantra we are invoking our own innate wisdom 13.287; for retentive memory, understanding of the Dharma, eloquence, power of speech 4.192

the effects of invoking him
he goes to extreme lengths to free bodhisattvas from obsessive remorse 14.183; to aid clarity in writing 26.250–1;

a retentive memory, scriptural knowledge, understanding, power of exposition 2.174

see also
Sangharakshita's initiation, *see under* Sangharakshita V/*sādhanas* and initiations

Manjula (Mrs Mitter's residence) v21

Mañjunātha (name of Mañjuśrī) 2.173

Manjunatha, Dharmachari v24

Manjuraja, Dharmachari v24

Mañjuśrī *see* Mañjughoṣa

Manjusri Thero (Sri Lankan painter) 7.445, 7.616 (n485)

Mañjuśrī-Buddhakṣetra-guṇa-vyūha 14.176

Mañjuśrī-mūla-kalpa 2.174

Manjuvajra, Dharmachari 17.110, v24

Mankazi Lama (Darjeeling) v20

Manmad, India 9.293, 9.300–1

Mann, Thomas 26.380

Mannerheim, Field Marshal v22

manners and etiquette breach of etiquette at the Hampstead Buddhist Vihara 23.21–2; Buddhist should cultivate good manners 6.xxxi, 12.403–4, 12.486–7; courtesy at a Thai airport 24.33; courtesy between followers of different religions 15.670–1, 15.676–9; courtesy paves the way for friendly communication 12.404; domestic, public, and religious 10.180; the link between ethics and good manners is very Buddhistic 4.337, 6.xxxi, 22.427; genuine belief, not just saying something as spiritual good manners 19.538–9; good manners a feature of popular Buddhism 2.232; hypocrisy: the politeness of an official to the man he imprisoned 4.338; manners and conventions as skilful means 19.255; manners need not be formal, one just needs general politeness 12.403–4; more conventional people may be better at observing courtesies 4.320; not doing harm, or causing annoyance or inconvenience, to other people 4.336–7; section of the Vinaya on etiquette 13.413; to talk of etiquette rather than rules is to reduce natural morality to conventional morality 13.413; the value of good manners is not to be underestimated 3.538

Manning, Cardinal 11.339, 12.228

Manoharā (*kinnarī*) 2.332–3

manomayakāya (mind-made body) the body through which one has supersensory experience 17.622; Pāli canon refers to it in the list of psychic powers 1.254–5, 1.443, 13.299, 17.622; traditional similes for its production 1.167; association with Lokottaravādin thinking 1.256–8; Sangharakshita experiences it in an 'out-of-body' experience 23.130

mano-vijñāna *see* eight *vijñānas*

Man-shu-shi-li 2.173

Mantegna, Andrea 23.255, 23.257, 23.259, 23.511 (n288), 24.273, 24.676 (n333)

Mantranaya *see* Mantrayāna

mantras

introduction
descriptions 3.671 (n291), 11.287–90, 16.166–7; etymology of 'mantra' 3.671 (n291), 11.287, 13.287–8, 16.166–7; origins 16.182–3; the symbolism of mantric sound 13.287–91; it is customary not to translate mantras 11.288, 26.233; meanings 5.631, 10.174; connection with the throat-centre 4.314; mantras contrasted with *dhāraṇīs* 16.497

definitions
a string of syllables from the Sanskrit alphabet 11.288–9, 13.289–90, 19.32; not susceptible to conceptual analysis 11.289, 13.290; the sound symbol of a Buddha or bodhisattva 11.288, 11.290, 13.290, 14.515, 16.167; given by the guru at initiation 11.290, 13.290–1, 26.700; a group of words or sounds imbued with spiritual power 26.698; phrases used to invoke the dormant spiritual forces within our minds 16.167; a short and simple prayer 17.418

notes on mantras
being given a mantra in a dream or in a meditation 13.291; the expression of inner realization in speech 1.512; hearing all sounds as mantras 5.607; how do they spark off a particular quality? 16.183; if you repeat the mantra, the Buddha or bodhisattva will be there 17.418; as important a part of *sādhana* as visualization? 5.628, 5.630; it has to be repeated, or its power will be lost 11.290, 13.291; *japa* (Hinduism) meant to go on day and night 7.100; like calling someone's name – you invoke them and they appear 4.314, 13.290; one traverses the Vajrayāna path with the help of

a mantra 26.699; poetry as a kind of mantra 26.211–12, 26.394; the power of a mantra 17.418; repeating a mantra once in Kalimpong like a hundred times elsewhere 22.468–9; a slender thread of contact with reality 1.578; speech simplified into *mantra* 7.320; their efficacy is not just about sonic vibrations (Govinda) 11.288, 13.288, 22.30; to teach others you need many books, but for yourself one mantra may suffice 14.348; a way of keeping in touch with one's ideals 3.309

chanting and reciting mantras
the brahmins who tried to kindle fire through reciting mantras 19.62–3; calling up our own inner forces 13.287; can mantra chanting produce weighty karma? 17.526; can you enter *dhyāna* while reciting a mantra? 5.595–6; a catalyst for the inner feeling 11.288; chanting mantras for healing 18.311; chanting mantras to work with turbulent energies 18.78–9; chanting them softly is just as efficacious as chanting louder 14.535; and *dhyāna* 5.631–2; the effect of chanting mantras 13.291, 18.430; the effect of repetition 5.461, 22.29–30; a good way of using energy 9.531; if you neglect to repeat it, its energy is lost 13.291; an *inner* sound 11.288; an integral part of the life of Triratna 13.415–16; an integrating effect 5.601; it's very important to be wholehearted about it 14.515; Malaysian nuns chanting, like birds skimming above the waves 24.36–7; occupies an extremely important place in the Tantra 13.288–9; the recitation is only a means to the subtle internal experience 13.288; to get rid of Māra 5.351; to retain a meditative state of mind while out and about 18.423–4; a way into devotional practice 4.298, 4.306; a way of freeing the mind from convoluted thinking 14.515

see also
individual mantras, *see under* the relevant Buddha or bodhisattva; *śūnyatā* mantra, *see oṃ svabhāva …*; visualizing a mantra, *see under* visualization during the practice

Mantrayāna (or Mantranaya) can the power it generates be used to protect Buddhism? 26.700; the earlier name for the Vajrayāna 13.288; the exoteric Tantra 13.22; School of Tantric Buddhism 1.384–5, 11.290–1, 16.359; the *mantrayāna* and the *bodhisattvayāna* 26.699; the Mantrayāna and the Pārimitāyāna 11.290–1, 13.288–9, 26.698; what is the *mantrayāna*? 26.698–9

Manu appears at the dawn of history and gives laws for society (Hinduism) 12.320–1; 'the Manu, the Buddha, the Guru, and the Tertön' 12.317–36; mentioned in the *Dhammapada* 15.42, 15.745 (n20); prepares the way for the Buddha 12.321; the progenitor of mankind (Hinduism) 7.570 (n132); Sangharakshita advised to act as Manu for the new Buddhists in India 12.320–1, 26.560

Manusmṛti advice about the way a father should treat his son 3.539, 15.412, 16.297; barbaric rules for the Shudra and Untouchable castes 6.612, 9.50, 10.23, 10.309, 10.625; the burning of the *Manusmṛti*, *see under* Mahad; 'even an infant king must not be despised … for he is a great deity in human form' 3.62–3; attitude to women 9.68

Mao Zedong 9.69, 26.654

maps Great Britain 24.xi; Maharashtra 9.167; New Zealand 24.x; North-eastern Himalayan Region, 1950s 22.xii; Sangharakshita's European Journey 23.2–3; Sangharakshita's Kalimpong 22.xiii; Spain 24.xii; Buddhism is a map of the human territory 3.7; a map to find our way around the maze which is ourselves 12.284; the map as a metaphor for incomplete truth 1.208; can the scriptures really act as a 'map' for one's spiritual life? 17.106–10

Māra

who is he?
brief introduction 15.744 (n4), 16.627 (n349); who or what is Māra? 11.400–2; baleful star in the firmament of man's delusion 7.327; corresponds to Satan, but there's a difference in principle 12.191; 'devil' is too strong, he is just a trickster 15.178, 18.149; embodiment of evil 3.52; embodiment of *saṃsāra* 3.277; 'the first lawyer' 12.188; 'friend of negligence' 10.617; he is cunning and resourceful, but can be defeated 15.178; he is a mischievous rather than an evil spirit 26.153–4; in a sense he rules over the whole of conditioned existence 11.402; rendered harmless as soon as he is recognized 26.154; the shadow in Jungian terms 12.190; vanquished by ridicule 26.154

his attacks on Siddhārtha
Māra's hordes 2.36, 3.277, 7.172, 11.396, 12.186–7; the attempt by Māra's daughters to seduce him 3.277, 11.396, 12.187–8; 'The Conquest of Māra' (poem) 25.256; described in the *Sutta-Nipāta* 14.57, 15.733; the victory over Māra 3.52, 10.260, 11.396, 11.403–6, 12.187; Māra's challenge: 'What right have you to sit here?' 9.381–2, 12.188, 13.308, 16.380; resembles Milton's description of the temptation of Jesus 24.573; a version in the story of Barlaam and Josaphat 13.661

the four Māras
(1) Māra of death (*maccu-māra*) 3.52, 11.400–1, 11.403, 26.645; (2) Māra of conditioned existence (*khanda-māra*) 26.645–6; (3) Māra of defilements (*kleśa-māra*) 3.52, 9.381, 11.401, 11.403–5, 26.645, 26.657; (4) Māra Pāpiyān (*devaputta-māra*, the Evil One) 11.402, 11.405–6, 15.178, 26.645

his appearances in the Pāli canon
the Buddha teaches the Dharma in an assembly of *māras* 12.526; a collection of sayings on Māra in the *Saṃyutta Nikāya* 3.84; convincing the forest renunciant of his superiority 4.554–5; the flower-tipped arrows of Māra (*Dhammapada*) 15.14, 15.745 (n8); he could not stop the wheel of the Dharma from rolling 8.227, 9.384; he intervened so that the Buddha returned with an empty bowl 1.228; Māra 'found no trace' of Vakkali 15.593; 'Māra has been overcome, the battle has been won' 10.524; Māra overthrows one as the wind blows down a weak tree (*Dhammapada*) 14.587; 'Māra retreated, sad and discomfited' 15.178; Meghiya is attacked by Māra 18.367; not even Māra could shake your faith (real Going for Refuge) 3.329, 12.505; perhaps he stopped Ānanda from asking the Buddha to live longer 10.584–5; scattering the armies of Māra (*Udāna*) 10.433–5; a story in which Māra is converted and assumes the form of the Buddha 14.68; he suggests to the Buddha that he should attain *parinibbāna* 10.584, 10.587; undefeated by Māra (*Maṅgala Sutta*) 15.453

his appearances in Mahāyāna sūtras
he could trick a bodhisattva into believing he was irreversible 2.169; how to tell Māra's from the Buddha's teachings 14.237; the deeds of Māra (related to studying the Perfection of Wisdom) 14.144; Māra's attempts to mislead the irreversible bodhisattva 14.145; 'the Māras who play the devil are all bodhisattvas' 16.525–6; outsmarted by Vimalakīrti 16.512–13; in the *Śūraṅgama-samādhi Sūtra* 25.143, 26.545–6, 26.662

Māra in our world
the Buddha's message can't be delivered in Māra's language 12.455–6; his influence in the 20th century 26.618; if monks stray from their meditation they get caught by Māra 19.341; Māra and astrology 22.307; Māra and his agents will stop at nothing to roll back the wheel of Dharma 23.365; our world-system is tough, with Māra's influence dominant 14.484; possible rebirth as a *devaputra* Māra 26.657; the power of the group is the power of Māra 11.359

our own encounters with Māra
the battle with the hindrances 15.178; being overcome by lethargy and sleep, one falls into his power 10.532–3; causing distractions in meditation 5.351–2; the danger of being attacked 18.34; he may let us go on retreat, but keep hold of our minds 18.177; his effect on our resolutions 8.191; if you recognize him, you see him as a state of your own mind 18.27; one should always be on one's guard 15.366–7; the reactive mind 5.309, 15.178; reciting a mantra to get rid of him 5.351; standing up to Māra 5.350–2, 18.149; tricking Māra into fighting for righteousness 8.191; the voices of Māra and the Buddha, temptation and resolve 15.402–3

Sangharakshita and Māra
his appearance in a short story, *Four Visitors* 26.616–20, 26.662–3; a poisoned arrow from Māra's bow 22.214; a vision of an old man's head 5.350–1, 20.114, 21.298–300, 26.618–19; Māra on the Tube train 4.546–7, 13.597, 26.565, 26.657

Marathi *Buddhayan*, *see Buddhayan*; Dharmananda Kosambi (writer in Marathi), *see* Kosambi; Buddhist literature

available in Marathi 9.218, 10.295; distinctive sound 10.255; translations of Sangharakshita's works into Marathi 9.170, 10.181, 10.299

Marathwada v9

Marc, Franz 24.588

Marcion 13.523, 13.622–3, 13.641–2

Marcus (English Sangha Trust) v23

Marcus Aurelius 12.134, 12.406

mārga* and *phala (path and fruit) analogy with karma and *vipāka* 15.641, 15.644; analogy with wisdom and compassion 15.644–5; correspond to the third and fourth noble truths 2.102; and the four noble persons 10.146, 15.527, 15.643; a psychological basis for the distinction 15.642, 15.644; of Stream Entry 1.176–7, 2.146, 15.641–2

Marichi, Dharmacharini v24

Marion and Dermot (Canvastown) 24.85–6

Mark, King 25.406

Marlowe, Christopher 14.15, 14.297, 20.62

Marma-kalikā Tantra *see* tantras/works

Marpa (the Translator) 'a Buddha disguised in human form' 19.336–7; an extraverted thinking type 18.145; 'had experienced the mother-like Essence of Mind' 18.64; a layman 11.571; and Milarepa, *see under* Milarepa/life story; Nāropā rejects his gold 16.625 (n321); the Pith-Instructions given by Marpa to Milarepa 18.593–4; a rather peppery character 18.110; he requires a disciple to give everything, even a lame goat 12.18–19, 19.530; why he is called the Translator 18.185

Marratt, Dr Howard 11.508

marriage

marriage and Buddhist practice
cultivating contentment in marriage 15.276; four qualities of husband and wife (Pāli canon) 14.49; if you're married, talk with other married sangha members about their life 17.364; married gurus 18.410; the place of marriage in your personal mandala 18.508–9

Buddhist marriage
the bodhisattva's marriage a 'pious fraud' to convert 1.442; ceremony 2.231, 4.115, 15.703–4, 26.560; dissolving marriage 4.115, 13.457–8, 18.378; not seen as a religious sacrament or legally enforceable 1.534, 3.371, 4.114–5; no rigid or universal pattern of marriage relationship 3.371; polyandry 1.534, 1.633 (n426), 4.115, 13.458, 21.329–30; polygyny 13.458; practising Buddhism in the context of marriage 7.178–9, 18.212–13; Order members getting married 15.414–15

Indian
caste system can be destroyed by intermarriage 9.355, 10.363; 'deceitful' marriage 9.525; dowry system 9.192, 9.217, 9.265, 10.20; early marriage 9.438; an elopement 22.454–6, 23.384; ending the tradition of getting into debt through marriage settlement 10.187; *lagna-vidhi* (marriage ceremony) 9.335–6, 26.560; love marriages and arranged marriage 10.412; marriage between Buddhists 10.414; *saptapadas* 9.335, 9.567 (n309)

notes on marriage
the Cathars were against marriage as a sacrament 8.423; communication difficulties in marriage 19.20; desired but feared 25.81; for the sake of close human companionship 2.607; hatred between husband and wife 17.269; an idealized view of marriage 23.98; in traditional cultures, you marry in order to produce sons 15.413–14; is marriage really a result of free choice? 18.457; the legal institution of marriage 3.528; a married man is like a donkey tethered to a post 26.29; a monk who refused an offer of marriage 22.273–4; monogamy 3.566; no marriage in heaven 16.392; not without its compensations 24.386; people who get married again and again, following the same pattern 18.276; resentment is a notable feature of many marriages 17.646–7; the 'silence of marriage' 23.99; a Spanish wedding 24.423–4; what is a good husband? 19.278; why a marriage break-up can be so acrimonious 15.311; why are some marriages so unhappy? 18.208–9; why secular people like to have a church wedding 17.638; wives as being less important than sons 15.413–14; you don't spiritualize a sexual coupling with holy words 18.428

see also
Nanda's marriage, *see under* Nanda

Marshall, Don 24.81

Marsyas the satyr 10.721–2 (n488)

Martin, Jim 23.197–8

Martin, Kingsley 23.202

Martin, P. W. 23.130

Martini, Simone v13, v24

martyrs the bodhisattva suffers, but there is no suggestion of martyrdom 4.14; Christian martyrs 4.316, 13.266–7, 13.631; martyrdom and Freud's death wish 8.127

Marvell, Andrew brief introduction 23.542 (n500); 'Annihilating all that's made/ To a green Thought in a green shade' 24.83; association with Highgate 23.473; 'The Garden' 26.397; 'Time's winged chariot drawing near' 26.293

Marx, Karl Dr Ambedkar on Marx 9.11, 9.69, 9.508; conflict with Christianity 10.347; and Hegel 20.83, 22.210; history in terms of economics and class conflict 3.423–4, 10.167, 10.347–8; *Das Kapital* 22.209

Marxism Dr Ambedkar's views on Marxism, *see under* Ambedkar/on politics; anticipated by Buddhism (Ambedkar) 9.412; asks good questions of Buddhists 4.442–3; battles of logic between Buddhists and Marxists 12.241–2; a *bhikkhu* attempting to convert Buddhists to Marxism 8.320; Conze's Marxist studies 8.538; discredited 11.603–4; Marxism has some features of a religion 10.71; as one of the alternatives before mankind 13.513; 'Religion is the opium of the people' – not as negative as it might sound 10.72–3; in Russia 17.44; the young Sangharakshita's response to Marxism 20.83, 22.209–10; to say that life is wholly determined by economics is to go to extremes 10.348; 'Why bother about religion?' 10.58; world-view 3.6

Mary *see* Virgin Mary

Mary I, Queen ('Bloody Mary') 8.170, 13.549

Mary Queen of Scots 20.27

Mary, Queen (consort of George v) 22.14

Masaccio, Tomasso 13.646–8, 23.314, 23.523 (n359), 24.273, 24.676 (n333)

Masala Dosai, Guru! 20.358–9

Mascarenhas, Father v13, v22, v23

masculine and masculinity (*puruṣendriya*) among secondary qualities of *rūpa* 2.97–8; *ḍākinīs* and *dharmapālas*: feminine and masculine energies 19.408–9; the demonization of masculinity 11.613; developing the whole range of human qualities, 'masculine' and 'feminine' 11.582; difference between Gurkhas and Newars the difference between masculine and feminine 7.345; don't emasculate yourself spiritually for the sake of being a 'good Buddhist' 4.444; feminine and masculine are very different mentalities and may need different spiritual practices 12.283; 'feminine' and 'masculine' Buddhist art 22.349; 'feminine' and 'masculine' in the symbolism of the stupa 13.163; *The Hazard of Being Male* 24.541–4; *heruka* and *ḍākinī* 18.373; the ideal of the warrior, but warriors can be of either sex 18.104–5; knowledge of a woman's unrealized 'masculine' side through Tantric practice 13.90; masculine beauty 23.278; masculine and feminine are two, individuality is the Dharma-door 16.548; masculine and feminine in the mandala of the five Buddhas 18.601; masculine forces (white channel) 19.31; masculine potency 2.156; the masculine principle and the jewel 22.28; represents compassion in Buddhist iconography 18.373; seeing the form and hearing the mantra: active and passive, 'masculine' and 'feminine' 26.39; a shift from feminine to masculine values in Judaism 19.414; *upāya*, wisdom-inspired activity personalized as masculine 7.139; and *vīrya* 4.118, 4.142–4; and yin and yang 16.163

Masefield, John 7.450, 26.393

Masefield, Peter 10.422

masks *see* persona

Maslow, Abraham 16.94

Masolino 13.647–8

Mass Movement Buddhist Brotherhood 9.422

massage 18.611

master and servant relationship *see* servant

mastery *aiśvarya* (autonomy) 10.592, 10.719 (n467); 'ascertaining' rather than 'mastering' the Dharma 11.253; 'the bodhisattva should master just one virtue: compassion' 2.125–6, 5.199–200; breaking a vow shows that you're not master of yourself 18.487; the idea of selfhood connected with mastery or ownership 1.172; the idea that if one understands the words one has mastered the meaning 18.167; if you think you've mastered the Dharma, how can you reverence it? 11.56–7, 18.167; 'Let my possessions be lost ... but never mastery of the mind' 4.380; master, practise, meditate upon, and spread these truths 2.29; mastery of Buddhist philosophy requires experiencing the primordial truth to which it points

19.354; 'May I master all dharmas' 4.81–3; Milarepa's mastery of *prāṇa* 19.30; Siddhārtha masters the teachings of the teachers he consults 3.51, 10.257–8; the Tathāgata exercises mastery with the body 18.75; why should you master all the teachings? for the benefit of others 18.413–14; you don't have to master all the scriptures to get the Buddha's complete message 18.495

Mātaṅgī (*Śūraṅgama Sūtra*) 13.358–60

Mātaraṃgara *see* Tarpa Nagpo

material things dependence on others for material things 18.387–8; full-timers dependent on part-timers for material things, but *only* material things 18.388; if you devoted the same energy to spiritual life as to material things, success would be assured 4.150; Jagdish Kashyap 'simply did not bother with material things' 20.444

see also
āmisa-pūja (worship with material things), *see under* devotion/ritual; giving material things, *see under dāna*; possessions

materialism (materialistic way of life) don't draw too sharp a distinction between materialistic West and spiritual East 13.489–90; being unconsciously influenced by friends with materialistic ideas 18.152; combination of materialism and piety 17.211; the forces of materialism in the modern world 10.389, 12.654; the hateful materialism of the West 24.401; in our society it can even make good business out of anti-materialist impulses 17.657; Marx showed that objective material conditions are important 10.347; material progress is a good thing, but spiritual progress is even more important 10.346–7; the materialism of Tibetans 15.684; materialistic prosperity is not satisfying 9.284; spiritual materialism 17.170–1, 17.210–11, 17.594, 17.656; technology replaces magic in the materialistic East 15.682–5; to withstand materialism, the Buddhist world must stand together 8.182–5

materialism (philosophy) materialism as a philosophy of life 7.166–7; materialism and Ātmanism: opposite poles of thought, but with similarities 7.165–8; the belief that life does not exist before birth or after death 7.165, 17.469; Bishop Berkeley saw materialism as synonymous with atheism 1.368; both East and West 9.47; denial of the continuity of empirical experiences 7.165–7; Guest's *Dialectical Materialism* 22.210; Lama Govinda speaks against a materialist interpretation of the effect of mantras 22.30; limitations 7.167; the Mahāyāna accused of materialism 8.183–4; materialist's limitations in understanding the Dharma 1.18; to believe that consciousness can be explained by brain function is materialism 8.581; *see also* Cārvakas; Lokāyatikas

mathematics the beauty of mathematical equations 15.577; Brahminical ritual and the development of arithmetic and geometry 16.363; mathematicians may be moved by the concept of infinity, but it leaves most of us cold 13.284; variables in the mathematics of character 7.271

Mathur, J. C. 7.424

Mathuran sculptures *see under* images

Matics, Marion introduction 4.268–9, 4.692 (n223); *Entering the Path of Enlightenment*, *see under Bodhicaryāvatāra*/translations

Mātṛceṭa 1.335, 11.43

mātṛkadharas 2.197, 14.72

mātṛkas (Pāli *mātikas*, matrices) Abhidharma 2.197, 7.502, 14.72–3; the Buddha himself sets up matrices for future discussion 14.85; the difference in approach from the *suttas* 14.80

mātṛkās (the Mothers) 18.469

mātsarya *see* avarice

matter the Abhidharma's investigation of what we would call matter 12.145; the belief that nothing exists except matter 9.229; disproving the existence of matter 1.368–9; Māra saying that there's nothing but matter 5.350–1, 20.114, 21.298–300, 26.618–19; the permanent possibility of sensation (Mill) 17.404; why do we think that matter exists? 1.369; in the world of matter, there is no unchanging material unit 7.153; materialism wrongly posited matter as the unifying factor of consciousness 19.237; to say that matter is evil is to say that it is not material 26.48; *see also under* Yogācāra/One Mind

mātugāma (womenfolk) 2.347

maturity the Buddha and the bodhisattva mature or ripen living beings 16.463, 19.24; feeling no attachment may be nihilism, not spiritual maturity 17.371; the five things that conduce to spiritual maturity, *see under Udāna*/Meghiya; people are a mixture of mature and immature 19.114–17; spiritual immaturity and maturity, *see Dhammapada*/chapters 5 and 6; the spiritually mature know that the

world is like a mirage 17.358–9; 'There is no companionship with the spiritually immature' 10.650, 15.385

Mau, India 20.399

Maudgalyāyana (Moggallāna)

his life
birth 1.256; birthplace (Kul) 7.427, 20.460; conversion, *see under* Sāriputta; ordination at the Bamboo Grove 2.24, 2.687 (n258); and real Going for Refuge 10.387; sense of humour 10.405; his murder 4.14; sacred relics, *see* sacred relics

Pāli canon references
a section on him in the *Saṃyutta Nikāya* 3.84; he practises mindfulness of the body (*Udāna*) 10.512–13; his definition of noble silence 26.203; the Buddha advises him on how not to fall asleep in meditation 19.614 (n155); he negotiates with a supporter about a change of arrangements 10.493, 10.495; Abhidharma texts ascribed to him 14.83

Mahāyāna references
his visits to various worlds (*Mahāvastu*) 14.70; in the *Vimalakīrti-nirdeśa* 16.502; in the *White Lotus Sūtra* (one of four elders) 14.115, 16.41–2

magical or psychic powers
do not include guaranteeing someone's faith in the Three Jewels 10.495; he perceives an impure monk in the assembly (*Udāna*) 10.557, 10.562; Sāriputta praises his psychic abilities 10.535; a princess with greater magical powers than him (Mahāyāna *sutra*) 14.184

see also
Sāriputta

Maugham, W. Somerset 15.411, 22.277, 22.600 (n224)

Maung Maung Ji, U 8.643, v22

Maupassant, Guy de 25.81

Maurice, St 13.631

'May all beings be happy' *see sabbe sattā sukhi hontu*

māyā as deceit, *see* deceit; as illusion, *see* illusion

māyā-citta 16.544–5

Māyādevī (Siddhārtha Gautama's mother) sources of her story 3.628–9 (n20); the Buddha taught her the Abhidharma, *see under* heavens/Heaven of the Thirty-Three; dream of a white elephant 9.364; Siddhārtha's birth 1.256, 1.612 (n212), 3.22; her death 3.22; why did she have such a short life? 10.546–7; her statue at Lumbini 20.421

Māyājāla Tantra *see under* tantras/works

Māyavāda 9.229

Mayayalis 20.264–5

'Maybe so, friend' *see* Upāka

Mazu 8.487

McAuley, Anne *see* Akasati

McBride, Dick v24

McCullers, Carson 24.374, 26.380

McCullough, Rev. Joseph v23

McDonald, Lesley 24.27, 24.617 (n65)

McEwen, Diana 24.200

McGee, Michael *see* Vipassi

McGilchrist, Iain 26.xiv

McGough, Roger 25.321–2

McKechnie, J. F. *see* Silacara

McLuhan, Marshall 'The medium is the message' 11.258, 23.122; the medium is *not* the message 13.438, 14.514–15

McPherson, D. J. v8

meaning

traditional references
'seeing the meaning of it' (*Udāna*) 10.556–7; explicit (*neyārtha*) and implicit (*nītārtha*) 3.355, 15.227, 16.579–81, 17.488–9; knowledge of meaning (*artha-pratisaṃvid*) 16.489–90; relying on the meaning, not the expression, *see under* four reliances; meaning is alone with itself (*vivikta*) and the cause of Nirvāṇa 14.208; a glimpse of the meaning of Milarepa's song 18.615

words and meaning
being preoccupied with words and missing the meaning 19.158–9; 'I understand the words, but I don't feel I understand the meaning' 4.249; the idea that if one understands the words one has mastered the meaning 18.167; insisting on 'understanding' a sentence before acting, you would never act 14.566; often people study not the meaning, but just the words 18.382; people find it very difficult to appreciate that one means what one says 18.347; sharp distinction between words and meaning 14.207–8; study words and their meanings carefully 8.272–3; words in conventionally meaningful patterns may not mean much to us 13.123

our quest for meaning
art gives both pleasure and meaning 26.165–6; if you study your own life, you may see the unfolding of a certain meaning 18.279; making the effort to develop positively, your life becomes more meaningful 17.435; the meaning of the experience of death 4.331; the meaning of meaning 2.639, 18.383; meaning must be meaning *for you* 16.533; the meaning of life is to be found only beyond life 26.13; our quest for meaning is our quest for ourselves 16.533; the thread of meaning running through our lives 15.94

mythical meanings
looking for rational meanings of poetic or archetypal images is limiting 19.563–4; read Mahāyāna *sūtras without thinking of their meaning* (Yinkuang) 24.533; poetic, imaginative 16.580–1; the realm of myth is a realm of indefinable meanings 16.528

meaninglessness 'Better than a thousand meaningless words collected together ...' 3.282–3, 12.33, 12.37; the doing of good is meaningless apart from the ability to do evil 7.245–6; in terms of life and practice, it's meaningless to think of taking in lots of religious traditions 18.381; if you teach the Dharma a lot, it can all become a bit meaningless 18.482; meaningless and meaningful life 7.322–3, 20.133; the meaninglessness of words 23.472; 'meaningless word-knowledge' 18.185; a world of perfectly meaningless 'Buddhist activities' 24.138

means to an end all Zen practices are means to an end 13.342–3; any term or concept is a means to an end 15.186; asceticism is a means to an end 26.158; Buddhist doctrines are a means to the end of Enlightenment 14.608; the Church saying that the end justifies the means 8.153, 8.253; the Dharma as a means, not an end 2.59, 7.244, 7.433, 10.141, 14.318, 14.440–1; discipline is a means to an end, not an end in itself 23.187; the end is the extreme of the means 13.75, 19.100, 25.83; ethics as a means to an end 3.245–6, 3.320–1, 7.257; life is a means to an end – the end being *bodhi* 7.320; the parable of the raft, *see* raft; 'No hurried path of success, forcibly cut by the greed of result, can be the true path' 2.112; sacrificing the end to the means is a common human error 8.196; the spiritual life has no goal, the means is the goal 7.412, 18.164–5; things that are a means to an end easily become ends in themselves 8.276; using an evil means to a good end will have disastrous results 19.129; 'We want all pleasant ends, but will use no harsh means' 25.83–4; what are meant to be means to an end become ends in themselves 19.134–5

meat cruel implications of eating meat 1.499–500; eating meat out of mental confusion 16.305; example of what may be pleasant for oneself but involves suffering for others 3.213–14; a goat cooked at Lumbini: violation of the first precept 20.420; how Tibetans justify eating meat 4.111–12, 19.331, 19.527; insistence of Burmese monks at the Sixth Council on eating meat and fish 22.232; 'like devouring one's own relatives ...' 14.203–4; meats prohibited by the Vinaya (human flesh, tiger flesh, etc.) 4.112; 'One who takes flesh kills the seed of great compassion' 14.236; origin of Untouchability in the eating of beef 9.87–90; Pāli canon extract which shows that eating beef was common in ancient India 1.160; Rechungpa's offerings of meat for Milarepa 19.515; 'shedding a tear for a deceased cat while relishing a leg of lamb' 23.239; some religions sanction it 17.195; Thai Buddhists' rationalizations about eating meat 17.586, 23.367–8; 'wilful addiction to flesh diet' 11.481

see also
Laṅkāvatāra Sūtra/chapter 8; not eating meat, *see* vegetarianism

mechanical Buddhism cannot be practised mechanically 9.193–4, 9.266, 17.306; disappointment at the mechanical practice of Buddhism 9.268; hindrances tend to arise when we react mechanically to situations 15.172–3; the mechanical approach of the Pāli canon 15.235; 'penny-in-the-slot' mind 11.23; recitation of the Refuges and Precepts, *see under* Going for Refuge/the Buddhist tradition/a formality; a middle way between pseudo-originality and mechanical repetitiveness 4.280–1; the *niyamas* guard against a tendency to see karma in a mechanical way 3.xiv; non-violent action on an intellectual basis can be mechanical rather than a flaming passion 7.373; practice of the Dharma becomes mechanical 19.584; primitive man had no mechanical sense of time 3.424; responding mechanically to sensory stimuli 17.102–3; spiritual life is not a mechanical process 1.133; the system of meditation: an organic, living system, not a dead, mechanical one 5.29; take care that making everyday activities into practices doesn't become mechanical 19.329–30; the tendency of

spiritual practices to become mechanical 11.37–8; thinking that observing the outward forms of religion mechanically will suffice 17.633; when you cultivate the five spiritual faculties, you're not seeing a mechanical universe 17.118

Medalla, David v24

medhā (sagacity) 17.131, 17.726 (n138)

medhī *see under* stupa

media celebrities in the media 25.57; expert in seizing the attention and manipulating the emotions 15.288; global media makes us more aware of world problems than were people in the past 3.615, 15.174–5; mass media give trivialities an importance they don't possess 26.82; media input can lessen our ability to deal with boredom creatively 15.174; media speculation about coming events 19.270–1; pandering to lust for sex and crime 26.115; the power of the visual medium, not to be misused 24.40; reduce input 12.473–5, 15.174, 15.287–8, 19.544–5, 26.62; if there were no radios, no newspapers, we would 'know' very little 13.345

median nerve *see* central channel

Medici, Cosmo de' 23.297, 23.314, 23.523 (n359)

Medici, Lorenzo de' 23.314, 23.523 (n359)

medicine

alternative therapies
acupuncture 23.84, 23.129–30, 24.337–9; aromatherapy 24.568; Ayurvedic medicine 24.114; Bach flower remedies 26.457–8; homoeopathy 22.106; practising them as a substitute for practising the Dharma 24.327–8

medical treatment
the advantages of modern medicine 24.332; effect on mental clarity 16.407; ethics of treatment dependent on experimenting on animals 16.406–7; pain relief when dying 16.407; should be in accordance with the laws of nature 16.408; should be in accordance with spiritual principles 16.406–7

practising medicine
'I wished I could practise medicine' (Sangharakshita) 10.1, 10.317–18, 27.1075; the responsibility of doctors and nurses for their patients 15.323; Sangharakshita assists at an operation 22.449; should a patient be warned of approaching death? 8.142–4; the very real connection for a doctor between Buddhism and medicine 24.332

medicine in Buddhist tradition
dosa as a medical term 10.451; medicine of gallnuts and cow's urine traditionally allowed the monk 3.590, 16.406; wise use of medicine (as monastic requisite) 1.149; are vitamin tablets medicine or food? 21.397, 22.312; aspect of monastic studies 2.197; medically trained Tibetan monks 13.51; medicine that has been blessed by a guru 19.366; medicine from Chattrul Sangye Dorje 25.443

medicine as metaphor
the Buddha's teaching as medicine for the five poisons 26.645; the corpse meditation: strong medicine 1.155; the Dharma as medicine 16.192, 16.201–2, 26.645; gaining more skill and experience after Enlightenment, like a doctor after qualification 15.469; the golden light as spiritual medicine 16.290; if the medicine becomes poisonous, where will you turn for treatment? 17.630; no more necessary to do all forty meditations than to take all medicines 1.161, 10.172; the teaching of *śūnyatā* is intended as a medicine for the cure of all attachments 3.237

Medicine Buddhas Bhaiṣajyaguru, *see* Bhaiṣajyaguru; eight Medicine Buddhas 16.193; seven Medicine Buddhas 12.228

medieval (Middle Ages) the age of faith – but was it real faith? 17.44; Arabic learning in the monasteries of medieval Europe 7.85; Dance of Death (medieval Christianity) 2.85, 13.230–1, 26.297; the dangers and significance of travel in medieval Tibet 18.325–6; feudal system 3.524, 11.697, 18.505; giving up weapons in medieval Tibet a huge step 18.98–9; the hardship of life in medieval times 19.96; 'medieval' as a pejorative term 13.425–6; the medieval idea of degree, or hierarchy (the 'great chain of being') 12.463; the monks of medieval Japan who fought in their own armies 7.443; reading was rare in medieval times 3.515; the Roundheads' destruction of the artistic heritage of medieval England 24.567; Sangharakshita joked he had a medieval cast of mind 13.425; scepticism and fanaticism 15.565

meditation

WHAT IS MEDITATION?

introduction
all serious Buddhists should meditate 8.200, 8.254, 10.392; the poem

'Meditation': 'a summary of the whole process' 6.xxvii–xxix, 25.3–4, 25.41–9; a basis for taking the initiative and developing positivity 18.574–5; the basis is dualistic 2.282; the development of new levels of consciousness 13.73; development *par excellence* 5.635; the distinction between mundane and transcendental meditation is very important 26.199; ideally a natural, spontaneous expression of how you feel 5.284–5; the second stage of the threefold path 3.247, 3.333–53; 'Meditation' (analysis of Sangharakshita's poem) 25.3–4, 25.41–9; meditation is the heart of Buddhism 8.200, 11.498; meditation lies at the heart of the spiritual life 13.71; meditation really involves getting down to the bedrock of the mind 3.227, 17.xxv; meditation was popularized by the Maharishi 12.645; more of an art than a science 3.351; a natural state 5.284–5, 18.31; no such thing as meditation, only methods of meditation 11.153; not many people think of it as bringing fundamental change 15.113–14; the principal method of Buddhist practice 8.550; its significance is not just psychological but primarily spiritual 3.9, 23.37; something dynamic, challenging, shattering 3.107; something to be practised and experienced, not talked and read about 3.335; source of energy and inspiration 9.242, 9.267; its value emphasized in Buddhism 7.125; we have a daily solitary retreat when we meditate 12.474–5; what meditation really is 11.111–27

definitions and descriptions
as well as mindfulness it includes the eight *vimokṣas* and the nine *samāpattis* 8.584; the basic building block 18.275; the basis of transformation 8.611; the direct method of raising the level of consciousness 2.387; calm (*śamatha*) and clear vision or insight (*vipaśyanā*) 5.417, 5.420–1, 5.423–4, 25.44; a clearing of the decks for action 15.221; essentially something to be practised 11.112; a field of creativity 12.637–8; the gathering, directing, and channelling of energy 15.217; a gathering of skilful mental states 5.435; 'glorious gem' (*Ratana Sutta*) 15.64; it is essentially the willing of the Good 26.75; a kind of activity 19.212, 26.63; the main avenue to other dimensions 5.52; the meditative life is the blissful life 8.440; the persistent and methodical attempt to see reality within 13.354; practices leading to states of consciousness above the ordinary mind 4.148; transformation of consciousness 3.123, 19.57; persuading the mind to move towards skilful activity 15.170; principal terms used in connection with meditation 4.501–2; a process of clarifying the mind 4.146; a raising of the level of consciousness 11.461, 19.57; its real aim is to transform consciousness 1.561; the royal road to Enlightenment 5.375, 9.115, 12.57; a savoury dish: nourishing, something you'll die without 19.440; the seed of the Dhamma Revolution 9.202–3; the spearhead of a reorientation of one's whole being 2.261; the systematic expansion of awareness or consciousness 3.335; the transcendence of self 5.656; unified and heightened consciousness 19.451; the uninterrupted production of skilful mental states 5.644–5, 5.649, 5.650–1, 11.131, 26.46; a union of purified emotion and clarified intelligence 4.146; always concentrating on something, in meditation we concentrate on the right thing 12.148; working directly on the mind 11.120

meditation in the Buddhist tradition
Buddhism grew out of meditation 5.29; Buddhist festivals and activities should include meditation 8.293–4; continuing to meditate after becoming an *arhant* 10.538–9; meditation and the Noble Eightfold Path 13.71; Sāriputta meditates without the thought 'I am meditating' 3.409; in early Buddhism, practice and decline 2.200–1, 15.734–5; Buddhaghosa collected the Buddha's teachings on meditation in the *Visuddhimagga* 17.441; the bodhisattva's practice of meditation 4.161; the approaches of the three *yānas* 7.508–9; for all Buddhist schools meditation is a fundamental practice 13.71; the importance of relating traditional accounts to one's own experience 5.250–1; one of the three 'items of meritorious action' 11.306; three stages in the practice of meditation (Abhidharma) 14.83; traditional division into *śamatha* and *vipaśyanā* 3.350–1, 5.426, 15.84, 15.109; Nyingma lamas guided by what came to them in their meditation 13.24; today in the East most Buddhists don't meditate 15.735–6; a revival of interest in meditation 8.254–5

meditation in other spiritual traditions
the connection between non-theistic religion and meditation 12.10; Conze's comparison of Buddhist meditation with Christian mysticism 4.513; a non-Buddhist can meditate 5.380

meditation in Triratna
criticism of the developmental model 11.688–9; meditation and the beginning

of the FWBO 9.201–2; Mitras and meditation 9.308; Sangharakshita leads a 'meditational workshop' at a conference 24.204–5; Sangharakshita's first experiment in guided meditation 23.37–8, 27.1071; system of meditation, *see* meditation/methods/system

learning to meditate
anybody can learn to meditate 25.141; books on meditation 4.519–20, 4.711 (n339), 19.461; books on meditation can be misleading 8.255, 11.112–13; the demand for meditation 11.113; if you can't learn from a teacher, choose a simple practice and go carefully 8.255–6; it's crucial to understand the difference between right and wrong meditation 8.254–6; more interest in the West now than when Buddhism was introduced 3.191, 26.257–8; learning meditation solely from books isn't enough 3.339, 15.103; the need for a personal teacher 3.340, 5.378, 8.200, 8.255, 15.103; some people are natural meditators, but that is rare 25.44–5; the tradition of oral teaching, the difficulty of learning from books 1.379; we need not put off learning to meditate until we have learned to be mindful 3.286; you learn a little, then modify your ideas as you go along 17.288

teaching meditation
if you are a meditator, if you are creative in that way, you can teach 12.645; meditation interviews 23.139; it's more than just teaching a technique 11.481; not all who teach it are qualified 11.113; once you have had a meditative experience, you want to share it 12.645; in prison 10.xli; those who have found it difficult are often the best teachers 17.303; an unbroken tradition? 5.35–6; you just need to have some experience to pass on to others 8.686 (n138)

group meditation
an ancient practice, mentioned in the Pāli canon 10.559–60; Sangharakshita leads for the first time 23.133–4; those present are sharing in a higher reality 10.561

the purpose of meditation
the aim of meditation described in terms of the four *dhyānas* 5.242; the aim of meditation is to transform oneself, not to have good meditations 26.47; clarity about why one meditates 17.616–17; goals change as your practice develops (parable of the magic city) 16.43; a lot depends on the intensity of your initial sense of purpose 5.387–8, 15.221–2; your intention to meditate may be at variance with the purpose of your life 5.387–8; important because of Buddhism's emphasis on direct personal experience 12.56–7; in the second *dhyāna*, one's purpose in life has been established 5.252; in a daily practice, keeping your comprehension of purpose takes work 5.389; it is absolutely necessary to the process of examining the mind 17.438; keeping your objective firmly in mind 5.699; a means to an end: wisdom 1.168–70, 3.248–9; meditating to achieve a positive state of mind 15.361; one does not sit to meditate, one sits to sit 2.112; the only way to realize the Dharma 8.219; the opportunity to enter further dimensions of mind 17.341; the permanent dissolution of the whole stream of thoughts 19.188; preparation for insight 15.83; the progressive self-transformation of one's total being 11.499; relating the practice of meditation to your own needs 19.57; to attain wisdom 17.306; to make us more concentrated, unified beings 17.116–17; to see oneself more clearly 25.91; to see reality within 13.354–6; to train the mind and thereby transform consciousness 15.299; to weaken the fourth and fifth fetters 3.421

mistaken ideas about meditation
it is more than just mindfulness 8.583–4; it is not a dreamy, drifting state 5.651, 11.499, 17.82; it is not making the mind a blank 5.52, 5.228–9, 8.424, 8.578, 11.112, 11.499; it is not the forcible fixing of attention 15.221; it is not just concentration, but also being positive, creative, contented, etc. 5.50; lots of people think that meditating is not doing anything 11.112, 18.268; 'meditating all the time' – a misconception 17.543, 18.498; it is not 'trance' 11.112, 17.118, 17.124

why do we need to meditate?
because we realize that insight hasn't arisen 12.542, 12.566; claiming to be in continuously skilful states without meditating 5.645; the fact that we need to meditate is a sign that something has gone wrong 5.284; having cultivated the previous *nidānas*, you do not need to 'meditate' 2.113; if we are mentally confused, we have to go back to meditation 12.566; psychological: search for peace of mind 3.335–6; spiritual: the desire or aspiration for Enlightenment 3.336

alternatives to meditation
better sweep a floor egolessly than meditate with the thought 'I am meditating' 7.284; formal meditation isn't necessarily needed for the arising of insight 19.451; indirect

methods, *see* indirect methods; insights are not limited to meditation 5.431–2; 'Maybe meditation isn't your way' 5.644; meditation is not the only way of raising the level of consciousness 18.359; patterns of behaviour that meditation doesn't affect 16.114; people who think of meditation as the only Buddhist practice 11.116–17, 16.127; the relationship between art and meditation 21.251; talking can have the same effect on one's mental state as meditation 10.530; unless your work is your meditation, your meditation is not meditation 26.18; when your energies are united, you're meditating, whether formally or not 18.579–80

METHODS OF MEDITATION

general points about methods
according to character type 2.83–4, 4.518–19, 5.46, 5.390–1, 12.280, 22.510; asking for a method that gives Enlightenment quickly without effort 19.284–5; best to adopt a systematic method 15.105; best not to chop and change 5.613–14, 18.405; better to practise one method for thirty years than thirty methods for a year 5.613–14; better to take one step in the right direction than a thousand in the wrong direction 8.256; Buddhaghosa's analysis: we must know exactly what we need to develop 12.280–1; formless meditation 11.688; four qualities to be 'made to grow' correspond to four of five basic methods 10.531–2; getting distracted by others' opinions as to what practice you should be doing 17.681; just take up a single meditation 5.50; many methods 1.207; placing too much faith in a particular method 17.681; three progressive stages: *śamatha*, *samāpatti*, *samādhi* 3.351–3; you can do any practice if you make an effort, regardless of temperament 5.390–1; you can't just sit down and meditate, there's a systematic technique 15.514–15; you can't practise meditation in a general way, you need specific methods 12.467

three main levels
introduction 3.120–3, 3.246–50, 5.654–6, 11.120–7; (1) integration or concentration of mind 3.120–1, 3.246, 3.617, 5.654–5, 11.20–4; (2) *dhyānas*, intensification, expansion 3.121–2, 3.246, 3.617, 5.655, 11.124–6; (3) insight into the true nature of existence 3.122, 3.246–7, 3.617, 5.656, 11.126–7

the system of meditation (Sangharakshita's teaching)
introduction 5.xxxiii–iv; source 5.xxii, 5.37; Sangharakshita's reason for devising the system as he did 5.607–8; an early version 5.28–9; the different stages fade into each other like the colours of the rainbow 13.71; any parallel in Tibetan Buddhism? 5.37; doing all the practices in the course of a day 5.490; full outline in five great stages 5.42–6, 13.71–3; full outline in four stages 5.29–35; how do the foundation (*mūla*) yogas fit into the system? 5.540–1; an organic, living system, not a dead, mechanical, artificially created one 5.29; and the 'path of no steps at all' 11.54, 26.47; and the path of regular steps 5.28, 5.40–2; and the prostration practice 5.540–1; too general? 5.46; wanting other methods without having fully explored the system of meditation 5.614; Western Buddhists' need for 'classical' systems of meditation 23.37; you can't just sit down and meditate, you have to follow a system 12.52

techniques
the anti-creative force manifests when meditation becomes about technique 12.644; every technique works if you practise it 11.85; the Mahāyāna and Vajrayāna rely on the Theravāda for methods 5.461; meditation cannot be reduced to special techniques or professional expertise 2.112, 11.481; meditation on sound 14.197; mistrust of special techniques 18.326; it's necessary to guide unfoldment, but one should let it grow naturally 18.31; not just a question of the application of techniques 2.260–1, 3.272; one needs to be wary of the idea of a meditation 'technique' 3.351; people who claim that their technique is the only one 11.85, 11.113–14; role of techniques in meditation 2.112–13; seeing meditation as a technique, not realizing what it really is 19.57; twenty-five methods of controlling the mind through meditation 14.197

PREPARATION

conditions for meditation
becoming able to meditate under almost any conditions 18.630–1; being in ideal conditions but not meditating 18.484; celibacy 2.371; colours for a meditation space 5.302; conditions for the practice of *dhyāna*, including renunciation and solitude 1.442; the effect of the weather on meditation 4.575, 24.107; meditating in the open air 18.629–30; meditating in solitude 15.102; meditating when tired 18.555; meditating with others 10.274–5, 15.102–3; practising meditation while travelling 19.346, 19.549–50; the vihara as the place to practise meditation 9.464; you have to have faith that you really can 5.336

ethics
traditional perspectives 1.146–9; before you start meditating, take a look at how you behave in daily life 15.343; connection with the mind precepts 2.387; ethical work 3.339, 3.617; meditation is impossible without the purification of morality 1.145; meditation needs a basis of ethics 10.172, 15.345; one's whole life needs to be a preparation for meditation 3.273, 3.617

preparing for meditation
contact with beauty 18.159; checking your mental state 5.283–4; closing your eyes 17.120; described in the *Amitāyurdhyāna Sūtra* 1.332; devotional exercises 3.340, 6.xxviii; exercise 3.339; getting in touch with your body 5.302–3, 15.429–30; look after your mental state all day 5.393; looking after one's health 3.617; enough sleep, but not too much 5.294, 5.305–6, 5.332–4; meditating with the eyes open 17.543; mindfulness 1.150, 3.339, 15.104; practices to free the mind of guilt 2.105; the preliminaries, if mastered, are half the battle 13.75; preparatory exercises (list) in the *Samādhirāja Sūtra* 14.193; preparing for an individual meditation session 3.273; reciting verses 5.388; refinement of the emotions through the fine arts 3.617; remembering an hour or two before that you're going to meditate 5.50; setting up your meditation space 4.42–3; simplifying your life 3.617; solitude 1.442; three things: purpose, determination, making sure you're rested 5.388; controlling food, sex, and sleep 3.337–8; study of the Dharma and other things 3.617; suppression of hindrances 1.153; and work 5.639–40, 5.648

the effects of preparation
good preparation can cushion the shock of meditation 5.365, 5.366; if you prepare yourself thoroughly, you are already practising 3.340, 5.386–7, 13.75, 15.345; insufficient preparation 5.336; is it worth sitting if you're not properly prepared? 5.294; to the extent that your preparation is perfect, your meditation will be perfect 5.293

WORKING IN MEDITATION

posture
the arising of physical ease 17.122; as described in the *Satipaṭṭhāna Sutta* 15.103–4; correcting 5.304; finding a stable and comfortable posture 15.104; if you are sleepy in meditation, check your posture 15.171; no virtue in maintaining a painful posture 10.503; selecting cushions 5.304–5; sitting like a mountain 10.511–12; *vajrāsana* 1.385; when the mind is deep in meditation the posture automatically changes 1.144, 5.303; 'When your body is rightly posed' 18.251

effort
alternating between exertion and relaxation, work and meditation 26.19; the callouses on Milarepa's buttocks from all his hours of meditation 18.xvii; *dhyāna* becomes so enjoyable that you don't have to make an effort 5.270–1; don't have a sort of 'moral holiday' between periods of practice 19.322–3; effort and receptivity 15.387; the effort is to remove the hindrances, *dhyāna* is natural 4.160; even if you're apparently meditating eight hours a day you can still be treading water 17.676; learning to broaden the scope of your emotional awareness 15.312; making the effort to meditate as preparation for external Buddhist life 22.309–10; meditating as though someone was standing over you with a sword 5.388–9; meditation is hard work (*kammaṭṭhana*, place of work) 12.607; meditation is the major manifestation of effort in the spiritual life 1.564; meditation should be enjoyable, not a hard grind 5.386, 5.392–3, 15.118; one may not be 'doing' much, but a lot is happening 4.36; right effort in meditation exemplified by the positive *nidānas* 5.392–3; Siddhārtha recollects his experience under the rose-apple tree, *see under* Siddhārtha; some meditation depends on conscious effort and some arises spontaneously 1.563; to begin with, most of the effort is to avoid the five hindrances 15.105–6; vigorous and creative practice 15.83; willed effort 3.272–3, 5.368; wise, gentle, smooth, regular effort 5.392; working on reducing wandering thoughts, ideas, worries 12.475; working in meditation with the subtle energy system 18.322

regularity
the cumulative effect of regular practice 15.364, 17.459–60; determination to meditate 5.328, 5.336–7, 5.385, 5.387–9, 12.417–18, 19.557; the *dhyānas* are within the reach of everybody who meditates regularly 26.46; different rhythms for different people 5.691–2; if you're busy with Dharma activities, keep up your meditation 19.550–1; it's important to refresh our practice from time to time 12.644; importance of regularity 5.375–6, 5.378–9; the important thing is consistency, not the occasional brilliant achievement 4.149; keeping up your practice helps to strengthen your motivation 12.382; meditate regularly 18.167–8; 'Meditate until you die' – because you love the

process so much 18.164–5; not just every day, but the same time every day 5.379; one good meditation isn't enough, you have to keep on meditating 18.321; outside the sangha it might be difficult to keep up your practice 15.657–8; the value of daily absorption in a higher state of consciousness 12.555; we need to practise regularly, not just when we feel like it 12.467; without regular meditation, our spiritual life has no sheet anchor 26.75; a young woman in India who meditated sitting on a shelf 12.513–14

discipline
a disciplined approach to preparation 15.104; how disciplined you should be depends on your temperament 5.376; is there a danger of becoming too disciplined in meditation? 5.377–8; it's dangerous to meditate only when you feel like it 5.376; learning some self-discipline will support your meditation practice 15.173; meditation disciplines the unruly mind 19.110; no 'shoulds' 5.328; not accepting uncritically whatever 'comes' in meditation 21.506; you can force someone to sit, but you can't force them to meditate 18.357–8; you should go to your morning meditation under virtually any circumstances 18.618

resistance
'Again and yet again work on whatever estranges you from meditation!' 5.393–4; the anti-creative force in meditation 12.644; breaking through resistance 13.171, 18.618; dealing with not wanting to meditate 5.373–7; from those parts of you that don't want to change 5.698; the gravitational pull 3.247–8; meditating when you don't feel like it 4.150, 5.373–5, 5.381–2, 10.602; naturally the mind revolts when we try to meditate 10.226; something on a deeper level feels threatened 5.693–4; resistance to going beyond a certain point 5.695; resistance to your higher purpose 15.94

talking about meditation
don't talk too freely about your meditation 5.383–5, 18.421–2, 18.476–7; don't talk about your practice too much 5.608–9; it can be helpful to talk about one's efforts to practise 5.384–5; Tibetan Buddhists rarely talk or write about meditation 13.92

THE EFFECTS OF MEDITATION

during meditation
'All the spirit's storm and stress is stilled into a nothingness' 6.xxix; eidetic images 12.172, 19.28; glimpses of reality 11.103, 12.25–6; light that comes from the mind (*mano-vijñāna*) 12.175; the removal of emotional blockage, leading to weeping 11.200; seeing lights and hearing sounds 12.25; sensitivity to atmosphere 18.23; telepathy, recollections of previous lives 3.122; 'A thousand brilliant hues arise' 6.xxviii–xxix; time travel 17.403, 18.545; visionary experiences 3.122, 10.506, 12.172

after meditation
'After Meditation' (poem) 25.307; be quiet for a while 15.364; ending the meditation 5.307–10; the 'ensuing *dhyāna* stage': the after-effect of successful meditation 18.72; the gains of meditation can easily be lost 15.177–8; guard against Māras waiting to rob you of the effect of meditation 5.309; how the world seems after meditation 17.124; it can be so tangibly and immediately beneficial as to feel like sustenance 18.50; 'Refreshed, we rise ...' 6.xxix; you may briefly have awareness with no mental activity 19.192; you may feel hungry 18.634

ongoing effects
the advantages of meditation (*Samādhirāja Sūtra*) 14.193; changing as a result of meditation 5.251; dealing with becoming more sensitive through meditation practice 4.542; even if you lose everything, you have inner resources to draw on 17.341; even within painful experience there will be a deep happiness 15.221; feeling balanced, poised, calm 10.638; how meditative consciousness differs from ordinary consciousness 11.148–9; integration 16.544, 18.522; it gives the strength to break through caste conditioning 10.lviii–ix; it helps one maintain the creativity of the dream state into waking life 26.46; it helps you communicate the Dharma 17.268; a natural flowing together of all one's energies 11.148–9; the old self is modified to an extreme degree 5.364; one's interests and desires are led upwards towards beauty 15.128; a pleasurable experience of liberated energy 11.149; turning away from sense pleasures on the basis of meditative experience 17.513–14; we should go forth to the *rūpaloka*, the world of beauty 12.559; literally to save the world 4.582; makes the mind more flexible 19.89–90; a means of developing enthusiasm 9.200–1; meditation as weighty karma 3.107, 5.269, 15.92, 15.108; meditation helps you establish what you really want to do 18.522; one who meditates sees the world differently from one who does not 12.169; it enables you to make the transition from intellectual

understanding to insight 5.425; it slows down reactivity 4.508; people underestimate what they can learn from meditation 5.624; Perfect Vision arising through meditation 1.481; rewards of meditating 4.622, 5.380; supernormal faculties developed through meditation 3.122; unifies one's energies and puts them behind the effort to see 5.424–5; a way of bringing about the *parāvṛtti* 12.177; what one meditates upon, that one becomes 14.174

meditation and power
it generates a tremendous 'thought-power' 4.607–8; it is a powerful thing, with important consequences for the meditator 17.264; the mind is in a very active, powerful, dynamic state 5.651; a power to help dispel the cloud of suffering 4.582

progress and success
introduction 5.684–99; 'Achievement in meditation is the sprout' (Milarepa) 18.292–3; blocked by the emergence of resistance 5.693–4; breaking through in meditation through intense practice 13.171–2; expectations 5.685; having 'good' meditations but not seeming to make much progress 4.149; if you think, 'Gosh, I'm getting on well today', there goes your meditation 14.454, 15.729–30; if your meditation isn't going well, you may need to go back to ethics 12.566–7; not just climbing a mountain, but also unfolding like a lotus 5.687; noticing change 5.684–5; it can be difficult to keep track of progress 5.687; reasons for lack of success 5.336–7; self-confidence is the key 5.453, 25.142; sometimes people have their best experience after the final bell has rung 5.405; sometimes you're not sure whether it is doing you any good 15.358–9; to succeed, you must want to succeed – but success is guaranteed 4.150; you can find yourself concentrated when you're not in the mood for meditation 15.220

going deeper, going higher
advanced practices 5.686–7; ambition to get hold of esoteric practices a waste of time 5.50; the difference between meditating and trying to meditate 3.107, 5.363–4, 5.384–5; experiencing the exchange of self and other in deep meditation 4.616–17; gaining higher meditative experience is a process of natural growth 5.392–3; going deeper 5.698–9; greed for more advanced practices 15.344; has a tonic effect on your whole system 19.384; to go deeper, one must *want* to go deeper 4.150; meditating on the fact that the world as we know it is unreal 2.81; scratching the surface with a little meditation will not reveal the Buddha within 26.479; a sign of attaining higher states is no longer wondering about attainment 9.522; when meditating (in the *dhyānas*), one is leading an angelic, androgynous life 2.371; when you are *really* meditating, you are being active 19.582; when you really get into meditation, you don't feel sensations of pain 19.583

time
the afternoon is when one is most likely to feel sluggish 4.574–5, 4.578, 5.351–2, 5.678–9; can there be a wrong time to meditate? 19.555; how long should one meditate for? 5.375–6, 5.379–80, 17.226; meditation transcends time and space 2.41; quality is more important than quantity 5.54; time travel in meditation 17.403, 18.545; what time of day to meditate 4.574–5, 4.577–9; which practice to do if you don't have much time 5.686–7

meditation diary
purpose of keeping a meditation diary 5.356–9, 15.364, 17.262; Sangharakshita keeps a diary 5.357, 20.207, 20.261, 22.300–2, 25.46–8

DEALING WITH DIFFICULTIES IN MEDITATION

fear
can be terrible 5.364; contact with spiritual friends can help 5.364; extreme experiences 5.364, 5.366–7; facing fear in meditation 26.75; fear at the dying down of the turmoil of thoughts 18.452; fear of going beyond a certain point 5.695; if you resist giving in to the fear, the experience passes away 13.73; overcoming fear 4.96–7, 5.363–7; on solitary retreat 5.367; reassuring to know that the Buddha-to-be himself had the experience 12.620; the touch of *śūnyatā* 5.32, 26.48

pain
dealing with pain 10.227–8, 10.502–4; when you really get into meditation, you don't feel sensations of pain 19.583; you don't have to suffer in meditation 10.228

distractions
dealing with distractions 16.543–4; distracting thoughts 19.257; distraction through sense perception 17.680; due to deep-seated tendencies 5.394; getting caught up in negative mental states 17.681; Māra causing distractions 5.351, 11.402; meditation is essentially easy, the problem is distraction 17.678; memories and fantasies 3.567; there's a strange side of the mind that almost wants to be distracted 5.394; three distinct states of mind with

regard to distractions 18.46–7; you can't deal with them through force of will 3.272

hindrances and obstacles
egoistic, grasping attitude 4.504, 15.222, 19.56–7; five hindrances, *see* five hindrances; going through the motions of meditating 5.293, 5.335–7, 15.532, 19.57; meditating for show 19.465; mentioned in a book by the Dalai Lama 8.611; most practices don't lead directly to higher states but remove the obstacles 4.160; people who say they are Buddhists but don't meditate 18.498–9; relationships as a hindrance to meditation (Śāntideva) 4.522–4; your lifestyle may be holding you back 8.211–12, 15.509

other difficulties
difficulties in meditating 19.90; energy going inward rather than out to the object of meditation 17.683–4; if you think it's easy, you have never seriously tried to practise it 8.200; if you're just concerned to escape an aspect of your experience, you won't get far 17.369; laziness prevents continuity of concentration in meditation 17.533–4; losing one's 'edge' 4.181–2; one should not rush ahead 5.40; over-thinking meditation 19.194; struggling with meditation 25.44–5

dangers
what are the dangers of meditation? 4.503–5, 4.509; caution about meditation for young children 4.503; concerns about the insight meditation movement, *see under* vipassanā movement; danger of being catapulted into an experience for which you are not ready 5.365; danger of 'self-hypnosis' 4.502–3; danger for someone with schizophrenia 4.504–5; is there a danger of becoming too disciplined in meditation? 5.377–8; meditation is 'dangerous for Westerners' 3.456, 4.503–4, 5.367–8, 23.48; the main danger is trying to do too much too soon 4.504, 5.368; possibility of madness? 5.363–5, 23.71; of *prāṇāyāma*, *see under prāṇāyāma*

limitations of meditation
even meditation isn't enough, wisdom is needed 4.371; it doesn't automatically lead to insight 5.450; it is not enough to produce an artistic renaissance 26.258

MEDITATION AND OTHER ASPECTS OF LIFE AND PRACTICE

meditation and pleasure
even meditation doesn't guarantee pleasure every time you practise it 17.396; individualistic enjoyment of higher states (Ambedkar) 9.114–15; it's important to associate meditation with enjoyment 5.375–7, 17.226; losing enthusiasm for practice 1.554–5; the meditator must not allow meditative bliss to overpower mindfulness 2.109; a very pleasant experience 12.543; we should never be attached to meditation for its pleasurable sweetness 7.95; you may need to bridge the gap between meditation and how you relate to pleasure 15.157

meditation and thinking
the *bardo* of meditation: gaps between thoughts 12.200; discursive thoughts 5.337–8, 10.606; the elimination of discursive thought 13.72–3; one can't separate meditation and clear thinking 4.146; watching thoughts rioting in the playground of our mind 12.261, 17.538

meditation and everyday life
carrying the effects into the rest of life 5.308–9; the effect of lifestyle on meditation 5.290, 15.171–2; it's hard to meditate in the midst of busy, worldly life 4.527–8, 5.651–2; layman's practice 1.441–2; make sure you get away on retreat 5.652; remain alert and mindful during everyday activities to support your meditation 5.652; almost entirely oriented towards the mundane, no use spending half an hour going the other way 2.261; mindfulness in everyday life will help concentration in meditation 15.172; people like the idea that meditation spills into everyday life, but it's often the other way round 18.499; the states of mind of our daily life are the states we have to address in meditation 15.222–3; sustaining the practice in between meditation sessions 19.321; to begin with, practice will be most effective away from everyday activity 4.160–1; use your meditation creatively, not just to sort out the problems of daily life 14.520

meditation and dreams
analogy between meditation and dreams 12.172–3; meditations practised in the dream state 12.199–200

meditation and the physical body
the connection between mind and body remains even in higher stages 17.393; the experience is of the body as well as the mind 18.75–6; meditation reminds us not to identify ourselves only with the physical body 12.555; the need for physical activity 5.643–5; sustaining a flow of skilful mental states while active 5.645, 5.649–50; withdrawal of the mind from the physical senses 5.323–5, 11.148, 13.71, 13.354; when you meditate deeply you aren't aware of the body 3.338

meditation and action
alternating meditation and external activity 4.463–4; it's difficult to meditate in the midst of activities 4.527–8; meditation combines with action in the world 18.77; meditation is action 17.64, 26.63; most people are inclined either towards activity or towards meditation 5.644, 5.648–9

meditation and study
alternating between meditation and study 5.438; choice between meditation and study 4.568–9; it's best to do both, but if you have to choose, choose meditation 18.486; it's not enough to meditate, we do have to study 5.463–4, 17.573–4; meditation or study? a surprising answer from the 1st century CE 8.465–6, 10.436; a phase of study followed by a phase of meditation 4.568–9; Tibetan lamas who are both scholars and meditators 13.108

meditation and death
death is a state of enforced meditation 5.34, 18.154, 26.49; meditation is a kind of death, death is a kind of meditation 12.206, 12.555–6; meditation is a preparation for death 18.154; when we truly meditate we die 5.34

questions
are there patterns that meditation can't change? 5.653; can meditation cure illness? 5.595–6; does meditation cause alienation? 4.105; if in the end we forget the self, what is the use of meditation? 10.223; is sitting watching a fire meditation? 5.49; is there a meditating type? 12.282; why does a Buddha meditate? 14.401–2, 19.421–6; why is a cave an ideal place to meditate? 4.542, 18.41–2; why do we fall so quickly from the heights of meditation? 3.247–50; writing instead of meditating? 5.636–7

see also
for specific practices, *see* each practice; antidotes to the five poisons, *see under* five *kleśas*; beginner's mind; *bodhicitta* practice; concentration; contemplation of decay; *dhyānas*; experience of the *vimokṣas*, *see under* eight *vimokṣas*; hindrances (*nivaraṇas*), *see* five hindrances; *kasiṇa* practice, *see* ten *kasiṇas*; on the loathsomeness of food, *see under* food; meditation as one of the six perfections, *see under* perfections/six perfections/(5); meditation and psychotherapy, *see under* psychotherapy; recollection of death, *see under* death/recollecting death; *sādhana*, *see* visualization; *samādhi*; *samāpatti*; *śamatha*; Sangharakshita's practice, *see under* Sangharakshita V/meditation; six element practice; Tantric meditation, *see under* Tantric Buddhism; Vipassanā meditation movement, *see* Vipassanā; *vipaśyanā* practices, *see vipaśyanā*; visualization; walking meditation; *yoga-nidrā*; in Zen, *see under* Zen/practices

Meditation school *see* Zen

Meditation Sūtra *see Amitāyur-Dhyāna Sūtra*

mediums a claim that after his death and rebirth, Dharmapala communicated via a medium 23.368; Molly the medium 25.374

Medlock, Julie 8.662

Medripa (or Maitrīpa) 19.172

meekness can lead to people attacking you 4.477–8; most people seem to think that being Buddhist means being meek 4.444; Sangharakshita's realization that he had been too meek as a Buddhist monk 4.444–5; self-confident, energetic people won't feel at home in a meek sangha 4.469

Meera (Kalimpong girl) v22

Megha (brahmin, also called Sumedha) 14.70

Megha, Dharmacharini v24

Meghiya (at one time the Buddha's companion) *see under Udāna*/other key teachings

Mehta, Ardeshir (Dr Mehta's son) v21, v23, v24

Mehta, Dr Dinshaw

life story
early years 21.600–1; a Parsi 12.692; body-building and agnostic phase 22.297–8; association with Gandhi 21.600–1, 22.291, 23.349; in conversation with a Seventh Day Adventist 15.264–5; and Dinoo Dubash 21.466–8, 22.282–4; for

some people an intimidating and alarming figure 23.337; his appearance 23.337; his opposition to the caste system 22.303; likening himself to the Buddha 21.615; 'Buddha hairstyle' 21.552, 21.614; a naturopath 22.283; photographs 22.294, 22.338; references to Buddhism 21.499; social conscience 22.303; his son, *see* Mehta, Ardeshir; spiritual life 21.601–2; last years 21.618–19

guidance
'attachment to the positive, not detachment from the negative' 10.513, 18.332–3; Chattrul Sangye Dorje's view on 'guidance' 22.374; directs Dr Mehta to open a branch of the Society in Poona 22.292; belief he was guided directly by God 21.466–7, 21.601–2, 22.284–5, 23.337–9, 26.668; this guidance cannot be accepted as infallible 21.505–6; 'having taken refuge in the Buddha, I need no other guidance' 21.571; Sangharakshita accepts only what accords with Buddhist principles 21.520, 21.522, 22.299, 22.356; the Scripts 22.284, 22.286–7, 22.296, 22.357–8

the Society of Servants of God
introduction 7.612 (n446), 21.466–7, 22.284–6; Christmas Humphreys speaks to the Society 22.359; a fire during a lecture 26.622; *Living Silence* (publication) 21.499, 21.503, 21.530, 21.543, 21.550, 22.296; Nature Cure Clinic in Poona 22.291–303, 23.349; opening of Poona centre 7.421–2, 22.292–4; Sangharakshita gives talks at the Bombay centre 10.118–19, 22.285–6, 24.12

and Sangharakshita
introduction 21.599–619; first meetings 21.602–3, 22.284–7; contact during Sangharakshita's visit to India in 1979 24.13; discussions about meditation 22.286, 22.298–9, 22.303; a kind of friendship 21.603–9, 22.298; help with Sangharakshita's work with the new Buddhists in India 21.608; 'I had grown very fond of him' 23.339; contrasts in meditation experience 21.612–13; Sangharakshita had 'a high sex potential' (according to Dr Mehta) 23.196; a visit cut short by Sangharakshita's urgent feeling he should go to Nagpur 22.356–60; 'With much of what he said about meditation I was in complete agreement' 22.298–9

Mehta, Gulbehn (Gool, Dr Mehta's wife) v21, v22, v23

Mehta, Phiroz v23

Mehta, Zubin 24.589

melancholy melancholy in Chinese poetry 18.52–3; 'Veil'd Melancholy has her sovran shrine' 3.13

melioristic definition 2.675 (n121); the word borrowed from George Eliot 2.90, 26.10; description of Buddhism 2.90, 26.10

Melling, David 24.311

Mellor, Philip 13.369–512

Melville, Herman 25.53, 26.332

Memling, Hans 23.257, 23.511 (n291), 24.450

Memnon 25.359

memorization of the Buddha's teachings *see* oral tradition

memory

the nature of memory
the connection between memory and emotion 15.87; crucial to an orally transmitted culture 16.363; how is memory possible? 18.289–90; it can play strange tricks 24.141–2; a Dickens story that illustrates the importance of memory 15.85–7; 'Life's memories are … the original work of an artist' 22.xv, 22.3; memory yields to pride 16.314; truth is made memorable when it finds poetic expression 13.644; without memory we cannot experience anything fully 15.85–7

in Buddhist tradition
Ānanda's memory, *see under* Ānanda/ the recorder of the Buddha's teachings; the Buddha created lists to help people remember the teachings 10.230; the Buddha praises Soṇa Koṭikaṇṇa for his good memory 10.573; Early Buddhist teachings in verse form to aid memory 14.20, 15.347; a *bhikkhu* who became an *arhant* but couldn't memorize a single Dharma verse 8.119; *sati* (or *smṛti*) translated as memory 15.85, 17.540–1; *vāsanā* ('habit-energy') corresponds to memory 14.209; a good memory bestowed on the preacher of the Dharma by Sarasvatī 16.368; Mañjuśrī invoked for a retentive memory 2.174; the story of a boy with a wonderful memory for the teachings 10.230–1

notes on memory
don't allow yourself to forget the Dharma, take notes 17.261–2; 'If a young man forgets his hat, no one thinks anything of it' 24.346; losing memory as we get older 17.541; memory and ethics 15.86–7; Mnemosyne, muse of memory 16.363; the point of memory loss 17.540–1; the purpose of retrieving repressed memories

15.87–8; remembering insight 5.432, 16.355; remembering where you were when you had an intense experience 18.400–1; Sangharakshita's strong visual memory 23.182; setting up conditions for retrieving memory 17.540

see also
learning the *sūtras* by heart, *see under* heart; memory of previous lives, *see under* rebirth/how it works

Memphis, Bull of 25.287

men beautiful young men 20.344, 26.471, 26.562–3, 26.594–9; cultures in which men fight to defend their honour 18.101; if a man has disadvantages due to gender, let him recognize that 18.148; knowledge of a man's unrealized 'feminine' side through Tantric practice 13.90; male friendship 11.583–4, 13.452, 13.618, 23.438, 24.542–4; images for a married man and an unmarried man 26.29; men's drive to find out where they stand in relation to other men 18.17–18; restaurant customers in Italy and India mostly male 24.297–8; there is nothing wrong with being a man 12.667–8; *Therīgāthā* verses about how men are not to be trusted 17.218; men and women, *see under* women

Menander (Greek dramatist) 24.295, 24.680–1 (n360)

Menander, King *see* Milinda

Mencius 3.427

Mendelssohn, Felix 20.31, 26.501

mental activity contemplating the Dharma without mental activity 5.438–9; deep concentration without mental activity 5.438; of an Enlightened one 5.421–3; unconscious mental activity, *see viññāna-sota*; very subtle mental activity 16.161; when you are completely absorbed, there is no mental activity 10.602–3

mental chatter 1.574, 15.117

mental concomitants *see caitta-dharmas*

mental events (Sanskrit *caittasikas*, Pāli *cetasikas*)

classifications
described in the Āgamas and Nikāyas 14.89; the Abhidharma's first attempt to classify them 14.88–9; *cetasikas* are preceded by *cittas* (first verse of *Dhammapada*) 15.422; divided into three groups: omnipresent and two types of defiled 14.89; the full list of 51 mental events (Mahāyāna Abhidharma) 17.699–701; Sarvāstivādin analysis of 46 mental functions or events 12.148, 17.446; Theravādin count of 52 *cetasikas* 1.102, 14.79, 17.446; the Abhidharma's list is not exhaustive 17.697

and mind
the distinction between mind and mental events an operational concept 17.493–4; five functional co-relations 17.495–7; going beyond the distinction 17.494; the relationship between mind and mental events 17.489–93; they are whatever correspond to the mind 17.500

omnipresent (sarvatraga) mental events
listed (*vedanā*, *saṃjñā*, *cetanā*, *sparśa*, *manaskāra*) 17.501; summary of how they function 17.501–31; they constitute the perceptual situation 17.501; two are passive, three are active 17.530; *see also* individual mental events

object-determining (viniyata) mental events
summary 17.532–48; a progressive series 17.547

positive mental events
summary 17.549–90; as subjects for reflection 17.588–90; connections with *dharma-vicaya* 17.550; eight occasions for their arising 17.589–90; faith the first to be enumerated 15.650, 17.550; positive mental events tend to integrate with each other 17.550; remember that they are not entities, and there is overlap between them 17.588; their wholesomeness 17.588; they produce skilful actions and also arise as a result of skilful actions 17.589; they tend to arise together 17.576

negative mental events
summary 17.591–682; five characteristics 17.591–2; seven occasions for their arising 17.593–4; six basic emotions (*mūlakleśas*) 17.596–642; twenty *upakleśas* 17.643–82

unclassifiable mental events (aniyatas)
why they are unclassifiable 17.683; account of the events 17.683–90

see also
mental states

mental illness an affinity between intense mental suffering and Enlightenment 13.134; mental illness can be determined only in relation to understanding of mental health 5.663; danger of losing mental balance due to forcible breath control 20.324; dementia 25.447; feeling ill and suffering from one's psychic state 5.657, 5.659–70, 12.225–6, 13.396; helping people in mental distress 4.71; and meditation 4.503; mental breakdown as a result of alienated awareness 12.267–8; more fear of insanity in the West than

in India 11.9, 16.278–9; more people suffer from mental health problems in the West than in the East 12.92–3; 'neurosis' can be a healthy symptom of rebellion 12.101; 'No one seems really normal' (of Buddhist circles in England in 1965) 23.72; people who are unwell are sometimes more spiritually successful 17.164; Sangharakshita and the case of a mentally ill novice 23.74–5; seeking help to alleviate one's mental suffering 5.659–70; schizophrenia 4.504–5, 4.548, 18.442, 23.102; the world of the tormented beings, a state of acute mental suffering 13.130

mental objects 1.110, 3.159, 14.314, 15.160–89, 17.542–3

mental states

INTRODUCING MENTAL STATES

their nature
how they emerge into consciousness 15.200; they cannot be illustrated in pictures or described in words 7.244; described in the *Satipaṭṭhāna Sutta* 15.160–3; always the product of definite conditioning factors 15.242; from instant to instant you are a mental state arising upon the previous one 19.376; karmic consequences are the natural consequence of your mental state 17.56–7; everything can change, and mental states are no exception 15.178; affected by external factors 16.223, 19.527; greatly influenced by other people 15.369; associated with different planes of consciousness 11.130–1; higher mental states associated with light and jewels 16.259

taking care of your mental state
assessing the ethical status and karmic significance of a mental state 15.160–3; be careful not to exaggerate your mental states 18.581–2; becoming aware of mental states 15.170; a Buddhist's basic concern is the transformation of mental states 18.511–12; discriminating between them is not an end in itself 15.166; heeding the ethical implications of mental states 17.679; look after your mental state all day 5.393; taking responsibility for your mental states 5.349, 17.433, 19.273; we need to scrutinize our mental state from moment to moment 15.242–3; your state of mind is within your control 15.178

NEGATIVE AND POSITIVE MENTAL STATES

introduction
confusing positive mental states with negative ones 17.670; how negativity arises 17.593–4; a lot of negativity is positiveness gone sour 4.595–6; most of us have a quantum of negativity 17.646, 17.665–6; the negativity of modern life 4.595; negativity wastes energy at a catastrophic rate 4.133; sense stimulation gives occasion for undesirable states, but it is not a cause 17.98–9; some negative mental states have a life of their own 18.441; they have an effect on both mind and body 17.289–90; the word negative is often emotionally loaded 17.235, 19.290; you put yourself in negative mental states, so don't blame others 4.368–9

hanging onto the negative
accusing someone of negativity 17.235; don't increase it by using language better suited to other cultural contexts 4.622–3; hanging on to negativity 5.349; indulging negativity 18.79; people are often looking for a chance to be negative 4.418; the unskilfulness of spreading an unskilful mental state 15.371–2; wanting to be negative 15.351, 19.35–6; we don't need to explore our negativity exhaustively 14.573–4

developing and sustaining positive states
quantum of positivity 17.777 (n584); the positive *nidānas*, *see* twelve positive *nidānas*; stabilizing a positive mental state 17.308; they won't be achieved through bypassing difficult ones 15.231–2; to enjoy them, pay attention to your everyday activities 15.298; we owe it to ourselves and others to be emotionally positive 3.270

dealing with negative mental states
channelling negativity into something where it cannot cause harm 17.666; the demands of the objective situation get you out of negative subjectivity 4.286–7; don't inflict them on others 4.595; emphasize developing the positive rather than crushing the negative 10.524–5; if you find yourself in a situation that has a negative effect, run away 15.369; making positive use of negativity 4.467; overcoming negative states leads to positive mental events 17.590; the patience of the positive outlasts the obstinacy of the negative 19.36; the positive is a great dissolver of the negative 14.574; relating in the love mode to people in negative states 15.351; they must be transformed, not just pushed away 17.369; to come to understand reality, one must be free of negative mental states 17.438; until *prajñā* arises, they could reassert themselves 17.597

see also
analysis, *see dharmas*/analysis; four right efforts; investigation of mental states,

see dharma-vicaya; seven *visuddhis/citta visuddhi*; skilful mental states, *see under* skilful; unskilful mental states, *see under* unskilful

Mephistopheles *see* Goethe

merchants the Buddha's lay disciples included merchant bankers 1.543; the merchant in the desert 9.264; *seṭṭhi* (Sanskrit *śreṣṭhin*) 10.499; Tapussa and Bhallika, *see* Tapussa and Bhallika; Visākhā, *see* Visākhā

mercy at the mercy of every passing whim and fancy 18.489; 'Inaction in a deed of mercy becomes an action in a deadly sin' 8.215, 13.609; 'Mercy I asked, mercy I found' 2.238, 15.363–4; 'Wisdom with Mercy met' 25.181

Meredith, George 1.23

merit

introduction
what is merit? 19.220; the importance of accumulating merit for all Buddhists 26.644–5; merit alone will not prompt you to seek liberation 17.160–1; not a reward, but the result of actions, like exercising for bigger muscles 14.423; accumulated over a series of lives 19.44; take the opportunity to make merit before you die 18.551

the Buddhist tradition on merit
great importance is attached to making merit 15.402; the holy person as a field of merit 19.220–1; the more advanced the one receiving offerings, the more merit 15.538–9, 19.537; pure and impure merit 16.331–2; red merit and white merit 17.772 (n542); three immeasurable accumulations of merit 14.185; traditionally you can build up a store of merit 14.422–3; the Buddha's appearance is impressive due to his merit (Mahāyāna view) 4.20; merit and the *sambhogakāya* 15.397–8; you must have merit to hear the *Sūtra of Golden Light* 16.336; 'treading the path of merits' (Milarepa) 18.343

actions that bring merit
copying texts 20.332; *dāna* (giving) 2.214–15, 13.86; developing faith in the Tathāgata's eternal life 14.127; giving alms to wanderers 10.479; hearing the *Sūtra of Golden Light* 16.382–3; making material gifts 14.446–7; making offerings 19.311; making offerings to the monastic sangha 15.647–8, 15.652; offering the whole universe 13.86; reading, reciting, copying, expounding the *White Lotus Sūtra* 14.127, 16.44; reciting Samantabhadra's name 14.177; 'special bright pure actions' 17.590; teaching the Dharma 14.446; teaching or studying the *Diamond Sūtra* 14.468–9, 14.480–2; the wish to help limitless beings in limitless worlds 17.306

what results from merit?
does merit always guard against misfortune? 16.421; having contact with a spiritually developed person 18.570; making merit to counterbalance bad karma from unskilful deeds 4.291; merit and the social order 16.427; offerings will accrue to you 19.357; one can accumulate merit without wisdom 19.47–8; rebirth in Sukhāvatī through Amitābha's compassion, not merit 1.334, 1.341; riches sprang to meet Dharmākara when reborn, due to immense merit 1.329; seeking your reward in heaven is spiritual materialism 17.170–1; a store of merit as a basis for spiritual practice 15.395–6

the bodhisattva's merits
immeasurable merit 14.421; they give the gift of their merits 3.368–9; they need a foundation of merit 19.44–5; they see their actions, and their own merit, as empty 14.417; they should acquire merit spontaneously 14.502

problems with merit
accruing a stock of merit 4.101, 4.678 (n124); doing meritorious deeds for the sake of fame 19.484; ethical formalism 2.152; hoarding merit 1.303; it's dissipated by anger 15.367; the oppression of gaining merit 16.322; selling merit 4.101, 4.600, 14.423; lay spiritual practice reduced to the acquisition of merit 15.98, 15.647–50; taking merit literally 1.414; undue emphasis on it leads to the neglect of other objects of charity 2.215; we stand in the way of our own accumulation of merit 14.424

transference of merit (pariṇāmanā)
as a bodhisattva you don't want to mark yourself off as more virtuous than others 3.368–9; at the end of visualization practice 5.583, 13.97, 16.180; counters individualism 4.101–2; dedicating one's merit to Enlightenment 16.331–2; faint echo in Christianity 4.600; at the highest level, becomes the bodhisattva ideal 4.47–8; for the bodhisattva, possible only on the basis of insight into *śūnyatā* 2.270; the ideal of every Buddhist 4.599; the metaphysical problem of donating merit to the Enlightenment of all 14.144; one of the most important teachings in the whole of Buddhism 2.269; paves the way for taking the bodhisattva vow 1.511;

in the Perfection of Wisdom scriptures 2.269–70; it's about inner attitude, not literal transfer 11.284; someone who sold his merit 1.414; this practice should accompany us all along the spiritual path 2.270; the traditional conclusion to any Mahāyāna practice 18.102; transference of merit and the eternal happiness radiated by all the Buddhas 8.452; very difficult to do 11.283–4; whenever you perform any skilful action, dedicate your merit to Enlightenment 2.269–70

see also
in the Sevenfold Puja, *see under* devotion/ puja and ritual; *puṇya*; rejoicing in merits

Merlin 25.97–100, 25.359, 25.438, 25.439, 25.452

Merton, Thomas introduction 22.611–12 (n308); life and death 20.464; he could not distinguish words and concepts from realities 8.491–2; met and was impressed by Chattrul Sangye Dorje 12.437; *Seeds of Contemplation* 13.627–8, 21.345; he inspires Sangharakshita to practise overcoming the egoistic will 13.628, 20.463–4, 22.394–5; *The Seven Storey Mountain* 20.463, 21.345; *Thomas Merton on Zen* (review) 8.490–2

Meru, Mount *see* Sumeru

Merupradīparāja, Buddha 16.456

Meshram, Shri 10.97

Messaien, Olivier 26.258

metaphor all language is metaphorical 13.122, 19.436–7; the danger of military metaphors 18.104–5; the danger of taking metaphors literally 1.83, 4.199, 16.133, 18.606–8; the danger of taking the metaphor of the path too literally 4.199–200, 26.206–7; the idea of 'seeing' another person is metaphorical 19.122; the limitations of metaphor 18.282–3; a metaphor may be taken literally, a paradox never 26.207; metaphor offers us a clue to the nature of reality 14.589, 26.70; metaphor used by poets, prophets, and spiritual leaders 26.209–10; metaphorical language is indispensable 11.659; the metaphors and similes of the *suttas* 14.42; metaphors and similes as vehicles of religious instruction 26.105; psychological metaphors 19.371; reality is metaphorical 26.70; Sangharakshita's shock of delight on first meeting a metaphor 20.10, 20.496, 26.392; taking care when using metaphors 18.286; trying to explain something through metaphors 18.282

metaphors and similes (a selection)

THE THREE JEWELS

the Buddha
a clear window through which the light of reality shines 4.171; the first to hatch from a clutch of eggs 3.61; like a crystal sphere cut into facets to reveal its beauty 5.596–7, 13.304, 18.601–2; like the moon, which only appears to wax and wane 14.238; the moon reflected in different pools 14.212; what he communicated was a handful of leaves 4.3, 7.50, 25.xxxviii

Buddhas and Tathāgatas
Buddhas incalculable as the sands of the Ganges 1.44; deep, immeasurable, unfathomable, like the ocean 2.44, 10.141, 10.449; his magic power like thistledown on the wind 1.255; like the sun arising to dispel darkness 1.53

the bodhisattva
the *bodhicitta* like lightning in a dark sky 4.282; the *bodhicitta* arises like finding a jewel on a dungheap 1.420, 2.126, 4.42, 4.44, 10.145; an elephant plunging into one lotus pool after another 4.135; the glow-worm and the sun: the confidence of *śrāvakas* and bodhisattvas 1.230; like a mother with her baby 17.193; like the rainbow when light passes through a prism 1.261; plunging into the worst hell like wild geese into the lotus pond' 4.582–3, 4.631

Enlightenment
an avalanche 1.48; the dewdrop slipping into the shining sea 4.80; the possibility like the moon reflected in agitated water 7.311

reality
the clear light of the Void 18.43–4; denying *śūnyatā*'s truth like a man on a horse denying he is on horseback 7.213, 10.158; the endless view like removing the window of a Japanese house 19.184–5; like a stained-glass window 5.606–7; trying to penetrate *śūnyatā* with the intellect like a gnat penetrating a ball of steel 14.468

insight
a flash of lightning 1.176; a sharp knife 18.574

the Dharma
as difficult to grasp rightly as a water snake 1.78, 18.180; a work of art that ranges up and down the whole gamut of colours 1.31; a stream or river 9.451–3, 9.455–8

the Sangha
like a greenhouse 3.312; like a lifeboat 19.347, 19.360; like mountaineers roped together 25.34

SPIRITUAL LIFE

Buddhism and Buddhist life
the false and true Buddhist: the donkey and the horse 9.273–5; a great river 2.39; a vast network of golden lotuses 11.88

spiritual life and practice
battleground 3.294, 18.103; a depth charge 2.282; like climbing a greasy flagpole 4.200, 4.213; a space probe launched from the Earth 2.263; weaving the thread of the teachings into cloth 18.136–7

meditation
dhyāna like the first stage of a rocket 4.521; the *dhyānas* like the sun's rays filtering through deep water 4.154; *śamatha* is like a picture drawn with coloured chalks 18.512; *vitakka* and *vicāra* like scouring a pot 9.200, 16.601 (n119), 17.689

the mind
an iceberg and a mountain 3.334; like a child crying at a broken sandcastle 4.431; the one mind like a great expanse of pure, clear water 2.275; pure awareness like a musician immersed in a symphony 15.202–3; tie the mad elephant of the mind to the pillar of the Dharma 4.384–5; a whirling firebrand: how senses perceive objects 17.406–7

consciousness
can be inferred from its functions, like the wind from swaying trees 14.187; a seed 14.187–8

mindfulness
the tailor who puts the garment of our practice together 18.83–4; like playing a musical instrument 15.83; like carrying a bowl of oil filled to the brim 4.480; pick it up again like a hero picking up their sword 4.479

ethics
like embroidery, a matter of delicate and sensitive craftsmanship 18.84; morality is like the launch pad of a rocket 3.245

faith
like the rising sun 1.286–7; like a man jumping across a river (Nāgasena) 1.289–90; those who walk in faith like a calf carried across a stream 1.291

praśrabdhi
like a bee within a flower 3.288, 15.117; like an elephant stepping into a huge lake 3.269, 12.161

other positive mental states
compassion springs up in the Void as a lotus in water 1.239; inspiration like a series of interconnected reservoirs 15.156; making people happy like a rain cloud watering the dry land 17.182; non-attachment like thistledown blown on the wind 17.562; *prīti* (Pāli *pīti*) like a balloon 3.267, 3.288, 9.297; *upekṣā* like a mountain 3.289, 9.299

LIFE AND THE WORLD

the self, ego
ego like an unwanted, faithful dog 7.406; ego a metaphor, like the 'it' in 'it's raining' 19.111; the empirical self is as necessary to the Buddhist as clay to the potter 14.462; practising non-violence while clinging to self is like rowing a boat tied to the shore 7.375

negative mental states
'adding to the cemeteries' (metaphor for craving and ignorance) 10.607–8; cutting the root of craving, like cutting the banana plant 18.579; resist slothfulness as one who leaps up when a snake is in their lap 4.480; subduing the army of the five poisons 18.103; trapped by craving like fish in the mouth of a net 10.617–18; using dirt to get rid of dirt 17.366, 17.494

conditioned things, phenomena
'All *dharmas* spontaneously freed as mists of rain vanish into air' 18.596–7; as delicately contingent as a candle in the wind 14.506; the chariot as a simile of the composite nature of being 1.100; *dharmas* like the reflection of the moon in water 2.154; letting go of the conditioned as a fisherman lets go of a poisonous snake 3.276; a mirage in the desert 14.208, 14.562

life
like a desert 9.453; as precarious as a single hair of a horse's tail on the verge of breaking 18.564; the turtle putting its head through a yoke in the sea 1.418, 4.367, 7.170, 13.139

the world, the universe
cloud, firebrand, moon in the ocean … 14.204; a bazaar 18.566–7; a rainbow 19.234; a ring produced by a firebrand 14.204, 17.350–1; *saṃsāra* like an ocean 1.42–3; stars unfolding like flowers 25.181; struggling towards pleasure like a dog in a treadmill 7.47

see also
the Buddha's teaching to be tested as gold in the fire, *see under* gold; the drum of the Deathless, *see under* deathless; finger pointing to the moon, *see* finger; the Dharma compared to the great

ocean and its qualities, *see under Udāna*; 'Housebuilder, I have seen you', *see Dhammapada*/chapter 11; humanity as a bed of lotuses, *see under* Brahmā Sahāmpati's request

metaphysics

metaphysics
the four logical positions on the metaphysical status of things 17.384–5; in a traditional society everything is linked with ideas of a metaphysical order 3.10–11; the metaphysical problems that arise from taking language too literally 19.437; no metaphysical principles running the universe 14.444; quasi-metaphysical objectivity 26.369; making a poetic statement, not a metaphysical explanation 18.285; the gestalt is not a metaphysical entity, not static or inert 18.282; someone who tied himself in metaphysical knots he could not unravel 26.606; the term 'ontological' is synonymous with the Western concept 'metaphysical' 10.545; we don't necessarily need arguments to convince us of the truth 4.571; you don't solve bad metaphysics with irrationalism 14.422; British disinclination for metaphysics 4.571, 4.578

introduction to Buddhism and metaphysics
there are no metaphysical statements in Buddhism 14.468; the Buddha had no views on metaphysical subjects 3.164; the Buddha's metaphysical teachings 7.229; many practising Buddhists don't think much about metaphysics 17.570; Buddhism is no more a metaphysical dualism than a metaphysical monism 26.645–6; the ethics of Buddhism are founded upon its metaphysics 7.33, 7.35; the dangers of the metaphysics of potentiality 16.61–2, 17.92–5, 17.97–8; the interpolation of practise into metaphysics: because Buddhism means practice 3.370; investigating the most general facts and principles of reality 4.647; little point in exploring metaphysical subtleties in the early stages of practice 16.21; applying metaphysical teachings psychologically can lead to alienation 12.268; the *vajra* represents the metaphysical base 12.186

Early Buddhism
'metaphysical reticence' 10.507, 14.553–4; it leaves open metaphysical questions with no practical implications 15.634; it goes too far in saying the Buddha said not to think about metaphysics 17.570; metaphysical interpretation of the *dharmakāya* 1.252

Mahāyāna
metaphysical interpretation of *kṣānti* 14.192; metaphysical interpretation of the parable of the raft 1.265; the *Bodhicaryāvatāra* on Madhyamaka metaphysics 1.322; we shouldn't allow Śāntideva to be too metaphysical 4.571, 4.578–9; Nāgārjuna transposed rejection of views from metaphysical to logical mode 1.313–15; the Perfection of Wisdom's metaphysical approach to Nirvāṇa 1.253

doctrinal categories
immanence: deep metaphysical waters 15.632–3; it is from a metaphysical point of view that the conditioned is illusory 14.505; metaphysical aspects of eternalism and nihilism 17.624; metaphysical implications of conditioned co-production 16.20; metaphysical implications of the Middle Way 14.240–1; the metaphysical problem of donating merit to the Enlightenment of all 14.144; a 'plurality' of Buddhas is metaphysical, not numeral 14.583; renunciation as a purely metaphysical position 19.201; seeing the *dharmakāya* in metaphysical terms 18.86; self and non-self are equally real empirically and equally unreal metaphysically 2.159; *śūnyatā* is the metaphysical aspect of *anattā* 7.213; *vairāgya* the consequence of a profound 'metaphysical' cognition 2.117; the Void has no metaphysical or ontological status 19.237; the whole of existence as one great Buddha: on the fringes, metaphysically 4.589

method and doctrine 'Buddhism as Doctrine and as Method' 22.268–9; confusing method and doctrine 15.129–30; distinction 1.122–31, 1.206–7, 1.293–4, 1.295, 17.593; divorced from doctrine, method collapses into conventional religiosity 1.404; doctrine and method 22.xvii; *dukkha* as an example 13.129–30; the Madhyamaka school: not so much a doctrine as a method 1.312; Mahāyāna approach 1.242–3; reflection on the repulsiveness of the body is method rather than doctrine 17.218; Tantric Buddhism is method rather than doctrine 1.374

methods always check whether the methods you recommend are working for people 4.102; better to practise one method for thirty years than thirty methods, each for a year 5.613–14; Buddhism has definite methods 10.156; in the end the methods of doctrine and faith converge 18.133; indirect methods, *see* indirect methods; methods and materials of Dharma study

1.22–31; methods of making a bridge between ordinary existence and spiritual life 16.231; methods to get the emotions flowing freely 4.256; methods to obtain freedom 9.342–3; the middle way between spatio-analytical and dynamic-synthetical methods 1.103; the Tantra's awareness of the relative validity of its methods 1.387; you can't practise meditation and mindfulness in a general way, you need specific methods 12.467; Zen's unorthodox methods 7.125

see also
meditation/methods; methods of teaching the Dharma, *see under* Dharma III/methods of communicating; the Buddha's teaching methods, *see under* Buddha III/the Buddha as teacher; gradual and sudden methods, *see* gradual, sudden

metonomy 1.388

mettā (Sanskrit *maitrī*)

translation of mettā
cognate with *mitta* (Pāli) or *mitra* (Sanskrit), 'friend' 12.457, 15.251; disinterested love 15.314–15; 'friendliness' translates it better than 'love' 15.312; literally means 'friendliness' 1.158; loving-kindness is perhaps the best translation 10.652; not a strong enough word 2.361, 5.174; translating it as love is misleading 1.157–8, 9.483–4, 12.457, 15.252–3

introduction
description 1.502, 9.323, 16.599 (n102); the fundamental positive emotion 17.186; the importance of *mettā* 10.653

what mettā is like
an ardent good will 15.251–3; the bliss of a warm and expansive heart 15.258; blissfully ecstatic 15.254; expansive 5.218–19, 15.328–31, 15.336–7, 15.340; fraternity 9.186; freedom of heart 2.315, 14.54–5; impersonal, impartial 5.164–6, 5.184–5, 15.251, 15.300, 15.314–15, 15.330, 17.186; it has the taste of freedom and delight 15.331, 15.341; 'the Sublime Abiding' 15.330

images and metaphors
compared to a mother's love for her only child 11.102, 14.57, 15.321–4, 26.690; it 'burns and shines and blazes forth' 15.253; like the sun shining upon whatever its rays touch 5.165–6, 15.325–6

descriptions of mettā
a cause of expansion in others 15.331; a cherishing, protecting, maturing love 15.315; a down-to-earth care for all living beings equally 15.251; a form of mindfulness 15.329; good will that is free from self-interest 15.312, 15.340, 17.342; a high ideal 15.344; imaginative identification with others 2.361, 5.174–6; an intense and warm desire for the happiness of other beings 11.733; it has a degree of wisdom 15.322; it includes intelligent objectivity 15.323; it includes openness and receptivity 5.189; it is something that must be *lived* 26.23; the most powerful force in the world 7.452; the normal human state 15.345; an outward movement *of* the self rather than *from* the self 15.336–7; powerful, but not a coercive power 15.329; a rational emotion 15.254–6; the response to be expected from one human being to another 5.174, 15.255–6; seeing someone's weaknesses and still appreciating their inner beauty 15.293–4; a spiritual rather than a psychological quality 15.311; the synthesis of reason and emotion 15.258; there is by definition something active about it 15.252

what mettā is not
not limited by time or space 15.299; not mere ratiocination, but involves one's whole being 21.314; not necessarily a reciprocal emotion 15.314; not weak but very strong 1.502, 9.192, 9.517, 9.521, 10.652, 15.253–4; not woolly 15.300; to try to use it to make people like us is a misunderstanding of its nature 17.188

mettā in relationship to other mental states
the Buddha's *mettā* is experienced as compassion 5.200; distinguished from *pema* (Sanskrit *prema*) and *sneha*, *see under pema*; it becomes compassion when faced by suffering 5.158, 5.171–2, 9.323, 9.537, 11.733–4; it becomes *muditā* when you become aware of someone's happiness 5.172, 5.203, 11.734; the difference between *mettā* and the *bodhicitta* 4.86; the difference between *mettā* and romantic love 17.668–9; *mettā* and *śraddhā* (faith) 5.158, 11.155, 15.327–8; getting irritated with people for spurning our '*mettā*' 17.188; hatred is the enemy of *mettā* 15.303; *mettā* and *kṣānti* 4.390–1; *mettā* and non-violence 2.361, 5.174–6, 17.583; *mettā* and the *bodhicitta* 14.556, 17.186; its near enemy is attachment, and its far enemy is anger 10.173

the effects of mettā
anyone within the range of your *mettā* will become its object 14.561; attraction to another person for their sake, not just your own 5.170–1; friendships can develop out of *mettā* 15.251–2; if *mettā* is present, force is unnecessary 3.450; the influence

of *mettā* 15.329–30; it is not an irresistible force, people can reject it 17.188; it must be expressed in action 1.533; it protects one from harm 17.189; people may not be sensitive to your *mettā* 15.330; it saves you from emotional ups and downs, but isn't that boring? 5.155–6

reflections on mettā
beauty and *mettā* 5.592–3, 13.279, 14.516, 17.222, 26.68; the bodhisattva's wisdom includes *mettā* 14.516; a Buddha has the same attitude of *mettā* towards beings whatever they do 15.319–20; a down-to-earth attitude towards *mettā* 16.134; the ethical foundations of *mettā* 15.268–96; feeling *mettā* but having the potential for hatred 18.606; the fullest experience of *mettā* is in the context of friendship 15.332; the irony of advocating *mettā* in an aggressive way 8.133; is it unconditional love? 5.146–8, 15.319–20; it expresses itself in different ways according to the nature of our relationships 15.315–16; it is of central ethical importance 8.452; it is very different from sexual feeling 26.28; it should be our natural state of mind 5.284; it should be reciprocal 5.171; the limitations placed on *mettā* by the sense of a separate self 15.336–7; a man with schemes to improve people's lot, but no *mettā* 7.327–8; *mettā* cannot be forced 17.188; *mettā* in everyday life 15.343–4; the test of *mettā* 5.203, 9.521–2; unskilful action estranges one from *mettā* 17.172; we all have potential for *mettā* 3.344

mettā and the Buddhist path
the average Buddhist is not usually noticeably radiating *mettā* 19.229; confidence in people's goodwill towards you 16.315; a Dharma teacher's most important qualities are inspiration and *mettā* 17.182–3; the eight virtues of *mettā* (Mahāyāna) 17.187–8; good works ... not worth a sixteenth part of *mettā*, the heart's release 2.315, 14.54–5; ideally the Buddhist should feel *mettā* towards everyone they meet 2.569–70; in Buddhism, *mettā* isn't left to chance, but consciously developed 1.502; inclusion as a topic in the *Patisambhidā-magga* 14.73; it is in the spiritual life that we should expect to find it exemplified 7.327; *mettā* and the first precept 1.533, 9.215; *mettā* and the path of regular steps 15.344–5; *mettā* made it possible to start a new Buddhist movement 10.195–6; the spiritual community is based on *mettā* 3.450–1, 15.298, 15.332; without *mettā* in the sangha, no chance of the *bodhicitta* arising in its midst 17.186

mettā, insight, and beyond
can one be liberated through *mettā*? 17.186–7; the cultivation of *mettā* as a path to insight 15.341; feeling constant *mettā* is tantamount to Stream Entry 5.185; insight arising from *mettā* 5.172–3, 15.252, 15.335–8; liberation through love (*mettā*) 17.186–7; *mahāmaitrī* 3.451, 15.257; only when *mettā* is permeated by insight do our emotions go beyond the self 15.336; taking *mettā* towards insight 15.338–41; to miss the link between *mettā* and insight is to miss the point of *mettā* 15.340

mettā bhāvanā

INTRODUCING THE PRACTICE

introduction
brief description 4.74, 5.52–3, 10.173, 10.196, 10.207, 10.393, 11.153–5, 11.701, 12.495–6; the cultivation of powerful, focused positive emotion 3.125; the foundation for the other *brahma vihāras* 10.173, 11.155; fundamentally it is a practice of transformation 15.316; a guide to recovering our inheritance of joy 15.345; it has two aspects: internal intensification and external radiation of love 1.158; it's about your emotional attitude towards living beings, including yourself 5.380; the need for a methodical approach 15.299–300; one of the most important and effective methods of personal development 11.153; a path of irregular and regular steps 15.277, 15.344–5; a positive example of the power of thought 26.700; representative of the four right efforts 17.456; a *śamatha* practice 5.33; take it seriously and you'll have your work cut out for the next twenty years 19.544

different versions of the practice
sources 1.157, 1.606 (n137), 3.684–5 (n382), 9.517; the Buddha's instructions in the *Karanīya Mettā Sutta* 15.297–332; Buddhaghosa's instructions, *see under* Buddhaghosa/*Visuddhimagga*/*brahma vihāras*

the history of the practice
one of four 'things that are to be made to grow' (*Udāna*) 10.531; on the list of 'Hīnayāna' perfections 1.257; expression of an other-regarding attitude 15.236–7; Subhūti became an *arhant* on the basis of the *mettā bhāvanā* 14.452; Mahāyāna attitude towards it 5.216; eulogized in the *Mahāparinirvāṇa Sūtra* 14.240; cultivated by bodhisattvas seeking to preserve the *White Lotus Sūtra* 16.47; Atīśa encouraged

the practice 12.577; taught by S. N. Goenka 5.445; undervalued in Theravāda Buddhism 5.111, 5.188, 5.215, 15.236, 15.338, 18.514; Anagarika Dharmapala's practice 6.606, 8.94, 8.103

Sangharakshita and the mettā bhāvanā
his own practice 5.36–40; he leads the practice for the first time 23.37–8; why he emphasized the practice 5.126

what is the practice like?
different from everyday experiences of love and affection 5.212; it implies the *bodhicitta* 4.39, 5.189; not about thinking vaguely beautiful thoughts 3.125; not an *idea* of a feeling, but the actual feeling 1.398, 3.343, 5.183, 7.329; not the suppression of natural affections but their universalization 1.426

purposes of the practice
the aim of the practice 5.164–6, 15.302–8; all religions say 'Love your neighbour', but the *mettā bhāvanā* shows how 10.156, 10.173; antidote to hatred 3.125, 3.342–4, 4.74, 5.29, 5.326, 9.494–5, 17.543, 19.227; changing hatred into loving-kindness 11.404, 13.173; egolessness 15.338; getting in touch with strong positive emotion 5.173; helps us shift from power mode to love mode 3.576–7; it may help to assuage the wandering mind 15.116; it only works if you really do become concerned about others' welfare 17.693; no practice is more supportive of the observance of the first precept 17.183; not just to feel good in oneself but to develop a positive attitude towards others 17.644–5; practising it for your own benefit will limit the practice 15.340; should make a difference to one's outlook and behaviour 4.585; to break through negative emotions 11.13; to develop mindfulness and loosen the grip of self-centredness 8.579; to dispel irritation 17.183; to sort out communication difficulties 5.149; a support to studying the Perfection of Wisdom 14.516; to become entirely equanimous in your attitude of loving-kindness 15.318

effects of the practice
benefits 9.516–17, 9.521; can it take you all the way to Enlightenment? 5.188–9; could it confer material blessings? 5.177; does it have an objective effect? 5.178–9; eleven benefits from practising *mettā* (Pāli canon) 4.394, 9.517, 10.725 (n511), 17.189; Govinda has a vision on account of doing it 3.209; helping people by developing *mettā* towards them 4.69; inculcating a positive mental state in another person 5.177–9; it brings a lightness to your being 15.329–30, 15.331; *mettā* should go on expanding, renewing itself 15.328; one starts to shift one's habitual reaction to people in a positive direction 17.504; the seed of Buddhahood is present in every small act, word, or thought 15.326; teaching people the practice is a step towards world peace 12.348; traditionally, rebirth in one of the higher realms 15.341–2; transcending usual self-interest 5.52–3, 15.326, 15.340; weakening the fifth fetter 3.421; you protect yourself from thoughts of enmity 18.80; you feel an airy and weightless joy 15.331; you will naturally *see* beauty in people 13.279

general advice about the practice
be careful not to practise it with an un-*mettā*-like attitude 9.517; don't force it 5.617; don't let it become 'that old *mettā bhāvanā*' 12.422; hate types (*dveṣa-carita*) should practise it 10.173, 12.280; how to develop more feeling 5.182–4; it can become over-sentimental 12.496, 18.582; it is beneficial for arrogant and complacent people 15.276; it's important to keep in touch with what you really feel 11.268; it's a mistake to approach it as an elementary exercise 15.341, 15.344; *mettā* and nostalgia 5.173–4; a perspective from the *Satipaṭṭhāna Sutta*: contemplating others' mental states 15.165; preparatory conditions (*Karaṇīya Mettā Sutta*) 15.260–96; try to bring warmth into actual relations with people 5.175, 15.344

to whom mettā is directed
directing *mettā* to a specific person 5.149; for the dead 5.179–82; for the dying 5.176–7; for those who are reborn 5.181; for people who 'aren't really there' 5.184–5; the practice counteracts any prejudice against certain types of people 15.300; Order *mettā bhāvanā* 17.42, 24.32

difficulties with the practice
a beautiful practice, though some people find it difficult 4.74; getting tired of practising it 15.341; if you feel resistant to it, that's a good reason to do it 17.183–4; if you find it difficult, it's important to keep going 12.24–5; if you resist it, you may need friends to help you 17.255; leaving it in the shrine-room 15.343–4; the man who lost his temper when interrupted while 'radiating *mettā*' 5.175–6, 8.133, 17.645; the practice is not easy, but rewarding 1.502; surprising that people find it difficult 5.173; tendency to drift away from the practice 5.138–9; why *mettā* is such a challenge 15.306

the mettā bhāvanā and other meditations
as one of the *brahma vihāras*, *see* four *brahma vihāras*; interleaving the practice with the six element practice 5.184; *mettā* balances the mindfulness of breathing 5.460, 12.496; *mettā* is more difficult than mindfulness, but more creative 5.608; *mettā* and mindfulness the twin pillars of practice 12.651, 12.680; *mettā* as an insight practice 18.513–14; in the system of meditation 5.31; in visualization practices, *see under* visualization

THE METHOD

introduction
method 3.342–4, 3.576, 5.109–11, 9.204–5, 9.375–6, 9.470, 15.301; going back to earlier stages to strengthen *mettā* 5.138, 5.148; what is the point of going through the stages? 5.165–6

first stage
developing *mettā* towards yourself is very important 10.173; drop the habit of self-criticism 15.309; feeling *mettā* for oneself is the keystone of contentment 15.309–10; goodwill towards ourselves is the basis 18.521–2; learning to feel *mettā* for yourself by realizing that others love you 15.308–9; misunderstanding what it means 5.127–8; recapture a feeling of joy 5.182; self-love, *see* self-love; a springboard for the practice, not an end in itself 15.340; we should have *strong* feelings of *mettā* towards our own self 26.23; what to do if you find it difficult 5.184, 15.429–30, 17.184; working on feelings about past abuse 18.444; you can't really feel *mettā* for others unless you feel it for yourself 11.267; you start here because to be contented you need a positive appreciation of yourself 15.277

second stage
beyond the distinction between self and other 5.186–8; can you choose the Buddha as your friend? 5.133–4; dealing with erotic feelings 5.131–3; the first stage flows into the second 15.310; isn't this stage rather exclusive? 15.310–12; the person chosen should be a living person of the same sex 1.159; starting with the second stage 17.184; think back to when you were happy together 5.182–3

third stage
choosing the person you're going to focus on 5.139; the value and challenge of this stage 15.312–15; relating to people from whom you can expect nothing 15.120–1

fourth stage
bearing in mind that there is no self, no underlying person 15.318–19; a challenge 10.lx–xi, 15.315; choosing a politician 5.149–50; danger of changing it from an emotional to a psychological exercise 5.147–8; difficulty in choosing a person 5.149–50, 15.430; do you strengthen your enemy's power by doing the practice? 9.517, 9.521; don't give up on someone you find difficult 17.185; don't think of *mettā* for an enemy as a sort of power over them 15.329; grapple with the idea of this person as an 'enemy' 15.317–18; 'I found it hard to wish happiness to those who were beating us' 10.xli; if strong negative feelings are aroused, go back to an earlier stage 15.317; putting relatives in the fourth stage 15.305; the role of reflection 15.316; a test of your *mettā* 5.147–8, 15.318–19; transforming the energy of hatred 15.316; a very useful stage 9.204–5; we put all thoughts of enmity aside 9.376; wishing them well whatever they have done 15.318

fifth stage
at the beginning, extending mettā to self, friend, neutral person, enemy 15.325; adopting a universal attitude 16.132; although your focus shifts, your attention remains constant 15.325; considering different categories of beings 15.301; could one start with the fifth stage? 5.127–8; at the end of the stage, *mettā* should persist without being specifically directed 5.185; developing *mettā* towards your children 15.324; equality of *mettā*: the arising of equanimity (*upekkhā*) 5.172, 5.210, 15.322, 15.433; extending benevolence to the universe as a whole 13.271; genuinely feeling equal love towards all 15.338; giving more time to this stage 17.184; a hint of the bodhisattva ideal in the phrase 'all sentient beings' 3.376; the idea of 'all beings' 15.325; identifying ourselves with all living things 12.353, 12.409; 'impersonal' *mettā* 17.511; important to include specific people 5.158–9; in love with everybody, or everything 5.618; in this way your heart becomes bigger 10.196; including animals 8.256–7, 9.323, 9.522–3, 10.171, 11.701; including the gods 11.701; including your parents 3.599, 5.156–8, 16.297; including your teacher 5.157; *mettā* for beings of all sorts and sizes (*Karaṇīya Mettā Sutta*) 15.298–300; *mettā* towards the whole of existence, even rocks and stones 19.504; not just a little *mettā* thinly spread over everything, like workhouse jam 5.618; reflection as part of the practice 15.339; removing the barriers between self and other 5.188, 15.325; sending *mettā* to all the quarters 15.299, 15.301; to develop *mettā* towards all

living beings, you must see them positively 19.540–1; we have to love humanity as ourselves 12.343; we need to overcome our likes and dislikes to feel *mettā* for all 5.206–9; we should direct *mettā* towards the whole of the sangha 12.680; 'we will suffuse the whole world with loving thoughts' 4.121; your *mettā* shines on all beings like the sun 15.325–6

Mettā Sutta (*Sutta-Nipāta*) *see Karaṇīya Mettā Sutta*

Mettānisaṃsa Sutta *see Aṅguttara Nikāya*/Book of the Elevens

Metz, France 23.247–8

Mexico bloodthirsty gods 26.297; conquest of Mexico 13.602; the Virgin Mary worshipped in Mexico 13.602

Mhow 9.40

Miccaka 13.341

micchā-diṭṭhis (wrong views)

introduction
brief introduction 10.684–5 (n168), 19.619–20 (n190); etymology 2.390; the importance of the distinction between right and wrong view in Buddhism 11.160; there is nothing worse than wrong views 17.259

definitions
the absence of right view 7.522; a conceptual concretization of an unskilful attitude 19.106; one-sided accounts of the true nature of existence 9.229; the presence of eternalist and nihilist views 7.522–3; the word has the same denotation as 'heterodox' but not the same connotation 7.524

the nature of wrong views
manifestations of either eternalism or nihilism 1.137, 14.572–3; aspects of ignorance 3.193; the difference between holding a wrong view and confused thinking 19.106; an expression of covetousness or hatred 2.390; held in accordance with an unacknowledged emotional bias 14.572; intellectual counterpart of lust-and-hate 1.19; intensification of craving and ignorance gives rise to a fresh crop of false views 10.608; like poor sight, weak, blinkered, and distorted 11.159; nihilism is the source of innumerable wrong views 17.243; not intellectual convictions, but unconscious assumptions 3.193; rationalizations of desire 1.20; a rationalization of a wrong attitude, as much emotional as cognitive 14.572; a right view to which you cling turns into a wrong view 17.259; seen as a *micchā-diṭṭhi* only in the light of a higher truth 10.612; self-view is the fundamental wrong view underlying all the others 17.619; symptomatic of wrong desires 8.231; they affect all aspects of life 17.196; they are catching 17.259; two kinds: those of non-Buddhists and those of heretical Buddhists 7.524; they usually underpin the way we look at the world 17.629; what is technically a wrong view may serve a skilful purpose 17.630–1

the forms they take
belief in God as a wrong view, *see under* God/God and Buddhism; disguised as a kind of universalism 17.618; even the view of non-self is wrong 17.383; 'idols of the theatre' (Bacon): wrong views systematized into systems of belief 12.656; the 'private life *micchā-diṭṭhi*' 10.570; they are rationalized as isms and ologies 11.160; thinking that the difference between Nirvāṇa and *saṃsāra* is real 1.267; thinking that the *khandhas*, separately or collectively, are the self 13.393; the wrong view that there is nothing after death, and therefore no *karma vipāka* 17.245; wrong views about Buddhism 9.265–6; wrong views about livelihood 17.194–5; wrong views about the spiritual life have deep roots 17.602; wrong views in the form of political ideologies 12.616–17; the wrong views of the worldly person 1.107–8

the Buddha's naming of wrong views
actions don't have consequences 2.391, 12.616, 17.594, 17.635–40; everything happens by chance, is made by God, is the result of fate 3.292, 10.249; *issara-nimmāna-vāda* (belief in a creator God) 2.695 (n338), 10.138, 11.361; refusal to recognize the possibility of liberation 17.639–40; there are no beings who have realized higher spiritual development 17.594; there are no living beings higher than sexually dimorphous man 2.391, 12.616; there is no such thing as the spiritual life 2.391; 62 kinds of wrong view, *see Dīgha Nikāya/Brahmajāla Sutta*

wrong views in Buddhist tradition
the Buddha's teaching does not provide a platform for false views 17.369; the refutation of wrong views placed at the forefront of the Tipiṭaka 10.587; confirmed wrong view (*niyata-micchā-diṭṭhi*) is weighty karma 7.523; relationship with the term *duppañña* 16.557–8; one of the *mūlakleśas* (Abhidharma) 17.617–42; through Buddhist history contradictory

opinions have been vigorously opposed 7.382–3; wrong views and the tenth precept 2.390–4; Buddhists criticizing the wrong views of other religions 7.382–3, 22.529

the consequences of wrong views
as long as they are not abandoned, they reinforce unskilful mental states 2.393; being overcome or 'ruined' by wrong views 10.532–3; escapism due to false view 7.220; they conduce to what is distasteful … and painful 7.523; low status 17.245; rebirth 7.523; right view, good rebirth, wrong view, bad rebirth, 'no view', Nirvāṇa 17.245; they can result in violence 7.383–4, 22.529; they have a disastrous effect on our spiritual life and also on our worldly life 12.616–17; wrong view leads to *niraya* (downfall) 12.475

modern micchā-diṭṭhis
discuss the Dharma in terms of right views, not fashionable false views 2.393–4; many of the views we encounter are quite inconsistent with the Dharma 12.476; obsession with the idea that people are equal 17.640, 18.439; the obstacle in bringing the Dharma to the West 11.522; refusing to face up to the fact of failure 19.343–4; regarding every mistake as a stage of development 19.343; taking the hammer of right view to fashionable *micchā-diṭṭhis* 11.612–14; that there is nothing after death 17.245; we must become aware of how we are affected by them 2.393

dealing with one's own wrong views
abandon them by eradicating the unskilful mental states that produce them 2.392; communication with those with greater positivity and clarity 2.392–3; dealing with them through emotions and through intellect 18.450–1; Dharma study 2.392, 19.508; eradication of false view that things and persons are ultimately real 2.128; let us test all views in the fire of our own reason and experience 12.617; meditation practices 2.392; renunciation of wrong views 1.20; transferring animosity towards people to annihilation of one's wrong views 4.151–2; the wrong views behind morally evil behaviour must be demolished 26.678; you can see through them, then bring them back through doubt 3.293, 10.250

tackling other people's wrong views
bodhisattvas should be able to rid all beings of their wrong views 17.465; the difficulty of refuting wrong views 10.587; dismantling wrong views 3.xiii–xiv; in tackling them, you have to understand why people say what they say 19.106–7; speaking out against wrong views 4.126; to expose wrong views requires practice, intelligence, alertness, and confidence 10.587; they are to be corrected by discussion, not force 11.360–1; the yogi pouncing on them like a hawk 19.76

freedom from wrong views
ceto-vimukti, freedom from wrong views 3.277; when all false views are abandoned, wisdom shines forth 2.393

see also
purifying the mind of wrong views, *see* seven *visuddhis*/*diṭṭhi visuddhi*; topsy-turvy views, *see* four *viparyāsas*

Michael, archangel 13.360, 13.583, 16.358, 25.499–500

Michael, Trevor 24.27, 24.611 (n45)

Michelangelo Blake's drawing of the Laocoon statue 26.386; Convivi, *Life, Letters, and Poetry* 24.316; *David* 26.264; he expresses his vision in a transformative way 26.246; his appearance at the height of the Italian Renaissance 3.58; friendship with Tommaso Cavalieri 24.316; his works among the supreme achievements of Western culture 12.392; *Pietà* 23.307; sculptures in Florence 23.313–14; Sistine Chapel frescoes 3.100, 13.573, 23.308, 26.246, 26.475; the sublimity of his work 14.472; a work now in Munich said to have inspired him 24.587

Michener, James A. 26.308–9

microcosm and macrocosm 7.159, 7.400, 13.438, 19.216, 26.51; an individual Order member is a microcosm of the Order, but cannot represent it 14.542

microscope 19.216

middha (torpor or drowsiness) energy going inward rather than out to the object of meditation 17.683–4; sloth and torpor as hindrance to meditation, *see under* five hindrances; *thīna* is its mental equivalent 17.683; as an unclassifiable mental event (*aniyata*, Abhidharma) 17.683–8

Middle Ages *see* medieval

Middle Country 2.748 (n709), 14.620 (n154)

middle way (*madhyama mārga*)

WHAT IS THE MIDDLE WAY?

introduction
brief introduction 10.135–6; its definition is a matter of exceptional difficulty 1.137,

19.281; each formulation of the Buddhist path is a 'middle way' 3.294; it's how Buddhism sees the world, just common sense 17.626; let us set forth as pilgrims upon the Middle Way 7.418

the nature of the middle way
at each level the opposites become more seductive, more 'spiritual' 1.137; attaining through it a larger conception of truth 7.40; the attitude of its true follower: to find the truth and be receptive to it 17.632; Hermetical correspondence between higher and lower modalities 1.138; if you tend to compromise, your middle way can become a *micchā-diṭṭhi* 14.572; it involves neither moral compromise nor intellectual eclecticism 7.299; not a 'golden mediocrity' but the embodiment of the 'spiral' principle 2.103; not so much between extremes as above them 7.363; a path between and above all mind-made dualities 7.357; taking it literally is spiritually disastrous 7.298–9

where it sits in the Dharma tradition
each formulation of the Buddhist path is a 'middle way' 3.294; co-extensive with the Dharma 1.138; taught in the Buddha's First Discourse at Sarnath 1.136, 10.608; the fourth noble truth as middle way 1.136–40; in the Mahāyāna: the Mādhyamikavāda and the Madhyāntavāda 7.532–5; in principle identical with *śūnyatā* 7.300; the path to Enlightenment is a middle way 11.481; rebirth and the middle way 1.109, 2.14–15, 12.690; a synonym for the goal of the disciple's career 1.137; the bodhisattva ideal 7.44; characteristic feature of the Madhyamaka school 1.313; the Dalai Lama's résumé of the Middle Way 8.504–5; the FWBO's first twenty years on the middle way 12.385–95

TRADITIONAL APPLICATIONS OF THE PRINCIPLE (THREE LEVELS)

introduction to these three levels
Sangharakshita's standard teaching 12.387

(1) ethics
between self-mortification and self-indulgence 10.247, 10.609, 13.138, 17.624–5; in the Buddha's day, these two extremes were quite clear-cut 10.609; the Buddha's practice of the middle way in this respect 9.399–400, 12.620; the middle way is neither ignoring one's unskilful side nor indulging it 10.608–9; neither extreme constitutes the way to Enlightenment 7.520; relationship to eternalism and nihilism 1.139–40, 11.497, 17.624–5; and repression 7.290; self-affirmation and self-denial 11.496–9; straying from the middle way in the *White Lotus Sūtra* 16.195; these extremes tend to turn into each other 11.497

(2) psychology
between affirmation and negation 1.119; between eternalism and nihilism 1.74, 1.137–9, 7.197, 7.532–5, 9.398–9, 10.597, 12.387, 17.242, 17.624, 19.375; between idea of an unchanging soul and the idea that we have no soul 12.387; between materialism and *ātmavāda* 7.166–8, 10.142; in psychology 1.139; regarding what happens after death 2.14–15, 7.165–6, 10.609, 19.375

(3) metaphysics
between existence and non-existence 10.609, 19.280; between ultimately real and illusory 17.624; between *satkāryavāda* and *asatkāryavāda* 10.142; Enlightenment transcends existence and non-existence 17.242, 17.251; the truth of your existence: neither unchanging existence nor non-existence 19.376; all things are becoming 7.153, 12.387; in philosophy 1.138–9, 9.397–8; refusing to think of reality in terms of existence and non-existence 1.363; *śūnyatā* interpreted in terms of the Middle Way 14.181

OTHER APPLICATIONS OF THE PRINCIPLE

the middle way between …
formalistic monasticism and lax laicism 12.389; accepting and rejecting the teachings of other faiths 2.246; anxiety about activities and a spaced-out state of mind 14.519; authoritarianism and individualism 16.553; belief that no progress is possible and belief in automatic progress 10.347; 'Buddhism says you must do this' and 'Buddhism says anything goes' 10.609; changing outer conditions and work on the mind 7.238–9, 10.348; conformity and rebellion towards parents 12.390–2; making no effort at all and intellectually directed effort 2.111–12; dependence and independence 7.261; dismissing the means to Enlightenment as superfluous and clinging to them 7.264–5; hedonism and asceticism 15.287, 24.467; an ideal that is too abstract and one that is too low 19.182; individualism and conformity 18.35; letting emotions go where they want and suppressing them 5.618; matters of life and death 17.244; mindfulness and spontaneity 16.300; pseudo-originality and mechanical repetitiveness 4.280–1; remembering death and becoming too preoccupied with it

19.103; seeing lower and higher evolution as same or different (*pratītya-samutpāda*) 3.13; self-consciousness and spontaneity 14.581–2; spatio-analytical and dynamic-synthetical methods 1.103; sympathy and solitude 26.142; ultimately real and illusory (five *skandhas*) 17.626; unthinking acceptance and unthinking rejection of culture 12.392–4

other manifestations of the middle way in the Buddhist movement, acceptance or rejection of tradition 9.402–3; in ceremonies, a combination of richness and simplicity 24.531; in relation to views 1.61, 1.138; karma a middle way between determinist and casualist views 7.585 (n220); a middle way leading to the stability and harmony of the sangha 10.580–1; not easy to follow a middle path between blocking and free expression 5.133; in social life 9.400–2; speech: a middle way between knowledge and ignorance of someone 18.216; truth is the middle way between exaggerating and minimizing 14.573; with respect to moral rules and religious observances 12.27

Middle Way (magazine) founded (1925) 10.139; a link between British Buddhists 12.73; Clare Cameron as editor, *see* Cameron; 'The Future of the Sangha in the West' (Walpola Rahula) 8.460; gave Sangharakshita the impression of a thriving Buddhist movement 11.518–19; model of conscientious editing 8.155; perhaps Sangharakshita would have edited it if life had gone a different way 26.583; reports of Sangharakshita's teachings at the summer school 23.33–4; review 8.375–6; Sangharakshita's articles, *see under* Sangharakshita XIII/articles; 'Wesak 1954' 8.138–9; 'Wesak 1965' 23.122

Middleton Murry, John short introduction 23.542 (n498); biographies 26.333; his life 26.332–3; acquisition of books 24.140; English literature began with the rejection of Catholicism 13.511, 26.259; 'To discover that within myself which I must obey' 2.401; the metabiological sciences 12.87; 'The Isolation of Katherine Mansfield' 13.385–6; and D. H. Lawrence 8.545–6, 26.332; as literary critic 26.333–6; 'The Nature of Poetry' 26.335; opponent of T. S. Eliot 26.332; 'Romantics and Tradition' 13.511; *Son of Woman*, a study of D. H. Lawrence 23.473, 24.525; Newman 'believed in God but he didn't like (trust) him' 15.620, 17.336, 17.552

midwives friends are like midwives, who draw forth what is waiting to be born 8.578; Socrates the 'Great Midwife', bringing ideas to fruition 18.301

Mijiao Zong 1.384

Milarepa

INTRODUCING MILAREPA

introduction
brief account 1.630 (n398), 3.652 (n176), 18.60–1; the meaning of his name 18.196; the archetypal example of the Sahajayāna 18.417; ascetic attitude in a Mahāyāna context 18.215; compared to Thoreau 24.52–3; compared to St Augustine 18.160–1; compared to St Francis 13.625, 18.xi, 18.xvi, 18.160; considered a bodhisattva 2.181; an exemplar of a particular presentation of the ideal 18.221–2; an example of a faith-follower 17.333; an example of how human beings can change 3.180; the greatest poet and yogi of Tibet 2.213, 13.27; the living embodiment of the Dharma 18.340; one of the most interesting and vivid figures in the history of religion 13.26; how can he have been a *samyak-sambuddha*? 26.699; it's not possible to know who he is 19.418; whatever he does is an expression of his Enlightenment 19.230–1; his place in world history 18.3–4; Sangharakshita reads his poems at a poetry reading in London 23.124; his material poverty and spiritual wealth 18.50, 18.96, 18.217–18; iconography 13.214, 18.4; illustration 13.214

biography
introduction 1.636 (n447), 4.662 (n20); Milarepa tells Rechungpa his life story 18.xvi, 19.303–7; *The Life of Milarepa* 18.xii, 18.xvi, 18.98, 22.444, 24.396–7; faith can arise through reading about his life 3.299; leafing through his biography

with a box of chocolates 1.553, 16.285, 19.96; Sangharakshita inspired by this 'masterpiece of religious biography' 18.xii, 20.151; plays and a film 18.xiii

LIFE STORY

early life
the tragedy of his childhood 13.26–7, 18.60–1; learning the darker arts of the Tantra, black magic 18.32, 18.64, 18.362; he must gain Enlightenment or go to hell 4.292, 4.448, 15.93, 17.467–8, 18.61, 18.128–9

Marpa, his guru
he functioned like the Perfection of Wisdom 14.488; no question of choosing a guru: 'To hear his name caused my skin to tingle' 18.65; Marpa's response when Milarepa asked him for teachings 18.113; Marpa's strict method of teaching Milarepa 12.18, 14.488, 15.747 (n38); he got him doing difficult and even dangerous things 13.176; 'I reduced myself to powder in his service' 18.61; Milarepa, in solitude, longs for his guru 18.13–15; Marpa gives Milarepa the Formless Ḍākinī Dharma Series 18.364; Marpa appears to Milarepa in the form of a lion 18.19; Marpa visualized above Milarepa's head 18.92; Milarepa prays to Marpa to bless Rechungpa 18.314, 18.379–80; he 'put himself into the hands of Marpa' 18.383; 'When with my Guru Marpa on that steep hill' 18.400–1; the Pith-Instructions given by Marpa to Milarepa 18.593–4; the ordeal of building towers 12.18, 14.488, 17.555, 18.61, 18.269

his life as a solitary yogi
a song which gives a brief biography 18.379, 18.383–98; the stages of his development 18.300–1; having repented of his wickedness, free from guilt 18.160–1; when faith arose in him, he didn't like its implications 17.553; his sister is concerned about his status 18.108, 18.561; he was almost naked and lived on a diet of nettles 13.27, 15.119; compared with Tsongkhapa 12.511, 17.376; he was never a monk in a technical sense 18.196, 18.333; his lifestyle 19.254–5; his loneliness 18.13–15; his life is spontaneous and free of obstruction 18.66; his nakedness 18.xvii, 18.133–4, 18.219, 18.221, 19.249–64; nothing holds him back because there is no-one to be held back 18.73; the robber ('I've never found anything even in daylight!') 13.27, 18.139, 18.341–2; people's offerings of gold to him 18.375–6; singing in his sleep 19.320; his heart 'turns into numerous small birds' 19.25; when his cooking-pot broke 13.27, 24.426; his old age 18.489–90, 19.367–8; he was apparently poisoned 4.14, 19.464; his final teaching 7.475; his disciples quarrel over his relics after his death 16.141

lineage of transmission
from Vajradhāra 1.276, 7.475; lineage in the true sense 18.314–15; founder of the Kagyu school, *see under* Tibetan Buddhism/schools

HIS CHARACTER AND QUALITIES

character
beyond time and space 18.532; the *bodhicitta* ('Friend Bodhi-Heart') is his companion 18.225–6; born from the union (*yab-yum*) of wisdom and compassion 18.296–7; he adds to the beauty of the mandala 18.447; he doesn't care that he's not scholarly 19.521; he doesn't care what people think of him 18.461, 19.466; his enjoyment of singing and speaking, and relishing of silence 18.48; experiences no separation between 'self' and 'world' 18.128; he has realized the *dharmakāya* 19.318–19; he is always in touch with the higher realization 19.176–7; he lives in the present 18.340; he meditates whatever he is doing 19.427; his faith is integral to what he is 18.30; his family is the Sangha 18.296–8, 18.394; he has no need of books 18.458–9; he has disposed of the concepts of *saṃsāra* and *nirvāṇa* 18.397; he has given up the sense of possession 18.219; he has transcended words and concepts 18.395; he is not attached to his native place 19.252; his body 19.41–2, 19.517; not a conformist or an individualist, but an individual 18.136; sleeping like a bird 19.318, 19.320; spiritual relationships are more important than family ones 19.253; a visual person 18.437–8; like a wheel-turning king 18.50; whatever he says is right speech 18.538–9; will not conform to others' standards 19.260

qualities
animism 19.504; compassionate 18.33, 18.268, 18.354, 18.588; confident 18.45; Enlightened 18.615, 19.23; equanimous 18.48, 18.53–4; fearless 18.52, 18.92; full of energy 18.340; happy 18.296, 18.328–45; joyful, whatever the conditions 4.316, 18.45–8, 18.129, 18.345, 19.177; mastery of *prāṇa* 19.30; mindful 18.10–13; non-attached 18.394; nothing can impede him 19.64–6; outside time 18.69; persevering 18.20; playful 19.14; positive 18.54; receptive 18.593–4; self-respecting 18.136; a simple, direct, almost childlike person 18.196; single-

minded 19.8; uncompromising 18.221, 18.246, 18.561–2, 18.617, 18.620, 18.638–9, 19.261, 19.463; unpopular 19.464

MIRACLES, PRACTICES, TEACHINGS

miracles and magic
creation of extra bodies 19.62, 19.119–20; the difference between Milarepa's miracles and supernormal powers 19.120; flying 19.75–6, 19.113, 19.121; performing the *abhijñās* 19.62–5; he transforms himself into seven *repas* 19.419–21; his body, speech, and mind become the three *kāyas* 19.23; he produces a phantasmagoria of himself 19.38; producing a hailstorm by magical power 18.547; Rechungpa disparages Milarepa's miracles 19.77; walking on water 18.63–4, 18.108–9

practices
the bodhisattva vow 18.215; the callouses on his buttocks from all his hours of meditation 18.xvii; devotion 18.117; the four initiations of Dem Chog 18.65; guru yoga 18.15, 18.92; held together by simplicity of faith and honesty of purpose 18.117; his practice and his way of life is his teaching 18.32–3; *mahāmudrā* 18.13, 18.29–30, 18.61; meditating in a tiger's cave 18.41, 18.51–2; meditating for years in a closed-up cave 18.326–8; mindfulness 18.9–12; offering the mandala 18.125–6; renunciation 18.80, 18.126–7; the 'Samādhi of Guru-Union' 18.63; the six yogas of Nāropā 13.28, 18.65; *tummo* heat 13.28, 18.49–50, 18.65, 18.89–91, 19.257; *yuganaddha* 19.258

his metaphorical possessions
'a horse of Prāṇa-Mind' 18.73; the boots of spiritual practice 18.80–1; a jacket of inner heat 18.89–91; instead of a hat, the guru on the crown of his head 18.92; his ornament is his devotion to the Dharma 18.96; the temple of his direct spiritual experience 18.124–5; cloth woven from the *bodhicitta* into 'dignified and altruistic trousers' 18.136–7

teachings
blending consciousness and the unconscious 19.323; emphasis on personal experience 18.228; '*Gurus, Devas, Ḍākinīs* – Combine these into a single whole and worship that' 7.305; his genius in being able to teach different kinds of people 18.255; 'No profounder teaching can I give you in my life' 19.111–12; plain straightforward Buddhism – or just common sense 18.565; the three delights 18.417–20

DISCIPLES

introduction
disciples were attracted to him though he lived in remote places 18.526; Drigom Repa 19.171–2, 19.491; eight heart-disciples 18.59–60, 18.97, 18.143, 19.171–2; 'establishing disciples on the path' 18.xvi; he is always concerned to instil a sense of urgency in his disciples 18.154; his two chief disciples 19.510; Gampopa, *see* Gampopa; Rechungpa, *see* Rechungpa; Sang Jye Jhab, an unsatisfactory disciple 18.187; son-disciples and heart-disciples 19.171–2; variety of disciples 18.xv; women disciples 16.335, 19.471

Sangje Jhap, the shepherd disciple
'The Shepherd's Search for Mind' 18.224–55; his curiosity about the nature of mind 18.224–47; his character 18.228–9, 18.234, 18.238; his name 18.238; he meditates for seven days 18.247–8; his attainment of 'superlative experience' 18.254

Shiwa Aui, the young aristocrat
'Meeting at Silver Spring' 18.57–190; Milarepa's dream of a *ḍākinī* predicts his meeting with his disciple 18.58–9, 18.146; their meeting 18.62–73; the character of the young aristocrat 18.62–4; his original name was Dharma Wonshu 18.150; 'karma-exhausted' 18.60, 18.71; his recognition of Milarepa as his teacher 18.68–70; one of Milarepa's eight heart-disciples 18.143; he offers gifts to Milarepa 18.70–142; he asks for ordination 18.97–8; the big step of giving up his weapons 18.97–101; he decides to commit suicide 17.338, 18.142–4; Milarepa accepts him as his disciple 18.155; he is sent for training to the translator Bhari Lotsawa 18.156–9; his initiations 18.159; he is given the name Repa Shiwa Aui 18.159; his transformation from sensualist to renunciant 18.159–60, 18.185–7; his vows 18.161; Milarepa's teachings to him 18.149–85; the merit gained by his family through his practice 18.186; he asks a question about Rechungpa's practice 19.552–3; served Milarepa until his death, and gained Enlightenment himself 18.187

THE HUNDRED THOUSAND SONGS (*MILA GRUBUM*)

introduction
contact with Milarepa's mind, which is much greater than ours 4.353; contain the essence of Buddhism 9.109; continuing the tradition of the *vajragītā* of the Tantric

masters 13.179; 'hundred thousand' means 'many' or 'collected' 13.27, 18.xii, 18.3; Kagyu text 2.555–6, 11.372; in principle canonical 14.263; the songs have antecedents in Indian literature 13.115; still sung today 18.4–5; studied in Triratna 11.377; the style in which the songs were sung 18.xviii–xix; a union of the emotional and the intellectual 14.451; they express the truths and experiences of authentic Buddhist practice 18.6; were the songs Milarepa's own? 18.432–3; whoever wrote them down must have been a great poet 18.4, 19.76; seminars on the songs 2.743 (n685), 18.xii, 18.xiii–iv; an inspiring example, even if they don't offer us a realistic lifestyle 18.33, 18.223; inspiration to the Triratna Buddhist Community 2.555, 12.368

songs and stories
brief introduction to a selection of songs 18.xv–vi; 'Milarepa's Eight Wonderful Examples' 18.xi; Challenge from a Wise Demoness 19.418; a song of happiness 18.328–45; a song with similarities to *Pilgrim's Progress* 18.80; The Tale of Red Rock Jewel Valley 18.7–37; song of spiritual friendship 18.13–15; the five Indian demons and how Milarepa deals with them 18.21–32; 'Everybody needs the Dharma' 9.170, 11.367–8, 18.589–90; The Meeting at Silver Spring 18.55–190; The Shepherd's Search for Mind 18.193–255; 'Song of the *Bardo*' 18.82–6; Milarepa's First Meeting with Rechungpa 18.265–347; The Challenge of the Logicians 18.349; Rechungpa's Third Journey to India 18.349–433; Rechungpa's Repentance 13.176–7, 19.5–167; Heartfelt Advice to Rechungpa 19.169–300; Rechungpa's Journey to Weu' 19.301–510; The Song of Meeting and Parting 19.501–9; 'Rechungpa's Departure' 19.511–89

translations
Drinking the Mountain Stream (trans. Kunga Rinpoche and Brian Cutillo) 18.xvii; *The Message of Milarepa* (Clarke) 18.xi–xii; 'Mila Repa and the Novices' (Snellgrove) 18.41; *The Hundred Thousand Songs of Milarepa* (Chang) 18.xii–xiii; *The Hundred Thousand Songs of Milarepa: a new translation* (Stagg) 18.xiii

Milinda (or Menander), King a college named after him 9.566 (n291); *Milinda-pañha*, *see Questions of King Milinda*

milk living together 'like milk and water blended' 12.606–7; milk put in the skin of a dog (Kumārila Bhaṭṭa) 8.359–60, 10.624; the milk-drinking heron leaves the water (*Udāna*) 10.649–50; the milkmaid who spilled the milk 19.9; moving closer to ageing and death like a calf drinking its mother's milk 10.617–18; the quintessence of milk and nectar (Milarepa) 18.117; Satyapriya organizes milk distribution for children 20.289, 20.291; 'the Vedas are the cows, the Upanishads the milk, the teaching the butter' 18.220; the wish-fulfilling tree produced from the cosmic ocean of milk (Hinduism) 16.398

Mill, John Stuart cut off from poetry 16.532–3; 'exhilarating in the extreme' 20.446; matter is the permanent possibility of sensation 17.404

Millais, John Everett *Bubbles* 12.643, 18.119; *The Blind Girl* 26.670

Millar, Colin v24

'millennium' 6.602, 11.623, 12.592–3

Miller, Arthur 24.390–1

Miller, Donald (Dharmadhara) 8.656

Miller, Henry 14.140, 23.234–5, 26.238

Miller, Stuart 13.452

Millet, Jean-Francois 23.265, 23.514–15 (n308)

Mills, Laurence *see* Khantipālo

Mills, Mrs 23.239

Mi-lo Fu ('Laughing Buddha') China the chief centre of his worship 1.335; introduction 22.575 (n47); Maitreya in the form of a medieval Chinese monk 2.182

Milosz, Czeslaw 24.577

Milton, John

introduction
experience of inspiration from outside 19.141; for Milton angels had an objective existence 13.591; he came to terms with the failure of his life's work 14.491; his inspiration like a great furnace 26.69; his superb artistry 24.572; his works among the supreme achievements of Western culture 12.392; 'of the Devil's party without knowing it' (Blake) 13.592, 18.78; 'Our language sunk under [Milton]' (Addison) 14.292; *Poetical Works*, a much-loved copy 24.515; there are no 'mute inglorious Miltons' 26.18

Paradise Lost
the angel Abdiel: 'Among the faithless, faithful only he' 3.569, 8.191; angels 13.583; angels merging 'Easier than Air with Air' 4.690–1 (n215), 24.517; begins with the invocation of the heavenly

muse 3.513; the 'bright essence create' 1.261; comparison with Dante's *Divine Comedy* 13.583; description of God 13.590; description of the archangel Raphael 13.584, 13.596, 26.471, 26.616; description of Satan 13.591–2; doctrinal elements are part of the story 13.669; an epic poem 13.592; 'Evil, be thou my Good' 26.618; the fall of Mulciber 13.595–6; fascination with the story as part of cultural, not religious, heritage 25.19; 'For me its characters existed only in Milton's imagination' 13.582, 13.584; God is not an attractive character 13.584; 'the greatest poetic experience of my life' 20.36, 26.392; has claim to be the most important work in English literature 26.22; has the quality *kāvya* 26.332; 'heroic valour, firm and unmoved' 26.153; illustrations by William Blake 13.592, 24.519; an imaginative statement of the whole dilemma of modern man 26.22; Lucifer denounced by Abdiel 3.569; 'Millions of spiritual creatures walk the earth' 1.32; 'The mind is its own place, and in itself/ Can make a heaven of hell, a hell of heaven' 17.497; a mixture of human and supernatural beings 13.583; once acceptable Sabbath reading 14.69; 'Paradise Lost' (Sangharakshita's poem) 25.386; rebel angels 13.583, 13.591–2; the rebel angels invent artillery 4.449, 15.139; rebel angels have to reduce their size 1.273; refurbishment of the Bible narratives 14.66; Sangharakshita's response to reading 13.529, 13.582–3, 20.36, 26.397; Satan, an attitude of chronic individualism 3.606; Satan, the fallen angel 13.591–2; Satan is the hero of the poem 13.592; Satan 'looks through the horizontal misty air/ Shorn of his beams' 14.98; 'the verdurous wall of Paradise up sprung' 22.319

Paradise Regained
the character of Jesus seems at times more like the Buddha 24.572–3; 'Dusk faces with white silken turbans wreathed' 20.12; its excellence as a narrative poem 24.572–3; an illustration by William Blake 24.574; 'With winning words to conquer willing hearts' 7.383

Areopagitica
'all the airs and madrigals that whisper softness in chambers' 7.283; 'A good book is the precious life-blood of a master-spirit' 19.70; has the quality *kāvya* 26.332

Sonnets
'How soon hath Time, the subtle thief of youth' 26.294; 'Licence they mean when they cry liberty' 13.462; 'On the late Massacre in Piedmont' 13.580–1, 26.476–7; 'sad Electra's poet' 23.244; 'They also serve who only stand and wait' 13.588; 'Who loves [liberty], must first be wise and good' 13.463

other works
Comus 2.319, 24.572; *Il Penseroso* 14.523; *Lines written on the Morning of Christ's Nativity* 7.46; *Lycidas* 26.439, 26.732 (n334); *Of Education* 26.394; *Samson Agonistes* 10.112; *Tetrachordon* 13.462

mīmāṃsā *see under* four *iddhipādas*

Mīmāṃsās *see under* Hinduism

Minakshi 20.232

mind

WHAT IS THE MIND LIKE?

what is the mind?
according to the Buddha's teaching there is no limit to the human mind 17.437; an activity, not a *tabula rasa* 17.499; Buddhist psychology conceives of it as experienced by direct perception 17.438–9; it cannot really be described, but it helps to try to describe it 17.493; it constructs from its perceptions a world of objects 12.175; it is not a thing, but consists solely in its activities 17.434; the most interesting thing about us 12.138; no more real in an ultimate sense than anything else 18.44; not a fixed abode, though it tends to try to settle down 18.562–4; nothing more than a complicated machine (Abhidharma)15.187–8; nothing more than the sum total of mental states 19.235; the raw material, the stuff of Enlightenment 18.234; a process, not a thing – not a *tabula rasa* but a force, an energy 12.99; what is mind? 16.270; that which perceives an object 17.690; universal mind (behind the evolutionary process) 12.86–7; *xin* (Mr Chen's explanation) 13.350; words for mind: *xin*, *citta* 11.21, 13.350–1; your mind is not a blank, but is full of *micchā-diṭṭhis* 19.508

the nature of mind
Milarepa's shepherd disciple tries to find out about his mind 18.226–55; what colour is it? what shape is it? where is it? 18.234–6; constantly moving, but where does its energy come from? 18.235–6; the dynamic aspect of mind (*cetanā*) 17.521; for the mind to wander is natural 17.97–8; if nothing in the mind was not previously in the senses, no memory of past lives 26.85; it has a hindering factor that prevents us from seeing things as they

are 14.209; its nature is to go wherever it wants to go 15.170; like a kaleidoscope 17.xvii–xviii, 17.xx, 17.xxiv; the mind is not just in the head 17.xviii; 'My mind is a theatre' 25.447; not a passive registering of things, but a reaching out (Abhidharma) 17.498; one sees the mind by not seeing 13.363–4; our minds are often more of a democracy than a kingdom 25.357; the open, ungraspable nature of mind (*cittata*) 17.493, 18.338; the true nature of mind is what is true about it in every mental state 19.97; to see the true nature of mind is hard 19.97–8; the mind cannot be located anywhere (*Śūraṅgama Sūtra*) 13.362–4; there is no difference between the 'Eastern mind' and the 'Western mind' 11.373; to understand the nature of mind, meditate on it for twelve years 18.247; what is the difference between mind and *vitarka*? 17.690; you only see your own mind when there's no mind to see 19.103

qualities of mind
butterfly mind 17.371; capable of mingling truth and falsehood 8.599; flexibility 15.274, 19.89–90; flighty 16.303; freedom of mind 3.277, 18.138, 26.154; illusionary (*māyā-citta*), relatively real, like *kliṣṭā-mano-vijñāna* 16.544–5; insubstantiality of mind 1.175; it can expand and then revert to its previous state like a stretched piece of elastic 8.441; it has no central nucleus that persists unmodified 7.153; intoxication of mind 16.299; the natural spontaneity of the mind 18.231; not wholly independent of external conditions 7.239; nothing is quite as the mind thinks, but the way it perceives things is useful 18.179; restless 17.66; a rigid mind tends to invite tragedy 19.86; self-luminous 17.410–11; short-lived and can't really settle down in anything 18.562–3; the silence of the mind 1.574; a tendency to spread out over the sense objects and become unconcentrated 7.358; 'the trembling, unsteady mind, which is difficult to guard' 10.226, 18.231; wandering mind (*bhantacitta*) 10.532, 15.116–17, 17.97

what the mind does
all terror and frustrations come from the mind 17.476; as we dwell on something we make it come into being 25.104–5; the beautiful flights of the mind 26.686; experiences are produced by mind, *see under Dhammapada*/ chapter 1; the mind has a certain responsibility for its own ideas 19.195; 'Mind produces the triple world' 14.209; the mind should not be misled by its own creations 19.239; the mind's action, now dark, now light 19.455–6; suffering caused by the mind 18.236, 18.237; the three family protectors correspond to the three functions of the mind 2.173; whatever world we find ourselves in owes its origin to ideas in the mind 17.476

purity of mind
acting with a pure mind (*Dhammapada*), *see Dhammapada* verse 2; by nature pure, but has adventitious defilements 1.84, 1.275, 1.364, 2.130, 7.527, 10.439–40, 11.656–7, 13.389–90, 17.95, 19.97; emergence of the pure mind 5.9; the ethical status of an action determined by the degree of purity of the mind 7.373; the impure mind perceives the world as of desire and therefore suffering 7.412; it is in the purified mind, if anywhere, that we will find the Buddha 25.33; 'My mind became full of peace and purity' 5.56, 20.144–5; prejudice reigns in all minds that have not been purified 1.34; the pure mind is just like a mirror – but not passive 18.603–4; the pure mind creates Buddha-fields that are pure 2.78; the pure mind perceives the world as the Pure Land 7.411; a pure singleness of mind without defilements 17.494–5; purification of the mind, *see Dhammapada* verse 183; indispensable to the understanding of traditional teachings 1.21; Vajrasattva represents the ultimate inherent purity of the mind 4.193, 13.84

discriminating mind
its polarizing activity imposes pairs of opposites on pure Voidness 7.299; transcending the conceptual activity of the discriminating mind 7.300

mind and matter
a continuity of awareness patterned in different ways 15.138; human beings are an amalgam of mind and matter (*nāma-rūpa*) 7.137; mind and body, *see under* body; symbols for the two poles of the perceptual situation 17.482–3; the universe of mind and matter 7.153

conscious mind
'the otherness that lies beyond the boundaries of man's conscious mind' 26.169; and the unconscious, *see under* unconscious; tries to force the decision to gain Enlightenment on the rest of the psyche 3.40–1; we can pass from the conscious mind to the superconscious (*dhyānas*) 10.349–50

rational mind
both rational mind and unconscious need to be involved in spiritual life 1.494, 16.67; the breakthrough when it gives up 18.189; the danger of its misunderstanding Nirvāṇa 14.553; it cannot understand Enlightenment 3.31, 3.181; one penetrates beyond it by exhausting its resources 17.616–17; only when reason is confounded can we enter the wisdom that goes beyond 14.xiv; it needs an explanation 16.259; the rational mind has achieved so much, but we need to break through it 11.8–9; to be suspended while listening to the *White Lotus Sūtra* 16.39; some truths cannot be perceived by it 3.114; what transcending the rational mind involves 26.188; ways of breaking through the rational mind 11.14–16; Zen gives it a slap in the face 11.9

images and metaphors
the clinging mind like a short-lived sparrow in the woods 18.262, 18.562–3; *ḍākinīs* represent the free-moving energies of the mind 13.236; like a clear blue sky, free of clouds of conceptualization 1.586; like an iceberg and a mountain 3.334; a mad monkey 4.385; 'to pass through the door of the mind to other regions of experience' 4.488–9; 'quieting the pool of troubled thought which is the mind' 4.339; tie the mad elephant of the mind to the pillar of the Dharma 4.384–5; the wild horse of the mind 15.286

WHAT THE MIND CAN DO

the mind's potential
all the Buddhas and bodhisattvas are to be found within one's own mind 13.83–4; all true understanding comes from your own mind 18.619; bodhisattvas who correspond to the mind's three main functions 2.173; both the world of suffering and the Realm of Truth are in the mind 7.274; Buddhas and bodhisattvas are the manifestation of our own true mind 5.34; consequences of mind-volitions 2.70–1; however far the mind reaches out into the universe, there is further to go 17.385; if our future lies anywhere, it lies in the mind 3.479; it has the *potential* to embark on the higher evolution 3.479; it is ridiculous for the mind to try to realize Buddhahood 13.364; 'The mind is its own place, and in itself/ Can make a heaven of hell, a hell of heaven' 17.497; our saṃsāric mind perfumed by Suchness 26.498; spiritual progress is possible because the mind can change 7.153, 9.399, 19.235; 'There is no Buddha other than one's mind' 19.283–4; 'the treasury within your mind' 18.569; wasting your mind's potential on futile intellectual activities 17.66

the effects of the world on the mind
the effect on your mind of the way you live 5.290; if your mind is right, no real ill can come from outside 10.536; made clear and tranquil by a beautiful environment 7.337; 'When world ceases, mind ceases, when mind ceases, world ceases' 14.606

MIND REACTIVE AND CREATIVE

introduction
brief account 11.164; at every moment the mind can choose to act either reactively or creatively 11.21–2, 17.434–5; comparing the experience of a shopping trip with reactive or creative mind 17.102–3; full talk 11.19–38; the individual has to choose each time whether to be reactive or creative 15.500; moving from reactive to creative mind is a difficult transition 11.38, 11.164; the reactive person tends to be predictable, the creative person unpredictable 15.504–5; switching from reactive to creative mind 11.32, 19.238

reactive mind
attachment to worldly pleasures a product of the reactive mind 18.130; its characteristics: conditioned, mechanical, repetitive, unaware 11.22–4; checking the reactive mind by being 'like a piece of wood' 4.382–3; conventional mind posits a permanent unchanging mind 19.234–5, 19.237; cutting through the root of the reactive mind 4.556; 'devouring' (Blake) 12.644, 12.646; does not act, but only *re*acts to external stimuli 23.428; drifting on the winds and tides of the world 15.233; the ego as a reactive way of functioning 17.344–5; goes between extremes 4.283; hindrances tend to arise when we react mechanically to situations 15.172–3; how can you be reactive and creative at the same time? 18.271; how to stop it: the sudden method and the gradual method 12.157–8; if you're sure how someone will behave, they must be essentially reactive 14.551; learning not to react to feeling with craving, *see under vedanā*; Māra 5.309; not just non-creative, it can be *anti*-creative 12.641–4; the psychology of the reactive mind 12.156–7; relative mind is capable of functioning either reactively or creatively 23.428; repeating the same patterns again and again 18.276–7; *saṃsāra* is nothing more or less than our own reactive mind 18.177; symbolized by the wheel of life 11.26–30; whatever happens, is our reaction cyclical or progressive? 3.279; the value of mindfulness for switching from reactive

to creative mind 19.238; when *vedanā* is experienced, be creative: don't let the reactive mind in 12.646

creative mind
creates where there is no possibility of creativity 11.25, 23.xvi, 23.428; goes from creation to further creation 4.283; the *bodhicitta* is the creative mind *par excellence* 4.283; how can you be reactive and creative at the same time? 18.271; how it functions demonstrated by the seven Enlightenment factors 11.35; in a creative state you feel free and open, expansive and flowing 17.344; independent, spontaneous, responsive, and aware 11.24–6, 23.428; it doesn't necessarily find expression in works of art 11.25; its freedom 11.25; its part in productive personal relations 11.25–6; loves where there is no reason to love 11.25, 23.xvi, 23.428, 26.76; the optimism of the creative mind 11.25, 26.76; the 'path' is the creative mind itself 15.233; the positive *nidānas*: the creative mind taken to its highest degree of development 17.357; responding creatively to experience gives us the chance to come off the wheel of life 17.504; refusing to react and instead responding with a healthy mental attitude 2.103; slices through likes and dislikes 18.131; symbolized by the path 11.30; using the mind creatively 17.260–1; the value of mindfulness for switching from reactive to creative mind 19.238; its vitality 11.26; when *vedanā* is experienced, be creative: don't let the reactive mind in 12.646

RELATIVE AND ABSOLUTE MIND

relative mind
a leap in the dark from relative to absolute mind 13.355; relative mind may function either reactively or creatively 11.21, 23.428

absolute mind
all conditioned things are phenomena of the unconditioned reality of absolute mind 2.67; breaking through to it through the six element practice 3.350; Buddhist conception not to be confused with that of the Advaita Vedanta 14.200; the concept grows out of the concept of emptiness 14.200; necessary to speak of it as empty, to prevent misunderstanding 2.130; in the *Śūraṅgama Sūtra* 1.356; is reflected in all things, just as all things are reflected in absolute mind: *vajra* 1.385, 14.219; *pariniṣpanna*, *see* three *svabhāvas*; pure awareness within which subject–object distinction does not exist 11.21, 13.355–6; sole reality 1.368; and the unreal imagination 1.369; Yogācāra: how the seemingly objective universe evolved from absolute mind 1.351; Zen points to absolute mind 13.354

WORKING WITH THE MIND

introduction
the aim is the meeting of mother-mind and son-mind 18.64; the appeal of Buddhism is to the mind 7.41; the Buddha developed a system of mind development 7.238–9; Buddhists are more concerned with the mind's heights than its depths 3.334–5; clarity of mind is hard to achieve 15.115; food for the mind 10.231; looking after your mind is like keeping your house in good repair 17.676–7; looking inward to the hidden treasure of the mind 15.277

knowing your mind
can one know one's own mind without external help? 17.107–8; becoming more familiar with the workings of the mind 17.xvi; the Buddha leads Ānanda to an understanding of the mind 1.356; 'direct pointing to the mind', *see under* Zen/teachings; how can you understand your own mind? 18.230–1; 'Know your own Mind completely ... like water meeting with water' 1.306; looking at the mind 13.351–7; maybe you've never looked there before 12.233; observe your mind to formulate your view 19.212; receiving teachings from your own mind 18.182; studying the way your mind works 19.338; using the mind to watch the mind 17.xviii–xix, 18.343–4; why can't you know the mind? 18.231

awareness of mind
awareness of the unwholesome content of the mind 1.411; awareness of what you are thinking 3.285, 3.309, 9.294; by looking into the mind we make it still and calm 17.282; it is difficult to find an honest witness of one's own mind 19.459; observing how fickle and easily distracted the mind is 26.657; people want to avoid awareness and lose their mind 19.86–7; shifting attention from the objects of the senses to our subjective experience 17.xix; we should be watching our minds all the time 17.xvi–xvii, 17.xx; where is the mind? not necessarily in the head 17.xviii, 18.545–6

control
controlling the mind is like riding a horse 4.354; creating a positive attitude of mind, not just checking negative tendencies 4.354; mental processes depend on conditions we can't control 1.172; think in aesthetic terms, like an artist having control

of his material 4.355; 'to stop a mind that comes and goes is happy' 18.345; why can't you stop the mind when you want to? 18.229–30

meditation
developing emptiness of mind 14.197; meditation makes the mind more flexible 19.89–90; in meditation the mind is in a very active, powerful, dynamic state 5.651; the mind has to be prepared before insight can arise 5.409–10, 15.83; the more concentrated it becomes, the more deeply it can penetrate Truth 7.358; *samādhi* and the transcendence of mind 26.199; *śamatha* actualizes all the positive potentialities of the mind 5.425; the scattered mind is unified by meditation 5.424–5

one-pointedness
one-pointedness of mind can be practised in everyday life 1.1534, 3.289; making your mind one-pointed through *śamatha* in order to develop insight 18.399

purification
citta visuddhi, *see under* seven *visuddhis*; keeping the non-defiled mind clean 18.323; the point of the Vajrayāna 5.556; purified by practising the mind precepts (Ambedkar) 9.287; as you purify your mind, you can think clearly 10.249; we cannot purify the mind through spiritual practice 4.193

changing your mind
acting upon it by manipulating breath and seminal fluid (Tantra) 1.375; bringing into existence a new mind 10.197–8; 'Clear your mind of cant' 4.244, 25.372, 26.484; the cultivation of beautiful states of mind 25.46; direct mind action 4.573; making our negatively conditioned mind into a positively conditioned mind 12.466–7; poetry strengthens the mind 26.190; transforming ('stretching') the mind through art 26.188–90; what you talk about shows the extent of your mind's transformation 18.539

freeing the mind
experiencing the mind outside time 19.84–5; glimpsing the mind that is neither subject nor object 18.232–4; going forth in respect of the mind 12.558–60; mind dissociated from the *skandhas* to become free 18.614–15; reality as the support of the emancipated mind 2.43

see also
defiled-mind-consciousness, see eight *vijñānas/kliṣṭā-mano-vijñāna*; Enlightened mind; malleability, *see* malleable; mind and body, *see under* body; mind and mental events, *see under* mental events; One Mind, *see under* Yogācāra/doctrines; mind as sixth sense, *see under* senses; states of mind, *see* mental states; superconscious mind, *see dhyānas*; unconscious; unskilful, *see* mental states/unskilful; *vajracitta*

Mind Only (*cittamātra*) *see* Yogācāra/doctrines/One Mind

mind-as-such *see cittata*

mindfulness (*sati, smṛti*)
WHAT MINDFULNESS IS

descriptions
analysing motives before allowing them to influence conduct 1.151; becoming aware of mental states 15.170; being aware within your present state of mind, whatever that is 15.220; a certain pliancy of mind 15.106; the characteristic virtue of the thinking part of our make-up 3.324; an intelligent, responsive awareness to ever-changing conditions 15.97, 15.214; it harmonizes and unifies every aspect of Buddhist practice 15.83; the meaning of *satipaṭṭhāna* 15.82, 15.747 (n34); mindfulness is not 'soberness' 17.79–80; more important than *dāna* and *śīla* 4.380; one aspect is 'looking into the mind' 17.282; the only way (*ekayāna*) 1.218; the practice of being present with the whole of your experience 17.369; the protector of inner calm 17.96; the qualities of mindfulness 1.569; true mindfulness is relaxed and emotionally warm 17.256; 'The way to immortality' (*Dhammapada*) 7.118, 17.581

mindfulness in the Buddhist tradition
all the most important formulations of the teaching include it 17.86–7; 'bringing mindfulness to the fore' (*Udāna*) 10.511; the Buddha's words to Ajātasattu 1.150; Buddhism stresses mindfulness in a way no other religions do 17.85–6; the danger of speaking of Buddhism almost exclusively in terms of mindfulness 17.87–8; 'the direct way' (*Satipaṭṭhāna Sutta*) 15.79–81, 15.243; a distinctively Buddhist emphasis 3.312; for the Mahāyāna a key practice only at the start of spiritual life 17.456; four abodes of mindfulness 1.324; four establishments of mindfulness (*smṛtyupasthāna*) 14.83; the heart of Buddhist practice 3.71, 17.539; one of the five object-determining mental events (Abhidharma) 17.535; perhaps awareness is a better term than mindfulness 17.88; recognized as fundamental to Buddhist growth 15.79–80; 'Set up mindfulness

in front of you' 15.104, 15.173; the seven *bodhyaṅgas* arise from establishing mindfulness 15.225; *satipaṭṭhāna* included as a topic in the *Patisambhidā-magga* 14.74; the teaching the Buddha gives Bāhiya is pure mindfulness 10.461–2; a topic in the *Śāriputra-abhidharma-śāstra* 14.74; bringing mindfulness alive in a modern western context 15.xvii; to be Buddhist is to be mindful, to be mindful is to be a Buddhist 17.87

images and metaphors
like carrying a bowl of oil filled to the brim 4.480; like playing a musical instrument 15.83; the nectar of mindfulness 18.51; the tailor who puts the garment of our practice together 18.83–4

the use and effects of mindfulness
antidote to doubt and distraction 5.29; desirable everywhere, like salt in cooking, like the prime minister in state functions 17.84–5; freeing the conscious mind from the influence of the unconscious 10.349; integration through mindfulness 11.731–3; it can bring a halt to our unskilful mental and emotional states 15.242; it can resolve possible conflict between *dāna* and *śīla* 4.116–17, 4.386–7; it creates harmony between the different aspects of ourselves 5.30–1; it encourages skilful states to grow 17.xxiii; it makes us more efficient in daily life 10.150; it may slow us down a bit 11.731–2; it protects the mind from excitedness 17.81; 'Life proceeds at a pace like that of a mild and majestic elephant' 1.151; mindfulness in the face of death 8.144; 'Mindfulness is always useful' 10.151, 10.158, 10.356, 10.368, 11.478, 11.626, 12.25, 13.328, 17.82, 17.84–5, 23.37; the most trivial occasion of life is invested with a halo of sanctity 1.151; preparation for meditation 1.150, 3.339; steering change through mindfulness 15.243; switching from reactive to creative mind 11.32, 19.238; you can never have too much mindfulness 1.293, 3.309, 9.214, 13.328, 17.60

PRACTICE

introduction
'Am I being mindful?' 15.214; a completely mindful person has no subconscious 10.151; ethical attentiveness 15.90–1; be honest with yourself about your actual experience 10.158, 15.220; it needs to be balanced by joy 17.79–83; learning to enjoy mindfulness for its own sake 15.118–19; mindfulness has to have its phases 4.603; pure mindfulness 10.462–4; secular practice 2.561; through the practice, insight unfolds of its own accord 15.206; you need specific methods 12.467

mindfulness in everyday life
be mindful while enjoying pleasure, or it will lead to suffering 18.151; bearing in mind *all the time* the true nature of our situation 3.324; the benefit of pausing between activities 5.77–8; can one be mindful in a busy life? 5.76–8; clear comprehension of daily activities (*Satipaṭṭhāna Sutta*) 15.97, 15.113–22; continuity throughout the day 5.399, 17.xx; developing more awareness of unskilful actions 16.311; every action should be done with full mindfulness 10.158; everyday activities turned from hindrances into helps 1.151; everyday mindfulness 3.289; guarding the gates of the senses, *see under* senses; is it possible to drive and talk at the same time? 23.114; mindful eating, *see under* food; mindfulness and sexual activity 17.215; mindfulness in everyday life will help concentration in meditation 15.172; paying attention to the small details of life 4.68, 15.97; to be practised whatever we are doing 3.286, 9.295; recognize what you notice about yourself and adjust accordingly 18.11; some experiences are incompatible with mindfulness 17.100–1; there can be no time off from mindfulness 15.210–11; we can be mindful in all circumstances, but meditation is key 15.83–4; you can fall asleep mindfully 15.97

mindfulness and meditation
concentration continues the work of mindfulness, but they are quite different 17.114; don't allow meditative bliss to overpower mindfulness 2.109; going directly from mindfulness to wisdom 10.151; how mindfulness helps us meditate 10.151; meditation is more than just mindfulness 8.583–4; mindfulness as a transition to meditation 10.158; remain mindful even with the experience of *śamatha* 19.159; walking meditation as a way of prolonging mindfulness 5.82–3

mindfulness of mental processes
examining mental states without being fully mindful of them 17.679; 'In unwavering mindfulness you should have a firm belief' 19.234–5, 19.238, 19.246; mindfulness of mental processes is particularly demanding 18.11; recollection of the six sense bases and their objects 15.199–211, 18.10–11

mindfulness of the present moment
awareness of the present moment is crucial to self-transformation 15.85;

being aware moment to moment of whether our action is beneficial or harmful 17.265; it's nonsense to talk about remaining in the present all the time 11.657; living in the present 7.285–7, 17.xviii, 18.340; make the most of each moment of mindfulness 15.214; mindfulness is not only about the present, it involves memory 15.85–8; strictly speaking there is no present moment in which to live 17.406

mindfulness and memory
it reminds you of the value of things 17.91; it's useful to think of mindfulness as an act of remembering 17.90–1; mindfulness is not only about the present, it involves memory 15.85–8; *sati* (or *smṛti*) translated as memory 15.85, 17.90–1, 17.536

conditions for mindfulness
conditions 4.480–1; do pain-relieving drugs affect mindfulness? 16.407; 'easily generated by living with a master' 4.381; 'In what circumstances may the practice of mindfulness exist?' 4.480–1; it needs the support of other practices 17.456; our mindfulness should includes being mindful of the conditions that support it 15.214; to practise the higher levels of mindfulness, you need the support of the sangha 17.111

losing mindfulness
being mindful of having lost mindfulness 15.213–14; if you lose it, habitual patterns of greed and aversion are likely to take over 15.96–7; if you relax your effort, think of the opportunity you are letting slip 18.155; lack of mindfulness in Triratna 12.382, 12.403; lapses of mindfulness 17.537; losing it through being pleased with yourself 17.663–4; losing it through drinking 3.323, 9.216, 13.401; losing it through getting carried away 16.300; losing it through wanting to be right 18.172; losing it when you're talking 10.473–4; pick it up again like a hero picking up their sword 4.479; restoring it by 'full recollection of the pain of hell' 4.381; suffering the consequences of lack of awareness 15.214, 17.292; you can lose it when you are pleased with your progress 15.213–14, 18.142–3

difficulties with mindfulness
being 'mindful' without really being alive 12.268, 23.463; does it exclude bounciness? 4.602; getting stiff and self-conscious 16.300–1; it's difficult to begin with, but becomes easier to sustain 15.243; mistaking alienated awareness for mindfulness 4.602, 10.463; a stage of lifelessness between old motives and new ones 23.463; you can have too much of the wrong sort of mindfulness 17.88

mindfulness and balance
being mindful and also free and joyful 4.602–3, 5.76, 16.300, 18.581–2; in the five spiritual faculties, *see under* five spiritual faculties; mindfulness and spontaneity 14.582, 16.301–2, 17.266–7; mindfulness is pivotal to Buddhism because balance is pivotal to Buddhism 3.310; perhaps mindfulness *can* go to extremes and needs balance 17.82–3; you can be carried away mindfully, as when playing music 15.615

FOUR FOUNDATIONS OF MINDFULNESS (OR AWARENESS)

introduction
description 3.285–6, 3.309, 3.469, 9.294, 10.150–1, 10.158, 10.206, 11.32, 11.36–7, 17.87; Pāli canon sources 3.85, 3.667 (n263), 11.369, 15.82–4, 17.87; continuous awareness 11.498; develop them for seven days and become an *arhant* or a non-returner 15.238–9; don't imagine anything static, they involve dynamic development 15.82; establishing them cultivates the conditions for refined states of consciousness 14.82; four dimensions of awareness, *see under* awareness; considered by some to be a self-sufficient path 17.456; in the first stage of the path of five stages 17.456; they are not progressive stages, all four are equally foundations 10.622; a twofold awareness: 'clearly comprehending and mindful' 15.100; we need to practise these kinds of awareness to become truly individual 3.60

(1) mindfulness of the body
awareness of the body and its movements 1.572–3, 3.309, 9.294, 11.121, 11.731, 15.114, 17.537; a *bhikkhu* has control over his hands and feet (*Dhammapada*) 20.122; be careful about your gestures 12.586; contemplating the body (*Satipaṭṭhāna Sutta*) 10.512, 15.82, 15.101, 15.111, 15.119–22, 15.243; a crucial aspect of awareness 3.285; described in the *Bodhicāryāvatāra* 4.384; doing one thing at a time 1.567–9, 5.681, 15.114–15, 26.17; doing things slowly, you may get more done than someone who looks busy 1.573; the foundation of all other forms of awareness of self 12.260, 17.537; giving a talk, pay attention to how you dress and your personal appearance 12.586; involves all six senses, including the mind 10.512–13; it is difficult, but brings Nirvāṇa very close 10.513; the Japanese tea ceremony, *see* Japanese

Buddhism/festivals; Mahākaccāna practises mindfulness of the body (*Udāna*) 10.621–2; mindful eating, *see under* food; the mindful performance of all bodily actions 11.36; the man who forgot where he'd left his umbrella, *see under* parables; 'A monk is self-possessed …' (*Sāmaññaphala Sutta*) 1.150; practising this, one becomes aware of lapses of mindfulness 17.537; reflection on the body, *see under* body; taking as much care of other people's body as of our own 15.120–1; 'watching' one's bodily movements can lead to alienation 17.103–4; you can be mindful and still act quickly 17.104–5

(2) mindfulness of feelings
introduction 1.573–4, 9.294, 12.261; as we become more aware, it will be clearer what leads to positive emotion 15.159; at first it may not be obvious that we need to make an effort to do this 3.285; the effect of becoming aware of our emotions 17.537; becoming more aware of passing emotional states, we're less likely to act impulsively 11.732; it is very important to be aware of our feelings 15.151–2; learning to broaden the scope of your emotional awareness 15.312; once you acknowledge a feeling there is a possibility of transforming it 19.395; the poet must be aware of their feelings at all times 26.138; to be aware of one's feelings one must allow oneself to experience them 11.36–7; we become clearly conscious of our passing moods 11.121; whether pleasant, painful, or neutral, *see under vedanā*

(3) mindfulness of thoughts
as we become more aware of them, our thinking becomes more purposeful 17.538; often we do not really think, we just allow thoughts to drift through 1.574, 17.538; one should know exactly where the mind is, from minute to minute 3.285, 3.309, 11.121; includes being aware of whether they are rooted in skilful or unskilful states 11.37; what are you really thinking? 9.294, 11.732, 12.261–2

(4) mindfulness of the Dharma (one's ideals, mental objects)
reciting a mantra is a means of keeping in touch with one's ideals 3.309; being aware of one's potential future state of freedom and spontaneity 11.37; a very important kind of mindfulness 9.294

see also
appamāda; as one of the five spiritual faculties (*indriyas*), *see under* five spiritual faculties; as one of the seven *bodhyaṅgas*, *see under* seven *bodhyaṅgas*; awareness; and the fifth precept, *see under* precepts/five precepts; four dimensions of awareness (self, things, other people, reality), *see under* awareness; four (Tantric) mindfulnesses, *see* four mindfulnesses; levels, *see under* awareness; Perfect, *see under* Noble Eightfold Path/stages; mindful eating, *see under* food; mindfulness of breathing; mindfulness of purpose; Sangharakshita's practice, *see under* Sangharakshita V/personal practice; unmindfulness; watching the senses, *see under* senses; *The Way of Mindfulness*, *see* Soma, Bhikkhu; 'With mindfulness strive', *see* Buddha/I life story/last words; the young man and the umbrella, *see under* umbrella

mindfulness of breathing (*ānāpānasati*)

introduction
brief description 10.392; commentary 15.101–112; antidote to distraction 3.124–5, 3.341–2, 4.73, 5.29, 11.405, 15.116, 19.227; as an insight practice 15.109–12; balances the *mettā bhāvanā* 5.460, 12.496; contrast between secular practice and practice in a Buddhist context 5.662–3; and the four foundations of mindfulness 17.456; in the system of meditation 5.30–1; and integration 5.30; it and the *mettā bhāvanā* are the twin pillars of practice 12.651, 12.680; it can take us a very long way 12.651; it may not help if you are in an alienated state 5.105; a psychological method: requires no specific knowledge of Buddhism 5.30; recommended for deluded types 2.392, 12.280; a *śamatha* practice 5.33; the starting point for the practice of mindfulness 5.30, 12.650–1, 15.101; take it seriously and you'll have your work cut out for the next twenty years 19.544; why practise it? 5.30–1, 9.516

canonical sources
Ānāpānasaṃyutta 3.675–6 (n312); *Ānāpānasati Sutta* 3.675 (n312); *Satipaṭṭhāna Sutta* 3.675 (n312), 15.101–112; *Mahāsatipaṭṭhāna Sutta* 1.156, 3.675 (n312)

its Buddhist history
said to be the meditation the Buddha was doing when he gained Enlightenment 8.119, 15.102; one of four 'things that are to be made to grow' (*Udāna*) 10.531; one of the ten recollections 1.155–6, 17.541; 'setting up mindfulness before him' (*Udāna*) 10.511, 10.581–2; Buddhaghosa's *Visuddhimagga* 3.676 (n312), 9.516; resemblance between Christian meditation and the mindfulness of breathing 8.126; a support to studying the Perfection of

Wisdom 14.515; difference from Hindu *prāṇayāma* 9.203, 9.375

method
description 3.341–2, 9.203–4, 9.375; best to adopt a systematic method 15.105; counting the breaths 3.676 (n312), 5.65, 15.104–5, 15.106–7; keeping the mind on the breath like tethering a calf with a rope (Buddhaghosa) 15.106; the fourth stage 5.65–7, 5.325, 10.582, 15.107–8; like a carpenter sawing wood 15.107; how the practice changes as it develops 15.108, 17.114–15; ending the practice 5.66

working in the practice
it can make one over-sensitized or alienated, needs to be balanced with *mettā* 12.496; the effect of wilful practice of the mindfulness of breathing 12.496; finding it boring 5.67–8, 12.422; how can concentrating on a sense object lead beyond the *kāmaloka*? 5.570–1; it isn't difficult to concentrate on the breathing, the problem is distraction 17.678; moving into the *dhyānas* 5.571; the point is not to think about the breath, but simply to be aware of it 3.341; practising it when you have a cold 9.520–1; sustaining the practice between meditation sessions 19.321

see also
New Burmese Method of Satipaṭṭhāna, *see* vipassanā movement; Sangharakshita's practice, *see under* Sangharakshita V/ meditation

mindfulness of purpose

introduction
the meaning of *sampajañña* (Sanskrit *saṃprajanya*) 15.100, 17.540; a connection with the Buddha's last words 18.411; a crucial aspect of the practice of mindfulness 3.324; remembering what is really important 17.xviii, 17.539–40; remembering why we became Buddhists 10.322; a sense of moral continuity 15.90–1; you have to be clear about what your main purpose is 19.265; Sangharakshita learns mindfulness of purpose 5.39

its nature
a balancing and integrating quality that permeates every area of experience 15.100; continuity of purpose over time 3.564–5, 3.567–8; a directed effort to strengthen the process of growth 15.95; directed, purposeful thinking 15.191–2, 17.538, 19.193–4; it prompts you to ask, 'Why on earth am I doing this?' 15.214; it supports *apramāda* 17.581; once aware of your higher purpose, you can never forget it completely 15.94, 17.540; *saṃprajanya* (total awareness) in the *Bodhicaryāvatāra*) 4.378–87; should not be confused with rushing or being greedy for results 5.389; useful in both day-to-day living and the fulfilment of your life's ambition 15.214–15; without it we just base our actions on habit 15.96–7

the practice
apply clarity of purpose to whatever you're doing 5.389; awareness of what you are doing and why you are doing it 15.360–1; developing mindfulness of purpose 15.89–100; any activity, however small, can be done with a sense of purpose 15.97; applied to eating 15.361; develop the habit of recollecting your goal often and deeply 15.96; an effective way to preserve it is to develop spiritual friendship 17.541; enter every activity having formed a clear intention 15.96; a festival is a reminder of the main purpose of human existence 11.419; formulating your long-range spiritual strategy 10.605; 'Is what I am doing really helping me in the direction of Enlightenment?' 3.256; persistently eliminating thoughts, words, and deeds inimical to one's purpose 7.117–18; sustaining mindfulness of purpose on a trip to town 18.422–4; treating all your practices as means to a specific end 3.420; we need constantly to remind ourselves why we are following the path 17.460

see also
lack of mindfulness of purpose, *see asaṃprajanya*

Mindoling Doong Rimpoche 8.659, 22.511, 22.624 (n385)

Mindon-min, King 14.253

mind-turning reflections *see* four mind-turning reflections

Minerva 25.378

minimization truth is the middle way between exaggerating and minimizing 14.573; we tell lies, exaggerate, minimize, or embroider 2.376–7

minorities any minority finds itself in a difficult position 3.483; being in a minority of one doesn't necessarily mean you're more of an individual 26.40; a threat to any minority is a threat to Buddhism 26.74

Mirabehn (Madeleine Slade) 22.179

miracles

introduction
associated with the Sacred Relics 21.197; the Buddha is against the performance

of miracles 3.76, 3.463, 16.451; the Buddha explains that the only useful miracle is instruction in the Dharma 3.76; the Buddha teaches the *devas* 4.16; Christian, *see under* Christianity/doctrines and beliefs; contrast between Buddhist and Christian miracles 1.168, 4.12–13, 9.344–5; the falling of untimely blossoms beneath the twin *sāl* trees 2.29, 4.10, 11.451–3, 13.145–6; Milarepa walks on water 18.63–4, 18.66; the miracle of instruction 3.686 (n394), 8.655, 14.38; Padmasambhava is falsely accused, and delivered by a miracle 22.509; people resorted to the miraculous to convey Padmasambhava's greatness 22.472; *prātihārya* (miraculous event) 4.16, 12.618; produced by collective faith 21.197–8; 'the real miracle is when someone starts following the light path' (the Buddha) 3.463, 12.619; in the *Sūtra of Golden Light* 16.258, 16.260, 16.261

the twin miracle
depiction at Kanheri 12.184; an exhibition of supernormal power 14.111; fire and water symbolism 12.183–5, 12.619; is one to take it literally? 10.37; performed at Śrāvastī 14.400; source, *see Dhammapada* commentary and *Mahāvastu*; symbol of the integration of the self at a higher level 10.654, 12.619; symbol of *yuganaddha* 12.184; *yamaka prātihārya* 12.618

mirages the bodhisattva sees all phenomena like a mirage in the desert 14.562; the body is like a 'mirage-city' 18.558–9; existence compared to a mirage 4.181, 5.187, 14.562, 16.452; the five *skandhas* are like a mirage 17.359; for the bodhisattva, self and other are like a dream, a mirage 4.181; if you've seen through something, you withdraw from it, like seeing a mirage in the desert 26.32; like a mirage, the qualities we attribute to the wrong things do exist elsewhere 17.359–60; like a mirage, the world is there in a sense 17.384; Nirvāṇa like a mirage 17.380–1; objective things, whether material or mental, are like a mirage 14.208, 14.562; the phenomena that appear to consciousness likened to a mirage 17.379–80; the spiritually mature know that the world is like a mirage 17.358–9

Mirandola, Pico della 26.284, 26.723–4 (n227)

Miró, Joan 24.372, 26.379, 26.441

mirrors be like a mirror, reflecting everything without distortion 12.158; by looking into the mirror of the Dharma you can see your spiritual blemishes 19.152–3; the empty mirror: an unconstrained consciousness 17.346–8; the guru holds up a mirror to you 19.570–1; interconnectedness explained using candles and mirrors 16.22; the mind in its purity is just like a mirror – but not passive 18.603–4; mirror, mirror on the wall 25.358; the mirror of the Dharma 3.627 (n13), 3.650 (n156); 'mirroring' (Zen practice) 11.375–6, 23.164, 26.603–4; mirror-like awareness is compatible with concentration 17.123; mirror-like wisdom, *see under* five *jñānas*; the mirror of Suchness is kept bright and clean 1.354; a mirror that implies revelation by *ḍākinīs* 19.566; 'Mirrors' (poem) 25.326; mirrors reflecting myriad worlds in Vairocana's Tower 14.224; polishing a stone to make it into a mirror 8.487, 10.439–40; the reflection of the Absolute in the mirror of individual consciousness 1.283; the relative *ālaya* like a mirror to which reflections stick 18.605–6; the senses are a mirror 19.192–4; the silver-bright mirror of the Tantric Precept 18.324; the wheel of life is like looking into a mirror 3.347–8, 13.128–41; you see an 'I' in the *skandhas* like seeing a reflection in a mirror 17.346–8

Mirza Ghiyath Beg 23.412

misery differences of nationality causing misery 21.69; giving up worldly miseries and taking up spiritual happiness 26.64; the misery of feeling so restricted by circumstances one cannot grow 16.71; nature 'cares nothing for the misery of man' 20.103; selfishness, the root cause of human misery 7.273–5; some religions advise giving up pleasures, but better to give up attachment to misery 17.396–7

misogyny teachings that appear misogynistic may be method, not doctrine 17.218–19; was Sangharakshita a misogynist? 21.476–8

Misra, Pandit Paramahans v22

missionaries

Buddhist
attempts to introduce the Buddhism of other countries to Nepal 7.349; conflict between monastic rule and 'missionary' activity 4.568; *dhammadūta* is a better word 9.332; Dharmapala, the greatest Buddhist missionary of our times 8.3, 8.51, 8.110; missionary activity of monks 2.212; Order members are not like Christian missionaries 4.446–7; should a Buddhist missionary be involved in politics? 9.333; Theravāda missionaries outnumbering Mahāyāna ones 14.554–5;

today Buddhists do very little missionary activity 8.277–8

Christian
see under Christianity/the spread of Christianity

mistakes

the nature of mistakes
everyone makes them, even the Buddha 3.20, 3.90, 4.360; nations commit the same mistakes as their people 8.212; 'Think it possible you may be mistaken' (Cromwell) 7.247–8, 16.40; to live we must act, so we are bound to make mistakes 17.434

mistakes about mistakes
the danger of thinking you can't be mistaken 16.40; 'Mistakes are very important to a Buddhist' – a misapprehension 8.148; regarding every mistake as a stage of development 19.343

our own mistakes
accepting your own mistakes 4.360; if you have made a mistake, admit it, confess, and apologise 10.398; overcoming the tendency to refuse to admit one has made a mistake 11.400; thinking you've got nothing more to learn 4.128, 16.40

mistakes in everyday life
complacent lethargy is not to be mistaken for blissful peace 15.219; doing something with part of yourself thinking you're doing it with the whole 19.276; imagining you are being a true individual when you are being individualistic 13.464; lack of imagination can be mistaken for fearlessness 14.474, 16.278; leave other people free to make their own mistakes 14.578; leaving one's children alone to make their own mistakes 16.202; mistakes when bringing up children 3.543–4; thinking that *siddhis* will make you more successful in worldly life 19.460; unskilful action comes from getting carried away and making mistakes 16.299; the view that happiness consists in the full satisfaction of desires 7.116

mistakes about Buddhism
assuming that Buddhism says that life is painful under all circumstances 2.90; assuming that the Dharma is bound up with a certain form of words 2.51; clinging to your idea of right view as if it were fixed 18.172; Going for Refuge 'in the secrecy of one's own heart' 15.738–9; the idea that pain in meditation shows that insight is being achieved 23.73; identifying Buddhism with one or another of its expressions 13.326; imagining that the concept of emptiness exempts you from activity 7.414; imagining you've seen the truth 17.376; theoretical knowledge mistaken for wisdom 1.225; thinking of the life of service *or* the life of contemplation 7.155–6; thinking you can practise spiritually without changing how you live 15.114; thinking that the *dhyānas* are the goal of spiritual life 2.108; thinking that it is concerned only with the removal of suffering 1.132

mistakes about Enlightenment
'Cessation of thought-processes mistaken for quiescence of infinite mind' 5.228–9, 5.421–3; imagining that Enlightenment represents the end of development 16.524, 17.459; mistakenly thinking you're Enlightened 4.586–7; mistaking limited mystical experience for the whole truth 10.596; mistaking psychic illumination for transcendental wisdom 18.251; mistaking *śamatha* experience for Enlightenment 19.159; mistaking a thought about reality for insight into reality 19.165; thinking of emptiness as the self-nature or own-being of *dharmas* 1.268

mistletoe and the Druids 13.274, 25.320; severing the sacred mistletoe with a sickle of gold 7.365; symbolism 16.373–4

Mistri, Mrs Rasma v21, v22

Mithraism 13.374

Mitra (Triratna) *see* Triratna II/people involved/sangha/becoming a Mitra

Mitra (god of Vedas) 16.419

Mitrata (magazine) 2.737 (n654), 5.xxvi

Mitter, Mrs Charu (Kalimpong) v21, v22

Mitty, Walter 1.538, 4.60

Mnemosyne, muse of memory 16.363

mockery 10.506

modanā (blending) 2.105

modern life

the nature of modern life
an age that believes in progress 7.162–4; a complicated and distracting thing 11.419; a complicated machinery of supply and demand 7.325; the conditioned pursues the conditioned relentlessly 16.394; cultural conditioning that emphasizes feeling and experience 11.81; the death of beauty 26.131–2; feverish pace 8.290–1, 11.731–2; incompatible with maintaining dhyānic consciousness 18.499; it seems almost designed to drain energy and dissipate positivity 15.151–2; its whole trend is against wisdom teachings 14.434; loss of anchorage in tradition 1.21; many factors

have risen between us and Enlightenment 14.399; the mobility of modern life and its effects 14.471, 18.276, 18.332, 18.336; *Paradise Lost* is an imaginative statement of the modern dilemma 26.22; 'a tuneless age' 25.257; the ugliness of modern life 10.368, 26.131–2; a very dull and routine affair 11.77; a wasteland 25.146

people
alienation from nature 12.217, 15.236, 18.22–4, 25.54; bad manners 6.xxxi; burdened with more knowledge and less wisdom than our forefathers 1.231; can't tell the difference between good and bad art 26.378; dead in life 8.265; do people feel despair? 18.556–7; extreme individualism 25.105; for all our 'knowledge', we grope and stumble in the dark 7.418; a great chasm between conscious and unconscious 12.217–18; lack of attachment may be due to alienation and lack of feeling 18.331–2; modern man is an incurably restless creature 7.147–8; negativity 4.595; our 'sick hurry and divided aims' 11.49–50; overdeveloped intellect and underdeveloped emotion 26.130; people find it difficult to put down roots 19.361; too emotionally exhausted to respond to the ideal 18.274; the vividness and vigour of emotional and intellectual life 26.118; no longer sure who or what we are 12.264; not adept at dealing with strong emotion 15.343; yet to understand the necessity of loneliness 8.260; why people are out of touch with their feelings 15.150

modern attitudes
antagonism towards religion 7.217, 26.130; a greater emphasis on rights and a decreasing emphasis on duties 25.63; life, even spiritual life, is about doing what you feel like doing 17.638; past heroes are now villains 25.431; suspicion of logical argument 17.375; we don't rejoice in merits enough 18.377; we don't worry about losing things because they can be replaced 18.334–5

what is needed
the appeal of Buddhism to the modern mind 7.127–9; looking for experiences that make us feel more alive 11.78–9; the need for clear thinking 11.625; the religion of art 26.196; time to be still and feel our own existence 12.82; to break through anti-spiritual tendencies we need the bodhisattva ideal 26.56; where are the modern heroes? 25.57

see also
modern world, *see under* world

modernism definition 13.424; Buddhist modernism 13.435–9; distinction from modernity 13.449; the FWBO is far from embracing modernism 13.509; in Christianity 7.34, 7.549–50 (n30), 13.424–7; is Sangharakshita modernist? 13.424–6; modernism in 20th century arts 26.378–80

modesty *apagabbho* (modesty) 15.284–5; appreciation of modesty 17.208; sexual modesty one of the last fetters to be broken, according to Indian belief 20.361; somewhat more positive than humility 18.514

Moggallāna *see* Maudgalyāyana

Moggalliputta Tissa 14.85–6

moha *see* delusion

Mohammed claims for him (Ambedkar) 9.424, 10.33–40; a depiction of his ascent to heaven 26.218; distinguished from the Buddha 9.94, 12.134; 'If you have a loaf of bread, sell half and buy a rose' [hyacinth in original] 22.432; an illustration in the *Children's Encyclopaedia* 26.689; never explained that speaking about the delights of heaven was only skilful means 3.167; Night Journey through the heavens to the Throne of God 2.644, 26.262, 26.689–90; the prophet of Islam 12.53–4; a strange experience in relation to a beautiful youth 5.618; use of metaphor 26.209

Moharram *see under* Islam

Mohini the Deluder 20.365–6

mokṣa (Pāli *mokkha*, freedom, deliverance) epithet of Nirvāṇa 1.69; Hindu understanding of 9.539

mokṣadatta 9.424–5, 10.35

Mokshajyoti, Dharmachari (Bryan Stevens) v24

Mokshapriya, Dharmachari (Garry Pierpoint) brief introduction 24.671 (n311); film-maker 2.739 (n659), 24.256, 24.319, 24.320

Moksharaja, Dharmachari v24

Moktan, Dhanman v21, v22

Moktan, Inspector T. v22

Molière 17.285, 17.739 (n256)

moments

the present moment
applying ourselves to meeting its demands 17.204; awareness of it is crucial to self-transformation 15.85; even when we

desire to be aware in it, the mind flings us into past and future 8.575; how we shape ourselves in it is what's important 17.212–13; in a state of neurotic desire, we need to get back to it 13.133–4; looking beyond it 25.22; past and future are both revealed in it 14.219; strictly speaking there is no present moment 17.406

every moment
each of us is falling from eternity 17.611; expresses the whole of one's personality 19.231; is unique, but it's easy to forget this 16.439–40; make the most of each moment of mindfulness 15.214; the mind can choose to move either reactively or creatively 11.21–2, 17.434–5; presents us with an opportunity to choose what to do 15.174; you are presented with the ultimate truth 16.184

at any moment
be aware whether what you are doing is beneficial or harmful 17.265; we are as close to Enlightenment as we shall ever be 4.213; you could breathe out and not breathe in again 2.536, 18.565

from moment to moment
'the beautiful is that which from moment to moment is always new' 18.159; sangha is something we bring into being 8.551; we need to scrutinize our mental state 15.242–3

reflections on moments
bringing the whole of our life up to the level of its highest moments 1.482; 'Even in one and the same moment, things are and are not the same' 7.195; the smallest moment of life is stronger than death 8.156; 'the intersection of the timeless moment' 3.145; a moment of pure awareness when you wake up in the morning 5.398, 19.192, 19.395; no moment is irreducible 17.367; not a moment to be lost to disseminate the Dharma 8.272; re-experiencing a moment in childhood: a transcendence of time and space 17.402–3

see also
the *bardo* of the moment of death, *see under bardo*

momentum after the Point of No Return the momentum of old thoughts continues 19.237–8; importance of maintaining momentum in one's practice 3.305; Stream Entry: the creative, outward-looking momentum of your being 17.345

monasteries (Buddhist) came to be repositories of the learning and culture of the age 2.197, 2.213; centralization and size in medieval India 3.407, 7.459–60, 9.237, 12.237–8; development 2.189–90, 3.406; the eighteen faults of a monastery 2.201; monks of different schools sharing the same monastery 1.246, 4.23, 7.490; Tibetan, *see under* Tibetan Buddhism/monastic life

monastic formalism *see* formalism

monastic–lay split *see under* sangha

monastic life

the traditional life
picture of it in the *Chapters* 2.201; conflict between monastic rule and 'missionary' activity 4.568; contradictory ideals 2.191; curriculum of monastic studies 2.197–8; eremitical and coenobitical 2.188–92, 7.496; for young monks, could involve travel to learn from different *ācāryas* 2.198; four kinds of purity 1.146–9; a happy life 4.628–9, 11.590, 16.392, 17.337–8, 19.74; it obviously involves giving up something 1.274; King Milinda's questions about it 2.191; *muṇḍaka* (shaven-headed ascetic) used as a contemptuous expression 10.623; obligations, *see under* Vinaya/*prātimokṣa*; ordination, *see under bhikkhu*/ordination; organizational structure 9.146; relation between master and disciple 2.196–7; requisites, *see* eight requisites; robe and bowl the two wings of the monastic life 1.152, 16.405; shaving the head 10.535; supports (*nissayas*), *see* four supports; vows 2.604–7; wise use of dwelling 1.149

changes
can be more faithfully pursued in India than in Buddhist countries 1.229; degenerated from a spiritual adventure to a safe investment 1.228; hypocrisy of monastic life 1.229; 'sham monks' 2.629–34; the Vajrayāna abandoned it 4.23; flouting monastic conventions 17.633–4; in the East it can be a very comfortable life 25.76; Sangharakshita's change of attitude to monastic life 23.27–8; without commitment to growth, it becomes a mundane institution 15.98

reflections
the idea of it can unsettle people 2.638; right livelihood provides an alternative arrangement 11.187–8; spiritual development is not synonymous with monastic life 10.629; we need an assertion of the monastic ideal in the best sense 16.394

monasticism coenobitical monasticism of the Theravāda and Sarvāstivāda 2.192; development from eremitical to

coenobitical 2.189–91, 7.497, 12.238; genuine monasticism replaced by formal monasticism 11.389; impossible to identify spiritual life exclusively with 1.244, 2.432; monastic interpretation of the Dharma failed to do justice to its depth and universality 2.205; the monastic order as 'the basis of Buddhism' 21.303; a narrow and rigid monasticism can be turned into Buddhist respectability 18.135; overvaluation of monasticism 11.388–9; pattern varies little from one part of the Buddhist world to another 2.193; period in Buddhist history when the spiritual life was identified with monastic life 12.238; placed at the centre of Buddhist life, instead of Going for Refuge 12.666; Sangharakshita would like to see a revival of Sūtra-style monasticism 2.604, 2.628; Triratna Buddhist Order neither monastic nor lay, *see under* Triratna III/life in the Order; the *Vinaya-vastu* deals with coenobitical monasticism 7.500

Monchanin, Father 13.557, 22.145

mondō *see under* Zen

money

what is money?
agreeing to treat banknotes as if they had value 17.196; the demon money, a power which has got out of control 12.333–4; like muck, the better for being spread 4.102, 16.402; money is power 10.489, 26.480; the mystery of quantitative easing 12.694–5; no such thing as money 26.480; a strange, protean thing: everything except money 16.402; we all make use of it without really knowing what it is 11.604

attitudes to money
being able to afford a holiday but not a Dharma book 18.376–7; Christian: 'Give until it hurts' 16.402–3; helping to relieve suffering for money 24.349; 'I never really bothered about money' 25.133; not spending too much on clothes or travel or frivolous things 12.554–5, 12.671; nothing wrong with money if used properly 9.286; people think the Dharma shouldn't be sullied by money 16.402; the squandering of public money 25.301

making money
ethical considerations are often not allowed to get in the way 12.670; if you use it to make money, your vocation can become a profession 18.119; incompatible with contentment 1.152; the Stock Exchange and the banks: 'This is what we're up against' 11.465, 12.333

giving money
being asked to give money reveals someone's true attitude to giving 4.611–12; giving money for the Dharma 18.113–14, 18.376–7; giving money is often the best way to practise *dāna* 14.417; insistence in the Tantra on offerings in hard cash 4.611; money is wasted in the name of *dāna* 8.175; rationalizations about giving money away 19.552

money and spiritual life
The Buddha on Wall Street 11.765 (n323); Buddhist activities as a means of making money 7.246, 19.491; financial independence is important for a spiritual movement 9.491–2, 19.464–5; living ethically saves money 10.644; *Mindfulness and Money* 11.765 (n323); misunderstanding about money and the spiritual life 18.114; personal finance and its implications for practice 11.604, 11.765 (n323); spiritual life is difficult, so people reduce it to external practice and money 19.278

not handling money ('gold and silver')
Mahāyāna view 22.103, 22.584 (n100); monks who abstain from contact with physical money but write cheques 7.263; Sangharakshita's practice, *see under* Sangharakshita V/monastic lifestyle

see also
giving, *see dāna*; poverty; wealth and prosperity, *see* prosperity

Mongkut, King 15.712, 15.774–5 (n270)

Mongolia Mongolian shamanism 8.517–18; Buddhism instigated by Pakpa, of the Tibetan Sakya school 13.29; influenced by Madhyamaka 1.323; formidable scholarship 13.40; the kind of Buddhism practised 2.548; perhaps Buddhism became widespread too quickly 19.486; politics played a part 8.518–19; the Third Dalai Lama brought the Mongols back to Buddhism 13.40; *The Religions of Mongolia* (review) 8.517–19

mongoose 13.166–7

Monier-Williams, M. 4.653, 8.41

monism 16.449

monks

what is a monk?
what defines a monk? 2.604–7; etymology of English word 16.391; in Buddhism, the word has a broader meaning than in English 3.407; a glorious spiritual parasite 16.391; he devotes all his energies to the Dharma 16.390–3, 16.404, 16.405; has

given up responsibility for supporting himself 15.278, 16.404; has overcome the world 16.393; in many ways the life of a monk is the best possible kind of life 11.389; traditionally remembered and preserved the teachings 13.339; they should appear to come from another world 26.36; under no pressure to be useful 18.120; what does he give in return for his support? 3.591, 15.365–6; with his bowl and robes is like a bird with two wings 1.152, 16.405; the main audience in Early Buddhist texts, contrast with Mahāyāna 1.272–3; the monk in the *Sūtra of Golden Light* 16.390–4, 16.401, 16.403–6

becoming a monk
'Come, O monk!' (ordination at the Buddha's time) 11.420, 15.507; becoming a monk for social reasons 11.570; confusion of Going for Refuge with becoming a monk 2.433; rigid adherence to the Vinaya is all that is expected of him 1.227–8; young monk or disciple (*antevasika*) 2.196, 15.667; in Buddhist countries being a monk becomes a sort of profession 17.111

a monk's life
as advisers 2.216–17, 3.410, 4.67; altruistic activity 2.213; angelic 16.392; attachment to particular families (for support) 15.284–5; bad luck to see a monk first thing in the morning 16.397; belief that monks can manipulate occult forces 2.215; chastity 2.604–5, 2.634–5, 11.570; commitments after ordination 13.339; daily routine 3.589–90; duties and rights of a young monk 2.196–8; fortune-telling 3.583; insurance against natural disasters 2.216; keeping up appearances 19.470; lazy 4.438, 4.443; lodging (*sayanāsana*) 16.406; meditation 2.200–1, 5.420, 19.341; needs spiritual friends 2.606–7; poet-monks 2.213; and politics 7.440–1; possessions 3.590; practice of threefold path 2.204; preachers of the Dharma 2.212; preaching to women 4.348; prevented from displaying psychic powers 3.584; receiving offerings from women 13.474, 13.497–8; 'robes' 16.404; status 2.608; they become deeply attached to their cloisters 8.312; unhealthy from lack of exercise 15.280; walking with downcast eyes 4.383–4, 15.173, 21.14–15

'good' monks and 'bad' monks
the Buddha foresees monks who will one day disgrace the sangha 14.189, 14.194–5; a bad monk, a bad Buddhist, and a bad man 22.130–1; a good Buddhist but a bad monk 2.581–2, 2.587–8; one can be a good monk and a bad Buddhist, and *vice versa* 2.433; 'a collection of rogues in yellow robes' 23.399; a monk who had the makings of a good Mitra 24.21; monks suspected of committing offences against criminal law 7.440–1; a young woman who fell in love with a monk 19.471

status
individual monk 'submerged in the sangha' 1.275; senior monks who don't insist on protocol 20.419; seniormost nun subordinated to juniormost monk 2.602–3; strictly speaking, 'Mahāyāna monk' represents a confusion of categories 7.473; subservience to people in authority 17.212

monks and spiritual life
assuming he is leading a spiritual life because he wears a robe and follows rules 12.389; being a monk often conceals a very real worldliness 1.442; 'Is Buddhism for monks only?' (a fictional dialogue) 7.177–89, 22.364; keeping up the pretence of being a monk while not keeping the rules 18.487; the monk who carried a girl over a stream, *see* parables and stories; not all monks are committed to the ideal of Enlightenment 16.393; not a monk who happens to be a Buddhist, but a Buddhist who happens to be a monk 2.607; regarded as a national asset, an insurance against calamities 2.216; talking about monks gives a wrong impression of Buddhist life 26.43; you can technically be a monk but be busy with worldly things 10.629

see also
bhikṣu; monks and lay people, *see under* lay people

monkeys apology for destroying the apes' habitat 25.447; the cries of monkeys: touching melancholy in Chinese poetry 18.52–3; the export of monkeys for vivisection 8.213–15; the god Hanuman, *see* Hanuman; the mind as a mad monkey 4.385; a monkey cradling her dead baby 20.313–14, 26.424; the monkey and the kitten 4.138, 7.366; 'monkey land', land of no men 19.519; monkey and typewriter theory of evolution 12.85; monkeys living free in the mountains, but trapped if they wander lower 19.341; Nanda ungallantly compares his former lover to a mutilated monkey 2.83, 10.505, 12.615; the partridge, the monkey, and the elephant 14.64; the small blue monkey 25.305; symbol of *vijñāna* on the wheel of life 1.108–9, 2.75; Tibetan belief that humans are descended from Avalokiteśvara and a monkey 2.65

Monkey (*Journey to the West*, Wu Cheng'en) *see under* Xuanzang

monlam (path of speech, Tibetan) 18.319

monogamy *see under* marriage

Monorhita 13.342

monotheism intolerance is characteristic of all forms of monotheism 4.124; the Jews came to recognize their god as the only god 19.414–15; the question of when and where monotheistic ideas emerged 14.602; that of Thomas Aquinas is not necessarily more developed than that of a tribesman 14.602

monsoon *see* rainy season

monsters if one does not dream, one becomes a monster 26.19; the mask slips to reveal the face of a monster 20.225–6; Mr Bounderby in *Hard Times*, a monster of ingratitude 3.601; monster of death, *see under* wheel of life

Montaigne, Michel de 3.47, 3.633 (n42), 24.567–8

Montessori schools 21.458, 21.462

Monteverdi, Claudio 24.589

Monticelli, Walter 17.xv

moods being in such a good mood that you feel like blessing everything 19.503–4; being taken over by a mood 3.488; *ḍākinīs* as moods 13.238–9; different moods at different times of day 20.187; going through the motions of devotion to get into a devotional mood 4.296, 15.706–7; if you don't feel in the mood to do a puja, you should probably do it 17.417–18; a mood of spiritual exaltation 2.415; a poem is the embodiment of a certain mood 1.144; relationship between scent and mood 16.559, 20.34; working creatively with moods 18.53

Mookerjee, Ashutosh 8.xx

Mookerjee, Babu Neel Comal v8

Mookerjee, Dr H. C. 8.167–8, 8.680 (n99)

Mookerjee, Nirodanath v8

Mookerjee, Dr Satkari 1.372, 20.135

Mookerjee, Dr Shyam Prasad an opponent of Dr Ambedkar in Parliament 10.76; president of the Maha Bodhi Society 9.208–9, 9.502, 21.416, 21.433, 22.65

Mookerji, Dr (Governor of West Bengal) 22.9

moon

moon and sun
as part of stupa symbolism 13.162–3; 'as the sun and moon never stop to brighten one small place' 18.215; as visualized in the offering of the mandala 13.262; in Buddhist cosmology 16.346; lunar and solar energies brought together 18.76–7; the myth that they were produced from the eyes of Avalokiteśvara 2.17; 'neither moon nor sun', *see under Udāna*/other key teachings

moon worship
invasion of her sacred space 25.447; lunar divinities 16.189–90; lunar symbolism in the stupa 16.149–51; we no longer appreciate the moon as an object of wonder 25.54; worship of the new moon (like the worship of bodhisattvas) 1.395, 14.181

the phases of the moon
full-moon festivals remind us to maintain harmony with nature 11.395; lunar influences on trees and plants 4.576; *uposatha* (new moon and full moon days) 1.146

poems
'The Moon of Beauty' 25.168; Sangharakshita's moon poems 25.xlii, 25.231, 25.255, 25.272, 25.287, 25.289, 25.294; Shelley's Moon 26.169

the moon of Enlightenment
the Buddha's different forms like the moon reflected in different pools 14.212; the Buddha compared to the moon 14.238, 26.125; the face and body of the Tathāgata shining like the autumn moon 1.327; the Full Moon of Enlightenment 25.176; the possibility of Enlightenment like the moon reflected in agitated water 7.311

other moon metaphors
the *bodhicitta* like the full moon 4.31; the conceptual symbols of Buddhism are like the moon's reflection 10.159; *dharmas* like the reflection of the moon in water 2.154; freed from clouds 2.627; *lalanā* corresponds to the moon 18.76; the world like the moon reflected in the ocean 14.204; good will like the moon's radiance, which shines and burns and flashes forth 2.315; one should feel that one's influence upon others is beneficent, like moonlight 13.82

see also
finger pointing to the moon, *see* finger

Moonasinghe, Mrs 22.63

Moonies 17.40, 17.711 (n43)

Moore, David *see* Ratnaketu

Moore, George *The Brook Kerith* 12.696, 13.650–2; *Conversations in Ebury Street* 24.541; *Conversations of a Young Man* 24.541; *Esther Waters* 24.540–1

Moore, Tom 26.114

moral crusaders *see under* ethics/general ethical considerations

moral rearmament movement *see* Buchman

morality (*śīla*) *see* ethics

More, Sir Thomas 1.539, 12.77, 12.355

more and more of less and less a little Dharma goes a long way 11.728; better to know a few works thoroughly than a lot superficially 26.42; the essence of the Dharma for you can be contained in a single verse 18.495; focus on a very few texts or teachings 4.147, 25.133; for your own benefit a few teachings are enough, but you need more to help others 18.413–14; how much, if anything, do you need to know about Buddhism to be a Buddhist? 17.391; if there's too much to practise you end up not practising anything 4.618; the inevitably encyclopedic nature of Buddhism 11.508–9; our practice is not to fill ourselves with teachings but to make ourselves fit to receive them 18.117; a principle of Triratna 11.376, 19.544–5; a single verse could be the whole teaching for a particular person 18.370; take one teaching and it contains all the rest 19.215–16; there is a great deal that we can safely ignore 26.42; we need less Dharma knowledge than we think 17.xix, 17.332; what we should take to heart from Milarepa's teaching 18.183; you don't need a lot of initiations or Dharma books to make your practice effective 18.167–8; you've got your work cut out, so keep things simple 18.381

Morel, Lady Ottoline 19.256–7

Morgan, Kenneth W. (*The Path of the Buddha*) aim of the book 2.434; edited by a Christian minister 8.363; book review 8.363–5; 'Buddhism in China and Korea' (Tsukamoto) 8.364; 'Buddhism in Japan' ((Hanayama) 8.364; 'Buddhism in Theravāda Countries' (Nayaka Thera) 8.364; 'Buddhism in Tibet', by Lobsang Lhalungpa 2.435, 8.236–7, 8.364, 22.265; 'Development of Mahāyāna Beliefs' (Yamaguchi) 8.364; 'The Fundamentals of Theravada Buddhism' (U Thittila) 2.720 (n535), 8.364; 'Origin and Expansion of Buddhism' (Bhikkhu Kashyap) 2.720 (n535), 8.363–4, 22.265; 'Unity and Diversity in Buddhism' (Nakamura) 8.364

Mori, Masatoshi Gensen 7.43

Morris, Chris 24.241

Morris, Peter 8.583

Morris, William introduction 26.649–50; 'the idle singers of an empty day' 26.209; *News from Nowhere* 12.355, 26.649–52, 26.661

Morrison, Robert *see* Sagaramati

Morse, Father 21.353–7

Mortimer, Roger 24.558–9

mosques *see under* Islam

mother

mother and child
the bodhisattva relates to all beings as a mother relates to her child 17.193; the child does not know the mother as a person 1.520; having children doesn't necessarily get in the way of spiritual life 11.581; her function is to worry 16.297–8; *mettā* like a mother's love for her only child 11.102, 14.57, 15.321–4, 26.690; a mother doesn't feel a difference between herself and her children 5.187–8; opportunity for insight given by childcare 5.638; she takes responsibility for her children 15.323; tendency to objectify other people, as a baby does its mother 12.262

our relationship with our mother
doing things to shock Mummy 19.258–9; fear of losing her love 16.307; the misfortune of having an affectionate mother 15.411; a monk not rescuing his mother for fear of contact with a woman 11.319; probably the most important emotional experience of our life 16.102; affects us for the whole of our life 3.521; pleasing mother 15.418–19; seeing an old woman being assaulted and realizing she is your mother 13.81, 17.193; why a boy has to be taken from his mother 15.411, 15.420, 15.480

mother as symbol or goddess
may represent craving in Buddhist myth 3.35; mother goddess (Hindu)10.46; mother-light (*dharmakāya*) and son-light 18.251; mother-mind and son-mind 18.64; Tārā as virgin, mother, and queen 5.581; virgin motherhood is a symbol found in many religions 12.106–7; worship of female gurus as Mother 3.550, 20.197

see also
Terry Delamare's sculpture, *see under* Delamare; mother and father, *see* parents; the Mothers (*mātṛkās*), *see mātṛkās*

motives and motivation

the world's motivations
it isn't the world that draws us away from the path, but our own motivation 15.174; it's craving that motivates us most of the time 12.623, 15.154; the motivation for work is hunger 18.294; reasons for lack of motivation in the modern world 12.379–80; we are usually motivated by what we think is pleasant or painful 10.482–3; the world is motivated by unskilful thoughts 11.130

one's own motivation
being aware of your own motivations 3.469; developing one's own motivation for the spiritual life 17.472; don't put off helping until your motivation is pure 4.89, 17.287; examine your motivation for leaving your family 10.456–7; how to strengthen your motivation to do more for the Dharma 12.381–3; if you don't feel like doing something, should you do it? 5.646–7, 10.604–5; meditation is about exposing one's motives to oneself 3.227; motivation will arise as long as we just get on with the job 17.576; not wanting to acknowledge our attitudes, we rationalize our motives 2.55–6; one is not always aware of one's motivations 17.597; to strengthen motivation, avoid distractions 12.381; unconscious motives 10.348–9

right motive (for Buddhist practice)
altruistic orientation of the motivation to gain Enlightenment 3.452; ask yourself what in Buddhism appeals to you and examine your motives 16.201; Buddha-pride as motivation 18.82; of decisive importance for the practice of the six perfections 1.425; emphasized in Buddhism 1.15; for studying Buddhism 1.13–14, 1.20, 19.106; having no egoistic motive for doing anything, one is free to respond 17.521–2; the heart of the Dharma will be revealed only to those who have cultivated right motive 1.21; the key of right motive opens the portals of the Palace of Wisdom 1.22; merit: the layman's motivation 2.214–15; more important than external consequences 21.314; motivation for seeking ordination 17.287, 19.247–8; motivation comes from faith 18.273; motives for engaging in Dharma activities 18.591–3; the only right motive for becoming a Buddhist 8.205; our motives change as we go along 10.551, 17.288; a stage of lifelessness between old motives and new ones 23.463; three motivations 11.282; the traditional motivation is a good rebirth, but that may not suit us 17.467–72; we need powerful, vivid images if we are going to be strongly motivated 19.26

wrong motive
attraction to Buddhism for the wrong reasons 1.19–20, 17.629–30; don't try to rebut an argument by questioning the person's motives 19.292–3; instructing someone in the Dharma with a wrong motive 18.421; meditating with mixed motives 5.373–5; practising the precepts with unskilful motivation 19.455–6; psychoanalysis suspects people's motives 4.317, 4.604; questioning someone's motives 17.235–6, 17.660–1; there's nothing that you cannot do with the wrong motive 18.361; wanting something from spiritual practice unconnected with its true purpose 3.420

Moung Hpo Myhin (Dharmapala's advisor) 8.91

mountains

physical mountains
the conquest of Mount Everest 22.11–12; crossing the Alps: of psychological and spiritual significance 23.249–50; defiled by trash 25.447; a discussion about mountaineering and Buddhism 22.196–7; 'golden in laughing sunlight' 25.218; Mount Egmont (New Zealand) 24.512–13; Mount Kailash 14.538, 22.12, 25.429; Mount Kanchenjunga, *see* Kanchenjunga; mountain people wondering why people like looking at mountains 11.196; mountains are alive, and sacred 22.12; 'Mountains are mountains and trees are trees' (Zen) 14.396, 14.496; the mountains of Nepal 20.440; mysterious mountains 25.211; a rainy day in the mountains 25.244; sacred mountains of China 2.224, 2.692 (n312); St Bernard ignoring the Alps on the way to Rome 13.279; Wang Wei sings of mountains, mists, and streams 7.437; 'The Young Hills' 25.292

metaphorical and symbolic mountains
Dr Ambedkar like a mountain 10.129–30; the archetypal journey like a spiral path up a mountain 26.273; becoming steadfast like a mountain 14.193; the Buddha and a group of *bhikkhus* sitting 'like mountains' 10.511; the Copper-Coloured Mountain 8.524, 18.304; the oceans and mountains of the cosmos, *see* cosmology; dream mountains 11.685, 26.460, 26.681;

exchanging mountains for the Pure Land 25.349; great men are like mountains 9.172–3; heights and depths symbolized by a mountain 12.22; Krishna lifting a mountain with one finger 10.255; 'the practitioner, like a mountain, does not tremble' 10.511–12; the precipitous ascent of the spiritual life 23.463; reverence is like looking up at a great mountain 15.426–7; sitting like a mountain 10.511–12; spiritual life is like crossing one mountain after another 19.396; spiritual progress is like climbing a mountain, and also unfolding like a lotus 5.687; *upekṣā* is like a mountain 9.299

Mountbatten, Lord 20.190, 23.202, 23.501 (n224)

Mozart, Wolfgang Amadeus *Don Juan* 24.441; he would hear the whole of a symphony in a moment, then write it down 17.609, 18.282; one of Sangharakshita's favourite composers 20.73, 23.173, 26.502, 26.505; his awe-inspiring final symphonies 2.644; hearing *Eine Kleine Nachtmusik* in India 26.504; his first symphony evidence of rebirth 26.22; his genius 15.194; his works among the supreme achievements of Western culture 12.392; moved beyond the conventions of the time 3.58; a performance of *The Magic Flute* 24.385; said that the pauses were the most important part of his music 7.322, 12.557–8; Sangharakshita writes a stanza on Mozart 26.503–4

mrakṣa (slyness-concealment) *see under* concealment

Mṛcchakaṭikā (Sanskrit drama) 9.85

Mucalinda the serpent king has the same name as a species of tree 10.470; and the *kuṇḍalinī* or *caṇḍālī* 2.37, 12.190; 'Mucalinda' (poem) 25.398–9; shelters the Buddha from the rain 2.37–8, 3.596, 10.469–70, 12.189–91

mud 'The bigger the heap of mud (or clay), the bigger the Buddha' 4.467, 25.73

muditā (sympathetic joy) appreciation of the happiness even of those who seem to be set against you 15.326–7; between spiritual friends 4.176; a deepening experience 15.256–7; happiness in others' happiness: a characteristically Buddhist emotion 1.505–6; at the heart of the spiritual community 3.451; *mettā* becomes *muditā* when you become aware of someone's happiness 5.172, 5.197, 5.199, 11.734; near enemies 5.204, 10.174, 26.78; rejoicing in merits, *see* rejoicing in merits; responding positively to people's pleasure in their own achievements 4.319–20; without *muditā* there is envy 5.203

muditā bhāvanā *mettā* clothed in the bright, dancing colours of *muditā* 15.327; rejoicing in people's happiness 5.197, 10.174; some people find it easier than the *karuṇā bhāvanā* 5.204–5

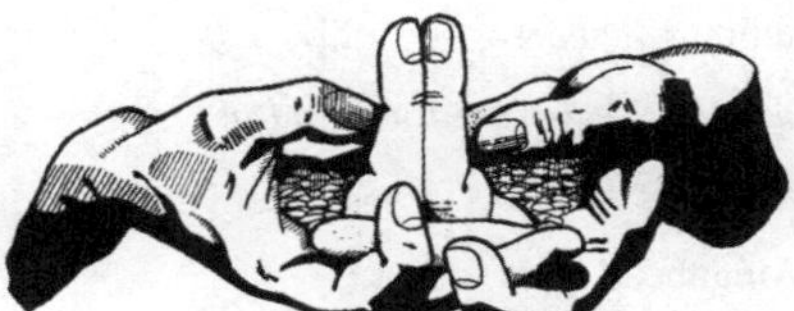

mudrās (gestures)

introduction
the meaning of the word *mudrā* 1.521, 19.271; action simplified into *mudrā* 7.320; the extension of Perfect Vision to the fingertips 1.512–13; Dudjom Rimpoche demonstrates *mudrās* 22.509; a *mudrā* is essentially Enlightenment expressed by the hands 13.306; spiritually significant movements (Tantra) 1.374–5; offering the mandala *mudrā* (illustration) 13.266; gesture of salutation representing the jewel in the lotus 16.179–80; artists who don't use the correct *mudrās* 8.132

the mudrās of the five Buddhas
come from incidents in the Buddha's life 9.381–6, 13.302–3; illustration 13.303; relationships between the *mudrās* of the five Buddhas of the mandala 13.311, 18.600

abhaya (fearlessness)
'Fear not!' 9.367, 9.385, 13.230; associated with Tārā 12.660–1; associated with Amoghasiddhi 12.216–17, 13.310; the Buddha reassuring his disciples 13.302;

statues with that gesture 2.156, 3.53–4, 10.259

bhūmisparśa (earth-touching)
a Buddha image with that gesture 9.418; calling the earth goddess to witness 9.381–2, 12.188, 12.213, 13.302, 13.308–9, 16.380; *mudrā* of Akṣobhya 12.213, 13.308; *mudrā* of Kṣitigarbha 2.181

dharmacakrapravartana (turning the wheel of the Dharma)
connection with Dr Ambedkar 9.383–5; from the Buddha's 'turning of the wheel of the truth' 12.212, 13.302, 13.306, 23.361–2; associated with Vairocana 4.207, 12.212, 13.306, 16.124

dhyāna (meditation)
Buddha images with that gesture 9.382–3; the *mudrā* of Amitābha 11.293, 12.215, 13.310; 'a prescribed attitude in which to meditate' 4.489

varada (giving)
association with Ratnasambhava 12.214, 13.309; the giving of the highest and best 9.385; the Buddha offering the gift of the Dharma to the world 13.302; represents unlimited generosity 13.309

mudrās (seals), see four *mudrās*

mudu (tender) 15.273–4

Mugabe, Robert 26.654

Muir, Dexter 24.82

Muir, Edwin 24.597–8

Mukherjee, Inspector v22

mūla yogas (foundation *yogas*) *see* four *mūla* yogas; individual practices

Mulagandhakuti *see* Sarnath

mūlakleśas *see under* mental events/ negative mental events

Mūlamadhyamakakārikā text, *see under* Nāgārjuna; commentary, *see under* Āryadeva, Candrakīrtī

Mūlasarvāstivādin Vinaya 2.195, 2.200, 7.528, 14.33–4

Mūlaśoka (translator) 14.242

Mullan, Bob 24.312, 24.319

Müller, F. Max *Chips from a German Workshop* 8.536–7; an early translator of Sanskrit texts, but did not live the religions they described 7.87; editor of *Sacred Books* 7.449; introduction 7.576 (n162), 7.618–19 (n500); meeting with Anagarika Dharmapala 8.54; translation of the *Rig Veda* 8.536–7, 12.70; translations of Pure Land *sūtras* 1.333–4, 12.70; visited by Swami Vivekananda 7.87

Mullick, Rajendra 22.59

Mullin, Glen H. 24.310–11

Multscher, Hans 24.594

Mulund, India 10.141

Mumba Devi 20.383

Mumbai (Bombay)

introduction
the beauty of the city should be given more importance 9.444–5; a fine city 9.14; 'the future of Buddhism in Bombay seems full of hope' 21.507; impressions of the city (1979) 24.9–10; deterioration 9.244; noise and crowds 10.291, 10.305; pollution 9.498, 11.562; monstrous buses 24.103; the sub-worlds of the city 22.280; unrest caused by the demand for a separate Maharashtra state 22.295; World Religion Day 22.280

places in the city
airport 24.99–100, 24.119–21; Dr Ambedkar's residence, 'Rajagriha' 9.14, 10.4–5, 10.127; Bahujana Vihara, Parel 10.335; Buddha Society 22.267, 22.272; Dadar railway station 9.238, 9.251, 24.110; Chetana's bookshop 24.11–12, 24.606 (n20); Currey Road 9.235, 9.562n; Elephanta 24.10, 24.605 (n16); Flora Fountain 22.139, 22.295; 'Harijan Colony' at Khar 22.288; Juhu Beach 24.118–19; Marine Drive 21.459, 24.10; Mumba Devi temple 20.383; Nair Hospital 22.267; Nare Park 9.72; Parsis 12.691–2; Presidency Mahar Conference 9.60; Prince of Wales Museum 24.12; Royal Asiatick Society 9.67; Theosophy Hall 9.244, 9.563n, 10.162

Siddharth College of Arts and Sciences
founding 10.667 (n44); inauguration of the Pāli Union 10.140; librarian (S. S. Rege) 10.660; named by Dr Ambedkar 9.63; Sangharakshita meets Dr Ambedkar there 9.16, 10.5; Sangharakshita speaks there in 1959 10.126–30; great work 9.286; meditation classes at the college 10.lix–lx

Worli
Japanese temple 9.67, 9.507, 10.121, 10.335, 13.50–1, 22.271, 23.333, 24.9–10; Sangharakshita speaks at Dr Ambedkar's request 9.18, 9.260–1, 9.405, 10.7–8, 10.336, 22.288–9; later talks 19.260–9, 10.122, 10.151–2, 10.295, 10.335–52, 23.333, 23.339–40, 23.348; an unexpected visit 23.348; Worli seen through Terry's eyes 23.339–40

Sangharakshita
his arrival there as a soldier 20.109; connections with the city 9.404–5; stays in Bombay during his wandering days 20.381–3; public talks 10.118–23, 10.149–55, 21.571–2, 23.333, 25.119–20; schedule December 1959 (facsimile) 10.132; visits the city in 1979 24.9–13, 24.24–5

see also
Kanheri Caves, *see under* caves; Maha Bodhi Society, *see under* Maha Bodhi Society/branches

Mumonkan (*The Gateless Gate*) 48 koan, verse, and commentary 2.555, 8.499; the Great Death 3.658 (n218); 'Has a dog Buddha nature?' 8.499, 13.356, 13.699 (n161); the masters who appear in the koan 8.499; review 8.498–501; spiritual life is like climbing a greasy flagpole 4.200, 4.213

muṇḍaka (shaven-headed ascetic, 'bald-pate') 10.623, 14.19

mundane (*laukika*) awareness of the limitations of the mundane 17.676; the dross of mundane experience is transmuted into the gold of transcendental experience 7.403; every mundane thought, word, and deed is individualistic 1.232; in the last analysis the duality between mundane and transcendental disappears 19.49; it's easier to be fascinated by the mundane than the transcendental 17.692; *laukika* in contrast to *lokuttara* 1.232, 10.586, 16.607–8 (n178), 26.198–9; the limited nature of mundane goals 15.95; mundane and transcendental morality 11.313–14; *samādhi* the last of the *laukika nidānas* 2.113; *śamatha* experiences are mundane (*laukika*), not transcendental (*lokuttara*) 8.440–1; the transcendental does not negate the mundane 14.496; the tree of mundane existence, to which Buddhism lays the axe of Wisdom 7.300; uniting the best of the mundane with the transcendental 19.44, 19.47, 19.52–3; you can't refine yourself out of the mundane world altogether 17.695

muni related to the Sanskrit term *mauna*, silence 3.591–2; *muni* as the original term used for the Buddha's disciples 3.592, 11.320; sometimes 'monk', sometimes sage 3.591

Munindra, Brahmachari v20, v21

Münthe, Axel 22.276, 22.599–600 (n221), 23.303–4

murder against the nature of things that a Buddha should be killed 4.14; assassination of the Sri Lankan prime minister 7.567 (n121), 8.283–4, 8.474, 22.458, 26.576; the Buddha's disciples are accused of murder 10.539–41; can an enlightened being kill out of compassion? 14.183, 14.188, 20.333; castes whose dharma is to murder 10.55; the concentration of a murderer is very different from true mindfulness 1.91; the crime of passion 18.208, 18.309–10; an extreme example of breaking a precept 16.433; how does the act of intentional killing shorten one's life? 17.293; if you feel like murdering someone but you don't do it, you are not being a hypocrite 11.268; jealousy comes from a basic insecurity which can lead to murder 17.655–6; of Moggallāna 4.14; a murdered man in New Zealand 24.494; 'Neither kill nor cause to kill' 2.359; the potentiality to commit murder is in all of us 25.75; rejection of the golden rule: behave towards others as you wish them to behave towards you 2.359; the outward expression of a state of mind dominated by hatred 1.143; Thai monk charged with murder and robbery 2.551; 'We who have seen men murdered' 25.270

see also
King Ajātasatru's murder of his father, *see* Ajātasatru; murder of parents as heinous crime, *see* five heinous crimes

Murillo, Bartolomé Estaban 13.598, 24.441

Murray, Gilbert (translator) 24.396

Murti, M. R. 9.69

Murti, T. R. V. 2.129, 2.671 (n84), 8.209, 8.535

Murugam, Tamil god of war 20.246

Mus, Paul 22.223

Muses analogy with *adhiṣṭhāna* 16.519; the *ḍākinī* as a Muse 18.59; a dream of an angry woman on the phone: a muse-type figure 13.239–40; can one invoke the Muses so vigorously that one can't hear them singing? 16.519; the higher self 3.513; invoking the Muse 11.151; nine Muses 16.363, 24.399; poetic inspiration from outside 19.141, 25.65; reading is not a Muse 25.337; serving the Muse 25.414; the White Goddess, the poet's Muse 25.433

Muses, Charles 8.365–6

music

what is music?
born of silence 7.322; made of auditory impressions 3.511

Western classical music
gratitude towards composers as spiritual friends 3.602–3; the influence of Buddhism on Western music has been negligible 7.451; inspiration from classical music 11.371; lifts our emotions to a high pitch of intensity 26.114; learning to enjoy 9.444; Nazis who committed atrocities and also enjoyed classical music 26.396; *opera seria* 24.182–3, 24.655–6 (n235)

other Western music
a fantasy about the kind of music radio networks could play 25.320; pop music 7.266, 11.196, 25.433

a refining influence
it can develop sensitivities, refine emotions, and open the way to meditation 12.672; learning to listen to music 12.260, 17.536–7; refining one's musical taste 5.511, 15.157–8

the music of different spiritual traditions
the Bauls, mendicant singers of mystic songs 7.461; Tantric song form (*vajra-gīta*) 18.5; Tibetan music 11.228–9, 18.5; the use of music in Christian liturgy 11.227–8; Vedic hymns 16.362

music in Buddhism
the Buddha's appreciation of music 26.124; Aśvaghoṣa the musician 13.132; instrumental music accompanying Tibetan ceremonies 8.532; *Carpe Diem*, Buddhist oratorio 11.466–7; the music of the Dharma in the Pure Land 1.333

music and spiritual life
finding the Dharma in music 22.465; the melody of impermanence 2.74, 3.382, 13.131–2; it may convey distant echoes of the truth 16.285; it's wrong to say that religion is found in musty books, not in flowers or music 7.283; Perfect Vision arising from an experience of music 1.481; sacred music as a path to the divine 22.294; to communicate spiritual values, music needs the aid of words 26.377–8; using music in pujas 11.227–9; we could experience it as a revelation that would transform our life 16.285; we have access to the *rūpaloka*, the archetypal realm, through music 12.559; we should be careful about the kind of music we sing 12.558; wisdom, compassion, and the metaphor of a lute 25.286

music as metaphor
analogy between the pianist practising scales and the Buddhist learning doctrines 2.60; let your life be a heroic symphony 8.157; the silence in the mind like that after the last notes have died away 24.66

see also
Indian music, *see under* India/Indian life and customs; individual composers; Sangharakshita's experience of music, *see* Sangharakshita XII/music

musicians buskers 26.564; completely absorbed in playing 15.731; discipline and improvisation 4.485–6; keen ear 3.507; mindfulness like playing a musical instrument 15.83; probably only a musician could listen to music with commitment 16.285; pure awareness like that of a musician immersed in a symphony 15.202–3; *samādhi* like the absorbed experience of the musician or the lover 11.34; a song by Pañcasika the celestial musician 26.121–3; you can be carried away mindfully, as when playing music 15.615

musing 7.228, 18.499, 25.84

muṣitasmṛtitā *see* unmindfulness

Muslim invasion of India *see under* Indian Buddhism

Muslim League 20.169–70, 22.59

Muslims *see* Islam

Muvattupuzha, South India 20.255–327

Muzhou 8.488

Myanmar (Burma)

history
Theravāda Buddhism 2.548, 3.407; *Sāsanavaṃsa* or *Thathanawin* (history of the Buddhist Order in Burma) 2.667 (n46); a copy of the Tipiṭaka **seized by** King Aniruddha 7.443; the Sixth Buddhist Council, *see under* councils; problem caused by compromise with Confucians 12.516; Buddhist resurgence associated with Ledi Sayadaw 7.445; Anagarika Dharmapala visits 8.37–8, 8.43; wartime experience of a Burmese refugee 22.277; Burma World Buddhist Mission 22.130; gift of Buddhist artefacts from China 7.446; Dr Ambedkar visits 9.11, 9.70, 9.119; acknowledgement of Dr Ambedkar's conversion 9.133; *Burma* (a nation in the making, 1958) 8.382; tolerance of Muslims (1953) 8.124–5; persecution of Rohingya Islamic minority (2013) 26.687, 26.691–2

royal family
Prince Ata 12.124; King Thibaw, who executed relatives by elephant-trampling 12.124–5, 15.521, 21.126; Queen Supayalat v21

Buddhist texts
Bishop Bigandet's compilation of texts 12.70; Buddhist scriptures carved on

marble 14.253; difference between Burmese and Thai Tipiṭaka 14.253; 'Burmese' Pāli 21.109; *Sangāyanā* publications 8.182–3; *The Light of the Dhamma* 8.155, 22.171

Buddhist practice
the animistic element (worship of Nats) 7.144, 11.247–8, 26.667; attitudes to vegetarianism 8.124–5, 17.585; a Burmese visitor in London 26.601–2; conservatism 1.222; *devas* 21.132–4, 21.136; devotion 21.197; meditation tradition 15.736; method of Satipaṭṭhāna 1.156, 1.225; money spent on shrines to glorify the giver 8.175; morality based on laws of Manu? 16.434; New Year's Day festival 2.229; rest houses for pilgrims at holy sites in India 7.465

monastic matters
a Burmese *mahāthera* of Sangharakshita's acquaintance 22.26, 22.28; dispute about how robes should be worn 4.186, 13.105; 'nuns' neglected, not being considered as providing merit 2.215; robe-giving ceremony 3.406; 'spreading Buddhism' by teaching people to eat fish and write Burmese 12.252–3; a young monk who refused an offer of marriage 22.273–4

see also
Sangharakshita's Burmese preceptor, *see* U Chandramani; vipassanā movement

Myers, L. H. 20.111

Mylapore *see under* Madras

myrobalan 16.620 (n276)

Myron 23.296, 23.307, 23.518 (n232)

Mysore, India 20.364–74

Mysorean, The (magazine) 22.178

mystery

the mystery of life
at the root of things there is an unfathomable mystery 7.37; concepts are vital, but they do not exhaust the whole of life's mystery 15.137; everything is unfathomable if you study it 25.133; this is how Job sees it 16.86; life charged with mysterious potency 7.322–3; like waking up in a strange inn, not knowing how you got there 3.7; the mysteriousness of life and death 3.4–6, 3.95; the mystery of existence 25.487, 26.306; the mystery of one's own spiritual life 3.232; a sudden communion between mystery and mystery 26.336; *śūnyatā* is a synonym for the indefinable mystery of the true nature of things 13.119; 'take upon's the mystery of things' (*King Lear*) 15.137; when the questioner realizes that he himself is the question, that question is a mystery 8.575; 'a world of mysteries and magnitudes' 25.175

the mystery of the Dharma
Buddhism is essentially trying to communicate a mystery 12.106; Buddhism is thousands of things, all with the same mysterious seal 2.53; the Dharma on which the Buddha depends is a mystery to the unenlightened 26.631–2; even when the teachings are familiar to us, they are still a mystery 25.133; the mysterious 'preachings' of the *dharmakāya* 14.259; the mysterious thread of unity that runs through the fabric of things 3.469; whatever we learn, the Dharma is always essentially a mystery 3.232

the mystery of Enlightened beings
the Buddha as a very mysterious 'personality' 12.657; the mysterious practical activity of the Enlightened mind 1.536, 12.216; a mysterious vision of the Buddha 14.438; the mystery of the bodhisattva's 'renunciation' of Nirvāṇa 7.291; the *tathāgatagarbha* reveals reality's mysterious immanence 2.43

the mystery of …
the *arūpa dhyānas* 5.249–51; death 15.145; egoless activity 7.376; how ideas emerge into consciousness 7.137; impermanence 15.183; the land of Uḍḍiyāna 22.474; love 7.58, 25.379, 25.483, 25.497; mountains 25.211; Nirvāṇa 12.657; poetry 26.335; *rūpa* 15.134, 17.445; Sangharakshita 2.529–30; skilful means 16.497; *śūnyatā* 3.231–2, 13.119, 25.248; the universe as seen by modern science 25.133; the world of a Mahāyāna *sutra* 16.237–8, 16.440

mystical experience analogies with aesthetic experience 26.327–8; mistaking limited mystical experience for the whole truth 10.596; mystical Buddhism 12.515–16; 'mystical' an unsatisfactory word 1.480; the Path of Vision arising as a result of 1.480; the range of the mystical in Buddhist psychology, mythology, and the stages of the Path 8.440; the third *dhyāna* 5.241; of William Blake 7.400; the world transfigured 4.245

mysticism the Buddha emphasized both rational and mystical approach 12.515; the clouds of a vague universalist mysticism 23.40; Conze's comparison of Buddhist meditation and Christian mysticism 4.513; dark night of the soul 7.101, 7.580 (n195), 17.109, 17.724 (n116); as defined by Agehananda Bharati 8.435–7; 'holy

indifference' 4.489; 'to me as a Buddhist, terms such as mystic and mysticism are alien, even repugnant' 4.640; mysticism and different faiths 7.369–70; mysticism in poetry 26.137; nothing wrong with reading the classics of Christian mysticism 13.337; the relation between mystical illumination and speculative thought 24.431; 'seeing the inward in the outward' 7.102; and science 4.642–3; theology is to mysticism as literary criticism is to poetry 26.45; Theravāda rationalism tinged with mysticism, Mahāyāna mysticism tinged with rationalism 12.515, 26.367; the Tibetans are mystical in the true sense 13.109–10; Western *bhikkhus* hostile to the Mahāyāna but drawn to Christian mysticism 23.24–5

mystics attest to the existence of absolute reality 12.86; the Christian mystic loves God for his own sake, not for the sake of reward 7.391; devotional and philosophical 7.97; the mystic's perception of a subtle brilliance 15.239; falling in love with the object of their devotion 5.618; get into difficulties when they interpret their experience in terms of God 14.460; *Manual of a Mystic* 8.34; speak of seeing everything as being lit up from within 13.120; theistically inclined, believing that their experiences come from God 16.98

Mystics and Scientists Conference 24.6

myths and mythology

the history of myth
definition of mythology 13.583; the difference between myths and legends 12.108; originated towards the end of prehistory 3.425; myths remoulded in Axial Age 3.427–8; fertility myths replaced nature myths 3.426; every people has a mythology of its own creation 13.583; allegorization of myths 16.103–5; myth as opposed to history 16.526–34; modern interest in myth influenced by Jung 11.15, 12.508

the nature of myth
the creation of a whole people, not any individual 4.37, 13.583, 26.486; emerge out of spiritual necessity 4.37; help to enlist cooperation of unconscious energies 3.41; much of what is thought of as history is really myth 26.72; multi-layered 16.105; not untrue, but have a higher spiritual, poetic truth 4.262, 12.182; psychological experiences and spiritual truths, not to be taken literally 12.108–9; a realm of indefinable meanings 16.528; they emerge when people's feelings are not supported by the existing state of affairs 4.37

connecting with myth
bringing one's feeling into exploring myths and finding connections 4.196; engagement can help one break through the rational mind 11.15–16; the heart is moved more powerfully by a myth than by an argument 1.325; the importance of a mythic aspect to life 25.100; literal belief in myths 12.106–7, 16.528; to invoke the power of mythological figures you have to be interested in them 16.358; Sangharakshita's earliest connections 20.23; try connecting with the mythical level of things in general 4.196; working out on the historical plane something of archetypal significance 4.36

and Buddhism
in the process of emerging in the Pāli canon 4.37; early Buddhists did not distinguish between historical and mythological 7.491, 16.241; mythological beings in a Mahāyāna *sūtra* 16.464; in Buddhist history it was first history, then myth 13.302; images belonging to Buddhist mythology that have nothing to do with doctrine 7.437; the language of myth 4.148, 12.102–11, 16.417; the mandala of myth 18.318; Dr Ambedkar's realization of the value of myth 9.110–11; how as Western Buddhists will we engage in the creation of myth? 4.37–8; might Western Buddhism adopt Greek mythology? 19.128, 19.410; the mythic life of the sangha 4.37; myths of the Buddha, *see under* Buddha II/symbols and myths; spiritual life needs both myths and rational thought 12.106, 16.67; the relevance of a study on Plato's myths to Sangharakshita's understanding 24.537; we have access to the *rūpaloka*, the archetypal realm, through myths 12.559; Western scholars tend to disregard myths and legends 11.15, 12.182

see also
Christian mythology, *see* Christianity/ myths and parables; Greek mythology, *see under* Greece (ancient); Irish mythology, *see under* Ireland; Norse mythology, *see* Norse; personal myth; symbolism

N

Nabokov, Vladimir 3.514, 3.478

Naciketas *see under* Upanishads

Nāḍi Kāśyapa *see* Kāśyapa brothers

nāḍīs the channels within which energies move 19.52, 19.284; the *nāḍīs* and *prāṇas* dispel drowsiness and distractions 19.155; a subtle network of vital forces 18.76; there's no faster way than *nāḍī* and *prāṇa* practice 19.284–5; Tsa (Tibetan) 19.411

Nag, Dr Kalidas 8.635, v20, v21, v22

Nagabodhi, Dharmachari brief introduction 24.643 (n181); editor of the *FWBO Magazine* and *Golden Drum* 9.241, 9.290, 11.565; foreword 2.xi–xviii; *Jai Bhim!* 9.xv, 10.xlviii, 10.87, 10.338, 12.379; in India with Sangharakshita 9.241, 9.290, 10.286; interviews Sangharakshita 11.518–28, 11.545–611; launches *The Taste of Freedom* 24.381; move to Croydon 15.517; move to Sheffield 24.385–6; on a 1974 seminar 14.xv; president of FWBO centres 12.631; as publisher 14.320–1; Sangharakshita tells him his wishes in the event of his death 24.340–1; seminars on the *Bodhicaryāvatāra* 11.699; 'Signs of the Times' 24.366

Nāgāhvaya 17.466

Nagaloka *see under* Nagpur

Nagapriya, Dharmachari 3.644–5 (n122 and n123)

***Nāgarī* script** *see devanāgarī*

Nāgārjuna (author of the *Bodhicittavivaraṇa*) 4.28

Nāgārjuna (Madhyamaka metaphysician)

LIFE STORY

biography
brief introduction 1.309–10, 8.678–9 (n92), 17.153, 23.526 (n372); the derivation of his name 1.309; by temperament analytical 1.360; he seems to have kept his wisdom and devotion in separate compartments 14.431; his friendship with the Andhra king Sātavāhana 1.309; he was vulnerable to the dangers of developing wisdom without meditation 1.349; how much do we really know about him? 12.562–3; one of the greatest philosophers the world has ever known 10.327; parallel to St Jerome 26.303; worship of the Buddhas Amitābha and Maitreya 1.324, 1.336

his place in the Buddhist tradition
allegedly referred to in the *Laṅkavatāra Sūtra* 14.203, 17.466; association with Padmasambhava 8.523; belief that Maitreya's advent will be preceded by Nāgārjuna's return 2.179; a bodhisattva of the second *bhūmi*, according to one tradition 17.412; could be regarded as the second founder of Buddhism 1.310; the founding father of both Madhyamaka and Pure Land School 1.324, 1.337, 13.45; the greatest figure in Mahāyāna Buddhism 1.309, 16.239; founder of the Madhyamaka school 13.342, 17.325, 17.450; association with the monastic centre Nāgārjunikoṇḍa 14.135; Indian patriarch of the Zen school 13.342; in some ways the most important Buddhist philosopher 6.xxx; an interpreter of one level of reality to another 26.302–3; one of the six ornaments of India 17.464–6; the most important figure in Indian philosophy 8.209; sometimes confused with a much later Nāgārjuna, a Tantric initiate 1.302; a watershed between Hīnayāna and Mahāyāna 2.181; ordination lineage

in Tibet 7.473–4; why should a cultured Englishman not be acquainted with his work? 20.61

how he received the Perfection of Wisdom from the nāgas
brief account 1.309, 8.210, 12.29, 14.xiv, 16.16–17; depicted on a raft receiving books from a *nāga* maiden 12.29, 14.135, 14.345–6; a kind of translation 26.239; possible historical explanation 1.310, 14.135–6; rediscoverer of the Perfection of Wisdom teachings 13.342; the symbolism of the legend 14.346, 17.325, 26.303; a thangka of Nāgārjuna and the *nāga* princess 6.xxx

HIS TEACHINGS

his challenges to other schools
attack on *asatkāryavāda* and *satkāryavāda* 1.315–16, 14.607, 17.637, 19.435; challenge to non-Buddhist schools 17.362; his philosophy not nihilistic, but ultimately positive and affirmative 23.319–20; the Perfection of Wisdom – to counter dogmatism, literalism, and scholasticism 1.310; refutation of the Abhidharma's analysis of *dharmas* 17.367–8; refutation of the *kṣānikavāda* 17.367, 17.748–9 (n314)

his relationship to the literary tradition
connection with the Prajñāpāramitā 14.135, 14.346; the earliest Perfection of Wisdom *sūtras* are considered to pre-date him 14.346; he published the Prajñāpāramitā *sūtras* 14.137, 17.153; he quoted the *White Lotus Sūtra* 1.302, 14.106; his writings sometimes referred to as Mahāyāna Abhidharma 7.503; which Prajñāpāramitā and other Mahāyāna *sūtras* did he know? 1.302

his logical methods
attempts to prove the non-existence of the self by logical argument 17.373–8; an audacious project, comparable to that of Parmenides 17.450; by remorseless logic, he annihilates both object and subject 7.126; dialectical method 1.314–21; he demonstrated that all views are inapplicable because self-contradictory 1.313; he exposed contradictions in Buddhist doctrines *when taken literally* 1.316; he transposed the rejection of all views from metaphysical to logical mode 1.313–15; his method compared to that of Socrates 1.312; propositions refuted by themselves when carried to logical conclusions 1.312

on śūnyatā
the Buddha's *khandavāda* logically suggests Nāgārjuna's *śūnyavāda* 7.132; emptiness of the composite (*saṃskṛta-śūnyatā*) 1.120; he affirmed the 'existence' of *śūnyatā* 8.443; he designated *pratītya-samutpāda* as *śūnyatā* 7.199; his approach anticipated in an early Mahāyāna *sūtra* 14.181; intended as a medicine for the cure of all attachments 3.237; the middle way in principle identical with *śūnyatā* 7.300; to misunderstand it is to be poisoned by the only medicine that can cure you 17.389; *see also* Nāgārjuna/works/ *Mūlamadhyamakakārikā*

on causation
refutation of *satkāryavāda* and *asatkāryavāda* views 1.314–16, 14.607; showed that causation and *pratītya-samutpāda* are ultimately unreal 1.316–17

other aspects
the essential nondifference between Buddhas and all beings, oneself and others 4.587–8; the ten perfections and the four abodes of mindfulness 1.324; two paths: self-reliance and dependence on the Buddhas' compassion 1.324, 1.400–1; the 'unthinkability' of reality 19.373

WORKS

brief entries
works can be divided into three categories: authentic, doubtful, and spurious 1.310; *Bhavasaṃkrānti Sūtra Vṛtti* 1.311; *Catuḥstava*: a kind of hymn in four parts 1.311; commentaries on Prajñāpāramitā *sūtras* 14.137; *Daśabhūmikavibhasa*: deals with the ten stages of the bodhisattva's career 1.311; *Discourse on the Transcendendality of the Bodhicitta* 4.241; *Dvādaśanikāya Śāstra*: important in China and Japan 1.311; *Ekaśloka Śāstra* 1.311; *Large Prajñāpāramitā Sūtra*, *see Large Prajñāpāramitā Sūtra*; *Prakaraṇa* 1.311; *Suhṛllekha* (*Friendly Epistle*) 1.309, 1.311, 17.663; *Śūnyatāsaptati*: on the doctrine of Emptiness 1.311; *Vaidalya Sūtra* 1.311; *Vigrahavyāvartanī* 1.311; *Yuktiṣaṣṭikā* 1.311

Mahāprajñāpāramitā (or Mahā-prajñā-pāramitopadeśa) Śāstra
cites the *Vimalakīrti-nirdeśa* 14.156; *trimaṇḍala-pariśuddha* (threefold circle of purity) 2.366, 4.104, 17.202, 17.734 (n204); a 'wealth of useful information' 1.311, 1.615 (n254); a work of encyclopedic content, existing in Chinese translation 14.146–7; Ramanan, K. Venkata, *Nāgārjuna's Philosophy* 23.319–20

Mūlamadhyamakakārikā
introduction 1.310–11, 6.xxx, 16.239; 'Being and non-Being should both be

rejected 8.211; 'Better to be attached to a self as high as Mount Sumeru, than to the idea of *śūnyatā*' 3.237, 4.693 (n227), 14.459–60, 18.179, 18.371, 19.241; can be regarded as a commentary on the Perfection of Wisdom 14.348; chapter 25, examination of Nirvāṇa – 13 verses quoted 1.317–19; commentaries include Candrakīrti's *Prasannapadā*, *see* Candrakīrti; contrast with Maitreyanātha's *Madhyāntivibhāga* 1.363; denying *śūnyatā* is like a man on a horse denying he is on horseback 7.213, 10.158; 'Everything exists on account of emptiness' 7.200, 14.607, 17.723 (n109); exposes inconsistencies of *āyatanas*, *skandhas*, and six *dhātus* 1.320; the foundational text of the Madhyamaka school 17.153; if cause and effect are identical or different, causation is impossible 14.607; makes it clear that Nāgārjuna does not propound any 'view' 19.372–3; the middle path 1.363, 7.200, 7.533–4; modern commentaries 17.758 (n397); a good idea to read the text itself, along with modern commentaries 17.465–6; of pivotal importance in the development of Indian thought 1.311; the relative truth is the means to the realization of the absolute truth 1.206, 1.348; senses and sense organs 17.751 (n335); translation by Jay Garfield 17.321–2; use of the *catuṣkoṭi* 10.690 (n202); the wise do not make plans (i.e. set up *saṃskāras*) 17.475; the world cannot really come to an end 17.387, 17.750 (n323)

PRECIOUS GARLAND OF ADVICE FOR THE KING

about the text
introduction 17.153–2, 17.323; its name (*Rājaparikathā-ratnamālā* or *Ratnāvalī*) 17.153; a classic of Tibetan literature 17.157; cultivates seeds present in earlier works 17.157; it is a general survey of the Mahāyāna 17.465; a guide to living in accordance with Mahāyāna principles 17.153; its theme: practising ethics and attaining wisdom 6.xxx, 11.723, 17.153–4; it was composed in Sanskrit as a literary text 17.154; it would originally have been chanted 17.417; probably authentic 1.311; provides the basis for part of Śāntideva's *Bodhicaryāvatāra* 17.417; it describes the two aspects of the bodhisattva's life: wisdom and compassion 8.507; the Tibetan translation includes explanations 17.155–6; Sangharakshita's commentary 17.xvi–xvii, 17.149–418; a summary of the text 8.506–7; translation by Jeffrey Hopkins 8.506–8 (review), 17.322; a *vade mecum* of the Mahāyāna, both theoretical and practical 8.507

Chapter 1
summary 8.506; the devotional beginning 17.326–7; ethics as the basis of wisdom 17.158; 'Having analysed well all deeds of body, speech, and mind' 17.xx, 17.265–7; high status and definite goodness 17.160–2; happiness, freedom, pleasure 17.164–6; the folly of unskilful action 17.170–1, 17.172–3; the ten precepts 17.175–9; right livelihood 17.193–7; generosity 17.198–202; the third precept 17.214–17; skilful speech 17.228–30; unskilful speech 17.236–9; eternalism and nihilism 17.241–51; self-mortification 17.251–5; intoxication 17.255–6; the mind precepts 17.257–9; the *brahma vihāras* 17.262–4; pride, jealousy, anger 17.279; the results of actions 17.292–6; fear of the doctrines of definite goodness 17.323–5, 17.339–41, 17.352–5; wisdom and faith 17.334–8; 'I' and 'mine' 17.342–52; Nirvāṇa 17.355–7; emptiness 17.357–61; existence, non-existence, time, and the world 17.362–9; 'delighting in a base' 17.369–72; the non-existence of the self 17.373–8; the elements 17.373–81; 'honouring the honourable' 13.270, 17.275–7; generating the Dharma, not just understanding of the Dharma 17.334

Chapter 2
summary 8.506; the impermanence of life 17.162–4; the pointlessness of unskilful activities 17.171–2; the bodhisattva ideal 17.173–4; the four *saṃgraha-vastus* 17.174–5; fear and power 17.179–83; the ugliness of the conditioned 8.506, 17.217–21; contemplation of beauty 17.221; the path of truth 17.230–6, 17.239–40; intoxicants and gambling 17.256–7; the 32 major marks 8.506; truth and illusions 17.382–91; the production of an illusory elephant 17.385–7, 19.596 (n33); 'Those who gladden embodied beings' 4.97, 17.182–3

Chapter 3
summary 8.506; happiness is beneficial 17.166–70; the fruits of kindness 17.185–90; the practice of giving 8.506, 17.203–5; giving the Dharma 17.205–8; cultivating the mind 17.260–2; developing a new world 17.296–9; 'A bodhisattva stays for a limitless time in the world' 4.61; merit and wisdom 8.506

Chapter 4
summary 8.506–7; advice to the king as king 8.506–7; healthy self-interest 17.190–3; the businessman's guide to

giving 17.209–13; pain and pleasure 17.299–304, 17.392–409; no mind 17.410–13; a vigorous defence of the Mahāyāna 8.507

Chapter 5
summary 8.507; forsake anger 17.268–71; pride 17.271–7; ignoble motives 17.277–9; attachment 17.281–6; hidden intentions 17.286–8; the consequences of mental states 17.288–91; merit, wisdom, and all good qualities 17.304–9; 'Along the way all pleasures' 4.62; practices to be engaged in and faults to be given up 8.507; a wish to help others motivated by desire 4.89; a Sevenfold Puja 8.507, 17.414–17

Nagarjuna Training Institute *see under* Nagpur/Nagaloka

Nāgārjunikoṇḍa (monastic centre) association with Nāgārjuna 8.163, 14.135; campaign to stop its flooding in an irrigation scheme 8.163–4, 8.210, 8.680 (n95); poem 25.263

Nagas (non-Āryans) 9.121

nāgas they represent inspiration from the depths 11.151; the *Large Prajñāpāramitā Sūtra* preserved in their region 14.145; on Mount Meru 16.344; a *nāga* princess who transforms herself into a male bodhisattva (*Lotus Sūtra*) 14.110, 14.122; the *nāga* that resides in Lake Anavatapta 14.539; spirit of the waters, the depths 14.539

see also
as elephants, *see under* elephants; as dragons, *see* dragons; as serpents, *see under* snakes; *nāga* princess who gave Nāgārjuna the Perfection of Wisdom, *see under* Nāgārjuna

Nāgasamāla (the Buddha's companion at one time) 10.649–50

Nāgasena *see Questions of King Milinda*

Nagercoil, India 20.244

Naginda *see* Dinesh

Nagpur

Buddhism in the city before Dr Ambedkar's conversion
Buddha Society (founded in 1944) 10.97, 10.98–9, 10.374, 22.163; Vaiśākha Purṇimā celebrated (1946) 22.163; followers of Dr Ambedkar (1954) 22.158; Sangharakshita's first visit (1954) 10.374, 22.154–65; its significance as the place where the Dhamma Revolution started 9.121, 10.376–7

Diksha Bhumi
conversion ceremony in 1956, *see under* Ambedkar/conversion to Buddhism; photographs 10.2, 10.92; a place of pilgrimage 10.97–8, 10.112–13, 10.677 (n128); disputes over the Diksha Bhumi 8.270–1, 10.364, 24.138, 24.639 (n162); celebrations of the anniversary of Dr Ambedkar's conversion 10.liii; visit in 1966 23.355

Sangharakshita's visit after Dr Ambedkar's death
his instinct to go to Nagpur then 10.10, 10.17, 22.357–60; the news of Dr Ambedkar's death 9.21–2, 9.176, 9.405–6, 10.11, 10.312, 10.375, 22.361; condolence meeting 9.22–3, 9.176–7, 9.406, 10.11, 10.18, 10.313, 10.375, 22.362–3; eyewitness accounts 10.xxxvii–viii, 10.96–7; talks in the different localities 9.468, 10.12, 10.98–105, 23.18–19; A. R. Kulkarni's account of the whole visit 10.95–105

Sangharakshita's later visits
visits in the 1960s 9.157, 10.149, 10.177, 10.376, 23.355–7; gives a talk at Nagpur Central Jail 23.355; reasons for not visiting the city in the 1980s 10.363–4, 10.376; return in 1992 10.liv, 10.372–398; encourages Nagpur people to use their energy for the Dharma 10.389; a last message to the people of Nagpur 10.392

Nagaloka
instigated at Sangharakshita's suggestion 10.lv–vi; Nagarjuna Training Institute 10.lv–lix, 10.lxii; Ashok Dhammaduta programme 10.li; support from Taiwanese Buddhists 10.li; Walking Buddha 10.lv, 10.lvi; photographs 10.xxxiv, 10.lv

Triratna
bookshop 10.405; numbers of Order members 10.387, 10.405, 10.704 (n339)

places in the city
Bahadma 22.160–1; Dharampeth 22.155; IAS training institute 10.381–2; Kamptee 10.104–5; Mahar ghettoes 9.123; Mahendra Nagar 10.383; Municipal Corporation 9.133–4; Ramakrishna Mission 22.155–6, 22.164–5; Science College 22.156, 22.157–8; Sitabaldi 22.156–7; Theosophists' lodge 22.156

Naidu, Sarojini

introduction
brief introduction 7.56–7, 7.556 (n70); association with Gandhi 7.56; on the committee that chose the Indian flag 8.xxviii; eager to live life and not merely to study it 7.60–1; influence of Persian poetry

7.58; love poetry 7.61–2; her nephew Jairaj 22.279–80; poem recited at the opening of the Indian National Congress 7.60; politics 7.56, 7.59; she can enter all temples and find the same God in every one 7.59; sonnets to Gandhi and Jinnah 7.57

The Sceptred Flute
folk songs 7.59; 'Give me to drink each joy and pain' 7.60; 'Haste, O wild-bee hours' 7.58; 'Her life is a revolving dream' 7.57; 'Hourly this subtle mystery flowers anew' 7.58; the last part gives expression to all she has learned about life 7.61–3; O Death, I cannot die!' 7.61; 'O I am tired of strife and song' 7.56; 'Valmiki's heroes bold' 7.57; Sangharakshita's article on *The Sceptred Flute* 7.13, 7.55–63, 21.436, 21.478

naiḥsargika-patayantika* or *nissaggiya-pācittiya (forfeiture, expiation) *see under vinaya*/offences

Nair, Dr Anandrao (Bombay philanthropist) v22

Nair, Kumaran (Muvattupuzha lawyer) 20.272–7

Nair, Ramana (caretaker of Muvattupuzha ashram) 20.260

nairātmya (twofold *śūnyatā*) of all *dharmas* (*sarvadharma-nairātmya*) 1.264–72, 2.88, 5.439, 7.155, 7.505, 14.495–6, 15.184, 18.246; of the so-called individual (*pudgala-nairātmya*) 1.266–7, 2.88, 5.438, 7.505, 15.184, 18.246; the reification of *dharmas* limits it to *pudgala-nairātmya* 15.184; two *nairātmyas* in the *Laṅkāvatāra Sūtra* 14.213

Nairs (group of Hindu castes of South India) in Travancore 20.251, 20.282; matrilineal society 20.286; Nair women kept as concubines by Nambudiri men 20.285–6

naiṣkramya (non-desire) *see* renunciation

Nakamura, Dr Hajime Buddhism is 'not a system of philosophy but a path' 8.604; 'The Peace Concept of Buddhism' 8.399; 'Unity and Diversity in Buddhism' 8.364

Nakayama, Rev. Riri (Shin Buddhism) 20.462

nakedness and nudity Allen Ginsberg and the naked truth 13.243, 19.260, 25.93; the *dharmakāya* depicted as a naked Buddha figure 4.204–5; embarrassment about nakedness 19.250–1, 19.256; even literal nakedness is not without significance 13.242; the Immaculate Fruit of Nakedness 19.165; Milarepa's nakedness 18.xvii, 18.4, 18.133–4, 18.219, 18.221, 19.249–64; naked ascetics 10.589; 'Naked we came into the world/ And naked will go out' 25.423; the nakedness of the *ḍākinī*, because she has nothing to hide 13.217, 13.240; natural, unselfconscious nudity 18.634–5; nudity for shock value in the arts 18.634, 19.258; religious nudity 18.634–5, 20.361; the spiritual significance of nakedness 13.179; truth in its nakedness 13.282; the unacceptableness of nudity in some cultures 19.249–50; the *vajrakula*, the authentic, naked community 13.178–9

Nakula's parents (Pāli canon) 14.49

Nala Sopara *see* Suppāraka

Nālaka Sutta *see Sutta-Nipāta*

Naḷakapāna Sutta *see under Majjhima Nikāya*

Nālandā crest 12.317, 12.335–6

Nalanda University history 3.173, 20.461; association with Nāgārjuna 1.309; Xuanzang's visit 2.201, 7.428, 9.390, 12.238, 20.460–1; Silabhadra (Xuanzang's teacher) 20.461; destruction (1197) 1.322, 20.461; the burning of the library 1.381, 12.243, 14.264, 25.10–11; thousands of monks burned alive 12.243; imagining how it would have been 7.428–9; its heyday 2.191, 8.244, 9.390, 12.238; ruins 20.460–1; Museum 7.429; the Nalanda Pāli Postgraduate Institute 12.430–1, 21.38, 22.16, 22.320, 23.124, 23.368; Dr Ambedkar mentions Nalanda 9.117; Sangharakshita visits 7.427, 20.460–1, 22.387, 23.368–9; 'Nalanda Revisited' (sonnet) 25.274; Jagdish Kashyap there 12.430–1, 22.16, 22.320, 23.124

nāma one of the five *dharmas* (categories) 14.213; *nāma-rūpa*, *see* psychophysical organism

namaskar 10.xliv

Nambudiri caste *see under* brahmins

name-giving ceremony *see under* ceremonies

names Milarepa's name signifies his unique nature as an individual 18.68–9; the net of names (concepts) 17.379; the power of a word, a name, a mantra 17.418; taking a new name on commitment to the spiritual life 18.150–1; the Tibetan approach to names 13.31; to ask someone's name is because you want to know them 18.238; useful, but have no ultimate validity 4.578–9

Namgyal Institute of Tibetology *see under* Sikkim/Gangtok

Namgyal, Palden Thondup *see* Sikkim/ Maharaj Kumar

Namgyal Rimpoche *see* Ananda Bodhi

namkaran-vidhi (child's naming ceremony) *see under* ceremonies

namu myōhō renge kyō Nichiren's teaching 16.59, 16.593 (n56); chanted at Japanese temple in Rajgir 20.462; those chanting it in a Bombay temple didn't understand it 9.261, 9.266, 9.507, 22.271

ñāṇa-dassana visuddhi *see* seven *visuddhis*

Ñāṇamoli, Bhikkhu *The Illustrator of Ultimate Meaning* (*Paramatthajotikā*) 10.230–1; *The Life of the Buddha* 2.553, 2.741 (n676), 6.xxv

Nanda (or Sundarananda) he becomes the Buddha's disciple through force 3.557–8; his ordination on his wedding day 3.689 (n437); he visits the dove-footed nymphs 2.82–3, 10.504–7, 12.614–15, 26.314, 26.596–7, 26.665; higher beauty 10.505–6, 11.588, 14.310, 15.128, 15.157, 23.317, 26.597; the significance of the episode 2.82, 10.505–6, 12.615, 18.371; what 'dove-footed' means 10.505

Nanda, B. R. 10.55

Nanda, Shri Gulzarilal 7.422, v22, 22.294

Nandawansa, Venerable 22.98

Nanded, India 9.387–8

Nandiya (Anuruddha's companion) 3.635 (n55), 3.670 (n287)

Nandy, Dr (Dharmapala's physician) 8.71–2

Nangwa, Sherab *see* Prajnaloka

Nan-in (Japanese master) 11.278–9, 17.208, 17.735 (n206)

Nanjio, Rev. B. 1.328, 1.616 (n259, n260), 14.254

Napoleon Bonaparte defeated at the battle of Waterloo 10.222, 24.149; his exile 26.277; his soldiers using the Sphinx for target practice 26.476; his tomb: glorification of the spirit of war 26.277–8; *Napoleon on board the Bellerophon* 26.661; view of Goethe: 'Look, there is a man!' 3.501

Nārada (Hindu divine sage) 7.95, 7.578 (n177)

Narada Thera introduction 8.674 (n64); *Abhidhammattha-saṅgaha: An Outline of Buddhist Philosophy* 1.102–3, 7.540–1, 8.119; 'A Buddhist monk is not allowed to appreciate beauty' 21.397, 22.148; his view that vitamin tablets were food 21.397, 22.312; maintained that *bhikkhus* were not allowed to peel their own bananas 22.348; maintained that he was superior to the Dalai Lama 22.354; *A Manual of Abhidhamma* 19.597–8 (n40; in Nepal 21.280–1, 21.300–4; narrow formalism 21.280–1, 21.300–4, 21.392–3, 22.312–15; a novice given to him for training 21.448; on the Sacred Relics tour 21.267, 21.392–3, 21.396–8; a visit to Kalimpong 22.312–15

Narada, U 15.736

Narain, Professor A. K. 12.430–1

nārapuṃgava 4.469

narasīha (Sanskrit *narasiṃha*) 4.469, 9.365, 11.383, 11.757 (n214)

Narasu, P. Lakshmi 7.158, 7.160–1, 7.590 (n259), 9.63

Narayan (host in Bangalore) 20.349–51

Narayan, Swami 9.450

Nārayāna (another name for Viṣṇu) 16.396

Narayana Guru 20.295

Narayanmani 22.323–4

Nardeo (Nepali student) 23.379

Narendrayaśa 14.190

Nargis, Miss (film star) 21.409–10, 22.281–2

Narokhachö *see* Vajrayoginī

Nāropā

introduction
his biography 18.382–3; given a hard time by his teacher Tilopa 18.382–3; Rechungpa debates his teachings 19.172; rejects Marpa's gold 16.625 (n321)

the six yogas of Nāropā
introduction 13.28, 18.65; (1) *tummo* heat 13.28, 18.65; (2) realizing the illusory nature of personality 13.28, 18.65; (3) dream yoga 13.28, 17.340, 17.744 (n292), 18.65; (4) comprehending the clear light of the Void 13.28, 18.65; (5) gaining Enlightenment in the *bardo* 13.28, 15.592, 18.85–6; (6) transference of consciousness at the moment of death 13.28, 18.65

Nāropāda (one of the eighty-four *siddhas*) 1.382

narva bolta 9.506

Nātaputta *see* Mahāvīra

Natarajan, Dr (also Nataraja Guru) v20, v22

nātha (protector) 16.288

Nātha (the form of Avalokiteśvara worshipped in Sri Lanka) 2.175

national costume *see* traditional costume

nationalism contrast between nationalism and patriotism 12.342–3; cultural chauvinism 24.460–1; the curse of modern history 12.342; group egocentricity 24.461; group loyalty 3.436; involving religion in nationalist ceremonies 19.263; the pride of nationalism 17.275; war threatens the world again because nations imagine themselves to be separate entities 7.274

nationality attachment to one's native land 19.252; being held responsible for the actions of your government 14.543; differences of nationality causing misery 21.69; in the sangha differences of caste and nationality should actively be discouraged 10.565; less important than it used to be 3.441; 'One's native land is the dungeon of the devil' (Milarepa) 18.151–2; necessity to accept? 9.524, 9.532; now the whole world is divided into nation states 19.519; Sangharakshita's personal views, *see under* Sangharakshita I/introduction; today there is no land over which no state exercises sovereignty 18.454; the value of leaving one's native country 9.330–1, 9.371–2, 12.553–4, 18.331; you think of *my* native land, but nothing in the whole world is yours 18.219

nations a nation's progress is analogous to that of the individual 8.212; nations commit the same mistakes as the people of whom they are made up 8.212

natural morality *see under* ethics/ethics in the Buddhist tradition

nature

its nature
a constant round of birth and death, bloom and fade 17.378; cyclical 4.578, 16.383; innocent 4.108; nature as *saṃsāra* 16.387–8; nature's lust for reproduction 10.652, 16.302; not dead, but alive with many voices 1.28; tranquil 5.309, 15.257

beauty
appreciating the beauty of nature 18.158–9, 26.185–7; the beauty of autumn 7.335–7; the beauty of the natural world in the Book of Job 13.540–1; the gap between emotion and reason bridged through natural beauty 8.445

power
awe 2.644; enjoying the energy of the natural world 26.653; fear of the natural world 18.42; floods, typhoons, and tidal waves 8.266; if your attitude towards the forces of nature is positive, they will cooperate 10.647; man insignificant in the midst of nature 26.284; monks as insurance against natural disasters 2.216; nature is governed by 'power' 8.447; 'nature red in tooth and claw' 8.447; the power of natural forces 18.12; the sublimity of wild natural forces 14.473; the wonders of nature have the power to draw awareness to them 15.158

a teacher
counterbalance excessive thinking through contact with Nature 26.37; 'I will read the Book of Nature' 25.186; it can remind us of the greater mandala 14.519–20; learning from nature 18.182, 18.619, 19.69; nature's encouragement to aspire 25.277; receptivity to nature 1.572, 13.456; teaches us the transitoriness of things – but we refuse to learn 7.131; 'Tongues in trees, books in the running brooks' 18.182, 18.619, 19.69

harmony and appreciation
appreciation of nature for its own sake 16.387; awareness of nature 3.469; the energies that find their expression in nature also exist in us 13.273; full-moon festivals remind us to maintain harmony with nature 11.395; an imaginative identification between man and nature 26.243; it can't be transformed, but our attitude to it can be 16.386; nature tamed, symbolized by the lion 26.286–7; not to be repressed but recognized, not rejected but assimilated 13.359–60; one can be in sympathy with nature without being sentimental 26.243–4; pagan sense of connectedness with the life of the earth 4.108, 26.14; seeing natural sights without grasping 19.192; simple pleasure from contact with nature 19.92–3; there is no wound man can give that nature cannot heal 25.492; the value of nature is its very valuelessness 26.186–7; we must remember that we are a part of nature 12.84–5, 13.272, 15.136; when you lose a sense of wonder at nature, you are dying 8.265

alienation and destruction
alienation from nature in modern life 12.217, 15.236, 18.22–4, 25.54–5; country people may be out of touch with nature 11.196; exploiting nature 10.647,

26.243; man ruining Nature's peace 25.237; Nature's indifference to humanity 20.103, 26.186–7; a poem apologising for mankind's destruction of the natural world 25.50–9; wasting natural resources 16.386–7; within human beings nature has got out of control 16.394

Buddhism and nature
the Buddha and his disciples lived in the midst of nature 10.452, 15.136, 26.242; the Buddha's appreciation of the beauty of nature 26.128–9; attainment of insight in response to the natural world 1.154; nature in relation to a higher principle: Enlightenment 16.388–9; the Path of Vision arising as a result of an experience of nature 1.480; the colour green as a symbol of nature 13.282; practising forbearance in relation to the weather 4.120

religious and artistic responses
primitive idea that through sacrifices you keep nature stable 10.517; religion saturates and sanctifies the whole of nature 7.284; in the theistic religions God is in a sense Nature 15.618–19; the celebration of the coming of spring in the Song of Solomon 13.543; Christian attitude to nature 4.108; the consequences of the view that God created Nature for man 8.xxiii–iv; nature is fundamentally spiritual (Blake) 8.558; the Romantic movement a protest against the Newtonian picture of nature 15.139; 'The art itself is nature' (Shakespeare) 12.84; the poet's observation of Nature 26.136; the artist recreates nature 5.598

see also
animals; environment; Mother Nature, *see under* earth goddess; Sangharakshita's love of nature, *see under* Sangharakshita VI/ emotional life; spirits, *see under* paganism; trees

naturopathy 16.408, 20.445

Nautanwa, India 20.418–19

navakata (making new) 11.74

ñāyapaṭipanno *see under Tiratana Vandanā*

Nazism group loyalty 15.489; in horror comics 8.208; how could a civilized people like the Germans have produced it? 26.538, 26.677; a Nazi teacher 26.501; Nazis could commit atrocities and at the same time enjoy Beethoven and Bach 26.396; parallel between the Inquisition and the Nazi Gestapo 8.422; the view behind Nazi atrocities 8.xxiii

near and far enemies explanation of terms 3.690 (n443), 19.612–13 (n140); Buddhism's near enemies can be more dangerous than its far ones 8.599; of compassion 5.200–1, 10.173; of confidence 14.405; of contentment 15.275–6; of faith 17.43; of *kalyāna mitratā* 12.540–1; of *mettā* 1.159, 10.173, 15.314; of fidelity 3.567–8; of tolerance 10.83; of peacefulness 10.83; of playfulness 19.397; of *muditā* 5.204, 10.174, 26.78; of *upekkā* 10.174

Nebesky-Wojkowitz, Rene de 12.435, 21.87, 21.253, 21.317–19

nectar *see amṛta*

needs

material and personal needs
behind many of our interests is a psychological need 19.48; the body clamours for what it needs 4.532; distinguishing between healthy needs and neurotic craving 10.605; do you give yourself what you need? 18.521–2; even on solitary retreat you are not free of needs 17.16; fulfilling our legitimate needs 10.605; happy is the man whose needs and wants coincide 26.12; human needs 15.309–10; importance of meeting material needs 9.340; it is quite dangerous to get too far away from your needs 19.50; liking someone because they fulfil a need we have 3.593–4; making a pattern according to the nature of your needs 17.15; responding to objective needs from within the greater mandala 14.519; the needs of the objective situation and your personal needs 17.614; sexual needs 3.527; a skilful act is an expression of will-to-growth rather than neurotic need 26.18; taking the needs of all the aspects of yourself into account 10.605; two kinds of need, unhealthy and healthy 3.593; when you have a strong need, at least you experience yourself 18.334

spiritual needs
adapting the teachings to our needs 3.169; the Buddha taught according to different needs 9.359; find out which texts are most suited to your spiritual needs 14.269; material difficulties and spiritual needs 10.123; the need for an individual teaching tailored to your needs 18.393; the need of boundless love 25.210; Nirvāṇa can become a projection of our mundane needs 3.229; organizing our life to meet our spiritual needs 5.691–2; relating the practice of meditation to your own needs 19.57; very often people don't want to be taught the lesson they need 18.493; we are

attracted to texts that seem relevant to our spiritual needs 16.247–8

others' needs
the bodhisattva doesn't separate others' needs from their own 17.661; concerning yourself with others' needs, you see your attachment to your own 17.206; the individual can't gain his desired end unless he is aware of others' needs 1.237; often our needs clash with those of other people 12.605; our only need before helping others is to love ourselves and feel loved 14.415; practise thinking about others' needs 14.414–15, 17.204; responding to others' needs 5.187, 11.597; taking responsibility for yourself makes you more responsive to others' needs 15.290–1; they are very great, and one may not have the resources to meet all of them 18.593; we think about our own needs carefully, less so those of others 17.204

negative and negativity negative presentation of Buddhism, *see under* Buddhism I/ways of describing it; emotions, *see under* emotions; mental states, *see* mental states/negative

Nehru, Jawaharlal ('Pandit') introduction 8.679–80 (n95); celebrates the 2,500th Buddha Jayanti 22.304–5; decided that the flag and seal of India should be Buddhist symbols 8.323; a friend of Buddhism 8.249, 8.322–3; harsh criticism of Nehru 24.528; and Dr Ambedkar 9.8, 9.10, 9.68, 9.75; letter forbidding Sangharakshita's entry into Tibet 21.199–201; meets the Eminent Buddhists from the Border Areas 22.344–5; at Sanchi 21.393–4; speaks out against astrology 8.304; view of the Buddha 9.450, 9.573 (n375); visits Anandamayi's ashram 20.190–1; visits the Ramakrishna Mission in Singapore 7.109; welcomes the Sacred Relics to India 8.322–3, 21.171; his death 8.322–3

Nehru, R. M. and Mrs Nehru 22.248

neighbourhood or access concentration (*upacāra-samādhi*) what is it? 5.230; almost any practice will carry you into it 5.84; could one develop insight on that basis? 5.461; the experience of approaching the first *dhyāna* 17.122–3; has an integrating effect on the whole psychophysical organism 5.458–9; reached through various of the forty *kammaṭṭhānas* 1.160–2; returning to it from the *dhyānas* 1.165, 5.278–9; a state in which meditation becomes lighter and more enjoyable 15.108; and the ten recollections 1.156

Neild-Smith, Penny 2.403

neither monastic nor lay *see under* sangha/monastic–lay split

Nelson, Horatio 19.410, 26.588–9

nembutsu (chanting Amitābha's name) *see under* Amitābha/devotion

nemesis 15.214

Neminath, Acharya 8.228–9, 22.305

neoclassical style 16.327

neo-orthodoxy 4.127

Neoplatonism

introduction
brief introduction 24.684 (n382), 25.594–5 (n101); the major spiritual tradition of the West 2.537, 13.374; an alternative Western tradition 13.374; how it developed 26.366–8; inspired by Plato's *Parmenides* 16.589 (n30); influenced by Egyptian magic and symbolism 13.292–3; connection with Sufism 3.429; 'Studies in Neoplatonism' 24.311

ideas and themes
beauty 13.279; the idea of the 'One' 14.583, 26.368–9; on Homer's *Odyssey* 8.607; in English poetry 26.398–9; in Renaissance art 26.245; the sea of materiality 26.397; sense experience as only part of the spectrum of human experience 5.51; soma, psyche, pneuma 2.335; Spirit and Soul 25.82, 25.85; theurgy 13.292–3

Neoplatonism and Buddhism
affinities between Neoplatonism and Buddhism 2.537, 13.374; comparison between its three hypostases and the three *svabhāvas* 26.590; it contributed spiritual impulses from the Buddha to Christianity 2.11–12, 7.485; little comparative study 13.374

Sangharakshita
first encounters with Neoplatonism 20.20, 26.366, 26.590; the book he wanted to write about it 26.590; 'The Neoplatonists' (poem) 25.401

see also
Cloud of Unknowing; Dionysius; the eye could not behold the sun …, *see* Plotinus; Iamblichus; Dean Inge's writings, *see* Inge; Marsilio Ficino, *see* Ficino; 'On Beauty', *see* Plotinus; Thomas Taylor, *see* Taylor

Nepal

history and people
history 20.424; a young Tibetan disciple of Milarepa's warns against visiting Nepal 18.137; Rana regime overthrown 20.435,

21.104, 21.264–5, 21.277–9, 21.292; kings 21.270, 21.273; pride in Tenzing Norgay 22.11–12; education 20.427, 21.280–1; police agents 20.435; government officials 20.439; Gurkhas 7.344–5; Nepalese prostitutes 25.119

caste system
and Buddhists 7.346–7, 20.436, 20.438; the caste of cooking 20.436–7; had the force of law 9.349–50, 20.433, 20.437–8; Hindu sacrifice of buffaloes at Dussehra 10.46; the 'Land of the Four Colours and Thirty-Two Castes' 20.436–7; Nepali bhikkhus with caste prejudice 9.175

Buddhism
'Glimpses of Buddhist Nepal' 7.341–54; the spread of Buddhism to Nepal 9.496; *anātma* doctrine opposed by the Rajpurohit ('Māra') 21.298–300; the atmosphere gives a sense of the eternal Dharma 7.342–3; attempts to introduce the Buddhism of other countries to Nepal 7.349; a beautiful evening puja in Patan 7.349–50; copies of the *White Lotus Sūtra* found there 14.108, 16.35; devotional singing 21.272; holy places 7.341–2; laws designed to stamp out Buddhism 20.438–9; mixed up with Hinduism 7.346–7, 14.435; multiplicity of temples, shrines, and artefacts 7.344; Nepalese collection of nine Mahāyāna *sūtras* (listed) 14.100; Newar Buddhists 7.344–5, 11.305, 20.432–3, 21.264–5, 21.283–4; reform and revival 7.347–51; relationship between Buddhists and Hindus 7.346–7; stupas 16.148, 16.157; traditional 2.549, 7.341, 7.349–50, 21.294–6; a visit to a traditional Buddhist family 7.352–4; translations of texts into Nepali 8.659–60, 21.348, 21.503, 21.531

Sangharakshita visits
first visit, soon after ordination 9.280–1, 9.468, 9.489, 9.501, 20.419–41, 21.263–4; realizing the strength of caste prejudice 9.349–50; visit with the Sacred Relics 21.264–306; warns against Christian missionaries 21.278–80

Kathmandu
Bodhnath 8.601, 21.284–5; Dr Ambedkar speaks there 9.11, 9.21, 9.407, 9.526; Ananda Kuti Vihara 21.271, 21.281, 21.300; Maha Bodhi temple, Patan 7.344; Narayanhiti 21.270–1; Pashupatinath, temple 21.274–5; Shantiniketan (vihara) 7.351–4; Singha Durbar 21.289–91; Swayambunath 7.341, 7.351, 12.574, 21.288–9, 21.304; travel advice 21.512–13; visit of Sacred Relics 21.269–92; a writer's disillusionment 8.601–2

Lalitpur (Patan)
architecture 21.286–8; Gyabal Vihara 21.294–6; Sangharakshita speaking there (photo) 21.294; visit of Sacred Relics 21.293

Tansen (Palpa)
Ananda Vihara 20.429–30, 20.440; Assistant Commander-in-Chief (Purohit Guru) 20.438–9; Atīśa's visit 12.574; Commander-in-Chief 20.435–6, 20.440; flinging rice at the Buddha's face: the offerings of busy housewives 10.241–2, 20.432–3; Mahachaitya Vihara 15.xi–xii, 20.430–40; Sangharakshita's visit to teach the Dharma 20.429–40, 23.16

other places
Bhadgaon (Bhaktapur) 21.296–7, 21.304; Butaol 9.280, 9.468, 20.426–7, 20.441, 23.16; Dumrai 20.429; Mashyam 20.428–9; the Terai 11.305, 20.422–3; western Nepal 8.354; *see also* Lumbini

Neptune 16.385

Netaji Day 23.408

Nettippakaraṇa (para-canonical Pāli work) refers to the positive *nidānas* 10.432; 'There is agitation for one who is dependent' 10.724 (n505); translated by Bhikkhu Ñāṇamoli as *The Guide* 10.705 (n351)

Neumann, Erich 23.419

neurosis

observations about neurosis
the ego is neurotic individuality 18.219; if you've got faith you can't be neurotic 14.557; it is not healed by time 26.25; 'neurosis' can be a healthy symptom of rebellion 12.101; our neuroses bring all kinds of rationalizations in their wake 17.629; the whole idea of possessing things is neurotic 18.218

craving
arising out of a feeling of emptiness 17.398–9; the discomfort of neurotic attachment produces further craving 15.231; eat without neurotic craving 3.370, 4.113, 4.74; neurotic craving is wanting something the situation can't give you 18.207; neurotic craving for company 26.24; neurotic craving to move 18.340–1; not much point in giving up sex when neurotic craving is still there 26.30; self-indulgence is a constant pandering to neurotic cravings 10.608; worldly desire is a sort of neurotic craving 19.156

neurotic ...
celibacy 11.587–8; desire (hungry ghosts) 13.130, 17.285; emotional dependence 18.300; insecurity 17.199; interest in Buddhism 18.359; love 17.656; motivation for running a Buddhist group 17.60–1; need for experience 11.79; obsession 19.396; preoccupation with what is going to happen 18.460–1; rituals 11.207; self-concern 26.23; sexual desire 4.75, 5.510, 11.538–40, 26.30; speech 10.581; thinking 10.462–3, 19.193–4; neurotic activity, *see under* activity/problems

Neusner, Jacob 13.402, 13.480

neutral neutral *dharmas* (*avyākata*) 12.146, 14.79; the senses are karmically or ethically neutral 19.191; *vedanā* can be pleasant, painful or neutral, *see under vedanā*; very few lifestyles are neutral in character 2.352

Never Direct (bodhisattva) *see under White Lotus Sūtra*/characters in the *sūtra*/Sadāparibhūta

Neville, Derek 21.338, 21.481

new *see* newness

New Age the Age of Aquarius 8.574, 8.586, 12.622, 17.242–3, 17.737 (n123), 24.201, 24.216; the Mind Body Spirit Festival 17.52, 18.428–9; new age beliefs might be a good starting point for an inquiry into the Dharma 18.412; a New Age group called Centre 23.416; New Age ideology 8.586; New Age universalism 17.52

New Buddhists (in India) *see under* Dalits

New Burmese Satipaṭṭhāna method *see under* vipassanā movement

New Delhi *see* Delhi

New Forest 6.619, 25.329, 26.610–11

New Man 'The New Man speaks' 11.410–19; a possible translation of *arhant* 15.7

new society 'The Positive Group and the New Society' 3.452–8; Sangharakshita's definition 3.456; the reason for founding a new Buddhist movement 3.455; why would one want to establish a new society? 19.520; giving up old ways 9.225, 9.265; Dr Ambedkar's wish to create one 9.182; comparison between old and new society 11.179; the emergence of a new society 24.196; the FWBO (Triratna) as the nucleus of a new society 11.179–80, 26.20; helping to create one 9.194; making the transition from the old society via a Buddhist centre 3.462; in India 2.516, 9.241, 9.508; the nucleus: communities, right livelihood, centres (the 'three Cs') 3.613, 12.468–9, 18.34–5; an oasis within worldly society 18.35; and the Pure Land, Sukhāvatī 3.453–6; supportive of the individual 9.285; in the West 2.516, 9.241, 9.508; we go for Refuge from the old society to a completely new kind of society 3.452; we need a new kind of Buddhist culture 15.282; your strength as an individual strengthens the new society 3.464

new start any goal becomes a new starting point 17.356–7; a fresh start every time we are reborn 16.283; through confession 16.312; true openness allows you to make a fresh start 10.570; *see also* beginner's mind

New Wisdom School *see* Madhyamakavāda

New Year celebrations 2.179, 2.219, 4.108; resolutions 8.190–3, 8.311, 16.313; a time for reflection on past and future 8.311

New Zealand

introduction
gold rush 24.78; greenstone 24.79, 25.353; industrial activity 24.81; isolated country life 10.329, 24.494–5; marriage 9.336; sheep (the 'white death') 24.51; skeletons of trees 13.228; tree plantations 24.51–2; urbanization 24.513; wildlife 24.68

Māoris
making cloth 24.79–80; Maori-style church 24.510–11; Māori writings 24.563, 24.565–6; wars 24.49–50, 24.618 (n69)

FWBO *(Triratna) activities*
Gotami goes to New Zealand 4.320; the first ordinations in New Zealand (1975) 24.92, 24.617 (n65); misunderstandings about ordination 24.74, 24.93–5; ordination retreat 1979 24.33, 24.48–51; favourable conditions for the spiritual life 11.94–5; mentioned on a tour of India 9.301, 9.492; wandering in New Zealand talking about the Dharma 17.402–3; Sudarshanaloka 24.513–14, 24.565, 24.734–5 (n628)

Sangharakshita visits
brief reference 10.276, 12.543; longer account 24.8–64; 'Letters from New Zealand' 24.490–514, 24.490–577; between Auckland and Wellington 24.28–30, 24.32–3, 24.51, 24.493, 24.510–13, 24.555; from Christchurch to Dunedin 24.67–70; from Christchurch to Auckland 24.75–88; South Island travels

24.51–2, 24.495–509; 'After Visiting New Zealand' (poem) 25.415

Auckland
Buddhist Centre 24.5, 24.27–8, 24.545, 24.574; the city at night like a Pure Land 24.97; a criticism of Sangharakshita's approach 24.167; a rainbow 26.671; Sangha Day 24.549; the sangha's energy stimulated by making jack-in-the-boxes 17.72; Sangharakshita at Suvarnaketu community (1979) 24.8–9, 24.26–7, 24.33, 24.88, 24.91, 24.98; Sangharakshita visits 24.545–54; Saranadipa community 24.513, 24.545; a sense of being part of the same movement as the 'Friends' in England 24.96; three talks, 'The Ideal of Human Enlightenment' (1975) 11.94–6; three talks, 'A New Buddhist Movement' 24.91–2, 24.95, 24.629 (n121); Waitakere Hills 11.95; Wesak 1979 24.95–6

Christchurch
FWBO (Ratnaloka) and community 24.47, 24.67, 24.74–5, 24.87, 24.617 (n65); Sangharakshita visits 24.35, 24.47–8, 24.67, 24.87

Wellington
the city 24.32, 24.493; Buddhist Centre 24.31–2, 24.510, 24.555, 24.563

other places
Canvastown 24.85–6; Clevedon 24.49–50; Dunedin 24.47–8, 24.71–3; Invercargill 24.493–5, 24.555; Jerusalem 24.510–11; Kapiti 24.32, 24.614 (n52); Lake Taupo 24.29, 24.51; Moeraki Boulders 24.69–70; Mount Egmont 24.512–13; Murchison 24.83–4, 24.507–8; Nelson (and Buddhism) 24.84–5, 24.627 (n115), 24.508–9; Northland tour 24.573; Oamaru 24.68–9; Otago (name) 24.140, 24.640 (n165); Otago Peninsula 24.71–2; Otoroganga 24.29, 24.32; Pancake Rocks 24.80; Picton 24.87, 24.509–10; Puketapu hill 24.70, 24.624 (n94); Queenstown and Arrowtown 24.501–3; Rātana temple 24.510; Shantytown 24.77–8; Wānaka, Hāwea, Haast, and Hokitika 24.503–6; W(h)anganui 24.88, 24.510, 24.628 (n116)

Newars devotional songs 20.434; devotion to Sangharakshita and Buddharakshita, as visiting monks 20.440; Refuges and Precepts 20.425–6, 21.9; of Kalimpong 20.471, 21.8–10, 21.30–2, 21.206, 21.210, 22.236; in Nepal, *see under* Nepal/ Buddhism; religious practices 21.41

newcomers (to Buddhism) *see* beginners

Newlin, Henry John 23.417–18

Newman, Cardinal John Henry brief introduction 23.504–5 (n241); *Arians of the Fourth Century* 13.534, 23.208; empathy with his agonizing over his religious difficulties 23.208; *Essays Critical and Historical* 23.208; 'He believed in God but he didn't like (trust) him' 11.340, 15.620, 17.336, 17.552; Sangharakshita is shown his rooms 13.562; sermons 12.519

newness the absolute newness of a work of art 26.174; beauty is 'that which, from instant to instant, is always new' 17.462, 26.174; 'Behold, I make all things new' 7.163, 13.428; bringing into existence a new mind 10.197–8; Buddhism is familiar (along with a sense of newness) 16.217–18; the coming into existence of a new order 26.18; every time we meditate is a completely new experience 16.439; in ancient India, wandering was the only way of learning anything new 10.478; it isn't easy to communicate a new idea or experience using the old words 10.467–8; 'Make it new' (Pound) 13.428; *navakata* (making new) 11.74; 'New' (poem) 2.538–9, 13.427–8, 25.lii–liv, 25.313; the new isn't necessarily better than the old 13.425–6; keeping Buddhism new 10.480; horizontal and vertical newness 13.428; we all respond with approval to the word 'new' 11.181–2

news and newspapers 'All news is gossip' (Thoreau) 15.174; a completely made-up story 23.89; endless speculation 19.270; generally bad literature 26.183; how valuable is a newspaper really? 18.376–7; the idea that spiritual people don't read newspapers 15.491–2; if there were no radios, no newspapers, we would 'know' very little 13.345; *Indian Mirror* 8.41, 8.632; purveyors of pseudo-artistic trash 26.115; reading about suffering and then turning to the sports pages 13.81; reading the *Daily Telegraph* and the *New Statesman* 23.89, 23.321, 23.526 (n374); realizing that newspapers have their own agenda 22.213; Sangharakshita's period of abstaining from reading newspapers 22.209; Sangharakshita's rare reading of a newspaper 8.147; seeking for a paper to catch up with the news after a period of seclusion 24.406; they stimulate negative emotions 11.6; to find out the truth about national and international events is not easy 24.148–9; when you read the paper, do you really feel the suffering of those you read about? 18.590; why read them? 9.532, 12.382

Newsome, David 24.389

Newton, Isaac Blake's view of Newton 8.561, 15.139, 16.630 (n364), 17.117–18, 19.178–9, 26.350; he 'cast a dark shadow over the spiritual radiance of the universe' 17.115, 17.117–18; he may have been insane, but modern science is based on his world-view 19.180; how he boiled his watch instead of an egg 17.114, 17.117; in quest of the theory of gravitation 1.52; the Romantic movement a protest against the Newtonian picture of nature 15.139

neyārtha *see under* meaning/explicit and implicit

Ngawang, Sherab *see* Prajnaloka

ngöndro *see* offering the mandala

nhamdog (Tibetan) ceaseless flow of thoughts 19.187; the complete stopping of the waterfall 19.200; the dissolving of the *nhamdog* into the *dharmakāya* 19.188; perhaps equivalent to *cittadhārā* 19.187

Nhu, Mme *see under* Vietnam

nibbidā *see nirdeva*

nibbuta (allayment) 1.69

niceness being 'nice' but feeling hostile 4.419–20; the problem of pseudo-Buddhist niceness 4.420–1

Nichiren introduction 16.593 (n56); death anniversary 2.228; identified himself with the bodhisattva Viśiṣṭacāritra 2.182; teaching reverence for the *White Lotus Sūtra* 2.225, 16.59

Nichiren Buddhism in Japan 3.442–3; degenerated into religion as revelation 7.370; reverence for the *White Lotus Sūtra* 2.225, 16.59; at the Japanese temple in Bombay 22.271

Nicholas of Cusa 7.103, 7.581 (n198)

Nicholas, Douglas 26.418

Nicholson, Richard (Marco Pallis's friend) 21.160–1, 23.240

nidāna (category of text) 14.25, 17.571

***nidāna* chain meditation** description of the practice 3.129–31, 3.346–8; antidote to delusion or ignorance 2.392, 4.80–1, 5.29, 19.227; every Buddhist should be acquainted with the twelve links 3.204; as an insight practice 18.513; a reflection on the workings of the law of karma 4.81; a way of breaking up individuality 5.32; a way to overcome ignorance 11.404

Nidānakathā (biography of the Buddha) attributed to Buddhaghosa 2.13, 12.182; the four sights 3.630 (n27); introduction to the commentary on the *Jātakas* 2.13; published as *Buddhist Birth Stories, see* Rhys Davids, T. W.; Queen Maya 3.628–9 (n20); Siddhārtha and the rose-apple tree 3.629n; Siddhārtha's supposed disgust at sleeping dancing girls (a misattribution) 2.33

nidānas (links) the *nidānas* and the *niyamas* 12.547–8; reflection, *see nidāna* chain meditation; a topic in the *Śāriputra-abhidharma-śāstra* 14.74; twelve cyclical *nidānas, see* twelve cyclical *nidānas*; twelve positive *nidānas, see* twelve positive *nidānas*; twenty-four *nidānas, see* twenty-four *nidānas*

Niddesa accorded canonical status by the Theravādins 14.55; ascribed to Śāriputra 14.73; association with the Abhidharma 14.73; commentary on the *Sutta-Nipāta* 14.55

Nidhikaṇḍa Sutta merit for good deeds 4.678 (n124); Sangharakshita's translation 15.xiii, 15.69–70

Nietzsche, Friedrich

introduction
Nietzsche's life and work 3.493–504, 16.375; his view intellectual, not the product of transcendental realization 3.502; the most devastating critic of itself that the human race has ever produced 3.502; philosophy a misnomer 3.494; reading him: making out the landscape of human existence by flashes of lightning 3.495; Sangharakshita's hero 20.68

Thus Spoke Zarathustra
introduction 3.496–9; 'Aphorisms should be peaks' 26.4; description of inspiration 2.645; a literary fiction 14.399; 'Man is the cruellest animal' 26.654; a 'nay-sayer' to life 7.218; one should choose one's enemies with care 4.412; Sangharakshita's first reading 3.493, 20.100, 26.577; it's significant that it's presented as poetry rather than philosophy 17.620; the shepherd's round-dance 25.144; 'To tell the truth and to shoot well with arrows' 2.376

sayings and thoughts
aphorisms 3.494–5, 26.3–4, 17.620; 'Baptize the worst in yourself as the best' 17.655; 'beyond good and evil' 7.377; *The Birth of Tragedy* 3.494; enemies are really friends 16.525; 'giving style to one's character' 3.500; 'God is dead' 3.497, 12.44; humanity as a bridge between the beast and the overman 3.499; the Last Man 3.498; 'Live dangerously' (*The Gay Science*) 19.57, 19.593 (n20); 'A man never

flies so high as when he doesn't know where he is going' 4.500; memory yields to pride 16.314; 'One must know what one wants, and that one wants' 15.610; Socrates' activity was destructive 19.182–3; the superman (Übermensch, overman) 3.61, 3.496–503; 'a transvaluation of all values' 2.140, 2.284, 10.620; *The Twilight of the Gods*: 'philosophizing with a hammer' 26.479; vision of overcoming ourselves 3.498, 3.503–4, 12.623; Will to Power 3.501–2; 'your bad love of yourself' 26.25

nigama **Tantric tradition** 10.46

niganṭhas *see under* ascetics

Nigg, Walter 13.628–9

Nightingale, Florence introduction 1.630 (n399); 'The first requirement of a hospital is that it should do the sick no harm' 18.285; her life an inspiration 3.509, 26.490; hero-worship 3.47; photographic portrait 24.359; rebelled against her female conditioning 4.597–8; rejoicing in her merits 1.509, 26.490

nihilism (*uccheda-diṭṭhi*, *ucchedavāda*)

introduction
definition 17.241; nihilism leads to an unhappy rebirth 17.244, 17.250; the philosophical expression of aversion to the world 17.250; psychological, metaphysical, and ethical aspects 17.624–5; a rationalization of self-hatred 17.243–4, 17.250; self-mortification as an expression of nihilism 17.251–2; the source of innumerable wrong views 17.243; the worst tendencies of spiritual ignorance 17.243

nihilist views
alignment with hedonism 1.138; the belief that unskilful action does not result in suffering 17.250; feeling no attachment may be nihilism, not spiritual maturity 17.371; feeling that nothing is worthwhile 5.433; a nihilist refuses to accept that things are causally connected (Nāgārjuna) 17.250; no life after death, actions neither good nor bad, everything happens by chance 7.523, 17.241–2

nihilism and Buddhism
is Buddhism nihilistic? 1.72–80, 17.362–3, 17.444; teachers of nihilism at the time of the Buddha 1.75; Vacchagotta the Wanderer 14.461; guarding against annihilationism 14.461, 15.230; in the *Precious Garland* 17.241–5; the idea that Buddhism seeks to save the individual by destroying him 13.393; the annihilation doctrine that after death a Tathāgata no longer exists 1.75; a bodhisattva sees that living beings have no reality without falling into nihilism 17.411

nihilism in relation to Dharma teachings
and the fetter of personality-view 2.146; in relation to *pratītya-samutpāda* 7.495; opposed and destroyed by the *animitta vimokṣa-mukha* 2.122; the *śūnyavāda* (way of emptiness) and nihilism 7.126, 17.360–1

nihilism and eternalism
all extreme or one-sided views are manifestations of eternalism or nihilism 1.137; better to be eternalist than nihilist 17.250–1; eternalist and nihilist ways of approaching death 17.243–3; the 'twin roads' steep and perilous? 19.393; the Buddha divides schools of philosophy into eternalists and nihilists 7.196; the Buddha said if you have to choose, eternalism is better 17.243; extreme views 1.88, 14.461; important to be aware of our own tendency in this respect 3.202; in relation to what happens after death 19.375–6; middle way between them, *see under* middle way; 'two learned kings' (*Dhammapada*) 15.41

see also
vibhava-tṛṣṇā (craving for non-existence), *see under tṛṣṇā*

niḥsvabhāva (devoid of determinate nature) 2.89

nijīvatā 1.99

Niṃbārka 1.166

nimitta one of the five *dharmas* (categories) 1.267, 14.213; *parikamma-nimitta* (preparatory image) 1.161; *uggaha-nimitta* (acquired image) 1.161; *paṭibhāga-nimitta* (reflex image) 1.162; the whole

structure of subjective ideas and concepts 2.121

nimmita Buddhas 1.255–6

Nin, Anäis 11.634, 23.472, 23.541 (n496)

nine *samāpattis* (attainments) *see under samāpattis*

nipako (prudence, discretion) 15.288–9

nipuṇa (subtle) 17.324

nirāmisa 15.155–6

niraya (downfall) 3.605, 12.475

nirdaya *see* cruelty

Nirgranthas *see under* Jainism

nirguṇa-brahman *see* Śaṅkara

Nirmāṇa-Buddha 14.211–12

nirmāṇakāya *see trikāya*

nirodha (extinction, cessation) *see* cessation

nirukti *see* etymology

Nirvāṇa (Pāli *Nibbāna*)

INTRODUCTION

the word
etymology 3.223, 7.509, 10.614, 14.553, 15.58, 15.229; misunderstandings of the idea of 'extinction' 15.451; such terms can be used only provisionally 13.348; the word is a noun derived from a verb 19.204

synonyms
the Deathless (*amata*) 1.171, 11.412, 15.57, 26.473; not definitions but descriptions, symbolical indications of the ineffable 1.131; infinite radiant consciousness 2.130; list of synonyms in Pāli tradition 1.69; the Unconditioned 3.234; the third noble truth is equivalent to Nirvāṇa 2.122; *upekṣā* 4.532

DESCRIPTIONS AND DEFINITIONS

introduction
general introduction 3.222–9; descriptions are not definitions but signposts 7.510; four main modes of definition: positive, symbolic, paradoxical, negative 14.552–4; in a sense it doesn't matter what we call it 26.369

positive descriptions and conceptions
all positive statements about Nirvāṇa are analogies, not to be taken literally 3.235; attraction to Nirvāṇa 15.567–8; the embodiment of wisdom and compassion 7.510; as fourth *lakṣaṇa*: 'Nirvāṇa alone is peace' 2.82, 2.89, 2.92, 26.11; the four positive aspects of Nirvāṇa 14.234; imperishable bliss 26.159; it possesses the opposite characteristics to the *lakṣaṇas* 16.11; a living process that continues beyond time 17.357; 'Nirvāṇa is' (Nāgasena) 1.226; not to be conceived of as a 'Blessed Rest' into which you retire 14.554; the positive approach is open to misinterpretation 14.554; positive conceptions of Nirvāṇa in Mahāyāna Buddhism 1.242–3; positive descriptions in the Pāli canon 1.73–4, 1.80, 3.632–3n; the quintessence of Buddhism 7.157; a state not of deprivation but of fulfilment 17.380; a state of absolute illumination, infinite love, unrestricted freedom 7.510; the quiet calm of Nirvāṇa 14.153; a spiritually (as distinct from conceptually) positive state 1.72–3; stable (*dhuva*) 7.191; state of harmonious and beneficent activity 2.102; state of matchless security 1.15; supreme bliss (*Dhammapada*) 2.124, 3.235, 7.68–9, 7.120, 7.191, 11.85–6, 18.90, 19.424; in the *Udāna* the Buddha makes it as clear as words can what Nirvāṇa is 10.632–3, 26.369; *viramānanda* (bliss arising from Nirvāṇa) 2.91; we have to speak of it as an objective reality, but beware of excessive literalism 26.368–9; without Nirvāṇa as a positive 'entity' there could be no escape from *saṃsāra* 10.634

negations and negative conceptions
introduction 1.68–72; 'The abandonment of all is Nirvāṇa' (Śāntideva) 4.358; aloofness from the mundane led to emphasis on negative aspects of religious life 1.68; the entire cessation of becoming 1.83; the cessation of suffering 24.331; described in terms of what it is not 1.67–8, 1.114, 2.123, 10.459, 10.632–6, 15.229, 16.389; the drawback with the negative approach 14.553; early translators took these terms literally, gaining a pessimistic view of the Dharma 15.229; far from being a negative state 7.509–10, 15.229–30; it is unfortunate that so much is made of the negative side 10.635; it 'lies in the surrender of all things' (*Bodhicaryāvatāra*) 7.150; Mahāyāna criticism 1.317; Nāgārjuna's characterization in negative terms 17.355; neither an entity nor a subjective state of mind 10.566–7; nihilistic views of Nirvāṇa 1.72–3, 1.77–8; Nirvāṇa as the cessation of suffering 17.368; Nirvāṇa as non-experience 11.86; not an object to be grasped or an individual possession 1.179; not a state of mere non-existence 1.114, 22.143; nothing can be predicated of it 1.82; better to think in crudely positive terms than purely negative

ones 10.635; Hīnayāna 1.225–6, 16.63–4; mistaken view of 'Nirvāṇa as a state of absolute annihilation 1.72, 15.230; people sometimes think, 'How dreary! Just a great blank nothing' 12.218; viewed in terms of the cessation of the saṃsāric process 1.226; whatever the world is not 2.123

other descriptions
all that can be said is that certain beliefs and practices conduce to its achievement 26.159; a breakthrough to something you couldn't envisage 17.233; coolness 15.451; the four kinds of Nirvāṇa 14.215; merely a psychological state, according to scholars 1.34; non-self 3.234–5; only an operational concept 19.236; ontological meanings 7.510; a scientific explanation: the alienated intellect at work 19.181–2; sole absolute truth 1.83; 'a subjective state of freedom', contrasted with *dharmakāya* 24.397; the supreme object of the *dharmakāya* 7.510; wisdom utterly divorced from action is called *nirvāṇa* 7.139

epithets and images
list of epithets 1.80, 2.132; *asaṃskṛta-dharma* 1.69, 1.171, 1.267; the bodhisattva helps all beings to enter the city of Nirvāṇa 8.452; 'a city razed to the ground': Candrakīrti's nihilist description 14.407–8; compared with all lesser satisfactions, Nirvāṇa is as the sun to shadows 1.129; the delightful stretch of level ground 1.81–2; the Buddha depicts it in the concretest forms and the strongest colours 1.83; the infinite light (*amitābha*) which shines within 7.510; an island in the flood 1.82; like a mirage 17.380–1; the Ocean of Nirvāṇa 25.195; the symbolic approach is attended by few misinterpretations 14.553; 'where the Silence lives' 1.171

Nirvāṇa's paradoxes and mysteries
beyond conception 12.657; beyond reasoning (*atakka-avacara*) 1.209; beyond time and space 16.389; beyond words and description 10.101; the dangers of the paradoxical approach 14.553; even in Nirvāṇa there is to be no settling down 17.574; even when you have gained it, nothing has happened 14.598; ineffable 1.63–72, 1.206, 1.242; inexpressible 1.65; is it the final step on the spiral path?, *see under* twelve positive *nidānas*/twelfth *nidāna*; it cannot be defined 1.317; it won't be what you imagined, but that doesn't mean you've been deceived 17.233; meaning is the cause of Nirvāṇa 14.208; 'near' or 'far' depending on how the Dharma is viewed 1.122–3; neither Ens nor non-Ens 1.317–19; Nirvāṇa is attained, but nobody attains it 7.495; Nirvāṇa remains the same whether people realize it or not 10.566–7; not easy to see 10.633–4; not something that can be attained 1.347; the solution of an insoluble contradiction 7.45; to be attained by means of a non-attainment 2.131, 26.207; to speak of it as the cessation of defilements is self-contradictory 1.320; a vanishing point that we call Nirvāṇa 17.356

HISTORY

the Buddha
gives rousing talks about Nibbāna (*Udāna*) 10.632–6; his 'conception' of Nirvāṇa 1.68; insisted on the necessity of personal realization of Nirvāṇa 2.203; renders Nirvāṇa practicable 1.51; said very little about Nirvāṇa 1.579, 2.120, 15.230; speaks about Nirvāṇa when the *bhikkhus* are listening attentively 10.632–3; gave both symbolic and conceptual indications of Nirvāṇa 1.84; it is untrue to say that he invariably remained silent on the subject 1.68

in Early Buddhism
abstract and conceptual indications of Nirvāṇa in the Pāli canon 1.84; disciples bear witness to their attainment of Nirvāṇa 1.180; two rival groups with different ways of seeing Nirvāṇa 1.83; 'Hīnayāna' ideal 16.7, 16.63; the 'metaphysical reticence' of early Buddhism 10.507, 14.553–4; the term is used more in Early Buddhism than in the Mahāyāna 19.199; Abhidharma analysis of Nirvāṇa 1.225–6; is the Abhidharma necessary to the attainment of Nirvāṇa? 8.118–19, 8.129–30; the eternal and unconditioned element (Abhidharma) 14.91; correlations of its meaning 2.120–1; literal use of language 1.234; regarded Nirvāṇa as an objective reality 17.548; Sarvāstivādin conceptions 1.319; it began to be seen as a state that could really be possessed 1.232–3

in the Mahāyāna and later traditions
sharp distinction between 'Hīnayāna' and 'Mahāyāna' 1.258; shift from goal of 'Hīnayāna' Nirvāṇa to perfect Buddhahood – the magic city 16.43; distinction between the *nirvāṇa* of the *arhant* and that of the bodhisattva 19.199; points of agreement between Hīnayāna and Mahāyāna 1.65; the Element of the Buddha exists in everyone, hence the wish for Nirvāṇa 1.283; evoked by the *Sukhāvatī-vyūha Sūtras* 2.132; separation of Nirvāṇa from *bodhi* 8.620; Sukhāvatī distinct from or identical to Nirvāṇa? 1.344; Nāgārjuna's examination of Nirvāṇa 1.317–19; for the Vajrayāna Nirvāṇa without pleasure isn't

the real Nirvāṇa 19.383; 'a monstrous conception' (view of early Western writer on Buddhism) 7.32

NIRVĀṆA IN PRACTICE

Nirvāṇa in spiritual life
accessible from everywhere (*sabbato pabhaṃ*) 7.169; at the moment of death 1.345–6; attainable here and now 1.345; if you understand completely why you want to reach it, you've reached it 3.228–9; insight gained through contemplating the idea of Nirvāṇa 2.262–3; it can become a projection of our mundane needs 3.229; mindfulness of the body brings Nirvāṇa very close 10.513; not reached with the *visuddhis* or without them 3.290–1; in practical terms, spoken of as an object 10.566–7; in reality only one way to Nirvāṇa 1.404; probably best to think in terms of growing into Nirvāṇa 10.635; through self-surrender 1.346; 'To live in *Nibbāna* is Dhamma' (Ambedkar) 9.287–8; we try to use it to settle problems that can only be resolved through awareness 3.227

the path to Nirvāṇa
always has a positive and a negative aspect 16.63; the Dharma as the only means of attaining Nirvāṇa 8.204; easy and difficult path 1.341; the eradication of negative states and cultivation of positive counterparts 9.345, 16.63; even the bird and the flower will not be excluded 7.121, 7.585 (n218); expressed in terms of the positive *nidānas* 1.114–20, 17.357; goal and path are both *śūnyatā* and *apraṇihita* 2.122; in the fullness of its undimmed glory, Nirvāṇa dawns at last 2.150; no accumulation of karma can get you to Nirvāṇa 26.52; only one way to Nirvāṇa 1.217–18, 14.117; the realization of Nirvāṇa depends upon conditions ascertained by the Buddha 1.133; temptation to think that it can be a personal gain 1.404–5

different kinds of Nirvāṇa
the difference between Nirvāṇa and Supreme Perfect Enlightenment 26.698; *kleśa nirvāṇa* (the cessation of greed, hatred, and delusion) 1.131, 2.122, 3.223, 16.63; *skandha nirvāṇa* (extinction of psychophysical existence) 3.223, 3.658 (n216), 7.168, 11.403; Nirvāṇa without remainder (*apratiṣṭhita-nirvāṇa*) 10.566–7, 14.407–8, 14.456, 14.596, 17.355–6, 17.574, 17.770–1 (n521); the Nirvāṇa which is established (*pratiṣṭhita-nirvāṇa*) 14.596

Nirvāṇa and the bodhisattva
asked about Nirvāṇa, they bring compassion into their reply 2.168–9, 4.65, 4.189; for a bodhisattva, Nirvāṇa is a failure 4.188, 26.8; for the bodhisattva the Nirvāṇa of the Hīnayāna does not exist 2.167; the bodhisattva is a synthesis of *nirvāṇa* and *saṃsāra* 4.92; individual Nirvāṇa not the ultimate objective of the bodhisattva's career 1.258; renunciation of an exclusive Nirvāṇa 7.41, 14.551

Nirvāṇa and śūnyatā
empty of the whole cause–effect process 14.561; the Mahāyāna equated emptiness and Nirvāṇa 1.268; Nirvāṇa as the state or principle of *śūnyatā* 1.253; realization of *śūnyatā* not indispensable for the attainment of Nirvāṇa 1.321

questions and discussion
all talk about Nirvāṇa is from ignorance 7.44; can Nirvāṇa be attained, or is speaking that way an operational concept? 19.47; if everybody gets the same teaching, why don't they all attain Nirvāṇa? 11.359–60; is Nirvāṇa identical with the Vedantic *ātman*? 7.211–3; is Nirvāṇa included in conditioned co-production? 1.116–18, 7.197–200; is it the goal? 1.72–3, 3.224–9, 11.310; is it the last stage of the path of conditioned co-production? 1.116–18, 1.266; questions about it are not to be asked or answered glibly 12.121–2, 18.357; a wanderer who ate rose-apples ... asked 'What is Nirvāṇa?' 1.69, 1.72–3, 2.122; wanting to discuss Nirvāṇa suggests not thinking about practising the Dharma 18.413; we can talk about Nirvāṇa, but not in any way that defines it 17.356; 'What is the counterpart of Nibbāna?' 3.68; 'What is Nirvāṇa?' 1.63, 2.120, 3.222–4

misunderstandings and mistakes
even silence about it might be misunderstood 1.82; it isn't a sort of spiritual retirement home 17.356; it isn't to be dismissed as a sort of antisocial selfishness 8.460; Makkhali Gosāla's eternalist views about Nirvāṇa 17.242; the mistake of realizing Nirvāṇa in the Hīnayānic sense 1.270–1; mistaken belief that the analysis of *ātman* is sufficient for its attainment 1.267; mistaking the word Nirvāṇa for an understanding of it 13.347; misunderstanding about the idea of Nirvāṇa as 'extinction' 15.451; nihilist and eternalist views of Nirvāṇa 17.242; the danger of the rational mind misunderstanding 14.553; thinking of Nirvāṇa as the object of personal attainment 26.208; to one to whom the

world is everything, Nirvāṇa is nothing (Schopenhauer) 17.362; wrong beliefs about Nirvāṇa 1.138

NIRVĀṆA AND *SAṂSĀRA*

contrasts
making the transition from the one to the other 16.394; Nirvāṇa attractive and fascinating, *saṃsāra* unpleasant and disappointing 18.129; Nirvāṇa cannot wait for *saṃsāra* to exhaust itself 26.8; opposite principles 16.388; to aspire to *nirvāṇa* simply strengthens the bonds which bind one to *saṃsāra* 7.413

connections
both are possibilities in the same reality 1.120, 7.167, 7.202, 7.203–4; for the Enlightened person there is no difference 19.65; the Mahāyāna equated the two 1.268; Nirvāṇa does not come by prolonging or ceasing the saṃsāric process 10.523; Nirvāṇa viewed in terms of the cessation of the saṃsāric process 1.226; penetrating into the nature of *saṃsāra*, one catches sight of Nirvāṇa 2.121; perfectly interwoven in a living vision of non-duality 18.102; their essential no-difference 14.592; they are both absolutes, but nonetheless connected 11.312–13; they are dependent on each other 1.268, 17.368; they are not eternally distinct realities 17.365; thinking there is a real difference points in the direction of egoism 1.267; the two-in-oneness of *saṃsāra* and *nirvāṇa* 13.75; ultimate emptiness of distinction 2.118–19, 3.236–7, 3.254, 7.45, 7.139, 14.205, 18.84; without Nirvāṇa as a positive 'entity' there could be no escape from *saṃsāra* 10.634; you cannot regard them as being ultimately two things 19.379

operational concepts
alike thought-constructions 1.306; disposing of these concepts disposes of the basis of the spiritual life 18.395–8; leading a spiritual life involves positing a dichotomy between *saṃsāra* and Nirvāṇa 26.498

the bodhisattva
charts a course between the extremes of *nirvāṇa* and *saṃsāra* 7.139; has passed beyond the duality between *saṃsāra* and *nirvāṇa* 17.411; realizes that they are discriminations of the mind 2.166–7; a synthesis of *nirvāṇa* and *saṃsāra* 4.92, 17.609; though free from *saṃsāra*, does not settle down in *nirvāṇa* 14.456

beyond both
'disposing of' *saṃsāra* and *nirvāṇa*: the Bliss-Void 18.415–16; only absolute freedom if one is free from both *saṃsāra* and *nirvāṇa* 2.118

Nirvāṇa Sūtra 2.125

nirvāṇa-dhātu ('sphere of extinction') 2.43

'Nirvanization' 10.515, 10.614, 16.449, 19.204

nirveda (Pāli *nibbidā*, withdrawal, repulsion) an attitude of sitting loose to life 12.164; letting go of the conditioned as a fisherman lets go of a poisonous snake 3.276; must be conjoined with compassion (Tsongkhapa) 2.116; a serene withdrawal, not to be confused with psychological disgust 2.115, 12.164; in the positive *nidānas*, *see under* twelve positive *nidānas*; talk conducive to *nibbidā* 10.530; the urge to withdraw 2.161

nirvikalpa-samādhi 1.166

nirvṛtti mārga (path of the inner life) 7.357–63

niṣkāma-karma yoga 9.102, 11.119, 16.413

niṣprapañca (inexpressible, non-delusion) Nirvāṇa inexpressible 1.65; the negation of all the categories of relative existence 7.132; Sangharakshita's first encounter with the term 7.587 (n234)

niśraya (Pāli *nissaya*, period of spiritual tutelage) *see under* ordination/*bhikṣu*

Nissanka, Sri Wijeyeratna (Sri Lankan politician and poet) 7.445, 21.280

nissaraṇa *see* escape

nissatta (without permanent essence) 1.99

nissayas **or** ***niśrayas*** *see* four supports

nītārtha *see under* meaning/explicit and implicit

Nityabandhu, Dharmachari (Michal Balik) Sangharakshita's amanuensis 13.523, 22.xxi; poems to him 25.442, 25.444, 26.455; interpreter in Kraków 26.448, 26.450–1; studying with Sangharakshita 11.685, 26.455–6; a holiday in Shropshire 26.463–4

Nityabodhananda, editor of the *Vedanta Kesari* 7.6, 20.228

nityakarma *see under* brahmins

Nityaswarupananda (Ramakrishna Mission) v21, v22

Nivāpa Sutta *see under* *Majjhima Nikāya*

nivaraṇa *see* five hindrances

Nivedita, Sister 22.179

nivṛta ('blown out') 4.608

Niwa, Fumio 24.532

Nixon, Ronald *see* Prem, Sri Krishna

niyamas *see* five *niyamas*

Niyogi, Dr M. B. 23.355

niyutas 1.327

Nizam of Hyderabad 9.55

no man's land (Tibetan) 19.519–20

Nobel, Johannes 14.242, 16.243

nobility 26.370–1

Noble Eightfold Path
(Pāli *aṭṭhāṅgikamagga*,
Sanskrit *aṣṭāṅgikamārga*)

INTRODUCTION

basic information
brief description 1.134, 4.645, 5.707 (n21), 7.219, 11.498, 12.27, 15.57; a cumulative process 1.588–90; it can be telescoped into right thought, right word, and right deed 7.117; it leads to the liberation of suffering 7.219; Path of Righteousness (Ambedkar) 9.141

etymology and translations
is 'holy' or 'noble' a better translation of *ārya*? 1.477–8; *aṅga* (shoot) suggests the path is more like a growing thing than a ladder 1.478, 1.590; the term perfect (*samyak*) is not to be taken literally 1.475–6

the path in Buddhist history
the Buddha's first teaching (?) 3.76, 3.281, 9.304; the subject of the Buddha's last teaching (to Subhadda) 1.178, 10.678 (n130); canonical source 1.126, 3.281, 9.328, 9.567 (n304), 11.369; the list almost certainly devised by the Buddha himself 4.334; as depicted in the Pāli texts, rather a negative affair 1.227; the path and the Ārya-sangha 1.178; for Hīnayāna, the whole spiritual training, Mahāyāna adds the perfections 1.134; in the Abhidharma 14.80, 14.81; 'right-hand path' 1.81; the eleventh of Dr Ambedkar's conversion vows 9.541; intended for the laity (Ambedkar) 9.147; Appleton's *On the Eightfold Path* (a Christian account of Buddhism) 23.215; the circumstances in which Sangharakshita's talks on the subject were given 12.366–7

its relationship to other Dharma teachings
comparison with the parable of the jewel in the garment 16.172; correlation with the six perfections 1.424–5; an elaboration of the threefold way 1.134, 11.306, 11.498; the fourth of the four noble truths 1.134–6, 1.477, 3.281, 9.213; relationship to the ten precepts 2.349–50

following the path
each step of the path is based on the truth of conditionality 15.250; the eight parts are to be practised both successively and simultaneously 11.498; every step of the path has been undervalued 1.581; in a sense we are following all the stages all the time 1.589–90; in a way the spiritual life is not at all like following a path 1.589; its aim is to bring the whole of our life up to the level of its highest moments 1.482; not following eight sequential steps, but developing eight factors 17.110; not like climbing a ladder but like rising up as the sap rises through a tree 16.123; reflect on how to put the path into practice 18.168; through following it we close the gap between ourselves and the Buddha 9.248; when a monk has a spiritual friend, he will cultivate the Noble Eightfold Path 26.632

THE PATH OF VISION (SEEING) AND THE PATH OF TRANSFORMATION

introduction
brief introduction 16.610 (n198); a natural division of the path 1.479–80; as they unfolded in the Buddha's experience 3.596–7; sources 1.178, 3.653 (n181), 3.666 (n259); the distinction between the two 3.595–6, 11.192–3, 19.17, 19.42; if the Buddha is vision, Padmasambhava is transformation 12.334; as experienced by Ruciraketu in the *Sūtra of Golden Light* 16.263–4; illustrates the relationship between heights and depths 12.26–7; initial vision and gradual transformation 3.282; like climbing a mountain 1.490–1; the Path of Seeing and Stream Entry 2.141, 2.146; a path of two stages 11.385; relationship to reason and emotion, conscious and unconscious 12.107–8

in practice
involve more and more of yourself, don't go through the motions 19.276, 19.278–9; through study you could contact vision, but you need transformation too 19.132; to move from vision to transformation, your heart must be in it 11.193–4; transforming self and world in accordance with Perfect Vision 23.110; transformation is harder because the unconscious is harder to transform 12.107–8; two are needed because of the problem of how to translate knowledge into being; why the path of vision is short and the path of

transformation is long 12.322; you may have had a vision, but you still have to work at transforming yourself 18.173; you have a vision and transform your life in accordance with it 1.476, 5.394; after some vision you need to make some headway on the path of transformation 11.279

A TWOFOLD PATH, MUNDANE AND TRANSCENDENTAL

distinction between the two
introduction 1.473–6; an important distinction 1.8–9; the distinction depends on whether it is practised by Āryans or worldlings 1.136; all enumerations of the path have a mundane and a transcendental section 11.313; analogy with bodhisattva vow 3.367; consequences of not understanding the difference 1.476, 15.595–7; imagine the two paths end to end, to form a path of sixteen stages 1.475; Pāli canon source 15.597

the Transcendental Eightfold Path
description 3.282–4; *bhāvanā*: the transformation is to be made through meditation 2.141; actual knowledge comes only with the attainment of the transcendental path 8.591; the first step: Stream Entry 2.141; the Path of Transformation: from Stream Entrant to *arhant* 2.141, 12.107–8; transcendental morality 11.314

THE STAGES OF THE PATH

introduction
brief summary 3.282–4; full account 1.473–591

(1) right view or understanding, perfect vision (sammā-diṭṭhi/samyak-dṛṣṭi)
etymology and translations 1.478–9; brief description 3.282; introduction 1.477–91; 'right understanding' and 'perfect view' are feeble equivalents to *samyak-dṛṣṭi* 2.127; the first step of the Noble Eightfold Path 1.135, 3.281; first glimpses of vision 1.480–1, 3.35–6, 9.454, 18.580; however vision arises, we must cherish it and allow it to transform us 1.481, 4.272; in relation to Going for Refuge 15.686; it could arise through humiliation 14.490, 26.61; it isn't about the study of the doctrine, it is a *vision* 1.482–3; of crucial importance 12.616, 23.77; the difference between right view and perfect vision 1.474–5, 7.521–2, 11.160, 11.653–4; doctrine held in common by Theravāda and Mahāyāna 7.531; five kinds of right understanding, mundane, transcendental, and intermediate 7.522; experienced through art, music or poetry 3.36, 3.262; our flashes of right view derive from the Buddha's Perfect Vision 11.160–1; like rain 16.123; related to knowledge and vision of things as they really are 3.275; as right view, *see* right view; perfect vision is an understanding of doctrine transformed into insight 1.135, 23.77; to begin with, right view is just a conceptual understanding 12.616; safeguard your original vision 12.679; having had the experience, seeking to communicate Perfect Vision 11.653–4; a total, integral vision 10.595–6; a true understanding of the meaning and purpose of life 11.498; View, Practice, Action, Fruit, *see* view; why wisdom comes first 1.169; you're likely to arrive at Perfect Vision through practice, not constant questioning 17.571; *see also* right view

(2) right or perfect emotion or resolve (samyak-saṃkalpa)
etymology and translations 1.21, 1.135, 1.494–5; brief description 3.282; introduction 1.492–511; the development of non-attachment, love, and compassion 11.498; emotions are not perfect if they are not expressions of perfect vision 1.495–6; comprises non-greed, non-hatred, non-injury 1.21; mediates between Perfect Vision and the other six stages 1.495; negative aspects 1.496–500; positive aspects 1.500–505; right emotions not backed up by right understanding are superficial and unreliable 7.271; the transformation of our entire emotional and volitional nature 3.282; why it is the second step 11.194; the volitional counterpart of right understanding 1.135, 1.494; *see also* faith, compassion, *mettā*, etc.

(3) right or perfect speech (samyag-vāc)
brief description 1.135, 3.282–3; introduction 1.512–25; the Buddha's philosophy of right speech 12.31–8; described in the *Aṅguttara Nikāya* 8.173; the fact that speech has a stage of the path to itself shows its great importance 1.513–14; four levels of skilful speech, *see under* speech/four levels; most Buddhist expositions are superficial and moralistic 1.515; the transformation of speech by perfect vision and perfect emotion 1.515; whatever a yogi says is right speech 18.538–9; *see also* speech

(4) right or perfect action (samyak-karmānta)
definition 1.135; etymology 1.526; brief description 3.283; introduction 1.526–37; practice of the five precepts 11.498; the characteristic virtue is *ahiṃsā* 7.118–20; that act in which the total self is involved,

symbolized by Amoghasiddhi 1.536–7; external behaviour may be the same, but very differently motivated 1.532; conscious discipline on the mundane Path, spontaneous on the transcendental Path 3.282; right action cannot proceed from wrong feeling, or from wrong thinking 7.270–1; sexual ethics 13.453; the spontaneous expression of perfect vision and perfect emotion 1.530; *see also* ethics; precepts; action

(5) right or perfect livelihood (samyag-ājīva)
brief description 1.136, 3.283, 11.498; introduction 1.538–51; the inclusion of this stage of the path shows the importance given to livelihood 3.582; as a stage of the Transcendental Eightfold Path 3.283; a shift from the transformation of individual to collective life 1.540; stands for the creation of an ideal society 1.540–3; the economic aspect of the path, but why not include political and social aspects? 1.543; wrong livelihood, *see* wrong livelihood mentioned in the Pāli canon 1.546–7; livelihood in the modern sangha 1.547–51; *see also* right livelihood; wrong livelihood

(6) right or perfect effort (samyag-vyāyāma)
etymology 1.552–3; brief description 1.136, 3.283–4, 11.498; introduction 1.552–66; the background: the higher evolution 1.564–6; the sixth stage of the path, but it enters at every stage 1.136. 3.283–4; the transformation of the individual will 1.552; twofold: general and specific (the four right efforts) 1.554–64; unremitting spiritual work on oneself 1.554, 19.328, 25.83–4; watching an unskilful thought like a cloud in the sky is a way of applying right effort 11.689; *see also* effort; four right efforts

(7) right or perfect mindfulness or awareness (samyak-smṛti)
etymology 1.567; brief description 3.284, 11.498; introduction 1.567–78; four foundations of mindfulness, *see* mindfulness/four foundations; means constantly bearing in mind the four noble truths 7.117–18; special emphasis in Triratna 13.456; *see also* awareness; mindfulness

(8) right or perfect concentration or samādhi (samyak-samādhi)
brief description 3.284, 11.498; introduction 1.579–88; it's crucial to understand the difference between right and wrong meditation 8.254–6; a serious distortion to think that the path culminates in 'concentration' 1.580, 1.588; the fruition of the whole Path of Transformation 1.581; not just exercise of understanding and will but the transformation of the total psyche 2.112; *see also samādhi*; meditation

noble truths *see* four noble truths

Nobodaddy 8.559–60, 26.348

Noguchi, Yone 8.30

noise the Buddha remonstrates with some noisy *bhikkhus* (*Udāna*) 10.508–9; in the city 12.474; the Buddha speaks of noisy cities 10.330, 10.702–3 (n315); noise and crowds in India 10.291, 10.305; noise pollution 10.291, 12.474, 16.387, 24.465–6

nominal better a small committed Order than a large nominal one 2.519; if you don't practise it, your knowledge of Buddhist philosophy is only nominal 19.446; nominal practice of religion 3.41–2; the nominal temple 19.467–9; people would rather have a nominal guru than a real one 19.462–3; societies where everybody is nominally Buddhist 19.474; you can't be a nominal Buddhist 19.468

nominalism (philosophy) definition 14.645 (n413); the Buddhist position on perception is nominalist 14.420, 14.439–40; *dharmas* have only a nominal existence 2.88–9

non-attachment (*alobha*, non-greed) absolute non-attachment to worldly things is an integral part of the bodhisattva ideal 1.399; along with non-hatred and non-deludedness, the three wholesome roots 17.566; as one of the positive mental events (Abhidharma) 17.561–3; becoming non-attached doesn't mean losing one's feelings 17.507; *bodhi* defined as 'true non-attachment' 14.570; a bodhisattva trains himself in non-attachment to all *dharmas* 14.141; developing non-attachment through giving 4.460–1; generosity is intrinsic to non-attachment 17.562; it may sound negative, but it is about serenity and confidence 17.562; it's a state of individuality, independence, freedom, and creativity 17.562–3; means attachment to something higher 10.492; non-greed an aspect of Perfect Emotion 1.21; can be confused with indifference and alienation 17.509, 18.331–3, 18.336–7; non-attachment has no meaning unless you're full-bloodedly capable of attachment 18.337; positive attachment is attachment that is a basis for non-attachment 19.241; projecting the goal of Enlightenment as

non-attachment 14.570; three levels of non-attachment 17.574; the traditional image is thistledown blown on the wind 17.562

non-binary 2.372

non-conceptual *see under* concepts

non-craving 16.447

non-cruelty (*avihiṃsā*) introduction 1.498–500; it assimilates into compassion 8.452; a person given to cruelty has non-cruelty to lead him upwards 11.658; *see also* non-violence

non-deludedness or non-delusion (*amoha*) as a positive mental event 17.566–74; how *amoha* arises 17.567; it's cultivated through studying the Buddha's teachings 17.571; *niṣprapañca*, *see niṣprapañca*; relationship to *prajñā* 17.568–70

non-desire (*naiṣkramya*) *see* renunciation

non-discrimination 1.346–7

non-duality

what is it?
the Buddha's robe of non-duality is not a mere patchwork of opposites 7.299; *āryajñāna* is non-dual awareness 12.560; explained in the *Vimalakīrti-nirdeśa* 16.457, 16.535–50; only one non-dual reality of which nothing can be predicated 1.306; inconsistent to maintain that the non-dual is related to anything (Vedānta) 7.131–2; philosophically the idea presents an insurmountable difficulty 14.592–3; to understand it we must change the structure of our consciousness 14.593; you have to express non-duality in terms of duality 19.49, 19.448; two-in-oneness, *see yuganaddha*

examples
conditioned and unconditioned 18.85; the bodhisattva's realization of non-duality 7.140; Enlightenment is a state of non-duality 15.592, 17.483; introvert and extravert distinction transcended by non-dual experience 22.248; the Mahāyāna's assertion that reality is Non-Dual 1.274; the non-duality of conditioned and Unconditioned 4.587–91; the non-duality of *śūnyatā* and *rūpa* 5.523; *saṃsāra* and *nirvāṇa* perfectly interwoven in a living vision of non-duality 18.102; speech as the spontaneous expression of the non-dual state 18.48; *śūnyatā*: 'the clear non-dual Shine' (Conze) 16.581

practice
along with non-dualistic view you must have non-dualistic practice 19.379–80; attempts to try to apply the doctrine directly failed 1.274; looking into consciousness in a non-dualistic way 18.242; moving in the direction of non-duality 14.479; overcoming the duality between conscious and unconscious 12.30; Tantric Buddhism based on non-dualist philosophy 7.401; to make spiritual progress, we have to make dualistic distinctions 14.591, 18.85; visualizing a bodhisattva: a taste of non-duality 5.607; when 'in the seen is only the seen' consciousness opens into non-dual awareness 15.205; with the practice of non-duality there is no right path or wrong path 18.51; you might understand the theory, but your being is based on duality 19.506

non-egoistic attitude the future of Triratna will need a stream of non-egoistic spiritual energy 12.600; *nairātmya* (non-ego) of all *dharmas*, *see nairātmya*; thinking of others is an important step towards being non-egoistic 17.345; two ways of developing: devotion and self-awareness 7.407–8; *see also* selflessness

non-existence craving for non-existence, *see under tṛṣṇā*; existence and non-existence, *see* existence/existence and non-existence

non-exploitation a fundamental principle of the ethical and spiritual life 3.592; 'let the silent sage move about the village as the bee goes taking honey from the flower' 3.589–94; should ideally hold good in all the relationships of life 3.581; 'so let the wise person live in the world' 3.592; has psychological and spiritual implications which cover all personal relationships 3.592; related to the second precept 3.582

non-greed (*alobha*) *see* non-attachment

non-harm *see ahiṃsā*

non-hatred (*adosa*, *adveṣa*, *avyāpāda*) an aspect of Perfect Emotion 1.21, 1.497–8; its characteristics 17.563–4; it is different from *mettā* 17.566; a positive mental event (Abhidharma) 17.563–6; suffering does not have to produce hatred 17.564; along with non-attachment and non-deludedness, the three wholesome roots 17.566

non-human beings gathered to hear the *Ratana Sutta* 15.63–6; gnomes, undines, salamanders, sylphs (alchemy) 15.139; how can they place themselves at the service of

the Dharma? 16.350–2; kept under control by the four great kings 16.349

see also
individual names (*gandharvas*, *asuras* etc.); nature spirits, *see under* paganism

non-production 14.562, 14.583

non-returner (*anāgāmin*) introduction 2.141, 3.412, 15.239–40; as a 'bodhisattva of the path' 4.179–80; breaks fourth and fifth fetters 1.178, 2.148–9, 3.254, 3.420–1; described in the *Ratana Sutta* 15.64; experiences craving in the form of desire for existence in the *rūpaloka* or *arūpaloka* 17.597; gravitational pull of the Unconditioned predominant 3.254; the Mahāyāna version 15.240; reborn in the pure abodes (*Suddhavāsa*) 1.177, 1.341, 2.148–9, 3.254, 15.239–40, 15.526–7, 16.345

nonsense the *Diamond Sūtra* a breath of nonsense 14.480–2; it's nonsense to talk about remaining in the present all the time 11.657; the no-nonsense guru 13.176–8; nonsense has an attraction for people who don't want to stop and think clearly 17.66

non-utilitarianism *see under* utilitarianism

non-violence (*ahiṃsā* or *avihiṃsā*)

WHAT IS IT?

introduction
it should be universal in practice and in application 3.319, 7.119; non-violence and *mettā* 2.361, 5.174–6, 17.583; non-violence and world peace 3.613–14, 7.236–9; non-violence as distinct from quietism (Ambedkar) 9.47; the principles of violence and non-violence have always been at work 12.354, 26.55; the principle can be applied to many of the world's problems 3.319, 8.453; the 'problem' of *ahiṃsā* 7.372–7; fear of non-violence 17.353; theoretical questions about it without the context of practice are confusing 7.372; there's more to it than one might think 17.583

its nature
the characteristic virtue of the active part of man 7.118–19; conduct will be non-violent when the consciousness behind it is non-egotistic 7.376; the external expression of an internal realization 7.373; it resolves itself into compassion 7.377; may be defined as love in action 3.319, 7.119; a principle of Light 12.354–5; you get people who wouldn't hurt a fly 13.135

its history in Buddhism
in some ways the fundamental principle of Buddhism 1.532–3, 3.318–20; not the Buddha's only teaching 8.179–80, 9.108, 9.426; the Buddha's belief in it 9.68; and the *Mettā Sutta* 7.119–20; carrying a water strainer to avoid harming life in water 17.583, 17.584; a distinction between the non-violence of the monk and of the householder 8.449–50; an aspect of Perfect Emotion 1.21; one of the eleven positive mental events (Abhidharma) 8.451–2, 17.582–7; Hindu non-violence a result of Buddhist influence 10.48; Buddhism spread by non-violent means 7.237, 9.236, 9.341, 9.472, 9.496; Aśoka's conversion to non-violence 9.120; Buddhism wields only the sword of wisdom against only one enemy, ignorance 7.443; the highest rule of Dharma is not to cause harm (*Mahāvastu*) 2.332, 2.358, 3.318–19; Buddhists have rather taken it for granted 17.582–3; the non-violence of the Dhamma Revolution 9.411–13, 9.427

in other traditions
Ahiṃsa: Non-violence in Indian Tradition (review) 8.447–53; comparing the meanings of *ahiṃsā* in different Indian systems of thought 8.448; the difference between Buddhism and Christianity 7.444; Gandhi and non-violence 7.119, 8.453; non-violence of *satyāgrahis* 9.221; practised towards all beings, or only towards non-violent beings? 8.449; the Vedic tradition makes exceptions 8.449; *see also* Jainism

NON-VIOLENCE IN PRACTICE

Buddhist practice
ahiṃsā is a state of love, so practising it means cultivating that state 7.373; Dalit reluctance to practise non-violence 10.302; the eradication of ignorance and the cultivation of wisdom 7.373; exaggerated importance may be attached to vegetarianism 17.586–7; how far you go with it will depend on your sensitivity 17.584; non-violence and the first precept 1.532–3, 3.318–20, 9.215, 17.583; non-violent action on an intellectual basis can be mechanical 7.373; practice while clinging to self is like rowing a boat tied to the shore 7.375; sincerely try to practise it, and you will end practising every other Buddhist virtue 3.319; to follow the principle is to be brought into the heart of the spiritual life 26.55; to live in accordance with it is to be fully a human being, or even an angel 12.354, 26.55; working for the welfare of others

by every means in our power 7.119; you can't perfect it, but you can cultivate your intention 4.355–6

Buddhist failures to practise non-violence
a predicted 'sword-interval' (Pāli canon) 11.322, 12.747 (n400), 19.597 (n37); Buddhism has not always been non-violent 7.11, 7.443; in modern times some Buddhists have degenerated into violent action 26.631; Thai monks sprinkling holy water on guns for Vietnam 12.252

protests
a plea for non-violence at a student demonstration in America 23.461; protest against nuclear war must be non-violent 12.346–7; to achieve peace, disputes need to be settled non-violently 12.353; a contrast between violence and non-violence 21.272

see also
precepts/first precept; vegetarianism

Norfolk, England Abhirati community, *see* Abhirati; Besthorpe 20.83–4, 24.141–2, 26.429–30, 26.586; Blickling Hall 24.239–40; Castle Acre 19.493; *Five Norfolk Worthies* 26.586–90; Norwich, *see* Norwich; Padmaloka, *see under* Triratna IV/retreat centres; Sangharakshita's Norfolk relations 20.84, 26.429–31; Tittleshall 21.597

Norgay, Tenzing 22.11–12

Norm and normative 5.175, 9.538, 12.112, 12.150, 15.255

Norse mythology 19.410, 22.14

north the cold grey old North Sea 24.157; contrast between the art of southern and northern Europe 26.255–6; the Buddha lay with his head to the north and his feet to the south 11.452, 12.357; a journey from north to south 26.263–4

North, Professor and Mrs 22.52

Northern Ireland 9.472

Norwich Julian of Norwich, *see* Julian; the Buddhist sangha includes many families 9.438; Sangharakshita reads poems about friendship at the centre 24.403, 24.464; the Buddhist centre team working together harmoniously 12.309; visiting the centre 26.565

no-self *see anātman*

nostalgia 5.173–4, 12.276–7, 17.401–3

Nosu, Kosetsu 10.699 (n274)

not taking the not-given *see under* precepts/second precept

no-thing-ness *see under dhyānas/arūpa*

'not-two' (*advaya*) absolute and relative *bodhicitta* 4.34; the *bodhicitta* as an initial experience of wisdom and compassion as one, not two 4.515; the bodhisattva's realization 2.159; Mahāyāna conception 1.268; the nature of the 'not-two doctrine' (*Vimalakīrti-nirdeśa*) 13.348–9; the reason for saying 'not-two' rather than 'one' 16.449; *śūnyatā* and *rūpa* 5.523, 19.371–2; the term avoids the risk of a fixed and final conception of reality 18.44; you cannot regard *saṃsāra* and *nirvāṇa* as ultimately two things 19.379

Nottingham, England 12.534, 24.580

noumenal everything possesses a diamond or noumenal aspect 7.400–1; noumena do not exist 1.99; try to view relationships in their noumenal (diamond) aspect 7.402; you realize that the noumenal and the phenomenal are one 13.97–8

noumenalism *see ātmavāda*

Novalis (Philipp Friedrich von Hardenberg) introduction 22.591 (n161); *Henry von Ofterdingen* 24.568; *Hymns to the Night* 24.568; Lama Govinda's belief that he had been Novalis in a previous life 12.688, 26.256; 'Poets and priests were one in the beginning' 22.180, 25.478

novice bodhisattva *see under* bodhisattva/four kinds of bodhisattva

Noyes, John Humphrey 24.486–7

Nu, U (Burmese Prime Minister) v8

nuclear war *see under* war

nudity *see* nakedness

numinous 17.135, 17.727 (n148)

nuns *see bhikkhunīs*

Nya Non 18.137, 18.140–1

Nyams and rTogs (Tibetan) 18.299

Nyanaponika, Venerable

introduction
introduction 8.694 (n222), 15.xx; interned in India during the war 6.617; analysis of Abhidharma 1.110, 1.224–5; and the Buddhist Publication Society, Kandy 8.275; comments on the Burma method of Satipaṭṭhāna 1.156, 1.225; *The Five Mental Hindrances and Their Conquest by Buddhist Spiritual Training* 1.153; *The Four Sublime States: Brahma-Vihara* 8.383–4

The Threefold Refuge assessment 2.485–8, 7.740–2; an attempt to revive the practice of Going for Refuge in the Theravāda 2.566; Sangharakshita's seminar on the text 2.484–8, 15.xx–xxi, 15.541–743

Nyanatiloka Thera brief introduction 7.565 (n111); on the Abhidharma 1.223–4, 14.89–90; *The Buddha's Teaching of Egolessness* (review) 8.379–80; on the difference between *mārga* and *phala* 1.177; on the four noble truths 1.121; on Nirvāṇa 1.77; on *saṃsāra* 1.130

Nyāya school of Indian logic 17.519–20

Nyingma *see under* Tibetan Buddhism/ schools

O

oak *see under* trees

obedience 'God's thundering commands are to be obeyed' 11.338, 12.228; 'He beat upon the wall / Till Truth obeyed his call' (Yeats) 15.520, 16.266; 'he sighed as a lover, obeyed as a son' 21.365; obedience in theistic religions 15.617–21; Sangharakshita decides to obey his teacher in all things 13.628, 20.463–4, 22.394–5; three kinds of disciple: disobey, obey, and know without being told 12.19; 'To discover that within myself which I *must* obey' 2.401

obeisance *see* prostrations

Obeyesekere, Gananath 13.403

object and subject, *see* subject–object; with the arising of *prajñā* one gets as close to an object as one can possibly get 17.547

objectifying objectifying a situation by talking about it with a friend 17.614–15; seeing yourself and others as objects (Fromm) 12.277; tendency to objectify other people, as a baby does its mother 12.262; the value of confession is that you objectify what you have done 16.313

objective situation the demands of the situation get you out of your negative subjectivity 4.286–7; the needs of the objective situation and your personal needs 11.451, 17.614; the objective situation is the same, but you're not worried about it in the same way 10.578; responding to the objective situation 4.91, 5.187; the situation may require you to carry on working when you're tired 18.617

objectivity

reflections on objectivity
a breakdown of the notion of objective truth 12.350–3; Enlightened or not, you see the same object, but you interpret it differently 16.453; grammar gives something quasi-metaphysical objectivity 26.369; how the seemingly objective universe evolved from absolute mind 1.351; if you don't regard ideas as yours, if an idea is attacked, you don't get upset 10.489; if you see someone objectively, you will never find them boring 18.159; it isn't wrong to discriminate, but our discrimination must be objective 17.282; no objective reason to be more concerned with our suffering than others' 4.569–70; objective evaluation of taste 18.131–3; objective facts are in their true nature infinite and boundless 14.143; objectively there is no difference between yourself and others 4.472–3; a puja has to have an objective orientation 18.321; the Pure Land: mutual experience of Enlightenment in objective terms 18.305–6; recognizing objectively that there are positive forces at work in the universe 4.317; there is no such thing as scholarly objectivity 15.197–8; we are completely non-objective 10.483; what is really a state of mind can appear as an objectively existing world 2.79

practising objectivity
be careful not to evaluate when you should be describing 17.233–4, 17.236, 19.289–90; be more objective 4.624; being objective even on the everyday level is difficult 12.655; being sceptical about our own objectivity 15.293; characteristic of a true individual 3.468; difference between necessary, objective thinking and worry 10.462; *mettā* includes intelligent objectivity 15.323; objective, skilful discussion 10.603; objectivity about criticism 3.546–7; practise different ways of looking at the same thing 5.512; responding to objective needs 14.519, 19.193; thinking about something objectively can be frustrating and takes courage 17.626; with spiritual practice one's views become more objective 17.168

seeing yourself objectively
a detached and objective attitude towards the body 4.609; friendship helps one to get an objective perspective on oneself 15.91; look after yourself objectively, without attachment 4.633; seeing oneself objectively 3.564, 15.91–2; self-awareness: the ability to be objective about yourself 3.469; telling your life story can help you become more objective 15.91–2

see also
objective and subjective, *see under* subjective

objects all objects of perception are transformations of consciousness 1.377; destruction of attachment to objects 1.100; difference between crafted and mass-produced objects 18.71; don't allow your thinking to be ruled by the apparent objects of your perception 14.417; in

modern life, attachments are spread over easily replaceable objects 19.13, 19.19; mental objects, *see* mental objects; objects are like floating clouds, like sea foam, like a reflection 14.192; objects of concentration, *see under* concentration; the objects of craving: the senses 1.111; places and objects can develop an atmosphere 14.463–5; seeing yourself and others as objects (Fromm) 12.277; Tantric ritual objects made of bone 13.243; we often treat other people not as persons but as objects 12.262; we imagine that sense-objects give us pleasure 18.158

obligation doing what you 'ought' to do 10.604; exploiting people through their sense of obligation 18.121; feeling under obligation 16.330

O-Bon ritual, *see under* Japan

obscurations the blue sky represents freedom from all obscurations 13.282; emotional obscuration 18.449–50; intellectual obscuration, wrong conceptions of reality 18.449–50; when the obscurations are removed through practice, the absolute mind shines forth 1.364

obsessions Buddhism does not encourage morbid obsession with suffering 1.132; 'the happiness which arose in me, could not obsess my mind' 2.108, 18.581; isn't talk of *dhyāna* rather self-obsessed? 5.450; a neurotically extrovert attitude 19.396; obsession with the idea that people are equal 18.439; Rechungpa's obsession with getting his books back 19.58–62, 19.74, 19.87

obstacles

obstacles we may meet
as we fail to see things as they are, there must be a hindering factor in our mind 14.209; the biggest obstacle to our search for Enlightenment is craving 12.623; doing something for the first time and meeting the most formidable obstacles 1.52; egoism is 'the only real obstacle to the realization of Truth' 20.362; the greatest obstacle to knowledge is to think that we know 13.346; ignorance is the root of all obstacles to the spiritual life 18.180; obstacles to Enlightenment 1.99, 23.18; *micchā-diṭṭhis* are the real obstacle to bringing the Dharma to the West 11.522; negative emotions: one of the biggest obstacles to the spiritual life 12.391; possible future obstacles to the Triratna Buddhist Community 12.598–9; the self is the sole obstacle to the 'attainment' of happiness 7.412, 26.53; two kinds: for those who are trying to become Enlightened and those who are not 19.65–6

overcoming obstacles
Dr Ambedkar had the strength to break through them 9.367–8; breaking through obstacles to our development 11.4–5; confession as a way of overcoming obstacles to growth 16.290, 16.508; the *dharmapālas* as breakers down of inner obstacles to Dharma practice 19.407; to the Enlightened person *saṃsāra* is no obstacle at all 19.64–5; learning to use life's adversities by conquering them 8.265; obstacles almost always arise, so you need the *vīrya* that does not turn back 17.577; obstacles are only relatively real 18.621; obstacles to friendship 12.458; removing the obstacles to receptivity 4.224; to be able to help living beings you need to have no obstacles 19.66

obstinacy the blind, egoistic obstinacy that keeps the whole saṃsāric process going 19.18; the cat's unteachable obstinacy 19.17; the obstinacy of self-will 19.16–18, 19.36–7; the patience of the positive outlasts the obstinacy of the negative 19.36; Rechungpa's obstinacy 19.58–62, 19.75, 19.87; Sangharakshita's obstinacy 20.72, 20.379; sometimes preference is just obstinacy 19.60

occult forces 2.215–6 3.409–10; *Literature and Occult Tradition* 22.141; occultist 20.25; precepts relating to occultism 11.317; properties of blood 21.446; use of pendulum 21.443

oceans *see* seas

Ockenden Venture 2.404, 2.712 (n471), 12.367

Odantapuri University 7.425, 9.390, 13.10

Odisha *see* Orissa

Odyssey *see under* Homer

Oedipus 16.423

offences all the more serious according to whom it is committed against 4.364; five heinous crimes, *see* five heinous crimes; monastic 2.194–5; *see also under* Vinaya/ *prātimokṣa*

offering goddesses eight offering goddesses 13.257, 13.262, 16.345–6; embodied prayers 19.143; illustration 13.257; in the Green Tārā practice 26.671; on Mount Meru 16.345–6; visualized on the Refuge Tree 13.208–9

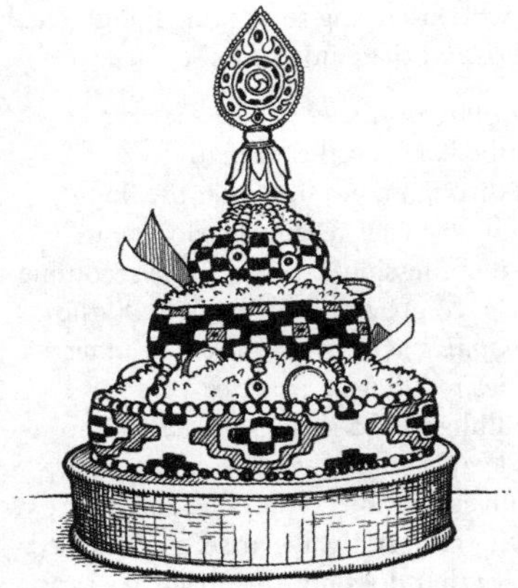

offering the mandala (*ngöndro*) one of the foundation yogas 13.85–6, 13.260, 18.125, 18.446; how the practice is done 13.85–6, 13.262–6; an act of the imagination 13.263; an expression of overwhelming gratitude to the Three Jewels 13.260; great offering, middle offering, and little offering 12.20; mantra 13.263; Milarepa's practice 18.125–6; *mudrā* 13.264, 13.266; illustrations 13.264–6; in offering the mandala, you acknowledge the true value of the teaching 18.125; offering verses 13.266, 17.1; offering the universe to the Buddhas and bodhisattvas 1.408, 13.86–7, 13.260–2, 18.446–7; in puja 1.408, 16.343; recitation of an esoteric sevenfold puja 13.262–3; in this context, 'mandala' means a symbolic representation of the universe 13.85–6; it signifies willingness to give, to surrender 13.86; to be done 100,000 times 13.263

offerings

THE BUDDHIST TRADITION

Early Buddhism
kings who offered their kingdoms to the Buddha 13.86; the Buddha encourages the Vajjians to keep up offerings at ancient shrines 14.463; offerings to the dead (*Tirokuḍḍa Sutta*) 15.67–8; Theravādin offerings 13.252–3; Thai monks receiving offerings from women 13.474, 13.497–8

Mahāyāna
Mahāyāna offerings 13.253–7; in the *Bodhicaryāvatāra* 4.290; the gods' offerings make a jewelled canopy (*White Lotus Sūtra*) 14.129–30, 16.50; marvellous offerings made in Vairocana's Tower 14.224–5

Tantric offerings
internal: 'the flower of the senses' 13.258–9; external 13.259; secret 13.259–60; Rechungpa's offering of meat to Milarepa 19.515, 19.527; offerings in hard cash 4.611, 19.530

the three traditional offerings (flowers, candles, incense)
reflections on the offerings 1.408, 9.324, 9.461, 13.252–3; expression of gratitude 13.417; in the verses of the Sevenfold Puja 11.234–41

seven (or eight) offerings
the Indian tradition of the honoured guest 1.507–8, 11.237–9, 13.254–6, 26.494; the Buddha as the unexpected guest (*atithi*) 1.508, 11.238, 13.256, 18.430, 26.494; the seven 'external' offerings 13.417; the eighth offering, music 1.507; illustration 13.256; symbolized by bowls of water 1.508, 13.255, 26.494; Tibetan offerings on special occasions 26.494

THE NATURE OF OFFERINGS

offerings made
bhojana-dāna (food offering) 2.212, 22.26–7, 22.28, 22.93, 22.99, 22.109, 23.364; food and drink (in the puja) 11.237; flowers 3.340, 4.297–8, 8.161–2, 9.461, 11.234, 13.252–3, 20.259; garlands 11.234–5; material wealth for the Dharma 18.113–15; mind-made flowers 14.143; offerings made during a puja 11.242–4; oneself 18.188; the senses 13.258–9; various kinds of offerings 13.417

offerings to whom or to what?
monks refusing offerings 19.482–3; to the guru 19.529–30; to the household shrine 2.229, 26.494; to local spirits at *caityas* (folk shrines) 10.452; to people at ordinations and other ceremonies 13.417; to people leading a genuinely spiritual life 19.499

purpose of offerings
as a form of generosity 1.501; in the hope of merit 19.311, 19.537; let the Buddhist maker of resolutions make offerings 8.193; to neutralize bad karma 4.399; to strengthen devotion 11.453

reflections and stories
Buddhists can't make offerings in the Karle caves 8.295; flinging rice at the Buddha's face: hurried offerings in Nepal 10.241–2, 20.432–3; if your merits are great, offerings will accrue to you 19.357; in principle, offering a single flower sets you on the path to Buddhahood 14.114, 16.41;

making offerings isn't the be-all and end-all of Buddhist life 13.270–1; making offerings may be unfamiliar to Westerners 11.239; offering three hundred pots of food is less than an instant of love 17.185–6

see also
offering the *mandala*; *prasad* (food offering), *see under* food

O'Keeffe, Georgia 24.524

ola leaves 19.367

Olcott, Col H. S. and the *Maha Bodhi* journal 8.38, 8.41; connection with Anagarika Dharmapala 8.18–34, 8.56; conversion to Buddhism 8.18; designed a Buddhist flag 22.92; Theosophist activities in Ceylon 7.444, 8.17–34

old age awareness of the issue of succession 11.600–1; the blind old king riding bravely to meet Death 25.411; the cause of old age 1.91; forbearance towards 4.120; a form of *duḥkha* 3.210; 'growing old unknown to my friends' 24.397; John Freeman's last poem 24.558; how can we ignore the fact of old age? 7.116; 'If a young man forgets his hat, no one thinks anything of it' 24.346; in old age the Buddha said that he was only free of pain when in *dhyāna* 15.156, 19.422; losing memory as we get older 17.541; an old people's home 24.252–4; moving closer to ageing and death like a calf drinking its mother's milk 10.617–18; old age in *Piers Plowman* 24.539–40; Perfect Vision arising in old age 1.481; represents history (Vimalakīrti) 16.526–7; a tendency to be conservative about travel as one gets older 11.14; as one of the four sights, *see* four sights; 'When patrons grow old their faith soon wears out' 19.477; why should the Buddha be subject to old age and death? 4.205

see also
old age, sickness, and death, *see under* four sights; one of Yama's three messengers, *see* Yama; Sangharakshita's old age, *see* Sangharakshita III/old age, sickness, and death

old people ancient harpies staggering off a coach 24.133; Buddhism is not for 'old ladies' (of both sexes and all ages) 1.553; choosing to look after the elderly is about personal choice 18.149–50; the conceit of the old 18.489; English old ladies natter about death, having come to terms with it 24.127–8; even little old ladies have to become lions in Buddhism 4.469; helping old people 4.70; an old woman who dies in the night in a Milarepa story 18.549–71; some old people are unreasonably independent 18.387; treated badly by younger people with power over them 26.658; the young getting impatient with the old 17.523

old pine tree *see* Eicho

Oldenberg, Hermann 7.191–3, 9.338

Olson, Eric T. 8.615

Olympics 12.674–5

oṃ (seed syllable) the abstract universal 16.176, 16.186; could be heard in the Virupaksha Guha cave 20.338; difficulty of chanting *oṃ* in India because of Hindu associations 9.538–9; the goal of the path 10.144, 10.174; in a psychedelic experience 23.468; primordial sound 3.80; relationship to *hūṃ* 10.147, 16.176, 16.186

oṃ āḥ hūṃ head, throat, and heart 19.30; no question of translating it 19.134; represent the seeds of the *trikāya* 18.293, 19.30; visualized in the guru yoga 13.219; visualization 16.135

oṃ maṇi padme hūṃ *see* Avalokiteśvara/mantra

oṃ svabhāva-śuddhāḥ sarvadharmāḥ svabhāva-śuddho 'haṃ (*śūnyatā* mantra) 5.33, 5.489, 5.604–5

oṃ vajra bhūmi āḥ hūṃ 13.263

Omar, Mullah Mohammed 26.475–6

Omiya (watch-repairer) 21.436, 22.105, 22.110, 22.113–14

omniscience Brahmā neither omniscient nor omnipotent 1.158; the Buddha and omniscience, *see* Buddha II/characteristics/omniscience

once-returner (*sakṛdāgāmin* or *sakadāgāmin*) introduction 2.141, 3.412; as a 'bodhisattva of the path' 4.179–80; described in the *Ratana Sutta* 15.64;

weakens fourth and fifth fetters 1.177, 2.147–8, 3.253, 3.420–1, 12.28

One Mind or Mind-Only doctrine (*cittamātra*) *see under* Yogācāra

one taste (*ekarasa*) *see under Udāna*/the great ocean

Oneida Community 24.486–8

one-pointedness (*cittass'ekagattā*, *ekagrata* or *ekaggatā*) etymology 1.149, 5.238; an example from the Buddha's life 3.288–9, 9.298; always useful 10.356, 23.37; as *dhyāna* factor 5.238, 9.200; the flowing of all the energies towards a single point 4.513, 5.654; any object may serve as the basis for its development, but some are special 1.153–4; definition of *samādhi* 1.149, 3.306; *samādhi* is healthy one-pointedness (*kauśalya-ekāgratā-citta*) 2.109

ontology the Buddha's wisdom in bypassing ontology 8.620; in Buddhism there are no ontological principles 10.545; Buddhism's pseudo-ontological statements 19.224; conflict between emptiness (ontologically) and the struggle for Enlightenment 14.146; confusion of ontology with epistemology (Upanishads) 8.619; the danger of appropriating ontological Buddhahood as a sort of mental possession 14.143, 19.98; the difference between the ontological and the – 26.84; the irreversible bodhisattva doesn't take anything seriously, ontologically speaking 14.501; of the *Diamond Sūtra* 10.165, 14.150; for Buddhism there is no question of an ontology as distinct from an epistemology 8.442–3; the ontological aspect of *śūnyatā* 14.150–1, 14.409–10; the ontological meaning of Nirvāṇa 7.510; it's not that *saṃsāra* and *nirvāṇa* are ontologically identical 19.65; *śamatha* experiences have no ontological content 8.441; saying the Buddha was Enlightened is not strictly an ontological statement 19.231; the term 'ontological' is synonymous with the Western concept 'metaphysical' 10.545; thinking of the Transcendental in ontological terms 19.38; the Void has no metaphysical or ontological status 19.237; the Buddha's ontological status, *see under* Buddha IV/who is the Buddha?/identifying him

opanayiko *see under Tiratana Vandanā*

open air the Buddha's open air life 11.452, 14.398, 15.136–7, 26.242; Buddhism had its origins in the open air 26.242; living more in the open air helps one's positivity 11.13

openness

openness to the Dharma
Buddhism must be approached with openness, or you will learn nothing 19.106; instead of saying 'Drop the ego', let yourself open up a little 17.345; opening up to spiritual experience 11.279; openness to *adhiṣṭhāna* 19.285; openness to deeper realities 17.xxii; openness to receive the teaching, shown by generosity 18.115; remaining open to the teaching that is all around you, wherever you are 18.182; a willingness to consider something new 9.515

openness with other people
committed friendship requires openness 15.311; cultivating openness needs to be taken seriously 16.316; the difficulty of being truly open 25.89; even a fraction of openness may be enough 19.86; fear of being open 10.570–1, 16.316; having enough confidence in our friends to be open with them 17.652; it's helpful to have a few friends to whom you can say absolutely anything 18.516; it's a strain not being totally open 16.314–15; it's very important to be open with one another 10.217; knowing we will die, we should be open and direct with one another 19.104; misusing the language of openness 17.234, 19.289–92; 'open up the thatch': if you open up you will be protected 10.559, 10.570–1; openness in communication 16.315; openness is only possible with somebody who has the same ideals as you 18.516; openness and *mettā* 5.189; openness to the *ḍākinī* – keeping in communication with spiritual friends 18.318; openness to people can make it possible for them to change 17.239; the Tantric attitude is of complete openness 19.532–3; true openness allows you to make a fresh start 10.570–1; we are rarely completely open – but we can be 18.515–16; with your spiritual friends you're used to being completely open 18.420–1

opportunities

taking opportunities
appamāda: a kind of zeal that never lets an opportunity go by 15.210–11; the Buddha's meeting with Upāka reminds us to take opportunities 10.262–3, 11.415; every moment presents us with an opportunity to choose what to do 15.174; 'Gather ye rosebuds while ye may' 18.151; Milarepa makes the most of any

opportunity 18.47, 18.560; opportunity translated as *kṣetra* 4.435; the oppression of opportunity 16.322; planet Earth has a wonderful opportunity 10.315; take full advantage of your spiritual opportunities 26.532; turning a difficulty into an opportunity 17.302

opportunities to take
being perfectly open 18.515; boredom is an opportunity 17.399; Buddha images give us an opportunity of developing devotional feelings 18.431; clear up misunderstandings 19.104; good conditions for Dharma practice 4.365–7, 10.322, 11.409, 15.365, 19.244–5; opportunities for insight 5.637–8; opportunities to spread the Dharma 8.267–8; the opportunity to change 18.640; practising *dāna* 18.271; living in a situation that is conducive to your development 3.464; relaxing the effort to be mindful, you let slip a wonderful opportunity 18.155; time with spiritual friends 18.425, 18.567; unemployment as an opportunity 15.366; what's the use of staying in a cave unless you make use of it? 19.557; with insight, you can enter the *dhyānas* whenever there is an opportunity 18.575–6

the opportunity of death
create merit before death 18.551; we have to prepare for it *now* 23.93; opportunities for liberation in the *bardos* after death 12.199–205; the time of death being uncertain, make the most of chances to hear the Dharma 9.291; the time of death can be a wonderful opportunity 12.201–2, 18.250

see also
eight opportunities; human life/rare opportunity; retreat/solitary retreat

opposites

Buddhism and opposites
the Buddha's robe of non-duality is not a mere patchwork of opposites 7.299; Buddhism points out the opposite of everything to which we cling 7.35; the Dharma is always expressed in terms of opposites 16.542

pairs of opposites
are created by the mind 7.299–300, 16.547–8, 22.29; expressed by the jewel in the lotus 22.29; horizontal and vertical pairs of opposites 12.21–2; and Dharma-doors in the *Vimalakīrti-nirdeśa* 16.543–9; the reactive mind swings between them 10.637, 18.343; we divide things into dichotomies for practical purposes 5.523–4

beyond opposites
the only way we can go 'between' opposites is by rising 'above' them 7.299; a state of consciousness beyond all pairs of opposites 10.464–5; *śūnyatā* transcends all apparent oppositions 7.505

the union of opposites
Enlightenment is the union of opposites at the highest possible level 12.185, 19.29; the need to unite those great opposites, heights and depths 12.29; opposites are not to be eliminated, but reconciled within a higher unity 26.38; symbolized by the *vajra* 13.183–6

see also
kliṣṭa-mano-vijñāna, see under eight *vijñānas*; complete reconciliation of all opposites, *see yuganaddha*

opposition 'Opposition is true friendship' 16.525; some people are stimulated by opposition 4.424

oppression Milarepa is not oppressed by solitude 18.42–3; the oppressions (*saṃkaṭa*) of life (*Sūtra of Golden Light*) 16.319–25; caste oppression 10.59–60

optimism the bodhisattva is serene, cheerful, and optimistic 1.440, 4.135; the events of the 20th century have shattered Western political optimism 11.270; Kṣitigarbha the embodiment of spiritual optimism 2.181; the Mahāyāna's optimism about our spiritual condition 14.483–5; a note of optimism in poetry 26.398; optimism about the potential of Buddhism in the modern world 9.511, 16.434; the optimism of the creative mind 23.xvi, 26.76; an optimistic Mahāyāna *sūtra* 14.195; the radical optimism of Buddhism 12.526, 15.81; Śāntideva's spiritual optimism 4.320–1; the world continues to be optimistic, but its ideals are degenerate 17.692

oral tradition (of passing on Dharma teachings)

introduction
brief account 15.3, 15.179–80; introduction 14.18–27; ancient India had an orally transmitted culture, symbolized by Sarasvatī 16.363; a *bhikkhu* who became an *arhant* though he couldn't remember one verse of the Dharma 8.119; the Buddha created an agency to preserve his teachings: the sangha 8.245; the Buddha wrote nothing, all his teachings were oral 7.498, 10.229–30, 13.336, 14.18, 15.179; the Buddha's disciples learned his teachings by heart 10.230,

14.20; a gradual process 3.83; importance for accuracy of clear pronunciation 10.576, 20.409; in the days before writing, the learned man was the man who had heard much 15.403–4; in India, memories could preserve teachings for a hundred generations 1.379; specialization: learning and passing on a section of the teachings 2.197; it meant that people were given exactly the spiritual teachings they needed 4.147; teachings were passed on from teacher to pupil over generations 3.77–8; a tremendous feat 10.575–6, 13.339; versification to help memorization 14.20, 15.347; the recitation of a new text in recent years 14.258

saṅgīti (chanting together) in the Early Buddhist tradition
etymology 7.521; recitation at *poṣadha* days 1.146, 2.187, 2.200, 10.559–61, 14.20; Ānanda's part 3.364, 9.356, 10.435–6, 14.400, 15.179, 16.36–7, 16.233–4; at the First Council 2.188, 4.660 (n9), 10.435–6, 10.706 (n358), 15.180, 16.234, 22.170; people pooled all that they remembered the Buddha saying 4.334–5; responsibility for maintaining the tradition, and its effect on the sangha 2.188–9; the faithfulness of oral transmission is something we could learn from 10.576; Śāriputra's organization of a *saṅgīti-paryāya* so that 'this holy life may persist' 14.20–1; congregational chanting came to be seen as a guarantee of authenticity 14.21; the *suttas* were lodged in the mind through recitation 15.180; Theravādin claim that their version was chanted at Rājagṛha after the *parinirvāṇa* 14.21; all the teachings handed down were systematized as the Abhidharma 12.140–1; the tradition continued for hundreds of years 14.21–2, 16.240; transition to a literary tradition, *see* scriptures/canonical literature

in the Mahāyāna
could the Mahāyāna *sūtras* have been transmitted orally? 1.326; relationship of texts to the oral tradition insoluble 2.51; the scriptures represent different strands of the oral tradition 16.241–2; in the *White Lotus Sūtra* 16.39

in Tibetan Buddhism
a great reservoir of oral teachings 18.469–70; many teachings are still transmitted exclusively by oral means 14.258–9; the oral tradition of the *lama gyupas* 13.48; the primacy of personal, oral teaching over mere book learning 18.14; Rechungpa as a reciter of stories from the *sūtras* 18.306–7

orchestra example of balance between effort and receptivity 16.519; an orchestra as a spiritual community 26.31

Order members (Triratna or Western Buddhist Order or TBM) *see under* Triratna III

ordinary life *see* everyday life

ordinary person *see pṛthagjana*

ordination, Buddhist

what is ordination?
what ordinations have in common is the Three Jewels 11.68–70, 11.135, 11.420, 26.32; full formal expression to one's commitment to the Three Jewels 11.396; the Buddhist ritual of ordination is richer in significance than generally supposed 8.350; it is not an achievement that sets you above other Buddhists 18.176; being committed to Dharma practice without the formal rite of ordination 18.176–7; reflects two things: going forth and joining the spiritual community 3.461–2, 11.133–4; reflections on its true meaning 21.521; a rich and fruitful growing thing 12.423; a subject that preoccupied Sangharakshita 23.142

ordination at the time of the Buddha
ordination at the Buddha's time: 'Come, O monk!' 11.420, 15.507; Subhadda's ordination, an example of ordination at the time of the Buddha 11.454–5; the Vinaya says you can be ordained if you are old enough to scare crows 2.193, 13.31

saṃvara (ordination)
difference between *saṃvara* and Tantric initiation (*abhiṣeka*) 2.447–8, 7.478; lay brother or sister, monk or nun, bodhisattva 7.473, 13.338–9; literally means restraint, control, obligation, vow, binding 2.448, 7.478, 11.68; *śrāmaṇera, bhikṣu, sthavira* 21.96; a unifying rather than a dividing factor in Buddhism 2.448, 23.143

see also
abhiṣeka; *bhikkhu* ordination, *see under bhikkhu*; *bhikkhunī* ordination, *see under bhikkhunī*; bodhisattva ordination (*bodhisattva-saṃvara*), *see under* bodhisattva/bodhisattva career; Mahāyāna ordination, *see under* Mahāyāna/what is the Mahāyāna?; ordination in the three *yānas*, *see under yānas*/'Hīnayāna', Mahāyāna, Vajrayāna/introduction; ordination within the Triratna Buddhist Order, *see under* Triratna III/ordination; Sangharakshita's, *see* Sangharakshita V/ordination; women's ordination, *see* women/ordination

O'Regan, Terry 2.403

organizations and organizing Buddhism before organization 10.480–1, 10.561; Buddhist organizations are simply the fruitful communication of the individuals involved 23.161; Buddhist organizations must remember that it is the human being that matters 18.121–2; Buddhist organizations must be run by Buddhists 9.212, 11.173–4, 11.381, 11.383, 23.437; Buddhism cannot be spread by purely organizational means 9.526; disillusionment with Buddhist organizations 11.381–2; the founding of Buddhist organizations in the West 12.72–3; how does a tolerant organization protect itself from an intolerant one? 4.127; organizational activity 4.569; organizer and organized are two: cooperation is the Dharma-door to non-duality 16.548; the organization of the sangha 10.480; people complain about organizations without considering the difficulties 16.478; some people are organized by temperament and others are non-organized 14.523, 17.280

orientalists 3.188, 9.46

Origen introduction 12.740 (n338), 17.759 (n402); dared to say that Satan would be saved 12.513, 12.526; his conception of hell: a purgatory 13.573–4; one of the most attractive figures in the history of Christianity 13.573; St Pachomius' criticism 13.629; story that Jesus was the son of a Roman soldier 13.568, 13.718 (n341); Traductionism: belief in pre-existence before physical birth 17.468–9

original face 13.141, 16.92–3

originality being different is not the same as being original 15.194; characterized by ceaseless productivity 11.25; claimed by the artist who doesn't acknowledge the cultural heritage 3.606; finding a middle way between pseudo-originality and mechanical repetitiveness 4.280–1; Mahāyāna *ācāryas* not original thinkers but systematizers of traditional teachings 1.366–7; originality would seem to be the prerogative of genius 13.345; in poetry, based on tradition 7.59; rarity of original thought 3.302–3; 'There is nothing original here' (Śāntideva) 4.280; Tibetan artists regard striving for originality as an aberration 13.59; we attach importance to it, but in the past it was foreign to people's thinking 14.399–400; you can only produce something original if *you* are original 12.637, 26.374

Orissa (Odisha), India modern Odisha 10.lvi–vii; merchants from Orissa, *see* Bhallika

Oriya Encyclopaedia *see under* Sangharakshita XIII/articles

Orlovsky, Peter 13.612, 22.566–8, 23.123, 25.93

ornaments it's a virtue to be ornamental as well as useful 14.522; Milarepa's ornament is his devotion to the Dharma 18.96; thangkas as drawing room ornaments 19.466, 22.477; ten ornaments of the Buddhist, *see* ten ornaments

Orpheus Orpheus and the modern bard 25.254, 25.257; 'Orpheus in the Underworld' (sonnet) 25.312; a plan for a long poem about Orpheus 24.399; the poet's kin 25.359; Rilke's sonnets 4.593, 4.713–14 (n360); visiting the underworld 25.405

orthodoxy

introduction
definitions and etymology 7.271, 7.517; the belief that someone is so obviously wrong that they cannot be reasoned with 4.127; clinging to orthodoxy, being closed to any other way of looking at things 16.82; negatively defined as 'opposed to heretical and heterodox' 7.522; not making the term wider than necessary 7.524, 7.528; orthodoxy in Christianity 7.521; orthodoxy in relation to natural and conventional morality 7.529–30, 7.544–5; 'orthodoxy is my doxy and heterodoxy is your doxy' 8.172; *see also* neo-orthodoxy

in Buddhism
definition 2.557, 7.524–5; the literal equivalent of right view 2.556–7, 7.520–1; 'The Meaning of Orthodoxy in Buddhism' 2.556–7, 7.514–46, 23.225, 23.434–5; often defined in terms of belief in formulas 7.521; an orthodox Buddhist is one for whom Going for Refuge is primary 2.557–8; doctrinal orthodoxy 7.531–43; a need to return to doctrinal fundamentals 7.271–2; scriptural orthodoxy 7.528–9; Theravāda claim to be the most orthodox 2.556, 7.516–17, 7.530–45, 23.22; Theravādin orthodoxy 22.312–15; the Abhidharma became a disastrous deviation from orthodoxy 7.539; the different ways in which different Buddhist schools are unorthodox 2.558–66; orthodox Buddhists shocked by modern discoveries 13.427; the Orthodoxy Police (parody)

8.133–5; principle in the Triratna Buddhist Community 2.556–67

Orwell, George (Eric Blair) a connection with the Kazini 21.483, 22.415; Big Brother 15.538; Newspeak 2.376, 12.352

oscillations and fluctuations how inspiration fluctuates 18.540–2; oscillation between animal level and level of reasoning 7.421–2; oscillation between pleasure and pain 3.260; physical energy in a state of oscillation 16.144; Sangharakshita's oscillation between extremes 20.68; subtle oscillations between existence and non-existence, Enlightenment and non-Enlightenment 15.223; Westerners' fluctuating interest in karma and rebirth 4.403; you can handle oscillations by placing yourself in stable surroundings 18.541–3

Osiris *see under* Egypt

Ossian 2.35, 2.668 (n56)

Otani, Kocho 8.123–4

other people

introduction
who or what are 'other people'? 12.604–5; what does living for others really mean? 12.9–10

the challenge of other people
being poisoned by other people's negative emotions 11.6, 22.416–17; forbearance towards other people 4.121, 26.81; 'Hell is other people' 4.121; but heaven and purgatory are other people too 12.602; importance of learning how to get on with others 9.189; most of the people you meet entertain false values 4.524–5; temptation to give up on people in despair 4.187–8; the test of our practice is how we relate to the challenge of 'other people' 3.521; they can be very trying, foolish, weak, and misguided 4.189; we must bear with other people, and they must bear with us 26.66; you take a risk every time you approach another person 14.490

being positive
all religions say 'love others', but Buddhism teaches a method 10.156, 10.173; are we becoming more positive but ignoring the difficulties of others? 10.73; be positive towards others in spite of all their failings and your own 4.180; delighting in someone for what they are, you will never find them boring 18.159; how strange that we do not naturally wish others the deepest happiness! 15.308; inculcating a positive mental state in another person through *mettā* 5.177–9; *mettā* is attraction to another person for their sake, not just your own 5.170–1; the *mettā bhāvanā* only works if you really are concerned about others' welfare 17.693; positive feelings must be expressed frequently, fully, and unmistakably 24.383; to be positive towards others most of the time is a big thing 5.185–6

kindness and consideration
the difficulty of doing good to others without harming or irritating them 8.535; to 'Enlighten all beings', start by being kind to them 4.69; if we live a simple life, there will be more for other people 10.396; not doing harm, or causing annoyance or inconvenience, to other people 4.336–7; reaching out to people who are neglected by others 10.86–7; taking as much care of other people as we do of ourselves 15.120–1; what makes people behave with so little consideration for others? 24.440; why should others have to pay the price for your self-expression? 15.494

feeling for others
as well as feeling *with* people, it is important to feel *for* them 4.68; freedom to be *for* others 8.579; it is difficult to enter into another person's experience 17.304; learn to treat people with sympathy, sensitivity, and awareness 11.439; one shouldn't treat people just from a subjective point of view 19.540; putting yourself imaginatively in the place of others 10.476, 10.544, 17.523; showing respect for people's feelings 25.17; some people naturally feel the sufferings of others, while others don't 4.571; *see also* empathy

ethics
ethical acts performed with the sense that others have an absolute existence 1.435; ethics is not just about our own mental state but about how we treat others 11.723–4; giving is the natural interchange of one's energy with that of others 26.35; refusing to recognize that one's relationship with others has an ethical dimension 17.637

others and spiritual life
being sensitive to the degree of Enlightenment in others 4.365; being with other people with a common spiritual objective 12.605–6; communicating the Dharma without being suspected of being a Buddhist 19.207; having confidence in someone else's potential 15.364; if the Dharma element is not there, sooner or later there will be trouble 18.214; it is so important

to make the Buddhist path known to others 15.94–5; once Enlightened, you experience others in a completely different way 17.483; projecting spiritual life onto other people 18.520; spiritual practice is done here in this world, *together* with other people 12.605–7; through spiritual practice we become more sensitive to other people 4.571; use the recollection of death to keep up good relations with other people 19.104; we do our spiritual practice here in this world, together with other people 12.605; we don't always appreciate the progress made by other people 15.364–5

knowing other people
be careful not to develop a formula and apply it to everybody 16.25; be reluctant to come to a value judgement about somebody 10.591; the difficulty of knowing someone near and dear to you 1.520, 15.164; don't assert your way of seeing them over their way of seeing themselves 4.248–9; don't jump to conclusions 10.500–1, 11.441–2, 19.282; it's difficult even for a Buddha to fathom the human mind to its depths 4.360; getting to know another human being is like exploring another world 26.25; getting to know other people more deeply 19.106–8; knowledge of another person is a way of knowing yourself 18.215; impossible to understand quickly or easily 4.41; it's always advisable to reserve one's judgement 19.538; it's difficult to know someone else's state of mind 15.164–5, 19.282, 19.555; it's difficult to see the truth about someone and communicate it to them 17.240; it takes a long time to get to know another person 10.590, 19.100, 19.282; it takes time to find out whether you can rely on someone 15.601–2; the only way is through appreciative attention 14.582; people are mysterious 25.133; they're usually an extraordinary mixture 19.115; to know another person is difficult, so don't rush in with advice 19.355, 19.491; we think we know what is best for others, but we rarely do 17.179; you can't know someone simply through what they have done or said 18.112; you can't ever be sure how somebody is going to act 3.139–40, 18.382; you don't know how they're going to develop 11.661

our effect on others
analysing someone, you may forget the effect on them of what you say 17.661; be careful about how your views affect others 17.259; getting in the way of other people acting 10.604; if you seek the good of others, you must understand what that good is 15.323; the more we develop, the more creative will be our effect on others 15.237; one should feel that one's influence is beneficent, like moonlight 13.82; telling someone a difficult truth, make sure you have their welfare at heart 17.240; the unskilfulness of frightening others 17.180; whatever we do to other people, we are in the long run doing to ourselves 3.106; when you hurt other people, you cause sorrow to the Buddhas 4.435

others' effect on us
adjusting to other people's views at the expense of your own convictions 18.461; can we put ourselves completely in the hands of another person? 18.383–6; if you're not developed your mental state is greatly influenced by other people 15.369; gratitude to others for what they do for us 5.154–5; not caring what other people think about you 19.466; often other people can see more of your potential than you can yourself 18.284; other people don't want you to change 9.418; other people have an effect on us 12.473–4; our dependence on other people 12.653, 15.176–7; the positive effects on us of association with others 11.13, 11.119; studying your mental states and realizing they are not caused by other people 5.672; they introduce us to ourselves, positive and negative 3.400; they tend to see us in a habitual way 11.48; until you're a bodhisattva, worldly people affect you more than you affect them 18.152; we get to know ourselves best in relation to others 3.400–1; we should not expect from others more than they can give 18.16

a sense of separation
the fact that others are others mean that you are isolated, lonely 18.16; it is difficult to get out of contact with other people 19.210; moving beyond narrow concerns to a wholehearted engagement with others 17.698; others are ultimately unreal 1.440; they play an important part in our lives and we can't get on without them 12.602; the true individual is not psychologically dependent on other people 3.470–1; trying to break down class barriers to relate to others as individuals 26.73; unless one can live alone one can't really live with other people 26.27, 26.29; you alone can have your experience, another person's will be quite different 14.593; you are not responsible for other people 14.578; you are only in contact with others through the medium of your own perception 5.179

difficulties
discarding respect for convention may be rationalizing contempt for others 17.667; expressing hatred under the pretext of encouraging others 18.104–5; fooling other people can be dangerous, but fooling oneself is fatal 26.83; interpreting one's own behaviour positively, other people's negatively 19.573; liking someone because they fulfil a need we have 3.593–4; misjudging other people 19.107; misunderstanding people 18.286; often the way we treat other people is due to lack of imagination 5.153, 17.598; the problems of being attached to people 18.330–1; projecting yourself onto another person 18.309–10; regarding others as possessions 10.490; secret joy in others' misfortune 1.505–6; some people don't see others as human 15.138; tendency to want to label other people 3.142; treating another person like a child 5.171; unable to take out your resentment on others, you take it out on yourself 10.524–5; we often treat other people not as persons but as objects 11.439, 12.262; you don't have control over a promise if it involves other people 19.364; your liking of other people mustn't be dislike of yourself 26.25; Zen stories and the tendency to laugh at the stupidity of others 17.279

see also
altruism; awareness or mindfulness of other people, *see under* awareness/four dimensions; empathy; helping other people, *see* helping others; others' needs, *see under* needs; serving others, *see under* service

other shore crossing to the other shore by raft 9.374, 16.514; the way to the other shore of the great ocean of this world of relativity 1.385

other-power (*tariki*)

introduction
brief introduction 3.651 (n165); Amitābha and other-power 1.346–7, 4.138; the irruption into the universe of a factor that confronts our ego-consciousness 1.332; can be included in the framework of conditionality 1.134; it has its place, but we cannot solely rely on it 11.689; and *kṣānti* 4.138–41; self-surrender to the Buddhas and bodhisattvas 4.49, 4.293–4; in the Shin sect of Japan 1.134, 1.199, 1.208, 4.138; in the *Smaller Sukhāvatī-vyūha Sūtra* 1.332; to surrender to it is to transcend the distinction between subject and object 1.346–7

and jiriki (self-power)
the bodhisattva practises both 4.141; a contradiction? 1.208–9, 4.138; each involves the other 4.140; for the Chinese Pure Land school, self-power and other-power are not incompatible 24.533; *jiriki* denies itself, *tariki* affirms the other 7.44; the monkey and the kitten 4.138, 7.366; must go hand in hand, otherwise, religion as a way of life founders 1.348; a polarity in the spiritual life, *kṣānti* and *vīrya* 4.138; reconciled in the bodhisattva ideal 7.44; self-power for the spiritually less advanced, other-power for the more advanced 24.534; Shōdōmon and Jōdomon, *see under* Pure Land Buddhism; which approach one adopts doesn't matter 4.140; the two paths have a common goal, but they won't work together 17.390

other-regarding *see* altruism

Ottama, U 9.56

ottappa (fear of blame) *see apatrapya*

Otto, Rudolf 17.135, 17.727 (n148)

Ouija board 20.351–3, 20.375

Oujen *see* Uḍḍiyāna

Ouspensky, Pyotr Demianovich 22.617 (n340), 23.180, 23.490 (n128)

outsiders Edward Conze as an outsider 17.41–2; the Gnostic idea of being 'a stranger here' 14.492, 23.111, 25.87; the outsider in Trollope's novels 26.581; Sangharakshita as an outsider 23.111, 26.319–20, 26.572–82

Ouyang Jingwu 8.605

Ouyi Zhixu 8.480

overcoming

the challenge
being honest about the limitations we need to overcome 18.147–8; there is so much to be overcome 11.407; the aspects of oneself that need to be overcome 11.4; the difficulties an artist has to overcome 26.193–4; 'I have overcome the world' 16.393; 'Nature is often hidden, sometimes overcome, seldom extinguished' 21.344; 'What the Buddha overcame, we too can overcome' 4.50, 11.293

things to be overcome
'Overcome anger with non-anger' 7.173; attachment to the body 1.155; desires 26.12; Māra 10.522, 10.524; the self, *see under* self/getting rid of the self; selfishness, the root cause of human misery 7.273–5;

sexual craving 17.217–19; the wrong view that one has a fixed self 17.623

ways of overcoming
all spiritual practices will help you to overcome desire for approval 18.639; the *bodhicitta* has the power to overcome evil 4.268, 4.270; the Buddha overcomes spiritual individualism 11.406–7; contemplation of decay overcomes fear 3.346; cultivate contentment to overcome craving and hatred 17.271; helping someone overcome depression can be exhausting 19.550; how the *kleśas* are overcome 11.403–5; love is the only force strong enough to overcome hatred 3.319; the *nidāna* chain to overcome ignorance 11.404; professional help may be needed to overcome alienated awareness 12.268; the search for a practice to overcome the egoistic will 13.628, 20.463–4, 22.394–5; spiritual friends can help you overcome weaknesses 19.153; the *upekkhā bhāvanā* to overcome likes and dislikes 5.206–9; the way to overcome arrogance is to reflect on the Dharma 17.607; 'Wheresoever desires arise, there must they be overcome' 7.171

overman *see under* Nietzsche

overwhelmed alleviating suffering without being overwhelmed by it 4.52; developing positivity so that you feel like a radiant lamp, not overwhelmed by darkness 18.575; the *Diamond Sūtra* an overwhelming experience 2.408, 14.371; an island that no flood can overwhelm 15.580; overwhelmed by the problems of the world 3.616; the overwhelming effect of the Dharma 9.247–8; people were overwhelmed by the Buddha 2.291–2, 9.247, 12.306, 13.249–50; *prīti* 'a driving and even overwhelming emotion' 2.106; sometimes we may feel overwhelmed in our Dharma practice 11.408; your positive ideas can be overwhelmed by reactive tendencies 19.61

Ovid 7.391

Owen, Wilfred 26.395

own-being *see svabhāva*

ownership adhering to the principle of generosity 2.369; connection with paying 16.403; 'Even his self is not his own', *see under Dhammapada*/chapter 5; freedom from ownership 10.489; love is incompatible with a sense of ownership 2.365; *see also* possessions

Oxford academic Oxford an exclusive, conventional, and snobbish place 23.56; Ashmolean Museum 23.124, 23.206; Balliol College: 'I am the Master of this College' 1.197, 17.605; 'home of lost causes' 23.55; the monastic atmosphere of the colleges 23.124; Movement or Group 3.419, 11.207–8, 12.253; Sangharakshita speaks at Linacre House 10.185, 23.81; Sangharakshita speaks to the University Buddhist Society 23.55; a Tibetan refugee in Oxford 23.129; Chögyam Trungpa in Oxford 23.129; a visit to Edward Conze 12.169–70, 23.55–6

P

pabbajjā as going forth, *see* going forth; as ordination, *see under bhikkhu*/ordination

pabhassara (luminous) 1.84

Pabodhana, Dharmachari 11.xiii–xiv, 17.152, 18.xiv

Pabongkhapa Rimpoche 8.659, 8.663–4, v22

paccataṃ veditabbo viññuhī *see under Tiratana Vandanā*

paccaya 1.602 (n93)

paccaya-sannissita-sīla 1.146, 1.149,

paccayākāras *see* twenty-four *paccayākāras*

Pachomius, St 13.629

Pachow, Dr 8.643, 22.126

pacifism 12.357

pācittiya *see under* Vinaya/prātimokṣa

Padam Bahadur (cook) v22

Padmadaka, Dharmachari 26.456

Padmākara 7.507

Padmaloka men's retreat centre *see under* Triratna IV/retreat centres

Padmanabhapuram, India 20.246

Padmanarteśvara 2.178, 13.310

Padmanathan, R. A. v22

Padmapāṇi 4.84, 5.202, 9.313, 11.292, 26.233–4, 26.384, 26.697

Padmapani, Dharmachari brief introduction 24.608 (n31); in India 24.20; painter of the Windhorse fresco 10.199, 10.694 (n233)

pada-parama (literalist) 8.620

Padmaraja, Dharmachari v24

Padmasambhava

INTRODUCING PADMASAMBHAVA

introduction
introduction 2.743–4 (n685), 11.293–4, 12.195–6; his name means 'the Lotus Born' 12.288, 12.317; his appearance 11.294, 13.11, 13.21; as Guru 12.319, 12.323–5; his extraordinary supernormal powers 1.383; he used his magical powers to spread the Dharma 10.448; many-sided: sage, scholar, magician, dancer 13.21; the most distinctive and colourful figure in Tibetan Buddhism 12.295; one of the most remarkable figures in the entire history of Buddhism 13.9; called Urgyen Padmasambhava 22.473–4; the Rainbow-Bodied One 26.673; people resorted to the miraculous to convey his greatness 22.472; the 'Second Buddha' 12.318–19, 13.20–1, 14.263; referred to in Tibet as Guru Rimpoche 13.21; one of the eighty-four *siddhas* 1.381–3, 7.507, 19.214; of the lotus family 13.310

what he represents
he doesn't represent energy in a one-sided psychological way 5.622; human consciousness face to face with death, fear, reality (cremation ground) 13.247; a spiritual reality 22.472; the subduer of the primordial forces in our own unconscious mind 12.325; symbol of the *nirmāṇakāya* 19.201; tackles the gods and demons not just of Tibet, but of the whole world 12.323; the transforming principle 12.334

forms
eight forms 6.xxii–xxiii, 13.20–1, 22.475–6, 26.235–6; *heruka* form 13.247; his *ḍākinī* form, Siṃhamukta 13.244–5; *tertöns* regarded as partial manifestations of Padmasambhava 12.299; as Tubka Shunukyuwa 8.525

iconography and emblems
iconography 12.285–6; eagle's or vulture's feather 12.334, 19.76; skull cup 12.334–5, 19.571; staff 12.335, 26.236; *vajra* (diamond sceptre) 19.571, 22.106

depictions
eight thangkas bought in Kalimpong 6.xxii–xxiii, 22.475–6; illustration 13.190; images 12.285–6, 21.95, 21.214, 22.27, 22.106; a silver image made by Kachu Rimpoche 22.471, 26.228

practice
in the guru yoga 5.562, 13.217; imitating Padmasambhava 19.55; offering a prayer to him in the *chöd* practice 13.268; Padmasambhava mantra 11.288, 14.535; visualized on the Refuge Tree 11.714–15, 13.205–7

inspiration
awe-inspiring 23.132; caves in which the Precious Guru meditated 22.468; people resorted to the miraculous to convey his greatness 22.472; Tamang followers of Padmasambhava 22.265–6, 22.467–9; a teacher of the Dharma needs a Padmasambhava-like quality 16.369; you can admire Padmasambhava without following him 18.223

and Sangharakshita
first encounter, in Darjeeling 8.520, 12.285–6, 21.95, 21.214, 22.27, 22.466–7, 26.673; the figure on a thangka given to him by Jamyang Khyentse 24.12; auspicious purchase of Nyingma texts 2.443; eight thangkas of Padmasambhava bought in Kalimpong 6.xxii–xxiii, 22.475–6; a poem to Padmasambhava 'like a little *sādhana*' 25.xxix, 25.419; receives the *abhiṣeka* from Kachu Rimpoche 2.442, 12.441, 22.469, 22.472–3; strongly drawn to the figure 23.19; 'very much alive in my own life and that of the Order' 26.673; Padmasambhava standing behind him during a talk 23.152, 26.673–4

HIS LIFE STORY

outline of his life
brief account 8.522–4, 12.286, 12.317; his birth from a lotus 1.382, 8.522, 12.288, 19.55, 22.473–4; association with Amitābha 1.382, 8.522, 12.288; association with Amritsar 1.382; his ordination by Ānanda 8.522; he is falsely accused, and delivered by a miracle 8.522, 22.509; he learned astrology from Mañjuśrī 8.522; his education in many Asian countries 12.288–9; contact with Nestorian Christians and Manicheans 3.431–2, 11.297, 12.289; encounters with *dharmapālas* 19.407–8; at the University of Odantapuri 7.425; visits to Bodh Gaya and Nepal 12.290; he is said to have established the Dharma in several countries 8.523; his life interwoven with those of King Aśoka, Nāgārjuna, and Āryadeva 8.523; known by different names at different stages of his career 8.525; departure for the Land of the Rākṣas 12.290, 12.318, 24.161

his female disciples and encounters with ḍākinīs
his accomplished female disciples 16.335; Mandāravā 8.522, 12.199, 13.21; Yeshe Tsogyal 8.521, 13.21; meditates in cremation grounds with the *ḍākinīs* 8.522, 12.289, 12.294, 13.224, 13.247; a *ḍākinī* swallows him, then gives him the Avalokiteśvara initiation 12.287, 22.471

his journey to Tibet
one of the most famous and fateful visits in Buddhist history 12.290; his impact on Tibet 13.10–11; his meeting with the King of Tibet said to have taken place in Kalimpong 22.468; how he came to be invited to Tibet 12.290–1; his visit to Tibet the central event in his life 8.522; he spent 111 years there, we are told 8.523; the building of Samye monastery, *see under* Tibetan Buddhism/monastic life/Samye; the founder of the Nyingma school of Tibetan Buddhism 1.383, 12.298, 13.11; ordination lineage 7.473–4

his conversion of the gods and demons of Tibet
what the legends tell us 12.291–2; what does bringing the demons under control mean? 11.715, 13.9–10, 19.411; Padmasambhava didn't suppress them, but harnessed their energies 18.24–5; the integration of irrational forces 12.292–4; we must harness the same forces in our own culture 11.715, 13.273

Pure Lands
the Copper-Coloured Mountain 8.524, 18.304; Uḍḍiyāna (Urgyen, Oujen), *see* Uḍḍiyāna

HIS TEACHINGS AND WORKS BY AND ABOUT HIM

teachings
the *atiyogayāna* is his special teaching 12.298; 'The books and teachings which you do not practise – give them up!' 4.147; difficult to say much about his teachings 12.295; divided the path to Enlightenment into nine *yānas* 12.296–8, 13.21–3; his works regarded by

Nyingmapas as canonical 14.263; on the sufferings of the six realms 8.524; 'When the iron birds fly in the sky ...' 12.196, 12.300, 12.720 (n144)

Life and Liberation of Padmasambhava (Padma bKa'i Thang)
a description of the text 8.521–4; Nyingma *terma* 2.555, 8.521; advice to the three fortunate women 5.299–302, 5.393–4, 5.423–4, 5.523–4, 24.161; the *ḍākinī* called Adamantine Conqueror of Demons 12.325; Tarpa Nagpo ('Black Salvation') or Mātaraṃgara, see Tarpa Nagpo; book review 8.520–6; comparison to Blake's 'Prophetic Books' 8.521; describes how after every Buddha comes a Guru 12.319; descriptions of *ḍākinīs*, the primordial forces to be subdued 12.324–5; gives a sense that Padmasambhava has come to the West 8.526; inspiration to the Triratna Buddhist Community 2.555; comparable to Italian romantic epics and Arthurian romances 8.521; pervaded by a sense of impermanence and yearning faith 8.526; richness of imagery 2.555

other works
symbolical biographies 1.145, 8.522–4, 12.286–7, 22.108; *The Tibetan Book of the Great Liberation, see under* Evans-Wentz; *The Lotus-Born* (Yeshe Tsogyal) 19.593 (n19); an account of his life that doesn't do him justice 8.345–6; literature about Padmasambhava 8.520–1

see also
Going for Refuge and Prostration practice; Padmasambhava Day, *see under* festivals; *termas*

Padmasiddhi, Dharmachari v24

Padmasuri, Dharmacharini brief introduction 24.650 (n213), 24.656 (n237), 24.703 (n456); leading retreats in India 10.l; a link with Sangharakshita's mother 24.186, 24.378; ordination 24.172; working as a nurse in India 10.l–li

Padmavajra, Dharmachari brief introduction 24.607 (n27); 'Going for Refuge in India' 24.366; in India 10.xl–xli, 10.lx, 10.194, 24.14, 24.19–20, 24.104–9, 25.xxiv–v; member of the Preceptors' College 12.597, 12.631; on Sangharakshita's poems 25.xxiv–xxxi; on the *Udāna* seminars 10.422; photograph 10.194

Padmottara, Buddha 14.175

paganism

HISTORY

pre-Christian and non-Christian
when powers of the earth served religion and forces of religion blessed the earth 23.265; Aztec mother goddess 13.602; Celtic paganism nearly destroyed by the Romans 4.107; the Giant of Cerne Abbas 19.410, 19.615 (n160); the Great Mother of the Mediterranean lands 13.601; Green Men at Rosslyn Chapel 24.584; Indian people's closeness to their pagan roots 13.272; originally all gods were gods of the soil 19.414; a woman who worshipped a milestone 13.272; not all sweetness and light 4.107; the word 'pagan' in a translation of Milarepa 18.441

and Christianity
St Augustine's conversion of the British from paganism 12.75; destruction of pagan symbols 19.67; Easter a pagan festival 3.231; Jesus's associations with the pagan god of harvest 16.163; our old pagan roots destroyed by Christianity 4.105–6, 12.253–4; the old gods were not destroyed but repressed 12.295; the overthrow of paganism mentioned by Dr Ambedkar 9.104; a pagan atmosphere in a Roman Catholic cathedral 23.253; pagan gods and goddesses seen as devils 13.595; pagan temples converted into Christian places of worship 23.310–11; in some ways Christianity was an improvement 4.107; the Virgin Mary acquired some of the attributes of the pagan Great Mother 13.601–2

the need for revival
the basic energies that find their expression in nature also exist in us 13.273; the British countryside has been denuded of gods 19.413; freedom from Christian conditioning in moral matters 12.254; losing our emotional connection with our pagan past 19.410–11; praise to our patient Mother Earth 25.177; a positive attitude towards Nature and towards oneself as part of Nature 26.14; a revival of paganism 4.106–7, 12.254–5; the Romantic movement a reassertion of pagan values 15.139

a combination of paganism and Buddhism?
'before Buddhism can thrive, paganism must be revived' 12.254–5; equating bodhisattva worship with polytheism reduces Buddhism to a pagan cult 2.172; how to be achieved? 4.107–9; perhaps if we make contact with the old gods, they will protect the Dharma 12.295

NATURE SPIRITS

introduction
the relationship of the Buddha to nature spirits 3.597–8; Burmese Buddhists worship Nats, spirits of wood and water 26.667; a purge of nature spirits in Judaism 19.414; the *yakkha*, an awe-inspiring natural force 10.451

tree spirits (rukkha-devatā)
the Buddha's gratitude to the tree under which he gained Enlightenment 3.597–8; dryads 15.139; their communication with the Buddha's disciples 10.452–3, 19.413; the personification of the psychic atmosphere of a place 18.22; a tree spirit is threatened by a creeper 10.708 (377); worshipping tree spirits 10.647

Pagare, H. M. 10.123

pagoda 16.150–1, 16.156, 19.41–2

pain

the nature of pain
association with the body means the possibility of pain 18.557–8; could pain be due to past karma? 10.502–4; the desire to be rid of pain contributes to it 17.507; the distinction between physical and mental pain 3.184; if you're really happy you can experience pain and not be worried by it 19.583; pain arising from making too much effort 10.228; a sensation, and hence indefinable 1.127; we tend to concentrate on pain to the exclusion of everything else 4.315

examples from Buddhist tradition
the Buddha's backache 3.184, 10.236, 14.238; in old age the Buddha was only free of pain when in *dhyāna* 15.156, 19.422; for Milarepa, an opportunity to experience the unconditioned nature of joy 18.47

pain and spiritual practice
'If it hurts it must be doing me good' is not a Buddhist attitude 10.503, 15.450; if you find the idea of hells too much, transfer it to painful experiences in this life 4.372; in a sense you don't feel the pain, because it doesn't absorb all your attention 4.391; the more you develop, the more pain and suffering are eliminated 19.426; 'Pain shall be transmuted into joy …' 23.446; pain transformed into joy 4.316–17; seek to learn from painful situations rather than run away from them 8.526; when the pain caused by craving is eliminated, one is left with bliss 19.126; with practice, even within painful experience there will be a deep happiness 15.221; you don't have to suffer pain in order to make progress 10.228, 17.252

see also
dukkha; pain and pleasure, *see under* pleasure

Pain, Colonel J. R. 10.139, 12.71

Paine, Thomas 8.560, 26.349, 26.587–8

painters *see* artists

painting *see under* art/works of art

Paiśāci 16.591 (n38)

pakati-sīla *see under* ethics

Pakistan 20.168–71, 21.69, 21.104–6

Pakudha 1.74

pāla 16.288

palace Indra's palace, where you can find everything you could desire 16.346; the key of right motive opens the portals of the Palace of Wisdom 1.22; 'The Palace of Art', *see under* Tennyson; the palace as mandala 12.221, 18.525; the path and the palace as alternative symbols of spiritual life 18.525; scrambling up the tree of one's intellect to try to reach the Palace of the Dharma 1.184; Siddhārtha's palaces, *see under* Siddhārtha/upbringing

Palestine 3.427, 3.429, 12.248

Pāli based on a dialect spoken close to the time of the Buddha 9.480; 'Burmese' 8.119–20, 21.109, 22.171; a 'dead' language 9.316; delight of being able to study the Buddha's teaching in 'his own words' 20.445–6; dictionary 1.97, 12.70; grammar 20.445; getting bogged down in studying Pāli grammar 10.123, 19.132–3, 25.9–10, 26.560–1; not the name of a language at all 7.499, 14.12; reasons for chanting the Refuges and Precepts in Pāli 19.133; relationship of Pāli literature to that of other languages 14.289; Sangharakshita learns Pāli 15.5–5, 20.328–9, 20.445–6; the Theravāda's insistence that the Buddha spoke Pāli 14.13–14; the word means 'a line of the sacred text' 7.499, 14.12

Pāli canon

introduction
brief introduction 3.161, 10.424–5, 15.4; historical and spiritual importance 16.531–2; how the teachings were collected 10.435–6; gratitude to its compilers 15.234; first committed to writing 1.326, 4.24, 13.339–40, 14.101, 14.341; much of it is in verse 26.128; written in three kinds of Pāli

10.220; the nine *aṅgas* of the Pāli canon 14.23–5; most of our physical evidence for the Pāli canon is very recent 8.618

its features
the Buddhism it describes belongs to the realm of historical reality 16.529; descriptions of *devas* intervening in the spiritual life of *bhikkhus* 19.413; the Buddha's *rūpakāya* and *dharmakāya* 1.254–6, 13.300–1, 16.60; far from deficient in teachings of a positive character 1.227; an idea of how the ideas in the Buddha's teaching evolved 8.618–21; imprecision in the use of terms 1.86; in it one sees myths in the process of emerging 4.37; insists on real Dharma practice, not the outward trappings 18.520; it describes the career of the disciple 1.96; it seems intended more for monks than lay people 1.272; it tends to describe the path in terms of extinction 1.120; its style and structure reflect its origin in the oral tradition 14.22–3, 15.180; no reference to Enlightenment as experience 11.73; not much requires explanation, and the Buddha explains where needed 11.719; not the sole criterion of what is and what is not Buddhism 7.499; our main source of early Buddhist teachings, but not the definitive record 1.185; our principal source of information about the Buddha 6.xxv; strangely silent with regard to meditation methods 1.379; teachings which are present in the Pāli canon but little regarded 1.84–5; the world of the Pāli canon 22.462–3

its vivid picture of the Buddha's life and times
a vivid sense of the Buddha as he appeared to people 17.402, 25.11; if choosing one Pāli work to get this sense, choose the *Udāna* 10.641; the light it sheds on India at that time 14.301; read its accounts of the Buddha's life slowly, mindfully, and imaginatively 26.635–6; replete with allusions to contemporary events and conditions 14.98, 16.236, 16.529; source of biographical information about the Buddha 17.402, 26.511; through its older sections the Buddha can become a living figure for us 11.717; you feel that a real historical period is being described 10.465–6

the flavour of the Pāli canon
an altruistic element 4.5–6; contains little trace of what the Mahāyāna calls the Hīnayāna 17.547; delicacy and refinement 1.240; examples of compassion 1.236; expressions of faith in the Buddha 1.240; free from ordinary human passion 1.240; mainly conceptual 12.210–11; mechanical approach 14.23, 15.235–6; nature as a living presence 15.136; poetical in spirit 26.128; rich in mythical and legendary material 4.37; set in a down-to-earth world 14.396; some parts thrill with quiet enthusiasm or glow with serene happiness 1.240; traces of the ideal of beauty 13.279

considering its authenticity
all the teachings are there, but their implications took time to develop 14.351–2; claims that the Pāli canon is the only canonical literature 7.31–2, 11.379, 14.341; it transmits the Buddha's words more faithfully than any other source 7.226–7; literally the word of the Buddha? 17.157; Pāli fundamentalists among Western Buddhists 11.379; pure chance that the Pāli canon was the version of the teachings preserved 15.184

compared with Mahāyāna sūtras
both have an outward-going basis 16.29; general comparison 14.96–100, 14.341–2, 16.235–7; continuity of development between *Nikāyas* (and *Āgamas*) and the *sūtras* 14.96; Mahāyāna *sūtras* more profound? 16.59–60; Mahāyāna *sūtras* supply an element missing from Pāli texts 16.532; some Pāli texts strangely anticipate the Mahāyāna 7.526–7; a very different atmosphere, but the same teaching 7.529; whereas Pāli literature is a cosmos, Sanskrit literature is a chaos 1.277; written down at around the same time 1.326

translation, study, ritual
the critical study of Pāli literature 10.219–21; the effect of the ceremonial chanting of Pāli texts 15.436; influence of Protestantism on early Western translators 11.207–8; little higher criticism applied 2.627; the need to be able to assess translations 15.373–4; studied in the Triratna Buddhist Community 12.368

Sangharakshita and the canon
an idea for an anthology of its poetic presentations of the Dharma 10.569; studying the Pāli scriptures in his old age 11.690; suggestions for a chronology of the Pāli canon 8.131, 22.170–3; suggests a uniform system of referencing quotations 8.130–1

see also
individual *nikāyas* (within which *suttas* are listed); oral tradition; Sanskrit equivalent, *see Āgamas*; Abhidharma/Abhidharma Piṭaka; Sutta Piṭaka; Tripiṭaka; Vinaya Piṭaka

Pali Text Society 12.70, 12.706 (n40), 13.357

Palladio, Andrea 23.257, 23.512 (n293)

Pallas Athene born from the head of Zeus 16.385; a calmly beautiful bas-relief 23.285; compared to Mañjuśrī 16.385; her bird the owl 25.397; in the story of the golden apples 26.469–70; statue of Hercules and Pallas Athene at Olympia 23.299; statue in Munich 24.588; statue in Naples 25.512

Pallis, Marco (Thubden Tendzin)

introduction
accompanies the Sacred Relics 21.208; admires the good looks of a student 22.338; asked to leave Kalimpong because of support for Tibetan resisters 21.228, 21.544; influenced by René Guénon 23.121; generosity 21.315; musician 21.160, 23.121; mysteriousness 21.160, 21.228; a pedantic talk at Wesak 23.122; Universalist 21.161

his friendship with Sangharakshita
began with the reading of *Peaks and Lamas* 20.151, 21.159; meetings in Kalimpong 21.159–63, 21.228–30; gives Sangharakshita funds to set up a new centre in Kalimpong 22.378; he sends Sangharakshita Buddhist books from London 22.224–5, 25.132–3; helps Sangharakshita communicate with Tibetans 21.176; he visits the vihara 8.664; meetings in London 23.121, 23.240

works
the bodhisattva ideal 'the presiding idea of Tibetan Buddhism' 3.133–4, 13.38; *Peaks and Lamas* 7.462, 8.399, 20.150–1, 21.68, 21.179; 'Sikkim Buddhism Today and Tomorrow' 21.195, 21.205; 'Some Aspects of a Buddhist Education' 8.643, 22.125

Palmer, Samuel 19.600 (n59)

Palmerston, Lord 24.359

pamojja *see* joy

pāṇātipāta 2.358–9

pañca-gati (five 'goings') 2.73

pañcāṅga-praṇama (prostrations) *see under* devotion/physical expressions

Pañcasikha the *gandharva* (Sanskrit Pañcaśikha) celestial song 26.121–3; in the *Mahāgovinda Sutta* 26.474; association with Mañjuśrī 2.173, 26.474

pañcasīla *see* precepts/five precepts

Pañcaviṃśatisāhasrikā *see Perfection of Wisdom in 25,000 lines*

Panchamas 9.31

panchang-pranam 9.338, 9.507

panchayat 22.410–12

Panchen Lama brief introduction 2.747 (n704), 22.609 (n296); the Chinese insistence on his equal status with the Dalai Lama 2.572–3, 13.39; emanation of Amitābha 13.39, 22.487; his arrival in India 13.39, 22.364–5; the reincarnation of the first abbot of Tashi Lhunpo 13.36

Panchgani, India 9.207, 10.161

Pāṇḍaravāsinī brief description 17.729–30 (n166); appears in verses to Tārā 17.146; also known as White Tārā 12.222; Amitābha's consort 1.263, 12.222, 13.315; insulated in purity, like the illustration of the fourth *dhyāna* 13.315; it is said that her robe is on fire 19.570; light red in colour 13.315

pandas 22.345

Pande, Govind Chandra 2.627, 2.755 (n775)

Pandit-ji *see* Chatterjee

Panggang Rimpoche 23.335–6

Pāṇini (grammarian) 16.35

pañña *see prajñā*

pañña-vimutti *see under vimukti*

paṇṇati-sīla *see under* ethics

paññattis 19.85, 19.597–8

Paññavaddho 23.47

pansil 2.410–11, 2.419, 2.438, 12.302, 20.102

Pant, Apa B. 8.664, v22, 23.376, 23.415

pantheism introduction 9.228–9; cosmic pantheism 14.459; one should be careful to avoid naive pantheism 5.597; sometimes the emptiness of all *dharmas* is interpreted as a sort of pantheism 14.603; two ways to look at pantheism 14.603

pāpa (evil) 16.290

pāpadeśanā (confession of faults) *see under* devotion/Sevenfold Puja/confession

Papini, Giovanni 7.88, 7.577 (n167)

para (further shore) 1.69, 15.58

pāra (beyond) 1.69

parables and stories

introduction
humanity has always loved stories 14.61; 'intelligent people through a parable reach understanding' 12.110–11, 16.215; as a method of teaching the Dharma 9.226–7, 10.238; 'once upon a time' (*bhūtapubbam*) 10.596; parables of the *suttas* 14.42; teaching the Dharma through telling stories 15.445–6; an anthology of stories would correct any impression that Buddhism is dry 10.569; some of the Buddha's stories have been taken too literally 10.596; stories as vehicles of religious instruction 26.105; they can be more illuminating than pages of psychological analysis 2.71; they support faith 9.110; they take place outside time 16.171

animal stories
the deer who need to stay safe up in the mountains 18.34; the donkey who said he was a cow 3.401, 9.192–3, 9.273; the fish and the turtle 10.685–6 (n175); the fox who lost his tail 19.358; the frog and the elephant 15.423–4, 16.299; the great fish Timiratipiṅgala finds room in the great ocean 14.91; Indra and the squirrel 3.305, 10.356; the ocean frog and the frog in the well 1.198, 9.372, 10.256, 26.105–6, 26.110; the parrot who let out his natural squawk 12.96, 18.249; realizing that one is grasping a snake, not a fish 2.116; the snake who could neither swallow a frog nor throw it up 10.490, 11.279, 15.94

stories about men and boys
the bliss of a man who travels through the desert and bathes in a lake 2.107–8; the boy scout who helped an old lady across the road 15.323; a foolish man and a mad elephant 18.632–3; the greedy brahmin 9.288; John and the path of irregular steps 11.59–62; the king who couldn't concentrate for seven days 3.271–2; a king who is convinced by a wise man that there is no point in conquest 19.337–8; an old man and a young man help victims of a famine 16.12–14; a man who caused an accident and interpreted the result as a miracle 17.63–4; the man who forgot where he'd left his umbrella, *see under* umbrella; the merchant in the desert 9.264; the wise physician and the prohibited cure 14.235; the young man who learned compassion through chess 1.504–5, 8.496

stories about women
Queen Vaidehī's vision of the Pure Land 1.332–4, 3.454–5, 3.571–2, 14.172–3, 20.464; the housewife who served boots to her ungrateful family 17.201; Kisā-Gotamī and the mustard seed 3.357–8, 9.233–4, 14.18; the milkmaid who spilled the milk 19.9; realizing that a woman being assaulted is your mother 13.81, 17.193; the serving girl and the rolling pin 9.522; the woman and the fish-basket 16.470–1; the woman who prayed to Amitābha 3.249–50, 16.201–2; the woman who worshipped a dog's tooth 2.71, 13.198–9, 19.327; a woman who worshipped a milestone 13.272; the woman who said she would go mad with no-one to talk to 21.449

stories about monks, gurus, sages, and disciples
the Daoist sage who went fishing without using any bait 14.518–19; the disciple who began with a strip of cloth and ended up with a farm 18.199–201; the guru who tied a kitten to a post 19.55; a guru whose 'greatness' was just inconsiderate behaviour 19.161–2; a monk who occupied a cell for forty years but never noticed its frescoes 13.279; the monk who ran to help a woman catch her train 4.86–7, 14.556; the monk who carried a girl over a stream 2.71, 8.496; the monk who gained Enlightenment on seeing a leaf fall 3.272; the monk who told bandits a lie to save someone 3.323, 7.118; the Zen master who told his disciple to be careful climbing down a tree 10.532

a few more stories
the ancient way to the ancient city 1.53–4, 1.81, 3.18, 10.567, 11.408–9; lovers who respond completely differently to a beggar 15.164; a Tibetan caravan is attacked by bandits 18.99–100; a parable of the good ship FWBO (in 2003) 26.453–5; the

poisoned arrow 1.112, 4.374, 16.93–4, 16.192, 18.442; the robbers who carve you limb from limb 1.437, 4.121, 8.200, 13.577, 14.475; the twentieth blow 2.282–3, 11.13, 12.177–8, 12.626, 14.456–7; the two paths 1.81–2

see also
the blind men and the elephant, *see under Udāna*; *Jātakas*; the parable of the raft, *see* raft; *White Lotus Sutra* parables, *see under White Lotus Sutra*

Paracelsus 8.560, 20.63

paracittajñāna *see* telepathy

Paradise 20.112

Paradise Lost *see under* Milton

paradox

introduction
as a description of the spiritual life 2.130; as an approach to reality 16.329; describing an ineffable state by juxtaposing contradictory attributes 2.130; a metaphor may be taken literally, a paradox never 26.207; paradoxes are needed to do justice to the non-conceptual nature of Reality 7.489; paradoxes are useful because you can't take them literally 19.242; transformed by the Mahāyāna into meditation subjects 1.82; truth standing on its head to attract attention 16.132, 26.200; used to describe the indescribable 26.201

paradoxes of the Buddhist tradition
the Buddha lived at a time and place, but manifests something beyond time and space 18.86; the paradoxes of the Buddhist scriptures are real contradictions 26.200; if the Dharma is inexpressible, how is it to be taught? 16.450; all is renounced for others so that all may be renounced 4.624; Buddha nature – 'you' and not 'you' 4.271; the bodhisattva as living paradox 26.202; the bodhisattva leads beings to Nirvāṇa with no perception of beings to save 1.395–6, 2.159, 7.154–5, 7.409, 10.165; in the Perfection of Wisdom 2.131, 3.87, 3.220, 7.489, 11.14, 14.xiv, 14.583–4, 16.329, 26.200–2; translogical matters can only be expressed in paradoxes (*Diamond Sūtra*) 14.467; Prajñāpāramitā-like paradox in the *Gaṇḍavyūha Sūtra* 14.225–6; in Zen Buddhism 2.131

doctrinal paradoxes
dhyāna is both active and passive 17.123–4; Enlightenment is an experience in which there is neither subject nor object 12.614; the existence and evident absence of the self 17.375; the experience of *prajñā* 17.547; the only affirmation of the Absolute possible is the negation of all affirmations 7.132; only that which has no support is truly supported 1.438–9, 14.477, 26.83; *śūnyatā*: known by not knowing 10.160; the sense of doing without a doer 10.602–3

paradoxes of life
he only is happy who does not care for happiness 7.412; life, but nobody lives it, suffering, but nobody suffers 7.133; the more we grasp pleasure, the more we find we are holding onto pain 17.506; most people spend their life in pursuit of things they do not want 7.294; the paradox of life and death 12.396; the paradoxes of modern science 17.375; the paradoxical nature of human self-delusion 17.163; to get what you want, you have to forget all about wanting it 17.208; you're not really free if you're at the mercy of every passing whim and fancy 18.489

paradoxes of spiritual life
cutting off ties will be your best companion 18.621; egos coming together with the objective of achieving egolessness 12.605–6; if you open up you will be protected 10.559, 10.570–1; inspiration and spontaneity come from discipline and regular practice 17.459–60; keeping the non-defiled mind clean 18.323; the more we strive to be spiritual, the more unspiritual we become 7.413; religion, intended to eradicate reason, has become an agent for augmenting it 7.281; to aspire to *nirvāṇa* simply strengthens the bonds which bind one to *saṃsāra* 7.413; to be truly free one has to escape not only from bondage but from liberation 2.56; to want to become a Buddha is the surest way of remaining ordinary 7.412; the warrior ideal in the context of the ideal of the flower 18.106; we can only get rid of ignorance because it is not there 17.408; you can't get rid of the ego until you've got an ego to get rid of 4.511; you can't realize the true mind, and yet the possibility of realizing it exists 18.233; you only see your own mind when there's no mind to see 19.103

pārājikas (defeats) *see under* Vinaya/*prātimokṣa*

Parakamma, King 4.24

Parakramabahu, King 8.468

Paramabandhu, Dharmachari 26.663

Paramabodhi, Dharmachari v24

paramānanda (bliss arising from the *dhyānas*) 2.91

Paramārtha Vasubandhu's biographer 1.365; introduction of Yogācāra school into China 1.371; *Diamond Sūtra* translation 14.151; *Śūraṅgama Sūtra* translation 14.197, 14.260; *Sūtra of Golden Light* translation 14.241

Paramartha, Dharmachari his life and travels with Sangharakshita v24, 26.408, 26.456–7, 26.738 (n372); friendship with Sangharakshita 24.307, 24.403, 26.542–51, 26.548–9, 26.581–2, 26.625–7; he goes to New Zealand to care for his mother 26.548–9, 26.581–2; poems to his partner Deji 25.453, 25.459; a letter to Paramartha 26.542–51; on a visit to Suffolk with Sangharakshita 26.507–14; his poem to his brother 25.427; poems to him 25.xxxv, 25.394, 25.405, 25.453, 25.454

paramārtha-satya (Pāli *paramattha-sacca*, absolute truth) *see* two truths

Paramashanti, Dharmachari v24

paramātman *see under ātman*

Paramatthajotikā *see under* Buddhaghosa

Parami, Dharmacharini 4.ix–xiv, 12.674, 24.312, 24.685 (n386), 26.549

pāramitās *see* perfections

Pāramitāsamāsanāma 17.575

Pāramitāyāna (or Pāramitānaya) 11.290–1, 13.288–9, 16.359, 26.698

paranoia hatred arising from paranoia 17.601; hungry ghosts project their paranoia onto others 19.497; imagining that people disapprove of us 17.652; paranoia and imagination 11.724; paranoia as projection 17.258–9; the paranoia of absolute rulers 17.258–9

parasambhoga 1.262

parasol symbolism 3.48; in the *Vimalakīrti-nirdeśa* 4.31, 14.158, 16.455, 16.465–6

parassa cetopariya-ñāṇa *see* telepathy

paratantra *see* three *svabhāvas*

parātmaparivartana (substitution of self and others) *see under* self/and other

parātmasamatā (equality of self and others) *see under* equality

parāvṛtti (turning about in the deepest seat of consciousness) brief introduction 13.235; all our ways of looking at things turned topsy-turvy 2.276, 12.174; in the *Bodhicaryāvatāra* 4.370; comes about in the *ālaya vijñāna* 2.280, 12.176, 17.486–7; compared to the *bodhicitta* 4.261; a great death and rebirth 17.481; how do we bring it about? 2.281–3, 12.174–7, 12.177–8; implies that Enlightenment is sudden – but the preparation takes a very long time 2.284–5; as knowledge and vision of things as they really are 3.275; in the *Laṅkāvatāra Sūtra* 1.358, 2.276–7, 3.88, 4.691 (n218), 10.620, 12.174, 14.210, 14.315; profound spiritual experience 26.347; synonymous with conversion 12.174; takes place when one realizes the illusory nature of the ego 14.315; a talk on the subject in 1966 23.232; the teaching draws attention to the fact that intellectual understanding is not enough 2.283–4

parāvṛtti-vijñāna (evolving consciousness) *see* eight *vijñānas*

Parbhani, India 9.379

parents

RELATING TO YOUR CHILDREN

having children
becoming a parent is easy, but being a good parent is very difficult 3.532; creativity as spiritual childbirth 26.316–18; the desire to have children 11.577, 11.581; seeing and getting between future parents in the *bardo* of rebirth 12.205; there are many other beings in the world who need our help 11.580–1; in Hinduism, it's a sin not to have children 12.245–6; a woman who desires to have a child is exhorted to pray to Avalokiteśvara 2.176

bringing children up
fifteen points for Buddhist parents 3.532–44; all aspects of parenting to be done in a loving spirit 3.544; attachment to children brings sorrow 10.651–2; bringing them up in a loving, peaceful, and supportive atmosphere 26.658; children don't just belong to their parents 3.537; could join a parent-teacher association 12.488; difference between mother's and father's attitude 15.418–20; they need bodily contact 4.562; they need consistency 16.429; the duty of a friend to show concern for our dependants 3.574; 'The first principle of good parenting is to let the child alone' 18.184; the importance of believing what children say 19.20–1; 'Let a child feel your healthy, hot anger' (Lawrence) 15.432; the middle way between being too easy-going and being too strict 9.440; opportunities for insight in childcare 5.638; parents are divine kings on a small scale 16.428–9; parents' power over children 26.656–8; power mode

in relation to children 16.433, 16.434; punishment 9.523; restrict television 3.535–6, 26.359; socializing 3.537–8, 17.638; a spirit of mutual giving between parents and children 3.593–4; training children (advice given in India) 10.161; treating children as friends 3.539; try to learn to feel as much for your neighbour's child as for your own 26.71; the welfare of your child is not necessarily the same as what they want 15.293; why should any parent torture their own child? 26.656

education
caring for the environment 3.541; confused thinking about what children should be taught 3.532; don't be afraid to teach them the Dharma 3.533; don't talk down to children 12.586; the most important thing about education is that it does no harm to the child 18.285; must be taught awareness of other people 9.439–40; the need for moral guidance 8.176–7; parents as teachers 3.70, 3.603; parents' duty to bring up their children in knowledge and practice of the Dharma 22.94; should learn rights and duties as citizens 9.440; respecting other people's property and considering other people's feelings 3.537, 26.71; teach them that actions have consequences 16.428–9; teach them empathy 1.498, 3.542–3, 10.477, 26.71; teach them not to be cruel to other living beings 1.498–9, 10.477; teach them to speak properly 3.539

RELATING TO YOUR PARENTS

attitude to parents
blaming them 3.600, 18.521–2; clear up any misunderstandings and express appreciation 19.104; the crucial relationship from an ethical point of view 17.637–8; the importance of developing positive feelings 3.599, 4.328–9, 9.447–8; finding a middle way between conformity and rebellion 12.390–2; forgive your parents if necessary 18.510; generation gap 18.509–10; 'A good man always loves his parents' (Gurdjieff) 16.297; gratitude 3.599–601, 16.297, 25.423; growing away from your parents as a result of spiritual growth 12.390; ingratitude 3.601, 3.607; internalized parent 12.390; it is hardly possible to have a neutral attitude 26.25; it's in your own best interests to have a good relationship 15.409, 16.296–8; a lot is invested in the relationship, so try to make it positive 12.391–2; making a break while maintaining a positive connection 15.410–12, 16.107; *mettā* towards them 3.599, 5.156–8, 16.297; monks' resentment at being handed over to the sangha by their parents 19.475; one's parents often give bad advice 19.355; psychological ties 19.521; relationship improved through spiritual practice 13.451; seeing them in perspective 3.37; sons' ill treatment of their parents 18.210; when parents have died 16.297; when visiting one's parents, danger of slipping back into infantile attitudes 3.37; killing one's parents, *see* five heinous crimes

advice from the Buddhist tradition
five ways of ministering towards parents (*Sigālaka Sutta*) 3.600; imagining your parents in the Going for Refuge and Prostration Practice 13.212; support of parents (*Maṅgala Sutta*) 15.407–9; 'You have no mother and no father to take care of you' 11.442–3

reflection that all living beings have been one's mother and father
a belief that the Tibetans feel in their bones 13.80–1; bonds of solidarity 2.161–2, 25.297; 'a cause of regret to abandon any being, for all have been our kindly parents' 5.152–5; 'I accept the infinite world of living beings as my mother, father ...' 2.207; even if you don't find the argument convincing, develop the attitude 13.81, 19.540; a helpful reflection for modern people? 5.153–5, 18.506; not an argument we find easy to accept in the West 19.539–40; one of the three types of Tantric practice 22.510; reflecting on this, generosity becomes an ever-expanding circle 1.426; suggests a strong belief in the reality of rebirth 18.506, 19.540; in *The Three Chief Paths* 17.427; a way of overcoming indifference to the world's suffering 13.81

parikalpita *see* three *svabhāvas*

parikamma-nimitta *see nimitta*

pariṇāma (transformation) 14.215

pariṇāmanā (transference of merit) *see under* merit, Sevenfold Puja

parinibbāyati ('Nirvanize') 10.614, 15.373

parinirvāṇa *see under* Buddha

Parinirvāṇa Day *see under* festivals

pariniṣpanna *see* three *svabhāvas*

pariññā (penetration) 14.90

Paris *see under* France

Paris (son of Priam) 26.469–70

pārisuddha *see under* ordination/*bhikkhu*

pariṣuddhi (ceremony of confession) 2.189, 2.199

pārisuddhi sīlas *see* four *pārisuddhi sīlas*

***paritrāna* ceremonies** *see under* festival, celebrations, and ceremonies

paritrāṇa sūtras 15.xii–xiii, 20.434

parivrājaka (mendicant, wanderer) *see* wanderers

pariyesanā *see under ariyapariyesanā*

Parmenides introduction 7.595–6 (n297); the denial of the existence of the world of appearance 7.194; his Eleatic method compared to that of Nāgārjuna 17.450

Parr, Stephen *see* Ananda

Parratt, Raymond 26.418

Parrinder, Edward 12.115

Parsis *see* Zoroastrianism

Pārśva 13.341–2

Parthenon 2.644, 23.284–5

parties giving offence at a tea party 19.255; hard to imagine having a party as part of a Buddhist festival 16.370–1; 'I felt like Alice at the Mad Hatter's tea party' 23.355; leaving party in Kalimpong 23.398; mindful people at a party would make it disintegrate 17.100–1

Pārvatī (Hindu goddess) 7.428, 7.612 (n451), 10.46

pasāda (sensitivity) 14.80

Pāsādika Sutta *see under Dīgha Nikāya*

Pascal, Blaise 'Extremes meet' 11.497; 'If Cleopatra's nose had been shorter the history of the world would have been different' 8.73; a grain of dust can destroy us if it gets in the wrong place 4.76; Pascal's wager 13.531, 13.715 (n302); 'The eternal silence of these infinite spaces terrifies me' 14.504

Pasenadi, King (Sanskrit Prasenajit) discusses with Queen Mallikā whether there is anyone dearer to one than one's own self 10.543–6; employs spies disguised as ascetics 10.588–93; ruler of Kosala 2.25, 10.472–3; example of a sincere follower who does not gain insight 3.674 (n306); he has confidence in the Buddha 10.540; he is convinced he is the poorest man in Śrāvastī (Mahāyāna *sūtra*) 14.185; he has some business to do with Visākhā 10.498; his faith in the Buddha traced in the *Majjhima Nikāya* 14.41; his rivalry with King Bimbisāra of Magadha (*Udāna*) 10.472–3; he offers oil to recluses and brahmins 10.487; the same age as the Buddha 10.589; his daughter Pure Giving (in a Mahāyāna *sūtra*) 14.183–4

Pasolini, Pier Paolo 13.650, 16.504

passaddhi *see praśrabdhi*

passion the Buddha sees beings tormented by feverish longings born of passion 10.521–5; the crime of passion 18.208, 18.309–10; the *ḍākinī* is that which arouses your passion for the Dharma 18.371, 18.425; from passion to greed to infatuation to addiction to intoxication 10.616–17; 'One who loves the Dharma passionately, progresses' 13.274–5; the Pāli canon free from ordinary human passion 1.240; a path for the dust of passion 1.58; pure passion 7.402–3; 'stupid and silly actions done by people befuddled and victimized by passion' 4.407; 'little dust of passion on their eyes', *see under* Brahmā Sahāmpati's request; to be truly Buddhist, our involvement with the Dharma must be truly passionate 26.57; unless you love the Dharma passionately, you cannot live the life of renunciation authentically 18.133

see also
mahā-rāga; five *kleśas*; a reliable teaching will lead towards dispassion, *see under* Mahāpajāpati Gotami

passivity

the nature of passivity
the ego is still there even in a passive person 15.387–8; embarking upon family life is usually a passive thing 18.457; everything we experience is either something that happens to us or something we do 17.476–8; the passive enjoyment of the art-lover 26.181; the passivity of heaven and hell 19.580; people think of themselves as busy, but there may be an underlying passivity 19.582; the root of *saṃsāra* is our own passive attitude 19.580

its difference from other states
the difference between being passive and being blocked 15.387–8; the difference between passivity and receptivity 15.387, 15.551–3, 19.581, 26.65; the lives of the gods are blissful, but passive 1.444; passivity is at best a pleasurable state, happiness is active 19.583, 26.63; what people think of as activity is often just passivity 19.582

passivity and Buddhism
the Buddha was against passivity in respect of the good 15.387; Buddhism seen as a passive, negative, gutless tradition 3.45,

3.287; Buddhists should be not passive but the embodiment of energy 3.287; ironically, people think of meditation as a form of passivity 19.582; paradoxically, *dhyāna* is both active and passive 17.123–4; the passive role of the Buddha's disciples 26.181–2

passivity and the spiritual life
ask yourself at any time of the day whether you are being active or passive 19.581; the goal is create a Pure Land, not endlessly consume spiritual goodies 17.243; never become passive in a situation where you are under pressure 18.456; no passengers in the spiritual life 14.577; passively expecting spiritual experience 11.82–4; passivity is the complete antithesis of spiritual life 18.456–8; preparation is not an entirely passive thing 25.85; to make progress, start experiencing yourself as acting rather than acted upon 26.63

past

going back into the past
action may not be based on the afflictions of the past 10.622; an attempt to be objective about the past that has no hope of success 3.423; being haunted by ghosts of the past (*White Lotus Sūtra*) 16.70; a crystal ball showing the past 25.403; do you need to go back into the past to resolve unskilful mental states? 18.442–5; the ghost, Yesterday 25.308; the individual must be liberated from the past 13.468; it can be helpful to keep a diary, to keep a clear view of the past 17.402; meeting people who know you as you are now, not stuck in the past 18.204; no question of a return journey in the sense of going back into the past 16.100–1; the past is in the mind 25.390; some people dwell on the supposed joys of the past 17.401–2; we automatically edit the past when we think about it 17.402; 'Yesterday's Blossoms' (poem) 25.402; you may need to go back a bit, but concentrate on looking forward 18.444

past, present, future
as Buddhists we have to look beyond past, future, and even present 25.22; an experience neither past nor present, a process outside time 18.613; the fact that actions have consequences connects us to both past and future 11.657; imagination loses itself in the future and in the past 7.285; linking with past and future helps us break out of the cocoon of the present 17.403; past, present, and future are only relatively real 17.405; past and future the product of our ethical decisions 17.637; past and future they exist only as concepts 8.289–91; a poet's sources may have their roots in the past or in the present 7.57

see also
Dīpaṅkara (the Buddha of the past); *Remembrance of Things Past, see under* Proust

Paston Letters 12.697

Paṭacārā 8.119

Pāṭali, India (*Udāna*) 10.641–8

Pāṭaligāma or Pāṭaliputra (modern-day Patna) 10.646–8, 18.24

Patan *see* Nepal/Lalitpur

patanīya-dharmas 2.194

Patañjali 8.255, 8.442, 8.456

Patañjali yoga sūtras 7.99

pātayantika *see under* Vinaya/*prātimokṣa*

Patel, Sardar Vallabhbhai 20.191

Pater, Walter introduction 26.748 (n445); description of the *Mona Lisa* 14.99; high priest of the Aesthetic Movement 26.488; *Studies in the History of the Renaissance* 26.332

path

THE BUDDHIST PATH

introduction
Buddhism as a path or way 4.644–6; what it's basically about 5.45–6; the One Way taught by the Buddha 26.49; only one way to the destruction of suffering 1.218; a unified way: what the path is in principle 15.80–1; one spiritual path for all: 'Hīnayāna' and 'Mahāyāna' are not distinct paths 4.40–1; the Dharma is the underlying principle of all paths 1.51; the aim of the Buddhist path is the transformation of consciousness 15.98; to understand what Buddhism is we must understand the path in principle 4.647–9; the conception of the path is inseparable from a sense of values 11.658; it finds vivid and concrete embodiment in actual human lives 4.646; it represents a combination of realism and positivity 15.232–3; the simultaneous practice of relative and absolute Truth 1.426; 'One path leads to prosperity, quite another to Nibbāna' (*Dhammapada*) 7.171–2; a path of human development 9.212, 19.125; the precepts: the path of self-effort that underlies all forms of Buddhism 26.669–70; a practical path 9.469–70, 9.494–5, 10.152; 'a hacked path, roughly made, through densest

jungle' 25.xxxix, 25.278; 'the Buddha's path will lead me to the Buddha's shining land' 25.290

the path and the goal
the Dharma is concerned with two things: the goal and the path 11.385; different conceptions of the goal 11.72; the goal is implicit in the path 18.164–5; the goal of the path: Nirvāṇa 7.359; not the achievement of goals but the unfoldment of potentialities 2.111; the path and the goal 11.309–10; 'The Path is one for all, the means to reach the goal must vary with the Pilgrims' 7.363; 'path' and 'goal' are discontinuous 4.200–1; the path is the goal 25.83; 'Walking this path you shall make an end of suffering' 4.644; 'You have understood the way' 14.60, 26.296–7

different ways of describing the path
conceptual formulations 11.30–1; different descriptions 11.72; different formulations 3.242–3, 3.294, 4.644–9, 7.495, 7.507; the architectonic of the path does not vary 7.507; all enumerations have a mundane and a transcendental section 11.313; historically Buddhism has not developed a path of beauty, but it could 26.665; horizontal and vertical models: hierarchy or path 14.312; the journey from conditioned existence to Unconditioned existence 3.244; arts transformed (through Zen) into paths to Enlightenment 2.555; the path connecting the wheel of life to the mandala of the Five Buddhas 1.484; the path of dependence on the Buddhas' compassion 1.324; the path of direct experience 19.377–8; the path of skilful means (*upāyamārga*) 18.407; seeing the faults of conditioned existence as a way to Enlightenment 4.593; serving others as a path of spiritual development 4.18; the Tantric path to Enlightenment 13.113–318; three paths of wisdom, devotion, and service, relating to thought, emotion, action 7.303; three stages: integration, positive emotion, spiritual death 11.730–6; the two-in-one path of wisdom and compassion 18.102; five stages: mindfulness, positive emotion, vision, transformation, compassionate activity 5.42–6; the five things that conduce to maturity amount to a path of development 10.531; the way of contemplative insight (*vipassanā-dhura*) 2.143; the way of study (*ganthadhura*) 2.143; the way to Enlightenment is the present experience without interpretation 10.463–4; if descriptions of the path seem schematic, take a more imaginative approach 15.230

the progressive path
essentially an ascending series of mental factors or mental states 4.648, 7.495; the path of the Higher Evolution 2.293–4, 3.477, 9.249, 13.515; the grand conception of the progressive path 1.119; Hīnayāna, Mahāyāna, Tantrayāna successive stages of a single path (Atīśa) 1.361; its basic principle: process of reaction in a progressive order 2.101–2; you can't develop a higher stage of the path fully before a lower stage 26.50; the three *yānas* (*śrāvakayāna* etc.) as grades of one path 1.362

WALKING THE PATH

the right path
doubting whether you are on the right path 15.360; how to check that you're on the right path 19.187; how the validity of the path is to be ascertained 8.611; is it possible to know whether you're on the right path? 4.200–1; 'No hurried path of success ... can be the true path' 2.112; the path is the same for all, only the stages differ 10.171; with the practice of non-duality there is no right or wrong path 18.51; there isn't a definite path because you always have to consider your mental state 19.273; you can't ensure you're on the right path by doing the right things 19.273, 19.275

starting out
setting yourself on the right path 15.400; we have to start from where we are 17.370; what starts us upon the path? 10.157–8; you can't compel anyone onto the spiritual path 18.357

following the path
are we really following the path? 9.272; Buddha-nature is innate within us, but we have to follow a path to realize it 4.9; easier to find success following the spiritual path than in the world 4.292–3, 4.323; fear of anything that holds us back from following the path 17.180; if you're of sluggish temperament, think in terms of following the path 18.525; it is not enough just to understand the Dharma, you must follow the *mārga* 10.247; no aspirant ever follows one path or one method exclusively 7.127; once on the path, conflict between rational and emotional is virtually resolved 26.77; there is always a next step 13.135; thinking that it means avoiding pain is spiritual selfishness 1.132, 7.391; to follow it we need our spiritual friends, like mountaineers roped together 25.34; why don't we attain emancipation without the

bother of following the path? 1.363–4; without a path, no progress 3.398; you traverse the whole path in a sketchy way, then do it again more thoroughly 4.475; you'll feel deeply happy because you're doing the best thing you could do 12.626

possible obstacles
don't come to a stop at any particular stage of the path 4.520; doubt is essentially resistance to the positive spirit of the path 15.176; if you're not happy following the spiritual path, how will you be happy? 17.338; one is not following the path if one feels forced to follow it like a driven sheep 17.435; on the spiritual path be careful not to compromise 19.261; through acting unskilfully we lose sight of the path away from suffering 17.172; turning the spiritual path into the mundane path leaves you no way out of corruption 18.175

MORE PERSPECTIVES ON THE PATH

the path within
the esoteric path 7.357, 7.359–60, 26.49; the path is in the mind 10.152–3, 15.233; the path is not out there, we *are* the path 17.435; the path of the inner life (*nirvṛtti mārga*, esoteric path) 7.357–63; the pilgrim is the path 11.656; 'Thou canst not travel on the Path before thou hast become the Path' 4.646, 7.359, 10.153; we have to 'make the path become' 7.359; we *develop* the path 17.435

what the path is not
not a set of rules that you can stick to mechanically 15.97; not a straightforward progression 4.277; not a vague, general process, but a specific action according to character type 12.280–1

the path as metaphor
calling it a journey is only a manner of speaking 3.254; the danger of understanding the metaphor too literally 26.206–7; the idea of the bodhisattva following a path is a metaphor 4.199–200; the path is only a figure of speech, but a useful one 11.659; reminds us that the Dharma is something to be practised 3.294; in a way the spiritual life is not at all like following a path 1.589

the path as symbol
all things can be symbols of the Liberation Path if you can see them that way 18.619–20; the path and the mandala as alternative symbols 18.525, 18.584, 19.436–7; the symbol of the path is repeated with every conceivable variation 7.297–8

images of the path
balancing the model of the path with the model of unfolding 4.201–3; Buddhas and bodhisattvas as personifications of the stages of the path 1.243; the image of the path means different things to different religions 15.81; Nietzsche's 'tightrope over an abyss' 3.503; a poetic description of the path rising up from the wheel of life 11.167; the spiritual path as the progressive brightening of *śūnyatā* 19.199; the spiritual path as a mythical journey 4.646, 18.80, 26.262–6; similarity and difference to the stages in the growth of a plant 11.64

long or short?
following 'the short path' does not mean skipping stages 16.183; the path takes a very long time 17.458; the shortest and swiftest path from the present instant to the end of the quest 7.173; the Tantra is a short and easy path only if practised long and hard enough 13.74

easy or difficult?
the 'difficult' path and the 'easy' path 1.324, 1.400–1; the difficulty of finding the path from the world of the gods or the hell realm 18.557; once you have come into contact with the path, can you never fall back? 16.291; the Vajrayāna is called the easy path because you don't have to give up bliss 19.379; we generally think of the path in terms of struggle and effort 18.584

gradual or sudden?
progress on the path is not sudden but gradual (Pāli canon) 1.176; there is no such thing as the quick path and the slow path (Huineng) 16.183

transcendental path (lokuttara-magga)
all Buddhist teachers should emphasize the transcendent nature of the path 11.656; the *dharmas* that make up the transcendental path are called *anāsrava dharmas* 18.295–6; gained by *prajñā* 2.147; Milarepa's happiness through following the transcendental path 18.296; the irreversible part of the spiral path, *see under* twelve positive *nidānas*; a path of perpetual self-transcendence 11.656; a strong will to follow the transcendental path 15.94; to follow it, one must turn one's back on the *arūpa dhyānas* 1.165; the unbiased and empty belong to the transcendental path, the imageless does not 2.122

see also
bodhisattva path; fourfold path; *magga-amagga-ñāṇa-dassana visuddhi*, *see under* seven *visuddhis*; *mārga* and *phala* (path

and fruit); middle way; Noble Eightfold Path; path of five stages (Sarvāstivāda), *see* five stages; Path of Seeing (the path of Stream Entry), *see under* Noble Eightfold Path/the Path of Vision; Path of Vision and Transformation, *see under* Noble Eightfold Path; path of purification, *see* seven *visuddhis*; to Enlightenment, *see under* Enlightenment/the path; spiral path, *see* twelve positive *nidānas*; threefold way; Vajrayāna; the view, the path, and the fruit; the way of emptiness, *see śūnyavāda*

path and fruit *see mārga* and *phāla*

path of five stages (Early Buddhism) from *dāna* to *vimukti* 2.204; precursor to the path of the *pāramitās* 2.207

path of five stages (Sarvāstivāda) (1) path of accumulation (*saṃbhāra-mārga*) 17.455–7; (2) path of preparation or practice (*prayoga-mārga*) 10.430, 17.457–8; (3) path of seeing (*darśana-mārga*) 17.458; (4) path of cultivation (*bhāvanā-mārga*) 17.458; (5) path of no more learning (*niṣṭhā-mārga*) 17.459

the path of regular and irregular steps

introduction
brief introduction 4.494–5, 19.618 (n183); full lecture 11.53–71; the importance of the distinction 11.54–5; a teaching of the Tendai (Tiantai) school 4.495, 11.54; the stage by stage teaching of the Mahāyāna 4.459; recommended by Nāgārjuna 17.268; and the path of five stages (Sarvāstivāda) 17.459; and the five stages of the spiritual path 5.44–5; and the system of meditation 5.28, 5.40–2; nobody, not even the Buddha, follows the path as the scriptures describe it 17.109; the path of no steps at all 11.54, 18.637, 26.47

the path of regular steps
setting yourself on the path of regular steps 15.400; spiritual progress is not automatic but takes a regular sequence of steps 2.100; we start practising the path of regular steps by going for Refuge 11.67–8; the Dharma is *opanayiko*, a path of regular steps 15.507–10; in the early days of Buddhism you could follow the path of regular steps 15.508–9; the five spiritual faculties as a path of regular steps 17.83–4; regular steps towards weakening the ego 18.636–7; the *Heart Sūtra* as a path of regular steps 14.365–6; *mettā* and the path of regular steps 15.344–5; one goes about the spiritual life methodically 15.514–15; a path of regular steps described in the *Maṅgala Sutta* 15.400, 15.406; Atīśa starts following the path of regular steps 12.565, 12.567

the path of irregular steps
most people have to start with the path of irregular steps 11.62, 15.508–9; Buddhism in the 'permissive' sixties: the path of irregular steps 11.586; following the path of irregular steps usually involves forcing the process 11.66; indiscriminate Tantric initiations: the path of irregular steps gone mad 19.488; John and the path of irregular steps 11.59–62; Siddhārtha Gautama on the path of irregular steps 5.392

making the transition from irregular to regular
how to get back to the path of regular steps 12.565–7; making the transition 11.62–3, 11.66–7; Milarepa's shepherd disciple moves from irregular to regular steps 18.237, 18.247–9; the path of irregular steps leading to the path of regular steps 15.507–8; you can't develop a higher stage of the path fully before a lower stage 11.66, 26.50

Path of Vision and Path of Transformation *see under* Noble Eightfold Path

pathetic fallacy 4.243, 4.689 (n210)

pathos a hymn to Green Tārā 1.336; the Indian *rasa* 26.325–6; in literature 26.371–2; in a poem about a dog 24.564

paṭibhaddacitta 10.490

paṭibhāga-nimitta *see nimitta*

pāṭi-desanīya 1.410, 2.195

patience *see kṣānti*

paṭigha *see* malice

Pāṭika Sutta *see under Dīgha Nikāya*

pāṭimokkha *see under* Vinaya Piṭaka

pāṭimokkha-saṃvara-sīla *see under* four *pārisuddhi sīlas*

patipadā-ñāṇa-dassana visuddhi *see* seven *visuddhis*

patisambhidā *see under* four *pratisaṃvids*

Patisambhidāmagga (*The Path to Analysis*) 11.309, 14.73–4, 14.79, 16.626–7 (n336)

paṭisandhi *see pratisandhi*

patisanthāra ('spreading before') *see* six *gāravas*

Patmore, Coventry 20.145, 26.193, 26.339

Patna India (ancient Pāṭaliputra) 7.424, 20.458–9

patriotism contrast between nationalism and patriotism 12.342–3; 'locality patriotism' 9.331–2; link between patriotism and religion in Sri Lanka 8.464, 8.471–2, 8.475; 'Patriotism is not enough' (Edith Cavell) 12.343; patriotism is not incompatible with peace, though peace goes beyond patriotism 12.343; the patriotism of the poet Michael Drayton 24.560; 'Then and Now' (poem) 25.431

patron Buddhas 19.404–5

patronage dangers of patronage 9.393; royal patronage of Buddhism (a reason for its decline) 9.390–1, 9.393, 12.238–9, 19.481–2

patterns

the pattern of your life
all the time we are creating patterns according to our state of mind 18.270; energy locked away in habitual patterns of thought, feeling, and behaviour 18.77; deep in communication, you become aware of someone's total pattern 18.285–6; individuality grows clearer, like the pattern on a lamp as it's turned up 14.451, 16.131; our whole life is the working out of a pattern, a gestalt 18.279–87; life like unrolling a Persian carpet to see the pattern 18.283; making a pattern according to the nature of your needs 17.15; mind and matter: a continuity of awareness patterned in different ways 15.138–9; we impinge on the world in accordance with the pattern which is ourselves 16.475; we impose upon reality an arbitrary pattern 19.241; we tend to set up the same patterns for ourselves again and again 18.276–7, 26.168–9; writing or telling one's life story shows the pattern 15.91–2, 18.283; your particular pattern links with a larger pattern 18.280–1; rebirth as the repetition of an old pattern 17.350, 17.475; You asked, 'What is this transient pattern?' 20.xvii

changing the pattern
are there patterns that meditation can't change? 5.653; breaking reactive patterns 17.434; decide which spiritual pattern to involve yourself with 17.570–1; the Dharma is intended to be a grid (pattern) that frees you from grids 19.241; how to tackle reactive patterns of behaviour 4.286–7, 16.114–5; pointing out one's friend's reactive patterns 5.653; renunciation: creating another pattern of behaviour 4.423; the whole pattern's got to change 4.508

the pattern of Buddhist life
the pattern of Buddhist life 3.298–9; the pattern of the spiritual life 15.154–5; precepts are not rules, but patterns of ethical behaviour 1.531, 2.341, 3.318, 3.370; patterns of morality 11.315–20; the life of every Buddha follows a standard pattern 4.59, 10.546–9; the pattern of a *bhikkhu*'s daily life at the time of the Buddha 10.582; in the lives of great Buddhists a noble pattern emerges 15.93–4; the mandala of the five Buddhas a beautiful and meaningful pattern 13.316; Western Buddhism is unlikely to follow any existing pattern 3.169

other patterns
the artist organizes the chaos of sense impressions into patterns 3.511, 26.113; beautiful patterns in Islamic art 26.245; mandala-like patterns produced by musical sounds 18.283; in the lives of all great men, there is a certain pattern 10.127; the pattern of the world's sorrow 4.311–12; people who love bringing facts together and forming them into patterns 12.274

Paṭṭhāna-pakaraṇa ('Treatise of Origination', Abhidharma text) introduction 14.91–3; 'a card index in which every card dances' 14.91; has enormous prestige in Theravāda circles 14.91; origin story 14.91; the pinnacle of the Abhidharma Piṭaka 14.78

Paul, St brief introduction 2.694 (n329); belief in hell 13.573; classification of the human being into body, soul, and spirit 12.33; conversion 2.238; 'being all things to all men' 1.448, 16.479; denounced rival Christian teachers 13.596; denunciation of homosexuality 13.611–12; disparagement of Diana of the Ephesians 13.602; 'Doing evil that good may come of it' 26.292, 26.724 (n231); 'going from glory to glory' 16.109; 'the good that I would I do not, but the evil which I would not, that I do' 1.493; in the novel *The Brook Kerith* 12.696, 13.651–2; it would have been better if Christianity's emphasis had been on the sayings of Jesus rather than those of St Paul 12.696; letters 12.695–6, 13.573; the peace that passes all understanding 13.283, 23.98; 'To the pure all things are pure' 7.99; 'Put on the whole armour of God' 13.595, 17.575

Pauling, Chris *see* Vadanya

paurāṇika (ancient or old) 7.342

Pausanius 23.293, 23.517 (n330)

pauses and empty spaces 7.322–3; have a pause between activities to refresh yourself with pure awareness 5.399; Mozart said that the pauses were the most important part of his music 7.322, 12.557–8

Pāvā, India dissension among the bhikṣus of Pāvā 14.82; the town where the Buddha ate his last meal 2.29, 3.117–18, 10.639

Pavitrananda, Swami 20.128–9, 20.301

Pawar, R. D. 10.143

Payne, Francis 12.72

Payne, Muriel 4.690–1 (n215), 12.704 (n25), 14.656–7 (n501), 26.561–2

peace

the nature of peace
immovable peace 5.213; peace is a fire 26.53; peace more cool than the moonlight is 25.195; peace springs naturally from duties quietly done 7.279; the peace that passes all understanding 13.283, 23.98; the shining peace of Ramana Maharshi's *darshan* 20.343; an atmosphere of deep peace at a Hindu festival 22.336; a state of mind purified of antagonism 7.451; symbolized by a circle 5.213; tendency to think of peace as weak and colourless 5.169

peace and Buddhism
the abode of peace (*santaṃ padaṃ*) 15.261–2; an aspect of the ultimate goal 15.262; the Buddha as an exemplar and teacher of peace 7.236–7, 12.338–9; Buddhism's association with peace 7.443–4, 7.451, 8.261–2; exceptions to Buddhism's peaceful record 7.443, 8.692 (n209), 26.631; the difference between Buddhism and Christianity 7.444; Buddhism tends towards peace of mind and heart, and peace in the world 7.278, 13.447; the calming, pacifying aspect of the Enlightened mind 13.282–3; *dharmas* are peaceful from the beginning 16.449; the goal as a state of utter peace 2.124–5, 5.213; a golden Buddha and an echo within: 'Peace unto all beings' 7.74–6; 'Nirvāṇa alone is peace' 2.82, 2.89, 2.92, 26.11; only the Dharma will and can bring true peace 26.538; peace and interpenetration 7.274; peace at the seat of intensest bodhisattva activity 7.141; peaceful 7.237, 9.236, 9.496; peaceful Buddha and bodhisattva forms 13.69–70; spread by peaceful means 7.486; Subhūti (the Buddha's disciple): a dweller in Peace 14.450

peace and Buddhist practice
an atmosphere of peace in the shrine-room 22.239; it's difficult to experience peacefulness without thinking how peaceful it is 5.398–9; laziness is the near enemy of peacefulness 10.83; peace of mind 3.336, 15.310; *samādhi* is the pool of peace 25.33; the vibrant peace of *upekṣā* 1.506–7, 5.212–13

the achievement of peace
abortion and peace 27.1073; between faiths 7.146; the dove of peace and the serpent of selfishness 7.274; how to bring it about, through outer or inner change? 7.237–8; if peace is not universal it is not peace 7.452; if peace is to be achieved, we have to identify ourselves with both parties 12.343–4; to achieve peace, disputes need to be settled non-violently 12.353; we vaguely hope we can achieve peace without giving up violence 12.360; world peace, *see under* world

peacocks *see under* birds

Peak District, England 24.384–5

Peake, Mervyn 24.365

Peanuts Group 23.124, 23.493 (n152)

Pearce, Malcolm v24

pearl gates of pearl in Revelation 1.539, 13.532; the 'Hymn of the Pearl', *see under* Gnosticism; 'My Pearl' (poem) 25.401; a pillar of pearl (precept) 2.378

pebble the child who picks up pebbles and calls them gems 7.34; the pebble of life which we fail to see as the precious stone it is 16.251

Pedong 12.3, 21.21–2, 21.444

Peleus 26.469, 26.481–2

pema (Sanskrit *prema*, sticky attachment) essentially a social emotion 15.314; in the *Dhammapada* 1.158, 4.526, 4.711 (n343); distinguished from *mettā* 1.158–9, 3.576, 3.603, 4.526, 5.169–72, 11.701, 15.313–15; the near enemy of *mettā* 15.314; a sort of infatuation which can be very painful 10.652

Pema Tsedeun, Princess (of Sikkim) 'Coocoola' 21.35; first meeting 21.24; Jamyang Khyentse Rimpoche stays at her house, Arunachal 22.403–4; possessor of beauty, charm, intelligence, and vitality 21.29; rebukes the French nun for bothering Jamyang Khyentse Rimpoche 22.399; related to the Sikkimese Maharajas 3.233, 21.142, 22.241

Pemalingpa (Bhutanese *terton*) 24.388

PEN ('Poets, Essayists, Novelists' society or club) what it is 10.682 (n154), 22.598

(n216), 26.760–1 (n549); magazine 7.457; Bombay branch 10.131, 10.134–5, 22.268; Sangharakshita might have joined it in another life 26.584

penance 16.510

pendulum 21.443

Pentheus, King 24.291, 24.679–80 (n352)

people 'The People' (poem) 25.301; 'The people that walked in darkness have seen a great light' 10.319; religion is 'the opium of the people' 10.70–4; 'Where there is no vision the people perish' 11.161, 25.144; *see also* human life; other people

People's Education Society founded by Dr Ambedkar 9.8, 10.128, 10.168; Aurangabad 9.302–3, 9.312, 9.320; the college in Bombay, *see* Mumbai/Siddharth College; Colleges of Art, Science, Commerce, and Law 9.441; in Mahad 9.286, 9.292; published Dr Ambedkar's works 9.224; relationship with Triratna (TBMSG) 10.298–9

perception as *skandha* (*samjñā*) 1.174; becoming indifferent to objects of perception 7.358; bringing a responsive awareness to what we perceive 15.136; all objects of perception are transformations of consciousness 1.377; all objects of perception have no real, ultimate existence 10.165, 18.574; association with Amitābha 1.263; the beginning of the world is 'perceived' when there's no one to perceive it 13.567; bodhisattvas do not mistake perceptions for reality 14.440; the process of perceiving a tree 10.231; don't allow your thinking to be ruled by the apparent objects of your perception 14.417; a double barrier between us and reality: perceptions and words 14.421; the five sense *vijñānas* as five 'perceptions' (Guenther) 17.484; 'If the doors of perception were cleansed ...' (Blake) 15.205–6; individualizing perception 17.499; the mind constructs from its perceptions a world of objects 12.175; nothing is quite as the mind thinks it is, but the way it perceives things is still useful 18.179; once subject and object are transcended, perceptions are 'forsaken and gone' 14.601; perceiving a flower 15.134; perceiving the non-existence of something 17.519–20; perception through the five senses plays no part in *samādhi* 17.543; perceptions with no relation to an objectively existing object: dreams, meditation 12.171–3; pure perception 5.398; we have a common perception to the extent that we have a common karma 17.483; we mistakenly posit behind what we perceive a definite fixed entity 14.420; we should refer not to having a perception of a thing, but only to having a perception 1.368; a whirling firebrand as a metaphor for how senses perceive objects 17.406–8; without perceiving 1.71

see also
perception and non-perception, *see under dhyānas*/fourth *arūpa dhyāna*; perception as *skandha*, *see samjñā*

perceptual situation the five omnipresent mental events 17.501–31; the objective content of the perceptual situation 2.97, 13.151, 15.134, 17.445, 17.479, 17.501; the perceptual situation 2.97, 13.151, 15.134, 17.xix–xx, 17.377, 17.482–3, 17.515

perfect action, effort, emotion, livelihood, mindfulness, samādhi, speech, vision *see under* Noble Eightfold Path

Perfect Net *see under Dīgha Nikāya*/*Brahmajāla Sutta*

perfection the 'cult of self-perfection' 13.385–6; in life 9.287; not an absolute value or a fixed condition 26.176; not being able to achieve perfection, we can still do the best we can 7.246–7; not perfect, but enough (poem) 25.331–2; we can't be expected to be perfect, we just need to keep watch over ourselves 18.11–12; you can't be objectively perfect, but only subjectively perfect 4.355–6

Perfection of Wisdom or Perfect Wisdom (*prajñāpāramitā*)

INTRODUCTION

the origins of the Perfection of Wisdom
introduction to the tradition 3.358–62; its name means the wisdom that goes beyond all duality 14.345; the Buddha 3.358–9, 14.317–18; foreshadowed in the Pāli canon 10.464–5, 10.523; Prajñāpāramitā-like paradox in the *Gaṇḍavyūha Sūtra* 14.225–6; the tradition arose to challenge the Abhidharma's literalism 3.359, 14.344; the Buddha preached it to his mother, *see under* heavens/Heaven of the Thirty-three

its place in the Buddhist tradition
called 'The Dark Wisdom' in Chinese translation 14.514; the heart of Mahāyāna Buddhism 1.70; of the six perfections, received by far the most attention 1.425; a strong influence on Tibetan Buddhism and Zen 14.367; studied deeply by Tibetan *geshes* 13.45, 13.106–7; worship of the Perfection of Wisdom 2.224–5

what it is like
the antidote to self-seeking 1.303; beyond logic 1.209–10; beyond the subject–object distinction 14.536; comparison with Sophia, the Divine Wisdom 13.603–4, 14.343; concerned with seeing *śūnyatā* everywhere, at all times 1.489; description in negative terms 1.70–1; elusive 1.65–7, 14.535–6; free from all determinations 1.73; it breaks down the dualistic basis of religious life 14.104; it is to be found and nourished within yourself 14.536; it may be powerful and thrusting 14.535; it may come softly, gently, unobtrusively 14.xvi, 14.534–5; it has the flavour of irrelevance 14.481; its demands are to be met only by a heroic spirit 14.537; Mañjuśrī's description of its qualities 1.70–1; not supposed to be useful in any way we can understand 14.524; the spiritual faculty that intuits *śūnyatā* 16.232; there are no gradations between Perfect Wisdom and our words and thoughts 14.585; what makes a bodhisattva a bodhisattva 16.232; when a Buddha 'thinks', Perfect Wisdom comes into operation 14.536–7

its doctrines
the unconditioned identity of the conditioned and the Unconditioned 1.305, 14.361; *śūnyatā* is its principal theme 1.305, 3.233, 4.161, 16.16; it is taught for no other purpose than to make everybody happy 14.537; it teaches the emptiness of *dharmas* 14.104; its field of enquiry: the career of a bodhisattva 14.513

its methods and approaches
coursing in the Perfection of Wisdom 14.547; its counteraction of an intellectual emphasis may not apply in the West today 14.442; it relentlessly hunts down our attempts to reify concepts 14.606–7; its logic of contradictions 1.268, 3.220; metaphysical approach to Nirvāṇa 1.253; not an intellectual teaching: they use thought to undo thought 14.513–15; paradox 2.131, 3.87, 3.220, 7.489, 11.14, 14.xiv, 14.583–4, 26.200–2; as a spiritual faculty 3.233; switching between Absolute and relative points of view 14.447–8; a warning not to impose on reality the categories of understanding 1.304

the bodhisattva's practice
the bodhisattva gains Enlightenment only by relying on Perfect Wisdom 14.363; going all out for Enlightenment while realizing that no one attains it 11.14; they should train in the perfection of wisdom 1.73; they are urged to deliver sentient beings who do not exist 1.348, 7.489, 11.14; they take emptiness for the basis 1.269

connecting with it
applying our rational mind to it takes us to the edge of reason 14.xiv; the danger of thinking we have grasped it 14.376, 14.583–4; devotion is part of preparing to become receptive to it 14.437; if you are not shaken by its teachings, probably you haven't understood them 14.598; one might find that one has a mysterious affinity with it 14.483; practising it needs a firm foundation in ethics and meditation 11.66; through practising meditation, both mindfulness and *mettā* 14.515–16; to be approached with respect 14.352, 14.567; to bring it alive, translate it into myth, symbol, images, metaphor 14.589; you need a good teacher 14.566–7

PERFECTION OF WISDOM LITERATURE

introduction
brief introduction 3.232–3, 3.359–60, 7.501, 10.163–4, 14.319; the scriptures of perfect wisdom 1.299–309, 14.133–55; the largest group of Mahāyāna *sūtras* 14.342–3; twenty-seven (or thirty-five) *sūtras* extant 14.133–4, 14.345

their history
the Buddha's prophecy about their place of origin 14.135; the legend of their origin, *see under* Nāgārjuna/life story; composition in four phases 1.299–300, 14.133–55, 14.345–7; commentaries and sub-commentaries 1.300; condensation into *dhāraṇis* and mantras 1.301, 2.216, 14.154; a continuity from the *Sutta-Nipāta* of the Pāli canon 14.137, 14.351; the dating of texts is difficult 14.134–5; if the Buddha did not preach them, whoever did was a spiritual genius 14.137; likely to have originated among the Mahāsaṅghikas 14.135; the medieval Indian mode of communication does not suit them 14.514–15; the oldest text is the *Perfection of Wisdom in 8,000 Lines* 1.300, 14.135, 14.345; published by Nāgārjuna 14.137; spiritual (as distinct from textual) authenticity of Perfection of Wisdom scriptures 14.139; to be understood in a context of literalism and scholasticism 1.307; traditionally classified in terms of length 14.134; the use of an exalted teaching as a lucky charm 2.216; association with Mañjuśrī, who holds the book to his heart 2.174; a work that is as much a tantra as a *sūtra* 14.154; is all their intellectual juggling really necessary? 14.584; could we develop Western versions? 14.514

what the texts are like
aim to awaken a joyous emotional response 14.533; composed of words that lead beyond words 14.xiv; 'dangerously disorienting to the unwary student' 3.361, 14.321; an example of the scientific sort of Buddhist literature 14.110; faithful to the spirit of the Buddha's teaching 14.318–19; quite simple, but addressed to bodhisattvas 1.302–3; their task is to demolish the conceptual framework they rest on 14.514; they can be misconstrued 1.72; they challenge literalistic thinking 3.361, 14.318–19, 14.321; they encourage us to take our understanding beyond the intellectual 3.361; they speak the language of concepts to transcend all concepts 14.467–8, 16.16; they tower over 'Hīnayāna' *sūtras* like the Himalayas over foothills 14.137

their contents
absolute altruism is conjoined with the realization of no-self 14.150; Akṣobhya is practically the only Buddha to appear in them 13.315, 14.138; the 'hidden meaning' (*saṃdhā*) 14.153; reality cannot be expressed in terms of existence or non-existence 19.377; the inconceivable nature of the Buddha 22.124; startling and paradoxical teachings 14.153, 14.583; they deal with just one topic: *śūnyatā* 1.305, 3.233, 7.501, 14.345, 14.347–8, 14.467–8, 16.16; they exemplify the true meaning of the Dharma Refuge 14.133

studying the Perfection of Wisdom
if we think we understand what's being said, we haven't begun to understand 14.584; obstacles that may arise 14.144

translations
Chinese translations 14.138; translated by Dr Edward Conze, *see under* Conze; Xuanzang translations 14.134, 14.138; *see also under* individual works

individual sūtras
Aṣṭadaśa, see Perfection of Wisdom in 18,000 lines; *Aṣṭasāhasrikā, see Perfection of Wisdom in 8,000 lines*; *Daśasāhasrikā, see Perfection of Wisdom in 10,000 lines*; *Diamond Sūtra* (*Vajracchedikā*), *see Diamond Sūtra*; *Ekākṣari, see Perfection of Wisdom in One Letter*; *Heart Sūtra, see Heart Sūtra*; *Kauśikaprajñāpāramitā, see Kauśikaprajñāpāramitā*; *Large Prajñāpāramitā, see Large Prajñāpāramitā*; *Pañcaviṃśatisāhasrikā, see Perfection of Wisdom in 25,000 lines*; *Prajñāpāramitāstotra, see under* Rāhulabhadra; *Ratnaguṇa-saṃcayagāthā, see Ratnaguṇa-saṃcayagāthā*; *Saptaśatikā, see Saptaśatikā*; *Śatasāhasrikā, see Perfection of Wisdom in 100,000 lines*; *Selected Sayings of the Perfection of Wisdom, see under* Edward Conze; *Svalpākṣarā* ('in a few syllables'), *see Svalpākṣarā*

commentaries and summaries
introduction 14.348; *Abhisamayālaṃkāra, see under* Maitreyanātha; *Mahāprajñāpāramitā Śāstra, see under* Nāgārjuna; *Prajñāpāramitā Śāstra, see under* Chinese Buddhism/literature

see also
goddess, *see* Prajñāpāramitā; mantra (*gate gate pāragate pārasaṃgate bodhi svāha*), *see under Heart Sūtra*

Perfection of Wisdom in One Letter
(*Ekākṣari*) 1.301, 12.104, 14.347

Perfection of Wisdom in 150 lines
(*Adhyardhaśatikā*) 14.154–5

Perfection of Wisdom in 500 lines
(*Suvikrāntvikrāmi-paripṛcchā*) 14.153, 14.303

Perfection of Wisdom in 700 lines *see Saptaśatika*

Perfection of Wisdom in 8, 000 lines
(*Aṣṭasāhasrikā*)

introduction
brief introduction 3.87, 16.16; introduction to the text, chapter by chapter 14.138–45; the transmission of the text to Ānanda 14.145; an early Mahāyāna *sūtra* 16.239; the oldest Perfection of Wisdom text 1.300, 14.135, 14.345; its composition took 200 years 14.138; parts included in the *Large Prajñāpāramitā* 14.146; written down at the same time as the Pāli canon 14.101–2; Haribhadra's commentary, the *Āloka*, *see* Haribhadra; the *Ratnaguṇa-saṃcayagāthā* is a verse summary 1.300, 14.145, 14.345; translations 14.138; one of nine *sūtras* venerated in Nepal 14.100; a copy presented to Sangharakshita by the Dalai Lama 22.371

characters in the text
Ānanda 14.143, 14.145; Maitreya 14.143; Pūrṇa Maitrāyaṇīputra 14.141; Śakra, the king of the gods 14.143; Śāriputra 14.139, 14.143; Subhūti 1.66–7, 2.157, 3.55–6, 14.139–43

topics in the sūtra
the attributes of Tathāgatahood applied to all *dharmas* 14.144; the attributes of Perfect Wisdom 14.144; the conditioned identity of conditioned and Unconditioned 14.139; the deeds of Māra 14.144;

distinction between poetry and the word of the Buddha 2.168; everything is like a magical illusion or a dream 14.143; an exalted teaching is made to function as a lucky charm 2.216; how the Buddha knows the world and minds of sentient beings 14.144; 'a mother who has many children' – an example of exaggeration 2.32; the nature of *dharmas* 1.66–7, 14.138–9; Subhūti's rhapsody on the Suchness of the Tathāgata 14.144; transference of merit 2.269, 14.144

the bodhisattva
the nature of the bodhisattva 14.140–1; the bodhisattva's marriage a 'pious fraud' for the conversion of others 1.442; conjuring a ghost to depart – or is it a trick of Māra? 2.169; the great armour of a bodhisattva 14.141–2; the heroic bodhisattva takes his family on a fearful journey 2.157, 3.55–6; how a bodhisattva should stand in Perfect Wisdom 14.143; how bodhisattvas help beings 14.144; how one first aspires to become a bodhisattva 2.156; the past deeds of bodhisattvas who fail in Perfect Wisdom 14.144; placing oneself and all beings in Suchness 1.230

irreversible bodhisattvas
compassion in replying to questions about the Dharma 2.168–9, 4.65, 18.588; Māra's attempts to mislead the bodhisattva 14.145; they never wonder whether they are an irreversible bodhisattva 4.189, 15.241; observe the ten precepts 2.333

Sadāprarudita, 'Ever Weeping' (bodhisattva)
always weeping because he is constantly moved by the Dharma 14.470; goes East in search of the Perfection of Wisdom 4.646, 14.138; worship of the Perfection of Wisdom 2.225

worship of the Perfection of Wisdom
the Buddhas' expression of gratitude for the Perfection of Wisdom 3.360, 14.319; hymn to Prajñāpāramitā (quoted in full) 3.362, 14.321–2; produces infinitely more merit than worshipping the Buddha's relics 14.144; a tower built as a shrine for the Perfection of Wisdom 2.224–5; worship of the book 4.307

Perfection of Wisdom in 10, 000 lines
(*Daśasāhasrikā*) emerged from the second of the four phases 14.346–7; its special feature is a collection of definitions of terms 14.147

Perfection of Wisdom in 18, 000 lines
(*Aṣṭadaśa*) introduction 1.300, 14.147; emerged from the second of the four phases 14.346–7; part of the *Large Prajñāpāramitā* 14.146

Perfection of Wisdom in 25, 000 lines
(*Pañcaviṃśatisāhasrikā*) introduction 14.146–7; part of the *Large Prajñāpāramitā* 14.146; emerged from the second of the four phases 14.346–7; the bodhisattva does not relish the *dhyānas* 1.443; the confidence of the bodhisattva: comparison between the glow-worm and the sun 1.230; a dialogue between Subhūti and the Buddha 9.143; distinction between mundane and transcendental practice of perfections 1.425, 1.433–4; how does the bodhisattva develop the recollection of the Buddha? 2.44–5; the ten *bhūmis* 14.227; commentary (*Abhisamayālaṃkāra*), *see* Maitreyanātha; commentary (*Mahāprajñāpāramitā Śāstra*), *see under* Nāgārjuna

Perfection of Wisdom in 100, 000 lines
(*Śatasāhasrikā*) enumerates the stages of the path 1.447; part of the *Large Prajñāpāramitā* 1.300, 14.146; tradition it was retrieved from the *nāgas* by Nāgārjuna, *see under* Nāgārjuna/life story

perfections (*pāramitās*)

introduction
all the perfections may be regarded as skilful means (*upaya*) 7.45, 14.188; and the *Jātakas* 2.16, 14.63, 14.65; a common path for all followers of the Buddha 2.452; practised by the Buddha for countless lives 4.21; a revised edition of the series of stages from *dāna* to *prajñā* or *vimutti* 2.204, 2.207; spiritual progress said to be more rapid on the Mantranaya than on the Pāramitānaya 13.288–9; the thirty functions of the *pāramitās* 14.186

THE SIX PERFECTIONS

introduction
brief description 10.175–6, 11.385; general introduction 1.422–45, 3.367–75, 8.199–201, 16.8–12; a 'glowing account' 22.144; summary of practice 16.8–12; sources 3.678 (n335); Dr Ambedkar as a practitioner of the six perfections 10.318–19; the benefits to be derived from *dāna* and *śīla* 14.193; all other-regarding virtues 7.46; the bodhisattva spirit makes them not dead dogmas but transcendental realities 1.426; the path of the bodhisattva 9.249, 9.396–7; Buddhahood is to be gained by the actual practice, not abstract contemplation 7.329; can be thought of in three pairs 3.375; correlation with the Noble Eightfold Path 1.424–5; degrees of practice 1.425; determination to practise

them is good preparation for Buddha Day 8.199; developing the perfections; distinction between mundane and transcendental practice 1.425, 1.433–4; explained in Beatrice Suzuki's *Mahāyāna Buddhism* 7.45; faith expresses itself as the first two *pāramitās* 2.105; the first five represent a calming down (*samādhi*) of the conditioned nature 4.550; the foundation stones of the Mahavihara in Poona 10.354–7; manifested by Dhardo Rimpoche 22.543; not really perfections unless associated with *prajñā* 1.434–5, 2.164; one of the most popular lists 4.336; patience and vigour later additions to the bodhisattva's four practices 1.424, 1.446; a perfectly balanced and comprehensive scheme of spiritual development 16.12; perhaps the noblest way of life ever proposed to humanity 16.12; practised by the Buddha over many lifetimes 9.382, 12.188, 16.380, 19.314; practising one a day, and all six on Sunday 4.618, 10.620–1; practising the first five to accumulate vast merit 19.46; practising them is the expression of our own deepest need 14.418–19; relationship to the *bodhicitta* 3.367–75, 4.55, 14.412; represented by the windhorse 19.439; right motive is of decisive importance 1.425; taught by the Tibetan lama 12.17; and the two accumulations (*puṇya* and *jñāna*) 17.463; Vimalakīrti's practice 16.480

(1) dāna pāramitā
introduction 1.426–35, 3.367–9, 16.8–9; antidote to greed 8.199; commentary on the perfection of giving (Dhammapala) 14.657 (n502); difference between transcendental and mundane giving 1.433–4; giving as an expression of our innermost nature 14.418; giving natural, spontaneous, inexhaustible 4.104, 14.421; giving the embodiment of all six perfections 14.416–17; not for worldly benefit, but for the sake of Enlightenment for all 10.175; not a *pāramitā* unless conjoined with wisdom 18.275; the practice of giving conjoined with the experience of reality 4.104; Śāntideva puts his finger on the perfection of giving 4.358–9, 8.174; a threefold circle of purity (*trimaṇḍala-pariśuddha*) 2.366, 4.104, 17.202; why it is the first *pāramitā* 4.93; *see also dāna*/traditional kinds of giving

(2) śīla pāramitā
introduction 3.369–71, 4.116–17, 16.9–10; egolessness as the basis 1.435–6; the indispensable foundation of the spiritual life 8.199; it becomes a perfection when united with wisdom 11.307; it is a perfection if the precepts are observed without ego-sense 10.175; *see also* ethics

(3) kṣānti pāramitā
introduction 1.436–9, 3.372, 16.10; patient acceptance 2.164; in the *Bodhicaryāvatāra* 4.388–437; in the *Diamond Sūtra* 14.475–9; much more than forbearance 8.200; *see also kṣānti*

(4) vīrya pāramitā
introduction 1.439–41, 3.372–3, 16.10–11; exertion for the benefit of all beings 2.164; of great importance 9.396; in the *Bodhicaryāvatāra* 4.438–87; having become patient, one should become heroic 4.470; it strikes a more active note 8.200; not a *pāramitā* unless conjoined with wisdom 1.434–5, 2.164, 18.275; in a sense all the other *pāramitās* depend on *vīrya* 4.132, 4.444; *see also vīrya*

(5) samādhi pāramitā (sometimes dhyāna)
introduction 1.441–4, 3.373, 16.11; anticipated in the Pāli canon 1.257; difference from meditation as a stage of the threefold way? 1.441; meditation not for peace of mind or to get to heaven, but for the benefit of all 4.160; paired with *prajñā pāramitā* in the *Sutra of Huineng*, *see Sūtra of Huineng*; at least a temporary getting away from the world 4.566; *see also samādhi*; *dhyāna*; meditation

(6) prajñā pāramitā
introduction 1.444–5, 16.11–12; considered in terms of the five wisdoms 3.373–5; the most important of the *pāramitās* 1.425, 1.444, 4.104; the glory of Buddhism alone 8.201; paired with *samādhi pāramitā* in the *Sutra of Huineng*, *see Sūtra of Huineng*; said by the Mahāyāna to be the only *pāramitā* 2.164, 11.307, 18.275; *see also* Perfection of Wisdom

THE TEN PERFECTIONS

introduction
summary 1.445–50; Dr Ambedkar's enumeration 9.141–2; associated of *hūṃ* with the last four *pāramitās* 10.151, 10.176; the Buddha's practice 8.232; canonical reference 1.401; correlation with the bodhisattva *bhūmis* 1.446–54, 4.645–6; Anagarika Dharmapala's practice 8.100–4; four added to the original list of six 2.164; influence of the decimal system? 1.447; Milarepa's jewels 18.295; taught by Nāgārjuna 1.324

(7) upāya-kauśalya-pāramitā (perfection of skilful means)
the bodhisattva is expected to be 'all things to all men' 1.448; equivalent to

compassion 2.164; includes the four *saṃgraha-vastus* and the four *pratisaṃvids* 1.449, 10.147, 10.176, 11.699; *see also* skilful means

(8) praṇidhāna-pāramitā (perfection of vow)
its importance in the eyes of Mahāyānists 1.449; not to rest until all are delivered 10.147, 10.176; its reappearance reminds us that the *bodhicitta* grows with progress 2.164

(9) bala-pāramitā (perfection of strength or power)
twofold: a group of five and a group of ten powers 1.449–50; strength, especially spiritual 10.176; the universalization of the vow 2.164

(10) jñāna-pāramitā (perfection of knowledge)
the subtlest type of *prajñā* 2.164–5; the four *śūnyatās* 10.176; differs from the perfection of wisdom only in name 1.450; Nirvāṇa in *saṃsāra*, the jewel in the lotus 10.147

see also
the bodhisattva's practice, *see under* bodhisattva/the practice of the perfections

perfume and fragrance the Buddha-land 'Sweetly Perfumed with All Perfumes' 16.554–5, 26.498; the Dharma like an invisible perfume in a musty chamber 1.22; the Dharma taught by perfume 16.458, 16.554, 16.558–63, 26.498; the fragrance of *devas* in a house in Kalimpong 11.236–7, 21.132–6; the fragrance of compassion 25.214; *gandharvas* live on perfume 16.348; Mulagandhakuti ('Original Perfumed Chamber' Vihara), *see* Sarnath; pure perfume of the Void 25.219; purifying effect of the fragrance of the food provided by Vimalakīrti 16.555–6; the fragrance of wild thyme 23.291; pine-scent 25.391, 25.435; the spiritual significance of perfume 24.567–8; smelling a perfume that isn't physically there 13.291; subtlety of perfume, symbol for something intangible 16.559; symbolizes compassion 16.560–1; ultimate reality 'perfumes' conditioned existence 4.33, 7.317, 7.400, 13.313, 16.560–1, 22.16–17, 25.32, 26.498; *vāsanā*, a perfuming energy that leaves its essence in the things it has perfumed 14.209; *see also* incense

Pericles 23.296, 23.518 (n232)

Periyar, Padamlal (student) v21

permissiveness Buddhism in the 'permissive' sixties 11.586; not necessarily beneficial 24.292; 'permissive' society 12.255

Perrers, Alice 24.538

persecution where there is persecution there is fanaticism and dogmatism 7.145–6; Buddhism has often been persecuted, but has not retaliated with persecution 7.127; carried out by Christians, *see under* Christianity/Roman Catholic Church; of Manicheans 3.432; the violence engendered by intolerance, directed against the thinker as well as the thought 7.380; why did Buddhism not resort to persecution to spread its teachings? 7.383

Perseus Cellini's statue 23.313; Perseus and Medusa 26.22, 26.481; the son of Zeus and Danaë 26.481

perseverance 'Be determined and persevering' – it's important to be both 18.411; the Buddha's life teaches us the quality of perseverance 10.259; constant perseverance in stern renunciation 7.358; 'Should there be great drowsiness, persevere in thine efforts' 5.678–80

Persia *see* Iran

persistence meditation: the persistent and methodical attempt to see reality within 13.354; persisting through challenges 18.161–2; sometimes we think we're being patient when we're only being persistent 26.34; *vīrya* as steady persistence 3.305

persona ('mask') Blake was 'a man without a mask' 19.122, 24.176; Allen Ginsberg as a man without a mask 24.176, 25.93; can be reinforced by wearing a particular style of dress 3.40; confession helps us live without a mask 25.95; 'The Mask' (poem) 25.88–96, 25.309; the mask donned for social purposes 23.108; only when we are alone are the masks down 8.260; a persona is safe if it represents you as less than you are 19.122; the persona of Tibetan lamas 19.122; pride is a mask 18.141; taking off your mask can be a revolutionary activity 25.95; time to lay aside the masks 25.323; worn because we are afraid of being seen as we are 3.40; writers who didn't have a persona 19.122

personal experience *see under* experience

personal myth 18.318–19

personal practice the practice you actually do is the Dharma as far as you are concerned 18.496; personal practice isn't enough, you need a whole way of life to support it 15.475, 15.477; for personal

practice, any approach that expresses genuine devotion is justified 4.305

personal precepts *see under* precepts/practising the precepts

personal responsibility *see under* responsibility

Personalist Group 23.104, 23.489 (n127), 23.217–18

personality

what is personality?
Buddhist analysis of personality into *skandhas* 1.109, 1.173; a complex and compound thing 1.175; a continuity of a series of experiences, subjective and objective 7.209; human beings are usually a number of personalities fighting for supremacy 26.258; 'merit-produced' personality 16.132; mistaken idea that though personality is unreal its constituent elements are real 1.304–5; none of the phenomena of personality can be regarded as the self 1.172–3; a pejorative view of personality 13.459–60; a rainbow interfusion, like the colours of a pigeon's neck 7.301–2, 26.129; the rational and the emotional are its two aspects 15.607; any given moment expresses the whole personality 19.230–1; will is the key component 7.301–3

effects of personality
being influenced by likes and dislikes of personality 15.516–17; literature an expression of the literary personality or of the whole personality 10.154; a powerful personality creates around them a world that reflects their values 17.298; in Western philosophy, the philosopher's personality translated into thought 7.77

personality and spiritual practice
even in pursuit of spiritual training one can entrap oneself further in personality 18.31; exhausting struggles between the 'higher' and 'lower' aspects of personality 7.401; a harmonious development of cognitive, conative, and affective aspects necessary 1.240; if one aspect is transformed, all will be transformed 7.303; one's personality is not set in stone 18.145–6; realizing the illusory nature of personality (one of Nāropā's six yogas) 13.28; the sublimation of all the forces of personality in the direction of Enlightenment 13.22; trying to be a personality in the sense of a Selfless Person 13.462; ultimately every aspect of personality must be cultivated 7.303–5; when teaching the Dharma, don't try to impress people with your personality 19.499; when you go for Refuge you do so with your whole personality 15.606–7, 18.383

Enlightened personality
all personalities are embraced by the One Personality, the primordial Buddha 7.304–5; egolessness of personality 1.270, 7.302; personality and the goal are not incompatible 2.128–9; the personality of an Enlightened being 1.252; the *vajracitta*: personality in its highest aspect 26.51; visualization of Enlightened qualities as personalities 7.303–4; when it becomes egoless, it shines with wisdom, compassion, and skilful activity 7.302

personality-view (*satkāya-dṛṣṭi*) *see* ten fetters/first fetter

perspective arousing positive emotion in someone to give them a wider perspective 19.514; the Buddha saw things not from a limited perspective, but as they are 12.547; Buddhist philosophy discloses awe-inspiring perspectives 7.486; confession helps you to experience your karma in a different perspective 4.314–15; cosmic perspectives of the background to the Dharma are similar to those of astronomy 1.39, 2.62–3; failure to view the Dharma in correct perspective 1.37–43; from the perspective of the gods the loveliest human face is repulsive 2.83; from the perspective of reality the attainment of a goal becomes absurd 18.44–5; historical perspective on Buddhism 4.22–3, 10.554–5; 'walking past the mortuary puts life in perspective' 10.lxii; the way we look at things exerts a strong influence on how they appear to us 17.xix; whether your life has been long or short, it's the same from the perspective of death 4.427; while doing a specific task, keep in mind the wider perspective 19.524

perversities *see* four *viparyāsas*

pessimism (in relation to Buddhism)

arising from the 'negative' description of Nirvāṇa
too subtle for some Early Buddhists to understand 1.72; there needs to be something positive to attract you 10.635, 12.218, 14.553; had a profoundly negative influence 15.229

idea that Buddhism is pessimistic and joy-destroying
an impression when Buddhism first reached the West 12.618; in reality Buddhism is not pessimistic or optimistic, but melioristic 2.90; Lama Govinda's

refutation of the criticism 2.108–9; extraordinary given its emphasis on positive states 2.90, 3.270

is the teaching about suffering pessimistic?
being reluctant to accept the truth of *dukkha* 3.213, 7.48; the point is not to dwell on suffering morbidly but to see what it is telling us 7.390–1; the charge arises from a misunderstanding about method and doctrine 1.124–5, 15.227–8; it could be considered so if it stopped short at the first noble truth 2.90, 7.390; no, it opens the door to progress 10.158

Petavatthu 14.68

Peter, Brother 21.352–3

Peter, Prince, of Greece 8.643, 12.435–6, v21, 22.125–6

Peter, St 13.552–3, 13.647–8

Petit, Hilla 12.320, 23.348, 23.376, 26.557–60

Pettit, Cyril 23.197–8

Peunkhang Rimpoche 22.491–2

Phabongkhapa Rimpoche 17.425

Phadampa Sangye his teachings in *The Tibetan Book of the Great Liberation* 8.347; introduced the *chöd* practice into Tibet 4.362, 13.268

Phagpa (Tibetan master) 4.123

phala (fruit) difference between *mārga* and *phala* 1.177, 2.146; the five effects (*pañca-phala*) 14.212; *mārga* and *phala* correspond to the third and fourth noble truths 2.102; the view, the path, and the fruit 19.211

phantasmagoria 1.355, 19.38

Phelps, Kathy v23

phenomena

the nature of phenomena
definitions, Greek and Buddhist 1.98–9; emptiness of phenomena 1.138, 1.305–6; internal as well as external 1.102; it is impossible to imagine a phenomenal thing existing in splendid isolation 7.132; the existence of phenomena is indistinguishable from our perception of them 1.351; not simple but composite 1.99–100; over and above its conditions and parts, no phenomenon exists 2.87; right view: understanding the conditionality of all phenomena 7.521; they arise in dependence upon a multiplicity of conditions 1.102, 1.231

all phenomena
the acceptance of their egolessness and impersonality 8.200; 'all phenomena are holy books' 19.69–70; Buddhas can express themselves through all the phenomena of existence 19.33; Buddhism does not teach that they are all reducible to one 16.449; if ever one was unchanging, all the others would be too 7.194; their outstanding feature is that they are conditioned 3.94; they could all be symbols of the Liberation Path, if seen that way 18.619–20

the phenomenal world
distinguished from the ontal world and the ideal world 1.98; Impressionism as an illustration of the nature of phenomenal existence 1.104; the Mahāyāna identifies it with the Absolute 1.268; to the worldling, it seems to be composed of real 'things' 1.104

perspectives from the Buddhist tradition
phenomena and *pratītya-samutpāda* 1.91–3, 1.102–3, 16.20; the Early Buddhist view that they are realities 1.264–5; analysed until they disappear 1.308; knowledge of phenomena in their appearance and reality (*dharma-pratisaṃvid*) 1.449; the phenomena that appear to consciousness likened to a mirage 17.379–80; the Perfection of Wisdom view 1.305–6; the Tantra sees reality as both transcendent to and immanent in phenomena 1.385

see also
dharmas

Pheunkhang, Mr (husband of Princess Pema Tsedeun) 3.233, v22

Phidias 3.427, 23.296, 23.518 (n232), 24.265, 24.673 (n320)

Philip II (of Spain) 24.412–14

Phillips, Anna v23

philology 1.17–18

philosopher's stone 16.221

philosophy

THE NATURE OF PHILOSOPHY

where it starts
the starting-point 7.386–9; philosophy begins with a sense of wonder (Plato) 4.212, 11.44, 12.306, 18.287; philosophy means 'love of wisdom', but it's really a craze or passion 12.551; it means love of wisdom, but it suggests something thought rather than seen 11.158; the love of wisdom for its own sake 15.314; all philosophizing begins with the experience of pain 7.389; people philosophize for the same reason they eat – because they feel

dissatisfied 7.389; begins its investigations with only one assumption: that knowledge is possible 7.190; a philosophy cannot be founded on reasons 26.76; psychological starting point 1.123; suffering from the lack of a philosophy of life 5.663–4; everyone has a philosophy of some kind 3.7, 3.58

what it does
all philosophies can guide and sustain all people of all periods of history 7.81; distinctions between philosophy and other branches of knowledge 7.190; endeavouring to comprehend the whole of existence 7.191; it 'is developed to conceptualize the ideal aspirations of a people' 8.604; it should suggest extra dimensions of things 18.287; it shows us how important it is to investigate the causes of things 3.261, 7.115; it takes for its object all time and all existence 4.647; the philosopher as 'the spectator of all time and all existence' (Plato) 7.191, 7.387; philosophers' attempts to analyse the universe 17.439–40; philosophy as a substitute for religion 12.45; philosophy titillates the rational surface of our being, poetry stirs it to its depths 1.347; a quest for truth, and the instrument of the quest is reason 10.142; the rational construction of reality 26.45

systems
attempts to build ever more elaborate systems 7.385; developed by Nietzsche's predecessors 3.494; fixed and unchanging: time and existence frozen 7.385–6; incorrect because partial (the blind men and the elephant) 9.227–8; philosophers building systems in accordance with subjective preferences 7.386–8; the problem with a system that expresses eternity in terms of time 7.386; theism 9.228

studying philosophy
any school of philosophy could ossify into an academic system 19.374; in the past all philosophies were religious, but then secular philosophies arose 10.344; secular philosophies 10.344–50; fallacy that linguistic convention about change denotes a real distinction between things 2.87; 'How many angels can dance on the head of a pin?' 14.76; many 'philosophical' difficulties are really linguistic difficulties 19.437; philosophical schools make the error of investing concepts with ultimate reality 17.368; philosophies arising from rationalization of belief in self 17.619–20; studying philosophy but never committing oneself to its practical implications 15.523; Westerners should acquaint themselves with Eastern philosophy 12.51

Sangharakshita's study of philosophy
logic: 'one of the most fascinating … stretches of the intellectual terrain' 20.446; studies with Bhikkhu Kashyap 20.446; Neo-Hegelianism 20.81, 20.83; Schopenhauer 20.83; troubled by problems of philosophy 20.159–60

BUDDHIST PHILOSOPHY

is philosophy the right word?
is Buddhism a philosophy? 7.24–5, 7.191, 8.604; not a very suitable term 4.647, 10.142; it should always go together with religion and be called Dharma 7.388; the logical connection between Buddhism as philosophy and as religion 7.202–3; 'Philosophy and Religion in Original and Developed Buddhism' 7.190–206

the essentials
the starting point is the Buddha's spiritual experience 8.498, 19.353; the central philosophy 10.142–3; the fundamental philosophy is *śūnyatā* 19.158; the only possible philosophical starting-point is suffering, *dukkha* 7.388; philosophy and the five *skandhas* 4.28; why the Buddha made *anattā* the ultimate philosophical foundation 7.374; principles 4.637–8; *The Buddhist Philosophy of Universal Flux*, *see* Mookerjee; *Essentials of Buddhist Philosophy*, *see* Takakusa

its nature
the Buddha gave to philosophical problems a purely pragmatic value 7.50, 7.69; the synoptic nature of the Buddha's thought (the blind men and the elephant) 7.197; Buddhism is neither a monism nor a pluralism 4.166; a communication by rational means of a reality already experienced 8.498; the conceptual formulation of the non-conceptual content of wisdom 7.509; an intelligible process of organic growth 7.199–200; it discloses awe-inspiring perspectives 7.486; it shifts the emphasis from the cognitive to the affective mode of experience 7.388; its emphasis is on seeing things as processes rather than entities 19.238; the Middle Way in philosophy 9.397–8; vast, profound, and sometimes very technical 12.515

history
Early Buddhist and Mahāyāna, but no Vajrayāna 18.407–8; the struggle between Buddhism and the abstract noun 3.398; pluralistic realism, absolutism, and idealism

all flourished in turn 7.488; in some Buddhist circles the study of philosophy became an end in itself 8.498; 'Philosophy and Religion in Original and Developed Buddhism' 1.120, 7.190–206, 15.637; *The Psychological Attitude of Early Buddhist Philosophy*, *see* Govinda

practice
Buddhism is not just learning philosophy, but changing our lives 3.370; if you don't practise it, your knowledge of it is only nominal 19.446; the need to take it literally to begin with 19.38–9; no need to take a philosophical position to lead the spiritual life 10.598; you are not a philosophical innocent, your mind is full of *micchā-diṭṭhis* 19.508; you only master it once you've experienced the truth to which it points 19.354

OTHER SYSTEMS OF PHILOSOPHY

Indian
its central concern the nature of man and how to transcend the present situation 8.456; considers all philosophical points of view to be equally valid 7.387; contrast between Indian and Western philosophy 7.77–8; *darśana* (view) is the key to Indian philosophy 7.78, 11.158; depends on the ancient thought of the Vedas, Upanishads, and Vedānta 8.604; emphasis on principles rather than on persons 7.77, 7.80; history 7.77–80; includes religion, work, and art 7.79; interest of Western philosophers in Asian philosophy 8.606; it has much in common with modern existentialism 8.457; the Sāṃkhya school, *see* Sāṃkhya; the six schools of classical Indian philosophy 11.158, 17.44, 17.712 (n52); truth is one, sages only call it variously 7.78; *Companion Encyclopedia of Asian Philosophy* (review) 8.603–6; *Yoga and Indian Philosophy* (review) 8.454–8

Greek
emergence in the Axial Age 3.427; it begins with the cosmological speculations of the Milesian school 8.456; to begin with, the Greeks' development of reason was rather 'brittle' 15.743; the passionate pursuit of beauty, truth, and goodness 26.104; philosophical spiritual communities 3.428–9; Eleatic philosophers 7.195; *A Critical History of Greek Philosophy* 7.195–6; see *also* individual Greek philosophers

Western (post-Greek)
all pre-Kantian philosophy is called pre-critical 10.597; British philosophy has virtually no connection with Christianity 12.77; 'Buddhism and Contemporary Western Philosophy' (Jayatilleke) 8.399; compared to the blind men who tried to describe the elephant 7.77–8; beginning with a quest for objectivity, later addressed the existential situation 8.456; ideas of self 8.613–14; in modern times has become a barren study detached from a way of life 26.104; often the personality of the philosopher translated into the language of thought 7.77; often speculative 19.353; 'at Oxford all they're interested in is linguistic analysis' 11.530, 12.170, 23.55–6; saw philosophy and religion as different things 7.387

see also
nihilism; plenism

Philpot, Glyn Warren 24.379

Phooley, Mahatma Jyotirao 9.438

photography Dhardo Rimpoche was very fond of photography 12.434; an exhibition of photographic portraits 24.358–9; Paramartha's dislike of photography 24.444; Sangharakshita takes up photography (1970) 23.469–71

***phowa* practice** the *phowa* practice of Amitābha 12.449; transference of consciousness (one of the six yogas of Nāropā) 13.28

phrenology 11.734–5, 26.637–8

Phrom, Ven. Maha 10.131, 10.138

physician the Buddha as a physician 3.213; the parable of the good physician, *see under White Lotus Sūtra*/parables

Picasso, Pablo 'Art is a lie that makes us realize truth' 26.4; *Guernica* 24.410

Pierpoint, Garry *see* Mokshapriya

pigs 'diamond sow', *see* Vajravārāhī; most human beings are content to be human beings, as a pig is content to be a pig 26.173; the pig at the hub, *see under* wheel of life; wallowing arrogantly in the world like a pig in his sty 19.494

pilgrimage focal points: Canterbury in the Middle Ages, Shakespeare's birthplace today 14.465; Heaven is a pleasant interlude in a pilgrimage of more serious import 2.86, 26.47; it may be better to stay at home and get on with your meditation 19.339; let us set forth as pilgrims upon the Middle Way 7.418; monks on pilgrimage: 'a motley collection of rogues in yellow robes' 23.399; Muslim pilgrims on the road between Bombay and Poona 24.104; no distinction between path and pilgrim 10.153; observing vegetarianism while

on pilgrimage 8.223–4; of Sudhana in the *Gaṇḍavyūha Sūtra*, *see Gaṇḍavyūha Sūtra*; paying respect to holy places 1.407, 4.324–5; the pilgrim is the path 11.656; to places associated with the Buddha's life, *see* four holy places; to places associated with great national figures 14.463; to the sacred mountains in China 2.224; Tibetan pilgrims 7.415–18, 19.335, 20.455–6; visiting Triratna centres 10.397; *The Way of the Pilgrim* and *The Pilgrim Continues His Way* (Russian works) 23.332; we are all bound on the same pilgrimage 7.364–5

Pilindavaccha 10.514

Pillai, Kesava (Muvattupuzha lawyer) v20

Pillai, Krishna (Muvattupuzha postal service) v20

Pillai, Shankara (ashram cook and manager) v20

Pindar 3.427, 23.288, 23.298

Piṇḍola Bhāradvāja 10.537–8

Piṅgiya (the Buddha's disciple) 1.287–9, 4.709 (n333)

Pinturicchio 13.637

Piombo, Sebastiano del 24.273, 24.676 (n333)

Pippala Cave *see under* Rajgir

Pirith Potha 8.532–3

pirivena 8.472, 23.42, 23.481 (n73)

piśācas (vampires) 16.346

Pisanello 23.255, 23.511 (n288)

Pistis Sophia *see under* Gnosticism

Piṭakas *see* Tripiṭaka

Pith-Instructions contrast between written words and direct teachings 19.460–1; the cow is Buddhism, the milk is the Vajrayāna, the butter is the Pith-Instruction 18.408; an example of skilful means 19.204; the one-sentence Pith-Instruction 18.186; giving Pith-Instructions is a very specific kind of teaching 19.204; they will come if you are well-versed in Buddhist principles and find a reliable guru 19.577–8; the instruction given by the guru directly to the disciple 19.388; it's through love and compassion that you can convert the Dharma into Pith-Instructions 19.204–5; many of the Buddha's teachings were Pith-Instructions 19.205–6; a personalized application of the Dharma 18.xvii, 18.162, 18.262, 18.408, 19.202; the Pith-Instructions given by Marpa to Milarepa 18.593–4; the Pith-Instructions of Reason and the Scriptures 19.202–3; the quintessential teachings of the Vajrayāna 19.129; Rechungpa thinks instructions are fine as long as they tell you to do what you want to do 19.365; you need someone to boil down the ocean of the teaching into a few drops 19.461–2; you need three things: the general teaching, the Pith-Instruction, and your own judgement 18.408

pīti *see prīti*

pity the difference between compassion and pity 12.661; 'Justice and Pity' (poem) 25.437; *kāruṇya rasa* (pity in Indian aesthetics) 24.564; looking down on people in a pitying way does no good at all 4.52; near enemy of compassion 5.201; 'Pity melts the mind to love' 26.613; in Shaw's play *Candida* 5.201; sometimes what passes for compassion is pity, which makes things worse 4.193; Stephan Zweig's *Beware of Pity* 12.661

Piyadassi, Ven. photographs 11.474, 23.33; *The Book of Protection* (review) 8.531–2; *The Seven Factors of Enlightenment* 8.383

Piyasilo (Malaysian monk) 24.617 (n64)

planets discerning planets from far stars 14.605–6; planetary conjunctions may have an influence, but they are not determining factors 19.269–70; the planets' dance of joy about the sun 25.497; theologians on the possibility of life on other planets 8.157; wish to live on a planet where friendship is the rule of life 25.454

planning arrange things provisionally and flexibly 19.525; don't tie your life up too much even with positive plans and schemes 19.522; having to have your life planned in advance 18.460–1; developing a plan to become more ethical 10.222–3; 'I believe in rebirth, but I'm planning for *this* life, not the next' 4.404; only commit yourself to a plan that can absorb all your energies and interests 19.522–4; planning our lives away 11.10; plans can only be provisional 17.475, 24.402

plants *see* flowers and plants

Platform Sūtra *see Sūtra of Huineng*

Plato

his life
introduction 7.570–1 (n133); his academy 3.560, 26.367; the gulf separating Plato from the average man (Nietzsche) 3.499; he died for others 12.9, 12.701–2 (n7)

work and sayings
the philosopher as 'the spectator of all time and all existence' 7.191, 7.387; 'Philosophy begins with a sense of wonder' 4.212, 11.44, 12.306, 18.287; comparison of Buddhist discourses with Platonic dialogues 14.36–7; the denial of the existence of the world of appearance 7.194; doctrine of reminiscence 16.61; for him the animal elements are excluded from the human essence 8.613; his Ideas 'an unearthly ballet of bloodless categories' 14.85, 26.163; his view that educating a pupil is also an education for the teacher 18.419; he knew that sense experience is only part of the spectrum of human experience 5.51; myths 24.537; truth flashes upon the soul, 'like a flame kindled by a leaping spark' 3.164; universals 14.589; view of the universe as alive 4.15

his influence
influence on Christianity and Islam 7.486; influence on Renaissance Europe 26.314; philosophical debate as to whether the existence of universals is real or notional 16.133; Plato and Platonism are inseparable 7.77; the revival of Platonism (Renaissance) 23.297; 'Western philosophy is little more than a series of footnotes to Plato' (Whitehead) 3.427; Sangharakshita's first reading of Plato 20.61

Republic
introduction 23.491 (n130); the guardians 15.538, 15.767 (n206); the idea of justice 12.463; Plato's dream of an ideal society 1.539; the prisoners in the cave 2.641–2, 2.756–7 (n789), 11.709–10, 26.106–8, 26.110; the sun as a symbol of the Good 13.61, 13.676 (n22)

Symposium
Alcibiades compares Socrates to a satyr 10.619, 10.721–2 (n488); the ascending scale of beauty 13.279, 14.310, 19.24, 26.137–8; 'A Crumb from the Symposium' (poem) 25.270; Eros as a daemon or intermediary 18.158; the infinite and universal realm of poetry and Truth 26.136–7; the myth of the people seeking their 'other half' 23.111, 23.491–2 (n140); Plato learned about Eros from Diotima 2.691 (n303), 26.312–15, 26.316–18, 26.665; Plato on beauty 25.232; progressive refinement of love 5.511, 5.618, 5.756 (n583); recommendation to read 12.406

other works
Apology of Socrates, *Ion*, and *Meno* 23.286; *Dialogues* 1.312; *Euthyphro* 24.362, 24.389; *First Alcibiades* 23.311, 23.521 (n351); *Parmenides* 16.23, 16.588–9 (n30); *Phaedo* 24.389; *Phaedrus* 24.389, 25.4; *Theaetetus* 4.212, 11.44, 12.306, 18.287

play and playfulness an antidote to over-mindfulness 16.301; the bodhisattva's life becomes a sort of play, a sort of spontaneous manifestation 4.240; competitiveness in the spiritual community should be playful, not about power 18.17–19; even while doing your best to succeed, remember it's essentially a game 14.523; the free play of the Transcendental 19.24; frivolity is the near enemy of playfulness 19.397; if you don't allow space to your irrational, playful side, it will creep in somehow 19.25; in our society we have divorced work from play, but they can go together 18.392, 24.66; the *Lalitavistara*'s account of the Buddha's life as 'child's play', *see Lalitavistara*; not taking oneself too seriously 4.137–8; perhaps we don't play hard enough 11.407; the play of the irreversible bodhisattva 14.501; the playful and inexhaustible manifestation of the Enlightened mind 18.48; play is not necessary, which is why it's necessary 14.521–2; the playful arts (*lalitakalā*) 14.521; playfulness on a transcendental level 19.51; playwords 18.66; work is the companion, but play is the lover 25.400

pleasure

what is pleasure?
not in itself unskilful 15.158; not the same thing as happiness 17.166, 19.584; 'pleasures are like poppies spread' 26.398; positive emotion is pleasurable and at the same time skilful 26.77; the pursuit of pleasure is the only rational purpose in life (Epicurus) 17.507; really a by-product of something else 17.507; 'that which one wants to feel again' 17.505–6; a *vipāka*, neither skilful or unskilful 18.528, 19.93, 19.381

the importance of pleasure
a certain amount is a tonic, but don't try to squeeze pleasure out of a situation 17.507; the element of pleasure is important for a human being 19.91; healthy pleasure is very nourishing 19.384; one can say we need pleasure, but it's better to say we need happiness 19.583–4; pleasure is an essential part of human, and spiritual, life 17.301–2; pleasure is our life, pleasure is our energy 19.381; we are largely ruled by pleasure, and we can't function well without it 18.129; we have to be honest about the importance we give to pleasure 17.302

worldly pleasures
bodhisattva Fugen Bosatsu, as a courtesan, teaches those addicted to pleasure 1.448–9; dangerous to deprive oneself based on a rational understanding of Buddhism 16.284; some religions advise giving them up, but better to give up misery 17.396–7; they are all conditioned, so they don't essentially differ from one another 16.284; they are unsure and impermanent 17.363; the unsatisfactoriness of pleasant worldly experiences 18.589; the universe's ceaseless pursuit of pleasure 7.47; you don't have to take occasional hankerings seriously 18.446–7; you don't have to try them all out to make sure! 16.284

the downsides of pleasure
aesthetic pleasures don't necessarily reflect the golden light 16.285; an emphasis on pleasure may discourage the development of *mettā* 5.126; fear of losing pleasure 3.214–15; mental pleasures: ways we distract ourselves from the tedium of life 17.393; for mundane pleasures we forgo the deeper pleasures of spiritual life 17.300; the pleasures of flesh and brain are fleeting 7.47, 7.51; sensual pleasures don't satisfy any more than a meatless bone satisfies a dog 14.42; 'To indulge in luxury and pleasure is the cause of poverty and death' 18.472; when we realize the fact of *dukkha*, the pleasures of the senses lose their relish 7.50–1; when you love pleasure you'll go after it at all costs 19.493; why sacrifice real happiness for transitory pleasure? 17.163

pleasure and pain
elusive 17.506; the human attitude to them is complex 17.302; the human state involves both 2.95, 19.497–8; even pleasant things, being ephemeral, are potentially sources of pain 1.128–9; inseparable (*The Prophet*) 1.129; the same body that can experience pleasure can also experience pain 10.482; interconnectedness 2.90–1; made by oneself or by another? 10.599; the more we grasp pleasure, the more we find we are holding onto pain 17.506; Nāgārjuna shows that they are less real than we assume 17.394–401; Nāgārjuna's challenge to seeking pleasure and avoiding pain 17.409; *nirāmisa*: a mode of feeling beyond pleasure and pain 15.155–6; a novel in which attempts to make life perfect lead to sensitivity and pain 17.395; one can experience both at the same time 17.511; our infatuation with pleasures prevents us from seeing the fact of suffering 7.388–9; equally unreal 17.405–6; pain now and pleasure later or *vice versa*, both perpetuate *saṃsāra* 10.608; pleasure is only succeeded by pain because of attachment 10.497–8; rapid alternation of pain and pleasure 17.506; we are dominated by what we think is pleasant and what we think is painful 10.482–3; we forget that pleasure is bound up with pain 10.497–8; we take a surrender of pleasure to be pain 17.409; what we take for pleasure is slight amelioration of pain 17.397

pleasure, attachment, and craving
better to not be attached to pleasure, but there's nothing unskilful in pleasure itself 19.493; the danger is when pleasure becomes the basis for craving or attachment 15.533; freeing oneself from attachment to pleasure 17.405; pleasure and craving 18.527–30, 19.380–4; attachment to sense pleasures 1.112; attachment to worldly pleasures a product of the reactive mind 18.130; what makes pleasure lead to craving? 19.92–3

the complexities of pleasure
although we run after it for a million years, we shall never find it 7.48; from an absolute perspective pleasant experience is *dukkha*, but it is still pleasant 17.592; if you're tense in anticipation, it spoils the enjoyment 19.387; it is tied up with anxiety because we are afraid of losing it 2.91; the more we acquire, the less enjoyment our 'pleasures' bring 17.394; most things we label 'pleasure' are really a mixed experience 17.400–1; occasional pleasures easily turn into regular indulgences 17.253; pleasure comes not from sense-objects, but from engaging our energies 18.158; tainted by repressed awareness that we enjoy it at someone else's expense 2.91; we don't enjoy our pleasures as much as we imagine we do 17.397–8

further perspectives on pleasure
art gives both pleasure and meaning 26.165–6; even pleasant experiences can only be enjoyed for a certain amount of time 17.505–6; expressing positive energy is always pleasurable 15.217; Faust and the desire for pleasure 17.397–8; our capacity for delight in simple pleasures in childhood 18.130; passivity is at best a pleasurable state, happiness is active 19.583, 26.63; physical and mental pleasure are inseparable 17.393; the pleasure given by the arts educates the heart and mind 26.99; pleasure is not something to be feared 8.446; the pleasure of the direct expression of emotion 18.610; pleasures that give rise

to skilful mental states 19.584; the purest physical pleasure: a cup of cold water on a hot day 17.393; simple pleasure from contact with nature 19.92–3; unpleasant experience can become pleasant, an acquired taste 17.506; we rarely experience pleasure through more than one sense organ at a time 17.394–5

giving up pleasure
'If you want Buddhahood, forget all pleasures of this life' 19.585; giving up the desire for pleasure 19.90–4; if you give up pleasures indefinitely, your spiritual life will dry up in the end 19.384; it's more like giving up worldly miseries and taking up spiritual happiness 26.64; lay Buddhists unable to give pleasures up yet 4.564–5; unwise to advise giving it up for the sake of spiritual pleasures to come 17.301; you don't necessarily get closer to happiness by depriving yourself of pleasure 19.244

pleasure in the Buddhist tradition
the pleasure the Buddha experienced could not lay hold of his mind 2.108, 17.528, 18.581; the possibility of enjoying pleasures and remaining unattached (Pāli canon) 17.221; 'stuck on pleasure's ties' (*Udāna*) 10.616–17; the Theravādin attitude to pleasure 19.384; Nāgārjuna argues that pleasure is unreal 17.403–9; pleasure and *śūnyatā* 17.404; the Tantra advocates shunning sexual pleasure 1.391–2; the Vajrayāna's attitude to pleasure 18.528–30, 19.379–84; four stages of bliss (Vajrayāna) 2.91

pleasure and spiritual practice
be mindful of pleasure and try to unite its energy with insight 19.379; be mindful while enjoying pleasure, or it will lead to suffering 18.151; challenge yourself to move beyond your habitual sources of pleasure 15.158; developing a more refined sense of pleasure (*dharmachanda*) 18.129–30; don't make pleasure the criterion for what you do 10.483; faith distinguished from pleasure 17.552–3, 17.672–3; few practitioners would cite spiritual experiences as their greatest pleasures 17.301; finding pleasure outside the objects of craving 17.271; the hedonic element is an essential part of the quest 8.446; in friendship one is ready to sacrifice one's own pleasure for that of another 7.293; in touch with the *bodhicitta*, you can amuse yourself with sensuous pleasures 14.188; learning to share our pleasures 18.130; turning away from sense pleasures on the basis of meditative experience 17.513–14; pleasure in the *dhyānas* 4.152–3, 4.482; pleasure is to be enjoyed, but not made the occasion of clinging 19.380–1; the pleasure of equanimity 4.153; seeing that pleasures have their limitations, you're not attached to them 15.449; trying to realize non-self, not pleasant feelings 17.511–12

see also
pleasant feeling, *see under vedanā*; pleasure and pain as worldly winds, *see* eight worldly winds

plenism 7.126

Plethon, Gemistos 23.296–7

pliability or pliancy *see* flexibility

Pliny the Elder 24.284–5

Plotinus

introduction
brief introduction 23.524 (n362); his teacher was Ammonius Saccas 26.368; apparently had no interest in ritual 13.292; a balance between rationalism and mysticism 26.367; his influence 26.666; his 'lineage' 26.367–8; the idea of emanation 12.463; 'Phraseology and Imagery in Plotinus and Indian Thought' 13.374; 'Plotinus and Vijñānavāda Buddhism' 13.374; Sangharakshita (at one time) could make very little of most of his writings 23.317; *Select Works of Plotinus* (trans. Thomas Taylor) 23.317; spiritual community founded by Plotinus 3.560; *The Philosophy of Plotinus*, *see* Inge

Enneads
the collection of writings put together by Plotinus' student Porphyry 23.524 (n363), 24.362; different translations 23.316–17; *Fourth* and *Fifth Enneads* 24.396; inspiring 26.366; 'Never did the eye see the sun unless it had at first become sun-like' 3.58, 4.33, 16.533; 'On Beauty' 14.311, 23.317–18, 26.596, 26.665–6; Sangharakshita's reading 24.311, 26.590

pluralism 17.362

pluralistic realism Radhakrishnan on the subject 7.539, 12.143, 17.444; Sarvāstivādin Abhidharma 1.103, 1.221, 7.539–40, 12.143, 14.360, 17.443–4; an attempt to explain the difference between *Sutta* and Abhidhamma 1.224; countered by the doctrine of the twofold *nairātmya* 2.88

Plutarch introduction 26.751 (n467); on the history of Egypt 26.494; *Isis and Osiris* 23.427, 23.537 (n461); *Lives* 23.245, 23.260, 23.385

Pluto 16.385

Poe, Edgar Allan 22.276, 22.600 (n222)

poetry

the nature of poetry
all great poetry is incantation, a kind of mantra 26.211–12; the essence of poetry is imagery 26.208–10; 'emotion recollected in tranquillity' (Wordsworth) 26.144; the magic of poetry 26.420; the most fully developed form of art 26.165; the mystery of poetry 26.335; 'The Nature of Poetry' (Murry) 26.335; the natural language of the soul 26.386; no poetry without intellectual content, but the two are not identical 22.269; plea for a vivid realization of the poetic nature of speech 26.70; a poem is a whole and its parts are inseparable 26.133, 26.212; poetry as a kind of mantra 26.211–12, 26.394; 'the poetry is in the pity' (Owen) 26.395–6; it expresses the personality of the poet 26.134; it is the literature of power *par excellence* 14.304; it is rooted in nursery rhyme and prophecy 25.433; 'simple, sensuous, and passionate' (Milton) 26.394; simultaneously expression and communication 1.191

what poetry can do
besides expressing the poet's emotions it communicates his sense of values 26.165–6; the cries of monkeys: touching melancholy in Chinese poetry 18.52–3; develop our sensitivities, refine our emotions, and open the way to meditation 12.672; get closer to reality than prose 19.238–9; how poems achieve vitality and the shock of delight 26.171; lift us out of the littleness of our being into an infinitely deeper, wider life 26.140; lyric poetry lifts our emotions to a high pitch of intensity 26.114; it 'enlarges the circumference of the imagination' (Shelley) 26.190; it is the mediator between the 'real' and the 'Ideal' 24.169, 25.36; perhaps for us poetry is 'whatever helps us to grow' 9.198; philosophy titillates the rational surface of our being, poetry stirs it to its depths 1.347; some types enlarge our sympathies 26.114; the spiritual function of poetry (Aurobindo) 26.118–20; 'A verse may find him who a sermon flies' (Herbert) 26.394; a way to communicate with the unconscious 12.106, 12.179, 12.181

what poetry means
don't lessen the impact of poetic images by giving them rational meanings 19.563; it's impossible to dissociate its emotional impact from its 'meaning' 26.118; making a poetic statement, not a metaphysical explanation 18.285; not *about* existence but *is* itself a new kind of existence (Rilke) 21.434; paraphrasing a poem takes you further away from it 19.563; a poem means what it says 14.302, 19.563, 26.68; 'poems don't tell you what to do' 26.395, 26.399; poetry is not about anything except itself 19.71; poetry isn't a guide in the way the Dharma is 26.395; searching for moral messages in poetry 26.394–5

poetry and Buddhism
the Buddha's prophecy about discourses by poets in the future 14.136; in Buddhism we need to use language poetically rather than scientifically 19.447; at a certain level, poetry and the Dharma are the same thing 21.78–9, 26.393; comparison of English and Zen poetry 17.322; the Dharma is probably closer to poetry than science 14.549; the discovery that teaching poetry *is* teaching Buddhism 21.77–9, 21.434; distinction between poetry and the word of the Buddha 2.168; no need to choose between Buddhist scriptures and English poetry 22.464; poetic descriptions of the goal 2.131–2; the poetry of the Mahāyāna *sūtras* 16.532; take the Buddha's statements poetically rather than scientifically 19.242; using Western poetic expressions to express Buddhist ideas and truths 16.138

poetic subjects
mysticism in poetry 26.137; poems rejoicing in merits 26.399; the poetry of common things 25.240; the poetry of friendship 25.407; reflections on transitoriness in poetry 13.228; truth is made memorable when it finds poetic expression 13.644; wisdom in poetry 25.239

reading poetry
bringing feeling to your reading of poetry 19.179; could it lead to *dhyāna*? 5.641–2; feed the soul with poetry 25.453; giving oneself to the poem 22.465; a kind of meditation 15.259; learning poetry by heart 26.393, 26.439; learning to enjoy poetry 9.444; 'Read aloud, all poems are good poems' 25.404; reading a poem, you move from words to experience 19.452; reading a wonderful poem by a poet of whom we haven't heard 12.526; reading poetry all day might only produce a few moments of exhilaration 17.396; to read exalted poetry is an initiation into a new mode of being 26.140; 'We are all poets when we read a poem well' 26.191

writing poetry
the contrast between writing poetry and writing prose 16.532; a poem is the embodiment of a certain mood 1.144;

Rilke's description of writing poetry 26.171–2; theory behind poetic practice 25.433; 'When Inspiration cracks the moulds of verse' 25.278; writing a poem, it's 'us' writing, but it's not 'us' 4.265

criticism and appreciation
critique of modern poetry 14.xii, 14.293–4; did Sangharakshita expect his disciples to appreciate poetry? 26.393, 26.399–400; 'English poetry's on its last legs' 25.433; for Poetry your heartstrings are the only stuff 25.288; gratitude towards poets 3.602; grief at the loss of Sappho's poems 25.285; 'Histories make men wise and the study of the poets makes them witty' 10.474; literary criticism is concerned primarily with the *enjoyment* of poetry 26.320–1; losing the capacity to enjoy poetry 16.532–3; perhaps only in the field of poetry have the English been truly great 26.21; 'Poetry is a great thing, a great thing to me' 25.391; theology is to mysticism as literary criticism is to poetry 26.45; 'tired lyrists of a tuneless age' 25.257; when poetry ceases to be enjoyed it is no longer poetry 26.68

poetic forms
alexandrines 22.89, 22.582 (n90), 25.350; ballads 25.334, 26.394; blank verse 15.xiii; the different genres of poetry 26.139; haiku 21.23–4, 21.94; Indian poetry 7.54–63; in poetry substance and form coalesce 26.133–4; metre in Indian poetry 26.331; metric poetry has a mantra-like effect 26.394; nursery rhymes 25.426–7, 25.433, 26.394, 26.439; the poetic image 26.208–10; rhythm in poetry 26.210–11; Vedic hymns 16.362

see also
Sangharakshita's poetry, *see under* Sangharakshita XIII/writing poetry; Sangharakshita's reading of poetry, *see under* Sangharakshita XII/reading/poetry

poets

what the poet is
'the best but live what once the poet dreamed' 25.359; 'the hierophants of an unapprehended inspiration' 26.209; the poet's kin are Memnon, Orpheus, Merlin 25.359; 'Poets and priests were one in the beginning' 22.180, 25.478; poets are born, not made (Horace) 26.133; poets as spiritual friends 3.603; the kinship between prophet and poet 26.178; a self-centred man can never be a great poet 26.140; 'What a fantastic creature is the poet' 25.228; the world's interpreter 25.359

the qualities of the poet
observational powers 26.135–6; the personality of the poet 26.134; receptiveness and creativity 26.171; rooted in the objective world as the plant is rooted in the soil 26.170; sensitivity to words 3.507; sympathy 26.139–40; they mean exactly what they say 14.302, 19.563, 26.68

advice for the poet
'Advice to a Young Poet' 2.424, 21.435–6, 26.xvi, 26.92, 26.133–47; develop observation, sensitiveness, sympathy, solitude, reflection 26.134–42; 'Do not offer your poem to a man who is not a poet' 8.496; don't earn your living from other kinds of writing 26.142–3; be aware of your feelings at all times 26.138; familiarity with music and painting enlarges the scope of poetry 26.146; living the poet's life 26.141–4; read the poetry of others, from your own culture and other countries 26.145–6; the risks of not being a poet and being one 25.456

the poet's way
may experience inspiration from within or from outside 4.131, 19.141; persists in seeing the universe as alive 15.139; 'The Poet' (poem) 25.414; the poet is not always fully conscious of what he is doing 26.3–4; 'the poet views the expanse of the whole universe' 14.295; 'The Poet's Reply' (poem) 25.192; poets as prophets, prophets as poets 26.209–10; practice of reflection 26.144–5; 'The real poet is the one who is able to write poetry in prose' 26.331; the religious teacher's advantage over the poet in communication 14.16; responds to the world beyond 26.137; the secularism of great English poets 12.76; should be familiar with the philosophy of aesthetics 26.146; subtilizes emotions through the asceticism of art 26.137–8, 26.170; the true poet seeks to enrich and refine his experience 26.170–1

the writing process
how he produces 'not a fourth note, but a star' is known only to the poet 26.144; learning poetic technique 26.146–7; 'The poet listens for the inevitable word' 25.436; a poet's sources may have their roots in the past or in the present 7.57; poetic inspiration as a kind of madness (Plato) 25.4; the 'poetic' state of mind, out of which poems emerge 24.168–9; uses ordinary words to communicate something new 16.138

a miscellany of poets
Buddhist poets 2.213; the Lake Poets 24.143–4, 24.640 (n168); 'The Minor

Poets' 25.lix, 25.412; 'The Modern Bard' 25.254; Romantic poets 12.698, 16.387

see also
Beat Poets; individual poets; Sufi poets, *see under* Sufism

Point of No Return introduction 3.250–3, 19.606 (n100); the Āryasaṅgha consists of all those who have passed this point 15.641; beyond the Point of No Return 15.636, 19.237–8; does one ever reach a point when there is nothing more to do? 18.268; the eighth positive *nidāna* as the Point of No Return 3.252–3, 4.182–3, 4.650, 12.163; 'knowledge and vision of things as they really are', *see* knowledge and vision; synonymous with Stream Entry 3.251–3, 13.432, 15.467; your transformation of craving has to be made irreversible 12.627; *see also* irreversibility

pointing-out ceremony *see under* Mahāmudrā

Points of Controversy *see Kathā-vatthu*

poison being poisoned by someone's negative emotions 22.416–17; grasping a poisonous snake: metaphor for the *lakṣaṇas* 3.276; 'handling poison' (metaphor in *Dhammapada*) 15.367–8; if the medicine becomes poisonous, where will you turn for treatment? 17.630; unskilful mental states are dangerous things, like poison 15.367; poison and antidote: an interdependent duality 17.368; poisoned arrow 1.112, 4.374, 16.93–4, 16.192, 18.442; pot of poison 16.398–9; shun evil like poison 15.367; spewing up poison (impurities) 10.450–1, 16.292–3; struggle between the golden light and one's inner poisons 16.290–1

see also
five *kleśas*; three roots; trade in poisons, *see under* wrong livelihood

Pol Pot 26.654

Poland famous Poles 26.450; Polish history 26.446, 26.451; Sangharakshita's visit to Kraków 26.404, 26.446–52; 'In Kraków' (poems) 25.442; Triratna activities 26.7439–40 (n384)

polarization between coveting subject and coveted object 2.386; between immanence and transcendence 20.234; between men and women 15.530; between the twin ideals of world-fulfilment and world-renunciation 1.274, 20.234–5; the discriminating mind's polarizing activity imposes pairs of opposites on pure Voidness 7.299; is not polarized in the way most communication is 15.527–8; one of the aims of the Vajrayāna is depolarization 15.529; sexual polarization 2.371–2, 15.528–30

police Ananda Bodhi investigated by the police 23.85–7; a fervent admirer of the police in London 23.128; the police station in Kalimpong 21.122–3; a policeman discusses the Dharma while on traffic duty 12.399; Sangharakshita required to register with the police in India 20.269

politeness *see* manners

political correctness 4.127, 26.74

politics

democracy
definition 8.462; Dr Ambedkar anchored his conception of it in the Buddha's *mettā* 10.xxvii–xxviii; 'an attitude of respect towards one's fellow man' (Ambedkar) 9.106; Athenian democracy 10.65; in Buddhist and non-Buddhist countries 7.439; the degenerate ideals of modern liberal democracies 17.692; means equality before the law, not that everyone is equal 15.715; imposing democracy on the spiritual community 8.583; in a modern democracy, does anyone really feel free? 10.65; 'No volcano … is a greater revolution than this' 9.xxi; probably the best form of government humanity has devised 11.612; to apply the word to the Buddha is a confusion of thought 8.462; triumphs over autocracy in Nepal: a good thing? 21.277–8

politics between nations
European federalism 2.612–14; the failure of communication between superpowers 12.349–53; political contact between countries doesn't go deep enough 12.79

politicians and political movements
all grumbling, prevaricating, and propaganda 4.595; based on the concept of separate, mutually exclusive ego-entities 7.278, 13.448; the first aim of a politician should be to tell people the truth 17.231; local politics 22.111; people believe politics cannot solve the world's problems 9.284; political propaganda 7.266; the politician on the platform 25.300; protection of political leaders by the four great kings 16.356; socialism 11.604; subsidiarity 14.543; ultra left-wing and right-wing groups 15.489; why don't politicians tell the electorate the truth? 17.230–1

the state
it is the function of the state to help its citizens lead an aesthetic life 26.184; the

power of the corporate state over the individual 11.356–7; the state controls people by manipulating their negative emotions 26.20; a state is governed by a combination of force and inertia 26.20; the state should be organized to enable people to lead good lives 7.239

power
about who coerces whom 3.447, 16.477; fear of losing political power 3.214–15; like a hawk attacked by other hawks for the meat it is carrying 3.215; politicians tend to create *asura*-like worlds 17.298; the power mode 16.433; the welfare state 10.449, 12.380–1, 17.269, 18.335

government
being held responsible for the actions of your government 14.543; by righteousness: the Dharmarāja 1.541; Christians seeking laws to compel non-Christians to conform to their ideas 11.361; controls everything 9.284–5; the corporate state is the group *par excellence* 11.356–7; difficult task 16.478; the equitable distribution of resources 2.368–9; the form likely to be most in accord with the Buddha's teaching 7.438–9; government power in totalitarian regimes 26.654; the ideal embodied by the wheel-turning king (*cakravartin raja*, *dharmarāja*) 7.512; ideally no need for it because we would take responsibility for ourselves 16.478; 'May the government be righteous' 7.259; must uphold the moral and spiritual law 7.438–9; petty regulations 17.269; relationship to the Sangha 7.439–41; religious people giving their blessing to government or royal activities 19.463; should promote the welfare of the people, including animals 7.512; the squandering of public money 25.301; a time has come when we cannot get away from government 19.519–20; you can get away from home, but not the state 11.624

UK parliament
a Mitra who was a Member of Parliament 25.129; political orators 23.89; Sangharakshita visits Parliament 23.87–9; Sangharakshita quoted in Parliament 13.468, 26.640; the 'white heat of technological revolution' 23.87; 'You've never had it so good' – a shameful slogan 23.61, 23.87

Buddhism and politics
introduction 7.437–41; analogy between statesmanship and building a Buddha-land 16.477; beware of importing political terms into a spiritual context 11.690; the Buddha advises the *bhikkhus* of Śrāvasti to stop talking about politics 10.471–4; the Buddha refrained from commenting on politics 7.438; in the Buddha's day there was no politics in the modern sense 10.65; difficult political conditions for Dharma practice 4.100–1, 12.490; an inspiration for politics in Asia 7.452; involvement of Buddhists in politics 9.332–3, 9.532, 16.433–4; monks and politics 2.217, 7.441, 26.576; on the political plane, Buddhism does not take sides 7.452; the political implications of Buddhism in the modern world 7.451–2; should a Buddhist 'missionary' be involved in politics? 9.333; spiritual values must be given concrete expression, which may involve politics 25.125–6; too much emphasis on politics in the Buddhist movement in India 10.169; what would happen if a member of the sangha gained political power? 16.433; why did Buddhism not use political influence to enforce religious conformity? 7.383; why is politics not part of the Noble Eightfold Path? 1.543

personal politics
Buddhists should try to live their political life in accordance with the Dharma 7.439; constant activity in pursuit of politics is laziness 4.132, 17.534, 18.390, 19.582; the idea of private vices as public benefits 11.604; it's easier to criticize politicians than conduct our affairs in line with our values 17.231; one should try to see the ethical principles involved 1.541–2; the view that any kind of problem is someone else's fault 11.604; when you practise the Dharma, you might find your political views changing 10.630; why do people feel the need to pay lip service to political ideals? 19.247

Sangharakshita
'I will not be a pawn in the game of politics' 25.186; little interest in politics 23.87; thoughts about getting involved in politics 10.77–8; political views about Britain's position at the end of the Second World War 20.153–4; 'To a political friend' 25.166; a visit to the British Parliament 23.87–9

Pollock, Jackson 14.436

pollution environmental pollution, *see under* environment; noise pollution, *see under* noise; ritual pollution, *see under* Hinduism/and Hindu practice

Polo, Marco 23.258, 23.513 (n299)

polyandry *see under* marriage/Buddhist marriage

Polyclitus 24.265, 24.673 (n320)

polytheism 2.172

Pomfret, Clive *see* Kevala

pomposity 19.131

Ponnabalam 20.122

Pontius Pilate 13.570, 13.649, 13.650

Poona, India (Pune)

Buddhism
established 9.157; Buddha image installed at new temple (1954) 9.119; mass conversion ceremonies 10.160–1; progress 9.169–70, 10.283–4; training course in Buddhism, 1961 10.179–80, 23.488 (n118); Buddhist localities and the caste system 24.17; TBMSG (Triratna) 9.169–71, 24.19, 24.23, 24.53, 24.619 (n76); the *sangha-kṣetra* 10.255

Mahavihara and Dapodi
architects 10.367; its beauty 10.366, 10.404; the ethical basis 10.355; the foundation of the six perfections 10.354–7; heroic accomplishment 12.490, 12.737 (n316); keeping the Mahavihara beautiful 10.366; medical centre 10.317–18; men's community 10.368; photograph 10.192; a place of pilgrimage 10.367–8; Sangharakshita lays the foundation stone 10.lii, 10.354–7; Sangharakshita speaks there (1983) 10.xlix–l, 10.316–25; Sangharakshita's delight at the finished centre 10.liv; the whole complex in accordance with Dr Ambedkar's vision 10.354

other Buddhist places
the Poona District Buddhist Women's Association 10.161–2, 10.166, 10.181–2, 10.401; girls' hostel, Vishrantwadi 10.401–3, 10.405, 10.413; Ambedkar Housing Society 9.169, 24.14–16, 24.607 (n26)

other aspects of the city
Ahalyashram 24.17, 24.19; Camp 23.352, 23.528 (n395); the city of the Peshwas 23.349, 23.350; Debu Road temple 9.11, 9.71; a guru in Poona 26.693–4; Maharashtra Untouchable Youths' Conference 9.59; Pimpri 9.189, 10.210; Range Hills 10.168, 10.199; Sinhagad Fort 10.xlvi, 10.219, 24.20–1; Yerawada 10.204

Sangharakshita
'one of my favourite places in India' 22.295; visits the city for the first time 22.292–303; Dharma talks 9.169–206, 10.144, 10.160–1, 10.166–9, 10.193–284, 23.350; a very strong connection with the city 9.406–7; visits the city in 1966 23.349–53

see also
Nature Clinic and Society of the Servants of God, *see under* Mehta

Pope, Alexander 'the feast of reason and the flow of soul' 3.71, 3.639 (n78); 'guide, philosopher, and friend' 7.124, 7.149, 21.84; 'Hope springs eternal in the human breast' 7.162; 'Know then thyself, presume not God to scan' 26.398–9; 'A little learning is a dangerous thing' 1.198; 'Men not afraid of God, afraid of me' 17.560–1; 'Most women have no characters at all' 24.461; 'See, from the brake the whirring pheasant springs' 24.151; 'To err is human, to forgive divine' 26.647; translation of Homer's *Odyssey* 7.554 (n62)

Pope, Joan 23.166

popes *see under* Christianity/Roman Catholic church

Popper, Karl 8.617, 11.532

popularity the Buddha praises Ānanda's friendliness and popularity 3.179; the need of most religions to be popular 19.468; popularity of art 3.515; popular Buddhism, *see under* Buddhism III/an overview of the history; popular views only remain popular so long as a total truth has not been discovered 10.612; the popularity of Zen 12.224–5; popularizing meditation 12.645

porāṇacariyas ('former teachers') 3.603

pornography magazines in Italy 24.304; pornographic films 17.181, 26.362–3; related to sexual misconduct 13.446

Porphyry of Tyre brief introduction 23.525 (n365); *Against the Christians* 24.522; he put together Plotinus' *Enneads* 23.524 (n363); *Launching-Points to the Realm of Mind* 24.361–2, 24.389; life of Plotinus 3.560; *On Abstinence from Animal Food* 23.427

poṣadha* or *uposatha the Buddha says that he will no longer participate in *uposatha* days 10.557, 10.562; in early days, recitation of *prātimokṣa* in the sense of Dharma verses 1.146, 2.187; in coenobitical monasticism, recitation of monastic code 2.199; became a ceremony of confession (*pariṣuddhi*) 2.189, 2.199; connection with meditation 2.200; lay followers practise eight precepts on *poṣadha* days 2.204; originally suggested by King Bimbisāra 10.559; regular meetings first mentioned in the *Udāna* 10.559; two parts: group meditation and recitation of Dharma 2.200, 10.559–61; abolition of the meditation part 2.201

Poseidon 23.286–7, 23.289

positivity

a positive life
life can be positive although it involves unpleasant things 15.147; the patience of the positive outlasts the obstinacy of the negative 19.36; the positivity of the creative mind 11.25–6; the positivity of the gods 16.354; there is a dreadful lack of positivity in many people's lives 15.237; there must be a positive side to spiritual life 10.523, 18.129; we may be inclined towards the positive from a previous existence 17.589

developing positivity
association with positive people can help 11.13; better think of attachment to the positive than detachment from the negative 10.513; emphasize developing the positive 10.432, 10.525; having a positive base for your spiritual development 15.396, 15.399; it's quite easy to be positive 4.289; motivation to be positive needs reference to the transcendental 16.354; to be positive is absolutely essential to spiritual life 15.237

challenges
cynicism arises when one lacks positivity to guard against it 11.553; difficulty in taking something positive at face value 4.602; distinguishing between the genuinely positive and what gives satisfaction 16.354; repression: gender and class conditioning 4.597–8; thoughtlessly showing off your 'positivity' at someone else's expense 5.201; truly positive energy can be more difficult to deal with than negative energy 18.78

see also
mettā; positive emotions, *see under* emotions; positive mental states, *see under* mental states

possession 'possession by demons' – literal or psychological? 18.441–2; by spirits or demonic entities 4.542–3, 4.546–9, 16.305; the demon or Māra on the Tube train 4.546–7, 13.597–8; Jesus casts out demons from those possessed 13.594–5; the story of someone who was possessed: 'I am not talking to a human being' 4.544–5; a study of spirit-possession in Africa 4.548–9

possessions

Buddhist tradition
it is the duty of a friend to watch over our property when we are neglectful 3.574; an *arhant* finds it difficult to possess anything apart from his robe and bowl 10.630; in the *Dhammapada*, *see Dhammapada*/chapter 5; don't 'dispute over others' goods' 19.357; 'Let my possessions be lost ... but never mastery of the mind' 4.380; Milarepa lets go of grasping at his few remaining possessions 18.9–11

the problems of possessions
attachment 3.199, 17.284; the greater a man's possessions, the less likely he is to be contented with them 1.152; having possessions is a source of trouble 10.485–6, 18.218; the hoarding orientation (Erich Fromm) 12.276–7; in traditional societies, wealth is kept in the form of property 18.94–5; intellectual possessions 10.489; intoxication 15.423–4; making someone ashamed to enjoy something so you can enjoy it yourself 17.659; the more we acquire, the less enjoyment our 'pleasures' bring 17.394; the more you possess, the more you have to defend 18.187; no satisfaction to be gained from possessions 18.296; these days possessions are easy to get, so losing them doesn't matter 18.334–5, 19.13; regarding others as possessions 10.490, 18.219; sadness associated with the possessions of the dead 22.86; spending too much on cosmetics and clothes 12.554–5; the suffering of having them 10.489

what can we possess?
even the possessor of a thousand shirts can only wear one at a time 17.394; everything we could cling to is liable to be taken away 18.13; in the last resort we have no possessions, so ultimately we have no self 1.173; nothing really belongs to you 8.199; the whole idea of possessing things is neurotic 18.218; you can't take it with you when you go 18.472

giving them up
appreciate beauty, but relinquish desire to possess it 17.271; attachment lessened through faith 3.264; giving possessions away for the sake of the Dharma 18.219–20; giving them up 1.497; giving up the sense of possession 18.219; greed for acquisition attenuated 7.360; whatever can be possessed can be given away 4.95

happiness without them
Enlightenment isn't anyone's possession 18.314–15; the freedom of letting go of possessions 17.202; freedom from possessions: with no 'I' there is no 'mine' 10.489; if you don't have anything, there's no fear of losing it 18.341–2; in a spiritual community, should everything be common

property? 19.551–2; the less you own, the happier you are 10.488–90; the quiet generosity of those who possess almost nothing 18.115–16

Sangharakshita
finds himself acquiring possessions despite having gone forth 22.188; experience of living without possessions 10.489

see also
akiñcana ('without possessions')

possessiveness antidote: generosity, and contemplating impermanence 17.657; any kind of possessiveness goes against the spirit of the second precept 17.199; *my* home, *my* wife, *my* son – but nothing in the whole world is yours 18.219; possessive love 15.253, 15.254; towards children 3.538–9; towards a sexual partner 13.238–9

possums 24.79

postponement the bodhisattva's 'postponement' of Enlightenment, *see under* bodhisattva/bodhisattva activity; easy to make the mistake of postponing one's spiritual endeavours 7.169; make the best use of your opportunities, don't postpone things 18.555

posture *see under* meditation/working in meditation

Potalaka (Avalokiteśvara's abode) *see under* Avalokiteśvara

Potaliya Sutta *see under Majjhima Nikāya*

potential

human potential
the bigger the heap of mud, the bigger the Buddha 4.467, 25.73; the heart's possibilities 7.307, 25.274; the most beautiful aspect of a human being is their spiritual potential 15.130–1; the possibilities far transcend what they're usually considered to be 5.51; a vision of possibilities 11.167; we can make our lives sublime 8.234; the whole idea is new to a lot of people 18.569; 'Within me sleep potencies unfathomably deep' 25.175

references in the Buddhist tradition
the Buddha's vision of human potential, see Brahmā Sahāmpati's request; Buddhism has great confidence in the potential of the individual 11.359–60; the first precept covers not hindering people's potential for development 17.178; the *ālaya-vijñāna* recognizes reality as the principle of potentiality 2.43; the possibility of transformation represented by Avalokiteśvara 13.228; *tathāgatagarbha* as a reification of the principle, *see under tathāgatagarbha*; the terrific spiritual potential of Milarepa's shepherd disciple 18.234

latent potential
all the latent potentialities of the individual galvanized and integrated 1.389; change contains the potentiality for development 11.29; confidence in one's own potential 17.576; denial of one's own spiritual potential 4.78, 4.248; bodhisattvas are within us, potentially 13.287; having confidence in someone else's potential 15.364; having 'potential' for hatred doesn't mean it's present in you unconsciously 18.606–7; illness because one's potential is buried in the business of living 12.227; insights hold the potential for transformation 2.296; latent spiritual-creative powers 7.268; most people involved in Triratna only use a fraction of their potential 4.445–6; positive emotions are latent within you 14.533–4; the potentiality for evil is in all of us 25.75–6; we have the potential to modify our habit-volitions to promote growth 17.474; within each of the six realms there is the potential for development 13.135

realizing potential
freedom to realize our potential 8.579; friendship is richly endowed with the potential for spiritual development 7.294; the person you have the potential to become if you make the right kind of effort 13.317; realizing our potential will take a great deal of time and effort 4.33; the type of person who aims at the development of all their potentialities 12.277

see also
Enlightenment/potential

pots four kinds of disciple compared to four kinds of pot 17.160; giving up the space element: the simile of the broken pot 5.482; Milarepa's broken cooking-pot 13.27, 24.426; recognizing a 'not-pot' 17.520; 'swallowing the pot of poison' 7.99, 7.580 (n190), 16.398–9; the upside-down pot – lack of receptivity 17.160, 18.115, 18.117; *vitakka* and *vicāra* like scouring a pot 9.200, 16.601 (n119), 17.689

Poṭṭhapāda Sutta *see under Dīgha Nikāya*

Pound, Ezra 'Literature is language charged with meaning to the utmost possible degree' 14.296, 26.321; 'Make it new' 13.428; overrated 26.339

poverty

the poor
the attitude to the poor of rich people in India 17.212; the charity that shines from the huts of the poor 25.239; eating rice balls offered to the dead in after-death ceremonies 4.478; the poor exploited by the rich 3.581; in India 10.lvii, 20.109–10, 22.42–3, 23.337; poor people fare better in a 'primitive' society than in a competitive one 4.449–50; the poor man in the parable of the return journey 16.88–9; the poor seldom worry about their poverty 3.214

giving to the poor
create a shrine-room before setting up a soup kitchen 14.447; direct energy to practical help rather than sentimental lamentations 23.337; importance of meeting material needs 9.340; Mahāyāna precept against giving nothing to the destitute 2.208; one has to be able to afford to be altruistic 4.90

attitudes to poverty
Buddhism does not sanctify poverty, but it also does not sanctify materialism 10.389; 27.1074; Christian tendency to think of poverty as a virtue 10.347; it suggests that God is not pleased with you (missionaries say) 17.19–20, 21.354–5; Langland's feeling for the poor and respect for their faith 24.540; 'one should not preach religion to a man with an empty stomach' 9.340; poverty is not a virtue 10.125; religion must not ennoble or sanctify poverty 9.106–7, 9.400, 9.426, 10.362, 10.389; St Francis was wedded to Lady Poverty 13.624; Sangharakshita found that to be a poor *bhikkhu* was thought a disgrace 18.333; voluntary poverty 27.1074

mental poverty and riches
the ability to feel wealthy even in the humblest circumstances 17.201; absolute spiritual poverty 7.397; achievements to express inner abundance, not compensate for inner poverty 26.15; Milarepa's material poverty and spiritual wealth 18.50, 18.96; a miser will always feel poor 17.208; spiritual poverty 4.358, 7.397; 'To indulge in luxury and pleasure is the cause of poverty and death' 18.472

Powell, J. Enoch 4.355, 4.440

power

power in the sense of force
'Absolute power corrupts absolutely' 13.555, 22.338; being drunk with power 16.299; imbalance or disparity of power 26.654–6; lack of power brings corruption in the form of envy and disgruntlement 17.654–5; the power of authority 3.447, 15.618; putting the fear of God into people, gratifying a desire for power 17.181–2; trying to defeat people by argument is a way of using power 18.354

power in the context of Buddhism
the *bodhicitta* (and the bodhisattva) as a power 14.575; consciousness is a sort of power 4.379; the difference between reverence and respect for power 15.717, 15.719–20; the fundamental principle of my philosophy that power and value do not coincide 26.83; the gentleness of spiritual power 14.534–5; Māra's power is illusory 15.178; *mettā* is powerful, but it is not coercive 15.329; the *mettā bhāvanā* is a positive example of the power of thought 26.700; the motive power of the spiritual life 10.174; people are governed by power until they develop reflexive consciousness 8.447–8; power and the Tantra 1.374; the power aspect of Enlightenment 7.397; power has no place in the spiritual community 15.619; the power of the four great kings 16.353; power sharing in the spiritual community? 8.583; purity is power 26.53; truthfulness is a power capable of producing tangible results 2.169, 15.501; why did Buddhism not use its political power to compel conversion? 7.382–3

other uses of the word
all rights are based upon power 26.19; every living being possesses power 2.361–2; exercise of power, skilful or unskilful, is pleasurable 26.657–8; nature is governed by 'power' 8.447; parents' power over children 26.656; power and indecisiveness 17.613; power and sexuality 17.216; the power of the group 3.438; the power of ideas 12.465; the power of the visual medium 24.40; the power of a word, a name, a mantra 17.418; your power should be the function of your being 26.20

see also
God of power, *see under* God; the power of Vajrapāṇi, *see under* Vajrapāṇi; in the Roman Catholic church, *see under* Christianity/Roman Catholic; the Will to Power, *see under* Nietzsche

power mode abandoning the power mode 2.365, 17.583, 26.66; based on and controlled by the love mode 16.433, 16.434; being tempted to switch from love mode to power mode in argument 18.354–5; exerting authority on the basis of seniority 15.537; getting what we want in a situation that involves other people

3.577; a great deal of life in society is based on it 17.583; in dealing with people who are not individuals the use of power may be necessary 15.537–8; it includes emotional blackmail 11.701–2, 17.583; means to relate to other living beings in terms of violence 2.361–2; no use of the power mode in friendship 11.702; short-term use of the power mode 16.434; the spiritual life as learning to switch from the power mode to the love mode 26.56; within the spiritual community 2.362, 8.582–3, 16.433–4, 17.584; must be subordinated to the love mode 2.362, 12.415; switch from the power mode to the love mode in as many areas of life as possible 2.362–3; *see also* love mode

powerlessness 9.284–5, 18.456–8

***poya* days** 2.204, 11.317, 21.370

prabhāva 14.444

Prabhāvyūha (bodhisattva) 16.503

Prabhūtaratna (Abundant Treasures) *see under White Lotus Sūtra*/the structure of the *sūtra*

Prabuddha Bharata *see under* Ramakrishna Mission

practical

Buddhism's practicality
what is Buddhism? – an essentially practical question 4.8–9; it is essentially practical 7.117, 10.156–8, 17.106; a practical path 9.469–70, 9.494–5, 10.152; in practical terms the sangha means we help one another 9.215; the practical usefulness of the Dharma 7.228, 17.106, 18.375–7; the Theravāda leaves open metaphysical questions with no practical implications 15.634; Buddhist history: transition from practical to theoretical 14.93; Chinese Buddhism is practical and earthy 4.578, 4.624; the Vajrayāna 'a working out of the Madhyamaka in practical terms' 19.372; the mysterious practical activity of the Enlightened mind 1.536, 12.216; Sangharakshita was concerned with Buddhism both theoretically and practically 12.67; Western Buddhism will perhaps develop in a simple, practical, earthy way 4.578, 4.624

practical doctrines
the Buddha gives a practical Dharma talk to some villagers 10.642–6; the whole of Buddhism, theoretical and practical, is founded upon conditionality 3.182; the bodhisattva ideal: the practical aspect of tradition 1.397, 1.445, 3.429, 13.515–16; for all practical purposes Buddhism is dualistic 15.634–5; the goal is described as though personal for practical reasons 2.129; in practical terms, Nirvāṇa is spoken of as an object 10.566–7; the purpose of the *anattā* teaching is entirely practical 3.492; Tibetans follow the bodhisattva ideal in an intensely practical way 13.109–10; we divide things into dichotomies for practical purposes 5.523–4; words and concepts cannot define suchness, but designate it for practical purposes 7.299

practical practices
attend to others' practical needs before spiritual ones 4.67, 4.72; devotion is a practical and realistic response to the nature of things 18.117; directing energies to practical help rather than sentimental lamentations 23.337; does the Mahāyāna's claim to altruism make a practical difference? 4.86; the practical question is at what point one's Going for Refuge is effective 10.486; practical wisdom (*nipako*) 15.288–90; the Refuge Tree: the whole conception of refuge and its practical application 13.208; the six element practice is more practical and concrete than meditating on *śūnyatā* 5.32; specific, practical vows 4.65

being practical
Dr Ambedkar was practical 9.172; doing things that are practically embodied, you see where you have gone wrong 18.277; for all practical purposes it's just this life that matters 4.372–3; language was created for practical purposes, not philosophical discussion 10.144; make sure time spent with friends is not all devoted to practical matters 14.520; some people live much more in ideas than in practical reality 19.287; studying philosophy but never committing oneself to its practical implications 15.523; Tibetans are practical, down-to-earth 13.4, 13.109–10; Sangharakshita realized that he was more practical than he thought 21.170–1; transition between aesthetic contemplation and practical activity 14.523–4; why our theoretical understanding and practical realization isn't commensurate 1.390

practice *see* spiritual practice

pradāśa (spite or defensiveness) 17.651–3

Pradhan, Bhaichand 8.660, 21.236–7

Pradhan, Gopal and Madan Kumar v21, v22

Pradhan, Moti Chand v21, v22

Pradhan, Parashmani v21, v22

Pradhan, Rudramani v21

pradhāna (Saṃkhya) 4.424–5

pragmatism the Buddha gave to philosophical problems a purely pragmatic value 7.50, 7.69; the Buddha's pragmatic attitude to Vacchagotta's questions 13.394; of the Dharma 7.50, 7.69, 7.434; the pragmatism of the English – a link with Buddhism 12.74–5; the pragmatism of traditional Dharma study 7.487; we need a balance between vision and pragmatism 4.62–3

Prague 25.405

praise the Buddha praises his disciples for their special qualities 3.179, 4.170–1, 18.132, 18.222; the Buddha praises Soṇa Koṭikaṇṇa for his good memory and fine voice 10.573; the Buddhas reveal their true self if they are praised 4.176; if your happiness is dependent on others' praise, you are in an insecure position 4.432; looking for praise reveals a lack of confidence in what you have done 18.165; in modern life, you can't praise anything wholeheartedly 4.595; 'In Praise of Water' (poem) 25.289; overpraise (to get something out of someone) 17.659; praise of the rain and the earth 25.177; praise for Sangharakshita (as a young *bhikṣu*) 22.178–81; praise for Siddhārtha's going forth 25.273; praising others insincerely 17.662; in Rilke's poems 4.594, 4.713–4 (n360); saying nothing in praise of those who practise the spiritual life: dishonesty by omission 17.661–2; St Francis's *Canticle of the Sun* 4.594; surely all who practise the Dharma to a superlative extent are worthy of praise 2.649; true praise of Dr Ambedkar 10.343; in the West, we need much more praise and appreciation 4.622; whatever the tongue utters is his praise 7.80

see also
appreciation; rejoicing in merits; praise and blame, *see under* eight worldly winds; praise of the Buddha, *see under* Buddha IV/ responses to the Buddha

prajñā (Pāli *paññā*)

introduction
introduction 16.606–7 (n171), 17.545–6; the intellectual and doctrinal side of Buddhism 3.303; includes all the doctrines of Buddhism 7.434–5; the approach to Buddhism represented by *prajñā* 3.303

the word
analytical appreciative understanding or discrimination (Guenther) 14.516, 17.545; etymology 3.356, 14.317, 14.343, 17.132; a mere word 1.308; wisdom an inadequate translation 2.127; translated 'gnosis' 13.438; 'right thinking' (Ambedkar) 9.143; used in the sense of 'understanding' 16.557–8; similarity to Macmurray's definition of reason 15.255; a primarily intellectual word, but not in the ordinary dualistic sense 1.347; it is of feminine gender, so wisdom is spoken of as female 14.343, 19.434; it came to mean something different in the Mahāyāna 1.447

its nature
emptiness 1.306; the experience is paradoxical 17.547; the faculty that 'tastes' mind that is neither subject nor object 18.233; it issues forth from *bodhi* and will return to it 7.139; it arises only in the concentrated mind 7.358; it means knowledge of reality 14.343–4; the most difficult method of stilling the turbulence of the wild winds of desire 7.125–7; seeing things as they really are 3.301; seeing the true nature of all conditioned things 2.114; 'Soul-wisdom' 26.198; the spirit of *prajñā* 11.481; symbolized by light 9.324; the three *yānas* see it in different ways 17.546–7; when taken to extremes, can become dry, merely academic knowledge 3.303–4; with the arising of *prajñā* one gets as close to an object as one can possibly get 17.547; with *prajñā* one sees the skilful, unskilful, and neutral as they are 17.545; without it, one cannot 'see' (the blind men and the elephant) 9.227–8

how it is developed
the contemplation of any phenomenal object can develop *prajñā* 19.70; developed by meditation on conceptual formulations: Buddhist philosophy 10.142; four kinds of knowledge to be cultivated for the attainment of *prajñā* 17.545–6; in the absolute sense not to be gained, but don't relinquish efforts to gain it 1.306–7; it can arise equally in dependence on all three levels of wisdom 12.541–3; it can arise under any circumstances whatsoever 4.533; *dhyāna* is indispensable to it 1.257; moving from insight to *prajñā* 14.564–5; can art produce *prajñā*? 7.436–7; produced from the coalescence of clarified intelligence and purified emotions 7.242

where it fits into formulations of the path
as one of the five object-determining mental events 17.545–6; as one of the five spiritual faculties (*indriyas*) 1.291, 1.293, 3.301–4; as one of the six perfections, *see under* perfections; in the three levels of wisdom, *see* three levels of wisdom;

the third stage of the threefold way, *see* threefold way

its relationship to other doctrinal categories
avidyā in the sense of lack of *prajñā* 17.607–8, 17.610; difference between gnosis and *prajñā* 16.238; difference from *jñāna* 1.587–8, 3.356–7, 14.317; different from Nirvāṇa 17.547–8; distinction from *vijñāna* 14.559; gives access to the transcendental path, when based upon *śīla* and *samādhi* 2.147; the five *jñānas* are the five aspects of fully developed *prajñā* 10.176; the great difference between *dhyāna* and *prajñā* 4.511; the incommensurability of *puṇya* and *prajñā* 14.468–9; learning without *prajñā* (*prajñā* without compassion) is like a sword in the hand of a man (Ambedkar) 3.354, 9.231; *mahā-prajñā* and *mahākaruṇā* 2.125, 13.330–1; must be accompanied by *śīla* and *karuṇā* 9.143, 9.231; needs to be balanced by faith 1.293, 3.301, 3.304, 9.325; *prajñā* and *upāya* 7.137–41; the relationship between *vidyā*, *prajñā*, and *jñāna* 17.610–11; its relationship to non-deludedness 17.568–9; relationship with *vipaśyanā* and knowledge and vision of things as they really are 2.114; *samādhi* and *prajñā* 7.140, 17.611; and *śūnyatā* 3.301–2, 3.233, 18.66

see also
wisdom; insight

prajñā (female partner in Tantric practice) 13.89–90

Prajñā (translator) 14.152, 14.217

Prajñācakra (translator) 14.152

prajñā-cakṣus *see under* five eyes

Prajnaloka (Sherab Nangwa, or Rigdzin Wangpo) brief introduction 24.666 (n285); acted as interpreter for Sangharakshita 12.447; his main theme was the fickleness of women 22.450; is operated on by Jivaka 22.449–50; ordination 8.662, 26.229; photograph 22.449; lunch with Kachu Rimpoche 23.383; the shrine where he lived in Kalimpong 26.229–30; translates for Dilgo Khyentse Rimpoche 23.409; translations 8.660; a Tibetan whom Sangharakshita ordained 12.447, 22.447; he was left to look after his baby 22.446–9; his death 24.237, 26.230

Prajnananda, Dharmachari (Mark Bowden) 17.8

Prajnananda, Venerable (Lucknow) 21.111

Prajñāpāramitā *sūtras* *see* Perfection of Wisdom

Prajñāpāramitā ('mother of all the Buddhas') the acme of transcendental wisdom personalized as feminine 7.139; comparison with Sophia, the Divine Wisdom 13.603–4, 14.343; descriptions 3.362, 14.155; mantra (*oṃ āḥ dhiḥ hūṃ svāhā*) 11.294, 14.365; the mother of bodhisattvas 7.139, 16.457; the 'mother of the Conquerors' (Jinamātā) 14.537; 'the Mother's deep tenets' 14.566–7; Rāhulabhadra's hymn to her 1.66; Śāriputra's hymn (quoted in full) 3.362, 14.321–2; *sādhana* 14.155; 'self-arising Wisdom' 19.434; teachings personified as a goddess 1.301, 14.347; visualization 1.301; the word *prajñā* is of feminine gender, so wisdom is spoken of as female 14.343, 14.535–6, 19.434; *gate gate pāragate pārasaṃgate bodhi svāha, see under Heart Sūtra*

Prajñapti-śāstra ('Treatise of Designations') 14.83–4

prajñaptisat 17.445

prajñās *see* five female Buddhas

Prajñātāra 13.342

prajñā-upāya *see* Tantric Buddhism

prajñāvimukta ('wisdom-liberated one') 2.145

prajñā-vimukti *see under vimukti*

Prakaraṇa *see* Nāgārjuna

Prakaraṇa-pāda (Abhidharma work) 14.88, 14.93–4

Prakasha, Dharmachari 24.6, 24.604 (n12)

Prakrit introduction 16.590–1 (n38); 'unpolished' vernacular language 3.206, 16.365; difference from Sanskrit 16.365–6; a link with Buddhist Hybrid Sanskrit 14.349

prakṛti (in Hindu philosophy) nature or matter 12.278; *puruṣa-prakṛti* dualism 7.194–5, 7.596 (n299), 10.53, 12.278, 22.29; supposed to consist of three *guṇas*: *sattva*, *rajas*, and *tamas* 10.53

prakṛti ('the natural') 16.364–5

Prakrti (low-caste girl) 9.142, 10.672–3 (n86)

Prakṛti (in *Śūraṅgama Sūtra*) 13.358–60

pramāda *see* heedlessness

pramāṇas (sources of knowledge) 19.185–6

prāmodya *see* joy

pramuditā (joyful) *see under* ten *bhūmis*

prāṇa the active energy that gives support to awareness 18.322; directing the *prāṇa* into the central channel 18.411; 'a horse of Prāṇa-Mind' 18.72, 18.322, 19.437–8; in the Kālacakra Tantra 1.386; Lung (Tibetan) 19.411; Milarepa's mastery of *prāṇa* 19.30; the *nāḍis* and *prāṇas* dispel drowsiness and distractions 19.155; psychophysical energies 18.76; there's no faster way than *nāḍi* and *prāṇa* practice 19.284–5

prāṇayāma all right if the desired results are achieved 4.355; dangers 4.505–6, 20.125, 20.317–18, 20.324; difference from the mindfulness of breathing 9.203, 9.375; effect of the practice on Buddharakshita 23.17; one needs a teacher and the right sort of environment 4.505; perhaps what Milarepa refers to as 'yogic madness' 18.177–8; Sangharakshita's abnormal experiences as a result of the practice 20.125

praṇidhāna (resolve, aspiration) 7.295, 19.421

praṇidhāna-pāramitā (perfection of vow) 1.449

praṇidhānas *see* vows; bodhisattva vow

prapañca (proliferation) brief description 17.730 (n167); the Buddha contemplates the abandonment of *prapañca* 10.621; definition in Prajñāpāramitā 14.146; the manifold grasping 7.587 (n234); the sword of *prapañca*-free *jñāna* 17.147; in the thought only the thought 10.462–3

prāpti **and** *aprāpti* 14.362

prasad *see under* food

Prasad, Dr Rajendra v8, v22

Prasad, Tilak 22.105, 22.110

Prasadacarin, Dharmachari 17.xv

Prasadavati, Dharmacharini v24

praśaṃsā (eulogy, hyperbolical praise) 5.199, 14.465

Prāsaṅgika school 1.321–2, 8.504–5

Prasannapadā *see* Candrakīrtī

Prasannasiddhi, Dharmachari (Daren de Witt) v24

Prasenajit, King *see* Pasenadi

Prasit, Phra Maha v23

praśrabdhi (Pāli *passaddhi*) as one of the eleven positive mental events (Abhidharma) 17.577–9; calming down and concentration of energy 15.219–20, 17.578; changeless, timeless bliss 11.34; flow and pliancy 17.579; having reached this stage, you should dwell in *dhyāna* whenever you meditate 15.221; like a bee within a flower 3.288, 15.117; like an elephant stepping into a huge lake 3.269, 12.161; a state of extreme refinement and delicacy of feeling 2.106; a state of peace 10.370; twofold: of the mind and the body 2.106, 17.578–9

see also
as one of the seven *bodhyaṅgas*, *see under* seven *bodhyaṅgas*; in the positive *nidānas*, *see under* twelve positive *nidānas*

prāthana (path of speech) 18.319

pratibhāna-pratisaṃvid 16.491

prātideśanīya *see under* *vinaya*/offences

pratigha *see* anger

prātihārya (miracle) *see* miracles

pratijñā *see* Ambedkar/conversion/twenty-two vows

prātimokṣa (*pāṭimokkha*) *see under* Vinaya Piṭaka

Prātimokṣa Sūtra 14.30–1

pratisaṃvids *see* four *pratisaṃvids*

pratisandhi (Pāli *paṭisandhi*, 'relinking consciousness') 1.108–9, 2.75, 2.95, 2.254, 3.196–8

pratisāraṇa *see* four great reliances

pratītya-samutpāda (Pāli *paṭicca-samuppāda*)

introduction
general introduction 1.88–97; the basic Buddhist doctrine 7.493; traditional statements 1.89–90; it includes in its majestic sweep every object of the phenomenal universe 7.270; it teaches that

things are mutually dependent 14.608; 'one thing leads to another' 22.133; a phenomenological approach 16.20–1; a revolutionary idea 12.153; translations 4.647; 'conditioned co-production' coined by Conze 4.676 (n105), 16.587 (n24), 17.710 (n38)

and the Buddha
the basis of all his teachings 2.251, 3.9; his distinctive discovery 1.74; his vision on the night of his Enlightenment 4.647–8, 4.701 (n278); the conceptualized formulation of the content of his Enlightenment 7.192; the teaching he had in mind when considering whether to teach the Dharma 7.191–2; contradictory accounts 1.93–4; 'He who sees conditioned co-production sees the Dharma ...' 1.97, 7.493; 'Deep indeed is this Causal Law ...' 1.90–1, 1.95–6, 3.92, 17.389, 17.750 (n325); the Āryan disciple's knowledge of the Law 1.96; Reality = Becoming = *paṭicca-samuppāda* 7.203; is Nirvāṇa included in conditioned co-production? 1.116–18, 7.197–200

'cyclic' and 'spiral' modes or trends of conditionality
introduction 1.117–20, 3.13–14, 4.312, 7.202–6; of the two trends, it is up to us to decide which to seek 7.206

further applications
in the early stages of spiritual life, concentrate on impermanence as an application 16.21; the four noble truths as an extension of the principle 1.94–5, 1.120–2, 3.14; the Buddha applied it to the most salient and striking experiences of life 1.93–4; developing insight into the dependently arisen nature of *vedanā* 10.482; applied to different groups of phenomena 1.91–3; applied to the process of evolution 3.12–14, 13.431; applied to *dharmas* 14.495–6; the *nidāna* chain illustrates the principle in terms of human existence 3.346–7; the sciences assume its truth 7.190; Darwin applied the principle to the origin of species 12.153; Freud applied it to the workings of the subconscious mind 12.153

reflections on the principle
the outstanding feature of all phenomena is that they are conditioned 3.94; phenomena arise in dependence upon a multiplicity of conditions 1.102; causation can be described neither in terms of identity nor in terms of difference 3.197; all things arise dependently ... yet they are neither existent nor non-existent 16.466; it is neither exclusively mundane nor exclusively transcendental 15.637; it teaches not a real causal relation between entities but their mutual dependence 1.316; things exist not as adamantine essences but as causally determined dynamic processes 8.618; there's no such thing as independence 4.424; metaphysical implications 16.20; the universe is not so much subject to this law as an expression of it 7.153

the doctrine in Buddhist history
in the Pāli canon 1.90–3, 1.96, 1.116, 3.175–8, 4.676 (n105); in the Abhidharma 14.83; doctrine held in common by Theravāda and Mahāyāna 7.631; and *anattā* 7.191, 7.195, 7.495; in the Mahāyāna designated as *śūnyatā*, *vijñāna*, and *ālaya-vijñāna* 7.199–200; the *śūnyatā* doctrine and *pratītya-samutpāda* 1.267, 1.316, 7.193, 7.199, 15.637, 16.21; Nāgārjuna insists that the doctrine is only relatively real 1.316, 14.608, 17.246–8; and the Yogācāra 7.193; Śāntarakṣita made it the basis of his exposition of the Dharma 7.193

Sangharakshita and conditioned co-production
the subject of his second ever article on Buddhism 12.494; the teaching drew his attention during his wandering days in India 20.302; his view of spiritual life as dynamic criticised 21.114

see also
the Abhidharma's list of causal conditions, *see Paṭṭhāna*; Dhammadinnā's analysis, *see* Dhammadinnā; the spiral path, *see* twelve positive *nidānas*; this being, that becomes

pratyakṣa (experience) 26.198

pratyātmagocara (inner perception)
'the field or sphere of experience' 19.374; preferred to *bodhi* as a term for Enlightenment in the *Laṅkāvatāra Sūtra* 11.74, 12.173, 13.492

pratyāya *see* four conditions

pratyeka-bodhi 2.267

pratyekabuddha (Pāli *paccekabuddha*)
what is a *pratyekabuddha*? 10.553–4; definition in the *Puggala-Paññatti* 2.150, 14.81; different schools' views on Enlightenment of 1.85–6; Enlightened but not articulate 19.204–5; as one of the nine holy persons 2.150–1; one with the maximum of conscious thought but the minimum of thought-expressive activity 7.138; *pratyeka-bodhi* gained without an instructor 2.267, 3.401; 'privately enlightened ones' did live before the Buddha 1.57; really just a doctrinal

category 15.472–3; Reginald Ray's account 3.681 (n360); said to practise the *brahma vihāras* 4.86; the Sarvāstivāda said you could choose whether to be a bodhisattva or a *pratyekabuddha* 12.504–5; selfishness as compared to bodhisattvas, in the Mahāyāna view 1.213, 1.230, 14.103; three kinds of Enlightenment: *arhant*, *pratyekabuddha*, *sammāsambuddha* 15.465

pratyekabuddhayāna *see under yānas*

pravāraṇā* or *pavāraṇā (confession at the end of rains retreat) 2.199, 3.405

pravṛtti mārga (outward-circling path) 7.357–8

Praxiteles 3.427, 23.299, 23.518 (n334)

prāyaścittika *see under* Vinaya/*prātimokṣa*

prayer

why do people pray?
why do we pray? 4.130, 19.139–40; a cry for help 12.95; one is usually driven to prayer when things are going badly 4.313; a parrot who recited God's name, but in danger gave his natural squawk 12.96, 18.249; prayers for salvation in return for tea 20.43; praying for the removal of difficulties: a very human tendency 12.95–6; continual prayer (Christianity) 7.101; as a boy, Sangharakshita prayed to the Buddha, Christ, and Mohammed in turn 20.44; 'seeing' the prayers of worshippers in the cathedral at Luxembourg 23.247, 24.104

isn't prayer to God?
if there is no personal God, what becomes of prayer? 12.10; the difference between Buddhist and Christian prayer 4.131, 19.141–2; it doesn't necessarily have theistic connotations 4.129, 19.139; if you feel like praying, go ahead – work out the theology later 4.130–1, 19.140, 19.509; to cut yourself off from prayer might be to cut yourself off from your emotions 19.143

prayer in Buddhism
introduction 1.412–13; an aspiration for qualities we do not yet possess 4.130; underlying philosophy 5.178; very different from meditation 4.130, 19.140; don't just recite the words, ask yourself what they mean 18.319; the difference between invocation and evocation 18.319–20; the *ḍākinīs* are embodied prayers 19.143; no such thing as petitionary prayer in Buddhism 4.130, 4.313, 9.461, 24.360–1; prayer to the Three Jewels: an attitude of receptivity 18.319; in the *Sūtra of Golden Light* 16.276; Tibetans use the phraseology of prayer 19.71; a mantra is in a way a short and simple prayer 17.418; 'O my own immediate holy guru' 13.219–20; 'Prayer is not perfect when the monk is aware of himself and of praying' 7.155

praying to Buddhas and bodhisattvas
the request is needed because of the limitations of language 19.139–40; they are as much outside oneself as within 4.131; what is one expecting when one asks for spiritual protection? 4.312–13

prayoga-mārga *see under* five stages

Pré, Gerald du 13.416

preaching the Dharma *see under* Dharma III/methods of communicating

preceptor helping someone to choose a *sādhana* practice 5.620–1; precepts taken from them 2.343; Sangharakshita as preceptor, *see under* Sangharakshita VIII/as personal teacher; Sangharakshita compares his experience of his different preceptors 2.455–6; traditional relationship between preceptor and disciple 2.196–7; in Triratna, *see under* Triratna III/ordination ceremonies; *upādhyāya* (*upajjhāya*), *see under bhikṣu*/ordination/the life of the newly ordained

precepts

INTRODUCTION

what are the precepts?
concrete applications of principles whose spirit no amount of rules can express 10.564; guidelines 19.557–8; how an Enlightened being would behave 1.530–1; not rules, but principles or patterns of behaviour 1.531, 2.341, 3.318, 3.370, 13.411, 17.176; the path of self-effort that underlies all forms of Buddhism 26.669–70; they guide the application of ethical principles to all aspects of life 4.110; promises 12.485; taught by all religions 7.124; training principles 3.370, 17.176–7

their importance
the importance of sets of rules does not mean that *śīla* is just ethical formalism 1.142; incense symbolizes their widespread influence 9.324; the lowest common denominator, but often seen as the highest common factor 2.324; necessary not only to the spiritual life but to the maintenance of society 7.124; the precepts are more important than more glamorous teachings 3.331–2; the reason for practising them 7.187–8; the relationship between Refuges and Precepts

2.323–5, 9.187; they're not just about our own mental state, but about how we treat others 11.723–4; those observed by all Buddhists are more important than monastic precepts 2.345

the precepts in Buddhist tradition
the Buddha permitted the abolition of minor precepts and rules 9.98, 12.678; bodhisattva precepts, *see* bodhisattva/precepts; the difference between bodhisattva precepts and *śrāvaka* precepts 14.186; they are common to all branches of Buddhism 1.141, 9.332; Mahāyāna adoption of 'Hīnayāna' precepts in a Mahāyāna spirit 2.209; precepts according to level of spiritual development 11.315–17; *śikṣāpadas* (Pāli *sikkhāpadas*, training rules) 2.340, 2.342–3, 2.349, 2.591, 2.607, 14.80, 14.82; breach of *śikṣāpadas* 2.580, 2.586–7, 2.589–90, 2.593–4, 2.598, 2.635; special days for the observance of precepts in Buddhist countries 1.141–2; thirty-two precepts (*dharmas*) in a Mahāyāna *sūtra* 14.185

PRACTISING THE PRECEPTS

personal practice
are you really observing them? 9.192; better to take a small number of precepts which you fully intend to observe 18.487; calling them 'training principles' doesn't let us off the hook 17.176–7; finding the precepts inspiring 2.341, 13.411; practising the precepts according to one's level of sensitivity 19.560; reflect on the precepts as the touchstone for your practice 18.167; looking at yourself in the mirror of the precepts 18.324; the Tibetans say it's better to practise one precept properly 13.53, 18.487–8; *upadeśa* (individual instruction) 18.393–4; we need to pay attention to the subtle ways we evade their spirit 17.233

negative and positive forms of the precepts
the negative forms don't mean abstaining from evil without doing good 1.142; the precepts aren't only about ceasing to do evil, they also inspire us to act positively 17.200; significant that negative formulations are better known 1.522; you begin with the practice of the 'negative' precepts 7.182–5

personal precepts
the Kadam precept, the teaching addressed just to you 18.393; a lot of the scriptures are personal precepts which we are overhearing 17.106; 'The precept of the Lama is more important than the scriptures and commentaries' 8.528; Zen stories and sayings are essentially precepts 8.497

the difficulty of practising the precepts
difficulty of practising them 7.182–5; our desires being strong, it's not surprising that we can't always observe them 1.141; to observe them, we have to find pleasure and beauty outside objects of craving 17.271; why might they seem dull? 7.184–6; *see also* Pith-Instructions

breaking precepts
a boy ground into dust by a *vajra* for not observing the precepts 14.235; breaking a precept to a disastrous extent places one beyond the Order 16.433; difference between breaking precepts out of desire and out of hatred 2.389, 14.186; going through the motions of practising the precepts 19.455–6; if you're sitting still doing nothing, at least you're not breaking any precepts 18.342; it's easy to forget basic things like the precepts, but we do so at our peril 3.331; precepts broken by Tantric teachers out of compassion 1.200–1; a world of difference between intending to follow the precepts and doing so 18.101

FIVE PRECEPTS (*PAÑCASĪLA*)

introduction
brief description 1.141, 2.669 (n69), 7.124, 9.19, 9.215–16, 9.265–7, 9.463–4, 9.475, 10.249, 26.669; fuller introduction 3.318–24; listed in English and Pāli 2.653; listed in their negative formulation 2.653, 3.318, 11.256; listed in their positive forms 2.653, 3.321, 11.256; canonical sources 3.662 (n243), 3.668 (n275), 3.673 (n299), 16.584 (n9); an aspect of the Noble Eightfold Path 11.498; the bodhisattva's practice of the five precepts 16.9–10; the ethical minimum required of all Buddhists 8.199–200, 8.205; finding loopholes in their practice 8.313; mentioned in the Abhidharma 14.82; observing them scrupulously without cultivating their positive counterparts 11.480; the practice of lay Buddhists 11.317; the primary school stage of spiritual education 7.187; they all involve other people or other beings 25.116; they can be regarded as good resolutions: promises, not commandments 8.192; they deal with a class of actions to be completely eschewed 7.409

(1) undertaking to refrain from taking life (pāṇātipātā veramaṇi)
introduction 2.357–63; literally 'abstain from violence to breathing beings' 18.183; what does the first precept really mean? 18.183–4; every time you breathe in you take life, but the practice avoids intentional harm 4.355–6; the most important

manifestation of Going for Refuge 2.358; it is the first precept because it allows people to grow in their own way 18.183–4; it means abstention from injuring living beings, not just killing 8.452; this principle runs very deep and is very significant 2.357–8; Pāli canon description 2.330; a pillar of diamond 2.363; abortion 8.610, 13.451, 15.482–3, 17.196; avoiding cruel occupations 8.450; the bodhisattva is careful not to injure even the humblest of living beings 16.9; a broad precept, and everyone decides how to practise it 19.560; can an Enlightened being kill out of compassion? 20.333; broken at Lumbini 20.420; explanation of the Pāli terms 17.178; expression of the love mode 2.361–3; hunting as a breach of the first precept 17.179–80; if we can think of being violent towards someone, we have lost the ethical perspective 17.644; includes not taking animal life 7.124, 11.481, 13.608, 26.669; it covers environmental concerns 26.669; it covers harm of all sorts, including preventing people from realizing their potential 17.178; killing is the most serious offence against natural morality 13.608–9; the *mettā bhāvanā* to support it 17.183; one given to killing living beings has abstention from killing to lead him upwards 11.658; one who habitually breaks this precept without guilt sinks below truly human level 13.609; as *pārājika* (defeat) 3.408; respect the individuality of others 17.178–9; 'reverence for life' (Schweitzer) 16.9; Triratna's special emphasis on the first precept 13.453–4; the weighty karma of deliberately taking life 3.107; why should killing be wrong? 2.358–9; positive counterpart: *mettā* 1.533; the vigorous expression of an imaginative identification with others 2.361; *see also* non-violence

(2) undertaking to refrain from taking the not-given (adinnādānā veramaṇi)
introduction 2.364–9, 9.215–16; Pāli canon description 2.330; a pillar of gold 2.369; the precept means far more than it appears to mean at first sight 17.198; and gratitude 2.367; any kind of possessiveness goes against the spirit of the precept 17.199; includes taking someone's time or energy 2.366–7, 17.198; and indebtedness 2.367–8; involves abstention from any kind of dishonesty 1.533; it implies abstaining from economic exploitation 26.669; a lotus whose spirit told a monk not to steal its scent 26.243; not giving into exploitation and still keeping the second precept 17.199; one given to taking what is not given has abstention to lead him upwards 11.658; practising it involves faith that you will receive what you need 17.198–9; related to the idea of non-exploitation 3.582; 'taking the not given' is not just a roundabout way of saying 'not stealing' 3.582; why is it wrong to take from multinationals in an unfair system? 3.320–1, 3.323; as *pārājika* (defeat) 3.408–9; principle of non-appropriation 3.320–1; rationalizing stealing 9.272; taking the not-given by taking the Dharma while holding onto the ego 18.188; violence in respect of property 2.364; the way it is worded suggests that ethically speaking there is no such things as rights 26.19; positive counterpart: generosity (*see under dāna*)

(3) undertaking to refrain from sexual misconduct (kāmesu micchācārā veramaṇi)
introduction to the precept 2.370–3, 9.216; Pāli canon description 2.330; a pillar of crystal 2.373; the essential meaning of the precept 11.567; advising prostitutes to 'do the best they can' with the third precept 25.119–20; adultery in the mind has karmic consequences 2.70–1; adultery isolates 25.104; behaving sensitively and mindfully in one's sexual relations 26.669; the Buddha makes it clear that this comprises rape, abduction, and adultery 1.534; the consequences of adultery 17.294, 25.105; cultivating stillness, simplicity, and contentment 3.321–2, 15.276; does it include prostitution? 11.567; the ethics of promiscuity 3.566; flirtation and the third precept 17.216; a form of taking the not-given 17.214; a narrow view of the precept in the Buddhist East 11.567–8; one should aim for a provisional identification with one's psycho-physical sex 2.373; pornography 13.446; the precept is about what we do with our sexuality in the broadest sense 17.216; principle of chastity 3.321–2; seen within the context of Buddhist cosmology 2.370–3; sexual ethics 13.453; using our sexuality to get what we want 17.216; what the precept meant in ancient India and means today 17.214–17; positive counterpart contentment (*saṃtuṣṭi* or *santuṭṭhi*), *see* contentment; the third Tantric precept 11.574

(4) undertaking to refrain from false speech (musāvādā veramaṇi)
introduction to the precept 2.375–8; Pāli canon description 2.330; a pillar of pearl 2.378; being believed when telling

a lie 26.79; the consequences of telling lies 17.236–7; difficult to practise 2.377, 9.463–4; emotional blackmail 17.234; false speech based on unconscious bias 17.234–5; false speech often hides behind jargon 17.234; includes not spreading fake news 26.669; making a misleading though factually accurate statement 11.480; practising the precept includes not sponsoring misleading advertising 26.669; principle of truthfulness 3.322–3; the difficulty of practising this precept 9.463–4; speech that is false because one's experience of oneself and the world is false 18.139; speech which is rooted in craving, hatred, or fear 1.534; 'There is no wrong that cannot be committed by a lying person' 2.376; 'those who speak falsely go to hell' 10.539; positive counterpart: truthfulness (*satya*) 1.534; psycho-spiritual jargon 17.234–5; speech based on assumptions 17.236; we confuse objective facts with our subjective interpretation 17.233–4, 17.236; *see also under* speech/four levels of skilful speech

(5) undertaking to refrain from taking drink and drugs that cloud the mind (Pāli *surāmerya-majja-pamādaṭṭhānā veramaṇi*); abstaining from taking or dealing in drugs 26.669; as Buddhists we seek to keep our minds clear 10.395; if you neglect this precept you may break all the others 8.226–7, 10.249; in much of the Buddhist world drinking is an accepted part of social life 8.313; does it mean complete abstention from alcohol, or moderation? 1.535, 3.323, 17.255–6; mentioned by Nāgārjuna in the *Precious Garland* 17.255–7; mentioned in the *Jātakas* 2.333; more to this precept than the question of drinking 3.324, 16.10; positive counterpart: mindfulness (*sati*) 1.535, 9.216, 16.10; the reason for taking the precept 9.216; why this is not included in the ten precepts 11.258

TEN PRECEPTS (*DAŚA-ŚĪLA, KUSALA-DHAMMAS*)

introduction
for the first four precepts, *see* five precepts above; brief description 1.141, 2.669 (n69), 9.51–2, 9.287, 9.310, 11.308–9; full account 2.307–96; approaching them imaginatively 17.176–7; the consequences of practising and not practising them 11.321–3; the difference between the five and ten precepts is fundamental 11.257; a different set of ten precepts taken by the *śrāmaṇera* 11.258, 11.747 (n117); guidelines for serious Dharma practice 17.228; in Pāli and English 2.311–12; observed by people of different socio-religious classes 2.347–8; known by a variety of names, but the content is always the same 2.340; to be learned from a teacher, which is why they are 'taken' from a preceptor 2.343; like opening up ten channels for the water of *cetanā* to flow into 17.529; listed in their negative and positive forms 11.256–7; and lifestyle 2.351–3; mentioned by Dr Ambedkar 9.287; the norm of ethical behaviour for all human beings 2.348; a path of practice, not a list of rules 17.176; as principles of ethics 2.339–41; Sangharakshita's reasons for speaking about them 2.318; in society 16.477; taken by the lay brother or sister 13.338–9; the ten petals of a magnificent flower 2.396; ten pillars of precious stone which support the edifice of the Dharma 2.318, 2.395, 13.444; their use in the Triratna Buddhist Order represents a new departure 11.258; they could be called the ten skilful intentionalities, or the ten creativities 17.528–9; and total transformation 2.335–8; why the fifth precept (of the five) is not included in the ten precepts 11.258; you must love them before they will seem worthy of your love 2.319

their history
canonical sources (Pāli and Mahāyāna) 2.326–334, 3.690–1 (n448), 17.175–6; positive precepts taught to Cunda the silversmith 2.313, 2.330–1, 3.632n; relationship to the Noble Eightfold Path 2.349–50; *mūla-prātimokṣa*: the discipline that supports individual liberation 2.344–8, 2.491–2, 17.268; as rules of training (*śikṣāpadas*) 2.342–3, 17.176; *śrāmaṇera*, *see* precepts/monastic; the ten ways of skilful actions (Buddhaghosa) 11.309; *cetanā* classified in terms of the ten precepts (Abhidharma) 17.528–9; doctrine held in common by Theravāda and Mahāyāna 7.531; Nāgārjuna spells out the consequences of not observing the three mind precepts 17.258; Atīśa encouraged their practice 12.577

the four speech precepts
why four? 2.375, 17.228–9; speech precepts 3.690–1 (n448); if you truly observe these precepts your speech *is* Going for Refuge 11.258; they emphasize the importance of communication in the spiritual life 11.258; four progressive levels of human communication, *see under* speech/four levels; listed in Nāgārjuna's *Precious Garland* 17.228

(5) undertaking to refrain from harsh speech (pharusa-vācāya veramaṇi)
introduction to the precept 2.379–82; abstention from coarse speech 2.379–80; being aware of the person to whom one is speaking and their response 17.229; being pierced with speech like an elephant in battle pierced with arrows 10.540; the consequences of harsh speech 17.237; extra mindfulness required during a debate 17.229; harsh speech can be appropriate, if spoken with positive intention 18.361–2; a pillar of amber 2.380; Pāli canon description 2.331; positive counterpart: kindly, affectionate speech 2.380, 17.229; *see also under* speech/four levels of skilful speech/affectionate

(6) undertaking to refrain from frivolous speech (samphappalapā veramaṇi)
introduction to the precept 2.381–2; Pāli canon description 2.331; abstain from spending too much time on small talk 17.229–30; this doesn't mean bringing in Buddhism in an artificial way 2.382, 17.229; a pillar of silver 2.382; speech can be truly meaningful only when life is meaningful 2.381; we should try to take seriously people in the habit of talking frivolously 17.238; *dhammakathā*, *see dhammakathā*; positive counterpart: meaningful speech; *see also under* speech/four levels of skilful speech/helpful

(7) undertaking to refrain from slanderous speech (pisuna-vacāyā veramaṇi)
introduction to the precept 2.383–4; the consequences of slanderous speech 17.237; not speaking so as to bring about a quarrel between others 2.383–4; not speaking when you know someone is being slandered 17.662; Pāli canon description 2.330, 2.383; a pillar of opal 2.384; positive counterpart: harmonious speech 2.384; *see also under* speech/four levels of skilful speech/harmonious

the mind precepts: introduction
these three precepts have a transcendental significance 11.257; overcoming subtle mental intoxications 11.258

(8) undertaking to refrain from covetousness (abhijjhāya veramaṇi)
introduction to the precept 2.385–7; meaning of *abhijjhā*: a mental state of brooding over 2.385–6; Pāli canon description 2.331; a pillar of emerald 2.387; the result of covetousness is that you get what you don't want 17.258; positive counterpart: tranquillity 2.386–7

(9) undertaking to refrain from malevolence or hatred (byāpādā veramaṇi)
introduction to the precept 2.388–9; the intent to harm brings fear 17.258; meaning of *vyāpāda* (Pāli *byāpāda*): wishing evil 2.388; Pāli canon description 2.331; a pillar of ruby 2.389; transforming hatred into compassion 7.383, 22.529; positive counterpart: compassion 2.386–7; *see also* compassion

(10) undertaking to refrain from wrong views (micchādiṭṭhiyā veramaṇi)
introduction to the precept 2.390–4; Pāli canon description 2.331; a pillar of sapphire 2.394; transforming ignorance into wisdom 7.383, 22.529; positive counterpart: wisdom 2.393–4; *see also micchā-diṭṭhis*

OTHER SETS OF PRECEPTS

eight precepts
the five precepts plus three additional rules 1.142; listed 2.654; brahmacarya 11.536; no special ceremony to take them 15.711; observed by lay people on *poya* (*poṣadha*) days 2.204, 11.317, 21.370; practised by monks 27.1074; refrain from sleeping in high and luxurious beds 19.275, 21.370; what does the eighth precept (about theatrical performances) mean? 26.120–1

monastic precepts (saṃvara-sīla)
introduction 1.535–6; recited on *uposatha* days 1.146, 2.187; how the number of precepts is worked out 1.633–4 (n427); lay followers who protect precept-observing monks with sword and stick 14.236; for novice monks 1.142, 3.408; for ordained monks 3.408–9; monks who are observing the precepts expelling those who are not 14.236; most are not additional precepts, but more thorough or specific applications 2.345; abstaining from music and 'improper shows' 23.173, 23.175; *pārājikas* (defeats) 3.408–9; some of them have no ethical significance 2.345

ten precepts taken by the śrāmaṇera on pravrajyā ordination
introduction 2.193, 2.350, 20.409–10; brahmacarya 11.536; listed 2.655; practised by layman 2.591; rule of not handling money, *see under* money

Tantric precepts
the list of precepts 26.8; the effort to avoid misusing the energy of others 15.217, 18.79; respect the individuality of others 17.178–9; taking someone's time or energy 2.366–7, 17.198; the third Tantric precept 11.574

three grades of morality ('Tract on Śīla')
lesser, relating to precepts of body and speech but not mind 11.315–16; middle, relating to 'cutting away the bond formed by a life of comfort' 11.316; greater, relating to beliefs and practices 11.316–17

see also
ethics

Precepts of the Gurus *see under* Gampopa

precious stones *see* jewels

precious things *see* seven precious things

predictable the more deeply you can rely on someone, the less predictable they become 14.551; the more reactive a person, the more predictable 15.504–5, 26.22; setbacks as reminders of the unpredictable nature of *saṃsāra* 18.47; the unpredictable nature of a creative writer 15.505; upon Enlightenment, you'll be joyful, or unpredictable 18.254

predictions

general
don't make predictions based on guesswork 19.357–8; how does a Buddha foretell future events? 14.493–4; a prediction about Mr Chen's life 22.537; prediction of a Renaissance based on the discovery of oriental culture 7.88, 12.79, 14.287–9; prediction of Siddhārtha's future 3.23–4, 14.608; the prediction that the sangha would deteriorate due to women's ordination 2.27, 11.642–5

predictions to Enlightenment (vyākaraṇa)
and the bodhisattva vow 2.163, 4.66; doesn't mean that the bodhisattva is sure to gain Enlightenment 4.66; in the *Avadānas* 14.67; of no importance to Śāntideva 1.422; perhaps a survival of the view that the bodhisattva ideal is not universally applicable 1.422; Tarpa Nagpo is predicted to Buddhahood 8.525; *see also under White Lotus Sūtra*/the structure of the *sūtra*

preferences Abhidharma analysis of likes and dislikes 17.505–6; appreciating sense experience free from the imposition of likes and dislikes 15.286; an ascetic who, not picking and choosing, ate a finger that fell into his bowl 17.585; being influenced by likes and dislikes of personality 15.516–17; the Enlightened mind sees things with no preferences 12.214–15; equanimity comes about when you have the same positive feelings towards all 15.432–3; freeing oneself from the tyranny of likes and dislikes 15.119, 18.130–3; the personal limitations of human beings: prejudices, preferences 12.655; philosophers building systems in accordance with subjective preferences 7.386–8; picking and choosing your frustrations 19.167; practising the *upekkhā bhāvanā* to overcome likes and dislikes 5.206–9; preferences arise from chopping reality into bits 14.409; refrain from insisting on your preference while being honest about what you prefer 18.36; some preferences are matters of principle 18.131; sometimes preference is just obstinacy 19.60; Western Buddhists' tendency to pick and choose between teachings 11.58, 11.209; young children are very honest about their likes and dislikes 15.432

pregnancy the Buddha's blessing and a healthy pregnancy (*Udāna*) 10.493–8; 'conversion through pregnancy' 21.364–6, 21.426, 22.25–6; mindfulness during pregnancy 9.364–5; the pregnancy of a Kalimpong girl 22.451–8; a wanderer tries to help his pregnant wife (*Udāna*) 10.487–8

prehistory dinosaurs 24.494; Neolithic Venus 16.386; nomadic life of early man 3.425; our descent from apes 11.271; primitive humanity 3.424–5; the beauty of the world 13.165–6; the mysteriousness of life and death 3.4–5, 3.95; slow rate of change 9.178–9; virtually coterminous with the history of humankind 3.425

prejudice caste prejudice, *see under* caste system; don't confuse natural morality with prejudices about right and wrong 4.110; emotions confused with prejudice 1.495–6; Enlightenment is freedom from all delusion, all prejudice 3.31; the *mettā bhāvanā* counteracts any prejudice one has against certain types of people 15.300; the need to remove racial prejudice from society 12.408–9; the personal limitations of human beings: prejudices, preferences 12.655; prejudice against Buddhism 19.207; reigns in all minds that have not been purified 1.34

preliminary meditations *see* four preliminary meditations

Prem, Sri Krishna (Ronald Nixon) introduction 22.590 (n159); devoted to the service of the Asian peoples 22.179; Sangharakshita corresponds with him 20.184; *The Yoga of the Bhagavad Gītā* 20.61

prema see pema

premonitions 19.84–5, 20.85–6

preparation ethical preparation 25.86; for the arising of the *bodhicitta*, *see under bodhicitta*/arising; if you prepare yourself thoroughly, you are already practising 15.345; the importance of preparation in the spiritual life 3.272–3, 4.42–3, 13.75, 25.83; for meditation, *see under* meditation; not an entirely passive thing 25.85

Pre-Raphaelites short introduction 24.670–1 (n307); colour in their work 2.609–10, 13.284, 26.218, 26.441; and the German masters 24.592; a Kalimpong sunset like a Pre-Raphaelite painting 18.158; Lady Lever Art Gallery, Port Sunlight 24.381; pleasurable patterns but not much deeper communication of values 26.245; 'pre-Raphaelite tendencies' 24.251; Sangharakshita discusses them with Lilavati 24.712 (n491); they set out to create beauty 25.121–2, 26.395

present

living in the present
'Living in the Present' 7.285–7; all we actually experience is the present 8.289–91; applying ourselves to meeting the demands of the present moment 17.204; being contented, you're consciously in the present 15.428; being in the present: not lost in the concerns of the present, but simply being aware 17.401; beginning to live in the present in the true spiritual sense 8.291; the difference between spiritual and mundane ways of living in the present 7.286–7; the eternal now 7.286, 11.11, 19.84; the ever-faithful Present 25.308; finding in the present an inexhaustible satisfaction and perennial joy 7.286; the present is – and isn't 25.390; if your reflexive consciousness is weak, you may find it easy to live in the present 15.359; in a state of neurotic desire, we need to get back to the present moment 13.133–4; it's nonsense to talk about remaining in the present all the time 11.657; responding creatively to the present 17.406; strictly speaking there is no present moment in which to live 17.406; Milarepa living in the present 18.340; mindfulness is the practice of being present with the whole of your experience 17.369; not karma but how we shape ourselves in the present moment is what's important 17.212–13; the way to Enlightenment is the present experience without interpretation 10.463–4

past, present, and future
as Buddhists we have to look beyond past, future, and even present 25.22; even when we want to be in the present moment, the mind flings us into past and future 8.575; an experience neither past nor present, a process outside time 18.613, 19.84–5; 'I have no before or after, neither beginning nor end' 26.53; linking with past and future to break out of the cocoon of the present 17.403, 17.598; mindfulness is not just about the present moment, but involves memory 15.85–8; so-called present experience actually consists of the 'present' plus the 'past' 24.4; past, present, and future are only relatively real 17.405; past and future are revealed in the present moment of illumination 14.219

pressure being pressured into doing what is wrong 25.120–1; fulfilling family or 'tribe' duties from personal choice, not group pressure 18.149–50; the monk is under no pressure to be useful 18.120; most people are religious not from an urge from within, but collective pressure from without 7.148; non-violent pressure (about nuclear weapons) must be brought to bear 12.346–8; not feeling pressured when people try to pressure you 17.563; one member of the sangha cannot pressurize, bully, or manipulate another 14.578; never become passive in a situation where you are under pressure 18.456; social pressure keeps us immersed in trivial pursuits 3.35; solitary retreat: an opportunity to be free of external pressures 5.637; spiritual friends should never exert pressure 18.456

pretas *see* hungry ghosts

pretence *see* deceit

Priapus 24.292

Price, Arnold discusses Buddhism with Sangharakshita on a pub crawl 20.101; perhaps friendship would have continued if Sangharakshita had stayed in England 26.583; writes to Sangharakshita in Singapore 20.150–1, 21.159

priceless jewel *see under White Lotus Sutra*

pride or conceit

introduction
pride is the basic error, and all spiritual practices are meant to tackle it 18.639; *māna* as arrogance as distinct from pride 17.604; pride is a mask 18.141; it produces a troubled mind 19.517–18

pride as a poison
associated with the human realm of the wheel of life 4.77; having a strong sense of

'I', 'me', 'mine' 3.134, 3.348; comparing oneself with others 13.183; one of the more intellectual of the *kleśas* 18.450

comparing oneself with others
canonical reference 13.686–7 (n78); denying that anybody could be superior 4.525; don't attach too much importance to your own strengths 4.41; feeling superior, inferior, or equal to others 1.178, 1.180, 4.78, 13.183, 18.450; an inflated idea of oneself, arrogance 17.604; insisting on being equal 17.273; real humility is not to think of oneself as superior, inferior, or equal 18.511; skilful and unskilful comparisons 17.273–4; we should be very grateful to have people to look up to 17.274–5

perspectives from the Buddhist tradition
conditioning of pride and arrogance (*Udāna*) 10.514; Mahāyāna precept against vaunting one's own qualities and disparaging others 2.208; three distinct types (*Bodhicaryāvatāra*) 4.623–4; Rechungpa suffers from pride 18.437–43, 18.468–71; a young man renounces worldly pride 18.71, 18.73

boasting
about one's good actions 4.319; of your achievements, whether or not they represent any attainment 17.605; giving without boasting 1.432–3, 4.103; overemphasizing one's abilities 17.274; Rechungpa boasts about his experiences 18.468–70

spiritual pride
apologising for the ego as an inverted form of conceit 18.81–2; better sweep a floor egolessly than meditate thinking proudly 'I am meditating' 7.284; don't think 'This skilful action is going to help *me* gain Enlightenment' 2.270; each stage of the path involves conceit only eradicated by attaining the next stage 2.149; the good qualities you have developed can lead to complacency and pride 17.285; monks comparing the 'purity' of their ethics with the 'impurity' of others 7.263; pride in your level of spiritual attainment 18.399–400, 18.405–6; pride in your morality 1.436; priding oneself on one's spiritual achievements 18.468–9; self-conceit may be increased by spiritual victories 1.303; using the teachings in a way that increases pride 19.178–83; Yalahankar Swami exposes pride 14.489, 20.356

other forms of pride
being an authority on an academic subject may lead to conceit 18.168–9; being proud of weaknesses 17.606; the conceit of the old 18.489; humility is just as much a form of egotism as pride 4.78, 14.489, 20.362; intoxication 16.298–9; memory yields to pride 16.314; people will take pride in whatever brings them attention 17.273; pride dressed up as self-depreciation 17.273; pride in learning 18.480; pride in qualities you have, or imagine or pretend you have 17.273; the pride of nationalism 17.275

getting rid of pride
antidote, *see under* six element practice; be proud of nothing except destroying pride 4.467; curbed by prostrations 1.407; giving up pride 10.520–1

Buddha-pride, vajra pride
a form of *apatrāpya* 17.275; *hrī* as Buddha-pride 17.558; as motivation 18.82; pride at being born into the Buddha's family 4.275–6, 4.359, 4.464–5, 4.613; pride in the activity of the *bodhicitta* 4.623; using pride to help you keep your resolutions 8.191; the Vajrayāna concept 14.451, 17.275

see also
as the eighth fetter, *see under* fetters; feeling inferior, *see* inferior

Priestley, J. B. 24.574

primal scream 4.605

primitive carry your basic and primitive emotions along with you 16.102; a curse is a very serious thing, especially among primitive peoples 18.309; the ignorance of primitive humans 3.424–5, 3.468; incorporation into Buddhism of primitive tree worship 2.222; poor people fare better in a 'primitive' society than in a competitive one 4.449–50; 'primitive beliefs about reality' 2.127; the primitive folklore of our indigenous culture 13.273; primitive humanity is reproductive, modern humanity is productive, the individual is creative 3.471; primitive idea that through sacrifices you keep nature stable 10.517; primitive man had no mechanical sense of time 3.424; primitive superstitions about good luck and bad luck 15.382–3; the responsiveness to the environment of primitive cultures 18.21–2; unconscious conditioning derives largely from the exigencies of primitive life 3.425

primordial Abundant Treasures, the primordial, eternal Buddha 16.152; *ḍākinīs*, the primordial forces to be subdued by Padmasambhava 12.324–5; the mother-mind, the original, primordial

mind 18.64; the primordial Ādibuddha, *see* Ādibuddha; the primordial dualism of earth and sky 16.385; the primordial error that 'self' represents an eternal, unchanging ego-identity 7.327; the primordial forces of the collective unconscious, subdued by Padmasambhava 12.323–32; primordial sound 3.79–80; space, the primordial energy 16.145

Princess, the (Burma Raja's wife) 21.130–6, 22.204–7, 22.380

principle, path, accomplishment 19.411

principles

introduction
the meaning of the word principle, which has much in common with Dharma 2.339; the modern search for spiritual principles 10.154–5; modernist attempts to 'personalize' matters of principle 13.375–6; concern with facts rather than principles 2.51, 7.486–7; relating things to their principles 4.82

Buddhist principles
Buddhism delineates principles but leaves their application to the individual 11.185; Buddhism is based on principles which admit of no exception 10.171; in Buddhist countries laws do not always spring from Buddhist principles 16.434; it's important to know them thoroughly and be convinced of their truth 2.245; principles of Buddhist philosophy 4.637–8; the principles of the Dharma are few, and can be explained in a few pages 7.333; reformulating them in terms of lay life 12.123–6; they need to be defended 2.649

sticking to your principles
any Buddhist has to fight to sustain their principles 3.534; be slow to take a stand on anything other than a real matter of principle 13.137; behaviour based on principles opposite to those professed 2.80–1; the difficulty of sticking to your principles 19.463–4; even at the cost of life itself 10.168, 16.198; if you accept principles, you should feel a responsibility to put them into practice 18.111; 'impossible to retract an opinion I believed to be true, even to save my life' 20.379; people respond to clear-cut principles, lived out and expressed with conviction 18.153; principles' bearings on the spiritual life of the individual 1.6; and remaining on friendly terms with people 18.502; wherever your interests take you, carry your Buddhist principles with you 4.82; your duty relates to the principles you believe in and the situation you're in 26.73

see also
knowledge of principles (*dharma-pratisaṃvid*), *see under* four *pratisaṃvids*; precepts as principles, *see under* precepts/introduction; *indriyas*; 'twelve principles of Buddhism', *see under* Christmas Humphreys

Prinsep, James 9.46

prison 'all beings in the Three Realms enslaved in a prison of fire' 18.588–90; being compelled to adhere to the caste system under threat of imprisonment 20.438; being imprisoned by the importance we give to being successful 18.101–2; the freedom of Enlightenment like release from prison 2.56, 10.262, 11.384, 13.192–3; human life like a prison 11.709–10; hypocrisy: the politeness of an official to the man he imprisoned 4.338; if you are imprisoned, be careful that it does not deprive you of your mental freedom 18.458; Merlin imprisoned in a cell of glass 25.439; the prison of the mind 1.88; Tomo Geshe Rimpoche's imprisonment in Lhasa 22.493–5; our self-imprisonment on the wheel of life, our death-in-life 3.348; we realize the extent to which we were imprisoned only when we attain release 16.448

prisoners Angulimala Buddhist Prison Chaplaincy 2.753 (n763), 12.489; helping prisoners 2.753 (n763), 4.70–1, 11.119, 12.489; how to treat prisoners 8.506–7, 16.615 (n234); the politeness of an official to the man he imprisoned 4.338; the prisoners in the cave, *see under* Plato/*Republic*; a young man who faithfully visited his father in prison 23.195

prīti (rapture, Pāli *pīti*)

its nature
translated 'rapture' 15.218; similar to enthusiasm 10.370; a driving and even overwhelming emotion 2.106; a positive state grounded in mindfulness 15.218; five degrees 3.266–7, 11.33, 12.160–1; listed by Buddhaghosa 2.106, 3.662 (n245), 3.667 (n270), 15.219; inner nourishment 18.50; Buddhaghosa's image of the balloon or silken bag 3.267, 3.288, 9.297

its arising
a sign that energy is on the move 15.219; it can arise in everyday life 15.220; in puja, or Dharma study, or friendship, or appreciating art 10.370; when you see a beautiful sunset or hear a beautiful piece of music 12.161; an experience of the body as well as of the mind 2.260; in second *dhyāna* 3.307; the sense of relief at the

release of blocked energy 2.105–6, 3.268, 15.218; a temporary but necessary stage 15.219; levitation brought about by excess of *prīti* 3.267–8

see also
as one of the seven *bodhyaṅgas*, *see* seven *bodhyaṅgas*; as a *dhyāna* factor, *see* five *dhyāna* factors; in the positive *nidānas*, *see under* twelve positive *nidānas*/(4)

private life are Order members entitled to a private life? 13.399; the arising of the *bodhicitta* as a private and personal experience 1.422; escaping into a private world: rural life, mystical or aesthetic experience, fantasies, madness 12.394; how can I think of withdrawing into private spiritual experience when others are suffering? 2.272; the imbalance between public and private life 13.384–6; life cannot be compartmentalized into professional conduct and private life 7.511–12; *pratyekabuddha* (private or solitary Buddha), *see pratyekabuddha*; the 'private life *micchā-diṭṭhi*' 10.570; the Western tendency to withdraw into the world of private concerns 2.516

Priyananda, Dharmachari brief introduction 24.604 (n13), 24.611 (n45), 24.647 (n199); accompanies Sangharakshita in India (1979) 10.194, 24.9–25; arrives in New Zealand with Sangharakshita 24.8; his brother Tony 24.8; leads ordination retreat in New Zealand 24.33; publisher 14.xx; runs a temple in Malaysia for six months 24.617 (n64)

priya-vāditā (loving speech) characteristic of the bodhisattva 16.486–7; expression of wisdom 16.486; as a *saṃgrahavastu*, *see* four *saṃgrahavastus*; *see also under* speech/four levels of skilful speech

problems

introduction
the difference between a problem and a difficulty 3.551, 4.245, 16.255; insoluble on their own level 7.299; all problems are reducible to the problem of how to escape suffering 7.114; often we don't see that we create our problems 17.434; two kinds of problem: doctrinal and personal 3.552; be aware of the limitations of language, to avoid artificial problems 18.608; setbacks as reminders of the unpredictable nature of *saṃsāra* 18.47

the central problem of the spiritual life
the difficulty of keeping the ego-sense out of spiritual practice 7.406–10; how to translate knowledge into being 11.192; that our energy is dissipated 1.390, 4.133–4, 5.571, 7.292–3, 18.77; that our knowledge is only superficial 12.22–3; that the means to Enlightenment becomes an object of attachment 1.303; need emotional equivalents for intellectual understanding 1.494, 11.193–4, 12.110–11

psychological problems
can be solved by friendship and spiritual nourishment 16.114, 26.78; Indian Buddhists find it hard to understand the problems of Western Buddhists 10.42; is lack of faith a psychological problem? 18.273; people coming to Sangharakshita with psychological problems 12.91–3; sometimes so-called psychological problems are spiritual problems 16.114

the problem of …
ahiṃsā 7.372–7; communicating the Dharma 18.57–8; communication 12.152; confusing alienated awareness with integrated awareness 12.259; death 3.95–6, 12.356–61, 23.91–3; eliminating the sense of separative selfhood 7.406; greed, hatred, and delusion 15.81; how to combine reason and emotion 26.76; human suffering 3.261–2, 7.126–7; what to do with our lives 12.355

solving problems
expecting a guru or teacher to solve your problems 3.552–3; getting what we want does not solve our problems 18.187; a glimpse of something beyond the problem-oriented mode 14.403; solving the problem of desire, you solve the problem of love 7.291; solving the problem of egoless activity 7.408–9; solving the problem of human suffering 26.299; be clear about your own problems, then you can help others with theirs 17.615; Siddhārtha sees the answer to the problem that had tormented him 12.134; solving Ruciraketu's problem (*Sūtra of Golden Light*) 16.253–61; Enlightenment offers the only lasting solution 15.261

see also
koan, *see under* Zen; world problems, *see under* world

processes the bodhisattva sees all bodily states and processes with complete equanimity 4.563; demons as inner processes 19.411; the digestive processes 2.65; the five *skandhas* are not separable components but five sets of processes 15.188; important not to identify thought processes with consciousness 5.229; liberation consists in seeing processes rather than things 17.355; the mind's tendency

to refer to processes as if they were things 17.248–9; the mindful observation of our own mental processes 17.260; the processes going on in the physical body 10.231; seeing things as processes rather than entities 1.175, 17.248–9, 19.238; *skandha nirvāṇa* (the extinction of the processes of psychophysical existence), *see under* Nirvāṇa/ Nirvāṇa in practice; thought processes, *see under* thoughts; the whole universe is a network of processes 3.216–17

Proclus *Elements of Theology* 24.389; influence on Dionysius? 13.585–6; inspiring only in small doses 26.366; *On the One* 20.81

procrastination coming to a decision to procrastinate 19.165; if we really wanted Enlightenment in the future, we would really want it now 17.354; make the best use of your opportunities, and don't postpone things 18.555; not putting off tomorrow what one can do today 7.285; 'O procrastinating one, who thinketh not of the coming of death' 12.208; 'Only by instant action can you succeed!' 18.153; putting off practice of the Dharma to another life 12.689–90; putting off practice until one has found the 'right teaching' 18.473–4; wasting our life 7.172; *see also* postponement

Procrustean bed what it is 8.690 (n182); the mutilation of Buddhism by those trying to prove it is part of Hinduism 8.231; the Procrustean bed of Hegel's dialectic 7.387–8

profane *see under* sacredness

profundity the *bardo* is one of the most profound aspects of Buddhism 12.197; a bodhisattva unafraid of profound teachings 14.166; the bodhisattva ideal: a profound conception of the inmost nature of things 7.44; the Buddha answers brahmins' questions on profound themes 2.205; 'Buddhism the most profound and fundamental antithesis to Christianity' 7.366; Buddhist philosophy is vast, profound, and sometimes very technical 12.515; the Dharma is called profound because it goes beyond ideas of existence and non-existence 17.364; the Dharma 'profound and hard to see' 1.90–1, 3.175, 3.181, 17.324; don't ask glib questions about profound things and expect an answer on the spot 21.121–2; don't try to explain profound teachings if you have only partial knowledge 19.356–7; Enlightenment: an overflowing of profound love and compassion 3.32, 22.285; 'The Essence of Profound Meaning' 22.504–7; friendship is of the most profound possible significance 7.295; *gambhira-dharma-kṣānti* (patient acceptance of the profound Dharma) 14.192; Going for Refuge a profound inner experience 2.7, 3.397, 22.461; the *Heart Sūtra* is 'one of the finest and most profound spiritual documents of mankind' 1.70, 1.444; the human heart is more profoundly moved by ideals than doctrines 1.397; in the modern world best to discuss profound questions in secular language 12.117; leisured and subtle discussion of profound questions 12.121–2, 22.373–4; 'No profounder teaching can I give you in my life' (Milarepa) 19.111–12; 'one of the best and most profound talks I had ever given' 22.286; 'the profound Buddha region', a world in itself 16.243–4; 'the profound Madhyamaka' 17.325; a profound 'metaphysical' cognition 2.117; a profound spiritual lesson: 'Love Dharma, for Dharma is Truth' 20.332; the profundity of the Mahāyāna 14.142–3, 16.59–60, 16.232; the profundity of the teaching has nothing to do with written language 1.222; *samādhi*: a little practice induces profound experience 2.113; *termas*: highly important teachings which exert profound influence 12.300; the *Udāna* verses strike a profound, solemn, impassioned, and serene note 14.53; who is to judge what is profound? 16.59

progress can be achieved only in the realm of the spirit 7.164–5; contrasted with change 7.163–4; distinction between evolution, progress, and development 13.465–6; human progress is not automatic 10.346; the idea of progress discovered in the 19th century 12.464; the modern world believes in progress 7.162–4; make sure that your progress is spiritual as well as material 10.389–90; many think they believe in progress who only believe in change 7.163; material progress is a good thing, but spiritual progress is even more important 10.346–7, 15.510; middle way between belief that no progress is possible and belief in automatic progress 10.347; only on the spiral path is progress assured 11.271; progress in civilization won't carry on indefinitely 11.271; spiritual progress, *see* spiritual progress; the theory of evolution has led to a widespread belief in progress 10.346–7; an un-Buddhistic conception 1.221; we are less confident of human history as uninterrupted progress than we used to be 12.593

progressive *anupubbi-kathā* (progressive discourse) 8.592–3, 10.551–2; the bodhisattva ideal is progressive, ready to adopt fresh formulations as necessary 1.394–5; the Buddha taught in a gradual, progressive way 8.256, 8.592–3, 10.551; the *dhyānas* represent the progressive unification of consciousness 2.110; every skilful mental state has an inbuilt tendency to transcend itself 18.207; history as the progressive manifestation of Spirit (Hegel) 3.423; a monk who was only Buddhist to the extent that Buddhism could be seen as 'progressive' 22.214; the *nidānas*: cyclical, progressive and regressive, irreversibly progressive 4.650; *opanayiko* (progressive), *see under Tiratana Vandanā*; the progressive refinement of love (Plato) 5.511; the spiritual life is nothing but a progressive attenuation of the ego-sense 7.302; the three *yānas* seen as progressive ascent 7.479; the threefold way, a progressive path 3.354, 7.257; whatever happens, is our reaction cyclical or progressive? 3.279

projection

introduction
how it works 15.305; the nature of psychological projection 13.352–3; it's not easy genuinely to project 15.391

kinds of projection
accusing someone of projecting 17.234, 19.292; being attracted to the exotic 13.494; habitual projection of negativity 17.665; not projecting the internal onto the external 18.614; paranoia as projection 17.258–9, 19.497; projecting the evil that is within ourselves 26.654; projection in communication 1.520, 3.140, 25.96; projection of higher castes onto lower castes 12.223; projection of the whole of yourself onto another person 18.309–10; romantic attachment and projection 17.224–7; sexual pleasure is often bound up with mental projections 17.393

projection in religious life
as a Buddhist, avoid playing up to people's projections 17.657–8; religious or spiritual projection 11.83–4, 12.524–5, 13.353, 16.96; Nirvāṇa can become a projection of our mundane needs 3.229; monks the focus of the projections of the laity 19.310, 23.424; people's projections onto Sangharakshita 11.686, 12.524; projecting spiritual life onto other people 18.520; projection of unconscious reaction against Christianity 11.339–40; Rechungpa projects his negative qualities onto Milarepa 18.531, 19.15; worship and projection 15.390–2; Zen calls for a withdrawal of all projections 13.353

working with projections
bringing our projections into awareness 15.307–8; a father-substitute may be necessary for a while 3.551; a single-sex situation helps one develop qualities normally projected 26.26

positive projection in spiritual practice
moving from projecting the *deva* 'out there' to experiencing the *deva* 'in here' 15.496; in Vajrayāna practice it occupies an important place 19.412–13; visualization as positive projection 19.412–13

prolongation could the presence of a *ḍākinī* prolong a lama's life? 22.404–6; craving usually expresses itself as a desire to prolong pleasure 19.383; eternity considered as transcending time rather than infinitely prolonging it 4.204, 4.210; Nirvāṇa does not come about either by prolonging or by ceasing the saṃsāric process 10.523; practices that prolong consciousness into the dream state 19.307; walking meditation as a way of prolonging mindfulness into the ordinary world 5.82–3; could the Buddha's life have been prolonged?, *see* Buddha I/last days/length of life

Prometheus the age of Prometheus 3.425; the myth of Prometheus 12.108, 24.674 (n323); *Church and Ethics After Prometheus* 2.613–14; depiction on a sarcophagus 24.266–7; *Prometheus Unbound*, *see under* Shelley

promiscuity 3.566, 11.322

promises doing something you've said you'll do requires a firm resolution 19.286–7; it's important to keep them, so don't make them lightly 4.484, 12.485, 18.487, 19.524; Going for Refuge and taking the precepts are promises 12.485, 19.57–8; if our self-awareness is weak, we will not be able to keep a promise 3.565; keeping the promises we make to our friends 3.574, 11.699; keeping promises requires individuality 12.485; promising to do something means actually doing it 17.696, 19.57; you don't have control over a promise if it involves other people 19.364, 26.60; a promise (*samaya*) to do your practice 19.385

promptness the Buddha was of a prompt, decisive character 11.440–1; in expressing appreciation 4.594, 4.596; the importance of prompt action 4.468

pronunciation importance for the oral tradition of accuracy of pronunciation 10.576, 20.409; Sangharakshita's struggle with pronunciation at his ordination 2.419, 11.388, 12.302–3, 20.409; suggestion that Burmese pronunciation of Pāli was incorrect 8.119–20, 22.171

proof dreams are proof that something can be perceived without objective reality 12.172; no need to prove the non-existence of God 9.344–5, 10.150; proof of karma 3.111–12, 3.115; proof of rebirth, *see under* rebirth/doubts and proofs; 'proving' spiritual attainment 18.108–9; rational proof of Enlightenment 1.285; what is the proof that the scriptures are the authentic word of the Buddha? 1.326–7, 16.240; whether we are practising the Dharma cannot be proved, only demonstrated by how we live 7.264

propaganda art and spiritual life: more subtle than using the arts as religious propaganda 26.69; the Buddha was the most successful propagandist the world has ever seen 2.25; Christian propagandists with the answer to everything 19.109; political propaganda 4.595, 7.266

property children should learn to respect other people's property 3.537; in a democratic country, a more equitable distribution of property achieved through legislation 2.368; giving and sharing 2.364; in traditional societies, wealth is kept in the form of property 18.94–5; it is the duty of a friend to watch over our property when we are neglectful 3.574; lack of respect for public property 18.335; moral life interpreted in terms of the accumulation of moral property 1.436; owning a property is a source of worry 18.334; property is theft (Proudhon) 2.368; violence in respect of property 2.364; *see also* possessions

prophecies the Buddha foresees monks who will one day disgrace the sangha 14.189, 14.194–5; the Buddha's prophecy about what would happen to his *śūnyatā* teachings 14.136; prophecies about the future Buddha's return 21.49–51; a prophecy that the 2,500th Buddha Jayanti would mark a revival for Buddhism 8.216, 22.315; 'When iron birds fly in the sky …' 12.196, 12.720 (n144), 12.300

prophets Jewish prophets 3.427, 12.134; the kinship between prophet and poet 26.178, 26.209; 'A prophet is not without honour, but in his own country' 22.298; prophets hearing 'the voice of God' 11.151; prophets or messengers of God 7.366; *The Prophet*, *see* Gibran

proportion be careful that your thinking doesn't develop disproportionately 26.38; keeping a sense of proportion 4.136–8; saying 'You're *always* doing that' suggests having things out of proportion 17.652

prose the danger of translating poetry into prose 14.301, 14.304; poetry can get closer to reality than prose 19.238–9; shift from prose to poetry 16.532

prosperity and wealth

getting wealthy
amassing wealth unethically but without breaking conventional ethical codes 3.582; the Christian idea that prosperity shows that God favours you 17.19–20, 21.354–5; creation of wealth 16.413; even the possessor of a thousand shirts can only wear one at a time 17.394, 18.568; material wealth 16.396–7; material prosperity and success 18.101–2; production of wealth by work 16.411–12; seeking wealth by wealth 17.659; there's nothing wrong with prosperity, you can make good use of it 19.509; in traditional societies, wealth is kept in the form of property 18.94–5

problems of wealth
the intoxication of wealth 16.299; inequalities of wealth in the world 10.396; monasteries paying more attention to wealthier people 19.478–9; not satisfying 9.284, 18.568; rich people afraid of becoming poor 3.214; wealth and poverty 21.224–5

inner wealth
the ability to feel wealthy even in the humblest circumstances 17.201; the inexhaustible richness of the potentialities of the human heart 7.307

Dhammapada references
'Contentment is the greatest wealth' 1.152, 18.96; 'Even his self is not his own. How then … wealth?' 1.173, 10.146, 10.455, 10.490, 18.219; 'Even though a man be richly attired … living a holy life, he is a *bhikkhu*' 1.244, 2.203, 2.432, 2.451, 2.591; 'One path leads to worldly prosperity, quite another to Nibbāna' 7.171–2

elsewhere in the Buddhist tradition
one could say that Siddhārtha's wealth was a disadvantage 10.236; the Buddha uses the prospect of wealth to encourage people to live ethically 10.645; 'Faith is the wealth here best for man' (*Sutta-Nipāta*) 1.290;

no riches can compare with the Tathāgata 15.63; the wealth of the Enlightened mind 12.214, 18.59; the wealth of the Dharma 18.334; Dharmākara's merits so immense that riches sprang to meet him when reborn 1.329; 'A rich man seldom enjoys the wealth that he has earned' (Milarepa) 18.568; Milarepa's material poverty and spiritual wealth 18.50, 18.96

in India 10.297
in ancient India 10.478; Indian symbolism 16.87–8; Lakṣmī represents prosperity, wealth, economics 16.399, 16.411; Śrī as goddess of wealth 16.399, 16.410; stress of Hinduism on prosperity 16.398; greater prosperity of new Buddhists 10.19, 10.303–4, 10.314–15, 10.407–8, 27.1075

see also
Jambhala (bodhisattva of riches); possessions

prostitution being forced into prostitution 25.118–21, 25.260; a Biblical harlot 13.545–6; bodhisattva Fugen Bosatsu, as a courtesan, teaches those addicted to pleasure 1.448–9; the Buddha teaches young men looking for a thieving courtesan 2.687 (n258), 15.269; the ethics of prostitution 11.567; the Great Whore of Babylon 13.555; not associating with prostitutes 4.545; the concubines who practised the Dharma 10.627–8; a fight over a courtesan 10.607–8; Indian view of the conduct of unmarried women 15.485; Japanese enslavement of Korean 'comfort women' 26.677; in Kalimpong 22.45; Nepalese prostitutes 25.119; Sangharakshita gives a talk to prostitutes in Mumbai 25.119–20; in Thailand 13.470–2, 13.489; Upagupta and the courtesan 14.68

prostrations *see under* devotion/physical expressions

protection asking the Buddhas and bodhisattvas for spiritual protection 4.312–13; the Buddha protects people from an experience for which they are not ready 14.183; Buddhist practice as a source of protection 18.80–1; an eagerness to be protected and cherished 4.470–1; desire for magical protection from holy men 10.496–7; the Dharma is protected by practising it 19.406; 'the Dharma protects him who practises the Dharma' 10.570; it may be that you are protected by grace waves in the sense of being open to positive influences 18.98; not Going for Refuge but just seeking the Buddha's protection in worldly life 19.484–5; protecting the mind is more important than protecting the body 18.80–1; protecting one's spiritual practice 17.561; protection from enemies 18.636; seeing the Buddha image as a source of blessing and magical protection 2.229–30; theme of the *Sūtra of Golden Light* 16.341–94; a young man offers Milarepa protection, but it is no such thing 18.137–9

protection ceremonies *see under* ceremonies

protectors the Buddhas and bodhisattvas as protectors 11.252, 11.263, 11.269, 17.561; *dhāraṇīs* taught to the bodhisattva by benevolent deities to protect him 1.449; present world-period protected by Amitābha and Avalokiteśvara 1.263; protectors of the Dharma, *see dharmapālas*; protectors of the world, *see lokapālas*, or (in another sense) *see hrī*; three family protectors, *see* three family protectors; translates two different Sanskrit words, *pāla* and *nātha* 16.288

protest 'Everything flows', a protest against the abstract Being of the Eleatic philosophers 7.195–6; it is important to protest against any misrepresentation of the Dharma 4.127, 8.xxiv, 24.206; Luther's protests against the sacramental system of the Church 18.428, 18.520; Mahāyāna teachings may be protests against taking earlier doctrines literally 1.221–2; the Mahāyāna's protest against the concept of Stream Entry 4.38; *pratītya-samutpāda* a protest against the static conception of Upanishadic thinkers 7.195; the Protestants' protest against the 'trade' of religion 10.593; protests against nuclear war must be non-violent 12.346–7; protests at the proposal to name a university after Dr Ambedkar 10.xli, 24.23; the Sahajayāna's protest against a literal-minded interpretation of the Tantra 1.386–7, 19.274; the Vajrayāna as a movement of protest against monastic formalism 19.109; the *White Lotus Sūtra*'s protest against the contradictions of a merely intellectual approach 1.218; *see also* activism

Protocols of the Elders of Zion 24.73, 24.625 (n99)

Proudhon, Pierre-Joseph 2.368

Proust, Marcel *Remembrance of Things Past* 17.402, 17.751 (n331), 26.491; self-isolation 26.354

pṛthagjana **or *puthujjana*** ('ordinary person', 'worldling') 'The worldling is like a madman' 4.711 (n342), 5.659, 12.229, 16.192–3, 26.75; two kinds of human

being: *pṛthagjana* and *āryan* 10.140–1, 10.235, 11.160, 14.312; also *bahujana* ('manyfolk') 2.138; argument that they possess no real knowledge refuted 14.86; ceasing to be one 2.115; characteristics 2.138–9; daring to sit in judgement on the wisdom of Buddhas and bodhisattvas 11.484; described in the Abhidharma 14.81; does not understand the luminosity of mind 1.84; the fool 2.139; governed by sense-based instincts and impulses 17.11–13; is not an individual 3.434; the morality of the *pṛthagjana* 11.314; one whose view of existence is limited, restricted, and distorted 11.160; progressing from *pṛthagjana* to Stream Entrant 14.312; the sangha stands in relation to society as the *ārya* stands in relation to the *pṛthagjana* 13.515; showing worldlings the Dharma 1.123; to the worldling, the phenomenal world seems to be composed of real 'things' 1.104; a worldly person can't tell whether someone is Enlightened 19.282; the wrong views of the worldly person 1.107–8

prudence (*nipako*) 15.288–89, 17.67

pseudo-Dharma 18.172

pseudo-egalitarianism *see under* egalitarianism

pseudo-liberalism asserting the value of all religious form 13.424; the belief that fairness can be achieved by unfair means 26.74; denial that there is such a thing as ethics 13.413; one of the difficulties facing Western Buddhism 11.521–2; its extreme form is political correctness 26.74; the word judgemental is pseudo-liberal jargon 13.413

pseudo-spiritual claptrap 8.437; consumerism 3.327; a *ḍākinī* is not a pseudo-spiritual girlfriend 12.314, 17.638, 18.371; exoticism 11.82–3; projection 11.83–4; technism 11.85

psyche what the word means 16.270; all systems of spiritual culture founded on a dualistic philosophy create a split in the psyche 7.401; effort to grow needs to be directed towards the whole psyche 2.112, 3.41

psychedelic experience *see under* drugs

psychic centres *see chakras*

psychic experiences Miss Albers' 20.168; Sangharakshita's, *see under* Sangharakshita VI/spiritual and supernatural experiences; Padmasambhava seen standing behind Sangharakshita during a talk 23.152, 26.673–4

psychic powers dismissed as impossibilities 1.33; Sangharakshita was once asked to teach someone how to develop them 3.584–5, 8.626, 22.434, 22.438; monks are prohibited from displaying them or promising them to others 3.584; *see also* supernormal powers

psychoanalysis the bringing of the unconscious into consciousness, id into ego 12.99–100; Buddhism and psychoanalysis 12.91–101, 12.228; confession 16.269; continuous free association 5.658–9; dismissal of religious ritual 11.207; Freud's development of psychoanalysis 10.348–9; may help one to come to terms with childhood trauma 14.573; in the *Nanda Jātaka* the Bodhisattva functions like a psychoanalyst 8.378–9; 'neurosis' can be a healthy symptom of rebellion 12.101; in the parable of the return journey, a comparison with psychoanalysis 16.97; a psychiatrist with problems 26.27; it knows the difficulty of knowing ourselves 12.233–4; there's almost no end to the process of going back, even to past lives 18.443; to think you will always need your analyst isn't encouraging from a Buddhist point of view 16.113; through drawing 22.253–4; undermines rejoicing in merits by suspecting people's motives 4.317, 4.605; a weakness to think in terms of adjusting to existing conditions 12.100–1

psychological types introduction 12.270–84; in the *Bhagavad Gītā* (*sattva*, *rajas*, *tamas*) 12.277–8; differentiated according to stage of development and which faculty is strongest 12.281; do the two sexes represent different psychological types? 12.282–3; the four humours 12.271–2; Freud's three stages 12.272, 12.281; Erich Fromm's theory about how the individual relates to the world 12.275–7; help us to understand ourselves and know what we must do to evolve 12.281–2; Karen Horney's theory of personality types 12.273–4; Carl Jung's psychic functions 12.273–5, 12.281; a map to find our way around the maze which is ourselves 12.284; is there a meditating type? 12.282; Wilhelm Reich's theory 12.273; is there a religious type? 12.282; William Sheldon on psychological types 12.281, 12.724–5 (n194); should you follow the line of least resistance or try to develop your weaker qualities? 12.283–4; Theravāda: six psychological types to which human beings belong 1.161

see also
character types (*caritas*), *see* Buddhaghosa/*Visuddhimagga*/character types; *Puggala-Paññatti* ('Designation of Human Types')

psychology

aspects of psychology
the assumption that the deeper you go, the worse it becomes 4.605; attraction to psychology can be a distraction 16.114; the danger of using the language of psychology 10.440–1; do we need to know why we are as we are? 18.442–3; depth psychology 3.334, 11.658; difference between psychological and spiritual 3.336, 4.620–3, 15.588, 16.270, 18.443; friendship as the panacea for psychological problems 26.78; the growth of psychology in the West 12.138; the image as a vehicle of psychological truth 2.132; the limitations of the psychological model of development 17.670–1; looking beyond psychology 5.355; 'No psychological solutions for psychological problems' 4.268; may not envisage the possibility of change 15.523; psychological breakthrough (compared with the breakthrough of the *vajra*) 13.171–2; responding to people's psychological suffering 10.86–7; sometimes so-called psychological problems are really spiritual problems 16.114

Buddhist psychology
Abhidharma contributions to Buddhist psychology 14.79, 14.93–4; the Abhidharma goes beyond psychology 17.649; aspects of Buddhist psychology (lecture series) 12.138–234, 12.366; Anagarika Dharmapala's contribution to Buddhist psychology 8.58; *citta-niyama*, *see under* five *niyamas*; depth psychology of the Yogācāra 12.166–78; extends to supernormal states 12.147; in using the term, beware of limiting your conception of Buddhism 17.436; the middle way in psychology 9.398–9; perhaps we should rely more on Buddhist psychology 4.604; a psychology that explores the heights and depths 7.486, 12.21–30; in a sense there's no such thing as Buddhist psychology 12.139, 17.433; it has no purpose other than to be put into practice 17.433; simply all of Buddhism's teachings about the nature and functioning of mind 12.139–40; subtler and more comprehensive than Western psychology 7.229

psychology and Buddhism
behaviourist psychology different from Buddhism 12.656; Buddhism is firmly grounded on the facts of psychology 8.262; dialogue between psychology and Buddhism 12.138–9; find ways to express Buddhism in psychological terms 12.117–18; growth of psychology in the West as preparation to meet Buddhism 3.333–4; how are psychological techniques useful in the context of spiritual practice? 16.113–15; bringing in current psychological ideas to FWBO classes 11.550–1; the FWBO (Triratna) getting a bit sick with psychological analysis 4.603–6; Sangharakshita not especially sympathetic to the psychological approach 11.549–50

psychophysical organism (*nāma-rūpa*)
comprises the five *skandhas* 3.198, 10.231; designed to shield us from the impact of reality 12.201; development 3.130; the five *skandhas* are inadequate to describe its complexities 15.187–8; the five skandhas divided into *nāma* and *rūpa* 15.187; mind and matter are dynamically related 7.137; one way of analysing the human being 2.335; the equivalent in a Buddha is *dharmakāya* and *rūpakāya* 2.336

see also
five *skandhas*; as fourth *nidāna*, *see under* twelve cyclical *nidānas*

psychotherapy

introduction
the reason for psychotherapy 5.659; whether it is helpful depends on its view of human beings 4.71–2, 12.227–8, 14.574; achieving breakthroughs in psychotherapy 13.171–2; advice to 'let out' negative emotions, but nothing said about positive ones 4.595–6; applies to those who 'suffer from their psychic state' (Jaspers) 5.657, 12.225–6; building up your psychological strength 15.270–1; co-counselling 19.555; group therapy situations can be unhelpful 14.574; has a number of methods but no underlying philosophy of existence 5.661–2; help with emotional neediness 15.283; may be helpful in the short term, but no need to explore negativity exhaustively 14.573–4; the purpose of retrieving repressed memories 15.88; regarding every mistake as a stage of development, a modern wrong view 19.343; the therapist simply helps you to mobilize your own powers 12.232; two kinds: adjustment therapy and character therapy 12.226–7

Buddhism and psychotherapy
common ground 12.227–9; psychotherapeutic and Buddhist ideas of mental health are different 17.164;

psychotherapy and meditation 5.653–65; Zen and psychotherapy 12.224–34

Ptolemy, Claudius 23.310, 23.521 (n349)

pubbenivāsānussati (remembrance of former births) *see under* rebirth/how it works

public life Buddhist ethics evidently not influential in public life 24.498–9; the Buddhist incognito in public life 12.126–7; participation in public life and the development of individuality 11.635; women in public life 11.635–6

public speaking the Buddha as the inventor of the public talk 10.551–2; Dharma talks, *see under* Dharma III/Dharma teachers; it can help one build up confidence 11.635; overcoming fear of it 16.28; potential for humiliation 14.491; *nirukti-pratisaṃvid* 16.490; Sangharakshita's public talks, *see under* Sangharakshita X

publishing and publishers Buddhist Publication Society, Kandy 8.275–6, 8.383–4, 8.694 (n221); Bukkyō Dendō Kyōkai 14.9; Burns, Oates & Washbourne 23.52; Chetana Ltd., Bombay 8.662, 24.101; Dharma Publishing 11.608, 24.491; difference between transcript and original recording 16.565; inaccuracy of publishers' blurbs 16.491–2; G. A. Natesan and Co., Madras 8.382; Rider 23.51; Tharpa Publications 14.xiii; Windhorse Publications 24.384–5, 24.474; Wisdom Publications 8.567

pudgala (person) analysis resolves into *dharmas* 2.89, 17.248; the Buddha as *pudgala* 17.631; no unchanging substantial entity 2.99; one should rely on the Dharma, not on any person 16.576–8; said to be devoid of selfhood because no element does not arise from external conditions 1.266; a topic in the *Śāriputra-abhidharma-śāstra* 14.74

pudgala-nairātmya *see nairātmya*

Pudgalavādins although the school has not survived, it was important in its day 17.632; believed in the real existence of the *pudgala* or person 7.490, 17.631; refuted by other schools, but no one questioned their ability to gain Enlightenment 7.490, 17.631–2; termed heretical 7.524, 17.631; split from the Sthaviravādins 7.497, 13.44; why did they introduce their doctrine? 17.632

Puggala-Paññatti (*Designation of Human Types*) 14.80–1

puja *see* devotion/puja and ritual

Pukkusa the Malla 2.29, 9.565 (n286), 13.144

punarbhava *see under* rebirth/tradition/introduction

punarjanman *see under* rebirth/tradition/Hindu ideas

punctuality the duty of an employee to be punctual 3.588; of the English 10.101, 10.239, 23.36; 'Few things tend more to alienate friendship than a want of punctuality ...' (Hazlitt) 24.561; Sangharakshita reproved for being two minutes late 9.499, 11.542–3, 23.36, 25.382

puṇḍarīka (white lotus) *see under* lotuses

Pundarika *see under* Triratna I/early days

punishment based on the power mode 16.433; better to think in terms of discipline 16.510; capital punishment 3.319, 7.119, 12.76; of children 9.523, 20.490, 23.95; eternal 16.78; fear of punishment 3.322, 11.260, 16.306–7; harsh punishment of transgressing *bhikkhus* in 17th-century Thailand 2.634–5; it's very dangerous to regard oneself as the instrument of punishment 26.59; and karma: no question of punishment or reward 3.100, 17.57; no question of law and punishment within a Buddhist order 16.433; punishment of sin 3.99–100; stoning to death 11.336; suffering as the punishment of God 16.86; training is not punishment, but a means to achieve a particular end 17.254

puṇya etymology of *puṇya*: 'merit' and 'virtue' 4.47; distinction between *puṇya* and *jñāna* 19.46–8; the humiliation that springs from *puṇya* 14.487–91; the incommensurability of *puṇya* and *prajñā* 14.468–9; *puṇya karma*, the skilful atmosphere you create around yourself 15.396–7, 18.244–5; *puṇya* is the quality of your being brought about by skilful actions 15.401–2; *see also* merit

Puṇya (the Buddha's disciple) 3.290–1

Punya, Dharmachari v24

puṇyabhūmi 9.315

puṇyadevatā *see under* guardian angel

Punyamala, Dharmacharini v24

Puṇyamitra 13.342

puṇyanumodanā (after-death ceremony) *see under* funerals

puṇyanumodanā *see* rejoicing in merits

Puṇyaraśmi 14.189

puṇya-sambhāra **and** ***jñāna-sambhāra*** *see* two accumulations

Punyasri, Dharmacharini v24

Punyayaśas 13.342

puppets 14.187

Purāṇas introduction 7.601 (n337); arguably modelled on Mahāyāna *sūtras* 10.50; you don't get any sense of human historical life 10.465; *Bhāgavata Purāṇa* 7.233; *Skanda Purāṇa* 21.437

pure abodes *see under* heavens

pure awareness absolute mind is pure awareness within which subject–object distinction does not exist 13.355–6; acting out of the depths of pure awareness 11.7; aesthetic appreciation is akin to resting in pure awareness 17.227; awareness of reality 11.101; a basis for insight as long as the awareness is integrated, not alienated 5.209, 5.400; cultivate towards all experiences an attitude of pure awareness 12.158; have a pause between activities to allow it to come through 5.399; like that of a musician immersed in a symphony 15.202–3; Locanā the embodiment of clear awareness 13.315; moments of pure awareness 15.201; pure, bright, clear awareness 10.606, 18.322; sometimes experienced first thing in the morning 5.398, 19.192, 19.395

Pure Giving, Princess 14.183–4

Pure Land (Buddha-field, Buddha-land)

what is a Pure Land?
archetypally ideal conditions for Dharma practice 2.553–4, 3.455; based on the principle that thoughts can give rise to things 17.296; Buddha-field (*buddha-kṣetra*) 3.243–4, 16.463; a Buddha can create one through infinitely powerful volition 17.479; a Buddha's wisdom and compassion create a Buddha-field 17.298; the endless harmonies of all the Buddha-fields 2.154; Enlightenment as a 'social experience' 18.305–6; the ideal environment to practise the Dharma 1.339–41, 17.243, 17.297; a field of living beings (*Vimalakīrti-nirdeśa*) 16.467, 16.473; flowers of jade and crystal flecked with gold 25.372; a form of *rūpaloka* 14.454–5; how they accomplish 'the buddha-work' 16.563–4; in what sense does a Buddha-field exist? 14.454–6; it provides for all conducive conditions for the attainment of Enlightenment 1.340; no work there, and whatever you need appears 17.297, 19.26; the product of a bodhisattva's intense aspiration 17.297; the qualities of an ideal Buddha-country 1.327; the sphere of spiritual authority of a Buddha 1.339, 14.167, 16.460–1; 'There is a land more lovely' (poem) 25.389; within a single flower of the Pure Land there are whole universes 19.216

in Buddhist literature and tradition
described in the Pāli canon 1.183; depictions 16.184–5; anticipation of the Pure Land in the *Dīgha Nikāya* 16.57; Queen Vaidehī is taught to visualize it 1.332–4, 3.454–5, 3.571–2, 14.172–3, 20.464; described in the *White Lotus Sūtra* 14.120–1, 16.45; the *Diamond Sūtra* on the creation of harmonious Buddha-fields 14.453–6; mentioned in Nāgārjuna's *Precious Garland* 17.296; numerous as the sands of the Ganges 1.239; owes something to Iranian influences 16.57; Sarvagandhasugandhā, where the Dharma is taught by perfume 16.554–6, 16.558; the Vajrayāna view 17.299; the Zen approach to the Pure Land 7.43; a talk on the Pure Land 23.79

building the Buddha-land
art as an analogy 16.476; how to build 16.467–78; built by bodhisattvas 16.467, 16.470–4; built with living beings 16.473; the goal is to be a creator of a Pure Land, not a consumer of spiritual goodies 17.243; has to be a joint creation 16.471; making a Pure Land out of a suffering world 25.349; the merit of a bodhisattva may be great enough to create a Pure Land 1.342; the principle is the power of positive thinking 17.297–8; statesmanship 16.477; what do we have to do with building a Buddha-land? 16.474

pure and impure Pure Lands
ours is an example of an impure Buddha-field 14.167; pure and impure 2.78, 16.462–3, 16.468–9, 17.298; purifying 16.463, 16.470–1; impure inhabited by beings from the six realms, pure by gods and men 1.339, 2.78, 14.167

rebirth in the Pure Land
'as the petals open see the wonders of Sukhāvatī' 25.421; described by Shinran 1.345; described in the *sūtras* 1.334; exchanging mountains for the Pure Land 25.349; how to ensure rebirth in a Pure Land 17.298; 'If one wishes to reach the Pure Land, he must first purify his mind' 2.78; the kinds of beings who will be reborn in the Buddha's Pure Land 14.158–9; 'the new-born lotus smiles beside the crystal fountains' 25.345; Pure

Lands created by a group of beings reborn together 14.455, 17.479; those born there are dazzled by its beauty and can hear and see the Buddha 14.168; what would cause you to be reborn in a Buddha-field? 14.455–6

our world transformed into a Pure Land
building a Pure Land may be beyond us, but we can set our own goals 15.95–6; description of our world as a future Pure Land 16.168–9; our task is to create it on this earth 3.455; people find it very difficult to live in a Buddha-land 16.463; the pure mind perceives the world as the Pure Land 7.411, 17.299; in Ruciraketu's dream 16.265; thinking of your surroundings as the Pure Land 16.181; wanting to bring distractions into the Pure Land 16.471; in the *White Lotus Sūtra* 16.45, 16.66, 16.189; the woman and the fish-basket 16.470–1; you are creating a world around you all the time 17.299

the Pure Land as metaphor or symbol
the Pure Land as mandala 18.525; a symbol of the *dharmadhātu* 3.244; the ten precepts as the bodhisattva's Buddha-field 2.334

other things compared to Pure Lands
Auckland at night like a Pure Land 24.97; a bookshop as a kind of Pure Land 12.492; 'I felt that I was in the Pure Land' 24.117; India as the *buddha-kṣetra* 10.254; puja as a foretaste of the Pure Land 11.241; the Pure Land of Amitābha, *see* Sukhāvatī; *see also* Pure Land *sūtras*

Pure Land schools of Buddhism
introduction 1.336–48; alternative names (White Lotus, Short Cut, White Path) 1.337–8; association with the *Tibetan Book of the Dead* 12.204; based on the Pure Land *sūtras* 14.176, 16.18; Chan (Zen) and Pure Land Buddhism not incompatible 24.533; and chanting Amitābha's name, *see under* Amitābha; difference between Indo-Chinese and Japanese forms 1.338; doesn't stress the master–disciple relationship 24.533; founders 1.337; inspiration and guidance from 2.553–4; it seems to have arisen out of a sense of spiritual despair 17.298–9; the main aim of (Chinese) Pure Land Buddhism is rebirth in a Buddha Land 24.534; Shōdōmon (path of self-power) and Jōdomon (path of other-power) 7.553 (n50), 24.533; Sukhāvatī a central feature of the Pure Land schools 17.298; the letters of Yinkuang (modern patriarch in China) 24.533

Pure Land (also Happy Land) *sūtras*
introduction 14.166–78; the basis of the Pure Land school 14.176, 16.18; part of the laity's creative response to exclusion from the spiritual life 14.168; represent the Mahāyāna's elucidation of the true meaning of sangha 14.168, 14.184–5; speak the language of images 16.18; *sūtras* that describe Pure Lands of Buddhas other than Amitābha 14.175; teach simple faith in the saving power of the Buddha's vow 14.104; translations 1.333–4, 16.624 (n313); *see also Akṣobhya-vyūha*; *Amitāyur-Dhyāna Sūtra*; *Guān Jing*; *Karuṇā Puṇḍarīka*; *Sukhāvatī-vyūha Sūtras*

Purfurst, William *see* Kapilavaddho

purification bathing not in the Ganges but in the Dharma 1.62; through confession 16.325, 16.509; ethical preparation 25.86; history as periods of purification and decay 13.440; instantaneous and gradual purification of the *āsravas* 14.215; Milarepa is purified by building towers for Marpa 12.18; nothing to do with time 9.538; purification of defilements on the Tibetan Buddhist path 12.296–7; purifying the defilements like removing a stain from a pure white cloth 26.642; purifying the soul 25.267; purifying and refining sensuality as a stage in spiritual practice 18.157–9; threefold: body, speech, and mind 2.330–1, 9.51–2, 9.287; and the *tummo* heat practice 19.570; 'using tradition to purify Buddhism' 13.439–40, 13.470; the way to purification: recognition, no blame, change 26.537; we purify ourselves by realizing we have never been impure 5.33–4, 4.193, 26.50, 26.52; you can't be purified by objects with good vibes 18.428–9; you don't become pure by bathing (*Udāna*) 10.457–8;

see also
'No one can purify another', *see Dhammapada*/chapter 12; purification of mind, *see under* mind/working with the mind; Vajrasattva practice, *see under* Vajrasattva

purisapuggalā 3.416

purities *see* seven *visuddhis*

purity

aspects of purity
the word 'purity' 5.115; of a buddha-field 16.468–9; *dāna*: a threefold circle of purity 2.366, 4.104, 17.202, 17.734 (n204); one of three aspects of Enlightenment 12.546–7; pure of all concepts, pure of conditionality 5.33; path of purity, in

the *Dhammapada* 1.171; 'Pure are your eyes' (hymn to the Buddha) 16.466; 'pure experience' 19.377; pure and radiant consciousness 1.84; purity of heart 5.211; purity and integration 19.385; purity is power 26.53; symbolized by the lotus 16.32–3; 'To the pure all things are pure' (St Paul) 7.99; Tārā represents complete purity 5.581; the *vajra* is absolutely pure 13.167, 13.169

pure by nature
'All *dharmas* are pure by nature, I too am pure by nature' 5.33, 5.489, 5.604–5, 16.17; you are pure from the beginningless beginning 5.33–4, 5.537, 26.52; the idea that we are pure by nature may come as a positive shock 5.34; 'fundamental purity' means that you can become pure if you make the effort 17.98; the danger of thinking that you are pure already 10.439–40, 17.98; natural purity is only an operational concept 17.98; the idea of a pure self at the mundane level is a defilement 13.390–1; the self-purity of the senses 19.191

becoming pure
purity and impurity depend upon one's own efforts 12.135; it does not come about by ritual ablutions 10.457–8; four kinds of morality consisting in purity 1.146–9

see also
pure awareness; purity mind, *see under* mind/what is the mind like?; *śubha*

Purna, Dharmachari 9.480–1, 17.72, v24

Pūrṇa Maitrāyaṇīputra (the Buddha's disciple) praised by the Buddha as the foremost of preachers 14.118, 16.185; his encounter with Vimalakīrti 14.161–2, 16.506–7; in the Perfection of Wisdom 14.141; prediction to Enlightenment in the *White Lotus Sūtra* 14.118, 16.43, 16.168–9

purohit 16.415

purpose beware of the idea that our purpose is to fill our time with useful activities 18.120; four purposes of the holy life 14.49; mindfulness of purpose, *see* mindfulness of purpose; the problem of what to do with our lives 12.355; the purpose of meditation, *see under* meditation/what is meditation?; religious activity with no clear purpose 7.148; we can have no higher purpose than being ourselves 18.120; wanting something from spiritual practice that has nothing to do with its true purpose 3.420

puruṣa (Hinduism) the archetypal man and the creation of the universe 4.589; that atom of divinity through which man attains union with the soul of the universe 7.41; the Buddha as Cosmic Person 4.589–90, 14.426–7; pure spirit 12.278; *puruṣa-prakṛti* dualism 7.194–5, 7.596 (n299), 10.53, 12.278, 22.29

puruṣendriya (masculinity) 2.97

Pūrvamīmāṃsāka doctrine (Hinduism) 7.100

pūrvanivāsāsānusmṛti *see abhijñās*

Puruṣa Sūkta 9.77

pūrvapraṇidhāna *see* bodhisattva vow

pūrvaśrama 20.232

Pushkar 9.486

pūtanās (fever-spirits) 16.346

puthujjana (worldling) *see pṛthagjana*

Pyarelal, Lalla (Sangharakshita's host in Kasauli) v20

Pye, Michael 24.193, 24.660 (n250)

Pyle, Ernest v23

Pythagoras 3.427, 3.429, 3.560

Q

Qin Shi Huang 25.10

qualities appreciate people's positive qualities without dwelling on their weaknesses 26.80; associate with people who appreciate your qualities 17.654; the better the work of art, the more fully it communicates spiritual qualities 18.132; compassion and wisdom have each other's qualities, if you look deeply enough 18.373–4; the first step towards developing a quality is realizing you don't have it 26.26; four qualities needed to preserve the *White Lotus Sūtra* 16.47; four qualities possessed of which one may hope for bodhisattvahood 14.189; four qualities to be 'made to grow' (*Udāna*) 10.527, 10.531–2; four qualities wherefrom the bodhisattva gains encouragement 14.189; the good qualities you have developed can lead to complacency and pride 17.285; the nature of the spiritual life: developing balancing qualities 4.41; needed by a spiritual teacher 1.448–9, 16.485–91, 17.307; pride in qualities you have, or imagine or pretend you have 17.273; the qualities we attribute to the wrong things do exist elsewhere 17.359–60; the recollection of the world's unpleasant qualities 18.128; spiritual qualities are developed gradually 11.396–7; spiritual qualities carried over from previous lives 18.543–4; works of art that show us the qualities of humanity 26.370–1; the disciples' qualities praised by the Buddha, *see* disciples/of the Buddha

Quảng Đức, Thích *see under* Vietnam

quantity Buddhism sees quality as more important than quantity 8.198, 8.205, 8.307; in meditation, quality is more important than quantity 5.54; the modern tendency to value quantity over quality 8.137, 12.32; *The Reign of Quantity and the Signs of the Times* 12.32; 'The worship of quantity is the worship of Mammon' 8.xxiv, 8.197

quarrels family quarrels 10.323; harmonious speech, not speaking so as to bring about a quarrel between others 2.383–4; humanity as quarrelsome through their views 10.600; 'Those who do realize [that we are heading for death] will compose their quarrels', see Dhammapada/chapter 1; the quarrel at Kosambi 3.77, 10.323–4; quarrel between Joe Cann and Ani-la ('the French nun') 22.236–8; a quarrel in a neighbouring hotel room 24.298; the quarrel over the Buddha's relics 16.141–2, 16.153; quarrelling in the sangha 9.195–6; quarrels in the name of religion 7.90; quarrels over the Diksha Bhumi 10.364; *see also* arguments

Quartermaine *see* Haslemere

queens the grief of three queens 22.13–14; the marriage of the red king and the white queen 12.184–5; the precious queen 13.262; the queen bee and the hive mind 18.227–8; Tārā as virgin, mother, and queen 5.581

quest the beauty of the spiritual quest 12.551; boredom leading to spiritual search 13.351–2; Buddhahood existing within the spiritual aspirant as the impulse behind their quest 7.312; the continuity of the religious quest 7.212; *dharmachanda* powers us on our spiritual quest 12.550; incorporating our deeper energies into the spiritual quest 12.335; our quest for meaning is our quest for ourselves 16.533; philosophy is a quest for truth, and the instrument of the quest is reason 10.142; quest as projection 5.352; the quest for holiness 26.44; noble and ignoble quest, *see under ariyapariyesanā* and *Majjhima Nikāya/Ariyapariyesanā Sutta*

questions

the Buddha
if he was asked a question three times, he would always answer 10.458–9, 10.462, 12.157; he says of a disciple, 'He did not bother me with questions about the Dharma' 10.578; he says there are four different ways of answering a question 4.335–6; 'How can the ego get rid of itself?': the sort of question he didn't think useful 17.349; the way the Buddha answers questions 18.357

questions and Buddhist tradition
'How may the mortal obtain the immortal Brahmā world?' 3.209, 3.579; 'What is the one thing?' 10.230–1, 13.31; Abhidharma analysis in catechism form 14.84–5, 14.90–1; questions and non-questions in the *Śāriputra-abhidharma-śāstra* 14.74; as

Buddhism developed, people asked more sophisticated questions 14.351–2; the *ālaya vijñāna* is one of the most obscure questions of Buddhist thought 18.282; Mahāyāna *sūtras* of the *paripṛcchā* (question) type 14.188–9; bodhisattvas bring in compassion when answering a question 2.168–9, 4.65, 18.588; the bodhisattva doesn't allow the terms of the question to limit the reply 14.417–1; 'Wouldn't you rather be practising the Dharma?' 8.593–4; in Zen, abstract questions become concrete and existential 13.356–7

asking questions about the Dharma
the nature of questions about the Dharma 9.327–8; abstract questions can only be answered in the abstract 5.273–4; asking the same question can elicit a different answer if you have changed 14.473; the Dharma is not the source of answers to what are really scientific questions 8.586–8; many pseudo-questions arise out of naive realism 10.598; don't ask glib questions and expect an answer just like that 18.357, 21.121–2; intellectual people need answers before they can start spiritual life 10.577; leisured and subtle discussion of profound questions 12.121–2, 22.373–4; questioning the wise should be an extension of questioning oneself 17.261; people usually ask questions in order *not* to receive an answer 13.356–7; people want ready-made 'Buddhist' answers for their questions 17.627–8; refining your questions because you don't want an answer 19.151; the spiritual life is a kind of interrogation of reality 17.260

answering questions
handling insensitive questions about one's practice 18.422; if you're teaching a Dharma class, it's the tough questions that are interesting 4.419; learning to answer questions spontaneously 13.362; the Roman Catholic Church is swift to supply answers 3.6; teams asking and answering questions on the Dharma on retreat 23.136–7

real questions
profitable questions for reflection 10.598; Dr Johnson's existential question 26.484; if it is a real question for you, you will think hard and get a breakthrough 4.245; real questions spring out of one's own experience, even one's own conflict 4.147; when you realize that you yourself are the question, such a question is a mystery 8.575; conditioned mind questions, but Unconditioned mind doesn't need answers 17.355

Sangharakshita and questions
asking myself, 'Why did the Buddha teach this particular doctrine?' 1.7, 19.295, 26.43; being asked a question and seeing that the question was utterly meaningless 23.472; inane questions 23.356; at least half those he was asked were based on literalistic misunderstandings 14.321; an occasion when the Buddha answered his questions 22.301–2

see also
unanswerable or undetermined, *see* undetermined questions; 'What do you teach?', *see* Mahāpajāpatī Gotami

Questions of King Milinda (*Milinda-pañha*) in Dr Ambedkar's *The Buddha and His Dhamma* 9.139; faith: the 'jump', like a knowledgeable man jumping across a river 1.289–90, 4.474; King Milinda's questions about monastic life 2.191; 'Nirvāṇa is' 1.226; not even ostensibly *Buddhavacana* 14.253; the obvious contrast of ideals of the sangha 2.191; 'What is the mark of vigour?' 17.70; why there can only be one Buddha in a world system at a time 19.312–13; wisdom is like a lamp 17.726 (139)

quietism the doctrine of the quiescence of *dharmas* has never led to quietism 1.269; non-violence as distinct from quietism 9.47; the quietism of Mme Guyon 13.626, 26.203

quietness absorption in quiet and evenmindedness is the true happiness 18.343; certain pages of the Pāli canon thrill with quiet enthusiasm 1.240; contemplation of decay: a quiet, almost gentle seeing of the facts as they are 4.536; eating should be quiet, peaceful, even meditative 4.113; in the vihara you can sit quietly 9.464; the need for a settled and quiet place to practise meditation 20.248; peace springs naturally from duties quietly done 7.279; quiet reflections that lead to insight 5.431; the quietest hints can have the force of commands 18.110; 'quieting the pool of troubled thought which is the mind' 4.339; the quietness of the countryside 10.329; 'the sweet but selfish rest of quiet wilds' 1.213; this side of Enlightenment, always make provision for withdrawal and quiet 4.532; 'to the sleeping woods all night/ Singeth a quiet tune' 1.153; *see also* silence

quincunxes 12.218

Quirk, Bill 24.50

Quirk, Bonnie *see* Vajrasuri

Quittner, Mrs 23.232

R

Rabten, Geshe his life story 8.515–16; he described a Tibetan monastery as being like a factory 8.517, 17.686; his upbringing on a farm in Tibet 8.515, 18.273–4; his practical teachings 8.516; *The Life and Teachings of Geshe Rabten* (review) 8.515–17

race Buddhism's good will to all, irrespective of race 23.438; the Buddhist should feel *mettā* towards everyone they meet, irrespective of race 2.569–70; the Dharma can be applied to all people whatsoever 7.158; the Dharma must break down barriers between one race and another 10.351; 'miscegenation' 24.442–3; in the realization of the highest truth, difference of race and caste is obliterated 7.103; in theosophy, friendship between people of different races, national and religious backgrounds 22.144

Racine, Jean 22.89, 22.582 (n90), 25.350

racism Black Panthers' action 23.459–61; Commission for Racial Equality 26.428; encouraged by horror comics 8.207; the need to remove racial prejudice from society 12.408–9; in the sangha differences of caste and nationality should actively be discouraged 10.565; to include someone in too conscious a way is to exclude them 11.641

Radha (Hindu goddess) 20.175, 20.188

Radha (of Kalimpong) v22

Radhakrishnan, Sarvepalli introduction 7.571–2 (n137); Sangharakshita encounters him 20.122–3; argued that the Buddha did not teach the *anātman* doctrine 12.62; and the Buddha Jayanti celebrations 22.305; a candidate for the presidency of the Maha Bodhi Society 22.65–7; criticized for having misrepresented *citta* 21.393–4; 'A Divided Inheritance' 8.382–3; Gautama the Buddha 16.300; pluralistic realism 7.539, 12.143, 17.444; six *darśanas* 7.78; lectures Tibetan lamas on the Mahāyāna 22.344; not a reliable interpreter of Buddhism 10.75; overstates the case for Buddhism being part of Hinduism 8.348; 'respect and appreciation for all faiths' 22.305; on the secular state 8.228–9; suggests Upanishadic influence on early Buddhism 10.545–6; thinks that *anattāvāda* is really *attavāda* 7.130, 7.586 (n229)

radiaesthesia 22.106, 22.110

Radiance of the Sun and Moon, Buddha 16.195

radical communication with spiritual peers is radical 18.420; the Dhamma Revolution involves radical change in every aspect of life 9.410, 9.511, 10.25; equal ordination for men and women is radical, historically speaking 12.667; friends can find it hard to accept that you have radically changed 4.271; just sitting: radical receptivity 5.xxxiv; Nietzsche's view of human beings is too radical and demanding 3.499; the radical optimism of Buddhism 12.526; the radical protest of Buddhism 4.38; radically different conception of Enlightenment 1.268, 4.25; receptivity means being prepared for a radical change to one's whole way of looking at things 4.128; to imagine radically changing involves letting go of our idea of self 3.418; understanding the Dharma is not enough, there must be a radical transformation 2.284; violence is a radical assertion of separative selfhood, based on a strong sense of 'I' 3.318, 3.320; when one places the Buddha at the centre, a radical reorganization takes place 2.324–5

radio bad manners on the radio 6.xxxi; 'the blessed influence of Jinas': like tuning the radio 4.272; 'Mr Wireless' (poem) 25.448; Sangharakshita interviewed for the BBC's *Prayer for the Day* 24.360; Sangharakshita listening to the radio 12.649, 12.674; in Sri Lanka, radio used to broadcast Buddhist programmes 7.65

Radu Rimpoche 23.335

raft (parable) full text 1.202–3, 7.518–19; introduction 3.165–6, 7.312–15; abandoning the raft 1.308; all doctrines are just components of the raft 3.232; carrying the raft: religion has repeatedly made this mistake 7.159, 13.437; clinging to a remnant of a raft while hurling abuse at those who are crossing 7.314; connection with Green Tārā 13.315; crossing the river of suffering to the other shore of peace 9.374; the Dharma as a means to an end 1.203, 2.59, 3.359, 3.394, 7.244, 7.433, 7.520, 10.141, 10.627, 14.318, 14.440, 23.77; the Dharma is something to leave behind, not take with you 7.158,

7.228, 16.514, 26.160; illustrates that doctrine has only a provisional value 22.268; in the *Diamond Sūtra* 14.440–1; later in the Buddhist tradition people made themselves at home on the raft 14.318; lazily thinking that you can discard it without bothering to make use of it at all 17.675; leaving righteous (and unrighteous) ways behind 1.203, 14.440; the Mahāyāna's metaphysical interpretation 1.265, 14.441; the moral applies to the Dharma as a whole and to each stage of the path 7.313; Perfection of Wisdom texts make us see that a raft is just a raft 14.321; the principle of the raft 19.241; spirit and letter 11.481; the spirit of the Dharma best served by modifying the raft as needed 1.189; the teaching must not be allowed to be a devaluation of the Dharma 14.441; treating the raft as though it were a permanent fixture of this shore 1.222, 11.37–8; the 'vessel of the Supreme Jinas' 14.575; we don't worship the raft, or repeat 'raft', but use it to cross the river 9.300; while some people are making a raft, the wise have already crossed the river 7.315, 10.643, 10.648

rāga (passion, cupidity-attachment) *abhijjhā* roughly synonymous 2.386; difference from *lobha* 17.596; literally colour, hue, dye 2.386; one of the six basic emotions (Abhidharma) 17.596–8

Raha, Ashok 22.54–5

raho 'nuśāka-bhikṣu (privy admonisher) 2.194, 8.353

Rāhu 22.506

Rāhula (the Buddha's son) the Buddha's admonitions to him 2.26; a curious story of his birth being delayed 8.481–2; in the *Dhammapada Commentary* 16.627 (n346); he is born and named, his name meaning 'a fetter' 3.24–5; encounter with Vimalakīrti 16.511; is ordained by Śāriputra and Maudgalyāyana 2.26; his view of the Buddha: 'How pleasant is thy shadow, O Śramaṇa!' 2.11; myth that he descended from heaven 14.188; predicted to Enlightenment in the *White Lotus Sūtra* 14.119

Rahula (Ambedkarite Buddhist) 24.114

Rahula, Walpola introduction 8.459–30; advocate for the involvement of the Sinhalese monastic sangha in politics 7.567 (n112), 23.327–8; *The Heritage of the Bhikkhu* 7.567 (n121), 8.459–76, 15.727, 23.327, 23.526 (n377); Sangharakshita's meetings with Rahula 8.459, 20.121–2, 23.327; translation of *What the Buddha Taught* into Gujarati 8.662

Rāhulabhadra 1.66

Rāhulata 13.342

Rai Bahadur Densapa v22

Rai, Sanumati 21.237

Rai, Sri Krishna Bahadur 8.656

rain 'All *dharmas* spontaneously freed as mists of rain vanish into air' 18.596–7; 'as on roses falls the rain' 6.xxix; the Buddha compared to a storm cloud pouring rain on the earth 26.126; depressing for some people 4.575; the ego is a metaphor, like the 'it' in 'it's raining' 19.111; the emperor commands the monk Jojin to make rain 2.216; 'every blade of grass feels with pain the sting of rain' 7.388, 25.220; explanation of process without subject: 'it is raining' 9.343–4, 10.453; Indra, god of rain and thunderstorms 16.418; may compassion pour down like rain 25.214; the rain of the Dharma mustn't go down the drain of intellectual curiosity 8.535; literature: 'like mist and rain, it permeates and nourishes' 14.295; the *nirmāṇakāya* like rain from the cloud of the *sambhogakāya* 4.204; a positive response to the fact that it is raining 11.580; praise to the rain 25.177; the rain of the Dharma must not be acid rain mixed with anti-Dharmic elements 3.314, 12.516; rain on Glastonbury Tor 25.504; a rainy day in the mountains 25.244; 'the sky god was raining' 10.453; *see also* rainy season

rainbows

visible rainbows
on the occasion of Sangharakshita's going forth 20.226, 22.185, 23.13, 26.671–2; rainbow-coloured light issues from the Sacred Relics 14.464, 21.197; a rainbow accompanies the start of the writing of the *Survey* 22.184–5; rainbows on Hampstead Heath – the effect of a psychedelic trip 23.466; at an ordination retreat in India, 1979 24.107; a rainbow in Auckland 26.671; a rainbow for Sangharakshita's 90th birthday 26.550, 26.674; a rainbow fragment, 'symbol of my life' 25.268

rainbows in Dharma practice
the different stages of meditation fade into each other like rainbow colours 13.71; the light of the *bodhicitta* through prisms (bodhisattvas) creating rainbows 1.261, 4.57; Padmasambhava, the Rainbow-Bodied One 26.673; in the Pure Land 2.132; the 'rainbow-body' 18.535, 19.42;

rainbow light in a thangka 22.407; rainbow plumes 25.185; rainbow-coloured clouds 13.204, 13.293; the rainbow track of the Windhorse 25.339; the rainbows of the offering goddesses in the Green Tārā practice 26.671; reality like the appearance and disappearance of divine images like rainbows 2.133; spiritual life a rainbow interfusion, like the colours of a pigeon's neck 7.301–2, 26.129; spiritual practices like refracting rainbows from the mandala of the five Buddhas 13.305; the *sambhogakāya* like a cloud surrounded by rainbows 4.204; the Void a bright white light containing all the colours of the rainbow 18.74

symbolic rainbows
'The rainbow became for me a symbol of the spiritual path' 25.268, 26.672; a narrow band of our experience spectrum: a rainbow with only one colour 17.341; conventional existence is like a rainbow 19.234; culture is a rainbow bridge thrown from the material world to the spiritual world 26.66; it means different things in different cultures 26.672; the rainbow of hope 25.275; the rainbow spectrum of our experience 17.xxi–xxii; symbol of the gay rights movement 26.672; symbol of hope 22.455; a symbol of spiritual life, and spirituality itself 26.672; Tibetans believe it to be an auspicious sign 20.226

in art and literature
in Holman Hunt's *The Scapegoat* 2.609, 2.612, 26.670; in Millais's *The Blind Girl* 26.670; 'My heart leaps up when I behold a rainbow in the sky' 26.670

raincloud (parable) *see under White Lotus Sūtra*/parables

Raine, Kathleen on Blake 26.385–6; on Buddhism and beauty 26.382–3; conversation with Sangharakshita 24.314, 24.686 (n390), 26.382–91; *Defending Ancient Springs* 24.404; the magazine *Temenos* 26.382; 'Memory of Sarnath' 26.391

rainy season

introduction
an evocation of the Indian rainy season 16.116–17; the Buddha spent twenty-five rainy seasons in Śrāvastī 14.401; early sangha settled during rainy season, then sought permanent lodgings 2.189–90, 12.237–8; everything growing after the rainy season 11.367; joy at the coming of the monsoon 4.97, 16.117, 17.182; Sangharakshita's affection for the rainy season 12.508; the sun shining after the rainy season 25.273

rainy season retreat (Sanskrit varṣāvāsa, Pāli vassāvāsa)
introduction 3.404–6; a time for monks to spend time together 16.272–3; apologies and confession after the retreat (*pravāraṇā*) 1.410, 3.405, 16.272–4; the Buddha observes the rainy season retreat for the last time 13.145; full-timers and part-timers during and after 3.405–6; in Kalimpong 21.40, 21.566–7; it began so that the Buddha's followers wouldn't damage young crops 8.264; lost its early significance, but developed into a valuable retreat 2.199; the nature of it for monks and lay people 8.264; part of the rhythm of Buddhist life 8.264; a phase of inner activity after a very active period 4.462; *pravāraṇā* (or *pavāraṇā*) at the end of the retreat, *see pravāraṇā*; 'Rainy Season Retreat' 22.458; wanderers would stay in one spot 12.508, 14.398; Sangharakshita's rainy season retreats 12.235–6, 20.439, 21.40

Raipur Ashram 20.211–18

Rajagopalachari, Sri C. 8.214

rajas (dust, impurity) 10.503

rajas (quality) *see under guṇas*

Rajasiddhimuni, Chao Kun 8.336, 23.43

Rajasimbha, King (Sri Lanka) 8.468

Rajasthan 9.158, 9.486–98, 10.157, 10.296

Rājataraṃgiṇī 12.563, 13.30

Rajbhoj, P. N. 9.64–5, 10.381, 23.349, 23.353

Rajgir, India (Pāli Rājagaha, Sanskrit Rājagṛha) Bamboo Grove 2.24, 10.447, 20.462; the Buddha visits soon after his Enlightenment 2.24; capital of kingdom of Magadha 20.464; the chanting of the Dharma there after the *parinirvāṇa* 14.21; Dharma talks for village workers 7.429, 20.462; encounter with an American Vaishnava 20.462–3; Japanese Buddhist Temple 7.429, 20.461–2; Bhikkhu Kashyap and Sangharakshita visit 7.429, 20.461–3; once a magnificent city 7.431; Pippala Cave 7.430, 20.462, 23.368; Roman Catholic mission 20.463; Sangharakshita visits with Terry 23.368; in the *Sūtra of Golden Light* 16.244; in the *Udāna* 10.447–9; *see also* Vulture's Peak

Rajgopal (host in Bangalore) 20.350–3, 20.355–59

Rajneesh, Bhagwan Shree introduction 24.606–7 (n24); an FBI investigation 24.258, 24.305; *No Water No Moon: Reflections on Zen* (review) 8.492–4; a Rajneesh follower in India 24.13; 'You submit yourself and I'll do the rest' 15.663

rākṣasas (flesh-eating demons) introduction 17.740 (n265); ruled by Vaiśravaṇa 16.346; Padmasambhava teaches them on the Copper-Coloured Mountain 8.524, 18.304; trampled on by the wrathful deities 17.317

Raleigh, Walter 26.293–4

Ralpacan (king of Tibet) 13.12–13

raṃ 26.621

Ram Das (Maharashtra saint) 9.199

Ram, Kanshi 9.499, 9.527, 10.xlviii

Rama claimed to be an incarnation of God 12.134; conquest of Ravana in Lanka 9.120; Hanuman the devotee of 16.361; mantra 20.325–6

Ramachandra Rao, S. K. 22.141

Ramakrishna, Sri

introduction
his life 7.84, 7.576 (n165), 7.106–7, 22.578 (n62); awareness and practice of the unity of religion 7.89–91; complete identification with others 7.89–90; his difficulty in detaching his mind from God 7.102; worships at the feet of a prostitute 7.102; his followers represented at a Buddhist gathering 9.450; *Paramahaṃsa* (Great Indian Swan) 7.88, 7.577 (n166); Sangharakshita's admiration for him 7.15, 7.88–91; Sangharakshita has a vision of him 20.311; statue at Belur Math 20.131

stories and sayings
a foolish man and a mad elephant 18.632–3; the frog and the elephant 16.299; how your sins become crows and fly back to you 3.194; the parrot who recited God's name, but in danger let out his natural squawk 12.96, 18.249; rowing the boat to mid-stream 3.252, 4.141; 'To conquer an army you need many weapons, but to commit suicide a pin is enough' 14.348

Ramakrishna Mission

introduction
establishment 9.116; perhaps modelled on *bhikṣu sangha* 9.116–17; caste prejudice 20.202; *Prabuddha Bharata* (magazine) 7.7; criticism (Agehananda Bharati) 8.437–8; Vivekananda's brother rails against it 20.136

Calcutta
Belur Math 20.131, 20.135; Dakshineshwar 7.106, 20.131; Institute of Culture 20.130–1, 20.135–7, 20.160–4, 21.157, 22.75–6

other branches
Benares 20.386; Kalady Ashram 20.252, 20.253–4; Malaysia 7.106–13; Singapore 7.107–12, 20.141; Trivandrum 20.247–52

Sangharakshita
visits in Calcutta 20.130–1; visits in Singapore 20.141; assists with literary work in Calcutta 20.160–4; involvement in Sri Lanka 7.14–15, 20.117–26; reading publications stimulated attraction to the spiritual life 20.123–4; stay at Muvattupuzha Ashram 20.255–327; 'recoiled from the Mission like one … about to step on a snake in the dark' 20.164

Ramana Maharshi brief introduction 4.691 (n217), 7.589 (n257); appearance 20.336; caste distinctions observed at his ashram 10.41, 10.44, 14.565, 19.164, 20.336; Sangharakshita (then Dharmapriya) stays at the ashram 9.347, 20.336–48; taking his *darshan* 1.524, 15.442–3, 20.341–3; had experience of the *arūpa dhyānas* but not wisdom 14.565; photograph 20.342; 'There is no such thing as *my* realizations or *your* realizations' 7.155; 'Try to see where 'I' starts' 4.376; what he said to his disciples before he died 10.492; the story of the twentieth blow, *see under* parables and stories

Ramanan, K. Venkata 23.319–20

Rāmānuja 1.166

Rāmayāṇa influence on Dr Ambedkar 9.111; Rāma and the squirrel 3.670–1 (n288); Sītā 7.58, 7.559 (n81); tradition of telling the story 15.445

Ramdas, Swami, of Kanhangad

introduction
against caste 20.321; Anandashram 20.321, 20.328–34, 26.576; devotees 20.330–1; a *jñānin* rather than a *bhakta* 20.332; photograph 20.323; regard for Ramana Maharshi and Sri Aurobindo 20.334; teaching through 'transcendental comedy' 20.329; view that the enlightened man could even take life 20.333; 'Why is it that people don't make progress in the spiritual life?' 3.398, 20.330; writings 20.319–21, 20.329, 20.332

and Sangharakshita (then Dharmapriya)
first visit 9.347, 20.321–6; Ramdas's advice 20.322–4; he gives Dharmapriya the Avalokiteśvara mantra 20.325–6; longer stay 20.328–34; a profound spiritual lesson: 'Love Dharma, for Dharma is Truth' 20.332

Ramkinkar (sculptor) 22.54

Rampa, Lobsang introduction 22.436, 22.617 (n339); Jivaka his disciple 3.584, 22.436–7, 23.388–9; *The Third Eye* 3.584, 8.255, 8.409, 8.626, 8.692 (n204)

Ramprasad Sen 7.61, 7.563 (n100)

Ramsingh 22.378–9

Rana, Keshab Shamser Janga Bahadur 21.291–2

Rana, Mohan Shamser Janga Bahadur 21.277–9, 21.281–2

Rand, Yvonne 24.473–5, 24.482

Rani, Devika 22.147–8, 26.222

Rao, Miss (Kalimpong) 21.225–8, v22

Rao, Mr (Miss Rao's brother) 22.201–2

Rao, Mrs (Kalimpong) 21.225–8, v22

Rao, P. R. Ramachandra 8.210

Raphael (angel) 13.583–4, 26.471

Raphael (artist) introduction 24.676 (n333); in Naples; frescoes at Siena 13.637; *School of Athens* 23.308, 23.519–20 (n343)

rapture *see prīti*

rarity the appearance of a Buddha is a rare event 1.44, 1.327; breakthrough through meditation and nothing else is quite rare 5.635; the cherishing, protecting, maturing love meant by the first precept is quite rare 2.361; living in a situation that is conducive to your growth is a rare opportunity 3.464; men will rarely make any sacrifice except for the sake of gain 7.96; 'Rarely, rarely, comest thou, Spirit of Delight' 3.512; reading was rare in medieval times 3.515; reflection is quite rare 3.303; some rare people seem able to lead a spiritual life by sheer instinct 4.90; Stream Entry became rarer after the Buddha's *parinirvāṇa* 2.298, 9.254; understanding is common, but practice is rare 18.107–8; *see also* human life/the rarity of birth as a human being

rasa Datta's sonnets on four *rasas* 26.325–6; the difference between emotion and *rasa* 26.326–7, 26.362; the qualities of *rasa* (relating to the taste of freedom) 10.567, 11.51–2; *rasa* and mystical experience 26.327–8; the *rasa* of pathos 26.325–6; *rasa-śāstra*, 'aesthetic relish' 10.567; the *rasas* of Indian literary criticism 26.325–8; *rasika*, the 'taster' or 'enjoyer' of *rasa* 26.166, 26.187, 26.324; *see also* taste

rasanā *see under* central channel

Rashk, Arjundev v21, 21.414 (photo), v22

Rashtriya Swayamsevak Sangh 9.122

Rāṣṭrapāla-paripṛcchā Sūtra 14.189

Ratana Sutta in Dr Ambedkar's puja book 9.71–2; 'the Buddha is highest and best' 9.385; 'Look lovingly upon the race of men' 13.271–3; metrical form 15.xiii; Sangharakshita's translation 15.xiii, 15.63–6; a Stream Entrant has no more than seven further rebirths 2.696 (n348), 3.661 (n233); 'The supreme Buddha praised pure meditation, which gives instantaneous results' 5.292–4; Three Jewels 3.662 (n242)

Rātana, Tahupōtiki Wirema 24.510, 24.733 (n622)

Ratanasara, Venerable (Sinhalese monk in London) 8.336, v23

Rathavinīta Sutta *see under Majjhima Nikāya*

rationalism being rational and being rationalistic are very different things 22.158; better to have the weeds of superstition than the sterile garden of rationalism 12.105; Christianity's rationalist assaults upon other faiths 7.85; the idea that the Buddha was an early Indian rationalist 12.618; if wisdom is strong but faith weak 1.293; the *Kālāma Sutta* rejects rationalism 1.60; mistaking rational comprehension for actual realization 1.222, 1.349; Western rationalism's devaluation of ritual 11.206–7; Theravāda rationalism tinged with mysticism, Mahāyāna mysticism tinged with rationalism 12.515, 26.367; why should the gods of Tibet, or any gods, dislike rationalism? 12.293–5

rationality

humans and rationality
Aristotle defined Man as a rational animal 3.479; human beings are desiderative rather than rational 1.123–4, 7.392; human beings are not rational, and it would be irrational to expect them to be 12.11; if Man was a rational animal, knowing would be indistinguishable from doing 7.392; people aren't rational, and in some ways it is good that they are not 18.171; there is less rational thinking going on than we think: the X factor 14.557–8

rational understanding of the Dharma
any rational grasp of truth is provisional, but necessary 15.198; mistaking rational comprehension for actual realization 1.222, 1.349, 2.113, 7.532; a dangerous basis on which to deny oneself all pleasures 16.284–5; misses out the desire for the Eternal 21.450; rational proof of Enlightenment 1.285; is a *bhikkhu*'s view of the world really 'sweetly rational'? 17.68; Sangharakshita's approach became as much rational as emotional 23.15

the rational and other dimensions
Going for Refuge: emotional, rational, volitional 2.487, 12.536–41, 15.607, 15.615, 15.727–9; it's limiting to look for rational meanings of poetic or archetypal images 19.563–4; life has an archetypal dimension that will always elude rational consciousness 4.36; nothing that is amenable to rational analysis will satisfy us for long 17.686; philosophy titillates the rational surface of our being, poetry stirs it to its depths 1.347; religion must do more than scratch the rational surface 1.124, 7.392; Sanskrit is highly rational, but the text may not have a rational meaning 14.349–40; spiritual life needs both myth and rational thought 12.106–8, 16.67; we cannot live in the realm of rational thought alone 13.418; we may 'know' something only with the rational part of ourselves 1.494

see also
emotion/emotion and reason; rational guilt, *see under* guilt; rational mind, *see under* mind/what is the mind like?

rationalizations

introduction
don't underestimate the rationalization people are capable of 18.366; accusing someone of rationalizing 17.234, 19.293–4; dressing up emotions as reasons 14.557–8; not wanting to acknowledge our attitudes, we rationalize our motives 2.55–6; rationalizing what you want to do with a lot of reasons for doing it 19.334; the unconscious is not fooled by the rationalizing conscious mind 3.214, 23.195–6

rationalizations
desultoriness by rationalization 17.682; family life rationalized as unselfish 15.476–7; fixed self-view is the rationalization of ordinary human egotism 26.188; the law of karma used as a rationalization for social injustice 15.681; nihilism a rationalization of self-hatred 17.243–4; our desires and neuroses bring all kinds of rationalizations in their wake 17.629; rationalizing hatred 19.107; rationalizing stealing 9.272; rationalizations about giving money away 19.552; rationalizations of desire 1.20

rationalizing and religion
belief in God is the result of rationalization 26.155; philosophical and religious views as rationalizations of limited perceptions 10.598–9; 'Life is my teacher' 18.632; the rationalizations of pseudo-teachers 19.430; rationalizing belief in self into the basis of a philosophy or religion 17.619; religious teachings as rationalizations of craving 12.99, 12.711 (n76); wrong views are rationalized as isms and ologies 11.160; any systematically worked-out view may be a rationalization 17.620

rationalizing and Buddhist practice
the bodhisattva ideal as a rationalization for attachment to the world 3.133, 13.38; don't rationalize your failure to study 25.14; rationalizations about renunciation 16.285, 19.331; 'I don't want to do that

– it'll get in the way of my development' 11.451, 18.591; Rechungpa rationalizes 18.490; saying 'I don't feel inspired to do this' is a rationalization for laziness 17.576; supernatural beings as rationalizations of the fears of pre-Buddhist India 26.153; Thai Buddhists' rationalizations about eating meat 17.586, 23.367–8

Ratnabandhu, Dharmachari v24

Ratnacchattra 16.572

Ratnadevi, Dharmacharini (Luise Holtbernd) v24

Ratnadharini, Dharmacharini 24.397

Ratnadvīpa (Place of Jewels) *see under White Lotus Sūtra*/parable of the magic city

Ratnagarbha, Dharmachari 26.xix, 26.351–73

Ratnagotravibhāga *see under* Sāramati

Ratnaguna, Dharmachari general entries v24; brief introduction 24.634 (n148); *The Art of Reflection* 24.634 (n148); *Great Faith, Great Wisdom* 1.616 (n261), 2.742 (n679), 16.607 (n176), 24.634 (n148); member of the Council 12.632

Ratnaguṇa-saṃcayagāthā

introduction
comes down to us through Haribhadra's recension 1.300, 14.145; an early Mahāyāna *sūtra* 14.532–3; it expounds the teaching in the form of chains of similes 14.145; its first two chapters are the oldest Perfection of Wisdom material 14.345; its single subject is the career of the bodhisattva 14.513; verse summary of *The Perfection of Wisdom in 8,000 lines* 1.300, 14.145, 14.345; written in Buddhist Hybrid Sanskrit 14.349; Sangharakshita's commentary 4.226–7, 4.230–1, 14.320, 14.532–608

the text
the full text 14.525–31; the opening of the *sūtra* 14.532–3; 'Call forth as much as you can of love, of respect, and of faith!' 3.361, 14.533–7, 18.262; the five skandhas 14.548–50, 14.561–2, 14.587–8, 14.600; 'No wisdom can we get hold of' – so what are we trying to do? 14.547; 'Without a home they wander' 14.548–52; the bodhisattva discovers that all *dharmas* are empty 14.560–8; the nature of the bodhisattva 14.569–78

Ratnākara (or Ratnakūṭa) in the *Vimalakīrti-nirdeśa* 16.455, 16.464; asks how to build a Buddha-land 16.467; sings the Buddha's praises 14.158, 16.466

Ratnaketu, Buddha (later standardized as Ratnasambhava) appears in Ruciraketu's house in the *Sūtra of Golden Light* 16.258, 16.261

Ratnaketu, Dharmachari (David Moore) introduction 24.611 (n45); a banner of victory for Dhardo Rimpoche 10.408–9; in New Zealand 24.27, 24.97

Ratnakūṭa Sūtras introduction 7.502, 14.179–89; and the absence of being 3.660 (n227); appeared over several centuries 14.179–80; Chinese translations 14.180; contain traces of the Buddha's original teaching 4.19; half of them are of the *paripṛcchā* (question) type 14.188–9; their original nucleus connected with the Mahāsaṅghika school 14.188; 'a small encyclopedia of Mahāyāna Buddhism' 14.179; *sūtras* associated with *śūnyatā* 14.181

Ratnamala, Dharmacharini 26.566

Ratnaman (Kalimpong) v21

Ratnapāṇi, bodhisattva 2.172, 5.624–5, 13.309

Ratnaprabha, Dharmachari brief introduction 24.662 (n268); general entries 24.210, 24.238; guide to reading aphorisms 26.3–5; writing a book 12.379

Ratnapriya, Dharmachari (Christer Starck, later Maharatnapriya) v24

Ratnasambhava brief description 4.207; his animal is the horse (association with the Buddha's going forth) 13.309; association with Ratnapaṇī 2.172; the Buddha of the jewel family 13.166, 13.309; his appearance in the *bardo* after death 12.203; his emblem is the jewel,

the wish-fulfilling gem 4.207, 12.214, 13.166, 13.309; his golden colour links him with the earth 12.214; in a Five Buddha *caitya* in Nepal 20.430; in the mandala of the Five Buddhas 3.374, 4.207, 12.214–15, 13.309, 18.599; and the Mirror of Equality 19.152; represents the beauty, richness, and abundance of the Enlightened mind 12.214; as *sambhogakāya* 2.42

see also
his *mudrā* (gesture), *see under mudrās*; wisdom of sameness (*samatā-jñāna*), *see under* five *jñānas*

Ratnaśikhin (Buddha) 16.390

Ratnasuri, Dharmacharini brief introduction 24.668 (n299); general entries v24; conducts ordinations in India 2.733 (n628), 10.lii

Ratnāvalī *see under* Nāgārjuna

Ratnoccaya (in the *Sūtra of Golden Light*) 16.389–90

Ratnolkānāma-dhāraṇi (Mahāyāna *sūtra*) 17.553

Rattle, Simon 24.589

Rattu, N. C. 9.123, 9.126

Ratzinger, Joseph v13

Rauf, Mrs v23

Raut, Dr Santosh I. *see* Maitriveer

Rāvaṇa (Buddhism) a great disciple of the Buddha 2.277; in the *Laṅkāvatāra Sūtra*, *see under Laṅkāvatāra Sūtra*

Ravana (Hinduism) 2.277, 9.120

Rawlinson, Andrew 8.626–9

Rawnsley, Mary *see* Sulochana

Ray, Annada Shankar (novelist) 22.55

Ray, Irene (Kalimpong) 21.156–7, 22.77, 22.131

Ray, Leela 22.55

Ray, Reginald A. (*Buddhist Saints in India*) the act of Going for Refuge loses its central position 4.677 (n110); the Buddha's instructions about building a stupa over his remains 13.684 (n62), 16.599 (n107); laymen, settled monastics, and forest renunciants 3.407; legendary elements of the Buddha's life 2.552–3; *pratyekabuddhas* 3.681 (n360); two-tiered model of Buddhism 2.560–1; Sangharakshita reads 24.573; a meeting with Sangharakshita 24.490, 24.522

ṛddhi (Pāli *iddhi*, supernormal power) definition 4.465–6, 15.58, 17.729 (n159); a topic in the *Patisambhidā-magga* 14.73–4; refined and powerful 'magical' energy generated by meditation experience 4.607; not necessarily magical power, the same word can refer to royal power 10.586, 14.539; the *ṛddhi* of the king 11.152–3; synonym for *anubhāva* 14.539; a topic in the *Śāriputra-abhidharma-śāstra* 14.74; *see also siddhis*; six *abhijñās*

ṛddhipādas *see* four *iddhipādas*

reactive mind *see* mind/mind reactive and creative

reactivity breaking out of the cycle of reactivity 15.205; Buddhism says: 'Don't just react. Act!' 19.582; your old reactive self may rise up in rebellion 19.82–3; confusing reactivity with creativity 4.340; the essence of reactivity 19.18; how can a reactive process evolve into a higher process? 18.279–80; one's conventional life and one's relationships are sustained by reactivity 4.508; reactive relationships 4.523–4; slowed down by meditation 4.508; thinking you're being spontaneous when you're just being reactive 4.340

Read, Carveth 20.446

Read, Herbert art communicates a sense of values 26.166; 'Art is an attempt to create pleasing forms' 3.510, 26.166; art stretches the mind 4.353, 26.187; 'Beauty is a unity of formal relations among our sense perceptions' 26.167; on Middleton Murry 26.333–4; the work of art is in some sense a liberation of the personality 26.191

readiness the *bodhicitta* takes you over when you are ready 4.241–2; the Buddha assesses who present is ready to receive his teaching 10.551; the Buddha protects people from an experience for which they are not ready 14.183; don't commit yourself to something for a specific period until you're ready 19.362–3; if you aren't ready to die, leave the Mahāmudrā alone 18.246; in the past, disciples were given teachings when their teachers thought they were ready 10.440; dangers of introducing people to teachings for which they are not ready 16.55–6; it's dangerous to read teachings that you're not ready for 17.390, 19.241; it's no longer possible to keep people from teachings until they're ready 16.75–6; not being ready to live in a community 19.275; 'not yet ready to be a full-time meditator' 22.448; only leave home when you're ready 9.535; readiness for ordination, *see under* Triratna III/

ordination; readiness to sacrifice one's own pleasure for that of another 7.293; ready to plunge into the heart of the sun that is the Perfection of Wisdom 14.352; tendency to grab at spiritual practices before being ready for them 5.609; the Vajrayāna is dangerous territory to wander into before you're ready 19.331; you are drawn to a teaching when you are ready for it 14.483

reading

NOTES ON READING

the value of reading
becoming a reader: an analogy with going for Refuge 15.574–5; can you enter *dhyāna* through reading a novel? 5.640–2; an imaginative and sympathetic identification with a larger consciousness 4.353; intelligent reading can be a matter of asking questions 17.260; knowing whether it is worth continuing reading a book 15.294; reading a difficult book compared to *śamatha* and *vipaśyanā* 19.451; reading plays aloud 4.354; reading that stimulates positive emotion and energy 15.159; reading that shakes you so much that you are never the same again 14.598; we go beyond our ordinary consciousness 3.515; 'We are all poets when we read a poem well' 26.191

caveats
'Who runs may read' 16.75, 18.246; be selective in your general reading 12.418, 12.474; consuming books as a sort of indulgence 17.672–3; even reading good books doesn't help us much, and most books are bad 26.42; if you read a book in a negative state it won't make any impression 17.678; reading as distraction 26.42; 'Some of us, including myself, read far too much' 25.11–12; sometimes people read a lot because what they read doesn't mean much to them 18.382; *vīrya* lost in reading 15.217

READING BOOKS ON BUDDHISM

what to read?
there are so many books, where do you start? 4.618; how to choose what to read 8.495, 25.11–12; don't read teachings that you're not ready for 17.390, 19.241; distinguish between books that inform and books with feeling 11.650, 12.538; eschew books which are merely *about* Buddhism 8.141; perhaps only start reading having had some higher spiritual experience 14.349; read books that concentrate on the basic teachings 25.11; be careful of books written from an academic point of view 14.348, 15.559; 'Reading some books, you'd think the Buddha-Way ... ran smooth and white' 25.278; read *sūtras* like any work of the imagination 16.443; importance of reading canonical literature 8.141, 13.337–8, 14.8, 14.271, 25.11; Western Buddhists seem to read anything rather than the scriptures 13.337, 14.300–1; reading the scriptures, *see under* the scriptures and us

how much do you need to read?
better a thorough knowledge of a few than a superficial knowledge of many 26.42; four kinds of readers 22.xvi; if we read a lot, we can be tempted to think we understand Buddhism 11.55–8; not much, but read the same things again and again 4.249, 4.352–3, 18.458–9, 25.12; one needs only to read and thoroughly assimilate a single verse 7.332; reading just a few books is enough 10.394, 10.400; select, even specialize 25.11–12; to teach others you must read a lot, but for yourself one mantra may suffice 14.348; we may start with enthusiasm, but after a while the wonder wears off 14.404; you don't need a lot of them to make your practice effective 18.167–8

is reading sufficient, or do you need a teacher?
traditionally, one must study a text with a teacher 13.339–40, 17.156; *lung* (permission to read, Tibetan tradition) 7.543, 13.340, 22.406; the difficulty of learning from books 1.379; learning from a teacher compared with reading a book 1.26–7; better read English classics than read Buddhist books without guidance 14.348; seek specific instructions, not just general teaching from books 19.461–2; you need a sort of living book 19.462

reading and practice
in the early days in the West, people's 'Buddhist' life was mainly reading 4.351, 11.378; 'The books and teachings which you do not practise – give them up!' 4.147; the letter learned from books, but the spirit transmitted heart to heart 7.543; allowing oneself to be moved by a book's power 14.304; ending up reading about meditation and never practising it 15.103; the Dharma cannot be understood by reading books but only by practising it 26.105; 'for one busy with recitations, books are an impediment to *samādhi*' 2.201; if what you read is not put into action, reading may hinder your practice 18.168; people read and then don't feel the need to practise 19.506–7; reading scriptures aloud in a ritual context 22.226, 25.11; reading about Buddhism is no use

without reflecting on it 9.230–1, 22.438; ultimately what we want is not book learning but spiritual awakening 11.716

reading in the Buddhist tradition
the *Divyāvadāna* refers to the *reading* of the Dharma for the first time 14.22; the merit of reading the *White Lotus Sūtra* 14.127, 16.44

see also
Sangharakshita's reading, *see under* Sangharakshita XII/reading

Reading University 11.19

realism alternative translation to eternalism, *see under* eternalism; in philosophy 14.420; pluralistic, *see* pluralistic realism

reality

THE NATURE OF REALITY

descriptions
atakkāvacara (beyond thought) 1.17, 9.398; both existent and non-existent 1.363; greater than any description, so any description is misleading 17.233; ineffable 1.119, 2.131, 7.299; it has unity in difference and difference in unity 4.31; it is not elsewhere that its nature becomes apparent, but here and now 17.353; it transcends 'real' and 'unreal' 4.146; logically indescribable 10.142; in reality all dualisms are transcended 14.361; its metaphorical nature 21.434; the natural laws of reality 8.xxiv; it manifests through the evolutionary process 12.86–7; its nature is revealed only to insight or wisdom 8.441; mysterious immanence 2.43; not a homogeneity but a harmony 7.167; not only static but dynamic, both wisdom and compassion 1.346; the principle of potentiality 2.43; reality is metaphorical 26.70; the revelry of reality 5.596–8; the texture of reality 3.205–6; totality and all-embracingness 2.43; unique, indefinable essentiality 2.43; the 'unthinkability' of reality 19.373; viewed as static or dynamic 1.119; wisdom and compassion coalesce in non-dual reality 17.694–6

what reality is not
not a sort of cosmological principle present in the world 14.603–6; the position that it is unchanging is logically indefensible 7.194; the wrong idea that it is the dust to which everything is reduced 17.444

Buddhist perspectives on reality
reality is not really a Buddhist word 3.205; taking on trust basic teachings about the nature of reality 17.33; emphasis on the value of direct, personal experience of reality 12.56–7; fully realized by the Buddha and revealed in and through him 2.43; Buddhist doctrines are symbols, intellectual supports to realize reality 1.303; teachings don't describe Reality but show the direction in which to seek it 7.244; alienation from reality represented by the three root poisons 2.252; 'Existence (or Reality) = Change (or Becoming)' 4.647

reality in Buddhist history
two tendencies: seeing reality in terms of emptiness, or in terms of mind 14.199–200; implications of early Buddhist conception made explicit by the Mahāyāna 1.65; the nature of reality as conceived by Buddhist philosophy 7.317; the development of different terms for reality viewed from different angles 2.43; how transcendental realities became identified with conceptual formulations 1.232; for Nāgārjuna neither positive nor negative, for Maitreyanātha positive 1.364; Mahāyāna: Emptiness, Suchness, Sameness, or Consciousness is the sole reality 1.268; the Mahāyāna asserted that reality is the Non-Dual 1.274; the setting up and discarding of one indication of reality after another 1.83; through the *Diamond Sūtra* we make contact with reality 14.373; reality and the *trikāya* doctrine 1.250; the Tantra sees it as both transcendent to phenomena and immanent in them 1.385

absolute reality
existence is neither absolutely real nor absolutely unreal 16.452–3; mystics attest to its existence 12.86; symbolized by the colour white 13.68; the world is not to be mistaken for absolute reality 17.626

reality and other Dharma terms
Buddhism is very rich in words for ultimate reality 4.189; knowledge of reality means seeing things in terms of *dharmas* 14.344; *lokuttara* (beyond time and space) 9.398; *prajñā* means knowledge of reality 14.343–4; Reality = Becoming = *paṭicca-samuppāda* 7.203; the term 'not-two' avoids the risk of a fixed conception of reality 18.44; two kinds: conditioned (*saṃskṛta*) and unconditioned (*asaṃskṛta*) 3.206–8

images and metaphors
apprehending reality through imagery, symbols, myths, metaphors 14.589; better to think of reality as colourful than as colourless 13.284, 19.25; its dynamic aspect symbolized by the flowering bowl 7.397; the flow of reality 19.377;

the golden thread that connects us to reality 4.171–2; the more vivid, poetic, and colourful our idea of reality the better 13.284–5; like the unclouded sky 14.361–2; like a stained-glass window 5.606–7; metaphor offers us a clue to the nature of reality 14.589; metaphors for reality relating to the elements 14.589–90; symbols *are* reality 5.598; symbols, treated as reality, turn from helps into hindrances 1.303–4; thought of in terms of light: positive effects and limitations 16.108–9; the *vajra* represents the splitting of reality that takes place all the time 13.181–2

REALITY IN PRACTICE

thinking about reality
mistaking a thought about reality for insight into reality 19.165; reducing things to intellectual formulas represents an attenuation of reality 18.287; thinking should be a springboard for the experience, not an end in itself 19.166; thinking that thoughts *are* reality, we mistake the finger for the moon 19.377; thought is incommensurable with reality and reality with thought 26.85

analysing reality
eradication of the false view that things and persons are ultimately real 2.128; the formless is not necessarily closer to reality than that which has form 18.88; one can't really chop reality into little bits 14.409, 17.493–4; seen as an object from within the framework of the dualistic mind 19.142–3; described as a subject or object of perception 17.410

reflections on reality
apparent contradiction between space-type and time-type models of reality 4.203; archetypal reality 16.529, 16.532; the idea of a self is a fiction obscuring awareness of reality 17.249; if there are degrees of reality, there must be degrees of spiritual experience 12.12–13; religion is adaptation *to* reality, not adaptation *of* reality 7.133; subject and object are suffused by the light of reality 18.614; philosophy is the rational construction of reality 26.45

reality and concepts
assuming that if reality isn't among concepts it will be found nowhere 17.379; conditioned consciousness attempts to catch reality in the net of concepts 17.379; danger of converting concepts of relative validity into entities of ultimate reality 1.224; distinction between concepts and realities 1.72, 2.114, 26.84; ideas can give us no idea of reality 14.588; if we start taking statements about reality literally we go off the rails 14.605; no concepts, no words, can possibly apply to reality 3.219; nothing can be said about reality 13.348; paradoxes are needed to do justice to its non-conceptual nature 7.489; reality can be mediated as much by images as by concepts 19.189; unmediated, unbound by concepts 18.66; while we are dealing with concepts we are not dealing with ultimate reality 14.547; words and concepts distort reality as much as they express it 7.331

reality and words
don't take attempts to express reality literally, but try to see the point of them 4.204; a double barrier between us and reality: perceptions and words 14.421; it cannot be spoken of either as subject or as object 17.548; no concepts, no words, can possibly apply to reality 3.219; no language can come up to the truth and force of reality (Hazlitt) 24.562; not to be expressed in terms of existence and non-existence 1.139; to speak about reality, one has to turn it into subject and object 18.614; words and concepts distort reality as much as they express it 7.331; 'words are not the highest reality' 1.238–9

approaches to reality
as we get more deeply into the spiritual life, our sense of reality changes 26.57; beauty as an intermediary between unreality and reality 5.586, 18.158; the Dharma's principal function is to make us aware of reality –but what is reality? 26.361; *dhyāna* experience allows one to contemplate reality 4.159, 4.494; the importance of a non-wilful approach to reality 19.387; literature as a means of access to reality 26.329–30; negative, affirmative, and paradox 16.328–9; the point of contact is neither thought nor feeling, but can be spoken of as either 4.516; prepare to encounter a reality that transcends anything you had imagined 16.223; reached by bringing all the bands of the spectrum of consciousness together 17.341; the Real is not to be attained by a series of increments of the unreal 1.332; to come to true understanding, one must be free of negative mental states 17.438; we cannot confront reality directly, art is the medium 26.22

reality and us
coming face to face with reality after death 3.110–11, 16.39; fear of reality 16.39, 16.216; how do we glimpse reality? 2.262–3, 11.506; it breaks into our cosy existence 9.35–6; it is to be experienced in the midst of ordinary life 14.xv; learning

to accept reality 16.216; mundane reality has to be allowed to exist on its own level 14.496; one can contact it directly from the dream state 19.305–6; one must experience everything, all the time, under its *vajra* aspect 13.180; our psychophysical organism is designed to shield us from its impact 12.201; 'Reality Telegrams' (poem) 25.362–5; the reality towards which we are progressing is not foreign to us, or we to it 4.32–3; the shattering experience of reality 13.171–2; spiritual life is a kind of interrogation of reality 17.260; throughout our life, our ordinary mind shelters us from reality 3.110; we are attracted to it like moths to a flame, but then we swerve away 10.610; we're related to it directly and indirectly 4.171–2, 11.505–6; we impose an arbitrary pattern upon it 19.241; who we are in relation to reality 12.43

the experience of reality
the bodhisattva's connection with reality described in terms of the elements 14.590; 'dwelling inwardly in the true nature of reality' 16.47; full realization of ultimate reality 11.115–16; pure inspiration from the experience of reality itself 18.180; upon Buddhahood, reality flows through you, and you are reality 12.234; when the Eye of Reality opens 25.309

see also
conventional reality, *see under* three *svabhāvas*; *dharmakāya*, *see under trikāya*; distorted view of reality, *see* four *viparyāsas*; 'Humankind cannot bear very much reality', *see under* T. S. Eliot; *jñeyāvaraṇa* (wrong conceptions of reality), *see under* two veils

realization

the highest realization
all Buddhas teach the same thing, because they have all realized the same reality 14.474; the Buddha insisted on the necessity of personal realization of Nirvāṇa 2.202–3; the *arhant*: realization of the ideal under limitations of time and space 16.7, 16.26; Buddhism is based upon the realization of emptiness 7.278, 13.447; complete realization 19.286; direct realization of the highest spiritual truth (Hakuin, *Sūtra of Wei Lang*) 2.555; the historical Buddha can't fully express his realization due to limits of history 4.191; a non-realization 1.268; *prajñā* is the realization of *mahā-śūnyatā* 3.236–7, 3.301–2; the realization of the absolute truth 1.206, 1.265, 1.269, 1.307, 1.348; the realization of one mind 1.260, 3.87; the realization of the essential non-difference of the universe and the Absolute 1.306; the realization of your true nature 19.387; realizing the *dharmakāya* 2.43, 19.318–19; the realm of *dharmas*, *śūnyatā*, the One Mind, the *ḍākas* and *ḍākinīs* 17.133; Milarepa is always in touch with the higher realization 19.176–7; the Dharma of words and speculation is the same as the Dharma of realization 19.88; 'There is no such thing as *my* realizations or *your* realizations' 7.155

the way to realization
the archetypal bodhisattva: the ideal in the process of realization within space 4.191; contradictory doctrines could lead to the same realization 1.208–210, 1.215; the doctrine of Going for Refuge is to facilitate the realization of the ideal 1.400; doctrines are not definitions of reality but intellectual supports for realization 1.303; faith in Amitābha as a condition for the realization of Nirvāṇa 1.345; if we realized a fraction of what we understand we'd be Buddhas on the spot 26.45; if the will is bent towards the realization of unity, thought and action will follow 7.140; in order to realize wisdom you have to go outside time 19.435–6; the relative truth is the means to the realization of the absolute truth 1.206, 1.348; right view is only relative, but must be upheld as the means to realization 1.206; the view that realization of *śūnyatā* not indispensable for attainment of Nirvāṇa 1.321; *vinaya*: way of life conducive to realization of the Dharma 2.18; Buddhist art designed as a means of spiritual realization 7.510

the effects of realization
the bigger the heap of passions you start with, the greater your realization 4.467; the bodhisattva's compassion radiates from his realization of non-duality 7.140; compassion is how one acts when one has a deep realization of non-selfhood 12.9; *dukkha* can only end on the basis of a realization of the Unconditioned 10.635–6; the deeper the realization, the broader and stronger the outflow of energy 26.17; mantra: the expression of inner realization in speech 1.512; religion based on realization smiles at criticism 7.145; if 'my' realization is real then 'I' must be a reality 1.232; in the realization of the highest truth, difference of race and caste is obliterated 7.103; *sahajānanda* (bliss from realizing non-duality of conditioned and Unconditioned) 2.91; we should have courage of our transcendental realizations 1.209; the wisdom of the realization of a dynamic Becoming 7.375

obstacles
confusing realization of primordial truth with concepts that communicate it 19.354; egoism is 'the only real obstacle to the realization of Truth' 20.362; mistaking rational comprehension for actual realization 1.222, 2.113; why our theoretical understanding and practical realization isn't commensurate 1.390

realizations of a less transcendental kind
how to sustain a realization brought by painful experience? 4.13; non-violence: the external expression of an internal realization 7.373; peace can only come through a realization of interconnectedness 7.274; Nietzsche's view not the product of transcendental realization 3.502

see also
without the realization of *śūnyatā* Vajrayāna visualizations are vulgar magic, *see under* Chen

reason

notes on reason
the distinction between intellect and reason (Macmurray) 15.255; the 18th-century idea of reason 12.463; how can reason be supreme in all human affairs? 26.76; it is an element of faith 1.283, 1.284–6; it is not reasonable to expect people to be reasonable 18.171; to begin with, the development of reason can be rather 'brittle' 15.743

the Dharma and reason
a reasonable teaching 3.397–8, 9.96–7; explicitly stated to be *atakkāvacara*, 'beyond reason' 1.17, 1.209, 8.589, 11.8; an ocean whose depths are not to be plumbed by reason alone 8.599; the Buddha emphasized the rational as well as the mystical approach 12.515; 'Let any reasonable man come to me, and I will teach him the Dharma' 3.562, 15.362

reason and experience
Buddhism upholds the equal validity of reason and experience 26.198; accepting only what agrees with reason and our own experience 21.505; harmony between genuine experience and valid reasoning 18.416; reason and the scriptures (and experience) must be balanced 18.416, 19.186, 19.203; reason deals with matters of experience 19.186–7

taking reason as far as you can
'Follow your reason as far as it will take you' (Huxley) 8.588–9; the Dalai Lama has faith in reason, and a willingness to use it to its limits 8.505; the instrument of the quest for truth 10.142; the superconscious is beyond reason, but does not contradict it 26.199; we can only go beyond reason when at the limits of our thinking 17.376–7; you overrun the positions of reason, you don't retreat from them 14.xiv, 14.422

beyond reason
'Reason dies in giving birth to ecstasy' 14.358–9, 25.82; concentrating more on intuition's undertones than on reason's overtones 7.133; reason is self-contradictory (Nāgārjuna) 1.209–10, 1.313, 10.143, 26.199; reason overcome by the will of God 15.620–1; Sangharakshita's life determined by impulse and intuition, not reason and logic 2.406; why not try doing something without finding a reason for it first? 14.556–7

see also
reason and emotion, *see under* emotions/ introduction; reason and faith, *see under* faith/aspects of faith

rebellion after a retreat your old reactive self may rise up in rebellion 19.82–3; 'Buddhism is the rebel child of Hinduism' 10.279–80; dangerous for the artist to think of himself as a rebel 26.359–60; the middle way between conformity and rebellion towards parents 12.390–2; 'neurosis' can be a healthy symptom of rebellion 12.101; a rampaging rebel is not necessarily a proto-individual 11.195; a rebel co-opted by the establishment 24.535–6; rebel angels, *see under* Milton/ *Paradise Lost*; the rebellion of the ego 18.367–8; the rebellious disciple 18.363–8; *saṃsāra*: just going on bearing things, never rebelling 19.580

rebirth

THE TRADITION

introduction
brief introduction 10.136; one of three (or four) possible views about what happens after death 17.468–9; *punarbhava* ('again-becoming') is the technically correct term 2.14, 3.198, 10.160

the Buddhist tradition
the Buddha accepted rebirth 8.565, 8.575–6; 'Destroyed is rebirth for me' (the Buddha) 1.95; Siddhārtha's vision of beings reborn in accordance with their karma 3.32, 3.115; did the Buddha teach karma and rebirth? 4.373, 4.405, 12.689, 17.467; the Buddha never suggested that a good rebirth was a worthy goal 17.212–13; the goal of Buddhist practice is release from the endless round of rebirth 8.565;

in the *Jātakas* 16.471–2; in the *Ratana Sutta* 15.65; positive rebirth as a result of listening to the *Sūtra of Golden Light* 16.382–3; rebirth as an excuse for putting off Dharma practice 12.689–90, 17.471; no school of Buddhism has questioned rebirth 3.114–15, 8.565; the sense in which Buddhism teaches rebirth 2.14; the Tibetan belief in the rebirth of spiritually advanced teachers 2.182–3, 3.134; the traditional doctrine needs reformulation 3.112–13; why Buddhism speaks of 'rebirth' rather than 'reincarnation' 3.198, 17.242

relationship to Dharma teachings and concepts
the *ālaya-vijñāna* 12.176, 18.290–2; *anātman* 3.111, 9.343–4; the middle way 1.109, 2.14–15, 12.387, 12.690; *pratītya-samutpāda* 1.109, 3.192–204; *saṃskāras* 1.108; the twelve cyclical *nidānas* 1.112, 2.253–5, 3.201

Hindu ideas of rebirth
Dalits told by caste Hindus that their suffering was due to bad karma 4.396, 4.400; first reference in *Brihadaranyaka Upanishad* 3.96; like putting on a new set of clothes (*Bhagavad Gītā*) 3.196–7, 7.165, 19.375; *punarjanman* (reincarnation), Hindu term 2.14, 10.160

Western responses
agnosticism with respect to rebirth 8.577; association with theosophists 17.31; attitude to rebirth 4.402–5; belief in a future life may comfort Westerners, but it does not reassure a true Buddhist 17.163; Christmas Humphreys' belief that he had lived in ancient Egypt 17.31, 23.41; Eastern and Western conceptions of rebirth 3.190–2, 12.689–90; a footballer ridiculed for trying to make sense of reincarnation 25.16–17; the idea of karma and rebirth struck early Western Buddhists forcibly 12.464; karma and rebirth in Western Buddhism 3.188–92; many prefer to keep an open mind on the subject 8.565–6; *Rebirth and the Western Buddhist* 8.xxxvi, 8.565–7; today people are more interested in the here and now 3.192, 17.32–3, 17.471–2; a poem on rebirth by John Masefield 7.450, 7.619 (n507); traditionally people practise Buddhism for a good rebirth, but that may not suit us 17.467–72; we have much to lose from failing to take the teaching seriously 8.566; women who claimed they had been Cleopatra in a past life 17.31, 23.41

philosophical reflections
asking what exactly is passed on at rebirth is just the mind reifying away 14.608; death and rebirth like ripples on your phenomenal surface 4.331; extreme views about rebirth 3.196–7, 19.375–6; rebirth takes places, but nobody is reborn 1.109, 3.198, 7.495, 10.142, 10.160, 19.376; the 'self' that is reborn is neither the same nor another 4.629–30; what is reborn? 1.109, 2.93–4, 3.196–7; whatever passes from one rebirth to the next is not separate from the *skandhas* 14.439

DOUBTS AND PROOFS

doubts about rebirth
Ajita Keskambalī tells Ajātasattu there is no such thing 12.757; all one needs is a faith in the conservation of spiritual values beyond death 4.63; for all practical purposes it's just this life that matters 4.372–3; if you can't accept it, make the most of this life 4.367–8, 4.372–3, 12.689–90; 'an indefensible hypothesis' (view of early Western writer on Buddhism) 7.32; is it possible to be a Buddhist and not believe in rebirth? 12.689–90, 17.27–8, 17.32; materialist view that there is no continuity of lives 7.165; Milarepa as a model for those who have difficulty with the idea 17.467–8; settling the question as to whether the Buddha taught it 26.695–6; we have to ask ourselves whether we accept the idea 12.690

evidence
are people interested in evidence? 17.29–32; attempts to verify empirically 2.15–16, 3.111–12, 4.403–4, 12.687–8, 17.29; the Buddha's evidence 3.115, 12.689; Dhardo Rimpoche and Lama Govinda's recollections 12.688; the doctrine becomes clear in higher states of consciousness 3.114, 17.45–6; evidence for rebirth 8.566–7; a feeling that comes from life experience 17.469–71; the idea follows logically from the tenet that actions have consequences 17.468; if nothing in the mind was not previously in the senses, no memory of past lives 26.85; it may be hard to prove, but other beliefs are harder to accept 17.30, 17.468–9; it's not necessary to prove rebirth in order to work for Enlightenment 4.402; Mozart as evidence for rebirth 26.22

HOW IT WORKS

what happens?
according to the *Tibetan Book of the Dead* 3.110–11, 12.205; causal continuity: like a flame feeding on successive bundles of fuel 2.14; the continuity of a process 19.375–7; how can it be explained? 9.343–4; how it happens 1.108–9;

preparing for rebirth through holy living and holy dying 8.142–4; the process (*utpatti-bhāva*) 1.112; the process of rebirth likened to the building of a house 18.269–30; rebirth as the repetition of an old pattern 17.350, 17.475; 'relinking consciousness' (*pratisandhi*) 1.108–9, 2.75, 2.95, 2.254, 3.196–8; volitional drives take an appropriate physical embodiment 17.473–4; we may have an inclination towards the positive from a previous existence 17.589; what is 'reborn' is the continuously changing stream of psychical energy 2.93–4, 26.52; who or what exactly is reborn? extreme views 3.196–8

karma and rebirth
introduction 3.107–115; Ajita Keskambalī tells Ajātasattu that there is no such thing 12.757; the creative power of skilful actions 1.342; the doctrine can be invigorating 17.472; the fact of rebirth does not entail ethical linkage between one existence and the next 8.576; it's possible to accept the principle of karma within a single lifespan 17.472; karmic effects on rebirth 1.108, 2.71–2, 3.107–9, 13.36–7; never a straightforward matter 17.208; no Buddhist teacher has ever suggested that belief in it might be a wrong view 17.468; not karma but how we shape ourselves in the present moment is what's important 17.212–13; a point of connection between 'Hīnayāna' and Mahāyāna 26.695; practising Buddhism without belief in karma and rebirth is difficult 3.113–14; rebirth from mixed karma 15.373; rebirth in different realms 2.73, 2.95, 16.419; rebirth in Sukhāvatī does not imply the suspension of karma 1.344; rebirth takes place on account of the residue of greed, hatred, and delusion 13.36–7; continuity of karma from one life to another 7.121

remembering former lives
if you can't remember recent events, why expect to remember past lives? 17.49–50; Lama Govinda's belief that he had been Novalis 12.688, 26.256; remembering them 16.282–3; a supernormal power (*abhijñā*) 1.167, 2.15, 3.115, 7.712–13 (n54); it would convince you of the truth of rebirth 17.26; as a child Dhardo Rimpoche could remember them 12.431–2, 12.688; why not see death as wiping the slate clean? 17.244

why are we reborn?
because of sexual desire 11.572–3; because we have not realized Essence of Mind 13.361–2; because our minds are dominated by the *kleśas* 11.401; because we want to be embodied 10.482; the cause of rebirth 1.91; clinging 18.612; our thoughts, words, and deeds 17.173; wrong views 7.523; *kāma-rāga* (desire for sensuous experience) 3.421, 15.65, 17.14; the residue of craving, aversion, and ignorance 2.253–4, 3.131; rebirth-producing volition 1.112; so long as there is an ego ... 17.475, 26.168; *tṛṣṇā* (craving) 3.199

WHERE ONE WILL BE REBORN

introduction
acting with the minimum of conscious thought one hurls oneself into rebirth 7.138; actions leading to rebirth in heaven or hell 14.67–8; beggars as guarantors of favourable rebirth 17.211; being reborn with those one has known before 17.480; the effect of ethical behaviour on rebirth 11.321; a fresh start every time 16.283; how we spend our time as an indicator of future rebirth 17.526–7; an over-literal idea 17.286; into different spheres of phenomenal existence 1.112; in the *kāmaloka*, *rūpaloka*, or *arūpaloka* according to fetters broken 2.148; in the realms of the wheel of life 2.73, 2.95, 13.283, 16.419; spiritual qualities carried over from previous lives 18.543–4

aspirations for one's next birth
bhikkhus piously hoping to be reborn in the days of Maitreya 8.280; the goal of Buddhism is not to be reborn at all 3.195, 8.565; rebirth as a Buddhist 15.687–91; in a time and place in which you can encounter a Buddha 4.8; into a situation where the Dharma is known 19.474–5; the spiritual community being reborn together 16.471–2; a vow to be reborn in more favourable circumstances 18.147–8

rebirth in heaven or as a god
the bodhisattva does not desire rebirth among the gods 1.443–4; by apparitional birth 15.342; seeking your reward in heaven is spiritual materialism 17.170–1; the Buddha warned that these realms were temporary 3.315–16; the craving for heaven leads only to rebirth 2.149; desire for rebirth in the celestial realms (*Dhammapada*) 15.55, 15.746 (n27); a god's rebirth as a king 16.420; through *dhyāna* 17.525; through following the path of the ten right actions 2.333; in the Pure Abodes (*śuddhāvāsa*) 2.148–9; rebirth as a god 1.32, 2.372, 11.323, 16.427; rebirth in Sukhāvatī, *see under* Sukhāvatī; a reward for virtuous deeds 1.32, 2.214–15, 5.434–5, 10.608, 16.420

rebirth in the human realm
desire for rebirth there (*Dhammapada*) 15.55, 15.746 (n27); if you are reborn as a human being, your karma is rather mixed 15.373; it is unlikely that those who have been human will not be reborn human 13.139, 17.524; reflexive consciousness is unlikely to be lost 16.291

other possibilities
being reborn as a *devaputra* Māra 26.657; rebirth as an animal 2.93–4, 16.291–2, 17.525; rebirth in hell 2.333, 16.282, 17.525, 26.700; rebirth in humble circumstances as a result of arrogance 17.606; rebirth in the lower realms 17.170; nihilism leads to an unhappy rebirth 17.244; noisy deathbed scenes may jeopardize the dying person's chance of happy rebirth 2.231–2; rebirth in multiple forms 17.522–3; rebirth as a spirit fox 14.593, 18.85; unfortunate rebirths 2.156; unskilful behaviour resulting in a bad rebirth 17.294

REBIRTH AND BEYOND

voluntary rebirth
imagine being reborn throughout the immense period of the bodhisattva career 4.60; out of compassion 13.37–8; there was nothing to cause the Buddha to be reborn 3.142; the path of the bodhisattva 3.132–4; wouldn't the Buddha want to be reborn in the world out of compassion? 4.205, 11.403

contact with the reborn
mettā for those who are reborn 5.181; remaining in contact with someone after they are reborn 4.558

rebirth and merit (puṇya)
good works undertaken for rebirth not worth a sixteenth part of *mettā* 2.315; if you get a good rebirth through merit, do you then aspire to insight? 17.160–1; rebirth in heaven as a reward for virtuous deeds 2.214–15; rebirth in the higher realms as a result of practising *mettā* 15.341–2; the only aspiration of lay people 2.204

endless rebirths
all sentient beings are undergoing a process of transmigration 14.203; immense number of lives 1.39; the flood of tears 1.130–1; one has been both a man and a woman many times 2.372; reflecting that all beings have been one's parents in past lives, *see under* parents; the rounds of rebirth 7.49, 11.253–4; *saṃsāra*: frightful sequence of rebirths 1.130; the world has been born and died thousands of times, and must do so again 7.343

the end of rebirth
seeing that any kind of existence is relative, there is no more rebirth 17.411; the Buddha would only be reborn out of compassion, not compulsion 11.403; by eradicating craving for continued individual existence 26.159; freedom from rebirth 3.190; how to go beyond rebirth? 3.97; it ceases with the eradication of volitions 2.123; no action based upon the conception of 'I' means no rebirth 17.351; recognizing the clear light of reality 11.17, 12.201–2, 16.96, 16.108, 18.250, 18.570–1; right view, good rebirth, wrong view, bad rebirth, 'no view', Nirvāṇa 17.245; that is the aim 8.565; with a fraction of your effort over many lives you could gain Enlightenment 4.629

see also
citta-santāna (psyche-continuum, mind-stream); the length of time between death and rebirth, *see under bardo*/introduction; rebirth in the Pure Land, *see under* Pure Land; rebirth in Sukhāvatī, *see under* Sukhāvatī; Sangharakshita's acceptance of rebirth, *see under* Sangharakshita III/life story; spiritual rebirth

receptivity

the nature of receptivity
Ākāśadhātviśvarī represents unlimited spiritual receptivity 13.313; characteristic of the true individual 3.468; communication and receptivity 18.58; the difference between passivity and receptivity 15.387, 15.551–3, 19.581; the difference between receptivity and submission 15.663; a feminine ideal, receptive and cooperative 18.105; it doesn't necessarily mean agreeing 19.581; it means being prepared for a radical change to your way of looking at things 4.128; like a lightning conductor 4.43–4; receptivity and *mettā* 5.189; receptive orientation (Erich Fromm) 12.276; receptivity to those above us in the spiritual hierarchy 4.174, 18.318; true receptivity to other people requires us to see them as they really are 15.164

the need for receptivity
the importance of receptivity 19.219; find the truth and be receptive to it, even if it threatens everything … 17.632; it supports awareness 17.xxi; receive rather than take, give rather than impose, share rather than divide 26.35; spiritual receptivity leads to valuable spiritual experiences 21.505; to be receptive to the wise, we need a personal

relationship with them 15.293; to get an inkling of what a symbol means, we have to be receptive to it 13.119, 13.123; until you're receptive to the spiritually superior, no progress is possible 12.14; without it, spiritual progress cannot be maintained 4.129; without a measure of it you will not really understand anything 17.261; without the students' curiosity and receptivity, no teaching can take place 11.277–8

the Buddha and receptivity
he assesses who present is ready to receive his teaching 10.551; he told his disciples they should be willing to learn 2.28; receptive listening to the *Buddhavacana* 22.226

receptivity to the Dharma
appreciating hearing the Dharma but still not being receptive to it 18.163; needed if one is to really hear the Dharma 4.359–60, 14.403; 'It requires a disciple possessing merit to receive the teaching' 18.244–5; you need to be receptive to the Dharma 4.359–60, 11.175–6, 14.403, 15.436; as long as the ego is there, one cannot receive the Dharma 18.188; being healthy doesn't necessarily make you more receptive 17.163–4

receptivity to …
the advent of the guru 3.557; archetypal symbols 12.180–1; the *bodhicitta* 4.49, 4.224; the Buddha's influence 4.7–8; the golden light of the transcendental 16.435; grace waves 4.139; higher things 17.261; the influence of a bodhisattva 16.230; the inner teaching 18.290; nature 1.572, 13.456; particular works of art 26.265–6; positive influences 18.98; spiritual friends 4.43; the teacher 17.50; the *trikāya* 18.89; the truth 16.55; the truth of the *White Lotus Sūtra* 16.61

developing and expressing receptivity
appealing to the bodhisattvas makes you more receptive 4.313; don't fill yourself with teachings but to make yourself fit to receive them 18.117; an inquiring mind: that's all you need 18.234; prayer to the Three Jewels: an attitude of receptivity 18.319; through prayer 4.129; devotion is part of preparing to be receptive to the Perfection of Wisdom 14.437; one of the most receptive audiences I have ever encountered 24.237; through the Sevenfold Puja 1.510, 11.223, 11.274–6; the receptiveness and creativity of the poet 26.171; receptivity in meditation 15.111–12, 15.387; removing the obstacles to receptivity 4.224; shown by placing your head to someone's feet 16.381; training in receptivity to art 26.98; sometimes you are unable to handle the experience 11.279; we need to go on being receptive 11.276–7; you can open yourself to spiritual forces, but *you've* got to respond 4.302

lack of receptivity
an arrogant or complacent person cannot be receptive 15.276; the difficulty of teaching an unreceptive audience 16.64; full of your own imagined attainments, you close your ears to the Buddha 16.64; going through the motions of accepting it as an ideal 19.289; being full of your own views: the overflowing cup 11.278–9, 17.208; if you don't want to be receptive, not even the Buddha can change that 11.277–8; lack of receptivity of those who walk out, *see under White Lotus Sūtra*/the structure of the *sūtra*; passivity is not to be mistaken for receptivity 26.65; pseudo-receptivity 18.423; the right not to be receptive to Buddhism 4.248

see also
influence; practice of *kṣānti*, *see under kṣānti*

Rechabites 20.2, 26.417

Rechung Rimpoche (reincarnation of Rechungpa) introduction 22.491; a good friend of Sangharakshita's in Kalimpong 18.433; hairs from his guru's head ('Like a dog's hair!') 19.366, 22.491; moves to Holland 8.663, 23.72, 23.75; Sangharakshita gives him a thangka 11.713; Sangharakshita takes on a helper on the Rimpoche's advice 22.521–2; Sangharakshita teaches him English 8.663; shows Sangharakshita his translation of a Tibetan medical text 23.240

Rechungpa (Milarepa's disciple)

HIS LIFE STORY

introduction
summary of the account of Rechungpa in the *Hundred Thousand Songs* 18.259–61; as an artist 18.260; biographies of Rechungpa 18.261, 19.509; compared to Gampopa 18.260–1; he belongs to the Kagyu lineage 19.388; his early life as a reciter of stories from the *sūtras* 18.306–7; his family's opposition to his discipleship with Milarepa 18.306–10; he contracts leprosy 18.309–13; his experience seems typical of the spiritual life 18.346; he becomes a professor at Sha 19.509; his relationship with the Lady Dembu 19.90, 19.418, 19.509, 19.513–14, 19.534, 19.552–3; how his story ended 19.588–9; eventually he has disciples in Weu 19.335–6; he wrote Milarepa's biography 18.xvi, 19.303–7

his character
desire for pleasure and comfort 18.260, 18.560–1, 18.566, 19.90–4, 19.400; different aspects of him alienated from one another 18.441–2, 19.90–1; easily distracted 19.7–11; even as a Stream Entrant he still needs Milarepa's guidance 19.510; a faith-follower 18.308–9; a greed type 18.561; he lacks the bodhisattva spirit 19.16; he thinks too much 18.540; he wants his own way 18.406, 19.7–8, 19.15–22, 19.36, 19.365; he's like a young horse that needs training 18.346; he has some supernormal powers but lacks insight 19.117–18; he oscillates between spiritual and mundane states of mind 18.540, 18.543; his love of travel 19.400; a mixture of skilful and unskilful qualities 18.470, 19.114–17; naive 18.406; not very integrated 19.307–8, 19.340; not a very stable character 19.113–14; obstinate and stubborn 18.261, 19.58–62, 19.75, 19.87; proud 18.437–44, 18.468–71, 19.15; rather extreme 19.144; resentful 19.12–13, 19.18, 19.35–7, 19.58–9; restless 19.339; uncomplicated 18.308; unreasonably independent 18.387

his relationship with Milarepa
brief account 18.xvi, 18.261–2; their first meeting 18.305–7; an authentic relationship 19.223–6; Rechungpa won't ask permission or take advice 18.323, 18.364–9, 18.550; Rechungpa's desire for Milarepa's approval 18.363–4, 19.365; Milarepa's faith in Rechungpa 18.381–2; one of Milarepa's two chief disciples 18.433, 19.115; Rechungpa thinks he is equal to or better than Milarepa 18.438–41, 18.549; Milarepa questions his motivation 18.463–4; the devotion of a disciple combined with the rebelliousness of a son 18.491; Rechungpa tries to teach Milarepa how to teach him 18.492–3; what matters is the depth of their relationship, not exchange of gifts 18.519; Rechungpa resists Milarepa's influence 18.538–9; he begins to realize that he isn't Milarepa's equal after all 18.546–7; Milarepa questions Rechungpa about his spiritual experience 18.573–4; Milarepa becomes stricter with him 18.621; Rechungpa projects his negative qualities onto Milarepa 19.15; the relationship becomes painful 19.91; their 'father–son' relationship 19.27, 19.114, 19.123; Rechungpa comes to see Milarepa as he really is 19.123–4; assumptions that Rechungpa is the greater of the two 19.311–12, 19.417, 19.430–3, 19.553; Milarepa advises Rechungpa to control his mind 19.337; Rechungpa refuses Milarepa's advice 19.363–5, 19.390–1; Milarepa says he will never forsake Rechungpa 19.390–1; Rechungpa asks for Milarepa's help 19.391–400; is it possible for Rechungpa to exceed Milarepa? 19.416–17; they will never be parted 19.419–21; Milarepa's sadness when Rechungpa leaves 19.428–9; Milarepa says that Rechungpa should leave him 'to benefit sentient beings' 19.574

HIS STORY AS TOLD IN THE *HUNDRED THOUSAND SONGS OF MILAREPA*

first journey to India
Milarepa's advice before he leaves 18.321–3; he returns cured of his illness 18.326–8, 18.346

'Third Journey to India'
Rechungpa wants to go to learn logic 18.351–63; Milarepa advises against, but stays in communication 18.363–74; Milarepa sets the journey in a more altruistic perspective 18.369, 18.374; Rechungpa is delighted to get his own way 18.403–6; Rechungpa is clearly out of touch with the spiritual life 18.419; where Rechungpa goes in India and who he meets 18.431–2, 18.466–70; he boasts about his experiences 18.468–70

'The Story of the Yak-Horn'
Rechungpa wants Milarepa to recognize him as an equal 18.438–42; he has acquired the teachings, but hasn't really 'got' them 18.491; Rechungpa's misunderstanding about the Dharma 18.527–30; he projects greed and hatred onto Milarepa 18.531; Milarepa takes shelter in the yak-horn 18.531–47; an old woman dies and Milarepa teaches Rechungpa a lesson 18.549–71; Rechungpa makes progress, but has an inflated idea of it 18.580–5; Rechungpa's mind is straightened out 18.616–17; Rechungpa has to decide what he is going to do 18.625–6

'Rechungpa's Repentance'
Rechungpa watching the play of goats 19.9–11, 19.77–80; Milarepa burns his books 18.xvii, 19.12–14; Rechungpa's resentment and hostility 19.14–18, 19.35–7; his obsession with getting his books back 19.58–62, 19.74, 19.87; a sudden upwelling of faith in Milarepa 19.113–15; Rechungpa's first teaching: he explains how to 'win' a dispute: 19.148–56

'Heartfelt Advice to Rechungpa'
Milarepa interrupts a discussion Rechungpa is having 19.171–248;

Milarepa gives Rechungpa some advice 19.173–248; Milarepa meets some patrons who are horrified by his nudity 19.249–64; returning from the village, Rechungpa finds the door shut 19.265–300; Rechungpa sings a song which Milarepa calls 'quotations' 19.266–89

'Rechungpa's Journey to Weu'
Rechungpa has dreams and asks Milarepa to tell his life story 19.303–7; their patrons think Rechungpa is better than Milarepa 19.308–17; Milarepa's dreams 19.318–333; Rechungpa's reasons for wanting to go to Weu 19.334–50; Milarepa advises him that he shouldn't roam until he's ready 19.341–63; Rechungpa compares the journey to the spiritual life 19.370–89; he makes claims about himself 19.388–9; Milarepa teaches his patrons a lesson 19.427–509

'Rechungpa's Departure'
Rechungpa gives some jade to a beggar and leaves Lady Dembu 19.513–14; Rechungpa's offerings of meat for Milarepa expand to fill a whole valley 19.515; he doesn't have an offering for the Tantric initiation 19.533; Rechungpa's confession 19.548–53; Milarepa interprets Rechungpa's dreams 19.561–73

reciprocity all human relationships are reciprocal 11.699; any interaction between people involves both giving and receiving 17.202; *apatrāpya* can be reciprocal 17.560; *mettā* should be reciprocal 5.171; one's attitude to someone on the same level as oneself 4.174; real giving is receiving 26.35; 'Reciprocity' (poem) 25.245; rights and duties are not only reciprocal but complementary 7.277–80, 12.603–4; *shù* (Confucian term for reciprocity) 8.448

reciting Ānanda asks the Buddha to recite the *pāṭimokkha* (*Udāna*) 10.557, 10.561; the benefits of hearing the Dharma being recited 8.532; it's not enough just to recite the Going for Refuge verses 5.541, 10.260, 12.305–6, 15.626; an esoteric sevenfold puja recited when offering the mandala 13.262–3; the Great Dhāraṇī recited by Mañjuśrī 13.359–60; to free yourself of guilt, burn incense before a Buddha image and recite *sūtras* 1.509; importance of correct pronunciation when reciting the Tipiṭaka 8.119–20; the merit of reciting Samantabhadra's name equals that of visualizing the Tathāgata 14.177; the merits of reciting the *White Lotus Sūtra* 14.127, 16.44; an offence for a monk to make a layperson recite the *suttas* 2.204, 16.54; the parrot who recited God's name, but in danger let out his natural squawk 12.96, 18.249; Rechungpa as a reciter of stories from the *sūtras* 18.306–7; reciting the bodhisattva vow 100,000 times 12.19–20, 13.81–2; reciting a prayer without thinking about what the words mean 18.319; reciting verses or mantras before sleep 17.686; the Root Verses recited before meditation 5.388; scriptures recited to invoke occult forces 2.216; Upāli recited the Vinaya Piṭaka at the First Council 14.186; the *White Lotus Sūtra* recited to bring rain 2.216; 'Who recites the Amitābha mantra?': a Zen question 18.239

see also
reciting mantras, *see under* mantras; reciting Refuges and Precepts, *see under* Going for Refuge/the Buddhist tradition

recklessness reckless driving 15.358; as negative mental event (*auddhatya*), *see under* restlessness

recognition the essence of religion is to recognize the Divine everywhere in the universe 7.86–7; getting so far away from yourself that you can't recognize yourself when you see it 4.271; if you recognize Māra, you see him as a state of your own mind 18.27; it is not easy to know whether someone is an *arhant* 10.590, 19.100, 19.282; no infallible criterion by means of which the unenlightened can recognize the Enlightened 26.49; people who failed to recognize the Buddha 14.431–2, 22.463; recognizing an irreversible bodhisattva, *see under* bodhisattva/bodhisattva hierarchy; refusal to recognize someone as deserving of respect 12.13–14, 15.714–20; to the extent that you are individual, you can recognize someone else as being more individual 15.717; we must recognize ourselves as essentially spiritual beings 7.308; a worldly person can't possibly tell whether someone is Enlightened 19.282, 26.49

recollection of the Buddha description of the practice 1.577; Buddhaghosa's description 4.701 (n279); calling to mind what one has heard about the Buddha 17.541; a good antidote to the passions 4.381; how does a bodhisattva develop the recollection of the Buddha? 2.44–5; meditating on the Buddha 10.207; one of the ten recollections (*anussatis*) 4.381, 4.519, 4.701 (n279), 4.710 (n337); perhaps similar to awareness of the presence of God 13.627; a way to keep the attention focused on the idea of the Buddha 17.89–90

recollection of death meditation *see under* death/recollecting death

recollection of impurity *see* contemplation of decay

recollection of purpose *see* mindfulness of purpose

recollection of the six elements *see* six element practice

recollections (*anussatis*) *see* ten recollections

red associated with the Tantric rite of fascination 13.280, 19.23; association with speech, communication 19.32; the colour of blood and hence the colour of life 13.280; the colour of love and compassion 2.389, 13.67; the colour of Enlightened passion (*mahā-rāga*) 13.280–1; total involvement with the spiritual life 13.242; Vajrayoginī 13.217, 13.240; Virūpākṣa (great king) 16.346

Redgrave, Vanessa 24.403

refinement

refinement and spiritual practice
the first five *pāramitās* are a refinement of the whole conditioned nature 4.550; the refinement of the *dhyānas* 4.494, 19.424–5; the lotus: the refined energies needed to do the work of the Three Jewels 19.438–9; *praśrabdhi* is a state of extreme refinement and delicacy of feeling 2.106; the refined energy of a spiritually developed person 19.327; the spiritual life cannot be a refined kind of selfishness 17.694–5, 19.315; what we are trying to do in all our practice is to refine consciousness 18.157–9

refinement and culture
through culture 3.617, 12.24, 12.672, 15.157–8, 16.375, 18.158, 19.469, 26.99–100; the refined language of culture 16.366–7; refining one's taste in music 5.511, 15.157–8; no spiritual life is possible without culture in the sense of refinement of spirit 3.368

refining emotions
one communicates with the more refined emotional side of oneself 19.409; through beauty 5.43, 15.157, 19.349; leading the emotions to more and more refined objects 19.228; through natural surroundings 18.158–9; by practising the *brahma vihāras* 10.173; as preparation for meditation 3.617; refining coarse emotions 4.134; refining desire 5.510–11, 11.588; shifting the focus of your emotional energy to more refined pleasures 15.154; only the more refined emotions can be absorbed into one's spiritual life 16.370; to make the link with the higher self 19.28; through contact with a *ḍākinī*, inner or outer 12.314–15

refinement of ideas
doctrines to be refined to such transparency that Enlightenment shines through 2.61; the refined concepts of the Madhyamaka 19.373–4; refining ideas 19.216; refining your questions because you don't want an answer 19.151

refined world
bliss is not to be rejected but refined 19.52, 19.196, 19.379; gradually refining gross energy 17.75; the mundane at its most refined 19.47, 19.49; our enjoyments are to be refined rather than given up 19.379; refinement of worldly pleasures 18.129–33; the progressive refinement of the heavens 16.344–5; you can't refine yourself out of the mundane world altogether 17.695

see also
refining gold, *see under* gold

reflection

the practice of reflection
it's difficult 15.191; could be more of a seeing than a reflection 5.449; moving between contemplating the Dharma and *dhyāna* 5.438–9; musing: a sort of contemplative reflecting 25.84; our reflections should be our own, not just a game of rearranging concepts 4.147; profitable questions for reflection 10.598; tending the sacred fire of reflection 26.145; reflecting on texts while copying them out 4.179; the time for reflection 25.402; Order members need to study and reflect more 24.391–3; the poet's practice of reflection 26.144–5; to practise Buddhism effectively we need to learn to reflect 15.191; reading about Buddhism without understanding the need for reflection 22.438; walking meditation as an aid to reflection 15.190; reflection on solitary retreat 5.668–9; turn aspects of the Dharma over in your mind whenever you can 17.207; association of certain reflections with certain actions (Vajrayāna) 19.329–30; you move from words to experience, like reading a poem 19.452; Sangharakshita copied passages into notebooks as material for reflection 20.260–1

purposes of reflecting on the Dharma
the contemplation of any phenomenal object can develop *prajñā* 19.70; deep concentration without mental activity 5.438; developing insight 5.431, 5.448, 17.543; giving a talk after a long process of reflection 12.581; helps to break the fetter of doubt 15.207; it lessens the

strength of egotism 10.601–2; to keep up contact with spiritual experience 4.272; to overcome arrogance 17.607; reflection on impermanence to get rid of egoism 10.532; reflective meditation is a way of translating thoughts into the language of feeling 8.575

subjects for reflection
visionary experience 5.44; an aspect of the Dharma leading to; the beauty of the state of non-craving 16.447; conceptual formulations 4.145; contradictions 16.469; the positive mental events 17.588–90; everything that happens to you 22.xvii; what you've been studying 12.418, 19.449; the breath 15.110–12; the doctrine of mutual interpenetration 16.21–2; exchange of self and other 4.617; the five *skandhas* (*Satipaṭṭhāna Sutta*) 15.181–2; infinity of consciousness 4.80, 16.447; the past 15.91, 25.22–3; the suffering inflicted by human beings 26.677–8; the *Gārava Sutta* 26.627–32; no-thing-ness 16.447; the teaching that every human being is potentially a Buddha 4.176; the rarity of human birth and the suffering of human beings 1.417–19; the body as empty 2.144; dependent origination, the four noble truths, the three characteristics 20.302, 23.14–15; the web of causes and conditions 10.601–2; *śūnyatā* 5.523, 16.21; aphorisms for reflection (Batchelor) 8.575

see also
as *cintā-mayī prajñā*, *see under* three levels of wisdom; four mind-turning reflections; reflecting on the six elements, *see* six element practice; reflection on the *lakṣaṇas*, *see under* three *lakṣaṇas*; reflections on self and other, *see under* self/self and other

reformation

Buddhist
Buddhism has had four major reformations and is due for a fifth 12.116–18; what might a reformation be in the context of Buddhism? 12.115

the Protestant Reformation
Augsburg Confession 24.591; because the Roman Catholic Church wouldn't be reformed 15.712; brought freedom to choose one's religion 8.408; the Dissolution of the Monasteries 26.509; its effect on European religion 11.74–5; an end and a beginning 8.225; from the Reformation a breakdown of the traditional synthesis of knowledge 10.154; Henry VIII instigates the Reformation in England 13.551, 26.509; its essence was that you couldn't be saved by going through the motions 19.278; inaugurated by Martin Luther 12.114, 13.550, 19.278; a protest against the 'trade' of religion 10.593; questioned the value of the sacramental side of religion 3.194; a reaction against the religious despotism of the Middle Ages 7.86; weakened the Catholic Church 9.318

refuge 'Be ye islands unto yourselves, refuges unto yourselves' 2.142, 2.593, 7.50, 7.268, 15.583; a castle is the ultimate material refuge, and the ultimate expression of fear 18.49; derived by Buddhaghosa from *sarati*, 'to crush' 15.646; green as the colour of refuge 13.282; the idea of refuge 13.194; the language of refuge used in Buddhism since early times 2.727–8 (n600); a Refuge doesn't just improve conditions in *saṃsāra*, but enables you to transcend them 15.587–8; the term is liable to be misunderstood 11.468; *see also Dhammapada*/chapter 14; Going for Refuge; Three Refuges

Refuge Tree the Buddha on the Refuge Tree 11.717–18; depictions of the Refuge Tree 13.209–11; Anagarika Dharmapala on the Triratna Refuge Tree 8.xvii; female figures 13.209; the books on the Tree 11.718–20; getting to know the figures on the Refuge Tree 11.714–21, 12.539; if you can't see the Tree clearly, at least feel that it is there 13.211; the value of the inspiring lives of the figures on the tree 11.717, 11.720–1; illustrations 13.206, 13.210; a Refuge Tree with Vajradhara at the centre 24.315; represents the whole conception of refuge and its practical application 13.208; a thangka of a Tsongkhapa Refuge Tree 11.713; the Tree imagined rising up above the wheel of life 11.167; Triratna Tree of Refuge and Respect 11.713–21, 13.209–10, 22.xx–xxi; visualized in the offering of the mandala practice 13.262; visualization of the Refuge Tree 13.77–8, 13.204–11; you are yourself a significant figure in the

depiction of the Tree 13.208–9; *see also* Going for Refuge and Prostration Practice

refugees modern refugees 3.441; Tibetan, *see under* Tibet/people

Refuges and Precepts *see under* Going for Refuge/the Buddhist tradition

Refuges *see* Three Refuges; Going for Refuge

Rege, S. S. 10.660

regret a cause of regret to abandon any being 5.152–5; confession a heartfelt pouring forth of regret 4.46–7; as desire lessens, regret, hope, and fear diminish 7.285; giving without regret 1.432–3, 4.103; sometimes you regret what you're doing even while you're doing it 15.172; to be out of harmony with the Three Jewels is a great cause of regret 18.483; the important thing is to get on with Dharma practice and not waste time in regrets 22.477; wandering thoughts are the cause of all regrets 18.559; what would you regret not doing before you die? 16.302

regularity of meditation, *see under* meditation/working in meditation; if you do puja, do it regularly 11.221; regular Dharma study 1.27; regular lifestyle 12.381, 15.154; regular steps, *see* path of regular and irregular steps

Reich, Wilhelm popularity 4.605, 4.606; character armour 12.273, 19.90, 19.598 (n44), 23.108; orgasm 23.172, 23.323; theory of character types 12.273

reification

the way we reify things
asking what exactly is passed on at rebirth is just the mind reifying away 14.608; the nature of language has a reifying tendency 19.238–9; the reification of abstract thought 14.362; it is possible to reify Buddhism too much 14.434; the mind's tendency to refer to processes as if they were things 17.248–9; the Perfection of Wisdom relentlessly hunts down our attempts to reify concepts 14.606–7; real koan must be distinguished from playing around with reified concepts 14.422; reification is the child of literalism 8.620; there is a danger of reifying any abstract noun 11.656; the way we reify things is a direct reflection of our belief in the fixed self 17.383; we insist on reifying even the most obviously insubstantial aspects of our experience 17.408; we usually start off by thinking that there are things called emptiness and absolute mind 19.39

subjects of reification
the *bodhicitta* 4.263, 14.594; the concept of sameness 16.449; *dharmas* 15.183–4; karma 8.620; the *ālaya* 18.291; the non-existence of *dharmas* 14.439; suchness 14.595; *tathāgatagarbha* 14.175, 14.211

Reijn, Eric van 24.568–70

reincarnation the Dalai Lamas are the descendants (reincarnations) of the third abbot of Ganden 13.36; identifying reincarnations 'seems an inexact science' 8.608; Jamyang Khyentse one of five reincarnations of the original Khyentse Rimpoche 22.487, 22.554; Khubilghanic succession 13.36; resemblance between Ananda Metteyya and Sangharakshita – reincarnation? 23.41; Tibetan 'incarnations' who didn't think they were reincarnations at all 19.359, 22.491–2; a Tibetan teacher reincarnated as a Spanish boy 8.608; why Buddhism speaks of 'rebirth' rather than 'reincarnation' 3.198, 17.242; *see also* rebirth

Reis, Mafalda 23.442–4, 23.446

rejection accepting what is useful from tradition and rejecting what is not useful 9.402–3; the awareness that comes with rejection by a partner 17.225; bliss is not to be rejected 19.52; the characteristic of desire is to grasp one thing and reject another 7.411; a middle way between accepting the world on its own terms and rejecting it 12.394–5; the monk who rejected art as 'the product of greed, hatred, and delusion' 12.393; rejecting anything is almost always a sign of negative emotion 12.391; rejecting the idea of an 'essence' of Buddhism 13.509; *see also* 'as the ocean rejects a dead body' *under Udāna*/great ocean

rejoicing in merits (*puṇyanumodanā*)

what is it?
an expression of *mettā* and also faith in the teaching 11.267, 15.224; the difference between ordinary appreciation and rejoicing in merits 18.494; not just seeing the good side of people, but expressing it 4.593; one of the principal forms of kindly speech 2.380; recognizing objectively that there are positive forces at work in the universe 4.317; the Vajrayāna practice of acting out rejoicing in merits 18.377

its effects
antidote to hatred 2.389; balances confession 4.317; counters tendency to envy and greed 11.266, 16.329–30; gives one strength, inspiration, and

encouragement 1.412, 4.47, 16.329; helps us to move towards seeing people as they really are 15.164–5; teaches how wholesome roots can be transmuted into Enlightenment 14.144; makes you realize that you are not alone in this world, spiritually speaking 1.510; people who regularly rejoice in others' merits are at peace with themselves 11.267

rejoicing in merits as a practice
a pleasurable thing, so why be reluctant? 4.429–31; appreciating one's own good qualities 4.318; appreciating people's good qualities 4.68, 4.593–4; deliberate cultivation of rejoicing in merits 4.430–1, 26.17; everyone in a positive situation has played their part in creating it 19.536; expressing appreciation promptly 4.594, 4.596; the fewer merits we have, the more reason to rejoice in those of others 16.330; finding it difficult 4.594, 10.542, 16.330; it is a weakness of modern life that we don't do it enough 4.47, 4.317, 18.377; Order members should rejoice in each other's merits 12.481–2; poems rejoicing in merits 26.399; rejoice impersonally, like rejoicing that the sun is shining 11.266; rejoicing in one's own merits without egotism 10.542; repression stops people from rejoicing in the merits of others 11.268; *Sadhu!* 4.317, 4.695 (n241), 15.708, 15.774 (n269)

examples from the tradition
the Buddha explains to Cunda how to rejoice in someone's merits 4.695 (n241); the Buddha rejoices in the merits of his disciples 4.170–1, 10.573, 10.576, 18.222; rejoicing in the Buddha's merits 1.509, 11.269, 16.326; Upasena rejoices impartially in his own merits and those of others 10.541–2

rejoicing in the merits of ...
inspiring people: spiritual and secular heroines, and ordinary people 1.509–10; the noble lives of others 11.266; even those who seem to be set against you 15.326–7; all manifestations of the ideal, even those you don't follow 18.222–3; Dhardo Rimpoche 25.392; someone who has died 11.734; those who communicate the Dharma 11.734

see also
in the Sevenfold Puja, *see under* devotion/ Sevenfold Puja

relationships

introduction
what is the most important relationship in your life? 18.508–9; relationships are inevitable, but with whom, and of what kind? 18.507–9; the relation between human beings like the movement of dancers 7.276–7; emotional sustenance from our relationships 17.271; every human relationship has a self pole and an other pole 12.604–5; the assumption that 'relationships' means sexual relationships 13.445; 'People matter: relations between them don't matter much' 4.523; necessary for human development 3.400–1; not only reciprocal but complementary: rights and duties 7.277–80, 12.603–4

positive relationships
awareness of the nature and quality of your relationships 3.469; the best ones are based on sincerity, straightforwardness, mutual trust, confidence 26.27; ethical relationships are based on responsible attitudes 15.533; non-exploitation in relationships 3.592–4; in a sense a healthy relationship ceases to be a relationship 17.565

relationships and spiritual life
any personal relationship could get in the way of our spiritual growth 3.528; distinction between *kalyāṇa mitratā* and 'mundane' personal relationships 4.522–4; it's spiritual relationships that are valuable, not worldly ones 18.297–8; the modern retreat from religion to personal relationships 26.397; one's most important relationship is with one's source of inspiration 18.504–5; positive relationships have their value, but a spiritual relationship is different 26.28; putting yourself in someone else's hands: an unconditioned relationship 18.386; relationships as a hindrance to meditation (Śāntideva) 4.522–4; try to view relationships in their noumenal (diamond) aspect 7.402

complexities
attachment in relationships 15.313–14; the effort needed to develop positive elements in a relationship 19.116; missing someone 19.428–9, 23.59–61; mutual dependence and exploitation the basis of most human relationships 3.592–3; our relationships contain more than a little self-interest 15.313; people are at cross purposes because they do not really know each other 1.520; sentimentalizing reactive relationships 4.523–4; sustained by reactivity 4.508; investing all our emotional energies in one person 19.19; without the Dharma to refer to, relationships of any kind tend to end in disaster 18.214

relationships in different cultures and faiths in ancient Greece 3.523–4; in Confucianism 3.523, 11.696–7; in medieval Europe (feudal) 3.524, 11.697, 18.505

the network of relationships
introduction 3.521–609, 11.695–8, 13.450–1; our whole life could be seen as a network of personal relationships 12.602–3; the importance of having a network of long-standing relationships 18.336–7; only two relationships in modern life 3.527; the value of having a range of relationships 13.450–1; between employer and employee 3.581–8, 18.506–7, 26.654; between the layperson and ascetics and brahmins 3.591; between master and servant 3.524–6, 18.506, 22.522; between teacher and pupil 3.526–7; between siblings 3.527; economic relationships 3.581–2, 3.588; a working relationship with no thought of who does what 10.603

see also
family, *see under* family; friendship; 'horizontal' and 'vertical', *see under kalyāṇa mitratā*/the basis; with parents, *see under* parents; sexual relationships, *see* sexual relationships; *Sigālaka Sutta*, *see Dīgha Nikāya/Sigālaka Sutta*

relative truth *see* two truths

relativism ethical relativism 1.200–1, 7.377, 15.291, 15.488–9; the present time in world history is one of intense relativism 15.489–90

relativity the idea of relativity 12.464; of space and time, *see under* time/and space

relaxation alternating between exertion and relaxation, work and meditation 26.19; an attitude of sitting loose to life 12.164; being determined in a relaxed way 5.389; 'existential' relaxation 19.136; 'I decided to 'relax' for a while' 24.162; in the depth of relaxation you touch that which you are all the time 19.387; the Mahāmudrā's relaxed attitude: a key to the realization of your true nature 19.387; meditative absorption, a direct experience of relaxation and tranquillity 17.263; 'My mind is always at ease and non-doing' 18.613; no need to emphasize relaxation in the early days of the FWBO 18.584; one could speak in terms not of getting rid of craving, but of just relaxing 18.584; 'relax – do not force your mind or body' 5.299–302; relaxing through drinking a little wine (in early FWBO days) 14.573, 17.257, 19.331–2; relaxation at the deepest level of one's being 18.451–2; relaxing the ego 5.300–1; relaxing a little doesn't mean giving up effort altogether 18.638; relaxation while working 5.301–2; a state of complete spontaneity (Mahāmudrā) 19.136–7; on retreat, a combination of relaxation and alertness 23.134; you can't *make* yourself relax 5.300, 18.584

relevance all Dharma teachings are good, but they are not equally relevant here and now 19.545–7; the Buddha's teaching about mutual relationship is relevant to social life everywhere 12.604; fundamentalists' insistence on the observation of irrelevant rules 7.262–3; it's important to be able to discern what is relevant to oneself 18.517–18; to accept the Buddha Jewel as an ideal is to acknowledge its relevance to us 3.393; there needs to be some element of the Dharma that is not 'relevant' to us at all 14.481; we are attracted to texts that seem relevant to our spiritual needs 16.247–8

reliance *see* self-reliance

reliances *see* four reliances

relics do relics really have spiritual power? 19.327; the tendency of the church to preserve relics 16.158; the human desire to preserve relics is a forgivable failing 16.141, 16.158; *śarīras* – the pearl-like relics of great yogis 16.158–9, 18.535, 22.395; Tibetan and Chinese practice of mummifying the teacher 16.159; worship of relics in Buddhism 16.142, 16.154, 22.92–3; the Buddha's, *see under* Buddha/I life story/last days; Sacred Relics of Sāriputta and Moggallāna, *see* Sacred Relics

religion

WHAT IS RELIGION?

the word
discomfort with using the word 'religion' 16.500, 26.43; it means one thing for Buddhists and another for followers of other religions 10.350–1; its original meaning akin to the Buddhist understanding of faith 17.554; the vagueness and ambiguity of this protean word 26.151; the word 'religion' is very troublesome 10.252

definitions
the achievement of a state of psychological wholeness 12.43, 12.46; a catalogue of the states of mind and actions recognized as religious (Aldous Huxley) 26.151–62; a collective designation for all the individual religions 12.42; the difficulty of definition 26.151–2; the encouragement of the individual to develop spiritual

qualities 15.81; human dissatisfaction finds expression as religion 7.114–15; it is what you are prepared to die for, it is your life 10.342; it originated when the first rogue met the first fool (Voltaire) 12.41; 'morality touched by emotion' (Matthew Arnold) 11.75; no such thing as religion 13.429; not acceptance of creed or dogma, the achievement of a series of experiences 7.357; not remote from life, but life become conscious of its tendency to develop 16.99; to recognize the Divine everywhere in the universe 7.86–7, 7.575 (n161); religion is always conservative, it would seem 16.365; self-transcendence is the true meaning 4.656; a shout, a shake, to wake us up 16.170; 'a system of belief in worship of God' leaves out non-theistic religions 12.135; those who say all religions are gates to Heaven are hypocrites 7.88; total concern with what is of ultimate value 12.43; the truly religious life is the life of egolessness 26.163; what in your heart of hearts you most deeply believe 10.340–1; what the individual does with his solitariness 12.40–1, 12.82, 15.705–6

descriptions
adaptation *to* Reality, not adaptation *of* Reality 7.133; are religions always embedded in social and cultural realities? 13.376–7; association with gloom 1.506, 11.155; the balance between subjective and objective 15.707; based on fear 26.155; built into the very structure of Reality 7.317; can be regarded as either solar or lunar 16.163; concern should be not with converts, buildings, proofs, but with evolving beings 12.90; the essential religious question 3.209; they try to justify their teachings to the intellect and recommend them to the feelings 26.164; the fundamental religious state of mind is a sense of absolute fearlessness 26.162; the giving of buns and blankets 1.428; gold mixed with ore 26.13; intended to eradicate reason, it has become an agent for augmenting it 7.281; is religion escapism? 7.217–24; it must have both a private and a public aspect 15.705–6; it need not be identified exclusively with 'religious experience' 11.305; the masses use it in an irreligious, semi-magical way 12.47; it must penetrate the desiderative depths of the psyche 1.124, 7.392; it's wrong to say it's found in musty books, not in flowers or music 7.283; most people unfortunately consider themselves excluded 7.283–4; the nearer to a religion's geographical centre, the nearer to its spirit (Conze) 13.106; not for everyone, but for those who have developed some self-awareness 12.45–7; nothing in religious life is truly esoteric except spiritual experience 7.359; often just part of *saṃsāra* 19.468–9; 'the opium of the people' 10.72–3; purports to bring freedom but keeps us enslaved 16.499–500; religion is essentially the experience of egolessness 26.14; religions arising from rationalization of belief in self 17.619–20; religions have their own mythologies 13.583; a religion's unworldliness is its greatest asset 8.539; religious consciousness is not a separate kind of consciousness 26.14; there are antinomies in any religion 7.39–40; truth and righteousness are more important than externals (the Buddha) 1.274; two trends: focus on the present life and focus on the hereafter 7.169; the universal perspective of the parable of the burning house 16.76–8; we are all bound on the same pilgrimage 7.364–5; what relief does it give the downtrodden? (Ambedkar) 10.58; the world's spiritual traditions 11.19

religion in theory and in practice
all religious people face a terrible gulf between theory and practice 1.493–4; burning a little incense at the shrine of religion 12.23; combination of materialism and piety 17.211; conventional religiosity has become quite flat and stale 12.44–5; ethics strips religion down to its essentials 7.173; the extremes of altruistic and solitary practice 7.149–50; if religion is not inherent in ordinary life, there is something amiss 14.419; if we practised our religions, would argument between us cease? 7.146, 7.588 (n246); is the goal of religious endeavour impossible to achieve? 7.168; it isn't easy to reform an established religion 15.712; it often has nothing to do with spiritual life, but is a matter of group politics 15.622–3; looking for distraction in religion 19.468–9; making a great show of practising religion 14.419; most are religious not from inner urge, but collective pressure 7.148; nominal practice of religion 3.41–2; people's behaviour can be based on principles opposite to those they profess 2.80–1; quarrels in the name of religion 7.90; religious activity with no clear purpose 7.148; religious projection 16.96; religious teachings as rationalizations of craving 12.99, 12.711 (n76); society has the habit of regarding certain actions as religious in themselves 7.283; theory is one thing, practice another 7.391; the truest religious action is one with no feeling that 'I am the doer' 7.408; we have enough to make us hate, but not enough to make us

love one another 10.283, 26.195; in the West we have no tradition of being taught religion in a practical way 17.606–7; whatever beliefs people profess, their behaviour is usually similar 19.229; why do people feel the need to pay it lip service? 19.246–7

common features
'all religions different manifestations of the Supreme Reality': no Buddhist could agree 8.167; asks who we are in relation to ourselves, other humans, and ultimate reality 12.42–3; the continuity of the religious quest, not equation of doctrines 7.212–13; every religion believes it's right, but they differ in how they treat those who disagree 17.21–2; from every religion we can learn something 7.146; influenced by secular philosophies 10.344–50; the image of the path means different things to different religions 15.81; recognize that the eradication of egoism is the central task of spiritual life 7.405–6; the view that all religions teach the same thing is itself intolerant 11.670–1; wherever produced, all can guide and sustain all people of all periods of history 7.81

art and culture
art and philosophy as substitutes for religion 12.45; art and religion overlap 25.26, 26.148; can attract people to religion, but become an end in itself 19.469–70; culture is the greatest friend of religion and also its greatest enemy 19.469; every creative writer is the founder of a new religion 26.67; relationship between religion and culture 13.507–9; art may allow some to experience the values in the past mediated by religion 26.195; a religion's art tends to flourish or decline with the religion 22.266; religious literature has two modes, one intellectual, the other emotional 14.109–10

Buddhism as a religion
Buddhism as an institutional religion 2.185; Buddhism is Religion in its classical and archetypal form 26.161–2; Buddhism proclaims freedom from religion 26.155; Buddhist teachers concerned with the functions of 'respectable' religion 18.164; Buddhists should stop letting other religions tell them what they 'really' believe 22.78; communicating the Dharma to someone who is suspicious of religion 19.207; the discrepancies between Buddhism and other religions 26.154–62; if any religion could cope with modern scientific needs, it would be Buddhism 1.471; is Buddhism a religion? 12.94; an international religion 7.430; it fulfils the requirements of religion (Ambedkar) 9.104–8; 'not a religion in the full sense of the word' 3.44–5; respect for the followers of other religions 10.279, 15.669–71; seeing that the truth is beyond words distinguishes it from other religions 7.331; some people prefer to think of it as a philosophy 15.250

THE STUDY OF RELIGION

historical developments
the continuity of Western religious life disrupted by Christianity 4.107; the development of religion, East and West 7.84–91; differences of religion dividing families in the 19th century 12.464; the effect of Darwin's theory of evolution 11.75; the effect of the Reformation on European religion 11.74–5; evolutionary thinking and the development of religion 4.22; the historical development of spiritual communities 3.428–33; the history of religion is the history of the mind or heart of man 7.364; the personalist understanding of religious significance 13.399, 13.428–9; religion doesn't develop 14.602; religion has repeatedly made the mistake of 'carrying the raft' 7.159, 13.437; the *saṃskāras* of the religious experiences of humanity still live within us 7.364–5; shows how often the spirit has been confused with the letter 7.158–9; split from secularism in the West 16.128–9; spread by the growth of empire 7.86–7; when earth's powers served religion and religion's forces blessed the earth 23.265; the World's Parliament of Religions (1893) 8.44–5, 8.47–9, 10.280

comparative religion
building correlations between religions arise from a fear of missing out 14.602; cannot work out the form Western Buddhism will take 14.270; making sense of Buddhism, we may understand our former religion better 2.245; comparison of one religion with another cannot but misrepresent them 26.630; consolidated in the West in the 19th century 7.84–8; difficult for one religion to operate with the concepts of the other 11.298, 11.496; early monastic study of comparative religion 2.197; an idea about why clergymen are interested in it 17.106; inaugurated by the Buddha in the *Brahmajāla Sutta* 7.364; inaugurated in Europe by Roger Bacon 7.85–6, 7.364; new interest among people in finding out about other faiths 12.129–30; the question of when and where monotheistic ideas emerged

14.602; replacing sectarian religious instruction with comparative religion 12.51–2; Snellgrove's reflections 8.602; some religions are more advanced than others 16.77; the study of the evolution of our own consciousness 7.365; study of the way religions have influenced each other 8.126–7; tolerance of Buddhism for other religions 15.265; the ultimate truths of other religions symbolize something beyond the material 14.459; Western teachers of Eastern religions 8.628–9; you can't understand your own religion except in relation to others 12.130

RELIGIOUS ISSUES IN THE MODERN WORLD

modern developments
all religions are under pressure from the changes brought by scientific methods 8.280–1; coming to terms with higher criticism and scientific discovery 13.427; for many, art is replacing religion 26.329

is religion necessary?
'Is religion necessary?' 12.39–48; just think of becoming a human being, no need to bring in religion 10.252; spiritual renewal need not be Christian 8.430–1; suffering from lack of religion 5.665–6

not feeling the need
getting by without religion 12.45; in modern life people are indifferent to religion 12.44–5; is there a religious type? 12.282; modern antagonism towards religion 7.217; 'Most men are really atheists' 7.88

choosing a religion
assessing the truth of different religions 2.246; being told what to believe 7.267; conscious individual commitment 15.711–12; diversity on the basis that a human being is first and foremost a human being 9.351; eclecticism usually involves an evasion of the real issues 12.52; freedom to choose 9.118–19, 9.184; following the religion in which you were born 12.50, 12.52; how to decide between the rival claims of religious teachings 1.60; if you will only change to a religion that's the same as your old one, why change? 14.602; in practice, it's meaningless to think of taking in lots of religious traditions 18.381; it 'cannot be taught, it can only be caught' 9.446, 26.56; 'passing over' into a different religion and returning to your own with new insights 8.432; requirements of religion (Ambedkar) 9.104–8, 9.181–6; should we be free to choose our own religion? 12.50–1; taking up an Eastern religion as a substitute for Christianity 26.256–7; we have more freedom to choose than ever before 8.408–9

decline or renewal
it will decline if it doesn't have capable preachers (Ambedkar) 16.185; loss of faith in religion 9.181, 12.47–8; many religions lose their hold because they ask us to believe impossibilities 10.169; the modern retreat from religion to personal relationships 26.397; on the decline 10.185; religions that have gone rotten with age are good for compost, not food 26.13; a religious tradition can never be regarded as higher than it was when it began 8.457; the sphere of religion has shrunk 1.28–9; updating religion 8.609; we may not like to think that a religion can be wiped out, but it can 13.103; Western religion in a state of decay 13.511

THEISTIC AND NON-THEISTIC RELIGIONS

theistic
introduction 9.228; the assumption that morality requires belief in God 8.281–2; authority in theistic religions 12.228, 15.617–21; the *Brahmajāla Sutta*'s critique of theism 13.435, 14.603; Christianity is the theistic religion *par excellence* 11.296; come from the construction of pseudo-ontologies 8.441; criticism of theistic religion 13.412–13; the Dalai Lama makes a distinction between theistic and non-theistic religions 12.677; the danger of theism represented by the sixth and seventh fetters 2.149; don't mistake Mahāyāna Buddhism for a kind of theism 7.535–7, 14.602–3; draw a distinction between the human mind and the 'mind of God' 17.437; have no self-critique 16.515; in the theistic religions God is in a sense Nature 15.618–19; list of theistic religions 11.296, 12.42; modern difficulty in accepting theistic religion 12.55; not influential in the India of the Buddha's day 10.517, 14.601; the Perfection of Wisdom brushes off the theistic viewpoint 14.601; popular religion satirized 26.397; referred to in the Pāli canon 10.517; theistically inclined mystics believe that their experiences come from God 16.98; theists can struggle to understand why God lets them suffer 15.370; tend to be corrupted by power and authority 3.447–8; in the West we're brought up to think that religion is necessarily theistic 12.94

non-theistic
an ancient idea 12.7; Buddhism as non-theistic, *see under* Buddhism I/what

Buddhism is not; the connection between non-theistic religion and meditation 12.10; humanistic religions 12.42, 12.227–8; list of non-theistic religions 11.296, 12.42; non-theistic religions 12.94, 12.135; religion does not necessarily imply belief in God 8.282

UNIVERSAL AND ETHNIC RELIGION

ethnic religion
brief introduction 12.42; belong to the lower evolution 12.244; contrasted with missionary religion 26.13; depend on a particular place 10.245; a group (ethnos) by definition 3.447, 12.54, 12.243, 16.364; has no one founder and no individual followers 12.243; Hinduism as an ethnic religion, *see under* Hinduism; list of ethnic religions 11.296, 12.54; one cannot be converted to an ethnic religion 12.54–5, 12.243; turning Buddhism into an ethnic religion: the worst of betrayals 8.471; values that ensure the survival of the group 12.243

universal religion
brief introduction 12.42; appears in the context of an ethnic religion 12.249–50; belongs to the higher evolution 12.244–5; Buddhism and Christianity as universal religions 11.295–6; Buddhism is the sole non-theistic universal religion 12.55; ideally has no place for power 3.447; may express itself in cultures, but is not identified with them 12.244; the religion of any individual at any time or place, potentially 12.243–4; its true purpose is to produce Buddhas 3.478; theistic and non-theistic 12.55; traditionally concerned with the higher evolution 3.483–4; very few people are capable of truly following one 12.251; you must be personally converted 12.244

relationship between ethnic and universal
conflict between them 10.443, 10.447; degeneration of universal into ethnic 3.443, 3.483–4, 8.471, 12.250–3, 12.644, 22.93; ethnic integrated with universal 13.274; relation between them 23.178; Sarasvatī represents their coming together 16.367; transition from ethnic to universal 9.100; universal has its roots in ethnic 12.253; universal has to make use of ethnic elements 16.162; universal speaks the language of ethnic culture 16.367

RELIGIONS OF REVELATION AND DISCOVERY

religions of revelation
Buddhism is not a 'revealed religion' in this sense 14.453; degeneration of certain Buddhist sects into 7.370; emphasize the weakness and sinfulness of human nature 7.366; examples of religion as revelation 7.368; their faith in infallibility leads to fanaticism and persecution 7.366–7; founders regarded as prophets or messengers of God 7.366; place responsibility for salvation on the shoulders of the Other 7.368

religions of discovery
examples of religion as discovery 7.368; the founder is simply one who shows the way 7.367; hold that the way of truth can be discovered by unaided human effort 7.367; inspire by appealing to innate strength and goodness 7.367; require not blind faith but clear-sighted understanding 7.367; tolerant 7.367

the relationship between the two
considered in relation to the Buddha's threefold way 7.369; the intellectual formulation of a spiritual difficulty we all face 7.365; the psychological basis of their divergence 7.368; 'Religion as Revelation and as Discovery' 7.364–71, 26.690; religion as revelation is included in religion as discovery 7.371

FURTHER PERSPECTIVES ON RELIGION

alternative traditions
in Christianity, *see under* Christianity/further perspectives; fringe religious groups 3.6; Voltaire's advice on starting a new religion 11.382

personal religion
both private and personal *and* objective and public 13.399; characterized in personalistic terms 13.399; choosing between one's religion and death 16.198; your 'own' religion is not necessarily the one you were born into 8.433; the view that religion is a personal and private matter 13.398–402; the woman who changed her religion seventeen times 3.6–7

problems with religion
the anxiety and guilt traditionally associated with it 15.331; conventional religiosity is a hindrance to Enlightenment 3.256; criticism of religion 7.145, 16.515, 19.546; the danger of institutions and activities becoming ends in themselves 18.164; destruction of religion as an end in itself 14.362–3, 16.505; distinction between personal and institutional religion 1.191–202, 1.227; the *Heart Sūtra* eliminates religion considered as an end in itself 14.362–3; how do we make sure that religion does not crush the individual? 16.500; if you feel that someone's religion

is damaging them, how do you deal with that? 11.671; the minute you start invoking power, it ceases to be religion 15.623; misunderstanding of other religions 7.87; 'one should not live by trading on religion' 10.593; people thinking that if you don't belong to their religion they must hate you 10.283; perhaps sticking to conventional religious forms will prove to be unrealistic 26.7; persecution 15.623, 16.198; quarrels in the name of religion 7.90; religion based on realization smiles at criticism 7.145; religious organizations that interpret success in terms of numbers 8.xxiv; religious zeal as a disguise for ill-nature 8.172; representatives of an old religion will always try to keep you inside it 10.280; repressive religions are afraid of emotion 7.290; some get carried away by the desire for numbers 19.468; split between faith and reason 14.443; those founded on a dualistic philosophy create a split in the psyche 7.401; transcendental critique 16.499–516; we don't like changing deep-rooted religious assumptions 12.10; we should have outgrown conventional religiosity 16.394; the weakness of religious people who have repressed their energy to be 'good' 18.78

pseudo-religions
Christianity could be considered to be a pseudo-religion 17.18–19; Communism as a pseudo-religion 17.18; people totally dedicating themselves to pseudo-religious groups 15.489–90; teachings which pass as religious but are not at all 16.78, 19.546; uncritical acceptance of the unprovable, leading to persecution and fanaticism 7.145

modern sects
Children of God 17.40, 17.711 (n43); what people look for in a sect 17.40

reluctance *arhants*' and bodhisattvas' reluctance to meet Vimalakīrti 16.455, 16.501–14; modern reluctance to respect or revere superior spiritual qualities 4.168, 4.345; one should be reluctant to come to a value judgement about somebody 10.591; rejoicing in merits is a pleasurable thing, so why be reluctant? 4.429–31; sometimes it would be better to make more effort, but don't force yourself too often 10.604–5; an unwillingness to find out about things, because of reluctance to change 3.293, 10.250

Rembrandt van Rijn depictions of the qualities of humanity 26.370; his genius 15.194; 'the most wretchedly painted signboard ... show that a Rembrandt once lived in the world' 3.58; the *Flayed Ox* 26.362–3; *Philosopher in Meditation* 26.268

remorse confessing with a heart on fire with remorse 1.411; confession to eliminate remorse and replace it with delight 2.259, 3.265–6; 'Don't become one who is later remorseful' (the Buddha) 3.670 (n287); Mañjuśrī goes to extreme lengths to free bodhisattvas from obsessive remorse 14.183; purged through the practice of generosity and ethics 2.105; to be distinguished from irrational guilt 2.260

ren (or *jen*, human-heartedness) *see under* Confucius

Renaissance, the in certain respects the art of the Renaissance represents a decline 24.273–4; challenge of Christian ideas 14.443; difference between Western and oriental renaissance 14.288–9; inspiration from Renaissance sources 26.252; Sangharakshita's early response to the Renaissance 20.32; prediction of a Renaissance inspired by oriental culture 7.88, 12.79, 14.287–9, 26.201, 26.256–9; the keen eye for individuality of the Renaissance 23.315; Neoplatonic philosophy in Renaissance art 26.245; the recovery of the classics of Greece and Rome 14.287–8; the revival of Platonism 23.297; the stream of religious tradition began to flow outside the Church 13.511; Symonds's *The Renaissance in Italy* 13.550, 20.32, 23.249–50; when people started emancipating themselves from the tutelage of religion 16.128

Renan, J. E. 2.627

Rennyo 2.566, 2.746 (n698)

renunciation (Sanskrit *naiṣkramya*, Pāli *nekkhamma*)

the nature of renunciation
active demonstration of what we know to be true 7.97; unless you renounce attraction to life, whatever you do won't be Dharma practice 8.593; you give up what is relatively satisfying for what is truly satisfying 17.363; it is significant only if it reflects an inner experience 18.36; learn to renounce during your life and you will be happy in the hour of death 8.199; the living symbol of the truth that we have no self 1.173; as necessary to attaining perfect love as to attaining perfect knowledge 7.95; no spiritual development without renunciation 12.479–80; the spirit of renunciation renders fruitful all one's religious observances 26.33; renunciation

of 'mine' is not possible without renunciation of 'me' 1.414; understanding the hollowness of every kind of mundane existence 1.308; Brother Lawrence's renunciation 9.96–7; renunciation in Hinduism 19.201

some perspectives from the Buddhist tradition
the begging-bowl as a symbol of renunciation 7.397; the Buddha's great renunciation 3.461; 'Renounce what lies in the future, give up that which is past …' (*Dhammapada*) 7.285; polarization between world-fulfilment and world-renunciation 1.274, 20.234–5; Enlightenment achieved by renouncing self-desires and views based on them 1.20; all is renounced for others so that all, including others, may be renounced 4.624; Vimalakīrti's perspective 16.511; more merit from accepting the *Diamond Sūtra* than renouncing everything 14.480–1; the bliss of renunciation represented by Padmasambhava's skull cup 12.335; Milarepa on the subject of what you don't need 18.618–22; Milarepa renounces attachment in order to enjoy freedom 18.54; the views of the different *yānas* 19.330–1

giving things up
be careful how you use the language of giving up 18.215; begin to enjoy being a Buddhist before you give up too much 16.285; being selective about what one wants to give up 18.493; the bodhisattva ideal is more inspiring 4.62; do you have to give things up? 4.455–7; don't use the need for enjoyment to rationalize not giving up anything at all 16.285; giving things up or transforming them? – views of different schools 19.330–1; giving up ideas of 'I' and 'mine' 7.361; giving up smoking 4.423, 4.617, 10.223, 17.303; in what sense can one 'give up the world'? 18.316; it need not involve hardship if you are in contact with spiritual friends 17.364; lay people not yet willing to give up pleasures 4.564–5; men will rarely make any sacrifice except for the sake of gain 7.96; monastic life obviously involves giving something up 1.274; the monk doesn't 'give up the world' 15.492–3; not giving up, but growing up 1.497; rationalizations about renunciation 16.285, 19.331; regarding giving something up as self-denial rather than training 17.253; the sense in which the Tantra doesn't require one to give anything up 17.595; suggestions of things to give up 12.479; trying to develop spiritually without giving up one's affluent lifestyle 11.613; to give up small pleasures in the hope of enjoying greater ones later is a gamble 17.301

the practice
experimenting with depriving oneself of sense satisfaction 5.677; ethics as a continual renunciation of the self 26.111; constant perseverance in stern renunciation 7.358; outer and inner renunciation 7.397; every Buddhist needs to think more in terms of renunciation 12.479–80; 'Since I started taking Buddhism seriously, what have I given up?' 1.496; pleasure from a life of renunciation 17.226–7; priding oneself on one's abstentions 7.281; to live the life of renunciation authentically, love the Dharma passionately 18.133; to renounce everything is necessary, but what about your wish to help others? 4.568–9; we can't always wait for things to drop away 12.480; you suffer at first, but after a while it becomes easy 4.423; Westerners respond better to growth and development than renunciation 19.200–1

things that could be given up
no single pattern of renunciation 1.497; attachment to the body 1.155; caste 9.532–3; consciousness 5.483; consumerism 16.412; drinking 3.323, 9.410; egoism and selfishness, all sense of 'I' 1.237, 3.579, 7.406; everything 11.132; the group 3.461; meat 1.357, 3.370, 4.111, 10.49; narrow, exclusive attachment for the sake of a wider vision 18.215; old ways 9.225, 9.265, 10.257; possessions 1.497, 8.199; the sense of possession 18.219; 'renouncing a gift' 14.478; smoking 4.423, 4.617, 10.223, 17.303; space: the simile of the broken pot 5.482; the toys and tales of childhood 3.36, 18.589; turmoil 18.452; worldly commitments 4.455; wrong views about Buddhism 9.265–6

see also
the bodhisattva's 'renunciation' of liberation *under* bodhisattva/bodhisattva activity; giving up; going forth; Siddhārtha Gautama/going forth

Renxiaowen, Empress 14.260

repa ('cotton-clad one') 18.462, 19.177, 19.366

repentance a 'bad' man shattered into humility and repentance 7.407; Milarepa's 18.160–1; Rechungpa's 13.176–7, 19.5–167

repetition the belief that a single heartfelt repetition of Amitābha's name is enough 24.540; the constant repetition of positive

actions is very important in Buddhism 17.525; developing concentration through mantra repetition 5.461; don't approach life as endless repetition 15.504–5; don't be afraid of repeating yourself in a talk, but let it be intentional 12.588–9; the effect of mantra repetition 22.29–30; mechanical repetition of Refuges and Precepts, *see under* Going for Refuge/taking the Refuges and Precepts; mistaken omission of 'unnecessary repetitions' from the Pure Land *sūtras* 1.333–4; occult forces invoked through repetition of the Sacred Word 2.215–16; repeating the bodhisattva vow 100,000 times 13.81–2; repeating the same patterns again and again 18.276–7; repetitions in the scriptures for emphasis 14.456; the symbol of the path or way is repeated with every conceivable variation 7.297–8; 'There is nothing whatever which is difficult after repetition' 4.423; the value of repeating verses over and over again 14.481–2; the Vajrayāna emphasizes the value of repetition 13.81–2

reporting in (Triratna practice) 24.162, 24.356, 24.645 (n193)

representation an individual Order member can't represent the Order 14.541–2; if you are really a Buddhist, you can't represent Buddhism 14.542–3

repression calmness can be the result of repressed energy 15.219; to deal with hindrances to meditation, *see under* five hindrances; energy locked away in habitual patterns 18.77; experiencing anger or desire is better than repressing it 17.599; Freud's view of how emotions are repressed 5.657–8, 10.608, 12.265–6; no negative mental states should ever be repressed 26.65; the idea of repression 12.464; it stops people from rejoicing in the merits of others 11.268; the purpose of retrieving repressed memories 15.88; religious people may be weak because to be 'good' they have repressed their energy 18.78; repression as an antidote to mental hindrances 1.560, 4.382; the repression of devotional feelings in a secular society 14.534; repression of negative emotions 3.487, 12.265–6; repression of positive emotions 4.256–7, 4.597–8, 14.533–4; repressions uncovered during analysis or therapy 15.150, 16.97; repressive religions are afraid of emotion 7.290; self-torture is like repression in the Freudian sense 10.608; without instinctual repression there could be no civilization (Freud) 24.463–4; you need not repress a feeling, but you may have to control its expression 15.494

Reps, Paul (*Zen Flesh, Zen Bones*) Hakuin and the child 11.283, 14.490; the story of the monk who carried the girl across the stream 2.71, 8.496; the story of the overflowing cup 11.278–9, 17.208; the story of the young man and the umbrella 3.286, 9.295, 12.260–1

repulsion from the mundane through wisdom, from the transcendental through compassion 1.419; innumerable forms of attraction to pleasure and repulsion from pain 7.392; *nirveda* (Pāli *nibbidā*), *see nirveda*

repulsiveness of the body *see aśubha bhāvanā*

reputation defence of Sangharakshita's reputation 1966) 23.403; hypocrisy: attachment to our faults and also to our reputation 17.284–5; the importance of keeping a good reputation when living in a village 10.644; it's said that reputation is one of the last attachments to be given up 11.283, 18.461

requisites *see* eight requisites

resentment (*upanāha*) at class inequality 15.716–17; at a sense of powerlessness in society 18.457–8; Burns' character 'nursing her wrath to keep it warm' 17.645; in modern society, people have everything they need and still feel deprived 17.269–70; dealing with resentment in family life 18.455–6; feeling resentful when someone dies 17.564; if anger is unexpressed, it becomes resentment or even hatred 15.303, 17.268–9; if imprisoned, even unjustly, don't give way to resentment 18.458; if you allow yourself to be exploited, sooner or later you will resent it 26.17; if you're not getting the respect you want 19.517–18; it needs to be checked in the early stages, before it gets too strong 17.646–7; leading to inactivity 10.604; the less committed should feel resentful towards the more committed 26.44; the nature of resentment 19.35–6; a notable feature of many marriages 17.646–7; often not based on anything people have done 15.305; Rechungpa's resentment 19.12–13, 19.35–7, 19.58–9; resentment at modern life expressed in criminal activities 11.78; resentment left over from childhood 14.573, 15.305, 19.58–9; resentment of the welfare state 17.269; as an *upakleśa* (Abhidharma) 17.645–6; we feel we have a right to our resentment 17.646; you can't take out your resentment on other people, so you take it out on yourself 10.524–5

resilience human nature is highly resilient even under difficult circumstances 4.423

resistance emotional resistance expressed by energy-sapping doubt 14.586; best confronted 17.418; ceasing to offer any resistance to the *kleśas* 17.676–7; to being helped out of a negative state 17.669; to being on retreat 5.382; to the *bodhicitta* 4.263–4; to change 3.293–4, 4.150, 15.520; to facing the challenge of existence 13.356–7; disguising a 'won't' as a 'can't' 5.692; to making any effort 5.679–80; many of us have a deep resistance to clarity in our approach to the Dharma 17.391; in meditation, *see under* meditation/working in meditation; powerful measures are needed to break through one's resistance to impermanence 15.180–1; to pressure 17.459; sloth is the weight of one's existence resisting further evolving 26.47; unconscious resistance to change you are consciously trying to make 17.255

resolution and resolve admit unskilful action, try to make up for it, resolve not to do it again, and forget it 3.265; the bodhisattva's resolve to rescue all beings 2.158–9; the Buddha resolves to worship the Dharma principle – why? 3.66–7; confession is not breast-beating, but a realistic appraisal and a resolve to do better 4.46; confession must include resolution to change 16.313; doing something you've said you'll do requires a firm resolution 19.286–7; firm resolution is the opposite of *vicikitsā* (doubt, the second fetter) 19.286–7; if you haven't made a firm resolution you don't get very far 19.286; make a resolution to do something specific to help spread the Dharma 8.192–3; making a resolution in front of a shrine 8.193; New Year resolutions 8.190–3, 8.311, 16.313; *praṇidhāna* (resolve, aspiration) 7.295; in relation to sin, have awareness, contrition, and resolve to change 1.411; the need to resolve an attitude of infantile dependence 12.232; the one thing to be concerned with: your resolve to gain Buddhahood 19.131; resolving to gain Enlightenment for the benefit of all 8.201; to turn over a new leaf 16.313; vows are taken to strengthen one's resolve 1.421, 4.65; you can't resolve your doubts theoretically and then start on the spiritual life 10.577–8

resources even if you lose everything, you have inner resources to draw on 17.341; exhausting the spiritual resources you have built up 19.550; giving oneself: not to be practised before one has developed the inner resources 3.369; inner resources 18.300; the need for resources to spread the Dharma 8.176; people's needs are very great, and one may not have the resources to meet all of them 18.593; replenishing your spiritual resources 19.550; using as few of the earth's resources as possible 12.670; think of yourself as a resource for the world 17.204; wasting natural resources 15.283, 16.386–7

respect an attitude of interest, openness, warm curiosity 17.261; a bodhisattva precept to show respect for your seniors in bodhisattva ordination 13.56; combination of respect and affection: contrast in India and the West 4.610–11; different people's ways of showing respect to the Buddha 4.295, 9.337–8, 11.250; feel the respect that you genuinely feel, whether for the Hīnayāna or the Mahāyāna 4.349; for the followers of other religions 10.279, 15.669–71; for the Three Jewels 4.326–7; for others who have more knowledge than you in your field 4.345–6; ideas, institutions, and practices are not necessarily worthy of respect due to mere antiquity 2.648; parents, teachers, elders, and the truly great should be shown respect 2.599, 10.273, 12.678–9; pay the greatest respect to even the slightest manifestation of something spiritual 4.435; refusal to recognize someone as deserving of respect 12.13–14, 15.714–20; respect towards members of the Sangha 17.261; showing respect for people's feelings 25.17; showing respect to the Three Jewels 15.668–9; to place something on your head is a sign of respect 13.107, 19.568; Tibetans' great respect for books and images 13.107; those who demand respect will never feel they are getting enough 17.208; we assume that the more we know about people, the less we will find to respect 17.276; in the West teachers are not greatly respected 17.606

see also
reverence; self-respect; for the robe, *see under* robes; lack of respect, *see* disrespect

respectability became all-important in the industrial age 18.101; Buddhist teachers concerned exclusively with the functions of 'respectable' religion 18.164; Christmas Humphreys' concern to adhere to middle-class respectability 23.404, 23.406; conflation of self-respect and respectability 18.134; the difference between respectability and virtue 4.110; if Buddhists agree to become 'respectable', Buddhism ceases to be Buddhism 18.135; a narrow and rigid monasticism can be turned into Buddhist respectability 18.135;

submission to group norms 18.134–6; Tantric Buddhism's abandonment of respectability 1.201

respiration-mindfulness *see* mindfulness of breathing

responsibility

personal responsibility
an aware attitude will be a responsible, ethical one 13.456; the Buddha takes responsibility for a situation, though not of his making 11.441; developing your own sense of responsibility 15.266–7; an ethical relationship with someone involves a responsible attitude 15.533; every individual is responsible for their own destiny 4.124; it means keeping your word 17.696; the mind has a certain responsibility for its own ideas 19.195; the responsibility of the true individual 3.473, 16.428; self-surrender and giving up responsibility 15.661–2; take a teacher's advice seriously, but take responsibility for yourself 17.308; to make any situation creative for yourself and others 3.473; in the spiritual context you can't hand over responsibility to someone else 14.541; using the *anātman* doctrine to avoid personal responsibility 17.625; you are not responsible for other people 14.578

taking responsibility for ...
your actions 11.262–3, 13.609, 16.323, 16.427; your conclusions 17.626; the effect of what you say 17.190–1; putting your principles into practice 18.111; taking care of yourself 15.289–90; who you really are 18.147–8; your egotism 19.111; your feelings 15.159; your spiritual life 18.98; your own growth 3.473, 11.147, 19.284; your own life 19.580; your own life, growth, happiness 26.12; the situations you find yourself in 15.174–5; your decisions and experience 15.290–1; your enjoyment 18.130; your thoughts, words, and actions 10.141; your own faith 10.495; your own mental states 5.349, 17.433, 19.273

responsibility for others
a mother takes responsibility for her children 15.323; the family man's responsibilities in ancient India 10.449, 10.485; Going for Refuge involves responsibility to others 14.446; the responsibility of doctors and nurses for their patients 15.323; to stop a person acting in case they act wrongly takes away their responsibility 7.245

taking on responsibilities
it means doing what you say you'll do 17.696–7; should involve both altruism and support for one's development 4.91; for preserving and disseminating the Dharma 8.271–2; for spreading the Buddhist movement 9.242; handing on responsibility for ordination 2.512–13

wider responsibilities
being held responsible for the actions of your government 14.543; failure to accept responsibility in modern society 16.431–2; ideally no need for government because we would each take responsibility 16.478; if everyone bears their share of responsibility, no room for authoritarianism 26.75; people don't want to carry the 'burden' of responsibility 11.147, 12.232–3; responsibility to act to avert global catastrophe 17.471–2; teaching responsibility towards the environment 9.440, 9.445–6

see also
Order members taking on responsibility, *see under* Triratna III/Order members

responsiveness communication in its most mature sense is mutual responsiveness across a chasm 18.16–17; creative mind: independent, spontaneous, responsive, and aware 11.24–6, 23.428; mindfulness: an intelligent, responsive awareness to ever-changing conditions 15.97, 15.214; responsiveness to the natural environment 18.21–2, 18.52–4; responsiveness to others' needs 15.290–1; the sangha as 'a vital mutual responsiveness' 2.247–8, 2.461–2, 23.xvi

rest the bodhisattva unable to rest so long as one grain of dust remains undelivered 7.317; if you have become attached to activity for its own sake, it's time to have some time off 4.479; 'resting one's mind at ease' 18.584; 'the sweet but selfish rest of quiet wilds' 1.213; the vow not to rest until all are delivered 10.147, 10.176; we know no rest, but we move not an inch forward 12.154; in the whole universe there is nowhere we can rest forever 7.49, 7.51

restlessness (*auddhatya*) getting restless when there is nothing to do 5.645; modern man is an incurably restless creature 7.147–8, 19.361; hankering after a different meditation practice 19.339–40; if you have a restless temperament, think of the spiritual life in terms of a static symbol 18.525; refusal to accept ourselves and our condition 15.277; restlessness in the spiritual life 18.346; as *upakleśa* (recklessness or ebullience) 17.670–1; *vīrya* is not to be confused with restlessness 1.293, 3.305–6, 4.478–9; why can't we

stay contented? 10.475, 15.201; you have everything you need where you are, but you still want to go elsewhere 19.339; you move because you are not happy where you are 18.340–1; as the ninth fetter, *see under* fetters; restlessness and anxiety as a hindrance, *see* five hindrances

results action directed towards securing the best possible results for oneself and others 2.340; the Buddha the inheritor of the results of actions performed during many lives 1.49; Buddhism infallibly produces the right results 3.14; contrasting attitudes to getting spiritual results 18.363; in Dharma practice, don't think in terms of results 11.736; the irreversible bodhisattva's truthfulness can produce tangible results 2.169; just sitting helps people to get away from a result-oriented attitude 5.404–5; mindfulness of purpose should not be confused with being greedy for results 5.389; mistakenly thinking one has experienced the truth of non-self, with painful results 12.267–8; no need to wait until after death to experience the results of positive action 9.287–8; 'The supreme Buddha praised pure meditation, which gives instantaneous results' 5.292–4; you get results after you put all your energy into something, fail, and give up 18.189; you will see the results of your practice in this lifetime 3.162, 10.156, 10.244–5

see also
karma-vipāka; the results of effort, *see under* effort; *sandiṭṭhiko*, *see under Tiratana Vandanā*

retreat centres (Triratna) *see under* Triratna IV

retreats (*shibir* in India)

GOING ON RETREAT

notes on retreats
the first ever Buddhist retreat (the Buddha's five disciples) 9.383; in England pre-FWBO 23.118, 23.132–41; FWBO's early retreats, *see under* Triratna I/early days; if necessary, stop all Buddhist centre activities so everyone can go on retreat 4.528–9; the traditional Tibetan long retreat 13.74–5; the lay equivalent of monastic retreats 12.125; meditation retreats 10.214; resistance to going on retreat 5.382; retreats for gay men 26.xiv; international retreat 12.674; poems written on retreat 25.310–11

what retreats are like
it can take a day or two to unwind 5.300–1; we often arrive on retreat in a very battered state, psychologically 5.694; 'a week bathed in a special kind of atmosphere' 23.137; keeping the *dhyāna* experience all day 18.595–6; held in the countryside because it is quiet 10.330; the need for retreat conditions 19.527; on a small scale a retreat is a new world 11.184–5; absorbed in retreat life, you don't feel the need of distractions 19.254

silent periods
'a very good atmosphere prevailed' 23.136; poems about silence on retreat 25.361, 25.367, 25.435; benefits and difficulties 9.519–20, 10.214; energizing effect 15.153; to calm down over-exuberance 18.581

why go on retreat?
the advantages of going on retreat 10.331–3; the purpose of going on retreat 15.153; can help us to change 9.377–8; the effect of positive conditions 4.183, 5.683, 11.117, 11.184, 15.153; supportive conditions allow change without much effort 5.252; making the most of the opportunity 4.366; the transformative effect of retreats 11.184, 12.554; past and future fade into the background 17.401; sometimes we find out what is really keeping us going from day to day 15.154; raise the level of consciousness 11.462; what about an occasional retreat from social activities? 12.125; physical conditions favourable for mental detachment 4.566

possible complexities
finding a balance between mindfulness and free-flowing energy 15.732–3, 16.300, 17.80; Māra may let us go on retreat, but not let go of our minds when we're there 18.177; falling in love with someone while leading a retreat 19.342; flirting on retreat 19.465

organizing a retreat
simply organizing a programme creates harmony 4.98; why not have a non-organized retreat with no programme? 14.523; the team running a retreat an example of the sangha in action 12.625; teams asking and answering questions on the Dharma 23.136–7

after the retreat
the dangers of throwing yourself back into worldly life 18.34; forgetting how good the experience is 5.450–1, 19.82–3, 19.217; very easy to lose the experience on return home 4.380, 14.520, 18.583; your old reactive self may rise up in rebellion 19.82–3

SOLITARY RETREATS

introduction
first suggestion that Order members should do solitary retreats 4.530–1, 4.535; what do people get out of solitary retreats? 5.671–2; have a solitary retreat every year 12.418–19; should be part of one's personal programme 5.637; should literally be solitary 5.669; be clear about whether you're going on retreat or on holiday 5.673–4, 19.492; is it enough just to be alone? 4.550–1; are surroundings important? 5.675; people imagine that solitary retreat is just masochism 17.303; Sangharakshita's in the ashram at Raipur 20.217; strange ideas about solitary retreats 5.669; we have a daily solitary retreat when we meditate 12.474–5

length of retreat
how long? 5.673, 5.675; be away for long enough to forget about worldly life 19.253; Milarepa's long retreat 18.328; three-year retreat 5.669–70

an opportunity
to have an intensified experience of yourself 5.673; to be free of external pressures and get to know yourself 5.637; to be still and feel your own existence 12.82; to contact deeper creative energies 5.682; to deal with unskilful reactions 5.671–2, 5.675–7; to do one thing at a time 5.681–2; to experience yourself by yourself 5.670, 12.419; to experiment with depriving oneself of sense satisfaction 5.677; to reflect 5.668–9; to see the extent to which you are dependent on company 15.176–7; to realize your mental states are not caused by other people 5.672; to reduce input 12.474; to see whether you're going through the motions 19.276–7; to strengthen your individuality 5.680; to think creatively about the situation to which you will be returning 15.177; making the most of the opportunity 19.557

preparation
general advice 5.670–1; best not to go when you're tired 5.672; setting up conditions 15.177; sorting out problems before you go 5.682

during the retreat
having a daily programme 5.674–5; whether or not to do formal practices 4.550–1; having a particular theme 4.617–18; different phases 5.677; keep it simple 5.668; meeting fear 5.367, 16.279–80; drowsiness 5.678–80; *dhyāna* 5.682; giving up meditation while in solitude 18.484; a relief 12.419; even in ideal conditions you might lack the inspiration to use them 15.154; even on solitary retreat you are not free of needs 17.16; feeling in contact with spiritual friends on solitary retreat 17.42; feeling that the spiritual community is watching you 19.277; unskilful mental states can arise despite the absence of sense stimuli 17.99; working creatively with moods 18.53; seeking diversions 19.491–3; advice about returning home 15.177–8

return journey *see under White Lotus Sūtra*/parables

Revata (the Buddha's disciple) 10.577–9

Revata (Buddhaghosa's teacher) 3.289

revenge 13.574, 25.xxxvii, 25.416, 26.381

reverence (*gārava*, homage)

introduction
awe might be a better translation 15.426; the difference between reverence and respect for power 15.717, 15.719–20; the difference between reverence and worship 15.425–7; reverence can be offered only to what you do not understand 17.276, 18.167; reverence is the guardian angel of our human world (Shakespeare) 24.575

natural reverence
the Buddha's reverence for the Dharma 3.65–9, 4.168, 4.346; Buddhists aim to cultivate a spirit of reverence 3.62–4; children's natural tendency to admire 15.715; faith arises when with *mettā* we look up to one who is more spiritually developed 9.323; honouring God's gifts in other men (Blake) 17.275; humility naturally comes with reverence 17.605; 'I think continually of those who were truly great' 7.423, 25.57, 26.399, 26.632; the instinct to revere is deep-rooted in the human psyche 2.213–14, 4.347, 26.629; looking for someone to look up to 4.346–7; looking up to men and women at a higher point of development 25.56–7; a pleasure to see the esteem in which one scientist held another 24.212; recollecting the lives of the sages 16.283; reverence for the Three Jewels 8.529; revering one's teacher 17.277; Sangharakshita's natural tendency to venerate 13.425, 22.xxi, 26.628–9; for spiritual teachers 3.63; we should be grateful to have people to look up to 17.274–5; we should reverence life as much as possible 4.111; becoming capable of genuine homage 15.720

reluctance to revere
better to have sacred cows, even literally, than to hold nothing sacred 26.36; modern

reluctance to revere spiritual qualities 4.168, 4.345, 15.714–20, 17.275–7; putting someone on a pedestal is not true respect 4.347, 15.719, 26.81; there are a lot of people who want to be looked up to, even if they're not worthy of it 4.347; 'There is now no reverence for any thing' (Coleridge) 15.392; the veneration of *bhikkhus* by lay people is bad for them 2.599–601

see also
devotion; six *gāravas*

Revill, Bill 12.128, v23

revolutions and revolutionary awareness is revolutionary 26.20; the Beatles were revolutionary 15.492; Chinese Cultural Revolution 26.477; political and national revolutions 8.588, 9.408–9; Green 9.409–10; neutralizing the revolutionary by incorporating him into the establishment 15.492; William Morris believed that non-violent revolution was impossible 26.650–1; properly understood, Buddhism is revolutionary 26.20; taking off your mask can be a revolutionary activity 25.95; 'There is no revolutionary like an old revolutionary' 26.74; those who prefer evolution to revolution 26.18; the true revolutionary does not play other people's games 26.18; *see also* Dhamma Revolution; Industrial Revolution, *see under* industry

revulsion in the positive *nidānas* (but revulsion isn't quite the right word) 3.75–6; upon gaining insight, you experience revulsion (spiritual, not psychological) 3.218; a response to seeing that everything conditioned is marked by the three *lakṣaṇas* 3.218; Sangharakshita's, on witnessing dancers in Darjeeling 20.132–3; at the unpleasantness of the body, *see aśubha bhāvanā*

reward don't reward yourself for periods of practice by permission to be unskilful 19.322–3; how you reward yourself is a sign of what your values are 19.323; Judaeo-Christian ethics: punishment of sin and reward of virtue 3.99–100; no harm in thinking in terms of the rewards of meditation 4.622; a man goes through the city on an elephant offering a reward for one Dharma verse 10.263; the *mettā bhāvanā* is not easy, but rewarding 1.502; paradoxically, for reward you have to forget about reward 17.208; of rebirth in heaven 3.315; the rewards of meditation 4.622, 5.380; spiritual rewards are subtle and complex 17.301; in life, not just after death 9.287–8

Rexroth, Kenneth 8.415–20

Reynolds, Sir Joshua 13.585

Rgyan-Drug Mchog-Gnyis (on Tibetan thangkas) 8.402–3

Rhea 16.386

rhetoric anthimeria (rhetorical device) 12.723 (n172); the art of inducing people to accept what you say 13.477; charisma is 'the rhetoric of the person' 13.477; the dominant interest of Mahāyāna *sūtras* is not rhetorical but spiritual 1.333; 'Take rhetoric and wring its neck!' 11.202, 13.476, 13.711 (n270), 26.78; when giving a Dharma talk, don't get carried away with your own rhetoric 17.658

Rhine, J. B. 2.33, 2.667 (n51)

rhinoceros 2.191, 4.469, 4.707 (n314)

Rhys Davids, Mrs Caroline A. F.

her life and work
introduction 2.754–5 (n775), 4.397–8, 7.569 (n126); the Abhidharma's 'one notable constructive contribution to knowledge' 14.91; description of an Abhidharma work as 'ten valleys of dry bones' 14.89; her difficulty in understanding what meditation is and why people do it 4.489, 4.708 (n320); her translation of *samādhi* as 'musing' 7.228, 17.578, 18.499; her literary style 4.397; on the importance of the positive *nidānas* 1.114, 7.204; the influences on her view of Buddhism 4.397–8; pioneering work on the higher criticism of the Pāli canon 2.627; on the thirty-two marks 14.426; took the first step in a new consideration of Buddhist history 7.72

Buddhism: a study of the Buddhist Norm
disciples who 'tell of their gain', but do not bring in the ego 7.154; exposition of the five *niyamas* 3.672 (n296), 4.399, 16.596 (n78), 16.621 (n285); Sangharakshita reads 20.302, 23.14; Sāriputta meditates without any thought of attainment 7.154; translation of Dharma as 'the Norm' 9.538, 15.255

other works and translations
Book of the Kindred Sayings (introduction) 14.47–8; *Dhammasaṅgaṇi, A Manual of Buddhist Ethics* (trans.), *see Dhammasaṅgaṇi*; *Outlines of Buddhism* 7.204; *Points of Controversy*, *see Kathā-vatthu*; *Sakya or Buddhist Origins* 14.14; *Theragāthā* (introduction) 26.128

Rhys Davids, T. W. introduction 7.619 (n501); how he developed an interest in Buddhism 3.188; meets Anagarika Dharmapala 8.46; founded the Pali Text

Society 12.70; on Buddhist ordination 11.455; on the *Jātakas* 3.86, 3.643 (n100), 14.63; *Buddhist Birth-stories* 3.628 (n20), 3.629 (n21), 3.630 (n25), 3.633 (n48); *Buddhist India* 10.478; translation work 7.449, 12.70

rhythm in the sangha a rhythm of expansion and contraction 8.263–4; observing the natural rhythm of your energies 5.352; one should try to follow the rhythm of one's natural interest 4.569; regular meditation: different rhythms for different people 5.691–2; rhythm in poetry 26.210–11; rhythm is the law of life 8.263; the rhythm of spiritual life 5.691–2, 15.357; the seasonal rhythm of life 4.577; writing poetry: 'out of the silence ... there arose a certain rhythm' 23.xxv–xxvi, 24.168, 25.35

ribus (relics) removed from an ancient stupa by Chattrul Sangye Dorje 12.436, 22.395, 25.443; Tomo Geshe Rimpoche distributes *ribus* 22.493–4

Richard the Lion-Heart 17.462

Richard of St Victor 14.358–9, 25.82

Richardson, Samuel 12.697

riches *see* prosperity

Ricketts, Mike 2.403

rickshaw pullers avoiding rickshaws on principle 19.261, 21.368; hard work 3.585; Sangharakshita's experience of travelling in a rickshaw 3.586, 19.261

Riding, Laura 25.433

Ridley, Nicholas 13.549

Rieker, Hans-Ulrich 8.395–6, 8.701 (n277)

Rievaulx Abbey 13.618, 24.386–7

Rig Veda *see under* Vedas

right action, aspiration or resolve, concentration, effort *see under* Noble Eightfold Path

right livelihood

GENERAL INTRODUCTION

traditional perspectives
the traditional meaning of right livelihood 13.454; 'lightweight' livelihood (*sallahukavutti*) 15.284; purity of monastic livelihood (*ājīva-saṃvara-sīla*) 1.146, 1.148; the Cathars' practice of a form of right livelihood 8.424

the ethics of right livelihood
does no harm to others or oneself 3.371, 9.441, 11.117–18, 15.415, 17.194; ethical stockbroking 16.412; ethics apply to livelihood as much as to private life 7.511; 'give what you can, take what you need' 11.603–4, 15.361, 16.391; moving towards right livelihood 10.630; to practise it we may have to question our attitude to work 15.281–2; right livelihood and Buddhist economics 16.400; we all have to work, so right livelihood is an integral part of the spiritual life 11.186; work should involve no exploitation of others and no degradation of oneself 4.114; your work can be right livelihood if you work honestly and conscientiously 1.548; don't employ another person to do work you don't want to do oneself 17.194

characteristics of right livelihood
what constitutes right livelihood? 1.548; allows time for Dharma and cultural activities 9.441; communicating the Dharma as right livelihood 18.176; difficult to practise strictly 19.473; earning our living in a way that doesn't lower our state of consciousness 11.117–18; it helps us to change 9.377; it should benefit ourselves and others 17.194; William Morris's ideal 26.650; should allow time for study, meditation, contact with friends 4.114; as support for meditation 3.617; take it seriously and you'll have your work cut out for the next twenty years 19.544; work you would do regardless of the pay 17.197

TEAM-BASED RIGHT LIVELIHOOD

established in the FWBO
'it occurred to me that we had to develop right livelihood' 11.715; a surprise development 11.596–7; how it began 3.622–3, 9.283, 9.437, 9.491–2, 9.505, 10.215–16, 11.465, 12.496–7; making a start 1.551; in the early days; a whole world within a world 11.524–5; possibility of starting in India? 9.267, 9.531; the most difficult thing undertaken by the FWBO (Triratna) 12.407; emphasis on right livelihood 11.376, 12.670–1

purposes
summary 11.186–8, 11.465, 13.455; (1) material support for workers 3.623, 11.186, 12.607–8, 12.670–1, 13.455, 16.413; (2) Buddhists work together 3.623, 9.491, 11.186–7, 12.469, 12.608, 12.671, 13.455, 17.72; (3) a working situation conducive to spiritual progress 16.413; (4) ethical 3.623, 11.187, 12.469, 12.608, 12.670, 13.455; (5) support for Buddhist activities 3.623, 9.491–2, 11.187, 12.609, 12.671, 13.381, 13.455, 15.517, 16.413

notes on team-based right livelihood
'always very close to my heart' 12.681; an alternative arrangement to the traditional life of the *bhikkhu* 11.187–8; an alternative to work that harms one's development and exploits others 3.623; a positive alternative work situation 3.371; organized on cooperative principles 9.241, 16.413; can have no positions of authority 3.446; consideration of business ethics 13.455; danger of losing perspective 15.99; going out of fashion 12.671; list of businesses 9.505, 12.607, 13.455; living and working together 12.608–9; the most positive situation one could have 12.671; an opportunity for insight 26.353; proves that one can reject an economic system geared to material gain 15.197; rules in the sense of agreed ways of doing things 19.559; saying you're going on retreat and then going on holiday 19.353; vegetarian restaurants as right livelihood 13.454, 13.709 (n252); while doing a specific task, keep in mind the wider perspective 19.524; you can get a lot of tough work done in a relaxed atmosphere 14.520

see also
Windhorse Trading; work; wrong livelihood

right mindfulness *see under* Noble Eightfold Path

right motive *see under* motivation

right speech *see under* Noble Eightfold Path

right view or right understanding (*sammā-diṭṭhi* or *samyak-dṛṣṭi*)

definitions
how to define right view 11.655; who decides what is right view? 11.654–5; three definitions 7.521; five kinds of right understanding, mundane, transcendental, and intermediate 7.522; 'orthodoxy' is the literal equivalent 2.556–7, 7.520–1

its nature
a benign and open perspective infused with the Buddha's teachings 17.xix; a non-view, held provisionally as a means to the attainment of Enlightenment 2.391; not a closed system of ideas but a skilful attitude provisionally adopted 17.618; right view (like good sight) is powerful, unlimited, and undistorted 11.159–60; views expressing a mental state with no covetousness, hatred, and delusion 2.390; our flashes of right view derive from the Buddha's Perfect Vision 11.160–1; right view distinguished from perfect vision 1.474–5, 7.521–2, 7.531, 11.160, 11.653–4

its importance
why emphasize right view? 11.653–4; 'abstract ideas' may not seem to impinge on 'real life', but right view is necessary 3.292; cherish right view: no right view, no Perfect Vision 12.475; the crucial importance of 'right doctrine' 7.524; importance of right view 1.112, 11.653–4; cultivating right view 3.281; only relative, but must be upheld as the means to realization 1.206; without right view there is no basis for right action 17.618

right view and wrong view
absence of right view is *micchā-diṭṭhi* (wrong or false view), *see micchā-diṭṭhis*; the importance of the distinction 11.160; taking the hammer of right view to fashionable *micchā-diṭṭhis* 11.612–14; a dogmatic or clinging attitude turns right views into wrong views 17.259, 17.631; to cling to your idea of right view as if it were fixed is a mistake 18.172; right view, good rebirth, wrong view, bad rebirth, 'no view', Nirvāṇa 17.245

see also
under Noble Eightfold Path/the stages of the path

righteous indignation 1.557–8, 17.601–2

rights and duties all rights are based upon power 26.19; the Buddha spoke of duties, not rights 26.588; Buddhist ethics cannot be grounded on the concept of rights 8.611, 26.19; difference between ethical and legal rights 13.451; the duties and rights of a young monk 2.196–8; duties unite, rights divide 7.278, 13.447; if everyone did their duty, there would be no need to speak of rights 7.280, 12.603–4, 13.446, 26.73; if we only perform our duties, won't our rights be trampled on? 7.279; in modern life there's more emphasis on rights and less on duties 25.63; it is duties that must be performed, rather than rights demanded 7.277, 26.588; the remedy for injustice is insistence not on one party's rights, but on the other's duties 7.279, 26.73; rights exist only within the group: within the spiritual community there are only duties 26.73; 'Rights and Duties' 7.276–80; 'rights' is not an ethical concept 13.451; teaching children their rights and duties as citizens 9.440; there can be a conflict between different rights 26.588; in the West the discourse of rights has been carried to absurd lengths 12.603; when a monk

feels it is his civic duty to get involved in politics 7.441

rigidity giving is 'superior to any form of rigid discipline' (Śāntideva) 4.354; a narrow and rigid monasticism can be turned into Buddhist respectability 18.135; a rigid mind tends to invite tragedy 19.86; rigidity of mind 19.59–60; thinking of karma in a rigid, literalistic way 4.301

Rilke, Rainer Maria brief introduction 24.713–14 (n500); 'beyond all that is comprehensible and embraceable here' 26.176; poetry is not *about* existence but *is* itself a new kind of existence 21.434; his philosophy of love 26.172–3; 'After Rilke' (poem) 25.359, 26.101; 'An Archaic Torso of Apollo: 'change your life' 26.xiv, 26.116–17, 26.166, 26.173; *Notebooks of Malte Laurids Brigge* 26.166–7, 26.171–2; his capacity of experiencing unknown modes of being 26.137; *Duino Elegies* 8.491, 26.150, 26.240, 26.268; *Orpheus Sonnets* 4.593, 4.713–14 (n360); sonnet on the Buddha 7.450; 'Spanish Trilogy' 24.398

Rimbaud, Arthur *Le Bateau ivre* 26.373; delight in Rimbaud 20.113, 26.737 (n365); 'a season in Hell' 26.453; 'a soul raged in her child' 23.97

Rimé tradition 12.437, 12.734 (n289), 22.554

rimpoche (meaning) 13.50

Rinchen Terdzö *see under termas*

Rinchen Zangpo ('the great translator') 12.575–6

Rinkingpong 22.490, 22.501

Rinzai 8.496

Rinzai school *see under* Zen

rishis *see under* Vedas

risk artists risk unpopularity 3.472, 3.510; the bodhisattva is willing to take risks 16.421; the Buddha had to risk unpopularity 3.472; commitment involves risk 17.46–7; an element of risk to being truly human (Nietzsche) 3.499; having faith and taking risks go hand in hand 17.47; perhaps it's better to be pedantic than risk compromising the ideal 19.463; testifying to your attainment is a risky procedure 14.450–1; to express yourself is to take a risk 18.278; why risk one's precious human life on dangerous sports like rock-climbing? 24.503; you cannot go through life without taking risks 17.47; you need to risk the humiliation of failure to be successful 14.489–91

Risshō Kōsei Kai (Buddhist Laymen's Association) 24.62, 24.622 (n86)

ritual *see* devotion

Ritualist controversy (Christianity) 11.208

River Valley Age 3.425–6

rivers

metaphorical rivers
Dr Ambedkar created steps down to the river of Dhamma 9.458; 'As the rivers lose their names in the great ocean ...' 2.691–2 (n305), 9.473, 9.574n; aspiration: like a man jumping across a river (Nāgasena) 1.289–90; the cold ice of dogmatism blocks the river of life 7.145; the Dharma like a stream or river 2.39, 9.451–3, 9.455–8, 14.539; Enlightenment is like a river flowing into an ocean we can't see 3.145–6; everything, sooner or later, will flow away, like the water of a great river 13.147; the five spiritual faculties illustrated by a man jumping across a river 4.474; the 'four violent rivers' (Brahmaputra, Sutlej, Indus, Karnali) 17.427, 17.754 (n355); life is like a river flowing faster and faster 24.89; selling water by the river 10.626; Swami Ramdas received confession like an ocean receiving the waters of a river 20.325; the threefold path as a river 3.252; the twenty-four *nidānas* like rain filling up the streams, rivers, and seas 1.116; you don't step into the same river twice 7.596 (n300), 12.422

physical rivers
apology for polluting them 25.447; the beauty of a cremation by the river 12.221, 15.143, 22.202–3; Brahminical rituals performed on the bank of the Sarasvatī river 16.362–3; how the emaciated Siddhārtha fell into a river 3.631 (n32); kingfishers and dragonflies by a river in Surrey 20.100–2; Niagara Falls 2.644; 'O limpid river in the evening air' 25.157; 'a primrose by the river's brim' 1.29

see also
Ganges; Jambu; Rohiṇi; Sarasvatī; Teesta; Thames, *see under* London; using a raft to cross the river, *see* raft

rjes-gnang 7.477

R. K. Films v21, v22

robbers *see* bandits

Robert of Anjou 24.278–9, 24.677 (n377)

Roberts, Peter Alan 10.685 (n174), 18.261

Robertson, Trisha *see* Rupachitta

robes

the Buddha
given robes of cloth-of-gold 2.29, 13.144; refused a gift of robes: more merit in giving them to the sangha 3.395; would have worn rags 3.50

robes at the Buddha's time
originally ordinary clothes discoloured with earth (*gerua-mati*) 12.237, 16.404; the monk whose robe is torn by robbers 10.649; Piṇḍola Bhāradvāja, the rag-robe wearer 10.537–8; robes in the *Dhammapada* 9.271, 15.43; wise use of robes (as monastic requisite) 1.149; robe and bowl: the two wings of the monastic life 1.152, 16.405; giving of robes after the rainy season retreat, *see kaṭhinacīvaradāna*

later traditions
Pāṇḍaravāsinī's robe on fire 19.570; the goddess Śrī gives robes to the monk (*Sūtra of Golden Light*) 16.404; Theravādin and Tibetan compared 21.177; Tibetan robes 13.52

robes today
for Theravādin lay people, unthinkable for a monk to wear civilian clothes 23.188; an elaborate collection of ecclesiastical robes 23.52–3; the robe of the Secret Order of the Potala 22.436, 23.388–9; respect for the robe 2.600–1, 19.262, 19.309, 19.490; a monk's robe can be four or five times as costly as that of a layman 21.377; yellow robes drying in the sun, like the petals of a celestial flower 9.279, 20.115; robes in the Triratna Buddhist Order (WBO) 24.363; Sangharakshita's wearing of robes, *see under* Sangharakshita V/monastic lifestyle

how robes are worn
ticīvara 9.316, 9.566 (n301); how robes are traditionally worn 14.400–1; controversy in Burma over whether the shoulder is covered or not 4.186, 13.105; different ways robes are worn in Sri Lanka 12.428, 20.447–8; Jagdish Kashyap struggles to wear his robe properly 12.429; Milarepa learns a lesson from his flyaway robe 18.9–10; a monk on a strict way of wearing robes: 'I am doing this to please fools' 23.198

better not to wear robes?
the belief that robes have nothing to do with Buddhism 23.190; the true Buddhist 'wears the yellow robe within' 23.190, 23.322; in a way wearing a robe is a form of mask 25.90; robes get in the way of communication 24.54; it's possible to practise the Dharma seriously without a special costume 18.520; one is not necessarily a true *bhikkhu* because one wears a robe 2.560, 23.323; seeing people in robes may be off-putting 12.127; they can give the wrong impression that Buddhism belongs to the remote past 9.316

Robinson, Eileen *see* Sister Vajira

Robinson, John (Bishop of Woolwich)

introduction
brief introduction 23.505 (n246); appearance in a TV programme 24.319; moving in the direction of Buddhism? 12.10–11, 12.94, 12.120, 23.211; what can Buddhists learn from the Bishop of Woolwich? 12.113

Honest to God
introduction 12.2–11, 13.561; courage and originality 12.5–7; the 'ground of being' 19.141; the 'man for others' 12.8–10, 23.211; perhaps influenced a dream 26.679; the traditional image of God must go 12.130, 12.135

The New Reformation?
introduction 12.114–28; on atheism 12.6–7, 23.210–11; passing reference to the Buddha 12.8; starting not with God, but with human beings 12.120

Sangharakshita
'Buddhism and the Bishop of Woolwich' 12.2–11, 12.112, 12.533–4, 13.561, 23.210–12; 'Buddhism and the New Reformation' 12.112–28, 23.241; he meets the bishop 12.112, 12.130, 13.561–2, 23.212–15

Robinson, Richard 14.180, 21.339

Robinson, Ruth 23.214–15

Rochefoucauld, Duc Francois de la 15.311, 15.755 (n109)

Rock, Dr Joseph v21

Roerich, Dr George introduction 21.33–4, 22.615–16 (n331); the publication of a lecture 21.53–4; *The Blue Annals* (translation) 21.51, 21.622 (n11), 22.125; the French nun betrays his secret 22.427–8; in Kalimpong v21, v22, 26.221; the translation of Buddhist texts into Tibetan 7.514–15; 'Vanaratna – the Last of the Great Panditas' 8.643, 22.125

Roerich, Helena founder of Agni Yoga 26.222; her psychic presence 21.34, 21.49, 21.319–20, 26.222

Roerich, Nicholas his paintings 7.451, 26.222; his devotion to the cult of Maitreya 21.49, 26.222; sets for Stravinsky's *Le Sacre du Printemps* 7.451

Roerich, Svetoslav v22, 26.222

Rogers, Mike 2.403, v23

Rohiṇi, River 12.338–9

Roiger, Heinz v24

Rolfe, Frederick 23.258, 23.512 (n295)

Rolland, Romain 8.156–7, 20.117

Rome *see under* Italy

Roman Catholicism *see under* Christianity

Romans destruction of Celtic paganism 4.107; seeing nothing shocking about crucifixion 26.675–6; they had skeletons at their feasts, to remind them of mortality 13.228

Romantic poets *see under* poets

Romantic movement 15.139, 24.568, 24.587, 26.255–6

Ronaldshay, Lord 8.64

Rongzom Chökyi Zangpo 14.518

Ronsard, Pierre de 23.452, 23.539 (n474)

Roof, Simmons and Marcia 8.665, v22

Root Verses of the Six Bardos *see under* *bardos*

roots

roots from the Buddhist tradition
the Buddha on going back to the roots of his words 14.350–1; 'digging out the root of grief' 10.492; four *viparyāsas*: attitudes as deeply rooted almost as sentient existence 2.81; 'Here are the roots of trees. Sit down, meditate' 1.236, 3.53, 14.19, 18.368; the root of desire is ignorance 7.126; young elephants poisoned by unwashed lotus roots 17.447, 19.296, 21.552–3

rootedness
the advantages of putting down roots 18.332, 18.336; in modern life people find it difficult to put down roots 19.361; in India, people's roots go back thousands of years 12.254; root yourself in your practices and efforts rather than a particular place 19.362; a difference between putting down spiritual roots and cultural or social roots 19.362; the bodhisattva rooted in the true nature of Dharma 14.587–8; the poet is rooted in the objective world as the plant is rooted in the soil 26.170; 'the soul roots deeper' 25.lvii

more roots
Buddhism is a great tree with wide branches and deep roots 12.111; the tree of Buddhist revival can only grow as high as its roots are deep 8.218–19; Dr Ambedkar's search for roots 9.74; the FWBO's role is radical, in the sense of returning to roots 13.440; the leaves return to the root 7.297; our pagan roots destroyed by the advent of Christianity 4.106–7, 12.253–4; the root error of humanity is abstraction 7.325–6; 'The Root Speaks' (poem) 25.39, 25.71–8, 25.229, 26.60; at the root of things is an unfathomable mystery 7.37, 25.133; roots in the sky 4.37, 10.620, 14.590; never any flower of human achievement but some great sorrow lay at its root 7.389; leaving our roots behind means growing beyond them, not severing them 26.60; don't keep tearing yourself up by the roots to see if you have grown 17.267

see also
three unskilful or unwholesome roots, *see* three roots; three wholesome roots

Roper, Rosi 26.458

rosanā (flash of rage) 15.302–3

rosary *see mālā*

rose-apple tree Siddhārtha's experience under a rose-apple tree, *see under* Siddhārtha Gautama/upbringing; the wanderer who ate rose-apples 1.69, 1.72, 2.122

Rosicrucianism 13.374, 20.64, 20.65–7

Rossetti, Christina 11.635, 26.490

Rossetti, Dante Gabriel brief introduction 24.688 (n395); Sangharakshita's admiration 20.36, 20.51, 24.547, 26.392, 26.661; connection with Blake 26.485, 26.661; underrated 26.339; *The Blessed Damozel* 2.64, 24.400, 24.511; 'Dante in Verona' 26.660; painting *Dante's Dream* 24.547, 24.584–5, 26.660; 'Hand and Soul' (story) 26.253; and *The Rubáiyat of Omar Kháyyám* 26.661; 'Sister Helen' 26.439; translation of early Italian poets 26.445

round going round and round, like a wheel going round and the ratchet never gripping 19.216–17; the long and weary round of life after life and death after death 7.49; a perfectly round sphere on a perfectly flat plane 3.219; the round of birth and death 1.39, 1.113, 1.130–1, 17.378

Round Table *see under* Arthur

Round Table Conferences 9.6, 9.7

Rousseau, Jean-Jacques the dissipation of a naive Rousseauistic view of human nature 26.376; idealization of infancy

8.586; pseudo-Rousseauism, the idea of a pure self enslaved by socially imposed beliefs 13.388–9; Rousseauism as a form of secular humanism 13.407; the view that the organization of society oppresses the individual 11.195–7

routines the daily routine of a monk 3.589–90; the danger of the whole of Dharma life becoming a routine 10.241–2; the deadening routine of daily life 10.241; developing a routine to sustain effort 19.438; how to stop Dharma practice from becoming a routine 19.457; the need for unprogrammed time 11.515; our daily routine should be such that we are strengthened, not weakened 16.207; the inner enemy of routine 10.240–2; routine is one of the biggest enemies of the Dharma 10.240–2; seem to drive all the freshness and spontaneity out of life 16.439; sooner or later external circumstances disturb spiritual routine 25.77; in the West we are dominated by routine 3.297; Sangharakshita's daily routine, *see under* Sangharakshita V/personal practice

Rovelli, Carlo 26.xvi, 26.686–7

Rowe, Nicholas 24.390

Roy, A. 8.604–5

Roy, Dr B. C. 8.165–6, 22.70

Roy, Dilip Kumar (musician) 22.77

Roy, Jamini 8.367

Roy, Kshitish 22.56

Roy, M. N. (Marxist thinker) 8.605

Roy, Sri S. N. v22

rubáiyát 1.382; *see also* Fitzgerald

Rubens, Peter Paul v24, 26.95–6

Ruciraketu (bodhisattva) *see under Sūtra of Golden Light*

Ruciraketu, King *see under Sūtra of Golden Light*/other characters

Rudd, Robbie 26.417–19

rudeness Christians' rudeness to followers of other faiths 15.671; don't let people think that Buddhists are rude 12.404; if people are rude when you're teaching the Dharma, you may have to respond firmly 4.359–60; if you don't want to dilute the Dharma, sometimes you have to be a bit rude 12.660–1; in the name of spontaneity 4.337

Rudio, René 23.401, 23.417

Rudra *see* Tarpa Nagpo

rukkha-devatā *see under* nature/nature spirits

rules the Buddha didn't sit down and draw up a list of rules 10.563–4; Buddhist morality is more about growth and progress than about rules 15.291; can become an external conformity, neglecting the spirit 10.563; in the Buddha's time, common mental states and ideals more important than common rules 10.561; it is quite possible to observe all the monastic rules and still be on the wrong path 19.558; at first, many *arhants* and few rules, then many rules and few *arhants* 10.480, 10.563–4, 19.262; laying down rules is always a sign of decline 10.563–4; rules in the Triratna Buddhist Community 19.558–60; rules and guidelines 19.557–8; rules give stability to life 17.573; the third fetter is about fear of breaking the rules, but why is one afraid of that? 17.635; *see also* Vinaya Piṭaka

Rumi, Jalāl ad-Dīn Mohammad coming across his work 26.688; constantly creating 12.645; 'I died as a mineral and became a plant' 7.583 (n211); 'In truth everything and everyone/ Is a shadow of the Beloved' 16.588 (n29); *Masnavi* 24.360

Rummindei *see* Lumbini

rūpa (form)

qualities
all the processes going on in the physical body 10.231; cohesion, undulation, radiation, and vibration 2.97, 13.151–2, 15.133–5; knowable through the senses (unlike other aspects of experience) 15.134; material qualities (Abhidharma) 1.102–3; masculinity, femininity, and gesture: not just 'matter' 2.97–8; not matter but a congeries of events of the 'material' order 1.173; primary and secondary material phenomena 1.174, 2.97, 15.183; *rūpa* as *mahābhūta* 2.97; thought is a power, an energy, which produces *rūpa* 17.479–80

as one of the five skandhas
introduction 1.173–4, 2.97–8; on the wheel of life 2.75; reflecting on *rūpa* as one of the five *skandhas* 15.181

analysed in the Abhidharma
in the *Dhātu-kathā* 14.84; the elements are the first four items on a list of subdivisions of *rūpa* 15.133; English translations of *rūpa* 15.133–4; 'the enormous quantity of matter that we perceive around us' 14.504; 'Form is not the self' 10.719 (n467); freeing the mind from the notion of *rūpa* 2.144; the mystery of *rūpa* 15.134, 17.445; 'objective

content of the perceptual situation' 2.97, 13.151, 15.134, 17.445, 17.479

see also
Heart Sūtra/śūnyatā and *rūpa*

Rupachitta, Dharmacharini (Trisha Robertson) v24

rūpakāya ('form body') the Buddha's physical phenomenal appearance 3.150; distinction from *dharmakāya* 3.150–1, 16.60–1; discussion of meaning of term 1.253–4; subdivision into *sambhogakāya* and *nirmāṇakāya* 1.261

rūpaloka *see under trailokya*

rūpaprasāda ('sensitivities') 2.97

Rupawate, Dadasaheb 10.xliii, 23.351, 24.25, 24.611 (n44)

Rushdie, Salman 12.477, 12.736 (n309), 26.248

Ruskin, John brief introduction 23.512 (n295); depictions of Apollo 4.685–6 (n188), 14.429; 'Ode on Venice' 23.512 (n295); a picture in Sangharakshita's flat 26.406; 'it is impossible to trace [a life] steadily through successive years' 22.xvi, 22.281; his relationship with his father 26.372; Ruskinian reflections 23.274; sued by James Whistler 12.581; support for Turner 26.255, 26.721–2 (n207); three architectures 25.377, 25.594 (n92)

Russell, A. J. 21.540–1

Russell, Bertrand Dr Ambedkar on Russell 9.46–7, 9.199; D. H. Lawrence's attempt to persuade him to join a spiritual community 8.545; mistaken idea that the Buddha was a rationalist like Russell 12.618; not necessarily greater than Plato 13.425; 'Of the great religions of the world, I prefer Buddhism' 7.450, 7.610 (n512)

Russell, George William ('Æ') 22.141

Russia black market in Bibles 9.349; Buddhism in Russia 2.549; Communism 9.409; effect of the weather on the people 4.576; embrace of Orthodox Christianity 24.530; the heroes of labour praised in the Soviet Union 18.390; 'A Hundred Years of Russian Art' 24.372; 'Icons from Moscow' exhibition in London 24.580; Khrushchev and the Cuban missile crisis 23.87; massacre by Stalin 26.654; not founded as secular state 9.349; Revolution 9.409; Russian translation of the *Dhammapada* 23.158; Sangharakshita's love for the Russian people 22.210–11; shift from Christianity to Marxism 17.44

Rustomji, Nariman K. 22.248

Rutherford, Lord Ernest 24.86

Ryan, Colonel John Warren Swale ('Swale') v21, v22

Ryōkan 2.555, 14.3, 18.105

S

Sabarimalai, India 20.318

sabbapāpassa akaraṇaṃ 3.242

Sabbāsava Sutta *see under Majjhima Nikāya*

sabbe dhammā anattā *see anātman*

sabbe saṅkhāra aniccā *see* impermanence

sabbe saṅkhāra dukkha *see dukkha*

sabbe sattā sukhi hontu ('May all beings be happy') ideally expresses the heartfelt wish of all Buddhists 1.502, 3.270, 10.283; it includes animals 8.256, 9.323; the *Karaṇīya Mettā Sutta*'s version 15.297–8; the motto of Buddhism 9.186, 10.171, 10.318, 11.733

śabda 26.330

sacca 15.404

Saccaka (debater at the Buddha's time) 2.716 (n492), 13.683 (n57)

Saccavibhaṅgha Sutta *see under Majjhima Nikāya*

Sachen Kunga Nyingpo 19.404

Sachin (student, Sachindra Coomar Singh)

introduction
character and appearance 21.73–4; at college 22.311; falls ill 22.68–9, 22.250–1; his family in Calcutta 22.68, 22.131, 22.166; musician 21.77; studies poetry 2.424, 21.433–5, 22.18–19, 22.112, 25.xlvii; like a character in *Black Narcissus* 21.73

friendship with Sangharakshita
deepening friendship 21.435, 22.19; daily life 22.224–7; dedicatee of *The Veil of Stars* 25.483; they go to Calcutta 22.58–9, 22.62, 22.68–9, 22.231; 'Life in the Hills' 8.645; Darjeeling 21.91, 22.18–27; Sangharakshita's intimacy with his family 21.344, 22.112, 22.113 (photo); a trip to Shantiniketan 22.49–56; they go to Bombay 22.267–73

sacramental commercialized sacramentalism 18.428–9; life's sacramental character 7.295; the sacrament of marriage, *see under* marriage; the sacramental actions of the Tantra 1.374–5; sacramental work 18.427; sexual sacramentalism 1.390–2; Luther's protests against the Church's sacramental system 18.428, 18.520; pseudo-sacramentalism 19.532; the Tantra's sexual sacramentalism 1.391; the way to sacramentalize eating and drinking 18.427–8

sacred footprint *see śrīpāda*

sacred places *see* holy places

Sacred Relics of Sāriputta and Moggallāna

their tour of India
returned by the Victoria and Albert Museum 10.93, 16.156, 20.453, 21.27, 21.171; Prime Minister Nehru welcomed them to India 8.322–3, 21.171; all India rose to welcome them 8.235; the atmosphere surrounding them 14.464; in Bihar 7.423, 20.459; in Darjeeling 21.214; in Gangtok 21.189–202; in Kalimpong 8.650, 21.173–203, 21.206–15, 21.214 (photo), 22.34; miracles associated with them 21.197; rainbow-coloured light issues from them 14.464, 21.197; re-enshrinement at Sanchi 9.14, 16.156, 21.172; their return symbolizes the return of Buddhism to India 7.423, 7.466

Sangharakshita
he and Jagdish Kashyap visit them in Benares 20.453, 21.172; accompanies their tour around India 21.170–215; accompanies them to Nepal 21.263–306; personal attitude towards the Sacred Relics 21.198

sacredness

reflections
better to have sacred cows, even literally, than to hold nothing sacred 26.36; copying sacred texts as an act of merit 20.332; the 'open secret', the sacred mystery of the

universe (Goethe) 26.178; the sacredness of trees 14.462–3, 16.149, 26.390–1; a sense of reverence for sacred things 1.407

sacred and profane
art may be either sacred or profane 7.436–7; both sides have instances of obscurity of purpose 7.148; a flower is sacred, a tree holy, if you look at it with an illumined mind 7.284; mindfulness obliterates the distinction 1.151; in the present age, things sacred are subordinated to things profane 7.310–11, 11.484; the sacredness or profaneness of a thing depends on the state of mind it inspires 7.283

see also
holy places; the sacred book, *see under* books

sacrifice animal sacrifice, *see under* animals; Brahminical sacrifice, *see under* brahmins; no part of Buddhist terminology 16.205–6; self-sacrifice, *see* self-sacrifice

Ṣaḍakṣarī ('possessing six syllables') 16.178

Sadāparibhūta ('Never Direct') *see under White Lotus Sūtra*/characters in the *sūtra*

Sadāprarudita ('Ever Weeping', bodhisattva) *see under Perfection of Wisdom in 8,000 lines*

ṣaḍāyatana *see* six bases

saddhā *see* faith

Saddhajivini, Dharmacharini (Pam Cooper) 24.249

Saddhaloka, Dharmachari 14.320

saddhamma (or *saddharma*) etymology 16.32, 16.51, 17.159; the true, real, good Dharma 11.246; Dr Ambedkar's threefold classification: Dhamma, Not-Dhamma, and *Saddhamma* 9.143, 10.351; the difference between Dhamma and *saddhamma* 10.351

Saddhanandi, Dharmacharini 25.39–148, 26.550

saddhānusārin *see* faith follower

Saddharma-Laṅkāvatāra *see Laṅkāvatāra*

Saddharma Puṇḍarīka Sūtra *see White Lotus Sūtra*

Saddhatissa (at Sangharakshita's ordination) 21.108

Saddhatissa, Venerable contribution to the Buddhist movement in Britain 8.336–7, v23; translation of the *Sutta-Nipāta* 15.xviii–xix

saddhāvimutta 1.291

saddhivihārika 2.196

sādhana Buddhist, *see* visualization practice; Indian use of term 7.578 (n175)

sadhu *see* wanderers

Sadhu Lama 22.259–60

Sadhu! 4.317, 4.695 (n241), 15.708, 15.774 (n269)

Sādhumati (Good Thoughts) *see under* ten *bhūmis*

sadisa-paṭibhāga 1.120

sadism 8.208, 11.79, 15.303

sadness the difference between sadness and depression 18.556; Milarepa's sadness when Rechungpa leaves 19.428–9; 'the note of eternal sadness' 26.397; 'sad mortality o'ersways their power' 1.231; the sad song of the cuckoo 18.53; sadness without suffering 10.492; sadness upon thinking of the experiences of life as a passing dream 18.556; 'Your sadness is my sadness, friend' 25.275

Sadutsnag, Yugyel (Kalimpong) 21.166–7

Sagar, Keith 8.541–51, 24.174, 26.319

Sagaramati, Dharmachari brief introduction 24.634 (n149); general entries v24; in Manchester 24.130; critique of Beni Barua 7.597 (n307); *Nietzsche and Buddhism* 12.550; scholarly advice 17.431–2

sages *ācāryas*: sages who had realized the transcendental import of the *sūtras* 1.298; 'The Brahmas and the Sages' (poem) 25.451–2; Chinese sages 3.427; 'Himalayan Sages' (poem) 25.183; the homely mysteriousness of a Daoist sage 7.396; it is in the nature of the sage to be unrecognized 18.68; legends that sages' meditations keep the world going 4.582; 'let the silent sage move about the village as the bee goes taking honey from the flower' 3.589–94; listening carefully to the words of the sages 17.50–1; recollecting the lives of the sages 16.283; the sage and the emperor 1.492–3, 3.241–2, 7.134, 7.292; and the symbolism of space 16.146–7; 'True sages and scholars are always in accord' 19.541–3; truth is one, sages only call it variously 7.78

saguṇa-brahman 1.166

Saha, Sri Ganapati 7.424

Sahā-world (*sahāloka*) *see under* world/ Buddhist perspectives

sahaja the immanence of Dharma 19.266–7; literally 'born with', natural, innate, spontaneous 1.386, 19.258, 19.267, 19.387; 'poised in the natural realm of Immanence' 18.344; the *sahaja* state 14.521; Tantric Buddhist word for the Unconditioned 3.206; the teaching of the innate-born wisdom 18.249

sahajānanda 2.91

Sahajayāna 1.384–7, 18.417, 19.273–4

sahajiya (inborn vital heat) 18.91

sāhitya 26.330

Sai Baba 8.608

śaikṣa (rule) *see under* Vinaya/other sets of rules

śaikṣa (learner) *see sekha*

Śailendrabodhi (translator) 14.190

saints approach to confession 4.309–10; beatification of a young priest in Naples 24.280; 'Better a live sinner than a dead saint' 26.34, 26.488–9; contrast in depiction of angels and saints 16.7–8; the English have produced very few saints 12.77; grim depictions of Christian saints 15.352–3; it's said that a real sinner is more likely than an ordinary person to become a saint 4.449; the odour of sanctity 11.237; tortured experience 19.426; truth embodied in the lives of saints 25.389; *see also* individual saints

Sakka, king of the gods (Sanskrit Sakra) sends Pañcika the *gandharva* musician to sing for the Buddha 26.122–4; disguises himself as a weaver to give almsfood to Mahākassapa 10.515–16; the Buddha as Sakka 1.49–50; in the *Perfection of Wisdom in 8,000 Lines* 14.143; in the *Vimalakīrti-nirdeśa* 16.571–2; in other Mahāyāna *sūtras* 14.176, 14.185; *see also* Indra

Sakkapañha Sutta *see under Dīgha Nikāya*

sakko (capable) 15.269–70

sakṛdāgāmin *see* once-returner

śaktis 1.389

Sakura (first FWBO centre) *see under* Triratna I/first FWBO centre

sakya (Tibetan) 13.28

Śākya Seng-ge 22.476

Śākya Trinity 2.180

Śākyadhitā 10.402

Śākyamuni

introduction
'(silent) sage of the Śākya tribe' 3.591, 14.494; a Buddha in whom *jñāna* predominates 12.512; continues to work in the world in the form of Avalokiteśvara 4.190; his miraculous deeds and victory over the Six Pandits 8.528; it is vital that he becomes a living figure and exemplar for us 11.690

previous lives
as bodhisattva Sadāparibhūta 4.418; as Prince Candracchattra 16.572–4; as Prince Gedrun 8.528

his place in the tradition
central figure of the Hīnayāna 1.262; positive and negative aspects of the bodhisattva ideal he exemplifies 14.189; became the ideal, archetypal Buddha in texts like the *White Lotus Sūtra* 13.302; one of the eight forms of Padmasambhava 13.20–1

devotion
paid to him in Mātṛceṭa's *Śatapañcāśatkastotra* 1.335; Atīśa encouraged his worship 12.578; not worshipped as main object of faith by any Mahāyāna school 1.335, 13.301–2; visualized on the Refuge Tree 13.78, 13.205; *sādhana* 26.636–7

Śākyamuni mantra (oṃ muni muni mahāmuni śākyamuni svāhā)
it reminds us of the Buddha's qualities 9.520; reciting it to get a sense of the Buddha as spiritual friend 26.636; Tibetan version 11.289

see also
Buddha (Gautama); and Amitābha, *see under* Amitābha; as *nirmāṇakāya*, *see under trikāya/nirmāṇakāya*; in the *Sūtra of Golden Light*, *see under Sūtra of Golden Light*/other characters; in the *Vimalakīrti-nirdeśa*, *see under Vimalakīrti-nirdeśa*/chapter 1, chapter 3; in the *White Lotus Sūtra*, *see under White Lotus Sūtra*/the structure of the *sūtra*

Śākyaprabha (authority on the Vinaya) 8.403

Śākyas or Śākyans conflict with the Koliyans over water 7.238, 9.140, 10.260, 12.338–9; laid claim to the Buddha's relics 16.141; republic 2.25; Siddhārtha Gautama's tribe 3.21–2; when attacked, they offered no resistance – history's first pacifists 12.357

Śākyas (clan of monks in Chinese Buddhism) 10.565–6

Sāl Grove *see* Kusinārā

***sāl* trees** *see under* trees

Saladin 17.462

Sāleyakka Sutta *see under Majjhima Nikāya*

Śālistamba Sūtra 7.632 (n603)

sallahukavutti 15.284

Sallekha Sutta *see under Majjhima Nikāya*

Salome 25.376

salt imbibing the guru's words like salt into water 18.593–4; mindfulness is desirable everywhere, like salt in cooking 17.84–5; the Salt March 23.347, 23.582 (n387); the taste of freedom like the salt in the ocean, *see under Udāna*/great ocean

Saltaire, England 24.584

Salutation to the Three Jewels *see Tiratana Vandanā*

salutations (*vandanā*) *see under* devotion/physical expressions

salvation *anātman* the keystone of the arch of salvation 7.133; the bodhisattva ideal the salvation of all sentient beings 7.41; the bodhisattva never tires of working for universal salvation 4.85–6; desire for salvation (*vairāgya*) 10.175; Enlightenment is not about individual salvation 3.245–6, 4.21–2; four kinds of people: caring for their own salvation, others' salvation, both, or neither 10.146; the four noble truths contain all schemes of salvation 7.126; of the bodhisattva 7.44–5; 'My passion shall burn as the flame of Salvation' 7.61; salvation by faith and works (Christianity) 13.531, 20.44; Tārā, Lady of Salvation 4.657

Salzberg, Sharon 24.473

Salzillo, Francisco 24.458, 24.461

samacitta 14.192

Samacitta, Dharmacharini 11.722–3, 17.152

samādhi

etymology and definitions
introduction 11.63–4; untranslatable 3.352, 11.498, 16.11; the wholesome concentration of the mind on a single object 1.150; literally the state of being firmly fixed 1.149, 1.580, 3.306, 16.610 (n196); different meanings in Theravāda and Mahāyāna 1.580, 4.501, 7.508, 13.330; how to express it when language derives from the experience it transcends? 26.199–200; it has a narrow denotation and a wide connotation 1.149–50; lower and higher degrees of the same experience 1.581; its meaning in modern Indian languages 15.463; 'musing', Mrs Rhys Davids' inadequate translation 7.228, 18.499; a state of total integration and absorption 11.34; three levels of meaning 2.109, 16.11

the nature of samādhi
drawing all of oneself together into a single focus of energy 3.306; 'The food of *samādhi* is sufficient to sustain one' 18.620; an uninterrupted flow of positive mental states 9.206; the harmonization of all one's energies 4.513; the indispensable basis for wisdom 7.257, 18.594; in its fullness, an aspect of Enlightenment 1.585–8, 3.353; it arises naturally when you are perfectly happy 15.221; it can't be acquired forcibly or artificially 2.260–1; like the absorbed experience of the musician or the lover 11.34; not an end, but a means 7.229; perception through the five senses plays no part in it 17.543; the pool of peace 25.33; *samādhi* and culture 7.436; *samādhi* and the transcendence of mind 26.199; the spirit and the letter 11.481

its relationship to other aspects of the Buddhist tradition
Buddhism is rich in methods to develop it 7.257; the heart and centre of the Buddhist spiritual life 7.508; was the Buddha always in *samādhi?* 5.447, 5.743 (n431); *avitakka samādhi* 10.606; ethics: thought simplified into *samādhi* 7.320; an ever-present mental state (Abhidharma) 12.148; as one of the object-determining mental events (Mahāyāna Abhidharma) 17.542–5; how *śrāvakas*, *pratyekabuddhas*, and bodhisattvas face its happiness 1.259; it needs to be balanced with *vīrya* 1.293, 3.307–8, 9.214, 17.82–3, 19.551; perfect or right concentration, *see under* Noble Eightfold Path; the bodhisattva and the twenty-five *samādhis* 14.239; in the *Samādhirāja Sūtra* 14.193

distinctions
samādhi and *prajñā* 21.506; concentration and establishment in Enlightenment 1.580, 1.588; *samādhi* and *dhyāna* 2.109–10, 9.205–6; *samādhi* and mindfulness 1.150

see also
meditation; concentration; the ensuing *samādhi*, *see under dhyāna*/a guide

to *dhyāna*; as one of the five spiritual faculties, *see under* five spiritual faculties; as one of the seven *bodhyaṅgas*, *see under* seven *bodhyaṅgas*; as one of the six *pāramitās*, *see under* perfections/ six perfections/(5); as one-pointedness (*citass'ekaggatā*), *see* one-pointedness; *lokuttara* (transcendental) *samādhis*, *see* three *vimokṣa-mukhas*; in the positive *nidānas*, *see under* twelve positive *nidānas*; *upacāra-samādhi*, *see* neighbourhood concentration

samādhi-prajñā 4.501

Samādhirāja Sūtra 2.567, 14.100, 14.190–5

samādhis *see* three *vimokṣa-mukhas*

Sāmagāma Sutta *see under Majjhima Nikāya*

samaṇa 12.522

samānārthatā *see* exemplification

sāmaṇera *see* under *bhikkhu*/ordination/ lower

Samaññaphala Sutta *see under Dīgha Nikāya*

Samantabhadra (bodhisattva) the universally beneficent 16.233; appears with Mañjuśrī and the Buddha in the Śākya Trinity 2.180; association with Emeishan, a sacred mountain in China 2.224; in the *Avataṃsaka Sūtra* (vows) 2.454; in China and Japan he rides a white elephant 2.180; Japanese form, Fugen Bosatsu, appears as a courtesan 1.448–9, 14.182; a figure in Ipoh, Malaysia, with an expression of mysterious dignity 24.43; in the *Gaṇḍavyūha Sūtra* 1.355, 2.179, 14.218, 14.226–7; iconography 2.180; one of a group of eight bodhisattvas 2.172; reciting his name brings as much merit as visualizing the Tathāgata 14.177; Samantabhadra's ten vows 14.226–7; in the *White Lotus Sūtra* 2.179, 14.128, 14.177; associated with Vairocana 2.172

Samantabhadra (Buddha) as Ādibuddha, visualized on the Refuge Tree 13.208; revered by the Nyingmapas 22.462; symbolizes the *svabhāvikakāya* 19.201

samanta-cakṣus *see under* five eyes

Samantamukha 2.176

Samantamukha-parivarta 14.108–9

Samantha 26.610–12

samāpattis ('attainments')

introduction
Sangharakshita's special use of the term 1.639 (n468); 'I don't nowadays generally use that term' 4.501; two uses of the term 4.496; dimensions of consciousness 4.514; four *arūpa-samāpatti* 14.83; nine *samāpattis* (attainments) 8.584; and psychedelic experience 4.514; and self-hypnosis 4.502

experiences as a result of concentration
visions, sounds, smells, changes in sense of weight and heat 1.583–4, 3.352; subtle senses: clairvoyance, clairaudience 1.584; joy, bliss, ecstasy, flashes of insight 1.585; they vary from person to person 15.108

samatā-jñāna *see under* five *jñānas*

śamatha (Pāli *samatha*)

introduction
alternative translations 1.582, 5.425; the limitations of *śamatha* 8.440–2; meditation practice pertaining to the four *dhyānas* 4.497; makes you so concentrated that you only have the thoughts you want to have 5.418; mistaking *śamatha* experience for Enlightenment 19.159; the importance of retaining mindfulness 19.159; the pacification of unskilful states and the attainment of the *dhyānas* 17.186–7; *samādhi* and *prajñā* 7.140, 17.611; the state of mind of the god realm 13.130; three levels 1.582, 3.351–2, 4.497, 4.501; what *śamatha* means for the Mahāyāna 17.187; and the Yogācāra 19.373

ŚAMATHA AND *VIPAŚYANĀ* (INSIGHT)

introduction
all meditation practices have *śamatha* and *vipaśyanā* aspects 15.109, 18.512–14; alternating the two kinds of practice until they merge 15.339; both are needed for full liberation 17.187; bliss and insight 18.416; calm and insight (or clear vision) 5.417, 5.420–1, 5.423–4, 11.155–6, 25.44; Siddhārtha left his teachers because they could teach him *śamatha* but not *vipaśyanā* 8.442; Nyams and rTogs (Tibetan) 18.299

distinction
the distinction 1.168, 3.351; inability to distinguish between them 8.442; one of Buddhism's most basic distinctions 8.439; the doctrinal formulation is the bridge between the two 19.452; sometimes too sharply differentiated 4.497, 4.619; stopping and seeing 1.354; the relation between them compared to reading a difficult book 19.451; roughly analogous to bliss and *śūnyatā* 19.155; *śamatha* is

like a picture drawn with coloured chalks, insight fixes the picture 18.512; *śamatha* refines conditioned individuality, *vipaśyanā* helps us see through it 5.33, 5.418, 26.48

in practice
vipaśyanā without *śamatha*?, *see* insight/how to gain insight/'dry' insight; deepening *vipaśyanā* once *śamatha* has been established 5.429; deepening *vipaśyanā* without the need for more formal practice of *śamatha* 5.428–9; emphasizing *vipaśyanā* at the expense of *śamatha* 8.584, 8.620–1; how much *śamatha* is enough before we go on to cultivate insight? 5.430; is *vipaśyanā* more difficult than *śamatha*? 5.462; making your mind one-pointed through *śamatha* in order to develop insight 18.399; the mind is cleansed and refined through *śamatha* and thus able to develop insight 5.410; people often take up *vipaśyanā* practices with insufficient *śamatha* preparation 17.768 (n489); *śamatha* experience as the basis for *vipaśyanā* 8.441; to try to eliminate *śamatha* is to misrepresent the Buddha's teaching 5.445; *vipaśyanā* should grow quite naturally out of *śamatha* 4.497; visualization practices a combination of *śamatha* and *vipaśyanā*, *see under* visualization/introduction; when having a strong *śamatha* experience, directing the mind towards *vipaśyanā* 5.602; within the context of *śamatha*, *vipaśyanā* arises (*Sūtra of Golden Light*) 16.261; with no insight, *śamatha* can become dull and drowsy 19.159

samatha-yānika 1.168

samaya (Tantric vow) the bond between guru and disciple created by initiation 26.700; breach of *samaya* is said to have potentially terrible consequences 26.700; entering an agreement or contract 7.476–7, 18.325; corresponds to *prātimokṣa* and *bodhisattva-śīla* 7.476; it is rare to find someone who really keeps the *samaya* 19.458; like a castle, the *samaya* gives strength and structure to your spiritual life 19.397–8; the Tantric vow or pledge: your promise to your *yidam* 19.385

samayasattva *see under* visualization

Samayatāra *see under* Tārā

samayavimukti *see under vimukti*

sambhogakāya *see under trikāya* doctrine

sambodhi 1.131, 2.116

sambodhicarya 14.521

saṃbodhicitta 4.268

sambodhyaṅgas 14.81

saṃdhā ('hidden meaning') 14.153

Saṃdhinirmocana Sūtra introduction 14.200–1; absolute mind 2.67; association with the Yogācāra 12.168; difficult of access 1.352; 'Explication of Knots' 12.168; 'Material help is not sufficient 1.428–9; says that the Buddha's teaching is a *miśra* (mixed) Dharma 26.548; a verse on the *ālaya-vijñāna* 14.200–1; translations 13.337, 14.200; Sangharakshita and the *sūtra* 24.573, 26.545

Samding Dorje Phagmo (female *tulku*) 12.16, 13.53, 18.109

Samdup, Mrs Rose 15.383, 21.238–42

sameness of all *dharmas* (*sarvadharma-samatā*) 1.268, 3.236–7, 7.505, 14.192; Buddhist preference for the expression 'not-two' 16.449; *ekalakṣaṇa-samādhi*: everything is in its ultimate depths the same 1.587; the sole reality 1.268; *see also* five *jñānas*/wisdom of equality

Saṃghabhadra 17.756 (n379)

saṃgrahavastus *see* four *saṃgrahavastus*

sāmisa 15.156

saṃjñā (perception) as omnipresent mental event 17.514–20; as *skandha* 2.75, 2.98, 14.420, 15.181–2; our propensity for *saṃjñā* 17.547; and the twelve positive *nidānas* 17.519; *see also* perception

Saṃjñāya (*yakṣa*) 16.245

Śaṃkara *see* Śaṅkara

saṃkaṭa *see* oppressions

Sāṃkhya (school of Brahminical philosophy) introduction 7.596 (n299); Āryadeva's application of the dialectical method to it 1.321; the Buddha's refutation of it described in the *Buddhacarita* 17.440; close in spirit to the philosophy developed by the Buddha 17.439; its connection with the Abhidharma 17.439–40; founded by Kapila 17.439; *pradhāna* and *ātman* 4.424–5; *puruṣa-prakṛti* dualism 7.194–5, 10.53, 12.278, 17.362; *satkāryavāda* view 1.314, 17.362, 17.775 (n572); state of liberation (*kaivalya*) 10.53; they conceived of consciousness as a sixth sense 17.439; they first thought in terms of the five elements 17.439

sammā-diṭṭhi *see* right view

sampajañña *see* mindfulness of purpose

Sampasādanīya Sutta *see under Dīgha Nikāya*

saṃprajanya *see* mindfulness of purpose

Sampson, Clare v23

saṃsāra

introduction
has no perceptible beginning in time 1.39, 16.388–9; driven by the forces of greed, hatred, and delusion 3.244; world of suffering 1.130–1, 7.274, 11.272; its cyclical nature 2.252, 12.593–4, 16.388, 19.122; nothing but our own reactive mind 18.177; nature as *saṃsāra* 16.387–8; not seeing its limitations 19.10; its root is our own passive attitude 19.580; round of conditioned existence 7.494; without end 26.208

its nature
absorbed in watching it unfold, you can forget the purpose of your existence 19.9–10; action utterly divorced from wisdom is called *saṃsāra* 7.139; essentially an expression of compulsiveness 17.633; gross, turbulent, and mutually conflicting energies 2.102; in a sense everything within it is unsatisfactory, but it is not completely negative 17.592; it never takes a holiday 18.177; kept going by blind, egoistic obstinacy 19.18; pain and pleasure both perpetuate *saṃsāra* 10.608; religion is often just part of it 19.468–9; setbacks as reminders of its unpredictable nature 18.47; 'still lingering in the realm of action' 19.177–8; 'The things of this samsaric world are all illusion, like a dream' 5.602–8; those in its bondage don't see anything wrong with it 10.617; we can remain in *saṃsāra* indefinitely if we want to 7.261, 26.52

images and symbols
the sea of birth and death 18.582; torrent in which worldly beings struggle 1.241; waves on the ocean 1.42–3; terrible waters infested with the sharks of birth and death 7.68; a jungle 11.407; a long road 19.398; a precipice 4.331; Māra the embodiment of *saṃsāra* 3.277, 11.401; the burning house 9.358; the wheel of life 3.243

Buddhist teachings about it
aversion can be useful if directed towards *saṃsāra* 17.290; *avidyā* is its root 17.610; being repelled by its ugliness 18.580; Buddhism divides it into three planes or *lokas* (see *trailokya*) 1.159; Buddhism sees what it is really like, but trusts the power of positive forces 4.267–8; described in the first two noble truths and the twelve cyclical *nidānas* 7.494; the Dharma is concerned to inculcate aversion to and renunciation of it 1.124; fall from higher to lower states within *saṃsāra* 16.100; 'near' or 'far' depending on how the Dharma is viewed 1.122–3; reflection on its shortcomings 1.130, 5.547; a Refuge doesn't just improve conditions, but enables you to transcend them 15.587–8; seeing through *saṃsāra*'s imperfections 10.549, 18.580; a spiritual community is a sort of hermitage in the middle of *saṃsāra* 19.341; the Tantra say we need to experience it on higher and higher levels 18.416; the powerful energies that produce it are to be channelled towards Enlightenment 19.378

freedom from it
cessation 2.102; free from *saṃsāra*, you become free within *saṃsāra* 18.45; if one is in the *saṃsāra* out of compassion, one doesn't experience it as *saṃsāra* 4.473; in the ultimate sense there can be no abandonment of *saṃsāra* 1.268; move from *saṃsāra* to Sukhāvatī 3.453; to find true happiness, you have to be convinced you won't find it in *saṃsāra* 19.242–4; to the Enlightened person *saṃsāra* is no obstacle at all 19.64–5

see also
Nirvāṇa/ Nirvāṇa and *saṃsāra*

saṃskāras (Pāli *saṅkhāras*, karma formations) Abhidharma analysis 1.174, 2.98–9; one aspect equivalent to *saṃskṛta-dharma* 2.67; definitions 1.108, 5.755 (n570); double meaning of the word – may relate to the first verse of the *Dhammapada* 2.67; entering *dhyāna* one experiences first *saṃskāra*, then *vedanā* 17.527–8; important equation: karma = *cetanā* = *saṃskāras* 2.68, 17.520–1; *karma-cetanā* and rebirth 1.108; likened to actions committed while drunk 17.434; as one of the five *skandhas* 15.182; *prāpti* and *aprāpti* 14.362; of the religious experiences of humanity 7.364–5; the root of the reactive mind 4.556; the *saṃskāra* of happiness 19.583; translated 'volitions' or 'willed action' 2.75, 3.195; 'underlying bases of conditioned existence' (Śāntideva) 4.556; *vedanā* combines with *saṃskāra* to produce emotion 15.150; the wise do not make plans (i.e. set up *saṃskāras*) 17.475; the workings of karma 15.182

see also
volitions; as second *nidāna*, *see under* twelve cyclical *nidānas*

saṃskṛta *see* composite

saṃskṛta-dharmas *see under dharmas*

saṃskṛta-śūnyatā *see under śūnyatā*/four *śūnyatās*

saṃskṛti ('the perfected') 3.206, 16.364–5

saṃtuṣṭi *see* contentment

saṃvara (ordination) *see under* bodhisattva/bodhisattva career

Śaṃvara (Dem Chog, Tantric deity) consort of Vajravārāhī 19.592 (n10); emanation of the Buddha Akṣobhya 19.592 (n10); four initiations of Dem Chog 18.65; and Milarepa 19.37; an offering to Dem Chog 19.537; Shiwa Aui is given the initiation 18.159

saṃvaṭṭa (involution) 1.40

saṃvega (to be shaken by the Dharma) 14.471

saṃvṛti-satya or *sammuti-sacca* (relative truth) *see* two truths

samyag-ājīva, samyag-dṛṣṭi, samyag-vāc, samyag-vyāyāma, samyak-karmānta, samyak-samādhi, samyak-saṃkalpa, samyak-smṛti *see* Noble Eightfold Path

samyak-dṛṣṭi *see* right view

samyak-sambodhi 13.297, 17.360–1

samyak-sambuddha (*sammāsambuddha*) Infinitely Creative One 15.469; one of the nine holy persons 2.151; Perfectly Enlightened One 15.58, 15.464; the prefix *sammā* implies completeness, universality 10.170, 15.470; three kinds of Enlightenment: *arhant*, *pratyekabuddha*, *sammāsambuddha* 15.465; what is a *samyak-sambuddha*? 26.699–700

Samye Ling (Scotland) 25.92

Samye monastery *see under* Tibetan Buddhism/monastic life

saṃyojanas *see* ten fetters

Samyuktāgama 14.550, 14.654 (n486)

Saṃyutta Nikāya

introduction
description 3.84–5, 14.43–7; an impressionistic account of the content of the first part 14.45–6; the difference between the first part and the other four 10.426, 14.44–6; emphasis on the thirty-seven *bodhipakṣya-dharmas* 14.47; overlap with the *Aṅguttara Nikāya* 14.44; tedious multiplication of *suttas* 14.47; translation by Bhikkhu Bodhi 14.9

FAMOUS *SUTTAS*

Brahmāyācana Sutta (6.1)
Nirvāṇa beyond the reach of reasoning (*atakkāvacara*) 1.209; Brahmā Sahāmpati's request, *see* Brahmā Sahāmpati; 'There are beings with but little dust in their eyes' 1.181, 12.188–9, 18.57, 23.366; vision of humanity as a bed of lotuses, *see under* Brahmā Sahāmpati's request; 'Wide open are the doors to the Deathless' 3.74, 3.640 (n80)

Gārava Sutta (6.2)
the Buddha wonders whom he can honour and respect 3.65, 4.168, 4.346, 19.316; the Buddha decides to honour and respect the Dharma 26.627–8; it is imperative to live revering that which is greater than oneself 22.xxi; the Buddha is giving us an example of how we should live 26.632

Upanisa Sutta (12.23)
the twenty-four *nidānas* like rain filling up the streams, rivers, and seas 1.116, 3.663 (n246); the twelve cyclical *nidānas* 1.116, 3.654 (n187), 3.676 (n316); the twelve positive *nidānas* 1.116, 2.103, 3.639 (n75), 3.654 (n184), 4.705 (n303), 7.205, 10.431; *pratītya-samutpāda* 1.91–3, 1.96, 1.115–16; 'This being, that becomes' 1.89, 2.700 (n374), 7.152

Anurādha Sutta (22.86)
'I teach only suffering and the end of suffering' 1.78, 3.213, 7.115, 7.134, 7.222, 26.158–9; impossible to describe the Buddha's state after death 2.43–4, 3.645 (n126), 13.393, 14.408, 14.583; a Tathāgata is incomprehensible 1.64, 1.75

the Fire Sermon (Āditta-pariyāya Sutta, 35.28)
beautiful and terrible words: everything is burning 7.223; in T. S. Eliot's *The Waste Land* 7.450; the mind is burning 3.687–8 (n421); seen in the Buddha's spiritual vision 16.70; a similar passage in the *Udāna* 10.522; taught at Gayā Head 2.24, 10.457

Dhammacakkappavattana Sutta (56.11)
the *sutta* has a unique position in the Pāli canon 1.35; the Buddha's first discourse 2.22–3, 3.395, 3.680–1 (n355), 11.417; probably an informal talk rather than a 'sermon' 22.331; extremes of materialism and Ātmanism 7.167; 'the five aggregates subject to clinging are suffering' 3.655 (n189), 3.657 (n206); the four noble truths 1.36, 1.127, 1.477, 8.589–91, 16.613 (n219); the middle way between self-mortification and self-indulgence 13.681–2 (n49), 26.158; the Noble Eightfold Path 1.126, 3.281, 9.328, 9.567 (n304); the second noble truth: craving for existence or non-existence 8.675–8 (n69), 17.243; Koṇḍañña has attained the knowledge 1.37, 2.295, 2.700 (n372), 10.620; the

shout of the gods 1.36–7; the Wheel of the Dharma set rolling 1.36–7, 9.384, 16.613 (n221); association with the wheel-turning *mudrā* 12.212; omission by scholars of the *sutta*'s conclusion 1.35–7

ON THE BUDDHA

the Buddha

he realized a forest, but disclosed a handful of leaves 4.3, 7.50, 25.xxxviii, 11.307, 25.131–2; observation of the twelve links of conditioned existence 4.701 (n278); finding the path to the ancient city 1.53–4, 3.18, 11.408–9; 'In regard to things unheard before, there arose in me light' 1.86, 7.600 (n331), 12.519; his prophecy about what would happen to his *śūnyatā* teachings 14.136; the difference between the Buddha's Enlightenment and his disciples' 3.61, 26.181–2

famous sayings

'Friendship is the *whole* of the spiritual life', *see under kalyāṇa mitratā*; 'He who is concentrated sees things as they really are' 1.168, 17.127; 'He who sees conditioned co-production sees the Dharma' 7.493; 'He who sees the Dharma sees me' 1.251, 3.150, 3.191, 7.493; 'Here are the roots of trees. Sit down, meditate' 3.53, 3.635 (n55); 'In this six-foot body is the origin and dissolution of the universe' 7.170, 10.597, 13.567; 'Within this body is the arising and passing away of the world' 10.597; 'Mindfulness is always useful' 10.151, 10.158, 10.356, 10.368, 11.478, 11.626, 12.25, 13.328, 23.37; 'Why do you harp on "being"?' 1.100

the Tathāgata

the marvellous powers of the Tathāgatas 1.255; the Tathāgata exercises mastery with the body 18.75; the Tathāgata who causes a way to arise is like the sun arising in darkness 1.52–3

TEACHINGS AND THE PEOPLE WHO RECEIVED THEM

stories, similes, metaphors

'By faith the flood is crossed' 1.290, 25.15; the definition of a *kalpa* 1.39–40, 2.671 (n88), 4.60, 19.593 (n16); a lotus whose spirit told a monk not to steal its scent 26.243; the blind turtle puts its head through a yoke in the sea 1.418, 4.367, 7.170, 13.139; images for the five hindrances 1.559, 11.122–3; monkeys living free in the mountains, but trapped if they wander lower down 19.341; *nāgas* descending from pool to pool compared to seven *bojjhaṅgas* 3.663 (n246); similes to suggest the vastness of infinite space 2.63, 2.671 (n85); tending the sacred fire and the light of inner practice 2.264–5

doctrines

the Dharma is that which is profitable to oneself as well as to others 7.256; form is not the self 10.592, 10.719 (n467); the three *lakṣaṇas* (Pāli *lakkhanas*) 1.175–6, 3.656–7 (n200), 16.585 (n13); four *iddhipādas* (bases of psychic power) 10.717 (n451); four kinds of attachment 3.199–200; four kinds of nutriment 22.285, 22.601–2 (n233); five hindrances 13.72, 13.677 (n27); five spiritual faculties (*indriyas*) 1.281, 3.669 (n281); four right efforts 16.585 (n11); the burden of the five *khandhas* 13.386–7; incalculable is this round of birth and death 1.39, 1.130–1; none of the five *skandhas* is self 11.755 (n201); the six sense bases 1.556; discussion of seven elements (*dhātu*), including the *subha* 4.270, 4.692 (n225); middle way between nihilism and eternalism 14.572, 14.656 (n500); 'Neither here nor there nor in between exist' 10.462, 10.638; Nirvāṇa: the cessation of *lobha*, *dosa*, and *moha* 3.223, 16.63; Nirvāṇa the delightful stretch of level ground 1.81–2; Noble Eightfold Path 3.653 (n181); ten fetters 3.684 (n377), 13.710 (n263); non-karmic factors in human experience (addressed to Sīvaka of the Top-Knot) 8.577; reference to an intermediate state 10.638, 10.723 (n504); the 'self' that is reborn is neither the same nor another 4.629–30, 4.715 (n369); Stream Entry 3.85, 4.666 (n50), 16.614 (n230); a Stream Entrant has no more than seven further rebirths 2.263, 2.696 (n348); whether Buddhas come or not, one thing stands: the relatedness of this to that 15.266, 15.754 (n103)

practice

a bigger mistake to identify oneself with the mind than with the body 3.216, 17.687; conceit: thinking of oneself as superior, equal, or inferior 4.77–8, 13.183, 18.450; eating 'only for the purpose of crossing over suffering' 24.725 (n573); the effect of wrong views on rebirth 7.523; the fate of actors 1.547, 15.371; the fate of those who exacerbate lust, hatred, and delusion 8.208; full development of the five spiritual faculties makes one an *arhant* 7.489; the senses find refuge in the mind as sixth sense, the mind finds refuge in mindfulness 17.543; mindfulness of breathing 3.675 (n312), 3.694 (n478); Moggallāna's definition of noble silence 26.203; ordination a rich and fruitful growing thing 12.423; questioning the

purifying power of ceremonial bathing 26.179, 26.714 (n130); there is agitation for one who is dependent 10.638, 10.724 (n505); thirty-two kinds of frivolous talk 2.381, 8.467, 12.33; ways to 'denourish' the hindrances to meditation 1.637 (n453); when a monk has a spiritual friend, he will cultivate the Noble Eightfold Path 26.632; 'wordy warfare': how one should *not* speak in discussion 8.169, 8.172, 22.171

people
Akkosaka Bhāradvāja, a brahmin who insulted the Buddha 3.606, 3.693–4 (n477); Anāthapiṇḍaka meets the Buddha for the first time 1.635 (n439); the suicide of Godhika 8.451; how Mahākassapa met the Buddha 2.698 (n363); 'Māra retreated, sad and discomfited' 15.178, 15.752 (n77); King Pasenadi's discussions with the Buddha 3.674 (n306); Sāriputta meditates without thinking 'I am meditating' 1.179, 3.409, 4.592, 7.154, 14.552; Susīma's ascetic practices for the wrong reason 10.519; ten brahmins meet the Buddha and, as a result, go forth 2.699 (n365); the Buddha speaks of Uṇṇābha's faith 1.286–7; Vacchagotta the wanderer's unanswerable questions 9.479, 9.574–5 (n385); Māra 'found no trace' of Vakkali 15.593; Vaṅgīsa's poetry 3.84, 26.124–6; a wanderer who ate rose-apples … asked 'What is Nirvāṇa?' 1.69, 1.72–3, 2.122; Yamaka learns that the Tathāgata is 'not to be apprehended' 1.75

Sanankumāra (Brahmā) 5.218, 26.472–4

sanātana (Pāli *sanantana*, eternally true, of universal applicability) definition 9.315; 'The Sanantana-Dhamma' 9.312–20; the Dharma's principles are true at all times and in all places 1.55–6, 7.115, 8.181; the feeling of that quality which one gets in Nepal 7.342–3; simply means *paurāṇika* (ancient or old) 7.342

Śānavāsa (Ānanda's disciple) 13.341

Sanchi, India archaeological area 21.395–6; Chetiyagiri Vihara 21.172, 21.396; Great Stupa 2.222, 3.628n, 16.155; a man in a yellow satin suit recruiting for his sangha 7.484, 12.374; Mulagandhakuti 21.396; re-enshrinement of relics of Śāriputra and Maudgalyāyana 8.223–4, 9.14, 16.156, 21.172, 21.390–6; Sangharakshita and Lama Govinda stay there 21.392–401

Sandaka Sutta *see under Majjhima Nikāya*

sandhis *see* three *sandhis*

sandiṭṭhiko *see under Tiratana Vandanā*

Sang Jye Jhab *see under* Milarepa/disciples

Saṅgāmaji (the Buddha's disciple) 10.454–7

Sangamner 9.292, 10.143

sangha

introduction
full introduction 2.137–232; meanings of the word *sangha* 2.137, 3.395, 3.671 (n293), 4.380, 9.482–3; Buddhism *is* essentially a spiritual community 3.429; the community of all those who are treading the path together 11.90; the community of those who stand in spiritual relation to the Buddha 2.138; a community which encourages the development of skilful mental states 11.130; different levels and meanings of *sangha* 3.390, 9.250; an integral part of the Three Jewels at every level 3.429; 'The Meaning of Spiritual Community' 11.128–40; a model for the ideal society 10.348; the nucleus of an ideal community 13.515; the ideal of sangha: the spiritual family 11.442–3, 17.363; it does not belong among the *dharmas* 14.492; it brings the *Buddhavacana* to life 3.90; its members are individuals, so it is not a group 11.134, 11.224; no sangha without Dharma, and no Dharma without Buddha 25.107, 25.109, 26.511; primarily the community of those who go for Refuge 2.450, 3.401, 11.68, 11.134; stands in relation to society as the *ārya* stands in relation to the *pṛthagjana* 13.515; the *vajrakula*, the community dedicated to the direct experience of reality 13.178–9; what commitment to the Sangha means 11.385; you cannot be born into the spiritual community 3.444

THE HISTORY OF THE SANGHA

the Sangha of the Buddha's time
the Buddha's deliberate decentralization of authority 7.438; the Buddha regarded the sangha as his spiritual family 2.138; the Buddha saw the sangha's importance from the beginning 3.395; the Buddha wanted his disciples to share any honour he received 3.395; conditions under which the Buddha says it will prosper, *see under* Vajjians; created by the Buddha to preserve his teachings 8.245; created to preserve the freedom and democracy of the Kshatriyas? 10.501; a deeply moving sight 12.308–9; developments in the sangha 10.480; a dispute breaks out in the Order 3.77; donations from wealthy followers 2.24–5; the early Buddhist conception of the sangha was twofold 13.195; the

first formation of the sangha 9.220; 'He wanted that His followers should be flames' 25.286; the historical development of the spiritual community 3.428–32; 'I do not consider that I lead the sangha' 2.28, 9.306, 10.580, 25.107; people of all castes and classes joined the Buddha's sangha 2.25; spontaneous unity 25.107; the tradition of homeless wanderers was adopted 15.278–9; 'Why did the Buddha start a Sangha?' (Ambedkar) 10.270; wanderers formed the early sangha 3.461, 10.479, 15.278; without the sangha the Dharma would quickly have been forgotten 8.245

the split in the Sangha after the Buddha's time
at the Second Council (the 'Vaiśāli schism'), *see under* councils; between Sthaviravāda (or Theravādins) and Mahāsāṃghikas 1.186–9, 2.205–6, 7.497; between doctrines and compassion 3.363–5, 4.9, 4.18; development of two paths for two goals 2.204, 26.207; distinction between absolute truth and relative truth 1.83; division into Theravāda and Sarvāstivāda 2.192, 3.407–8; into sects and factions 7.273–5, 7.497; *saṅghabheda*, *see saṅghabheda*

Mahāyāna sangha
introduction 1.272–6; the bodhisattva sangha 2.207, 2.153–84; Buddhas and bodhisattvas and those who aspire to be like them 13.196–7; does not exclude the *arhants* 2.155; leading members occupy the foreground 1.275; monastic and lay 1.238, 1.274, 2.207, 7.505, 9.255; and the *mahāsaṅgha* 2.207; revivified and enlarged conception of the Buddha's spiritual family 2.152; the Tibetan sangha 13.43–57

supporting the sangha
a Buddhist should not support those who are disseminating false doctrines 1.427–8; lay support for monastic sangha, *see under* lay people; state support for the spiritual community 3.587

unity in the sangha
Dr Ambedkar emphasized the sangha's fundamental unity 9.147; could mirror to a war-torn world a faint image of a realm of peace 7.275; the spontaneous unity of the Buddha's sangha 25.107; what constitutes the unity of the sangha, and what prevents unity? 12.456–7

the future of the sangha
being reborn together 16.471–2; the Buddha makes a prophecy about monks who will one day disgrace the sangha 14.189; the future of Buddhism in the West depends on a united spiritual community 3.xi–xii; the future of the sangha 10.261–75; if too many people fall away, the whole sangha will decay 12.679; it needs at least some people whose Going for Refuge is transcendental 15.658–9; its precariousness in a precarious world 11.269–73; a network of spiritual communities could perhaps influence world events 3.619; the spiritual survival of the sangha 3.398–9

MONASTIC–LAY SPLIT

equality between monastics and lay people
Ambedkar's administering of Refuges and Precepts asserted unity 9.131; the bodhisattva ideal as an expression of that equality 14.166–7; at the time of the Buddha 2.202–3, 10.484–7; both being equally the Buddha, the one cannot be superior 1.275; the laity as much Buddhists as the monastic order 23.144; no difference between them (Ambedkar) 2.496, 2.597–8, 9.141; reformulating the principles of Buddhism in terms of lay life 12.123–6; spiritual equality: 'even though a man be richly attired …' 2.203; surely all who practise the Dharma to a superlative extent are worthy of praise 2.649

distinction
Dr Ambedkar on the subject 9.146, 9.147; the bedrock on which the edifice of Theravāda spiritual life is founded 2.592; Buddhaghosa assumes a split in his definition of Going for Refuge 15.647; created conflict in the English sangha in the 1960s 23.xv–xvi, 23.143–5; crops up again and again in Buddhist history 16.496; the difference between the two (Ambedkar) 9.112–14, 9.130–1; a difference in degree of commitment means a difference of duties 11.475–6; the difference is in relation to sexual activity 11.570; enshrined in the *Buddhavacana* 14.167; monks coming to be regarded as the 'real Buddhists' 12.388–9, 12.666, 13.411–12; for the Jōdo Shinshū the dichotomy has no relevance 8.624; for Theravādins, first-class and second-class Buddhists 2.299, 2.597, 9.254; the difference is between those who go for Refuge and those who don't 2.299, 10.385; divisions in Buddhist countries 12.388; its existence in modern India 15.486–8; the Mahāyāna transformed the distinction 14.167; a mistake to identify the sangha exclusively with the monastic community 11.136; the split is not between monastics and lay, but between more and less committed 15.98; people

attach a lot of importance to external differences 19.229–30, 19.308–10; perhaps it was necessary in the early days, but there was a cost 15.280; relationship between monks and lay people, *see* lay people/and *bhikkhus*; reasons why there shouldn't be a split 19.473; is a renunciant 'better' than a layman? 9.165, 9.340, 20.234–5; Sangharakshita's attempt to bridge the gap 2.449; separation a cause of the disappearance of Buddhism from India 9.390, 9.392; their separation according to the Theravāda 2.559–60; the Theravāda introduced the separation of monks from laity to the West 23.143; the traditional distinction becomes quite unfeasible 19.472–3; the traditional pattern need not be perpetuated 23.144; the two groups need not have the same relation to politics 7.438; unlikely to be perpetuated in the Buddhist movement in England 11.476; the Vajrayāna and Tibetan tradition doesn't distinguish 2.445–6, 16.496, 19.384; the weak spot of Buddhism, as identified by Dr Ambedkar 10.129; which is the *upāsaka* and which is the *bhikkhu*? 10.225

full-timers and part-timers
be cautious about speaking in such terms 10.486; became monks and lay people 3.406–7; Dharmapala an example of a lay (for most of his life) full-time worker for Buddhism 8.110; during and after rainy season retreat 3.405–6; full-timers dependent on part-timers only for material things 18.388; FWBO (Triratna) conception 3.414–15, 9.225, 9.319–20; modern Buddhists can be full-time and also work 15.281–2

neither monastic nor lay
an alternative: the full-time or effective sangha 3.414–15; Dr Ambedkar's solution 9.131–2; let us do away with divisions between monastic and lay Buddhists 26.56; middle way between purely monastic and 'born Buddhist' 2.470; shift of embodiment of sangha ideal from lay supporters to Vimalakīrti 2.207; Shinran described himself as being neither a monk nor a layman 2.562; U Thittila: at heart neither monk nor layman but simply a Buddhist 2.411; the traditional pattern need not be perpetuated 23.144; Triratna Buddhist Order, *see under* Triratna/Order/lifestyle; we may live in one way at one time, and the other at another time 8.577–8; we need a Buddhism that is neither, but based on the centrality of Going for Refuge 11.613; whether you live at home or have gone forth, you must practise 15.649

expulsion or suspension
introduction 2.194–5; breaking a precept disastrously places one beyond the Order 16.433; keeping out disruptive and welcoming positive energies 16.353

THE TRADITIONAL SANGHA

hierarchies of the sangha
introduction 3.403–15; Āryasaṅgha, monastic sangha, *Mahāsaṅgha* 13.43; laymen, monastics, forest renunciants 3.407; traditional categories 3.406–13; twofold: *āryas* and non-*āryas* 11.650–1, 12.538–9

Āryasaṅgha (ārya-pudgalas or ariya-puggalas)
brief introduction 3.410–13, 9.250, 10.146, 15.58; *adhiśīla*, *adhicitta*, *adhiprajñā* 1.446; all those who have passed the point of no return 15.641; awareness of their characteristics (*Dhammapada*) 15.41, 15.745 (n19); characterized by the quality of wisdom or insight 3.411; contrasting conceptions in Hīnayāna and Mahāyāna 1.273, 2.138; correlation with the bodhisattva *bhūmis* 1.446; correlation with the threefold way 1.446; disappearance into the legendary past 2.214; four noble paths (four *ārya-mārgas*) 12.27; the first three possible in lay life, but to become an *arhant* you had to go forth 10.628; hierarchy, *see under* hierarchy; in the Hīnayāna schools became a subdivision of the *bhikṣu-sangha* 2.152; holy persons, *see* holy persons; in the *Tiratana Vandanā*, *see under Tiratana Vandanā*; etymology of *ārya* 3.410; learning about their lives, developing feeling for them, aspiring to be like them 12.539; in practice represented by the *bhikṣu* sangha 7.496; intermediate between Buddhahood and unenlightened humanity 3.410–11; outlined in the Pāli canon 1.178, 3.413; the spiritual aristocracy of Buddhism 7.230; the third of the Three Jewels 1.178–9, 2.246–7, 3.326, 9.128–9; *see also* Stream Entrant; once-returner; non-returner; *arhant*

bhikṣu/bhikṣuṇī sangha
brief introduction 2.247, 3.407–10; fuller introduction 2.185–201; Dr Ambedkar's wish to reform 9.118, 9.190; *āvāsa* (local group or chapter of *bhikṣus*), *see āvāsa*; the Buddha's reasons for establishing it (Ambedkar) 9.113–14; ceremonial recitation of sacred texts for magical purposes 2.216; a convenient means of livelihood for idle people: the tragedy of the sangha 1.229; corporate acts: *poṣadha*, *varṣāvāsa*, *pravāraṇā*, *kaṭhina* 2.198–200; destruction

of the sangha 9.340; disrespect to the sangha 9.131; duties 3.409–10; ecclesiastical corporation 2.138; eleemosynary (subsisting on charity) and eremitical (being recluses or hermits) 7.496; ethical precepts, *see* precepts/monastic; failing to live up to ideals 8.246, 9.115; the field of merit 2.214, 15.647–8; of the four quarters 2.188, 2.189; givers of worldly advice, *see* monks/advisers; and Jesuits (Ambedkar) 9.116–17, 9.318–19; joining the sangha for dubious reasons 8.246–7, 10.519–20; and lay people, *see* lay people/and monks; may have a higher spiritual standard in non-Buddhist countries 1.229; membership does not signify a particular depth of Going for Refuge 3.408; a model for other Buddhists 9.113–14; in modern times the need to make it clear what a member of the sangha is 8.247; the monastic sangha 'the only constant factor in the history of Buddhism' (Conze) 8.245; need to reform (Ambedkar) 9.112–18, 9.190; the oldest religious order in the world (except perhaps the Jains) 7.496; one-sidedly monastic 9.391; praised at the expense of other groups 2.649; and ownership of property 9.114; responsibilities 2.198–200; terms sangha and *bhikṣu* sangha 2.226, 10.100, 10.676–7 (n123); three duties: to practise, preserve, and preach the Dharma 7.230, 8.245; three stages of development 2.189–90; through the ages monks have kept the lamp of the Dharma burning 8.245–6; too weak to cope with modern threats to Buddhism 9.319; united by a common way of life, the precepts 3.408; 'without a monastic order Buddhism has no backbone' (Conze) 3.410; in worldly affairs 2.216–17; *see also* monastic life; monks; *bhikkhus*; *bhikkhunīs*; ordination

mahāsaṅgha
caturvarga 2.138; all those who go for Refuge 3.407, 9.483; coincidence with the bodhisattva sangha in the Mahāyāna 2.207; the entire Buddhist community 2.138, 2.453, 7.497, 9.433; some more experienced than others 9.474–5; the spiritual community of the four directions and the three times 3.458; we go for Refuge to the whole Buddhist community 2.247

THE SANGHA (OR SPIRITUAL COMMUNITY) IN PRACTICE

introduction
all Buddhists should get to know one another as well as they can 12.81; 'The blaze of spiritual practice of those on the same path is happy' 3.402; based on *mettā* 3.450–1, 15.298, 15.332; Buddhists are all one family 9.422; the 'couple' is the enemy of the spiritual community 8.548–9; by definition the sangha is very small 3.440, 3.619; the defining principle: freedom to grow 3.440; the environment for the development of the five spiritual faculties 3.312; four characteristics of the spiritual community 8.547–51; gathering in large numbers 3.399, 3.413, 7.438, 12.412, 12.675–6; going for Refuge is the uniting factor that creates a sangha 15.599; the ideal society on a small scale 1.550; ideally consists of developing individuals 3.390; it is extremely difficult to explain its nature 2.474; a living network of friendship and communication 15.293; maintaining harmony in a larger sangha 15.517; members of the spiritual community are necessarily active by definition 11.138; neither 'we' nor 'I' 11.224; no one in the sangha has any special position 25.107; an orchestra as a spiritual community 26.31; 'all together putting forth energy, resolute, always with strong effort' 11.429; the Russian term *sobornost* is a clue to its nature 2.474, 4.656, 23.209; the sangha as 'a vital mutual responsiveness' 2.247–8, 2.461–2, 23.xvi; the sangha cannot be represented, even by a guru 14.541–3; the sangha is not a group 8.549, 10.573, 11.224, 13.485, 17.559, 26.7; sangha is something we bring into being from moment to moment 8.551; a sense of belonging 8.189; the spirit of sharing 10.273–4; the spiritual community is ideally an anarchy 14.543; the spiritual community must have a common ideal and method of practice 8.549–50; the spiritual life is a cooperative venture 14.456; a spiritual movement can have a teacher, but not a leader 25.107, 26.31; spiritual family 9.195; taking care of one another in the sangha 11.442–4; there's no such thing as a sangha regardless of the people in it 18.498, 19.361; a 'third order of consciousness' 2.474–5, 4.278, 4.656–7, 12.676; unfailing kindness in all the relationships within the sangha 11.444; the *Vimalakīrti-nirdeśa* as an elucidation of the true meaning of sangha 16.156; why the sangha has to be based on a common understanding of the Dharma 25.108–9; within the sangha, change should be in the context of continuity 12.677–8; you can almost forget about the Dharma if you're in contact with a sangha 15.610–11

images and metaphors
finding one's place in the mandala of the sangha 4.98; it has a dream life, or a mythic life, of its own – deep

roots in the sky 4.37; led on the path to Enlightenment by the bodhisattva 4.657; like a greenhouse, to nurture the spiritual faculties 3.312; a mandala and its guardians 4.97–8, 16.352–3; like roses blooming on a single rose bush 11.507; like a spiritual family in which everybody gets what they need 4.177; the sangha likened to a football team 9.304–5; the spiritual community, in whatever form, is like a lifeboat 19.347, 19.360; the unfolding of a pattern of overlapping individuals 18.286

creating sangha
all you need is people 16.473; analogous to building the Pure Land or Buddha-land 1.339–40, 16.471–8; the importance of the creation of sangha in the West 12.81; it can be founded only on the basis of complete individual freedom 18.488–9; it is to be found wherever there are individuals who have gone for Refuge 11.135–6; to create a sangha, you need individuals 3.438–9

joining the sangha
as a way of working towards solving world problems 3.618; if you are a Buddhist, you are part and parcel of the sangha 15.649–50; if you want to join the sangha, you want to go for Refuge 15.668; joining the sangha, then drifting away (as the ocean rejects a dead body) 10.564–5; making the transition to the spiritual environment of the sangha 17.39–41; not necessarily joining an organized body or living with others 3.618; open to everyone who can make a commitment 3.457, 11.135; seeking out spiritual fellowship 15.608; transition from the world to the world within the world, the sangha 17.111–12; two separate phases: going forth from home and joining the sangha 3.461, 11.133; what you want is a spiritual family, not a substitute social family 17.40–2; when you join, you give up your separate identity 9.195; you join the sangha by leaving the group 3.459–64

communication in the sangha
a basis of Going for Refuge, without attaching too much importance to our differences 26.82; becoming aware of other people's states of consciousness 15.166; being on good terms with your spiritual brothers 18.511; Blake's words about mutual forgiveness as a motto 26.649; challenges us to live out what we know conceptually and shows us what we know 17.307; complete transparency in the sangha 11.137–8, 11.386; connecting the sangha through magazines and journals 8.188–9; criticizing the sangha without realizing that one is oneself part of it 18.475; disharmony in the sangha 2.522–3, 12.456–7, 21.202–3; disputes due to differences of temperament 18.171; even the most junior member has an equal voice 15.412; harmony in the sangha 3.90, 10.580–1, 12.676–7, 18.15; hatred between members of the sangha 17.269; if everyone is covering up, there's no real communication 10.570; keep the channels of communication open and spiritual seniority will be clear 15.534–5; learning to relate (sometimes painfully) on the basis of what we have in common 11.138; mutual inspiration 17.189–90; people within it will do what they can to spark off real communication 3.439; we have to be careful not to bring pressure to bear on anyone 17.184; what's the use of being in a sangha if you don't try to communicate? 19.557; within the sangha we can be ourselves 11.136–8; working together in the sangha helps communication 15.517, 17.72; you should be able to own up to all your unskilful thoughts and feelings 11.268

how does the sangha function?
building a bridge between the world and the spiritual community 11.139–40, 11.272–3; a common spiritual framework: ideal and path (Buddha and Dharma) 3.439; decision-making in the spiritual community 18.35–6; eating together as a spiritual community 18.426–8; it keeps your faith alive 15.657, 17.71; hospitality and devotion to members of the spiritual community 15.534; how does the authentic spiritual community sustain itself? 18.175; an important function of the sangha is letting people know they are cared for 17.185; the importance of helping one another 9.194–5, 14.414–15; imposing democracy on the spiritual community 8.583; it has to be independent so that it can stick to its ideals 19.464–5; it has to distribute work so that no one has to exhaust themselves working 18.203; it is impossible for one member to pressurize, bully, or manipulate another 14.578; it should encourage people to change 17.239; members are not obliged to do anything for the world 11.139; regarding the spiritual community as a convenience to your own development 11.286; relating to each other on the basis of the spiritual ideal 11.136–7; respect towards members of the Sangha 17.261; the sangha and the power mode 8.582–3, 15.619, 16.433–4; sharing possessions in the spiritual community

19.551–2; sometimes we're more interested in what someone can do than who they are 11.439; the team running a retreat an example of the sangha in action 9.304–7, 12.625; there should be a place for those devoted to more intensive practice 12.679–80; what do its members do for themselves, one another, and the world? 11.136–40; without *mettā* in the sangha, no chance of the *bodhicitta* arising in its midst 17.186

the sangha and the group
are we looking for a spiritual community or a group? 3.441, 3.442–3; it battles (non-violently) with the group and may one day overcome it 3.432–3; being able to leave shows you haven't turned the sangha into a group 5.680; don't use the Buddhist community as a community substitute 12.68–9, 12.81, 19.361; individual and group are two, and the sangha is the entrance to non-duality 16.548; it can't be a flock of sheep under a shepherd, nor sheep going their own way 10.580–1; Milarepa's craving turns the sangha into a gathering of hungry ghosts 18.27; the sangha can alternate between spiritual community and group 19.361; the sangha cannot cut itself off from the group entirely 3.444, 11.272–3; the sangha is companionship that helps you grow, not a group to conform to 18.35; the sangha is not a group, not a cosy place to be 10.573; the sangha tends to degenerate and become a group 3.440, 15.498; the sangha's effect on the group 3.440–4, 3.619; the sangha's purpose is the opposite of the aims of the group 3.440; the spiritual community can be vulnerable to the gravitational pull of the group 3.443; the Triratna Buddhist Order is not a group, but a spiritual community 2.568

love and power in the sangha
no question of law and punishment within a Buddhist order 16.433; positive emotion is at the heart of the spiritual community 3.451; the sangha is based not on power but on *mettā* 3.450–1; the sangha can have no representing, official positions, authority 3.446; the sangha cannot coexist with power 3.447; the spiritual community is not a power structure 11.185; the spiritual community sometimes supports complacency and lack of care 18.164; trust within the sangha 3.488, 10.332, 10.571, 16.315; we should direct *mettā* towards the whole of the sangha 12.680; what would happen if a member of the sangha gained political power? 16.433

why we need a sangha
to help each other develop spiritually 3.438, 5.252; its presence in the world can counter the forces of destruction 7.512; it can be trusted to provide you with what you need 17.327; it is a world within a world 1.340; it encourages freedom of thought, freedom to grow 3.440; it gives us the chance of inhabiting the *dharmadhātu* 3.402; it gives us the opportunity to serve others 3.401; it helps us become aware of what is going on in us 3.488; it helps us to maintain genuine interest in the Dharma 18.542; it provides a safe environment for self-disclosure 3.488; it's where we begin to transform our lives 18.37; no one else can practise for us, but practising with others is best 3.578, 10.267–8, 11.703; not all Western Buddhists recognize the sangha's importance 3.396; rejoicing in its merits 11.269; the sangha and the arising of the *bodhicitta* 3.451, 4.30, 11.285; to be able to talk with others with experience of the way of life we're considering 17.364; to bring about the integration of Buddhism into society 3.624, 11.468; to help us with the difficulties of the spiritual life 11.138–9; to provide an emotionally positive, open-ended base 17.370; to sustain our faith and our Going for Refuge 15.657–9, 15.738; for companionship and support 12.514; we wouldn't get far on our own 4.173–4, 12.67–8, 12.622; to help transform our emotional nature 1.511; without it, no future for Buddhism in the West 3.xi–xii; we need it until we have insight 19.347, 19.359–63; we should associate with those who will support our practice of the Dharma 17.308–9; we will develop more easily and enjoyably with others 11.385–6; you rely on others and they rely on you 11.442–3

see also
esoteric Sangha refuge, *see under* three esoteric refuges; and the positive group, *see* group/positive group; as Refuge, *see* Going for Refuge/Going for Refuge to the Sangha; the Sangha Jewel, *see under* Three Jewels

Sangha Sabha (Council of Buddhist Monks of Great Britain) 8.336–8, 23.42–4, 23.198

saṅghabheda the emperor Aśoka warns against schism 23.360; Devadatta attempts to cause, *see under* Devadatta; distinction between unskilful *saṅghabheda* and skilful division of the sangha 3.638 (n70); one of the five heinous crimes, *see* five heinous crimes; trying to create

divisions in the Sangha is an offence against it 4.311

Sanghadeva, Dharmachari 26.406, 26.659

Sanghadevi, Dharmacharini centre president 12.632; conducts ordinations 2.733 (n628); member of the Preceptors' College 12.597, 12.631; at Mañjughoṣa stuti *sādhana* retreat 26.663

saṅghadisesa 2.195, 2.628–30

saṅgha-karmas (Pāli *sanghakammas*, corporate acts of the sangha) 2.193, 2.198–200

Sanghamittā (historical) 2.222

Sanghamitta, Dharmacharini 15.437

Saṅghānandi 13.342

Sangharakshita

contents for this section

(I) life story 1: from birth to departure for India (1925–1944): introduction – early years – in the Second World War. (II) life story 2: India 1944–1964: going forth – wandering days – in Kalimpong – Kalimpong places of residence – Triyana Vardhana Vihara. (III) life story 3: return to the West (1964–2018): return to England (1964) – Triratna (FWBO) years – places of residence – travels – old age, sickness, and death. (IV) family: ancestry – father – mother – other relatives. (V) Buddhist life: early years – ordination – personal practice – meditation – *sādhanas* and initiations – monastic lifestyle. (VI) inner and emotional life: spiritual and supernatural experiences – spiritual life – influences and inspirations – emotional life. (VII) identity: temperament and characteristics. (VIII) Dharma teacher: thinking about the Dharma – becoming a teacher – as personal teacher – study seminars. (IX) Dr Ambedkar and the Dhamma revolution. (X) public speaking: giving talks – talks in India before Dr Ambedkar's conversion – teaching tours among the new Buddhists in India (1956–1992) – talks elsewhere in the world. (XI) people. (XII) cultural life: art – works of art seen – theatre – music – reading – books read. (XIII) writings, translations, and editing: the writing experience – early writings, aphorisms, and other genres – articles – book reviews – writing poetry – *A Survey of Buddhism*: publication history – publication history of other titles – translations. (XIV) photographs and portraits. (XV) gifts and possessions

(I) LIFE STORY 1: FROM BIRTH TO DEPARTURE FOR INDIA (1925–1944)

INTRODUCTION

summary

brief account of his life 9.466–9, 10.311–12, 11.169–73, 12.493–8, 12.681–4, 23.8–20; life a single stream of activity, though located in different places 8.xxxvi–vii, 21.474; checking the growth of the 'Sangharakshita Legend' 12.385; his life described in flowers 25.282; 'I'm just living my life' 11.558–9, 11.692; overall experience of life positive 22.199; reflecting on life 26.591; what might have been if life had turned out differently 26.582–5

birthday (August 26th)

childhood birthdays 20.14, 20.504; 40th 23.147–8; 54th 24.89; 60th 24.238–42, 24.243, 24.249; 64th 24.403; 65th 24.405–6; 70th 2.546; 71st 24.518; 75th 11.660, 12.630, 25.22, 26.403–4; 77th 26.455; 78th 26.463; 80th 11.685; 90th 18.xi, 25.39, 26.549–50, 26.576, 26.674; 93rd 25.xxxii–iii; the same day as the feast day of St Josaphat 23.307

names

changes of name over the years 26.532; Dennis Lingwood: 'I never liked my Christian name' 23.111–12, 26.531–2; Dharmapriya 7.5, 20.207, 20.332; Sangharakshita 2.749–50 (n724), 20.410; giving up the title 'Maha Sthavira' 13.499; Imji Gelong (the English monk) 13.31, 22.224, 22.498; Urgyen 13.499, 22.473–4, 23.19, 23.319, 26.673

nationality

(almost) 'ashamed of being English' 20.159, 23.61; destruction of identification papers 2.414, 12.652, 20.225, 20.269, 22.560–1, 23.13; 'I cannot feel that I owe an exclusive loyalty to any nation or race' 20.230, 22.13; 'In principle I belong no more to one part of the world than another' 24.3–4; 'Much as I might believe I had no nationality, plenty of people believed I did' 22.560; in India, treated as a representative of Britain 3.446

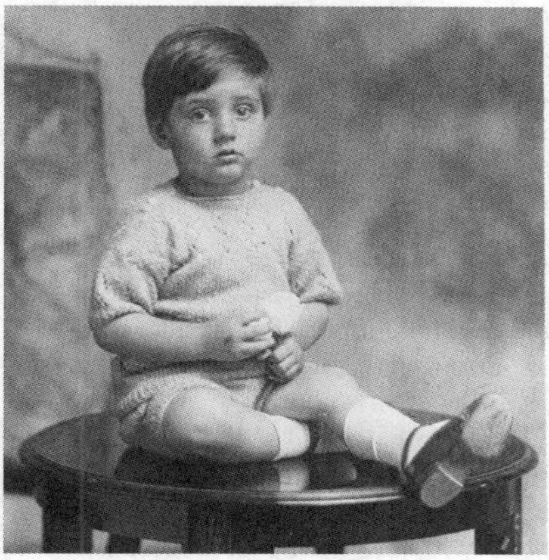

EARLY YEARS

birth
refusal to cry 20.480; baptism 20.20; birthchart 2.405–6, 22.306–7; a connection with Ananda Metteyya? 20.4, 23.41; a dream when young of a dead boy – memory of a past life? 26.678

childhood
brief introduction 9.277–8; 'Strange that someone like me should emerge from those surroundings' 12.681; described in poetry ('The Awakening of the Heart') 25.463–8; earliest memories 20.4–5, 26.432; christening 20.5; attraction to the Far East 13.495, 20.61; curio collection, *see under* Sangharakshita/XV/possessions; the effect of a film about African wildlife 25.52; at home alone 26.426; memories evoked by smell 26.491; holidays 20.33, 25.455; libraries, *see* libraries; and nature 20.27, 20.28–9; nightmares 20.482; moving house to Streatham 20.34, 26.419, 26.501–2; artwork 20.35–6, 26.582, 26.661–2; pets 26.418; shopping 26.426–8; Sunday best and social niceties 18.134; taking photographs 26.532; 'Then and Now' (poem) 25.431; Tooting 20.4–33, 20.37, 20.480

childhood illnesses and injuries
accidents 26.415, 26.429–30, 26.432–4; an experience of injustice in hospital 13.609; flu 26.433; removal of tonsils 13.609, 23.217, 26.434; an operation to remove a swelling 26.435; in hospital with scarlet fever 20.16–17, 26.421, 26.435; confined to bed at home 9.487, 12.493, 14.xi, 20.18–25, 23.8–9, 26.421, 26.435; occultist's vision of his future 20.25; the change in character brought about by confinement 13.529–30, 23.9, 26.573; convalescence 20.26–7; diagnosis reversed 20.24

education
infant and junior school 20.5–7, 20.29–32, 20.490, 26.419–21, 26.500; learning to draw 20.490; languages 20.64, 20.70; mathematics 20.39, 20.46; music lessons 26.501; self-education 9.487, 20.22–4, 20.38, 20.46, 20.61–4, 20.70, 26.217–18; sex education 13.610; teacher's warning voice 25.434; teachers 20.29–32, 20.37–8, 26.661; Tooting Public Library 20.32, 20.38, 23.9–10, 26.484; transfer to 'better' school 20.38–40; first experience of art 26.217–18, 26.661–2

other people
friends 20.5, 20.35, 20.40, 20.46–52, 20.481, 20.491, 26.417–19, 26.684; neighbours 20.39, 20.481, 26.413–17; rescuing another boy from bullies 26.418, 26.573; natural craving to belong to a group 20.41; shocked at hearing someone swearing 13.607; a glimpse of Princess Elizabeth 22.14; a dream of a boyhood friend on Wimbledon Common 26.684; early love 20.41–2, 26.420–1; 'I used to tell people I would never marry' 26.591–2; inability to understand how adults could keep talking 10.581, 19.493–4; family, see Sangharakshita/IV

games and festivals
chess 20.40; Christmas 20.12, 20.14, 20.502–4; cowboys and Indians 20.34; 'Dancing Round the Maypole' 25.430–1; Derby Day 20.7–8; grottoes 20.491–2; Guy Fawkes Day 20.8, 26.419; dressing up 20.5; pantomime, Santa Claus, fair, circus, zoo 26.421–4; playing the dulcimer 26.499; sailing a model yacht 25.xlviii, 25.249, 26.425; toy farm 26.427; toy soldiers 26.427; toy telephone 26.433

religion in early life
asking the question 'How big is God?' 26.475, 26.479; attraction to the Virgin Mary 13.598–9; Sunday School 13.527, 20.20; Boys' Brigade 7.12–13, 13.530–1, 13.609–10, 20.40–4; first encounter with the mystical (Neoplatonism in *Hypatia*) 20.20; the atheist schoolteacher 20.39–40; fascination with angels 13.585; first experiences of moral sensibility 13.606–10; regret at selfish behaviour 20.71–2; being told off for firing his water pistol at a cat 26.655–6; the Lord's Prayer 26.647; 'heart on fire with devotion to Christ' 20.44; prayed to the Buddha, Christ, and Mohammed in turn 13.531, 20.44; purchase of a small Buddha image 2.408, 12.681–2, 20.38, 26.495; writing a 'Life of Siddhārtha Gautama', *see* Sangharakshita/writings; at 13 or 14, made no clear distinction between

poetry and religion 24.547; 'I realized that I was not a Christian', *see under* Christianity/ Sangharakshita's relationship 12.493, 20.63–4, 23.10; Rosicrucianism 20.64, 20.65–7; universalism 7.12–16

adolescence
'What do you want to be when you grow up?' 26.582, 26.591; craving for emotional intoxication 20.72–3; discovering his sexuality 13.610; thoughts of being an artist 20.27–8; responses to music 20.72–3; listening to the wireless 20.72, 26.502

see also
reading, *see under* Sangharakshita XII/cultural life; writing, *see under* Sangharakshita/XIII

IN THE SECOND WORLD WAR

evacuation to Barnstaple
the outbreak of war 13.531–2, 20.45; a sense of being an outsider 26.573–4; a stay at the vicarage 13.585, 20.46–50; conflict with a Wesleyan landlady 20.50–3; school in Barnstaple 20.48

stay in Torquay
contact with Christianity 13.532; library 20.61–4; discovery that he was not a Christian, *see under* Christianity/ Sangharakshita's relationship; a little girl who took a fancy to him 15.432; lodgings with the 'insanely houseproud' Mrs Baker 20.56–7, 20.59–60; happy lodgings with Mr and Mrs French and Gwen 20.60; friendship with Mary French 20.60; work at Parkes' Coal Company 20.58–9, 20.64–5, 23.10

return to London (1941–2)
'among the most important years of my present existence' 20.68; discovery of Buddhism, *see under* Sangharakshita/V Buddhist life; getting out into the wider world 15.420; house destroyed by bomb 20.103–4, 23.10, 25.468, 26.485; mystical experiences 20.73–4, 23.10; National Gallery visits 20.71; work at London County Council 20.75–87, 23.10; through a colleague's plain speaking, learns to discuss taboo subjects 20.76; relationship with Sonia 20.78–9, 20.106

army life
conscription 9.13, 9.278, 12.683, 20.88, 23.10, 26.576–7; 'I ought never to have allowed myself to become conscripted' 4.285–6, 20.150; what might have happened if he hadn't been conscripted 26.583–5; 'could not deflect the master current of my being' 20.96; drinking black and tans 20.99; fellow soldiers 20.94–6; friend Ernie 20.91–2, 20.94–5, 20.99, 20.107–108, 20.140, 20.153; Harry the Ticker 12.416, 20.95–6; training 20.91–99, 26.577; study of Buddhism during army life 20.101–2; transformed from Outsider to Insider 26.577

India
childhood excitement at prospect of meeting Indian people 20.12; learned about through reading as a child 9.487; 'just like my own home' 9.176, 10.294, 12.508; memories of India evoked by smell 26.492–5; pleasure at the prospect of posting to India 12.683; sense of destiny to have been posted there 20.105; sea journey 20.107–9; army life in India 20.110–137; first impressions 9.278–9, 9.488, 20.109–113, 25.115; on the lookout for some vestige of Buddhism 9.278–9; visit to Calcutta and Darjeeling 20.130–7

Ceylon (Sri Lanka)
Buddhism seemed dead, or at least asleep 9.279; contact with Buddhists 9.488; the Ramakrishna ashram 20.117–29, 23.11

Singapore
time spent there during the war 20.138–57 (photo 20.156); contact with Chinese Buddhists 9.279, 9.488; policy of non-cooperation 20.153–6; camp conditions 20.154–5; day off for Vaiśākha Purṇimā Day 20.156; non-cooperation after VJ Day 20.153–4; demobilization (or 'desertion') 20.157, 23.11–12

early days after demobilization
staying in Calcutta 20.152–72, 23.12; attends All-India Dharma Parishad (aged 21) 9.279, 9.449–50, 20.173–8, 23.12–13; attends a Hindu wedding 20.181–2

(II) LIFE STORY 2: INDIA 1944–1964

GOING FORTH

what it was like
brief description 2.499, 9.279, 12.545–6, 20.225–6, 23.13; disillusionment with worldly life and organized religion 2.412–13, 12.551–2; destruction of ID papers 2.414, 12.652, 20.225, 20.229, 22.208, 22.560–1; rainbows appeared as he set out on foot 20.226, 22.185, 23.13, 26.671–2; robes dyed with *gerua-mati* 2.413, 20.225; realization of change of status: people prostrating at his feet 20.228–9

reflections
anniversaries 12.545–6, 12.652; reflections on the experience 2.415–16; did not realize the distinction between going forth and

bhikṣu ordination 2.413–14; differences from Siddhārtha's going forth 12.551–2; following the personal example of the Buddha 2.413, 12.552; motivations 12.652; the only thing from which he did not go forth was his mother tongue 22.208; an Outsider, in the world, but not of it 26.575; sticking to the principle of going forth 22.209

WANDERING DAYS

introduction
brief account 9.13, 9.279, 9.467, 9.488, 9.501, 12.683, 23.13–14; full account 20.226–441; *see also* Buddharakshita

the wandering life
the burden of carrying one's possessions 20.241–3; came to know and love India 12.652; difficulty of meditating en route 18.629, 19.361, 20.248–9; feet blistered through walking on hot sand 20.382–3; 'for the first time in my life I wished I possessed fewer books' 20.243; 'a freelance wandering ascetic' 12.652–3; homelessness 22.186; long-haired and long-bearded 22.152; wandering from place to place was very distracting 19.361

Indian lifestyle
bathing Indian style 20.176–7, 20.258, 20.304–5; first stay in Indian household 20.161–2; learns to cook 20.216–17; learns to eat with his fingers 20.119; sanitary habits 20.235–6; simple life 20.304; sleeping conditions 19.96

caste
challenged to declare caste 3.142, 9.280, 11.353, 12.245, 20.267–9, 20.306; caste discrimination 20.194–5; enumerated as a Hindu by religion and a Buddhist by caste 21.168–9; insists on receiving food from a low caste woman 20.399–400; a woman persuaded to give water despite her caste 20.415

the route
decision to walk from Cape Comorin to the Himalayas 20.230; Cape Comorin 7.165, 7.591–2 (n268), 20.237–42; from Cape Comorin to Trivandrum 20.243–6; Trivandrum (staying at the Ramakrishna Mission) 20.247–52; from Trivandrum to Muvattupuzha 20.252–4; Muvattupuzha (where he stayed for a year) 20.255–327; Mangalore (Swami Ramdas' ashram) 20.321–34, 26.575–6; Tiruvannamalai (Ramana Maharshi's ashram) 20.335–48; Bangalore (Yalahankar Swami's ashram) 20.349–63; excursion to Mysore 20.364–74; excursion to the Divyagiri mountains 20.375–80; Bombay 20.381–3; from Bombay to near Lucknow 20.383–6; Benares (Varanasi) 20.386–8; walking from Benares to Sarnath 20.388–9, 23.16; Sarnath 20.388–91; back to Benares 20.392–5; Benares to Kusinārā 'through the curtain of fire' 20.396–401, 23.16; from Kusinārā to Lumbini 20.414–9; crossing the Nepali border to Lumbini 20.419–21

Anandamayi's ashram
full account 20.183–210; first impressions 20.183–4; devotional meetings 20.185–90; caste distinctions 20.194–202; spiritual flirtation 20.197–8

Muvattupuzha ashram
full account 20.255–327; description 20.256–8; devotional practice 20.258–60; food 20.260, 20.288; staff 20.260, 20.288–9, 20.297–8; support by subscription 20.265–6, 20.305–6; benefits of visiting local people 20.266; ideal conditions for meditation 20.288; Satyapriya organizes milk distribution for children 20.289, 20.291; public meetings and town events 20.292–4; idea for an Industrial School at 20.296–7, 20.300; fasting 20.303–4; reflecting on the Dharma 2.414, 23.14–15; appearance of hungry ghosts 20.310; Krishna's vision 20.312–15; leaving the ashram 20.327

Ramana Maharshi's ashram
full account 20.336–48; glimpse of a beautiful young man 20.344; meets the Shankaracharya of Puri 20.343–4; Ramana Maharshi's *darshan* 20.341–3; Virupaksha Guha cave 20.337–48; vision of Amitābha, *see* Sangharakshita V/spiritual experiences/visions; spiritual change symbolized by the temple bell 20.340–1

see also
the quest for ordination, *see under* Sangharakshita V/study and travels with Bhikkhu Kashyap, *see under* Kashyap

IN KALIMPONG

arrival
summary of the time there 11.171–2, 23.17–19; first sight of the town 20.467–69; arrival 9.13, 9.281, 9.468, 9.501, 20.467–71; 'Stay here and work for the good of Buddhism' 9.281, 9.468, 9.489, 9.501, 10.3, 12.430, 20.470, 21.7–8, 21.474, 22.388, 23.17; its bright colours: 'a world of jewels' 11.171; concern about the state of religion in the town 21.161

starting Buddhist activities
time to start paying attention to the spiritual needs of others 21.24; how

was I to start working for the good of Buddhism? 9.281, 9.468, 21.35–6; the bodhisattva ideal a support 2.455, 22.541–2; perhaps better advised to join forces with an established organization? 21.367; feeling that no-one understood him or sympathized with his aims 2.424

Young Men's Buddhist Association (YMBA), *Kalimpong*
founding 8.649, 21.36–8, 23.17; Activities Committee 21.243–4; Kalimpong branch of the Maha Bodhi Society 8.650, 8.655, 21.427–31, 22.62; caste prejudice against its members 21.82; fundraising 21.100–1, 21.138–43, 21.316; disharmony between helpers 21.81, 21.144–6; financial difficulties 21.316–17, 22.102–4, 22.118–19; photograph 21.219; recreational activities 21.59, 21.63, 21.314, 22.189; Aniruddha shuts it down 21.115–16; Banshilal's Godown 21.138–9; writing to Dr Ambedkar about it 9.13, 9.502, 10.3

tutorial classes
meeting a need 21.59–62; exam anxiety 21.95; demand for classes 22.46–7; at the Dharmodaya Vihara 21.95, 22.232–3, 22.249; teaches Bhumiveda, a Thai layman 22.43–5; students 4.610, 15.640, 16.401, 21.15–16, 21.70–8, 21.219 (photo), 21.431–2, 22.184; teaches the abbot of the Tharpa Choling Gompa 8.663, 22.511; teaches Aniruddha, a Newar monk 22.43–5, 22.225; teaches Durgaprasad v22; teaches Rechung Rimpoche 8.663; teaching Sachin poetry, *see* Sachin; Tibetan students 8.663, 21.327–8

involvement with the community
assists at an operation 22.449; Miss Barclay's cremation, *see* Barclay; celebration of Anagarika Dharmapala's birth anniversary 22.34; charcoal-burners 25.236–7; finding independence day celebrations upsetting 19.263; giving offence at a tea party 19.255; jeered at by the Christian boys at Dr Graham's Homes 22.137–8; adviser in the love affairs of Kalimpong 22.446–56; local politics 22.111; neighbours 21.148–59; presides at prize-giving ceremonies in the area 22.196–7; a rumour that he had been asked to leave Kalimpong 23.373; rumoured to be a Communist spy 13.559, 21.54, 22.25–6; takes steps to avoid a political meeting 22.211–13; the visit of the Sacred Relics, *see* Sacred Relics; with Dhardo Rimpoche he faces a threat of Chinese invasion 12.434–5

wider involvement with Buddhism in India
Dr Ambedkar, *see* Sangharakshita/IX; magazine *Stepping-Stones*, *see Stepping-Stones*; Maha Bodhi Society, *see under* Maha Bodhi Society

personal life
alternation between periods of activity and retreat time 4.462; *annus mirabilis* 21.548, 22.379–80, 23.18; daily routine 22.224–8, 22.241, 22.248–9, 23.132; the Dalai Lama visits 8.651, 21.529–30, 22.368–72; experience of generosity 16.9; financial matters 22.88–9, 22.102–4, 22.118–19, 25.133; the first seven years 22.388–9; going for alms 21.11–15, 21.41, 22.215; memories 23.205; the scents of Kalimpong 26.493–4

KALIMPONG PLACES OF RESIDENCE

Dharmodaya Vihara
first living there 21.17–19; 'as though I had settled there for good' 21.95; made to leave 21.115–24; painful memories of the place 22.43, 22.204

Burma Raja's guest cottage
life there 21.124–69; Burma Raja's great kindness 22.204

The Hermitage
life there 21.216–42; Cleopatra the cat 21.317; games room 22.7; the garden 22.5, 22.190; move from chalet to bungalow 21.319–20; neighbours 21.323–4; octagonal shrine-room 21.217–18, 21.219 (photo), 21.261–2, 21.430, 22.16; passersby 21.320–1; staff 21.322–7; the unhappy driver who lived in the garden 22.189; walking the gravel path 15.190, 21.321–2, 22.190, 25.238, 25.591–2 (n62); leaving the Hermitage 22.187–90

Craigside
life there 22.187–98; *dāna* party 22.190; blessed by Dhardo Rimpoche 22.192–3; leaving Craigside 22.263–4

Everton Villa
moving there 21.503, 22.264; gardening 21.534; the ghost of a Bengali lady 22.323–4; leaving the villa 21.535, 22.377–9, 22.389–90

TRIYANA VARDHANA VIHARA

establishing the vihara
aims and objectives 8.652–3; arrangements to purchase 8.651, 22.378–9; description 8.654–5, 22.378, 22.390; dedicated to the total Buddhist tradition 8.652, 22.376; Dhardo Rimpoche blesses the vihara 23.381; guest cottage 22.433–4; a banner of victory on the roof, *see* Kachu

Rimpoche; how the vihara was organized 8.655; a letter to Dinoo Dubash outlining plans 21.534–6; to be a 'semi-monastic' community 21.535, 21.537; Friends of the Triyana Vardhana Vihara 23.82–3, 23.324; funds raised 21.524–5, 21.546; founder-donors 8.664; helpers at the vihara 22.512–14, 22.520–4; library 8.660–1; moving in 21.547, 21.549, 22.380; Chattrul Sangye Dorje names it 8.653, 12.437, 22.376–7, 22.390, 22.393–4; dedicatory verses 8.653, 22.376–7, 22.394; the 'Monastery Where the Three Yānas Flourish' 23.18; part of worldwide Buddhist revival 8.652

life at the vihara
account of activities at the vihara 8.649–665; daily meditation and puja 8.657; life there was very simple 12.636; farming the land 21.551, 21.553, 22.429–33, 22.524, 24.463, 26.530–1; a growing community 21.552, 21.560, 21.572–3; raising funds for upkeep and support from England 23.82–3; a robbery 22.562; the vihara cat 22.441; vihara cooks 22.523–4; publications 8.659–60; support from the Maha Bodhi Society 8.655; taken seriously by other monks once he owned a property 15.717–18

festivals and ceremonies
first Vaiśākha Pūrṇimā celebration 8.658; Dharmacakra Day 8.658; festival celebrations 8.657–9; full-moon day pujas 8.657; celebration of Anagarika Dharmapala's birthday 8.658; Tsongkhapa's death anniversary 8.659; ordinations at the vihara 8.655–6; the planting of a bodhi tree 22.543–4, 25.302

visitors
list of visitors 8.656–7, 8.663–5; Sister Amita Nisatta 8.664, 22.518–20; Amritlal Bechardas of Ahmedabad 8.657; John Blofeld 8.664; Dharmadhirarajamahamuni (Thai abbot) 8.664; Dupchen, an orphan who lived at the vihara 22.440–1; John Driver 8.664; Maurice Frydman 8.665, 23.376; Christmas Humphreys 8.664; Jamyang Khyentse's visit and blessing 8.663; Jivaka, *see* Jivaka; Khantipālo, *see* Khantipālo; Bhikṣus Khemasiri and Sugatapriya 8.656; Ladakhi boys on holiday 23.363; Dr Leiventhal 8.664; D. R. Maheshkar of Poona (Dharmarakshita) 8.657; P. T. Namgyal, Maharajkumar of Sikkim 8.664; Namzey, Kachu Rimpoche's nephew 22.472; Pabongkhapa Rimpoche 8.663–4; Marco Pallis 8.664; Apa B. Pant 8.664; Hilla Petit 23.376; Tijang Rimpoche's visit and blessings 8.663; Dr Tom Schmidt 8.664–5; Mr and Mrs Simons Roof 8.665; Dr N. C. Sinha 8.665; Devapriya Valisinha 8.664; serving tea to incarnate lamas 13.54–5; students from different parts of the Buddhist world 8.657; visiting monks 22.514–15; a Western visitor who came to appreciate Buddhist ritual 11.215

leaving the vihara
leaving party 23.398; monks from the Lower Tantric College to be installed there 23.409; the sale of the vihara 21.595, 21.598

departure from Kalimpong
saying goodbye 23.375; he did not intend ever to leave 7.xx, 11.172, 11.518, 11.545, 21.573, 22.560–1; disrupted his network of relationships 18.336; 'I left as sane as when I arrived, unfortunately' 25.389; the isolation of working in that context 7.27; once he had left India, he didn't really miss it 11.527; positive memories 25.134; why didn't he stay? 9.156–7, 9.329–30, 9.469, 23.59–61

(III) LIFE STORY 3: RETURN TO THE WEST (1964–2018)

RETURN TO ENGLAND (1964)

the decision to return
invited by the English Sangha Trust 2.457, 9.157, 11.172, 11.518, 21.578–80, 22.560, 23.19–20; Khantipālo's view that he had a responsibility to the Buddhist movement in England 11.545; having kept in touch with developments while in India 11.546; had had the impression of a thriving Buddhist movement 11.518–19, 11.546; awareness of difficulties in the Buddhist movement in England 11.171–2; 'among the most demanding and spiritually rewarding years of my life' 13.382; travel from India 21.581–2, 21.586, 21.588–9; arrival 23.5–7

what it was like to return
changes in England 11.461, 12.129, 18.152–3, 23.57–8, 23.61–2, 26.237; felt no need to 'adjust' 23.57; given a watch: 'I had become the prisoner of time' 9.499, 11.543, 23.36; little knowledge of life in the workaday world 23.191; the smells of London 26.495; re-engaging with Western culture 12.634–5, 26.237–8; return was at just the right time 12.654; thoughts about getting involved with politics 10.77–8

working for the Dharma
it was my duty to help spread the Dharma in England 22.561, 23.71; the first six months 'the busiest of my life' 21.591, 23.223; came to feel very much part

of the English Buddhist scene 23.329; what Buddhism in Britain was like then, *see under* Western Buddhism/Buddhism in Britain; effort to unite Buddhist organizations 23.44–5, 23.49–50, 23.144, 23.200–1, 23.326; at the Hampstead Buddhist Vihara, *see* Hampstead Buddhist Vihara; 'Head of the English Sangha' 8.336, 23.43–4, 23.402, 23.403, 23.423; his reception ('The Ballad of the Return Journey') 25.382; 'Are you allowed to speak to people?' (journalists' question) 11.142, 18.316, 23.89; 'Who sent you?' (journalists' question) 4.643, 10.211, 12.246, 12.524, 23.89; talks at the Buddhist Society and the Hampstead Buddhist Vihara 23.49; treated as a representative of Buddhism 3.446–7; provincial groups 11.172, 12.137, 12.138, 12.364, 23.44–5, 23.141, 23.176, 23.197–8, 23.220; people's projections onto him 11.686, 12.524; presenting the Dharma in an accessible way, but not 'adapting' it 12.635, 13.378–9; reciting the Refuges and Precepts, Wesak 1964 12.304–5; summer schools, *see under* Buddhist Society

the decision to stay permanently in the West
a clear choice 11.173; difficult to say when the decision was made 23.325; 'I could work for the good of Buddhism more effectively in England' 23.325–6; the plans for his return he made before leaving for India 11.495; advantages and disadvantages 23.326–7; reflecting on the decision at Sarnath 23.362; advised not to return 11.172, 11.520, 11.547, 12.364–5, 23.376–8, 23.407, 26.441–2; some of those opposed to his return were not Buddhists 11.173; realizing the need for a new Buddhist movement, *see under* Triratna I/founding; support for Sangharakshita 23.385, 23.400–7; replying to Goulstone's letter 23.385–6; his teachers' support 11.519, 23.385, 23.409, 23.422; bringing books and thangkas back from India 23.394, 23.408; determination to create a pattern of life and work like that in India 23.331–2; the importance of fulfilling the promise to return 26.441–2; returning for good in 1967 2.466, 23.416; Centre House 23.416–17; a letter to friends and supporters 23.420–3; the intention: to make known the Buddha's Path to Enlightenment 23.423; would Western Buddhism be a fringe cult or the centre of ordinary people's lives? 23.424; his dismissal by the English Sangha Trust 11.xx, 23.425, 23.432–7; aloneness at this time 11.xx; in the wilderness (or desert) 2.610–12, 13.633–4

a flat in Highgate
moving there with Terry 23.440; art school friends (English Mystical painters) 26.612; a drama group that met there 24.582; incense parties 24.567, 26.495–6; Saturday nights at the Prince of Wales pub 26.604–5; two *rūpas* that created a strong atmosphere 14.463; visitors 26.601–6; leaving Highgate 23.473

TRIRATNA (FWBO) YEARS

early years
contact with leading Western Buddhists 2.547; finding time for everything 5.691; founding the Triratna Buddhist Order, *see under* Triratna/founding; handing on responsibilities, *see under* Triratna II/Sangharakshita's role; a period of expansion (1970) 23.451; teaching at Yale (1970) 23.453–62; returning from America to find Order members running classes well 23.462; didn't consider returning to India 11.552

sabbatical in Cornwall (1973)
reasons for the sabbatical 4.463, 11.514–17, 11.552; how he saw the Order at that time 2.474; no extended contact with the Movement for a year 4.225; 'Four Gifts': a challenge 25.139, 25.147; sensing a cloud emanating from Order members 4.572; the *Udāna* seminar 10.420–3; the positive consequences 11.525–6

later years
on retreat on the Isle of Arran (1977) 11.532; a very busy period (1980s) 24.6–7; 'a strong sense of dissatisfaction with the way I was functioning' 24.306–7; *annus horribilis*, 'the most difficult year of my life' (2003) 26.447, 26.453–64; relationship with the rest of the Buddhist world

2.543–74, 11.669–70; interfaith activities 13.562; 'retirement' plans 11.660, 11.692, 12.378–9, 12.397–8, 12.491, 12.600–1, 12.632–3; years of achievement, happiness, and fulfilment 11.736

see also
Triratna II/Sangharakshita's role

PLACES OF RESIDENCE

Padmaloka
settling there 11.562–3; he buys plates adorned with peacocks for use there 24.104; description of life there 24.6, 24.150–9; love of Padmaloka 24.187–8, 24.354; his study 12.382, 24.146; he visits and sees improvements 12.580; poems about Padmaloka 25.liv–lix, 25.344–5, 25.457; the wild geese and the cuckoo 26.438–9

flat at Sukhavati (London Buddhist Centre)
connections with the community 24.186–7; the flat is redecorated 24.371; listening to the blackbird 26.438–9; 'Neighbours' (poem) 25.384–5; 'The people of Bethnal Green' 25.385; the tree outside the window 13.227–8, 24.xxiv, 24.66; staying there after having moved to Madhyamaloka 26.455

Guhyaloka
daily routine 24.395–400; a favourite place 26.455; his cottage 24.578, 26.446; imagining himself to be in ancient Greece 24.399; like living in a kind of Buddha-land 24.394–5; like living in one of the sacred mountains of South India 24.400; poems about Guhyaloka 25.xxxvii, 25.lx, 25.391, 25.424–5, 25.435; a serious illness while there 24.330–5; an untrue rumour about his attitude to Guhyaloka 24.333–4; staying there with Paramartha 24.393–406, 24.463–4; enfolded by Guhyaloka's calm 24.601–2; plans to spend more time there 12.398

Madhyamaloka
moving there 24.578–9, 26.456–63; account of his life there 26.403–6; sitting on the patio in the sunshine 12.637; a room with a view 26.438–9; pictures on the door 26.466

Adhiṣṭhāna
naming the place 26.408; the move to Adhiṣṭhāna 26.543–4; suggestion for a painting set at Adhiṣṭhāna 26.663; the Urgyen Annexe 26.579–80

other residences and plans
a brief stay in a wooden caravan in New Zealand 24.48–9; Castle Acre, Norfolk 19.493; Norfolk, London, and North Wales the three points of a triangle 24.310; a plan to retire to the south of France 5.24, 24.187–92; a plan to share a house with friends in Suffolk 5.24, 24.190–2; idea of going to live in the United States 24.324; Il Convento, Italy, *see under* Il Convento

TRAVELS

visits to different countries
visit to India with Paramartha (1990) 24.402; visit to India with Terry Delamare (1966) 23.325–414, 24.506–7; travelling through Europe with Terry 23.242–321, 26.237–8, 26.266–7, 26.417; Sangharakshita as navigator 23.247; at ease travelling alone 24.xxi; wishes to visit New Mexico and Istanbul 11.627; lecture tours in India, *see* Sangharakshita IX/ Dr Ambedkar; *see also under* individual countries

flying
first flight 21.265–9; a flight from London to Pisa 24.222, 24.254–5; a nightmarish flight to 'Calvary' 26.674–5; flying from India to the UK 24.121–2

modes of travel in India
by car from Bombay to Poona 24.13–14; the difficulties and delights of travelling in India 10.291–3; by pony 22.470; a hazardous journey between Calcutta and Kalimpong 22.167; train travel 21.104–6, 22.135–6, 22.154–5, 22.165–6, 22.267, 23.176–7, 23.336, 23.349, 23.353, 24.110–11

holidays in Britain
childhood holidays 20.33, 25.455; North Wales 24.132–3; the North of England 24.582–4; a visit to Yorkshire 23.45, 24.384–8, 24.584; Shropshire 26.463; Somerset 26.546–8; Suffolk 26.507–14; the West Country 26.615–16

OLD AGE, SICKNESS, AND DEATH

illness and injury
acupuncture 23.84, 23.129–30, 24.337–9, 26.458, 26.461–2; advice from doctors in the Order 26.463; altitude sickness in Italy 23.301; a bad cold and fever on tour in India, 1966 23.344, 23.348–50; a bout of fever in Calcutta 22.230; bronchitis in Bombay 11.562; a day of stomach upset (India) 24.23; depleted by illness in Assam 22.90–101; Dhardo Rimpoche's concern that he shouldn't be held back by threat to life force 22.562; an encounter with a nurse who could 'see' that he had cancer 23.84, 24.337; feeling ill due to old age 24.503; fever in Calcutta 21.542; fever in Italy 23.260; flu at Padmaloka 24.374;

gall-bladder complaint 21.591; heart attack 26.404–5; 'heart condition' 20.16–27, 20.88; high blood pressure 24.307–9, 24.320, 24.602, 26.458, 26.463; a high fever in India (1979) 24.112–16; his friends are concerned about his health 22.249, 23.229–30; in hospital with pneumonia, feeling comfortably close to death 26.645; illness on retreat at Keffolds (1970): life and death in the balance 12.246, 23.464–5; illness during a tour of Maharashtra, 1981–2 10.296; illness in 1957 leading to cancellation of winter tour 21.551; illness in England in 1965 due to over-work 23.165; illness in the winter of 1962 21.573; illness in the winter of 1963 21.583; the influence of his childhood illness 23.8–9; inheriting his mother's strong constitution 25.67; insomnia 11.685, 12.686, 26.404–5, 26.456–64, 26.543–4; jaundice: tries naturopathy at Bhikkhu Kashyap's suggestion 20.445; the need to avoid stress 24.320; macular degeneration 11.686, 12.649, 12.674, 24.xv, 26.393, 26.404, 26.440–1; prostate operations 24.330–54; receiving initiations with a raging toothache 12.438, 22.402; seasickness 24.87, 24.520; severe illness in Spain 24.330–5; should have taken more exercise when young 9.442; sickness on first visit to Nepal 20.427–30; stung by scorpion 20.305; a sudden collapse in Birmingham 26.461; toothache at a summer school 23.151; toothache in Kalimpong 21.531; toothache in Spain 24.444–5; unwell in Malaysia 24.39; *see also under* Sangharakshita I/early years

old age
'Death stares me in the face' 25.348; enjoying old age 11.671; the experience of old age 9.169, 11.686; feeling ill due to old age 24.503; his carers 26.658; ideas about how to spend his time 11.618; identifying with a depiction of the Buddha in old age 26.635–6; 'I'm an old fogey' 25.57; in the form of a man in a grey cloak 25.390; 'It's as though the last 75 years have been a dream' 12.630; 'an old man with tired bones and a heart empty of desires' 25.444; one of the happiest periods of his life 26.658; plan to write more poems in old age 12.398; realization that old age is a stage of life in its own right 12.698–9; reflecting on the past 25.22–3; 'Sangharakshita At Seventy' 11.xxiii, 11.615–29; still driven 25.xli, 25.450; 'Up and down the gravel path: an update' 25.460; the white lotus in old age 25.282; Yama's messenger arriving in celebratory form 24.238

death
'At Death's Door': visiting his burial site 26.659–60; 'The Dance of Death' 25.415; how would he like to be remembered? 11.672; 'I have been close to death more than once in my life' 26.645; in hospital with pneumonia, feeling comfortably close to death 26.645; people talking about his death 11.628; preparations for death 11.671, 24.337, 24.340, 24.343; his death 7.xvi, 10.lxiv, 25.lv, 26.409; requests for his funeral 11.628, 26.506; his funeral 25.xxx–xxxi, 25.lv, 26.767 (n618); his burial mound 26.xvii, 26.767 (n618); people looking for other teachers after his death 11.668

rebirth
acceptance of karma and rebirth 4.404, 12.684–5; aspiration to be reborn in the Pure Land? 25.345, 25.349, 25.421, 25.453; assumption of having been Buddhist in previous lives 12.684; 'I believe in rebirth, but I'm planning for *this* life, not the next' 4.404, 11.628–9; 'I hope to remain in contact with the Dharma' 11.692; perhaps Sangharakshita was the reincarnation of Ananda Metteyya? 23.41; threatened with rebirth as a dwarf 22.171; was he previously born in Tibet? 25.216–17

(IV) Family

ANCESTRY

introduction
documents about the Lingwood family 26.509–10, 26.514–28; Norfolk relations 20.84, 26.429–30; searching for ancestors in Suffolk 26.508–14; family photographs 24.127; reflections on his ancestry 26.530–3; relatives who emigrated to Canada 26.525–6; St John's, a house associated with the Lingwood family 26.509–10, 26.520–1; his own descendants will be not biological but spiritual 26.530, 26.533; a sense of belonging to his family 26.573

great-grandparents
great-grandfather (mother's side) 20.12, 24.127, 24.521; great-grandfather (father's side) 26.508–9, 26.526–7; great-grandmother (father's side) 13.526, 26.430–1, 26.513–14, 26.526–7, 26.567

grandfather (father's father)
photograph 20.2; a book that belonged to him 26.527; Suffolk origins 20.3, 20.486, 26.527–8; work at the War Office 20.3, 20.486, 26.528; death 20.486, 26.528–9

step-grandfather (father's stepfather)
travelled with the merchant navy 20.4, 26.552; his character 26.552–4

grandfather (mother's father)
clarinettist 20.12, 20.500; Hungarian 20.500, 22.248

grandmother ('Nana', father's mother)
Sunday morning visits 20.1–3; the place she was born 20.83–4; spending time with Nana 20.99, 26.429–31; she voted Conservative 26.571; her house 26.570; parting from her 20.105–6; first marriage 20.2, 26.529; second marriage 20.3, 20.487, 26.428; suicide 23.30–1; the inheritance of her house 23.31

parents
considered themselves Christian 9.487, 13.525; did not swear 13.607; their first meeting 20.489, 26.529, 26.556, 26.569; 'I loved them, but I loved the Dharma more' 23.27; estrangement 20.70, 20.88, 20.89–90, 23.27, 25.66; his wish to see them again after twenty years in India 23.20, 23.28; they gave him their blessing when he went to India 20.129, 23.27, 25.62; sense of duty and pleasure 13.606–7; severing connection with them while in India 21.344, 23.27; very fortunate to have such parents 25.69

FATHER (PHILIP LINGWOOD)

his life
birth 20.3, 20.485, 26.529; upbringing 26.529, 26.554–5; appearance 20.3, 20.487; a countryman at heart 13.607, 25.67–8; working for a jeweller 26.555; pleasures 13.607; politics 20.9, 26.571; religious views 20.21; storyteller: 'his secret ambition was to be a writer' 20.488; his second wife, Florrie 23.30–1, 23.205

wartime experience
First World War 20.488–9, 26.529, 26.555; Second World War 20.46, 20.68–9, 20.104, 23.10; war injuries 25.68, 26.433, 26.529, 26.555–6; trained as a French polisher 26.529, 26.556

character
hot-tempered 20.3–4; sociable 20.71; common sense and courage 20.25; cheerful disposition 25.68; unselfish 20.4; a just man 20.89; fond of teasing 26.426, 26.567; in the poem 'The Family Reunion' 25.67–9, 25.449; 'Let them enjoy themselves. They are only young once.' 26.431

and Sangharakshita
happy memories of talking together 3.535; the teaching of a prayer 13.525–6; childhood excursions with him 22.14, 26.425–6; accompanying him to the pub 15.420, 20.88, 20.90; spending time with him 14.420; hearing his son was to be a monk, wrote 'Your life is your own' 9.501, 20.129, 25.62; Sangharakshita's closeness to him 25.68; visiting him in the 1960s 23.30, 23.205, 23.240, 25.62–3

MOTHER (FLORENCE, NÉE KETSKEMETY)

life
early years 26.566–9; city born and bred 13.607, 25.67; in old age, reminisces about her life as a young girl 10.328; during the First World War 26.568–9; work 20.71; character 20.4, 20.71, 20.72; in the poem 'The Family Reunion' 25.66–7, 25.449; war work 26.529; nights at the cinema: 'We had a really good cry' 14.471; a trip to the pantomime 26.421–2; relationship with sisters 20.11; religious views 20.21–2; relationship with Sid 20.71, 20.74, 20.88–9, 20.99, 23.28; leaves the family 20.88–9; three marriages 26.529; 2.739 (n660); photographs 23.29, 24.357; playing the piano 26.499, 26.568; pleasures 13.607; her teeth removed 26.433–4; concern for people of India 21.596, 24.185–6; link with Padmasuri 24.186; in hospital after a fall 24.325–7, 24.330; serious illness 24.230–3

her death
a reminder that we may die at any moment 2.536; 'The prospect of her death fell like a black shadow across my heart' 24.357; she talked of wanting to die 24.357; psychic awareness of her death 24.375, 26.625–7; her death 24.375–7; her funeral, at which Sangharakshita spoke 24.377–9

and Sangharakshita
argument about schooling 20.54, 20.56; hears that he is to return to England 21.578, 23.28; hopes that his being a

monk won't prevent him from seeing her 20.129, 25.62; reads his memoirs 24.181; meets him again after twenty years 23.28, 25.62–3; he buys a figure of Guanyin for her 23.130, 23.147; establishing a deep and genuine understanding 24.231–3; his love for her 20.89–90, 26.434; letters 25.380; their relationship 25.66–7; attends London Buddhist Society Wesak celebration 20.102; his visits to her 23.147, 23.240, 23.429, 24.145, 24.160, 24.162, 24.185, 24.230–3, 24.242–3, 24.306, 24.357–9; she visits the London Buddhist Centre 24.180–2, 24.185; she visits Padmaloka 24.185

OTHER RELATIVES

sister Joan
childhood games 20.5, 20.7, 26.428; her dancing career 25.61, 25.69–70, 25.449; dolls 26.428; in a dream 26.680; her happy disposition 25.70; knocked down by a car 26.434; evacuated to Chichester in the war 20.46, 26.574; a holiday together 20.88; joins ATS 20.99, 20.104–5; lived in a gypsy caravan 23.29, 25.69, 25.449; quarrelling over music 20.72; response to her parents' estrangement 20.89; in contact while Sangharakshita was in India 25.62; meeting her again after twenty years 18.204, 23.29–30; she reads Sangharakshita's memoirs 24.181; visits the London Buddhist Centre 24.180–2; visits Padmaloka 25.69; her husband Eddie 23.30, 23.147, 23.429, 25.70; her death 25.69–70

aunts
Dick 26.433; Dolly 20.501; Dorothy 26.552; Fanny 20.24, 26.430; Helen (godmother) 13.526, 23.31, 26.531; Hilda 20.501; Jessie 20.10–11, 20.497–9, 20.502; Kate 20.10–11, 13.527, 20.496–9, 20.502, 24.124, 26.499, 26.542–3, 26.567; Kath 13.532, 20.45–6, 20.57, 20.99; Louie 26.431; Luke 26.430; Noni 20.3–4, 20.483, 20.485, 20.487–8, 20.496, 26, 429–30

uncles
Bert 20.501; Charles 20.45, 20.53, 20.57, 20.99, 20.104, 20.485, 23.31, 26.552–3; Charlie 20.498, 26.570–1; Dan 20.498, 26.567, 26.570–1; Dick (Kets) 20.12, 20.132–4, 20.159–60, 20.501, 24.124, 24.232, 24.242–3, 24.251–4; Harry 20.501–2; Jack 13.526–7, 20.501, 24.122–8, 26.499, 26.568; Leonard 26.431, 26.569–70; 'Uncle' Tom (godfather) 13.526, 20.482–3, 20.501–2, 26.416–17, 26.417–18, 26.531–2; Tom (mother's brother) 26.568

cousins
Gillian 24.123; Peter 24.123; Dorothy 20.485; John 26.570

nephews
David 23.29; John (and wife Tynia) 23.29, 24.231, 24.326, 24.357, 24.375, 24.377

niece Kamala (later Kay)
news of her birth 21.344; visits 23.240, 23.429; Sangharakshita names her Kamala 23.147; visits the London Buddhist Centre 24.180–2; at her mother's funeral 25.69–70; great-niece Anna 24.377

(V) BUDDHIST LIFE

introduction
'I am a *Western* Buddhist' 13.669–70; why I am a Buddhist 10.342

EARLY YEARS

discovery of Buddhism through reading
awoke me to the existence of something I had forgotten 14.xi–xii, 20.85, 23.110; contact with Buddhism was contact with the depths of my own being 16.218; his keen response to beauty helped him realize he was a Buddhist 23.317–18; I am a Buddhist, and I always have been 2.407, 9.13, 12.59, 12.493, 12.624, 13.534, 20.85; I had an intuitive apprehension that this was the truth 12.59; I never questioned the validity of that initial insight 7.xvii, 14.xii; a natural affinity with Buddhism 25.xlviii, 26.638; as a result of my reading I had gone for Refuge to the Dharma 2.408; a sort of spiritual falling in love 20.301–2; the *sūtras* converted me 9.487; at that time there were very few books available in English 12.611; This is what I really believe 9.278, 12.682; these texts gave me my first glimpse of Perfect Vision 3.389, 11.170

London Buddhist Society (1943–4)
in my early years as a Buddhist I was very much alone 9.467, 11.170, 25.34; *The Middle Way*: an advert at the back of a book 12.59–60; first meeting 20.100–1; attending the society during the war 11.652, 12.544; *Concentration and Meditation* 12.682; first takes Refuges and Precepts (*pansil*) from U Thittila 2.410–11, 12.301–2, 20.102; meditating during an air raid 3.326–7, 9.278, 12.494, 12.682–3, 20.101; Wesak celebration, 1944 20.102, 23.121

during army years
study of Buddhism during army life 20.101–2; first experience of a Buddhist temple (in Delhi) 20.115, 23.410; on the

lookout for some vestige of Buddhism 9.278–9

during wandering years in India
Hindu teachers more impressive than Buddhist ones 20.301; although people were unable to teach, nonetheless he learned 1.147; isolation in Hindu environment intensified awareness of Buddhism 2.414–15, 20.301; faith in Buddhism: from instinctive attraction to reasoned conviction 20.301–2; attention drawn to conditioned co-production, four noble truths, three *lakṣaṇas* 20.302; 'homesick' for Buddhism after living for so long in the midst of Hinduism 20.346; 'I lived like an Indian sadhu' 11.170; fantasy of living as a monk at Sarnath 20.346; seeing Buddhas at Kanheri: 'once again I was under the protection of Buddhism' 20.382; for attitude to Hinduism, *see under* Hinduism

Tibetan Buddhism
first encounter with Tibetan Buddhists 21.176–9; contact with Tibetan Buddhists 2.440–6, 2.500, 13.117; discusses Tibetan Buddhism with Lobsang Lhalunga 22.234–5; first impressions of Tantric Buddhism: 'a jungle' 11.679–80, 13.92, 13.116–17, 17.685–6, 21.176–8; first visit to a Tibetan monastery, *see under* Ghoom; he declared he would make a study of Tantric hats 11.13.117; studying the Tantra in earnest 13.117; Tibetan teachers among those coming to India 11.171

teachers and gurus
Chattrul Sangye Dorje, *see* Chattrul Sangye Dorje; Mr Chen, *see* C. M. Chen; Dhardo Rimpoche, *see* Dhardo Rimpoche; Dilgo Khyentse Rimpoche, *see* Dilgo Khyentse Rimpoche; did any of them use the 'sudden method'? 16.183–4; greatly inspired by them, but doesn't represent their lineages 11.666; his training, the basis for the FWBO 13.470; Jagdish Kashyap, *see* Kashyap; Jamyang Khyentse Rimpoche, *see* Jamyang Khyentse Rimpoche; Kachu Rimpoche, *see* Kachu Rimpoche; keeping in touch with 'my kind teachers' 23.60; keeping in touch with them through *sādhanas* 11.691, 11.720; looking up to them 26.629; spiritually speaking, they would always be in touch with me, and I with them 23.398; spiritual teachers of exceptional attainments 22.560–1; 'they are at the back of my mind all the time' 26.228; 'what they were was more important to me than what they said' 11.720–1; 'wherever I go I shall carry the memory of their great kindness' 26.443; writing a book about them (*Precious Teachers*) 11.691

Zen
appreciation deepened through practice of other forms of Buddhism 13.324; personal connection with Zen 13.323–5

see also
going forth, *see under* Sangharakshita II/ going forth

ORDINATION

desire for ordination
'unbearably intense' 20.346; 'so great we would have prostrated ourselves the whole distance' 20.395; 'time to regularize my position' 2.499; prepared by two years as a wanderer 9.501; walking to Sarnath in search of ordination 20.388–9; request refused 2.418, 9.280, 9.467, 9.488, 9.501, 20.390–1, 22.208, 23.16, 23.358–9; aimlessness after refusal 20.392–4

sāmaṇera ordination at Kusinārā
on Bhikkhu Kashyap's advice, walking to Kusinārā 20.395–401; U Chandramani's agreement 2.417–18; ceremony an ordeal 20.408–10; pronunciation more important than understanding 2.419, 11.388, 12.302–3, 20.409; 'We felt we would die rather than be guilty of the smallest infringement' 20.410; naming 2.749–50 (n724), 20.410; a very positive occasion 2.419; took place on the anniversary of the Buddha's Enlightenment 23.16; a connection with Dr Ambedkar 9.280, 9.467–8, 9.501; important role of the Dharma Mata (mother in religion) 20.411, 22.259; shown how to lacquer his begging bowl 20.413; thought in terms of becoming a monk rather than Going for Refuge 2.418; the hostility of a brahmin 10.446–7; a Christian priest's shock at the respect paid to him as a novice monk 11.251

bhikṣu ordination
becoming an Outsider 26.576; in danger of confusing commitment and lifestyle 2.499; the culmination of a process of spiritual discovery 2.579–80; 'I wanted to be a *real* monk, not a hanger-on' 21.96–8; 'I was a monk because I wanted to identify myself with Buddhism as fully as I could' 21.343; praise for Sangharakshita (as a young *bhikṣu*) 22.178–81

bhikṣu ordination ceremony at Sarnath
the ceremony 2.420–2, 21.106–8; emphasis on the four reliances (*nissaya*) of the monk 2.421; an experience of the Sangha refuge 2.421–2, 2.583; 'I experienced an extraordinary sense of peace' 2.579, 2.583, 21.109; no recollection of reciting the Refuges and Precepts 12.303; nowhere in the ceremony was there provision for Going for Refuge 2.421; the *bhikkhus* who refused his first ordination attended this one 22.60–1; U Chandramani unable to attend 2.748–9 (n713); photograph 21.110; inter-*nikāya* 2.751 (n735); presence of a Ladakhi lama, Kusho Bakula 2.756 (n783); the two Burmese *bhikkhus* who attended it 2.582; revisiting Sarnath six years later 22.332

technical invalidity of bhikṣu ordination
an act of betrayal 2.611; because the chapter was inquorate 2.623; did those present really think it was valid? 2.586–7, 2.588; 'affected the whole course of my life as a Buddhist' 22.331–4; a good thing for spiritual development in the long run 2.581–2, 2.611; most of the *bhikkhus* present were in breach of rules 2.582, 2.628–9; no alternative to seek ordination elsewhere 2.589; shock of discovering that it was invalid 2.580–1, 21.520–1, 22.332–4; so what had happened during the ceremony? 2.583–4

bodhisattva ordination
preparation 2.455; reasons for taking the ordination 2.585–6; didn't include vows: 'I felt I had enough on my plate' 4.197; its effects 2.456; preceptor Dhardo Rimpoche 2.455–6, 12.435, 13.587, 22.420, 22.541–4, 23.18

THE BASIS OF PERSONAL PRACTICE

Going for Refuge
early experiences of formal Going for Refuge 2.479, 2.499, 12.301–5; an early article on the subject (1945) 7.67–70; centrality 1.408–10, 11.388, 16.63, 21.343–4, 23.160, 23.437–8; history 2.403–503, 2.611; later developments anticipated in earlier teachings 2.460–1; looking up to the Buddha, Dharma, and Sangha 26.629; analysis of writings on the subject in *A Survey of Buddhism* 2.429–33; realizing the Buddhist community's need for a concrete spiritual basis 23.160

ethical practice
'My head full of the Perfection of Wisdom, I didn't think about practice' 4.75–6, 4.284–5; becomes vegetarian, *see under* vegetarianism; opposition to violence: should never have joined the army 4.285–6, 20.150; perplexed by ethical questions 20.159; refusing an invitation on Buddhist principle 10.279; taking care to observe the effects of speech 20.306–7; when I was young I was more interested in 'what is' than 'what to do' 17.569

confession
confession to Dhardo Rimpoche 16.274; experience during ordination retreat 16.273–4; disappointment at the perfunctory ceremony as a Theravādin monk 21.300–1, 26.642; confession of weaknesses to Swami Ramdas 20.325; when close to death, confessing unskilful actions 26.647–8

faith and devotion
a Buddhist not just inwardly but in terms of outward activities 3.614–15; daily devotions 22.224; experiencing devotion towards himself: 'What had I done to deserve it?' 22.165; faith in the Buddha who creates Sukhāvatī 4.640; faith in Buddhism remains unshaken despite ordination refusal 20.394; faith in the Mahāyāna attitude 18.347; intense love and devotion for the Buddha 22.301, 25.198–9; 'Let my life burn like incense/ Before thy precious shrine' 25.219; looking up to the Three Jewels and the geniuses of Buddhist history 26.629; love of decorating shrines 4.299, 20.259, 20.311; 'my view of current world problems is … a confession of faith' 3.614–15; devotional feelings at Lumbini 20.421, 25.196–7; prayer to Tārā 25.293; reciting the *Tiratana Vandanā* 21.429; 'Secret Worship' (poem) 8.161–2; turned against Hindu worship 4.299–300, 20.259–60

Dharma study and reflection
enjoyment of the study of logic 14.90, 20.446; with Jagdish Kashyap, *see under* Kashyap; with Mr Chen, *see under* Chen; the Pure Land *sūtras* 2.554; reflection on the suffering inflicted by human beings 26.677–8; reflections on the question of why Buddhism disappeared from India 12.236–7; studying Pāli: delight of studying the Buddha's teaching in 'his own words' 20.445–6; studying the Pāli scriptures in

old age 11.690; with Nityabandhu 11.685, 26.455–6; with Paramartha 26.544–6, 26.548

retreats
in the ashram at Raipur 20.217; eager to observe a rainy season retreat soon after ordination 20.439; favourite time for writing 11.171; in Kalimpong: the atmosphere and effects of the rainy season retreat 12.235–6, 21.40

reflection
a deliberate practice 24.322, 24.324; on dependent origination, the four noble truths, and the three characteristics 23.14–15; reflecting on things for many years before writing them down 26.250

mindfulness
helped in the practice by needing to be so careful when ill as a child 23.9; learning to be mindful 5.39, 22.403; strength and continuity of mindfulness 23.xvii

daily routine
in Kalimpong 22.224–7, 22.241, 22.248–9, 22.526; at Il Convento 24.225–7; at Guhyaloka with Paramartha 24.395–400, 24.404; the need for some unprogrammed time (1973) 11.515; at Padmaloka 24.156–7; a wish for a simple life 25.315; with Paramartha in London 24.321–2, 24.356, 24.391

the need for sangha
practised in isolation 3.389, 4.346, 4.409, 12.60, 12.377; desire for contact with other Buddhists 2.428, 2.499, 2.583; came to appreciate the value of the sangha 3.390; the encouragement of practising with someone else 12.68; wasn't lucky enough to join the Western Buddhist Order 5.614, 11.652, 12.377, 12.544; 'had I been the only Buddhist in the world, I could have followed no other path' 20.301

MEDITATION

making a start
meditations and initiations: introduction 5.xxix–xxx; early experiments with meditation 23.11; Shankara's method 20.113–14, 20.125; first experience 'too delicate and delicious for words' 20.207; where and from whom he learned to meditate 5.xxi–ii

practising meditation
conditions for meditation in India 18.629, 18.631; discovers the need for a settled and quiet place to practise 20.248; finding meditation difficult 22.226–7; growing faith and confidence in meditation 22.227; making a special effort to deepen meditation practice 22.299–303; an ascent into a more colourful world 25.42–3; progress in meditation 5.37–8; regular meditation practice 22.103; meditation diary 5.357, 20.207, 20.261, 22.300–2, 25.46–8; agreed with much of what Dr Mehta said about meditation 22.298–9; a 'positive peace' 22.300–1; 'not yet ready to be a full-time meditator' 22.448; an expression of creativity 12.640; sometimes it came naturally, sometimes it was a struggle 25.44–5; system of meditation, *see under* meditation; time spent meditating in Kalimpong 22.475

sustaining the practice
experiences of insight 20.302, 22.227, 23.15; on returning to London, little time for personal meditation 23.132; did he stop meditating? 5.428–9; deepening *vipaśyanā* without the need for formal practice 5.428–9; practised meditation all his life and clearly realized much 5.xxxii

ānāpānasati (mindfulness of breathing)
consults Anandamayi about the practice 20.207; daily practice 22.224, 23.132; learns it from Bhikkhu Soma and first practises it 5.36, 12.495, 20.144–5, 25.45–6; a new technique produces intense *prīti* 22.448; 'for long the sheet anchor of my spiritual life' 20.145, 22.403

mettā bhāvanā
discovering its importance 5.39–40; helped to balance the practice of mindfulness 5.39; perhaps started practising it after taking up the Green Tārā practice 5.38; 'to some extent I had to discover it' 5.36–7

other practices
abnormal experiences as a result of *prāṇāyāma* 20.125; practice of hatha yoga 20.303; Going for Refuge and Prostration Practice 2.443, 22.475, 22.528, 23.132, 26.673; cremation ground practice 3.346; *mūla yogas* 22.474–5; six element practice 5.484

SĀDHANAS AND INITIATIONS

mantras
Avalokiteśvara mantra given by Swami Ramdas 20.325–6; chants the Avalokiteśvara mantra in response to black magic 22.261; experience of chanting the Vajrasattva mantra, *see under* Vajrasattva/mantra

Green Tārā
an affinity with Green Tārā 22.374–5, 22.395; initiation 5.754 (n554), 12.436, 12.659–60, 22.374–5, 22.392–3, 25.443, 26.228; the effect of doing the practice

26.670; given two versions, depending on time available 5.584, 13.98; initiations from three teachers 12.661; handed on to Order members 12.660; marks a new phase of spiritual life 22.375–6, 26.668–9; orders a thangka to aid his practice 22.375; the practice and generosity 5.xxx; and the *mettā bhāvanā* 5.38; the rainbows of the offering goddesses 26.671; the transcendental counterpart of my mundane nature 22.374–5

Vajrasattva
introduced by Kachu Rimpoche 22.473; given the Hell-Annihilator *sādhana* by Dudjom Rimpoche 22.504–7; asks for a simpler version of the practice 22.507; 'the energy seemed to come like a ray of light from him to me' 13.161–2; doing the practice with Terry Delamare 23.xviii–xix, 23.139–40; resolution to do the practice every day 23.147

Avalokiteśvara, Vajrapāṇi, Mañjughoṣa, and Green Tārā
ceremony 2.685 (n238), 12.438, 22.402; Jamyang looked up as though seeing them sending blessings 12.438, 22.402, 23.390, 26.228; seeing a correspondence between the four practices 26.663–4; the transmission of the essence of the great masters 22.407

other sādhanas
Amitāyus 22.473; fourfold *abhiṣeka* of Ekajaṭī, Rāhu, and Vajrasādhu 22.506; Jambhala and Kurukullā 12.448–9, 22.555–7; Padmasambhava 2.442, 12.441, 22.469, 22.472–3, 26.673; White Tārā initiation 12.435, 12.662, 22.420, 22.562; *sādhanas* translated by John Driver 2.174–5, 2.685 (n238), 22.403, 22.506–7; time devoted to such practices 23.132

MONASTIC LIFESTYLE

introduction
experiencing both the benefits and the defects 11.692; a human being who went for Refuge and happened to live monastically 2.456; seen by Tibetans as 'an antiquated figure out of the remote past' 21.178; 'I had no wish to give up the monastic life' 22.307; in many ways the life of a monk is the best possible kind of life 11.389; 'The life of a Buddhist monk in the West is not easy' 12.80; realization that he had often been too meek as a Buddhist monk 4.444–5; separating himself from monastic formalism 23.xv

going for alms
going for alms after ordination 20.414–18; the first time was of unprecedented importance in our lives 20.417; the agony of alms with chillies 20.338; being jeered at 20.421–2; the joy of those giving alms 20.426; having lived on alms, Sangharakshita wanted to give alms 23.303; in Kalimpong 21.11–15, 21.41, 22.215; sharing his almsfood 21.15; 'The Message of the Bowl' 25.204–5; showed how dependent we are on others 12.653

not handling money
stopping handling it 20.388; it simplified life greatly 16.401–2; refused ordination as a consequence 9.280, 9.467, 20.390, 22.208; giving up the practice 10.489, 21.42, 22.102–3, 22.208–9, 27.1074

wearing robes
attempts to gather charred cloth to make robes 20.386; changing back into robes on return from a trip round Europe 23.322–3; colours clothes with *gerua-mati* on the occasion of going forth 20.225; considered exotic in the West 25.382; reproved for wearing shabby robes 3.50, 18.333, 18.562, 21.376–7; out in London in his robes: ''Ere comes Julius Caesar!' 23.174; people making obeisance to him because he was wearing robes 20.228–9; reasons for deciding not to wear robes on return to the West 12.524–5, 17.634; returning to India and changing back into robes 24.11, 24.14; the transition from wearing robes back to civilian clothes 11.665–6, 23.188–91; wearing robes as a signal that he was not a layman 25.90–1; wearing robes 'for ceremonial purposes' 4.644, 12.524

other aspects of practice
abstaining from reading newspapers 22.209; going barefoot 20.426, 20.432, 20.439; jeered at for wearing spectacles 20.421–2; not eating after mid-day 10.473, 20.428–9, 22.225, 23.165; *brahmacarya* 11.569, 22.306–7; walking with downcast eyes 21.14–15; worrying that playing ping-pong might be frowned upon 21.75

experimenting with giving up monastic lifestyle
beginning to be less rigid in observance 23.175, 23.322, 23.394; allowing his hair to grow 12.524, 15.713, 17.634, 23.322–3, 25.90–1, 25.382; 'I knew myself to have been no less a monk when in civilian clothes' 23.323; people asking whether he was monk or layman 25.402; sometimes living more like a monk, sometimes more like a layman 2.611; 'in the West, shaven heads tend to get in the way of communication' 24.54; giving up celibacy 27.1073

(VI) Inner and emotional life

spiritual and supernatural experiences

experiences
consciousness struggling to free itself of the body 20.73; feeling of being insubstantial in a world of ghosts 20.74; abnormal experiences due to practising *prāṇāyāma* 20.125; 'Extraordinary experience of Transcendental' 23.183, 23.387; after Ambedkar's death, 'an impersonal force' 11.xix–xx, 21.523, 22.364; a near-death experience (from acupuncture) 23.129–30, 24.337–9; life and death in the balance 23.464–5; a love and peace so strong that it was unbearable 22.302; a golden Buddha and an echo from deep within: 'Peace unto all beings' 7.75–6; putting questions to the Buddha and receiving answers 22.301; awareness of an Indian friend who had died 26.627; strange circumstances around his mother's death 26.625–7; experiences of people after their death 4.559, 26.622–3, 26.674; premonitions (or clairvoyance) 19.84–5, 20.85–6, 20.215–16, 22.278; telepathy 4.553–4; receiving a transfer of energy 'like dirty dishwater' 19.327; looking at gemstones almost a spiritual experience 24.322; an exalted state of consciousness after giving the fourth *Survey* lecture 22.145

presences and sensations
the atmosphere in the trees at Broomhouse Farm 4.540–1, 26.624; the atmosphere at the Colosseum 18.312, 23.310; downward pressure from an upper room 21.34, 21.49, 21.319–20, 26.222; a Presence (bodhisattva?) in Bombay while writing the *Survey* 22.278–9; a Presence in Nagpur after Dr Ambedkar's death 9.23, 10.17–18, 22.363; sensations of a light trying to break through 22.302; sensations of vastness and emptiness 22.302; a sense of the four great kings gathered around him 16.357; sense of really being present in the India of the Buddha's day 17.402–3; a sinister presence in a room at Rivendell 26.625

non-human beings
an attack by *devas* 26.624–5; *devas* and the scent of roses 21.136; an encounter with an *asura* 26.621–2; experiencing someone who had been taken over by a demon 26.623–4; Māra as the head of an old man 5.350–1, 20.114, 21.298–300, 26.618–19; Māra on the Tube train 4.546–7, 13.597–8, 26.565; hungry ghosts 20.310; the voice of an angel 13.591, 26.611, 26.617–18; a young man talking about black magic surrounded by green flames 22.261

visions
Amitābha 5.xxx, 12.683–4, 20.345, 23.15, 26.225–6, 26.576; an apparition of a dead friend in a pit 5.xxx, 12.438–9, 11.455–7, 23.387–91; the Buddha as Ganesha 20.208; a Buddha image shining with a green light 14.464, 19.327–8, 21.460; a dream-vision of a kind of initiation 26.224–5; flowers of flame and jewels of light 22.302; landscapes and patterns 20.208; Satyapriya 20.215–16; Sri Ramakrishna 20.311; the Virgin Mary 20.208

spiritual life

devotion, faith, joy
attraction to the spiritual life 20.123–4; communicating the Dharma 'one of the great joys of my life' 22.528, 23.xvi; deeply moved by devotional practice in Nepal 21.295–6; faith found expression in poems 25.47; a gift of thangkas an incitement to live the spiritual life 21.230–1; Maitreya statue at Ghoom portended dedication of life to the Dharma 20.134; 'most of the time quite ecstatic' 23.xvii; 'The only refuge for him who aspires to true perfection is the Buddha alone' 22.76; though devoted to the Dharma, could I have made the supreme sacrifice? 22.517

realizations
could singing a hymn at school have instilled the truth of impermanence? 26.294; convinced that external activity and inner experience are not incompatible 22.247–8; 'I *knew* that I would die' 22.199, 23.91; seeing the shadow of mortality 25.470; a new insight into the nature of Zen 22.247–8; realizing that 'the responsibility for my life and actions was mine alone' 22.212

experiences
first encounter with the mystical (Neoplatonism in *Hypatia*) 20.20; a period of uninterrupted reflection on the Dharma 20.302, 23.14–15; *annus mirabilis* (in Kalimpong) 22.379–80; the bursting through of 'secret life' 23.182–4; experience of the eight worldly winds 2.499, 25.425; the effect of a talk on Buddhism and beauty (1947) 21.439, 26.383; 'Extraordinary experience of Transcendental' 23.183; revulsion at the idea of food 26.452; the spiritual experiences of writing 11.675–7; the consolation of the Dharma at a time of ill health 11.685

questions
constantly asking 'Why did the Buddha say this?' 1.7, 26.43; how to go beyond the ego? 26.668–9; 'What is the cause of *śūnyatā*?' – a koan 21.187–8; what caused the disappearance of Buddhism from India? 12.236; what was the significance of worldly activities for spiritual life? 22.118; 'Who am I?' 8.613

practices
early struggles with meditation and mindfulness 11.552–3, 25.44–5; learning a lot from small incidents 15.718; practice of the teaching 'In the seen only the seen' 22.336; praise and criticism an opportunity to develop evenness of mind 11.664; the practice of doing the teacher's will rather than his own 13.628, 20.463–4, 22.394–5; the search for a practice to overcome the egoistic will 13.628, 20.463–4, 22.394–5; 'following my guru's example' 22.407; resolving to sustain idealism 24.401

elements of spiritual life
the rainbow became for me a symbol of the spiritual path 25.268, 26.672; the central place of the bodhisattva ideal 7.22–3, 21.179; drawn to transcendental beauty rather than disgusted by the conditioned 22.199; the inspiration of the spiritual hierarchy 14.312–14; my own spiritual project inseparable from that of the Movement 25.84; Padmasambhava 'was to occupy a permanent place in my spiritual life' 22.467; the mysterious land of Uḍḍiyāna was my true home 22.474; the *Śūraṅgama-samādhi Sūtra* 'became a permanent part of my spiritual life' 26.546; identification with Tiresias 25.420

self-assessments
'the Bodhichitta flowers in me' 25.xli, 25.302; the ego disintegrating in meditation 25.81; 'My mind's a silver awning …' 25.351; 'My Secret Garden' (poem) 25.393; 'My spiritual life has not been angst-ridden – perhaps it should have been more so' 26.397; 'I am much worse than people think I am, and also much better' 26.34; 'I cannot live without this belief, and I would rather die than give it up' 10.342; 'I had not yet succeeding in integrating East and West' 22.186, 26.392–3; 'I sense within this "being" a "not-being" more profound' 25.435; 'I was being changed …': the temple bell at Arunachala 20.341; 'I would experience an intense joy' 21.322; 'I've never had any sort of doubt' 11.552; 'My mind is a theatre' 25.447; 'Now it is time to be myself' 25.319; 'So near the goal, and yet so far away!' 25.348

the pattern of spiritual life
not just a progression, but an unfolding 21.259; a personal synthesis of modern culture and ancient spiritual tradition 21.425; a strict sense of duty in earlier life, then more trustful of intuition 4.485; a similar spiritual journey to members of the Triratna Buddhist Order 2.584–6; resolved upon a life of renunciation 20.128; a change: rational understanding of the Dharma as strong as emotional response 23.15; a suggestion that his spiritual life followed a similar pattern to Shinran's 24.529; time to start paying attention to the needs of others 21.24, 25.44, 25.115–16; contact with Ambedkar's followers brought in social involvement 25.125; a new phase: taking up mantra recitation and visualization 22.375–6, 26.668–9; a change of attitude to monastic life 23.27–8; being technically not a *bhikkhu* contributed to spiritual development 2.581; a shift in the centre of spiritual gravity 23.185

INFLUENCES AND INSPIRATIONS

Buddhist works and teachings
Avataṃsaka Sūtra ('The Vows of the Bodhisattva Samantabhadra') 22.541; Barua's 'Buddhism as Personal Religion' 7.25, 20.124; the *Bodhicaryāvatāra* 22.129; the bodhisattva ideal 2.454–5, 7.22–3, 20.124, 22.541–2, 23.17–18; Conze's *Buddhist Wisdom Books* 8.387; the *Dhammapada* 15.5; the *Diamond Sūtra*, *see under Diamond Sūtra*; Emerson's 'Thoreau' 24.52; *Laṅkāvatāra Sūtra* 22.375; Mahāyāna *sūtras* 19.350, 25.lix; *Platform Sūtra*, *see under Sūtra of Huineng*; the *Prajñāpāramitā* and the *Bodhicaryāvatāra* 22.234–5; the *Śikṣā-samuccaya* 22.541, 23.17; the *Sutta-Nipāta*, the *Udāna*, and the *Itivuttaka* 2.552, 22.320; Vasubandhu's *Thirty Stanzas on Representation Only* 20.101; Yamamaki's *Systems of Buddhistic Thought* 20.101

Western literature and writers
William Blake 13.639–40, 26.649; Marsilio Ficino 2.536; Thomas Merton 20.463–4, 22.394–5; Plotinus' *Enneads* 26.366; Rilke on poetry, and Sophocles: 'a permanent part of my thinking' 21.434; Shelley 25.xlvii, 26.398; Thomas Taylor the Platonist 2.536, 23.317

people and archetypal figures
Anagarika Dharmapala 8.3–4; Dhardo Rimpoche 11.666; Lama Govinda 11.563, 21.258; Hercules 23.269;

Huineng 11.715–16; Milarepa 20.151; Padmasambhava, *see under* Padmasambhava; St Catherine of Siena 13.634–8, 26.387; St Jerome 2.526–7, 13.633–4, 26.267–8; Sri Ramakrishna 7.15; Yalahankar Swami 4.78, 14.489, 20.362; Zhiyi 11.716–17

other inspirations and influences
the Himalayas 21.436–7; in old age: the Dharma, his teachers, the Buddha 11.690; an incident which was to affect the whole course of my life as a Buddhist 22.351; the influence of childhood illness 23.8–9; the influence of friendship with Terry Delamare 23.xviii, 23.94; the inspiration to write 26.250; Mount Kanchenjunga 23.17; 'not many living people I admire' 11.626; the spiritual hierarchy 14.312–14; 'The teachers on the Refuge Tree inspire me to do what I can for the Dharma' 11.720–1

EMOTIONAL LIFE

aesthetic experiences
'Beauty was Truth, Truth Beauty' 24.547; Bhaja caves lit up by the evening sun 26.390; chrysanthemums 20.34; cool night air after a hot Indian day 20.113; 'I only looked at something fair' 25.163; music, *see under* Sangharakshita XII; poetry 12.672, 20.36; the Renaissance palaces of Florence 23.xviii, 23.314, 23.317–18; seeing the lights of Port Said 20.108; the Taj Mahal 22.340–1; Tirumal Nayak's palace 20.233; 'a trembling that is all delight' 23.318

animism
in childhood 20.484; 'the great white peak [Kanchenjunga] seemed to speak to me' 20.470; 'The grey clouds are my friends' 25.446; 'How wonderful it was to feel oneself alive in a world of living things!' 24.38; a lost essay: 'In Defence of Animism' 26.390; mountains are alive 22.12; the stars: 'How flashingly alive they were!' 24.82; trees as living presences 20.444

aspirations
a poet and a poor man will I be 25.239; a prayer for the Enlightenment of all, made on the Vulture's Peak 20.466; affinity with an old recluse: 'wings fluttering within me' 20.222; to live at Sarnath sweeping the temple steps would be the height of happiness 20.346

emotional experiences
after Terry's death 'I wept every day for six months' 23.446; a beautiful young man on the Underground 26.562–3; a childhood response to kittens 26.418; childhood terror 26.427; coming to understand the depth of his feeling for Terry 23.149–50; deeply affected by the story of the thousand-armed Avalokiteśvara 26.599; deeply moved by a pastoral scene in Greece 23.265; the effect of early classical sculptures 23.299; an exhilarating sense of spaciousness in Seville 24.437; feeling that words have no meaning at all 23.472; the fragrance of wild thyme, a memento of Greece 23.291; the experience of chrysanthemums in the garden in childhood 20.34; grief so deep that it is dumb 25.281; happiest when spreading the Dharma in India 11.691–2; haunted by the terrorist attacks of 9/11 26.479–80, 26.688; horror and dread at the pantomime as a child 26.422; joy at knowing how much difference to people Buddhism has made 11.671–2; joy's fountain 25.xxxiv, 25.163; a monkey cradling her dead baby 20.313–14, 26.424; on the grief of three queens 22.13–14; on witnessing the distress of Dr Ambedkar's followers 9.22; an ordination in Ahmedabad: 'I felt that I was in the Pure Land' 24.117; the most difficult and painful years of my whole life 24.308–9; 'my exultant twenty-five-year-old heart' 22.322; 'The prospect of [my mother's] death fell like a black shadow across my heart' 24.357; directing emotional energies to practical help, not sentimental lamentations 23.337; saddest when Terry Delamare committed suicide 11.692; sadness at being the object of abuse and hostility 11.665, 22.172; sharing deeper thoughts and feelings 22.323; the sight of midgets at the fair 26.423; a time of being unable to cry due to medication 26.682; the torments of love 25.xxxv

gratitude
for access to the profound thoughts of Zhiyi 8.480; for *The Door of Liberation* 8.529; to all those who made a stay at Guhyaloka possible 24.403; to all who had assisted him during a hospital stay 24.354; to Madame Blavatsky 20.64; to Buddharakshita, for helping him to adopt a Buddhist life 20.444; to Burma Raja and the Princess 21.220; to Carter for the initiation into erotic bliss 26.608; to Clare Cameron for her criticism of his poetry 22.183; to Edward Conze 11.535; to Dhardo Rimpoche 4.253; to Dharmachari Sarajit 23.447; to editors and publishers 22.384; to have been brought up speaking English 26.531; to his parents 25.69; to his teachers 22.384, 26.629; to Samuel Johnson 3.598; to Shakespeare

3.602; to Mother Vipassana 22.259; to Samacitta 11.722–3; to the translators of the *Diamond Sūtra* and the *Platform Sūtra* 3.361, 14.320; to the swamis in Sri Lanka for enthusiasm for spiritual life 20.119; to Tooting Public Library 26.484; to Vidyadevi 6.xxvii, 11.722; towards Sangharakshita 3.607–8, 10.xl, 24.242; verses of acknowledgement 25.331–2

heroes
boyhood heroes 26.628; Beethoven, Ludwig van 20.68; Blake, William 26.484–6; Cavell, Edith 26.490; Coleridge, Samuel Taylor 26.486–7; Elizabeth I 26.490; Johnson, Samuel 26.483–4; Lawrence, D. H. 26.489–90; Nietzsche, Friedrich 20.68; Nightingale, Florence 26.490; Strindberg, August 20.68; Teresa, Mother 27.1075; Wilde, Oscar 26.487–9

love of nature
bamboo grove 22.431–2; the beauty of a riverside cremation 12.220–1; the beauty of autumn 7.335–7, 22.322; the beauty of a London morning 23.226; the breath of the Antarctic wastes 24.72, 24.494; 'I could not see where the mountains ended and the sky began' 7.74; Cape Comorin 20.237, 20.239; celebration of trees 25.lvi; contact with the elements (an open-air shower) 24.398–9; contact with nature in New Zealand 24.75–87; Devon countryside 20.50; an evening at an Indian ashram 20.215; the fall in New England 24.470; the Himalayas 21.436–8; the Italian seashore 23.262; kingfishers and dragonflies by a river in Surrey 20.100–2; the awe-inspiring landscape of the Himalayas 18.158–9; 'I found myself wishing I knew more about the mysteries of nature' 24.70; 'I loved all flowers for their beauty' 22.433; love of animals 25.52, 26.418; love of the sea 26.508, 26.589; a magical Indian sunset, through the iridescent haze of pollution 10.292; a moonlit night by the Ganges 20.384–5; mountains of Nepal 20.428, 20.440; moving insects out of the way before lying on the ground to sleep 10.xxxix; the natural world of Guhyaloka 24.393–5; New Zealand's South Island 24.496–7; a Norfolk winter landscape 4.225; the rainy season 21.40; reptiles and amphibians 20.27, 20.28–9, 20.484, 26.418; the sea at Shoreham 23.243; a Spanish sunrise 12.383–4; the sphere of Sangharakshita I 20.451; spring in Bihar 7.427, 20.457; trees as living presences 20.444; the view of Mount Kanchenjunga 12.235; 'it was as though the trees were my silent companions' 21.322; watching goats in India 20.218

dreams
childhood nightmare of a cross 13.525–6; an angry woman on the phone 13.239–40, 17.687; Paramartha 25.454; bookshops 26.681; a deserted church 26.679–80; an angry black bull 26.681; an English woodland where *arhants* lived 26.683–4; Auntie Kate 26.542–3; Mallika 26.543; a dead boy – memory of a past life? 26.678; changing Buddhist 'churches' into something else 25.64–5; dreaming of the same place many times 26.683; dreams in a cathedral-type space 26.459–60; being in a group of monks before a shrine 11.685, 25.64, 26.459; business deals and space travel 26.682; initiation and ordination 26.682; mountains and sea and sky 11.685, 26.460, 26.681; London 26.543, 26.680–1, 26.683; casting out demons 23.263; a Greek or Roman party 23.319; Kachu Rimpoche 23.319; jewels and Dhardo Rimpoche 23.110; his parents 25.60–1, 25.64; tea shops, children, and animals 26.681; two hermitages or ashrams and a secret path 12.685–6, 23.184, 26.223–5, 26.678–9; dreams recalling another life 12.687; dreams of his teachers when handing on responsibility for the Order 11.691, 12.686, 25.64; hearing beautiful music in a dream 26.460; jewels in dreams 23.110, 26.459; 'My heart was held within an Angel's hands' 25.361; one of every three dreams in India, speaking Hindi 24.395; wonderful archetypal dreams during a time of insomnia 12.686, 26.459–60

(VII) Identity

TEMPERAMENT AND CHARACTERISTICS

facets and forces
'the forces in my personality ... would have ripped me apart' without the Three Jewels 7.xvii; oscillation between extremes 20.68; a complex person, a mystery 2.529–30, 26.637–41; his funny side 24.711–12 (n491); 'I have presented a different personality at different stages of my career' 12.512; 'I was still far from knowing myself' (in Kalimpong) 21.170–1; liable to fluctuations of mood 22.184; limitations: 'one can hardly be of all temperaments' 2.531, 11.663; 'My life has many facets' 24.148; 'Perplexed between the East and West' 26.392; 'Himavantavasi': 'an extension of my personality' 22.69; no illusions about himself 2.530

conflict between Sangharakshita I and Sangharakshita II
introduction 20.449–52; arose under conditions of 'settled peace' 15.xii; they used to alternate in the course of a single

day 22.30–1; had not yet succeeded in integrating 'East' and 'West' 22.186; the process of reconciling them 22.464–5, 25.103, 26.90–2, 26.98–9; a connection with Hesse's *Narziss and Goldmund* 24.576; a division in his psyche reflected in his unpublished early novel? 26.444; a fruitful tension between religious absolute and artistic absolute 26.247–9; how other people saw the two Sangharakshitas 25.86; maybe there were more than two 25.86; no real conflict about his interest in poetry 11.553; 'The Poet is the truest Sage, the Sage the sweetest Poet' 25.231; in relation to the founding of the FWBO 26.248; a resolution in old age 25.110; 'A true ascetic he cannot be, for his lips are stained with poesy' 25.192

direction
'My life is a dance in which every movement is planned yet spontaneous' 25.403; life determined by impulse and intuition, not reason and logic 2.406, 11.584–5; a strong sense of direction, but no particular plans 11.548–9; 'the whole force of my being had a definite direction from the beginning' 12.681

fearlessness
couldn't retract an opinion I knew to be true, even to save my life 20.379; courage 26.535–6; insists on meeting a Nepalese official on the same level, risking jail 20.439; at time of violence in India 20.169–70; when hungry ghosts appeared 20.310

duty and discipline
endurance 25.424–5; 'For you the blithe "I want to", For me the grave "I ought"' 25.400; leading a disciplined life came naturally 23.187; a methodical and tidy mind 5.576, 13.92; a strong sense of duty 12.491

reserve
the checking of spontaneous physical expression of feelings 23.9; feelings buried in reticence 23.60–1; 'I have sometimes bleated like a sheep when I should have roared like a lion' 4.445

conservatism
appreciation of courtesy and orderliness 24.33; a gradualist, socially and politically 26.639; a collector 26.639; 'I love the old more than the new' 13.425–6, 26.639; love of continuity 25.liv; a medieval cast of mind 13.425; a reluctant revolutionary 11.549; a traditionalist 11.549; unprogressive 24.80; a well-developed sense of history 11.554

separateness
aloneness 11.xx, 11.598; a desire to avoid attention as much as possible, to be inconspicuous 23.189; feeling of separateness and difference 23.9; given a free choice, he would have preferred to spend his time in solitary retreat 24.3; 'The less I have had to do with other people, the easier I have found things' 11.553; 'I lived in two worlds, one shared with others, the other all my own' 13.529–30; an outsider 23.111, 26.319–20, 26.572–82

in relation to others
'bump of veneration': natural tendency to revere 11.735, 22.xxi, 26.628–9, 26.637–8; capacity to be bored 24.156; diplomatic 22.315, 22.344, 23.162–3; efforts to bring harmony 21.484–5; extremely impressionable as a young man 13.533; forthright 22.346–7; generosity 5.xxx; had a sharp tongue as a child 19.154; obstinacy 20.72, 20.379; outspoken 8.xxvii, 26.435; selfishness (in adolescence) 20.71–2; sympathy with others' difficulties 10.306–7, 11.554, 11.596, 20.213–14, 21.228, 22.22–5, 25.275; a well-developed faculty of distrust 12.483

creativity
drawn more to the arts than the sciences 2.531–2, 11.663, 26.638; imaginal faculty 26.268; imagination 7.8–9, 23.61; a lover of beauty, both bodily and spiritual 23.317–18; one for whom 'the visible world exists' 23.182; poetic temperament 7.16, 22.179–80; sensitivity 22.184, 26.464; someone whose life was an expression of creativity 11.559, 12.640–1

a few more glimpses
capacity for gratitude, *see under* Sangharakshita VI/emotional life; cheerfulness and depression 22.86; clear thinking 11.553; cosmopolitan 26.638; by nature fond of detail 26.467; equally at home in England and India 10.294; fiery radicalism 25.liv; a good organizer 26.638; no charisma 11.663; optimistic 12.408; realizing that he was more practical than he thought 21.170–1; tearfulness 23.446, 26.464; tendency to think that the world was a pleasant, happy place 4.415–16; upward aspiration 25.xlviii, 26.638

others' views
'an unfathomable, fascinating, and somewhat scruffy friend' 10.xliv–v; had 'a high sex potential' (according to Dr Mehta) 23.196; naivety (according to other people) 21.231, 21.238; accused of being impractical 22.183; the 'Enemy of the Church' 8.xxvii, 21.363–4; described as

having charismatic (or personal) authority 13.469, 13.472–3; 'intellectual powers, supreme efficiency, and advanced spiritual awareness' 23.xix

sexuality
he first reads about homosexuality 13.610–11, 22.57; discovering his homosexuality 13.610–11, 26.xv–xvi, 26.577; the first time someone talked to him about homosexuality 22.56–7; giving expression to feelings 26.578; rumours of his alleged homosexuality 23.402; the sense of being an Outsider 26.577–8; giving up celibacy 27.1073; sexual experimentation 11.584–5; what might have happened if he hadn't gone to India 26.584–5; the wish to make his sexual orientation public 26.442; confession in relation to unskilful sexual activity 26.647–8

(VIII) Dharma teacher

thinking about the dharma

elements of thought
a change with regard to the three *yānas* 6.xxvi; contact with Dr Ambedkar and awareness of Buddhism's social dimension 10.xxxi; could an Enlightened man take life? – a dilemma for years 20.333; the development of thinking 7.21; development of thinking about and experience of Going for Refuge 2.401–503; dropping a teaching on Lama Govinda's advice 22.30; on early Buddhist and Mahāyāna conceptions of the self 7.40, 7.553 (n46); 'finding out what I really thought of Buddhism' (through writing the *Survey*) 1.6; on Going for Refuge 2.450, 2.500, 11.383, 11.388, 15.xxi, 21.343–4, 23.160, 26.669; gradual realization that Buddhism was the higher evolution 13.516–17; *The Hazard of Being Male*: 'astonishingly close to my own thinking' 24.541–2; interest is spiritual, doctrinal, metaphysical, not psychological or social 11.549–50; later thinking implicit in earlier 2.433; 'my thinking is still changing' 11.649, 12.535; *pratītya-samutpāda* a part of his thinking and teaching from the early days 12.494; the relationship between Buddhist concepts and the realization behind them 11.653–4; the fundamental principle of my philosophy is that power and value do not coincide 26.83

ecumenical attitude
the principle of ecumenism 2.547–56; an equally high regard for all Buddhist traditions 24.276; a link with the Rimé tradition 12.437; saw myself not as a follower of this or that school, simply a Buddhist 21.245–6

becoming a teacher

soon after ordination
a visit to Nepal 20.419–41, 21.263–4; administering the Refuges and Precepts for the first time 12.303, 20.425–6

Dharma activity in India
'working for the good of Buddhism' in Kalimpong, *see under* Sangharakshita II/in Kalimpong; Dr Ambedkar and the Dhamma Revolution, *see* Sangharakshita IX; 'Eminent Buddhists from the Border Areas' tour, *see* Eminent Buddhists; 'I am not a sort of oracle' 9.327–8; 'It was not going to be easy to revive Buddhism in the land of its birth' 21.169; *Maha Bodhi* journal, *see* *Maha Bodhi* journal; and the Maha Bodhi Society, *see* Maha Bodhi Society; the talks on which the *Survey* was based, *see under* Sangharakshita XIII/writings

Dharma activity in the West
invited to return to England, *see under* Sangharakshita III/return to England; the founding of the FWBO (Triratna), *see under* Triratna; aloneness as a Dharma teacher 11.598

the altruistic dimension
considering the needs of those 'with little dust on their eyes' 24.3; 'I felt that I was not a person but an impersonal force' 11.xix–xx, 21.523, 22.364; 'I wished I could practise medicine as well as teaching the Dharma' 10.1, 10.317–18, 27.1075; a life of service 25.44; people coming to him with their problems 12.91–3, 12.232–3; time to start paying attention to the needs of others 21.24, 25.44, 25.115–16; times when I felt that a higher power was acting through me 26.670; 'working for the good of Buddhism', *see under* Sangharakshita II/in Kalimpong

experiences of teaching
asked to teach someone how to develop psychic powers 3.584; attitude to giving advice 18.623; 'Before deciding you disagree with me, clarify your understanding of what I've said' 26.4; communicating the Dharma one of his great joys 22.528, 23.xvi; teaching poetry the same as teaching the Dharma 12.672–3, 21.78–9, 22.464–5, 26.393; first time leading a group retreat 23.133–5; has he ever used the 'sudden method'? 16.184; 'I am inclined to doubt my own explanation' (re will power and the *dhyānas*) 5.269; 'I may not have as much time to finish my work as I had previously supposed' 23.465; 'I want disciples who are bold, self-confident,

and independent' 26.80; leading a 'meditational workshop' at a conference 24.204–5; talking about the Dharma as though it had just been revealed 17.402–3; using knowledge of the coal industry as skilful means 18.414

intentions
natural tendency to emphasize the positive aspects of spiritual life 26.638; not trying to 'adapt' the Dharma, just to make it understandable 13.379, 13.423; presenting the Dharma in terms accessible to a Western audience 12.635; sharing his enthusiasm 14.xvi

subjects and contexts
the essence of his teaching: human spiritual development 11.730–6; practices he emphasized 6.xxii; system of meditation, *see under* meditation/methods; tackling the subject of karma and rebirth 4.404–5; teaches at Yale University 4.296, 9.446–7, 12.656, 23.453–62; teaching at the Buddhist Society's summer school 23.32–4; teaching the four *mūla yogas* to the 'Three Musketeers' 23.231–2; teaching meditation 5.xxiii–iv, 5.xxix; teaching the new Buddhists in India, *see* Sangharakshita IX; teachings he particularly emphasized 6.xxi–xxii; tends to teach in terms of the humanities rather than the sciences 2.531–2, 11.663; the three fetters in his teachings 13.363–4; 'Was it any part of my work for the Dharma to be used as an Aunt Sally?' 24.75

AS A PERSONAL TEACHER

as preceptor
conducting ordinations at the vihara in Kalimpong 8.655–6; ordains Prajnaloka (a Tibetan) in Kalimpong 12.447, 22.447; gives the bodhisattva ordination 23.232; gives the Refuges and Precepts to Miss Delannoy (the 'French nun') 22.15; gives the *śrāmaṇera* ordination to Eric (ordained as Viriya) 23.236–7; for the Triratna Buddhist Order (WBO), *see under* Triratna II/Sangharakshita; ordains Anna Phillips as Amritapani at Biddulph 23.139, 23.145–6; ordains an 'eight-precept lay Buddhist' (first ordination in England) 23.118; did he expect his disciples to appreciate poetry? 26.393, 26.399–400

what kind of teacher?
the basis of his 'authority' as a teacher 11.655, 11.667; I would rather not apply the word 'guru' to myself 2.529, 11.666; people projecting power onto him 11.686; a spiritual friend, or even just a friend 2.529, 11.666

means of communication
at least half questions based on literalistic misunderstandings 14.321; checking what he really said 15.415; deliberately choosing an extreme example 13.473; elucidator or translator of the Dharma 2.525–7, 4.601, 11.xvi, 23.xvi–xvii, 26.268; film and video, *see under* films; getting to know him 26.xiii–xiv; he amuses himself by giving 'Zen-like' responses to a questioner 26.452; 'If forbidden to speak of Buddhism in Buddhist terms, I could use Christian terms' 26.387; international communication 24.158; the joy of relating to someone simply as friend to friend 23.112; letters 2.533, 12.411–12, 12.698, 24.325, 24.361; postcards 2.535, 23.295, 23.364, 24.11, 24.21, 24.39, 24.67, 24.88, 24.90–1, 24.272, 24.298, 24.361, 24.422; principal means the spoken and written word 2.532–5, 22.528, 23.xvi; shift from traditional Buddhist expressions to 'the way I see things here and now' 4.600–1; talks and lectures, *see* Sangharakshita X/ public speaking; telephone calls 24.325; with leading figures in the Western Buddhist world 24.484–5; writings, *see* Sangharakshita XIII/writings; non-verbal means 2.535

personal interviews
at the Hampstead Buddhist Vihara 2.457, 23.194–5; in a curtained-off space at Sakura 12.366; on early retreats in England 23.239; in Birmingham 26.406; dissatisfied with the formal interview as a way of communication 24.155–6; available to 'anyone who wants to talk to me about anything' 24.158–9; in New Zealand 24.546; may become more selective 24.324–5; would rather call them individual meetings 24.314

STUDY SEMINARS

introduction
how the seminars were conducted 5.xxii–iv, 15.xvi, 17.xi–xii, 18.xiii–iv; participants 18.xiv–xv; photographs 10.420, 17.xii; Sangharakshita's approach to editing them 11.723; transcription 5.xxvi, 17.xi–xiii, 18.xiv; edited for publication 8.xv, 17.xii–xiii, 17.6, 18.641–2 (n8); wish for them to be edited and published 2.532–3, 10.215, 11.525, 12.398

texts studied
'The Advice Given to Three Fortunate Women' 24.161; 'Conditions of the Stability of the Order' 24.31; *Dhyāna for Beginners* 5.xxxi, 24.362; *Diamond Sūtra* 14.320; *The Duties of Brotherhood in Islam* 26.688; *The Endlessly Fascinating*

Cry (*Bodhicaryāvatāra*) 4.225–7, 4.233–7; *Heart Sūtra* 14.320; *The Jewel Ornament of Liberation* 24.172, 24.225, 24.255–6; *Maṅgala Sutta* (*Auspicious Signs*) 15.xx; *Meghiya Sutta* 24.371; *Mind in Buddhist Psychology* (*Necklace of Clear Understanding*) 17.xvii, 17.431; 'An Ode on Friendship' (Johnson) 24.315; 'On the Death of Dr Robert Levett' (Johnson) 24.314–15; *Outlines of Mahāyāna Buddhism* 14.xv; 'The Precepts of the Gurus' 24.159; 'Questions and Answers at the Buddhist Society of New South Wales' 24.58; *Ratnaguṇa-saṃcayagāthā* 4.226–7, 14.xv–xvi, 14.320, 17.xvi–xvii; on *sādhanas* 5.xxxi–ii; *The Songs of Milarepa* 18.xii, 18.xiii–iv; *Sūtra of Huineng* 24.321; *Sūtra of Forty-Two Sections* 24.28, 24.93; *The Threefold Refuge* 2.484, 2.566, 24.66; *The Tibetan Book of the Dead* 24.159–60; *Tiratana Vandanā* (*Salutation to the Three Jewels*) 15.xx; the *Udāna* (two seminars) 10.421–3; *The Way to Wisdom* 17.xvii, 17.6–9, 24.184

(IX) Dr Ambedkar and the Dhamma revolution

beginning of involvement
Sangharakshita first becomes aware of Dr Ambedkar 10.3–4, 10.15, 20.452; Dr Ambedkar encourages him to be more active 10.30–2, 21.90–1; connection 9.xii–xiii, 9.13–24, 9.207–11, 9.260, 9.281, 9.317, 9.405, 9.468, 9.489, 9.502–4; correspondence 10.4, 10.15, 10.31–2, 21.89–90, 21.415; Dr Ambedkar's letter to Sangharakshita (facsimile) 10.30

meetings with Dr Ambedkar
'After my contact, I became much more aware of the social dimension' 10.xxxi; 'among the happiest memories of my whole life' 10.336; first meeting, in Bombay 8.xx, 9.14–16, 10.4–5, 10.15–16, 21.415–16, 22.287; second meeting, at Siddharth College 9.16–17, 10.5–8, 10.16, 22.287–8; Dr Ambedkar asks Sangharakshita to give a talk 9.17–18, 10.7–8, 10.336; third meeting, in Delhi 9.19–21, 9.503, 10.9–10, 10.17, 22.352–3, 23.354; 'the greatest man I ever met in all my life' 10.lxiv, 10.360; Dr Ambedkar said Sangharakshita was one of two *bhikṣus* to be trusted 9.549 (n4)

the conversion
Dr Ambedkar asked Sangharakshita about how to convert 9.17, 9.209, 9.502, 10.7, 22.288; haunted by the plight of the Dalits 22.160–1; not present at the conversion ceremony 9.19, 10.19, 10.374, 22.350, 23.354; the message he sent to be read out at the ceremony 22.350; writings in support of Dr Ambedkar's conversion 22.350–2

Dr Ambedkar's death
a strong urge to go to Nagpur 10.10, 10.17, 22.357–60; in Nagpur at the time of Dr Ambedkar's death 8.651, 9.405–6, 9.503–4, 10.96–105; condolence meeting 9.22–3, 9.210, 9.223, 9.406, 9.503–4, 10.10–12, 10.18, 10.313, 10.375, 21.523, 23.354; eyewitness accounts 10.xxxvii–viii, 10.96–7; Sangharakshita's assessment of the occasion 22.363–4; 'over the crowd hung an enormous Presence' 9.23, 10.17–18, 22.363; 'I felt that I was not a person but an impersonal force' 11.xix–xx, 11.523, 22.364; 'I tried to clarify for them what Buddhism meant' 10.290; A. R. Kulkarni's account of the visit 10.95–105; talks and giving *diksha* in Nagpur localities 10.12, 10.18, 10.313, 10.375–6; a special feeling for the people of Nagpur 10.376, 23.355

teaching the Dharma to Dr Ambedkar's followers
'allowing myself to be a channel for something beyond me' 11.687; being given river water to drink because the Dalits could not use the well 25.124; ceremoniousness and garlands 10.193–4, 10.239–40, 10.305–6, 12.487, 24.17; documentary film: *In the Footsteps of Ambedkar* 10.lii, 10.liii–iv, 10.353, 24.312; explaining what Going for Refuge really meant 12.304; a fellow feeling because they were New Buddhists, like him 25.125; founded the Poona District Buddhist Women's Association 10.181; the happiest period of his life 11.691–2; his influence because he was an Outsider, as they also were 26.578–9; reason for attraction to the movement of conversion 3.296; sense of closeness to the new Buddhists because of shared Going for Refuge 2.437–9; similar approach to Buddhism 2.496–7, 10.xliii; Subhuti's description 9.xiii–xv; talks and tours, *see under* Sangharakshita/public speaking; a way of serving the Buddha 25.124–5; the development of Triratna (TBMSG), *see under* Triratna I/Triratna in India

(X) Public speaking

giving talks

the experience of giving talks
'allowing myself to be a channel for something beyond me' 11.687; communicating the Dharma through speaking one of the great joys of my life 22.528; deep fulfilment 22.xix–xx; enjoyment of giving talks 23.78; 'I beat

the drum of the Dharma vigorously and without compromise' 23.79; 'I was possessed by a passion for spreading the Dharma by the spoken word' 23.90; an exalted state of consciousness produced by giving a talk 13.132, 23.xvii; 'getting the feel of an audience was so tangible as to be almost physical' 22.143; the intense atmosphere during a talk about the *bardos* 23.93; 'one of the best and most profound talks I had ever given' 22.286; one of the most receptive audiences I have ever encountered 24.237; spending part of a talk correcting the person who introduced it 22.270–1; 'thousands of people really wanting to hear what you have to say' 10.296; 'The words that came from my lips were not really mine' 26.670

reflections on the nature of giving talks
the difference between a prepared lecture and an extemporary talk 24.129–30; different styles of speaking in India and in England 10.301, 24.18; dissatisfaction with the talk as a medium of communication 24.92; the effects of recorded talks years later 12.533–4; effectiveness of communicating the Dharma by spoken word 22.528, 23.xvi, 23.78; giving a talk after a long process of reflection 12.581; giving up giving talks 12.473, 12.534, 12.545; Lama Govinda advises him to speak less and write more 23.414; in principle, no less a way of being productive than writing 23.226; the Indian appetite for long talks 10.306; lectures showed the audience the seriousness of the enterprise 23.463; people walking out of talks 12.583–4; people were struck by his youth when he first gave talks in India 22.165; preferring to speak last, to correct mistakes of previous speakers 23.121; the process of preparing a talk 12.363–4; is 'talk' or 'lecture' the better description? 12.533; would rather present a paper than give a talk 12.534

TALKS IN INDIA BEFORE DR AMBEDKAR'S CONVERSION

places
at All India Dharma Parishad (aged 21) 20.174; Buddha Jayanti in Kalimpong 22.9–11; finding himself teaching 'in the wrong way' in Calcutta 16.507; first sermon in Hindi 22.31; a funeral sermon 22.36; in Kalimpong 21.83–4; a lecture in Bangalore on *The Voice of the Silence* 22.147; in Bombay, 1955 22.268–71; in Lucknow, a talk on the bodhisattva ideal which baffled students 21.114–15; speech at the World Fellowship of Faiths 22.77–8; talks at the Maha Bodhi Society which weren't taken seriously 19.295–6; talks for the Tamang Buddhists of Kalimpong 22.265–6; talks in Nagpur (1954) 22.155–65; talk in Nagpur on Buddhism and culture 10.99; to the Maitri Sangha (Bengali) 22.9; to the population of Muvattupuzha 20.265; at Santiniketan 21.507, 21.509; Satyapriya mortifyingly undermines a talk 20.294–5; speaking to a crowd in Kausali on Indian Independence Day 20.222–3

themes
'Buddhism and God' 22.68; 'The Differences Between the Principles of Buddhism and Hinduism' 22.153; 'How to Develop Discrimination' 22.32; 'Inspiration – Whence?' (talk in Bombay) 12.692, 22.269; 'Love and Devotion in Buddhism' 22.285; 'The Meaning of Buddhism and the Value of Art' 22.77; 'Practical Buddhism for the Layman' 22.73; 'The Recollection of Death' 22.89, 22.230; 'The Spiritual Path in Buddhism' 22.164–5; a talk on the Buddha's 'Song of Victory' 22.190; the talks on which the *Survey* is based, *see under* Sangharakshita XIII/published writings; on Buddhism and Christianity 20.291–2; 'Who is a Buddhist?' 22.111

TEACHING TOURS AMONG THE NEW BUDDHISTS IN INDIA (1956–1992)

1950s and 60s
brief account 9.156–7, 9.504, 10.12, 10.19–20, 12.319–20, 21.572; talk notes 10.116–184; advised to act as Manu (lawgiver), not Dharma teacher 12.320–1, 26.560; the conditions in which the talks were given 10.xxxviii–ix, 10.xliii; cutting down on preaching tours 22.475; didn't avoid talking about complex subjects 12.587; evocative description of a visit to a village in Maharashtra 7.467–9; 'My lectures had far more impact than I realized at the time' 24.16; on one occasion introduced as the pope 24.18, 24.608 (n30); teaching Buddhism and removing misunderstandings about it 10.20; people would remember the talks years later 10.xl, 12.526; a tour of over seven months giving over 200 lectures 10.178, 23.19; a hiatus in the work due to the conversion movement's politicization 23.327; saying goodbye and promising to continue to help 23.327; 1966 talks in Bombay 23.333, 23.339–40

themes
are Hinduism and Buddhism the same? 10.117; what the *Diksha* movement means 10.124; the bodhisattva ideal 10.122, 10.125; the impact of conversion on Indian

life 10.125–6; the origin of Buddhism 10.132–3; Hīnayāna and Mahāyāna 10.133–4; Tibetan Buddhism 10.134–5; the middle way 10.135–6; Tantric Buddhism 10.136; karma and rebirth 10.137; atheism 10.138; Buddhism in England 10.139–40; the central philosophy of Buddhism 10.142–3; Buddhism and God 10.150; mindfulness 10.150–1; *oṃ maṇi padme hūṃ* 10.151–2, 10.174–6; literature and ethics 10.153–4; Buddhism today 10.156–7; practical Buddhism 10.157–9; *anātman* and *śūnyatā* 10.159–60; duties of *upāsakas* and *upāsikas* 10.161; the *Diamond Sūtra* 10.162–6; the great life of Dr Ambedkar 10.167–9; the universality of Buddhism 10.170–2; 'What is Dharma?' (Kalimpong) 8.660; 'What it Means to Become a Buddhist' 10.7–8, 10.336, 22.289–90

1979 talks
brief description 10.xliv–vi, 10.191; letter to the Order about the tour 24.9–25; the talks themselves 10.191–284; driving home the Dharma with a sledgehammer 24.18; 'I found I could carry on from where I had left off' 24.16–17; Lokamitra deputizes as a speaker 24.113, 24.115; loudspeakers blaring with film music 24.17; questions and answers in Poona 24.105–6

1981–2 teaching tour
brief description 9.158–9, 10.liv–lvi, 10.305–6; the talks themselves 9.163–539; conditions in which talks were given 10.292, 10.295; described in *Jai Bhim!* 10.xlviii; enjoyment of preparing and giving talks 10.294, 10.296; itinerary 10.294–5; location map 9.167; reflections on the tour 10.286–304

last visits
1983 10.xlix–l; 1991–2 (final visit to India) 10.liv–vi

talks in Britain
early talk on 'The Inferiority of Women' 20.83, 21.478; 'Buddhism and the Problem of Death' 26.505; 'A Case of Dysentery': 'a change from spiritual this and transcendental that' 11.432–44, 26.658; first public poetry reading 23.124; first talks under the auspices of the FWBO 12.366–7, 12.653; 'The Higher Evolution of Man' 13.517, 23.463; 'The Higher Evolution of the Individual' 23.463; 'The Individual and the World Today' 13.379; list of talks given 23.544–5; in London in the 1960s (before the FWBO) 23.49, 23.78–80, 23.90–2; talks about Dr Ambedkar's work 10.3–14, 10.286–315, 23.81, 24.204; talks on the occasion of the first ordinations in the WBO 2.468–9; 'The Meaning of Conversion in Buddhism' 2.460–5, 23.79–80, 23.117; 'Mind Reactive – and Creative' 23.427–8; at Oscott College, Birmingham 13.562; 'The Psychology of Ritual' 13.420; 'Religion and Caste in India' 23.330; a sermon at King's College Cambridge 12.519, 16.211–23; talks in Cambridge, *see under* Cambridge; talks in Oxford, *see under* Oxford; talks translated into sign language 24.246; 'Transforming Self and World' 10.xxxix

TALKS ELSEWHERE IN THE WORLD
Berlin 12.602–27, 26.451; Cairo 23.415; Kraków 26.450–1; Malaysia, *see under* Malaysia; Singapore, aged 21 4.318, 7.19–20, 9.501, 20.149; United States, *see under* United States

(XI) PEOPLE

friends
Ramzam Ali, a Muslim friend 26.692–4; Ananda (Dharmachari) 2.404, 12.396, 12.653, 25.420–1, 26.352, 26.611; Ayya Khema, see Ayya Khema; Ernie (Army friend) 20.91–2, 20.94–5, 20.99, 20.107–108, 20.140, 20.153; Tan Keng Lock in Singapore 20.142–3; The Venerable Siak Hiong Hiup in Singapore 20.142–3; Banerjee, Rabindra Kumar, *see* Buddharakshita; Brooks, Kevin 23.465–70, 23.473, 23.543 (n501), 24.241, 24.666 (n289); Cameron, Clare, *see under* Cameron; Cann, Joe, *see under* Cann; Delamare, Terry, *see under* Delamare; Driver, John 22.403, 22.503; Dubash, Dinoo, *see under* Dubash; Frydman, Maurice (friend in Bombay), *see* Frydman; Hipkin, John 23.152–5, 23.402–5; Iyer, Venkateshwara (Muvattupuzha lawyer), *see under* Iyer; Govinda, Lama Anagarika, *see under* Govinda; Junius, Michael 22.324; Kazi, Sonam Topgay 22.337; the Kazi and Kazini of Chakhung 21.483–5, 22.413–15, 22.478–86, 23.378–9; Khamtul Rimpoche 22.490–1, 23.336; Khantipālo 12.635–7, 22.526–8; Lhalungpa, Lobsang Phuntsok v21; Nair, Kumaran (Muvattupuzha lawyer) 20.272; Narayanmani and Taranath 22.323–4; Nityabandhu (Michal) 26.450–2, 26.455–6, 26.463–4; Pallis, Marco 20.151, 21.159–63, 21.228–30, 23.121, 23.240; Paramartha, *see under* Paramartha; Mr Pheunkhang 22.190; Pillai, Kesava (Muvattupuzha lawyer) 20.272; 'Poems For Four Friends' 25.305; Rashk, Arjundev 21.399, 21.413–15, 22.266–7, 22.275–8, 23.304; Rechung Rimpoche 18.433, 23.75; Roof, Simmons and Marcia

22.324–8; Roper, Rosi 26.458; Sivalibodhi 24.117; Theosophist friends Rie and Sten von Krusenstierna 10.276, 20.147–8, 24.56–64; Thich Thien Chau 22.515, 23.193, 23.228–30; Sachin, *see* Sachin; Saddhanandi 26.550; Schlaum, Blanca 20.194; Shewalay, Professor, *see* Shewalay; Singh, Gurkipal 20.222; Sonam Topgay (Kalimpong) v21, v22, v23; Tomo Geshe Rimpoche, 'the most mysterious person I have known' 22.493, 23.397, 26.230; Vaidyasekara 22.324; Vivekananda, Bhikkhu, 'one of my closest friends at that time' 12.635, 12.647, 23.365; Willmott, Antoinette 23.145; Yhonzone, S. 22.337–8

friendship
desire for friendship 7.13; the deaths of old friends 24.237–8; the essence of the Buddhist life is communicated through friendship 21.475; my experience shows it is better to keep sexual relations and friendship separate 26.639; friends behaving badly through jealousy 21.560; 'Friendship is a great thing to me' 25.391; friendship with people of different religions 9.348; friendships with a wide range of people 22.xviii–xix; 'I never like to break with a friend' 21.571; keeping up a personal life through reading, writing, and friendship 25.92; lonely longing for the Friend (poem, 'Many were the friends ...') 25.226–7; making a point of introducing friends to one another 21.485; not missing friends when separated from them, because of a vivid imagination 23.61; 'one of the great blessings of my life that I have had so many good friends' 12.640–1; one's real friends remain a part of one's consciousness 21.473, 21.589; wish to live on a planet where friendship is the rule of life 25.454; with friends in the New Forest 26.611

intimate relationships
asking for forgiveness 25.230, 26.647–8; 'happy because we were together' on Westminster Bridge 25.276; a kiss under the desk with Daphne Taylor 20.490, 26.420; in love with Gladys Gown at school 26.420–1; I never felt that I had found my 'other half' 23.111; love poems 25.222–5, 25.230, 25.255, 25.258–9, 25.264, 25.287, 25.379, 25.483–98; 'Nature had not meant me for a lover' 20.88; reading the Book of You 25.327; sexual experimentation 11.584–5; sexual relationship with Carter 26.608; sharing a bed with Kati 26.604–5; Sonia 20.78–9, 20.84, 20.87–8, 20.106; about to have sex with a woman, heard a voice say 'Don't' 13.591, 26.611, 26.617–18; 'When I was very young I used to tell people I would never marry' 26.592; confession of unskilfulness in sexual activity 26.647–8

correspondence
keeping in contact with Buddhists in other places 22.457; with Jack Austin 11.546, 21.338; with Adrienne Bennett 11.546; with Clare Cameron, *see* Cameron; with Edward Conze 11.531–2, 11.546; with Alexandra David-Néel 6.609; with Dinoo Dubash 21.457–619; with Lama Govinda 11.560–4; with Christmas Humphreys 11.542; with Ayya Khema 24.484–5, 26.408, 26.536–9; with Nityabodhananda, editor of the *Vedanta Kesari* 20.228; with the Shankaracharya of Puri 20.177; with Bhikkhu Soma 20.449, 20.451; with Sri Krishna Prem 20.184

meetings
with Dr Ambedkar, *see* Sangharakshita IX; visits the Arya Maitreya Mandala in Germany 12.584; with Ashok, a young man of Ahmedabad 20.180; with the Bishop of Woolwich 12.112; with the Dalai Lama 22.354, 22.365–6, 22.371; visits Edward Conze in Oxford 12.169–70, 23.55–6; with Pandit-ji 20.178; with Rabindra Kumar Banerjee (later Satyapriya) 20.146; with Ramana Maharshi 20.337; with Reginald Ray 24.490, 24.522; with Sangharatana Thera 20.453; with the Shankaracharya of Puri 20.177, 20.343; with Swami Ramdas 20.322–5; with Trungpa Rimpoche 12.494; with Yalahankar Swami 20.359

women
an account of Sangharakshita, women, and friendship (Kalyanaprabha) 21.476–9; early talk on 'The Inferiority of Women' 20.83, 21.478; 'For me women have always been friends, not sex partners' 26.611; he founded the Poona District Buddhist Women's Association 10.181; noticing a contrast between Western and Indian women 23.5–6; the position of women in Buddhism 10.161, 10.182–4; women on study seminars 18.xv

(XII) Cultural life

art

childhood encounters with art
introduction to art 20.24; National Gallery visits during the war 20.71; first experience of art 26.217–18; first meeting with an artist 20.39; ruthless passion for art 20.68

practice of art
as a child 13.585, 20.27–8, 20.35–6, 20.39, 20.48; drawing angels 13.585; painting the

Virgin Mary 13.598; photography v24 (see index under 'Sangharakshita'); sketches of historical figures 20.27–8; taking up painting and photography (1970) 23.469–71; thoughts of becoming an artist 20.29, 20.36

appreciation of art
'colour has always been important to me' 26.441; Contemporary Art Fair at Olympia 24.322; reflections on art 3.510; when wandering in India, love of art revived by the art gallery at Trivandrum 20.248

WORKS OF ART SEEN

Bellini
The Burial of Christ 24.419; *Transfiguration* 24.274

Blake
Christ Refusing the Banquet 24.574; illustrations to the Book of Job 13.536, 26.485

Botticelli
Christ on the Mount of Olives 24.450; at the Prado 24.410; at the Uffizi 17.222–3, 23.313

Bruegel, Pieter the Elder
Parable of the Blind 24.274–5; *The Triumph of Death* 24.410

Burne-Jones
The Beguiling of Merlin 25.438, 25.452; *The Golden Stairs* 26.661–2

Caravaggio
St Jerome 23.308; *St John the Baptist* 24.420

El Greco
The Agony in the Garden (school of El Greco) 26.308, 26.675; *The Baptism of Christ* 24.409, 26.308; *The Burial of Count Orgaz* 24.417–18, 26.308–18; *The Coronation of the Virgin* 13.588, 24.421; *El Espolio* 24.419; *The Immaculate Conception* 24.421; *Map of Toledo* 24.422; *The Martyrdom of Saint Maurice* 24.413; *Portrait of a Painter* 24.441; *The Resurrection of Christ* 24.409, 26.308; *St Andrew* 24.421; *St Bernardino* 24.422; *St Ildefonso* 24.413; *St Jerome* 24.415; *St John the Baptist* 24.421; *St John the Evangelist* 24.421; *St Joseph and the Infant Christ* 24.421; *St Maurice and the Theban Legion* 26.308; *St Peter* 24.413, 24.421; *The Storm over Toldeo* 26.308

Goya
The Arrest of Christ 24.419; *The Burial of the Sardines* 24.416; 'disappointing' 24.409

Leal, Valdés
Defeat of the Saracens at Assisi 24.441; *Temptation of St Jerome* 24.441

Leonardo da Vinci
The Last Supper 13.648–9, 23.254; *Portrait of a Lady with an Ermine* 26.448

Mantegna
Enthroned Madonna and Child with Saints 23.255; frescoes in Padua 23.259

Martini, Simone
Annunciation 13.599–600; painting of St Louis of Toulouse crowning his brother 24.274

Michelangelo
Pietà 23.307; Sistine Chapel frescoes 23.308

Murillo, Bartolomé Estaban
Adoration of the Shepherds 24.441; *Immaculate Conception* 13.598, 24.441; 'a revelation' 24.441; *St Thomas of Villanueva Distributing Alms* 24.441

Salzillo
sentimental holy figures 24.461; sculpture of St Jerome 24.458

Titian
Bacchus and Ariadne 26.218; *Crucifixion* 24.419; *Pope Paul III* (including illustration) 24.274–6; portrait of Pier Luigi Farnese 24.264; *Sacred and Profane Love* 23.308; *Salome* 25.376

Velázquez
Immaculate Conception 13.598; *Las Meninas* 24.409, 24.410–11; *Portrait of Cardinal Borja* 24.420; portrait of Pope Innocent X 3.508; portraits of dwarfs 24.460

Veronese
Feast in the House of Levi 23.258; *The Temptation of St Anthony* 25.376

Zurbarán, Francisco de 24.415
Apotheosis of Saint Thomas Aquinas 24.441; *Saint Hugo in the Carthusian Refectory* 24.441

other artists and works A – C
Acker, Hans (stained-glass) 24.595; *Apollo Belvedere* 23.308; bad art 24.83–4; the *Barbarini Faun* 24.587; Bernini sculptures 23.308; Berruguete's *Auto da Fe* 13.666–7, 24.410; Bosch's *The Garden of Earthly Delights* 24.409, 24.413; Boyd, Arthur 24.534; Bronzino's *An Allegory of Time and Love* 23.219–20; Buffalmacco's *The Triumph of Death* 24.224; Burra, Edward 24.251; Cairos' *Herodias with the Head of John the Baptist* 23.257; Cameron's *Portrait*

of an Unknown Woman (illustration) 24.358; Carpaccio, Vittore, *The Lion of St Mark* 25.377; Caulfield, Patrick 24.134; Caxton in his workshop 26.662; Cellini's statue of Perseus 23.313; the *Charioteer*, the *Two Brothers*, and *Antinous* (at Delphi) 23.276–8; Chevalier, Nicholas, *Buddha's Renunciation* 24.536; Chinese snuff bottles 24.384; Colantonio's *St Jerome in his Study* (including illustration) 24.276–7; Collins, Cecil (angels) 26.240; Cologne School of Painting 24.369; Cranach the Elder's *Venus and Cupid* 23.308; Cranach the Younger's *Martin Luther and Philipp Melanchthon* 24.591–2

other artists and works D – H
della Vecchia's *St Sebastian* 23.257; Dix, Otto 26.379; Donatello's statue of Erasmo da Narni 23.259; Doré's depiction of Satan 13.593; Dossi's *Circe* 23.308; Duccio's *Maestà* 13.634, 13.646; the Ephesian Artemis 23.305–6; Epstein, Jacob 26.379; Erasmus (portrait) 24.275; Etty, William 24.386; Farnese Hercules 23.305; Fra Angelico's *Annunciation* 13.599; frescoes at Burghley House 24.383–4; German masters 24.592; Ghiberti's baptistery doors, Florence 23.312; Ginés, José, *Massacre of the Innocents* 24.416; Giorgione's *Tempest* 23.258; Giotto's frescoes in Padua 13.593–4, 13.646, 23.259; Gormley's *Angel of the North* 24.584; Greek and Roman works in Munich 24.587–8; Grosz, George 26.379; Guercino paintings 24.586; William Hogarth's paintings 3.508; Holbein's *Dance of Death* 13.230, 26.297; Holiday's *Dante and Beatrice* 24.547; Holman Hunt's *The Scapegoat* 2.609–10, 24.65, 24.134, 26.465, 26.670

other artists and works I – R
Isenheim Altarpiece 26.675–6; Kandinsky, Wassily v24, 26.379; the Laocoön 23.308, 23.519 (n343); Len Lye's kinetic sculptures 24.510; Maderno's *St Cecilia* 23.308; Magritte, Rene 26.379; Marc's *Blaue Reiter* 24.588; Masaccio's frescoes in Florence 13.646–8; Masolino's work in Florence 13.647–8; Millais, *The Blind Girl* 26.670; Millet's *Angelus* 23.265; Miró, Joan 24.372, 26.379; Multscher, Hans, *Man of Sorrows* 24.594; Myron's statue of the *Discobolus* 23.307; Orchardson's *Napoleon on board the Bellerophon* 26.661; paintings of Naples 24.271; Persian miniature paintings 13.284, 26.218; Philpot's *Melampus* 24.379; Piazzetta's *Ecstasy of St Francis* 23.257; Picasso's *Guernica* 24.410; Pinturicchio and Raphael's frescoes at Siena 13.637; Pisa fresco of Satan 13.593; Pompeii fresco from the house of Terentius Neo (illustration) 24.288; Pre-Raphaelites, *see* Pre-Raphaelites; Praxiteles' statue of Hermes carrying Dionysus 23.299; Raphael's *School of Athens* 23.308, 23.519–20 (n343); Ravenna mosaics 23.260–1, 26.237, 26.389; Rossetti's *Dante's Dream* 24.547, 24.584–5, 26.660; Rubens' *The Feast of Herod* 24.585–6

other artists and works S – Z
Savoldo's *Tobias and the Angel* 13.589–90, 25.375; Schaffner's choir altar in Ulm 24.594; Schiavone, Andrea, *The Adoration of the Magi* 25.376–7; sculptures at the archaeological museum in Athens 23.289; Simberg, Hugo, *The Wounded Angel* 26.240; Spanish artists 24.416; Spinello Aretino fresco 13.597; Syrlin's figures from classical antiquity 24.594–5; Tintoretto 13.649, 23.255, 24.586; *the Triumph of Death* (Pisa) 26.298; Turner's *Bridge of Sighs, Ducal Palace and Custom-House, Venice* 2.609, 2.612; van der Berch's St Christopher 24.369; van der Weyden's *The Magdalen Reading* 24.451; van Gogh: 'I realized I did not really like him' 24.371; Vanni's *St Catherine* 13.635; *Venus de Milo*: a disappointment 23.452; Watts, *The Eve of Peace* 24.73; Wright, Joseph, of Derby 24.379; Wyspianski's mural in Kraków 26.449; Zeitblom, scenes from the life of St Valentine 24.592

THEATRE

introduction
Sangharakshita's acting as a child 20.37, 26.501; going to a pantomime as a child 26.421–2; 'a love for the stage which I never felt for the screen' 20.86; theatre going in London (1942) 20.86

Shakespeare plays seen
Cymbeline 24.582; *Henry* VIII 24.581–2; *King John* 13.553–4; *Measure for Measure* 24.581; *The Merchant of Venice* 20.37, 24.582; *Richard* II 24.312; *Richard* III 24.318; *The Tempest* 24.582; *Twelfth Night* 24.582

other performances seen
Leslie French, *Everyman* (ballet) 13.658–9, 15.375–6, 20.86; Chekhov, *The Cherry Orchard* 24.390; Goldsmith, *She Stoops to Conquer* 24.582; Ibsen, *The Wild Duck*, 24.390; Miller, *The Crucible* 24.390–1; Rowe, *The Tragedy of Jane Shore* 24.390; Sherman, *A Madhouse in Goa* 24.403; Strindberg, *Master Olof* 24.373; Synge, *Riders to the Sea* 24.582; Synge, *The Shadow of the Glen* 24.582; Webster, *The Duchess of Malfi* 24.390; Williams, *A*

Streetcar Named Desire 24.390–1; Yeats, *Purgatory* 24.582

MUSIC

music in early life
childhood experience 20.14, 20.31–2; Caruso and Gershwin 20.14, 20.504, 26.501; *Fingal's Cave* 20.31; Gilbert and Sullivan 20.37, 26.501; addiction 20.72–3; attempts to translate experience of music into poetry 20.72, 26.503–4; Bach's *Toccata and Fugue in D Minor* 20.72, 26.503; 'I would practically lose consciousness of my body' 20.72–3; 'Music swept me to heights of ecstasy that even poetry could not' 23.173; playing the dulcimer 26.499; regretting not learning to play an instrument 26.499; singing 26.499–501; 'Whistling in the Dark' 26.422

music later in life
the music of Walt Disney's *Fantasia* in Singapore 26.504, 26.670; in India, did not miss listening to music 22.148–9; response to the monastic rule of 'abstaining' from music 23.173; Chinese music 20.140; a music student in Kalimpong 22.325; Tibetan trumpets 25.237; 'The Wandering Singer' 25.170–1; a passionate love for classical music 23.10, 23.173; the silence in the mind after the last notes have died away 24.66; listening to Christian music 13.669; listening to music with Terry 26.505; competition for his attention between music and poetry 26.503; exploring the whole heritage of Western music 26.505; a gift of gramophone records 22.148–9, 22.188, 25.331–2; the 'Friendship Duet' from *The Pearl Fishers* played at a poetry reading 24.360; hearing beautiful music (like *Spem in Alium*) in a dream 26.460; music requested for his funeral 26.505

Indian music
response to the first recital he heard 7.95–7; appreciation of Indian classical music 7.14, 7.81–3, 20.120–1; 'I have not tried to grasp it with my mind, but to open my heart to its influence' 7.83; learning to listen to it 7.14, 7.81–3; a recital of devotional music 22.77; comparison between Indian and Western music 7.83; Sachin's singing 21.77; unsure of propriety of listening to Indian film music 20.350

performances heard
American Indian flute music 24.519; Bartók's *Bluebeard's Castle* 24.589; Bavarian State Opera 24.589; a beautiful melody in Naples 24.262; David Earl's Cello Concerto 24.589; a cello recital at Khadiravani community, Croydon 24.249; Wagner's *Ring* cycle 23.xvii, 23.173–4; early music concert at the Purcell Room 24.372; gypsy music in Poland 25.442, 26.447–8; *The Magic Flute* 24.385; Monteverdi, Claudio, *Coronation of Poppea* 24.589; organ music in Metz 23.248

composers
Beethoven, *see* Beethoven; Chopin 23.173, 26.448; Grieg, Haydn, Elgar 23.173; Handel, *see* Handel; Haydn 20.73, 24.521, 24.589, 26.503; Liszt 24.537, 24.555; Mozart 23.173, 24.157, 26.502, 26.504

READING

introduction
'always a great reader' 25.327; audiobooks 26.581; biography 'one of my favourite forms of literature' 13.624; insatiable appetite for reading 14.xi–xii, 20.68; five literary heroes 26.481–90; how reading led to Buddhism 25.25–6; 'I am not a scholar, just well read' 11.602; 'I readily took on the mood of whatever book I was reading' 13.533; keeping up a personal life through reading, writing, and friendship 25.92; looking up from books to see the shadow of mortality 25.468–70; 'Myself into his book I hurled' 25.405; on the value of reading the classics 12.406; reading is not a Muse 25.337; responding to fictional characters as though they existed 13.582–3; some of us, including myself, read far too much 25.11–12; listening to the radio 12.649, 12.674; newspapers, *see under* newspapers; discerning the Dharma in Western literature 22.464–5; 'Books have always been my constant companions and friends' 24.515; reading psychology 4.605–6; discovering American writers 22.276; admiration for women writers 11.634–5; reading Christian literature became necessary 23.216; 'What have their contents told me, these volumes old and stout?' 25.423

early reading
learned to read from newspapers and the Bible 20.9–10, 20.495–6; as a child 'I was absolutely immersed in my reading' 10.340–1; shock of delight on meeting a metaphor for the first time 20.10, 26.392; childhood reading of poetry 20.36, 26.392; reading while confined to bed as a child 20.18–20; reading at school 26.419–20; overview 20.20–4, 25.25; its influence on his literary style 7.xix; learning to love the good life from the classics 20.61; fiction the branch of literature read least in teenage years 20.81, 23.10; 'Why should

I limit myself to Europe?' 9.278, 10.341, 20.61, 25.26; taste in reading as a teenager 23.9–10; reading on Buddhism, *see under* Sangharakshita V/Buddhist life/early years

reading when living in India
copied passages into notebooks, as material for reflection 20.260–1; a period of stopping reading in favour of Dharma practice 25.471–3; 'amid the simplicities of Arunachala books seemed out of place' 20.339; freedom to read while studying with Bhikkhu Kashyap 20.449; didn't have many books in Kalimpong, but read a few again and again 4.249

reading poetry
first experience of reading poetry 20.10; competition for his attention between music and poetry 26.503; conversation with Kathleen Raine 24.314, 24.686 (n390); early responses to the magic of poetry 26.392, 26.420; finding listening to people reading poetry excruciating 26.393; learning poetry by heart 26.439; poetry an inspiration before contact with the Dharma 12.672; hard to say whether he appreciated poetry more as poetry or religion 20.63, 26.393; poetry read with 'a strange troubled intensity of emotion' 20.108; reading Christian poetry 13.669; 'Poetry is a great thing, a great thing to me' 25.391; poetry would go through him 'like a spear' 25.xlv, 26.392; a poetry reading on friendship 24.359–60, 24.379, 24.381, 24.403

book collection
partly destroyed in bombing 20.104; books taken to India 20.107–8; Buddhist collection in India extended by books sent from London 22.224–5; books brought back to the UK from India 15.xi; books left behind in England 20.105, 23.31, 23.40; books collected in Australia 24.536; books sent back to England from America 24.527; bookshops, *see* bookshops; 'One day I must leave you, my old friends' 25.404

BOOKS READ
These lists relate to Sangharakshita's descriptions of reading these works, but references to many of them (and many others) will also be found elsewhere in the concordance.

early reading
Alice's Adventures in Wonderland 20.16–17; classic children's books 26.420; comics 20.22, 23.8; Corelli, Marie, *The Mighty Atom* and *Jane* 26.575; *Everybody's* 26.416; Joan Grant's *Winged Pharaoh* 20.37, 26.466–7; Hornung's *Raffles* 26.574–5; Kingsley's *The Heroes* 26.482; Lang's *Fairy Books* 23.8; *My Life in Time* 26.574; *The Story of the Iliad* 26.482

Harmsworth's Children's Encyclopaedia
every one of its sixty parts became familiar 23.8; an illustration of Mohammed 26.689; 'the image of the Buddha stuck in my mind' 12.681, 26.218; infinite riches in a little room 13.528–9, 20.22–4; learning about Egypt 26.466; the life of the Buddha 9.487; my first experience of art 26.217–18; on heroes 26.482; opened up for me all the treasures of the human spirit 26.416; section on India 9.487

biographies and autobiographies
Omraam Mikhael Aivanhov 24.531; Henri-Frederic Amiel's *Journal Intime* 8.149–51; Paul Bowles 24.374; Brittain, Vera, *Testament of Friendship* 26.637; Browne, Thomas, *Religio Medici* 20.52, 26.587; Coleridge (Richard Holmes) 24.563; Coleridge, *Biographia Literaria* 26.487; *Cecil Collins: The Quest for the Great Happiness* 24.316–17; composers 20.70; *The Shadow of Dante* 24.546; Davies, *Autobiography of a Super-Tramp* 24.389; Abdullah Dougan, *40 Days* 24.576–7; Diderot's *Memoirs of a Nun* 20.51; El Greco 24.570–1; Elizabeth I 13.550, 24.xxii; St Francis 13.624–5; Mme Guyon 13.626; *Mahatma* (on Gandhi) 22.276; Gide, Andre, *If It Die* 22.166; *Conversations with Goethe* 22.464; Graves, Robert 25.433; *Life of Johnson* 20.51, 23.137, 26.483; Johnson's *Lives of the Poets* 26.483; Elias Kazan 24.389; Father Ronald Knox 24.374; Philip Larkin 26.440; *Son of Woman* (D. H. Lawrence) 23.472–3; *Lorenzo in Taos* (D. H. Lawrence) 24.525, 26.489; Charles Webster Leadbeater 24.213; Franz Liszt 24.537; Carson McCullers 24.374; *Michelangelo: Life, Letters, and Poetry* 24.316; *Miro* 24.372; Moore, George, *Confessions of a Young Man* 24.541; Münthe, *The Story of San Michele* 22.276, 23.304; Nightingale, Florence 26.490; Santayana, *Persons and Places* 24.518; Savonarola 13.550, 13.626–7; Sri Chaitanya 7.563 (n99); Sri Ramakrishna and Swami Vivekananda 20.117; 'Thoreau' (Emerson) 24.52–3; Thoreau, *Walden* 24.519; Lionel Trilling 24.374; *The Prophet Armed: Trotsky 1879–1921* 24.157; Simone Weil 24.374; Wells, H. G., *Experiment in Autobiography* 23.473; Oscar Wilde 13.617; Wilde, *De Profundis* 26.489; Tennessee Williams 24.374; *Yeats: The Man and the Masks* 24.404

Buddhism
Aris, Michael, *Hidden Treasures and Secret Lives* 24.388; Arnold, *Light of Asia* 20.107; Aśvaghoṣa, *Awakening of Faith in the Mahāyāna* 20.332, 26.576; *Avataṃsaka Sutra* ('The Vows of Samantabhadra') 2.454, 22.541; *Buddhism in Australia* 24.373–4; *A Buddhist Bible* 20.151; Carrithers, *Forest Monks of Sri Lanka* 2.589; Carus, *Gospel of Buddha* 7.548 (n23); Caxton's *The Golden Legend* 13.653–62; *Dhammapada* 20.115; *Diamond Sūtra* 2.407, 7.548 (n23), 12.59, 12.493, 20.85, 23.10; Evans-Wentz's *Tibetan Yoga and Secret Doctrine* 20.340; Fields, Rick, *How the Swans Came to the Lake* 24.374; Friedman, Lenore, *Meetings with Remarkable Women* 24.373; Gampopa, *The Jewel Ornament of Liberation* 2.425, 2.440–2; Hari Singh Gour's *Spirit of Buddhism* 22.163; Hearn, *Gleanings from Buddhafields* 7.549 (n29), 13.495; *Laṅkāvatāra Sūtra* 7.548 (n23), 20.74, 22.241; Ling, Trevor, *The Buddha* 15.381; Lopez, *Buddhism in Practice* 24.515–16; *Majjhima Nikāya* 20.302, 23.14, 24.515; Müller, *Chips from a German Workshop* 8.536; Mullin, *Death and Dying* 24.310; Pallis, *Peaks and Lamas* 20.150–1; Ramanan, *Nāgārjuna's Philosophy* 23.319–20; Ray, Reginald, *Buddhist Saints in India* 24.573; Mrs Rhys Davids 4.397–8, 20.302, 23.14; *Saṃdhinirmocana Sūtra* 24.573, 26.545; Śāntarakṣita, *Tattvasaṅgraha* 20.260, 23.14; Śāntideva, *Bodhicaryāvatāra* 24.516–17; Śāntideva, *Śikṣāsamuccaya* 2.454, 22.541; *Shinran: An Introduction to His Thought* 24.529; Simpson, *The Meaning of Evolution* 23.399; Sinnett, *Esoteric Buddhism* 20.63; Snellgrove, *Indo-Tibetan Buddhism* 24.311; Sogyal, *The Tibetan Book of Living and Dying* 26.460; *Śūraṅgama-samādhi Sūtra* 26.545–6; *Sūtra of Wei Lang* 2.408, 7.548 (n23), 12.493, 20.85, 23.40, 24.321; Suzuki, D. T. 13.324, 20.302, 22.141, 22.247–8, 23.206; Thomas, E. J. 22.141; *Tibet's Great Yogi Milarepa* 20.151; Vasubandhu, *Thirty Stanzas on Representation Only* 20.101; Geshe Wangyal, *Door of Liberation* 4.264–5; Watanabe and Iwata, *The Love of the Samurai* 24.388–9; *White Lotus Sūtra* 7.548 (n23); Willis, Janice Dean (ed.), *Feminine Ground* 24.389; Woodward, *Some Sayings of the Buddha* 15.xi–xii, 20.434; Yamamaki, *Systems of Buddhistic Thought* 7.548 (n23), 20.101; Yinkuang's letters, *Pure-Land Zen and Zen Pure-Land* 24.533–4

Christianity
Aelred of Reivaulx, *Spiritual Friendship* 13.618–19, 24.387; Arseniev, Nicholas 23.209; Asch, *The Nazarene* 13.650; St Augustine, *Confessions* 23.207; the Bible, *see under* Bible; books on the Second Vatican Council 2.457–8, 23.209–10; Butler, Samuel, *The Fair Haven* 13.533; *The Cloud of Unknowing* 23.332; Creighton, Mandell, *History of the Papacy* 13.550, 20.32; Dionysius the Areopagite 13.585–6, 23.207; Faber, Geoffrey, *The Oxford Apostles* 23.208; Geering, Lloyd, *Tomorrow's God* 24.499–501, 24.563; Gibbon, Edward, on Christianity 13.533; Griffiths, Bede, *The Golden String* 13.557; Julian of Norwich, *Revelations of Divine Love* 26.587; Merton, Thomas 20.462–3; Newman, John Henry 13.534, 23.208; Nigg, *Warriors of God* 13.628–9; *Philokalia* (Orthodox) 23.209; Robinson, *Honest to God*, *see* Robinson; Schweitzer, *The Quest of the Historical Jesus* 13.643; *The Secret Instructions of the Jesuits* 20.52; Solovyov, Vladimir, *Lectures in Godmanhood* 13.603, 23.209; Stanley, *Lectures on the History of the Eastern Church* 23.208; Voltaire, *Selected Works* 13.533; Ware, Timothy, *The Orthodox Church* 23.209; *The Way of the Pilgrim* and *The Pilgrim Continues His Way* 23.332; Whichcote, Benjamin, *Aphorisms* 24.389

Hinduism
Bhagavad Gītā (Edwin Arnold's translation) 7.559 (n81), 20.62; Devaraja, N. K., *An Introduction to Śaṅkara's Theory of Knowledge* 24.546; Gandhi, *Hind Swaraj* 22.159; *Hindu Scriptures* 7.559 (n81), 20.62; *Katha Upanishad* 7.41, 24.546; Prem, *The Yoga of the Bhagavat Gītā* 20.61; Ramakrishna Mission publications 20.123–4; Shankara, *Aparokṣānubhūti* 20.113; *Song of Dattatreya* 20.340; Swami Ramdas, *Mother Krishnabai* and *In Quest of God* 20.319–21; Upanishads 20.62, 23.311; Vedic hymns 20.62; Yogananda, *Autobiography of a Yogi* 21.582; *Yoga-Vāsiṣṭha* 20.260

other spiritual traditions
Collins, Rodney 23.135; Corbin, Henri 26.688; *Dao De Jing* 20.87; Huainanzi, *Tao, the Great Luminant* 23.40; Iamblichus, *The Egyptian Mysteries* 23.136, 23.494 (n162); Jain *Dhammapada* 20.449; Kabir, *Dijak* 20.449; Kazemi, *Common Ground Between Islam and Buddhism* 26.688–92; King, *The Gnostics and Their Remains* 24.248; the Koran

26.687; *Liezi* (Daoism) 20.332; Schimmel, Annemarie, *Mystical Dimensions of Islam* 24.311; Spiegelberg, *The Religion of No-Religion* 20.332; Swedenborg, *Heaven and Hell* 20.60; Blavatsky's *Isis Unveiled* 13.533–4, 14.xi, 14.298, 20.63–4, 23.10; Annie Besant and C. W. Leadbeater, Theosophist writings 20.148; Walker, Kenneth, *Venture with Ideas* 22.276; *Zhuangzi* (Daoism) 20.332

classics
Aeschylus 20.51, 23.287, 23.292–3, 24.396; Aristophanes 23.288, 23.298; Aristotle, *Ethics* 23.301; A. H. Armstrong, *An Introduction to Ancient Philosophy* 23.311; Bulwer-Lytton, *The Last Days of Pompeii* 20.19–20, 23.8, 23.304; Chapman's *Homer* 20.49, 23.xviii; Cicero 24.294; *The Essential Works of Stoicism* 23.288; Euripides 23.243–4, 23.269–70, 23.279–81, 23.286, 23.297, 26.238; Homer, *Iliad* 20.49, 23.266–7, 26.482; *Homeric Hymns* 24.396; the *Life of Aristides* 23.245; Melling, *Understanding Plato* 24.311; Newsome, David, *The Two Classes of Men* 24.389; Pindar, *Odes* 23.288, 23.298; Plato 23.286, 23.311, 24.300, 24.362, 24.389, 24.537; Plutarch 23.245, 23.260, 23.287, 23.427; Seneca, *De Beneficia* and *De Consolatione* 13.611, 20.61; Sophocles 23.300; Virgil, *Aeneid* 24.396

early Western literature
Beowulf 12.641–3; Dante 20.84, 23.314, 24.546–8; Langland, *Piers Plowman* 24.538–40

fiction
Ackerley, A. J., *We Think the World of You* 24.389; American fiction 24.374, 24.389; Austen, Jane 11.634; Balzac, *Séraphita* 24.96–7; Bowles, Paul, *Let It Come Down* 24.362; Brontë, Charlotte, *Jane Eyre* 20.19–20, 23.8; Capote, Truman 26.380; Cather, Willa, *Death Comes for the Archbishop* 24.389; Cervantes, *Don Quixote* 22.464; Dickens, Charles 22.464, 23.8, 24.555–7; Dostoevsky, *The Brothers Karamazov* 22.120; Eliot, George 11.634; Faulkner, William 22.276, 24.389; Forster, E. M. 26.380; Gide, Andre 22.135–6; Gissing, George, *Born in Exile* 24.374; Goldsmith, Oliver 24.582; Hamsun, Knut, *Mysteries* 24.397; Hemingway, *The Old Man and the Sea* 22.276; Hesse, Hermann 24.575–6, 26.380; Holtby, Winifred 26.637; Ihimaera, Witi 24.563, 24.565–6; Johnson, Mike, *Dumb Show* 24.548–9; James, Henry 23.260, 24.374; King, Francis, *A Domestic Animal* 24.389; Kingsley, *Hypatia* 20.20, 23.8; Klíma, Ivan 26.380; Lawrence, D. H. 24.373, 24.525, 26.380, 26.489–90; Lowry, Malcolm, *Under the Volcano* 24.323, 24.374, 26.380; Macaulay, Rose 11.634; Mann, Thomas 26.380; McCullers, Carson 26.380; Moore, George, *Esther Waters* 24.540–1; Myers, *The Near and the Far* 20.111; Nin, Anäis 11.634, 23.472; Niwa, Fumio, *The Buddha Tree* 24.532; Novalis, *Henry von Ofterdingen* 24.568; Rossetti, 'Hand and Soul' 26.253; Shikibu, Murasaki, *The Tale of Genji* 11.634, 23.472; Stapledon, *Star Maker* 3.381, 22.463; Thackeray, *The History of Henry Esmond* 22.464; Tolkien, *The Lord of the Rings* 25.100, 26.625; Tolstoy, *Anna Karenina* 22.464; Trelawny, Edward John, *Adventures of a Younger Son* 24.571–2; Trollope, *The Prime Minister* and *Dr Thorne* 26.581; Vonnegut, Kurt, *Slaughterhouse Five* 24.526; West, Nathanael 26.380

drama
Calderón, Pedro, *La Vida es Sueño* 24.410; Goethe, *Faust* 20.49; Goldsmith, *She Stoops to Conquer* 24.582; Dr Johnson, *Irene* 20.51; Jonson, Ben 20.62; Maeterlinck, Maurice 7.557 (n73); Marlowe, Christopher 20.62; Noh Plays of Japan 20.61; Shakespeare 24.313, 24.374, 24.574–5; Wilde, Oscar 22.141, 26.488

poetry
Ariosto, *Orlando Furioso* (trans. Hoole) 20.51; Arnold, Matthew 20.452; Attar 26.687; Baudelaire, Charles 20.113, 25.73; Baxter, James K., *Collected Poems* 24.549–54; Betjeman, John 26.379; Bridges, Robert 20.124, 26.379; Burns, Robert 22.464; Campbell, Alistair Te Ariki 24.563–5; Cavafy, C. P. 23.472; Davies, W. H., *Collected Poems* 24.389; de la Mare, Walter 26.379; Donne, John 20.100; Ernest Dowson, 'Cynara' 20.108; Drayton, Michael, *The Baron's Wars* 24.558–61; Dryden's *Alexander's Feast* 26.373; Freeman, John, *Last Poems* 24.577–8; George, Stefan 25.279; Ginsberg, Allen 22.567–8; Graves, Robert 26.379; Gunn, Thom 25.xl; Hafez 25.26, 26.687; Heine, Heinrich, 'The North Sea' 26.508; Herrick, Robert 20.100; Johnson, Samuel, 26.483; Kalidasa, *Śakuntala* and *Meghadūta* 20.62; Keats, John 20.36; Larkin, Philip 26.379, 26.439–40; Lawrence, D. H. 23.257; Li Bai 25.26; Manley Hopkins, Gerard, 20.108, 26.379; Milton, John 13.529, 13.582–4, 20.36, 24.515, 24.572–3; Mitchell, Adrian, *For Beauty Douglas* 24.374; Morris, William, 'The Haystack in the Floods'

20.108; Naidu, Sarojini, *The Sceptred Flute* 7.13, 7.55–63; Rimbaud, Arthur 20.113, 26.373; Rossetti, Christina 11.635; Rumi 7.583 (n211), 26.687; Russell, George William ('Æ') 22.141; Shakespeare, 'Venus and Adonis' 25.25; Shelley 21.78, 21.434, 22.54–5, 22.112, 25.xlvii, 25.25, 26.373; Solovyov, Vladimir 13.603; Spenser, *The Faerie Queene* 22.464; Tagore 7.562 (n98); Tennyson, Alfred Lord 20.29–30, 20.56; Thayumanavar (Tamil poet and mystic) 7.572 (n143); Urdu love poems 22.41; Whitman's 'Passage to India' 23.300; Wilde, Oscar, poems 26.488; Yeats, W. B. 22.141, 26.379

essays
Beerbohm, Max, *Works and More* 24.557; Browne, *Hydriotaphia* 20.52; Carlyle, *On Heroes and Hero-Worship* 26.482; Dr Johnson, essays in *The Rambler* and *The Adventurer* 20.51, 26.483; *Spectator* essays 22.101

literary criticism
Eliot, *The Use of Poetry and the Use of Criticism* 22.30; Moore, George, *Conversations in Ebury Street* 24.541; du Pin, Patrice de la Tour, *The Dedicated Life in Poetry* 24.389; Priestley, J. B., *Literature and Western Man* 24.574; Raine, Kathleen, *Defending Ancient Springs* 24.404; Saurat, Denis, *Literature and Occult Tradition* 22.141; Swinburne, *William Blake* 20.332, 26.484–5; Swinnerton, Frank, *The Georgian Literary Scene* 24.557

art and cinema
My Pilgrimages to Ajanta and Bagh (Dey) 21.402; Fuller, Peter, *Theoria: Art and the Absence of Grace* 24.313, 24.374; Tarkovsky, Andrei, *Sculpting in Time: Reflections on the Cinema* 24.389

Neoplatonism
Ficino, Marsilio, *Commentary on Plato's Symposium on Love* 24.389; Inge, Dean, *The Philosophy of Plotinus* 23.328, 24.248, 24.361, 26.590; Plotinus, *Enneads* 23.316, 24.396, 26.590; Porphyry 23.427, 24.361–2, 24.389, 24.522; Proclus, *Elements of Theology* 24.389; 'Studies in Neoplatonism' 24.311

philosophy
Bergson, *Creative Evolution* 7.599 (n321); Bradley, F. H. 20.446; Guest, *Dialectical Materialism* 22.210; Hegel 20.70, 20.107, 23.40; Jaspers, Karl, *Way to Wisdom* 23.311; Kant, *Critique of Pure Reason* 7.551 (n39), 20.70, 24.248; Kierkegaard, *Fear and Trembling* 20.124; Mill, John Stuart 20.446; Nietzsche, *Thus Spoke Zarathustra* 3.493, 20.100; Read, Carveth 20.446; Reijn, Eric van, *The Epistles of the Sincere Brethren* 24.568–70; Schiller, *Formal Logic* 20.446; Schopenhauer 20.61; Weil, Simone, *The Need for Roots* 24.374; Wilson, Colin 23.111, 23.332, 26.572

psychology
Bly, *A Little Book on the Shadow* 24.362; Carpenter, Edward, *The Intermediate Sex* 13.610; Ellis, Havelock, *The Psychology of Sex* 13.610–11; Goldberg, Herb, *The Hazard of Being Male* 24.541–4; Hillman, James 24.389, 24.397; Hodgkinson, Liz, *Sex is Not Compulsory* 24.313; Hopcke, Robert H., *Jung, Jungians, and Homosexuality* 24.389; Kennedy, Pagan, *The First Man-Made Man* 11.710; Kübler-Ross, Elisabeth, *On Death and Dying* 24.310; Neumann, *The Origins and History of Consciousness* 23.419; Watts, Alan, *Psychotherapy East and West* 23.332

history
Barzini, *The Italians* 23.312; Burckhardt, *Civilization of the Renaissance in Italy* 23.312; Chinese history and culture 20.70; Donnelly, *Atlantis* 20.32; Hill, Christopher, *Milton and the English Revolution* 24.193; *The Pelican History of Greece* 23.287; Segal, *The Crisis in India* 23.316; Symonds, *The Renaissance in Italy* 20.32, 23.249–50; Wells, H. G., *A Short History of the World* 2.408

politics
Dobbs-Higginson, *Asia Pacific* 24.509, 24.563; Engels, *The Conditions of the Working Class in England* 25.121; Lenin, *The State and Revolution* 22.210; Marx, *Das Kapital* 22.209; Milosz, Czeslaw, *The Captive Mind* 24.577; Powell, Enoch, *No Easy Answers* 4.440

science
Hawking, *A Brief History of Time* 26.xvi, 26.686; Jeans, *The Mysterious Universe* 26.685; reading in connection with the Higher Evolution 23.472–3; Rovelli, *Reality Is Not What It Seems* 26.xvi, 26.686–7

travel
Dickens, Charles, *American Notes* 24.78; Michener, James A., *Iberia* 26.308–9; Miller, Henry, *The Colossus of Maroussi* 23.234–5, 26.238; Shukman, Henry, *Savage Pilgrims: on the Road to Santa Fe* 24.518–19

see also
films

(XIII) Writings, translations, and editing

This section covers references to writings rather than the writings themselves (otherwise the whole of the Complete Works would need to be included). For a chart locating writings within the Complete Works, see Bibliography pages 1060–3

THE WRITING EXPERIENCE

introduction
authorial names 7.5–6, 22.69–70; only one of his books conceived as a book (1990) 2.533–5; giving priority to writing in later years 11.526–7, 11.558, 11.563, 11.603, 11.617; hard to say whether he was a Buddhist who wrote or a writer who was a Buddhist 26.639; he continued to write through his life 8.xxxvii; he said his writings wouldn't be taken seriously until 200 years after his death 24.xxiii; the influence of his early reading on his writing style 7.xix; in later life 7.xxi; literary legacy 6.xxiii; 'I never show what I am writing to anybody, and never discuss it' 26.69; keeping up a personal life through reading, writing, and friendship 25.92; 'my writings are like my children' 25.23; 'reading my books, you are very much in contact with me' 2.534; why early writings stressed the Mahāyāna, later the Pāli scriptures 6.xxv; some facility with writing, but not a 'popular' writer 11.663; writings on ethics 13.443–4; writing to participate in public debate 26.640–1

style
literary style 7.xix, 26.587; changing prose style 25.li; his writing style considered 'flowery' 26.300; learning (at school) not to use long words for their own sake 20.56, 20.261; the only writer he ever wanted to imitate was Sir Thomas Browne 26.587

writing process
devoting mornings to literary work 22.191, 22.224, 23.51, 23.223, 24.157; doing justice to the many-layered, many-faceted nature of experience 24.xxvi; enjoyment of writing 9.174, 26.639; entering a spiritual dimension through writing 11.673–7; it requires concentration, in the same way as meditation 11.675–6; 'I have always sought to give expression to what I genuinely thought and felt' 26.639–70; 'I have never found it difficult to write, only to begin writing' 23.469; taking care to understand the words used 25.7; meditating on Mañjuśrī for clarity 26.250–1; the rainy season a favourite time for writing 11.171; reflecting on things for many years before writing them down 26.250; the significance of mistakes in writing 26.282; walking up and down until a difficulty had been resolved 26.585; the wish that he had written down more about his spiritual experiences 17.262

unwritten books
autobiography 26.587; a biography of the Buddha 26.590–1; a book that would clarify his terminology 11.619; a commentary on the bodhisattva precepts 2.537; a commentary on 'The Veil of Stars' 2.537; comparative study of Buddhism and Christianity 13.521; *Five Norfolk Worthies* 26.586–90; 'Reason and Emotion in English Literature' 26.537; the relationship between Buddhism and Neoplatonism 2.537, 26.590; a supplement to the *Survey* 2.537; writing plans (1977) 11.526

EARLY WRITINGS, APHORISMS, AND OTHER GENRES

early writings
drama 20.36–7; loss of early manuscripts 23.31, 23.40; novel (unpublished) 20.88, 24.417, 24.525, 26.444, 26.489; publication 7.6–8; poetry 20.36, 20.89, 26.582–3, 26.661; short stories 20.37; short story set in ancient Egypt 26.467–8; a synopsis of *The Spanish Tragedy* 20.56; theses in the manner of Proclus' *On the One* 20.81; 'Of Tombs and Sepulchres' 20.52; while studying with Jagdish Kashyap 7.23–4

aphorisms
composition of a new aphorism 15.701; a guide to reading his aphorisms 26.xv, 26.3–5

devotional texts
dedication ceremony 3.521, 12.366, 23.429; Sevenfold Puja 11.218–19, 11.235; Threefold Puja 11.746 (n107)

memoirs
an autobiographical poem, 'Sri Pada' 25.25–34; Jivaka encourages him to write them 20.475–6, 22.459; mostly outer life, some inner life, almost no secret life 23.182; not autobiography but memoirs 20.477, 26.443, 26.591; the process of writing memoirs 11.676–7; their closeness in style to novels 26.443–4; wondering who the 'I' was who had all those experiences 8.613; intention to write 12.397–8

travel letters
a distinctive 'scrambled' literary form 24.4; literature was unable to keep up with life 24.7; a selection from the totality of experience 24.148

short stories
The Antique Dealer 25.554–68; *The Artist's Dream* 24.372, 25.xxx, 25.544–53, 26.252–3; *The Cave* 24.371–2, 25.569–86; *Four Visitors* 26.616–20, 26.662–3; *The Parable of the Talking Buddha* 25.540–3; *The Two Roses* 25.524–32; *The White Lotus* 25.533–9; 'Is Buddhism for Monks Only?' 7.177–89, 22.364, 22.608–9 (n294); an idea for a short story about a cathedral's images coming to life 26.273–6, 26.282; the Orthodoxy Police (parody) 8.133–5; publication history 25.523

other genres
diaries 5.357, 20.207, 23.71–2, 23.74, 23.110, 23.140, 23.182–3, 23.186–7; letters 21.472–3, 21.560; literary criticism 26.319–39; polemical writing 22.458; satire 22.10

ARTICLES

early articles
'The Disestablishment of the Church of England' 20.56; first ever article on Buddhism, 'The Unity of Buddhism' 7.xviii, 7.3–4, 12.494; second article, on *pratītya samutpāda* 12.494; 'A Note on *Anattā*' (1949 article) 7.207–14, 20.228; 'The Life of Siddhārtha Gautama the Buddha' 2.408, 7.xvii, 20.37; at 21, had been writing articles on Buddhism for several years 9.488; articles in full 7.1–248

The Middle Way
first submission 20.87; Middle Way articles 7.31–51, 7.64–76; 'Twenty Years After: Impressions of Buddhism in England' 23.33–4, 23.37

Oriya Encyclopaedia articles
commissioned 2.3, 20.476, 21.572, 21.575–6, 22.460–1; looking for a publisher in London 23.51; *The Three Jewels* 2.3, 2.450, 20.476, 22.461, 23.224; *The Eternal Legacy* 14.5, 20.476, 22.461, 23.224; *The Heritage of Buddhism* (incomplete) 26.585; there were to have been five books, but only two were written 26.585–6; unpublished articles 22.462

other articles
article on the *anātman* doctrine in the *Vedanta Kesari* 20.228; *Aryan Path* contributions 22.133; in *The Buddhist* (English Sangha Association) 11.475–99, 13.495–6; commissioned to write for the OUP's *The Legacy of India* 26.585; *Buddhism in England* 11.485–7, 12.60; *Maha Bodhi* journal articles, *see under Maha Bodhi* journal; 'The Bodhisattva Ideal' 22.627 (n401; 'Buddhism and Science' 7.161, 13.436–8; 'Philosophy and Religion in Original and Developed Buddhism' 1.120, 7.24, 7.206, 15.637; 'Where Buddhism begins – and Why It Begins There' 1.123

editor of magazine articles
Bhikkhu Kashyap's *Buddhism for Everybody* 20.452; *The Buddhist* (magazine) 11.473, 23.83, 23.118, 23.134–5, 23.144; Chetana's *The Buddhist Library* series 8.662, 24.101; *Living Silence* 21.499, 21.503, 21.531, 21.543, 21.550, 22.296; *Lumbini*, a magazine 22.214; *Maha Bodhi* journal, *see under Maha Bodhi* journal; *Stepping-Stones*, *see Stepping-Stones*

BOOK REVIEWS

introduction
summary 8.xxxii–vi; why does one write book reviews? 8.571, 8.599; *Aryan Path* 8.xxxv, 8.343–54, 22.107, 22.133; *Times Higher Education Supplement* reviews 8.xxxvi

Conze, Edward
Buddhism: its Essence and Development 8.343–4; *Buddhist Scriptures* (compiler and translator) 8.387–8; *A Buddhist Students' Manual* 8.390–1; *Buddhist Wisdom Books* 8.387; *Selected Sayings from the Perfection of Wisdom* 8.386–7; *Thirty Years of Buddhist Studies* 8.534–5; *Further Buddhist Studies* 8.536–40; *Vajracchedikā Prajñāpāramitā* 8.387

14th Dalai Lama
The Buddhism of Tibet and the Key to the Middle Way 8.504–5; *Transforming the Mind: Teachings on Generating Compassion* 8.611–12

Piyadassi
The Book of Protection 8.531–2; *The Seven Factors of Enlightenment* 8.383

Schloegl, Irmgard
and Ayya Khema 26.536; *The Wisdom of the Zen Masters* (trans.) 8.495–7; *The Zen Way* 8.489–90

Snellgrove, David
Asian Commitment 8.600–2; *Himalayan Pilgrimage* 8.353–4

Wickramasinghe, Martin
Oldest Short Stories of India 8.378–9; *The Jātaka Stories and the Russian Novel* 8.378–9

reviews of Buddhist books A – F
Allen, G. F. (ed.), *Buddhist Wisdom for the West* 8.361–3; Batchelor, Stephen, *Buddhism Without Beliefs* 8.xxxvi, 8.571–99; *Buddha Jayanti* special publications

8.367–8, 8.369–70, 8.373, 8.375–6; Buddharakkhita (trans.), *Dhammapada* 8.385–6; *Buddha's Life by Modern Indian Painters* 8.367; *Buddhist Sculptures and Monuments* 8.349, 8.366–7; *Burma* (a nation in the making) 8.382; Chou, *T'ai Hsu, His Life and Teachings* 8.374; Cleary (trans.), *The Blue Cliff Record*, volume 1 8.484–9; David-Néel, Alexandra, *The Secret Oral Teachings in Tibetan Buddhist Sects* 8.349; Dhammaratana, U, *Buddha and Caste System* 8.359–60; Tu Lun (trans.), *The Essentials of the Dharma Blossom Sūtra* (vol. 1) 8.477–83; Evans-Wentz, W. Y., *The Tibetan Book of the Great Liberation*, 8.344–8, 22.107–8, 22.471–2; Fa-hsien, *A Record of Buddhist Countries* 8.374–5

reviews of Buddhist books G – M
Gabb, W. J., *The Goose is Out* 8.370–1; Gallagher and Shear, *Models of the Self* 8.613–16, 12.584–5; Ganhar, J. N. and P. N., *Buddhism in Kashmir and Ladakh* 8.380–1; Gethin, Rupert, *The Foundations of Buddhism* 8.623–5; Glasenapp, Helmut von, *Vedānta and Buddhism* 8.383; Gombrich, Richard, *How Buddhism Began* 8.xxxvi, 8.617–22; Gyaltsen, Yeshe, *Mind in Buddhist Psychology* 8.508–11; Heissig, Walther, *The Religions of Mongolia* 8.517–19; Horner, I. B., *Ten Jātaka Stories* 8.392–3; Humphreys, Christmas, *The Wisdom of Buddhism* 8.394–5; Lama Govinda, *Foundations of Tibetan Mysticism* 8.391–2; Hoffman, Helmut, *The Religions of Tibet* 8.351–3; Hunt, Ernest Shinkaku, *An Outline of Buddhism* 8.372; Jayatilleka et al., *Buddhism and Science* 8.383–4; Jivaka, *An English Buddhist in a Tibetan Monastery* 8.398–9; Keown, Damien, *Contemporary Buddhist Ethics* 8.609–11; Lang, David Marshall, *The Wisdom of Balahvar – A Christian Legend of the Buddha* 8.397–8; Leggett, Trevor, *The Tiger's Cave* 8.494; Levy, Paul, *Buddhism: A Mystery Religion?* 8.350; Mahinda, Bhikkhu, *The Blue Print of Happiness* 8.360–1; Malalasekera, G. P., *Encyclopaedia of Buddhism* 8.400–2; Merton, *Thomas Merton on Zen* 8.490–2; Muses, Charles, *East-West Fire: Schopenhauer's Optimism and the Laṅkāvatāra Sūtra* 8.365–6

reviews of Buddhist books N – Y
Nāgārjuna and the 7th Dalai Lama, *The Precious Garland* 8.506–8; Nyanaponika, *The Four Sublime States: Brahma-Vihara* 8.384; Nyanatiloka, *The Buddha's Teaching of Egolessness* 8.379–80; *Places of Buddhist Interest* 8.349; Rabten, Geshe, *The Life and Teachings of Geshe Rabten* 8.515–17; Rahula, Walpola, *The Heritage of the Bhikkhu* 8.459–76, 15.727; Rajneesh, Bhagwan Shree, *No Water No Moon: Reflections on Zen* 8.492–4; Ray, Reginald, *Buddhist Saints in India* 2.553; *Rgyan-Drug Mchog-Gnyis* (on Tibetan thangkas) 8.402–3; Rieker, Hans-*Ulrich, Beggar Among the Dead* 8.395–6; Soni, Dr R. L., *Life's Highest Blessing* (on the *Maṅgala Sutta*) 8.384–5; Tagore, *Buddhadeva* 8.366; Tucci, Giuseppe, *The Religions of Tibet* 8.513–15; Trungpa, Chögyam, *Visual Dharma: The Buddhist Art of Tibet* 8.530–1; Vaswani, T. L., *In the Footsteps of the Buddha* 8.368–9; Wangyal, Geshe, *The Door of Liberation* 8.527–9; Watts, Alan W., *The Way of Zen* 8.388–90; Willson, Martin, *Rebirth and the Western Buddhist* 8.xxxvi, 8.565–7; Yamada, Koun (trans.), *The Gateless Gate* 8.498–501; Yeshe Tsogyal, *The Life and Liberation of Padmasambhava* 8.520–6; Yung Hsi, *The Commentary on the 'Formless Gatha'* 8.371–2

reviews of non-Buddhist books
Bharati, Agehananda, *The Light at the Center* 8.434–46; Brown, Mick, *The Spiritual Tourist* 8.607–8; Carr and Mahalingam, *Companion Encyclopedia of Asian Philosophy* 8.603–6; Chari, A. S. R., *Veganism and Why?* 8.370; Dunne, John S., *The Way of All the Earth: An Encounter With Eastern Religions* 8.431–3; *Gandhi Marg* 8.382–3; Guirdham, Arthur, *The Great Heresy* 8.420–5; Jenkins, Daniel, *The British: Their Identity and Their Religion* 8.429–31; Rawlinson, Andrew, *The Book of Enlightened Masters* 8.626–9; Rexroth, Kenneth, *Communalism* 8.415–20; Sagar, Keith, *Life of D. H. Lawrence*, 8.541–51, 24.174; Tähtinen, Unto, *Ahiṃsa: Non-violence in Indian Tradition* 8.447–53; Tulsidas, *Rāmacaritamānasa*, 8.xix, 8.357–8; Werner, Karel, *Yoga and Indian Philosophy* 8.454–8

WRITING POETRY

introduction
'the Cinderella of my writings' 2.534, 25.xxi; spiritual autobiography 2.423, 2.535, 25.xxii, 25.xliv, 25.49, 26.640; 'I've been creative in that way, whatever their objective value' 12.640; 'in it there is a great deal of me, perhaps more than in my prose' 2.535; gives expression to thoughts and feelings that could find no other outlet 2.423; 'I do not care at all/ About writing any more poems' 25.xxx, 25.336; 'I remember very few of my poems' 25.23;

'I write poetry' 25.329; 'it was the poet in Sangharakshita that led him to the religious life' 22.180; my poems are like my children 25.23–4; advised to stop writing 16.406, 20.436; poetry not incompatible with the spiritual life (Swami Ramdas) 20.451; reflecting on his poems 25.xxiii; guides to Sangharakshita's poetry 25.xxiv–lx

becoming a poet
becoming a poet 20.36; first attempt at writing poetry 20.35, 26.582; the first poem was about a lark 23.244, 25.xlv; inspired by *Paradise Lost* to write an epic 20.36; attempts to translate experience of music into poetry 20.72, 26.503–4; trying to write poetry (teenage) 20.100, 25.xlv

later writing
written en route to India 20.108; written at Muvattupuzha ashram 20.289; writing haiku in Kalimpong 21.23–4, 21.94; a poem traced on the ground in charcoal 21.437; 'Sangharakshita II' destroys poems written in India 20.452; poems written in retreat 25.310–11; only one poem written in first two years after return to England 23.226; a plan for a long poem about Orpheus 24.399; plan to write more poems in old age 12.398

the experience of writing poetry
all my poems come spontaneously 26.380–1; the arising of a 'poetic' mood 24.167–9; a balancing factor to mindfulness 5.39; 'my poems just emerge, and I don't always know where they've come from' 25.23; poetry 'strewn with rocks of prose' 25.284; some poems need work and others come more spontaneously 25.46; waiting for the Muse 2.538; 'Whatever I allowed my mind to rest upon became a poem' 24.168; writing poetry: 'out of the silence ... there arose a certain rhythm' 23.xxv–xxvi; 'I used to feel that a poem ought to have a message to it' 26.219; 'it's difficult to be a modern poet in English' 25.xlvi

genres, themes, influences
influence of Shelley 25.xlvii–l; influence of Tagore 21.94; influence of Yeats 22.181, 25.xlvii; poems about India 22.182; poems about poets 25.xlvi; six sonnets on the six realms of existence 24.169; 'Chinese' poems 2.404, 25.310; epigrams 25.423, 25.445; experimental poetry 26.640; what stars mean in the poems 25.78

responses
Clare Cameron's reading of the poetry 20.103, 22.183, 26.583; praise for the poems 22.179–82; reviewed by I. B. Horner 22.182; Ginsberg's surprise that a radical Buddhist should write traditional poetry 26.640; comparisons to Walter de la Mare 22.181–2; 'I'll write my poems for my friends, for those who love me' 25.243; no one to share poems with 25.380; poems read for five short TV programmes for Wesak 24.388; the poems and Triratna 25.49

publication
difficulty of getting them published 21.507; first poems published in India 21.89–90; published in the *Illustrated Weekly of India* 21.250, 22.103; *Messengers from Tibet and Other Poems* 8.650, 20.103, 22.181–3; translation into French 26.445; *The Call of the Forest* 26.380–1; *Conquering New Worlds* 24.388; *The Enchanted Heart* 15.xiii, 24.177–8, 24.653 (n224), 25.xxv

origins of and reflections on individual poems
'Advent' 25.xxvi, 25.39, 25.79–87; 'An Apology' 25.50–9, 25.447; 'Argosies' 25.xlviii, 25.249; Arthurian poems 25.97–110; 'The Awakening of the Heart' 22.186, 25.xliv–xlv, 25.li, 25.463–73, 26.392; 'Birds and Their Gods' 26.439; 'The Bodhisattva' 4.243, 21.89–90; 'The Bodhisattva's Reply' 22.42–3, 25.xxv–xxvi, 25.40, 25.111–29, 25.260–1; 'The Call of the Forest' 25.xlii–xliii, 25.137, 25.408–9; 'The Caves of Bhájá' 24.234–7, 25.505–11; 'The Family Reunion' 25.39, 25.60–70, 25.449; 'Four Gifts' 18.xviii, 25.138–48, 25.335; 'The Fragrance of Compassion' 25.xl; 'The Great Things of Guhyaloka' 25.lx, 25.391; 'The Guardian Wall' 13.587, 14.312–14; 'Hercules and the Birds' 25.4, 25.20, 25.512–20; 'Himalayan Sages' 8.646; 'I Want to Break Out' 25.xxxiii, 25.xxxv, 25.309; 'Immensities' 25.xlix, 25.262; 'In the Woods are Many More' 25.xxxviii, 25.130–7, 25.241; 'Invocation' 22.182; 'It is not love that seeks to bind ...' 26.666; 'Life is King' 26.445; literary influences on his poems 25.xliv–lx; 'Love and Duty' 25.97–10, 25.438–9, 26.439; 'The Mask' 25.88–96; 'Meditation' 6.xxvii–xxix, 25.3–4, 25.41–9; 'Messengers from Tibet' 21.52, 22.181; 'The Minor Poets' 25.lix; 'Mountain Mist' 22.182; 'New' 2.538–9, 13.427–8, 25.lii–liv; 'On Glastonbury Tor' 23.469, 26.612–13, 25.xxix, 25.xxxvi, 25.liii, 25.499–504, 26.640; 'The Only Way' 21.474; 'Padmasambhava' 25.xxix; Persian quatrains 20.96; 'The Pilgrim' 26.439; a poem about Dr Johnson 26.490; 'The Twin Towers', a poem about '9/11' 25.452, 26.480, 26.688; poem about the Taj Mahal 22.340–1; 'Revenge' 25.xxxvii,

25.23–4, 25.416, 26.381; 'The Root Speaks' 25.39, 25.71–8, 26.60; 'St Francis and the Birds' 24.242; 'St Jerome in the Desert' 13.633; 'Scapegoat' 26.465; 'The Scapegoat' 2.610–11, 24.169, 25.350–1, 26.465; 'The Scholars' 25.xxxiii–iv, 25.4–21, 25.286; 'Secret Worship' 8.161–2; 'Siddhārtha's Dream' 12.685; 'The Silver Spoon' 25.444, 26.455; 'The Six Elements Speak' 25.xxx–xxxi, 25.440–1; 'Song' 25.xlvii; 'Splendor Solis' 25.55–6, 25.418; 'Sri Pada' 25.24–34; 'The Time Has Come' 25.xxviii; poem to Sophia Wadia 21.479, 25.298–9; a sonnet on the Himalayas and Norfolk 24.169; 'Spring' 25.xli; three Polish poems 26.447; 'Taking Refuge in the Buddha' 2.423–6, 2.439, 8.xxvii, 21.429, 22.143, 25.xxxvii–viii, 25.250–1; 'Tobias and the Angel' 13.589–90; 'The Unseen Flower' 25.xxvii, 25.215; 'Village India' 21.89–90, 25.212–13; 'Waiting in the Car' 23.226; 'The White Calf' 25.xxxvi; 'The Wind' 25.xli, 25.450; 'Your sorrow is my sorrow, friend …' 22.454–5

The Veil of Stars
the argument that prefixes it 25.481–2; a critique of the poem 25.xlix–l; influenced by Tagore 25.xxviii, 25.l; Lama Govinda's introduction 22.180, 25.l, 25.477–80; Padmavajra on the experience of reading it 25.xxvii–viii; the poem itself 25.483–98; the torments of love 25.xxxv

A SURVEY OF BUDDHISM: PUBLICATION HISTORY

introduction
brief account 2.427–33, 21.544; aims 1.6–7, 22.142–3; ascertaining the keywords of Buddhism and their meanings 22.459; concerned to see Buddhism in its depth and breadth 2.428; the most comprehensive and systematic of my writings on Buddhism 2.427; opportunity to find out what Buddhism really meant to me 1.6, 2.427, 22.142; a tremendous intellectual and spiritual effort 22.143; 'I had not yet worked out the implications of Going for Refuge' 2.428–9; the section on the bodhisattva ideal 2.429–30, 22.144; later analysis 2.427–33; a retrospective 1.7–11; limitations 1.8–10, 2.428, 2.719 (n522); not originally conceived as a book 2.534

based on a lecture series
invitation to give the lectures 1.5–6, 8.650, 9.563n; preparation 22.142–3; preceded by the reading of 'Taking Refuge in the Buddha' 22.143; giving the lectures 22.143–6; as I spoke and they listened, time almost stood still 22.xx, 22.145; the book grew out of the lectures 23.78–9

writing the Survey
starting to write the book, accompanied by a rainbow 22.184–5; writing it while also learning about Tibetan Buddhism 2.434–5; getting absorbed 22.190–1; 'Why are you wasting your time on that old-fashioned stuff?' 22.214; making progress 22.265; a Presence (perhaps connected?) experienced while writing 22.278–9; typescripts for correction 22.276

publication and editions
original publication 1.5, 21.543; changes for later editions 1.xix; American edition 24.174; second edition 8.661; a new cover for the third edition (designed by Terry Delamare) 23.112; Dharmapriya's help with the fifth edition 24.174

translations
into French 23.451; into German and Spanish 26.446; into Polish 26.446–7

reception
admirers of the *Survey* 23.70; John Blofeld an admirer 21.589, 22.503; known in America 11.607; praised by Edward Conze 21.543; reviews 1.5, 1.10, 21.558, 22.380

PUBLICATION HISTORY OF OTHER TITLES

preparation for publication
having a book published is one of the most satisfying experiences 22.182; not recasting talks in more 'literary' form 13.321; transcription 24.188, 24.315, 24.658 (n244); *Mitrata* 24.27, 24.612 (n46), 24.658 (n244); appeal for editors 2.533, 2.737–8 (n653, 654); Spoken Word Project 11.729, 15.xvi, 24.658 (n244), 24.687 (n393); seminars, *see* Sangharakshita VIII/study seminars

Ambedkar and Buddhism
reasons for writing the book 10.89, 10.359–60; the only work (at that time) conceived and written as a book 2.534; summary of the book 10.360–3; Dr Ambedkar and Going for Refuge 2.494–7

Flame in Darkness (A Biographical Sketch)
censored by a Hindu at the Maha Bodhi Society 9.211, 19.464, 21.386–9; the commissioning of the work 8.xv, 21.367–8; criticized for inaccuracy 21.439–40; '*I had discovered Dharmapala*' 21.381, 22.61; previous biography rejected 21.371–2; the writing process 8.89–91, 21.370–81, 21.573; the successful conclusion of the work 9.14; prohibited in Vietnam 16.196; revisiting the book 24.401

The Eternal Legacy
answers the need for a guide to the *Buddhavacana* 14.5; began as a series of articles 14.xiii, 20.476; date of publication postponed 24.250; dedicated to translators of *Diamond* and *Platform Sūtras* 3.361, 14.320; the launch 14.xiii; no substitute for the study of canonical texts 14.270–1; not meant for scholars 14.xvi, 14.6; origin of the title 14.3; originally *The Heritage of Buddhism* 8.661; 'writing it, I felt myself transported to another world' 22.462–3

The Rainbow Road (The Thousand-Petalled Lotus)
various editions 2.740 (n665); original title *The Golden Pilgrimage* 8.661; first ten chapters cut, then reinstated 20.477–8; 'haunted by the ghost of my unfinished autobiography' 23.469; the process of writing 20.476, 22.459–60; title 20.477

The Three Jewels
accepted for publication 2.3–4, 21.592; first expression of the realization that Going for Refuge is central 2.450–2; origin in articles for the *Oriya Encyclopaedia* 2.3, 2.450, 20.476; preparing the book for publication 23.224; subtitle 2.4; Doubleday edition 23.469; a copy discovered in a bookshop in Australia 24.xxii; known in America 11.607; translated into Finnish 26.214; translated into German 24.531

other titles A – F
'Advice to a Young Poet' 2.424, 21.435–6, 26.xvi, 26.92, 26.133–47; *Alternative Traditions* 8.xxxv–vi, 8.407, 8.410–14; *Aspects of Buddhist Morality* 2.319, 11.305–25, 13.443; 'A Bird's-Eye View of Indian Buddhism' 2.452–3, 7.485–513, 22.461, 26.585; 'The Bodhisattva Principle' 24.203; *The Buddha's Noble Eightfold Path* (*Vision and Transformation*) 12.366–7, 13.443, 24.35–6; *Buddhism and Blasphemy* 11.326–47, 13.468, 24.619–20 (n77), 24.53, 24.142, 26.640; 'Buddhism and Art' 21.463, 21.497, 21.528, 21.531, 22.364; 'Is Buddhism for Monks Only?' 21.497, 21.528, 21.531; 'Buddhism in the Modern World' 7.453; 'Buddhism, World Peace, and Nuclear War' 10.87, 26.640; *Crossing the Stream* 8.662, 24.11–12, 24.101; 'Cultural and Political Implications of Buddhism for the Modern World' 22.249; *Dear Dinoo* 12.691–9; *The Drama of Cosmic Enlightenment* 12.492, 12.500; *The Endlessly Fascinating Cry* 4.228–31; *The Essence of Zen* 13.321, 21.596, 24.250; *The Essential Sangharakshita* 6.xxiii–xxvii, 11.722, 11.730; *Extending the Hand of Fellowship* 2.543, 24.533–4, 24.549; *Forty-Three Years Ago* 2.577, 2.619–50, 2.638, 2.752 (n752), 24.489; *From Genesis to the Diamond Sūtra* 11.691, 26.442; *The FWBO and 'Protestant Buddhism'* 13.xv–xvii, 26.252

other titles G – M
The Glory of the Literary World 12.363, 14.xii–xiv, 24.249–51; 'The Goal of Life's Endeavour' 20.302; 'Great Buddhists of the Twentieth Century' 6.600–21, 12.561–2, 24.549; 'Is Buddhism For Monks Only?' 8.660; 'Is a Guru Necessary?' 2.528–9; *The History of My Going for Refuge* 2.534, 12.396–7; *Human Enlightenment* 11.94–140, 24.174, 24.208, 24.371, 24.670 (n303); *Know Your Mind* 17.431–2; 'Krishna's Flute' 7.13, 21.436, 21.478; *Living Beautifully* (*Dhammapada* chapter 9) 15.xx, 15.347–77; *Living Ethically* 6.xxx, 11.722–3, 17.151–2, 26.405; *Living Wisely* 17.151, 26.405; *Living With Awareness* 11.685, 15.xvi–xviii, 26.458; *Living With Kindness* 11.685, 15.xviii–xix; 'The Meaning of Buddhism and the Value of Art' 8.660, 22.77, 22.465, 26.92–4; 'The Meaning of Orthodoxy in Buddhism' 2.556–7, 7.546, 8.661, 23.225, 23.434–5; *Mind Reactive – and Creative* 23.427–8; 'A Modern View of Buddhism' 7.19–20; *A Moseley Miscellany* 26.406–8, 26.549–50; *Moving Against the Stream* 12.634, 24.579, 26.441–2; *My Relation to the Order* 2.507, 24.380

other titles N – W
'The Nature of Buddhist Tolerance' 7.378–84, 22.529–30; *New Currents in Western Buddhism* 11.350–92, 24.91–2, 24.629 (n121), 24.160, 24.388; 'Ordination and Initiation in the Three Yanas' 2.447–8, 7.471–84, 8.661, 23.142; 'Paradox and Poetry in *The Voice of the Silence* 26.92; pamphlets 21.496–7; 'The Path of Regular Steps and the Path of Irregular Steps' 11.53–71, 24.225; *Peace is a Fire* 24.208, 26.9–53, 26.214; *Precious Teachers* 22.xxi, 22.383–4, 26.442–3; 'The Religion of Art' 22.180, 22.465, 26.92–5; *The Taste of Freedom* 24.360, 24.381, 24.665 (n279); *The Ten Pillars of Buddhism* 2.534, 11.560, 13.444; *The Threefold Refuge* 2.484–8, 2.566; *Travel Letters* 24.251; 'Wanted: A New Type of Bhikkhu' 2.448–9, 8.xxxii, 8.327–30, 8.661, 10.271; 'Wanted: A New Type of Upāsaka' 2.448–9, 8.xxxii, 8.331–5, 8.661, 10.271; *Was the Buddha a Bhikkhu?* 2.617, 24.489; *What is the Dharma?* 3.xii, 24.580; *Wisdom Beyond Words* 14.xiv–xvi, 14.320–1, 14.327–38

TRANSLATIONS

by Sangharakshita
the *Dhammapada* 23.469, 24.371; an esoteric sevenfold puja recited when offering the mandala 13.262–3; the 'Flower-Garland Hymn to the Goddess Tārā' 17.141–7; mandala offering verse 17.1; invocation to the wrathful deities 17.317–18; organization of Nepali translations 8.659–60, 21.348, 21.503, 21.531; revised version of the *Sūtra of Wei Lang* 24.321, 24.371; 'The Three Chief Paths', *see* Tsongkhapa/'Three Chief Paths'; verse translations of *paritrāṇa sūtras* 15.xii, 20.434

of Sangharakshita's work
need for translators 2.534; into Finnish 11.xvi–xvii; into French 23.451; into German and Spanish 26.446; into Marathi 8.660, 9.170, 10.181, 10.408, 10.704–5 (n345); into Polish 26.446–7; *Mensch? Gott? Buddha* 24.600; a translation refused for publication because its author was a Buddhist 8.539; works translated into many languages 3.xii, 26.446

(XIV) PHOTOGRAPHS AND PORTRAITS

family and army life
aged 3 20.6; aged 5 20.13; with mother, and sister Joan 20.55; in Torquay 20.66; army life 20.114; in Singapore, 1946 20.139; with army unit, Singapore 1946 20.156

in India
with Banerjee and Swami Bhaswarananda 20.148; Dharmapriya addressing the crowd, Indian Independence Day 1947 20.224; with Buddharakshita after ordination, 1949 20.412; with Buddharakshita and Shakyananda in Nepal, 1949 20.431; *bhikṣu* ordination ceremony 21.110–11; speaking to a crowd in Kausali on Indian Independence Day 20.224; speaking in Kalimpong 21.174; reception for the Sacred Relics 21.211; with Lama Govinda 21.257; speaking in Nepal 21.294; with Raj Kapoor and Arjun Dev Rashk 21.414; with Sachin's family 22.113; with friends and visitors in Kalimpong 22.229; with other Western Buddhists in Kalimpong 22.251–2; leading the Buddha Jayanti procession through Kalimpong 22.316; with Dhardo Rimpoche 22.343, 22.345; with Kachu Rimpoche 22.400; with Jivaka at the Triyana Vardhana Vihara 22.437; ordaining Prajnaloka in Kalimpong 22.449; with Khantipālo 22.527; with Dilgo Khyentse Rimpoche 22.556; at the Triyana Vardhana Vihara 22.561; with the Bhutanese royal family and Marco Pallis 23.120; with Dr Mehta 23.338; with the Dalai Lama 23.341; giving the Refuges and Precepts, Ahmedabad 23.344; with Li Gotami, Lama Govinda, and Terry 23.413; with Mrs Ambedkar, 1988 10.6; giving a talk in Ahmedabad, 1965 10.155; with the Poona Buddhist Women's Association 10.162; with Padmavajra, Yuvaraj, Lokamitra, and Virabhadra in India, 1979 10.194; after the ordination retreat at Sinhagad (1979) 24.22; with Bakula, Dharmarakshita, and Lokamitra after ordinations in India 10.xlv, 24.22

back in the West
at the Hampstead Buddhist Vihara 23.22, 23.50; Buddhist Society Summer School 11.474, 23.33; with Maurice and Ruth Walshe 23.64; in the Little Bus 23.113; at Stonehenge 23.115; with Christmas Humphreys 23.35; with the Three Musketeers 23.133; with Terry 23.230; in Athens (1966) 23.284; at Viriya's ordination 23.237; with Terry in Cairo 23.415; with Ben Guntersame at Yale 23.455; with Kevin Brooks 23.466; camping in Cornwall (1970) 23.471; Cambridge 1973: 'an unfathomable, fascinating, and somewhat scruffy friend' 10.xlv; on the *Udāna* seminar in Cornwall, 1974 10.420; at his desk at Padmaloka, 1970s 11.472; with Allen Ginsberg (1979) 24.177; Padmaloka, 1980s 11.2; with Croydon Order members (mid-1980s) 24.255; at the San Francisco Buddhist Center (1993) 24.483; at Tārāloka (2007) 11.694; with Tarahridaya, 2018 10.lxiv

portraits
by Alison Harper (Lilavati) 24.361, 24.391–2; by Paramabodhi 24.329

(XV) GIFTS AND POSSESSIONS

gifts
a brown woollen cloak is made for him 23.203; Christmas Humphreys gives him a watch 9.499, 11.542–3, 23.36; the Dalai Lama's gifts 22.371; Dhardo Rimpoche's parting gifts 23.398; the gift of a crystal lotus 24.250; a gift of the *Encyclopaedia Britannica* 24.400; a gift of gramophone records 22.148–9, 22.188; the gift of a piece of the Berlin Wall 24.361; the gift of a sandalwood Buddha 24.336; the gift of a silver spoon 25.444, 26.455; gifts from Chattrul Sangye Dorje 25.443; gifts from Paramartha 26.581; an illustrated history of London 24.238; 'Indian lotus tree' china 24.403; a *mere* of New Zealand jade 24.574; a mosaic picture of a female

head 24.249; a silver crystal ball 24.143, 24.146; a single *mālā* bead 18.116, 22.337; violets 25.336

possessions
his childhood wish to inherit his godfather's stuffed fox 20.482–3, 26.417; being cheated when buying minerals in Pompeii 24.296–7; books and other things brought back from Kalimpong 23.394; buying pottery in Pisa 24.223–4; cigarette cards 26.639; coin collection 26.639; collection of semi-precious stones and minerals 24.188, 24.456, 26.221; curios 20.1–2, 20.32, 20.38, 20.483–5, 21.232–3, 24.452–3, 26.553–4, 26.639; the difficulty of buying clothes 23.190–1; Dr Johnson's *Dictionary* 24.251; the experience of living without possessions 10.489; finds himself acquiring possessions despite having gone forth 22.188, 23.394; having to curb the tendency to acquire things 26.639; a meditation mat bought in Greece 23.297; money given by his godfather 26.417; postcard collection 26.425; stamp collection 26.418–19, 26.639; taken seriously by other monks once he owned a property 15.717–18

thangkas
eight thangkas of Padmasambhava 6.xxii–xxiii, 22.475–6; a gift of a thangka 21.230–1; giving away a thangka of the Refuge Tree 13.78; having to sell his thangkas 22.118–19; he orders a thangka of Green Tārā to aid his practice 22.375; a Mañjughoṣa thangka given by Jamyang Khyentse Rimpoche 22.406–7

Sangharatana Thera, Venerable M.
brief introduction 24.665–6 (n285); Sangharakshita first meets him 20.453; apologizes for the refusal to grant Sangharakshita ordination 23.359; attendant to Anagarika Dharmapala 8.69; construction of a vihara at Śrāvastī, *see under* Śrāvastī/Jeta Grove; dismay at Hindu takeover of Bodh Gaya 20.454–5; feels the need to flatter lay people 19.481; had a magnificent bass voice 23.361; his connection with Sangharakshita 8.672 (n47); invites Sangharakshita to Sarnath 21.97–8; at Sarnath when Sangharakshita and Terry visit in 1966 23.359; voluble and eccentric 22.130; welcomes the Eminent Buddhists to Sarnath 22.331–2; his death 24.237

Sanghasena, Dhammachari 10.liii, 12.573–4

Saṅghavarman 1.328

saṅghāvaśeṣa (suspension) *see under vinaya*/offences

Sanghavasi, Aiem v23

saṅgīti (chanting together) *see under* oral tradition

Saṅgīti Sutta *see under Dīgha Nikāya*

Saṅgīti-paryāya (Abhidharma)
introduction 14.81–2; attributions 14.82; resemblances to *Dīgha Nikāya suttas* 14.81–2; the text says it was written after the Second Council 14.82; translated by Xuanzang 14.82

Sangpo, Geshe 21.191

Sañjaya Belaṭṭhiputra 2.24

Śaṅkara (Śaṃkara, Shankara, Shankaracarya)

his life
introduction 7.568 (n124); birthplace at Kalady 20.253

and brahman
meditation on *brahman* 7.96; *Nirguṇa Brahman* 1.166, 1.269, 9.228–9; inquiry into *brahman* 7.95; the purport of the Vedānta is *brahman* 7.78; the universe only appears to emanate from *brahman* 14.592

and Buddhism
accused the Buddha of nihilism 1.74; borrowed method and conclusions from Madhyamaka school of Buddhism 1.323; did he have a role in the disappearance of Buddhism from India? 9.389; incorporated elements of Buddhist monasticism into Hinduism 20.235; was he a Buddhist in disguise? 7.72, 7.370

views and works
adhyāsavāda 7.131, 7.586–7 (n231); commentary on the *Brahma Sūtras* 14.109; commentary on *Kaṭha Upaniṣad* 7.578 (n179); the denial of the existence of the world of appearance 7.194; Devaraja, N. K., *An Introduction to Śaṅkara's Theory of Knowledge* 24.546; 'Few practise, while many understand' 7.97; the idea of Christianizing his philosophy 13.557; the meaning of *dharma* 13.569; 'If there is a God, it is the absolute seen through the veil of nescience' 12.7; on animal sacrifice 8.450; on the nature of reality 16.454; proposes supreme goal of human existence 1.166; quotes the *Manusmṛti*'s barbaric statements about Shudras approvingly 10.624; *satkāryavāda* view, incorporated into Vedānta 1.314; *Upedeśasāhasrī* 7.566 (n112); vindication of Advaita Vedānta 7.72

Sangharakshita
practises meditation method 20.113; studies 20.124

Śaṅkhacūḍa, King 14.159

saṅkhāra *see* composite or compounded

Sankrityayan, Rahul 7.448, 7.617–18 (n496), 21.75–6, 21.449

sannyasin **or** ***saṃnyāsin*** 7.95, 9.112–13

Sanlun Zong **or** ***Sanron-Shū*** 1.311

Sanskrit

introduction
Anglicized version of *saṃskṛta*: 'beautifully put together' 3.206; Bengali love of compound Sanskrit words 20.261; 'the language of the gods' (*devabhāṣa*) 9.36, 14.448; *saṃskṛti* ('the perfected'), contrasted with *prakṛti* 16.364–5; the Sanskrit equivalent of the Pāli canon 7.501; difference from Prakrit 3.206, 16.365–6; the Buddha didn't forbid the monks to teach the Dharma in Sanskrit 16.365; 'negative' words may have positive meanings 14.448; relationship to Hindi 9.480–4; spoken by educated, cultured people 16.365; 'Untouchables' not permitted to learn 9.36; a highly rational language, but the text may not have a rational meaning 14.349–40; however articulate it is, it cannot express the Unconditioned 14.448

works
Mahāvyutpatti (Sanskrit dictionary) 16.342; *Mṛcchakaṭikā* (Sanskrit drama) 9.85; only one historical work in classical Sanskrit literature, the *Rājataraṃgiṇī* 12.563, 13.30; Mahāyāna *sūtras* written down in Sanskrit 16.365–6; very early material is preserved in the original Sanskrit 1.612 (n200); whereas Pāli literature is a cosmos Sanskrit literature is a chaos 1.277; relationship of Sanskrit literature to that of other languages 14.289; translations of Sanskrit books reached the West 7.87; 'uncollected' Sanskrit texts 7.528–9

Buddhist Hybrid Sanskrit
a distinct and separate language 9.357; close to Prakrit, the vernacular language 14.349; comparison with pure Pāṇinian Sanskrit 14.107–8; disparaging it would be like Addison disparaging Shakespeare 14.349; *sūtras* written in it 14.107, 14.190, 14.349, 16.35, 16.239

Pure
comparison with Buddhist Hybrid Sanskrit 14.107–8; follows the rules laid down by Pāṇini 14.349, 16.35

Vedic
preserved in an archaic form due to the sacredness of the Vedas 16.365; the Buddha forbade the monks to teach the Dharma in *chandas*, Vedic Sanskrit 16.365; Sanskrit developed out of Vedic 3.161; Vedic and anti-Vedic 16.367

santa (peace) 15.261–2

Santacitta, Dharmacharini (Jane Evans) 24.316, 26.463

santāna (flux) 26.188

Śāntarakṣita

life story
introduction; founded the Yogācāra-Svātantrika Madhyamaka 1.323; accepted the Yogācāra as relative truth 1.371; at the University of Odantapuri 7.425; *Tattvasiddhi*: philosophical defence of Tantric practices 1.382

in Tibet
co-founder with Padmasambhava of Tantric Buddhism in Tibet 7.193, 12.290–5, 13.9–10; 'my doctrine is to follow whatever is proved correct …' 12.293; his presentation of the Dharma angered the gods of Tibet 12.291–3, 12.318, 13.9; he was a great man, but could not overcome unconscious resistance to Buddhism 13.10; instigated the coming of Padmasambhava 12.291, 12.318, 13.9; ordination lineage in Tibet 2.745 (n696), 7.473–4

Tattvasaṅgraha ('Compendium of Principles')
a masterpiece of Indian Buddhist dialectics 20.260; establishes the author's own tantra, known as the Tantra Yogācāra 12.291; exposes the inconsistency of doctrines and doctrinal categories 1.322–3, 12.291; a kind of encyclopedia of refutations 1.323; test the Buddha's words like gold in the fire, *see under* gold; makes *pratītya-samutpāda* the vehicle of his exposition 7.193

Santayana, George *Egotism in German Philosophy* (and a romantic episode) 20.78, 24.518; The Last Puritan 24.520; 'not one of my favourite philosophers' 24.518; *Persons and Places* 24.518; *Platonism and the Spiritual Life* 24.518; *Scepticism and Animal Faith* 24.518

Śāntendriya (bodhisattva) 16.546

santi (stillness) 1.69

Śāntideva

life
his intense confession of sin 1.411; *In the Footsteps of the Buddha* (résumé of life and teachings) 8.368–9; knows both the heights and depths of spiritual experience 1.322; from western India 4.629

BODHICARYĀVATĀRA

introduction
an example of devotion 8.146; it contains the essence of Buddhism 9.109; the Buddhist counterpart of St Augustine's *Confessions* 24.516; it looks directly at hard truths, (sin, hell), but they are transcended by spiritual optimism 4.321; one of the brightest gems of Mahāyāna literature 1.322, 22.129; one of the sublimest statements of the bodhisattva ideal 4.224; paradoxes and inconsistencies at every turn 4.426; possible link with the *Dhammapada* 4.378; read the text as a practical guide 17.465; Marion Matics' guide 4.436, 4.551; Śāntideva's way of putting things is not always appropriate for beginners 4.623; says little about *dāna* and *śīla*, perhaps because they were well covered elsewhere 4.339; the Sevenfold Puja derived from the text 1.406, 1.413, 2.429, 4.45, 11.216, 13.705 (n220); shows that the Mahāyāna never went to the extreme of anti-intellectualism 1.240; studied by the Kadam school 12.578; summary of worldly life 4.627–8; especially good for the strong craving type 4.623; 'There is nothing original here' 4.280; a union of the emotional and the intellectual 14.451; a valuable source of information on Madhyamaka metaphysics 1.322

Sangharakshita's and Triratna's teachings on the text
grew out of the *Survey* 1.9; seminar on the *Ratnaguna-saṃcayagāthā* an important supplement 4.226–7; study retreat at Abhirati, Tittleshall, Norfolk 4.225–7, 21.597; studied in Triratna 11.377; Nagabodhi's seminars 11.699

translations
available translations 4.230; *Entering the Path of Enlightenment* (Marion Matics) 4.226, 4.384, 11.219; *The Path of Light* (L. D. Barnett) 1.411, 1.620 (n323), 15.218, 22.129, 23.55; translation by Stephen Batchelor 11.219; translation by Adrienne Bennett 8.636, 11.218–19, 23.55; translation by Kate Crosby and Andrew Skilton 24.516–17

Chapter 1: Praising the Thought of Enlightenment
commentary 4.239–89; the arising of the *bodhicitta* 4.239–79; like finding a jewel on a dungheap 1.420, 2.126, 4.42, 4.44, 10.145; 'Like lightning in a dark sky, the thought of the world may be turned to good' 4.282; 'Sometimes an act of evil takes great strength, but goodness is without effort' 4.289

Chapter 2: Confession of Evil
commentary 4.290–332; based on Nāgārjuna's *Precious Garland* 17.417; confession of faults 1.411, 4.47, 4.310–12, 4.324–32; 'In order to grasp this jewel of the mind, I offer …' 4.217; many kinds of offerings 11.235; places associated with bodhisattvas 4.324; resemblance to the confession verses of the *Sūtra of Golden Light* 16.268; Śāntideva calls himself an 'animal', but this may be unfair to animals 4.325–6; 'What essence has remained mine from things I once enjoyed?' 18.131; the would-be bodhisattva 'becomes without fear of being or becoming' 4.48, 4.293–4

Chapter 3: Grasping the Thought of Enlightenment
commentary 4.357–62; 'The abandonment of all is Nirvāṇa' 4.358, 7.150; 'the caravan of humanity moving along the road of being …' 4.361; *dāna* 4.357–62; the devotee implores the Enlightened Ones not to disappear 1.413; 'I would be a protector for those without protection …' 4.360–1; 'I would be … a magic jewel, an inexhaustible jar, a powerful spell …' 4.361; 'May I be a guide to the helpless' 7.150; 'May I be an inexhaustible treasure …' – a passage of matchless beauty 1.415–16; 'May I be for all beings the healer of pain!' 8.368–9; offerings 4.290

Chapter 4: Vigilance in the Thought of Enlightenment
commentary 4.363–77; 'the Dharma should not be spoken to a woman without a man present' 4.347–8; making use of good conditions 4.365–7; not teaching the Dharma to someone who is not behaving respectfully 4.342; the passions as illusion 4.373–7; related to the *chöd* practice 4.362

Chapter 5: Guarding of Total Awareness
commentary 4.378–87; all terror and frustrations come from the mind 17.476; 'being like a piece of wood' 4.340, 4.382–3; instead of covering the earth with leather, wear shoes 4.379, 18.80; resolving the conflict between *dāna* and *śīla* 4.116, 4.385–7

Chapter 6: The Perfection of Patience
commentary 4.388–437; on anger 4.405–8, 4.424–7, 15.316; as a child cries at a broken sandcastle, the mind reacts to losing praise and fame 4.431; enemies 4.407–17; if you don't want to practise patience, Śāntideva's arguments will irritate you 4.433; the irrationality of jealousy 17.280; 'One's enemies are to be prized and treasured' 4.410; one of the original and attractive parts of the whole work 4.418; people who give you a hard time are helping you practise *kṣānti* 17.566; Śāntideva's ingenious arguments can be curiously irritating 17.376; to understand all is to forgive all 4.425; your attacker brought the stick (or sword), but you brought the body 4.119–20, 4.409, 4.425, 10.600, 15.440, 17.172

Chapter 7: The Perfection of Strength
commentary 4.438–87; description of hell 4.476; the elephant the image of *vīrya* 4.468–9; the elephant plunging from one lotus pool to another 1.440, 3.287–8, 9.297, 23.223; energy in pursuit of the good 1.439, 3.287, 3.304, 3.372, 4.132, 9.213–14, 9.297, 10.369, 16.584 (n10); 'In vigour lies Enlightenment' 1.440; practising *dāna* step by step, from giving vegetables to self-sacrifice 4.457–60; Śāntideva tries to make a positive use of negativity 4.467

Chapter 8: The Perfection of Contemplation
commentary 4.488–634; 'All sorrows are ownerless' 4.571, 4.630; 'Attachment to the self … is the reason that sorrow has power over anyone' 4.570; breaking down the barrier between self and other 3.574, 11.698–9; Buddhahood takes a fraction of the effort of millions of years of rebirths 4.629; the Compassionate Ones plunge into hell like geese into a lotus pond 4.582–3, 4.631; contemplation of the ten stages of decomposition of a corpse 4.536; the essential advice: be more objective, imaginative, empathetic, and less selfish 4.624; a false calculation to think that there is an 'I' 4.629; 'Fortunate are those on delightful rock terraces …' 4.629; 'I've got to get the self before it gets me' 4.634; mutual transcendence of egotism 4.633–4, 12.638; no reason to be more concerned with our own than with others' suffering 4.569–70, 15.237; 'passing through the door of the mind' 4.488–9; relationships as a hindrance to meditation 4.522–4; Śāntideva is basically trying to talk us into being more unselfish 4.634; Śāntideva identifies himself with the other 4.633; Self-anti-self 4.614–16, 4.619–20; 'Since fear and sorrow are pleasing neither to me nor another …' 4.569–70; we shouldn't allow him to be too metaphysical 4.571, 4.578–9

Chapter 9: Perfection of Understanding
exchanging self and other (*parātma-parivartana*) 2.360–1, 3.574, 4.607, 4.613–17, 8.432; 'monkhood is imperfectly established' 24.516–17; 'sense organ and object separated by a space' 24.517

ŚIKṢĀSAMUCCAYA

introducing the text
compiled from Mahāyāna *sūtras* 9.137; *Gaganagañja Sūtra* quoted 7.41; it quotes the *Gaṇḍavyūha Sūtra* 14.217; quotation of passages from the *Vimalakīrti-nirdeśa* 4.552, 14.157, 16.445; quotes *sūtras* that don't now exist elsewhere 1.322, 14.100; Sangharakshita and the text 2.454, 21.23, 22.541, 22.627–8 (n402), 23.17; studied by the Kadam school 12.578

quotations
avoid anger at all costs 4.74; the *bodhicitta* arising even when the heresy of individuality as high as Mount Sumeru 4.272–3; the bodhisattva needs to master just one virtue: great compassion 1.504, 2.125–6, 5.199; the bodhisattva's resolve to rescue all beings 2.158–9; *bodhisattva-śīla* 2.208; description of giving 8.174, 14.657 (n502); five spiritual faculties as successive stages of the path 1.291–2, 7.491; the qualities of one possessing faith 1.292; 'What is the nature of name?' 4.578–9; 'Whatever is well said, that is the word of the Buddha' 3.168, 3.394, 7.434, 9.198

śāntināyaka (the one who leads to peace) 15.262, 15.267

santindriyo 15.286

Santiniketan *see under* Tagore

Śāntipāda 1.382

santuṭṭhi *see* contentment

Sanyal, Phani Bhusan 20.136, 20.160, v22

Sappho 25.285

Saptaśatikā-prajñāpāramitā (Perfection of Wisdom text) 'as taught by Mañjuśrī' 14.153, 14.181; beings taught as non-beings 26.202; Mañjuśrī's description of the qualities of the Perfection of Wisdom 1.70–1; translated by Edward Conze 8.534

sāra (the essence of the matter) 10.450

Sarada Devi (the 'Holy Mother') introduction 7.579 (n189); her picture on the shrine 20.121; a little girl went to visit her and was disappointed 12.525;

'The pure mind sees everything pure' 7.99; Sangharakshita visits her shrine: 'I steeped myself in its tranquillity' 20.136

Saradananda, Swami 20.124

Sarahapāda (Saraha) introduction 2.686 (n252); one of the eighty-four *siddhas* 7.507; *tulkus* 2.182; *Dohākośa* (*Treasury of Songs*) 1.27, 1.306, 1.382, 13.179

Sāramati (*ācārya*) (*Ratnagotravibhāga*) the bodhisattva: 'Like a fire his mind constantly blazes up' 1.396, 8.xvii, 8.95, 20.124; the Element of the Buddha in everyone 1.275, 1.283, 13.389; and Plotinus 13.374; Sāramati's best-known work 1.371; the stains of adventitious defilements 13.389

Saramati, Dharmachari (Alan Sponberg) chaired a talk given by Sangharakshita 12.492; ordination 12.492; studied with Professor A. K. Narain 12.430–1

śaraṇa 3.397, 15.646, 15.650, 18.563–4

śaraṇa-gamana *see* Going for Refuge

Saranankara, Venerable v22

Sarasvatī or Saraswati (goddess) appearance 16.361, 16.396; and Calcutta 22.59; description 16.372–3; etymology: the name of a river 16.362; goddess of learning 16.361–2, 20.296; hymn 16.372–3, 16.384; inspiration from Saraswati 21.403; Mañjughoṣa's consort 16.376; memory and the muses 16.363, 16.368; personifies the orally transmitted culture of ancient India 16.363; popularity in India 16.384; seated on a white *haṃsa* (goose) 16.361; in the *Sūtra of Golden Light* 16.360–77; and Vāc, goddess of speech 16.363; worship 16.361, 16.371, 16.411

Sarasvatī (river) 16.362–3

Saraswati (aspirant) v21.84–5

Sarichak *see under* Bihar

Śāriputra-abhidharma-śāstra 14.73–4

Sāriputta (Sanskrit Śāriputra)

introduction
birth 1.256; birthplace 7.429, 7.612 (n453), 20.461; a brahmin by birth 12.522; describes Nirvāṇa 1.69; difference between Pāli canon and Mahāyāna versions 1.271, 16.537; *Dharmasenāpati*, 'commander-in-chief' 3.49, 10.496, 12.522; Enlightened 1.271; foremost for wisdom 3.179; an example of a doctrine-follower 17.333; saw Nirvāṇa as the goal of the spiritual life 1.72–3; and real Going for Refuge 10.387; successful teacher 4.20, 10.535

his spiritual quest
initially a follower of Sañjaya Belaṭṭhiputra 2.24; he and Moggallāna set out together 3.93, 3.173, 4.698 (n260), 12.511; gains insight on hearing the truth of *pratītya-samutpāda* from Assaji (Aśvajit) 1.89, 2.24, 3.93, 3.174–5, 7.192–3, 7.493, 8.73, 8.119, 9.142, 11.163, 12.464, 12.542; his lifelong gratitude to Aśvajit as his first teacher 18.93; ordination at the Bamboo Grove 2.24, 2.687 (n258)

and Moggallāna (Maudgalyāyana)
'I couldn't even see a mudsprite!' 10.535; Moggallāna remarks how Sāriputta does not lay claim to spiritual attainment 3.409; their temperaments compared 10.535–6, 12.511; they rejoice in each other's merits 10.535–6

meditates
even after becoming an *arhant* 10.538–9; is hit on the head by a *yakkha*, but doesn't notice 1.639 (n469), 10.534–5, 18.25; reviews his own calm 10.542; without the thought 'I am meditating' 1.179, 3.409, 4.592, 7.154, 14.552; similar example from the Christian tradition 7.155; sitting like a mountain 10.511–12

in the Pāli canon
association with the Abhidharma 12.143, 14.73, 14.76, 14.82, 14.83; being reborn with the Buddha in the *Jātakas* 16.471–2; the Buddha has backache and asks Śāriputra to teach in his stead 3.184, 10.236; communicates Enlightenment to Bhaddiya the dwarf 10.613–16; consoles Anāthapiṇḍada on his deathbed 2.204; declares the Buddha the greatest of the Enlightened Ones 1.54, 1.293, 3.144; discusses the seven *visuddhis* with Puṇya 3.290–1; enters into conversation with a precocious child 10.496; explains what kind of conduct makes skilful states grow 2.328–9; has his limitations 10.614–6; says that certain teachings are not communicated to householders 2.204; Vaṅgīsa speaks verses in praise of him 26.125; and the wanderer who ate rose-apples 1.69, 1.72–3, 2.122

in the Mahāyāna sūtras
defeated in discussion by an eight-year-old girl 14.183; in the *Heart Sūtra* 1.70, 14.358–9; hymn to Prajñāpāramitā, *see* Prajñāpāramitā; in the Prajñāpāramitā 14.139; a princess refuses to show him any respect 14.184; in the *Vimalakīrti-*

nirdeśa 14.161, 16.457, 16.501–2, 16.535–9, 16.552–5; in the *White Lotus Sūtra, see under White Lotus Sūtra*; used to represent the *arhant* ideal as a kind of spiritual individualism 1.271

see also
relics, *see* Sacred Relics

Sariputta (Swiss novice) 23.367

śarīras *see under* relics

Sarkar, Benoy Kumar 20.135

Sarnath (Isipatana)

history
where the Buddha first taught 3.74–6, 9.141, 9.365, 10.263–4, 16.124, 20.388–9, 23.361–2; a place of refuge for wild creatures 22.331; Muslim invasion 20.390; excavated by British archaeologists 9.237; the site plundered for building materials 16.567

Mulagandhakuti ('Original Perfumed Chamber' Vihara)
Anagarika Dharmapala builds the vihara 8.66, 8.67, 8.194, 10.699 (n274), 20.390, 22.331; opening 8.69–70; nineteenth anniversary of its opening 21.97–8; pictures of the Buddha's life 10.260, 10.699 (n274), 23.360; relics of the Buddha presented to Sarnath 8.69–70, 21.191; Sangharakshita's *bhikṣu* ordination, *see under* Sangharakshita V/ordination; visited by the Eminent Buddhists 22.331–2

other buildings and features
Aśoka column 20.390, 23.360; beautiful images in the museum 26.384; Buddha image 23.361–2; Buddhist temple 9.419; Burmese temple 21.106–7, 22.332; Chaukambhi Stupa 20.389; Dhamekh Stupa 22.331; an Industrial School 8.58–9; Ladakhi rest house 23.363; Maha Bodhi High School 22.518; Tibetan gompa 23.363

visiting Sarnath
visiting Sarnath 21.511–12, 23.358–65; evening puja 23.361–2; a funeral at Sarnath 23.362–3; hippies begging at Sarnath 23.364; Jivaka in Sarnath 22.441–3; 'Memory of Sarnath' (Kathleen Raine) 26.391; pilgrimage to Sarnath 2.223, 22.331–4; Sangharakshita gives a talk there 23.362

see also
Maha Bodhi Society, *see under* Maha Bodhi Society/branches; Sangharakshita is refused ordination there, *see under* Sangharakshita V/ordination

Saroj 20.163–4

Sartre, Jean-Paul 2.100, 4.121, 8.616

Sarum House *see* Croydon Buddhist Centre/Aryatara

Sarvabuddhaḍākinī *see* Vajrayoginī

sarvadharma-nairātmya *see* egolessness

sarvadharma-samatā *see* sameness

sarvadharma-śūnyatā, 'emptiness of all *dharmas*' *see under śūnyatā/śūnyatā* as concept

Sarvagandhasugandhā Buddhaland ('Fragrant with all Fragrances') 16.457–8

sarvam asti 1.188

Sarvamitra, Dharmachari 11.xvi–xxiv

Sarvanivaraṇaviṣkambhin (bodhisattva) 2.172

Sarvasattvapriyadarśana (bodhisattva) *see under White Lotus Sūtra*/characters

Sarvāstivāda (school of early Buddhism)

introduction
brief introduction 2.675 (n120), 7.504–5; known as the Vaibhāṣikas 7.504; ordination 2.745 (n696), 7.472–3; coenobitical monasticism 2.192; most widespread and important of the early schools of Buddhism 1.188; emergence of Buddha image 2.222; the emergence of specifically Sarvāstivāda ideas 14.87; they produced one of four systematic transmissions of the doctrine 13.340; list of countries it's practised in 3.408, 7.473

relationship to the Buddhist tradition
split from the Sthaviravādins 7.497, 13.44; foundation laid in the *Vijñāna-kāya* (Abhidharma work) 14.87–8; and Asaṅga 1.364; not a rival to other thought systems but an expression of advanced insight 7.509; analysis incorporated into Yogācāra 1.370; influence on Mahāyāna 1.188; how it relates to Tibetan Buddhism 2.745 (n696), 8.503, 13.12, 13.44

views and teachings
cause and effect (*asatkāryavāda*) 1.314–15; conception of Nirvāṇa refuted 1.319–20; doctrine of *sarvam asti* ('everything exists'), after which it is named 1.188; equal validity of *śrāvakayāna, pratyekabuddhayāna, bodhisattvayāna* 1.214; introduction of *prāpti* and *aprāpti* as a category of the *saṃskāras* 14.362; karmic concatenations 17.479; pluralistic realism 1.103, 2.88; starting to treat *dharmas* as ultimately real 1.221, 7.539–40, 12.143; and *rūpakāya*

1.253; *samayavimukti* 2.145; saw *vyākaraṇa* as prediction to Enlightenment 14.24; identification of thousands of kinds of faith- and doctrine-followers 2.152; the theory of the four conditions (*pratyāya*) 14.88; thesis that past, present, and future *dharmas* are equally real 14.87; thought it possible for the disciple to aspire to Buddhahood 1.188; twelve *aṅgas* (categories of texts, *dharmapravacana*) 14.25, 17.571; separation of act from intention to act 8.620; view of conditioned and Unconditioned as two mutually exclusive realities 3.236; view of death and rebirth 2.76

see also
Abhidharma and Sarvāstivādin thought, *see under* Abhidharma/Abhidharma Piṭaka; *Abhidharmakośa*, *see under* Vasubandhu; and *gotrabhū*, *see under gotrabhū*; *Mahāvibhāṣāśāstra*; origins of the wheel of life, *see* wheel of life/introduction; path of five stages; *Samyuktāgama*; Vasubandhu; *vinaya* rules, *see under* Vinaya/the history of the Vinaya

Sarvodaya movement *see under* Bhave, Vinoba

sāsana what it is 8.670 (n23); the Buddha says that his *sāsana* will last longer than those of previous Buddhas 14.434; can the *sāsana* be made new or reformed? 14.86; is practice or learning the basis of the *sāsana*? 8.465, 10.706 (n359); reinvigorated by the sixteen *arhants* 2.316

Sasanaratna, Dharmachari (Derek Goodman) v24

Sasanasiri, Venerable (Sarnath) v23

Sāsanavaṃsa *see under* Myanmar

sassata-diṭṭhi *see* eternalism

śāstras (commentaries) *alaṃkāras* 1.361–2, 2.440; difference from *sūtras* 26.197; School of the Three Śāstras 1.311; systematic 13.340; written by *ācāryas* 1.298, 1.311, 26.197

Sastri, N. Aiyaswamy 7.537

śāśvatavāda *see* eternalism

Satan (or Lucifer) as a dragon beneath the feet of the Virgin Mary 13.598; Bible stories 12.513, 18.27; Dante's description of Satan 13.592–3; depictions of Satan 13.593–4, 13.649; entered into Judas Iscariot 13.594; he complained when the Virgin Mary opened the back door to hell 13.601; 'If Satan cast out Satan, he is divided against himself' 18.27; Irenaeus said that the theology of others was the result of Satan's inspiration 13.596; Lucifer and the celestial hierarchy 1.16; Māra corresponds to Satan, but there's a great difference 12.191; Origen dared to say that Satan would be saved 12.513, 12.526; Satan the Accuser (Blake) 8.559; 'Satan finds work for idle hands to do' 15.350; 'Satan himself is transformed into an angel of light' (St Paul) 13.596

see also
in *Paradise Lost*, *see under* Milton; temptation of Jesus, *see under* Jesus

Śatapañcāśatkastotra *see* Mātṛceṭa

Satara, India 9.40, 9.42, 9.179

Śatasāhasrikā *see Perfection of Wisdom in 100,000 lines*

Sātavāhana dynasty 1.309, 17.153

śaṭhya *see* dishonesty

sati (Sanskrit *smṛti*) *see* mindfulness

satipaṭṭhāna *see* mindfulness

Satipaṭṭhāna Sutta *see under Majjhima Nikāya*

satire Hogarth's satires are deadly accurate 3.508; popular religion satirized 26.397; Sangharakshita's satirical sketch on Brahmanism 22.10

sati-sampajañña the meaning of the term 15.99–100; difference from consciousness 9.514–15; *see also* awareness

satisfaction

real satisfaction
compared with all lesser satisfactions, Nirvāṇa is as the sun to shadows 1.129; finding in the present an inexhaustible satisfaction and perennial joy 7.286; happiness comes not from satisfying craving, but from not having it at all 10.474–5; real satisfaction is possible only outside time 17.408; the real source of satisfaction is within oneself 17.507, 18.218; sometimes mediocre satisfaction blocks the path of true satisfaction 16.286

what won't satisfy
cosmic ignorance endeavours to satisfy its ceaseless craving for pleasure 7.47; experiences are rarely satisfying in themselves 26.13; experimenting with depriving oneself of sense satisfaction 5.677; even the best of things can't give permanent satisfaction to the human heart 2.121; the mistaken view that happiness consists in the full satisfaction of desires 7.116; no satisfaction to be gained from possessions 18.296; nothing conditioned

can fully satisfy the deepest longings of the human heart 4.51; pleasure from conditioned things can't satisfy our longing for the Unconditioned 3.215; sexual satisfaction is short-lived 11.575–6; Siddhārtha's father attempts to satisfy his son with a pleasurable life 3.24–5, 10.256; thieves are *preta*-like people who are never satisfied with what they have 17.294; you can never be satisfied 18.207

satisfactions of different kinds
an aesthetic satisfaction from contemplating the good 15.349; 'an emotional satisfaction that no argument could be allowed to disturb' 20.217; having a book published is one of the most satisfying experiences 22.182; most people are satisfied with themselves as they are 26.172–3; if you find worldly life satisfactory, it may be hard to get into the spiritual life 18.557

see also
dissatisfaction; *dukkha* (unsatisfactoriness)

Satkāryavāda (school of thought) *see under* cause and effect

satkāya-dṛṣṭi *see under* fetters

satori *see under* Zen

satsangh (Hinduism) 4.173, 11.119, 20.123–4

Satterthwaite, Keith v23

satthā devamanussānaṃ ('teacher of gods and men') 1.33, 3.69, 15.495–6, 26.603

sattva (quality) *see under guṇas*

Satya Sai Baba 26.229–30

Satyadevi, Dharmacharini (Verne Barrett) v24

satyāgraha 9.562 (n239)

satyagrahis 9.6, 9.49, 9.221

Satyalila, Dharmacharini 14.xx, 26.659

Satyaloka, Dharmachari v24

Satyapriya (previously Rabindra Banerjee) *see* Buddharakshita

Satyasiddhi school 1.252–3

saumanasya (joy) 2.98

Saurat, Denis 22.141

Sautrāntikas *asatkāryavāda* 1.314; criticized by Candrakīrti 1.322; not a rival to other systems of thought but an expression of successively advanced insight 7.509; Śāntarakṣita thought their views could be accepted as relative truth 1.322; they produced one of four systematic transmissions of the doctrine 13.340; Vasubandhu incorporates Sautrāntika views in his work 7.504–5

sāvadya 16.545

sāvaka *see śrāvaka*

sāvakasaṅgho *see under Tiratana Vandanā*

Savarnas 9.28

Sāvatthī *see* Śrāvastī

savikalpa-samādhi 1.166

Savitri *see under Mahābhārata*

Savoldo, Giovanni, Girolamo 13.589–90, 25.375

Savonarola, Girolamo 13.550, 13.626–7, 23.315, 23.523–4 (n359)

Sayadaw, Ledi 7.445

Sayadaw, Mahasi 23.73, 23.485 (n98)

Sayadaw, U Kawinda 2.717–18 (n506), 2.748–9 (n713)

sayanāsana (place to sleep) 16.406

scapegoat making someone a scapegoat in the name of humour is very unskilful 17.653; the projections of the Church 11.340–1; Sangharakshita being made a scapegoat 2.609–12, 26.465; 'Scapegoat' (poem) 25.328; *The Scapegoat* (painting) 2.609–10, 24.65, 24.134, 24.169, 26.255, 26.465; 'The Scapegoat' (poem) 2.610–11, 24.169, 25.350–1, 26.465

Scarfe, Gerald 8.446

scent *see* smell; perfume

scepticism Buddhism is not sceptical 11.110; doubt is an inflexible attitude of scepticism and indecision 15.207; the scepticism of the West 11.110, 17.556, 24.401; scepticism and fanaticism in the Middle Ages 15.565; a place for faith and a place for healthy scepticism 16.553; a middle course between credulity and scepticism 8.607–8; if wisdom is strong but faith weak 1.293

schadenfreude 1.505–6, 15.311–12

Schaffner, Martin 24.594

Schayer, Stanislaw 7.366

Scheduled Castes *see under* Dalits

Scheduled Castes Federation (SCF) 10.8, 10.667 (n46), 22.287, 22.289

Schelling, Friedrich 26.487, 26.747–8 (n442)

Scherk, Mike *see* Dharmapriya

Schiavone, Andrea 25.376–7

Schiller, F. C. S. concept of a beautiful soul 7.33, 7.549 (n27); *Formal Logic*: 'hilarious' 20.446; friendship with Goethe 26.365; *Letters on the Aesthetic Education of Man* 12.695, 12.758 (n489), 26.363

Schimmel, Annemarie 24.311

schizophrenia 4.504–5, 4.548, 18.442, 23.102

Schlaum, Blanca 20.194–5, 20.198–9

Schloegl, Irmgard 8.489–90, 8.495–7

Schmidt, Dr Tom 8.664–5

scholars and academics

the nature of academia
Dr Johnson's definition of 'scholar' 25.5; an academic is not an intellectual 26.45; academic methodology 13.388, 13.429, 13.447, 13.481; the academic mind delights in a sticky web of 'contradictions' 7.310, 11.483; academic Oxford an exclusive, conventional, and snobbish place 23.56; academic study as an example of *khitta* ('contracted' state) 15.162–3; 'Academics in their ivory tower' 25.423; being an authority on an academic subject may lead to conceit 18.168–9; concerned more with facts than with principles 2.51; the importance of declaring an interest 13.406, 13.430; the irrationality of scholars 14.557; the scholar who uses his learning to engage in controversies with other scholars 19.545; a scholar's work described as 'the last ounce of dust in desiccation' 5.248, 23.225; 'The Scholars' (poem) 25.xxxiii–iv, 25.4–21, 25.286; symbolized in the parable of the return journey 16.97; there is always some subjective element at work 15.197–8; they should declare personal interests 13.406; the very greatest scholars are never intellectually arrogant 21.114

scholars of Buddhism
the academic approach is hostile to the possibility of Enlightenment 7.310, 11.483; academic knowledge has its own value, but it is not going for Refuge 3.326; academics in the field of Buddhism 25.5–6; dry approach 9.230–1; how Gerald Scarfe might depict a scholar in the field of Buddhist studies 8.446; kept going not by their interest in Buddhism but by other things 19.50–1; many understand the words without understanding the meaning at all 4.249, 25.8; philology: bad philology, good doctrine, good philology, bad or no doctrine 1.17–18; scholarship in the early days of Buddhism in the West 25.6; 'scientific' study is useful as long as its limitations are recognized 2.51; the spirit and the letter 1.222, 1.227, 16.579; their different views of it are like the blind men examining the elephant 12.103; they often treat it as a game that has no bearing on spiritual life 26.43; they sometimes insist on interposing themselves between reader and text 14.348; unable to see it in its breadth and depth 1.6–7; understanding language no qualification for teaching spiritual significance 1.18; useful academic work in Tibetan studies 17.453; what is the role of the scholar in reading a Mahāyāna text? 17.156–7; why should it be necessary to subject Buddhism to academic analysis? 13.506

aspects of Buddhism scholars may question
cannot believe that the Dharma was rediscovered by the Buddha 1.56; dismissal of the reality of supernatural beings 1.33–4; may claim that only their own branch of Buddhism is valid 1.198; some scholars ignore 'mythical' elements of the Buddhist scriptures 1.56, 11.15; Western scholars' scepticism about *termas* 12.300

scholarship and Buddhist practice
academic study as a substitute for practising the Dharma 24.327–8; *bhikkhus* who become academics 19.486–7; Buddhism best understood and expounded by those who accept and practise it 1.25; difference between academic study and commitment to the Three Jewels 2.470; the difficulty scholars find in 'passing through the door of the mind' 4.488–9; the formidable scholarship of Mongolian Buddhists 13.40; having exhaustive knowledge about Buddhism does not make one a Buddhist 11.467; interpolating practice into metaphysics may be questioned, but Buddhism means practice 3.370; the more 'scholarly' a Buddhist is, the more the need to base himself on practice 26.58; 'Nothing is more shameful than a learned Buddhist who neglects his meditation' 18.486; Sakyapas are distinguished for their scholarship 13.29; scholars need to practise the Dharma 9.39

being both scholar and Buddhist
Conze was a Western scholar who actually practised Buddhism 6.620; scholars in Triratna 11.601; 'True sages and scholars are always in accord' 19.541–3; Tsongkhapa was both scholar and saint, a rare combination 13.30

being a Buddhist without being a scholar
don't feel inferior because you're not scholarly 19.521–2; a peasant with faith more likely to understand than a scholar without 7.310, 11.483, 17.331; qualifications have little to do with ability to understand the Dharma 9.339; Sangharakshita: 'I am not a scholar, just well read' 11.602; we mustn't be either dry-as-dust intellectuals or cotton candy Buddhists 12.515

scholasticism the bodhisattva ideal's exemplification prevents it from degenerating into scholasticism 2.155–6; danger for the doctrine-follower of sinking into scholasticism 2.142; Hīnayāna Buddhism and scholasticism 1.222–5, 1.277, 1.310; Madhyamaka doctrine sank into scholasticism 1.374; Nāgārjuna's dialectical method liable to degenerate into 1.350; Perfection of Wisdom to be understood in the context of tendency towards 1.307; purely formal elaboration of existing doctrinal patterns 2.152; the tendency of all forms of Buddhism towards scholasticism 8.312, 18.497

School of Economic Science 23.105, 23.106, 23.173

School of the Three Śāstras (*Sanlun Zong, Sanron-Shū*) 1.311

schools *see* education

schools of Buddhism *see under* Buddhism III/schools and sects; *see also* individual schools

Schopenhauer, Arthur

introduction
all great art contains an element of self-transcendence 7.403, 26.21; Amiel's reading of Schopenhauer 8.149–51; challenged the academic and professional conception of philosophy 26.104; a work of Edward Conze modelled on Schopenhauer 8.536; declared himself a Buddhist 7.449, 8.149; made an approach to the Dharma 16.375; *East-West Fire: Schopenhauer's Optimism and the Laṅkāvatāra Sūtra* (review) 8.365–6; his 100th death anniversary 8.284–5; the influence of his writings on the introduction of Buddhism to Europe 8.285; the male human form more beautiful than the female 23.289, 23.516–17 (n326); parallel between aesthetic and mystical experience 17.608; 'wisdom literature' 14.343; Sangharakshita and Schopenhauer 20.61, 20.83

Die Welt als Wille und Vorstellung (The World as Will and Representation)
comparison to karma-process and action process 2.76; popularized a version of Buddhism all over Europe 7.449; predicts a Renaissance from oriental culture 7.88, 12.79, 14.287–9, 26.102, 26.256–9; to one to whom the world is everything, Nirvāṇa is nothing 17.362; 'we see something as beautiful when we see it without desire' 12.613, 15.533, 17.222

Schroeder, Wolfgang *see* Dayaraja

Schumacher, E. F. 11.533–4, 16.399–400

Schwarte, Thomas *see* Amritavacha

Schwarzenegger, Arnold 24.461–2

Schweitzer, Albert 2.627, 13.643, 16.9

science

history
Newton may have been insane, but modern science is based on his world-view 19.180; split from humanities 3.6; the modern scientific attitude as protest against medieval Christianity 26.103–4; split between religion and science 14.443; the idea of science in the modern sense discovered in the 19th century 12.464; the sufferings of the world are probably greater than before scientific discovery 7.115

modern science
āsura-like? 4.449; an attempt to understand life by the alienated intellect (Blake) 19.180, 26.77; danger of search for knowledge without ethical considerations 16.351; an exceptionally intelligent and unpretentious scientist 24.210–11; less biased towards materialism than it was 2.33; brings about higher standard of living 9.413; creates big cities 9.413–14; devotes its attention to material ancestry, disregarding spiritual existence 1.42; has given us knowledge of the 'how' of existence, but not the 'why' 7.148; the sciences assume the truth of causation, but don't consider why life exists 7.190; if you try to eliminate the subjective element you end up with science 15.707; the mystery of the universe as seen by modern science 25.133; the paradoxes of modern science 17.375; quantum physics seen as treating the whole of existence 24.209; scientific institutions give us our faith now 17.44; 'scientific' understanding without feeling 19.178; scientists and the emotional side of life 26.130; this is the age of science 10.169; the 'white heat of technological revolution' 23.87; Sangharakshita's early attitude towards science 20.23–4

Buddhism and science
'Buddhism and Science' (1948 article) 7.157–61; *Buddhism and Science* (Jayatilleka) 8.383–4; belief that Buddhism will regenerate science in the West 7.37; Buddhism differs from science in using emotion as well as intellect 4.642–3; Buddhism is uncommitted to dogmas that conflict with scientific facts 8.280; Buddhism neither agrees nor disagrees with the results of science 10.226; the comparison is an *upāya* 1.39; if any religion could cope with scientific needs, it would be Buddhism (Einstein?) 1.471; is scientific insight the same as Buddhist insight? 26.687; modern Buddhists taking the name of science in vain 26.685; no conflict between them 22.158; they agree that nothing in the world is solid 22.29–30; investigating the links between them 24.196; religion as discovery sees science as a friend 3.367; science and Dharma practice 8.582; to appeal to science on behalf of Buddhism is to appeal to authority 17.330–1; they are not in disagreement (Ambedkar) 9.425–6; the truth of Buddhism as a whole does not coincide with the truth of science 13.438; their truths do not coincide, but they share a similar spirit 7.159–60

Buddhist tradition and modern science
attempts to verify rebirth scientifically 2.15–16, 3.111–12; Buddhist teachings do not conflict with the discoveries of science 7.128; Buddhists free to reject doctrines that conflict with modern science (Ambedkar) 9.426; claims that scientific inventions were anticipated by the Buddha 12.104–5, 17.329–30; the Dharma is not the source of answers to scientific questions 8.586–8; *dharmas* and atoms 14.344, 17.443–4, 24.213–14; discrepancies 2.64–6; the *manas* is the scientific mind, though great scientists also possess imagination 12.559; no question of proving the truth of Buddhism through anticipations of science 13.438; nothing in Buddhism hinders us from discarding obsolete science in the scriptures 2.65; the origin of the universe is a matter for science, not religion 10.138; science and the *niyamas* 3.98–99; uncertainty about conveying Buddhism in accordance with scientific terminology 13.438

is Buddhism scientific?
is Buddhism scientific or non-scientific? 4.642–3; adopting a truly scientific attitude towards Buddhist scriptures 2.34; the Buddha was the embodiment of the scientific spirit 7.160; it doesn't resist the evidence of the senses, but that doesn't make it scientific 3.10; it inclines to a traditional, pre-scientific viewpoint 3.10; it is scientific in that it is based on reason and observation, not authority 26.685; it is a scientific religion in the full sense of that term 7.128; it's dangerous to present Buddhism as being more scientific than Christianity 19.541–2; it's a misnomer to call Buddhism a scientific religion, but there is an analogy 12.56; naive assertions of the scientific character of Buddhism 13.436; 'scientific' approach to ethics 14.547; scientific study of Buddhism 1.16–18, 1.22–3; spiritual and scientific knowledge are entirely different 17.330; verification for oneself: the real scientific attitude to Buddhism 9.528–9; the FWBO accused of being unscientific 13.416, 13.438–9

poetry, beauty, science
art can heighten consciousness more than science can 7.436; the beautiful flights of the mind of poetry and science 26.686; the bodhisattva should learn all arts and sciences 4.81, 18.414; Buddhism is probably closer to poetry than science 14.549; in Buddhism we need to use language poetically rather than scientifically 19.447; the link between beauty and truth: scientists in search of 'elegant' truths 13.279; Rovelli brings poetry and science close together 26.686; take the Buddha's statements poetically rather than scientifically 19.242

science fiction and the archetypal 16.533; comparison between science fiction and Mahāyāna *sūtras* 3.381, 12.503, 16.37, 16.237, 22.463; fantasies will all come true 25.320; taking the works too seriously 17.63

Scientific Buddhist Association 13.416

Scientology 17.40, 17.711 (n43)

Scotland has its own social and cultural realities 13.373; twelve Buddha images to go to different parts of Scotland 24.583; steel strike in 1980 24.149, 24.641 (n173); *see also* Dhanakosa *under* Triratna IV/ retreat centres; Edinburgh; Glasgow

Scott, Mary v21

Scott, Paul 25.110, 26.353–4

Scott, Sir Walter his house Abbotsford 18.276; *Redgauntlet* 12.697; underrated 26.339; writing in the midst of family life 26.355

scriptures

INTRODUCING THE BUDDHIST SCRIPTURES

introduction
summaries 3.83–9, 7.499–503, 8.220, 12.31; what is a scripture? 16.233; the written records of the *Buddhavacana* 14.11; the specific purpose of Buddhist literature 14.xiii, 14.302; do not possess spiritual authority 7.334, 16.443; authoritative only as slices of enlightened human experience 19.186; not an infallible revelation from God 9.109–110, 16.443; alternative formulations, not different teachings 18.370, 19.215; each text serves people from particular cultures at particular times 14.xvii; a larger canonical literature in more languages than any other tradition 8.220; probably the most valuable of all the oriental literature yet discovered 14.290; without them we would know very little about the Buddha 14.264–5; a vast collection 10.163; reasons why there are so many 7.333, 14.251, 14.268–9; schools of Buddhism developed in association with particular texts 13.16; three great collections of sacred literature, all invested with canonical authority 7.525–6; what was lost due to the Muslim invaders of India 14.264

the nature of the scriptures
among the supreme flowerings of the human spirit 7.486; in ancient Buddhist literature, every word contributes to the meaning 17.159; bequeathed by the Buddha out of compassion as an eternal legacy 14.271; the Buddha's message is simple, but has been elaborated for different people 18.495; Cave of Treasures 14.xviii, 14.271; emphasis on the cognitive 5.268; every Buddhist scripture is a Book of the Dead 16.262; far horizons and limitless vistas 1.38; in some ways like a pharmacopoeia with cures for all 14.268–70; like a river forever receiving more water 14.257–8; literature 'writ large' 14.xiii, 14.293; a lot of the scriptures are personal precepts which we are overhearing 17.106; a millennium-long crystallization of orally transmitted teachings 14.26; only a fraction of the Buddha's infinite knowledge 4.3; a progressive revelation from the Dharma's inexhaustible reservoir 14.xvii; record of the life and teaching of a 'common man' 9.109; repetitions for emphasis 14.456; slices of experience rather than revealed knowledge 18.632; tremendous sources of inspiration 12.382; value primarily spiritual, also a useful version of the history of India 7.503

reflections on the texts
as literature of knowledge and literature of power 14.303–4; can it be described as 'literature'? 14.290, 14.292–3, 16.240; literature *par excellence* 14.291; reflections on Buddhist literature *as literature* 14.290–304; the early texts speak the language of reason, the later the language of myth 12.108; positive emphasis of oldest scriptures 3.46; 'must make the language in which it is produced live' (Ambedkar) 9.111; monks as the preservers of the correct interpretation of texts 13.339; influence on Western culture 14.267; Zen makes use of scriptures without becoming attached to them 13.343

the way they were written down
'Thus have I heard' 14.99, 14.399, 15.179, 16.36–7, 16.234; introduction 1.184, 2.197, 3.78, 3.83, 13.339, 14.293, 16.34–5, 16.242–3; the *Mahāvaṃsa* explains why the Dharma was written down 14.22, 14.293; the *Divyāvadāna* refers to the *reading* of the Dharma for the first time 14.22; they were written on strips of ola leaf 19.367; committing teachings to writing a sign of spiritual deterioration 1.222; Pāli canon first written down at the Fourth Council at Alu-vihāra 4.24; we don't know the order in which texts were written down 14.25–6; the haphazard way Buddhist texts have come down to us 14.83; textual criticism separating earlier and later passages 2.50; don't assume that texts written down earlier must be more genuine 14.26; the order in which they appear corresponds to spiritual progression 14.27; a shift towards the writing down of esoteric teachings 14.27; in the future new texts may come to light 14.258

a Buddhist 'Bible'?
Dr Ambedkar's views 7.332, 9.108–11, 9.136; assessment of the need for a Buddhist Bible 7.331–4; Buddhism possesses not one sacred book but many 7.525–9, 12.520, 14.14; and the Christian Bible: connotations very different 7.332–3, 9.110; need for a Buddhist 'gospel'? 9.109; in fact Buddhism possesses a number of 'gospels' 7.333–4, 10.466; it might aid the rapid spread of Buddhism, but it would not in truth be Buddhism 7.333; Dwight Goddard's *Buddhist Bible*, *see under* Goddard; to create an infallible authority would pollute the pure Dharma with dogmatism 7.334; Westerners don't like the idea 9.538; why Buddhism doesn't

have a single body of scriptures 11.508; would involve rejecting some characteristic features of the Dharma 7.334

complexities
contradictory passages in the scriptures 19.165; confusion between the spirit and letter of sacred texts is ruinous 14.207–8; discarding obsolete science in the scriptures 2.65; fundamentalist approach 2.50–1; the idea of Buddhist texts being blasphemous 11.329; recited to invoke occult forces 2.216; a tendency to read later meanings back into earlier texts 10.555; Theravādin view of two blocks, one a faithful recension and the other forgeries 14.26; they should not be invoked to justify unBuddhistic practices 14.265; what about texts that seem to conflict with morality? 1.145, 9.99–100; what is the proof that they are the word of the Buddha? 1.326–7, 16.240

TRANSLATION

the nature of translation
in many languages right from the beginning 7.498–9, 14.13; comparison between scholarly translations and translations by Buddhists 1.23–4; mistaken omission of 'unnecessary repetitions' from the Pure Land *sūtras* 1.333–4; the issues of choosing or coining words to translate Buddhist texts 7.515; some words untranslatable 16.565; the value of the use of beautiful language 16.444; much care is taken to systematize and coordinate terms 7.515–16; need a sifting process to isolate the really useful texts 17.453

translations into different languages
pioneered by Eugene Burnouf 3.654 (n185); into Nepali 21.236–8; into Tibetan 7.514–15; into modern languages 14.15, 14.266–7; plea to have translations into Indian languages 8.220–2, 22.310; into Chinese 1.326, 16.444; the whole of it is becoming available in Japanese and English 14.266–7; into Western languages 3.188, 13.337; into many languages 7.498–9; great quantities of translations 7.393–4

THE SCRIPTURES AND US

what to read and how
reading them is indispensable, but where to begin? 14.8; the purpose of reading Buddhist literature 14.xvii–xviii; be careful not to 'condition' your experience to fit the manuals 17.108–9; how to choose what to read 14.xvii; how to read it: for enjoyment, as a whole, and for its own sake 14.300–2; often unattractive and difficult, but make the effort to read them 13.337; one needs only to read and thoroughly assimilate a single verse 7.332; no need for a Buddhist to read all Buddhism's vast literature 7.332–3, 10.327; no need to choose between Buddhist scriptures and English poetry 22.464; reading for ulterior purposes 14.301–2; insight experiences from reading 5.640; there is much that cannot be conveyed by words 14.296–7

what part can they play in our spiritual life?
a crystallization of somebody else's experience, no substitute for our own 12.232; Buddhist texts label experience, to be related to one's own experience 4.158; can they really act as a 'map' for one's spiritual life? 17.106–10; going through them, very little seems relevant to one's experience 17.108–9; balance reason, the scriptures, and personal experience 18.416, 19.186, 19.203; have to become part and parcel of our whole way of thinking, feeling, experiencing 4.36; the importance of relating traditional accounts to one's own experience 5.250–1; meditation or the scriptures? a surprising answer from the 1st century CE 8.465, 10.436; more truly canonical the more deeply they move us 14.303; nobody, not even the Buddha, follows the path in the order they describe 17.109–10; practice is to be judged by whether it is in accordance with the scriptures 14.265; prayer that 'I may enter deeply into the *sūtra*-treasure' 2.5; reading them aloud in a ritual context 22.226, 25.11; their existential effect 14.xvii; unless we read them, we cannot understand and practise the Dharma 14.300; Western Buddhists have to relate them to their own spiritual lives 14.270; you have to find out which best suit your spiritual needs 14.269; you need a knowledge of it to understand and practise Buddhism 8.141, 14.271

studying the scriptures
which should we study? 11.718–20; an invitation to explore the world of Buddhist literature 14.xvi; best way of studying 1.26; the serious student needs a general idea of the literature as a whole 14.265–6; it's not a prescribed text on which we are going to be examined 14.300; no one can study them all 13.16; adopting a scientific attitude towards scriptures 2.34; only personal contact with an Enlightened teacher absolves us from study 13.338; rely on scriptures of definitive or explicit meaning 3.355, 16.579–81; to be studied with reference to the tradition from which it sprang 14.17; an understanding of Buddhism goes with a knowledge of the sacred books 14.7; we need a

teacher to help us find our way 3.89–90, 13.339–40, 17.156–7, 19.172–4; we need a tradition of study and interpretation to avoid misunderstanding 17.454; Western Buddhists should make more effort to study the scriptures 13.337–8; you don't have to master them all to get the Buddha's complete message 18.495; Zhiyi represents the spirit of inquiry into the scriptures 11.717

copying
the merits of copying the *White Lotus Sūtra* 14.127, 16.44; the novice bodhisattva copies out texts while reflecting deeply on them 4.179; a copy of the Kangyur made with ink from the dust of precious stones 14.255; 'your skin for paper … your bones for a pen' 2.213; copying sacred texts as an act of merit 16.44, 20.332

see also
Abhidharma; *abhūtadharma* ('marvellous events'); *Āgamas*; *Aṅguttara Nikāya*; anthologies, *see under* Sutta Piṭaka; *Avadānas*; *Buddhavacana*; *Dhammapada*; *Dīgha Nikāya*; *gātha*; *geya*; individual texts; *Jātakas*; learning the *sūtras* by heart, *see under* heart; Mahāyāna *sūtras* (and also individual *sūtras*); oral tradition; *Majjhima Nikāya*; Pāli canon; individual *Nikāyas*; reading/books on Buddhism; *Saṃyutta Nikāya*; Sanskrit uncollected texts, *see under* Sanskrit; *śāstras*; 'a special transmission outside the scriptures', *see under* Zen/teaching; *suttas* (Sanskrit *sūtras*); tantras; Tripiṭaka; *Udāna*; Vinaya; worship of scriptures, *see under* books

scrofula 16.424

Scruton, Roger 26.xiv

Seale, Bobby 23.459, 23.540 (n481)

search Siddhārtha's quest, *see ariyapariyesanā*; going in search when what you're looking for is near at hand 18.519–20; 'I wish I had a companion in my search for the Way' 18.656–7 (n153); modern literature in search of wholeness 10.154; out of a sense of dissatisfaction we might start looking for something 11.79–80, 12.624, 13.396; the modern search for spiritual principles 10.154–5; search for a guru 3.561, 9.250; we don't know what we're looking for – that's the beauty of it 3.262; *see also* quest

seas and oceans

the ocean of saṃsāra
the *ālaya* compared to the ocean, and *vāsanā* to the wind blowing across it 14.210; human birth: the blind turtle in the middle of the sea 1.418, 4.367, 7.170, 13.139; human life like a wave of the ocean 7.165; 'Not in the sky, nor in the … sea … can one escape the fruits of one's evil deeds' 7.221; the ocean of misunderstanding 10.587; objects are like floating clouds, like sea foam, like a reflection 14.192; phenomenal existence a vast ocean of changes in which not anything is changed 7.133; phenomenal reality a great ocean without beginning and without end 12.593–4; *saṃsāra*, the sea of birth and death 18.582; the twenty-four *nidānas* like rain filling up the streams, rivers, and seas 1.116

the ocean of Enlightenment
the *arhant*'s association with the ocean 1.310; the bodhisattva plunging into the ocean of Enlightenment 14.548; the dewdrop slipping into the shining sea 4.80; the Dharma as an ocean 8.599, 10.569, 11.706–7, 17.595; if the *dharmakāya* is the ocean, conditionality is the waves 14.607; 'the light that never was on sea or land' 7.451; 'More than the seas he gave his blood, more than the stars his eyes' 1.430; the Tathāgata is deep, immeasurable, unfathomable, like the ocean 2.44, 10.141, 10.449; the visualized form emerging and disappearing like a leaping fish 5.583, 5.600

the ocean of practice
Dudjom Rimpoche was like a great ocean: calm depths and a sparkling surface 22.508; Malaysian nuns chanting, like birds skimming above the waves 24.36–7; receiving confession like an ocean receiving the waters of a river 20.325; seeing oneself as full of faults and others as oceans of virtue 4.592–3

the symbolic sea
the churning of the cosmic ocean 7.580 (n190), 16.398, 22.179, 22.589–90 (n158); the great fish Timiratipiṅgala finds room in the great ocean 14.91; symbol of the unconscious 14.346; 'Voyaging through strange seas of Thought, alone' 1.52

the sea, the sea
the cold grey old North Sea 24.157; 'the deep and dark blue ocean' 2.644; how the seas and oceans formed 8.265–6; the ocean wild and dark 25.287; poems about the sea 26.393–4; Sangharakshita's love of the sea 26.508, 26.589; the sea at Shoreham 23.243; the sea figures in the imagination of all English people 26.393–4, 26.589; the shipping forecast 26.589; 'the waves of the sea', in a psychedelic experience 23.468; the wine-dark sea 23.264

see also
the oceans of the Buddhist cosmos, *see under* cosmology; qualities of the great ocean, *see under Udāna*/great ocean

seasons impermanence seen in the changing seasons 3.345; the seasonal rhythm of life 4.577; *see also* individual seasons

Sebastian, St 13.631, 23.257, 25.308

Second Council (Buddhism) *see under* councils

Second Vatican Council 2.457–8, 12.4, 13.552, 13.555

Second World War

general entries
experience of a Burmese refugee 22.277; 'froze the blood in the veins of humanity' 7.163; involvement of India 9.8, 9.62; London 20.68–7, 20.82–3, 23.62, 25.155; Poland 26.446, 26.451; the politeness of Polish officers 12.404; political views about Britain's position at the end of the war 20.153–4; Sangharakshita's experience, *see under* Sangharakshita I/Second World War; spreading 'alarm and despondency' ('Dismal Jimmy') 11.201, 17.181; 'We who have seen bombs fall' 25.270

Germany
damage in the war and restoration 24.597–8; extermination of Jews, homosexuals, and Roma 11.270, 26.677; the Holocaust 3.449, 11.270, 26.33, 26.677; the birds still don't sing in Belsen 18.312; Nazis who committed atrocities and were also highly cultured 11.270, 26.396; the Nuremberg Trials 10.56, 20.150, 26.396; remorse after the war 24.498

Japan
a book attempting to show that the Japanese were victims, not aggressors 26.602; cruelty 26.677; enslavement of Korean 'comfort women' 26.677; invasion of Singapore 7.110–11; Japanese conduct suggest that Buddhist ethics were not influential in public life 24.498–9; no apology until 1998 26.602; occupation of Burma 22.600 (n225); prisoner-of-war camp 26.538; Siam-Burma Death Railway 7.111; VJ Day 20.153, 26.504

secrets *bhikkhus* who break the Vinaya secretly 7.263; the secrets of the universe are fathomed 1.354; the secret of success in the spiritual life 7.413; each grain of dust contains the secrets of the universe 1.353–4; ethics makes intelligible the secrets of spirituality 1.144; 'The great secret of morals is love' 2.360, 15.249, 17.598, 26.139, 26.189–90; a mistake to think of Going for Refuge 'in the secrecy of one's own heart' 15.738–9; 'keeping the *ḍākinīs*' teaching secret' 18.475–6; keeping secrets in polite society 19.256–7; secrets: 'loved by women, brahmins, and the holders of false doctrines' 9.419; the secret of bodhisattvahood 2.155; Mijao Zong (School of the Secret Teaching) 1.384; 'My Secret Garden' (poem) 25.393; the Open Path and the Secret Path (Blavatsky) 1.404–5, 7.361, 26.207; the 'open secret', the sacred mystery of the universe (Goethe) 26.178; the secret of the Buddha's radiant happiness 3.315, 7.120; 'The Secret' (poem) 25.226; the secret feast (Tantra) 18.424–6, 19.485–6; the secret of bondage is also the secret of liberation 1.113; the secret of love is love 25.498; secret joy in others' misfortune 1.505–6; 'secret life' 23.181–5, 23.387; the secret of spiritual life 26.132; the secret of spiritual practice 7.302; secret teachings 7.359–60; the secret of work: 'seeing the inward in the outward' 7.102–3; thinking the brahmins had secret teachings which the Buddha made available is a misreading 10.625; the word 'secret' in a book title 11.181–2; 'Work out the secret of your blood' 25.277

sectarianism in Buddhism, *see under* Buddhism III/in Northern Ireland 11.670; sectarian organizations tend to express negative emotions 16.76; what it means 11.670

sects Buddhist schools and sects, *see under* Buddhism III/is Triratna a sect? 11.670; modern sects, *see under* religion/further perspectives

secularism and the secular

introduction
dictionary definition of secular 8.228; Sangharakshita's dislike of the word 'secular' 16.137; growth of secularism in the West 16.128–9; a purely secular culture is a contradiction in terms 16.355

secularism
America is officially secular, but not totally 9.351; the secularism of the British arts 12.76–7; the secularism of the English 12.75–7; the secularism of Shakespeare's plays 12.76; the secularized modern world 12.563

the spiritual and the secular
secular culture as the bearer of spiritual values in the West 13.511; secular practice of mindfulness 2.561, 5.662–3;

'secular spirituality': spiritual without being traditionally religious 16.137–8; secularized version of the jewel motif: man is fundamentally good 16.222; separation between religious and secular: a 'ruthless division' 1.28; in the past all philosophies were religious, but then secular philosophies arose 10.344; in the modern world, best to discuss profound questions in secular language 12.117; the influence on Christianity of secular philosophies 10.344–50; religion in a secular state 9.349, 9.352–5; 'trans-ethnic religion' superseded by secular modes of thought 24.500–1; we have to discuss ethics in secular terms 12.117

Buddhism and the secular
it flourishes in a secular state 9.355; it has no means of enforcing uniformity of action in secular life 7.439; it has to learn to speak modern secular language 12.117–18; Christmas Humphreys saw the Buddhist Society as secular 23.404; the difference between secular gatherings and Dharma activities 10.209, 12.676; popular Buddhism and communication between secular and spiritual worlds 2.218; blessing the activities of secular life 15.703–4; a rationalistic view of Buddhism similar to secular humanism 21.450; using the Dharma as a sort of secular profession 10.593; the bodhisattva's study of secular subjects and trades 4.81; Sangharakshita's approach is almost the opposite of secular 15.xviii; without insight, the bodhisattva ideal degenerates into secular humanism 2.160

see also
India as a secular state, *see under* India/politics

security (and insecurity) anxiety about the future suggests insecurity within yourself 19.269; finding security in a set of views 17.629–30; generosity comes from psychological security 17.199; insecurity can lead to dogmatism 16.82; illusory security 18.66; the insecurity of a spiritual life based on supporting *bhikkhus* 2.592–4; a link with craving, aversion, and delusion 11.129–30; living with insecurity 3.499; the consequence of social insecurity is the search for security of love 13.386; Nirvāṇa a state of matchless security 1.15; not feeling the need for security 10.630–1; wanting certainty, people are apt to believe teachers with very definite views 17.627; persistent doubt suggests insecurity 10.578; security is insecurity 26.83; there's no security in going through the motions 19.274–5; there is no security to be found in any fixed belief or way or life 19.273; we need a provisionally secure base 17.370

seduction the attempt by Māra's daughters to seduce Siddhārtha 3.277, 12.187; be wary of being seduced by charismatic purveyors of Enlightenment 8.578; being seduced by the attractions of the middle-class lifestyle 12.555; we want the transcendental to coax, even seduce us 13.284, 14.597, 19.25

seed syllables *see* individual seed syllables

seeds around the seed of 'I' develops the world of 'mine' 17.342; the birth of the seed of Buddhahood 5.44; the *bodhicitta* like a seed 2.165; the bodhisattva can enclose Mount Sumeru in a mustard seed 14.164, 16.451; the comparison of consciousness to a seed 14.187–8; 'Faith is the seed' 10.331–2, 13.571, 15.625, 17.17–19, 26.648–9; the FWBO was not a blueprint but a seed 26.580; good seeds, bad seeds, and Buddha seeds in the six realms 13.135–40; Kisā Gotamī and the mustard seed, *see* Kisā Gotamī; pure and impure seeds stored in the *ālaya-vijñāna*, *see under* eight *vijñānas*; the sangha as the seed of a new world 11.189; the seed of awakening hidden in the heart 7.316–17; the seeds of degeneration were present in Christianity from the beginning 3.430; the seed of the Dharma 1.57; the seed of Enlightenment within 15.568–9; 'The seeds for the possible worlds are concepts' 17.475; the seeds of spiritual development 14.594; the symbol of the seed 18.282; the transcendental seed 25.381

seeing things as they are *see* knowledge and vision of things as they really are

seeing through if you've seen through something, you withdraw from it 26.32; insight is not seeing into, but seeing through 18.579; you can see through wrong views, then bring them back through doubt 3.293, 10.250; seeing through the conditioned to the Unconditioned 3.274–5, 15.576; seeing through the mind, you see that there's no subject–object distinction 18.236; seeing through *saṃsāra*'s imperfections 18.580; seeing through the self 4.621–2, 17.383, 17.391; *vipaśyanā* helps us see through our conditioned individuality 5.33, 5.418, 26.48

Segal, Ronald 23.316

sekha* or *śaikṣa (learner) 14.81, 14.88

Sekha Sutta *see under Majjhima Nikāya*

sekhiya *see under* Vinaya/other sets of rules

Sela Sutta *see under Majjhima Nikāya*

self (*attā* or *ātman*)

INTRODUCTION

terms and definitions
difference between psychological and spiritual conceptions of the self 4.620; different teachers' teachings about the self 3.489–90; if you get too scrupulous about the term, you are taking it too literally 14.549; Jung's definition 3.491, 16.173; negative and positive uses of the term 3.491

basic questions
can you really dispose of the concept of the self? 18.396; who am I? 3.489, 3.490, 3.497, 8.613–17, 17.66, 17.623; why do we believe we have a certain identity over time? 8.613–14

the experience of selfhood
the alienated self, a fictitious, rather ghostly little self 10.602; a bundle or jumble of selves 3.486, 3.501, 5.30, 5.655, 11.120–1, 19.81–2, 19.98, 26.39; 'the burden of self' 13.384–97; the characteristic of desire is to love self and hate not-self 7.411; desires form a knot of psychic energies which seek to remain tied as the 'self' 8.492; don't hate yourself, but see through your experience of selfhood 4.621; extreme fear can lead to a disintegration of our sense of self 17.180; a false idea of ourself which we try to live up to 16.279; feeling of selfhood: this is *my* Enlightenment 2.268; feeling like a speck of selfhood floating on the hostile waters of what is not self 7.273; for us our self is the centre of the universe, and that's why we act selfishly 12.614; an instant when you wake up and don't know who you are 5.398–9; keeping hold of the 'rope' of the self 9.456; making claims: '*I* did that!' 3.409; our experience shows us that the self does exist 17.375; the overall self comes into existence only with the practice of mindfulness 11.121; people place a lot of their sense of existence on their sense of self 19.293; the phenomenal fact of the sense of selfhood 8.614–15; refusing to experience part of oneself does not mean that it has ceased to exist 3.488; seeing self as agent: 'the success is all due to me' 10.601; the self is the sole obstacle to the 'attainment' of happiness 7.412, 26.53; a strong sense of self even in the *arūpa dhyānas* 17.608; a subtle sense of self only disappears completely upon Enlightenment 14.413; taking the self as the absolute reality of things has a negative effect on experience 15.335; our self is extensive, but the amount we let ourselves experience is small 11.497, 12.266; the self tries to appropriate the non-self to fill its inner emptiness 2.386; violence a radical assertion of separative selfhood 3.318, 3.320

ideas about the self
the assumption of the self's ultimate validity 17.619; the claim of the waking self to be the whole of us 17.341; the idea of a pure self enslaved by socially imposed beliefs 13.388; the idea of a pure self at the mundane level is a defilement 13.390–1; the idea of a self is a fiction obscuring awareness of reality 17.249; the idea of self as self-contradictory 17.377–8; the idea of selfhood associated with mastery or ownership 1.172; the impression that there is a real self to be liberated 2.159, 26.52; *Models of the Self* (book review) 8.613–16, 12.584–5; the self we guard so jealously is no more than an idea 15.263; a sequence of many selves, like a string of pearls 8.615; theoretical knowledge of the unreality of the self is useless 1.402; no need to drop the concept of 'self' as long as we are clear that it is only operational 14.549; understanding that the separate self is no more than an idea 15.337; Western emphasis on self 13.385; Western (cross-disciplinary) ideas of self 8.614–16; what one thinks of as self is a tiny fraction of limitless multidimensional consciousness 17.522; what we think of as our self is just an ever-changing flow of mental states 17.454, 17.697–8

the history of Buddhist teaching on 'self'
the *ālaya-vijñāna* doctrine explains how we take the illusory self to be real 17.488; *anātman* (*anatta*), *see anātman*; avoiding the question of whether the self exists or not 11.755 (n201); the Buddha's silence when asked if the self exists 13.393–4; the Buddha's teaching about self 7.539, 13.393–4; in the *Dhammapada* 1.173, 3.48, 3.294, 3.502; the goal is to go beyond the individual self, not regress from it 17.625; none of the five *skandhas* is self 11.755 (n201); a one-sided account of the Buddha's teaching on self 13.392–4; the 'self that has become cool' (*abhinibbutatta*) 10.515; the six senses are not self 11.755 (n201); 'There is no other dearer than the self' (*Udāna*) 10.543–6; Stream Entry: an achievement of the self? 4.40; Abhidharma analysis 1.103, 1.267, 12.149; early

Buddhist and Mahāyāna conceptions of the self 7.40, 7.553 (n46); the Mahāyāna starts from the 'non-self' 1.403; the Mahāyāna's use of 'great self' (*mahā-atma*) 3.234, 3.235, 3.659 (n226); Nāgārjuna's attempts to prove the non-existence of the self by logical argument 17.373–8; the Prajñāpāramitā as the antidote to self-seeking 1.303; things are mutually dependent and therefore lack 'selfhood' 14.608

THE DELUSION OF SELF

no unchanging self
as we are now, we cannot dictate to our future selves 4.44; the Buddha negated the Brahminical idea of a permanent, unchanging self 3.492; the error that 'self' is an eternal, unchanging ego-identity, not just a label 7.327; the ethics of actions performed with the false view of an unchanging self 1.435; everything about one's 'self' is subject to change 4.666 (n52); the false conception that the word 'self' denotes an unchanging entity 26.153; fixed self-view, *see under* ten fetters/first fetter; how does the conception of an unchanging subject arise? 7.209; the idea of individuality is incompatible with the idea of an unchanging self 19.234–5; the idea that the self can persist unchanged through spiritual experiences 26.206; if the self was really unchanging, human growth would be impossible 17.444; it means identifying with a cross-section of the flow of *skandhas* 17.625; it's not that we never have a self, but we always have a *new* self 11.48; no unchanging substantial entity 2.99; not 'no-self', but 'no unchanging self' 19.375; not ultimate but only provisional 11.497; one of the basic doctrines 12.657; our so-called self is really a stream of mental states and processes 19.376; the point is that we do not have an *unchanging* self 2.264, 7.165; the rationalization of ordinary human egotism 26.188; relating this truth to the practice of the *mettā bhāvanā* 15.318–19; the self is in a state of constant flux 3.492; the 'self' that is reborn is neither the same nor another 4.629–30; a tendency to think that the world changes, but 'I' persist unchanging 7.208–9; there *can* be no unchanging self 3.17; thinking of the self as having experiences but remaining unchanged 16.122; two reasons why the *anātman* doctrine denies the existence of an unchanging self 11.364; we are not an absence of self, but an absence of *fixed* self 17.625–6

wrong belief in a separate self
attachment to a belief in a permanent unchanging self 3.200; attenuated through spiritual practice until it disappears 7.360; can we really deduce from the stream of impressions a self that 'has' them? 15.206–7; a cold, hard, tight knot of separate selfhood 11.6; conflict between people and nations comes from this wrong belief 26.168–9; our constant reaffirmation of the *skandhas* as substantial gives rise to the self 17.475; the ego is simply the wrong idea of separate individuality 26.167–9; eight ways we may misinterpret our experience (*Diamond Sūtra*) 14.438–40; Enlightenment is the cessation of this delusion 1.179; eradicating the false view that things and persons are ultimately real 2.128; a 'good' man's core of separative selfhood may be harder than a 'bad' man's 7.407; 'The idea of a self is Mount Meru' (Huineng) 2.77; if there was a permanent self, one could not go a step along the path 7.133, 7.213; if you forget the self's unreality, you degenerate into spiritual individualism 1.404; the illusory self is created by the conventional mind 19.234–5; the individual self is the innermost citadel of separateness 7.412, 26.51; the limitations placed on *mettā* by the sense of a separate self 15.336–7; as long as you have that belief you always feel lonely 18.17; makes the *arhant* ideal unattainable 7.362; an obstacle to Enlightenment 1.99; our wrong notion of a separate self does not correspond to the facts 14.408; rationalizing belief in self into the basis of a philosophy or religion 17.619–20; rebirth is one of its effects 26.168; the root of ignorance 7.374–6; the root-illusion that prevents us from seeing things as they really are 7.360, 26.53; the illusion that we are individual selves, separate ego-identities 7.360, 7.374–6, 7.383, 26.53; it produces selfishness, the cause of all wickedness and misery 7.374; phenomenal existence is based on this wrong assumption 1.232; saying that there is no self is in some contexts miserable sophistry 2.529; seeing what is not possessed of unchanging selfhood as being so 12.613–14; the 'self' is not a thing, but a limitation that is removed 10.470; to identify with a self is to be susceptible to the arising of hatred 15.306–7; understanding that the separate self is no more than an idea 15.337; the unreality of the self means not that we are less than we thought, but we are more 11.497

what is not the self
the body is not the self 1.172; the emptiness of self revealed through mindfulness 10.622; 'Form is not the self' 10.719 (n467); however big the 'self', the Buddhist would say 'this is not my self' 14.458–9; the mind is not the self 1.172–3; the mind misinterprets impressions as a separate, real self 12.175; none of the phenomena of personality can be regarded as the self 1.172–3; *pudgala* (person) is devoid of selfhood 1.266; the *skandhas* are not the self 3.217; there is no person apart from their actions 15.318–19; what is devoid of self nature is said to be empty 1.267; when we say the self is empty, we must be clear what we're talking about 14.461

self and non-self (or not-self)
the *bodhicitta* abolishes the tension between self and not-self 17.192–3; equally real empirically and equally unreal metaphysically 2.159; even the view of non-self is wrong 17.383; the cessation of the distinction 1.64; compassion is how one acts when one has a deep realization of non-selfhood 12.9; lose their ordinary meanings in the sublimer realms of spiritual experience 1.133–4; mistakenly thinking one has experienced the truth of non-self 12.267–8; a paradox: the existence and evident absence of the self 17.375; trying to realize non-self, not pleasant feelings 17.511–12

GETTING RID OF THE SELF

attachment to self
attachment to your image of yourself 17.285; better than attachment to the idea of *śūnyatā* 3.237; conflict between attachment to self and rejection of self 13.396; contemporary attachment to self means no interest in Buddhism (Mellor) 13.394–5; our guarding of the self is the root cause of our suffering 15.263; 'the reason that sorrow has power over anyone' 4.570; self-hatred may reinforce one's emotional investment in the self 17.250; *śūnyatā* is the cure for every form of attachment to self 3.237; we fear death because we cling to 'self' 15.147, 23.92

abandonment of self
an alternative: the development of individuality 3.59; becoming tired of the old self 3.224–5, 16.227–8; 'Forgoing self, the Universe grows "I"' 5.656, 7.46, 26.141; if in the end we forget the self, what is the use of meditation? 10.223; little to be gained from renouncing the self unless you can imagine transforming it 17.364; not *gaining* Enlightenment *for* the self, but the death *of* the self 7.291; quite out of the question for most of us 3.60; we need to develop a self before we can realize the non-self 3.60, 17.630–1; we refuse to accept that it can happen 3.255

annihilation (or elimination) of self
all fear is ultimately fear of annihilation of self 18.46; analogy with waking up from a dream 10.470; be careful not to take this too literally 10.470–1; danger of not getting rid of the self but replacing it with another 3.234–5; discard the illusory self, but it is not helpful to attempt to destroy the empirical self 14.461; the first and last duty of the Buddhist 7.312; getting rid of the habit of the old self 11.48; the goal according to the Theravāda 15.338; 'hacking off great bleeding lumps of self' 3.490, 10.524, 23.35; liberation is not so much of the self as from the self 7.412, 26.53; it may be more helpful to think of expanding the limited circle of self-interest 17.342; more helpful to speak in terms of growth and development 10.471; not 'self-effacement', but absorbing the empirical self in the higher self 4.278–9; the problem of eliminating belief in a self 7.406; to produce a new self, there has to be a death of the old self 3.418; replacing the self by a creative orientation of becoming 15.340; the self can reinstate self at any moment whatever you do 15.739; the touch of *śūnyatā* feels like death to the conditioned self 5.32, 26.48; what is to be destroyed is the wrong view that the *khandhas* are the self 13.393; when the centre of the self expands to infinity 7.412, 26.51

overcoming the self
Akṣobhya represents overcoming the self 18.598–9; consciousness can either contract around a 'self' or break out of that view of things 17.348; Nietzsche states the need to overcome ourselves, but doesn't say how 3.503–4; by learning to be dissatisfied with ourselves (Nietzsche) 3.498

seeing through the self
don't hate yourself, but see through your experience of selfhood 4.621; the only way to see through it is to be to some extent free from attachment 17.383; to do so, we need to understand Dharma teachings correctly 17.391

working on the 'self' through spiritual practice
as faith strengthens, one becomes less self-centred 3.264; attenuation of the ego-sense 7.362; attenuation through

the six element practice 3.348–50; be careful not to use the idea of no self to create alienation 3.488; confession: disillusionment with self 16.304; don't concern yourself with the reality or otherwise of the self 3.491; ethics as a continual renunciation of the self 26.111; finding a map to find our way around the maze which is ourselves 12.284; if we don't confess the evil we've done, we're hanging on to the old self 16.293; incorporating the self into higher experience 16.520; in meditation the old self is modified to an extreme degree 5.364; the need to integrate all one's 'selves' 3.418–19, 3.486; the purpose of spiritual practice is to remove the illusion of separate selfhood 7.360, 26.53; realizing that what you have thought of as you is not there 5.365; re-evaluating the self 19.155; reflecting, 'How real is the self with which I identify?' 17.378; renunciation is the living symbol of the truth that we have no self 1.173; spiritual life is nothing but a loosening of the bonds of selfhood 7.412; spiritual progress is a perpetual ascent through an unending series of 'selves' 7.166; to realize the self's ultimate emptiness, try to be a little less selfish 15.339; transformation from self-affirmation to self-negation 7.302–3

SELF AND OTHER

introduction
all our experience takes place within the framework of this dichotomy 17.693; equality of self and other (*parātmasamatā*), *see under* equality; no distinction between oneself and others 3.31, 7.155–6; self-reference and other-reference in religions 7.149–50

causes and effects of the distinction
belief in the real existence of self or other is a source of bondage 2.159, 26.52; the dichotomy that is the real obstacle to Enlightenment 23.18; false conception of 'self' and 'other' as separate leads to painful states 7.222; finding safety in a self, we fear threat from what we perceive as other 18.139; loneliness is based on the duality of self and other 18.54; the more you possess, the more fixed the boundary 18.187; 'One single self we shall tame' ('Hīnayāna') 1.231

reflections
reflecting on whether there is really any difference between self and other 15.339; seeing self-agency and the agency of others as an arrow 10.600–1; self and others, beings and things, are ultimately unreal 1.440; 'thinking of ourselves' in the context of family 13.461–2; we are separate from each other, but there isn't a hard and fast division 17.522; what does living for others really mean? 12.9–10; who we are in relation to others: Buddhism's view 12.43; wisdom is realizing what benefits self and others 17.165

overcoming the distinction
acting for others' welfare without a fuss 18.179; any unselfish act acknowledges the interconnectedness of self and other 17.696; on the arising of the *bodhicitta* you see that in reality there is no distinction 17.192–3, 23.18; as you progress, you are less and less able to discriminate 4.591; be careful not to build up barriers with concepts which are meant to pull them down 15.335; behind every friendship is the denial of the selfish individual will 7.293–4; the bodhisattva ideal: 'self' and 'other' become indistinguishable 4.221–2; by realizing *śūnyatā* 16.232; combining work on self-development with work for others' welfare 15.237, 18.77; the Dharma door to non-duality is the imagination 11.726; genuinely seeing no difference between yourself and others 14.501; helping others, *see* helping others; no objective reason to be more concerned with our own suffering 4.570; one realizes as a matter of *fact* that there is no difference 17.694; perhaps the best way to approach reality is via the other 17.693–4; the purpose of all Buddhist schools 4.666 (n52); reflecting that objectively there is no difference 4.472–3; removing self, 'you' are there, but equally identified with all the other 'yous' 10.470; Śāntideva tries to close the gap 4.630; securing the best possible results for oneself and others 2.340; seeing oneself as full of faults and others as oceans of virtue 4.592–3; seeing that there is no difference between our own interests and those of others 15.337; tension between the two begins to lessen 4.180–1; thinking of others is an important step towards being non-egoistic 17.345; through friendship 3.574, 11.698–9; through the *mettā bhāvanā* 5.186–8; through practising ethics 3.321; transfer your consciousness to other people and as it were become them 4.633–4; Upasena rejoices impartially in his own merits and those of others 10.541–2; we can only solve our own problems by taking others into account 4.91–3; when you and others are suffering, choose to help the other 4.579–80

exchange of self and other (parātma-parivartana)
in the *Bodhicaryāvatāra* 2.360–1, 4.607, 4.613–17, 8.432; in the *Sigālaka Sutta* 3.574, 11.698–9

transcendence of self and other
the experience of self and other permeated by something that transcends both 4.180; for the bodhisattva, these categories are like a dream, a mirage 4.181; a level where self and other are not experienced as we usually do 12.605; the perfection of equanimity 15.223–4; Stream Entry, *bodhicitta* 4.40, 23.17–18

self and world
the integration of the outer world and the non-clinging self 18.102; made by oneself or another? 10.599; Milarepa experiences no separation between 'self' and 'world' 18.128; transforming self and world, *see under* transformation

FURTHER PERSPECTIVES ON 'SELF'

the empirical self
absorbing the empirical self in the higher self 4.278–9; annihilating self, the empirical self is still 'there', but as part of a larger whole 10.470; as necessary to the Buddhist as clay to the potter 14.462; awareness of the changing empirical self 17.537; distinguishing between the illusion of self and the reality of our empirical being 14.506; don't attempt to destroy the empirical self, but refine it 14.461–2; an 'impure likeness': like you, but not your 'true self' 4.282–3; Śāntideva on the fundamental delusion, not the empirical self 4.615; not a fixed entity (the Buddha) 3.492; taking the empirical self by surprise 4.267; through our practice we are hammering the rock of the empirical self 12.178; we *do* have a self as the sum total of our activities, our thinking etc. 14.461; until we are Enlightened we need to 'make the self strong' 17.630–1

being yourself
be yourself when giving a talk (but what is this 'self'?) 12.584–5; being in touch with yourself, knowing who and what you are 12.637; boredom is connected with not being able to be yourself 17.400; keep faith with your better self 4.363–4; Order members being 'good Buddhists' and not being themselves 4.603; a harmful pseudo-Rousseauist version of 'being oneself' 13.388–9; look carefully at what you think of as your better self 17.655; the need to have friends with whom you can be yourself 25.89–90; Siddhārtha overcame Māra by being himself 11.405–6; sometimes it's better not to 'be yourself' 25.93–4; the starting point of the 'real you' 4.259–60; suppressing aspects of yourself because you want approval 19.17; to thine own self be true (Shakespeare) 3.563; trying to live up to a false idea of ourself 16.279; we can have no higher purpose than being ourselves 18.120; we tend to withhold our total 'selves' 4.598; within the sangha we can be ourselves 11.136–8; you best imitate your teacher by being yourself 14.568; you differ from others simply by being yourself 3.470; you yourself are the justification for your existence 14.522

the true self
the *bodhicitta* 4.283; the Buddha-nature within: 'you' and 'not you' 4.271; contact with the true self is the most important thing in one's life 16.173; the Dharma is there to help us see ourselves more clearly 17.342; don't let work become an escape from your true self 15.284; in the Jungian rather than the Vedantic sense 16.173; symbolized by the jewel 16.173–4; we shouldn't be too afraid of that sort of language 4.283

new self
creating a new self compared to building a house 18.271–2; faith as the creator of the new self 18.275; how terrible it would be to be stuck with your old self for ever! 15.147; the new self born out of the conflicts of the old 12.219; our past selves live on in our present self 2.415–16; to produce a new self, there has to be a death of the old 3.418; unconditioned 18.275

HIGHER SELF AND LOWER SELF

higher self
Buddhism does not speak of Enlightenment in terms of a higher self 12.614; clinging to a 'higher self' more dangerous than attachment to the empirical ego 7.211; and the dangers of language of potentiality 16.111; does it have a guiding function in one's life, like a guardian angel? 16.110; don't posit some absolutely real 'big self' to which you go forth 17.341; never loses its awareness of the lower self (a windowed chamber) 16.94–5, 16.110; in the parable of the return journey 16.91–8; positive emotion is the bridge between the lower and the higher self 19.28; represented by one's 'genius' 3.513; to be cultivated 3.491; Buddhism never calls the possibilities that surpass our everyday self a higher self 11.497; why do we not hear its voice more often? 16.111

lower self
in the parable of the return journey 16.91–8; positive emotion is the bridge between the lower and the higher self 19.28; some selves are lower than others 16.111; to be eradicated 3.491

see also
anātman; fixed self-view (*satkāya-dṛṣṭi*), *see under* ten fetters; learning to love oneself, *see* self-love; surrender of self, *see* self-surrender; Upanishadic view of self, *see under* Upanishads; Vedāntic view of self, *see under* Advaita Vedānta

self-absorption 15.221

self-agency 10.601

Self-anti-self (*Bodhicāryāvatāra*) 4.614–16, 4.619–20

self-awareness

what is it?
the ability to be objective about yourself 3.469; cannot be inherited 3.482; it distinguishes at least some human beings from animals 12.46; it includes awareness of death 3.568–9; it involves a degree of separation from the present 3.565; it reconciles self-consciousness and spontaneity 14.581–2; life has swept us onto the shores of self-consciousness to fend for ourselves 3.482; 'shining like a brilliant lamp, pure and bright as a flower' 18.252; the starting point of the higher evolution 3.14

becoming self-aware
as soon as you become aware of your self you have changed 15.167; developed by the true individual 3.468–9; developing the levels of self-awareness 1.572–5, 3.285, 3.469, 9.294; effort is impossible without self-awareness 12.46; if we are self-conscious, it is only in the most vague and intermittent way 3.435; in relation to another person, tested by separation 3.568; one cannot be what one should be by closing one's eyes to what one is 26.34; one's own behaviour should be the primary object of one's scrutiny 4.25; our task is to clarify and intensify self-awareness 3.491; religion is for those who have developed some self-awareness 12.45–7; it requires at least some of one's relationships to be continuous 3.566; makes it possible for us to make a promise 3.565; seeing ourselves as others see us, as an object of awareness 3.565, 19.317; self-integration 5.43; the spiritual life is the progressive intensification of self-awareness 12.69; 'An unexamined life is not worth living' 18.164; a way of developing a non-egoistic attitude 7.408; we need to learn whether what we are doing is helping us to grow 19.544; you are aware of your own motivations, able to be objective about yourself 3.469

see also
awareness/four levels; consult your own experience, *see under* experience; mindfulness; reflexive consciousness, *see under* consciousness/four levels

self-centredness *see* selfishness

self-confidence *see under* confidence

self-consciousness (social) getting stiff and self-conscious 16.300–1, 17.82–3; unhelpful self-consciousness 16.330–1; the wrong kind of self-consciousness 15.613–15, 15.729–30

self-consciousness (stage of evolution) *see under* consciousness/four levels

self-control *see under* control

self-criticism *see* criticism

self-deception about how well you could get on outside the group 3.459; beware of thinking that you are not among the 'weaker brethren' 4.555; an element of self-deception in the way we justify our addictions 17.257; any form of wage slavery must involve an element of self-deception 17.196; spiritually incapacitating 17.215; thinking you will do something 'just this once' 15.362

self-deprecation 17.654

self-development Buddhism: a non-theistic system of spiritual self-development 12.57; combining work on it with work for others' welfare 15.237, 17.693, 18.77; for most people the route is through meditation 3.617; Goethe one of the noblest examples 23.473; helping others as a way of escaping its demands 18.592–3; Judaism, Christianity, and Islam have no scheme of systematic self-development 7.369; the most demanding aspect is what one does to support meditation practice 3.617; necessary for any kind of activism to be successful 3.617; no such thing without concern for others 1.237, 3.245–6, 4.591, 16.6, 17.692–4; a practical way of working towards solving the world's problems 3.617; *see also* growth and development

self-discipline *see under* discipline

self-disclosure the sangha provides a safe environment 3.488; it is essential to human health and happiness 11.440

self-discovery the attempt to discover oneself (Shils) 13.385; 'To discover that within myself which I *must* obey' 2.401; the value and dangers of self-discovery (Mellor) 13.392–3

self-effacement annihilating self not 'self-effacement', but absorbing empirical self in higher self 4.278–9; considered a virtue in the past 14.400; getting rid of ego-clinging should not be confused with feeble self-effacement 18.81–2

self-hatred *see under* hatred

self-help *see* self-reliance

self-identification *see* identification

self-indulgence 'accepting yourself' can be rather self-indulgent 12.480; aesthetic self-indulgence: 'The Palace of Art' 26.149–51; avoid the extreme of self-indulgence, but don't go to the other extreme 10.609; is Buddhism self-indulgent? 4.441–2; a constant pandering to neurotic cravings 10.608; don't allow your openness to be self-indulgent 10.571; faith and compassion as emotional self-indulgence 15.612–15; and the middle way, *see under* middle way; the mistake of thinking that freedom means doing just as you like 10.567; 'self-affirmation' 11.496–9; a self-indulgent idea of what development is 17.671; self-indulgent wacky behaviour 18.178; we need to avoid extravagance in all its forms 16.207; indulging ourselves without considering the consequences is a failure of imagination 17.598

self-interest breaking out of or expanding the closed circle of self-interest 17.342; *dhyāna* is a vast improvement on everyday self-interest, but still self-referential 15.336; practising the *mettā bhāvanā* helps one transcend self-interest 5.53, 15.312–15, 15.340, 17.342; our relationships contain more than a little self-interest 15.313; skilful action's freedom from narrow self-interest 15.263–4; there is nothing wrong with healthy self-interest 17.192

selfishness

the nature of selfishness
the cause of all wickedness and misery 7.273–5, 7.374; the ego as a selfish way of functioning 17.344–5; difference between selfish and unselfish feeling 12.612–13; for us our self is the centre of the universe, and that's why we act selfishly 12.614; self-defeating 17.208; the dove of peace and the serpent of selfishness 7.274; 'the sweet but selfish rest of quiet wilds' 1.213, 7.361; this self-centred world as the demon Tarpa Nagpo 12.331, 12.333–4; unwillingness to face new experiences 16.589 (n33), 26.169; we are naturally selfish 3.579; 'What do you mean, that was selfish? Everyone is ultimately selfish' 15.176

examples
ordinary friendship is usually a bit selfish 10.394; is it selfish to leave your family? 10.455–6; 'the greediest and most selfish person I had ever met' 22.257–8; the natural selfishness of youth 18.63; a self-centred man can never be a great poet 26.140; a selfish attitude can be erected into a philosophy of selfishness 19.105; selfishness in sexual relationships 14.414–15, 18.208–9, 19.514; using the power mode 3.577

spiritual selfishness
concentrating on 'individual liberation' is not selfish in the long run 17.268; more of a danger in monastic than in lay life 14.414; of the *arhant* ideal as it developed 1.403; of disciples and *pratyekabuddhas* as compared to bodhisattvas (Mahāyāna) 1.230; the idea that Buddhism is selfish 3.245, 5.209–10, 17.191–2; Nirvāṇa isn't to be dismissed as a sort of antisocial selfishness 8.460; of one who goes forth 7.217; regarding the spiritual community as a convenience to your own development 11.286; selfishness can take a spiritual form, salvation for oneself alone 10.146; the spiritual life cannot be a refined kind of selfishness 17.694–5, 19.315; the supposed selfishness of the pseudo-*arhant* 7.361; thinking following the path means avoiding pain is spiritual selfishness 1.132, 7.391; whatever the context, one may adopt a self-regarding or an other-regarding attitude 4.25

overcoming it
be less selfish 4.624; crossing from individual selfish existence to selfless wisdom and compassion 7.253; eliminated by dedicating merit to Enlightenment 16.332; as faith strengthens, one becomes less self-centred 3.264; if you have exhausted your selfishness, you become unselfish 19.200; the *mettā bhāvanā* loosens the grip of self-centredness 8.579; no distinction between altruism and selfishness 17.190–1; in spiritual friendship you try to get beyond your selfishness 7.293–4, 12.669; through the conscientious performance of one's duties 7.277; to realize the self's ultimate emptiness, try to be a little less selfish 15.339; we are urged to overcome it 7.273–5

self-knowledge

its nature
'Know thyself' 8.259, 12.461–2, 13.351, 19.97–100; a rare and difficult thing 19.99–100; true self-knowledge must include self-love 17.668; unflinching self-knowledge 8.585–6; 'We are greater than we know' 11.497; we're not usually clear about what is shaping what we do, feel, and think 17.11

why do we need it?
a freedom that arises from knowing oneself 17.434; the importance of knowing ourselves 1.555; to make a vow, you need to know yourself 17.169–70, 19.397–8; to speak the truth, we must know ourselves 1.518–19; 'he who knows himself is near to knowing God' 7.98; test the Buddha's teachings in the light of your knowledge and experience 7.128; we must know exactly what practices we need, almost from hour to hour 12.280–1; you can know what your ideal is only when you know yourself 22.293; you need to know what your feelings are and the effect things have on you 19.350

developing it
it's difficult, so you need friends and teachers 25.74; get to know yourself on solitary retreat 5.637; exercise your own judgement based on your self-knowledge 15.289; the importance of honesty with oneself 1.555; knowing others is a way of knowing yourself 18.215; observe your mind to formulate your view 19.212; the sangha is there to help us know ourselves better 3.401; seeing oneself more clearly through meditation 25.91; it tends to be achieved late in life 12.461–2; we get to know ourselves best in relation to other people 3.400–1; your life reveals yourself to yourself 18.280

selflessness of the *arhant* 1.182; the Buddha taught utter selflessness 7.275; developed by doing the six element practice 11.405; the difficulty of being truly selfless 15.336; of Enlightenment 7.296; the more you appreciate beauty, the more selfless you become 26.244; not separable from insight 17.208; progression from egoism to selflessness 26.111; the spirit of selflessness 15.322; there is a place for selflessness, but not for grim conditions 15.309–10

self-love accept your mistakes 4.360; appreciate your own good qualities 4.318; at the root of shamelessness and lack of respect is lack of self-love 17.667–9; being less concerned with oneself and loving oneself are not incompatible 26.23; being on good terms with oneself 2.259; charity begins at home but does not end there 1.426, 7.327–9; having a positive attitude towards oneself as part of Nature 26.14; if you feel you don't deserve to be happy, look into that 5.184; if you feel positively about yourself you are going to look after yourself 17.189; an important function of the sangha is to let us know that we are cared for 17.185; indulgence in habits that harm health indicates lack of self-love 5.126; it's difficult to recognize that one lacks self-love 17.668; it is part of your responsibility towards others to take care of yourself 15.289–90; look after yourself objectively, without attachment 4.633; nothing wrong with healthy self-love, but remember that others feel the same 10.544; our only need before helping others is to love ourselves and feel loved 14.415; positive self-regard can come from realizing that others love you 17.668; practise loving kindness towards yourself by eating wholesome food 4.112; true self-knowledge must include self-love 17.668; unless you love yourself you can't love others 26.27; why is it hard to love oneself? 5.125–6; *see also mettā bhāvanā/* method/first stage

self-mortification (self-torture) the Buddha regarded it as an extreme to be avoided 8.451; is burning oneself un-Buddhistic? 8.451, 16.205–6; even while doing ascetic practices, one's ego-sense may stay intact 7.406; an expression of nihilism 17.251–2; the Jains approved of it 8.451; like repression in the Freudian sense 10.608; the practice of patience isn't anything like as bad 4.391; no excuse for describing Buddhism as a system of self-torture 8.146; not a spiritual error we are in danger of falling into 3.40; self-denial 11.496–9; virtuous actions done for the sake of heaven can lead to the extreme of self-torture 10.608; Westerners confuse self-mortification and self-discipline 17.253–5; of the worshippers of Durga 4.390; and the middle way, *see under* middle way; Siddhārtha Gautama's practice of austerities, *see under* Siddhārtha

self-nature *see svabhāva*

self-possession 1.151–2

self-power (*jiriki*) difficult path of self-reliance 1.324; emancipation through one's own efforts 7.41, 12.97; and the Jōdu Shinshū school 2.562, 3.168, 3.651 (n165); and the Theravāda 1.199; the Triratna Buddhist Order follows the path

of dependence on self-power 2.562; and *vīrya* 4.138–41; you can open yourself to spiritual forces, but *you've* got to respond 4.302; and Zen 1.208, 4.138; and other-power (*tariki*), *see under* other-power

self-preoccupation 4.68

self-regarding (aspect of the spiritual life) 4.87–117

self-reliance and self-help according to Milarepa, you can get everything you need from your own spiritual life 18.620–1; the bodhisattva can lead the way, but we have to follow on our own two feet 14.577; the Buddha said 'Don't rely on anyone outside yourself' (*Dhammapada*) 12.97; can harden into self-sufficiency, creating difficulties for the disciple 1.133; the difficult path of self-reliance 1.324, 1.400–1; don't depend on others for things you could do for yourself 18.387; don't rely on an outside source for something you should be developing within yourself 18.300; finding things out for yourself 18.228; in the early days we very much rely on others to support our Going for Refuge 15.560–1; learning to stand on your own feet 12.232–3; no such thing as self-sufficiency, even for a Buddha 11.277–8; people sometimes need a period of dependence 26.44; self-help is one of the fundamental principles of Buddhism 12.135; self-reliance was the keynote of Dr Ambedkar's work 10.103; someone's death reminds us that we have to rely on our own efforts 10.324–5; in the spiritual life, it's important to come to your own conclusions 19.164–5; think for yourself 10.246–7, 17.626; unless we are self-reliant, we cannot 'abide islands unto ourselves' 2.592–3; what can we learn on our own and what do we need help to discover? 18.xviii; we are our own saviour 10.141; we should take Refuge both in ourselves and in the Dharma 7.317

self-respect Buddhism has given the Dalits back their self-respect 10.303, 10.314–15; Chinese people have great self-respect 4.318–19; *hrī*, *see hrī*; Milarepa's self-respect 18.136

self-sacrifice

reflections
do not give up your principles, even at the cost of sacrificing life 10.168; friendship: a readiness to sacrifice one's own pleasure for that of another 7.293; 'If all is to be sacrificed by me, it is best that it be given to beings' (Śāntideva) 4.358; if we take Buddhism seriously, we may be required to make sacrifices 4.100–1; in working for others' happiness you don't have to sacrifice your own 19.547; men will rarely make any sacrifice except for gain 7.96; a mother will lay down her life for her child 15.322; not many of us want to sacrifice ourselves at all 13.270; practising *dāna* step by step, from giving vegetables to self-sacrifice 4.457–60; it earns less merit than teaching a stanza of the *Diamond Sūtra* 14.468–9; skilful and unskilful motivations for self-sacrifice 17.191; could we give our lives for the Dharma? 10.271, 10.342, 12.573, 16.198, 22.517; when helping others, beware of a sense of self-sacrifice 18.592

examples
Atīśa's acceptance of a shorter life for the sake of the Dharma 12.572–3, 12.578; story of being unable to choose who should be sacrificed to bandits 15.322; self-immolation of Vietnamese monks 3.54, 16.195–7, 22.516–18, 23.211; Dr Ambedkar 10.168; Shakyananda and Sanghasena, who taught the Dhamma in India 12.573–4; Jñānaprabha's sacrifice of himself so that Atīśa could come to Tibet 12.571–2; a young monk offering himself in the place of a condemned man 8.157–8

see also
chöd practice; in the *Jātakas*, *see under Jātakas*

self-surrender the best way of getting rid of fear 15.735; the Buddha never spoke of a complete surrender of self 8.128–9; to the Buddhas and bodhisattvas 4.49, 4.293–4; can we put ourselves completely in the hands of another person? 18.383–6; to the compassion of Amitābha 1.346; conflict between incorporating and surrendering 16.520; to the Divine – but what if we are not convinced that it *is* the Divine? 21.506; expressed in the *Bodhicaryāvatāra* 1.415; and giving up responsibility 15.661–2; Going for Refuge and surrender of self 2.486–8, 15.660–79, 15.698, 15.722–3, 15.733–40; ordination as self-surrender 15.660–1; to other-power 1.346–7; puja as a way of self-surrender 4.294; the Religion of Art: surrender to the Beautiful 26.98, 26.174; requires a lot of effort 4.302; in the Sevenfold Puja, *see under* devotion/ Sevenfold Puja; the surrender of at least a little independence 5.259; the surrender of the egoistic will 15.662–3, 18.189; a surrender of person to person 2.365, 26.66; surrendering oneself to meditation experience 13.73

self-torture *see* self-mortification

self-transcendence all great art contains an element of it 7.403, 26.21; expressed in its highest form by the bodhisattva 3.17; harmonious speech leads to mutual self-transcendence 1.523, 12.37; in meditation 5.656; the naturally self-transcending nature of the conscious being 4.202; in relation to love 7.402–3; self-transcending immortality 3.208–9; self-transformation paves the way for it 11.499; spiritual practice is whatever conduces to it 26.129; sympathy is closely allied to it 26.140; the threefold way is a path of perpetual self-transcendence 11.656; the true meaning of everything that goes by the name of religion, spiritual life 4.656; what the evolutionary principle is all about 3.17, 4.655–6

self-transformation *see under* transformation

self-view *see under* ten fetters/first fetter

self-will blind, obstinate self-will 19.17–18; breaking through self-will 19.166–7; coming up against one's self-will is the start of the spiritual struggle 19.21; determination is very different from self-will 19.16; the koan is a mechanism to beat down your self-will 19.16; not being believed when speaking the truth challenges your egoistic will 19.19–20; the silence of self-will 26.203–4; when your self-will is frustrated you experience how egoistic you are 19.16, 19.167

Selkirk, Alexander 18.454, 18.660 (n177)

semantics 3.489–91, 14.86, 14.566

Semele 12.523, 12.741–2 (n350)

semi-monastic *see under* lifestyle

sems nyid *see cittata*

Sen, Narendra Nath v8

Senauke, Hozan Alan 26.691–2

Seneca born in Córdoba 24.427, 24.434; *De Beneficia* and *De Consolatione* 13.611, 20.61; 'Harm cannot befall the wise man' 10.536; the influence of his 'ethical sublimity' on the young Sangharakshita 20.61, 24.427; 'Life is nothing but a preparation for death' 10.320; recommendation to read his letters 12.406

Sengcan (Zen patriarch) 13.342, 14.659 (n521)

Sennett, Richard v13

sense experience the beauty we experience through the senses is not the highest beauty available to us 15.131; a degree of sense experience is compatible with spiritual experience 5.643; experimenting with depriving oneself of sense satisfaction 5.677; its influence on our minds 3.422; the material view that only sense experience provides valid knowledge 19.185; only part of the total spectrum of possible human experience 5.51–2; withdrawal from sense experience 5.641–3; you have to be aware of sense impressions and their effect on you 15.210–11

see also
kāma-rāga (desire for sense experience); in the seen, only the seen, *see under Udāna*/Bahīya

sense of humour *see* humour

sense of shame *see hrī*

sense-organs (*ṣaḍāyatana*) *see* six bases

senses

what are the senses?
awareness of things through the six senses (including the mind) 10.231; *ṣaḍāyatanas* (six sense organs), *see under* twelve cyclical *nidānas*; the six senses the bases for our experience of the external world 3.198

the senses in Buddhist tradition
ānanda (bliss arising from the senses) 2.91; the five senses and the five spiritual faculties (both *indriyas*) 3.297, 17.13; craving for experience through the senses (*kamāsrava* or *tṛṣṇā*) 1.111, 3.278; five (or six) sense consciousnesses, *see* eight *vijñānas*; 'in the seen, only the seen', *see Udāna*/Bāhiya; *kāmacchanda*, *see kāmacchanda*; sense consciousness 11.32; a whirling firebrand: how senses perceive objects 17.406–8

the innocence of the senses
'allowing the senses to return to their original nature' 18.344–5; karmically or ethically neutral 19.191; the self-purity of the six senses 19.191; sense stimulation gives an occasion for undesirable states, but it is not a cause 17.98–9; the senses are a mirror 19.193; sensing is innocent, the trouble is craving 10.610–11, 15.200–1, 15.286–8, 18.345

being controlled by the senses
the extent to which our lives are shaped by sense-based instincts 17.11–13; modern life multiplies the distractions from the sensory world 15.152, 17.44; most of the time we are controlled by and identify with the senses 3.298; they dominate before one takes up spiritual life 1.280; through them

the mind reaches out to things and can't easily be deflected 17.101–2

control or restraint of the senses
applying a Dharma perspective to whatever is happening through our senses 17.xix; 'guarding the gates of the senses' 1.148, 1.556–7, 10.512–13, 15.289, 17.101–2; liberty, according to the Buddha 10.520; limiting sense experience 12.473–5, 15.174, 15.287–8, 19.544–5; one of the four kinds of morality (*indriya-saṃvara-sīla*) 1.146; Pāli canon reference 1.148; practice leads to an unblemished happiness 1.148; taking control of your responses to sensory stimuli 17.102–3

the senses and pleasure
attachment to sense pleasures 1.112; experimenting with depriving oneself of sense satisfaction 5.677; pleasure comes not from sense-objects, but from engaging our energies 18.158; turning away from sense pleasures on the basis of meditative experience 17.513–14; we rarely experience pleasure through more than one sense organ at a time 17.394–5; when we realize the fact of *dukkha*, the pleasures of the senses lose their relish 7.50–1

mind as sixth sense
conceived of by the Sāṃkhya school 17.439; how the mind sense works 10.231, 15.168–9, 19.195; the idea of mind as sense organ is a corollary to the 'perceptual situation' 17.484; in meditation 17.543; and the *mano-vijñāna* 17.484–5; mental activity 3.511; the mind regarded as sixth sense is our everyday mind 1.556; mindfulness of the body involves all six senses, including the mind 10.512–13; one of the 'six spheres of contact' 10.512; of all six senses it is the mind that is the origin of craving and attachment 15.286; an organ of sense with its own mental objects (*dharmas*) 1.110, 3.159; the senses find refuge in mind as sixth sense, and it finds refuge in mindfulness 17.543

the senses and meditation
dhyāna: insensibility with regard to sense perceptions 4.489; how can concentrating on a sense object lead beyond the *kāmaloka*? 5.570–1; imagining the space left behind if one abstracts oneself from the senses 4.156; the mind tends to spread out over sense objects and become unconcentrated 7.358; perception through the five senses plays no part in *samādhi* 17.543; recollection of the six sense bases and their objects 15.199–211, 18.10–11; to enter the higher *dhyānas* is to enter a state of sensory deprivation 4.154, 5.641–3; turning away from sense experience in meditation 5.324–5; the withdrawal of consciousness from the senses like the setting sun 12.215, 13.310; the withdrawal of the mind from the physical senses 13.71

going beyond the senses
developing new senses 16.565–6; knowledge that is not derived from the senses 3.11; letting go of sense experience 19.156; the life of the senses is not left behind, but gathered into the life of the spirit 7.297; the subtle counterparts of the senses 13.291; turning them inside out, like a glove, to merge into a single inner sense 7.358; we have other, different kinds of sensory 'skin' 17.510

offering the senses
dedicating them to Enlightenment 13.258–9; puja is the consecration of the senses to the attainment of Enlightenment 1.408

reflections on the senses
after death you have desires but no senses through which to satisfy them 17.15; art begins with sensory impressions 3.511; biological instincts seem to come before the senses 17.13–14; if nothing in the mind was not previously in the senses, no memory of past lives 26.85; in dreams, vivid sensuous impressions without objective stimulus 1.368–9; the evidence of the senses viewed in the light of vision, insight, imagination 3.11; the more aware you are the more sensitive you are to sense impressions 15.287; the objects of the senses are neither absolutely real nor absolutely unreal 17.384; the 'ratio of the senses' (Blake): the split-off intellect 17.484; sense impressions do not imply the existence of matter 1.368

see also
individual senses; perception

sensitivities (*rūpaprasāda*) 2.97

sensitivity

sensitive matters
sensitivity (*pasāda*, Abhidharma) 14.80; every living thing feels and is sensitive, and they are all connected 4.541; a sensitive, almost reverential attitude towards one's environment 10.647; to living things 4.542; losing sensitivity in the city 4.545; a novel in which attempts to make life perfect lead to sensitivity and pain 17.395; psychic sensitivity 18.311–12; the poet's sensitiveness 26.136–9; the sensitiveness of the artist 3.507–8, 26.169; sensitivity to

atmosphere 18.23; sensitivity to criticism 18.278

becoming more sensitive
beware of being precious about your sensitivity 10.571; dealing with becoming more sensitive through meditation practice 4.542; the more aware you are, the more sensitive to sense impressions 15.287; awareness is very sensitive, very alive 5.400

ethical sensitivity
developing ethical sensitivity 16.311–12; practising the precepts according to one's level of sensitivity 19.560; how far you go with the practice of non-violence will depend on your sensitivity 17.584; being sensitive to judgement passed upon you by the wise 15.417–18

sensitivity towards others
being sensitive to the degree of Enlightenment in others 4.365; learning to judge how to speak to someone 4.359–60; sensitivity to the joys and sorrows of others 8.452; sensitivity to tension between people 18.311; take care not to tread upon hearts 25.231; through spiritual practice we become more sensitive to others 4.571, 4.581–2; to tell when someone is speaking the truth 2.377

sensuality the *Dhammapada* can hardly be accused of a tendency to sensuality 2.124; purifying and refining one's sensuality as an intermediate stage in spiritual practice 18.157; St Augustine, from sensualist to saint 18.160; the word carries an element of moral condemnation, influenced by Christianity 18.160–1

sentient beings

all sentient beings
the significance of the phrase 'all sentient beings' 3.376–7; they all depend on food 10.230–1; they are capable of Buddhahood 13.135; they are destined for Enlightenment 13.516; they are undergoing a process of transmigration 14.203; commitment to the happiness of all sentient beings 13.271; 'All the Buddhas and all sentient beings are nothing but the One Mind 12.170–1; dedication to their Enlightenment (bodhisattva ideal) 1.259, 1.422, 3.376, 7.41; the sweet fruit of [unselfish] love is liberation for all sentient beings 7.291; the bodhisattva treats them as his friends 1.426; a hint of the bodhisattva ideal in the phrase 3.376

love, happiness, suffering, and existence
the Buddha's actions were the overflow of his love for sentient beings 22.285; observing the suffering of sentient beings 2.271–2, 4.51–2; 'A bodhisattva who breaks precepts out of desire [still] holds sentient beings in his embrace' 2.389, 4.702 (n283), 14.185–6, 16.614 (n232); bodhisattvas are urged to deliver sentient beings who do not exist 1.348, 7.489, 11.14; how the Buddha knows the world and minds of sentient beings 14.144; the 'I'-concept is the root cause of the suffering of sentient beings 7.273; 'May sentient beings possess happiness with its causes' 5.197, 5.719 (n179); harmony arises when looking with compassion on the suffering of sentient beings 7.347; Buddhism does not see sentient beings as divided into different forms of life 2.93–4

see also
living beings

sentimentality the bodhisattva is no sentimentalist 2.156, 4.84, 4.243, 5.202; compassion must never be confused with sentimental pity 2.125, 4.193; the cynic feels less than is justified, the sentimentalist more than is justified 26.23; directing energy to practical help rather than sentimental lamentations 23.337; don't indulge in Buddhist sentimentalism 4.244; Emile Boin's diatribe against sentimentality 23.239; feeling sentimental and lovey-dovey 18.582; one can be in sympathy with nature without being sentimental about it 26.243–4; sentimentalizing a beggar 19.538; sympathy should be robust, not sentimental 10.571

separateness an experience of 'yourself' as not separateness but the blissful Void 18.54; nothing is really and truly separate 14.409; war threatens the world because nations imagine themselves to be separate entities 7.274

see also
separate selfhood, *see under* self/the delusion of self; Sangharakshita's sense of separateness, *see under* Sangharakshita VII/characteristics

separation the bitter wine of separation 25.446; the bodhisattva experiences no separation between 'self' and 'world' 18.128; from what one likes is suffering, *duḥkha* 3.212; in a sexual relationship 3.568–9, 3.572

seriousness all serious Buddhists should meditate 10.392; celibacy is to be seriously considered by the time you're 45 12.402; don't take reading too seriously 16.57; Stream Entry is a serious ideal for every Buddhist 18.578; if we take Buddhism

seriously, we may be required to make sacrifices for our ideals 4.100–1; frivolity as a way of avoiding facing things seriously 19.397; not taking oneself too seriously 4.137–8; rebirth is a pleasant interlude in a pilgrimage of more serious import 2.86; the seriousness of the enterprise of being a Buddhist 23.463; the seriousness with which Christianity was believed in 17th century Britain 4.125; 'Since I started taking Buddhism seriously, what have I given up?' 1.496; taking the bodhisattva ideal seriously 18.463

sermon Fire Sermon, *see under Saṃyutta Nikāya*/famous *suttas*; the meaning of the word 12.519; some of the greatest English literature takes the form of sermons 12.519

serpent *see* snake

servant–master relationship the best and worst masters, from a Tibetan point of view 22.522; historically 3.525–6, 16.106; Sam Weller and Mr Pickwick 3.525–6; in a spiritual context 16.105–7

service few are great enough to serve 26.81; for most of us the spiritual path is about humble, everyday tasks of service 26.17; the idea is alien to us, because of the collapse of the idea of hierarchy 4.174; he only can serve who is free of the thought 'I serve' 7.414; 'He who wishes to serve me, let him serve the sick' 4.11, 9.195, 11.443; in India, a greater understanding of personal service 4.609–10; living a life of service 25.40, 25.44, 25.140–1; serving others as a path of spiritual development 4.18, 27.1075; the sangha gives us the opportunity to serve others 3.401; 'just as the earth and other elements are serviceable …' 11.282; serving the Muse 25.414; serving spiritual friends 4.174–5; serving your spiritual teacher 16.106; some people don't like to think of themselves as servants 25.141; even when one is a bodhisattva, the universe is full of Buddhas whom one can serve 4.175; to think of the life of service *or* the life of contemplation is a mistake 7.155–6; the transformation of action into service 7.302–3

seṭṭhi (merchant) 10.499

settling down the bodhisattva not settling down in any particular ideas 14.563; the Buddha exhorts his disciples not to settle down in views 14.549; don't just settle down and accept limitations 19.279; even in Nirvāṇa there is to be no settling down 17.574; the mind is not a fixed abode, though it tends to try to settle down 18.562–4; Nāgārjuna tries to stop us from settling down in ourselves 17.378; the natural tendency is to settle down at ever lower levels 8.312–13; not settling down in spiritual individualism 2.270; settling down in a partial experience of Enlightenment 16.524; settling down in a way that is committed and also provisional 17.371; the spiritual life is so rewarding at all levels it's tempting to stay put where you are 17.675–6; though free from *saṃsāra*, the bodhisattva does not settle down in *nirvāṇa* 14.456; we like to settle down in the familiar 14.409–10, 18.204–5; we should use concepts but not settle down in them 14.417; we try to settle down in the world although there is nothing to settle down in 17.370

sevanā 15.384

seven (symbolism) 2.37–8

seven *bodhyaṅgas* (Pāli *bojjhaṅgas*)

introduction
outlines 2.126, 3.284–9, 4.648–9, 9.293–300, 10.368–70, 11.31–5, 16.280–1; etymology 3.285, 9.294; Pāli and Sanskrit terms 2.679 (n161); emerge like the petals of a flower from the bud 15.225; they collectively illustrate the way the creative mind functions 11.35; sequence 16.280–1; the states that arise from establishing mindfulness more firmly 15.225; contemplating them 'externally' 15.224; resemblance to the twelve positive *nidānas* 15.224–5, 15.579; three discourses on them 8.532; a useful checklist of one's spiritual progress 15.225; using them to help us scrutinize our mental state 15.242–3; *see also* individual *bodhyaṅgas*

sources
Pāli canon 3.667 (n265), 11.369; *Satipaṭṭhāna Sutta* 15.212–26; *Dhammapada* 15.19; Abhidharma 14.80, 14.83, 14.84; *Sūtra of Golden Light* 16.280–1; *Samādhirāja Sūtra* 14.193

(1) sati (mindfulness, awareness)
self-awareness 3.285–6, 11.31–2; classical forms of mindfulness 10.369; the sequence begins with the question 'Am I being mindful?' 15.214; whatever we do, we must do it with a clear mind 9.294–5

(2) dharma-vicaya (investigation of mental states)
ascertaining the ethical status of experience 15.161–2; discriminating between states of consciousness is not an end in itself 15.166; the distinctions the mind makes 18.179; distinguishing between what in the mind is reactive and what is creative 11.32;

the importance of making clear distinctions 10.369; a simple but creative shift of attention 18.53; we have to keep watch over the mind 3.286–7, 9.295–6; we need to know what helps or hinders its arising 15.215–16

(3) vīrya (energy)
elimination of the bad and cultivation of the good 10.369; like an elephant plunging between lotus pools 3.287–8, 9.296–7; with increased awareness energy is released 11.32–3; working with energy 15.216–17

(4) prīti (rapture)
like a silken bag full of air, so light and free 3.267, 3.288, 9.297; a turning point of the spiritual life 10.369–70; a sign that energy is on the move 15.217–19; five degrees of rapture 11.33

(5) passadhi or praśrabdhi (tranquillity)
calming down 3.288, 9.297–8, 15.219–21; a state of peace 10.370; the concentration of vital energy 18.90–1; transition from the psychosomatic to the mental-spiritual level of experience 11.34

(6) samādhi (concentration)
start with one-pointedness 3.288–9, 9.298–9; absorption in positive mental states 10.370; far more than the cultivation of *dhyāna* 15.221–3; the spontaneous merging of all the energies of the psyche 11.34

(7) upekṣā (equanimity)
being like a mountain 3.289, 9.299; complete imperturbability 10.370; you no longer distinguish between self and other 15.223–4; difference from *upekṣā* as an aspect of *vedanā* 17.508–9; in this context, synonymous with Enlightenment itself 3.289; a state of poise and equilibrium 11.34–5

seven days the Buddha sitting under the bodhi tree for seven days: literal or symbolic? 10.427–8; 'the commotion will only last seven days' 10.539–40; developing the foundations of mindfulness for seven days is enough to reach the goal 15.238, 15.242; the king who couldn't concentrate for seven days 3.271–2

seven jewels (or treasures) of the universal monarch (also seven precious things) their causes expounded 14.84; in Buddhist cosmology 13.262, 16.346; in the *Diamond Sūtra* 14.445–7, 14.500; Milarepa possesses them as inner treasures 18.50

seven kinds of followers (faith-follower, one freed by faith, etc.) 2.737 (n651), 4.709 (n333), 8.621

seven *visuddhis* (purities)

introduction
outline 3.289–95, 4.645; introduced in the *Rathavinīta Sutta* ('relay of chariots') 3.290–1, 10.248, 10.578–9; the basis of Buddhaghosa's *Visuddhimagga* 10.578; path of purification 4.292; remind us that the Buddhist path is a path of beauty 3.295, 10.248

(1) sīla visuddhi
paying attention to your ethical life 3.291; encompasses the five precepts 10.249

(2) citta visuddhi
a central purpose of meditation 3.291; getting rid of unskilful states of mind, akin to *dharma-vicaya* 3.292

(3) diṭṭhi visuddhi
purifying the mind of wrong views 3.292, 9.287; you see that you can gain control over your own life 10.249–50

(4) kankhāvitaraṇa visuddhi, 'crossing over by the overcoming of doubt'
Revata reviews his own purification by overcoming doubt 10.577–8; an unwillingness to find out about things, because of reluctance to change 3.292–3, 10.250

(5) magga-amagga-ñāna-dassana visuddhi, 'knowledge and insight into what is the path and what is not the path'
you need to commit yourself to a particular line of approach 3.293–4; a very important stage 10.250

(6) patipadā-ñāna-dassana visuddhi, 'knowledge and vision of the path'
the battleground of the spiritual life 3.294; the next step is to actually tread the path yourself 10.250

(7) ñāṇa-dassana visuddhi, 'knowledge and insight'
fills you with energy and enables you to work for the benefit of others 3.294, 10.251

Sevenfold Puja *see under* devotion/puja and ritual

Sevitabbāsevitabba Sutta *see under Majjhima Nikāya*

sex (biological)

introduction
differentiation into sexes as part of the process of 'evolution' 1.42; not just physical difference, but closely associated with differences of mental outlook 12.283

sexual dimorphism
and *brahmacarya* 2.605; no separation into male and female in the *rūpaloka* 2.371; transcended in meditation 2.371

sexual orientation
the Buddha made no pronouncements about sexual orientation or behaviour 3.322; the Buddhist should feel *mettā* towards all, irrespective of orientation 2.569–70, 23.438; labelling people 'heterosexual' or 'homosexual' 11.583

see also
bisexuality; homosexuality; lesbianism; sex change, *see* transsexuality

sexual activity

introduction
the X factor in most people's lives 17.12, 19.475–6; disproportionate attention given to it 11.587; food and sex are likely to arouse almost everyone's interest 15.154; not necessarily unskilful on its own level 17.638; one doesn't need sex to keep in touch with one's emotions 26.28; the wrong view that everyone needs sexual experience 17.215–16

sexual desire
the cause of rebirth 11.572–3; contemplation of decay an antidote for neurotic sexual desire 4.75, 5.510–11; attraction can be emotional, not sexual 17.217; different responses of men and women 11.577; the emotions connected with sex are unskilful but strong 26.79; even a healthy sexual impulse pertains to a lower level of consciousness 1.10; fear of sexual feelings 17.216–17; a hindrance to spiritual development 24.247; were the monks who painted the images at Ajanta free of sexual desire? 17.226, 21.403; in relation to the subject–object distinction 15.525–6; is sexual desire always craving? 11.573–4; liberating in the direction of self-transcendence (Tantric Buddhism) 7.402–3; no connection with the energies symbolized by the *ḍākinī* 18.425; carried away by sexual passion, we lose the ability to imagine others' feelings 17.598; putting it onto one's spiritual ideal 5.619; refining desire by contemplating beauty 5.511; restraining by concentrating on the repulsive aspects of the body 1.160, 15.125–6; the sex drive is very powerful 11.572–3; sexual craving 17.218–21, 17.271; to the extent that one is dominated by the sex-instinct one is not an individual 26.29

psychological and religious conditioning
freedom from Christian conditioning with regard to sex 12.254; Freud's three stages of sexual development 12.272; clamping down on bodily sensations associated with sex 3.487; the guilt that surrounds sex makes people spiritualize it 17.638–9; in some religions God blesses sex 11.572; living in a culture that overvalues sex 11.586–7; absence of sexual game-playing in India 24.18, 24.116; the effect of contraception on attitudes to sex 11.586–7; being sexually blocked 17.638, 17.776 (n573); 'sex in the head' (D. H. Lawrence) 5.619; sexual instinct (Freud) 10.349; sexual modesty one of the last fetters to be broken, according to Indian belief 20.361; sexual needs not only biological but also psychological 3.527; neurotic and non-neurotic sexual activity 11.538–40, 26.30; turning to the excitement of sex 11.78; using sex to satisfy the neurotic need for change 1.534; viewed from the standpoint of Theosophy 21.446–7

sex itself
does it give energy? 11.574; if your sex life is restricted you need more simple bodily contact 4.562; fetishism 12.230; finding sex distasteful 23.99, 23.172; a gross outlet for emotion 26.194; not much help in developing communication 11.585; orgasm 11.574–5; sexual energy 19.52–3, 19.412; sexual pleasure is often bound up with mental projections 17.393; sometimes when people think they want sex, they just want bodily contact 4.562–3; a source of satisfaction? 11.575–6; a story of sexual incompatibility 23.99; Sangharakshita's army colleagues talking about sex 20.96

sex and spiritual life
'Sex and the Spiritual Life' 11.567–90; complexity 27.1073–4; Buddhism is unique in saying that sex can be an obstacle to spiritual life 11.572–3; the events which led to the Buddha's framing the monastic rule about abstention 14.30; if there was another saṃsāric force as strong, no hope of Enlightenment 3.321, 11.571; if you're serious about spiritual life you'll need to overcome sexual desire 11.573; is a promiscuous lifestyle ethical? 3.566; energy trapped in sexual channels is unavailable for spiritual life 1.390; the effect of sexual activity upon one's state of mind 17.215; abstention from sex does not in itself constitute spiritual progress 1.10; can the sexual act possibly be conducive to spiritual life? 1.390; restraint as preparation for meditation 3.337; no point avoiding sex if you can't find pleasure elsewhere 17.226–7; not associating with prostitutes as a matter of spiritual hygiene 4.545; the important

thing is to bring a spirit of non-harming to our sexual activities 3.322; behaving sensitively and mindfully in one's sexual relations 26.669; a modest sex life compatible with the aim of attaining Stream Entry 17.221; does faith in the Three Jewels come into it? 17.639; for the average Western Buddhist, the question of sex is touchy 11.540

the Buddhist tradition
failure to abstain from sexual intercourse as a *pārājika* (defeat) 3.409, 14.30; a nun questions whether certain activities amount to a Vinaya breach 22.194–5; monks who don't keep their vows 2.580–2, 2.588, 21.20, 21.38; a text predicting unskilful conduct leading to 'the world falling into promiscuity' 11.322; sexual gratification progressively refined in the realms of the gods 16.344–5; sexual symbolism of the Tantra, *see under* Tantric Buddhism/ doctrines and practices; even the married bodhisattva is required to abstain from sexual intercourse 1.442; a bodhisattva as a courtesan to teach those addicted to carnal pleasure 1.448–9; the Tantra advocates shunning sexual pleasure 1.391–2

sexo-yogic practices
in the *anuyogayāna* 12.297–8; discussion with Terry 23.171–2; 'Can you do it with a boy?' 22.568; takes the sexual situation (a paradigm of polarization) and refines it 15.528–30; 'a partner qualified in Mudrā' 18.418; 'Tantric practice with a lady' 19.553

see also
brahmacarya; celibacy; monogamy, *see under* marriage; the place of sex in one's life, *see under* sexual relationships; polyandry, *see under* marriage; sexual ethics, *see under* precepts/third precept

sexual misconduct *see under* precepts/third precept

sexual and romantic relationships

their nature
can be like the realm of the hungry ghosts 13.130; destructive love, 'noble pathos' 26.371–2; a form of organized *kāmacchanda* 5.348; a group of two (*égoïsme à deux*) 3.39; like a lobster pot, easy to get into but difficult to get out of 26.79; the myth (in Plato) of people seeking their 'other half' 23.111, 23.491–2 (n140); not really giving yourself to another person, just striking a bargain 19.534; someone as one's 'other half' 8.548, 17.224; their diamond or *vajra* aspect 7.402–3; there might be intimacy but not much honesty 15.164

romantic love
the difference from *mettā* 17.668–9; different kinds of romantic love 25.106; it is neurotic and should be shaken off 17.656; romantic attachment and projection 17.224–7

danger
of emotional dependence 1.10; of hindering one's development as an individual 3.39; an obstacle to friendship 12.458, 24.542–4; of overloading 3.525

modern tendency to glorify the sexual relationship
misunderstanding of *yab-yum* forms 16.376; specific to Western culture and our own time 3.524–5, 11.697–8; we should steer clear of that tendency 3.322, 13.449–50; the institutionalization of sexual relationships 3.528

the place of the relationship in your life
better not to live with your sexual partner 11.579; can one's sexual partner be one's best friend? 11.576; fidelity 3.566–8, 11.579–80; how do you know when you're over-investing? 11.578–9; if your most important relationship is with your partner 18.505, 18.508–9; in one's personal mandala 11.578–80, 11.587, 12.488, 13.449–50, 18.509, 19.475; most people tend to over-invest in this type of relationship 26.28; not to be idealized or romanticized 17.215; non-continuous or promiscuous 3.566; over-valuation of the sexual relationship 11.577–8, 17.638; tendency to overload the sexual relationship 3.525, 13.450

problems
complicated relationships in Kalimpong 22.324–5, 22.408–13, 22.417–18; advising on the love affairs of Kalimpong 22.446–56; a scandalous relationship in Assam 22.39; seeing evidence of your partner's infidelity 18.579; selfishness in sexual relationships 14.414–15, 17.215, 18.208–9, 19.514; people may think they're disenchanted when they just want a change 10.456–7; experiencing a break-up 11.538–40, 17.506; staying together out of hatred 17.600; attachment leading to hatred 17.564; the awareness that comes with rejection 17.225; why am I doing this? 5.348, 17.220–1

and spiritual life
compassion is a sort of enemy to this kind of relationship 19.514; the 'couple' is the enemy of the spiritual community 8.548–9; living in separate communities 11.579–80; the long-distance relationship as a stage

in spiritual development 24.517; raising a relationship from the *kāmaloka* to the *rūpaloka* 24.517; relationships as a threat to spiritual progress 26.28

sexuality definitions 13.449–50; in modern times immorality tends to be associated with sexuality 15.204; using our sexuality to get what we want 17.216

shadow *anābhāsa* (imagelessness, shadowlessness) 14.219; Bly's *A Little Book on the Shadow* 24.362; compared with all lesser satisfactions, Nirvāṇa is as the sun to shadows 1.129; 'How pleasant is thy shadow, O Śramaṇa!' 2.11; in Jung, *see under* Jung/archetypes; 'In truth everything and everyone/ Is a shadow of the Beloved' (Rumi) 16.588 (n29); 'The lengthened shadow of a man/ Is history' 3.423, 3.685 (n383); Mahars not allowed to let their shadow fall on a caste Hindu 10.309; 'They that sit in the shadow of death' 7.68

Shaga Dawa *see under* Tibetan Buddhism

Shagabpa, Mr and Mrs 21.361–2

Shahn, Ben 2.77

Shahnameh *see* Ferdowsi

Shaivism 7.72

Shakespeare, William

introduction
ability to realize with absolute conviction the life of another human being 3.508; compared with Addison 14.349; Charles Darwin lost his capacity to enjoy Shakespeare 16.532; claim that he is 'the creator of human nature as we know it' 3.602; the development of his personality 26.258; enriched the English language 12.241; the exchange of parts of speech, 'anthimeria' 12.723 (n172), 19.239; his genius 15.194; gratitude towards Shakespeare 3.602; had no problems with limitations of language 16.579; 'He was not of an age but for all time' (Ben Jonson) 8.298; hierarchy in Shakespeare 12.463; his works among the supreme achievements of Western culture 12.392; kingship in the history plays 16.423; lived in a very creative age for dramatic poetry 3.58; saying Buddhism is part of Hinduism like saying Shakespeare 'copied' his plays 2.58–9; Shakespeare surrounded by his characters: analogy with the *sambhogakāya* 15.397–8; Shakespeare's birthplace 14.465; the secularism of his plays 12.76; '... like reading Shakespeare by flashes of lightning' 3.495, 13.73, 19.450; the unpredictable nature of his writing 15.505; we cannot appreciate Shakespeare unless there is something of Shakespeare in us 3.58

As You Like It
'Tongues in trees, books in the running brooks' 18.182, 18.619, 19.69; 'Whoever loved, that loved not at first sight?' 23.149

Cymbeline
cruelty to animals can lead to cruelty to human beings 24.575; a Kabuki-style performance 24.582

Hamlet
once Hamlet has seen the ghost he's a changed man 3.275; going to see the Russian film of the play 23.175; his decision not to kill Claudius 13.574–5; his noble qualities 26.371; 'Imperious Caesar, dead and turned to clay' 15.144; 'My sea-gown scarfed about me' 19.239; 'Nothing good or bad but thinking makes it so' 1.142; Ophelia's death 25.xlviii; 'That sleep of death' 16.262; 'There's the rub' 8.153; 'This above all: to thine own self be true' 3.563; 'To be or not to be' 16.86; 'the fell incensèd points of mighty opposites' 12.344; the play within a play 26.326; superior to *Gorboduc* 13.425; 'There's a divinity that shapes our ends' 25.406; 'There's such divinity doth hedge a king' 16.423; Tibetans might enjoy it 22.114; 'Words, words, words' 18.382; Yorick's skull 4.76

Henry IV part 2
Shakyananda 'the Buddhist Falstaff', 'the lion of the south' 10.liii, 12.573; 'Uneasy lies the head that wears a crown' 16.423

Henry V
Laurence Olivier's film 23.206; 'singing masons building roofs of gold' 26.195; the wording of the death of Falstaff 8.625, 8.708 (n346)

Julius Caesar
the fickle mob 23.461; 'As fire drives out fire, so pity pity' 23.55

King John
its historical significance 13.553–4; a production in Stratford 13.553–4; winter's icy fingers 25.lvi

King Lear
an archetype of family life 18.210–11; if King Lear had attained Stream Entry there would have been no tragedy 16.423; ingratitude 'sharper than a serpent's tooth' 15.253; like King Lear's fool, a fool may have things to say 17.238; 'take upon's the mystery of things' 15.137; 'The thunder would not peace at my bidding' 12.723 (n172)

Macbeth
'cabined, cribbed, confined' 7.217; 'Full of sound and fury, signifying nothing' 7.328, 21.43; has the quality *kāvya* 26.332; 'Out, out, damned spot' 15.376; 'the perilous stuff that weighs upon the heart' 1.412; 'the primrose way to the everlasting bonfire' 17.549–50; 'sound and fury' 24.298

Measure for Measure
a favourite play 24.581; 'Condemn the fault and not the actor of it?' 15.318–19; 'Man, proud man, dressed in a little brief authority' 15.424; 'What we fear of death' 3.211

The Merchant of Venice
a performance 24.582; 'All that glitters is not gold' 13.653; 'the badge of all our tribe' 7.247; 'glassy essence' 26.140; the three caskets and a version of the Buddha's life 13.653, 13.657–8, 13.663; 'Still quiring to the young-ey'd cherubins' 24.82; 'thick inlaid with patines of bright gold' 1.39, 22.203, 24.400; Sangharakshita plays Shylock 20.37

Othello
'He hath a daily beauty in his life/ That makes me ugly' 17.280, 17.654; the woman who shouts that Desdemona is innocent 14.517

Richard II
a performance 24.312; the horror of banishment 17.185; 'I wasted time and now doth time waste me' 3.419

Sonnets
'bare ruined choirs' 22.86; distribution of ten million copies 25.320; 'Like as the waves make towards the pebbl'd shore' 26.293; 'Lilies that fester smell far worse than weeds' 1.443, 26.631; 'Sad mortality o'ersways their power' 1.231; 'When to the sessions of sweet silent thought' 23.15, 24.360

The Tempest
part of a strange sequence of writing 15.505; a performance with an interesting Ariel 24.582; Ariel 13.582; 'the dark backward and abysm of time' 3.32, 7.342, 23.310

other works
Henry VIII 24.581–2; *A Midsummer Night's Dream* 7.297; *The Phoenix and the Turtle* 2.365–6; *Richard III* 24.318; *Romeo and Juliet* 23.255; *Timon of Athens* 2.369; *Twelfth Night* 24.582; *The Two Noble Kinsmen* 15.505, 24.374; 'Venus and Adonis' 25.25; *The Winter's Tale* 12.84

***shakti* cult** *see under* Tantra/Hindu

Shakti and Shiva *see under* Shiva

Shakyananda, Dhammachari 10.liii, 12.573

Shakyananda, Venerable (disciple of U Chandramani) 20.430, 20.431 (photograph), 20.438–9, 20.440

shamanism 12.185, 13.10, 24.380, 26.178

Shambhala, King of 21.49

shame covering up what you consider shameful 19.259–60; feeling ashamed of nudity 19.250, 19.258; a human being should be ashamed not to attempt that which is difficult 11.408; 'Nothing is more shameful than a learned Buddhist who neglects his meditation' 18.486; in a positive sense, *see hrī*; Western Buddhists sometimes feel ashamed of the Buddha 4.465

shamelessness (*āhrīkya*) at its root is lack of love for oneself 17.667; knowing that what you are doing is unskilful, but doing it anyway 17.666–7; as *upakleśa* (Abhidharma) 17.666–7

Shandao 1.337

***shang shang* bird** 13.311

Shankar, Ravi 26.258

Shankara or Shankaracharya (non-dualist philosopher and reformer) *see* Śaṅkara

Shankaracharya (of Puri) 9.348, 20.175–7, 20.343–4

Shankaracharya (of Puri, rival to the other one) 8.168, 22.78

Shankaracharyas (of Shringeri Math) 9.348, 20.369–73, 20.371, 23.16

Shantananda, Swami Saraswati 23.105

Shāntarakṣita *see* Śāntarakṣita

Shantavira, Dharmachari copy-editor 5.xxii, 12.693, 13.523, 14.xx, 14.9, 14.320, 17.xv, 17.152, 17.432, 18.xviii, 26.xix; in Sheffield 24.384

Shantideva *see* Śāntideva

Shantideva, Dharmachari (Stephen Hall) v24

Shantigarbha, Dharmachari 26.374–81

Shantiniketan *see under* Tagore

Shantipada, Dharmachari v24

Shantiprabha, Dharmachari (Adrian Macro) 5.xxxv, v24

sharing because we live at this time, we share the world's problems 12.113–14; the bodhisattva shares himself with people 16.487; the Buddha wanted his disciples to share any honour he received 3.395; the Buddha's advice to the Vajjians: share everything 10.273–4; Buddhism has always stressed that knowledge should be shared with everyone 1.501; collective consciousness shared by individuals with the same spiritual ideals 4.656; different backgrounds and lifestyles but a shared commitment 10.387, 12.665; the difficulty of living in a society whose values you do not share 4.524–5; the duty of employers to share extra profits with the employee 3.587; sharing possessions with others 19.552; simple consciousness is the level of consciousness we share with animals 3.480; if we live a simple life, there will be more for other people 10.396; once you have had a meditative experience, you want to share it 12.645; Sangharakshita shares his almsfood 21.15; the sharing of Going for Refuge with others 2.471–2, 2.524; the spirit of sharing in the sangha 10.273–4; receive rather than take, give rather than impose, share rather than divide 26.35; when you attain insight you want to share it with others 17.348–9

Sharma, Dr Naga Raja 8.228

Sharples, Jim *see* Vipula

Shastri, Lal Bahadur (Indian Prime Minister) 12.79, 12.709 (n59), 23.202

Shastri, Shantibhikshu 22.52–3

shaving the head *see under* monastic life

Shaw, George Bernard brief introduction 23.532 (n419); Sangharakshita reads at school 20.39–40; Gandhi's assassination 'shows it is dangerous to be too good' 10.540–1; *Back to Methusaleh* 23.371; *Candida* 5.201; *The Devil's Disciple* 15.431; *Man and Superman* 2.359, 26.504

Shear, Jonathan 8.613

sheep Christianity compares people to sheep, the Buddha to nobler animals 10.201; 'I have sometimes bleated like a sheep when I should have roared like a lion' 4.445; one is not following the path if one feels forced to follow it like a driven sheep 17.435; the sangha can't be a flock of sheep under a shepherd, nor sheep all going their own way 10.580–1; 'Sheep May Safely Graze' 23.261; the tiger and the sheep 10.167, 10.236–8; the 'white death' in New Zealand 24.51

Sheffield, England 12.681, 24.384–6

Sheldon, William 12.281, 12.724–5 (n194)

Sheldrake, Dr Rupert v24

Shelley, Percy Bysshe

introduction

he didn't create a protective persona 19.122; relationship between Shelley and Godwin 26.223–3; in revolt against conventional morality 3.512; his powers of observation 26.135; 'an ineffectual angel' (Arnold) 25.350; his early death 11.448; Sangharakshita's reading 22.54–5, 22.112, 25.xlvii–xlviii, 25.25, 26.373; a source of inspiration 25.xlvii, 26.398; appreciation for Shelley in India 22.54–5; the exhilarating effect of his poetry 8.19, 26.114; his poems among the greatest treasures of English literature 25.xlvii, 26.398; his poetry is religious in sentiment, though non-religious in subject 26.164; influence on Anagarika Dharmapala 8.19–20; influence on Sangharakshita's poetry 25.xlvii–l; a Western equivalent of a

dharmapāla? 19.410; Trelawny's *Records of Byron, Shelley and the Author* 24.571

Adonais: an elegy on the death of John Keats
its strong effect 25.25, 26.373; 'the contagion of the world's slow stain' 7.352; 'the soul of Adonais' 25.lix; 'that unrest which men miscall delight' 2.124, 8.190; 'waged contention with their time's decay' 2.182; 'wedge sublime' (the pyramid of Caius Cestius) 23.347

A Defence of Poetry
'the best and happiest moments' 14.xii, 8.458, 14.293, 21.23; 'The great secret of morals is love' 2.360, 15.249, 17.598, 26.139, 26.189–90; a poem is 'the very image of life expressed in its eternal truth' 8.458; poets are 'the hierophants of an unapprehended inspiration' 8.458, 26.209; poetry 'enlarges the circumference of the imagination' 26.190; 'regions of light and fire' 13.418

Ode to a Skylark
the only way to share the poet's experience is to read the poem 19.70; beautiful in the highest sense of the term 26.396; 'Hail to thee, blithe Spirit!' 19.595 (n29); Indian students loved its similes 16.327; a symbol of the upward aspiration of the human spirit 23.244, 26.23; 'We look before and after, and pine for what is not' 7.285; its wings are reason and emotion 26.132

Prometheus Unbound
the dialogue between the moon and the earth 25.25; 'forms more real than living man' 5.598; 'I must hurry, whirl and follow' 26.169; 'My soul is an enchanted boat' 25.xlviii; the poem's influence on Dharmapala 8.20; 'The Poet's Dream' 26.135

other works
The Cloud 12.672–3, 21.78–9, 22.464–5, 26.393; *Epipsychidion* 1.158; *The Necessity of Atheism* 11.343, 11.754 (n191); *Ode to the West Wind* 20.54, 21.434, 22.19, 26.211; *The Sensitive Plant* 22.86, 26.399; 'the enchanted heart' 25.151; *Julian and Maddalo* 26.660–1; 'Nothing in this world is single' 7.194, 7.304, 7.399; *Rarely, rarely, comest thou, Spirit of Delight* 3.512; *The Triumph of Life* 25.lix; 'Worlds on worlds are rolling ever' 1.43

shells the bodhisattva emerging from the eggshell of ignorance 3.231; insight is like making a hole in the shell of the mundane 19.435; Nāgārjuna shattered the hard shell of literalism in which Buddhism was imprisoned 1.316; 'Shells' (poem) 25.317

Sherman, Martin 24.403

Shewalay, Prof. N. M. 10.123, 19.132–3, 25.9–10, 26.560–2

shibboleths 19.446–7

shibir *see* retreat

shikantaza *see* just sitting

Shikibu, Murasaki 11.634, 23.472, 23.541–2 (n497)

Shils, Edward v13

Shin Buddhism *see* Jōdo Shinshū

Shin Yeung (Kah Tong) 24.35–6, 24.44–5, 24.54–5

Shingon Shū 1.388, 4.589

Shinje (the Lord of the Dead) 8.559

Shinran Shonin

life
death anniversary 2.228; described himself as being neither a monk nor a layman 2.562; taught by Genko 1.328; initiated into the Amitābha mantra by Honen 1.344; not to be accused of being an innovator 1.346; renunciation of monastic vows 1.344–5, 1.348; a suggestion that Sangharakshita's spiritual life followed a similar pattern 24.529

teachings
all we should seek to attain is an awakening of faith in Amitābha 1.345, 7.42; insights into his teaching in a novel, *The Buddha Tree* 24.532; *An Introduction to His Thought* (Ueda and Hirota) 24.527; other-power (*tariki*) 1.346–8, 1.617 (n273), 3.651 (n165), 11.688; saw Sukhāvatī as synonymous with Nirvāṇa 1.341, 1.345; *Shinshu Shogyu* 1.345–7; *Tanni Shō*: 'Even the good man will be saved. How much

more so the evil man!' 1.199; taught that death and Nirvāṇa were synonymous 1.345–6; a transposition from the intellectual to the emotional mode 1.325, 1.347

Shinshu Shogyu 1.345–7

Shintoism contact with Buddhism when the Dharma spread to Japan 7.144; an ethnic religion 12.248; influenced by the Buddha 2.11, 7.485; its relationship with Buddhism is very interesting 12.248

Shiva (Śiva) seems destructive, but represents the potential for transformation 13.228; appears (as Mahādeva) in a hymn to Tārā 17.146; an attempt to show that Aṅgulimāla was a worshipper of Shiva 8.621; awe-inspiring images 26.383; the bel tree is sacred to Shiva, part of a marriage ceremony 21.41; the cremation ground the domain of 16.71; in the Hindu *trimūrti* (the Destroyer) 16.364, 17.729 (n162); the Himalayas 'the congealed laughter of Shiva' 21.437; the quarrelling of Shiva's ghosts and Vishnu's demons 22.239; Lord of Benares 20.387; Maheshwara, (Shiva) 25.458; makes the love god Kāmadeva invisible 17.691–2, 25.458; Nīlakaṇṭha ('blue-throated') 7.99, 7.580 (n190), 16.398, 26.642; represented in Kathmandu 21.275; said to represent non-Aryan beliefs 19.414; *Śaiva Tantra* 10.46; seduced by Mohini the Deluder 20.365–6; the Shiva-lingam 20.351, 24.76; Shiva and Shakti 22.29; Shiva worship 20.296; Shivaratri 20.162; Sri Aurobindo said to be like Shiva 20.334; takes possession of an impersonator 20.162; trident 19.366–7

Shiwa Aui *see under* Milarepa/disciples

shock doing things to shock Mummy (an attitude which may persist into adulthood) 19.258–9; good preparation can cushion the shock of meditation experience 5.365, 5.366; having a spiritual breakthrough when one has had a shock 11.17; the idea that we are pure by nature may come as a positive shock 5.34; nudity for shock value in the arts 18.634, 19.258; recognition of the truth of *dukkha* comes not as a pleasant diversion but a terrible shock 1.124, 7.392; shock of delight 20.36, 26.392, 26.400; the shock of a holy monk told to have sex: 'Why should I be shocked?' 12.223; shock may have nothing to do with awakening 26.362; the shock of a reversal of standard Buddhist terminology 14.234–5; Sangharakshita's shock at discovering that his ordination was invalid 2.580–1, 21.520–1; Tibetans are shocked to hear the follower of one religion running down another 12.137, 13.111; to make spiritual progress, people need to experience a few unpleasant shocks 17.161

Shōdōmon (path of self-power) *see under* Pure Land Buddhism

shoes a Hindu guru chooses shoe-cleaning as a method of teaching 20.356–7; instead of covering the earth with leather, wear shoes 4.379, 18.80; the indignity in India of beating someone with a shoe 22.441, 23.389; the symbolism of leaving your shoes outside the shrine-room 12.541; taking off your shoes on holy ground (Bible) 25.17–18; a willingness to put oneself in other people's shoes 4.68, 5.175–6, 11.724

Sholapur, India 9.404

'shopping around' 11.xxii, 12.566

Shoreham, Sussex 20.33, 23.242–3, 26.532

Short, Miss (Kalimpong) 21.358–63

Short Cut *see* Pure Land school

Shōtoku Taishi introduction 2.686 (n250); considered as bodhisattva 2.182; observation of his death anniversary 2.228; patron of Buddhism in Japan 2.182, 2.228; perhaps he didn't fully realize the potential of the Dharma as a catalyst for social change 7.512

Shravasti *see* Śrāvasti

Shrine of Wisdom (Fintry Trust) 23.317, 23.525 (n366)

shrines

the shrine-room
the atmosphere in shrine-rooms 19.328; the symbolism of leaving your shoes outside 12.541; an imaginative and archetypal component to spiritual life 10.506–7; how to sit in the shrine room 11.233–4; responding to the beauty of the shrine 11.233; making a resolution in front of a shrine 8.193; create a shrine-room before setting up a soup kitchen 14.447; the word shrine should be used for the whole space, not the image table 11.232; a shrine should not be called an altar 11.232–3; good behaviour within, then letting yourself go outside 14.465; the neglect of a shrine-room 23.137; the pros and cons of eating in the shrine-room 18.426–8

decorating shrines
decorating a shrine in Kalimpong 22.237–9; make preparing the shrine a labour of love 11.233; Sangharakshita's love of decorating shrines 20.259, 20.311; Hinduization of a Buddhist shrine 7.461, 22.97–8; choosing a beautiful Buddha image for a shrine 11.232; making a green shrine for Tārā 5.570, 13.292; use colours related to the figure to whom the shrine is dedicated 5.570; taking good care of the shrine 9.419–20; a book to represent the Dharma jewel 16.59; placing symbols of the *trikāya* on the shrine 11.226; should be simple and aesthetic, but need not be plain 19.128; when decorating a shrine, aim for a rich but simple beauty 11.222

personal shrines
household shrines 2.229–30; every Buddhist home should have one 8.193; every serious practitioner should maintain one 1.406–7; stand for the presence of the Unconditioned in the midst of the conditioned 2.229

Shrivastava, Prof. S. N. L. 7.207–13

Shuddhavajra, Dharmachari v24

Shudras one of the designations for 'Untouchable' 9.31; in Hindu law books, termed a graveyard 9.554 (n77); punished for listening to the Vedas 10.186; 'to be despised' (Tulsidas) 8.xix, 8.358, 20.199; *Who Were the Shudras?* (Ambedkar) 9.76–7, 10.361; *see also* Dalits

Shukman, Henry 24.518–19

Siam *see* Thailand

Sibyls 20.103, 24.595

sickness

sickness, cures, and spiritual experience
becoming irritable when you are ill 17.282; can meditation cure illness? 5.595–6; choosing to look after the sick 18.149–50; failing to sympathize with the sick because you are in good health 17.303; 'The first requirement of a hospital is that it should do the sick no harm' 18.285; human beings psychically and spiritually sick 12.228; serious illness can bring intense spiritual experiences 11.16–17, 13.137; people who are unwell are sometimes more spiritually receptive 17.164; Perfect Vision arising through nursing the sick 1.481; spewing up impurities 10.450–1; spiritual benefits from illness 21.579; types of people who can be cured of illness 14.239

in the Buddhist tradition
ancient Indian ideas about the origin and treatment of disease 14.244, 16.246; 'He who would wait on me, let him wait on the sick' 11.443; the four noble truths based on a medical formula 5.660, 12.98, 12.228, 16.192, 19.227; a form of *duḥkha* 3.210–11; Enlightenment like recovery from illness 13.192–3, 14.42; a bodhisattva precept not to neglect the sick 13.57; chapter on curing sickness in the *Sūtra of Golden Light* 16.406; Vimalakīrti: 'I am sick because beings are sick' 12.228–9, 14.163–4, 16.456, 16.521–3

dysentery
the Buddha had an attack of dysentery 15.369; the Buddha tends a monk with dysentery 4.11, 9.194–5, 10.260, 11.161, 11.432–44, 14.414, 26.658

leprosy
a leper's finger falling into Mahākassapa's bowl 17.771 (n534); a man who thought the only good cause was to help lepers 4.72, 17.285, 25.52; a missionary who looked after lepers 21.354; Rechungpa contracts leprosy 18.309–13; Suppabuddha the leper 10.549–56, 10.672 (n86)

other illnesses
AIDS 11.586, 11.622, 12.408; Sitala, goddess of smallpox 10.46, 16.385, 20.233–4; a swami with hydrocele 22.77; psychosomatic illness 18.535–6

see also
looking after the sick, *see under* helping others; mental illness; one of Yama's three messengers, *see* Yama; Sangharakshita's, *see* Sangharakshita III/old age, sickness, and death; sickness as one of the four sights, *see* four sights

siddha (Tantric sage) the ideal of the Vajrayāna 7.506, 11.319; a man who is so much in harmony with the cosmos that he is under no constraint whatsoever 7.506; a sort of Tantric sage 4.466; Tantric *siddhas* 'went forth' from monastic life 10.629, 18.496; *see also* eighty-four *siddhas*

Siddhārtha Gautama, who became the Buddha

introduction
brief account of his early life 2.19–20, 3.261, 7.143, 12.131; his life described in the *Mahāvastu*, *see Mahāvastu*/volume 2; a vivid description of the events of Siddhārtha's life 22.152

conception
reborn from the Tuṣita *devaloka* 1.190, 1.324, 2.18, 2.179, 4.136–7, 13.570–1;

the Buddha-to-be descends in the form of a white elephant 13.570; the Buddha-to-be emanates a ray that descends into his mother's womb 4.136; could not have taken place as the result of sexual intercourse 1.256; his mother's dream of the white elephant 9.364

birth
celebrated in Japan with a Flower Festival 2.227–8; date 2.19; in the Kṣatriya caste 3.23, 3.49; at Lumbinī 2.19, 3.21, 10.261; 'non-material' 1.256; into the Śākyan tribe 3.21; takes seven steps in each of the directions, and lotuses spring up 2.38, 11.15, 11.738 (n20); the tradition that he was born from his mother's side 10.35–6; tradition that the baby was bathed by the four *lokapālas* 2.228

upbringing
he was brought up in Kapilavastu 17.439; astrologers predicted his future 13.655; the prediction of the sage Asita: a great warrior or a great sage 3.23–4; he was raised by his aunt, Mahāprajāpati Gautami, *see under* Mahāpajāpatī Gotami (Pāli); experience under the rose-apple tree 2.20, 2.110–11, 3.22–3, 5.391–3, 15.222, 18.31; education 3.23; probably could not read or write 2.20, 3.23; warrior training 2.19, 3.23, 3.49, 12.529; his delicate and luxurious upbringing 2.20; 'he had everything, but in a sense he had nothing' 12.624; mansions and dancing girls 2.20, 3.24, 9.191, 10.256; one could say that his wealth was a disadvantage 10.236–7; he had to prove himself by fighting Yaśodharā's kinsmen 3.49; 'The Wounded Swan' 25.200–1; his father's efforts to bind him with pleasure 3.25, 3.34–5, 10.256; his marriage and son 2.20, 3.24–5, 25.491

the decision to go forth
four sights, *see* four sights; disgust at sleeping dancing girls (a misattribution) 2.33; his disgust at a life of luxury 1.58; his struggle to make the decision 3.208

going forth (leaving home)
brief account 10.257, 12.133, 12.359, 12.546, 12.620; the archetypal going forth 11.132–3; no alternative 3.29; 'because of trouble and disturbances': the source of Dr Ambedkar's account 10.221; becomes a *parivrājaka* 2.186; different accounts 10.221–2, 11.397–8; the event related dramatically 3.460; echoes in the story of Josaphat's 'going forth' 13.661; following the time-honoured Indian custom 1.58, 2.20; for us, symbolized going from the old life to the new life 10.257; a great turning point 9.219; heroic, a great wrench 3.49–50; leaving his family 3.29, 11.397, 13.445; praise for his going forth 25.273; 'The Quest' (sonnet) 25.272; sources of the story 3.630–1 (n29), 3.685–6 (n393), 10.221; symbolized by the horse 9.365; it was the beauty of the fourth sight that moved him to go forth 12.551; an undisputed fact 10.221–2; a victory over his attachment to the group 11.398; wasn't it selfish to leave his wife and son? 10.456, 17.191–2; what age was he when he left home? 8.481–2

he exchanges clothes with a beggar
the beggar's delight 3.29; not just an external but an internal change 9.191; a similarity with Josaphat's story 13.661; symbolizes the giving up of social identity 3.40; symbolizes the giving up of the old way of life 10.257

the search
he became a *parivrājaka* (mendicant) 3.460; his search for teachers 1.58, 3.29–30; he employed the principle of trial and error 1.58–9; he was on the path of irregular steps 5.392

his first teachers
he knew there was something beyond all they knew 3.29–30; he left them because they could teach him *śamatha* but not *vipaśyanā* 8.442; his experience of *dhyāna* under the instruction of his teachers 1.166, 2.21, 5.391; his gratitude to them 3.597; leaving them because they couldn't teach him the highest truth 10.257–8; leaving them a victory over spiritual complacency and spiritual ambition 11.398–9; the incident teaches us that however much we learn, we can learn more 10.258; his instinct to teach them the Dharma 11.413–14

overcoming his fear in the jungle
he didn't try to escape it 3.51, 12.620; from this we can learn to let go of our fear 10.258–9; he didn't rationalize his fear, but subdued and conquered it 26.153; he was victorious over fear 11.399

his practice of austerities
canonical source 3.634 (n50); the *devas* offer him celestial nourishment, but he refuses 10.448, 22.285; the five fires 25.252; following a widespread tradition 12.620; he tried many methods which failed 1.58; images of his emaciation 3.51, 3.634 (n51); no sage had gone further 2.21; simply perverse or impressive? 3.52; self-mortification 1.166, 9.219–20, 9.399–400; symbolizes an attempt to gain Enlightenment by force of will 3.40–1;

their fame 'spread like the sound of a great bell' 3.30

giving up austerities
abandoning both self-affirmation and self-denial 11.496–7; he realizes that they are taking him in the wrong direction 3.30, 3.472; a victory over the tendency to refuse to admit one has made a mistake 11.400

his five disciples leave him
their disappointment and disgust 2.21, 3.30; Siddhārtha's courage in giving up their expectations 3.52, 3.472; symbolism of being prepared to be alone on the spiritual path 3.41; loneliness and solitude 1.59, 12.620

he arrives at Bodh Gaya (then Uruvelā)
he is given milk-rice to eat by Sujātā 3.31, 3.42, 9.400, 10.437, 25.256; milk from a goatherd 25.252; a grass-cutter gives him *kuśa* grass to sit on 3.31, 3.42; he sits to meditate 2.21, 3.30–1, 12.133–4;

his memory of his experience under the rose-apple tree
he recollects his childhood experience 2.21, 3.30–1, 18.31, 25.xlv; the memory's decisive effect 2.21, 2.110–11, 5.391–3, 15.222; important knowledge goes hand in hand with innocence 18.31; time stood still – a miracle or symbolic? 3.22–3

his resolve to reach the goal
a six-year search 12.133–4; 'Let blood dry up, let flesh wither away' 3.52, 4.370–1, 5.389, 10.259, 11.16; others' doubts do not trouble him 2.21, 25.256–7; teaches us the quality of perseverance 10.259; for the next part of the story, *see* Buddha I/ Enlightenment

see also
Lalitavistara Sūtra; his father, *see* Śuddhodana Gautama; his mother, *see* Māyādevī; four sights; his teachers, *see* Āḷāra Kālāma and Uddaka Ramaputta; 'Discourse on the Great Renunciation (Going Forth)', *see Abhiniṣkramaṇa Sūtra*; Māra attacks him, *see under* Māra

Siddhatmananda, Swami 20.119–24, v22

Siddhiratna, Dharmachari (Graham Sowter) 23.473, 23.543 (n501), v24

siddhis (success or perfection, sometimes *ṛddhi*) if you get yourself into a skilful way of life, *siddhis* will come without effort 19.578–9; mistakenly thinking that *siddhis* will make you more successful in worldly life 19.460; Perfection's Road 19.393; Tārā as the source 17.143; two kinds, mundane and spiritual (Enlightened) 4.466, 19.214, 19.386–7, 19.459; as (mundane) supernormal powers, *see* supernormal powers; supreme Enlightenment 19.387

Sigālaka* or *Sigālovāda Sutta *see under Dīgha Nikāya*

sights *see* four sights

significance the cosmic significance of the bodhisattva ideal 3.376; distinguishing which incidents of the Buddha's life are of spiritual significance 19.54–5; in a certain state of mind, everything you see has significance 13.120; painting is born of empty space, and derives its significance therefrom 7.322; the simple life glows with significance, the unessential having melted away 7.320–1; one has got to be able to see in the guru what is of universal significance 19.120–1; the significance of ceremonies 24.530–1; the significance of images can change 26.273–6; trying to find more significance in our daily lives: what the spiritual life is about 13.120; ultimately nothing is any more significant than anything else 13.120; you don't imbue something with spiritual significance using external religious symbols 18.428

Sīha, General 8.141, 8.677 (n77)

Sikhī Buddha 1.45

Śikhin (god) 16.468

Sikhism introduction 9.348; Dr Ambedkar's attraction to it 9.57; invitation to Dr Ambedkar to become a Sikh 9.56; Sangharakshita sees millionaire Sikhs in Kasauli 20.219–20; worship of the book, *Adi Granth* 4.306–7, 16.58–9

sikkhā *see* six *gāravas*

Sikkim

general entries
Buddhism in Sikkim 7.464, 21.195–7, 22.243–4, 22.248; the *dewan* of Sikkim 17.84–5; Maharani of Sikkim v22; Pemayangtse Gompa 2.445, 12.440, v22; politics 22.480–4, 23.119, 23.203–4; a 'protectorate' 22.261, 22.596 (n202); Rangpo 22.242; Rumtek Gompa 22.413–14; the Sacred Relics visit Sikkim 21.189–202; Sikkimese Buddhist art 22.349; Sikkimese death ceremony 2.231

Gangtok
Enchay Gompa 22.247; Namgyal Institute of Tibetology 8.402; the Residency 22.319; Sir Tashi Namgyal High School 22.247; 2,500th Buddha Jayanti celebrations 22.318–19; Sangharakshita gives Dharma

talks there 21.195–6, 22.245–6, 22.321–2, 22.470; the 'village capital' 22.242; the visit of the Sacred Relics 21.189–202, 21.569, 22.240

Maharaja of Sikkim (Sir Tashi Namgyal)
introduction 21.583–4; his funeral 21.581

Maharaj Kumar (Palden Thondup Namgyal)
celebration of Vaiśākha Purṇimā in Kalimpong 8.658; complaint about the installation of a giant statue of Hanuman 22.483; first Buddhist president of the Maha Bodhi Society 8.xxi, 9.209, 10.76, 22.64–7; his guru was always drunk, but he was said to be very wise 13.177, 19.160–1; invites Sangharakshita to visit Gangtok 22.240–9; Kachu Rimpoche performed his coronation ceremony 12.442; marriage to Hope Cooke 22.485–6; the Kazi and Kazini's hatred for him 22.414, 22.482–4; patron of the Triyana Vardhana Vihara 8.664; Sangharakshita protests against his plans for the slaughter of animals 22.485–6; sends Sangharakshita food offerings 22.248; Sangharakshita visits him in London 23.203; deposed 24.179

śikṣa (education) 1.430, 2.342–3; *see also* education

śikṣāpadas (Pāli *sikkhāpadas*, rules of training) *see under* precepts/introduction/ Buddhist tradition

Śikṣāsamuccaya *see under* Śāntideva

Śikṣānanda (translator) 14.201–2, 14.217

śīla *see under* ethics

sīla visuddhi *see* seven *visuddhis*

Silabhadra (Xuanzang's teacher at Nālanda) 20.461

Silabhadra, Dharmachari (Tony Bowall) 2.737 (n653), 17.431, v24

Silabhadra, Venerable (Bengali monk) 8.635, v21, v22

Silacara or Silachara, Bhikkhu (J. F. McKechnie) introduction 7.590 (n260); Scottish Buddhist monk 21.348; *Buddhism for the Beginner* translated into Nepali 8.659–60; translation of the *Majjhima Nikāya* 7.590 (n260)

Siladasa, Dharmachari v24

Śīladharma (translator) 14.227

Silaprabha, Dharmacharini (Eve Gill) v24

śīlavrata-parāmarśa *see under* ten fetters/ third fetter

Silburn, Lilian 22.251–3 (photograph), 22.256

silence

the Buddha and silence
beyond the Buddha's smile there is only silence 26.385; he communicates in silence with a group of previously noisy *bhikkhus* 10.510–11; his practice of remaining silent on his almsround 12.157; he remained silent from Enlightenment until death, *see Laṅkāvatāra Sūtra*/chapter 7; his silence about the limits of the world 17.387; his silence when asked about the fourteen inexpressibles 13.393–4, 17.624; sitting in silence with a crowd of monks 2.200, 3.77, 15.103, 16.274–5; tells monks to talk about the Dharma or observe silence 10.472–5, 10.517–21, 10.561, 15.191; he taught through silence 9.226, 11.162; the term *muni* is related to the Sanskrit term *mauna*, silence 3.591–2, 11.202, 14.494

noble silence (ariya-mona)
Anuruddha and his friends live their daily lives in silence 12.606; the Buddha's noble silence, so little understood 7.132; Moggallāna's definition 26.203; the noble silence of the second *dhyāna* 17.624, 26.203

the practice of silence
the benefits of observing silence 9.519, 11.202; conserving energy by observing silence 4.134, 18.482; Dharma practice requires periods of silence and solitude 7.239; difficulties of observing silence 9.519, 10.214; going forth from speech into silence 12.557–8; an important spiritual discipline 11.202; one should be able to maintain inner silence 15.191; silence can be a form of communication 12.557, 14.515; thinking of the ideal in terms of silence 11.320; we need to make more time for silence in our lives 1.524; silence on retreat 23.136; a vow of silence 7.406; a way of freeing the mind from convoluted thinking 14.515

resistance to silence
'The eternal silence of these infinite spaces terrifies me' 14.504; people value words, not silence 13.344; Satyapriya is nearly driven mad by attempts to practise silence 20.375–8; talking to the cat 9.520; a woman who said she would go mad with no one to talk to 13.347

inner silence
in the silence of the heart speaks the voice that makes all things known 7.134; learn the value of silence: not just physical

silence, but the silence of the mind 13.347; only when the egoistic will is 'silent' will the True Sound be heard 7.323; retire within and feel the whisper vibrating through the silence there 7.268; the silence of self-will 26.203–4; the silence of the mind 1.574; 'The Voice of Silence' (sonnet) 25.276

silence and emptiness
entrance to non-duality 16.548–9; silence about Nirvāṇa might be misunderstood 1.82; silence and emptiness are the most important parts of life 7.322; the silence of *śūnyatā-śūnyatā* 4.163

Sangharakshita and silence
experiencing the silence of Ramana Maharshi 1.524; 'The Face of Silence' (poem) 26.595; the profound silence of Terry's flat 23.171; the hush of a Tibetan monastery 7.75; the intense silence of a stay in Shropshire 26.463; the silence of the hills 25.492–3; the silence of a hospital ward 24.351–2; a silence out of which comes a wordless rhythm from which poems emerge 24.168; 'there seemed to be between us and all round us a great ocean of silence' 26.548; wrapped in silence at Guhyaloka 25.435

different kinds of silence
different kinds of silence 16.549; Eternal Finger on the lip of Being (poem) 25.xxxv, 25.361; flashes of silence 1.524; four kinds: of sound, of desires, of thoughts, of the will 26.203; 'The Gospel of Silence, in forty volumes' (Carlyle) 1.525; listening to the silence 16.203; Milarepa relishes silence 18.48; a misunderstood silence 23.174; the noble silence of the second *dhyāna* 17.624; not mere absence of sound, a living silence 1.523–5; silence full of sound 7.141; the silence of the heart 7.134, 25.167; the silence of wisdom 3.592, 9.226; a silence of words, a silence of desires, and a silence of thoughts 7.323; the towers of silence 12.692

see also
thunder-like silence of Vimalakīrti, *see under Vimalakīrti-nirdeśa*/chapter 9; *The Voice of the Silence*, *see* Blavatsky

Silendrabodhi (translator) 14.242

Siliguri 21.566–7, 22.20, 22.22

silk a piece of silk cut in half by a sword 17.462; *prīti* like a balloon or silken bag 3.267, 3.288, 9.297; time taken for a piece of silk to wear away a rock, *see kalpa*

śilpa (Pāli *sippa*) 10.521, 15.404

silver Cunda the silversmith, *see* Cunda; gift of a silver spoon 25.444, 26.455; the lost piece of silver 16.221; 'My mind's a silver awning ...' 25.351; not handling gold and silver, *see under* money; a pillar of silver 2.382; a silver image of Padmasambhava 22.471, 26.228

sīmā *see under* bhikkhu/ordination/ceremony

Simberg, Hugo 26.240

Simeon Stylites, St 4.200, 4.687 (n192)

Siṃha, bodhisattva 16.545

Siṃhamukta, the lion-headed *ḍākinī* 13.244–5

siṃhanāda *see* lion/lion's roar

similes *see* metaphors and similes

Simmonds, Paul v24

simplicity

of lifestyle
anger is the product of frustrated desire, so a simpler lifestyle may help 17.271; the attention we give the body is often unnecessary, even harmful 12.554–5; before we can reduce life to its essentials we must determine what the essentials are 7.320; the Buddha said we need four things: food, clothing, shelter, medicine 10.395–6; in the Buddha's day 10.561, 14.398–9; dealing with one thing at a time in old Tibet 18.220; easier to live simply in a residential community 12.670; if one tries to live simply, craving will be diminished 12.608; and the monastic precepts 2.606; living simply but with no aspiration 18.176; a refined simplicity, like a Zen garden or a Greek vase 2.606; simplicity is the key word 16.207; you might want to simplify your lifestyle as you start to practise the Dharma 10.630–1

the simple life
glows with significance, the unessential having melted away 7.320–1; goodness, truth, and beauty 7.321; is dedicated solely to the attainment of Supreme Wisdom 7.320; a wish for a simple life 25.315; you can only lead a simple life if you remember what life is really for 26.34; a simpler life as a result of faith 3.264; simplifying one's life as support for meditation 3.617; two advantages: we will be more contented, and there will be more for other people 10.396; a visit to a traditional Buddhist family in Nepal 7.352–4; we should try to see not how much we can consume, but how little we can live on 10.396; when working in a right livelihood business 12.607–8, 12.670–1; with practice your contentment will not be dependent on living simply 15.288

other forms of simplicity
keep ceremonies simple 19.535; misled by the apparent simplicity of the Dharma, people stay on the surface 12.34; simplicity's purpose is not to let the business of living get in the way of what's important 26.34; simple people 25.231

see also
a reliable teaching will lead towards simplicity, *see under* Mahāpajāpati Gotami; simplicity and the third precept, *see under* precepts

Simpson, George Gaylord 23.399, 23.535 (n448)

***siṃsapā* leaves** 4.3, 7.50, 25.xxxviii, 25.131–2

sin belief in 'sin' is nothing but a stumbling block 16.508; believing that you are basically wicked will inhibit your practice of the Dharma 17.166; 'Better a live sinner than a dead saint' 26.34, 26.488–9; confessing 'sins' as obstructions to Enlightenment 4.309–10; don't be morbidly preoccupied with it: have awareness, contrition, and resolve to change 1.411; five deadly sins (Buddhism), *see* five heinous crimes; a human being is not by definition a miserable sinner 2.99; the idea of sin weakens the individual 13.468; in Buddhism, ignorance, not sin, is the root evil 17.134; 'Inaction in a deed of mercy becomes an action in a deadly sin' 8.215, 13.609; a real sinner more likely than an ordinary person to become a saint 4.449, 4.467; Śāntideva's intense confession not of original sin, but of his own acts 1.411; term to be avoided because of Christian connotations 16.290; 'Thinking one is a terrible sinner is a very unhealthy state to be in' 3.265; unpardonable 1.334; the Vajrasattva practice is undertaken for the purification of sins 13.82–3; in the West, with our background of sin and guilt, we need much more praise and appreciation 4.622; Christian view (original sin), *see under* Christianity/Christian beliefs

sincerity effective Going for Refuge 3.329, 12.666; for one seeking to understand and explain the Dharma sincerity is not enough 8.599; if we all sincerely practised our religion, inter-religious argument would cease 7.146, 7.588 (n246); it is an employee's duty to be sincere and trustworthy 3.588; a sincere man is often one who has deceived himself 7.327; to one who is sincere, Buddhism marks the beginning of a great spiritual adventure 7.186; a sincere follower of the Buddha who does not gain insight 3.674 (n306); sincerely try to practise non-violence, and you will end practising every other Buddhist virtue 3.319; we can learn from the sincerity of the Tibetans 13.110, 18.62–3; we are full of ideas we do not truly think and emotions we do not sincerely feel 7.266–7; the world truly needs peace, but does not sincerely desire it 7.278–9

sinfulness (*sāvadya*) 16.545

Singapore Chinese in Singapore 20.139–40; a flying visit 24.55; Ramakrishna Mission, *see under* Ramakrishna Mission; Sangharakshita's first visit 7.17, 9.279, 9.488, 20.138–57; in the Second World War 7.110–12, 20.141–2, 26.504

Singh, Beena (Sachin's sister) 22.201

Singh, Gurkipal 20.222

Singh, Gurubaksh 7.447–8, 7.617 (493)

Singh, Ishwar 8.367

Singh, Dr Ravi (Sachin's father) v22

Singh, Mrs (Sachin's mother) v22

Singh, Miss (Sachin's cousin) v22

Singh, Sachindra Coomar *see* Sachin

Singh, Sardar Baldev v22

Singh, Setu v22

Singh, Tilakdhari Prasad v21

Singha, Jaideva 12.741 (n342)

singing and songs at the celebration of Sangharakshita's ninetieth birthday 18.xi; choirs at Buddhist centres 12.558; lusty hymn singing 20.42–3; Milarepa's songs,

see under Milarepa/*Hundred Thousand Songs*; singing suggests freedom of communication and inspiration 18.462; to get the emotions flowing freely 4.256; the songs (*vajragītā*) of Tantric masters 13.179; 'This is not the time for singing' 25.402; 'The Wandering Singer' 25.170–1; we should be careful about the kind of music we sing 12.558

single-sex idea conducive to growth, but the two wings of the Order mustn't drift too far apart 12.402; connected with ideas of communication, spiritual friendship, Going Forth, androgyny 2.517; enhanced spiritual fellowship in a situation free from inter-sex tensions 24.95; living and working with people of the same sex 14.520; need of monks for a 'closed' spiritual community 2.607; not at first envisaged in Triratna 11.520–1; not a principle: method, not doctrine 2.710 (n445); helps one develop qualities which are normally projected 26.26; to progress on the path, single-sex situations are indispensable 2.372; single-sex activities lessen opportunities for sexual misconduct 2.372, 24.247; a respite from sexual polarization 2.372; and those who are attracted to people of their own sex 2.709–10 (n445); to help men and women relate to one another as individuals 26.29; women and men may need to take up different spiritual practices 12.283; women in single-sex situations 26.284

Sinha, Dr N. C. 8.665

Sinha, Malla 22.272

Sinhadevi, Dharmacharini 11.633–46, 12.486

Sinnett, A. P. *Esoteric Buddhism* 20.63; *The Occult World* 8.20; 'The only refuge for him to aspire to true perfection is the Buddha alone' 8.xx, 8.21, 8.90, 22.76; Theosophist activity 8.21, 8.23

sippa *see śilpa*

Siraj ud-Dauluah 22.59

Siri Rahula *see* Thotagamuwe

Sirinivas, Ven. Nayaka Mahāthera 20.419

Sistine Chapel *see under* Italy/Rome

Sisyphus 2.261, 2.696 (n347)

Sītā *see under Rāmayāṇa*

Sitala (goddess of smallpox) 10.46, 16.385, 20.233–4

Sitaram, Mr 21.386–8

situation

your situation
avoid any feeling that you're trapped in the family situation 18.455–8; developing a clearer understanding of it 17.260; don't try to squeeze pleasure out of it 17.507; ethics are about being less bound by one's present situation 17.598; learning to see its complexity 17.626; making it creative for yourself and others 3.473; mindfulness is bearing its true nature in mind *all the time* 3.324; in a situation that has a negative effect on you, run away 15.369; seek to learn from painful situations rather than run away from them 8.526; it is usually possible to change it 15.117; no choice of starting point, but we can choose what to make of it 17.434; objectify it by talking about it with a friend 17.614–15; practising contentment in an unsatisfactory situation 15.289–90; seeing that a 'negative' situation is actually positive 4.418; there is no foolproof situation because into it you bring the fool 19.363; wanting something that it can't give you 18.207; when it's no longer helping you to grow, be ready to move on 17.371; wrongly thinking that by changing it you can escape suffering 7.220; you can't be deceived if you enter a situation with integrity 26.35; your duty relates to the principles you believe in and your situation 26.73

situations
any situation is conditioned and impermanent 17.371; avoiding the truth of the immediate situation 15.272; the Buddha concerned with the realities of the human situation 1.123; death: the paradigm of the inescapable situation 15.376–7; even the closest friends may perceive the same situation differently 24.433; everyone in a positive situation has played their part in creating it 19.536; gaining Stream Entry in a workaday situation 5.638; 'having' an experience is really a situation in which perception takes place 13.151; helping someone to extricate themselves from a harmful situation 19.514; living in a situation that is conducive to growth is a rare opportunity 3.464; Milarepa sees his situation with creativity 18.13; a potentially vajric situation 13.172; thinking any situation guarantees spiritual progress is formalism 19.362; *upekṣā*: the ability to take in the whole situation 18.53–4; work as an intensive situation in which insight could arise 13.172

see also
crucial situation, *see under* cremation ground; objective situation

Sitwell, Edith books found in New Zealand 24.574; her maid reports that she isn't busy, 'only writing' 3.506–7, 18.267; 'The Coat of Fire', partly derived from *The Tibetan Book of the Dead* 7.450; sensitivity to words 3.507

Sitwell, Osbert 3.506–7

Sitwell, Sacheverell 24.417, 26.307–8, 26.444

Sīvali (*arhant*) 2.229

Sivalibodhi, Bhikkhu 24.117

Sivaraksa, Sulak 12.516

Sivis, king of the *see under Jātakas*/stories about humans

six *abhijñās* (Pāli *abhiññas*)

introduction
1.166–8, 2.750 (n728), 14.648 (n440), 22.612 (n310); list 1.167, 3.645 (n125); in the Abhidharma 14.83; Buddhist tradition takes them both literally and symbolically 19.62–3; canonical reference 4.709–10 (n334); the *chaḷabhiñño* (possessor of the six superknowledges) 14.81; developed by the preacher of the *White Lotus Sūtra* 14.128; and the *dhyānas* 1.170, 3.122; experienced in the *manomayakāya* 17.622; how they relate to the Enlightenment experience 14.493; magic power of the Tathāgata 1.255; to be mastered by the bodhisattva 1.443; Milarepa performs the *abhijñās* 19.62; all mundane except the last, and thus spiritually insignificant 1.167–8; not desirable, or to be exhibited to impress or 'convert' people 1.167; some people apparently go all the way to Enlightenment without developing them 1.584; three experienced by the Buddha in the course of Enlightenment 2.111

see also
manomaya (mind-formed body); divine ear (*dibba-sota*), *see* clairaudience; telepathy; remembrance of former births, *see under* rebirth/how it works; divine eye (*dibba-cakkhu*/*divya-cakṣus*), *see under* five eyes; destruction of the *āsavas*, *see* three *āsravas*

six bases or sense organs (*ṣaḍāyatana*) includes the mind in the ordinary sense 10.512; symbolized by the empty house on the wheel of life 2.75, 2.254; without objects to perceive, the sense organs cease to be sense organs 17.404; as fifth *nidāna*, *see under* twelve cyclical *nidānas*

six element practice

INTRODUCING THE PRACTICE

introduction
brief description 11.404–5; sources 3.647 (n138), 3.676–7 (n318), 4.675 (n102), 5.484–5, 19.617 (n175); in use in the Buddha's time 5.35; an insight (*vipaśyanā*) practice 5.32–3, 5.485, 15.110, 18.513, 19.453; Sangharakshita received the practice from Yogi Chen 5.484; 'The Six Elements Speak' (poem) 25.xxx–xxxi, 25.440–1

its nature
the contemplation of the incessant flux of the elements 15.136; an effective practice, which is why one resists it 5.482; Milarepa integrates the elements into non-dual awareness 18.66; a minute examination of the components of our material existence 14.418; not to be understood in too rational a way 5.481–2, 5.484; the practice and spiritual death 5.32–3; probably not to be done outside the retreat situation 5.483, 5.490; a sort of introduction to *sādhana* 5.486, 5.605; and the *śūnyatā* mantra 5.489; a sort of *śūnyatā* meditation 5.32; more practical and concrete than meditating on *śūnyatā* 5.32; stripping away the elements to nothing, like the core of the banana tree 17.382–3; when we die, 'our' elements will disperse across the universe 15.111

the purpose of the practice
counteracts the poison of conceit 3.136, 3.348–9, 4.78, 5.29, 10.532, 11.404–5, 19.227; to overcome the wrong view that one has a fixed self 17.623; preparation for ordination 2.387, 5.485, 5.489; a reminder of death 11.448; develops selflessness 11.405; directly attacks the notion of an ego 19.453; it dissolves the idea of one's own individuality in a narrow sense 4.80; eradicates covetousness 2.387; eradicates delusion 2.392

THE PRACTICE ITSELF

method
method 3.134–6, 3.348–50, 4.78–80; in the system of meditation 5.32–3, 5.486, 5.490; the stupa as the basis 13.64; different forms of element practice 5.486–7; interleaving the practice with the *mettā bhāvanā* 5.184; why are the stages in the order they are? 5.483; 'Death and the Bodhisattva Trainings' studied as preparation 24.310–11

(1) earth
the earth element within and without 3.134–5; ashes to ashes, dust to dust

4.78; the sense of 'I' starts to lose its firm outlines 3.349

(2) water
everything fluid within us and in the world 3.135; giving it back 4.78; the dissolving of 'I' 3.349

(3) fire
let the heat element in me go back to the universe 3.135; its source is the sun 4.79; the cooling of the passion of 'I' 3.349

(4) air
the borrowed breath of life 3.135, 3.350; finally giving back the breath 4.79; we share with all breathing beings the same body of air 15.111

(5) space
ākāśa 3.350; the arbitrariness with which things occupying space are divided up 19.239–40; merging with the vast space around 4.79; giving up space: the simile of the broken pot 3.135–6, 5.482; and the infinity of space 5.485

(6) consciousness
clear, bright consciousness 5.485; it resolves itself into a higher and wider consciousness 3.350; even one's consciousness is not really one's own 3.136, 17.623; freed from limitations 5.485; 'giving back' ideas that you normally think of as your own 19.39–40; giving up consciousness 5.483; reflection on infinity of consciousness 4.80, 16.447; 'self' is a tiny fraction of limitless multidimensional consciousness 17.522; withdrawing from the different levels 4.79

see also
individual elements; stupa visualization, *see under* stupa

six *gāravas* 3.69–71

Six Pandits 8.528

six *pāramitās* or perfections *see under* perfections

six realms *see under* wheel of life

six senses *see* senses

sixteen the age of 16 is reckoned to be the prime of life 18.238–9; good works undertaken for rebirth not worth a sixteenth part of *mettā*, the heart's release 2.315; the significance of bodhisattvas being depicted as 16 years old 2.316, 18.238; the 16 *arhants* 2.316; symbolic associations of the number 2.315–16

sizar 16.106

Skanda Purāṇa *see under Purāṇas*

Skandhakas *see under* Vinaya Piṭaka/other sets of rules

skandhas (Pāli *khandhas*) *see* five *skandhas*

skeletons a Nepalese nun who had a vision of her dead brother as a skeleton 20.434; the Romans had skeletons at their feasts, to remind them of mortality 13.228; seeing people as walking skeletons 15.572; skeletons on the escape route from Burma to India 22.277; 'You delight in a village full of walking skeletons' 4.627; *see also* bones

skilful (*kuśala*)

WHAT IS SKILFULNESS?

introduction
definition 9.187, 11.129, 17.164; associated with disinterestedness, friendliness, and wisdom 11.308; *kuśala* is a very important term meaning 'clever, skilful, expert' 2.340, 15.262–3; *kuśala* makes it clear that intelligence is required for skilful action 11.129, 15.349–50; the meanings of *kuśala* and ethics coincide 2.340; using the words skilful and unskilful rather than good and evil 11.129; 'skilful' is not necessarily equivalent to 'healthy' 17.164; applicable only to karma-producing volitions and associated mental phenomena 1.142; positive emotion is pleasurable and at the same time skilful 26.77; you can suffer evil but stay skilful 15.368–70

distinctions
the avoidance of harmful emotions and the cultivation of positive ones 15.263; the difference between skilful and unskilful (*akuśala*) 9.271–2, 9.296, 17.636; the error of not distinguishing between lower and higher orders of skilfulness 17.639; the difference between delighting in the skilful and in the unskilful 15.350–1; not being able to distinguish between skilful and unskilful (*avidyā*) 17.607; receive what is skilful and reject what is unskilful 12.480–1, 26.61

SKILFUL MENTAL STATES

introduction
characteristics of a skilful mental state 15.263–4; characterized by contentment, love, understanding, and clarity of mind 3.102; characterized by harmony of consciousness 15.115; confidence in one's ability to develop skilful states 2.260; every skilful mental state has an inbuilt tendency to transcend itself 18.207; in skilful states we act out of awareness and empathy 15.263; *śraddhā* (faith) is present

in them all 1.291, 17.43, 17.557, 18.207, 26.36

skilful states in meditation
claiming to be in continuously skilful states without meditating 5.645, 18.498; a gathering of skilful mental states 5.435; intensification of skilful mental states 5.650–1; the uninterrupted production of skilful mental states 5.644–5

developing and developed skilful states
the bodhisattva wants to share his skilful mental states 15.371–2; the cultivation of beautiful states of mind 25.46; mindfulness encourages skilful states to grow 17.xxiii; the sangha encourages their development 11.130; the *vīrya* needed to bring about wholesome *dharmas* 17.69–70; we can't always have skilful mental states before we do skilful things 11.267; without insight they are vulnerable to circumstances 18.512; whatever skilful mental states you develop, you can spark off in others 4.95

SKILFUL ACTION (*KUŚALA-KARMA*)

what is it?
action directed towards the best possible results for oneself and others 2.340; action free from craving, hatred, and confusion (delusion) 1.530, 7.508; action is skilful or unskilful not according to rules but according to state of being 3.102; being active in the skilful sense 18.423; its defining characteristic is freedom from narrow self-interest 15.263–4; the definition of a skilful act 26.18; motivated by generosity, love, compassion, and understanding 1.530, 7.508; whether an action is skilful depends on the state of consciousness 15.90

how does it come about?
the Dharma is a force that makes possible your skilful activities 15.631; Enlightened beings do not have to try to act skilfully, it's their nature 14.440; can be performed by all beings 16.425; it's sometimes hard to do something evil, easier to do good 4.289; no conflict between what you know you should do and what you actually do 18.459; positive mental events produce skilful actions 17.589; we can't always have skilful mental states before we do skilful actions 11.267; what is skilful for one person may not help another 15.291

its Buddhist history
acts performed by a king 16.424; Buddhist history is a living tapestry of skilful actions 11.315; its benefits are attested and exemplified by the great Buddhist saints 15.93; does Buddhism advocate skilful action as a mean to one's own ends? 3.245; feeding the poor, providing for the sick, digging wells, planting shady trees 3.315; there is no good deed that falls outside the scope of the Way 16.41

consequences
the basis for developing a connection with the transcendental 16.354; can it be good to do the right thing for the wrong reason? 5.373, 11.430; the creative power of skilful actions 1.342; doing something skilful, you feel that you are on the side of life 15.351; the foundation of any higher spiritual experience 15.90; clarity of mind 17.613; good works undertaken for rebirth not worth a sixteenth part of *mettā* 2.315; happiness 16.419; karma 2.70, 15.395–9, 15.90; perfect work comes from the unification of pure wisdom and pure deeds 26.19; present skilfulness will bring us future joy 3.317; *punya* (merit) is the quality of your being brought about by skilful actions 15.401–2; the pure seeds of the *ālaya vijñāna*, *see under* eight *vijñānas*; rebirth in heaven realms 3.315, 3.324; Sāriputta explains what kind of conduct makes skilful states grow 2.328–9; skilful actions eventually bear positive fruit 15.92; to counterbalance unskilful action 4.291–2

things to watch out for
good deeds that produce too acute an awareness of your own goodness 7.282; don't think 'This skilful action is going to help *me* gain Enlightenment' 2.270; is what you are doing really the most skilful thing at this moment? 18.51; performing 'good' actions egotistically binds you to the wheel of life 7.409–10; skilful actions done for approval pave the way for unskilful actions 18.165

see also
skilful mental states, *see under* mental states

skilful means (*upāya-kauśalya*)

notes on skilful means
the term's appearance in the Pāli canon 16.626 (n330); be careful about promising people worldly success as a skilful means 19.460; don't make arguments based on teachings that someone has yet to accept 4.407; don't confuse skilful means with capitulation to the group 19.261; identical with compassion 7.457; distinguishing between skilful means and conformity to mental conditioning 19.526; learning the array of teachings to place them at others' disposal 18.413–14; prematurely adopting 16.231; truthful speech and

skilful means 17.232–3; use whatever knowledge you've got to establish contact with people 18.414; using any medium you can to communicate the Dharma 19.206; viewed from the perspective of *śūnyatā*, any term or concept is an *upāya* 15.186–7; we ourselves must become skilful means 16.497–8

the Buddha
adopts the appearance and speech of those he is talking to 2.647, 12.523–5; he protects people from an experience for which they are not ready 14.183; he teaches according to the different needs of different people 9.359; his communication 4.21; his message is simple, but has been elaborated for the sake of different people 18.495

and the Mahāyāna
why does the Mahāyāna hold skilful means in such high regard? 16.481–4; the bodhisattva's practice, the seventh *pāramitā* 1.395, 1.448–9, 16.481–5; the Buddha's earthly career and *parinirvāṇa* were skilful means 1.250, 4.85, 14.188; in the parable of the burning house 14.115, 16.74, 16.83–4, 17.232–3; preaching the Dharma as skilful means (*Sūtra of Huineng*) 7.34; a *sūtra* on the subject of skilful means 14.188; Vimalakīrti's 'liberative technique' 16.479–81; Mañjuśrī goes to extreme lengths to free bodhisattvas from obsessive remorse 14.183; wisdom and skilful means as the twin aspects of the Buddha's teaching 1.122; the all-performing wisdom of Amoghasiddhi 3.374–5

examples
black magic? 18.361–2; the categories of Buddhist thought 14.409; comparison of Buddhism with science 1.39; cultivating goodness 7.35; *dhāraṇis* 16.496–7; manners and conventions 19.255; Pith-Instructions 19.204; popular Buddhism 2.218; tolerance 7.384; wearing appropriate clothes 19.526

see also
the Buddha's teaching to Kisāgotamī, *see* Kisāgotamī; perfection of skilful means, *see* perfections/seventh perfection; *pratisaṃvids* (analytical knowledges), *see* four *pratisaṃvids*; *saṃgrahavastus*, *see* four *saṃgrahavastus*

Skilton, Andrew (ex-Dharmachari Sthiramati) brief introduction 17.7, 24.635 (n149); in Manchester 24.130, 24.134–5; *Bodhicaryāvatāra* translation 24.516–17; *A Concise History of Buddhism* 4.664–5 (n36)

skull and skull-cup *see under* bones

sky

the symbolism of the sky
all gods are sky gods 16.385; the Dharma taught by means of 'lights in the sky' 16.563; 'The Mind is like the sky' 7.336–7; the 'path of the sun' (*Dhammapada*) 15.28, 15.745 (n12); primordial dualism of earth and sky 16.385; reality is like the unclouded sky 14.361–2; roots in the sky 4.37, 10.620, 14.590; the sky of the One Mind in which *ḍākinīs* dance 12.294; the sun shining from a cloudless sky 18.614; symbolizes *śūnyatā* 5.603–4

blue sky
Akṣobhyā's dark blue colour is like the midnight sky without any stars 12.213; the beauty of the blue autumn sky 7.336; the blue sky of Tibet and its contribution to Tantric visualization 26.221; the Buddha like the sun shining in a clear blue sky 26.125; the *dharmakāya* like the pure blue sky 4.204; how can you wish the blue sky health and fortune? 19.503; the mind like a clear blue sky, free of clouds of conceptualization 1.586; in the New Forest 25.329; nothing but dark blue sky above one's head and brown earth beneath one's feet 24.105; represents freedom from all obscurations 13.282; symbol of *śūnyatā* 5.603–4, 13.67, 13.204, 19.454; visualizing the blue sky at the start of visualization practices 5.488–9

sky-dancers *see ḍākinīs*

sky-father 19.141

Slade, Madeleine *see* Mirabehn

slavery Abraham Lincoln and the end of the slave trade 1.534 (n443), 1.546, 'all beings in the Three Realms enslaved in a prison of fire' 18.588–90; always condemned and prohibited in Buddhist countries 3.582–3; being a slave to work 18.294; Buddhist countries condemn and prohibit slavery 3.582–3; declared unethical in the Pāli canon 1.546; the Biblical story of Israel's bondage and oppression 16.220; in ancient Greece 15.278; religion purports to bring freedom but keeps us enslaved 16.499–500; 'the slave-labour of the hungry' (Milarepa) 18.294; slavery as wrong livelihood 1.546, 3.582–3, 12.670, 13.454; slavery of Dalits 9.135, 9.222; we are slaves to our unaware and ignorant desires 16.220

sleep awareness of having been asleep 17.518; clear consciousness shines through sleep 1.151–2; Dharmapala's practice with

regard to sleep 8.12; effect of meditation on sleep 3.337–8, 17.686; fondness for sleep despite the reality of death 4.471–2; getting the right amount of sleep for meditation 5.294, 5.305–6, 5.332–4; hatred takes away one's sleep 17.602; one sleep pattern is not more virtuous than another 17.684; praise of sleep (*Don Quixote*) 3.338; preparing yourself for sleep 19.322; the purpose of sleep 3.338; reciting verses or mantras before sleep 17.686; if you sleep too comfortably, it may be hard to get up 19.95–6; living one's life, even one's spiritual life, in a sleep of unawareness 11.24, 26.47; not really 'unification with the essence' (as suggested) 8.457–8; sleep as a *bardo* state 19.321–2; sleeping in is unskilful 19.97; sleep is a recuperative state 17.684; sleeping well is one of the eleven benefits of practising *mettā* 4.394, 17.602; sleep on solitary retreat 5.679–80; the symbolism of sleep 16.170–1, 16.218; taking sleep for granted 16.252; you can fall asleep mindfully 15.97; *see also* tiredness

sleepiness *see* drowsiness

sloth the adversary of *vīrya* 4.470–1; if you have a sluggish temperament, think of the spiritual life in terms of an active symbol 18.525; how does sloth arise? 4.470–1; one should resist slothfulness as one who leaps up when a snake is in their lap 4.480; sloth is the weight of one's existence resisting further evolving 26.47

see also
laziness; sloth and torpor in meditation, *see under* five hindrances

Small, Bill v22

Smaller Sukhāvatī-vyūha Sūtra *see under Sukhāvatī-vyūha Sūtras*

Smaragdine Tablet *see under* Hermes Tresmegistus

Smart, Christopher 26.332

Smart, Ninian 13.403–5

smell the Big Cat house at London Zoo 26.424; dogs' sense of smell 16.559, 26.498; the far-spreading effect of incense scent as a metaphor for spiritual practice 13.253; the fragrance of *devas* in a house in Kalimpong 11.236–7; the importance of the sense of smell 24.567, 26.491–8; its indirect nature 16.558; the language of smells and scents 26.497–8; the least well developed of all our senses 16.559; 'Lilies that fester smell far worse than weeds' 1.443, 26.631; a lotus whose spirit told a monk not to steal its scent 26.243; a means of communication 16.561–2; memories evoked by smell 26.491–8; the odour of sanctity 11.237; personal 16.561–2; relationship between scent and mood 11.235–6, 16.559, 20.34; the smell of death 16.562; *see also* perfume

smile the smile of the Buddha 11.492, 25.403; beyond the Buddha's smile there is only silence 26.385; Dilgo Khyentse Rimpoche's sweet smile 12.447, 12.450; giving someone a smile 25.114; 'the new-born lotus smiles beside the crystal fountains' 25.345; bodhisattvas address others with smiling countenances 2.154; the smile of the *arhant* 4.137, 12.146; the sun-smile of Enlightenment 25.257; a single smile of beauty 26.189; the beatific smile of the young man in the hut 26.595, 26.597–8

Smith, Stevie 26.398

Smith, Sydney 1.524, 17.394–5

smoking attitude of traditional Buddhists to smoking 21.181; giving up smoking 4.423, 4.617, 10.223, 17.303; regarded as a sin in the Boys' Brigade 13.609–10; Sangharakshita as a smoker 3.537; unskilfulness of dealing in tobacco 3.583

smṛti *see* mindfulness

snakes and serpents

snake facts
among the few beings not present at the *parinirvāṇa* 14.233; eaten by peacocks 25.396

snake similes and symbols
the Dharma is as difficult to grasp rightly as a water snake 1.78, 18.180; realizing that one is grasping a snake, not a fish (Buddhaghosa) 2.116; rejecting one's weaknesses like a man throwing off a snake 8.586; resist slothfulness as one who leaps up when a snake is in their lap 4.480; the energies of the unconscious in their positive, creative aspect 2.37–8, 12.189–90; the rope of clinging cut, the *bardo* disappears 'like the uncoiling of a snake' 18.612–13; the serpent: one who has destroyed the *āsavas* 1.309–10, 14.346; 'a serpentine movement through incalculable dimensions' 14.140; Ananta the cosmic serpent (Hinduism) 16.398, 26.641; Sesh, the Cosmic Snake (Hinduism) 25.458

cobras
a cobra in a basket remains a cobra still 25.445; a cobra who was the companion of an ascetic 20.331; the disciple who

had to meditate with a 'cobra' in his lap 20.354–5; Jagdish Kashyap's *mettā* tested by a cobra? 9.521

see also
at the hub of the wheel of life, *see* wheel of life; Mucalinda the serpent king, *see* Mucalinda; *nāgas* as elephants or dragons, *see* elephants and dragons; the serpent maiden and Nāgārjuna, *see under* Nāgārjuna/life story; the snake who swallowed a frog, *see* parables and stories

sneha (affection, attachment) 4.526, 4.570

Snellgrove, David

introduction
introduction 21.564; he adopts Cambodian children orphaned by the Khmer Rouge 8.602; his gift for friendship 8.601; his visit to Kalimpong 22.81

works
Asian Commitment (review) 8.600–2; *Buddhist Himalaya* 2.174, 21.560; *Himalayan Pilgrimage* (review) 8.353–4; *Indo-Tibetan Buddhism* 8.602, 24.311; 'Mila Repa and the Novices' 18.41; translation of the *Hevajra Tantra* 12.104, 12.210

Snow, C. P. 3.6, 3.625 (n2), 4.523

Snow-White 25.358

Snyder, Gary 4.383, 22.566, 22.630 (n418)

sobornost a clue to the nature of the spiritual community 2.474, 23.209; expressive of collective consciousness 4.656; the term in a book by Timothy Ware 23.209

social conventions *see* convention

social identity giving it up, symbolized by Siddhārtha's exchange of clothes with a beggar 3.40; think clearly about it 9.533

social life Buddhists should try to live their social life in accordance with the Dharma 7.439; the giving of gifts emphasized in social life 1.533; is it impossible for the bodhisattva to conform to the conventions of social life? 1.442; modern social life doesn't involve much in the way of friendly communication 18.152; one-parent families may give children a sense of alienation from social life 10.73–4; the Pāli canon's insistence on the importance of being at ease socially 10.644–5; the pull of joining the social whirl 16.287–8; the Pure Land: Enlightenment as a 'social experience' 18.305–6; social pressure keeps us immersed in trivial pursuits 3.35

social work the bodhisattva ideal is not to be equated with the secular concept of social service 8.460–1; 'Buddhist monks ought to be social workers' 21.86; a good thing to do, but not Buddhism's main thing 4.440–1; practising social work as a substitute for practising the Dharma 24.327–8; teaching the Dharma is more meritorious 14.446

socialism 11.604, 26.488

society

what is society?
definition 11.459; composed of true individuals and statistical individuals 13.458–9; the family as model of society 16.428–9; it needs shared values 26.74; its insistence on self-control 11.195, 16.434, 19.261; the need for a pluralistic society 26.74; three aspects: social, political, and economic 1.541–3

traditional society
the context for Dharma study 1.25–6; description of a traditional civilization 1.27–8; everything linked with ideas of a metaphysical order 3.10–11; studying the Dharma in a non-traditional society 1.29–30; supports those engaged in spiritual activity 4.94; supports the ordinary group member 15.488; it is easier to live a Buddhist life in a traditional society 7.395

the moral order
introduction 16.428–35; assumption that society's ethics must be Christian 12.406–7; a collapse accompanied by sexual promiscuity and incest 11.322–3; collapse when 'the king overlooks an evil deed' 16.429–32; creating a moral society 16.428; modern breakdown 4.105, 16.431–2, 16.434; restoration through the spiritual community 16.432–4; positive effects when upheld by the king 16.435, 16.477; society held together by law or morality (Ambedkar) 9.104, 9.181; there will always be a minority who try to harm others 26.73; why should the social order be a moral order? 11.321–2, 16.427

the individual and society
society seen as insignificant compared to the individual 13.385; danger of becoming more positive but ignoring the difficulties of society 10.73; education must enable the individual to function as a member of society 26.71; we cannot isolate ourselves from society 3.622; we exist as individuals, but also as members of society 4.89

modern society
complexity 16.432; escape is no longer possible: modern societies will not leave anyone alone 18.34; the higher our standard of living, the more control society has over us 11.356–7; 'permissive' 12.255; resentment, because it gives us everything without telling us how to use it 17.269–70; some emotions need to be suppressed in everyday society 11.194–5; those of different ideologies must see the need for peaceful coexistence 26.74

difficulties
alienation 18.335; fragmentation 13.392; living in a society whose values you do not share 4.524–5; shifting responsibility for one's actions from self to society 13.389; you can't live in an unethical society without being besmirched by it 1.540; young people's sense of frustration 18.457–8, 26.194

changing society
Buddhist view of social reform 13.390; burning up old ways 9.225; the Dhamma revolution in India shows that it's possible 10.315; Dharma practice will bring about a complete change 9.525–6; to alleviate poverty 9.340; transforming society 1.540–3; we must work to make actual changes in society 10.315; to support the individual 7.239, 9.285, 10.207; the value of art to the whole community 26.194; through establishing single-sex communities 15.473–4; we should appreciate the positive features of the existing society 12.488; what happens when societies come into contact with one another 15.488–9; wish to change it 9.508

society and the spiritual community
how the sangha stands in relation to society 13.515; maintaining a society in which the spiritual community can flourish 11.271–2; progressing from society to the positive group 18.359; the sangha must keep in contact with the wider society 11.272–3; social helpfulness of Buddhism 7.127; society at the time of the Buddha 1.543; society should be directed by the Dharma 7.239

ideal society
introduction 1.538–40; Buddhism stands for its creation 1.540; Buddhism's social ideals 7.511–2; sangha as model 1.550, 9.114, 10.348; Sukhāvatī as an archetype 1.539

see also
new society; Western society

Society of Servants of God *see under* Dr Mehta

Socrates

his life
emergence in the Axial Age 3.427; his own greatest work of art 3.471; it is doubtful whether he was an agnostic 8.588; notoriously ugly 10.619, 19.182; his daimon 13.591, 13.720–1 (n380); the 'Great Midwife', bringing ideas to fruition 18.301; Nietzsche's view that Socrates' activity was destructive 19.182–3; sentenced to death for 'corrupting' the youth of Athens 26.179–80; his death 3.472, 3.524, 15.348

methods
catechetical method 8.169; his dialectical method compared to that of Nāgārjuna 1.312; his logical arguments are sometimes less than compelling 17.376; Plato's reconstructions of Socratic dialogues 10.552; to begin with, his development of reason was rather 'brittle' 15.743

teachings
'An unexamined life is not worth living' 18.164; his definition of the good man, who 'produces' virtue (*arete*) 15.404–5; his ethical theory fails to consider 'the irrational parts of the soul' 11.192, 26.164; 'Socrates is a man' (syllogism) 19.186–7; 'To know the good is sufficient' 11.192

Soft, Dr Madhuram v21, v22

Sogen, Yamakami 1.186, 1.609 (n166), 4.495, 4.590, 7.200–2

Sogyal Rimpoche 23.384, 23.533 (n432), 26.460

Sokkhasobhano, Preah Maha 21.468

Solanki 24.100, 24.118

solar symbolism *see under* sun

solitude

notes on solitude
art as what a man does with his solitude 26.67; the challenge of finding solitude 15.102; an essential human need 5.670; fear of being alone 8.260; 'He who can bear to live alone is either a beast or a god' 7.276; is anyone ever absolutely on their own? 15.707; joy in solitude, and in society 19.518; a middle way between sympathy and solitude 26.142; outer and inner solitude 26.141; if you spent your whole life on a desert island, you'd never really know yourself 3.400; the solitude of the writer 25.110, 26.141, 26.353–5; 'the thick solitude of crowds' 22.457; the value of solitude 8.259–60; sometimes more solitude in the city than in the countryside 19.492–3

solitude and spiritual life
being secluded from the world can mean not solitude, but sangha 17.112; Dharma practice requires periods of silence and solitude 7.239; the limitations of solitary practice 3.401; meditating in solitude 1.442, 4.533–6, 15.102, 18.621; giving up meditation while in solitude 18.484; practising Buddhism in isolation 3.390, 17.41–2, 17.711 (n41); 'Religion is what the individual does with his solitariness' 12.40–1, 12.82, 15.705–6, 26.67; solitary forms of spiritual life 7.149

solitude in the Buddhist tradition
the Buddha (and an elephant) go to the forest 10.323–4, 10.429, 10.536–7, 14.401; the true solitude of which the Buddha speaks in the *Khaggavisāṇa Sutta* 8.260; 'Wander alone, as the horn of the rhinoceros is single' 2.191, 4.707 (n314), 8.259–60, 14.56, 26.156; Milarepa is not oppressed by solitude 18.42–3

see also
the Dharma conduces to solitude, not company, *see under* Mahāpajāpatī Gotami; hermit lifestyle, *see under* hermits; solitary Buddhas, *see pratyekabuddha*; solitary retreat, *see under* retreats

Solomon, King 13.544

Solovyov, Vladmir brief introduction 23.290, 23.505 (n244); fetishism 12.230; *Lectures in Godmanhood* 13.603, 23.209; and Sophia, the Divine Wisdom 13.603–4

Soma, Bhikkhu advises Sangharakshita to stop writing poetry 16.406, 20.436; advocates traditional medicine 16.406; compared to a swami 20.301; teaches Sangharakshita *ānāpānasati* 12.495, 20.144; unconventional views for a Theravādin 20.144; *The Way of Mindfulness* 15.xvii

Some Sayings of the Buddha *see under* Woodward

Sona, Dharmachari brief introduction 24.622 (n88); centre president 12.632; established FWBO Stockholm 24.6, 24.153; member of the Preceptors' College 12.597, 12.631; at Padmaloka 24.65, 24.152–3

Soṇa Koḷivisa (the Buddha's disciple) advised to tune the spiritual faculties like a lute 1.293, 7.489, 9.561 (n232), 26.635; overdoes walking meditation 5.80

Soṇa Koṭikaṇṇa (the Buddha's disciple) wants to go forth, but is advised by his teacher to wait 10.572–3; is ordained 10.572; learns Dharma verses by heart, to the Buddha's pleasure 10.572–6, 14.20

Soṇadaṇḍa Sutta *see under Dīgha Nikāya*

Song of the Four Mindfulnesses *see under* Tsongkhapa/works

Songtsen Gampo (first religious king of Tibet) 7.512, 12.290, 13.6–9

Soni, Dr R. L. 8.384–5, 9.70

Sonia 20.78–9, 20.84, 20.106

sons

Buddhist references
the Buddha as Father, the Dharma as Mother, and the Sangha as son 2.138; 'Even his self is not his own. How then a son?' 1.173, 10.146, 10.455, 10.490, 18.219; Saṅgāmaji, who left his wife and son 10.454–7; 'You are my own true sons, born of my mouth' 2.138, 8.476, 11.108, 14.444, 19.171–2; the tradition in Buddhist countries for the eldest son to become a monk 19.475

other traditions and references
the desire for a son 18.209–11; if you have surmounted your attachment even to your son, you are free indeed 10.455; in Hinduism and Chinese culture 10.455; in traditional cultures, you marry in order to produce sons 15.413–14; the misfortune of having a really affectionate mother 15.411; mother-light (*dharmakāya*) (or father-light) and son-light 18.251; mother-mind and son-mind 18.64; the prodigal son 16.90, 16.220; a son leaving his parents in tribal life 15.410, 15.480; sons' ill treatment of their parents 15.408, 18.210; 'Which of you, if your son asks for bread, will give him a stone?' 1.22

relationship between fathers and sons
advice about the way a father should treat his son 3.539, 15.412, 16.297–8; father and son in the *White Lotus Sūtra*, *see White Lotus Sūtra*/myth of the return journey; Lord Chesterfield's letters to his son 12.697; 'the love of a father for his son is very strong, piercing the heart' 10.256; 'Oh that my son might experience peace of mind such as this!' 4.16, 10.287, 12.309, 12.676; the traditional relationship 18.505–6; using the language of father and son in a religious context 18.315–16

see also
Rāhula (the Buddha's son)

Soothill, W. E. description of the *Lotus Sūtra* 3.377–8, 14.110–11; translation

of the *White Lotus Sūtra* 8.479, 14.110, 16.36

Sopāka (the Buddha's disciple, 'Untouchable') 9.142, 10.672 (n86)

Sophia (the Divine Wisdom) 13.603–4, 14.343, 26.388

sophistication as Buddhism developed, people asked more sophisticated questions 14.351–2; Buddhism's sophisticated use of language 19.437; from our sophisticated viewpoint we have to hunt for a real feeling for the life of things 15.138; a sophisticated response to Buddhist teachings in the West may trivialize them 17.454; the Tibetans' unsophisticated acceptance of Buddhism had spiritual advantages 17.454

sophistry 7.196

Sophocles emergence in the Axial Age 3.427; *Antigone* 16.85, 23.300; Buddhist elements in his plays 21.431; 'Call no man happy until he is dead' 6.601

Sopp, Thomas *see* Abhayada

Soratha (the Little Monk) v22

Soren, Lakhindar 10.lvi–ix

Sørensen, Alfred ('Mr Emptiness' or Sri Sunyata) 21.87–8, 24.528

Sorenson, Lord 23.202

sorrow 'All sorrows ... are ownerless' 4.571, 4.630; 'The ashes of all my heartaches ...'25.222; 'Attachment to the self ... is the reason that sorrow has power over anyone' 4.570; *daurmanasya* (form of *vedanā*) 2.98; a heavy atmosphere of greed and sorrow in big cities 4.571–4; nearly all our sorrows come from seeing only one aspect of life 8.224–5; patterns of the world's sorrow 4.311–12; the ploughshare of sorrow 8.156; sensitivity to the joys and sorrows of others 8.452; 'Since sorrow comes from my own offences, why should I be angry elsewhere?' 4.426; the sorrow that takes away the sorrow of the world 4.429; never any flower of human achievement but some great sorrow lay at its root 7.389, 26.11; those who are attached to a hundred things have a hundred sorrows 10.651–2; when you hurt beings, you indirectly cause sorrow to the Buddhas 4.435; 'When you are sorrowful, look again in your heart ...' (*The Prophet*) 1.129; 'Your sorrow is my sorrow, friend ...' 22.454–5; *see also* sadness

Sorrowless Giving, Princess 14.184

sotāpanna *see* Stream Entrant

sotāpatti *see* Stream Entry

Sōtō Zen *see under* Zen/schools

soul

Buddhism and 'soul'
a word with un-Buddhistic connotations 7.202; to deny the 'soul' in its poetic sense would put Buddhism in a false light 14.460; a middle way between the ideas of an unchanging soul and no soul 12.387; Buddhism is not merely the daydream of a beautiful soul 7.33; doubt: a soul-corroding unease 4.185–6; 'in the soul two aspects may be distinguished' 7.202; 'I feel my body and soul break forth/ Like the crushing of an egg' 18.605

different views of the soul
Christian analysis of human being into body, soul, spirit 2.335; eternalist view of the soul (Christianity) 17.624; immortality of the soul (Christianity) 2.85; union with the soul of the universe (Hinduism) 7.41; what profit to 'gain the whole world, and lose his own soul?' 16.173; flowers develop a 'soul' as a result of attention paid to them 8.423; truth flashes upon the soul 'like a flame kindled by a leaping spark' (Plato) 3.164

human soul
the holy ground of the human soul 25.xxxiv, 25.17; human life as a vale of soul-making 12.698, 26.399; Goethe: 'a beautiful soul' (Schiller) 7.33, 7.549 (n27); 'only a beautiful soul can perceive beautiful colours' 21.162; seeing with the eye of the soul 23.318; soul is reticulated into souls 26.84; 'soul-wisdom' 7.359, 26.198; we are miserable because we have denied the aspirations of our souls 7.307; to love the body but not the soul or spirit is perversion 12.230; Jogis, gatherers of the souls of the dead 11.456–7, 12.439, 23.391

poetic soul
feed the soul with poetry 25.453; poetry is the natural language of the soul 26.386; the adventures of the soul among books 26.335; 'the feast of reason and the flow of soul' 3.71; 'Ah, what a dusty answer gets the soul' 1.23; hieroglyphics of the soul 25.239; 'Letters mingle souls' 12.694, 21.457, 25.421; 'My soul between the feeling and the thought' 25.286; 'No coward soul is mine' 2.418; 'A soul raged in their child' 23.97; 'Yet shall my soul burn upward like a fire' 25.271

see also
dark night of the soul, *see under* mysticism

sound the communication of the Dharma through sound 8.531–2; of the Dharma in a pure Buddha-land 16.462; the fame of Siddhārtha's austerities 'spread like the sound of a great bell' 3.30; fear removed by the sound of the golden drum 16.276–9; 'Full of sound and fury, signifying nothing' 7.328, 21.43; hearing all sounds as mantras 5.607; 'a light in sound, a sound-like power in light' 16.267; meditation on sound 14.197; only when the egoistic will is 'silent' will the True Sound be heard 7.323; primordial sound 3.79–80; the ravishingly beautiful sounds of Vairocana's Tower 14.224; transformation through sounds and movements 1.374; 'the unstruck sound' 2.130; visualization: the convergence of a light symbol and a sound symbol 16.179; 'What is the sound of one hand clapping?' 1.210, 16.591 (n40); words are sounds associated in varying degrees with conceptual meaning 3.511; *see also* sound symbols *under* mantras/definitions

south contrast between the art of southern and northern Europe 26.255–6; 'a beaker full of the warm South' 23.275; the Buddha lay with his head to the north and his feet to the south 11.452, 12.357; a journey from north to south 26.263–4

South America conquest of Mexico 13.602; photographs of Peru 24.422; Protestants tortured to death in Colombia 7.380, 8.116

Southall, Derek 23.197

Southwold, M. 13.436

Sowter, Graham *see* Siddhiratna

space

element (ākāśa)
associated with the colour blue or gold and a flaming jewel shape 13.153, 16.147; correlated with the psychic centre at the top of the head 16.147; space is light and light is space 13.152

symbolism
halfway between matter and spirit or consciousness 16.145, 16.160; the sage 16.146–7; the higher dimension within which all movements take place 16.146; in the stupa reflection about freeing energy 13.154–5

notes on space
the arbitrariness with which things occupying space are divided up 19.239–40; an aspect of consciousness 17.385; compared to the Mahāyāna 14.142; the Dharma taught by means of empty space 16.563; finite or infinite? 2.63, 10.597, 16.161; imaginal space 13.152; imagining the space left behind if one abstracts oneself from the senses 4.156; insight is a spatial term 18.607; methods of realizing that space is a concept 18.544–6; the need for personal space 4.538–9; not a thing, but a way in which you experience things 17.385, 18.544; one's inner visionary experiences take place within an inner, imaginal space 13.152; space in the fourteen inexpressibles 17.384–5; space is curved (Einstein) 19.437; space programme 26.39; the subjectivity of space 10.597; its vastness is conveyed by the scriptures imaginatively 2.63; the space within which is the universe 16.341; spatial metaphors 13.122; wisdom, like space, does not break or crack 14.600

see also
six element practice; sphere of infinite space, *see under dhyānas/arūpa*; and time, *see under* time

Spain

notes on Spain
general impressions 24.464–7; a cardinal is annoyed at tolerance of non-Catholics in Spain 8.117–18; chains of prisoners of the Moors 24.422; *churros* 24.409, 24.446; Civil War 24.412, 24.466; clothes 24.466–7; the FWBO in Spain 24.467; a hope of a romantic journey disappointed 24.406; migration of Jews 24.720 (n543); travels in Spain 24.402, 24.405, 26.446; Spanish Civil War 24.412; the Spanish royal family 24.449–50; Spanish television 24.426; vegetarian food 24.408–9, 24.410, 24.431

cities
Alicante 24.462; Castile–La Mancha 24.407–8; Córdoba 24.426–34, 24.581; Granada 24.443–56; Madrid 13.666–7, 24.408–17, 26.308; Murcia 24.456–61; Seville 24.434–43; Toledo 24.416–24, 26.308–9

see also
Akashavana and Guhyaloka, *see under* Triratna IV/retreat centres

Spalding, Frances 24.316

spark the bodhisattva benefits people by sparking them off 16.487, 17.175; the bodhisattva vows: sparks struck from the bodhisattva's total being 4.57–8; the Buddha taught those who had 'quite forgot their ancient Spark' 25.402; the spark of the *ḍākinī* 12.314–15; fearlessness is not so much given as sparked off 4.95; how

do mantras spark off a particular quality? 16.183; human life: a spark of pleasure between the terminals of two eternities of non-existence 7.311; insight sparked off in communication 19.328; intellectual knowledge is like a motorcar: it needs the motivating spark of devotion 2.243; in the spiritual community people try to spark off real communication 3.439; noticing which Buddhas spark you off 19.43; one is not really human unless one has a spark of awareness 26.7; reflexive consciousness is what sparks off the whole process of spiritual growth 15.215; the spark of Enlightenment 15.570; spiritual experience can be sparked off by others, but you need something to be sparked off 18.300; symbols spark off developments in our spiritual life 13.123; transmission as a sparking off 19.402–4, 19.529; truth flashes upon the soul 'like a flame kindled by a leaping spark' 3.164; whatever skilful mental states you develop, you can spark off in others 4.95

sparśa (contact) a particular transformation in the sense faculty 17.529–30; as omnipresent mental event 17.529–30; *see also under* twelve cyclical *nidānas*

Spartacus 26.675–6

spatial and temporal models *see under* time/and space

special the disciples praised by the Buddha for their special qualities 3.179, 4.170–1, 18.132, 18.222; no special set of conditions for death 3.128; a special correspondence between the human condition and Buddhahood 2.96; thinking you are a special person who needs special teachings 18.473–4; you don't need special conditions for Dharma practice 18.342, 18.473–4;

see also
eight special conditions (*garudhammas*); the eighteen special qualities of a Buddha; 'a special transmission outside the scriptures', *see under* Zen/Zen teachings

specialization we live in the era of the specialist 3.5–6; from the Reformation a breakdown of knowledge into specializations 10.154; our line of spiritual practice must be specialized, but our general approach should be broad 13.326

***Spectator* essays** *see under* Addison

speculation arriving at general conclusions from limited experience 10.612; the Buddha did not encourage speculation 7.134, 13.566; the Buddha taught the three *lakṣaṇas* for pragmatic reasons, not as a speculative sport 7.50; the Buddha wanted us to form a picture of suffering, not indulge in abstract speculations 1.128; Buddhism's critique of speculative views 13.435; Buddhist doctrines are not speculative, but state the conditions of spiritual progress 10.158; Buddhist thought is not the speculations of unenlightened Buddhists 3.81; the Dharma is not speculative philosophy or a set of theories 7.256; don't let the Mahāyāna's fondness for speculation steer you too far from experience 14.605; media speculation about coming events 19.270–1; the One Mind is something to be experienced, not just discussed and speculated about 12.173; speculation, creed, and dogma lead to doubt, hesitation, uncertainty 7.145; speculation on where the *kleśas* come from – the poisoned arrow? 4.374; speculation about the origin of the universe is irrelevant 13.566; speculation about what is behind what we perceive is futile 14.420

speech

INTRODUCTION

speech in the Buddhist tradition
a *bhikkhu* who 'has no need to talk to people' (*Udāna*) 10.502–3; the Buddha as one who speaks only to help beings 17.342; the Buddha clearly attached great importance to speech 12.33; description of Ariyan speech 8.173; *dhammakathā*, talk about the means to Enlightenment, *see dhammakathā*; 'words well spoken' (*Maṅgala Sutta*) 15.406; 'Whatever the Buddha said was well said' 3.168, 3.394, 7.434; 'Whatever is well said, that is the word of the Buddha', *see under Buddhavacana*; 'All Dharmas are your speech' (Milarepa) 19.32–3; Mañjughoṣa mantra repeated for eloquence and power of speech 4.192; Nāgārjuna's advice about speech 17.308; the speech of the bodhisattva 2.154, 16.486–7; speech simplified into *mantra* 7.320; *vāc*, 'creative speech' 16.363; Vagīśvara, 'Lord of Speech', *see* Vagīśvara; *vajra* speech 19.43, 19.295

reflections on speech
choosing the right time to speak 8.xxiv, 8.173, 17.231–2, 19.556; communication of knowledge through speech 19.32; the difficulty of skilful speech 9.275, 9.420; the most difficult precept to practise 12.556; don't parrot others' words, but speak from personal experience 17.308; enjoyment of speech 18.48; freedom of speech 4.125, 4.127; getting upset

or elated about what is said stops you from assessing the truth of it 11.334; the importance of speaking properly 3.539; it distinguishes human beings from other forms of life 1.514, 12.33; Freudian slips 5.658; it's important to speak out when the Dharma is misrepresented 4.127, 8.xxiv, 24.206; a middle way between knowledge and ignorance of a person 18.216; the poetic nature of speech 26.70; purification of speech 9.287; speaking with boldness, courage, and wit 1.449, 16.491; the spontaneous expression of the non-dual state 18.48; taking responsibility for the effect of what you say 17.190–1, 17.661; to be a Buddhist means to act, to speak out 8.xxxii; what you talk about shows how much your mind has been transformed 18.539; words cannot be recalled, and one has to live with the consequences 22.491

speech and thought
it's difficult to control speech because it is so close to thought 2.375; speech is important, being intermediate between body and mind, action and thought 2.374; thought leaps to speech 25.248; ultimate truth can be neither thought about nor spoken about 17.383

mindfulness of speech
avoid wrong speech when giving a Dharma talk 12.585; be aware of what you are saying and whether it is worth saying 17.308; be mindful of your speech when in large gatherings 12.556; the effects of losing mindfulness when you're talking 10.473–4; sometimes it's best to say nothing at all 11.202; in speech we waste energy and time, lose mindfulness, express fixed views 18.162–3; *see also* right speech

talking too much
a Buddhist conference as a talking shop 8.154–5; craving for talk 19.493; if you talk and talk without reaching a conclusion, you don't have to take action 3.293; nattering monks are told to talk about the Dharma or stay quiet 10.472–5, 10.517–21; people talk far too much 1.524, 13.347; positive communication can turn into sociable talkativeness 19.550; sometimes we talk to avoid communication 12.557; in spiritual life, the more important something is, the less there is to say 1.579–80; talking exhausts energy, but real communication heightens it 4.482, 18.478, 18.482; why do people go on talking? 10.581, 19.493–4; a woman who talked too much because she had something on her mind 15.116–17

going beyond speech
'He who knows does not speak, he who speaks does not know' 7.37, 7.44; 'a mystery beyond the grasp of speech' 25.379; some things, though they can be experienced, transcend thought and speech 13.348; speech is transcended by the Perfection of Wisdom 1.66; the ultimate experience is beyond the reach of speech 1.64; *see also* silence

UNSKILFUL SPEECH

introduction
the consequences of unskilful speech 17.236–8; to deal with negative speech, just stop it 11.202

abusive speech
the Buddha explains how to deal with it 3.76, 3.546–7, 4.119; don't run down or defame others 17.308; it's only words 4.427; speaking in dispraise of the Three Jewels 11.332–5; whatever people say to or about you, don't bother 4.394

gossip
gossip at the vihara in India 9.420, 9.464; 'All news is gossip' (Thoreau) 15.174; Buddhist gossip 19.478; the consequences of gossip 17.237; dealing with gossip 24.215–16; gossip about Sangharakshita and Terry 23.432, 23.434, 23.438; gossip at the Hampstead Buddhist Vihara 23.138; gossiping nurses 24.349; it's best to say nothing in response 18.517; it spreads poison 11.201; malicious gossip 15.350; slanderous gossip 19.525; someone who was no gossip 23.69; superficial gossip is not *dharmakathā* 10.474

frivolous speech
after meditation or puja 5.307–8, 5.310; its draining effect 17.229–30; the consequences of useless speech 17.237–8; foolish talk 19.380; 'Here may no idle word be spoken' 11.651, 12.541; the Pāli scriptures list 32 kinds, but now we have thousands 2.381, 12.33; trivial speech 18.567

other kinds of unskilful speech
critical 4.317–18, 11.201, 16.505; cruel 1.499; depressing 12.36–7; 'dismal-jimmyism' 11.201, 17.181–2; frightening 17.180–1; grumbling 11.200–1; harsh 9.274, 9.420, 10.395, 15.273, 24.528–9; meaningless 16.490; nagging 11.201–2; neurotic 10.581; rough 2.374–5; spontaneous 13.360; swearing 10.395, 13.607, 13.609–10; talking about religion emptily 17.627, 18.183–4, 19.399; useless 19.522

FOUR LEVELS OF SKILFUL SPEECH

introduction
overview 1.515–25; aspect of the Noble Eightfold Path 11.498; each deeper than the one preceding 1.516, 12.34, 17.229; most contemporary expositions of Buddhism present this in a superficial way 12.33; what did the Buddha mean by this teaching? 19.295

(1) truthful speech
introduction 1.516–19; always spoken to another person 12.35; always to speak the truth 9.216; being able to hear the truth is as important as being able to tell it 17.239–40; being straightforward and honest in all our dealings 17.231; a breakdown of the notion of objective truth 12.350–3; the Buddha speaks the truth in the sense of ultimate reality 14.477–8; the Buddha's choice of a court case as an illustration of truthfulness 2.376, 3.322; develop awareness and sensitivity to tell when someone is speaking the truth 2.377; direct and open 9.445, 10.217; don't hold back, but don't upset people for the sake of it 15.273, 16.505; don't keep anything in your heart which you don't let out 10.217; exaggerated speech, *see* exaggeration; the Houyhnhnms (Swift) had no word for 'lie' 3.322; if you feel that someone isn't being honest, gently tackle them about it 10.570; if your thoughts aren't subject to craving and hatred, your speech is truthful 18.139; importance of factual accuracy 1.516–17, 2.376–7, 9.445, 10.576, 12.34; in childhood we are naturally honest, but we learn to hide things 18.140; involves saying what we *really* think – but do we know? 1.517–18, 12.34–5; we may need to give up truthfulness for the sake of a greater virtue 3.323, 7.118; modern life gives many temptations to bend the truth 3.323; most of us live with a kind of background dishonesty 18.140; Newspeak (Orwell) 2.376; not being believed when speaking the truth 2.377, 19.19–20, 26.79; not spreading fake news 26.669; one can only speak the truth to one person 21.457, 26.45; people find it very difficult to appreciate that one means what one says 18.347; the rectification of terms (Confucius) 2.376; unskilful not to tell the truth when this might remove misunderstanding 3.322; telling the truth is a relief 1.518–19, 12.35; in some countries speaking the truth is not allowed 10.271; to speak the truth we must clarify our ideas, be honest, be ourselves 1.518–19; speaking spontaneously, with one's own voice, is very rare 13.360; speaking, thinking, and acting the truth 9.267; speaking the truth is very difficult 2.377, 10.271, 12.35; a statement is no more true because someone believes it strongly 19.292; 'There is no wrong that cannot be committed by a lying person' 2.376; trustful and open communication in the spiritual community 16.315; 'Truth is immortal (or deathless) speech' 13.644, 14.293, 19.294–5; truthful speech and skilful means 17.232–3; truthfulness is a power capable of producing tangible results 2.169, 15.501; the utterance of truth in the full sense is a really powerful thing 15.500–1; when filling out forms, difficulties around declaring caste status 9.523–5; we should never (directly or indirectly) consent to what we know is false 7.118; we must be honest about what we believe, or what is freedom of speech worth? 4.125; we tend to bend the facts in the direction we'd like them to go 1.517; we tell lies, exaggerate, minimize, or embroider 1.517, 2.376–7, 3.322, 12.34; when you are dying you can speak the truth without fear 15.376–7; why don't politicians tell the electorate the truth? 17.230–1; without truthfulness there's no commerce, justice, politics, society 2.375–6, 3.322

(2) affectionate, loving, kindly speech
introduction 1.519–21; avoiding rough or harsh speech 10.395, 12.403, 12.416; gentle, courteous, and polite speech 2.380; gracious speech (*Mettā Sutta*) 15.273; kindly speech between friends 3.573, 3.575, 3.579, 11.698; kindly speech is like the warm rays of the rising sun 2.380; one of the four *saṃgrahavastus* (*priya-vāditā*) 1.449, 16.486–7, 17.174–5; means being aware of another person, not just our reactions to them 1.519–21, 12.36, 17.229; in the *Maṅgala Sutta* 15.441; kindly speech within the Order 12.416; speak with a kindly awareness of the hearer and how they might feel 17.308; tone of voice 17.174–5

(3) helpful or meaningful speech
introduction 1.521–2; aim to make sure that whatever you say is meaningful and helpful 17.230; articulate speech 24.212; communicating difficult truths 17.240; constructive criticism 1.521–2, 17.652–3; Lama Govinda an exemplar of constructive speech 12.36–7; not formal speech about the Dharma, but is itself a means to Enlightenment 2.381–2; say what is actually useful, not just what people will find agreeable 17.308; speak methodically and with discretion 17.308; speaking to promote the spiritual growth

of the other person 1.521, 12.36; see the good and positive, not just the negative 1.521–2; speech can only be meaningful when one's life is meaningful 2.381; study words and their meanings carefully 8.272–3; the time has to be right, the other person receptive, and we ourselves positive 17.232

(4) harmonious speech
introduction 1.523–3; the fullest experience of it takes place between Enlightened human beings 17.230; leads to mutual self-transcendence 1.523, 12.37; not saying yes all the time 1.522; culminates in silence 1.523–5, 17.230; speech that transcends selfhood 17.230

see also
Perfect Speech; right speech, *see under* Noble Eightfold Path; speech precepts, *see under* precepts

Spencer, Herbert introduction 10.691–2 (n216); 'his idea of a tragedy was a theory killed by a fact' 8.242, 12.274; he coined the phrase 'the survival of the fittest' 10.691 (n216); three kinds of knowledge 10.171

Spender, Stephen 'I think continually of those who were truly great' 7.423, 25.57, 26.399, 26.632

Spenser, Edmund

introduction
brief introduction 23.488–9 (n121); 'Every sweet with sour is tempered still' 20.14, 20.504; love poetry 23.98

The Faerie Queene
reading it in India 22.464; has the quality *kāvya* 26.332; 'Isis church' 24.529; 'Sleep after toyle, port after stormie seas' 7.46, 13.283

Sphinx Napoleon's soldiers using it for target practice 26.476; tells the secret 25.320; 'The Sphinx' (Wilde) 26.488

Sphuṭartha *see* Yaśomitra

Spiegelberg, Frederic 20.332

Spinello Aretino 13.597

Spinoza, Baruch (Benedict)

introduction
brief account of his life 7.553–4 (n54); his early death 11.448–9; 'substance' 1.269, 16.449; wonderment that there should be anything rather than nothing 8.575; axioms he thought self-evidently true 7.387; 'despite their learning they have gone far astray' 8.230

Ethics
'Everything endeavours to persist in its own being' 26.168; 'God is an absolutely infinite substance with infinite attributes' 4.203, 14.603; hatred is a feeling of pain and an idea of its cause 15.304, 17.269, 17.503; love is a feeling of pleasure and an idea of its cause 17.503, 26.172; 'The love with which we love God' 7.44

spiral the archetypal journey like a spiral path up a mountain 26.273; Enlightenment as a spiral 14.596; with insight, circling thoughts become a spiral 19.237; the middle way is not a 'golden mediocrity' but the embodiment of the 'spiral' principle 2.103

spiral path *see* twelve positive *nidānas*

spirit the flame of the spirit 8.265; the scale of spirit 14.309; Spirit in the Neoplatonic sense 25.82

spirit fox 14.593, 18.85

spirit guides 23.199, 23.231

spirit and letter

introduction
'the letter which killeth and the spirit which giveth life' 7.159, 13.437; the history of religion shows how often they have been confused 7.158–9; interdependent 2.59; Jesus emphasizes the spirit rather than the letter of morality 13.614; rules can become an external conformity, neglecting the spirit 10.563; scholars 1.222, 1.227, 16.579

various applications
getting in touch with the spirit of the Sevenfold Puja 11.222; learning the spirit of the precepts 2.343; convey what someone has said accurately in spirit and letter 2.377; spirit and letter on the threefold way 11.480–1; the spirit and letter of the monastic rule of eating by noon 22.225; spirit and letter of translation 14.15; universalism: not comparing the letters of traditions, but seeking the spirit 26.15; letter and spirit in the Vinaya 7.263–4

in Dharma study and practice
rely on the spirit (*artha*) as opposed to the letter (*vyañjana*) 14.297; Buddhism is the exhilarating exaltation of the spirit above the letter 7.331; the living spirit must vivify the letter 14.17; to communicate the Dharma you need both letter and spirit 2.23, 14.366; the spirit can be studied in the light of the letter 1.240; the letter can be learned from books, but the spirit must be transmitted from heart to heart

7.543; they are both needed on the path to Enlightenment 11.481; a fine line to be drawn between spirit and letter 17.157; avoiding confusing the letter and the spirit 1.449; the importance of transmitting both spirit and letter of sacred texts 14.207–8, 14.266; conflict between the spirit and the *stress* on the letter 2.591; desire for an easier practice, to practise the letter and neglect the spirit 7.185; forced to choose, a Buddhist should have the strength to choose the spirit 1.240; technically in the school of the spirit, you may still practise only the letter 4.25

in the Theravāda
it includes both the spirit and the letter of the Buddha's teaching 4.19; slavish dependence on the letter 1.239–40, 7.471, 7.540; Theravāda depends on the letter, Mahāyāna on the spirit 7.541–2; *bhikkhus* unfaithful to the Dharma's spirit but having regard for its letter 8.468

in the Mahāyāna
more importance attached to spirit than letter 1.239, 14.26, 14.101, 16.390; later schools were faithful to the spirit of the teaching, if not always the letter 7.121

spirit of place 18.21–4

spiritual (the word) an important aspect of its meaning is unified being 14.443; distinction between spiritual and psychological 4.620–3, 11.128–9, 15.588, 16.270, 17.436–7, 18.443; distinction from transcendental 11.131, 16.271, 17.436–7; *nirāmisa* could be translated 'spiritual' 15.155; not to be used in a vague, woolly way 16.271; pay the greatest respect to the slightest manifestation of something spiritual 4.435; the rainbow as a symbol of spirituality 26.672; for Sangharakshita the word has two meanings 11.674; to be understood as meaning whatever conduces to Enlightenment 12.150–1

spiritual bypassing forgetting what you have to do to achieve your beautiful spiritual ideas 25.74–5; the group is a basic human need which cannot simply be bypassed 3.444; positive mental states will never be achieved through bypassing difficult ones 15.231–2; the term might be used by people more interested in psychology than spiritual practice 25.75

spiritual community *see* sangha

spiritual death

the experience
destruction of what you are so that you are free to become what you can be 16.504; 'I go to Eternal Death!' (Blake) 26.486; if we do not confess evil done, we are hanging on to the old self, refusing to die 16.293; it really means unselfishness 11.735–6, 26.169; the happy, healthy individual you have become must die 5.32; in Hinduism 3.461; members of the sangha are prepared to die in order to be spiritually reborn 11.134; the discriminating mind commits suicide 7.37; only those who experience death in life can experience life in death 26.83; to produce a new self, there has to be a death of the old self 3.418, 5.43–4; those used to being close to death can be close to the spiritual path 18.245; the Transcendental obliterates the mundane 25.82; transformation as a model for the spiritual life: death and rebirth 16.227; what we are looking for 16.227; plunging into the heart of the sun that is the Perfection of Wisdom 14.352; when you see the truth, you die, when you die, you see the truth 5.44; without sacrifice there is no resurrection 8.156

in the Buddhist tradition
at the foot of the bodhi tree Siddhārtha died and the Buddha was born 3.149; Dabba Mallaputta attains final *nibbāna*, a sort of spiritual death 10.653–6; 'you start feeling a bit singed and in danger of being burned up' (*Udāna*) 10.610; transcendental wisdom (the *vajra*) destroys us as we are at present 13.170–2, 14.373–4; the colour black stands for spiritual death 13.283; the great death (Zen) 3.149, 3.230, 12.174

in relation to aspects of Dharma practice
every Buddhist scripture is a Book of the Dead 16.262–3; spiritual death and the first fetter 3.418; spiritual death and the spiral path 5.41–2; in terms of the *parāvṛtti* (turning about) 2.276, 17.481; if you're not prepared to die, you cannot become a bodhisattva 16.262–3; 'Death and the Bodhisattva Trainings' 24.310–11; meditation on *śūnyatā* 4.162, 5.32–3, 5.44; if you aren't ready to die, leave the Mahāmudrā alone 18.245–6

meditation
meditation as spiritual death 5.34, 12.206; the third stage of the system of meditation 5.xxxiv; the six element practice 5.32–3, 5.44; when we truly meditate we die 5.34; 'All the spirit's storm and stress/ Is stilled into a nothingness' 25.43; visualizing a Buddha or bodhisattva: you as you will be if you allow yourself to die 5.33, 26.50

right now?
we have to be prepared to experience spiritual death at any time 16.263; we

may think we want insight right now, but do we really? 17.354; are we prepared for spiritual death? (*Diamond Sūtra*) 14.408–9; facing dissolution of the mind 25.502; fear of the death of the ego 17.339, 17.354

Enlightenment
the 'experience' of Enlightenment is more like death 3.149; not *gaining* Enlightenment *for* the self, but the death *of* the self 7.291; the touch of *śūnyatā* feels like death to the conditioned self 26.48

in a negative sense
most so-called humanity today is dead in life 8.265; our self-imprisonment on the wheel of life, our death-in-life 3.348; the slow death of aspiration caused by the five poisons 3.123

spiritual development *see* growth and development

spiritual experience

its nature
a difficult thing to communicate 11.303; a living and electric thing, utterly indefinable 7.144; it can be expressed in terms of concepts, but is not identical with these 1.259, 1.482; it catches up with doctrinal knowledge 4.500; it flowers in the depths of your being and penetrates to your fingertips 13.306; 'It is foolish to expect too much advance information' 8.539; Buddhism's emphasis on the supreme value of spiritual experience 26.104–11; five different aspects of a single crucial spiritual experience 2.301, 2.483; its relationship with sense-experience is analogical 2.54; spiritual experience is three-dimensional, the intellect two-dimensional 26.201; trying to translate its subtleties into the coarse language of thought 7.134

your own spiritual experience
firm footing is to be found only in one's own spiritual experience 10.599; making it the centre of your existence 18.541; an experience which can be kept to oneself is not the same as one communicated 2.465; not being able to accept one's spiritual experience 4.267; the test of whether it is spiritual is whether you can call it 'my' experience 7.360–1; how can I think of withdrawing into private experience when others are suffering? 2.272; the importance of keeping in contact with spiritual experience 4.272

the process
Buddhism is above all a way of life that leads to spiritual experiences 7.143–4; if there are degrees of reality, there must be degrees of spiritual experience 12.12–13; the esoteric path in the heart-depths of spiritual experience 7.359–60, 26.49; external activity and inner spiritual experience need not be incompatible 22.247–8; people undergoing suffering may have intense spiritual experiences 13.137; no one, not even the Buddha, can literally hand on their spiritual experience 13.161; spiritual receptivity leads to valuable spiritual experiences 11.279, 21.505; the chain leading from spiritual experience to tolerance 7.145

difficulties
the difference between craving and aspiring for spiritual experience 11.80–1; expecting to be given a spiritual experience 11.80–5; grabbing spiritual experience 11.81; the idea that the self can persist unchanged through spiritual experiences 26.206; a subtle ego-sense attaching itself to spiritual experience 18.580–2; superimposing on spiritual experience our limited linear modes of thinking 10.614; you attain some genuine experience but then your ego intervenes 18.174

spiritual faculties *see* five spiritual faculties

spiritual friendship *see kalyāṇa mitratā*

spiritual hierarchy *see under* hierarchy

spiritual individualism *see under* individualism

spiritual life

INTRODUCTION

what is the spiritual life?
the *bodhicitta* at work 4.265; change, development, growth 16.439; an active, strenuous, even militant life 11.407; an adventure with no end in sight 17.413; an attempt to escape 13.191–2; bringing about a state in which the whole tendency of our being is expansive 15.341; built into the very structure of Reality 7.317; a constant dissolving of the stream of thoughts into the *dharmakāya* 19.188; a continual progression to ever higher states of consciousness 11.116; essentially a process of growth 15.578–9; the free life 16.471; a willed process of becoming 7.204; everything in it exists for the sake of the Three Jewels 13.43; Going for Refuge is the root, the foundation, the absolute bedrock 26.32; in a way it is unnatural 17.97; it became identified with monastic life in Buddhist history 2.203; it is governed by the spiral mode of conditionality 2.252; it is strange to us 11.42–3; learning to switch from the

power mode to the love mode 26.56; only possible because the unreal imagination exists 1.363; may be seen as cessation or development 7.151; above all else 'the marriage of heaven and hell' 12.29; in the highest sense the spiritual life is an illusion 14.592; its essential definitive qualities 2.552; a kind of interrogation of reality 17.260; a life devoted to the development of skilful mental states 11.130; a loosening of the bonds of selfhood and egoity 7.412; radical transformation 13.236, 16.227; the achievement of something highly positive 10.635; non-violence is at its heart 26.55; a progressive attenuation of the ego-sense 7.302; the progressive intensification of self-awareness 12.69; a recapitulation of the history of Buddhism 1.393; seeking the truth and learning to live by it 17.231, 26.16; self-transcendence is its true meaning 4.656; shifting the focus of your emotional energy to more refined pleasures 15.154; a spontaneous welling-up of spiritual energy (*līlā*) 14.521; not only seeing clearly but also functioning smoothly 18.322; thinking of it in terms of breaking through 11.4–5; transformation is implicit in its every aspect 15.114; trying to find more significance in our daily lives 13.120; finding your true place in the mandala 18.447; we need criteria for the spiritual life 16.575; wisdom in the process of becoming Perfect Wisdom 14.359

what it is not
better not to present it in predominantly negative terms 17.291, 17.295–6; for Buddhism it is a question not of goodness or piety, but of skill 15.262–3; if you conceive it as a means of attaining eternal bliss, you have not understood 7.412, 26.53; impossible to identify exclusively with monasticism 1.244, 2.432; it cannot be a refined kind of selfishness 17.694–5, 19.315; it doesn't depend on chance or fate, it's about our own efforts 8.202; it is not all introspection and self-evaluation 15.120; not a flight from the things of the 'world' to the things of the 'spirit' 7.401; not a little chipping away, but a complete turning about 2.275–6, 12.174; no question of regimentation 16.127; not a mechanical process 1.133; suffering is not integral to spiritual life 15.353; there are no passengers in the spiritual life 14.577; wrong views about having deep roots and needing to be dug out with patience 17.602

the purpose of the spiritual life
connecting it with worldly gains distracts us from its true purpose 17.263–4; the development of the individual 15.266–7; the eradication of egoism 7.405–10, 26.668; in the highest sense purposeless 7.409; its ultimate goal is the Unconditioned 2.149; it is an end in itself and doesn't have to be justified in worldly terms 14.522, 18.121; Stream Entry is the real turning-point in one's spiritual life 15.240–1; to expand the centre of the self to infinity 7.412, 26.51; to get away from becoming 10.523; to grow and develop 11.87–8, 17.363

images and metaphors
a battlefield 1.111–12, 3.294, 4.372, 18.103; different metaphors to describe it 18.105; horizontal and vertical models 14.313; it has all sorts of beautiful colours 13.284; like a castle, the *samaya* gives it strength and structure 19.397–8; like climbing a greasy flagpole 4.200; like crossing one mountain after another 19.396; like the gradual training of a young horse 2.343, 4.460–1; like suddenly tuning into a new radio station 4.272; models of the spiritual life 16.227; one should not think too literally in terms of an exclusively linear model 18.280; the path and the palace as alternative symbols 18.525; a precipitous ascent 23.463; racing forward and at the same time keeping absolutely still 4.203; the rainbow 26.672; a real framework 17.408; the rhythm of spiritual life 5.691–2, 15.357; symbols are full of energy and give birth to spiritual life in us 13.123; unfolding like a flower or climbing a mountain? 4.202; we are the soil in which the plant of spiritual life will grow 12.513; where the true wish-fulfilling jewel is to be found 19.73; a wondrous game 19.73

necessary elements of spiritual life
acting with compassion 25.116; awareness of the consequences of one's actions 26.61; Buddhism and art 26.117; being free to choose how to be here and now 17.212–13; communication 11.258; confession 16.319, 26.62; friendship 24.360; devotion 2.242; the concepts of *saṃsāra* and *nirvāṇa* 18.395–8; the distinction between *jñāna* and *vijñāna* 3.356, 14.315–16; the *dhyānas* 4.156; a dualistic approach 4.162, 14.591; emptiness 14.607; joy 15.118, 17.336; ethics 8.199; faith 17.335, 25.47; going forth 22.209; gratitude and thanksgiving 4.257; the higher hedonism 8.445; violence to the aspects of oneself that need to be overcome 11.4; the simultaneous expansion of understanding and emotions 26.132; nature 16.387; will 11.650, 12.538, 26.62; practicality 18.152; physical work 18.391; pleasure 17.301–2;

preparation 3.272–3, 4.42–3, 13.75, 25.83; right livelihood 11.186, 11.376; a sense of wonder 11.44; imagination 10.506–7; positivity 15.237; operational concepts 18.397–8; beauty 12.308; art 26.130–1; regular meditation 26.75; your heart must be in it 11.193–4

LIVING THE LIFE

how spiritual life begins
aim to precipitate the arising of the *bodhicitta* from the start 2.270; being drawn by the ideal's beauty, or repelled by *saṃsāra*'s ugliness 18.580, 22.199; building up your psychological strength 15.270–1; with the activation of one's energies 13.157; the idea that you need to have a lot of worldly experience before embarking on it 17.215–16; if you have a happy, prosperous life, you may not want to hear about it 19.495; it *may* start with anguish, but that is not the only way 8.581–2; it's better to draw people into spiritual life than drive them into it 15.573; with conversion 2.238; after seeing the whole saṃsāric process 10.549; what people need when they first become interested in spiritual life 17.159; when we enter upon it, we take our place in a hierarchy 12.13–14; when we wake up to the fact that we are asleep 11.24; with your own experience of unsatisfactoriness 18.400; you need to be, or become, a capable human being 15.269–71; you can't resolve your doubts theoretically and then start 10.577–8

living the spiritual life
balancing the five spiritual faculties 26.629; causality in the spiritual life 25.77; a combative approach 18.104–5; commitment is always commitment to the unknown 16.448; commitment means you become 'without fear of being or becoming' 4.48; committing oneself to the spiritual life 11.50; creating an edge 25.77; the early stages are a struggle between lower and higher impulses 7.358; the emphasis may shift from time to time 19.546–7; growth and development a positive way of thinking about it 19.227; in the spiritual life everybody becomes kin 15.416; it includes the life of the senses 7.297; it is usually a very gradual process 15.363–4; it involves positing a dichotomy between *saṃsāra* and Nirvāṇa 26.498; it should include sorting out things from the past 4.329; it's a happy life, but the struggle to get into it isn't necessarily happy 15.360, 17.252–3; as we get more deeply into the spiritual life, our sense of reality changes 26.57; no need to take a philosophical position to lead the spiritual life 10.598; the wise aren't supernatural, they've just got on with leading the spiritual life 10.648; one can be a true friend only to the extent that one has a spiritual life 17.328; only when you start can you tell what helps and what doesn't 12.370; people who aren't trying to lead a spiritual life can't judge those who are 10.591; periods of internal activities, then external 4.461–4, 4.568–9; a phase of stupidity: less reactive but not yet spontaneous 4.382–3; setting up the conditions for the attainment of Enlightenment in one's life 17.589; some rare people seem able to lead a spiritual life by sheer instinct 4.90; the spiritual life is to develop heroes, not pussycats 19.360; there's a definite method of going about it 15.514–15; to begin with it's difficult because you don't know yourself or what to do 25.74; transitional phases 14.599; uncomfortable because you are no longer papering over discomfort with distractions 15.232; we immediately come up against attachment 14.570; the whole of our spiritual life contributes to clarity of mind 17.613

your own spiritual life
the *bodhicitta*: not just 'my' subjective idea of the goal of 'my' spiritual life 4.263; based not on what one believes about oneself but on what one knows 2.592, 2.622–3; it should be a natural expression of how you feel 5.295; it must be for the benefit of all 19.315; make progress every day, but don't bother about exactly where you are 4.500–1; no one can live our spiritual life for us 4.43; not *gaining* Enlightenment *for* the self, but the death *of* the self 7.291; taking responsibility for one's own spiritual life 18.98; to determine the next step you need not just faith but a definite goal 18.272–3; what do you get out of the spiritual life? 5.251; working out priorities 5.692–2; you are trying to work out an ideal in, or *as*, your spiritual life 18.282

balance in the spiritual life
altruistic and self-regarding aspects 4.87–92, 7.149–50; the art is to be mindful and at the same time spontaneous 16.300; balance of emotion and intellect, introvert and extrovert 1.294; developing balancing qualities 4.41, 26.129; essential to cultivate faith to achieve a balanced approach 23.151; the idea of balancing reason and faith is not useful 14.442–3; it needs both the rational and unconscious aspects of human nature 16.67; making provision for all aspects 5.691–2; the need to unite the heights and depths 12.29

the spiritual life and the emotions
engaging the emotions with spiritual practice 17.685; few desires are so negative that they cannot be connected with some aspect of it 4.152; genuine emotional involvement requires much more time than intellectual involvement 26.45; one should not be afraid to feel 13.242; lower emotions transmuted into higher ones: its motive power 10.174; no more possible without emotion than without understanding 7.290; no spiritual life without positive emotion 5.188; not being afraid of emotion, but using it to the advantage of the spiritual life 7.290; sublimated desire generates the energy to keep the spiritual life going 26.130; there must be some aspect of your spiritual life in which you feel devotion 4.297; unless we transform our emotional nature, for us there is no spiritual life 1.511

enjoying the spiritual life
enjoyment is not a luxury, but central 18.133; few practitioners would cite spiritual experiences as their greatest pleasures 17.301; for the sake of little pleasures we forgo the deeper pleasures of the spiritual life 17.300–3; for some it has its own appeal, with no further motivation needed 17.472; to really enjoy yourself, get involved with the spiritual life 19.67, 19.73; the importance of the positive approach 10.513, 10.523, 26.638; lack of interest is one of the greatest difficulties, so pleasure is important 5.327; only joy will keep us going 18.133; the sheer adventure of the spiritual life 16.487; it has to be interesting and fun 19.22; looked at from the outside, spiritual life might not look like much fun 17.381; we have to be honest about how much spiritual joy we experience 17.302; we need plenty of encouragement 16.230; you can't force people to lead a spiritual life, they've got to want to 5.252, 18.357; you can't have a cold or a dry spiritual life 12.514; you won't get far without inspiration, the breath of the *ḍākinī* 18.180; you need to think of it as something you can enjoy 15.155; you should get as much enjoyment from it as from mundane life 19.379

effort and energies in the spiritual life
a conscious effort to break away from entanglements and murkiness 13.191–2; incorporating our deeper energies into the spiritual quest 12.335; integrating primordial forces, so that it glows with the energy of the *ḍākinīs* 12.324; the more we strive to be spiritual, the more unspiritual we become 7.413; Nanda's lack of zest for spiritual life 2.82–3; not an armchair life, but active and dynamic 1.553; one needs all the time to be making a definite effort 4.44; only a little of our energy goes into it 4.133; passivity is its complete antithesis 18.456–8; Sangharakshita's view of spiritual life as dynamic criticized 21.114; the subjugation and transfiguration of all the energies of our consciousness 12.336; the transformation of psycho-spiritual energy is its central business 13.162; trapped in sexual channels, our energy may be unavailable for spiritual life 1.390; you can use the competitive spirit to get yourself to make more effort 13.136–7

CHALLENGES

the central problem of the spiritual life
finding emotional equivalents for our intellectual understanding 1.494, 12.111, 15.154–5; conserving and unifying our energies 1.390, 4.133–4, 5.571; how to translate knowledge into being 11.192; our knowledge is only superficial, we don't know in the depths 12.22–3; when the means to Enlightenment becomes an object of attachment 1.303

difficulties in the spiritual life
all kinds of ideologies by which we may be ensnared 12.654–6; anyone can come to a standstill 19.457; attempting to combine sexual activity and spiritual life 17.215; belief in God stultifies our spiritual life 12.96–7; the different obstacles faced by men and women 17.219; doubt and indecision lie at the root of our difficulties 17.615–17; guilt can poison or vitiate our spiritual life 1.509; how to deal with a spiritually barren period 26.58; if we're trying to live a spiritual life, the world may not give us an easy time 12.623; if you are anxious about the spiritual life, something has gone wrong 17.254; ignorance is the root of all hindrances and obstacles 18.180; at the beginning it's difficult to know yourself and know what you need to do 25.74; it is not necessarily easy or free from suffering 14.487; lack of wholeheartedness 15.208; negative emotions are one of the biggest obstacles 12.391; no reason to think of spiritual life as difficult and worldly life as easy 4.48–9, 4.292–3; sex is an obstacle to spiritual life 11.572–3; spiritual life is difficult, so people reduce it to external practice and money 19.278; the more we struggle to eliminate the ego-sense, the stronger it becomes 7.407; there is a force that is holding or even pulling us back all the time 15.359; there will always be ups and

downs 26.80; typical setbacks 18.346; uncomfortable at first, but it's worth it to get rid of the great difficulty 4.370; until Stream Entry, it is bound to be a struggle 2.250; we have to confront its demands 17.363; you may experience real suffering and at the same time feel deeply happy 17.338

dangers of the spiritual life
beware of taking too soft a view of it 11.407; the danger of its becoming ego-centred 4.500; the danger of treating the ideal in a drily analytical fashion 2.155; the danger that it may become associated with fear and revulsion 18.129; ethical formalism is one of its greatest enemies 2.366; if we regard the relatively real as illusory our spiritual life falls to the ground 14.576; one must be on one's guard against humbug 18.429; there is no safe way of living the spiritual life 19.57; valuing psychology over ethics, spiritual life can becomes refined aestheticism 17.694–5

opposition to the spiritual life
compromise is the enemy of the spiritual life 26.63; the externality that threatens to grind it out of existence 7.267–8; conflict between ego-centred intellect and transpersonal spiritual life 12.217–18; deliberately forgetting it 4.272; it is under attack and needs to be defended 2.649–50

SUPPORT AND SUCCESS

supportive conditions for spiritual life
art as a support 1.262, 21.250–1; creating favourable conditions 4.481; a healthy basis to feel that everything is alive 13.272; it needs supportive conditions 7.259–61, 12.554; meditation, study, work, puja, communication 10.213–18; positive conceptions of reality efficacious as supports 1.243; the recollection of death 18.551; the spiritual life is a cooperative venture 14.456; supportive conditions allow change without much effort 5.252; you shouldn't be too dependent on them 11.618

success in spiritual life
can we reach a point from which we will not regress? 2.261; conceiving of it in terms of worldly success 19.460; constant mindfulness of emptiness is the secret of success 7.413; success would be assured if you put in the energy you give to material things 4.150; remember that people in a much worse condition have succeeded 4.448; people with success in the world are well placed to take up the spiritual life 4.450–1

spiritual materialism *see under* materialism

spiritual practice

what is spiritual practice?
all practice is dualistic, though its goal is non-dualistic 2.282, 14.591–2; any observance, method, or exercise conducive to skilful mental states 11.130; if you are rooted in reality your practice is the way you live 14.588; it is actuated by a desire to escape from something 7.218; a form of psychological conditioning 12.467; like a depth charge 2.282; a source of protection 18.80–1; weaving the thread of the teachings into cloth 18.136–7; whatever conduces to expansion of consciousness, self-transcendence 26.129

the purpose and effect of practice
all spiritual practices will help you to overcome desire for approval 18.639; can you see immediate results of practice? 15.502–5; the far-reaching effect of spiritual practice 13.253; it brings happiness 17.168; it must develop all the 'faculties' of human personality 26.129; its aim is to redirect the cyclic flow of semi-conscious volitions 15.205; a mistake to imagine you can practise without changing 15.114; one of its fruits is clarity: seeing things as they are 17.168; practice without understanding that in reality no one practises anything is dangerous 1.403; practices serve a purpose that lies beyond them 2.265, 17.306; to change the mind 12.466–7; to tackle pride 18.639; to overcome fear of change 16.110; to remove the illusion of separate selfhood 7.360, 26.53; the redirecting of the will 7.302; replenishing your spiritual resources 19.550; we need to pay specific attention to its other-regarding aspects 15.236–7; we tend to want something from it that has nothing to do with its true purpose 3.420

choosing the right practice
any practice will do, as long as you do it 18.473; don't be too precious about it 18.192–3; latch onto whichever form of practice seems most inspiring and helpful 11.221; the main thing is to start actually practising 4.618; suitability depends on adapting the practice to the character of the practitioner 7.313; the temptation of the transcendental sweet shop 11.62; we should practise teachings that correspond to the stage we have reached 11.65

what do you need to be able to practise?
bringing the enjoyment of daily life into spiritual practice 15.155; engaging the emotions with spiritual practice 17.685;

freedom from energy-sapping doubt 14.586; it is perhaps surprising how little we need to know 18.184; no spiritual practice will do you any good unless you put your heart into it 11.711–12; powerful commitment 18.161; protecting one's practice 17.561; a sense of urgency, in a positive context 19.245; there is not some kind of separate religious faculty we bring to it 14.443; we need specific, concrete practices 12.467; you are carried along in your practice by your faith 17.336, 17.554–5; you can practise the Dharma without a special costume 18.520; you don't need a lot of initiations or Dharma books 18.167–8

day to day practice
altruism stops the ethical dimension from being crowded out by the psychological 17.645; the day to day application of your practice 19.455; doing things for others, you are surely moving towards the aim of spiritual practice 17.694; five things to practise every day 5.45–6; hang on to your practice 19.418; look after your practice as you look after your body 17.306; make whatever you are doing your spiritual practice 18.153–4; the need for constant practice 7.99–100; our line of practice must be specialized, but our approach should be broad 13.326; the practice you actually do is the Dharma as far as you are concerned 18.496; to be done regularly, not just when you feel like it 12.467; you have to work out your practice in a detailed manner 19.380

theory and practice
all practice should be performed in a cheerful and easy-going manner 14.451; danger that your preoccupation with the Unconditioned is purely theoretical 15.576; having understood what is skilful, one still has to put the theory into practice 17.569–70; if you accept principles, you should put them into practice 18.111; one can amass knowledge about Buddhism while hardly practising it at all 18.107–8; thinking you're qualified to practise what you understand intellectually 18.517–18; wanting to discuss Nirvāṇa suggests not having begun to think about practice 18.413; you can only find out whether a teaching is helpful in practice 12.369–70

are you really practising?
believing you're practising when you're not 19.276; determination to practise the Dharma 19.223, 19.245; drifting from one 'deep and meaningful' practice to another 17.681–2; feeling that your practice is 'not good enough' 16.488; going through the motions of spiritual practice 3.420, 3.457–8, 17.306, 19.456; objecting to spiritual practice because of its imagined discomforts 17.302–3; ostentatious spiritual practice 19.465; out of touch with your practice, it's hard to appreciate what others are doing 11.267; practice that heightens the ego-sense is unspiritual 7.375; review your practice, but not too often 17.571; talking about 'my spiritual development' is a reduction of truly spiritual practice 15.340; the tendency of spiritual practices to become mechanical 11.37–8; the test of Dharma practice: the parrot that squawked 18.249–50; we are not Buddhist unless we practise 10.158

practising alongside other people
be tolerant towards others' spiritual practice 18.222; the true test is how we relate to the challenge of 'other people' 3.521; we practise here in this world, together with other people 12.605

spiritual progress

what is spiritual progress?
Buddhist doctrines state the conditions of spiritual progress 10.158; in what does it really consist? 3.400; it depends on the emergence of the five spiritual faculties 17.10–13; it is possible because the mind can change 7.153, 9.399, 19.235; like a space probe launched from the Earth 2.263; not just climbing a mountain, also unfolding like a lotus 5.687; one must distinguish spiritual from material progress 15.510; 'One who loves the Dharma passionately, progresses' 13.274–5; a perpetual ascent through an unending series of 'selves' 7.166; progress is impossible if there is an unchanging self 7.213; the three *yānas* seen as progressive ascent 7.479; we are all participating in the process of cosmic Enlightenment 16.77

making progress
as you progress, you stop distinguishing between helping yourself and helping others 14.555; as you progress, your path converges with that of others 16.76–7; as you progress, your practice becomes more and more specific 18.413; being open to positive influences enables you to make progress 18.98; the beginning of progress is to know that we do not know 13.346, 14.403; if we can feel real concern for the needs of others, we have made some progress 17.204; in meditation, *see under* meditation; it begins when you come up against self-will 19.16; make sure

that your progress is spiritual as well as material 10.346–7, 10.389–90; often those who concentrate on basic teachings make the most progress 15.198; progress depends on our own efforts 10.346; said to be quicker on the Mantranaya than on the Pārimitānaya 13.288–9; single-sex situations are indispensable 2.372; spiritual life is usually a very gradual process 15.363–4; there is no limit if you are single-minded 15.242; to make progress, people need to experience a few unpleasant shocks 17.161; try to stretch yourself and go a little further all the time 19.279; we have to make dualistic distinctions 18.85, 18.179; we need to intervene positively in the way we experience the world 15.153; when you become a bit more advanced, don't look down on your early efforts 25.74; the wrong idea that to make progress we will have to suffer 17.166; you may make as much progress with one practice as with another 18.392–3

what supports progress
the ability to persist through challenges 18.161–2; being honest about the limitations we need to overcome 18.147–8; the best time to make progress is when you are sick and suffering (Hakuin) 15.393, 15.395; exploring the path with others in complete harmony and honesty 2.462; Going for Refuge in the presence of the sangha 4.66; once your direction is established, you don't need conceptual support 5.252; the qualities needed for spiritual progress 17.335; short-term goals give us something to work on and a measure of progress 15.96; sticking to a long list of dos and don'ts doesn't guarantee progress 18.324; there is no situation in which progress is guaranteed 19.362; we don't always appreciate the progress made by other people 15.364–5; we must know *exactly* what we need to do to help us go forward 12.280–1; without strong positive emotion no progress is possible 26.25; you don't have to suffer pain in order to make progress 10.228, 17.252; you have to start where you are 18.284, 25.74

measuring progress
comparing your spiritual progress with that of others 18.17–19; the concept of the breaking of fetters gives us a way to measure progress 4.185; danger of comparing people in terms of their spiritual progress 4.41; don't keep tearing yourself up by the roots to see if you have grown 17.267; every year there should be some discernible progress 15.509; forget all about making progress 5.46; going beyond the idea of progress 18.397; however much we learn, we can learn more 10.258; make some progress every day, but don't bother exactly where you are 4.500–1; no need to fuss about one's spiritual progress 19.578–9; observing the progress of a spiritual friend 15.363; the seven *bodhyaṅgas* as a checklist of progress 15.225; signs of spiritual progress 12.25–6; steady and systematic 3.411; when you are pleased with your progress, you can lose mindfulness 18.142–3

not making progress
are you making progress or are you stuck? 18.51; the difficulty of making spiritual progress 4.181–2; having 'good' meditations but not seeming to make much progress 4.149; if you're not making progress, consider what is holding you back 8.211–12; if you're not making progress, go back to fundamentals 12.565–7; if you have fixed self-view, no progress is possible 15.519–20; it may be because we don't act with the whole of ourselves 11.50; it's no use blaming conditions or lifestyle 12.566; making little progress due to lack of *vīrya* 4.132–3, 4.474; to make progress, start experiencing yourself as acting rather than acted upon 26.63; not to advance is to go back 7.100; the 'person incapable of progress', *see icchantika*; relationships as a threat to spiritual progress 26.28; settling for limited progress 17.682; the story of the twentieth blow, *see under* parables and stories; unless we become integrated there is no real progress 5.30–1; we may not seem to be progressing, but we will, through sustained effort 3.305; why don't people seem to make spiritual progress? 3.398; without a path, no progress 3.398; without positive emotion there is no progress 11.155, 19.28; a woman who had been trying for forty years, but 'hadn't got anywhere' 2.244, 26.558–9; you refuse to commit yourself, so you get nowhere 2.297

spiritual rebirth

introduction
the birth of the seed of Buddhahood 5.44; the Buddha's spiritual rebirth 10.261; desire to emerge like a butterfly from the chrysalis of our old conditions 16.227; Going for Refuge as spiritual rebirth 2.7, 11.384, 22.461; 'healing powers descend and bless' 25.43; integration is a rebirth of the whole personality 17.119; members

of the sangha are prepared to die in order to be spiritually reborn 11.134; positive symbolism of fire: change, transformation, spiritual rebirth 16.70; and the spiral path 5.41–2; in terms of the *parāvṛtti* (turning about) 2.276, 12.174, 17.481; transformation as a model for the spiritual life: death and rebirth 16.227; we have to give birth to the young hero, that is, to ourselves 12.193; when we go for Refuge to the Buddha we are spiritually reborn 25.29; visualization of a Buddha or bodhisattva 5.33–4

symbols
the cave 4.542; fire 16.70; the lotus 4.207, 12.220; the mandala, symbolizing the new self born out of the conflicts of the old 12.219; spring 25.29

see also
new self, *see under* self/further perspectives on 'self'

spiritualism Sangharakshita perceives the dangers of spiritualism 20.351, 20.352–3; Sangharakshita's mother's interest in it 20.21; Satyapriya and the Ouija board 20.351–3; it might be a good starting point for an inquiry into the Dharma 18.412

spite *see pradāśa*

Sponberg, Alan *see* Saramati

spontaneity

introduction
the Sanskrit for spontaneity is *sahaja* 19.258; opening up, becoming free-flowing 19.156; the natural spontaneity of the mind 18.231; the essence of spiritual inspiration 18.119; *anubhogacarya*, the life of spontaneity 14.521, 18.254; spontaneity and *adhiṣṭhāna* 16.520; the spontaneity of the true individual 3.470; without spontaneity, there is no life 3.297

Enlightened spontaneity
'All *dharmas* spontaneously freed as mists of rain vanish into air' 18.596–7; Siddhārtha's experience under the rose-apple tree 2.111, 15.222; the Buddha's life as like child's play 16.18; the Buddha's actions were the spontaneous overflow of his love 22.285; *bodhi*: uninterrupted creativity and spontaneity 13.298; the bodhisattva's spontaneity 4.135–6, 4.240, 14.411, 14.501–2; Enlightenment as complete spontaneity: the Vajrayāna view 19.258–9; the life of wisdom is the spontaneous life 14.556; Milarepa's life is spontaneous and free of obstruction 18.66; perfect spontaneity 1.586–7; the spontaneity of the Enlightened person 11.11; the spontaneity of the Transcendental 19.24–5, 19.156; a state of poise and balance and at the same time spontaneous action 18.344; waking up to being a Buddha releases tremendous spontaneity 12.234; the all-performing wisdom of Amoghasiddhi 3.374–5, 4.166

spontaneity in the Buddhist tradition
the Mahāmudrā 18.253–4, 19.156; the spontaneity of Nyingma lamas 12.298–9; Dudjom Rimpoche's spontaneity 22.508; a state of complete spontaneity (Mahāmudrā) – difficult to achieve 19.136–7; spontaneity of the way Buddhism began in the West 7.449

the practice of spontaneity
acting spontaneously in everything we do 11.7–8, 18.122; beneficial activities spontaneously manifesting with no ego-sense 7.409; paradoxically, it comes from discipline and regular practice 17.268, 17.459–60; to learn it, you just do whatever occurs to you 18.253–4; a day-to-day commitment may feel more spontaneous than a vow 19.146–7; devotion must involve an element of joy and spontaneity 15.604–5; ideally we should act spontaneously, without self-recrimination 17.166; if you get rid of desires and clinging, joy will spontaneously arise 19.579; notice your spontaneous reaction when you ask yourself what you want to do 19.395; responding spontaneously to others' needs 5.187, 22.374; speaking spontaneously 13.360, 18.48; spontaneity and the spiritual life 5.285; spontaneous compassionate activity when the ego-sense is removed 5.44, 7.376; spontaneous ethics 14.547; spontaneous understanding 18.444; trying to develop a free-flowing spontaneous attitude 14.410; trying to surprise someone into spontaneity 19.556

mindfulness and spontaneity
blended with mindfulness 16.301–2; the idea that mindfulness curbs spontaneity 11.626; mindfulness and spontaneity 14.582, 16.301–2, 17.266–7; true self-awareness reconciles self-consciousness and spontaneity 14.581–2; you may have a 'stupid' phase – less reactive but not yet spontaneous 4.382–3; you may start off 'like a piece of wood', but the wood must start flowering 4.340

obstacles and confusions
'being yourself' is not to be confused with spontaneity 12.487; the difference between true spontaneity and reactive behaviour 4.340, 17.266, 19.258–9; rudeness in the

name of spontaneity 4.337; we are less free to think and feel spontaneously than at any time in history 7.266; dominated by routines and responsibilities, how can you be spontaneous? 3.297; the Dharma's crystallization: a spontaneous act becomes a laborious chore 14.436

sports

introduction
bungee jumping 24.503; future Dharma practitioners may be those whose energies have been aroused by sport 18.412; golf 24.471; listed in the Pāli canon 16.236; a sense of a team rather than oneself 10.603; why risk one's precious human life on dangerous sports like rock-climbing? 24.503; wrestling 20.140–1

football
football hooligans 11.195; a footballer ridiculed for trying to make sense of reincarnation 25.16–17; sangha likened to a football team 9.304–5, 9.307, 9.310–11; the tribal excitement of a football match 11.79

spring 'Alas, that Spring should vanish with the Rose!' 21.291–2; the Buddha walks through the Magadha countryside one spring morning 10.310; the celebration of the coming of spring in the Song of Solomon 13.543; crocus 25.221; the loveliness of spring 25.284; the month of May 25.341; orchids of spring 2.130; 'Peach-bloom, each Springtide, fills my heart with grief' 25.281; 'Spring' (poem) 25.302; spring buds 25.336; spring 'comes slow up this way' 23.133; spring festival 18.379; spring flowers 24.150; spring in Bihar 7.427, 20.457; in youth and in riper years 25.285

Springheel Jack (missionary) 21.357

squirrel Indra and the squirrel, *see under* parables and stories; the old grey squirrel 25.307; Princess Irene's squirrel 21.319, 25.258

śraddhā (Pāli *saddhā*) in Buddhism, *see* faith; in Hinduism 7.96

Śraddhāpa, Dharmachari 14.xix–xx, 14.327–36

śramaṇa-brāhmaṇa *see brāhmaṇa-śramaṇa*

śramaṇakāraka-dharmas (duties of an ascetic) 2.194

śramaṇas (Pāli *samaṇa*) definition 3.643 (n109); antagonism with *brāhmaṇas* 20.234–5; language 16.367; *samaṇa* and *bhikkhu* as overlapping terms for alms-mendicants 10.479

śrāmaṇera (male novice) ordination, *see under bhikkhu*/ordination; *prātimokṣa* 2.345; precepts, *see under* precepts/other sets of precepts

śramaṇerikā (female novice) 2.345

śrāvaka (Pāli *sāvaka*, hearer, listener) definition 16.616 (n241); attains a stage of holiness having heard about the path from a Buddha or his disciple 1.213, 2.267; disrespect to 16.303; the first characteristic of a good disciple is that he listens 12.296; 'hearer': one who is completely receptive 15.512–13, 15.551, 17.208, 19.219; hears not only with the ear, but also within 2.266, 15.436; makes no attempt to communicate their experience 2.267; *sāvaka-bodhi* 1.85–6, 2.266–7; as compared to bodhisattvas, in the Mahāyāna's view 1.230; *śrāvaka* mind 16.545

śrāvakayāna *see under yānas*

Śrāvastī (Pāli Sāvatthī, present-day Balampur)

introduction
associations with the Buddha's life 16.567; the attachment to pleasure of the people of Sāvatthī 10.616–18; called the City of Wonders because the Buddha performed the 'twin miracle' there 14.400; the setting of the *Diamond Sūtra* 14.400–1; where the Buddha spent twenty-five rainy seasons 14.401; described by Trevor Ling 15.381

Eastern (or East) Park (the house of Migāra's mother)
donated by Visākhā 15.381; in the *Udāna*, *see under Udāna*/settings

Jeta Grove, Anāthapiṇḍika's Park
the addition of a *dharmasala*, as recorded in the *Udāna* 10.471–2; the Buddha's headquarters 15.381; Sangharatana's construction of the Nava Jetavana Vihara 10.472, 10.710 (n390); the donation of the park, *see under* Anāthapiṇḍika; the excavation of the Jeta Grove 10.472; setting in the *Udāna*, *see under Udāna*/settings; the setting for the *Gaṇḍavyūha Sūtra* 14.218–19; setting for the *Small Sukhāvatī-vyūha Sūtra* 1.331

Śreṇika (the wanderer) 14.549–51, 14.654 (n486)

Śrī (goddess) birth as a goddess 16.409; as a goddess of agriculture 16.409; as a goddess of wealth 16.399; in the *Sūtra of Golden Light*, *see under Sūtra of Golden*

Light; worship 16.410, 16.395–6; *see also* Lakṣmī

Sri Gauranga Press 22.120–1, 22.132

Sri Lanka (Ceylon)

NOTES ON SRI LANKA

history
the idea that a Sinhalese had to be a Buddhist 8.463, 8.471; King Dutugamunu (2nd century BCE) 7.512, 8.463–5; King Valagamba (also Vaṭṭhugāmini, 1st century BCE) 8.465, 14.22; Kassapa V 2.225; King Mahinda IV (10th century CE) 8.466; King Rajasimbha I (of Kandy) 8.468; King Parakramabahu the Great 8.468; Catholic conversion and persecution by the Portuguese (1505) 8.468; Dutch occupation (1658–1796) 8.468–9; Catholic riots 8.19; Christian control 8.471–2; drinking 7.64–5, 8.55–6; link between patriotism and religion 8.464, 8.471–2, 8.475; British rule 8.469–70; Christian missionaries 8.5–6, 8.27, 8.470; the Panadura Controversy (encounter between Buddhism and Christianity) 8.16–17; Dharmapala's ideas for the regeneration of the nation 8.61–2; Muslim–Buddhist Riots 8.63; independence (1948) 8.473; great insurgency (1971) 8.473, 8.475; conflict between Sinhalese and Tamils 24.245, 24.667 (n294)

politics
'Religio-Nationalism in Sri Lanka' 8.459–76; banning alcohol from state functions 8.227; nationalizing denominational (Christian) schools 8.285–6; Prime Minister assassinated by a monk 7.567 (n121), 8.283–4, 8.474, 22.458, 26.576; the first woman Prime Minister in history (Sirimavo Bandaranaike) 8.283–4

culture
practice of visual arts and literature 8.467–8; Sinhalese classical poetry 25.176, 25.591 (n55); Siri Rāhula, the best classical Sinhalese poet 2.213; Buddhist contributions to culture 7.445; D. H. Lawrence in Ceylon 8.543–4

HISTORY OF BUDDHISM IN SRI LANKA

history
Buddhism was brought by Mahinda 2.228, 8.462–3, 15.184–5; Sanghamittā brings a cutting of the bodhi tree to Sri Lanka 2.222; the Buddha's footprint at Adam's Peak 2.223, 25.27; Sumana, the deity of Sripada (Mount of the Holy Footprint) 8.216; Pāli canon first written down at the Fourth Council at Alu-vihāra 4.24; the writing down of the Tipiṭaka (1st century BCE) 8.465; preservation of the Pāli canon 14.35; belonged to the oldest Mahāyāna school, according to Dharmapala 8.41; in the *Laṅkāvatāra Sūtra* 1.358–9; all three *yānas* once flourished 7.483; *bhikkhus* accompanied the army into battle (2nd century BCE) 8.464–5; extinction of the *bodhisattva-saṃvara* and *abhiṣeka* lineages 7.483; suppression of Vetulyavāda (quasi-Mahāyānist movement) 22.169; practice of Theravāda Buddhism 3.407; Buddhists having to live under Christian marriage and divorce laws 8.399; Hardy's study of monastic life 12.69–70; religio-nationalism 8.463–5, 8.475; promotion by post-colonial government 8.xxviii; revival 7.444–5, 8.472–6; Hikkaduwa Siri Sumangala Nayaka Thera 8.7; 'modernist' Buddhism 13.403, 13.427

Mahāvaṃsa
introduction 7.569 (n125); composed by Mahānāma 8.467–8; dates of the Buddha's life 7.491, 11.491; explains why the Dharma was written down 14.22, 14.293; the origins of Sri Lanka 2.667 (n40); Sanghamittā brings a cutting of the bodhi tree to Sri Lanka 2.222; Sinhalese kings sponsored celebrations on full moon days 2.226; the statement of the eight *arhants* 8.464; Tamil records tell a different story 7.72

other texts
Cūḷavaṃsa 2.225; *The Book of Protection* (*Pirith Potha*) 8.532–3

monasteries and temples
administration and maintenance 8.467; *pirivenas* 8.472, 23.42, 23.481 (n73); Abhayagiri 4.24; Avukana Buddha Statue 8.139; Bambalapitiya temple 20.125–6; Mahāvihāra 4.24; Mandalārāma 8.465, 10.706 (n359); Kandy, Temple of the Tooth 9.63, 20.126–8, 23.11; Vidyodaya Pirivena Maligakanda 8.7, 8.51; Vidyalankara Pirivena (University of Kelaniya) 7.72, 7.567–8 (n122), 12.428

Sangharakshita visits
first visit 9.279, 9.488, 20.116–29; Wellawatta (Colombo), Ramakrishna Mission ashram 20.116–26, 23.11; Vidyalankara Pirivena 20.122; experience of travelling in a rickshaw 3.586; invited there to write a biography of Dharmapala (but doesn't go) 22.135; musical events 7.82; not allowed to enter, having destroyed identification papers 2.414, 20.229–30, 23.13

the state of Buddhism
an evocation of Sri Lankan Buddhism 1.192–4; 'Impressions of a Buddhist Country Today' (1945) 7.64–6; departed from real Buddhist principles a long time ago 10.413; Buddhism subordinated to the state 8.463; Buddhism as a living tradition disappeared long before the British came 8.472; exclusion of non-rational elements 12.105–6; traditional or 'a live thing'? 9.66; 'If Ceylon is Buddhist, cannibals are Christian' 7.14, 7.71; literature dry and dull, suggested spiritual deadness of Buddhism 20.124; mechanical recitation of the Going for Refuge formula 15.692–700, 15.710; the dying out of the significance of individual Going for Refuge 15.694, 15.709–10; the teacher as just one who imparts information 15.727; *dāna* wasted 8.175; the reason why meditation almost died out in Sri Lanka 8.465–6; spiritually moribund 21.204

bhikkhus
became the intelligentsia 15.557; becoming more political than spiritual 8.473–5; betrayal of the spirit of Buddhism 8.475–6; 'the cap-wearing *bhikkhu*' 17.634; unfaithfulness to the spirit of the Dharma, regard for its letter 8.468; European 7.65; more interested in meditation than good works 7.65; most *bhikkhus* have no clear idea of their religion 7.65; different Nikāyas 2.193, 2.688 (n269), 12.428; chanting of *suttas* on the radio 15.437; a heritage of shame 8.475–6; in thrall to the laity 17.587; forest-dwelling monks 8.475; Jagdish Kashyap and the *anattā* doctrine 3.492, 12.428–9, 17.630, 19.446–7, 20.447; a lot of monks have been pushed into ordination 17.587; 'meditate all the time' – a misconception about meditation 18.498; most *bhikkhus* don't meditate 15.735–6; on pilgrimage: 'a motley collection of rogues in yellow robes' 23.399; political activities (5th to 18th century CE) 8.468; 'sitting on a treasure … the value of which they do not understand' 12.429, 20.448; some resentful to have been handed to the sangha by their parents 10.267, 19.475; take on secular education, medicine, and law 8.466; tendency to undermine 'mere faith' 15.723–4; their participation in politics 8.283–4; think that puja and worship is just for lay people 14.431, 19.125

popular Buddhism
festivals 2.226–8, 7.65; orthodox Buddhists shocked by modern discoveries 13.427; Buddhist programmes on the radio 7.65, 15.437; *dasasilamata* ('ten precept nuns') 2.744 (n689); *pirith* (protection) ceremony 8.532, 22.250–1; stupas 16.150, 16.157; Buddhists accuse a painter of polluting the Buddha 21.398–9; un-Buddhistic practices (observed by Dharmapala) 8.27; Hindu temples (*kōvil, devālaya*) 7.72, 12.105–6, 19.226–7, 20.122; Tamil god Muruka (or Skanda) 7.72; worship of Nātha, a form of Avalokiteśvara 2.175; worship of Vishnu as a protector of the Dharma 26.667

Buddhist World
its fundamentalist nature 21.245–7; 'arguing by abuse' 8.171–2, 22.171–2; attacks Sangharakshita and Dr Malalasekera 8.172, 8.682 (n113), 22.168–78, 23.158; Sangharakshita's parody 8.135

other publications
The Buddhist (magazine founded by Dharmapala) 8.28–9, 8.399; *The Buddhist* (YMBA magazine) 7.7, 8.138, 8.373; the *Bosat* 8.138, 8.376; *Ceylon Daily News Vesak Annual* 8.139; free literature distributed by the Buddhist Publication Society, Kandy 8.275–6; *Sinhala Bauddhaya* (Maha Bodhi Society publication) 8.64

in relation to Buddhists elsewhere
an ancient poem predicting the spread of the Dharma over the earth 8.216; contact with the Buddhists of Japan 8.30–4; Dr Ambedkar visits 9.10, 9.65–7, 9.119; acknowledgement of Dr Ambedkar's conversion 9.133; no response to an appeal for help with Buddhist revival in India 22.271; contrast with Tibetan Buddhism 1.192–7

see also
Dharmapala, Anagarika; Dharmapala, Bhikkhu; *Forest Monks of Sri Lanka, see* Carrithers; formalism; Jagdish Kashyap's experience in Sri Lanka, *see under* Kashyap

Srimala, Dharmacharini brief introduction 24.650 (n212); conducts ordinations in India 2.733 (n628), 10.lii; *Mitrata* 2.737 (n654), 24.658 (n244); member of the Preceptors' College 12.597, 12.631; on retreat at Padmaloka 24.172

Śrīmāla, Queen 14.175

Śrīmāladevi-siṃhanāda (Queen Śrīmāla's 'Lion's-Roar') 14.175; her Buddha-field 14.175; her ten vows 14.175; she teaches *ekayāna* and the *tathāgatagarbha* 14.175

Śrīmati (*Gaṇḍavyūha Sūtra*) 14.221–2

Sringeri, India 20.367

śrīpāda (Pāli *siripāda*, the Buddha's footprint) be prepared to see the Buddha's footprints in unlikely places 25.33; the Buddha's footprint at Adam's Peak 2.223, 25.27; footprints in different parts of the Buddhist world 2.223; Sangharakshita's poem 'Sri Pada' 25.24–34; wherever the Buddha leaves his footprints there is an efflorescence of culture 25.27–8; worship 2.222–3, 16.156, 26.476

Śrīsambhava (*Gaṇḍavyūha Sūtra*) 14.221–2

srotāpanna *see* Stream Entrant

śruta-mayī prajñā *see under prajñā*

St Clair, William 24.584

St John, John 15.392

Stace, Walter Terence 7.195–6, 7.596 (n301)

Stagg, Christopher 18.xiii

stagnation *see styāna*

stained-glass reality like a stained-glass window 5.606–7; in Ulm Cathedral 24.595

stains 'the contagion of the world's slow stain' 7.352; purifying the defilements like removing a stain from a pure white cloth 26.642; the 'shadow side' – not a romantic shadow but a smelly stain 16.304; the stains of adventitious defilements 13.389; 'Worst of all stains is the stain of ignorance' (*Dhammapada*) 7.126

Stalin, Joseph 26.654

Stanley, Arthur Penrhyn 23.208

Stapledon, Olaf 3.381, 22.463

Starck, Christer *see* Ratnapriya

stars 'At the birth of a child or a star there is pain' 3.210, 20.409; brightness obscured by city smoke 25.447; A brilliant star appeared on the horizon and has vanished' (re Ambedkar) 10.97; concepts can wreak havoc, like a constellation of malignant stars 7.326; the Evening Star 25.239; following the Buddha: 'kinship with a star' 25.286; 'How flashingly alive they were!' 24.82; 'I wonder if tonight I shall see the stars' 25.444; logic cannot reach *brahman* any more than a ladder can reach the stars 7.79; 'Love which moves the sun in heaven, and all the stars' 7.61; 'love's flight among the stars' 25.229; Māra: a baleful star in the firmament of man's delusion 7.327; 'More than the seas he gave his blood, more than the stars his eyes' 1.430; 'not a fourth [third] note but a star' 2.162, 26.144; the Southern Cross 24.82; *Star Maker* 3.381, 22.463; 'As stars, a fault of vision, as a lamp ...' 2.81, 16.623 (n308); their meaning for different poets 25.75–6; 'to see the stars after the sun has risen' 2.81; standing for spiritual aspirations 25.77–8; stumbling to the stars 25.215; 'unbounded as the stars' 26.391; stars unfolding like flowers 25.181; the virtue of the stars 17.58–9; 'What can the stars do?' (*Jātaka*) 22.278

starting points cultural Going for Refuge is not to be depreciated, it's a starting point 3.328; even thinking that one is Enlightened might be a starting point 18.412–13; 'May I deliver all beings from difficulties': a pragmatic starting point 4.66–7; the mindfulness of breathing as the starting point for the practice of mindfulness 5.30, 12.650–1; self-awareness is the starting point of the higher evolution 3.14, 3.477; spiritualism and other potential starting points for an inquiry into the Dharma 18.412; the starting point of the 'real you' 4.259–60

state *see under* politics/government

states of mind *see* mental states

statesmanship 16.477

status

spiritual status
bhikkhus' certainty about their superior status 22.332, 22.338–9; *bhikkhunīs*' desire for equal status with *bhikkhus* 2.602–3; dropping hints about our social or spiritual status 17.286–7; spiritual status cannot be conferred 4.198; the danger of 'pride of priesthood' 18.176; don't make use of your spiritual development to aggrandize yourself 10.448; make a clear distinction between spiritual attainment and ecclesiastical position 19.359; a monk

Stepping
Stones
Vol. 1
No. 1
JULY 1950.
Contents
YOUNG MEN'S BUDDHIST ASSOCIATION, KALIMPONG

17.196–7; the Dharma student should abstain from activities which stimulate the lower mind 1.30; in dreams, vivid sensuous impressions without objective stimulus 1.368–9; effective Going for Refuge is a means of stimulating real Going for Refuge 4.197; the mildly stimulating effect of a brief trip into town 18.424; some people are stimulated by opposition 4.424; spiritually stimulating friendship 13.203; taking control of your responses to sensory stimuli 15.288, 17.102–3; work stimulates energy 17.71–4

Stoicism acceptance of death at Pompeii 24.293; *apatheia* 2.117; *The Essential Works of Stoicism* 23.288, 23.516 (n325)

Stonehenge Sangharakshita's visit 12.254–5, 23.113–16, 23.115 (photograph); reopened 25.320; we may not feel any continuity with the people who built it 4.105, 12.254–5

Stonyhurst College 24.365–6

stopping the complete stopping of the waterfall 19.200; stop doing anything until you know what you want to do 4.483–7, 5.647; stopping and seeing 1.354; stopping positive ideas from 'floating away' 17.89–91; stopping the process of reacting to feeling with craving, *see under vedanā*/gap; stopping the wheel 2.256, 3.243; sudden method of stopping craving 2.256–9

stories *see* parables and stories

storms a bush surviving a storm 25.242; a demon-created storm, a metaphor for ego-clinging 18.12; 'Indra's cows' (storm clouds) 13.167; stillness of wisdom, storm of activity realized as twin aspects of emptiness 7.140–1; *The Storm over Toldeo* 26.308; Turner going out to sea during a storm 14.473

Story, Francis (Anagarika P. Sugatananda) *The Case for Rebirth* 2.662 (n7), 12.687–8; English director of the Burma World Buddhist Mission 22.130; a rationalistic neo-Theravādin 22.130

Stowe, Harriet Beecher 22.276, 22.600 (n222)

Strachan, Francoise v23

Strachey, Lytton 3.47

straightforwardness the Abhidharma is not really mysterious but quite straightforward 12.140; confession of faults a straightforward acknowledgement 2.260; Milarepa teaches plain straightforward Buddhism – or just common sense 18.565; being straightforward was considered very important by Tantric yogis 19.385–6; the straightforward and upright person (*Mettā Sutta*) 15.272–3; thinking you're being straightforward when you're just being insensitive 15.273

strange Buddhism is 'strange, exotic, colourful, weird, mysterious' 4.644, 13.495; how strange that we do not naturally wish others the deepest happiness! 15.308; it seems strange that anything should continue to exist at all 14.506–7; memory can play strange tricks 24.141–2; the revival of Buddhism is one of the strangest events in the history of religions 7.446–7; space and time are strange things 24.147; the strangeness of the *Dharma-Vinaya* 10.569, 11.42–4, 11.707; the Transcendental is strange to us 11.xvii, 11.42; 'Voyaging through strange seas of Thought, alone' 1.52

strangers the Buddha is a stranger in an ultimate sense 11.xvii, 11.43; confession to a stranger 16.318; Hindus questioning strangers aggressively about their background 20.263–4; preparing for the arrival of the Stranger 25.80–1, 25.184; Sangharakshita's sense of being a stranger 23.111; the Stranger in the Gnostic tradition 14.492, 23.111, 25.87

Stratford-upon-Avon 24.581–2

Stravinsky, Igor 7.451

Strauss, C. T. 8.48

Strauss, D. F. 2.627

Strauss, Richard 12.643, 26.505–6

Strawson, Galen 8.614–16

stream *mahā-rāga*: a stream of positive feeling flowing from the heart of Enlightenment 13.281; 'one whose stream

goes upward' (to Nirvāṇa) (*uddhaṃsoto*) 15.33, 15.745 (n14); one stone divides the whole stream 26.33; the spiritual life a dissolving of the stream of thoughts into the *dharmakāya* 19.187–8, 19.200; 'the wise have crossed the stream' 7.315

Stream Entrant (*srotāpanna*) definition 3.412, 16.614 (n230), 17.635–6 (n212); described in the *Ratana Sutta* 15.64–5; as a 'bodhisattva of the path' 4.179–80; can never forsake the Dharma, because they have *become* the Dharma 9.445–6; someone who took full advantage of Buddhist centre facilities could become a Stream Entrant 12.377–8; has broken the first three of the ten fetters 2.263, 9.252, 15.518; has not more than seven lives to pass through before attaining Nirvāṇa 1.177, 2.263, 15.64, 15.207; one, or rather two, of the eight holy persons: attainment of the path and its fruit 2.146, 15.518; progressing from *pṛthagjana* to Stream Entrant 14.312; reborn into the spiritual family of the Buddha 2.140; the Stream Entrant *lives* his or her knowledge 15.337; a Stream Entrant who loses the will to live 15.369; subtle awareness of being a Stream Entrant vanishes on becoming a once-returner 2.149; three kinds of Stream Entrant (Abhidharma) 15.163; until you're a Stream Entrant, you could resile from the spiritual life 11.586

Stream Entry (*sotāpatti*)

introduction
introduction to the term 15.58, 16.589 (n34); path and fruit 1.176–7, 2.146, 10.146, 15.641; 'Entering the Stream' 2.250–65; how it is to be attained is what the Dharma is meant to explain 3.252; a decisive shift towards the positive 15.341; it is crucially important 15.531–2; the real turning-point in one's spiritual life 15.240–1; a serious and achievable ideal for every Buddhist 3.256, 4.87, 11.450, 18.578; distinction from simply having come into contact with the golden light 16.291; the permanent and far-reaching nature of spiritual experience 2.301, 2.483; the creative, outward-looking momentum of your being 17.345; seems to refer to the self's achievement, but the 'achievement' is liberation from ego 4.40; a transvaluation of values 2.140

history
canonical references 3.661 (n235), 16.590 (n34), 16.614 (n230); in the *Saṃyutta Nikāya*, *see Saṃyutta Nikāya*/doctrines; 'Better is the fruit of entering the Stream than sole sovereignty over the earth' 2.140; became rarer after the Buddha's *parinirvāṇa* 2.298, 9.254; having 'gone upstream' (*uddhaṃsota*) an earlier classification 15.33, 15.467, 15.518; four constituents of Stream Entry 14.82; a concept which solidified and was negated by the protest of the Mahāyāna 4.38; a certificate confirming Stream Entry 23.73

achieved by breaking the first three fetters
insight sufficiently powerful to break them 1.177, 9.253; because the Path of Stream Entry is also the Path of Seeing 2.146–7; looking at the experience objectively 2.263; three fetters broken at once 2.297–8, 15.206; because the gravitational pull of the Unconditioned is stronger 3.253–7; a standard by which to measure our progress 4.185–7; the fetters are permanently broken 5.426–7, 15.523–4; getting to the heart of the theory 11.xix; a taste of freedom 11.47–51

equivalences
and the *bodhicitta* 4.38–41, 4.264, 11.285–6; and the arising of insight 16.589 (n32), 19.450; corresponds to the psychological phenomenon of religious conversion 2.140; feeling constant *mettā* is tantamount to Stream Entry 5.185; the first step of the transcendental Eightfold Path 2.140–1; and Going for Refuge 2.296–7, 15.532; the opening of the Dharma Eye 9.253; the Path of Seeing 2.141, 2.146; transcendence of self and other 4.40

irreversibility
compared with the Mahāyāna view of irreversibility 4.184–5; described as the Point of No Return 3.250–3, 13.432, 15.467; now irreversibly bound for Enlightenment 4.182–3, 16.291; until this point, spiritual life is bound to be a struggle 2.250; whatever you do henceforth can only be creative 18.268

until Stream Entry
always the danger of practising the Dharma the wrong way 19.56–7; gaining Stream Entry in a workaday situation 5.638; mistakenly thinking that Stream Entry is being achieved 23.73; a modest sex life is compatible with the aim of attaining Stream Entry 17.221; a positive, creative, supportive environment is indispensable 12.315; vigour is always necessary 17.70

after Stream Entry
the faith needed to go beyond Stream Entry 17.70–1; having attained it, you cannot be regarded as having failed in life 16.423; the subtle 'I' sense that persists 4.187; you still have to be careful in your practice 19.510

strength building up your psychological strength 15.270–1; choosing between letter and spirit, a Buddhist should have the strength to choose the spirit 1.240; don't attach too much importance to your own strengths 4.41; '... Nowadays it is the strong who need help' 15.538–9, 26.5, 26.35, 26.489; the elephant as a symbol of strength 9.366; 'Hast thou given the horse strength?' 13.540–1; having no emotional strength behind one's action 19.470; in English, difficulty of associating strength with positivity 5.169; 'A disciplined life gives strength' 16.207, 16.552, 20.281; the *samaya* gives strength and structure to your spiritual life 19.397–8; strength, directed by love, changes the world 25.519–20; to strengthen motivation, avoid distractions 12.381; there is no feeling of joy without a feeling of strength 26.35; use your warrior's strength to fight the inner, spiritual battle 18.103, 18.106; vows taken to strengthen one's resolve 1.421, 4.65; you have to estimate your own strength to sustain life in the city 4.583, 19.342; your strength as an individual strengthens the new society 3.464; strengthening faith, *see under* faith/development of faith

strenuousness the bodhisattva putting on the armour of strenuousness 4.60, 4.69; the spiritual life is an active, strenuous, even militant life 11.407; strenuous spiritual practice 7.172

Strindberg, August 14.151, 20.68, 24.373

strīndriya (femininity) 2.97

striving the bodhisattva courses in the idea of non-attainment while striving to attain 1.269; the cessation of all striving 18.451; in reality there is no striving and no attainment 7.45

Strong, John S. 3.653 (n177), 16.599 (n109)

structure like a castle, the *samaya* gives strength and structure to your spiritual life 19.397–8; people need structure 5.378; religion is built into the very structure of Reality 7.317; the structure of language 10.159; the structure of the Triratna Buddhist Community 19.545; the structure of the whole system of practice 1.154; the whole structure of Buddhism stands or falls with the doctrine of *anattā* 7.130; without structure the individual can't be creative 19.545

struggle the artist's struggle 26.363–4; being honest about one's struggles to live in accordance with one's vision 16.488; the Buddha gained Enlightenment through struggle and mistakes 3.20, 11.400; between Buddhism and the abstract noun 3.398; between the golden light and one's inner poisons 16.290–1; between the lower and the higher impulses of one's nature 7.358, 7.401, 26.37; Buddhism exhorts us to perform our duties rather than struggle for our rights 7.280; coming up against one's self-will is the start of the spiritual struggle 19.21; in the early stages of any spiritual career there has to be a struggle 18.32; in practical terms, life is a constant struggle 11.273; Sangharakshita's early struggles with meditation and mindfulness 11.552–3, 25.44–5; the more we struggle to eliminate the ego-sense, the stronger it becomes 7.407; *saṃsāra*: the torrent in which worldly beings struggle 1.241; Siddhārtha's struggle to decide to go forth 3.208; the spiritual life is happy, but it may be a struggle to get into it 15.360; the struggle for survival 12.379–80; the struggle to transform craving 12.626; to struggle with oneself is not easy 12.489; the universe struggling away from pain like a dog in a treadmill 7.47; unless you love the Dharma passionately, sexual renunciation is a struggle 18.127; we generally think of the path in terms of struggle 18.584

stubbornness *see* obstinacy

study

APPROACHING DHARMA STUDY

approach
correct and wrong attitudes to study 1.15–16; studying Buddhism as a 'subject' separate from one's life and experience is impossible 11.508; crucial to all Dharma study is our attitude and our intention 17.460; four stages: words, ideas, meaning, experience 18.382; four knowledges 17.567; the ideal method 1.23–4; the ideal student 1.20–1; learning key terms 1.24, 2.60; a methodical approach to study 15.96; methods and materials 1.22–31; sectarian and synoptic approaches 7.487; *sikkhā* (study) as a *gārava* (object of reverence) 3.70; what intellectual study of Buddhism would cover 11.509–10; whatever we learn, it is always essentially a mystery 3.232

traditional approach
the way (or burden) of study (*ganthadhura*) 2.143, 4.568; predominantly pragmatic, Buddhism being known from within 7.487; in the early sangha study would have been recitation and memorization 3.404; traditional society as a support

for study 1.27–8; early monastic study of comparative religion and secular subjects 2.197; in later Indian Buddhism, study and meditation were considered incompatible 2.201; is practice or learning the basis of the *sāsana*? 8.465, 10.706 (n359); the value Mahāyāna Buddhists place on scriptural studies 7.543; the history of Buddhist studies in the West 3.396, 7.449

'scientific' approach
limited to aspects of Dharma susceptible of intellectual understanding 1.16–17; not irreconcilable with the traditional approach 1.18; 'pseudo-scientific' approach: attempts to demonstrate Buddhism's inferiority 7.487; tends to accumulate facts rather than illuminate principles 7.486–7

study of canonical literature
study it with reference to the tradition from which it sprang 14.17; the critical study of Pāli literature 10.219–21; study of Mahāyāna texts must be preceded by study of the Pāli canon 1.184; study of Pāli, Sanskrit, Tibetan, and Chinese in modern India 7.447; Western Buddhists should make more effort to study the scriptures 13.337–8; commentary must itself be creation, or it is not even commentary 26.45; we need a tradition of interpretation so that texts aren't misunderstood 17.454; wisdom in the context of understanding the scriptures 18.118

caveats
isolating aspects of the Dharma and giving them Western names can distort it 12.139; the modern student may think of Dharma study as one activity among many 1.29; 'no greater menace than a mere grammarian set loose on a sacred text' 8.539; objective and subjective difficulties of studying Buddhism in the West 11.508–10; obstacles that may arise when studying the Perfection of Wisdom 14.144; often people study not the meaning, but just the words 18.382; presenting experiences that you only know about from study 4.551; pride in learning might lead one astray 18.480; unhelpful ways of answering the question 'What is Buddhism?' 25.15–17

DHARMA STUDY AS A PRACTICE

introduction
a demanding discipline 11.508; the devotion to study of the novice bodhisattva 4.178–9; could a non-Buddhist student with a sense of the spiritual understand it better? 1.18; the Dharma must seem the dominating influence of the whole of life 26.43; includes intellectual study, personal practice, and contact with the sangha 11.509–10; it can be a practice, but you have to go on to reflect and meditate 17.535; moving from clarity to uncertainty and back to clarity 19.101; people who think that study is the only Buddhist practice 16.127–8; a phase of study followed by a phase of meditation 4.568–9; receiving teachings from Dharma study 18.182; study and the three levels of wisdom 17.567; study and the three temperaments 25.12–15

why do we need to study?
don't rationalize your failure to study 25.14; Dharma study is probably essential, in balance with other practices 17.573–4; Dharma study's importance to the development of insight 19.449; even immersed in a Buddhist lifestyle, you still need to study 19.508; festivals and celebrations are all very well, but study is needed 8.243; how far can one get without study? 4.350–1; the importance of study 1.169–70, 9.267–8; in the Buddha's day, people didn't study the Dharma 4.351; no good being 'deep and mystical' and thinking we can skip study 2.244; only after some Dharma study do you realize you can't take words literally 19.508; only personal contact with an Enlightened teacher absolves us from it 13.338; Order members need to study and reflect more 24.391–3; to know the Dharma, we have to study it 2.244, 10.393–4; a way of strengthening motivation 12.382; why and how to study the Abhidharma 17.447, 17.476; without study, concentration is no more use than a pencil to one who can't write 1.170; you don't have to study Buddhism before you can start practising it 1.482; you need to study to remove the wrong views already in your mind 19.508

purposes of Dharma study
the cultivation of non-deludedness 17.567, 17.571; it helps us to change 9.376–7; it is one way to cherish the doctrine 12.454; it subserves the quest for holiness 26.44; it will be fruitful only if we have some hankering after the spiritual life 1.21; the joy of studying the Dharma 4.448; only one motive: the hope that through it Enlightenment may be attained 1.15–16; studying different schools, you encounter contradictions 13.327–8; as support for meditation 3.617; to support the faith that comes from practice 18.185

limitations
the dangers of dry, abstract study 19.50–1; intellectual study has its limits, but don't

underestimate its importance to insight 15.198; the limitations of intellectual study 1.22–3, 2.244–5; studying without meditation or spiritual practice makes you a pompous preacher 19.131; not much point in studying the Dharma if you can't think clearly 12.475–6; a poet who was eager to live life and not merely to study it 7.60; through study you can contact vision, but you need transformation too 19.132; ultimately what we want is not book learning but spiritual awakening 11.716; you could study and still miss the essence of the matter 19.158

quantity and quality
general knowledge of scriptures and detailed knowledge of key texts 14.266; the inevitably encyclopedic nature of Buddhism 11.508–9; it is not necessary to study a lot of books 10.394; no need to study all the scriptures to understand Buddhism 14.267–8, 18.369–70; to handle the mass of material we need an approach like Zhiyi's 8.483; studying the Dharma with discrimination 17.447; there is no end to study: you can't study everything before practising anything 19.132–3; trying to learn more without having practised what you have already learned 18.370; we should have a thorough knowledge of a number of key texts 12.454

the study of ourselves
the Dharma student must recapitulate in his spiritual life the history of Buddhism 1.393; Dharma study is self-study, to be applied to ourselves 12.83; interesting, because it's the study of your own life 9.377; relating study to our own spiritual life 14.xvii, 14.270

tips
approach the Dharma as though you had never approached it before 12.40–1; abstain from activities which stimulate the lower mind 1.30; ask yourself what the words mean, and what the meaning means 18.383; avoid books which are merely 'about' Buddhism 1.23; be careful not to develop an exam mentality 9.230, 9.328; carry your Buddhist principles with you 4.82; discuss Buddhism in the language of Buddhism 2.393, 12.61; it's important to find texts that really move you 18.372–3; know doctrinal principles thoroughly and be convinced of their truth 2.245; reflect on what you've been studying 12.418, 19.449; study a little and deeply rather than skimming through a lot 19.131–2; study words and their meanings carefully 8.272–3

STUDYING WITH OTHERS

teachers and friends
ideally with one's teacher 17.567; learning from a teacher as compared with reading a book 1.26–7; the primacy of personal, oral teaching over mere book learning 18.14; study with the help and companionship of spiritual friends 18.xvii, 16.578; the Tibetan tradition of studying a text with a teacher 7.543, 17.156; we must come to our own conclusions 9.230–1; we should study with a *kalyāṇa mitra* 9.376–7; what can we learn on our own and what do we need help to discover? 18.xviii

study groups
what a study group is like 10.214–15; asking questions and discussion is the best way to understand the Dharma 10.394; the best size for a study group 18.479; communication in study groups 18.478–9; debate that is only words doesn't do anything to get you off the wheel of life 19.177; discussion without inner understanding is like dogs barking at each other 19.178–9; dull discussions may be because people are being 'nice' but feeling hostile 4.419–20; 'It may be better when it is worse' 18.480; meet regularly in small groups 9.465; not just reading, but reflecting on what we've read and discussing it with others 12.454; positive discussion can prepare you for the arising of insight 10.530; the purpose of a study group: to arouse energy 18.479–80; regular group study 1.27; the value of collective Dharma study 18.xvii

see also
study and meditation, *see under* meditation/meditation and other aspects of life

Stukeley, William 8.560, 26.349

stupa (Pāli *thūpa*)

introduction
etymology 16.140, 16.151; considered to be the most important of all Buddhist

symbols 16.151; origins and history of the stupa 13.147–50, 16.140–43; burial mound 13.63–4, 13.149, 16.141–2, 16.149; built by Aśoka 16.143, 16.155

the Buddha
his instructions about his own stupa 13.149–50, 16.142; eight stupas built over his relics 13.148, 16.153–4; a stupa marks the spot where the Buddha gazed at the bodhi tree 3.596; stupas at places associated with the Buddha's life 16.567–8; dedicating a stupa to the Buddha better than dedicating it to world peace 14.447

scriptural references
in the *Kathā-vatthu* 16.143; in the *Mahāvastu* 2.221, 16.155; in the Theravāda Tipiṭaka 2.221; in the *White Lotus Sūtra* 16.140, 16.143–4, 16.151–2

stupa worship
Chaityavādins 16.154–5; the cult of stupa worship 13.251, 14.144, 16.142–3; in the *Kathā-vatthu* 16.143; in the *Mahāvastu* 2.221, 14.144, 16.155; imagining what it would have been like 16.568; from relic worship to stupa worship 16.154; from stupa worship to the Buddha image 4.298

architectural forms
a great variety of forms 1.192, 16.139; Chinese pagodas 16.150, 16.156; Japanese, in England 9.507–8; Nepalese *chaityas* 13.157, 16.148, 16.157, 20.430, 21.286; Sinhalese *dagoba* 16.150, 16.157; Thai 16.157; Tibetan (*chorten*) 13.63–4, 13.162–3, 16.150, 16.157; recommendations about stupas in the West 16.156–7; illustration 13.142

parts of the stupa
association with colours and geometric shapes 13.63, 13.153, 16.599 (n112); the different correspondences don't always fit together 16.162; hemisphere (*garbha* or *aṇḍa*) 13.150, 16.150; square base (*medhī*) 16.150; higher cube (*harmika*) 13.150, 13.157, 14.479, 16.148, 16.149, 16.151, 16.161–2; spire (*kunta*) 13.150, 16.150, 16.162; moon, sun, and flaming jewel 13.162–3, 16.151; the flaming drop at the tip of the Tantric stupa 13.163, 16.151

symbolism
the Buddha's *parinirvāṇa* 3.137–8, 13.149–50; correlation with the path of the Higher Evolution 16.163; the five elements 13.63, 13.150–5, 15.139, 16.144–7; lower and higher evolution 16.163; the progressive liberation of energy 16.147; reminder of death 3.138; solar and lunar 16.149–51, 16.163; a synthesis of the opposite poles of our being 16.149; a three-dimensional symbol of the Buddha's teaching 13.150; in the Tantra, the stupa came to be a symbol of the world within 13.153; symbolism of the Tantric stupa 16.139–64; the vase of initiation 13.157–62; the whole material universe 13.153; yin-yang 16.148–9, 16.150–1

visualization
introduction 3.136–7; a form of six element practice 4.78, 13.64; as a concentration exercise 5.486–7; could it be made into an insight practice? 5.488; description of the practice 5.572; the origin of the practice 5.573

stupidity karmic cause 2.72; a 'stupid' phase of spiritual development: no longer reactive but not yet spontaneous 4.382–3; 'stupid and silly actions done by people befuddled and victimized by passion' 4.407

styāna (Sanskrit, Pāli *thīna*) gloominess or stagnation 17.669; it's difficult to get out of it, though exercise may help 17.669; a state in which things get worse without our doing anything to make them worse 26.59; stiffness, dryness of mind 19.90, 19.598 (n43); *thīna* is the mental equivalent of *middha* (torpor) 17.683; as an *upakleśa* (Abhidharma) 17.669; *see also* *thīna-middha* (sloth and torpor) *under* five hindrances

Stylites, St Simeon 7.406, 7.611 (n444)

Subāhu (bodhisattva) 16.544

Subbalakshmi (South Indian singer) 20.350

Subha, Inspector 21.122, 21.123

Subha, a young brahmin 7.434, 7.519

Subhā (a nun in the *Therīgāthā*) 4.557, 4.712 (n349), 15.126–7, 15.129

śubha definitions 2.82, 4.269–70, 5.510; a fusion of goodness and beauty 4.269; a link with the *brahma vihāras* 5.592, 17.222; *see also* beauty

Subha Sutta *see under Dīgha Nikāya*

Subhadda (or Subhadra, the Buddha's last disciple) the Buddha insists on seeing him 2.30, 3.77, 13.147; the Buddha's teaching to him 1.178, 10.678 (n130); the story in the *Mahāparinirvāṇa Sūtra* 14.241; his ordination 11.454

subha-dhātu 4.692–3 (n225)

Subhadra, Dharmachari (Andy Friends) v24

Subhadramati, Dharmacharini 25.xxxii–iii

subharo (easily supported) 15.xix, 15.277–82

Subhūti (the Buddha's disciple)

in the Pāli canon
foremost among those worthy of gifts 10.607; foremost among those who dwell in peace 14.450–1; foremost among those who dwell remote 10.606–7; attains non-discursive concentration – a link with *śūnyatā* and the *Diamond Sūtra* 10.605–7; he became an *arhant* on the basis of the *mettā bhāvanā* 14.452

in Mahāyāna texts
in the *Diamond Sūtra*, *see under Diamond Sūtra*; in the *Perfection of Wisdom in 8,000 lines* 1.66–7, 2.157, 3.55–6, 14.139–43; in the *Perfection of Wisdom in 25,000 lines* 14.227; in the *Vimalakīrti-nirdeśa* 3.679 (n338), 16.502; in the *White Lotus Sūtra* (one of four elders) 14.115, 16.41–2

Subhuti, Dharmachari

his life
brief introduction 2.731–2 (n627); his mother born in New Zealand 24.88, 24.628 (n116); as a young man 4.234–5, 4.236–7; in the early days of the FWBO 11.729; is baffled by karma 4.402–3; attends seminar on the *Bodhicaryāvatāra* 4.225; at Mañjughoṣa stuti *sādhana* retreat 26.663; resilience and resourcefulness 24.190–1; conducts ordinations for the first time 2.510–12, 12.379; develops a post-ordination process 12.419–21; farewell supper on the eve of his departure for Greece 24.163–5; as Sangharakshita's secretary 24.229, 24.665 (n282); cares for Sangharakshita when he is ill at Guhyaloka 24.330–5; gives a talk at the opening of the Nottingham Buddhist Centre 12.534; talks on friendship 12.458; visits to chapters 2.515; 'witnessing someone else's Going for Refuge, my own is called into question' 2.512; introduces a book launch 26.549–50; lectures on Going for Refuge retreats 2.515; member of the Preceptors' College 12.597, 12.631; centre president 12.632; 'Subhuti has his style and I have my own' (Sangharakshita) 2.547

Buddhism for Today
Sangharakshita's joy at seeing it published 11.557, 24.206–8; a landmark 11.557; Christmas Humphreys' interest in the book 11.544; 'Bowing Before the Buddha' 13.416; on Christianity 13.430–1, 13.457; criticism of theistic religion 13.412–13; on culture 13.482–3, 13.502; on the higher evolution 13.430–3; the limitations of Buddhist societies 13.510; on the nuclear family 13.457; on the purpose of the FWBO 2.516; on relationships 13.445–6; on therapeutic blasphemy 13.468; on Western interest in Buddhism 13.493, 13.498

other works
writing books 12.379; books published 24.662 (n264); articles on the ordination process 2.513–14; *Bringing Buddhism to the West* 11.619, 11.621; *The Buddhist Vision* 11.640–1; 'Going for Refuge and Spiritual Friendship' 24.366; 'Have We Friendship in the Order?' 24.379; 'Relationships with Other Buddhists' 2.547; *Remorse and Confession in the Spiritual Community* 2.707 (n421); *Sangharakshita: A New Voice in the Buddhist Tradition* 2.722 (n549), 2.735 (n639), 11.623, 12.535; *Seven Papers* 5.xxiv–v, 14.327, 26.405; *Women, Men and Angels* 26.4

subject–object distinction or duality

the apparent distinction
all so-called objective things, whether material or mental, are like a mirage 14.208; awareness differentiates subject and object 14.420; in the subject–object framework, we get at what is within via what seems outside 19.412; the *kliṣṭa-mano-vijñāna* constructs a dualistic world 12.175; the logical prespective 7.208–11; no object without a subject, no subject without an object 17.404; ordinary experience is based on it 2.275, 12.173–4, 17.481; our experience has subjective and objective poles 17.479–80; *saṃsāra* and Nirvāṇa separate within the subject–object framework 16.389; still operates whether Buddhas and bodhisattvas thought to be outside or within 4.131; where there is a perceiving subject there is an object, a world 16.388; the whole thing is about the ego 18.241–2; without breaking it down there can be no peace of heart or happiness on earth 7.273–4

transcending the distinction
how to do it 15.526; Dharma transcends it 15.584; in communication through empathy 17.521; the experience becomes more diaphanous 19.142–3; the further one progresses, the harder it is to dichotomize one's experience 7.360; the line where they meet replaced by a crack through which light shines 3.481; mitigated in a 'poetic' state of mind 24.169; not as hard and fast a distinction as we had perhaps supposed 5.179; seeing through the mind, you see that there's no distinction 18.236; in the fourth *arūpa*

dhyāna 1.563, 4.157, 4.531; in relation to the fourth and fifth fetters 15.524–6; the realm of sense perception, breaking down the subject–object distinction 17.510; a state of awareness in which there is no distinction 18.344; through the eight emancipations 16.447; through Vajrayāna sexo-yogic practices 15.528–39; through visualization practice 15.529, 16.187; to be transcended in all its forms 18.416; a tremendous change required 2.275; to get closer to reality, operate in terms of both subject and object 15.704–5; transcending even the subtle potentiality of subject–object relation: the *ālaya* 4.511; the transformation of 'objective' into 'subjective' 19.199; the ultimate aim, but you can't do it immediately 18.640; very difficult 19.103; we are held back from this realization by mind-made fetters 15.210; we can't refine it out of existence 17.695; we have to transcend the object just as much as the subject 15.237; you can't grapple with it, or think about it – you can only stop 18.231; you make subjective that which was formerly to you objective 19.199

beyond the distinction
absolute mind: pure awareness within which the distinction does not exist 13.355–6; *āryajñāna*: knowledge without a subject and without an object 12.560; the Buddha transcends the subject–object distinction 11.101, 12.530–1; the absolute *ālaya*, free from subjectivity and objectivity 17.486; emptiness and the unreal imagination 1.363; it narrows and disappears 7.359; our only refuge is at the feet of the Buddha, above the dualism 2.424; perceptions are 'forsaken and gone' 14.601; Perfect Wisdom is beyond it 14.536; reality cannot be described as a subject or object of perception 17.410; something beyond it to which one directs prayers and aspirations 4.131, 19.142–3; subject and object suffused by the light of reality 18.614; if there is no object, there's no subject either 12.172–3; the mind which is neither subject nor object 18.232–4; when the distinction disappears, consciousness remains 1.364; when it is transcended, the 'world' ceases 13.567

subjective

introduction
the *bodhicitta*: not just 'my' little subjective idea of the goal of 'my' spiritual life 4.263; Nirvāṇa is neither an entity nor a subjective state of mind 10.566–7; a person with no subjective mental states, whose awareness is just a mirror 19.192–3; philosophers building systems in accordance with subjective preferences 7.386–8; subjective idealism, *see* Berkeley; *śūnyatā* is the nature of reality, and *prajñā* is its subjective counterpart 18.66; truth can be subjective 17.390; when the *bodhicitta* has arisen, you still act, but you will not be subjectively disturbed 19.193; the whole structure of subjective ideas and concepts 2.121

subjective and objective
a balance between subjective and objective approaches to the spiritual life 10.12–13, 10.41–2; *dhyāna*: 'subjective' equivalents of corresponding planes of 'objective' existence 7.228–9; the difference between subjective and objective knowledge 2.640–2; eliminate subject, you get science, eliminate the positive, music: balance them, religion 15.707; personality: a continuity of a series of experiences, subjective and objective 7.209; the Sevenfold Puja has a subjective and an objective aspect 11.223; subjective and objective aspects of art 25.165–6; subjective and objective Going for Refuge 11.451; what is understood as objective transformed into what is experienced as subjective 19.199; *vīrya*: objective (helping others) and subjective (the four right efforts) 3.304; wrong notion of objective and subjective existence 1.370; you can't be objectively perfect, but only subjectively perfect 4.355–6

sublimation being cruel to yourself prevents the process of sublimation occurring 10.524; how to sublimate the emotions 26.131; if one can sublimate one's sexual feelings and live happily celibate, that is best 12.402; Kṣitigarbha is the principle of spiritual sublimation 2.180; one cannot just cut off unsublimated energy 10.507; spiritual life's main concern: the sublimation of desire and reorientation of emotion 1.390, 26.130–1; sublimation and the artistic experience 25.172–3; the sublimation of all the forces of the personality in the direction of Enlightenment 13.22; the sublimation of anger represented by Vajrapāṇi 13.174; the Tantra seeks to bring about sublimation of desire through sexual sacramentalism 1.391; Vajrapāṇi corresponds to power, sublimated volition 2.173

sublime what is the sublime? 14.472; the sublime bodhisattva ideal 4.221, 8.369; the contemplation of beauty gives rise to love, and when sublime, to faith 2.554; the courage to be inspired by sublimity

14.473; however sublime a teaching, it is meaningless unless it can effect radical transformation 8.483; 'The most sublime act is to set another before you' 2.361; the sublime beauty of Buddhahood 2.554; sublime images of Hindu gods 26.383; the sublime moves us in a way that the simply beautiful cannot 14.472; 'the sublime Yogācāra' 17.325; the sublimer realms of spiritual experience 1.133–4; the sublimity of the Dharma 14.471–2, 14.474; the sublimity of wild natural forces 14.473; we can make our lives sublime 8.234; wisdom sublime and awe-inspiring 14.xvi; *see also* *brahma-vihāras* (sublime abodes)

submission the difference between submission and receptivity 15.663; submission to authority in the contemporary world 15.489; submission to group norms 18.134–6

submissiveness 4.469, 4.477–8

subsidiarity 14.543

substantialism in relation to *dharmas* 2.88; the Abhidharma came to stand for the very substantialism the Buddha rejected 1.305; the author of the *Vijñāna-kāya* shows he's in no danger of lapsing into substantialism 14.87–8; all words indicative of existence have for Buddhism a disagreeably substantialist flavour 2.55; Buddhism is not substantialist 14.603; immanence: one doesn't want to adopt a substantialist or eternalist outlook 19.387; investing things with a reality they don't possess 19.39

subtlety

this subtle mystery
nipuṇa (subtle) 17.324; Buddha-nature is extremely subtle 14.237; communication can be so subtle as to be telepathic 1.576; Dilgo Khyentse Rimpoche 'subtly impressive' 12.451; a fire doesn't go out, but passes from a gross to a subtle state 10.655–6; 'Hourly this subtle mystery flowers anew' 7.58; language is a subtle, elastic thing 12.118; the subtler an emotion grows, the less adequate normal means of expression 26.136–7; the subtlety of perfume, symbol for something intangible 16.559; the subtleties of spiritual experience and the coarse language of thought 7.134

subtle mind, subtle energy
the *arūpa dhyānas* render the mind subtler and more 'transparent' 2.110; consciously checking emotions to allow them more subtle expression 26.138; does all experience include some kind of subtle vocalizing? 5.629; the same Buddha viewed with different subtleties of perception 2.45–6; subtle mental activity and insight 4.514, 16.161; subtle senses: clairvoyance, clairaudience 1.584; the subtlest type of *prajñā* 2.164–5; in the third *dhyāna* even subtle mental activity dies away 5.243; working in meditation with the subtle energy system 18.322

subtle teachings and practices
the Buddha thought his teaching too subtle to be communicated 17.324; the subtlety of the Buddha's psychological teachings 7.229; early Buddhists' quest to understand the mystery of impermanence 15.183; the subtle and delicate nature of visualization 5.581; systems of correspondences are subtle, complex, and changing 19.43

subtleties to be pinned down
all experience short of Enlightenment is a subtle form of suffering 1.486; the *arhant* has a subtle self-awareness to be overcome by the bodhisattva ideal 2.149–50; the Buddha warned of Atmanism's subtlety 7.211; the five hindrances can be very subtle 5.337, 18.11; the removal of the subtle 'I' sense that persists after Stream Entry 4.187; transcending even the subtle potentiality of subject–object relation 4.511

see also
subtle body, *see under* body/from a spiritual perspective

Sucandrima, King (*Kinnari Jātaka*) 2.332–3

success

being successful
always dangerous 17.272; even while doing your best to succeed, remember it's a game 14.523; imprisoned by the importance we give to being successful 18.101–2; it is wise sometimes not to be too openly successful 10.541; not without its drawbacks 26.16; people's qualities may only be recognized when they become successful 15.717–18; success and material prosperity 18.101–2; successful people in worldly terms are well placed to take up the spiritual life 4.450–1; very few people succeed in life, even on their own terms 15.478

success and other people
people's motives for joining a successful sangha 10.519; seeing self as agent: 'the success is all due to me' 10.601; the success of a venture is due to everybody's cooperation 19.536; why be angry at someone else's success? 4.430

success in the spiritual life
assured if you devoted the energy to it you give to material things 4.150; conceiving of spiritual life in terms of worldly success 19.460; confusion between ecclesiastical success and spiritual attainment 18.561–2; constant mindfulness of emptiness is the secret of success 7.413; depends on establishing a disciplined and committed lifestyle 15.97; easier to find success on the spiritual path than in the world 4.292–3, 4.323; how can I even think of not being successful? 4.363; if we don't really try we won't be successful 11.407; never forget that people in a much worse condition than you are have succeeded 4.448; 'Only by instant action can you succeed!' 18.153; success in Mahāyāna practice depends on realizing that success is impossible 1.239; the success of a Buddhist sect depends on its containing Enlightened people 7.313–14; 'To be humble is to succeed'? 18.511; when teaching, it should be the Dharma in you that is the success, not you 19.499; worldly success does not necessarily equate with spiritual success 17.164

see also
siddhis

Sucharita, Dharmacharini (Lee Carter) v24

Suchindram, India 20.244–5

suchness (thusness, *tathatā*) all things exist in a state of suchness 7.505; an analogy between perfuming clothes and the perfuming of Suchness 22.17; and *anātman* 2.89; be careful not to imply that it is some kind of 'stuff' 14.595; the bodhisattva stands firmly in it 2.167; the absolute truth 1.265; '*Dharma-niyāmatā* indicates suchness' 16.84; the mirror of Suchness is kept bright and clean 1.354; a mistake to think of emptiness as the self-nature or own-being of *dharmas* 1.268–9; a more 'positive' synonym for the Void 2.168; one of the five *dharmas* (categories) 14.213; our saṃsāric mind perfumed by it 26.498; the positive counterpart of *śūnyatā* 14.595; reveals reality's unique indefinable essentiality 2.43; the sole reality 1.268; the spiritual life and suchness 11.325; Subhūti's rhapsody on the suchness of the Tathāgata 14.144; it expresses the impossibility of defining or describing anything 14.502–3, 14.595; used by Aśvaghoṣa 14.502; words and concepts cannot define it, but designate it for practical purposes 7.299

sudarśana* or *sudassī (world) 2.148

sudden how to stop the reactive mind: the sudden method and the gradual method 12.157–8; instantaneous and gradual purification of the *āsravas* 14.215; *Laṅkāvatāra Sūtra* not a gradual but an abrupt realization of the truth 14.207; method of stopping craving 2.256–9; sometimes change is very sudden 4.271–2; sudden breakthrough 18.613; suddenly realizing the absurdity of worrying 4.203, 18.12; there is no such thing as the quick path and the slow path (Huineng) 16.183; when someone close to you dies suddenly, life starts teaching you about impermanence 18.560–1

see also
gradual; Enlightenment, *see under* Enlightenment/the path/quick and slow routes

suddhavāsa* or *śuddhāvāsa (pure abodes) *see under* heavens

suddha-vipassanā *see* insight

Suddhodana Gautama (the Buddha's father) appalled at the prediction that Siddhārtha might become a sage 3.24; attempts to satisfy his son Siddhārtha with a pleasurable life 3.24–5, 10.256; leader of the Śākyans 3.21; 'the love of a father for his son is very strong, piercing the heart' 10.256; in *The Light of Asia* 1.46; reproaches the Buddha for begging in the streets of Kapilavastu 13.461

Sudhana *see under Gaṇḍavyūha Sūtra*

Sudhanu, Prince (*Jātakas*) 2.332–3

Sudhir 20.178–82, 20.201

Sudinna (monk) 14.30

***sudṛśa* or *sudassā* world** 2.148

Sudurjaya (Very Difficult to Conquer) *see under* ten *bhūmis*

Suez Canal 20.108–9

Suez Canal crisis 14.543, 22.341

suffering *see dukkha*

Suffolk, England 20.486, 26.507–33

Sufism

history and thoughts
introduction 3.429–30; and beauty 13.279; contributed spiritual impulses from the Buddha to Islam 2.11–12, 7.485; derivation of ideas 3.429; different kinds of spirit at different times of day 5.351; an ambiguous relationship with orthodox Islam 3.429; Ibn Arabi's meeting with Averroes 24.431; the influence of Buddhism and Vedānta on primitive Islam 7.370; knowledge that sense experience

is only part of the spectrum of human experience 5.51; legends that sages' meditations keep the world going 4.582; similar doctrine to the pure love of Mme Guyon 13.626; speaks of Reality in terms of light 16.108; 'Beget the man you need' 17.190, 18.205; Sufi tombs in Maharashtra 10.293; Sufis falling in love with the object of their devotion 5.618; viewed with suspicion by more orthodox Muslims 7.369; the writings of Henri Corbin 26.688

Sufi poets
ghazals 7.61, 7.563 (n101); Hafez, Attar, and Rumi 25.26, 26.687, 26.770 (n651); 'If there is Paradise upon the face of the earth, it is here' 20.112, the Sufis of medieval Iran were true poets 26.209

Sugandhakūṭa, Buddha 16.554–6

Sugata 3.315, 10.198, 14.404, 14.548, 15.477–8

Sugatadasa 21.448–9

Sugatananda, Anagarika P. *see* Story, Francis

Sugatapriya (of Assam) 8.656, 22.513, 22.520

Suhṛllekha (Friendly Epistle) 1.309, 1.311, 17.663

suicide 'To conquer an army you need many weapons, but to commit suicide a pin is enough' 14.348; the discriminating mind commits suicide 7.37; the French nun considers suicide 22.197; Japanese suicide epidemic between the wars 8.127; Milarepa's disciple Shiwa Aui considers suicide 17.338, 18.142–4; monks who committed suicide 3.346, 4.67, 4.360, 15.589; Rechungpa (Milarepa's disciple) has suicidal thoughts 19.113–16; the suicide of Godhika (*Saṃyutta Nikāya*) 8.451; the suicide of humanity 12.340–1; the suicide of Dhammachari Mahadhammavira 24.233–8; the suicide of Sangharakshita's grandmother 23.30–1; suicide rates in modern times 5.659; of Terry Delamare 4.560, 23.443–6; Terry's friend Ivan commits suicide 4.543–5, 23.116–17, 26.623–4; you can't take out your resentment on other people, so you take it out on yourself 10.524–5; *see also* *tṛṣṇā*/craving for non-existence

Sujātā (who offered Siddhārtha milk-rice) 3.31, 9.400, 10.437

Sujata (Sara Boin) *see* Boin, Sara

Sujiva, Śrāmaṇera *see* Khantipālo

sūkaramaddava 10.639–40

sukha can be mistaken for having realized God, or Brahman, or the ultimate goal of life 2.108; description in Buddhaghosa's *Aṭṭhasalini* 2.107–8; enjoyed by the Buddha 1.64; has various meanings in Buddhism 3.269; important to cultivate detachment towards it, as the Buddha did 2.108, 18.581; non-hedonic spiritual happiness 2.107; *sukha* is painful (*dukkha*) because it has its limitations 15.449; the word is used in two ways: as a sensation, pleasure, and as a *saṃskāra*, happiness 19.583

see also
bliss; happiness; as a *dhyāna* factor, *see* five *dhyāna* factors; in the positive *nidānas*, *see under* twelve positive *nidānas*; of third *dhyāna*, *see under dhyānas*/four *rūpa dhyānas*

Sukhāvatī

the Pure Land of Amitābha
described in the *sūtras* 1.328–31, 16.18, 16.462–3; all its symbols proclaim the original teaching of the Buddha 1.183; aspiring to be born there 13.310, 15.240; brief introduction 1.539–40; a central feature of the Pure Land schools of China and Japan 17.298; distinct from Nirvāṇa 1.344; easier to attain to Enlightenment from this land than from anywhere else 7.43; faith in the Buddha who creates Sukhāvatī 4.640; in relation to Padmaloka 25.lviii–lix; an expression of the relative truth 1.344; and Indra's Net 7.274; a kind of cosmic sangha 1.340–1; introducing into your life a little of the essence of Sukhāvatī 18.121; neither mundane nor transcendental 1.341; one petal of Amitābha's paradise 25.372; our world transformed into 7.274; penultimate or final goal? 1.341; Queen Vaidehī's vision of Sukhāvatī 1.332–4, 3.454–5, 3.571–2, 14.172–3, 20.464; visualization 1.329–31

rebirth in Sukhāvatī
because of repeating Amitābha's name 1.328–9, 7.123–4; on the basis of one repetition of Amitābha's name at the moment of death 7.124; on the basis of keeping in mind Amitābha's name 14.171–2; despite having committed the five heinous sins 7.42–3; gestation in the calyx of a lotus 7.42–3; through meditation 1.333–4, 14.174; not through merit but through Amitābha's compassion 1.341, 15.240

Sukhavati (London) *see under* London Buddhist Centre

Sukhāvatī-vyūha Sūtras ('Array of the Happy Land')

introduction
in the earlier group of Mahāyāna *sūtras* 16.239; difference between the two: rebirth in Sukhāvatī through merit or grace? 1.331–2, 14.171–2; evocation of Nirvāṇa 2.132; they came to light in Japan in the 19th century 14.168; a very different atmosphere from the Pāli canon, but the teaching is the same 7.529; Ratnaguna's commentary, Śraddhāpa's translation 1.616 (n261), 2.742 (n679), 16.607 (n176); Śāntideva refers to them 4.476; Vasubandhu's commentary 9.149

Larger
introduction to the *sūtra* 1.327–31, 14.168–71; Amitābha appears 14.171; Avalokiteśvara 2.175; date of composition 1.326–7, 14.168–9; the causes leading to rebirth in the Happy Land 14.170–1; description of the bodhisattva's career 1.329, 1.401; description of the Pure Land 14.169–70; Dharmākara's 48 vows, *see under* Amitābha/history and myth; Great Vow of Amitābha 2.745 (n693); Pure Land imagery anticipated in the Pāli canon 1.183, 4.37, 16.57; in the Ratnakūta group of Mahāyāna *sūtras* 7.502; the reason for the *sūtra*'s jewels and flowers, light and colour 14.170; spontaneous birth in the Pure Land 14.171; translations 1.328, 14.168, 14.189; unpardonable sins 1.334; one of the most gorgeous writings in world literature 1.329

Smaller
introduction 1.331–2, 14.171–2; its special teaching: birth in the Pure Land is from thinking of Amitābha's name 14.171–2; birds created by Amitābha to sing the Dharma 1.343; the invocation of Amitābha's name 1.340; Mañjuśrī 2.174

Sukitti, Ven. (Thai monk) 10.131, 23.364

sukkha-vipassanā *see* insight

Sullivan, Harry Stack 12.93

Sully, Duc de 15.172

Sulochana (Order member, Mary Rawnsley) 4.225, 4.233–4

Sumangala (peasant) 9.142

Sumaṅgala (Pāli canon) *see under Theragāthā*

Sumangala Thera (monk at Bodh Gaya) v8

Sumaṇgala, H. (Sri Lanka) 7.444

Sumangala, M. 8.336

Sumangala Nayaka Maha Thera v8

Sumatidārikā-paripṛcchā (Mahāyāna *sūtra*) 14.185

Sumatikīrti *see* Tsongkhapa

Sumatra 12.567, 12.569

Sumedha (Gautama Buddha in a previous life) brief introduction 8.690 (n183); his vow to attain Enlightenment 1.45, 13.299, 26.697–8; predicted to Enlightenment by the Buddha Dīpaṅkara 2.17, 8.232, 14.70, 14.143, 14.650 (n451); the *Diamond Sūtra*'s comment on the tradition 14.452–3, 14.492–4

Sumedha (Order member) 4.559

Sumedha (protégé of Anand-ji) *see* Jayadev

Sumeru or Meru, Mount the Buddha likened to Mount Sumeru 16.464; 'The idea of a self is Mount Meru' (Huineng) 2.77; in Buddhist cosmology, *see under* cosmology; 'Hermits upon Mount Meru or Everest' (Yeats) 7.450; the bodhisattva can enclose the mountain in a mustard seed 14.164, 16.451; a man as huge as Sumeru (*Diamond Sūtra*) 14.458–9; spinal column identified with Mount Sumeru by the tantras 2.67; the Tantras identify Mount Sumeru with the spinal column 2.67; a view of self as high as Sumeru 3.237, 4.272–3, 4.693 (n227), 14.459–60, 18.179, 18.371, 19.241

Sumerupradīparāja (Tathāgata) 14.164

Sumitra, Dharmachari v24

summer the red roses of summer 25.lv; summer afternoon 25.240; the summer rose 25.221; summer schools, *see under* Buddhist Society; a sweet singing bird in his summer array 25.281

sun

physical sun
Bhaja caves lit up by the evening sun 24.390; a fiery-gold sunrise on a flight in India 24.9; the invigorating sunshine of Poona 24.105; our dependence on his bounty 25.427; shining after the rainy season 25.273; shining from a cloudless sky 18.614, 25.307; the strong friendly sun – perhaps the best thing in India 24.9; the sun as an intelligent entity 24.531; sunbathing 24.398; sunshine is vitalizing 4.575, 11.13; a total eclipse at Cape Cod 23.456–7

solar divinities
Apollo 16.190; Ra, the Egyptian sun god 23.56; Sūrya, the sun god 16.418, 20.460

the sun in the Buddhist tradition
Buddhism a solar religion 16.163; the Buddha (or Tathāgata) as the sun 1.53, 16.464, 26.125; dispelling the forces of evil like the sun lighting up the whole sky (*Udāna*) 10.434–5; the place where the sun rises and the place where the sun sets (Pāli canon) 14.49; 'to see the stars (conditioned things) after the sun has risen' 2.81; Mañjughoṣa, kind sun of speech 25.56; Amitābha and the setting sun 12.215; concentrating on the setting sun in the *Amitāyurdhyāna Sūtra* 1.332; identified in the tantras with the spinal column 2.67; *rasanā* corresponds to the sun 18.76; yellow the colour of sunlight and the Tantra 13.67; Tantric tradition associated with sun worship 10.46; if the world 'with all its suns and galaxies' is everything, Nirvāṇa is nothing 17.362

sun similes and metaphors relating to Buddhist practice
the *bodhicitta* is like the sun 2.165, 4.33; the dawning sun of Buddhism in the West 12.383–4; the *dhyānas* like the sun's rays filtering through deep water 4.154; *dukkha*: a cloud has to float across the face of the sun 26.12; the effect of love on others' spiritual being like the sun on their physical being 2.361; faith is like a sunflower turning towards the sun 21.463; the glow-worm and the sun 1.230, 10.611–12, 25.495–6; kindly speech is like the warm rays of the rising sun 2.380; love 'impartial as the sun' 4.165, 25.203; *mettā* shines on all beings like the sun 15.325–6; rejoice in merits impersonally, like rejoicing that the sun is shining 11.266; the Sun of Truth 1.239; compared with all lesser satisfactions, Nirvāṇa is as the sun to shadows 1.129

other uses of sun imagery
'Eternity's sunrise' (Blake) 17.506, 26.598; 'Splendor Solis' (poem) 25.55–6, 25.418; 'The sun shines out to light us after death' (Aristophanes) 23.290; 'You remind me of whatever's like the sun' (poem) 25.287

solar symbolism
in Buddhist cosmology 16.346; circumambulation's association with the solar cult 19.329; cosmic solar symbolism 2.222; the golden drum 12.384, 16.264, 16.266; a golden door into the higher world 16.266; in the stupa 16.149–51; the sun as a symbol 25.56; the sun's limitations as a symbol of Reality 16.108; a symbol of God 12.181, 13.61; a symbol of the Good (Plato) 13.61; Vairocana, *see* Vairocana

sun and moon
as part of stupa symbolism 13.162–3; as visualized in the offering of the mandala 13.262; 'as the sun and moon never stop to brighten one small place' 18.215; the myth that they were produced from the eyes of Avalokiteśvara 2.176; solar and lunar energies brought together 18.76–7

see also
'the eye could not behold the sun …', *see under* Plotinus; 'neither moon nor sun', *see Udāna*/other key teachings

Sunayaka, Dharmachari v24

Sundarananda *see* Nanda

Sundarī (woman wanderer) 10.539–40

Sundarika-Bhāradvāja (brahmin) 2.665 (n30)

Sunīdha, government minister of Magadha 10.642

Sunīta the sweeper in Dr Ambedkar's account of the Buddha's life 9.142; in the *Theragāthā* 8.15, 8.670 (n34), 10.672 (n86)

Śūnya Puruṣa 7.461

śūnyatā (*suññata*, emptiness, the Void)

WHAT IT IS – AND ISN'T

what the word means
although its spiritual content is positive, the word connotes the negative: an absence 14.594; etymology and translations 3.231; don't be misled by 'voidness' or 'emptiness' 4.161, 16.232, 19.446; the prefix *mahā-*, *see mahā-*; *śūnyatā* is a mere word 1.308; *tathatā* (suchness) is its positive counterpart 14.595; translated as 'nothingness' 3.231; translated as 'openness' 5.523; voidness, nothingness, death 5.32, 26.48; the word really means 'empty of all concepts' 16.21, 19.377

descriptions
the absolute truth 1.265; the death of everything conditioned 26.48; emptiness and activity are not two but one 7.362; emptiness of 'self' 7.375; 'Everything exists on account of emptiness' (Nāgārjuna) 7.200, 14.607; free of all dualities (but what does this mean?) 18.43–4, 26.387–8; identical with the indefinability of the real nature of things 1.65; indicates reality's transcendence over the world of phenomena 2.43; in each particle of dust the reason of *śūnyatā* is perceivable 1.354; indefinable 14.560; the ineffable non-dual Reality which transcends all apparent oppositions 7.505; non-different

from *prajñā* 1.306–7; not 'conditioned' or 'compounded' of anything 15.58; the 'object' of *prajñā* 14.181; the open dimension of being (Guenther) 5.43, 5.523, 14.560, 18.294, 19.38; Perfect Wisdom is the spiritual faculty that intuits *śūnyatā* 16.232; a possible parallel with the dark night of the soul 7.101; the principle of unrestrictedness 18.294; reality as the realm of *śūnyatā* 17.133; the sole reality 1.268, 1.321; *śūnyatā* is the nature of reality, and *prajñā* is its subjective counterpart 18.66; it supports meditation and makes Enlightenment possible 1.363; a term for the total process of conditionality 15.637; the undifferentiated continuum of the Void 19.236, 19.258; the union of bliss and emptiness 13.75, 17.364, 18.61, 19.155, 19.196–7; a vast spectrum of experiences 3.233; the Void has no metaphysical or ontological status 19.237; we can be positively drawn even to the ineffable emptiness of *śūnyatā* 18.129

the nature of śūnyatā
the activity of emptiness is ever serene and harmonious 7.409; alive with unleashed energy, bright and beautiful 18.74; its nature is not to be a particular thing with a fixed identity 18.44; the middle way between existence and non-existence 9.398; a mystery 3.231–2, 13.119, 25.248; it can be known by the negation of all concepts 14.347; it pulsates with spiritual life 7.375; it represents the possibility of complete transformation 17.95; it resolves the tension between the claims of compassion and renunciation 4.567–8; it makes everything possible 7.200, 18.294–5; seeing the empty character of the universe as plainly as a leaf 1.356; that which cannot be put into thought 10.606

śūnyatā and compassion
the activity of emptiness is compassion 7.413, 26.50; the *bodhicitta* is characterized by perpetual emptiness 4.29; all *dharmas* are *śūnyatā* and therefore *karuṇā* 1.391; compassion is based on the realization of emptiness 14.562; compassion is the dynamic aspect of *śūnyatā* 7.457, 26.204–5; compassion springs up in the emptiness when you are not there 25.215; compassion springs up in the Void as a lotus in water 1.239; compassion which has *śūnyatā* for its object 5.202; emptiness, activity, and compassion: one thing seen from three points of view 7.413; emptiness and compassionate activity two sides of the same coin 7.375–6; don't think that the concept of emptiness exempts you from compassion 7.414; non-difference 16.522; the overflowingness of the 'seeming void' is compassion 7.361–2; *śūnyatā*, endowed with the essence of compassion, is the absolute *bodhicitta* 2.162, 4.31; the transcendental activity of emptiness manifests in the world as compassion 7.377, 26.50

symbols and images
blue sky 5.603–4, 13.67, 19.454; a bright white light containing all the colours of the rainbow 18.74; the clear light of the Void 13.28, 18.43–4, 18.570–1; 'the clear non-dual Shine' 16.581; the 'fine warehouse of *śūnyatā*' (Milarepa) 18.294–5; the flowering bowl: the dynamic aspect of Reality 7.397; the *brahma vihāras* passing through the fires of *śūnyatā* 15.339; the great armour of *śūnyatā* 14.572; an illusory elephant made to appear by a magician 14.501, 16.452–3, 19.79; the Light of the Void shines through positive conceptions of reality 1.243; the purifying flames of *śūnyatā* 14.571–2; represented by the colour blue 13.67; the skull on Padmasambhava's staff representing insight into *śūnyatā* 26.236; the *vajra* the most widely current Tantric synonym for *śūnyatā* 1.385

what śūnyatā is not
a mistake to think of it as the self-nature or own-being of *dharmas* 1.268; no kind of substance or thing 14.467, 14.603; not annihilation or nothingness 7.375, 15.230, 18.179; not a theory, doctrine, or philosophy 3.231–2; not a thing to be described, more like a mode of being 14.561; not to be apprehended by means of any thought-construction, however subtle 1.306; one should not think of it in terms derived from sense- and mind-experience 10.165

the impossibility of describing it
how is it possible to make any declaration regarding it? 7.132; the inadequacy of words to express it 3.232, 3.238, 9.345–6, 16.21; the last word uttered by Buddhism before it passes beyond thought and speech 7.300; to speak about it we have to do violence to language 14.467; we have to be cautious about even trying to say anything about it 15.187

ŚŪNYATĀ AS CONCEPT AND TEACHING

śūnyatā as a concept
avoid taking the notion too literally 4.163–4; conflict between emptiness (ontologically) and the struggle for Enlightenment 14.146; contrast with the

idea of a personal God 7.92; emptiness is only a concept, a word, but really there is nothing to be said 1.490; emptiness of all concepts 16.21, 19.377; emptiness of the concept of emptiness 16.11–12; the Perfection of Wisdom doesn't allow the intellect to play around with *śūnyatā* 14.467–8; the principle of causality is the chief conceptual formulation of *śūnyatā* 1.343; *śūnyatā* can be known by the negation of all concepts 14.347; trying to penetrate *śūnyatā* with the intellect like a gnat trying to penetrate a ball of steel with its proboscis (Zen) 14.468; the utter emptiness of all 'I'-concept 7.274; viewed from its perspective, any term or concept is an *upāya* 15.186–7; what is it that posits *śūnyatā*? 15.634

śūnyatā as a teaching
Bodhidharma's teaching: 'Vast emptiness and nothing meritorious within' 12.531; a bodhisattva precept: don't instruct an unprepared person in *śūnyatā* 13.56, 14.576; the Buddha declares that he no more teaches than *śūnyatā* does 14.239; the central tradition of Buddhism 8.535; the concept of absolute mind grows out of the concept of emptiness 14.200; the counterbalance to the teaching on *śūnyatā* is the Yogācāra's 'Mind Only' 18.74; the difference between Buddhist doctrine and Hindu or Western conceptions 1.268–9; the *Heart Sūtra* is a restatement of the four noble truths in the light of emptiness 14.152; if it is not clearly understood, the result is an ego-based life 17.391; it can only be perceived when all previous modes of thinking have been abandoned 15.187; it does not remove the need for other Buddhist teachings 15.187; it is to existence as a whole what *anātman* is to the individual 10.160; the metaphysical aspect of *anattā* 7.213; ontological, psychological, logical, and soteriological aspects 14.150–1, 14.409–10; a refined, precise, intellectual concept 4.145; the *śūnyatā* doctrine and *pratītya-samutpāda* 1.267, 1.316, 7.193, 7.199, 15.637; *śūnyatā* interpreted in terms of the Middle Way 14.181; the teaching is intended as a medicine for the cure of all attachments 3.237

the history of śūnyatā
the Buddha used the term in a general way, and the Mahāyāna developed it 14.350–1; the Buddha's prophecy about what would happen to his *śūnyatā* teachings 14.136; in early Buddhism 4.163, 14.136; Madhyamaka interpretations 16.20; Mahāyāna Buddhism's background 1.243, 5.33; Mañjuśrī tests an eight-year-old girl's understanding of *śūnyatā* 14.185; the main theme of the Perfection of Wisdom *sūtras* 4.161, 14.136; in the *Diamond Sūtra*, *see under Diamond Sūtra*; in the *Heart Sūtra* 1.70, 14.360–1; *Ratnakūṭa sūtras* associated with *śūnyatā* 14.181; in the *Sūtra of Golden Light* 14.243, 16.245; twenty kinds of *śūnyatā* according to the Prajñāpāramitā 14.560; it is used by the Madhyamaka to undermine all concepts 17.326; the Yogācāra saw Reality in terms not of *śūnyatā*, but of the One Mind 16.20–1; the Vajrayāna is concerned with the direct experience of *śūnyatā* 17.546

the emptiness of all dharmas (sarvadharma-śūnyatā)
introduction 1.265–6; applying the principle of *pratītya-samutpāda* to *dharmas* 14.495–6; all *dharmas* are *anattā* 1.172, 7.152; all things are empty but that does not mean that they do not exist 18.179; all things are equally *śūnyatā* 2.117, 19.191; the basic view of the Madhyamaka 19.371; the basis of every transcendental thought, word, and deed 1.232; because all *dharmas* are *śūnyatā*, they are *karuṇā* 1.391; the Buddha is identical with emptiness 14.495; cannot be expressed in words 1.65–6; bodhisattvas are convinced that all *dharmas* are empty and abide in the same state 14.193; the discovery of their emptiness is non-rational 14.560; don't think of *dharmas* as being made of a sort of stuff called emptiness 1.269; the emptiness of phenomena coincides with the emptiness of Nirvāṇa 1.305; in the *Heart Sūtra* 1.70, 14.360–1; in *śūnyatā* no *dharmas* exist 14.361–2; locus of the teaching of the Perfection of Wisdom 1.305, 14.104, 14.345; the Madhyamaka doctrine that countered Sarvāstivādin eternalism 7.540; the Mahāyāna's answer to the Abhidharma's literalism 14.344–5, 14.440, 17.448–9; the Mahāyāna's reassertion of the primacy of universal conditionality 1.267; Milarepa recommends meditating on this for twelve years 18.247; ontologically 10.165; phenomena as non-different from *śūnyatā* 1.305–6, 1.321; reducing *dharmas* to *śūnyatā* 14.500; 'some beings are more empty than others' (*Diamond Sūtra*) 14.498; sometimes interpreted as a sort of pantheism 14.603

mistakes and misunderstandings about śūnyatā
'Better to be attached to a self as high as Mount Sumeru than to the idea of *śūnyatā*' 3.237, 4.693 (n227), 14.459,

18.179, 18.371, 19.241; denying the truth of *śūnyatā* is like a man on a horse denying he is on horseback 7.213, 10.158; imagining that the concept of emptiness exempts you from activity 7.414; misunderstanding it may reduce Buddhism to materialism or nihilism 14.459–60; thinking of emptiness as the self-nature or own-being of *dharmas* 1.268; thinking that there is an actual thing called emptiness 19.39; to misunderstand *śūnyatā* is to be poisoned by the only medicine that can cure you 17.389; to prevent misunderstanding we need to speak of absolute mind as empty 2.130; 'the trap of nothingness': the danger of thinking of *śūnyatā* nihilistically 15.374, 18.179

THE PRACTICE OF *ŚŪNYATĀ*

reflections and meditations
becoming familiar with emptiness 17.168; can become abstract, six element practice more concrete and practical 5.32; comprehending the clear light of the Void (one of Nāropā's six yogas) 13.28; constant mindfulness of emptiness is the secret of success in the spiritual life 7.413; developing emptiness of mind 14.197; developing insight into *śūnyatā* on the Tibetan Buddhist path 12.296; meditation on *śūnyatā* 5.707–8 (n22); practising awareness of *śūnyatā* 1.577; reflecting on the *Heart Sūtra* 5.523; reflecting on the body as empty 2.144; reflection on *śūnyatā* 16.21; the remembrance of emptiness increases one's power of spiritual activity 7.413; seeing everything as *śūnyatā* 18.599–600; systematic 5.523; to confront the reality of *śūnyatā* can be terrifying 17.337; to start with, just focus on impermanence, which does ultimately imply *śūnyatā* 16.21; transmuting rejoicing in merits into Enlightenment through emptiness 14.144; *vipaśyanā* practice 5.32–3; in visualization practice, *see* visualization/and emptiness; 'What is the cause of *śūnyatā*?' – a koan for Sangharakshita 21.187–8; you can't just 'contemplate the Void', you need actual practices 18.636–7; you have to learn to control the *kleśas* to see their fundamental emptiness 13.174

śūnyatā as a basis
the basis of transference of merit 2.270; the bodhisattva takes it for the basis 1.269; emptiness makes spiritual life possible 14.607; growth in holiness is essentially growth in emptiness 7.375, 26.53; take the tranquillity of *śūnyatā* as a basis to transform your whole life 5.394

realizing śūnyatā, and its effect
after a glimpse of *śūnyatā* the tendency is to become estranged from it 5.394; brightening *śūnyatā* 19.197–9; the Buddha can be 'seen' only in the same way that *śūnyatā* is to be 'realized' 1.307; the experience of *śūnyatā* 14.561; give up even ideas like 'Buddha' and 'bodhisattva' if *śūnyatā* is to be realized 10.165; having realized emptiness you are incapable of acting unethically 7.377; in realizing *śūnyatā* the bodhisattva transcends the self–other distinction 16.232; no such thing as an unrealized *śūnyatā* 19.198–9; realizing *śūnyatā* and experiencing wine as the nectar of Enlightenment 19.332; renouncing group identity in favour of the freedom of absolute emptiness 18.139; the touch of *śūnyatā* feels like death 26.48; the view that realizing *śūnyatā* is not indispensable for attaining Nirvāṇa 1.321; we can radiate love only from egolessness, from *śūnyatā* 12.458; the wisdom will be the Voidness, the Voidness the wisdom 18.222; without realizing *śūnyatā* Vajrayāna visualizations are vulgar magic, *see under* Chen

FOUR *ŚŪNYATĀS*

introduction
description 2.118–19, 3.233–8, 4.161–3, 10.160, 16.11–12; a brief introduction to the meditation practice 1.270, 18.398–9; the concluding mantra of the *Heart Sūtra* could refer to them 4.163; different kinds of *śūnyatā* 1.305, 3.233, 4.161; do they magnify the literalism they were elaborated to quash? 4.163–4; keys to unlock the experience the Buddha had 18.399; not different kinds of reality, but deeper stages of penetration into reality 4.161; reflection on them to gain insight 19.453

(1) the emptiness of the conditioned (saṃskṛta-śūnyatā)
introduction 3.234–5, 12.163; corresponds with what Buddhaghosa calls *visabhāga-paṭibhāga* 1.120, 7.201; the 'emptiness of the composite' (Nāgārjuna) 1.120, 7.200; the flux of relative existence is without what only the Conditioned can give 4.161–2; it is devoid of the characteristics of the Unconditioned 1.488, 2.118; and 'knowledge and vision of things as they really are' 12.163; emptiness of self 3.217; emptiness of the *skandhas* 3.217

(2) the emptiness of the Unconditioned (asaṃskṛta-śūnyatā)
introduction 3.236, 12.163; emptiness of the incomposite (Nāgārjuna) 1.120; it is devoid of the characteristics of the

conditioned 1.488, 2.118; on account of *śūnyatā* or unrestrictedness everything becomes possible 7.200; devoid of the unsatisfactory, impermanent, and unreal nature of the conditioned 4.162; and 'knowledge and vision of things as they really are' 12.163

(3) the great emptiness (mahā-śūnyatā)
introduction 3.236–7; emptiness of the distinction between conditioned and Unconditioned 1.489–90; emptiness of distinction between *saṃsāra* and *nirvāṇa* 2.118, 3.236–7, 3.254, 4.162; how a bodhisattva becomes irreversible 4.188; *prajñā* is the realization of *mahā-śūnyatā* 3.236–7, 3.301–2; exemplified by the Perfection of Wisdom literature 2.118; it is the 'great void' because we are all afraid of disappearing into it 4.162; *vimutti* corresponds to 2.118–19; you awake from the dream of dualistic thinking 4.188, 14.591–2

(4) the emptiness of emptiness (śūnyatā-śūnyatā)
introduction 3.237–8; emptiness itself is empty 17.380; rejection of the concept of emptiness 2.118, 4.162–3; not a sort of stuff out of which *dharmas* are made 1.269; the most appropriate expression of it is to say nothing 1.490, 2.118, 3.238; meditation 1.270, 1.308–9; *śūnyatā* itself has to be discarded 14.440; taught to counter the tendency to cling 23.320; thunderous silence 1.490, 2.118, 4.163; the Void is itself void 7.361, 7.413, 16.449

see also
one of the three *vimokṣas*, *see* three *vimokṣas*; in Perfection of Wisdom texts, *see* Perfection of Wisdom and individual texts; *śūnyatā* mantra, *see oṃ svabhāva…*; *śūnyatā* and *rūpa* (emptiness and form), *see under Heart Sūtra*; twofold *śūnyatā*, *see nairātmya*; visualization and emptiness, *see under* visualization/doing the practice

Sunyata, Sri *see* Sørensen

Śūnyatāsaptati *see* Nāgārjuna

śūnyavāda (way of emptiness) another name for the Madhyamaka 17.360; is also the way of compassion 7.362; it can be mistaken for nihilism, but is really neither eternalistic nor nihilistic 17.360; it seems nihilistic to those whose reality is wholly mundane 17.362–3; its followers have *samyak-sambodhi* as their declared aim 17.360–1; to misunderstand it is to be poisoned by the only medicine that can cure you 17.389; logically nihilistic but spiritually plenistic 7.126; the path seen as the way of emptiness 7.357; the progressive attenuation of the ego-sense 7.361

supaṭipanno *see under Tiratana Vandanā*

Supayalat, Queen *see under* Burma

superconscious *dhyāna* and the superconscious 11.124, 11.149; difference between a superconscious and a transcendental state 20.206; four levels: animal, rational, superconscious, transcendental 22.293; the superconscious is beyond reason, but does not contradict it 26.199

superficiality aesthetic experience can be superficial and untransforming 16.285; if our emotions are tied up with worldly life, our Dharma life can only be superficial 26.57; people go very much by outward appearances 10.618–19; most Buddhist expositions of Perfect Speech are rather superficial 1.515, 12.33; one of the curses of the modern age 11.49–50, 19.459; our knowledge is only superficial, we don't know in the depths 12.22–3; our usual type of consciousness tends towards superficiality 17.xviii–xix; people judge others by quite superficial standards 19.308–10; religion summed up as the giving of buns and blankets 1.428; right emotions not backed up by right understanding are superficial and unreliable 7.271; the Roman Catholic church demands superficiality 19.278; spreading one's attention across the enjoyments of modern life 15.152–3; superficial communication 19.107; as the third fetter, *see under* ten fetters/third fetter

superiority acknowledging that some people are better than others in certain respects 18.132; brahmins' belief in their superiority over other castes 1.501, 12.239; don't assert superiority over someone having a difficult time 26.24; an inflated idea of oneself, imagined superiority 17.604; Māra convincing a forest renunciant of his superiority 4.554–5; ordination is not an achievement that in itself sets you above other Buddhists 18.176; taking charge of a spiritual institution does not imply spiritual superiority 18.18; we should be very grateful that we are *not* superior to all others 17.274–5; *see also* pride/thinking of oneself as superior, inferior, or equal

superman *see mahāpuruṣa*

supernatural beings the Buddha lived in a world populated by supernatural beings 15.136; *devas* and *brahmās* belong

to the natural world 2.34; even if their existence were disproved, the basic truths of the Dharma would remain unshaken 26.153; in Buddhism the supernatural is natural 12.522; perhaps rationalizations of the fears of pre-Buddhist India 26.153; references to them in scriptures dismissed by modern scholarship 1.33–4, 2.33–4; *see also* non-human beings

supernatural experiences suggest that the laws of nature are more profound than we usually think 26.229–30; Sangharakshita's supernatural experiences, *see under* Sangharakshita/VI

supernormal powers or faculties (*siddhis* or *iddhis*)

notes on supernormal powers
the powers of Bhaddiya the dwarf 10.618; the difference between Milarepa's miracles and supernormal powers 19.120; difference between supernormal and supernatural powers 10.36–7; don't misuse your magical powers 10.448; encouraging that the accounts of them are not wholly mythical 20.309; their existence supports the Buddhist belief in the creative power of thought 1.342; not regarded as very important in Buddhism, except in the Tantra 4.517; regarded as dangerous in the early days of Buddhism in Britain 4.517; Satyapriya's experience of clairaudience 20.308–9; some Enlightened beings develop them, others don't 19.423; of Tomo Geshe Rimpoche 1.342–3; unhealthy fascination with supernormal powers 3.584

the Buddha's supernormal powers
Dr Ambedkar on the subject 9.95–7; churned-up water becomes clear when he wants a drink 10.639; he uses his divine eye 10.456; he uses 'magic' to unblock a well 10.622–7; his powers once dismissed as invention, but science now less biased towards materialism 2.33; his psychic powers are natural, and can be developed by anybody 2.34; he crosses the Ganges by means of supernormal power 10.643, 10.648; he teaches the *devas* 4.16–17; magical powers 16.450; Uruvelā Kāsyapa is unimpressed by his powers 2.23

see also
arising on the basis of the fourth *dhyāna*, *see under dhyānas*/four *rūpa dhyānas*; six *abhijñās*

superstition better to have the weeds of superstition than the sterile garden of rationalism 12.105; devotion can go to extremes, to become superstition, fanaticism, or intolerance 3.301; infiltration into Buddhism of superstitious rites and beliefs 2.220; superstitions about good and bad luck 15.382–3, 16.397; superstition as defined by Francis Bacon 12.655; superstitions about breaking a Buddha image 22.7–8; superstitious beliefs as an aspect of the third fetter 17.633; a symbol can become a superstition 7.283; Westerners sometimes think that devotion is childish or superstitious 3.301

Suppabuddha (the leper) *see under Udāna*/people/the Buddha's disciples

Suppāraka, India (modern Nala Sopara) 10.459–60

Suppavāsā (the Buddha's disciple) 10.493–8

Suppiya (the Buddha's disciple, 'Untouchable') 9.142, 10.672 (n86)

Suppiya, a critic of the Buddha 3.76, 3.546–7, 11.333

support

material support
being easily supported (*subharo*) 15.xix, 15.277–84; a financially self-supporting Buddhist movement 9.491–2, 10.300–1; giving to support the Dharma 9.393, 15.402, 18.375–7; giving to support the sangha 1.427–8; gratitude for the support we are given 17.201; householders' support for wanderers 10.648, 15.278–9; lay people's support for monks, *see under* lay people; material support for those committed to spiritual life 18.121–2; state support for the spiritual community 3.587, 15.365–6; supporting others to practise is not enough, you need to practise yourself 15.650; to ask people to support you, you need faith and yearning for the Dharma 19.352–3; we should support people to live a Buddhist life 18.121; what does a monk give in return? 3.591, 15.365–6; you've no right to be supported until you've destroyed your inner cravings 19.357

supportive conditions for spiritual practice
art as support to the spiritual life 1.262; the Buddhist movement exists to support the development of the individual 3.457 culture supporting spiritual growth 13.483–4; a healthy person's principal support is always from within 26.29; *kalyāṇa mitra* supports the development of the emotions 9.443–4; society supportive of the individual 4.94, 7.239, 9.285, 10.207; supportive conditions allow change without much effort 5.252; supportive conditions for a hermit lifestyle are hard to find today 18.33–4; a supportive environment is indispensable

until you enter the Stream 12.315; supportive karma 2.72, 3.109–10; the need to set up positive conditions to support practice 4.183, 12.315, 18.36; three levels of practice: in supportive, unsupportive, and whatever conditions 18.84; we need the support of the sangha 12.514, 14.456, 15.738, 17.308–9

supportive Dharma practices
the active energy that gives support to awareness 18.322; the bodhisattva ideal a support to 'working for the good of Buddhism' 2.455, 22.541–2; the bodhisattva vow as a support to the *bodhicitta* 4.65–6, 14.412, 18.161; the Buddha gives guidance in doubt, support in crisis, impetus in stagnation 2.11; 'Dharma' comes from a root 'to support' 1.28, 1.99, 12.501, 16.369; *dhyāna* as a support for *prajñā* 1.444; intellectual supports for realization 1.303; the *mettā bhāvanā* as a support for the observance of the first precept 17.183; positive conceptions of reality are efficacious as supports 1.243; precepts: the discipline that supports individual liberation 2.344–8, 2.491–2; the purpose of learning is to support the faith that comes from practice 18.185; reality as the support of the emancipated mind 2.43; support for insight 5.421–2, 5.629–30; the ten precepts support the edifice of the Dharma 2.395; we need doctrinal supports to begin with 14.547; you need a conceptual support for your Dharma practice 19.508

support for meditation
art as support for meditation 3.617; classical 'supports' of concentration 1.159–60; learning some self-discipline will support your meditation practice 15.173; support for meditation 1.363, 3.617, 5.635, 5.652

supporting others
anaññaposī (not supporting anyone) 10.449, 10.454; support for artists 4.94–5; support for New Buddhists in India 7.465, 9.xiii, 9.118–19, 9.155–6; support of parents (*Maṅgala Sutta*) 15.407–9

no support
the Buddha's teaching is 'baseless' in the sense of unsupported 17.369; a Buddhist should not support those who are disseminating false doctrines 1.427–8; don't look to others to support your image or experience of yourself 18.388; giving 'unsupported' 14.416–24; going out into the world without spiritual support 19.347; patience unsupported by anything 1.437–8, 14.476; 'That which is supported has no support' (*Diamond Sūtra*) 1.438–9, 14.477, 26.83

see also
four supports; *subharo* (easily supported); in right livelihood, *see under* team-based right livelihood

suppression the ability to suppress the expression of emotions enables us to practise the precepts 19.17; be careful to direct positive feelings rather than suppress them 5.617; finding a middle way between letting emotions go where they want and suppressing them 5.618; human beings' suppression: we can't fully be ourselves 4.598–9; *mettā*: not the suppression of natural affections but their universalization 1.426; Padmasambhava didn't suppress the demons of Tibet, but harnessed their energies 18.24–5; suppressing aspects of yourself because you want approval 19.17; suppressing desire is appropriate to sense-desire (*kāmacchanda*), but not *dharmachanda* 7.306–7; suppressing energy 4.598–9; the suppression of hindrances 1.153; you can't suppress your own better nature indefinitely 4.267

supra-individual or supra-personal after Ambedkar's death: 'I felt I was not a person but an impersonal force' 11.xix–xx, 21.523, 22.364; 'allowing myself to be a channel for something beyond me' 11.687; the arising of the *bodhicitta*: supra-individual, but not collective 4.30, 11.285, 14.575; the bodhisattva as a 'supra-personal' stream of spiritual energy, cosmic force 4.63, 7.155, 16.229; the supra-personal emotions associated with devotion 11.228–9; 'A wind was in my sails' 25.xli, 25.450; 'The words that came from my lips were not really mine' 26.670

Śūraṅgama Sūtra (The Buddha's Great Crown Sūtra')

introduction
brief summary 1.355–6; description 13.358–63; influence on Zen 2.555; predominantly psychological and discursive 1.355; in principle canonical 14.260; translations 13.337, 14.197–8, 14.260; Sangharakshita compares his experience to the *sūtra*'s description of consciousness 20.73

the content of the sūtra
Ānanda is rescued from the charms of Prakṛti by Mañjuśrī 13.358–60; the Buddha asks Ānanda questions to be answered spontaneously 13.360–1; Ānanda sees the Buddha's beauty 12.307–8,

13.361, 15.556, 15.721, 17.337, 25.31; the Buddha shows Ānanda that his mind cannot be located anywhere 13.362–4, 18.544; 'each one's mind was co-extensive with the universe' 1.356; 'Great Crown' *dhāraṇi* 2.691 (n301); paradoxical description of Nirvāṇa 1.71–2; twenty-five methods of controlling the mind through meditation 14.197

Śūraṅgama-samādhi Sūtra ('Sūtra of the Heroic Advance') introduction 14.195–7; it is beyond time and space 26.546; Dṛḍhāmati asks how the bodhisattva manifests wonderful qualities without entering Nirvāṇa 14.195; the gods offer the Buddha miraculous lion thrones 14.195–6; Māra's appearance in the *sūtra* 25.143, 26.545–6, 26.662; the practice of the *śūraṅgama-samādhi* 14.196–7; Sangharakshita and Paramartha study the *sūtra* 26.545–6; translations 14.195

Surata (bodhisattva) 14.185

Surata, Dharmachari brief introduction 17.6; in India 10.xxxix; member of the Preceptors' College 12.631

Surata-paripṛcchā 14.184–5

surface allowing one's real desires to surface 4.151–2; consciousness like the surface waves, unconscious like the ocean depths 12.179; Dudjom Rimpoche was like a great ocean, with calm depths and a sparkling surface 22.508; the dust on the surface of the mind 18.323; experiencing reality in one aspect leaves you sliding on the surface 14.589; it's not enough to scratch the rational surface of the mind, we need to drop a depth charge 12.323; a meaning deeper and more acceptable than the surface meaning 16.103; misled by the apparent simplicity of the Dharma, people stay on the surface 12.34; philosophy titillates the rational surface of our being, poetry stirs it to its depths 1.347; religion must do more than scratch the rational surface 1.124, 7.392; scratching the surface with a little meditation will not reveal the Buddha within 26.479; the 'surface experience of *dhyāna*' compared to the depth of *prajñā* 18.251–2; we create patterns as we move over the surface of things 18.283

Surrealism 22.269

surrender *see* self-surrender

surroundings Dr Ambedkar grew up in beautiful surroundings, but an ugly social system 10.400; are surroundings important on solitary retreat? 5.675; as a Buddhist you shouldn't be too strongly affected by them 11.618; can we surround ourselves with conditions that support our spiritual aspirations? 18.36; combating ugliness in one's surroundings 26.183, 26.192; having a harmonious effect on one's surroundings 4.98; importance of keeping our surroundings beautiful 9.444–5; 'It seems strange that someone like me should emerge from those surroundings' 12.681; living in surroundings not conducive to stillness, simplicity, and contentment 18.34; Milarepa makes best use of a beneficial environment 18.41–2; taking care of one's surroundings 9.445–6; thinking of your surroundings as the Pure Land 16.181; through developing positivity, you feel more powerful than your surroundings 18.575; you can handle oscillations by placing yourself in stable surroundings 18.541

Survey of Buddhism *see under* Sangharakshita XIII

Sūrya, the sun god 16.418, 20.460

Suryaprabha, Dharmachari (Terry Williams) 2.739 (n659), 24.385, 24.706 (n476)

Susambhava, King 16.389–90

Sushila, Anagārikā (Tansen, Nepal) 20.430, 20.433–4

Susiddhi, Dharmachari 17.8, 24.136, 24.658 (n158)

susikkhito 15.406

suśīla 11.307

Susthitamati-paripṛcchā 14.181, 14.182–3

Sutherland, Graham 26.478

Sūtra of the Buddha's Bequeathed Teachings 14.230

'Sūtra of Complete Enlightenment' 14.250

Sūtra of Forty-Two Sections introduction 14.60; the first canonical text to be translated into Chinese 14.60; 'It is hard to help others towards Enlightenment according to their various needs' 4.67; 'Of all the lusts and desires, there is none so powerful as sexual inclination' 3.321, 11.572; one flame being lit from another 12.646, 12.753 (n444); seminar 24.28, 24.93; the span of a man's life a single breath 14.60, 26.296–7; story about the Buddha's response to verbal abuse 4.119

Sūtra of Golden Light (*Suvarṇaprabhāsa Sūtra*)

introduction
introduction 14.241–5; summary of the *sūtra*'s contents 16.244–6; chapter by chapter description 14.242–4; the chapters classified into three groups 14.244–5; full commentary 16.227–435; no summary could do justice to its spirit of fervent devotion 16.246; written in Buddhist Hybrid Sanskrit over many years 14.241–2, 16.239–40; compared with the *Bhagavad Gītā* 16.424–5; a Tantric development in the *sūtra* 16.260; translations 14.241–2

the nature of the sūtra
its distinctive teaching: transformation of self and world 16.247; draws into its orbit all the principal Mahāyāna teachings 14.244–5; disorganized 16.246–7, 16.369; has a spiritual unity despite seeming like a transcendental ragbag 14.244, 16.246–7; it requires a lot of explanation and interpretation 11.719–20; it is held together by the spiritual needs of the individual 16.247; favours the affirmative approach 16.329; Jātakas in the *sūtra* 14.244, 16.246; one of nine *sūtras* venerated in Nepal 14.100; a popular text 14.241; a *dhāraṇi* 14.245, 16.369; 'the profound Buddha region', a world in itself 16.243–4; sense of time in the *sūtra* 16.288; really the *sūtra* is just the *sūtra* talking about the *sūtra* 16.243, 19.71

Ruciraketu (bodhisattva)
his history 16.253; he questions why the Buddha has such a short life 14.242, 16.244–5, 16.253–61; his house expands and four Buddhas appear in it 14.242, 16.257–61; the four-Buddha mandala, suggesting a slight Tantric development 16.260–1; his dream of the golden drum 14.242, 16.245, 16.253, 16.262–7, 16.287–8; an example of true individual 16.308; his experience of the Path of Vision and the Path of Transformation 16.263–4; the *bodhicitta* arises 16.288; takes the bodhisattva vow 16.288–9; becomes a king 16.414–15

the golden drum and its meaning
compared to the sun 12.384; it has many meanings 16.263–5; its Brahmā voice 16.281; fulfils wishes 11.565, 16.283, 16.286; removes fear 16.176–9

golden light
bringing the world under the influence of the golden light 12.395; and the earth goddess: separate principles within the subject–object framework 16.389; effect of the golden light 16.287–8; once you've come into contact with it, you won't forget it 16.291; spiritual food or medicine 16.290; struggle between the golden light and one's inner poisons 16.290–1; submitting to the golden light 16.358; to communicate it, a language is needed: the refined language of culture 16.366–7

confession section
has a poetic quality 4.47; 'literature of power' 14.303; the nucleus of the *sūtra* 16.243; of Ruciraketu 16.293–4; the spiritual significance of confession 16.268–337, 24.383; 'creating light for one another' 16.335; verses spoken by the golden drum 14.242–3, 16.267–8

the four great kings
appear in chapter 6 of the *sūtra* 14.243, 16.347; extol the virtues of the *sūtra* 16.347; four promises 16.347, 16.355–6; nourished by the *sūtra* 16.347, 16.353–5; as protectors 16.288, 16.346–53

Sarasvatī
'Buddhism and Culture' 16.359–77; what is a Hindu goddess doing in a Buddhist scripture? 16.364

Dṛḍhā (earth goddess)
'Nature, Man, and Enlightenment' 16.378–94; exemplifies many of the characteristics of Mahāyāna Buddhism 16.228, 16.233; expounding the *sūtra* makes her more powerful 16.355, 16.382; the *sūtra* nourishes her 16.383; people will turn to the *sūtra* through the earth goddess's promise 16.382

Śrī
'Buddhist Economics' 16.395–413; her birth as the goddess 16.409; hymn of praise to Śrī 16.384; promises to equip the preacher of the Dharma 16.395, 16.399, 16.401–6; promises to give 16.400, 16.410–11; worship 16.409

Brahmā, the teacher of the gods
'The Moral Order and Its Upholders' 16.415–31

other characters who appear in the sūtra
Balendraketu, King 16.414–5; Brahmin (Kauṇḍinya) 16.258, 16.372; Jalavāhana the physician 14.244, 16.246; Ruciraketu, King 16.414–15; Śākyamuni 16.409, 16.414; Susaṃbhava, King 16.389–90; Varendraketu, King 16.415

India
Indian aesthetics 16.326–7; Indian ideas about the origin and treatment of disease 14.244, 16.246; the language of Indian cosmology 16.367

magic, miracles, and Dharma teachings
magic (or Tantric ritual) 14.245, 16.370; miracles 16.258; the ten precepts 2.334; brief account of *śūnyatā* 14.243, 14.303

preaching, hearing, protecting
the monk who preaches the *sūtra* 16.389–93; why the monk is the preacher 16.393–4; listening to the *sūtra* produces merit that guarantees positive rebirth 16.382–3; protection 16.341–94; Saṃjñāya the *yakṣa* promises to protect the *sūtra* 14.243

praise, aspiration, worship
aspirations for the welfare of all living beings 16.276, 16.333–4; the praise of the Tathāgatas 14.244; prayers 16.276–89; Sevenfold Puja 11.219, 16.267–8, 16.275; hymns of praise to the Buddha 16.246, 16.326, 16.328; worship of the Buddhas 16.326, 16.328; predictions to Buddhahood 14.243–4, 16.246

Sūtra of the Great Merit of Foremost Purity 14.260, 14.628 (n275)

Sūtra of Huineng (*Platform Sūtra, Sūtra of Wei Lang*)

THE *SŪTRA*

introduction
original edition of the *Sūtra of Wei Lang* 23.40; an edition brought out by Christmas Humphreys 24.321; emphasis on direct realization of the highest spiritual truth 2.555; the entire system of Buddhist training according to Huineng 13.331; inspiration to the Triratna Buddhist Community 2.555, 12.368

content
'The profundity of the teachings … has nothing to do with the written language' 1.222; 'the child who picks up pebbles and calls them gems' 7.34; the 'formless *gāthā*' 8.371–2, 18.364; gradual and sudden Enlightenment 3.146, 16.183; it deals with *śūnyatā* 11.170; 'The idea of a self is Mount Meru' 2.77; 'Let us take refuge to the Three Gems within our mind!' 2.408, 15.580–2; the *samādhi* of one characteristic and the *samādhi* of evenmindedness 1.587

jñāna or samādhi and prajñā
like the light and the lamp 1.587–8, 3.357, 4.166–7, 13.329–30, 14.317; the idea that *samādhi* just means concentration leads to confusion 1.588; *samādhi* is the quintessence of *prajñā*, while *prajñā* is the activity of *samādhi* 7.140; what *samādhi* and *prajñā* mean in this context 13.330–1

SANGHARAKSHITA AND THE *SŪTRA*

first reading (then called the Sūtra of Wei Lang)
'I realized I was a Buddhist' 2.499, 9.13, 9.278, 9.382; 'Contact with Buddhism was contact with the depths of my own being' 16.218; my first glimpse of Perfect Vision 11.170; going for Refuge to the Dharma 2.408; 'My debt to it is incalculable' 24.321; 'Whenever I read the text I would be thrown into a kind of ecstasy' 20.85

later readings
conducts a seminar on the text 24.321; gives Terry Delamare a copy of the *sūtra* 22.107; gratitude to the translator 3.361; work on a revised version 24.321, 24.371

see also
Huineng's biography, *see under* Huineng

Sūtra of the Lord of Healing (*Bhaiṣajyaguru Sūtra*) brief introduction 12.228, 14.175, 22.571–2 (n22); its translator presents Sangharakshita with a copy 22.15[illegible]; twelve great vows 1.335, 14.175, 16.194, 22.557

Sūtra of Perfect Enlightenment 4.496

Sūtra Piṭaka *see* Sutta Piṭaka

Sūtralaṃkāra *see* Maitreyanātha, Asaṅga

sūtras *see suttas*

Sutta-Nipāta

introduction
description 14.55–9; its appearance in Sanskrit texts 14.56; the archaic parts of the text are in verse 10.425–6; down-to-earth approach 14.514; the text is cited elsewhere in the Tipiṭaka, attesting to its age 14.55; a commentary on the text (the *Niddesa*) accorded canonical status 14.55; it shows the essence of Buddhism 9.109; glimpses of the *bhikṣu* sangha 2.188; index of similes 26.210; inspiration and guidance from the text 2.552, 22.320; it comes as close as anything in the canon to telling us what the Buddha said 17.157; link with the *Dhammapada* 14.57; a mixture of early and late material 15.258; oldest and greatest of the anthologies 14.55; portions of the text in the *Mahāvastu* 14.71; translation 15.xviii–xix; a very important work 10.57

chapter 1: uraga-vagga ('snake chapter')
introduction: an extract from a seminar 11.536–40; thought to be the work of a single gifted poet-author 14.56; (1.1) *Uraga Sutta* a true monk sloughs off bonds like a snake his worn-out skin

14.56; (1.2) *Dhaniya Sutta*: the business of secular living 14.56; (1.3) *Khaggavisāṇa Sutta* (*Rhinoceros Sutta*): 'Wander alone, as the horn of the rhinoceros is single' 2.191, 4.707 (n314), 8.259–60, 14.56, 26.156; (1.4) *Kasi-Bhāradvāja Sutta*: 'Faith is the seed' 10.331–2, 13.571, 15.625, 17.17–19, 26.648–9; Kasi-Bhāradvāja and the Buddha discuss ploughing 3.76, 10.330–2, 14.56, 18.294, 25.174–5, 26.648–9; (1.5) *Cunda Sutta*: describes four different types of monk 14.56; (1.6) *Parābhava Sutta*: a dialogue with a female deity on the factors leading to spiritual deterioration 14.56; 'One who loves the Dharma passionately, progresses' 13.274–5; (1.7) *Vasala Sutta*: a brahmin is asked if he really knows what makes an outcaste 14.19; the Buddha redefines the meaning of *vasala* (caste) 13.699 (n163), 23.178, 23.499 (n206); caste 1.634 (n433); doesn't contain the whole of the Buddha's teaching 8.205; one becomes a brahmin not by birth but by deeds 8.358, 10.xxvi, 12.727 (n218), 14.56; social comment 8.532; (1.9) *Hemavata Sutta*: two deities chant the praises of the Buddha 14.57; (1.10) *Āḷavaka Sutta*: the acceptance of the guiding ideal 15.663–5; the conversion of a fierce demon 14.57; 'Faith is the wealth here best for man' 1.290; (1.11) *Vijaya Sutta*: the repulsiveness of the human body 14.57; (1.12) *Muni Sutta*: the description of the sage 14.57

chapter 2: cullavagga
introduction: biographical ballads and encounters with brahmins 14.57; (2.8) *Nāva Sutta*; worshipping the man from whom one learns the Dharma 22.385

chapter 3: mahāvagga
(3.1) *Pabbajjā Sutta*: Siddhārtha's going forth 8.481, 9.478, 10.221, 10.696 (n249), 14.57; (3.2) *Padhāna Sutta*; Siddhārtha's temptation by Māra 14.57, 15.733; (3.4) *Pūralāsa Sutta*: the Buddha says that he doesn't belong to any particular caste 1.634 (n433), 13.699 (n163); Sundarika-Bhāradvāja exclaims on the effect of the Dharma 9.248; Sundarika-Bhāradvāja becomes a monk 2.665 (n30); (3.5) *Māgha Sutta*: Māgha becomes a lay disciple 2.665 (n30); (3.6) *Sabhiya Sutta*: Sabhiya praises the Buddha 14.57; *vīrya* compared to a horse 19.438; (3.7) *Sela Sutta*: the Buddhas reveal their true selves if they are praised 4.176; Sela praises the Buddha 14.57; (3.9) *Vāseṭṭha Sutta*: the true brahmin 14.57; (3.10) *Kokālika Sutta*: description of hell 14.57; (3.11) *Nālaka Sutta*: Asita's encounter with the infant Siddhārtha 3.629 (n23), 9.140

chapter 4: aṭṭhakavagga
introduction: anticipates the Madhyamaka doctrine 7.527; the Buddha answers brahmins' questions on profound themes 2.205; as close as we can get to the Buddha's original teaching 10.575; corresponds to the *Arthapāda Sūtra* of the Chinese canon 7.527; Hare's translation 19.374; how the text is arranged 14.57; the language and the thought is very difficult 10.575; no description could do its stanzas justice 14.57–8; and the Perfection of Wisdom 14.137, 14.351; Soṇa Koṭikaṇṇa learns the verses by heart 10.573–6, 14.20; a very difficult chapter 19.374; (4.5) *Paramaṭṭhaka Sutta*: a source of a rather austere type of Buddhism 8.362; (4.10) *Purābheda Sutta*: description of the *arhant* ('truly man-of-calm') 1.181–2; making no comparison with others as superior, inferior, or equal 18.660 (n176); (4.14) *Tuvaṭaka Sutta*: how does a monk become 'cool'? 14.58; (4.15) *Attadaṇḍa Sutta*: there is nothing in this world that is solid at base 14.549, 14.654 (n485)

chapter 5: pārāyanavagga
introduction: summary of the chapter 14.58–9; brahmin Bāvari and his students visit the Buddha and ask him a question 2.689–90 (n288); the Buddha answers brahmins' questions on profound themes 2.205; the language and the thought is very difficult 10.575; (5.6) Upasīva's questions: 'man of naught' 3.144, 4.358; 'There is no measuring of man' 2.43; 'When all conditions are removed,/ All ways of telling are removed' 1.65, 2.43, 3.143–4; (5.10) Kappa's questions: 'The Way to the Beyond': the Buddha tells Kappa about an island of refuge 1.82

Pārāyana Thuti Gātha (epilogue)
Piṅgiya, an example of someone freed by faith 4.709 (n333); Piṅgiya's faith in the Buddha 1.287–9, 14.59

see also
Karaṇīya Mettā Sutta; *Ratana Sutta*; *Maṅgala Sutta*

Sutta (or Sūtra) Piṭaka

introduction
brief description 14.252; anthologies 2.553, 3.84, 9.137–8, 14.43–60; contrast with the Vinaya Piṭaka 1.184–5, 2.627–8; comparison between Pāli canon *suttas* and Mahāyāna *sūtras* 14.96–100; the content is of two kinds, Hīnayāna and Mahāyāna 14.35, 14.96; the Pāli collection

was preserved intact in Sri Lanka 14.35; difference between Burmese and Thai versions 14.253

collections (Nikāyas in Pāli, Agamas in Sanskrit)
brief introduction 7.501, 14.35; *Aṅguttara Nikāya, see Aṅguttara Nikāya*; *Dīgha Nikāya, see Dīgha Nikāya*; *Majjhima Nikāya, see Majjhima Nikāya*; *Saṃyutta Nikāya, see Saṃyutta Nikāya*; *Khuddaka Nikāya, see Khuddaka Nikāya*

dialogues or discourses (Dīgha and Majjhima)
comparison with Platonic dialogues 14.36–7; 'composed for Buddhist hearers, and not for Western readers' 14.37; the effect of congregational chanting 14.37; like a Bach fugue 14.36; their appeal is through the ear to the heart rather than through the eye to the intellect 14.37; use of metaphors, similes, and parables 14.41–2

suttas (Sanskrit *sūtras*)

introduction
definition 1.297, 3.652 (n170), 7.500–1, 16.233–4; meaning of *sutta* (literally 'thread') 7.500, 9.357, 12.501, 16.33, 16.235, 16.441; a reason to dispense with the term 16.443; a literary record of a discourse or dialogue of the Buddha 14.342; misleading to think of them as 'scriptures' 16.441; the Buddha could be said to have invented the public discourse 10.551–2; perhaps the most important and characteristic of Buddhist literary genres 7.500; literary compositions, but perhaps suggest the Buddha's teaching style 10.552; records of oral communication 16.441–2; *suttas* preached by disciples 14.261; Zhiyi's classification of the *sūtras* 10.554–5, 11.716–17; one of the nine *aṅgas* of the Pāli canon 14.23; 'Hīnayāna' and 'Mahāyāna' 7.501–2, 16.235–7; difference from *śāstras* 26.197; difference in approach from Abhidharma *mātikas* 14.80

reflections
learning to read *sūtras* 16.443–4; 'The outer phenomena suffice for one's Sūtras' 18.619, 18.621–2; certainly more useful to us than 'outer phenomena' 18.632–3; Rechungpa as a reciter of stories from the *sūtras* 18.306–7; sources of inspiration, not 'texts you have to slog your way through' 16.443–4; a revelation issuing from the depths of the Enlightened consciousness 16.33; the tradition derived from *termas* is the 'near' tradition (that from *sūtras* is 'far') 12.299; when we read a *sūtra* we are in contact with a higher level of being 14.342

see also
Mahāyāna *sūtras*; *paritrāṇa sūtras*; scriptures

Suttavibhaṅga *see under* Vinaya

Suvajra, Dharmachari brief introduction 2.732 (n627), 17.7, 24.635 (n149); biography of Dhardo Rimpoche 12.435; conducts ordinations for the first time 2.510–12, 12.379; entries in Sangharakshita's travel letters v24; his meeting with Sundri Vaswani 21.617; member of the Preceptors' College 12.597, 12.631; one of Sangharakshita's carers 26.549

Suvajri, Dharmacharini (Ann Gill) v24

Suvarṇaprabhāsa Sūtra *see Sūtra of Golden Light*

Suvarṇaratnākaracchatrakūṭa (Buddha) 14.244

Suvikrāntvikrāmi-paripṛcchā *see Perfection of Wisdom in 500 lines*

Suyāma gods 16.344–5

Suzuki, Beatrice Lane (*Mahāyāna Buddhism: A Brief Outline*) description of the celebration of the Buddha's birthday in Japan 2.227–8; the *Nirvāṇa Sūtra* 2.125; the O-Bon ritual 2.232; read by Sangharakshita in his youth 7.548 (n23); the six perfections 7.45

Suzuki, D. T.

introduction
a great Buddhist 6.621; influence on the development of Buddhism in the West 12.72, 23.46; 'antirationalism and antinomianism' 8.610

Outlines of Mahāyāna Buddhism
tantalizing glimpses of the world of the Mahāyāna 20.302; the *bodhicitta* is not an individual affair 4.689 (n207); the bodhisattva never becomes tired of working for universal salvation 4.85–6; maintains that the *dharmakāya* is personal 2.45; one who understands the nature of *bodhicitta* sees everything with a loving heart 4.70; the three *svabhāvas* 19.232; translation of *sambhogakāya* 2.41; Vasubandhu's four factors 4.49–50

Studies in the Laṅkāvatāra Sūtra
a discourse on a certain kind of religious experience 1.357; *anābhogacaryā* 18.647 (n81); 'a perpetual upholding of the intuitive element in religion' 14.206–7; *pratyātmagocara* 19.374; Vipāka-Buddha 14.212

Essays in Zen Buddhism: First Series
the Buddha holds up a flower and Mahākāśyapa understands 14.16; Zen verse attributed to Bodhidharma 14.611 (n27)

Essays in Zen Buddhism, third series
the *Avataṃsaka* 1.353–4; the *bodhicitta* 2.160; Japanese Buddhism 7.442–3; Samantabhadra 2.179

Manual of Zen Buddhism
the bodhisattva's four vows 2.163; ox-herding pictures 2.707 (n420)

other writings
familiarizing students with Zen 1.210–1; 'East and West': contrast between Tennyson and a Zen poet 17.331–2; the endless view, like removing the window of a Japanese house 19.184–5; essays on the *Gaṇḍavyūha Sūtra* 1.355, 14.226; *Essays in Zen Buddhism* 20.302; *The Essence of Buddhism* 1.243, 13.400; *Mysticism: Christian and Buddhist* 4.640; translates *citta* as 'soul' 13.351; translation of the *Laṅkāvatāra Sūtra* 2.276, 2.279, 13.337, 14.202; 'What is Zen?' 8.362; wisdom and compassion are 'the twin pillars of the whole edifice of Buddhism' 3.158; Zen anecdotes 8.497; *The Zen Doctrine of No Mind* 23.206

see also
Awakening of Faith in the Mahāyāna, *see under* Aśvaghoṣa

Suzuki, Ven. Sochu 25.305

svabhāva (own-being, self-nature) all phenomena are without self-nature or substantiality 7.193; all things are devoid of self-nature: a basic Buddhist teaching 19.37; the *anātman* doctrine just warns us not to abstract an entity behind it 14.461; to be dependent means to be devoid of own-being 1.267; emptiness of *svabhāva* 4.666 (n52); a Mahāyāna teaching 17.448; a mistake to think of emptiness as the self-nature or own-being of *dharmas* 1.268; reality is contemplated as having no self-nature 4.159; realizing that something is devoid of self-nature doesn't mean you experience it less vividly 19.40; seeing into one's own nature 13.358; things have no unchanging essence 18.84

svabhāvas *see* three *svabhāvas*

svabhāvikakāya and the fourth Tantric initiation 13.91; the foundation or unifying element of the *trikāya* 14.428, 19.201, 19.215; means the 'self-existent body' or 'self-existent personality' 13.91; symbolized by the Buddha Samantabhadra 19.201

svāhā 4.163, 11.289

svākkhāto ('well taught') *see under* *Tiratana Vandanā*

Svalpākṣarā (Perfection of Wisdom 'in a few syllables') 14.154

svasambhoga 1.262

Svātantrika school 1.321

Swadipa, Dharmachari 26.507, 26.514, 26.754 (n494)

swan *see under* birds

Sweden FWBO activities start 9.171, 9.189, 9.319, 9.492; FWBO Stockholm established 24.6; interest in Buddhism in Sweden (1954) 8.136; St Bridget 13.638; Swedenborg, *see* Swedenborg; Uppsala Cathedral 13.639

Swedenborg, Emanuel brief introduction 13.638–9, 24.629–30 (n123); buried in Uppsala 13.639; influence on Blake 8.560; *Arcana Celestae* 20.64; every man has both an internal and an external 7.581 (n197); *Heaven and Hell* 13.639, 20.60; Swedenborgian philosophy in Balzac 24.96

Swift, Jonathan *Gulliver's Travels* 3.322; Dr Johnson's *Life of Swift* 26.371–2; 'We have enough religion to make us hate, but not enough to make us love one another' 10.283, 26.195

Swinburne, Algernon essay on William Blake 20.332, 26.484–5; 'Hertha' 12.188, 16.386; satirization of the Christian establishment 11.343, 11.754 (n191); Swinburnian rhythms 24.396

Swinnerton, Frank 24.557

Switzerland 23.249, 23.316

swords Avalokiteśvara brings the sword of knowledge to the *asuras* 2.74, 3.382, 13.132; Blake's 'destructive sword' 26.652–3; Buddhism wields only one sword, the sword of wisdom 7.443; Christian conversion by logic and the sword 7.85; Chu La Swordsmanship 19.156; 'The Dharma-farer destroys the hosts of Māra with the sword of wisdom' 3.54; don't teach the Dharma to one carrying a sword 4.116, 4.342, 4.359; a dreadful 'sword-interval' (Pāli canon) 11.322, 12.747 (n400), 19.597 (n37); if you've lost your mindfulness, pick it up again, like a hero picking up their sword 4.479; Mañjughoṣa wields the sword of knowledge 1.432, 2.174, 3.54, 10.81,

11.292, 13.367, 17.462; meditating as though someone was standing over you with a sword 5.388–9; learning without *prajñā* (or *prajñā* without compassion) is like a sword in the hand of a man (Ambedkar) 3.354, 9.231; spreading the gospel of love by means of the sword 7.384, 22.529; the 'Sūtra of How to Kill with the Sword of Wisdom' 14.181, 14.182–3; the sword of *prapañca*-free *jñāna* 17.147; the sword of wisdom like Saladin's sword, which can cut in two a piece of silk that falls onto it 17.462; the sword of wisdom used to kill the *kleśas* 25.445; your attacker brought the stick (or sword), but you brought the body 4.119–20, 4.409, 4.425, 10.600

Śyāmaka 14.71

syllogisms 8.169, 19.186–7

symbols and symbolism

definition
what is a symbol? 13.118–23; a symbol is not a sign 13.118; 'that which by custom or convention represents something else' 13.61; something on a lower level representing something on a higher level 13.61; a visible sign of something invisible 12.181; we tend to devalue the word 'symbol' 5.598

meaning
beware of explaining symbols in a purely conceptual way 13.121; dwelling on the meaning of symbols 13.121; not understanding a symbol but allowing yourself to be changed by it 16.175; 'reading' signs and symbols 14.566; symbols do not have a meaning in a cut-and-dried sense 16.172; symbols have many meanings and are more than all their meanings 16.264; need to study them deeply to understand their complexity 16.350; a real symbol doesn't symbolize anything, it *is* something, it *is* reality 5.598; symbols are not concepts, so their meaning cannot be exhausted conceptually 13.118; to get an inkling of what a symbol means, we have to be receptive to it 13.119

the nature of symbols
cultural language of symbols 16.373–4; everything we do is symbolical, or at least expressive 18.269; everything we see is symbolic 13.120; hieroglyphics of the soul 25.239; 'huge cloudy symbols of a high romance' 13.120; Mahāyāna *sūtras* indicate transcendental realities by poetic symbols 1.355; some people respond to symbols more than others 5.556–7; some things are more symbolic than others 13.120–1; the strength of the Vajrayāna is its symbols 26.38; a symbol can become a superstition 7.283; symbols are like dreams 13.118; they are full of energy and give birth to spiritual life in us 13.123; they work on us and transform us if we are receptive to them 13.123

relating to symbols
all things could symbolize the Liberation Path, if you see them that way 18.619–20; an example of how to approach a symbol 13.118–19; associations mustn't be just intellectual 13.120–1; can words lead us to a deeper experience of symbols? 13.122–3; engagement with myths and symbols helps break through the rational mind 11.15–16; how to develop a feeling for a symbol 13.121–2; in the West we suffer from a dearth of symbols 13.70; learning to speak the language of symbols 4.148; modern interest in symbolism is perhaps influenced by Jung 12.508; swinging the emphasis from the symbol to the thing symbolized 7.284; we each need to explore what makes something symbolic for us personally 13.121; we have access to the *rūpaloka*, the archetypal realm, through symbols 12.559; we have a thirst for symbolism, but a special effort is needed to grasp it 11.679, 13.116

examples of symbolism
symbols of life and growth 16.120–2; the symbolism of colours 13.280–7; the symbolism of mantric sound 13.287–91; the symbols of Tibetan art 13.61–70; for specific symbols, *see* relevant entries

Symonds, John Addington 20.32, 13.550

Symons, Arthur 7.63, 7.564 (n106)

sympathetic joy *see muditā*

sympathy etymology 1.234; causes of lack of sympathy 17.303–4; a middle way between sympathy and solitude 26.142; the person who wears the shoe knows where it pinches 17.304; should have a robust, bracing quality 10.571, 18.624–5; poetry and fiction can enlarge our sympathies 26.114; sympathizing with something to such an extent that one disagrees with it 26.5; sympathy for someone having a difficult time 26.24; sympathy is closely allied to self-transcendence 26.140; the sympathy of the poet 26.139–40; understanding is impossible without sympathy 7.368; the workplace as an opportunity for developing sympathy 26.141–2; *see also* Tennyson/painless sympathy with pain

syncretism 'I don't believe in mixing Buddhism with other religions for a purely theoretical syncretism' 12.369; an error to interpret Tantric Buddhism as a syncretist movement 1.373; generally evidence of enervation 1.323

synecdoche 1.115

Synge, J. M. 24.582, 26.332

synoptic thought 7.197, 12.65, 13.326

synthesis analysis and synthesis 1.102; beware the premature synthesis 19.52, 26.83; the bodhisattva a living contradiction, a synthesis of *nirvāṇa* and *saṃsāra* 4.92; of Buddhism 1.360–1, 13.408; creating a personal synthesis of modern culture and ancient spiritual tradition 21.425; the four noble truths: the briefest synthesis of the entire doctrines of Buddhism 1.121; Maitreyanātha's attempts to conciliate various tendencies of Buddhism 1.360–1; of reason and emotion, meditation and action, self and other, wisdom and compassion 18.77; the synthesis of yin and yang is Enlightenment 16.151

Syrlin, Jörg the Elder 24.594–5

systematization the Abhidharma not a distortion of the Dharma, but an attempt to systematize it 1.223, 12.141–2; four systematic presentations: Vaibhāṣikas, Sautrāntikas, Vijñānavādins, Mādhyamikas 13.340; Mahāyāna *ācāryas* not original thinkers but systematizers of traditional teachings 1.366–7; Mahāyāna schools pass through three stages: dogmatism, systematization, scholasticism 1.297; systematic texts 13.340; systems of classification 7.84–5; in translations, much care is taken to systematize and coordinate terms 7.515–16; the value of realizing that spiritual systems aren't neat and tidy 17.685–6; wrong views systematized into erroneous systems of belief (Bacon) 12.656

Szagun, Gisela *see* Jinamata

T

taboos fear of breaking a taboo 21.225; and the regulation of emotion 26.131; as a young man Sangharakshita learns to discuss taboo subjects 20.76

tabula rasa 12.99, 17.499

Tagore family of Calcutta 22.578 (n63)

Tagore, Abanindranath (artist) 7.448, 7.618 (n497), 8.367

Tagore, Debendranath 21.154

Tagore, Pratima Devi v21, v22

Tagore, Rabindranath

introduction
introduction 7.562 (n98); birth centenary 8.298–9; brought up in the liberal theism of the Brahmo Samaj 8.299; discovered the Bauls, mendicant singers of mystic songs 7.461; endlessly creative 12.645; friend of Buddhism 8.298–9; the greatest figure in modern Bengali literature 21.43; his drama *Natir-Puja* adapted from a Buddhist story 14.68; a man of peace 8.299; 'My passion shall burn as the flame of Salvation' 7.61; omitted from an encyclopedia of Asian philosophy 8.605; a poet rather than a philosopher 8.299; songs sung 7.82

his influence on Sangharakshita
discovery of his writings 21.93–4; influence on Sangharakshita's poetry 8.696 (n241), 25.xxviii

Shantiniketan, the Abode of Peace
how it was founded 22.51–2; Cheena Bhavan (Sino-Indian studies) 22.52–4; educates protégés of Dharmapala 8.69; Kala Bhavan (school of art) 22.54; motto 22.576 (n52); Sangharakshita is first told about it 21.155; Sangharakshita gives talks there 21.507, 21.509, 22.52, 22.320–1; Sangharakshita visits 22.51–6; visited by James K. Baxter 24.554

Gitanjali
'I know I shall love death, because I have loved life' 4.76, 8.224–5, 12.195; 'narrow domestic walls' 7.273, 7.399

other works and sayings
Buddhadeva (review) 8.366; *Fruit-Gathering* 21.94; 'the idolatry of geography' 10.387; 'Life's memories are not life's histories, but the original work of an artist' 22.xv, 22.3; 'No hurried path of success, forcibly cut by the greed of result, can be the true path' 22.112; 'One solitary tear hanging on the cheek of time' 22.340; *Stray Birds* 21.94, 25.xxviii; 'We hasten to gather our flowers' 1.129; writings on Buddhist themes 7.447, 8.299

Tagore, Rathindranath v21

Tähtinen, Unto 8.447–53

t'ai chi ch'uan 5.67, 11.118, 11.561–2

Tais (Buddhists of Assam) *see under* Assam

Taiwan *bhikṣuṇī* ordination 3.408; funding of Dhamma projects in India 10.li

Taixu introduction 7.619 (n479), 24.615 (n55); devotion to the revival of Chinese Buddhism 7.444–5, 8.605, 12.594; a great Buddhist 6.621, 24.36; Mr Chen was his disciple 22.536; *T'ai Hsu, His Life and Teachings* (review) 8.374

Taj Mahal *see under* Agra

Takakusa, Junjirō (*Essentials of Buddhist Philosophy*) common action-influence creates the universe itself 2.77; the five *niyamas* 2.70; Tendai school 4.495

taking the initiative 'I'm capable of doing it, so why should I leave it to other people?' 4.477; Buddhists should take the initiative with people: for time is short 4.446–7; essentially a mental attitude 18.423; in spreading Buddhism 9.395; is living in the city conducive to an initiative-taking attitude to one's mental states? 18.423; it's extremely important 9.303–6; making your own luck 15.385–7; with the hindrances, it is essential to keep the initiative 15.174; on the basis of positive mental states developed through meditation 18.574–5; protects one from distractions 18.423–4; spiritual initiative ultimately rests within one's own volition 7.367; symbolized by the bull 9.356

taking things for granted don't take the bodhisattva for granted 11.277; don't take the Buddha for granted 11.277; if we take things for granted, we deprive ourselves of a rich source of satisfaction 17.202; a reason for ingratitude 3.606, 4.250; Sangharakshita being taken for granted 21.516–17; taking beauty for granted

18.159; taking sleep for granted 16.252; we take it for granted that we can be aware 16.252

takkikā (speculators) 10.612

Takuan, Master 8.496

Talapuṭa (actor-manager) 1.547, 7.523, 15.371

Tallis, Thomas 26.460

tāṃ (Tārā's seed syllable) 5.580, 13.94

Tamang Buddhist Association 22.27

Tamang Buddhists introduction 7.462–3, 21.30–1, 21.92–3, v22; *gompa* in Darjeeling, *see under* Darjeeling; *gompa* near Kalimpong 22.468

Tamang, Captain v22

tamas (quality) *see under guṇas*

Tambimuttu, Meary James Thurairajah 7.445, 7.616 (n489)

tame being ready to be tamed 15.493; the Buddha like an alert, perfectly tamed elephant 4.706 (n313); the earth goddess represents the same forces as Māra's daughters, now tamed 12.188; ego-clinging makes life painful, but is a demon which can be tamed 18.12; Padmasambhava tames the demons of Tibet 12.291–4; shrill despairing cry: 'One single self we shall tame' ('Hīnayāna') 1.231; taming the lion the symbol of man's taming his own nature 26.286–8; the tameness of wild animals in Buddhist lands 1.427

Tamerlane 26.297

Tamil god Muruka (or Skanda) installed in Sri Lankan Buddhist temples 7.72; the language taught to Agastya by Avalokiteśvara 26.225

Tan Yun-Shan, Professor 22.53–4

tanden 5.67

taṇha (craving) *see tṛṣṇā*

Taṇhaṅkara Buddha 1.45

Tanka, Master 8.497

Tanluan 1.337

Tannhäuser 25.428

Tanni Shō *see* Shinran/teachings

Tansen 9.280, 9.468

Tantra six Tantric traditions in India 10.46; Buddhist, *see* Tantric Buddhism; Hindu 1.388–9, 10.45–6, 20.148

tantras (Buddhist texts)

INTRODUCING THE TANTRAS

what are they?
description 14.246–50; etymology of the word tantra 7.503, 12.210, 14.248–9; the most highly esoteric of the canonical texts 7.503; in Buddhism, usually specifically the Vajrayāna scriptures 12.210; means of transmission 14.250; can only be taken up after receiving the appropriate *abhiṣeka* 7.503, 14.247; four classes: *Kriyā*, *Caryā*, *Yoga*, and *Anuttara* 1.381; tantras and sexual practice 1.391–2; the tantras and the eighty-four *siddhas* 14.249–50; identify Mount Sumeru with the spinal column 2.67; Nyingma tantras 13.23; a Perfection of Wisdom text that is as much a tantra as a *sūtra* 14.154; to be studied with a teacher 12.104; Western approach to tantras 14.248

their history
Dudjom Rimpoche explains the lineage of tantras 22.509; the tantras as *Buddhavacana* 1.379, 12.577, 14.249; said to have been preached directly by the *dharmakāya* 14.249; taught at the same time as the *sūtras*, but on a different plane, some say 7.623 (n531); many tantras perished in the flames of Nālandā 1.381; originally written in Sanskrit, but most only extant in Tibetan 12.210, 14.246; freelance Tantric teachers gave them a bad name in Tibet 12.570, 12.576; their emergence represented not a degeneration but a rebirth of Buddhism 12.219

their nature
a chaotic jumble of images, archetypes, and cryptic instructions 12.211; essentially manuals of actual practice 14.247; reservations about trying to explain them 14.247–8; virtually unintelligible without commentary 14.247; vast difference between literal meaning and symbolical interpretation 1.380; largely unexplored and difficult to understand 1.378

WORKS

Guhyasamāja Tantra (Tathāgataguhyaka) 'esoteric integration' 1.380, 7.503; an *Anuttara* tantra 1.381; a connection with the Prajñāpāramitā and the *Bodhicaryāvatāra*? 22.234–5; correlations (of elements etc.) with the five Buddha mandala 2.706 (n418); date 14.249; esoteric integration of body, speech, and mind with that of the Tathāgata 1.380; production of mind-made body 1.167; one of nine texts venerated in Nepal 14.100, 14.246; only found in the Tibetan canon 7.527; Sangharakshita is instructed in

the text by Dhardo Rimpoche 22.234–5; Tsongkhapa's commentary 17.423

Hevajra Tantra
among the best-known tantras 7.503; practices to be undertaken before starting the *Hevajra* 7.490; date 14.249; Conze's review 12.104, 12.210–11; a flow of images, concepts, practices, descriptions, and advice, all mixed up 12.211; 'if someone unworthy should *see* this book' 14.247–8; innate bliss 2.91; Milarepa initiated into the practice 18.65; when you travel, to be hidden in the hair or under the arm 14.247, 19.367; taking an 'untouchable' as sexual consort 12.223; translated into English by Snellgrove 12.104, 12.210

Kālacakra Tantra
'wheel of time' 7.503; contains references to Mecca and Islam 14.249; date 14.249; on the Ādibuddha 7.536; *prāṇa* 1.386

other tantras
Ādibuddha Tantra 1.392; *Cakrasaṃvara Tantra* 7.503; *Marma-kalikā Tantra* 1.392; *Māyājāla Tantras* 7.503, 22.508–9; the Tantra Yogācāra 12.291; *Vajrabhairava Tantra* 7.503

Tantric Buddhism ('the Tantra')

WHAT IS TANTRIC BUDDHISM?

introduction
brief introduction 10.136; longer introduction 1.373–93; *Buddhist Himalaya*: 'its account of Tantric Buddhism is the best I know' 21.560; difficult to summarize, because it deals with particulars 1.378; 'Magical Buddhism' 1.296, 26.699

descriptions
aims to reveal the transcendental aspect of all phenomena of consciousness 7.403; among the five spiritual faculties, it represents vigour 1.374; aware of the instrumental function and relative validity of its methods 1.387; based on a non-dualistic philosophy 7.401; based on the symbolic meaning of everything 3.10; a complex of gardens 13.117–18; emphasis on direct experience 13.285; an esoteric teaching 1.378; its goal is the transmutation of body, speech, and mind into *trikāya* 7.506–7, 17.546; great passion and great anger as synonyms for Enlightenment 3.235; in it Buddhism finds its efflorescence and constant rejuvenation (Guenther) 1.374; it seeks to reveal to us our essential nature through symbols 13.118–22; 'a jungle' 13.92, 13.116–17, 17.685–6, 21.176–8; the practical side of Buddhism 1.374; represents the faculty of *vīrya* 2.549; a short and easy path if practised long and hard enough 13.74; a system associating Buddhas and bodhisattvas with mantras, colours etc. 1.376–7; the union of wisdom and compassion is its work 13.184; view of the universe 1.375, 1.388; *upāyamārga*, the path of skilful means 18.407

questions
the Tantra asked, if transcendental realities were reflected in the world, where? 1.376; is it based on an experimentally verifiable principle? 1.391; should Western Buddhists bother with Tantric teachings? 18.494–5; why does it have so many forms and colours? 13.285–7

how it sees things
the conditioned seen in its ultimate depth is the Unconditioned 3.658 (n212); don't fight with or flee mundane things, but see them in their diamond aspect 7.401–2; reality is not only transcendent to phenomena but immanent in them 1.385; its view of interpenetration 1.376, 1.388; sometimes it professes to have a non-dualistic basis, but it doesn't 15.635; we need to realize both eternity and time simultaneously 4.211; the world is not a hindrance but a help to Enlightenment 1.375

misunderstandings
an error to interpret it as a syncretist movement 1.373; it may look relaxed, but it is a knife-edge path 17.595; a mistake to think of it as a degeneration of Buddhism 1.377, 1.381; misunderstandings about the Tantra 4.505–6, 13.19

HISTORY

India
ācāryas included in the Tantric succession 1.382; Assam as a centre of Tantric Buddhism 22.91; Atīśa 12.565, 12.576–7; the *Avataṃsaka Sūtra* a link between Yogācāra and Tantra 1.376; four phases of development 1.384–5; Mantrayāna, *see* Mantrayāna; Vajrayāna, *see* Vajrayāna; Kālacakrayāna 1.384, 1.386; Sahajayāna 1.384–7, 18.417, 19.273–4; pseudo-Tantric schools 1.274

historical features
contrast with non-Tantric schools 1.199–200; indissolubly connected with Mahāyāna teaching 1.377; lineage 13.215; some methods now regarded as Tantric may be part of the original teaching 1.241; Tantric Buddhism and the Yogācāra 1.373

its spread to other countries
the Tantric tradition in Tibet 11.678–9; for Tibetans the most sacred stage in the development of Buddhism 13.19; Westerners will need to make a special effort to understand it 13.116–17

DOCTRINES AND PRACTICES

ethics
abandonment of respectability 1.201; an Enlightened person may act unethically out of compassion 1.200–1; the sense in which one doesn't have to give anything up 17.595; the Tantric form of the bodhisattva ideal 4.607; unconventional Tantric acts 13.176–8, 19.160–4

meditation
bringing the 'breath' (*prāṇa*) into the central channel 18.76; identifying with the deity at the centre of the mandala 14.461; it cannot be practised without a guru 13.89; meditations of the Inner and Outer Tantra 5.576–7, 13.91–2; *sādhanas*, *see* visualization practice/*sādhanas*; why did Dhardo Rimpoche reveal its secrets? 22.235

energy and the body
becoming sensitive to subtle energies 15.216; the body invested with sacredness 1.375; correspondence between higher and lower manifestations of energy 18.77; energy is primary 18.74, 18.79; neither creates conflict in the psyche nor dissipates its psychic energies 7.401; spiritual life starts with the activation of one's energies 13.157; Tantric practice relies on energy, positivity, and inspiration 18.181

Tantric ritual
all implements are *vajra*, imbued with the sense of ultimate reality 13.180; based on a system of correspondences, like Neoplatonist theurgy 13.292; importance of sacramental actions: mantras and *mudrās* 1.374–5; mantra chanting occupies an extremely important place 13.288–9; the means of implementing Mahāyāna philosophy 13.293; puja a scientific way of producing internal by way of external change 1.377; the secret or sacramental feast 18.424–6, 19.485–6; in the *Sūtra of Golden Light* 14.245; Tantric ritual has a strong aesthetic appeal 18.157; the *vajra* in Tantric ritual 13.186–7; *vajrapuṣpa*, the flower of Tantric ritual 13.180

symbolism and the arts
the colours of Tantric Buddhist art 13.284–5; creative symbols of Tantric Buddhism 13.115–318; Jungian archetypes 12.191; mandala of the five Buddhas one of its most beautiful and meaningful patterns 13.316; the songs (*vajragītā*) of Tantric masters 13.179; the symbolism of the 'low-caste woman' 13.359, 13.699 (n163)

sexual symbolism
introduction 1.388–92; devaluation 21.231–2; intercourse with a virgin or 'low caste maiden' 1.385–6, 12.223; depicts the inseparableness of wisdom and compassion 1.389–90; sexual sacramentalism 1.390–2; to think that anything 'Tantric' must be erotic is misleading 4.506; *yab-yum* figures (figures in sexual union), *see yab-yum*

Anuttara Yoga Tantra
mind-made body 1.167; one of four *yogas* 13.91; preparation 3.332

the union of bliss and emptiness
bliss is just as important as emptiness 19.197; the culmination of the entire Tantric path 19.197

prajñā-upāya
synonymous with *kāla-cakra* 1.386; four reflections: cosmic, Buddhological, individual, social 1.388–9; phenomena reflecting wisdom and compassion in indissoluble union 1.388; represented by female and male figures embracing 7.345; in the Tantra *upāya* is the term for compassion 1.448

texts and commentaries
introduction to Tantric works 1.380–1; biographies must be interpreted not literally but symbolically 1.378; *Cittaviśuddhiprakaraṇa*, *see* Āryadeva; an element of the Tantra appears in the *Sūtra of Golden Light* 16.260

see also
the Formless Ḍākinī Dharma Series, *see under ḍākinī*; tantras, *see* tantras; *An Introduction to Tantric Buddhism*, *see* Dasgupta; *Tattvasiddhi*, *see* Śāntarakṣita; *sahaja*; *abhiṣeka*; Tantric guru, *see under* guru; transmission of the Dharma, *see under* transmission/Tantric; *vajra* or diamond aspect, *see under vajra*; work as the Tantric guru, *see under* work/work and the Buddhist tradition

Tantric precepts *see under* precepts/other sets of precepts

Tantric rites *see* four Tantric rites

Tantric yogi being straightforward considered very important 19.385–6; the 'elephantine work' of the yogi 18.419–20; fearlessness and unconventionality 18.420–1; his hardships enable him to see how experience is not 'out there' but one's response 18.138; liberated by those

practices by which others are bound 7.402; unconventional 19.386–7; the yogi sees all beings with the eye of absolute equality 7.102

Tao Te Ching *see* Laozi/Dao De Ching

Taoism *see* Daoism

tapas (Pāli *tapo*, literally 'heat') etymology 15.447, 17.457–8; intensive practice (Buddhism) 10.332, 10.430; as part of the path of five stages 17.457–8; self-torture (Hinduism) 10.332; *see also* asceticism

Tapussa (Sanskrit Trapuṣa) *see under* Bhallika

Tārā, bodhisattva

INTRODUCING TĀRĀ

introduction
description 11.292–3; a bodhisattva appearing in female form 12.375, 12.572; not 'female' any more than Mañjughoṣa is 'male' 4.192; neither young nor old 2.178; the many colours of Tārā 13.285; sometimes placed at the centre of the mandala 18.602; a manifestation of the *dharmakāya* 12.572

her name
'the saviouress' or 'the star' 1.503, 5.577, 12.375, 13.92, 13.315; 'she who ferries across' 12.375, 13.92, 13.315; in Tibet Jetsun Dolma, 'The Faithful Dolma' (or Drölma) 2.178, 5.577, 13.92

her family
belongs to the family of Amitābha 5.578–9, 13.93, 17.147; Avalokiteśvara's daughter 1.263; born from a lake of Avalokiteśvara's tears 1.503, 2.178, 4.193, 5.577–8, 13.92–3, 16.177–8, 17.144

her nature
the embodiment or quintessence of compassion 5.577–8; approachable and compassionate, so may help with worldly affairs 2.229; Lady of Salvation, who delivers from all dangers 4.657; maternal qualities 2.178; Samayatāra, the embodiment of fidelity 3.572; she helps people to help themselves 11.293, 13.315; she will overlook all mistakes in ritual 13.292

devotion to Tārā
Atīśa encouraged her worship 12.578; worshipped in many countries 2.178; *Devotion to Tārā* 23.270, 23.515 (n315); finding yourself attracted to Tārā 13.308; prayer to Tārā 25.293; hymns to Tārā 13.97; the 'Flower-Garland Hymn to the Goddess Tārā' 17.141–7; on household shrines 2.229; if you hear Tārā's voice advising you, also consult your spiritual friends 12.572–3; on the Refuge Tree 13.209; a standing Tārā image with a beautiful face 22.476

Tārā mantra
oṃ tāre tuttāre ture svāhā 5.582, 13.96, 14.535; a series of modulations of the name Tārā 11.290; Tibetan pronunciation 11.288–9; her seed syllable (*bīja*), *tāṃ* 5.580, 13.94

GREEN TĀRĀ

introduction
the bodhisattva of fearlessness and spontaneous helpfulness 22.374; the consort of Amoghasiddhi 12.222, 13.315; a member of the action or karma family 13.311; correspondence with Avalokiteśvara, Vajrapāṇi, and Mañjughoṣa 26.663–4; Green Tārā and the fourth *lakṣaṇa* 26.665–6; in the *Āryatārā-bhaṭṭārikānāmāṣṭottaraśatakastotra* 1.336, 24.394; she was Atīśa's *yidam* 12.572

names
Dolma Jang-gu or Drölma (Tibetan) 12.660, 13.92; Khadiravaṇi Tārā 12.660, 13.93; Śyāma Tārā 12.660

iconography
description 5.580–1, 13.95; her blue lotuses represent the Buddhas of the three periods of time 13.69; her tiara represents the five wisdoms 13.69; one foot in meditation posture, the other ready to step into the world 13.69–70; illustrations 13.314, 17.142; her *mudrā* (fearlessness), *see mudrās*

qualities
compassionate action 6.xxix, 12.660–1; the *samādhi* of pure beauty associated with Green Tārā 26.664; that form of Tārā concerned with pacification and salvation

from danger 13.68; virgin, mother, and queen 5.581

visualization practice
description 5.578–83, 13.93–7; seeing and hearing everything in terms of Tārā 5.616–17; simplified practice 5.584, 13.97–8; start by connecting Tārā with ordinary objects, colours, and sounds 13.292; offering goddesses 26.671; women's and men's reasons for choosing the practice 5.622, 13.246; making a green shrine 5.570, 13.292; you start to experience the spiritual equivalent of greenness 13.287; your connection with Tārā is more important than seeing her 10.lxv; for many years one of Sangharakshita's main practices 26.663

OTHER FORMS OF TĀRĀ

White Tārā
one of the most popular forms 1.336; 108 mantras for Sangharakshita 25.xxxiii; also known as Pāṇḍaravāsinī 12.222; 'The Crystal Rosary' (poem) 25.304; the development of a white form of Tārā as she became a more central figure 13.305–6; her seven eyes, signifying the way compassion is informed by awareness 4.193; the symbolism of her three lotuses 16.121–2; a similarity to the Virgin Mary 24.511; smiling down on Sangharakshita and Dhardo Rimpoche 22.562; Dhardo Rimpoche and Sangharakshita work together on a *sādhana* 23.382; 'White Tārā' (poem) 25.417

twenty-one Tārās
a group of twenty-one emanations of Avalokiteśvara 1.336; a form of taking Refuge in the Sangha 5.578; a mandala of twenty-one Tārās 12.662, 18.603; the Tārā of Healing 18.311; Vajratārā, of the colour of gold 17.145

see also
Kurukullā (Red Tārā); Sangharakshita's initiations, *see under* Sangharakshita V/ *sādhanas* and initiations

Tarahridaya, Dhammacharini 10.lxiv–v

Tarajyoti, Dharmacharini 14.xx, 17.xv, 17.152, 26.xix

Tārāloka women's retreat centre *see under* Triratna IV/retreat centres

Taranath (Nepali friend) 22.323, 22.325

Tāranātha (Tibetan scholar) 2.182, 2.686–7 (n252), 13.29

Taranatha, Dharmachari v24

Tarashri, Dharmacharini 25.383

tariki *see* other-power

Tarkovsky, Andrei 24.389, 24.582

Tarpa Nagpo ('Black Salvation', Mātaraṃgara, Rudra) full quotation of the text describing him 12.325–31; precis 8.525–6; an example of individualism 3.606; he becomes Mahākāla and is predicted to Buddhahood 8.525; he lurks in the depths of the collective unconscious 12.331–2; he *is* this self-centred world 12.331, 12.333–4; similar figures in the Western tradition 12.331–2

taste the 'action-of-one-taste' 19.191; a matter of personal experience 2.641, 10.568; a more concrete term for experience 19.191–2; refining one's tastes 18.131–3; taste of freedom, *see under* *Udāna*/great ocean; *see also rasa*

Tathāgata

definition
'thus gone' or 'thus come' 2.116, 3.643 (n108), 12.528, 14.502; one who acts as he speaks and speaks as he acts 3.322, 12.528

his nature
deep, immeasurable, unfathomable, like the ocean 2.44, 10.141, 10.449, 10.655; free of the *skandhas*, cut off at the root like a palm-tree stump 2.44; his fructifying power 14.539; his wisdom cannot be measured by the yardstick of human intelligence 1.20; immanent and transcendent 14.211; incomprehensible 1.307, 2.43; ineffable 1.64; like the sun among glow-worms 10.611–12; like the sun arising to dispel darkness 1.53; neither arises nor does not arise 2.44; no riches can compare with him 15.63; non-different from *śūnyatā* 1.307–8; similes 1.275; speaks the truth in the sense of ultimate reality 14.477–8

references and descriptions in the tradition
after death 1.64, 1.75, 1.307, 2.43–4, 10.655–6, 17.621; the attributes of Tathāgatahood applied to all *dharmas* 14.144; a Bodhisattva should be honoured far more than a Tathāgata 14.181; the bodhisattva should worship the Tathāgata 14.153; the body of the Tathāgata 1.255, 16.494–5, 18.75; born from the ten precepts 2.334; myriad names, even those of non-Buddhist deities and designations of reality 1.261; has explained the origin of those things which proceed from a cause 1.90, 3.93; difference from *arhant* 1.52; element of Tathāgatahood present in all, 'like a treasure hidden in the soil' 1.275; 'In this very life a Tathāgata is not to be regarded as existing in truth' 13.393; not

to be attended to through the *skandhas* or the thirty-two marks 2.44–5, 14.550; the praise of the Tathāgatas in the *Sūtra of Golden Light* 14.244; Subhūti's rhapsody on the Suchness of the Tathāgata 14.144; Vimalakīrti's description 16.569–71; the five Buddhas called the five Tathāgatas 13.304; the merit of developing faith in the Tathāgata's eternal life 14.127

ten powers and four confidences
attributed to the Buddha by his disciples 3.144; *cetovimutti* and *paññavimutti* as the tenth power 3.665 (n255), 13.695–6 (n142); the power of knowing rightly where all paths of conduct lead 1.59

see also
contemplation of the virtues of the Tathāgatas, *see under* Vasubandhu/doctrines

tathāgata-dhātu the element of Buddhahood 16.561; Buddhahood reflected in the heart of every sentient being 7.400; not to be confused with *bodhicitta* 1.416–17; the seed of Enlightenment 15.569

tathāgatagarbha (womb of Enlightenment, Buddha-nature) and the *ālaya vijñāna* 14.210–11; a helpful approach 14.594; in the *Mahāparinirvāṇa Sutra* 3.659 (n223), 14.237; unless the doctrine is related to the Noble Eightfold Path, it can be misleading 3.9; the idea of the true, real, or great self 3.659 (n223), 14.237; not to be confused with the non-Buddhist idea of the supreme self 14.200; the danger of thinking one is 'already Buddha' 10.438–40, 11.657, 11.689, 14.594, 17.390, 17.594; Queen Śrīmāla's teaching on the doctrine 14.175; a reification of the principle of potentiality 14.175; reveals reality's mysterious immanence 2.43

Tathāgatagarbha Sūtra 11.689

Tathāgataguhyaka *see* tantras/works/*Guhyasamāja Tantra*

tathatā *see* suchness

Tattvasaṅgraha *see under* Sāntarakṣita

Tatz, Mark 24.483

Tāvatiṃsa-devaloka *see under* heavens

Taxila University 9.117

Taylor, Daphne 26.420

Taylor, Jeremy 12.519

Taylor, Reverend Richard 24.510–11

Taylor, Rosa 23.45

Taylor, Thomas (Neoplatonist) introduction 2.740 (n662), 23.525 (n362); influence on Blake 8.260, 26.349; Sangharakshita drawn to him 2.536; translation of Orphic hymns 26.494; translation of Plotinus 23.317

TBMSG *see under* Triratna I/Triratna in India

Tchaikovsky, Pyotr Ilyich 20.73

tea Atīśa wrote a poem in praise of Tibetan tea 12.574–5; Chinese monasteries that serve the best tea to the wealthiest visitors 19.478–9; a cup of tea for Bhante 24.xxii; cups of tea at Indian funerals 13.223; 'the cups that cheer but not inebriate' 22.23, 23.275; a hierarchy of tea cups for Tibetan lamas 13.54–5; the Japanese tea ceremony 1.572–3, 4.113; the overflowing cup 11.278–9, 17.208; a tea estate near Darjeeling 22.20–5; tea for the Dalai Lama 22.368–9; Thien Chau gives Sangharakshita tea after lectures 23.230; the Tibetan monastery whose tea urn still contained a drop from Tsongkhapa's day 17.695

teachers (spiritual)

the nature of the teacher
difference between spiritual teacher and one who imparts information 15.727; in communication, the religious teacher has an advantage over the poet 14.16; needed to guide us through teachings 3.89–90; teacher as archetype or exemplar 5.563–4; qualities needed 1.448–9, 16.485–91, 17.307; invites you to share his life 26.68; their spiritual teaching never fully expresses their realization 11.720–1; unwise for any Buddhist to teach others just because they feel like it 16.29; a training course for Dharma teachers 8.279; we don't any longer need teachers who stand for a religious absolute 26.248–9; monks as both spiritual and secular teachers 2.212–13; Zen teachers may pick on someone, but this is a dangerous approach 17.653; *The Book of Enlightened Masters* (Western spiritual teachers) 8.626–9; the different kinds of Enlightened teachers 18.222

looking for a teacher
how to recognize a good teacher 14.567–8; looking for the right teacher 18.405–6; attractive Dharma teachers 19.498–500; learning from lots of different teachers 19.544–5; teachers can appear in many forms: your own mind, Dharma study, nature 18.182; wanting certainty, people are apt to believe those with very definite

views 17.627; 'When the disciple is ready the master will be there' 1.27, 1.510

different kinds of teacher
parents 3.70, 3.601, 12.427; school teachers called 'guru' in India 3.70; the title commands reverence 3.69–70; in the West teachers are not greatly respected 17.606; artists, composers, and writers as spiritual teachers 3.602–3

traditions
in the past, a teacher would just teach you what you needed to know 15.508–9, 19.507; living with the teacher (Indian tradition) 15.667–8; traditional teacher–student relationship 1.26–7; 'serving the learned' 18.409; a disciple who asked for a teaching every twenty years 19.507, 19.619 (n189); the production of liturgies for disciples' use is traditional 13.419; in some Buddhist traditions the *dharmakāya* in human form 1.422; the bodhisattva has a teacher and aspires to have disciples 13.22; a bodhisattva precept to work for your own circle of disciples and students 13.57; Tibetan and Chinese practice of mummifying teachers 16.159

relating to the teacher
relationship between teacher and disciple 2.248; 'I make profound obeisance to the Teachers' 11.249; including your teacher in the *mettā bhāvanā* 5.157; gratitude towards one's teachers 3.601–2; reverence for one's teacher 3.63; one must be aware of him as a spiritual person 1.576; one should rely on the teaching, not the person who teaches 3.355; can your level of awareness be raised by the touch of a teacher? 9.528; seeing the teacher as the head of a group 15.564; arrogance: 'My teacher is better than your teacher' 17.606; people often try to teach their teachers 18.492–3, 19.258, 19.465–6; you need to be receptive to the teacher 17.50; students' curiosity and receptivity is needed for teaching to happen 11.277–8; a teacher's problem: literal-minded people want literal answers to literal questions 26.83; take their advice seriously, but take responsibility for yourself 17.308; no need to worry that without your teacher you are going to stop learning 18.182; we can't be with our teacher all the time, but we can be with our friends 11.703, 11.705

see also
guru; Tantric teacher, *see vajraguru* under guru/gurus of different traditions

Teachings of the Compassionate Buddha *see* Burtt

techniques (meditation) *see under* meditation/methods/techniques

technology children taking to new technology 24.424–5; electronic devices 15.152; the growth of modern technology and the power of the state 11.356–7; psychologically, magic may be better for you than technology 15.685; technology replaces magic in the materialistic East 15.682–5

teenagers *see* young people

Teesta, River 22.19–20, 25.283

teeth Jesus said of a dead dog, 'What beautiful teeth!' 1.521–2; 'Laughter that shows the teeth is madness' 4.137, 12.450, 15.372; 'nature red in tooth and claw' 8.447; the removal of mother's teeth 26.433–4; 'Sharp Tooth' 23.173; 'sharper than a serpent's tooth' 15.253; Temple of the Tooth, Kandy, 9.63, 11.208–9, 20.126–8, 23.11; the woman who worshipped a dog's tooth 2.71, 13.198–9, 19.327

teisho 8.500

Tejamitra, Dharmachari v24

Tejananda, Dharmachari (John Wakeman) brief introduction 17.7; 'Faith, Devotion and Ritual' 13.418

Telegu brahmins 20.368–9

teleology 1.565, 3.476, 14.433

telepathy the Buddha's telepathy 12.110; communication can be virtually telepathic 1.576; it develops when it's really useful 4.554; empirically verifiable 12.110; it happens, but no need for experiments to prove it 4.553; the highest level of transmission (Vajrayāna) 1.523; of Kachu Rimpoche 12.440–1, 22.326–8, 22.397–8; mind transmission of the Jinas 3.82; Sangharakshita's telepathy 4.553–4; supernormal power (*parassa cetopariya-ñāṇa* or *paracittajñāna*) 1.167, 22.328; of Vimalakīrti 16.535

television being selective about what we watch 12.474; does not improve the mental state of the viewer 3.536; a distraction 12.421; the first time Sangharakshita watched television 23.147; a good medium but not well used 26.359; in the homes of Buddhists in Maharashtra 24.23; is our current cultural decline due to television? 14.434; restrict television-watching for children 3.535–6, 26.359; the man who threw his television set from the Eiffel Tower 1.497; people watching television in hospital 24.351; Sangharakshita appears

on Thames Television's *Night Thoughts* 24.243–8; Sangharakshita participates in a programme asking 'Why are we here?' 24.319–20; Sangharakshita reads poems for five short TV programmes for Wesak 24.388; Spanish television 24.426; switching it on without being aware of what we are doing 15.172–3; is there a connection between television and violence? 3.535–6; Thai monks' favourite television programme 22.514; turning on the television when bored 11.78, 15.174, 18.334; wasting time watching third-rate television programmes 10.322, 12.355

temperament can be changed: 'giving style to one's character' 3.500; differences of religious temperament 2.143; different images appeal to people of different temperaments 14.589–90; different kinds of giving depending on temperament 17.202; different temperaments need different approaches to the Dharma 4.372, 7.127; the very different temperaments of different Enlightened beings 12.511–12; disputes in the spiritual community due to differences of temperament 18.171; gurus should communicate *through* their temperament, not just express it 14.567–8; *lobha-carita* (artistic temperament) 21.496; modified through communication 3.555; organized and non-organized 14.523, 17.280; sluggish or overactive? 18.525; study and the three temperaments (faith-follower, doctrine-follower, body-witness) 25.12–15; the three temperaments and the three levels of wisdom 25.14–15; will stay more or less the same right up to the point of Enlightenment 3.180; *see also* Buddhaghosa/character type

temperance 20.21

Templars 11.340

Temple, Shirley 15.443

temples of the body a pagoda on each floor of which is a shrine to a Buddha 19.41–2; building a Buddhist temple in an English style 13.273–4; an enclosed sacred space 16.350; the four great kings as temple guardians 16.346, 16.350; the nominal temple, not a spiritual centre but just part of local social life 19.467–9; a poet who can enter all temples and find the same God in every one 7.59; Samye monastery's temple to Avalokiteśvara 12.292; a symbol of Buddhism 18.525; Temple of the Emerald Buddha, Bangkok 19.470; 'The Temple of Sunyata' (Govinda) 21.147; temples of Nepal 7.344; Tibetan temples 13.64–6, 16.327–8, 21.214–15, 22.467–8; a Western Buddhist temple should include motifs of indigenous significance 18.25; 'Within the temple of your body is your own Buddha mind' 18.613–19

see also
at Buddhist holy places, *see* individual places; *devālaya*, *see* Sri Lanka/temples; Hindu temples, *see under* Hinduism; the temple of Apollo at Delphi, *see under* Apollo

temporal and spatial models *see under* time/and space

temporary all the apparently solid objects in the universe are temporary condensations of energy 2.86, 26.48; *dhyāna*: a temporary state 4.566, 18.575, 19.448–9; don't mistake temporary states for Enlightenment 19.159; the five *skandhas* are temporary condensations of energy 14.548; *pratītya-samutpāda*: a temporary coming together of factors 17.246; rebirth in heaven is temporary 3.315–16, 7.120–1, 13.578; *śamatha* states are temporary 8.441; *samayavimukti* (temporary emancipation) 2.145; second *dhyāna*: the temporary dissolving of the stream of thoughts 19.188; system of temporary ordination for young men 2.210–11

temptation for a bodhisattva, to stay in the higher realms of meditation 4.522; don't deliberately expose yourself to temptation 4.384; keep away from it until you have a lot of experience of spiritual life 7.99; modern life gives many temptations to bend the truth 3.323; resisting modern values and temptations 3.39, 3.621; Siddhārtha's temptation by Māra 14.57, 15.733; the temptation of the transcendental sweet shop 11.62; to believe something because it feels comfortable 12.655; to stay in higher meditative realms 4.521–2; to stay in the peaceful countryside rather than going back to help people in the city 4.521–2; Triratna's future: possible obstacles and temptations 12.598–9; the would-be bodhisattva's temptation to give up on people in despair 4.187–8; the temptation of Jesus in the wilderness 3.449, 13.554, 13.594

ten *bhūmis*

introduction
brief description 17.752 (n341); list 2.16–17, 2.170, 4.669 (n67); sources 3.579 (n341); terms obviously symbolic and poetic rather than scientific 2.170; among them all the more important doctrines and practices are distributed 2.170; the

bodhisattva passes through this series of stages 1.401, 2.16–17, 3.375, 4.645–6; correlation with the Āryasaṅgha 1.273, 1.446; correlation with the perfections 1.446–54; as the fourth stage of the path of five stages, which takes aeons to complete 17.458; language cannot distinguish between them 1.450; the Mahāyāna's hierarchy 14.571; the *bodhicitta* manifesting through them like gold refined and made into a crown 4.177–8; references in the *Lalitavistara* and the Perfection of Wisdom 14.227; the *samādhis* and *dhāraṇis* attained at each stage 14.186–7; Tārā reaching the end of them 17.143

detailed description
(1) *Pramuditā* (Joyful) 1.450–1, 4.197; (2) *Vimalā* (Immaculate) 1.451; (3) *Prabhākari* (Illuminating) 1.451, 2.170; (4) *Arciṣmati* (Blazing) 1.451–2; (5) *Sudurjaya* (Very Difficult to Conquer) 1.452, 2.170; (6) *Abhimukhī* (Face-to-Face) 1.452–3, 4.184; (7) *Dūraṃgamā* (Far-Going) 1.453; (8) *Acalā* (Immovable) 1.258–60, 1.439, 1.453–4, 4.323, 14.228–9, 14.500–2; (9) *Sādhumati* (Good Thoughts) 1.454; (10) *Dharmameghā* (the Cloud of the Doctrine) 1.454, 4.584, 14.237

see also
Daśabhūmika Sūtra

ten fetters (*saṃyojanas*)

INTRODUCTION

what they are
brief description 3.253, 4.667 (n54), 10.146; the word *saṃyojana* 11.710; canonical references 2.697 (n349), 2.701 (n375), 3.662 (n238), 3.684 (n377), 4.667 (n54), 9.559n, 16.595–6 (n75), 19.594 (n21); five 'lower' fetters 2.148, 15.50, 15.746 (n24); five 'higher' fetters 15.530; they don't give us the full picture, but can be useful 3.254; there is no definitive list, but the list of ten comes from the Abhidhamma 15.203; the list is not to be taken too literally 15.209–10; the metaphor is misleading 15.204; how fetters arise 15.203; comparison with the chain forged by Jacob Marley 15.205

breaking the fetters
all the time we are either breaking or reinforcing them 15.205; breaking the fetters and becoming an *arhant* 1.178, 7.223; 'breaking fetters' may suggest sudden breakthrough, but progress is gradual 3.420; one becomes an *arhant* upon breaking all ten fetters 3.254; naming the fetters broken gives us little idea of the *ariyapuggalas*' true nature 10.569; the overlap between the hindrances and the fetters 15.203–4; right view and the breaking of the fetters 15.207

THE FIRST THREE FETTERS (OF TEN)

introduction
description 2.146–7, 2.263–5, 3.253–7, 9.252–3, 15.518–23, 15.532, 21.27–8; habit, vagueness, and superficiality 11.xviii–xix; scientific psychology, conventional religion, academic philosophy 15.523, 17.633; liberation from them 13.463–4; in Sangharakshita's teachings 13.363–4; various kinds of spiritual blindness or ignorance 2.146; these first three are called intellectual fetters 15.206, 15.208, 19.510, 21.28; wrong belief concerning the nature of individuality 1.177

breaking the first three fetters
characterizes the true individual 3.416–20; described in the *Ratana Sutta* 15.65; do you break the fetters and thus develop insight, or *vice versa*? 4.41; is possible for anyone within their present lifetime 3.256; it is crucial to break them, so approach them from every angle 17.633; many minor liberations to be achieved on the way 13.464; and gaining Stream Entry, *see under* Stream Entry; related to path and fruit 15.642; to break one is to break all three 15.206, 18.578; they are broken by becoming creative, clear, and committed 11.50, 11.712

FIRST FETTER (FIXED SELF-VIEW, *SATKĀYA-DṚṢṬI*)

what it is
'Am I stuck with a fixed idea of who and what I am?' 17.348; the belief that I am I, fixed and final 4.185, 15.519; the belief that 'I' am real: the biggest mistake of all 2.263–4; the belief that there is a self that does not change 15.206–7, 19.234–5, 24.94–5; translated 'personality-belief' 3.417; habit 11.47–8, 15.355, 17.633; the fundamental wrong view underlying all the others 17.619

its nature
an attitude that blocks change and inhibits growth 9.252; the challenge of this fetter 11.710–11; connected with *anutpattika-dharma-kṣānti* 14.501–2; eternalism and nihilism 2.146, 3.417; if you have this view, no progress is possible 15.519–20; keeping hold of the 'rope' of the self 9.456; Milarepa detects the arising of fixed self-view 18.11; the negation of the spiritual path 3.255; unless it is broken, there's a strong sense of self even in *arūpa dhyānas* 17.608; it is very difficult to imagine

oneself different 2.297; not an intellectual viewpoint but a deeply-rooted attitude 3.417–18, 15.206; the rationalization of ordinary human egotism 26.188; a refusal to accept the possibility of change or progress 2.297, 3.254–5, 15.519; subtler forms of self-view recur at more advanced stages 15.211; twenty forms of self-view associated with the five *skandhas* 17.620–1; the way we reify things directly reflects our belief in a fixed self 17.383

breaking the fetter
the first fetter to be broken 2.264; creativity: getting out of the habit of being a particular kind of person 11.49; if we can convince ourselves that the 'self' is illusion, the fetter is broken 15.207; the six element practice overcomes it 17.623; understanding that the separate self is no more than an idea 15.337; we are free to remake ourselves as we wish 11.710

SECOND FETTER (DOUBT AND INDECISION, *VICIKITSĀ*)

what it is
'doubt' is an inadequate translation 12.27–8; not so much doubt as doubtfulness 2.264; a culpable state of uncertainty 2.146–7, 9.252–3; vagueness 11.xix, 11.49, 17.633; doubt and indecision are two sides of the same negative mental event 17.612; doubt and indecision with regard to the Dharma 17.612; doubt with regard to the Three Jewels 17.632; one of the *mūlakleśas* (Abhidharma) 17.612–17; connection with *mrakṣa* (slyness-concealment) 17.648; the enemy of effective Tantric practice 18.181

its nature
essentially resistance to the positive spirit of the path 15.176; an inflexible attitude of scepticism and indecision 15.207; it lies at the root of our difficulties with spiritual life 17.615–17; lack of integration 3.418–19; not intellectual doubt, but unwillingness to commit oneself 2.147, 2.264, 3.255, 3.418; not wanting to know what one thinks, so one doesn't have to act 17.290–1; avoiding it by remaining in a dark cloud of unawareness 17.613; in relation to the gravitational pull 17.612; in your heart of hearts you don't want to find out the truth 11.711; refusing to commit yourself, you get nowhere 2.297, 15.522; a soul-corroding unease 4.185–6; an unwillingness really to find out about things 10.250; 'Whatever you do, don't wobble' 17.612; why we are indecisive about trivial things 17.612–13; wilfully incomplete or hesitant acceptance of the Doctrine 1.177; wondering whether to let go of the 'rope' of self 9.456–7; highly educated people tend to suffer from it 3.293

breaking the fetter
it must be overcome, or your will is paralysed 10.250; commitment frees us from dithering 4.293; don't keep your options open for too long 12.484–5; doubt is not conclusively abolished until ignorance is abolished 15.209–10; faith brings relief and clarity to the undecided mind 17.551; firm resolution is the opposite of *vicikitsā* 19.286–7; it eventually gives way under pressure of understanding and reflection 15.207; clarity: clear thinking 11.49, 17.613–17

THIRD FETTER (DEPENDING ON RULES AND RITUALS *AS ENDS IN THEMSELVES*, *ŚILAVRATA-PARĀMARŚA*)

what it is
brief introduction 19.594 (n21); attachment to moral rules ... as ends in themselves 1.177, 23.178; 'clinging to ethical formalism and conventional religion' 17.633; 'dependence on moral rules and religious observances' 4.186, 9.193–4; the emphasis is on *as ends in themselves* 3.419; superficiality 11.49–50, 17.633, 19.275–6, 19.459; the fetter is *irrational dependence* on ritual, not ritual itself 11.208; often mistranslated and misunderstood 2.147, 2.264–5; a philosophical term designating all manner of thinking or speculation 7.172; a form of attachment 1.112, 3.200, 17.633; conventional morality, conventional religion 3.419, 15.522; conventional piety: not a sufficient means to Enlightenment 11.27

its nature
a comfortable acquiescence in ceremonial routine 8.312; the danger of the whole of Dharma life becoming a routine 10.241–2, 19.456–7; a fidelity to one's practice that is not questioned enough 15.207; going through the motions but remaining unchanged 15.520–2; your heart is not in what you are doing 2.297, 11.711–12; it's about fear of breaking the rules, but why is one afraid of that? 17.635; just saying the words may make no impression on the mind 13.82; not just about ritual: a lack of wholeheartedness throughout spiritual life 15.208; pretending to let go of the 'rope' of self 9.457; a reminder that there is no safe way of practising the Dharma 4.186–7; society has the habit of regarding certain actions as religious in themselves 7.283; something isn't with spiritual significance using external religious symbols 18.428;

sometimes what we are practising is a counterfeit Dharma 16.82–3; a split between external observances and your inward state of being 2.298, 9.253, 19.57; such attachment to observances binds us more securely to *saṃsāra* 17.633; thinking a lot of oneself on account of being good 4.186; thinking any situation guarantees spiritual progress 19.362; thinking that observing the outward forms mechanically will suffice 17.633; to rely on rules and rituals places a barrier between us and reality 14.421; way of avoiding the real practice of religion 7.185; the wrong belief that any external observance suffices to attain salvation 2.147; rules can become an external conformity, neglecting the spirit 10.563

examples
an extreme example: dispute about how exactly to wear one's robe 4.186; flinging rice at the Buddha's face: hurried offerings in Nepal 10.241–2, 20.432–3; reciting a prayer without thinking about what the words mean 18.319; the scriptures give the example of tending the sacred fire 2.264–5

breaking the fetter
commitment: acting with the whole of oneself 11.50; ask yourself, 'What am I really doing?' 10.242, 15.610; 'Is what I am doing helping me in the direction of Enlightenment?' 2.265, 3.256; not giving up rules, but following them without attachment 4.186; one should follow a middle path 21.27

FOURTH TO TENTH FETTERS

fourth and fifth fetters (kāma-rāga and vyāpāda)
most people don't even begin to work with these fetters 15.530; to understand what they're like, consider the subject–object distinction 15.524–6; the Vajrayāna tackles them quite effectively 15.531; emotional fetters, more difficult to break 2.147–8, 12.28, 15.524, 19.510; tackling them involves dismantling the overall framework of ignorance 15.525; weakening them 1.177, 3.253, 3.420–1; breaking them 1.178, 2.148, 3.256, 15.208

sixth and seventh fetters (rūpa-raga and arūpa-raga)
the desire for continuing existence 15.208; relate to the plane of archetypal form and formless plane 3.254; stand for the danger of theism 2.149; breaking them 2.149

eighth, ninth, and tenth fetters
māna (conceit) 1.178, 2.149, 4.187; *auddhatya* (Pāli *uddhacca*) (restlessness) 1.178, 2.149, 15.208–9; *avidyā* (Pāli *avijjā*, ignorance) 1.178, 2.149–50, 15.209–10

ten impurities 1.155, 17.543

ten *kasiṇas*

introduction
brief description 1.154–5; the practice goes back to the Buddha's day 5.569; among the forty *kammaṭṭhānas* 1.154, 4.519; an insight practice 18.513; a method of enhancing our appreciation of beauty 12.615; suitable for hate types 2.83; preparation for *dhyāna* 5.643; preparation for visualization practice 5.568–9; pure sense experience without reaction 5.643

the meditation practice
the stages of the practice 1.161–2, 5.566–8, 5.570–1, 10.176; choosing a colour 1.154–5, 5.567–9; traditionally involved making a disc from flowers 5.569; described in the *Amitāyurdhyāna Sūtra*: the setting sun, water and ice 1.332–3; and neighbourhood concentration 5.230; one cannot develop concentration in all its stages through the practice 17.543

ten kinds of knowledge 14.94

ten ornaments of the Buddhist 10.391–8

ten *pāramitās* *see under* perfections

ten powers of a Tathāgata *see under* Tathāgata

ten precepts *see* precepts/ten precepts

ten recollections (*anusattis*) introduction 1.155, 4.701–2 (n279); the practice of any one of them leads to Nirvāṇa 4.701–2 (n279); practices that help to recollect the mind 17.541; mindfulness is the most important 1.155–6; recollection of morality 11.306; among the forty *kammaṭṭhānas* 1.155, 4.519

see also
recollection of the Buddha; recollection of death, *see under* death/recollecting death

Tendai (or Tiantai) school 4.495, 4.520, 11.54, 11.89, 25.207

tenderness the aching tenderness of seeing the white calf 25.207; Avalokiteśvara's face alive with tenderness and compassion 2.176; beware of being precious about tender feelings 10.571; the bodhisattva practises four virtues: creative adjustment, morality, tenderness, sacrifice 1.354; 'tender as a flower and hard as a diamond' (Clare Cameron) 20.100, 21.480; the tender-heartedness of Dr Ambedkar 9.322, 10.339

Tendufla, Mr 21.259–60

Tendulgar, Dinanath Gopal 22.276, 22.600 (n221)

Tendzin, Thubden *see* Pallis, Marco

Tengyur *see under* Tibetan Buddhism/ literature

Tenno and the umbrella *see under* umbrella

Tennyson, Alfred Lord

introduction
brief introduction 23.489 (n122); he said that the peace of God came into his life when he married 23.98; he deliberately kept people at a distance 19.122; hero-worship of Tennyson 3.47; contrast between Tennyson and a Zen poet 17.331–2; Sangharakshita's appreciation of Tennyson 20.29–30, 20.56

Idylls of the King
how Lancelot and Guinevere are portrayed 25.106; a model for Sangharakshita's Arthurian poems 25.99; 'We needs must love the highest when we see it' 2.292, 9.248

In Memoriam
'cast as rubbish to the void' 8.6, 8.164; 'painless sympathy with pain' 4.52, 4.581, 7.290, 16.523, 17.304, 17.511; 'There lives more faith in honest doubt' 2.146–7, 3.418; 'little systems that have their day' 2.249; 'nature red in tooth and claw' 8.447

The Lotos Eaters
'all things ripen toward the grave' 7.51; the gods 12.355, 24.302; has the quality *kāvya* 26.332; the mood of the poem 26.395; 'the roof and crown of things' 1.32

'The Palace of Art'
aesthetic self-indulgence 26.149–51, 26.173–4, 26.338; escape into aesthetic experience 12.394; Oscar Wilde's resemblance to the 'Glorious Devil' 26.488; realizing the lack of an ethical element 25.110

other works
the blackness of ash-buds in March 26.136, 26.709 (n66); 'English Lullaby' 26.420; 'Flower in the crannied wall' 1.376, 7.45, 14.219, 17.271, 17.331; 'The Lady of Shalott' 20.29–30, 20.56, 26.395; 'Like summer tempest came her tears' 22.197; 'Locksley Hall' 7.452–3; 'Sweet and Low' 26.500; 'the ringing plains of windy Troy' 26.262

tension creative tension between the individual and the group 11.355–6; a fruitful tension between different sides of Sangharakshita 26.247–8; if you're tense in anticipation of a pleasure, it spoils the enjoyment of the pleasure 19.387; the Mahāyāna brought about an easing of tension between mundane and transcendental 1.274; psychological tensions in the family 11.188–9; Śāntideva might be in favour not of relieving tension but of letting it build up 4.310; sensitivity to tension between people 18.311; tension between religious and artistic absolutes 26.248–9; the tension between the claims of compassion and renunciation 4.567–8; tension between the *manas* and the relative *ālaya* 12.218; tension between withdrawal and involvement 2.271–4, 15.281

Teresa of Avila, St introduction 2.681 (n193), 7.581 (n196); a difference between her devotional mysticism and the intellectual mysticism of Eckhart 2.143; uses a bee metaphor to caution against excessive self-absorption 13.392–3; her personal diary 24.413; 'Pots and pans are my instruments of prayer' 7.102

Teresa, Mother 27.1072–4

termas

introduction
definition 17.705 (n2); association with Padmasambhava 8.523–4, 12.196–7, 12.295–6, 12.299–300; dismissed by Western scholars as forgeries 14.262–3; eighteen kinds of *termas* 12.332; found in Sikkim 22.470; hidden in the body of Tarpa Nagpo 8.526, 12.333; highly important teachings which exert profound influence 12.300; not just books or material objects, you can have mind *termas* 12.332; Padmasambhava describes where they will be found 8.523–4; teachings entrusted to *mātṛkas* and *ḍākinīs* 18.469; the *Tibetan Book of the Dead*, *see Tibetan Book of the Dead*; the transforming principle adapted to specific circumstances 12.333; Western scholars' scepticism about *termas* 12.300, 13.23

collected edition (Rinchen Terdzö or Rinchen Terdzer)
introduction 11.372, 12.299–300; regarded as canonical 12.196; the 'near tradition' 12.299, 14.263; new edition instigated by Dilgo Khyentse Rimpoche 12.719 (n143); 64 'concealed scriptures' from the Nyingma tradition 13.23–4; part of the basis of Tibetan Buddhism 2.555, 22.462; 'unearthed works' 14.262

terms *see* words

tertön 'treasure-revealers' 14.262; Pemalingpa (Bhutanese *tertön*) 24.388; the person who finds the exact remedy for the concrete situation 12.334; 'taker out' of *termas* regarded as partial manifestations of Padmasambhava 12.299, 12.332–3

test experiment to test the mental states of Zen monks 5.400; how is fidelity tested? 3.568–9, 3.570–2; the means to Enlightenment to be determined by the test of experience 7.520; spiritual personalities claiming they are exhibiting anger as a test 4.614; submit all teachings to the test of personal experience 7.128, 7.381, 10.171, 10.691 (n215); the test of Dharma practice 18.249–50; the test of whether any experience is spiritual is whether one can call it 'my' experience 7.360–1; tests of *mettā* 5.147–8, 5.203, 9.521; 'test my words as the goldsmith tests gold in the fire', *see under* gold; the true test of spiritual practice is how we relate to the challenge of 'other people' 3.521; weigh and test all the thoughts and emotions that come pouring in 7.268

Tevijja Sutta *see under Dīgha Nikāya*

Tevijjavacchagotta Sutta *see under Majjhima Nikāya*

Thackalay, India 20.295–6

Thackeray, William Makepeace associations with Calcutta 22.59, 22.578 (n61); *The History of Henry Esmond* 22.464; *Vanity Fair* 3.46

Thailand (Siam)

the country
Bangkok 19.470, 24.33; Buddhism the official religion 9.350; the king is 'Protector of All Religions' 3.15, 9.350; King Mongkut 15.712, 15.774–5 (n270); *coup d'état* 22.44; an Indian connection with Thailand 22.99; abortion rate 8.610; prostitution, with monks involved in procurement 13.470–2, 13.489; Anagarika Dharmapala visits 8.50; Mr Chen in Thailand 22.541

Thai Buddhism
Theravāda Buddhism 2.548, 3.407; revival of Buddhism 7.445–6; emphasis on merit-making 13.382; depiction in *What the Buddha Never Taught* 13.382; Dhammayuttika Nikāya 15.712, 15.774–5 (n270); royal family links with the Buddhist Society in London 23.157; paintings in which the Buddha's disciples are identical to him 14.567

practice
celebration of Buddha Jayanti 8.249–50; politics 23.163; rationalizations about eating meat 17.586, 23.367–8; Thai Buddhists who find the idea of God ridiculous 4.126, 12.622; lay support of the English Sangha Trust 13.381–2; no word for God 13.565; *sammā arahaṃ* meditation 2.144

monastic tradition
maechis ('nuns') 2.601–2; *bhikkhunī* tradition revived 2.688–9 (n274); *bhikkhus* 'simply uneducated farmers in yellow robes' 2.645; *bhikṣus* taught new Buddhists to prostrate to them as though teaching Buddhism 2.458; *bhikkhus* teaching the Dharma through story-telling 15.445–6; ordinations 2.630–1; tonsure ceremony 2.230–1; forest monasticism 13.410, 13.423; generous gifts to monks, including televisions 22.514; harsh punishment of transgressing *bhikkhus* in the 17th century 2.634–5; a monk charged with murder and robbery 2.551; monks blessing guns destined for Vietnam 12.252, 17.111; monks not permitted to say or do anything against the government 18.339; monks receiving offerings from women on a white cloth 13.474, 13.497–8; scandals involving monks 2.551; Thai monks at the Hampstead Buddhist Vihara 23.43, 23.162–3; transferring Thai Buddhism to Britain 13.508

holy sites
the beauty of its eight principal places of worship 8.139; the Buddha's footprint 2.223; Emerald Temple, Bangkok 19.470; stupas 16.157

see also
Royal Thai Pāli canon, *see under* Tripiṭaka/Pāli Tipiṭaka

Thakur *see* Sri Ramakrishna

Thales 3.427

thangkas the brilliant colours of a thangka and what they represent 13.66–8; derived ultimately from someone's meditation 13.67; the effect of a guru blessing a thangka 19.326; eight thangkas of Padmasambhava bought in Kalimpong 6.xxii–xxiii, 22.475–6; a gift to Sangharakshita 21.230–1; Kham-style thangkas 26.236; Sangharakshita has to sell his thangkas 22.118–19; Sangharakshita orders a thangka of Green Tārā to aid his practice 22.375; a mandala of Amitāyus 24.315; a Mañjughoṣa thangka given by Jamyang Khyentse Rimpoche 22.406–7; the process of

producing a thangka 13.60–1, 26.226; Refuge Tree thangkas 11.713, 13.78, 24.315; *Rgyan-Drug Mchog-Gnyis* (on Tibetan thangkas) 8.402–3; a thangka of Nāgārjuna and the *nāga* princess 6.xxx; a thangka of a white *ḍākinī* 25.443; thangka painters should ideally meditate on the figure they are painting 26.598; thangkas as drawing room ornaments 19.466; thangkas brought out of Tibet by refugees 6.xxx, 22.476–7; the two haloes of the Buddha represent the two accumulations 14.425, 17.463; a Vajrapāṇi thangka with an erect penis 21.231–2

Tharchin, Mr (editor of the *Tibet Mirror*) v21, v22

Tharpa Choling Gompa *see under* Kalimpong

Tharpa Publications *see under* publishing

Tharpe Delam ('The Easy Path to Emancipation') introduction 22.622 (n370); Sangharakshita discovers it among texts bought in the bazaar 2.443, 22.474; discussion with Dilgo Khyentse Rimpoche 22.555

Thatcher, Margaret 5.149–50, 24.359

Thaton 7.443

Thay, Venerable Phoe 20.143

Thayumanavar (Tamil poet and mystic) 7.572 (n143)

theatre an actress whose performance terrified people with the prospect of changing their lives 26.166–7; 'idols of the theatre' (Bacon): wrong views systematized into erroneous systems of belief 12.656; the revival of poetic drama 26.375; separation between actors and audience 14.517; the theatre at Pompeii 24.295; 'Towards a Buddhist Theatre' 24.254; Sangharakshita's theatre-going, *see under* Sangharakshita XII

Thein Maung, U 22.72

theism *see* religion/theistic and non-theistic

theistic religion *see under* religion

Theocritus 20.61

Theognis of Megara 14.343

theology Christian theology, *see under* Christianity/theory and practice; the English have never shone in the field of theology 12.77; if you feel like praying, go ahead, and work out the theology later 4.130–1, 19.140, 19.509; four kinds: episcopal, monastic, scholastic, seminary 21.122–3; lay theology 12.125–6; theology of evolution 3.625n; theology is to mysticism as literary criticism is to poetry 26.45

theory difference between theoretical knowing and knowing in our very bones 12.612, 15.358; becoming engrossed in theory is as unhelpful as woolly thinking 4.147; the danger of theoretical understanding 18.167; impossible to keep people away from theoretical knowledge as was possible in the past 5.41–2; theory and practice well balanced 9.274; theoretical analysis is sometimes a means not of understanding facts but escaping from them 1.127; Buddhism is above all else practical, not theoretical 10.157, 11.369–70; there's no such thing as a purely theoretical understanding of Buddhism 15.553; you can't find out whether a teaching is helpful in theory, but only in practice 12.369

Theosophical Society brief history 23.481–2 (n76); accuses the Maha Bodhi Society of hostility 21.439; Adyar 8.22–3, 8.29, 8.34, 8.51, 20.228, 21.439; Agni Yoga 26.222; aims to create a nucleus of universal brotherhood 12.81; Benares 20.387–8; Annie Besant's leadership 8.24; Buddhist Society originally the Buddhist Lodge of the Theosophical Society 10.139, 23.46; founding in the USA 12.70; motto: 'There is no religion higher than Truth' 21.439; familiarized people with the idea of Buddhism as a living religion 9.46, 12.71; *Sandaresa* (magazine) 8.28, 8.62; schisms 8.51, 8.54–5; Singapore 20.147–50; Sri Lanka 8.20–9

Theosophy

introduction
an alternative Western tradition 13.374; belief in karma and rebirth 17.31–2; Christmas Humphreys was 'basically a Theosophist' 10.56; communication about Buddhism in India 9.46; described the Buddha as 'a sort of oriental Jesus' 13.296–7; Hinduizing and Christianizing tendencies 22.134; the 'original' theosophy of Mme Blavatsky 22.134; people of different races and national and religious backgrounds on terms of friendship 22.144; Robert Crosbie's *The Friendly Philosopher* 22.140; in Sri Lanka 8.17–34; the term *Dhyāni* Buddhas 13.304, 13.692–3 (n123); vitiating influence of Krishnamurti 21.58, 23.46

Sangharakshita
response to *Isis Unveiled* 12.493, 14.xi, 14.298, 20.63–4, 23.10; prejudice against Theosophy 20.147; Theosophist friends Rie and Sten, *see under* Krusenstierna

Theragāthā (or *Sthavira-gātha*)

introduction
brief description 14.34, 14.59–60; compared to Keats and Shelley 26.128; comparison with *Therīgāthā* 14.59–60; included as part of the *gātha*, one of the nine *aṅgas* of the Pāli canon 14.24; inspiration and guidance 2.552; poetry 26.386

stories
a leper's finger falling into Mahākassapa's bowl 17.771 (n534); Dhammika: 'the Dharma protects him who practises the Dharma' 10.718 (n453); Lakuntaka Bhaddiya Thera 3.105–6; Sappaka, who was sent into ecstasy by the beauty of a white bird and a dark cloud 26.242; the stories of Sumaṅgala, Sopāka, and Upāli 10.672 (n86); Subhūti became an *arhant* on the basis of the *mettā bhāvanā* 14.452; Sunīta the sweeper 8.15, 8.670 (n34), 10.672 (n86); Vaṅgīsa, the Buddha's poet disciple 13.644, 14.293, 19.294–5, 26.124

therapies alternative therapies, *see under* medicine; Buddhism could be described as a therapy 12.98–9; colour therapy 5.570; drifting from one personal growth therapy to another 17.681–2; how can the prostration practice be regarded as 'therapy'? 10.441; primal therapy 4.605; psychotherapy, *see* psychotherapy

Theravāda Buddhism

THE HISTORICAL THERAVĀDA

its nature
general characteristics: harmlessness, kindness ... 2.552; 'rationalism tinged with mysticism' 12.515, 26.367; regards the Mahāyāna as a degeneration 1.249; tendency to formality and dignity 4.86–7; tendency to underrate faith 4.516; tends to miss the inspiring nature of the Buddha 15.548; emphasis on monasticism 2.558–62; orthodoxy 22.312–15; attitude to pleasure 19.384; refusal to accept that anything in their tradition has changed or could change 15.697; sangha tends to be identified with monastic community 3.429; shut up between the pages of a book 1.222

history
split from Mahāsāṃghikas 1.186–9; Vibhajyavādins (analysers), alternative name 4.336, 14.23–4; coenobitical monasticism 2.192; insistence on rigid observance of the Vinaya 1.147–8; has only recently begun to translate texts from Pāli 16.15; lineage 7.472–3; *vinaya* rules 2.196; efforts to enlarge the sphere of Buddhist influence 1.345

approach to the Dharma
it has always been concerned with verbal accuracy 16.240; claim that the Pāli canon is the only canonical literature 14.341; insistence that the Buddha spoke Pāli 14.13–14; view that some canonical literature is forged 14.26; veneration for the Abhidharma Piṭaka and the *Mahāsatipaṭṭhana Sutta* 2.225; includes the spirit as well as the letter of the Buddha's teaching 4.19; metaphysical questions left open when they have no practical implications 15.634; helpful teachings for Triratna 2.552–3; take the Theravāda for daily practice and the Mahāyāna as a guide to the ideal 4.62–3

aspects of doctrine
attitude to compassion: just one state of mind among others 1.235; the bodhisattva ideal 1.214, 1.257, 16.29–30; view of death and rebirth 2.76, 3.196; view of the *mettā bhāvanā* 5.215; view of the material body of the Tathāgata 1.253; the twenty-nine Buddhas 1.45

and other Buddhists
courteous discussion between the Theravādins and their opponents 14.86; difference in style from Vajrayāna 16.327; doctrines held in common with other Buddhists 7.531–40; emphasis on one's own efforts (contrast to Jōdo Shinshū school) 1.199

MODERN THERAVĀDA

introduction
countries where it's practised 2.548–9, 3.407, 7.473, 11.372; efforts to enlarge sphere of influence 1.345; criticisms 1.10–11, 2.433, 2.720 (n533)

characteristics
aggressive fundamentalism 21.246; bigotry, exclusiveness, and authoritarianism 14.14; conformity with public opinion 19.263; conservative 1.186–7, 1.222; qualifies the devotional by the intellectual 15.629

approach to the Dharma
correcting what it regarded as misrepresentations of the Dharma 14.85–6; insistence that only their form of Buddhism is orthodox 1.187; literal-minded reading of scriptures 7.525, 7.541, 21.248; losing sight of the positive side of the Buddhist tradition 15.567–9, 15.579; maintain that it is impossible to tread the Path in the present age 7.370;

narrow literalistic definition of the Dharma 15.646; putting off practice of the Dharma to another life 12.689–90; tendency to ignore the mythical aspect of literature 4.37; they believe the age of *arhants* is past 15.585–7; they go too far in saying that the Buddha said not to think about metaphysics 17.570; unorthodoxy 2.558–62

practice
choice between bodhisattva path and *arhant* path 1.397; hampered by lack of awareness of the beauty of the Unconditioned 2.84–5; insistence that progress on the path depends on one's own efforts 1.199; negative view of Nirvāṇa 15.338, 16.63–4; neglect of the practice of meditation 1.225; regarding compassion as just another wholesome mental state 1.235; *śīla* accompanied by strong sense of separate selfhood 1.435; tendency to privilege intellectual over devotional approach 15.557–8, 19.126–7; to avoid danger, best to avoid pleasure 19.384; undervaluation of the *mettā bhāvanā* 5.111, 5.188, 5.215, 15.236, 15.338, 18.514

and the Mahāyāna
an attitude of blind fury 7.538; considers Mahāyāna doctrine unorthodox 1.247, 4.24; difference of opinion about accordance with the scriptures 7.541; living evidence of the need for the Mahāyāna movement 1.187, 1.221; Mahāyānists have more right view than modern Theravādins 7.532; pride in 'flawless' morality as compared to the 'degeneracy' of Mahāyānists 1.436; Western *bhikkhus* hostile to the Mahāyāna but drawn to Christian mysticism 23.24–5

monastic matters
confusion of Going for Refuge with becoming a monk 2.433, 2.560; introduction into the West of the rigid separation of monks from laity 23.143; a forgiving attitude to monks' breaches of chastity rules 11.570; monk says that he is not allowed to appreciate beauty 2.84, 21.397, 22.148; monks tend not to be emotionally involved in Buddhism 15.557–8; ordination identified exclusively with monastic ordination 23.143; preoccupation with keeping up the faith of the laity 2.152; rigid adherence to matters of conventional morality 7.544–5; system of temporary ordination 2.210–11; unnecessary insistence on the difference between monk and layman 2.299

see also
Early Buddhism; ethical formalism, *see under* formalism; triumphalism; vipassanā (insight meditation) movement, *see* vipassanā movement

Therīgāthā (or *Sthavirigathā*) introduction 14.24, 14.59–60; comparison with *Theragāthā* 14.59–60; inspiration and guidance 2.552, 5.622; Kisā Gotamī and the mustard seed 3.357–8, 9.233–4, 14.18; Paṭacārā 8.119; Subhā, who plucked out her eyes 4.557, 4.712 (n349), 15.126–7, 15.129; poetry 26.386; preserved by *bhikkhus* 11.645; verses about how men are not to be trusted 17.218; verses by Mahāpajāpatī Gotami 11.428–9

Thetis 26.469, 26.481–2

Thibaw, King *see* Burma

Thích Minh Châu 22.515, 22.517

Thich Nhat Hanh on a panel at the European Buddhist Union 26.536, 26.757 (n519); *The Miracle of Mindfulness* 12.405

Thích Quảng Đức *see under* Vietnam

Thích Thien Châu 22.515, 22.517, 22.520, 22.562

Thien *see* Zen

thieves *see* bandits

Thig Le *see bindu*

thīna (Pāli) *see styāna* (Sanskrit)

thīna-middha *see* five hindrances/sloth and torpor

things are neither loathsome nor attractive, they are as they are 4.579; as they really are, *see* knowledge and vision of things as they really are; no things exist apart from their attributes 14.439–40; personalizing things so that they are not just things but 'spirits' 13.273; *see also dharmas*; phenomena

thinking

the practice of thinking
do we really know what we think? 1.518, 10.246, 12.35; all your thinking should have an aim 15.195; the importance of learning to think 12.475–6; the quality of your thinking is important because it has an effect 19.86; directed, purposeful thinking 15.191–2, 19.193–4; the power of positive thinking 17.297–8; setting aside time for thinking 15.192; freeing yourself from associative thinking 15.194–5; don't allow your thinking to be ruled by the apparent objects of your perception 12.417; thinking about

something objectively can be frustrating and takes courage 17.626; we have to know what we are thinking from moment to moment 9.294; the capacity for directed thinking is a characteristic of the integrated personality 15.193

clear thinking
after insight the thinking process functions more purposefully 19.151–2; as you purify your mind, you can think clearly 10.249; a condition for spiritual growth 3.314, 12.515; the difficulties of clear thinking 12.655, 15.191–2; the expression of thoughts clarifies them, and opens them to scrutiny 18.278; get things as clear as you can, but recognize that there are other dimensions 18.287; it's important to clarify issues of all kinds 2.517–18; inseparable from meditation 4.146; a means of overturning wrong view 12.617; of crucial importance for avoiding the arising of negative mental events 17.594; a particular need in modern times 11.625; people's inability to think clearly is surprising 11.553; some people seem to think that clear thinking isn't in the spirit of the Dharma 17.391; there isn't much point in studying the Dharma if you can't think clearly 12.475–6; thinking clearly about Buddhist doctrines and practices 17.616–17; to clear away doubt and indecision 17.615–17; we have to rely on relative truth for the purpose of clear thinking 17.383; we need to challenge one another to think more clearly 4.145, 15.192–3; unclear thinking is one of the main difficulties in bringing the Dharma to the West 11.521; the whole of our spiritual life contributes to clarity of mind 17.613; writing helps one to develop clear thinking 15.193

woolly, sloppy, muddled thinking
the difference between holding a wrong view and confused thinking 19.106; muddled thinking 11.521, 11.624; sloppy thinking should be challenged 4.442, 4.443; sloppy thinking may hinder one's spiritual development 4.145; the world is full of woolly thinking 11.167

excessive, convoluted, anxious thinking
constant thinking: a habit to fill periods of calm 19.151–2; counterbalance excessive thinking through contact with Nature 26.37; excessive thinking is pathological 26.37; how can we free our minds from a tendency to convoluted thinking? 14.515–16; much of our thinking is just needless anxiety 11.149; neurotic thinking 10.462–3, 19.193–4; freedom from neurotic thinking 10.606; clinging to the turmoil of thoughts 18.452; when we are truly happy we tend not to think more than necessary 11.149

rational thinking
logical thinking 15.195–6; rational thinking 15.198; there is less rational thinking going on than we think 14.557–8; breaking through rational thinking 11.14–16; thinking without *prajñā* can do a lot of harm 9.231; we only go beyond reason when we have arrived at the limits of our thinking 17.376–7

thinking and feeling
be careful that your thinking doesn't develop disproportionately 26.38–9; the higher thinking faculty 3.11, 11.205; in a healthy person feeling and thinking are virtually identical 15.257; it is hardly possible to think without emotion 14.573; saying 'I feel' instead of 'I think' 17.235, 19.291–2

creative thinking
collaborative thinking 15.192–3; creative power of thought 1.342; requires the bringing together of intellect and emotion 19.189

learning to think for oneself
according to Buddhism you must question everything 9.494; if we cultivate awareness, our thinking becomes our own 12.261–2; people would rather have absolute certainty than think for themselves 17.626–7; the second level of wisdom 9.230; thinking for oneself in the modern world 9.443, 12.617; usually emancipation from the group occurs via independent thinking 26.40–1

thinking and other people
accepting that others think differently from you 17.53–4; thinking of others is an important step towards being non-egoistic 17.345

thinking and the Dharma
don't superimpose on spiritual experience your limited linear modes of thinking 10.614; thinking about reality as a springboard for the experience, not an end in itself 19.166; transformed by *śamatha* experience 5.420; understanding the Dharma is more like eating than thinking 10.568; the 'unthinkability' of reality 19.373

see also
thought

third order of consciousness *see under* consciousness/the nature of consciousness

thirst the most pressing of the physical appetites 18.51; *tṛṣṇā*, *see tṛṣṇā*

thirteen *vihāras* ('abodes') **of the Mahāyāna path** 4.646

thirty-two marks of a superman *see under mahāpuruṣa*

Thirty-three, gods of the *see* heavens/Heaven of the Thirty-three

Thirty-five Buddhas 14.185

thirty-seven *bodhipakṣya-dharmas* introduction 1.423; listed 12.466; the Buddha's teaching to his disciples 2.126, 12.466; confusion between literal and symbolic interpretations of the same terms 1.423; in the *Udāna* 10.568; emphasis in the *Saṃyutta Nikāya* 14.47; doctrine held in common by Theravāda and Mahāyāna 7.531; four *iddhipādas* 10.568; five spiritual faculties and five powers 1.279, 10.568; offering thirty-seven candles to symbolize them 8.55, 13.252; practices recommended to the *śrāvakas* 1.86; what is striking about them is that they are all things to be done 10.568, 12.466

this being, that becomes the fundamental principle of Buddhism 3.92–4; *imasmiṃ sati* ... Pāli verse 1.89, 2.700 (n374); 'the origin of those things which proceed from a cause' 1.90, 3.93, 3.174, 11.163; 'Whatever arises ... arises in dependence on conditions ...' 12.152–3; in dependence upon A, B arises 5.266, 7.495, 10.160; the Buddha saw this in the course of his Enlightenment 11.162–3; canonical references 10.427–33, 17.710 (n38); the credo of Buddhism 3.94; the deepest nature of things 7.152; on ancient monuments throughout the Buddhist world 1.89, 3.94, 3.175, 11.163; expresses the nature of change 3.12–13, 4.647–8; the most important formulation of Buddhist philosophy 10.142; not a theory of causation 10.142, 14.607–8; Aśoka commanded the sangha to hear and learn this doctrine 7.193; whether Buddhas come or not, one thing stands: the relatedness of this to that 15.754 (n103)

see also
Aśvajit tells Śāriputra the phrase, *see under* Śāriputra/spiritual quest; *pratītya-samutpāda*; twelve cyclical *nidānas*; twelve positive *nidānas*

Thittila, Sayadaw U (Burmese monk) brief introduction 2.714 (n483); 'Buddhism: the Path to Wisdom' 8.362; 'The Fundamental Principles of Theravada Buddhism' 2.720 (n535); Sangharakshita first takes Refuges and Precepts from him 2.410–11, 20.102–3, 20.404; at heart neither monk nor layman but simply a Buddhist 2.411; president of the Sangha Sabha 8.336, 23.43–4; worked as a stretcher-bearer in the war 2.411, 20.201

Thomas Becket, St 24.369, 24.698 (n438)

Thomas, Dylan 26.398, 26.615

Thomas, E. J.

general entries
introduction 22.587 (n130); *The Life of the Buddha as Legend and History* 2.36; 'New Year Resolutions' 8.643

The History of Buddhist Thought
definition of *vedalla suttas* 14.25; summary of *Kāraṇḍavyūha Sūtra* 1.336; *Laṅkavatāra Sūtra* 1.351, 1.357–9; the twelve *aṅgas* of the Sarvāstivādin school 14.25

Thomas, Edward 24.360

Thomas, George *see* Tonypandy

Thomas, St (apostle) 13.663

Thomas, Gospel of *see under* Gnosticism

Thomas à Kempis he said he would rather feel compunction than know the definition of it 17.106; *The Imitation of Christ* 19.53, 19.593 (n18)

Thomson, James ('B.V.') criticism of Christianity 11.343, 11.754 (n191); 'Spring' 24.151–2; underrated 26.339

Thönmi Sambhota 13.8

Thor 19.410

Thoreau, Henry David brief introduction 24.619 (n74); comparison between Thoreau and Milarepa 24.52–3; Emerson's 'Thoreau' 24.52–3; *Walden* 15.174, 24.519, 26.398

thorn getting rid of the thorns of hatred in our hearts 25.32; a rose set round with thorns 25.282; using one thorn to get rid of another 18.637

Thorndike, Sybil 23.202

Thorpe, Jeremy 23.156, 23.202

Thotagamuwe Siri Rahula Thera (Sri Lankan poet) 2.213, 2.690 (n295), 7.442

Thoth *see under* Egypt

thought

the nature of thought
where do thoughts come from? 19.195–6; not limited by time and space 3.565; a power, an energy, which produces *rūpa*

17.479–80; is thought dependent on physical energy? 24.347–8; distinction between thoughts and things 1.72, 26.84; it produces a karmic result even if not acted on immediately 17.264; to a certain extent a more fundamental fact of existence than action 7.137–8; thought is incommensurable with reality and reality with thought 26.85; thoughts can give rise to things 17.296

Buddhist thought
the Abhidharma categorized existence for the first time in Buddhist thought 14.93; the *ālaya vijñāna* is one of the most obscure questions of Buddhist thought 18.282; *Avataṃsaka Sūtra* the consummation of Buddhist thought 14.216; conditionality is perhaps the most important principle of Buddhist thought 12.21; the endeavour to transcend antinomies constitutes the history of Buddhist thought 7.39; the Enlightened mind's attempt to communicate through concepts 3.81; fingers pointing to the moon 14.584; the hardening of the categories of Buddhist thought 2.131, 4.38; not the speculations of unenlightened Buddhists 3.81; the *trikāya*, one of the finest flowers of Buddhist thought 2.39; the two truths are fundamental to all schools of Buddhist thought 1.83

freedom of thought
freedom to make up one's mind 26.19; in the *Kālāma Sutta*, *see Aṅguttara Nikāya/Book of the Threes*; the sangha encourages freedom of thought, freedom to grow 3.440; unlike other religions, Buddhism has always encouraged freedom of thought 8.297

original thought
have you ever had a truly independent thought? 3.302–3, 11.23; original thought is very rare 11.23; our heads are full of ideas we do not truly think 7.266–7

wandering thoughts
bhantacitta (wandering mind) 10.532, 15.116–17, 17.97; the cause of all regrets 18.559; the elimination of wandering thoughts 12.261; the teachings of the Great Bliss will 'burn all wandering thoughts' 19.155; in meditation, watching thoughts rioting in the playground of our mind 12.261, 17.538

concentrated thought
as we become more aware of thoughts, our thinking becomes more purposeful 17.538; becoming so concentrated that you only have the thoughts you want to have 5.418; in the thought only the thought 10.462–3; 'a man in his wholeness, wholly attending' 14.291, 15.198, 15.257; Perfect Vision arising from deep thought 1.481; thought simplified into *samādhi* 7.320; thoughts a lower form of energy than the energy of meditation 4.481; we have to learn to see where thoughts come from and where they go 1.574

thought processes
their cessation in meditation doesn't mean that the mind goes blank 5.228–9, 5.422–3; don't identify thought processes with consciousness 5.229; the *manas* is the faculty of abstract thought 12.559; three kinds: fragmented, developed to support insight, communicating insight 5.421–2

discursive thought
a basis for developing insight 5.429; the disappearance of discursive conceptual thinking 10.606; in meditation 5.337–9, 13.72–3

the power of thought
the creative power of thought 1.342; the *mettā bhāvanā* is a positive example of the power of thought 26.700

limitations
the danger of being preoccupied with thoughts and missing the meaning 19.158–9; every unskilful thought seems by nature to be self-perpetuating 18.207; failing to distinguish thoughts from things, and words from thoughts 13.347; often we're not sure what we think 18.278; the limitations of thought force us into contradictions 7.133; the oppression of foolish thought 16.321; restraining 'anti-Dharma' thoughts is easier said than done 19.110–11

beyond thought
consciousness of that which cannot be put into thought 10.606; existence and experience transcend the capacity of thought fully to express them 19.377; going through the day without thought isn't necessarily transcending concepts 18.398; it's difficult to experience peacefulness without thinking how peaceful it is 5.398–9; 'one whose thoughts have been burned up like incense' 10.606; some things, though capable of being experienced, transcend thought and speech 13.348; trying to translate subtle spiritual experience into the coarse language of thought 7.134

thought and reality
beyond the Point of No Return, no more reactive thoughts 19.237–8; contact with reality: neither thought nor feeling, but can

be spoken of as either 4.516; the Perfection of Wisdom teachings use thought to undo thought 14.515; regarding the fictions of thought as having an independent real existence 7.325–6; the relation between mystical illumination and speculative thought 24.431; thinking that thoughts *are* reality, we mistake the finger for the moon 19.377; transcending the conceptual activity of the discriminating mind 7.300; the transformation of thought into wisdom 7.302–3; ultimate truth can be neither thought about nor spoken about 17.383

see also
distracting thoughts, *see under* distractions; flow (or stream) of thoughts, *see citta-santāna*; laws of thought, *see under* logic; thinking; thought and action, *see under* action/reflections on action; thought of Enlightenment, *see bodhicitta*

thought-constructions cessation 1.64, 1.307; conditioned and Unconditioned *dharmas* are alike mere thought-constructions 1.306; currents in the great ocean of this world of relativity 1.385; *see also* concepts

thoughts, words, and deeds to harmonize thoughts, words, and deeds and raise them higher 7.141; the impressions left by our thoughts, words, and deeds since beginningless time 14.209; we limit ourselves by our own thoughts, words, and actions 10.141; your own thoughts, words, and deeds will eventually free you 7.219

thousand-petalled lotus 14.239, 16.561, 18.76

Thrangu Rimpoche 2.567

threads discerning a clear thread running through your life 15.91–2; the golden thread of the *bodhicitta* 13.587; the golden thread that connects us to reality 4.171–2; mantra: a slender thread of contact with reality 1.578; the mysterious thread of unity that runs through the fabric of things 3.469; Sangharakshita's Going for Refuge: a process of discovery with a thread of continuity 2.498–502; the thread of meaning running through our lives 15.94; weaving the thread of the teachings into cloth: a metaphor for spiritual practice 18.136–7; *see also suttas*

threats an arrogant person fears anything that threatens their fixed idea of who they are 15.275–6; the Buddha threatened by a *yakkha* 10.453–4; Dhardo's concern that Sangharakshita shouldn't be held back by threat to life force 22.562; feeling threatened by someone's energy 17.660; find the truth and be receptive to it, even if it threatens everything you have based your life on 17.632; patience when people annoy or threaten us 15.263; Sangharakshita threatened with rebirth as a dwarf 8.682 (n113), 22.171; something on a deeper level feels threatened by meditation 5.693–4; the threat of hell 15.621–2; the threat of war 4.95–6, 7.274, 22.557; threats to Buddhism in the 20th century 9.319; threats to the integrity of the Order 22.327; a tree spirit is threatened by a creeper 10.708 (n377); we fear threat from what we perceive as other 18.139

three aims (well-being, happy rebirth, Enlightenment) 16.331–2

three (or four) *āśravas* (Pāli *āsavas*)

introducing the āśravas
brief introduction 15.57, 18.295; Pāli canon sources 1.170, 1.639 (n470), 3.665–6 (n257); early use of the term 10.450; etymology 1.585, 12.164; the mind set round with wisdom is quite free from the biases 2.28; relationship with the five poisons 18.449; they must be removed because they obstruct and waste energy 12.534; instantaneous and gradual purification 14.215

descriptions
summary 1.585–6; (1) *avidyāśrava*, poison or bias of the mind towards spiritual ignorance 3.32, 3.278, 12.164; (2) *bhavāśrava*, craving for conditioned existence 3.32, 3.278, 12.164; (3) *kāmāśrava*, craving for experience through the senses 3.32, 3.278, 12.164; (4) *diṭṭhāsava*, the mental poison of wrong views 3.665 (n257), 18.449

knowledge of the destruction of the āśravas (āsravakṣaya-jñāna)
the emphasis is on *knowledge* 2.119, 10.542; the end of the path? 3.68–9, 3.278; higher spiritual experience viewed negatively 7.151; a negative description of *samādhi* 1.586; in the positive *nidānas*, *see under* twelve positive *nidānas*; Siddhārtha Gautama's experience 1.95, 2.22, 2.111, 2.119, 3.32–5, 10.434; sometimes preface by understanding of the four noble truths 1.170; as a supernormal power 1.167; what that experience is like 17.519; Yamaka's wrong view of the experience 1.75

three Cs 3.613, 12.468–9, 18.34–5

three characteristics of conditioned existence *see* three *lakṣaṇas*

Three Chief Paths *see under* Tsongkhapa

three endurances of the Dharma 17.735 (n207)

three esoteric refuges introduction 4.175, 12.312–15, 13.197–204, 18.418, 18.496; the addition of the *dharmapāla* 19.408; and the three exoteric refuges 12.313–15, 19.221–2; '*Gurus, Devas, Ḍākinīs* – Combine these into a single whole and worship that' 7.305; not to be mystified 18.496–7; they are not in addition to the original Three Refuges 13.204; the three roots: lama, *yidam*, and Dharma protector (Tibetan Buddhism) 2.565–6, 18.317; visualized on the Refuge Tree 13.77–8; the guru as esoteric Buddha Refuge 2.481, 4.175, 12.17, 12.313, 19.221–2; *yidam* as esoteric Dharma refuge 2.481, 4.175, 12.312–15, 13.200–2; *ḍākinī* as esoteric Sangha refuge 13.237

three family protectors correspond to the three functions of the mind 2.173; emanate other bodhisattvas from themselves 2.177–8; embodiments of the three principal aspects of Enlightenment 26.232; visualizing them 7.304, 12.297; *see also* Mañjuśrī; Avalokiteśvara; Vajrapāṇi

Three Jewels

introduction
simple description 3.394–6, 9.380, 10.199–200, 11.134–5, 11.175, 11.394; description in the Threefold Puja 2.462; canonical references 3.662 (n242); how did they come to be spoken of as the Three Jewels? 13.166; difference between 'jewels' and 'refuges' 2.241–2, 10.266–7, 15.547; how the Three Jewels become the Three Refuges 15.577–87; their colours 9.536, 10.199–200; their appearance the expression of the essence of existence 7.317; the highest values of human existence 11.134–5; the lifeblood of Buddhism 14.103; they are wonderful 11.43–4; the most precious of all non-material things 3.395, 11.395; the three highest values of Buddhism 2.241; one value looked at from three points of view 16.175; they constitute Buddhism 1.250, 2.8; everything in the spiritual life exists for their sake 3.395, 13.43; everything in Buddhism relates to them 11.394–5; all are essentially Unconditioned 16.547; they represent the possibility of complete liberation from suffering 2.241–2

devotion to the Three Jewels
Avataṃsaka Sūtra prayer 2.5; the *ḍākinī*'s self-abandonment to the Three Jewels 13.242; devotion to them 2.220–6, 15.328; feeling strongly and deeply about them 14.471; fidelity to them 3.572, 14.471; homage by prostration to the Three Jewels 15.669, 15.672–3; honouring them 17.277; reverence for them 8.529; their preciousness to us 25.31; Sangharakshita's evidently the first book dedicated to them 2.8; three festivals rejoicing in them 11.395–6

difficulties
being out of harmony with the guru, and thus with the Three Jewels 18.483; doubt with regard to the Three Jewels 17.632; disrespect to them 4.326–7, 16.303; speaking in dispraise of the Three Jewels 11.332–5

the Three Jewels in practice
can the Three Jewels be seen as 'within our mind'? 15.580–2; contemplating the Three Jewels 14.586; difference between academic study and commitment 2.470; in the end we must ourselves *become* the Three Jewels 2.250; organizing one's life around the Three Jewels 2.461; to go from *dhyāna* to *prajñā*, invoke the Three Jewels 18.252; they are what all ordinations have in common 26.32; they will do their bit if you do yours 18.20

how they relate to each other
the Buddha the centre, the Dharma the radius, and the Sangha the circumference 2.137; the Buddha as Father, the Dharma as Mother, and the Sangha as son 2.138; the Buddha gained Enlightenment, taught the Dharma, his followers the Sangha 3.395–6; the Buddha … works through the Dharma to create the Sangha (Sukhāvatī) 4.640; no duality between any two of them 16.547; no Sangha without Dharma, no Dharma without Buddha 25.107, 25.109, 26.511; you can't treat any of them without reference to the others 14.104

how they appear in the tradition
understanding them in accordance with tradition 1.409; three of the six *gāravas*, objects of respect 3.69; manifested in all three *yānas* 11.255; Mahāyāna doctrines concerning them 1.250–64; Mahāyāna precept against speaking ill of the Triratna 2.208; the Mahāyāna's elucidation of their true meaning 14.103–4; the bodhisattva ideal as a restatement of the Sangha Jewel 14.166–7; the *White Lotus Sūtra*'s evocation 14.132; carried to the world by the windhorse 10.199–200, 19.438–9; the Supramundane Jewels (Milarepa) 18.294–5; essence of mind (Huineng) 2.408; the Three Treasures (Chinese tradition) 11.394

see also
commitment; esoteric, *see* three esoteric Refuges; faith in the Three Jewels, *see under* faith; Going for Refuge; salutation to the Three Jewels, *see Tiratana Vandanā*

three *lakṣaṇas* (Pāli *lakkhanas*)

introduction
brief introduction 1.486, 9.231–3; fuller account 1.170–6, 2.81–92, 3.209–17, 7.47–51; the facts of the *lakṣaṇas* are basic and obvious 7.50; conditioned existence and the three *lakṣaṇas* 2.87, 3.220–1, 3.234; even the *dhyānas* are inherently painful, transitory, and insubstantial 1.444; the first two are mundane, the third both mundane and transcendental 7.538; by no means best understood when understood most literally 2.87; the Buddha taught them for pragmatic reasons, not as a speculative sport 7.50; illustrated by the changing colour of a leaf 2.87–8; the teaching drew Sangharakshita's attention during his wandering days 20.302; 'The Three Marks' (poem) 25.295

canonical references
summary 16.585 (n13); in the *Dhammapada* 1.171, 2.81–2, 3.657 (n200), 9.562 (n246); in the *Udāna* 3.657 (n200); in the *Saṃyutta Nikāya* 1.175–6

relationship to other teachings
the first three of the four *viparyāsas* 2.81, 3.281; the three *vimokṣas* 2.114–5; the four Dharma *mudrās* 12.754–5 (n456); proclaimed by the symbols of Sukhāvatī 1.183

the relationship of impermanence to the other two
the most important of the three *lakṣaṇas* 9.232; intermediate between the other two 2.85; logically prior to the other two 1.171; points to the fact that the whole universe is a network of processes 3.216–17; the other two *lakṣaṇas* are contained within it 11.446; underlying impermanence is the law that all things are interdependent (*anattā*) 7.49

reflections and insight
contemplating the *lakṣaṇas* as a way to insight 2.262, 4.498, 11.126, 19.453; as the first of four levels of wisdom 16.11; as one of Vasubandhu's four factors 4.50–1; connection with reflection on the breath 15.110–11; knowledge and vision of things as they really are 3.274–5; through the three doors of liberation (*vimokṣa-mukhas*) 1.165, 5.524

fourth lakṣaṇa
the ugly or repulsive 26.665; association with Green Tārā 26.665–6; 'Nirvāṇa alone is peace' 2.82, 2.89, 2.92, 26.11

three levels of wisdom

introduction
descriptions 3.302–3, 3.357, 9.229–31, 10.176, 10.197–8, 12.515, 15.511, 16.11, 17.128; as a hierarchy 4.169; if we don't develop the first two levels, we will not be able to develop the third 17.573; impermanence in relation to the three levels of wisdom 17.129–30; method of cultivating non-deludedness 17.567; need to be practised more by Order members 21.393; *prajñā* (insight) can arise equally in dependence on all three levels of wisdom 12.541–3; important to make distinctions between the levels we've experienced 3.303; related to the jewel in the lotus 16.186–7; the three levels are continuous 17.130; the three temperaments and the three levels of wisdom 25.14–15; to develop *prajñā* is to follow this path 17.611

sources
canonical sources 3.670 (n284), 3.677 (n324), 3.683 (n370), 4.683 (n170), 16.585 (n12); Buddhaghosa's explanation 1.169; described by Conze 17.127; mentioned in the *Abhidharmakośa* 17.725 (n128)

(1) śruta-mayī prajñā (hearing)
the aim is to get a clear conceptual idea of how things are 3.411; insight may arise on the basis of what we hear or read, but if not, we need to reflect 12.542; it is what you have to do first, the necessary basis 9.229, 15.511; listening to the Dharma with one's whole being 10.197; study can be a method of practice, but you have to go on to reflect and meditate on it 17.535; the understanding one gets from Dharma study with a teacher 17.567; you are sufficiently interested and receptive to listen 3.302; you can tell when a book on Buddhism has been written at this level 17.128–9

(2) cintā-mayī prajñā (reflection)
emphasized by Dr Ambedkar 10.197; if insight doesn't arise when we reflect, we need to meditate 12.542; thinking for yourself 9.230; a more substantial understanding 15.511; quite rare 3.303; Dharma talks based on the second level of wisdom, not just the first 17.129; turning the teachings over in your own mind 3.411, 17.567; working out the implications of the Dharma yourself 3.302

(3) bhāvanā-mayī prajñā (meditating)
the development of mind 9.231; based on reflections in a higher state of consciousness 3.302; bringing into existence a new mind 10.197–8; coincides with the highest level of *samādhi* 16.11; experiencing the truth for yourself 15.511; 'finding out and knowing directly' 13.491; not conceptual, but direct insight 3.411, 7.509; and the four levels of *śūnyatā* 16.11–12; has access to both levels of existence (composite and incomposite) 13.438; sees that the true nature of human existence is development 9.232; understanding or intuition 17.567; what makes a Buddha a Buddha 3.357, 9.231; you don't just bring in a technical aid to help you develop it 17.130; you've become one with the object of your creative thinking 17.129–30

Three Musketeers v23

three *puṇya-kriyā-vastūni* (Pāli *puñña-kiriya-vatthuni*) 11.306

Three Refuges brief description 3.396–7, 9.474–5, 23.437–8; *tisaraṇa* (Sanskrit) *triśaraṇa* explanation 9.547; the approach to the Three Refuges of the three *yānas* 13.195–204; in the *Dhammapada* 13.195; difference between 'jewels' and 'refuges' 2.241–2, 10.266–7, 15.547; doctrine held in common by Theravāda and Mahāyāna 7.531; 'Everything can be changed except the Three Refuges' 10.576, 17.634; how the Three Refuges destroy fear (Buddhaghosa) 15.647; not an authority 19.285; refuge from what? from suffering 2.241–2; relationship to precepts 9.187; they will never fail 18.20

see also
Three Jewels; Going for Refuge; three esoteric Refuges

three roots (root poisons, *akuśala-mūlas*)

introduction
the most elementary classification of all (*Satipaṭṭhāna Sutta*) 15.162; a primitive formula 2.70; their arising from pleasant, painful, and neutral feelings 17.512–13; canonical reference 13.686 (n77); connection with three character types (Buddhaghosa) 17.602; described in a Tibetan source 11.129–30; variants of the three poisons (*rāga, pratigha, māna*) 17.596; universal problems 15.81

their nature
the driving force of our existence 4.73; the forces that drive *saṃsāra* 3.244; becoming a devil under their influence 26.657; the fate of those who exacerbate them in others 8.208; heedlessness produced by them 17.677; pleasure gives rise to greed, pain to hatred, neutral feelings to delusion 2.121–2; one does not find anything that can cause them in the ultimate sense 14.192; a stream running through the hearts of men and through our world 7.253; they can't be separated, arising from the same primordial alienation from reality 2.252; they produce unskilful actions 1.142–3, 16.419; unenlightened human beings are dominated by them 26.479; the world is burning with them 16.70

getting rid of them
the essence of the Dharma life is their eradication 5.256, 7.221–2; confessing them 16.304; breaking the chains of folly, hate, and greed 25.381; it's hard for us to imagine being free of them, but we have to try 12.547; inner struggle between the poisons and the golden light 16.290–1; overcoming them 5.347–8; through spiritual practice one is able gradually to eliminate them 13.37; to be skilful means to act, speak, and think so as to move away from them 17.164; Nirvāṇa is their extinction 2.122, 13.571

see also
greed, hatred, delusion; at the hub of the wheel of life, *see under* wheel of life

three roots (esoteric counterpart to the Three Refuges) *see* three esoteric Refuges

three *samādhis* *see* three *vimokṣa-mukhas*

three *sandhis* of the wheel of life 2.255, 12.156–7; correlation with the *bardos* 12.197–8; points at which we can disengage from the reactive cycle 15.228

three *svabhāvas*

introduction
brief description 14.505–6, 19.232; the analogy with the rope that is perceived as a snake 14.214, 14.506; comparison with the three hypostases of Neoplatonism 26.590; the distinction is pragmatic, ultimately only the One Mind exists 1.370; the five *dharmas* represent an alternative classification 14.214; important to distinguish between *paratantra* and *parikalpita* 14.576; in the *Laṅkāvatāra Sūtra* 14.214; related to the two kinds of truth (*satya*) 14.214; Vasubandhu explains the difference between the three: a piece of wood and an elephant 1.370; a Yogācāra threefold division (Suzuki) 19.232

(1) parikalpita-satya
illusory reality 1.265; that which is perceived to exist but does not exist at all 19.232; two kinds of illusion 14.506

(2) paratantra-satya
contingent reality 1.265; it's real, but not *absolutely* real 19.232–6; conventional reality is divided up in arbitrary ways 19.240–1; conventionally valid ideas 19.233

(3) parinispanna-satya
that which is absolutely real 19.232–3; absolute knowledge 14.506; corresponds to absolute mind 1.370

three unskilful or unwholesome roots *see* three roots

three *vimokṣa-mukhas* (doors to Enlightenment, *lokuttara samādhis*, *vimokṣa-dvāras*)

introduction
brief description 3.219, 16.447; sources 3.658 (n213); references in the *Sūtra of Huineng* 1.587; reference in the *Gaṇḍavyūha Sūtra* 14.222; the bodhisattva should know them 14.153; correspondence with the *lakṣaṇas* and *viparyāsas* 2.114–15, 2.121–2, 5.524, 19.453; doors of liberation 26.664–5; the unbiased and empty belong to the transcendental path, the imageless does not 2.122; a fourth *vimokṣa*, pure beauty Tārā 26.664

(1) apraṇihita (Pāli appaṇihita)
the door of the unbiased or directionless 1.165; association with Avalokiteśvara 26.664; a mental state without any inclination in any direction 3.219, 12.506; perfect spontaneity 1.586–7; like a perfectly round sphere on a perfectly flat plane 3.219, 26.83; having no egoistic motive for doing anything, one is free to respond 17.521–2; having nowhere to go, the mind stays where it is 4.159; in meditation, ready to roll in any direction 10.638; realized through reflecting on the unsatisfactoriness of conditioned existence 3.220; the 'unbiased' because of its complete immunity to the three poisons 2.122

(2) animitta
the door of the signless or imageless 1.165; to the Unconditioned bypassing words, thoughts, concepts 2.121, 3.219, 12.505–6, 26.478; association with Vajrapāṇi 26.664; the mind like a clear blue sky, free of clouds of conceptualization 1.586; opposes and destroys eternalism and nihilism 2.122; reality is contemplated as being devoid of all conceptual constructions 4.159; realized through reflecting on the impermanence of conditioned existence 2.121, 3.220; a very distinctive experience 12.505–6

(3) śūnyatā or suññata
the door of emptiness 1.165, 12.505; association with Mañjughoṣa 26.664; connected with the *ekalakṣaṇa-samādhi*, seeing everything as ultimately the same 1.587; connection between insubstantiality and emptiness 2.89–90; the Mahāyāna emphasized this more than the other two gateways 5.524; must be careful not to be misled by the literal translation 'voidness' or 'emptiness' 16.232; you see that everything is transparent, nothing has any self-identity 3.219–20; reality is contemplated as having no self-nature 4.159; realized through reflecting on the conditioned as devoid of self 3.220

three wholesome roots 17.566, 17.574

three worlds *see trailokya*

three *yānas* (ways) *see yānas*

threefold knowledge (*tevijja*) memory of past lives, ability to see others' karma, release of mind 1.78–9, 3.115; the Buddha's revalorization of the term 10.438; a group of *bhikkhus* realize the three knowledges 10.711–12 (n409)

Threefold Lotus Sūtra 8.479, 16.52

Threefold Way (or path, *triśikṣā*)

introduction
brief description 7.434–5, 7.507–9, 9.187, 9.249, 10.152, 11.63–4, 13.330, 16.219; full account 1.136–82, 3.315–62; the most important and fundamental division of the path 11.63; spirit and letter on the threefold way 11.480–1; such a path not present in religions of revelation 7.369; called 'old-fashioned' 22.214

history
early version (*Udāna*) 10.434; the Buddha's last teachings 2.28, 3.354, 4.334, 4.644–5, 7.507, 8.92, 11.306; Ānanda teaches Subha the threefold way 7.434, 7.519; held in common by Theravāda and Mahāyāna 7.531; recognized by all schools of Buddhism 8.254; the six perfections as an expanded version 1.425; practised by monks only 2.204

its nature
all the methods of Buddhism can be included under one of its headings 22.269; domestic life incompatible with the threefold way 1.340; a path of perpetual self-transcendence 11.656; a progressive path 3.354, 7.257; stepping stones to cross the stream 7.254; symbolized by

the windhorse 19.438–9; to be followed vigorously while reflecting that in reality one can do nothing 1.348

practising the path
consolidate each stage before proceeding to the next one 11.65–6; four kinds of mental objects to concentrate on 17.542–3; liberates one from the conception of things as mutually exclusive ego-entities 7.382; purifying the mind by means of it 26.642; talk of it is helpful 10.530; practice without understanding that really no one practises anything is dangerous 1.403

see also
ethics and the threefold way, *see under* ethics/ethics in the Buddhist tradition

threshold guardians of the threshold 16.352; hope that humanity will pause upon the threshold of a third world war 7.280; 'humanity clamouring for admission on the threshold of the Divine' 20.127

Thubden (Tibetan novice in Kalimpong) v22, v23

Thubten Chodron v24

Thucydides 3.427, 23.518 (n332)

thugs (assassins) 10.55

Thūna, India 10.622–3

thūpa *see* stupa

Thurman, Robert A. F. 16.444–5

'Thus have I heard' 14.99, 14.399, 15.179, 16.36–7, 16.234

thusness (*tathatā*) *see* suchness

Ti Rimpoche 13.40

Ti-tsang *see under* Chinese Buddhism

Tiantai (or Tendai) school 4.495, 4.520, 11.54, 11.89, 25.207

Tibet

HISTORY

introduction
Tibetans, being history-minded, have produced many historical works 13.30; Hoffman, Helmut, *The Religions of Tibet* 8.351–3; Tucci, Giuseppe, *The Religions of Tibet* 8.513–15

the introduction of Buddhism
the introduction of Buddhism to Tibet took 500 years 13.6; the political motives involved in the introduction of Buddhism 8.514; an obstacle to Buddhism's adoption was the difference between India and Tibet 13.3–6; 7th to 9th century CE, Buddhism introduced and established 12.570; giving up weapons in medieval Tibet was a huge step 18.98–9

the reign of Songtsen Gampo
the decision to introduce Buddhism to Tibet 13.7; centralized administration and embarked on social and cultural reform 13.6–8; introduction of weaving, masonry, and carpentry 13.7; prohibition of blood sports 13.7; the building of the Jokhang and Ramoche in Lhasa for his two wives 13.7–8; the building of the first Buddhist temples in Tibet 13.8; invention of the Tibetan alphabet 13.8; translation of Indian Buddhist scriptures 13.8; the Dharma by no means well established 12.290

the reign of Trisong Detsen
the years of his reign 12.286; Śāntarakṣita and Padmasambhava bring Buddhism to Tibet 8.523, 12.290–4, 13.9–11; the building of Samye monastery, *see under* Tibetan Buddhism/monastic life/Samye; the 'seven men on trial', the first seven Tibetans to be ordained 12.292, 12.294, 13.10; the 'Council of Lhasa' (or Samye Debate) 13.11–12, 13.673 (n1); the *triyāna* character of Tibetan Buddhism established 1.246, 13.12, 13.44; Śāntarakṣita brought the Sarvāstivādin monastic ordination to Tibet 2.745 (n696)

the reign of Ralpacan
a glossary (the *Mahāvyutpatti*) produced 13.12; a permanent commission for the translation of scriptures set up 12.570, 13.12–13; after Ralpacan's assassination, Buddhism almost wiped out 12.570–1, 13.13

the reign of Yeshe-Ö (Jñānaprabha)
Atīśa is invited to restore Buddhism in Tibet (11th century CE) 12.571, 13.13; the king is kidnapped, but the ransom gold funds Atīśa's journey 12.571–2, 13.13–14; Atīśa's visit to Tibet, *see under* Atīśa; a renaissance for Buddhism 13.14, 18.3–4

the next phase
after the destruction of Indian monasteries, monks sought refuge in Tibet 18.402; in Milarepa's day Tibetans would go to India for teachings 18.326; there was quite a lot wrong with Buddhism in Tibet in Milarepa's time 19.584; the political power of the Shakya school in the 13th century 4.123, 13.29–30; Buddhism perhaps became widespread too quickly 19.486; the Fifth Dalai Lama took over the temporal rule of Tibet (17th century) 13.40–1; the Younghusband expedition to Tibet 13.41

the Chinese invasion
the Tibetans used the rite of destruction to try to halt it 22.372, 26.700; advance on Lhasa 13.100, 21.104; damage to monasteries 13.33; destruction of the Jokhang and the Ramoche 13.7–8; first challenge to Buddhism in Tibet in nearly a thousand years 13.14; the flight of the Dalai Lama, *see under* Dalai Lama/ Fourteenth; grim tragedy 8.309, 27.1072; the inhumanity with which Buddhism was rooted out 8.314; occupation 22.209; Sangharakshita and Dhardo Rimpoche speak against the invasion 22.549–50; a spiritual community has been almost wiped out 11.270; the Tibetans' armed struggle against the Chinese 22.558; a base for incursion into India? 8.308–9; the effect of Marxist Communism 12.616–17; a Tibetan prisoner of the Chinese 22.493–5

recent times
change in Tibet in the 20th century 12.400, 13.100–2; growing interest in Tibetan Buddhism in the West 8.503–4; spreading the Dharma to other countries 11.607, 14.554, 19.209, 19.532–3; the old Tibet is gone 8.503, 13.102

GEOGRAPHY AND PLACES

introduction
the austere beauty of the Tibetan landscape 18.158–9; clutter of temples 16.327–8; danger of robbery when travelling in Tibet 16.165; Din Ri 18.137; *maṇi* walls 16.165–6; Nya Non 18.137, 18.140–1; Tibetan architecture determined by climate 13.62; the vivid colours of the Tibetan landscape 13.66

Lhasa
a pilgrimage to Lhasa 22.259–60; the visit of a Jesuit priest in the 18th century 11.297; circumambulating the city 19.335; the Jokhang 13.7–8; medical college 13.51; politics 4.338; the Potala 1.412, 13.41, 13.62; the Ramoche 13.7–8; Tantric colleges 13.48

Manasarovar, Lake (Anopatapta, Anavatapta)
Atīśa's visit 12.574; Lama Govinda's description 12.574; the *nāga* that resides in the lake 14.539; in the *Ratnaguṇa-saṃcayagāthā* 14.538–9

TIBETAN PEOPLE

brief introduction
civilization 'exists in fossilized form' (Toynbee) 3.424; an evocation of Tibet and Tibetan Buddhism 1.194–6, 16.165; a pastoral way of life 13.3–4

the character of Tibetan people
aggressive 13.4–5; contrasted with Indian people 10.38, 13.3–5, 19.399; courteous 22.427; hardy, fond of pleasure, keenly curious, sincere: good material for the Dharma 18.62–3; Indian people are considered irreligious by Tibetans 17.556, 17.627, 19.399; logically-minded 21.362; materialistic 15.684; mystical in the true sense 13.110; positive attitude towards parents 18.506; practical, down-to-earth 13.4, 13.109–10; shocked to hear the follower of one religion running down another 12.137, 13.111; Tibetan officials 22.498–500; tolerance 13.110–11; the virile and energetic genius of the Tibetan people 7.397

Khambas (Khampas)
generosity 13.53; income divided between the Dharma, pleasure, and household 16.401; Khamba guerrillas 18.99–100, 21.357, 22.558–9; fondness for cowboy films 18.99; a typical Khampa 21.328–9; warrior-like nature 13.4–5, 18.99

refugees in Kalimpong
a sizeable population 21.441; anxiety that they would have to leave after the Chinese incursion into India 22.551; arrival leads to a rise in property prices 21.535, 21.537–8, 22.263; the change in young men after their arrival, from traditional to modern 13.101–2; the more refugees arrived, the more Christian missionaries came 21.353–4; a refugee has to sell his thangkas 6.xxii–xxiii, 22.475–6; Tibetan officials wanted to keep refugees under their control 12.435; 'Tibetan Refugee' (poem) 25.297

refugees elsewhere
in India 2.551, 8.319–20, 12.435, 13.102–3, 22.469, 23.335–6, 23.400; in Oxford 23.129; scholarships for students 22.342; selling precious artefacts in Calcutta 23.400; thangkas and images brought out of Tibet by refugees 22.476–7

CULTURE

architecture
gompa 13.62; stupa (*chorten*) 13.63–4, 15.150, 16.157, 16.165; three-storeyed temple, symbolizing the *trikāya* 13.64–6, 21.214–15, 22.267–8

art
the aim is to put the viewer in touch with the One Mind 13.61; almost entirely religious 13.59–60; the art of Tibet is based on the spirituality of Buddhism 8.531; artist monks 13.52; the 'demoniacal' in Tibetan Buddhist art 8.117; an exhibition in the West 26.236, 26.719 (n186);

iconography popular in the West 2.556; influenced by India, Nepal, China 13.58–9; inspiring and invigorating 18.372; numberless vigorous and fearful forms 7.397; six categories of Tibetan Buddhist art 8.531; the symbols of Tibetan art 13.61–70; thangkas, *see* thangkas; Tibetan artists regard striving for originality as an aberration 13.59–60; *Visual Dharma: The Buddhist Art of Tibet* (review) 8.530–1; wood blocks 21.232–3

beliefs and myths
astrology 19.268–9; dragons guard the gold in the earth 15.138; human beings are descended from Avalokiteśvara and a monkey 2.65; the rebirth of incarnate lamas 3.134; Śākyamuni continues to work in the world in the form of Avalokiteśvara 4.190; demons 12.435, 21.318; exorcism 4.548, 19.550; medicine 13.51, 16.193–4; oracles 18.228, 22.551

culture
the influence of Buddhism on Tibetan culture 7.442, 11.679; Lama Dances 12.438, 13.108, 19.384, 22.399; the singing of Milarepa's songs 18.4–5; Tibetan culture is, or was, a culture of faith 17.556; Tibetan music 18.5, 11.228–9; Tibetan tea 12.574–5; Tibetan trumpets 25.237; Tibetans are great cinema-goers 18.99, 22.114–15; traditional costume 21.193

customs and traditions
customs relating to the guru 5.564–5; hats 5.565, 13.32–3, 13.117; hierarchy and precedence 13.54–5; sky burial 15.142–3; the tradition of lowering one's umbrella as a sign of respect 4.342

language and literature
alphabet 12.570, 13.8; the feeling that Tibetan has some mystic quality 19.133; the Gesar epic 13.59, 13.675–6 (n21); love poems by the 6th Dalai Lama 13.59; relationship of Tibetan literature to that of other languages 14.289; the structure lends itself to verse 18.5; written language created so that Buddhist texts could be translated 13.8, 16.15

proverbs
'If it isn't difficult, it isn't religion' 12.655; 'You can make yourself comfortable in hell if you go about it the right way' 4.423, 23.10

see also
conversion of demons to Buddhism *under* Padmasambhava/life story/conversion; Bön religion, *see* Bön; books, *see under* books

Tibet Mirror 21.164

Tibetan Book of the Dead (*Bardo Thödol*)

introduction
brief introduction 2.743 (n685), 3.655 (n190), 17.708 (n23); meaning of *Bardo Thödol* 12.197; 'Liberation by Hearing in the Intermediate State' 5.34, 12.202; a Nyingma *terma* 2.555, 12.197, 12.300, 13.23–4; association with the Pure Land school 12.204; first English translation 12.197; 'also a book of the living' (Govinda) 12.206, 16.107; every Buddhist scripture is a Book of the Dead 16.262; translations 5.212–13, 13.168, 22.247

influences
its influence on Lama Govinda 14.263; Jung's response to the text 12.197; a passage mentioned in a poem by Edith Sitwell 7.450; among three texts most popular with Western Buddhists 14.268–9; inspiration to the Triratna Buddhist Community 2.555; seminar 24.159–60

notes on content
paints a vivid picture of the intermediate process 2.76; the *bardo* is much of the book's subject matter 3.196; to be taken literally or symbolically? 16.107–8; psycho-spiritual symbolism 12.194–208; the journey from death to rebirth 3.110–11, 12.201–6, 16.532, 23.93; the departed consciousness can be helped by the positive thoughts of the living 4.560; fear of Reality at the point of death 16.39, 12.201–2; the clear light of reality (the void) 11.17, 12.201–2, 16.96, 16.108, 18.250, 18.570–1; teaches that all are phenomena of the unconditioned reality of absolute mind 2.67; 'This mind of yours is inseparable luminosity' 2.672 (n93); the order in which the Buddhas appear 8.558; the sublimity of the wrathful deities 14.472; spiritual death 16.262–3; richness of imagery 2.555

see also
bardos; Root Verses of the Six Bardos, *see under bardos*

Tibetan Buddhism

INTRODUCTION

what kind of Buddhism is it?
a direct continuation of Indian Buddhism 8.503, 13.58, 13.105–6, 13.115–16; essentially the Buddhism of the Pala dynasty transported to Tibet 8.503; a form of Sarvāstivāda Buddhism 3.408; influenced by Madhyamaka 1.323; a combination of Sarvāstivāda, Madhyamaka, and Yogācāra 8.503; almost a blend of Madhyamaka and Yogācāra

17.451–2, 19.373; predominantly Tantric, especially as encountered in the West 2.564; the Tantric tradition in Tibet 11.678–9; a magnificent and rich synthesis of the total Buddhist tradition 13.112; unsophisticated acceptance of Buddhism had spiritual advantages 17.454; ‘Lamaism’ (archaic term) 8.514–15; Rimé tradition 12.437, 12.734 (n289), 22.554; the future of Tibetan Buddhism (as seen in 1966) 13.99–112

its nature
brief introduction 2.555–6, 10.134–5, 11.372, 17.155; a balanced approach 13.108–9; both highly intellectual and deeply devotional 13.106–8; comparison with Roman Catholicism 13.110; a constant effort to appease powers which are feared 8.514; freedom of emotion 19.124–5, 19.428; the intellectual and emotional aspects of religious life are not divided 13.107–8; ‘a jungle’ 13.92, 13.116–17, 17.685–6, 21.176–8; kindness and compassion 4.86, 14.555–6; it has made original contributions of great value 17.155; its strength is its symbols 26.38; ‘a striking lack of social compassion’ 8.514; the sunlit rationality of the Dalai Lama’s approach 8.505; viewed as black magic by a Christian missionary 21.357

Westerners and Tibetan Buddhism
inspiration for the Triratna Buddhist Community 2.555–6, 12.368; sometimes Westerners are confused by Tibetan culture 11.598–9; what can Westerners learn from it? 13.105–12; Sangharakshita first meets Tibetan Buddhism 13.116–117, 21.176–8

TEACHINGS AND STUDY

teachings and beliefs
belief that all the *yānas* were the personal teaching of the Buddha 13.200; the bodhisattva ideal, *see under* bodhisattva ideal/history/in Tibetan Buddhism; even the Tibetans can be misled by externals 13.161; Going for Refuge 2.435–6, 12.296, 12.305, 13.80; Going for Refuge and the arising of the *bodhicitta* 2.564–5, 2.567; interest in advanced teachings 18.167, 19.531; soteriological goals 8.514; the teaching a current of spiritual energy (*adhiṣṭhāna*) descending from above 12.14; three kinds of suffering: pain, change, conditioned existence 17.427, 17.754 (n358); three lines of lineage: mind-lineage, sign-lineage, word-lineage 3.82, 14.16–17; Tibetan Buddhists are surrounded by symbols 13.70; Tibetans may not have heard of the historical Buddha 12.180–1, 12.507–8, 13.20–1

Dharma study
mode of discussing profound questions 12.121–2, 22.373–4; no Tibetan would study a text without authorization from their preceptor 7.543; scholastic debate 13.47, 17.465, 18.168; texts are explained and interpreted by one’s teacher 17.156

LITERATURE

introduction
the sacred canon 1.211–12; Tibetan attitude to the Sacred Scriptures 14.262–3; Abhidharma 14.84; the academic work on Tibetan texts of Japanese scholars 17.453; all schools accept the same scriptures as canonical 13.19; books on Tibetan Buddhism in the West 8.503–11; ‘Death and the Bodhisattva Trainings’ 24.310; *Eight Verses on Transforming the Mind* (Langri Thangpa) 8.611–12; *Kadamthorbu* 8.528, 8.593; *lung* (permission to read) 12.340, 22.406; the *Maṇi Kabum* 10.227, 13.8; *Vinayavastu* 2.200

Tengyur
compiled by Buton 13.29, 14.261; mainly commentaries and treatises by distinguished *ācāryas* 7.525, 13.20; the ‘remote tradition’ 14.263; 225 volumes 13.19, 14.261–2; what it includes 14.262; works of Padmasambhava 14.262; works on dance studied by Jamyang Khyentse Rimpoche 12.437–8

translations
Kāraṇḍavyūha Sūtra reputedly the first Buddhist text translated into Tibetan 2.176; *Laṅkāvatāra Sūtra* 14.202; Nāgārjuna’s *Precious Garland* 17.155–7; the translation of Buddhist texts into Tibetan 7.514–15, 12.570; standardization of translation of Buddhist terms into Tibetan 13.12–13; *Samādhirāja Sūtra* 14.190; *Śūraṅgama-samādhi Sūtra* 14.195; *Sūtra of Golden Light* 14.242; *The Tibetan Dharmapada* 15.59; translations at the time of Padmasambhava 8.523; translations by Rinchen Zangpo 12.575

see also
Kangyur, *see under* Tripiṭaka; the *Lam-rim chen-mo* and the *sNgags-rim chen-mo*, *see under* Tsongkhapa/works; *termas*, *see termas*; *Tharpe Delam*, *see Tharpe Delam*

PRACTICE

ethics and precepts
bodhisattva precepts 13.56–7; *prātimokṣa* (*so sor thar pa*) means ‘individual liberation’ 2.344

vegetarianism
the Dalai Lama is not vegetarian 22.365; observed during pujas 4.112; Tibetan attitudes to vegetarianism 10.50, 17.586, 19.50, 19.331, 19.528, 22.365; belief that a killed animal can be diverted to a better rebirth 4.111–12, 19.331, 19.527

meditations, reflections, initiations
levitation 3.268; meditating before starting the day's work 13.98; modern neglect of preliminary practices 5.541; Tantric meditation 5.574–85; practising Tantric meditation without a guru is a contradiction in terms 5.575–6; Tibetan Buddhism derives its meditation from the Vajrayāna 13.12, 13.73; Tibetan Buddhists rarely talk or write about meditation 13.92; in Tibetan Buddhism meditation lies at the heart of the spiritual life 13.71; Tibetan Buddhists reflect on death and decay in a very positive spirit 4.537–8; traditional long retreat (three years, three weeks, three days, three hours) 13.74–5; visualization of the chakras 16.135

devotional practice
appealing to the bodhisattvas 4.312–13; devotional response to an image of the Buddha 4.177; enormous amounts spent on butter lamps 8.175; great respect for books and images 13.107; importance of physical contact with sacred objects 21.194; Jambeyang, name for Mañjuśrī 2.173; Jetsun Dolma, 'The Faithful Dolma' (Tārā) 2.178, 13.92; mantra chanting 13.98; offended by a Buddha image which 'chopped his head in two' 21.56–7; offerings to the shrine 26.494; prayer 19.71, 19.130–40; pilgrimage to holy places 2.223, 7.415–18, 13.54, 13.79, 20.455–6; prostrations 13.79; seven (or eight) offerings 13.255; Tibetan incense 26.495; worship of the three family protectors 2.173; *yab-yum* figures regarded as extremely sacred 4.143

rituals and ceremonies
accompanied by instrumental music 8.532, 11.228–9; alcohol used in Tibetan ritual 13.25, 22.399; the exoticism (to Westerners) of a Tibetan puja 11.229; light refreshments 11.229; long-life ceremony 10.585; symbolically significant 11.209

festivals
the Great Prayer Festival 24.310; New Year celebrations (horse races in Maitreya's honour) 2.179, 2.219, 4.108; Shaga Dawa (celebration of the Buddha's Enlightenment) 2.227

LAY PEOPLE AND LAMAS

lay life and practice
a constant coming and going between houses and monasteries 13.55; divide income between needs, pleasure, and Dharma 13.53, 16.401, 18.62–3, 21.329; home shrines 13.54; inspired by *Jātakas* 3.86; meditation and mantra chanting 5.576, 5.584–5, 13.53; names 13.31, 18.150; take the Dharma very seriously 18.301–2; better to practise one precept properly 13.53, 18.487–8; women in Tibetan Buddhism 13.54, 24.389; worship of the three family protectors 2.173

lamas
introduction 12.12–20; the art of weather-making 13.643; both scholars and meditators, like a mix of Bertrand Russell and St John of the Cross 13.108; difference between spiritual attainment and ecclesiastical status 19.359; disastrously regarded as infallible 2.565; exorcism is almost a full-time occupation for some lamas 19.550; the lama as a fourth Jewel of Buddhism 13.49; 'lama' translates the Sanskrit *uttama*, 'superior' 13.49; a lama who taught effectively despite his disreputable behaviour 13.177–8, 19.162–3; lamas invited to sit with *bhikkhus* 22.332; lamas in relation to the three *yānas* 12.15–18; lamas who live in a grand style, impressive and elevating 18.157; may or may not be monks 3.408, 12.14; no difference in attainment between married and celibate lamas 2.445–6, 11.571; not to be confused with *bhikṣus* 3.408; often don't bother to teach the Refuges and Precepts 19.489; publicity claiming authority for lamas 15.720; referred to not by name but by title 25.92; 'to be without a lama is to be no better than an animal' 19.71; the persona of Tibetan lamas 19.122; their encyclopaedic knowledge 13.108; the view that authority rests with the lama 11.655; Vinaya 14.30–1; 'Your movement's all right, but you haven't had teachings from lamas' 19.522

tulkus and incarnate lamas
belief that some lamas could postpone Enlightenment 17.411; the bodhisattva's manifestation as a *tulku* 2.183; Buddha-nature's compassion aspect brought out in the *tulku* doctrine 7.397; careful scrutiny of incarnate lamas 10.38; some confusion about whether *tulkus* are incarnate lamas 12.16–17, 22.487; discovery of *tulkus* 2.183, 3.134; the doctrine emphasizes the compassion aspect of the Buddha-nature 7.397; etiquette with respect to incarnate

lamas 22.521–2; an incarnate lama who became a Christian 22.492; 'incarnations' who didn't think they were reincarnations at all 19.359, 22.491–2; matters of protocol 22.498–9; might their special qualities come from their exceptional upbringing? 22.488; only one female *tulku* (Samding Dorje Phagmo or Dorje Lamo) 12.16, 13.53, 18.109; progress through the six stages of monastic training 13.49; and rebirth 2.182–3; returning to their previous monasteries 17.411–12; a series of personalities dedicated to Enlightenment through a succession of lives 2.182; some lines start from a historical figure, some from an archetypal bodhisattva 2.182–3; the practical wish to know exactly where a bodhisattva would be reborn 12.16; they don't come into the structure of lama training 13.49; *tulkus* who are *śrāmaṇeras* 22.490–1; the view that very few *tulkus* are really incarnate bodhisattvas 17.412; the word corresponds to the Sanskrit *nirmāṇakāya* 2.182, 22.487

MONASTIC LIFE

life in the monastery
the architecture of the *gompa* 13.62; attitude to work 15.279; curfew 13.50; embroidery 4.288; 'like a factory' (Geshe Rabten) 8.517, 17.686; 'going with boys' in monasteries 13.612, 22.521; the monastery whose tea urn still contained a drop from Tsongkhapa's day 17.695; music and chanting in liturgical services 13.50–1; the secular power of religious communities 8.514

Samye monastery
built after the model of the Odantapuri Monastery in India 13.10; on Atīśa's visit he found texts that were no longer available in India 12.577; consecration 12.294; destroyed by the Chinese 13.10; the first Buddhist monastery in Tibet 12.292, 12.725 (n201); built by Śāntarakṣita and Padmasambhava 12.292, 12.317–18, 13.10; Rechungpa wants to visit the temple 19.334–5; the Samye Debate 13.11–12, 13.673 (n1); its symbolic design, with a temple to Avalokiteśvara 12.292

other monasteries
Drepung 2.191, 13.33, 22.476; Dungkar Gompa 1.342–3, 26.229; Ganden 13.33, 13.36, 13.40; Ghoom monastery, *see under* Ghoom; Reting, near Lhasa, founded by Drömton 12.578; Sera 8.516–17, 13.33; Tashi Lhunpo 13.35–6; Tholing, Ngari, Atīśa's headquarters in Tibet 12.574–7; Tsaparang, *see under* Govinda

SCHOOLS OF TIBETAN BUDDHISM

introduction
brief introduction 19.404; extensive account 13.15–34; the schools are distinctive, but not exclusive 13.15–17; the schools cannot be distinguished as either Tantric or non-Tantric 13.19; how the schools arose 13.16–17; the suffix '*-pa*' means 'man' or 'person' 13.17; the tolerance of the schools for each other 13.110–11; 'unreformed' and 'reformed' schools 13.17; what the schools have in common 13.17–20

Gelug (New Kadampa)
introduction 13.30–4; based on the Kadam school 12.579; classification of the Kangyur 14.256; connection with the original Indian Buddhist literature 17.451–2; continued to flourish after Tsongkhapa's death 13.35–6; the Dalai Lama's affiliation with the Gelug school 13.35–6; differs from the other schools only in being more exclusively monastic 7.482; doctrine that the three *yānas* are successive stages of a single path 1.361; faith in the power of logic to convey the truth of the Dharma 17.376; formalized debate is very popular with the Gelugpas 13.47; founded by Tsongkhapa 1.383, 2.182, 13.17, 13.30–2, 13.214–15, 23.382; *Lam-rim chen-mo* and *sNgags-rim chen-mo*, *see under* Tsongkhapa/works; lineage 19.404; Mañjughoṣa an important figure 17.463; an overemphasis on scholastic studies 8.517; of purely Tibetan origin 13.17; the 'reformed' school 13.17; Refuge Tree 11.713, 13.215; Sangharakshita's friendships with Gelugpas 1.10; the school of the Dalai Lamas 12.579; take tantras on wine and sexual intercourse symbolically 1.383; tease the Nyingmapas about the power of their initiations 13.111, 18.498; tend to consult the literature before acting 12.299, 13.24, 17.376; tradition of public debate 18.168; Vajrabhairava their tutelary deity 2.178, 19.405; the 'Virtuous' school 13.30, 13.32, 23.382; 'Yellow Hat' monks 13.32–3, 21.177–8

Kadam school
founded by Atīśa 12.578, 19.404; based on the word (*ka*) of the Buddha 12.578; begun by Dromtön, Atīśa's disciple 8.528, 12.577–9; ecumenical, paid particular attention to six non-canonical works 12.158–9; the history of the lineage 8.528; the Kadam precept, the teaching addressed just to you 8.528, 18.393; *Kadamthorbu* 8.528, 8.593; the basis for the Gelug school 12.579

Kagyu
introduction 13.26–8; its basic view is that *śūnyatā* and *rūpa* are not-two 19.371; emphasis on inspiration and personal experience 17.376; emphasis on practice as opposed to books and words 13.27–8, 18.168, 18.180, 18.380; emphasis on speaking to people deeply, their irrational side as well 19.109; free expression of positive emotion 19.125; its highest teaching is the *mahāmudrā* 18.65; Kagyupas do not bother about monastic ordination 18.177; offshoots called the Black Hats or White Hats 13.32; rejection of the tradition of scholastic debate 18.168; the resolution of disputes in the lineage 19.149–51; three levels of ethical practice 18.84; the six yogas of Nāropā 13.28; the unconventional behaviour of the gurus of the lineage 13.177, 19.160; the wearing of the *repa* (cotton garment) 13.27, 18.462; Karma Kagyu (sub-school of the Kagyu) 2.747 (n704)

the 'whispered lineage' (Kagyu)
founded by Milarepa 13.26–8, 13.214, 18.14, 18.65, 18.168, 18.186, 19.339, 19.569; pure inspiration 18.180; Vajradhāra to Tilopa to Nāropā to Marpa to Milarepa 1.276, 7.475, 19.404; why it is called 'whispered' 13.26, 18.96

Nyingma
introduction 13.20–6, 22.462; the 'Old Style' school 1.383, 12.298, 13.20, 23.382; the disastrous consequences of Nyingma literalism 1.383; don't look *back* to the Buddha, but look *up* 22.467; Dudjom Khyentse Rimpoche's book on its history and teachings 12.443; the emphasis of the practice is on the Vajrayāna 13.23; an emphasis on meditation 13.24; founded by Padmasambhava 1.383, 12.298, 13.11, 19.404, 23.382; guardian deities 22.506–7; incorporated indigenous traditions from the Bön cult 1.383; inspiration from the Yogācāra 17.451; made a great thing of handing on esoteric teachings 18.498; the nine *yānas* are the basis of Nyingma practice 13.21–3; the nature of Nyingma lamas 12.298–9, 13.24–6, 18.177; Nyingma tantras 13.23; Padmanarteśvara their tutelary deity 2.178; practise *ati-yoga* (Dzogchen) 12.299; the 'Red Hat' tradition 12.298, 13.32; revere Samantabhadra 22.462; the richest form of Tibetan Buddhism 13.21; *rinchen terma*, *see termas*; the symbolism of the 'Four Bodies' 19.201; take tantras on wine and sexual intercourse literally 1.383; they made a living experience of the Abhidharma 17.494; the 'unreformed' school 22.473; underestimation of the Nyingma 1.9–10

Sakya
introduction 13.28–30; Büton 13.29; and Drokmi 13.28; founded by Könchok Gyalpo 13.28; Kublai Khan 13.29–30; lineage 19.404; Phagpa (or Pakpa), the head of the school 4.123, 13.29–30; political power 13.29; *sakya* in this context means 'tawny earth' 13.28; Sakyapas are distinguished for their scholarship 13.29; succession between two branches of the same family 13.28–9; they converted the Mongols to Buddhism 13.29

Zhiche ('Pacification')
founded by Phadampa 4.362

MONKS AND NUNS

monks
Sarvāstivādin monastic ordination brought to Tibet by Śāntarakṣita 2.745 (n696); artist monks 13.52; called *trapas* (or *drapas*), 'students', because they study all their lives 12.14, 13.50; belong to the Sarvāstivāda *nikāya* 13.44; *dubdor* (fighting monk) 22.521; lifestyle 13.50–2; medically trained monks 13.51; (1) *genye* (Tibetan *upāsaka*) 12.14, 13.44–5; (2) *getsul* (Tibetan *śrāmaṇera*) 12.14, 13.45, 22.520; (3) *gelong* (Tibetan *bhikkhu*) 7.481, 7.483–4, 12.14, 13.45; (4) *geshe* 8.515–16, 13.45–8, 17.573, 19.374; (5) *lama gyupa* ('the lama of the lineage') 13.47–8, 13.50; (6) *khenpo* ('abbot', equivalent to *upādhyāya*) 7.474, 13.48–50; 'Rimpoche' ('precious one') refers to the fourth, fifth, and sixth classes of monk 13.50; robes 13.52; Tibetan monks take an intense interest in the Vinaya 7.481–2; to speak of a 'married monk' is a confusion 12.14; *tulkus*' progress through the six stages of monastic training 13.49; two lineages of ordination 7.473–4

nuns (genyen, Tibetan equivalent of upāsikā)
the order of nuns died out 18.42; there were never fully ordained *bhikṣuṇīs* in Tibet, just *genyemas* and *getsulmas* 13.52; three kinds of nun 13.52–3

see also
chöd practice; Dalai Lama; Dzogchen; fortune-telling; four *mūla yogas*; how Buddhism came to Tibet, *see under* Tibet/history; gurus/*vajraguru*; *yānas*/nine *yānas*; *sādhana* practice, *see* visualization; sexo-yogic practices, *see under* sexual activity; Tantric initiation, *see abhiṣeka*; the Yogācāra and Tibetan Buddhism, *see under* Yogācāra

Tibetan wheel of life *see* wheel of life

ticīvara *see under* robes

tidiness 9.420, 9.445–6, 23.168–9

Tiepolo, Giovanni Battista 23.257, 23.511 (n291), 24.599

tigers apology for destroying their habitat 25.447; doubt as a tiger to be killed (*Dhammapada*) 15.41, 15.745 (n18); footprints spotted 20.380, 20.398; 'I felt as if I were a tiger cub' 18.582; Milarepa meditates in the tiger-cave of Singa-dzong 18.41–2, 18.51–2; the starving tigress, *see under Jātakas*; the tiger and the sheep (illustrating the strength and potential of human beings) 10.167, 10.237–8; the tiger in the deep forest 19.340; 'The tigers of wrath are wiser than the horses of instruction' 18.78; 'Tyger, Tyger, burning bright' 19.563

tightrope correspondence between Nietzsche's 'tightrope over an abyss' and the Buddhist path 3.503; tightrope between pleasure without craving and non-craving without eliminating pleasure 19.382

Tijang Rimpoche 8.659, 8.663

ṭīkās 1.299

Tilak, Bal Ganghadar v24

Tillett, Gregory 24.213

Tillich, Paul 12.5, 12.701 (n3)

Tillopāda 1.382

Tillyard, E. M. W. 12.76

Tiloka (founder of Kagyu school) 1.276

tiloka *see trailokya*

Tilopa 18.382–3

time

the nature of time
what is time? 3.112; Buddhism as a meditation on time 26.296; any moment is infinitely divisible 17.367; the 'dark backward and abysm of time' 3.32, 7.342, 23.310; it belongs to the mundane world, not ultimate truth 17.365, 17.468, 19.435; it passes by more and more quickly 24.89; a *paññatti*, a concept (Abhidharma) 19.85; part of our structure of consciousness 26.49; part of our way of perceiving reality 14.606, 19.85; the relativity of time 14.162; there is only ever just one time 16.439; threefold: past and future (conceived) and present (perceived) 8.289; 'Time, like an ever-rolling stream ...' 26.294, 26.500–1; we divide it into minutes, but is it really divided at all? 17.494; we perceive the world in terms of time, but in reality there is no coming or going 17.365; we tend to think that everything must have a beginning in time 16.388

our perception of time
breaking through mechanical time 11.9–10; could there be a wrong time to listen to the Dharma? 15.437–9; humans are conscious of the passing of time in a way animals aren't 15.304; 'It was as though time stood still' 23.264, 24.67, 26.589; organic time and clock time 11.9–10, 11.16; primitive man had no mechanical sense of time 3.424; Sangharakshita is given a watch 9.499, 11.542–3, 23.36; experience of travelling (imaginatively) back in time 7.342; the feverish pace of modern life 8.290–1; the oppression of time 16.322; self-consciousness involves a degree of separation from the present 3.565; a sense of ancient time in Nepal 7.342–4; a sense of ourselves as continuous entities moving through time 15.306; 'We have forgotten the passing of days and hours' 2.404, 25.310

images and symbols
'footprints in the sands of time' 8.232; images for time 26.294–5; *kāla-cakra* (wheel of time) synonymous with *prajñā-upāya* 1.386; Krishna as the All-Destroyer, Time 10.56; prisoner of time 9.499, 11.543, 23.35; St Jerome's hourglass 26.292–3, 26.295–6; time as a healer 26.25; time in English poetry 26.293–6

the use of time
Dr Ambedkar' example of how to use time well 10.322; the amount of time spent preparing food 17.11–12; the benefit of pausing between activities 5.77–8; beware of the idea that our purpose is to fill our time with useful activities 18.120; choosing the right time to speak 8.xxiv, 8.173, 17.231–2, 19.556; continuity of purpose over time 3.564–5, 3.567–8; dealing with one thing at a time in old Tibet 18.220; devoting one's limited time to helping those who are doing a lot for the world 19.539; don't wait until you have more time, do it now 17.163; giving one's time 1.500; the gods face the problem of what to do with their time, as do we 12.355; how best to use our time 9.530, 25.113; how we spend our time as an indicator of future rebirth 17.526–7; making the best possible use of every hour still remaining to me 23.465; the more time-saving devices one has, the more pressed for time one becomes 8.290;

'Only by instant action can you succeed!' 18.153; periods of internal activities, then external 4.461–4; a phase of study followed by a phase of meditation 4.568–9; time is short, but that is no reason for being in a hurry 26.49; make best use of time to practise the Dharma 10.322–3, 11.652, 12.543, 19.244–5; when morality is pure and clear consciousness established, not a minute is wasted 1.151; the art of life is being able to do one thing at a time 5.681, 26.17; the unskilfulness of taking time from another person 2.366

wasting time
clinging to one-sided views is a waste of time 10.598; don't waste time with spiritual friends talking about trivial things 18.567; the French nun is horrified to be told she needs to learn to waste time 14.520–1; get on with Dharma practice and don't waste time in regrets 22.477; if you mean to attain Stream Entry, there is no time to waste 15.210–11; it's a pity to waste time on anything that doesn't enhance the quality of one's life 26.68; no time to waste 18.489; some phases are not a 'stage of development', but just a waste of time 19.343; practices are ultimately a waste of time (Zen) 13.364; there is no time in life for misunderstandings 26.82; through procrastination 7.172; 'I wasted time and now doth time waste me' (*Richard II*) 3.419; wasting someone's time 17.198; wasting time with trivial pursuits 10.322, 12.355

time and space
the absolute *bodhicitta* transcends time and space 4.31; the archetypal bodhisattva: the ideal in the process of realization within space 4.191; the function of the *bodhicitta* is to transcend spatial–temporal models 3.16–17; the Buddha manifests something beyond time and space 18.86; determined by consciousness 2.67; the Dharma is not limited by space or time 10.245–6; Enlightenment beyond time and space 3.146, 19.34; existence determined by time and space 16.527; the expression 'outside space and time' is self-contradictory 19.436; the gestalt is in terms of space what the continuum is in terms of time 19.239–40; of God's attributes only two are known to us: space and time (Spinoza) 4.203; going beyond time and space 16.101; if discussions about time and space go over your head, don't worry 19.436; it's very difficult for us to think in non-spatial terms 18.607; methods to realize the relativity of time and space 18.544–5; *mettā* is not limited by time or space 15.299; Nirvāṇa is beyond time and space 16.389; not easy to reconcile the language of time with the language of space 4.33; not objective realities, but forms of our perception 2.63, 3.149, 17.385; the path implies time, the mandala implies space 18.584, 19.436–7; re-experiencing a moment in childhood transcends time and space 17.402–3; represented in the *White Lotus Sūtra* 16.65; space and time are strange things 24.147; the *Śūraṅgama-samādhi Sūtra* is beyond time and space 26.546; there are infinitely more attributes of which we know nothing 14.603; time and space are in the mind 18.545, 19.84–5; time and space disappear (*Gaṇḍavyūha Sūtra*) 14.219; time, like space, is curved 26.49; vastness of sphere of mundane existence in time and space 1.38; we inevitably arrive at either a spatial or a temporal model of reality 4.203; we speak in space- and time-bound language 18.607, 19.436–7

outside time
an encounter with someone outside time 18.69; an experience neither past nor present, a process outside time 18.613; going outside time: seeing your original face before you were born 13.141, 16.92–3; how can the transition from dualism to insight be a matter of time? 16.112–13; however far back we go in time, we never reach where our ignorance began 16.219; in order to realize wisdom you have to go outside time 19.435–6; parables take place outside time 16.171; real satisfaction is possible only outside time 17.408

time and Enlightenment
Enlightenment takes place outside time 19.435; Nirvāṇa is a living process that continues beyond time 17.357; one does not attain Enlightenment either slowly or quickly 13.11–12; the timeless nature of Enlightenment symbolized by the Ādibuddha 18.94

see also
kalpa; time and eternity, *see under* eternity

time of day different moods at different times 20.187; what time of day to meditate 4.574–5, 4.577

timeless every moment is timeless, because every moment is unique 18.159; 'the intersection of the timeless moment' 3.145; the timeless nature of Enlightenment, symbolized by the Ādibuddha 18.94

Timiratipiṅgala (the great fish) 14.91

Timmins, Freddie 26.418

Tinnevelly, India 4.625–6, 20.235

Tintoretto (Jacopo Comin) 23.255, 23.511 (n288), 24.586, 26.253

Tiphupa (Dipupa) 18.518–19

Tipiṭaka *see* Tripiṭaka

Tiratana Vandanā (Salutation to the Three Jewels)

INTRODUCTION

the Pāli text
in the *Mahāparinibbāna Sutta* 2.343, 3.627 (n13), 15.493, 19.600 (n60); Buddhaghosa's discussion of the text 3.650 (n156), 19.600 (n60); not everyone likes chanting it in Pāli 19.134; Pāli text in full 15.458–60

Sangharakshita and the text
haunted by the words 'May grace abound and victory!' 2.426; he recited it every morning 2.425–6, 21.429; his translation 15.xii, 15.458–60, 20.434; seminar (*Salutation to the Three Jewels*) 15.xx, 15.457–540

SALUTATION TO THE BUDDHA

introduction
homage to the Buddha 1.179, 1.282–3; opening salutation 15.461–71; Going for Refuge to the Buddha 15.497; Buddhas of past, present, and future 15.498; 'by the power of this truth' 15.500–1; reciting it gives a sense of the Buddha being our spiritual friend 26.636

the terms used
bhagavato 15.461–2; *arahato* 15.462–3; *sammāsambuddhassa* 15.463–9; *vijjā-caraṇa-sampanno* (the one fully endowed with knowledge and practice) 2.127, 15.471–5; *sugato* (or *sugata*) 3.315, 10.198, 14.404, 14.548, 15.477–8; *lokavidū* 12.528, 15.491–3; *anuttaro purisadammasārathi* 2.343, 2.706 (n419), 15.493–4; *satthā devamanussānaṃ* (teacher of gods and men) 1.33, 3.69, 15.495–6, 26.603

SALUTATION TO THE DHARMA

introduction
introduction to the text 10.242–7, 15.501–12; asking yourself what the words really mean 10.242; in just a few words it gives us a clear idea of the nature of the Dharma 3.160; the well-known formula 7.229, 7.493; what is meant by 'Dharma' in this context 15.501

(1) svākkhāto bhagavatā dhammo (well-communicated)
the Dharma of the Blessed One 15.501–2; the many ways the Buddha communicated the Dharma 3.160–2, 10.243–4; the outcome of the Buddha's spiritual experience 10.156

(2) sandiṭṭhiko (immediately apparent)
can you see immediate results of practice? 15.502–5; you will see the results of your practice in this lifetime 3.162, 10.156, 10.244–5

(3) akāliko (not connected with time)
the culture may be different, but the Dharma is the same 3.162, 10.245–6; always fresh, appropriate, relevant 25.30–1; never out of date 10.156–7, 15.505; principles which are true in all times and all places 1.55, 9.314; the word used in the *Dhammapada* 15.505–6

(4) ehipassiko ('come and see', of the nature of a personal invitation)
come and taste it for yourself 10.568; an invitation to explore the world of Buddhist literature 14.xvi; learning to understand what we need to learn 3.xv; make the experiment, live the life: all that Buddhism asks us to do 7.128, 11.110; to be verified for yourself 3.15, 3.162–3, 10.246–7, 10.331–2, 12.136; no one can experience reality for us 10.141; no one can practise the Dharma for you 10.267–8, 11.703; the original Pāli is very forceful 15.506–7; a scientific approach 22.157–8

(5) opanayiko (progressive, leading forward)
both spiritual and material 10.156; demonstration of the Dharma's progressive effect 9.293; the Dharma is progressive in the cultural and spiritual sense 3.163, 10.247; a path of regular steps 15.507–10

(6) paccataṃ veditabbo viññūhi (to be understood individually, by the wise)
part of the central tradition of Buddhism 13.492; if it isn't experienced personally, it isn't really the Dharma 15.510–11; nobody else can practise it for you 3.163, 10.247; no one can purify another of ignorance 10.156; take things on trust only provisionally 15.510–11

SALUTATION TO THE SANGHA

introduction
the eight holy persons, *see under* holy persons; the Sangha *vandana* 15.539

the terms used
sāvakasaṅgho 15.512–13; *supaṭipanno* 15.513; *ujupaṭipanno* 15.513–14;

ñāyapaṭipanno 15.514–15; *sāmīcipaṭipanno* 15.515–17; *aṭṭha purisapuggalā* 15.518, 15.642–3; *āhuneyyo, pāhuṇeyyo* 15.534; *añjalikaraṇīyo* 15.534–8; *punnakkhettam lokassa'ti* (a field of merit for the world) 15.580–1, 19.220–1

Tiratanaloka women's retreat centre *see under* Triratna IV/retreat centres

tiredness and exhaustion becoming tired of the old self 16.227–8; being exhausted and worn away by work 4.627, 18.201–3; the bodhisattva never becomes tired of working for universal salvation 4.85–6; carrying on when you feel tired 18.617–18; don't allow yourself to get too tired 5.387; exhausting the spiritual resources you have built up 19.550; exhausting struggles between the 'higher' and 'lower' aspects of personality 7.401; exhaustion is a typically modern complaint 18.338; feeling fresh and rested despite exertion 22.364; the long and weary round of life after life and death after death 7.49; meditating when tired 18.555; in modern times people may be too emotionally exhausted to respond to the spiritual ideal 18.274; 'O I am tired of strife and song' 7.56; the spiritual community distributes work so that no one has to exhaust themselves 18.203; talking exhausts energy, but real communication heightens energy 4.482; the tiredness of people one sees in the city 18.424; tiredness on solitary retreat 5.678–80; trying to communicate with people can be exhausting 19.550; sloth and torpor, *see under* five hindrances

Tiresias 25.420

Tirokuḍḍa Sutta 15.xiii, 15.67–8

tīrthika, tīrthakara ('ford-maker') 7.524

Tirumal Nayak 20.232–3

Tiruvannamalai, India 20.335–48

tisaraṇa **or** ***triśaraṇa*** *see* Three Refuges

Tisch, Bernie *see* Gunapala

Tissa (the Buddha's cousin) 1.81–2

Tissa Buddha 1.45

Titian (Tiziano Vecelli) *Bacchus and Ariadne* 26.218; his genius 15.194; a great colourist 26.253, 26.441; the idealization of women in his paintings 24.461; *Sacred and Profane Love* 23.308; *Salome* 25.376; various references v24; in Verona 23.255

Tittleshall *see under* Norfolk

toddy-tappers 20.283–4

toilets an Italian toilet 23.253; Ucchuṣma, the deity of the toilet 18.426

tolerance

etymology, definitions, meanings
the ability to accept difference with the difference giving rise to unskilful states 11.671; an aspect of *kṣānti* 4.123–7; connection with Atlas, from Greek mythology 7.379; no word for tolerance in Sanskrit or Pāli 4.169, 7.378–9, 7.384; not vague or woolly 4.124; really a modern word for *upāya*, skilful means 7.384; sometimes confused with pseudo-egalitarianism 4.126

in Buddhism
because Buddhists are convinced of the relativity of their own doctrines 22.268; Buddhism has been persecuted, but has not retaliated with persecution 7.127, 11.360; Buddhist reformations without force or bloodshed 12.116; a characteristic of the English, so a point of affinity with Buddhism 12.75; 'everybody ... free to follow the form of Buddhism they like best' 4.123, 13.29–30; has carried tolerance of what did not belong to it to an extreme 2.220; the idea of tolerance struck early Western Buddhists forcibly 12.464; indifference is the near enemy of tolerance 1.428, 10.83; maintained tolerance for indigenous faiths in the countries to which it spread 7.144; the nature of Buddhist tolerance 7.378–84, 8.xxiii–v, 22.529–30; Buddhism is prepared to respect and even admire other spiritual leaders 2.243; tolerance does not mean condoning untruth and error 8.204; tolerance of Buddhist schools for one another 1.205–6, 7.439, 10.282, 21.245; *Tolerance, a Study from Buddhist Sources* 22.528; the tolerance of Tibetan Buddhists 13.110–11; tolerance towards other religions 7.127, 7.439, 12.137, 15.265, 15.670–1, 17.21, 26.58; a tolerant and peaceful record 9.472, 9.495–6, 10.171, 16.72; why is Buddhism so tolerant? 7.142–5, 7.318, 9.183, 11.360

other interpretations of tolerance
Christian tolerance a product of impotence and indifference 7.381; confusing and misleading ideas in Hinduism 22.528–9; how does a tolerant belief protect itself from an intolerant one? 4.127; the ideal of tolerance in society 26.74; a mixed blessing: example of unhelpful tolerance in Nepal 7.346–7

the practice of tolerance
accepting that the other person has the right to think differently from you 17.53; based on a realization that all beings are a network, parts of one body 4.405; be tolerant towards others' spiritual practice, not discounting their efforts 18.222; because everybody has to find out the Truth for themselves 3.14–15, 12.136; the chain leading from spiritual experience to tolerance 7.145; for beliefs that contradict your cherished convictions 3.379–80; it doesn't mean intolerance 1.428; to be tolerant does not mean you have to agree with what others say 12.677; tolerance of human frailty 13.477–8

Tolkien, J. R. R. (*The Lord of the Rings*) *asuras* like orcs 2.372; the Black Riders looking for the hobbits at Bree 24.135; and desire to contact the archetypal 16.533; the finger of Mordor 24.43; Sangharakshita reads the book 25.100, 26.625; Sauron compared to Tarpa Nagpo (of the Tibetan tradition) 12.332

Tolstoy, Leo *Anna Karenina* 22.464, 25.104; his wife's help with copying out his work 26.366; his works among the supreme achievements of Western culture 12.392

Tomo Geshe Rimpoche created a vision of Maitreya 1.342; his character 26.230; his fondness for his pets 26.230; his monastery at Ghoom, with its image of Maitreya 13.78, 20.134; imprisonment in Lhasa 22.493–5, 23.397, 26.230; Lama Govinda's guru 6.616, 22.493, 22.496–7; photograph 22.496; his residence in Kalimpong 21.213, 23.397; his vision of lotuses materialized so they could be seen by other people 1.342–3, 26.229; his friendship with Sangharakshita 22.493, 23.397, 26.230; Sangharakshita gives him a Refuge Tree thangka 13.78; celebrating Tsongkhapa at the Triyana Vardhana Vihara 8.659; visits the Triyana Vardhana Vihara 8.663; Sangharakshita and Terry visit him (1966) 23.397–8; his tomb at Dungkar Gompa 1.342–3

Tondo, Niccola di 13.637

Tonypandy, Viscount (George Thomas) 24.244–6

Tooting *see under* London

topsy-turvy views *see* four *viparyāsas*

tormas 22.472–3

torpor (*middha*) *see* five hindrances/sloth and torpor; *see also middha*

Torquay, Devon 18.414, 20.54–67, 23.10

tortoise 25.380

torture 'arguing by torture' 8.170; Christian martyrs feeling joyful even when tortured 4.316; Protestants tortured to death in Colombia 7.380, 8.116, 8.170; self-torture, *see* self-mortification; the worst form of human suffering 26.653

totalitarianism 26.20, 26.654

touch can your level of awareness be raised by the touch of a teacher? 9.528; feeling a breeze that is not blowing 13.291; need for bodily touch 4.562; the touch of *śūnyatā* 5.32, 26.48; *see also* senses

touching the earth the Buddha touches the earth with his big toe (*Vimalakīrti-nirdeśa*) 16.468; *mudrā*, *see mudrās*

Toynbee, Arnold 3.424, 23.202

tradition the effect on the artist of the breakdown of tradition 22.269; the idea of religion as a special form of tradition lost its appeal for Sangharakshita 21.161; finds expression in culture 7.394–5; the knowledge gained by the wise and transmitted to their disciples 7.394; Marco Pallis's views on tradition 21.161; distinction between Tradition and tradition 13.469–74, 13.497–8; tradition can be good or bad 10.154; tradition was once innovation 26.20; traditional authority and charismatic authority 13.468–74; using tradition to purify Buddhism 13.439–40; the question of what is traditional and what is not 13.466–8

traditional costume Burmese 21.127–8; and caste or nationality 21.69; Indian preference for Western dress 21.68–70; Sangharakshita came to see that the issues involved weren't simple 21.161; of

students in Kalimpong 21.100; of Tibet 21.193

traditional society *see under* society

Traductionism 17.468–9

tragedy the Book of Job comes close to being a tragedy 16.423; Elizabeth and Jacobean tragedy 24.182–3; the grief of three queens: a quality of archetypal tragedy 22.13–14; a happy ending is not necessarily an artistic disaster 24.183; an insight contributed by the West 16.422–3; pre-Euripidean Greek tragedy 14.109; a rigid mind tends to invite tragedy 19.86; the tragedy is not that we don't get what we want, but that we get it 26.11; the tragedy of life 3.96; the Path of Vision arising as a result of tragedy 1.480

Traherne, Thomas introduction 16.617 (n249); *Centuries of Meditation* 16.327; 'the dirty devices of this world' 13.31, 17.470

trailokya (Pāli *tiloka*)

introduction
brief description 4.683 (n171), 2.370, 12.370; the meaning of *trailokya* 10.xlvii–viii; the triple world 14.209; an inner imaginal journey through the three realms 26.271–3; the Abhidharma distribution of *cittas* (mental states) among the three *lokas* 12.147; 'all beings in the Three Realms enslaved in a prison of fire' 18.588–90; all planes of conditioned existence 14.309; beauty is usually experienced on the level of the *kāmaloka* or *rūpaloka* 13.279; as a hierarchy 4.169, 14.309; casting aside the bodies of the three worlds 25.194, 25.591 (n57); correspondence with *dhyānas* 2.66–7; desiring the conquest of the three worlds 4.477; each of the *lokas* has a state of consciousness as its subjective counterpart 1.159; experience of craving in the three *lokas* 17.597; even the blissful higher realms are painful compared to Enlightenment 18.589; the mystical in the *trailokya* 8.440; 'the Three Kingdoms are jeopardized by desires' 18.171

kāmaloka (world or plane of sensuous desire)
god realms in the *kāmaloka* 16.344–5; going forth from the *kāmaloka* to the *rūpaloka* 12.558–9; how can concentrating on a sense object lead beyond the *kāmaloka*? 5.570–1; inhabitants 2.66; Māra rules over it 11.402; raising a sexual relationship from the *kāmaloka* to the *rūpaloka* 24.517; the transition from the *kāmaloka* to the *rūpaloka* 2.105, 4.154; turning from the *kāmaloka* to the *rūpaloka* 17.512–14; seen as relatively ugly 2.83–4; we are at home in it, and find it hard to leave even for the pleasure of *dhyāna* 4.153–4; we'll be stuck in it without delight in the beauty of the Unconditioned 2.84–5; the world 11.130–2

rūpaloka (world of form, archetypal realm)
a Buddha-field as a form of *rūpaloka* 14.454–5; inhabitants 2.66; no such thing as sexual dimorphism 2.371; a plane of skilful action and *dhyāna* 11.131; rebirth in the *rūpaloka* 2.73; seen as relatively beautiful 2.83–4; accessed through dreams, the arts, images, myths, symbols, imagination 12.559; where your experience is purely awareness of light 15.239; the world of pure beauty 12.559

arūpaloka (formless world)
inhabitants 2.66; rebirth in the *arūpaloka* 2.73

Trailokya Bauddha Mahasangha Sahayak Gana (TBMSG) *see* Triratna I/Triratna in India

Trailokya Vijaya 3.48, 3.633 (n44)

Trailokyavijaya (bodhisattva) 2.172

training the Buddha as *purisadamma-sārathi* (the charioteer for the training of persons) 2.343; as used by the Buddha, 'training' means not a set of rules but a whole ideal 10.563–4; Greek *askein* (or *ascesis*): we need such a term to express that aspect of spiritual life 4.122, 17.253–4; spiritual friendship a training in egolessness 3.579, 7.293–6, 12.458; spiritual life as training a mettlesome young horse 2.707 (n420); training is not punishment, but a means to achieve a particular end 17.254

see also
gradual training, *see under* gradual; training-rules, *see* precepts

trance of Krishna, the small boy at Muvattupuzha ashram 20.312–15; meditation is not 'trance' 4.584, 11.112, 17.118, 17.124

tranquillity of the bodhisattva 1.269; compassion must be matched by inner tranquillity 4.393; green the colour of peace, calm, and tranquillity 2.387, 13.67, 18.59; the mind made clear and tranquil by a beautiful environment 7.337; the positive counterpart of abstention from covetousness 2.386–7; the tranquil beauty of the life of the Enlightened One 7.33; the tranquillity of nature 15.257;

through friendship we perceive the pure and tranquil lineaments of Enlightenment 21.476; a valley with intense tranquillity 20.341

transcendence Buddhahood is both immanent and transcendent 25.33; friendship is a mutual transcendence of egotism 12.638; polarization with immanence 20.234; self-transcendence, *see* self-transcendence; transcending the human predicament 16.79

transcendental

the term
the use of that terminology 5.266; translation of *lokuttara* (*lokottara*) 3.236, 16.271, 25.144; Sangharakshita always uses it in the sense of *lokuttara* 11.619; the danger of reifying it 11.656; it means transcending the distinction between subject and object 3.481

the Transcendental and the mundane
absolute discontinuity of transcendental and mundane 1.332; the awakening of faith: a reflection of the transcendental in the mundane 18.280; in the last analysis the duality between them disappears 19.49; it's easier to be fascinated by the mundane than the transcendental 17.692; mundane and transcendental morality 11.313–14; *śamatha* experiences are mundane (*laukika*), not transcendental (*lokuttara*) 8.440–1; the transcendental obliterates the mundane 25.82; the transcendental does not negate the mundane 14.496; uniting the best of the mundane with the transcendental 19.44, 19.52–3

the nature of the Transcendental
all conceptual formulations and verbal expressions are symbolical 1.238; gold leaf in works of art, the transcendental breaking through 13.284; it is strange to us 11.xvii, 11.42; it shines just as brightly through myth as through concepts 1.326; its colourful, vibrant aspect 18.372–3; the light in which we see it is also the light in which it sees us 3.481; logical contradiction is the safest way to communicate it 26.207; no words can apply to it 14.585; spontaneity 19.156

relating to it
every transcendentally inspired thought, word, and deed is non-individualistic 1.232; if discussions about it go over your head, don't worry 19.436; if you lose sight of the transcendental element, you lose sight of Buddhism 26.57; the *Kālāma Sutta* is not an invitation to question its existence 1.60; Mahāyāna inspiration from transcendental sources 1.276; the memory of a transcendental experience can sustain one, but only for a time 16.355; positive motivation only possible with reference to it 16.354; those who refuse to accept its existence can never hope to understand the Dharma 1.18; we don't want it just to convince us we want it to coax, even seduce us 13.284, 19.25; you need a personal connection with someone who has experienced it 16.354

approaching it
attraction to it through wisdom, repulsion from it through compassion 1.419–20; can it be approached through the *brahma vihāras*? 5.217–18; contact with reality is made when the mind in *dhyāna* turns to the transcendental 4.159; the goal described as transcendental 11.656; having a glimpse of a glimpse 25.144; to go for Refuge effectively you must intend to aim for the transcendental 11.257; the Tantra asked: if transcendental realities are reflected in the world, where? 1.376; the threshold of the Transcendental 26.280

distinctions
difference between a superconscious and a transcendental state 20.206; discerning higher realms from the transcendental 14.605–6; distinction between spiritual and transcendental 11.131, 16.271, 17.436–7; it's understandable to confuse 'God' with the Transcendental 14.605–6

the Transcendental
compassion a purely transcendental force 1.387–8; the nature of the Buddhas is wholly transcendental (Lokottaravādin doctrine) 1.189–90; transcendental consciousness 3.480–1; the transcendental body of the bodhisattva 1.259; transcendental *ḍākinīs* 18.370–1; the transcendental life is realizing that in the absolute sense the self is unreal 1.402; transcendental *samādhis* 4.159; the Unconditioned as the transcendental 3.236; *vajra*: prefix which denotes transcendental significance 1.385–6; transcendental path, *see under* path/more perspectives

Transcendental Meditation (TM) 12.645, 15.588, 19.460, 23.107

transference of merits *see under* merit

transformation

the aim of transformation
the aim of the Buddhist path is the transformation of consciousness 15.98; the aim of meditation is to transform oneself, not to have good meditations 26.47; made

possible by the principle of conditionality 15.81; the nine transformations 14.215; the philosophical basis of the possibility of transformation 5.352–3; transformation as a model for the spiritual life: death and rebirth 16.227

what is transformed?
Buddhism has to transform every aspect of our lives 26.20; negative mental states must be transformed, not just pushed away 17.369; the potential effect of aesthetic experience 16.285; the transformation of desire 25.248; the transformation of energy 13.173; the transformation of the ordinary human being into a Buddha 18.605; transformation is implicit in every aspect of spiritual life 15.114; transformation must be external as well as internal 19.213; transforming psycho-spiritual energy is the central business of the spiritual life 13.162; the transformation of turbulent energies within the psyche (*dharmapālas*) 19.408; the Vajrayāna belief that everything can be transformed, even killing 19.331; we've got to transform everything with which we come into contact 12.336

the process of transformation
the basis of transformation is meditation 8.611; beauty as an agent of transformation 18.158; brought about by the *parāvṛtti* 2.281; the chakras as the basis for transformation 19.37, 19.40–1; the five wisdoms make the process more concrete 18.606; general and specific transformation: Vision and Transformation 19.42; from ordinary consciousness to meditative consciousness 16.259; human life is a transformation of energy by a process of intermediate steps 2.101–2; insights hold the potential for transformation 2.296; is awareness transformative? 17.539; making change into transformation 13.228, 15.81; Michelangelo expresses his vision in a transformative way 26.246; once you acknowledge a feeling there is a possibility of transforming it 19.395; the spiritual community is where we begin to transform our lives 18.37; transformation through awareness 1.575; transforming the mind through art 26.188–9; that understood as objective transformed into that experienced as subjective 19.199

self-transformation
awareness of the present moment is crucial to self-transformation 15.85; a Buddhist's basic concern is the transformation of mental states 18.511–12; the difficulty of transforming oneself 12.107–8, 16.488; expecting some sort of magic to transform you 18.520; Goethe on self-transformation 11.463; love and passion transformed to brilliance and bliss 25.278; the miracle of self-transformation 12.619; one is transformed specifically, down to the last detail 19.41–2; it paves the way for self-transcendence 11.499; symbols work on us and transform us if we are receptive to them 13.123; transforming your life by doing justice to what you are and what you wish to be 17.364

transformation of self and world
by transforming our level of awareness, we transform the world we live in 15.128; determination to act to transform ourselves and our bit of the world 10.315; the message of Padmasambhava 12.335–6; one foot in the world and one in the spiritual dimension 1.550; Order members seek to transform self *and* world 2.516; in accordance with Perfect Vision 23.110; in the *Sūtra of Golden Light* 16.227–435; what the Buddhist way of life is about 16.228; transformation of world, *see under* world

total transformation
the difficulty of total transformation 19.18–19; Going for Refuge to the Three Jewels must find expression in total transformation 2.325; the point of the Vajrayāna 18.535, 19.42; *śūnyatā* represents the possibility of complete transformation 17.95; supported by *dhyāna* 18.576; the ten precepts and total transformation 2.335–8; through meditation 19.57; your vision starts transforming every aspect of your experience 5.44

Transformation, Path of *see under* Noble Eightfold Path

transience life is transient, but it is also beautiful 26.241–2; penetration into the truth of the transience of all phenomena 1.171; 'Transience' (poem) 25.221; 'When the transiency of life strikes deeply into one's heart' 18.554; You asked, 'What is this transient pattern?' 20.xvii; *see also* impermanence

transition between aesthetic contemplation and practical activity 14.523–4; Enlightenment does not involve a transition of a real person 1.268; experience of the six element practice may help the transition to universal consciousness 4.80; how can the transition to insight be a matter of time? 16.112–13; how to make the transition from the old society to the new

3.462; human beings represent something transitional (Nietzsche) 3.499; 'lightning-like transitional stage' between average person and Stream Entrant 2.142; making the transition from external to internal life 18.302–3; the point of transition from the ignoble quest to the noble quest 7.151; the transition between sensation and craving: the battlefield of the spiritual life 1.111–12; a transition from group existence to the spiritual community 2.415; transition from intellectual understanding to embodied experience 16.186; the transition from the *kāmaloka* to the *rūpaloka* 2.105; the transition from *vijñāna* to *jñāna* 16.186; the transition from the wheel to the spiral 2.259; transition from the world to the world within the world, the sangha 17.111–12; the transition to the second *dhyāna* 5.229; the transitional phases of one's spiritual life 14.599; walking meditation as a transition from spiritual practice to the ordinary world 5.82–3

transitoriness all things are transitory 7.48–9; Buddhism doesn't have a monopoly on transitoriness 18.565; desire for the transitory is doomed to disappointment 7.307; even the *dhyānas* are inherently painful, transitory, and insubstantial 1.444; hell exists in the Buddhist ethical system, but transitory, not eternal 3.316, 16.282; 'It is after the manner of transitoriness' 18.xi; only one exceptionally deep in love with life will find it sweeter for its transitoriness 1.129; our infatuation with transitory pleasures prevents us from seeing the fact of suffering 7.388–9; *see also* impermanence

translation definitions 13.505; the beauty of the language [of a translation] has its own value 16.444; the best translations are re-creations of the meaning of the original 26.445; bringing something up from the depths or down from the heights 26.238–9; collaboration of scholar and sage 19.542; 'cultural translation' (Mellor) 13.505–6; the danger of translating poetry into prose 14.301, 14.304; even a clumsy translation by someone with insight can open the reader's Dharma eye 1.23–4; every language is unique, so completely faithful translation is hardly possible 26.445–6; the expression of one mode or degree of knowledge in terms of another 13.505; how does one translate knowledge? 26.301–5; the impact on Buddhism in the West of new translations 17.453–4; an individual, even solitary activity 26.305; the meaning of translator 2.525–6; the only way you can translate Dharma is to *become* Dharma 11.xix; Sangharakshita as (metaphorical) translator 2.526–7, 11.xvi–xvii, 23.xvi–xvii; spirit and letter of translation 14.15; standardization of translation of Buddhist terms into Tibetan 13.12–13; to translate is to interpret 14.328, 26.302; translating Buddhist terms into English 8.596–7; translating what one has experienced in the heights or depths 25.li, 26.305; translation as a journey 11.xvii–xviii; *see also* Jerome, St

translations of Buddhist texts *see under* scriptures/translation

transmission can Enlightenment really be transmitted? 19.402–4; and the eighty-four *siddhas* 7.507; four transmissions: ordination, the scriptures, the doctrine, the spirit of Buddhism 13.338–43; the Heart-Doctrine transmitted from the Buddha to his disciples 7.360; knowledge gained by the wise and transmitted to their disciples 7.394; the letter can be learned from books, but the spirit must be transmitted heart to heart 7.543, 18.181; like the planting of a seed 13.215–16; like a relay of flaming torches 14.453; one has to be cautious when using the language of transmission 18.314–15; the place of transmission in Buddhism 19.402–4; a spiritual chain reaction, not the handing down of an object or role 18.93–4; in Tantric Buddhism 3.82, 14.16–17; there is not some *thing* that is passed on 14.453; the transmission of the essence of the great masters 22.407; transmission of the Dharma through words 3.82; the transmission of energy from one person to another 19.327–8; a transmission of spiritual power from guru to disciple 13.88–9; the *vidyādharas*' transmission of the Dharma 3.82; what is transmitted? 13.216

see also
lineage; *abhiṣeka*; telepathy; oral transmission of teachings, *see* oral tradition; the 'whispered transmission', *see under* Tibetan Buddhism/schools; Zen

The Transmission of the Lamp of the Dharma 12.675

transmutation 1.391

transparency the *arūpa dhyānas* render the fully conscious mind subtler and more 'transparent' 2.110; complete transparency in the sangha 11.137–8, 11.386; doctrines are to be refined to such transparency that Enlightenment shines through 2.61; Mahāyāna doctrine is transparent 1.239;

the mind is limpid 18.236; through the door of emptiness you see that everything is transparent 3.219–20; the transparency of consciousness 8.616

transpersonal forms (horizontal and vertical) 13.385, 13.391–2, 13.420, 13.458–9, 13.471

transport (a random mixture) bicyclists in Edwardian costume 24.387; a cart pulled by women and girls 22.99–100; the effect on consciousness of the speed of aeroplane travel 8.290–1; first flight in an aeroplane 21.265–9; the steam train at Darjeeling 13.101, 18.63, 21.331; travel by bullock-cart 7.468, 10.xxxix, 10.xliii, 10.143, 22.96

transsexuality the difficult journey from one gender to the other 26.655; one should aim for a provisional identification with one's psycho-physical sex 2.373; one should not think of oneself as a man or a woman in any absolute sense 2.372; a bodhisattva who changes to female and back to male, to 'liberate the lustful' 14.182; *The First Man-Made Man* 11.710; Jivaka's sex change 11.710, 22.434–6, 22.439, 22.519–20, 23.388; a little girl transforms herself into a boy (in a Mahāyāna *sūtra*) 14.183–4; a *nāga* princess who transforms herself into a male bodhisattva (*Lotus Sūtra*) 14.110, 14.122; not so much the body but the mind that has to be transformed 11.710; Princess Sorrowless Giving changes her female body into a male one 14.184; Śāriputra changed from male to female and back (*Vimalakīrti-nirdeśa*) 14.164–5, 16.538–9, 22.435; spiritual significance of sex change 16.538–9; spontaneous sex changes described in the Pāli canon 22.435, 22.616–17 (n338); the transformation of Avalokiteśvara into female form 1.336, 2.175, 7.124, 26.599, 26.655

transvestites 23.196

trap Ajātaśatru's fear that Jīvaka is leading him into a trap, *see under* Ajātasattu; avoid any feeling that you're trapped in the family situation against your will 18.455–8; energy trapped in sexual channels 1.390; the sexual relationship like a lobster pot, easy to get into but difficult to get out of 26.79; even in pursuit of spiritual training one can entrap oneself further in time, place, personality 18.31; 'the trap of nothingness' 18.179; trapped by craving like fish in the mouth of a net 10.617–18; we need to make sure we are not falling into the trap of consumerism 10.lxii

Trapuṣa *see* Tapussa

Travancore, South India (Kerala) Maharaja of Travancore 20.249–51; Sangharakshita stays in Travancore for a year and a half 20.241 et seq.; 'unseeability' in Travancore 10.186, 20.284

travel broadens the mind 9.371–2, 9.373; crossing the Alps: of psychological and spiritual significance 23.249; the dangers and significance of travel in medieval Tibet 18.325–6, 19.367; the difficulty of meditating while travelling 19.346; gives one the experience of isolation 4.530–1; and going forth 12.556–7; helps one see the limitations of one's own conditioning 3.39, 3.468; much enjoyed in modern times 3.441; the ocean frog and the frog in the well, *see* parables and stories; the pleasure and beauty of travelling by air 19.93–4; practising meditation while travelling 19.549–50; the speed of modern travel can't be good for us 18.337; a tendency to be conservative about travel as one gets older 11.14; travel gave Dr Ambedkar a universal outlook 9.372; travel 'with a humble and merry mind' 18.325; in ancient India, young monks might travel to learn from different *ācāryas* 2.198; is travel helpful to spiritual development? – pros and cons 19.346–8; a way of overcoming one's conditioning 11.13–14; why do you really want to go to (say) Italy? 19.347–8

Trāyastriṃśa Heaven (Pāli Tāvatiṃsa) *see* heavens/of the Thirty-three

treasure Abundant Treasures (Buddha), *see under White Lotus Sūtra*; all spiritual treasures are dug up from the depths of the Enlightened mind 12.214; the element of Tathāgatahood is present in all, 'like a treasure hidden in the soil' 1.275; the 'golden treasure underground' 19.497; the hidden treasure of the mind 15.277; in Indra's palace 16.346; 'May I be an inexhaustible treasure ...' 1.415–16; mind-treasures 22.538; *Nidhikaṇḍa Sutta* ('The Buried Treasure'), *see Nidhikaṇḍa Sutta*; 'One's enemies are to be prized and treasured' 4.410; prayer that 'I may enter deeply into the *sūtra*-treasure' 2.5; spiritual treasures (*ariyadhanas*) 11.306, 14.81; the seven treasures of a universal monarch 14.84; 'Where your treasure is, there will your heart be also' 16.98, 16.346, 25.103

trees

TRADITIONAL AND SYMBOLIC TREES

trees in the Buddhist tradition
the major events of the Buddha's life took place beneath trees 4.10, 10.330, 15.137, 26.242; rose-apple tree 1.69, 1.72, 2.20, 2.110–11, 3.23, 5.391–3, 15.222, 18.31; bodhi tree, *see* bodhi tree; 'The Tree of Wisdom' (a poem for Wesak) 25.252–4; the Buddha under the goatherd's banyan tree 10.437; the twin *sāl* trees 2.29, 4.10, 11.451–3, 13.145–6; Buddhism compared to a tree 1.63, 1.394, 12.111; 'Here are the roots of trees. Sit down, meditate' 1.236, 3.53, 18.368; Vacchagotta, having shed his false views, feels like a *sāl* tree 'pure in its strength' 1.77; 'As the wind blows down a weak tree' (*Dhammapada*) 14.587–8; joyfully rising to the height of seven palm trees 14.183; the incorporation into Buddhism of primitive tree-worship 2.222; 'Mountains are mountains and trees are trees' (Zen) 14.396, 14.496; the Mucalinda tree 10.470; one of the most important Buddhist symbols 12.111; the Zen master who told his disciple to be careful climbing down a tree 10.532

symbolic and metaphorical trees
Brother Lawrence sees a tree as a demonstration of the power of God 7.94; the Christian cross 12.186; consciousness inferred from its functions like the wind from swaying trees 14.187; a flower is sacred, a tree holy, if you look at it with an illumined mind 7.284; identifying Buddhism with one of its forms like identifying an oak with an acorn 26.10; a spiritual experience spreads through your being like sap through a tree 13.306; the tree of mundane existence, to which Buddhism lays the axe of Wisdom 7.300; a tree is a wonderful symbol, but it cannot be a teacher 18.632–3; the world tree or cosmic tree 12.185–6; Yggdrasil, the world ash 12.186

TREES AND REFLECTING ON THEM

introduction
celebration of trees 25.lvi; the deep silence of innumerable trees 22.322; the effect of the loss of forests 18.23, 25.52; Forestry Commission 24.51; happy trees near Padmaloka 18.23; the hostile atmosphere among a group of trees 4.540–1, 18.23; Indian trees 20.457; living presences 20.444; lunar influences on trees and plants 4.576; much better to worship a tree than not to worship anything 26.390; planting trees in cities 18.23; rainforests being cut down 25.52; sacred trees 14.462–3, 16.149, 26.390–1; trees as companions 4.534, 21.322; unimaginative planting of conifers in Britain 24.51

reflecting on trees
description of the process of perceiving a tree 10.231; 'A fool sees not the same tree that a wise man sees' 19.80; an object possessing certain attributes 7.326; reflecting on impermanence through observing a tree 13.227–8, 24.xxiv, 24.66; the changes of a tree: origination and decease 7.195–6; skeletons of trees in the New Zealand bush 13.228; 'The Stricken Giant' (a fallen tree) 25.359; the teaching of the leaves that change must come to all 25.195; a tree that is too big to be used 14.524, 19.219; trees in poetry 25.lvi; utilitarian and aesthetic responses to a beautiful pine tree 1.571, 14.517; we say that we see a tree, but what do we really see? 12.171

PARTICULAR TREES

bamboos
the beauty of bamboos 22.431–2, 25.217, 25.237; 'bending the bamboo the other way' 15.124, 15.129; farming bamboos 22.431; to paint bamboos, learn to see bamboos 1.571–2, 26.249

bananas
bhikkhus not allowed to peel their own bananas 22.348; cutting the root of craving, like cutting the banana plant 18.579; the simile of the banana tree, which has no core 17.382

mango groves
how Ambapāli gave the Buddha a mango grove, *see* Ambapāli; Meghiya's wish to meditate in a mango grove, *see under* *Udāna*/Meghiya; the nature of Indian mango groves 10.528, 11.702

oak trees
associated with the oracle of Zeus 23.266; 'The Oak and the Ivy' (poem) 25.387; oak could be used as part of an English Buddhist shrine 13.274, 18.25

pines
'An old pine tree is preaching wisdom' 1.28, 7.395, 26.243; pine-scent 25.391, 25.435; pine trees at Guhyaloka 25.424

other trees
acacia trees (associated with Tārā) 12.660; chestnut 25.306; cypresses ('black flames') 24.292, 24.295; flame-of-the-forest trees 22.295; hawthorn 25.438; holly 25.436; manuka tree 24.84; oranges 22.429–31, 23.383; plantain trees 19.476–7; *sāl* trees 4.10; silver birches 25.380, 25.444; *uḍumbara* tree 8.177, 8.683 (n115); willow 25.306

see also
Refuge Tree; roots in the sky, *see under* roots; tree spirits, *see under* nature/nature spirits

Trelawny, Edward John 24.571–2

Trethong, Mr T. 8.661, 17.xxvi, 17.422, 17.425

Trevelyan, Sir George v24

Tribe, Anthony *see* Anandajyoti

tribes the effect of environmental destruction on tribal people 25.58; membership of a tribe 9.352; one's kinsmen as a tribe with reciprocal duties 18.149–50; pleasing the elders of the tribe 15.418–19; a son leaving his parents in tribal life 15.410, 15.480; tribespeople in India, *see* Adivasi

Tribhuvan, king of Nepal v21

trident *khakkhara* (monastic staff), *see khakkhara*; symbolism of Padmasambhava's trident 12.335; *triśūla* (yogi's trident, associated with Shiva) 19.366–7

Trijang Rimpoche v22

***trikāya* doctrine**

INTRODUCTION

summaries
brief 1.250, 3.664 (n251), 4.651, 7.455–6, 7.505, 13.64, 13.307, 16.590 (n35), 21.563; summarized by Charles Eliot 1.260; slightly fuller account 18.86–7

what kāya means
'personality' is better than 'body' 13.299; don't take the translation 'body' too literally 19.222; means something like 'person' (without personality), akin to *hypostasis* 12.507; identifying *kāyas* gives a more concrete grasp of what is being described 19.201; not 'body' as opposed to 'mind', but the whole psychophysical aggregate 2.182

descriptions
one of the finest flowers of Buddhist thought 2.39; not 'three bodies' but one Buddha-nature functioning on three levels 4.204; the product of supreme creativity 18.293; the three 'magic bodies' (Milarepa) 18.86–7

reflections
the bodhisattva's transmutation into the *trikāya* 2.169; as body, speech, and mind, potentially present in every human being 21.215; one must beware of being led astray by words about the doctrine 2.45; sometimes we contact it in dreams, meditation, or aesthetic experience 4.208; 'To that Trikāya which is the true nature of all Dharmas … I make obeisance' 13.262; unless we understand it, much of the tradition is likely to remain obscure 2.39; why the *trikāya* doctrine is important 22.321

symbols and metaphors
a flower viewed by a child, a botanist, and a poet 2.40–6; Padmasambhava's staff 12.335; placing symbols of the *trikāya* on the shrine 11.226; represented by the three seed syllables *oṃ āḥ hūṃ* 18.293; the three-floored Tibetan temple 21.214–15, 22.467–8

history
stages of its evolution 1.251–8; correspondences in the *Laṅkāvatāra Sūtra* 14.212–13; the development of the *trikāya* 13.300–2; developed by the Yogācārins 2.39, 2.42–3, 16.61; doctrine not accepted by Hīnayānists 2.151; to regard it as a theistic development is a pernicious error 2.42; *trikāya* doctrine in the Mahāyāna 1.251–4; not taught explicitly in the 'early' Mahāyāna *sūtras* 2.171; how it emerged in later Mahāyāna *sūtras* 16.60–1; included in the five *kāyas*, *see* five *kāyas*; as depicted in Vajrayāna Buddhism 4.204–5; the Vajrayāna aims to transmute body, speech, and mind into the *trikāya* 7.506, 17.546; the 'Four Bodies': *trikāya* plus *svabhāvikakāya* 13.91, 14.428, 19.201, 19.214–15, 19.336–7; the *trikāya* and the *vidyādhara* 7.472; Milarepa's body, speech, and mind become the three *kāyas* 19.23

correlations and comparisons
the Christian Trinity and the Hindu *trimūrti* 16.77; body, speech, and mind 1.380, 2.169, 2.336, 7.506, 13.90–1, 18.87, 19.319, 21.215; the three *bardos* between death and rebirth 12.205; the first three of the four Tantric initiations 13.90–1; three types of conditionality 4.650–2

the trikāya doctrine and the Buddha
according to this, the Buddha is not merely a human being, but reality itself 1.250; the Buddha during his earthly lifetime is all three *kāyas* 4.208, 10.118; the Buddha of the *White Lotus Sūtra* in relation to the *trikāya* doctrine 14.131; each of the *kāyas* preaches the Dharma on its own plane 14.259; gives expression to the Buddha's transcendental compassionate activity 2.128; Going for Refuge to all three *kāyas* 11.255; the same Buddha viewed with different subtleties of perception 2.45–6; the *trikāya* and the Buddha's *parinirvāṇa* 7.455–6; visualizing the Buddha in his three *kāya* forms 1.284; the ordinary person's name and form in a Buddha is *dharmakāya* and *rūpakāya* 2.336

distinction between the three kāyas
distinction between *kāyas* 16.27; the *nirmāṇakāya* and *sambhogakāya* two veils hung before the *dharmakāya* 18.88; no line of distinction, any more than there is between colours of the rainbow 2.46; perhaps not advisable to distinguish too sharply 16.61; they can be distinguished but they're not really separate 19.201

(1) NIRMĀṆAKĀYA (RŪPAKĀYA)

introduction
the central figure of the Hīnayāna 1.262, 1.276; literally 'body of transformation' 19.319; popularization of the term 2.40–1; *tulku* is the Tibetan equivalent 2.182; 'your actual being here and now' (Guenther) 19.230–1

perspectives on the nirmāṇakāya
denial that the Buddhas possess a *rūpakāya* 14.194; the form in which the Buddha preaches the *suttas* of Early Buddhism 14.99; he comes in direct contact with the world of suffering beings 14.212; the historical Buddha as *nirmāṇakāya* (depictions) 4.205, 13.64–5; most people make use only of their senses, so this is the best understood *kāya* 2.41; the *nirmāṇakāya* is either of this kind or that kind, but not of all kinds 18.222; the perception of a mind darkened by negative emotions and wrong views 2.45; *rūpakāya* in the *Diamond Sūtra* 14.497; the Sevenfold Puja as a *nirmāṇakāya* puja 11.225–6; sphere of influence limited 16.461; symbolized by Padmasambhava 19.201; that body in which the Buddha communicates with ordinary human beings 19.319; teachings confined to a short period 14.259; today perhaps we need to pay more attention to the historical Buddha 12.507–8; what is the relationship between Enlightened being and physical body? 17.623; what we conventionally think of as a Buddha 18.68

and the sambhogakāya
every *nirmāṇakāya* is the reflection of one particular *sambhogakāya* 1.263; like rain from the cloud of the *sambhogakāya* 4.204; *nirmāṇakāya* overshadowed by *sambhogakāya* in Tibetan Buddhism 12.507; *sambhogakāya* emerges from splitting *rūpakāya* into gross and subtle forms 1.261

and the dharmakāya
the *nirmāṇakāya* is the *dharmakāya* as perceived by ordinary folk 1.262, 7.455; the Buddha is to be identified not with his *rūpakāya* but with his *dharmakāya* 1.307; Pāli texts distinguished between *rūpakāya* and *dharmakāya* 12.506–7; the *White Lotus Sūtra* emphasizes the *dharmakāya* 12.507–8

(2) SAMBHOGAKĀYA

etymology and definitions
'body of mutual enjoyment': possible reasons for the name 2.41, 4.206; the Buddha's 'glorious body' 1.264, 2.41; more helpful to translate it as the ideal or archetypal Buddha 13.301

descriptions
the aspect of the Buddha which communicates with bodhisattvas and Buddhas 16.461; the Buddha beyond space and time, with the perfections of historical Buddhas 4.206; the dominating figure of the Mahāyāna 1.262, 1.276; the embodiment of the perfection of speech 19.319; the full manifestation of all possible aspects of Enlightened experience 18.222; the ideal of Enlightenment outside any historical context 4.63; represents the ideal of Buddhahood as existing without limitations 16.27; a subtle and mysterious doctrine 22.321; the 'thirty-two marks' 14.428

perspectives on the sambhogakāya
Amitābha or Amitāyus one of the most important forms 2.42, 7.455–6; an analogy with Dickens or Shakespeare surrounded

by their characters 15.397–8; aspects include the Five Jinas or Buddhas, *see* mandala of the Five Buddhas; attributes of boundless effulgence and unlimited longevity 7.455; difference between images released from subconscious and *sambhogakāya* 2.42; emergence in the later Mahāyāna 16.61, 18.86; a glorious company, classified into five Buddha 'families' 1.263; the form in which the Buddha teaches Mahāyāna *sūtras* 1.272–3, 14.99; it's a sort of *puṇyakāya*, a 'merit body' 15.397; its roots in the element of spiritual friendship in the Enlightenment experience 11.437; not perceived in the same way as external objects or mental pictures 2.42; perceived in many ways: peaceful, fascinating, stern, even terrible 2.42; the reality it represents is accessible only by imagination 18.88; renders the Buddha ever present, always accessible 18.86–7; reveals the Mahāyāna *sūtras*? 16.52–3, 16.241; seeing the guru's *sambhogakāya* 19.120–1; two aspects: private and for others 2.669 (n63); twofold: *svasambhoga* and *parasambhoga* 1.262; an uninterrupted stream of eloquence 14.259; what is speech in ordinary beings is the *sambhogakāya* in a Buddha 19.43

images and depictions
like a cloud surrounded by rainbows 4.204; depicted as a richly apparelled Buddha 4.205; depicted on the middle floor of a three-storeyed temple 13.65; symbolized by the thousand-armed Avalokiteśvara 19.201

meditation on the sambhogakāya
as far ahead as we can see: the basis of visualization practices 18.87; the Buddha as perceived by a mind disciplined by long practice of meditation 2.45; to be meditated on as *śūnyatā* 10.118; seen when attention is withdrawn from the senses 2.41

and the dharmakāya
Buddhahood with and without form, the two being non-different 18.88; the route to the *dharmakāya* is through the *sambhogakāya* 18.87; the *sambhogakāya* is the *dharmakāya* as perceived by bodhisattvas 1.262

(3) DHARMAKĀYA

the term
its meaning 1.251–3, 4.189; metaphysical interpretation (late Hīnayāna) 1.252; chiefly *prajñā* (early Mahāyāna) 1.253; it has no name 21.559; use of the term in the *Laṅkāvatāra Sūtra* 14.211

definitions and descriptions
authentic contact with the essence of the Buddha 19.222–3; the Buddha as existing in the dimension of eternity 3.150; the embodiment of the infinite merits of the Buddhas 14.194; the embodiment of the perfection of mind 19.319; endowed with bliss, permanence, self, and pure beauty 14.236; the highest reality as actually embodied 19.187; if the *dharmakāya* is the ocean, conditionality is the waves 14.607; the mother-light 18.251; an ontological reality, contrasted with *nirvāṇa* (Lhalungpa) 24.397; the principle through which everything is woven into the *dharmadhātu*'s harmony 14.604; the real, true, genuine, ultimate Buddha 4.208; reality fully realized by the Buddha and revealed in and through him 2.43; that which is eternally real, the 'body of spiritual truth' 3.275

perspectives on the dharmakāya
it can only be described by paradox or a 'thunderous silence' 7.456; concept brought into prominence by the *White Lotus Sūtra* 16.60; the conception shifted from doctrinal to metaphysical terms 18.86; contact with an archetypal bodhisattva is contact with the *dharmakāya* 12.572–3; contact with it can occur under mysterious circumstances 14.438; the dissolving of the *nhamdog* into the *dharmakāya* 19.188; the emptiness of the *dharmakāya* 14.561; the eternal reality of the *dharmakāya* 14.230, 14.233; 'From the Dharma should one see the Buddhas ...' (*Diamond Sūtra*) 4.208–9; the gestalt: product of your self over many lives and action of *dharmakāya* 18.282; however depraved, a human being has some reflection of the *dharmakāya* 18.286; in what sense is the *dharmakāya* personal or impersonal? 2.45; it manifests to the extent that any individual is Buddha-like 14.604; its vulnerability to quasi-theistic or pantheistic interpretations 14.604–5; limitations disappear to such an extent that the Buddha himself disappears 16.27; its mysterious 'preachings' transcend all limitations 14.259; not to be characterized by words or signs, not even *nirvāṇa* 14.194; Nirvāṇa is the supreme object of the *dharmakāya* 7.510; object of devotion 1.324, 1.346; the principle of harmony 14.605; a positive counterpart to the *anātman* doctrine 14.604; quasi-religious conception wherein wisdom and compassion are united 1.243; recognized

from the beginning of Buddhism 2.43–4; the reflection of the *dharmakāya* in the individual 18.281–2; the tantras said to have been preached directly by the *dharmakāya* 14.249; the teacher considered to be the *dharmakāya* in human form 1.422; to be in contact with the Buddha is to be in contact with the *dharmakāya* 14.437; transcends time and space 12.507; Vasubandhu's interpretation 1.252

images and symbols
depicted as a naked Buddha figure 4.204–5, 13.65; illustrated in the *White Lotus Sūtra* 4.209–10; like the pure blue sky 4.204; represented by the stupa 2.221; symbolized by Amitābha 1.324, 19.201

the Buddha and the dharmakāya
the Buddha should be identified with the *dharmakāya*, not the physical body 16.512; a Buddha's knowledge has no limit and there is no communication 16.461–2; no difference between the Buddha and one with *prajñā* who sees him as he is 2.45

the dharmakāya in practice
all *sādhanas* are aspects of the *dharmakāya* 22.403; allowing the ego to be dissolved into the *dharmakāya* at the time of death 18.250; the *dharmakāya* and the perfection of *vīrya* 1.440; realizing the *dharmakāya* 19.318–19

see also
bodhisattvas of the *dharmakāya under* bodhisattva/bodhisattva hierarchy; *dharmakāya* and *sambhogakāya*, *see under trikāya/sambhogakāya*

trimaṇḍala-pariśuddha 2.366, 4.104, 17.202, 17.734 (n204)

Triṃśikā-vijñapti *see* Vasubandhu

trimūrti *see under* Hinduism

Triple Gem *see* Three Jewels

triple world *see trailokya*

Tripiṭaka (Pāli Tipiṭaka)

introduction
etymology of the term 13.335–6, 14.28; regarded as *Buddhavacana* 13.336, 14.289; three different recensions of essentially the same material 7.526–8, 14.266; the Tripiṭaka is a living, growing thing 14.257–8; recited to invoke occult forces 2.216

Pāli Tipiṭaka
brief introduction 1.184–5, 7.499, 9.271, 12.210, 12.520, 13.335–6, 14.251–3; Abhidharma Piṭaka, *see* Abhidharma/Abhidharma Piṭaka; almost all translated into English, thanks to the Pali Text Society 13.357, 14.253; the balance of the content of the three collections 17.572; editions in different countries 14.253; the incongruity of imagining that the Buddha was the author of all three Piṭakas 8.130; rehearsed at the Third Council 14.85; in relation to the Tibetan and Chinese canons 7.527, 13.336; Royal Thai edition 7.446, 7.617 (n490), 9.271, 11.372, 13.336, 14.253; Sanskrit equivalent (*Agamas*), *see* scriptures/*Agamas*; Sutta (Sūtra) Piṭaka, *see* Sutta Piṭaka; as viewed in Theravādin countries 7.525, 14.14, 14.252–3; Vinaya Piṭaka, *see* Vinaya Piṭaka; what is in the three 'baskets' 14.28–9, 14.252; inclusion in Dr Ambedkar's anthology 9.139; *see also* Pāli canon

Kangyur (Tibetan Tripiṭaka)
introduction 11.372, 14.255–6; the 'Translated Word of the Buddha' 7.503; a collected edition of whatever *sūtras* were available 14.100; compiled by Büton 13.29; contains the Tripiṭaka and the four great Tantras 7.525; the *Diamond Sūtra* is popular in Tibet 13.45; first printed edition appeared in Beijing 14.255; Gelug classification 14.256; includes only canonical works, others being collected in the Tengur 14.261–2; includes Perfection of Wisdom, *Saddharma Puṇḍarīka*, *Laṅkāvatāra* 13.19–20; one copy made with ink from the dust of precious stones 14.255; 100 or 108 volumes 13.19; in relation to the Chinese and Pāli canons 7.527; the 'remote tradition' 14.263; revered as a canon 14.256; tantras 14.246

Chinese Tripiṭaka (San Zang)
brief introduction 11.372, 13.336, 14.253–5, 24.620 (n78); venerated as canonical in China and Japan 7.525–6; Abhidharma section includes works by Indian *ācāryas* 14.254, 14.261; catalogues 14.253; a collected edition of whatever *sūtras* were available 14.100; contains 1,662 independent works 11.372, 13.336, 22.54; in relation to the Tibetan and Pāli canons 7.527, 13.336, 14.261–2; inclusion of *Sutta-Nipāta* material 14.56; a literary and bibliographical collection rather than a canon 14.254–5; *Ming Tripiṭaka* in Penang 24.55; *Taishō Shinshū-Daizōkyō* 14.255, 22.54; three out of the original twelve collections survive 14.253; Yogi Chen read all 1,656 works twice 12.443, 23.383

triratna *see* Three Jewels

Triratna Buddhist Order and Community *previously* (*Friends of the*) *Western Buddhist Order* (FWBO), *Trailokya Bauddha Mahasangha Sahayak Gana* (TBMSG)

contents for this section
(I) history: the founding – early days – Triratna in India. (II) the form Triratna took: introduction – characteristics and principles – teachings and practices – the people involved – further developments – anniversaries – Sangharakshita's role. (III) the Order: what is the Order? – ordination – ordination ceremonies – life in the Order – Order members – the Order and the wider world. (IV) institutions: Buddhist centres – retreat centres.

(I) History

THE FOUNDING

a new Buddhist movement
a new kind of Buddhist movement was needed 2.459, 4.413, 9.489–90, 10.26; 'Do you know what this means?' 11.172–3, 12.364–5, 23.376–7, 24.506; reasons for founding 2.470, 3.455, 9.211, 9.240–1, 9.469, 9.490, 10.383–5; the field was fertile, but it needed cultivating 11.519–20; the beginning of a new tradition? 19.417; inadvertently helped by enemies 4.412–13, 11.xxi; founded in the same year that homosexual acts were decriminalized 26.580, 26.672; it nearly didn't come into existence at all 12.386; a means to support the new movement in India 9.xiii; not a blueprint but a seed 26.580; the Order's coming into existence little short of a miracle 2.530; an organization which would not be an organization 11.382; predictions that it would peter out 14.307; Sangharakshita's role, *see* Triratna II/ Sangharakshita role; why it was called a 'movement' 11.350

the basis for the new movement
brief introduction 9.281–3, 9.435–8, 9.490–2; communication and friendship were central 11.663; a departure from Eastern Buddhist tradition 2.468, 11.376; the English context in which it was founded 11.378–9; first ordinations, *see under* Triratna III/ordination; framing the constitution: you can't be a member unless you're a Buddhist 4.458; Going for Refuge to the Three Jewels 10.266, 11.388, 11.662; in the context of the development of British Buddhism 13.465–6; the need for a new kind of sangha that takes Buddhism seriously 2.470, 10.271, 11.174; no membership, not a 'society' 2.303–4, 9.239, 9.245–6, 9.469, 10.385, 11.383, 12.497; only one thing needed: human beings who go for Refuge 10.270, 11.383; not perpetuating the old corrupt way of doing things 15.712–14; not a pinnacle but a foundation 13.466; an order, not a society 2.466–7, 2.519, 11.174, 11.386, 11.469, 11.61–2, 12.374; it would have to be free of homophobia if friendship was to flourish 23.438; a shared process: it depended on people wanting to be ordained 2.524; the sharing of Going for Refuge with others 2.471–2, 2.524; a similar approach to that of Dr Ambedkar 2.496–7, 10.xliii; was the idea to create a *distinctively* Western Buddhism? 11.377–9; why did the new Buddhist movement take the form it did? 2.466–8; why it was called the Friends of the Western Buddhist Order 11.350–92

first FWBO *centre, Sakura*
Sangharakshita's first visit to the shop 23.130–1; in Monmouth Street, London 12.386, 23.426; the As You Like It café next door 26.565; references to Monmouth Street in Dickens 12.365, 12.729 (n241); like the early Christian catacombs 11.461, 11.728, 12.495; dedication ceremony, *see* dedication ceremony; marked the birth of the Friends of the Western Buddhist Order 23.431; named the 'Triratna meditation centre and shrine' 12.366; played an important part in the history of British Buddhism 23.131, 23.429; the seed from which everything sprang 11.351; set on fire 26.607–8; 'striving to make a little room in people's minds for faith and hope' 25.420; what the centre was like 11.727–8, 12.365–6, 12.650, 23.430; meditation classes 3.620–1. 9.201–2, 9.490, 10.195, 11.461–2, 11.728, 12.495–6, 12.650–1, 23.430; why it started with meditation 5.xxxi, 10.213, 12.495–6; first Wesak celebration (photograph) 23.430; Zen Study Class 23.430

EARLY DAYS

introduction
brief account 10.204–5; developing an altruistic aspect of practice 2.471, 4.461; difficulty in taking something positive at face value 4.602; emphasis that you didn't have to be highly educated 11.716; much like the early days of Buddhism 4.351; not using people's neurotic energy to get things done 17.61; the Order bloomed lotus-like from the mud of the metropolis 2.404–5; two or three dozen people who took Buddhism seriously 11.174; a very joyful

time 12.663–4; what made it possible? *mettā* 10.195–6

the historical context
the atmosphere of the sixties 5.xxxii, 10.83, 11.729, 24.319; flow of energy 4.607; friendship was talked about a lot, but there was little around 12.540; getting a bit sick with psychological analysis 4.603–6; helped by the experimental spirit of the times 12.654; no need to emphasize relaxation in the early days 18.584; people relaxing with a little wine 14.573, 17.257, 19.331–2; tendency to disrespectful behaviour in the name of informality 4.345–6; 'we tend to get the misfits in our sort of group' 4.329; were lots of hippies involved? 11.550–1

firsts
first right livelihood businesses, *see under* right livelihood/team-based; first talks under the auspices of the FWBO 12.366–7, 12.653; Pundarika, the first Buddhist centre (Archway) 11.525, 17.76, 17.719 (n83); Sangharakshita's welcome to newcomers in the first *FWBO Newsletter* 11.503–4

early retreats
raised level of consciousness 3.621; Easter retreat 1968 3.xi–xii, 23.443; the effort to keep a balance of freed energies and mindfulness 18.581; first communication exercises 9.518, 12.651; the first time someone other than Sangharakshita led a puja 11.557–8, 12.367; for some the most important events of the year 23.464; living in a completely Buddhist fashion 9.436–7, 9.490; people's sadness at having to leave 9.282, 9.437, 12.496, 12.651–2; showed that conditions are important 12.652; showed that the Dharma really works 11.728

first residential communities
Aryatara (Sarum House), *see under* Croydon; emerged from people's experience of retreats 3.622, 9.283, 9.437, 9.491, 11.464, 12.496; Sangharakshita forms the first men's community 23.473, 24.241, 24.666 (n289); men's and women's communities 9.505; set up by squatting in derelict properties 12.496, 12.654, 12.664

activities
communication exercises, *see* communication exercises; fundraising 4.612–13, 9.491–2, 9.505, 12.663; growing interest in Dharma study 4.350–1; in the early days people didn't feel grateful 15.433–4; speakers' classes 12.377; a wish for a women's vihara and retreat centre 11.645

TRIRATNA IN INDIA (*PREVIOUSLY TRAILOKYA BAUDDHA MAHASANGHA SAHAYAK GANA, TBMSG*)

how it began
introduction 13.500–1; Sangharakshita's wish for it to happen 11.527; founding 2.490, 9.307, 10.313–14, 21.595; funding 10.li, 24.24; Dharma work in the villages 10.413–14; fired by the vision of Dr Ambedkar 2.497, 10.83; it grew from the connections Sangharakshita made with Dr Ambedkar's followers 26.652; Lokamitra's work, *see* Lokamitra; the name TBMSG 9.165–6, 9.214, 10.xlvii–viii, 10.314, 11.174–512.370; the new Buddhists were looking for support from outside India 11.591–2; a one-hundred-percent Buddhist movement 9.307; Sangharakshita was the link 11.663–4; structures established in the West suit the situation in India 10.418, 11.664, 24.24

growth
areas for growth 10.417–18; assessment after ten years 11.591–4; rapid growth 10.298, 10.359, 10.404–5, 11.664; in maturity as well as numbers 10.416; the most active Buddhist organization in India 11.562; actively teaching the Dharma 10.416; ceremoniousness 12.487; decision to replace 'Upasaka' with Dhammachari 9.165

ordinations
ordination training 10.liv, 10.lxv, 10.366; first ordination retreat (1979) 9.286, 10.xlvi, 10.290, 24.xix–xx, 24.20–2, 24.106–9; photographs 10.xlv, 24.22; men's ordinations conferred by preceptors other than Sangharakshita 24.256; ordination at Ahmedabad 24.117; ordinations at Bhaja 10.xlix, 10.lii, 10.352; first ordinations of women by women 10.lii; numbers of Order members (in Nagpur) 10.387, 10.704 (n339); women Order members 10.413; contact between Indian and Western Order members 10.89–90, 10.417–18, 11.596; Order members' delight to have meaning and purpose in their lives 10.416–17

activities
the danger of getting too involved in ceremonies that bless secular life 15.702–3; hostels 10.358, 10.366, 10.399–400, 10.401–3, 10.415; Nagarjuna Training Institute 10.lv–lix, 10.lxii; Ashok Dhammaduta programme 10.li; publications, *see under* Triratna/publications; retreats (*shibir*) 9.377–8, 9.418; first women's retreat (photo) 10.l; trying to fulfil Dr Ambedkar's vision of a

new Buddhist movement 10.362; women's community 10.366

challenges
the nature of traditional Indian society 15.486–8; their work in difficult conditions is an inspiration to Buddhists in the West 11.593–4

(II) The form Triratna took

introduction

stages of development
its arising seems like a miracle 12.543; first sympathy for Buddhist ideals, then bringing conduct into line 11.586; an Indra's net 2.513; an assessment of progress after six years 11.514–16; development was organic 11.662; is it a sect? 11.6760–1; Order members like trainee gardeners 11.516; the FWBO after seven years of existence 4.227, 21.595; reflections after ten years 11.518–28; reflections after twenty-five years 11.595–605, 12.385–95, 14.307–8; over the years it came to understand its own nature 11.143–4; stage of development in 1981–2 9.171, 9.224–5; its growth is by no means complete (after nearly thirty years) 12.535

names
summary of changes 24.xiv; named by Sangharakshita 9.166; nomenclature 9.165–6; originally the Friends of the Western Sangha 23.xiii, 23.474 (n3); calling the movement the 'Friends' 4.586; changing the name to Triratna 11.661, 12.370, 12.730 (n246), 12.405, 26.511; translation of *triratna* 9.166; the first centre was called the 'Triratna meditation centre and shrine' 12.366; the significance of 'Western' 11.70, 12.373–4, 12.498, 13.379; why *Friends* of the Western Buddhist Order? 12.374; why Friends of the Western *Buddhist* Order? 11.371; Order names, *see under* Order/ordination/private

images and metaphors
a tree, a bed of lotuses, a garden, a road, a raft 12.462; a branch of a mighty tree 2.548; a stream of spiritual energy that deeply transforms 12.336; a temple 12.462–3

five pillars of the FWBO (Triratna)
introduction 2.612, 12.461–72, 14.308; (1) ideas 2.515–18, 12.463–5, 14.308; (2) practices 6.xxii, 12.466–7; (3) institutions 6.xxii, 12.468–9, 12.639–41; (4) experiment 12.469–71; (5) imagination 12.472

six distinctive emphases
introduction 2.725 (n582), 26.405; the emphases were needed because of the movement's expansion 26.580; (1) centrality of the act of Going for Refuge 10.266, 10.268, 11.383, 11.388, 12.596, 12.665–7, 14.308, 15.695; 'Everything can be changed except Going for Refuge' 10.576, 17.635; (2) a unified Order 2.467, 11.469–70, 12.498, 12.667–8; (3) a non-sectarian approach 9.362, 11.470, 11.713–14, 12.368–9, 12.668–9; (4) the importance of spiritual friendship 12.669–70, 12.675, 26.639; (5) right livelihood 12.670–1; (6) the spiritual value of the arts 11.620–1, 12.672–3, 13.502, 26.99, 26.356–9

characteristics and principles

characteristics and attitudes
'alternative'? 11.551; approach of decentralization 24.485; approaches derived from different traditions 11.376; attitude to Christianity 13.490, 13.501, 13.503; attitude towards sex 26.28; activities a cooperation between meditation and psychotherapy 5.665; based on what is fundamental in the Buddhist tradition 11.455; a basis for true individuality 13.465–6; Blake's words about mutual forgiveness would be a suitable motto 26.649; a *Buddhist* organization 12.386–7, 12.497–8; the establishing of a Western Buddhist tradition 13.409; creating a helpful structure 19.545; draws what is helpful from all Buddhist traditions 9.362, 12.368–9; an embodiment of the *bodhicitta* 4.278; going back to what is central from what is peripheral 11.599; 'I see the FWBO as never standing still' 11.590; inspired by the Tendai school? 4.495, 11.89; it certainly does not 'explore existing religious channels in new ways' 13.512; it looks forward, not back 11.352; it seeks to make the Buddha's teaching available to as many people as possible 26.650; it tries to see Buddhism from the Buddhist point of view 11.379; it started in the West, but is not 'Western' 13.380–1; 'Western' in the sense of being concerned with the world of today 13.379; its role is radical, in the sense of returning to roots 13.440; not identified with any one school of Buddhism, but not eclectic 11.376–7, 11.470; 'just a Buddhist movement, plain and simple' 12.368; relationship to Western culture 13.484; unwillingness to compromise 4.444–5, 15.671, 24.167

areas of principle
basic view (following Madhyamaka): primacy of experience over thoughts 19.371–2; clarity of Dharma teaching 11.608, 11.687–8; clear thinking 2.517–18; demolishing the wrong views

that undergird morally evil behaviour 26.678; the development of an ecological dimension 12.409–10; devotional approach 24.61–2; facilities for spiritual practice 12.377–8; financially self-supporting 10.272, 12.497, 13.381, 19.464–5, 19.479; follows the middle way 12.387–95; ecumenical principle 2.547–56, 5.xxix, 12.500; Going for Refuge 2.515–16, 10.266, 10.268–72, 11.376, 11.469, 11.599, 12.465, 24.485; Going Forth 2.517, 12.545–60; the higher evolution 12.465; importance of good relationship with parents, *see under* parents; it offers four gifts to the modern man and woman 11.144–90, 25.138–48, 25.325; leverage for social change 13.440; more and more of less and less 11.376, 19.544–5; moving in the direction of celibacy 13.452–3; the new society 2.516–17, 11.179–80, 19.520; not mixing Buddhism with Christianity or other things 24.485; positive conditionality 12.465; right livelihood 11.376; service 27.1075; single-sex idea, *see* single-sex idea; special emphasis on the first precept 13.453–4; emphasis on sangha 11.608, 11.687–8; spiritual friendship 2.517, 11.602, 12.465, 12.675, 13.451; vegetarianism 13.454; whatever has the taste of freedom 11.51

TEACHINGS AND PRACTICES

meditation practices
list of practices 12.467; the mindfulness of breathing and the *mettā bhāvanā* the twin pillars 11.376, 12.650–1, 12.680; why are visualization practices limited to the Order? 19.28

ritual and devotion
based on traditional practices 13.419; chanting is an integral part of religious life 13.415–16; salutations and offerings 13.415–18; *see also* devotion/puja; Going for Refuge and Prostration practice; dedication ceremony

teachings
a *miśra* (mixed) Dharma 26.548; the Noble Eightfold Path 13.453–6; people teach different things, but within the same framework 19.544–5; a re-presentation of the Dharma 19.51–2; Triratna's synthesis of the Dharma 19.543–4

inspirations
Mahāyāna *sūtras* 2.553, 12.368; the need for inspiration in the Order 24.462; Pāli texts 12.368; the principal source of inspiration is the Buddha and his teachings 11.371; Pure Land Buddhism 2.553–4; the *Udāna* 10.422, 11.377; the study of Buddhist texts drawn from all sources 11.377; the Theravāda 2.552–3; Tibetan Buddhism 2.555–6. 12.368; a time when what was primary in Buddhism was treated as such 13.440; useful insights from *The Fall of Public Man* 13.385; Western classical music 11.371; the whole of the Buddhist tradition, the only approach possible 12.368–9, 12.668–9; Western writers like Blake, Goethe, Plato 11.370–1, 12.369, 26.649; Zen 2.554–5

ceremonies and festivals
emphasize Going for Refuge 19.535; festivals, *see under* festivals; to mark arrivals and departures, taking and leaving office 12.486; that combine richness with simplicity, aesthetic appeal with significance 24.531; Triratna ceremonies should not just be about blessing the activities of secular life 15.701–4: performing funerals 15.702–3; rejoicing in merits at a funeral 11.734

arts
appreciation of the arts 13.502; arts events 11.620–1; choirs (with choirmasters) at Buddhist centres 12.558; developments Sangharakshita wanted to see 11.621; films, *see under* films/FWBO; a poetry reading at Brighton 24.128–9; reflections on what makes a successful event 24.161; relationship to Western culture 13.484

publications
Buddhayan 11.562, 24.27; *Dakini* (later *Lotus Realm*) 11.631–46; *Dharma Life* 24.xx, 11.647–92; *FWBO Newsletter* 11.501–64, 21.595, 24.25, 24.156, 24.612 (n46); *The FWBO Puja Book* 13.418–19; *Golden Drum* 11.565–630, 12.383, 12.488; Indian publications 9.170, 10.liv, 10.295, 10.299; *Mitrata* 24.27, 24.612 (n46), 27.1069–70

THE PEOPLE INVOLVED

the sangha
conception of the full-time or effective sangha 3.415, 9.225, 9.319–20; different degrees of involvement: Friend, Mitra, Order member 11.390–1, 12.374; fundamentally a network of friendship 12.645–6; gathering in large numbers 12.675–6; it's good for balance that we have our two wings, Western and Indian 10.12; it is very important that our sangha is classless and supranational 10.565; people's failings can be surprising, but they do make sincere effort 11.553–4; the positive group has a definite place 11.392, 24.128; scholars in Triratna 11.601; spiritual friendship is a cornerstone 12.457–8; we need a movement that

transcends national and cultural barriers 10.90; we're very fortunate to have some very creative people 12.673

getting involved
attracting people who have been successful in the world 4.450–5; being a Friend (*sahayak*) 9.308, 9.545, 10.268, 11.178, 11.391; communicating ideas 12.465; the difficulty of making the transition from interest to commitment 24.58; friendliness draws people to Triratna 12.457–8; 'I don't believe in encouraging people to give up their worldly commitments' 4.455; people are sometimes just looking for group acceptance 15.421; reaching out to black women and gay people 11.596; reaching out to those who need the Dharma 10.86–7, 12.489; self-confident, energetic people won't feel at home in a meek sangha 4.469; some people make contact by the merest fluke 12.543–4; what attracts people? 11.598–9, 12.669; working for the Movement 15.402; young people 9.437–8

women in Triratna
the advantages for women of communal living 8.418; encouraging women to accept responsibilities 11.640; equal ordination for women and men 2.467–8, 12.667; facilities for growth and development 12.376; have just the same responsibilities as men 10.222; the importance of their participation in Triratna's public life 11.635; the positive atmosphere created by a women's Order convention 12.591; retreat centres, *see under* Triratna/IV; Triratna offers women more freedom and scope than the women's movement 24.73; wish for more women's facilities 11.645–6; wish to see more women Order members 11.645, 12.402; women ordained by women 2.733 (n628), 10.lii; women's ordination process 11.636, 12.375–6; women's ordinations 24.172; women's retreats held at Padmaloka 24.171–2

becoming a Mitra (Dhammamitra)
introduction 2.304–5, 9.246; explanation of term 9.165, 9.545; commitments 2.304, 4.688 (n204), 9.246, 9.308, 10.388, 10.700 (n282), 11.391, 12.312, 19.559, 21.486, 24.604–5 (n14); friendship with Order members 9.308; Mitra ceremony 11.178, 11.391, 18.378; you can stay a Mitra for as long as you like 11.178

relations with the wider world
attitude to parents, culture, and the world 12.390–5; characteristics in common with the rest of the Buddhist world 12.664–5; contact with non-Buddhists as potential Buddhists 19.482; contributions to Western Buddhism? 11.597–600; influence 11.600; must play an active part in combatting racial prejudice 12.408–9; we have a duty to communicate the Dharma 11.600

FURTHER DEVELOPMENTS

expansion
after an easy start, the prospect of moving into more difficult areas 11.554–5; ambition to have centres in the holy places in India 11.527; better a small committed Order than a large nominal one 2.519; broadening out: what that means 11.555; envisaging the expansion of the movement 24.158; everything should go on expanding all the time 19.417; expansion led to the need for the talk on the six distinctive emphases 26.580; the movement must expand if it is the real thing 5.218–19; the growth of a new society, a new world 26.20; growth into hundreds of lotuses 2.530–1; hopes for expansion 11.xxiii, 11.522–5; 'I see the FWBO as never standing still' 11.590; the idea of expansion into Far Eastern countries 11.528, 15.742; if it isn't growing as fast as it could, that suggests lack of motivation 18.593; isn't dilution inevitable? 11.555; the 1970s the decade of expansion 14.xvi; expansion in the 1980s 11.174, 11.729; numbers 2.510, 2.522, 2.546, 12.664; the objective to make the Movement a world within a world 11.527; possible expansion into Eastern Europe 24.361; activities in Poland 26.7439–40 (n384); rapid expansion wouldn't do much good 18.362–3; the slow pace of expansion 11.551–2; spreading to countries across the world 10.272, 11.524, 12.489, 12.554, 13.500; it started in the West, but is not 'Western' 13.380–1; there could be a tremendous expansion 12.400–1; we should go to places where we can most fruitfully employ our energy 11.619; 'where once a seed was, now a tree' 25.420

changes seen and needed
any disappointments? 11.514–15, 11.595, 11.662–3, 11.736; beginning to know ourselves 12.462; lectures, retreats, and study groups improving 24.173; more emphasis on the arts 11.663, 12.405–6; more emphasis on right livelihood and fundraising 12.407; need for more effective publicity 12.407–8; need to adapt to changing conditions 12.470–1; need to develop before being labelled 19.52; a parable of the good ship FWBO (in 2003) 26.453–5; possible improvements 11.663;

reaching out to people who need help 11.595–6; we need continuity between old and new ways 12.471, 12.677–8, 19.211

dangers, shortcomings, challenges
be careful not to degenerate into something weak and wishy-washy 10.14; the challenge of the four gifts 25.147–8; consumer mentality 15.433–4; contemporary ideologies that are inimical to the Dharma 11.603, 11.612–14; a drift towards the personal and away from public service 10.13; finding it difficult to see the wood for the trees 24.207; gratitude for and disappointment in the FWBO 12.386; 'In certain respects the FWBO falls below the standards of the outside world' 24.212; it might face difficult conditions in the world 11.616; lack of mindfulness 12.382, 12.403; more attention should be paid to *dāna* (giving) 12.467; more demands could be made on Western Order members 10.416; perhaps we place too much importance on having good conditions 11.622–3; a period of upheaval (2003) 26.458; pseudo-Buddhist niceness 4.420–1, 4.445; shortcomings 9.539; take care not to talk about a new society while living like everyone else 19.229; taking refuge within the movement as an escape from society 10.73; too growth-oriented and not sufficiently other-oriented 18.592–3; unmindfulness 11.625–6; we don't have a strong enough sense of Śākyamuni 11.690; we're always up against the five poisons 11.603

critique of the FWBO
accused of antipathy to tradition 13.471–2; accused of being unscientific 13.416, 13.438–9; called modernist 13.424; criticized for emphasis on friendship and puja 13.416; 'Protestant Buddhism' 13.367–512; contrast with the English Sangha (Trust) 13.381–3, 13.407–23; misrepresentations 13.426, 13.480–5, 13.491–2, 13.501–4; rational and irrational criticism 11.664–5; said to be suspicious of ritual 13.413–23; sexual ethics 13.443–53; the Buddha's rejection of self as a stick with which to beat the FWBO 13.394

future
assured if enough members of the sangha safeguard their vision 12.679; 'Buddhism and the Future of India' 22.270; clues to the final nature of Western Buddhism? 11.557; hope for progress on the path to Enlightenment 11.669; 'I feel confident the FWBO will go in the right direction' 11.690; if Order members stay committed to embodying the Three Jewels, it will survive 11.688; the hope of attracting talented and highly skilled people 11.557; possible obstacles and temptations 12.598–9; until there are sufficient Stream Entrants, the whole thing could just dissolve 11.586; will need a stream of non-egoistic spiritual energy to manifest through people 12.600; a wish for Triratna to spread to Eastern Europe and South America 12.489; a wish to see more 'quantum leaps' 11.556–7

ANNIVERSARIES

FWBO
20th 12.385–95 23rd 24.382; 25th 11.466; 40th 12 649–50, 12.678; 41st 12.676; 42nd 11.727; 50th 3.xvi

Western Buddhist Order
1st 11.4; 16th 2.315–17, 2.396; 19th 12.363; 20th 2.403, 2.502, 12.397–410; 21st 24.327; 22nd 2.507, 2.509, 24.380, 24.382–3; 25th 2.577, 14.307; 28th 2.543, 2.545; 40th 12.663

SANGHARAKSHITA'S ROLE

founder
previously his idea was to reform the old movement, not start a new one 11.548; 'At the beginning it was just me' 9.490, 11.549, 11.557–8, 12.364, 12.386; being sent into the wilderness led to the founding 2.611, 12.364–5; being a good organizer, he founded an Order rather than a looser structure 26.638; bringing in current psychological ideas 11.550; and the 'conflict' between Sangharakshitas I and II 26.248–9; glad that the FWBO had been brought into existence 24.139; 'Hard to believe that I was its founder' 2.531; 'I didn't found the Order single-handed' 2.523–4; 'I didn't have a detailed or precise idea' 11.143, 11 548–9, 11.617, 11.662; 'I didn't have a vision, but went step by step' 11.662; 'I wanted to start something new and vigorous' 10.194–5; the ideas had been forming for a while 11.548; an offering of four gifts 11.144–90, 25.138–48, 25.325; an onerous responsibility 2.531; just part of the scope of his Dharma life 11.616–17; reflecting on the founding of the movement thirty years later 24.506–7; reflected in the story *The Artist's Dream* 26.253; a reluctant revolutionary 11.549; striving to infuse new life and energy into the movement 25.463; under no illusion that he was the most suitable person 2.530, 11.687; 'a vast, overshadowing Consciousness that through me founded the Order' 2.531; what he meant (in 2009) by a 're-founding' of the Order 26.673;

what would he have done differently? 11.663

relationship to the Order
full account 2.509–39; admiration for Order members 11.626–7; communication with Order members 2.521, 2.532–7, 12.411–12; the Order should not be Sangharakshita writ large 2.531–2, 11.663; the Order's importance to him 2.520–3, 24.382–3; the painfulness of conflict and disharmony in the Order 2.522–3, 12.676–7; people projecting power onto him 11.686; as preceptor 2.523; he put more energy into the Order than into anything else in his life 2.522; how do Order members see him? 11.666; 'I expect every Order member to do better than I have ever done' 12.377, 12.545; 'I never thought of myself as leading the Order' 11.690; a spiritual friend, or just a friend 2.527–8, 11.666; styles of communication 2.533–6; it 'bears the hallmarks of my personality' 26.637

how he functioned
as elucidator or translator of the Dharma 2.525–7, 11.687; as 'a channel for something beyond me' 11.687; he directed his mind to whatever was needed 11.554; visiting Buddhist centres 11.526, 11.627, 24.582–3; his historical sense gave him a very long-term view of the Movement 11.554; 'I feel more and more that the best thing I can do is write' 11.526–7, 11.558; 'If I talk about something for long enough it often happens' 19.85; 'My own spiritual project has been inseparable from that of the Movement' 25.84; the pitfalls of selectively following his example 5.614; 'a strong sense of dissatisfaction with the way I was functioning' 24.306–7

handing on responsibilities
sabbatical (1973): the first step towards handing on 11.514–16; confidence in senior Order members 11.601, 12.481; confidence in public preceptors 12.597; continuance of the Order assured 24.314; dreams relating to it which could be important to the Order 12.686; early expression of the wish to hand on (1977) 11.525; plans to hand on 2.536; represented by the publication of Subhuti's book 24.207–8; for headship of the Order 2.748 (n706), 12.597–8, 12.630–2, 25.107–8, 26.403–4; for ordinations 2.510–12, 4.274, 11.557–8, 12.376–7, 12.378–9, 12.398–400, 24.256, 24.314; 'handing on', not 'stepping down' 11.686; he wanted to be free to be a disruptive influence 11.687; an important step 2.546; his 75th birthday a watershed 11.660; how he felt about the process 11.661; list of those to whom responsibility was first handed on 12.597; like one lamp being lit from another 2.511; 'My work will be done when the Order is no longer dependent on me' 12.401; withdrawing from organizational responsibilities 11.603, 11.618, 24.324; plans for handing on responsibilities 12.490–1; the only way the Movement could grow 12.377; to the College of Public Preceptors 11.615–16, 12.631–2, 25.109; urgency about withdrawing from responsibilities 24.308; wish to 'supervise' at least two stages of succession 11.600–1; withdrawing from responsibilities, not people 24.324–5

legacy
a threefold legacy: Dharma teachings, spiritual practices, institutions 6.xxi–xxii; two further aspects: material and literary 6.xxii–xxvi

(III) The Order

WHAT IS THE ORDER?

introduction
the commitments of an Order member 9.493; a free association of committed individuals 11.389–90; it can be a model for a self-contained 'Western' Buddhist world 26.631; men and women take equal responsibility 2.467, 10.222; not a group but a spiritual community 2.568; is the Order a lineage? 11.667–8; it is not a legal entity and has no legal existence 11.177; the Order as a dance 25.145; a paradigm for the integration of Buddhism into Western society 11.469; positive emotion is the lifeblood of the Order 26.24; the reasons for the original name (Western Buddhist Order) 11.70–1; a rich and fruitful growing thing 12.423; the spiritual fellowship of the Order 24.31; their main object must be real Going for Refuge 10.387, 12.372; we should be prepared to live and die for one another 11.443; why the Order is at the heart of Triratna 12.369–70

a unified order
based on a common understanding of the Dharma 25.108–9; a bond with other Order members, whether friends or not 4.524; could there be a 'monastic–lay' split? 11.556; different lifestyles and levels of commitment 2.467, 11.555, 12.498; the influence of Order members working together 12.309, 12.625, 25.128; it does not identify itself with any one form of Buddhism 11.470; the

living, joyful spiritual fellowship of those practising the Teaching 3.457; equal ordination for men and women 2.467–8, 12.667; one of the six distinctive emphases 2.467, 11.469–70, 12.498, 12.667–8; one Order with Eastern and Western 'wings' 10.417–18; open to all, whatever nationality, race, sexuality, or class 12.668, 12.675, 13.452, 26.638, 26.672; there is a lot of coherence 11.689–90; unified in three important respects 11.469–70; we can provide an example of how human beings can get on together 25.58–9; Western Order members can learn a lot from those in India 10.lxiv, 10.87, 10.89; what would keep it together after Sangharakshita's death? 11.669

the Order as the thousand-armed Avalokiteśvara
aspiring to be a tiny reflection of this figure 11.517; at the highest level the Order as the embodiment of the *bodhicitta* 12.405; and the third order of consciousness 2.474–5; each hand holds a different implement 2.532; every day realizing more that we are a hand of Avalokiteśvara 2.502, 12.414–15, 26.655; the myth of the Order 12.472; not just a figure of speech, to be taken seriously, even literally 12.599; operating in accordance with compassion 12.415; a stream of non-egoistic energy manifesting through people 12.600; when will the Order become a recognizable reflection? 2.316

nomenclature
originally *upāsaka* or *upāsikā* 9.165; *mahā-upāsaka* or *upāsikā*: senior lay brother or sister, originally seen as part of ordination structure 2.469; changed to Dharmachari or Dharmacharini 2.489–93, 2.729 (n612), 9.165, 9.539; change first adopted in India 2.501–2, 24.xiv; early sign of Sangharakshita's thinking 2.449; the meaning of Dharmachari 2.339, 2.491 9.544, 13.498; scriptural references 2.491; why the name was changed 2.491–2, 24.5

ORDINATION

introduction
brief explanation 2.732–3 (n628); based on knowledge, not belief in technical validity 2.596; the beginning of a process, not a culmination 12.420; the mythical journey towards ordination 26.272–3, 26.279; one joins the Order by Going for Refuge to the Three Jewels 11.175; a parallel in the Pāli canon 11.454–5; a resonance with Nyanaponika's description of self-surrender 15.740; speeding up ordination 4.421; men's ordination process developed at Padmaloka 2.513–18; women's ordination process 11.636, 12.375–6

first ordinations
the ceremony 2.403–5, 2.466, 3.xi, 12.367–8, 23.440; emphasis on the bodhisattva ideal 2.471; exhortation to the first Order members 3.xi–xii; photograph 23.441; sharing of Sangharakshita's understanding of the Three Jewels 2.471–2; the shrine 2.404; talks 12.371; what people wore 12.368; what had happened? 2.404–5; what was expected of an Order member 2.468–9, 2.489

development of ordination
originally four grades 2.468–9, 12.371; one ordination 2.346–7, 2.492, 2.481, 2.598, 12.371; originally conceived of as a lay Order 11.178; consideration of a kind of monastic ordination 11.523–4

characteristics of Triratna ordination
effective Going for Refuge 2.481, 10.486, 12.312, 12.666; emphasis on Going for Refuge 11.469, 12.371–2; equal ordination for women and men 11.469–70, 11.641, 12.368, 12.498, 12.667; is it recognized by other Buddhists? 2.595–6; it represents self-surrender, total commitment 15.660–1, 15.737, 15.740–1

seeking ordination
confusion between desire for ordination and commitment to the Three Jewels 24.93; how one becomes an Order member 11.390–1; motivation for seeking ordination 19.247–8; not a promotion 12.416–17, 17.672; not an object that one can appropriate without undergoing change 24.94–5; you don't have to wait until your motives are completely pure 11.430, 17.287; you have to ask, not just wait for it to happen 11.276

training for ordination
discharging all debts 2.368; Going for Refuge groups 2.514, 2.734 (n633); Going for Refuge retreats 2.514; having a glimpse of a glimpse of the Transcendental 25.144; how long it takes 12.500–1; it is not easy to become an Order member 9.510–11, 10.269, 10.388, 12.389; *kalyāṇa mitra* system 2.514, 4.274; moving to another country to prepare for ordination 12.554; one should not commit oneself without serious thought 25.63; Order members need to communicate a clear idea of the Order 2.518; ordination teams 2.512; it is presumptuous to speak of 'preparing people for ordination' 4.274; six element practice 2.387; deepening provisional Going for Refuge until effective 2.515–16, 12.596; Sangharakshita reflects on his similar spiritual journey 2.584–5; study of *The Ten Pillars of Buddhism* 13.444; taking up the Going for Refuge and Prostration practice 2.514

readiness for ordination
assessment of readiness for ordination 2.304, 2.512, 4.273–4, 12.399–400; being angry at not being considered ready 11.430; being prepared to put as much energy as you can into Going for Refuge 11.430; in a sense you are ordained when you are not yet ready 15.507–8; the time it takes to become ready varies a lot 11.179; wondering what one has to do to be considered ready 17.672

ordination retreats
a case for making a long journey to get there 26.263; in India 9.286, 10.xlvi, 10.290, 24.xix–xx, 24.20–2, 24.106–9; in New Zealand 24.33, 24.48–51; an opportunity for change 15.363; in Spain 12.738 (n323); in Tuscany, *see under* Il Convento

ORDINATION CEREMONIES

introduction
brief description 24.609 (n38); the beauty of the ceremony 2.305, 9.246; the two phases represent the subjective and objective elements of Going for Refuge 15.705; two phases reflect going forth and joining the sangha 3.461–2; why have a ceremony? 18.378

preceptors
devotion and gratitude to one's preceptors 26.630; Order members could ordain as many people as Sangharakshita did 12.400; Sangharakshita as preceptor, or preceptor's preceptor 2.523; preceptors' part in the ordination ceremony 12.498–9

private ordination
choosing a *sādhana*, *see under* visualization/Buddhas and bodhisattvas; new name 12.499, 13.499–501, 13.502–3, 18.150–1; name chosen to emphasize qualities needed in the Order 24.171; the Refuges and Precepts 11.175–6, 12.498–9; why it is a private ceremony 11.176

public ordination
Going for Refuge in the presence of the sangha 4.66, 11.176, 12.499; offerings to people being ordained 13.417; reflections on a pre-FWBO ordination ceremony 23.145–6; ritual recognition that someone is effectively Going for Refuge 12.597; solemnity and joy 24.171

College of Public Preceptors (and Council)
the establishment of the College 2.546, 2.740–1 (n667), 12.597, 12.631–2, 26.403–4; the appointment of more preceptors 11.689; it should speak with one voice 25.109; no need for a single head of the Order 11.690; people withdrawing and others being admitted 11.667–8; responsible for ensuring harmony and fidelity to Sangharakshita's teachings 11.668; spiritual leadership 25.108; they began by living together, to learn to function as a team 11.661; what should the College of Public Preceptors do? 11.616; why a College and Council rather than one person? 11.615

ordination vows
'For the benefit of all beings' 10.lxiii; ordination represents a promise 12.485; 'With loyalty to my teachers' 2.525

taking the ten precepts
because Going for Refuge must find ethical expression 12.499; change to the wording of the positive precepts 2.703–4 (n396); extra precepts a personal choice representing more intensive practice 2.347, 15.700–1; in this way the whole being is purified 9.309–10; as '*mūla-prātimokṣa*' 2.346–7, 2.492–3; reasons for choosing this particular set of precepts 2.305, 2.346–7; their use in the Order represents a new departure 11.258; they lay down the basic principles 19.559–60

kesas
at the first WBO ordination ceremony 2.404; encouraging men to make their own *kesas* 4.287–8; an exhibition of Japanese *kesas* 24.529–30; 'an outward and visible sign of an inward and spiritual grace' 14.542; what a *kesa* is 9.546, 11.176; to be worn with pride 25.91; what the colours of the Three Jewels represent 9.536; what the strings represent 9.531; robes 24.363

post-ordination process
the need for a process 12.419–21; finding out what you want to do in the Order 19.99–100

LIFE IN THE ORDER

chapter meetings
description 2.730–1 (n626); chapter discussions 12.481; confession in chapter meetings 25.95, 26.642–3; good to have a mix of people in a chapter 11.556; important to attend regularly 12.412–13, 12.679; the responsibility of Order members to keep each other up to scratch 11.556; 'spiritual workshops' 2.510, 12.412; Subhuti's visits to chapters 2.515; a venue within which one can be completely open 25.95

Order weekends
attending them and preparing for them 12.413; the third ever men's Order weekend 11.432

Order conventions
the first Order convention 12.580; 'gathering in large numbers' 2.317; a good time to make an effort towards real Going for Refuge 12.597; the need for periods of silence 12.557; Order convention 1989 (at Stonyhurst College) 24.365–6; Order convention 1999 12.591; at Bodh Gaya (2009) 6.xxi, 11.718; at Bodh Gaya (2018) 10.lxiii (photo)

lifestyle
are Order members entitled to a private life? 13.399, 25.63; could there be a 'monastic–lay' split? 11.556; Order members getting married 15.414–15, 25.63; Order members should be able to relate to one another despite different lifestyles 26.31; originally conceived of as a lay order 11.176; constantly questioning commitment and lifestyle 12.389; are there rules? 19.558–60; different backgrounds and lifestyles 2.305, 2.467, 10.387, 11.176–7, 12.665; those studying or meditating full-time may be supported by right livelihood 11.188

neither monastic nor lay
anticipated in Sangharakshita's transition from being a monk 25.91; treated as 'lay' by Theravādins 2.560; neither a monastic nor a lay movement and Order 11.464, 11.469–70; to us, being a layman or monk is just a matter of lifestyle 11.662; simply people who commit themselves to the Dharma 12.498; the Order doesn't divide into those who practise celibacy and those who don't 13.452–3; if you go for Refuge, you practise whatever your socio-religious position 15.649 19.473

anagārikas
the emergence of *anagārikas* 2.469; all Order members move in the direction of *brahmacarya* 13.452–3; *anagārika* ceremony 19.534–5; an expression of Going for Refuge 2.643; having more will hold the two wings of the Order together 12.402; in a sense they correspond to *bhikkhus* and *bhikkhunīs* 12.373; moving towards the *rūpaloka* 2.608; growth in numbers 2.561, 11.587, 11.597; a place for monasticism in the Order 2.561; status no different from that of any other Order member 2.608; to be seriously considered by the time you're 45 12.402; they are still citizens 11.624; vow of chastity or celibacy 2.305, 2.608–9

status
no need for anyone to claim superiority 15.535–7; respect is due to the elders in the Order 11.602–3, 12.678–9; 'senior' Order members 12.37[illegible], 12.481–2, 15.535–6

practices and activities
discussions about organizational matters 10.561; giving Dharma talks 12.377, 12.487, 17.129; the importance of Order members keeping in contact with each other 11.177; meditation practices 5.52–3; not all Order members are involved with Buddhist centres 11.390; Order *mettā bhāvanā* 17.42, 24.32; the 'Order Office' v24; the path of dependence on self-power 2.562; a place for *vipassanā* in the traditional sense 2.561–2; relating to other Order members on the basis of Going for Refuge 11.179; 'reporting in' 24.162, 24.356, 24.645 (n193); relationship to the Triratna Buddhist Community (FWBO) 11.177–8; *Shabda* (newsletter) 2.521, 2.736 (n644), 12.413–14, 12.477, 12.482, 12.736 (n310), 24.361; sick and aged Order members being cared for 26.658; writing books 12.379

ORDER MEMBERS

what are Order members like?
a comparison with the knights of the Round Table 2[illegible].99–100; contrasted with *bhikkhus* 9.17[illegible]–4; a difference between how they appear to the movement and to their relatives? 24.125; an individual Order member is a microcosm of the Order, but cannot represent it 14.542; mistakenly assumed to be laity 2.560; Order members as disciples 2.524; their different lifestyles and nationalities 11.390; they are not like Christian

missionaries 4.446–7; they can be very busy 11.617; they look like ordinary people 9.493; they should be meditative and also active 4.464; the very different temperaments of different Order members 12.512; they wear the ordinary 'lay' dress of their society 2.347, 2.492

advice for Order members
attend chapter meetings and Order weekends 12.412–13; avoid distractions 12.421–2; be careful to pass on what you have heard accurately 10.576; be mindful of your speech when in large gatherings 12.556; be more ceremonious 12.486–7; be well read and comb the scriptures for insights 11.602; don't be too fussy about where you'd like to do your Dharma work 11.618; don't give yourself too easy a time 25.77; don't keep too many options open too long 12.484–5; don't misuse the developmental model 12.404–5, 12.478–9; communication of the Dharma by charisma is not encouraged 13.477; cultivate good manners 6.xxxi, 12.403–4, 12.486–7; don't argue, discuss 12.483–4, 26.82; get involved in local politics 10.77–8, 12.488–9; place a greater emphasis on the bodhisattva ideal 12.405; be more mindful 10.84, 12.382, 12.403; develop more vision, more imagination, a broader view 12.404; don't accept yourself 8.584–6, 12.480–1, 15.520, 15.523, 26.61, 26.537; distinguish fact from value judgement 12.477; have an annual solitary retreat 4.530–1, 4.535, 12.418–19; just do your best to live up to the ideal to which you've committed yourself 25.94; keep alive and deepen your Going for Refuge 11.602; keep beginner's mind 12.422–3; keep up Dharma study 10.436, 12.418; keep up your *sādhana* 12.417–18; keep your promises 12.485; be heroic 12.489–90; be kind to Mitras 12.416–17; be kind to other Order members 12.404, 12.415; learn a foreign language 12.556–7; live up to your commitment, but avoid playing up to people's projections 17.657–8; look up to the Buddha, to spiritual teachers, and all the truly great 26.632; make sure that your motive for being in the Order stays pure 11.430; move towards complete *brahmacarya* 12.487–8; operate in the love mode 12.415; participate in the post-ordination process 12.419–21; take the precepts (especially speech) more seriously 12.403, 12.416–17; practise the *mūla* yogas 5.555–6; the project is to bring your life into harmony with the Dharma 25.103; read *Shabda* 12.482; reduce input 12.473–5, 15.174, 15.287–8, 19.544–5, 26.62; rejoice in one another's merits 12.481–3; remember you're a citizen 11.624, 12.488–9; resolve disputes and restore harmony 12.598–9; study the classics 12.405; identify with the Order as a whole 12.414–15; report in to *Shabda* 12.413–14; see the altruistic dimension of Going for Refuge more clearly 12.405; seek to move from effective to real Going for Refuge 12.596–7, 12.600; take more initiative with people 4.446–7; take pride in the Order 12.483; think clearly 12.475–6; think more in terms of renunciation 12.479–80; think of others, especially those who need the Dharma 12.489; trust one another 12.483; work together harmoniously 11.xxiii

taking on responsibility
advice on strengthening motivation to take responsibility 12.381–3; encouraging women to accept responsibilities 11.640; for ordinations 2.510–12, 2.732–3 (n628), 12.376–7, 12.378–9, 12.597; responsibility and the spiritual hierarchy 11.617; why don't more Order members take on responsibilities? 12.379–81

potential problems for Order members
being 'good Buddhists' and not being themselves 4.603; concern about Order members risking their lives in dangerous sports 24.503; conflict and disharmony should be resolved 2.522–3, 12.456–7, 12.676–7; the dangers to Order members of 'having a career' 24.327–8; dismay that for some, idealism had become a dirty word 24.393, 24.401; everyone knows the teachings, but does everyone live up to them? 10.84; in a false position when they behave as though they are not really Buddhist 2.570–1; Order members in India seem more fired up than those in the UK 10.83–4; putting yourself out of harmony with the Order 15.418; using only a fraction of their potential 4.445–6; tension in the Order 25.108–9; they need to study and reflect more 24.391–3; threats to the integrity of the Order 24.327; unmindfulness 11.625–6; why aren't Order members full of enthusiasm for the Dharma? 10.84

leaving and rejoining the Order
because of disagreement on fundamentals 11.667; the dropping of names from the Order register 2.518–19; reasons why people leave the Order 2.518; re-ordination 2.519; withdrawal of Order members in the early days 12.372

THE ORDER AND THE WIDER WORLD

the relation of the Order to the rest of the Buddhist world
'Extending the Hand of Fellowship' 2.543–74; ecumenism 2.547–56; essentially a relation with individuals 2.502, 2.546; important to feel part of the Buddhist world 2.548; investigating links with Buddhist and other spiritual groups 24.195–6; 'the less the FWBO is involved with 'Buddhist groups' the better' 24.167; orthodoxy 2.556–67; part of the rising wave of Buddhism in the context of world decline 12.595; part of a worldwide Buddhist movement 11.688; personal contact 2.568–74

relating to other Buddhists
do not allow yourself to be put in a false position 2.570–1; do not be misled by labels 2.572–3; as individuals 2.568–9; look for the deepest common ground 2.571–2; on a shared basis of Going for Refuge, not religious status 2.560

outward-looking
the aim is to transform the world, not just find a niche within it 11.377; disappointment that it has not done more 12.386; other-regarding aspect: seek to transform self *and* world 2.516, 12.373; responding to the needs of the world 12.380–1, 18.592–3; should try to get in contact with people with drink problems 24.154; we need to raise our voices against the harm being done in the world 25.58; what does Triratna offer the world? 11.669; the wish that it should project itself more 11.525

(IV) INSTITUTIONS

introduction
brief introduction 6.xxii, 9.504–5, 12.468–9; discouragement of any creeping paralysis of institutions 17.635; intended purely to help us move in the direction of Enlightenment 11.690; the nucleus of the new society 3.613, 18.34–5; they can act as a demonstration of the Dharma 19.507–8; the three Cs (centre, community, 'co-op') 3.613, 12.468–9, 18.34–5; institutions as a field of creativity 12.639–40; we need our institutions because we need other people, and they need us 12.469

BUDDHIST CENTRES

the basis
best to have many small centres 9.393; building our own Buddhist centres 11.623–4, 19.128; charging for Dharma classes 18.377; don't worry about starting small 11.728; each centre is legally and financially autonomous 3.623–4, 11.177, 11.569, 24.485; how to go about developing a new centre 15.95–6; number of centres 12.375; when planning a new centre, keep your plans flexible 19.525

the purpose of a Buddhist centre
best use of centres 9.420–1; compared to the Temple of Isis at Pompeii 24.294–5; the nucleus of a new society 3.456, 3.623; people come along for one reason and stay for another 10.551; the purpose of the centre 12.468–9, 25.141; a spiritual research station, not the equivalent of the parish church 12.128; to find out what a centre is like, you have to come and see for yourself 15.506

centre activities
all sorts of activities are run 2.303, 9.245, 9.504–5; an alternative to activities that merely pass the time 3.623; choirs (with choirmasters) at Buddhist centres 12.558; developing friendships at the Buddhist centre 12.539–40; examples of activities 11.139–40; the meditation practices taught 10.206–7, 10.213–14, 25.141; participating in all activities 11.478; the presence of Dharmacharinis is important 11.636

participating in centre life
helping out at the centre 4.458–60, 18.592–3; if necessary, stop all activities so everyone can go on retreat 4.528–9; make newcomers feel welcome 4.338, 11.238–9, 12.60–1, 12.487, 12.539, 12.680; the symbolism of leaving your shoes outside the shrine-room 12.541; taking full advantage of facilities, you could be a Stream Entrant 12.377–8; visiting centres as a kind of pilgrimage 10.397

advice about centres
a Buddhist centre should have a happy, friendly, and peaceful atmosphere 17.182; the danger of mere socializing 11.651, 12.540–1; make sure the social element is serving the Dharmic purpose 19.467–8; make sure its significance doesn't become purely cultural 19.469–70; centres could get involved with local politics 10.77–8, 12.488–9; centres could take more interest in the local community 10.87; don't use the Buddhist group as a community substitute 12.68–9, 12.81; it should be an oasis of awareness and kindness 11.651, 17.299; using the centre as a community substitute is fine on its own level 10.74

those who run the centre
the chair is the focal point for the whole centre 12.486; the chair should perhaps

stay in post for a long time 18.336; officiating at a centre, you are the embodiment of the ethical ideal 15.353; presidents 12.631–2

see also
individual centres *under* place name

RETREAT CENTRES

introduction
retreat centres should be simple and should not suggest domesticity 19.96

Adhiṣṭhāna
introduction 24.754 (n760); named by Sangharakshita 26.408; Sangharakshita's move to Adhiṣṭhāna 26.543–4; the building project 26.544; an Order gathering 25.xxxii; a seminar and exhibition on William Blake 26.659

Akashavana, women's retreat centre in Spain
introduction 2.735 (n635); ordination retreats 12.738 (n323)

Aryaloka Retreat Center, New Hampshire
established 12.375; Sangharakshita visits 12.426, 24.469–70, 24.486, 24.516–20

Bhaja retreat centre, India
near the Bhaja caves 12.375; architecture 10.405; banner of victory 10.408–9; 'Bhaja, 1983' (poem) 25.374; building the centre 10.xlix (photograph), 10.406; congratulations on the achievement 10.334; first women's retreat (photograph) 10.l; the opening of the centre 10.326–34; the opening of the shrine hall 10.404–9; ordinations 10.xlix; photograph 10.xlix; relationship to Bhaja caves 10.405–6; Sangharakshita's last visit 10.liv

Dhanakosa, Scotland
Sangharakshita's visit 24.583

Guhyaloka, men's ordination retreat centre in Spain
brief introduction 2.717 (n498), 15.744 (n3); a black cat at Guhyaloka 24.394–5; could the community grow vegetables? 24.463; Dhardo Rimpoche's stupa 26.455; and the men's ordination process 2.514, 12.500; might the improvement to the road mean a loss of seclusion? 24.406; Sangharakshita staying there, *see* Sangharakshita/life story/Triratna years; struggle to create facilities 24.333; wildlife and nature 24.393–5

Hsüan Tsang retreat centre (previously Bordharan), Wardha, India
opening 10.liv, 10.393 (photograph); support from Taiwanese Buddhists 10.li, 10.liv

Padmaloka men's retreat centre
introduction 2.728 (n604), 11.562; set up in 1976 24.171; the 'abode of the lotus' 24.104; Aloka's paintings 2.735 (n637); archives 12.398; the atmosphere during retreats 24.163; candle workshop 24.152, 24.154, 24.157; changes (1985) 24.6; the community as it was in its early days 15.477, 24.152–6; development of men's ordination process 2.513–18; its name evokes Sukhāvatī 25.lviii; an owl down the chimney 24.151; ordinations at Padmaloka 24.170–1, 24.172, 24.314; poems about Padmaloka 25.liv–lix, 25.344–5, 25.457; the woods near Padmaloka seem very happy 18.23; summer 24.65–6, 24.145–6; library 12.418; Olle Mallander's visit 26.215–16; Order–Mitra event (1980) 24.173; Sangharakshita and Padmaloka, *see under* Sangharakshita III/places of residence; stupa to Dhardo Rimpoche 25.457; summer retreats 1979 24.159–60; Tiger, the community cat 24.151; winter and early spring 24.150–1; women's retreats held there 24.171–2

Rivendell
Sangharakshita visits 26.625

Sudarshanaloka (Tararu), New Zealand
Sangharakshita names the centre 24.734–5 (n628); the enshrining of Dhardo Rimpoche's ashes in the stupa 24.513–14, 24.565

Tārāloka women's retreat centre
introduction 2.733 (n629), 12.738 (n323); working to establish it 24.248, 24.649 (n203); named by the women who founded it 12.375; an impressive achievement 11.645; international retreat 12.674; opening of the Tārā shrine 12.659–62; seminar on the *Heart Sūtra* 14.xv; the women creating the retreat centre as a world of Tārā 12.375; and the women's ordination process 12.375–6, 12.500

Tiratanaloka women's ordination retreat centre
introduction 2.733 (n629)

Vajraloka meditation centre (Tyn-y-ddol)
the creation of the centre 10.214; early team and aspirations 5.xxxv, 24.311; dedicated to meditation and celibacy 2.371; Sangharakshita visits 24.6, 24.67, 24.132–3, 24.311; mentioned in India 12.375; work on the building 5.xxix, 5.xxxiii–v

see also
team-based right livelihood, *see under* right livelihood; communities, *see* community/residential

Triratna Grantha Mala Marathi publications 9.170

triśaraṇa *see tisaraṇa*

Triśatikāya Prajñāpāramitāya Kārikā-saptati *see* Asaṅga

Trisong Detsen *see under* Tibet/history

Tristan and Isolde 25.406, 25.595 (n104)

triśūla *see* trident

Trisvabhāvanirdeśa *see* Vasubandhu

triumphalism of the Church 2.458, 23.306–7, 23.310; at the Hampstead Buddhist Vihara 2.458–9, 13.415; creeping into *Maha Bodhi* editorials 2.458, 22.311; of the Theravāda 2.50, 2.458–9, 2.495, 13.414–15

Trivandrum, India 20.247–52

trivial art viewed as trivial 3.506–7; concerned with trivial things, are you missing the possibility of Enlightenment? 18.155; bitter disputes often arise over trivialities 13.137; don't waste time with spiritual friends talking about trivial things 18.567; the 'Hīnayāna' Nirvāṇa taught for those bent on the enjoyment of trifling things 14.117–18; mass media give trivialities an importance they don't possess 26.82; social pressure keeps us immersed in trivial pursuits 3.35; *taking* the Refuges – a trivialization 2.241, 3.397; through mindfulness, the most trivial occasion of life is invested with a halo of sanctity 1.151; trivial speech 10.581, 18.567, 19.493–4; triviality is one of the greatest disasters that can happen to us 26.82; wasting time with trivial pursuits 10.322, 12.355, 26.68; Zen can be trivialized: 'the witty word among the teacups' 8.488, 17.454

triyāna *see yānas*/three

Triyana Vardhana Vihara *see under* Sangharakshita II

Trollope, Anthony 20.81, 26.581, 26.595–6

tṛṣṇā (Pāli *taṇha*, craving, literally 'thirst')

introduction
roughly synonymous with *abhijjhā* 2.386; almost always used in a negative sense 12.550; canonical reference for three types of *tṛṣṇā* 8.675–8 (n69); in *Nietzsche and Buddhism* 12.550; it's doubtful if we can eliminate *tṛṣṇā* 12.550–1; and libido 12.99; the origin of rebirth and suffering 3.199; religious teachings as rationalizations of *tṛṣṇā* 12.99, 12.711 (n76)

craving for sensuous experience (kāma-tṛṣṇā or kamāsrava)
craving for a particular form, sound, etc. 1.111, 3.199; craving for experience through the five senses 3.278; we have to learn to experience sensations without allowing craving to arise 3.202–3

craving for continued existence (bhava-tṛṣṇā or bhava-taṇhā)
craving for any form of conditioned existence 3.278; association with *sassatavāda* (eternalism) 1.111, 3.202, 14.572, 17.243; the cause of rebirth 26.159; craving for heaven 3.199; craving for eternal life leads to continued rebirth 2.149; thirst for being 25.194

craving for non-existence (vibhava-tṛṣṇā or vibhava-taṇhā)
the desire for oblivion 3.199; associated with *ucchedavāda* (nihilism) 1.111, 3.202, 14.572, 17.243–4; related to Freud's death wish 8.127, 12.99; such a desire is a fact of human nature 8.127–8

see also
craving; as eighth *nidāna*, *see under* twelve cyclical *nidānas*

true nature alienation from one's true nature (*White Lotus Sūtra*) 16.91–2, 16.173, 16.200; 'dwelling inwardly in the true nature of reality' 16.47; the Enlightened mind understands the true nature of everything, as a mirror reflects objects 4.155; a human being's true nature is to develop 9.232–3, 16.71; insight into the true nature of existence 3.122, 3.246–7, 3.617, 5.656; insight into the true nature of phenomena 1.87–8; insight into the true nature of reality 5.417; instead of running from happiness into guilt or intoxication, understand its true nature 3.227; the jewel symbolizes our own true nature 16.173–4; the Mahāmudrā's relaxed attitude: a key to the realization of your true nature 19.387; mindfulness implies bearing in mind *all the time* the true nature of our situation 3.324; penetrating your own true nature, you emerge into Buddhahood 12.234; to see the true nature of mind is hard 19.97–8; seeing the true nature of all conditioned things 2.114; the true nature of the Dharma cannot be comprehended abstractly, only through experience 10.568; the true nature of levels of concentration 2.144; *see also* human nature

Trungpa, Chögyam brief introduction 23.494 (n158), 24.653 (n223); accepts an invitation to teach meditation at Biddulph

23.206; departs for America 23.440, 25.92; disagreement with Akong Rimpoche 25.92; and Allen Ginsberg 24.176–7; living in Oxford 23.129; photographs 11.474, 23.33; a poem to Trungpa 25.xxviii, 25.92, 25.323; his reputation 19.163; *The Tibetan Book of the Dead*, *see under Tibetan Book of the Dead*/translations; Sangharakshita's meeting with him 12.494, 23.129; the 'Three Musketeers' become his disciples 23.407; *Visual Dharma: The Buddhist Art of Tibet* (review) 8.530–1

trust an attitude of faith and trust towards life 14.596; cannot be forced 16.315; confession requires trust 10.570–1, 16.315–16, 18.516; confidence that someone you trust will act from the love mode 18.387; an employee's duty to be trustworthy 3.588; faith, trust, and pleasure 17.552–3; losing trust in existence 18.579; mutual trust and confidence 26.27; Cardinal Newman believed in God but didn't trust (like) him 15.620, 17.336, 17.552; only an integrated person can be trusted 17.697; 'Put not your trust in princes' 12.239, 17.552; take things on trust only provisionally 15.510–11; takes time to develop 16.316; trusting politicians 17.231; trusting the power of positive forces 4.267–8; with trust, explanations are unnecessary, but without it, explanations are useless 26.81; within the spiritual community 10.571, 16.315; you can completely trust only one whose virtues can survive any circumstances 17.327

truth

the nature of truth
beyond words and concepts 7.331; birthless and deathless, only the Truth endures 7.343; divine revelation or human discovery? 9.63; indescribable, hence a matter for personal experience 1.206; ineffable 1.64–5; it can appal 25.358; it can be subjective 17.390; it does not seek to please anybody 7.133; it may be eternal, but its manifestations are not 1.231; it naturally communicates itself 10.624–5; it often seems not liberating but an imprisonment 16.96–7; only the Buddhas can understand it in its fullness (*White Lotus Sūtra*) 16.39–40; a sort of gestalt, a whole, complete in itself 10.595–6; subject to the vicissitudes of fortune 1.50; 'Truth is immortal (or deathless) speech' 13.644, 14.293, 19.294–5; 'The Truth is the whole' 2.50, 7.44, 7.385, 8.225

find the truth
and be receptive to it, even if it threatens everything you have based your life on 17.632; and then live by it 17.231, 26.16; be prepared for it to transcend anything you had imagined 16.223; embodied in the lives of saints and seers 25.389; insight into Truth gives a feeling of certitude 7.145; it has to be approached gradually 16.39; knowledge of what is ultimately valid and how it is to be obtained 17.546; more likely to be with the individual than with the group 26.42; openness to truth 5.43; 'a wild crane cries out the Truth' 26.243; you are presented with the ultimate truth every moment of your life 16.184; you don't get the truth by adding together what different people have said 10.595–6

images
the Buddha as embodiment and symbol of the truth 11.492–3; the ascent to truth is a slope, not a precipice 7.78; map as metaphor for incomplete truth 1.208; a path that guides 25.203; the ship of truth 2.17; the sun of truth 1.239; workshops in which truths are manufactured 26.195

reflections on truth
Beauty is not merely Truth, but Goodness as well 26.196; beauty may or may not be truth, but truth is certainly beauty 12.308; a breakdown of the notion of objective truth 12.350–3; distinction between scientific truth and poetic truth 12.182; Hīnayāna conception of Truth in effect merely rational 1.221, 7.542; saying 'Truth is everywhere' may be an excuse for not studying or practising 10.626; the truth doesn't scorch you as fiercely as the suffering when you ignore it 26.46; truth is one, sages only call it variously (Indian philosophy) 7.78; truth that is repeated becomes untruth, or another truth 26.7; trying to escape from the truth 13.356–7; the unimpeded progress of truth 2.5; what is the truth about the current and historical events we hear about? 24.148–9; without knowledge of truth, our world is a dry and barren place 16.219

see also
absolute truth and relative truth, *see under* two truths

truthfulness *see under* speech/four levels of skilful speech; *see also* honesty

Tsa *see nāḍīs*

Tsangnyön Heruka 1.636 (n447)

Tsaparang *see under* Govinda, Lama

Tsedeun, Princess Pema *see* Pema

Tsering, Ang (Sherpa cook) v21, v22

Tsering, Lha ('Long-Lived Deva') v21, v22

Tseten Tashi 21.194–6, 22.243, 22.246

Tshering, Topsher 21.36

Tsongkhapa (*Sumatikīrti, Jetsun Tsongkhapa, Je Rimpoche*)

HIS LIFE

introduction
his life story 2.681 (n194), 13.30–2, 17.423–5; literally 'the man from the onion valley' 13.31; he became a *śrāmaṇera* aged 7 13.31; an example of a doctrine-follower 2.143, 17.333; founder of the Gelug school of Tibetan Buddhism, *see under* Tibet/schools; he studied and synthesized all the teachings 13.31–2; the reformer of Tibetan Buddhism 13.30; his nephew Gendun Drup 13.35–6; a great organizer 13.30; higher ordination 13.32; and Madhyamaka 1.323; referred to in *The Necklace of Clear Understanding* 17.466; he named Guṇaprabha and Śākyaprabha authorities on the Vinaya 8.403; his death 13.33; celebration of his death anniversary 8.659, 13.33–4, 22.510–11, 23.395–6; a 600-year-old tea urn which still contained a drop from Tsongkhapa's day 17.695

his status as a revered figure
both scholar and saint – a rare combination 13.30; compared with Milarepa 12.511, 17.376; considered as a bodhisattva 2.182, 13.34; iconography 13.214; illustration 13.215, 17.425; in the guru yoga 5.562; on household shrines 2.229; regarded as a manifestation of Mañjuśrī 2.182, 13.34, 13.214; a thangka of a Tsongkhapa Refuge Tree owned by Sangharakshita 11.713; his depiction 13.34

HIS WORKS

introduction
summary 17.423–4; 'The human body, at peace with itself' 2.676 (n126); hymn of praise to the Buddha 8.528; *Lam-rim chen-mo* 2.440, 13.33, 13.106, 17.423, 17.533–4; *sNgags-rim chen-mo* 2.440, 13.33, 17.423; *Song of the Four Mindfulnesses* 8.508; the teaching of the combination of withdrawal and compassion 2.116, 18.52; a work revealed to him by Mañjuśrī 8.508

The Three Chief Paths (Lam Gyi Gtso Bo Rnam Gsum)
introduction 17.424; commentary by the Fourth Panchen Lama 8.529; full text 17.426–8; a copy presented to Sangharakshita by the Dalai Lama 22.371; Geshe Wangyal's commentary 17.421, 17.753 (n346); study groups in Bombay 10.131; the themes of the text 8.529; translation into English at the Dalai Lama's request 8.529, 8.661, 10.131, 17.422; withdrawal and the *bodhi*-mind 2.116, 17.424

Tu Fa Shun 1.353

Tu Lun, Ven. 8.477–83

Tubka Shunukyuwa 8.525

Tucci, Giuseppe introduction 8.674 (n63); 'one of the greatest scholars whom Buddhist studies has yet produced' 8.513; 'Buddha Jayanti' 8.373; 'The Demoniacal in the Far East' 8.117; *On Some Aspects of the Doctrines of Maitreya(nātha) and Asaṅga* 1.350–1, 1.360–2; *The Religions of Tibet* (review) 8.513–15; *Secrets of Tibet* 21.422; visit to Tsaparang, Tibet 21.422

Tukloji Maharaj 22.163

tulkus *see* Tibetan Buddhism/*tulkus*

Tulsidas (*Rāmacaritamānasa*) hostility to Buddhism 8.358; the hot air of devotional frenzy 26.164; Sangharakshita's review of a new translation 8.xix, 8.357–8; Shudras should be despised, brahmins worshipped 8.xix, 8.358, 9.26, 20.199

***tummo* heat** (Sanskrit *caṇḍālī*) one of the six yogas of Nāropā 13.28; burning up impurities 19.569; corresponds to chakras and *caṇḍālī* 16.121, 19.439; Alexandra David-Néel's description 24.113, 24.623 (n135); developing *tummo* 12.297–8, 18.91; explained to Sangharakshita by Dhardo Rimpoche 19.570; the heat generated is perceptible to other people 19.439; Milarepa's practice 13.28, 18.49–50, 18.65, 18.89–91, 19.257; not

just literal heat, but conjoined with the bliss and contentment of the Void 18.90–1; not just a subjective experience, but an actual change in temperature 18.536, 19.570; practised by Sangharakshita's teachers 19.569; the practice makes you feel you're enveloped in warm garments 18.620; connection with purity 19.569–70; *śamatha* and *vipaśyanā* forms of the practice 19.439–40, 19.569–7; similarity to *tapas* 15.447; the syllable *āḥ* visualized 18.321–2; the wearing of the *repa* (cotton garment) 13.28, 18.462, 19.366

Tun Hla Oung 21.245–7, 21.416, 22.168–9

turban the Dharma not to be taught to one wearing a turban 4.116, 4.342; on fire 1.124, 7.392

Turkestan 2.180

Turkey Constantinople (Istanbul) 11.627, 13.603, 13.622, 24.530; Manuel II Paleologus, Emperor of Byzantium 15.624; Ottoman Empire 26.450; Yeats on Byzantium 26.386

Turner, J. M. W. *Bridge of Sighs, Ducal Palace and Custom-House, Venice* 2.609, 2.612, 2.752 (n752), 26.465–6; capturing the dramatic qualities of the elements 26.254; a certain way of looking at the landscape 5.642; colour in his work 13.284; *Fire at Sea* 26.254; going out to sea during a storm 14.473; a great genius who took no notice of criticism 26.254–5; his works among the supreme achievements of Western culture 12.392, 12.615; mythological paintings 26.254; Ruskin's support for Turner 26.255, 26.721–2 (n207); the secular nature of his paintings 12.76; Turneresque dreams 11.685

Turner, Leslie 21.44–5

Turner, Phyllis 23.231

'turning about in the deepest seat of consciousness' *see parāvṛtti*

turtles putting its head through a yoke in the sea 1.418, 4.367, 7.170, 13.139; set free at Chinese Buddhist festivals 1.427

Tuscany *see under* Italy

Tuṣita Heaven (*devaloka*) *see under* heavens

twelve *āyatanas* (six sense bases and their objects) introduction 15.200, 17.404; contemplating them (*Satipaṭṭhāna Sutta*) 15.199–211, 18.10–11; difference between *sutta* and Abhidharma descriptions 14.80; doctrine held in common by Theravāda and Mahāyāna 7.531; inconsistencies exposed 1.320; in the Abhidharma 14.79, 14.83, 14.84; only mental constructions 1.267; they are empty of independent existence, so only relatively real 17.404

twelve cyclical *nidānas*

INTRODUCTION

description
description of links 3.192–200, 4.649, 7.494; wheel of life (brief) 2.74–6, 2.253–4, 3.129–31, 3.347, 11.28–9, 11.166, 12.155–6, 12.646, 13.127–8, 13.140; on wheel of life (full) 1.106–113; sometimes five or ten links are enumerated 17.759–60 (n412); why are twelve links enumerated? 1.105–7; most modern authors mention just twelve links 19.576

sources
the links derive from the Buddha's experience 4.701 (n278), 10.428–9, 17.476; canonical 3.653–4 (n184), 3.676 (n316), 19.614 (n151); Buddhaghosa's account, *see under* Buddhaghosa; different traditions enumerate different numbers of links 1.105, 3.193; doctrine held in common by Theravāda and Mahāyāna 7.531; the Hīnayāna fastened their attention on the cyclical *nidānas*, ignoring the spiral 1.226; in the *Sūtra of Golden Light* 16.281

reflections
developing an understanding of them on the Tibetan Buddhist path 12.296; how can a reactive process evolve into a higher process? 18.279; can be taken literally or symbolically 3.200–1; the cyclical mode of conditionality governs the *saṃsāra* 2.252, 16.388; the spiral path is the symbol of the creative mind 11.30; we mostly live this way: we know no rest, but move not an inch forward 12.154; we should know the twelve links by heart 3.204, 19.577; whatever happens, is our reaction cyclical or progressive? 3.279

how the process works
cyclic reaction between opposites 1.117–19, 3.13, 3.97, 3.184–5, 12.153–4; direct and reverse order (*anuloma* and *pratiloma*) 1.107, 10.433; action process and result process 1.111, 2.75–6, 3.201–2, 5.516, 15.527; a sequence of three lives, past, present, and future 2.76, 2.255, 3.201, 12.156, 17.478

breaking the chain
introduction 3.202–3, 10.152; disengaging from the reactive cycle: the aim of our

practice 15.228; the gap between feeling (*vedanā*) and craving (*tṛṣṇā*), *see under vedanā*; a sudden and an abrupt method 2.256–9; the circle tries to become a spiral 16.383–4; trying to see the point of origin 4.377; really seeing the process of passing from one state to another, we become free 13.140

THE TWELVE NIDĀNAS

(1) avidyā
ignorance 3.193–4, 12.155, 15.471–2; the starting point of the entire teaching 1.107–8; the blind, egoistic obstinacy that keeps the whole saṃsāric process going 19.18; may be enumerated first, but underlies all the *nidānas* 5.516; no actual beginning to the chain 3.193; a blind man with a stick 2.75, 2.253, 19.18

(2) saṃskāras
karma formations 2.253–4, 3.194–6, 12.155; and first *nidāna*: like drunkenness and acts committed when drunk 1.108, 3.195–6, 17.434; a potter with a wheel and pots 2.75, 2.253

(3) vijñāna
the initial seed of consciousness 2.75, 2.254, 12.155; what is reborn? 1.108–9; 'relinking consciousness' (*pratisandhi*), *see pratisandhi*; symbolized by a monkey in a flowering tree 2.75, 2.254

(4) nāma-rūpa
the psychophysical organism 2.254, 3.198, 12.155; the five *skandhas* 1.109, 3.198, 10.231; symbolized by a boat with four passengers 2.75, 2.254, 15.200, 17.502

(5) saḍāyatanas
the six sense organs, six bases 12.155; the bases for our experience of the external world 3.198; complex network of conditions 1.109–10; the transition to *sparśa* 17.530; symbolized by a house with five windows and a door 2.75, 2.254, 15.200

(6) sparśa
contact 3.198, 12.155; a combination of organ, object, and impression 1.110; symbolized by a man and woman embracing 2.75, 2.254

(7) vedanā
feeling: pleasant, painful, or neutral 1.110, 3.199, 12.155; represented by a man with an arrow in his eye 2.75, 2.254; for the transition between feeling and craving, *see under vedanā*

(8) tṛṣṇā (Pāli taṇhā)
craving 3.199; the flame of desire 1.110–11; three kinds of *tṛṣṇā*, *see under tṛṣṇā*; represented by a woman offering a drink to a man 2.75, 2.254

(9) upādāna
clinging, attachment 3.199, 12.156, 19.58–9; four kinds of grasping 1.112; represented by a man gathering fruit 2.75, 2.254

(10) bhāva
becoming 2.75–6, 12.156; not parturition, but development in the womb 1.112–13; the *bardo* according to some schools, the period in the womb according to others 3.200; represented by a pregnant woman 2.75, 2.254

(11) jāti
birth 2.254, 3.200, 12.156; rebirth on one of three planes 1.112; represented by a woman in childbirth 2.76, 2.254

(12) jarā-maraṇa
old age, disease, and death 2.254, 3.200, 12.156; 'this whole mass of suffering' 1.113; just facts 15.147; represented by a man carrying a corpse 2.76, 2.254

see also
nidāna chain meditation; names of individual links; points at which effect process becomes cause process, *see* three *sandhis*

twelve great acts in a Buddha's life *see under Lalitavistara Sūtra*/introduction

twelve positive *nidānas* or links (spiral path)

INTRODUCING THE SPIRAL PATH

introduction
brief description 1.115, 3.67, 7.494–5, 11.45–7, 12.647, 17.519; full description 2.101–19, 2.258–62, 3.258–95, 12.158–65; canonical references 1.116, 2.103, 3.203, 3.654 (n184), 17.747 (n305); referred to in a para-canonical work, the *Nettippakaraṇa* 10.432; not included in the *Survey* 1.8

a rediscovered teaching
ignored for many years 15.568, 15.579, 16.64; why did the tradition lose sight of this vital teaching? 10.431–2; Sangharakshita's discovery of the teaching 1.114–19, 13.516–17; Dr Beni Madhab Barua's account 1.116–20, 10.432, 10.614, 26.174–6; Mrs Rhys Davids's account 1.114, 1.116, 4.676 (n106), 10.432, 16.64; 'an oasis of affirmation in the midst of an arid desert of negation' 1.114, 7.204; a

talk on the positive *nidānas* in Glasgow 23.177–8

the twelve links as the spiral path
the spiral mode governs the spiritual life 2.252; an ascending series of mental states 4.648, 12.154; development of factors, one augmenting another 1.119, 3.13–14, 3.97–8, 3.278–9; the creative mind taken to its highest degree of development 17.357; the growth of consciousness leading to Enlightenment 15.229–30; the path of the Higher Evolution 2.476–7, 13.432–3, 13.517; resemblance to the seven *bodhyaṅgas* 15.224–5, 15.579; the outward-moving spiral 17.xxv; a positive approach to spiritual life 3.xiv–xv, 3.203–4, 10.513; the positive *nidānas* as the path to Nirvāṇa 1.114–20, 17.357; the rationale of the spiritual life 1.119, 3.67; the mystical (third to seventh *nidānas*) 8.440; and spiritual death and rebirth 5.41–2; a switch-over from the cyclical to the spiral type of conditionality 11.xxii, 11.32; without them the spiritual path has no rationale 3.203–4

the practice of the path
embarking on the spiral path: opening up to a new way of being 15.205; don't take the stages too literally, *samādhi* is present all the time 5.275; the gradual method 2.258–60, 10.562–3, 12.158; how can a reactive process evolve into a higher process? 18.279; a natural flow from one stage to the next 3.278–9, 5.392–3; going from happiness to happiness 4.475; not exclusively associated with sitting and meditating 10.613; progress is not a matter of egoistically willed achievement 2.112; cultivate the previous *nidāna* fully, or the present one will be a caricature 2.113; to the extent that we identify with the spiral trend, we 'escape' the cyclical trend 4.312; whatever happens, is our reaction cyclical or progressive? 3.279

path divides into two sections, mundane and transcendental
introduction 3.67–8, 4.649–50, 15.638–40; the reversible part of the spiral 4.182, 15.635–6, 16.383–4; succumbing to the gravitational pull 2.261; beyond the point of no return 15.636; the irreversible part of the spiral path 13.432–3

THE TWELVE POSITIVE LINKS

(1) duḥkha (Pāli dukkha)
from suffering to faith 1.115, 2.103–4, 2.258, 3.260–2, 4.419, 5.660–1, 12.625; faith is the first movement of creativity 19.580–1; for the gap between feeling (*vedanā*) and craving (*tṛṣṇā*), *see under* twelve cyclical links

(2) śraddhā (Pāli saddhā)
faith 1.115, 2.104–5, 2.258–9, 3.263–5, 12.159–60

(3) prāmodya (Pāli pāmojja)
joy 1.115, 2.105, 2.259–60, 3.265–6; the natural consequence of faith is joy 18.143; at this stage we may feel great devotion, and a clear conscience 12.160

(4) prīti (pīti)
rapture 1.115, 2.105–6, 2.260, 3.266–7, 12.160–1; marks the transition from the *kāmaloka* to the *rūpaloka* 2.105

(5) praśrabdhi (Pāli passaddhi)
calming down 1.115, 2.106, 2.260, 3.268–9, 12.161

(6) sukha
bliss 1.115, 2.107–9, 2.260, 3.269–70, 12.161–2

(7) samādhi
concentration 1.115, 2.109–113, 2.260, 3.271–4; after the preceding *nidānas*, a little practice brings profound experience 2.113; last of the *laukika* (mundane) *nidānas* 2.113; not just concentration, but perfect wholeness at a very high level of awareness 2.260; present with increasing intensity throughout 5.275

(8) yathābhūta-jñānadarśana
knowledge and vision of things as they really are 1.115, 2.262, 3.274–5, 16.589 (n32), 12.163; the crucial *nidāna* 3.68, 11.46–7, 12.163; as the Point of No Return 3.252–3, 4.182–3, 4.650, 12.163; synonymous with *vipaśyanā* 2.113–14; transition from cyclical to spiral mode 13.432; it is essentially an experience 2.113; you're not safe until you reach the Point of No Return 15.639–40

(9) nirveda (Pāli nibbidā)
withdrawal 1.115, 2.115–17, 3.275–6, 12.164

(10) vairāgya (Pāli virāga)
dispassion 1.115, 2.117, 3.276–7, 12.164

(11) vimukti
freedom 1.115, 2.118, 3.277–8, 12.164, 13.463, 16.446; corresponds to the third of the four *śūnyatās* 2.118–19; not what we ordinarily think of as freedom, but goes far beyond that 11.46–7; the stage of absolute compassion 2.119

(12) āsravakṣaya-jñāṇa
knowledge of the destruction of the *āsravas* 1.115, 2.119. 3.278, 12.164;

what the experience is like 17.519; is the twelfth *nidāna* the last? 1.116–20, 3.68–9, 10.614–15, 11.309, 15.226, 15.230, 15.466–70, 19.576, 26.174–6

see also
individual links

twenty-two vows *see under* Dr Ambedkar/ conversion

twenty-four causal conditions (Abhidharma) 1.110, 14.91–3

twenty-four *nidānas* two sets of twelve *nidānas* forming a continuous series 4.649–50; between them they cover *saṃsāra* and *nirvāṇa* 19.576–7; to know these and the four noble truths is to know the whole rationale of Buddhism 19.577; the twenty-four *nidānas* like rain filling up the streams, rivers, and seas 1.116; *see also* twelve cyclical *nidānas*; twelve positive *nidānas*

twenty-four *paccayākāras* 14.80

twin miracle *see under* miracles

two accumulations *puṇya-sambhāra* (merits) and *jñāna-sambhāra* (knowledge) 18.415–16; correspondence with *ceto vimutti* and *pañña vimutti* 17.187; one can accumulate merit without wisdom 19.47–8; 'postponing' Enlightenment for the sake of accumulating merit 19.46–7; and the six *pāramitās* 17.463; the union of the two accumulations 19.47; symbolized by a bird's two wings 19.566; the two haloes in a Tibetan thangka represent them 14.425, 17.463; why accumulate merit as well as knowledge? 19.44–7

two truths

introduction
the egolessness of all *dharmas* 1.264–72; discussion with Sonam Topgay 23.204–5; Śāntarakṣita's acceptance of the views of different schools as absolute and relative truth 1.322

absolute truth (paramārtha-satya)
in early Buddhism, just the doctrines of Buddhism 1.264–5; corresponds to *pariniṣpanna* 14.214; ultimate truth can be neither thought about nor spoken about 17.383

relative or conventional truth (saṃvṛti-satya)
the categories of Buddhist doctrine represent only relative truth 10.165; corresponds to *parikalpita* and *paratantra* 14.214; the danger of forgetting about provisional truth altogether 13.420–2; indispensable means to absolute truth 1.206, 1.265, 1.269, 1.274, 1.307, 1.348, 14.576; if we regard the relatively real as illusory our spiritual life falls to the ground 14.576; the only way to understand any Buddhist doctrine is to identify it as relative truth 17.383; the 'something' which is negated in negative descriptions of *śūnyatā* 1.266; Sukhāvatī is an expression of relative truth 1.344; we have to rely on relative truth for the purpose of clear thinking 17.383

distinction between absolute and relative
the absolute truth can only be realized in dependence on the relative truth 26.201; the absolute truth is the absolute truth of the relative truth 14.594, 26.85; fundamental to all schools of Buddhist thought 1.83; led to a rupture between two rival groups in the sangha 1.83; Mahāyāna teachings conscious of their own relativity 1.239; the path to Enlightenment lies in their simultaneous practice 1.426; in practice observed by the Buddha 1.82–3; really the truth is neither absolute nor relative 26.387–8; ultimately no distinction 16.454

two veils (two coverings)

jñeyāvaraṇa
veil of false assumptions, ignorance, obstructing true knowledge 1.270, 2.56; intellectual obscuration, wrong conceptions of reality 18.449–50; 'primitive beliefs about reality' 2.127; removing the veils of ignorance 7.91

kleśāvaraṇa
veil of passions 1.270, 2.55–6; emotional obscuration 18.449–50; unhealthy affectivity 2.127; Buddhahood reached by piercing these two veils 7.505

two-in-oneness *see yuganaddha*

Tyddyn Rhydderch, Wales introduction 24.658 (n243); Sangharakshita spends three months there 24.6, 24.188; a stay with Paramartha 24.306, 24.310

Tyn-y-ddol *see* Triratna IV/retreat centres/ Vajraloka

Tyrtaeus 20.61

U

ubhayatobhāgavimukta ('doubly liberated one') 2.145

uccheda-diṭṭhi or *ucchedavāda* *see* nihilism

Ucchuṣma, the deity of the toilet 18.426

Udāna

INTRODUCING THE *UDĀNA*

introduction
brief description 14.53–4, 16.235; etymology of *udāna* 10.425–6, 11.411–12, 13.179, 14.24, 26.128; archaic Buddhism 10.435, 10.466–7, 14.53; down-to-earth approach 14.514; a vivid picture of what it was like to be alive in the Buddha's day 10.465–6, 10.641; the history of the text 10.425–6; inspiration and guidance from the *Udāna* 2.552, 22.320; it comes as close as anything in the canon to telling us what the Buddha said 17.157; one of the nine *aṅgas* of the Pāli canon 14.24; references to Indian mythology 10.466; the relationship between prose and verse 10.426–7, 10.435, 10.490, 14.54; Sangharakshita's seminars 10.421–658; studied in Triratna 11.377

the way the text was compiled
a bit like a gospel 10.466, 10.588; the compiler wants to leave us with a positive impression 10.656; the compilers' priorities 10.435–6; put together with literary skill 10.445, 10.490, 10.541, 10.648, 10.655; a sense of chronological sequence 10.588, 10.641; the structure chosen 10.465–6; the verses strike a profound, solemn, impassioned, and serene note 14.53; *udānas* included in the Mūlasarvāstivādin Vinaya 14.34; verse form suggests heightened inspiration 18.5–6

translations
by F. L. Woodward 10.422; translation of the verses by Dhivan Thomas Jones 10.419–656

SETTINGS

Śrāvastī
could the monks who compiled the *Udāna* have been from Śrāvastī? 10.465–6; the Eastern Park (house of Migāra's mother) 10.498–9, 10.557–72, 10.588–93, 10.651–3; the Jeta Wood (Anāthapiṇḍika's Park) 10.443–5, 10.454–7, 10.459–65, 10.471–7, 10.477–93, 10.502–13, 10.517–21, 10.537–41, 10.543–8, 10.556–9, 10.572–6, 10.581–2, 10.593–607, 10.610–22, 10.632–8, 10.655–6; the addition of a *dharmasala* 10.471–2

other settings
Anupiya 10.500–1; Bodh Gaya (Uruvelā) 10.427–43, 10.469–71, 10.521–5; the Buddha travels among the Mallas 10.622–7; Cālika Hill 10.526–32; Gayā Head 10.457–8; Kosambī 10.536–7, 10.627–31; Kuṇḍiya 10.493–8; Kusinārā (the *sāl*-tree grove of the Mallas) 10.532–3; Pāṭali 10.641–8; Rājagaha, the Squirrels' Feeding Ground 10.445, 10.447–51, 10.514–17, 10.534–6, 10.541–2, 10.549–56, 10.579–81, 10.653–5, 10.607–9; Vesāli in the Great Wood 10.583–8

THE TEXT

general observations
anticipation of later doctrinal developments 10.549; the clarification of the spiritual ideal – almost the first thing the Buddha does 10.446–7; the first appearance of *devas* in the text 10.447–9; the Buddha appears with a group of disciples 10.443–5; the development of the sangha 10.479, 10.574; the emergence of doctrines in the text 10.552–3; the first appearance of disciples in the text 10.444, 10.480; the first mention of Going for Refuge 10.553; a glimpse of the future of Buddhism 10.648; 'seeing the meaning of it' 10.556–7; the sun (the Buddha and his teaching) and the glow-worms 10.611–12; suggests the background of cosmic development in which Buddhas appear 10.547

connections with other texts
a verse which also appears in the *Dhammapada* 10.534; a passage similar to the Fire Sermon 10.522; the Perfection of Wisdom in the *Udāna* 10.523; a verse which appears in many other texts 10.637–8, 10.724 (n505)

a miscellany of Dharma teachings:
the eight holy persons 4.683–4 (n172), 10.569; the four noble truths 10.552; the fourfold sangha 3.683 (n371); *lakṣaṇas* or *lakkhanas* 3.657 (n200), 16.585 (n13); on Nirvāṇa 10.632–6; 'One who sees holds on to nothing' 10.627, 10.631, 10.633–4; one-sided views 10.594–605; the thirty-seven *bodhipakṣya-dharmas*, *see under* thirty-

seven *bodhipakṣya-dharmas*; what makes a true Brahmin? 10.xxvi, 10.430, 10.436–44; 'This being, that becomes' 10.427–33; there must be a positive side to spiritual life 10.523; how to know if someone is an *arhant* 10.590, 19.100, 19.282; cessation of pain 1.68; abandoning proliferation 10.621

THE PEOPLE OF THE UDĀNA

the Buddha's experiences
the bliss of Enlightenment 10.262, 10.469–71; the week after Enlightenment 10.427–43; Mucalinda the serpent king shelters the Buddha from the rain, *see under* Mucalinda; the Buddha is threatened by Ajakalāpaka the *yakkha* 10.451–4; the Buddha comments on some ascetics and their ceremonial ablutions 10.457–8; the Buddha and an elephant seek solitude 10.323–4, 10.429, 10.536–7, 14.401; the Buddha reviews his state of mind 10.593–4; the Buddha talks about his mother's length of life 10.546–8; Ānanda fails to ask the Buddha to live longer 10.583–8; the Buddha crosses the Ganges by means of supernormal power 10.643, 10.648; the Buddha's telepathy 12.110; villagers block a well, but cannot stop the Buddha from drawing water 10.622–7; Māra suggests to the Buddha that he should attain *parinibbāna* 10.584, 10.587; earthquake 3.100–1, 10.584, 10.588; his last meal 10.639–41

the Buddha's advice to bhikkhus
advice about handling criticism 10.477–83; a *bhikkhu* who goes around calling other *bhikkhus* outcastes 10.514–5; the *bhikkhus* are accused of murder 10.539–41; nattering monks should talk about the Dharma or observe silence 10.472–5, 10.517–21; noisy *bhikkhus* 10.508–11; a monk is ejected from a *poṣadha* day meditation 2.200, 10.557, 10.570–2

the experiences of lay people
the addictions of the people of Sāvatthi 10.616–18; boys tormenting animals 1.498–9, 3.688 (n429), 9.573n, 10.476–7, 10.556–7, 16.429; the Buddha and his followers respected by people living nearby 10.477–8; the Buddha talks with Visākhā 10.498–9, 10.651–3; the Buddha's blessing and a healthy pregnancy 10.493–8; the Buddha and the cowherd 10.533–4; the Buddha gives villagers tips on the benefits of practising ethics 10.641–6; the Buddha meets a businessman 10.483–7; the Buddha reflects on agitation 10.637–8; a meeting with a grieving father 10.490–3; the death of Visākhā's granddaughter 3.77, 10.651–2; an encounter with a married wanderer 10.487–90; an encounter with Saṅgamaji and his former wife 10.454–7; a haughty brahmin 2.663 (n19), 10.436–43; King Pasenadi's spies 10.588–93; King Pasenadi and Queen Mallikā talk 10.543–6; two factions fight over a courtesan 10.607; a wanderer tries to help his pregnant wife 10.487–8; women of the harem gain insight (*Udāna*) 10.627–9

the lives of the Buddha's disciples
Bhaddiya 'the dwarf' 10.618–19; Dabba Mallaputta's final *nibbāna* 10.653–6; Devadatta decides to break away 10.579–81; Kassapa and the *devas* 10.447–51, 10.515–7; Mahākaccāna and Soṇa Koṭikaṇṇa 10.572–6; Piṇḍola the rag-robe wearer 10.537–8; Saṅgāmaji, who left his wife and son 10.454–7; Suppabuddha the leper 3.77, 4.660 (n7), 9.142, 10.549–56, 10.562, 10.672 (n86); Upasena rejoices in merits 10.541–2; a *yakṣa* hits Sāriputta on the head, but he doesn't notice 1.639 (n469), 10.534–6, 18.25

meditations
Aññāta-Koṇḍañña contemplates his release by the destruction of craving 10.619–21; a *bhikkhu* who endured pain in meditation 10.502–3; Bhaddiya, the *bhikkhu* who said 'Ah, what bliss!' 10.500–1; the Buddha contemplates the abandonment of *prapañca* 10.621; the Buddha reviews his state of mind 10.593–4; Cūḷapanthaka meditates 10.581–2; Mahākaccāna practises mindfulness of the body (*Udāna*) 10.621–2; mindfulness of the body 10.621–2; Revata meditates 10.577–9; Sāriputta and Moggallāna meditating 10.511–13, 10.538–9; Subhūti meditates 10.605–7

BĀHIYA OF THE BARK-CLOTH

introduction
brief account 3.663 (n248), 12.157–8; the full story 10.458–65; his life by the seashore at Suppāraka 10.460, 10.708–9 (n384); an explanation of his 'bark garment' 10.460; he wonders whether he is an *arhant* (word used in early Buddhist sense) 10.458–9; a *devatā* appears to him 10.461; he urgently asks the Buddha for a teaching 10.458–9, 10.461–2

'In the seen, only the seen'
introduction 5.757 (n600); full commentary 10.459–64; a similar passage in the *Saṃyutta Nikāya* 10.709 (n386); attachment to what we *see* and hear 10.610–11; consciousness opens out into non-dual awareness 15.205; 'Don't react' 2.257–8, 12.158; the eye is simply seeing, the ear is simply hearing (Milarepa) 18.345; give up the mental

commentary, the ego-based 'thereby' 15.202; if our minds were pure, there would be nothing to pacify 15.286; it sounds simple, but if you have tried it, you know how difficult it is 15.202–3; a reminder in meditation 15.220; the path is in the mind 10.152; Sangharakshita's practice of the teaching 22.336; the teaching the Buddha gives Bāhiya is pure mindfulness 10.461–2

other aspects of the teaching
'Neither here nor there nor in between exist …' 10.463, 10.724 (n505); a person with no subjective mental states, whose awareness is just a mirror 19.192–3; 'When who you are … is not defined by that' 10.463–4

Bāhiya's response and what happened next
he became Enlightened 4.660 (n7), 10.151, 10.459, 12.157–8; 'a wise man who did not vex me in the matter of Dharma-teaching' (the Buddha) 10.464; his death (killed by a cow) and burial under a stupa 10.464; his destiny 10.459, 10.464–5; the verse: 'Where water, earth, heat, air no footing find …' 10.459, 14.53

THE GREAT OCEAN

introduction
the setting of the Buddha's telling of the parable 11.39–40; Mahā-Moggallāna's ejection of one of those present 11.40; the senses in which the *Dharma-Vinaya* is strange and wonderful 11.42–4

(1) like the ocean bed
training in the Dharma is gradual 1.176, 8.592, 10.145, 10.388, 10.562–3, 11.707; the path is a path of regular steps 11.40

(2) as the ocean doesn't go beyond its boundaries
bhikkhus don't transgress the training 10.563–4; their commitment to the *Dharma-Vinaya* is absolute 11.40

(3) as the ocean rejects a dead body
the sangha throws out one not conforming to the ideal 10.564–5; the sangha rejects those who are not truly leading a spiritual life 11.40–1

(4) as rivers lose their separate identity in the ocean
compared to joining the sangha 2.691–2 (n305), 9.195, 9.473, 10.565–6, 11.41, 12.521

(5) as the ocean does not grow or diminish
Nirvāṇa is not a limited quantity 10.566–7; the condition of Nirvāṇa neither increases nor decreases 11.41

(6) like the ocean, the Dharma has one taste (ekarasa): freedom
the taste of freedom 7.157, 9.183, 11.41, 13.463, 14.20, 16.446; the taste of the Dharma is all one taste, so the form doesn't matter 19.60; the Dharma's sole function 1.16, 1.50, 3.277–8, 10.141; freedom can be understood on many levels 11.707; the life-giving waters of the truth 1.219; one could also say that the Dharma's one taste is of growth and development 10.567; what does the Buddha mean by the *taste* of freedom? 10.568, 11.50–1; what is it freedom from? 2.56, 3.277, 12.164, 16.125; freedom from and freedom to 10.567; the word translated as taste is *rasa* 10.567, 11.51–2, 16.125

(7) a great ocean full of jewels
the Dharma and its practices compared to 10.568, 14.346; the *Dharma-Vinaya* contains many types of spiritual teachings 11.41–2

(8) the abode of vast creatures
the Āryasaṅgha 1.310, 3.412, 10.569, 14.346; it contains Stream Entrants, bodhisattvas, *ḍākinīs*, and all kinds of great beings 11.42; better to think of the *ariyapuggalas* this way than as a list of fetters broken 10.569–70; mysterious beings 25.137

OTHER KEY TEACHINGS

the blind men and the elephant
the full story 10.594–605; the abandonment of views 26.160; the Buddha explains what it means 11.719; the Buddha as critical philosopher 7.197; applied to Western philosophers 7.77; celebrated story 14.54, 16.16; a contrast between infinite and narrow consciousness 26.108–10; the dangers of a one-sided approach to the truth 10.170, 12.102–3; different approaches to Buddhism of modern writers 2.49; the elephant represents the nature of existence 9.227–8; mistaking the part for the whole 10.595–6; one of the most important parables in the whole Pāli canon 10.596

Meghiya
the whole story 10.526–32; Meghiya's walking meditation 5.80; he wants to meditate in a mango grove 3.577–8, 10.526–8, 11.702–3, 18.367; the Buddha asks him not to go 10.528, 17.342; the Buddha teaches him five things that conduce to spiritual maturity 3.578, 10.527; a definite sequence, amounting practically to a path of development 10.531; (1) spiritual friendship 3.578,

10.529, 11.703; (2) follow the training rules 3.578, 10.529–30; (3) seek out Dharma talk (*dharmakathā*) 3.578, 10.530; (4) abandon unskilful states and cultivate skilful states 3.578, 10.531; (5) develop wisdom 3.578, 10.531; four qualities to be 'made to grow' 10.527, 10.531–2

'neither earth nor water ... neither moon nor sun'
beyond all pairs of opposites 10.464–5; makes it clear that Nirvāṇa has a positive content 1.68, 10.632–3; negative descriptions of the goal 2.123; the same teaching to be found in the *Ariyapariyesanā Sutta* 10.633; an unborn, unbecome, uncreated, unconditioned, uncompounded 13.193, 16.389; this teaching comes close to the Perfection of Wisdom 10.465; the *udāna* at the end of Bāhiya's story 10.459, 14.53; the very basis of escape from the conditioned 1.68, 14.54, 16.389, 26.369; where Dharma practice starts 8.581–2

commentary
'adding to the cemeteries' (metaphor for craving and ignorance) 10.608; commentary on *abhinibbutatta*, the 'self that has become cool' 10.515; discussion of the monks' ulterior motives for going for alms 10.519; an explanation of Bāhiya's 'bark garment' 10.460; explanation of *issara* 10.592; explanations of *sakesu dhammesu* 10.453; on the formless 10.606; interpretations of *aññāta* 10.449; on the term *kaṅkha* (uncertainty) 10.577; on the term *upadhi* 10.481–2

see also
Nanda

Udānavarga an anthology roughly corresponding to the *Dhammapada* 12.578–9, 14.52–3, 15.4; contains the collected verses of the *Udāna* 10.429, 14.53; studied by the Kadam school 12.578; 'There is no agitation for one who has no dependence' 10.724 (n505); Tibetan translation 15.59

Udaya, Dharmachari 24.8, 24.26, 24.611 (n45)

Uddaka Rāmaputta (Udraka Rāmaputra) his teaching inadequate rather than wrong 1.58; taught Siddhārtha how to reach the sphere of neither-perception-nor-non-perception 1.166, 2.21; the Buddha's instinct to teach him the Dharma 11.413–14

uddhacca-kukkucca *see* five hindrances/ restlessness and anxiety

uddhaṃsoto ('one whose stream goes upward') 15.33, 15.467, 15.745 (n14)

Uḍḍiyāna (also Urgyen, Oujen) Atīśa is said to have visited the land of Uḍḍiyāna and practised with the *ḍākinīs* 12.565; Milarepa wishes to meet people there 18.217, 18.302; Padmasambhava's Pure Land 18.217, 18.304; perhaps located in the Swat valley of modern Pakistan 18.304; the place in northwest India associated with Padmasambhava 26.673; Sangharakshita's true home 22.474

Udena, King 10.627

***uḍumbara* tree** 8.177, 8.683 (n115)

Udumbarika-Sīhanāda Sutta *see under Dīgha Nikāya*

UFOs 16.564, 24.491

uggaha-nimitta *see nimitta*

ugliness Dr Ambedkar grew up in beautiful surroundings, but an ugly social system 10.400; *aśubha bhāvanā, see aśubha bhāvanā*; the beauty or ugliness of a face depends on mental and emotional state 26.594; being repelled by *saṃsāra*'s ugliness as a way to the spiritual life 18.580, 22.199; Bhaddiya is teased for his ugliness 10.618–19; combating ugliness in one's surroundings 26.183, 26.192; grotesque old harpies 24.133; a karmic consequence of anger (or hatred) is to make you ugly 4.390, 17.281, 17.602; in Tantric legend ugly old women are sometimes *ḍākinīs* in disguise 13.203–4; ugly modern buildings 23.243; the ugliness of city life 26.184–5; the ugliness of modern life 10.368, 26.131–2; the ugliness of Socrates 10.619, 19.182; with *mettā*, even an ugly person can seem beautiful 13.279

see also
aśubha; seeing what is ugly as beautiful, *see under* four *viparyāsas*

Ugra-paripṛcchā 14.189

uju (upright) 15.271–3

ujupaṭipanno *see under Tiratana Vandanā*

Ukraine 25.444

Ulhasnagar, India 9.270

umbrella the ceremonial umbrella that crowns the whole mandala 13.262; the man (Tenno) who couldn't remember where he'd left his umbrella 3.286, 9.295, 12.260–1; not preaching the Dharma to someone carrying an umbrella 4.342, 4.359; precious umbrella, in Buddhist

cosmology 16.346; solar symbol 16.149; and the stupa 13.150, 16.149; symbol of the Buddha 3.49, 3.137, 7.123, 16.156; symbol of sovereignty, a king or elder, or the cosmic refuge tree 3.48–9, 4.342, 16.162, 16.371

unawareness *see* ignorance

uncertainty *see under* certainty

unchanging the assertion that the universe is an unchanging 'block-universe' disproved 7.194; nothing has any unchanging essence 18.179; the obstacle of belief that terms such as *attā* refer to unchanging realities 1.99; tendency to think that the world changes, but 'I' persist unchanging 7.208–9; an unchanging element at the heart of becoming would make change impossible 7.153; *see also* self/unchanging self; change

uncompounded 13.193, 16.389, 17.546; *see also asaṃskṛta*; Unconditioned

Unconditioned (*asaṃskṛta*)

introduction
the use of that terminology 5.266; perhaps we shouldn't speak of it as though it were a thing 15.636; description: the negative way and the affirmative way 16.328–9; Conze's article 1.102, 22.124–5

traditional references
'When all conditions are removed,/ All ways of telling are removed' 1.65, 2.43, 3.143–4; in the *Udāna* (uncompounded) 16.389; synonym for Nirvāṇa 3.234; among the ultimate elements of existence categorized by the Abhidharma 14.93; *mahā-atma*, the 'great self' (Mahāyāna) 3.234, 3.235; *niḥsvabhāva* (devoid of determinate nature) 2.89; the *dharmadhātu* 3.243; *sahaja*: Tantric Buddhist word for the Unconditioned 3.206

the nature of the Unconditioned
characteristics 3.234; beautiful 2.82, 2.84–5, 15.568, 16.329; inexpressible 16.328–9; insubstantial 2.89; beyond words 26.478; blissful, permanent, and ultimately real 4.161; reality in its eternal, unconditioned aspect 13.282

the Unconditioned in practice
becoming absorbed in it 3.238; danger that preoccupation with the Unconditioned is purely theoretical 15.576; doctrine-follower and faith-follower approaches 15.569–70, 15.575, 15.579–80; going for Refuge to the Unconditioned 15.653–7; the gravitational pull of the Unconditioned 3.249, 3.252

see also
asaṃskṛta; conditioned; the conditioned in pursuit of the Unconditioned, *see ariyapariyesanā*; uncompounded

unconscious

introduction
Freud's 'discovery' of the unconscious 10.348–9; the idea of the unconscious 12.464; the idea of the unconscious mind is only a metaphor 18.606–7; our unconscious conditioning from the exigencies of primitive life 3.425; unconscious motives 10.348–9; symbolized by the ocean 14.346; unconsciously being a little child, or even a baby 26.37

the relationship between conscious and unconscious
conflict 10.349, 12.218; split 3.487–8, 5.658–9, 12.217–18; the surface waves and the ocean depths 12.179; higher consciousness appropriating the contents of the unconscious 12.221; integration into something clear, rich, and colourful 19.307; the light of consciousness burning the surrounding darkness 12.220; mindfulness can free the conscious mind from the influence of the unconscious 10.349; overcoming the gulf between them 12.223; related to the path of vision and the path of transformation 12.107–8; ritual reduces the tension 11.212; symbolized by an iceberg, a mountain 12.22; the unconscious influences the conscious mind more than we realize 10.349; the unconscious is not fooled by the rationalizations of the conscious mind 3.214; unconscious resistance to change you are consciously trying to make 17.255

practice
Siddhārtha's victory over his unconscious mind 12.187; the Mantranaya directed to the unconscious depths 13.289; energies enlisted by myth and symbol, imagination and devotion 3.41; the *ḍākinī* offers a way of integrating one's unconscious contents 13.239–40, 18.59; developing unconscious qualities through visualization 5.581; a completely mindful person has no subconscious 10.151; the roots of the great tree of Buddhism must go deep into our unconscious 12.111; guilt when the unconscious knows that our pleasure is at someone's expense 3.214; subduing and integrating primordial forces 12.325; as a true individual, you are not the victim of your own unconscious urges 3.470; the value of repetition, to penetrate the unconscious mind 13.81–2

see also
collective unconscious, *see under* Jung; *viññāna-sota* (stream of unconscious mental activity)

unconventionality Dr Ambedkar's unconventionality 12.561–2; Jagdish Kashyap's unconventional manner of teaching 12.431, 20.446–7; mistakenly looking for unconventionality in a teacher 19.161; Nyingma lamas tend to be a bit unconventional 12.298–9; unconventional 'Tantric acts' 13.176–8, 19.160–4; the unconventionality of the Tantric yogi 18.420–1, 19.385–6

understanding

introduction
a metaphorical term: 'standing under' 13.122; 'scientific' understanding 19.178; spontaneous understanding 18.444; alienated understanding and understanding with feeling 19.178–80; 'To understand all is to forgive all' 4.425; 'Few practise, while many understand' 7.97

limited understandings
the idea that if one understands the words one has mastered the meaning 18.167; it isn't easy to understand oneself or other people 19.98–101; it's refreshing to have something you don't understand 14.481; one can love people only as far as one understands them 26.65; preferring to believe there are some things we *don't* understand 25.247; remind yourself constantly that your understanding is limited 17.412–13; we are involved in something we do not fully understand 18.83; the disciple cannot really understand the actions of the guru 18.112; understanding is impossible without sympathy 7.368; why do people struggle to understand a straightforward point? 26.80

your own understanding
all true understanding comes from your own mind 18.619; keep going back to what you think you understand 18.183; translating rational understanding into lived experience 15.95; without receptivity you will not really understand anything 17.261; understanding within 19.178–80, 19.184–5

understanding Buddhism
the *Heart Sūtra* represents the deepening of a limited understanding 14.366; conceptual symbols to move from intellectual to intuitive understanding 18.399; a flash of understanding, but not permanent insight 19.217; if we realized a fraction of what we understand we'd be Buddhas on the spot 26.45; if we think we understand Buddhism, we do not understand it *at all* 11.56–8; to understand Buddhism's truths is to act on them 15.553; Sangharakshita's approach as much rational understanding as emotional response 23.15; shape your understanding to Buddhism, not Buddhism to your understanding 7.310, 11.483; teaching that is as far from everyday understanding as one can get 17.325; an understanding of Buddhism goes with a knowledge of the sacred books 14.7; we do not realize the extent to which we understand but do not practise 18.183

see also
Buddhism II/knowledge; intellectual understanding; right understanding, *see* right view

undetermined questions (*avyākṛtavastūni*)

introduction
brief account 17.384–5; canonical references 13.684 (n61), 17.750 (n322); listed 17.750 (n322); four questions which become fourteen through formulaic treatment 17.384, 17.621; twelve illustrate the four logical positions on metaphysical status 17.384–5; why ten are more usually counted than fourteen 17.750 (n322); pairs of antinomies 10.598; the Buddha's silence 17.622; the Buddha had no views on metaphysical subjects 3.164; sometimes the Buddha considered people's questions unanswerable 9.479; the Pāli texts say that the Buddha refused to answer them for two reasons 1.79–80; evidence of the Buddha's awareness of the limitations of words 14.15–16; getting side-tracked from the main issue 4.376; Nāgārjuna on the fourteen inexpressibles 17.384–5

notes on some of the questions
does a Buddha exist after death? 1.64–5, 1.75, 3.116, 3.143, 4.205–6, 13.149, 17.621; the universe: finite, infinite, both, neither? 2.63, 10.596–7, 17.384–5, 17.641–2; whether the mind and the body are the same or different 10.225–6, 17.621–3; the wrong view of belief in a creator God 10.138, 17.641–2; 'How can the ego get rid of itself?': an example of an unhelpful question 17.349; whatever the answer is, you can still practise the Dharma 10.226, 10.597–8

unemployment 9.531, 15.365–6

unenlightened bridging the gap between Enlightened and unenlightened mind 12.152; the difficulty of expressing Enlightenment to the unenlightened 3.158, 3.178, 3.181–2; encouraging

unenlightened minds to grow in the direction of Enlightenment 13.280; the Enlightened mind in communication with the unenlightened mind 2.58; the experience of all unenlightened beings: seeing things as they are not 2.55; the hierarchy of the unenlightened being right up to the Enlightened Buddha 4.171–98; if we are unenlightened, we need to be aware of it 15.163–4; in our unenlightened state, we are in no position to look down on the *arhant* 4.87, 4.631; only through ignorance do we think of ourselves as unenlightened 1.347; an unenlightened Buddhist is still a Buddhist 19.129; when the unenlightened man becomes Enlightened, what changes? 11.114–15; the world: the total sum of unenlightened human activities 16.359

unfathomable at the root of things there is an unfathomable mystery 7.37; individuality is unfathomable and inexhaustible 3.468; Sangharakshita: 'an unfathomable, fascinating, and somewhat scruffy friend' 10.xliv–v; the Tathāgata is unfathomable, like the ocean 2.44, 10.141, 10.449; 'to have fathomed the fathomable, and quietly to revere the unfathomable' 11.57; the unfathomable individual 14.580–6; we have become much too ready to speak about the unfathomable 11.57

unfolding balancing the model of the path with the model of unfolding 4.201–3; if you study your own life, you may see the unfolding of a certain meaning 18.279; imagine yourself growing in a garden, unfolding your petals 18.105; the lotus unfolds gradually, like the bodhisattva 10.175; the Mahāyāna: a movement not of innovation but of development and unfoldment 1.247; meditation techniques can guide, but one should allow unfolding to happen naturally 18.31; the path: not achievement of conscious goals but harmonious unfoldment of potentialities 2.111; the Path of Vision and the Path of Transformation unfolding in the Buddha's experience 3.596–7; personal myth is more than inner unfoldment 18.318–19; Sangharakshita comes to see spiritual life as not just a progression, but an unfolding 21.259; sometimes you may feel as though you are unfolding like a flower 4.202, 5.687; the spiritual community: the unfolding of a pattern of overlapping individuals 18.286; the unfolding of the golden flower of Awakening 7.171; wisdom: a complete harmonious unfoldment of all the aspects of the human being 12.283–4

ungraspableness ungraspable experience 7.37; the open, ungraspable nature of mind (*cittata*) 17.493, 18.338

unhappiness associated with traditional religion 15.331; awareness of unhappiness is transformative 16.286; cruelty to others may arise from one's own unhappiness 10.477; everybody wishes that unhappiness could be removed 4.631; it is unhappiness that makes us think 26.11; setting up a goal of happiness to get away from unhappiness is ineffective 3.225–8; what is it, at bottom, that makes us unhappy? 3.228; we are miserable because we have denied the aspirations of our souls 7.307; whether or not there is a remedy for unhappiness, there is no need to worry 4.422–3; why are some marriages so unhappy? 18.208–9

unicorns 4.196, 17.544

unification the bodhisattva ideal is the principal unifying factor of the whole Buddhist tradition 1.397, 2.432; concentration is a unifying, synthesizing activity 17.116–17; the *dhyānas*: the progressive unification of consciousness 2.110; mindfulness harmonizes and unifies every aspect of Buddhist practice 15.83; represented by the Tantric stupa 13.163; unifying consciousness (after analysing it) 19.236–7

see also
means of unification, *see* four *saṃgrahavastus*; unification of energies, *see under* energy/working with energy

unified meditation: unified and heightened consciousness 19.451; a single unified focus of attention 7.358–9; a unified way is emphasized throughout the Buddha's teaching 15.80–1; Triratna as a unified Order, *see under* Triratna III/what is the Order?

union the achievement of the union of wisdom and compassion is the work of the Tantra 13.184; Enlightenment: the union of opposites at the highest possible level 12.185, 19.29; indissoluble union of wisdom and compassion (the Tantra) 1.388–90, 19.33–4; meditation is a union of purified emotion and clarified intelligence 4.146; Milarepa is born from the union (*yab-yum*) of wisdom and compassion 18.296–7; practices for developing the union of wisdom and compassion 13.22; the Tantra's application of interconnectedness to sexual union 1.388, 1.389–90; intellect and emotion 14.431; bliss and emptiness 13.75, 18.61,

19.155, 19.196–7; fire and water: the marriage of the red king and the white queen 12.184–5; the highest conscious thought and the acme of thought-expressive activity 7.138–9; the union of opposites symbolized by the *vajra* 13.183–6; the union of wisdom and compassion gives birth to the *bodhicitta* 18.296–7; wisdom (*prajñā*) and skilful means (*upāya*) 19.29, 19.33; *see also yab-yum*

uniqueness awareness of your own uniqueness 3.469; the Buddha a unique being 7.227; a Buddha is *relatively* unique 12.593; discriminating wisdom: you see the unique features of every individual thing 13.182–3, 18.599–600; each individual living being is in some way unique 17.474; the Enlightened mind sees not only the unity of things but also their uniqueness 4.166; every moment is timeless, because every moment is unique 18.159; every moment of our life is unique, but it's easy to forget this 16.439–40; for Christians, Jesus is unique, the incarnate *logos* 12.592, 13.567; the giving of fearlessness is a uniquely Buddhist conception 1.429; hatred is a uniquely human quality 15.303–4; the historical uniqueness of the Dharma 1.56–63; Milarepa's name signifies his unique nature as an individual 18.68–9; reality's unique indefinable essentiality 2.43; the true individual is unique, unrepeatable 14.581; words and concepts a medium for a unique and ineffable experience 2.59

United States of America

Buddhism
the acid rain of the Dharma 3.314, 11.610–11, 12.516; American Buddhist Order 23.458; the 'Americanization' of Buddhism 11.606–7; cotton candy Buddhism 11.610, 12.515; Dharma Publishing, *see under* publishers; family orientation 11.607–8; the number of Buddhists in the US (1955) 8.158; the first ever celebration of Vaiśākha in the United States (1897) 8.55; the first person to receive the Refuges and Precepts in America 8.48; Going for Refuge 2.563, 2.567, 11.609–10, 12.506; *Golden Lotus* (magazine), *see Golden Lotus*; San Francisco Zen Center 12.492, 24.482, 24.485; Sangharakshita's impressions from a visit 11.606–11; strong in the United States 10.265; Tibetan Buddhism an increasing influence 11.606–7

resident and visiting Buddhists
Dharmapala's response to Niagara Falls 8.10; Dilgo Khyentse Rimpoche 12.450; Geshe Wangyal in rural America 23.458; Dr Ambedkar studies at Columbia University 9.4

Triratna (FWBO) in America
Aryaloka, *see* Triratna/retreat centres; first ordinations 12.492; flourishing 9.171, 9.189, 9.492, 24.491–2; hopes for FWBO activity there 11.628; Rocky Mountain Buddhist Center, Missoula 24.520, 24.736 (n644); the sangha in Maine 3.xii; San Francisco Buddhist Center 11.607, 24.481–3; Sangharakshita's writings known 11.607

Sangharakshita visits
attends a conference in Tucson, Arizona (1994) 24.468–77; personal talks with people in the sangha 12.457–8; plans to visit 12.543, 24.402; talk at the San Francisco Zen Center and in Seattle and Missoula 12.492–3; tours of the west and south-west 11.627, 24.477–81, 24.490–2, 24.522, 26.677; D. H. Lawrence's ranch 24.522–6, 26.444, 26.677; teaches at Yale 9.446–7, 11.531, 12.656, 23.453–62, 26.676; talk in Amherst 23.457

politics and history
the Pilgrim Fathers 19.519–20; Revolution 9.408; the American fight against Communism 22.517; the assassination of John F. Kennedy 22.517–18, 24.148; America's part in the persecution of Buddhists in Vietnam 8.318–19; support of coup in Vietnam 13.561; Black Panther Party 23.459–61; Chappaquiddick 24.148; Minutemen and Weathermen 23.460; Watergate 24.148; the terrorist attacks of 9/11 25.452, 26.479–80, 26.688

American people
a big place: no wonder Americans think big 24.470; discovering American writers 22.276; generosity 4.255; 'I saw that America is a new civilization, alien to that of Europe' 23.459; *Letter from America* 12.695; material prosperity 21.67; Native Americans 24.525

other religions and communities
American communes and intentional communities 8.416; officially secular, but not totally so 9.351; Oneida Community, *see* Oneida Community; Self-Realization Fellowship (Los Angeles) 21.582–3; the World's Parliament of Religions (Chicago, 1893) 8.44–5, 8.47–9, 10.280

places and wildlife
American bison 25.53–4, 25.447; Amherst 23.457–8; Concord 24.520; Desert Museum, Tucson 24.475; the fall in New England 24.470; Hawaii 8.49, 8.74; New York 23.458–9, 23.462; San Francisco

11.608, 24.484, 24.491, 24.526–7; Seattle 24.491, 24.529–31; a total eclipse at Cape Cod 23.456–7; Walden Pond 24.519–20; wildlife 24.475, 24.481

unity

unity: the Enlightened perspective
the Enlightened mind sees things in their unity and their diversity 3.374; Buddhism sees reality as having unity in difference and difference in unity 4.31; unity doesn't obliterate difference, and difference doesn't obscure unity 12.215–16; the aim is not to reduce all difference to unity, but to see things as interfused 14.409; *anattā* envelops the whole world in a cloak of unity and love 7.133; positing a ground of unity beneath all states of consciousness 19.236; *Avataṃsaka Sūtra* sees that both unity and diversity are just concepts 16.21

the importance of unity among Buddhists
importance of unity among Buddhists 9.268, 10.282–3, 8.xxv; the Dalai Lama declares it to be essential 23.335; Dharmapala's work for the unity of Buddhism 8.110; essential for the Buddhist revival in India 10.169; the great weakness of the Buddhist world is lack of unity 8.217–18, 22.308; let's have no divisions: monastic and lay, men and women, different schools 26.56; 'Live united' (Dhardo Rimpoche) 12.456–7; the need for a common life in the Dharma 7.273–5; only a united Buddhism can contribute to the building of a united world 8.218; a plea for unity 8.245; the spiritual basis is far more important than superficial differences 8.182–5; to withstand materialism, the Buddhist world must stand together 8.182–5; we shouldn't allow anybody from outside Buddhism to divide us 10.282–3; what unites us is more important than what divides us 6.621

the basis of Buddhist unity
'The Unity of Buddhism': Sangharakshita's first article 7.31–6; unity stems from the Buddha 11.690; all schools of Buddhism aim at Enlightenment 1.202, 7.488; the bodhisattvas participate in one *bodhicitta*: the source of their unity 4.57; could devotion to Maitreya be a unifying factor in modern Buddhism? 1.324; let Buddhists unite in the task of implementing the Buddha's teaching 8.272; monastic and lay united through a common spiritual objective 2.452; Going for Refuge as the basis of unity 2.346–7, 2.451–2, 2.463, 26.56; the three *yānas* give a firm ground for unity 7.479; the transcendental unity of all forms of Buddhism 1.202–11, 22.143; its unity is not rational but transcendental 7.489

unity in the wider world
duties unite, rights divide 7.278, 13.447; modern man has no unifying principle 10.154; unity of East and West 7.91, 10.341–2; the unity of religions 7.89–91, 7.103, 7.212–13; unity is strength 8.182–5, 8.218

see also
unity in the sangha, *see under* sangha/the history of the sangha

universal perhaps only an individual can be universal 16.132; philosophical debate as to whether the existence of universals is real or notional 16.133; the term universal can be misleading 16.132–3; there's no such thing as the universal from a spiritual point of view 16.133

universal consciousness *see under* consciousness

universal religions *see under* religion

universalism 'all religions are different manifestations of the Supreme Reality': no Buddhist could agree 8.167; the clouds of a vague universalist mysticism 23.40; contention that all benefactors of humanity are bodhisattvas 2.183–4; difference between universalism and the Christian term Universalism 16.595 (n71); 'falling among the universalists' 22.78; fixes systems of belief into patterns which have to rely on intellectual resemblances 16.78; Hindu universalism 22.67; Miss Rao the universalist 22.200; New Age universalism 17.52; not comparing the letters of different traditions, but trying to get through to their spirit 26.15; of René Guénon 21.159, 21.161; and the Ramakrishna Mission 21.159; and Sangharakshita 7.12–16, 7.68, 7.70, 7.565–6 (n112), 22.67; taught by the parable of the burning house? 16.77–8; to assert the value of all religious forms comes close to pseudo-universalism 13.424; wrong views disguised as a kind of universalism 17.618

universality

the universal nature of the Dharma
all Buddhists are a universal family 9.359–60; all the ways are different aspects of the path to perfect Buddhahood 16.76; as distinct from history 1.31–7; good will irrespective of race, nationality, social position, gender, or sexual orientation 23.438; the culture may be different, but the Dharma is the same 10.245–6; it can

be practised wherever living beings with intelligence are found 2.64; it speaks to all as individual human beings 8.552, 26.9, 26.341; no limitation or one-sidedness 10.170; suited to all sorts and conditions of mind 7.33; universal in the fullest sense, including whatever beings are elsewhere in the cosmos 3.377; universal in origin, appeal, principle, practice, attitude, ideal, and application 10.170–2; a universal religion 12.246–7

aspects of universality
insight into the universality of death (Kisā-Gotamī) 3.357–8, 9.233–4; the universality of outlook of the Mahāyāna *sūtras* 2.553; the universality of suffering 7.389

universals 16.186

universe

creation of the universe
axiomatic to Buddhism that *saṃsāra* has no beginning 14.606, 16.388; Buddhist perspectives 14.605–6; no Buddhist text attributes to the Buddha the creation of the universe 2.129; Christian view 16.388; created by collective consciousness-volition 2.77; the *Kāraṇḍavyūha Sūtra* describes how Avalokiteśvara created the world 2.176; God spins the whole universe out of himself (Hindu view) 9.229, 10.233; Hindu myth 16.398; 'the whole universe is one person': the cosmic *puruṣa* 4.589

origin of the universe
evolution (and involution) according to Buddhist tradition 14.84, 16.388; it arises in dependence on consciousness sullied by subject–object (Yogācāra) 10.143; a matter for science, not religion 10.138; the origin of the universe cannot be perceived, the Buddha said 13.567; speculation about the origin of the universe is irrelevant 13.566; an inexorable impulsive will to live, as at the origins of the Universe (Tucci) 8.117; where it came from is not a question that concerns the Dharma 10.234

the nature of the universe from a Buddhist perspective
accounts of the universe a product of craving and ignorance 26.154; completely empty of all separate selfhood 7.382; energy that coagulates into separate forms of life 17.522; not static but as dynamic 7.208; a gigantic system of correspondences 1.376, 26.209; however far the mind reaches out into the universe, there must be further to go 17.385; it is struggling away from pain towards pleasure, like a dog in a treadmill 7.47; its positive energies need to be nourished by the transcendental 16.353; its grosser energies will cooperate with the proclaiming of the Dharma 16.356; like any other conditioned thing it is not a self-existent reality 17.385; 'the universe is an ethical universe' 3.100; natural morality is an integral part of the order of the universe 1.145, 8.201; one gigantic process of becoming 3.475, 12.84; replaces mechanistic view with one that has meaning 3.11; seeing clearly the empty character of the universe as plainly as a leaf 1.356

perspectives from the Buddhist tradition
depiction of the traditional Buddhist model 24.243; prefigured that of modern astronomy 7.128; 'In this six-foot body is the origin and dissolution of the universe' 7.170, 10.597, 13.567; like a motion picture (Abhidharma) 14.91; it underwrites the bodhisattva vow 4.66; the Mahāyāna refined the Abhidharma vision of the universe 17.450–1; consists only of ideas (Vasubandhu) 1.351; the Yogācāra addresses the question of whether the universe is eternal or not 17.641–2; the seemingly objective universe evolved from absolute mind 1.351, 1.364, 1.369; a bodhisattva whose scream was heard all over the universe 4.605; through one object the secrets of the universe are fathomed (*Avataṃsaka Sūtra*) 1.353–4; a measure of time: a galactic system ground up into ink (*White Lotus Sūtra*) 14.112; the stupa symbolizes the whole material universe 13.153; divided into 'womb-element' and 'diamond-element' (Tantra) 1.388

the Buddha and the universe
the Buddha is said to have gained Enlightenment at the central point 12.186; the Buddha's compassion embraces it 2.128, 25.262; the highest being in the universe is an Enlightened human being 15.81; not all universes are fortunate enough to have a Buddha 16.460–1; perhaps it would prevent the Buddha from being killed 4.14

the universe is alive
be on friendly terms with the universe 13.272–3; seeing the universe as alive 4.14–15; the universe is alive, magically so 15.136–9; one could not gain Enlightenment in a universe conceived of as dead 15.138–9

the universe and us
faith: the response of what is ultimate in us to what is ultimate in the universe 12.159; the universe we know and love (our native land) puts heart into our ideals 13.274; we're active participants in consciousness, not receivers of messages

from a fixed universe 15.136; we are part of the evolving universe 12.84; we experience everything in the universe as possessing colour 13.283–4; cultivating the five spiritual faculties, you don't see a mechanical universe 17.118; loosening bonds of self, the universe seems a delightfully free and fluid interplay 7.412; every atom of the universe reflected in my heart 25.497

Western views
Indo-Tibetan and Western 'useful for different purposes' 16.343, 19.505–6, 22.497; modern Western view of the universe 16.343; block-universe 7.194, 7.385; the mystery of the universe as seen by modern science 25.133; philosophers' attempts to analyse the universe 17.439–40; 'the poet views the expanse of the whole universe' 14.295; the Ptolemaic universe 23.310, 23.521 (n349); science presents an inspiring vision, a contrast with the static picture of religions 12.84; scientists treat the universe as a discrete entity with boundaries of some kind 17.385; the universe of science exists in space and time, that of Buddhism also in depth 2.65

other views
ancient Indian belief in beings inhabiting a 'multi-storey' universe 3.141, 16.342; identifying the whole universe with your body (Upanishads) 14.459; Christian theologians on the possibility of life on other planets 8.157

see also
cosmology; cannot be said to be either infinite or finite, *see* undetermined questions; evolution in the *Aggañña Sutta*, *see under Dīgha Nikāya*; offering the universe, *see under* offering the mandala; three-tiered universe (*trailokya*), *see trailokya*

unknown the artist's contact with 'unknown modes of being' 26.169–70; dimensions of consciousness unknown to our everyday self 14.462; 'growing old unknown to my friends' 24.397; if one always tries to explain the unknown by the known, one will never learn anything 26.83; the known lives from the Unknown 25.291; fear of the unknown 14.566, 17.370; we try to understand the unknown with the help of the known 12.526; you always commit yourself to the unknown 14.550, 14.566, 14.602, 16.448, 26.31

unmindfulness (*muṣitasmṛtitā*) Buddhism speaks of unmindfulness rather than sin, disobedience, and guilt 16.90, 16.300; does unmindfulness have karmic consequences? 17.524; a fault that gives rise to a multitude of further faults 17.282; in a sense it's forgetfulness of oneself 17.678; unmindful eating 11.625–6, 18.426; Newton's concentration led to unmindfulness 17.117; a problem in the Triratna community 11.625–6; why are people unmindful? 10.84; as *upakleśa* (Abhidharma) 17.677–8; you start becoming unmindful when things are going well 10.532, 15.640; for the story about the man and the umbrella, *see* umbrella

Uṇṇābha (brahmin disciple of the Buddha) 1.286–7

unnatural in a way the spiritual life is unnatural 17.97

unorthodox in Buddhism, no one is consigned to hell for holding unorthodox views 7.490; Mahāyāna teachings may seem unorthodox, but they appear in germinal form in Pāli scriptures 1.247; unorthodox methods of Zen 7.125, 13.333; unorthodox views of the Theravāda 7.540–1

unpleasantness of the body *see aśubha bhāvanā*

unpopularity Dr Ambedkar was unpopular because he spoke the truth 10.271; the artist risks unpopularity 3.472, 3.510; the Buddha had to risk unpopularity 3.472; Milarepa's unpopularity 19.464; of the true individual 3.472–3

unreal antithesis between *sāra* and *asāra*, 'real' and 'unreal' 10.450; beauty an intermediary between unreality and reality 18.158; a Buddha may appear remote, even a little unreal 2.214; the Buddhist 'Gnostic' concludes that all things are unreal 7.126; cause and effect unreal: a thought-construction imposed upon existence 1.316; conditioned and unconditioned *dharmas*: not a distinction between real and unreal 12.144, 17.443; the essence of transcendental life is realizing that the self is unreal 1.402; if the unreality of others is lost sight of, the ideal degenerates into profane sentiment 1.404; many books 'about' Buddhism have an air of unreality 15.578; meditating on the unreality of the world 2.81; Nāgārjuna argues that pleasure is unreal 17.403–9; phenomenal existence is neither absolutely real nor absolutely unreal 16.452, 17.626, 19.233–4; the Real is not to be attained by a series of

increments of the unreal 1.332; self and others, beings and things, are ultimately unreal 1.440; the Vinaya is truly observed by one who knows that *dharmas* are unreal 14.162; *see also abhūtaparikalpa* (unreal imagination)

unreasonable complaining that the guru's teachings are unreasonable 18.493; if you believe in the interconnectedness of all beings, it's unreasonable to be angry 4.405; '*Me? Unreasonable?*' 22.412; reasonable and unreasonable dependence 18.387–9, 19.360

unsatisfactoriness *see dukkha*

'unseeability' 10.186, 20.284

unseen the glorious unseen nightingale 25.266; the seen lives from the Unseen 25.291; 'The Unseen Flower' 25.xxvii, 25.215

unselfishness any unselfish act acknowledges the interconnectedness of self and other 17.696; being unselfish involves taking on responsibilities 17.696–7; Buddhism is based upon unselfishness 7.278, 13.447; the conventionally 'bad' man or woman may be sympathetic and unselfish 7.282; the difference between selfish and unselfish feeling 12.612–13; family life rationalized as unselfish 15.476–7; 'I never knew anyone to whom unselfishness was so natural' (Sangharakshita's father) 20.487; if you have exhausted your selfishness, you become unselfish 19.200; it's not enough to feel unselfish, you have to *be* unselfish 17.694; openness to new experiences, willingness to die for the sake of being born anew 26.169; realizing the truth of egolessness simply means being truly and deeply unselfish 15.339; 'Remain unselfish till the endless end' 26.207–8; Śāntideva tries to talk us into being more unselfish 4.634; spiritual death really means practising unselfishness 11.735–6; spiritual friendship is a training in unselfishness 3.579, 10.394, 11.705; the sweet fruit of [unselfish] love is liberation for all sentient beings 7.291; *see also* egolessness

unshakeable faith 3.329, 12.505, 15.771 (n235), 18.219

unskilful (*akuśala*)

INTRODUCTION

what is unskilfulness?
using the words skilful and unskilful rather than good and evil 11.129; being clear about the difference between skilful and unskilful 9.271–2; compared to Christian notion of sin 13.577; it has no place in the *dhyānas* 1.118; present unskilfulness is almost certain to result in future suffering 3.317; unskilful factors never let up 16.322–3; at home you just go on multiplying whatever is unskilful (Milarepa) 18.206; the world without unskilfulness is an experience of complete clarity 19.192; all our suffering is *indirectly* the result of past unskilful volitions 17.173

attitudes to unskilfulness
delighting in being unskilful 15.350–1; disentangling yourself from the unskilful 15.421; don't reward yourself for practice by permission to be unskilful 19.322–3; knowing that what you are doing is unskilful, but doing it anyway 17.666–7; receive with approbation what is skilful, and reject what is unskilful 12.480–1; take care not to bring a judgemental attitude to unskilfulness 17.xxiv; the unskilful in oneself is not to be accepted 8.584–6; the wilful refusal to acknowledge a distinction between skilful and unskilful 17.636

UNSKILFUL MENTAL STATES

introduction
list of 57 unskilful mental states (Nāgārjuna) 17.268; *aśraddhā* (absence of faith) is present in every unskilful state of mind 18.207; the 'contracted' or 'shrunken' state (*khitta*) 15.162–3; holding back energy is unskilful 18.79; resentment, hatred, and enmity: the most unskilful states 17.268–71; malice is the most unskilful of all mental states 16.296; all the phenomena of hell are created by one's own mental states 4.369; pushing them under the carpet (alienated awareness) 12.267; the suffering we cause ourselves through our mental states 4.51–2; to the extent that you have unskilful states, you're not a Buddhist 15.651–3; they are brought about by unsatisfactory conditions 15.289–90; they are dangerous things, like poison 15.367; they are painful and lead to painful experiences 18.559; they drive the wedge of self-interest between things 15.263; they have an inbuilt tendency to degenerate 18.207–8; the true brahmin is one who has banished evil states 10.439; we don't realize the extent to which we pander to them 5.675–7; why give yourself a hard time by indulging in unskilful mental states? 5.349; your own unskilful mind can do you more harm than any foe 10.534

dealing with unskilful states
awareness, contrition, resolve to eliminate 1.411; consciousness of the goal enables you to free yourself from them 18.443; the goal is their complete and permanent eradication 2.122; how to help someone tackle their unskilful mental states 17.652–3; if you have a vision, you don't need to know the cause of your unskilful state 18.443; in the *dhyānas* unskilful mental states are temporarily suspended 18.575; just observing an unskilful state may not get rid of it 17.456; the need to withdraw from sense stimuli to study negative mental states 17.99; noticing their arising is a step towards overcoming them 17.270; the permanent destruction of unskilful mental states 15.651–2; prevented from arising through mindfulness of the body 10.622; the vigorous abandonment of unskilful states of mind 10.531; watching an unskilful thought like a cloud in the sky 11.689; weakened by *śīla* 1.144; with the help of a skilful mental state: one thorn to remove another 18.637

UNSKILFUL ACTION

where does it come from?
all sorts of factors in the world almost oblige us to behave unskilfully 16.323–4; being pressured into doing what is wrong 25.120–1; inevitably our actions are nearly always unskilful 1.145; getting carried away and making mistakes 16.299; greed, hatred, and delusion 1.142–3, 1.530, 2.70, 11.308, 13.577, 16.419; performed under duress 16.320; the shock of someone doing something unskilful in a beautiful way 15.352; the tendency to act unskilfully is very powerful 15.359; why can't we act in accordance with what we know is right? 1.493–4

consequences
it hinders one's progress and undermines one's happiness 16.508–9, 17.163; it leads to suffering, but this shouldn't be made a threat 15.621–2; karma 2.70, 3.102; the mental state that produces unskilful action can lead to unhappy situations 10.476; nihilism dangerously believes that unskilful action does not result in suffering 17.250; the regret experienced when bad deeds have unpleasant consequences 17.290; not perceiving its disastrous consequences 16.300; unskilful actions produce suffering 16.419, 17.294

dealing with it
admit it, try to make up for it, resolve not to do it again, and forget it 3.265; be careful not to let unskilful actions become habits 15.354; becoming aware of its unskilfulness has an energizing effect 15.216; don't allow yourself to do something unskilful 'just this once' 15.362; fear of confessing it 16.317; having broken the fetters, your unskilfulness won't go beyond a certain point 18.579; important not to feel comfortable with it 16.311; it is not enough just to hold back from unskilful action 18.79; it's sometimes hard to do something evil, easier to do good 4.289; reflect on the sheer pointlessness of unskilful activities 17.171–2; riding the impulse to unskilfulness 17.xxiii; skilful actions performed to counterbalance unskilful ones 4.291–2; we must cease to do evil before we learn to do good 1.145; what if what you want to do is unskilful? 18.285; you can't abandon bad actions unless you have dealt with unskilful attitudes 19.109; you simply need to make sure that you're not doing the wrong things 19.579

see also
confession; karma

Untouchables and Untouchability *see* Dalits

untruthfulness not just telling lies, but refraining from speaking the truth when this might remove ignorance 7.118; tolerance does not mean condoning untruth and error 8.204; truth that is repeated becomes untruth, or another truth 26.7; *see also* dishonesty; false speech, *see under* precepts/fourth precept

unwise attention 15.170, 15.204

unworldliness 'A religion's unworldliness is its greatest asset' (Conze) 8.539; *sāmisa* and *nirāmisa*, worldly and unworldly feeling 15.156; 'unworldly individualism' 13.387

upacāra-samādhi *see* neighbourhood concentration

upādāna *see* attachment, grasping; as ninth *nidāna*, *see under* twelve cyclical *nidānas*

upādāyarūpa 2.97

upadeśa (individual instruction) 14.25, 17.571, 18.393–4

upadhi 10.481–2, 10.486

upādhyāya (Pāli *upajjhāya* (preceptor) *see under bhikkhu*/ordination/the life of the newly ordained

Upagupta patriarch of the Zen school 13.341; spiritual teacher of the Emperor Aśoka 13.341, 14.68; a story in which

he converts Māra, who assumes the form of the Buddha 14.68; Upagupta and the courtesan 14.68

Upāka the Buddha meets him on the road from Bodh Gaya 2.22, 7.600 (n332); the Buddha's first utterance to humanity 11.414–15; the Drum of the Deathless 16.610–11 (n199); 'May it be so, friend' 3.693 (n477), 13.683 (n57); for him the Buddha wasn't a refuge 15.547; the incident shows that one must be careful to take opportunities 10.262–3, 11.415; a similar meeting between the Buddha and Doṇa 3.647 (n139); 'Whom should I point out as my teacher?' 15.48, 15.746 (n23)

Upakkilesa Sutta *see under Majjhima Nikāya*

Upāli Sutta *see under Majjhima Nikāya*

Upāli the barber (the Buddha's disciple) among the 'Low and the Lowly' to be converted (Ambedkar) 9.142, 10.672 (n86); expert in the Vinaya 14.162, 16.507; recited the Vinaya Piṭaka at the First Council 14.186; encounter with Vimalakīrti 14.162, 16.507–9

Upāli the householder (the Buddha's disciple) 2.701 (n378)

Upāli-paripṛccha Sūtra 'A bodhisattva who breaks precepts out of desire ...' 2.389, 4.702 (n283), 14.185–6, 16.614 (n232); confession to the Thirty-five Buddhas 14.185

Upanishads (Upaniṣads)

introduction
brief description 3.658 (n211), 7.569 (n128), 7.572 (n139), 23.521 (n351); emergence in the Axial Age 3.427, 11.355; the confusion of ontology with epistemology 8.619; a disciple who asked for a teaching once every twenty years 19.507, 19.619 (n189); it may appear that the Upanishads contradict each other 7.78–9; they include no personalities 7.78; 'the Vedas the cows, the Upanishads the milk, the teaching the butter' 18.220, 18.408

and Buddhism
Upanishadic influence on early Buddhism? 10.545–6; *pratītya-samutpāda* a protest against the Upanishads' *anattā-brahman* conception 7.195; mentioned by Śāntideva 4.490; claim that the Buddha's teaching is identical 7.234

teachings
analysis of human being into five *kośas* 2.335; association with the language of potentiality 16.62; *ātman* and *aiśvarya* 10.592–3; doctrine of one basic substance 14.603; *esanā* 3.208, 10.637; identifying the whole universe with your body 14.459; *neti, neti* ('not this, not that') 14.347; view of *ātman* 3.217, 10.545–6; the wise man as 'trackless' 7.73

Bṛhadaraṇyaka Upaniṣad
'from the unreal to the real' 7.133; perception of rebirth 3.96, 10.50, 10.671 (n82)

Chāndogya Upaniṣad
on rebirth 10.671 (n82); a conversation between a brahmin and his wife about the self 10.545–6

Īśopaniṣad
'The door of the Truth is covered by a golden disc' 12.384

Kaṭha Upaniṣad
commentary by Śaṅkara 7.578 (n179); Naciketas 7.96, 7.578 (n179); the *puruṣa* 7.41; Sangharakshita reads 24.546; 'They go from death to death who see difference, as it were, in it' 7.131; translations and poems 7.578 (n179)

Mundaka Upaniṣad
God produces the universe like a spider spinning thread 9.229, 10.233

Śvetāśvatara Upaniṣad ('White Horse')
the 'green parrot with red eyes' 23.311

Taittiriya Upaniṣad
bliss 8.438–9; the *kośa* system 14.429

upāsaka* or *upasīka basis of relationship with *bhikṣu* 16.106–7; duties of *upāsakas* and *upāsikas* (i.e. new Buddhists in India) 10.161; glossary explanation of terms 9.547; lay ordination 13.338–9; originally simply a disciple of the Buddha who stays at home 10.484–5; term once used in the Triratna Buddhist Order 2.489–93, 2.729 (n612), 9.165, 9.539; the Tibetan tradition recognizes five kinds of *upāsaka* 7.477; *upāsaka* and *upāsikā prātimokṣa* 2.345; *see also* lay people

upasampadā (*bhikṣu* ordination) *see under* ordination/*bhikṣu*

upāsana (Vedānta) 7.78, 7.572 (n142)

Upasena Vaṅgantaputta (the Buddha's disciple) 10.541–2

Upasīva 1.64

upāya issues forth from *bodhi* and will return to it 7.139; and *prajñā* 7.137–41; in the Tantra, the term for compassion 1.386, 1.448; wisdom-inspired activity, personalized as masculine 7.139

Upaya *see* Boin, Emile

upāya-kauśalya *see* skilful means

upāya-kauśalya-pāramitā *see under* perfections/ten perfections/(7)

Upāyakauśalya Sūtra 24.483

upāyamārga (the path of skilful means) 18.407

Upedeśasāhasrī (Śaṅkara) 7.566 (n112)

upekkhā bhāvanā 5.189, 5.206–10, 10.174

upekṣā (Pāli *upekkhā*, equanimity)

its nature
the ability to take in the whole situation 18.53–4; absorption in quiet and even-mindedness is the true happiness 18.343; does not exclude happiness, but takes it to a higher level 5.211; even more pleasurable than pleasurable states of mind 4.153; a faint reflection of the utter peace of the Goal 2.125; it has an intense, definite, dynamic character 5.212–13, 15.257; like a mountain 3.289, 9.299; not the absence of something, but a quality in its own right 1.507; not indifference 26.26; not separate from positive emotion, but the culmination of it 5.244; similar to the wisdom of equality 5.215; the strength that comes from complete emotional integration 17.582; synonym for Nirvāṇa 4.532; tranquillity or peace 1.506–7, 4.532, 5.212–13, 15.257

traditional references
on the list of 'Hīnayāna' perfections 1.257; as one of the eleven positive mental events 17.581–2; reference in the *Maṅgala Sutta* 11.35; near and far enemies 10.174; *virāga*: much more than psychological equanimity 2.117; Buddhaghosa's story of a decision as to who should be sacrificed to bandits 15.322; the bodhisattva sees all bodily states and processes with equanimity 4.563; the equanimity of Milarepa's mind in all circumstances 18.48

developing it
Buddhism should inculcate the same attitude to all 10.171; the aim of the *aśubha bhāvanā* 4.564; arises upon the equalization of *mettā* 5.172, 5.197; at the heart of the spiritual community 3.451; in the fourth *dhyāna* 5.244, 17.582; a cure for levitation 3.267–8; the danger of its being regarded as indifference 5.209–10; it comes about when you have the same positive feelings towards all 15.432–3; three levels: 'hedonic indifference', positive mental event, Nirvāṇa 17.508–9, 17.582; in its perfected form, you no longer make distinctions between self and others 15.223

see also
as one of the seven *bodhyaṅgas*, *see* seven *bodhyaṅgas*; *upekkhā bhāvanā*

uposatha *see poṣadha*

upside-down the *bodhicitta* turns everything upside down 4.261–2; the need for isolation to turn your views upside-down 4.530; the turning about, *see parāvṛtti*; turning yourself upside-down is a good Buddhist way of looking at things 14.590; upside-down pot, *see under* pots; views, *see* four *viparyāsas*

urgency Bāhiya's sense of urgency about his need for a Dharma teaching 10.461–2; commitment to following the Buddha with urgency and determination 25.29; creating an edge in spiritual life 25.77; the Dharma practised in modern India with an edge, a sense of urgency 10.303; it can be hard for young people to feel a sense of urgency 19.104; Milarepa instils a sense of urgency in his disciples 18.154; to practise the Dharma you need a sense of urgency, in a positive context 19.245; the urgency of the human predicament 16.79

Urgyen Pure Land, *see* Uḍḍiyāna; Sangharakshita's name, *see under* Sangharakshita I/names

ūrṇā (between the Buddha's eyebrows) 16.38–9, 19.32, 19.592 (n8)

Urthona (Blake) 8.556

Urthona (Buddhist arts magazine) 26.xix, 26.99, 26.351–400

Uruvelā Bodh Gaya, *see* Bodh Gaya; the Buddha goes forth to teach there 1.181, 2.23; centre of the Jaṭilas, fire-worshipping ascetics 2.23; the place of the Buddha's Enlightenment (Bodh Gaya) was near there 2.21

Uruvelā Kāśyapa (fire-worshipper) *see* Kāśyapa brothers

Uṣas (goddess of the dawn) 16.418

usefulness

being useful
be useful, but only within the larger context of complete uselessness 26.16; beware of the idea that our purpose is to fill our time with useful activities 18.120; even in the sangha we may consider people primarily in terms of their usefulness 11.439; it's a virtue to be ornamental as

well as useful 14.522, 26.16; 'making yourself useful' 17.204; the mandala of usefulness, surrounded by the mandala of myth 18.318; the monk is under no pressure to be useful 18.120; resist the impulse to make a commodity of yourself 18.122; try to be too big to be used 14.524, 26.16

the usefulness of Dharma teachings accepting the useful in Buddhism and rejecting what is not useful 9.402–3, 18.495; the Dharma is not just a source of interesting and useful ideas 3.326; devotion is there to be useful, not to use us 3.419; the fetters don't give us the full picture, but can be useful 3.254; 'Mindfulness is always useful' 10.151, 10.158, 10.356, 10.368, 11.626, 12.25, 13.328, 17.82, 17.84–5, 23.37; the only useful miracle is instruction in the Dharma 3.76; the Tibetans' emphasis on the usefulness of the Dharma 18.375–6

the usefulness of other things assessed concepts are useful, but they can become dangerous 7.326; the Devil fulfils a useful role 4.412; 'How can the ego get rid of itself?': not a useful question 17.349; the most useful book in the world, scriptures aside, is the dictionary 12.476; different ideas of the universe 'useful for different purposes' 16.343, 19.505–6, 22.497; internal enemies are useful 4.467; it can be useful to get drunk once or twice in the early stages of your development 4.603; nothing is quite as the mind thinks, but the way it perceives things is still useful 18.179; 'scientific' study of Buddhism useful as long as its limitations are recognized 2.51; the symbols of the path and the mandala are useful in different ways 18.525; the usefulness of communication exercises 9.518–19, 12.38; the usefulness of institutions 12.468; the usefulness of words 17.249

uselessness be useful, but only within the larger context of complete uselessness 16.522–4, 26.16; the other monks don't care for the monk with dysentery because he is useless to them 11.439; to be a Buddhist in name only is worse than useless 26.56; useless speech 19.522; wisdom is essentially useless 15.314–15

uṣmagata 10.420

uṣṇīṣa (bodhic protuberance) 16.151

usury 13.616

utilitarianism creativity will find its own uses, so don't try to direct it 18.119–20; follies that serve no purpose 18.276; non-utilitarianism 16.387; upsurge at the time of the industrial revolution 16.387; utilitarian and aesthetic responses to a beautiful pine tree 1.571, 14.517; the utilitarian nature of work 18.294; we are not here *for* anything 14.522, 18.120; we should not seek to use things, but just enjoy them 14.518–24

Utopia *see* More, Thomas

utpala (blue lotus) *see under* lotuses

Utpaladok (nun) 8.528

utpatti (the production of the form in visualization) 18.320

utpatti-bhāva *see under* rebirth

uttama aṅga 16.381

Uttara, Dharmachari v24

Uttarakuru (continent) 16.342

Uttarapāthaka (Hīnayāna school) 2.152

V

Vāc (goddess) 16.363

Vacchagotta the wanderer the Buddha's silence when Vacchagotta asked if the self exists 9.574–5 (n385), 13.393–4, 14.461; his spiritual evolution traced in the *Majjhima Nikāya* 2.698–9 (n363), 14.41; his questions to the Buddha 1.75–7, 3.647 (n140), 13.393–4

vāda (as a suffix) 4.567

Vadanya, Dharmachari (Chris Pauling) v24

Vagīśvara, 'Lord of Speech' 2.173, 3.90–1

vagueness if we are self-conscious, it is only in the most vague and intermittent way 3.435; the *mettā bhāvanā* is not about thinking vaguely beautiful thoughts 3.125; the path is not a vague, general process, but specific action 11.370, 12.280–1, 15.83; the term spiritual is not to be used in a vague, woolly way 16.271; the vagueness and ambiguity of the word 'religion' 26.151; we are vague when we don't want to decide 11.49; we vaguely hope that we can achieve peace without giving up violence 12.360; as a fetter, *see under* ten fetters/second fetter

Vaibhāṣikas *see* Sarvāstivāda

vaidalya (Pāli *vedalla*) 14.25, 14.72–3

Vaidalya Sūtra *see* Nāgārjuna

Vaidehī, Queen her vision of the Pure Land 1.332–4, 3.454–5, 3.571–2, 14.172–3, 20.464; exemplar of fidelity in the way she keeps her husband alive 3.571, 20.464; imprisoned by Prince Ajātasatru 3.453, 3.571; she asks the Buddha how his life has been connected with Devadatta's 3.454

Vaiḍūryaprabha *see* Bhaiṣajyaguru

Vaihinger, Hans 19.102

Vaijapur 9.321, 9.567n

vaipulya sūtras *see under* Mahāyāna *sūtras*

vaipulyas among the texts of the Sarvāstivāda 17.571

vaira (enmity, Pāli *vera*) 2.388

vairāgya (Pāli *virāga*) the consequence of a profound 'metaphysical' cognition 2.117; described in the *Maṅgala Sutta* 2.117; desire for salvation 10.175; epithet of Nirvāṇa 1.69; like Māra's weapons turning to flowers 2.117, 3.277, 12.164; talk conducive to *virāga* 10.530; as one of the positive *nidānas*, *see* twelve positive *nidānas*; a reliable teaching will lead towards dispassion, not passion, *see* Mahāpajāpati Gotami

Vairocana (Dainichi)

introduction
brief introduction 26.724 (n228); description 4.207, 12.212–13, 16.124–5; associated with Samantabhadra 2.172; being gradually transformed into Vairocana (Tibetan Buddhism) 12.297; connection with Mañjughoṣa 13.307; Dainichi 16.124; head of the Tathāgata or Buddha family 13.307; his appearance in the *bardo* after death 12.203; his emblem, a golden wheel 4.207, 12.203; his popularity in Japan 13.306; in a Five Buddha *caitya* in Nepal 20.430; Mahāvairocana presides over the Shingon Shū 1.388, 12.212; in the mandala of the Five Buddhas 3.374, 4.207, 12.212–13, 13.306–8, 18.600; as *sambhogakāya* 2.42, 4.207; symbolism of his white colour 12.213

associated with the lion
link with the lion's roar of the Buddha 13.307; throne supported by lions 12.203, 16.125, 26.289

sun symbolism
the Buddha of Sun-like Splendour 16.232; the dissemination of the truth in all directions 16.124–5; the Illuminator because he illuminates reality as the sun illuminates the heavens 4.164, 12.212; in Indian Vedic times Vairocana was an epithet of the sun 13.306, 18.600;

prefigured in the Pāli canon 10.435; the sun of the spiritual universe 13.306

see also
Ākāśadhāteśvarī (his consort); his *mudrā*, *see under mudrās*; knowledge or wisdom of the *dharmadhātu*, *see under* five *jñānas*; wrathful bodhisattva form, *see* Acala

Vairocana's Tower *see under Gaṇḍavyūha Sūtra*

Vairotsana 8.523

Vaiśakha Pūrṇimā for the festival, *see* festivals/Buddha Day; the night of the Buddha's Enlightenment 3.31, 7.454, 20.102

Vaiśālī (Pāli Vesālī) the Buddha bids farewell to Vaiśālī 2.29; the Buddha visits the Hall of the Gabled House 10.508–9; the Cāpāla Shrine 10.586; home of Vimalakīrti 16.457, 16.458, 16.481, 16.555; Vesāli in the Great Wood (*Udāna*) 10.583–8; the *Vimalakīrti-nirdeśa* originated there 14.156–7; Yasoja and a group of *bhikkhus* spend the rainy season there 10.509–10; *see also* councils/Second Council ('Vaiśālī schism')

Vaiśeṣika school of Brahminical philosophy 1.321, 17.362, 17.776 (n572)

Vaiṣṇavism Bengal Vaiṣṇavism 20.188; includes *bhikkhus* and *bhikkhunīs* 'fallen upon evil days' 7.71; a possible parallel with the dark night of the soul 7.101; Sangharakshita wrote an article on the subject 7.563 (n99); why did Buddhism ally itself with Vaiṣṇavism? 7.72

Vaiśravaṇa (great king) 16.346

Vajira, Sister (Eileen Robinson) 22.519–20

Vajjians

introduction
Ajātaśatru plans their destruction 2.28, 7.438; the Buddha encourages them to keep up offerings at ancient shrines 14.463

the Buddha's advice about the conditions under which the sangha will prosper
introduction 2.28, 3.398–9, 7.438, 12.675–80; (1) regular assembly in large numbers 2.317, 3.398–9, 3.413, 7.438, 10.209, 12.412, 12.675–6; (2) gathering and dispersing in harmony 10.273, 12.676–7; (3) no change to any accepted practice or formulation 12.677–8; (4) elders must be respected 10.273, 12.678–9; (5) no backsliding 12.679; (6) within the sangha there should be a place for those practising more intensively 12.679–80; (7) members of the sangha should welcome new members 12.680; (8) share everything 10.273–4; (9) meditate together 10.274

vajra (Tibetan *dorje*)

introduction
detailed introduction 13.164–89; illustration 13.164; a ritual implement 13.186–7; diamond sceptre 13.189, 22.106; the most widely current Tantric synonym for *śūnyatā* 1.385; prefix to other terms, to show their transcendental significance 1.385–6, 13.178–80; Akṣobhya's emblem 4.207, 12.213, 13.170, 13.308; *vajra* body, speech, and mind 19.30, 19.43

physical description
full description 13.174, 13.176; the *makaras* (mythological beast) on the *vajra* 13.184–5; the meaning of the central sphere 13.180; the meaning of the two lotuses 13.180–2

qualities
holding the *vajra*, you become what you truly always were 13.187; it bursts through limitations, like Vimalakīrti 16.504; it is absolutely pure 13.167, 13.169; it is not really an external thing but a quality you possess 13.168; like a diamond, it can cut everything, but nothing can cut it 12.213, 13.167; thunderbolt qualities 13.167–9

symbolism
dual symbolism: diamond and thunderbolt 13.167–9; the circle of *vajras* around the mandala 12.220; crossed *vajras* on which the universe rests 16.341; jewel symbolism 16.175; a Tantric symbol but prefigured earlier in Buddhist history 13.169–70; the splitting of reality that takes place all the time 13.181–2; the transcendental element, the metaphysical base 12.186, 12.220; transcendental wisdom that cuts through conditioning 14.373–4; *yab-yum* figures symbolized by *vajra* and lotus, or *vajra* and bell 13.313

associations
the *devanāgarī* alphabet, symbols of all *vajra* teachings 19.32; the Perfection of Wisdom 13.170–1; *vajra* family 13.309; the *vajrāsana* 13.169–70; Vajrapāṇi's association with the *vajra* 2.177, 13.174–5; a boy ground into dust by a *vajra* for not

observing the precepts 14.235; Nietzsche's 'philosophizing with a hammer' a dim reflection 26.479

the vajra or diamond aspect of existence
the diamond path 7.399–404; the diamond aspect of sexual relationships 7.402–3; everything possesses a diamond or noumenal aspect 7.400–1, 10.136; one must experience everything, all the time, under its *vajra* aspect 13.180

see also
viśvavajra (double *vajra*)

***vajra* brothers** 18.15

***vajra*-bell** *see vajraghaṇṭa*

Vajrabhairava form of Yamāntaka 2.178; tutelary deity of the Gelugpas 2.178, 19.405; in the *vajra* family 13.309

Vajrabhairava Tantra 7.503

vajrabodhi (Enlightenment) 13.178

Vajrabodhi (Hampstead Buddhist Vihara) v23

Vajrabodhi (Buddhist missionary to China) 1.383–4

Vajrabodhi, Dharmachari 4.442, 11.xviii, 24.49, 24.618 (n68)

vajrācārya 1.385, 12.17

Vajracchedikā *see Diamond Sūtra*

vajracitta 7.400, 13.178, 26.51

Vajradaka, Dharmachari 4.225, 4.236, 12.663, v24

Vajradevi, Dharmacharini 17.xv–xxv

Vajradhara Buddha (Dorje-Chang) iconography 18.94; lineage of the Kagyu school 1.276, 13.187, 18.94, 19.149–51, 19.402; Milarepa appears as Dorje-Chang 19.23; a Refuge Tree with Vajradhara at the centre 24.315; the teacher of Tilopa 18.383

vajra-dhātu (diamond-element, diamond world) 1.388, 7.401, 26.51

Vajra-dhvaja Sūtra *see Diamond Banner Sūtra*

Vajradipa, Dharmachari (Roger Jones) v24

Vajragarbha (bodhisattva) 14.128–9

vajraghaṇṭa (vajra-bell) 1.385, 13.180–1, 13. 313

vajragītā 13.179, 18.5

vajraguru (or *vajrācārya*) *see under* guru/gurus of different traditions

vajrakanya 1.385

vajrakāya 1.385, 1.443

vajrakula 13.204, 13.178–9

Vajrakumara, Dharmachari *see* Dunlop, Mark

Vajrakuta (Blaenddol) 24.6, 24.604 (n12)

Vajraloka meditation centre *see under* Triratna IV/retreat centres

Vajramala, Dharmacharini 10.409

Vajrananda, Dharmachari v24

Vajrapāṇi, bodhisattva

introduction
his name means 'thunderbolt in hand' 11.292; iconography 4.192, 13.173; illustration 13.175, 17.316; Sangharakshita' response to the figure 21.230; and the *vajra* 2.177, 13.173; depicted wielding a lasso 14.658 (n517); a Vajrapāṇi thangka with an erect penis 21.231–2

forms
peaceful (*śānta*) form 2.177; swine-faced form 8.525; wrathful (*krodha*) form 2.177, 3.54, 11.17–18, 26.232–3

what he represents
annihilation of all mental constructions 26.479; power 2.173, 4.192, 5.424; sublimation of anger 13.174; symbol of breaking through 11.17–18; trampling on ignorance and craving 13.173; the transformation of action into energy or skilful means 7.303–4

his place in the tradition
his legend and literature 1.336; association with Akṣobhya 2.172; Avalokiteśvara reveals to him the 108 names of Tārā 1.336; correspondence with Avalokiteśvara, Mañjughoṣa, and Green Tārā 26.663–4; Lord of Might

4.657; the Lord of the Thunderbolt (in the *Bodhicaryāvatāra*) 4.330; Tibetan names: Dorje-lek-pa, Chagna Dorje 2.177; one of a group of eight bodhisattvas 2.172; one of the three 'family protectors' in Tibetan Buddhism 7.304, 11.292; largely superseded by Mahāsthāmaprāpta in the Far East 2.180

see also
Sangharakshita's initiation into the practice, *see under* Sangharakshita V/ *sādhanas* and initiations

Vajrapushpa, Dharmacharini chair of the Karuna Trust 10.li; editor of *Lotus Realm* 11.631

vajrapuṣpa (flower of Tantric ritual) 13.180

Vajrasādhu v22

Vajrā-samādhi Sūtra 14.198

vajrāsana (meditation posture) 1.385

vajrāsana (*bodhimaṇḍa*, Tibetan *dorje den*) all the Buddhas of the past sat on that same spot 13.169–70; Siddhārtha places himself there to gain Enlightenment 9.381, 16.380; not really a place but a state of mind 16.503; the central point, the spiritual centre of the universe 1.32–3, 12.186, 12.220; the transcendental foundation of attainment 19.398

Vajrasara, Dharmacharini 11.647, 11.685–92

Vajrasattva

introduction
iconography 4.193, 13.83; illustration 13.188; association with death 5.xxx, 5.34, 11.455–7, 12.438–9, 23.387–91; and confession 16.325; horse-faced form 8.525; a hundred wrathful and peaceful emanations of Vajrasattva 22.508; in Japan known as 'the Subduer of the Three Worlds' 2.633n; the 'sixth Buddha', in relation to the mandala of the five Buddhas 13.83, 22.504; visualized on the Refuge Tree 13.208; making a white shrine 5.570

and purification
Dudjom Rimpoche connects the practice with a *Dhammapada* verse 5.555–6; realizing that ultimately you have never been impure 5.533–4, 5.537, 13.187–9, 26.52; a positive shock for anyone brought up in a guilt-ridden culture 5.34; the practice is undertaken for the purification of sins 13.82–3; purifies those who have broken their vows 22.504; represents the ultimate inherent purity of the mind 4.193, 13.84; spewing up your impurities 10.450–1; you see that you are a pure being in a pure world 16.325

mantra
to purify oneself of thinking that one is not intrinsically pure 4.193; how it appears in visualization 13.187; the aim is to recite it 100,000 times 13.85; at least recite it twenty times a day 5.556; chanting it on Parinirvāṇa Day 11.455; Jamyang Khyentse Rimpoche explains the mantra's efficacy 12.438, 22.407, 23.390–1; recite the mantra at the end of whatever other practice you do 5.556; reciting the Vajrasattva mantra when someone has died 22.407; Sangharakshita chants it to help a dead friend out of a pit 5.xxx, 11.455–7, 12.438–9, 23.387–91

visualization practice
description 5.537–8, 12.20, 13.84–5, 13.187–9, 16.325; if you can't do anything else, do the Vajrasattva practice 5.555–6; as *mūla yoga* 5.540–1, 12.20, 13.82–5; a purely Tantric practice 13.82; the purgative effect of the practice (sometimes in dreams) 14.487; symbolism of visualizing the figure above your head 16.381; and the system of meditation 5.541; Terry Delamare does the practice 23.xviii–xix, 23.139–40; *Māyājāla sādhanas* 22.503–9

'Confounder of Hell' (or 'Confounder of Narak')
E MA O! verses 2.211–13; 'The Essence of Profound Meaning' 22.504–7; a somewhat similar passage in the *Udāna* 10.632

see also
Sangharakshita does the practice, *see under* Sangharakshita V/*sādhanas* and initiations

Vajrasuri, Dharmacharini (Bonnie Quirk) v24

Vajratārā (bodhisattva) 17.145

Vajratara, Dharmacharini 14.xi–xviii

Vajravārāhī (Dorje Phagmo, 'diamond sow') consort of Śaṃvara 19.592 (n10); Milarepa's patron 18.519, 19.405

Vajrayāna Buddhism

descriptions
brief introduction 4.664 (n33), 7.506–7; called the easy or blissful path because it doesn't require you to give up bliss 19.379; concerned with arousing and applying energies 18.371; consists simply of skilful means 18.408; dangerous territory for anybody to wander into before they are ready 19.331; entirely concerned with experience 18.408; the heroic path 19.382; its magical aspect 2.215; a movement of protest against monastic formalism 19.109; the path of direct experience 13.176, 19.377–8; a vast array of practices: rainbows refracted from the mandala 13.305; the way to the other shore of the great ocean of this world of relativity 1.385; without *śūnyatā* the Vajrayāna's visualizations are vulgar magic, *see under* Chen; a working out in practical terms of the Madhyamaka, some say 19.372; the *yāna* of experience and practice 12.312–15, 18.74–7; the *yāna* of expression of body as well as speech and mind 18.377

reflections
it may be especially applicable now because of the need to engage energies 18.417; our understanding of its myths and symbols is held back by literal-mindedness 18.88; the path on which you may appear mad, or like an animal, or like a ghost 13.176; you don't enter upon the Vajrayāna unless the *bodhicitta* has arisen 18.463

history
it irrupted into the Mahāyāna 16.369; it reasserted the primacy of direct spiritual experience 17.465; it took over all sorts of indigenous deities 19.413–14; Atīśa practised it for years, but was not satisfied with his progress 12.565; became widespread too quickly in Tibet 19.486; the emphasis of Nyingma practice is on the Vajrayāna 13.23; there were great teachers who were not monks 11.571; married lamas 11.571; *see also* Tantric Buddhism/ history

and the other yānas
difference in style from Theravāda 16.327; traversing the teachings of Early Buddhism and the Mahāyāna first 19.331; comparison with the approaches to energy of the other *yānas* 18.416–17; differs from the Mahāyāna more in method than in doctrine 7.506, 18.74

its goal
the direct experience of one's own essential nature 18.75; it sees Enlightenment as magical 19.214; the meeting of the mother-mind with the son-mind 18.64; *prajñā-upāya*, the unity of wisdom and compassion 1.386; the purification of mind (Dudjom Rimpoche) 5.556; the transmutation of body, speech, and mind into those of the Tathāgata 7.506

its ideal
the lama (or guru) as fourth refuge 1.409, 12.17; the *vidyādhara* or *siddha* 4.23, 4.664 (n33), 7.472, 7.506

emphases
the body 18.75–6; the intimate and personal link between teacher and disciple 14.402; practice, experience, and realization 18.417; the strength of the Vajrayāna is its symbols 26.38; the total transformation of body, speech, and mind 18.535, 19.42; the total unification of energy 18.411–12; the value of repetition, to penetrate the unconscious mind 13.81–2

teachings
attitude to monasticism 4.23, 19.384; belief that everything can be transformed, even killing 19.331; Enlightenment as complete spontaneity 19.258–9; the guru's important place 7.507, 19.173–4; may have incorporated the eight *vimokṣas* 2.144; systems of correspondences 19.33, 19.43

the body and the senses
attitude to the body 13.78–9; attitude to drinking 19.331–3; attitude to pleasure 18.528–30, 19.379–84; body, speech, and mind associated with three psychic centres 1.514–15; concretizes the Dharma in direct experience of the body 18.74–5; emphasis on the body 18.75–6; four stages of bliss 2.91, 2.124; higher hedonism 19.379; our worldly enjoyments are to be blended with the spiritual 19.379; the passions transformed from hindrances to helps 1.385–6; to practise the Vajrayāna safely you need some preliminary asceticism 19.382; telepathy 1.523

practices and meditations
accelerated practice 7.506–7; aim to attain a state of purity and translucency of mind to reflect the Truth 7.509; the ancient Buddhist picture of the universe the symbolism for practice 16.343; association of certain reflections with certain actions 19.329–30; based on symbolism of five

Buddha families 2.172; confrontation of negative emotions 5.394; the emergence of new bodhisattvas 4.194; facing the *kleśas* directly by visualizing the wrathful form of a bodhisattva 5.353; the four *mūla yogas* are the entrance to the Vajrayāna 13.76, 13.86–7; include mantra recitation and visualization of Buddhas and bodhisattvas 7.508–9; inner yogas 18.76; intended to transform energy 5.352–3; mantra recitation develops concentration 5.461; one traverses the Vajrayāna path with the help of a mantra 26.699; offering food and drink to the gurus, *devas*, and *ḍākinīs* 19.325–6; tackling the fourth and fifth fetters 15.528–30

see also
abhiṣeka; *dharmapālas*; three esoteric Refuges; Sahajayāna, *see under* Tantric Buddhism/history/India; Tantric Buddhism

Vajrayoginī description 13.217, 13.240–3; illustrations 13.218, 13.241; in the guru yoga 13.217; sometimes placed at the centre of the mandala 18.602; as Sarvabuddhaḍākinī, 'the ḍākinī of all the Buddhas' 13.240; in Tibetan called Narokhachö 13.240

Vajrayogini (Order member, Nel In't Veld) 4.295, 4.485, 4.694 (n234)

Vajrayudha (*siddhācarya*) 2.174–5

Vakkali (the Buddha's disciple) followed the Buddha around 3.150, 3.191, 3.649 (n151); on his deathbed desired to see the Buddha 1.251; Māra 'found no trace' of Vakkali 15.593

vakratā 26.330

Valentinius (Gnostic teacher) 13.596

Valentino, Rudolph 23.301

Valéry, Paul 8.194

Valisinha, Devapriya general entries v8, v9, v20, v21, v22, v23; brief history 21.567–8; attendant to Anagarika Dharmapala 8.71; involvement with the Dharma mission in England 8.67; on the board of the *Maha Bodhi* journal 8.636; visit to Kalimpong 8.664

Vallabha Acharya 1.166, 9.450, 9.573 (n370)

values

a sense of values
definition of values 26.378; the conception of the path is inseparable from a sense of values 11.658; the fundamental principle of my philosophy: power and value do not coincide 26.83; how you reward yourself is a sign of what your values are 19.323; if values do not exist one must create them 26.33; the arts as bearers of values 26.194, 26.376–8, 26.396; making a choice between values set in opposition to each other 18.103; mindfulness reminds you of the value of things 17.91; society needs a set of shared values 26.74; the value of nature is its very valuelessness 26.186–7

group and modern values
Christ's teachings attack group values 12.249; consumerism eroding the values of the traditional Buddhist world 2.551; the difficulty of living in a society whose values you do not share 4.524–5; the difficulty of resisting modern values and temptations 3.39, 3.621; values that ensure the survival of the group 12.243; we almost always accept the values of the groups to which we belong 3.435

spiritual values
an almost pathological state of antagonism to spiritual values 18.504; the conservation of spiritual values beyond death 4.63; Atīśa emphasized ethical and spiritual values 12.576–7; Buddhism's values eroded by the behaviour of some of its traditional custodians 2.551; a household shrine is a constant reminder of higher spiritual values 2.230; not being wholly devoted to the Dharma because you value something else more 25.103; there can be no healthy culture without a basis in transcendental values 16.355; Stream Entry: a transvaluation of values 2.140; the Three Jewels: the three highest values of Buddhism 2.241, 2.477, 16.175; in the world today, we need courage to uphold spiritual values 12.518

Vāmācāra (Hinduism) 7.72, 7.568 (n123)

Vāmana 26.331

Vammika Sutta *see under Majjhima Nikāya*

Van Buren, Mr 24.337–9

van Gogh, Vincent 24.292, 24.371, 24.680 (n355)

vandalism breaking off armfuls of flowering branches 8.287; destruction of bluebell woods 25.456; the destruction of 'superstitious' art by Puritans 26.276, 26.476–7; it seems to stem from alienation from society 18.335; Napoleon's troops firing at the Sphinx 26.476; two kinds of vandalism: wanton and principled 26.476–8; vandalism of the Kanheri caves by a film crew 8.287–8, 8.300; vandalism of the Karla caves 8.294–6, 8.300–2, 22.458; vandalism of works of art 26.477–8

vandanā (salutation) *see under* devotion/physical expressions

Vaṅgīsa (the Buddha's poet disciple) the Buddha praises him for his verses 26.125–6; he speaks verses in praise of Sāriputta 26.125; in the *Saṃyutta Nikāya* 3.84, 26.124–6; reproduced the *Buddhavacana* in stanza form 14.20, 15.347; 'Truth is immortal (or deathless) speech' 13.644, 14.293, 19.294–5

Vangisa, Dharmachari at first WBO ordination ceremony 12.372, 24.582

vanity human vanity 25.240–1; Vanity Fair 18.567, 18.665 (n208); *The Vanity of Human Wishes* 26.483

Vanni, Andrea 13.635

varada 'highest giving' 9.385; *mudrā, see under mudrās*

Varanasi *see* Benares

varaññū ('one who knows') 9.385

Varendraketu, King 16.415

vargas *see* four *vargas*

Varkala, India 20.295

Varma, Prince Norodom Sihanouk 22.231

Varnas, four 9.28–31, 9.77–8

Varrier community (Travancore) 20.287

Varrier, Krishna 20.287

varṣāvāsa *see* rainy season retreat

Varuṇa (god of Vedas) 16.419

vasala (caste) *see Sutta-Nipāta*/1.7

vāsanā (habit-energy) 1.369, 14.209–10

Vasari, Giorgio 13.649

vase of immortality *see amṛta kalaśa*

Vāseṭṭha (brahmin disciple of the Buddha) 2.692 (n305), 3.76–7

Vassakāra (government minister of Magadha) 10.642

Vasubandhu

INTRODUCTION

life story
Asaṅga's brother 1.365, 17.449; his biographer was Paramārtha 1.365; founder of the Vijñānavāda school 13.342; the greatest theoretician of the Yogācāra (Vijñānavāda) school 1.351; he lived and worked in north-west India 17.447; Indian patriarch of the Zen school 13.342; one of the founders of the Pure Land school 1.337; one of the six ornaments of India 17.464–6; the only *ācārya* who enjoyed equal prestige in Hīnayāna and Mahāyāna 1.365; in old age he moved from the Sarvāstivāda to the Yogācāra 1.365, 7.504–5, 17.447, 17.449; originator of the ordination lineage that went to Tibet 7.473–4; and the Sautrāntika 7.504

doctrines and teachings
he accepted the whole Buddhist tradition 1.367; and Bishop Berkeley 1.368–9, 12.78; attitude to devotion 1.373; designation of *pratītya-samutpāda* as *jñāna* 7.199; four factors towards the arising of the *bodhicitta, see under bodhicitta*/arising/four factors; the universe consists only of ideas (*vijñaptimātratā*) 1.351, 1.367–9

WORKS

Abhidharmakośa (Treasury of Abhidharma)
the Abhidharma's culminating phase of complete systematization 14.95; Buddhist cosmology 16.342; definition of *sparśa* (contact) 17.529; doctrine of *sarva asti* 2.675 (n120); explains the *Mahāvibhāṣāśāstra* 7.504–5; explanations of *dharmakāya* 1.252; exposition of the Abhidharma 1.365, 12.143, 14.254; enumeration of *dharmas* 1.103; the foundation of a school called the Kusha Shū 1.365; incorporates Sautrāntika views 7.504–5; the planes of existence 2.672 (n90); temporary emancipation 2.145; ten precepts 17.528; three levels of wisdom 17.725 (n128)

Abhidharmakośa-bhāsya
a critique of Sarvāstivādin points with which he no longer agreed 1.365, 17.449; it gives the impression of a vigorous discussion that carried on for centuries 17.451; planes of existence 2.709 (n443)

Trimśikā-vijñaptimātratā (Thirty Stanzas on Representation Only)
an attempt to show that there is no material substance, only ideas exist 1.368; eight *vijñānas* 2.698 (n357); influenced Sangharakshita deeply 20.101; the most authentic and important of Vasubandhu's works 1.366, 1.368; ten commentaries 1.366, 17.453; the third level of wisdom 17.127, 17.725 (n129); 'Where there is nothing to grasp there is no more grasping' 1.368; Xuanzang's commentary 17.453

other works
Abhidharmakośa-vyākhyā 2.143; *Bodhicittotpādasūtra* (four factors), *see under bodhicitta*/arising; commentary on Asaṅga's *Mahāyānasaṃgraha* 1.366; commentary on the *Diamond Sūtra* 14.148–9, 14.372, 14.416; commentary on Maitreyanātha's *Madhyānta-Vibhānga* 1.366, 17.489; *Nirvāṇa-śāstra* 14.231; *Pañcaskandhaprakaraṇa* 17.500; *Trisvabhāvanirdeśa* 1.366, 1.370–1; *Vimśatikā-Kārikā* 1.369

Vasuṃdhara *see* Jagatīmdhara

Vasumitra possible composer of the *Dhātu-kāya* 14.88; earliest historian of Buddhism 13.342; patriarch of the Zen school 13.341; reported the belief that the Buddha was always in *samādhi* 5.743 (n431)

Vasumitra, Dharmachari (David Boxer) v24

Vaswani, Hira v21, v22

Vaswani, Jashan P. 21.616

Vaswani, Sadhu 21.616

Vaswani, Sundri v21, v22, v24

Vaswani, T. L. 8.368–9

Vātsīputrīyas 1.174

Vaṭṭhugāmini, King 14.22

Vatthūpama Sutta *see under Majjhima Nikāya*

Vaughan, Henry 2.679 (n171), 17.470, 23.103

Veale, Philip *see* Arthadarshin

vedalla *see vaidalya*

vedanā (feeling)

introduction
sāmisa and *nirāmisa*, worldly and unworldly feeling 15.156; *vedanā* combines with *saṃskāra* to produce emotion 15.150; *vedanā* as the result of karma 1.151, 15.304, 17.504; *vedanā* is passive, arising as a result of conditions 15.150–1, 15.304, 17.478–9

in Buddhist teaching
analysed in the Abhidharma 14.84; contemplation of *vedanā* described in the *Satipaṭṭhāna Sutta* 15.149–59; the feeling tone of our experience of *vipāka* 17.502; an omnipresent mental event 3.199, 17.502–14; as *skandha* 1.174, 2.75; five kinds of *vedanā* 2.98

feeling and emotion
the close link between feelings and emotions 15.151–2; the difference between *vedanā* and emotion 15.150–1, 15.252, 17.503–4; feeling is passive, but emotion is active 17.503; feeling is the raw material out of which emotion is produced 17.503

the gap between feeling (vedanā) and craving (tṛṣṇā)
at this point, maintain awareness and don't let the reactive mind come in 12.646; with awareness one can enjoy pleasant feelings without letting craving arise 17.507; the battlefield of the spiritual life 1.111–12; the beginning of the spiral path 2.103, 2.256–9, 3.202–3, 3.259–60, 11.35–6, 12.157–8; don't try to get rid of craving by getting rid of pleasure 19.381; finding the gap between pleasure and craving 18.527–8, 19.383; how craving arises 15.200–1; learn to feel *vedanā* and not let craving arise 2.256–9, 3.202–3, 10.151, 12.157–8, 15.287; the movement from passivity to activity 17.478, 19.581; the opportunity to create fresh karma 17.478; the practice is to keep returning to the bare feeling 15.151; stopping the process of reacting to feeling with craving 2.256–8; there is a 'fall of man' every time craving arises in dependence on feeling 1.111, 16.101; usually craving arises so quickly that we can't separate it from feeling 19.382–3; *vedanā* is something that happens to us, *tṛṣṇā* is something we do 17.503–4; whether we allow feeling to develop into craving depends on how we channel *cetanā* 17.530

pleasant, painful, or neutral
the arising of the three poisons from these feelings 17.512–13; awareness of whether feelings are pleasant, painful, or

neutral 3.285, 3.309; dealing with these experiences 15.150–2, 17.504–9; the six sense bases 1.110; in *vedanā* as *skandha* 1.174, 2.98, 10.231; no pain in higher planes 3.199; one can experience both pleasure and pain at the same time 17.511; oscillation between pleasure and pain 3.260; what is neutral *vedanā*? 15.152, 17.508–9

further classifications of vedanā
physical and mental 17.509–10; subjectivistic and transpersonal 17.510–12; according to which sense organ gives rise to the feeling 17.512; whether it sustains attachment to or disentanglement from mundane experience 17.512

vedanā in practice
developing insight into the dependently arisen nature of *vedanā* 10.482; entering *dhyāna* one experiences first *saṃskāra*, then *vedanā* 17.527–8; it is how we deal with our feelings that is of crucial importance 15.304–5; learning to create positive karma even while experiencing pain 15.151; *nirāmisa*: a mode of feeling beyond pleasure and pain 15.155–6; reflecting on *vedanā* as one of the five *skandhas* 15.181; turning from the *kāmaloka* to the *rūpaloka* 17.512–14

Vedānta *see* Advaita Vedānta

Vedanta Kesari (magazine) 7.6–7, 20.228, 23.207

Vedantic Buddhism of the Buddha *see* Jennings

Vedas

introduction
are they 'the imaginative creations of poets'? 8.458; 'declaration of Truth' 9.63; Buddhist history would have been very different if it had included them 13.623; have no human author 10.34, 19.187; regarded as revealed works 14.374; regarded as an independent source of valid knowledge 19.185; Shudras punished for listening to them 10.186; *vegadu* (in Vedas versed) 10.438; 'the Vedas are the cows, the Upanishads the milk, the teaching the butter' 18.220, 18.408; Vedic hymns 16.362, 20.62; Vedic Sanskrit 16.365; the Vedic tradition makes exceptions in relation to the practice of non-violence 8.449; the full span of life is a hundred years, according to tradition 10.584–5; gods personifications of natural phenomena and spiritual qualities 16.418–19; Jagdish Kashyap's disillusionment with the Vedas 12.427–8

Rig Veda
an ardent admirer 20.370–1; claimed to contain instructions to build a nuclear bomb 17.330; claimed to include modern scientific discoveries 20.370–1; hymns to Indra 13.167; the myth of the 'cosmic man' and the origin of the four castes 9.77, 12.239, 14.426; translated by Max Müller 12.70; truth is one, sages only call it variously 7.78

rishis
celestial scientists who made inspiring discoveries 7.77; said to have 'seen' the mantras or hymns of the Vedas 7.570 (n131); stories of *rishis* 3.248

Vedic sacrifice
criticized in the Pāli texts 10.45; the Vedic injunction to sacrifice animals 8.450; *yajñas* and *yāgas* 9.100, 10.45–6

Vedehikā (of Sāvatthi) 9.522

vegadu 10.438

vegetarianism

Buddhism and vegetarianism
the Buddha did not insist on vegetarianism 4.111, 10.49, 17.585; vegetarianism came to India due to the influence of Buddhism and Jainism 10.48–9; an obvious application of the first precept 10.630, 12.660, 13.454; sometimes exaggerated importance is attached to it 17.586–7; if you are not vegetarian, are you really a Buddhist? 17.584; Chattrul Sangye Dorje's insistence on vegetarianism 12.660–1; Dharmapala was a lifelong vegetarian 8.94; regarded as unBuddhistic by a Thai abbot 23.367–8; sticking to your principles 19.462–3; attitudes of different Buddhist cultures 1.201, 4.111–12; vegetarian restaurants as right livelihood 13.454; the virtues of growing vegetables 24.463

Laṅkāvatāra Sūtra
giving up meat 1.357, 3.370, 4.111, 10.49; 'It is not true that meat is proper food ...' 17.585; 'like devouring one's own relatives ...' 14.203–4

becoming vegetarian
becoming vegetarian during festivals and on pilgrimage 4.112, 8.222–4, 22.310; a bodhisattva tries to be vegetarian 16.9; a butcher who became vegetarian through an apparent miracle 22.31; the environmental effect of vegetarianism 25.58; giving up meat 9.523; the link with animals shown by evolution has led people to become vegetarian 10.346; influencing the society you live in by being vegetarian 17.585; moving towards vegetarianism 1.499–500,

4.111; not something you impose on yourself, but arises out of natural feeling 5.285; if one looked at what it meant to eat meat, one would not eat it 17.195; as preparation for meditation 3.338; Sangharakshita becomes vegetarian 4.284–5, 4.476, 17.569, 20.149, 24.56; to eat or not eat eggs 8.125; *Veganism and Why?* (book review) 8.370; vegetarian pub in Suffolk 26.510; Porphyry's *On Abstinence from Animal Food* 23.427

difficulties with vegetarianism
beef-eating and Untouchability 9.84–91; Buddhists in India sometimes feel that vegetarianism is a Hindu thing 10.81–2; Burmese attitudes to vegetarianism 8.124–5, 17.585; the Dalai Lama is not a vegetarian 22.365; the difficulty of being vegetarian in Tibet 19.50, 19.527–8; monks bringing fish to eat at an event where none is provided 8.xxxi; monks' excuses for not being vegetarian 4.112, 10.49; separate tables for vegetarians and non-vegetarians at the summer school 23.34; someone who regarded prawns as vegetables 24.61; vegetarian food in Spain 24.408–9, 24.410, 24.431; finding vegetarian food in Italy 24.272; Tibetan attitudes to vegetarianism 10.50, 17.586, 19.50, 19.331, 19.528, 22.365; tolerance of non-vegetarianism 8.124–5; don't make meat-eaters feel uncomfortable 17.285; don't think that if someone isn't vegetarian they can't be on the spiritual path 18.222

veil (*āvaraṇa*) *see* two veils

Vekhanassa Sutta *see under Majjhima Nikāya*

Velázquez, Diego introduction 7.564 (n104); *Immaculate Conception* 13.598; *Las Meninas* 24.409, 24.410–11; *Portrait of Cardinal Borja* 24.420; portrait of Pope Innocent X 3.508; power of psychological penetration 24.460

Venice *see under* Italy

Venkata Rao, M. A. v22

Venus Aphrodite, *see* Aphrodite; Botticelli's *Birth of Venus* 26.592–3; Palaeolithic 16.386, 26.592–3; *Venus de Milo* 23.452

vera *see vaira*

Verdi, Giuseppe 24.589

Verlaine, Paul 11.202, 13.476, 13.711 (n270), 26.78

vernacular everyone should learn the Dharma in their own language, *see under* language/and Buddhism; Prakrit, *see* Prakrit

Veronese, Paolo 23.255, 23.258, 23.511 (n288), 25.376

Veronica (the witch) v23

Verrocchio, Andrea del great man of Florence 23.314, 23.523 (n359); *Tobias and the Angel* 4.99, 13.589, 26.269

Vesālī *see* Vaiśālī

Vessabhū Buddha 1.45

Vessantara, Dharmachari brief introduction 24.672 (n311); at Vajraloka 5.xxxv; president of FWBO centres 12.631; *Puja and the Transformation of the Heart* 13.418; leading men's ordination retreats 24.256, 24.672 (n311); reading of Milarepa commentary 18.xiv

Vessantara, Prince *see under Jātakas*

Vetulyavāda 22.169

via affirmativa 1.119, 2.124, 7.44

via negativa 1.67, 1.119, 2.124, 7.44

Vial, Alf v23

vibhajyavādin (epithet of the Buddha) 4.335–6, 14.23

Vibhajyavādins (Early Buddhist school) 4.336, 14.23–4

Vibhaṅga (Abhidharma work) 14.79–80

Vibhāṣā 1.365

'vibrations' (or vibes) 4.272, 4.538, 18.428–9

vicāra *see vitarka-vicāra*

Vichitr, Phra Maha 8.336, v23

vicikitsā (doubt and indecision) *see* ten fetters/second fetter

Vico, Giambattista 24.265, 24.673 (n319)

victim a feeling of victimization coming from unacknowledged ill will 17.258; Feminism's tendency to see woman as victim and man as victimizer 11.639; refuse to be the victim of circumstances 15.174–5; socialism's tendency to see people as victims 11.604; 'stupid and silly actions done by people befuddled and victimized by passion' 4.407; as a true individual, you are not the victim of your own unconscious urges 3.470

Victor (Hampstead Buddhist Vihara) v23

Victoria, Queen 17.65, 26.290

Victorians conditions of workers in Victorian England 25.121–2; conventional morality compared to Theravāda 19.384; taste for hero-worship 3.46–7

victory brings out the worst in people 21.278; *The Buddha's Victory* 11.394–409; over oneself 1.112; Siddhārtha's victory over Māra 3.52, 10.260, 11.396, 12.187; a talk on the Buddha's 'Song of Victory' 22.190; 'That Enlightened One whose victory is irreversible' 4.182–3; 'the victory of Yama' – allegorical 19.122; the words 'May grace abound and victory!' haunted Sangharakshita 2.426; *see also* banner of victory

vidarśana (synonymous with *vipassanā*) 7.472

Videha (continent) 16.342

Viḍūḍabha (King of Kosala) 12.357, 12.729 (236)

vidyā aesthetic appreciation, a relishing of things 14.516–17, 15.472; appreciative awareness 17.608–9, 17.773 (n551), 19.219; the basic, original awareness 17.610; with it, everything one does is to transform the everyday world 17.608–9; Indian term for *śruta-mayī prajñā* 9.229; intrinsic awareness: within us, within our reach, all the time 17.611; it is what perceives 'pure fact' 17.493; the relationship between *vidyā*, *prajñā*, and *jñāna* 17.610–11; transcendental cognition 2.127

vidyādharas (knowledge-holding deities) appearance in the *bardo* after death 12.204; the ideal of the Vajrayāna 7.472, 7.624 (n535); Illumination Holder 19.219; transmission of the Dharma 3.82, 14.17; transmuted into the *trikāya* 7.472

Vidyadevi, Dharmacharini compiler of *The Essential Sangharakshita* 6.xv–xx, 6.xxiii–xxvii, 11.722, 11.730; concordance compiler ('harmless drudge') v27; correspondence 26.403–9, 26.456; *Golden Drum* interview 11.615–29; prefaces and forewords 3.xi–xvi, 5.xxi–xvii, 14.xix–xx, 15.xxii, 18.xi–xix, 18.259–63, 25.xxi–iii; and the Spoken Word Project 2.737–8 (n654), 6.xxx, 11.723, 17.152, 17.431, 24.687 (n393); *Urthona* article 26.392–400

vidyā-guru (Hinduism) 18.508

Vidyalankara Pirivena *see under* Sri Lanka

Vidyārājas 17.317

Vidyaruchi, Dharmachari 26.544

Vidyasri, Dharmacharini 2.734 (n633), v24

Vidyavati, Dharmacharini v24

Vidyutprāpta-paripṛcchā 14.181–2

Vietnam

Buddhism
bhikṣunī ordination 3.408; a *bhikṣunī* who wanted to start a world organization of Buddhist nuns 23.327; a combination of Chan and Pure Land Buddhism 16.197, 23.124–5; influence of the *White Lotus Sūtra* 16.197; Mahāyāna Buddhism 2.549; Sarvāstivāda Buddhism 3.408; Van Hanh Buddhist University 15.500; wax burned on the head at the time of bodhisattva ordination 16.197, 16.206

history
Catholic regime 8.314–21, 13.559–61, 16.196–7, 22.515–17, 23.124; America's part in the persecution of Buddhists 8.318–19; Diệm government 8.315–19, 13.559–61; Mme Nhu 2.636, 8.318, 13.561, 22.517; Vietnam War 12.252, 22.517, 23.229

self-immolation of monks
monks 'barbecuing' themselves (Mme Nhu) 2.636, 13.561, 22.517; practice of bodhisattva-like generosity 3.54; Thích Quảng Đức 12.702 (n7), 13.560–1, 16.195–7, 22.516–18; they died for others 12.9, 23.211; what we can learn from them 16.197–8

view (philosophy) the basic view of the Mahāyāna: thought is not adequate to existence 19.377; the basic views of various schools 19.371; the Madhyamaka view is the ultimate view because it is a non-view 19.373; a finger pointing to the moon 19.446; the theoretical basis of your practice, your philosophy 19.446; there's no view which you can be sure won't ossify into an academic system 19.374; what is the basic view of the Triratna Buddhist Order? 19.371–2; a word-conditioned view that doesn't flow out of experience 19.446–8

the view, the path, and the fruit (or view, practice, action) 19.157–8, 19.211, 19.371, 19.380, 19.411

views (Pāli *diṭṭhi*, Sanskrit *dṛṣṭi*)

introduction
etymology of *dṛṣṭi* 1.479; the word *diṭṭhi* without a qualifier is always negative 15.333–4; an analogy between views and vision 11.158–60; a conceptual formulation to which you adhere as though

it had absolute value 15.334; deeply ingrained convictions connected with deep conditioning 19.18; no view can express reality 15.334; we assume that our view of things is always correct 17.233–4; your view is not quite the same as your gestalt 19.212

views and how we relate to them
attachment to views 1.112, 3.199–200; constructed because we think we know when we don't 16.449; the difference between healthy conviction and attachment to views 3.199–200; distorted views 16.200; a dogmatic attitude turns right views into wrong views 17.259, 17.631; finding security in a set of views 17.629–30; 'He that complies against his will is of his own opinion still' 15.197, 18.360; full of your own views – the overflowing cup 11.278–9, 17.208; humanity quarrelsome through their views 10.600; our views of ourselves and the world are based largely on stereotyping 17.238; philosophical and religious views as rationalizations of limited perceptions 10.598–9; views based on limited experience are popular until a total view is discovered 10.612; we shouldn't abuse people on account of their views 25.17

images
the bandits of bigotry 19.393; a finger pointing to the moon 15.334, 19.446; a forest of views, a wilderness of views, a tangle of views 10.605

the Buddha
abjured all views transposed from metaphysical to logical mode 1.313; exhorts his disciples not to settle down in views 14.549; uprooted the jungle of views of his time 1.61–2; has no views 2.391, 3.164, 3.549, 15.334, 17.617

views and the Buddhist tradition
five *dṛṣṭis* (views) 14.89; the Madhyamaka the negation of all views 19.372–3; Nāgārjuna demonstrated that views are self-contradictory 1.313; the absence of being becoming a dogmatic view 3.660 (n227); right view, good rebirth, wrong view, bad rebirth, 'no view', Nirvāṇa 17.245

views and Buddhist practice
a Buddhist has a duty to clarify views that do not accord with the Dharma 8.xxiv; Buddhists should state their views clearly 4.124–5; the distinction between wrong and right view is of supreme importance 11.160; distinguishing between views that help us towards the goal and views that don't 15.334; the ethical dimension of views 8.xxiii–iv; observe your mind to formulate your view 19.212; one can realize having no views only by taking one's stand upon right views 17.618; views can be constructed from *śamatha* experiences 8.441; when you start practising, you might find your political views changing 10.630

one-sided views
the blind men and the elephant 2.49, 9.228, 10.594–8; Buddhism brings out the darker side of life to correct our one-sided view of it 2.90–1; clinging to one-sided views is a waste of time 10.598; dogmatic insistence on them leads one to sink in midstream 10.599; not seeing adherence to one-sided views as a hindrance to insight 10.600–1

abandoning views
the abandonment of views 26.160; the culmination of wisdom is freedom from all views 26.52; the 'endless view': the clearing up of all misunderstandings 19.184–5; views of the universe to be abandoned 26.154

see also
eternalism; nihilism; fourteen inexpressibles, *see* undetermined questions; right view; *satkāryavāda* and *asatkāryavāda*, *see under* cause and effect; topsy-turvy views, *see viparyāsas*; *uccheda-diṭṭhi*, *see* nihilism; wrong views, *see micchā-diṭṭhis*

Vig, Rohit 24.555

viggāhika (wordy warfare) 8.169, 8.172, 22.171

vigilance continual vigilance is necessary to guard against the gravitational pull 19.61; unsleeping vigilant attentiveness 7.172, 15.210–11; until Enlightenment has been attained, you've always got to be vigilant 4.532; vigilance in the thought of Enlightenment 4.363–77; vigilance with regard to distractions 18.47

vigour *see vīrya*

Vigrahavyāvartanī *see* Nāgārjuna

vihāras **('abodes') of the Mahāyāna path** *see* thirteen *vihāras*

viharas (monasteries) *see* Hampstead Buddhist Vihara, London Buddhist Vihara, Triyana Vardhana Vihara

Vijaya, Dharmachari v24

Vijayadashami *see under* Hinduism/festivals

vijjā-caraṇa-sampañña 2.127, 15.471–5

vijñāna (Pāli *viññāna*)

introduction
description 16.602–3 (n135); etymology 2.278, 3.355; Abhidharma analysis 1.174, 2.99, 14.84; awareness of things through the six senses (including the mind) 10.231; the collective term for all our evanescent mental states 1.173; discriminates an object as being of a particular type 2.278; distinction from *prajñā* 14.559; equated with *pratītya-samutpāda* 7.199; in the Pāli *suttas*, six classes of consciousness are distinguished 1.174; transition to *jñāna* 16.186

as skandha
introduction 2.99; and Akṣobhya 1.376; 'the life force that holds things together' 14.439; as part of a reflection on the five *skandhas* 15.182; steering the boat of the *skandhas* on the wheel of life 2.75, 17.502

see also
consciousness; *jñāna*; eight *vijñānas*; as third *nidāna*, *see under* twelve cyclical *nidānas*

Vijñāna-kāya (Abhidharma work) 14.87–8

Vijñānavāda *see* Yogācāra

vijñaptimātra 1.351, 1.367–9

Vijñaptimatratā-siddhi 1.371

vikalpa 14.213

Vikramaśīlā (monastic university, India) introduction 12.745–6 (n387); destruction 8.523, 9.390; Atīśa's time there 12.569–72

vikṣepa *see* distraction

Vilasak (Kalimpong novice monk) 22.191

village life the beauty of Indian villages 26.183–4; Dalits still forced to live outside the village 9.416, 10.309; *The Deserted Village* 10.129–30; the desire to get away to the city 10.329, 11.196; don't idealize the village 11.196, 18.202; the ethics of village life 10.644–5; 'global village' 4.639, 12.129–30; hard to be independent in a village 9.413–4; 'let the silent sage move about the village as the bee goes taking honey from the flower' 3.589–94; in the village the caste system is very strong 10.329; life in an Indian village 3.296–7, 7.467–9; the practice of magic in an Indian village 13.277–8; 'Village India' (poem) 21.89–90, 25.212–13; 'you delight in a village full of walking skeletons' 4.627; you see life at very close quarters in a village 18.212

Vimalā (Immaculate) *see under* ten *bhūmis*

Vimaladatta-paripṛcchā 14.181, 14.183–3

Vimalakirti, Dhammachari 10.367, 24.109, 24.366, 24.631 (n133)

Vimalakīrti-nirdeśa

INTRODUCTION TO THE TEXT

outlines
brief introduction 16.17–18; an outline of the text, chapter by chapter 14.158–66, 16.454–9; subtitle: *acintya-vimokṣa*, the 'inconceivable emancipation' 14.164, 16.445; the text is named by the Buddha in the text itself 14.166, 16.459

what is it like?
'After Reading the *Vimalakīrti-nirdeśa*' (poem) 25.349; a beautiful balance between concepts and images 14.431, 16.17–18; elucidation of the true meaning of sangha 14.156, 14.184–5; emphasis on lay people 16.65; includes many genres 16.440; magical events express poetic, mythic meaning 16.580–1; it teaches the Dharma through magical action 16.450–4; inaccuracy of publisher's blurb 16.491–2; literature of power 14.303; a world where all the familiar landmarks are removed 16.440; written mainly in prose 14.157–8

history
one of the older Mahāyāna *sūtras* 14.156, 16.239, 16.444; originated in Vaiśālī 14.156–7; relationship to the *White Lotus Sūtra* and the Perfection of Wisdom 14.157; in the Ratnakūta group of Mahāyāna *sūtras* 7.502; not really a *sūtra*? 16.442–3; original Sanskrit lost 16.445; cited by Nāgārjuna 14.156; commentary 16.439–582; popularity in China 16.444; influence on Zen 2.555; translations 13.337, 13.697 (n146), 14.156–7, 16.444–

5, 21.313; Sangharakshita's lectures on the text 24.160–2

introduction to Vimalakīrti
he might have been a historical personage 14.157; his origin 16.569; the meaning of his name 16.442; a bodhisattva who lives like a layman 11.571, 14.104, 16.455; the characteristics of his house 16.456; he is 'all things to all men' 2.479–81; his effect is like that of the main character in Pasolini's *Theorem* 16.504; his practice of the six perfections 16.480; his purpose: to purify living beings and make the light of wisdom shine 16.569; his skilful means ('liberative technique') 16.479–81; the embodiment of the lay Buddhist ideal 2.207; imitating Vimalakīrti 16.495–6; his magical powers 16.450–1, 16.555; he is like a *vajra*, bursting through limitations 16.504; telepathy 16.535
Dharma themes
the Dharma-door to non-duality 11.726, 16.541–9; four *pratisaṃvids* (analytical knowledges) 16.488–92; four reliances 3.677 (n321), 16.575–82; four *saṃgrahavastus* (elements of conversion) 16.485–8; skilful means (liberative technique) 14.164, 16.483–4

THE TEXT

chapter 1
opening 16.464–9; Āmrapalī's Park 14.158, 16.454, 16.464, 16.529; Śākyamuni Buddha's appearance 16.454–5; the Licchavi youths and their 500 parasols 4.31, 14.158, 16.455, 16.465–6; the Buddha is praised by Ratnākara (or Ratnakūṭa) 14.158, 16.466; building a Buddha-land 14.159, 16.467–78; the ten precepts as the Buddha-land 2.334; Śāriputra asks why the Buddha's Buddha-field should be impure 14.159, 16.468–9; the Buddha reveals the universe as made of jewels 14.159, 16.468; this chapter may originally have formed a separate *sūtra* 14.159

chapter 2
Vimalakīrti is introduced 14.160, 16.479–81; he is a bodhisattva who appears as a layman out of skilful means 16.492–3; the physical body compared with the body of a Tathāgata 16.494–5; he becomes sick, as a skilful means 14.160–1, 16.501

chapters 3 and 4
the Buddha asks disciples to call on Vimalakīrti 16.455, 16.501–2; the *arhants* and bodhisattvas are reluctant to meet Vimalakīrti 14.161–3, 16.455, 16.501–14; eating without desire, hatred, or folly (advice to Subhūti) 3.679 (n338)

chapter 5
Vimalakīrti makes everything in his house disappear 14.163, 14.164, 16.521; Mañjuśrī visits Vimalakīrti 2.173, 13.348–9, 14.163, 16.456, 16.518–34, 22.350; 'I am sick because beings are sick' 12.228–9, 14.163–4, 16.456, 16.521–3; the encounter between Mañjuśrī and Vimalakīrti 2.207, 16.521–34; a mural illustrating the scene 16.517–18; the life of a bodhisattva is the union of wisdom and skilful means 14.164

chapter 6
Śāriputra worries about where everybody is going to sit 14.164, 16.535; 'Did you come for the sake of the Dharma or for a chair?' 16.536–7; the house is filled with lion-thrones 14.164, 16.537; a bodhisattva whose scream was heard all over the universe 4.605; a discourse on the Inconceivable Emancipation 14.164, 16.537

chapter 7
how a bodhisattva should regard living beings 16.537–8; Śāriputra and the goddess 14.164–5, 16.537–9; Śāriputra is changed from male to female and back again 14.164–5, 16.538–9; Vimalakīrti's house is a pure Buddha-land 16.463; a belief in a personality as high as Sumeru 4.693 (n227)

chapter 8
beautiful verses about the true family of the Buddha 14.165, 16.457, 16.539–41

chapter 9
the climax of the *sūtra* 14.165; the Dharma-door of non-duality 14.165, 16.541–9; Vimalakīrti's 'thunderous silence' 1.490, 2.54, 2.118, 7.456, 13.348–9, 14.165, 16.457, 16.549–50

chapter 10
Śāriputra worries about when lunch will be 16.457, 16.552–5; Mañjuśrī restrains the bodhisattvas through supernatural power 16.554–5; the Buddha-land of Sugandhakūṭa 16.554–6; a bodhisattva brings ambrosia and feeds the entire assembly 14.166, 16.457, 16.555–6; the Dharma taught by perfume 16.458, 16.554, 16.558–63, 26.399; the Buddha explains to Ānanda all the ways the Dharma can be taught 16.563–4

chapter 11
Vimalakīrti arrives in Āmrapalī's Park to pay homage to the Buddha 14.166, 16.563

chapter 12
Vimalakīrti manifests Akṣobhya's Buddha-field, Abhirati 14.166

chapter 13
Dharma-worship 16.571–4; Indra praises the teaching 16.458

chapter 14
two types of bodhisattva: fond of literary ornament, unafraid of profound teachings 14.166; promises to protect the *sūtra* 14.166; the text is named by the Buddha 14.166, 16.459

Vimalamitra, Dharmachari v24

Vimalamitra (Indian monk-scholar) 8.523

Vimalamitra (translator) 14.152

Vimalasuri, Dhammacharini 10.lii

Vimalo (German *bhikkhu*) 8.336, v23

vīmaṃsā (Sanskrit *mīmāṃsā*, investigation) *see under* four *iddhipādas*

Vīmaṃsaka Sutta *see under Majjhima Nikāya*

Vimānavatthu 14.68

vimokkha* or *vimokṣa introduction 16.446; inclusion as a topic in the *Patisambhidā-magga* 14.73; *see also* eight *vimokṣas*; freedom

vimokṣa-mukhas (doors to liberation) *see* three *vimokṣa-mukhas*

Viṃśatikā-Kārikā *see* Vasubandhu

vimukti (Pāli *vimutti*)

introduction
explanation 16.446; the word occurs throughout the Pāli scriptures 13.463–4; epithet for Nirvāṇa 1.69; fourth stage of spiritual development 16.446; freedom from both *saṃsāra* and *nirvāṇa* 2.118; in the positive *nidānas*, *see under* twelve positive *nidānas*; liberation from the first three fetters 13.463; means freedom from restrictions imposed by our own minds 2.127; *samayavimukti* (temporary emancipation) 2.145

ceto-vimukti (Pāli cetovimutti) and prajñā-vimukti (Pāli paññavimutti)
introduction 17.733–4 (n196); correspondence with *puṇya-sambhāra* and *jñāna-sambhāra* 17.187; distinction between the two 2.145, 13.330, 13.695–6 (n142); the tenth of the ten powers of a Tathāgata 13.695–6 (n142); *ceto-vimukti* (freedom of heart and mind) 1.349, 3.277, 12.164, 16.446; how they are achieved 17.186–7; *prajñā-vimukti* as emancipation through wisdom 1.291, 2.145, 17.187; *prajñā-vimukti* as freedom from wrong views 3.277, 12.164, 16.446, 17.187

see also
four *vimuttis* (faith, ethics, meditation, wisdom); freedom; *prajñāvimukta* ('wisdom-liberated one'); *ubhayatobhāgavimukta*

Vimuktisena (of Madhyamaka School) 1.323

Vinaya Piṭaka (monastic law)

INTRODUCING THE VINAYA

introduction
the meaning of *vinaya* 2.186, 7.499, 15.406; common property of all schools 1.184–5; Dr Ambedkar's study of the Vinaya 9.64; the original nucleus was probably a primitive Buddha-biography 7.500, 13.336, 14.69–70; Tibetan monks take an intense interest in the Vinaya 7.481–2, 13.45

what is in the Vinaya?
brief introduction 14.252; can it be taken to be the Buddha's own words? 11.568; a complex and elaborate body of monastic law, requiring a lifetime's study 2.622; 'manners, customs, opinions, knowledge, ignorance, superstitions, hopes, fears' 7.500, 14.29; rules plus historical, biographical, and anthropological material 3.84; the rules include good manners 6.xxxi; its rules were specific applications of the ethical precepts 17.572–3

THE HISTORY OF THE VINAYA

early history
the Buddha permits the abolition of minor precepts or rules 9.98, 12.678; don't imagine the Buddha compiling a list of dos and don'ts 7.262, 10.563–4, 11.426, 19.558; at first, many *arhants* and few rules, later, many rules and few *arhants* 10.480, 10.563–4, 19.262; an intensification of the training rules observed by the laity 2.607; laid down in accordance with situations that developed 10.563–4, 14.236; not a fixed code of discipline 8.461–2; originally compiled to distinguish the teachings from their practical application 17.572

how it developed
rules of different Buddhist schools 1.146–8, 2.195–6; seven recensions, one Pāli and six translated from Sanskrit 14.29–34; similarity between Theravādin and Sarvāstivādin Vinayas 1.185; two great divisions: *Prātimokṣa* and *Skandhakas*

2.189–90, 7.496, 14.29; the *Mahāvastu* a Vinaya work of the Lokottaravādins 7.500, 14.69, 16.155; Sarvāstivādin Vinaya 2.195; Mūlasarvāstivādin Vinaya 2.195, 2.200, 7.528, 14.33–4; not a unitary composition 2.627–8; Sanskrit Vinaya 7.499–500, 14.30–3; Chinese Vinaya 14.30; Tibetan Vinaya 14.30, 14.31; application of the higher criticism to Vinaya literature 2.627; conflict between the spirit of the Dharma and the *stress* on the letter 2.591; cruel punishment in Thailand for transgressions 2.634–6; the Kaṭhina ceremony as a reminder of the importance of the Vinaya 8.306–8

Theravādin Vinaya
as preserved in the *Sutta-vibhaṅga* 1.146, 16.611 (n206); the structure of their Vinaya Piṭaka 14.30–1; *Cullavagga khandaka* 11 describes the recitation of the Theravādin canon 14.21; division of rules into matters of natural and conventional morality 7.530; rainy season conduct 21.621 (n7); section on etiquette (*Cullavagga*) 13.413

Mahāyāna
introduction 1.146–8; *bodhisattva-śīla, see* bodhisattva/precepts; criticism of monks for not observing it 1.244; includes 'Hīnayāna' precepts' 2.208–9; Guṇaprabha and Śākyaprabha, called authorities on the Vinaya by Tsongkhapa 8.403; the Mahāyāna evolved a Vinaya for both monastic and lay 2.207–9; Mañjuśrī asks why Vinaya regulations are necessary 14.186; observed in addition to the 'Hīnayāna' Vinaya 4.24; rewriting the Monastic Code in the spirit of the Mahāyāna 11.319; sprang up in India and Tibet 4.24; 'There is no Vinaya in the Mahāyāna' – a misunderstanding 7.481; in Tibet 2.208, 7.481; the Vinaya superseded (according to a *sūtra*) 14.185

THE PRACTICE OF THE VINAYA

number of rules
227 (or 263) rules for monks 2.344, 11.426, 19.558, 19.612 (n202); *bhikkhus*' lack of understanding of the rules 2.622; *bhikṣuṇīs* observe 311 rules 2.196, 2.602–3, 11.318, 11.426; monastic precepts (*saṃvara-śīla*), *see under* precepts/introduction; no amount of rules can express the spirit of the principle 10.564, 19.558

different sets of rules
bhikṣu and *bhikṣuṇi prātimokṣa* (rules for wanderers) 2.345, 3.83–4; *mūla-prātimokṣa, see under* precepts/ten precepts/introduction; rules for novices (*śramaṇera, śramaṇerikā*) 2.345; *śikṣāpadas* (Pāli *sikkhāpadas*), *see under* precepts/introduction/Buddhist tradition; *upāsaka* and *upāsikā prātimokṣa* 2.345

practising the Vinaya
fundamentalists' insistence on the observation of irrelevant rules 7.262–3; how to apply the rules 16.552–3; investigate why rules were made and whether they serve their original purpose 7.265; legalistic 2.624, 2.628; list of topics covered 14.31–2; a nun asks whether certain activities amount to a breach of the Vinaya 22.194–5; the principle behind them 4.340; relaxing the rules for the sake of the Dharma 4.117, 4.386–7; rigid adherence to the *vinaya* is all that is expected of the monk 1.227–8; taking a moral stand on matters that are not Vinaya rules 17.587; the Vinaya is truly observed by one who knows that *dharmas* are unreal 14.162

PRĀTIMOKṢA (PĀLI PĀṬIMOKKHA)

etymology and meaning
etymology 2.344; 'obligation' 10.562; one of the most important terms in Early Monastic Buddhism 2.344; 'bond of union': original meaning in the early days of Buddhism 2.187, 10.529; *prātimokṣa* (*so sor thar pa*) means 'individual liberation' in Tibetan tradition 2.344

introduction
originally not a set of rules but a verse summary of the teaching 10.560–1; 150 or 152 *śīlas* (rules) 2.194, 2.195, 2.344, 11.317–18; 227 rules of the *prātimokṣa* 2.702 (n387), 19.621 (n202); seven categories of offence 2.194–5; adopting the rules isn't artificial – just behaving like everyone around you 10.529–30; concerned with mental attitudes only in that intention is a factor 7.477; corresponds to the *samaya* of Tantric Buddhism 7.476; four *nissayas* (reliances), *see* four supports; 'individual liberation', according to a Tibetan tradition 2.344; Pāli and Sanskrit versions are in substantial agreement 14.33; *parivrājaka* conventions become *prātimokṣas* 2.188; a *prātimokṣa* preserved in the *Dhammapada* and *Dīgha Nikāya* 2.187; recitation on *uposatha* (*poṣadha*) days 1.146, 7.496, 10.559, 10.716 (n441), 14.31; took the place of Going for Refuge in some parts of the Buddhist world 2.345; together with the *Skandhakas* constitutes the complete Vinaya 11.318; Vinaya (spiritual ideal) became Abhivinaya (body of rules) 2.203

pārājikas ('defeats')
brief introduction 2.687 (n256); how the first rule was introduced 14.30; abstention from sex, theft, murder, making false claims 2.187, 3.408–9, 13.339; identical with *patanīya-dharmas* 2.194; permanent expulsion 2.194–5, 2.634–5, 23.188; training-rule of abstention from sexual activity 2.605, 13.612

pācittiya (or pātayantika, prāyaścittika)
confession 1.410; different numbers of rules 2.195; making a layperson recite the *suttas* (*pācittya* 4) 2.204, 16.54; teaching a woman the Dharma without a man present (*pācittya* 5) 4.347–8; 'looking at armies' (*pācittya* 48) 18.105; kindling a fire (*pācittya* 56) 18.390; rules about how a monk can obtain food 14.401

other categories of offence
saṅghāvaśeṣa or *saṅghadisesa* (suspension) 2.195, 2.628–30; *aniyata* 2.195; *naiḥsargika-patayantika/nissaggiya-pācittiya* (forfeiture, expiation) 2.195; *prātideśanīya/pāṭi-desanīya* (confession) 1.410, 2.195; *adhikaranaśamatha/adhikaraṇasamatha* 2.195

OTHER SETS OF RULES

śaikṣa (sekhiya or sekhīya), rules for both bhikṣu and śramaṇera
different numbers of rules 2.195–6; little more than a code regulating manners and behaviour 7.530; 'sitting well-restrained': not wriggling your toes (*sekhīya* 5) 4.695–6 (n245); don't teach the Dharma to one with an umbrella (*sekhīya* 57) 4.342, 4.359; don't teach the Dharma to one carrying a sword (*sekhīya* 59) 4.116, 4.342, 4.386; don't teach the Dharma to one wearing sandals (*sekhīya* 62) 2.707–8 (n427); don't teach the Dharma to one wearing a turban (*sekhīya* 66) 4.116, 4.386

Skandhakas (Chapters)
to an extent superseded the *prātimokṣa* 2.189–90; different recensions of the same material 2.192; draw a picture of monastic life 2.201; together with the *prātimokṣa* constitutes the complete Vinaya 11.318; the rule against putting a begging-bowl on bare ground 12.429, 20.447

eating rules
abstention from garlic 2.208, 19.559; according to the monastic rules, one should not eat 'at the wrong time' 23.479 (n60); are vitamin tablets medicine or food? 21.397, 22.312; breaking the rule is a minor offence, but lay people tend to see it as serious 23.188; broken 21.212, 21.374–5; finish eating by noon 10.473, 16.551–3, 19.455–6, 22.225, 22.314–15; a monk who practised the rule over-zealously 17.283–4; the principle is moderation in eating 23.188; prohibited meats (human flesh, tiger flesh, etc.) 4.112; rules about how a monk can obtain food 14.401; things that *bhikkhus* are not to do when they eat 6.xxxi; the translation of monastic rules about eating in terms of lay life 12.124; zealous application of the rules 22.348

rules on ordination
bhikkhu ordination 2.594–5; ordination discussion 2.594–5; the quorum needed to carry out an ordination 2.623–4, 2.628–30, 2.754 (n770); rules for valid ordination in the Middle Country 2.748 (n709); you can be ordained if you are old enough to scare crows 2.193, 13.31

other rules
a monk shouldn't beg for alms outside a wine shop or a brothel 18.394; a monk not rescuing his mother because it would be contact with a woman 11.319; one is supposed not to shave one's head without shaving one's face 17.587; a rule stating that monks should not live near a frontier 18.187; rule about hair length 15.713, 15.775 (n271)

THE STORIES OF THE VINAYA

the Buddha's biography
his life story 7.500, 12.109, 12.712 (n86); considers whether the Dharma is too difficult to teach, *see* Brahma Sahāmpati's request; first discourse 2.22–3, 3.75, 3.680–1 (n355), 9.383–4, 10.263–4, 11.447; incidents in his life 13.696 (n145); affirms that women are capable of the highest spiritual attainment 16.334–5; cares for a monk with dysentery 4.11, 9.194–5, 10.260, 11.161, 11.432–44, 14.414; demonstrates psychic powers to the Kassapa brothers 2.668 (n54); dismisses the monks who want to guard him 4.14, 12.216; how to respond when somebody sneezes 19.608–9 (n112); how he spent the first four weeks after Enlightenment 10.705 (n346); *Jātakas* in the Vinaya Piṭaka 14.66; like the first chick to hatch from a clutch of eggs 3.61, 11.108; 'the love of a father for his son is very strong, piercing the heart' 10.256; 'O monks, I am freed from all bonds, human and divine ...' 4.20, 15.464–5; 'Wide open are the doors to the Deathless' 1.90, 3.74, 3.176–7, 7.153, 23.367; the world is burning 16.70

Anāthapiṇḍika
'Did you say *Buddha*?' 1.284, 13.683 (n57); the Buddha's gradual teaching to

him 8.592; 'Come, Sudatta' 2.687 (n258); donation of the Jeta Grove 2.687–8 (n262), 8.671 (n44); fabulously wealthy 4.351, 4.698 (n260); gains insight on meeting the Buddha 3.664 (n248)

Devadatta
downfall, death, and rebirth 3.63; psychic powers 2.666 (n36), 10.36; offers to lead the sangha 3.63, 4.13, 9.305–6, 10.580, 14.541; schism in the sangha 4.661 (n15); rolls a boulder towards the Buddha 2.27, 3.63, 4.13–14, 15.93, 15.368–9, 16.616 (n244); sets a mad elephant to attack the Buddha 2.27, 3.63, 4.13, 10.260, 13.280, 17.188

the monk who had dysentery
the Buddha and Ānanda care for him 4.11, 9.194–5, 10.260, 14.414; 'You must be brother and sister, mother and father, to one another' 4.11, 14.414; the other monks admit that the monk was of no use to them 4.11, 4.69; monks criticized for sitting in silence 9.520, 9.577 (n401); monks who committed suicide 3.346, 4.67, 4.360, 15.589; Rāhula's entry into the Order 2.665 (n34)

Sariputta and Moggallāna
Aśvajit communicates conditioned co-production to Sariputta, *see under* Sariputta; they receive 'ordination': 'Come, *bhikkhu*' 2.687 (n258)

other Vinaya stories
Ambapāli meets the Buddha 16.624 (n310); Soṇa Koḷivisa and his walking meditation 5.80, 5.712 (n79), 7.489; Mahāpajāpatī Gotami's question, 'What do you teach?', and her request for ordination, *see under* Mahāpajāpatī Gotami; Tapussa and Bhallika, the two merchants who were the Buddha's first disciples, *see* Bhallika; a tree god speaks to a monk 10.608 (n376); Viśākha 8.671 (n44); Yasa 2.33, 2.667 (n47), 4.698 (n260), 9.142, 10.264; young men (looking for a courtesan) who 'received the going forth' 2.687 (n258), 15.269

DHARMA TEACHINGS AND HISTORY IN THE VINAYA

Dharma teachings
anattā doctrine 3.687 (n407); eight *garudhammas* 2.751 (n743); list of games 16.606 (n168); the qualities of the great ocean, *see under Udāna*/great ocean; Noble Eightfold Path 3.653 (n181), 9.567n; 'the origins of those things which proceed from a cause' 1.90, 16.507; 'This being, that becomes' 7.192–3; young elephants poisoned by unwashed lotus roots 17.447, 19.296, 21.552–3

the history of Buddhism
the Buddha urges the sixty disciples to teach the Dharma, *see under* disciples/of the Buddha; the Buddha says that his *sāsana* will last longer than those of previous Buddhas 14.434; everyone should be taught the Dharma in their own language 3.161–2, 7.393, 7.498, 8.220–2, 9.480, 10.244, 14.13, 16.15–16, 16.365, 22.10; account of the First Council 4.660 (n9), 10.706 (n358)

Vinaya-saṅgīti *see under* councils/First Council

Vinita (Sinhalese monk) 23.75–6

viniyata 17.532–48

viññāna *see vijñāna*

viññāna-sota (stream of unconscious mental activity) 12.99, 12.710–1 (n72)

violence (*hiṃsā*)

introduction
the most extreme form that unethical behaviour can take 2.359; the Jains enumerate 432 types of *himsā* 8.448; an ignoble passion 13.619; affiliation to hatred, and to ignorance 7.373; a principle of Darkness 12.354–5; why should killing be wrong? 2.358–9; Buddhism precludes the use of violence to advance its tenets 7.384, 22.529; a contrast between violence and non-violence 21.272; more common than the cherishing love developed by the first precept 2.361

how it develops
all deeds of violence were once hateful thoughts 1.533, 3.319, 22.529; the assumption that intolerance is sure to be followed by violence 22.529; due to sensuous craving (Pāli canon) 7.238; is there a connection between watching television and violence? 3.535–6; turning to violence to relieve boredom 11.79; young people's sense of frustration leading to violence 18.457–8

types of violence
against women in India 10.lvii, 10.lxii, 20.382–3; a brutal atmosphere at the Colosseum 23.255, 23.310; Buddhist monks encouraging violence in Myanmar 7.11, 26.687; friendliness not incompatible with *seeming* violence (Mahāyāna *sūtra*) 14.236; in respect of property 2.364; not believing someone when they are telling the truth 2.377; on the increase in cities 11.358; sex and violence in horror comics 8.206–7; towards another human being 3.318, 17.644; the violence of the Church

13.622; violence to the aspects of oneself that need to be overcome 11.4; violent films 17.181, 17.666

how to stop it
the Buddha wished to cut it at its root rather than tackle its manifestations 8.452; only by uprooting the ego-sense 7.374; we vaguely hope we can achieve peace without giving up violence 12.360

see also
power mode; non-violence

vipāka *see karma vipāka*

Vipāka-Buddha 14.212

vipallāsas (Sanskrit *viparyāsas*) *see* four *viparyāsas*

vipassanā (Sanskrit *vipaśyanā*) *see* insight

Vipassana, Mother (U Chandramani's disciple) 20.403, 20.406, 20.409, 20.411, 22.258–9

vipassanā movement (insight meditation movement)

introduction
differences between Sangha Association and Buddhist Society 11.547, 23.23, 23.45–9; concerns about the practice in the 1960s 1.9, 17.253, 23.23, 23.38, 23.45–6, 23.66, 23.70–1; danger of being catapulted into an experience for which you are not ready 5.365, 5.367; is *dhyāna* regarded as a detour? 5.445; discursive reviewing of doctrines with minimal concentration 5.458; 'dry' insight', *see under* insight/how to gain insight; its leaders take the practice out of its Buddhist context 2.561; the method can lead to alienation 5.459–60

New Burmese Method of Satipaṭṭhāna
origins in Myanmar 2.561, 7.532, 11.740–1 (n47); not given an unqualified endorsement 1.9; a remarkable revival 1.156; system of grades, exams, and certificates 2.112; discussions about the controversial new technique 23.367; Lama Govinda's critique 11.740–1 (n47); claimed to lead directly to insight 1.225; tendency to think that this is the only effective meditation practice 11.85

vipassanādhura (the way or burden of insight) 2.143, 4.568

Vipassī Buddha and the four sights, in the *Dīgha Nikāya* 3.630 (n27); his *pāṭimokkha* (*Dhammapada* verses) 10.560; place in lineage 1.45

Vipassi, Dharmachari (Michael McGee) v24

Vipaśvin Buddha 2.176

vipaśyanā **meditation practices** all insight meditation practices are methods of coping with the fear of death 26.75; alternation between *dhyāna* and *vipaśyanā* 5.438–9, 5.446, 5.464, 18.576–7; confine *vipaśyanā* practice to the retreat situation 5.427–8; consciousness being drawn to the opposite of what one is trying to realize 17.680–1; really attend to phenomena, then you can develop insight into them 19.69–70; reflecting on the fact of death can take you a long way 19.453; six element practice as *vipaśyanā* practice 5.32–3, 5.485; *vipaśyanā* meditation practices 3.351; visualization as *vipaśyanā* practice 5.32–3; watching the rise and fall of mental events: what is meant by *vipaśyanā* meditation 17.550; where does clinging come from? – an insight exercise 4.376–7

see also
insight; *vipaśyanā* and *śamatha* practices, *see under śamatha*

Vipula, Dharmachari (Jim Sharples) 17.72, 17.717 (n77), v24

Vipulakirti, Dharmachari 18.xi

Vipulananda, Swami 7.14, 7.82, 20.119–23

Virabhadra, Dharmachari brief introduction 24.606 (n23), 24.635 (n149); during Sangharakshita's visit to India (1979) 24.13, 24.19–20; practises medicine in India 10.l–li, 10.367, 24.6

virāga *see vairagya*

viramānanda 2.91

Virgil (*Aeneid*) discrepancies in the character of Aeneas 24.548; Dryden's translation 26.469; Hermes in the poem 26.469; recommendation to read 12.406; 'return and gain the cheerful skies' 23.253; 'Smooth the descent, and easy is the way' 1.25

Virgin Mary

in Christian doctrine
the Annunciation 4.99, 13.599–600; 'the handmaid of the Lord' 13.600, 18.105; Mother of God 13.598–9; the Immaculate Conception 13.601–2; the myth of the virgin birth 12.106–7, 13.568–9, 13.576; at the Crucifixion 13.599; her death (Dormition) 13.600; the Assumption 13.600; crowned Queen of Heaven 13.588, 24.421; became a fourth member of the Trinity 13.601

myths, worship, resonances
Black Madonna 24.590; her appearances to saints and ordinary people 13.600–1; she opened the back door to hell 13.601; story that her house was carried by angels to Loreto 13.505; churches dedicated to her 13.601–2; acquired some of the attributes of the pagan Great Mother 13.601; worshipped in Mexico 13.602; in a New Zealand mission 24.511; a poem by James K. Baxter 24.552–3; likeness to Guanyin 26.599; a similarity to White Tārā 24.511; the appeal of the *ḍākinī* to women: very different from Mary 13.244; Swami Agamananda publishes an attack on Mary 20.298–9

depictions
Botticelli's *Madonna of the Magnificat* 26.593; depicted as a goddess 26.593; depictions in art 13.588, 13.598–601, 26.471; in El Greco's *The Burial of Count Orgaz* 26.310, 26.316; pseudo-religious art of sensually attractive Madonnas 26.164

Sangharakshita and Mary
he paints a picture of her 13.598, 26.593; his attraction to her 13.598–9; a short story, *Four Visitors* 26.616–20, 26.662–3; his vision of her 13.599, 20.208

viriya *see vīrya*

Viriya (Eric before ordination) 11.494, v23, 23.237 (photograph)

virtue

Buddhist virtues
the bodhisattva's practice: creative adjustment, morality, tenderness, sacrifice 1.354; the bodhisattva should master just one virtue: compassion 2.125–6, 5.199–200; the Buddhist path in Dr Ambedkar's version: purity, righteousness, virtue 9.141; cheerfulness from being aware of following the path of virtue 2.105; giving is the basic Buddhist virtue 1.500; gratitude: very much a Buddhist virtue 3.360–1; *kṣānti* is one of the most beautiful of all the Buddhist virtues 3.372; literacy: almost a Buddhist virtue 2.213; mindfulness is the characteristic virtue of the thinking part of our make-up 3.324; the six perfections are all other-regarding virtues 7.46

the Buddha and virtue
the Buddha 'adorned with virtues' 17.326–7; the Buddha praises Ānanda's virtues 2.30, 3.118; compared to those of a majestic elephant 4.706–7 (n313); contemplation of the virtues of the Tathāgatas 2.273, 4.52–3; it is not possible to know the end of the Buddha's virtues 16.328

notes on virtue
action is not a virtue in itself 19.355; Christianity's tendency to think of poverty as a virtue 10.347; the difference between respectability and virtue 4.110; an enumeration of virtues will never reveal the secret of bodhisattvahood 2.155; etymology of *puṇya*: 'merit' and 'virtue' 4.47; our tendency is to see others' faults rather than virtues 18.112; seeing oneself as full of faults and others as oceans of virtue 4.592–3; a virtue carried to extremes becomes a vice 7.325; we may need to give up truthfulness for the sake of a greater virtue 3.323, 7.118; you can completely trust only one whose virtues can survive any circumstances 17.327

see also
five spiritual faculties; friendship can only exist between virtuous persons, *see* Aristotle; good and goodness

Virūḍhaka (great king) 16.346

Virūpākṣa (great king) 16.346, 16.351–2

vīrya (Pāli *viriya*)

introduction
etymology and definitions 4.132, 4.339, 17.58–9, 17.574–5; the foundation of everything 4.474; innate vigour 17.68; signifies both energy and masculine potency 2.156; *vīrya* and 'masculinity' 4.118, 4.141–3; it lends itself to the excitement of doing things 17.81; its nature is to go on and on 17.577; objective (helping others) and subjective (the four right efforts) 3.304–5; in conjunction with the perfection of wisdom it becomes a cosmic force 1.440

traditional references
five stages of *vīrya* 17.575–7; as one of the eleven positive mental events (Abhidharma) 17.574–7; synonyms in the *Dhammasaṅgaṇi* 1.439; difference between Early Buddhism and Mahāyāna conception 1.439–40; Śāntideva on *vīrya* 4.438–87; 'What is the mark of vigour?' 17.70; and self-power–other-power 4.138–41

energy in pursuit of the good
what is 'the good'? 1.439, 3.372, 4.132, 10.369; directing our active energy in conscious pursuit of the good 15.155; energy in pursuit of the good of self and others 10.176; using energy for another purpose is not *vīrya* 3.287, 3.304, 9.297, 17.574–5; activity in pursuit of politics and business is laziness 4.132, 17.534, 18.390, 19.582; 'enthusiasm for the good'

9.213–14; Anagarika Dharmapala's tireless energy in doing good 8.25–6, 8.41–2; it has an essentially ethical reference 17.670; working for the Dharma 10.396–7, 11.89–90, 14.xvi, 14.522–3, 16.207

vīrya and other mental states
an active state of being developed by mindfulness and *dhamma-vicaya* 15.216–17; follows on from faith 18.274–5; there is no vigour without faith 17.70; balanced with *kṣānti* 4.132, 4.141, 4.143; balanced with *samādhi* 1.293, 3.305–6, 9.214, 19.551; not to be confused with neurotic activity or restlessness 4.478–9, 17.60–2; and enjoyment 9.297, 15.217; its adversary is sloth 4.470–1

images
an elephant the image of *vīrya* (Śāntideva) 4.468–9; the 'heavy armour' of *vīrya* 17.575–6; symbolized by the horse or Windhorse 9.275, 9.366–7, 10.200–2, 19.438

the practice of vīrya
how is vigour cultivated? 17.68–70; activity is the condition of growth (Ambedkar) 9.47; becoming aware of where *vīrya* can be lost and found 15.217; the energetic practice of the perfections 1.440; one never rests on one's laurels 8.226, 11.617, 17.577; making little spiritual progress due to lack of *vīrya* 4.474; steady persistence 3.305; in the transcendental practice, self and others, beings and things, ultimately unreal 1.440; *vīrya* and the four right efforts 1.374, 1.440. 3.304, 8.200, 16.10–11; what to do with an excess of *vīrya* 17.62

the need for vīrya
especially at the beginning of the spiritual life 4.141; for the development of all the *pāramitās* 16.164; for the practice of all the disciplines leading to Enlightenment 16.11, 16.280; obstacles almost always arise, so you need the *vīrya* that does not turn back 17.577; until Stream Entry vigour is always necessary 17.70; 'In vigour lies Enlightenment' 1.440; without *vīrya*, the bodhisattva will attain to nothing but defeat 4.469; you've got to be making constant effort, like juggling, or propping a house up 17.70

a Buddhist characteristic
we mustn't forget the *vīrya* aspect of Buddhism 4.444–7; don't curb your courage and confidence for the sake of being a 'good Buddhist' 4.444; Buddhists can be gentle, but also sure, determined, confident 4.444, 12.216–17

vīrya and the bodhisattva
contrast with the practice of the *śrāvaka* 1.439–41; the embodiment of energy 2.156, 3.372; like an elephant plunging from one lotus pool to another 1.440, 3.287–8, 9.297; their *vīrya* is not a question of will 14.588

see also
energy; as one of the five spiritual faculties, *see under* five spiritual faculties; as one of the four *iddhipādas*, *see under* four *iddhipādas*; as one of the seven *bodhyaṅgas*, *see under* seven *bodhyaṅgas*; as one of the six perfections (*pāramitās*), *see under* perfections; Indra and the squirrel, *see under* parables and stories

visabhāga-paṭibhāga 1.120, 7.200–1

Visākha (husband of the Buddha's disciple Dhammadinnā) 3.68

Visākhā ('Migara's mother') talks to the Buddha about a difficult conversation with King Pasenadi 10.499; contributed lavishly to the Buddhist cause 2.25, 4.454, 8.49, 8.671 (n44); donation of East Park to the Buddha 15.381; the death of her granddaughter 3.77, 10.651–3; her idea that nuns should wear bathing dresses 10.498–9, 19.250, 19.262; why she was called Migāra's mother 10.498

Vishnu (or Viṣṇu, also called Nārayāna) appears in a hymn to Tārā 17.146; the Buddha said to be an *avatāra* 3.151–2, 7.228, 7.253–4, 8.122, 9.18, 9.46, 9.265, 9.365, 13.569, 22.96, 22.152; the Buddha's footprint at Bodh Gaya appropriated as that of Vishnu 2.223; consort of Lakṣmī 16.396; however much Shiva's ghosts and Vishnu's demons quarrel, the two gods remain friends 22.239; an image of the god sleeping (later described in a poem) 21.276, 21.626 (n66), 25.458; the king of Nepal as an incarnation 21.270; lion-headed 9.365; the Preserver in the Hindu *trimūrti* 16.364, 17.729 (n162; Ramana Maharshi said to be like Vishnu 20.334; takes the form of Mohini the Deluder 20.365–6; the ten *avatāras* of Vishnu 13.569; worshipped in Sri Lanka as a protector of the Dharma 26.667

Vishvantara, Dharmacharini 25.xxxii–xliii

Vishvapani, Dharmachari biography of the Buddha 6.xxv–xxvi; editor of *Dharma Life* 11.647, 11.653–9; 'The Literary Influences on Sangharakshita's Poetry' 25.xliv–lx

vision the Buddhist vision is of constant transformation 16.488; can be communicated through images and

through concepts 1.483; dwelling on visionary experience 5.44; emotional freedom to respond to an ideal or vision is what produces faith 18.273; giving oneself to the Buddha's vision, to live and die for it 11.384; difficulty of living up to the vision of the ideal 16.488; intelligence: a sort of mundane vision 15.564–5; a picture in one's mind of what one is aiming for 4.62; of reality 5.43; seeing with the eye of the soul 23.318; 'vision merely mine' 25.159; vision springs out of your own experience 19.207; we need a balance between vision and pragmatism 4.62–3; we need a vision 25.143–4; 'Where there is no vision the people perish' 11.161, 25.144

see also
Path of Vision and Path of Transformation, *see under* Noble Eightfold Path; Perfect Vision, *see under* Noble Eightfold Path

visions a Muslim who had visions of the Buddha 14.438; *samāpatti*, *see samāpatti*; Sangharakshita's, *see under* Sangharakshita VI/spiritual experiences

Viśiṣṭacāritra or Jōgyō (bodhisattva) 2.182, 2.686 (n251)

visualization (of Buddhas and bodhisattvas, *sādhana*)

INTRODUCTION

what is a visualization practice?
basic description 1.207, 2.273; the aim of the practice is the development of unconscious qualities 5.581; akin to an experience of your guardian angel? 16.111–12; all *sādhanas* are aspects of the *dharmakāya* 22.403; Atīśa explains that all *sādhanas* are in principle the same 12.575–6; although you perceive the visualized figure as object, it is subjective 17.544–5; the convergence of a light symbol and a sound symbol 16.179; the practices follow a pattern also found in the Pure Land *sūtras* 2.554; visualizing the innumerable Buddhas as practice of *kṣānti* 14.193; visualization of Enlightened qualities as personalities 7.303–5

why do the practice?
why visualize an Enlightened being? 5.621–3; it engages one emotionally and thus integrates 5.601; facing the *kleśas* directly by visualizing a wrathful form 5.353, 13.173–4; gaining insight through visualization 4.145–6, 5.465, 5.601; Going for Refuge in visualization practice 5.578–9, 13.93–4; having meditated on the Buddhas, one will not shrink from them after death 23.93; a means of approach to the Absolute 5.600; realizing one's transcendental nature 1.385; a way of getting beyond the ego 22.374–5, 22.394–5

the nature of the practice
appealing to the bodhisattvas 4.313; as you 'change' the object, you change yourself 17.544; a creative process 5.591, 12.638, 17.544–5; in relation to the *sambhogakāya* 2.42, 18.87; merging with the heart of the Buddha or bodhisattva 4.53; not perceived in the same way as external objects or mental pictures 2.42; objectification and assimilation, likened to the artistic process 3.516; painting a picture in the mind's eye 25.42–3; resolution of the tension between subject and object 15.529, 16.187; seeing the Buddha as actually present in a glorious form 2.41–2; spiritual death and rebirth 5.33–4, 26.50; the subtle and delicate nature of visualization 5.581; tapping the energy of the Void 18.320; the transformation of subject and object 16.187; trying to experience yourself as that which you're trying to become 5.591, 5.612; types of practice for 'middling' and 'superior' practitioners 22.510; visualization as positive projection 19.412–13

the practice in the Triratna Buddhist Order
it comes with *adhiṣṭhāna* (blessing), not *abhiṣeka* 4.266; regular practice of one's *sādhana* 12.417–18; why are visualization practices limited to the Order? 19.28; Western forms may develop 5.609

sādhana and other meditation practices
in the system of meditation 5.33–4; and the *kasiṇa* practice 1.154, 5.568; and the *brahma vihāras* 5.592–3; and *mettā* 5.592–3, 5.608; the six element practice as an introduction to *sādhana* 5.486, 5.605

choosing a sādhana
better to allow your preceptor to choose, or leave it to chance 5.619, 13.202; choosing a male or female figure 5.622; a form that corresponds to a quality you need or to which you are drawn 13.287; the form that makes Buddhahood most real to you 19.405; the main thing is to make a start 5.620, 13.202; people tend to think in psychological terms 5.622; the tradition recognizes that you are usually drawn to a particular figure 13.308; your *yidam* is chosen by your unconscious needs 13.203

beauty
the beauty of the figure is what holds you to begin with 5.592–3; their beauty is expressive of the qualities they embody

13.279; it engages your emotional energies 5.601; the contemplation of the beautiful aspect of reality 5.586; a more ideal form of beauty 5.345–6

in Tantric Buddhism
introduction 5.574–85; elaborate forms of colour devices 1.154; in combination with *pūjā* 1.377; *kriyāyoga tantrayāna* 13.22; *sādhana* as written text 1.381; to learn that all objects of perception are transformations of consciousness 1.377; why are there so many colours and forms? 13.285–7

both śamatha and vipaśyanā
how the practice potentially has both aspects 5.448, 5.461, 5.585–6, 19.453–4; a combination of *śamatha* and *vipaśyanā* 4.618–19, 5.426, 18.512–13; to begin with, a pretty picture, but then you reflect on its significance 18.512–13; compared to falling in love with someone and then finding out about them 5.595; visualization and the *dhyānas* 5.594–6, 5.630–1

samayasattva (conventional being) and jñānasattva (knowledge-being)
an important distinction 5.614–16; falling in love with the *samayasattva* 5.618; 'getting rid of' the *samayasattva* to allow the *jñānasattva* to arise 5.448; tuning in to the *jñānasattva* through the *samayasattva* 4.8, 17.544–5

DOING THE PRACTICE

beginning the practice
beginning the practice with the *śūnyatā* mantra 5.489; the blue sky 5.488–9, 5.603–4, 19.454, 26.221; the production of the form (*utpatti*) 18.320; visualizing oneself as the figure or visualizing the figure in front of one 16.187

colours
the importance of the visualization of colour 16.259; to begin with, one may see only an undifferentiated patch of colour 5.572, 13.287; the colour of a visualized form is often a key to its significance 13.67, 13.287; haloes of coloured light surrounding the Buddha or bodhisattva 16.260; visualizing colours one has never seen before 4.57; the colour of a visualized form is often an important key to its significance 13.67

visualization and mantra
the combination of visualization and mantra chanting 13.291–2; which is more important? 5.628–9; seeing the form and hearing the mantra: active and passive 26.39; subtle vocalization 5.629–30

mantra visualization
not just a visualization exercise but a spiritual practice 19.33; clockwise and anti-clockwise 5.582, 13.96, 19.329; see it moving fast if you're sleepy, slowly if you're restless 5.582

the figure
the Buddha's form as you perceive it represents the mundane in its perfection 18.416; concentration remaining constant while one focuses on different details 17.542; discursive activity while visualizing 5.628–9; evocation and invocation 18.319–20; the form emerging and disappearing like a fish leaping from the sea 5.583, 5.600, 13.96; the relation between a painting of a figure and visualizing them in meditation 13.288; a taste of non-duality between conditioned and Unconditioned 5.607; repetition of verses 14.481–2

and emptiness
dissolving the figure back into *śūnyatā* 13.85, 13.96; form and emptiness in the practice 5.599–600, 5.603–6; how do you imagine a form as being *śūnyatā*? 5.604–5; meditating on the voidness of the visualized form 1.377; the *śūnyatā* mantra recited at the start of the practice, *see under* mantras; the *śūnyatā* meditation as part of the practice 5.579–80; visualizing the form and the voidness at the same time 5.583

after the practice
seeing all beings as the bodhisattva and hearing all sounds as mantras 5.607; continuing to visualize oneself as the bodhisattva after the practice 16.187–8; making connections with the *sādhana* in everyday life: don't force it 5.616–17

ADVICE ABOUT THE PRACTICE

advice
being inhibited by the form 16.112; better not to practise just as a concentration exercise 5.598–9; can the relationship with one's *yidam* be sexual? 5.619; doing two visualization practices 5.610–11, 22.403; don't talk about your visualization practice too much 5.608–9, 16.187, 18.421; if you have to choose, choose visualization over mindfulness or *mettā* 5.608; is visualization a sidetrack? 5.445; just doing the practice to alter psychological and emotional states limits it 5.607; make your own investigations 5.624–5; start by connecting the figure with ordinary objects, colours, and sounds 13.292; *thinking* the visualization as well as *seeing* it 5.629–30; is the visualization more important than the mantra? 5.628; difference between

producing an eidetic image and feeling for the figure 5.598–9, 19.28; wanting a visualization practice for acquisitive reasons 5.40; you get from the practice what you put into it 19.28

difficulties with visualizing
if you can't see the figure, at least feel that it is there 13.211; taking up a different kind of practice 5.612–13; training oneself to visualize 5.611–12; why do some people find visualization difficult? 5.556–7; if you can't visualize well, you tend to focus on the mantra 5.628; if you find visualization difficult, recite the mantra for a similar effect 5.601; your connection with Tārā is more important than seeing her 10.lxv

see also
visualizing the Buddha, *see under* Buddha IV/responses; individual Buddhas and bodhisattvas, *see* individual figures; *yab-yum* figures, *see yab-yum*; vulgar magic without the realization of *śūnyatā*, *see under* Chen/teachings

visuddhi epithet for Nirvāṇa 1.69; etymology: 'brightness, splendour, excellence' 3.295; *see also* seven *visuddhis*

Visuddhimagga ('Path of Purity') *see under* Buddhaghosa

Visuddhisara (Burmese monk) v22

Viśvapaṇī (bodhisattva) 2.172

viśvavajra (double *vajra*) introduction 13.186; Amoghasiddhi's emblem 4.207, 12.216, 13.186; crossed *vajras* on which the universe rests 16.341

Vitakkasaṇṭhāna Sutta *see under Majjhima Nikāya*

vitalism 3.476, 12.85–7

vitality artists' energy flows with extraordinary vitality 3.509; Buddhism's spiritual vitality 14.251; most people live far below the level of their optimum vitality 11.33; a princess with vitality 21.29; the spiritual vitality of the Mahāyāna 1.276; the vitality of the creative mind 11.26

vitarka-vicāra apprehension and investigation of an object 5.242; like seizing a pot with one hand and scouring it with the other 9.200, 16.601 (n119), 17.689; and the development of insight 16.161; how they relate to *saṃjñā* 17.518; the second *dhyāna* is a state free from *vitarka* and *vicāra* 17.125; they may be positive or negative 17.689–90; thinking *of* and *about* an object 5.238; as unclassifiable mental events (*aniyatas*) 17.689–90; *vicāra* is 'going around and around the subject' 4.491; what is the difference between mind and *vitarka*? 17.690

Vivaldi, Antonio 26.505

vivaṭṭa (evolution) 1.40

Vivekananda, Phra (Thai *bhikkhu*) 10.149, 10.160, 10.169, 12.635, 12.647, 22.525, 23.365

Vivekananda, Swami

his life
introduction 7.559–60, 9.573 (n373), 22.578 (n62); established the Ramakrishna Mission 9.116; at the World's Parliament of Religions in Chicago 8.48, 8.166, 10.280; admiration of his oratory 18.363; drinking wine at dinner parties 21.387; criticism of him 8.437–8, 9.211; Anagarika Dharmapala's defence of him 8.33, 21.386–7; 'spirit guide' of Rajgopal's family 20.375; visited Max Müller in Oxford 7.87; Vivekananda's Rock, Cape Comorin 20.239; Sangharakshita's involvement with the Vivekananda Society (Sri Lanka) 20.117

teachings and sayings
'The Buddha taught simply "Be good and do good"' – a silly thing to say 7.524; 'Buddhism is the rebel child of Hinduism' 10.279–80; caused harm by teaching *prāṇāyāma*? 20.125; on the *gopīs* and Krishna 7.93; 'Hinduism killed Buddhism with a loving embrace' 8.xx; 'Malabar is a mad-house!' 20.298; 'Most men are really atheists' 7.88; prayer as 'shopkeeper's love' 17.171, 17.732 (n185); scathing about people referring to 'Lord Ramakrishna' 10.442; spoke of the weakness of the Indian people 7.58; his story of the ocean frog and the frog in the well, *see* parables and stories; 'You are not sinners, you are divine' 14.460

Vivian (and Merlin) 25.438, 25.452

Vivien (Terry's girlfriend) v23

vivisection 8.213–15

voice 'After the fire a still small voice' 14.535; Bhaddiya 'foremost of those who have a sweet voice' 10.615; of Brahmā 16.281–2; busy listening to your own voice you won't hear the *ḍākinī* within 18.178–9; 'Nature is not dead but alive with many voices' 1.28; symbolizing the creation of the world by God 26.204; the voice of the devil 15.620; *The Voice of the Silence*, *see* Blavatsky, H. P.; the voice within 7.266–9; 'the warlike voice of authority' 22.126;

Sangharakshita hears the voice of an angel 13.591, 26.611, 26.617–18

voidness (or the Void) *see śūnyatā*

volition a committed volition to perpetual self-transcendence 3.17; impeded and unimpeded 2.127; rebirth-producing volition 1.112; sublimated, correspondence with Vajrapāṇi 2.173; varying degrees of volition brought to an action 17.589; volition and action 3.99; volition is a creative force 17.479; *see also javana*

volitions (*saṃskāras*) the aim of spiritual practice is to redirect the cyclic flow of semi-conscious volitions 15.205; the consequences of mind-volitions 2.70–1; as second *nidāna* 3.195–6; the Buddha is free from volitions 3.142; blindly stumbling 3.130; skilful and unskilful volitions determine rebirth 2.71–2, 3.142, 3.195, 17.473–4; volitions have varying degrees of intensity 2.71; we have the potential to modify our habit-volitions to promote growth 17.474; *see also saṃskāras*, *cetanā*

Voltaire his advice about how to start a new religion 11.382; 'Religion originated when the first rogue met the first fool' 12.41; *Selected Works* 13.533

volunteers failing to do what you promised through lack of integration 17.696–7; giving a talk on the bodhisattva ideal, then not finding volunteers to wash up 18.163

Vonnegut, Kurt 24.526

voraciousness 18.559

Voragine *see* Jacobus

vows (*praṇidhana*)

making (or taking) a vow
what making a vow involves 17.169–70; if you are really determined, why is a vow necessary? 19.146; learning how to make and keep vows 2.343, 4.56–7, 18.161; to make a vow, you need to know yourself 17.169–70, 19.397–8; it is customary to make vows at the time of initiation 18.161; a mutual vow between guru and disciple, or between spiritual friends 18.146–7; taking a vow before a shrine, one draws to oneself the protection of *apatrāpya* 17.561; taking a vow of celibacy 19.145; taking a vow requires a high degree of integration 17.170, 19.145; to make a vow is to keep it 17.169; to take a vow and 'live up to it all your life' is not easy 19.144–5; to take a vow the disciple's commitment must be beyond question 18.162; a vow should relate to something very specific 19.145–6; a vow to be reborn in more favourable circumstances 18.147–8; a day-to-day commitment may feel more spontaneous 19.146–7

breaking vows
better not to make a vow than to make it and fail to keep it 4.476–7; breaking a vow shows that you're not master of yourself 18.487; the consequences of breaking vows 18.161; Vajrasattva purifies those who have broken their vows 22.504

vows in the Buddhist tradition
bodhisattva vow, *see* bodhisattva vow; Dharmākara's 48 vows, *see under* Amitābha/history and myth; 'King of Vows Concerning the Good Life' 14.227; Samantabhadra's ten vows 14.226–7; Shiwa Aui's vows 18.161; Queen Śrīmāla's ten vows 14.175; the vow of Bhaiṣajyaguru Vaidūryaprabha 1.335

vrata 2.147

Vrindavana 16.73

Vulture's Peak (Gṛdhrakūṭa) introduction 16.591 (n41); historical and symbolic 3.378, 16.38; imagining the Buddha there 7.431–2; and King Bimbisāra 7.431; where the Mahāyāna *sūtras* were taught 1.297, 14.112, 14.182, 16.241; in the *Sūtra of Golden Light* 16.244; in the *White Lotus Sutra* 3.91, 14.112–13, 14.127, 16.38, 20.465; setting of the *Perfection of Wisdom in 8,000 Lines* 14.138; setting of the Pure Land *sūtras* 1.327, 14.168, 14.172; the scene of the *Samādhirāja Sūtra* 14.191; the opening of the *Śūraṅgama-samādhi Sūtra* 14.195; Bhikkhu Kashyap and Sangharakshita visit 7.430–2, 20.464–6, 22.387; Sangharakshita visits with Terry 23.368; chairlift 25.325

vyādha (huntsman) 2.388

vyādhi (sickness) 2.388

vyākaraṇa (Pāli *veyyākaraṇa*) as explanation, one of the *aṅgas* of the Pāli canon 14.23–4, 17.571; as prediction to Enlightenment, *see under* prediction

vyākhyās 1.299

vyañjana 14.297; *see also* spirit and letter

vyāpāda *see* aversion

Vyāsa 16.85

vyūha (Pāli *viyūha*) 14.169

W

Waddell, David 2.403

Waddell, Laurence (*The Buddhism of Tibet*) references to 'Buddha fiendesses' 13.68, 17.313; Sangharakshita's view of the book 4.239, 8.365, 12.103

Wadia, Shri B. P. 1.5, 9.563 (n254), 22.139, 22.267

Wadia, Mme Shrimati Sophia brief introduction 9.563 (n254), 24.610 (n43); born in Colombia 22.587 (n131); dedicatee of *A Survey of Buddhism* 1.5, 2.289; editor of the *Aryan Path* (which is how Sangharakshita met her) 22.133–4; introduces a talk on the *Diamond Sūtra* 10.162; introduces a talk on Going for Refuge 2.289, 9.244; poem to her 21.479, 25.298–9; Sangharakshita stays with the Wadias in Bangalore 22.139–50; Sangharakshita gives lectures at their house 22.268–70; Sangharakshita consults her about his book of poems 22.183; Sangharakshita visits her (1979) 24.25; not hearing from her any more 21.596; what she was like 22.140

Wadkin, John *see* Lalitavajra

wages see under work/the world of work

Wagner, Richard introduction 23.498 (n199); the 'complete artwork' 26.377–8; *The Ring* cycle 12.188, 16.380–1, 23.xvii, 23.173–4

waking up a Buddhist vibrates with wakefulness to life 3.296; getting rid of the sense of self is like waking up from a dream 10.470; life is like waking up in a strange inn, not knowing how you got there 3.7; waking up to the truth of things, as from a dream 3.36; reaching a higher level of consciousness is like waking up in the morning feeling really happy 18.298; waking up to the fact that you are Buddha 12.234, 13.364; we purify ourselves by waking up to the fact that we have never been impure 4.193; a moment of pure awareness when you wake up in the morning, *see under* pure awareness; requires a great deal of effort 13.364; wake up, for life in this world is short (Dharmapala) 8.57; 'Wake up! Wake up!' says Zen 13.364; when you wake up in the morning, notice how you feel about the coming day 19.395–6

Wala Tsandra 18.313, 18.322–3

Waldensians (Waldenses) 8.416, 13.580–1

Wales FWBO presence in Wales 13.373; retreat centres, *see under* Triratna IV/ retreat centres; Rhyl 24.133

Waley, Arthur 7.450, 25.26

Walford, Lee 17.xv

Walker, Kenneth 22.276, 22.599 (n221)

walking meditation (*caṅkamana*) introduction 5.79–86; an aid to reflection 15.190–1; an alienated experience of walking 10.602; Aristotle's practice 5.80; the Buddha described as walking up and down and meditating 5.644; the Buddha explains its benefits 5.81, 5.712 (n80); learning to make the transition from spiritual practice to the ordinary world 5.82–3; over-zealous (Soṇa) 1.293, 5.80; problems of too analytical an approach 5.85; and reflection leading to insight 5.465; walking and chanting 5.81–3, 5.644

Walshe, Maurice introduction 23.484 (n93); general entries v23; chairman of the English Sangha Trust 11.495; *Dīgha Nikāya* translation 23.439; photographs 23.50, 23.64

Walshe, Ruth introduction 23.484–5 (n94); classes at the vihara 11.494–5; general entries v23; photograph 23.64

Walter, Harriet 24.390

wanderers brief introduction 9.546; the life of a *parivrājaka* (Pāli *paribbājaka*) 3.404–6, 3.460, 10.477–9, 15.278–9; the Buddha-to-be as a wanderer 3.460, 9.191, 10.479; community: the earliest sangha 2.186–8, 12.237; conventions became *prātimokṣas* 2.188; discouraged from getting attached to particular families 15.284–5; giving alms to wanderers meritorious 10.479; most of the Buddha's disciples recruited from the wanderers 3.461, 10.479, 15.278; six groups of wanderers in the Buddha's day 10.479; *śramaṇa* wanderers contrasted with settled *brāhmaṇas* 10.488; wanderers with families 10.487–8; wandering was the only way of learning anything new 10.478; becoming a wanderer means changing 9.191; ethical conduct 2.186–7; householders should support wanderers before making offerings to *devas* 10.648; improper to question a sadhu about his

previous stage of life (*pūrvaśrama*) 20.232; a king who goes forth as a wanderer when his barber finds his first grey hair 18.13; 'the monk is pure who goes' 3.404; 'one who has gone forth' 2.186; a source of advice 10.479; the story of a Nepalese wanderer 21.304–5; style of dress 12.237; Sundarī, a woman wanderer 10.539–40; variety of views held by wanderers 10.594, 10.596–7; wanderers of other views (than those of the Buddha) 10.477–8, 10.539–41, 10.611–12

wandering as a lifestyle 12.237–8, 19.549; can you usefully increase your experience by wandering? 19.360–3; wandering from place to place can be very distracting 19.361, 19.549; wandering may not be advisable unless you have insight 19.346–60; wandering mind 10.532, 15.116–17, 17.97; wandering the *bardo* 18.83–4; wandering through the realms of conditioned existence 8.558–9; wandering thoughts, *see under* thought

Wang Wei 7.437, 7.613–4 (n464)

Wangchuk, Jigme Dorji *see under* Dorji

Wangpo, Rigdzing *see* Prajnaloka

Wangyal, Geshe

introduction
brief introduction 2.744 (n685), 22.585 (n108), 23.539–40 (n479); Sangharakshita meets him in Kalimpong 8.527, 22.119, 22.192; his Buddhist centre in America 8.527, 23.458

The Door of Liberation
book review 8.527–9; a collection of precepts 8.528; discussion of *mettā* 5.164–6; gratitude for the book 8.529; 'If you do not meditate on impermanence in the early morning, by midday you will have many desires' 4.265, 8.528; 'If you do not renounce activity, do not say you are a great meditator' 5.643–7; inspiration to the Triratna Buddhist Community 2.555, 12.368; the text is pervaded with a deep reverence for the Three Jewels 8.529; Tsongkhapa's *Three Chief Paths* 8.528–9, 17.421, 17.753 (n346); 'Wouldn't you rather be practising the Dharma?' 8.593–4

Wanshiv, Dadasaheb 24.21

war

views of war
what the Buddha said 8.141, 8.677 (n77); Dr Ambedkar's view 9.47; Einstein's view 9.497; 'ancestral voices prophesying war' 22.341; no question of justifying any war 3.583; not a favourite subject for poetry 26.393; an unhealthy interest in the progress of war 18.105; what is war but mass murder? 8.212

religious views
by refusing to wage righteous war a Kṣatriya incurs sin (*Bhagavad Gītā*) 8.449; 'Every war is an inspiration for Christians' (Dharmapala) 8.15; the Catholic Church and war 8.152–3; pseudo-Christian justification of war 8.129; religious 9.472

causes and nature of war
it comes from the wrong belief in separate selfhood 26.168–9; it should be no surprise that the world is full of conflicts 15.306; in a war setting, facilities of communication are used for non-communication 12.340; life isn't valued so much in wartime – a biological significance? 16.302; mass destruction between people who do not know one another 12.340; men come home in body bags 25.445; nations imagine themselves to be separate entities 7.274; a novel in which the youthful hope of a conscript may end in a distant death 24.541; two extreme views about the causes of war 7.237–8

ceasing war
hope that humanity will pause upon the threshold of a third world war 7.280; if peace is to be achieved, we have to identify ourselves with both parties 12.343–4; it would be precluded by the practice of *ahiṃsā* 7.119

wars in history
war has the same features throughout history 12.339; a Byzantine Emperor whose purpose was to avoid war 15.624; Napoleon's tomb: glorification of the spirit of war 26.277–8; Cold War 8.298, 22.209, 23.87; military build-up in the Kalimpong area 22.557–8; invasion of Kuwait 24.406

nuclear war
Buddhism, World Peace, and Nuclear War 10.87, 12.338–62; Campaign for Nuclear Disarmament 10.87; the Cuban missile crisis 23.87; the dangerous world of the Cold War and the atom bomb 8.298, 25.228; a soldier makes a nuclear threat 22.557; non-violent pressure must be brought to bear on governments and citizens 12.346–8; nuclear weapons (and also conventional ones) must be abolished 12.341, 12.353; the failure of communication between superpowers 12.349–50; fatalism about atomic war 19.86; our fear of it appears absurd (in the context of the vastness of time) 7.343; protest against Polaris missile systems

23.493 (n152); the *Rig Veda* is claimed to contain instructions to build a nuclear bomb 17.330; setting an example of impartiality, love for humanity, and non-violence 12.348–9; those opposing it must learn to speak with one voice 12.345–6, 12.350; weapons as deterrent 3.583; while nuclear weapons don't affect our everyday life, we can forget about them 10.87–8; teaching people the *mettā bhāvanā* could have an effect 12.348; the threat of nuclear war 7.512, 8.261–2, 9.497, 12.360–1, 12.408, 26.376; it would mean the suicide of humanity 12.340–1; we have to assume that nuclear holocaust is not inevitable 12.344–5; whether or not nuclear war is averted, we will all have to die 12.356–7; is it worth delivering humanity only to fall victim to worthless pursuits? 12.355

Ward, Timothy 13.382

Warder, A. K. 26.326–8

Wardha, India Anand Kausalyayan visits 21.449–50; Hsüan Tsang retreat centre, *see under* Triratna IV/retreat centres; opening of the boys' hostel 10.358

Ware, Timothy Kállistos 23.209, 23.505 (n242)

Warhol, Andy 26.360

Warren, Henry Clarke 9.137, 10.263

warrior the Buddha and his followers: 'We fight for *śīla*, *samādhi*, *prajñā*, *vimukti*' 3.49–53, 11.407; Buddhism's use of the metaphor of the warrior 18.104; masculine ideal – but warriors can be of either sex 18.105–6; the sole armour of a warrior of the Dharma was reason, his only weapon persuasion 7.383; use your warrior's strength to fight the inner, spiritual battle 18.103, 18.106; the warrior ideal and the ideal of the flower 18.106; warrior-like nature of Tibetan Khambas 18.99; *see also* Siddhārtha/the Buddha's warrior training

waste don't waste good conditions for Dharma practice 4.365–7, 10.322; negativity wastes energy at a catastrophic rate 4.133–4; the preciousness of human life wasted 7.131, 10.322; the waste of food 10.322; a waste of time to think of developing the *bodhicitta*, but you can set up the conditions 4.43; wasted energy 3.372, 4.133–4; *see also* time/wasting time

Waste Land, the the 'other country' of the parable of the priceless jewel 16.219; T. S. Eliot's poem, *see under* Eliot

Watanabe, Tsuneo and Iwata, Jun'ichi 24.388–9

Watchmaker, Mrs 23.351

water

element
associated with the colour white and the shape of a sphere 13.153, 16.147; correlated with the psychic centre at the solar plexus 16.147; *kasiṇa* visualization of water and ice 1.332; 'Meditation Upon Water' 8.xxxi, 8.265–6; 'In Praise of Water' (poem) 25.289; reality flows through the bodhisattva's veins 14.590; Chu (water) 19.156

symbols and metaphors
the Amitābha mantra like a narrow white path between fire and water 1.338; the Buddha walking in the air emitting fire and water, *see under* miracles/twin miracle; compassion springs up in the Void as a lotus in water 1.239; the cosmic golden lotus floating on the waters of existence 12.220; every drop of the Dharma is precious, like water in the desert 9.291; the experience of the *dhyānas* is like the sun's rays filtering through deep water 4.154; the experience of the one mind is like a great expanse of pure, clear water 2.275; fire and water are cosmic opposites: alchemy 12.184–5; flowing like water to the sea 25.164; 'If you won't get under the shower you can't complain if it isn't wetting you' 26.60; 'Know your own Mind completely ... like water meeting with water' 1.306; *lalanā* corresponds to water 18.76; moon in water 2.154; physical energy in a state of oscillation 16.144–6; the possibility of Enlightenment like the moon reflected in agitated water 7.311; psychical energy in a state of limited mobility 13.154, 13.155, 16.145–6; *saṃsāra*: terrible waters infested with the sharks of birth and death 7.68; the so-called normal person 16.146; symbolized in the stupa 16.150; the union of fire and water: the red king and the white queen 12.184–5

water stories
Ānanda took water from an 'Untouchable' woman 10.260, 14.68–9; the battle of the Śākyas and the Koliyans over water 7.238, 9.140, 10.260, 12.338–9; brahmins try to stop the Buddha from drawing water 10.622–7; water churned up by wagons becomes clear when the Buddha asks for a drink 10.639; purification of water with the products of the cow 9.49, 9.221; 'How wonderful! How miraculous! I draw water and I carry fuel.' 14.397, 16.252; Sangharakshita persuades a woman to give him water despite her caste 20.415

see also
images for the *dhyānas*, *see under* *dhyānas*; four *rūpa dhyānas*; images for the hindrances, *see under* five hindrances; in the six element practice, *see under* six element practice

Waterloo (battle) 10.222, 24.149

Waterton, Connie 23.141

Watkins, Alfred 24.70, 24.624 (n95)

Watts, Alan introduction 7.552–3 (n44), 8.700 (n274); Sangharakshita's reservations about Watts 7.553 (n44); 'This is IT!' 4.163; *Psychotherapy East and West* 23.332; *The Spirit of Zen* 7.40, 7.45; *The Way of Zen* 2.698 (n359), 8.388–90

Watts, George Frederic 24.73, 24.625 (n100)

Watts, Isaac a rose in winter: essence without existence 13.582; 'Time, like an ever-rolling stream' 26.294

Watts-Dunton, Theodore, *Aylwin* 24.310, 24.683 (n378)

way *see* path

way of life *see* lifestyle

Way to the Beyond 1.82

Wayman, Alex 2.706 (n418), 18.494–5

weakness

one's own weaknesses
an attempt to cover up your weaknesses is a serious matter 19.152–3; be open about your weaknesses 19.153–4; being compassionate to your weaknesses 10.524–5; being proud of weaknesses 17.606; beware of the tendency to think that you are not among the 'weaker brethren' 4.555; being stopped from doing something by a weak and reluctant part of yourself 10.605; confessing weaknesses 16.289–90; 'cry no more that you are weak' 25.185; a fine line between acknowledging your weaknesses and indulging them 17.657–8; get impatient with your weaknesses and failings 4.368; hanging on to your weaknesses 17.647–8; not allowing your weaknesses to be questioned 17.666–7; pay attention to your weakest faculty 3.311, 12.25; recognizing our weaknesses is the first step towards removing them 7.182; reflecting that alongside one's weaknesses are the seeds of real spiritual qualities 14.594; rejecting one's weaknesses like a man throwing off a snake 8.586; spiritual friends can help you overcome weaknesses 19.153, 19.407; using your *dharmapāla* aspect to be hard on your own weaknesses 19.407

other people's weaknesses
appreciate people's positive qualities without dwelling on their weaknesses 26.80; 'Let not his frailties be remembered, he was a very great man' 24.582; Milarepa's mettle even in a moment of weakness 18.20; people are not deliberately wicked, but weak 16.320; in real friendship you don't bolster up each other's little weaknesses 18.389; seeing someone's weaknesses and still appreciating their inner beauty 15.293–4

human weakness
'marks of weakness, marks of woe' 3.228, 11.78, 18.424; religions of revelation emphasize the weakness of human nature 7.366; some concession must be made to human weakness 18.638; tolerance of human weakness 13.477–8; a weak character: yielding too easily to the impressions of the moment 3.567; why is our concentration so weak? 1.569

weaknesses and strengths
dogmatism arises if faith is strong but wisdom weak 1.293; it can be hard to distinguish weaknesses from strengths 19.154–5; knowing your own strengths and weaknesses 19.360; *mettā* is not weak but very strong 1.502, 9.192, 9.517, 9.521; our daily routine should be such that we are strengthened, not weakened 16.207; the strong helping the weak 26.655; the tyranny of the weak over the strong 10.471; weakness in relation to the guru's strength 18.410; weaknesses springs from strengths 7.324–5

weakness and spiritual life
religious people can be weak because to be 'good' they have repressed their energy 18.78; in the sangha we have to be careful not to put pressure on weaker people 17.184; using the bodhisattva ideal an excuse for a weak and cowardly life 1.443; we have to be careful that our Buddhism doesn't become weak and wishy-washy 10.14; a weak point of much Buddhism is the lack of a concrete spiritual basis 23.160; the weakness of the Buddhist world is lack of unity 8.217–18, 22.308

weaknesses of modern life
it is a weakness of modern life that we don't rejoice in merits enough 18.377; the weakness of our attachments being spread over many things 19.19

reflections
'I believe that it is a weakness to believe anything ... or nothing' 7.38; humility is the pride of the weak 26.61; intellectual rigour can become a weakness if not balanced by faith 3.304; 'Don't waste time helping the weak ...' 15.538–9, 26.5, 26.35, 26.489; to overcome evil, what is needed is the *bodhicitta* 4.268, 4.270; sometimes thought is luminous, but action is weak 7.138; the weak cannot be joyful 26.35

wealth *see* prosperity

weapons a collection of live shells 26.553; giving up weapons in medieval Tibet a huge step 18.98–9; love is the most powerful weapon in the world 3.319; manufacture and trade in a form of wrong livelihood 1.546–7, 3.283, 3.583; nuclear weapons, *see under* war/nuclear war; Māra's weapons turn to flowers 3.277; wielded by wrathful deities 17.318

weather effect on different cultures 4.576–8; effect on meditation 4.575; in India, meditation carrying on despite a hailstorm 24.107; practising forbearance in relation to the weather 4.120; saying 'It's raining' is fact, but saying 'The weather is bad' is value judgement 12.477; the Tibetan art of weather-making 13.643

Weber, Max 13.468–9

Webster, Geoffrey 2.403

Webster, John 24.390

Webster's New International Dictionary *see under* dictionaries

Wee (Malaysian aspirant) 21.84–5

weeds *see under* flowers and plants

weeping after Terry's death 'I wept every day for six months' 23.446; crying in meditation 11.200; the effect of meeting the Tantric guru 18.67; in the first *dhyāna* 4.152; the mind reacting to the loss of praise and fame like a child crying at a broken sandcastle 4.431; weeping at Dickens' novels, and enjoying 'a good cry' at the cinema 14.471; a time of being unable to cry due to medication 26.682; weeping at the Buddha's *parinirvāṇa* 4.10, 16.295; weeping is quite common in Tibetan Buddhism but rare in other Buddhist schools 19.124–5

see also
Ānanda weeps on losing the Buddha, *see under* Ānanda/his friendship with the Buddha; Sadāprarudita, 'Ever Weeping', *see under Perfection of Wisdom in 8,000 lines*; Subhūti weeps in the *Diamond Sūtra*, *see under Diamond Sūtra*/the text

Wei Lang, Sūtra of *see Sūtra of Huineng*

weight Going for Refuge as if a great weight had been lifted 3.330; sloth is the weight of one's existence resisting further evolving 26.47; a Tibetan king ransomed for his weight in gold 12.571–2, 13.13–14; to practise the Dharma, we have to go against the weight of our conditioning 12.455

weighty karma *see under* karma/kinds of karma

Weintrob, Dr 22.73

Weiss, Peter 23.175

welfare aspiration for the welfare of all living beings (*Sūtra of Golden Light*) 16.276, 16.333–4; Avalokiteśvara concerned with the welfare of his devotees 2.176; *bahujana hitāya*, *see* 'for the welfare of the many'; combining work on self-development with work for others' welfare 15.237, 18.77; the Enlightened mind devotes itself to the welfare of all beings 4.166, 12.217; Enlightenment for the welfare of all beings 3.245–6, 4.21–2; looking after the welfare of our friends 3.574, 3.579, 11.698; the products of the cow like one who strives for his own welfare and that of others 14.50; take an active interest in the welfare of your fellow citizens 7.439; there is no spiritual welfare state 17.243; welfare state, *see under* politics/government; your friend won't see your welfare in quite the same way you do 15.293

wells the ocean frog and the frog in the well 1.198, 9.372, 10.256, 26.105–6, 26.110; villagers block a well, but cannot stop the Buddha from drawing water 10.622–7; Sangharakshita persuades a woman to give him water despite her caste 20.415

Wells, H. G. short introduction 23.542 (n498); *Experiment in Autobiography* 23.473; *Men Like Gods* 1.539; *The Outline of History* 1.542; prophecies 8.123, 8.675 (n67); *A Short History of the World* 2.408

Wendy-Kūṭadanta 23.173–4

Wénshū 2.173

Werblowsky, R. J. Zwi v13

Werner, Karel 8.454–8

Wertham, Dr Frederic 8.206–9

Wesak *see* festivals/Buddha Day

Wesley, John his religion seemed different from the Methodism of Sangharakshita's boyhood 23.208–9; his impressive personality and methods 10.85–7; liked to remind his congregations that they were grovelling worms 18.120; a parallel with Zen 12.4, 23.208

West, the

spiritual life
alternative spiritual traditions 13.373–5; *The Book of Enlightened Masters* 8.626–9; caution about committing oneself to a religious cause or person 17.307–8; continuity of religious life disrupted by Christianity 12.253; for a long time all cultures and communities were 'officially' religious 16.128; good conditions for Dharma practice 3.313–14; the greatest task is to explain the difference between *jñāna* and *vijñāna* 3.356, 14.315; in some ways the situation is worse than that of the Dalits in India 10.315; interest in meditation 3.191, 26.257–8; lacks traditional underpinning 24.401; modern Western man must recognize himself as an essentially spiritual being 7.308; people need some awareness of the culture and philosophy of the East 12.51; 'Perplexed between the East and West' 26.392; rationalist and secular outlook of society gives us a thirst for myth and symbol 13.116; secular culture the bearer of spiritual values 13.511; secularism 16.128–9; spiritual void in Europe 2.612–14; unanimity of religious ideals in East and West 7.105; we don't like to think of anybody as being spiritually superior 12.13; we have no tradition of being taught religion in a practical way 17.606–7; we suffer from a dearth of symbols 13.70

lifestyle
comfortable life 17.253; confusion and chaos 16.351; distractions 10.251; materialism, cynicism, scepticism, and indifferentism 17.556, 24.401; need to find ways of integrating the Dharma with Western culture 3.45; not so sharp a distinction between materialistic West and spiritual East 13.489–90; we should support people just to live a Buddhist life 18.121

West London Buddhist Centre 24.329

West, Mae 18.479

West, Nathanael 26.380

Western Buddhism

EARLY HISTORY

nineteenth century
introduction 3.188–92, 7.449–50, 10.139, 12.69–71; the Buddha's teaching impinging on thoughtful minds 8.149; Buddhist characteristics to replace lost Christian faith 3.190; early translators 7.449–50, 12.69–71; scholarship in the early days of Buddhism in the West 25.6; Ananda Metteyya, *see under* Bennett; the forcible effect of Buddhist ideas 12.464; the impact of *The Light of Asia* 7.449, 10.139, 11.76, 12.71; initial reception as a religion of ethics or 'experience' 11.76; little reference to meditation 3.191; T. W. Rhys Davids 3.188; Schopenhauer's influence 7.449, 8.285; strange ideas about the Buddha and Buddhism 12.618

twentieth century
'Buddhism in England' 12.67–81; remarkably, the British converted themselves to Buddhism 11.485, 12.71; developments in the UK in the 1950s 21.339–40; Anagarika Dharmapala's mission to London 8.65–6, 10.139; *The British Buddhist* (journal) 8.66, 8.107; influence of D. T. Suzuki 12.72; Alexandra David-Néel one of the first Westerners to take Buddhism seriously 6.609; interest in Buddhism in Europe (1954) 8.136, 8.138–9; mission of Sinhalese *bhikṣus* 8.67; founding of Buddhist organizations 12.71–3; Buddhist Society founded (1924), *see* Buddhist Society; misunderstandings about the nature of Buddhism 26.102–4; preserving South-east Asian Buddhism in a hot-house 8.151; role of the Theosophical Society 10.139, 12.70–1; signs of increasing interest (1955); *Buddhist Wisdom for the West* (1956) 8.361–3; Theravāda and Zen the most popular 11.76; Western artists influenced by Buddhism 7.451

BUDDHISM IN BRITAIN IN THE 1960S

Buddhist movement
sectarianism 16.127–8; low calibre 12.80–1; adoption of a narrow-minded approach to rules 15.712–13; the beginnings of a native-born sangha (1965) 11.475; Buddhist organizations 11.382; the circles around Sangharakshita in 1966 23.193–201; diluted by many other beliefs 23.199–200; a distinctive Western Buddhism in the process of emergence 11.489–90; ethical formalism 17.634; individualistic 15.565–6; 'I realized that something was seriously wrong with

British Buddhism' 12.305; run by people who did not really believe in Buddhism 10.384–5, 11.173–4; polarization within the British Buddhist movement 23.48; the Sangha Sabha (Council of Buddhist Monks) 8.336–8; the size of the Buddhist movement in the 1960s 12.74, 23.199–200; the struggle to give up Christianity 11.378, 23.199–200; a time of crucial importance 23.71; unlikely to adopt the traditional pattern of monastic and lay 11.476; would Western Buddhism be a fringe cult or the centre of ordinary people's lives? 23.424; why did only Sangharakshita found an order at that time? 11.386–8; the FWBO provided a more adequate basis 13.465–6; 'May the Dharma continue to spread in England!' 23.71; what it was like 27.1071–2

meditation
great interest in meditation 23.37, 27.1071; meditating in a dangerously alienated way 12.267–8, 17.88–9, 23.45, 23.71–3; most people had hardly heard of meditation 12.623; a need for the practice of 'classical' systems of meditation 23.37, 27.1071; a warning that more than five minutes was dangerous 3.456, 4.504, 11.378, 23.48

what people were like
Buddhism was just a philosophy, or a hobby 9.241; no contact with Buddhism as a way of life 12.58–9; difficulty of making contact with Buddhists 12.60–1; what was missing was the sangha 10.265; 'No one seems really normal' 23.72; only a few people were actually practising Buddhism 11.174; English Zen students who refused to join in with a puja 11.375; Pāli fundamentalists 11.379; people's 'Buddhist' life was mainly reading 4.351, 11.378; they didn't change, or want to change 11.174; they didn't talk about being a Buddhist 10.630, 11.378, 11.605, 12.540, 19.500; 'I'm a Buddhist, but I'm just like everybody else' 11.174, 12.392–3; they read a lot, but didn't practise much 4.351, 11.378; people thought of Buddhism as arid, dull, and lifeless 19.126

THE FUTURE OF BUDDHISM IN THE WEST

'Western' Buddhism?
'Western' in the sense of practising the Dharma in modern conditions 12.498; seeing a Western Buddhist might show people that they could do that too 19.309–10; some are merely Westerners who have adopted the Buddhism of another country 23.xvii; it is 'British Buddhism', not 'English Buddhism' 13.373

signs of growth
'I believe in the future of Buddhism … in the West' (written in 1944) 7.37, 24.xxii; 'a distinctive Western Buddhism is already emerging' (1966) 23.238; will it ever be able to make an impact? (1966) 12.74; Buddhism starts to be practised seriously (1974) 11.53; Buddhism is not yet really known in the West at all (1976) 26.10; a connection with the number of books available 3.389–90; attended by serious difficulties 2.603; growing in the West but declining in the East 12.595; growth of interest in Buddhism 7.486–7; it has not really begun to communicate through Western culture 8.553; Padmasambhava comes to the West 8.520–6; rapid growth 12.137; Buddhism becoming acclimatized 13.496–7; starting to understand the nature of the challenge 23.180; strong in the United States and Europe 3.327, 10.265; English Buddhism a sturdily independent growth 11.485–6; there is almost too much Buddhism in the West 11.62; the dawning sun of Buddhism in the West 12.383–4

potential
Buddhism could fill the spiritual void in the West 2.614; clues to the final nature of Western Buddhism? 11.557; consolidating the influence of the Dharma in the West 12.609; the effect of the availability of translated literature 14.269–70; the establishing of a Western Buddhist tradition 13.409; for it to succeed, people need to be inspired with a positive ideal 15.571; its future will be assured if Western Buddhists take responsibility for it 12.79–81; appeal for a critical spirit in Western Buddhism 7.73; the integration of Buddhism into society 3.621–2, 3.624, 11.461–6; introducing Buddhist ideas into Western intellectual discourse 3.624, 11.463; the future assured if Western Buddhists take responsibility for it 12.79–81; made possible by the collapse of Christian constraints 13.377–8; no guarantee of the Dharma's inevitable decline or automatic progress 8.574; the test will be creating our own cultural forms of Buddhism 12.77–8; we are fortunate to be free to practise Buddhism 4.100–1, 12.573

Westerners' reasons for attraction to Buddhism
why do people become Buddhist? 9.283–5, 9.469–72, 9.493–7, 13.395–7; attraction to Tantric initiation 2.566; British audiences like to be given a complete picture (Govinda) 3.304; Buddhism is a system of spiritual life without a personal God

10.205–6, 12.55–6; Buddhism offers us the possibility of developing as human beings 10.206; attraction to meditation 10.206–7; Buddhism teaches social improvement 10.207; Buddhist art 10.207–8; characteristics of the English which may mesh with Buddhism 12.74–9; Mr Chen's list of reasons 22.540; spiritual friendship 10.208–9; exoticism 11.82–3, 13.493–6; modern Buddhists no longer looking for what attracted people in the past 3.190–2; an element of cultural rebellion? 13.510–12; desire for freedom to develop oneself 13.410–12; dissatisfaction and a sense of lack 13.396; it can feel not foreign but strangely familiar 16.217–18; likely to appeal to left-wing intellectuals? 13.410; people adopt Buddhism for many reasons, not all rational or clear 13.395–6; those who feel 'at home' within the framework called Buddhism 2.7; the three most popular texts 14.268–9; we are attracted to texts that seem relevant to our spiritual needs 16.247–8

what is needed
the communication of fundamental Buddhist ideas 3.624; it will only take root when Buddhists feel as well as think 12.295; myth, imagination, emotions 16.129–30; engagement with the imagery of Buddhist tradition 4.35–6; more study of the scriptures 13.337–8; the practice of 'classical' systems of meditation 23.37; a sense of responsibility to develop Buddhism in the West 12.79–81; study of the canonical literature and relating it to our spiritual lives 14.270; to address Buddhism's central concern, emptiness (Conze) 8.535; more devotion 15.626; more intensity 13.171; not an 'interpretation' of the Dharma 13.378–9; the creation of sangha 3.396, 12.81; drawing on the teachings deeply and adapting them to our needs 3.169; richness and colour 19.126–8; to assimilate Buddhism's spiritual influences and communicate in our own way 4.281; to make Buddhism a living experience 6.617; Western Buddhist institutions 11.463–4

how might Western Buddhism develop?
it will depend on the actual lives of individual Buddhists 14.270; perhaps in a rather simple, practical, earthy way 4.578, 4.624; unlikely to follow any existing pattern 3.169; we are capable of creating our own form of Buddhism 11.486–7; we are fortunate to be able to be full-time Buddhists and also work 15.281–2; 'Western Buddhists, make your choice' 25.399

challenges
difficulties facing Western Buddhism 11.521–2; Buddhism shouldn't be identified with philosophy or psychology 12.117–18; compared to traditional Buddhist countries we are at a disadvantage 18.148; Buddhism presented as an exotic curiosity 11.509; to distinguish the essential in Buddhism from the nonessential 12.78; it isn't easy to be a Buddhist in the West 8.598, 11.362, 12.128; the life of a Buddhist monk in the West is not easy 12.80; *micchā-diṭṭhis* are the real obstacle to bringing the Dharma to the West 11.522; objective and subjective difficulties 11.508–10; pseudo-spiritual consumerism 3.327; sometimes the Dharma is disguised by Eastern culture 11.598; a sophisticated response to Buddhist teachings may trivialize them 17.454; taking too soft a view of the spiritual life 11.407; becoming more positive while ignoring the social difficulties of others 10.73; thinking of appeal to 'the intellectual classes' an error 7.241, 7.243–4, 23.58–9; a Western example of *navakata*, a kind of heresy 11.74; will Westerners always have a superficial understanding of Buddhism? 11.670

WHAT CAN WESTERN BUDDHISM LEARN FROM EASTERN BUDDHISM?

Eastern Buddhism in the West
what is the relation between Western Buddhists and Eastern Buddhism? 11.371–7; the introduction of many types 11.375–6, 11.485–6, 12.115–16, 12.610–1; problems with Eastern Buddhists teaching in the West 11.83, 12.119, 15.555–7, 23.136; often what they bring is Buddhist culture rather than Buddhism 26.67; the idea of monks as the backbone cannot survive in the West 8.609–10

engaging with all traditions
learning from all the oriental traditions 13.104; practising the same Dharma as Buddhists throughout the ages 12.373–4; we need what is essential in all schools 11.89; studying and learning to appreciate all schools of Buddhism 13.325–6; a synthesis, but not a jumble 13.111–12; recognizing, honouring, and deriving inspiration from all 12.369; we are fortunate to have access to the Dharma in all its forms 12.579, 14.352

Buddhism in India
comparison between Buddhism in India and in the West 9.240–3, 10.12–14, 10.41–2; learning from Indian Buddhists 10.13–14; features in common with Indian Buddhists 9.506–8; inspired by the life and teachings of Dr Ambedkar 10.337

learning to distinguish
concerned with ultimate issues, not Eastern trappings 12.78, 13.104–5; can't be limited to one form of Eastern Buddhism 11.372–3, 14.267; the problem of indiscriminate Tantric initiations 19.488; must learn to distinguish Buddhism from Eastern culture 11.374–6; a feeble replica of any form of Eastern Buddhism is not what is needed 11.486; the Theravāda's introduction of the rigid separation of monks from laity 23.143; the *triyāna* system of Tibet and Tiantai Buddhism of China as possible models 11.89; questioning the *triyāna* conception 11.599; Western Buddhists need a self-contained Buddhist world of their own 26.630

WHAT MIGHT BE DIFFERENT?

mythology and archetypes
how will we engage in the creation of myth? 4.37–8; looking for Western equivalents to Buddhist archetypal figures 19.410–11; no reason why new bodhisattva forms should not emerge 4.194, 5.609; reasons for resistance to Buddhist myth and legend 11.76; might create a new mythology or perhaps adopt Greek mythology 19.128; hopefully patterns will spring up and we'll start actually believing something 19.413

devotion
how will we treat images? 4.304; book worship might be a bit artificial 4.307–8; it's a mistake to play down the devotional side 15.550–1; will we retain image worship? 4.298–9; Westerners' warm response to devotional practice 12.24; developing forms of devotional practice 4.296–300; building a Buddhist temple in an English style 13.273–4, 18.25; dismissive attitudes to ritual 11.205–8, 13.418

what teachings?
don't be too concerned about what is relevant to us in the West 14.481; new ways of presenting the Dharma 23.180; perhaps we could develop the Buddha's teaching about beauty 14.311; need to express Buddhist vision in a more imaginative and effective way 16.137; we may conclude that it would be unimaginative to stick to traditional forms 16.129; more inspiration from some canonical texts than others 14.268; we need much more praise and appreciation 4.622

potential directions
better to let ourselves be a bit less 'careful' 16.327; better to think of cultivating virtues than correcting faults 17.291, 17.296; is magic a helpful way of thinking about the Dharma? 4.374–5; not out to defend organized Buddhism 4.444; reflection on the foulness of the body perhaps not suitable 15.130; the rule subordinating women to men 2.602–3; should we bother with Tantric teachings? 18.494–5; the traditional view of karma may not be acceptable 4.395–6, 4.402–3; Westerners respond better to growth and development than renunciation 19.200–1; we may not need the Perfection of Wisdom's attack on intellectualism 14.442

language
adopting the language of a high-culture élite might not help 16.138; if Buddhism is to spread in the West, it needs to speak in familiar terms 12.120; the danger of using the language of psychology 10.440–1; the development of new (non-Sanskrit?) terms 4.585–6; the language of Buddhism becoming part of Western vernacular 11.xviii; need to develop a completely indigenous yet faithfully Buddhist language 16.138; needs to speak a secular language 12.117; newcomers put off by traditional Buddhist language 16.137; no need to use Tibetan, Chinese, or Japanese terms 19.134

CHALLENGES FOR WESTERN BUDDHISTS

characteristics
always looking for short cuts 13.74–5; grabbing at spiritual practices before being ready for them 5.609, 11.62; not fond of metaphysics 4.571, 4.578–9; perhaps one in twenty actually tries to practise Buddhism 11.58; tendency to pick and choose between teachings 11.58, 11.209

beyond Christianity
quite a high proportion are ex-Roman Catholics 17.556; ex-Catholics and ex-Protestants 17.639–40, 24.366; getting rid of Christian conditioning 10.277, 11.106–7, 11.378, 17.337, 18.443; guarding against Christianity 16.416; the struggle to give up Christianity 23.199–200; sympathy with alternative traditions of the West 13.375

areas of difficulty
can feel ashamed of the Buddha 4.465; confusion of self-mortification and self-discipline 17.253–5; difficulty about expressing generosity and gratitude? 4.251–7; for the average Western Buddhist, the question of sex is touchy 11.540; may struggle with hierarchy in Buddhism 4.169;

regarding the guru only as the bearer of an archetype 5.565

see also
Western Buddhism and culture, *see under* culture/Buddhism and Western culture; European Buddhist Union; Sangha Saba; Sangharakshita starts new movement, *see* Triratna

Western Buddhist *see under* Western Buddhist Order (Clifton)

Western Buddhist Order (founded by Robert Stuart Clifton) introduction 8.123, 8.674–5 (n66), 13.370, 21.339–43, 22.53; approbation of Prince Patriarch Kocho Otani 8.123–4; its publication the *Western Buddhist* 8.123–4, 8.155, 22.173, 23.53–4; recognizes Sangharakshita as a member 21.340–1; Sangharakshita's doubts about the Order 21.340; ordained as priests rather than monks 21.343; did not see ordination in terms of Going for Refuge 21.342–3

Western Buddhist Order (founded by Sangharakshita) *see under* Triratna Buddhist Order

Western culture *see under* culture

Western literature *see under* literature

Western society *āsura*-like in its competitiveness 4.449–50; becoming more supportive to Buddhism 11.605; perhaps we have forgotten basic human kindness 4.68; individualism 13.458–64; 'The Integration of Buddhism into Western Society' 11.459–70; the integration of Buddhism involves changing society 3.621–2, 11.462–3; its rationalist and secular outlook gives us a thirst for myth and symbol 11.679, 13.116; Sangharakshita's Indian students viewed Western ways as the future 21.67; similar to ancient Indian society with its trends and fashions 10.612; Western dress 21.69–70; wrong views 10.612; *see also* society

Weston, Tim 17.152

Westward, Leonard 26.418

Weyden, Rogier van der 24.450–1

Whalen, Philip v24

whales affected by plastic pollution 25.53; the killing of whales 25.51, 25.53, 25.447; peacefully grazing in *Moby Dick* 25.53

'What do I really want to do?' *see under* action/deciding what to do

wheel and spiral *see under* conditionality

wheel of life

introduction
brief description 1.483, 2.74–7, 2.252–4, 3.243, 12.356, 13.37, 17.731 (n181); full account 2.68–79, 11.26–30, 11.165–7, 12.154–7, 13.124–41; it gives a graphic illustration of karma and *karma-vipāka* 17.476–8; illustration 13.124, 17.477; it shows past, present, and future lives, *see under* twelve cyclical *nidānas*; only partly Tantric and only partly symbolic 13.125; origins 2.73–4, 3.653 (n183), 13.679–81 (n43)

THE FIRST AND SECOND CIRCLES

the hub of the wheel
the cock, the pig, and the snake 11.165, 12.154, 13.125; symbolizing the three root poisons 2.74, 2.252, 3.202–3, 3.347–8, 4.73, 11.401; they bite each other's tails because of the poisons' interconnectedness 2.252, 11.27; we need to see in the hub our own animal nature 13.128–9; the objectivization of the poisons in the mind 2.77

black and white circle showing beings rising and falling
ascent into heaven, descent into hell 2.74, 11.165, 13.125–6; recognizing oneself in that state 3.348; the ethical life and the unethical life 12.155; a choice – evolution or regression – is before us every minute 11.27, 13.129, 15.500

THE THIRD CIRCLE: THE SIX REALMS

introduction
description 2.74, 11.165–6, 12.155, 13.126–7; the colours associated with rebirth in the six realms 13.283; in non-human realms unhealthy volitions are more likely to arise than healthy ones 2.95–6; reflection of our own mental states 3.348; the six realms considered as *bardos* 18.83;

the six realms considered as states of mind 11.28, 13.129–30, 17.497; creating the six realms 16.478; as a hierarchy 14.309–10; 'The Realms of Existence' (poem) 25.354–6; release from falling into the three lower realms 18.220; 'The six realms are jeopardized by desires' 18.171–2; they are not permanent 17.497–8; the potential for development: good seeds, bad seeds, and Buddha seeds 13.135–40; the appearance of Avalokiteśvara reminds us of potential 13.228

(1) animal realm
Avalokiteśvara brings a book 2.74, 3.382–3, 13.134, 14.291, 26.300–1; can be helped through contact with human beings 2.96; the animals are depicted as having a peaceful existence 13.126–7; a state of purely sensual indulgence 13.130

(2) asuras (titans)
Avalokiteśvara (or the Buddha) brings the sword of knowledge 2.74, 3.382, 13.132; fighting the gods for the possession of the wish-fulfilling tree 13.126, 26.641; have the least potential for Enlightenment of beings in the six realms 13.136–7; an aggressive, competitive state of mind 13.130

(3) god realm
Avalokiteśvara plays the melody of impermanence 2.74, 3.382, 13.131–2, 26.397; conflict with *asuras* 11.323, 16.427, 16.439; the difficulty of finding the spiritual path from there 13.137–8, 18.557; an experience of pleasure without pain 2.95, 19.497–8; for a Buddhist a respite, not a way of life 13.138, 24.302; the gods are born there through positive karma 2.73, 16.354; the gods' potential for Enlightenment is small 13.137–9; what prompts those born with high status to seek liberation? 17.160–1; a state of relaxation and repose 13.130; they don't want to realize that what they are enjoying is impermanent 19.496; where every wish is instantly gratified 13.126

(4) hell realm
Avalokiteśvara gives the beings there ambrosia (*amṛta*) 2.74, 3.383, 13.134; the difficulty of finding the spiritual path from there 18.557; an experience of pain without pleasure 2.95; the only hope for beings in hell: Enlightenment 2.96, 13.134; a state of acute mental suffering 13.130; Yamarājā, the King of Death, holds the mirror of karma 13.126

(5) human realm
Avalokiteśvara appears bearing a staff and begging-bowl 2.74, 3.383, 13.135; the clearness of mind and the goad of discontent to see Enlightenment 4.448; an experience of both pleasure and pain 2.95, 18.557; human activities 13.127; in relation to karma and *karma-vipāka* 2.95–6; a truer picture would have the human realm at the centre 2.94–6; an aware, human state of mind, which 'human beings' rarely experience 13.130–1

(6) hungry ghosts (pretas, revenants)
Avalokiteśvara (gives them food and drink they can consume 2.74, 3.383, 13.133–4, 19.59; so miserable that they cannot think about the Dharma 19.497–8; suffering all the time from ravenous hunger 13.126

THE MONSTER AND THE BUDDHA

the monster or demon of Impermanence and Death
description 2.76, 11.167; coming face to face with the fact of impermanence 11.29, 13.140; the Buddha could face him 12.359–60; he holds in his grasp the whole of conditioned existence 12.356; his crown of skulls 13.128; the Māra of conditioned existence 26.645–6; a reminder that the realms of the wheel are not permanent 17.497–8; why he represents Impermanence 2.85

the Buddha
pointing the way beyond the wheel 2.76, 11.30, 11.167, 26.646; direct experience of what we truly are 13.140–1; the path to Enlightenment 13.128; beyond birth and death 12.361; a description of the path the Buddha is pointing out 11.167; the hare in the moon: the Bodhisattva 13.141

REFLECTIONS ON THE WHEEL

the mirror
like looking into a mirror 3.347–8, 13.128–41; 'a portrait of myself' (Ben Shahn) 2.77; seeing Enlightenment in the mirror 13.140–1; a graphic illustration of human life 2.254–5; can be taken to mirror the everyday process of actions and consequences 3.200–1; it represents the reactive mind 11.26–30; shows the whole process of cyclical action and reaction 3.185, 3.279

the prison
the chain of events which binds us to the wheel of saṃsāric existence 7.223; any status within the wheel is still imprisonment 17.245; the Buddha-to-be realized he was binding himself to the wheel of life 3.208; debate doesn't do anything to get you off the wheel of life

19.177; an impure Buddha-field 1.339, 2.78; no longer bound, you can still choose to be reborn: the bodhisattva ideal 13.37–8; oscillation between pleasure and pain 3.260; performing 'good' actions with ego binds you to the wheel of life 7.409–10; rebirth in the wheel of life 2.73, 2.95, 13.36–8, 16.419; wandering through the realms of conditioned existence 8.558–9

ways beyond the wheel
the path that connects the wheel to the mandala of the Five Buddhas 1.484; responding creatively to experience 17.504; setting up fresh karma 17.478; stopping the wheel 2.256, 3.243; we will need more than ethics 3.324; the whole purpose of spiritual life is to get away 10.523

see also
Blofeld/*The Wheel of Life*; the twelve links around the edge of the wheel, *see* twelve cyclical *nidānas*

Wheel of the Dharma *see dharmacakra*

Wheeler, Owen 26.418

wheel-rolling or wheel-turning king *see under* king

wheel-turning gesture *see under mudrās*

Whichcote, Benjamin 24.389

whims 4.484–5

Whinnery, Steve v24

Whistler, James 2.757 (n791), 12.581

white associated with the Tantric rite of pacification 13.280, 19.24; the colour of centrality 13.282; Dhṛtarāṣṭra (great king) 16.346; represents the absolute reality that transcends time 13.68; represents the calming, pacifying aspect of the Enlightened mind 13.282–3; represents purity 13.67, 13.282; white depictions of Buddhas or bodhisattvas depict their absolute aspect 12.213; a white dot against a black background 26.84

White Lotus Sūtra (*Saddharma Puṇḍarīka Sūtra*)

ABOUT THE *SŪTRA*

introduction
introduction to the *sūtra* 3.87, 3.178, 3.377–81, 16.38–50, 16.213–16; etymology of title *Saddharma Puṇḍarīka Sūtra* 12.501–2, 16.32–3; how to approach studying the *sūtra* 8.482–3; its subject matter is the *sūtra* itself 14.132; symbolic significance of the name 16.51–2; the words *Saddharma Puṇḍarīka* connote much more than a title 14.132

its place in Buddhist history
one of the oldest Mahāyāna *sūtras* 8.477, 14.103, 16.239; dated to the 1st century CE 8.477, 14.106, 16.34; written down at the same time as the Pāli canon 14.101–2; probably no direct connection with the teaching of the historical Buddha 4.19; represents a transition from Early Buddhism to the Mahāyāna 14.104–5; four conditions for the *sūtra*'s becoming fully appreciated in the West 8.482–3

its interaction with Buddhist cultures
association with the Tiantai school 8.478, 13.16; devotion to the *sūtra* in Japan 2.225, 3.443; discovery of copies in Nepal, central Asia, Kashmir 14.108, 16.35; its images and symbols not yet part of our mentality as Western Buddhists 4.36; its position in the Far East is like that of the Bible in the West 14.109; influence on Buddhism in China and other countries 16.197; Nichiren's teaching of reverence for the *sūtra* 16.59; one of nine *sūtras* venerated in Nepal 14.100; presented with other *sūtras* as the *Threefold Lotus Sūtra* 8.479, 16.52; quoted by Nāgārjuna 1.302, 14.106; recited to bring rain 2.216

the form the sūtra takes
a lengthy *sūtra* 12.501; a remarkable synthesis of all the imaginative elements 14.110; poetry mixed with Prakritisms, prose in classical Sanskrit 12.509, 14.107–8, 16.35; it presents in dramatic and parabolic form the main truths of the Mahāyāna 7.502; two recensions of the text 14.108; interpolations 14.130

translations
3.643 (n103), 16.591 (n39); appraisal of the available translations 8.478–9; one of the first Buddhist scriptures to be translated into a European language 8.478; by Eugene Burnouf 3.654 (n185), 8.478; by Bunnō Katō and William Soothill (*The Threefold Lotus Sūtra*) 8.479, 16.36; Hendrik Kern's translation into English 8.375, 8.478–9, 13.337, 16.36; Kumārajīva's Chinese version 8.479, 14.108–9, 16.35; by W. E. Soothill 8.479, 14.110, 16.36; Conze's translation (of chapter 5) 8.479, 8.482, 8.534–5; chapter 12 of Kumārajīva's Chinese version 14.121–2; Chinese translations 14.108–9, 16.35; Tu Lun, *The Essentials of the Dharma Blossom Sūtra* (vol. 1) 8.477–83; need for a new translation 8.482

commentaries
need for access to the traditional commentaries 8.482; Sangharakshita's commentary 16.3–224; the Tiantai school's fivefold discussion of the principles of the *sūtra* 8.480–2

THE NATURE OF THE *SŪTRA*

what is it like?
an affirmation of the transcendental quintessence of the Dharma 1.218; an atmosphere of miracle and marvel 16.19; the Buddha Jewel predominates 14.132; it blossoms forth like a lotus in the midst of the world 12.502; it speaks the language of images, myths, and symbols 12.503, 16.18; like science fiction 3.381, 12.503, 16.37; a sort of transcendental sound and light show 16.19; no need for specialist knowledge to understand it 16.208–9; not quite what one imagines a Buddhist scripture to be like 3.381; an object of devotion 14.132; a protest against the contradictions of a merely intellectual approach 1.218; 'a spiritual drama of the highest order' (Soothill) 3.377–8, 14.110–11; to be interpreted allegorically? 16.104–5; when you read the *sūtra*, how do you feel? 16.66; the whole *sūtra* is a symbol of life and growth 16.120

Sangharakshita and the sūtra
an awareness of its importance and meaning 22.302; full commentary 16.3–223; a series of lectures in 1970 12.500, 12.503; reads in his young days 7.548 (n23); reads two chapters before an operation 24.343; a sermon in Cambridge 16.211–23; talks in Mumbai 9.260–9, 22.271

TEACHINGS

introduction
the *sūtra* doesn't contain much doctrine 14.109–10, 16.209; two main themes: *ekayāna* (one way) and the Buddha's eternal life 8.477–8; how do the two main themes go together? 16.58; adapted to suit the varying capacities of different people 16.42; the Buddha's *parinirvāṇa* as skilful means 4.85, 7.456, 16.199; cosmic evolution 13.516; the ideal Buddhist is depicted as ardently devoted to the *sūtra* 14.132; if anyone offers a single flower, they are on the path to Buddhahood 14.114, 16.41; the interdependency of provisional and actual teachings 8.481; its evocation of the Three Jewels 14.132; the Pure Land 16.45, 16.168–9; the *sūtra* attempts to convey the meaning of infinity through images 14.112, 16.38; the *sūtra*'s use of the term *arhant* 18.172

the Buddha's eternal life
his transcendental compassionate activity unlimited by space and time 2.128; the *dharmakāya* speaking 4.209–10, 16.60–1; in truth he is neither born nor passes away 8.477–8; it is the Buddha principle speaking 16.198–9; perhaps today in the West we need the opposite teaching 12.506–8; the primordial Buddha 16.152; in the *sūtra* the Buddha's declaration produces a tremendous effect 16.49

ekayāna, one goal for all
the *sūtra*'s main teaching 14.555; made clear by the parable of the burning house 1.215–18; the distinction of paths due to differences of temperament and ability 2.168, 16.214–15; different ways of looking at the same path 4.41, 16.40–1, 16.76–8; the *yānas* an expedient device 8.477, 14.113–14; two more parables to explain further 14.116–18; all Buddhists follow the same path 12.503–5, 16.62–3; Buddhayāna 7.362, 9.359–60, 14.116; the idea of different goals a false antithesis 14.571; adopting the *sūtra*'s position 11.255

THE STRUCTURE OF THE *SŪTRA*

the beginning: the Buddha's call
he proclaims the Dharma on the Vulture's Peak 3.91, 14.112–13, 16.38; a ray of light issues from between his eyebrows 14.111–13, 16.38–9, 19.32, 19.592 (n8); he explains the difficulty of understanding the Truth 16.39–40

the walking out of the disciples
five thousand leave in dismay 2.155, 14.110, 14.113, 16.40, 16.68, 16.214; dramatization of the rejection of the truth 16.64; lack of receptivity 4.127–8; a situation with parallels in the modern Buddhist world 2.155; 'Now the assembly is quite pure' 16.40

predictions to Enlightenment
Ānanda 14.119; Devadatta 3.63, 12.513, 14.122; Mahāprajāpatī Gautami 14.122–3, 16.46–7; none for lay people 16.65; Pūrṇa Maitrāyaṇīputra 14.118, 16.43, 16.169; Rāhula 14.119; Śāriputra 1.271, 3.379, 14.114, 16.41, 16.215; the four elders 14.117; Yaśodharā 14.122–3, 16.46–7

protecting and preaching the sūtra
the four qualities that bodhisattvas preserving the *sūtra* must have 14.123, 16.47; merits of listening to the *sūtra*

and demerits of disparaging it 14.119, 16.49–50; can the *sūtra* be a full path to Enlightenment? 16.58–9; the qualities needed to preach the *sūtra* 14.119–20; receptivity to the *sūtra* 16.61; the merits of reading, reciting, copying, expounding the *sūtra* 14.127, 16.44; penetrating and discoursing on the meanings of the *sūtra* 14.128; the preacher will develop the six *abhijñās* 14.128; promises to preach the *sūtra* 14.129, 16.50; *dhāraṇis* to protect the *sūtra* 14.130

the Pure Land
many Buddhas are summoned to the Sahā-world 14.120, 16.45; the world is made into a Pure Land to accommodate the Buddhas 14.120–1, 16.45; our own world as a future Pure Land 16.168–9; no distinction between men and women 16.169; contact between human world and the world of the gods 16.169; no suffering 16.169

the stupa of the Buddha Abundant Treasures (Prabhūtaratna)
the stupa appears 3.379–81, 14.120–1, 16.44–6, 16.143–4, 16.152, 16.159; the two halves of the sūtra are divided by the appearance of the stupa 16.140; Śākyamuni and Abundant Treasures sitting together 14.111, 16.46, 16.65, 16.151–2; the Buddha asks who will preach the *White Lotus Sūtra* 14.121, 16.46; stupa worship 16.154–6, 16.205; the stupa disappears 14.130, 16.50

the appearance of the irreversible bodhisattvas
irreversible bodhisattvas appear from the space below the earth 14.124, 16.198; how can Śākyamuni have trained all those bodhisattvas? 4.209–10, 14.124–5, 16.198; they'll protect *sūtra* 'in the evil age to come' 12.747 (n400), 14.123, 16.47–8, 19.597 (n37)

the Buddha Śākyamuni proclaims his eternal Enlightenment
in this *sūtra* he becomes the ideal, archetypal Buddha 13.302; he is eternally Enlightened 4.209–10, 14.125–6, 16.60–1, 16.199; it is no longer the historical Buddha speaking 10.118, 16.48–9; he reveals himself as a cosmic principle, reality itself 14.104, 16.48–9; on the level of eternity the Buddha is always preaching the *sūtra* 4.206, 16.203; the merit of developing faith in the Tathāgata's eternal life 14.127; he encircles the universe with his tongue 2.128, 14.129, 16.104; a vision of infinite Buddhas 14.129; 'The Tathāgata's Infinite Life' (chapter 15) 14.130; this is not to be misunderstood as suggesting a theistic element 14.130–1; to be seen in relation to the *trikāya* doctrine 14.131

later chapters (21–26)
perhaps annexed to the *sūtra* later 14.130, 14.176; devoted to various bodhisattvas 14.176–7; translation of the Avalokiteśvara chapter (24th) 8.375

the end of the sūtra
the inhabitants of distant worlds see the Sahā-world revealed, like the ocean depths 16.50; Śākyamuni's final exhortation to preserve and promulgate the *sūtra* 14.130; the gods' offerings make a vast jewelled canopy 14.129–30, 16.50; all the worlds interpenetrate, and become one harmonious Buddha-field 16.50

PARABLES AND STORIES

introduction
the great glory of the *sūtra* 8.478; 'intelligent people through a parable reach understanding' 12.110–11, 16.215; their minor details are not to be applied too literally or pressed too far 14.131; often depicted in painting and sculpture 8.478; unsurpassed in the entire range of Buddhist literature 14.112

the burning house
the story 9.357–8, 14.114–15, 16.68–9, 16.215; the text quoted 1.215–17; symbolism 9.358–60, 14.115, 16.69–80; compared to Siddhārtha's palace life 3.35; compared to Dr Ambedkar's response to Hindu society 9.360–2; does it teach escapism? 16.78–9; the father in the story is not to be taken to be the creator of mankind 14.131; houses that resembled the ruined mansion 22.192, 22.247; Milarepa uses a similar image 18.588; it doesn't say that the end justifies the means 16.83–4; the parable should not be

taken literally, but interpreted carefully 17.232–3; richly suggestive 1.219; suggests the double significance of the Mahāyāna 1.219–20; resolution of three *yānas* into one, *ekayāna* 1.217–18, 2.168; skilful means 14.115, 16.74, 17.232–3; trying to get out of the burning house 19.360; is it teaching universalism? 16.76–8; its effect on the four elders in the *sūtra* 14.115, 16.41–2

the return journey
told by Mahākāśyapa 14.115, 16.41–2, 16.86; the story 14.115–16, 16.87–90; symbolism 14.115, 16.91–8; and the story of the prodigal son 16.90; and the 'Hymn of the Pearl' 4.646, 16.91, 16.170, 16.220; not a journey back into the past 16.100–1; difference from the jewel in the garment 16.171

the raincloud (the herbs and plants)
the story 10.211–12, 11.367, 14.116, 16.116–38; text quoted 12.509–10, 16.117–20; symbolism 16.124–30; the symbol of the plant added to the symbol of the journey 16.123–4; and the fructifying power of the Tathāgata 14.539; illustration of the Higher Evolution 2.476; it is important that we should feel ourselves living, growing 11.87, 16.130; we all grow in our own way 3.178–9, 9.453, 10.211–12, 11.87, 11.367, 14.116, 16.464

the magic city
the story 14.117–18, 16.42–3; applied to meditation 16.43; the journey to Ratnadvīpa (Place of Jewels) 14.118, 16.42–3; symbolism 14.118, 16.43

the jewel in the garment
the story 16.43, 16.169–73, 16.216–223; quoted text 14.118–19, 16.169–70, 16.213; symbolism 14.119, 16.170–81; difference from the myth of the return journey 16.171; the exchange of the jewel: transforming theory into practice 16.221–2; 'Jewel of Enlightenment stitched in the hem of poverty' 25.207; what the jewel represents 16.173–4, 16.220–1; the removal of the jewel 16.222–3; don't be misled by an over-literal reading of the parable 16.218, 16.221; you realize that you were unknowingly a Buddha from the very beginning 18.44–5

the good physician
the story 14.126–7, 16.199–200; symbolism 4.205–6, 7.456, 16.200–3; the Buddha had to die so that his disciples could become independent 10.324–5

other stories
the parable of the sun 14.116, 16.124–5, 16.464; the wheel-rolling king and the crest jewel 14.123–4, 16.47–8; two parables that explain the three *yānas* 14.116–17

CHARACTERS IN THE *SŪTRA*

Avalokiteśvara
Akṣayamati's hymn of praise to him 1.336, 2.176, 14.177, 16.178–9; his chapter originally an independent *sūtra* 14.130, 16.176–7; his appearance as Samantamukha 2.176; he delivers those who call on his name from dangers 2.176; one of the main canonical sources of his cult 2.176; one of the symbols of the Mahāyāna in the *sūtra* 16.168

Bhaiṣajyarāja (Buddha)
he offers spells for the protection of the *sūtra* 14.130; his appearance in the *sūtra* in bodhisattva form 16.194–5; the bodhisattva (Sarvasattvapriyadarśana) who burned himself as an offering 8.451, 14.121–2, 14.176, 16.195, 22.516; burning wax on oneself 16.197, 16.205–6, 20.407; could we give our lives for our spiritual principles? 16.198, 22.516–17; he declares his readiness to preserve the *sūtra* 14.122

Sadāparibhūta (Never Direct or Never Despise), bodhisattva
annoyingly told people they would be Buddhas 4.417–18, 4.690 (n213), 14.128–9, 14.484, 16.49–50; eventually became Śākyamuni 4.418, 14.129; not a very good psychologist 4.248–9, 4.418

Śāriputra
doubts a woman's spiritual capacity, is corrected by a *nāga* princess 14.110, 14.122; not a historical but a symbolical figure 1.271; speaks for those perplexed by the Buddha's teaching of the *ekayāna* 16.41, 16.215; predicted to become a Buddha 1.271, 3.379, 14.114, 16.41, 16.215; representative of the Hīnayāna 16.81–2; reproaches himself for having imagined he had attained Nirvāṇa 1.271

other characters
Gadgadasvara 14.130, 14.176; Mahābhijñājñānābhibhū (Tathāgata) 14.117; Mahākāśyapa 14.115, 16.41–2, 16.86; Mahākātyayāna 14.115, 16.42; Mahāmaudgalyayāna 14.115, 16.42; Mahāpratibhāna 14.120, 14.122; Maitreya 14.113, 14.124, 16.39; Mañjuśrī 2.173, 14.113, 14.122–3, 16.39, 16.47; a gifted *nāga* princess who transforms herself into a male bodhisattva 14.110, 14.122; Prajñākūṭa 14.122; Radiance of the Sun and Moon (Buddha) 16.195;

Samantabhadra (bodhisattva) 2.179, 14.128, 14.177; Subhūti 14.115, 16.42; Viśiṣṭacāritra (bodhisattva) 2.182, 2.686 (n251), 14.129

White Lotus school *see* Pure Land schools

White Path *see* Pure Land schools

White Tārā *see under* Tārā

White, Edmund 24.374

Whitehead, A. N. brief introduction 15.774 (n268); 'Religion is what the individual does with his own solitariness' 12.40–1, 12.82, 15.705–6; Western philosophy a series of footnotes to Plato 3.427

Whitehouse, Mary 10.499, 10.711 (n405), 18.634

Whitelaw, Bernie v23

Whitman, Walt brief introduction 22.276, 22.600 (n222), 24.714 (n500); compared with Allen Ginsberg 26.376; 'I Saw in Louisiana a Live-Oak Growing' 24.360; 'Passage to India' 23.300; *Sea Drift* 26.394; 'Song of the Open Road' 24.398; 'the terrible doubt of appearances' 17.378; 'When I give, I give myself' 2.364, 3.369, 4.93, 11.169, 16.8

Whittaker, Thomas 23.317

Whitwell, Richard 21.582

whole being compassion involves one's whole being 21.314; the *dhyānas* have the effect of resting one's whole being 5.418, 19.422–3; the *dhyānas* refine the whole being so that insight is able to develop 4.494, 5.418; in the second *dhyāna* the trend of your whole being is established 5.252; generosity as an attitude of one's whole being 4.93; insight: a suffusion of our whole being with reality 13.73; joining our hands at head, throat, and heart: a salutation with our whole being 1.514–15; listening to the Dharma with one's whole being 10.197, 15.436; meditation: spiritual growth of the whole being 2.260–1; the urge of one's whole being in the direction of Enlightenment 3.366; when you go for Refuge you do so with your whole being 15.606–7, 18.383; the whole of us is growing all the time 11.87–8

wholeheartedness being wholeheartedly committed to Dharma practice without the formal rite of ordination 18.176–7; celebrating festivals in a wholehearted way 18.379; committing yourself wholeheartedly to your practice, insight may arise at any time 18.154; find something to believe in, then you can do it with all your energy and enthusiasm 10.603–4; a lack of wholeheartedness throughout spiritual life 15.208; make an effort to give yourself wholly to what you are doing 15.115–16; in modern life, you can't praise anything wholeheartedly 4.595; we are not wholehearted either in skilful or in unskilful ways 19.19; whatever you are doing, do it wholeheartedly 11.50, 18.154; the wholeheartedness of Tibetan Buddhists 18.307; young people are often more wholehearted than older people 18.248

wholeness all five spiritual faculties must be regarded as one whole, which is *you* 17.59–60; Buddhism's emphasis on wholeness 15.625; don't mistake doing something with part of yourself for doing it with the whole of yourself 19.276; Enlightenment is acting with the whole of oneself 1.536; link with holiness 1.30, 7.305; 'a man in his wholeness, wholly attending' 14.291, 15.198; modern literature is aware of its limitations and in search of wholeness 10.154; religion is the achievement of a state of complete psychological wholeness 12.43; through ritual we become more whole 11.212; 'The Truth is the whole' (Hegel) 2.50, 7.44, 7.385, 8.225; the whole man or woman responding to reality 14.589; *see also* integration

Wickramasinghe, Martin 8.378–9

Wickremeratna, H. A. C. 8.138

widdershins 19.329, 19.612 (n134)

Wilber, Ken 24.208

Wilcocks, Dick 23.123–4

Wilde, Oscar

introduction
brief introduction 23.534 (n441); the Aesthetic Movement 26.149, 26.488, 26.710 (n82); and Andre Gide 22.588–9 (n150); he was destroyed by his alienation from society 13.617, 19.87, 19.598 (n41); Christmas Humphreys' father was a prosecutor at his trial 23.393; imprisonment for breaking the law prohibiting homosexuality 13.611, 26.149, 26.177; one of Sangharakshita's literary heroes 26.487–9; out of sympathy with the age in which he lived 26.488; resemblance to the 'Glorious Devil' in Tennyson's poem 26.488; a very moral writer 15.374; Ellmann's biography 26.375

essays
The Decay of Lying 26.488; *The Importance of Masks* 26.488; *The Soul*

of Man, see under Socialism 26.488; their influence on Sangharakshita 26.488–9

poems
The Ballad of Reading Gaol 19.598 (n41), 26.398; his poems have the quality *kāvya* 26.332; 'The Harlot's House' 26.488; 'Requiescat' 26.488; 'The Sphinx' 26.488

other works and quotes
aphorisms 26.488; 'The House Beautiful' (lecture) 26.395; 'I wish I had said that.' 'You will, Oscar, you will.' 2.644; *An Ideal Husband* 26.488; *The Picture of Dorian Gray* 1.544, 15.374, 17.281, 26.488; *De Profundis* 3.210, 20.409, 26.489; two tragedies: not getting what one wants, and getting it 17.258

wilderness a forest of views, a wilderness of views, a tangle of views 10.605; formerly you could go off and live in the wilderness, but now all land is owned 18.454; Jesus's temptation in the wilderness 3.449; the sangha as a garden in a wilderness 25.145–7; being sent into the wilderness led to Sangharakshita founding the FWBO 2.610–12, 12.364–5; the Wilderness of Word 25.194

Wildmind 5.xxiv

wilfulness better to grow in a natural way rather than forcing yourself 4.566; the difference between wilfulness and will 11.649–50, 12.537; effect of wilful practice of the mindfulness of breathing 12.496; the fool is the wilful person, motivated by egoistic will 15.385; the importance of a non-wilful approach to reality 19.387; the solution to the problem is not simply to take things easy 16.520; willed, forceful effort doesn't get you very far 10.507

Wilkes, Kathleen V. 8.615

will

what is will?
the constitutive essence of man 7.138; logically prior to thought, emotion, and action 7.301–2; not that man wills, but rather that will 'mans' 2.93, 26.52; free will 1.119, 26.18; 'There is no such thing as the will' 15.615–16, 26.16; gradations of will 7.138

will in spiritual life
faith and the will 17.35–7; from the depths come our energies of instinct, emotion, and will 12.23; doubt must be overcome or the will is going to be paralysed 3.293, 10.250; the goal seen in terms of will is a state of freedom from restrictions 2.127; Going for Refuge: emotional, rational, volitional 2.487, 11.94, 12.536–41, 15.607, 15.615, 15.727–9; if the will is bent towards unity, thought and action will follow 7.140; its true function is removing the obstacles to receptivity 4.224; 'the keen chisel of the will' 25.221; the role of determination and inspiration 18.618; the role of the will in spiritual practice 11.650, 12.538, 26.62; spiritual progress is not a matter of egoistically willed achievement 2.112; a strong will to follow the transcendental path 15.94; a transformative way of life seeks to turn the will the opposite way 7.302; the will plays a crucial part in the Buddhist life 11.650, 12.537–8; your performance will always fall short of your will not to harm 4.355–6

will and meditation
could the *dhyānas* be brought about by will power? 5.268–9; *dhyāna* a state of pure will 4.481; meditation is essentially the willing of the Good 26.75; perhaps the word 'will' implies too much effort 5.270

letting go of will
the bodhisattva never pits their will against the will of others 14.578; doing the Buddha's will 4.35; embracing someone else's will so that it becomes your own 4.34–5; friendship and the transformation of the will from selfish to selfless 7.293–6; 'He that complies against his will is of his own opinion still' 15.197, 18.360; it's not easy to give up your own will 4.302; let me be directed not by my egoistic will, but by the will to Enlightenment 4.49; only when the egoistic will is 'silent' will the True Sound be heard 7.323; pitting your will against that of a child 5.638; the surrender of the egoistic will 18.189–90; two kinds of giving up one's will 15.661–3; when you give up your own will, you really do have it 14.540

force of will
letting spiritual life grow naturally rather than forcing development 18.31; Siddhārtha's attempt to gain Enlightenment by it 3.40–1, 5.392; unflaggingly strenuous will-force: a weapon to scatter the hosts of Māra 7.172; we have to use willed effort sometimes 18.618; operating on will power tends to have a limit 18.618; you can't rely on it indefinitely 15.118; Beethoven at his worst is will pretending to be power 26.22; the will of God 7.97, 15.620–1

see also
cetanā; self-will; will to Enlightenment, *see bodhicitta*

will (last testament) 15.146

will to live the evolutionary process 7.47; in an Enlightened person, the will to live is replaced by compassion 10.585; taking care not to negate a child's will to live 19.20–1

William Rufus 25.329, 26.611

Williams, Charles 23.197

Williams, Isaac 16.592 (n53)

Williams, Paul 2.669 (n63), 13.669–70, 24.362

Williams, Raymond 13.479

Williams, Rowan 12.756 (n469)

Williams, Tennessee 24.374, 24.390–1

Willis, Janice Dean 24.389

Willmott, Antoinette v23

Willson, Martin 8.xxxvi, 8.565–7

Wilson, Colin brief introduction 17.717 (n73)23.491 (n138); *The Outsider* 17.66, 23.111, 26.572; *Beyond the Outsider* 23.332

Wilson, Harold 23.87

Wilson, Peter Lamborn 26.270

Winchester, England 4.638, 24.194, 24.203

wind the *ālaya* compared to the ocean, and *vāsanā* to the wind blowing across it 14.210; 'And the wind shall say: "Here were decent godless people"' 12.45; 'As the wind blows down a weak tree' (*Dhammapada*) 14.587; conditioned things are as delicately contingent as a candle in the wind 14.506; consciousness can be inferred from its functions, like the wind from the swaying of trees 14.187; drifting on the winds and tides of the world 15.233; energy, like the wind, bloweth where it listeth 11.515; magic power of the Tathāgata, like thistledown on the wind 1.255; non-attachment is like thistledown blown on the wind 17.562; *Ode to the West Wind* 20.54, 21.434, 22.19; sailing against the wind 17.366; stilling the turbulence of the wild winds of desire 7.125; wandering the *bardo*, we are buffeted by the winds of evil karma 18.83–4; 'The Wind' (poem) 25.xli, 25.450; wind or air burial 12.692; *see also* eight worldly winds

windhorse (Tibetan *lungta*)

depictions in art and poetry
London Buddhist Centre mural 9.275, 10.199–201, 10.200 (photograph); 'Song of the Windhorse' 25.338–9

symbolism
free but controlled energy 4.354; carries the Three Jewels 10.199–201, 19.438–9; the direction of all one's energies 13.309; represents the six *pāramitās* 9.275–6, 19.439; symbol of the threefold way 19.438–9

Windhorse Publications community in Sheffield 24.384–5; distribution in America 24.474

Windhorse Trading its success 11.465; started by Kulananda 24.6, 24.642 (n178); shop in Essen 24.601

windows the endless view, like removing the window of a Japanese house 19.184–5; the Enlightened person is like a clear window through which the light of reality shines 4.171; the higher self like a windowed chamber with a view onto the lower self 16.94–5; reality like a stained-glass window 5.606–7; rose windows like mandalas 12.218; the sense organs like an empty house with six windows 1.109, 2.75

wings the Dharma a bird, the two wings wisdom and compassion 3.355, 3.365, 9.231, 16.14–15, 19.566; a monk with his bowl and robes is like a bird with two wings 1.152, 16.405; wings folded like Baudelaire's albatross 22.103; 'Secret Wings' (poem) 25.185; *see also* thirty-seven *bodhipakṣya-dharmas*

winter 'here shall I dwell during winter …' – thus reflects the fool (*Dhammapada*) 7.171; a Norfolk winter landscape 4.225; the purity of winter 25.284; a rose in winter: essence without existence 13.582; 'The winter evening settles down' 20.11, 20.500; 'Winter in the Hills' 25.255; winter solstice 25.56; winter vignettes 25.306–7; winter's icy fingers 25.lvi, 25.344

Winternitz, M. 7.485, 14.37, 14.51–2, 14.65, 14.106, 14.177–8, 14.227

wisdom

introduction
etymologies and different terms: *vijñāna, jñāna, prajñā* 3.355–6; what wisdom is concerned with (Conze) 17.133; the beginning of wisdom is to know that we do not know 13.346, 14.403; only wisdom cuts through everything: in a sense *the* basic point of Buddhism 4.371; wisdom is realizing what benefits self and others 17.165

the nature of wisdom
direct insight into the truth 11.64; a dynamic understanding of experience that sees things as process 17.245; iconoclastic 26.479; it begins at home, in the body 17.389; it cannot arise without a cause 19.434; it disperses the darkness of delusion 17.131–2; it distinguishes between concepts and lived experience 17.307; it holds no views 2.393, 17.245; it is essentially useless 15.314–15; it lends itself to the excitement of discovery 17.81; it penetrates into *dharmas* as they are in themselves 1.87, 17.131; sublime and awe-inspiring 14.xvi; the knowledge that oneself and all other entities are empty of 'self' 7.375; no longer thinking in terms of dichotomies 5.523–4; the silence of wisdom 9.226; there is no such thing as wisdom, only wise individuals 17.306–7; there is nothing intellectual about it 14.444

in terms of what it is not
not comprehension of superior truths, but making truths the object of a concentrated mind 1.170; not the prerogative of philosophy alone 7.79–80; not a set of ideas, but an openness to aesthetic appreciation and love 14.xvi; wisdom and goodness are incompatible with individualism 13.463

relationship to other Dharma categories
always put in the context of understanding the scriptures 18.118; an understanding of the Four Noble Truths 9.213; connotations of wisdom in the *Dhammasaṅgaṇi* 17.130–1; it is designed to cut off the *kleśas* 17.131; wisdom and the *arhant* ideal 1.168–82; as one of the six perfections 3.373–5; the reciprocal relationship between ethics and wisdom 17.154; relationship with meditation 1.168–70, 17.136; and the arising of the *bodhicitta* 1.419–20

some distinctions
contrast between Gnostic and Buddhist views of wisdom 16.238–9; the difference between consciousness and wisdom 14.260; difference from knowledge 1.225, 1.170; distinguishing wisdom from mere cleverness 17.131; 'heart wisdom' and 'head wisdom' 19.542–3; learning transformed into wisdom 1.169–70; you can have wisdom without being an intellectual 17.135

images and symbols
the axe of Wisdom and the tree of mundane existence 7.300; the cloudless sky 18.603; a goad, because it spurs you on 17.131; like space, it does not break or crack 14.600; symbolized by light 9.324; like a blade 18.118; like a lamp 17.726 (n139); a butterfly, not a gloomy bird of prey 2.405, 26.265; represented by the feminine in Buddhist iconography 18.373

wisdom and other mental states
an affinity with hatred 4.392–3, 13.132–3, 18.577, 26.478–9; *dhyāna* is not enough, there must be wisdom too 18.252–3; 'Love cannot bear the burden of wisdom' 25.442; starting off on the path of wisdom, you have to bring in devotion 16.59; you can't have 'holiness' without wisdom 17.134–5

developing wisdom
awakening wisdom by appealing to the heart 26.198; in Buddhism not an intellectual pursuit but a spiritual one 15.197; developing a more 'embodied' wisdom by teaching the Dharma 17.307; ethics as the basis on which wisdom may be developed 17.158; in order to realize wisdom you have to go outside time 19.435–6; the key of right motive opens the portals of the Palace of Wisdom 1.22; 'No wisdom can we get hold of' – so what are we trying to do? 14.547; the purpose of meditation is to attain wisdom 17.306; pursuit of wisdom vitiated by domestic responsibilities 1.340; *samādhi* is the indispensable basis, but wisdom far transcends it 18.594; stages: entering the stream, once-returning, non-returning, Arhantship 1.176–7; transcendent and immanent approaches to wisdom 11.655–6; the transformation of thought into wisdom 7.302–3

the wisdom of Enlightenment
daring to sit in judgement on the wisdom of Buddha and bodhisattvas 7.311, 13.413; the Tathāgata's wisdom cannot be measured by the yardstick of human intelligence 1.20; wisdom utterly divorced from action is called *nirvāṇa* 7.139; 'The

wisdom will be the Voidness. The Voidness will be the wisdom.' 18.242

its effects
all limitations are removed by the experience of wisdom 18.594; the culmination of wisdom is freedom from all views 26.52; emancipation through wisdom (*paññavimutti*) 1.291; 'Harm cannot befall the wise man' 10.536; the wisdom of the wise undoing the harm done by the merely good 4.193, 13.69; the life of wisdom is the spontaneous life 14.556; liberation by wisdom 17.187; 'Wisdom shines bright from within' 18.594; perfect work comes from the unification of pure wisdom and pure deeds 26.19

the expression of wisdom
assuming that wisdom is better expressed in concepts than images 14.430–1; intelligence is the ability to express what wisdom sees 17.603; it may not take conceptual forms 17.134–5; loving speech as an expression of wisdom 16.486; wisdom in poetry 25.239

kinds of wisdom
'crazy wisdom' 18.178; irrational wisdom 26.266; Minerva's wisdom 25.378; practical wisdom 15.288–90; 'self-arising Wisdom' 19.434–6

see also
wisdom and compassion, *see under* compassion; and faith, *see under* faith/aspects of faith; knowledges of the five Buddhas, *see* five *jñānas*; perfection of wisdom, *see* Perfection of Wisdom; *prajñā*; *vijñāna*; *jñāna*; three levels, *see* three levels of wisdom; transcendental, *see jñāna*

wise, the

the qualities of the wise
ethical sensibility 15.294; they don't have a strong 'I'-sense 15.385; they don't indulge in acrimonious disputes 1.60; they don't make plans (i.e. set up *saṃskāras*) 17.475; they have crossed the stream 7.315; they take what they need and give what they can 3.592

assessments of the wise
a fool can give more advice in a day than a wise man can follow in a year 26.80; 'A fool sees not the same tree that a wise man sees' (Blake) 9.80; no magical attainments, they've just got on with the spiritual life 10.648; there is no such thing as wisdom, only wise individuals 17.306–7; to know someone, you must be a wise man and not a fool 10.590, 19.100; while some are making a raft, the wise have crossed the river (*Udāna*) 10.643, 10.648; 'The wise man can detect the flavour of the Dharma ...' (*Dhammapada*) 10.568; 'The wise man forges ahead ...' (*Dhammapada*) 9.367

learning from the wise
how do you know that 'the wise' really are wise? 15.292; acting in accordance with the testimony of the wise 1.60; associating with the wise 15.384; being sensitive to the judgement passed upon you by the wise 15.417–18; lack of respect for wise opinion (*anapatrāpya*) 17.667–9; not pursuing things for which the wise might censure you 15.291–3; only someone who is to some extent wise can learn from a wise man 18.516; questioning the wise should be an extension of questioning yourself 17.261; to be receptive to the wise, we need a personal relationship with them 15.293

wishes the difference between desires and real wishes 19.28; everybody wishes that unhappiness could be removed 4.631; the golden drum fulfils wishes 16.283, 16.286; 'He who wishes to serve me, let him serve the sick' 4.11, 9.195, 11.443; 'If one wishes to reach the Pure Land, he must first purify his mind' 2.78; if you follow the spiritual path your deepest wishes will be fulfilled 19.73; 'Oh for a Persian garden ...' 25.373; the unskilfulness of taking someone's energy against their wishes 2.367, 18.79

wish-fulfilling cow 13.261

wish-fulfilling jar 13.262, 19.73

wish-fulfilling jewel or gem (*cintāmaṇi*) a sort of Aladdin's lamp 4.361; gives us what we really desire: Enlightenment 13.166; held by bodhisattvas Kṣitigarbha and Ākāśagarbha 2.181; it is in the spiritual life that the true wish-fulfilling jewel is to be found 19.73; the ocean of the Buddha's words 17.595; symbol of the *bodhicitta* 10.145, 10.686 (n176), 16.174–5; symbol of Ratnasambhava 12.214; the true *cintāmaṇi* is the Enlightened mind itself 12.214; visualized in the offering of the mandala 13.262

wish-fulfilling tree (*kalpa-vṛkṣa*) Śāntideva's wish 4.361; fought over by the gods and the *asuras* 13.126, 26.641; held by Kṣitigarbha 2.181; produced from the cosmic ocean of milk (Hinduism) 16.398, 26.641; visualized when offering the mandala 13.261

witch burning of witches 11.340–1; Sangharakshita meets a witch 23.196–7; 'The Witch' (Yeats) 15.117–18

withdrawal

withdrawal (in the sense of nirveda)
the difference between disgust and withdrawal: getting rid of the snake 2.115–16; if you've seen through something, you withdraw, like seeing a mirage in the desert 26.32; must be conjoined with compassion (Tsongkhapa) 2.116, 17.424, 17.426–7, 18.52

the arising of the bodhicitta
the conjunction of serene withdrawal and compassion 2.116; together with withdrawal from the mundane produces Enlightenment 18.102; tension between withdrawal and involvement 2.271–4, 17.424; after apparent withdrawal, the bodhisattva continues to work for the good 1.443

withdrawal from the world
alternation between withdrawal and engagement 4.528–9; arhantship gained on complete withdrawal from all worldly concerns 7.504; if we withdraw from it perhaps we shall understand its teaching 7.134; this side of Enlightenment, always make provision for withdrawal and quiet 4.532; withdrawal from involvement in conditioned things 3.275–6; withdrawing from the world 25.176

withdrawal from the senses
withdrawal of the mind from sense experience 5.641–3, 13.71; like the setting sun 12.215; the need to withdraw from sense stimuli to study negative mental states 17.99; withdrawal of the mind's scattered forces into a focus of attention 7.358–9

psychological withdrawal
fear of the withdrawal of love 16.307; some people withdraw into spiritual individualism 2.272; the Western tendency to withdraw into the world of private concerns 2.516

see also
nirveda

Woden 19.410

Wolf at the Door 26.99

Wolsey, Cardinal 26.483, 26.507, 26.514

women

WOMEN IN THE BUDDHIST TRADITION

the Buddha
tells Ānanda how to behave in relation to women 8.444; his attitude towards women 9.68, 9.142, 11.426; disciples, *see under* disciples

women's spiritual capacity
affirmed by the Buddha 5.622, 10.627–8, 11.422, 11.426, 16.334–5; Buddhism is the only religion in which women can exercise all spiritual functions 16.335; even little old ladies have to become lions in Buddhism 4.469; the evidence of the Therīs 5.622; only Buddhism states that women can reach the highest attainment 16.335; disadvantages due to gender 18.148

the ordination of women
Ānanda made it possible for women to be ordained 2.27, 3.179, 11.421–2; eight special conditions for ordination 2.27, 11.422–8, 11.638–9; to overcome 'the gospel of inequality' (Ambedkar) 9.101; the Buddha's reluctance may relate to the need for an appropriate environment 10.628; seeking ordination for social reasons 11.426–7; would it cause a deterioration of the sangha? 2.27, 11.642–5; *bhikṣuṇī* ordination, *see under* bhikkunī; in Eastern countries getting ordained is very difficult 12.389, 12.669; was the Buddha being unfair in setting special conditions? 11.425–7; U Chandramani's ordination of many women 11.427; the position of women in Buddhism 10.161, 10.182–4

Early Buddhism
the Dharma should not be spoken to a woman without a man present 4.347–8; female frailty in the *Jātakas* 14.65; it would be wrong for a monk to pull his mother out of a pit 1.207; women as lovers of secrecy (Pāli canon) 9.419; monks receiving offerings from women on a white cloth 13.474, 13.497–8; precepts observed by *mātugāma* (womenfolk) 2.347; a rule that subordinates the most senior nun to the most junior monk 2.602–3; strong-minded women in the Pāli canon 10.496; 'Women in Early Buddhism', *see* Horner; women of the harem gain insight (*Udāna*) 10.627–9; women going to the temple because they are attracted to the monks 19.471, 19.476

Mahāyāna Buddhism
evil committed 'for a reason involving women' 16.303; a world with no distinction between men and women (*White Lotus Sūtra*) 16.169; 'May all women become men' (*Sūtra of Golden Light*) 16.334–5; Śāriputra's doubt about a woman's capacity answered (*Lotus Sūtra*) 14.110, 14.122

Tibetan Buddhism
the appeal of *ḍākinīs* to Western Buddhist women 13.244–6; in Tantric legend ugly old women may be *ḍākinīs* in disguise

13.203–4; knowledge of a woman's unrealized 'masculine' side through Tantric practice 13.90; Milarepa's view of women's spiritual aptitude 19.471; a monk whose theme was the fickleness of women 22.450; only one female *tulku* 12.16, 13.53, 18.109; women in Tibetan Buddhism 13.54, 24.389

REFLECTIONS

men and women
'Angels are to men as men are to women …' 26.4–5, 26.27; between men and women there will always be war, or at least tension 26.29; the cliché that women are more receptive than men 17.76–7; concepts of equality and inequality inappropriate 26.56; contrast between men's and women's Dharma talks 13.327; the danger of women disrupting men's friendships 24.542–4; different approaches to friendship 11.638; the different obstacles in the spiritual life faced by men and women 17.219; different responses to sexual desire 11.577; don't think of yourself as a man or a woman in any absolute or exclusive sense 2.372; Feminism's tendency to see woman as victim and man as victimizer 11.639; helping men and women to relate to one another as individuals 26.29; imagining a world where men can live without a wife, women without a master 25.454; irrationality in women and men 14.535–6, 19.108; let us do away with divisions between men and women Buddhists 26.56; the male human form more beautiful than the female 23.289, 26.594; men's emotional dependence on women 26.28; men's responses to a nude female statue in Córdoba 24.433; polarization between men and women 15.530; the pseudo-liberal idea that men and women must do everything together 11.521–2; sugar and spice, or frogs and snails and puppy-dogs' tails? 25.426–7; there is no immovable barrier to communication between them 11.639; to be at her best, a woman needs some masculine qualities 16.164; the unwanted attention of men 17.284; women have more beautiful faces than men 26.594; women in the sangha doing all the things men do 10.222; women should focus on their own development without comparing themselves to men 26.56; young men going to the temple to look at the women 19.476

women in India
a brahmin-born Buddhist woman in modern Ahmedabad 23.345; a cart pulled by women and girls 22.99–100; a contrast between Western and Indian women 23.5–6; disadvantages 10.403–4; encouragement to take an active part in Dharma life 9.400–1; full and perfect Indian womanhood 7.56, 7.58; a harmonizing influence in the early days of the Buddhist movement in Poona 10.401; ill treatment within Nambudiri caste 20.286; in India married women are regarded as bringers of good luck 16.397; *Manusmṛti* attitude towards women 9.68; Poona District Buddhist Women's Association, *see under* Poona; the position of women in Buddhism 10.161, 10.182–4; retreat in India (photograph) 10.l; violence against women in India 10.lvii, 10.lxii, 20.382–3; women's community in Pune 10.402–3

role models
Alexandra David-Néel showed what a really determined woman is capable of 6.610; friendship between women: Vera Brittain and Winifred Holtby as exemplars 26.637; positive spiritual role models: Tārā and the *ḍākinī* 5.622, 13.246; role models for Buddhist women in the West 24.373

further observations
avenues open to women 11.603; choosing to look after the sick and elderly 18.149–50; conditioning around the expression of feelings 4.597–8; reaching out to black women 11.596; 'Most women have no characters at all' (Pope, quoting Martha Blount) 24.461; positive discrimination in favour of women 11.639–40; St Catherine of Siena encourages women to be heroic 11.633–4; the satisfaction of seeing a woman as a head of state 8.283; 'What does a woman want?' (Freud) 22.221; woman as the embodiment of ideal beauty 26.593; a woman who found it difficult to accept herself as a woman 23.173–4; women in public life 11.635–6; women writers 23.472; women's clothes in Spain 24.467; women's difficulty with celibacy 17.219; women's friendships 11.637–8, 26.637

see also
feminism; *maechis*, *see under bhikkhunīs*; Sangharakshita and women, *see under* Sangharakshita XI/people; single-sex idea; women in Triratna, *see under* Triratna II/ the people involved

wonder four wonderful and marvellous things 14.24–5; 'How wonderful! How miraculous! I draw water and I carry fuel' 14.397, 16.252; 'How wonderful it was to feel oneself alive in a world of living things!' 24.38; in a Buddha's attributes there is nothing that is not wonderful

11.43; philosophy begins with a sense of wonder (Plato) 4.212, 12.306, 18.287; preserving a sense of wonder at the *gift* of the Dharma 14.403–4; the Three Jewels are wonderful 11.43–4; we've lost the wonder of it all 25.233; when you lose a sense of wonder at nature, you are dying 8.265; 'Wonders are many, and none is more wonderful than man' 16.85

wongkur *see under abhiṣeka*

wood 'being like a piece of wood' (*Bodhicaryāvatāra*) '4.340, 4.382–3; a piece of wood in the form of an elephant (Vasubandhu illustration) 1.370; 'Split the wood and there am I' (Gnostic) 16.22

Woodard, W. P. 8.154

Woodham-Smith, Cecil 26.490, 26.750 (n462)

Woodroffe, Sir John ('Arthur Avalon') 20.135, 20.148, 25.162, 25.591 (n54)

Woodward, F. L. *Manual of a Mystic* (trans.) 8.34; mistaken translation of *Aṅguttara Nikāya* passage as referring to 'great self' 3.659 (n226); *Some Sayings of the Buddha* 7.515, 9.137, 15.xi–xii, 20.434, 21.503; translation of the *Udāna* 10.422

Woolf, Virginia 25.410–11, 26.339

Woolwich, Bishop of *see* Robinson

Worcester, England 24.581

words

the Buddha's use of words
don't imagine that he carefully defined his terms 14.350–1; he gave new meanings to old words 9.480, 10.429, 10.438, 10.441–2; he used the best words he could find 19.452; he used old words but was not influenced by old teachings 2.58–9, 10.133, 23.178; his awareness of the limitations of words 14.15–16; his use of existing language 9.480; it isn't easy to communicate a new idea or experience using old words 10.467–8; 'putting new wine in old bottles' 1.62, 2.58–9, 9.480, 10.429, 23.178, 26.474; we may not find out what he meant from the roots of his words 14.350–1; words are the lowest level at which the Enlightened mind communicates 3.81

Buddhist terminology
adding Buddhist meaning to your usage of words 12.118; ascertaining the keywords of Buddhism 8.273, 22.458–9; beware of being led astray by words about the *trikāya* doctrine 2.45; beware of importing political terms into a spiritual context 11.690; careless use of Buddhist terms 7.515–17; the definitions of Buddhist terms were worked out over many years 14.350–1; developing new (non-Sanskrit?) terms to express the Dharma in the West 4.585–6; Dharma words with upper and lower cases 4.432; the effort to ascertain the key words of Buddhism and their meanings 22.459; if we don't practise the Dharma, it won't live, and we will only have words 12.455; if words to describe *bodhi* sound baffling – well, they are just words 13.298; the importance of a clear understanding of Buddhist terminology 8.272–3; literal and abstract terminology may confuse and vitiate spiritual strivings 26.188; Sangharakshita's wish to clarify his own terminology 11.619; shibboleths in Buddhism 19.446–7

teaching the Dharma through words
ācāryas' transmission of the Dharma through words 3.82, 14.17; Buddhism is not to be understood by words alone 14.17; Buddhism makes use of words but can never be reduced to them 11.418; 'the Dharma that is taught is only a collection of words and letters' 2.425; doing one's best with words 13.344; don't use fashionable terminology to communicate the Dharma 12.585; a kind of bodhisattva who is fond of diverse phraseology and literary ornament 14.166; a mistake to assume that the Dharma is bound up with a certain form of words 2.51; sometimes our being is not adequate to the words we say 4.6; using words to convey ideas, and ideas to point to spiritual experience 13.343; using words which are only quotations, not from personal experience 19.288–9

words and reality
'All words for things in use in this world must be left behind' 14.585; all words indicative of existence have a disagreeably substantialist flavour 2.55; 'All ways of telling are removed' 1.65, 2.43, 3.143–4; *animitta*: the approach to the Unconditioned by bypassing all words 3.219; a double barrier between us and reality: perceptions and words 14.421; 'how could liberation … be expressed in words?' (*Buddhacarita*) 17.741 (n268); thinking we 'know' reality when we have just understood the words 13.347; the truth is beyond words and concepts 7.331, 14.297; words are but signs, and should not be mistaken for realities 14.234; words are a medium for communicating a unique and ineffable

experience 2.59; 'Words are not the highest reality' 1.238–9; words aren't ultimately true 1.265; words can give us no idea of Enlightenment 3.250–1; words cannot define suchness, but designate it for practical purposes 7.299; the words that make up the Dharma hint at a certain kind of reality 19.452

words and meaning
being preoccupied with words and missing the meaning 19.158–9; 'Better than a thousand meaningless words...' (*Dhammapada*) 3.282–3; the experience that words don't mean anything at all 14.585, 23.472; 'I understand the words, but I don't understanding the meaning' 4.249; the idea that if one understands the words one has mastered the meaning 18.167; incomprehensible words on Glastonbury Tor 25.501; meaning is alone with itself, but words are bound up with discrimination 14.208; 'meaningless word-knowledge' 18.185; one should rely on the meaning, not on the expression, *see under* four reliances; people who trip you up with words because they don't want to understand 16.579; same words with different meanings 1.447, 1.474–5, 3.491, 9.482–3, 15.463–4; sharp distinction between words and meaning 14.207–8; sounds associated in varying degrees with conceptual meaning 3.511; to understand what 'Enlightenment' really means requires great imagination 4.6–7; the usefulness of words 17.249; 'We inherit words without questioning their meanings!' 10.xliv; we may put words into conventionally meaningful patterns, but they may not mean much to us 13.123; what do the words we use really mean? 4.145; 'Words, words, words': studying the words, not the meaning 18.382

etymology
bad etymology can still make good sense 15.646; knowledge of etymology (*nirukti-pratisaṃvid*) 1.449, 16.490–1; science of etymology (*nirukti*) 16.362

nouns
any word used as a noun apparently refers to a thing 17.248–9; devices to deal with the multitude of impressions, but can become dangerous 7.326–7; the struggle between Buddhism and the abstract noun 3.398; there is a danger of reifying any abstract noun 11.656

the limitations of words
can we describe even the colour of a rose? 2.54; caught up in endless words 19.131; the chances of misunderstanding words are very great 3.83; a culture often doesn't have a word for its most important principle 4.168–9; don't think that putting something into words expresses it fully 16.565; finding no word for beauty 25.237; getting the better of words for the thing one no longer has to say 17.249; how words check the flow of experience 17.248–9; the inability of words to express experience 7.37; the limitations of words to express beauty 14.15; to show their limitations, use different words for the same thing 18.285; they have their limitations 16.578–9; we rely too much on words 16.564–6; the Wilderness of Word 25.194; words cannot tell the whole story 18.262; 'Words defile' 25.404

taking words literally
Dharma study teaches us that we can't take words literally 19.508; if you start taking words literally, your view becomes 'word-conditioned' 19.446–8; words must be understood not literally but symbolically 1.234

words and clarity
do words conceal or reveal thought more? 7.378; the rectification of terms 3.489–91, 9.479; semantics 3.489–91, 14.86, 14.566; use words carefully, to convey what you really mean 5.651, 8.273; using words clearly to express concepts 4.145, 16.490–1; using words loosely, and using jargon, does not conduce to clarity 12.476, 26.70; we need to know what words mean, using the dictionary if necessary 12.476, 16.490, 25.6–8; words ... blur everything that they do not make more clear 26.4

the power of words
expressing thoughts and feelings in words clarifies and objectifies them 18.278; a few words are enough to say what the heart means 25.336; a few words can have a huge effect 8.73–5; the importance of words 9.479; *Littera Scripta Manet* (the written word *remains*) 23.414, 26.70; occult forces invoked through repetition of the Sacred Word 2.215–16; the power of a word, a name, a mantra 17.418; words can lose power through overuse 25.7; words spoken cannot be recalled, and one has to live with the consequences 22.491; words that make the heart beat faster 25.373

words and the poet
'The poet listens for the inevitable word' 25.436; the poet's sensitivity to the tones and rhythms of words 3.507

going beyond words
the Buddha holds up a golden flower, *see* flowers/golden flower; Milarepa's 'playwords': transcendence of thought and language 18.66; Nirvāṇa beyond words and description 10.101; *Prajñāpāramitā* literature is composed of words that lead beyond words 14.xiv; sometimes words transcend words, but don't let facility with them deceive you 13.122–3; the truth is beyond words 7.331, 14.297; the Unconditioned beyond words 26.478; using words to get free from words until we reach the pure wordless essence 8.498, 13.348, 14.325, 19.241, 19.447; Zen masters teach by actions so disciples don't get caught up in words 19.230

see also
the Buddha did not utter a single word, *see Laṅkāvatāra Sūtra*/chapter 7; *Buddhavacana*; language; 'No dependence on words and letters', *see under* Zen/Zen teachings; 'Test my words as the goldsmith tests gold in the fire', *see under* gold; translation

Wordsworth, William

introduction
one of the Lake Poets 24.640 (n168); appreciation of nature 16.387; idealization of infancy 8.586; his friendship with Coleridge 26.365–6; Dove Cottage 24.144; Rydal Mount 24.144–5; walking up and down a gravel path 25.591–2 (n62); his character in later life 19.121–2; he achieved a true vision 17.470; made some approach to the Dharma 16.375; definition of poetry: 'emotion recollected in tranquillity' 26.144; influence on Sangharakshita 25.xlv

'Immortality Ode'
studied in India 21.434, 22.19; 'the glory and the freshness of a dream' 26.447; 'Thoughts that do often lie too deep for tears' 26.137; 'trailing clouds of glory' 17.470

'Lines Written a Few Miles above Tintern Abbey'
expresses a state of calm close to what Buddhists experience in meditation 12.672; 'felt in the blood, and felt along the heart' 3.361, 11.73; 'little, nameless, unremembered acts of kindness and of love' 11.736; 'a sense sublime/ Of something far more deeply interfused ...' 17.557

'My heart leaps up'
'My heart leaps up when I behold a rainbow in the sky' 26.670; 'The child is father to the man' 3.148

The Prelude
'unknown modes of being' 26.169, 26.170; 'Voyaging through strange seas of Thought, alone' 1.52

sonnets
'November 1806' 20.49; 'Composed upon Westminster Bridge' 23.312–13, 24.71; 'We are greater than we know' 11.497; 'We must be free or die, who speak the tongue that Shakespeare spake' 2.434; 'The world is too much with us' 1.481

quotations from other poems
'Chatterton, the marvellous boy' 23.206; 'Every flower enjoys the air it breathes' 7.388; 'the light that never was on sea or land' 7.451; 'mighty poets in their misery dead' 11.448; 'the mighty stream of tendency' 16.595 (n72); 'O Blithe newcomer' 21.543; 'old, unhappy, far-off things' 23.109; 'One impulse from a vernal wood' 26.243–4; 'Our meddling intellect/ Mis-shapes the beauteous forms of things' 7.242; 'Peter Bell': 'a primrose by the river's brim' 1.29; 'the plan that pleased his boyish thought' 8.540; 'rocks, and stones, and trees' 1.28; 'A slumber did my spirit seal' 1.28; 'Stern daughter of the Voice of God' 7.277; 'To be young was very heaven' 23.xiv; 'We murder to dissect' 13.506; 'You must love him before he will seem worthy of your love' 2.319

work

THE WORLD OF WORK

introduction
three aspects of work: developmental, social, and productive 18.391; producer of wealth 16.411, 18.391; should be an expression of one's life, not simply the means to one's existence 26.72; we are conditioned by the work we do 11.7; it's important because we invest so much time and ego-identity in it 17.193–4

work and the Buddhist tradition
the Buddha describes the spiritual life in terms of work 3.76; the Buddha never did a day's work in his life 4.114; duties of employees (*Sigālaka Sutta*) 3.588–9; duties of employers (*Sigālaka Sutta*) 3.585–7, 12.603; *appakicco*, 'with little work' 15.284; crafts and trades of the Buddha's day (*sippa*, *vijja*) 10.520; the attitude to work in the early sangha 15.278–9; Tibetan Buddhists' attitude to

work 15.279; the great Tantric guru 4.91, 18.322; 'A day of no working is a day of no eating' 2.555, 8.487, 11.318, 12.497, 17.73; Zen attitude to work 15.279; some *bhikkhus* would love to work, but the lay people won't let them 17.73; careerlessness (of the monk) 2.606

quotations from Western writers
'Give a man a motive to work, and he will work' (Hazlitt) 24.562; 'There is no point in work unless it absorbs you like an absorbing game' (Lawrence) 19.26; 'Toil and grow rich ...' (Yeats) 15.117–18; what a horrible word 'worker' is (Chesterton) 18.390

do we have to work?
Dharma life may change your need for job security 10.630–1; feeling uncomfortable when someone else is not working 4.113–14, 18.389–90; the idea of a basic stipend provided by the government to everyone 3.587; if we work, it should be because we want to 18.121; in an ideal society no one would have to work for wages 4.114; the Indian attitude that work is inherently unspiritual 15.278–9; in a luxury culture, people should work because they want to 3.587, 15.366; living on the dole 12.380, 15.365–6; the motivation for work is hunger 18.294; our real work is to enjoy the universe 14.519; the Protestant (or Puritan) work ethic 4.113–14, 18.390, 23.187; a response to London workers streaming towards the City 26.612; too many people work on the basis of guilt and obligation 18.121; the time to take a holiday is when there's a lot of work to be done 4.484, 5.647; a tribe who didn't mind if some people worked and others just sat around 18.389; we have to work because we need to eat 17.11; work as little as possible 1.549–50, 3.371

physical work
the difficulty and toil of agricultural work 18.202–3; discomfort at the hard work of a rickshaw worker 3.586; helps you meditate and study better 10.215; physical work should be part of everyone's spiritual life 18.391; physical workers may think that mental work is not doing anything at all 18.267–8; the poet and manual labour 26.143; prejudice against physical work in ancient Greece and India 10.216, 15.404; *vīrya* in the form of physical work as a balancing factor to *dhyāna* 3.308; we should respect the worker, and not be ashamed of physical work 10.216, 15.404; workers on a tea estate about whose welfare Sangharakshita was concerned 22.22–5

industrial relations
best and worst masters, from a Tibetan point of view 22.522; disparity of power between employer and employee 26.654; a pay dispute in Kalimpong 22.249; trade unions 26.654; 'Unemployment leads to riots' 26.195; we may call someone a good worker because we over-value production 18.390

wages
the Buddhist ideal is to give what you can without thinking of *quid pro quo* 16.391; an element of deception in the way wages are set 17.196; working just for the taxman 18.568–9

REFLECTIONS ON WORK

the difficulties of work
exploitation at work 3.565–6, 25.121–3; being exhausted and worn away by work 4.627, 18.201–3; don't let work become an escape from your true self 15.284; feeling that work has been imposed on you 17.73; going round and round like dumb chained cattle 25.301; going through the motions of work 17.196; perceived as dull, repetitive, exhausting, and boring 11.77–8; the shift from working for the same firm all your life to modern mobility 18.336; we need to review what we are doing from time to time 15.99; work can be a form of *duḥkha* 3.211–12; work can have a terrible effect on body and mind 1.544–5; what to do if you don't enjoy your work 15.117–18

making the best of work
all work is worship 7.102; in Japan, work provides a group for people to belong to 3.442; no need to be afraid of work 10.216; opportunities for insight at work 5.637–8, 13.172; relaxing while working 5.301–2; the secret of work: 'seeing the inward in the outward' 7.102–3; simple work which leaves you free to think is best 18.391, 18.392; singing while working 18.392; 'Sometimes I think work is the greatest enjoyment in life' 26.72; we are near to heaven if we enjoy our work and our work is our life 26.17; work and play can go together 18.392, 24.66; work stimulates energy 17.71–4; you can get a lot of tough work done in a relaxed atmosphere 14.520

working with others
people who have no real work always interfere with that of others 26.15; the value of working with others 18.391; a

working relationship with no thought of what you do and what he does 10.603; the workplace as an opportunity for developing sympathy 26.141–2

work and ethics
any form of work involves deception, and even self-deception 17.196; choose an ethical occupation, or join a right livelihood business 12.670; the effect on your mind of your means of livelihood 1.544–5, 5.290; perfect work comes from the unification of pure wisdom and pure deeds 26.19; work and conventional morality 4.109–10; you don't just want a job, you want right livelihood 15.366, 17.194–5

vocational work
the caring professions 14.415; commitment to nursing 24.349; creative work 4.114

working for the Dharma
Buddhist activities as a means of making money 7.246; one shouldn't make a trade of the Dharma 10.593; sacramental work 18.427; seeing Buddhism in terms of work 11.89–90; working for the Dharma 10.396–7, 11.89–90, 14.xvi, 14.522–3, 16.207; working hard at the Dharma 18.316–18

work and meditation
alternating between exertion and relaxation, work and meditation 26.19; unless your work is your meditation, your meditation is not meditation 26.18; work as preparation for meditation 3.339

see also
right livelihood; wrong livelihood

world

WHAT IS THE WORLD?

introduction
the emptiness of the world, which contains nothing of real value 3.238; everything done in this world is the action of a mad person 12.229; scientific view 16.341; the total sum of unenlightened human activities 16.359; we may be worldly-wise, but we do not know the world as it really is 12.528; what is the 'world'? 16.341

origin
ancient Indian Buddhist view of the universe, *see under* cosmology; the Buddhist story of the origin of the world 1.41–2, 3.13, 16.100; the evolution of the world 8.265–6; taking the *Genesis* story literally 10.554; creation by God, *see under* God

the end of the world
according to Nāgārjuna, the world cannot really come to an end 17.387; legends that the world continues only because of meditating sages 4.582; 'When silence settles on the globe and man with all his dreams is dead' 25.404; why did the Buddha stay silent on the subject? 17.387; the world has been born and died thousands of times, and must do so again 7.343; 'Worlds on worlds are rolling ever' 1.43

images and metaphors for the world
a big madhouse 10.209; a cloud of fine particles of dust blown about by invisible winds 7.49; cloud, moon in the ocean … 14.204; like a ring produced by a firebrand 14.204, 17.350–1; the spiritually mature know that the world is like a mirage 17.358–9; like a bazaar 18.566–7

philosophical reflections on the world
the denial of the existence of the world of appearance 7.194; extreme view of the world as absolutely non-existent 2.81; how can the world exist if there is no past, present, or future? 17.365; how real is the world we see today? 17.378; like a mirage, the world is there in a sense 17.384; meditating on the fact that the world as we know it is unreal 2.81; the nature of the world is beyond categorization 17.387; not completely real but not absolutely unreal 16.452, 17.626, 19.233–4; real freedom is where there is no world and no freedom from the world 17.368; the world we see is not the fixed reality we take it for 17.403; the relationship between things we distinguish in the world is impossible to pin down 17.377; trying to ascertain whether it is finite or infinite is a mistake 17.385; whatever world we find ourselves in owes its origin to ideas in the mind 17.476; where there is a perceiving subject there is an object, a world 16.388; the world has no self-nature and has never been born 14.204; 'The world constantly is running down, and yet its sorrow never terminates' 4.311; the world of things is a reflex of people's deeds 1.342

BUDDHIST PERSPECTIVES ON THE WORLD

the Buddha and Early Buddhism
the *ālaya-vijñāna* doctrine explains how we take the illusory world to be real 17.488; the Buddha's silence about the limits of the world 17.387; Buddhism recognizes both the world's evil and the power of positive forces 4.267–8; it is burning with craving, hatred, and delusion 16.70; it consists

solely of the five *skandhas* 7.130–1; only the Buddha sees the true beauty of the world 12.616; a place where people are motivated by craving, aversion, and delusion 11.130–2; 'Tied up in confusion, the world is seen as agreeable in nature' (*Udāna*) 10.627, 10.631; when you become Enlightened the world is the same but you see it differently 17.483; the world is attached to the process of becoming 10.522–3; people are entranced by the sights and sounds of the world 10.610–11; the world is the illusory creation of an illusory self 17.328–9

Mahāyāna Buddhism
difficult and dangerous conditions for Dharma practice 4.100–1, 12.490; it's tough, with Māra's influence dominant 14.484; not just one world but a plurality, even infinity, of worlds 3.376–7; a future Pure Land (*White Lotus Sūtra*) 16.168–9; texts describe an ideal world, but we are left to work out the details 11.185; the oppression of the world 16.322; an impure Buddha-land, dirty, disagreeable, and dangerous 16.462; in the *Gaṇḍavyūha Sūtra*: a concrete world of glowing particulars 1.355; present world-period protected by Amitābha and Avalokiteśvara 1.263

Vajrayāna Buddhism
this self-centred world as the demon Tarpa Nagpo 12.331, 12.333–4; Tantric Buddhism sees it not as a hindrance but as a help to Enlightenment 1.375–6; the way to cross the great ocean of this world of relativity 1.385; the Enlightened mind operating in this deluded world through wrathful forms 13.68–9

the Sahā-world (sahāloka, our world)
bodhisattvas teaching there 16.48; in Buddhist cosmology, corresponds in part to the Milky Way 2.63–4; *sahā* means endurance or suffering 3.380, 16.45, 16.555, 19.580; purified in the *White Lotus Sūtra* 3.380, 16.45; the Dharma must be taught here using blunt language 16.556–7, 26.399; this ridiculous earth 25.454

bodhisattvas in the world
the *bodhicitta* an active force at work in the world 4.32; they are part of its 'spiritual economy' 13.39; they perceive it as a mock show without plunging into fear and madness 14.576; those who work here have to have strong compassion and determination 16.558

THE MODERN WORLD

what it is like
the age of science 10.169; becoming a smaller place through communication 8.267–8, 8.273–4, 16.76; chaos 16.351, 16.356; developed, undeveloped, and developing worlds 12.370; a difficult and dangerous place 11.71, 12.490; 'the dirty devices of this world' 13.31, 17.470; divided into nation states 19.519; dominated by greed, in need of the qualities of the *Dhammapada* 15.8; environment, *see* environment; ethical considerations not allowed to get in the way of making money 12.670; everyday activity lacks any clearly spiritual dimension 15.157; the forces of materialism 8.182, 10.389, 12.654, 17.556, 17.657; full of woolly thinking and wrong views 11.167–8; the growth of modern technology 11.356–7; high standard of living 11.272, 11.357; industrialization 11.522, 12.563; inequalities of wealth 10.396; it continues on its crazy course 25.445; it continues to be optimistic, but its ideals are degenerate 17.692; it multiplies the sensory world's distractions 17.44; life feels dull and routine 11.77; our 'knowledge' of it comes from the media 13.344–5; the pace of change 10.xxii, 10.328, 11.111; the passing of the 'world of yesterday' 11.351–2; population growth 11.356; population shift from country to city 10.328–9; the power of the corporate state over the individual 11.356–7; Ruskinian reflections on modern civilization 23.274; secularized, urbanized, competitive, consumerist, materialistic, violent 12.563; we *are* each the modern world, to a certain extent 11.81; what the world has gone through since the time of the Buddha 25.30; you can get away from home, but not the state 11.624

modern views and attitudes
a breakdown of the notion of objective truth 12.350–3; democratization, feminization, integration 11.612–14; evolution dominates the modern world 1.564, 3.10; intense relativism 15.489–90; the irreversibility of 'progress' 24.349–50; obsession with the individual 13.459, 13.464; organized religion is on the defensive 8.276; political correctness 26.74; rampant consumerism 12.654; reasons for lack of motivation 12.379–80; reluctance to revere superior qualities 4.168, 4.345, 15.714–20, 17.275–7; superficiality 11.49–50, 19.459; suspicion and fear, the inevitable result of the 'I'-

concept 7.274; today our head races ahead of our heart 15.558; wallowing arrogantly in the world like a pig in his sty 19.494; the whole contemporary world view is based on illusion 14.506

problems
because we live at this time, we share the world's problems 12.113–14; the biggest problem is the survival of the individual 11.352; bringing Buddhism to bear on world problems 8.262; a Buddhist view of world problems 3.613–19, 12.113–14; the collapse of the traditional way of life 8.181–2; damage to the imagination 26.240; the world of the Cold War and the atom bomb 8.298; dark and dangerous times in the world 4.637–8, 4.658, 17.471–2, 23.161–2; do problems come from the system or the nature of human beings? 11.183; essentially group problems 3.616; the forces of death and destruction need an equally strong creative response 4.638; frightening people about the world's problems 17.181; global media makes us more aware of them than people used to be 3.615, 15.174–5, 11.77; how to respond to them personally? 3.615–17, 11.77; individual development the only solution: four courses of action to take 3.616–18; list of world problems 3.615–16; living at a time of crisis in world history 8.272; might be influenced by a network of spiritual communities 3.619; no surprise that the world is full of conflicts, wars, and misunderstandings 15.306; not many grounds for optimism 12.408; the principle of non-violence can be applied to many of the world's problems 8.453; the problem with abstract analyses of world problems 3.613–14; so many terrifying things are going on that we can do without hell 4.447; threat of nuclear war, *see under* war/nuclear war; the warm glow of humanitarianism not enough to fuse differences into unity 7.271; we mustn't feel that we are living in a 'dark age' 11.272; we have to think what we can do to save it 25.57–8; we've got ourselves into a mess and we will need to get ourselves out of it 12.97

peace
to achieve it we need to see ourselves as citizens of the world 12.353; the Buddha's solution 7.239; Buddhism tends towards peace in the world 7.278, 13.447; better build a stupa to the Buddha than one to world peace 14.447; can only come through realizing interconnectedness 7.274; depends on restoring the notion of objective truth 12.350–3; the enormity of the problem makes us more aware of the problem of death 12.361; everyone wants world peace, but how to achieve it? 12.605; many religions and philosophies support it 3.614; middle path to solve the problem 7.236–9; in the modern world, peace can only mean world peace 12.341–2; monks employed to negotiate peace terms 2.217; one country that wants to fight can upset the peace of the world 11.271; talks that suggest that Buddhism can bring it about, but not how 3.613–14; teaching people the *mettā bhāvanā* could be a step towards it 12.348; the way to world peace 7.236–9; we can hardly imagine it 12.354–5; we must work for the abolition of all weapons 12.353; the world truly needs peace, but does not sincerely desire it 7.278–9

choices
the choice before us is one world or no world 12.342; the choice facing us: (higher) evolution or extinction 3.617; 'global village' 4.639, 12.129–30; planet Earth has a wonderful opportunity, but it's in a terrible position 10.315; the significance for the world of the peaceful Dhamma Revolution 9.431, 10.379; we are being brought closer and closer together 7.146, 7.236

transforming the world
anticipated by miracles (*Sūtra of Golden Light*) 16.261; 'A Blueprint for a New World' 11.181–9; Buddhism seeks to transform the world 16.223; can be brought about by people committed to spiritual development 16.359–60; changing the system or changing ourselves? 11.183; making a Pure Land out of a suffering world 25.349; neither accepting it on its own terms nor rejecting it, but transforming it 12.394–5; our desire to transform the world 16.228; part of the task of transforming ourselves 1.550; represented by the four great kings 16.357; the effect of retreats showed the need to transform world *and* self 12.554; strength, directed by love, changes the world 25.519–20; transforming the world into a spiritual community 11.182–9; usually people draw up a plan and then try to get everybody to adopt it 11.185; the world is not bad, or evil, or wrong, but its energies need to be transformed 12.335–6; we can change, help others to change, together change the world 26.57; we need to transform the world, not just find a niche within it 11.377; we try to put the world right, but it's easier to put ourselves right 4.379, 11.271–2

Buddhism in the modern world
best to discuss profound questions in secular language 12.117–18; bringing the world under the influence of the golden light 12.395; the Buddha's teaching should be applied to contemporary issues 23.161; 'Buddhism in the Modern World' (1956, 1959) 7.433–53, 10.119–21; Buddhism's independent attitude towards the external world 7.266–8; Buddhist world, *see* Buddhist world; the conflict between Buddhist traditions and the forces of the modern age 8.538; the Dharma is opposed to some aspects of modern thinking and belief 12.679; the FWBO 'Western' in the sense of being concerned with the world of today 13.379; if we're trying to live a spiritual life, the world may not give us an easy time 12.623; in modern times Buddhism can no longer be claimed to be peaceful 26.631; it belongs to future and present as well as past 9.313–14; it has no means of enforcing uniformity of action in secular life 7.439; it is up to every individual to choose their own way in spiritual life 15.282; it isn't easy to lead a spiritual life these days 12.654; it must be adapted to needs of modern life 9.316–20, 12.117; changing Buddhism in response to changing culture 12.115–18; could devotion to Maitreya be a unifying factor? 1.324; the danger of being smothered by information 'about' Buddhism 1.8; the importance of Buddhism as a spiritual teaching 7.512; only a united Buddhism can contribute to the building of a united world 8.218; the opportunities to spread the Dharma in the modern world 8.267–8; optimism about the potential of Buddhism 9.511, 16.434; the presence of the spiritual community able to counter the forces of destruction 7.512; restating the truths of Buddhism for the modern world 11.600; revival in India, *see under* Indian Buddhism; special clothes and words don't accord automatic respect 8.276; this is no time for Buddhists to be sitting back 4.447; to be a consumer of Buddhism is the antithesis of transformation 3.327; the idea of monks as the backbone of Buddhism cannot survive in the modern West 8.609–10; the Vajrayāna may be especially applicable 18.417; the versions of Buddhism peddled to the consumer society 18.135; we need Buddhism more desperately than ever 10.157, 11.144; we need courage as well as love to uphold spiritual values 12.518; we need the integration of the world into Buddhism, not Buddhism into the world 11.613; we need to balance ignorance, hatred, egotism with wisdom, love, selflessness 7.34; what does Triratna offer the world? 11.669; worldwide revival 8.652; you need a more solid prop than occasional enjoyment of the arts 26.396; you need spiritual support unless you have a degree of insight 19.347

OURSELVES IN RELATION TO THE WORLD

how we create the world
around the seed of 'I' develops the world of 'mine' 17.342; change your consciousness to see a different world, or see the world differently 26.84; it is a collection of raw materials to which you give form 18.269–70; the 'objective' world we perceive is really a state of mind 2.79; we create the world we live in 16.478, 17.xx, 17.299, 17.433, 17.497; 'When world ceases, mind ceases, when mind ceases, world ceases' 14.606; 'the whole world was a poem' 24.168, 25.36; with intrinsic awareness, everything one does transforms the everyday world 17.608–9; a world coming into existence through collective karma 17.479; the world we live in is the exteriorization of the thoughts we cherish 7.274; you create your world, the network of your desires 17.14–15

relating to the world
the beauty of the world (Rovelli) 26.686; by the very fact of living in the world we are up against it 16.324–5; easier to find success on the spiritual path than in the world 4.292–3, 4.323; the effects of the world on the mind, *see under* mind/what the mind can do; enjoying the world like a work of art 14.517, 26.64; experiencing the world without unskilfulness is complete clarity 19.192; getting to know another human being is like exploring another world 26.25; if you are contented, you can find delight in the world around you 15.310; a little insight sets you going against the grain of the world 17.164; overcoming indifference to the world's suffering 13.81; as perceived by the pure mind and the impure mind 7.411–12; the poet is rooted in the objective world as the plant is rooted in the soil 26.170; a positive way of seeing our physical interaction with the world 17.510; a sense of living in a world in which we are foreigners and aliens 16.220; thinking of oneself as a resource for the world 17.204; we impinge on the world in accordance with the pattern

which is ourselves 16.475; we may be dissatisfied with it, but are we dissatisfied enough? 11.182; we need to intervene positively in the way we experience the world 15.153; we should take from it no more than we need, and give what we can 15.283; we try to settle down in it, but there is nothing to settle down in 17.370; wrong views underpin the way we look at the world 17.629

giving up the world
the idea that religious people can have nothing to do with worldly affairs 15.492–3; if we withdraw ourselves from it perhaps we shall understand its teaching 7.134; in what sense can one 'give up the world'? 18.316; in the world but not of it 2.38, 7.291; middle way between accepting it on its own terms and rejecting it 12.394–5; the monk doesn't 'give up the world' 15.492–3; non-attachment could be confused with indifference 18.331–3, 18.336–7; seclusion from the world may mean not solitude, but the sangha 17.112

see also
modern life

World Fellowship of Buddhists

introduction
introduction 2.746 (n702), 21.515; prefigured by a gathering held by Dharmapala 8.186; inauguration 8.473; adoption of Buddhist flag 22.92; aims and objects 8.185; appeal to them to take up the cause of Vietnamese Buddhists 8.316–17; it must develop more cooperation between the Buddhists of the world 8.297–8; to be effective, it needs to translate resolutions into action 9.332, 23.160–2; Triratna involvement 2.568; *World Buddhism* 8.394

conferences
first conference (Sri Lanka, 1950) 8.185, 23.158; third conference (Myanmar) 8.186, 8.195, 23.159–60; fourth biennial conference in Kathmandu 21.512–13; fifth conference (review of a report) 8.393–4; sixth conference held in Cambodia 8.297–8, 23.162; seventh conference attended by Christmas Humphreys 23.159; such gatherings a waste of time 23.159–60; a talking-shop 8.154–5

World Fellowship of Faiths 22.77–8

World Religion Day 22.280

World's Parliament of Religions 8.44–5, 8.47–9, 8.166–8, 10.280

worldling *see pṛthagjana*

worldly life

living worldly life
Buddhism seems nihilistic to those immersed in worldly life 17.362–3, 26.44; Eastern monks see it as good, but know there is something more satisfying 4.565–6; the fragility of our hold upon worldly things 17.657; the (horizontal) imagination tethered to worldly activity 11.724–5; monks' advice on worldly affairs 2.216–17; motivated by craving, aversion, and delusion 11.130; our habitual grasping for worldly things 18.177; Śāntideva's caustic summary 4.627–8; the unsatisfactoriness of pleasant worldly experiences 18.589

dangers
after retreat, you may not see the dangers of throwing yourself back into it 18.34; the dangers of immersion in it 18.422–4; worldly people are likely to affect you more than you affect them 18.152

worldly life and spiritual life
connecting spiritual life with worldly gains distracts us from its true purpose 17.263–4; no objective reason for thinking spiritual life is difficult and worldly life easy 4.48–9; forgetting about worldly life 19.253–4; thinking you need worldly experience before embarking on spiritual life 17.215–16; thinking that *siddhis* will make you more successful in worldly life 19.460; if you find worldly life satisfactory, it may be hard to get into the spiritual life 18.557; seeking the Buddha's protection in worldly life 19.484–5; 'What is worldly? What is religious?' 10.629; you should get as much or more enjoyment from spiritual life 19.379

worldly winds *see* eight worldly winds

worms ants and worms requested to depart before the building of a temple 22.502; 'The cut worm forgives the plough' (Blake) 26.646; 'Many who are Buddhas today were once worms' – a convincing argument? 4.448; the true individual: an indefatigable earthworm undermining the foundations 3.619; John Wesley liked to remind his congregations that they were grovelling worms 18.120

worry *see* anxiety

worship *see* devotion

wounding a Buddha *see* five heinous crimes

Wozniak, Czarek 26.451–2

Wragg, Carl v23

Wragg, Violet she saw Padmasambhava standing behind Sangharakshita during a talk 23.152, 26.673–4; Sangharakshita's experience of her after her death 4.559, 26.622–3, 26.674

wrathful deities (*krodha*)

introduction
in the *vajra* family 13.309; *krodha* wrongly translated 'evil' 8.353; their sublime nature 14.472; the way they are depicted 13.68, 17.313; five *herukas* (wrathful forms of the five Buddhas) and the Ladies of Wrath 13.316; wrathful *ḍākinīs* 13.244–6; how the Enlightened mind can operate in this deluded world 13.68–9, 17.314–15; appearance in the *bardo* after death 12.204–5

meditating on them
invocation 17.317–18; why invoke and meditate on them? 13.258; a way to face the *kleśas* directly 5.353, 13.173–4; they put us in touch with primal energies 13.246; contemplated in an unskilful state they are threatening, in a skilful state sublime 14.473

symbolism
symbol of breaking through 11.17–18; symbolism of the flames that surround them 11.18, 16.71; manifestations of the destructive aspect of the Enlightened mind 13.68, 17.313, 19.24; their colour symbolizes the destruction of spiritual ignorance 13.68, 17.313

see also
Acala; Vajrapāṇi

Wrekin Trust ('Mystics and Scientists' conference) 4.638, 10.305, 10.701 (n302), 11.558, 24.194–217

Wright, Eric *see* Mangala

Wright, Joseph, of Derby 24.379

Wright, Murray *see* Guhyavajra

writers

observations
the difference between a writer's personality and their work 19.121–2; gratitude towards writers 3.602; an author may be dissatisfied, but that doesn't mean critics have the right to be 26.67; compromising for the sake of money 12.643–4; every creative writer is the founder of a new religion 26.67; one does not write a book, one writes sentences 26.67; one of the signs of a great writer is that even his bad work is interesting 26.68; prolific writers 12.645; the solitude of the writer 25.110, 26.141, 26.353–5; some are like comets, others like a lingering perfume 8.148; they are unpredictable 15.505; they use the same language as the ordinary person, but more expressively 3.57–8; what they write is what they actually think and really believe 18.347; writing as though with one eye fixed on an infinitely horrifiable public 19.258; sometimes claim originality without acknowledging the literary canon 3.606–7

writers and spiritual life
encouraging them to devote their talents to the service of the Dharma 8.188; the need for writers committed to the spiritual life and dedicated to their art 26.69; the spiritual development of great writers 26.258; they have to work on reducing input, just as meditators do 12.475; a writer, even a Buddhist writer, should be involved in public debate 26.640; writers on Buddhism should study it carefully 8.241–3

writing

writing about Buddhism
assimilating what you know and then writing it in your own way 4.281–2; certain words in a book title arouse curiosity: 'secret', 'magic', 'sex', 'Tantra' 13.276; of the monastic sangha 2.212; should ideally do justice to both its letter and its spirit 2.59; should use doctrinal terms, but not too literally 2.60–1; there shouldn't be any general articles on Buddhism written for the non-Buddhist reader 17.106; Western writers are conditioned to write about the stereotype of the lazy monk 4.438; without ascertaining its keywords it raises unnecessary dust 22.458; writing instructions is even more difficult than describing how to ride a bike 19.461

writing autobiography and biography
the difficulty of writing truthful biography 24.148; even the fullest autobiography is no more than a thin cross-section 24.148; 'It is impossible to trace [a life] steadily through successive years' 22.xvi, 22.281; 'Life's memories are not life's histories' 22.xv; make notes about your spiritual experiences, so you don't forget them 17.261–2; writing memoirs is the penance one performs for having lived – or not lived 26.68; writing or telling one's life story shows the pattern of one's life 18.283

the writing process
'always awakens within us something ... we failed clearly to recognize before' 13.367; authorship is an essentially solitary

business 26.69; creative writing is a spiritual discipline 26.69; first thoughts are not necessarily best thoughts 24.562; the importance of having a strong feeling for what you are writing about 5.249; writing down how you feel helps you to face up to it 18.453; writing helps one to develop clear thinking 15.193; 'Writing is in itself a joy' 14.294; you might want to write but not find it easy 15.361

notes on writing
a conflict with meditation? 5.636–7; considered profane in ancient Indian culture 16.363; the emergence of writing style 20.261; no need to use long words for the sake of it 20.56, 20.261; Wolf at the Door creative writing workshops 26.99; writing groups 26.357; writing no substitute for face-to-face communication, unless one writes a book 26.70; a maid reports that her mistress isn't busy, 'only writing' 3.506–7, 18.267

wrong livelihood acting of certain kinds 1.547; astrology and fortune-telling 1.547; animal slaughter 1.544–5, 3.583, 11.117–18, 13.454, 17.195; avoiding cruel occupations 8.450; confession of wrong livelihood 16.303; it frequently involves deception of some kind 17.194–5; production of harmful or frivolous things, boring, repetitive, non-creative work 1.548, 16.412, 17.194; selling drink 11.118; slavery 1.546, 3.582–3, 12.670, 13.454; trade in poisons, drugs, and cigarettes 1.546, 3.583, 12.670, 13.454; trading in weapons 1.546–7, 3.583, 11.118, 12.670, 13.454, 17.195; work that puts you under mental strain 1.548

wrong views *see micchā-diṭṭhis*

Wu Chien 22.503–4

Wu Daozi (poet-painter) 2.213, 2.690 (n297)

Wutaishan, sacred mountain 2.224

wuxin 1.354

Wuzhuo 8.488

Wycliffe, John 12.75, 12.707–8 (n49), 24.538

Wyspianski, Stanislaw 26.449, 26.736 (n358)

X

xenophobia 18.137–9

x-factor 14.557–8, 17.12–13, 19.475–6

Xianglin Chenguan 8.487

xin 13.350

Xuanzang (Hsüan Tsang)

introduction
brief introduction 2.686 (n245), 4.717 (n382); considered a bodhisattva 2.181; depicted in Chinese art 26.304; founder of the Faxiang Zong or Dharmalakṣaṇa school 1.371, 17.770 (n516); introduction of Yogācāra school into China 1.366, 1.371; Hsüan Tsang retreat centre named after him 10.liv–v; parallel to St Jerome 26.303–4; 'What heroism!' 7.32

his pilgrimage
it conformed to the pattern of the wandering of young monks 2.198; heard the story that Aśvaghoṣa was a great musician 13.132; saw 'Hīnayāna' and 'Mahāyāna' followers living together 1.246, 4.23, 7.490, 10.282; sees evidence of women's devotion to Ānanda at Mathura 4.712–13 (n352); sees 'the stupa of unblinking eyes' 3.596; visits Moggallāna's birthplace 7.427; visits Nālandā 2.201, 7.428, 9.390, 12.238, 20.460–1; fictionalized in *Journey to the West*, called *Monkey* 4.646, 4.717 (n382), 16.86, 26.262; *Great Tang Records on the Western Regions* 4.717 (n382), 9.570 (n346)

translations and commentaries
Abhidharma works 14.82, 14.83, 14.88, 14.93; *Diamond Sūtra* 14.151; *Doctrine of Mere-Consciousness* (*Cheng Weishi Lun*) 2.669 (n63), 17.452–3; *Heart Sūtra* 14.152; Prajñāpāramitā *sūtras* 14.134, 14.138; studies commentaries on the *Triṃśikā-vijñapti-kārikās* 1.366; *Vijñaptimatratā-siddhi* 1.371; *Vijñaptimātratāsiddhi-śāstra* 17.551, 17.561, 17.563, 17.565, 17.567–8; *Vimalakīrti-nirdeśa* 14.157, 16.444

Xuedou Chongxian 8.486

Xuyun, Master 6.621, 8.479–80, 24.533, 24.740 (n668)

Y

yab-yum the Ādibuddha as a *yab-yum* figure 13.65; Dem Chog 18.65; description of a wrathful Father-Mother image 1.197; 'father-mother' suggests a positive relationship with parents 18.506; illustration 13.312; images of figures in sexual union are regarded as particularly sacred 12.222, 13.313; misunderstanding 13.311, 16.376, 19.477; no erotic suggestion 13.313; perfect balance of 'femininity' and 'masculinity', wisdom and compassion 4.143; sometimes placed at the centre of the mandala 18.602; sometimes symbolized by *vajra* and lotus, or *vajra* and bell 13.313; symbolism 1.388; the union of wisdom and compassion 18.296–7, 19.517; visualizing *yab-yum* figures 12.297; *yab-yum* form of Mañjughoṣa never popularized 16.376–7

yācanā 1.412

yajñas* and *yāgsa *see under* Vedas/Vedic sacrifice

yak's tail 16.87–8, 21.53

yakṣa (Pāli *yakkha*) brief introduction 17.741 (n267); an awe-inspiring natural force 10.451; King Bimbisāra's rebirth as a *yakkha* 16.621 (n287); the Buddha called the great *yakkha* 10.451–2; the Buddha is asked if he is a *yakṣa* 3.141; the Buddha is threatened by Ajakalāpaka the *yakkha* (*Udāna*) 10.451–4; consumed by the wrathful deities 17.318; could be translated *daimon* 10.451; images of *yakṣas*, 'kindly demons' 26.388–9; early Mahāyāna Buddha images perhaps modelled on images of *yakkhas* 10.452; on Mount Meru 16.344; ruled by Vaiśravaṇa 16.346; Saṃjñāya the *yakṣa* promises to protect the *Sūtra of Golden Light* 14.243 16.245; a *yakṣa* hits Sāriputta on the head, and falls into the great hell 1.639 (n469), 10.534–5

Yalahankar Swami Sangharakshita's encounter with him 20.353–63, 23.16; appearance 20.360; his disciples' ordeals 20.354–5, 20.359–61; he exposes pride 14.489, 20.356; methods 20.356–7; said to be 600 years old 20.357, 20.360, 23.16; could he be Āryadeva? 20.361–2; strange message to 'the English saint' and his companion 20.379

Yale University *see under* United States

Yama or Yamarāja (lord of death) doesn't take bribes 10.321; his three messengers: old age, disease, and death 24.229–38; holds the mirror of karma in the world of tormented beings (hell) 13.126; the Yamarāja of hatred 17.317; 'the victory of Yama' (allegorical) 19.122

Yamaguchi, Susuma 2.124

Yamaka ('The Pairs', late Abhidharma work) introduction 14.89–91; 'many of its plays upon words ... appear rather strange, if not silly' 14.90; 'ten valleys of dry bones' 14.89

Yamaka (a monk with wrong views) 1.75

Yamamaki, Sogen 20.101

Yamāntaka, 'Destroyer of Death' 2.178–9

Yamarāja (lord of death) *see* Yama

yānas

'HĪNAYĀNA', MAHĀYĀNA, VAJRAYĀNA

introduction
brief description 11.678, 12.116, 12.167, 13.18, 13.115; fuller account 1.211–19; the three great phases of Indian Buddhism 7.503–4; the approach to the Three Refuges of the three *yānas* 13.195–204; the Three Jewels are manifested in all three 11.255; three restatements of the essentials of the Buddha's teachings 12.116; complexity of classifying Buddhist countries into the different *yānas* 7.482–3; each phase lives on in the next 2.448; each produced its own canonical literature 12.210, 14.249; each *yāna* finds its fullest expression in a specific type of ideal

7.472; each *yāna* has a fourfold process of development and decline 18.496–7; expression of the unity of Buddhism 7.490; a framework for the whole Buddhist tradition 7.479; literalism in the three *yānas* 19.49–50; metaphors describing the *yānas* 7.471–2, 7.480; in the Sevenfold Puja 11.291; 'Ordination and Initiation in the Three Yanas' 2.447–8, 7.471–84, 23.142; the three *yānas* see *prajñā* in different ways 17.546–7; and unity in Buddhism 7.479

the triyāna system in Tibetan Buddhism
Buddhism of the three *yānas* (*triyāna*) 5.574, 13.18–19; the *triyāna* synthesis is only found in Tibetan Buddhism 13.106; might offer a model for Western Buddhism 11.89; seen as successively higher teachings 1.246, 7.479–81, 12.15, 13.12, 19.49–50; declared by Atīśa to be successive stages of a single path 1.361, 13.19; Sangharakshita's thinking on the three *yānas* changed 6.xxvi; you're not necessarily on a higher path because practising a higher *yāna* 19.532; a useful framework, but should not be applied too rigidly 17.547; belief that all the *yānas* were the personal teaching of the Buddha 13.200; questioning the *triyāna* conception 11.599; the *triyāna* system came from a process of degeneration and revival 13.200; the division of the three *yānas* into nine 13.23; taught by Padmasambhava 12.296; introduction to the nine *yānas* 12.296–8, 13.22–3

ŚRĀVAKAYĀNA, PRATYEKABUDDHAYĀNA, BODHISATTVAYĀNA

introduction
the three vehicles 1.211–19; how each faces the happiness of *samādhi* 1.259; the *śrāvakayāna* and *bodhisattvayāna* can be seen as complementary 26.697; as successive grades of one path 1.362

in schools of Early Buddhism
term *yāna* (way or vehicle) recognized 1.213; why they recognized three *yānas* 1.213–14; the Buddha's teaching draws on all three 26.548; expressed the Hīnayāna's plurality of religious ideals 2.209; Sarvāstivāda view as equally valid 1.214; viewed as separate attainments 1.213–14, 1.403

in the Mahāyāna
how the Mahāyāna saw the *yānas* 1.214–18; the *bodhisattvayāna* and the *mantrayāna* 26.698–700; they symbolize different possible approaches to Enlightenment 16.40–1; three ways to Nirvāṇa (*Daśabhūmika Sūtra*) 1.258–9; later Mahāyāna texts see them as successive stages of one path 1.405

ekayāna
the three *yānas* converge in *ekayāna* 2.210; distinctive teaching of the *White Lotus Sūtra*, *see under White Lotus Sūtra/* teachings; Queen Śrīmāla's teaching on the doctrine 14.175; Maitreyanātha's teaching 1.360; prefigured in the Pāli canon 1.217–18; Buddhayāna 7.362, 9.359–60, 14.116; knowledge of how the *yānas* merge together (*Daśabhūmika Sūtra*) 16.489; in the *Mahāparinirvāṇa Sūtra* 14.238

Yasa (the Buddha's disciple) 2.23, 2.33, 4.698 (n260), 9.142, 10.264

Yasa (German novice) 23.367

Yashoda Ma 20.184–5

Yashodeva, Dharmachari v24, 26.549

Yashodhara (Ahmedabad Buddhist) 23.345, 23.347, 24.114

Yashomitra, Dharmachari v24

Yashpal (Hindi writer) 7.447

Yaśodharā Siddhārtha had to prove his worth to her relatives by combat 3.49; marriage 3.24; Siddhārtha's leaving 3.29, 11.397, 13.445; wasn't it selfish of Siddhārtha to leave her? 10.456, 17.191–2; her conversion to Buddhism 9.142; being reborn with the Buddha in the *Jātakas* 16.471–2, 18.147; predicted to Enlightenment in the *White Lotus Sūtra* 16.47; Siddhārtha's love 25.491; 'Yashodhara' (poem) 25.228

Yasoja (in the *Udāna*) 10.508–10

Yaśomitra 1.365

yathābhūta-jñānadarśana *see* knowledge and vision of things are they really are

Yatung 21.188, 21.200

Yeats, W. B.

introduction
as good a poet as Eliot 26.379; he rebuilt the ancient tower at Ballylee 18.276; on Byzantium as the perfect city 26.386; play readings 4.354, 4.699 (n263); *Purgatory* (one-act play) 24.582; reading Yeats 22.141; Yeats' influence on Sangharakshita's poetry 22.181, 25.xlvii; *Yeats: The Man and the Masks* 24.404

quotations
'An aged man is but a paltry thing' 12.595; 'All dreams of the soul …' 25.232; 'The

cataract smokes on the mountainside' 26.116; 'Hammer your thoughts into a unity' 25.304, 25.592 (n74); 'He beat upon the wall / Till Truth obeyed his call.' 15.520, 16.266; 'Hermits upon Mount Meru or Everest' 7.450; 'Myself must I remake' 15.520, 18.271; 'Nineteen Hundred and Nineteen' 25.xlix; 'Romantic Ireland's dead and gone' 24.467; 'Things below are copies' 1.28; 'Toil and grow rich ...' 15.117–18; 'Turning and turning in the widening gyre' 7.311; 'Wild Swans at Coole' 25.lv, 26.398; 'Wisdom is a butterfly/ And not a gloomy bird of prey' 2.405, 26.265

Yeats-Brown, Francis 8.65–6

yellow associated with the Tantric rite of prosperity 13.280, 19.24; the colour of growth, prosperity, and riches 13.67, 13.201; the colour of sunlight 13.67; Virūḍhaka (great king) 16.346; 'Yellow, glistering gold' (*Timon of Athens*) 2.369

Yellow Monk *see* Chodags, Thubden

Yemen 25.373

Yeola 9.54–5, 9.60, 9.222, 9.292, 9.370, 9.411

Yeshe De (translator) 14.242

Yeshe Tsogyal 8.521, 13.21, 19.593 (n19), 24.389

Yggdrasil 12.186

yidam (or *iṣṭa-devatā*) *yidam* means 'oath-bound', sometimes translated 'guarantor' 13.200; as esoteric Dharma Refuge 2.481, 4.175, 12.312–15, 13.200–2; can the relationship with one's *yidam* be sexual? 5.619; the centre of your attention, spiritually speaking 13.201; how to choose a *yidam*, *see under* visualization/choosing a *sādhana*; making the acquaintance of the *yidam* 13.201–2; the practitioner's particular characteristic expression of Buddha-nature 8.531; visualized on the Refuge Tree 13.207; your promise to your *yidam* that you will do the practice 19.385; *see also* visualization

Yijing (translator) 14.151, 14.241

yin and yang associations with the earth and the sky 16.129; associations with the stupa 16.148–9; dragon and phoenix 20.484; the jewel and the lotus 16.175; masculine and feminine qualities 16.163–4; their synthesis is Enlightenment 16.151

Yinkuang (Pure Land school patriarch) 24.533, 24.740 (n668)

yoga

introduction
etymology 13.75; the inner yogas of the Vajrayāna 18.76; the origin and purpose of yoga 8.456; union of wisdom and compassion 13.75; *Yoga and Indian Philosophy* (review) 8.454–8; yoga of the long *hūṃ* 8.558

hatha yoga
at the Buddhist centre 9.245; classic texts about yoga 20.303; its beneficial effects 9.442, 11.118; just a system of techniques 2.112; relationship between Western practice and Indian philosophy 8.454–5, 8.457; Sangharakshita practises yoga 20.303

see also
four *mūla* yogas; four principal yogas of Hinduism, *see under* Hinduism/Hindu practice

Yogācāra school (Vijñānavāda)

INTRODUCTION

what was the Yogācāra?
introduction 1.348–52, 1.359–73; 'the school of yoga': the reason for the name 1.350; the relationship between the names Yogācāra and Vijñānavāda 1.351; founded by Asaṅga and Vasubandhu 1.276; foundation story: texts from Maitreya 1.276, 1.359, 12.28, 12.169, 14.260, 17.463–4; descended from the heights 12.28; inspired by Maitreyanātha 1.301; traces of its origins in the *Samādhirāja Sūtra* 14.192; it began with *sūtras* 19.373–4; *alaṃkāras* the link between the Mahāyāna *sūtras* and the Yogācāra 1.361–2; association with the *Saṃdhinirmocana Sūtra* 12.168; the depth psychology of the Yogācāra 12.166–78; incorporation of Sarvāstivādin analysis 1.370; produced one of four systematic transmissions of the doctrine 13.340; four central doctrines 1.367–71; it gained many adherents in China and Japan 2.201; criticized by Candrakīrti 1.322; 'Plotinus and Vijñānavāda Buddhism' 13.374

its character
called 'the sublime Yogācāra' 17.325; devotional practice 1.373; emphasis on individual experience rather than scriptural authority 1.352; had a loose relationship with a wide variety of texts 1.352; an intuitive approach 7.506; its philosophy is epistemological and its method psychological 7.201; a mistake to call it 'subjective realism' 1.618 (n292); not a coherent body of teachings but a

movement 1.351; not philosophy in the Western sense 12.169–70; not a rival to other systems of thought but an expression of insight 7.509; Śāntarakṣita thought their views could be accepted as relative truth 1.322; talent for elaboration 1.265; in the end it became scholastic 19.374

meditation
great emphasis on the practice 1.350, 2.201, 7.506; did the One Mind idea place stress on meditation, or the other way round? 19.373–4; awareness of the *sambhogakāya* 2.42; became a theoretical interpretation of existence 1.374; so they saw things very differently from how other people saw them 12.169–70; a view of reality should attend to the nature of the world experienced in *samādhi* 2.42

One Mind or Mind-Only doctrine (cittamātra)
the basic view of the Yogācāra 19.371; anticipated in the Pāli canon 7.527; perceived by the Yogācārins in their meditations 1.368–9, 12.170; follows from the nondifference between Buddhas and ordinary beings 4.588; absolutely undifferentiated consciousness alone was real 1.84; in 'idealist' *sūtras* 2.130; the *Bhadrapāla-śreṣṭhi-paripṛcchā Sūtra* one of its sources 14.187–8; in the *Laṅkāvatāra Sūtra* 1.357, 2.679 (n170), 3.87, 7.502, 12.170, 14.204–5, 14.208–9, 19.374; in the *Śūraṅgama Sūtra* 1.356; something to be experienced, not just discussed and speculated about 12.173; this approach ensures that you get onto the path of meditation 19.374; can be understood epistemologically and metaphysically 12.171; demonstrated by disproving the existence of matter 1.368–9; it denies the reality of matter as a separate category from mind 17.450, 17.482–3; identified absolute mind with positive reality 1.364; the light of the One Mind experienced at the time of death 12.201–2; mind is no more real in an ultimate sense than anything else 18.44; counterbalance to the abstract teaching on *śūnyatā* 16.20–1, 18.74; ultimate reality by nature pure, perfect, and bright 1.353–4; the experience is like a great expanse of pure, clear water 2.275, 12.173; the universe consists only of ideas (*vijñaptimātra*) 1.351, 12.171–2; how the seemingly objective universe evolved from absolute mind 1.351, 1.364, 2.67; reality as the realm of the One Mind 17.133; there is only one *skandha*, *vijñāna* 17.482; a tremendous change to go from subject–object dualism to the One Mind 2.275–6; misunderstood and misrepresented 1.368; aphorisms about the One Mind 14.209

other views and doctrines
compared to the philosophy of Bishop Berkeley 1.351, 1.368, 12.172, 17.450; contribution to *trikāya* doctrine 2.39, 2.42–3, 16.61; the problem of the origin of apparently objective phenomena 1.103; phenomena's existence indistinguishable from our perception of them 1.351, 12.171–2; illusory and contingent reality 1.265; and *pratītya-samutpāda* (dependent origination) 7.193, 7.199; it addresses the question of whether the universe is eternal or not 17.641–2; mind-stream (*citta-santāna*) 19.237, 19.606 (n99); the universe arises in dependence on consciousness sullied by subject–object 10.143; *śūnyatā* is the nature of reality, and *prajñā* is its subjective counterpart 18.66; what determines ordinary knowledge 3.355

the Yogācāra and Tibetan Buddhism
how the Yogācāra relates to Tibetan Buddhism 8.503; a blend of Yogācāra and Madhyamaka 19.373; the *Avataṃsaka Sūtra* a link between the Yogācāra and Tantric Buddhism 1.376; an account of the Mind Only school by the Dalai Lama 8.612; the sky of the One Mind in which *ḍākinīs* and *ḍākas* dance 12.294; the aim of Tibetan art is to put the viewer in touch with the One Mind 13.61; the direct, immediate recognition of the One Mind (Tibetan Buddhist path) 12.298; 'All the Buddhas and all sentient beings are nothing but the One Mind' 12.170–1

see also
Asaṅga; eight *vijñānas*; and the Madhyamaka, *see under* Madhyamaka; three *svabhāvas*; Vasubandhu

Yogācāra-Svātantrika Madhyamaka 1.323

Yogācaryabhūmi *see* Asaṅga

Yogadarśana *see under* Hinduism

yogakkhema (*yogakṣema*, rest from exertion) 2.124

Yogananda 21.582

Yogaratna, Nepal 21.304–5

yoga-nidrā (yogic sleep) 20.221

yogas (Hindu philosophy) *see under* Hinduism

yogi (Tantric) *see under* Tantric yogi

Yogi Swami of Jaffna 20.123, 20.301, 20.357

yojana 10.569–70, 16.342, 19.593 (n16)

Yolmo *see under* local deities

Yongden, Lama 6.609

York, England 24.386

Yorke, Gerald a disciple of Aleister Crowley 18.xiii, 23.52, 23.197; giving a lecture 11.495; Sangharakshita writes to him from Kalimpong 23.379; helped to publish Sangharakshita's *The Three Jewels* 18.xiii, 23.51–2, 23.419–20; is relieved to see Sangharakshita on his return from India 23.419; work on the *Songs of Milarepa* 18.xii–xiii

Young Men's Buddhist Association (YMBA) its founding 21.82–3; Colombo 9.66; failed attempts to start branches in Darjeeling and Gangtok 21.234; in Kalimpong, *see under* Sangharakshita II/in Kalimpong

young people in the Buddhist East, young people have very little time for Buddhism 12.118–19; giving advice to young people 18.624; the intoxication of youth 2.36, 15.423, 16.298; it can be hard for young people to feel a sense of urgency 19.104; juvenile delinquency 26.131, 26.194; more interested in films than the Dharma 8.212–13; the natural selfishness of youth 18.63; never talk down to teenagers, who are as intelligent as any adult 18.238–9; reflecting on impermanence when you are young 13.228–9; sense of being lost 7.421; they should consider devoting themselves to Buddhism 1.549; when we are young we see the simple reality of things quite clearly 18.30–1; when we are young we think there will be time for piety and goodness when we are old 7.172; the young getting impatient with the old 17.523; young people are often more wholehearted than older people 18.248; young people in the FWBO 9.437–8; young people need the Dharma (Milarepa) 11.368, 18.589; young people's sense of frustration leading to violence 18.457–8

Younghusband, Sir Francis 1.427, 13.41

your way all participate in one *bodhicitta*, but express it in their own way 4.57; be careful not to think that your way of helping is the only way 4.72, 17.285, 25.52; don't assert your way of seeing people over their way of seeing themselves 4.248–9; don't be concerned with communicating the Dharma 'your way' 12.585; the first precept allows people to grow in their own way 18.183–4; a benefit of community life is that you can't always have things your own way 12.669–70, 19.21; in the modern world it is up to everyone to choose their own way in spiritual life 15.282; the rain falls on all alike, and we all grow in our own way 10.211–12, 16.126–9; the sangha can't be a flock of sheep under a shepherd, nor sheep all going their own way 10.580–1; sometimes people aren't happy that something has been done if it hasn't been done their way 18.352; when the Buddha speaks, everyone understands in their own way 16.281–2; wilfully wanting your own way 13.137, 18.363–4, 18.404, 18.406, 19.7–8, 19.15–22, 19.36–7, 19.73; you have to allow others freedom to grow spiritually in their own way 3.15

yourself

yourself as a spiritual being
believe the Dharma because you can verify it for yourself 3.15, 3.162–3; faith in the Buddha is inseparable from faith in yourself 17.37; having committed yourself to the spiritual life, there's nothing to worry about 4.48–9; it makes sense to decide which spiritual pattern to involve yourself with 17.570–1; questioning the wise should be an extension of questioning yourself 17.261; religion is what you yourself most deeply believe 10.340–1; take a spiritual teacher's advice seriously, but take responsibility for yourself 17.308; turning yourself upside-down is a good Buddhist way of looking at things 14.590; you can't be a spiritual friend to yourself 18.395; 'You don't even have to call yourself a Buddhist' 3.14; you don't have to keep tearing yourself up by the roots to see if you have grown 17.267; you yourself are responsible for your own faith 10.495

creating yourself
puṇya karma, the skilful atmosphere you create around yourself 18.244–5; whatever you are creating, you are really creating yourself 3.471; you yourself become the jewel in the lotus 16.181

working on yourself
better to grow in a natural way rather than forcing yourself 4.566; the desirability of controlling yourself 19.17; don't make use of your spiritual development to aggrandize yourself 10.448; expecting a sort of magic to transform you without having to work on yourself 18.520; give yourself wholly to what you are doing 15.115–16; having had the vision, you still have to work at transforming yourself 18.173; instead of saying 'Drop the ego', let yourself open up a little 17.345; integrated awareness is developed by learning to experience yourself more fully

3.488; if you prepare yourself thoroughly, you are already practising 15.345; it's sometimes better to make more effort, but don't force yourself too often 10.604–5; it's a useful exercise to look at the worst aspect of yourself positively 17.655; learning to feel *mettā* for yourself by realizing that others love you 15.308–9; looking at yourself in the mirror of the precepts you see what needs to be done 18.324; *mettā* is about your emotional attitude towards living beings, including yourself 5.380; no one can do puja on your behalf, you do it yourself 10.217; observe yourself and adjust accordingly 18.11–12; the spiritual life shouldn't be something you have to impose on yourself 5.285; at the start you need a strong sense of duty, later, you can let yourself go more 4.485; you can't *make* yourself relax 5.300

looking after yourself
cultivating *mettā* for all that lives, you protect yourself from thoughts of enmity 18.80; do you give yourself what you need? 18.521–2; don't deliberately expose yourself to distraction 4.384; have a pause between activities to refresh yourself with pure awareness 5.399; if you allow yourself to be exploited, sooner or later you will resent it 26.17; if you feel positively about yourself you are going to look after yourself 17.189; if you find yourself in a situation that has a negative effect on you, run away 15.369; it is part of your responsibility towards others to take care of yourself 15.289–90; look after yourself objectively, without attachment 4.633; practise loving kindness towards yourself by eating wholesome food 4.112; resilience: 'you can make yourself comfortable in hell' (Tibetan proverb) 4.423; taking the needs of all the aspects of yourself into account 10.605; to be contented you need a positive appreciation of yourself 15.277; whatever your situation, remind yourself that you are free to leave 18.458; why give yourself a hard time by indulging in unskilful mental states? 5.349; you can handle oscillations by placing yourself in stable surroundings 18.541

challenges to yourself
alienation: getting so far away from yourself that you can't recognize yourself 4.271; anxiety about the future suggests insecurity within yourself 19.269; breaking a vow shows that you're not master of yourself 18.487; don't allow yourself to do something unskilful 'just this once' 15.362; don't hate yourself, but *see* through your experience of selfhood 4.621–2; don't mistake doing something with part of yourself for doing it with the whole 19.276; 'It's very challenging to change yourself' 10.lxi; the suffering you bring on yourself when you ignore the truth 26.46; there is no fool-proof situation because into it you bring the fool: yourself 19.363; to cut yourself off from prayer might be to cut yourself off from your emotions 19.143; when you have a strong need, at least you experience yourself 18.334; you only afflict yourself by being envious 4.431; you ought to get a bit impatient with yourself sometimes 4.368; you reap the consequences of what you have allowed yourself to think 2.70–1; you *refuse* to make up your mind and commit yourself, so you get nowhere 2.297; you tend to draw to yourself karmically appropriate experiences 4.402

yourself in relation to the ideal
attachment to your ideal image of yourself 17.285; by going for Refuge to the Buddha, you gradually transform yourself into a Buddha 15.583; closing the gap between yourself and the Buddha 4.202; discovering Buddhism within yourself 4.352; Enlightenment: acting with the whole of yourself 1.536; experiencing the truth for yourself 15.511; following the Buddha's teaching means gaining his experience for yourself 19.403; freedom to close yourself to spiritual influence 4.247; just immerse yourself in the Dharma 11.736; trying to experience yourself as that which you're trying to become 5.591; visualizing yourself as Amitābha you contact hidden aspects of yourself 19.412; visualizing a Buddha: you as you will be if you allow yourself to die 5.33, 26.50; you can close yourself to the influence of a bodhisattva if you want to 4.247; you can open yourself to spiritual forces, but *you've* got to respond 4.302; 'You yourself must make the effort' 3.163, 9.475, 15.267, 15.546, 15.547–8

going beyond yourself
the dream is you, though a part of yourself you do not usually experience 26.84; an experience of 'yourself' as not separateness but the blissful Void 18.54; Mahāyāna *sūtras* transport you out of yourself into some higher realm 19.26; the more you give up yourself, the more perfectly yourself you become 5.656; opening yourself to the sublime 14.473; part of the value of aesthetic experience is that it lifts you out of yourself 16.285; thinking too much of yourself as you are now 14.481

yourself alone
depend on yourself, look within 13.351, 26.29; dependence on the very person you can't depend on: yourself 18.387; don't isolate yourself from everyday experience 15.288; don't look to outside sources for what you should be developing within yourself 18.300; education should teach you to think for yourself 9.443; experiencing yourself by yourself: an essential human need 5.670; finding things out for yourself 18.228; for spiritual companionship, live by yourself and practise meditation 18.621; if you are an individual you never really depend on anybody except yourself 19.284; if you spent your life alone on a desert island, you'd never really know yourself 3.400; separating yourself from the group 3.36–9, 3.460–1; solitary retreat: an intensified experience of yourself 5.673

yourself and other people
becoming yourself through communication 3.555; being with others as an escape from yourself 26.29; concerning yourself with others' needs, you realize how attached you are to your own 17.206; devoting yourself to the good of all must include yourself 17.191; don't depend on others for things you could do for yourself 18.387; don't look to others to support your image or experience of yourself 18.388; fear of confronting people with the truth of yourself as you really are 15.272; helping others, you are being a true friend to yourself 17.166; if you feel disappointed with yourself, look to your spiritual friends for help 25.33; if you try to harm another, you are really harming yourself 15.371; if you stay in the group you make it more difficult for yourself to evolve 18.485–6; in concealing something from others, you are also concealing it from yourself 17.648; in intense communication with somebody, they reflect you to yourself 19.571; objectively there is no difference between yourself and others 4.472–3; often other people can *see* your potential more than you can yourself 18.284; projecting the whole of yourself onto another person 18.309–10; putting yourself into the hands of someone else 18.382–6; radiating yourself out towards others, not holding anything back 3.369, 4.600–1; the responsibility to make any situation creative for yourself and others 3.473; sometimes a spiritual friend is a better friend to you than you are to yourself 18.521; taking responsibility for yourself makes you more responsive to others' needs 15.290–1; thinking of yourself as a resource for the world 17.204; to encourage others you need to be inspired yourself 17.189–90; to express yourself is to take a risk 18.278; you can't help helping others when you are truly helping yourself 26.17; you cannot help yourself without helping others, and *vice versa* 16.472–3, 21.314; you can't really feel *mettā* for others unless you feel it for yourself 11.267; you give fearlessness to others by being fearless yourself 16.27; you put yourself in negative mental states, no point in blaming others 4.368–9

see also
being yourself, *see under* self/further perspectives; self-knowledge; loving yourself, *see* self-love

youth *see* young people

Yuanwu Keqin 8.486

yuddhavijaya 9.120

yuganaddha ('two-in-oneness') the achievement of this union is the work of the Tantra 13.184; the Bliss-Void 19.196–7; a complete reconciliation and harmony of all opposites 18.299, 19.29; Milarepa's practice 19.258; the non-duality of wisdom and compassion 13.75, 18.51; reflected in all phenomena 1.388; the two-in-one path of wisdom and compassion 18.102; the two-in-oneness of *saṃsāra* and *nirvāṇa* 13.75; symbolized by the twin miracle 12.184; symbolized by the *vajra* 13.183–4

yugas 1.43, 27.1074

Yuktiṣaṣṭikā *see* Nāgārjuna

Yung His 8.371–2

Yunmen 8.487, 8.488

Yuvaraj, Dharmachari 10.194, 24.19–20, 24.609 (n34)

Z

Zaehner, Robert Charles introduction 13.713 (n292); *Evolution in Religion* 23.508 (n263); Sangharakshita's response 13.513–18, 23.227

Zagaya, Yetanapon U 2.749 (n713), 21.108

Zahavi, Dan 8.615

Zarathustra (Zoroaster) in the Axial Age 3.427, 11.355; founder of Zoroastrianism 12.248

zeal a kind of zeal that never lets an opportunity go by 15.210–11; missionary zeal 10.84–5; a monk who practised the eating rule over-zealously 17.283–4; over-zealous walking meditation 1.293, 5.80; religious zeal as a disguise for ill-nature 8.172

Zeb-un-Nisa (Persian poet) 7.58, 7.560 (n83)

Zeitblom, Bartholomäus 24.592

Zeitgeist it is easy to be affected by it, but it eventually passes over 14.509–10; the Zeitgeist of the Sixties suited Sangharakshita's project 23.xiv, 11.729

Zen Buddhism (also Chan, Dhyāna school, Thien)

THE HISTORY OF ZEN

introduction
etymology of the term 'Zen' 2.563, 13.329; brief description 12.230–1; the Buddha holds up a golden flower 1.523, 3.82, 4.148, 8.73, 8.484–5, 12.231–2, 13.341, 14.16; a form of Mahāyāna Buddhism 12.225; reaction against distinctively Indian modes of expression 2.32; Chan movement 19.372; Chinese Zen 13.331; a legacy from Chinese ethnic ideas 10.566; indirect inspiration and guidance from Zen 2.554–5; it probably arose among Chinese students of the *Laṅkāvatāra Sūtra* 2.555, 19.372; much of what we think of as Zen is merely Japanese 12.241; one could say that Zen had nothing to do with Japan 13.333; one of the most spiritually vital and creative periods in Buddhist history 8.487; formalism 1.11; iconoclasm 16.514, 26.57; it became quite rigid 14.436

schools
Rinzai 12.594, 13.342, 16.591 (n40); Sōtō Zen 2.112, 13.342

four kinds of Zen (or Chan)
(1) Tathāgata Chan: classic methods of concentration 13.329; (2) Patriarchal Chan: relates to the *Platform Scripture* 13.329–31; (3) Offspring Chan: as taught by Huineng's descendants 13.331; (4) Mouth Chan: mere talk or writing about Zen 8.494, 12.230, 13.331

Zen and the rest of the Buddhist tradition
Zen and Early Buddhism 19.48; Zen has no time for Abhidharma studies 8.624; connection with the *Heart Sūtra* 14.362; that aspect of Mahāyāna Buddhism that emphasizes meditation 11.498, 13.329, 13.354; is the view of Zen founded on Yogācāra? 19.372; Zen and the *Laṅkāvatāra Sūtra* 12.173; Chan (Zen) and Pure Land Buddhism 7.43, 24.533; divergence from Shin Buddhism 1.208, 17.390; the 'Council of Lhasa', Kamalaśīla's debate with a Chan monk 13.11–12; Zen and the Mahāmudrā 13.28, 19.272; correspondence with *atiyogayāna* (Tibetan Buddhism) 13.22–3; one can learn about Zen through practising other forms of Buddhism 13.324; study its special teachings in relation to what it shares with all Buddhist schools 1.184; very different from Indian Buddhism 11.513; Zen and Going for Refuge 2.563, 3.323, 12.506; better to speak in terms of Buddhism than Zen, or any school 8.496; danger of losing sight of Buddhist doctrine 14.435

ZEN AND THE WEST

Western encounters with Zen
armchair followers of 'Zen' in the West 8.497; being iconoclastic about Zen 26.57; books about Zen 2.284, 11.9, 13.332, 14.515, 14.576; disassociation of Zen from its traditional background 1.372; Mr Chen wept bitterly on reading a Western account of Zen 12.444, 13.331; a Christian assessment of Zen 8.500–1; a confused talk about Zen at the Buddhist Society summer school 23.34–5; Hannyakai (London Zen group) 23.420; Christmas Humphreys' 'Zen class' 23.35, 23.46, 23.69, 23.128; in danger of become a highbrow parlour game 8.371; San Francisco Zen Center, *see under* United States/Buddhism; sanctioning non-Buddhist teachers to teach Zen threatens its integrity 2.564; tendency to

identify with the master, not the disciple 8.497; three causes of misunderstanding 13.332–3; trivializing Zen as 'the witty word among the teacups' 8.488, 17.454; in the West it operates not in emptiness but in a vacuum 8.535; a Zen presentation at a conference in the USA 24.472–3; *The Zen Way* 8.489–90

Zen and Western culture
Alice in Wonderland isn't some kind of Zen text 14.481, 17.65–6; contrast between Tennyson and a Zen poet 17.331–2; a parallel with John Wesley 12.4; Don Quixote and Zen 17.64–7; Zen and psychotherapy 2.564, 12.224–34, 12.516–17; *Zen in English Literature and Oriental Classics, see* Blyth; Zen sayings likened to those of Nietzsche 3.495

Zen and Sangharakshita
Essence of Zen lectures 1.9, 13.321–64; he amuses himself by giving 'Zen-like' responses to a questioner 26.4452; 'I have the greatest admiration for Zen' 13.323; learning the spirit of Zen from Mr Chen 13.324–5; a new insight into the nature of Zen 22.247–8; response to the popularity of Zen 12.224–5

TEACHERS AND DISCIPLES

patriarchs
Six Chinese Patriarchs 13.342; the 28 Indian 'patriarchs' of the Zen school 13.341–2

masters
comparison between the insights of Milarepa and those of the Zen masters 18.13; encouraging their disciples not to mistake temporary states for Enlightenment 19.159; if you ask them for a teaching you take your life in your hands 11.275; laughing at the absurdity of ever imagining that they weren't Enlightened 4.203, 18.45; the master who told his disciple to be careful climbing down a tree 10.532; *mondō* (exchange between master and disciple) 13.356–7, 13.360–1; the Roshi ideal 11.320; teach by dramatic actions so their disciples don't get caught up in words 19.230; teachers may pick on someone deliberately, but this is a dangerous approach 17.653; Tokusan and the thirty blows 13.333, 13.696 (n144); trying to dispense with language 26.200; Zen masters who appear to be quite mad 11.279

transmission
sometimes understood in a literal, even materialistic way 14.453; lineage considered important for the acknowledgement of Enlightenment 19.403; lines of transmission 1.523, 13.342; the only thing that ultimately matters is the experience of Enlightenment 13.343; tends to be one-to-one 13.342, 18.97; Zen transmits the *bodhisattva-saṃvara* 7.483

ZEN TEACHINGS

characteristics
emphasis on direct experience 12.75; emphasis on wisdom rather than merit 19.48–9; emptiness of the concept of emptiness 16.11–12; the 'great death' 3.149, 3.230, 12.174; the 'great doubt' 17.378; iconoclasm 14.436, 16.514; it degrades Zen to think of it as a kind of irrationality 17.65–6; it gives the rational mind a slap in the face 11.9; it may profess to have a non-dualistic basis, but it doesn't 15.635; it says the experience it transmits cannot be expressed in words 7.125; paradox 2.131; realizing the truth through a flash of intuitive insight 7.125; rising above the intellect by the cultivation of 'contradictory' attitudes 1.210; the 'ruthlessness' of Zen 13.346

texts and commentaries
introduction 2.554–5; *The Awakening of Zen, see* D.T. Suzuki; *Blue Cliff Record, see Blue Cliff Record*; popular books on Zen 2.284, 13.332, 14.515, 14.576; *Ch'an and Zen Teaching, see* Luk; claims not to be based on any *sūtra* 2.554; *First Zen Reader, see* Leggett; a great quantity of literature, despite originally being a wordless transmission 8.485; how Zen scriptures arose 8.486; influence of the *Diamond Sūtra* 2.555, 10.164, 14.453, 19.372; influence of the *Laṅkāvatāra Sūtra* 2.276, 2.555, 4.591, 19.372; *Mumonkan* (*The Gateless Gate*), *see Mumonkan*; *On Having No Head, see* Harding; *Platform Sūtra, see Sūtra of Huineng*; the Sixth Patriarch tearing up the scriptures 12.233, 13.337–8, 19.372; *The Tiger's Cave, see* Leggett

verse describing Zen
the verse itself 11.20, 13.333–4; attributed to Bodhidharma 14.611 (n27); 'A special transmission outside the scriptures' 2.554, 8.485, 12.231–4, 13.335–43, 14.16, 14.266, 14.453; 'No dependence upon words and letters' 2.284, 12.232–3, 13.344–9; 'Direct pointing to the mind' 2.554, 3.334, 12.233–4, 13.350–7, 19.328; 'Seeing into one's own nature and realizing Buddhahood' 12.234, 13.358–64

PRACTICES AND LIFESTYLES

meditation
concerned not with *dhyāna* but with insight 5.400; emphasis on meditation 1.372, 2.563; experiment to test the mental states of Zen monks 5.400; meditating as though someone was standing over you with a sword 5.388–9; one does not sit to meditate, one sits to sit 2.112; *shikantaza*, *see* just sitting; some practitioners are critical of other meditation techniques 11.85; some teachers insist that pain is necessary, but it is not 10.503; walking meditation 5.82; why does Zen point to the mind? 13.354; you can force someone to sit, but you can't make them meditate 18.358

the arts
art 2.555, 5.642, 16.184–5; poetry 2.555; Zen aesthetic 16.326–7; Zen and creativity 16.475–6

other practices
all its practices are means to an end 13.342–3; alternative ways to insight 5.640; attitude to work 3.308, 15.279; 'mirroring' 11.375–6, 23.164, 26.603–4; rituals 11.209; unorthodox methods 7.125, 13.333; Zen and the art of statesmanship 16.477; Zen applied to the art of living 16.475

monastic life
a Confucian praises the etiquette in a Chan monastery 12.309; in Zen monasteries scriptures are studied and learned by heart 13.338; 'married monks' 15.7; monasticism 2.555, 18.358

KOAN (CHINESE *KUNG-AN*)

what they are
introduction 16.255–7; literally 'public documents', 'public case', 'public record' 8.486, 13.331; bypassing concepts with koan 8.499; commentaries (*teisho*) are 'encouragement talks' 8.500; difficult to transplant to the West 11.15; how koan work 8.500, 18.189; how Zen answers abstract questions 13.356–7; the *Diamond Sūtra* is a sort of elaborate koan 14.468; koan must be distinguished from playing around with concepts 14.422; a mechanism to beat down your self-will 19.16; paradox 2.131, 4.92; a real koan is something that really bothers us 4.245; a way of breaking through the rational mind 11.14–15; you don't need to go haring after koan 19.544

traditional koan
apparent contradiction between space-type and time-type models of reality 4.203; the body of a cow can pass through a door, but the tail cannot 8.248; can a blade of grass become Enlightened? 4.244–6; the goose and the bottle 1.210, 4.245, 4.689–90 (n212), 7.299, 14.468, 16.255–6, 17.366, 18.189; 'Has a dog Buddha-nature?' 8.499, 13.356, 13.699 (n161); 'If all things are reduced to the One, to what will you reduce the One?' 8.500; 'Juzhi's One Finger Chan' 8.493; '*mu*' 8.499, 16.256–7; three pounds of hemp 8.488; 'What are you carrying?' 5.600, 11.15, 16.255, 17.352; 'What is the sound of one hand clapping?' 1.210, 11.15, 16.591 (n40), 18.189; 'When you have reduced all things to the One Mind, to what will you reduce the One Mind?' 19.372; 'Who are you that is standing before me?' 'I don't know': Bodhidharma's koan 14.576; 'Who recites the Amitābha mantra?' 18.239; 'Why did Bodhidharma come from the West?' 13.356, 13.699 (n161)

SAYINGS AND STORIES

sayings
'The bigger the heap of mud (or clay), the bigger the Buddha' 4.467, 25.73; 'A day of no working is a day of no eating' 2.555, 8.487, 12.497, 17.73; 'Do not offer your poem to a man who is not a poet' 8.496; 'Don't just sling dirt about' 8.496; 'How wonderful! How miraculous! I draw water and I carry fuel.' 14.397, 16.252; 'If you meet the Buddha on the road, kill him' 14.362; 'Mountains are mountains and trees are trees' 14.396, 14.496; on neon signs 25.320; 'The painted picture of a dumpling does not take one's hunger away' 8.496; those used to being close to death can be quite close to the spiritual path 18.245; trying to penetrate *śūnyatā* with the intellect is like a gnat trying to penetrate a ball of steel with its proboscis 14.468; 'using the mind to seek for the mind' is useless 13.363; 'Wake up! Wake up!' 13.364; 'Whatever you do, don't wobble' 17.612; 'You are Buddha' 13.364

stories and metaphors
a jump from the top of the pole 16.93; Master Kendo secretly ate the scraps the young monks had wasted 8.496; kneeling in the snow 3.459; the monk who carried a girl over a stream 2.71, 8.496; the overflowing cup 11.278–9, 17.208; ox-herding pictures 2.343, 8.489; people's tendency to identify with the wise master, not the ignorant disciple 17.279; polishing a stone to make it into a mirror 8.487, 10.439–40; rebirth as a spirit fox 14.593, 18.85; seeing your original face before you were born 13.141, 16.92–3; selling

water by the river 10.626; Master Takuan does not invoke Amida 8.496; Master Tanka burns a statue of the Buddha for fuel 8.497; the man who, intending to be a priest, learned horse-riding and singing 19.104–5; the young man who learned compassion through chess 1.504–5, 8.496; Zen stories and sayings are essentially precepts 8.497

ATTAINMENTS AND MISUNDERSTANDINGS

satori
can occur in sleep 4.514; declarations of attainment (*kenshō*) 14.450–1, 14.576; flash of insight 12.25; gained when the bottom drops out of a bucket 5.449; how it arises 19.70; may be sudden, but the preparation takes a very long time 2.284; sudden Enlightenment 1.176

misunderstandings
confusion 8.494; its attraction for lazy people who think it needs no effort 17.675; mistaking expressions of Zen for Zen itself 13.333; mistaking the finger for the moon 13.333; confusing knowledge and understanding 18.518; pseudo-Zen 14.422, 17.594; trying to understand it apart from Buddhism 8.500–1, 12.225, 13.332–3; trying to understand it intellectually 13.332; *see also* beginner's mind; self-power

Zen Flesh, Zen Bones *see under* Reps, Paul

Zen Shū *see* Japanese Buddhism

Zeus appearing to Semele 12.523, 12.741–2 (n350); descending on Danaë in a shower of gold 26.481; and the fair Bithynian boy 25.258; and Ganymede 25.397; the father of Hercules and Perseus 26.481; his bird the eagle 25.397; hymn to Zeus accompanied by incense 26.494; in the *Iliad* 23.266–7; kills Asklepios, the god of healing 16.191; at Olympia 23.298–9; and Pallas Athene 16.385; Phidias' statue, one of the seven wonders of the world 23.298

Zhaozhou 8.487–8

Zhenyan Zong 1.384

Zhi Qian (translator) 14.138

Zhiche ('Pacification') school 4.362

Zhiyan (second patriarch of the Huayan school) 1.353

Zhiyi (Chih-I)

introduction
the founder of the Tiantai or Tendai school 4.520, 11.54; classification of the Buddha's teaching into five periods 8.483, 10.554–5, 11.716–17; he represents the spirit of inquiry into the Buddhist scriptures 11.717; the path of regular and irregular steps 4.495, 11.54; profound exposition of the *White Lotus Sūtra* 8.480–1; on the Refuge Tree 11.716–17

Dhyāna for Beginners
'*Dharma-niyāmatā* indicates suchness' 16.84; getting to grips with Māra 5.351; the middle way in principle identical with *śūnyatā* 7.606 (n376); recommended 4.519–20; recommends practices to free the mind of guilt 2.105, 14.486; Sangharakshita's seminar on the text 5.xxxi; studied in Triratna 11.377

Zhuangzi (or Zhuang Zhou) 3.427, 14.109

Zhuangzi (book) 8.362, 20.332

zodiac *see* astrology

Zoroastrianism brief introduction 12.52–3; perhaps the source of the Buddha's analysis of body, speech, and mind 2.337–8; caste prejudice 9.43–4; emergence in the Axial Age 3.427, 11.355; an ethnic religion with universal features 12.248; founded by Zarathustra Spitama 12.248; Parsis (or Parsees) 9.348, 12.691–2, 13.103, 21.510, 23.351; persecution of Manicheans 3.432; a philosophical religion 8.604; presence of Zoroastrians at Dharma Parishad 20.173; 'virtually extinct' 13.513

Zuinglius, Ulricus 7.39, 7.552 (n42)

Zurbarán, Francisco de v24

Zweig, Stephan 12.661

THE COMPLETE WORKS: A RETROSPECTIVE

THE BEGINNING

It was in 2003 that Sangharakshita made a will in which he requested his literary executors 'to bring out a complete uniform edition of all my writings, published and unpublished'. Ten years later, the literary executors, who were at that time Subhuti, Nagabodhi, Sagaraghosa, and me (Vidyadevi), met at the London Buddhist Centre to discuss how to respond to that request. The meeting had been instigated by Priyananda, then director of Windhorse Publications. He was keen and confident that Windhorse, which had already been Sangharakshita's publisher for many years, should undertake the publishing of what would become his *Complete Works*. Sagaraghosa met Sangharakshita several times to discuss what he thought should be included in the uniform edition, and a list was drawn up. Sagaraghosa's combination of publishing and mathematical experience meant that she could also work with Priyananda on financial projections. The next thing to do was to work out who would work on the project, how the writings should be organized, and how this ambitious project would be funded.

The literary executors asked Kalyanaprabha, soon to become an executor herself, to become an editor. As well as editing the magazine *Dakini* (later *Lotus Realm*, 'a new voice for Buddhist women'), in recent years she had worked closely with Sangharakshita on a number of his Ibis publications. 'Ibis' was a publishing enterprise he came up with

himself when for financial reasons Windhorse Publications could not take on publishing *Dear Dinoo*. Further Ibis publications – *Beating the Drum*, *Anagarika Dharmapala*, *Early Writings*, and *A Moseley Miscellany* – followed, and Kalyanaprabha played a key role in their production, including writing extensive endnotes and introductions, based partly on conversations with Sangharakshita. Trying to get a sense of the amount of work the new collection would involve, we eventually agreed that Kalyanaprabha and I would share the role of series editor. I had been involved for many years in a different part of Sangharakshita's publishing life, the Spoken Word Project, which edited Sangharakshita's talks and seminars into books. Jinananda and I worked together on this, the first books being *The Drama of Cosmic Enlightenment* and *Wisdom Beyond Words*, and this project, on which several editors worked, including Pabodhana, produced many books published by Windhorse from 1993 to 2013.

As this is a retrospective look at what we came to call the *Complete Works* (there was an initial debate about whether *Collected Works* would be better), I should mention that of course it really began long before its 'beginning', and involved the work of many people over many years, including editors, publishers, and transcribers. Part of the process of preparing the *Complete Works* was the transcription of previously unpublished texts; many thanks to the volunteers who helped to do that. The texts specially edited for this project include the previously unpublished lectures of Volumes 9, 10, and 12, as well as part of Volume 11, and seminars including 'Buddha and the Future of His Religion' (on Dr Ambedkar's book of that name), now in Volume 10, two *Udāna* seminars, edited into a single commentary, also in Volume 10, the commentary on *Dhammapada* chapter 9 (*Living Beautifully*) in Volume 15, and all the stories of Milarepa and Rechungpa in Volumes 18 and 19.

Having had quite different experiences of working with Sangharakshita on his books, Kalyanaprabha and I found that it was fruitful to bring together our approaches, though at times it was challenging to negotiate our different ideas. We worked with Priyananda to devise the structure of the series, and eventually settled on a series of 'baskets', each with a different theme. (We had wondered about chronological order, which some would have preferred, but in the end the themes gave us the flexibility we needed to organize a very wide

range of material.) Some of the literary executors were keen that it should be a sequence of small books, but from Windhorse's point of view, logistics demanded that we had no more than 26 volumes, which is why they are so very substantial. Dhammarati, Windhorse's long-time designer, came up with an elegant design that made these large volumes feasible – I have found the way the hardback copies lie flat when open on my desk very helpful – as well as finding striking and beautiful images for the covers. As I write this, Windhorse Publications is in the process of bringing out a series of the most popular books, to be based on the *Complete Works* editions, so we have ended up with both. Throughout the planning process we were able to be in dialogue with Sangharakshita himself, and that was very helpful.

How would the project be funded? In 2015 Mahamati, who had held various roles over many years, and was then closely involved with supporting Sangharakshita, headed a fundraising initiative, together with Amalavajra of the FutureDharma Fund, to raise money for the *Complete Works*. There was a very generous response, and on Sangharakshita's ninetieth birthday, in August 2015, more than the aimed-for £90,000 was handed over. Sangharakshita's reflections on that occasion, which was marked by the rainbows that attended many auspicious moments in his life, are to be found in Volume 26 (see pages 549–50 – and to find more of those auspicious moments, look up 'rainbows' in the concordance). The funds would go to the *Complete Works* and also to funding translations.

THE WORK

From then on, the work began. For the first couple of years we managed to bring out four volumes a year, and in later years (as circumstances changed) it was three. Work was delayed during the pandemic year of 2020. We decided that each group produced would include volumes from several different 'baskets', which is why they appeared in an apparently haphazard order. The first volume to be published was Volume 9, *Dr Ambedkar and the Revival of Buddhism I*, brought out on 14 October 2016 to coincide with the sixtieth anniversary of Dr Ambedkar's conversion.

Something else that proved to be rather haphazard was the question of what would appear in each volume. The problem – and it was a nice

problem to have – was that our author kept writing, right up until just before his death in 2018, so we needed to find room for these new essays. They went into Volume 26, so then we found homes for other material elsewhere, and in the end quite a few volumes were a little different from how they were first imagined. One small consequence of this is that I believe the list of the *Complete Works* that appears in the back of each volume is never completely accurate. Apologies for that – but at least in this volume there's a bibliography which shows in which volume each book is to be found (see pages 1060–3).

An important realization in these early stages was that the books would need quite full endnotes. Much of the text, especially that based on spoken teachings, contained unattributed quotations and references, and we saw that it could be underpinned by endnotes identifying sources, so this became a substantial part of editorial work. Indeed, in January 2016 we held a *Complete Works* working retreat in the course of which I asked several people to research endnotes, issuing what they said was a bit like an exam paper. I remember asking Dharmottara, a great friend of the project until her death in 2019, to research whether the Buddha could really have heard a lion roar (see Volume 3, note 57, for her answer). As we were at Adhiṣṭhāna, we had the use of the Sangharakshita Memorial Library, which contains the books that were Sangharakshita's own source material, and this proved very helpful for researching endnotes, both then and throughout the project. I spent many peaceful hours in the library myself searching for elusive references, and often called on Dhivan for his scholarly knowledge, especially of the Pāli canon. As the project developed, we were lucky to have the help of a searchable database set up by Pabodhana to log all the assembled endnotes so that we could reuse them as required. After that first occasion with the 'exam paper', editors tended to prepare the endnotes themselves, with the help of their scholarly friends. I'm afraid there are a few references we didn't find, but we did pretty well.

To get the work done, we were very fortunate to have the help of Kalyanasri and Shantavira, who have worked on every single volume. I first met Kalyanasri in the 1980s, when we were both part of a team of women ('Lion's Roar') who produced a periodical called *Mitrata*, which published series of booklets based on Sangharakshita's talks plus extracts from his seminars. Now she took on the substantial work of proofreading *Complete Works* volumes, remarkably reading each one

four times in the course of her work and not hesitating to question any aspect of what she read, bringing to the work her deep knowledge of Sangharakshita's writings. Shantavira has been involved with those writings even longer, having acted as Sangharakshita's copy-editor since the early 1980s and has been much appreciated for his meticulous and good-humoured approach to the work. Shantavira was assisted by Maitiu O'Ceileachair, who checked words in Pāli, Sanskrit, and other languages. The first few indexes were created by Roger Bennett, Windhorse's regular indexer, but all the rest were the creation of Satyalila, who took on the challenge of making *Complete Works* indexes unusually full and informative, and in her time on Index Mountain (as she called it) helped a friendly software developer to improve his indexing programme. It was Satyalila who came up with the image of the *Complete Works* remote scriptorium, each of us at work in our own part of the country – or in Pabodhana's case another country, as he was living in Hong Kong at the time. At Windhorse, meanwhile, we were in the very capable hands of Michelle Bernard, production controller, who kept her expert eye on all the many aspects of this enormous project. Tarajyoti, Windhorse's typesetter, who was ordained during the course of the project, coped with these great rivers of text with tremendous vigour, kindness, and flexibility. Steve Foot did the careful work of creating the eBook digital versions, and the unsung but important work of looking after subscribers and publicizing the series was handled by a succession of Windhorse staff: Giulietta Spudich, Pasadanita (also ordained during her time with the project), and Walter Monticelli.

So, did it all go smoothly? Well, no, it didn't. The whole project really owes its existence to Priyananda, whose initial enthusiasm and confidence set the process going, but the financial reality was even more challenging than anticipated. Subscribers to the *Complete Works* contributed so much to the viability of publication, but at a certain point, facts had to be faced, and we realized that more financial support would be needed if Windhorse was to continue to bring out the *Complete Works*. Thanks to more fundraising efforts (especially the work of Prajnaketu, who became a literary executor), and the wonderful generosity of donors, the work has been brought to completion. Priyananda retired part-way through the process, but his successor, Dhammamegha, has been just as committed to the project, and helped very much in the effort to complete it.

It was fortunate that Sangharakshita himself was able to be involved in the planning stages, and he lived to see the production of the first eight volumes before his death in October 2018. Editors and literary executors had grown used to consulting him about decisions and directions, but now we had to rely on each other, and that was a difficult adjustment to make at first. Another big change was when in 2018 Kalyanaprabha decided that she must withdraw as series editor. She has a hereditary eye condition, and her eyesight was deteriorating to the extent that close literary work was too much of a strain. She had just completed work on Volume 2, and before that Volume 1, two of the most demanding volumes in the whole series, and she went on to edit one more to help the project. Much gratitude is due to her for her work on those and four other volumes, as well as everything she contributed to the planning of the whole series. Very luckily, Pabodhana, veteran of Spoken Word editing, kindly agreed to take on the editing of some volumes, and in the end he edited four, each produced with characteristic imagination and flair. (His idea to include endnotes on all the Order members mentioned in Volume 24 is a particular highlight.)

We were also fortunate in the people who agreed to write forewords for the various volumes and made other contributions. Subhuti, Maitriveer Nagarjuna (Dr Santosh I. Raut), and Lokamitra brought their deep knowledge of the Buddhist movement in India to their work in Volumes 9 and 10, and Subhuti also gave a masterly account of *A Survey of Buddhism* and *The Noble Eightfold Path* in Volume 1. Nagabodhi, having been director of Windhorse Publications for many years, was well placed to introduce the collection of many works that is Volume 2, and the early works presented in Volume 7. Parami is well known for her devotion to the bodhisattva ideal, and brought it to her introduction to Volume 4, Kamalashila and Vajradevi brought their deep experience of meditation to Volumes 5 and 17, and Ratnaguna evoked his response to the Mahāyāna *sūtras* of Volume 16 with imagination and sensitivity. Dhivan brought Pāli scholarship to his foreword for Volume 15 and a love of art to his introduction to *The Religion of Art* in Volume 26, as well as contributing his translations of the verses of the *Udāna* and much scholarly advice to the commentary on the *Udāna* in Volume 10. Vajratara wrote a very thoughtful introduction to volume 14, which offers much food for thought about the reading of the *Complete Works* as a whole. Mahamati introduced Volume 13 with characteristic

sensitivity and clarity. Abhaya and Buddhadasa brought their personal experience to their lively introductions to the biographical works of Volumes 23 and 24, and Sarvamitra, a Finnish Order member, brought a refreshing and thoughtful perspective, with an eye on the future, to his foreword to Volume 11. Padmavajra, Vishvantara, and Vishvapani gave a range of insightful perspectives on Sangharakshita's poetry in Volume 25, and in the same volume Saddhanandi shared the experience of the 'living out of lineage' of her conversations with Sangharakshita on his poems. Maitreyabandhu combined his artistic sensibility and his love of Sangharakshita's teachings to his introduction to Volume 26, and Kalyanaprabha herself wrote the forewords for Volumes 8, 20, 12, and 22, expressing her deep engagement with Sangharakshita's life and teachings. (And I wrote the others: Volumes 3, 6, 12, 18, and 19.) The scholar Śraddhāpa contributed a thoughtful piece on the Perfection of Wisdom to Volume 14 and Ratnaprabha a very helpful reflection on how to read aphorisms to Volume 26, while several members of our Indian sangha – Lokamitra, Dharmarakshita, Jnanasuri, Maitreyaratna, Dhivya, Lakhindar, Amitamati, and Tarahridaya – movingly contributed to the introduction to Volume 10. Vessantara brought his extensive knowledge of Tibetan Buddhism to a helpful reading of part of the Milarepa commentary (Volumes 18 and 19). Aloka, who has been creating illustrations for Sangharakshita's writings since the 1970s, generously allowed us to include his drawings in Volume 13, and also this volume.

THE COMPLETION

So, the *Complete Works* are now complete. (Though of course calling them 'complete' was a hostage to fortune; they are sure to be not quite complete.) I don't know at what time in history you're reading this, or what the world is like in your time, but at the time I'm writing it, the world increasingly communicates through brief messages: 'sound bites' and 'text messages'. At the same time, we are drowning in a deluge of words. Powerful computer 'search engines' produce millions of words informing (or misinforming) us on any subject imaginable. A new interest, or concern, is AI, 'artificial intelligence', which can synthesize all this information to create, or simulate, writings in a way which may even bypass the self-expression of human beings altogether. Added to all that, this is a time in which there is such sensitivity to words and what

they mean that many 'culture wars' are in progress. In the UK, where I live, a commentator recently said that 'the country is evenly split on whether people are too easily offended or whether they should be more sensitive'. And into this world comes this series of hefty physical books (although they also have their digital equivalent), many of their writings originating from a time in which none of this was even dreamed of, and in place of a search engine they have such an old-fashioned means of finding information as a 'concordance' (a word that dates back to the fourteenth century).

But – who knows? – perhaps such a means of communication will turn out to be a portent of the future. As it happened, on the morning of Sangharakshita's death in 2018 I was visiting an exhibition of beautiful ancient books at the British Library in London, some dating back to the fifth century and still quite legible. For me, it was a deeply meaningful synchronicity. After all, I can't even access the words I trustingly stored on floppy disks thirty years ago. Maybe the printed word will outlast digital technology after all – or at least it may prove important to have made this provision in case it does, as I think Sangharakshita foresaw in his request to his literary executors. This brings to mind one of the endnotes it took me a long time to find, relating to the story of a time when 'a great king would send a man round the city on an elephant proclaiming a reward of half the kingdom to anyone who knew even a single verse of the Dharma, but there would be no one to come forward to claim the reward, because not even a single verse of the Dharma would be remembered any more, even for such a price' (*Complete Works* Volume 10, p. 263). I eventually found the reference in a work among the 'hundred books' in the Sangharakshita library which are those he brought back with him from India, and which in a real sense are where these *Complete Works* began. Words can't tell the whole story – look up 'words' in the concordance for some perspectives on this – but the words of the Dharma are precious nonetheless, and there are certainly plenty here that we could produce if anyone on an elephant came looking for them.

THE TIGER

I will finish this retrospective by remembering the trip to London I made in 2013 to meet with the other literary executors and Priyananda to

discuss this work. On that same trip I went to a wonderful exhibition at the Victoria and Albert Museum on 'Masterpieces of Chinese Painting', and in that exhibition was the painting reproduced on the cover of this volume, 'Itinerant Monk Accompanied by a Tiger'. This strange image caught my imagination, and all these years I have identified it with our work on the *Complete Works* project. On the monk's back is a sort of rucksack in which he is evidently carrying precious Dharma teachings, like those carried from India to China along the Silk Road in ancient days. From the *sūtras* incense smoke is rising. It's clearly a hard journey; the monk's face is creased with effort, and there is sweat on his brow. And accompanying him quite closely, with steady stride and determined, though crazy, expression, is a tiger…

When I looked into this, I discovered that there are many similar images, and that they may even reflect the unlikely reality that monks really did travel accompanied by tame tigers. But in this context, for me the monk stands for the effort, the weight, the journey that carrying the *Complete Works* has been, and the tiger represents whatever mysterious, playful but perilous element it is that accompanies such Dharma endeavour, the 'other' element that appears out of the forest of being of its own accord to bless and support our efforts, something wild yet benevolent – a kind of bodhisattva spirit, I suppose, or a supra-personal force, to use an expression Sangharakshita coined. So all our heartfelt thanks are due not just to everyone who has contributed in any way to this 'complete uniform edition', not just to Sangharakshita, who produced this extraordinary body of work, but also to that mysterious spirit, that elusive tiger, which has accompanied us, and accompanied him, on this long journey.

Vidyadevi
Herefordshire
July 2024

BIBLIOGRAPHY

For simplicity, this list is of books published in English and (mainly) in England. Books and pamphlets have also been published elsewhere, notably lectures published in booklet form under the Dhammamegha imprint by TBMSG (later Triratna) in India. Many translations have also been published in many countries.

BUDDHISM: INTRODUCTORY AND GENERAL WORKS

title	date	CW volume
A Survey of Buddhism: Its Doctrines and Methods Through the Ages	1957	1
The Three Jewels: The Central Ideals of Buddhism	1967	2
The Path of the Inner Life	1975	7
Buddhism and Blasphemy (booklet)	1978	11
Human Enlightenment: An Encounter with the Ideals and Methods of Buddhism	1980	11
Aspects of Buddhist Morality (booklet)	1980	11
The Essence of Zen	1983	13
The Bodhisattva: Evolution and Self-Transcendence (booklet)	1983	4
The Ten Pillars of Buddhism	1984	2
The Eternal Legacy: An Introduction to the Canonical Literature of Buddhism	1985	14
Ambedkar and Buddhism	1986	9

Going for Refuge (booklet)	1986	2
Buddhism, World Peace, and Nuclear War (booklet)	1986	6 + 12
Dialogue Between Buddhism and Christianity (booklet)	1986	11
The Heroic Ideal in Buddhism (booklet)	1986	3
The Meaning of Orthodoxy in Buddhism (booklet)	1987	11
Crossing the Stream	1987	7
Mind – Reactive and Creative (booklet)	1989	11
The Taste of Freedom: Approaches to the Buddhist Path	1990	11
The Buddha's Noble Eightfold Path*	1990	1
The Buddha's Victory	1991	11
Who is the Buddha?	1995	3
Tibetan Buddhism: An Introduction	1996	13
Buddhism for Today – and Tomorrow	1996	11
What is the Dharma?: The Essential Teachings of the Buddha	1998	3
The Bodhisattva Ideal: Wisdom and Compassion in Buddhism	1999	4
What is the Sangha?: The Nature of Spiritual Community	2000	3
Buddha Mind	2001	11

*Originally published as *Vision and Transformation*

COMMENTARIES ON BUDDHIST TEXTS

The Threefold Refuge	1984	15
The Way to Wisdom	1984	17
Auspicious Signs: a seminar on the *Maṅgala Sutta*	1988	15
The Drama of Cosmic Enlightenment: Parables, Myths, and Symbols of the *White Lotus Sūtra*	1993	16
Wisdom Beyond Words: The Buddhist Vision of Ultimate Reality	1993	14
The Inconceivable Emancipation: Themes from the *Vimalakīrti Nirdeśa*	1995	16
Transforming Self and World: Themes from the *Sūtra of Golden Light*	1995	16
Know Your Mind: The Psychological Dimension of Ethics in Buddhism	1998	17
Living with Awareness: A Guide to the *Satipaṭṭhāna Sutta*	2003	15
Living with Kindness: The Buddha's Teaching on *Mettā*	2004	15
The Yogi's Joy: Three Songs of Milarepa	2006	18
Living Ethically: Advice from Nāgārjuna's *Precious Garland*	2009	17
Living Wisely: Further Advice from Nāgārjuna's *Precious Garland*	2013	17

RITUAL, MYTH, AND SYMBOLISM

Ritual and Devotion in Buddhism: An Introduction	1995	11
Creative Symbols of Tantric Buddhism	2002	13

ART AND CULTURE

The Religion of Art	1980	26
Buddhism and William Blake (booklet)	1981	8 + 26
The Journey to Il Covento (booklet)	1984	26
St Jerome Revisited (booklet)	1985	26
The Glory of the Literary World (booklet)	1985	14
Alternative Traditions	1986	8
Buddhism and the West: The Integration of Buddhism into Western Society	1992	11
The Priceless Jewel	1993	16 + various others
In the Realm of the Lotus: A Conversation about Art, Beauty, and the Spiritual Life	1995	26

POETRY AND TRANSLATIONS

The Caves of Bhaja (booklet)	1985	25
Conquering New Worlds	1986	25
Hercules and the Birds and other poems	1990	25
Complete Poems 1941–1994	1995	25
The Call of the Forest	2000	25
Dhammapada: The Way of Truth	2001	15

MEMOIRS AND OTHER PERSONAL WRITINGS

Travel Letters	1985	24
The History of My Going for Refuge	1988	2
My Relation to the Order (booklet)	1990	2
Facing Mount Kanchenjunga: An English Buddhist in the Eastern Himalayas	1991	21
Forty-Three Years Ago: Reflections on my Bhikkhu Ordination	1993	2
Was the Buddha a Bhikkhu?	1994	2
In the Sign of the Golden Wheel: Indian Memoirs of an English Buddhist	1996	22

Title	Year	Volume
Great Buddhists of the Twentieth Century (booklet)	1996	6
The Rainbow Road From Tooting Broadway to Kalimpong*[2]	1997	20
Reflections on Going Forth (booklet)	1997	12
Through Buddhist Eyes: Travel Letters	2000	24
Moving Against the Stream: The Birth of a new Buddhist Movement	2003	23
From *Genesis* to the *Diamond Sūtra*: A Western Buddhist's Encounters with Christianity	2005	13
Precious Teachers: Indian memoirs of an English Buddhist	2007	22
Dear Dinoo: Letters to a Friend	2011	21
Anagārika Dharmapala (*part previously published as* Flame in Darkness)	2013	8

* Originally published as Learning to Walk (1990) and The Thousand-Petalled Lotus: An English Buddhist in India (1976)

ANTHOLOGIES AND APHORISMS

Title	Year	Volume
Peace is a Fire	1979	26
A Guide to the Buddhist Path	1990	various
A Stream of Stars	1998	26
The Essential Sangharakshita	2009	6
The Purpose and Practice of Buddhist Meditation	2012	5
Beating the Drum: *Maha Bodhi* Editorials	2012	8
Early Writings: 1944–1954	2014	7
A Moseley Miscellany: Prose and Verse 1997–2012	2015	8 + 25

THE TRIRATNA BUDDHIST ORDER

Title	Year	Volume
New Currents in Western Buddhism: The Inner Meaning of the FWBO	1990	11
The FWBO and 'Protestant Buddhism': An Affirmation and a Protest	1992	13
Extending the Hand of Fellowship: The Relation of the WBO to the Rest of the Buddhist World (booklet)	1996	22

For simplicity, this list is of books published in English and (mainly) in England. Books and pamphlets have also been published elsewhere, notably lectures published in booklet form under the Dhammamegha imprint by TBMSG (later Triratna) in India. Many translations have also been published in many countries.

ERRATA

VOLUME 1

p. 75: for 'four undetermined questions' read 'fourteen undetermined questions'.

p. 89: for '*Imasmiṃ sati, idaṃ hoti; imass' uppādā, idaṃ upapajjati*' read '*Imasmiṃ sati, idaṃ hoti; imass' uppādā, idaṃ uppajjati*'.

p. 97: for '*Ya ḥapratītyasamutpādaṃ*' read '*Yaḥ pratītyasamutpādaṃ*'.

pp. 136, 473, 665: for '*pṛthaflanas*' read '*pṛthagjanas*'.

p. 174: for 'ideas' gans of form, being regarded' read 'ideas being regarded'. And for 'sense-or sound' read 'sense organs of sound'.

p. 255: for 'Tuṣita heaven' read 'Heaven of the Thirty-Three'.

p. 256: No note has been provided for the reference to the *Dīgha Nikāya* at the top of the page, but the reference is evidently to *Dīgha Nikāya* 28 (iii.104), the details being supplied (according to Walshe) by the *Dīgha Nikāya* commentary. See M. Walshe (trans.), *The Long Discourses of the Buddha*, Wisdom Publications, Boston 1995, pp. 419 & 606.

p. 324: for 'Forty-nine vows' read for 'forty-eight vows'.

p. 603: note 111 should read 'For examples, see *The Religion of Art*, *Complete Works*, vol. 26, pp. 126–7.'

p. 633 note 426: for the first instance of 'polyandry' read 'polygamy', and for '2010' read '1935'.

p. 654: Going for Refuge index entry, remove p. 672.

VOLUME 2

p. 43: for 'world or phenomena' read 'world of phenomena'.

p. 145: for '*j778*' read '*paññāvimutti*'.

p. 162: for 'not a third note but a star' read 'not a fourth sound but a star' (quoting Browning's 'Abt Vogler').

p. 466: for 'March 1967' read 'February 1967'.

VOLUME 3

p. 209: for '*Majjhima Nikāya*' read '*Dīgha Nikāya*'.

p. 647 note 139: for '*Aṅguttara Nikāya* iii.223' read '*Aṅguttara Nikāya* ii.38'. The other page details are correct.

p. 647 note 143: for 'verse 1070' read 'verse 1059'.

p. 652: note 169 should read '*Ariyapariyesanā Sutta*, *Majjhima Nikāya* i.167–8. See Bhikkhu Bodhi (trans.), *The Connected Discourses of the Buddha*, Wisdom Publications, Boston 2000, p. 260; or I. B. Horner (trans.), *The Collection of the Middle Length Sayings*, vol. i, Pali Text Society, London 1976, p. 211.'

p. 653: note 178 should read 'See note 169.'

p. 666 note 260: for '*pṛthaflanas*' read '*pṛthagjanas*'.

p. 685: note 390 should read 'See Karl Jaspers, *The Origin and Goal of History*, Routledge and Kegan Paul, London 1953.'

VOLUME 4

p. 576: for 'on my way hack' read 'on my way back'.

p. 675 note 101: for 'vi.49' read 'iii.445' and in the Hare reference for 'p. 255' read 'p. 310'.

VOLUME 7

p. 149: Remove the two asterisks.

p. 531: for 'eighty major and thirty-two minor' read 'thirty-two major and eighty-four minor'.

VOLUME 8

pp. 123 & 124: for 'Hongwanji' read 'Honganji'.

p. 371: for 'Rev. Yung His' read 'Rev. Yung Hsi'.

p. 383: for 'K. N. Jayatilleka' read 'K. N. Jayatilleke'.

p. 456: for 'Aurobindo Ghosh' read 'Aurobindo Ghose'.

p. 546: for 'Ralph Gardiner' read 'Rolf Gardiner'.

p. 643: for 'G. Constant Loundsberry' read 'G. Constant Lounsberry'.

p. 643: for 'R. Kulkarni' read 'A. R. Kulkarni'.

p. 660: for 'Buddhism for Beginners' read 'Buddhism for the Beginner'.

VOLUME 10

p. xliii: for 'the real meaning insisted of the precepts' read 'the real meaning of the precepts'.

p. 139: for 'Spencer Hardy' read 'Spence Hardy'.

pp. 156 & 247: for '*opanayiko*' read '*opaniyiko*'.

p. 162: for 'Sophie Wadia' read 'Sophia Wadia'.

p. 186: for 'Śaṅkara's punishment' read 'Śaṅkara spelled out the punishment'.

p. 381: for 'Mr P. M. Rajbhoj' read 'Mr P. N. Rajbhoj'.

p. 545: for 'Dr Radhakrishna' read 'Dr Radhakrishnan'.

p. 597: for '*Dīgha Nikāya*' read 'Pāli canon'.

VOLUME 12

p. 97: omit 'called Kevaddha'.
p. 634: for '2001' read '2002'.

VOLUME 13

p. 163: for 'median nerve' read 'central channel'.
p. 342: for 'Pārśva ?President' read 'Pārśva, President'.
p. 453: for 'third step' read 'fourth step'.
p. 463: for 'four *dharma-skandhas*' read 'five *dharma-skandhas*'.

VOLUME 14

p. 85: for 'a bloodless ballet of unearthly categories' read 'an unearthly ballet of bloodless categories'.
p. 162: for 'Vasuṃdhara' read 'Jagatīṃdhara'.
p. 517: for 'and unlike the experience' read 'or like the experience'
p. 560: for 'open-ended dimension' read 'open dimension'.

VOLUME 15

p. 217: for '*ātāpa*' read '*tapas*'. The sources page is missing. The sources for this volume are: *Dhammapada* translation first published by Windhorse Publications in 2000; other translations previously published in *The Enchanted Heart*, Ola Leaves, 1980. *Living With Awareness* (first published by Windhorse Publications in 2003) is based on the transcript of a seminar on the *Satipaṭṭhāna Sutta* given in Tuscany in 1982. *Living With Kindness* (first published by Windhorse Publications in 2004) is based on the transcript of a seminar on the *Karaṇiyā Mettā Sutta* given at Padmaloka in 1978. *Living Beautifully* (*Dhammapada* chapter 9) was edited for *Complete Works* vol. 15 from the transcript of a seminar on that text held at Padmaloka in 1983. *Auspicious Signs* is the edited transcript of a seminar on the *Maṅgala Sutta* held in 1976, originally published by Ola Leaves in 1979 and published by Windhorse Publications in 1985. *Salutation to the Three Jewels* is the edited transcript of a seminar on the *Tiratana Vandanā* held in 1978, originally published by Ola Leaves in 1978 and published by Windhorse Publications in 1985. *The Threefold Refuge* is the edited transcript of a seminar held in 1978 and first published by Windhorse Publications in 1984.
p. 494: for 'a polarized and misunderstood Freudianism' read 'a popularized and misunderstood Freudianism'

VOLUME 16

p. 235: *abūtadharma* should read *adbhūtadharma*
p. 627: note 342 should read 'Blasphemy laws were abolished in England and Wales in 2008, and in Scotland in 2021, while Northern Ireland still maintains "blasphemy" provisions.'

VOLUME 17

p. 20: for 'righteous people' read 'richest people'.

p. 66: for 'There was also a bishop who wrote detective stories. That was George Birmingham, Bishop of Birmingham, who was well known as a writer of detective stories.' read 'There was also an Irish clergyman who wrote detective stories, George A. Birmingham, who published many stories in the first half of the twentieth century.'

p. 189: for 'The *Dhammapada* also has such a list' read 'Conversely, the *Dhammapada* lists the negative effects of unskilfulness.'

p. 424: for 'casual sequence' read 'causal sequence'.

p. 734 note 200: for '137–40' read '137–40, 309–10'.

p. 750 note 322: for 'always presented' read 'often presented'.

p. 765 note 462: for 'iii.196' read 'iii.415' and for 'p. 145' read 'p. 294'.

p. 774 note 559: Replace this note with 'See *Aggivacchagotta Sutta, Majjhima Nikāya* 72 (i.484–5); see Bhikkhu Ñāṇamoli and Bhikkhu Bodhi (trans.), *The Middle Length Discourses of the Buddha*, Wisdom Publications, Boston 1995, p. 591; or I. B. Horner (trans.), *The Collection of the Middle Length Sayings*, vol. ii, Pali Text Society, Oxford 1994, pp. 164–5.'

VOLUME 18

p. 189: for 'transcendental insight wit' read 'transcendental insight'.

p. 230: for 'It's the mind that tries to or pick up' read 'It's the mind that tries to catch or pick up'.

VOLUME 20

p. 516: for 'Life of 37, 51' read 'Life of Siddhartha Gautama 37'.

VOLUME 21

p. 402: for 'My Journeys to Ajanta and Bagh' read 'My Pilgrimages to Ajanta and Bagh'.

VOLUME 22

p. 146: for 'adverse to' read 'averse to'.

p. 524: for 'base voice' read 'bass voice'.

VOLUME 23

p. 568: In the right hand column, exchange the 7th and 8th lines.

VOLUME 24

p. 194: for 'King Arthur' read 'King Alfred'.

p. 519: for '1922' read '1992'.

p. 525: for 'literary influence of the novel' read 'literary influence on the novel'.

p. 535: for 'Robert Lindsay' read 'Norman Lindsay'.

p. 547: for 'Halliday' read 'Holiday'.

p. 620: note 79 connects the Hare Krishna movement with Maharishi Mahesh Yogi. There is, in fact, no such connection.

p. 779: for 'Lobstein, Anne (formerly Bancroft)' read 'Lobstein, Anne (later Bancroft)'

VOLUME 25

p. 15: for '*Sutta-Nipāta*' read '*Saṃyutta Nikāya*'

p. 427: The poem 'To C—' is by Dharmachari Paramartha, not Sangharakshita.

p. 588 note 22: for '*Sutta-Nipāta* 10.4' read '*Saṃyutta Nikāya* i.214 (10.12)'.

VOLUME 26

p. 78: for 'Arthur Rimbaud' read 'Paul Verlaine'.

p. 209: for 'unapprehended mystery' read 'unapprehended inspiration'.

p. 474: for '*Majjhima Nikāya*' read '*Dīgha Nikāya*'.

p. 504: for 'Byron' read 'Shaw'.

In Volume 6 (page 613), Volume 9 (page 181), and Volume 10 (page 24), Sangharakshita mentions that when Dr Ambedkar was a schoolboy he was given a copy of Edwin Arnold's *The Light of Asia*. But in the preface to his book *The Buddha and His Dhamma*, Ambedkar himself says that at 16 he was given by his mentor Dadaji Keluskar a copy of Keluskar's own book in Marathi, a life of the Buddha called *Gautam Buddha Charitra*, so Sangharakshita may have been mistaken. We know that in later life Dr Ambedkar owned two copies of *The Light of Asia*, but we don't know when he acquired or was given his first copy.

OMISSIONS

INTRODUCTION

Calling this uniform edition of Sangharakshita's writings his *Complete Works* was always going to give a hostage to fortune. We have done our best to make them complete, but there are omissions of various kinds. For one thing, I know that some people have assumed that this series includes all the seminars that Sangharakshita gave. However, while much seminar material is included in the *Complete Works*, this had mainly already been edited and published in book form, although some was edited specially for this series, as explained on page 1052. There are many more seminars, and at the time I'm writing this a project is under way to edit and publish the complete seminars as a companion series to the *Complete Works*.

An early publishing initiative in the FWBO (later Triratna) was *Mitrata*, a magazine for Mitras which began in 1975 (when it appeared monthly) and continued until 1990 (by which time it was quarterly). Many issues consisted of talks by Sangharakshita and extracts from his seminars, but others contained talks and essays by other Order members. Of the teachings of Sangharakshita published in *Mitrata*, many were re-edited and republished in book form and thus appear in the *Complete Works*, but some seminar extracts do not, so the publishing history is quite complicated. We didn't try to include writings published in *Mitrata* in the *Complete Works*, on the basis that almost all the content appears

elsewhere here, but any missing seminar material will be found in the complete seminars.

We combed Sangharakshita's archives to find unpublished writings, but the archives have not yet been fully catalogued, and we may have missed some items. Mahamati had the opportunity to consult Sangharakshita about previously unpublished work found in the archives, and there were a few things that Sangharakshita decided not to include. Also in the archives are Sangharakshita's letters, and in the future perhaps a selection may be published, if not a *Complete Letters*.

When planning the *Complete Works*, we decided to include previously unpublished talks, including some transcribed for this series. There were, however, a few recordings we knew about but could not find, and more may come to light. The interviews and conversations included have almost all been published in magazines, though the conversations on poetry in Volume 26 are published here for the first time, but video and audio recordings of other conversations and interviews exist, and one day they could perhaps be included in a new edition of the *Complete Works*.

Some omissions are deliberate. For example, in 1963 and 1964, Sangharakshita contributed a number of pieces to *Sangha* magazine, produced by the English Sangha Trust, but when we investigated these we found that they had been extracted from *The Three Jewels* and *The Eternal Legacy* (see volumes 2 and 14 of the *Complete Works*), and did not need to be included separately. Most of the articles written for the Buddhist Society's magazine, the *Middle Way*, are included in Volume 7 of the *Complete Works*, some among the early writings at the start of the book and others in the final section. A further *Middle Way* article, 'The "Legendary" Life of the Buddha', was produced from chapter 4 of *The Three Jewels*.

After Volume 9 had been published, we realized that a passage had been omitted from *Ambedkar and Buddhism*; it was included as an appendix to Volume 10, pp. 659–61, which explains where the passage fits into the text. And there are still three pieces that we are now aware have accidentally been omitted from the volumes of the *Complete Works*; the following summaries are intended to correct those errors. If you are interested in seeing the full versions, please contact the Urgyen Sangharakshita Trust.

The first of the missing pieces was commissioned by the *Middle Way* (issue XXXIX.3, November 1964) a few weeks after Sangharakshita's return to England in 1964. Asked to write about his impressions of Buddhism in his homeland, he felt that it was too early to say much, but said that what struck him most was the growth and expansion of the Buddhist movement since he left, but also its inadequacy compared to the total population, and 'the limited extent to which it impinges on national life and thought'. He said he intended this observation not to dampen enthusiasm, but to act as a challenge. After all, so much had been achieved in the previous twenty years. Still thinking of the Sangha in terms of ordained monks, he observed that there were now enough Western monks to constitute *the first Western branch of the Order in the history of Buddhism* (this observation in italics to emphasize its significance).

He noted the 'degree of joyous comradeship' at the Buddhist Society's summer school, and the affection and gratitude of the participants for Christmas Humphreys, the Society's founder, and also observed that 'a high proportion of Western Buddhists seem interested in meditation'. While acknowledging that this interest was natural in view of the 'alarmingly high incidence of mental strain and disorder', he said that it 'must always be borne in mind that the significance of Buddhist meditation is not merely psychological but primarily spiritual: its goal is Enlightenment'. At the summer school, he reports, 'I conducted an experiment in what I called guided meditation, the class progressing from one stage to another of *mettā bhāvanā* (development of love) practice as directed at five minute intervals by the voice of the instructor. Verbal directions were gradually reduced to a minimum until, in the last session, transition from one stage to the next was indicated merely by strokes of the gong. The experiment seemed successful, and it may be possible to apply the same technique to the teaching of other types of meditation. In any case, I feel strongly that there is a great need, among English Buddhists, for a wider and more intensive practice of the 'classical' systems of meditation, such as *mettā bhāvanā* and *ānāpānasati* (respiration mindfulness), which are common to all *yānas* and which constitute the indispensable foundation of the more advanced techniques. I also feel that less attention is paid than might be to the

devotional side of the Buddha's teaching.' And, he added, quoting one of his favourite sayings of the Buddha, 'Mindfulness is always useful.'

THE TIMELY RAIN

The second missing piece (published in the *Middle Way*, XXXIX.4, February 1965) is a review of *The Timely Rain: Travels in New Tibet*, by Stuart and Roma Gelder. Sangharakshita was clearly deeply dismayed by this work, whose authors' admiration for Communist China affects their account of their visit to Tibet, their bias leading them 'to make one of the most vicious attacks on Tibetan Buddhism that have appeared in print for a long time. They make it knowing nothing about Buddhism in any form and not caring to know.' For their information they rely on their Chinese mentors and 'a curious collection of authorities', all of whom are fiercely disapproving, uncomprehending, or otherwise unsympathetic, rather than turning to the work of 'anyone who has written of Tibetan Buddhism with respect or sympathy'. The review concludes sadly: 'All this is the climax of an attempt to highlight the achievements of the present, with its schools, hospitals, and roads, by contrasting them with the poverty, ignorance, and slavery of the past. Not unnaturally, the Gelders think that the Tibetans are better off under the new regime than they were under the old, happier without Buddhism than with it, and they would like us to be believe that the Tibetans think so too. Persecution of Buddhism? Quite unnecessary. "Even if the Communists had wished to do so there was no need to persecute the few harmless monks in worn-out clothes, stiff with dirt, who shuffled round the silent streets and altars which had once been alive with more than a thousand men." (p. 39) It is hardly necessary to read between the grim lines of passages like these to know what has happened to Buddhism in Tibet. Neither is it necessary to accuse the Gelders of deliberate lying in order to doubt the authenticity of their report. Timely or untimely, the rain that has fallen on Tibet is one of mingled blood and tears, and what they have written contains nothing to convince us of the contrary.'

ABORTION, PEACE, AND SO ON

The third missing piece, written in May 2017 (more than fifty years after the previous two) was published online but not in print. Entitled

'Abortion, Peace, and So On', but in fact mainly on the themes of celibacy and poverty, it was prompted by Sangharakshita's hearing on the radio a clip of an interview with Mother Teresa. 'In it she connected abortion and peace in an interesting way. I already knew of her attitude towards abortion, which of course was in accordance with Roman Catholic teaching, but the way in which she connected the practice of abortion with peace was new to me. Nor was that all. I was impressed by the sound of her voice and by the confident tone in which she expressed her views. For her, abortion was killing. It was the taking of a human life, even when that life was still in an embryonic form. War, too, was killing, in that it consisted in the taking of human life, regardless of who the combatants were. In principle, therefore, there was no difference between the killing that was abortion and the killing that was war, so that if we acquiesce in the one we acquiesce in the other, the implication being that we can hardly work for peace in the world without also working for the abolition of abortion. Mother Teresa apparently saw herself as working for both, the two being inseparable.'

While saying that he had never been an admirer of Mother Teresa, Sangharakshita remembered all too vividly the conditions in Calcutta which she and her helpers did their best to alleviate. Reflecting on the fact that Mother Teresa's order had far more women than men, it seemed to him that membership of the order (with its vows of chastity, poverty, and obedience) represented a kind of career opportunity for young Indian women of limited means. Going on to consider chastity or celibacy in general, he observed that for some Western Buddhists the question of to what extent celibacy is part of the spiritual life is debatable, and went on to say, 'I was a *bhikkhu* for some years and as such observed chastity. For much of that time, in fact, I was convinced that the monk was the true Buddhist and that therefore celibacy was an integral part of the spiritual life. Gradually I became less sure of this, and began to think that in certain circumstances one could be a true Buddhist without being celibate. In the end I gave up the practice of celibacy, and I gave it up without thinking that I was less a true Buddhist that I had been before. Yet I do not regret my years as a wandering ascetic and as a *bhikkhu*, which certainly gave an edge to my Dharma life at the time. Members of the Triratna Buddhist Order do not observe a vow of celibacy though they are free to practise celibacy if they wish, with or without taking a vow. In any case, the relation between sexual

activity and spiritual life is a complex and very personal one, in which one suit cannot fit all.'

Reflecting on this subject brought to mind the Brahma Kumaris or Divine Virgins who tracked Sangharakshita down in the hope of converting him to their Hindu faith, trying to persuade him that the Age of Gold (the Satya Yuga) was at hand, and that 'we shall all be living in beautiful houses in which the bathrooms will have taps of gold' (a notion which Sangharakshita thought rather vulgar). Not surprisingly, they did not practise poverty as did the Missionaries of Charity, and as do Buddhist monks. To the subject of poverty Sangharakshita now turned:

'Buddhist monks are limited to the possession of eight items: an alms bowl, three robes, a razor, a needle and thread, and a water strainer, which Jain monks consider a very liberal allowance. Though the individual Buddhist monk owns only eight things, groups of monks may hold moveable and immoveable property in common. Moreover, a Buddhist monk may not handle money, or listen to music, or use a high and wide bed. During my time as a *bhikkhu* I therefore lived very simply, going for alms and sleeping rough, and neither handling money nor listening to music. In my memoirs I have related how contaminated I felt when I was again obliged to handle money in the form of banknotes. Though I lived very simply, I did not have to look very far to see that many others were living more simply than I was. I was living simply out of choice but they were living simply because they had no choice. For me poverty meant freedom, while for them poverty meant slavery. This was especially the case with those who lived in sub-human conditions outside the caste system and who were oppressed, exploited, and victimized by the higher castes. They were prohibited from entering Hindu temples, denied education, and refused access to clean drinking water. Of the millions of such people Dr B. R. Ambedkar was the undoubted leader, and it was partly because Buddhism did not sanctify or ennoble poverty that in 1956 he led his people from Hinduism to Buddhism. Although the Buddha founded an order of monks and an order of nuns, there were many of his followers who continued to lead the household life, earning money or its equivalent and supporting their families. The Buddha was not against the creation of wealth provided this was done in accordance with the precepts of morality. Observers have noted that those followers of Dr Ambedkar who converted to Buddhism

have become, in the decades that followed, more advanced socially, educationally, and economically than those who did not convert. At the same time, it should be remembered that the achievement of material prosperity is not the highest object of human life.'

Observing that poverty, chastity, and obedience 'are not regarded as virtues in today's world', Sangharakshita concluded his reflections by considering the limitations of his teachings to Dr Ambedkar's followers: 'No doubt I was wholehearted in teaching the Dhamma to those followers of Dr Ambedkar who had converted to Buddhism, and in the course of ten years I must have given talks to millions of people in hundreds of cities, towns, and villages; but I was aware that what I was doing had its limitations. Everywhere I went there was poverty, malnutrition, and disease. I more than once wished that besides being a *bhikkhu*, I could also have been a doctor so that wherever I went I could not only have given talks on the Dhamma but also have been able to give medical treatment. Friends indeed once gave me a homeopathic outfit in the form of a wooden box containing bottles of tiny pills and a little book of instructions as to which pills had to be given for which illnesses. In the end I did not make use of the box as I was afraid of doing more harm than good, and in any case there was often no time, as my talks would carry on until late at night or the early hours of the morning. I am therefore all the more glad that there are people in Triratna who not only practise the Dharma but serve others in various capacities, though of course their service is part of their practice. Though we cannot always agree with Mother Teresa, perhaps we have something to learn from the work of the Missionaries of Charity. Nor is that all. Perhaps I shall have to consider adding Mother Teresa herself to my list of personal heroines.'

Vidyadevi
September 2024
Herefordshire

WINDHORSE PUBLICATIONS

Windhorse Publications is a Buddhist charitable company based in the UK. We produce books of high quality that are accessible and relevant to all those interested in Buddhism, at whatever level of interest and commitment. We are the main publisher of Sangharakshita, the founder of the Triratna Buddhist Order and Community. Our books draw on the whole range of the Buddhist tradition, including translations of traditional texts, commentaries, books that make links with contemporary culture and ways of life, biographies of Buddhists, and works on meditation.

THE TRIRATNA BUDDHIST COMMUNITY

Windhorse Publications is a part of the Triratna Buddhist Community, an international movement with centres in Europe, India, North and South America and Australasia. At these centres, members of the Triratna Buddhist Order offer classes in meditation and Buddhism. Activities of the Triratna Community also include retreat centres, residential spiritual communities, ethical Right Livelihood businesses, and the Karuna Trust, a UK fundraising charity that supports social welfare projects in the slums and villages of India.

Through these and other activities, Triratna is developing a unique approach to Buddhism, not simply as a philosophy and a set of techniques, but as a creatively directed way of life for all people living in the conditions of the modern world.

For more information please visit thebuddhistcentre.com

SANGHARAKSHITA.ORG

You can find out more about Sangharakshita's life, teachings, and the Buddhist movement he founded on his official website: sangharakshita.org